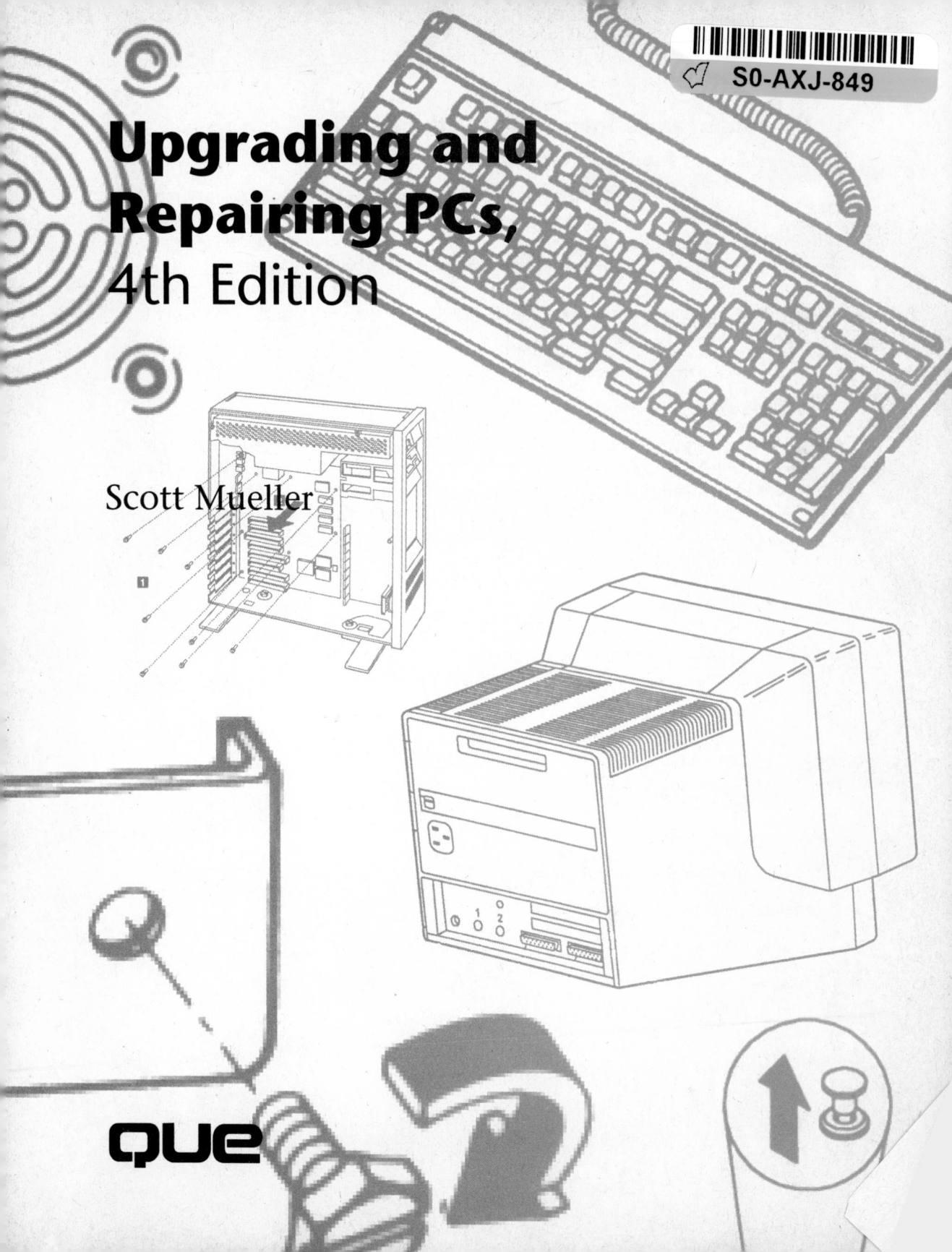

Upgrading and Repairing PCs,

4th Edition

Scott Mueller

que

Upgrading and Repairing PCs, 4th Edition

Copyright© 1994 by Que® Corporation

Library of Congress Catalog No.: 94-65316

ISBN: 1-56529-932-9

97 96 95 94   6 5 4 3 2 1

Interpretation of the printing code: the rightmost double-digit number is the year of the book's printing; the rightmost single-digit number, the number of the book's printing. For example, a printing code of 94-1 shows that the first printing of the book occurred in 1994.

Screen reproductions in this book were created using Collage Plus from Inner Media, Inc., Hollis, NH.

Publisher: David P. Ewing

Associate Publisher: Corinne Walls

Publishing Director: Brad R. Koch

Managing Editor: Michael Cunningham

Product Marketing Manager: Greg Wiegand

Dedication

This one is for my brother Brian, my best friend.

Hey Lip, anmedabondya!

Credits

Acquisitions Editor
Cheryl Willoughby

Product Directors
Stephanie Gould
Jim Minatel

Project Editor
Chris Nelson

Production Editor
Mike La Bonne

Editors
Danielle Bird
Fran Blauw
Geneil Breeze
Kelli M. Brooks
Gail Burlakoff
Theresa Mathias
Susan Ross Moore
Maureen Schneeberger
Kathy Simpson

Technical Editors
Todd Brown
Jerry Cox
Anthony Drewery
John Little

Figure Specialist
Cari Ohm

Book Designers
Paula Carroll
Amy Peppler-Adams

Cover Designer
Dan Armstrong

Acquisitions Assistant
Ruth Slates

Editorial Assistants
Jill Byus
Andrea Duvall

Production Team
Cameron Booker
Mona Brown
Stephen Carlin
Amy Cornwell
Mary Ann Cosby
Terri Edwards
Carla Hall
Aren Howell
Bob LaRoche
Elizabeth Lewis
Kaylene Riemen
Mike Thomas
Marcella Thompson
Tina Trettin
Donna Winter
Jody York

Indexer
Rebecca Mayfield

Composed in *Stone Serif* and *MCPdigital* by Que Corporation

About the Author

Scott Mueller is president of Mueller Technical Research, an international personal computer research and corporate training firm. Since 1982, MTR has specialized in the industry's most accurate and effective corporate technical training seminars, maintaining a client list that includes Fortune 500 companies, the U.S. and foreign governments, major software and hardware corporations, as well as PC enthusiasts and entrepreneurs. He has logged many thousands of miles presenting his seminars to thousands of PC professionals throughout North and South America, Europe, and Australia.

Mueller has many popular books, articles, and course materials to his credit, in addition to *Upgrading and Repairing PCs*, which has sold more than 600,000 copies in previous editions. He has authored several other books, produced video training tapes published by Learn Key, and written for monthly publications such as the *Troubleshooter*, from Landmark International.

As an internationally recognized seminar director and renowned authority in deciphering technical information, Mueller has developed and presented personal computer training courses in all areas of PC hardware and software. The seminars he conducts cover topics in all areas of PC hardware and data recovery, including upgrades, maintenance, troubleshooting, and repair. He is an expert in PC hardware, data-recovery techniques, local area networks, and major operating systems software including DOS, Windows, and OS/2. Mueller's seminars are available on an on-site contract basis and are conducted for a variety of organizations. Video presentations of Mueller's most popular seminars on PC troubleshooting and repair are available.

When he is not working on books or seminars, he can usually be found working in the garage on various performance car projects, testing the vehicles at the local drag strip, or showing them off at car shows and the local drive-in scene.

For more information about having Mueller put on a custom PC Troubleshooting or Data Recovery seminar for your organization, information about video availability, or just to ask questions, contact:

Mueller Technical Research
21718 Mayfield Lane
Barrington, IL 60010-9733
Phone: (708)726-0709
Fax: (708)726-0710
CompuServe ID: 73145,1566
Internet: 73145.1566@compuserve.com

If you have questions about PC hardware, suggestions for the next version of the book, or any comments in general, send them to Mueller via CompuServe or the Internet if at all possible. Correspondence through standard mail takes him much longer to answer!

Acknowledgments

This fourth edition is the product of a great deal of additional research and development over the previous edition. Several people have helped me with both the research and production of this book. I would like to thank the following people.

First, a very special thanks to my wife and partner, Lynn. This book continues to be an incredible burden on both our business and family life, and she has put up with a lot! Lynn is excellent at dealing with the many companies we have to contact for product information and research. She is the backbone of MTR.

Thanks to Lisa Carlson of Mueller Technical Research for helping with product research and office management. She has fantastic organizational skills that have been a tremendous help in managing all of the information that comes into and goes out of this office.

Thanks to all of the companies who have provided hardware, software, and research information that has been helpful in developing this book. Thanks to Joe Antonelli for feedback from the field about various products. Thanks also to Allen Wyatt, Steve Konicki, Steve Bosak, Barry Nance, and Keith Aleshire for assistance with updating several of the chapters under intense deadline pressure!

I would like to offer a special thanks to the people at Que who have made this book possible. First off, I would like to extend a special thanks to Brad Koch, who has been my main contact at Que and who has overseen this book through both this and the previous edition. Brad works incredible hours, is very dedicated, and is genuinely concerned with the quality and content of this book. I would also like to thank Cheryl Willoughby, who came on this project in the middle, but who has proven very enjoyable to work with. She oversaw the final deadlines and submissions, and her positive attitude and good nature really helped when the pressure was on. Thanks also to Chris Nelson, who did much of the editing and handling of the text once it was submitted. I have enjoyed working with you all!

Finally, I would like to thank all of the people who have attended the many seminars that I have given; you may not realize how much I learn from each of you and your questions! Also thanks to those of you who have written to me with questions and suggestions concerning this book; I welcome all of your comments. It may take me a while, but I do try to reply to every letter. Thanks also to those of you on the many CompuServe forums with both questions and answers, from which I have also learned a great deal.

Trademarks

Contents at a Glance

Introduction 1

**PC Hardware Introduction
and Overview** **7**

1 Personal Computer Background 9

2 Overview of System Features
and Components 15

3 System Teardown and
Inspection 25

Hardware Introduction

Primary System Components **79**

4 Motherboards 81

5 Bus Slots and I/O Cards 95

6 Microprocessor Types and
Specifications 159

7 Memory 227

8 The Power Supply 291

Primary System Components

Input/Output Hardware **325**

9 Input Devices 327

10 Video Display Hardware and
Specifications 375

11 Communications and
Networking 413

12 Audio Hardware 483

Input/Output Hardware

Mass Storage Systems **513**

13 Floppy Disk Drives and
Controllers 515

14 Hard Disk Drives and
Controllers 587

15 CD-ROM Drives 773

16 Tape and Other Mass-Storage
Drives 807

Mass Storage Systems

**System Assembly and
Maintenance** **833**

17 System Upgrades and
Improvements 835

18 Maintaining Your System:
Preventive Maintenance,
Backups, and Warranties 897

Assembly & Maintenance

**Troubleshooting Hardware
and Software Problems** **945**

19 Software and Hardware
Diagnostic Tools 947

20 Operating Systems Software
and Troubleshooting 975

Troubleshooting

IBM System Technical Reference Section   **1047**

21   IBM Personal Computer   1049
     Family Hardware

22   IBM PS/1, PS/ValuePoint,   1107
     and PS/2 System Hardware

23   A Final Word   1327

IBM Technical Reference

Appendixes   **1335**

A   PC Technical Reference   1337
     Section

B   Vendor List   1473

     Index   1505

Appendixes

Contents

Introduction   **1**

What Are the Main Objectives of This Book? 2
Who Should Use This Book? 3
What Is in This Book? 4

I PC Hardware Introduction and Overview   7

1 Personal Computer Background   9

Personal Computing History 9
The IBM Personal Computer 11
The IBM-Compatible Marketplace 14 Years Later 12
Summary 13

2 Overview of System Features and Components   15

Types of Systems 15
Documentation 20
    Types of Documentation 20
    Technical-Reference Manuals 21
    Hardware-Maintenance Manuals 22
    Obtaining Documentation 23
Summary 24

3 System Teardown and Inspection   25

Using the Proper Tools 25
    Hand Tools 25
    Soldering and Desoldering Tools 28
Using Proper Test Equipment 29
    Wrap Plugs (Loopback Connectors) 30
    Meters 30
    Logic Probes and Logic Pulsers 31
    Outlet Testers 31
    Chemicals 32
A Word about Hardware 33
    Types of Hardware 34
    English versus Metric 34
Disassembly Procedures 35
    Disassembly Preparation 35
    XT and Slimline Case Systems 39
    AT and Tower Case Systems 46
    PS/2 Systems 52
Summary 76

II Primary System Components   79

4 Motherboards   81

Replacement Motherboards 82
Knowing What to Look For (Selection Criteria) 83
    Documentation 85
    ROM BIOS Compatibility 85
    Using Correct Speed-Rated Parts 91
Motherboard Form Factors 92
Summary 94

5 Bus Slots and I/O Cards   95

What Is a Bus? 95
    The Processor Bus 96
    The Memory Bus 97
    The Address Bus 98
The Need for Expansion Slots 98
Types of I/O Buses 99
    The ISA Bus 100
    The Micro Channel Bus 106
    The EISA Bus 114
    Local Bus 120
    VESA Local Bus 122
    The PCI Bus 127
    The PCMCIA Bus 138
System Resources 141
    I/O Port Addresses 142
    Interrupts (IRQs) 143
    DMA Channels 146
    Memory 148
Resolving Resource Conflicts 151
    Resolving Conflicts Manually 152
    Using a System-Configuration Template 152
    Heading Off Problems: Special Boards 153
    The Future: Plug-and-Play Systems 155
Summary 157

6 Microprocessor Types and Specifications   159

Processor Specifications 159
    Data Bus 159
    Internal Registers 161
    Address Bus 162
    Processor Speed Ratings 163
Intel Processors 167
    8088 and 8086 Processors 167
    80186 and 80188 Processors 168
    286 Processors 169
    386 Processors 171
    386DX Processors 173
    386SX Processors 173

386SL Processors 174
386 Processor Clones 174
486 Processors 175
Overdrive Processors and Sockets 190
Pentium 203
IBM (Intel-Licensed) Processors 209
IBM SLC Processors 209
Blue Lightning Processors 210
Intel-Compatible Processors 212
Math Coprocessors 212
8087 Coprocessor 214
80287 Coprocessor 216
80387 Coprocessor 218
Weitek Coprocessors 219
80487 Upgrade 220
Processor Tests 221
Known-Defective Chips 221
Other Processor Problems 225
Heat and Cooling Problems 225
Summary 226

7 Memory   227

The System Logical Memory Layout 227
Conventional (Base) Memory 229
Upper Memory Area (UMA) 230
Extended Memory 255
Expanded Memory 258
Preventing ROM BIOS Memory Conflicts and Overlap 260
ROM Shadowing 260
Total Installed Memory versus Total Usable Memory 261
Adapter Memory Configuration and Optimization 264
Physical Memory 270
RAM Chips 271
Physical Storage and Organization 271
Memory Banks 273
Parity Checking 275
Single In-Line Memory Modules (SIMMs) 279
SIMM Pinouts 284
RAM Chip Speed 287
Testing Memory 288
Parity Checking 288
Power-On Self Test 288
Advanced Diagnostic Tests 289
Summary 289

8 The Power Supply   291

Power Supply Function and Operation 291
Power Supply Form Factors 293
Power Supply Connectors 295
The Power_Good Signal 299

Power Supply Loading 300
Power Supply Ratings 302
Power Supply Specifications 304
Power-Use Calculations 306
Leave It On or Turn It Off? 309
Power Supply Problems 310
Power Supply Troubleshooting 312
Digital Multi-Meters 313
Specialized Test Equipment 316
Repairing the Power Supply 321
Obtaining Replacement Units 322
Deciding on a Power Supply 322
Sources for Replacement Power Supplies 323
Summary...324

III Input/Output Hardware   325

9 Input Devices   327

Keyboards 327
Types of Keyboards..327
Keyboard Technology 333
Keyboard Troubleshooting and Repair 356
Reference Material 362
Mice 363
Mouse Interface Types 365
Mouse Troubleshooting 367
Trackpoint II 370
Game Adapter (Joystick) Interface 372
Summary...374

10 Video Display Hardware and Specifications   375

Monitors 375
Display Technologies 375
Monochrome versus Color 378
The Right Size 379
Monitor Resolution 379
Interlaced versus Noninterlaced 380
Energy and Safety 380
Monitor Buying Criteria 382
Video Cards 384
Color Graphics Adapter (CGA) and Display 386
VGA Adapters and Displays 391
Super-VGA (SVGA) 397
VESA SVGA Standards 399
XGA and XGA-2 399
Video Memory 402
Improving Video Speed 403

Video Card Buying Criteria 405
Video Cards for Multimedia 406
Adapter and Display Troubleshooting 410
Summary 411

11 Communications and Networking   413

Using Communications Ports and Devices 413
Serial Ports 413
Serial-Port Configuration 419
Modem Standards 420
Parallel Ports 438
Parallel Port Configuration 440
Detecting Serial and Parallel Ports with DEBUG 441
Testing Serial Ports 442
Testing Parallel Ports 444
Diagnosing Problems with Serial and Parallel Ports 444
Understanding the Components of a LAN 444
Workstations 445
File Servers 445
LAN Cables 446
Network Adapters 448
Evaluating File Server Hardware 452
Evaluating the File Server Hard Disk 453
Evaluating the File Server CPU 453
Evaluating Server RAM 453
Evaluating the Network Adapter Card 454
Evaluating the Server's Power Supply 455
Evaluating the Keyboard, Monitor, and Mouse 455
Examining Protocols, Frames, and Communications 455
Using Frames That Contain Other Frames 456
Using the OSI Model 457
Using Low-Level Protocols 459
Using Ethernet 460
Using Token Ring 463
Using the Fiber Distributed Data Interface (FDDI) 470
Using LAN Cables 472
Using Twisted Pair Cable 472
Using Coaxial Cable 474
Using Fiber Optic Cable 475
Using the IBM Cabling System 476
Connecting the Cables 477
Evaluating Fast Network Adapters 479
Summary 481

12 Audio Hardware   483

Sound Card Applications 483
Games 484
Multimedia 485
MIDI 486
Presentations 486

Screen Savers 487
Recording 487
Voice Annotation 488
Voice Recognition 488
Proofreading 489
Audio CDs 489
Sound Card Concepts and Terms 489
The Nature of Sound 489
Game Standards 490
Frequency Response 490
Sampling 490
8-Bit versus 16-Bit 491
The CD-ROM Connection 492
Sound File Formats 493
Compression/Decompression 494
Sound Card Characteristics 494
Compatibility 494
Sampling 495
Stereo versus Mono 495
CD-ROM Connector 496
Data Compression 496
MIDI Interface 497
Bundled Software 497
Multi-Purpose Digital Signal Processors 497
Sound Drivers 497
Connectors 498
Volume Control 499
Sound Card Options 499
Speakers 499
Microphone 501
Joysticks 502
MIDI Connector 502
Synthesizer 503
Sound Card Installation 503
Troubleshooting Sound Card Problems 505
Hardware Conflicts 505
Other Sound Card Problems 508
Summary 511

IV Mass Storage Systems   513

13 Floppy Disk Drives and Controllers   515

Development of the Floppy Disk Drive 515
Drive Components 516
Read/Write Heads 517
The Head Actuator 520
The Spindle Motor 521
Circuit Boards 522
The Faceplate 523

Connectors 523
Drive-Configuration Devices...525
The Floppy Disk Controller 532
Disk Physical Specifications and Operation 534
Disk Magnetic Properties..537
Logical Operation 539
Types of Floppy Drives 543
The 360K 5 1/4-Inch Drive 544
The 1.2M 5 1/4-Inch Drive 545
The 720K 3 1/2-Inch Drive 546
The 1.44M 3 1/2-Inch Drive 547
The 2.88M 3 1/2-Inch Drive 547
Handling Recording Problems with 1.44M 3 1/2-Inch Drives 548
Handling Recording Problems with 1.2M and 360K Drives 550
Analyzing Floppy Disk Construction 551
Floppy Disk Types and Specifications 553
Formatting and Using High- and Low-Density Disks 557
Caring for and Handling Floppy Disks and Drives 565
Drive-Installation Procedures 568
Drive Configuration 568
Physical Installation 573
Floppy Drive Installation Summary 576
Troubleshooting and Correcting Problems 577
Handling the "Phantom Directory" (Disk Change) 577
Handling Incorrect Media-Sensor Operation 579
Handling Problems Caused by Using Double-Density Disks
    at High Density 579
Handling Track-Width Problems from Writing on 360K Disks
    with a 1.2M Drive 580
Handling Off-Center Disk Clamping 580
Realigning Misaligned Drives 581
Repairing Floppy Drives 581
Cleaning Floppy Drives 582
Setting the Floppy Drive Speed Adjustment 583
Aligning Floppy Disk Drives 585
Summary..586

14 Hard Disk Drives and Controllers   587

Definition of a Hard Disk 587
Hard Drive Advancements 588
Areal Density 588
Hard Disk Drive Operation 589
The Ultimate Hard Disk Drive Analogy! 590
Magnetic Data Storage 591
Data Encoding Schemes 594
Encoding Scheme Comparisons 599
Sectors 601
Basic Hard Disk Drive Components 607
Hard Disk Platters (Disks) 608
Recording Media..609

Read/Write Heads 610
Read/Write Head Designs 612
Head Sliders 615
Head Actuator Mechanisms 615
Air Filters 627
Hard Disk Temperature Acclimation 628
Spindle Motors 629
Spindle Ground Strap 630
Logic Boards 632
Cables and Connectors 632
Configuration Items 634
The Faceplate or Bezel 634
Hard Disk Features 635
Actuator Mechanism 636
Head Parking 636
Reliability 638
Performance 638
Shock Mounting 649
Cost 650
Capacity 650
Specific Recommendations 652
Hard Disk Interfaces 652
The ST-506/412 Interface 654
The ESDI Interface 663
The IDE Interface 666
Introduction to SCSI 681
IDE versus SCSI 710
Recommended Aftermarket Controllers and Host Adapters 711
Hard Disk Installation Procedures 715
Controller Configuration 716
Physical Installation 721
System Configuration 722
Formatting and Software Installation 736
Disk Hardware and Software Limitations 761
Disk Interface Capacity Limitations 761
ROM BIOS Capacity Limitations 763
Operating-System Capacity Limitations 763
Hard Disk Drive Troubleshooting and Repair 764
17xx, 104xx, and 210xxxx Hardware Error Codes 764
Drive Spin Failure (Stiction) 767
Logic Board Failures 770
Summary 771

15 CD-ROM Drives   773

What Is CD-ROM? 773
CD-ROM, a Brief History 774
CD Technology 774
Inside Data CDs 775
What Types of Drives Are Available? 777
CD-ROM Drive Specifications 777

Interface 779
CD-ROM Disc and Drive Formats 780
Multimedia CD-ROM 786
Other Drive Features 787
Installing Your Drive 788
Avoiding Conflict: Get Your Cards in Order 788
External CD-ROM Hook-Up 794
Internal Drive Installation 795
SCSI Chains: Internal, External, a Little of Both ... 798
CD-ROM Software on Your PC 800
Software Loaded, Ready to Run 803
Media Player 804
Summary 805

16 Tape and Other Mass-Storage Drives — 807

Tape Backup Drives 807
The Origins of Tape Backup Standards 809
The QIC Standards 809
Common QIC Tape Backup Types 812
Newer High-Capacity QIC-Standard Drives 815
QIC-Tape Compatibility 816
Other High-Capacity Tape Drive Standards 817
Choosing a Tape Backup Drive 819
Tape Drive Installation Issues 821
Tape Drive Backup Software 824
Removable Storage Drives 826
Magnetic Media Drives 827
Floptical Drives 828
Magneto-Optical Drives 829
Write-Once Read-Many (WORM) Drives 831
Summary 832

V System Assembly and Maintenance — 833

17 System Upgrades and Improvements — 835

Upgrading Goals 836
Upgrading by Increasing System Memory 837
Conventional Memory 837
Extended Memory 838
Expanded Memory 838
Upgrade Strategies 839
Adding Motherboard Memory 839
Selecting and Installing memory Chips or SIMMs ... 839
Adding Adapter Boards 847
Installing Memory 847
Installing 640K on an XT Motherboard 850
Upgrading the ROM BIOS 853
Keyboard-Controller Chips 855
BIOS Manufacturers and Vendors 855

Alternatives to Upgrading the BIOS 857
Special ROM BIOS-Related Problems 858
Changes to an Existing BIOS 858
Upgrading Disk Drives 867
Upgrading a Floppy Disk Drive 867
Adding a High-Density Floppy Drive to an XT System 872
Adding a Hard Disk to a System 872
Speeding Up a System 873
Math Coprocessors 873
Main-CPU Upgrades or Replacements 876
Adding High-Performance Video 887
Adding a Hardware Reset Switch 888
Upgrading the DOS Version 892
Upgrading DOS the Easy Way 893
Upgrading DOS the Hard Way 894
Summary..895

18 Maintaining Your System: Preventive Maintenance, Backups, and Warranties   897

Developing a Preventive Maintenance Program 898
Active Preventive Maintenance Procedures 898
Hard Disk Maintenance 909
Passive Preventive Maintenance Procedures 915
Using Power-Protection Systems 924
Surge Suppressors (Protectors) 926
Phone Line Surge Protectors 927
Line Conditioners 927
Backup Power 928
Using Data-Backup Systems 930
Backup Policies 931
Dedicated Backup Hardware 934
Recommended Backup System 939
Purchasing Warranty and Service Contracts 939
Summary..943

VI Troubleshooting Hardware and Software Problems   945

19 Software and Hardware Diagnostic Tools   947

Diagnostic Software 947
The Power-On Self Test (POST) 948
What Is Tested? 948
POST Audio Error Codes 949
POST Visual Error Codes 950
I/O Port POST Codes 950

IBM Diagnostics 953
   IBM System Diagnostics 953
   IBM Advanced Diagnostics 956
General Purpose Diagnostics Programs 962
   AMIDiag 963
   Checkit Pro 963
   Micro-Scope 964
   Norton Diagnostics 965
   PC Technician 966
   QAPlus/FE 966
   Service Diagnostics 967
Disk Diagnostics 968
   Drive Probe 968
   Disk Manager 969
Data Recovery Utilities 970
   Norton Utilities 970
   Others 971
Configuration Utilities 971
   MSD (Microsoft Diagnostics) 971
   InfoSpotter 972
   SysChk 972
Windows Diagnostic Software 972
Shareware and Public-Domain Diagnostics 973
Summary 974

20 Operating Systems Software and Troubleshooting   975

Disk Operating System (DOS) 975
   Operating System Basics 976
   The System ROM BIOS 977
   DOS Components 979
   The I/O System and System Files 979
   DOS History 987
   The Boot Process 990
   How DOS Loads and Starts 991
   File Management 995
   DOS File Space Allocation 995
   Interfacing to Disk Drives 997
   DOS Structures 1003
   Potential DOS Upgrade Problems 1013
   Known Bugs in DOS 1017
   PS/2 BIOS Update (DASDDRVR.SYS) 1023
   DOS Disk and Data Recovery 1029
   The DEBUG Program 1040
   Memory-Resident Software Conflicts........................1043
   Hardware Problems versus Software Problems 1044
Summary 1045

VII IBM System Technical Reference Section   1047

21 IBM Personal Computer Family Hardware   1049

System-Unit Features by Model 1050
An Introduction to the PC 1050
PC Models and Features 1053
PC Technical Specifications 1054
An Introduction to the PC Convertible 1059
PC Convertible Specifications and Highlights 1061
PC Convertible Models and Features 1063
Memory Cards 1063
Optional Printers 1063
Serial/Parallel Adapters 1063
CRT Display Adapters 1063
Internal Modems 1064
Printer Cables 1064
Battery Chargers 1064
Automobile Power Adapters 1064
The IBM 5144 PC Convertible Monochrome Display 1064
The IBM 5145 PC Convertible Color Display 1065
An Introduction to the XT 1065
XT Models and Features 1068
XT Technical Specifications 1070
An Introduction to the 3270 PC 1075
3270 PC Models and Features 1075
The 3270 System Adapter 1075
The Display Adapter 1076
The Extended Graphics Adapter 1076
Programmed Symbols 1076
The Keyboard Adapter 1076
Software 1077
Windows 1077
Special Facilities 1077
The Significance of the 3270 1078
An Introduction to the XT 370 1079
XT/370 Models and Features 1079
An Introduction to the Portable PC 1080
Portable PC Technical Specifications 1082
An Introduction to the AT 1085
AT Models and Features 1088
AT Technical Specifications 1092
AT 3270 1097
The AT-370 1098
An Introduction to the XT Model 286 1098
XT Model 286 Models and Features 1100
XT Model 286 Technical Specifications 1101
Summary 1105

22 IBM PS/1, PS/ValuePoint, and PS/2 System Hardware   1107

Differences between the PS/x Systems 1107
   PS/2 1108
   PS/1 1109
   PS/ValuePoint 1109
   Ambra 1110
   The Major Differences 1110
   Micro Channel Architecture (MCA) Slots 1114
PS/2 System-Unit Features by Model 1116
   Decoding PS/2 Model Numbers 1117
   Differences between PS/2 and PC Systems 1130
   PS/2 Model 25 1130
   PS/2 Model 30 1139
   PS/2 Model 25 286 1148
   PS/2 Model 30 286 1153
   PS/2 Model 35 SX 1160
   PS/2 Model 40 SX 1165
   PS/2 Model L40 SX 1170
   PS/2 Model 50 1176
   PS/2 E 1184
   PS/2 Model 53 1188
   PS/2 Model 55 SX 1192
   PS/2 Model 56 SX, SLC, LS, and LS SLC 1199
   PS/2 Model 56 486SLC3, LS, and 57 486SLC3, M57 486SLC3
     Ultimedia 1204
   PS/2 Model 57 SX 1207
   PS/2 Model 60 1216
   PS/2 Model 65 SX 1223
   PS/2 Model 70 386 1230
   PS/2 Model 70 486 1238
   PS/2 Model P70 386 1242
   PS/2 Model P75 486 1249
   PS/2 Models 76, 77, and 77s Ultimedia 1254
   PS/2 Model 80 386 1260
   PS/2 Model 90 XP 486 1270
   PS/2 Model 95 XP 486 1275
PS/1 System-Unit Features by Model 1283
PS/ValuePoint System-Unit Features by Model...1298
   Support 1298
   System Features 1298
   Decoding ValuePoint Model Numbers 1299
   ValuePoint P60/D 1300
   ValuePoint Performance Series 1303
   ValuePoint Si Series 1306
PS/2 BIOS Information 1308
Summary of IBM Hard Disk Drives 1312
Summary...1326

23 A Final Word   1327

Manuals 1328
Machines 1330
Modems 1332
Magazines 1333
The Appendixes 1334
In Conclusion 1334

Appendixes   1335

A PC Technical Reference Section   1337

General Information 1338
    ASCII Character Code Charts 1338
    Hexadecimal/ASCII Conversions 1339
    Extended ASCII Keycodes for ANSI.SYS 1343
    EBCDIC Character Codes 1343
    Metric System (SI) Prefixes 1348
    Powers of 2 1348
Hardware and ROM BIOS Data 1349
    IBM PC and XT Motherboard Switch Settings 1350
    AT CMOS RAM Addresses 1350
    IBM BIOS Model, Submodel, and Revision Codes 1353
    Disk Software Interfaces 1355
Motherboard Connectors 1357
System Video Information 1358
    Monitor ID Pins 1360
Modem Control Codes 1361
Printer Control Codes 1368
DOS Disk Structures and Layout 1376
    DOS Boot Record 1378
    Directory Structure 1379
Hard Disk Drives 1379
    AT Motherboard BIOS Hard Drive Tables 1396
Troubleshooting Error Codes 1410
    ROM BIOS Port 80h Power-On Self Test (POST) Codes 1410
    AMI BIOS Audio and Port 80h Error Codes 1411
    Hewlett Packard POST and Diagnostics Error Codes 1420
    IBM POST and Diagnostics Display Error Codes 1424
    IBM SCSI Error Codes 1453
    DOS Error Messages 1460
IBM Technical Manuals and Updates 1462
    Guide to Operations and Quick-Reference Manuals 1462
    Hardware-Maintenance Library 1463
    Technical-Reference Library 1467
    Ordering Information 1471

B Vendor List   1473

Index   1505

Introduction

Welcome to *Upgrading and Repairing PCs*, 4th Edition. This book is for people who want to upgrade, repair, maintain, and troubleshoot computers. It covers the full range of IBM and IBM-compatible systems.

In addition, this book covers state-of-the-art hardware that makes the most modern personal computers easier, faster, and more productive to use. Hardware coverage includes systems based on the 486 and Pentium CPU chips, local bus technology, CD-ROM drives, tape backups, sound boards, PCMCIA devices for laptops, IDE and SCSI-interface devices, larger and faster hard drives, and increased system memory capacity.

The comprehensive coverage of the IBM-compatible personal computer in this book has consistently won acclaim. With the release of this 4th edition, *Upgrading and Repairing PCs* takes its place as one of the most comprehensive and easily used references on even the most modern systems—those based on cutting-edge hardware and software. The book examines personal computer systems in depth, outlines the differences among them, and presents options for configuring each system at the time you purchase it.

Sections of this book provide detailed information about each internal component of a personal computer system, from the processor to the keyboard and video display. The book examines the options available in modern, high-performance PC configurations, and how to use them to your advantage; it focuses on much of the hardware and software available today and specifies the optimum configurations for achieving maximum benefit for the time and money you spend. At a glance, here are the major system components and peripherals covered in this edition of *Upgrading and Repairing PCs*:

- Pentium, 486, and earlier central processing unit (CPU) chips

- The latest processor upgrade socket specifications

- Special bus architectures and devices including high-speed PCI (Peripheral Component Interconnect) and VL-Bus (Video Local), EISA (Extended Industry Standard Architecture), and MCA (Micro Channel Architecture)

- Plug-and-play architecture

- Larger, faster hard drives and hard drive interfaces, including IDE and SCSI

- Floppy drives, including 360K, 1.2M, 1.44M, and 2.88M drives

- New storage devices such as CD-ROM and magneto-optical drives

- Increased system memory capacity

- Large-screen Super VGA monitors and high-speed graphics adapter cards

- Peripheral devices such as CD-ROM drives, sound boards, and tape backups

- PCMCIA devices for laptops

- Multimedia

This book also shows you how to troubleshoot the kind of hardware problems that can make PC upgrading and repairing difficult. Troubleshooting coverage includes DMA channel and IRQ problems, and memory address conflicts. This book tells you how to avoid these kinds of problems, and how to make installing a new adapter board in your computer a simple plug-and-play operation. This book also focuses on software problems, starting with the basics of how DOS or another operating system works with your system hardware to start up your system. You also learn how to troubleshoot and avoid problems involving system hardware, the operating system, and applications software such as word processors or spreadsheets.

This book is the result of years of research and development in the production of my PC hardware, operating system, and data recovery seminars. Over the years I have personally taught thousands of people about PC troubleshooting, upgrading, maintenance, repair, and data recovery. This book represents the culmination of many years of field experience as well as knowledge culled from the experiences of thousands of others. What originally started out as a simple course workbook has over the years grown into a complete reference on the subject. Now you can benefit from this experience and research.

What Are the Main Objectives of This Book?

Upgrading and Repairing PCs focuses on several objectives. The primary objective is to help you learn how to maintain, upgrade, and repair your PC system. To that end, *Upgrading and Repairing PCs* helps you fully understand the family of computers that has grown from the original IBM PC, including IBM and IBM-compatible systems. This book discusses all areas of system improvement such as floppy disks, hard disks, central processing units, math coprocessors, and power-supply improvements. The book discusses proper system and component care; it specifies the most failure-prone items in different PC systems, and tells you how to locate and identify a failing component. You learn about powerful diagnostics hardware and software that enable a system to help you determine the cause of a problem and how to repair it.

The IBM-compatible microcomputer family is moving forward rapidly in power and capabilities. Processor performance increases with every new chip design. *Upgrading and Repairing PCs* helps you gain an understanding of each of the CPU chips used in IBM and IBM-compatible computer systems.

This book covers the important differences between major system architectures—the original Industry Standard Architecture (ISA), Extended Industry Standard Architecture (EISA), and Micro Channel Architecture (MCA). The most modern systems use special local bus architectures and adapter cards to get top speed from system peripherals like video adapter cards and hard drives. Besides ISA, EISA, and MCA, these local bus architectures include PCI (Peripheral Component Interconnect) and VL-Bus devices. *Upgrading and Repairing PCs* covers each of these system architectures and their adapter boards to help you make decisions about which kind of system you may want to buy in the future, and how to upgrade and troubleshoot such systems.

The amount of storage space available to modern PCs is increasing geometrically. *Upgrading and Repairing PCs* covers storage options ranging from larger, faster hard drives to state-of-the-art storage devices. In addition, this book provides detailed information on upgrading and troubleshooting system RAM.

When you finish reading this book, you should have the knowledge to upgrade as well as troubleshoot and repair almost all systems and components.

Who Should Use This Book?

Upgrading and Repairing PCs is designed for people who want a good understanding of how their PC systems work. Each section fully explains common and not-so-common problems, what causes problems, and how to handle problems when they arise. You will gain an understanding of disk configuration and interfacing, for example, that can improve your diagnostics and troubleshooting skills. You'll develop a feel for what goes on in a system so that you can rely on your own judgment and observations and not some table of canned troubleshooting steps. This book is for people who are truly interested in their systems and how they operate.

Upgrading and Repairing PCs is written for people who will select, install, configure, maintain, and repair systems they or their companies use. To accomplish these tasks, you need a level of knowledge much higher than that of an average system user. You must know exactly which tool to use for a task and how to use the tool correctly. This book can help you achieve this level of knowledge.

What Is in This Book?

Part I serves primarily as an introduction. Chapter 1 begins this part with an introduction to the development of the IBM PC and compatibles. Chapter 2 provides information about the different types of systems you encounter and what separates one type of system from another, including the types of system buses that differentiate systems. Chapter 2 also provides an overview of the types of PC systems that help build a foundation of knowledge essential for the remainder of the book. Chapter 3 discusses the physical disassembly and reassembly of a system.

Part II covers the primary system components of a PC. Chapter 4 begins this discussion of the components in a PC system by covering the motherboard. Chapter 5 continues this discussion by focusing on the different types of expansion slots and bus types found in PC systems. Chapter 6 goes into detail about the central processing unit (CPU), or main processor, including those from Intel as well as from other companies. Chapter 7 gives a detailed discussion of PC memory, from basic architecture to the physical chips and SIMMs themselves. Chapter 8 is a detailed investigation of the power supply, which remains as the primary cause for PC system problems and failures.

Part III is about input/output hardware and begins with Chapter 9 on input devices. This chapter includes coverage of keyboards, pointing devices, and the game port. Chapter 10 discusses video display hardware, including video adapters and monitors. Chapter 11 is a detailed discussion of communications and networking hardware, and Chapter 12 focuses on audio hardware, including sound boards and speaker systems.

Part IV is about mass storage systems and leads off with Chapter 13 on floppy disk drives and controllers. Chapter 14 is a detailed discussion of hard disk drives and controllers, including IDE and SCSI in depth. This information is invaluable when you install drives as either replacements or upgrades in a system, and if you troubleshoot and repair malfunctioning drives. Chapter 15 is about CD-ROM drives, and Chapter 16 covers tape and other mass storage drives.

Part V covers system assembly and maintenance. Chapter 17 discusses system upgrades and improvements. Chapter 18 covers system preventive maintenance, backups, and warranties.

Part VI covers troubleshooting and diagnostics and starts off with Chapter 19 on diagnostic tools. Chapter 20 covers operating system software and troubleshooting.

Part VII is a technical reference section that covers in considerable depth each IBM PC and PS/2 model and lists differences among individual versions of each system. Technical specifications for each system are highlighted in these chapters also. This information is useful not only for supporting actual IBM equipment, but also for IBM-compatible systems not supplied with extensive documentation. You learn how to compare systems with the IBM standard. This part begins with Chapter 21 on the IBM classic PC family hardware. Chapter 22 is a reference to the IBM PS/1, PS/Valuepoint, and PS/2 system hardware.

Appendix A provides an extensive PC technical reference section, including a variety of technical information tables. Appendix B provides an extremely detailed vendor list useful for finding suppliers and vendors of necessary hardware and software.

I believe that *Upgrading and Repairing PCs*, 4th Edition, will prove to be the best book of its kind on the market. It offers not only the breadth of IBM and compatible equipment, but also much in-depth coverage of each topic. This book is valuable as a reference tool for understanding how various components in a system interact and operate, and as a guide to repairing and servicing problems you encounter. *Upgrading and Repairing PCs* is far more than just a repair manual. I sincerely hope that you enjoy it.

Part I

PC Hardware Introduction and Overview

1 Personal Computer Background

2 Overview of System Features and Components

3 System Teardown and Inspection

Chapter 1

Personal Computer Background

Many discoveries and inventions have contributed to the development of the machine known today as the personal computer. Examining a few important developmental landmarks can help bring the whole picture into focus.

Personal Computing History

A modern digital computer is largely a collection of electronic switches. These switches are used to represent, as well as control, the routing of data elements called *binary digits* (bits). Because of the on or off nature of the binary information and signal routing used by the computer, an efficient electronic switch was required. The first electronic computers used vacuum tubes as switches, and although the tubes worked, they had many problems.

The tube was inefficient as a switch. It consumed a great deal of electrical power and gave off enormous heat—a significant problem in the earlier systems. Tubes were notoriously unreliable also; one failed every two hours or so in the larger systems.

The invention of the transistor, or semiconductor, was one of the most important developments leading to the personal computer revolution. The transistor was invented in 1948 by John Bardeen, Walter Brattain, and William Shockley (engineers at Bell Laboratories). The transistor, essentially a solid-state electronic switch, replaced the much less suitable vacuum tube. Because the transistor consumed significantly less power, a computer system built with transistors was much smaller, faster, and more efficient than a computer system built with vacuum tubes.

The conversion to transistors began a trend toward miniaturization that continues to this day. Today's small laptop (or palmtop) PC systems, which run on batteries, have more computing power than many earlier systems that filled rooms and consumed huge amounts of electrical power.

In 1959, engineers at Texas Instruments invented the integrated circuit (IC), a semiconductor circuit that contains more than one transistor on the same base (or substrate material) and connects the transistors without wires. The first IC contained only six transistors. By comparison, the Intel Pentium microprocessor used in many of today's high-end systems has more than 3.1 million transistors, and the successor to the Pentium, code named P6, will have more than 6 million transistors! Today, there are many ICs with transistor counts in the multi-million range.

In 1969, Intel introduced a 1K-bit memory chip, which was much larger than anything else available at the time. (1K-bits equals 1,024 bits, a byte equals 8 bits; this chip, therefore, stored only 128 bytes—not much by today's standards.) Because of Intel's success in chip manufacturing and design, Busicomp, a Japanese calculator-manufacturing company, asked Intel to produce 12 different logic chips for one of its calculator designs. Rather than produce the 12 separate chips, Intel engineers included all the functions of the chips in a single chip. In addition to incorporating all the functions and capabilities of the 12-chip design into one multipurpose chip, they designed the chip to be controlled by a program that could alter the function of the chip. The chip then was "generic" in nature: it could function in designs other than just a calculator. Previously, designs were hard-wired for one purpose with built-in instructions; this chip could read from memory a variable set of instructions, which controlled the function of the chip. The idea was to design almost an entire computing device on one chip that could perform different functions depending on what instructions it was given. The first microprocessor, the Intel 4004, a 4-bit processor, was introduced in 1971. The chip operated on 4 bits of data at a time. The 4004 chip's successor was the 8008 8-bit microprocessor in 1972.

In 1973, some of the first microcomputer kits based on the 8008 chip were developed. These kits were little more than demonstration tools and did little except blink lights. In late 1973, Intel introduced the 8080 microprocessor, which was 10 times faster than the earlier 8008 chip and addressed 64K of memory. This breakthrough was the one the personal computer industry was waiting for.

MITS introduced the Altair kit in a cover story in the January 1975 issue of *Popular Electronics* magazine. The Altair kit, considered to be the first personal computer, included an 8080 processor, a power supply, a front panel with a large number of lights, and 256 bytes (not kilobytes) of memory. The kit sold for $395 and had to be assembled. The computer included an open architecture bus (slots) that prompted various add-ons and peripherals from aftermarket companies. The new processor inspired other companies to write programs, including the CP/M (Control Program for Microprocessors) operating system and the first version of Microsoft BASIC.

IBM introduced what can be called its first *personal computer* in 1975. The Model 5100 had 16K of memory, a built-in 16-line-by-64-character display, a built-in BASIC language interpreter, and a built-in DC-300 cartridge tape drive for storage. The system's $9,000 price placed it out of the mainstream personal computer marketplace, dominated by experimenters (affectionately referred to as hackers) who built low-cost kits ($500 or so) as a hobby. The IBM system obviously was not in competition for this low-cost market and did not sell well. The Model 5100 was succeeded by the 5110 and 5120 before IBM introduced what we know as the IBM Personal Computer (Model 5150). Although the 5100 series preceded the IBM PC, there was nothing in common between these older systems and the 5150 IBM PC released later. The PC it turned out was very closely related to the IBM System/23 DataMaster, an office computer system introduced in 1980.

In 1976, a new company, Apple Computer, introduced the Apple I (for $695). This system consisted of a main circuit board screwed to a piece of plywood. A case and power supply were not included. Only a handful of these computers were made, and they reportedly have sold to collectors for more than $20,000. The Apple II, introduced in 1977, helped set the standard for nearly all the important microcomputers to follow, including the IBM PC.

The microcomputer world was dominated in 1980 by two types of computer systems. One type, the Apple II, claimed a large following of loyal users and a gigantic software base that was growing at a fantastic rate. The other type consisted not of a single system, but included all the many systems that evolved from the original MITS Altair. These systems were compatible with each other and were distinguished by their use of the CP/M operating system and expansion slots that followed the S-100 (for slots with 100 pins) standard. All these systems were built by a variety of companies and sold under various names. For the most part, however, these companies used the same software and plug-in hardware.

The IBM Personal Computer

At the end of 1980, IBM had decided to truly compete in the rapidly growing low-cost personal computer market. The company established what was then called the Entry Systems Division, in Boca Raton, Florida, to develop the new system. This small group consisted of 12 engineers and designers under the direction of Don Estridge. The team's chief designer was Lewis Eggebrecht. The division developed IBM's first real PC. (IBM considered the 5100 system, developed in 1975, to be an intelligent programmable terminal rather than a genuine computer, even though it truly was a computer.) Nearly all these engineers moved from working on the System/23 DataMaster project, a small, office computer system introduced in 1980 (and the direct predecessor of the IBM PC).

Much of the PC's design was influenced by the DataMaster's design. In the DataMaster's single-piece design, the display and keyboard were integrated into the unit. Because these features were limiting, they became external units on the PC—although the PC keyboard layout and electrical designs were copied from the DataMaster. Several other parts of the IBM PC system also were copied from the DataMaster, including the expansion bus, or input-output slots, which included not only the same physical 62-pin connector, but also the almost identical pin specifications. This copying was possible because the PC used the same interrupt controller and a similar direct memory access (DMA) controller as the DataMaster. Expansion cards already designed for the DataMaster could then be easily "ported" to the PC. The DataMaster used an Intel 8085 CPU, which had a 64K address limit, and an 8-bit internal and external data bus. This prompted the PC design team to use the Intel 8088 CPU in the PC, which offered a much larger 1M memory address limit, and had an internal 16-bit data bus, but only an 8-bit external data bus. The 8-bit external data bus and similar instruction set allowed the 8088 to be easily interfaced into the earlier DataMaster designs.

Estridge and the design team rapidly developed the design and specifications for the new system. In addition to borrowing from the System/23 DataMaster, the team also studied the marketplace, which also had enormous influence on the IBM PC's design. The designers looked at the prevailing standards, learned from the success of those systems, and incorporated into the new PC all the features of the popular systems—and more. With the parameters for design made obvious by the market, IBM produced a system that filled perfectly its niche in the market.

IBM brought its system from idea to delivery in one year by using existing designs and purchasing as many components as possible from outside vendors. The Entry Systems Division was granted autonomy from IBM's other divisions and could tap resources outside the company rather than go through the bureaucratic procedures required to use only IBM resources. IBM contracted out the PC's languages and operating system, for example, to a small company named Microsoft. (IBM originally had contacted Digital Research, which invented CP/M, but that company apparently was not interested in the proposal. Microsoft was interested, however, and since has become one of the largest software companies in the world.) The use of outside vendors was also an open invitation for the aftermarket to jump in and support the system. And it did.

On Wednesday, August 12, 1981, a new standard took its place in the microcomputer industry with the debut of the IBM PC. Since then, IBM has sold more than 10 million PCs, and the PC has grown into a large family of computers and peripherals. More software has been written for this family than for any other system on the market.

The IBM-Compatible Marketplace 14 Years Later

In the more than 14 years since the original IBM PC was introduced, many changes have occurred. For example, the IBM-compatible computer advanced from a 4.77 MHz 8088-based system to 100 MHz 486-based and 100 MHz Pentium-based systems—nearly *200 times faster* than the original IBM PC (in actual processing speed, not just clock speed). The original PC could have only two single-sided floppy drives that stored 160K each using DOS 1.0, whereas modern systems easily can have several gigabytes of hard disk storage. A rule of thumb in the computer industry is that available processor performance and disk storage capacity at least doubles every two to three years. Since the beginning of the PC industry this pattern has shown no signs of changing.

In addition to performance and storage capacity, another major change since the original IBM PC was introduced is that IBM is not the only manufacturer of "IBM-compatible" systems. IBM invented the IBM-compatible standard, of course, and continues to set standards that compatible systems follow, but it does not dominate the market as before. As often as not, new standards in the PC industry are developed by companies and organizations other than IBM. Hundreds of system manufacturers produce computers compatible with IBM's systems, not to mention the thousands of peripheral manufacturers with components that expand and enhance IBM and IBM-compatible systems.

IBM-compatible systems have thrived not only because compatible hardware could easily be assembled, but also because the primary operating system was available not from IBM, but from a third party (Microsoft). This allowed other manufacturers to license the operating systems software from Microsoft and to sell their own compatible systems. The fact that DOS borrowed the best functions from both CP/M and UNIX probably had a lot to do with the amount of software that became available. Later, with the success of Windows and OS/2, there would be even more reasons for software developers to write programs for IBM-compatible systems. One of the reasons that Apple Macintosh systems will never enjoy the success of IBM compatibles is that Apple controls all the software and does not license it to others for use in compatible systems. It is fortunate for the computing public as a whole that IBM did otherwise. The competition between manufacturers and vendors of IBM-compatible systems is the reason that such systems offer so much performance and capabilities for the money compared to other non-IBM compatible systems.

The IBM-compatible market continues to thrive and prosper. New technology will be integrated into these systems and enable them to grow with the times. Because of both the high value these types of systems can offer for the money and the large amount of software available to run on them, IBM and IBM-compatible systems likely will dominate the personal computer marketplace for perhaps the next 10 years as well.

Summary

This chapter traced the development of personal computing from the transistor to the introduction of the IBM PC. Intel's continuing development of the integrated circuit led to a succession of microprocessors and reached a milestone with the 1973 introduction of the 8080 chip. In 1975, MITS introduced the Altair computer kit, based on the 8080 microprocessor. IBM jumped into the personal computer market with the Model 5100 in 1975.

In 1976, Apple sold its first computers, followed in 1977 by the enormously successful Apple II. Because of its success, the Apple II played a major role in setting standards and expectations for all later microcomputers.

Finally, in 1981, IBM introduced its Personal Computer to a microcomputer world dominated by the Apple II and the computers that evolved from the Altair, which used the CP/M operating system. The IBM PC, designed with the needs of the market in mind and with many of its components produced by outside vendors, immediately set the new standard for the microcomputer industry. This standard has evolved to meet the needs of today's users, with more powerful systems that offer performance levels not even imagined in 1981.

Chapter 2

Overview of System Features and Components

This chapter discusses the differences in system architecture of IBM and compatible systems and explains memory structure and use. It also discusses how to obtain the service manuals necessary to maintain and upgrade your computer.

Types of Systems

Many types of IBM and compatible systems are on the market today. Most systems are similar to one another, but a few important differences in system architecture have become more apparent as operating environments such as Windows and OS/2 have increased in popularity. Operating systems such as OS/2 1.x require at least a 286 CPU platform on which to run. OS/2 2.x requires at least a 386 CPU. Environments such as Windows offer different capabilities and operating modes based on the capabilities of the hardware platform on which you run it. Knowing and understanding the differences in these hardware platforms will enable you to plan, install, and utilize modern operating systems and applications to use the hardware optimally.

All IBM and compatible systems can be broken down into two basic system types, or classes, of hardware:

- PC/XT class systems
- AT class systems

The term *PC* stands for Personal Computer, of course, while *XT* stands for eXTended. The XT is basically a PC system that includes a hard disk for storage in addition to the floppy drive(s) found in the normal PC system. These systems have an 8-bit 8088 processor and an 8-bit Industry Standard Architecture (ISA) Bus for system expansion. The *bus* is the name given to expansion slots where additional plug-in circuit boards can be installed. The 8-bit designation comes from the fact that the ISA Bus found in the PC/XT class systems can only send or receive 8-bits of data in a single cycle. The data in an 8-bit bus is sent along eight wires simultaneously in parallel.

More advanced systems are said to be *AT class,* which indicates that they follow certain standards first set forth in the IBM AT system. *AT* stands for Advanced Technology, which is the designation IBM applied to systems that first included more advanced 16-bit (and later 32- and 64-bit) processors and expansion slots. AT class systems must have any processor compatible with the Intel 286 or higher processors (including the 386, 486, and Pentium processors) and must have a 16-bit or greater expansion slot system. The bus architecture is central to AT compatibility; PC/XT class systems with upgraded processor boards that do not include the 16-bit or greater expansion bus do not qualify as true AT systems. The first AT systems have a 16-bit version of the ISA Bus, which is an extension of the original 8-bit ISA Bus found in the PC/XT class systems. Eventually a number of expansion slot or bus designs were developed for AT class systems, including those listed here:

- 16-bit ISA Bus

- 16/32-bit Enhanced ISA (EISA) Bus

- 16/32-bit PS/2 Micro Channel Architecture (MCA) Bus

- 16-bit Personal Computer Memory Card International Association (PCMCIA) Bus

- 16/32/64-bit Video Local (VL) Bus

- 32/64-bit Peripheral Component Interconnect (PCI) Bus

A system with any of these types of expansion slots is by definition an AT class system, regardless of the actual processor used. AT-type systems with 386 or higher processors have special capabilities not found in the first generation of 286-based ATs. The 386 and higher systems have distinct capabilities regarding memory addressing, memory management, and possible 32-bit-wide access to data. Most systems with 386DX or higher chips have 32-bit slots to take full advantage of the 32-bit data-transfer capabilities.

The ISA and MCA architectures were developed by IBM and copied by other manufacturers for use in compatible systems. Other expansion bus designs were independently derived by other companies. For years the ISA Bus dominated the IBM-compatible marketplace. When the 32-bit 386DX processor debuted, however, there arose a need for a 32-bit expansion slot design to match. IBM took the high road and developed the Micro Channel Architecture Bus, which has outstanding technical capabilities compared to the previous ISA designs. Unfortunately, IBM has had a difficult time marketing the MCA Bus due to problems with the high cost of manufacturing MCA motherboards and adapter cards, as well as the perceived notion that MCA is proprietary. Although it is not, IBM has not succeeded in marketing it as the new bus of choice, and it has remained largely a feature of IBM systems only. The rest of the marketplace has for the most part ignored MCA, although a few companies have produced MCA-compatible systems and many companies produce MCA expansion adapters.

Compaq, for example, was the primary architect of the Extended Industry Standard Architecture Bus. Realizing the difficulty IBM had in marketing its new MCA Bus, Compaq decided that the best approach would be to give the bus design away rather than to keep it as a Compaq-only feature. They feared a repeat of what IBM was going through in trying to get the MCA Bus accepted throughout the industry. After all, how many companies would market expansion cards for a new bus unique to Compaq systems? Compaq decided that others should share in their new design, and they contacted a number of other system manufacturers to see if they were interested in participating. This led to the EISA consortium, which in September 1988 debuted the Compaq-designed expansion bus: Extended Industry Standard Architecture (EISA). The system is a 32-bit slot for use with 386DX or higher systems.

Speculators said that EISA was developed to circumvent the royalties IBM charges competitors who use the ISA or MCA slot design in their systems. This speculation was false because EISA is an extension of the IBM-developed ISA Bus, and manufacturers of EISA systems must pay IBM the same licensing fees as do manufacturers of ISA or MCA systems. EISA was developed not to circumvent licensing fees, but to show technological leadership and to enable Compaq and other companies to have some design freedom and control over their systems. Whether EISA, an alternative to the IBM-designed MCA, becomes a useful standard depends on the popularity of systems that use the slot.

Unfortunately, EISA never achieved great popularity and sold in far smaller numbers than did MCA systems. There are fewer EISA expansion adapters than MCA adapters, as well. This failure in the marketplace occurred for several reasons. One is the high cost of integrating the EISA Bus into a system. The special EISA Bus controller chips add several hundred dollars to the cost of a motherboard. In fact, having EISA slots onboard can double the cost of the motherboard. Another reason for the relative failure of EISA was the fact that the performance it offered was actually greater than most peripherals it could be connected to! This incompatibility in performance was also true for MCA. The available hard disks and other peripherals could not transfer data as fast as the 16-bit ISA Bus could handle, so why use EISA, a still faster bus? Memory had already found its way off the standard bus and was normally installed directly on the motherboard via SIMMs (Single In-line Memory Modules). EISA complicated system installation and configuration whenever standard ISA boards were mixed with EISA boards. The standard ISA boards could not be controlled by the EISA configuration program required to configure the jumper and switchless EISA cards. In the years following EISA's introduction, it found a niche in high-end server systems because of the bus's increased bandwidth. For standard workstations, however, the EISA Bus has been superseded by VL-Bus and PCI.

The newest trend in expansion slots is the *local bus*. This type of bus is connected closely or directly to the processor. A problem with ISA and EISA is that the bus speed was locked in at 8.33 MHz, which was far slower than the processors. MCA offered greater performance, but it was still limited compared to the advancements in processors. What was needed were expansion slots that could talk directly to the processor, at processor speed, using all the bits the processor could handle. The first of the local buses to achieve popularity was the Video Local Bus, so named because it actually was designed for video adapters. The VL-Bus was created initially by NEC Corporation, who sought to include it in their systems to allow much faster video adapter functionality. Because NEC Corporation saw strength in numbers, they decided to give away the VL-Bus technology and to make it an industry standard. The Video Electronics Standards Association was formed and split from NEC to control the new VL-Bus and other standards. The inexpensive design and high performance of the VL-Bus made it a popular addition to the ISA Bus and even to some EISA systems. VL-Bus was defined as an extension connector to the ISA or EISA Bus and could be found only in systems with those buses.

Peripheral Component Interconnect Bus was created by Intel to be a new generation bus, offering local bus performance while also offering processor independence and multiple processor capabilities. Like so many of the other bus creators, Intel formed an independent organization to make the PCI Bus an industry standard in which all could participate. The PCI Committee was formed to administer this new bus and to control its destiny. Due to the superior design and performance of PCI, it has rapidly become the bus of choice in the highest performance systems. Over the next few years, we will probably see PCI unseat the ISA Bus and become the dominant bus architecture.

Chapter 5, "Bus Slots and Specifications," has more in-depth information on these and other PC system buses, including technical information, such as pinouts, performance specifications, bus operation and theory, and so on.

Table 2.1 summarizes the primary differences between a standard PC (or XT) system and an AT system. This information distinguishes between these systems and includes all IBM and compatible models.

Table 2.1	Differences between PC/XT and AT Systems	
System Attributes	**PC/XT Type**	**AT Type**
Supported processors	All Intel 80xx	286 or higher
Processor modes	Real	Real or Protected (Virtual Real on 386+)
Expansion-slot width	8-bit	16/32/64-bit
Slot type	ISA	ISA, EISA, MCA, PCMCIA, VL-Bus, PCI
Hardware interrupts	8	16 or more
DMA channels	4	8 or more
Maximum RAM	1 megabyte	16 or 4096 megabytes
Floppy controller	250 kHz Data Rate	250/300/500/1000 kHz Data Rate
Standard boot drive	360K or 720K	1.2M/1.44M/2.88M
Keyboard interface	Unidirectional	Bidirectional
CMOS setup/clock	No	Yes
Serial port UART	8250B	16450/16550A

This table highlights the primary differences between PC and AT architecture. Using this information, you can properly categorize virtually any system as a PC type or an AT type. A Compaq Deskpro, for example, is a PC system, and the Deskpro 286 and Deskpro 386 are AT-type systems. IBM's XT Model 286 is actually an AT-type system. The AT&T 6300 qualifies as a PC-type system, and the 6310 is an AT-type system.

You usually can identify PC and XT types of systems by their Intel-design 8088 or 8086 processors; many possibilities are available, however. Some systems have the NEC V-20 or V-30 processors, but these processors are functionally identical to the Intel chips. A few PC or XT systems have a 286 or 386 processor for increased performance. These systems have only 8-bit slots of the same system-bus design featured in the original IBM PC. The design of these slots includes only half the total DMA and hardware interrupts of a true AT design, which severely limits the use of expansion slots by different adapter boards that require the use of these resources. This type of system can run most software that runs under MS-DOS, but is limited in more advanced operating systems such as OS/2. This type of system cannot run OS/2 or any software designed to run under OS/2, nor can it run Windows 3.1 or greater. These systems also cannot have more than 1 megabyte of processor-addressable memory, of which only 640K is available for user programs and data.

You usually can identify AT systems by their Intel-design 286, 386, or higher processors. Some AT systems differ in the types of slots included on the main system board. The earlier standard called for 8/16-bit ISA slots compatible with the original IBM PC and AT. Other standards such as EISA, MCA, PCMCIA, VL-Bus, and PCI also would be found only in AT class systems. Most of these systems today would use 486 or Pentium processors.

PC systems usually have double-density (DD) floppy controllers, but AT systems must have a controller capable of high-density (HD) and double-density operation. Almost all current systems also have a controller capable of extra-high density (ED). These systems can run the 2.88M floppy drive. Because of the different controller types, the boot drive on a PC system must be the DD, 5 1/4-inch 360K or 3 1/2-inch 720K drives, but the AT needs the 5 1/4-inch 1.2M or the 3 1/2-inch 1.44M or 2.88M drives for proper operation. You can use a double-density disk drive as the boot drive in an AT system; the problem is that your boot drive is *supposed* to be a high-density drive. Many applications that run on only AT-type systems are packaged on high-density disks. The OS/2 operating system, for example, is packaged on high-density disks and cannot be loaded from double-density disks. The capability to boot and run OS/2 is a basic AT-compatibility test.

A subtle difference between PC/XT and AT systems is in the keyboard interface. AT systems use a bidirectional keyboard interface with an Intel 8042 processor "running the show." This processor has ROM built-in and can be considered a part of the total system ROM package. The PC/XT systems used an 8255 Programmable Peripheral Interface (PPI) chip, which supports only a unidirectional interface. A keyboard can be configured to work with only one of the interface designs. With many keyboards, you can alter the way the keyboard interfaces by flipping a switch on the bottom of the keyboard. Others, such as IBM's Enhanced 101-key keyboard, detect which type of system they are plugged into and switch automatically. The older XT and AT keyboards work with only the type of system for which they were designed.

The AT architecture uses CMOS memory and a real-time clock; the PC-type systems usually don't. (An exception is the PS/2 Model 30, which has a real-time clock even though it is an XT class system.) A *real-time clock* is the built-in clock implemented by a special CMOS memory chip on the motherboard in an AT system. You can have a clock added on some expansion adapters in a PC system, but DOS does not recognize the clock unless a special program is run first. The CMOS memory in the AT system also stores the system's basic configuration. On a PC- or XT-type system, all these basic configuration options (such as the amount of installed memory, the number and types of floppy drives and hard disks, and the type of video adapter) are set by using switches and jumpers on the motherboard and various adapters.

The serial-port control chip, Universal Asynchronous Receiver/Transmitter (UART), is a National Semiconductor 8250B for the PC-type systems; AT systems use the newer NS 16450 or 16550A chips. Because these chips differ in subtle ways, the BIOS software must be designed for a specific chip. In the AT BIOS, designed for the 16450 and 16550A chips, using the older 8250B chip can result in strange problems, such as lost characters at high transmission speeds.

Some differences (such as the expansion slots, the hardware interrupts, and the DMA channel availability) are absolute. Other differences, such as which processors are supported, are less absolute. The AT systems, however, must use the 286 or higher; the PC systems can use the entire Intel family of chips, from the 8086 on up. Other parameters are less absolute. Your own system might not follow the true standard properly. If your system does not follow all criteria listed for it, especially if it is an AT-type system, you can expect compatibility and operational problems.

Documentation

One of the biggest problems in troubleshooting, servicing, or upgrading a system is proper documentation. As with the system units, IBM has set the standard for the type of documentation a manufacturer makes available. Some compatible manufacturers duplicate the size and content of IBM's manuals, and other manufacturers provide no documentation at all. Generally, the type of documentation provided for a system is proportionate to the size of the manufacturing company. (Large companies can afford to produce good documentation.) Some of this documentation, unfortunately, is essential for even the most basic troubleshooting and upgrading tasks. Other documentation is necessary only for software and hardware developers with special requirements.

Types of Documentation

Four types of documents are available for each system. Some manuals cover an entire range of systems, which can save money and shelf space. You can get the following types of manuals:

- Guide-To-Operations (GTO) manuals (called quick-reference manuals for the PS/2)

- Technical-Reference (TR) manuals

- Hardware-Maintenance Service (HMS) manuals
- Hardware-Maintenance Reference (HMR) manuals

A Guide-To-Operations manual is included in the purchase of a system. For PS/2 systems, these manuals have been changed to Quick-Reference manuals. They contain basic instructions for system setup, operation, testing, relocation, and option installation. A customer-level basic diagnostics disk (usually called a Diagnostics and Setup Disk) normally is included with a system. For PS/2 machines, a special disk—the Reference Disk—contains the setup and configuration programs, as well as both customer-level and technician-level diagnostics.

For PC and XT types of systems, you can find listings of all the jumper and switch settings for the motherboard. These settings specify the number of floppy disk drives, math-chip use, memory use, type of video adapter, and other items. For AT systems, the basic diagnostics disk also has the SETUP routine (used to set the date and time), installed memory, installed disk drives, and installed video adapters. This information is saved by the SETUP program into CMOS battery backed-up memory. For PS/2 systems, the included disk (called the Reference Disk) contains the special Programmable Option-Select (POS) configuration routine and a hidden version of advanced diagnostics.

Technical-Reference Manuals

The Technical-Reference manuals provide system-specific hardware and software interface information for the system. The manuals are intended for people who design hardware and software products to operate with these systems or for people who must integrate other hardware and software into a system. Three types of Technical-Reference manuals are available: one is a Technical-Reference manual for a particular system; another covers all options and adapters; and a third covers the ROM BIOS interface. For PS/2 systems, one Hardware Interface Technical-Reference manual covers all PS/2 systems with updates for newer systems as they become available.

Each system has a separate Technical-Reference manual or an update to the Hardware Interface Technical-Reference manual. These publications provide basic interface and design information for the system units. They include information about the system board, math coprocessor, power supply, video subsystem, keyboard, instruction sets, and other features of the system. You need this information for integrating and installing aftermarket floppy and hard disk drives, memory boards, keyboards, network adapters, or virtually anything you want to plug into your system. This manual often contains schematic diagrams showing the circuit layout of the motherboard and pinouts for the various connectors and jumpers. It also includes listings of the floppy and hard disk drive tables, which show the range of drives that can be installed on a particular system. Power specifications for the power supply are also in this manual. You need these figures in order to determine whether the system has adequate current to power a particular add-on device.

The Options and Adapters Technical-Reference manual begins with a starter manual augmented with supplements. The basic manual covers a few IBM adapter cards, and supplements for new adapters and options are issued continually. These publications provide interface and design information about the options and adapters available for the various systems. This information includes a hardware description, programming considerations, interface specifications, and BIOS information.

The third manual is the BIOS Interface Technical-Reference manual. This publication provides basic input-output system (BIOS) interface information. This compendium covers every BIOS that has been available in IBM's systems. The manual is designed for developers of hardware or software products that operate with the IBM PC and PS/2 products.

Hardware-Maintenance Manuals

Each hardware-maintenance library consists of two manuals: a Hardware-Maintenance Service manual and a Hardware-Maintenance Reference manual. These are real service manuals that are written for service technicians. Although their intended audience is the professional service technician, they are very easy to follow and useful even for amateur technicians or enthusiasts. IBM and local computer retail outlets use these manuals for diagnosis and service.

For IBM systems, two sets of manuals are available. One set covers the PC, XT, Portable PC, AT, and PS/2 Model 25 and Model 30. The other manual set covers the PS/2 systems except Model 25 and Model 30: these systems are considered old PC or XT systems, rather than true PS/2 systems.

Manuals are purchased in starter form and then updated with supplements covering new systems and options. The PS/2 Model 25 and Model 30, for example, are covered by supplements that update the PC Maintenance Library; the PS/2 Model 80 is covered by a supplement to the PS/2 Maintenance Library.

The basic Hardware-Maintenance Service manual for the PC or PS/2 contains all the information you need to troubleshoot and diagnose a failing system. This book contains special flowcharts that IBM calls *Maintenance-Analysis Procedures* (MAPs), which can help you find a correct diagnosis in a step-by-step manner. It contains information about jumper positions and switch settings, a detailed parts catalog, and disks containing the advanced diagnostics. The Hardware-Maintenance Service manual is an essential part of a troubleshooter's toolkit.

Many technicians with troubleshooting experience never need to use MAPs. When they have a tough problem, however, MAPs help them organize a troubleshooting session. MAPs tell you to check the switch and jumper settings before the cables, to check the cables before replacing the drive or controller, and so on. This type of information is extremely valuable and can be generalized to a range of systems.

The basic Hardware-Maintenance Reference manual for the PC or PS/2 contains general information about the systems. It describes the diagnostic procedures and Field-Replaceable Unit (FRU) locations, system adjustments, and component removal and

installation. The information in it is useful primarily to users with no experience in disassembling and reassembling a system or to users who have difficulty identifying components within the system. Most people do not need this manual after the first time they
take down a system for service.

Obtaining Documentation

You cannot accurately troubleshoot or upgrade a system without a Technical-Reference
manual. Because of the specific nature of the information in this type of manual, it will
most likely have to be obtained from the manufacturer of the system. The IBM AT Technical Reference Manual, for example, is useless to a person with a Compaq Deskpro 486.
A person with a Deskpro 486 must get the specific manual for that machine from
Compaq.

A service manual is also a necessary item, but is not available from most manufacturers.
This type of manual is not nearly as system-specific as a Technical-Reference manual;
because of that, the service manuals put out by IBM work well for most compatibles.
Some information, such as the parts catalog, is specific to IBM systems and does not
apply to compatibles, but most of the IBM service manuals have general information.

Many knowledgeable reviewers use the IBM Advanced Diagnostics, included with the
Hardware-Maintenance Service manual, as an acid test for compatibility. If the system
truly is compatible, it should pass the tests with flying colors. (Most systems pass.) Many
manufacturers do not have or sell a book or disk equivalent to the IBM Hardware-
Maintenance Service manual. Compaq, for example, has a service manual, but does not
sell it or any parts to anyone who is not a Compaq-authorized dealer. Servicing or upgrading these systems therefore is more costly, and limited by how much your dealer
helps you. Buyers are fortunate that sufficient third-party diagnostics work with most
compatible systems such as the Compaq systems.

To get hardware-service documentation, contact the dealer who sold you the system and
then, if necessary, contact the manufacturer. (Contacting the manufacturer is often more
efficient because dealers rarely stock these items.) You can get any IBM manuals easily
from IBM. To order the IBM manuals, call this toll-free number:

>   1-800-IBM-PCTB (1-800-426-7282)

TB is the abbreviation for Technical Books. The service is active Monday through Friday,
from 8 a.m. to 8 p.m. Eastern time. When you call, you can request copies of the *Technical Directory*—a catalog listing all part numbers and prices of available documentation.
You also can inquire about the availability of technical-reference or service documentation covering newly announced products that might not be listed in the current
directory.

The process of obtaining other manufacturers' manuals might (or might not) be so easy.
Most larger-name companies run responsible service and support operations that provide
technical documentation. Others either do not have or are unwilling to part with such
documentation, to protect their service departments or their dealers' service departments

from competition. Contact the manufacturer directly, and the manufacturer can direct you to the correct department so that you can inquire about this information.

Summary

Apart from the overall similarity between IBM computers and their compatibles, important differences in system architecture exist. IBM and compatible computers can be broken down into PC/XT and AT categories. This chapter explained their differences, and a discussion about how to obtain the service manuals necessary for maintaining and upgrading your computer ended the chapter.

Chapter 3

System Teardown and Inspection

This chapter examines procedures for tearing down and inspecting a system. It describes the types of tools required, the procedure for disassembling the system, and the various components that make up the system. A special section discusses some of the test equipment you can use, and another section covers some problems you might encounter with the hardware (screws, nuts, bolts, and so on).

Using the Proper Tools

To troubleshoot and repair PC systems properly, you need a few basic tools:

- Simple hand tools for basic disassembly and reassembly procedures

- Diagnostics software and hardware for testing components in a system

- Wrap plugs for diagnosing serial and parallel port problems

- Test and measurement devices, such as Digital Multi-Meters (DMMs), that allow accurate measurement of voltage and resistance, and logic probes and pulsers that allow analysis and testing of digital circuits

- Chemicals, such as contact cleaners, component freeze sprays, and compressed air for cleaning the system.

In addition, you might also need soldering and desoldering tools for problems that require these operations. These basic tools are discussed in more detail in the following section. Diagnostics software and hardware is discussed in Chapter 20, "Software and Hardware Diagnostic Tools."

Hand Tools

It becomes immediately apparent when you work with PC systems that the tools required for nearly all service operations are very simple and inexpensive. You can carry most of the required tools in a small pouch. Even a top-of-the-line "master mechanic's" set fits inside a briefcase-sized container. The cost of these tool kits ranges from about $20 for a small-service kit to $500 for one of the briefcase-sized deluxe kits. Compare these costs to what might be necessary for an automotive technician. Most automotive service techs spend between $5,000 to $10,000, or more, for the tools they need! Not only are the tools much less expensive, but I can tell you from experience that you don't get nearly as dirty working on computers as you do when working on cars!

In this section, you learn about the tools required to make up a set capable of basic, board-level service on PC systems. One of the best ways to start such a set of tools is with a small kit sold especially for servicing PCs.

This list shows the basic tools you can find in one of the small "PC tool kits" sold for about $20:

> 3/16-inch nut driver
>
> 1/4-inch nut driver
>
> Small Phillips screwdriver
>
> Small flat-blade screwdriver
>
> Medium Phillips screwdriver
>
> Medium flat-blade screwdriver
>
> Chip extractor
>
> Chip inserter
>
> Tweezers
>
> Claw-type parts grabber
>
> T10 and T15 Torx drivers

You use nut drivers to remove the hexagonal-headed screws that secure the system-unit covers, adapter boards, disk drives, power supplies, and speakers in most systems. The nut drivers work much better than a conventional screwdriver.

Because some manufacturers have substituted slotted or Phillips head screws for the more standard hexagonal head screws, the standard screwdrivers can be used for these systems.

You use the chip-extraction and insertion tools to install or remove memory chips (or other, smaller chips) without bending any pins on the chip. Usually, you pry out larger chips, such as microprocessors or ROMs, with the small screwdriver. Larger processors, such as the 486 or Pentium chips, require a chip extractor if they are in a standard socket. These chips have so many pins on them that a large amount of force is required to remove them. The chip extractor tools for removing these chips distribute the force evenly along the chip's underside to minimize the likelihood of breakage.

The tweezers and parts grabber can be used to hold any small screws or jumper blocks that are difficult to hold in your hand. The parts grabber is especially useful when you drop a small part into the interior of a system; usually, you can remove the part without completely disassembling the system.

Finally, the Torx driver is a special, star-shaped driver that matches the special screws found in most Compaq systems, and in many other systems as well.

Although this basic set is useful, you should supplement it with some other small hand tools, such as:

Needlenose pliers

Hemostats

Wire cutter or wire stripper

Metric nut drivers

Tamper-proof Torx drivers

Vise or clamp

File

Small flashlight

Pliers are useful for straightening pins on chips, applying or removing jumpers, crimping cables, or grabbing small parts.

Hemostats are especially useful for grabbing small components, such as jumpers.

The wire cutter or stripper obviously is useful for making or repairing cables or wiring.

The metric nut drivers can be used in many clone or compatible systems, as well as in the IBM PS/2 systems, which all use metric hardware.

The tamper-proof Torx drivers can be used to remove Torx screws with the tamper-resistant pin in the center of the screw. A tamper-proof Torx driver has a hole drilled in it to allow clearance for the pin.

You can use a vise to install connectors on cables and to crimp cables to the shape you want, as well as to hold parts during delicate operations.

Finally, you can use the file to smooth rough metal edges on cases and chassis, as well as to trim the faceplates on disk drives for a perfect fit.

The flashlight can be used to light up system interiors, especially when the system is cramped and the room lighting is not good. I consider this an essential tool.

Another consideration for your tool kit is an ESD (Electro Static Discharge) protection kit. These kits consist of a wrist strap with a grounding wire, and a specially conductive mat also with its own ground wire. Using a kit like this when working on a system will help to ensure that you never accidentally zap any of the components with a static discharge.

The ESD kits, as well as all the other tools and much more, are available from a variety of tool vendors. Specialized Products Company and Jensen Tools are two of the more popular vendors of computer and electronic tools and service equipment. Their catalogs show an extensive selection of very high quality tools. These companies and several others are listed in Appendix B, "Vendor List." With a simple set of hand tools, you will be equipped for nearly every PC repair or installation situation. The total cost for these tools should be less than $150, which is not much considering the capabilities they give you.

Soldering and Desoldering Tools

For certain situations, such as repairing a broken wire, reattaching a component to a circuit board, removing and installing chips that are not in a socket, or adding jumper wires or pins to a board, you must use a soldering iron to make the repair. Even if you do only board-level service, you will need a soldering iron in some situations.

You need a low-wattage iron, usually about 25 watts. More than 30 watts generates too much heat and can damage the components on the board. Even with a low-wattage unit, you must limit the amount of heat to which you subject the board and its components. You can do this with quick and efficient use of the soldering iron, as well as with the use of heat-sinking devices clipped to the leads of the device being soldered. A *heat sink* is a small, metal, clip-on device designed to absorb excessive heat before it reaches the component that the heat sink is protecting. In some cases a pair of hemostats can be used as an effective heat sink when you solder a component.

To remove components originally soldered into place from a printed circuit board, you can use a soldering iron with a *solder sucker*. This device normally is constructed as a small tube with an air chamber and a plunger-and-spring arrangement. (I do not recommend the "squeeze bulb" type of solder sucker.) The unit is "cocked" when you press the spring-loaded plunger into the air chamber. When you want to remove a device from a board, you heat with the soldering iron the point at which one of the component leads joins the circuit board, from the underside of the board, until the solder melts. As soon as melting occurs, move the solder-sucker nozzle into position and press the actuator. This procedure allows the plunger to retract, and to create a momentary suction that inhales the liquid solder from the connection and leaves the component lead dry in the hole.

Always do the heating and suctioning from the underside of a board, not from the component side. Repeat this action for every component lead joined to the circuit board. When you master this technique, you can remove a small chip, such as a 16-pin memory chip, in a minute or two with only a small likelihood of damage to the board or other components. Larger chips with many pins can be more difficult to remove and resolder without damaging other components or the circuit board.

If you intend to add soldering and desoldering skills to your arsenal of abilities, you should practice. Take a useless circuit board and practice removing various components from the board; then reinstall the components. Try to remove the components from the board by using the least amount of heat possible. Also, perform the solder-melting operations as quickly as possible, and limit the time the iron is applied to the joint. Before you install any components, clean out the holes through which the leads must project, and mount the component into place. Then apply the solder from the underside of the board, using as little heat and solder as possible. Attempt to produce joints as clean as the joints that the board manufacturer performed by machine. Soldered joints that do not look "clean" may keep the component from making a good connection with the rest of the circuit. This "cold-solder joint" normally is created because you have not used enough heat. *Remember that you should not practice your new soldering skills on the motherboard of a system you are attempting to repair!* Don't attempt to work on real boards until you are sure of your skills. I always keep a few junk boards around for soldering practice and experimentation.

No matter how good you get at soldering and desoldering, some jobs are best left to professionals! For example, components that are surface mounted to a circuit board require special tools for soldering and desoldering, as do other components with very high pin densities. I upgraded my IBM P75 portable system by replacing the 486DX-33 processor with a 486DX2-66 processor. This would normally be a simple procedure (especially if the system uses a Zero Insertion Force or ZIF socket), but in this system the 168-pin 486DX chip is soldered into a special processor card! To add to the difficulty, there were surface mounted components also on both sides (even the solder side) of the card. Well, needless to say, this was a very difficult job that required a special piece of equipment called a *hot air rework station*. The hot air rework station uses blasts of hot air to simultaneously solder or desolder all of the pins of a chip at once. To perform this replacement job the components on the solder side were protected by a special heat resistant masking tape, and the hot air was directed at the 168-pins of the 486 chip while the chip was pulled out from the other side. Then the new chip was placed in the holes in the board, a special solder paste was applied to the pins, and the hot air was used again to simultaneously solder all 168 pins. The use of professional equipment like this resulted in a perfect job that cannot be told from factory original, and resulted in a perfectly operating 66 MHz system. Attempting a job like this with a conventional soldering iron would have probably damaged the very expensive DX2 processor chip as well as the even more expensive multilayer processor card.

Using Proper Test Equipment

In some cases you must use specialized devices to test a system board or component. This test equipment is not expensive or difficult to use, but can add much to your troubleshooting abilities. I consider wrap plugs and a voltmeter required gear for proper system testing. The wrap plugs allow testing of serial and parallel ports and their attached cables. A Digital Multi-Meter (DMM) can serve many purposes, including checking for voltage signals at different points in a system, testing the output of the power supply, and checking for continuity in a circuit or cable. An outlet tester is an invaluable accessory that can check the electrical outlet for proper wiring. This is useful if you believe the problem lies outside the computer system itself.

Logic probes and pulsers are not considered mandatory equipment, but they can add to your troubleshooting proficiency. You use the logic probe to check for the existence and status of digital signals at various points in a circuit. You use the logic pulser to inject signals into a circuit to evaluate the circuit's operation. Using these devices effectively requires more understanding of how the circuit operates.

Wrap Plugs (Loopback Connectors)

For diagnosing serial- and parallel-port problems, you need wrap plugs, also called loopback connectors, which are used to circulate, or "wrap," signals. The plugs enable the serial or parallel port to send data to itself for diagnostic purposes. Several types of wrap plugs are available. You need one for the 25-pin serial port, one for the 9-pin serial port, and one for the 25-pin parallel port (see table 3.1). Many companies, including IBM, sell the plugs separately, and IBM also sells a special version that includes all three types in one plug.

Table 3.1	Wrap Plug Types
Description	**IBM Part Number**
Parallel-port wrap plug	8529228
Serial-port wrap plug, 25-pin	8529280
Serial-port wrap plug, 9-pin (AT)	8286126
Tri-connector wrap plug	72X8546

The handy tri-connector unit contains all commonly needed plugs in one compact unit. The unit costs approximately $30 from IBM. Be aware that most professional diagnostics packages (especially the ones I recommend) include the three types of wrap plugs as part of the package; you may not need to purchase them separately. If you're handy, you can even make your own wrap plugs for testing. I have included wiring diagrams for the three types of wrap plugs in Chapter 11, "Communications and Networking." In that chapter you will also find a detailed discussion of serial and parallel ports.

Meters

Many troubleshooting procedures require that you measure voltage and resistance. You take these measurements by using a handheld Digital Multi-Meter (DMM). The meters can be analog devices (using an actual meter) or digital-readout devices. The DMM has a pair of wires, called test leads or probes. The test leads make the connections so that you can take readings. Depending on the meter's setting, the probes will measure electrical resistance, Direct-Current (DC) voltage, or Alternating-Current (AC) voltage.

Usually, each system-unit measurement setting has several ranges of operation. DC voltage, for example, usually can be read in several scales to a maximum of 200 millivolts, 2 volts, 20 volts, 200 volts, and 1,000 volts. Because computers use both +5 and +12 volts for various operations, you should use the 20-volt-maximum scale for making your measurements. Making these measurements on the 200-millivolt or 2-volt scales could "peg the meter" and possibly damage it because the voltage would be much higher than expected. Using the 200-volt or 1,000-volt scales works, but the readings at 5 volts and 12 volts are so small in proportion to the maximum that accuracy is low.

If you are taking a measurement and are unsure of the actual voltage, start at the highest scale and work your way down. Some better system-unit meters have an autoranging capability—the meter automatically selects the best range for any measurement. This type of meter is much easier to operate. You just set the meter to the type of reading you want, such as DC volts, and attach the probes to the signal source. The meter selects the correct voltage range and displays the value. Because of their design, these types of meters always have a digital display rather than a meter needle.

I prefer the small, digital meters. You can buy them for only slightly more than the ana-log style, and they're extremely accurate. Some are not much bigger than a cassette tape; they can fit in a shirt pocket. Radio Shack sells a good unit (made for Radio Shack by Beckman) in the $25 price range, which is only a half-inch thick, weighs 3 1/2 ounces, and is digital and autoranging as well. This type of meter works well for most if not all PC troubleshooting and test uses.

You should be aware that many analog meters can be dangerous to digital circuits. These meters use a 9-volt battery to power the meter for resistance measurements. If you use this type of meter to measure resistance on some digital circuits, you can damage the electronics because you are essentially injecting 9 volts into the circuit. The digital meters universally run on 3 to 5 volts or less.

Logic Probes and Logic Pulsers

A logic probe can be useful in diagnosing problems with digital circuits. In a digital cir-cuit, a signal is represented as either high (+5 volts) or low (0 volts). Because these signals are present for only a short time (measured in millionths of a second), or oscillate or switch on and off rapidly, a simple voltmeter is useless. A logic probe is designed to dis-play these signal conditions easily.

Logic probes are especially useful in troubleshooting a dead system. Using the probe, you can determine whether the basic clock circuitry is operating and whether other signals necessary to system operation are present. In some cases, a probe can help you cross-check the signals at each pin on an IC chip. You can compare the signals present at each pin to what a known, good chip of the same type would show—a comparison helpful in isolating a failed component. Logic probes can be useful in troubleshooting some disk drive problems by letting you test the signals present on the interface cable or drive-logic board.

A companion tool to the probe is the logic pulser. A pulser is designed to test circuit reaction by delivering into a circuit a logical high (+5 volt) pulse, usually lasting 1 1/2 to 10 millionths of a second. Compare the reaction to that of a known functional circuit. This type of device normally is used much less frequently than a logic probe, but in some cases can be helpful in testing a circuit.

Outlet Testers

Another very useful test tool is an outlet tester. These simple, inexpensive devices are sold at hardware stores which are used to test electrical outlets. You simply plug the de-vice in, and three LEDs will light in various combinations indicating whether the outlet is wired correctly. Although you might think that badly wired outlets would be a rare problem, I have actually run into a large number of installations where the outlets were wired incorrectly. Most of the time it seems the problems are with the ground wire. An improperly wired outlet can result in flaky system operations such as random parity checks and lockups. With an improper ground circuit, currents can begin flowing on the electrical ground circuits in the system. Because the voltage on the ground circuits is used by the system as a comparator to determine whether bits are 0 or 1, this can cause data errors in the system. Once, while running one of my PC troubleshooting seminars, I was using a system that I literally could not approach without locking it up. As I would walk by the system, the electrostatic field generated by my body would interfere with the system, and the PC would lock up with a "parity check" error message. The problem was that the hotel we were using was very old and had no grounded outlets in the room. The only way I could prevent the system from locking up was to run the class in my stocking feet, as my leather soled shoes were generating the static charge. Another symptom of bad ground wiring in electrical outlets is electrical shocks when touching the case or chassis of the system. This indicates that voltages are flowing where they should not be! This can also be caused by bad or improper grounds within the system itself as well. By using the simple outlet tester, you can quickly determine whether the outlet is at fault.

Chemicals

Chemicals can be used to help clean, troubleshoot, and even repair a system. For the most basic function, cleaning components and electrical connectors and contacts, one of the most useful chemicals is 1,1,1 trichloroethane. This substance, sometimes sold as "carbo-chlor," is a very effective cleaner. It can be used to clean electrical contacts and components, and will not damage most plastics and board materials. In fact, carbo-chlor can be very useful for cleaning stains on the system case and keyboard. New replacements for trichloroethane are being offered by many electronic chemical supply companies because it is being regulated along with other CFCs (Chloro-Floro-Carbons) such as freon.

A very unique type of contact enhancer and lubricant is on the market called Stabilant 22. This chemical is applied to electrical contacts and acts to greatly enhance the connection as well as lubricate the contact point. It is much more effective than conventional contact cleaners or lubricants.

Stabilant 22 is actually a liquid polymer semiconductor. It behaves like liquid metal, and conducts electricity in the presence of an electric current. It also serves to fill in the air gaps between the mating surfaces of two items in contact, which makes the surface area of the contact larger and keeps out oxygen and other contaminants which can oxidize and corrode the contact point.

This chemical is available in several forms. Stabilant 22 itself is the full strength concentrated version, while Stabilant 22a is a version diluted with isopropanol in a 4 to 1 ratio. An even more diluted 8 to 1 ratio version is sold in many high-end stereo and audio shops under the name "Tweek." Just 15ml of Stabilant 22a sells for about $40, while a liter of the concentrate costs about $4,000! As you can plainly see, stabilant 22 is fairly expensive, but very little is required in an application, and nothing else has been found to be as effective in preserving electrical contacts. An application of Stabilant can provide protection for up to 16 years according to the manufacturer, and is used by NASA on spacecraft electronics. Stabilant is manufactured and sold by D. W. Electrochemicals. You will find their address and phone number in the vendor list in Appendix B.

Stabilant is especially effective on I/O slot connectors, adapter card edge and pin connectors, disk drive connectors, power supply connectors, and virtually any connectors in the PC. In addition to enhancing the contact and preventing corrosion, an application of Stabilant lubricates the contacts, making insertion and removal of the connector easier.

Compressed air often is used as an aid in system cleaning. Normally composed of freon or carbon dioxide, compressed gas is used as a blower to remove dust and debris from a system or component. Be careful when you use these devices; some of them can generate a tremendous static charge as the compressed gas leaves the nozzle of the can. Be sure that you are using the kind approved for cleaning or dusting off computer equipment, and consider wearing a static grounding strap as a precaution. Freon TF is known to generate these large static charges; Freon R12 is less severe. Of course, because both chemicals are damaging to the ozone layer, they are being phased out by most suppliers. Expect to see new versions of these compressed-air devices with carbon dioxide or some other less-harmful propellant.

Caution

If you use any chemical with the propellant Freon R12 (dichlorodifluoromethane), *do not expose the gas to an open flame or other heat source*. If you burn this substance, a highly toxic gas called *phosgene* is generated. Phosgene, used as a choking gas in WWI, can be deadly.

Freon R12 is the substance used in most automobile air conditioner systems prior to 1995. Automobile service technicians are instructed *never* to smoke near air conditioner systems. By 1996, the manufacture and use of these types of chemicals have been either banned or closely regulated by the government, and replacements will have to be found. For example, virtually all new car automobile air conditioning systems have been switched to a chemical called R-134a. The unfortunate side effect of this is that all of these newer replacement chemicals are much more expensive.

Related to compressed-air products are chemical-freeze sprays. These sprays are used to quickly cool down a suspected failing component to restore it to operation. These substances are not used to repair a device, but rather to confirm that you have found the failed device. Often, a component's failure is heat-related; cooling it temporarily restores it to normal operation. If the circuit begins operating normally, the device you are cooling is the suspect device.

A Word about Hardware

This section discusses some problems you might encounter with the hardware (screws, nuts, bolts, and so on) used in assembling a system.

Types of Hardware

One of the biggest aggravations you encounter in dealing with various systems on the market is the different hardware types and designs that hold the units together.

For example, most system hardware types use screws that can be driven with 1/4-inch or 3/16-inch hexagonal drivers. IBM used these screws in all original PC, XT, and AT systems, and most compatible systems use this standard hardware as well. Some manufacturers might use different hardware. Compaq, for example, uses Torx screws extensively in most of its systems. A Torx screw has a star-shaped hole driven by the correct-size Torx driver. These drivers carry size designations, such as T-8, T-9, T-10, T-15, T-20, T-25, T-30, T-40, and so on. A variation on the Torx screw is the tamper-proof Torx screw, found in power supplies and other assemblies. These screws are identical to the regular Torx screws except that a pin sticks up exactly in the middle of the star-shaped hole in the screw. This pin prevents the standard Torx driver from entering the hole to grip the screw; a special tamper-proof driver with a corresponding hole for the pin is required. An alternative is to use a small chisel to knock out the pin in the screw. Usually, a device sealed with these types of screws is considered a complete, replaceable unit and rarely, if ever, needs to be opened.

The more standard slotted-head and Phillips-head screws are used by many manufacturers as well. Using tools on these screws is relatively easy, but tools do not grip these fasteners as well as hexagonal head or Torx screws, and the heads can be rounded off more easily than other types. Extremely cheap versions tend to lose bits of metal as they're turned with a driver, and the metal bits can fall onto the motherboard. Stay away from cheap fasteners whenever possible; the headaches from dealing with stripped screws aren't worth it.

English versus Metric

Another area of aggravation with hardware is that two types of thread systems are available: English and metric. IBM used mostly English-threaded fasteners in its original line of systems, but many other manufacturers used metric-threaded fasteners in their systems.

The difference becomes apparent especially with disk drives. American-manufactured drives use English fasteners; drives made in Japan or Taiwan usually use metric fasteners. Whenever you replace a floppy drive in an early-model IBM unit, you encounter this problem. Try to buy the correct screws and any other hardware, such as brackets, with the drive because they might be difficult to find at a local hardware store. The OEM's drive manual has the correct data about a specific drive's hole locations and thread size.

Hard disks can use either English or metric fasteners; you will need to check your particular drive to be sure.

Caution

Some screws in a system might be length-critical, especially screws used to retain hard disk drives. You can destroy some hard disks by using a mounting screw that's too long. A screw that is too long can puncture or dent the sealed disk chamber when you install the drive and fully tighten the screw. When you install a new drive in a system, always make a trial fit of the hardware and see how far the screws can be inserted in the drive before they interfere with components on the drive. When in doubt, the drive manufacturer's OEM documentation will tell you precisely what screws are required, and how long they should be.

Disassembly Procedures

The process of physically disassembling and reassembling systems isn't difficult. Because of marketplace standardization, only a couple of different types and sizes of screws (with a few exceptions) are used to hold the systems together, and the physical arrangement of the major components is similar even among systems from different manufacturers. Also, not many individual components are in each system. This section breaks down the disassembly and reassembly procedure into these sections:

- Case or cover assembly
- Adapter boards
- Disk drives
- Power supply
- Motherboard

This section discusses how to remove and install these components for several different system types. With regards to assembly and disassembly, it is best to consider each system by the type of case the system uses. For example, all systems with AT type cases are assembled and disassembled in much the same manner. Tower cases are basically AT-type cases turned sideways, so the same basic instructions would apply there as well. Most Slimline and XT style cases are similar and these systems are assembled and disassembled in much the same way as well. In the following section, disassembly and reassembly instructions are listed for several of the different case types, including standard IBM Compatible as well as several of the PS/2 systems.

Disassembly Preparation

Before beginning the disassembly of any system, several issues must be discussed. One is ESD (Electro-Static-Discharge) protection. Another is recording the configuration of the system, both with regards to the physical aspects of the system such as jumper or switch settings and cable orientations, as well as the logical configuration of the system especially with regards to things like CMOS settings.

ESD Protection. When you are working on the internal components of a system, you need to take the necessary precautions to prevent accidental static discharges to the components. At any given time, your body can hold a large static voltage charge which can easily damage components in your systems. Before I ever put my hands into an open system, I first touch a grounded portion of the chassis such as the power supply case. This serves to equalize the charge that both myself and the device are carrying. Some people would say that the charge is vented off to ground in this case, but not really. I never recommend working on a system with the cord plugged in because of the electrical hazard, as well as the simple fact that it is too easy to either power the system on at the wrong time or to simply forget to turn it off. It is too easy to drop tools and other things into systems while they are powered on, which would short out and possibly damage circuits. After destroying an adapter card because I accidentally plugged it in while the system was running, I decided that the only good way to ensure that the system is really off is to unplug it!

I have been told by some that if the system is not plugged in, the static charges cannot be vented off to ground. That is true, but the problem with static is not whether a device carries a charge or not, but only whether that charge suddenly flows from one device to another through the delicate logic circuits. By touching the system chassis, or any other part of the system's ground circuit, you equalize the charge between you and the system, which will ensure that no additional charge will pass from you to the IC chips. No matter what anybody says, you absolutely do not want the system plugged in!

A more sophisticated way to equalize the charges between you and any of the system components is to use the ESD protection kit mentioned earlier. This kit consists of a wrist strap and mat with ground wires for attachment to the system chassis. When you are going to work on a system, you place the mat next to or partially underneath the system unit. A ground wire is then clipped to both the mat and the system's chassis, tying the grounds together. Then you put on the wrist strap and attach that wire to a ground as well. Since the mat and system chassis are already wired together, you can attach the wrist strap wire to either the system chassis or mat itself. If you are using a wrist strap without a mat, clip the wrist strap wire to the system chassis. When clipping these wires to the chassis, be sure to use an area that is free from paint so that a good ground contact can be achieved. This setup insures that any electrical charges are carried equally by you and any of the components in the system, which will prevent the sudden flow of static electricity which can damage the circuits.

As you remove disk drives, adapter cards, and especially delicate items such as the entire motherboard as well as SIMMs or processor chips, you should place them on the static mat. I see some people put the system unit on top of the mat, but it should be along side so that you have room to lay out all the components as you remove them. If you are going to remove the motherboard from a system, be sure that you leave enough room on the mat for it.

If you do not have such a mat, simply lay the removed circuits and devices on a clean desk or table surface. Always pick up loose adapter cards by the metal bracket used to secure the card to the system. This bracket is tied into the ground circuitry of the card, and by touching it first you will prevent a discharge from damaging the components on the card. If the circuit board has no metal bracket, like a motherboard for example, carefully handle the board by the edges and try not to touch any of the components.

Caution

Some people have recommended that loose circuit boards and chips should be placed on sheets of aluminum foil. This is absolutely NOT RECOMMENDED and can actually result in an EXPLOSION! You see, many motherboard adapter cards and other circuit boards today have built-in lithium or nicad batteries. These batteries react violently when they are shorted out, which is exactly what you would be doing by laying such a board on a piece of aluminum foil. The batteries will quickly overheat and possibly explode like a large firecracker (with dangerous shrapnel). Because it is often not possible for you to know whether a board has a battery built into it somewhere, the simple warning is to NEVER place any board on any conductive metal surface like foil.

Recording Setup and Configuration. Before you power the system off for the last time to remove the case, you should find out several things about the system and record them. Often times when working on a system you will intentionally or accidentally wipe out the CMOS setup information. Most systems use a special battery powered CMOS clock and data chip that is used to store the system configuration information. If the battery is disconnected, or if certain pins are accidentally shorted, you can discharge the CMOS memory and lose the setup. The CMOS memory in most systems is used to store simple things such as how many and what type of floppy drives are connected, how much memory is in the system, and the date and time. A critical piece of information is the hard disk type settings. While the system or you can easily determine the other settings the next time you power on the system, the hard disk type information is another story. Most modern BIOS software can actually read the type information directly from most IDE and all SCSI drives. With older BIOS software, however, you have to explicitly tell the system the parameters of the attached hard disk. This means that you need to know the current settings for Cylinders, Heads, and Sectors per track. Some BIOS software indicates the hard disk only by a "type" number, usually from 1 through 47. Be aware that most BIOS programs use type 47 as what is called a user definable type, which means that the cylinder, head, and sector counts for this type were manually entered in and are not constant. These user definable types are especially important to write down, because this information may be very difficult to figure out later when you need to start up the system.

If you do not enter the correct hard disk type information in the CMOS Setup program, you will not be able to access the data on the hard disk. I know of several individuals who have lost some or all of their data because they did not enter the correct type information when reconfiguring the system. If this information is incorrect, the usual result is a `Missing operating system` error message when starting the system and the inability to access the C drive. Some of you might be thinking that you could just figure out the parameters by looking up the particular hard disk in a table. For example, I have included a table of popular hard disk drive parameters in Appendix A, and it has proven useful to me time and time again. Unfortunately, this only works if the original person setting up the system entered the correct parameters as well. I have encountered a large number of systems where the hard disk parameters were not entered correctly, and the only way to regain access to the data is to determine and to use the same incorrect parameters that were originally used. As you can see, no matter what, you should record the hard disk information from your setup program.

Most systems have the setup program built right into the ROM BIOS software itself. These built-in setup programs are activated by a hot key sequence such as Ctrl-Alt-Esc or Ctrl-Alt-S if you have a Phoenix ROM. Other ROMs prompt you for the setup program every time the system boots, such as with the popular AMI BIOS. With the AMI, you simply press the Delete key when the prompt appears on the screen during a reboot.

When you get the setup program running, record all the settings. The easiest way to do this is by printing it out. If a printer is connected, hit the Shift-PrintScreen keys and a copy of the screen display will be sent to the printer. Some setup programs have several pages of information, so you should record the information on each page as well. Many setup programs such as those in the AMI BIOS allow for specialized control over the particular chipset used on the motherboard. These complicated settings can take up several screens of information, however all should be recorded. Most will return all of these settings to a default state when the battery is removed, and you will lose any custom settings that were made.

MCA and EISA bus systems have a very sophisticated setup program that stores not only the motherboard configuration, but configurations for all of the adapter cards as well. Fortunately the setup programs on these systems have the ability to save the settings to a file on a floppy disk so that they can be restored later. To access the setup program for most of these systems, you will need the setup or Reference Diskette for the particular system. Many of the new PS/2 systems store a complete copy of the Reference Diskette on the hard disk in a hidden partition. When these systems boot up, you will notice that the cursor jumps over to the right-hand side of the screen for a few seconds. During this time, if you strike the Ctrl-Alt-Ins keys, the hidden setup programs will be executed.

Recording Physical Configuration. While you are disassembling a system, it is a good idea to record all the physical settings and configurations within the system. This includes jumper and switch settings, cable orientations and placement, ground wire locations, and even adapter board placement. Keep a notebook handy for recording these items, and write down all the settings. It is especially important to record all the jumper and switch settings on every card you remove from the system as well as the motherboard itself. If you accidentally disturb these jumpers or switches, you will know how they were originally set. This is very important if you do not have all the documentation for the system handy; and even if you do, undocumented jumpers and switches often do not appear in the manuals, but must be set a certain way for the item to function. It is very embarrassing, to say the least, if you take apart somebody's system and then cannot make it work again because you disturbed something. If you record these settings you will save yourself the embarrassment!

Also record all cable orientations. Most name brand systems use cables and connectors that are keyed so that they cannot be plugged in backwards, but most generic compatibles do not have this luxury. It is also possible to mix up hard disk and floppy cables; each cable should be marked or recorded as to what it was plugged into and the proper orientations. Ribbon cables will usually have an odd colored wire at one end which indicates pin 1. The devices that the cables are plugged into are also marked in some way to indicate the orientation of pin 1, and these should obviously match.

Although cable orientation and placement seems like a very simple thing, it is rare in my PC troubleshooting seminars that we get through the entire course without several groups having cable connection problems. Fortunately, in most cases (excepting power cables), plugging in any of the ribbon cables inside the system backwards rarely causes any permanent damage. Power and battery connections are a big exception to this, however, and plugging them in backwards will surely cause damage. In fact, plugging the motherboard power connectors in backwards or to the wrong plug location will put 12 volts where only 5 should be and can cause components on the board to explode violently. I know people with scars on their faces caused by shrapnel from exploding components. I always like to turn my face away from the system when I power it on for the first time! Plugging the CMOS battery in backwards can damage the CMOS chip itself, which is usually soldered into the motherboard, requiring replacement of the motherboard itself.

Finally, it is a good idea to record other miscellaneous items such as the placement of any ground wires, adapter cards, or anything else you might have difficulty remembering later. Some configurations and setups are particular to which slots the adapter cards are located in; it is usually a good idea to put everything back exactly the way it was originally. This is especially true for any MCA or EISA bus systems.

Now that we have made the necessary preparations and taken the necessary precautions, we can actually begin working on the systems.

XT and Slimline Case Systems

The procedure for disassembling the XT style or Slimline type case systems offered by most manufacturers is very simple. Only two tools are normally required: a 1/4-inch nut driver for the external screws holding the cover in place and a 3/16-inch nut driver for all other screws. Note that I almost always prefer to use a nut driver, although most of these screws have a Phillips type head embedded within the hexagonal head of the screw. Compared to a Phillips screwdriver, the nut driver can get a much better grip on the screw, and you are much less likely to strip it out.

Removing the Cover. To remove the case cover, follow these steps:

1. Turn off the system and unplug the power cord from the system unit.

2. Turn the system unit around so that the rear of the unit is facing you, and locate the screws that hold the system-unit cover in place (see fig. 3.1).

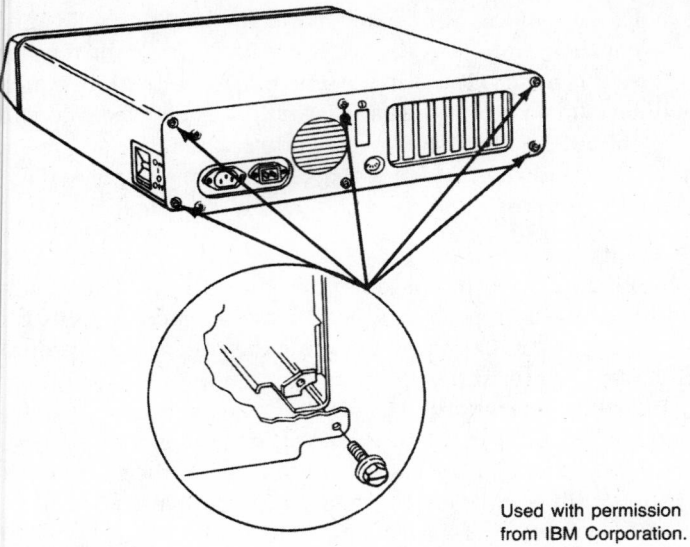

Used with permission
from IBM Corporation.

Fig. 3.1
The screws holding the XT-type case cover in place.

3. Use the 1/4-inch nut driver to remove the cover screws.

4. Slide the cover toward the front of the system unit until it stops. Lift up the front of the cover and remove it from the chassis.

To remove all adapter boards from the system unit, first remove the system-unit cover, as described earlier. Proceed as follows for each adapter:

1. Note which slots all the adapters are in. If possible, make a diagram or drawing.

2. Use the 3/16-inch nut driver to remove the screw holding the adapter in place (see fig. 3.2).

3. Note the position of any cables plugged into the adapter before removing them. In a correctly wired system, the colored stripe on one side of the ribbon cable always denotes pin number 1. The power connector is normally shaped so that it can be inserted only the correct way.

4. Remove the adapter by lifting with even force at both ends.

5. Note the positions of any jumpers or switches on the adapter, especially when documentation for the adapter isn't available. Even when documentation is available, undocumented jumpers and switches often are used by manufacturers for special purposes, such as testing or unique configurations.

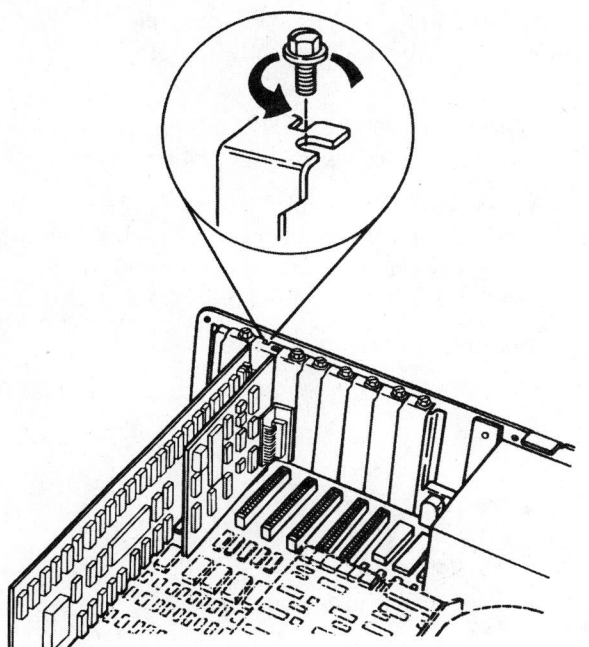

Used with permission
from IBM Corporation.

Fig. 3.2
Removing the screw that holds the adapter in place.

Jumpers and switches normally are named on the circuit board. SW1 and SW2 are used for switch 1 and switch 2, for example, and J1 and J2 are used for jumper 1 and jumper 2. If these jumpers or switches later are disturbed, you can return to the original configuration—as long as you noted it when the adapter was first removed. The best procedure usually is to make a diagram showing these features for a particular card.

Removing Disk Drives. Removing drives for XT or Slimline case systems is fairly easy. The procedures are similar for both floppy and hard disk drives.

Before you remove hard disks from the system, they should be backed up. Older drives should have the heads parked as well, but almost all newer drives automatically park the heads when the power is off. The possibility always exists that data will be lost or the drive damaged from rough handling. Hard disks are discussed in more detail in Chapter 14, "Hard Disk Drives and Controllers."

First, remove the cover and all adapters, as previously described. Proceed as follows:

1. Some systems have drive retaining screws on the bottom of the chassis. Lift up the front of the chassis so that the unit stands with the rear of the chassis down and the disk drive facing straight up. Locate any drive-retaining screws in the bottom of the chassis and remove them. On IBM equipment, you find these screws in XT systems with hard disks or half-height floppy drives (see fig. 3.3). These screws

might be shorter than others used in the system. You must reinstall a screw of the same length in this location later; using a screw that's too long can damage the drive.

2. Set the chassis flat on the table and locate the drive-retaining screws on the outboard sides of the drive. Remove these screws (see figs. 3.4 and 3.5).

3. Slide the disk drive forward about two inches and disconnect the power and signal cables from the drive (see figs. 3.6 and 3.7). In a correctly wired system, the odd-colored stripe on one side of the ribbon cable always denotes pin number 1. The power connector is shaped so that it can be inserted only the correct way.

4. Slide the drive completely out of the unit.

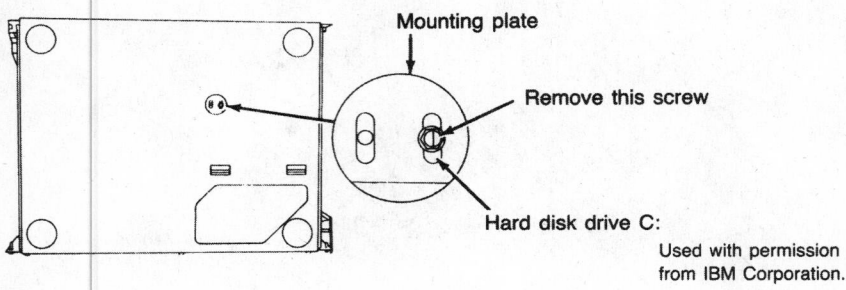

Mounting plate

Remove this screw

Hard disk drive C:

Used with permission
from IBM Corporation.

Fig. 3.3
Removing the retaining screws from the bottom of the chassis.

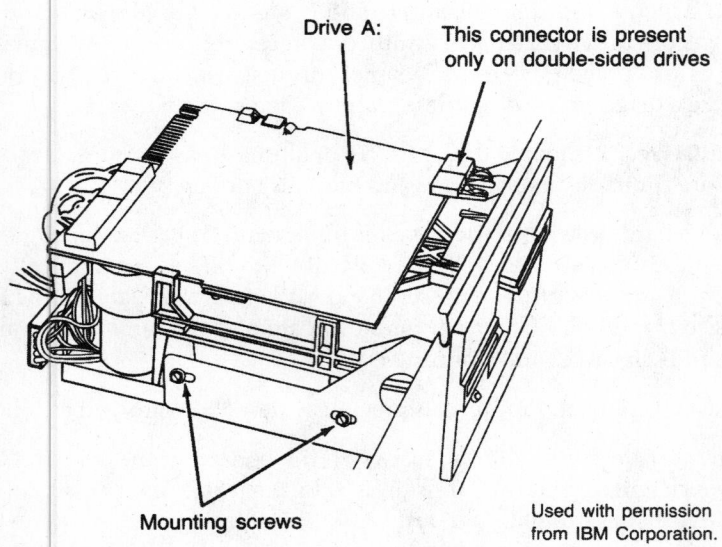

Drive A:

This connector is present
only on double-sided drives

Mounting screws

Used with permission
from IBM Corporation.

Fig. 3.4
Removing the retaining screws from the outboard sides of a floppy disk drive.

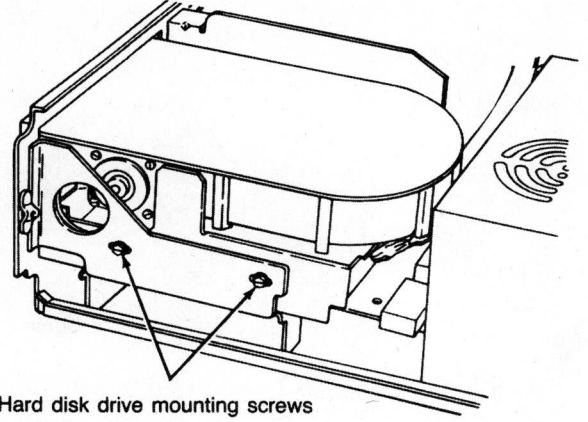

Hard disk drive mounting screws

Used with permission
from IBM Corporation.

Fig. 3.5
Removing the retaining screws from the outboard sides of the hard disk drive.

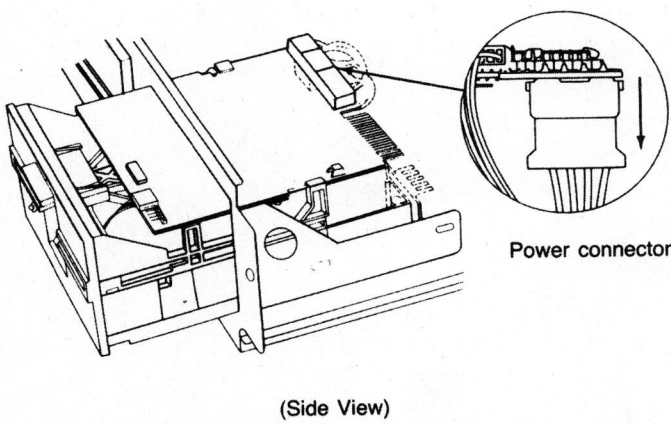

Power connector

(Side View)

Used with permission
from IBM Corporation.

Fig. 3.6
The power connector on a floppy disk drive.

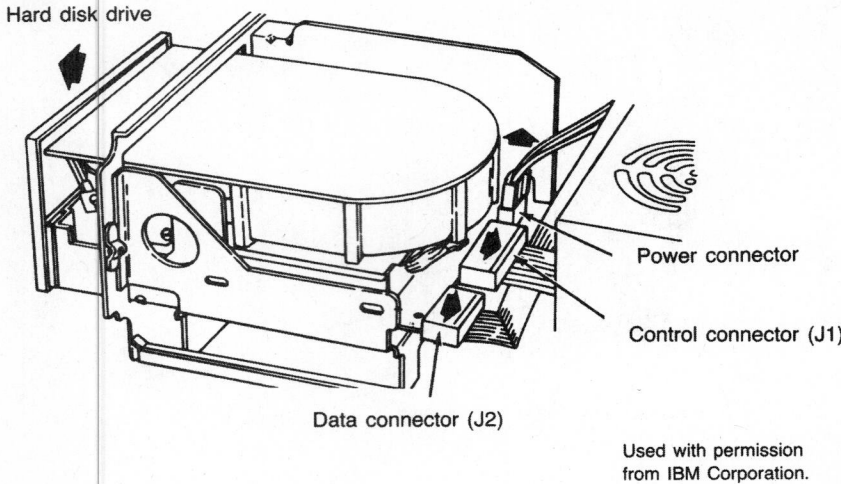

Hard disk drive

Power connector

Control connector (J1)

Data connector (J2)

Used with permission
from IBM Corporation.

Fig. 3.7
Disconnecting the power and signal cables from the hard disk drive.

Removing the Power Supply. In XT or Slimline case systems, the power supply is mounted in the system unit with four screws in the rear and usually two interlocking tabs on the bottom. Removing the power supply may require that you remove the disk drives before getting the power supply out. You will probably have to at least loosen the drives to slide them forward for clearance when you remove the supply.

To remove the power supply, first remove the cover, all adapter boards, and the disk drives, as described earlier. If sufficient clearance exists, you might not have to remove the adapter boards and disk drives. Proceed as follows:

1. Remove the four power-supply retaining screws from the rear of the system-unit chassis (see fig. 3.8).

2. Disconnect the cables from the power supply to the motherboard (see fig. 3.9). Disconnect the power cables from the power supply to the disk drives. Always grasp the connectors themselves; never pull on the wires.

3. Slide the power supply forward about a half-inch to disengage the interlocking tabs on the bottom of the unit. Lift the power supply out of the unit (see fig. 3.10).

Removing the Motherboard. After all the adapter cards are removed from the unit, you can remove the system board, or *motherboard*. The motherboard in XT and Slimline case systems is held in place by only a few screws and often several plastic standoffs that elevate the board from the metal chassis so that it does not touch the chassis and cause a short. The standoffs slide into slots in the chassis. *These standoffs should remain with the motherboard.* You do not have to extract these standoffs from the motherboard to remove it; you just remove the motherboard with the standoffs still attached. When you reinstall the motherboard, make sure that the standoffs slide properly in their slots. If one or more standoffs have not properly engaged the chassis, you might crack the motherboard when you tighten the screws or install adapter cards.

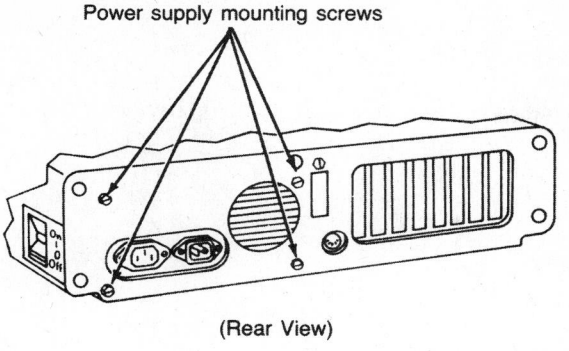

Power supply mounting screws

(Rear View)

Used with permission
from IBM Corporation.

Fig. 3.8
Removing the power supply retaining screws from the rear of the chassis.

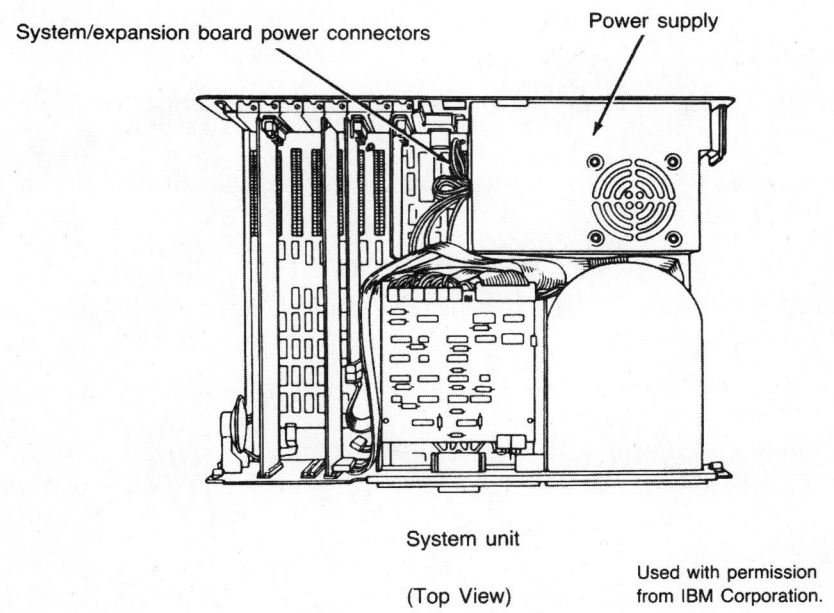

System/expansion board power connectors   Power supply

System unit

(Top View)

Used with permission
from IBM Corporation.

Fig. 3.9
Disconnecting the cables from the power supply to the motherboard.

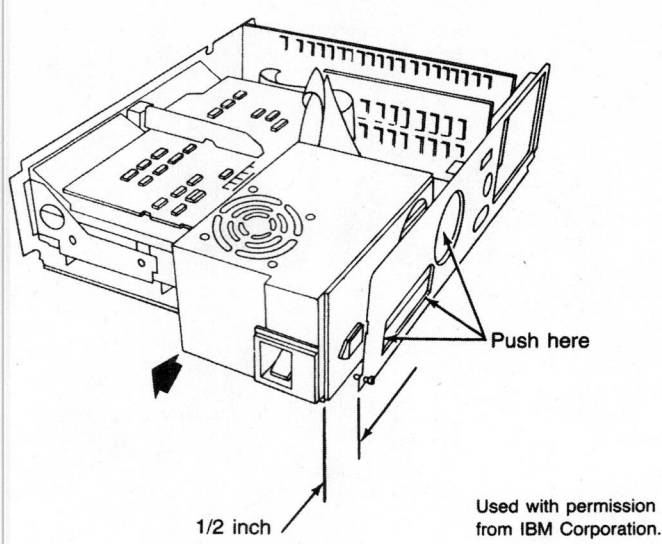

Push here

Used with permission
from IBM Corporation.

1/2 inch

Fig. 3.10
Sliding the power supply forward to disengage the interlocking tabs on the unit's bottom.

To remove the motherboard, first remove all adapter boards from the system unit, as described earlier. Proceed as follows:

1. Disconnect all electrical connectors from the motherboard, including those for the keyboard, power supply, and speaker.

2. Locate and remove the motherboard retaining screws.

3. Slide the motherboard away from the power supply about a half-inch until the standoffs have disengaged from their mounting slots (see fig. 3.11).

4. Lift the motherboard up and out of the chassis.

AT and Tower Case Systems

Disassembling an AT or Tower case system normally requires only two tools: a 1/4-inch nut driver for the external screws holding the cover in place and a 3/16-inch nut driver for all the other screws.

Most of the procedures are exactly like those for the XT or Slimline case systems. One difference, however, is that many AT case systems use a different method for mounting the disk drives. Special rails are attached to the sides of the drives, and the drives slide into the system-unit chassis on these rails. The chassis has guide tracks for the rails, which enables you to remove the drive from the front of the unit without having to access the side to remove any mounting screws. Normally the rails are made of plastic or fiberglass, but they can also be made of metal in some systems. A diagram showing how most of these rails are constructed can be found in Chapter 13, "Floppy Disk Drives and Controllers."

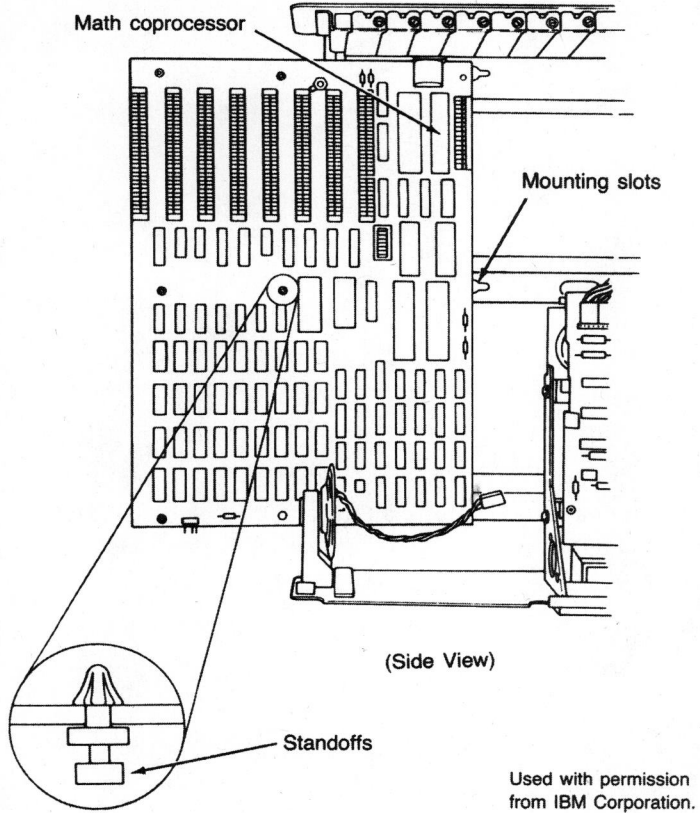

Fig. 3.11
Sliding the motherboard away from the power supply until standoffs disengage from mounting slots.

Removing the Cover. To remove the case cover, follow these steps:

1. Turn off the system and unplug the power cord from the system unit.

2. Turn the system unit around so that you're facing the rear of the unit. Locate the screws that hold the system-unit cover in place (see fig. 3.12).

3. Use the 1/4-inch nut driver to remove the cover screws.

4. Slide the cover toward the front of the system unit until it stops. Lift up the front of the cover and remove it from the chassis.

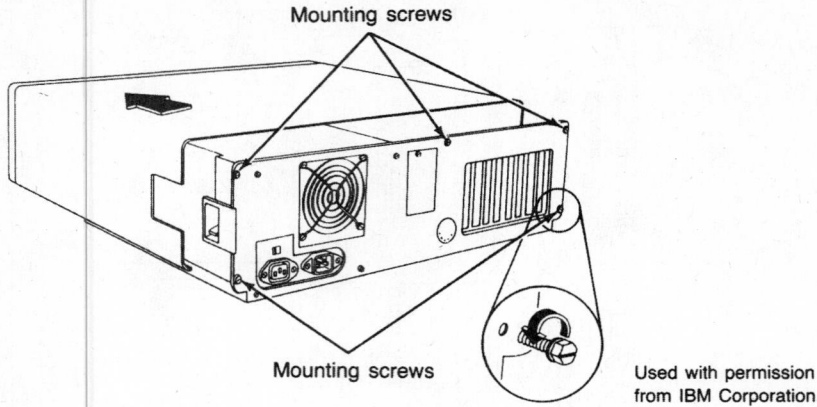

Mounting screws

Mounting screws

Used with permission
from IBM Corporation.

Fig. 3.12
Removing the screws that hold the AT case cover in place.

Removing Adapter Boards. To remove all the adapter boards from the system unit, first remove the system unit cover, as described earlier. Proceed as follows for each adapter:

1. Note which slot each adapter is in. If possible, make a diagram or drawing.

2. Use the 3/16-inch nut driver to remove the screw holding the adapter in place (refer to fig. 3.2).

3. Note the positions of any cables plugged into the adapter before you remove them. In a correctly wired system, the colored stripe on one side of the ribbon cable always denotes pin number 1. Some connectors have keys that enable them to be inserted only the correct way.

4. Remove the adapter by lifting with even force at both ends.

5. Note the positions of any jumpers or switches on the adapter, especially when documentation for the adapter is not available. Even when documentation is available, undocumented jumpers and switches often are used by manufacturers for special purposes, such as testing or unique configurations. It's a good idea to know the existing settings in case they are disturbed.

Removing Disk Drives. Removing drives from AT case systems is very easy. The procedures are similar for both floppy and hard disk drives.

Always back up hard disks completely and park the heads before removing disks from the system. Most newer drives (IDE and SCSI) automatically park the heads when powered off. A backup is important because the possibility always exists that data will be lost or the drive will be damaged from rough handling.

To remove the drives from an AT case system, first remove the cover, as described earlier. Proceed as follows:

1. Depending on whether the drive is a hard disk or floppy disk drive, it is retained by either a metal keeper bar with two screws or two small, L-shaped metal tabs each held in place by a single screw. Locate these screws and remove them, along with the tabs or keeper bar (see figs. 3.13 and 3.14).

2. Slide the disk drive forward about two inches, disconnect the power cables, signal and data cables, and ground wire from the drive (see figs. 3.15 and 3.16). In a correctly wired system, the colored stripe on one side of the ribbon cable always denotes pin number 1. The power connector is shaped so that it can be inserted only the correct way.

3. Slide the drive completely out of the unit.

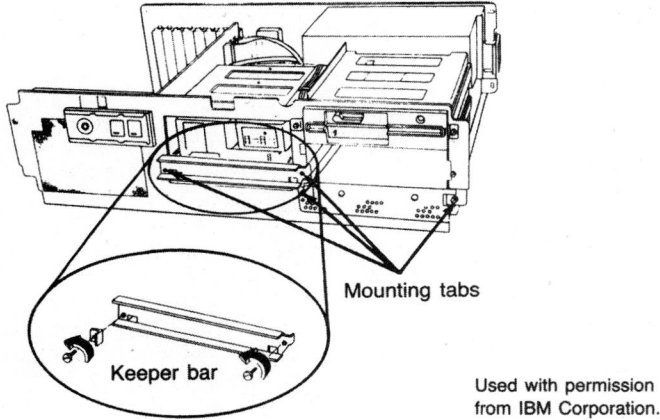

Mounting tabs

Keeper bar

Used with permission
from IBM Corporation.

Fig. 3.13
Removing mounting tabs and the keeper bar on a hard drive.

Removing the Power Supply. In AT case systems, the power supply is mounted in the system unit with four screws in the rear and usually two interlocking tabs on the bottom. Removing the power supply usually requires that you slide the disk drives forward for clearance when you remove the supply.

To remove the power supply, first remove the cover, loosen the disk drive mounting screws, and move the disk drive forward about two inches, as described earlier. Proceed as follows:

1. Remove the four power supply retaining screws from the rear of the system unit chassis (see fig. 3.17).

2. Disconnect the cables from the power supply to the motherboard (see fig. 3.18). Disconnect the power cables from the power supply to the disk drive. Always grasp the connectors themselves; never pull on the wires.

3. Slide the power supply forward about a half-inch to disengage the interlocking tabs on the bottom of the unit. Lift the power supply out of the unit.

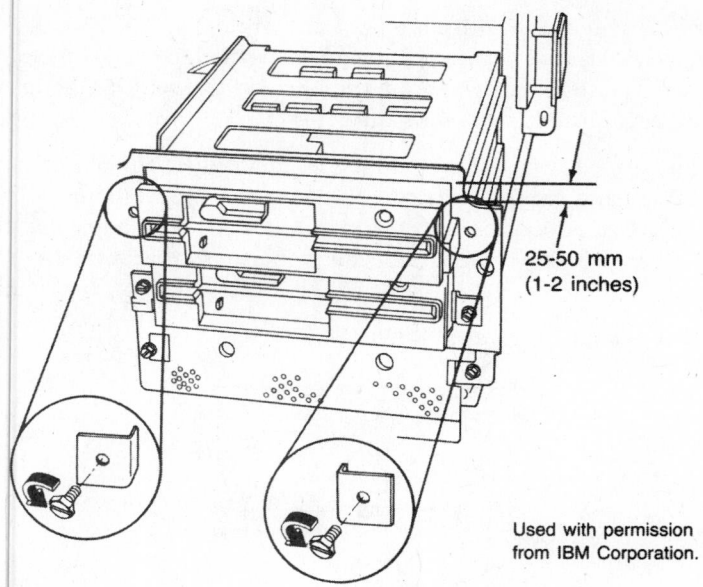

25-50 mm
(1-2 inches)

Used with permission
from IBM Corporation.

Fig. 3.14
Removing the mounting tabs on a floppy drive.

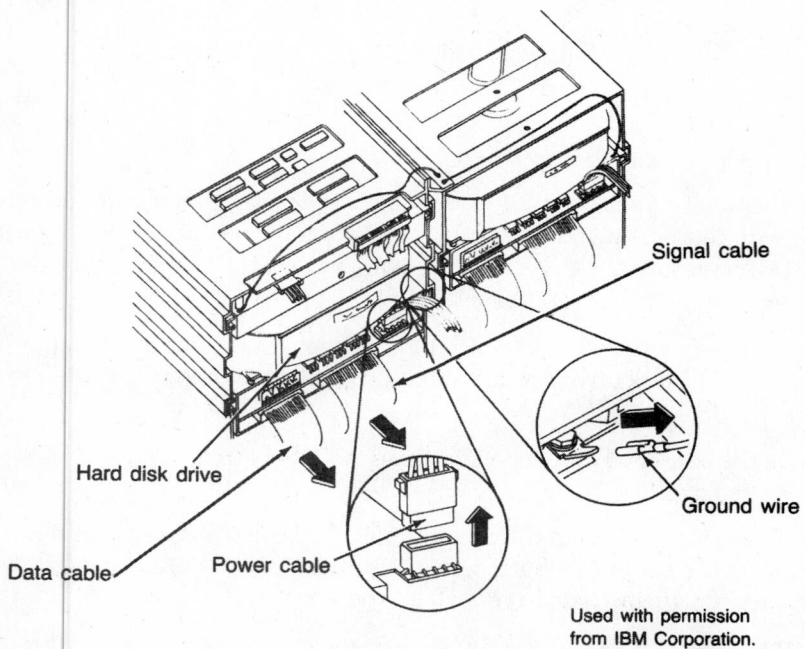

Signal cable

Hard disk drive

Ground wire

Data cable

Power cable

Used with permission
from IBM Corporation.

Fig. 3.15
Disconnecting the hard drive power cable, signal and data cables, and ground wire.

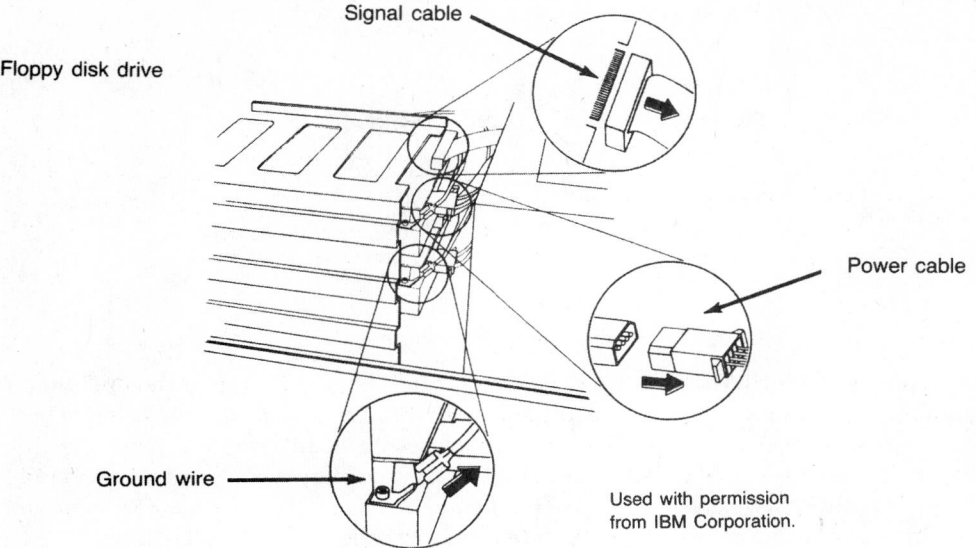

Fig. 3.16
Disconnecting the floppy drive power cable, signal cable, and ground wire.

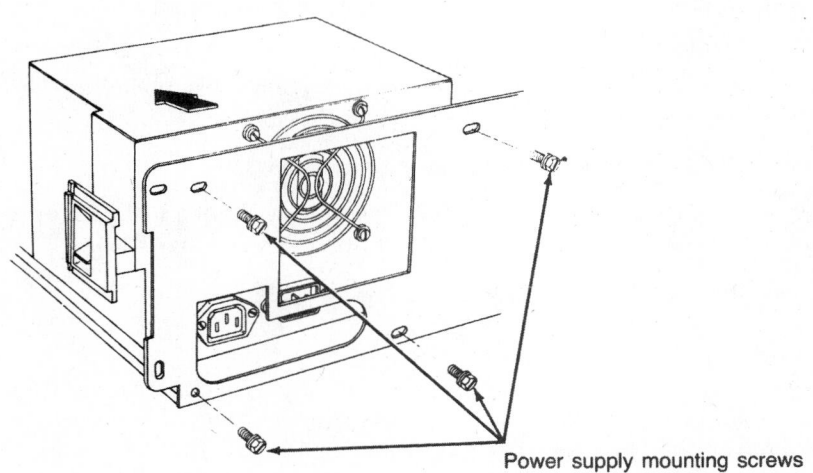

Fig. 3.17
Removing the power supply retaining screws from the rear of the chassis.

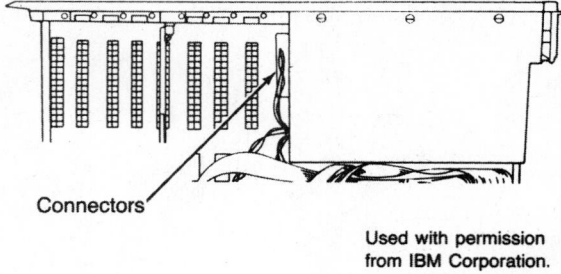

Connectors

**Used with permission
from IBM Corporation.**

Fig. 3.18
Disconnecting the cables from the power supply to the motherboard.

Removing the Motherboard. After all adapter cards are removed from the unit, you can remove the motherboard. The motherboard in AT case systems is held in place by several screws as well as plastic standoffs that elevate the board from the metal chassis so that it does not touch the chassis and cause a short. You should not separate the standoffs from the motherboard; remove the board and the standoffs as a unit. The standoffs slide into slots in the chassis. When you reinstall the motherboard, make sure that the standoffs are located properly in their slots. If one or more standoffs have not engaged the chassis properly, you might crack the motherboard when you tighten the screws or install adapter cards.

To remove the motherboard, first remove all adapter boards from the system unit, as described earlier. Proceed as follows:

1. Disconnect from the motherboard all electrical connectors, including those for the keyboard, power supply, speaker, battery, and keylock.

2. Locate and remove the motherboard retaining screws.

3. Slide the motherboard away from the power supply about a half-inch until the standoffs have disengaged from their mounting slots (see fig. 3.19).

4. Lift the motherboard up and out of the chassis.

PS/2 Systems

The disassembly of IBM's PS/2 systems is incredibly easy. In fact, ease of disassembly and reassembly is one of the greatest features of these systems. In addition to being easy to service and repair, they were designed to be assembled primarily by robots and automated machinery. This type of machinery does not handle conventional fasteners such as screws, nuts, and bolts very well. Most PS/2 systems therefore are assembled with a great deal of "snap together" technology. The screws that are used have a special self-centering design in which the screw end is tapered so that it is self-guiding, to mate with the threads in the hole. Automated robotic machinery then can insert and tighten the screws more easily and accurately, and without stripping the threads. This approach to construction makes these systems not only easier to assemble by machine, but also much easier for people to disassemble and reassemble.

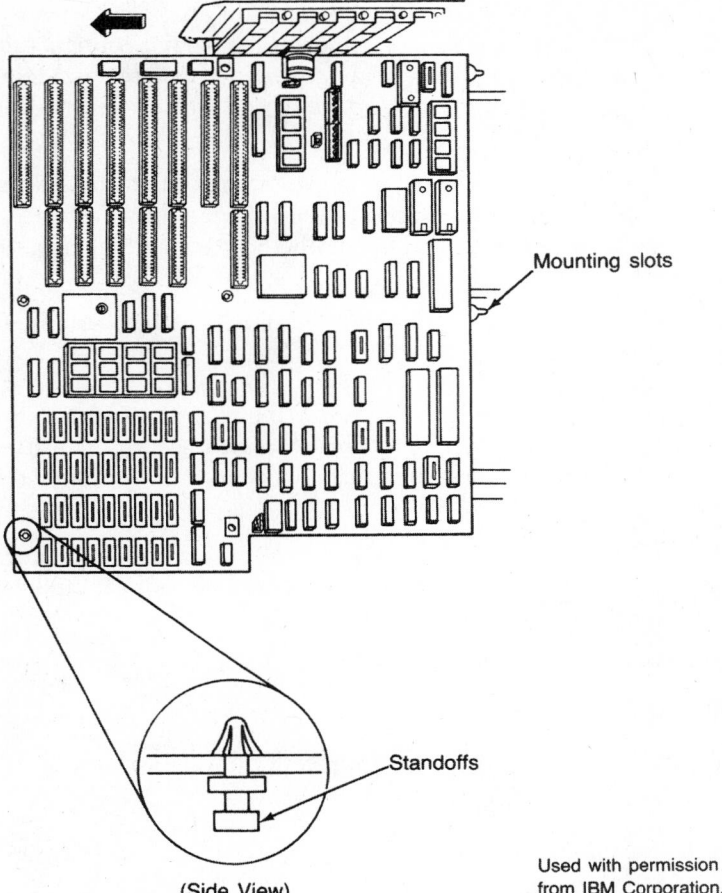

Mounting slots

Standoffs

(Side View)

Used with permission
from IBM Corporation.

Fig. 3.19
Disengaging standoffs from their mounting slots.

If you can disassemble one PS/2 system, you see how easily the others come apart as well, especially systems that are similar or identical physically. Although a variety of PS/2 designs exist, many of them are similar. The three primary original types of PS/2 chassis design are the 30/30-286/55 SX, the 50/70, and the 60/65/80. Other designs, including the 90, 95, and 35/40/57/76/77, are similar in many ways to the three primary types. Models 25 and 25-286 are unique in that they have a built-in display.

- Models 25 and 25-286 have a unique design with a built-in monitor.

- Models 30, 30-286, and 55 SX share a common chassis and mechanical design, although their circuit boards are different.

- The newer 35, 40, 56, 57, 76, and 77 systems physically are nearly identical to each other. Many of these different models even share motherboards.

■ Models 50, 50 Z, and 70 represent the "ultimate" in ease of disassembly and reassembly. These units have not a single cable in their default configuration and are snapped together almost entirely without conventional fasteners. Models 50 Z and 70 especially share many physical components and are difficult to tell apart from the outside.

■ Models 60, 65 SX, and 80 are full-size, floor-standing systems. These systems are virtually identical to each other from a physical standpoint and share most of their physical components, even though the motherboards are different.

■ The newer Model 90 is similar to the 50/70 systems in construction, but is unique in some ways. The newer Model 95 is similar to the 60/65/80 systems, but also differs in some ways.

The following section discusses, step-by-step, disassembly and reassembly procedures for the PS/2 systems. The three main system types each cover a section. The disassembly procedures for the three primary designs can be applied to the other, similar PS/2 system designs as well.

Models 30, 30-286, and 55 SX. This section describes the disassembly procedures for the PS/2 Model 30, Model 30-286, and Model 55 SX. The systems are modular in nature, and most of the procedures are simple.

Removing the Cover. To remove the system-unit cover, follow these steps:

1. Park the hard disk.

2. Turn off the system and unplug the power cord from the wall socket.

3. Disconnect all external options.

4. If the keylock option is installed, make sure that the lock is in the unlocked position and the key removed.

5. Loosen all four screws located at the bottom corners on the sides of the system. Slide the cover back and lift it up and away.

6. Remove the rear cover that covers the system's back panel. You remove this cover by loosening the screw on each corner of the rear cover on the back of the system. Pull the rear cover back and away from the system unit (see fig. 3.20).

Removing the 3 1/2-inch Floppy Disk Drive. The procedure for removing the floppy drive is very simple. Proceed as follows:

1. Remove the front cover (the bezel) from the drive by pushing down on the two plastic tabs on top of the bezel.

2. Pull the bezel off and away from the front of the system.

3. Disconnect the disk cabling by gently pulling the cable away from the drive.

4. Remove the plastic nails from each side of the drive bracket.

5. Press up on the plastic tab under the front of the drive.

6. Pull the drive forward out of the system (see fig. 3.21).

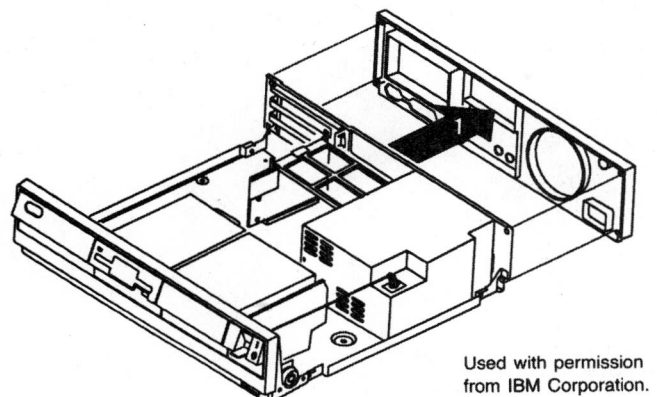

Used with permission
from IBM Corporation.

Fig. 3.20
Removing the rear cover (Models 30, 30-286, and 55 SX).

Removing the Hard Disk Drive. Before removing the hard disk, make sure that the heads have been parked. You can use the Reference Disk to perform this task. Simply boot the disk, and select the Move the Computer option from the main menu. If this option is not present, IBM supplied your system with only self-parking drives; you park them by simply turning off the power. Even if the option is present, you still might have a self-parking drive (refer to Chapter 14, "Hard Disk Drives and Controllers"). You can remove the drive by following these steps (which are similar to the steps for removing a floppy drive):

1. Remove the front cover (the bezel) from the drive by pushing down on the two plastic tabs on top of the bezel and pulling it off and away from the front of the system.

2. Disconnect the disk cabling by gently pulling the cable away from the drive.

3. Remove the plastic nails from each side of the drive bracket.

4. Press upward on the plastic tab under the front of the drive, and pull the drive forward out of the system.

Removing Adapters. To remove all adapter cards from the system unit, first remove the system-unit cover, as described earlier. Proceed as follows for each adapter:

1. Remove the screw from the bracket retaining the card.

2. Slide the adapter sideways out of the system unit (see fig. 3.22).

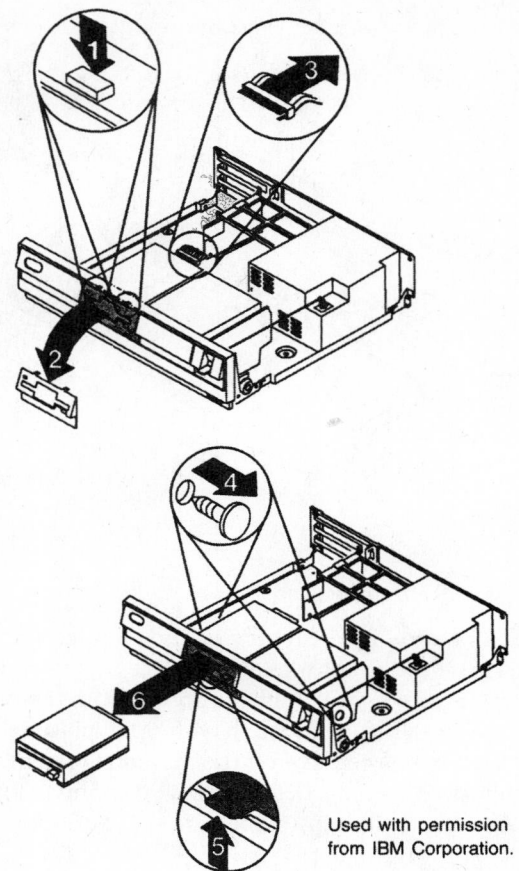

Used with permission
from IBM Corporation.

Fig. 3.21
Removing a 3 1/2-inch floppy drive (Models 30, 30-286, and 55 SX).

If you add new options, their installation might require that you remove the plastic insert on the rear panel. Also, if you add a 3/4-length adapter, you must adjust the sliding support bracket to support the adapter properly.

Removing the Bus Adapter. These systems have a bus adapter card that contains the slots. This adapter plugs into the motherboard. To remove the device, proceed as follows:

1. Push in on the two tabs on top of the bus adapter support.

2. Gently rotate the end of the support upward and disengage the tabs in the power supply.

3. Lift up and remove the bus adapter (see fig. 3.23).

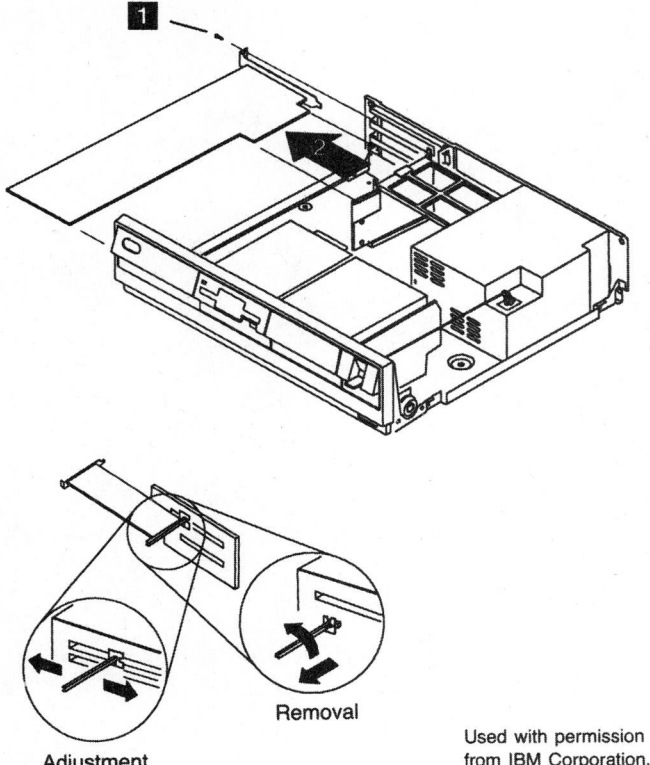

Adjustment   Removal

Used with permission
from IBM Corporation.

Fig. 3.22
Removing adapter cards (Models 30, 30-286, and 55 SX).

Removing the Power Supply. When you remove the power supply, first remove the rear cover and the bus adapter support, as described earlier. Proceed as follows:

1. Disconnect the power connector from the power supply to the motherboard by pulling the connector straight up.

2. Disengage the power-switch link from the power supply.

3. Remove the three screws that secure the power supply to the system frame. The screws are at the back of the power supply.

4. Gently slide the power supply toward the front of the system to disengage the power supply from the base of the frame.

5. Lift the power supply up and away from the unit (see fig. 3.24).

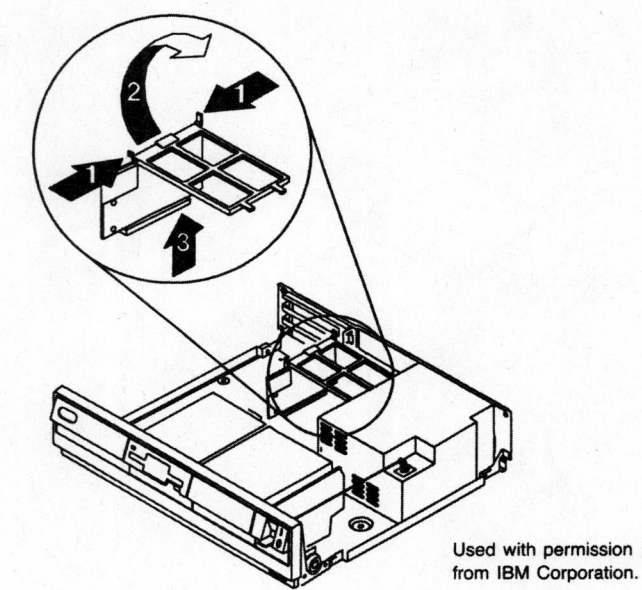

Used with permission
from IBM Corporation.

Fig. 3.23
Removing the bus adapter (Models 30, 30-286, and 55 SX).

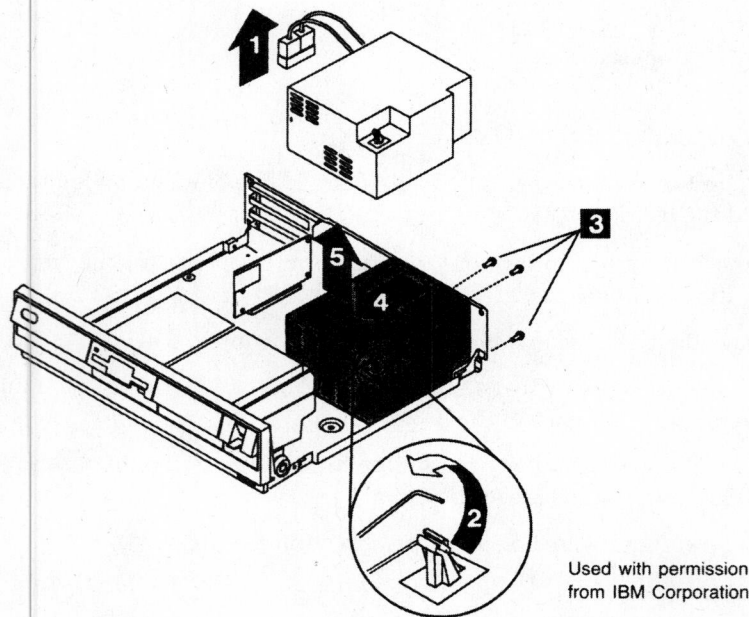

Used with permission
from IBM Corporation.

Fig. 3.24
Removing the power supply (Models 30, 30-286, and 55 SX).

Removing Single In-Line Memory Modules (SIMMs). One benefit of using single in-line memory modules (SIMMs) is that they're easy to remove or install. When you remove memory modules, remember that because of physical interference you must remove the memory-module package closest to the disk drive bus-adapter slot before you remove the package closest to the edge of the motherboard. To remove a SIMM properly, follow this procedure:

1. Gently pull the tabs on each side of the SIMM socket outward.

2. Rotate or pull the SIMM up and out of the socket (see fig. 3.25).

Caution
Be careful not to damage the connector. If you damage the motherboard-SIMM connector, you could be looking at an expensive repair. Never force the SIMM; it should come out easily. If it doesn't, you are doing something wrong.

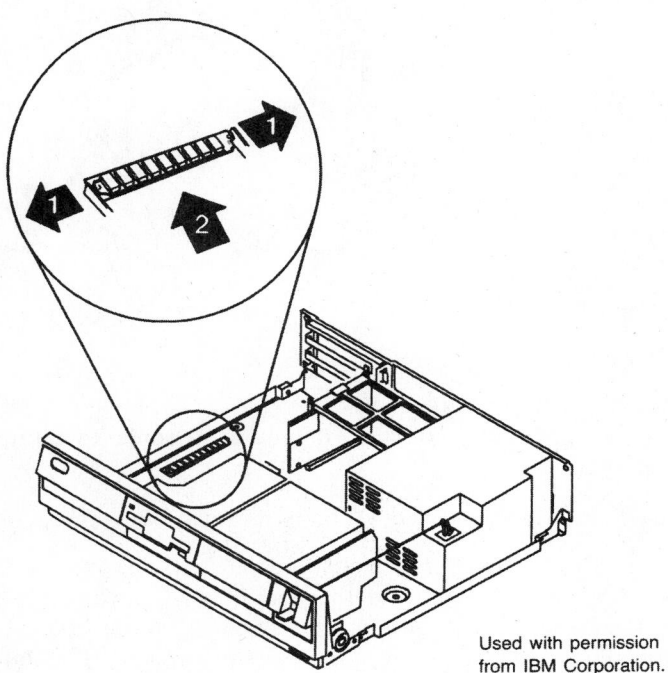

Used with permission
from IBM Corporation.

Fig. 3.25
Removing a SIMM (Models 30, 30-286, and 55 SX).

Removing the Motherboard. The motherboard is held in place by several screws, all of which must be taken out. Proceed as follows:

1. Remove all screws.

2. Carefully slide the motherboard to the left.

3. Lift the motherboard out of the system unit (see fig. 3.26).

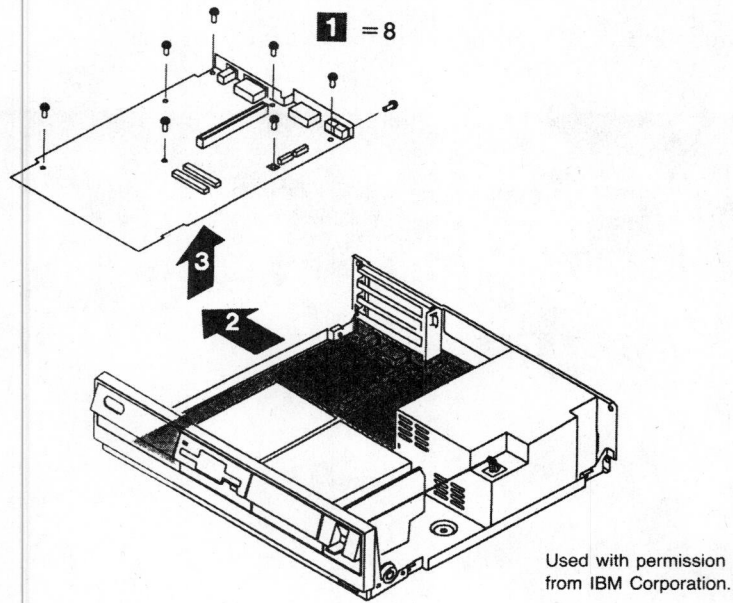

Used with permission
from IBM Corporation.

Fig. 3.26
Removing the motherboard (Models 30, 30-286, and 55 SX).

Models 50, 50 Z, and 70. This section describes the disassembly procedures for the PS/2 Model 50, Model 50 Z, and Model 70. These systems are modular in nature, and most of the procedures are simple.

Removing the Cover. To remove the system-unit cover, follow these steps:

1. Park the hard disk. Nearly all these systems come with self-parking hard disks; only the 20M drive used in the Model 50 does not. Self-parking drives require no manual parking operation. Because no parking program is necessary, the reference disks for the Model 70 do not have a head-parking program or menu selection.

2. Turn off the system and unplug the power cord from the wall socket.

3. Unlock the cover.

4. Loosen the two cover thumbscrews on the back of the system.

5. Slide the cover toward you and lift it off (see fig. 3.27).

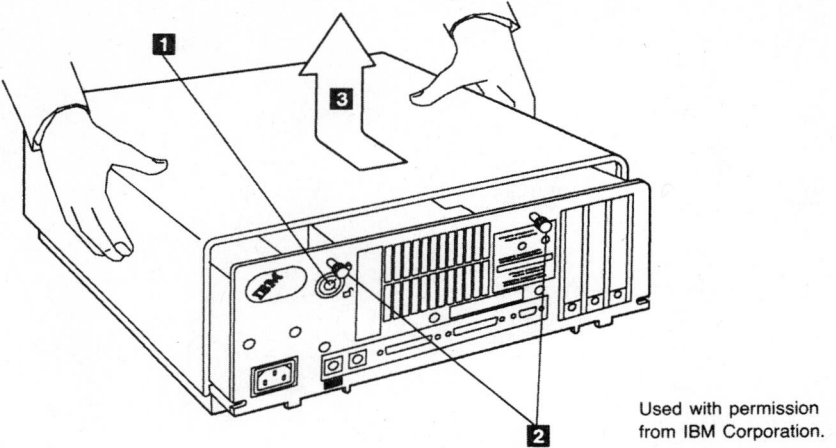

Used with permission
from IBM Corporation.

Fig. 3.27
Removing the cover (Models 50 and 70).

Removing the Battery-and-Speaker Assembly. The battery and speaker are contained in a single assembly. To remove this assembly, follow these steps:

1. To avoid accidentally discharging the battery, remove the battery from its holder before removing the battery-and-speaker assembly: bend the tabs on the holder toward the rear and pull the battery straight up. Remember to install this assembly before replacing the battery.

2. Push the tab on the bottom of the speaker unit to disengage the speaker assembly from the support structure.

3. Lift the entire battery-and-speaker assembly up and out of the system (see fig. 3.28).

Removing the Fan Assembly. The fan assembly in Model 70 systems is an integral part of the power supply. In these systems, the fan is screwed directly to the power supply. You remove the fan by removing the power supply.

In Model 50 systems, remove the fan assembly as follows:

1. Disengage the two plastic push-button tabs on either side of the fan assembly by prying them upward. If necessary, use the small pry tool located at the front, right corner of the system.

2. Pull the entire assembly up and out of the system (see fig. 3.29).

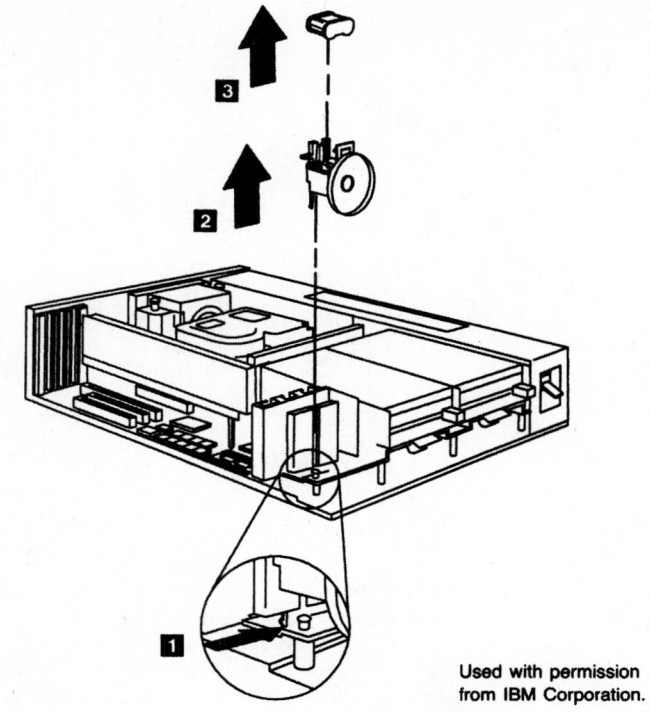

Used with permission
from IBM Corporation.

Fig. 3.28
Removing the battery-and-speaker assembly (Models 50 and 70).

Removing Adapters. An important part of removing adapter boards in these systems is to make a diagram of the adapter and cable locations.

Micro Channel bus systems such as the PS/2s remember exactly where each adapter card was located. Because of this, you should put all adapters back in the same slot from which they were removed. Otherwise, the CMOS memory configuration must be run to reconfigure the adapters in their new slots.

To remove the adapters, follow these steps:

1. Make sure that all cables are disconnected.

2. Loosen the retaining thumb screw at the base of the card bracket.

3. Grasp the option adapter and gently pull it up and out of the system unit (see fig. 3.30).

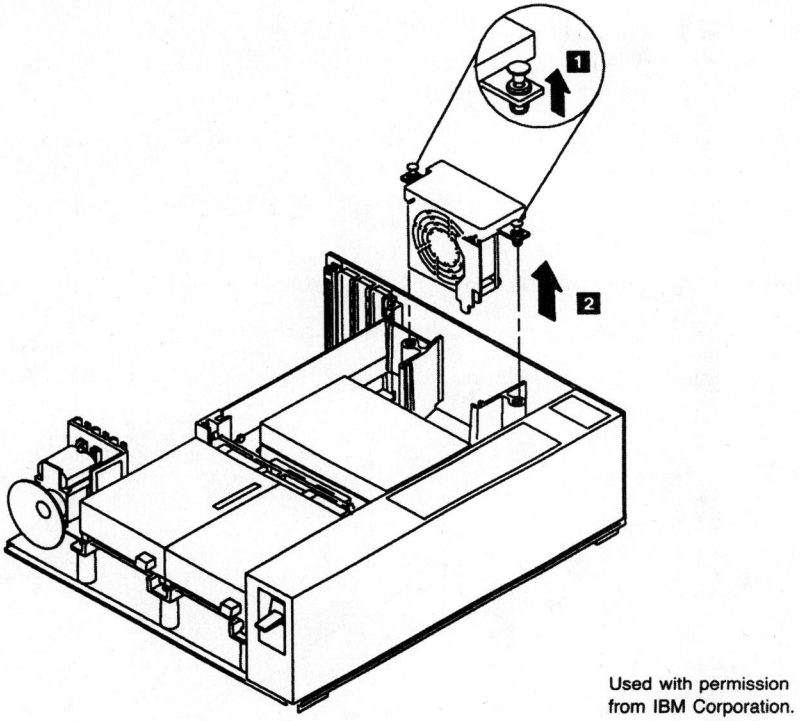

Used with permission
from IBM Corporation.

Fig. 3.29
Removing the fan assembly (Models 50 and 70).

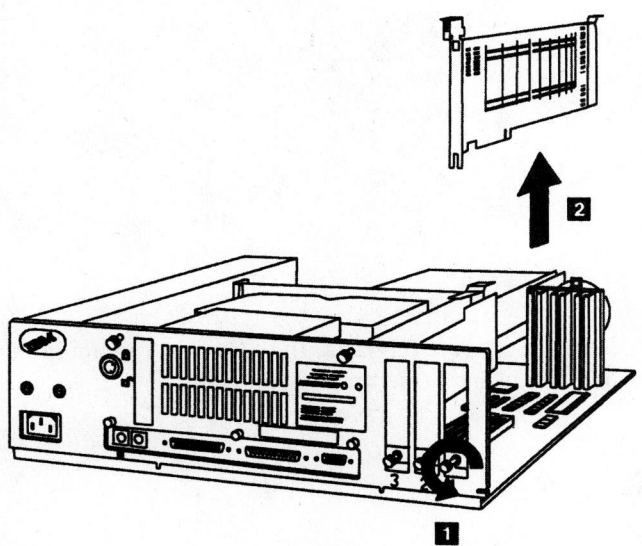

Used with permission
from IBM Corporation.

Fig. 3.30
Removing an adapter (Models 50 and 70).

Removing the 3 1/2-Inch Floppy Disk Drive. Removing floppy drives from 3 1/2-inch floppy disk drive systems is a simple task. Just push up on the tab underneath the floppy drive, and slide the drive out toward you.

Removing Fixed Disk Drives. Removing the hard disk from a fixed disk drive is almost as easy as removing a floppy drive. Before removing the hard disk, make sure that you've backed up all the information on the fixed disk and parked the heads. Follow these steps:

1. Press down the two plastic tabs on the side where the power supply is located.

2. Slide the fixed disk drive toward the power supply and up.

3. Grasp the adapter at each end, and gently pull the adapter up (see fig. 3.31).

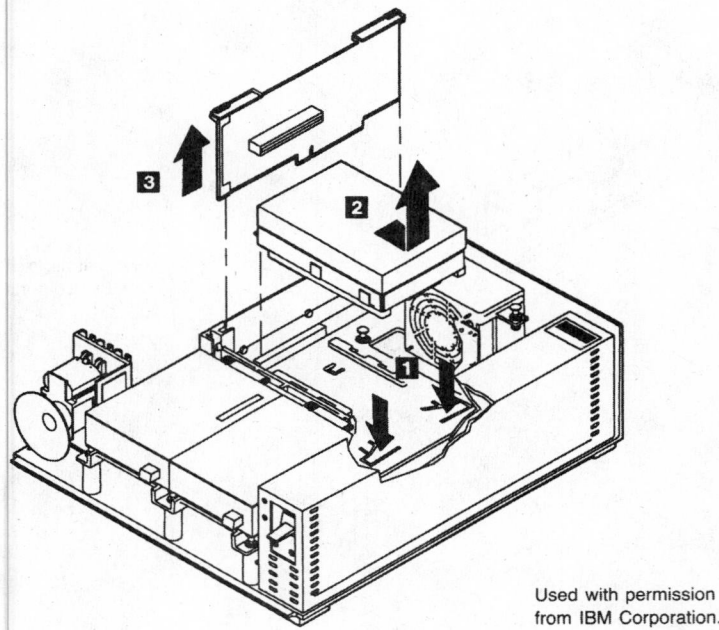

Used with permission
from IBM Corporation.

Fig. 3.31
Removing the fixed disk drive (Models 50 and 70).

Removing the Drive-Support Structure. To remove the support structure from the system unit, you first must remove these components:

Cover

Battery-and-speaker assembly

Fan assembly

Adapters

Floppy disk drives

Fixed disk drives

When these items have been removed, pull up all six white plastic push-button lock tabs, and lift the assembly up (see fig. 3.32). If necessary, you can use the small pry tool on the front, right side of the system to pry up the lock tabs.

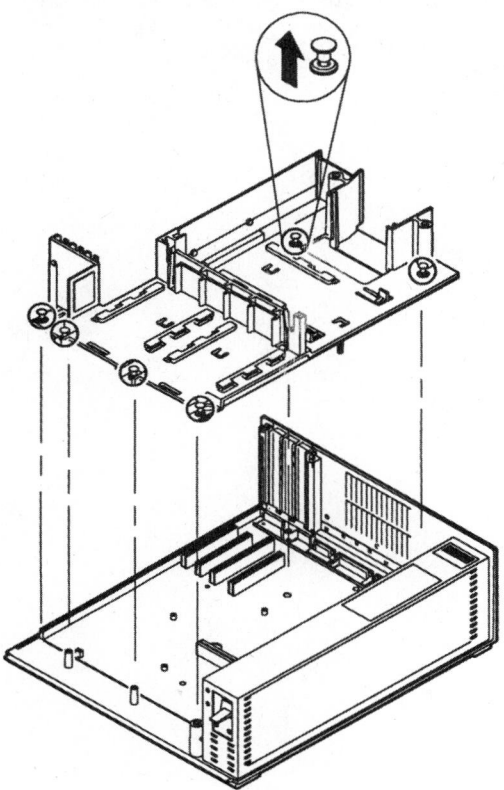

Used with permission
from IBM Corporation.

Fig. 3.32
Removing the drive-support structure (Models 50 and 70).

Removing the Power Supply. To remove the power supply, follow these steps:

1. Remove the screw on the front, left side of the system.

2. Remove the two screws on the back of the power supply.

3. Slide the power supply to the right, and remove from the system unit (see fig. 3.33).

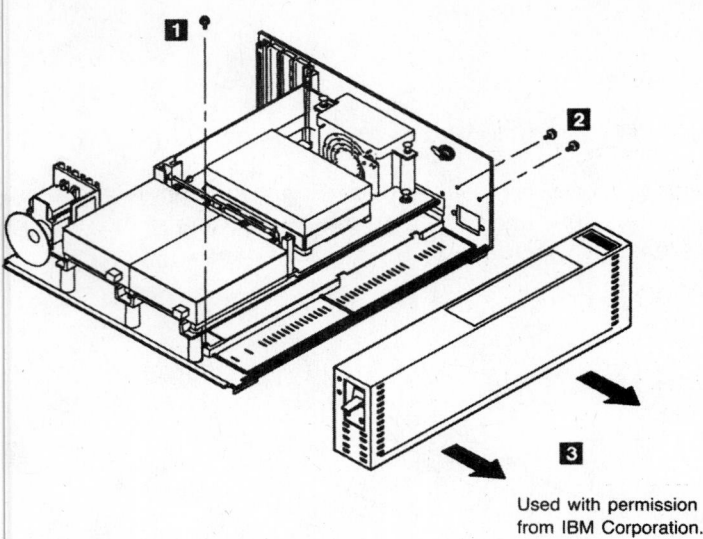

Used with permission
from IBM Corporation.

Fig. 3.33
Removing the power supply (Models 50 and 70).

Removing the Motherboard. To remove the motherboard from the system unit, you first must remove these components:

Cover

Battery-and-speaker assembly

Fan assembly

Adapters

Floppy disk drives

Fixed disk drives

Disk-support structure

Power supply

After you remove all these components from the system unit, removing the motherboard requires only these two steps:

1. Remove all six retaining screws (three on the back of the system unit and three on the motherboard).

2. Gently lift the motherboard up and out of the system (see fig. 3.34).

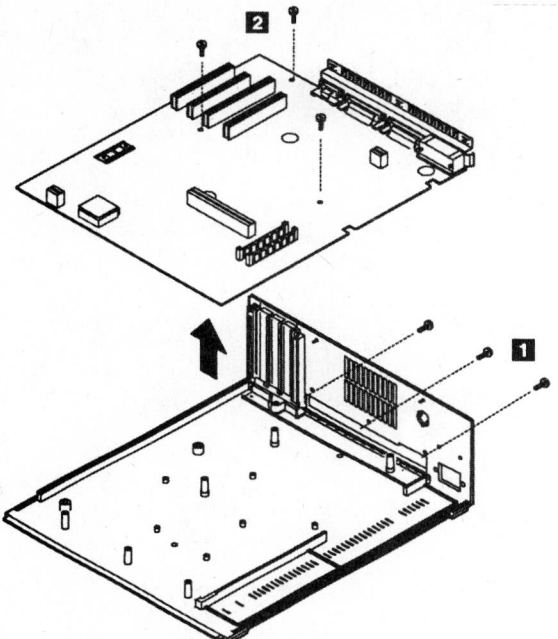

Used with permission
from IBM Corporation.

Fig. 3.34
Removing the motherboard (Models 50 and 70).

Removing Single In-Line Memory Modules (SIMMs). A benefit of using single
in-line memory modules (SIMMs) is that they are easy to remove or install. When you
remove memory modules, remember that, because of physical interference, you must
remove the memory-module package closest to the disk drive bus-adapter slot before
removing the package closest to the edge of the motherboard. To remove a SIMM properly, follow the steps shown for the 30, 30-286, and 55 SX (see fig. 3.35).

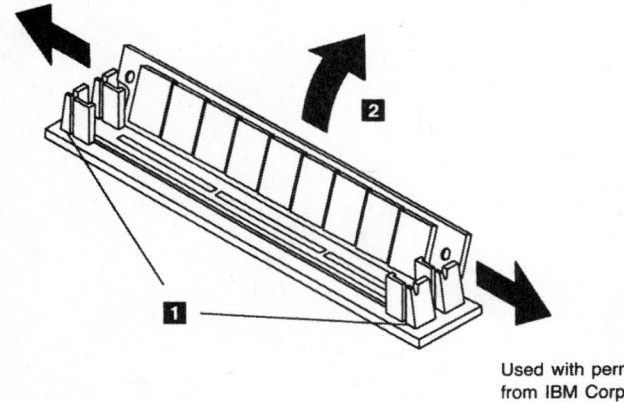

Used with permission
from IBM Corporation.

Fig. 3.35
Removing a SIMM (Models 50 and 70).

Caution

Be careful not to damage the connector. If you damage the motherboard-SIMM connector, you could have an expensive repair. Never force the SIMM; it should come out easily. If it doesn't, you are doing something wrong.

Models 60, 65 SX, and 80. This section describes the disassembly procedures for the PS/2 Model 60, Model 65 SX, and Model 80, These floor-standing PS/2 systems are not as easy to work on or as modular as the desktop systems, but they're still easy to service compared with the earlier PC- and AT-type systems. Most repair procedures do not even involve using any tools.

Removing the Cover. To remove the system-unit cover, follow these steps:

1. Park the hard disk. Because all Model 60, 65 SX, and 80 systems delivered from IBM include self-parking hard disks, no manual parking operation is necessary. The reference disks for these systems do not include a head-parking program or menu selection because they are unnecessary with self-parking drives.

2. Turn off the system, and unplug the power cord from the wall socket.

3. Disconnect all external options.

4. Unlock the cover lock.

5. Loosen the two cover screws on the side of the system.

6. Tilt the cover toward you.

7. Lift the cover up (see fig. 3.36).

Removing Adapters. An important part of removing adapter boards in these systems is to make a diagram of the adapter and cable locations.

Because Micro Channel bus systems remember where each and every card is located, you should put all adapters back in the same slot from which they were removed. Otherwise, the CMOS memory configuration must be run.

To remove the adapters, follow these steps:

1. Make sure that all cables are disconnected.

2. Loosen the retaining thumb screw at the base of the card bracket.

3. Grasp the option adapter, and gently pull it up and out of the system unit (see fig. 3.37).

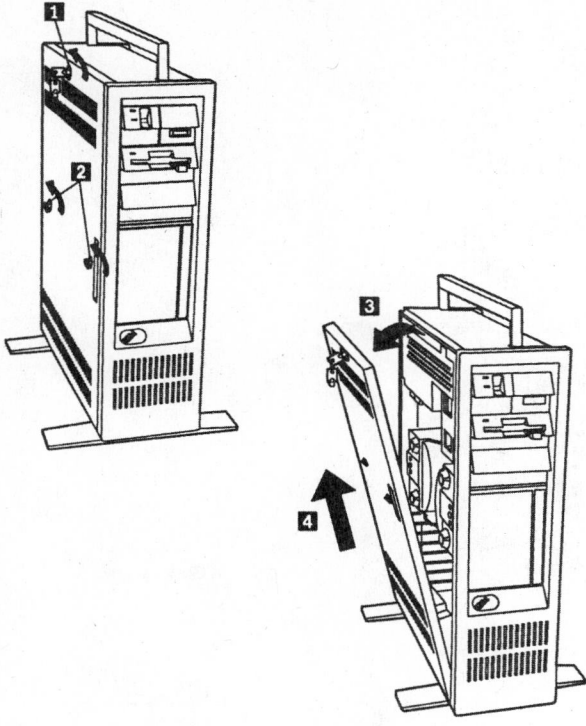

Used with permission
from IBM Corporation.

Fig. 3.36
Removing the cover (Models 60, 65 SX, and 80).

Removing the Battery-and-Speaker Assembly. The battery and speaker are contained in a single assembly. To remove this assembly, follow these steps:

1. To avoid accidentally discharging the battery, remove the battery from its holder before removing the battery-and-speaker assembly: bend the tabs on the holder toward the rear, and pull the battery straight up. Remember to install this assembly before replacing the battery.

2. Disconnect the battery-and-speaker assembly cable.

3. Push the tab on the bottom of the speaker unit to disengage the speaker assembly from the support structure (see fig. 3.38).

4. Lift the entire battery-and-speaker assembly up and out of the system.

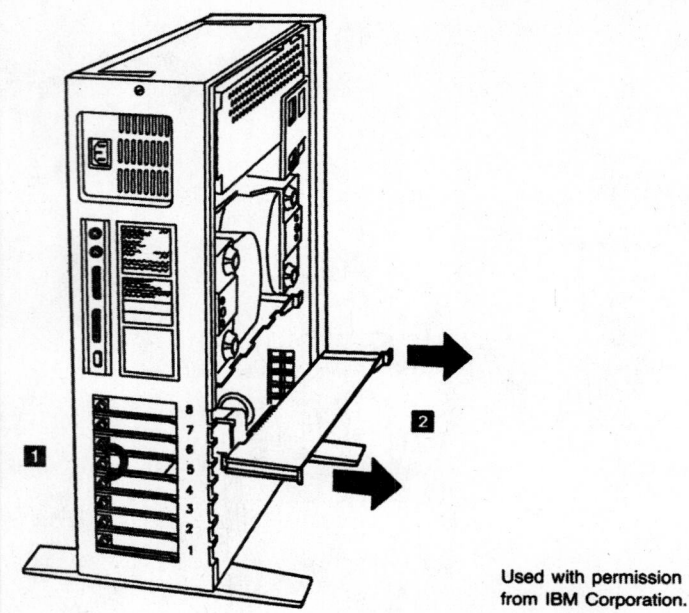

Used with permission
from IBM Corporation.

Fig. 3.37
Removing an adapter (Models 60, 65 SX, and 80).

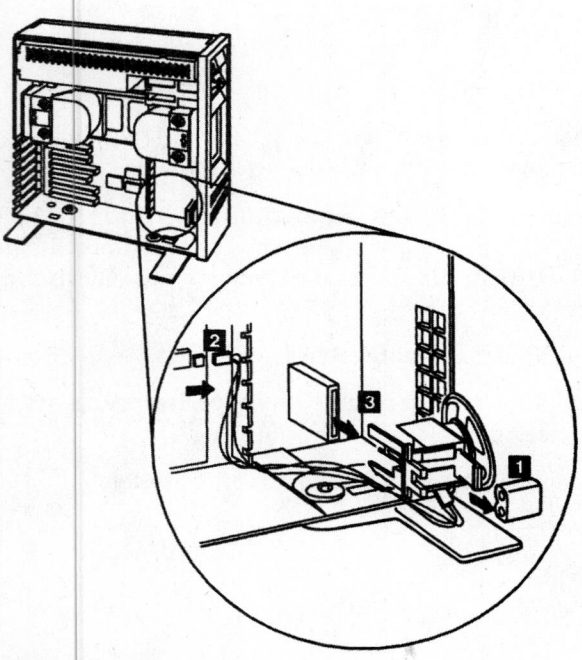

Used with permission
from IBM Corporation.

Fig. 3.38
Removing the battery-and-speaker assembly (Models 60, 65 SX, and 80).

Removing the Front Bezel. These models have a large front panel, or bezel, that you must remove to gain access to the floppy disk drives. The panel snaps off easily if you follow this procedure:

1. Grasp the bottom near the feet of the unit.

2. Pull out (see fig. 3.39). The bezel should snap off freely.

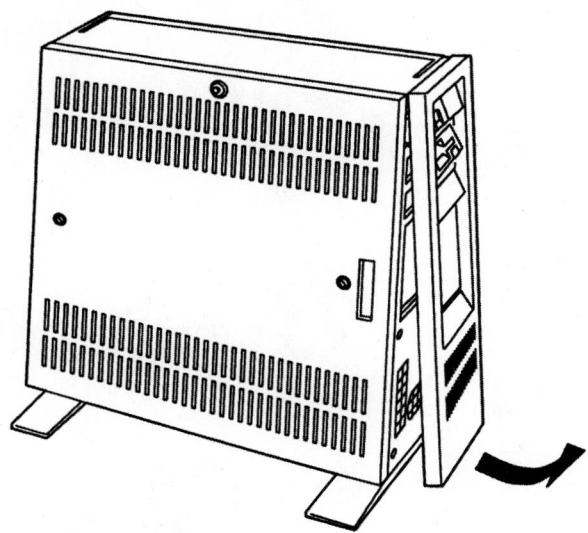

Used with permission
from IBM Corporation.

Fig. 3.39
Removing the bezel (Models 60, 65 SX, and 80).

Removing the Power Supply. To remove the power supply, you first must remove the cover and front bezel. Follow these steps:

1. Disconnect all cables from the power supply.

2. Remove the three screws that retain the power supply. One screw is near the power switch, and the other two are near the back of the supply.

3. Lift the power supply out the side of the unit (see fig. 3.40).

Removing Floppy Disk Drives. The floppy drives are located next to the power supply. Removing floppy drives from these systems requires only these two steps:

1. Push the tab underneath the floppy drive up while you simultaneously press a tab on the rear of the drive sideways.

2. Slide the drive out the front of the unit (see fig. 3.41).

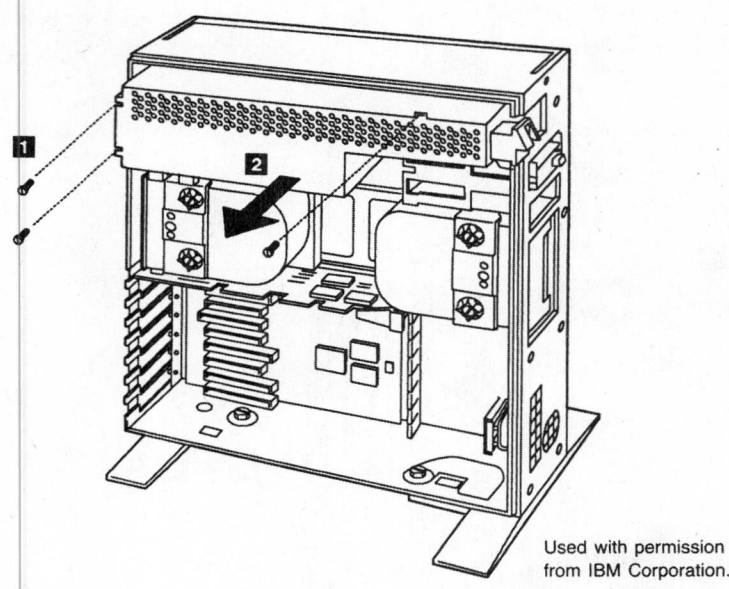

Used with permission
from IBM Corporation.

Fig. 3.40
Removing the power supply (Models 60, 65 SX, and 80).

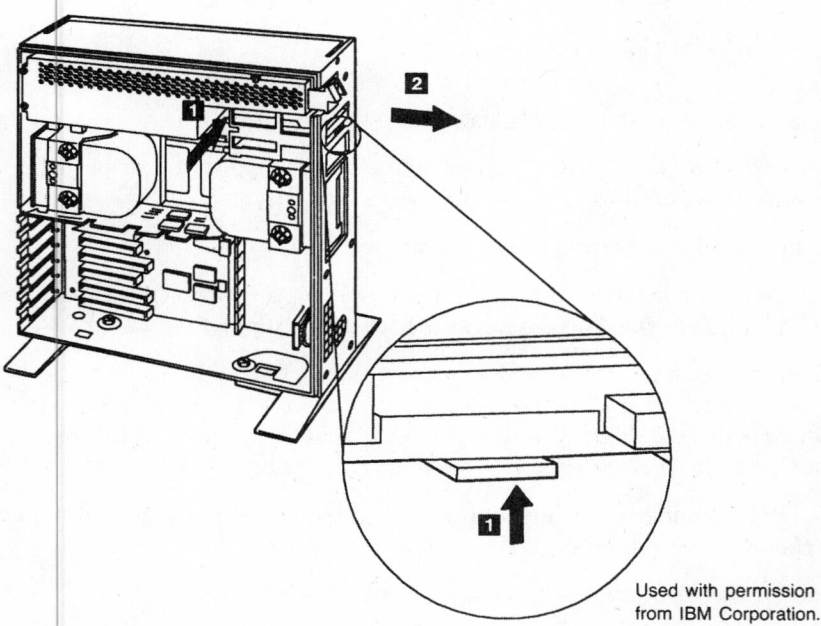

Used with permission
from IBM Corporation.

Fig. 3.41
Removing a disk drive (Models 60, 65 SX, and 80).

Removing the Floppy Disk Drive Cable Retainer. Floppy disk drive systems use a retainer to hold cables in place when the floppy drives are plugged in. To remove this cable retainer, follow these steps:

1. Press the tabs located on the side of the cable retainer.

2. Rotate the retainer out toward the back of the system unit.

3. Pull off the retainer (see fig. 3.42).

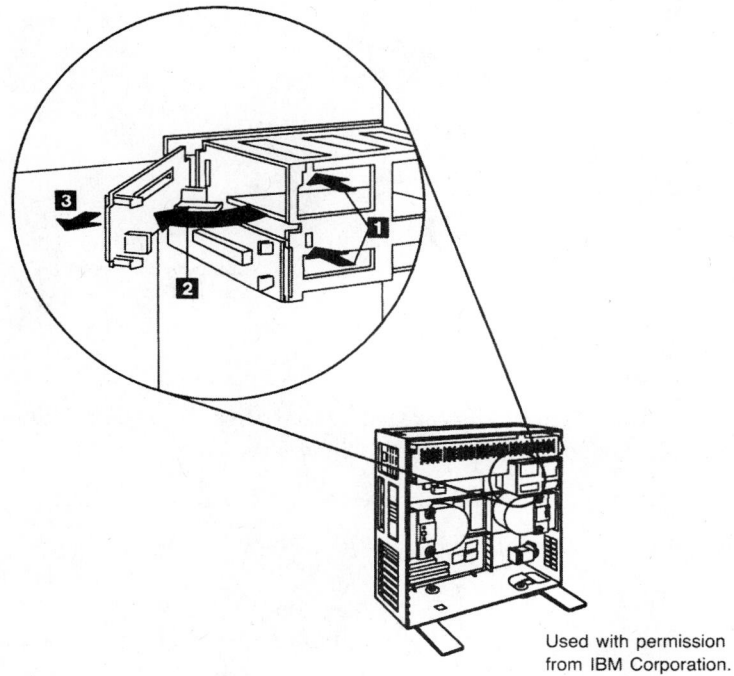

Used with permission
from IBM Corporation.

Fig. 3.42
Removing the disk drive cable retainer (Models 60, 65 SX and 80).

Removing the Second Hard Disk Drive. Make sure that you have a backup of the information on the drive before removing the disk. Follow these steps:

1. Disconnect the ground wire and all cables from the fixed disk drive.

2. Turn both thumb screws counterclockwise.

3. Remove the front bezel.

4. Slide the fixed disk drive out the front of the system unit (see fig. 3.43). Note that drive D must be removed before drive C because of physical interference.

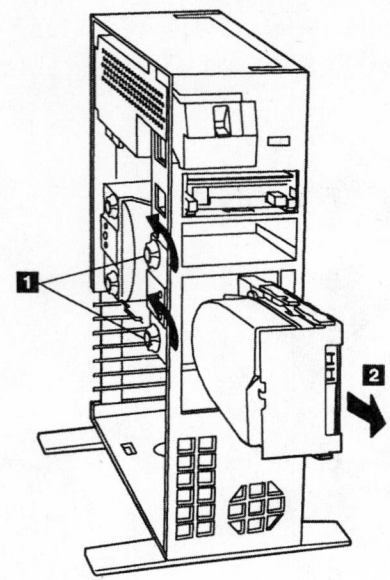

Used with permission
from IBM Corporation.

Fig. 3.43
Removing the second hard drive (Models 60, 65 SX, and 80).

Removing the Primary Hard Drive. Make sure that you have a backup of the information on the drive before removing the drive. Proceed as follows:

1. Disconnect the ground wire and all cables from the fixed disk drive.

2. Turn both thumb screws counterclockwise.

3. Remove the front bezel.

4. Slide the drive a little toward the front and lift the fixed disk drive sideways out of the system (see fig. 3.44). Note that drive D must be removed before drive C because of physical interference.

Removing the Hard Disk Drive-Support Structure. A large, metal hard disk drive support structure is used to clamp the hard disks in place. You must remove this structure in order to remove the motherboard. Follow these steps:

1. Remove the four screws located on the front portion of the structure.

2. Slide the structure forward, and lift it up and sideways out of the system (see fig. 3.45).

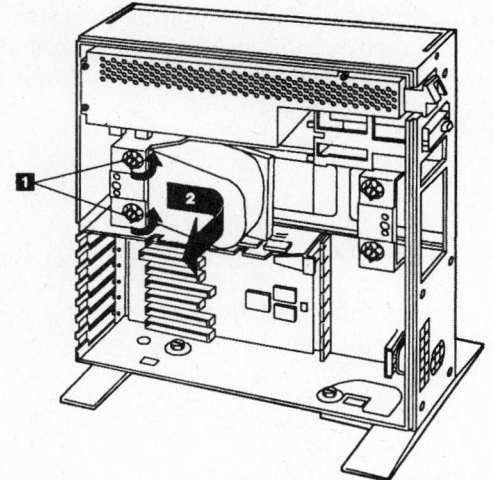

Used with permission
from IBM Corporation.

Fig. 3.44
Removing the primary hard drive (Models 60, 65 SX, and 80).

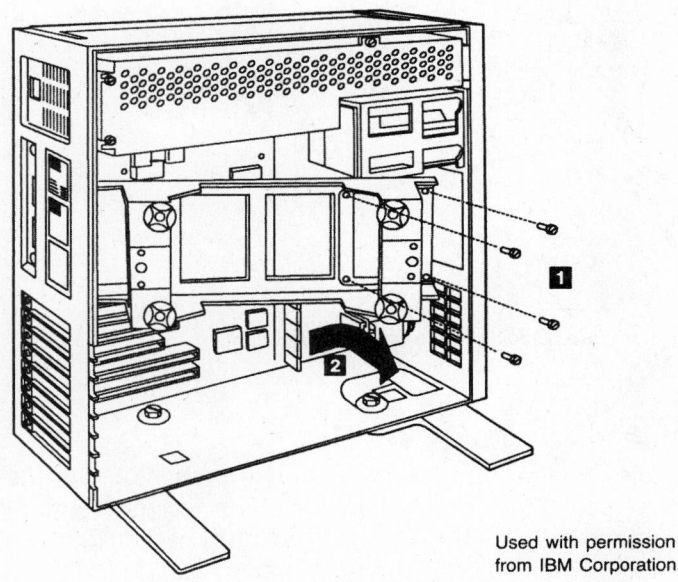

Used with permission
from IBM Corporation.

Fig. 3.45
Removing the fixed disk drive support structure (Models 60, 65 SX, and 80).

Removing the Motherboard. To remove the motherboard from the system unit, you first must remove the cover, any adapters, the fixed disk drives, and the fixed disk support structure. With these components removed from the system unit, removal of the motherboard requires these steps:

1. Disconnect all cables from the motherboard.

2. Remove all eight retaining screws.

3. Gently lift the motherboard up and out of the system (see fig. 3.46).

Now that you've examined the procedures for disassembling a system, let's move on to Chapters 4–8, which examine the different components that make up a system.

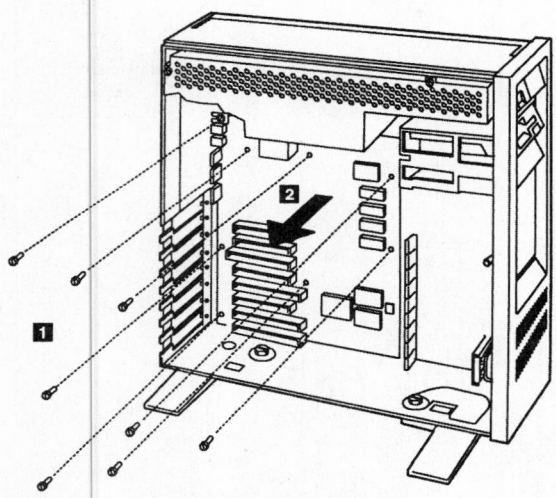

Used with permission
from IBM Corporation.

Fig. 3.46
Removing the motherboard (Models 60, 65 SX, and 80).

Summary

This chapter has discussed the initial teardown and inspection of a system and looked at the types of tools required, from simple hand tools to meters for measuring voltage and resistance. It mentioned some of the problems you might encounter with the actual hardware (screws, nuts, bolts, and so on) in a system.

The chapter also has discussed the physical-disassembly procedure and how to recognize the different components that make up a system. Emphasis was made on the preliminary steps taken before and during disassembly such as ESD protection and the recording of system setup information to ensure that the system works properly again when reassembled.

Different disassembly procedures were discussed based on the type of case used for the system. Most systems built using a particular style case such as AT and Tower cases, for example, are constructed in a similar fashion. Once you have worked on a system with one particular type of case design, most others with the same type of case are almost identical.

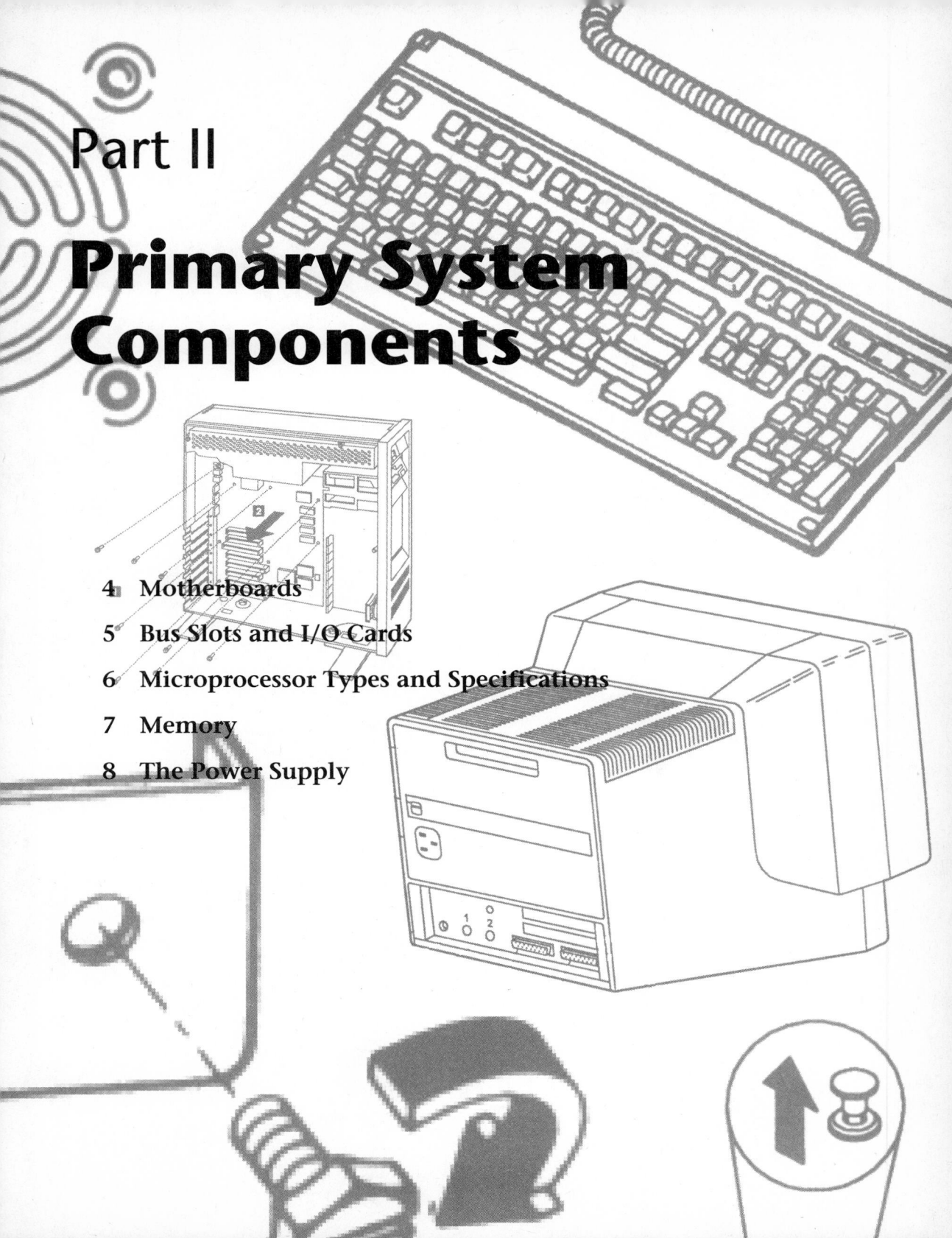

Part II

Primary System Components

4   Motherboards

5   Bus Slots and I/O Cards

6   Microprocessor Types and Specifications

7   Memory

8   The Power Supply

Chapter 4

Motherboards

Easily the most important component in a PC system is the main board or *motherboard*. The terminology can be confusing because IBM refers to the motherboard as a *system board* or *planar*. The terms motherboard, system board, and planar are interchangeable. Not all systems have a motherboard in the true sense of the word. In some systems, the components found normally on a motherboard are located instead on an expansion adapter card plugged into a slot. In these systems, the board with the slots is called a *backplane*, rather than a motherboard. Systems using this type of construction are called *backplane systems*.

Backplane systems come in two main types: passive and active. A *passive backplane* means the main backplane board does not contain any circuitry at all except for the bus connectors and maybe some buffer and driver circuits. All of the circuitry found on a conventional motherboard is contained on one or more expansion cards installed in slots on the backplane. Some backplane systems use a passive design which incorporates the entire system circuitry into a single mothercard. The mothercard is essentially a complete motherboard that is designed to plug into a slot in the passive backplane. The passive backplane/mothercard concept allows the entire system to be easily upgraded by changing one or more cards. Because of the expense of the high function mothercard, this type of system design is rarely found in PC systems. The passive backplane design does enjoy popularity in industrial systems which are often rack mounted.

An *active backplane* means the main backplane board contains bus control and usually other circuitry as well. Most active backplane systems contain all of the circuitry found on a typical motherboard except for the *processor complex*. The processor complex is the name of the circuit board that contains the main system processor and any other circuitry directly related, such as clock control, cache, and so forth. The processor complex design allows the user to easily upgrade the system later to a new processor type by changing one card. In effect it amounts to a modular motherboard with a replaceable processor section. Most modern PC systems that use a backplane design use an active backplane/processor complex. Both IBM and Compaq use this type of design in some of their high-end (server class) systems, for example. This allows an easier and generally more affordable upgrade than the passive backplane/mothercard design since the processor complex board is usually much cheaper than a mothercard. Unfortunately, since there are no standards for the processor complex interface to the system, these boards are proprietary and can only be purchased from the system manufacturer. This limited market and availability causes the prices of these boards to be higher than most complete motherboards from other manufacturers.

The motherboard system design and the backplane system design have both advantages and disadvantages. Most original personal computers were designed as backplanes in the late 1970s. Apple and IBM shifted the market to the now traditional motherboard with a slot-type design because this type of system generally is cheaper to mass-produce than one with the backplane design. The theoretical advantage of a backplane system, however, is that you can upgrade it easily to a new processor and new level of performance by changing a single card. For example, you can upgrade a system with a 486-based processor card to a Pentium-based card just by changing the card. In a motherboard-design system, you must change the motherboard itself, a seemingly more formidable task. Unfortunately, the reality of the situation is that a backplane design is often much more expensive to upgrade, and because the bus remains fixed on the backplane, the backplane design precludes more comprehensive upgrades that involve adding local bus slots for example.

Because of the limited availability of the processor complex boards or mothercards, they usually end up being more expensive than a complete new motherboard that uses an industry standard form factor. For this reason, I recommend staying away from any backplane system designs. In most cases a conventional motherboard design makes it much easier to obtain replacement components for repair or upgrade.

Another nail in the coffin of backplane designs is the upgradable processor. Intel has designed all 486 and Pentium processors to be upgradable to faster (usually called OverDrive) processors in the future by simply swapping (or adding) the new processor chip. Changing only the processor chip for a faster one is the easiest and generally most cost-effective way to upgrade without changing the entire motherboard.

Replacement Motherboards

Some manufacturers go out of their way to make their systems as physically incompatible as possible with any other system. Then replacement parts, repairs, and upgrades are virtually impossible to find—except, of course, from the original system manufacturer, at a significantly higher price than the equivalent part would cost to fit an IBM or clone system. For example, if the motherboard in my original IBM AT (or any AT Clone) dies, I can find any number of replacement boards that will bolt directly into the AT chassis, with my choice of processors and clock speeds, at very good prices. If the motherboard dies in your Compaq Deskpro, you'll pay for a replacement available only from Compaq, and you have virtually no opportunity to select a board with a faster or better processor than the one that failed. In other words, upgrading one of these systems is almost out of the question.

Knowing What to Look For (Selection Criteria)

As a consultant, I often am asked to make a recommendation for purchases. Making these types of recommendations is one of the most frequent tasks a consultant performs. Many consultants charge a large fee for this advice. Without guidance, many individuals don't have any rhyme or reason to their selections and instead base their choices solely on magazine reviews or, even worse, on some personal bias. To help eliminate this haphazard selection process, I have developed a simple checklist that will help you select a system. This list takes into consideration several important system aspects overlooked by most such checklists. The goal is to ensure that the selected system truly is compatible and has a long life of service and upgrades ahead.

It helps to think like an engineer when you make your selection. Consider every aspect and detail of the motherboards in question. For instance, you will want to consider any future uses and upgrades. Technical support at a professional (as opposed to a user) level is extremely important; what support will be provided? Is there documentation, and does it cover everything else?

In short, a checklist is a good idea. Here is one for you to use in evaluating any IBM-compatible system. You might not have to meet every one of these criteria to consider a particular system, but if you miss more than a few of these checks, consider staying away from that system. The items at the top of the list are the most important, and the items at the bottom are perhaps of lesser importance (although I think each item is important!). The rest of this chapter discusses in detail the criteria in this checklist.

Processor. A 486 motherboard should be equipped with a 486DX2- or DX4-type processor—the faster the better. The 486 processor should be an SL Enhanced version, which is standard on the most desirable DX4 models. A Pentium motherboard should only use the second generation 3.3v Pentium processor, which has a 296-pin configuration that differs physically from the 273-pin first generation design. All second generation Pentiums are fully SL Enhanced.

Processor Sockets. A 486 motherboard should have a ZIF (Zero Insertion Force) processor socket that follows the Intel Socket 3 or Socket 6 specifications. A Pentium motherboard should have one or two ZIF sockets that follow the Intel Socket 5 specification.

Motherboard Speed. A 486 motherboard should run at 33 MHz for maximum performance and compatibility. Switchable speed selection is a bonus and may allow other speeds to be selected as well. A Pentium motherboard should run at 60 or 66 MHz and be speed-switchable between these two speeds. All components should be rated to run at the maximum allowable speed.

Cache Memory. All motherboards should have a Level 2 cache onboard. 486 motherboards should have 256K and Pentium motherboards should have 512K for maximum performance. The Level 2 Cache should be of a Write-Back design, and must be populated with chips that are fast enough to support the maximum motherboard speed.

SIMM Memory. 486 motherboards should ideally use 72-pin SIMMs which support a single bank per SIMM. 30-pin SIMMs are acceptable for upgrade boards designed to reuse memory from older motherboards. Pentium motherboards must only use 72-pin SIMMs. The SIMMs should be rated at 70 ns or faster.

Bus Type. 486 motherboards should have an ISA (Industry Standard Architecture) bus with either two or three VL-Bus, or ideally three or more PCI local bus slots. Pentium motherboards should have an ISA or EISA primary bus with three or more PCI local bus slots.

BIOS. The motherboard should use an industry standard BIOS such as those from AMI, Phoenix, or Award. The BIOS should be of a Flash ROM design for easy updating, and support Enhanced IDE as well as 2.88M floppy drives. APM (Advanced Power Management) support should be built into the BIOS as well.

Form Factor. For maximum flexibility, the motherboard should come in a Baby-AT form factor. This will allow it to be installed in the widest variety of case designs.

Built-In Interfaces. Ideally a motherboard should contain as many built-in standard controllers and interfaces as possible (except video). A motherboard should have a built-in floppy controller that supports 2.88M drives, a built-in local bus (PCI or VL-Bus) IDE connector, one or two built-in serial ports (must use 16550A type UARTs), and a built-in parallel port (must be EPP or ECP compliant). A built-in mouse port would be a bonus, although one of the serial ports can be used for a mouse as well. A built-in SCSI port is a bonus as long as it conforms to ASPI (Advanced SCSI Programming Interface) standards. Built-in network adapters are acceptable, but usually an ISA slot card network adapter is more easily supported via standard drivers and is more easily upgraded as well. Built-in video adapters are generally undesirable, since there are better choices in external local bus video adapters.

Power Management. The motherboard should fully support SL Enhanced processors with APM (Advanced Power Management) and SMM (System Management Mode) protocols that allow for powering down various system components to different levels of readiness and power consumption.

Documentation. Good technical documentation is a requirement. Documents should include information on any and all jumpers and switches found on the board, connector pinouts for all connectors, specifications for cache RAM chips, SIMMs and other plug-in components, and any other applicable technical information. I would also acquire separate documentation from the BIOS manufacturer covering the specific BIOS used in the system, as well as the Data Books covering the specific chipset used in the motherboard. Additional data books for any other controller or I/O chips on-board are a bonus, and may be acquired from the respective chip manufacturers.

You may note that these selection criteria seem fairly strict, and may disqualify many motherboards on the market, including what you already have in your system! These criteria will, however, guarantee you the highest quality motherboard offering the latest in PC technology that will be upgradable, expandable, and provide good service for many years. Most of the time, I recommend purchasing boards from better known motherboard manufacturers such as Intel, Micronics, AMI, Acer, Alaris, and so on. These boards might cost a little more than others that you have never heard of, but there is some safety in the more well-known brands. That is, the more boards that they sell, the more likely that any problems will have been discovered by others and solved long before you get yours. Also, if service or support is needed, the larger vendors are more likely to be around in the long run.

Documentation

As mentioned, extensive documentation is an important factor to consider when you're planning to purchase a motherboard. Most motherboard manufacturers design their boards around a particular *chipset*, which actually counts as the bulk of the motherboard circuitry. There are a number of manufacturers offering chipsets such as Intel, Micronics, Opti, VLSI, Chips & Technologies, and others. I recommend obtaining the data book or other technical documentation on the chipset directly from the chipset manufacturer.

One of the more common questions I get about a system relates to the BIOS Setup program. People want to know what the "Advanced Chipset Setup" features mean and what will be the effects of changing them. Often they go to the BIOS manufacturer thinking that the BIOS documentation will offer help. Usually, however, people find that there is no real coverage of what the chipset setup features are in the BIOS documentation. You will find this information in the data book provided by the chipset manufacturer. Although these books are meant to be read by the engineers who design the boards, they contain all of the detailed information about the chipset's features, especially those that might be adjustable. With the chipset data book, you will have an explanation of all of the controls in the Advanced Chipset Setup section of the BIOS Setup program.

Besides the main chipset data books, I also recommend collecting any data books on the other major chips in the system. This would include any floppy or IDE controller chips, "super I/O" chips, and the main processor as well. You will find an incredible amount of information on these components in the data books. A word of warning: most chipset manufacturers only make a particular chip for a short time, rapidly superseding it with an improved or changed version. The data books are only available during the time the chip is being manufactured so if you wait too long you will find that such documents may no longer be available. The time to collect documentation on your motherboard is NOW!

ROM BIOS Compatibility

The issue of ROM BIOS compatibility is important. If the BIOS is not compatible, any number of problems can result. Several reputable companies that produce compatibles have developed their own proprietary ROM BIOS that works just like IBM's. These companies also frequently update their ROM code, to keep in step with the latest changes

II

Primary System Components

IBM has incorporated into its ROMs. Because IBM generally does not sell ROM upgrades or provide them for older systems (unless the upgrade is absolutely necessary, and IBM decides if that is the case), keeping current with an actual IBM system is more difficult than with most of the compatible systems on the market. The newer PS/2 systems do use a BIOS that is either stored on the hard disk, or contained in a Flash ROM that is easily updated via a floppy disk. If you have one of these systems, BIOS upgrade disks can be obtained via the IBM National Support Center (NSC) BBS. The number is listed in Appendix B. Also, many of the compatibles' OEMs (original equipment manufacturers) have designed ROMs that work specifically with additional features in their systems while effectively masking the effects of these improvements from any software that would "balk" at the differences.

OEMs. Many OEMs have developed their own compatible ROMs independently. Companies such as Compaq, Zenith, and AT&T have developed their own BIOS product, which has proven compatible with IBM's. These companies also offer upgrades to newer versions that often can offer more features and improvements or fix problems with the older versions. If you use a system with a proprietary ROM, make sure that it is from a larger company with a track record and one that will provide updates and fixes as necessary.

Several companies have specialized in the development of a compatible ROM BIOS product. The three major companies that come to mind in discussing ROM BIOS software are American Megatrends, Inc. (AMI), Award Software, and Phoenix Software. Each company licenses its ROM BIOS to a motherboard manufacturer so that the manufacturer can worry about the hardware rather than the software. To obtain one of these ROMs for a motherboard, the OEM must answer many questions about the design of the system so that the proper BIOS can be either developed or selected from those already designed. Combining a ROM BIOS and a motherboard is not a haphazard task. No single, generic, compatible ROM exists, either. AMI, Award, and Phoenix ship to different manufacturers many variations of their BIOS code, each one custom-tailored to that specific system, much like DOS can be.

AMI. Although AMI customizes the ROM code for a particular system, it does not sell the ROM source code to the OEM. An OEM must obtain each new release as it becomes available. Because many OEMs don't need or want every new version that is developed, they might skip several version changes before licensing a new one. The AMI BIOS is currently the most popular BIOS in PC systems today. Newer versions of the AMI BIOS are called *Hi-Flex* due to the high flexibility found in the BIOS configuration program. The AMI Hi-Flex BIOS is used in Intel, AMI, Alaris and many other manufacturer's motherboards. One special AMI feature is that it is the only third-party BIOS manufacturer to make its own motherboard as well.

Older versions of the AMI BIOS had a few problems with different keyboards and keyboard controller chips, and very early versions also had some difficulty with certain IDE hard disk drives. To eliminate these types of problems, make sure that your AMI BIOS is dated 04/09/90 or later, and has keyboard controller F or later. You will possibly have keyboard lockups and problems running Windows or OS/2 if you have an older keyboard controller chip.

To locate this information, power on the system and observe the BIOS ID string displayed on the lower left of the screen. The primary BIOS Identification string (ID String 1) is displayed by any AMI BIOS during the POST (Power-On Self Test) at the left bottom corner of the screen, below the copyright message. Two additional BIOS ID strings (ID String 2 and 3) can be displayed by the AMI Hi-Flex BIOS by pressing the Insert key during POST. These additional ID strings display the options that are installed in the BIOS.

The general BIOS ID String 1 format for older AMI BIOS versions is the following:

ABBB-NNNN-mmddyy-KK	
Position	**Description**
A	BIOS Option: D = Diagnostics built-in. S = Setup built-in. E = Extended Setup built-in.
BBB	Chipset or Motherboard Identifier: C&T = Chips & Technologies chipset. NET = C&T NEAT 286 chipset. 286 = Standard 286 motherboard. SUN = Suntac chipset. PAQ = Compaq motherboard. INT = Intel motherboard. AMI = AMI motherboard. G23 = G2 chipset 386 motherboard.
NNNN	The manufacturer license code reference number.
mmddyy	The BIOS release date, mm/dd/yy.
KK	The AMI keyboard BIOS version number.

The BIOS ID String 1 format for AMI Hi-Flex BIOS versions is the following:

AB-CCcc-DDDDDD-EFGHIJKL-mmddyy-MMMMMMMM-N	
Position	**Description**
A	Processor Type: 0 = 8086 or 8088. 2 = 286. 3 = 386. 4 = 486. 5 = Pentium.
B	Size of BIOS: 0 = 64K BIOS. 1 = 128K BIOS.
CCcc	Major and Minor BIOS version number.
DDDDDD	Manufacturer license code reference number: 0036xx = AMI 386 motherboard, xx = Series #. 0046xx = AMI 486 motherboard, xx = Series #. 0056xx = AMI Pentium motherboard, xx = Series #.

(continues)

II

Primary System Components

AB-CCcc-DDDDDD-EFGHIJKL-mmddyy-MMMMMMMM-N Continued	
Position	**Description**
E	1 = Halt on Post Error.
F	1 = Initialize CMOS every boot.
G	1 = Block pins 22 and 23 of the keyboard controller.
H	1 = Mouse support in BIOS/keyboard controller.
I	1 = Wait for <F1> key on POST errors.
J	1 = Display floppy error during POST.
K	1 = Display video error during POST.
L	1 = Display keyboard error during POST.
mmddyy	BIOS Date, mm/dd/yy.
MMMMMMMM	Chipset identifier or BIOS name.
N	Keyboard controller version number.

AMI Hi-Flex BIOS ID String 2:

AAB-C-DDDD-EE-FF-GGGG-HH-II-JJJ	
Position	**Description**
AA	Keyboard controller pin number for clock switching.
B	Keyboard controller clock switching pin function: H = High signal switches clock to high speed. L = High signal switches clock to low speed.
C	Clock switching through chip set registers: 0 = Disable. 1 = Enable.
DDDD	Port address to switch clock high.
EE	Data value to switch clock high.
FF	Mask value to switch clock high.
GGGG	Port Address to switch clock low.
HH	Data value to switch clock low.
II	Mask value to switch clock low.
JJJ	Pin number for Turbo Switch Input.

AMI Hi-Flex BIOS ID String 3:

AAB-C-DDD-EE-FF-GGGG-HH-II-JJ-K-L	
Position	**Description**
AA	Keyboard controller pin number for cache control.
B	Keyboard controller cache control pin function: H = High signal enables the cache. L = High signal disables the cache.

Position	Description
C	1 = High signal is used on the keyboard controller pin.
DDD	Cache control through Chipset registers: 0 = Cache control off. 1 = Cache control on.
EE	Port address to enable cache.
FF	Data value to enable cache.
GGGG	Mask value to enable cache.
HH	Port address to disable cache.
II	Data value to disable cache.
JJ	Mask value to disable cache.
K	Pin number for resetting the 82335 memory controller.
L	BIOS Modification Flag: 0 = The BIOS has not been modified. 1–9, A–Z = Number of times the BIOS has been modified.

The AMI BIOS has many features, including a built-in setup program activated by pressing the Delete or Esc key in the first few seconds of booting up your computer. The BIOS will prompt you briefly as to which key to press and when to press it. The AMI BIOS offers user-definable hard disk types, essential for optimal use of many IDE or ESDI drives. The newer BIOS versions also support Enhanced IDE drives and will auto-configure the drive parameters. A unique AMI BIOS feature is that, in addition to the setup, it has a built-in, menu-driven, diagnostics package, essentially a very limited version of the stand-alone AMIDIAG product. The internal diagnostics are not a replacement for more comprehensive disk-based programs, but they can help in a pinch. The menu-driven diagnostics does not do extensive memory testing, for example, and the hard disk low-level formatter works only at the BIOS level rather than at the controller register level. These limitations often have prevented it from being capable of formatting severely damaged disks.

An excellent feature of AMI is its technical support BBS. You will find the phone number listed in the vendor list in Appendix B. The AMI BIOS is sold through distributors, and any updates to the AMI BIOS or keyboard controller are available through Washburn and Co., also listed in the vendor list in Appendix B.

Award. Award is unique among BIOS manufacturers because it sells its BIOS code to the OEM and allows the OEM to customize the BIOS. Of course, then the BIOS no longer is Award BIOS, but rather a highly customized version. AST uses this approach on its systems, as do other manufacturers, for total control over the BIOS code, without having to write it from scratch. Although AMI and Phoenix customize the ROM code for a particular system, they do not sell the ROM's source code to the OEM. Some OEMs that seem to have developed their own ROM code started with a base of source code licensed to them by Award or some other company.

II

Primary System Components

The Award BIOS has all the normal features you expect, including a built-in setup program activated by pressing Ctrl-Alt-Esc. This setup offers user-definable drive types, required in order to fully utilize IDE or ESDI hard disks. The Power-On Self Test is good, and Award runs a technical support BBS. The phone number for the BBS is listed in the vendor list in Appendix B.

In all, the Award BIOS is high quality, has minimal compatibility problems, and offers a high level of support.

Phoenix. The Phoenix BIOS for many years has been a standard of compatibility by which others are judged. It was one of the first third-party companies to legally reverse-engineer the IBM BIOS using a "clean room" approach. In this approach, a group of engineers studied the IBM BIOS and wrote a specification for how that BIOS should work and what features should be incorporated. This information then was passed to a second group of engineers who had never seen the IBM BIOS. They could then legally write a new BIOS to the specifications set forth by the first group. This work would then be unique and not a copy of IBM's BIOS; however, it would function the same way. This code has been refined over the years and has very few compatibility problems compared to some of the other BIOS vendors.

The Phoenix BIOS excels in two areas that put it high on my list of recommendations. One is that the Power-On Self Test is excellent. The BIOS outputs an extensive set of beep codes that can be used to diagnose severe motherboard problems which would prevent normal operation of the system. In fact, this POST can isolate memory failures in Bank 0 right down to the individual chip with beep codes alone. The Phoenix BIOS also has an excellent setup program free from unnecessary frills, but that offers all of the features one would expect, such as user-definable drive types, and so on. The built-in setup is activated by typing either Ctrl-Alt-S or Ctrl-Alt-Esc, depending on the version of BIOS you have.

The second area in which Phoenix excels is the documentation. Not only are the manuals that you get with the system detailed, but Phoenix also has written a set of BIOS technical-reference manuals that are a standard in the industry. The set consists of three books, titled *System BIOS for IBM PC/XT/AT Computers and Compatibles*, *CBIOS for IBM PS/2 Computers and Compatibles*, and *ABIOS for IBM PS/2 Computers and Compatibles*. Phoenix is one of few vendors who has done extensive research on the PS/2 BIOS and has produced virtually all of the ROMs in the PS/2 Micro Channel clones on the market. In addition to being an excellent reference for the Phoenix BIOS, these books serve as an outstanding overall reference to any company's IBM-compatible BIOS. Even if you never have a system with a Phoenix BIOS, I highly recommend these books, published by Addison-Wesley and available through most bookstores.

Micronics motherboards have always used the Phoenix BIOS, and these motherboards are used in many of the popular "name-brand" compatible systems. Phoenix is also one of the largest OEMs of Microsoft MS-DOS. Many of you that have MS-DOS have the Phoenix OEM version. Phoenix licenses its DOS to other computer manufacturers so long as they use the Phoenix BIOS. Because of its close relationship with Microsoft, it has access to the DOS source code, which helps eliminate compatibility problems.

Although Phoenix does not operate a technical support BBS by itself, its largest nation-wide distributor does, which is Micro Firmware Inc. The BBS and voice phone numbers are listed in the vendor list in Appendix B. Micro Firmware offers upgrades to many systems with a Phoenix BIOS including Packard Bell, Gateway 2000 (with Micronics motherboards), Micron Technologies, and others.

Unless the ROM BIOS is truly a compatible, custom OEM version such as Compaq's, you might want to install in the system the ROM BIOS from one of the known quantities, such as AMI, Award, or Phoenix. These companies' products are established as ROM BIOS standards in the industry, and frequent updates and improvements ensure that a system containing these ROMs will have a long life of upgrades and service.

Using Correct Speed-Rated Parts

Some compatible vendors use substandard parts in their systems to save money. Because the CPU is one of the most expensive components on the motherboard, and many motherboards are sold to system assemblers without the CPU installed, it is tempting to the assembler to install a CPU rated for less than the actual operating speed. A system can be sold as a 33 MHz system, for example, but when you look "under the hood," you may find a CPU rated for only 25 MHz. The system does appear to work correctly, but for how long? If the company that manufactures the CPU chip installed in this system had tested the chip to run reliably at 33 MHz, it would have labeled the part accordingly. After all, the company can sell the chip for more money if it works at the higher clock speed. When a chip is run at a speed higher than it is rated for, it will run hotter than normal. This may cause the chip to overheat occasionally, which appears as random lockups, glitches, and frustration. I highly recommend that you avoid systems whose operation speed exceeds the design of the respective parts.

This practice is easy to fall into since the faster rated chips cost more money, and Intel and other chip manufacturers usually rate their chips very conservatively. I have taken several 25 MHz 486 processors and run them at 33 MHz, and they seemed to work fine. The Pentium 90 chips I have tested seem to run fine at 100 MHz. Although I might purchase a Pentium 90 system and make a decision to run it at 100 MHz, if I were to experience lockups or glitches in operation, I would immediately return it to 90 MHz and retest. If I purchase a 100 MHz system from a vendor, I fully expect it to have 100 MHz parts, not 90 MHz parts running past their rated speed! These days many chips will have some form of heat sink on them, which helps to prevent overheating, but which can also sometimes cover up for a "pushed" chip. If the price is too good to be true, ask before you buy: "Are the parts really manufacturer-rated for the system speed?"

To determine the rated speed of a CPU chip, look at the writing on the chip. Most of the time, the part number will end in a suffix of –xxx where the xxx is a number indicating the maximum speed. For example, a –100 indicates that the chip is rated for 100 MHz operation.

Motherboard Form Factors

There are several compatible form factors used for motherboards. The form factor refers to the physical dimensions and size of the board, and dictates what type of case the board will fit into. The types of motherboard form factors generally available are the following:

- Full-size AT
- Baby-AT
- LPX

The full-size AT motherboard is so named because it matches the original IBM AT motherboard design. This allows for a very large board of up to 12 inches wide by 13.8 inches deep. The keyboard connector and slot connectors must conform to specific placement requirements to fit the holes in the case. This type of board will fit into full-size AT or Tower cases only. Because these motherboards will not fit into the popular Baby-AT or Mini-Tower cases, and because of advances in component miniaturization, they are no longer being produced by most motherboard manufacturers.

The Baby-AT form factor is essentially the same as the original IBM XT motherboard, with modifications in screw hole positions to fit into an AT-style case (see fig. 4.1). These motherboards also have specific placement of the keyboard connector and slot connectors to match the holes in the case. Note that virtually all full size AT and Baby-AT motherboards use the standard 5-pin DIN type connector for the keyboard. Baby-AT motherboards will fit into every type of case except the low profile or slimline cases. Because of their flexibility, this is now the most popular motherboard form factor. Figure 4.1 shows the dimensions and layout of a Baby-AT motherboard.

Another popular form factor used in motherboards today is the LPX and Mini-LP form factors. This form factor was first developed by Western Digital for some of its motherboards. Although it no longer produces PC motherboards, the form factor lives on and has been duplicated by many other motherboard manufacturers. These are used in the Low Profile or slimline case systems sold widely today. The LPX boards are characterized by several distinctive features. The most noticeable is that the expansion slots are mounted on a *Bus Riser* card that plugs into the motherboard. Expansion cards must plug sideways into the riser card. This sideways placement allows for the low profile case design. Slots will be located on one or both sides of the riser card depending on the system and case design. Another distinguishing feature of the LPX design is the standard placement of connectors on the back of the board. An LPX board will have a row of connectors for video (VGA 15-pin), parallel (25-pin), two serial ports (9-pin each), and mini-DIN PS/2 style Mouse and Keyboard connectors. All of these connectors are mounted across the rear of the motherboard and protrude through a slot in the case. Some LPX motherboards may have additional connectors for other internal ports such as Network or SCSI adapters. Figure 4.2 shows the standard form factors for the LPX and Mini-LPX motherboards used in many systems today.

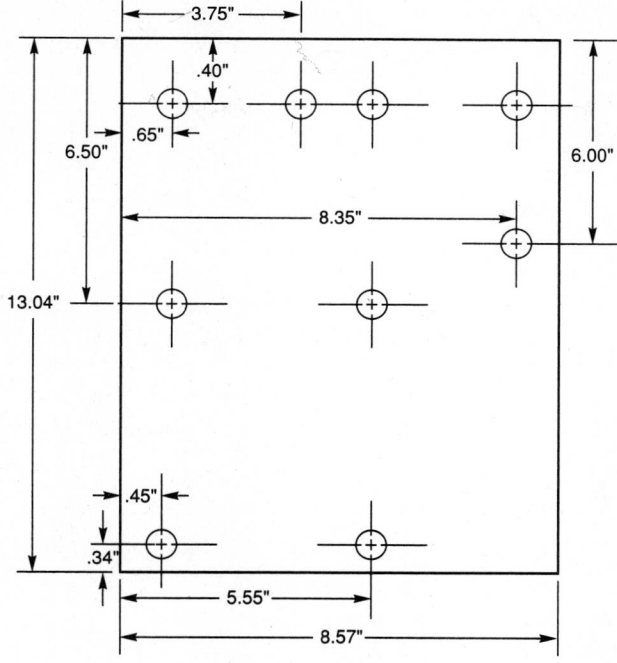

Fig. 4.1
Baby-AT motherboard form factor.

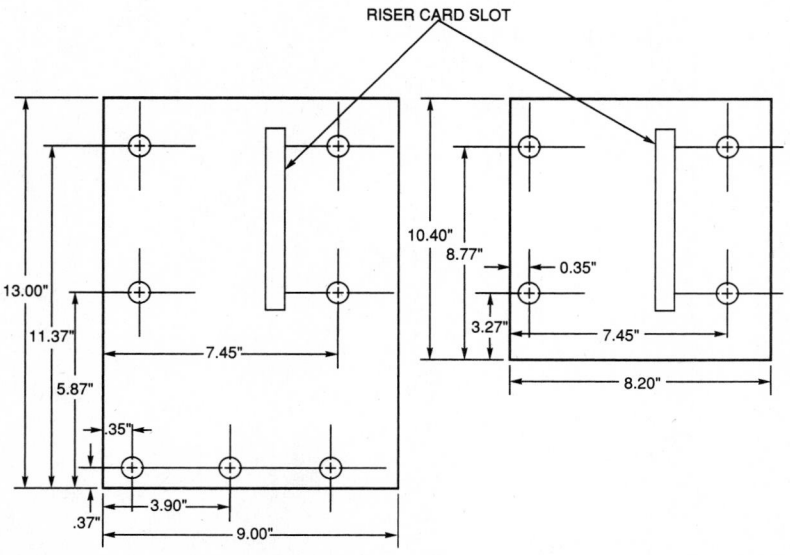

Fig. 4.2
LPX and Mini-LPX motherboard form factors.

There can be some differences between systems with LPX form factor motherboards, so it is possible to find interchangeability problems between different motherboards and cases. I usually do not recommend LPX style systems if upgradability is a factor since it is not only difficult to locate a new motherboard that will fit, but LPX systems are also limited in expansion slots and drive bays as well. Generally, the Baby AT configuration is the most popular and the most flexible type of system to consider.

Summary

The motherboard is obviously the core of your system, and is one component that you do not want to take lightly. There are hundreds of versions available, with a variety of different CPUs, speeds, features, and options. This chapter has covered the basics about different motherboards including a list of desirable features. Also discussed were the different form factors you will encounter and how they can affect other system options.

Chapter 5

Bus Slots and I/O Cards

At the heart of every system is the motherboard; you learned about various mother-boards in the preceding chapter. A motherboard is made up of components. The major component that determines how the motherboard actually works is called the *bus*. In this chapter, you learn about system buses. Specifically, you learn the following:

- What a bus is and what types of buses exist

- Why expansion slots are needed

- What types of I/O buses are used in PC systems

- What system resources are

- How adapter cards use system resources

- How to resolve conflicts among system resources

What Is a Bus?

A bus is nothing but a common pathway across which data can travel within a com-puter. This pathway is used for communication and can be established between two or more computer elements. A PC has many kinds of buses, including the following:

- Processor bus

- Address bus

- Memory bus

- I/O bus

If you hear someone talking about the PC bus, chances are good that he or she is refer-ring to the I/O bus, which also is called the *expansion bus*. Whatever name it goes by, this bus is the main system bus and the one over which most data flows. The I/O bus is the highway for most data in your system. Anything that goes to or from any device—in-cluding your video system, disk drives, and printer—travels over this bus. The busiest I/O pathway typically is to and from your video card.

Because the I/O bus is the primary bus in your computer system, it is the main focus of discussion in this chapter. The other buses deserve some attention, however, and they are covered in the following sections.

The Processor Bus

The *processor bus* is the communication pathway between the CPU and immediate support chips. This bus is used to transfer data between the CPU and the main system bus, for example, or between the CPU and an external memory cache. Figure 5.1 shows how this bus fits into a typical PC system.

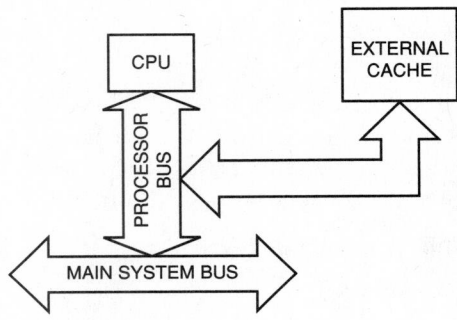

Fig. 5.1
The processor bus.

Not all PC systems have an external cache for the CPU; these caches typically are used only in high-end systems that use the faster 486 and Pentium chips. In many systems, therefore, the sole purpose of the processor bus is to communicate with the main system bus.

Because the purpose of the processor bus is to get information to and from the CPU at the fastest possible speed, this bus operates at a much faster rate than any other bus in your system; no bottleneck exists here. The bus consists of electrical circuits for data, for addresses (the address bus, which is discussed in the following section), and for control purposes. In a 486-based system, for example, the processor bus consists of 32 address lines, 32 data lines, and a few lines for control purposes. A Pentium system's processor bus has 64 data lines, 32 address lines, and associated control lines.

The processor bus operates at the same base clock rate as the CPU and can transfer one bit of data per data line every one or two clock cycles. Thus, a 486-based system can transfer 32 bits of data at a time, whereas a Pentium can transfer 64 bits of data.

To determine the transfer rate for the processor bus, you multiply the data width (32 bits for a 486 or 64 bits for a Pentium) by the clock speed of the bus (the same as the base clock speed of the CPU). If you are using a 66 MHz Pentium chip that can transfer a bit of data each clock cycle on each data line, you have a maximum instantaneous transfer rate of 528M per second. You get this result by using the following formula:

66 MHz × 64 bits = 4,224 megabits/second

4,224 megabits/second ÷ 8 = 528M/second

This transfer rate, often called the *bandwidth* of the bus, represents a maximum. Like all maximums, this rate does not represent the normal operating bandwidth; you should expect lower average throughput, even up to 25 percent lower. A system that has a 128M/second bandwidth (such as a 33 MHz 486 system), for example, typically may operate at a rate of 100 M/second. Other limiting factors (such as how fast the system bus can feed information to the processor bus) can conspire to lower the effective bandwidth even more.

The Memory Bus

The *memory bus* is used to transfer information between the CPU and main memory—the RAM in your system. This bus is implemented by a dedicated chipset that is responsible for transferring information between the processor bus and the memory bus. This chipset typically is the same chipset that is responsible for managing the I/O bus. Figure 5.2 shows how the memory bus fits into your PC.

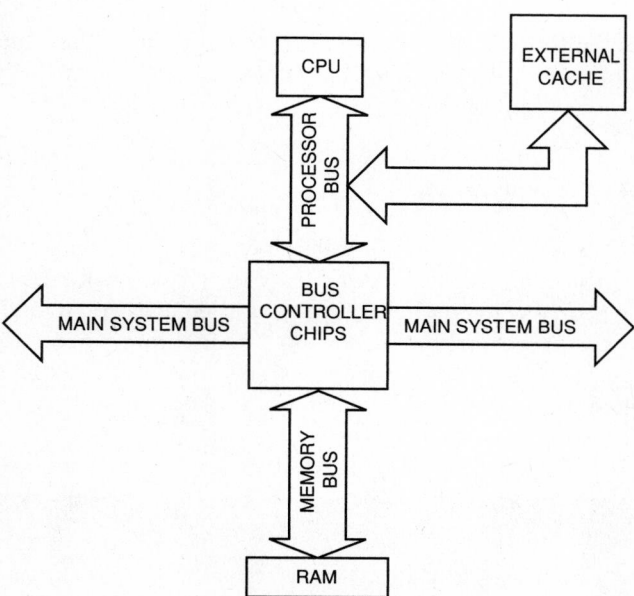

Fig. 5.2
The memory bus.

The information that travels over the memory bus is transferred at a much slower rate than the information on the processor bus, for two reasons: the memory bus has fewer data lines, and the memory chips cannot handle data as quickly as the CPU can. The chip sockets or the slots for memory SIMMs are connected to the memory bus in much the same way that expansion slots are connected to the I/O bus.

> **Caution**
>
> You should make sure that you purchase a system in which the data width of the memory bus matches the capabilities of the CPU. If a system has a 32-bit CPU, for example, you should insist that it also have a 32-bit memory bus. Likewise, in a Pentium system (which has a 64-bit CPU), you should insist on a 64-bit memory bus. Some Pentium systems, particularly the early ones, have a limited memory bus (32 bits); stay away from these systems. You typically can identify these systems by their names; they are touted as being "Pentium-ready" or "P5-ready."

The Address Bus

The *address bus* actually is a subset of the processor bus. Earlier in this chapter, you learned that the processor bus in a 486 or Pentium system consists of either 32 or 64 data lines, 32 address lines, and a few control lines. These address lines constitute the address bus; in most block diagrams, this bus is not broken out from the processor bus.

The address bus is used to perform operations on memory. The address bus indicates precisely where in memory the next operation will occur. The size of the memory bus is directly related to the amount of memory that the CPU can address directly.

The Need for Expansion Slots

The I/O bus enables your CPU to communicate with peripheral devices. The bus and its associated expansion slots are needed because basic systems cannot possibly satisfy all the needs of all the people who buy them. The I/O bus enables you to add devices to your computer to expand its capabilities. The most basic computer components, such as hard drive controllers and video adapter cards, can be plugged into expansion slots; you also can plug in more specialized devices, such as sound boards and CD-ROM drive interface cards.

> **Note**
>
> In some PC systems, some I/O capability is built into the motherboard. Some systems, for example, have the hard drive controller, SCSI port, serial ports, mouse port, and parallel printer ports built into the motherboard; in such a system, an expansion slot on the I/O bus is not needed. Nevertheless, these built-in controllers and ports still use the I/O bus to communicate with the CPU.

The number of expansion slots varies among computers. The original IBM PC had five expansion slots, for example, and the PC-XT had eight slots; to this day, virtually no PC systems have more than eight expansion slots. When the number of expansion slots increases, the distance between the slots decreases. Slots are approximately an inch apart in the original PC and only 0.8 inch apart in XT-series machines. Because of this design change, some of the extremely thick (*double-stacked*) expansion cards that fit well in a PC require two adjacent slots in most other systems.

Some PC systems provide only a single expansion slot on the motherboard. This slot typically is called a *riser-card slot*. The riser card in turn has expansion slots on its sides. Adapter cards are installed in the riser card, meaning that they are parallel to the motherboard.

Riser cards are used when a vendor wants to produce a computer that is shorter in height than normal. These computers usually are called "slimline," "low profile," or "ultra-thin." Even though this type of configuration may seem odd, the actual bus used in these systems is the same kind used in normal computer systems; the only difference is the use of the riser card.

Types of I/O Buses

Since the introduction of the first PC, many I/O buses have been introduced; most buses seem to have been introduced in the past several years. The reason is quite simple: faster I/O speeds are necessary for better system performance. This need for higher performance involves three main areas:

- Faster CPUs
- Increasing software demands
- Greater video requirements

Each of these areas requires the I/O bus to be as fast as possible. Surprisingly, a large number of PC systems shipped today (by some reports, as many as 75 percent) still use the same bus architecture as the IBM PC/AT. This situation is changing, however, as the types of systems sold demand different I/O bus structures, as the architectures mature, and as the cost of newer systems continues to plummet.

One of the primary reasons why new I/O-bus structures have been slow in coming is compatibility—that old catch-22 that anchors much of the PC industry to the past. One of the hallmarks of the PC's success is its standardization. This standardization spawned thousands of third-party I/O cards, each originally built for the early bus specifications of the PC. If a new, high-performance bus system is introduced, it must be compatible with the older bus systems so that the older I/O cards do not become obsolete. Therefore, bus technologies seem to evolve rather than make quantum leaps forward.

You can identify different types of I/O buses by their architecture. The main types of I/O architecture are:

- ISA
- Micro channel
- EISA
- Local bus
- VESA local bus
- PCMCIA bus

The differences among these buses consist primarily of the amount of data that they can transfer at one time and the speed at which they can do it. Each bus architecture is implemented by a chipset that is connected to the processor bus. Typically, this chipset also controls the memory bus (refer to fig. 5.2 earlier in this chapter). The following sections describe the different types of PC buses.

The ISA Bus

ISA, which is an acronym for *Industry Standard Architecture,* is the bus architecture that was introduced with the original IBM PC in 1982 and later expanded with the IBM PC/AT. ISA is the basis of the modern personal computer and the primary architecture used in the vast majority of PC systems on the market today. It may seem amazing that such an antiquated architecture is used in today's high-performance systems, but this seems to be true for reasons of reliability, affordability, and compatibility.

The ISA bus enabled thousands of manufacturers to build systems whose components (except for a few specialized parts) were interchangeable. Floppy drives that work in an IBM PC also work in IBM clones, for example, and video adapters that work in IBM ATs also work in IBM-compatible systems based on the 286 CPU chip.

Two versions of the ISA bus exist, based on the number of data bits that can be transferred on the bus at a time. The older version is an 8-bit bus; the newer version is a 16-bit bus. Both versions of the bus operate at an 8 MHz cycle rate, with data transfers requiring anywhere from two to eight cycles. Therefore, the theoretical maximum data rate of the ISA bus is 8M per second, as the following formula shows:

8 MHz × 16 bits = 128 megabits/second

128 megabits/second ÷ 2 cycles = 64 megabits/second

64 megabits/second ÷ 8 = 8M/second

The bandwidth of the 8-bit bus would be half this figure (4M per second). Remember, however, that these figures are theoretical maximums; because of I/O bus protocols, the effective bandwidth is much lower—typically by half.

The 8-Bit ISA Bus. This bus architecture is used in the original IBM PC computers. Although virtually nonexistent in new systems today, this architecture still exists in hundreds of thousands of PC systems in the field.

Physically, the 8-bit ISA expansion slot resembles the tongue-and-groove system that furniture makers once used to hold two pieces of wood together. An adapter card with 62 gold contacts on its bottom edge plugs into a slot on the motherboard that has 62 matching gold contacts. Electronically, this slot provides 8 data lines and 20 addressing lines, enabling the slot to handle 1M of memory.

Table 5.1 describes the pinouts for the 8-bit ISA bus.

Table 5.1   Pinouts for the 8-Bit ISA Bus

Pin	Signal Name	Pin	Signal Name
B1	Ground	A1	I/O Channel Check
B2	Reset Driver	A2	Data 7
B3	+5V	A3	Data 6
B4	IRQ 2	A4	Data 5
B5	–5V	A5	Data 4
B6	DMA Request 2	A6	Data 3
B7	–12V	A7	Data 2
B8	Card Selected (XT only)	A8	Data 1
B9	+12V	A9	Data 0
B10	Ground	A10	I/O Channel Ready
B11	Memory Write	A11	Address Enable
B12	Memory Read	A12	Address 19
B13	I/O Write	A13	Address 18
B14	I/O Read	A14	Address 17
B15	DMA Acknowledge 3	A15	Address 16
B16	DMA Request 3	A16	Address 15
B17	DMA Acknowledge 1	A17	Address 14
B18	DMA Request 1	A18	Address 13
B19	DMA Acknowledge 0	A19	Address 12
B20	Clock	A20	Address 11
B21	IRQ 7	A21	Address 10
B22	IRQ 6	A22	Address 9
B23	IRQ 5	A23	Address 8
B24	IRQ 4	A24	Address 7
B25	IRQ 3	A25	Address 6
B26	DMA Acknowledge 2	A26	Address 5
B27	Terminal Count	A27	Address 4

(continues)

Table 5.1	Continued		
Pin	**Signal Name**	**Pin**	**Signal Name**
B28	Address Latch Enable	A28	Address 3
B29	+5 VDC	A29	Address 2
B30	Oscillator	A30	Address 1
B31	Ground	A31	Address 0

Figure 5.3 shows how these pins are oriented in the expansion slot.

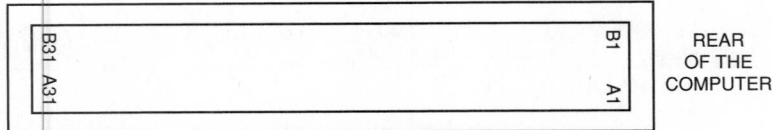

REAR OF THE COMPUTER

Fig. 5.3
The 8-bit ISA bus connector.

Although the design of the bus is simple, IBM never published full specifications for the timings of the data and address lines, so in the early days of IBM compatibles, manufacturers had to do their best to figure out how to make adapter boards. This problem was solved, however, as IBM-compatible personal computers became more widely accepted as the industry standard and manufacturers had more time and incentive to build adapter boards that worked correctly with the bus.

The dimensions of 8-bit ISA adapter cards are as follows:

4.2 inches (106.68mm) high

13.13 inches (333.5mm) long

0.5 inch (12.7mm) wide

In the XT or Portable PC, the eighth slot—the one closest to the power supply—is a special slot; only certain cards can be installed there. A card installed in the eighth slot must supply to the motherboard, on pin B8, a special card-selected signal, which few cards are designed to do. (The IBM asynchronous adapter card and the keyboard/timer card from a 3270 PC are two examples of cards that fit into the eighth slot.) Additionally, the timing requirements for the eighth slot are stricter.

The reason why this strange slot exists in the XT is that IBM developed the system to support a special configuration called the 3270-PC, which really is an XT with three to six special adapter boards installed. The eighth slot was designed specifically to accept the keyboard/timer adapter from the 3270 PC. This board needed special access to the motherboard because it replaced the motherboard keyboard circuitry. Special timing and the card-selected signal made this access possible.

Contrary to what many users believe, the eighth slot has nothing to do with the IBM expansion chassis, which was popular at the time of the PC-XT. The IBM expansion chassis is a box developed by IBM that looks like another system unit. Because the IBM XT has eight slots, one full-height floppy drive, and one full-height hard drive, the expansion chassis makes room for more expansion slots and for additional floppy and hard drives.

The 16-Bit ISA Bus. The second-generation 80286 chip can handle 16 bits on the I/O bus at a time, compared with 8 bits in older CPUs. The introduction of this chip posed a problem for IBM in relation to its next generation of PCs. Should the company create a new I/O bus and associated expansion slots, or should it try to come up with a system that could support both 8- and 16-bit cards? IBM opted for the latter solution, and the PC/AT was introduced with a set of double expansion slots. You can plug an older 8-bit card into the forward part of the slot or a newer 16-bit card into both parts of the slot.

> **Note**
>
> The expansion slots for the 16-bit ISA bus also introduced access keys to the PC environment. An *access key* is a cutout or notch in an adapter card that fits over a tab in the connector into which the adapter card is inserted. Access keys typically are used to keep adapter cards from being inserted into a connector improperly. The ends of the two expansion slots of the 16-bit ISA bus, when butted up against each other, serve the same purpose as an access key.

The second part of each expansion slot adds 36 connector pins to carry the extra signals necessary to implement the wider data path. In addition, one or two of the pins in the base portion of the connector (used for ISA cards) serve different purposes.

Table 5.2 describes the pinouts for the full 16-bit ISA expansion slot.

Table 5.2   Pinouts for the 16-Bit ISA Bus

Pin	Signal Name	Pin	Signal Name
B1	Ground	A1	I/O Channel Check
B2	Reset Driver	A2	Data 7
B3	+5V	A3	Data 6
B4	IRQ 9	A4	Data 5
B5	−5V	A5	Data 4
B6	DMA Request 2	A6	Data 3
B7	−12V	A7	Data 2
B8	−0 WAIT	A8	Data 1
B9	+12V	A9	Data 0
B10	Ground	A10	I/O Channel Ready

(continues)

Primary System Components

II

	Table 5.2	Continued		
Pin	**Signal Name**		**Pin**	**Signal Name**
B11	Memory Write		A11	Address Enable
B12	Memory Read		A12	Address 19
B13	I/O Write		A13	Address 18
B14	I/O Read		A14	Address 17
B15	DMA Acknowledge 3		A15	Address 16
B16	DMA Request 3		A16	Address 15
B17	DMA Acknowledge 1		A17	Address 14
B18	DMA Request 1		A18	Address 13
B19	DMA Acknowledge 0		A19	Address 12
B20	Clock		A20	Address 11
B21	IRQ 7		A21	Address 10
B22	IRQ 6		A22	Address 9
B23	IRQ 5		A23	Address 8
B24	IRQ 4		A24	Address 7
B25	IRQ 3		A25	Address 6
B26	DMA Acknowledge 2		A26	Address 5
B27	Terminal Count		A27	Address 4
B28	Address Latch Enable		A28	Address 3
B29	+5 VDC		A29	Address 2
B30	Oscillator		A30	Address 1
B31	Ground Access key		A31	Address 0 Access key
D1	Memory 16-bit chip select		C1	System bus high enable
D2	I/O 16-bit chip select		C2	Latch Address 23
D3	IRQ 10		C3	Latch Address 22
D4	IRQ 11		C4	Latch Address 21
D5	IRQ 12		C5	Latch Address 20
D6	IRQ 15		C6	Latch Address 19
D7	IRQ 14		C7	Latch Address 18
D8	DMA Acknowledge 0		C8	Latch Address 17
D9	DMA Request 0		C9	Memory Read
D10	DMA Acknowledge 5		C10	Memory Write
D11	DMA Request 5		C11	Data 8
D12	DMA Acknowledge 6		C12	Data 9
D13	DMA Request 6		C13	Data 10
D14	DMA Acknowledge 7		C14	Data 11
D15	DMA Request 7		C15	Data 12
D16	+5V		C16	Data 13
D17	Master 16-bit select		C17	Data 14
D18	Ground		C18	Data 15

Figure 5.4 shows how the pins are oriented in the expansion slot.

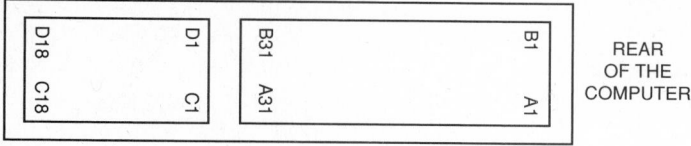

REAR
OF THE
COMPUTER

Fig. 5.4
The 16-bit ISA bus connector.

The extended 16-bit slots physically interfere with some adapter cards that have a *skirt*—an extended area of the card that drops down toward the motherboard just after the connector. To handle these cards, IBM left two expansion ports in the PC/AT without the 16-bit extensions. These slots, which are identical to the expansion slots in earlier systems, can handle any skirted PC or XT expansion card.

> **Note**
>
> Extended expansion slots were introduced years ago. Since then, virtually every manufacturer of expansion cards has modified its design so that the cards fit properly in the systems that are available today. Although card skirts are a thing of the past, you sometimes find them on older cards, such as those that you may pick up at a flea market or garage sale.

The dimensions of a typical AT expansion board are as follows:

4.8 inches (121.92mm) high

13.13 inches (333.5mm) long

0.5 inch (12.7mm) wide

Two heights actually are available for cards that are commonly used in AT systems: 4.8 inches and 4.2 inches (the height of older PC-XT cards). The shorter cards became an issue when IBM introduced the XT Model 286. Because this model has an AT motherboard in an XT case, it needs AT-type boards with the 4.2-inch maximum height. Most board makers trimmed the height of their boards; many manufacturers now make only 4.2-inch-tall boards so that they will work in systems with either profile.

32-Bit ISA Buses. After 32-bit CPUs became available, it was some time before 32-bit bus standards became available. Before MCA and EISA specs were released, some vendors began creating their own proprietary 32-bit buses, which were extensions of the ISA bus. Although the proprietary buses were few and far between, they do still exist.

The expanded portions of the bus typically are used for proprietary memory expansion or video cards. Because the systems are proprietary (meaning that they are nonstandard), pinouts and specifications are not available.

The Micro Channel Bus

The introduction of 32-bit chips meant that the ISA bus could not handle the power of another new generation of CPUs. The 386 chips can transfer 32 bits of data at a time, but the ISA bus can handle a maximum 16 bits. Rather than extend the ISA bus again, IBM decided to build a new bus; the result was the MCA bus. MCA (an acronym for *micro channel architecture*) is completely different from the ISA bus and is technically superior in every way.

IBM not only wanted to replace the old ISA standard, but also to receive royalties on it; the company required vendors that licensed the new proprietary MCA bus to pay IBM royalties for using the ISA bus in all previous systems. This requirement led to the development of the competing EISA bus (described later in this chapter) and hindered acceptance of the MCA bus. Another reason why MCA has not been adopted universally for systems with 32-bit slots is that adapter cards designed for ISA systems do not work in MCA systems.

> **Note**
>
> The MCA bus is not compatible with the older ISA bus, so cards designed for the ISA bus do not work in an MCA system.

MCA runs asynchronously with the main processor, meaning that fewer possibilities exist for timing problems among adapter cards plugged into the bus.

MCA systems produced a new level of ease of use, as anyone who has set up one of these systems can tell you. An MCA system has no jumpers and switches—neither on the motherboard nor on any expansion adapter. You don't need an electrical-engineering degree to plug a card into a PC.

The MCA bus also supports bus mastering. Through implementing bus mastering, the MCA bus provides significant performance improvements over the older ISA buses. (Bus mastering is also implemented in the EISA bus. General information related to bus mastering is discussed in the "Bus Mastering" section later in this chapter.) In the MCA bus mastering implementation, any bus mastering devices can request unobstructed use of the bus in order to communicate with another device on the bus. The request is made through a device known as the Central Arbitration Control Point (CACP). This device arbitrates the competition for the bus, making sure all devices have access and that no single device monopolizes the bus.

Each device is given a priority code to ensure that order is preserved within the system. The main CPU is given the lowest priority code. Memory refresh has the highest priority, followed by the DMA channels, and then the bus masters installed in the I/O slots. One exception to this is when an NMI (non-maskable interrupt) occurs. In this instance, control returns to the CPU immediately.

The MCA specification provides for four adapter sizes, which are described in table 5.3.

Table 5.3   Physical Sizes of MCA Adapter Cards

Adapter Type	Height	Length
Type 3	3.475"	12.3"
Type 3 half	3.475"	6.35"
Type 5	4.825"	13.1"
Type 9	9.0"	13.1"

Four types of slots are involved in the MCA design:

- 16-bit
- 16-bit with video extensions
- 16-bit with memory-matched extensions
- 32-bit

16-Bit MCA Slots. Every MCA slot has a 16-bit connector. This connector is the primary MCA slot design—the one used in all MCA systems. This 16-bit MCA slot has connectors that are smaller than the connectors in an ISA system. The slot itself is divided into two sections; one section handles 8-bit operations, and the other handles 16-bit operations.

Table 5.4 describes the pinouts for the 16-bit MCA connector. Pins B1/A1 through B45/A45 are responsible for 8-bit operations, and pins B48/A48 through B58/A58 handle 16-bit operations.

Table 5.4   Pinouts for the 16-Bit MCA Bus

Pin	Signal Name	Pin	Signal Name
B1	Audio Ground	A1	–CD Setup
B2	Audio	A2	MADE 24
B3	Ground	A3	Ground
B4	Oscillator	A4	Address 11
B5	Ground	A5	Address 10
B6	Address 23	A6	Address 9
B7	Address 22	A7	+5V
B8	Address 21	A8	Address 8
B9	Ground	A9	Address 7
B10	Address 20	A10	Address 6
B11	Address 19	A11	+5V
B12	Address 18	A12	Address 5
B13	Ground	A13	Address 4
B14	Address 17	A14	Address 3

(continues)

II

Primary System Components

Table 5.4	Continued		
Pin	**Signal Name**	**Pin**	**Signal Name**
B15	Address 16	A15	+5V
B16	Address 15	A16	Address 2
B17	Ground	A17	Address 1
B18	Address 14	A18	Address 0
B19	Address 13	A19	+12V
B20	Address 12	A20	−ADL
B21	Ground	A21	−PREEMPT
B22	−IRQ9	A22	−BURST
B23	−IRQ3	A23	−12V
B24	−IRQ4	A24	ARB 0
B25	Ground	A25	ARB 1
B26	−IRQ5	A26	ARB 2
B27	−IRQ6	A27	−12V
B28	−IRQ7	A28	ARB 3
B29	Ground	A29	ARB/−GNT
B30	−DPAREN	A30	−TC
B31	DPAR(0)	A31	+5V
B32	−CHCK	A32	−S0
B33	Ground	A33	−S1
B34	−CMD	A34	M/−IO
B35	CHRDYRTN	A35	+12V
B36	−CD SFDBK	A36	CD CHRDY
B37	Ground	A37	Data 0
B38	Data 1	A38	Data 2
B39	Data 3	A39	+5V
B40	Data 4	A40	Data 5
B41	Ground	A41	Data 6
B42	CHRESET	A42	Data 7
B43	−SD STROBE	A43	Ground
B44	−SDR(0)	A44	−DS 16 RTN
B45	Ground	A45	−REFRESH
B46	Access key	A46	Access key
B47	Access key	A47	Access key
B48	Data 8	A48	+5V
B49	Data 9	A49	Data 10
B50	Ground	A50	Data 11
B51	Data 12	A51	Data 13
B52	Data 14	A52	+12V
B53	Data 15	A53	DPAR(1)

Pin	Signal Name	Pin	Signal Name
B54	Ground	A54	–SBHE
B55	–IRQ10	A55	–CD DS 16#
B56	–IRQ11	A56	+5V
B57	–IRQ12	A57	–IRQ14
B58	Ground	A58	–IRQ15

Figure 5.5 shows how the connector for this card appears.

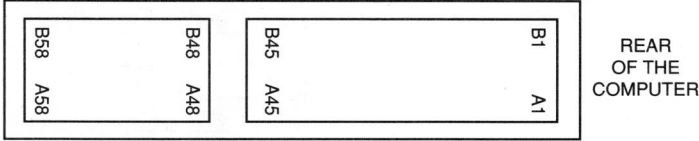

Fig. 5.5
A 16-bit MCA connector.

32-Bit MCA Slots. In addition to the basic 16-bit slot, MCA systems based on the 386DX or later CPU have several 32-bit slots that are designed to take advantage of the processors' increased communications and memory-addressing capabilities. Even though the 32-bit slot is an extension of the original MCA connector (as the 16-bit ISA slot is an extension of the 8-bit ISA design), this extension was designed at the same time as the rest of MCA. Therefore, because the extension connector was not an afterthought, the design is more integrated than the 16-bit extension in ISA systems.

Table 5.5 describes the pinouts for the 32-bit MCA connector. Pins B1/A1 through B58/A58 are exactly the same as in the 16-bit connector. Pins B59/A59 through B89/A89 are the 32-bit section.

Table 5.5	Pinouts for the 32-Bit MCA Bus		
Pin	**Signal Name**	**Pin**	**Signal Name**
B1	Audio Ground	A1	–CD Setup
B2	Audio	A2	MADE 24
B3	Ground	A3	Ground
B4	Oscillator	A4	Address 11
B5	Ground	A5	Address 10
B6	Address 23	A6	Address 9
B7	Address 22	A7	+5V
B8	Address 21	A8	Address 8
B9	Ground	A9	Address 7
B10	Address 20	A10	Address 6

(continues)

II

Primary System Components

Table 5.5	Continued		
Pin	**Signal Name**	**Pin**	**Signal Name**
B11	Address 19	A11	+5V
B12	Address 18	A12	Address 5
B13	Ground	A13	Address 4
B14	Address 17	A14	Address 3
B15	Address 16	A15	+5V
B16	Address 15	A16	Address 2
B17	Ground	A17	Address 1
B18	Address 14	A18	Address 0
B19	Address 13	A19	+12V
B20	Address 12	A20	–ADL
B21	Ground	A21	–PREEMPT
B22	–IRQ9	A22	–BURST
B23	–IRQ3	A23	–12V
B24	–IRQ4	A24	ARB 0
B25	Ground	A25	ARB 1
B26	–IRQ5	A26	ARB 2
B27	–IRQ6	A27	–12V
B28	–IRQ7	A28	ARB 3
B29	Ground	A29	ARB/–GNT
B30	–DPAREN	A30	–TC
B31	DPAR(0)	A31	+5V
B32	–CHCK	A32	–S0
B33	Ground	A33	–S1
B34	–CMD	A34	M/–IO
B35	CHRDYRTN	A35	+12V
B36	–CD SFDBK	A36	CD CHRDY
B37	Ground	A37	Data 0
B38	Data 1	A38	Data 2
B39	Data 3	A39	+5V
B40	Data 4	A40	Data 5
B41	Ground	A41	Data 6
B42	CHRESET	A42	Data 7
B43	–SD STROBE	A43	Ground
B44	–SDR(0)	A44	–DS 16 RTN
B45	Ground	A45	–REFRESH
B46	Access key	A46	Access key
B47	Access key	A47	Access key
B48	Data 8	A48	+5V
B49	Data 9	A49	Data 10

Pin	Signal Name	Pin	Signal Name
B50	Ground	A50	Data 11
B51	Data 12	A51	Data 13
B52	Data 14	A52	+12V
B53	Data 15	A53	DPAR(1)
B54	Ground	A54	−SBHE
B55	−IRQ10	A55	−CD DS 16#
B56	−IRQ11	A56	+5V
B57	−IRQ12	A57	−IRQ14
B58	Ground	A58	−IRQ15
B59	Reserved	A59	Reserved
B60	Reserved	A60	Reserved
B61	−SDR(1)d	A61	Ground
B62	−MSDR	A62	Reserved
B63	Ground	A63	Reserved
B64	Data 16	A64	−SFDBKRTN
B65	Data 17	A65	+12V
B66	Data 18	A66	Data 19
B67	Ground	A67	Data 20
B68	Data 22	A68	Data 21
B69	Data 23	A69	+5V
B70	DPAR(2)	A72	Data 24
B71	Ground	A71	Data 25
B72	Data 27	A72	Data 26
B73	Data 28	A73	+5V
B74	Data 29	A74	Data 30
B75	Ground	A75	Data 31
B76	−BE0	A76	DPAR(3)
B77	−BE1	A77	+12V
B78	−BE2	A78	−BE3
B79	Ground	A79	−DS32 RTN
B80	TR32	A80	−CD DS32
B81	Address 24	A81	+5V
B82	Address 25	A82	Address 26
B83	Ground	A83	Address 27
B84	Address 29	A84	Address 28
B85	Address 30	A85	+5V
B86	Address 31	A86	−APAREN
B87	Ground	A87	−APAR(0)
B88	APAR(2)	A88	−APAR(1)
B89	APAR(3)	A89	Ground

II

Primary System Components

Figure 5.6 shows how the connector for this card appears.

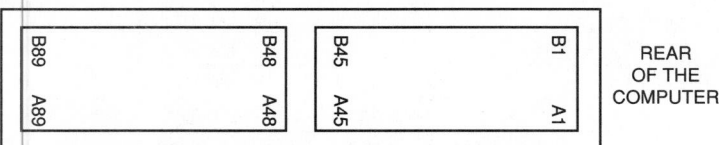

Fig. 5.6
The MCA connector.

Memory-Matched Extensions. Certain MCA systems (notably, IBM models 70 and 80) have bus extensions that support the operation of enhanced memory cards and support data transfer to those cards. These extensions are called *memory-matched extensions.*

The presence of memory-matched extensions varies from system to system. Some systems don't use the extensions at all; other systems include them on only one or a few slots. If one of your slots is equipped with these extensions, they will be on the end of the slot toward the rear of the motherboard (preceding pins B1 and A1 on your main MCA connector). You should refer to your system documentation to determine whether your system uses the extensions.

Table 5.6 details the additional pin-out specifications for the extensions.

Table 5.6	Additional Pinouts for the MCA Memory-Matched Extensions		
Pin	**Signal Name**	**Pin**	**Signal Name**
BM4	Ground	AM4	Reserved
BM3	Reserved	AM3	–MM cycle command
BM2	–MM cycle request	AM2	Ground
BM1	Reserved	AM1	–MM cycle

Figure 5.7 shows how this connector appears in your system.

MCA Video Extensions. The third type of MCA slot is a standard 16-bit MCA connector with a special video-extension connector. This special slot appears in almost every MCA system. This slot is designed to speed your video subsystem.

The MCA video-extension connector is positioned at the end of the slot toward the rear of the motherboard (before pins B1 and A1 on the main MCA connector). The connector takes advantage of special VGA circuitry built into the motherboard. MCA provides compatible high-resolution video adapters that have special access to this motherboard circuitry, so that the special circuitry does not have to be duplicated on the video card itself.

No matter what new type of video board you add to an MCA system, all your programs will run, because you never lose the built-in VGA circuits. In addition, the built-in VGA circuits do not have to be disabled if you add a newer video card. Your new card can coexist with the VGA circuits and even "borrow" some elements, such as the digital-to-analog converter. This arrangement (in theory) can make the add-on video boards less expensive, because they can rely on motherboard circuitry instead of providing their own.

Typically, only one slot in an MCA system has the video extensions. This arrangement makes sense, because a typical system has only one video card.

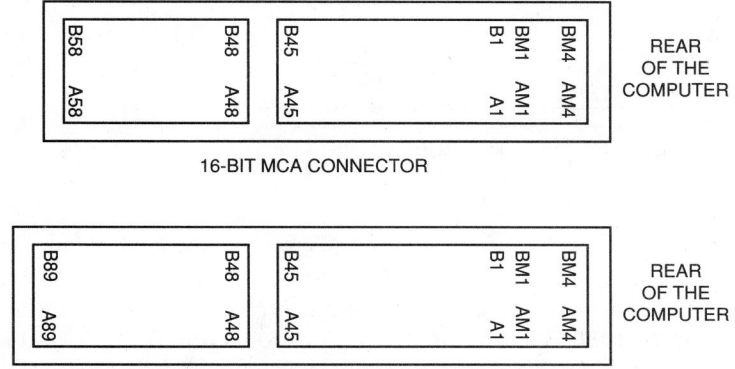

Fig. 5.7
The MCA connector with memory-matched extensions.

Table 5.7 describes the additional pinout connections for the slot with video extensions.

Table 5.7	Additional Pinouts for the MCA Video Extensions		
Pin	**Signal Name**	**Pin**	**Signal Name**
BV10	Esync	AV10	Vsync
BV9	Ground	AV9	Hsync
BV8	P5	AV8	Blank
BV7	P4	AV7	Ground
BV6	P3	AV6	P6
BV5	Ground	AV5	Edclk
BV4	P2	AV4	Dclk
BV3	P1	AV3	Ground
BV2	P0	AV2	P7
BV1	Ground	AV1	Evideo

Figure 5.8 shows what this slot looks like in your system.

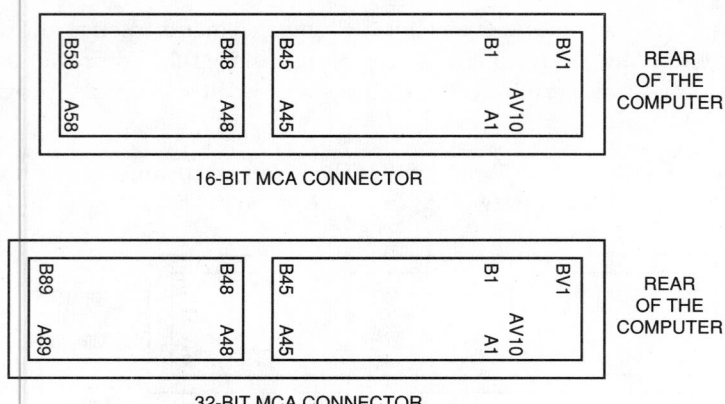

Fig. 5.8
The MCA connectors with video extensions.

The EISA Bus

EISA is an acronym for *extended industry standard architecture*. This standard was announced in September 1988 as a response to IBM's introduction of the MCA bus—more specifically, to the way that IBM wanted to handle licensing of the MCA bus. Vendors did not feel obligated to pay retroactive royalties on the ISA bus, so they turned their backs on IBM and created their own buses. The EISA standard was developed by leading computer manufacturers (minus IBM, of course) and supported by leading software companies. The first EISA machines started appearing on the market in 1989.

The EISA bus was designed as a successor to the ISA bus, although it has not turned out quite that way (as evidenced by the appearance of additional bus specifications). The EISA bus provides 32-bit slots for use with 386DX or higher systems. The EISA slot enables manufacturers to design adapter cards that have many of the capabilities of MCA adapters, but the bus also supports adapter cards created for the older ISA standard.

EISA provides markedly faster hard-drive throughput when used with devices such as SCSI bus-mastering hard drive controllers. Compared with 16-bit ISA system architecture, EISA permits greater system expansion with fewer adapter conflicts.

The EISA bus adds 90 new connections (55 new signals) without increasing the physical connector size of the 16-bit ISA bus. At first glance, the 32-bit EISA slot looks much like the 16-bit ISA slot. The EISA adapter, however, has two rows of connectors. The first row is the same kind used in 16-bit ISA cards; the other, thinner row extends from the 16-bit connectors.

To visualize the edge connectors on an EISA card, imagine that you are laying a 1-by-1-inch board on a 2-by-2-inch board in a lumberyard. The edge connector on an EISA board is about 0.2 inch longer than the connectors on an 8- or 16-bit ISA adapter board. The longest (and thinnest) connectors on an EISA card pass through the 16-bit part of the slot and make contact with the 32-bit connectors deeper in the slot.

The physical specifications of an EISA card are as follows:

> 5 inches (127mm) high
>
> 13.13 inches (333.5mm) long
>
> 0.5 inch (12.7mm) wide

The EISA specification calls for more than 45 watts at four different voltages to be available to each slot—a challenge to 200-watt or smaller power supplies, because it takes more than 325 watts to fully power the eight EISA slots in a system. Most EISA adapter cards, however, do not use the full 45 watts available to them; in fact, most cards use about the same amount of power as 8- and 16-bit ISA adapter boards.

The EISA bus can handle up to 32 bits of data at an 8.33 MHz cycle rate. Most data transfers require a minimum of two cycles, although faster cycle rates are possible if an adapter card provides tight timing specifications. The maximum bandwidth on the bus is 33M per second, as the following formula shows:

> 8.33 MHz × 32 bits = 266.56 megabits/second
>
> 266.56 megabits/second ÷ 8 = 33.32M/second

Data transfers through an 8- or 16-bit expansion card across the bus would be reduced appropriately. Remember, however, that these figures represent theoretical maximums. Wait states, interrupts, and other protocol factors can reduce the effective bandwidth—typically, by half.

Table 5.8 describes the pinouts for the EISA bus.

Table 5.8   Pinouts for the EISA Bus

Pin	Signal Name	Pin	Signal Name
B1	Ground	A1	I/O Channel Check
F1	Ground	E1	CMD
B2	Reset Driver	A2	Data 7
F2	+5V	E2	START
B3	+5V	A3	Data 6
F3	+5V	E3	EXRDY
B4	IRQ 9	A4	Data 5
F4	Unused	E4	EX32
B5	−5V	A5	Data 4
F5	Unused	E5	Ground
B6	DMA Request 2	A6	Data 3
F6	Access key	E6	Access key
B7	−12V	A7	Data 2

(continues)

Table 5.8 Continued			
Pin	**Signal Name**	**Pin**	**Signal Name**
F7	Unused	E7	EX16
B8	Zero Wait State	A8	Data 1
F8	Unused	E8	SLBURST
B9	+12V	A9	Data 0
F9	+12V	E9	MSBURST
B10	Ground	A10	I/O Channel Ready
F10	Memory I/O	E10	W/R
B11	Memory Write	A11	Address Enable
F11	LOCK#	E11	Ground
B12	Memory Read	A12	Address 19
F12	Reserved	E12	Reserved
B13	I/O Write	A13	Address 18
F13	Ground	E13	Reserved
B14	I/O Read	A14	Address 17
F14	Reserved	E14	Reserved
B15	DMA Acknowledge 3	A15	Address 16
F15	BE3	E15	Ground
B16	DMA Request 3	A16	Address 15
F16	Access key	E16	Access key
B17	DMA Acknowledge 1	A17	Address 14
F17	BE2	E17	BE1
B18	DMA Request 1	A18	Address 13
F18	BE0	E18	LA31
B19	Refresh	A19	Address 12
F19	Ground	E19	Ground
B20	Clock	A20	Address 11
F20	+5V	E20	LA30
B21	IRQ 7	A21	Address 10
F21	LA29	E21	LA28
B22	IRQ 6	A22	Address 9
F22	Ground	E22	LA27
B23	IRQ 5	A23	Address 8
F23	LA26	E23	LA25
B24	IRQ 4	A24	Address 7
F24	LA24	E24	Ground
B25	IRQ 3	A25	Address 6
F25	Access key	E25	Access key
B26	DMA Acknowledge 2	A26	Address 5
F26	LA16	E26	LA15

Pin	Signal Name	Pin	Signal Name
B27	Terminal Count	A27	Address 4
F27	LA14	E27	LA13
B28	Address Latch Enable	A28	Address 3
F28	+5V	E28	LA12
B29	+5V	A29	Address 2
F29	+5V	E29	LA11
B30	Oscillator	A30	Address 1
F30	Ground	E30	Ground
B31	Ground	A31	Address 0
F31	LA10 Access key	E31	LA9 Access key
H1	LA8	G1	LA7
H2	LA6	G2	Ground
D1	Memory 16-bit chip select	C1	System Bus High Enable
H3	LA5	G3	LA4
D2	I/O 16-bit chip select	C2	LA23
H4	+5V	G4	LA3
D3	IRQ 10	C3	LA22
H5	LA2	G5	Ground
D4	IRQ 11	C4	LA21
H6	Access key	G6	Access key
D5	IRQ 12	C5	LA20
H7	Data 16	G7	Data 17
D6	IRQ 15	C6	LA19
H8	Data 18	G8	Data 19
D7	IRQ 14	C7	LA18
H9	Ground	G9	Data 20
D8	DMA Acknowledge 0	C8	LA17
H10	Data 21	G10	Data 22
D9	DMA Request 0	C9	Memory Read
H11	Data 23	G11	Ground
D10	DMA Acknowledge 5	C10	Memory Write
H12	Data 24	G12	Data 25
D11	DMA Request 5	C11	Data 8
H13	Ground	G13	Data 26
D12	DMA Acknowledge 6	C12	Data 9
H14	Data 27	G14	Data 28
D13	DMA Request 6	C13	Data 10
H15	Access key	G15	Access key

(continues)

Table 5.8	Continued		
Pin	**Signal Name**	**Pin**	**Signal Name**
D14	DMA Acknowledge 7	C14	Data 11
H16	Data 29	G16	Ground
D15	DMA Request 7	C15	Data 12
H17	+5V	G17	Data 30
D16	+5V	C16	Data 13
H18	+5V	G18	Data 31
D17	Master 16-bit select	C17	Data 14
H19	/MACK0	G19	/MREQ0
D18	Ground	C18	Data 15

Figure 5.9, on the following page, shows the locations of the pins.

Bus Mastering. EISA uses a technology called *bus mastering* to speed the system. In essence, a bus master is an adapter with its own processor that can execute operations independently of the CPU. To work properly, bus-mastering technology relies on an *EISA arbitration unit*, most often called an *integrated system peripheral* (ISP) chip. The ISP enables a bus-mastered board to temporarily take exclusive control of the system, as though the board were the *entire* system. Because the board has exclusive control of the system, it can perform operations very quickly. A bus-mastering EISA hard drive controller, for example, achieves much greater data throughput with a fast drive than can controller cards that are not bus-mastered.

The ISP determines which device gains control by using a four-level order of priority. That order, in terms of priority, is:

- System-memory refresh
- DMA transfers
- The CPU itself
- Bus masters

A bus-mastering adapter board notifies the ISP when it wants control of the system. At the earliest possible time (after the higher priorities have been satisfied), the ISP hands control over to the bus-mastered board. The boards, in turn, have built-in circuitry to keep them from taking over the system for periods of time that would interfere with first-priority operations, such as memory refresh.

Automated Setup. EISA systems also use an automated setup to deal with adapter-board interrupts and addressing issues. These issues often cause problems when several different adapter boards are installed in an ISA system. EISA setup software recognizes potential conflicts and automatically configures the system to avoid them. EISA does, however, enable you to do your own troubleshooting, as well as to configure the boards through jumpers and switches.

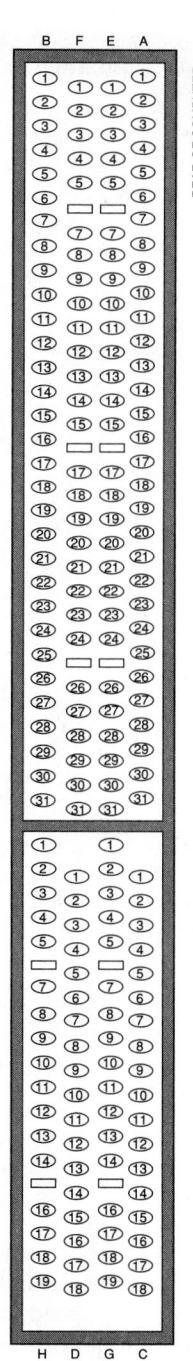

Fig. 5.9
The card connector for the EISA bus.

Local Bus

The I/O buses discussed so far (ISA, MCA, and EISA) have one thing in common: relatively slow speed. This speed limitation is a carryover from the days of the original PC, when the I/O bus operated at the same speed as the processor bus. As the speed of the processor bus increased, the I/O bus realized only nominal speed improvements, primarily from an increase in the bandwidth of the bus. The I/O bus had to remain at a slower speed, because the huge installed base of adapter cards could operate only at slower speeds.

Figure 5.10 shows a conceptual block diagram of the buses in a computer system.

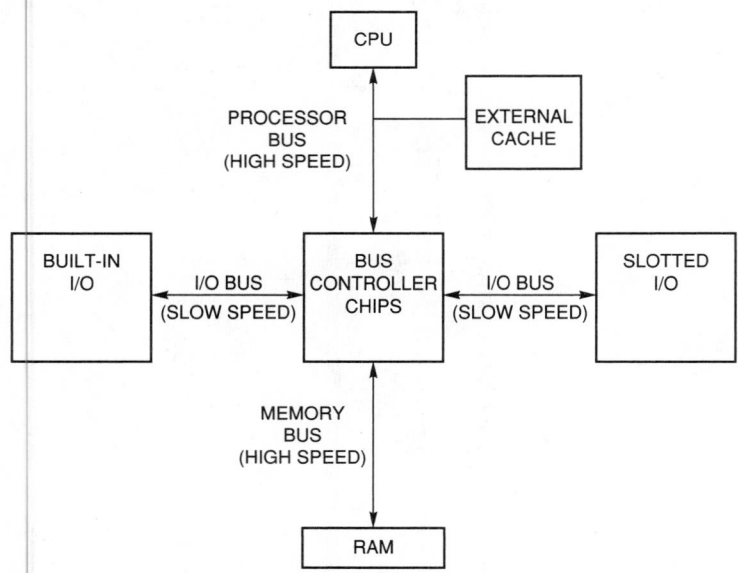

Fig. 5.10

Bus layout in a traditional PC.

The thought of a computer system running slower than it could is very bothersome to some computer users. Even so, the slow speed of the I/O bus is nothing more than a nuisance in most cases. You don't need blazing speed to communicate with a keyboard or a mouse, for example; you gain nothing in performance. The real problem occurs in subsystems in which you need the speed, such as video and disk controllers.

The speed problem became acute when graphical user interfaces (such as Windows) became prevalent. These systems required the processing of so much video data that the I/O bus became a literal bottleneck for the entire computer system. In other words, it did little good to have a CPU that was capable of 66 MHz speed if you could put data through the I/O bus at a rate of only 8 MHz.

An obvious solution to this problem is to move some of the slotted I/O to an area where it could access the faster speeds of the processor bus—much the same way as the external cache. Figure 5.11 shows this arrangement.

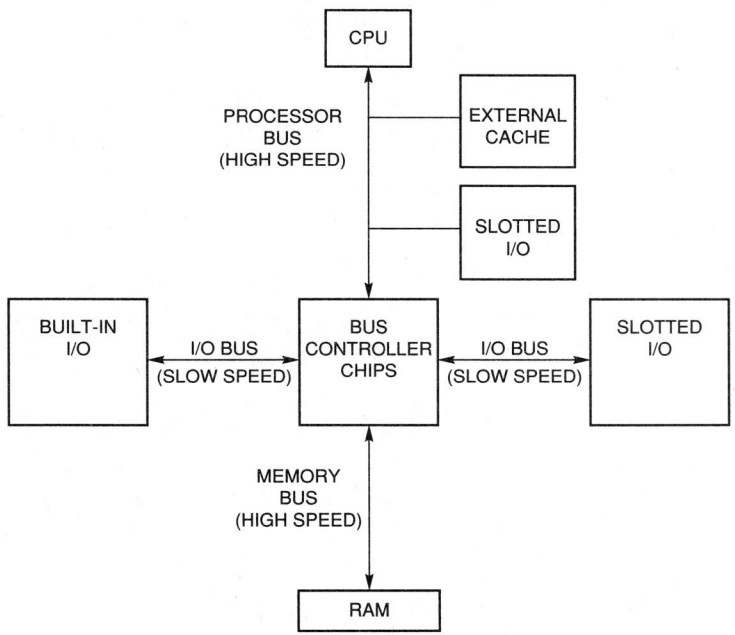

Fig. 5.11
How local bus works.

This arrangement became known as *local bus,* because external devices (adapter cards) now could access the part of the bus that was local to the CPU—the processor bus. Physically, the slots provided to tap this new configuration would need to be different from existing bus slots, to prevent adapter cards designed for slower buses from being plugged into the higher bus speeds that this design made accessible.

The first local-bus solution was introduced in 1992 as a joint effort between Dell Computer and Intel. Although the resulting system was very expensive (at first), it proved the feasibility of moving the video subsystem to the other side of the tracks, so to speak, where it could access the high speeds of the processor bus. This first pass at local bus became known, officially, as *i486 local-bus I/O.* By late 1992, the cost of local-bus systems began to decline, and many vendors began to offer similar systems.

> **Note**
>
> A system does not have to have a local-bus expansion slot to incorporate local-bus technology; instead, the local-bus device can be built directly into the motherboard. (In such a case, the local-bus-slotted I/O shown in fig. 5.11 would in fact be built-in I/O.) This built-in approach to local bus is the way the first local-bus systems were designed.

Local-bus solutions do not replace earlier standards, such as ISA and EISA; they are designed to augment those standards. Therefore, a typical system is based on ISA or EISA and has one or more local-bus slots available as well. Older cards still are compatible with the system, but high-speed adapter cards can take advantage of the local-bus slots as well.

Local-bus systems are especially popular with users of Windows and OS/2, because these slots are used for special 32-bit video accelerator cards that greatly speed the repainting of the graphics screens used in those operating systems. The performance of Windows and OS/2 suffers greatly from bottlenecks in even the best VGA cards connected to an ISA or EISA bus. Whereas regular VGA cards may be capable of painting 600,000 pixels per second on-screen, manufacturers of local-bus video adapters often claim that their cards can paint 50 million to 60 million pixels per second. Although performance typically is somewhat less in real-world situations, the increase in speed still is remarkable.

VESA Local Bus

At first, the local-bus slot primarily was used for video cards; this slot was where the bottleneck in top-of-the-line computer systems became apparent. Unfortunately, in late 1992, several competing local-bus systems were on the market, and each system was proprietary to its vendor. This lack of standardization hindered widespread acceptance of the local-bus solution.

To overcome this problem, the Video Electronics Standards Association (VESA) developed a standardized local-bus specification known as VESA Local Bus or simply VL-Bus. As in earlier local-bus implementations, the VL-Bus slot offers direct access to system memory at the speed of the processor itself. The VL-Bus can move data 32 bits at a time, enabling data to flow between the CPU and a compatible video subsystem or hard drive at the full 32-bit data width of the 486 chip. The maximum rated throughput of the VL-Bus is 128M to 132M per second. In other words, local bus went a long way toward removing the major bottlenecks that existed in earlier bus configurations.

Additionally, VL-Bus offers manufacturers of hard-drive interface cards an opportunity to overcome another traditional bottleneck: the rate at which data can flow between the hard drive and the CPU. The average 16-bit IDE drive and interface can achieve throughput of up to 5M per second, whereas VL-Bus hard drive adapters for IDE drives are touted as providing throughput of as much as 8M per second. In real-world situations, the true throughput of VL-Bus hard drive adapters is somewhat less than 8M per second, but VL-Bus still provides a substantial boost in hard-drive performance.

Despite all the benefits of the VL-Bus (and, by extension, of all local buses), this technology has a few drawbacks, which are described in the following list:

■ *Dependence on a 486 CPU.* The VL-Bus inherently is tied to the 486 processor bus. This bus is quite different from that used by Pentium processors (and probably from those that will be used by future CPUs). A VL-Bus that operates at the full rated speed of a Pentium has not been developed, although stopgap measures (such as stepping down speed or developing bus bridges) are available.

■ *Speed limitations.* The VL-Bus specification provides for speeds of up to 66 MHz on the bus, but the electrical characteristics of the VL-Bus connector limit an adapter card to no more than 50 MHz. If the main CPU uses a clock modifier (such as the kind that doubles clock speeds), the VL-Bus uses the unmodified CPU clock speed as its bus speed.

■ *Electrical limitations.* The processor bus has very tight timing rules, which may vary from CPU to CPU. These timing rules were designed for limited loading on the bus, meaning that the only elements originally intended to be connected to the local bus are elements such as the external cache and the bus controller chips. As you add more circuitry, you increase the electrical load. If the local bus is not implemented correctly, the additional load can lead to problems such as loss of data integrity and timing problems between the CPU and the VL-Bus cards.

■ *Card limitations.* Depending on the electrical loading of a system, the number of VL-Bus cards is limited. Although the VL-Bus specification provides for as many as three cards, this can be achieved only at clock rates of up to 40 MHz with an otherwise low system-board load. As the system-board load increases and the clock rate increases, the number of cards supported decreases. Only one VL-Bus card can be supported at 50 MHz with a high system-board load.

These drawbacks should not dissuade you from investing in a VL-Bus system; indeed, they provide an acceptable solution for high-speed computing. Many critics, however, complain that even though the VL-Bus is well suited to 486 systems, it is just that—a modified 486 system. These people contend that the VL-Bus is not adaptable or extensible, meaning that it does not work well for nonvideo needs and will not work well (without modification) for future generations of CPUs.

Caution

If you are contemplating the purchase of a local-bus system, you should make sure that it is a VL-Bus system. If the system instead uses a proprietary design, you may have a hard time finding adapter cards that take advantage of the local-bus slots. If you are convinced that another local-bus standard is superior, you should invest in the motherboard only after you ensure that you can buy video cards and hard drive adapters that take full advantage of the proprietary design.

Physically, the VL-Bus slot is an extension of the slots used for whatever type of base system you have. If you have an ISA system, the VL-Bus is positioned as an extension of your existing 16-bit ISA slots. Likewise, if you have an EISA system or MCA system, the VL-Bus slots are extensions of those existing slots. Figure 5.12 shows how the VL-Bus slots could be situated in an EISA system.

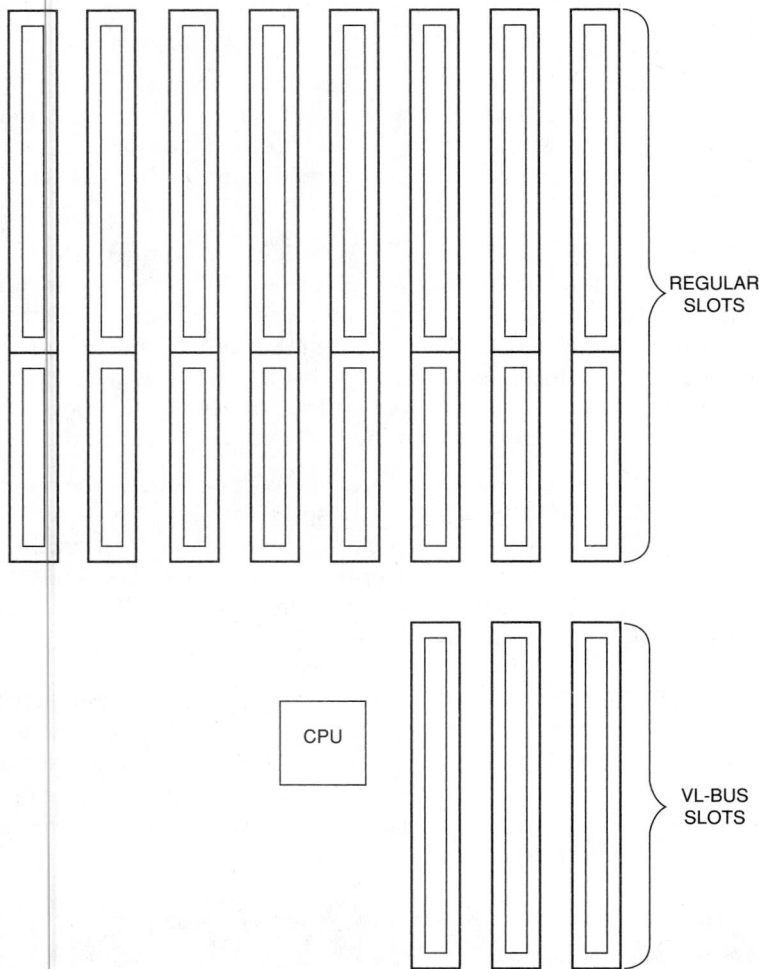

Fig. 5.12
An example of VL-Bus slots in an EISA system.

The VESA extension has 112 contacts and uses the same physical connector as the MCA bus. Table 5.9 describes the physical sizes of the various VL-Bus cards. (The sizes represent the main board only; the depths of the edge connectors are not included.)

Table 5.9 Size Specifications for Various VL-Bus Adapter Cards

System	Height	Length	Thickness
ISA	4.48"	13.4"	0.062"
MCA	2.95"	11.5"	0.063"
EISA	4.48"	13.4"	0.062"

The VL-Bus adds a total 116 pin locations to the bus connectors that your system already has. The complete pinout description for a VL-Bus card depends on which type of primary bus the VL-Bus is being used with. Table 5.10 lists the pinouts for only the VL-Bus connector portion of the total connector. (For pins for which two purposes are listed, the second purpose applies when the card is in 64-bit transfer mode.)

Table 5.10 Pinouts for the VL-Bus

Pin	Signal Name	Pin	Signal Name
B1	Data 0	A1	Data 1
B2	Data 2	A2	Data 3
B3	Data 4	A3	Ground
B4	Data 6	A4	Data 5
B5	Data 8	A5	Data 7
B6	Ground	A6	Data 9
B7	Data 10	A7	Data 11
B8	Data 12	A8	Data 13
B9	VCC	A9	Data 15
B10	Data 14	A10	Ground
B11	Data 16	A11	Data 17
B12	Data 18	A12	VCC
B13	Data 20	A13	Data 19
B14	Ground	A14	Data 21
B15	Data 22	A15	Data 23
B16	Data 24	A16	Data 25
B17	Data 26	A17	Ground
B18	Data 28	A18	Data 27
B19	Data 30	A19	Data 29
B20	VCC	A20	Data 31
B21	Address 31 or Data 63	A21	Address 30 or Data 62
B22	Ground	A22	Address 28 or Data 60
B23	Address 29 or Data 61	A23	Address 26 or Data 58
B24	Address 27 or Data 59	A24	Ground
B25	Address 25 or Data 57	A25	Address 24 or Data 56

II

Primary System Components

(continues)

Table 5.10	Continued		
Pin	**Signal Name**	**Pin**	**Signal Name**
B26	Address 23 or Data 55	A26	Address 22 or Data 54
B27	Address 21 or Data 53	A27	VCC
B28	Address 19 or Data 51	A28	Address 20 or Data 52
B29	Ground	A29	Address 18 or Data 50
B30	Address 17 or Data 49	A30	Address 16 or Data 48
B31	Address 15 or Data 47	A31	Address 14 or Data 46
B32	VCC	A32	Address 12 or Data 44
B33	Address 13 or Data 45	A33	Address 10 or Data 42
B34	Address 11 or Data 43	A34	Address 8 or Data 40
B35	Address 9 or Data 41	A35	Ground
B36	Address 7 or Data 39	A36	Address 6 or Data 38
B37	Address 5 or Data 37	A37	Address 4 or Data 36
B38	Ground	A38	Write Back
B39	Address 3 or Data 35	A39	Byte Enable 0 or 4
B40	Address 2 or Data 34	A40	VCC
B41	Unused or LBS64#	A41	Byte Enable 1 or 5
B42	Reset	A42	Byte Enable 2 or 6
B43	Data/Code Status	A43	Ground
B44	Memory-I/O Status or Data 33	A44	Byte Enable 3 or 7
B45	Write/Read Status or Data 32	A45	Address Data Strobe
B46	Access key	A46	Access key
B47	Access key	A47	Access key
B48	Ready Return	A48	Local Ready
B49	Ground	A49	Local Device
B50	IRQ 9	A50	Local Request
B51	Burst Ready	A51	Ground
B52	Burst Last	A52	Local Bus Grant
B53	ID0	A53	VCC
B54	ID1	A54	ID2
B55	Ground	A55	ID3
B56	Local Clock	A56	ID4 or ACK64#
B57	VCC	A57	Unused
B58	Local Bus Size 16	A58	Loc/Ext Address Data Strobe

Figure 5.13 shows the locations of the pins.

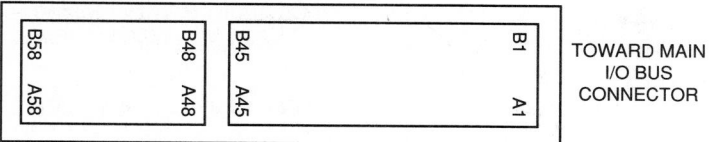

Fig. 5.13
The card connector for the VL-Bus.

The PCI Bus

In early 1992, Intel spearheaded the creation of another industry group which was formed with the same goals as the VESA group in relation to the PC bus. Recognizing the need to overcome weaknesses in the ISA and EISA buses, the PCI Special Interest Group was formed.

PCI is an acronym for *peripheral component interconnect bus*. The PCI bus specification, released in June 1992 and updated in April 1993, redesigned the traditional PC bus by inserting another bus between the CPU and the native I/O bus by means of bridges. Rather than tap directly into the processor bus, with its delicate electrical timing (as was done in local bus and VL-Bus), a new set of controller chips was developed to extend the bus, as shown in figure 5.14.

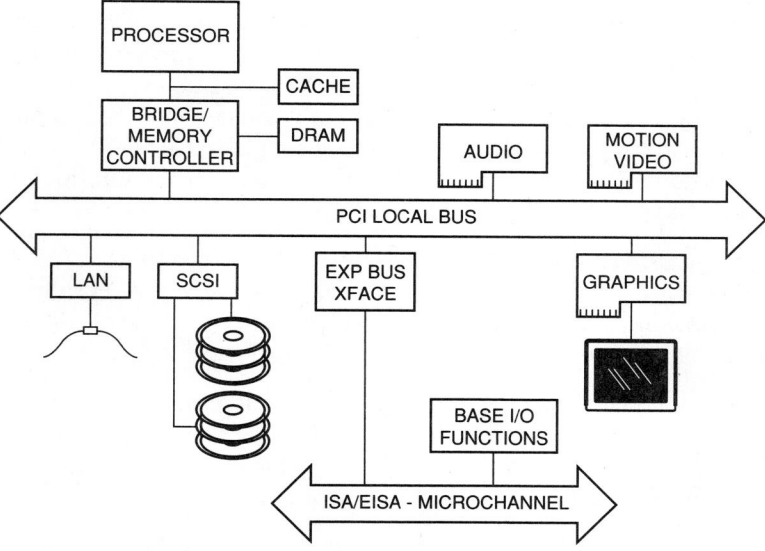

Fig. 5.14
Conceptual diagram of the PCI bus.

II

Primary System Components

The PCI bus often is called a *mezzanine bus* because it adds another layer to the traditional bus configuration. PCI bypasses the standard I/O bus; it uses the system bus to increase the bus clock speed and take full advantage of the CPU's data path. Systems that integrate the PCI bus became available in mid-1993 and have since become the mainstay high-end systems.

Although the PCI bus is the clear choice for Pentium-based systems, some critics have contended that for 486 systems, the VL-Bus is the winner because it is cheaper to implement. These critics base their contention on the fact that extra chips and pins are necessary to implement the mezzanine configuration inherent to PCI. This argument is incomplete, however; in reality, connecting an I/O chip to the VL-Bus requires almost twice as many pins as connecting it to the PCI bus does (88, compared with 47). Therefore, PCI versions of chips (the ones built into the motherboard) should be less expensive than the VL-Bus versions.

Information is transferred across the PCI bus at 33 MHz, at the full data width of the CPU. When the bus is used in conjunction with a 32-bit CPU, the bandwidth is 132M per second, as the following formula shows:

33 MHz × 32 bits = 1,056 megabits/second

1,056 megabits/second ÷ 8 = 132M/second

When the bus is used with a 64-bit CPU, the bandwidth doubles, meaning that you can transfer data at speeds up to 264M per second. Real-life data-transfer speeds necessarily will be lower, but still will be much faster than anything else that is currently available. Part of the reason for this faster real-life throughput is the fact that the PCI bus can operate concurrently with the processor bus; it does not supplant it. The CPU can be processing data in an external cache while the PCI bus is busy transferring information between other parts of the system—a major design benefit of the PCI bus.

A PCI adapter card uses a standard MCA connector, just like the VL-Bus. This connector can be identified within a computer system because it typically is offset from the normal ISA, MCA, or EISA connectors (see fig. 5.15 for an example). The size of a PCI card can be the same as that of the cards used in the system's normal I/O bus.

The PCI specification identifies three board configurations, each designed for a specific type of system with specific power requirements. The 5-volt specification is for stationary computer systems, the 3.3-volt specification is for portable machines, and the universal specification is for motherboards and cards that work in either type of system.

Table 5.11 shows the 5-volt PCI pinouts, and figure 5.16 shows the pin locations. Table 5.12 shows the 3.3-volt PCI pinouts; the pin locations are indicated in figure 5.17. Finally, table 5.13 shows the pinouts, and figure 5.18 shows the pin locations, for a universal PCI slot and card. Notice that each figure shows both the 32-bit and 64-bit variations on the respective specifications.

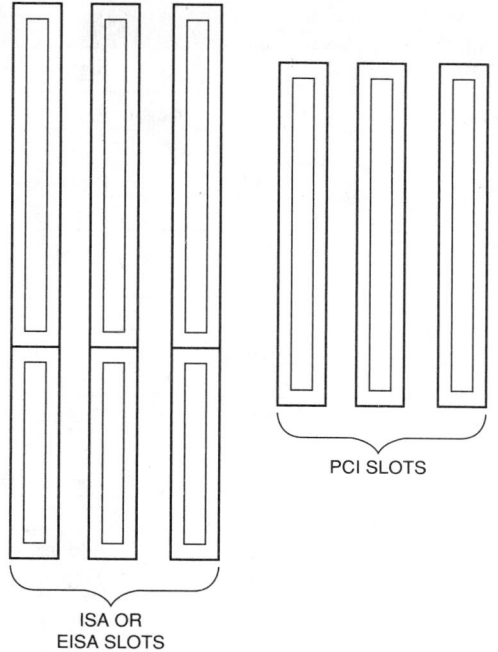

PCI SLOTS

ISA OR
EISA SLOTS

Fig. 5.15
Possible configuration of PCI slots in relation to ISA or EISA slots.

Note

If the PCI card supports only 32 data bits, it needs only pins B1/A1 through B62/A62. Pins B63/A63 through B94/A94 are used only if the card supports 64 data bits.

Table 5.11   Pinouts for a 5-Volt PCI Bus

Pin	Signal Name	Pin	Signal Name
B1	–12V	A1	Test Reset
B2	Test Clock	A2	+12V
B3	Ground	A3	Test Mode Select
B4	Test Data Output	A4	Test Data Input
B5	+5V	A5	+5V
B6	+5V	A6	Interrupt A
B7	Interrupt B	A7	Interrupt C
B8	Interrupt D	A8	+5V

(continues)

Table 5.11	Continued		
Pin	**Signal Name**	**Pin**	**Signal Name**
B9	PRSNT1#	A9	Reserved
B10	Reserved	A10	+5V I/O
B11	PRSNT2#	A11	Reserved
B12	Ground	A12	Ground
B13	Ground	A13	Ground
B14	Reserved	A14	Reserved
B15	Ground	A15	Reset
B16	Clock	A16	+5V I/O
B17	Ground	A17	Grant
B18	Request	A18	Ground
B19	+5V I/O	A19	Reserved
B20	Address 31	A20	Address 30
B21	Address 29	A21	+3.3V
B22	Ground	A22	Address 28
B23	Address 27	A23	Address 26
B24	Address 25	A24	Ground
B25	+3.3V	A25	Address 24
B26	C/BE 3	A26	Init Device Select
B27	Address 23	A27	+3.3V
B28	Ground	A28	Address 22
B29	Address 21	A29	Address 20
B30	Address 19	A30	Ground
B31	+3.3V	A31	Address 18
B32	Address 17	A32	Address 16
B33	C/BE 2	A33	+3.3V
B34	Ground	A34	Cycle Frame
B35	Initiator Ready	A35	Ground
B36	+3.3V	A36	Target Ready
B37	Device Select	A37	Ground
B38	Ground	A38	Stop
B39	Lock	A39	+3.3V
B40	Parity Error	A40	Snoop Done
B41	+3.3V	A41	Snoop Backoff
B42	System Error	A42	Ground
B43	+3.3V	A43	PAR
B44	C/BE 1	A44	Address 15
B45	Address 14	A45	+3.3V
B46	Ground	A46	Address 13
B47	Address 12	A47	Address 11

Pin	Signal Name	Pin	Signal Name
B48	Address 10	A48	Ground
B49	Ground	A49	Address 9
B50	Access key	A50	Access key
B51	Access key	A51	Access key
B52	Address 8	A52	C/BE 0
B53	Address 7	A53	+3.3V
B54	+3.3V	A54	Address 6
B55	Address 5	A55	Address 4
B56	Address 3	A56	Ground
B57	Ground	A57	Address 2
B58	Address 1	A58	Address 0
B59	+5V I/O	A59	+5V I/O
B60	Acknowledge 64-bit	A60	Request 64-bit
B61	+5V	A61	+5V
B62	+5V Access key	A62	+5V Access key
B63	Reserved	A63	Ground
B64	Ground	A64	C/BE 7
B65	C/BE 6	A65	C/BE 5
B66	C/BE 4	A66	+5V I/O
B67	Ground	A67	Parity 64-bit
B68	Address 63	A68	Address 62
B69	Address 61	A69	Ground
B70	+5V I/O	A70	Address 60
B71	Address 59	A71	Address 58
B72	Address 57	A72	Ground
B73	Ground	A73	Address 56
B74	Address 55	A74	Address 54
B75	Address 53	A75	+5V I/O
B76	Ground	A76	Address 52
B77	Address 51	A77	Address 50
B78	Address 49	A78	Ground
B79	+5V I/O	A79	Address 48
B80	Address 47	A80	Address 46
B81	Address 45	A81	Ground
B82	Ground	A82	Address 44
B83	Address 43	A83	Address 42
B84	Address 41	A84	+5V I/O
B85	Ground	A85	Address 40

II

Primary System Components

(continues)

Table 5.11	Continued		
Pin	**Signal Name**	**Pin**	**Signal Name**
B86	Address 39	A86	Address 38
B87	Address 37	A87	Ground
B88	+5V I/O	A88	Address 36
B89	Address 35	A89	Address 34
B90	Address 33	A90	Ground
B91	Ground	A91	Address 32
B92	Reserved	A92	Reserved
B93	Reserved	A93	Ground
B94	Ground	A94	Reserved

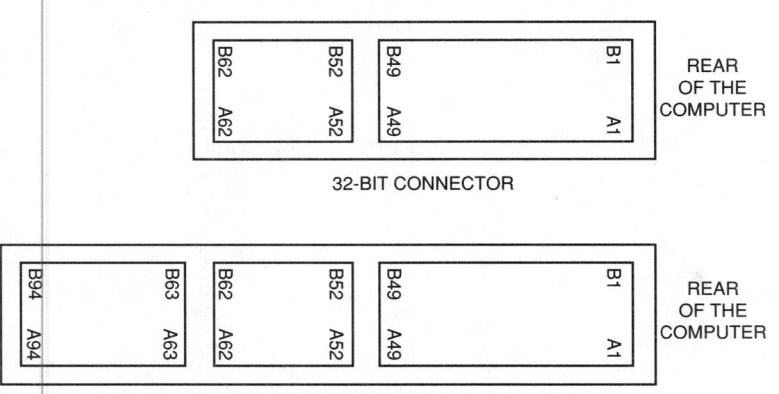

Fig. 5.16
The 5-volt PCI slot and card configuration.

Table 5.12	Pinouts for a 3.3-Volt PCI Bus		
Pin	**Signal Name**	**Pin**	**Signal Name**
B1	–12V	A1	Test Reset
B2	Test Clock	A2	+12V
B3	Ground	A3	Test Mode Select
B4	Test Data Output	A4	Test Data Input
B5	+5V	A5	+5V
B6	+5V	A6	Interrupt A
B7	Interrupt B	A7	Interrupt C
B8	Interrupt D	A8	+5V
B9	PRSNT1#	A9	Reserved

Pin	Signal Name	Pin	Signal Name
B10	Reserved	A10	+3.3V
B11	PRSNT2#	A11	Reserved
B12	Access key	A12	Access key
B13	Access key	A13	Access key
B14	Reserved	A14	Reserved
B15	Ground	A15	Reset
B16	Clock	A16	+3.3V
B17	Ground	A17	Grant
B18	Request	A18	Ground
B19	+3.3V	A19	Reserved
B20	Address 31	A20	Address 30
B21	Address 29	A21	+3.3V
B22	Ground	A22	Address 28
B23	Address 27	A23	Address 26
B24	Address 25	A24	Ground
B25	+3.3V	A25	Address 24
B26	C/BE 3	A26	Init Device Select
B27	Address 23	A27	+3.3V
B28	Ground	A28	Address 22
B29	Address 21	A29	Address 20
B30	Address 19	A30	Ground
B31	+3.3V	A31	Address 18
B32	Address 17	A32	Address 16
B33	C/BE 2	A33	+3.3V
B34	Ground	A34	Cycle Frame
B35	Initiator Ready	A35	Ground
B36	+3.3V	A36	Target Ready
B37	Device Select	A37	Ground
B38	Ground	A38	Stop
B39	Lock	A39	+3.3V
B40	Parity Error	A40	Snoop Done
B41	+3.3V	A41	Snoop Backoff
B42	System Error	A42	Ground
B43	+3.3V	A43	PAR
B44	C/BE 1	A44	Address 15
B45	Address 14	A45	+3.3V
B46	Ground	A46	Address 13
B47	Address 12	A47	Address 11
B48	Address 10	A48	Ground

II

Primary System Components

(continues)

Table 5.12	Continued		
Pin	**Signal Name**	**Pin**	**Signal Name**
B49	Ground	A49	Address 9
B50	Ground	A50	Ground
B51	Ground	A51	Ground
B52	Address 8	A52	C/BE 0
B53	Address 7	A53	+3.3V
B54	+3.3V	A54	Address 6
B55	Address 5	A55	Address 4
B56	Address 3	A56	Ground
B57	Ground	A57	Address 2
B58	Address 1	A58	Address 0
B59	+3.3V	A59	+3.3V
B60	Acknowledge 64-bit	A60	Request 64-bit
B61	+5V	A61	+5V
B62	+5V Access key	A62	+5V Access key
B63	Reserved	A63	Ground
B64	Ground	A64	C/BE 7
B65	C/BE 6	A65	C/BE 5
B66	C/BE 4	A66	+3.3V
B67	Ground	A67	Parity 64-bit
B68	Address 63	A68	Address 62
B69	Address 61	A69	Ground
B70	+3.3V	A70	Address 60
B71	Address 59	A71	Address 58
B72	Address 57	A72	Ground
B73	Ground	A73	Address 56
B74	Address 55	A74	Address 54
B75	Address 53	A75	+3.3V
B76	Ground	A76	Address 52
B77	Address 51	A77	Address 50
B78	Address 49	A78	Ground
B79	+3.3V	A79	Address 48
B80	Address 47	A80	Address 46
B81	Address 45	A81	Ground
B82	Ground	A82	Address 44
B83	Address 43	A83	Address 42
B84	Address 41	A84	+3.3V
B85	Ground	A85	Address 40
B86	Address 39	A86	Address 38

Pin	Signal Name	Pin	Signal Name
B87	Address 37	A87	Ground
B88	+3.3V	A88	Address 36
B89	Address 35	A89	Address 34
B90	Address 33	A90	Ground
B91	Ground	A91	Address 32
B92	Reserved	A92	Reserved
B93	Reserved	A93	Ground
B94	Ground	A94	Reserved

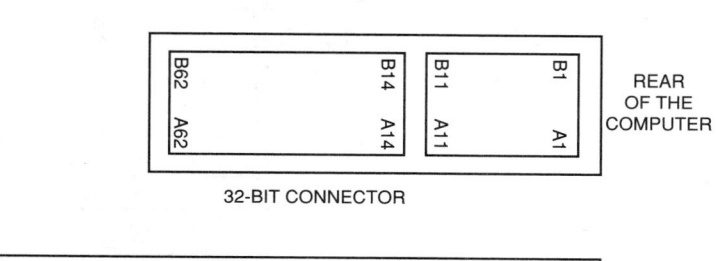

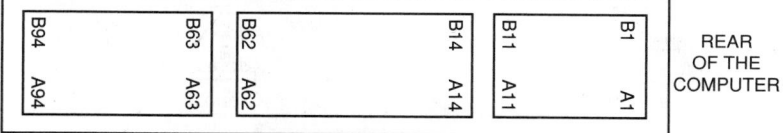

Fig. 5.17

The 3.3-volt PCI slot and card configuration.

Table 5.13	Pinouts for a Universal PCI Bus		
Pin	Signal Name	Pin	Signal Name
B1	–12V	A1	Test Reset
B2	Test Clock	A2	+12V
B3	Ground	A3	Test Mode Select
B4	Test Data Output	A4	Test Data Input
B5	+5V	A5	+5V
B6	+5V	A6	Interrupt A
B7	Interrupt B	A7	Interrupt C
B8	Interrupt D	A8	+5V
B9	PRSNT1#	A9	Reserved
B10	Reserved	A10	+V I/O
B11	PRSNT2#	A11	Reserved

(continues)

Primary System Components

Table 5.13 Continued			
Pin	**Signal Name**	**Pin**	**Signal Name**
B12	Access key	A12	Access key
B13	Access key	A13	Access key
B14	Reserved	A14	Reserved
B15	Ground	A15	Reset
B16	Clock	A16	+V I/O
B17	Ground	A17	Grant
B18	Request	A18	Ground
B19	+V I/O	A19	Reserved
B20	Address 31	A20	Address 30
B21	Address 29	A21	+3.3V
B22	Ground	A22	Address 28
B23	Address 27	A23	Address 26
B24	Address 25	A24	Ground
B25	+3.3V	A25	Address 24
B26	C/BE 3	A26	Init Device Select
B27	Address 23	A27	+3.3V
B28	Ground	A28	Address 22
B29	Address 21	A29	Address 20
B30	Address 19	A30	Ground
B31	+3.3V	A31	Address 18
B32	Address 17	A32	Address 16
B33	C/BE 2	A33	+3.3V
B34	Ground	A34	Cycle Frame
B35	Initiator Ready	A35	Ground
B36	+3.3V	A36	Target Ready
B37	Device Select	A37	Ground
B38	Ground	A38	Stop
B39	Lock	A39	+3.3V
B40	Parity Error	A40	Snoop Done
B41	+3.3V	A41	Snoop Backoff
B42	System Error	A42	Ground
B43	+3.3V	A43	PAR
B44	C/BE 1	A44	Address 15
B45	Address 14	A45	+3.3V
B46	Ground	A46	Address 13
B47	Address 12	A47	Address 11
B48	Address 10	A48	Ground
B49	Ground	A49	Address 9
B50	Access key	A50	Access key

Pin	Signal Name	Pin	Signal Name
B51	Access key	A51	Access key
B52	Address 8	A52	C/BE 0
B53	Address 7	A53	+3.3V
B54	+3.3V	A54	Address 6
B55	Address 5	A55	Address 4
B56	Address 3	A56	Ground
B57	Ground	A57	Address 2
B58	Address 1	A58	Address 0
B59	+5 I/O	A59	+V I/O
B60	Acknowledge 64-bit	A60	Request 64-bit
B61	+5V	A61	+5V
B62	+5V Access key	A62	+5V Access key
B63	Reserved	A63	Ground
B64	Ground	A64	C/BE 7
B65	C/BE 6	A65	C/BE 5
B66	C/BE 4	A66	+V I/O
B67	Ground	A67	Parity 64-bit
B68	Address 63	A68	Address 62
B69	Address 61	A69	Ground
B70	+V I/O	A70	Address 60
B71	Address 59	A71	Address 58
B72	Address 57	A72	Ground
B73	Ground	A73	Address 56
B74	Address 55	A74	Address 54
B75	Address 53	A75	+V I/O
B76	Ground	A76	Address 52
B77	Address 51	A77	Address 50
B78	Address 49	A78	Ground
B79	+V I/O	A79	Address 48
B80	Address 47	A80	Address 46
B81	Address 45	A81	Ground
B82	Ground	A82	Address 44
B83	Address 43	A83	Address 42
B84	Address 41	A84	+V I/O
B85	Ground	A85	Address 40
B86	Address 39	A86	Address 38
B87	Address 37	A87	Ground
B88	+V I/O	A88	Address 36

(continues)

II

Primary System Components

Table 5.13	Continued		
Pin	**Signal Name**	**Pin**	**Signal Name**
B89	Address 35	A89	Address 34
B90	Address 33	A90	Ground
B91	Ground	A91	Address 32
B92	Reserved	A92	Reserved
B93	Reserved	A93	Ground
B94	Ground	A94	Reserved

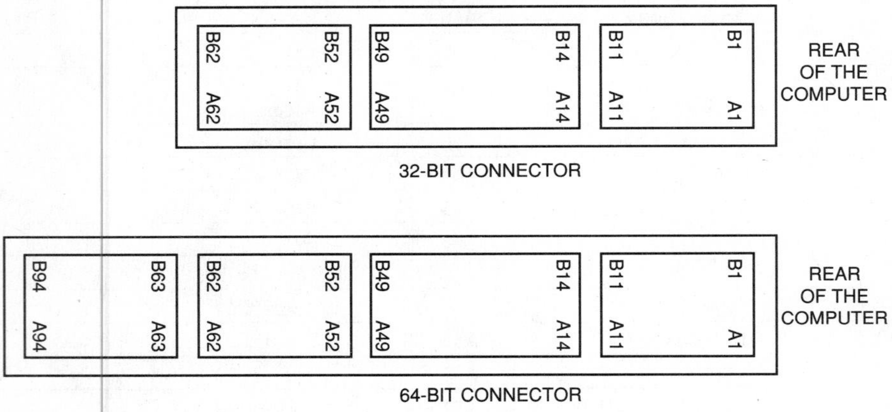

32-BIT CONNECTOR

64-BIT CONNECTOR

Fig. 5.18
The universal PCI slot and card configuration.

Notice that the universal PCI board specifications effectively combine the 5-volt and 3.3-volt specifications. For pins for which the voltage is different, the universal specification labels the pin simply *V I/O*. This type of pin represents a special power pin for defining and driving the PCI signaling rail.

The PCMCIA Bus

In an effort to give laptop and notebook computers the kind of expandability that users have grown used to in desktop systems, the Personal Computer Memory Card International Association (PCMCIA) has established several standards for credit-card-size expansion boards that fit into a small slot on laptops and notebooks.

The PCMCIA standards, which were developed by a consortium of more than 300 manufacturers (including IBM, Toshiba, and Apple), have been touted as being a revolutionary advance in mobile computing, because PCMCIA laptop and notebook slots enable you to add memory expansion cards, fax/modems, SCSI adapters, local-area-network cards, and many other types of devices. The idea behind PCMCIA is to enable you to plug any manufacturer's PCMCIA peripheral into your notebook computer.

The promise of the 2.1- by 3.4-inch PCMCIA 68-pin cards is enormous. Marketers envision not only memory expansion cards, tiny hard drives, and wireless modems (which already are available), but also wireless LAN connectors, PCMCIA sound cards, CD-ROM controllers, tape backup drives, and a host of other peripherals. Current PCMCIA devices cost considerably more than the same devices for ISA desktop systems. In version 2 of the PCMCIA card standard, devices can be longer, which will help manufacturers design some advanced peripheral cards.

PCMCIA has just one drawback: the standard has been followed loosely by manufacturers of computers and peripheral devices. If you purchase a laptop or notebook computer with an eye toward expandability, you must do your homework before buying the system; some devices that are advertised as being fully PCMCIA-compatible do not work with other systems that advertise themselves as being fully PCMCIA-compatible. If you already have a PCMCIA-bus computer, the only safe way to buy PCMCIA cards is to contact the device manufacturer and determine whether the device has been tested in your computer. Before you purchase a PCMCIA-compatible computer, you should get from the manufacturer a list of devices with which the computer will work.

In an effort to solve these compatibility problems, the PCMCIA has continued to establish standards. At this writing, in fact, four standards exist: PCMCIA Type I through Type IV. Even with all the PCMCIA types, compatibility problems remain, mostly because PCMCIA standards are voluntary; some manufacturers do not fully implement these standards before advertising their products as being PCMCIA-compatible. The standards have, however, helped make more and more PCMCIA computers and peripherals compatible with one another.

The following list describes the major features of the PCMCIA standards:

- *PCMCIA Type I*. The original PCMCIA standard, now called Type I slots, can handle cards that are 3.3mm thick. These slots work only with memory expansion cards. If you are shopping for a PCMCIA memory expansion card, check with your system manufacturer before buying to ensure that the card you buy will work with your system.

- *PCMCIA Type II*. PCMCIA Type II slots accommodate cards that are 5mm thick but otherwise have the same physical form factor as Type I cards. PCMCIA Type II slots also can be used with Type I cards because the guides that hold the cards are the same thickness; the center portion of the slot provides more room. Type II cards support virtually any type of expansion device (such as a modem) or LAN adapter.

- *PCMCIA Type III*. In late 1992, PCMCIA Type III was introduced. These slots, intended primarily for computers that have removable hard drives, are 10.5mm thick, but they also are compatible with Type I and Type II cards.

- *PCMCIA Type IV*. PCMCIA Type IV slots are intended to be used with hard drives that are thicker than the 10.5mm Type III slot allows. The exact dimensions of the slot have not yet been determined, but Type IV slots are expected to be compatible with Types I through III.

Table 5.14 shows the PCMCIA pinouts.

Pin	Signal Name
Table 5.14	**Pinouts for a PCMCIA Card**
1	Ground
2	Data 3
3	Data 4
4	Data 5
5	Data 6
6	Data 7
7	−Card Enable 1
8	Address 10
9	−Output Enable
10	Address 11
11	Address 9
12	Address 8
13	Address 13
14	Address 14
15	−Write Enable/−Program
16	Ready/−Busy (IREQ)
17	+5V
18	Vpp1
19	Address 16
20	Address 15
21	Address 12
22	Address 7
23	Address 6
24	Address 5
25	Address 4
26	Address 3
27	Address 2
28	Address 1
29	Address 0
30	Data 0
31	Data 1
32	Data 2
33	Write Protect (−IOIS16)
34	Ground
35	Ground
36	−Card Detect 1
37	Data 11

Pin	Signal Name
38	Data 12
39	Data 13
40	Data 14
41	Data 15
42	−Card Enable 2
43	Refresh
44	RFU (−IOR)
45	RFU (−IOW)
46	Address 17
47	Address 18
48	Address 19
49	Address 20
50	Address 21
51	+5V
52	Vpp2
53	Address 22
54	Address 23
55	Address 24
56	Address 25
57	RFU
58	RESET
59	−WAIT
60	RFU (−INPACK)
61	−Register Select
62	Battery Voltage Detect 2 (−SPKR)
63	Battery Voltage Detect 1 (−STSCHG)
64	Data 8
65	Data 9
66	Data 10
67	−Card Detect 2
68	Ground

System Resources

In various chapters in Parts II–IV, you learn about system resources. At their lowest level, these resources typically include the following:

■ I/O port addresses

■ IRQ numbers

- DMA channels
- Memory

These resources are required and used by many different components of your system. Adapter cards need these resources to communicate with your system and to accomplish their purposes. Not all adapter cards have the same resource requirements. A serial communications port, for example, needs an I/O port address and an IRQ number, whereas a sound board needs these resources and at least one DMA channel.

As your system increases in complexity, the chance for resource conflicts increases dramatically. You naturally have a conflict if you have two or three cards, each of which needs an IRQ number or an I/O port address. So that you can resolve conflicts, most adapter cards allow you to modify resource assignments by setting jumpers or switches on the cards.

I/O Port Addresses

Your computer's I/O ports enable you to attach a large number of important devices to your system to expand its capabilities. A printer attached to one of your system's LPT (parallel) ports enables you to make a printout of the work on your system. A modem attached to one of your system's COM (serial) ports enables you to use telephone lines to communicate with computers thousands of miles away. A scanner attached to an LPT port or a SCSI host adapter enables you to convert graphics or text to images and type that you can use with the software installed on your computer.

Most systems come configured with at least two COM (serial) ports and one LPT (parallel printer) ports. The two serial ports are configured as COM1 and COM2, and the parallel port as LPT1. The basic architecture of the PC provides for as many as four COM ports (1 through 4) and three LPT ports (1 through 3).

> ### Caution
>
> Theoretically, each of the four COM ports in a system can be used to attach a device, such as a mouse or modem, but doing so may lead to resource conflicts. For more information, see the discussion of resolving IRQ conflicts in "IRQ Conflicts" later in this chapter.

Every I/O port in your system uses an I/O address for communication. This address, which is in the lower memory ranges, is reserved for communication between the I/O device and the operating system. If your system has multiple I/O cards, each card must use a different I/O address; if not, your system will not be able to communicate with the devices reliably.

The I/O addresses that your ports use depend on the type of ports. Table 5.15 shows the I/O addresses expected by the various standard ports in a PC system.

Table 5.15 Standard I/O Addresses for Serial and Parallel Ports	
Port	**I/O Address**
COM1	03F8
COM2	02F8
COM3	03E8
COM4	02E8
LPT1	03BC
LPT2	0378
LPT3	0278

Besides your serial and parallel ports, other adapters in your system use I/O addresses. Quite truthfully, the I/O addresses for the serial and parallel ports are fairly standard; it is unlikely that you will run into problems with them. The I/O addresses used by other adapters are not standardized, however, and you may have problems finding a mix of port addresses that works reliably. Later in this chapter, in "Resolving Resource Conflicts," you learn some of the techniques that you can use to solve this problem.

Interrupts (IRQs)

Interrupt request channels (IRQs), or *hardware interrupts,* are used by various hardware devices to signal the motherboard that a request must be fulfilled. This procedure is the same as a student raising his hand to indicate that he needs attention.

These interrupt channels are represented by wires on the motherboard and in the slot connectors. When a particular interrupt is invoked, a special routine takes over the system, which first saves all the CPU register contents in a stack and then directs the system to the interrupt vector table. This vector table contains a list of memory addresses that correspond to the interrupt channels. Depending on which interrupt was invoked, the program corresponding to that channel is run.

The pointers in the vector table point to the address of whatever software driver is used to service the card that generated the interrupt. For a network card, for example, the vector may point to the address of the network drivers that have been loaded to operate the card; for a hard disk controller, the vector may point to the BIOS code that operates the controller.

After the particular software routine finishes performing whatever function the card needed, the interrupt-control software returns the stack contents to the CPU registers, and the system then resumes whatever it was doing before the interrupt occurred.

Through the use of interrupts, your system can respond to external events in a timely fashion. Each time that a serial port presents a byte to your system, an interrupt is generated to ensure that the system reads that byte before another comes in.

Hardware interrupts are prioritized by their numbers; the highest-priority interrupts have the lowest numbers. Higher-priority interrupts take precedence over lower-priority interrupts by interrupting them. As a result, several interrupts can occur in your system concurrently, each interrupt nesting within another.

If you overload the system—in this case, by running out of stack resources (too many interrupts were generated too quickly)—an internal stack overflow error occurs, and your system halts. If you experience this type of system error, you can compensate for it by using the STACKS parameter in your CONFIG.SYS file to increase the available stack resources.

The ISA bus uses edge-triggered interrupt sensing, in which an interrupt is sensed by a signal sent on a particular wire located in the slot connector. A different wire corresponds to each possible hardware interrupt. Because the motherboard cannot recognize which slot contains the card that used an interrupt line and therefore generated the interrupt, confusion would result if more than one card were set to use a particular interrupt. Each interrupt, therefore, usually is designated for a single hardware device, and most of the time, interrupts cannot be shared.

A device can be designed to share interrupts, and a few devices allow this; most cannot, however, because of the way interrupts are signaled in the ISA bus. Systems with the MCA bus use level-sensitive interrupts, which allow complete interrupt sharing to occur. In fact, in an MCA system, all boards can be set to the same interrupt with no conflicts or problems. For maximum performance, however, interrupts should be staggered as much as possible.

Because interrupts usually cannot be shared in an ISA bus system, you often run out of interrupts when you are adding boards to a system. If two boards use the same IRQ to signal the system, the resulting conflict prevents either board from operating properly. The following sections discuss the IRQs that any standard devices use, as well as what may be free in your system.

8-Bit ISA Bus Interrupts. The PC and XT (the systems based on the 8-bit 8086 CPU) provide for eight different external hardware interrupts. Table 5.16 shows the typical uses for these interrupts, which are numbered 0 through 7.

Table 5.16   8-Bit ISA Bus Default Interrupt Assignments

IRQ	Function	Bus Slot
0	System Timer	No
1	Keyboard Controller	No
2	Available	No
3	Serial Port 2 (COM2)	Yes (8-bit)
4	Serial Port 1 (COM1)	Yes (8-bit)
5	Hard Disk Controller	Yes (8-bit)
6	Floppy Disk Controller	Yes (8-bit)
7	Parallel Port 1 (LPT1)	Yes (8-bit)

External hardware interrupts often are referred to as *maskable interrupts*, which simply means that the interrupts can be masked or turned off for a short time while the CPU is used for other critical operations. It is up to the programmer to manage interrupts properly and efficiently for the best system performance.

If you have a system that has one of the original 8-bit ISA buses, you will find that the IRQ resources provided by the system present a severe limitation. Installing several devices that need the services of system IRQs in a PC/XT-type system can be a study in frustration because the only way to resolve the interrupt-shortage problem is to remove the adapter board that you need the least.

16-Bit ISA, EISA, and MCA Bus Interrupts. The introduction of the AT, based on the 80286 processor, was accompanied by an increase in the number of external hardware interrupts that the bus would support. The number of interrupts was doubled, to 16, by using two interrupt controllers, piping the interrupts generated by the second one through the unused IRQ 2 in the first controller. This arrangement effectively means that only 15 IRQ assignments are available, because IRQ 2 and IRQ 9 mirror each other.

Table 5.17 shows the typical uses for interrupts in the 16-bit ISA, EISA, and MCA buses.

Table 5.17 16-Bit ISA, EISA, and MCA Default Interrupt Assignments		
IRQ	**Standard Function**	**Bus Slot**
0	System Timer	No
1	Keyboard Controller	No
2	Second IRQ Controller	No
3	Serial Port 2 (COM2)	Yes (8-bit)
4	Serial Port 1 (COM1)	Yes (8-bit)
5	Parallel Port 2 (LPT2)	Yes (8-bit)
6	Floppy Disk Controller	Yes (8-bit)
7	Parallel Port 1 (LPT1)	Yes (8-bit)
8	Real-Time Clock	No
9	Available (appears as IRQ 2)	Yes (8-bit)
10	Available	Yes (16-bit)
11	Available	Yes (16-bit)
12	Motherboard Mouse Port	Yes (16-bit)
13	Math Coprocessor	No
14	Hard Disk Controller	Yes (16-bit)
15	Available	Yes (16-bit)

Because IRQ 2 now is used directly by the motherboard, the wire for IRQ 9 has been rerouted to the same position in the slot that IRQ 2 normally would occupy. Therefore, any board you install that is set to IRQ 2 actually is using IRQ 9. The interrupt vector table has been adjusted accordingly to enable this deception to work. This adjustment to the system provides greater compatibility with the PC interrupt structure and enables cards that are set to IRQ 2 to work properly.

Notice that interrupts 0, 1, 2, 8, and 13 are not on the bus connectors and are not accessible to adapter cards. Interrupts 8, 10, 11, 12, 13, 14, and 15 are from the second interrupt controller and are accessible only by boards that use the 16-bit extension connector, because this is where these wires are located. IRQ 9 is rewired to the 8-bit slot connector in place of IRQ 2, which means that IRQ 9 replaces IRQ 2 and therefore is available to 8-bit cards, which treat it as though it were IRQ 2.

Note

Although the 16-bit ISA bus has twice as many interrupts as systems that have the 8-bit ISA bus, you still may run out of available interrupts, because only 16-bit adapters can use any of the new interrupts.

The extra IRQ lines in a 16-bit ISA system are of little help unless the adapter boards that you plan to use enable you to configure them for one of the unused IRQs. Some devices are hard-wired so that they can use only a particular IRQ. If you have a device that already uses that IRQ, you must resolve the conflict before installing the second adapter. If neither adapter enables you to reconfigure its IRQ use, chances are that you cannot use the two devices in the same system.

IRQ Conflicts. One of the most common areas of IRQ conflict involves serial (COM) ports. You may have noticed in the preceding two sections that two IRQs are set aside for two COM ports. IRQ 3 is used for COM2, and IRQ 4 is used for COM1. The problem occurs when you have more than two serial ports in a system—a situation that is entirely possible, because a PC can support up to four COM ports.

The solution used by the PC—assigning IRQs among different COM ports—historically has been unsatisfactory. In reality, IRQ 3 is used for *even* COM ports, and IRQ 4 is used for *odd* COM ports. Therefore, COM2 and COM4 both share IRQ 3, and COM1 and COM3 both share IRQ 4. As a result, you cannot use COM1 at the same time as COM3; neither can you use COM2 at the same time as COM4. Why? If more than one device shares the same IRQ, neither one can signal the CPU to indicate that it needs attention.

When you install devices that use COM ports, you must ensure that no two devices will be using the same IRQ at the same time. This issue can be tricky. If a mouse is configured for COM3 (and IRQ 4), for example, you cannot use COM1 (which also uses IRQ 4) for another device, such as a modem. In this example, the mouse driver, when it is installed in memory from CONFIG.SYS or AUTOEXEC.BAT, takes control of the IRQ for which it is configured. If another device attempts to use the IRQ that the mouse uses, the resulting conflict could destroy data or lock up your system.

DMA Channels

DMA (*direct memory access*) channels are used by high-speed communications devices that must send and receive information at high speed. A serial or parallel port does not use a DMA channel, but a network adapter often does. DMA channels sometimes can be shared if the devices are not of the type that would need them simultaneously. For example, you can have a network adapter and a tape backup adapter sharing DMA channel 1, but you cannot back up while the network is running. To back up during network operation, you must ensure that each adapter uses a unique DMA channel.

8-Bit ISA Bus DMA Channels. In the 8-bit ISA bus, four DMA channels support high-speed data transfers between I/O devices and memory. Three of the channels are available to the expansion slots. Table 5.18 shows the typical uses of these DMA channels.

Table 5.18	8-Bit ISA Default DMA-Channel Assignments	
DMA	**Standard Function**	**Bus Slot**
0	Dynamic RAM Refresh	No
1	Available	Yes (8-bit)
2	Floppy disk controller	Yes (8-bit)
3	Hard disk controller	Yes (8-bit)

Because most systems typically have both a floppy and hard disk drive, only one DMA channel is available in 8-bit ISA systems.

16-Bit ISA DMA Channels. Since the introduction of the 80286 CPU, the ISA bus has supported eight DMA channels, with seven channels available to the expansion slots. Like the expanded IRQ lines described earlier in this chapter, the added DMA channels were created by cascading a second DMA controller to the first one. DMA channel 4 is used to cascade channels 0 through 3 to the microprocessor. Channels 0 through 3 are available for 8-bit transfers, and channels 5 through 7 are for 16-bit transfers only. Table 5.19 shows the typical uses for the DMA channels.

Table 5.19	16-Bit ISA, EISA, and MCA Default DMA-Channel Assignments	
DMA	**Standard Function**	**Bus Slot**
0	Available	Yes (8-bit)
1	Available	Yes (8-bit)
2	Floppy disk controller	Yes (8-bit)
3	Available	Yes (8-bit)
4	First DMA controller	No
5	Available	Yes (16-bit)
6	Available	Yes (16-bit)
7	Available	Yes (16-bit)

EISA. Realizing the shortcomings inherent in the way DMA channels are implemented in the ISA bus, the creators of the EISA specification created a specific DMA controller for their new bus. They increased the number of address lines to include the entire address bus, thus allowing transfers anywhere within the address space of the system. Each DMA channel can be set to run either 8-, 16-, or 32-bit transfers. In addition, each DMA channel can be separately programmed to run any of four types of bus cycles when transferring data:

- *Compatible*. This transfer method is included to match the same DMA timing as used in the ISA bus. This is done for compatibility reasons; all ISA cards can operate in an EISA system in this transfer mode.

- *Type A.* This transfer type compresses the DMA timing by 25 percent over the compatible method. It was designed to run with most (but not all) ISA cards and still yield a speed increase.

- *Type B.* This transfer type compresses timing by 50 percent over the compatible method. Using this method, most EISA cards function properly, but only a few ISA cards will be problem-free.

- *Type C.* This transfer method compresses timing by 87.5 percent over the compatible method; it is the fastest DMA transfer method available under the EISA specification. No ISA cards will work using this transfer method.

EISA DMA also allows for special reading and writing operations referred to as *scatter write* and *gather read*. Scattered writes are done by reading a contiguous block of data and writing it to more than one area of memory at the same time. Gathered reads involve reading from more than one place in memory and writing to a device. These functions are often referred to as *buffered chaining* and they increase the throughput of DMA operations.

MCA. You might assume that, because MCA is a complete rebuilding of the PC Bus structure, DMA in an MCA environment would be better constructed; this is not so. In the MCA specification, systems were designed around one DMA controller with the following issues:

- The DMA controller can only connect to two 8-bit data paths. Thus, it can only transfer one or two bytes per bus cycle.

- The DMA controller is connected to address lines 0 through 23 on the address bus. This means the DMA controller can only address up to 16M of memory.

- The DMA controller runs at 10 MHz.

The inability of the DMA controller to address more than two bytes per transfer severely cripples this otherwise powerful bus. Perhaps this is a part of the MCA specification that will be modified in future versions.

Memory

All adapters, to one extent or another, use memory. The type of memory that an adapter uses depends on the type of adapter card and what it is designed to accomplish. Some cards (such as video cards) consume part of your system memory as video buffers; other cards require memory in the ROM portion of your system. The following sections discuss these types of memory use.

System-Memory Use by Video Cards. A video adapter installed in your system uses some of your system's memory to hold graphics or character information for display.

Some adapters, including the VGA, also have on-board BIOS mapped into the system space reserved for such types of adapters (discussed in the following section). Generally, the higher the resolution and color capability of the video adapter, the more system memory that the video adapter uses. Most VGA or Super VGA adapters have additional on-board memory that is used to handle the information that is currently displayed on-screen and to speed screen refresh.

In the standard system-memory map, a total 128K is reserved for use by the video card to store currently displayed information. The reserved video memory is located in segments A000 and B000; each segment is 64K. The video adapter ROM uses additional upper-memory space in segment C000. The following list describes how each type of video adapter affects your use of memory:

- *Monochrome Display Adapter (MDA).* This adapter uses only a 4K portion of the reserved video RAM from B0000 through B0FFF. Because the ROM code that is used to operate this adapter actually is a portion of the motherboard ROM, no additional ROM space is used in segment C000.

- *Color Graphics Adapter (CGA).* The CGA uses a 16K portion of the reserved video RAM from B8000 through BBFFF. Because the ROM code that is used to operate this adapter is a portion of the motherboard ROM, no additional ROM space is used in segment C000.

- *Enhanced Graphics Adapter (EGA).* This adapter uses all 128K of the video RAM from A0000 through BFFFF. The ROM code that is used to operate this adapter is on the adapter itself and consumes 16K of memory from C0000 through C3FFF.

- *Video Graphics Array (VGA).* Standard VGA cards use all 128K of the video RAM from A0000 through BFFFF, as well as 32K of ROM space from C0000 through C7FFF.

- *PS/2 Video Adapter.* Certain models of the PS/2 incorporate a VGA adapter. This adapter uses all 128K of video RAM from A0000 through BFFFF. The ROM code that operates this adapter is on the adapter itself and consumes 24K of memory from C0000 through C5FFF.

Notice that the IBM PS/2 Display Adapter uses additional memory, called *scratch-pad memory*. This memory use was not documented clearly in the technical-reference information for the adapter. In particular, the 2K of memory used at CA000 can cause problems with other cards if they are addressed in this area. If you try to install a hard disk controller with a 16K BIOS at C8000, for example, the system locks up during bootup because of the conflict with the video-card memory. You can solve the problem by altering the start address of the disk controller BIOS to D8000.

In PS/2 systems that have the Video Graphics Array (VGA) or MultiColor Graphics Array (MCGA), the built-in display systems also use all 128K of the reserved video RAM space. Because these display systems are built into the motherboard, however, the control BIOS code is built into the motherboard ROM BIOS and needs no space in segment C000.

Using Video Memory

Some programs, such as memory managers, may play tricks with your system, such as trying to move drivers and other system software into memory that typically is used by the video adapter. Whether this situation causes problems depends on how heavily you tax your video card. If you use the high-resolution video modes available with many of the modern video cards, no memory in the video area may be left for anything else. Make sure that you know how your video adapter will be using memory before you arbitrarily decide that your memory manager can have it.

ROM BIOS Memory Areas. Many types of adapter cards use memory areas for their ROM BIOS controllers. These areas are necessary for programs that control the way that the adapter does its work. Typically, these areas begin at a segment address somewhere above C000.

The amount of memory consumed by an adapter's ROM is entirely up to the adapter. For this reason, you could install in your system two adapters that attempt to use the same ROM areas. In such a case, you need to change the address used by one of the cards (many cards now permit you to do this) or remove one of the cards.

Table 5.20 describes the typical ROM addresses used by various types of adapters. (You should not assume that this table lists all the possible addresses, however; it always seems that one more board out there uses a different area.)

Table 5.20   Default Memory Use by Various Adapter Boards

Adapter	Starting Segment	Amount Used
IBM EGA ROM	C000	16K
PS/2 VGA ROM	C000	24K
PS/2 VGA scratch RAM	CA00	24K
Most EGA/VGA ROMs	C000	32K
IBM XT 10M hard disk controller ROM	C800	8K
IBM XT 20M hard disk controller ROM	C800	4K
Most other hard disk controller ROMs	C800	16K
Token Ring network adapter ROM	CC00	8K
Token Ring network adapter RAM	D800	16K
LIM expanded memory adapter RAM	D000	64K

Notice that some of the listed adapter boards would use the same memory addresses as other boards, which is not allowed in a single system. If two adapters have overlapping ROM or RAM addresses, neither board operates properly. Each board functions if you remove or disable the other one, but the boards do not work together.

On many adapter boards, you can use jumpers, switches, or driver software to change the actual memory locations to be used. This procedure may be necessary to make the two boards coexist in one system.

A conflict of this type can cause problems for troubleshooters. If you install a Token Ring network card and an Intel Above Board (an EMS board) in the same system, and then use the factory-set default configuration with each one, neither adapter card works. You must read the documentation for each adapter to find out what memory addresses the adapter uses and how to change the addresses to allow coexistence with another adapter. Most of the time, you can work around these problems by reconfiguring the board or by changing jumpers, switching settings, or software-driver parameters. For the Token Ring card, you can change the software-driver parameters in the CONFIG.SYS file to move the memory that the card uses from D8000 to something closer to C4000. This change enables the two boards to coexist and stay out of each other's way.

Resolving Resource Conflicts

The resources in a system are limited. Unfortunately, the demands on those resources seem to be unlimited. As you add more and more adapter cards to your system, you will find that the potential for resource conflicts increases. If your system does not have a bus that resolves conflicts for you (such as an MCA or EISA bus), you need to resolve the conflicts manually.

How do you know whether you have a resource conflict? Typically, one of the devices in your system stops working. Resource conflicts can exhibit themselves in other ways, though. Any of the following events could be diagnosed as a resource conflict:

- A device transfers data inaccurately.
- Your system frequently locks up.
- Your sound card doesn't sound quite right.
- Your mouse doesn't work.
- Garbage appears on your video screen for no apparent reason.
- Your printer prints gibberish.
- You cannot format a floppy disk.

In the following sections, you learn some of the steps that you can take to head off resource conflicts or to track them down when they occur.

II

Primary System Components

> **Caution**
>
> Be careful in diagnosing resource conflicts; a problem may not be a resource conflict at all, but a computer virus. Many computer viruses are designed to exhibit themselves as glitches or as periodic problems. If you suspect a resource conflict, it may be worthwhile to run a virus check first to ensure that the system is clean. This procedure could save you hours of work and frustration.

Resolving Conflicts Manually

Unfortunately, the only way to resolve conflicts manually is to take the cover off your system and start changing switches or jumper settings on your adapter cards. Each of these changes then must be accompanied by a system reboot, which implies that they take a great deal of time. This situation brings us to the first rule of resolving conflicts: when you set about ridding your system of resource conflicts, make sure that you allow a good deal of uninterrupted time.

Also make sure that you write down your current system settings before you start making changes. That way, you will know where you began and can go back to the original configuration (if necessary).

Finally, dig out the manuals for all your adapter boards; you will need them. If you cannot find the manuals, contact the manufacturers to determine what the various jumper positions and switch settings mean.

Now you are ready to begin your detective work. As you try various switch settings and jumper positions, keep the following questions in mind; the answers will help you narrow down the conflict areas.

■ *When did the conflict first become apparent?* If the conflict occurred after you installed a new adapter card, that new card probably is causing the conflict. If the conflict occurred after you started using new software, chances are good that the software uses a device that is taxing your system's resources in a new way.

■ *Are there two similar devices in your system that do not work?* If your modem and mouse do not work, for example, chances are good that these devices are conflicting with each other.

■ *Have other people had the same problem, and if so, how did they resolve it?* Public forums—such as those on CompuServe, Internet, and America Online—are great places to find other users who may be able to help you solve the conflict.

Whenever you make changes in your system, reboot and see whether the problem persists. When you believe that you have solved the problem, make sure that you test all your software. Fixing one problem often seems to cause another to crop up. The only way to make sure that all problems are resolved is to test everything in your system.

As you attempt to resolve your resource conflicts, you should work with and update a system-configuration template, as discussed in the following section.

Using a System-Configuration Template

A system-configuration template is helpful, simply because it is easier to remember something that is written down than it is to keep it in your head. To create a configuration template, all you need to do is start writing down what resources are used by which parts of your system. Then, when you need to make a change or add an adapter, you can quickly determine where conflicts may arise.

To create a system-configuration template, mark eight columns on a piece of paper, and label each column as follows:

■ Subsystem

■ Use

■ Slot

■ IRQ Line

■ I/O Address

■ DMA Channel

■ Memory Used

■ Comments

Each row in the template represents a different system component. You definitely want to include standard components, such as video, COM1, COM2, LPT1, floppy controller, and hard drive controller. Don't forget to include other common components, such as tape drive, CD-ROM, scanner, SCSI port, and sound card.

Next, fill in each column of the template to reflect which resources are used by that component. Figure 5.19 shows an example of a filled-in system-configuration template. Remember that because every system is different, your system-configuration template probably will differ from the one in this example.

SYSTEM CONFIGURATION TEMPLATE

SYSTEM: JOHN SMITH
DATE LAST CHANGED: 10/4/94

SUBSYSTEM	USE	SLOT	IRQ LINE	I/O ADDRESS	DMA CHANNEL	MEMORY USED	COMMENTS
VIDEO	SUPER VGA	1				A0000 - BFFFF	
COM1		BUILT-IN	4	03F8			
COM2	MOUSE	BUILT-IN	3	02F8			
COM3	MODEM	4	4	03E8			INTERNAL MODEM CARD
COM4							
LPT1	LASER PRINTER	BUILT-IN	7	03BC			IRQ CONFLICT OK; NEVER USE BOTH AT ONCE
LPT2	DOT-MATRIX	BUILT-IN	7	0378			IRQ CONFLICT OK; NEVER USE BOTH AT ONCE
LPT3							
FLOPPY DRIVE	FLOPPY DRIVE	2	6	03F0 - 03F7	2	C8000	SAME CARD AS HARD DRIVE CONTROLLER
HARD DRIVE	HARD DRIVE	2	14	01F0 - 01F7		C8000	SAME CARD AS FLOPPY DRIVE CONTROLLER
SCSI PORT	CD-ROM, SCANNER	6	11	0330 - 0333	5	DC000	
SOUND CARD	SOUND BLASTER	7	5	0220	1		CAN'T CHANGE I/O ADDRESS
NETWORK ADAPTER	ETHERNET	5	10	02A0 - 02BF			MUST RECOMPILE DRIVERS IF SPECS CHANGED

Fig. 5.19
A sample system-configuration template.

Heading Off Problems: Special Boards

A number of devices that you may want to install in a computer system require IRQ lines or DMA channels, which means that a world of conflict could be waiting in the box that the device comes in. As mentioned in the preceding section, you can save yourself problems if you use a system-configuration template to keep track of the way that your system is configured.

You also can save yourself trouble by carefully reading the documentation for a new adapter board *before* you attempt to install it. The documentation details the IRQ lines that the board can use, as well as its DMA-channel requirements. In addition, the documentation will detail the adapter's upper-memory needs for ROM and adapter RAM.

The following sections describe some of the conflicts that you may encounter when you install today's most popular adapter boards. Although the list of adapter boards covered in these sections is far from comprehensive, the sections serve as a guide to installing complex hardware with minimum hassle. Included are tips on sound boards, SCSI host adapters, and network adapters.

Sound Boards. Most sound boards require two kinds of hardware communication channels: one or more IRQ lines, and exclusive access to a DMA channel. If you take the time to read your sound board's documentation and determine its communications-channel needs, compare those needs to the IRQ lines and DMA channels that already are in use in your system, and then set the jumpers or switches on the sound board to configure it for available channels, your installation will go quickly and smoothly.

One example of a potential sound-board conflict is the Pro Audio Spectrum 16 sound card. This card needs access to as many as two DMA channels—one for use by its own circuitry, and the other for SoundBlaster compatibility—and as many as two IRQ lines. Before installing this board, you must determine not only how you plan to use the board (thereby determining the IRQ lines and DMA channels that you will need), but also the available IRQ lines and DMA channels that the board can be configured to use.

The Pro Audio Spectrum 16 sound card is not singled out here because there is something unusual or particularly complex about the card; many high-end sound cards require a great deal of system resources.

SCSI Adapter Boards. SCSI adapter boards, like other advanced add-in devices for modern PCs, require considerable system resources. A SCSI host adapter board, for example, may require an IRQ line, a DMA channel, or a large chunk of unused upper memory for its ROM and RAM use.

Before installing a SCSI adapter, be sure to read the documentation for the card, and make sure that any IRQ lines, DMA channels, and upper memory that the card needs are available. If the card needs system resources that are already in use, use your system-configuration template to determine how you can free the needed resources before you attempt to plug in the adapter card. In addition, remember to set the jumpers or switches detailed in the card's documentation, and run any setup software that the device requires.

Multiple-COM-Port Adapters. Because COM ports are required for so many peripherals that connect to the modern PC, and because the number of COM ports that can be used is strictly limited by the IRQ setup in the basic IBM system design, special COM-port cards are available that enable you to assign a unique IRQ to each of the four COM ports on the card. For example, you can use such a card to leave COM1 and COM2 configured for IRQ 4 and IRQ 3, respectively, but to configure COM3 for IRQ 10 and COM4 for IRQ 11.

With a multiple-COM-port adapter card installed and properly configured for your system, you can have devices hooked to four COM ports, and all four devices can be functioning at the same time. For example, you can use a mouse, modem, plotter, and serial printer at the same time.

The Future: Plug-and-Play Systems

What does the future hold? Perhaps the most exciting development looming on the horizon is plug-and-play systems. The specifications for these systems are available, and the systems themselves should start becoming available late in 1994 or early in 1995. Specifications exist for ISA, PCI, SCSI, IDE CD-ROM, MCA, and PCMCIA systems and components.

Most users of MCA or EISA systems already know what *plug-and-play* means: it means that your computer senses any new adapter card on the I/O bus and makes the necessary adjustments to share resources without conflict. You never need to worry about I/O addresses, DMA channels, or IRQ settings.

As mentioned earlier, this sort of capability has been built into EISA and MCA buses for some time; the problem is that these are not the only buses on the market. Other buses (all of which are described earlier in this chapter) enjoy the lion's share of the PC market. As a result, most computer users must use the trial-and-error method of making their systems work properly. The plug-and-play specifications already in existence have perhaps the greatest impact on users of systems that have ISA buses. Their implementation promises a great boon for most PC users.

Plug-and-play is not only a hardware issue. For plug-and-play to work, three components are required:

- Hardware
- BIOS
- Operating system

Each of these components needs to be plug-and-play-compatible, meaning that it complies with the plug-and-play specifications.

The Hardware Component. The *hardware component* refers to both computer systems and adapter cards. The term does not mean, however, that you will not be able to use your older ISA adapter cards (referred to as *legacy cards*) in a plug-and-play system. You can use these cards; you just won't receive the benefits of automatic configuration, as you would if the cards were compatible.

Plug-and-play adapter cards will be able to communicate with the system BIOS and the operating system to convey information about what system resources are needed. The BIOS and operating system, in turn, will resolve conflicts (wherever possible) and inform the adapter cards which specific resources it should use. The adapter card then can modify its configuration to use the specified resources.

The BIOS Component. The *BIOS component* means that most users of existing PCs will need to update their BIOSs or purchase new machines that have plug-and-play BIOSs. For a BIOS to be compatible, it must support 13 additional system function calls, which can be used by the operating-system component of a plug-and-play system. The BIOS specification developed for plug-and-play was developed jointly by Compaq, Intel, and Phoenix Technologies. The latest version is 1.0A, dated May 5, 1994.

The plug-and-play features of the BIOS are implemented through an expanded power-on self-test (POST). The BIOS is responsible for identification, isolation, and possible configuration of plug-and-play adapter cards. The BIOS accomplishes these tasks by performing the following steps:

1. Disables any configurable devices on the motherboard or on adapter cards.

2. Identifies any plug-and-play ISA devices.

3. Compiles an initial resource-allocation map for ports, IRQs, DMAs, and memory.

4. Enables I/O devices.

5. Scans the ROMs of ISA devices.

6. Configures initial-program-load (IPL) devices, which are used later to boot the system.

7. Enables configurable devices by informing them which resources have been assigned to them.

8. Starts the bootstrap loader.

9. Transfers control to the operating system.

The Operating-System Component. The *operating-system component* can be implemented by a brand-new version (such as an update of DOS or Windows, or the upcoming Chicago version of Windows) or through DOS extensions. Extensions of this type should be familiar to most DOS users; extensions have been used for years to provide support for CD-ROM drives. Some sort of extensions are expected to be available before the end of 1994 to ensure plug-and-play compatibility.

It is the responsibility of the operating system to inform users of conflicts that cannot be resolved by the BIOS. Depending on the sophistication of the operating system, the user then can configure the offending cards manually (on-screen) or turn the system off and set switches on the physical cards. When the system is restarted, the system is checked for remaining (or new) conflicts, any of which are brought to the user's attention. Through this repetitive process, all system conflicts are resolved.

Summary

This chapter covered a great deal of ground, going from the general to the specific and from the conceptual to the actual. The information in this chapter enables you to understand how your system works, physically and logically. You learned the following:

- How buses are used in a computer system

- What a processor bus, memory bus, address bus, and I/O bus are

- How expansion slots fit into the architecture of your system

- How the major types of I/O buses (ISA, MCA, EISA, local bus, VL-Bus, and PCI) compare

- That system resources (including I/O addresses, IRQ lines, DMA channels, and memory areas) are limited

- How adapter cards rely on system resources to communicate with your PC and to do their work

- That system-resource conflicts can stop your adapter cards or your entire system from functioning properly

- That the MCA bus, the EISA bus, and (in the future) plug-and-play greatly simplify allocation of system resources

- That if your system does not resolve system-resource conflicts automatically, you must resolve them manually

II

Primary System Components

Chapter 6

Microprocessor Types and Specifications

Primary System Components

The brain of the PC is the processor, or Central Processing Unit (CPU). The CPU performs the system's calculating and processing (except for special math-intensive processing in systems that have a math coprocessing unit chip). The processor is easily the most expensive chip in the system. All the IBM PC and PS/2 units and IBM-compatibles use processors that are compatible with the Intel family of chips, although the processors themselves may have been manufactured or designed by various companies, including IBM, Cyrix, and AMD.

The following sections cover the processor chips that have been used in personal computers since the first PC was introduced more than a decade ago. These sections provide a great deal of technical detail about these chips and explain why one type of CPU chip can do more work than another in a given period of time. First, however, you learn about two important components of the processor: the data bus and the address bus.

Processor Specifications

Confusing specifications often are quoted in discussions of processors. The following sections discuss some of these specifications, including the data bus, address bus, and speed. The next section includes a table that lists the specifications of virtually all PC processors.

Data Bus

One of the most common ways to describe a processor is by the size of the processor's data bus and address bus. A *bus* is simply a series of connections that carry common signals. Imagine running a pair of wires from one end of a building to another. If you connect a 110-volt AC power generator to the two wires at any point and place outlets at convenient locations along the wires, you have constructed a power bus. No matter which outlet you plug the wires in to, you have access to the same signal, which in this example is 110-volt AC power.

Any transmission medium that has more than one outlet at each end can be called a bus. A typical computer system has several buses, and a typical processor has two important buses for carrying data and memory-addressing information: the data bus and the address bus.

The processor bus discussed most often is the *data bus*: the bundle of wires (or pins) used to send and receive data. The more signals that can be sent at the same time, the more data can be transmitted in a specified interval and, therefore, the faster the bus.

Data in a computer is sent as digital information, consisting of a time interval in which a single wire carries 5 volts to signal a 1 data bit or 0 volts to signal a 0 data bit. The more wires you have, the more individual bits you can send in the same time interval. A chip such as the 286, which has 16 wires for transmitting and receiving such data, has a 16-bit data bus. A 32-bit chip such as the 486 has twice as many wires dedicated to simultaneous data transmission as a 16-bit chip and can send twice as much information in the same time interval as a 16-bit chip.

A good way to understand this flow of information is to consider a highway and the traffic it carries. If a highway has only one lane for each direction of travel, only one car at a time can move in a certain direction. If you want to increase traffic flow, you can

Table 6.1   Intel Processor Specifications

Processor	CPU Clock	Std. Voltage	Internal Register Size	Data Bus Width	Address Bus Width	Maximum Memory
8088	1x	5v	16-bit	8-bit	20-bit	1M
8086	1x	5v	16-bit	16-bit	20-bit	1M
286	1x	5v	16-bit	16-bit	24-bit	16M
386SX	1x	5v	32-bit	16-bit	24-bit	16M
386SL	1x	3.3v	32-bit	16-bit	24-bit	16M
386DX	1x	5v	32-bit	32-bit	32-bit	4G
486SX	1x	5v	32-bit	32-bit	32-bit	4G
486SX2	2x	5v	32-bit	32-bit	32-bit	4G
487SX	1x	5v	32-bit	32-bit	32-bit	4G
486DX	1x	5v	32-bit	32-bit	32-bit	4G
486SL**	1x	3.3v	32-bit	32-bit	32-bit	4G
486DX2	2x	5v	32-bit	32-bit	32-bit	4G
486DX4	2-3x	3.3v	32-bit	32-bit	32-bit	4G
Pentium 60/66	1x	5v	32-bit	64-bit	32-bit	4G
Pentium 90/100	1.5-2x	3.3v	32-bit	64-bit	32-bit	4G

*The 386SL contains an integral-cache controller, but the cache memory must be provided outside the chip.
**The 486SL processor has been discontinued; instead, Intel now markets SL Enhanced versions of the SX, DX, and D
FPU = Floating-Point Unit (math coprocessor)
WT = Write-Through cache (caches reads only)
WB = Write-Back cache (caches both reads and writes)

add another lane so that twice as many cars pass in a specified time. You can think of an 8-bit chip as being a single-lane highway because with this chip, one byte flows through at a time. (One byte equals eight individual bits.) The 16-bit chip, with two bytes flowing at a time, resembles a two-lane highway. To move a large number of automobiles, you may have four lanes in each direction. This structure corresponds to a 32-bit data bus, which has the capability to move four bytes of information at a time.

Just as you can describe a highway by its lane width, you can describe a chip by the width of its data bus. When you read an advertisement that describes a computer system as being a 16-bit or 32-bit system, the ad usually is referring to the data bus of the CPU. This number provides a rough idea of the performance potential of the chip (and, therefore, the system).

Table 6.1 lists the specifications, including the data-bus sizes, for the Intel family of processors used in IBM and compatible PCs.

Internal Registers

The size of the internal register is a good indication of how much information the processor can operate on at one time. Most advanced processors today—all chips from the 386 to the Pentium—use 32-bit internal registers.

Integral Cache	Cache Type	Burst Mode	Integral FPU	No. of Transistors	Date Introduced
No	—	No	No	29,000	June 1979
No	—	No	No	29,000	June 1978
No	—	No	No	134,000	Feb. 1982
No	—	No	No	275,000	June 1988
0K*	WT	No	No	855,000	Oct. 1990
No	—	No	No	275,000	Oct. 1985
8K	WT	Yes	No	1,185,000	April 1991
8K	WT	Yes	No	1,185,000	April 1994
8K	WT	Yes	Yes	1,200,000	April 1991
8K	WT	Yes	Yes	1,200,000	April 1989
8K	WT	Yes	Optional	1,400,000	Nov. 1992
8K	WT	Yes	Yes	1,100,000	March 1992
16K	WT	Yes	Yes	1,600,000	Feb. 1994
2×8K	WB	Yes	Yes	3,100,000	March 1993
2×8K	WB	Yes	Yes	3,300,000	March 1994

ocessors are available in both 5v and 3.3v versions and include power-management capabilities.

Primary System Components

Some processors have an internal data bus (made up of data paths and of storage units called *registers*) that is different from the external data bus. The 8088 and 386SX are examples of this structure. Each chip has an internal data bus that is twice the width of the external bus. These designs, which sometimes are called *hybrid designs*, usually are low-cost versions of a "pure" chip. The 386SX, for example, can pass data around internally with a full 32-bit register size; for communications with the outside world, however, the chip is restricted to a 16-bit-wide data path. This design enables a systems designer to build a lower-cost motherboard with a 16-bit bus design and still maintain compatibility with the full 32-bit 386.

Internal registers often are larger than the data bus, which means that the chip requires two cycles to fill a register before the register can be operated on. For example, both the 386SX and 386DX have internal 32-bit registers, but the 386SX has to "inhale" twice (figuratively) to fill them, whereas the 386DX can do the job in one "breath." The same thing would happen when the data is passed from the registers back out to the system bus.

The Pentium is an example of the opposite situation. This chip has a 64-bit data bus but only 32-bit registers—a structure that may seem to be a problem until you understand that the Pentium has two internal 32-bit pipelines for processing information. In many ways, the Pentium is like two 32-bit chips in one. The 64-bit data bus provides for very efficient filling of these multiple registers.

Address Bus

The *address bus* is the set of wires that carry the addressing information used to describe the memory location to which the data is being sent or from which the data is being retrieved. As with the data bus, each wire in an address bus carries a single bit of information. This single bit is a single digit in the address. The more wires (digits) used in calculating these addresses, the greater the total number of address locations. The size (or width) of the address bus indicates the maximum amount of RAM that a chip can address.

The highway analogy can be used to show how the address bus fits in. If the data bus is the highway, and if the size of the data bus is equivalent to the number of lanes, the address bus relates to the house number or street address. The size of the address bus is equivalent to the number of digits in the house address number. For example, if you live on a street in which the address is limited to a two-digit (base 10) number, no more than 100 distinct addresses (00 to 99) can exist for that street (10 to the power of 2). Add another digit, and the number of available addresses increases to 1,000 (000 to 999) or 10 to the 3rd power.

Computers use the binary (base 2) numbering system, so a two-digit number provides only four unique addresses (00, 01, 10, and 11) calculated as 2 to the power of 2, and a three-digit number provides only eight addresses (000 to 111) which is 2 to the 3rd power. For example the 8086 and 8088 processors use a 20-bit address bus which calculates as a maximum of 2 to the 20th power or 1,048,576 bytes (1M) of address locations. Table 6.2 describes the memory-addressing capabilities of Intel processors.

Table 6.2 Intel Processor Memory-Addressing Capabilities					
Processor Family	**Address Bus**	**Bytes**	**Kilobytes**	**Megabytes**	**Gigabytes**
8088/8086	20 bits	1,048,576	1,024	1	—
286, 386SX	24 bits	16,777,216	16,384	16	—
386DX, 486, Pentium	32 bits	4,294,967,296	4,194,304	4,096	4

The data bus and address bus are independent, and chip designers can use whatever size they want for each. Usually, however, chips with larger data buses have larger address buses. The sizes of the buses can provide important information about a chip's relative power, measured in two important ways. The size of the data bus is an indication of the information-moving capability of the chip, and the size of the address bus tells you how much memory the chip can handle.

Processor Speed Ratings

A common misunderstanding about processors is their different speed ratings. This section covers processor speed in general and then provides more specific information about Intel processors.

A computer system's *clock speed* is measured as a frequency, usually expressed as a number of cycles per second. A crystal oscillator controls clock speeds, using a sliver of quartz in a small tin container. As voltage is applied to the quartz, it begins to vibrate (oscillate) at a harmonic rate dictated by the shape and size of the crystal (sliver). The oscillations emanate from the crystal in the form of a current that alternates at the harmonic rate of the crystal. This alternating current is the *clock signal*. A typical computer system runs millions of these cycles per second, so speed is measured in megahertz (MHz). (One hertz is equal to one cycle per second.)

Note

The hertz was named for the German physicist Heinrich Rudolph Hertz. In 1885, Hertz confirmed the electromagnetic theory through experimentation which states that light is a form of electromagnetic radiation and is propagated as waves.

A single cycle is the smallest element of time for the processor. Every action requires at least one cycle and usually multiple cycles. To transfer data to and from memory, for example, an 8086 chip needs four cycles plus wait states. (A *wait state* is a clock tick in which nothing happens to ensure that the processor isn't getting ahead of the rest of the computer.) A 286 needs only two cycles plus any wait states for the same transfer.

The time required to execute instructions also varies. The original 8086 and 8088 processors take an average of 12 cycles to execute a single instruction. The 286 and 386 processors improve this rate to about 4.5 cycles per instruction; the 486 drops the rate further, to 2 cycles per instruction. The Pentium includes twin instruction pipelines and other improvements that provide for operation at 1 cycle per average instruction.

Different instruction execution times (in cycles) makes it difficult to compare systems based purely on clock speed, or number of cycles per second. One reason why the 486 is so fast is that it has an average instruction-execution time of 2 clock cycles. Therefore, a 100 MHz Pentium is about equal to a 200 MHz 486, which is about equal to a 400 MHz 386 or 286, which is about equal to a 1,000 MHz 8088. As you can see, you have to be careful in comparing systems based on pure MHz alone; many other factors affect system performance.

How can two processors that run at the same clock rate perform differently, with one running "faster" than the other? The answer is simple: efficiency. Suppose that you are comparing two engines. An engine has a crankshaft revolution, called a cycle. This cycling time is measured in revolutions per minute (RPM). If two engines run the same maximum RPM, they should run the car at the same speed, right?

Wrong! Suppose that you're shopping for a fast family car, and you decide to compare the Ford SHO Taurus against the Chevrolet Impala SS. You stop first at the Ford dealership and look at the '95 SHO. You ask the dealer, "What's the engine speed at maximum power output?" The dealer tells you that the SHO has a 3.2-liter, 6-cylinder engine that puts out 220 HP at 6,200 RPM. You are impressed by the high RPM rating, and you record the information.

Then you see the Chevrolet dealer, who steers you toward a '95 Impala SS. You ask the same question about engine power and speed, and the dealer tells you that the Corvette-style LT1 5.7-liter, V-8 engine used in the SS puts out 260 HP at 5,000 RPM. You now figure that because the Ford engine turns 1,200 RPM higher when producing maximum power, it will propel that car much faster than the Chevrolet, the engine of which is turning only 5,000 RPM.

Actually, the car with the higher power output is faster, assuming that the cars weigh the same (which they do not). As you can see, these types of specification comparisons can be difficult to manage because of all of the other variables that can enter into the comparison. I would not compare two computer systems based solely on MHz any more than I would compare two cars on the basis of engine RPM.

You can see that comparing the performance of two vehicles based solely on engine RPM is inaccurate. You never would make such a comparison, because you know that many more factors than just engine speed determine vehicle speed and acceleration capability.

Unfortunately, we often make the same type of poor comparison in evaluating computers. Using engine RPM to compare how fast two cars can run is similar to using MHz to compare how fast two computers can run. A better specification to use when you are comparing the two vehicles would be engine horsepower, which is a measurement of the amount of work that each engine can perform. Then you would have to adjust the horsepower figure for the weight of the vehicle, the coefficient of drag, drive-line gearing, parasitic losses, and so on. In effect, too many other variables are involved for you to make any simplistic comparison, even if you first picked a more meaningful specification to compare than engine redline. The best way to evaluate which of the two vehicles is faster is through a road test. In a computer, the equivalent is taking some of your software and running *benchmarks*, or comparative performance tests.

The big V-8 engine in the Chevrolet does more work in each crankshaft revolution (or cycle) than the 6-cylinder engine in the Ford. In the same manner, a 286 or 386 can perform much more work in a single CPU cycle than an 8088 can; it's simply more efficient. As you can see, you must be careful in comparing MHz to MHz, because much more is involved in total system performance.

Comparing automobile engines by virtue of their horsepower output is a much more valid comparison than just RPM. What is needed is a sort of horsepower measurement for processors. To compare processors more accurately based on comparative "horsepower," Intel has devised a specific series of benchmarks that can be run against Intel chips to produce a relative gauge of performance. This is called the ICOMP (Intel COmparative Microprocessor Performance) index. The following tables show the relative power, or ICOMP index, for several processors.

Table 6.3 Intel ICOMP Index Ratings	
Processor	**ICOMP Index**
386SX-16	22
386SX-20	32
386SX-25	39
386SL-25	41
386DX-25	49
486SX-16	63
386DX-33	68
486SX-20	78
486SX-25	100
486DX-25	122
486SX-33	136
486DX-33	166
486SX2-50	180
486DX2-50	231
486DX-50	249
486DX2-66	297
486DX4-75	319
486DX4-100	435
Pentium 60	510
Pentium 55	567
Pentium 90	735
Pentium 100	815

The ICOMP index is derived from several independent benchmarks and is a stable indication of relative processor performance. Floating-point calculations are weighed in the ICOMP rating, so processors that have a built-in FPU (Floating-Point Unit) always have some advantage over those that do not.

Another factor in CPU performance is clock speed. Clock speed is a function of a system's design and usually is controlled by an oscillator, which in turn is controlled by a quartz crystal. Typically, you divide the crystal-oscillation frequency by some amount to obtain the processor frequency. The divisor amount is determined by the original design of the processor (Intel), by related support chips, and by how the motherboard was designed to use these chips together as a system. In IBM PC and XT systems, for example, the main crystal frequency is 14.31818 MHz, which is divided by 3 by an 8284 clock generator chip to obtain a 4.77 MHz processor clock speed. In an IBM AT system, the crystal speeds are 12 or 16 MHz, which is divided by 2 internally inside the 80286 to produce a 6 or 8 MHz processor clock speed, respectively.

If all other variables are equal—including the type of processor, the number of wait states (empty cycles) added to memory accesses, and the width of the data bus—you can compare two systems by their respective clock rates. Be careful with this type of comparison, however; certain variables (such as the number of wait states) can greatly influence the speed of a system, causing the unit with the lower clock rate to run faster than you expect, or causing the system with a numerically higher clock rate to run slower than you think it should. The construction and design of the memory subsystem can have an enormous effect on a system's final execution speed.

In building a processor, a manufacturer tests it at different speeds, temperatures, and pressures. After the processor is tested, it receives a stamp indicating the maximum safe speed at which the unit will operate under the wide variation of temperatures and pressures encountered in normal operation. The rating system usually is simple. For example, the top of the processor in my system is marked like this:

    A80486DX2-66

The *A* is Intel's indicator that this chip has a Ceramic Pin Grid Array form factor, which describes the physical packaging of the chip. The *80486DX2* is the part number, which identifies this processor as a clock-doubled 486DX processor. The *-66* at the end indicates that this chip is rated to run at a maximum speed of 66 MHz. Because of the clock doubling, the maximum motherboard speed is 33 MHz. This chip would be acceptable for any application in which the chip runs at 66 MHz or slower. For example, you could use this processor in a system with a 25 MHz motherboard, in which case the processor would happily run at 50 MHz.

Sometimes, however, the markings don't seem to indicate the speed. In the 8086, for example, *-3* translates to 6 MHz operation. This marking is more common in some of the older chips, manufactured before some of the marking standards used today were standardized.

A manufacturer sometimes places the CPU under a heat sink, which prevents you from reading the rating printed on the chip. (A *heat sink* is a metal device that draws heat away from an electronic device.) Although having a heat sink generally is a good idea, Intel designs its chips to run at rated speed without a heat sink.

Intel Processors

IBM-compatible computers use processors manufactured primarily by Intel. Some other companies, such as Cyrix and AMD, have reverse-engineered the Intel processors and have begun making their own compatible versions. IBM also manufactures processors for some of its own systems as well as for installation in boards and modules sold to others. The IBM processors are not reverse-engineered, but are produced in cooperation with and under license from Intel. The terms of IBM's agreement also allows IBM to make modifications and improvements to the basic Intel design. IBM uses these processors in their own systems, but also is allowed to sell the processors in boards they manufacture for other companies. IBM is not allowed to sell these chips raw, but must always install them in some type of board assembly.

Knowing the processors used in a system can be very helpful in understanding the capabilities of the system, as well as in servicing it. To fully understand the capabilities of a system and perform any type of servicing, you must at least know the type of processor that the system uses.

8088 and 8086 Processors

The original IBM PC used an Intel CPU chip called the 8088. The original 8088 CPU chip ran at 4.77 MHz, which means that the computer's circuitry drove the CPU at a rate of 4,770,000 *ticks*, or computer heartbeats, per second. Each tick represents a small amount of work—the CPU executing an instruction or part of an instruction—rather than a period of elapsed time.

In fact, both the 8088 and 8086 take an average 12 cycles to execute the average instruction. The 8088 has an external data bus 8 bits wide, which means that it can move 8 bits (individual pieces) of information into memory at a time. The 8088 is referred to as a 16-bit processor, however, because it features internal 16-bit-wide registers and data paths. The 8088 also has a 20-bit address bus, which enables the system to access 1M of RAM. Using the 8088, a manufacturer could build a system that would run 16-bit software and have access to 1M of memory while keeping the cost in line with then-current 8-bit designs. Later, IBM used the 8088 chip in the PC/XT computer.

IBM used the 8088 to put together the original IBM PC 5150-001, which sold for $1,355 with 16K of RAM and no drives. A similarly configured Apple II system, the major competition for the original PC, cost about $1,600.

The 8088 eventually was redesigned to run at 8 MHz—nearly double the speed of the original PC. The speed at which the processor operates has a direct effect on the speed of program execution. Later sections of this chapter cover the speeds of the CPU chips that are successors to the 8088.

> **Note**
>
> The real mode of 286 and higher CPU chips refers to the mode that these advanced chips use to imitate the original 8088 chip in the first PC. Real mode is used by 286 and higher CPU chips to run a single DOS program at a time, just as though systems based on these powerful chips are merely faster PCs. The additional modes of 286 and higher CPU chips are covered in subsequent sections of this chapter.

Computer users sometimes wonder why a 640K conventional-memory barrier exists if the 8088 chip can address 1M of memory. The conventional-memory barrier exists because IBM reserved 384K of the upper portion of the 1,024K (1M) address space of the 8088 for use by adapter cards and system BIOS (a computer program permanently "burned into" the ROM chips in the PC). The lower 640K is the conventional memory in which DOS and software applications execute.

In 1976, before the 8088 chip, Intel made a slightly faster chip named the 8086. The 8086, which was one of the first 16-bit chips on the market, addressed 1M of RAM. The design failed to catch on, however, because both the chip and a motherboard designed for the chip were costly. The cost was high because the system needed a 16-bit data bus rather than the less expensive 8-bit bus. Systems available at that time were 8-bit, and users apparently weren't willing to pay for the extra performance of the full 16-bit design. Therefore, Intel introduced the 8088 in 1978. Both the 8086 and the 8088 CPU chips are quite slow by today's standards.

IBM largely ignored the 8086 CPU chip until it manufactured the first PS/2 Models 25 and 30. Systems produced by many other manufacturers, such as the Compaq Deskpro and the AT&T 6300, had been using the 8086 for some time. The capability of the 8086 to communicate with the rest of the system at 16 bits gives it about a 20 percent increase in processing speed over an 8088 with an identical speed (in MHz). This improvement is one reason why IBM can claim that the 8 MHz, 8086-based Model 30 is 2-1/2 times faster than the 4.77 MHz, 8088-based PC or XT, even though 8 MHz is not more than twice the clock speed. This claim is the first indication of what a CPU chip with a wider data path can mean in terms of speed improvements.

80186 and 80188 Processors

After Intel produced the 8086 and 8088 chips, it turned its sights toward producing a more powerful chip with an increased instruction set. The company's first efforts along this line—the 80186 and 80188—were unsuccessful. But incorporating system components into the CPU chip was an important idea for Intel, because it led to faster, better chips, such as the 286.

The relationship between the 80186 and 80188 is the same as that of the 8086 and 8088; one is a slightly more advanced version of the other. Compared CPU to CPU, the 80186 is almost the same as the 8088 and has a full 16-bit design. The 80188 (like the 8088) is a hybrid chip that compromises the 16-bit design with an 8-bit external communications interface. The advantage of the 80186 and 80188 is that they combine on a single chip

15 to 20 of the 8086–8088 series system components, a fact that can greatly reduce the number of components in a computer design. The 80186 and 80188 chips are used for highly intelligent peripheral adapter cards, such as network adapters.

Although the 80186 and 80188 did provide some new instructions and capabilities, not much in those chips was new compared with the improvements that came later, in the 286 and higher chips. The 80186 and 80188 chips were difficult for systems designers to use in manufacturing systems that were compatible with the IBM PC. For example, these chips had DMA (Direct Memory Access) and Interrupt controllers built-in, but they were incompatible with the external controllers required for an IBM-compatible PC design. Slight differences in the instruction sets also caused problems when the 80186 and 80188 were supposed to emulate 8086 and 8088 chips. In addition to compatibility problems, the chips didn't offer much performance improvement over the earlier 8086 and 8088. In addition, the individual components that the 80186 and 80188 chips were designed to replace had become inexpensive, which made the 80186 and 80188 chips less attractive.

286 Processors

The Intel 80286 (normally abbreviated as 286) processor did not suffer from the compatibility problems that damned the 80186 and 80188. The 286 chip, introduced in 1981, is the CPU behind the IBM AT. You also can find 286 chips in IBM's original PS/2 Models 50 and 60 (later PS/2s contain 386 or 486 chips). Other computer makers manufactured what came to be known as *IBM clones*, many of these manufacturers calling their systems AT or AT-class computers.

When IBM developed the AT, it selected the 286 as the basis for the new system because the chip provided much compatibility with the 8088 used in the PC and the XT, which means that software written for those chips should run on the 286. The 286 chip is many times faster than the 8088 used in the XT, and it offered a major performance boost to PCs used in businesses. The processing speed, or *throughput*, of the original AT (which ran at 6 MHz) was five times greater than that of the PC running at 4.77 MHz.

For several reasons, 286 systems are faster than their predecessors. The main reason is that 286 processors are much more efficient in executing instructions. An average instruction takes 12 clock cycles on the 8086 or 8088 but an average 4.5 cycles on the 286 processor. Additionally, the 286 chip can handle up to 16 bits of data at a time through an external data bus that is twice the size of the 8088.

Another reason why personal computing received a major boost from the 286 chip is clock speed. AT-type systems are based on 6, 8, 10, 12, 16, and 20 MHz versions of the 286 chip. Earlier processors typically are available in versions only up to 8 MHz. Even if the clock speeds are the same—as in comparing a system that has an 8 MHz 8088 with a system that has an 8 MHz 286—the 286-based system operates roughly three times faster.

The 286 chip has two modes of operation: real mode and protected mode. The two modes are distinct enough to make the 286 resemble two chips in one. In real mode, a 286 acts essentially the same as an 8086 chip and is fully object-code-compatible with the 8086 and 8088. (A processor with *object-code-compatibility* can run programs written for another processor without modification and execute every system instruction in the same manner.)

In the protected mode of operation, the 286 truly was something new. In this mode, a program designed to take advantage of the chip's capabilities believes that it has access to 1G of memory (including virtual memory). The 286 chip, however, can address only 16M of hardware memory. When a program calls for more memory than physically exists in the system, the CPU swaps to disk some of the currently running code and enables the program to use the newly freed physical RAM. The program does not know about this swapping and instead acts as though 1G of actual memory exists. *Virtual memory* is controlled by the operating system and the chip hardware.

A significant failing of the 286 chip is that it cannot switch from protected mode to real mode without a hardware reset (a warm reboot) of the system. (It can, however, switch from real mode to protected mode without a reset.) A major improvement of the 386 over the 286 is the fact that software can switch the 386 from real mode to protected mode, and vice versa.

When the 286 chip was introduced, Intel said that real mode was created so that much of the 8086- and 8088-based software could run with little or no modification until new software could be written to take advantage of the protected mode of the 286. As with later Intel processors, however, it was a long time before software took advantage of the capabilities of the 286 chip. For example, most 286 systems are used as if they are merely faster PCs. These systems are run in real mode most of the time because the programs were written for DOS, and DOS and DOS programs are limited to real mode. Unfortunately, much of the power of systems based on the 286 chip is unused. In real mode, a 286 chip cannot perform any additional operations or use any extra features designed into the chip.

IBM and Microsoft together began the task of rewriting DOS to run in both real and protected modes. The result was early versions of OS/2, which could run most old DOS programs just as they ran before, in real mode. In protected mode, OS/2 provided true software multitasking and access to the entire 1G of virtual or 16M of physical address space provided by the 286. UNIX and XENIX also were written to take advantage of the 286 chip's protected mode. In terms of mass appeal, however, these operating systems were a limited success.

Little software that took advantage of the 286 chip was sold until Windows 3.0 offered Standard Mode for 286 compatibility, and by that time, the hottest-selling chip was the 386. Still, the 286 was Intel's first attempt to produce a CPU chip that supported *multitasking*, in which multiple programs run at the same time. The 286 is designed so that if one program locks up or fails, the entire system doesn't need a warm boot (reset) or cold boot (power off or on). Theoretically, what happens in one area of memory doesn't affect other programs. Before multitasked programs are "safe" from one another, however, the 286 chip (and subsequent chips) needs an operating system that works cooperatively with the chip to provide such protection.

In a way, this situation leads back to OS/2, which could provide protection but never caught on for the 286 in a big way. Although newer versions of OS/2 offer a graphical user interface similar to that of Windows—and although on 386 and newer systems, OS/2 offers full 32-bit processing for software that is designed to take advantage of it— OS/2 is nowhere near to replacing DOS as the operating system of choice on PCs and is nowhere near as popular as Windows. One reason why is the fact that few OS/2 applications have been developed, compared with the number of DOS and Windows programs.

Protected mode on a 286 enables multiple programs to run at one time only when those programs are specifically written for the operating system (or operating environment). To run several programs at the same time on a 286 in Windows, for example, each active program must be a Windows program (written specifically to run only under Windows).

Because of the virtual-memory scheme of the 286, the size of programs under operating systems such as OS/2 and UNIX can be extremely large. Even though the 286 does not address more than 16M of physical memory, the 286's virtual-memory scheme enables programs to run as though 1G of memory were available. But programs that require a great deal of swapping run slowly, which is why software manufacturers usually indicate the amount of physical RAM needed to run their programs effectively. The more physical memory you install, the faster 286-based systems running OS/2 or UNIX will work.

Windows 3.0, which is not a true operating system because it uses DOS for its underpinnings, provides only poor protection on a 286. Unruly programs still can crash the entire system. Windows 3.1 does a better job of implementing protection on a 286, but it still is far from perfect.

Although UNIX and XENIX provide support for the 286 chip's protected mode, these operating systems have found a following among a small group of extremely high-end computer users, primarily in academic or scientific settings.

386 Processors

The Intel 80386 (normally abbreviated as 386) caused quite a stir in the PC industry because of the vastly improved performance that it brought to the personal computer. Compared with 8088 and 286 systems, the 386 chip offers greater performance in almost all areas of operation.

The 386 is a full 32-bit processor optimized for high-speed operation and multitasking operating systems. Intel introduced the chip in 1985, but the 386 appeared in the first systems in late 1986 and early 1987. The Compaq Deskpro 386 and systems made by several other manufacturers introduced the chip; somewhat later, IBM used the chip in its PS/2 Model 80. For several years, the 386 chip rose in popularity, which peaked around 1991. Since then, the popularity of the 386 has waned; in the past year or so, it has virtually died out, due to the availability of inexpensive systems based on the 486 and Pentium CPU chips. The 386 had an extended life in the mainstream due in part to the use of the chip in extremely small, lightweight, and powerful laptop and notebook computers.

The 386 can execute the real-mode instructions of an 8086 or 8088, but in fewer clock cycles. The 386 was as efficient as the 286 in executing instructions, which means that the average instruction takes about 4.5 clock cycles. In raw performance, therefore, the 286 and 386 actually seemed to be about equal at equal clock rates. Many 286-system manufacturers were touting their 16 MHz and 20 MHz 286 systems as being just as fast as 16 MHz and 20 MHz 386 systems, and they were right! The 386 offered greater performance in other ways, mainly due to additional software capability (modes) and an incredibly enhanced Memory Management Unit (MMU).

The 386 can switch to and from protected mode under software control without a system reset, a capability that makes using protected mode more practical. In addition, the 386 has a new mode, called *virtual real mode*, which enables several real-mode sessions to run simultaneously under protected mode.

Other than raw speed, probably the most important feature of this chip is its available modes of operation, which are:

■ Real mode

■ Protected mode

■ Virtual real mode (sometimes called *virtual 86 mode*)

Real mode on a 386 chip, as on a 286 chip, is 8086-compatible mode. In real mode, the 386 essentially is a much faster "turbo PC" with 640K of conventional memory, just like systems based on the 8088 chip. DOS and any software written to run under DOS requires this mode to run.

The protected mode of the 386 is fully compatible with the protected mode of the 286. The protected mode for both of these chips often is called their *native mode* of operation, because these chips are designed for advanced operating systems such as OS/2 and Windows NT, which run only in protected mode. Intel extended the memory-addressing capabilities of 386 protected mode with a new memory-management unit (MMU) that provides advanced memory paging and program switching. These features are extensions of the 286 type of MMU, so the 386 remains fully compatible with the 286 at system-code level.

The 386 chip's virtual real mode is new. In virtual real mode, the processor can run with hardware memory protection while simulating an 8086's real-mode operation. Multiple copies of DOS and other operating systems, therefore, can run simultaneously on this processor, each in a protected area of memory. If the programs in one segment crash, the rest of the system is protected. Software commands can reboot the blown partition.

In simple terms, a PC with a 386 has the capability to "become" multiple PCs under software control. With appropriate management software, the 386 chip can create several memory partitions, each containing the full services of DOS, and each of these partitions can function as though it were a stand-alone PC. These partitions often are called *virtual machines*.

In 386 virtual real mode under software such as Windows, several DOS programs can be running at the same time as programs designed for Windows. Because the processor can service only a single application at a time by delivering a clock tick, Windows manages the amount of CPU time that each program gets by using a system called *time slices*. Because the 386 chip is so fast and because time slices are tiny fractions of a second, under Windows, all applications appear to be running simultaneously.

OS/2 exploits the multitasking capabilities of the 386 chip even more than Windows does. OS/2 2.x can simultaneously manage native OS/2 programs, DOS programs, and most Windows programs. These capabilities aren't available in lesser processors, such as the 286.

The 386 exploits protected mode much more effectively than the 286 does. The 386 can switch to and from protected mode under software control without a system reset. The 286 cannot switch from protected mode without a hardware reset.

Numerous variations of the 386 chip exist, some of which are less powerful and some of which are less power-hungry. The following sections cover the members of the 386-chip family and their differences.

386DX Processors

The 386DX chip was the first of the 386-family members that Intel introduced. The 386 is a full 32-bit processor with 32-bit internal registers, a 32-bit internal data bus, and a 32-bit external data bus. The 386 contains 275,000 transistors in a VLSI (Very Large Scale Integration) circuit. The chip comes in a 132-pin package and draws approximately 400 milliamperes (ma), which is less power than even the 8086 requires. The 386 has a smaller power requirement because it is made of CMOS (Complementary Metal Oxide Semiconductor) materials. The CMOS design enables devices to consume extremely low levels of power.

The Intel 386 chip is available in clock speeds ranging from 16 MHz to 33 MHz; other manufacturers offer comparable versions that offer speeds up to 40 MHz.

The 386DX can address 4G of physical memory. Its built-in virtual memory manager enables software designed to take advantage of enormous amounts of memory to act as though a system has 64 terabytes of memory. (A *terabyte* is 1,099,511,627,776 bytes of memory.) Although most 386 systems are built to accept 64M or less in RAM chips on the motherboard, some high-end computer users do take advantage of the 386 chip's capacity for 4G of physical memory, as well as its 64T virtual-memory potential.

386SX Processors

The 386SX, code-named the P9 chip during its development, was designed for systems designers who were looking for 386 capabilities at 286-system prices. Like the 286, the 386SX is restricted to only 16 bits when communicating with other system components. Internally, however, the 386SX is identical to the DX chip; the 386SX can handle 32 bits of data at the same time (compared with the 8 bits that the original IBM PC handled). The 386SX uses a 24-bit memory-addressing scheme like that of the 286, rather than the full 32-bit memory address bus of the standard 386. The 386SX, therefore, can address a maximum 16M of physical memory rather than the 4G of physical memory that the 386DX can address. The 386SX is available in clock speeds ranging from 16 MHz to 33 MHz.

The 386SX signaled the end of the 286 because of the 386SX chip's superior MMU and the addition of the virtual real mode. Under a software manager such as Windows or OS/2, the 386SX can run numerous DOS programs at the same time. The capability to run 386-specific software is another important advantage of the 386SX over any 286 or older design. For example, Windows 3.1 runs nearly as well on a 386SX as it does on a 386DX.

> **Note**
>
> One common fallacy about the 386SX is that you can plug one into a 286 system and give the system 386 capabilities. This is not true; the 386SX chip is not pin-compatible with the 286 and does not plug into the same socket. Several upgrade products, however, have been designed to adapt the chip to a 286 system. In terms of raw speed, converting a 286 system to a 386 CPU chip results in little performance gain, because 286 motherboards are built with a restricted 16-bit interface to memory and peripherals. A 16 MHz 386SX is not markedly faster than a 16 MHz 286, but it does offer improved memory-management capabilities on a motherboard designed for it, as well as the capability to run 386-specific software.

386SL Processors

Another variation on the 386 chip is the 386SL. This low-power CPU has the same capabilities as the 386SX, but it is designed for laptop systems in which low power consumption is needed. The SL chips offer special power-management features that are important to systems that run on batteries. The SL chip offers several sleep modes that conserve power.

The chip includes an extended architecture that includes a System Management Interrupt (SMI), which provides access to the power-management features. Also included in the SL chip is special support for LIM (Lotus Intel Microsoft) expanded memory functions and a cache controller. The cache controller is designed to control a 16K-to-64K external processor cache.

These extra functions account for the higher transistor count in the SL chips (855,000) compared with even the 386DX processor (275,000). The 386SL is available in 25 MHz clock speed.

Intel offers a companion to the 386SL chip for laptops called the *82360SL I/O subsystem*. The 82360SL provides many common peripheral functions, such as serial and parallel ports, a direct memory access (DMA) controller, an interrupt controller, and power-management logic for the 386SL processor. This chip subsystem works with the processor to provide an ideal solution for the small size and low power-consumption requirements of portable and laptop systems.

386 Processor Clones

Several manufacturers, including AMD and Cyrix, have developed their own versions of the Intel 386DX and SX processors. These 386-compatible chips are available in speeds up to 40 MHz; Intel produces 386 chips up to only 33 MHz. Intel does not offer a 386 chip faster than 33 MHz because that speed begins to tread on the performance domain of the slowest of its own 486 processors.

In general, these chips are fully function-compatible with the Intel processors, which means that they run all software designed for the Intel 386. Many manufacturers choose these "cloned" 386 chips for their systems because they are faster and less expensive than Intel 386 chips. (Intel developed its "Intel Inside" advertising campaign in the hope of enticing buyers with a promise of getting the real thing.)

The section on IBM processors discusses the Intel-compatible chips designed and sold by IBM. These chips are not quite comparable with the other Intel processor clones, because they actually use official masks and microcode licensed directly from Intel. This arrangement essentially gives IBM the full design of the chip to use in its present form or modify. Thus, the IBM processors are fully compatible with the Intel processors and often offer many enhancements that are not even available in the Intel versions.

486 Processors

In the race for more speed, the Intel 80486 (normally abbreviated as 486) was another major leap forward. The additional power available in the 486 fueled tremendous growth in the software industry. Tens of millions of copies of Windows, and millions of copies of OS/2, have been sold largely because the 486 finally made the graphical user interface (GUI) of Windows and OS/2 a realistic option for people who work on their computers every day.

Three main features make a given 486 processor roughly twice as fast as an equivalent MHz 386 chip. These features are:

- *Reduced instruction-execution time.* Instructions in the 486 take an average of only 2 clock cycles to complete, compared with an average of more than 4 cycles on the 386.

- *Internal (Level 1) cache.* The built-in cache has a hit ratio of 90 percent to 95 percent, which describes how often zero-wait-state read operations will occur. External caches can improve this ratio further.

- *Burst-mode memory cycles.* A standard 32-bit (4-byte) memory transfer takes 2 clock cycles. After a standard 32-bit transfer, more data up to the next 12 bytes (or 3 transfers) can be transferred with only 1 cycle used for each 32-bit (4-byte) transfer. Thus, up to 16 bytes of contiguous, sequential memory data can be transferred in as little as 5 cycles instead of 8 cycles or more. This effect can be even greater when the transfers are only 8 bits or 16 bits each.

- *Built-in (synchronous) enhanced math coprocessor* (some versions). The math coprocessor runs synchronously with the main processor and executes math instructions in fewer cycles than previous designs do. On average, the math coprocessor built in to the DX-series chips provides two to three times greater math performance than an external 387 chip.

The 486 chip is about twice as fast as the 386, which means that a 386DX-40 is about as fast as a 486SX-20. If given a choice between a 40 MHz 386 and a 20 MHz 486, I would go for the 486. The lower-MHz 486 chip not only will be just as fast (or faster), but also can easily be upgraded to a DX2 or DX4 processor—which would be two or three times faster yet. You can see why the arrival of the 486 rapidly killed off the 386 in the marketplace.

Before the 486, many people avoided GUIs because they didn't have time to sit around waiting for the hourglass, which indicates that the system is performing behind-the-scenes operations that the user cannot interrupt. (It was said, only partly in jest, that you could turn on your system in the morning, start Windows or OS/2, and then go make coffee for the office. By the time you got back to your computer, Windows or OS/2 might be finished loading.) The 486 changed that situation. Many people believe that the 486 CPU chip spawned the widespread acceptance of GUIs.

The 486 chip's capability to handle the GUI prompted sales of pricey hardware: faster and larger hard drives, faster video display boards and larger monitors, faster and better printers, optical storage devices, CD-ROM drives, sound boards, and video capture boards. A fortunate occurrence prompted by all this spending is the fact that hardware (and software) prices have been in a steep decline for several years.

With the release of its faster Pentium CPU chip, Intel began to cut the price of the 486 line to entice the industry to shift over to the 486 as the mainstream system. Now Intel is starting to cut the price of the Pentium as well. The 486 chip is available in numerous versions: with and without math coprocessors, in clock speeds ranging from 16 MHz to 100 MHz, with special power-management capabilities, and with 3.3-volt operation to save even more power.

Besides high performance, one of the best features of the 486 family of chips is upgradability. In most cases, you can enjoy a performance increase in a given 486 system simply by adding or changing to a faster CPU. Unfortunately, Intel has not explained this upgradability well. I have found it difficult to cut through the marketspeak to find out the technical issues behind the different 486 CPU upgrades—specifically, how they work and what the ramifications of these upgrades are.

In this section, you will find information that can dispel any misunderstandings you may have about the 486 chip versions and possible upgrades. The section explains all the available 486 processors, as well as the possible upgrades and interchanges. You will learn the differences between items such as the new DX2 and Overdrive CPUs, and you will learn which items are appropriate for a given 486-class system. The sections that follow cover the variations on the basic 486 chip.

The 486 Processor Family. Since the introduction of the original 486DX chip in April 1989, the 486 has spawned an entire family of processors. Although 486 processors share certain features, such as full 32-bit architecture and a built-in memory cache, the various members of the 486 family differ in certain features, as well as in maximum speeds and pin configurations. This section first breaks down the different 486 processors by their major types, speed differences, and physical configuration, and then describes each processor in depth. Following are the current primary versions of the 486:

- 486SX—486 CPU without FPU (Floating-Point Unit)

- 486DX—486 CPU plus FPU

- 486DX2—Double-speed (Overdrive) 486 CPU plus FPU

- 486DX4—Triple-speed 486 CPU plus FPU

In addition, most of these 486 chips are available in a variety of maximum speed ratings, varying from 16 MHz at the low end to 100 MHz for the fastest chips. The following table shows the maximum speed ratings of the 486 processors.

Table 6.4   Standard Intel 486 Processor Maximum Clock Ratings

Processor Type	Clock Speed in Megahertz (MHz)									
	16	20	25	33	40	50	66	75	83	100
486SX	×	×	×	×						
486DX			×	×		×				
486DX2					×	×	×			
486DX4								×	×	×

A processor rated for a given speed always functions at any of the lower speeds. A 33 MHz-rated 486DX chip, for example, runs at 25 MHz if it is plugged into a 25 MHz motherboard. Notice that the DX2/Overdrive processors operate internally at 2 times the motherboard clock rate, whereas the DX4 processors operate at 2, 2-1/2, or 3 times the motherboard clock rate. The following table shows the different speed combinations that can result from using the DX2 or DX4 processors with different motherboard clock speeds.

Table 6.5   Intel DX2 and DX4 Operating Speeds versus Motherboard Clock Speeds

Motherboard Clock Speed	16 MHz	20 MHz	25 MHz	33 MHz	50 MHz
DX2 processor speed	32 MHz	40 MHz	50 MHz	66 MHz	N/A
DX4 (2x mode) speed	32 MHz	40 MHz	50 MHz	66 MHz	100 MHz
DX4 (2.5x mode) speed	40 MHz	50 MHz	62.5 MHz	83 MHz	N/A
DX4 (3x mode) speed	48 MHz	60 MHz	75 MHz	100 MHz	N/A

Besides differing in clock speeds, 486 processors have slight differences in pin configurations. The DX, DX2, and SX processors have a virtually identical 168-pin configuration, whereas the Overdrive chips sold retail have either the standard 168-pin configuration or a specially modified 169-pin Overdrive (sometimes also called 487SX) configuration. If your motherboard has two sockets, the primary one likely supports the standard 168-pin configuration, and the secondary (Overdrive) socket supports the 169-pin Overdrive configuration. Most newer motherboards with a single ZIF (zero insertion force) socket support any of the 486 processors except the DX4. The DX4 is different because it requires 3.3 volts to operate instead of 5 volts, like most of the other chips.

If you are upgrading an existing system, be sure that your socket will support the chip that you are installing. In particular, if you are putting one of the new DX4 processors in an older system, you need some type of adapter to regulate the voltage down to 3.3 volts. If you put the DX4 in a 5v socket, you will destroy the (very expensive) chip!

II

Primary System Components

The 486-processor family is designed for high performance because it integrates formerly external devices such as cache controllers, cache memory, and math coprocessors. Also, 486 systems are designed for upgradability. Most 486 systems can be upgraded by simple processor additions or swaps that can effectively double the speed of the system. Because of these features, I recommend the 486SX or DX as the ideal entry-level system, especially in a business environment. Your investment will be protected in the future by a universally available, low-cost processor upgrade.

Internal (Level 1) Cache. All members of the 486 family include, as a standard feature, an integrated (Level 1) cache controller with either 8K or 16K of cache memory included. This cache basically is an area of very fast memory built into the processor that is used to hold some of the current working set of code and data. Cache memory can be accessed with no wait states, because it can fully keep up with the processor. Using cache memory reduces a traditional system bottleneck, because system RAM often is much slower than the CPU. This prevents the processor from having to wait for code and data from much slower main memory, therefore improving performance. Without the cache, a 486 frequently would be forced to wait until system memory caught up. If the data that the 486 chip wants is already in the internal cache, the CPU does not have to wait. If the data is not in the cache, the CPU must fetch it from the secondary processor cache or (in less sophisticated system designs) from the system bus.

You do not need special software or programs to take advantage of this cache; it works invisibly inside the chip. Because the cache stores both program instructions (code) and data, it is called a *unified cache*.

The organization of the cache memory in the 486 family technically is called a 4-Way Set Associative Cache, which means that the cache memory is split into four blocks. Each block also is organized as 128 or 256 lines of 16 bytes each.

To understand how a 4-way set associative cache works, consider a simple example. In the simplest cache design, the cache is set up as a single block into which you can load the contents of a corresponding block of main memory. This procedure is similar to using a bookmark to locate the current page of a book that you are reading. If main memory equates to all the pages in the book, the bookmark indicates which pages are held in cache memory. This procedure works if the required data is located within the pages marked with the bookmark, but it does not work if you need to refer to a previously read page. In that case, the bookmark is of no use.

An alternative approach is to maintain multiple bookmarks to mark several parts of the book simultaneously. Additional hardware overhead is associated with having multiple bookmarks, and you also have to take time to check all the bookmarks to see which one marks the pages of data that you need. Each additional bookmark adds to the overhead but also increases your chance of finding the desired pages.

If you settle on marking four areas in the book to limit the overhead involved, you have essentially constructed a 4-way set associative cache. This technique splits the available cache memory into four blocks, each of which stores different lines of main memory. Multitasking environments, such as OS/2 and Windows, are good examples of environments in which the processor needs to operate on different areas of memory simultaneously and in which a four-way cache would improve performance greatly.

The contents of the cache must always be in sync with the contents of main memory to ensure that the processor is working with current data. For this reason, the internal cache in the 486 family is a Write-Through cache. *Write-Through* means that when the processor writes information out to the cache, that information is automatically written through to main memory as well.

By comparison, the Pentium chip has an internal *Write-Back* cache, which means that both reads and writes are cached, further improving performance. Even though the internal 486 cache is Write-Through, the system still can employ an external Write-Back cache for increased performance. In addition, the 486 can buffer up to 4 bytes before actually storing the data in RAM, improving efficiency in case the memory bus is busy.

The cache controller built into the processor also is responsible for watching the memory bus when alternate processors known as Bus Masters are in control of the system. This process of watching the bus is referred to as Bus Snooping. If a Bus Master device writes to an area of memory that also is stored in the processor cache currently, the cache contents and memory no longer agree. The cache controller then marks this data as invalid and reloads the cache during the next memory access, preserving the integrity of the system.

An external *secondary cache* (Level 2) of up to 512K or more of extremely fast Static RAM (SRAM) chips also is used in most 486-based systems to further reduce the amount of time that the CPU must spend waiting for data from system memory. The function of the secondary processor cache is similar to that of the 486 chip's on-board cache. The secondary processor cache holds information that is moving to the CPU, thereby reducing the time that the CPU spends waiting and increasing the time that the CPU spends performing calculations. Fetching information from the secondary processor cache rather than from system memory is much faster because of the extremely fast speed of the SRAM chips—20 nanoseconds (ns) or less.

The following sections discuss the technical specifications and differences of the various members of the 486-processor family in more detail.

486DX Processors. The original Intel 486DX processor was introduced on April 10, 1989, and systems using this chip first appeared during 1990. The first chips had a maximum speed rating of 25 MHz; later versions of the 486DX were available in 33 MHz- and 50 MHz-rated versions. The 486DX originally was available only in a 5v, 168-pin PGA

(Pin Grid Array) version but now also is available in 5v, 196-pin PQFP (Plastic Quad Flat Pack) and 3.3v, 208-pin SQFP (Small Quad Flat Pack) as well. These latter form factors are available in SL Enhanced versions, which are intended primarily for portable or laptop applications in which saving power is important.

Two main features separate the 486 processor from older processors such as the 386 or 286: integration and upgradability. The 486DX integrates functions such as the math coprocessor, cache controller, and cache memory into the chip. The 486 also was designed with upgradability in mind; double-speed Overdrive are upgrades available for most systems.

The 486DX processor is fabricated with low-power CMOS (Complimentary Metal Oxide Semiconductor) technology. The chip has a 32-bit internal register size, a 32-bit external data bus, and a 32-bit address bus. These dimensions are equal to those of the 386DX processor. The internal register size is where the "32-bit" designation used in advertisements comes from. The 486DX chip contains 1.2 million transistors on a piece of silicon no larger than your thumbnail. This figure is more than four times the number of components on 386 processors and should give you a good indication of the 486 chip's relative power. The following table shows the technical specifications of the 486DX processor.

Table 6.6 Intel 486DX Processor	
Specifications	
Introduced	April 10, 1989 (25 MHz) June 24, 1991 (50 MHz)
Maximum rated speeds	25, 33, 50 MHz
CPU clock multiplier	1x
Register size	32-bit
External data bus	32-bit
Memory address bus	32-bit
Maximum memory	4G
Integral-cache size	8K
Integral-cache type	4-way set associative, Write-Through
Burst-mode transfers	Yes
Number of transistors	1.2 million, 1.4 million (SL Enhanced models)
Circuit size	1 micron (25, 33 MHz), 0.8 micron (50 MHz and all SL Enhanced models)
External package	168-pin PGA, 196-pin PQFP*, 208-pin SQFP*
Math coprocessor	Integral Floating-Point Unit (FPU)
Power management	SMM (System Management Mode) in SL Enhanced models
Operating voltage	5v standard, 3.3v optional in 208-pin SQFP models

PGA = Pin Grid Array
PQFP = Plastic Quad Flat Pack
SQFP = Small Quad Flat Pack
*The PQFP and SQFP models are SL Enhanced only.

The standard 486DX contains a processing unit, a Floating-Point Unit (math coprocessor), a memory-management unit, and a cache controller with 8K of internal-cache RAM. Due to the internal cache and a more efficient internal processing unit, the 486 family of processors can execute individual instructions in an average of only 2 processor cycles. Compare this figure with the 286 and 386 families, both of which execute an average 4.5 cycles per instruction, or with the original 8086 and 8088 processors, which execute an average 12 cycles per instruction. At a given clock rate (MHz), therefore, a 486 processor is roughly twice as efficient as a 386 processor; a 16 MHz 486SX is roughly equal to a 33 MHz 386DX system, and a 20 MHz 486SX is equal to a 40 MHz 386DX system. Any of the faster 486s are way beyond the 386 in performance.

The 486 is fully instruction-set-compatible with previous Intel processors, such as the 386, but offers several additional instructions (most of which have to do with controlling the internal cache).

Like the 386DX, the 486 can address 4G of physical memory and manage as much as 64 terabytes of virtual memory. The 486 fully supports the three operating modes introduced in the 386: real mode, protected mode, and virtual real mode. In real mode, the 486 (like the 386) runs unmodified 8086-type software. In protected mode, the 486 (like the 386) offers sophisticated memory paging and program switching. In virtual real mode, the 486 (like the 386) can run multiple copies of DOS or other operating systems while simulating an 8086's real-mode operation. Under an operating system such as Windows or OS/2, therefore, both 16-bit and 32-bit programs can run simultaneously on this processor with hardware memory protection. If one program crashes, the rest of the system is protected, and you can reboot the blown portion through various means depending on the operating software.

Built-In Math Coprocessor. The 486DX series has a built-in math coprocessor that sometimes is called an MCP (math coprocessor) or FPU (Floating-Point Unit). This series is unlike previous Intel CPU chips, which required you to add a math coprocessor if you needed faster calculations for complex mathematics. The FPU in the 486DX series is 100 percent software-compatible with the external 387 math coprocessor used with the 386, but it delivers more than twice the performance because it runs in synchronization with the main processor and executes most instructions in half as many cycles as the 386.

486SL. Intel originally announced a stand-alone chip called the 486SL. Now the SL as a separate chip has been discontinued, and all the SL enhancements and features are available in virtually all the 486 processors (SX, DX, and DX2) in what are called SL Enhanced versions. The stand-alone 486SL, therefore, has been discontinued. *SL Enhancement* refers to a special design that incorporates special power-saving features.

The SL Enhanced chips originally were designed to be installed in laptop or notebook systems that run on batteries, but they are finding their way into desktop systems as well. The SL Enhanced chips feature special power-management techniques, such as sleep mode and clock throttling, to reduce power consumption when necessary. These chips are available in 3.3v versions as well.

The following table shows the technical specifications of the 486SL processor.

Table 6.7   Intel 486SL Processor

Specifications

Introduced	November 9, 1992
Maximum rated speeds	25, 33, 50 MHz
CPU clock multiplier	1x
Register size	32-bit
External data bus	32-bit
Memory address bus	32-bit
Maximum memory	4G
Integral-cache size	8K
Integral-cache type	4-Way Set Associative, Write-Through
Burst-mode transfers	Yes
Number of transistors	1.4 million
Circuit size	0.8 micron
External package	168-pin PGA, 196-pin PQFP, 208-pin SQFP, 227-pin LGA*
Math coprocessor	Integral Floating-Point Unit (FPU), optional in some models
Power management	System Management Mode (SMM)
Operating voltage	5v standard, 3.3v optional in 208-pin SQFP models

PGA = Pin Grid Array
PQFP = Plastic Quad Flat Pack
SQFP = Small Quad Flat Pack
LGA = Land Grid Array
*The LGA version has been discontinued.

Intel has designed a power-management architecture called System Management Mode (SMM). This new mode of operation is totally isolated and independent from other CPU hardware and software. SMM provides hardware resources such as timers, registers, and other I/O logic that can control and power down mobile-computer components without interfering with any of the other system resources. SMM executes in a dedicated memory space called System Management Memory, which is not visible and does not interfere with operating-system and application software. SMM has an interrupt called System Management Interrupt (SMI), which services power-management events, and which is independent from and higher-priority than any of the other interrupts.

SMM provides power management with flexibility and security that were not available previously. For example, when an application program tries to access a peripheral device that is powered down for battery savings, a System Management Interrupt (SMI) occurs, powering up the peripheral device and reexecuting the I/O instruction automatically.

Intel also has designed a feature called suspend/resume in the SL processor. The system manufacturer can use this feature to provide the portable-computer user with instant-on-and-off capability. An SL system typically can resume (instant on) in one second from the suspend state (instant off) to exactly where it left off. You do not need to reboot, load the operating system, load the application program, and then load the application data. Simply push the suspend/resume button, and the system is ready to go.

The SL CPU was designed to consume almost no power in the suspend state. This feature means that the system can stay in the suspend state possibly for weeks and yet start up instantly right where it left off. While it is in the suspend state, an SL system can keep working data in normal RAM memory safe for a long time, but saving to a disk still is prudent.

486SX. The 486SX, introduced in April 1991, was designed to be sold as a lower-cost version of the 486. The 486SX is virtually identical to the full DX processor, but the chip does not incorporate the FPU or math coprocessor portion.

As you read earlier in this chapter, the 386SX was a scaled-down (some people would say crippled) 16-bit version of the full-blown 32-bit 386DX. The 386SX even had a completely different pinout and was not interchangeable with the more powerful DX version. The 486SX, however, is a different story. The 486SX is in fact a full-blown 32-bit 486 processor that is basically pin-compatible with the DX. A couple of pin functions are different or rearranged, but each pin fits into the same socket.

The 486SX chip is more a marketing quirk than new technology. Early versions of the 486SX chip actually were DX chips that showed defects in the math-coprocessor section. Instead of being scrapped, the chips simply were packaged with the FPU section disabled and sold as SX chips. This arrangement lasted for only a short time; thereafter, SX chips got their own mask, which is different from the DX mask. The transistor count dropped to 1.185 million (from 1.2 million) to reflect this new mask.

The 486SX chip is twice as fast as a 386DX with the same clock speed. Intel has marketed the 486SX as being the ideal chip for new computer buyers, because not much entry-level software uses the math-coprocessor functions. If you use software that *does* use or require the math coprocessor, you are well advised to stick with the DX series as a minimum.

The 486SX is available in 16, 20, 25, and 33 MHz-rated speeds, and it normally comes in a 168-pin version, although other surface-mount versions are available in SL Enhanced models.

II

Primary System Components

The following table shows the technical specifications of the 486SX processor.

Table 6.8   Intel 486SX Processor

Specifications

Introduced	April 22, 1991
Maximum rated speeds	16, 20, 25, 33 MHz
CPU clock multiplier	1x (2x in some SL Enhanced models)
Register size	32-bit
External data bus	32-bit
Memory address bus	32-bit
Maximum memory	4G
Integral-cache size	8K
Integral-cache type	4-Way Set Associative, Write-Through
Burst-mode transfers	Yes
Number of transistors	1.185 million, 1.4 million (SL Enhanced models)
Circuit size	1 micron, 0.8 micron (SL Enhanced models)
External package	168-pin PGA, 196-pin PQFP*, 208-pin SQFP*
Math coprocessor	None
Power management	SMM (System Management Mode) in SL Enhanced models
Operating voltage	5v standard, 3.3v optional in 208-pin SQFP models

PGA = Pin Grid Array
PQFP = Plastic Quad Flat Pack
SQFP = Small Quad Flat Pack
*The PQFP and SQFP models are SL Enhanced only.

Despite what Intel's marketing and sales information implies, technically, no provision exists for adding a separate math coprocessor to a 486SX system; neither is a separate math coprocessor chip available to plug in. Instead, Intel wants you to add a new 486 processor with a built-in math unit and disable the SX CPU that already is on the motherboard. If this situation sounds confusing, read on, because this topic brings you to the most important aspect of 486 design: upgradability.

487SX. The 487SX math coprocessor, as Intel calls it, really is a complete 25 MHz 486DX CPU with an extra pin added and some other pins rearranged. When the 487SX is installed in the extra socket provided in a 486SX-CPU-based system, the 487SX turns off the existing 486SX via a new signal on one of the pins. The extra key pin actually carries no signal itself and exists only to prevent improper orientation when the chip is installed in a socket.

The 487SX takes over all CPU functions from the 486SX and also provides math coprocessor functionality in the system. At first glance, this setup seems rather strange and wasteful, so perhaps further explanation is in order. Fortunately, the 487SX turned out simply to be a stopgap measure while Intel prepared its real surprise: the Overdrive processor. The DX2/Overdrive speed-doubling chips, which are designed for the 487SX 169-pin socket, have the same pinout as the 487SX. These upgrade chips are installed in exactly the same way as the 487SX; therefore, any system that supports the 487SX also supports the DX2/Overdrive chips.

When the 486SX processor was introduced, Intel told motherboard designers to install an empty 169-pin socket in the motherboard for a 487SX math coprocessor and originally called this socket a Performance Upgrade Socket. At first, the only thing that you could plug into this socket was what Intel called a 487SX math coprocessor. The strange thing was that the 487SX was not really a math coprocessor at all, but a full 486DX processor!

The only difference between a 487SX and a 486DX is the fact that the 487SX uses the 169-pin rearranged pinout. When you plug a 487SX into the upgrade socket, a special signal pin that was not defined before (interestingly, *not* the extra 169th one) shuts down the original 486SX CPU, and the 487SX takes over. Because the 487SX functionally is a full-blown DX processor, you also get the math coprocessor functions that were left out of the original 486SX CPU. That is one of the reasons why the 487SX is so expensive; you really are buying more than you think. The real crime is that the original CPU sits silently in the system and does nothing!

Even though the 487SX basically is the same as the 486DX, you normally cannot install a "regular" 486DX processor in the Overdrive socket, because the pin designations are not the same. (I used the word *normally* because some motherboards have a jumper selection to allow for the different CPU pin configurations.) Because the 486SX actually uses a 168-pin design similar to that of the 486DX (even though it normally is installed in a 169-pin socket), you may be able to install a regular DX chip in the SX socket and have it work, but this capability depends somewhat on the flexibility of your motherboard.

Although in most cases you could upgrade a system by removing the 486SX CPU and replacing it with a 487SX (or even a DX or DX2/Overdrive). Intel originally discouraged this procedure and recommended that PC manufacturers include a dedicated upgrade (Overdrive) socket in their systems, because several risks were involved in removing the original CPU from a standard socket. (The following section elaborates on those risks.) Nowadays, Intel recommends—or even insists on—the use of a single processor socket of a ZIF (zero insertion force) design, which makes upgrading an easy task physically.

DX2/Overdrive Processors. On March 3, 1992, Intel introduced the DX2 speed-doubling processors. On May 26, 1992, Intel announced that the DX2 processors also would be available in a retail version called Overdrive. Originally, the Overdrive versions of the DX2 were available only in 169-pin versions, which meant that they could be used only with 486SX systems that had sockets configured to support the rearranged pin configuration.

On September 14, 1992, Intel introduced 168-pin Overdrive versions for upgrading 486DX systems. These new processors, which represent the ultimate in PC performance, are available in new systems and also can be added to existing 486 (SX or DX) systems as an upgrade, even if those systems do not support the 169-pin configuration. When you use this processor as an upgrade, you simply install the new chip in your system, which subsequently runs twice as fast. (As the guy in *RoboCop* said, "I *like* it!")

The DX2/Overdrive processors run internally at twice the clock rate of the host system. If the motherboard clock is 25 MHz, for example, the DX2/Overdrive chip runs internally at 50 MHz; likewise, if the motherboard is a 33 MHz design, the DX2/Overdrive runs at 66 MHz. The DX2/Overdrive speed doubling has no effect on the rest of the system; all components on the motherboard run the same as they do with a standard 486 processor. Therefore, you do not have to change other components (such as memory) to accommodate the double-speed chip. In other words, you can achieve a significant performance gain simply by changing the CPU chip; you do not have to use faster (more expensive) motherboard circuitry.

The DX2/Overdrive chips are available in several speeds. Currently, three different speed-rated versions are offered:

- 40 MHz DX2/Overdrive for 16 MHz or 20 MHz systems

- 50 MHz DX2/Overdrive for 25 MHz systems

- 66 MHz DX2/Overdrive for 33 MHz systems

Notice that these ratings indicate the maximum speed at which the chip is capable of running. You could use a 66 MHz-rated chip in place of the 50 MHz- or 40 MHz-rated parts with no problem, although the chip will run only at the slower speeds. The actual speed of the chip is double the motherboard clock frequency. When the 40 MHz DX2/Overdrive chip is installed in a 16 MHz 486SX system, for example, the chip will function only at 32 MHz—exactly double the motherboard speed. Intel originally stated that no 100 MHz DX2/Overdrive chip will be available for 50 MHz systems—which technically has not been true since the DX4 can be set to run in a clock doubled mode and used in a 50 MHz motherboard (more information on that situation later in the chapter).

The only part of the DX2 chip that doesn't run at double speed is the *bus interface unit*, a region of the chip that handles I/O between the CPU and the outside world. By translating between the differing internal and external clock speeds, the bus interface unit makes speed doubling transparent to the rest of the system. The DX2 appears to the rest of the system to be a regular 486DX chip, but one that seems to execute instructions twice as fast.

DX2/Overdrive chips are based on the 0.8-micron circuit technology that was first used in the 50 MHz 486DX. The DX2 contains 1.1 million transistors in a three-layer form. The internal 8K cache, integer, and Floating-Point Units all run at double speed. External communication with the PC runs at normal speed to maintain compatibility.

The following table shows the technical specifications of the 486DX2/Overdrive processors.

Table 6.9 486DX2/Overdrive Processor

Specifications

Introduced	March 3, 1992
Maximum rated speeds	40, 50, 66 MHz
CPU clock multiplier	2x
Register size	32-bit
External data bu	32-bit
Memory address bus	32-bit
Maximum memory	4G
Integral-cache size	8K
Integral-cache type	4-Way Set Associative, Write-Through
Burst-mode transfers	Yes
Number of transistors	1.1 million, 1.4 million (SL Enhanced models)
Circuit size	0.8 micron
External package	168-pin PGA, 169-pin PGA, 196-pin PQFP*, 208-pin SQFP*
Math coprocessor	Integral Floating-Point Unit (FPU)
Power management	SMM (System Management Mode) in SL Enhanced models
Operating voltage	5v standard, 3.3v optional in 208-pin SQFP models

PGA = Pin Grid Array
PQFP = Plastic Quad Flat Pack
SQFP = Small Quad Flat Pack
*The PQFP and SQFP models are SL Enhanced only.

Besides upgrading existing systems, one of the best parts of the DX2 concept is the fact that system designers can introduce very fast systems by using cheaper motherboard designs, rather than the very costly designs that would support a straight high-speed clock. This means that a 50 MHz 486DX2 system is much less expensive than a straight 50 MHz 486DX system. In a 486DX-50 system, the system board operates at a true 50 MHz. In a 486DX2-50 system, the 486DX2 CPU operates internally at 50 MHz, but the motherboard operates at only 25 MHz.

You may be thinking that a true 50 MHz DX-processor-based system still would be faster than a speed-doubled 25 MHz system, and this generally is true, but the differences in speed actually are very slight—a real testament to the integration of the 486 processor and especially to the cache design.

When the processor has to go to system memory for data or instructions, for example, it has to do so at the slower motherboard operating frequency, such as 25 MHz. Because the 8K internal cache of the 486DX2 has a hit rate of 90 percent to 95 percent, however, the CPU has to access system memory only 5 percent to 10 percent of the time for memory reads. Therefore, the performance of the DX2 system can come very close to that of a true 50 MHz DX system and cost much less. Even though the motherboard runs only at 33.33 MHz, a system with a DX2 66 MHz processors ends up being faster than a true 50 MHz DX system, especially if the DX2 system has a good Level-2 cache.

Because the DX2 66 MHz chips are much cheaper than the straight 50 MHz DX models, the systems are cheaper as well. Additionally, the newer local buses operate best at 33 MHz and do not tolerate 50 MHz speeds without using buffering. All these factors have contributed to the elimination of true 50 MHz DX systems from most manufacturers' inventories.

Many 486 motherboard designs also include a secondary cache that is external to the cache integrated into the 486 chip. This external cache allows for much faster access when the 486 chip calls for external-memory access. The size of this external cache can vary anywhere from 16K to 512K or more. When you add a DX2 processor, an external cache is even more important for achieving the greatest performance gain, because this cache greatly reduces the wait states that the processor will have to add when writing to system memory or when a read causes an internal-cache miss. For this reason, some systems perform better with the DX2/Overdrive processors than others, usually depending on the size and efficiency of the external-memory cache system on the motherboard. Systems that have no external cache still will enjoy a near-doubling of CPU performance, but operations that involve a great deal of memory access will be slower.

At this writing, Intel has stated that it has no plans for a DX2/Overdrive chip for 50 MHz systems. Producing a speed-doubled Overdrive processor for 486DX-50 based systems would mean that the Overdrive chip would have to function internally at 100 MHz. Indirectly, Intel has solved this problem with the introduction of the DX4 processor.

Although the DX4 technically is not sold as a retail part, you can indeed purchase it from several vendors, along with the 3.3v voltage adapter that you need to install the chip in a 5v socket. These adapters have jumpers that enable you to select the DX4 clock multiplier and set it to 2x, 2.5x, or 3x mode. In a 50 MHz DX system, you could install a DX4/voltage-regulator combination set in 2x mode for a motherboard speed of 50 MHz and a processor speed of 100 MHz! Although you may not be able to take advantage of the latest local bus peripherals, you will, in any case, have one of the fastest 486-class PCs available.

Differences between DX2 and Overdrive Processors. One of the most common questions about the DX2/Overdrive processors is "What's the difference between a DX2 chip and an Overdrive chip?" Although the advertisements are somewhat misleading, the DX2 and Overdrive processor chips actually are the same thing. The real difference is the way that they are sold and the amenities that are (or are not included). The simple answer is that if the chip comes installed in a system, it's a DX2; if it comes in an Intel retail upgrade kit, it's an Overdrive processor.

Overdrive processors are DX2 chips that are sold as end-user-installable upgrades. Like math coprocessors, these processors are available at retail outlets and carry a limited lifetime warranty from Intel. Included with Overdrive processors are a user guide, a utilities disk, a chip-extractor tool and a grounding strap. Overdrive processors for 25 MHz and 33 MHz systems also include a heat sink, which already is attached to the top surface of the chip. Although not all systems have poor-enough air circulation to require the heat sink, its presence increases the number of systems that can use the Overdrive chips. Technical support direct from Intel is provided with each Overdrive processor.

DX2 chips are the raw CPUs, which are sold in quantity only to OEMs (Original Equipment Manufacturers), which install the chips in their systems as the primary microprocessors. The DX2 chips are sold in bulk and do not include the packaging, documentation, software utilities, extractor tool, and other items that are part of the retail package. DX2 chips also do not include a heat sink from Intel; it is up to the system manufacturer to determine whether a heat sink is needed for a particular application and to add one if it is needed.

The raw DX2 CPUs are classified by Intel as OEM products and are warranted only to the OEM or authorized Intel distributor for one year from the ship date. When that OEM or distributor sells the system or the CPU, that company extends the warranty to the purchaser. The warranty and support for a raw 486DX2 come from the company from which you purchase your system or the 486DX2 CPU, not from Intel.

"Vacancy." Perhaps you saw the Intel advertisements—both print and television—that featured a 486SX system with a neon Vacancy sign pointing to an empty socket next to the CPU chip. Unfortunately, these ads were not very informative, and they made it seem that only systems with the extra socket could be upgraded. When I first saw these ads, I was worried, because I had just purchased a 486DX system, and the advertisements implied that only 486SX systems with the empty Overdrive socket were upgradable. This, of course, was not true, but the Intel advertisements surely did not communicate that fact very well.

I later found out that upgradability does not depend on having an extra Overdrive socket in the system and that virtually any 486SX or DX system can be upgraded. The secondary Overdrive socket was designed simply to make upgrading easier and more convenient. What I mean is that even in systems that have the second socket, you can actually remove the primary SX or DX CPU and plug the Overdrive processor directly into the main CPU socket, rather than into the secondary Overdrive socket.

In that case, you would have an upgraded system with a single functioning CPU installed; you could remove the old CPU from the system and sell it or trade it in for a refund. Unfortunately, Intel does not offer a trade-in or core-charge policy; it simply does not want your old chip. For this reason, some people saw the Overdrive socket as being a way for Intel to sell more CPUs. Some valid reasons exist, however, to use the Overdrive socket and leave the original CPU installed.

One reason is that many PC manufacturers void the system warranty if the CPU has been removed from the system. Also, when systems are serviced, most manufacturers require that the system be returned with only the original parts; you must remove all add-in cards, memory modules, upgrade chips, and similar items before sending the system in for servicing. If you replace the original CPU when you install the upgrade, returning the system to its original condition will be much more difficult.

Another reason for using the upgrade socket is that if the main CPU socket is damaged when you remove the original CPU or install the upgrade processor, the system will not function. By contrast, if a secondary upgrade socket is damaged, the system still should work with the original CPU.

If you think that damaging the socket or chip are not valid concerns, you should know that it typically takes 100 pounds of insertion force to install a chip in a standard 169-pin screw machine socket. With this much force involved, you easily could damage either the chip or socket during the removal-and-reinstallation process.

Many motherboard manufacturers began using low-insertion-force (LIF) sockets, which typically require only 60 pounds of insertion force for a 169-pin chip. With the LIF or standard socket, I usually advise removing the motherboard so that you can support the board from behind when you insert the chip. Pressing down on the motherboard with 60 to 100 pounds of force can crack the board if it is not supported properly. A special tool also is required to remove a chip from one of these sockets.

Nowadays, nearly all motherboard manufacturers are using zero-insertion-force (ZIF) sockets. These sockets almost eliminate the risk involved in upgrading, because no insertion force is necessary to install the chip. Most ZIF sockets are handle-actuated; you simply lift the handle, drop the chip into the socket, and then close the handle. This design makes replacing the original processor with the upgrade processor an easy task. Because it is so simple to perform the upgrade with a ZIF socket, most motherboards that use such a socket have only one processor socket instead of two. This arrangement is a bonus: the unnecessary second socket does not waste the additional motherboard space, and you are forced to remove the otherwise-dormant original processor, which you then can sell or keep as a spare.

If a ZIF socket is not used, it is usually much easier to install an upgrade processor in an empty Overdrive socket than it is to remove the original CPU and then install the upgrade chip in the CPU socket. For these reasons, Intel now recommends that all 486 systems (SX and DX) use the two-socket approach or (more likely) use a single ZIF socket for the primary CPU as well as for any later upgrades.

Most single-socket systems can take any of the 486-family chips from the 486SX to the DX and the DX2/Overdrive. These boards usually have a set of jumpers or switches that enable you to select the type and speed of CPU that you are installing. In systems that have no second socket or ZIF socket, you may be more restricted in terms of the types of upgrades that you can install.

Some motherboards now include sockets beyond the original 169-pin Overdrive socket (now officially called Socket 1) for use in additional upgrades. These larger sockets can be both primary-CPU sockets and Overdrive sockets. This design not only accommodates the original 486DX or DX2 processor, but also allows for an upgrade to the next level of Overdrive CPU based on the Intel Pentium processors.

Overdrive Processors and Sockets

Intel has stated that all of their future processors will have Overdrive versions available for upgrading at a later date. As a result, Intel has developed a series of socket designs that will accommodate not only the original processor with which a system is shipped, but also the future Overdrive processor.

In many cases, the future Overdrive unit will be much more than just the same type of processor running at a higher clock rate. Although the original Overdrive series of processors for the 486SX and 486DX chip simply were clock-doubled versions of essentially the same chips, Intel plans Overdrive upgrades that go beyond this level. For example, the company already has designed Overdrive-style single-chip upgrades for DX2, DX4, and Pentium systems.

This new processor will require a larger socket than the original processor does; the additional pins are reserved for the new processor when it is ready. Intel is making available the pin specifications and some functions of the new processors so that motherboard designers can prepare now by installing the proper sockets. Then, when the Overdrive processor becomes available, all the end user will have to do is purchase it and install the new chip in place of the original one. To make the process easy, Intel now requires that all these sockets be of ZIF (zero insertion force) design.

Intel has created a set of six socket designs, named Socket 1 through Socket 6. Each socket is designed to support a different range of original and upgrade processors. The following table shows the specifications of these sockets.

Table 6.10   Intel 486/Pentium CPU Socket Types and Specifications

Socket Number	No. of Pins	Pin Layout	Voltage	Supported Processors
Socket 1	169	17x17 PGA	5v	SX/SX2, DX/DX2*
Socket 2	238	19x19 PGA	5v	SX/SX2, DX/DX2*, Pentium Overdrive
Socket 3	237	19x19 PGA	5v/3.3v	SX/SX2, DX/DX2, DX4, Pentium Overdrive, DX4 Pentium Overdrive
Socket 4	273	21x21 PGA	5v	Pentium 60/66, Pentium 60/66 Overdrive
Socket 5	320	37x37 SPGA	3.3v	Pentium 90/100, Pentium 90/100 Overdrive
Socket 6	235	19x19 PGA	3.3v	DX4, DX4 Pentium Overdrive

DX4 also can be supported with the addition of an aftermarket 3.3v voltage-regulator adapter.
PGA = Pin Grid Array
SPGA = Staggered Pin Grid Array

The original Overdrive socket, now officially called Socket 1, is a 169-pin PGA socket. Motherboards that have this socket can support any of the 486SX, DX, and DX2 processors, as well as the DX2/Overdrive versions. This type of socket is found on most 486 systems that originally were designed for Overdrive upgrades. Even if your system has only a 168-pin version (technically, not Socket 1), you still can get DX2 chips with the correct pinout to plug right in. You even can install a DX4 triple-speed processor in this socket by using a voltage-regulator adapter. The following figure shows the pinout of Socket 1.

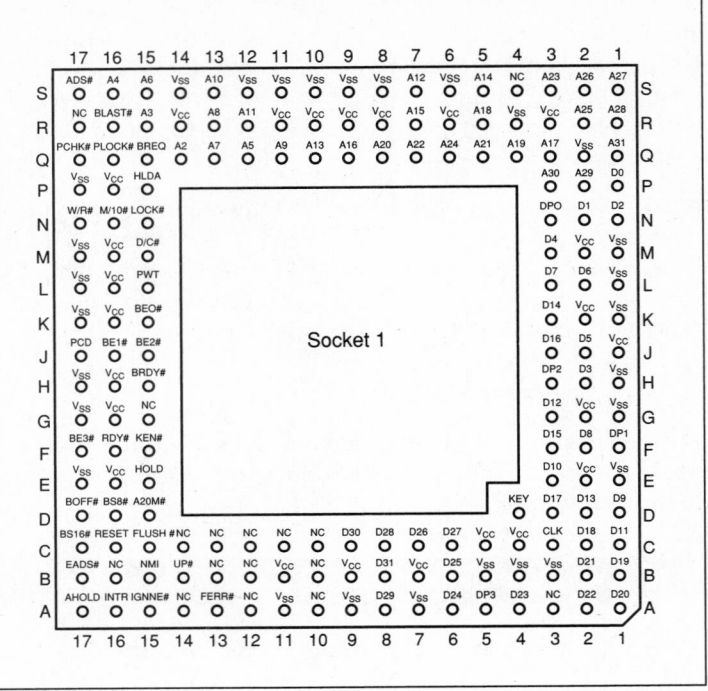

Fig. 6.1

Intel Socket 1 pinout.

The original DX processor draws a maximum 0.9 amps of 5v power in 33 MHz form (4.5 watts) and a maximum 1 amp in 50 MHz form (5 watts). The DX2 processor or Overdrive processor draws a maximum 1.2 amps at 66 MHz (6 watts). This minor increase in power requires only a passive heat sink consisting of aluminum fins that are glued to the processor with thermal transfer epoxy. Overdrive processors rated at 40 MHz or less do not have heat sinks.

When the DX2 processor was released, Intel already was working on the new Pentium processor. The company wanted to offer a 32-bit, scaled-down version of the Pentium as an upgrade for systems that originally came with a DX2 processor. Rather than just increasing the clock rate, Intel created an all-new chip with enhanced capabilities derived from the Pentium.

The chip, officially called the Pentium Overdrive Processor, is not available at this writing but is scheduled to be available by the end of 1994, which may be when you read this. This chip will have 236 pins and will plug into a processor socket with the 238-pin Socket 2 design. This type of socket will hold any 486 SX, DX, or DX2 processor, as well as the Pentium Overdrive.

Figure 6.2 shows the pinout configuration of the official Socket 2 design.

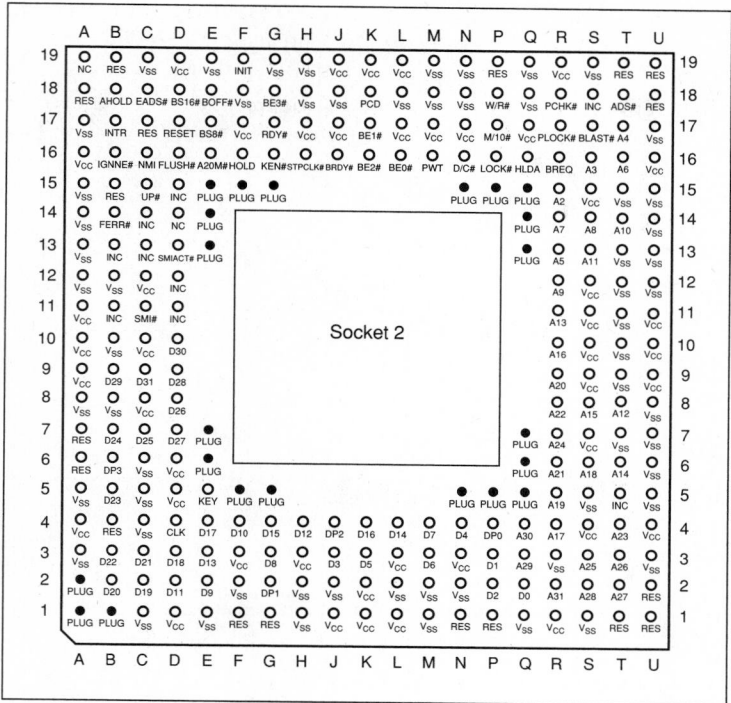

Fig. 6.2
238-pin Intel Socket 2 configuration.

Notice that although the new chip for Socket 2 is called Pentium Overdrive, it is not a full-scale (64-bit) Pentium; the chip is more like a Pentium SX. Most manufacturers that claim to have Pentium-ready systems really mean that their systems have a Socket 2 processor socket that will accommodate the Pentium Overdrive chip in the future.

Intel released the design of Socket 2 a little prematurely and found that the chip ran too hot for many systems. The company solved this problem by adding a special Active Heat Sink to the Pentium Overdrive processor. This active heat sink is a combination of a standard heat sink with a built-in electric fan. Unlike the aftermarket glue-on or clip-on fans for processors that you may have seen, this one actually draws 5v power directly from the socket to drive the fan. No external connection to disk drive cables or the power supply is required. The fan/heat sink assembly clips or plugs directly into the processor, providing for easy replacement should the fan ever fail.

Another requirement of the active heat sink is additional clearance—no obstructions for an area about 1.4 inches off the base of the existing socket, to allow for heat-sink clearance. In systems that were not designed with this feature, the Pentium Overdrive upgrade will be difficult or impossible.

Another problem with this particular upgrade is power consumption. The 5v Pentium Overdrive processor will draw up to 2.5 amps at 5v (including the fan) or 12.5 watts, which is more than double the 1.2 amps (6 watts) drawn by the DX2 66 processor. Intel did not provide this information when it established the socket design, so the company set up a testing facility to certify systems for thermal and mechanical compatibility with the Pentium Overdrive upgrade. For the greatest peace of mind, ensure that your system is certified compatible before you attempt this upgrade.

Figure 6.3 shows the dimensions of the Pentium Overdrive Processor and Active Heat Sink/fan assembly.

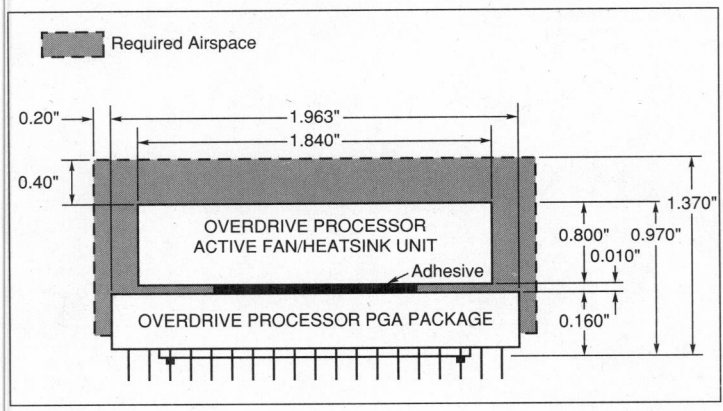

Fig. 6.3
Physical dimensions of the Intel Pentium Overdrive Processor and Active Heat Sink.

Because of problems with the original Socket 2 specification and the enormous heat the 5v version of the Pentium Overdrive Processor will generate, Intel came up with an improved design. The new processor, officially called the DX4 Overdrive Processor, actually is the same as the Pentium Overdrive processor, with the exception that it runs on 3.3v and draws a maximum 3.0 amps of 3.3v (9.9 watts) and 0.2 amp of 5v (1 watt) to run the fan, for a total 10.9 watts. This configuration provides a slight margin over the 5v version of this processor. The fan will be easy to remove from the Overdrive processor for replacement, should it ever fail.

To support both the new DX4 processor, which runs on 3.3v, and the 3.3v DX4 (Pentium) Overdrive processor, Intel had to create a new socket. In addition to the new 3.3v chips, this new socket supports the older 5v SX, DX, DX2, and even the 5v Pentium Overdrive chip. The design, called Socket 3, is the most flexible upgradable 486 design.

Figure 6.4 shows the pinout specification of Socket 3.

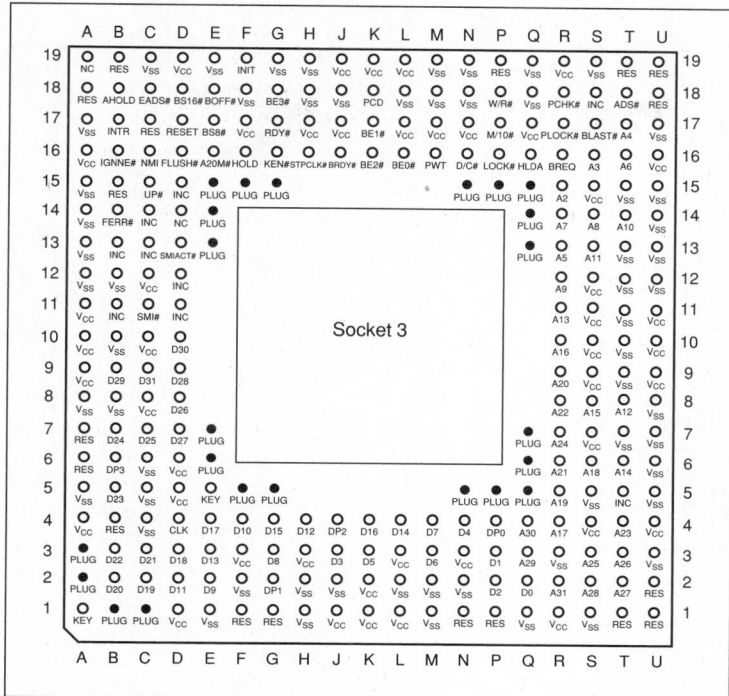

Fig. 6.4

237-pin Intel Socket 3 configuration.

Notice that Socket 3 has one additional pin and several others plugged compared with Socket 2. Socket 3 provides for better keying, which prevents an end user from accidentally installing the processor in an improper orientation. One serious problem exists, however: this socket cannot automatically determine the type of voltage that will be provided to it. A jumper is likely to be added on the motherboard near the socket to enable the user to select 5v or 3.3v operation. Because this jumper must be manually set, however, a user could install a 3.3v processor in this socket when it is configured for 5v operation. This installation will instantly destroy a very expensive chip when the system is powered on. It will be up to the end user to make sure that this socket is properly configured for voltage, depending on which type of processor is installed. If the jumper is set in 3.3v configuration and a 5v processor is installed, no harm will occur, but the system will not operate properly unless the jumper is reset for 5v.

The original Pentium processor 60 MHz and 66 MHz versions had 273 pins and would plug into a 273-pin Pentium processor socket—a 5v-only socket, because all the original Pentium processors run on 5v. This socket will accept the original Pentium 60 MHz or 66 MHz processor, as well as the Overdrive processor.

Figure 6.5 shows the pinout specification of Socket 4.

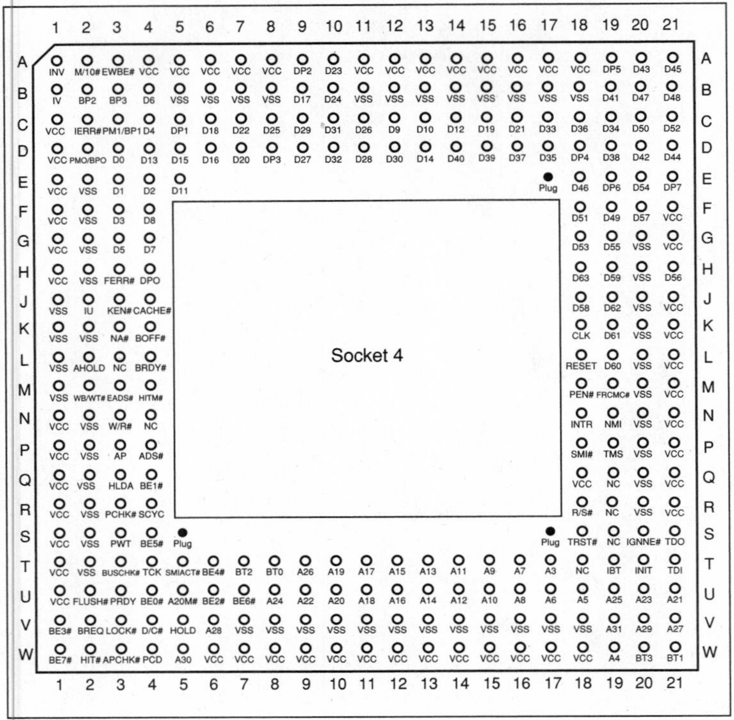

Fig. 6.5

273-pin Intel Socket 4 configuration.

Somewhat amazingly, the original Pentium 66 MHz processor consumes up to 3.2 amps of 5v power (16 watts), not including power for a standard active heat sink (fan), whereas the 66 MHz Overdrive processor that will replace it consumes a maximum 2.7 amps (13.5 watts), including about 1 watt to drive the fan. Even the original 60 MHz Pentium processor consumes up to 2.91 amps at 5v (14.55 watts). It may seem strange that the replacement processor, which likely will be twice as fast, will consume less power than the original, but this has to do with the manufacturing processes used for the original and Overdrive processors.

Although both processors will run on 5v, the original Pentium processor was created with a circuit size of 0.8 micron, making that processor much more power-hungry than the newer 0.6-micron circuits used in the Overdrive and the other Pentium processors. Shrinking the circuit size is one of the best ways to decrease power consumption. Although the Overdrive processor for Pentium-based systems indeed will draw less power than the original processor, additional clearance may have to be allowed for the active heat sink (fan) assembly that is mounted on top. As in other Overdrive processors with built-in fans, the power to run the fan will be drawn directly from the chip socket, so no separate power-supply is required for connection. Also, the fan will be easy to replace, should it ever fail.

When Intel redesigned the Pentium processor to run at 90 and 100 MHz, the company went to a 0.6-micron manufacturing process as well as 3.3v operation. This change resulted in lower power consumption: only 3.25 amps at 3.3v (10.725 watts). Therefore, the 100 MHz Pentium processor can use far less power than even the original 60 MHz version.

The Pentium 90/100 processors actually have 296 pins, although they plug into the official Intel Socket 5 design, which calls for a total 320 pins. The additional pins will be used by what officially is called the Future Pentium Overdrive Processor. This socket has the 320 pins configured in a Staggered Pin Grid Array, in which the individual pins are staggered for tighter clearance.

Figure 6.6 shows the standard pinout for Socket 5.

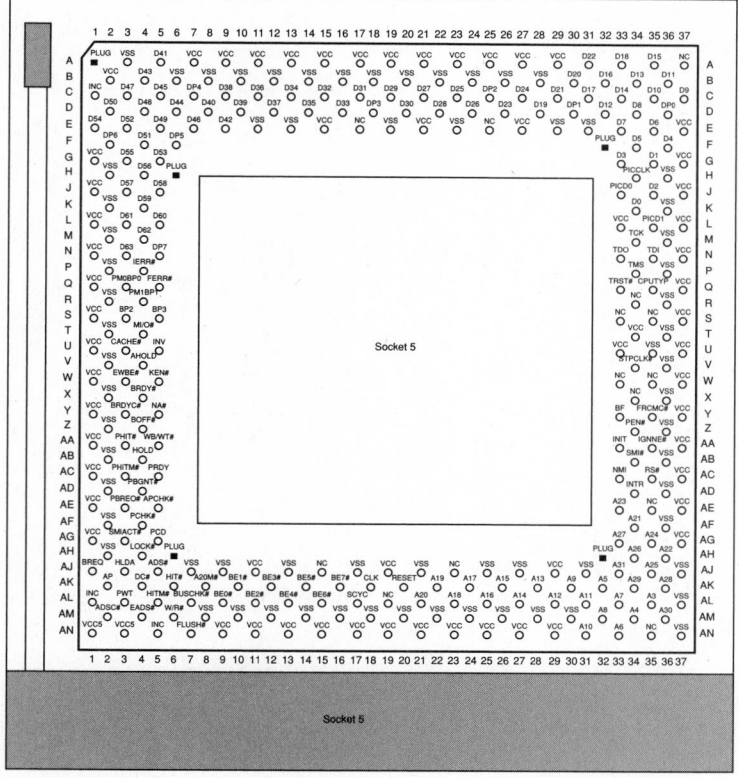

Fig. 6.6
320-pin Intel Socket 5 configuration.

The Future Pentium Overdrive Processor that eventually will use this socket will have an active heat sink (fan) assembly that will draw power directly from the chip socket. Intel has stated that this chip will require a maximum 4.33 amps of 3.3v to run the chip (14.289 watts) and 0.2 amp of 5v power to run the fan (1 watt), which means total power consumption of 15.289 watts. This amount is less power than the original 66 MHz Pentium processor requires, yet it runs a chip that is likely to be as much as four times faster!

The last socket is the newest design, which was created especially for the DX4 and the DX4 (Pentium) Overdrive Processor. Socket 6 basically is a slightly redesigned version of Socket 3, which has an additional two pins plugged for proper chip keying. Socket 6 has 235 pins and will accept only 3.3v 486 or Overdrive processors. Currently, this means that Socket 6 will accept only the DX4 and the DX4 (Pentium) Overdrive Processor. Because this socket provides only 3.3v, and because the only processors that plug into it are designed to operate on 3.3v, no chance exists that potentially damaging problems will occur, like those with the Socket 3 design. Most new 486-class systems that come with DX4 chips initially will use Socket 6. Figure 6.7 shows the Socket 6 pinout.

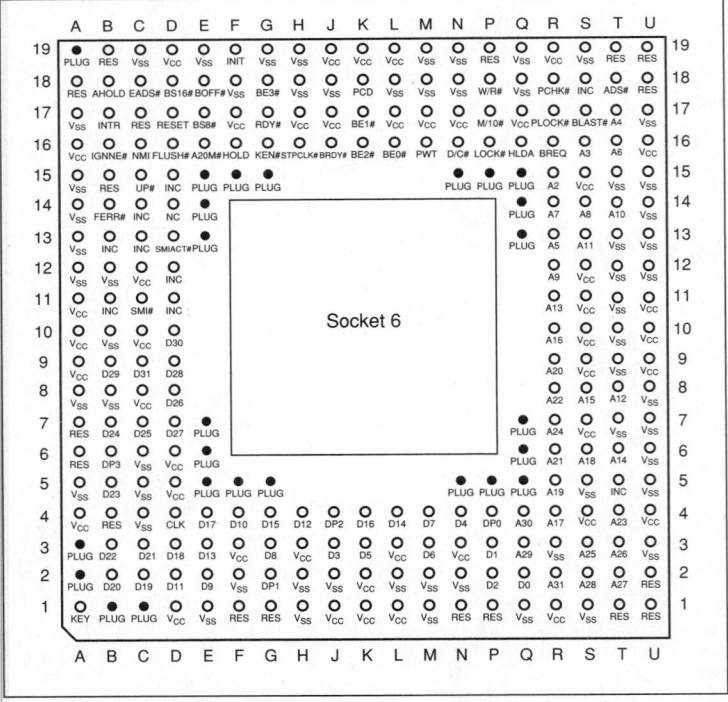

Fig. 6.7
235-pin Intel Socket 6 configuration.

The DX4 100 MHz processor can draw a maximum 1.45 amps of 3.3v (4.785 watts). The DX4 (Pentium) Overdrive Processor that eventually will replace that processor will draw a maximum 3.0 amps at 3.3v (9.9 watts) and 0.2 amp at 5v (1 watt) to run the fan, for a total 10.9 watts. Like all the other Overdrive processors that have active heat sink/fan assemblies, the processor has an easy-to-remove fan that can be replaced should it ever fail.

Overdrive Processor Installation. You can upgrade almost any system with an Overdrive processor. The most difficult aspect of the installation is simply having the correct Overdrive processor for your system. Currently, 486 Overdrive processors (which really are DX2 processors) are available for replacing 486SX and 486DX processors. The following table lists all the current and future Overdrive processors with their official Intel designations.

Processor Designation	Replaces	Socket	Heat Sink	Max. Power
486SX Overdrive	486SX	Socket 1	Passive	6 watts
486DX Overdrive	486DX	Socket 1	Passive	6 watts
486DX Overdrive	486DX	168-pin*	Passive	6 watts
Pentium Overdrive	486DX2	Socket 2 or 3	Active	12.5 watts
DX4 Overdrive	486DX4	Socket 3 or 6	Active	10.9 watts
Overdrive for Pentium	Pentium 60/66	Socket 4	Active	13.5 watts
Future Pentium Overdrive	Pentium 90/100	Socket 5	Active	15.289 watts

The 168-pin version is designed for the original 486DX socket, which is slightly different from the official Socket 1 design.

Three types of system configurations support the original 486 Overdrive (really DX2) processors:

- 486SX (Socket 1)
- 486DX (Socket 1)
- 486DX with standard 168-pin socket

Although Intel labels the Overdrive processors for SX or DX systems with a Socket 1 design, technically, the processors are exactly the same. The 168-pin version was specially created for systems that do not have the Socket 1 design, because it was created after the original 486DX systems were on the market. Many older 486DX systems will need this version of the Overdrive processor, which actually has the same pinout that is sold commercially as the DX2 processor, with the exception of the Intel-applied passive heat sink.

These Overdrive chips also are available in different speed ratings. You must select a version that is rated at least as fast as your motherboard will run. An Overdrive chip rated faster than is necessary will cost more but will work well; an Overdrive chip rated at a speed that is less than your motherboard will run will cause the chip to overheat and fail.

Most motherboards are speed-switchable, which means that if you currently have a 25 MHz 486SX system, you can upgrade to the 66 MHz Overdrive (or DX2) processor by first switching your motherboard to 33 MHz operation. If you leave the motherboard set at 25 MHz, the 66 MHz-rated chip would run at 50 MHz, but you would be missing out on potential performance.

To upgrade any 486SX or DX system that uses dual sockets—and therefore has a vacant Socket 1-type Overdrive Processor socket—you simply turn off the system, plug in the proper 169-pin Overdrive Processor, and turn the system back on. With the 169-pin versions designed for Socket 1, putting the processor in is literally impossible unless it is properly oriented with respect to pin 1. If you are using the 168-pin version that does not feature the key orientation pin, you must match the pin 1 indicator on the chip (usually a dot or a notched corner) with the appropriate designation on the socket (also a dot and/or notched corner). If you install the chip out of orientation, you likely will fry it when you power the system up.

To upgrade a system that has only a single processor socket, remove the existing processor and replace it with either a 169-pin (SX) or a 168-pin (DX) Overdrive Processor. If the system uses a ZIF (zero insertion force) socket, this procedure is very easy; otherwise, you must use a pry tool to remove the old chip.

Intel includes a pry-bar chip-extractor tool for removing the primary CPU, if that is necessary. You simply wedge the tool under one side of the chip and then pull to pry the chip partially out of the socket. You repeat this step for each of the chip's four sides. Then you can lift the loose chip out of the system and store it in a static-protective storage box (included with the Overdrive upgrade kit).

After you plug the Overdrive chip in, some systems require you to change jumper or switch settings on the motherboard to activate the chip. If you have an SX system, you also will have to run your system's setup program, because you must inform the CMOS memory that a math coprocessor is present. (Some DX systems also require you to run the setup program.) Intel provides a utility disk that includes a test program to verify that the new chip is installed and functioning correctly.

After verifying that the installation functions correctly, you have nothing more to do. You do not need to reconfigure any of the software on your system for the new chip. The only difference that you should notice is the fact that everything works nearly twice as fast as it did before the upgrade.

Upgrades that use the newer Overdrive chips for Sockets 2 through 6 are likely to be much easier, because these chips almost always go into a ZIF socket and therefore require no tools. In most cases, special configuration pins in the socket and on the new Overdrive chips take care of any jumper settings for you. In some cases, however, you may have to set some jumpers on the motherboard to configure the socket for the new processor.

Overdrive Compatibility Problems. Although you can upgrade most older 486SX or 486DX systems with the Overdrive processors, some exceptions exist. Four factors can make an Overdrive upgrade difficult or impossible:

- BIOS routines that use CPU-dependent timing loops
- Lack of clearance for the Overdrive heat sink (25 MHz and faster)
- Inadequate system cooling
- A 486 CPU that is soldered in rather than socketed

To start with one of the obvious exceptions, you cannot use a DX2/Overdrive process to upgrade a 50 MHz 486DX system, because Intel does not make a DX2 Overdrive that is rated to run at the 100 MHz internal clock rate. In that case, you can perform an upgrade that is not officially authorized by Intel but that works in most cases: purchase a raw DX4 processor and voltage-regulator adapter to install in the 50 MHz 486DX socket. The voltage regulator will have a jumper for configuring the speed of the DX4 to 2x, 2.5x, or 3x operation. In this case, you need to set the jumper to 2x for 100 MHz operation, which is the maximum for which the DX4 100 chip is rated.

Because this upgrade is not officially authorized by Intel, and because Intel does not even sell the DX4 chips through retail channels, Intel provides no warranty. Make sure that the vendor from which you purchase the DX4 chip will take it back in case it does not work.

Systems that come with DX2, DX4, or Pentium chips installed by the system manufacturer also are eligible for future Overdrive upgrades, which may not yet be available.

In some rare cases, problems may occur in systems that should be upgradable but are not. One of these problems is related to the ROM BIOS. A few 486 systems have a BIOS that regulates hardware operations by using timing loops, based on how long it takes the CPU to execute a series of instructions. When the CPU suddenly is running twice as fast, the prescribed timing interval is too short, resulting in improper system operation or even hardware lockups. Fortunately, you usually can solve this problem by upgrading the system's BIOS.

Another problem is related to physical clearance. All Overdrive chips for 25 MHz and faster systems have heat sinks glued or fastened to the top of the chip. The heat sink can add 0.25 inch to 1.2 inches to the top of the chip. This extra height can interfere with other components in the system, especially in small desktop systems and portables. Solutions to this problem must be determined on a case-by-case basis. Sometimes, you can relocate an expansion card or disk drive, or even modify the chassis slightly to increase clearance. In some cases, the interference cannot be resolved, leaving you only the option of running the chip without the heat sink. Needless to say, removing the glued-on heat sink will at best void the warranty provided by Intel and will at worst damage the chip or the system due to overheating. I do not recommend removing the heat sink.

The Overdrive chips can generate up to twice the heat of the chips that they replace. Even with the active heat sink/fan built in to the faster Overdrive chips, some systems do not have enough airflow or cooling capability to keep the Overdrive chip within the prescribed safe operating-temperature range. Small desktop systems or portables are most likely to have cooling problems. Unfortunately, only proper testing can indicate whether a system will have a heat problem. For this reason, Intel has been running an extensive test program to certify systems that are properly designed to handle an Overdrive upgrade.

Finally, some systems have the 486SX or DX chip soldered directly into the motherboard rather than in a socket. This method is used sometimes for cost reasons, because leaving out the socket is cheaper; in most cases, however, the reason is clearance. The IBM P75 portable that I use, for example, has a credit-card-size CPU board that plugs into the motherboard. Because the CPU card is close to one of the expansion slots, to allow for clearance between the 486 chip and heat sink, IBM soldered the CPU directly into the small card, making an Overdrive upgrade nearly impossible unless IBM offers its own upgrade via a new CPU card with the DX2 chip already installed. This situation did not stop me, of course; I desoldered the DX chip and soldered in a pin-compatible 168-pin DX2 processor in its place. I currently am installing a voltage regulator and DX4 processor.

To clarify which systems are tested to be upgradable without problems, Intel has compiled an extensive list of compatible systems. To determine whether a PC is upgradable with an Overdrive processor, contact Intel via its FaxBACK system (see the vendor list in Appendix B) and ask for the Overdrive Processor Compatibility Data documents. These documents list the systems that have been tested with the Overdrive processors and indicate which other changes you may have to make for the upgrade to work (a newer ROM BIOS or setup program, for example).

One important note about these compatibility lists: if your system is not on the list, the warranty on the Overdrive processor is void. Intel recommends Overdrive upgrades only for systems that are in the compatibility list. The list also includes notes about systems that may require a ROM upgrade, a jumper change, or perhaps a new setup disk.

Some IBM PS/2 486 systems, for example, may require you to use a new Reference Diskette when you install an Overdrive CPU. You can download the latest version of any PS/2 Reference Diskette from the IBM National Support Center Bulletin Board System (NSC BBS), which appears in the vendor list. A wise practice is to download the latest version of the Reference and Diagnostics diskettes for any PS/2 system before attempting a processor upgrade.

Notice that the files on the IBM NSC BBS are compressed Reference and Diagnostics Diskette images. To decompress and extract the files in the appropriate format, you need one or both of the following files:

FILENAME.EXT	Contents
LDF.COM	".DSK" file-extraction program
TGSFX.COM	".TG0" file-extraction program

These files contain programs that will create the Reference or Diagnostics Diskette from the compressed ".DSK" or ".TG0" files.

Pentium Overdrive for DX2 and DX4 Systems. In late 1994, the Pentium Overdrive Processor (code-named P24T) and the DX4 (Pentium) Overdrive Processor will be released. These chips will be virtually identical, except that the first one will run on 5v, whereas the DX4 version will run on 3.3v and consume slightly less power.

The Pentium Overdrive Processor will be required for systems that have a processor socket that follows the Intel Socket 2 specification. This processor also will work in systems that have a Socket 3 design, although the DX4 3.3v version (the DX4 Overdrive Processor) is much more desirable. Just make sure that if you are using a 3.3v processor, you have Socket 3 set for 3.3v operation. Plugging the 3.3v version of the Overdrive chip into the Socket 2 design will be impossible; special key pins will prevent improper insertion. If your system has a 3.3v-only Socket 6 design, the only Overdrive processor to get is the DX4 Overdrive Processor.

Besides a 32-bit Pentium core, these processors will feature increased clock-speed operation, due to internal clock multiplication, and will incorporate an internal Write-Back cache (standard with the Pentium). In essence, these Overdrive processors are Pentium SX chips, because they will have all the features of the real Pentium processors except the 64-bit external data bus; the external data bus of these Overdrive chips will be 32 bits instead. Even so, with the improved Pentium core, separate code and Write-Back data caches, higher clock speeds and other enhancements, these processors should nearly double the performance of the systems in which they are installed.

If you are purchasing a 486 motherboard with the idea of performing this Pentium-level upgrade in the future, make sure that your motherboard has a Socket 3 or Socket 6 design so that you can take advantage of the improved 3.3v version of the Pentium Overdrive Processor.

Pentium

On October 19, 1992, Intel announced that the fifth generation of its compatible microprocessor line (code-named P5) would be named the Pentium processor rather than the 586, as everybody had been assuming. Calling the new chip the 586 would have been natural, but Intel discovered that it could not trademark a number designation, and the company wanted to prevent other manufacturers from using the same name for any clone chips that they might develop.

The actual Pentium chip shipped on March 22, 1993. Systems that use these chips were only a few months behind.

The Pentium is fully compatible with previous Intel processors, but it also differs from them in many ways. At least one of these differences is revolutionary: the Pentium features twin data pipelines, which enable it to execute two instructions at the same time. The 486 and all preceding chips can perform only a single instruction at a time. Intel calls the capability to execute two instructions at the same time *superscalar* technology. This technology provides additional performance compared with the 486.

II

Primary System Components

The standard 486 chip can execute a single instruction in an average two clock cycles—cut to an average of one clock cycle with the advent of internal clock multiplication used in the DX2 and DX4 processors. With superscalar technology, the Pentium can execute many instructions at a rate of two instructions per cycle. Superscalar architecture usually is associated with high-output RISC (Reduced Instruction Set Computer) chips. The Pentium is one of the first CISC (Complex Instruction Set Computer) chips to be considered to be superscalar. The Pentium is almost like having two 486 chips under the hood. Table 6.11 shows the Pentium processor specifications.

Table 6.11 Pentium Processor Specifications	
Introduced	March 22, 1993 (first generation); March 7, 1994 (second generation)
Maximum rated speeds	60, 66 MHz (first generation); 75, 90, 100 MHz (second generation)
CPU clock multiplier	1x (first generation), 1.5x–2x (second generation)
Register size	32-bit
External data bus	64-bit
Memory address bus	32-bit
Maximum memory	4G
Integral-cache size	8K code, 8K data
Integral-cache type	2-Way Set Associative, Write-Back Data
Burst-mode transfers	Yes
Number of transistors	3.1 million (60/66 MHz), 3.3 million (75 MHz and up)
Circuit size	0.8 micron (60/66 MHz), 0.6 micron (75 MHz and up)
External package	273-pin PGA, 296-pin SPGA
Math coprocessor	Built-in FPU (Floating-Point Unit)
Power management	SMM (System Management Mode), enhanced in second generation
Operating voltage	5v (first generation), 3.3v (second generation)

PGA = Pin Grid Array
SPGA = Staggered Pin Grid Array

The two instruction pipelines within the chip are called the *u- and v-pipes*. The u-pipe, which is the primary pipe, can execute all integer and floating-point instructions. The v-pipe is a secondary pipe that can execute only simple integer instructions and certain floating-point instructions. The process of operating on two instructions simultaneously in the different pipes is called *pairing*. Not all sequentially executing instructions can be paired, and when pairing is not possible, only the u-pipe is used. To optimize the Pentium's efficiency, you can recompile software to allow more instructions to be paired.

The Pentium is 100 percent software-compatible with the 386 and 486, and although all current software will run much faster on the Pentium, many software manufacturers want to recompile their applications to exploit even more of the Pentium's true power. Intel has developed new compilers that will take full advantage of the chip; the company will license the technology to compiler firms so that software developers can take advantage of the superscalar (parallel processing) capability of the Pentium. This optimization is starting to appear in some of the newest software on the market. Optimized software should improve performance by allowing more instructions to execute simultaneously in both pipes.

To minimize stalls in one or more of the pipes, caused by delays in fetching instructions that branch to nonlinear memory locations, the Pentium processor has a Branch Target Buffer (BTB) that employs a technique called *branch prediction*. The BTB attempts to predict whether a program branch will be taken or not and then fetches the appropriate next instructions. The use of branch prediction enables the Pentium to keep both pipelines operating at full speed. The following figure shows the internal architecture of the Pentium processor.

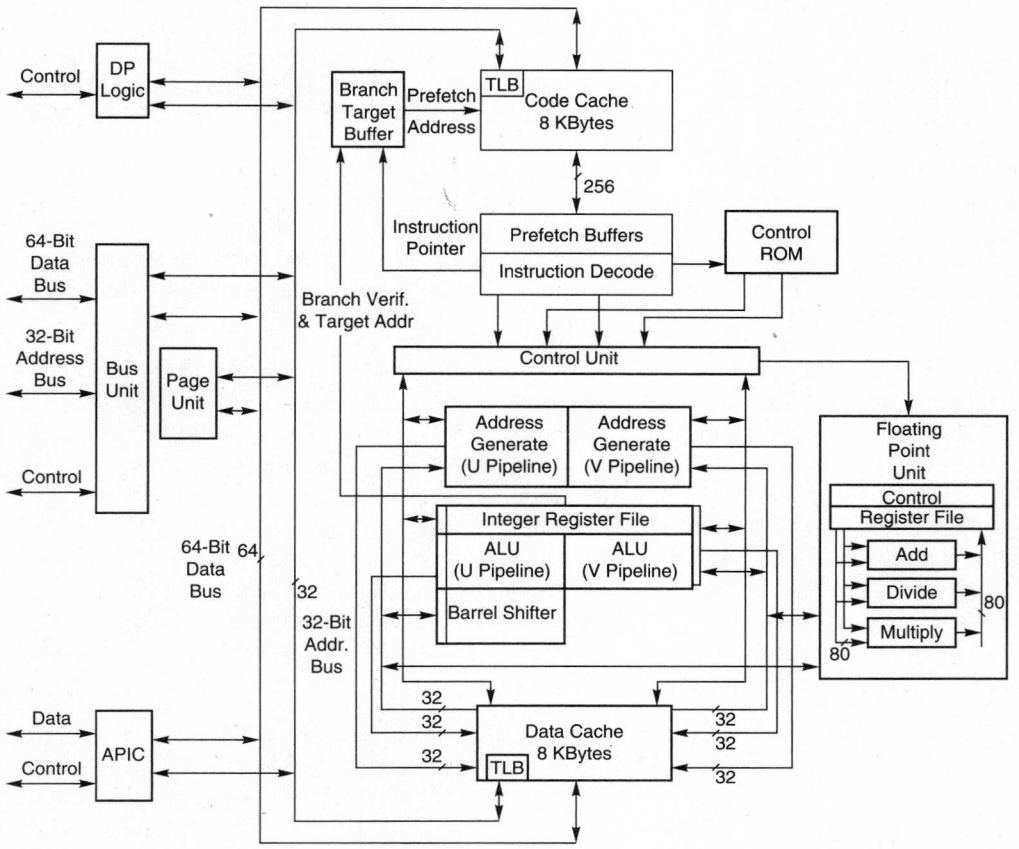

Fig. 6.8
Pentium processor internal architecture.

The Pentium has a 32-bit address bus width, giving it the same 4G memory-addressing capabilities as the 386DX and 486 processors. But the Pentium expands the data bus to 64 bits, which means that it can move twice as much data into or out of the CPU compared with a 486 of the same clock speed. The 64-bit data bus requires that system memory be accessed 64 bits wide, which means that each bank of memory is 64 bits.

On most motherboards, memory is installed via SIMMs (Single In-Line Memory Modules), and SIMMs are available in 9-bit-wide and 36-bit-wide versions. Most Pentium systems use the 36-bit-wide (32 data bits plus 4 parity bits) SIMMs—4 of these SIMMs per bank of memory. Most Pentium motherboards have 4 of these 36-bit SIMM sockets, providing for a total two banks of memory.

Even though the Pentium has a 64-bit data bus that transfers information 64 bits at a time into and out of the processor, the Pentium has only 32-bit internal registers. As instructions are being processed internally, they are broken down into 32-bit instructions and data elements, and processed in much the same way as in the 486. Some people thought that Intel was misleading them by calling the Pentium a 64-bit processor, but 64-bit transfers do indeed take place. Internally, however, the Pentium has 32-bit registers that are fully compatible with the 486.

The Pentium has two separate internal 8K caches, compared with a single 8K or 16K cache in the 486. The cache-controller circuitry and the cache memory are embedded in the CPU chip. The cache mirrors the information in normal RAM by keeping a copy of the data and code from different memory locations. The Pentium cache also can hold information to be written to memory when the load on the CPU and other system components is less. (The 486 makes all memory writes immediately.)

The separate code and data caches are organized in a two-way set associative fashion, with each set split into lines of 32 bytes each. Each cache has a dedicated Translation Lookaside Buffer (TLB), which translates linear addresses to physical addresses. You can configure the data cache as Write-Back or Write-Through on a line-by-line basis. When you use the Write-Back capability, the cache can store write operations as well as reads, further improving performance over read-only Write-Through mode. Using Write-Back mode results in less activity between the CPU and system memory—an important improvement, because CPU access to system memory is a bottleneck on fast systems. The code cache is an inherently write-protected cache, because it contains only execution instructions and not data, which is updated. Because burst cycles are used, the cache data can be read or written very quickly.

Systems based on the Pentium can benefit greatly from *secondary processor caches* (Level 2), which usually consist of up to 512K or more of extremely fast (20 ns or less) Static RAM (SRAM) chips. When the CPU fetches data that is not already available in its internal processor (Level 1) cache, wait states slow the CPU. If the data already is in the secondary processor cache, however, the CPU can go ahead with its work without pausing for wait states.

The Pentium uses a BiCMOS (Bipolar Complementary Metal Oxide Semiconductor) process and superscalar architecture to achieve the level of performance expected from the new chip. BiCMOS adds about 10 percent to the complexity of the chip design, but adds about 30 to 35 percent better performance without a size or power penalty. CMOS designs are running out of bandwidth at 66 MHz, and although CMOS can be made faster, a BiCMOS design provides room to go to 100 or 150 MHz and beyond. Intel probably will use the BiCMOS process in all future chip generations beyond the Pentium.

All Pentium processors are SL Enhanced, meaning that they incorporate the System Management Mode (SMM) to provide full control of power-management features, which helps reduce power consumption. The second-generation Pentium processors (75 MHz and faster) incorporate a more advanced form of SMM that includes processor clock control, which allows you to throttle the processor up or down to control power use. With these more advanced Pentium processors, you even can stop the clock, putting the processor in a state of suspension that requires very little power. The second-generation Pentium processors run on 3.3v power (instead of 5v), reducing power requirements and heat generation even further.

The Pentium, like the 486, contains an internal math coprocessor or Floating-Point Unit (FPU). The FPU in the Pentium has been rewritten and performs significantly better than the FPU in the 486, yet it is fully compatible with the 486 and 387 math coprocessor. The Pentium FPU is estimated to be 2 to as much as 10 times faster than the FPU in the 486. In addition, the two standard instruction pipelines in the Pentium provide two units to handle standard integer math. (The math coprocessor handles only more complex calculations.) Other processors, such as the 486, have only a single standard execution pipe and one integer-math unit.

First-Generation Pentium Processor. Currently, the Pentium is available in two designs, each with several versions. The first-generation design is available in 60 and 66 MHz processor speeds. This design uses a 273-pin PGA form factor and runs on 5v power. In this design, the processor runs at the same speed as the motherboard—in other words, a 1x clock is used.

The first-generation Pentium was created through an 0.8-micron BiCMOS process. Unfortunately, this process, combined with the 3.1 million transistor count, resulted in a die that was overly large and complicated to manufacture. As a result, reduced yields kept the chip in short supply; Intel could not make them fast enough. The 0.8-micron process was criticized by other manufacturers, including Motorola and IBM, which had been using 0.6-micron technology for their most advanced chips. The huge die and 5v operating voltage caused the 66 MHz versions to consume up to an incredible 3.2 amps or 16 watts of power, resulting in a tremendous amount of heat—and problems in some systems that did not employ conservative design techniques. Often, the system required a separate fan to blow on the processor, keeping it cool.

Much of the criticism leveled at Intel for the first-generation Pentium was justified. Some people realized that the first-generation design was just that; they knew that new Pentium versions, made in a more advanced manufacturing process, were coming. Many of those people (including the author of this book) advised against purchasing any Pentium system until the second-generation version became available.

A cardinal rule of computing is never to buy the first generation of any processor. Although you can wait forever, because something better always will be on the horizon, a little waiting is worthwhile in some cases.

Second-Generation Pentium Processor. Intel announced the second-generation Pentium on March 7, 1994. This new processor was introduced in 90 and 100 MHz versions, with a 75 MHz version for laptop and portable systems in development. The second-generation Pentium uses 0.6-micron BiCMOS technology to shrink the die and reduce power consumption. Additionally, these new processors run on 3.3v power. The 100 MHz version consumes a maximum 3.25 amps of 3.3v power, which equals only 10.725 watts. The slower 90 MHz version uses only 2.95 amps of 3.3v power, which is only 9.735 amps. The 75 MHz version probably will use about 6 watts of power and will function reasonably well in laptop and portable systems that run on batteries.

The second-generation Pentium processors come in a 296-pin SPGA (Staggered Pin Grid Array) form factor that is physically incompatible with the first-generation versions. The only way to upgrade from the first generation to the second is to replace the motherboard. The second-generation Pentium processors also have 3.3 million transistors— more than the earlier chips. The extra transistors exist because additional clock-control SL enhancements were added, as were an on-chip Advanced Programmable Interrupt Controller (APIC) and dual processor interface.

The APIC and dual processor interface are responsible for orchestrating dual-processor configurations in which two second-generation Pentium chips can process on the same motherboard simultaneously. Many of the new Pentium motherboards will come with dual Socket 5 specification sockets, which fully support the multiprocessing capability of the new chips. Already, software support for what usually is called Symmetric Multi-Processing (SMP) is being integrated into operating systems such as Windows and OS/2.

The second-generation Pentium processors use clock-multiplier circuitry to run the processor at speeds faster than the bus. The 90 MHz Pentium processor can run at 1.5 times the bus frequency, which normally is 60 MHz. The 100 MHz Pentium processor can run at a 1.5x clock in a system using a 66 MHz bus speed or at 2x clock on a motherboard that is running at 50 MHz. The future 75 MHz version reportedly also will use the 1.5x clock and, therefore, run on 50 MHz motherboards.

Currently, running the motherboard faster than 66 MHz is impractical because of memory and local-bus performance constraints. The fastest Pentium systems would combine the 66 MHz motherboard operation with a 1.5x clock and 100 MHz processor operation. If you think that 1.5 times 66 equals 99 and not 100, you may be right, but in nearly all cases, 66 MHz operation really means 66.6666 MHz actual speed.

Now that the second-generation Pentium processors have arrived, the time is right to purchase a Pentium system. The ideal system uses the second-generation 100 MHz processor with a 66 MHz motherboard.

Make sure that your Pentium motherboard includes two 320-pin processor sockets that fully meet the Intel 320-pin Socket 5 specification. These sockets enable you to add a second Pentium processor to take advantage of SMP (Symmetric Multi-Processing) support in the newer operating systems.

Also make sure that the motherboard can be jumpered or somehow reconfigured for 66 MHz operation, which will enable you to take advantage of future Pentium Overdrive processors that will support the higher motherboard clock speeds.

These simple recommendations will enable you to perform several dramatic upgrades without changing the entire motherboard.

IBM (Intel-Licensed) Processors

For many years, IBM and Intel have had a very close relationship, especially considering the fact that IBM is one of Intel's largest customers. The companies often enter into agreements to exchange technology and information. One such agreement involves the licensing of Intel's processors; IBM has a license to produce several of the Intel processors.

In a licensing agreement, Intel shares with IBM the original mask, or design, of the chip. A CPU chip mask, which is the photographic blueprint of the processor, is used to etch the intricate signal pathways into a silicon chip. Using this mask, IBM can produce the chip as Intel designed it or make modifications in the basic design. Normally, IBM must also share with Intel any modifications that it makes.

Restrictions often exist in the way that IBM can market these Intel-derived chips. Other manufacturers (such as AMD, Harris, and Siemens) licensed several of the older Intel processors up through the 286, but no manufacturer other than IBM has licensed the 386 and newer processor masks. The 386 and newer chips produced by companies other than Intel and IBM are reverse-engineered without Intel's blessing. In fact, Intel has been involved in drawn-out legal battles with several of the clone-processor manufacturers.

Several years ago, IBM licensed the 386 processor mask. The company since has produced several variations that include modifications of the basic Intel design, including some versions that also carry a 486 designation. Some of the IBM processors have few design changes; others have major differences that make the chip faster, less power-hungry, or both. Table 6.12 summarizes the IBM processors that are derived from Intel masks.

IBM SLC Processors

The IBM SLC processors are enhanced versions of the Intel 386SX that offer greater performance and lower power consumption. The SLC processors, which are based on the Intel 386SX mask, have the physical form factor and pinout of the 386SX, with some of the unused pins now being used for cache control.

Table 6.12   IBM Processor Specifications

Processor	CPU Clock	Std. Voltage	Internal Register Size	Data Bus Width	Address Bus Width
386 SLC	1x	5v	32-bit	16-bit	24-bit
486 SLC	1x	3.3v	32-bit	16-bit	24-bit
486 SLC2	2x	3.3v	32-bit	16-bit	24-bit
486 BL2	2x	3.3v	32-bit	32-bit	32-bit
486 BL3	3x	3.3v	32-bit	32-bit	32-bit

FPU = Floating-Point Unit (math coprocessor)

The IBM-enhanced chips have some 486 features (including the internal cache) and perform as well as, or even better than, a 486SX at a much lower cost. IBM states that the 386SLC chip is as much as 80 percent faster than the standard 386SX chip, which means that a 20 MHz 386SLC can outperform a 33 MHz 386DX system. The first system to use any of these custom IBM processors was the PS/2 Model 57; these processors now are used in other manufacturers' systems as well.

The SLC processors are often criticized for having only a 16-bit data bus and a 24-bit address bus. The address bus allows access to only 16M of memory, which is fine for most users. Users who need more memory, however, should look to the IBM Blue Lightning (BL) or to the Intel 486 processors and beyond, which provide a full 32 bits of memory addressing.

Although the SLC processors have only a 16-bit data bus, these processors still outperform many 32-bit chips because of the large (8K or 16K) internal cache. In fact, the 16K cache in the 486SLC performed so well that they changed the designation of the chip to 486. This chip performs about as well as an Intel 486 chip running at equal clock rates, even though the IBM version is only 16 bits and the Intel version is 32 bits. Because all the SLC chips have the full 486 instruction set, including the cache-control instructions, the designation is accurate.

The SLC2 version runs at twice the system speed (clock-doubled) and yet costs less than the standard Intel 486 chips while providing greater performance. You can find the 486SLC2 processor in many bargain-priced motherboards that offer nearly the performance of the Intel 486SX2 and DX2 processors for much less money. Although the IBM processors do not have a built-in math coprocessor, as some of the Intel processors do, most of the motherboards sold with the IBM processors include an Intel or Intel-compatible 387SX math coprocessor.

Blue Lightning Processors

The IBM BL (Blue Lightning) processors are based on the 386DX mask and are full 32-bit processors. These processors also support a full 32-bit memory addressing scheme, which means that they can support the same 4G memory as the Intel 486 processors.

Maximum Memory	Integral Cache	Burst Mode	Integral FPU	No. of Transistors	Date Introduced
16M	8K	No	No	955,000	October 1991
16M	16K	No	No	1,349,000	1992
16M	16K	No	No	1,349,000	June 1992
4G	16K	No	No	1,400,000	1993
4G	16K	No	No	1,400,000	1993

The IBM Blue Lightning was the first processor to run in clock-tripled mode, which is available in 25/75 MHz and 33/100 MHz versions. Notice that most 33 MHz systems actually run at 33.33 MHz, so a clock-tripled system effectively would run at 100 MHz.

All the IBM processors fully support power-management capabilities, and all of them are considered to be low-power (or green) processors. Due to their low power consumption and low-voltage design, these processors often are used in systems that meet the EPA Energy Star certification program, which sets standards for energy conservation and low power consumption in PC systems.

The SLC2 and BL processors are low-power units that run on 3.3 volts, due in part to IBM's superior chip-fabrication facilities. IBM reduced the die size and power consumption greatly by going to a 0.6-micron process for these chips. (This number refers to the minimum individual feature size on the chip mask. Intel did not use the a 0.6-micron process until the DX4 and Pentium chips were introduced.)

The original agreement with Intel was intended to prevent IBM from marketing its processors in the open market in competition with Intel. The agreement specifies that IBM cannot sell processors individually, but only as parts of modules. This restriction essentially means that the chip must be mounted on a circuit board of some type—which actually caused IBM to enter the motherboard and upgrade-board business.

Several companies have designed motherboards and processor upgrade boards that use the low-cost IBM processors. These boards are manufactured by IBM, but they often are designed by the companies for whom IBM makes them. Among the most popular of these motherboards are the Alaris motherboards, which use the IBM processors and an AMI BIOS; IBM manufactures these boards at its manufacturing plant in Charlotte, North Carolina.

It is important to note that for any of these products, IBM is acting as a subcontractor to the company that is considered to be the manufacturer; IBM is not responsible for the design, sales, or support of the products. Support must come from the (so-called) manufacturer, not from IBM.

Intel-Compatible Processors

Several companies—mainly AMD and Cyrix—have developed new processors
that are compatible with one or more of the Intel processors. These chips are fully
Intel-compatible, which means that they emulate every processor instruction in the
Intel chips. Most of the chips are pin-compatible, which means that they can be used in
any system designed to accept an Intel processor; others require a custom motherboard
design. Any hardware or software that works on Intel-based PCs will work on PCs made
with these third-party CPU chips.

AMD and Cyrix have developed their own versions of the Intel 386 and 486 processors
in a variety of speeds and configurations.

Cyrix markets a chip called the 486DRx2, which, the company states, can be used as a
direct replacement for a 386 chip in existing systems. Although the Cyrix chip lacks
some of the important features of the Intel 486, it gives a 386-based system many of the
benefits of the 486.

Math Coprocessors

The next several sections cover the math coprocessor. Each central processing unit
designed by Intel (and cloned by other companies) can use a math-coprocessor chip,
although the Pentium and 486 chips have a built-in math coprocessor. Coprocessors
provide hardware for floating-point math, which otherwise would create an excessive
drain on the main CPU. Math chips speed your computer's operation only when you
are running software that is designed to take advantage of the coprocessor.

Math chips (as coprocessors sometimes are called) can perform high-level mathematical
operations—long division, trigonometric functions, roots, and logarithms, for example—
at 10 to 100 times the speed of the corresponding main processor. Math chips also are
more accurate in these calculations than are the integer-math units built into the primary CPU. The integer units in the primary CPU work with real numbers, so they perform addition, subtraction, and multiplication operations. The primary CPU is designed
to handle such computations; these operations are not offloaded to the math chip.

The instruction set of the math chip is different from that of the primary CPU. A program
must detect the existence of the coprocessor and then execute instructions written explicitly for that coprocessor; otherwise, the math coprocessor draws power and does nothing
else. Fortunately, most modern programs that can benefit from the use of the coprocessor
correctly detect and use the coprocessor. These programs usually are math-intensive programs: spreadsheet programs; database applications; statistical programs; and some graphics programs, such as computer-aided design (CAD) software. Word processing programs
do not benefit from a math chip and therefore are not designed to use one.

Table 6.13 summarizes the coprocessors available for the Intel family of processors.

Table 6.13 Math Coprocessor Summary	
Processor	**Coprocessor**
8086	8087
8088	8087
286	287
386SX	387SX
386SL	387SX
386SLC	387SX
486SLC	387SX
486SLC2	387SX
386DX	387DX
486SX	487SX, DX2/Overdrive*
487SX*	Built-in FPU
486SX2	DX2/Overdrive**
486DX	Built-in FPU
486DX2	Built-in FPU
486DX4	Built-in FPU
Pentium	Built-in FPU

FPU = Floating-Point Unit
*The 487SX chip is a modified pinout 486DX chip with the math coprocessor enabled. When you plug in a 487SX chip, it disables the 486SX main processor and takes over all processing. This chip has been discontinued and is replaced by the DX2/Overdrive processor.
**The DX2/Overdrive is equivalent to the SX2 with the addition of a functional FPU.

Within each 8087 group, the maximum speed of the math chips vary. A suffix digit after the main number, as shown in table 6.14, indicates the maximum speed at which a system can run a math chip.

Table 6.14 Maximum Math-Chip Speeds	
Part	**Speed**
8087	5 MHz
8087-3	5 MHz
8087-2	8 MHz
8087-1	10 MHz
80287	6 MHz
80287-6	6 MHz
80287-8	8 MHz
80287-10	10 MHz

The 387 math coprocessors, as well as the 486 or 487 and Pentium processors, always indicate their maximum speed rating in MHz in the part-number suffix. A 486DX2-66, for example, is rated to run at 66 MHz. Some processors incorporate clock multiplication, which means that they may run at different speeds compared with the rest of the system.

The performance increase in programs that use the math chip can be dramatic—usually, a geometric increase in speed occurs. If the primary applications that you use can take advantage of a math coprocessor, you should upgrade your system to include one.

Most systems that use the 386 or earlier processors are socketed for a math coprocessor as an option, but they do not include a coprocessor as standard equipment. A few systems on the market don't even have a socket for the coprocessor because of cost and size considerations. Usually, these systems are low-cost or portable systems, such as older laptops, the IBM PS/1, and the PCjr. For more specific information about math coprocessors, see the discussions of the specific chips—8087, 287, 387, and 487SX— in the following sections.

Table 6.15 shows some of the specifications of the various math coprocessors.

Table 6.15	Intel Math Coprocessor Specifications				
Name	**Power Consumption**	**Case Min. Temp.**	**Case Max. Temp.**	**No. of Transistors**	**Date Introduced**
8087	3 watts	0°C, 32°F	85°C, 185°F	45,000	1980
287	3 watts	0°C, 32°F	85°C, 185°F	45,000	1982
287XL	1.5 watts	0°C, 32°F	85°C, 185°F	40,000	1990
387SX	1.5 watts	0°C, 32°F	85°C, 185°F	120,000	1988
387DX	1.5 watts	0°C, 32°F	85°C, 185°F	120,000	1987

Most often, you can learn what CPU and math coprocessor are installed in a particular system by checking the system documentation. The following section examines the Intel family of CPUs and math coprocessors in more detail.

8087 Coprocessor

Intel introduced the 8086 processor in 1976. The math coprocessor that was paired with the chip—the 8087—often was called the numeric data processor (NDP), the math coprocessor, or simply the math chip. The 8087 is designed to perform high-level math operations at many times the speed and accuracy of the main processor. The primary advantage of using this chip is the increased execution speed in number-crunching programs, such as spreadsheet applications. Using the 8087 has several minor disadvantages, however, including software support, cost, power consumption, and heat production.

The primary disadvantage of installing the 8087 chip is that you notice an increase in speed only in programs that are written to use this coprocessor—and then not in all operations. Only math-intensive programs such as spreadsheet programs, statistical programs, CAD software, and engineering software support the chip. Even then, the effects vary from application to application, and support is limited to specific areas. For example, versions of Lotus 1-2-3 that support the coprocessor do not use the coprocessor for common operations such as addition, subtraction, multiplication, and division.

Applications that usually do not use the 8087 at all include word processing programs, telecommunications software, database programs, and presentation-graphics programs.

To test the speed capabilities of the 8087 math coprocessor, two spreadsheets were created, each with 8,000 cells. The first spreadsheet used simple math tasks—addition, subtraction, multiplication, and division—split evenly among the 8,000 cells. The second spreadsheet used high-level math operations—including formulas that used SQRT, SIN, COS, and TAN calculations—throughout the 8,000 cells. The following table shows the recalculation times.

Spreadsheet	XT without 8087	XT with 8087
Sheet 1 (standard math)	21 seconds	21 seconds
Sheet 2 (high-level math)	195 seconds	21 seconds

The addition of an 8087 to a standard IBM XT did nothing for the spreadsheet that contained only simple math, but the 8087 calculated the spreadsheet that contained high-level math in one-tenth the time. (This also was the time it took both systems to calculate the spreadsheet that contained only simple math.)

If your spreadsheets consist of nothing but addition, subtraction, multiplication, and division calculations, before buying a math chip, you need to know whether the program that you use takes advantage of the math chip for simple calculations. Many new programs are designed to support the 8087 chip for these operations. Installing an 8087 can extend the useful life of a PC or XT, because the chip closes some of the performance gaps between PC- or XT-type computers and AT-type computers. In short, the chip is an asset whenever the software supports it.

The 8087 chip is inexpensive, costing as little as $50. Remember to purchase a chip with the correct maximum-speed rating; the 8087 must be rated to run at the same rate of speed as the CPU or faster, because the main CPU and the coprocessor must run in synchronization. In an IBM XT, for example, the 8088 and the 8087 run at 4.77 MHz. Look in your system documentation to find the speed at which your system will run the math chip.

Math chips are quite power-hungry because of the number of transistors included. A typical 8088 has only about 29,000 transistors, but the 8087 has about 45,000. (Nearly all the 45,000 transistors are dedicated to math functions, which is why the 8087 can perform math operations so well.) This figure translates to nearly double the calculating horsepower, as well as double the electrical power drain. In a heavily loaded PC, the 8087 could be the straw that breaks the camel's back: the power supply might be insufficient for the increased load. The chip draws nearly one-half amp of current.

Another problem is the amount of heat generated: 3 watts. A 75 MHz 486DX4 with 1.6 million transistors uses only 3.63 watts. This heat level generated in such a small chip can raise the temperature to more than 180° Fahrenheit. (The approved maximum temperature for most 8087s is 185°F.) For this reason, math coprocessor chips usually are made of ceramic.

Power and heat are not problems in XT or portable systems, because these systems are built to handle these situations. The PC, however, usually requires a higher-watt power supply with a more powerful cooling fan to handle the load. Power supplies are covered later in this chapter.

80287 Coprocessor

Imagine that two company employees have computers. One user has an IBM XT, and the other has a 6 MHz AT. Both employees use Lotus 1-2-3 as their primary application. The AT user delights in being able to outcalculate the XT user by a factor of three. The XT user purchases an 8087 math chip for $50 and installs it. The XT user then finds that the XT calculates many spreadsheets 10 times faster than before—or more than three times as fast as the AT.

This performance frustrates the AT user, who thought that the AT was the faster system. The AT user, therefore, purchases an 80287 for $50 and discovers that the AT is merely equal in speed to the XT for many spreadsheet recalculations. In a few situations, however, the XT may still outrun the AT.

Of course, the AT user wants to know why the 80287 chip did not make the AT superior to the XT, by a significant margin, for spreadsheet recalculations. (For "normal" processing, which does not use the math chip's high-level math functions, the AT holds its performance edge.) The answer is in the 80287 chip. For various design reasons, the 8087 chip has much more effect on the speed of the PC and XT than the 80287 has on the AT.

The 80287, internally, is the same math chip as the 8087, although the pins used to plug them into the motherboard are different. Because the AT has a healthy power supply and generous, thermostatically controlled fan cooling, the heat and power problems mentioned in the discussion of the 8087 generally don't apply to the 287. Internally, however, the 80287 and the 8087 operate as though they were identical.

Another reason is that the 80286 and its math chip are *asynchronous*, which means that the chips run at different speeds. The 80287 math chip usually runs at two-thirds the speed of the CPU. In most systems, the 80286 internally divides the system clock by 2 to derive the processor clock. The 80287 internally divides the system-clock frequency by 3. For this reason, most AT-type computers run the 80287 at one-third the system clock rate, which also is two-thirds the clock speed of the 80286. Because the 286 and 287 chips are asynchronous, the interface between the 286 and 287 chips is not as efficient as with the 8088 and 8087.

In summary, the 80287 and the 8087 chips perform about the same at equal clock rates. The original 80287 is not better than the 8087 in any real way—unlike the 80286, which is superior to the 8086 and 8088. In most AT systems, the performance gain that you realize by adding the coprocessor is much less substantial than the same type of upgrade for PC- or XT-type systems or for the 80386.

Some systems run the 80287 and the 8087 at the same speed. PS/2 Models 50, 50 Z, and 60 use circuitry that enables both the 80286 and 80287 to run at 10 MHz. The PS/2 Model 25-286 and 30-286, however, follow the standard AT-type design, in which the 286 runs at 10 MHz and the 287 runs at 6.67 MHz.

You must consult the system documentation to learn the speeds at which your system would run a 287 coprocessor, because the motherboard designers determine these specifications. Table 6.16 shows 80286 and 80287 clock speeds for most AT-type systems.

Table 6.16 80286 and 80287 Clock Speeds (in MHz)		
System Clock	**80286 Clock**	**80287 Clock**
12.00	6.00	4.00
16.00	8.00	5.33
20.00	10.00	6.67
24.00	12.00	8.00
32.00	16.00	10.67

How can you improve this differential in performance gain? One method takes advantage of the fact that the 80286 and the 80287 run asynchronously. You can install an add-in board that uses its own clock signal to drive the 80287 chip and therefore can drive the chip at any speed. Some companies have designed a simple speed-up circuit that includes a crystal and an 8284 clock generator chip, all mounted on special boards, some of which are not much bigger than the 287 socket. This special board, called a *daughterboard*, is plugged into the 287 socket; then the 287 is plugged in on top of the special board. Because such boards separate the crystal and clock generator from the motherboard circuitry, the daughterboard can run the 80287 at any speed you want, up to the maximum rating of the chip—8 MHz, 10 MHz, 12 MHz, or more—without affecting the rest of the system.

You could, for example, add one of these daughterboards to your old 6 MHz AT and run a 287 at 10 MHz. Without the daughterboard, the chip would run at only 4 MHz. The boards are available from many math-coprocessor suppliers. Using these boards is highly recommended if you run math-intensive programs. Remember that this type of speed increase does not apply to systems that use 8087 or 80387 chips, because these systems must run the math coprocessor at the same speed as the main CPU.

Intel has introduced new variations of the 80287 called the 287XL and 287XLT. (The original 287 has been discontinued; only the 287XL and XLT are available today.) The XL version is designed to be a replacement for the standard 287 math coprocessor. The XLT version is functionally identical to the XL but has a plastic leadless chip carrier (PLCC) case, which some laptop systems require.

These redesigned XL chips are patterned after the 387 instead of the 8087. The XL chips consume much less power than the original 287 chips, because they are constructed with CMOS technology. The XL chips perform about 20 percent faster than the original 287 at any clock rate as a result of their improved design. The design improvements extend to the instruction set, which includes 387 trigonometric functions that are not available with older 287 coprocessors.

The XL chips are available at only one speed rating: 12.5 MHz. The chips can be run at lower speeds on slower systems. Unlike the 287 daughterboards, these chips do not increase the clock speed of a math chip.

Many older diagnostics programs incorrectly identify the XL chips because they were designed after the 387 math chips. Some diagnostics simply indicate that the 287XL is a 387; other diagnostics incorrectly show a problem with the math coprocessor if a 287XL is installed. Intel provides a special diagnostics program called CHKCOP (which stands for CHecK COProcessor) that can test all its math coprocessors. You can get this program on disk from Intel's customer-support department or download it from the Intel BBS at (503) 645-6275.

After considering all these issues, if you decide to invest in a 287 chip, remember that only the XL or XLT versions are available now and that they are rated for up to 12.5 MHz operation. Adding the 287 to an AT is a good idea if the software that you use supports the chip. You also should consider using one of the math coprocessor-speedup daughterboards, which will run the newer XL chips at the maximum 12 MHz rating regardless of your system's clock speed. Otherwise, the benefits may not be enough to justify the cost.

80387 Coprocessor

Although the 80387 chips run asynchronously, 386 systems are designed so that the math chip runs at the same clock speed as the main CPU. Unlike the 80287 coprocessor, which was merely an 8087 with different pins to plug into the AT motherboard, the 80387 coprocessor is a high-performance math chip designed specifically to work with the 386.

All 387 chips use a low-power-consumption CMOS design. The 387 coprocessor has two basic designs: the 387DX coprocessor, which is designed to work with the 386DX processor; and the 387SX coprocessor, which is designed to work with the 386SX, SL, or SLC processors.

Originally, Intel offered several speeds for the 387DX coprocessor. But when the company designed the 33 MHz version, a smaller mask was required to reduce the lengths of the signal pathways in the chip. (A *mask* is the photographic blueprint of the processor and is used to etch the intricate signal pathways into a silicon chip.) Intel reduced the feature size from 1.5 to 1 micron. This action reduced the size of the silicon chip by 50 percent.

In addition to the size reduction, other design improvements were engineered into the new mask, resulting in a 20-percent improvement in processing efficiency. The 33 MHz version, therefore, outperformed other versions even at slower clock rates.

At the time, purchasing the 33 MHz version of the 387DX was a good idea (even for a 20 MHz 386 system), because the chip would run 20 percent faster than a 20 MHz 387. In October 1990, however, Intel upgraded the entire 387DX line to the improved mask, resulting in a 20 percent performance boost across the board.

You can easily identify these improved 387DX coprocessors by looking at the 10-digit code below the 387 part number. The older (slower) chips begin this line with the letter *S*, and the improved (faster) chips do not. Recently, Intel discontinued all its 387DX processors except the 33 MHz version, which, of course, always used the new design. (Remember that even though the chip is rated for 33 MHz, it runs at any lower speed.)

The 387SX coprocessors are designed to work specifically with 386SX, SL, or SLC processors. All versions of the 387SX use the improved mask design. When you select a 387SX for your system, be sure to purchase one that is rated at a speed equal to or higher than that of your CPU. Currently, Intel 387SX chips are available at speeds up to 25 MHz.

> **Note**
>
> Because Intel lagged in developing the 387 coprocessor, some early 386 systems were designed with a socket for a 287 coprocessor. Performance levels associated with that union, however, leave much to be desired.

Installing a 387DX is easy, but you must be careful to orient the chip in its socket properly; otherwise, the chip will be destroyed. The most common cause of burned pins on the 387DX is incorrect installation. In many systems, the 387DX is oriented differently from other large chips. Follow the manufacturer's installation instructions carefully to avoid damaging the 387DX; Intel's warranty does not cover chips that are installed incorrectly.

Several manufacturers have developed their own versions of the Intel 387 coprocessors, some of which are touted as being faster than the original Intel chips. The general compatibility record of these chips is very good. Intel has significantly reduced the prices of its own coprocessors, however, which means that these third-party chips usually are only a few dollars cheaper than the Intel version.

When the 387s were introduced, the Intel 33 MHz 387DX chips listed for more than $2,000. Today, you can buy the chip from various suppliers for as little as $90. The cost is so low that many people should consider making this upgrade. If the software that you run supports the chip, the performance gains can be very impressive.

Weitek Coprocessors

In 1981, several Intel engineers formed Weitek Corporation. Weitek has developed math coprocessors for several systems, including those based on Motorola processor designs. Intel originally contracted Weitek to develop a math coprocessor for the Intel 386 CPU, because Intel was behind in its own development of the 387 math coprocessor. The result was the Weitek 1167, a custom math coprocessor that uses a proprietary Weitek instruction set that is incompatible with the Intel 387.

The Weitek 1167 is not a single chip; it is a daughterboard consisting of several chip elements that plug into a special 112-pin Weitek socket. To use the Weitek processors, your system must have the required socket, which is incompatible with the 387 math coprocessor and 486SX processor enhancement sockets. The daughterboard includes a socket for an Intel 387 coprocessor so that both coprocessors can be installed in a system; as a result, software that runs either Weitek or Intel math instructions will work on such a system.

The 1167 was replaced in April 1988 by a single-chip version called the 3167. Many computers, such as the Compaq 386, contain a special socket that enables you to use a Weitek 3167 math coprocessor or an Intel 387DX. This socket has three rows of holes on all four sides. The inner two rows of pins are compatible with the Intel 387DX. If you want to install a 387DX in the special socket, however, you must use extreme caution to orient the chip correctly; otherwise, you could damage both the computer and the 387DX.

Read your system documentation to determine the correct procedure for installing the 387DX in your computer. Some computers, such as the Tandy 4000, use the Weitek socket but do not support the 387DX. Contact your computer manufacturer or dealer for more specific information.

Unfortunately, even if you have the socket for the Weitek processor, your software probably does not support it. As mentioned, your software must contain programming code that makes use of the specific capabilities of a math coprocessor.

Weitek introduced the 4167 coprocessor chip for 486 systems in November 1989. To use the Weitek coprocessor, your system must have the required additional socket. Before purchasing one of the Weitek coprocessors, you should determine whether your software supports it; then you should contact the software company to determine whether the Weitek has a performance advantage over the Intel coprocessor.

80487 Upgrade

The Intel 80486 processor was introduced in late 1989, and systems using this chip appeared during 1990. The 486DX integrated the math coprocessor into the chip.

The 486SX began life as a full-fledged 486DX chip, but Intel actually disabled the built-in math coprocessor before shipping the chip. As part of this marketing scheme, Intel marketed what it called a 487SX math coprocessor. Motherboard manufacturers installed an Intel-designed socket for this so-called 487 chip. In reality, however, the 487SX math chip was a special 486DX chip with the math coprocessor enabled. When you plugged this chip into your motherboard, it disabled the 486SX chip and gave you the functional equivalent of a full-fledged 486DX system.

Perhaps that somewhat strange marketing scheme is responsible for some of the confusion caused by the Intel advertisements that feature a 486SX system with a neon vacancy sign pointing to an empty socket next to the CPU chip. Unfortunately, these ads do not transmit the message properly. Few people seem to understand that the socket next to the CPU in a 486SX system is not a math-coprocessor socket, but an Overdrive socket.

Essentially, systems that have this extra socket have two processor sockets; however, you can use only one of them at any time. When you install a chip in the secondary socket, that chip takes over from the primary processor and puts the original processor to sleep.

Most newer 486SX systems use a surface-mounted PQFP (Plastic Quad Flat Pack) or SQFP (Small Quad Flat Pack) version that is permanently soldered to the motherboard. These systems still have a conventional processor socket of a specific design for new Overdrive processors. These Overdrive chips will contain all processing functions, including the math-coprocessor functions, and will shut down the 486SX when they are installed. Depending on the type of processor socket on the motherboard, you can install a DX2 or DX4 processor, or even a special version of the Pentium chip.

For more information on this subject, see the section on Overdrive processors earlier in this chapter.

Processor Tests

The processor is easily the most expensive chip in the system. Processor manufacturers use specialized equipment to test their own processors, but you have to settle for a little less. The best processor-testing device to which you have access is a system that you know is functional; you then can use the diagnostics available from IBM and other system manufacturers to test the motherboard and processor functions. Most systems mount processors in a socket for easy replacement.

Landmark offers specialized diagnostic software called Service Diagnostics to test various processors. Special versions are available for each processor in the Intel family. If you don't want to purchase this kind of software, you can perform a quick-and-dirty processor evaluation by using the normal diagnostic program supplied with your system.

Because the processor is the brain of a system, most systems don't function with a defective one. If a system seems to have a dead motherboard, try replacing the processor with one from a functioning motherboard that uses the same CPU chip. You may find that the processor in the original board is the culprit. If the system continues to play dead, however, the problem is elsewhere.

Known-Defective Chips

A few system problems are built in at the factory, although these bugs or design defects are rare. By learning to recognize one of these problems, you may avoid unnecessary repairs or replacements. This section describes several known defects in system processors.

Early 8088s. A bug in some early 8088 processors allowed interrupts to occur after a program changed the stack segment register. (An interrupt usually is not allowed until the instruction after the one that changes the stack segment register.) This subtle bug may cause problems in older systems. Most programmers have adopted coding procedures that work around the bug, but you have no guarantee that these procedures exist in all software programs.

Another problem is that the bug may affect the operation of an 8087 math coprocessor. Approximately 200,000 IBM PC units sold during 1981 and 1982 were manufactured with the defective chip.

Originally, in the 8087 math-coprocessor-chip package, IBM always included an 8088 to be installed with the math chip. This practice led to rumors that the parts somehow matched. The rumors were unfounded; IBM had simply found an easy way to prevent machines that used its 8087 chips from using the defective 8088. Because the cost of the chip was negligible, IBM included a bug-free 8088 and eliminated many potential service problems.

You can check the 8088 chip with diagnostic software, or you can identify a good or bad chip by its appearance. If you can open the unit to look at the 8088 chip, the manufacturer and copyright date printed on the chip provide clues about which version you have. An 8088 chip made by a manufacturer other than Intel is bug-free, because Intel began licensing the chip mask to other manufacturers after the bug was corrected. If a chip was manufactured by Intel, older (defective) parts have a 1978 copyright date; newer (good) parts have 1978 and 1981 (or later) copyright dates.

This marking on Intel 8088 chips indicates a chip that has the interrupt bug:

8088

(c)INTEL 1978

The following markings on Intel 8088 chips indicate chips on which the bug is corrected:

8088

(c)INTEL '78 '81

8088

(c)INTEL '78 '83

Many diagnostic programs can identify the chip. You also can identify the chip yourself by using DEBUG, which comes in DOS versions 2.0 and later. Just load DEBUG at the prompt, and enter the commands shown in the following example. The commands that you enter appear in boldface type; the DEBUG screen output is not. XXXX indicates a segment address, which varies from system to system.

A 100

[XXXX:0100] MOV ES,AX

[XXXX:0102] INC AX

[XXXX:0103] NOP

[XXXX:0104

T

AX=0001 BX=0000 CX=0000 DX=0000 SP=FFEE BP=0000 SI=0000 DI=0000

DS=XXXX ES=0000 SS=XXXX CS=XXXX IP=0103 NV UP EI PL NZ NA PO NC

XXXX:0103 90 NOP

—Q

The A 100 command tells DEBUG to assemble some instructions, of which three are entered. The T command then executes a Trace, which normally executes a single instruction, displays the contents of the 8088's registers, and then stops. The Trace command usually executes only one instruction. However, when the instruction is MOV to a segment register, as in this case, the Trace command should execute the second instruction before interrupting the program. The third instruction is a dummy no-operation instruction.

Look at the value shown by DEBUG for the register AX. If AX is equal to 0000, the processor has a bug. If AX is 0001, the second instruction in the test was executed properly, and the chip is good. If the second instruction is executed, DEBUG increments the value of the AX register by 1. In this example, after the Trace is executed, AX equals 0001, which indicates a good chip.

Note

If you try this test on a 286 or higher system, the test will fail; it is valid only for 8088s.

If you have an 8087 and a 4.77 MHz 8088 dated '78 or an 8088 that fails this test, you can get a free replacement 8088. Contact Intel customer support for the replacement. Only 4.77 MHz 8088 chips may need to be upgraded. The 8088-2 and 8088-1 do not require replacement. You also can purchase a replacement 8088 from most chip houses for less than $10. If you suspect that your chip is bad, a replacement is inexpensive insurance.

Early 80386s. Some early 16 MHz Intel 386DX processors had a small bug that you may encounter in troubleshooting what seems to be a software problem. The bug, which apparently is in the chip's 32-bit multiply routine, manifests itself only when you run true 32-bit code in a program such as OS/2 2.x, UNIX/386, or Windows in Enhanced mode. Some specialized 386 memory-management software systems also may invoke this subtle bug, but 16-bit operating systems (such as DOS and OS/2 1.x) probably will not.

The bug usually causes the system to lock up. Diagnosing this problem can be difficult, because the problem generally is intermittent and software-related. Running tests to find the bug is difficult; only Intel, with proper test equipment, can determine whether your chip has a bug. Some programs can diagnose the problem and identify a defective chip, but they cannot identify all defective chips. If a program indicates a bad chip, you certainly have a defective one; if the program passes the chip, you still may have a defective one.

Intel requested that its 386 customers return possibly defective chips for screening, but many vendors did not return them. Intel tested returned chips and replaced defective ones. The known-defective chips later were sold to bargain liquidators or systems houses that wanted chips that would not run 32-bit code. The known-defective chips were stamped with a 16-bit SW Only logo, indicating that they were authorized to run only 16-bit software.

Chips that passed the test, and all subsequent chips produced as bug-free, were marked with a double-sigma ($\Sigma\Sigma$) code, which indicates a good chip. 386DX chips that are not marked with either 16-bit SW Only or the designation have not been tested by Intel and may be defective.

The following marking indicates that a chip has not yet been screened for the defect; it may be either good or bad. Return a chip of this kind to the system manufacturer, which will return a free replacement.

> 80386-16

The following marking indicates that the chip has been tested and has the 32-bit multiply bug. The chip works with 16-bit software (such as DOS) but not with 32-bit, 386-specific software (such as Windows or OS/2).

> 80386-16
>
> 16-bit SW Only

The following mark on a chip indicates that it has been tested as defect-free. This chip fulfills all the capabilities promised for the 80386.

> 80386-16
>
> $\Sigma\Sigma$

This problem was discovered and corrected before Intel officially added DX to the part number. So if you have a chip labeled as 80386DX or 386DX, it does not have this problem.

Another problem with the 386DX can be stated more specifically. When 386-based versions of XENIX or other UNIX implementations are run on a computer that contains a 387DX math coprocessor, the computer locks up under certain conditions. The problem does not occur in the DOS environment, however. For the lockup to occur, all the following conditions must be in effect:

- Demand page virtual memory must be active.

- A 387DX must be installed and in use.

- DMA (direct memory access) must occur.

- The 386 must be in a wait state.

When all these conditions are true at the same instant, the 386DX ends up waiting for the 387DX, and vice versa. Both processors will continue to wait for each other indefinitely. The problem is in certain versions of the 386DX, not in the 387DX math coprocessor.

Intel published this problem (Errata 21) immediately after it was discovered, to inform its OEM customers. At that point, it became the responsibility of each manufacturer to implement a fix in its hardware or software product. Some manufacturers, such as Compaq and IBM, responded by modifying their motherboards to prevent these lockups from occurring.

The Errata 21 problem occurs only in the B Stepping version of the 386DX and not in the later D Stepping version. You can identify the D Stepping version of the 386DX by the letters DX in the part number (for example, 386DX-20). If DX is part of the chip's part number, the chip does not have this problem.

Other Processor Problems

Some other problems with processors and math coprocessors are worth noting.

After you remove a math coprocessor from an AT-type system, you must rerun your computer's SETUP program. Some AT-compatible SETUP programs do not properly unset the math-coprocessor bit. If you receive a Power-On Self Test (POST) error message because the computer cannot find the math chip, you may have to unplug the battery from the system board temporarily. All SETUP information will be lost, so be sure to write down the hard drive type, floppy drive type, and memory and video configurations before unplugging the battery. This information is critical in reconfiguring your computer correctly.

Another strange problem occurs in some IBM PS/2 Model 80 systems when a 387DX is installed. In the following computers, you may hear crackling or beeping noises from the speaker while the computer is running:

- 8580 Model 111, with serial numbers below 6019000
- 8850 Model 311, with serial numbers below 6502022

If you are experiencing this problem, contact IBM for a motherboard replacement.

Heat and Cooling Problems

Heat can be a problem in any high-performance 486 or Pentium system. The Intel DX2/66 consumes about 40 percent more power than a 33 MHz 486DX and generates correspondingly more heat. The Pentium generates even more heat. If your system is based on the DX2 or Pentium chip, you must dissipate the extra thermal energy; the fan inside your computer case may not be able to handle the load.

To cool a system in which processor heat is a problem, you can buy (for less than $20) a special attachment for the CPU chip called a heat sink, which draws heat away from the CPU chip. Many applications may need only a larger standard heat sink with additional or longer fins for a larger cooling area. Several heat-sink manufacturers are listed in Appendix B, the "Vendor List."

II

Primary System Components

I prefer clip-on heat sinks, but some are attached with a special adhesive. In many cases, you need to use a thermal transfer paste even if the heat sink is clipped on. This paste fills any small air gaps between the processor and the heat sink, providing a more effective transfer of heat.

Most of the Overdrive processors that Intel will be introducing over the next few years will have a built-in active heat sink, which includes a fan. Unlike the aftermarket add-on fans, these built-in fans will draw power directly from the processor itself and will not require additional connections.

Summary

This chapter covered what many people consider to be the primary component of a personal computer: the processor. Sometimes also called the Central Processing Unit (CPU) chip, this is the primary chip in the system. This chapter discussed the variety of processors that are available for IBM-compatible systems, including those made by Intel and other vendors. You now should have a much better appreciation of this component, including general functionality and especially how the different processors compare.

Chapter 7

Memory

This chapter looks at memory from both a physical and logical point of view. The chapter discusses the physical chips and SIMMs (Single Inline Memory Modules) that you can purchase and install. The chapter also looks at the logical layout of memory and defines the different areas and uses of these areas from the system's point of view. Because the logical layout and uses are within the "mind" of the processor, memory remains as perhaps the most difficult subject to grasp in the entire PC universe. This chapter contains much useful information that removes the mysteries associated with memory and enables you to get the most out of your system.

The System Logical Memory Layout

The original PC had a total of 1M of addressable memory, and the top 384K of that was reserved for use by the system. Placing this reserved space at the top (between 640K and 1024K instead of at the bottom, between 0K and 640K) led to what today is often called the *conventional memory barrier*. The constant pressures on system and peripheral manufacturers to maintain compatibility by never breaking from the original memory scheme of the first PC has resulted in a system memory structure that is (to put it kindly) a mess. More than a decade after the first PC was introduced, even the newest Pentium-based systems are limited in many important ways by the memory map of the first PCs.

Someone who wants to become knowledgeable about personal computers must at one time or another come to terms with the types of memory installed on their system—the small and large pieces of different kinds of memory, some accessible by software application programs, and some not. The following sections detail the different kinds of memory installed on a modern PC. The kinds of memory covered in the following sections include the following:

- Conventional (Base) memory
- Upper Memory Area (UMA)
- High Memory Area (HMA)
- Extended memory

- Expanded memory (obsolete)

- Video RAM memory

- Adapter ROM and Special Purpose RAM

- Motherboard ROM BIOS

Subsequent sections also cover preventing memory conflicts and overlap, using memory managers to optimize your system's memory, and making better use of memory. In an AT system, the memory map extends beyond the 1M boundary and can continue to 16M on a system based on the 286 or higher processor, or as much as 4G (4,096M) on a 386DX or higher. Any memory past 1M is called *extended memory*.

Figure 7.1 shows the logical address locations for an IBM-compatible system. If the processor is running in Real Mode, then only the first megabyte is accessible. If the processor is in Protected Mode, then the full 16 or 4,096 megabytes are accessible. Each symbol is equal to 1K of memory, each line or segment is 64K, and this map shows the first two megabytes of system memory.

```
      . = Program-accessible memory (standard RAM)
      G = Graphics Mode Video RAM
      M = Monochrome Text Mode Video RAM
      C = Color Text Mode Video RAM
      V = Video ROM BIOS (would be "a" in PS/2)
      a = Adapter board ROM and special-purpose RAM (free UMA space)
      r = Additional PS/2 Motherboard ROM BIOS (free UMA in non-PS/2 systems)
      R = Motherboard ROM BIOS
      b = IBM Cassette BASIC (would be "R" in IBM compatibles)
      h = High Memory Area (HMA), if HIMEM.SYS is loaded.

   Conventional (Base) Memory:

          : 0---1---2---3---4---5---6---7---8---9---A---B---C---D---E---F---
   000000: ................................................................
   010000: ................................................................
   020000: ................................................................
   030000: ................................................................
   040000: ................................................................
   050000: ................................................................
   060000: ................................................................
   070000: ................................................................
   080000: ................................................................
   090000: ................................................................

   Upper Memory Area (UMA):

          : 0---1---2---3---4---5---6---7---8---9---A---B---C---D---E---F---
   0A0000: GGGGGGGGGGGGGGGGGGGGGGGGGGGGGGGGGGGGGGGGGGGGGGGGGGGGGGGGGGGGGGGGG
   0B0000: MMMMMMMMMMMMMMMMMMMMMMMMMMMMMMMMMMCCCCCCCCCCCCCCCCCCCCCCCCCCCCCCCC
          : 0---1---2---3---4---5---6---7---8---9---A---B---C---D---E---F---
   0C0000: VVVVVVVVVVVVVVVVVVVVVVVVVVVVVVVVVaaaaaaaaaaaaaaaaaaaaaaaaaaaaaaaa
   0D0000: aaaaaaaaaaaaaaaaaaaaaaaaaaaaaaaaaaaaaaaaaaaaaaaaaaaaaaaaaaaaaaaa
          : 0---1---2---3---4---5---6---7---8---9---A---B---C---D---E---F---w
```

```
0E0000: rrrrrrrrrrrrrrrrrrrrrrrrrrrrrrrrrrrrrrrrrrrrrrrrrrrrrrrrrrrrrrrr
0F0000: RRRRRRRRRRRRRRRRRRRRRRRRRRRbbbbbbbbbbbbbbbbbbbbbbbbbbbbbRRRRRRRR

Extended Memory:

       : 0---1---2---3---4---5---6---7---8---9---A---B---C---D---E---F---
100000: hhhhhhhhhhhhhhhhhhhhhhhhhhhhhhhhhhhhhhhhhhhhhhhhhhhhhhhhhhhhhhhh

Extended Memory Specification (XMS) Memory:

110000: ..............................................................
120000: ..............................................................
130000: ..............................................................
140000: ..............................................................
150000: ..............................................................
160000: ..............................................................
170000: ..............................................................
180000: ..............................................................
190000: ..............................................................
1A0000: ..............................................................
1B0000: ..............................................................
1C0000: ..............................................................
1D0000: ..............................................................
1E0000: ..............................................................
1F0000: ..............................................................
```

Fig. 7.1
The logical memory map.

Note

To save space, this map is ended after the end of the second megabyte. In reality, this map continues to the maximum of 16M or 4,096M of addressable memory.

Conventional (Base) Memory

The original PC/XT-type system was designed to use 1M of memory workspace, sometimes called *RAM* (Random-Access Memory). This 1M of RAM is divided into several sections, some of which have special uses. DOS can read and write to the entire megabyte, but can manage the loading of programs only in the portion of RAM space called *conventional memory*, which at the time the first PC was introduced was 512K. The other 512K was reserved for use by the system itself, including the motherboard and adapter boards plugged into the system slots.

IBM decided after introducing the system that only 384K was needed for these reserved uses, and the company began marketing PCs with 640K of user memory. Thus, 640K became the standard for memory that can be used by DOS for running programs and is often termed the *640K memory barrier*. The remaining memory after 640K was indicated as reserved for use by the graphics boards, other adapters, and the motherboard ROM BIOS.

Upper Memory Area (UMA)

The term *Upper Memory Area* (UMA) describes the reserved 384K at the top of the first megabyte of system memory on a PC/XT and the first megabyte on an AT-type system. This memory has the addresses from A0000 through FFFFF. The way the 384K of upper memory is used breaks down as follows:

- The first 128K after conventional memory is called *video RAM*. It is reserved for use by video adapters. When text and graphics are displayed on-screen, the electronic impulses that contain their images reside in this space. Video RAM is allotted the address range from A0000-BFFFF.

- The next 128K is reserved for the software programs, or adapter BIOS, that reside in read-only memory chips on the adapter boards plugged into the system slots. Most VGA-compatible video adapters use the first 32K of this area for their on-board BIOS. The rest can be used by any other adapters installed. Adapter ROM and special purpose RAM are allotted the address range from C0000-DFFFF.

- The last 128K of memory is reserved for motherboard BIOS, the basic input-output system, which is stored in read-only RAM chips or ROM. The POST (Power-On Self Test) and bootstrap loader, which handles your system at bootup until DOS takes over, also reside in this space. Most systems only use the last 64K of this space, leaving the first 64K free for remapping with memory managers. The motherboard BIOS is allotted the address range from E0000-FFFFF.

Not all the 384K of reserved memory is fully used on most AT-type systems. For example, according to IBM's definition of the PC standard, reserved video RAM begins at address A0000, which is right at the 640K boundary, but this reserved area may not be used, depending on which video adapter is installed in the system. Some adapters do not use the area beginning at A0000, instead using a higher address. Different video adapters use varying amounts of RAM for their operations depending mainly on the mode they are in.

In fact, although the top 384K of the first megabyte was originally termed *reserved memory*, it is possible to use previously unused regions of this memory to load device drivers (like ANSI.SYS) and memory-resident programs (like MOUSE.COM), which frees up the conventional memory they would otherwise require. The amount of free UMA space varies from system to system depending on the adapter cards installed on the system. For example, most SCSI adapters and network adapters require some of this area for built-in ROMs or special-purpose RAM use.

Segment Addresses and Linear Addresses. One thing that can be confusing is the difference between a segment address and a full linear address. The use of segmented address numbers comes from the internal structure of the Intel processors. They use a separate register for the segment information and another for the offset. The concept is very simple. For example, assume that I am staying in a hotel room, and somebody asks for my room number. The hotel has ten floors, numbered from zero through nine; each floor has 100 rooms, numbered from 00 to 99. The hotel also is broken up into segments of ten rooms each, and each segment can be specified by a two-digit number from 00 to 99. I am staying in room 541. If the person needs this information in segment:offset form, and each number is two digits, I could say that I am staying at a room segment starting address of 54 (room 540), and an offset of 01 from the start of that segment. I could also say that I am in room segment 50 (room 500), and an offset of 41. You could even come up with other answers, such as that I am at segment 45 (room 450) offset 91 (450+91=541). That is exactly how segmented memory in an Intel processor works. Notice that the segment and offset numbers essentially overlap on all digits except the first and last. By adding them together with the proper alignment, you can see the linear address total.

A linear address is one without segment:offset boundaries, such as saying room 541. It is a single number and not comprised of two numbers added together. For example, a SCSI host adapter might have 16K ROM on the card addressed from D4000 to D7FFF. These numbers expressed in segment:offset form are D400:0000 to D700:0FFF. The segment portion is composed of the most significant four digits, and the offset portion is composed of the least significant four digits. Because each portion overlaps by one digit, the ending address of its ROM can be expressed in four different ways, as follows:

```
D000:7FFF =    D000     segment
          +    7FFF     offset
               -----
          =    D7FFF    total

D700:0FFF =    D700     segment
          +    0FFF     offset
               -----
          =    D7FFF    total

D7F0:00FF =    D7F0     segment
          +    00FF     offset
               -----
          =    D7FFF    total

D7FF:000F =    D7FF     segment
          +    000F     offset
               -----
          =    D7FFF    total
```

As you can see in each case, although the segment and offset differ slightly, the total ends up being the same. Adding together the segment and offset numbers makes possible even more combinations, as in the following examples:

```
D500:2FFF =    D500     segment
          +    2FFF     offset
               -----
          =    D7FFF    total

D6EE:111F =    D6EE     segment
          +    111F     offset
               -----
          =    D7FFF    total
```

II

Primary System Components

As you can see, several combinations are possible. The correct and generally accepted way to write this address as a linear address is D7FFF, whereas most would write the segment:offset address as D000:7FFF. Keeping the segment mostly zeros makes the segment:offset relationship easier to understand and the number easier to comprehend. If you understand the segment:offset relationship to the linear address, you now know why when a linear address number is discussed, it is five digits, whereas a segment number is only four.

Video RAM Memory. A video adapter installed in your system uses some of your system's memory to hold graphics or character information for display. Some adapters, like the VGA, also have on-board BIOS mapped into the system's space reserved for such types of adapters. Generally, the higher the resolution and color capabilities of the video adapter, the more system memory the video adapter uses. It is important to note that most VGA or Super VGA adapters have additional on-board memory used to handle the information currently displayed on-screen and to speed screen refresh.

In the standard system-memory map, a total of 128K is reserved for use by the video card to store currently displayed information. The reserved video memory is located in segments A000 and B000. The video adapter ROM uses additional upper memory space in segment C000.

The location of video adapter RAM is responsible for the 640K DOS *conventional memory barrier*. DOS can use all available contiguous memory in the first megabyte—which means all—of memory until the video adapter RAM is encountered. The use of adapters such as the MDA and CGA allows DOS access to more than 640K of system memory. The video memory *wall* begins at A0000 for the EGA, MCGA, and VGA systems; but the MDA and CGA do not use as much video RAM, which leaves some space that can be used by DOS and programs. The previous segment and offset examples show that the MDA adapter enables DOS to use an additional 64K of memory (all of segment A000), bringing the total for DOS program space to 704K. Similarly, the CGA enables a total of 736K of possible contiguous memory. The EGA, VGA, or MCGA is limited to the normal maximum of 640K of contiguous memory because of the larger amount used by video RAM. The maximum DOS-program memory workspace therefore depends on which video adapter is installed. Table 7.1 shows the maximum amount of memory available to DOS using the referenced video card.

Table 7.1 DOS Memory Limitations Based on Video Adapter Type	
Video Adapter Type	**Maximum DOS Memory**
Monochrome Display Adapter (MDA)	704K
Color Graphics Adapter (CGA)	736K
Enhanced Graphics Adapter (EGA)	640K
Video Graphics Array (VGA)	640K
Super VGA (SVGA)	640K
eXtended Graphics Array (XGA)	640K

Using this memory to 736K might be possible depending on the video adapter, the types of memory boards installed, ROM programs on the motherboard, and the type of system. You can use some of this memory if your system has a 386 or higher processor. With memory manager software, such as EMM386 that comes with DOS, that can operate the 386+ Memory Management Unit (MMU), you can remap extended memory into this space.

The following sections examine how standard video adapters use the system's memory. Figures show where in a system the monochrome, EGA, VGA, and IBM PS/2 adapters use memory. This map is important because it may be possible to recognize some of this as unused in some systems, which may free up more space for software drivers to be loaded.

Monochrome Display Adapter Memory (MDA). Figure 7.2 shows where the original Monochrome Display Adapter (MDA) uses the system's memory. This adapter uses only a 4K portion of the reserved video RAM from B0000-B0FFF. Because the ROM code used to operate this adapter is actually a portion of the motherboard ROM, no additional ROM space is used in segment C000.

```
     . = Empty Addresses
     M = Original Monochrome Adapter RAM
     m = Additional Memory used in VGA Monochrome Text Mode

         : 0---1---2---3---4---5---6---7---8---9---A---B---C---D---E---F---
0A0000: ................................................................
0B0000: MMMMmmmmmmmmmmmmmmmmmmmmmmmmmmmmmm..............................
```

Fig. 7.2

The Monochrome Display Adapter memory map.

Note that although the original Monochrome Display Adapter only used 4K of memory starting at B0000, a VGA adapter running in Monochrome emulation mode (Mono Text Mode) activates 32K of RAM at this address. A true Monochrome Display Adapter has no on-board BIOS, and instead is operated by driver programs found in the primary motherboard BIOS.

Color Graphics Adapter (CGA) Memory. Figure 7.3 shows where the Color Graphics Adapter (CGA) uses the system's memory. The CGA uses a 16K portion of the reserved video RAM from B8000-BBFFF. Because the ROM code used to operate this adapter is a portion of the motherboard ROM, no additional ROM space is used in segment C000.

```
        . = Empty Addresses
        C = Original Color Graphics Adapter (CGA) RAM
        c = Additional Memory used in VGA Color Text Mode

            : 0---1---2---3---4---5---6---7---8---9---A---B---C---D---E---F---
     0A0000: ................................................................
     0B0000: ....................................CCCCCCCCCCCCCCCCcccccccccccccccccc
```

Fig. 7.3

The Color Graphics Adapter (CGA) memory map.

The CGA card leaves memory from A0000-B7FFF free, which can be used by memory managers for additional DOS memory space. However, this precludes using any graphics mode software such as Windows. The original CGA card only used 16K of space starting at B8000, whereas a VGA adapter running in CGA emulation (Color Text) mode can activate 32K of RAM at this address. The original CGA card has no on-board BIOS and is instead operated by driver programs found in the primary motherboard BIOS.

Enhanced Graphics Adapter (EGA) Memory. Figure 7.4 shows where the Enhanced Graphics Adapter (EGA) uses the system's memory. This adapter uses all 128K of the video RAM from A0000-BFFFF. The ROM code used to operate this adapter is on the adapter itself and consumes 16K of memory from C0000-C3FFF.

```
        . = Empty Addresses
        G = Enhanced Graphics Adapter (EGA) Graphics Mode Video RAM
        M = EGA Monochrome Text Mode Video RAM
        C = EGA Color Text Mode Video RAM
        V = Standard EGA Video ROM BIOS
        R = Standard Motherboard ROM BIOS

            : 0---1---2---3---4---5---6---7---8---9---A---B---C---D---E---F---
     0A0000: GGGGGGGGGGGGGGGGGGGGGGGGGGGGGGGGGGGGGGGGGGGGGGGGGGGGGGGGGGGGGGGG
     0B0000: MMMMMMMMMMMMMMMMMMMMMMMMMMMMMMMMMCCCCCCCCCCCCCCCCCCCCCCCCCCCCCCCC
            : 0---1---2---3---4---5---6---7---8---9---A---B---C---D---E---F---
     0C0000: VVVVVVVVVVVVVVVV................................................
     0D0000: ................................................................
            : 0---1---2---3---4---5---6---7---8---9---A---B---C---D---E---F---
     0E0000: ................................................................
     0F0000: RRRRRRRRRRRRRRRRRRRRRRRRRRRRRRRRRRRRRRRRRRRRRRRRRRRRRRRRRRRRRRRR
```

Fig. 7.4

The Enhanced Graphics Adapter (EGA) memory map.

The original IBM EGA card only used 16K of ROM space at C0000. Aftermarket compatible EGA adapters can use additional ROM space up to 32K total. The most interesting thing to note about EGA (and this applies to VGA adapters as well) is that segments A000 and B000 are not all used at all times. For example, if the card is in a graphics mode, then only segment A000 would appear to have RAM installed, whereas segment B000 would appear completely empty. If you switched the mode of the adapter (through software) into Color Text mode, then segment A000 would instantly appear empty, and the last half of segment B000 would suddenly "blink on"! The Monochrome text mode RAM area would practically never be used on a modern system, because little or no software would ever need to switch the adapter into that mode. Figure 7.4 also shows the standard motherboard ROM BIOS so that you can get a picture of the entire UMA.

The EGA card became somewhat popular after it appeared, but this was quickly overshadowed by the VGA card that followed. Most of the VGA characteristics with regard to memory are the same as the EGA because the VGA is backward compatible with EGA.

Video Graphics Array (VGA) Memory. All VGA (Video Graphics Array) compatible cards, including Super VGA cards, are almost identical to the EGA in terms of memory use. Just as with the EGA, they use all 128K of the video RAM from A0000-BFFFF, but not all at once. Again the video RAM area is split into three distinct regions, and each of these regions is used only when the adapter is in the corresponding mode. One minor difference with the EGA cards is that virtually all VGA cards use the full 32K allotted to them for on-board ROM (C0000 to C7FFF). Figure 7.5 shows the VGA adapter memory map.

```
    . = Empty Addresses
    G = Video Graphics Array (VGA) Adapter Graphics Mode Video RAM
    M = VGA Monochrome Text Mode Video RAM
    C = VGA Color Text Mode Video RAM
    V = Standard VGA Video ROM BIOS
    R = Standard Motherboard ROM BIOS


         : 0---1---2---3---4---5---6---7---8---9---A---B---C---D---E---F---
  0A0000: GGGGGGGGGGGGGGGGGGGGGGGGGGGGGGGGGGGGGGGGGGGGGGGGGGGGGGGGGGGGGGGG
  0B0000: MMMMMMMMMMMMMMMMMMMMMMMMMMMMMMMMCCCCCCCCCCCCCCCCCCCCCCCCCCCCCCCC
         : 0---1---2---3---4---5---6---7---8---9---A---B---C---D---E---F---
  0C0000: VVVVVVVVVVVVVVVVVVVVVVVVVVVVVVVV................................
  0D0000: ................................................................
         : 0---1---2---3---4---5---6---7---8---9---A---B---C---D---E---F---
  0E0000: ................................................................
  0F0000: RRRRRRRRRRRRRRRRRRRRRRRRRRRRRRRRRRRRRRRRRRRRRRRRRRRRRRRRRRRRRRRR
```

Fig. 7.5
The VGA (and Super VGA) adapter memory map.

You can see that the typical VGA card uses a full 32K of space for the on-board ROM containing driver code. Some VGA cards may use slightly less, but this is rare. Just as with the EGA card, the video RAM areas are only active when the adapter is in the particular mode designated. In other words, when a VGA adapter is in graphics mode, only segment A000 is used; and when it is in color text mode, only the last half of segment B000 is used. Because the VGA adapter is almost never run in monochrome text mode, the first half of segment B000 remains unused (B0000-B7FFF). Figure 7.5 also shows the standard motherboard ROM BIOS so that you can get a picture of how the entire UMA is laid out with this adapter.

II

Primary System Components

IBM created VGA, and the first systems to include VGA adapters were the PS/2 systems introduced in April 1987. These systems had the VGA adapter built directly into the motherboard. Because IBM had written both the video and motherboard BIOS, and they were building the VGA on the motherboard and not as a separate card, they incorporated the VGA BIOS driver code directly into the motherboard BIOS. This meant that segment C000 did not have an on-board video ROM as in most of the compatibles that would follow. Although this may sound like a bonus for the PS/2 systems—they still had the additional ROM code—it was merely located in segment E000 instead! In fact, the PS/2 systems used all of segment E000 for additional motherboard ROM BIOS code, whereas segment E000 remains empty in most compatibles.

Many compatibles today have their video adapter built into the motherboard. Systems that use the LPX (Low Profile) motherboard design in an LPX- or Slimline-type case incorporate the video adapter into the motherboard. In these systems, even though the video BIOS and motherboard BIOS may be from the same manufacturer, they are always set up to emulate a standard VGA-type adapter card. In other words, the video BIOS appears in the first 32K of segment C000 just as if a stand-alone VGA-type card were plugged into a slot. The built-in video circuit in these systems can be easily disabled via a switch or jumper, which then allows a conventional VGA-type card to be plugged in. By having the built-in VGA act exactly as if it were a separate card, disabling it allows a new adapter to be installed with no compatibility problems that might arise if the video drivers had been incorporated into the motherboard BIOS.

When the VGA first appeared on the scene, it was built into the PS/2 motherboard. So that you could add VGA to other systems, IBM also introduced at that time the very first VGA card. It was called the PS/2 Display Adapter, which was somewhat confusing at the time because it was designed for standard ISA bus-compatible systems and not for the PS/2s, which mostly used the new Micro Channel Architecture bus and already had VGA built-in. Nevertheless, this card was sold to anybody who wanted to add VGA to their ISA bus system. The IBM VGA card (PS/2 Display Adapter) was an 8-bit ISA card that had the same IBM-designed video chip and circuits as were used on the PS/2 motherboard.

If you were involved with the PC industry at that time, you might remember how long it took for clone video card manufacturers to accurately copy the IBM VGA circuits. It took nearly two years (almost to 1989) before you could buy an aftermarket VGA card and expect it to run everything an IBM VGA system would with no problems. Some of my associates who bought some of the early cards inadvertently became members of the video card manufacturer's "ROM of the week" club! They were constantly finding problems with the operation of these cards, and many updated and patched ROMs were sent to try and fix the problems. Not wanting to pay for the privilege of beta testing the latest attempts at VGA compatibility, I bit the bullet and took the easy way out. I simply bought the IBM VGA card—PS/2 Display Adapter. At that time, the card listed for $595, but I could usually expect a 30 percent discount in purchasing it at the local computer store. That is still about as much as you would pay for the best Local Bus Super VGA cards on the market today. In fact, you can now buy basic VGA clone cards for less than $20 that are actually faster and better than the original IBM VGA card!

I remember purchasing the IBM VGA card, not only because it was so expensive, but also because the card actually proved somewhat difficult to purchase! When I arrived to buy it at my local IBM authorized retailer (after first calling to see that they had one in stock), I asked for it by name. I said: "I am here to purchase an IBM PS/2 Display Adapter." The salesman asked what type of system I was going to install it in. I replied that I was going to put it in the AT clone I had assembled. Then I met resistance! The salesman told me that I could not use that in my clone because it was designed for PS/2 systems only. I told him he was mistaken and that the card is in fact designed for any IBM-compatible system with an ISA bus and is supposed to give the system the same graphics capability of the new PS/2s. The salesman maintained that the card was only for PS/2 systems, and I finally had to say "Look, I have cash, will you sell me the card or not?" Lo and behold I emerged from the store victorious, with the card in hand!

Although the card worked very well, and although I never did find any compatibility problems, I did later run into some interesting problems with the memory use of this card. This was my first introduction to what I call *scratch pad memory* use by an adapter. I found that many different types of adapters may use some areas in the UMA for mapping scratch pad memory. This refers to memory on the card that stores status information, configuration data, or any other temporary type information of a variable nature. Most cards keep this scratch pad memory to themselves and do not attempt to map it into the processor's address space, but some cards do place this type of memory in the address space so that the driver programs for the card can use it. Figure 7.6 shows the memory map of the IBM PS/2 Display Adapter (IBM's VGA card).

```
  . = Empty Addresses
  G = Video Graphics Array (VGA) Adapter Graphics Mode Video RAM
  M = VGA Monochrome Text Mode Video RAM
  C = VGA Color Text Mode Video RAM
  V = IBM VGA Video ROM BIOS
  S = IBM VGA Scratch Pad memory (used by the card)
  R = Standard Motherboard ROM BIOS


        : 0---1---2---3---4---5---6---7---8---9---A---B---C---D---E---F---
0A0000: GGGGGGGGGGGGGGGGGGGGGGGGGGGGGGGGGGGGGGGGGGGGGGGGGGGGGGGGGGGGGGGGG
0B0000: MMMMMMMMMMMMMMMMMMMMMMMMMMMMMMMMCCCCCCCCCCCCCCCCCCCCCCCCCCCCCCCCCC
        : 0---1---2---3---4---5---6---7---8---9---A---B---C---D---E---F---
0C0000: VVVVVVVVVVVVVVVVVVVVVVVVV..SSSSSS........SS......................
0D0000: ................................................................
        : 0---1---2---3---4---5---6---7---8---9---A---B---C---D---E---F---
0E0000: ................................................................
0F0000: RRRRRRRRRRRRRRRRRRRRRRRRRRRRRRRRRRRRRRRRRRRRRRRRRRRRRRRRRRRRRRRRRR
```

Fig. 7.6
IBM's somewhat strange ISA-bus VGA card (PS/2 Display Adapter) memory map.

There is nothing different about this VGA card and any other with respect to the Video RAM area. What is different is that the ROM code that operates this adapter only consumes 24K of memory from C0000-C5FFF. Also strange is the 2K "hole" at C6000, and the 6K of scratch pad memory starting at C6800, as well as the additional 2K of scratch pad memory at CA000. In particular, the 2K "straggler" area really caught me off guard when I installed a SCSI host adapter in this system that had a 16K on-board BIOS with a default starting address of C8000. I immediately ran into a conflict that completely disabled the system. In fact, it would not boot, had no display at all, and could only beep out error codes that indicated that the video card had failed. I first thought that I had somehow "fried" the card, but removing the new SCSI adapter got everything functioning normally. I also could get the system to work with the SCSI adapter and an old CGA card substituting for the VGA, so I immediately knew a conflict was underfoot. This scratch pad memory use was not documented clearly in the technical-reference information for the adapter, so it was something that I had to find out by trial and error. If you have ever had the IBM VGA card and had conflicts with other adapters, now you know why! Needless to say, nothing could be done about this 2K of scratch pad memory hanging out there, and I had to work around it as long as I had this card in the system. I solved my SCSI adapter problem by merely moving the SCSI adapter BIOS to a different address.

As a side note, I have seen other VGA-type video adapters use scratch pad memory, but they have all kept it within the C0000-C7FFF 32K region allotted normally for the video ROM BIOS. By using a 24K BIOS, I have seen other cards with up to 8K of scratch pad area, but none—except for IBM's—in which the scratch pad memory goes beyond C8000.

As you can see in the preceding figures, each type of video adapter on the market uses two types of memory: video RAM, which stores the display information; and ROM code, which controls the adapter, must exist somewhere in the system's memory. The ROM code built into the motherboard ROM on standard PC and AT systems controls adapters such as the MDA and CGA. All the EGA and VGA adapters for the PC and AT systems use the full 128K of video RAM (not all at once of course) and up to 32K of ROM space at the beginning of segment C000. IBM's technical-reference manuals say that the memory between C0000 and C7FFF is reserved specifically for ROM on video adapter boards. Note that the VGA and MCGA built into the motherboards of the PS/2 systems have the ROM-control software built into the motherboard ROM in segments E000 and F000 and require no other code space in segment C000. Also note that you can often use your memory manager software (such as what comes with DOS) to map extended memory into the monochrome display area (32K worth), which can get you an extra 32K region for loading drivers and resident programs.

Adapter ROM and Special Purpose RAM Memory. The second 128K of upper memory beginning at segment C000 is reserved for the software programs, or BIOS (basic input-output system), on the adapter boards plugged into the system slots. These BIOS programs are stored on special chips known as read-only memory (ROM), which have fused circuits so that the PC cannot alter them. ROM is useful for permanent programs that always must be present while the system is running. Graphics boards, hard disk controllers, communications boards, and expanded memory boards, for example, are adapter boards that might use some of this memory.

On systems based on the 386 CPU chip or higher, memory managers like the MS-DOS 6 MEMMAKER, IBM DOS RAMBOOST, or aftermarket programs like QEMM by Quarter-deck, can load device drivers and memory-resident programs into unused regions in the UMA.

Video Adapter BIOS. Although 128K of upper memory beginning at segment C000 is reserved for use by the video adapter BIOS, not all this space is used by various video adapters commonly found on PCs. Table 7.2 details the amount of space used by the BIOS on each type of common video adapter card.

Table 7.2   Memory Used by Different Video Cards

Type of Adapter	Adapter BIOS Memory Used
Monochrome Display Adapter (MDA)	None - Drivers in Motherboard BIOS
Color Graphics Adapter (CGA)	None - Drivers in Motherboard BIOS
Enhanced Graphics Adapter (EGA)	16K onboard (C0000-C3FFF)
Video Graphics Array (VGA)	32K onboard (C0000-C7FFF)
Super VGA (SVGA)	32K onboard (C0000-C7FFF)

Some more advanced graphics accelerator cards on the market do use most or all the 128K of upper memory beginning at segment C000 to speed the repainting of graphics displays in Windows, OS/2, or other graphical user interfaces (GUIs). In addition, these graphics cards may contain 2M of on-board memory in which to store currently displayed data and more quickly fetch new screen data as it is sent to the display by the CPU.

Hard Disk Controller and SCSI Host Adapter BIOS. The upper memory addresses C0000 to DFFFF also are used for the BIOS contained on many hard drive controllers. Table 7.3 details the amount of memory and the addresses commonly used by the BIOS contained on hard drive adapter cards.

Table 7.3   Memory Addresses Used by Different Hard Drive Adapter Cards

Disk Adapter Type	Onboard BIOS Size	BIOS Address Range
IBM XT 10M Controller	8K	C8000-C9FFF
IBM XT 20M Controller	4K	C8000-C8FFF
Most XT Compatible Controllers	8K	C8000-C9FFF
Most AT Controllers	None	Drivers in Motherboard BIOS
Most IDE Adapters	None	Drivers in Motherboard BIOS
Most ESDI Controllers	16K	C8000-CBFFF
Most SCSI Host Adapters	16K	C8000-CBFFF

The hard drive or SCSI adapter card used on a particular system may use a different amount of memory, but it is most likely to use the memory segment beginning at C800 because this address is considered part of the IBM standard for personal computers. Virtually all the disk controller or SCSI adapters today that have an on-board BIOS allow the BIOS starting address to be easily moved in the C000 and D000 segments. The locations listed in table 7.3 are only the default addresses that most of these cards use. If the default address is already in use by another card, then you have to consult the documentation for the new card to see how to change the BIOS starting address to avoid any conflicts.

Figure 7.7 shows an example memory map for an Adaptec AHA-1542CF SCSI adapter.

```
    . = Empty Addresses
    G = Video Graphics Array (VGA) Adapter Graphics Mode Video RAM
    M = VGA Monochrome Text Mode Video RAM
    C = VGA Color Text Mode Video RAM
    V = Standard VGA Video ROM BIOS
    H = SCSI Host Adapter ROM BIOS
    R = Standard Motherboard ROM BIOS


        : 0---1---2---3---4---5---6---7---8---9---A---B---C---D---E---F---
  0A0000: GGGGGGGGGGGGGGGGGGGGGGGGGGGGGGGGGGGGGGGGGGGGGGGGGGGGGGGGGGGGGGGG
  0B0000: MMMMMMMMMMMMMMMMMMMMMMMMMMMMMMMMCCCCCCCCCCCCCCCCCCCCCCCCCCCCCCCC
        : 0---1---2---3---4---5---6---7---8---9---A---B---C---D---E---F---
  0C0000: VVVVVVVVVVVVVVVVVVVVVVVVVVVVVVVVVVVV.............................
  0D0000: ...........................................HHHHHHHHHHHHHHHHH
        : 0---1---2---3---4---5---6---7---8---9---A---B---C---D---E---F---
  0E0000: ................................................................
  0F0000: RRRRRRRRRRRRRRRRRRRRRRRRRRRRRRRRRRRRRRRRRRRRRRRRRRRRRRRRRRRRRRRR
```

Fig. 7.7
Adaptec AHA-1542CF SCSI adapter default memory use.

Note how this SCSI adapter fits in here. Although no conflicts are in the UMA memory, the free regions have been fragmented by the placement of the SCSI BIOS. Because most systems do not have any BIOS in segment E000, that remains as a free 64K region. With no other adapters using memory, this example shows another free UMB (Upper Memory Block) starting at C8000 and continuing through CBFFF, which represents an 80K free region. Using the EMM386 driver that comes with DOS, memory can be mapped into these two regions for loading memory-resident drivers and programs. Unfortunately, because programs cannot be split across regions, the largest program you could load is 80K, which is the size of the largest free region. It would be much better if you could move the SCSI adapter BIOS so that it was next to the VGA BIOS, as this would bring the free UMB space to a single region of 144K. It is much easier and more efficient to use a single 144K region than two regions of 80K and 64K respectively. Fortunately, it is possible to move this particular SCSI adapter, although doing so does require that several switches be reset on the card itself. One great thing about this Adaptec card is that a sticker is placed directly on the card detailing all the switch settings! This means that you don't have to go hunting for a manual that may not be nearby. More adapter card manufacturers should place this information right on the card.

After changing the appropriate switches to move the SCSI adapter BIOS to start at C8000, the optimized map would look like figure 7.8.

```
      . = Empty Addresses
      G = Video Graphics Array (VGA) Adapter Graphics Mode Video RAM
      M = VGA Monochrome Text Mode Video RAM
      C = VGA Color Text Mode Video RAM
      V = Standard VGA Video ROM BIOS
      H = SCSI Host Adapter ROM BIOS
      R = Standard Motherboard ROM BIOS


          : 0---1---2---3---4---5---6---7---8---9---A---B---C---D---E---F---
   0A0000: GGGGGGGGGGGGGGGGGGGGGGGGGGGGGGGGGGGGGGGGGGGGGGGGGGGGGGGGGGGGGGGG
   0B0000: MMMMMMMMMMMMMMMMMMMMMMMMMMMMMMMMMMMCCCCCCCCCCCCCCCCCCCCCCCCCCCCCCCCC
          : 0---1---2---3---4---5---6---7---8---9---A---B---C---D---E---F---
   0C0000: VVVVVVVVVVVVVVVVVVVVVVVVVVVVVVVVVVVVVHHHHHHHHHHHHHHHHHH...............
   0D0000: ................................................................
          : 0---1---2---3---4---5---6---7---8---9---A---B---C---D---E---F---
   0E0000: ................................................................
   0F0000: RRRRRRRRRRRRRRRRRRRRRRRRRRRRRRRRRRRRRRRRRRRRRRRRRRRRRRRRRRRRRRRR
```

Fig. 7.8
Adaptec AHA-1542CF SCSI adapter with optimized memory use.

Notice how the free space is now a single contiguous block of 144K. This represents a far more optimum setup than the default settings.

Network Adapters. Network adapter cards also can use upper memory in segments C000 and D000. The exact amount of memory used and the starting address for each network card vary with the type and manufacturer of the card. Some network cards do not use any memory at all. A network card might have two primary uses for memory. They are as follows:

- IPL (Initial Program Load or Boot) ROM

- Shared Memory (RAM)

An *IPL ROM* is usually an 8K ROM that contains a bootstrap loader program that allows the system to boot directly from a file server on the network. This allows the removal of all disk drives from the PC, creating a diskless workstation. Because no floppy or hard disk would be in the system to boot from, the IPL ROM gives the system the instructions necessary to locate an image of the operating system on the file server and load it as if it were on an internal drive. If you are not using your system as a diskless workstation, it would be beneficial to disable any IPL ROM or IPL ROM socket on the adapter card. Note that many network adapters do not allow this socket to be disabled, which means that you lose the 8K of address space for other hardware even if the ROM chip is removed from the socket!

Shared memory refers to a small portion of RAM contained on the network card that is mapped into the PC's Upper Memory Area. This region is used as a memory window onto the network and offers very fast data transfer from the network card to the system. IBM pioneered the use of shared memory for its first Token Ring network adapters, and now shared memory is in common use among other companies' network adapters today. Shared memory was first devised by IBM because they found transfers using the DMA channels were not fast enough in most systems. This had mainly to do with some quirks in the DMA controller and bus design, which especially affected 16-bit ISA bus systems. Network adapters that do not use shared memory will either use DMA or Programmed I/O (PIO) transfers to move data to and from the network adapter. Although shared memory is faster than either DMA or PIO for ISA systems, it does require 16K of Upper Memory Area space to work. Most standard performance network adapters use PIO because this makes them easier to configure, and they require no free UMA space; whereas most high performance adapters will use shared memory. The shared memory region on most network adapters that use one is usually 16K in size and may be located at any user-selected 4K increment of memory in segments C000 or D000.

Figure 7.9 shows the default memory addresses for the IPL ROM and shared memory of an IBM Token Ring network adapter.

```
      . = Empty Addresses
      G = Video Graphics Array (VGA) Adapter Graphics Mode Video RAM
      M = VGA Monochrome Text Mode Video RAM
      C = VGA Color Text Mode Video RAM
      V = Standard VGA Video ROM BIOS
      I = Token Ring Network Adapter IPL ROM
      N = Token Ring Network Adapter Shared RAM
      R = Standard Motherboard ROM BIOS


           : 0---1---2---3---4---5---6---7---8---9---A---B---C---D---E---F---
     0A0000: GGGGGGGGGGGGGGGGGGGGGGGGGGGGGGGGGGGGGGGGGGGGGGGGGGGGGGGGGGGGGGGG
     0B0000: MMMMMMMMMMMMMMMMMMMMMMMMMMMMMMMMMMCCCCCCCCCCCCCCCCCCCCCCCCCCCCCCC
           : 0---1---2---3---4---5---6---7---8---9---A---B---C---D---E---F---
     0C0000: VVVVVVVVVVVVVVVVVVVVVVVVVVVVVVVVVV.................IIIIIIII........
     0D0000: ...............................NNNNNNNNNNNNNNNNN.................
           : 0---1---2---3---4---5---6---7---8---9---A---B---C---D---E---F---
     0E0000: ................................................................
     0F0000: RRRRRRRRRRRRRRRRRRRRRRRRRRRRRRRRRRRRRRRRRRRRRRRRRRRRRRRRRRRRRRRR
```

Fig. 7.9
Token Ring network adapter default memory map.

I have also included the standard VGA video BIOS in Figure 7.9 because nearly every system would have a VGA-type video adapter as well. Note that these default addresses for the IPL ROM and the shared memory can easily be changed by reconfiguring the adapter. Most other network adapters are similar in that they also would have an IPL ROM and a shared memory address, although the sizes of these areas and the default addresses may be different. Most network adapters that incorporate an IPL ROM option can disable the ROM and socket such that those addresses are not needed at all. This helps to conserve UMA space and prevent possible future conflicts if you are never going to use the function.

Notice in this case that the SCSI adapter used in Figure 7.9 would fit both at its default BIOS address of DC000 as well as the optimum address of C8000. The Token Ring shared memory location is not optimum and causes the UMB space to be fragmented. By adjusting the location of the shared memory, this setup can be greatly improved. Figure 7.10 shows an optimum setup with both the Token Ring adapter and the SCSI adapter in the same machine.

```
  . = Empty Addresses
  G = Video Graphics Array (VGA) Adapter Graphics Mode Video RAM
  M = VGA Monochrome Text Mode Video RAM
  C = VGA Color Text Mode Video RAM
  V = Standard VGA Video ROM BIOS
  H = SCSI Host Adapter ROM BIOS
  I = Token Ring Network Adapter IPL ROM
  N = Token Ring Network Adapter Shared RAM
  R = Standard Motherboard ROM BIOS


        : 0---1---2---3---4---5---6---7---8---9---A---B---C---D---E---F---
 0A0000: GGGGGGGGGGGGGGGGGGGGGGGGGGGGGGGGGGGGGGGGGGGGGGGGGGGGGGGGGGGGGGGG
 0B0000: MMMMMMMMMMMMMMMMMMMMMMMMMMMMMMMMCCCCCCCCCCCCCCCCCCCCCCCCCCCCCCCC
        : 0---1---2---3---4---5---6---7---8---9---A---B---C---D---E---F---
 0C0000: VVVVVVVVVVVVVVVVVVVVVVVVVVVVVVVVHHHHHHHHHHHHHHHHHAAAAAAAAAAAAAAAA
 0D0000: IIIIIIII........................................................
        : 0---1---2---3---4---5---6---7---8---9---A---B---C---D---E---F---
 0E0000: ................................................................
 0F0000: RRRRRRRRRRRRRRRRRRRRRRRRRRRRRRRRRRRRRRRRRRRRRRRRRRRRRRRRRRRRRRRR
```

Fig. 7.10
Adaptec AHA-1542CF SCSI adapter with optimized memory use.

This configuration allows a single 120K Upper Memory Block (UMB) that can very efficiently be used to load software drivers. Notice that the IPL ROM was moved to D0000, which places it as the last item installed before the free memory space. This is because if the IPL function is not needed, it can then be disabled, and the UMB space would increase to 128K and still be contiguous. If the default settings are used for both the SCSI and network adapters, the UMB memory would be fragmented into three regions of 16K, 40K, and 64K, which would function but is hardly optimum.

Other ROMS in the Upper Memory Area. In addition to the BIOS for hard drive controllers, SCSI adapters, and network cards, upper memory segments C000 and D000 are used by some terminal emulators, security adapters, memory boards, and various other devices and adapter boards. Some adapters may require memory only for BIOS information, and others may require RAM in these upper memory segments. For information on a specific adapter, consult the manufacturer's documentation.

Motherboard BIOS Memory. The last 128K of reserved memory is used by the motherboard BIOS (Basic Input-Output System, which is usually stored in a read-only memory chip). The BIOS programs in ROM control the system during the boot-up procedure and remain as drivers for various hardware in the system during normal operation. Because these programs must be available immediately, they cannot be loaded from a device like a disk drive. The main functions of the programs stored in the motherboard ROM are as follows:

- *Power-On Self Test*, the POST, is a set of routines that tests the motherboard, memory, disk controllers, video adapters, keyboard, and other primary system components. This routine is useful when you troubleshoot system failures or problems.

- The *bootstrap loader* routine initiates a search for an operating system on a floppy disk or hard disk. If an operating system is found, it is loaded into memory and given control of the system.

- The *Basic Input-Output System* (BIOS) is the software interface, or master control program, to all the hardware in the system. With the BIOS, a program easily can access features in the system by calling on a standard BIOS program module instead of talking directly to the device.

Both segments E000 and F000 in the memory map are considered reserved for the motherboard BIOS, but only some AT-type systems actually use this entire area. PC/XT-type systems require only segment F000 and enable adapter card ROM or RAM to use segment E000. Most AT systems use all of F000 for the BIOS, and may decode but not use any of segment E000. By decoding an area, the AT motherboard essentially grabs control of the addresses, which precludes installing any other hardware in this region. In other words, it is not possible to install any other adapters to use this area. That is why most adapters that use memory simply do not allow any choices for memory use in segment E000. Although this may seem like a waste of 64K of memory space, any 386 or higher system can use the powerful Memory Management Unit (MMU) in the processor to map RAM from extended memory into segment E000 as an Upper Memory Block and subsequently use it for loading software. This is a nice solution to what otherwise would be wasted memory. Under DOS, the EMM386 driver controls the MMU remapping functions.

PC/XTSystem BIOS. Many different ROM-interface programs are in the IBM motherboards, but the location of these programs is mostly consistent. The following figures show the ROM BIOS memory use in segments E000 and F000.

Figure 7.11 shows the memory use in an IBM PC and XT with a Type 1 (256K) motherboard.

```
    . = Empty Addresses
    b = IBM ROM (Cassette) BASIC Interpreter
    R = Motherboard ROM BIOS


          : 0---1---2---3---4---5---6---7---8---9---A---B---C---D---E---F---
   0E0000: ................................................................
   0F0000: .........................bbbbbbbbbbbbbbbbbbbbbbbbbbbbbbbbbRRRRRRRR
```

Fig. 7.11
Motherboard ROM BIOS memory use in an original IBM PC and XT.

Figure 7.12 shows the memory use in an XT with a 640K motherboard as well as in the PS/2 Model 25 and Model 30. These systems have additional BIOS code compared to the original PC and XT. Note that Cassette BASIC remains in the same addresses.

```
    . = Empty Addresses
    b = IBM ROM (Cassette) BASIC Interpreter
    R = Motherboard ROM BIOS


          : 0---1---2---3---4---5---6---7---8---9---A---B---C---D---E---F---
   0E0000: ................................................................
   0F0000: RRRRRRRRRRRRRRRRRRRRRRRRRbbbbbbbbbbbbbbbbbbbbbbbbbbbbbbbbbRRRRRRRR
```

Fig. 7.12
Motherboard ROM BIOS memory use in IBM XT (Type 2) and PS/2 Models 25 and 30.

Figure 7.13 shows the motherboard ROM BIOS memory use in most PC- or XT-compatible systems. These systems lack the Cassette BASIC Interpreter found in IBM's BIOS.

```
    . = Empty Addresses
    R = Standard XT Motherboard ROM BIOS


          : 0---1---2---3---4---5---6---7---8---9---A---B---C---D---E---F:--
   0E0000: ................................................................
   0F0000: ...............................RRRRRRRRRRRRRRRRRRRRRRRRRRRRRRRRRR

   In compatible XT type systems, the BIOS length may vary, but 32K is common.
```

Fig. 7.13
Motherboard ROM BIOS memory use in most PC- or XT-compatibles.

AT System BIOS. Figure 7.14 shows the motherboard BIOS use in an IBM AT or XT-286 system.

```
      . = Empty Addresses
      b = IBM ROM (Cassette) BASIC Interpreter
      R = Motherboard ROM BIOS

            : 0---1---2---3---4---5---6---7---8---9---A---B---C---D---E---F---
    0E0000: ................................................................
    0F0000: RRRRRRRRRRRRRRRRRRRRRRRRRRRRRRRRRRRRRRRRRRRRRRRRRRRRRRRRRRRRRRRRR
```

Fig. 7.14
Motherboard ROM BIOS memory use in an IBM AT and XT-286.

Figure 7.15 shows the motherboard ROM BIOS memory use of most AT-compatible systems. These systems lack the IBM Cassette BASIC, but do usually include a built-in Setup program.

```
      . = Empty Addresses
      R = Standard Motherboard ROM BIOS

            : 0---1---2---3---4---5---6---7---8---9---A---B---C---D---E---F---
    0E0000: ................................................................
    0F0000: RRRRRRRRRRRRRRRRRRRRRRRRRRRRRRRRRRRRRRRRRRRRRRRRRRRRRRRRRRRRRRRRR
```

Fig. 7.15
Motherboard ROM BIOS memory use of most AT-compatible systems.

Note that the standard AT-compatible system BIOS uses only segment F000 (64K). In almost every case, the remainder of the BIOS area (segment E000) is completely free and can be used as UMB space.

IBM PS/2 ROM-BIOS. The motherboard BIOS memory use by PS/2 models with a 286 or higher processor, including ISA and MCA systems, is shown in figure 7.16. This shows that PS/2 systems use more of the allocated ROM space for their motherboard ROM BIOS. The extra code contains VGA drivers (PS/2 systems have built-in VGA adapters), and additional code to run the system in protected mode.

```
      . = Empty Addresses
      b = IBM ROM (Cassette) BASIC Interpreter
      R = Motherboard ROM BIOS

            : 0---1---2---3---4---5---6---7---8---9---A---B---C---D---E---F---
    0E0000: RRRRRRRRRRRRRRRRRRRRRRRRRRRRRRRRRRRRRRRRRRRRRRRRRRRRRRRRRRRRRRRRR
    0F0000: RRRRRRRRRRRRRRRRRRRRRRRRRRRRbbbbbbbbbbbbbbbbbbbbbbbbbbbbRRRRRRRRR
```

Fig. 7.16
IBM PS/2 motherboard ROM BIOS memory map.

Note that some of the newest PS/2 systems no longer have the Cassette BASIC interpreter in ROM. In those systems, additional BIOS code fills that area.

PS/2 Models with 286 and higher processors have additional Advanced BIOS code, to be used when the systems are running protected-mode operating systems such as OS/2. Non-PS/2 systems, that don't have the Advanced BIOS code, can still easily run OS/2, but must load the equivalent of the Advanced BIOS software from disk rather than having it loaded from ROM.

Some compatible systems with a SCSI hard disk and host adapter need a special protected-mode driver for the adapter to work under OS/2 because the on-board BIOS runs only in real mode and not in protected mode. IBM SCSI adapters, however, are unique in that they include both real- and protected-mode BIOS software on-board and operate hard disks under any operating system with no need for drivers. Again, this is not really that much of a bonus or feature because this same type of protected mode operating driver code can simply be loaded from disk (bootup occurs in real mode) during the OS/2 boot process. In fact, many of the Advanced BIOS routines originally in the PS/2 BIOS have been enhanced, so that many of the built-in BIOS routines are being discarded and superseded by loaded routines anyway. The way things have turned out, there is simply no inherent advantage to the Advanced BIOS code in the PS/2 systems.

IBM Cassette Basic. The ROM maps of most IBM compatibles equal the IBM system with which they are compatible—with the exception of the Cassette BASIC portion. This section examines the origins of Cassette BASIC (also called ROM BASIC) and investigates reasons why you would ever see this in a modern system. A variety of related error messages from compatible systems are explored as well.

It may come as a surprise to some personal computer users, but the original IBM PC actually had a jack on the rear of the system for connecting a cassette tape recorder. This was to be used for loading programs and data to or from a cassette tape. At the time the PC was introduced, the most popular personal computer was the Apple II, which also had the cassette tape connection. Tapes were used at the time because floppy drives were very costly, and hard disks were not even an option yet. Floppy drives came down in price quickly at the time, and the cassette port never appeared on any subsequent IBM systems. The cassette port also never appeared on any compatible system.

The original PC came standard with only 16K of memory in the base configuration. No floppy drives were included, so you could not load or save files from disks. Most computer users at the time would either write their own programs in the BASIC (Beginners All-purpose Symbolic Instruction Code) language or run programs written by others. Various versions of the BASIC language were available, but the Microsoft version had become the most popular. Having a Microsoft BASIC interpreter was essential in the early days of personal computing, yet these interpreters would take 32K of memory when loaded. That meant you would need 32K of RAM just for the language interpreter and additional memory for your program and data. To make the system cheaper and to conserve memory, IBM contacted Microsoft and licensed the MS-BASIC interpreter.

They then built the BASIC interpreter directly into the motherboard ROM BIOS, where it occupied the 32K address range F6000-FDFFF. This meant that although the system only came with 16K, you could use all 16K for your own programs and data because no additional memory was required to run the BASIC language interpreter. To save and load programs, this BASIC language was designed to access the cassette port on the back of the system.

If you purchased a floppy drive for your PC system, you would also need DOS (Disk Operating System) to run it. Because the BASIC built into the ROM on the PC motherboard did not have the code required to operate the floppy drive for storing and retrieving files, an extension or overlay to the ROM BASIC interpreter was located on the DOS disk. Called Advanced BASIC, or BASICA.COM, this program on the DOS disk was actually constructed as an overlay to the ROM BASIC, and would not function independently. Because no compatibles ever had ROM BASIC (no compatibles ever had a cassette tape recorder port either), the BASICA extensions found on the IBM DOS disks would not run in any compatible. At that time, there was no such thing as a separately available generic MS-DOS as there is today.

Compaq was one of the first to solve this problem. They went to Microsoft and licensed the DOS separately from IBM, thus producing their own version called Compaq DOS. On the Compaq DOS disks, they included a version of the Microsoft BASIC interpreter called GWBASIC.EXE (Graphics Workstation BASIC) that was complete as a stand-alone program. In other words, it was not constructed as an overlay for the ROM BASIC (which was absent from the Compaq), but was a version complete all by itself. This stand-alone GWBASIC version of the MS-BASIC interpreter would run on any system, IBM or compatible, because it did not depend on the existence of the ROM BASIC, as did IBM's BASICA program. In some strange way, perhaps the reliance of the IBM BASICA on the IBM ROM BASIC was one way to make the IBM PS/2 different from the compatibles. Because any compatible vendor could license the complete BASIC interpreter (and DOS as well) directly from Microsoft, the IBM ROM BASIC became an unimportant feature.

What is really strange is that IBM kept this ROM BASIC and BASICA relationship all the way through most of the PS/2 systems! The 486 PS/2 system I am using right now came standard with a built-in SCSI adapter and a standard 400M SCSI drive. (I have long since outgrown that drive and in fact have just installed a 4G drive in this portable machine!) And yet this system still has the ROM BASIC wasting 32K of space! I liken this to humans having an appendix. The ROM BASIC in the IBM systems is a sort of vestigial organ—a left-over that had some use in prehistoric ancestors, but that has no function today!

You can catch a glimpse of this ROM BASIC on IBM systems that have it by disabling all the disk drives in the system. In that case, with nothing to boot from, most IBM systems unceremoniously dump you into the strange (vintage 1981) ROM BASIC screen. When this occurs, the message looks like this:

```
The IBM Personal Computer Basic
Version C1.10 Copyright IBM Corp 1981
62940 Bytes free
Ok
```

Many people used to dread seeing this because it usually meant that your hard disk had failed to be recognized! Because no compatible systems ever had the Cassette BASIC interpreter in ROM, they had to come up with different messages to display for the same situations in which an IBM system would invoke this BASIC. Compatibles that have an AMI BIOS in fact display a confusing message as follows:

```
NO ROM BASIC - SYSTEM HALTED
```

This message is a BIOS error message that is displayed by the AMI BIOS when the same situations occur that would cause an IBM system to dump into Cassette BASIC, which of course is not present in an AMI BIOS (or any other compatible BIOS for that matter). Other BIOS versions display different messages. For example, under the same circumstances, a Compaq BIOS displays the following:

```
Non-System disk or disk error
replace and strike any key when ready
```

This is somewhat confusing on Compaq's part, because this very same (or similar) error message is contained in the DOS Boot Sector, and would normally be displayed if the system files were missing or corrupted.

In the same situations that you would see Cassette BASIC on an IBM system, a system with an Award BIOS would display the following:

```
DISK BOOT FAILURE, INSERT SYSTEM DISK AND PRESS ENTER
Phoenix BIOS systems will display either:
No boot device available -
strike F1 to retry boot, F2 for setup utility
```

or

```
No boot sector on fixed disk -
strike F1 to retry boot, F2 for setup utility
```

The first or second Phoenix message appears depending on exactly which error actually occurred.

Although the message displayed varies from BIOS to BIOS, the cause is the same for all of them. Two things can generally cause any of these messages to be displayed, and they both relate to specific bytes in the Master Boot Record, which is the first sector of a hard disk at the physical location Cylinder 0, Head 0, Sector 1.

The first problem relates to a disk that has either never been partitioned or has had the Master Boot Sector corrupted. During the boot process, the BIOS checks the last two bytes in the Master Boot Record (first sector of the drive) for a "signature" value of 55AAh. If the last two bytes are not 55AAh, then an Interrupt 18h is invoked, which calls the subroutine that displays the message you received as well as the others indicated or on an IBM system that invokes Cassette (ROM) BASIC itself.

The Master Boot Sector (including the signature bytes) is written to the hard disk by the DOS FDISK program. Immediately after you low-level format a hard disk, all the sectors are initialized with a pattern of bytes, and the first sector does NOT contain the 55AAh signature. In other words, these ROM error messages are exactly what you see if you attempt to boot from a hard disk that has been low-level formatted, but has not yet been partitioned.

Now consider the second situation that can cause these messages, and potentially your other problem causing the same message. If the signature bytes are correct, then the BIOS executes the Master Partition Boot Record code, which performs a test of the Boot Indicator Bytes in each of the four partition table entries. These bytes are at offset 446 (1BEh), 462 (1CEh), 478 (1DEh), and 494 (1EEh) respectively. They are used to indicate which of the four possible partition table entries contain an active (bootable) partition. A value of 80h in any of these byte offsets indicates that table contains the active partition, whereas all other values must be 00h. If more than one of these bytes is 80h (indicating multiple active partitions), or any of the byte values is anything other than 80h or 00h, then you see the following error message:

```
Invalid partition table
```

If all these four Boot Indicator Bytes are 00h, indicating no active (bootable) partitions, then you also see Cassette BASIC on an IBM system or the other messages indicated earlier depending on which BIOS you have. This is exactly what occurs if you were to remove the existing partitions from a drive using FDISK, but had not created new partitions on the drive, or had failed to make one of the partitions Active (bootable) with FDISK before rebooting your system.

In the latest PS/2 systems, IBM has finally done away with the ROM BASIC once and for all. DOS versions through 5.x from IBM included the BASICA interpreter, however with the introduction of DOS 6, IBM eliminated BASICA because the newer systems did not have the ROM portion anyway. Microsoft included GWBASIC in MS-DOS versions up to and including 4.x and eliminated it in later versions. All DOS 5 and higher versions (IBM and MS) have a special crippled version of the Microsoft QuickBASIC Compiler now included rather than GWBASIC or BASICA. The compiler is crippled so that you can compile programs in memory, but cannot create EXE files on disk. The run-time compiler executes virtually all the older interpreted BASIC programs, so newer systems have no need for the old GWBASIC or BASICA interpreters. If you want the full version of QuickBASIC that will compile a program and save it as an EXE file, you must purchase the full version of QuickBASIC.

ROM Versions. Over the years, the BIOS in various PC models has undergone changes almost always associated with either a new system or a new motherboard design for an existing system. There are several reasons for these changes. The introduction of the XT, for example, gave IBM a good opportunity to correct a few things in the system BIOS and also add necessary new features, such as automatic support for a hard disk. IBM retrofitted many of the same changes into the PC's BIOS at the same time.

Because an in-depth knowledge of the types of BIOS is something a programmer might find useful, IBM makes this information available in the technical-reference manuals sold for each system. A new ROM BIOS technical-reference manual covers all IBM systems in one book. Complete ROM BIOS listings (with comments) accompanied early IBM system documentation, but that information is not supplied for later IBMs.

Even if you aren't a programmer, however, certain things about system BIOS are important to know. IBM has had many different BIOS versions for the PC and PS/2 families. Sometimes a system has different versions of BIOS over the course of a system's availability. For example, at least three versions of BIOS exist for each of the PC, XT, and AT systems. Because a few important changes were made in the software stored in BIOS, knowing which BIOS is in your system can be useful.

To determine which ROM BIOS module is installed in your system, first check your system documentation. If you have a 386 or later system, a few lines of text at the top of your screen during the POST probably identifies the manufacturer, BIOS revision number, and date of manufacture. The BIOS version you have also may be indicated by the manufacturer's name, version number, and date encoded in the chip.

On IBM systems, the ROM BIOS contains an ID byte (the second-to-last byte). The value of the byte at memory location FFFFE (hexadecimal) corresponds to the system type or model. Table 7.4 shows information about the different ROM BIOS versions that have appeared in various IBM systems.

Table 7.4   IBM BIOS Model, Submodel, and Revision Codes

System Type	CPU Speed	Clock	Bus Type/ Width
PC	8088	4.77 MHz	ISA/8
PC	8088	4.77 MHz	ISA/8
PC	8088	4.77 MHz	ISA/8
PC-XT	8088	4.77 MHz	ISA/8
PC-XT	8088	4.77 MHz	ISA/8
PC-XT	8088	4.77 MHz	ISA/8
PC*jr*	8088	4.77 MHz	ISA/8
PC Convertible	8088	4.77 MHz	ISA/8
PS/2 25	8086	8 MHz	ISA/8
PS/2 30	8086	8 MHz	ISA/8
PS/2 30	8086	8 MHz	ISA/8
PS/2 30	8086	8 MHz	ISA/8
PC-AT	286	6 MHz	ISA/16
PC-AT	286	6 MHz	ISA/16
PC-AT	286	8 MHz	ISA/16
PC-XT 286	286	6 MHz	ISA/16
PS/1	286	10 MHz	ISA/16
PS/2 25 286	286	10 MHz	ISA/16
PS/2 30 286	286	10 MHz	ISA/16
PS/2 30 286	286	10 MHz	ISA/16
PS/2 35 SX	386SX	20 MHz	ISA/16
PS/2 35 SX	386SX	20 MHz	ISA/16
PS/2 40 SX	386SX	20 MHz	ISA/16
PS/2 40 SX	386SX	20 MHz	ISA/16
PS/2 L40 SX	386SX	20 MHz	ISA/16
PS/2 50	286	10 MHz	MCA/16
PS/2 50	286	10 MHz	MCA/16
PS/2 50Z	286	10 MHz	MCA/16
PS/2 50Z	286	10 MHz	MCA/16
PS/2 55 SX	386SX	16 MHz	MCA/16
PS/2 55 LS	386SX	16 MHz	MCA/16
PS/2 57 SX	386SX	20 MHz	MCA/16
PS/2 60	286	10 MHz	MCA/16
PS/2 65 SX	386SX	16 MHz	MCA/16
PS/2 70 386	386DX	16 MHz	MCA/32
PS/2 70 386	386DX	16 MHz	MCA/32
PS/2 70 386	386DX	16 MHz	MCA/32
PS/2 70 386	386DX	20 MHz	MCA/32

ROM BIOS Date	ID Byte	Submodel Byte	Rev.	ST506 Drive Types
04/24/81	FF	—	—	—
10/19/81	FF	—	—	—
10/27/82	FF	—	—	—
11/08/82	FE	—	—	—
01/10/86	FB	00	01	—
05/09/86	FB	00	02	—
06/01/83	FD	—	—	—
09/13/85	F9	00	00	—
06/26/87	FA	01	00	26
09/02/86	FA	00	00	26
12/12/86	FA	00	01	26
02/05/87	FA	00	02	26
01/10/84	FC	—	—	15
06/10/85	FC	00	01	23
11/15/85	FC	01	00	23
04/21/86	FC	02	00	24
12/01/89	FC	0B	00	44
06/28/89	FC	09	02	37
08/25/88	FC	09	00	37
06/28/89	FC	09	02	37
03/15/91	F8	19	05	37
04/04/91	F8	19	06	37
03/15/91	F8	19	05	37
04/04/91	F8	19	06	37
02/27/91	F8	23	02	37
02/13/87	FC	04	00	32
05/09/87	FC	04	01	32
01/28/88	FC	04	02	33
04/18/88	FC	04	03	33
11/02/88	F8	0C	00	33
?	F8	1E	00	33
07/03/91	F8	26	02	None
02/13/87	FC	05	00	32
02/08/90	F8	1C	00	33
01/29/88	F8	09	00	33
04/11/88	F8	09	02	33
12/15/89	F8	09	04	33
01/29/88	F8	04	00	33

II

Primary System Components

(continues)

Table 7.4 Continued

System Type	CPU Speed	Clock	Bus Type/ Width
PS/2 70 386	386DX	20 MHz	MCA/32
PS/2 70 386	386DX	20 MHz	MCA/32
PS/2 70 386	386DX	25 MHz	MCA/32
PS/2 70 386	386DX	25 MHz	MCA/32
PS/2 70 486	486DX	25 MHz	MCA/32
PS/2 70 486	486DX	25 MHz	MCA/32
PS/2 P70 386	386DX	16 MHz	MCA/32
PS/2 P70 386	386DX	20 MHz	MCA/32
PS/2 P75 486	486DX	33 MHz	MCA/32
PS/2 80 386	386DX	16 MHz	MCA/32
PS/2 80 386	386DX	20 MHz	MCA/32
PS/2 80 386	386DX	25 MHz	MCA/32
PS/2 90 XP 486	486SX	20 MHz	MCA/32
PS/2 90 XP 486	487SX	20 MHz	MCA/32
PS/2 90 XP 486	486DX	25 MHz	MCA/32
PS/2 90 XP 486	486DX	33 MHz	MCA/32
PS/2 90 XP 486	486DX	50 MHz	MCA/32
PS/2 95 XP 486	486SX	20 MHz	MCA/32
PS/2 95 XP 486	487SX	20 MHz	MCA/32
PS/2 95 XP 486	486DX	25 MHz	MCA/32
PS/2 95 XP 486	486DX	33 MHz	MCA/32
PS/2 95 XP 486	486DX	50 MHz	MCA/32

The ID byte, Submodel byte, and Revision numbers are in hexadecimal.
— = This feature is not supported.
None = Only SCSI drives are supported.
? = Information is unavailable.

The date that the BIOS module design was completed is important: It has the same meaning as a version number for software. (IBM later began to code an official revision number, as indicated in the last column of table 7.4) You can display the date by entering the following four-statement BASIC program:

```
10 DEF SEG=&HF000
20 For X=&HFFF5 to &HFFFF
30 Print Chr$(Peek(X));
40 Next
```

An easier way to display the date is to use the DOS DEBUG program. First run DEBUG at the DOS prompt by entering the following command:

DEBUG

ROM BIOS Date	ID Byte	Submodel Byte	Rev.	ST506 Drive Types
04/11/88	F8	04	02	33
12/15/89	F8	04	04	33
06/08/88	F8	0D	00	33
02/20/89	F8	0D	01	33
12/01/89	F8	0D	?	?
09/29/89	F8	1B	00	?
?	F8	50	00	?
01/18/89	F8	0B	00	33
10/05/90	F8	52	00	33
03/30/87	F8	00	00	32
10/07/87	F8	01	00	32
11/21/89	F8	80	01	?
?	F8	2D	00	?
?	F8	2F	00	?
?	F8	11	00	?
?	F8	13	00	?
?	F8	2B	00	?
?	F8	2C	00	?
?	F8	2E	00	?
?	F8	14	00	?
?	F8	16	00	?
?	F8	2A	00	?

Then at the debug "-" prompt, enter the following command to display the ROM BIOS date:

D FFFF:5 L 8

If you are interested in a ROM upgrade for your system, you can contact the motherboard or even the BIOS manufacturer, such as Phoenix, Award, or AMI. Occasionally, the BIOS may be updated to fix problems or add support for new peripherals.

Extended Memory

As mentioned previously in this chapter, the memory map on a system based on the 286 or higher processor can extend beyond the 1 megabyte boundary that exists when the processor is in real mode. On a 286 or 386SX system, the extended memory limit is 16M; on a 386DX, 486, or Pentium system, the extended memory limit is 4G (4,096M).

For an AT system to address memory beyond the first megabyte, the processor must be in *protected mode*—the native mode of these newer processors. On a 286, only programs designed to run in protected mode can take advantage of extended memory. 386 and higher processors offer another mode, called *virtual real mode*, which enables extended memory to be, in effect, chopped into 1 megabyte pieces (each its own real-mode session) and for several of these sessions to be running simultaneously in protected areas of memory. Although several DOS programs can be running at once, each still is limited to a maximum of 640K of memory because each session simulates a real-mode environment, right down to the BIOS and Upper Memory Area. Running several programs at once in virtual real mode, which is termed *multitasking*, requires software that can manage each program, keeping them from crashing into one another. OS/2 does this now, and the new Windows 4 will allow this as well.

The 286 and higher CPU chips also run in what is termed *real mode*, which enables full compatibility with the 8088 CPU chip installed on the PC/XT-type computer. Real mode enables you to run DOS programs one at a time on an AT-type system just like you would on a PC/XT. However, an AT-type system running in real mode, particularly a 386-, 486-, or Pentium-based system, is really functioning as little more than a turbo PC. The 286 can emulate the 8086 or 8088, but it cannot operate in protected mode at the same time.

Extended memory is basically all memory past the first megabyte, which can only be accessed while the processor is in protected mode.

XMS Memory. The extended memory specification (XMS) was developed in 1987 by Microsoft, Intel, AST Corp., and Lotus Development to specify how programs would use extended memory. The XMS specification functions on systems based on the 286 or higher and allows real-mode programs (those designed to run in DOS) to use extended memory and another block of memory usually out of the reach of DOS.

Before XMS, there was no way to ensure cooperation between programs that switched the processor into protected mode and used extended memory. There was no way for one program to know what another had been doing with the extended memory because none of them could see that memory while in real mode. HIMEM.SYS becomes an arbitrator of sorts that first grabs all the extended memory for itself and then doles it out to programs that know the XMS protocols. In this manner, several programs that use XMS memory can operate together under DOS on the same system, switching the processor into and out of protected mode to access the memory. XMS rules prevent one program from accessing memory that another has in use. Because Windows 3.x is a program manager that switches the system to and from protected mode in running several programs at once, it has been set up to require XMS memory to function. In other words, HIMEM.SYS must be loaded for Windows to function.

Extended memory can be made to conform to the XMS specification by installing a device driver in the CONFIG.SYS file. The most common XMS driver is HIMEM.SYS, which is included with Windows and recent versions of DOS, including DOS 6. Other memory managers, like QEMM, also convert extended memory into XMS-specification memory when you add their device drivers to CONFIG.SYS.

High Memory Area (HMA) and the A20 line. The High Memory Area (HMA) is an area of memory 16 bytes short of 64K in size starting at the beginning of the first megabyte of extended memory. It can be used to load device drivers and memory-resident programs, to free up conventional memory for use by real-mode programs. Only one device driver or memory-resident program can be loaded into HMA at one time, no matter its size. Originally this could be any program, but Microsoft decided that DOS could get there first, and built capability into DOS 5 and newer versions.

The HMA area is extremely important to those who use DOS 5 or higher because these DOS versions can move their own kernel (about 45K of program instructions) into this area. This is accomplished simply by first loading an XMS driver (such as HIMEM.SYS) and adding the line DOS=HIGH to your CONFIG.SYS file. Taking advantage of this DOS capability frees another 45K or so of conventional memory for use by real-mode programs by essentially moving 45K of program code into the first segment of extended memory. Although this memory was supposed to be accessible in protected mode only, it turns out that a defect in the design of the original 286 (which fortunately has been propagated forward to the more recent processors as a "feature") accidentally allows access to most of the first segment of extended memory while still in real mode.

The use of the High Memory Area is controlled by the HIMEM.SYS or equivalent driver. The origins of this memory usage are interesting because they are based on a bug in the original 286 processor carried forward to the 386, 486, and Pentium.

The problem started from the fact that memory addresses in Intel processors are dictated by an overlapping segment and offset address. By setting the segment address to FFFF, which itself specifies an actual address of FFFF0, which is 16 bytes from the end of the 1st megabyte, and then specifying an offset of FFFF, which is equal to 64K, you can create a memory address as follows:

```
      FFFF    segment
   +  FFFF    offset
   ------
   = 10FFEF   total
```

This type of address is impossible on a 8088 or 8086 system that has only 20 address lines and therefore cannot calculate an address that large. By leaving off the leading digit, these processors interpret the address as 0FFEF, in essence causing the address to "wrap around" and end up 16 bytes from the end of the first 64K segment of the first megabyte. The problem with the 286 and higher was that when they were in real mode, they were supposed to operate the same way, and the address should wrap around to the beginning of the first megabyte also. Unfortunately a "bug" in the chip left the 21st address line active (called the A20 line), which allowed the address to end up 16 bytes from the end of the first 64K segment in the second megabyte. This memory was supposed to be addressable only in protected mode, but this bug allowed all but 16 bytes of the first 64K of extended memory to be addressable in real mode.

Because this bug caused problems with many real-mode programs that relied on the wrap to take place, when IBM engineers designed the AT, they had to find a way to disable the A20 line while in real mode, but then re-enable it when in protected mode. They did this by using some unused pins on the 8042 keyboard controller chip on the motherboard. The 8042 keyboard controller was designed to accept scan codes from the keyboard and transmit them to the processor, but there were unused pins not needed strictly for this function. So IBM came up with a way to command the keyboard controller to turn on and off the A20 line, thus enabling the "defective" 286 to truly emulate an 8088 and 8086 while in real mode.

Microsoft realized that you could command the 8042 keyboard controller to turn back on the A20 line strictly for the purpose of using this "bug" as a feature that enabled you to access the first 64K of extended memory (less 16 bytes) without having to go through the lengthy and complicated process of switching into protected mode. Thus HIMEM.SYS and the High Memory Area was born! HIMEM.SYS has to watch the system to see if the A20 line should be off for compatibility, or on to enable access to the HMA or while in protected mode. In essence, HIMEM becomes a control program that manipulates the A20 line through the 8042 keyboard controller chip.

Expanded Memory

Some older programs can use a type of memory called *Expanded Memory Specification* or EMS memory. Unlike conventional (the first megabyte) or extended (the second through 16th or 4,096th megabytes) memory, expanded memory is *not* directly addressable by the processor. Instead it can only be accessed through a small 64K window established in the Upper Memory Area (UMA). Expanded memory is a segment or bank-switching scheme in which a custom memory adapter has a large number of 64K segments onboard combined with special switching and mapping hardware. The system uses a free segment in the UMA as the home address for the EMS board. After this 64K is filled with data, the board rotates the filled segment out and a new, empty segment appears to take its place. In this fashion, you have a board that can keep on rotating in new segments to be filled with data. Because only one segment can be seen or operated on at one time, EMS is very inefficient for program code and is normally only used for data.

Segment D000 in the first megabyte usually is used for mapping. Lotus, Intel, and Microsoft—founders of the LIM specification for expanded memory (LIM EMS)—decided to use this segment because it is largely unused by most adapters. Programs must be written specially to take advantage of this segment-swapping scheme, and then only data normally can be placed in this segment because it is above the area of contiguous memory (640K) that DOS can use. For example, a program cannot run while it is swapped out and therefore not visible by the processor. This type of memory generally is useful only in systems that do not have extended (processor-addressable) memory available to them.

The figure 7.17 shows how expanded memory fits with conventional and extended memory.

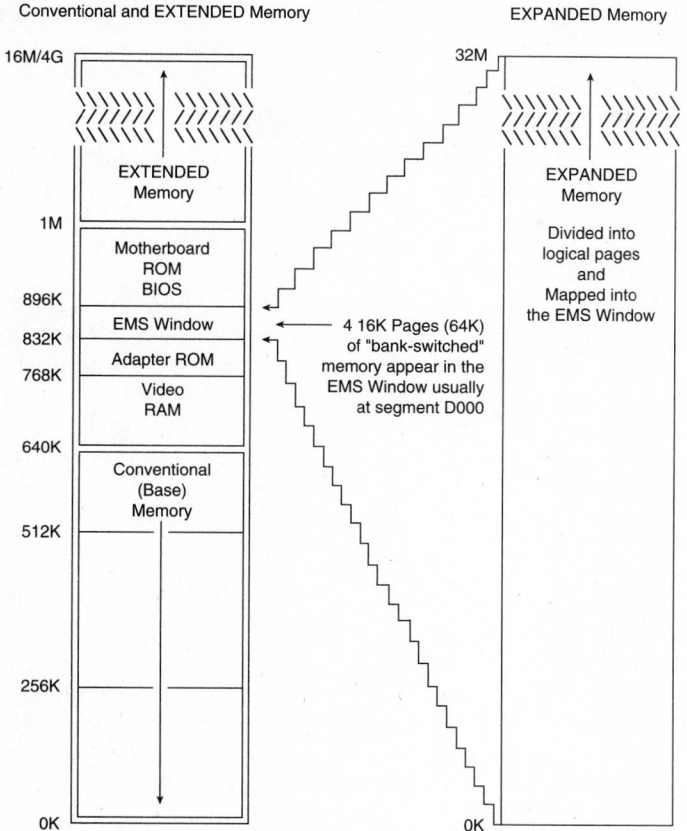

Fig. 7.17
Conventional, extended, and expanded memory.

Intel originally created a custom purpose memory board that had the necessary EMS bank-switching hardware. They called these boards *Above Boards*, and they were sold widely many years ago. EMS was designed with 8-bit systems in mind and was appropriate for them because they had no capability to access extended memory. 286 and newer systems, however, have the capability to have 15 or more megabytes of extended memory, which is much more efficient than the goofy (and slow) bank-switching EMS scheme. The Above Boards are no longer being manufactured, and EMS memory—as a concept as well as functionally—is extremely obsolete. If you have any antique software that still requires EMS memory, you are advised to upgrade to newer versions that can use extended memory directly. It is also possible to use the powerful Memory Management Unit (MMU) of the 386 and higher processors to convert extended memory to function like LIM EMS, but this should only be done if there is no way to use the extended memory directly. EMM386 can convert extended to expanded and, in fact, was originally designed for this purpose, although today it is more likely being used to map extended memory into the UMA for the purposes of loading drivers and not for EMS. The EMM386 driver is included with DOS versions 5 and newer as well as with Windows. If you have several versions on hand, as a rule, always use the newest one.

Preventing ROM BIOS Memory Conflicts and Overlap

As detailed in previous sections, C000 and D000 are reserved for use by adapter-board ROM and RAM. If two adapters have overlapping ROM or RAM addresses, usually neither board operates properly. Each board functions if you remove or disable the other one, but they do not work together.

With many adapter boards, you can change the actual memory locations to be used with jumpers, switches, or driver software, which might be necessary to allow two boards to coexist in one system. This type of conflict can cause problems for troubleshooters. You must read the documentation for each adapter to find out what memory addresses the adapter uses and how to change the addresses to allow coexistence with another adapter. Most of the time, you can work around these problems by reconfiguring the board or changing jumpers, switch settings, or software-driver parameters. This change enables the two boards to coexist and stay out of each other's way.

Additionally, you must ensure that adapter boards do not use the same IRQ (interrupt request line), DMA (direct memory access) channel, or I/O Port address. You can easily avoid adapter board memory, IRQ, DMA channel, and I/O Port conflicts by creating a chart or template to mock up the system configuration by penciling on the template the resources already used by each installed adapter. You end up with a picture of the system resources and the relationship of each adapter to the others. This procedure helps you anticipate conflicts and ensures that you configure each adapter board correctly the first time. The template also becomes important documentation when you consider new adapter purchases. New adapters must be configurable to use the available resources in your system.

ROM Shadowing

Computers based on the 386 or higher CPU chip, which provide memory access on a 32- or 64-bit path, often use a 16-bit data path for system ROM BIOS information. In addition, adapter cards with on-board BIOS may use an 8-bit path to system memory. On these high-end computers, using a 16- or 8-bit path to memory is a significant bottleneck to system performance. In addition to these problems of width, most actual ROM chips are available in maximum speeds far less than what is available for the system's dynamic RAM. For example, the fastest ROMs available are generally 150ns to 200ns, whereas the RAM in a modern system is rated at 60ns. Because ROM is so slow, any system accesses to programs or data in ROM cause many additional wait states to be inserted. These wait states can slow the entire system down tremendously, especially considering that many of the driver programs used constantly by DOS reside in the BIOS chips found on the motherboard and many of the installed adapters. Fortunately, a way was found to transfer the contents of the slow 8- or 16-bit ROM chips into much faster 32-bit main memory. This is called *shadowing the ROMs.*

Virtually all 386 and higher systems enable you to use what is termed *shadow memory* for the motherboard and possibly some adapter ROMs as well. Shadowing essentially moves the programming code from slow ROM chips into fast 32-bit system memory. Shadowing slower ROMs by copying their contents into RAM can greatly speed up these BIOS routines—sometimes making them four to five times faster. The shadowing is accomplished by using the powerful Memory Management Unit (MMU) in the 386 and higher processors. With the appropriate instructions, the MMU can take a copy of the ROM code, place it in RAM, and enable the RAM such that it appears to the system at exactly the same addresses where it was originally located. This actually disables the ROM chips themselves, which are essentially shut down. The system RAM that is now masquerading as ROM is fully write-protected so that it acts in every way just like the real ROM, with the exception of being much faster, of course! Most systems have an option in the system Setup to enable shadowing for the motherboard BIOS (usually segment F000) and the video BIOS (usually the first 32K of segment C000). Some systems will go farther and offer you the capability to enable or disable shadowing in (usually 16K) increments throughout the remainder of the C000 and D000 segments.

The important thing to note about shadowing is that if you enable shadowing for a given set of addresses, anything found there when the system is booting will be copied to RAM and locked in place. If you were to do this to a memory range that had a network adapter's shared memory mapped into it, the network card would cease to function. You must only shadow ranges that contain true ROM and no RAM.

Some systems do not offer shadowing for areas other than the motherboard and video BIOS. In these systems, you can use a memory manager such as EMM386 (that comes with DOS and Windows) to enable shadowing for any range you specify. It is preferable to use the system's own internal shadowing capabilities first because the system shadowing uses memory that would otherwise be discarded. Using an external memory manager such as EMM386 for shadowing costs you a small amount of extended memory, equal to the amount of space you are shadowing.

If you enable shadowing for a range of addresses and one or more adapters or the system in general no longer works properly, then you may have scratch pad memory or other RAM within the shadowed area, which is not accessible as long as the shadowing remains active. In this case, you should disable the shadowing for the system to operate properly. If you can figure out precisely which addresses are ROM and which are RAM within the Upper Memory Area, you can selectively shadow only the ROM for maximum system performance.

Total Installed Memory versus Total Usable Memory

One thing that most people don't realize is that not all the SIMM or other RAM memory you purchase and install in a system will be available. Because of some quirks in system design, the system usually has to "throw away" up to 384K of RAM to make way for the Upper Memory Area.

For example, most systems with 4M of RAM (which is 4,096K) installed show only 3,712K installed during the POST or when running Setup. This showing indicates that 4,096K – 3,712K = 384K of missing memory! Some systems may show 3,968K with the same 4M installed, which works out to 4,096K – 3,968K = 128K missing.

If you run your Setup program and check out your base and extended memory values, you will find more information than just the single total shown during the POST. In most systems with 4,096K (4M), you have 640K base and 3072K extended. In some systems, Setup reports 640K base and 3328K extended memory, which is a bonus. In other words, most systems come up 384K short, but some come up only 128K short.

This shortfall is not easy to explain, but it is consistent from system to system. I currently take six to nine hours of class time in my seminars to fully explore, explain, and exploit memory, but this explanation must be more brief! Say that you have a 486 system with two installed 72-pin (36-bit) 1M SIMMs. This setup results in a total installed memory of 2M in two separate banks because the processor has a 32-bit data bus, and one parity bit is required for every eight data bits. Each SIMM is a single bank in this system. Note that most cheaper 486 systems use the 30-pin (9-bit) SIMMs of which four are required to make a single bank. The first bank (or SIMM in this case) starts at address 000000 (the first Meg), and the second starts at 100000 (the second Meg).

One of the cardinal rules of memory is that you absolutely cannot have two hardware devices wired to the same address. This means that 384K of the first memory bank in this system would be in direct conflict with the Video RAM (segments A000 and B000), any adapter card ROMs (segments C000 and D000), and of course the motherboard ROM (segments E000 and F000). This means that all SIMM RAM that occupies these addresses must be shut off or the system will not function! Actually, a motherboard designer can do three things with the SIMM memory that would overlap from A0000-FFFFF, as shown in the following list:

■ Use the faster RAM to hold a copy of any slow ROMs (shadowing), disabling the ROM in the process.

■ Turn off any RAM not used for shadowing, eliminating any UMA conflicts.

■ Remap any RAM not used for shadowing, adding to the stack of currently installed extended memory.

Most systems shadow the motherboard ROM (usually 64K) and the video ROM (32K), and simply turn off the rest. Some motherboard ROMs allow additional shadowing to be selected between C8000-DFFFF, usually in 16K increments. Note that you can only shadow ROM, never RAM, so if any card (such as a network card for example) has a RAM buffer in the C8000-DFFFF area, you must not shadow the RAM buffer addresses or the card does not function. For the same reason, you cannot shadow the A0000-BFFFF area because this is the video adapter RAM buffer.

Most motherboards do not do any remapping, which means that any of the 384K not shadowed is simply turned off. That is why enabling shadowing does not seem to use any memory. The memory used for shadowing would otherwise be discarded in most systems. These systems would appear to be short by 384K compared to what is physically installed in the system. In my example system with 2M, no remapping would result in 640K of base memory and 1,024K of extended memory, for a total of 1,664K of usable RAM—384K short of the total (2,048K – 384K).

More-advanced systems shadow what they can and then remap any segments that do not have shadowing into extended memory so as not to waste the non-shadowed RAM. PS/2 systems, for example, shadow the motherboard BIOS area (E0000-FFFFF or 128K in these systems) and remap the rest of the first bank of SIMM memory (256K from A0000-DFFFF) to whatever address follows the last installed bank. Note that PS/2 systems have the video BIOS integrated with the motherboard BIOS in E0000-FFFFF, so no separate video BIOS exists to shadow as compared to other systems. In my example system with two 1M 36-bit SIMMs, the 256K not used for shadowing would be remapped to 200000-23FFFF, which is the start of the third megabyte. This affects diagnostics because if you had any memory error reported in those addresses (200000-23FFFF), it would indicate a failure in the FIRST SIMM, even though the addresses point to the end of installed extended memory. The addresses from 100000-1FFFFF would be in the second SIMM, and the 640K base memory 000000-09FFFF would be back in the first SIMM. As you can see, figuring out how the SIMMs are mapped into the system is not easy!

Most systems that do remapping can only remap an entire segment if no shadowing is going on within it. The video RAM area in segments A000 and B000 can never contain shadowing, so at least 128K can be remapped to the top of installed extended memory in any system that supports remapping. Because most systems shadow in segments F000 (motherboard ROM) and C000 (Video ROM), these two segments cannot be remapped. This leaves 256K maximum for remapping. Any system remapping the full 384K must not be shadowing at all, which would slow down the system and is not recommended. Shadowing is always preferred over remapping, and remapping what is not shadowed is definitely preferred to simply turning off the RAM.

Systems that have 384K of "missing" memory do not do remapping. If you want to determine if your system has any missing memory, all you need to know are three things. One is the total physical memory actually installed. The other two items can be discovered by running your Setup program. You want to know the total base and extended memory numbers recognized by the system. Then simply subtract the base and extended memory from the total installed to determine the missing memory. You will usually find that your system is "missing" 384K, but may be lucky and have a system that remaps 256K of what is missing and thus shows only 128K of memory missing. Virtually all systems use some of the missing memory for shadowing ROMs, especially the motherboard and video BIOS. So what is missing is not completely wasted. Systems "missing" 128K will find that it is being used to shadow your motherboard BIOS (64K from F0000-FFFFF) and video BIOS (32K from C0000-C8000). The remainder of segment C0000 (32K from C8000-CFFFF) is simply being turned off. All other segments (128K from A0000-BFFFF and 128K from D0000-EFFFF) are being remapped to the start of the fifth megabyte (400000-43FFFF). Most systems simply disable these remaining segments rather then take the trouble to remap them. Remapping requires additional logic and BIOS routines to accomplish, and many motherboard designers do not feel that it is worth the effort to reclaim 256K. Note that if your system is doing remapping, any errors reported near the end of installed extended memory are likely in the first bank of memory because that is where they are remapped from. The first bank in a 32-bit system would be constructed of either four 30-pin (9-bit) SIMMs or one 72-pin (36-bit) SIMM.

Adapter Memory Configuration and Optimization

Ideally, adapter boards would be simple "plug-and-play" devices that require you to merely plug the adapter into a motherboard slot and then use it. However, sometimes it almost seems that adapter boards (except on EISA and MCA systems) are designed as if they were the only adapter likely to be present on a system. Rather than adapter boards being plug-and-play, they usually require you to know the upper memory addresses and IRQ and DMA channels already on your system and then to configure the new adapter so that it does not conflict with your already-installed adapters.

Adapter boards use upper memory for their BIOS and as working RAM. If two boards attempt to use the same BIOS area or RAM area of upper memory, a conflict occurs that can keep your system from booting. The following sections cover ways to avoid these potential conflicts and how to troubleshoot them if they do occur. In addition, these sections discuss moving adapter memory to resolve conflicts and provide some ideas on optimizing adapter memory use.

Adding adapters to EISA and MCA systems is somewhat more simple because these system architectures feature *auto-configure adapter boards*. In other words, EISA and MCA systems work with adapters to determine available upper memory addresses, IRQs, and DMA channels and automatically configure all adapters to work optimally together.

How to Determine What Adapters Occupy the UMA. You can determine what adapters are using space in upper memory in the following two ways:

- Study the documentation for each adapter on your system to determine the memory addresses they use.

- Use a software utility that can quickly determine for you what upper memory areas your adapters are using.

The simplest way (although by no means always the most foolproof) is to use a software utility to determine the upper memory areas used by the adapters installed on your system. One such utility, Microsoft Diagnostics (MSD), comes with Windows 3 and DOS 6 or higher versions. You also can download MSD from the Microsoft BBS (see the vendor list for the number). This utility examines your system configuration and determines not only the upper memory used by your adapters, but also the IRQs used by each of these adapters. Many other utilities can accomplish the same task, but most people already have a copy of MSD—whether they know it or not!

After you run MSD or another utility to determine your system's upper memory configuration, make a printout of the memory addresses used. Thereafter, you can quickly refer to the printout when you are adding a new adapter to ensure that the new board does not conflict with any devices already installed on your system.

Moving Adapter Memory to Resolve Conflicts. After you identify a conflict or potential conflict by studying the documentation for the adapter boards installed on your system or using a software diagnostic utility to determine the upper memory addresses used by your adapter boards, you may have to reconfigure one or more of your adapters to move the upper memory space used by a problem adapter.

Most adapter boards make moving adapter memory a somewhat simple process, enabling you to change a few jumpers or switches to reconfigure the board. The following steps help you resolve most conflicts that arise because adapter boards conflict with one another:

1. Determine the upper memory addresses currently used by your adapter boards and write them down.

2. Determine if any of these addresses are overlapping, which results in a conflict.

3. Consult the documentation for your adapter boards to determine which boards can be reconfigured so that all adapters have access to unique memory addresses.

4. Configure the affected adapter boards so that no conflict in memory addresses occurs.

For example, if one adapter uses the upper memory range C8000-CBFFF and another adapter uses the range CA000-CCFFF, you have a potential address conflict. One of these must be changed.

Optimizing Adapter Memory Use. On an ideal PC, adapter boards would always come configured so that the upper memory addresses they use immediately follow the upper memory addresses used by the previous adapter, with no overlap that would cause conflicts. Such an upper memory arrangement would not only be "clean," but also would make it much more simple to use available upper memory for loading device drivers and memory-resident programs. However, this is not the case. Adapter boards often leave gaps of unused memory between one another, which is, of course, preferable to an overlap, but still is not the best use of upper memory.

Users who want to make the most of their upper memory might consider studying the documentation for each adapter board installed on their system to determine a way to compact the upper memory used by each of these devices. For example, if it were possible on a particular system, using the adapters installed on it, the use of upper memory could be more simple if you configured your adapter boards so that the blocks of memory they use fit together like bricks in a wall, rather than look like a slice of

Swiss cheese, as is the case on most systems. The more you can reduce your free upper memory to as few contiguous chunks as possible, the more completely and efficiently you can take advantage of the upper memory area.

Taking Advantage of Unused Upper Memory. On systems based on the 386 or higher CPU chip, memory-resident programs and device drivers can be moved into the upper memory area by using a memory manager like the DOS 6.x MEMMAKER utility or Quarterdeck's QEMM. These memory management utilities examine the memory-resident programs and device drivers installed on your system, determine their memory needs, and then calculate the best way to move these drivers and programs into upper memory, thus freeing the conventional memory they used.

Using MEMMAKER and QEMM is quite simple. Make a backup of your CONFIG.SYS and AUTOEXEC.BAT files so that you have usable copies if you need them to restore your system configuration, and then run either MEMMAKER from the DOS prompt or use the installation program on the QEMM diskette. Both programs install required device drivers in your CONFIG.SYS file, and then begin optimizing your memory configuration. Both do an outstanding job of freeing up conventional memory, although QEMM can free more conventional memory automatically than most other utilities. With careful fine-tuning, an individual using only the raw DOS HIMEM.SYS and EMM386.EXE drivers can perform feats of memory management that no automatic program can do!

The following sections cover using memory management software to optimize conventional memory, as well as additional ways to configure your system memory to make your system run as efficiently as possible. It is important to note that the DOS HIMEM.SYS and EMM386.EXE play an integral role in MEMMAKER's capability to move device drivers and memory-resident programs into upper memory. The next two sections describe using HIMEM.SYS and EMM386.EXE to configure extended and expanded memory.

Using HIMEM.SYS (DOS). The DOS device driver HIMEM.SYS, which has been included with Windows DOS 4.0 and higher, is used to configure extended memory to the XMS specification as well as to enable the use of the first 64K of extended memory as the High Memory Area (HMA). HIMEM.SYS is installed by adding a line invoking the device driver to your CONFIG.SYS file.

The XMS extended memory specification was developed by Microsoft, Intel, AST Corp., and Lotus Development in 1987 and specifies how programs can use memory beyond the first megabyte on systems based on the 286 CPU chip or higher. The XMS specification also allows real-mode programs (those designed to run in DOS) to use extended memory in several different ways.

Using EMM386.EXE (DOS). The program EMM386.EXE, which is included with DOS 5.0 and higher, is used primarily to map XMS memory (extended memory managed by HIMEM.SYS) into unused regions of the Upper Memory Area (UMA). This allows programs to be loaded into these regions for use under DOS. EMM386 also has a second-ary function of using XMS memory to emulate EMS version 4 memory, which can then be used by programs that need expanded memory. For more information on using EMM386.EXE, refer to Que's *Using MS-DOS 6* or your DOS manual.

MS-DOS 6.x MEMMAKER. You can increase the amount of conventional memory avail-able to software applications on systems based on the 386 chip and above by running the MS-DOS 6.x utility MEMMAKER. DOS 5 had the capability, using EMM386, to map extended memory into the Upper Memory Area so that DOS can load memory-resident programs and drivers into the UMA. Unfortunately, this required an extensive knowl-edge of the upper memory configuration of a particular system, as well as trial and error to see what programs can fit into the available free regions. This process was difficult enough that many people were not effectively using their memory under DOS (and Win-dows). To make things easier, when DOS 6 was released, Microsoft included a menu driven program called MEMMAKER that determines the system configuration and auto-matically creates the proper EMM386 statements and inserts them into the CONFIG.SYS file. By manipulating the UMA manually or through MEMMAKER and loading device drivers and memory-resident programs into upper memory, you can have more than 600K of free conventional memory.

Over the course of months or years of use, the installation programs for various software utilities often install so many memory-resident programs and device drivers in your AUTOEXEC.BAT and CONFIG.SYS files that you have too little conventional memory left to start all the programs you want to run. You may want to use MEMMAKER to free up more conventional memory for your programs. When you run the MEMMAKER util-ity, it automatically performs the following functions to free up more memory:

- Moves a portion of the DOS kernel into the high memory area (HMA)

- Maps free XMS memory into unused regions in the Upper Memory Area (UMA) as *Upper Memory Blocks* (UMBs), into which DOS can then load device drivers and memory-resident programs to free up the conventional memory these drivers and programs otherwise use

- Modifies CONFIG.SYS and AUTOEXEC.BAT to cause DOS to load memory-resident programs and device drivers into UMBs

Before running MEMMAKER, carefully examine your CONFIG.SYS and AUTOEXEC.BAT files to identify unnecessary device drivers and memory-resident programs. For example, the DOS device driver ANSI.SYS is often loaded in CONFIG.SYS to enable you to use color and other attributes at the DOS prompt as well as to remap the keys on your key-board. If you are primarily a Windows user and do not spend much time at the DOS prompt, then you can eliminate ANSI.SYS from your CONFIG.SYS file to free up the memory the driver is using.

II

Primary System Components

After you strip down CONFIG.SYS and AUTOEXEC.BAT to their bare essentials (it is advisable to make backup copies first), you are ready to run MEMMAKER to optimize your system memory. To run MEMMAKER, exit from any other programs you are running; start your network or any memory-resident programs and device drivers you absolutely need; and at the DOS prompt, type the following:

MEMMAKER

The MEMMAKER setup runs in two modes—Express and Custom. Express setup is preferable for those who want to enable MEMMAKER to load device drivers and memory-resident programs into high memory with the minimum amount of user input, unless they have an EGA or VGA (but not a Super VGA) monitor. If you have an EGA or VGA monitor, choose Custom Setup and answer Yes in the advanced options screen where it asks whether MeMMAKER should use monochrome region (B0000-B7FFF) for running programs. Use the defaults for the rest of the options in Custom Setup unless you are sure that one of the defaults is not correct for your system. Custom setup is probably not a good idea unless you are knowledgeable about optimizing system memory and particular device drivers and memory-resident programs on the system.

When MEMMAKER finishes optimizing the system memory, the following three lines are added to CONFIG.SYS:

```
DEVICE=C:\DOS\HIMEM.SYS
DEVICE=C:\DOS\EMM386.EXE NOEMS
DOS=HIGH,UMB
```

In addition, MEMMAKER modifies each line in CONFIG.SYS and AUTOEXEC.BAT that loads a device driver or memory-resident program now being loaded into UMBs. Various DEVICE= lines in your CONFIG.SYS are changed to DEVICEHIGH=, and various lines in your AUTOEXEC.BAT have the LH (LoadHigh) command inserted in front of them. For example, the line DEVICE=ANSI.SYS is changed to DEVICEHIGH=ANSI.SYS. In your AUTOEXEC.BAT, lines like C:\DOS\DOSKEY are changed to LH C:\DOS\DOSKEY. The DEVICEHIGH and LH commands load the device drivers and memory-resident programs into UMBs. MEMMAKER also adds codes to specify where in upper memory each program will be loaded. For example, after you run MEMMAKER, a statement like this might be added to your AUTOEXEC.BAT:

```
LH /L:1 C:\DOS\DOSKEY
```

The "/L:1" causes the resident program DOSKEY to load into the first UMB region. On many systems, MEMMAKER configures the system to free up 620K of conventional memory.

For detailed information on using the MEMMAKER utility, consult your DOS 6 manual or Que's *Using MS-DOS 6.2,* Special Edition. If you have MS-DOS, you can get help on MEMMAKER by typing **HELP MEMMAKER** at the DOS prompt.

IBM-DOS 6.x RAMBoost. The IBM-DOS 6.x RAMBoost utility, licensed from Central Point, which supplies some of the DOS 6 utilities, works much like MEMMAKER to free up additional conventional memory. After you make backup copies of CONFIG.SYS and

AUTOEXEC.BAT and strip down these files to only what you need to load, enter the following at the DOS prompt:

RAMSETUP

RAMBoost calculates the best way to load your memory-resident programs and device drivers into UMBs. RAMBoost gives results roughly equivalent to the MS-DOS 6 MEMMAKER utility. On many systems, it frees up 620K of conventional memory.

Third-Party Memory Managers. Although MEMMAKER and RAMBoost do a good job of freeing-up conventional memory on most systems, memory management utilities like Quarterdeck's QEMM, and Qualitas' 386MAX can do a better job on many systems with more complex configurations, and therefore, numerous memory-resident programs and device drivers. The following sections provide information about QEMM and 386MAX.

Quarterdeck QEMM. One of the strengths of QEMM is how simple it is to install and use. Before running the QEMM INSTALL program, make a backup of your CONFIG.SYS and AUTOEXEC.BAT files so that you have usable copies if you need them to restore your system configuration. Then exit any program you are running. At the DOS prompt, log in to the drive where the QEMM install diskette is located and run the INSTALL program. QEMM copies its files to the C:\QEMM directory (or another directory if you want).

Then the INSTALL program loads the Optimize utility, which calculates the upper memory needed for your memory-resident programs and device drivers and determines the proper region of upper memory for each. During this process, your system is rebooted several times (or when prompted, you may have to turn off your system and then restart it). When Optimize is finished, you can type **MEM** at the DOS prompt to find out how much free conventional memory your system has.

After QEMM is installed and running on your system, each time you add a memory-resident program or device driver, or any time you add or remove an adapter board (which might change the configuration of upper memory), you need to again run OPTIMIZE. For additional information on installing and running QEMM, and for troubleshooting help, consult your QEMM user manual.

One of the best features of QEMM is that it comes with a system configuration diagnostic utility called MANIFEST. This program is much like MSD, but offers more information and detail in many areas.

Qualitas 386MAX. Before running the 386MAX INSTALL program, make a backup copy of your CONFIG.SYS and AUTOEXEC.BAT files in case you need them later to restore your system. Then exit any program you are running, log in to the drive with the 386MAX install diskette, and run INSTALL. 386MAX copies its files to the C:\386MAX subdirectory (or any directory you choose). Then the INSTALL program loads the MAXIMIZE utility, which determines where in upper memory to place each memory-resident program and device driver.

II

Primary System Components

When MAXIMIZE finishes, you can type **MEM** at the DOS prompt to find out how much free conventional memory your system has.

As with MEMMAKER and QEMM, 386MAX uses codes to specify which region of upper memory each memory-resident program and device driver is loaded into. Whenever you add a new device driver or memory-resident program to your system, or when you add or remove an adapter, you must again run MAXIMIZE.

Physical Memory

The CPU and motherboard architecture dictates a computer's physical memory capacity. The 8088 and 8086, with 20 address lines, can use as much as 1M (1,024K) of RAM. The 286 and 386SX CPUs have 24 address lines; they can keep track of as much as 16M of memory. The 386DX, 486, and Pentium CPUs have a full set of 32 address lines; they can keep track of a staggering 4 gigabytes of memory.

When the 286, 386, 486, and Pentium chips emulate the 8088 chip (as they do when running a single DOS program), they implement a hardware operating mode called *real mode*. Real mode is the only mode available on the 8086 and 8088 chips used in PC and XT systems. In *real mode,* all Intel processors—even the mighty Pentium—are restricted to using only 1M of memory, just as their 8086 and 8088 ancestors, and the system design reserves 384K of that amount. Only in protected mode can the 286 or better chips use their maximum potential for memory addressing.

Pentium-based systems can address as much as 4 gigabytes of memory. To put these memory-addressing capabilities into perspective, 4 gigabytes (4,096M) of memory costing the going rate of about $30 per megabyte for fast (60 nanoseconds or less) RAM chips would total $122,880!! Of course, you could probably negotiate a much better price with a chip vendor if you planned to buy 4 gigabytes of SIMMs! Even if you could afford all this memory, the largest SIMMs available today are 72-pin versions with 64M capacity. Most Pentium motherboards have only four to eight SIMM sockets, which allows a maximum of 256M to 512M if all four or eight sockets are filled. Not all systems accept all SIMMs, so you might have a limitation of less than this amount for many Pentium and 486 systems.

On many systems, accessing RAM chips installed directly on a motherboard is faster than accessing memory through an expansion slot. Even without considering this speed advantage, you have the advantage of saving slots. The more memory chips you can get on the motherboard, the fewer adapter slots you need to use. A system that does not have a memory expansion slot faces a large reduction in speed if you use a memory expansion board made for a standard 16-bit slot.

Some 386 and 486 motherboards may have problems addressing memory past 16M due to DMA (Direct Memory Access) controller problems. If you install an ISA adapter that uses a DMA channel and you have more than 16M of memory, you have the potential for problems because the ISA bus only allows DMA access to 16M. Attempted transfers beyond 16M cause the system to crash. Most modern 486 motherboards enable you to install a maximum of 64M on the motherboard using four 16M SIMMs.

Because the PC hardware design reserves the top 384K of the first megabyte of system memory for use by the system itself, you have access to 640K for your programs and data. The use of 384K by the system results in the 640K conventional memory limit. The amount of conventional memory you can actually use for programs depends on the memory used by device drivers (such as ANSI.SYS) and memory-resident programs (such as MOUSE.COM) you load in your CONFIG.SYS and AUTOEXEC.BAT files. Device drivers and memory-resident programs usually use conventional memory.

RAM Chips

A *RAM chip* temporarily stores programs when they are running and the data being used by those programs. RAM chips are sometimes termed *volatile storage* because when you turn off your computer or an electrical outage occurs, whatever is stored in RAM is lost unless you saved it to your hard drive. Because of the volatile nature of RAM, many computer users make it a habit to save their work frequently. (Some software applications can do timed backups automatically.)

Launching a computer program instructs DOS to bring an EXE or COM disk file into RAM, and computer programs reside in RAM as long as they are running. The CPU executes programmed instructions in RAM. RAM stores your keystrokes when you use a word processor. RAM stores numbers used in calculations. The CPU also stores results in RAM. Telling a program to save your data instructs the program to store RAM contents on your hard drive as a file.

If you decide to purchase more RAM, you need the information on RAM chips and their speeds presented in the following sections to help ensure that you don't slow down your computer when you add memory.

Physical Storage and Organization

RAM chips can be physically integrated into the motherboard or adapter board in several forms. Older systems used individual memory chips, called *Dual In-line Pin* (DIP) chips, that were plugged into sockets or soldered directly to a board. Most modern systems use a memory package called a *Single In-line Memory Module* (SIMM). These modules combine several chips on a small circuit board plugged into a retaining socket. A SIPP, or Single In-line Pin Package, is similar to a SIMM, but it uses pins rather than an edge connector to connect to the motherboard. It would be possible to convert a SIPP to a SIMM by cutting off the pins, or to convert a SIMM to a SIPP by soldering pins on.

II

Primary System Components

Several types of memory chips have been used in PC system motherboards. Most of these chips are single-bit-wide chips, available in several capacities. The following is a list of available RAM chips and their capacities:

16K by 1 bit	These devices, used in the original IBM PC with a Type 1 motherboard, have a small capacity compared with the current standard. You won't find much demand for these chips except from owners of original IBM PC systems.
64K by 1 bit	These chips were used in the standard IBM PC Type 2 motherboard and in the XT Type 1 and 2 motherboards. Many memory adapters, such as the popular vintage AST 6-pack boards, use these chips also.
128K by 1 bit	These chips, used in the IBM AT Type 1 motherboard, often were a strange physical combination of two 64K chips stacked on top of one another and soldered together. True single-chip versions were used also for storing the parity bits in the IBM XT 286.
256K by 1 bit (or 64K by 4 bits)	These chips once were very popular in motherboards and memory cards. The IBM XT Type 2 and IBM AT Type 2 motherboards, as well as most compatible systems, used these chips.
1M by 1 bit (or 256K by 4 bits)	These 1M chips are very popular in systems today because of their low cost. These chips are most often used in SIMMs because of their ease of installation and service. (See the section entitled "Single In-Line Memory Modules (SIMMs)" for more information.)
4M by 1 bit (or 1M by 4 bits)	Four-megabit chips have gained popularity recently and now are used in many compatible motherboards and memory cards. They are used primarily in 4M and 8M SIMMs and generally are not sold as individual chips.
16M by 1 bit (or 4M by 4 bits)	16-megabit chips are gaining popularity in Pentium-based systems in which as much as 256 megabytes can be installed on some systems. The use of these chips in SIMMs allow for 16M or larger capacities for a single SIMM.
64M by 1 bit (or 16M by 4 bits)	64-megabit chips are the most recent on the market. These chips allow enormous SIMM capacities of 64M or larger! Because of the high expense and limited availability of these chips, you see them only in the most expensive systems.

Figure 7.18 shows a typical memory chip. Each marking on the chip is significant.

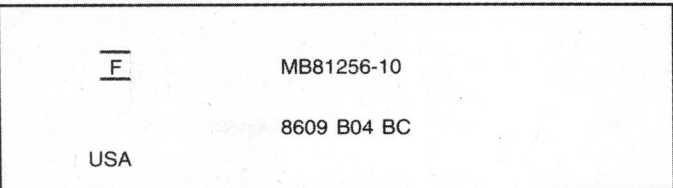

Fig. 7.18
The markings on a typical memory chip.

The -10 on the chip corresponds to its speed in nanoseconds (a 100-nanosecond rating). MB81256 is the chip's part number, which usually contains a clue about the chip's capacity. The key digits are 1256, which indicate that this chip is 1 bit wide, and has a depth of 256K. The 1 means that to make a full byte with parity, you need nine of these single-bit-wide chips. A chip with a part number KM4164B-10 indicates a 64K-by-1-bit chip at a speed of 100 nanoseconds. The following list matches common chips with their part numbers:

Part Number	Chip
4164	64K by 1 bit
4464	64K by 4 bits
41128	128K by 1 bit
44128	128K by 4 bits
41256	256K by 1 bit
44256	256K by 4 bits
41000	1M by 1 bit
44000	1M by 4 bits

Chips wider than 1 bit are used to construct banks of less than 9, 18, or 36 chips (depending on the system architecture). For example, in the IBM XT 286, which is an AT-type 16-bit system, the last 128K bytes of memory on the motherboard consist of a bank with only six chips; four are 64K-by-4 bits wide, and two parity chips are 1 bit wide, storing 18 bits.

In figure 7.18, the "F" symbol centered between two lines is the manufacturer's logo for Fujitsu Microelectronics. The 8609 indicates the date of manufacture (ninth week of 1986). Some manufacturers, however, use a Julian date code. To decode the chip further, contact the manufacturer if you can tell who that is, or perhaps a memory chip vendor.

Memory Banks
Memory chips (DIPs, SIMMs, and SIPPs) are organized in *banks* on motherboards and memory cards. You should know the memory bank layout and position on the motherboard and memory cards.

II

Primary System Components

You need to know the bank layout when adding memory to the system. In addition, memory diagnostics report error locations by byte and bit addresses, and you must use these numbers to locate which bank in your system contains the problem.

The banks usually correspond to the data bus capacity of the system's microprocessor. Table 7.5 shows the widths of individual banks based on the type of PC:

Table 7.5	Memory Bank Widths on Different Systems			
Processor	Data Bus	Bank Size (w/Parity)	30-Pin SIMMs per Bank	72-Pin SIMMs per Bank
8088	8-bit	9-bits	1	1 (4 banks)
8086	16-bit	18-bits	2	1 (2 banks)
286	16-bit	18-bits	2	1 (2 banks)
386SX, SL, SLC	16-bit	18-bits	2	1 (2 banks)
386DX	32-bit	36-bits	4	1
486SLC, SLC2	16-bit	18-bits	2	1 (2 banks)
486SX, DX, DX2, DX4	32-bit	36-bits	4	1
Pentium	64-bit	72-bits	8	2

The number of bits for each bank can be made up of single chips or SIMMs. For example, in a 286 system that would use an 18-bit bank, you could make up a bank of 18 individual 1-bit-wide chips, or you could use four individual 4-bit-wide chips to make up the data bits, and two individual 1-bit-wide chips for the parity bits. Most modern systems do not use chips, but instead use SIMMs. If the system has an 18-bit bank, then it likely would use 30-pin SIMMs and have two SIMMs per bank. All the SIMMs in a single bank must be the same size and type. As you can see, the 30-pin SIMMs are less than ideal for 32-bit systems because you must use them in increments of four per bank! Because these SIMMs are available in 1M and 4M capacities today, this means that a single bank has to be 4M or 16M of memory, with no in-between amounts. Using 30-pin SIMMs in 32-bit systems artificially constricts memory configurations and such systems are not recommended. If a 32-bit system uses 72-pin SIMMs, then each SIMM represents a separate bank, and the SIMMs can be added or removed on an individual basis rather than in groups of four. This makes memory configuration much easier and more flexible.

Older systems often used individual chips. For example, the IBM PC Type 2 and XT Type 1 motherboard contains four banks of memory labeled Bank 0, 1, 2, and 3. Each bank uses nine 64K-by-1-bit chips. The total number of chips present is 4 times 9, or 36 chips, organized as shown in figure 7.19.

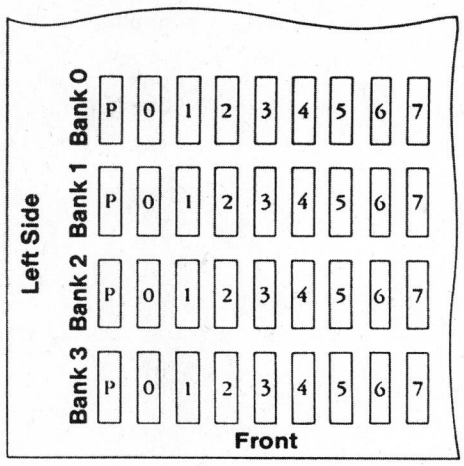

Top View of System Board

Fig. 7.19
A memory bank on a PC Type 2 or XT Type 1 motherboard.

This layout is used in many older 8-bit motherboards, including the Type 1 and 2 PC motherboards and the Type 1 and 2 XT motherboards. Most PC or XT clones also followed this scheme. Note that the parity chip is the leftmost chip in each bank on the XT motherboard.

The physical orientation used on a motherboard or memory card is arbitrary and determined by the board's designers. Documentation covering your system or card comes in very handy. You can determine the layout of a motherboard or adapter card through testing, but this takes time and may be difficult, particularly after you have a problem with a system.

Parity Checking

One standard IBM has set for the industry is that the memory chips in a bank of nine each handle one bit of data: eight bits per character plus one extra bit called the *parity bit*. The parity bit enables memory-control circuitry to keep tabs on the other eight bits—a built-in cross-check for the integrity of each byte in the system. If the circuitry detects an error, the computer stops and displays a message informing you of the malfunction. Some modern SIMMs have only three chips, however, with each chip handling three of the nine bits.

IBM established the *odd parity* standard for error checking. The following explanation may help you understand what is meant by odd parity. As the eight individual bits in a byte are stored in memory, a special chip called a *74LS280 parity generator/checker* on the motherboard (or memory card) evaluates the data bits by counting the number of 1s in the byte. If an even number of 1s is in the byte, the parity generator/checker chip creates a 1 and stores it as the ninth bit (parity bit) in the parity memory chip. That makes the total sum for all nine bits an odd number. If the original sum of the eight data bits is an odd number, the parity bit created is 0, keeping the 9-bit sum an odd number. The value of the parity bit is always chosen so that the sum of all nine bits (eight data bits plus one parity bit) is an odd number. Remember that the eight data bits in a byte are numbered 0 1 2 3 4 5 6 7. The following examples may make it easier to understand:

Data bit number: 0 1 2 3 4 5 6 7   Parity

Parity bit value: 1 0 1 1 0 0 1 1   0

In this example, because the total number of data bits with a value of 1 is an odd number (5), the parity bit must have a value of 0 to ensure an odd sum for all nine bits.

The following is another example:

Data bit number: 0 1 2 3 4 5 6 7   Parity

Parity bit value: 0 0 1 1 0 0 1 1   1

In this example, because the total number of data bits with a value of 1 is an even number (4), the parity bit must have a value of 1 to create an odd sum for all nine bits.

When the system reads memory back from storage, it checks the parity information. If a (9-bit) byte has an even number of bits with a parity bit value of 1, that byte must have an error. The system cannot tell which bit has changed, or if only a single bit has changed. If three bits changed, for example, the byte still flags a parity-check error; if two bits changed, however, the bad byte may pass unnoticed. The following examples show parity-check messages for three types of systems:

For the IBM PC: PARITY CHECK *x*

For the IBM XT: PARITY CHECK *x yyyyy (z)*

For the IBM AT and late model XT: PARITY CHECK *x yyyyy*

Where *x* is 1 or 2:

1 = Error occurred on the motherboard

2 = Error occurred in an expansion slot

yyyy represents a number from 00000 through FFFFF that indicates, in hexadecimal notation, the byte in which the error has occurred.

Where *(z)* is (S) or (E):

(S) = Parity error occurred in the system unit

(E) = Parity error occurred in the expansion chassis

An expansion chassis was an option IBM sold for the original PC and XT systems to add more expansion slots. This unit consisted of a backplane motherboard with eight slots, one of which contained a special extender/receiver card cabled to a similar extender/receiver card placed in the main system. Due to the extender/receiver cards in the main system and the expansion chassis, the net gain was six slots.

When a parity-check error is detected, the motherboard parity-checking circuits generate a *non-maskable interrupt* (NMI), which halts processing and diverts the system's attention to the error. The NMI causes a routine in the ROM to be executed. The routine clears the screen and then displays a message in the upper left corner of the screen. The message differs depending on the type of computer system. On some older IBM systems, the ROM parity-check routine halts the CPU. In such a case, the system locks up, and you must perform a hardware reset or a power-off/power-on cycle to restart the system. Unfortunately, all unsaved work is lost in the process. (An NMI is a system warning that software cannot ignore.)

Most systems do not halt the CPU when a parity error is detected; instead, they offer you a choice of either rebooting the system or continuing as though nothing happened. Additionally, these systems may display the parity error message in a different format from IBM, although the information presented is basically the same. For example, many systems with a Phoenix BIOS display these messages:

```
Memory parity interrupt at xxxx:xxxx
Type (S)hut off NMI, Type (R)eboot, other keys to continue
```

or

```
I/O card parity interrupt at xxxx:xxxx
Type (S)hut off NMI, Type (R)eboot, other keys to continue
```

The first of these two messages indicates a motherboard parity error (Parity Check 1), and the second indicates an expansion-slot parity error (Parity Check 2). Notice that the address given in the form `xxxx:xxxx` for the memory error is in a segment:offset form rather than a straight linear address such as with IBM's error messages. The segment:offset address form still gives you the location of the error to a resolution of a single byte.

Note that you have three ways to proceed after viewing this error message. You can press S, which shuts off parity checking and resumes system operation at the point where the parity check first occurred. Pressing R forces the system to reboot, losing any unsaved work. Pressing any other key causes the system to resume operation with parity checking still enabled. If the problem recurs, it is likely to cause another parity-check interruption. In most cases, it is most prudent to press S, which disables the parity checking so that you can then save your work. It would be best in this case to save your work to a floppy disk to prevent the possible corruption of a hard disk. You should also avoid overwriting any previous (still good) versions of whatever file you are saving, because in fact you may be saving a bad file due to the memory corruption. Because parity checking is now disabled, your save operations will not be interrupted. Then you should power the system off, restart it, and run whatever memory diagnostics software you have to try and track down the error. In some cases, the POST finds the error on the next restart, but in most cases you need to run a more sophisticated diagnostics program, perhaps in a continuous mode to locate the error.

The AMI BIOS displays the parity error messages in the following forms:

```
ON BOARD PARITY ERROR ADDR (HEX) = (xxxxx)
```

or

```
OFF BOARD PARITY ERROR ADDR (HEX) = (xxxxx)
```

These messages indicate that an error in memory has occurred during the POST, and the failure is located at the address indicated. The first one indicates the error occurred on the motherboard, whereas the second message indicates an error in an expansion slot adapter card. The AMI BIOS also can display memory errors in the following manner:

```
Memory Parity Error at xxxxx
```

or

```
I/O Card Parity Error at xxxxx
```

These messages indicate that an error in memory has occurred at the indicated address during normal operation. The first one indicates a motherboard memory error, and the second indicates an expansion slot adapter memory error.

Although many systems enable you to continue processing after a parity error, and even allow for the disabling of further parity checking, continuing to use your system after a parity error is detected can be dangerous if misused. The idea behind letting you continue using either method is to give you time to save any unsaved work before you diagnose and service the computer, but be careful how you do this.

Caution

When you are notified of a memory parity error, remember the parity check is telling you that memory has been corrupted. Do you want to save potentially corrupted data over the good file from the *last* time you saved? Definitely not! Make sure that you save your work to a different file name. In addition, after a parity error, save only to a floppy disk if possible and avoid writing to the hard disk; there is a slight chance that the hard drive could become corrupted if you save the contents of corrupted memory.

After saving your work, determine the cause of the parity error and repair the system. You may be tempted to use an option to shut off further parity checking and simply continue using the system as if nothing were wrong. Doing so resembles unscrewing the oil pressure warning indicator bulb on a car with an oil leak so that the oil pressure light won't bother you anymore!

IBM PS/2 systems have a slightly different way of communicating parity-check errors than the older IBM systems. To indicate motherboard parity errors, the message looks like this:

```
110

xxxxx
```

To indicate parity errors from an expansion slot, the message looks like this:

```
111

xxxxx
```

In these messages, the *xxxxx* indicates the address of the parity error. As with most IBM systems, the system is halted after these messages are displayed, thus eliminating any possibility of saving work.

Single In-Line Memory Modules (SIMMs)

For memory storage, most modern systems have adopted the single in-line memory module (SIMM) as an alternative to individual memory chips. These small boards plug into special connectors on a motherboard or memory card. The individual memory chips are soldered to the SIMM, so removing and replacing individual memory chips is impossible. Instead, you must replace the entire SIMM if any part of it fails. The SIMM is treated as though it were one large memory chip.

IBM compatibles have two main physical types of SIMMs—30-pin (9 bits) and 72-pin (36 bits)—with various capacities and other specifications. The 30-pin SIMMs are smaller than the 72-pin versions, and may have chips on either one or both sides. SIMMs are available both with and without parity bits. Until recently, all IBM-compatible systems used parity-checked memory to ensure accuracy. Other non-IBM-compatible systems like the Apple Macintosh have never used parity-checked memory. For example, Apple computers use the same 30-pin or 72-pin SIMMs as IBM systems, but Apple computers as a rule do not have parity-checking circuitry, so they can use slightly cheaper 30-pin SIMMs that are only eight bits wide instead of nine bits (eight data bits plus one parity bit) as is required on most IBM-compatible systems. They also can use 72-pin SIMMs that are only 32-bits wide rather than 36-bits (32 data bits plus 4 parity bits) as is required on most IBM compatibles. You can use the parity SIMMs in Apple systems; they will simply ignore the extra bits. If you use non-parity SIMMs in an IBM compatible that requires parity-checked memory, you instantly get memory errors, and the system cannot operate. If you service both IBM and Apple systems, you could simply stock only parity SIMMs because they can be used in either system.

Recently, a disturbing trend has developed in the IBM compatible marketplace. Some of the larger vendors have been shipping systems with parity checking disabled! These systems can use slightly cheaper non-parity SIMMs like the Apple systems. The savings amounts to about $10 per 4M SIMM, which can result in a savings to the manufacturer of about $20 for a typical 8M configuration. Because most buyers have no idea that the parity checking has been taken away (how often have you seen an ad that says "now featuring NO PARITY CHECKING"?), the manufacturer can sell its system that much cheaper. Because several of the big names have started selling systems without parity, most of the others have been forced to follow to remain price competitive. Because nobody wants to announce this information, it has remained as a sort of dirty little secret within the industry! What is amazing is that the 386 and higher processors all contain the parity circuitry within them, so no additional circuits are needed on the motherboard. It is solely the cost of the parity chips on the SIMMs that is being saved.

How can they do this? Well most newer motherboards have a method by which parity checking can be disabled to accommodate non-parity SIMMs. Most older motherboards absolutely required parity SIMMs because there was no way to disable the parity checking. Some newer motherboards have a jumper to enable or disable the parity circuitry. Some include this as a SETUP option, and some systems check the memory for parity bits and if they are not detected in all banks, parity checking is automatically disabled. In these systems, installing a single non-parity SIMM normally causes parity checking to be disabled for all memory. I have often found parity checking to be the first alert to system problems, so I am not thrilled that virtually all newer systems come with non-parity SIMMs. Fortunately, this can be rectified by specifying parity SIMMs when you order a new machine. If you don't specify parity SIMMs, then surely you will get the cheaper non-parity versions. Also make sure that your motherboard has parity checking enabled as well, because most are not coming configured with it enabled.

Figures 7.20 and 7.21 show typical 30-pin (9-bit) and 72-pin (36-bit) SIMMs, respectively. The pins are numbered from left to right and are connected through to both sides of the module. Note that all dimensions are in both inches and millimeters (in parentheses).

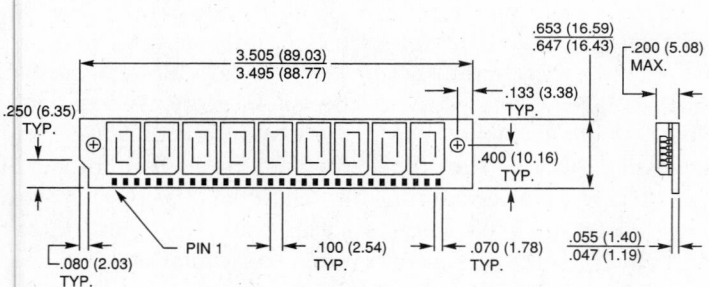

Fig. 7.20
A typical 30-pin (9-bit) SIMM.

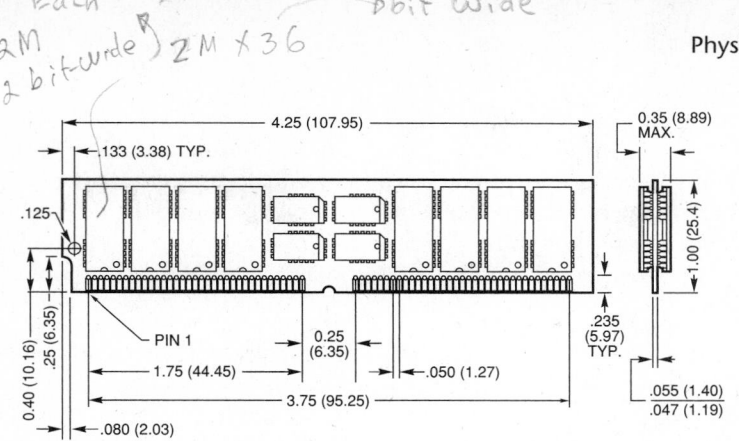

Each
2M
2 bit wide } 2M × 36 ← bit wide

Fig. 7.21

A typical 72-pin (36-bit) SIMM.

A SIMM is extremely compact, considering the amount of memory it holds. SIMMs are available in several capacities, depending on the version. Table 7.6 lists the different capacities available for both the 30-pin and 72-pin SIMMs.

Table 7.6 SIMM Capacities		
Capacity	**Parity SIMM**	**Non-Parity SIMM**
30-Pin SIMM Capacities		
256K	256K × 9	256K × 8
1M	1M × 9	1M × 8
4M	4M × 9	4M × 8
16M	16M × 9	16M × 8
72-Pin SIMM Capacities		
1M	256K × 36	256K × 32
2M	512K × 36	512K × 32
4M	1M × 36	1M × 32
8M	2M × 36	2M × 32
16M	4M × 36	4M × 32
32M	8M × 36	8M × 32
64M	16M × 36	16M × 32

Dynamic RAM SIMMs of each type and capacity are available in different speed ratings. These ratings are expressed in nanoseconds (billionths of a second, abbreviated ns). SIMMs have been available in many different speed ratings ranging from 120ns for some of the slowest, to 50ns for some of the fastest available. Many of the first systems to use SIMMs used versions rated at 120ns. These were quickly replaced in the market by 100ns and even faster versions. Today, you can generally purchase SIMMs rated at 80ns, 70ns, or 60ns. Both faster and slower ones are available, but they are not frequently required and are difficult to obtain. If a system requires a specific speed, then you can almost always substitute faster speeds if the one specified is not available. There are no problems in mixing SIMM speeds, as long as you use SIMMs equal or faster than what the system requires. Because often very little price difference exists between the different speed versions, I usually buy faster SIMMs than are needed for a particular application, as this may make them more usable in a future system that may require the faster speed.

Several variations on the 30-pin SIMMs can affect how they work (if at all) in a particular system. First, there are actually two variations on the pinout configurations. Most systems use a *generic* type of SIMM, which has an industry standard pin configuration. Many older IBM systems used a slightly modified 30-pin SIMM, starting with the XT-286 introduced in 1986 through the PS/2 Models 25, 30, 50, and 60. These systems require a SIMM with different signals on five of the pins. These are known as *IBM-style* 30-pin SIMMs. You can modify a generic 30-pin SIMM to work in the IBM systems and vice versa, but purchasing a SIMM with the correct pinouts is much easier. Be sure you identify to the SIMM vendor if you need the specific IBM-style versions.

Another issue with respect to the 30-pin SIMMs relates to the chip count. The SIMM itself acts as if it were a single chip of 9-bits wide (with parity), and it really does not matter how this total is derived. Older SIMMs were constructed with nine individual 1-bit-wide chips to make up the total, whereas many newer SIMMs use two 4-bit-wide chips and one 1-bit-wide chip for parity, making a total of three chips on the SIMM. Accessing the 3-chip SIMMs can require adjustments to the refresh timing circuits on the motherboard, and many older motherboards could not cope. Most newer motherboards automatically handle the slightly different refresh timing of both the 3-chip or 9-chip SIMMs, and in this case the 3-chip versions are more reliable, use less power, and generally cost less as well. If you have an older system, most likely it will also work with the 3-chip SIMMs, but some do not. Unfortunately, the only way to know is to try them. To prevent the additional time required to change them for 9-chip versions should the 3-chip versions not work in an older system, it seems prudent to recommend sticking with the 9-chip variety in any older systems.

The 72-pin SIMMs do not have different pinouts and are differentiated only by capacity and speed. These SIMMs are not affected by the number of chips on them. The 72-pin SIMMs are ideal for 32-bit systems like 486 machines because they comprise an entire bank of memory (32 data bits plus 4 parity bits). When you configure a system that uses a 72-pin SIMM, you can usually add or remove memory in single SIMM modules (except on systems that use interleaved memory schemes to reduce wait states). The 30-pin SIMMs are clumsy when used in a system with a 32-bit memory architecture because these SIMMs must be added or removed in quantities of four to make up a complete bank. A 386SX or a 286 system would require only two 9-bit SIMMs for a single bank of memory so the 30-pin SIMMs are a better match.

Remember that some 486 systems (such as the PS/2 90 and 95 systems) use interleaved memory to reduce wait states. This requires a multiple of two 36-bit SIMMs because interleaved memory accesses are alternated between the SIMMs to improve performance.

> **Note**
>
> A *bank* is the smallest amount of memory that can be addressed by the processor at one time and usually corresponds to the data bus width of the processor. If the memory is interleaved, then a virtual bank may be twice the absolute data bus width of the processor.

You cannot always replace a SIMM with a greater-capacity unit and expect it to work. For example, the IBM PS/2 Model 70-Axx and Bxx systems accept 72-pin SIMMs of 1M or 2M capacity, which are 80ns or faster. Although an 80ns 4M SIMM is available, it does not work in these systems. The PS/2 Model 55 SX and 65 SX, however, accept 1M, 2M, or 4M 72-pin SIMMs. A larger-capacity SIMM works only if the motherboard is designed to accept it in the first place. Consult your system documentation to determine the correct capacity and speed to use.

SIMMs were designed to eliminate chip creep, which plagues systems with memory chips installed in sockets. *Chip creep* occurs when a chip works its way out of its socket, caused by the normal thermal expansion and contraction from powering a system on and off. Eventually, chip creep leads to poor contact between the chip leads and the socket, and memory errors and problems begin.

The original solution for chip creep was to solder all the memory chips to the printed circuit board. This approach, however, was impractical. Memory chips fail more frequently than most other types of chips and soldering chips to the board made the units difficult to service.

The SIMM incorporates the best compromise between socketed and soldered chips. The chips are soldered to the SIMM, but you can replace the socketed SIMM module easily. In addition, the SIMM is held tight to the motherboard by a locking mechanism that does not work loose from contraction and expansion, but is easy for you to loosen. This solution is a good one, but it can increase repair costs. You must replace what amounts in some cases to an entire bank rather than one defective chip.

For example, if you have a 486DX4 with one 60ns 8M SIMM that goes bad, you could replace it for about $250 or less from chip suppliers who advertise in the computer magazines. This is certainly more expensive than replacing a single 256K chip costing about $2 each. Of course, 8M SIMMs are used on systems never designed for single chips. It would take 288 256K chips to equal the memory storage of one 8M SIMM. Troubleshooting a problem with a single SIMM device is much easier than troubleshooting 288 discrete chips. In addition, one SIMM is more reliable than 288 individual chips!

All systems on the market today use SIMMs. Even Apple Macintosh systems use SIMMs. The SIMM is not a proprietary memory system but rather an industry-standard device. As mentioned, some SIMMs have slightly different pinouts and specifications other than speed and capacity, so be sure that you obtain the correct SIMMs for your system.

SIMM Pinouts

Tables 7.7 and 7.8 show the interface connector pinouts for both 30-pin SIMM varieties, as well as the standard 72-pin version. Also included is a special presence detect table that shows the configuration of the presence detect pins on various 72-pin SIMMs. The presence detect pins are used by the motherboard to detect exactly what size and speed SIMM is installed. Industry-standard 30-pin SIMMs do not have a presence detect feature, but IBM did add this capability to its modified 30-pin configuration.

Table 7.7	Industry-Standard and IBM 30-Pin SIMM Pinouts	
Pin	**Standard SIMM Signal Names**	**IBM SIMM Signal Names**
1	+5 Vdc	+5 Vdc
2	Column Address Strobe	Column Address Strobe
3	Data Bit 0	Data Bit 0
4	Address Bit 0	Address Bit 0
5	Address Bit 1	Address Bit 1
6	Data Bit 1	Data Bit 1
7	Address Bit 2	Address Bit 2
8	Address Bit 3	Address Bit 3
9	Ground	Ground
10	Data Bit 2	Data Bit 2
11	Address Bit 4	Address Bit 4
12	Address Bit 5	Address Bit 5
13	Data Bit 3	Data Bit 3
14	Address Bit 6	Address Bit 6
15	Address Bit 7	Address Bit 7
16	Data Bit 4	Data Bit 4
17	Address Bit 8	Address Bit 8
18	Address Bit 9	Address Bit 9
19	Address Bit 10	Row Address Strobe 1
20	Data Bit 5	Data Bit 5
21	Write Enable	Write Enable
22	Ground	Ground
23	Data Bit 6	Data Bit 6
24	No Connection	Presence Detect (Ground)
25	Data Bit 7	Data Bit 7
26	Data Bit 8 (Parity) Out	Presence Detect (1M = Ground)
27	Row Address Strobe	Row Address Strobe
28	Column Address Strobe Parity	No Connection
29	Data Bit 8 (Parity) In	Data Bit 8 (Parity) I/O
30	+5 Vdc	+5 Vdc

Table 7.8   Standard 72-Pin SIMM Pinout

Pin	SIMM Signal Name
1	Ground
2	Data Bit 0
3	Data Bit 16
4	Data Bit 1
5	Data Bit 17
6	Data Bit 2
7	Data Bit 18
8	Data Bit 3
9	Data Bit 18
10	+5 Vdc
11	Column Address Strobe Parity
12	Address Bit 0
13	Address Bit 1
14	Address Bit 2
15	Address Bit 3
16	Address Bit 4
17	Address Bit 5
18	Address Bit 6
19	Reserved
20	Data Bit 4
21	Data Bit 20
22	Data Bit 5
23	Data Bit 21
24	Data Bit 6
25	Data Bit 22
26	Data Bit 7
27	Data Bit 23
28	Address Bit 7
29	Block Select 0
30	+5 Vdc
31	Address Bit 8
32	Address Bit 9
33	Row Address Strobe 3
34	Row Address Strobe 2
35	Parity Data Bit 2
36	Parity Data Bit 0
37	Parity Data Bit 1
38	Parity Data Bit 3
39	Ground

(continues)

Pin	SIMM Signal Name
40	Column Address Strobe 0
41	Column Address Strobe 2
42	Column Address Strobe 3
43	Column Address Strobe 1
44	Row Address Strobe 0
45	Row Address Strobe 1
46	Block Select 1
47	Write Enable
48	Reserved
49	Data Bit 8
50	Data Bit 24
51	Data Bit 9
52	Data Bit 25
53	Data Bit 10
54	Data Bit 26
55	Data Bit 11
56	Data Bit 27
57	Data Bit 12
58	Data Bit 28
59	+5 Vdc
60	Data Bit 29
61	Data Bit 13
62	Data Bit 30
63	Data Bit 14
64	Data Bit 31
65	Data Bit 15
66	Block Select 2
67	Presence Detect Bit 0
68	Presence Detect Bit 1
69	Presence Detect Bit 2
70	Presence Detect Bit 3
71	Block Select 3
72	Ground

Table 7.8 Continued

Note that the 72-pin SIMMs employ a set of four pins to indicate the type of SIMM to the motherboard. These presence detect pins are either grounded or not connected to indicate the type of SIMM to the motherboard. This is very similar to the industry-standard DX code used on modern 35mm film rolls to indicate the ASA (speed) rating of the film to the camera. Unfortunately, unlike the film standards, the presence detect signaling is not a standard throughout the PC industry. Different system manufacturers sometimes use different configurations for what is expected on these 4 pins. Table 7.9 shows how IBM defines these pins.

Table 7.9   72-Pin SIMM Presence Detect Pins

70	69	68	67	SIMM Type	IBM Part Number
N/C	N/C	N/C	N/C	Not a valid SIMM	N/A
N/C	N/C	N/C	Gnd	1 MB 120ns	N/A
N/C	N/C	Gnd	N/C	2 MB 120ns	N/A
N/C	N/C	Gnd	Gnd	2 MB 70ns	92F0102
N/C	Gnd	N/C	N/C	8 MB 70ns	64F3606
N/C	Gnd	N/C	Gnd	Reserved	N/A
N/C	Gnd	Gnd	N/C	2 MB 80ns	92F0103
N/C	Gnd	Gnd	Gnd	8 MB 80ns	64F3607
Gnd	N/C	N/C	N/C	Reserved	N/A
Gnd	N/C	N/C	Gnd	1 MB 85ns	90X8624
Gnd	N/C	Gnd	N/C	2 MB 85ns	92F0104
Gnd	N/C	Gnd	Gnd	4 MB 70ns	92F0105
Gnd	Gnd	N/C	N/C	4 MB 85ns	79F1003 (square notch) L40-SX
Gnd	Gnd	N/C	Gnd	1 MB 100ns	N/A
Gnd	Gnd	N/C	Gnd	8 MB 80ns	79F1004 (square notch) L40-SX
Gnd	Gnd	Gnd	N/C	2 MB 100ns	N/A
Gnd	Gnd	Gnd	Gnd	4 MB 80ns	87F9980
Gnd	Gnd	Gnd	Gnd	2 MB 85ns	79F1003 (square notch) L40SX

N/C = No Connection (open)
Gnd = Ground
Pin 67 = Presence detect bit 0
Pin 68 = Presence detect bit 1
Pin 69 = Presence detect bit 2
Pin 70 = Presence detect bit 3

RAM Chip Speed

Memory-chip speed is reported in nanoseconds (ns). (One *nanosecond* is the time that light takes to travel 11.72 inches.) PC memory speeds vary from about 10ns to 200ns. When you replace a failed memory module, you must install a module of the same type and speed as the failed module. You can substitute a chip with a different speed only if the speed of the replacement chip is equal to or faster than that of the failed chip.

II

Primary System Components

Some people have had problems when "mixing" chips because they used a chip that did not meet the minimum required specifications (for example, refresh timing specifications) or was incompatible in pinout, depth, width, or design. Chip access time always can be less (that is, faster) as long as your chip is the correct type and meets all other specifications.

Substituting faster memory usually doesn't provide improved performance because the system still operates the memory at the same speed. In systems not engineered with a great deal of "forgiveness" in the timing between memory and system, however, substituting faster memory chips might improve reliability. Faster RAM chips may improve your system performance also when the motherboard was designed for faster chips than the manufacturer installed. For example, if your motherboard was designed for 70ns chips, but the manufacturer installed cheaper 80ns RAM, you may get a slight performance boost from removing all the old RAM chips and installing faster ones. However, do not mix chip speeds by replacing only some 80ns chips with 70ns ones.

The same common symptoms result when the system memory has failed or is simply not fast enough for the system's timing. The usual symptoms are frequent parity-check errors or a system that does not operate at all. The POST also might report errors. If you're unsure of what chips to buy for your system, contact the system manufacturer or a reputable chip supplier.

Testing Memory

The best way to test memory is to install and use it, with your PC system acting as the testing tool. Numerous diagnostic programs are available for testing memory. Many advanced diagnostic programs are discussed in Chapter 20 "Software and Hardware Diagnostic Tools." Many of these programs, such as the Norton Utilities NDIAGS program, are very inexpensive and yet offer very complete memory diagnostic capabilities. One word of advice is that all memory testing should be done on a system booted from a plain DOS disk with no memory managers or other resident programs loaded.

Parity Checking

As mentioned previously, the memory chips handle eight bits per character of data plus an extra bit called the *parity bit*. Memory-control circuitry uses the parity bit to cross-check the integrity of each byte of data. When the circuitry detects an error, the computer stops and displays a message informing you of the malfunction. Parity checking is the first line of defense for memory and other system errors. Note that many newer systems are coming with non-parity SIMMs to save money. This eliminates parity checking, and increases the likelihood that errors go undetected.

Power-On Self Test

The Power-On Self Test (POST), which is in ROM, can be an effective test for problem memory. When you turn on your system, the POST checks the major hardware components including memory. If the POST detects a bad memory chip, it displays a warning. A more sophisticated disk-based program, however, usually does a better job.

Advanced Diagnostic Tests

A number of diagnostic programs can be used to test RAM chips and other system components. For example, Norton Utilities includes a utility called NDIAGS that tests RAM chips for defects. Other utility packages that can be used to test RAM chips are discussed in Chapter 20 "Software and Hardware Diagnostic Tools." For IBM computers, the Advanced Diagnostics Disk contains utilities that can be used to test your system RAM.

Such programs should be used any time you receive a memory parity error message, or a memory error in the POST (Power-On Self Test). Even if you do not receive error messages, if a properly running system suddenly begins locking up or if strange characters appear on-screen, you should run a good diagnostic program. Software diagnostics can help you spot trouble before a hardware problem destroys data.

Summary

This chapter discussed memory from both a physical and a logical point of view. The types of chips and SIMMs that physically comprise the memory in a PC system were discussed, and the logical arrangement of this memory was examined. The terms used to describe the different regions and the purpose for each region were covered. The chapter also looked at ways of reorganizing the system memory and taking advantage of unused areas.

II

Primary System Components

Chapter 8

The Power Supply

One of the most failure-prone components in any computer system is the power supply. You should understand both the function and limitations of a power supply, as well as its potential problems and their solutions.

Power Supply Function and Operation

The basic function of the power supply is to convert the type of electrical power available at the wall socket to that which is usable by the computer circuitry. The power supply in a conventional desktop system is designed to convert the 120-volt, 60 Hz, AC current into something the computer can use—specifically, both +5- and +12-volt DC current. Usually, the digital electronic components and circuits in the system (motherboard, adapter cards, and disk drive logic boards) use the +5-volt power, and the motors (disk drive motors and any fans) use the +12-volt power. You must ensure a good, steady supply of both types of current so that the system can operate properly.

If you look at a specification sheet for a typical PC power supply, you see that the supply generates not only +5v and +12v, but –5v and –12v as well. Because it would seem that the +5v and +12v signals power everything in the system (logic and motors), what are the negative voltages used for? The answer is not much! In fact, these additional negative voltages are not really used at all in modern systems.

Although –5v and –12v are indeed supplied to the motherboard via the power supply connectors, the motherboard itself uses only the +5v. The –5v signal is simply routed to the ISA Bus on pin B5 and is not used in any way by the motherboard. It was originally used by the analog data separator circuits found in older floppy controllers, which is why it was supplied to the bus. Because modern controllers do not need the –5v, it is no longer used, but still is required simply because it is part of the ISA Bus standard. Note that power supplies in systems with a Micro Channel Architecture (MCA) Bus do not have –5v. This power signal was not ever needed in these systems because they always used a more modern floppy controller design.

Both the +12v and –12v signals also are not used by the motherboard logic and instead are simply routed to pins B9 and B7 of the ISA Bus (respectively). These voltages can be used by any adapter card on the bus, but most notably they are used by serial port driver/receiver circuits. If the motherboard has serial ports built-in, then the +12v and –12v signals can be used for those ports. Note that the load placed on these voltages by a serial port would be very small; for example, the PS/2 Dual Async adapter uses only 35mA of +12v and 35mA of –12v (0.035 amps each) to operate two ports.

Most newer serial port circuits no longer use 12v driver/receiver circuits, but instead use circuits that run on 5v or even 3.3v only. If you have one of these modern design ports in your system, then the –12v signal from your power supply is likely to be totally unused by anything in the system.

The main function of the +12v power is to run disk drive motors. Usually a large amount of current is available, especially in systems that have a large number of drive bays such as in a Tower configuration. Besides disk drive motors, the +12v supply also is used by any cooling fans in the system, which of course should always be running. A single cooling fan can draw between 100mA to 250mA (0.1 to 0.25 amps); however, most newer ones seem to use the lower 100mA figure. Note that although most fans do run on +12v, most portable systems use fans that run on +5v or even 3.3v instead.

In addition to simply supplying power to run the system, the power supply also ensures that the system does not run unless the power being supplied is sufficient to operate the system properly. In other words, the power supply actually prevents the computer from starting up or operating until all the correct power levels are present. Each power supply completes internal checks and tests before allowing the system to start. The power supply sends to the motherboard a special signal, called Power_Good. If this signal is not present, the computer does not run. The effect of this setup is that when the AC voltage dips and the power supply becomes over-stressed or overheated, the Power_Good signal goes down and forces a system reset or complete shutdown. If your system has ever seemed dead when the power switch is on and the fan and hard disks are running, you know the effects of losing the Power_Good signal.

IBM originally used this conservative design with the view that if the power goes low or the supply is overheated or over-stressed, causing output power to falter, the computer shouldn't be allowed to operate. You even can use the Power_Good feature as a method of designing and implementing a reset switch for the PC. The Power_Good line is wired to the clock generator circuit (originally an 8284 or 82284 chip in the original PC/XT and AT systems), which controls the clock and reset lines to the microprocessor. When you ground the Power_Good line with a switch, the chip and related circuitry stop the processor by killing the clock signal and then reset the processor when the Power_Good signal appears after you release the switch. The result is a full hardware reset of the system. Instructions for installing such a switch in a system not already equipped can be found in Chapter 17, "System Upgrades and Improvements."

Power Supply Form Factors

The shape and general physical layout of a component is called the *form factor*, and items that share form factor are generally interchangeable. When a system is designed, the designers can choose to use one of the popular standard form factors, or they can "roll their own." Choosing the former means that a virtually inexhaustible supply of inexpensive replacements is available in a variety of quality and power output levels. Choosing to go the custom route means that the supply will be unique to the system and only available from the original manufacturer in only the model or models they produce. If you can't tell already, I am a fan of the industry-standard form factors!

The form factor of the power supply that a particular system uses is based on the case design. Four popular case and power supply types can be called "industry standard." The different types are as follows:

- PC/XT style
- AT/Tower style
- Baby AT style
- Slimline style

Each of these supplies are available in numerous different configurations and output levels.

When IBM introduced the XT, they used the same basic power supply shape as the original PC, except that the new XT supply had more than double the power output capability (see fig. 8.1). Because they were identical in external appearance as well as the type of connectors used, you easily could install the better XT supply as an upgrade for a PC system. Because of the tremendous popularity of the original PC and XT design, a number of manufacturers began building systems that mimicked the shape and layout of these IBM systems. These clones (as they have been called) could interchange virtually all components with the IBM systems, including the power supply. Numerous manufacturers have since begun producing these components, and nearly all follow the form factor of one or more IBM systems.

When IBM later introduced the AT, they created a larger power supply that had a form factor different from the original PC/XT. This system was rapidly cloned as well and to this day still represents the basis for most IBM-compatible designs. Hundreds of manufacturers now make motherboards, power supplies, cases, and so on that are physically interchangeable with the original IBM AT. If you are buying a compatible system, I recommend those that are form factor compatible with the IBM AT because you will have numerous motherboards and power supplies to choose from.

The compatible market has come up with a couple of variations on the AT theme that are popular today. One is the Tower configuration, which is basically a full-sized AT-style system running on its side. The power supply and motherboard form factors are the same in the Tower system as in the AT. The Tower configuration is not new, in fact even

II

Primary System Components

IBM's original AT had a specially mounted logo that could be rotated when you ran the system on its side in a tower configuration. The type of power supply used in an AT system is identical to that used in a Tower system. This type of power supply is called an AT/Tower form-factor supply (see fig. 8.2).

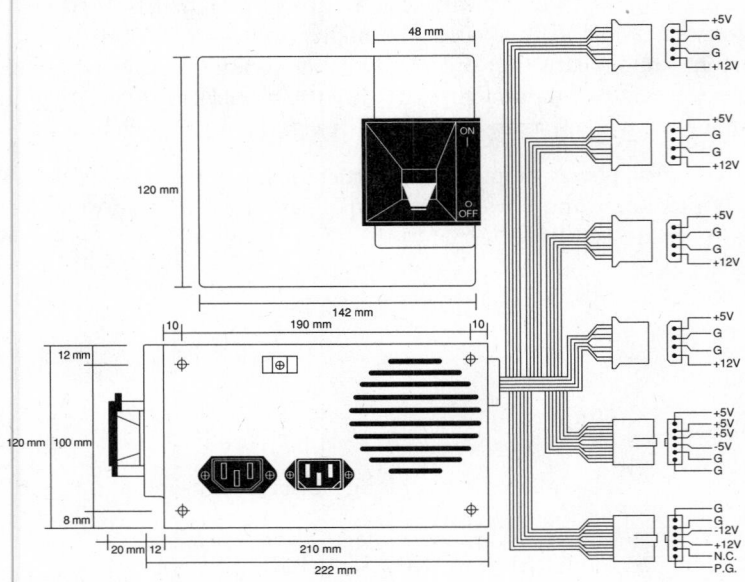

Fig. 8.1

PC/XT-style power supply.

Another type that has been developed is the so-called Baby AT, which is simply a shortened version of the AT system. The power supply in these systems is shortened on one dimension, however it matches the AT design in all other respects. These Baby AT-style power supplies can be used in both Baby AT chassis as well as the larger AT-style chassis, however the full size AT/Tower power supply does not fit in the Baby AT chassis (see fig. 8.3).

The fourth type of form factor that has developed is the Slimline (see fig. 8.4). These systems use a different motherboard configuration that mounts the slots on a "riser" card that plugs into the motherboard. The expansion cards then plug into this riser and are mounted sideways in the system. These types of systems are very low in height, hence the name "Slimline." A new power supply was specifically developed for these systems and allows interchangeability between different manufacturers' systems. Some problems with motherboard interchanges occur due to the riser cards, but the Slimline power supply has become a standard in its own right.

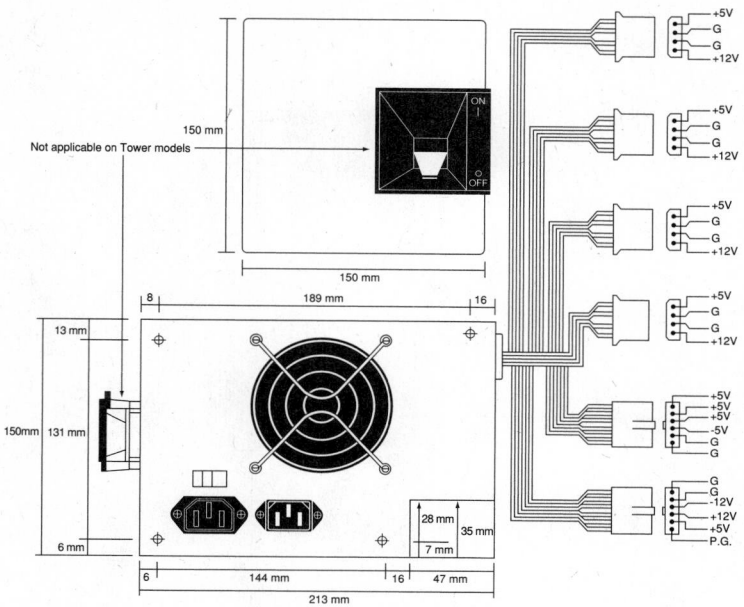

Fig. 8.2

AT/Tower-style power supply.

You will find it very easy to locate supplies that fit these industry-standard form factors. Several vendors who manufacture PC power supplies in all these form factors are listed later in this chapter. For proprietary units, you will likely have to go back to the manufacturer.

Power Supply Connectors

Table 8.1 shows the pinouts for most standard AT or PC/XT-compatible systems. Some systems may have more or fewer drive connectors, for example, IBM's AT system power supplies only have three disk drive power connectors, although most of the currently available AT/Tower type power supplies have four drive connectors. If you are adding drives and need additional disk drive power connectors, "Y" splitter cables are available from many electronics supply houses (including Radio Shack) that can adapt a single power connector to serve two drives. Make sure that your total power supply output is capable of supplying the additional power as a precaution.

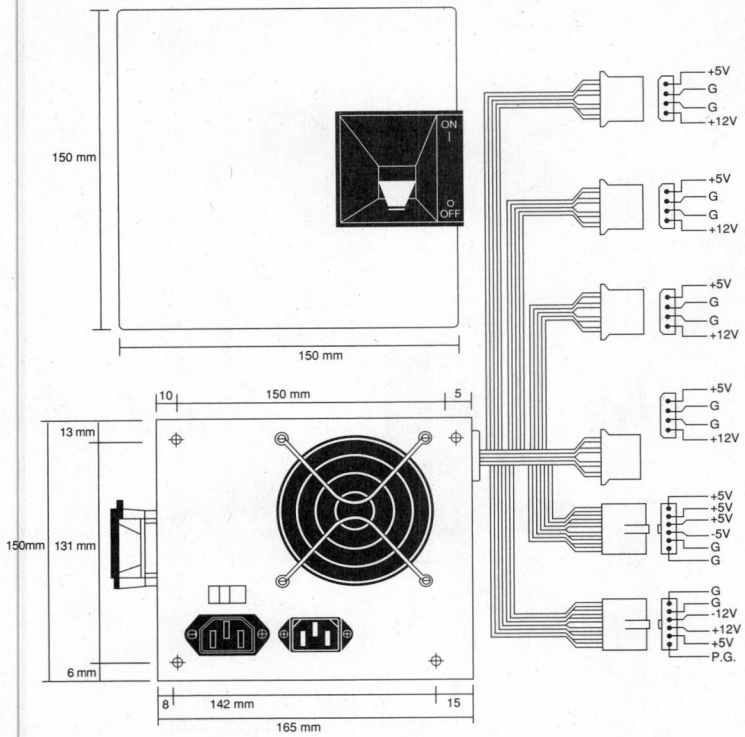

Fig. 8.3
Baby AT-style power supply.

Table 8.1 Typical PC-Compatible Power Supply Connections		
Connector	**AT/Tower Type**	**PC/XT Type**
P8-1	Power_Good (+5v)	Power_Good (+5v)
P8-2	+5v	Key (No connect)
P8-3	+12v	+12v
P8-4	–12v	–12v
P8-5	Ground (0)	Ground (0)
P8-6	Ground (0)	Ground (0)
P9-1	Ground (0)	Ground (0)
P9-2	Ground (0)	Ground (0)
P9-3	–5v	–5v
P9-4	+5v	+5v
P9-5	+5v	+5v
P9-6	+5v	+5v
P10-1	+12v	+12v
P10-2	Ground (0)	Ground (0)

Connector	AT/Tower Type	PC/XT Type
P10-3	Ground (0)	Ground (0)
P10-4	+5v	+5v
P11-1	+12v	+12v
P11-2	Ground (0)	Ground (0)
P11-3	Ground (0)	Ground (0)
P11-4	+5v	+5v
P12-1	+12v	—
P12-2	Ground (0)	—
P12-3	Ground (0)	—
P12-4	+5v	—
P13-1	+12v	—
P13-2	Ground (0)	—
P13-3	Ground (0)	—
P13-4	+5v	—

Note that the Baby AT and Slimline power supplies also use the AT/Tower pin configuration.

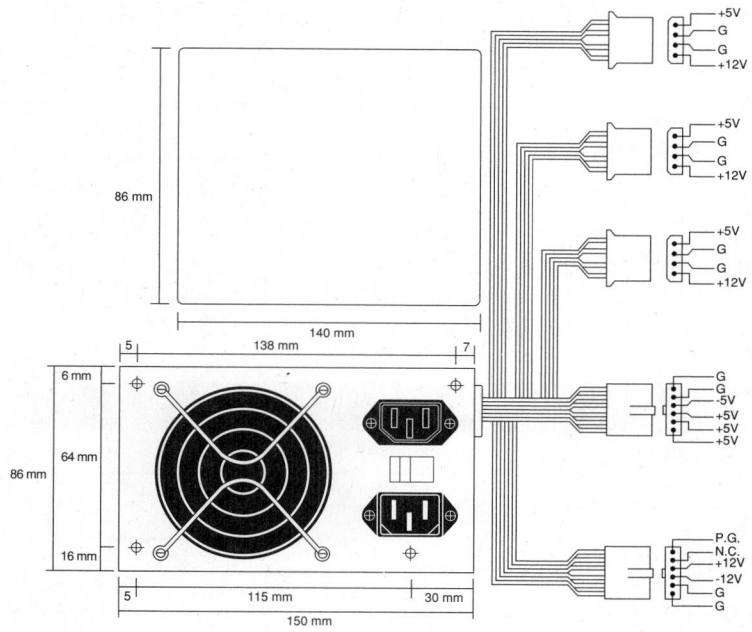

Fig. 8.4
Slimline-style power supply.

Although the PC/XT power supplies do not have any signal on pin P8-2, you can still use them on AT-type motherboards or vice versa. The presence or absence of the +5v signal on that pin has little or no effect on system operation. If you are measuring voltages for testing purposes, anything within ten percent is considered acceptable by many, although most manufacturers of high-quality power supplies specify a tighter 5-percent tolerance (see table 8.2). I prefer to go by the 5-percent tolerance, which is a tougher test to pass.

Table 8.2	Power Supply Acceptable Voltage Ranges			
Desired Voltage	**Loose Tolerance**		**Tight Tolerance**	
	Min. (–10%)	**Max. (+8%)**	**Min. (–5%)**	**Max. (+5%)**
+/–5.0v	4.5v	5.4v	4.75	5.25
+/–12.0v	10.8v	12.9v	11.4	12.6

The Power_Good signal has different tolerances than the other signals, although it is nominally a +5v signal in most systems. The trigger point for Power_Good is about +2.5v, but most systems require the signal voltage to be within the tolerances listed in table 8.3.

Table 8.3	Power_Good Signal Acceptable Range	
Signal	**Minimum**	**Maximum**
Power_Good (+5v)	3.0v	6.0v

A power supply should be replaced if the voltages are out of these ranges. A later section in this chapter details how to measure the power supply voltage and where to get replacement supplies as well.

Disk Drive Power Connectors. The disk drive connectors are fairly universal with regard to pin configuration and even wire color. Table 8.4 shows the standard disk drive power connector pinout and wire colors.

Table 8.4	Disk Drive Power Connector Pinout	
Pin	**Wire Color**	**Signal**
1	Yellow	+12v
2	Black	Gnd
3	Black	Gnd
4	Red	+5v

This information applies whether the drive connector is the larger Molex version or the smaller mini-version used on most 3.5-inch floppy drives. In each case, the pinouts and wire colors are the same. To determine the location of pin 1, look at the connector carefully, and you will usually see it embossed in the plastic connector body; however, it often is very tiny and difficult to read.

Note that some drive connectors may only supply two wires—usually the +5v and a single ground (Pins 3 and 4)—because the floppy drives in most newer systems only run on +5v and do not use the +12v at all.

Physical Connector Part Numbers. The physical connectors used in industry-standard PC power supplies were originally specified by IBM for the supplies used in the original PC/XT/AT systems. They used a specific type of connector between the power supply and the motherboard (the P8 and P9 connectors), as well as specific connectors for the disk drives. The motherboard connectors used in all the industry-standard power supplies have not changed since 1981 when the IBM PC appeared; but with the advent of 3.5-inch floppy drives in 1986, a new smaller type of drive power connector appeared on the scene for these drives. Table 8.5 lists the standard connectors used for motherboard and disk drive power.

Table 8.5 Physical Power Connectors		
Connector Description	**Female (on Power Cable)**	**Male (on Component)**
Motherboard P8/P9	Burndy GTC6P-1	Burndy GTC 6RI
Disk Drive (large style)	AMP 1-480424-0	AMP 1-480426-0
Disk Drive (small style)	AMP 171822-4	AMP 171826-4

You can get these raw connectors through the electronics supply houses (Allied, Newark, Digi-Key, and so on) listed in Appendix B, the "Vendor List." You also can get complete cable assemblies including drive adapters from the large to small connectors, disk drive "Y" splitter cables, and motherboard power extension cables from a number of the Cable and miscellaneous supply houses such as Cables To Go, the Cable Connection, Ci Design, and Key Power (see the vendor list).

The Power_Good Signal

The Power_Good signal is a +5v signal (+3.0 through +6.0 is generally considered acceptable) generated in the power supply when it has passed its internal self tests and the outputs have stabilized. This normally takes anywhere from 0.1 to 0.5 seconds after you turn on the power supply switch. This signal is then sent to the motherboard, where it is received by the processor timer chip, which controls the reset line to the processor.

In the absence of Power_Good, the timer chip continuously resets the processor, which prevents the system from running under bad or unstable power conditions. When the timer chip sees Power_Good, it stops resetting the processor, and the processor begins executing whatever code is at address FFFF:0000 (usually the ROM BIOS).

If the power supply cannot maintain proper outputs (such as when a brownout occurs), the Power_Good signal is withdrawn, and the processor is automatically reset. When proper output is restored, the Power_Good signal is regenerated, and the system again begins operation (as if you just powered on). By withdrawing Power_Good, the system never "sees" the bad power because it is "stopped" quickly (reset) rather than allowed to operate on unstable or improper power levels (which can cause parity errors and other problems).

In most systems, the Power_Good connection is made via connector P8-1 (P8 Pin 1) from the power supply to the motherboard.

A well-designed power supply delays the arrival of the Power_Good signal until all voltages stabilize after you turn the system on. Badly designed power supplies (found in *many* low-cost compatibles!) often do not delay the Power_Good signal properly and allow the processor to start too soon. The normal Power_Good delay is from 0.1 to 0.5 seconds. Improper Power_Good timing also causes CMOS memory corruption in some systems. If you find that a system does not boot up properly the first time you turn on the switch, but subsequently boots up if you press the reset or Ctrl-Alt-Del warm boot command, then you likely have a problem with Power_Good. This happens because the Power_Good signal is tied to the timer chip that generates the reset signal to the processor. What you need to do in these cases is to find a new high-quality power supply and see if it solves the problem.

Many cheaper power supplies do not have proper Power_Good circuitry and often just tie any +5v line to that signal. Some motherboards are more sensitive to an improperly designed (or improperly functioning) Power_Good signal than others. Intermittent startup problems are often caused by improper Power_Good signal timing. A common example occurs when somebody replaces a motherboard in a system, and then finds that the system intermittently fails to start properly when the power is turned on. This ends up being very difficult to diagnose, especially for the inexperienced technician, because the problem appears to be caused by the new motherboard. Although it seems as if the new motherboard may be defective, it usually turns out to be that the original power supply is poorly designed and either cannot produce stable enough power to properly operate the new board, or more likely has an improperly wired or timed Power_Good signal. In these situations, replacing the supply with a high-quality unit is the proper solution.

Power Supply Loading

PC power supplies are of a switching rather than linear design. This type of design is very efficient and does not need a large internal transformer. One characteristic of all switching type power supplies is that they do not run without a load, which means that you must have the supply plugged into something drawing +5v and +12v, or the supply does not work. If you simply have the supply on a bench with nothing plugged into it, the supply either burns up, or protection circuitry shuts it down. Most power supplies are protected from no-load operation and will shut down; however, some of the cheap clone supplies lack the protection circuit and relay and are destroyed after a few seconds of no-load operation. A few power supplies even have their own built-in load resistors so that they can run even though no normal load is plugged in.

According to IBM specifications for the standard 192-watt power supply used in the original AT, a minimum load of 7.0 amps was required at +5v and a minimum load of 2.5 amps was required at +12v for the supply to work properly. Because floppy drives present no +12v load unless they are spinning, systems without a hard disk drive often do not operate properly.

When IBM used to ship AT systems without a hard disk, they had the hard disk drive power cable plugged into a large 5-Ohm 50-watt sandbar resistor mounted in a little metal cage assembly where the drive would have been. The AT case even had screw holes (on top of where the hard disk would go) specifically designed to mount this resistor cage. Several computer stores I knew in the mid 80s would order the diskless AT and then install their own 20M or 30M drives, which they could get cheaper from other sources than IBM. They were throwing away the load resistors by the hundreds! I managed to grab a couple at the time, which is how I know the type of resistor they used.

This resistor would be connected between pin 1 (+12v) and pin 2 (Ground) on the hard disk power connector. This placed a 2.4-amp load on the supply's 12-volt output drawing 28.8 watts of power (it would get HOT!), thus enabling the supply to operate normally. Note that the cooling fan in most power supplies draws approximately 0.1 to 0.25 amps, bringing the total load to 2.5 amps or more. If the load resistor was missing, the system would intermittently fail to start up or operate properly. The motherboard draws +5v at all times, but +12v is normally used only by motors, and the floppy drive motors are off most of the time.

Most of the 200-watt power supplies in use today do not require as much of a load as the original IBM AT power supply. In most cases a minimum load of 2.0 to 4.0 amps at +5v and a minimum of 0.5 to 1.0 amps at +12v are considered acceptable. Most motherboards will easily draw the minimum +5v current by themselves. The standard power supply cooling fan only draws 0.1 to 0.25 amps, so the +12v minimum load may still be a problem for a diskless workstation.

Some high-quality switching power supplies, like the Astec units used by IBM in all the PS/2 systems, have built-in load resistors and can run under a no-load situation because the supply loads itself. Most of the cheaper clone supplies do not have built-in load resistors, so they must have both +5v and +12v loads to work.

II

Primary System Components

Tip

If you are setting up a "diskless" workstation, it is a good idea to install a load resistor, or the power supply may cause intermittent system problems. You can construct the same type of load resistor originally used by IBM by connecting a 5-Ohm, 50-watt sandbar resistor between pins 1 and 2 on a disk drive power connector. You only need to worry about loading the +12v power because the motherboard places a load on the +5v outputs.

If you want to bench test a power supply, make sure that loads are placed on both the +5v and +12v outputs. This is one reason that it is best to test the supply while it is installed in the system rather than separately on the bench. For impromptu bench testing, you can use a spare motherboard and hard disk drive to load the +5v and +12v outputs respectively. Information on building your own load resistor network for bench testing power supplies is covered later in this chapter.

Power-Supply Ratings

Most system manufacturers will provide you with the technical specifications of each of their system-unit power supplies. This type of information is usually found in the system's technical-reference manual and also is normally found on stickers attached directly to the power supply. Power supply manufacturers also can supply this data, which is preferred if you can identify the manufacturer and contact them directly.

Tables 8.6 and 8.7 list power-supply specifications for several of IBM's units, from which most of the compatibles are derived. The PC-system power supplies are the original units that most compatible power supplies have duplicated. The input specifications are listed as voltages; the output specifications as amps, at several voltage levels. IBM reports output wattage level as "specified output wattage." If your manufacturer does not list the total wattage, you can convert amperage to wattage by using the following simple formula:

Wattage = Voltage * Amperage

By multiplying the voltage by the amperage available at each output and then adding them up, you can calculate the total output wattage the supply is capable of.

Table 8.6	Power Supply Output Ratings for IBM "Classic" Systems				
	PC	**PPC**	**XT**	**XT-286**	**AT**
Minimum Input Voltage	104	90	90	90	90
Maximum Input Voltage	127	137	137	137	137
Worldwide Power (220v)?	No	Yes	No	Yes	Yes
110/220v Switch?	–	Switch	–	Auto	Switch
Output Current (amps): +5v	7.0	11.2	15.0	20.0	19.8
−5v	0.3	0.3	0.3	0.3	0.3
+12v	2.0	4.4	4.2	4.2	7.3
−12v	0.25	0.25	0.25	0.25	0.3
Calculated output wattage	63.5	113.3	129.9	154.9	191.7
Specified output wattage	63.5	114.0	130.0	157.0	192.0

Table 8.7 shows the standard power supply output levels available in industry-standard form factors. Most manufacturers that offer supplies have supplies with different ratings for each type of supply. Supplies are available with ratings from 100 watts to 450 watts or more. Table 8.7 shows the rated outputs at each of the voltage levels for supplies with

different manufacturer-specified output ratings. To compile the table, I referred to the specification sheets for supplies from both Astec Standard Power and PC Power and Cooling. Although most of the ratings are accurate, as you can see they are somewhat misleading for the higher wattage units.

Table 8.7   Typical Compatible Power Supply Output Ratings

Specified Output Wattage	100W	150W	200W	250W	300W	375W	450W
Output Current (amps): +5v	10.0	15.0	20.0	25.0	32.0	35.0	45.0
−5v	0.3	0.3	0.3	0.5	1.0	0.5	0.5
+12v	3.5	5.5	8.0	10.0	10.0	13.0	15.0
−12v	0.3	0.3	0.3	0.5	1.0	0.5	1.0
Calculated output wattage	97.1	146.1	201.1	253.5	297.0	339.5	419.5

Most compatible power supplies have ratings between 150 to 250 watts output. Although lesser ratings are not usually desirable, it is possible to purchase heavy duty power supplies for most compatibles that have outputs as high as 500 watts.

The 300-watt and larger units are excellent for enthusiasts who are building a fully optioned desktop or tower system. These supplies run any combination of motherboard and expansion card and a large number of disk drives as well. In most cases, you cannot exceed the ratings on these power supplies—the system will be out of room for additional items first!

Table 8.8 shows the rated output levels of IBM's PS/2 power supplies. IBM uses very high quality supplies in these systems. They are normally supplied to IBM by Astec, but other manufacturers have made IBM supplies as well.

Table 8.8   Power Supply Output Ratings for PS/2 Systems

Model	Part Number	Worldwide Power (220v)	110/220v Manual/Auto	Output Wattage
25	8525-xx1	Yes	Manual	90
	8525-xx4	Yes	Manual	115
30	8530-0xx	Yes	Auto	70
25 286	8525-xxx	Yes	Manual	124.5
30 286	8530-Exx	Yes	Manual	90
35 SX	8535-xxx	Yes	Auto	118
40 SX	8540-0xx	Yes	Manual	197
50	8550-0xx	Yes	Auto	94
55 SX	8555-xxx	Yes	Manual	90
57 SX	8557-0xx	Yes	Manual	197

(continues)

II

Primary System Components

Model	Part Number	Worldwide Power (220v)	110/220v Manual/Auto	Output Wattage
Table 8.8	**Continued**			
60	8560-041	Yes	Auto	207
	8560-071	Yes	Auto	225
65 SX	8565-xxx	Yes	Auto	250
70 386	8570-xxx	Yes	Auto	132
70 486	8570-Bxx	Yes	Auto	132
P70 386	8573-xxx	Yes	Auto	85
P75 486	8573-xxx	Yes	Auto	120
80 386	8580-xxx	Yes	Auto	225
	8580-Axx	Yes	Auto	242
	8580-Axx	Yes	Auto	250
90 XP 486	8590-0xx	Yes	Auto	194
95 XP 486	8595-0xx	Yes	Auto	329

Most power supplies are considered to be *universal*, or *worldwide*: they run on the 220-volt, 50-cycle current used in Europe and many other parts of the world. Most power supplies that can switch to 220-volt input are automatic, but a few require you to set a switch on the back of the power supply to indicate which type of power you will access. (The automatic units sense the current and then switch automatically.)

My PS/2 P75, for example, runs on both 110- and 220-volt power; all I have to do is plug it in, and the system automatically recognizes the incoming voltage and switches circuits accordingly. This is different from some other systems that run on both levels of power, but require you to flip a switch manually to select the proper circuits within the power supply.

Power Supply Specifications

In addition to power output, many other specifications and features go into making a high-quality power supply. I have had many systems over the years, and my experience has been if a brownout occurs in a room with several systems running, the systems with higher quality power supplies and higher output ratings always make it over power disturbances in which others choke. I would not give $5 for many of the cheap, junky power supplies that come in some of the low-end clone systems.

To get an idea of the expected performance from a power supply, you should know the specifications IBM dictates for all its PS/2 power supplies. This information comes from the *PS/2 Hardware Maintenance Manual* (#S52G-9971-01) and is an example of what a properly designed power supply should do. Keep in mind that Astec makes virtually all IBM PS/2 supplies, and it also makes supplies for a number of other high-end system vendors. IBM's specifications for its PS/2 power supplies follow:

> PS/2 power supplies operate continuously over two ranges: the first is from 90 to 137 VAC, and the second is from 180 to 265 VAC. The AC signal must be a sine

wave and have a maximum of 5-percent total harmonic distortion. Some units have an automatic voltage range selection feature whereas others require a switch be set to operate on either the 100v or 200v ranges.

PS/2 power supplies are protected from both input over and under voltages. If the input voltage goes over or under the acceptable range, the power supply shuts down until the power switch is recycled.

All PS/2 supplies have output over-current protection. This means that if more than a safe load is drawn from the supply, it shuts down until the power switch is re-cycled. This protection extends to short circuits as well. If any short is placed between an output and ground, or between any two outputs, the power supply shuts down until the power switch is recycled.

Most PS/2 power supplies have an automatic restart feature that causes the power supply to recycle automatically after an AC power outage. Beginning with products announced in October 1990, a three to six second delay was added to the restart time to allow any subsystems or peripherals enough time to reset before the system restarts.

IBM states that the PS/2 supplies sustain operation during the following power line disturbances:

- A 20-percent below nominal voltage (that is, 80 volts) brownout lasting up to two seconds repeated up to 10 times with a 10-percent duty cycle

- A 30-percent below nominal voltage (70 volts) brownout lasting up to .5 seconds repeated up to 10 times with a 10-percent duty cycle

- A 15-percent above nominal voltage (143 volts) surge lasting up to one second repeated up to 10 times with a 10-percent duty cycle

- A 400 Hz oscillatory (exponentially decaying) disturbance at the peak of the input line voltage that increases the line voltage by two times (200 volts) that occurs up to 100 times at three second intervals

- A transient pulse of 1.5 times the peak input voltage (150 volts) superimposed at the input voltage peak and repeated up to 100 times at three second intervals

IBM also states that their PS/2 supplies (or attached systems) are not damaged if any of the following conditions occur:

- A 100-percent power outage of any duration

- A brownout of any kind

- A spike of up to 2,500 volts(!) applied directly to the AC input (for example, a lightning strike or a lightning simulation test)

PS/2 power supplies have an extremely low current leakage to ground of less than 500 microamps. This safety feature is very important if your outlet has a missing or improperly wired ground line.

As you can see, these specifications are fairly tough and are certainly representative of a high-quality power supply. Make sure that your supply can meet these specifications. The vendors recommended in this chapter produce supplies that meet or exceed these specifications.

Power-Use Calculations

One way to see whether your system is capable of expansion is to calculate the levels of power drain in the different system components and then deduct the total from the maximum power supplied. This calculation might help you decide when to upgrade the power supply to a more capable unit. Unfortunately, these calculations can be difficult to make because many manufacturers do not publish power consumption data for their products.

It is very difficult to get power consumption data for most +5v devices including motherboards and adapter cards. Motherboards can consume different power levels depending on numerous factors. Most 486DX2 motherboards consume about 5 amps or so, but if you can get data on the one you are using, so much the better. For adapter cards, if you can find the actual specifications for the card, then use those figures; however, to be on the conservative side, I usually go by the maximum available power levels as set forth in the respective bus standards.

For example, consider the typical power consumption figures for components in a modern PC system. Most standard desktop or Slimline PC systems today come with a 200-watt power supply rated for 20 amps at +5v and 8 amps at +12v. The ISA specification calls for a maximum of 2.0 amps of +5v and 0.175 amps of +12v power for each slot in the system. Most systems have eight slots, and you can assume that four of them are filled for the purposes of calculating power draw. The following calculation shows what happens when you subtract the amount of power necessary to run the different system components.

5-Volt Power:			20.0 Amps
	Less:	Motherboard	−5.0
		4 slots filled at 2.0 each	−8.0
		3.5" and 5.25" floppy drives	−1.5
		3.5" hard disk drive	−0.5
Remaining power			5.0 amps

12-Volt Power:			8.0 Amps
	Less:	4 slots filled at 0.175 ea.	−0.7
		3.5" hard disk drive	−1.0
		3.5" and 5.25" floppy drives	−1.0
		Cooling fan	−0.1
Remaining power			5.2 amps

In the preceding example, everything seems okay for now. With half the slots filled, two floppy drives, and one hard disk, the system still has room for more. There might be trouble if this system was expanded to the extreme. With every slot filled and two or more hard disks, there definitely will be problems with the +5v, however the +12v does seem to have room to spare. You could add a CD-ROM drive or a second hard disk without worrying too much about the +12v power, but the +5v power will be strained. If you anticipate loading up a system to the extreme, for example as in a high-end multimedia system, then you may want to invest in the insurance of a higher output supply. For example, a 250-watt supply usually has 25 amps of +5v and 10 amps of +5v current, whereas a 300-watt unit has 32 amps of +5v power. These supplies would allow a fully expanded system and are likely to be found in full-sized desktop or tower case configurations in which this capability can be fully used.

Motherboards can draw anywhere from 4 to 15 amps or more of +5v power to run. In fact, a single Pentium 66 MHz CPU draws up to 3.2 amps of +5v power all by itself. Considering that dual 100 MHz Pentium processor systems are now becoming available, you could have 6.4 amps or more drawn by the processors alone. A motherboard like this with 64M of RAM might draw 15 amps or more all by itself. Most 486DX2 motherboards draw approximately 5 to 7 amps of +5v. Bus slots are allotted maximum power in amps as shown in table 8.9.

Table 8.9 Maximum Power Consumption in Amps per Bus Slot

Bus Type	+5v Power	+12v Power	+3.3v Power
ISA	2.0	0.175	N/A
EISA	4.5	1.5	N/A
VL-Bus	2.0	N/A	N/A
16-Bit MCA	1.6	0.175	N/A
32-Bit MCA	2.0	0.175	N/A
PCI	5	0.5	7.6

As you can see from the table, ISA slots are allotted 2.0 amps of +5v and 0.175 amps of +12v power. Note that these are maximum figures and not all cards draw this much power. If the slot has a VL-Bus extension connector, then an additional 2.0 amps of +5v power is allowed for the VL-Bus.

Floppy drives can vary in power consumption, but most of the newer 3.5-inch drives have motors that run off +5v in addition to the logic circuits. These drives usually draw 1.0 amps of +5v power and use no +12v at all. Most 5.25-inch drives do use standard +12v motors that draw about 1.0 amps. These drives also require about 0.5 amps of +5v for the logic circuits. Most cooling fans draw about 0.1 amps of +12v power, which is almost negligible.

Typical 3.5-inch hard disks today draw about 1 amp of +12v power to run the motors and only about 0.5 amps of +5v power for the logic. The 5.25-inch hard disks, especially those that are full-height, draw much more power. A typical full-height hard drive draws 2.0 amps of +12v power and 1.0 amps of +5v power. Another problem with hard disks is that they require much more power during the spinup phase of operation than during normal operation. In most cases, the drive draws double the +12v power during spinup, which can be 4.0 amps or more for the full-height drives. This then tapers off to normal after the drive is spinning.

The figures most manufacturers report for maximum power supply output are full duty-cycle figures, which means that these levels of power can be supplied continuously. You usually can expect a unit that continuously supplies some level of power to supply more power for some noncontinuous amount of time. A supply usually can offer 50 percent greater output than the continuous figure indicates for as long as one minute. This cushion often is used to supply the necessary power to start spinning a hard disk. After the drive has spun to full speed, the power draw drops to some value within the system's continuous supply capabilities. Drawing anything over the rated continuous figure for any long length of time causes the power supply to run hot and fail early, and can prompt several nasty symptoms in the system.

> **Tip**
>
> If you are using internal SCSI hard drives, then a very useful tip can ease the startup load on your power supply. The key is to enable the Remote Start option on the SCSI drive, which causes the drive to start spinning only when it receives a startup command over the SCSI bus. The effect is such that the drive remains stationary (drawing very little power) until the very end of the POST, and spins upright when the SCSI portion of the POST is begun. If you have multiple SCSI drives, they all spin up sequentially based on their SCSI ID setting. This is designed so that only one drive is spinning up at any one time and that no drives start spinning until the rest of the system has had time to start. This greatly eases the load on the power supply when you first power the system on. This tip is essential when dealing with portable type systems in which power is at a premium. I burned up a supply in one of my portable systems before resetting the internal drive to Remote Start.

The biggest causes of overload problems are filling up the slots and adding more drives. Multiple hard drives, CD-ROM drives, floppy drives, and so on can exact quite a drain on the system power supply. Make sure that you have enough +12v power to run all the drives you are going to install. Tower systems can be a problem here because they have so many drive bays. Also make sure that you have enough +5v power to run all your expansion cards, especially if you are using VL-Bus or EISA cards. It pays to be conservative, but remember that most cards draw less than the maximum allowed.

Many people wait until an existing unit fails before they replace it with an upgraded version. If you're on a tight budget, this "if it ain't broke, don't fix it" attitude works. Power supplies, however, often do not just fail; they can fail in an intermittent fashion or allow fluctuating power levels to reach the system, which results in unstable operation. You might be blaming system lockups on software bugs when the culprit is an overloaded power supply. If you've been running with your original power supply for a long time, you should expect some problems.

Leave It On or Turn It Off?

A frequent question that relates to the discussion of power supplies concerns whether you should turn off a system when not in use. You should understand some facts about electrical components and what makes them fail. Combine this knowledge with information on power consumption and cost, not to mention safety, and perhaps you can come to your own conclusion. Because circumstances can vary, the best answer for your own situation might be different depending on your particular needs and application.

Frequently powering a system on and off does cause deterioration and damage to the components. This seems logical, and the reason is simple but not obvious to most. Many people believe that flipping system power on and off frequently is harmful because it electrically "shocks" the system. The real problem, however, is temperature. In other words, it's not so much electrical "shock" as thermal shock that damages a system. As the system warms up, the components expand; and as it cools off, the components contract. This alone stresses everything, but in addition, various materials in the system have different thermal expansion coefficients, which means they expand and contract at different rates. Over time, thermal shock causes deterioration in many areas of a system.

From a pure system reliability point, it is desirable to insulate the system from thermal shock as much as possible. When a system is turned on, the components go from ambient (room) temperature to as high as 185 degrees F (85 degrees C) within 30 minutes or less. When you turn the system off, the same thing happens in reverse, and the components cool back to ambient temperature in a short period of time. Each component expands and contracts at slightly different rates, which causes the system an enormous amount of stress.

Thermal expansion and contraction remains the single largest cause of component failure. Chip cases can split, allowing moisture to enter and contaminate the chip. Delicate internal wires and contacts can break, and circuit boards can develop stress cracks. Surface-mounted components expand and contract at different rates from the circuit board they are mounted on, which causes enormous stress at the solder joints. Solder joints can fail due to the metal hardening from the repeated stress causing cracks in the joint. Components that use heat sinks such as processors, transistors, or voltage regulators can overheat and fail because the thermal cycling causes heat sink adhesives to deteriorate, breaking the thermally conductive bond between the device and the heat sink. Thermal cycling also causes socketed devices and connections to "creep," which can cause a variety of intermittent contact failures.

Thermal expansion and contraction not only affect chips and circuit boards, but things like hard disk drives as well. Most hard drives today have sophisticated thermal compensation routines that make adjustments in head position relative to the expanding and contracting platters. Most drives perform this thermal compensation routine once every five minutes for the first 30 minutes the drive is running, and then every 30 minutes thereafter. In many drives, this procedure can be heard as a rapid "tick-tick-tick-tick" sound.

In essence, anything you can do to keep the system at a constant temperature prolongs the life of the system, and the best way to accomplish this is to leave the system either on or off permanently. Of course, if the system is never turned on in the first place, it should last a long time indeed!

Now, although it seems like I am saying that you should leave all systems on 24 hours a day, that is not necessarily true. A system powered on and left unattended can be a fire hazard (I have had monitors spontaneously catch fire—luckily I was there at the time), is a data security risk (cleaning crews, other nocturnal visitors, and so on), can be easily damaged if moved while running, and simply wastes electrical energy.

I currently pay $0.11 for a kilowatt-hour of electricity. A typical desktop-style PC with display consumes at least 300 watts (0.3 kilowatts) of electricity (and that is a conservative estimate). This means that it would cost 3.3 cents to run this typical PC for an hour. Multiplying by 168 hours in a week means that it would cost $5.54 per week to run this PC continuously. If the PC were turned on at 9:00 a.m. and off at 5:00 p.m., it would only be on 40 hours per week and would cost only $1.32—a savings of $4.22 per week! Multiply this savings by 100 systems, and you are saving $422 per week; multiplied by 1,000 systems, you are saving $4,220 per week! Using systems certified under the new EPA Energy Star program (that is, "Green" PCs) would account for an additional savings of around $1 per system per week, or $1,000 per week for 1,000 systems. The great thing about Energy Star systems is that the savings are even greater if the systems are left on for long periods of time because the power management routines are automatic.

Based on these facts, my recommendations are that you power the systems on at the beginning of the work day, and off at the end of the work day. Do not power the systems off for lunch, breaks, or any other short duration of time. Servers and the like of course should be left on continuously. This seems to be the best compromise of system longevity with pure economics.

Power Supply Problems

A weak or inadequate power supply can put a damper on your ideas for system expansion. Some systems are designed with beefy power supplies, as if to anticipate a great deal of system add-on or expansion components. Most desktop or tower systems are built in this manner. Some systems have inadequate power supplies from the start, however, and cannot accept the number and types of power-hungry options you might want to add.

In particular, portable systems often have power supply problems because they are designed to fit into a small space. Also, many older systems had inadequate power supply capacity for system expansion. For example, the original PC's 63.5-watt supply was inadequate for all but the most basic system. Add a graphics board, hard disk, math coprocessor (8087) chip, and 640K of memory, and you would kill the supply in no time. The total power draw of all the items in the system determines the adequacy of the power supply.

The wattage rating can sometimes be very misleading. Not all 200-watt supplies are created the same. Those who are into high-end audio systems know that some watts are better than others. Cheap power supplies may in fact put out the rated power, but what about noise and distortion? Some of the supplies are under-engineered to just barely meet their specifications, whereas others may greatly exceed their specifications. Many of the cheaper supplies output noisy or unstable power, which can cause numerous problems with the system. Another problem with under-engineered power supplies is that they run hot and force the system to do so as well. The repeated heating and cooling of solid-state components eventually causes a computer system to fail, and engineering principles dictate that the hotter a PC's temperature, the shorter its life. Many people recommend replacing the original supply in a system with a heavier duty model, which solves the problem. Because power supplies come in common form factors, finding a heavy duty replacement for most systems is easy.

Some of the available replacement supplies have higher capacity cooling fans than the originals, which can greatly prolong system life and minimize overheating problems, especially with some of the newer high-powered processors. If noise is a problem, models with special fans can run quieter than the standard models. These types often use larger diameter fans that spin slower so that they run quietly while moving the same amount of air as the smaller fans. A company called PC Power and Cooling (see Appendix B, the "Vendor List") specializes in heavy-duty as well as quiet supplies; another company called Astec (see Appendix B) has several heavy-duty models as well. Astec supplies are found as original equipment in many high-end systems such as those from IBM, Hewlett Packard, and so on.

Ventilation in a system can be important. You must ensure adequate air flow to cool the hotter items in the system. Most processors have heat sinks today that require a steady stream of air to cool the processor. If the processor heat sink has its own fan, then this is not much of a concern. If you have free slots, space the boards out in your system to allow air flow between them. Place the hottest running boards nearest the fan or ventilation holes in the system. Make sure that adequate air flow is around the hard disk drive, especially those that spin at higher rates of speed. Some hard disks can generate quite a bit of heat during operation, and if the hard disks overheat, data is lost.

Always make sure that you run with the lid on, especially if you have a loaded system. Removing the lid can actually cause a system to overheat because with the lid off, the power supply fan no longer draws air through the system. Instead, the fan ends up cooling the supply only, and the rest of the system must be cooled by simple convection. Although most systems do not immediately overheat because of this, several of my own systems, especially those that are fully expanded, have overheated within 15 to 30 minutes when run with the case lid off.

If you experience intermittent problems that you suspect are related to overheating, a higher capacity replacement power supply is usually the best cure. Specially designed supplies with additional cooling fan capacity also can help. At least one company sells a device called a *fan card*, but I am not especially convinced these are a good idea. Unless the fan is positioned to draw air to or from outside the case, all the fan does is blow hot air around inside the system and provide a spot cooling effect for anything it is blowing on. In fact, adding fans in this manner contributes to the overall heat inside the system because each fan consumes power and generates heat.

The CPU-mounted fans are an exception to this because they are designed only for spot cooling of the CPU. Many of the newer processors run so much hotter than the other components in the system that a conventional finned aluminum heat sink cannot do the job. In this case a small fan placed directly over the processor can provide a spot cooling effect that keeps the processor temperatures down. One drawback to these active processor cooling fans is that if they fail, the processor overheats instantly and may even be damaged. Whenever possible, I try to use the biggest passive (finned aluminum) heat sink and stay away from more fans.

> **Tip**
>
> If you seal the ventilation holes on the bottom of the PC chassis, starting from where the disk drive bays begin and all the way to the right side of the PC, you drop the interior temperature some 10 to 20 degrees Fahrenheit—not bad for two cents' worth of electrical tape. IBM "factory-applied" this tape on every XT and XT-286 it sold. The result is greatly improved interior aerodynamics and airflow over the heat-generating components.

Power Supply Troubleshooting

Troubleshooting the power supply basically means isolating the supply as the cause of problems within a system. Rarely is it recommended to go inside the power supply to make repairs because of the dangerous high voltages present. Such internal repairs are beyond the scope of this book and are specifically not recommended unless the technician knows what he or she is doing.

Many symptoms would lead me to suspect that the power supply in a system is failing. This can sometimes be difficult for an inexperienced technician to see, because at times little connection appears between the symptom and the cause (the power supply).

For example, in many cases a "parity check" type of error message or problem indicates a problem with the supply. This may seem strange because the parity check message itself specifically refers to memory that has failed. The connection is that the power supply is what powers the memory, and memory with inadequate power fails. It takes some experience to know when these failures are not caused by the memory and are in fact power related. One clue is the repeatability of the problem. If the parity check message (or other problem) appears frequently and identifies the same memory location each time, then I would indeed suspect defective memory as the problem. However, if the problem seems random, or the memory location given as failed seems random or wandering, then I would suspect improper power as the culprit. The following is a list of PC problems that often are power supply related:

- Any power on startup failures or lockups.

- Spontaneous rebooting or intermittent lockups during normal operation.

- Intermittent parity check or other memory type errors.

- Hard disk and fan simultaneously fail to spin (no +12v).

- Overheating due to fan failure.

- Small brownouts cause the system to reset.

- Electric shocks felt on the system case or connectors.

- Slight static discharges disrupt system operation.

In fact, just about any intermittent system problem can be caused by the power supply. I always suspect the supply when flaky system operation is a symptom. Of course, the following fairly obvious symptoms point right to the power supply as a possible cause:

- System is completely dead (no fan, no cursor).

- Smoke!

- Blown circuit breakers.

If you suspect a power supply problem, some simple measurements as well as more so-phisticated tests outlined in this section can help you determine whether the power supply is at fault. Because these measurements may not detect some intermittent failures, you might have to use a spare power supply for a long-term evaluation. If the symptoms and problems disappear when a "known good" spare unit is installed, then you have found the source of your problem.

Digital Multi-Meters

A simple test that can be done to a power supply is to check the output voltage. This shows if a power supply is operating correctly and whether the output voltages are within the correct tolerance range. Note that all voltage measurements must be made with the power supply connected to a proper load, which usually means testing while the power supply is still installed in the system.

Selecting a Meter. You need a simple Digital Multi-Meter (DMM) or Digital Volt-Ohm Meter (DVOM) to make voltage and resistance checks in electronic circuits (see fig. 8.5). You should only use a DMM rather than the older needle-type multi-meters because the older meters work by injecting a 9v signal into the circuit when measuring resistance. This will damage most computer circuits! A DMM uses a much smaller voltage (usually 1.5v) when making resistance measurements, which is safe for electronic equipment. You can get a good DMM from many sources and with many different features. I prefer the small pocket-sized meters for computer work because they are easy to carry around. The following lists some features to look for in a good DMM:

- *Pocket Size.* This is self-explanatory, but small meters are available that have many if not all the features of larger ones. The elaborate features found on some of the larger meters are not really needed for computer work.

- *Overload Protection.* This means that if you plug the meter into a voltage or current beyond the capability of the meter to measure, the meter protects itself from damage. Cheaper meters lack this protection and can easily be damaged by reading current or voltage values that are too high.

- *Autoranging.* This means that the meter automatically selects the proper voltage or resistance range when making measurements. This is preferred to the manual range selection; however, really good meters offer both autoranging capability and a manual range override.

- *Detachable Probe Leads.* The leads can be easily damaged and sometimes a variety of differently shaped probes are required for different tests. Cheaper meters have the leads permanently attached, which means that they cannot easily be replaced. Look for a meter with detachable leads that plug into the meter.

- *Audible Continuity Test.* Although you can use the Ohm scale for testing continuity (0 ohms indicates continuity), a continuity test function causes a beep noise to be heard when continuity exists between the meter test leads. Using the sound, you can more quickly test cable assemblies and other items for continuity. After you use this feature, you will never want to use the ohms display for this purpose again!

- *Automatic Power Off.* These meters run on batteries, and the batteries can easily be worn down if the meter is accidentally left on. Good meters have an automatic shutoff that turns off the meter if no readings are sensed for a predetermined period of time.

- *Automatic Display Hold.* This feature allows the last stable reading to be held on the display even after the reading is taken. This is especially useful if you are trying to work in a difficult-to-reach area single-handedly.

- *Minimum and Maximum Trap.* This feature allows the lowest and highest readings to be trapped in memory and held for later display. This is especially useful if you have readings that are fluctuating too quickly to see on the display.

Although you can get a basic pocket DMM for about $30, one with all these features costs about $200. Radio Shack carries some nice inexpensive units, whereas the high-end models can be purchased from electronics supply houses like Allied, Newark, or Digi-Key (see Appendix B, the "Vendor List").

Measuring Voltage. When making measurements on a system that is operating, you must use a technique called *back probing* the connectors. This is because you cannot disconnect any of the connectors while the system is running and instead must measure with everything connected. Nearly all the connectors you need to probe have openings in the back where the wires enter the connector. The meter probes are narrow enough to fit into the connector alongside the wire and make contact with the metal terminal inside. This technique is called back probing because you are probing the connector from the back. Virtually all the following measurements must be made using this back probing technique.

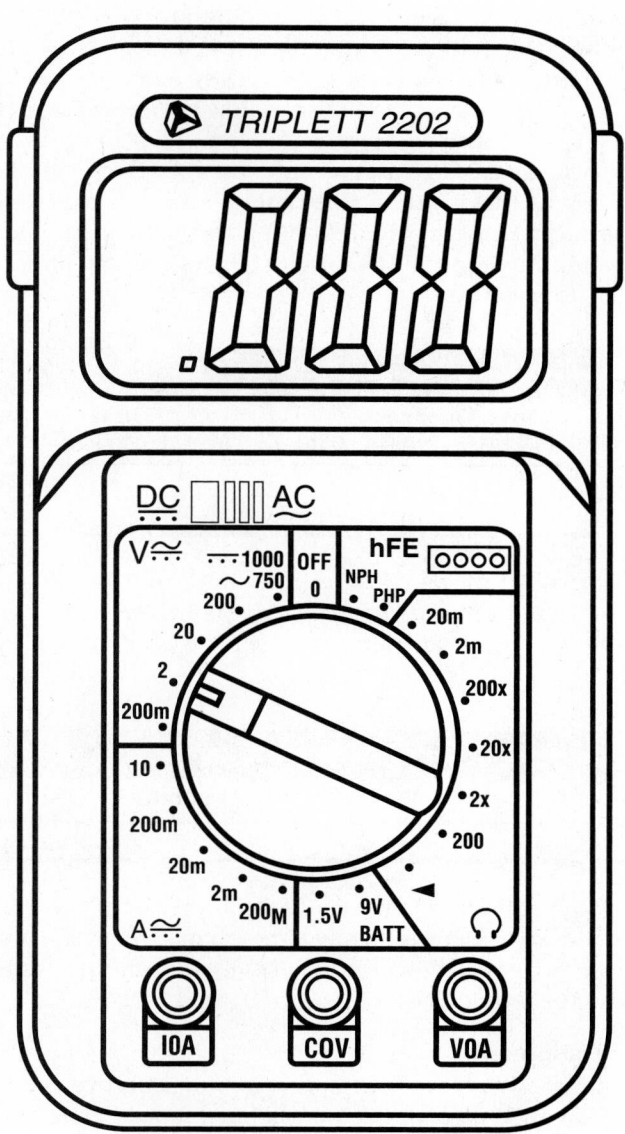

Fig. 8.5
A typical Digital Multi-Meter (DMM).

To test a power supply for proper output, first check the voltage at the Power_Good pin (P8-1 on most IBM-compatible supplies) for +3v to +6v. If the measurement is not within this range, then the system never sees the Power_Good signal and therefore does not start or run properly. In most cases, the supply is bad and must be replaced.

Continue by measuring the voltage ranges of the pins on the motherboard and drive power connectors (see table 8.10). Note that the exact pin specifications and acceptable voltage ranges may vary for different manufacturer's systems, however these figures are representative of most IBM-compatibles. Many follow the looser tolerance guidelines of accepting anything approximately 10 percent too low or 8 percent too high, especially for the –5v and –12v (negative) signals. I prefer to use tighter tolerances myself, and would only pass a supply that is within 5 percent or less of the correct voltages. Some manufacturers have even tighter tolerances on their systems, and in that case you should go by what the manufacturer specifies. Consult your system's technical reference manual for this information to make sure.

Table 8.10 Power Supply Acceptable Voltage Ranges				
Desired Voltage	**Loose Tolerance**		**Tight Tolerance**	
	Min. (–10%)	**Max. (+8%)**	**Min. (–5%)**	**Max. (+5%)**
+/–5.0v	4.5v	5.4v	4.75	5.25
+/–12.0v	10.8v	12.9v	11.4	12.6

The Power_Good signal has tolerances different from the other signals, although it is nominally a +5v signal in most systems. The trigger point for Power_Good is about +2.5v, but most systems require the signal voltage to be within the tolerances listed in table 8.11.

Table 8.11 Power_Good Signal Acceptable Range		
Signal	**Minimum**	**Maximum**
Power_Good (+5v)	3.0v	6.0v

Replace the power supply if the voltages you measure are out of these ranges. Again, it is worth noting that any and all power supply tests and measurements must be made with the power supply properly loaded, which usually means it must be installed in a system, and the system must be running.

Specialized Test Equipment

You can use several types of specialized test gear to more effectively test power supplies. Because the power supply is perhaps the most failure-prone item in PCs today, if you service many PC systems, it is wise to have many of these specialized items.

Load Resistors. If you want to bench test a power supply, you must make sure that loads are placed on both the +5v and +12v outputs. This is one reason that it is best to test the supply while it is installed in the system rather than separately on the bench.

For impromptu bench testing, you can use a spare motherboard and hard disk drive to load the +5v and +12v outputs respectively while you make voltage measurements or check overall system operation.

If you are frequently testing power supplies, then you may want to construct your own load resistors to make testing easier. In my shop, I often use one of the +12v load resistors originally installed in AT systems sold without hard disks. Although these are nice, they do not load the +5v signal, and often I want more than a 2.4-amp load on the +12v as well.

You can construct your own power supply load resistor network out of light bulbs. By wiring a set of light sockets in parallel, you can vary the load by adding or removing bulbs from their sockets. The type of bulb to use for a +12v load is the standard #1156 bulb used in many automobile exterior light assemblies. These bulbs are designed to run on +12v and draw approximately 2.1 amps of current or about 25 watts. Each bulb effectively acts as if it were a 5.7-ohm resistor. I recommend that you wire up at least four bulb sockets in parallel, mounted on a non-conductive breadboard. For testing high output supplies, you could wire up as many as eight sockets in parallel. It would be wise to have four disk drive connectors also wired in parallel in the same circuit to balance the draw from the supply. A single drive connector cannot handle more than a two-bulb (4-amp) load reliably. To use this load tester, plug the bulb loading network into the disk drive power connectors, and by adding or removing bulbs from their sockets you can control the load. With four bulbs installed, you have approximately an 8-amp load, which is good for maximum load testing of a standard 200-watt PC power supply rated for 8 amps of +12v output.

You will still need a +5v load as well. Unfortunately, a #1156 type bulb does not work well for a +5v load because each bulb only draws 0.875 amps at +5v (4.4 watts). Even eight of these bulbs would only draw 7 amps or 35 watts of +5v power. You could substitute a #1493 bulb instead, which draws about 2.75 amps at +5v or about 14 watts. You would still need eight of these bulbs, which would draw 22 amps at +5v, to perform a maximum load test on a standard 200-watt-rated PC power supply.

Perhaps a better solution than using bulbs is to use heavy duty wirewound resistors to construct a load network. For a +12v load, you could mount a series of 6-ohm 50-watt resistors in a parallel network with a toggle switch to bring each one into the circuit. Using a 6-ohm resistor would draw 2 amps or 24 watts exactly, so make sure that each switch is rated for 3 amps or more to be safe. As you switch each additional resistor into the circuit, the load increases by 2 amps or 24 watts. Note that the resistors are rated to handle up to 50 watts, which means we are simply being conservative. I might start this network off with a single #1156 bulb because the visual information from the light is useful. The fact that the light is lit means of course that power is available, and sometimes you can see voltage variations as changes in the brightness of the lamp as you switch in additional loads. This can give you a visual impression of how well the supply is performing.

This same type of setup can be used to create a +5v load network. In this case, I recommend you use 1-ohm 50-watt wirewound resistors in the same type of parallel network, with a switch for each resistor. You could start the network off with a single #1493 bulb for a visual indicator of power supply output, which would draw 2.75 amps or about 14 watts of power. Each 1-ohm 50-watt resistor draws 5 amps of +5v current or exactly 25 watts. Again, I would specify resistors with a 50-watt rating and a switch with a rating higher than 5 amps to be on the conservative side. A network of four of these resistors alone draws exactly 20 amps of power, which is exactly what the typical 200-watt PC power supply has to offer in +5v. By switching four of these resistors into the load, you could perform a full stress test on the supply. Add more, and you could test higher output supplies as well. Again it would be prudent to draw this through four disk drive connectors simultaneously so as to balance the load between the connectors. You also could get some motherboard (P8 and P9 type) connectors and draw the load through all the +5v pins on those connectors.

You can purchase all these components including wirewound resistors, bulbs, sockets, connectors, breadboard, and so on through electronics parts supply houses such as Allied, Newark, and Digi-Key (see the vendor list).

Variable Voltage Transformer. In testing power supplies, it is desirable to simulate different voltage conditions at the wall socket to observe how the supply reacts. A *variable voltage transformer* can be a very useful test device for checking power supplies because it enables you to have control over the AC line voltage used as input for the power supply (see fig. 8.6). This device consists of a large transformer mounted in a housing with a dial indicator to control the output voltage. You plug the line cord from the transformer into the wall socket, and then plug the PC power cord into the socket provided on the transformer. The knob on the transformer can then be used to adjust the AC line voltage seen by the PC.

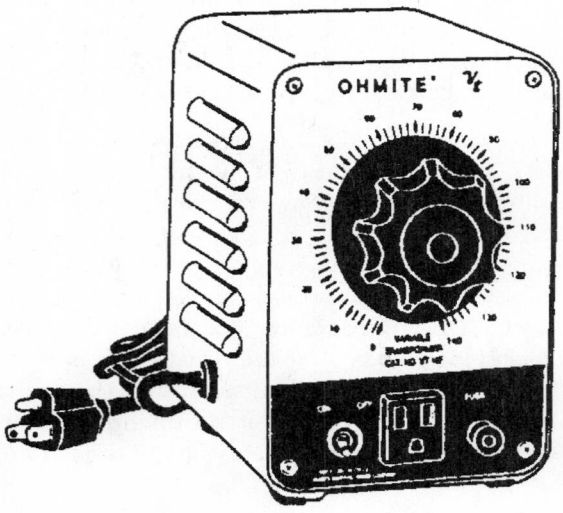

Fig. 8.6
A variable voltage transformer.

Most variable transformers can adjust their AC output from 0v to 140v no matter what the AC input (wall socket) voltage is. Some can even cover a range from 0v to 280v as well. You can use the transformer to simulate brownout conditions, enabling you to observe the PC's response. This enables you to check for proper Power_Good signal operation among other things.

By running the PC and dropping the voltage until the PC shuts down, you can see how much "reserve" is in the power supply for handling a brownout or other voltage fluctuations. If your transformer can output voltages in the 200v range, then you also can test the capability of the power supply to run on foreign voltage levels as well. A properly functioning supply should operate between 90v to 137v, but shut down cleanly if the voltage is outside that range.

An indication of a problem is seeing "parity check" type error messages when you drop the voltage to 80v. This indicates that the Power_Good signal is not being withdrawn before the power supply output (to the PC) fails. What should happen is that the PC simply stops operating as the Power_Good signal is withdrawn, causing the system to enter a continuous reset loop.

Variable voltage transformers are sold by a number of electronic parts supply houses such as Allied, Newark, and Digi-Key (see the vendor list). You should expect to pay anywhere from $100 to $300 for these devices.

PC PowerCheck. The PC PowerCheck card by Data Depot (see the vendor list) is an ISA bus plug-in card that can be used to easily test power supplies while in the system or on a bench. It has a series of LEDs that indicate over or under voltage conditions, noise, and transient spike occurrences. These indicators can be set up to run in real time, or to trap any anomalies and stay lit.

The PC PowerCheck card can connect to the system in two ways. The easiest way to use it is to plug it directly into a slot like any other adapter card. One caution is to make sure that you plug the card in the correct orientation; if you plug it in backwards, serious damage to the card and motherboard can result. No metal bracket is on the card, so it is possible to plug it in either way. You will make that mistake only once!

A second way to use the card is in a bench test mode. In this case, you remove the power supply from the system and plug it directly into the power connectors found on the card. The power connectors on the PC PowerCheck card are not keyed, so if your power supply has keyed connectors, they can be difficult to plug in. Also, you must make sure that the power supply connectors are plugged in the proper orientation. If you plug the connectors in backwards, you may destroy the card.

In the bench test mode, the card is substituting for the motherboard. The PC PowerCheck card has built-in load resistors, however they are very small, drawing only 0.5 amps of +5v and 0.1 amps of +12v current. These loads are certainly not enough to stress the supply and may not be enough in many cases for the supply to operate at all. In this case, additional load can be placed on the supply by plugging in a hard disk, or using custom-made load resistors.

The PC PowerCheck also has an LED to monitor the Power_Good signal, but to monitor that signal the power supply must be plugged in directly in the bench test mode. When plugged into a slot, the same LED then monitors the bus Reset line, which is controlled by the Power_Good signal giving you a secondary indication of Power_Good status.

The PC PowerCheck can be a useful tool in testing PC power supplies as installed in a system, especially for those unwilling to use a digital voltmeter. It is extremely useful for quick pass/fail testing such as on a PC assembly line. Supplies that fail the test can be quickly identified and replaced, and the defective units can be subjected to further testing without holding up the assembly process. The bench test mode is not as useful because additional loads must be placed on the supply for proper stress testing. In any mode, the LED indicators for noise, transients, and Power_Good/Reset are very informative, useful, and unique for this product.

PC Power System Analyzer. The most sophisticated power supply test device I have used is the PC Power System Analyzer from TCE (see Appendix B, the "Vendor List"). This is a portable toaster-sized piece of gear that comes in a padded case for transport that contains the Analyzer and all its accessories. This device sells for around $750 and performs three main functions, all of which are conducted with the supply still installed in the system unit.

The primary function is to load test the system. The PC Power System Analyzer comes with a bus adapter (for both ISA/EISA and MCA) that probes the power output and adds a couple of amps additional load to the +5v and +12v lines. Using this additional load in conjunction with the load of the system, it analyzes the capability of the supply to deliver the proper current.

The unit also performs a Power_Good timing test, which checks to see that the Power_Good signal arrives within the proper time span of 100 to 500 ms. Personally, I have seen many supplies that have problems with the Power_Good signal, and some motherboards are more sensitive to this than others. This unit quickly identifies these failing or improperly designed supplies.

The other tests are voltage tests. Both the power supply output as well as line (wall current) voltage are continuously tested, and minimums and maximums are recorded over time. Information from all the tests can be output to a printer via a parallel port on the unit. During voltage measurements, any anomalies are recorded along with the time of the occurrence, actual voltage values, duration of the failure, and additional information. The unit also has several LEDs to indicate failures or proper operation under the different tests.

The printout is excellent especially when you are servicing systems for others. When you have to explain to a customer how their power supply is failing, it gives you documentation to back you up.

The TCE Power System Analyzer is one of the most sophisticated and specialized pieces of test gear for power supplies. It can be used in PC service shops or assembly operations to quickly test and validate power supply function. Because it is portable, it also can easily be carried into the field for testing remote systems. It is more of a professional tool and is probably too pricey for the average end user.

Repairing the Power Supply

Actually repairing a power supply is rarely done anymore primarily because it is usually cheaper simply to replace the supply with a new one. Even high-quality power supplies are not that expensive relative to the labor required to repair them.

Defective power supplies are usually discarded unless they happen to be one of the higher quality or more expensive units. In that case, it is usually wise to send the supply out to a company that specializes in repairing power supplies and other components. These companies provide what is called *depot repair*, which means you send the supply to them; they repair it and return it to you. If time is of the essence, most of the depot repair companies immediately send you a functional equivalent to your defective supply, and then take yours in as a core charge. Depot repair is the recommended way to service many PC components such as power supplies, monitors, printers, and so on. If you take your PC in to a conventional service outlet, they often diagnose the problem to the major component, and then send it out to be depot repaired. You can do that yourself and save the markup the repair shop normally charges in such cases.

For those with experience around high voltages, it may be possible to repair a failing supply with two relatively simple operations; however, these require opening the supply. I do not recommend this; I am only mentioning it as an alternative to replacement in some cases. Most manufacturers try to prevent you from entering the supply by sealing it with special tamper-proof Torx screws. These screws use the familiar Torx star driver, but also have a tamper prevention pin in the center that prevents a standard driver from working. Most tool companies such as Jensen or Specialized (see Appendix B) sell sets of TT (tamper-proof Torx) bits, which remove the tamper-resistant screws. Other manufacturers rivet the power supply case shut, which means you must drill out the rivets to gain access. Again, the manufacturers place these obstacles there for a reason—to prevent entry by those who are inexperienced around high voltage. Consider yourself warned!

Most power supplies have an internal fuse that is part of the overload protection. If this fuse is blown, then the supply does not operate. It is possible to replace this fuse if you open up the supply. Be aware that in most cases in which an internal power supply problem causes the fuse to blow, replacing it does nothing but cause it to blow again until the root cause of the problem is repaired. In this case, you are better off sending the unit to a professional depot repair company. Appendix B lists several companies that do depot repair on power supplies and other components.

PC power supplies have a voltage adjustment internal to the supply that is calibrated and set when the supply is manufactured. Over time, the values of some of the components in the supply can change, thus altering the output voltages. If this is the case, you often can access the adjustment control and tweak it to bring the voltages back to where they should be. Several adjustable items are in the supply—usually small variable resistors that can be turned with a screwdriver. You should use a nonconductive tool such as a fiberglass or plastic screwdriver designed for this purpose. If you were to drop a metal tool into an operating supply, dangerous sparks and possibly fire could result, not to mention danger of electrocution and damage to the supply. You also have to figure out which of the adjustments are for voltage, and which are for which voltage signal. This requires some trial-and-error testing. You can mark the current positions of all the resistors, begin measuring a single voltage signal, and then try moving each adjuster slightly until you see the voltage change. If you move an adjuster and nothing changes, then put it back to the original position you marked. Through this process, you can locate and adjust each of the voltages to the standard 5v and 12v levels.

Obtaining Replacement Units

There may be times when it is simply easier, safer, or less expensive (considering time and materials) to replace the power supply rather than repair it. As mentioned earlier, replacement power supplies are available from many manufacturers. Before you can shop for a supplier, however, there are other purchasing factors you should consider.

Deciding on a Power Supply

When looking at getting a new power supply, there are several things you should take into account. First, consider the power supply's shape, or *form factor*. For example, the power supply used in the IBM AT differs physically from the one used in the PC or XT. Therefore, AT and PC/XT supplies are not interchangeable.

Differences exist in the size, shape, screw-hole positions, connector type, number of connectors, and switch position in these and other power supplies. Systems that use the same form-factor supply can easily interchange. The compatible manufacturers realized this and most began designing systems that mimicked the shape of IBM's AT with regard to motherboard and power supply configuration and mounting. As the clone market evolved, four standard form factors for power supplies became popular—the AT/Tower, Baby AT, Slimline, and PC/XT form factors. You can easily interchange any supply with another one of the same form factor. Earlier this chapter gave complete descriptions of these form factors. When ordering a replacement supply, you need to know which form factor your system requires.

Many systems use proprietary designed power supplies, which makes replacement difficult. IBM uses a number of designs for the PS/2 systems, and little interchangeability exists between different systems. Some of the supplies do interchange, especially between any that have the same or similar cases, such as the Model 60, 65, and 80. Several different output level power supplies are available for these systems, including 207-, 225-, 242-, and 250-watt versions. The most powerful 250-watt unit was supplied originally for the Model 65 SX and later version Model 80 systems, although it fits perfectly in any Model 60, 65, or 80 system. I have not found any company manufacturing aftermarket supplies for the PS/2 systems, probably because the IBM factory-supplied units are more than adequate for their intended application. Although these supplies are mostly made by Astec, they do not sell them directly because of contractual agreements with IBM. Traditionally, it is too expensive to purchase parts from IBM, so a great number of third-party companies are repairing and even reselling brand new IBM PS/2 power supplies (and other IBM parts) at prices greatly below what IBM charges for the same thing. Scan the "Vendor List" in Appendix B for some recommended vendors of these parts.

One risk with some of the compatibles is that they might not use one of the industry-standard form-factor supplies. If a system uses one of the common form-factor power supplies, then replacement units are available from hundreds of vendors. An unfortunate user of a system with a nonstandard form-factor supply doesn't have this kind of choice and must get a replacement from the original manufacturer of the system—and usually pay through the nose for the unit. Although you can find AT form-factor units for as little as $50, the proprietary units from some manufacturers run as high as $400. When *Popular Mechanics* magazine reviews an automobile, it always lists the replacement costs of the most failure-prone and replacement-prone components, from front bumpers to alternators to taillights. PC buyers often overlook this type of information and discover too late the consequences of having nonstandard components in a system.

An example of IBM-compatible systems with proprietary power supply designs are those from Compaq. None of its systems use the same form-factor supply as the IBM systems, which means that Compaq usually is the only place you can get a replacement. If the power supply in your Compaq Deskpro system "goes south," you can expect to pay $395 for a replacement, and the replacement unit will be no better or quieter than the one you're replacing. You have little choice in the matter because almost no one offers Compaq form-factor power supplies except Compaq. An exception is that PC Power and Cooling offers excellent replacement power supplies for the earlier Compaq Portable systems and for the Deskpro series. These replacement power supplies have higher output power levels than the original supplies from Compaq and cost much less.

Sources for Replacement Power Supplies

Because one of the most-failure prone items in PC systems is the power supply, I am often called on to recommend a replacement. Literally hundreds of companies manufacture PC power supplies, and I certainly have not tested them all; however, I have come up with a couple of companies whose product I have come to know and trust.

Although other high-quality manufacturers are out there as well, at this time I recommend power supplies from either Astec Standard Power or PC Power and Cooling (see Appendix B).

Astec makes the power supplies used in most of the high-end systems by IBM, Hewlett Packard, Apple, and many other name brand systems. They have power supplies available in a number of standard form factors (AT/Tower, Baby AT, and Slimline) and a variety of output levels. They have power supplies with ratings of up to 300 watts, and also now have power supplies especially designed for "Green" PCs that meet the EPA Energy Star requirements for low power consumption. Their "Green" power supplies are specifically designed to achieve high efficiency at low-load conditions. Be aware that high-output supplies from other manufacturers may have problems with very low loads. Astec also makes a number of power supplies for laptop and notebook PC systems and has numerous non-PC type supplies as well.

PC Power and Cooling has the most complete line of power supplies for PC systems. They make supplies in all the standard PC form factors used today (AT/Tower, Baby AT, PC/XT, and Slimline). Versions are available in a variety of different quality and output levels, from inexpensive replacements to very high-quality high-output models with ratings up to 450 watts. They even have versions with built-in battery backup systems and a series of special models with high-volume low-speed (quiet) fan assemblies. Their quiet models are especially welcome to people who can't take the fan noise that some power supplies emanate.

PC Power and Cooling also has units available to fit some of Compaq's proprietary designs. This can be a real boon if you have to service or repair Compaq systems because the PC Power and Cooling units are available in higher output ratings than Compaq's own; they cost much less than Compaq; and they bolt in as a direct replacement.

A high-quality power supply from either of these vendors is one of the best cures for intermittent system problems and goes a long way toward ensuring trouble-free operation in the future.

Summary

This chapter examined the power supply in great detail. You should now have an understanding of how the supply functions in the system and the characteristics of power supply operation. You should understand the function of the Power_Good signal and its role in the system. Also covered was troubleshooting power supply problems and using test equipment to check out power supply operation. I have always found that the power supply is the single most failure-prone component in a PC system, and the information presented here should help greatly whether you are building systems from scratch, upgrading existing systems, or repairing a system with a failing power supply.

Part III

Input/Output Hardware

9   Input Devices

10   Video Display Hardware and Specifications

11   Communications and Networking

12   Audio Hardware

Chapter 9

Input Devices

This chapter discusses *input devices*—the devices used to communicate with the computer. The most common input device is of course the keyboard, and this chapter discusses keyboards in depth. Also discussed are mice because they are now a standard requirement to operate a modern PC with a GUI (graphical user interface) such as Windows or OS/2. Finally, this chapter also discusses the game or joystick interface, used to input signals from joysticks, paddles, or other game devices.

Keyboards

One of the most basic system components is your keyboard. The keyboard is the primary input device and is used for entering commands and data into the system. This section examines the keyboards available for IBM and compatible systems. This section examines the different types of keyboards, how the keyboard functions, the keyboard-to-system interface, and finally keyboard troubleshooting and repair.

Types of Keyboards

Since the introduction of the original IBM PC, IBM has created three different keyboard designs for PC systems, which have become standards in the industry shared by the compatible manufacturers as well. The three primary keyboard types are as follows:

- 83-key PC and XT keyboard
- 84-key AT keyboard
- 101-key enhanced keyboard

This section discusses each keyboard type and shows its layout and physical appearance. Because most systems use the 101-key enhanced keyboard design, this version is emphasized.

83-Key PC and XT Keyboard. When the PC was first introduced, it had something that few other personal computers had at the time: an external detachable keyboard. Most other small personal computers had the keyboard built in, like the Apple II. Although the external design was a good move on IBM's part, its keyboard design was not without criticism. One of the most criticized components of the original 83-key keyboard is the awkward layout (see fig. 9.1). The Shift keys are small and in the wrong place on the left side. The Enter key also is too small. These oversights were especially irritating at the time because IBM had produced the Selectric typewriter, perceived as a standard for good keyboard layout.

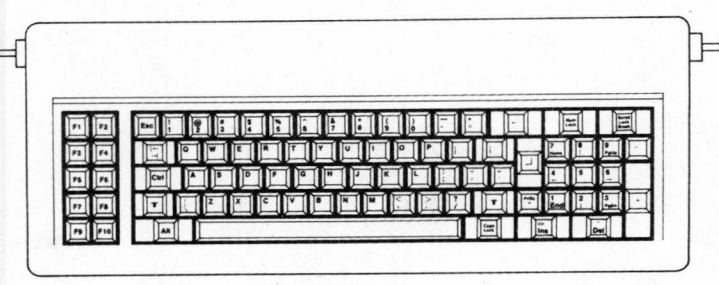

Fig. 9.1
PC and XT 83-key keyboard layout.

The PC/XT keyboard has a built-in processor that communicates to the motherboard via a special serial data link. The communication is one-way, which means that the motherboard cannot send commands or data back to the keyboard. For this reason, IBM 83-key keyboards have no LED indicator lights. Because the status of the Caps Lock, Num Lock, and Scroll Lock are maintained by the motherboard, there is no way to make sure that any LED indicator lights remain in sync with the actual status of the function. Many aftermarket (non-IBM) PC keyboards added the lights, and the keyboard attempted to keep track of the three functions independently of the motherboard. This worked in most situations, but it was entirely possible to see the LEDs become out of sync with the actual function status. Rebooting corrected this temporary problem, but it was annoying nonetheless. By eliminating the lights, IBM keyboards did not have this potential problem.

The original 83-key PC/XT keyboard is no longer used and is not electrically compatible with AT motherboards, although some aftermarket units may be compatible by moving an XT/AT switch usually found on the bottom of the keyboard.

84-Key AT Keyboard. When the AT was introduced in 1984, it included a new keyboard—the 84-key unit (see fig. 9.2). This keyboard corrected many problems of the original PC and XT keyboards. The position and arrangement of the numeric keypad was modified. The Enter key was made much larger, like that of a Selectric typewriter. The Shift key positions and sizes were corrected. IBM also finally added LED indicators for the status of the Caps Lock, Scroll Lock, and Num Lock toggles.

Fig. 9.2
AT 84-key keyboard layout.

These keyboards use a slightly modified interface protocol that is bidirectional. This means that the processor built into the keyboard can talk to another processor (called the keyboard controller chip) built into the motherboard. The keyboard controller on the motherboard also can send commands and data to the keyboard, which allows functions such as changing the keyboard typematic (or repeat) rate as well as the delay before repeating begins. The keyboard controller on the motherboard also scans code translations, which allows a much easier integration of foreign language keyboards into the system. Finally, the bidirectional interface can be used to control the LED indicators on the keyboard, thus ensuring that the status of the function and indicators are always in sync.

The 84-key unit that came with the original AT system is no longer used, although it does have the proper electrical design to be compatible with the newer systems. It lacks some of the keys found in the newer keyboards and does not have as nice a numeric keypad section, but many prefer the more Selectric style layout of the alpha-numeric keys. Also some prefer the ten function keys arranged on the left-hand side as opposed to the enhanced arrangement in which 12 function keys are lined up along the top.

Enhanced 101-Key (or 102-Key). In 1986, IBM introduced the "corporate" enhanced 101-key keyboard for the newer XT and AT models (see fig. 9.3). I use the word "corporate" because this unit first appeared in IBM's RT PC, which is an RISC (Reduced Instruction Set Computer) system designed for scientific and engineering applications; keyboards with this design are now supplied with virtually every type of system and terminal IBM sells. This universal keyboard has a further improved layout over that of the 84-key unit, with perhaps the exception of the Enter key, which reverted to a smaller size. The 101-key enhanced keyboard was designed to conform to international regulations and specifications for keyboards. In fact, other companies such as DEC and TI had already been using designs similar to the IBM 101-key unit even earlier than IBM. The IBM 101-key units originally came in versions with and without the status indicator LEDs, depending on whether the unit was sold with an XT or AT system. Now there are many other variations to choose from, including some with integrated pointing devices.

III

Input/Output Hardware

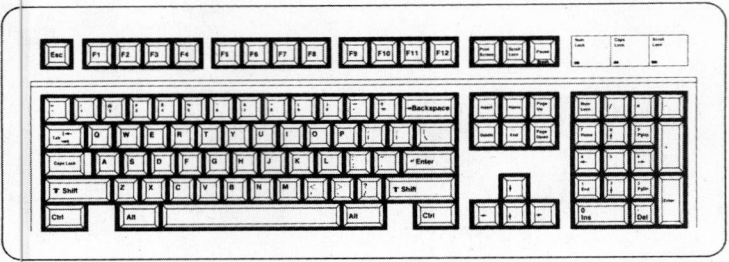

Fig. 9.3

101-key enhanced keyboard layout.

The enhanced keyboard is the current standard and is available in several different variations, but all are basically the same electrically and can be interchanged. IBM and its keyboard and printer subsidiary Lexmark have produced a number of versions including some newer ones with built-in pointing devices. Most of the enhanced keyboards attach to the system via the standard 5-pin DIN connector, but many newer ones come with cables for the 6-pin mini-DIN connector found on many newer systems including the IBM PS/2s and most Slimline compatibles. Although the connectors may be physically different, the keyboards are not, and you can either interchange the cables or use a cable adapter to plug one type into the other.

Because older PC/XT-style systems lack the bidirectional keyboard interface required to drive the LED indicators found on most enhanced keyboards, IBM even made models without these lights (Caps Lock, Num Lock, and Scroll Lock). These keyboards are the same as the others, but they are missing the small add-on circuit board used to drive the lights. If you use an older XT system with an enhanced keyboard that has the LEDs, they simply remain dark. Some compatible keyboard manufacturers have added circuitry internal to the keyboard that turns the LEDs on and off whenever you press the appropriate keys. In such a case, however, it is possible for the LEDs to get "out of sync" with the actual state of the toggles, which are actually maintained within the computer and not the keyboard.

The 101-key keyboard layout can be divided into the following four sections:

- Typing area
- Numeric keypad
- Cursor and screen controls
- Function keys

The 101-key arrangement is similar to the Selectric keyboard layout with the exception of the Enter key. The Tab, Caps Lock, Shift, and Backspace keys have a larger striking area and are located in the familiar Selectric locations. Ctrl and Alt keys are on each side of the space bar. The typing area and numeric keypad have home-row identifiers for touch typing.

The cursor and screen-control keys have been separated from the numeric keypad, which is reserved for numeric input. (As with other PC keyboards, you can use the numeric keypad for cursor and screen control when the keyboard is not in Num Lock mode.) A division-sign key and an additional Enter key have been added to the numeric keypad.

The cursor-control keys are arranged in the inverted T format. The Insert, Delete, Home, End, Page Up, and Page Down keys, located above the dedicated cursor-control keys, are separate from the numeric keypad. The function keys, spaced in groups of four, are located across the top of the keyboard. The keyboard has two additional function keys (F11 and F12). The Esc key is isolated in the upper left corner of the keyboard. Dedicated Print Screen/Sys Req, Scroll Lock, and Pause/Break keys are provided for commonly used functions.

Foreign language versions of the enhanced keyboard include 102-keys and a slightly different layout from the 101-key United States versions.

One of the enhanced keyboard's many useful features is removable keycaps. With clear keycaps and paper inserts, you can customize the keyboard. Keyboard templates are also available from IBM to provide specific operator instructions.

The enhanced keyboard probably will be on any desktop system IBM introduces for quite some time. It is currently the most popular design and does not show any signs of being replaced in the future. Because most compatible systems use this same type of keyboard, it is relatively easy to move from one system to another without relearning the layout.

Compatibility. The 83-key PC/XT is different from all the others and normally only plugs into a PC/XT system that does not use the motherboard-based 8042-type keyboard controller chip. This is definitely true for IBM's keyboards, but also is true for many compatible units as well. Some compatibles may be switchable to work with an AT-type motherboard via an XT/AT switch.

The 84-key unit from IBM works only on AT-type motherboards and does not work at all with PC/XT systems. Again, some aftermarket designs may have an XT/AT switch to allow for compatibility with PC/XT-type systems.

The enhanced keyboards from IBM are universal and auto-switching, meaning that they work in virtually any system from the XT to the PS/2 or any IBM-compatible by simply plugging them in. Some may require that a switch be moved on the keyboard to make it compatible with PC/XT systems that do not have the 8042-type keyboard controller on the motherboard. In some cases, you also may need to switch to a different cable with the proper system end connector, or use an adapter.

Although the enhanced keyboard is electrically compatible with any AT-type motherboard and even most PC/XT-type motherboards, many older systems will have software problems using these keyboards. IBM changed the ROM on the systems to support the new keyboard properly, and the compatible vendors followed suit. Very old (1986 or earlier) machines may require a ROM upgrade to properly use some of the features on the 101-key enhanced keyboards, such as the F11 and F12 keys. If the

III

Input/Output Hardware

individual system ROM BIOS is not capable of operating the 101-key keyboard correctly, then the 101-key keyboard may not work at all (as with all three ROM versions of the IBM PC); the additional keys (F11 and F12 function keys) may not work; or you may have problems with keyboard operation in general. In some cases, these compatibility problems cause improper characters to appear when keys are typed causing the system to beep, and general keyboard operation is a problem. These problems can often be solved by a ROM upgrade to a newer version with proper support for the enhanced keyboard.

If you have an IBM system, you can tell whether your system has complete ROM BIOS support for the 101-key unit: when you plug in the keyboard and turn on the system unit, the Num Lock light automatically comes on and the numeric keypad portion of the keyboard is enabled. This method of detection isn't 100 percent accurate, but if the light goes on, your BIOS generally supports the keyboard. A notable exception is the IBM AT BIOS dated 06/10/85; it turns on the Num Lock light, but still does not properly support the enhanced keyboard. All IBM BIOS versions dated 11/15/85 or newer do have proper support for the enhanced keyboards.

In IBM systems that support the enhanced keyboard, if it is detected on power up, Num Lock is enabled, and the light goes on. If one of the older 84-key AT-type keyboards is detected, then the Num Lock function is not enabled because these keyboards do not have arrow keys separate from the numeric keypad. When the enhanced keyboards first appeared in 1986, many users (myself included) were irritated upon finding that the numeric keypad was automatically enabled every time the system boots. Most compatibles began integrating a function into the system setup that allowed specification of the Num Lock status on boot. Unfortunately, IBM still does not have this feature in many PS/2 systems.

Some thought that the automatic enabling of Num Lock was a function of the enhanced keyboard because none of the earlier keyboards seemed to operate this way. Remember that this function isn't really a keyboard function—instead it's a function of the motherboard ROM BIOS, which identifies an enhanced 101-key unit and turns on the Num Lock as a "favor." In systems that cannot disable the automatic numeric keypad enable feature, you can use the DOS 6.0 or higher version NUMLOCK= parameter in CONFIG.SYS to turn Num Lock on or off as desired. If you are running an earlier version of DOS than 6.0, then you can simply use one of the many public domain programs available for turning off the Num Lock function. Placing the program command to disable Num Lock in the AUTOEXEC.BAT file turns off the numeric keypad each time the system reboots.

In an informal test, I plugged the new keyboard into an earlier XT. The keyboard seemed to work well. None of the keys that didn't exist previously, such as F11 and F12, were operable, but the new arrow keys and the numeric keypad did work. The enhanced keyboard seems to work on XT or AT systems, but does not function on the original PC systems because of BIOS and electrical interface problems. Many compatible versions of the 101-key enhanced keyboards have a manual XT/AT switch on the bottom that may allow the keyboard to work in an original PC system.

Keyboard Technology

The technology that makes up a typical PC keyboard is very interesting. This section focuses on all aspects of keyboard technology and design including the keyswitches, the interface between the keyboard and the system, scan codes, and the keyboard connectors.

Keyswitch Design. Several types of switches are used in keyboards today. Most keyboards use one of several variations on a mechanical keyswitch. A mechanical keyswitch relies on a mechanical momentary contact-type switch to make electrical contact in a circuit. Some high-end keyboard designs use a totally different nonmechanical design that relies on capacitive switches. This section discusses these switches and the highlights of each design.

The most common type of keyswitch is the mechanical type, available in the following variations:

- Pure mechanical
- Foam element
- Rubber dome
- Membrane

The *pure mechanical* type is just that, a simple mechanical switch that features metal contacts in a momentary contact arrangement. Often a tactile feedback mechanism— consisting of a clip and spring arrangement to give a "clickety" feel to the keyboard and offer some resistance to pressing the key—is built-in. A company called Lite-On manufactures this type of keyboard using switches from Alps Electric (see Appendix B, the "Vendor List"). Mechanical switches are very durable, usually have self-cleaning contacts, and normally are rated for 20 million keystrokes, which is second only to the capacitive switch. They also offer excellent tactile feedback.

Foam element mechanical switches were a very popular design in some older keyboards. Most of the older compatible keyboards, including those made by Keytronics and many others, use this technology. These switches are characterized by a foam element with an electrical contact on the bottom that is mounted on the bottom of a plunger attached to the key itself (see fig. 9.4).

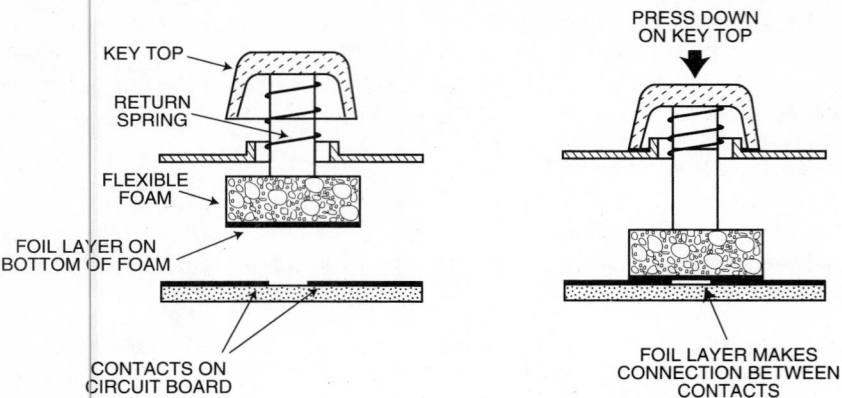

Fig. 9.4

Typical foam element mechanical keyswitch.

When the switch is pressed down, a foil conductor on the bottom of the foam element closes a circuit on the printed circuit board below. A return spring pushes the key back up when the pressure is released. The foam dampens the contact, helping to prevent bounce, but unfortunately gives these keyboards a "mushy" feel. The big problem with this type of keyswitch design is that there is often little in the way of tactile feedback, and systems with these keyboards often resort to tricks like clicking the PC's speaker to signify that contact has been made. Compaq used keyboards of this type (made by Keytronics) in many of its older systems, but perhaps the most popular user today is Packard Bell. Preference in keyboard feel is somewhat subjective, and personally I do not favor the foam element switch design.

Another problem with this type of design is that it is more subject to corrosion on the foil conductor as well as the circuit board traces below. When this happens, the key strikes may become intermittent, which can be frustrating. Fortunately, these keyboards are among the easiest to clean. By disassembling this type of keyboard completely, you usually can remove the circuit board portion, without removing each foam pad separately, and expose the bottoms of all the pads. Then you can easily wipe the corrosion and dirt off the bottom of the foam pads as well as the circuit board, thus restoring the keyboard to like-new condition. Unfortunately, over time, the corrosion problem will occur again. Using some Stabilant 22a from D.W. Electrochemicals (see Appendix B) is highly recommended to improve the switch contact action as well as to prevent future corrosion. Because of problems like this, the foam element design is not used much anymore and has been superseded in popularity by the rubber dome design.

Rubber dome switches are mechanical switches that are very similar to the foam element type, but are also improved in many ways. Instead of a spring, these switches use a rubber dome that has a carbon button contact on the underside. As you depress a key, the key plunger presses down on the rubber dome, causing it to resist and then collapse all at once, much like the top of an oil can. As the rubber dome collapses, the user feels the tactile feedback, and the carbon button makes contact between the circuit board traces below. When the key is released, the rubber dome re-forms and pushes the key back upward.

The rubber eliminates the need for a spring and provides a reasonable amount of tactile feedback without any special clips or other parts. A carbon button is used because it is resistant to corrosion and also has a self-cleaning action on the metal contacts below. The rubber domes are formed into a sheet that completely protects the contacts below from dirt, dust, and even minor spills. This type of design is the simplest, using the fewest parts. These things make this type of keyswitch very reliable and contribute to making rubber dome-type keyboards the most popular in service today.

If rubber dome keyboards have a drawback at all, it is that tactile feedback is not as good as many would like. Although it is reasonable for most, some prefer more tactile feedback than rubber dome keyboards normally provide.

The *membrane keyboard* is a variation on the rubber dome type in which the keys themselves are no longer separate, but are formed together in a sheet that sits on the rubber dome sheet. This severely limits key travel, and membrane keyboards are not considered usable for normal touch typing because of this. They are ideal in extremely harsh environments. Because the sheets can be bonded together and sealed from the elements, membrane keyboards can be used in situations in which no other type could survive. Many industrial applications use rubber dome keyboards especially for terminals that do not require extensive data entry, but are used to operate equipment such as cash registers.

Capacitive switches are the only nonmechanical type of switch in use today (see fig. 9.5). These are the Cadillac of keyswitches; they are much more expensive than the more common mechanical rubber dome, but also are more resistant to dirt and corrosion and offer the highest quality tactile feedback of any type of switch.

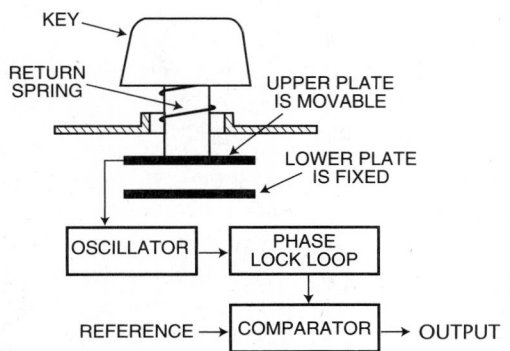

Fig. 9.5
A capacitive keyswitch.

A capacitive switch does not work by making contact between conductors. Instead, two plates usually made of plastic are connected in a switch matrix designed to detect changes in capacitance of the circuit.

When the key is depressed, the plunger moves the top plate relative to the fixed bottom plate. Usually a mechanism provides for a distinct over-center tactile feedback with a resounding "click." As the top plate moves, the capacitance between the two plates changes and is detected by the comparator circuitry in the keyboard.

Because this type of switch does not rely on metal contacts, it is almost immune to corrosion and dirt. These switches are very resistant to key bounce problems resulting in multiple characters appearing from a single strike, and are also the most durable in the industry—rated for 25 million or more keystrokes, as opposed to 10 to 20 million for other designs. The tactile feedback is unsurpassed because a relatively loud click and strong over-center feel normally are provided. The only drawback to this design is the cost. Capacitive switch keyboards are among the most expensive designs, but the quality of the feel and durability are worth it.

Traditionally, the only vendors of capacitive keyswitch keyboards are IBM and its keyboard division Lexmark, which is why these keyboards have always seemed to stand out from the rest.

The Keyboard Interface. A keyboard consists of a set of switches mounted in a grid or array called the *key matrix*. When a switch is pressed, a processor in the keyboard itself identifies which key is pressed by identifying which grid location in the matrix shows continuity. The keyboard processor also interprets how long the key is pressed and can even handle multiple keystrokes at the same time. A 16-byte hardware buffer in the keyboard can handle rapid or multiple keystrokes, passing each one in succession to the system.

When you press a key, in most cases the contact actually bounces slightly, meaning that there are several rapid on-off cycles just as the switch makes contact. This is called *bounce*, and the processor in the keyboard is designed to filter this or *debounce* the keystroke. The keyboard processor must distinguish bounce from a double key strike actually intended by the keyboard operator. This is fairly easy because the bouncing is much more rapid than a person could simulate by striking a key quickly several times.

The keyboard in an IBM-compatible system is actually a computer itself. It communicates to the main system through a special serial data link that transmits and receives data in 11-bit packets of information consisting of eight data bits in addition to framing and control bits. Although it is indeed a serial link (the data flows on one wire), it is not compatible with the standard RS-232 serial port commonly used to connect modems. The original PC/XT setup was a one-way connection; however, the AT design is bidirectional, which means that the keyboard can receive as well as send data. In this manner, the AT keyboard could be reprogrammed in several different ways.

The processor in the original PC keyboard was an Intel 8048 microcontroller chip, but newer keyboards often use an 8049 version that has built-in ROM, or other microcontroller chips compatible with the 8048 or 8049. For example, IBM has always used a custom version of the Motorola 6805 processor in its enhanced keyboards, which is compatible with the Intel chips. The keyboard's built-in processor reads the key matrix, debounces the keypress signals, converts the keypress to the appropriate scan code, and transmits the code to the motherboard. The processors built into the keyboard contain their own RAM, possibly some ROM, and a built-in serial interface.

In the original PC/XT design, the keyboard serial interface is connected to an 8255 Programmable Peripheral Interface (PPI) chip on the motherboard of the PC/XT. This chip is then connected to the interrupt controller IRQ1 line, which is used to signal that keyboard data is available. The data itself is sent from the 8255 to the processor via I/O port address 60h. The IRQ1 signal causes the main system processor to run a subroutine (INT 9h) that interprets the keyboard scan code data and decides what to do.

In an AT-type keyboard design, the keyboard serial interface is connected to a special keyboard controller on the motherboard. This is an Intel 8042 Universal Peripheral Interface (UPI) slave microcontroller chip in the original AT design. This microcontroller is essentially another processor that has its own 2K of ROM and 128 bytes of RAM. An 8742 version that uses EPROM (Erasable Programmable Read Only Memory) can be erased and reprogrammed. Often when you get a motherboard ROM upgrade from a motherboard manufacturer, a new keyboard controller chip is included because it has somewhat dependent and updated ROM code in it as well. Some systems may use the 8041 or 8741 chips, which differ only in the amount of built-in ROM or RAM, whereas other systems now have the keyboard controller built into the main system chipset.

In an AT system, the (8048-type) microcontroller in the keyboard sends data to the (8042-type) motherboard keyboard controller on the motherboard. The motherboard-based controller also can send data back to the keyboard as well. When the keyboard controller on the motherboard receives data from the keyboard, it signals the motherboard with an IRQ1 and sends the data to the main motherboard processor via I/O port address 60h just as in the PC/XT. Acting as an agent between the keyboard and the main system processor, the 8042-type keyboard controller can translate scan codes and perform several other functions as well. Data also can be sent to the 8042 keyboard controller via port 60h, which is then passed on to the keyboard. Additionally, when the system needs to send commands to or read the status of the keyboard controller on the motherboard, it does so by reading or writing through I/O port 64h. These commands are also usually followed by data sent back and forth via port 60h.

The 8042 keyboard controller also is used by the system to control the A20 memory address line, which controls access to system memory over one megabyte. This aspect of the keyboard controller is discussed in Chapter 7, "Memory."

Typematic Functions. If a key on the keyboard is held down, it becomes *typematic*, which means that the keyboard repeatedly sends the keypress code to the motherboard. In the AT-style keyboards, the typematic rate is adjustable by sending the keyboard processor the appropriate commands. This is not possible for the earlier PC/XT keyboard types because the keyboard interface is not bidirectional.

AT-style keyboards have a programmable typematic repeat rate and delay parameter. The DOS MODE command in versions 4.0 and later enables you to set the keyboard typematic (repeat) rate as well as the delay before typematic action begins. The default value for the RATE parameter (r) is 20 for IBM AT-compatible systems, and 21 for IBM PS/2 systems. The default value for the DELAY parameter is 2. To use the MODE command to set the keyboard typematic rate and delay, use the command as follows:

MODE CON[:] [RATE=r DELAY=d]

The acceptable values for the rate "r" and the resultant typematic rate in characters per second (cps) are shown in table 9.1.

Table 9.1	DOS 4.0+ MODE Command Keyboard Typematic Rate Parameters
RATE No.	**Rate ± 20%**
32	30.0cps
31	26.7cps
30	24.0cps
29	21.8cps
28	20.0cps
27	18.5cps
26	17.1cps
25	16.0cps
24	15.0cps
23	13.3cps
22	12.0cps
21	10.9cps
20	10.0cps
19	9.2cps
18	8.6cps
17	8.0cps
16	7.5cps
15	6.7cps
14	6.0cps
13	5.5cps
12	5.0cps
11	4.6cps
10	4.3cps
9	4.0cps
8	3.7cps
7	3.3cps
6	3.0cps
5	2.7cps

RATE No.	Rate ± 20%
4	2.5cps
3	2.3cps
2	2.1cps
1	2.0cps

Table 9.2 shows the values for DELAY and the resultant delay time in seconds.

Table 9.2 DOS MODE Command Keyboard Typematic Delay Parameters	
DELAY No.	**Delay Time**
1	.25sec
2	.50sec
3	.75sec
4	1.00sec

For example, I always place the following command in my AUTOEXEC.BAT file:

```
MODE CON: RATE=32 DELAY=1
```

This command sets the typematic rate to the maximum speed possible, or 30 characters per second. It also trims the delay to the minimum of 1/4 second before repeating be-gins. This command "turbocharges" the keyboard and makes operations requiring re-peated keystrokes work much faster, such as moving within a file using arrow keys. The quick typematic action and short delay can sometimes be disconcerting to ham-fisted keyboard operators. In that case, slow typists may want to leave their keyboard speed at the default until they become more proficient.

If you have an older system or keyboard, you may receive the following message:

```
Function not supported on this computer
```

This indicates that your system, keyboard, or both do not support the bidirectional interface or commands required to change the typematic rate and delay. Upgrading the BIOS, keyboard, or both may enable this function, but it is probably not cost-effective to do this on a very old system.

Keyboard Key Numbers and Scan Codes. When you press a key on the keyboard, the processor built into the keyboard (8048- or 6805-type) reads the keyswitch location in the keyboard matrix. The processor then sends a serial packet of data to the motherboard that contains the scan code for the key that was pressed. In AT-type motherboards that also use an 8042-type keyboard controller, the 8042 chip then translates the actual key-board scan code into one of up to three different sets of system scan codes, which are then sent to the main processor. It can be useful in some cases to know what these scan codes are, especially when troubleshooting keyboard problems, or when otherwise read-ing the keyboard or system scan codes directly in software.

When a keyswitch on the keyboard sticks or otherwise fails, the scan code of the failed keyswitch is usually reported by diagnostics software, including the POST (Power On Self-Test) as well as conventional disk-based diagnostics. This means that you have to identify the particular key by its scan code. Tables 9.3 through 9.7 list all the scan codes for every key on the 83-, 84-, and 101-key keyboards. By looking up the reported scan code on these charts, you can determine which keyswitch is defective or needs to be cleaned.

Note that the 101-key enhanced keyboards are capable of three different scan code sets, with Set 1 as the default. Some systems use one of the other scan code sets during the POST, including some of the PS/2 machines. For example, my P75 uses Scan Code Set 2 during the POST, but then switches to Set 1 during normal operation. This is rare, but useful to know if you are having difficulty interpreting the Scan Code number.

IBM also assigns each key a unique key number to distinguish it from the others. This is important when trying to identify keys on foreign keyboards, which may use different symbols or characters from the United States models. In the case of the enhanced keyboard, most foreign models are missing one of the keys (key #29) found on the United States version and have two other additional keys (keys #42 and #45) as well. This accounts for the 102-key total rather than the 101 keys found on the United States version.

Figure 9.6 shows the keyboard numbering and character locations for the original 83-key PC keyboard, and table 9.3 shows the scan codes for each key relative to the key number and character.

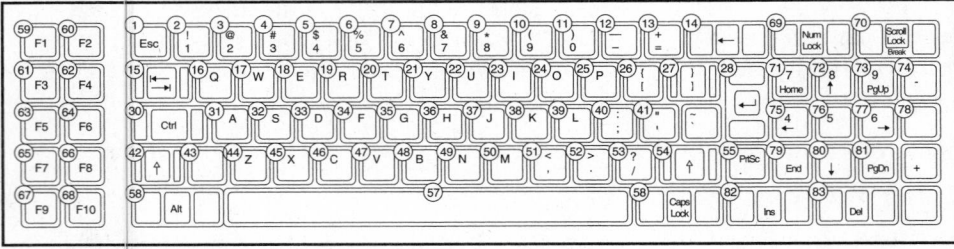

Fig. 9.6
83-key PC keyboard key number and character locations.

Table 9.3 83-Key (PC/XT) Keyboard Key Numbers and Scan Codes		
Key Number	**Scan Code**	**Key**
1	01	Escape
2	02	1
3	03	2
4	04	3
5	05	4
6	06	5

Key Number	Scan Code	Key
7	07	6
8	08	7
9	09	8
10	0A	9
11	0B	0
12	0C	-
13	0D	=
14	0E	Backspace
15	0F	Tab
16	10	q
17	11	w
18	12	e
19	13	r
20	14	t
21	15	y
22	16	u
23	17	i
24	18	o
25	19	p
26	1A	[
27	1B	]
28	1C	Enter
29	1D	Ctrl
30	1E	a
31	1F	s
32	20	d
33	21	f
34	22	g
35	23	h
36	24	j
37	25	k
38	26	l
39	27	;
40	28	'
41	29	`
42	2A	Left Shift
43	2B	\
44	2C	z
45	2D	x

(continues)

Input/Output Hardware

III

Table 9.3	Continued	
Key Number	**Scan Code**	**Key**
46	2E	c
47	2F	v
48	30	b
49	31	n
50	32	m
51	33	,
52	34	.
53	35	/
54	36	Right Shift
55	37	*
56	38	Alt
57	39	Space bar
58	3A	Caps Lock
59	3B	F1
60	3C	F2
61	3D	F3
62	3E	F4
63	3F	F5
64	40	F6
65	41	F7
66	42	F8
67	43	F9
68	44	F10
69	45	Num Lock
70	46	Scroll Lock
71	47	Keypad 7 (Home)
72	48	Keypad 8 (Up arrow)
73	49	Keypad 9 (PgUp)
74	4A	Keypad -
75	4B	Keypad 4 (Left arrow)
76	4C	Keypad 5
77	4D	Keypad 6 (Right arrow)
78	4E	Keypad +
79	4F	Keypad 1 (End)
80	50	Keypad 2 (Down arrow)
81	51	Keypad 3 (PgDn)
82	52	Keypad 0 (Ins)
83	53	Keypad . (Del)

Figure 9.7 shows the keyboard numbering and character locations for the original 84-key AT keyboard. Table 9.4 shows the scan codes for each key relative to the key number and character.

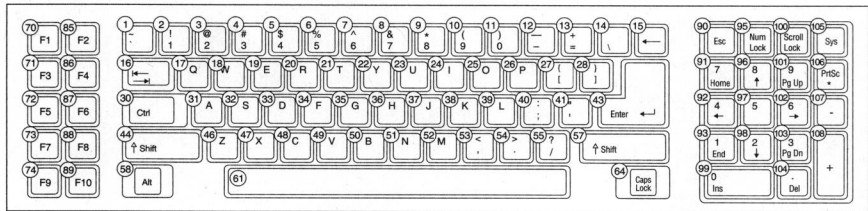

Fig. 9.7
84-key AT keyboard key number and character locations.

Table 9.4   84-Key AT Keyboard Key Numbers and Scan Codes

Key Number	Scan Code	Key
1	29	`
2	02	1
3	03	2
4	04	3
5	05	4
6	06	5
7	07	6
8	08	7
9	09	8
10	0A	9
11	0B	0
12	0C	-
13	0D	=
14	2B	\
15	0E	Backspace
16	0F	Tab
17	10	q
18	11	w
19	12	e
20	13	r
21	14	t
22	15	y
23	16	u
24	17	i

(continues)

Table 9.4	Continued	
Key Number	**Scan Code**	**Key**
25	18	o
26	19	p
27	1A	[
28	1B	]
30	1D	Ctrl
31	1E	a
32	1F	s
33	20	d
34	21	f
35	22	g
36	23	h
37	24	j
38	25	k
39	26	l
40	27	;
41	28	'
43	1C	Enter
44	2A	Left Shift
46	2C	z
47	2D	x
48	2E	c
49	2F	v
50	30	b
51	31	n
52	32	m
53	33	,
54	34	.
55	35	/
57	36	Right Shift
58	38	Alt
61	39	Space bar
64	3A	Caps Lock
65	3C	F2
66	3E	F4
67	40	F6
68	42	F8
69	44	F10
70	3B	F1
71	3D	F3

Key Number	Scan Code	Key
72	3F	F5
73	41	F7
74	43	F9
90	01	Escape
91	47	Keypad 7 (Home)
92	4B	Keypad 4 (Left arrow)
93	4F	Keypad 1 (End)
95	45	Num Lock
96	48	Keypad 8 (Up arrow)
97	4C	Keypad 5
98	50	Keypad 2 (Down arrow)
99	52	Keypad 0 (Ins)
100	46	Scroll Lock
101	49	Keypad 9 (PgUp)
102	4D	Keypad 6 (Right arrow)
103	51	Keypad 3 (PgDn)
104	53	Keypad . (Del)
105	54	SysRq
106	37	Keypad *
107	4A	Keypad -
108	4E	Keypad +

Figure 9.8 shows the keyboard numbering and character locations for the 101-key enhanced keyboard. Tables 9.5 through 9.7 show each of the three scan code sets showing the scan code for each key relative to the key number and character. Note that Scan Code Set 1 is the default; the other two are rarely used. Figure 9.9 shows the layout of a typical foreign language 102-key version of the enhanced keyboard, in this case a U.K. English version.

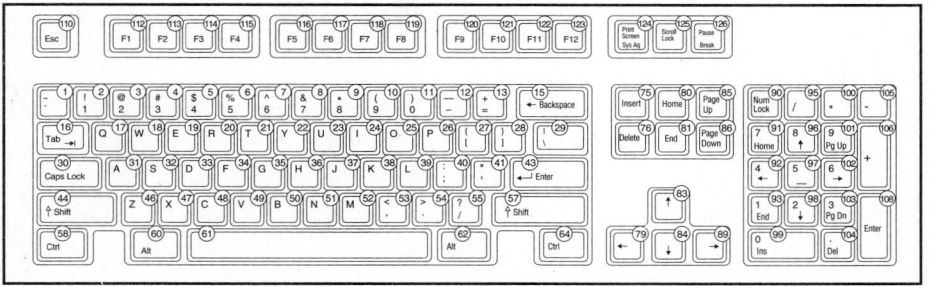

Fig. 9.8
101-key enhanced keyboard key number and character locations (U.S. version).

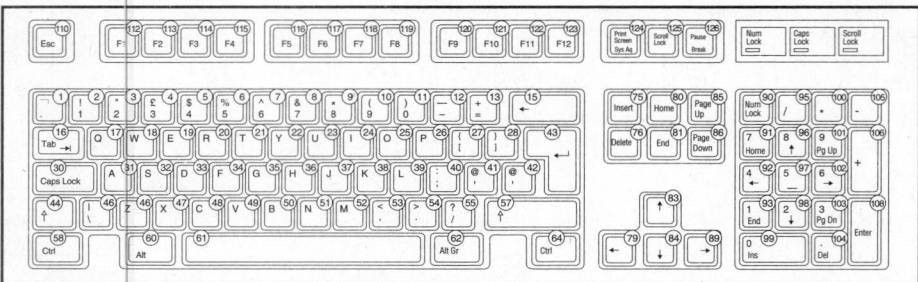

Fig. 9.9
102-key enhanced keyboard key number and character locations (U.K. English version).

Table 9.5	101/102-Key (Enhanced) Keyboard Key Numbers and Scan Codes (Set 1)	
Key Number	**Scan Code**	**Key**
1	29	`
2	02	1
3	03	2
4	04	3
5	05	4
6	06	5
7	07	6
8	08	7
9	09	8
10	0A	9
11	0B	0
12	0C	-
13	0D	=
15	0E	Backspace
16	0F	Tab
17	10	q
18	11	w
19	12	e
20	13	r
21	14	t
22	15	y
23	16	u
24	17	i
25	18	o
26	19	p
27	1A	[

Key Number	Scan Code	Key
28	1B	]
29	2B	\ (101-key *only*)
30	3A	Caps Lock
31	1E	a
32	1F	s
33	20	d
34	21	f
35	22	g
36	23	h
37	24	j
38	25	k
39	26	l
40	27	;
41	28	'
42	2B	# (102-key *only*)
43	1C	Enter
44	2A	Left Shift
45	56	\ (102-key *only*)
46	2C	z
47	2D	x
48	2E	c
49	2F	v
50	30	b
51	31	n
52	32	m
53	33	,
54	34	.
55	35	/
57	36	Right Shift
58	1D	Left Ctrl
60	38	Left Alt
61	39	Space bar
62	E0,38	Right Alt
64	E0,1D	Right Ctrl
75	E0,52	Insert
76	E0,53	Delete
79	E0,4B	Left arrow
80	E0,47	Home
81	E0,4F	End

(continues)

Table 9.5   Continued

Key Number	Scan Code	Key
83	E0,48	Up arrow
84	E0,50	Down arrow
85	E0,49	Page Up
86	E0,51	Page Down
89	E0,4D	Right arrow
90	45	Num Lock
91	47	Keypad 7 (Home)
92	4B	Keypad 4 (Left arrow)
93	4F	Keypad 1 (End)
95	E0,35	Keypad /
96	48	Keypad 8 (Up arrow)
97	4C	Keypad 5
98	50	Keypad 2 (Down arrow)
99	52	Keypad 0 (Ins)
100	37	Keypad *
101	49	Keypad 9 (PgUp)
102	4D	Keypad 6 (Left arrow)
103	51	Keypad 3 (PgDn)
104	53	Keypad . (Del)
105	4A	Keypad -
106	4E	Keypad +
108	E0,1C	Keypad Enter
110	01	Escape
112	3B	F1
113	3C	F2
114	3D	F3
115	3E	F4
116	3F	F5
117	40	F6
118	41	F7
119	42	F8
120	43	F9
121	44	F10
122	57	F11
123	58	F12
124	E0,2A,E0,37	Print Screen
125	46	Scroll Lock
126	E1,1D,45,E1,9D,C5	Pause

Table 9.6 101/102-Key (Enhanced) Keyboard Key Numbers and Scan Codes (Set 2)

Key Number	Scan Code	Key
1	0E	`
2	16	1
3	1E	2
4	26	3
5	25	4
6	2E	5
7	36	6
8	3D	7
9	3E	8
10	46	9
11	45	0
12	4E	-
13	55	=
15	66	Backspace
16	0D	Tab
17	15	q
18	1D	w
19	24	e
20	2D	r
21	2C	t
22	35	y
23	3C	u
24	43	i
25	44	o
26	4D	p
27	54	[
28	5B	]
29	5D	\ (101-key *only*)
30	58	Caps Lock
31	1C	a
32	1B	s
33	23	d
34	2B	f
35	34	g
36	33	h
37	3B	j
38	42	k

(continues)

Input/Output Hardware

III

Table 9.6	Continued	
Key Number	**Scan Code**	**Key**
39	4B	l
40	4C	;
41	52	'
42	5D	# (102-key *only*)
43	5A	Enter
44	12	Left Shift
45	61	\ (102-key *only*)
46	1A	z
47	22	x
48	21	c
49	2A	v
50	32	b
51	31	n
52	3A	m
53	41	,
54	49	.
55	4A	/
57	59	Right Shift
58	14	Left Ctrl
60	11	Left Alt
61	29	Space bar
62	E0,11	Right Alt
64	E0,14	Right Ctrl
75	E0,70	Insert
76	E0,71	Delete
79	E0,6B	Left arrow
80	E0,6C	Home
81	E0,69	End
83	E0,75	Up arrow
84	E0,72	Down arrow
85	E0,7D	Page Up
86	E0,7A	Page Down
89	E0,74	Right arrow
90	77	Num Lock
91	6C	Keypad 7 (Home)
92	6B	Keypad 4 (Left arrow)
93	69	Keypad 1 (End)
95	E0,4A	Keypad /

Key Number	Scan Code	Key
96	75	Keypad 8 (Up arrow)
97	73	Keypad 5
98	72	Keypad 2 (Down arrow)
99	70	Keypad 0 (Ins)
100	7C	Keypad *
101	7D	Keypad 9 (PgUp)
102	74	Keypad 6 (Left arrow)
103	7A	Keypad 3 (PgDn)
104	71	Keypad . (Del)
105	7B	Keypad -
106	E0,5A	Keypad +
108	E0,5A	Keypad Enter
110	76	Escape
112	05	F1
113	06	F2
114	04	F3
115	0C	F4
116	03	F5
117	0B	F6
118	83	F7
119	0A	F8
120	01	F9
121	09	F10
122	78	F11
123	07	F12
124	E0,12,E0,7C	Print Screen
125	7E	Scroll Lock
126	E1,14,77,E1,F0,14,F0,77	Pause

Table 9.7 101/102-Key (Enhanced) Keyboard Key Numbers and Scan Codes (Set 3)

Key Number	Scan Code	Key
1	0E	`
2	16	1
3	1E	2
4	26	3
5	25	4

(continues)

Input/Output Hardware

Table 9.7	Continued	
Key Number	**Scan Code**	**Key**
6	2E	5
7	36	6
8	3D	7
9	3E	8
10	46	9
11	45	0
12	4E	-
13	55	=
15	66	Backspace
16	0D	Tab
17	15	q
18	1D	w
19	24	e
20	2D	r
21	2C	t
22	35	y
23	3C	u
24	43	i
25	44	o
26	4D	p
27	54	[
28	5B	]
29	5C	\ (101-key *only*)
30	14	Caps Lock
31	1C	a
32	1B	s
33	23	d
34	2B	f
35	34	g
36	33	h
37	3B	j
38	42	k
39	4B	l
40	4C	;
41	52	'
42	53	# (102-key *only*)
43	5A	Enter
44	12	Left Shift

Key Number	Scan Code	Key
45	13	\ (102-key *only*)
46	1A	z
47	22	x
48	21	c
49	2A	v
50	32	b
51	31	n
52	3A	m
53	41	,
54	49	.
55	4A	/
57	59	Right Shift
58	11	Left Ctrl
60	19	Left Alt
61	29	Space bar
62	39	Right Alt
64	58	Right Ctrl
75	67	Insert
76	64	Delete
79	61	Left arrow
80	6E	Home
81	65	End
83	63	Up arrow
84	60	Down arrow
85	6F	Page Up
86	6D	Page Down
89	6A	Right arrow
90	76	Num Lock
91	6C	Keypad 7 (Home)
92	6B	Keypad 4 (Left arrow)
93	69	Keypad 1 (End)
95	77	Keypad /
96	75	Keypad 8 (Up arrow)
97	73	Keypad 5
98	72	Keypad 2 (Down arrow)
99	70	Keypad 0 (Ins)
100	7E	Keypad *
101	7D	Keypad 9 (PgUp)
102	74	Keypad 6 (Left arrow)

(continues)

III

Input/Output Hardware

Table 9.7	Continued	
Key Number	**Scan Code**	**Key**
103	7A	Keypad 3 (PgDn)
104	71	Keypad . (Del)
105	84	Keypad -
106	7C	Keypad +
108	79	Keypad Enter
110	08	Escape
112	07	F1
113	0F	F2
114	17	F3
115	1F	F4
116	27	F5
117	2F	F6
118	37	F7
119	3F	F8
120	47	F9
121	4F	F10
122	56	F11
123	5E	F12
124	57	Print Screen
125	5F	Scroll Lock
126	62	Pause

These key number figures and scan code tables can be very useful when troubleshooting stuck or failed keys on a keyboard. Diagnostics can report the defective keyswitch by the scan code, which varies from keyboard to keyboard as to which character it represents as well as the location.

Keyboard/Mouse Interface Connectors. Keyboards have a cable available with one of two primary types of connectors at the system end. Most aftermarket keyboards have a cable connected inside the keyboard case on the keyboard end and require that you open up the keyboard case to disconnect or test. Actual IBM enhanced keyboards use a unique cable assembly that plugs into both the keyboard and the system unit. This makes cable interchange or replacement an easy plug-in affair. A special connector called an SDL (Shielded Data Link) is used on the keyboard end, and the appropriate DIN (Deutsche Industrie Norm) connector at the PC end. Any IBM keyboard or cable can be ordered separately as a spare part. The newer enhanced keyboards come with an externally detachable keyboard cable that plugs into the keyboard port with a special connector, much like a telephone connector. The other end of the cable is one of the following two types:

■ Earlier systems use a 5-pin DIN connector.

■ PS/2 and most Low Profile compatible systems use a 6-pin mini-DIN connector.

Figure 9.10 and table 9.8 show the physical layout and pinouts of all the respective keyboard connector plugs and sockets.

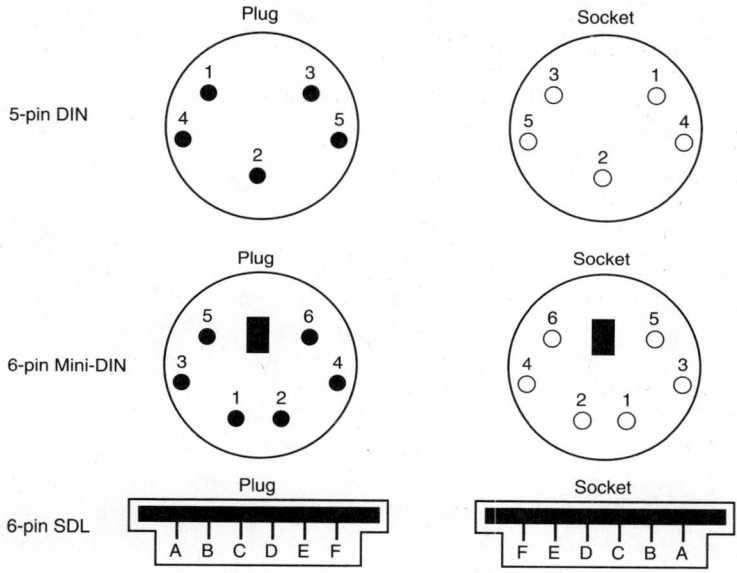

Fig. 9.10
Keyboard and mouse connectors.

Table 9.8 Keyboard Connector Signals			
Signal Name	**5-Pin DIN**	**6-Pin Mini-DIN**	**6-Pin SDL**
Keyboard Data	2	1	B
Ground	4	3	C
+5v	5	4	E
Keyboard Clock	1	5	D
Not Connected	—	2	A
Not Connected	—	6	F
Not Connected	3	—	—

DIN = German Industrial Norm (Deutsche Industrie Norm), a committee that sets German dimensional standards
SDL = Shielded Data Link, a type of shielded connector created by AMP and used by IBM and others for keyboard cables

Motherboard mouse connectors use the 6-pin mini-DIN connector and have the same pinout and signal descriptions as the keyboard connector; however, the data packets are incompatible. This means that you easily can plug a motherboard mouse (PS/2 style) into a mini-DIN keyboard connector, or plug the mini-DIN type keyboard connector into a motherboard mouse port; however, neither would work properly in this situation.

Keyboard Troubleshooting and Repair

Keyboard errors are usually caused by two simple problems. Other more difficult intermittent problems can arise, but these are also much more rare. The most common problems are as follows:

- Defective cables

- Stuck keys

Defective cables are easy to spot if the failure is not intermittent. If the keyboard stops working altogether or every keystroke results in an error or incorrect character, then likely the cable is the culprit. Troubleshooting is simple, especially if you have a spare cable on hand. Simply replace the suspected cable with one from a known working keyboard, and verify to see if the problem still exists. If it does, the problem must be elsewhere. You also can test the cable for continuity with it removed from the keyboard by using a DMM (Digital Multi-Meter). DMMs that have a built-in audible continuity tester make this procedure much easier to perform. Wiggle the ends of the cable as you check each wire to make sure that there are no intermittent connections. If you discover a problem with the continuity in one of the wires, replace the cable or the entire keyboard if that is cheaper. Because replacement keyboards are so inexpensive, sometimes it can be cheaper to replace the entire unit than to get a new cable!

Often you first discover a problem with a keyboard because the system has an error during the POST. Most systems use error codes in a 3xx numeric format to distinguish the keyboard. If you have any such errors during the POST, write them down. Some BIOSs do not use cryptic numeric error codes and simply state something like the following:

```
Keyboard stuck key failure
```

This message normally would be displayed by a system with a Phoenix BIOS if a key were stuck. Unfortunately, the message does not identify which key it is!

If your 3xx (keyboard) error is preceded by a two-digit hexadecimal number, this number is the scan code of a failing or stuck keyswitch. Look up the scan code in the tables provided in this section to determine which keyswitch is the culprit. These charts tell you to which key the scan code refers. By removing the keycap of the offending key and cleaning the switch, you often can solve the problem.

For a simple test of the motherboard keyboard connector, you can check voltages on some of the pins. Use figure 9.10 in the preceding section as a guide, and measure the voltages on various pins of the keyboard connector. To prevent possible damage to the system or keyboard, first turn off the power before disconnecting the keyboard.

Then unplug the keyboard and turn the power back on. Make measurements between the ground pin and the other pins according to table 9.9. If the voltages read are within these specifications, the motherboard keyboard circuitry is probably OK.

Table 9.9 Keyboard Connector Specifications			
DIN Connector Pin	Mini-DIN Connector Pin	Signal	Voltage
1	5	Keyboard Clock	+2.0v to +5.5v
2	1	Keyboard Data	+4.8v to +5.5v
3	—	Reserved	—
4	3	Ground	—
5	4	+5v Power	+2.0v to +5.5v

If your measurements don't match these voltages, the motherboard might be defective. Otherwise, the keyboard cable or keyboard might be defective. If you suspect the cable is the problem, the easiest thing to do is replace the keyboard cable with a known good one. If the system still does not work normally, then you may have to replace either the entire keyboard or the motherboard.

In some systems, such as many IBM PS/2s, the motherboard keyboard and mouse connectors are protected by a fuse that can be replaced. Look for any type of fuse on the motherboard in the vicinity of the keyboard or mouse connectors. Other systems may have a socketed keyboard controller chip (8042-type). In that case, it may be possible to repair the motherboard keyboard circuit by simply replacing this chip. Because these chips have ROM code in them, it is best to get the replacement from the motherboard or BIOS manufacturer.

A list of standard POST and diagnostics keyboard error codes is displayed as follows:

Error Code	Description
3xx	Keyboard errors
301	Keyboard reset or stuck-key failure (XX 301, XX = scan code in hex)
302	System unit keylock switch is locked
302	User indicated keyboard test error
303	Keyboard or system-board error; keyboard controller failure
304	Keyboard or system-board error; keyboard clock high
305	Keyboard +5v error; PS/2 keyboard fuse (on motherboard) blown
341	Keyboard error
342	Keyboard cable error
343	Keyboard LED card or cable failure
365	Keyboard LED card or cable failure
366	Keyboard interface cable failure
367	Keyboard LED card or cable failure

III

Input/Output Hardware

Disassembly Procedures and Cautions. Repairing and cleaning a keyboard often requires you to take it apart. When performing this task, you must know when to stop! Some keyboards literally come apart into hundreds of little pieces that are almost impossible to reassemble if you go too far. An IBM keyboard generally has these four major parts:

■ Cable

■ Case

■ Keypad assembly

■ Keycaps

You easily can break down a keyboard to these major components and replace any of them, but don't disassemble the keypad assembly or you'll be showered with hundreds of tiny springs, clips, and keycaps. Finding all these parts (several hundred of them) and piecing the unit back together is not a fun way to spend time. You also may not be able to reassemble the keyboard properly. Figure 9.13 shows a typical keyboard with the case opened.

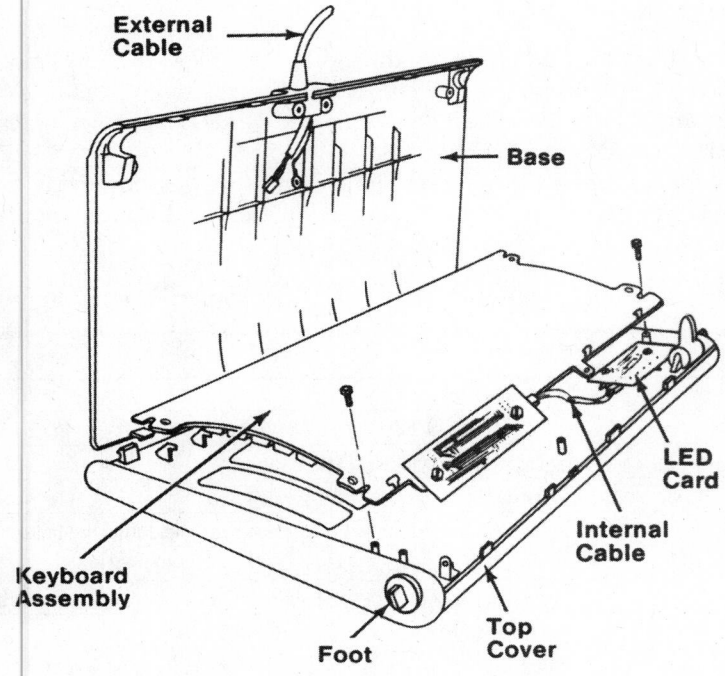

Fig. 9.11
Typical keyboard components.

Another problem is that you cannot purchase the smaller parts separately, such as contact clips and springs. The only way to obtain these parts is from another keyboard. If you ever have a keyboard that's beyond repair, keep it around for these parts. They might come in handy some day.

Most repair operations are limited to changing the cable or cleaning some component of the keyboard, from the cable contact ends to the key contact points. The keyboard cable takes quite a bit of abuse, and therefore can fail easily. The ends are stretched, tugged, pulled, and generally handled roughly. The cable uses strain reliefs, but you still might have problems with the connectors making proper contact at each end or even with wires that have broken inside the cable. You might want to carry a spare cable for every type of keyboard you have.

All keyboard cables plug into the keyboard and PC with connectors, and you can change the cables easily without having to splice wires or solder connections. With the earlier 83-key PC and 84-key AT keyboards, you must open the case to access the connector to which the cable attaches. On the newer 101-key enhanced keyboards from IBM and Lexmark, the cable plugs into the keyboard from the outside of the case, using a modular jack and plug similar to a telephone jack. This design also makes the IBM/Lexmark keyboards universally usable on nearly any system (except the original PC) by easily switching the cable.

The only difference, for example, between the enhanced keyboards for an IBM AT and an IBM PS/2 system is the attached cable. PS/2 systems use a tan cable with a smaller plug on the computer side. The AT cable is black and has the larger DIN-type plug on the computer side. You can interchange the enhanced keyboards as long as you use the correct cable for the system.

The only feasible ways to repair a keyboard are to replace the cable and clean the individual keyswitch assemblies, the entire keypad, or the cable contact ends. The individual spring and keyswitch assemblies are not available as a separate part, and disassembling the unit to that level is not advisable because of the difficulty in reassembling it. Other than cleaning a keyboard, the only thing you can do is replace the entire keypad assembly (virtually the entire keyboard) or the cable.

Cleaning a Keyboard. One of the best ways to maintain a keyboard in top condition is periodic cleaning. As preventive maintenance, you should vacuum the keyboard weekly or at least monthly. You also can use canned compressed air available at electronics supply houses to blow the dust and dirt out instead of using a vacuum. Before you dust a keyboard with the compressed air, turn the keyboard upside down so that the particles of dirt and dust collected inside can fall out.

On all keyboards, each keycap is removable, which can be handy if a key sticks or acts erratically. For example, a common problem is a key that doesn't work every time you press it. This problem usually results from dirt collecting under the key. An excellent tool for removing keycaps on almost any keyboard is the U-shaped chip-puller tool. You simply slip the hooked ends of the tool under the keycap, squeeze the ends together to grip the underside of the keycap, and lift up. IBM sells a tool specifically for removing

Input/Output Hardware

keycaps from its keyboards, but the chip puller works even better. After removing the cap, spray some compressed air into the space under the cap to dislodge the dirt. Then replace the cap and check the action of the key.

When you remove the keycaps, be careful not to remove the space bar on the original 83-key PC and 84-key AT-type keyboards. This bar is very difficult to reinstall. The newer 101-key units use a different wire support that can be removed and replaced much more easily.

Spills also can be a problem. If you tip a soft drink or cup of coffee into a keyboard, you don't necessarily have a disaster. You should immediately (or as soon as possible) flush out the keyboard with distilled water. Partially disassemble the keyboard and use the water to wash the components. (See the following section for disassembly instructions.) If the spilled liquid has dried, let the keyboard soak in some of the water for a while. Then, when you're sure that the keyboard is clean, pour another gallon or so of distilled water over it and through the key switches to wash away any residual dirt. After the unit dries completely, it should be perfectly functional. You may be surprised to know that you can drench your keyboard with water, and it will not harm the components. Just make sure that you use distilled water, which is free from residue or mineral content. Also make sure that the keyboard is fully dry before you attempt to use it, or some of the components might short out: water is a conductor of electricity.

Replacement Keyboards. In most cases, it is cheaper or more cost-effective to simply replace a keyboard rather than repair it. This is especially true if the keyboard has an internal malfunction or if one of the keyswitches is defective. Replacement parts for keyboards are almost impossible to procure, and in most cases the installation of any repair part is difficult. In addition, many of the keyboards supplied with lower cost compatible machines leave much to be desired. They often have a mushy feel, with little or no tactile feedback. A poor keyboard can make using a system a very frustrating experience, especially if you are a touch typist. For all these reasons, it is often a good idea to consider replacing an existing keyboard with something better.

Perhaps the highest quality keyboards in the entire computer industry are those made by IBM, or more accurately Lexmark. Several years ago IBM spun off its keyboard and printer divisions as a separate company called Lexmark. Lexmark now manufactures all IBM brand keyboards and printers and sells them not only to IBM, but to compatible vendors or even end users as well. This means that if you are lucky, your compatible system comes with a Lexmark keyboard, but if not, you can purchase one separately on your own.

Table 9.10 shows the part numbers of all IBM-labeled keyboards and cables. These numbers can serve as a reference when you are seeking a replacement IBM keyboard from IBM directly or from third-party companies. Many third-party companies sell IBM label keyboards for much less than IBM, in both new and refurbished form. Remember that you also can purchase these exact same keyboards through Lexmark, although they do not come with an IBM label.

Table 9.10 IBM Keyboard and Cable Part Numbers

Description	Part Number
83-key U.S. PC Keyboard assembly with cable	8529297
Cable assembly for 83-key PC Keyboard	8529168
84-key U.S. AT Keyboard assembly with cable	8286165
Cable assembly for 84-key Keyboard	8286146
101-key U.S. Keyboard without LED panel	1390290
101-key U.S. Keyboard with LED panel	6447033
101-key U.S. Keyboard with LED panel (PS/2 logo)	1392090
6-foot cable for enhanced keyboard (DIN plug)	6447051
6-foot cable for enhanced keyboard (mini-DIN plug)	61X8898
6-foot cable for enhanced keyboard (shielded mini-DIN plug)	27F4984
10-foot cable for enhanced keyboard (mini-DIN plug)	72X8537

Note that the original 83/84-key IBM keyboards are sold with a cable that has the larger, 5-pin DIN connector already attached. IBM enhanced keyboards are always sold (at least by IBM) without a cable. You must order the proper cable as a separate item. Cables are available to connect the keyboards to either the older system units that use the larger DIN connector or to PS/2 systems (and many compatibles) that use the smaller mini-DIN connector.

Recently, IBM has started selling complete keyboard assemblies under a program called "IBM Options." This program is designed to sell these components in the retail channel to end users of both IBM and compatible systems from other vendors. Items under the IBM Options program are sold through normal retail channels such as CompUSA, Elek Tek, Computer Discount Warehouse (CDW), and so on. These items are also priced much cheaper than items purchased as spare parts; they include a full warranty and are sold as complete packages including cables. Table 9.11 lists some of the IBM Options keyboards and part numbers.

Table 9.11 IBM Options Keyboards (Sold Retail)

Description	Part Number
IBM enhanced keyboard (cable w/DIN plug)	92G7454
IBM enhanced keyboard (cable w/mini-DIN plug)	92G7453
IBM enhanced keyboard, built-in Trackball (cable w/DIN plug)	92G7456
IBM enhanced keyboard, built-in Trackball (cable w/mini-DIN plug)	92G7455
IBM enhanced keyboard, integrated Trackpoint II (cable w/mini-DIN plug)	92G7461

The IBM/Lexmark keyboards use capacitive keyswitches, which are the most durable and lowest maintenance. These switches have no electrical contacts and instead rely on

III

Input/Output Hardware

changing capacitance to signal a keystroke in the switch matrix. This type of design does not have wear points like a mechanical switch, and has no metal electrical contacts, which makes it virtually immune to the dirt and corrosion problems that plague other designs.

The extremely positive tactile feedback of the IBM/Lexmark design is also a benchmark of comparison for the rest of the industry. Although keyboard feel is somewhat a personal preference issue, I have never used a keyboard that feels better than the IBM/Lexmark designs. I now equip every system I use with a Lexmark keyboard, including the many clone or compatible systems I use. You can purchase these keyboards through Lexmark or a Lexmark distributor for very reasonable prices. You can find IBM-labeled models available from advertisers in the *Processor* or *Computer Hotline* magazines (see Appendix B) selling for as little as $80 or less.

IBM/Lexmark also sells other versions for very reasonable prices. Many different models are available, including some with a built-in trackball or even the revolutionary Trackpoint II pointing device. Trackpoint II refers to a small stick mounted between the G, H, and B keys. This device is an IBM/Lexmark exclusive and was first featured on the IBM Thinkpad laptop systems, although they now sell the keyboards for use on compatibles and also are licensing the technology to others such as Toshiba. Note that this keyboard only comes with the mini-DIN type connectors for both the keyboard and Trackpoint II portions, and only works with a Motherboard (PS/2 type) mouse port.

Other manufacturers of high-quality keyboards are available. A company called Lite-On manufactures keyboards very similar in feel to the IBM/Lexmark units. They have excellent tactile feedback with a positive click sound as well. They are my second choice to a Lexmark unit. Maxi-Switch also makes a high-quality aftermarket keyboard used by a number of compatible manufacturers including Gateway. These also have a good feel and are recommended. Maxi-Switch also can make its keyboards with your own company logo on them, which is ideal for small clone manufacturers looking for name brand recognition.

Reference Material

If you are interested in more details about keyboard design or interfacing, a company called Annabooks (see Appendix B) publishes a book/disk package called *PC Keyboard Design*. This document defines the protocol between the keyboard and computer for both XT and AT types and includes schematics and keyboard controller source code. The kit includes a license to use the source code and costs $249.

Other excellent sources of information are the various technical-reference manuals put out by IBM. Appendix A contains a list of the important IBM reference manuals in which you can find much valuable information. This information is especially valuable to compatible system manufacturers, because they often do not put out the same level of technical information as IBM, and compatible systems are in many ways similar or even identical to one or more IBM systems. After all, that is why they are called "IBM compatible!" Much of my personal knowledge and expertise comes from poring over the various IBM technical-reference manuals.

Mice

The mouse was invented in 1964 by Douglas Englebart, who was at the time working at the Stanford Research Institute (SRI)—a think tank sponsored by Stanford University. The mouse was officially called an "X-Y Position Indicator for a Display System." Xerox later applied the mouse to its revolutionary Alto computer system in 1973. Unfortunately, at the time these systems were experimental and used purely for research. In 1979, several people from Apple, including Steve Jobs, were invited to see the Alto and the software that ran the system. Steve Jobs was blown away by what he saw as the future of computing, which included the use of the mouse as a pointing device and the graphical user interface it operated. Apple promptly incorporated these features into what was to become the Lisa computer and lured away 15 to 20 Xerox scientists to work on the Apple system. Although Xerox released the Star 8010 computer using this technology in 1981, it was expensive, poorly marketed, and perhaps way ahead of its time. Apple then released the Lisa computer in 1983, and it also was not a runaway success largely because of its $10,000 list price; but by then Jobs already had Apple working on the low-cost successor to the Lisa, the Macintosh. The Apple Macintosh was introduced in 1984; although it was not an immediate hit, the Macintosh has been steadily growing in popularity since that time. Many credit the Macintosh with inventing the mouse and GUI, but, as you can see, this technology was actually borrowed from others including SRI and Xerox. Certainly the Macintosh, and now Microsoft Windows and OS/2, have gone on to popularize this interface and bring it to the legion of IBM-compatible systems.

Although the mouse did not catch on quickly in the IBM-compatible marketplace, today the GUIs for PC systems such as Windows and OS/2 virtually demand the use of a mouse. Because of this, it is common for a mouse to be sold with virtually every new system on the market.

Mice come in many shapes and sizes from many different manufacturers. The largest manufacturers of mice are Microsoft and Logitech. Even though mice may come in different varieties, their actual use and care differ very little. The mouse consists of several components as follows:

- A housing that you hold in your hand and move around on your desktop
- A roller ball that signals movement to the system
- Several (usually two) buttons for making selections
- A cable for connecting the mouse to the system
- An interface connector to attach the mouse to the system

The housing is made of plastic and consists of very few moving parts. On top of the housing, where your fingers normally reside, are buttons. There may be any number of buttons, but typically in the PC world there are only two. If additional buttons are on your mouse, specialized software is required for them to operate. On the bottom of the housing is a small rubber ball that rotates as you move the mouse across the tabletop.

III

Input/Output Hardware

The movements of this rubber ball are translated into electrical signals transmitted to the computer across the cable. Some mice use a special optical sensor that detects movement over a grid. These optical mice have fallen into disfavor because they work only if you use a special grid pad underneath them.

The cable can be any length, but is typically between four and six feet long. (If you have a choice on the length of cable to purchase, go for a longer one. This allows easier placement of the mouse in relation to your computer.)

The connector used with your mouse depends on the type of interface you are using. Three basic interfaces are used, with a fourth combination device possible as well.

After the mouse is connected to your computer, it communicates with your system through the use of a device driver, which can be either separately loaded or built into the system software. For example, no separate drivers are needed to use a mouse with Windows or OS/2, but to use the mouse with most DOS-based programs requires a separate driver to be loaded. Regardless of whether it is built-in, the driver translates the electrical signals sent from the mouse into positional information and information that indicates the status of the buttons.

Internally, a mouse is very simple as well. The ball usually rests against two rollers, one for translating the X-axis movement and the other for the Y-axis. These rollers are usually connected to small discs with shutters that alternately block and allow the passage of light. Small optical sensors detect movement of the wheels by watching an internal infrared light blink on and off as the shutter wheel rotates and "chops" the light. These blinks are then translated into movement along the various axes. This type of setup is called an *Opto-mechanical mechanism* and is by far the most popular in use today (see fig. 9.12).

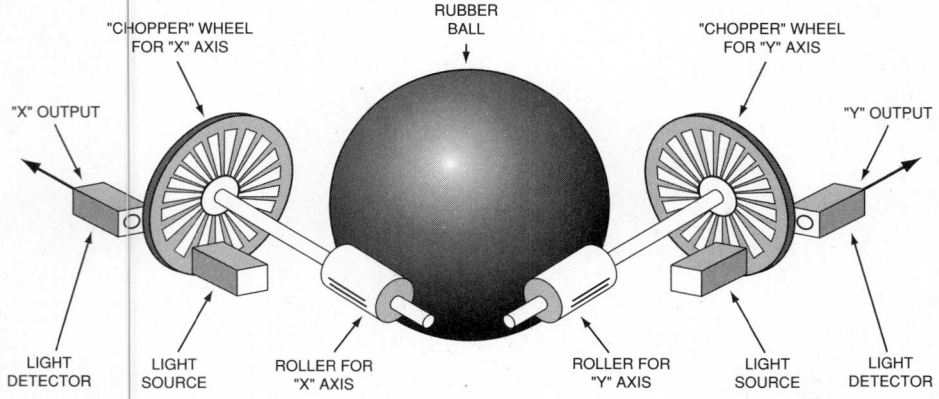

Fig. 9.12
Typical Opto-mechanical mouse mechanism.

The following sections explain the different types of mouse interfaces and how you can care for the mice.

Mouse Interface Types

Mice can be connected to your computer through the following three devices:

- Serial interface
- Dedicated motherboard mouse port
- Bus-card interface

Serial. A popular method of connecting a mouse to most older IBM-compatible computers is through a serial interface. As with other serial devices, the connector on the end on the mouse cable is either a 9-pin or 25-pin male connector. Only a couple of pins in the DB-9 or DB-25 connectors are used for communications between the mouse and the device driver, but the mouse connector typically has all 9 or 25 pins present.

Because most PCs come with two serial ports, a serial mouse can be plugged into either COM1: or COM2:. The device driver, when initializing, searches the ports to determine which one the mouse is connected to.

Because a serial mouse does not connect to the system directly, it does not use system resources by itself. Instead, the resources used are those used by the serial port to which it is connected. For example, if you have a mouse connected to COM2:, then it most likely uses IRQ3 and I/O Port Addresses 2F8h–2FFh.

Motherboard Mouse Port (PS/2). Most newer computers now come with a dedicated mouse port built into the motherboard. This was started by IBM with the PS/2 systems in 1987, so this interface often is referred to as a PS/2 mouse interface. Using this term should not imply that such a mouse can work only with a PS/2, but instead means that the mouse can connect to any system that has a dedicated mouse port on the motherboard.

A motherboard mouse connector usually is exactly the same as the mini-DIN connector used for newer keyboards. In fact, the motherboard mouse port is connected to the 8042-type keyboard controller found on the motherboard. All the PS/2 computers include mini-DIN keyboard and mouse port connectors on the back. Most compatible Slimline computers also have these same connectors for space reasons. Other motherboards have a pin-header type connector for the mouse port because most standard cases do not have a provision for the mini-DIN mouse connector. In that case, an adapter cable is usually supplied with the system that adapts the pin-header connector on the motherboard to the standard mini-DIN type connector used for the Motherboard Mouse.

Connecting a mouse to the built-in mouse port is the best method of connection because you don't lose any interface slots or any serial ports, and the performance is not limited by the serial port circuitry. The standard resource usage for a motherboard (or PS/2)

III

Input/Output Hardware

mouse port is IRQ 12 and I/O Port Addresses 60h and 64h. Because the motherboard mouse port uses the 8042-type keyboard controller chip, the port addresses are those of this chip. IRQ 12 is a 16-bit interrupt that is usually free on most systems, and must remain free on any ISA bus systems that have a motherboard mouse port because interrupt sharing is not allowed with the ISA bus.

Serial and Motherboard Mouse Port (PS/2). A hybrid type of mouse can plug into both a serial port and a motherboard mouse port connection. This combo serial-PS/2 mouse is the most popular type because it is more flexible than the other single design types. Circuitry in this mouse automatically detects which type of port it is connected to and configures the mouse automatically to work. These mice usually come with a mini-DIN connector on the end of their cable and also include an adapter between the mini-DIN to 9- or 25-pin serial port connector.

Sometimes people use adapters to try to connect a serial mouse to a motherboard mouse port, or a motherboard mouse to a serial port. This does not work and is not the fault of the adapter. If the mouse does not explicitly state that it is both a serial and PS/2 type mouse, then it does not work on either interface, but instead works only on the single interface for which it was designed. Most of the time, you find the designation for what type of mouse you have printed on the bottom of the mouse.

Bus. A bus mouse is typically used in systems that do not have a motherboard mouse port or any available serial ports. The name *bus mouse* is derived from the fact that the mouse requires a special bus interface board that occupies a slot in your computer and communicates with the device driver across the main motherboard bus. Although the use of a bus mouse is transparent to the user (there is no operational difference between a bus mouse and other types of mice), many people view a bus mouse as less desirable than other types because it occupies a slot that may be needed for other peripherals.

Another drawback to the bus mouse is that it is electrically incompatible with the other types of mice, and because it is not very popular, a bus mouse can be hard to find in a pinch. Also, the bus adapters are typically available for ISA slots only, and because they are always 8-bit cards, you are limited in the choice of non-conflicting hardware interrupts. A bus mouse also can be dangerous because it uses a mini-DIN connector just like the (PS/2) motherboard-type mouse, although they are totally incompatible. I have even heard of people damaging motherboards by plugging a bus mouse into a motherboard mouse connector.

Bus mouse adapter cards usually have a selectable interrupt and I/O port address setting, but the IRQ selection is limited to 8-bit interrupts only. This usually means that you must choose IRQ 5 in most systems that already have two serial ports because all the other 8-bit interrupts will be used. If you also are using another 8-bit only card that needs an interrupt, such as some of the sound cards, then you will not be able to run both devices in the same system without conflicts. All in all, I do not recommend bus mice and think they should be avoided.

One thing to note is that Microsoft sometimes calls a bus mouse an *Inport* mouse, which is its proprietary name for a bus mouse connection.

Mouse Troubleshooting

If you are experiencing problems with your mouse, you need only look in two general places—hardware or software. Because mice are basically very simple devices, looking at the hardware takes very little time. Detecting and correcting software problems can take a bit longer, however.

Hardware Problems. Several type of hardware problems can crop up when you are using a mouse. The most common is a dirty mouse, which is solved by doing some "mouse cleaning." The other relates to interrupt conflicts and is more difficult to solve.

Cleaning Your Mouse. If you notice that the mouse pointer moves across the screen in a jerky fashion, it may be time to clean your mouse. This jerkiness is caused when dirt and dust get trapped around the mouse's ball and roller assembly, thereby restricting its free movement.

From a hardware perspective, the mouse is a very simple device, and cleaning it also is very simple. The first step is to turn the mouse housing over so that you can see the ball on the bottom. Notice that surrounding the ball is an access panel that you can open. There may even be some instructions that indicate how the panel is to be opened. (Some off-brand mice may require you to remove some screws to get at the roller ball.) Remove the panel and you can see more of the roller ball, as well as the socket in which it rests.

If you turn the mouse back over, the rubber roller ball should fall out into your hand. Take a look at the ball. It may be gray or black, but it should have no visible dirt or other contamination. If it does, wash it in soapy water or a mild solvent such as contact cleaner solution or alcohol and dry it off.

Now take a look at the socket in which the roller ball normally rests. You will see two or three small wheels or bars against which the ball normally rolls. If you see dust or dirt on or around these wheels or bars, you need to clean them. The best way is to use a compressed air duster can to blow out any dust or dirt. You also can use some electrical contact cleaner to clean the rollers. Remember, any remaining dirt or dust impedes the movement of the roller ball and means that the mouse won't work as it should.

Put the mouse back together by inserting the roller ball into the socket and then securely attaching the cover panel. The mouse should look just like it did before you removed the panel (except that it may be noticeably cleaner).

Interrupt Conflicts. Interrupts are internal signals used by your computer to indicate when something needs to happen. With a mouse, an interrupt is used whenever the mouse has information to send to the mouse driver. If a conflict occurs and the same interrupt used by the mouse is used by a different device, then the mouse will not work properly, or it may not work at all.

III

Input/Output Hardware

Interrupt conflicts do not normally occur if your system uses a mouse port, but they can occur with the other types of mouse interfaces. If you are using a serial interface, interrupt conflicts typically occur if you add a third and fourth serial port. This is because in ISA bus systems, odd-numbered serial ports (1 and 3) are often improperly configured to use the same interrupts, as are the even-numbered ports (2 and 4). Thus, if your mouse is connected to COM2: and an internal modem uses COM4:, then they both may use the same interrupt, and you cannot use them at the same time. You may be able to use the mouse and modem at the same time by moving the mouse (or the modem) to a different serial port. For instance, if your mouse uses COM1: and the modem still uses COM4:, then you can use them both at once because odd and even ports use different interrupts.

The best way around these interrupt conflicts is to simply make sure that no two devices use the same interrupt. Serial port adapters are available for adding COM3: and COM4: serial ports that do not share the interrupts used by COM1: and COM2:. These boards allow the new COM ports to use other available interrupts, such as IRQ 10, 11, 12, and 15. I never recommend configuring an ISA system with shared interrupts; it is a sure way to run into problems later.

If you are using a bus interface and you suspect an interrupt problem, you can use a program such as Microsoft's MSD (MicroSoft Diagnostics) to help you identify what interrupt the mouse is set to. You get MSD free with Windows 3 or higher as well as MS-DOS 6.0 or higher. If you use OS/2 and/ or IBM DOS, you can still get MSD for free by downloading it from the Microsoft BBS (see Appendix B). Beware that programs such as MSD that attempt to identify IRQ usage are not always 100 percent accurate and usually require that the device driver for the particular device be loaded to work at all. After the IRQ is identified, you may need to change the IRQ setting of the bus mouse adapter or one or more other devices in your system so that everything works together properly.

If your driver refuses to recognize the mouse at all, regardless of what type it is, then try using a different mouse that you know works. Replacing a defective mouse with a known good one may be the only way to identify if the problem is indeed caused by a bad mouse.

I have had problems in which a bad mouse caused the system to lock right as the driver loaded, or even when diagnostics such as MSD attempted to access the mouse. You can easily ferret out this type of problem by loading MSD with the /I option, which causes MSD to bypass its initial hardware detection. Then run each of the tests separately, including the mouse test, to see if the system locks. If the system locks during the mouse test, you have found a problem with either the mouse or the mouse port. Try replacing the mouse to see if that helps. If not, you may need to replace the serial port or bus mouse adapter. If a motherboard-based mouse port goes bad, you either can replace the entire motherboard (usually expensive!) or just disable the motherboard mouse port via jumpers or the system setup program and install a serial or bus mouse instead. This enables you to continue using the system without having to replace the motherboard.

Software Problems. Software problems can be a little trickier than hardware problems. Software problems generally manifest themselves as the mouse "just not working."

In such instances, you need to check the driver and your software applications before assuming that the mouse itself has gone bad.

Driver Software. To function properly, the mouse requires the installation of a device driver. I normally recommend using the drivers built into the Windows or OS/2 operating environments. This means that no additional external driver is necessary. The only reason for loading an external driver (via CONFIG.SYS) is if you want the mouse to work with DOS applications.

If you need the mouse to work under standard DOS, in other words outside of Windows or OS/2, you must load a device driver either through your CONFIG.SYS file or your AUTOEXEC.BAT file. This driver, if loaded in the CONFIG.SYS file, is typically called MOUSE.SYS. The version that loads in the AUTOEXEC.BAT file is called MOUSE.COM. (It is possible that your mouse drivers have different names, depending on who manufactured your mouse.) Again, remember that if you only use a mouse under Windows or OS/2, no external drivers are required because the mouse driver is built-in.

The first step, then, is to make sure that the proper command is in your CONFIG.SYS or AUTOEXEC.BAT file to load the driver. If it is not, add the proper line, according to the information supplied with your mouse. For instance, the proper command to load the mouse driver through the CONFIG.SYS file for a Microsoft mouse is as follows:

```
DEVICE=\DOS\MOUSE.SYS
```

The actual working or syntax of the command may vary, depending on whether you are loading the device into upper memory and where the device driver is located on your disk.

One of the biggest problems with the separate mouse driver is getting it loaded into an Upper Memory Block (UMB). The older drivers—9.0 and earlier—require a very large block of 40K to 56K UMB to load into, and upon loading they shrink down to less than 20K. Even though they only take 20K or less after loading, you still need a very large area to get them "in the door."

The best tip I can give you with respect to these separate drivers is to use the newest 9.01 or higher drivers from Microsoft. This new driver works with any type of Microsoft-compatible mouse, which basically means just about anything. These new drivers are included free with IBM DOS 6.3 and higher, but surprisingly not with MS-DOS. Microsoft requires that you pay for an upgrade to the newer versions of the mouse driver and does not include the more recent mouse driver with MS-DOS! If you use version 9.01 or later, it will require less memory than previous versions and will automatically load itself into high memory as well. One of the best features is that it first loads itself into low memory; shrinks down to less than 20K; and then moves into a UMB automatically! Not only that, but the driver seeks out the smallest UMB that can hold it, rather than try only the largest as would happen if you use the DEVICEHIGH, LOADHIGH, or LH commands to load the driver. Previous versions of the driver could not fit into an upper memory block unless that block was at least 40K to 56K or larger in size, and would certainly not do it automatically. The enhanced self-loading capability of the mouse driver 9.01 and higher can save much memory space and is very much worth having. I hope that this type of self-loading and self-optimizing technique is used in other device drivers; it will make memory management much easier than it currently is.

After placing the proper driver load command in your CONFIG.SYS or AUTOEXEC.BAT file, reboot the system with the mouse connected and observe that the driver loads properly. If the proper command is in place and the driver is not loading, watch your video screen as your system boots. At some point, you should see a message from the mouse driver indicating that it is loaded. If, instead, you see a message indicating that the loading was not done, you must determine why. For example, the driver may not be able to load because not enough memory is available. After you determine why it is not loading, you need to rectify the situation and make sure that the driver loads. Again the new 9.01 or higher driver versions help greatly with memory problems.

It also is possible that some software requires a certain mouse device driver. For example, Microsoft is now up to mouse driver version numbers above 9.0. If you are using an older mouse driver and your application software requires a newer mouse driver version, the mouse will not work properly (or at all). In such cases, contact your vendor directly and request a mouse driver update. Often you can get these through the vendor's BBS or on CompuServe; however, Microsoft wants you to pay for its new drivers and does not make them available on its BBS. One shortcut around Microsoft is to use IBM DOS 6.3 or higher, which includes the new Microsoft driver for free.

Application Software. If your mouse does not work with a specific piece of application software, check the setup information or configuration section of the program. Make sure that you indicated to the program (if necessary) that you are using a mouse. If it still doesn't work and the mouse works with other software you are using, contact the technical support department of the application software company.

Trackpoint II

In April 1992, I attended the spring Comdex computer show in Chicago, and at one of the IBM booths was an enthusiastic gentleman with what looked like some homemade keyboards. These keyboards had a small rubber tipped "stick" that protruded from between the G, H, and B keys. I was invited to play with one of the keyboards, which was connected to a demonstration system. What I found was amazing! By pressing on the stick with my thumb or index finger, I could move the mouse pointer on the screen. The stick itself did not move and is not a joystick. Instead it had a silicone rubber cap that contained pressure transducers that measured the amount of force my finger or thumb was applying and the direction of the force and moved the mouse pointer accordingly. The harder I pressed, the faster the pointer moved. I could move the pointer in any direction smoothly, by slightly changing the direction of push. The silicone rubber gripped my thumb even though I had been sweating from dashing about the show. After playing around with it for just a few minutes, the movements became automatic—almost as if I could just "think" about where I wanted the pointer to go, and it would go there. After reflecting on this for a minute, it really hit me. This had to be the most revolutionary pointing device since the mouse itself!

This device occupies no space on a desk; does not have to be adjusted for left-handed or right-handed use; has no moving parts to fail or become dirty; and most important, does not require you to move your hands from the home row to use! This is an absolute boon for anybody who touch types.

The gentleman at the booth turned out to be Ted Selker, one of the actual inventors of the device. He and Joseph Rutledge together created this amazing integrated pointing device at the IBM T.J. Watson Research Center. When I asked him when such keyboards would become available, he could not answer. At the time, there were no plans for production, and he was only trying to test user reaction to the device. However, just over six months later on October 20, 1992, IBM announced the Thinkpad 700, which included the Trackpoint II integrated pointing device.

In final production form, the Trackpoint II consisted of a small, red silicone, rubber knob nestled between the G, H, and B keys on the keyboard. Two buttons are placed below the space bar to emulate the LH and RH mouse buttons for making selections. These buttons also can be easily reached without taking your hand off the keyboard. Research done by the inventors found that the act of removing your hand from the keyboard, reaching for a mouse, and replacing the hand on the keyboard takes approximately 1.35 seconds. Almost all this time can be saved each time the track point is used to either move the pointer or make a selection (click or double-click). The combination of the buttons and the positioning knob also allow drag and drop functions to be performed easily as well.

By the way, the reason the device was called Trackpoint II is that IBM had previously been selling a convertible mouse/trackball device called the Trackpoint. No relationship exists between the Trackpoint, which has since been discontinued, and the Trackpoint II integrated device.

Another feature of the Trackpoint II is that a mouse also can be connected to the system to allow for dual pointer use. In this case, a single mouse pointer would still be on the screen; however, both the Trackpoint II and the simultaneously connected mouse could move the pointer. This allows not only the use of both devices by a single person, but in fact two people can use both the Trackpoint II and the mouse simultaneously to move the pointer on the screen! The first pointing device that moves takes precedence and retains control over the mouse pointer on the screen until after completing a movement action. The second pointing device is automatically locked out until the primary device is stationary. This allows both devices to be used, but prevents each one from interfering with the other.

The Trackpoint II is obviously an ideal pointing device for a laptop system where lugging around an external mouse or trackball can be a pain. The trackballs and mini-trackballs built into some laptop keyboards are also very difficult to use and usually require removing your hands from the home row. Mouse and trackball devices are notorious for becoming "sticky" as the ball picks up dirt that affects the internal roller motion. This is especially aggravated with the smaller mini-trackball devices. But the benefits of the Trackpoint II are not limited to laptop systems. IBM/Lexmark now manufactures and sells desktop enhanced keyboards with the Trackpoint II device built-in. These new keyboards are also optional when purchasing a new PS/2 system. One drawback is that the Trackpoint II device in these keyboards initially worked only with systems that used a PS/2- or motherboard-type mouse connector. However, now the Trackpoint II enhanced keyboard is available in two versions. One interfaces via a motherboard mouse port (mini-DIN connector) and has a mini-DIN type keyboard connector as well. The other has a standard DIN keyboard connector and a serial connector for the pointing function. I have listed the part numbers for the IBM enhanced keyboard with the Trackpoint II in the section, "Replacement Keyboards," earlier in this chapter. You also can purchase these keyboards direct from Lexmark.

The Trackpoint II probably stands as the most important and revolutionary new pointing device since the original invention of the mouse in 1964 by Douglas Englebart at the Stanford Research Institute (SRI). As IBM licenses this technology to other manufacturers, you probably will see this device show up in many different systems. It is already available built into keyboards, which can upgrade many existing systems, and companies such as Toshiba are already using this IBM-developed technology in their own systems.

Game Adapter (Joystick) Interface

The game control or joystick adapter is a special input device that allows up to four paddles or two joysticks to be attached to a PC system. This function can be found on a dedicated ISA or MCA bus adapter card, or can be combined with other functions in a multifunction card. The game connector on the card is a female 15-pin D-Shell type socket (see fig. 9.13).

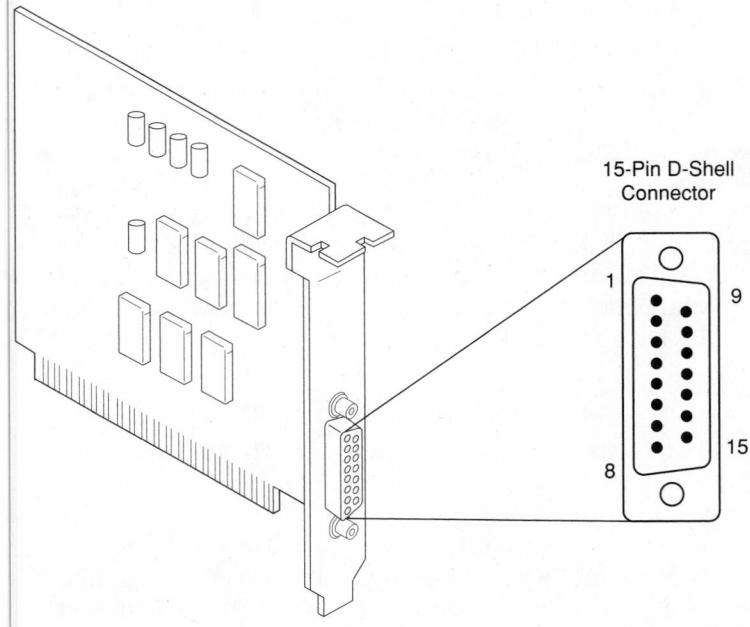

Fig. 9.13
Typical game adapter and 15-pin connector.

The game adapter can recognize up to four switches (called buttons) and four resistive inputs. Each paddle normally has one button and one knob controlling a variable resistor, whereas a joystick normally has two buttons and a central stick that controls two variable resistors. In a joystick, the variable resistors are both tied to the central stick; one indicates the relative vertical position (or x-coordinate), and the other indicates the relative horizontal position (or y-coordinate) of the stick.

Resistor inputs are variable from 0 to 100K ohms. The adapter converts the resistive value to a digital pulse with a duration proportional to the resistive load. Software can time these pulses to determine the relative resistance value. The game adapter does not use much in the way of system resources. The card does not use an IRQ, DMA channel, or memory, and requires only a single I/O address (port) 201h. The adapter is controlled by reading and writing data to and from port 201h.

Table 9.12 shows the interface connector pinout specification for a PC-compatible game adapter.

Table 9.12 PC-Compatible Game Adapter Connector			
Pin	**Signal**	**Function**	**I/O**
1	+5v	Paddle 1, Joystick A	Out
2	Button 4	Paddle 1 button, Joystick A button #1	In
3	Position 0	Paddle 1 position, Joystick A x-coordinate	In
4	Ground	—	—
5	Ground	—	—
6	Position 1	Paddle 2 position, Joystick A y-coordinate	In
7	Button 5	Paddle 2 button, Joystick A button #2	In
8	+5v	Paddle 2	Out
9	+5v	Paddle 3 and Joystick B	Out
10	Button 6	Paddle 3 button, Joystick B button #1	In
11	Position 2	Paddle 3 position, Joystick B x-coordinate	In
12	Ground	—	—
13	Position 3	Paddle 4 position, Joystick B y-coordinate	In
14	Button 7	Paddle 4 button, Joystick B button #2	In
15	+5v	Paddle 4	Out

III

Input/Output Hardware

Because this adapter actually reads resistance and easily can be manipulated with standard programming languages, the game adapter serves as a poor man's data acquisition board or real-time interface card. With it, you can hook up to four sensors and four switches and easily read the data in the PC.

Game adapters are available for ISA and MCA bus systems from a number of vendors. Consult the vendor list for some companies that may offer these types of adapters. Generally, the best place to look is one of the larger mail order system and peripheral vendors.

Summary

This chapter has examined all manner of standard input devices. Keyboards and pointing devices (usually mice) were covered in detail, as was a less known input device, the game interface. The next chapter covers video display hardware.

Chapter 10

Video Display Hardware and Specifications

Your monitor provides the link between you and your computer. Although you can get rid of your printer, disk drives, and expansion cards, you cannot sacrifice the monitor. Without it, you would be operating blind; you couldn't see the results of your calculations or the mistyped words on-screen.

The first microcomputers were small boxes that lacked displays. Instead, users waited for the final output to be printed. When the monitor was added, the computer became more attractive to a wider audience. This trend continues today with graphical user interfaces such as Microsoft Windows.

The video subsystem of a PC consists of two main components:

Monitor (or *video display*)

Video adapter (also called the *video card, video adapter*, or *graphics card*)

This chapter explores the range of available IBM-compatible video adapters and the displays that work with them.

Monitors

The monitor is, of course, the display located on top of, near, or inside your computer. Like any computer device, a monitor requires a source of input. The signals that run from your monitor come from video circuitry inside your computer. Some computers, such as the IBM PS/2 computers, contain this circuitry on the motherboard. Most systems, though, use a separate circuit board that is plugged into an expansion slot. The expansion cards that produce video signals are called video cards, video adapters, or graphics cards.

Display Technologies

A monitor may use one of several display technologies. By far the most popular is *cathode-ray tube* (CRT) technology, the same technology used in television sets. CRTs consist of a vacuum tube enclosed in glass. One end of the tube contains an electron gun; the other end contains a screen with a phosphorous coating.

When heated, the electron gun emits a stream of high-speed electrons that are attracted to the other end of the tube. On the way, a focus control and deflection coil steer the beam to a specific point on the phosphorous screen. When struck by the beam, the phosphor glows. This light is what you see when you watch TV or your computer screen.

The phosphor chemical has a quality called *persistence*, which indicates how long this glow will remain on-screen. You should have a good match between persistence and scanning frequency so that the image has less flicker (if the persistence is too low) and no ghosts (if the persistence is too high).

The electron beam moves very quickly, sweeping the screen from left to right in lines from top to bottom, in a pattern called a *raster*. The *horizontal scan rate* refers to the speed at which the electron beam moves across the screen.

During its sweep, the beam strikes the phosphor wherever an image should appear on-screen. The beam also varies by intensity in order to produce different levels of brightness. Because the glow fades almost immediately, the electron beam must continue to sweep the screen to maintain an image—a practice called *redrawing* or *refreshing* the screen.

Most displays have a *refresh rate* (also called a vertical scan rate) of about 70 hertz (Hz), meaning that the screen is refreshed 70 times a second. Low refresh rates cause the screen to flicker, contributing to eyestrain. The higher the refresh rate, the better for your eyes.

It is important that the scan rates expected by your monitor match those produced by your video card. If you have mismatched rates, you won't be able to see an image and may actually damage your monitor.

Some monitors have a fixed refresh rate. Other monitors may support a range of frequencies; this support provides built-in compatibility with future video standards (described in "Video Cards" later in this chapter). A monitor that supports many video standards is called a *multiple-frequency monitor*. One example is the NEC MultiSync 4FGe, which supports all popular video standards. Different vendors call their multiple-frequency monitors by different names, including multisync, multifrequency, multiscan, autosynchronous, and autotracking.

Phosphor-based screens come in two styles: curved and flat. The typical display screen is curved, meaning that it bulges outward from the middle of the screen. This design is consistent with the vast majority of CRT designs (the same as the tube in your television set).

The traditional screen is curved both vertically and horizontally. Some models use the Trinitron design, which is curved only horizontally and is flat vertically. Many people prefer this flatter screen because it results in less glare and a higher-quality, more accurate image. The disadvantage is that the technology required to produce flat-screen displays is more expensive, resulting in higher prices for the monitors.

Alternative display designs are available. Borrowing technology from laptop manufacturers, some companies provide LCD (liquid-crystal diode) displays. LCD displays have low-glare flat screens and low power requirements (5 watts versus nearly 100 for an ordinary monitor). The color quality of an active-matrix LCD panel exceeds that of most CRT displays. At this point, however, LCD screens usually are limited to VGA resolution and are very expensive; even a 10-inch screen costs thousands of dollars. There are three LCD choices: passive-matrix monochrome, passive-matrix color, and active-matrix color.

In an LCD, a polarizing filter creates two separate light waves. In a color LCD there is an additional filter that has three cells per each pixel—one each for displaying red, green, and blue.

The light wave then passes through a liquid-crystal cell, with each color segment having its own cell. The liquid crystals are rod-shaped molecules that flow like a liquid. They let light pass straight through, but an electrical charge alters their orientation, as well as the orientation of light passing through them. Though monochrome LCDs do not have color filters, they can have multiple cells per pixel for controlling shades of gray.

In a passive-matrix LCD, each cell is controlled by electrical charges transmitted by transistors according to row and column positions on the screen's edge. As the cell reacts to the pulsing charge, it twists the light wave, with stronger charges twisting the light wave more. Supertwist refers to the orientation of the liquid crystals, comparing on-mode to off-mode—the greater the twist, the higher the contrast.

Charges in passive-matrix LCDs are pulsed, so the displays lack the brilliance of active-matrix, which provides a constant charge to each cell. To increase the brilliance, some vendors have turned to a new technique called double-scan LCD, which splits passive-matrix screens into a top half and a bottom half, cutting the time between each pulse.

In an active-matrix LCD, each cell has its own transistor to charge it and twist the light wave. This provides a brighter image than passive-matrix displays, since the cell can maintain a constant, rather than momentary, charge. However, active-matrix technology uses more energy than passive-matrix. With a dedicated transistor for every cell, active-matrix displays are more difficult and expensive to produce.

In both active- and passive-matrix LCDs, the second polarizing filter controls how much light passes through each cell. Cells twist the wavelength of light to closely match the filter's allowable wavelength. The more light that passes through the filter at each cell, the brighter the pixel.

Monochrome LCDs achieve gray scales (up to 64) by varying the brightness of a cell or dithering cells in an on-and-off pattern. Color LCDs, on the other hand, dither the three color cells and control their brilliance to achieve different colors on the screen. Double-scan passive-matrix LCDs have recently gained in popularity because they approach the quality of active-matrix displays but do not cost much more to produce than other passive-matrix displays.

III

Input/Output Hardware

Many active-matrix LCDs, which are produced by such firms as Sharp Electronics Corp. and NEC Corp., do not pass quality-assurance tests in the factory because of failed transistors, resulting in low factory yields and higher prices.

In the past, several hot cathode ray tubes were needed to light an LCD screen, but portable computer manufacturers now use a single tube the size of a cigarette. Light emitted from a tube gets spread evenly across an entire display using fiber-optic technology.

Thanks to supertwist and triple-supertwist LCDs, today's screens let you clearly see the screen from more angles with better contrast and lighting. To improve readability, especially in dim light, some laptops include *backlighting* or *edgelighting* (also called *sidelighting*). Backlit screens provide light from a panel behind the LCD. Edgelit screens get their light from the small fluorescent tubes mounted along the sides of the screen. Some laptops exclude such lighting systems to lengthen battery life.

The best color displays are active-matrix or thin-film transistor (TFT) panels, in which each pixel is controlled by three transistors (for red, green, and blue). Active-matrix-screen refreshes and redraws are immediate and accurate, with much less ghosting and blurring than in passive-matrix LCDs (which control pixels via rows and columns of transistors along the edges of the screen). Active-matrix displays are also much brighter and can easily be read at an angle.

An alternative to LCD screens is gas-plasma technology, typically known for its black and orange screens in some of the older Toshiba notebook computers. Some companies are incorporating gas-plasma technology for desktop screens and possibly color HDTV (high-definition television) flat-panel screens.

Monochrome versus Color

During the early years of the IBM PC and compatibles, owners had only two video choices: color using a CGA display adapter and monochrome using an MDA display adapter. Since then, many adapter and display options have hit the market.

Monochrome monitors produce images of one color. The most popular is amber, followed by white and green. The color of the monitor is determined by the color of the phosphors on the CRT screen. Some monochrome monitors with white phosphors can support many shades of gray.

Monochrome monitors cost less than color models—typically about one-third to one-fourth the price of color models. A monochrome monitor is ideal for character-based applications: word processing, spreadsheet analysis, database management, and computer programming. Such monitors, however, may not work as well with Windows software as the more-expensive color monitors do. In addition, large monochrome monitors designed for specialized applications, such as desktop publishing and CAD/CAM, cost hundreds of dollars more than standard color monitors.

Color monitors use more sophisticated technology than monochrome monitors, which accounts for their higher prices. Whereas a monochrome picture tube contains one electron gun, a color tube contains three guns arranged in a triangular shape referred to as a *delta configuration*. Instead of amber, white, or green phosphors, the monitor screen contains phosphor *triads*, which consist of one red phosphor, one green phosphor, and one blue phosphor arranged in the same pattern as the electron guns. These three primary colors can be mixed to produce all other colors.

Although color monitors cost more than monochrome monitors, they are more versatile, enabling you to take advantage of color software for purposes such as presentations.

The Right Size

Monitors come in difference sizes, ranging from inexpensive (albeit rare) 12-inch monochrome monitors to 42-inch color monitors. The larger the monitor, the higher the price tag. The most common monitor sizes are 14, 15, 17, and 21 inches. These diagonal measurements, unfortunately, represent not the actual screen that will be displayed but the size of the tube. As a result, comparing one company's 15-inch monitor to another's may be unfair unless you actually measure the active screen area. One company's 15-inch monitor may display a 13.8-inch image, whereas another company's 14-inch monitor may present a 13.5-inch image.

Larger monitors are handy for applications (such as desktop publishing) in which the smallest details must be clearly visible. With a larger monitor, you can see an entire 8 1/2-by-11-inch page in a 100-percent view—in other words, what you see on-screen virtually matches the page that will be printed. This feature is called *WYSIWYG* (what you see is what you get). If you can see the entire page at its actual size, you can save yourself the trouble of printing several drafts before you get it right.

Monitors come in both portrait and landscape styles. The screen of a *portrait* (full-page) monitor is taller than it is wide, enabling you to view an entire page of a document. Portrait monitors differ from standard monitors in that they stretch image height to about 66 lines, enabling you to see the equivalent of a full printed page on one screen. A *landscape* (dual-page) monitor is the opposite of a portrait monitor, suitable for viewing two pages side by side at the same time.

Although most general-purpose monitors are landscape, monitors with this orientation are larger and wider—and usually more expensive—than portrait models. When you consider a portrait monitor, you should make sure that it supports your software. Some monitors require special video drivers to work with certain software packages.

Monitor Resolution

Resolution is the amount of detail that a monitor can render. This quantity is expressed in the number of horizontal and vertical picture elements, or *pixels*, contained in the screen. The greater the number of pixels, the more detailed the images. The resolution required depends on the application. Character-based applications (such as word processing) require little resolution, whereas graphics-intensive applications (such as desktop publishing and Windows software) require a great deal.

In a monochrome monitor, the picture element is a screen phosphor, but in a color monitor, the picture element is a phosphor triad. This difference raises another consideration called dot pitch, which applies only to color monitors. *Dot pitch* is the distance, in millimeters, between phosphor triads. Screens with a small dot pitch contain less distance between the phosphor triads; as a result, the picture elements are closer together, producing a sharper picture. Conversely, screens with a large dot pitch tend to produce less clear images.

Most monitors have a dot pitch between 0.25 and 0.52 millimeters. To avoid grainy images, look for a dot pitch of 0.28 millimeters or smaller for 12- and 14-inch monitors, or 0.31mm or smaller for 16-inch and larger monitors. Be wary of monitors with 0.39mm or greater dot pitches; for fine text and graphics, there is a lack of clarity.

Interlaced versus Noninterlaced

Monitors may support interlaced or noninterlaced resolution. In *noninterlaced* (conventional) mode, the electron beam sweeps the screen in lines from top to bottom, one line after the other, completing the screen in one pass. In *interlaced* mode, the electron beam also sweeps the screen from top to bottom, but it does so in two passes, sweeping the odd lines first and the even lines second; each pass takes half the time of a full pass in noninterlaced mode. Therefore, both modes refresh the entire screen in the same amount of time. This technique redraws the screen faster and provides more stable images.

Monitors that use interlacing can use lower refresh rates, lessening their cost. The drawback is that interlacing depends on the ability of the eye to combine two nearly identical lines, separated by a gap, into one solid line. If you are looking for high-quality video, however, you want to get a video adapter and monitor that support high-resolution, noninterlaced displays.

Energy and Safety

A monitor can save energy. Many PC manufacturers are trying to meet the Environmental Protection Agency's Energy Star requirements. Any PC-and-monitor combination that consumes less than 70 watts (35 watts apiece) can use the Energy Star logo. Some research shows that such "green" PCs can save each user about $70 per year in electricity costs.

Monitors, being one of the most power-hungry computer components, can contribute to those savings. Perhaps the best-known energy-saving standard for monitors is VESA's Display Power-Management Signaling (DPMS) spec, which defines the signals that a computer sends to a monitor to indicate idle times. The computer or video card decides when to send these signals.

If you buy a DPMS monitor, such as one of NEC's recent MultiSync models, you can take advantage of energy savings without remodeling your entire system. If you don't have a DPMS-compatible video adapter, some cards, such as ATI's (based on that company's mach32 chipset), can be upgraded to DPMS with a software utility typically available at no cost. Similarly, ViewSonic's energy-saving monitors include software that works with almost any graphics card to supply DPMS signals.

Another trend in green monitor design is to minimize the user's exposure to potentially harmful electromagnetic fields. Several medical studies indicate that these electromagnetic emissions may cause health problems, such as miscarriages, birth defects, and cancer. The risk may be low, but if you spend a third of your day (or more) in front of a computer monitor, that risk is increased.

The concern is that VLF (very-low-frequency) and ELF (extremely low-frequency) emissions somehow affect your body. These two emissions come in two forms: electric and magnetic. Some research indicates that ELF magnetic emissions are more threatening than VLF emissions, because they interact with the natural electric activity of body cells. Monitors aren't the only culprits; significant ELF emissions also come from electric blankets and power lines.

> **Note**
>
> ELF and VLF are not considered to be radiation; they actually are radio frequencies below those used for broadcasting.

These two frequencies are covered by the new Swedish monitor-emission standard called SWEDAC, named after the Swedish regulatory agency. In many European countries, government agencies and businesses buy only low-emission monitors. The degree to which emissions are reduced varies from monitor to monitor. The Swedish government's MPR I standard, which dates back to 1987, is the least restrictive. MPR II, established in 1990, is significantly stronger (adding maximums for ELF as well as VLF emissions) and is the level that you're most likely to find in low-emission monitors today.

A more stringent 1992 standard called TCO further tightens the MPR II requirements; in addition, it's a more broad-based environmental standard that includes power-saving requirements as well as emission limits. Nanao is one of the few manufacturers currently offering monitors that meet the TCO standard.

A low-emission monitor costs about $20 to $100 more than a similar regular-emission monitors. When you shop for a low-emission monitor, don't just ask for a low-emission monitor; also find out whether the monitor limits specific types of emission. Use as your guideline the two electromagnetic-emission standards described in this section.

If you decide not to buy a low-emission monitor, you can take other steps to protect yourself. The most important is to stay at arm's length (about 28 inches) from the front of your monitor. When you move a couple of feet away, ELF magnetic emission levels usually drop to those of a typical office with fluorescent lights. Also, monitor emissions are weakest at the front of a monitor, so stay at least three feet from the sides and backs of nearby monitors and five feet from any copiers—very strong sources of ELF.

Electromagnetic emissions should not be your only concern; you also should be concerned about screen glare. In fact, some antiglare screens not only reduce eyestrain, but also cut ELF and VLF electric (but not magnetic) emissions.

Monitor Buying Criteria

A monitor may account for as much as 50 percent of the price of a computer system. What should you look for when you shop for a monitor?

The trick is to pick a monitor that works with your selected video card. You can save money by purchasing a single-standard (fixed-frequency) monitor and a matching video card; for example, you can order a VGA monitor and a VGA video card. For greatest flexibility, get a multisync monitor that accommodates a range of standards, including those that are not yet standardized.

With multisync monitors, you must match the range of horizontal and vertical frequencies the monitor accepts with those generated by your video card. The wider the range of signals, the more expensive—and more versatile—the monitor. Your video card's vertical and horizontal frequencies must fall within the ranges supported by your monitor. The *vertical frequency* (or refresh/frame rate) determines how stable your image will be. The higher the vertical frequency, the better. Typical vertical frequencies range from 50 to 90 Hz. The *horizontal frequency* (or line rate) ranges between 31.5 kHz and 59 kHz.

To keep the horizontal frequency low, some video cards use interlacing signals, alternately displaying half the lines of the total image. On some monitors, interlacing can produce a pronounced flicker. For this reason, your monitor should synchronize to twice the vertical frequency of the video card. For example, the IBM XGA video standard uses a frame rate of 43.5 Hz. To match those signals, a monitor must accept a vertical frequency of 87 Hz and a horizontal frequency of 35.5 kHz.

When you shop for a VGA monitor, make sure that the monitor supports a horizontal frequency of at least 31.5 kHz—the minimum that a VGA card needs to paint a 640-by-480 screen. The VESA super-VGA (800-by-600) standard requires a 72 Hz vertical frequency and a horizontal frequency of at least 48 kHz. The sharper 1,024-by-768 image requires a vertical frequency of 60 Hz and a horizontal frequency of 58 kHz. If the vertical frequency increases to 72 Hz, the horizontal frequency must be 58 kHz. If flicker-prone interlacing is used, a 1,024-by-768 video card needs a monitor with a 43.5 Hz vertical frequency and a 35.5 kHz horizontal frequency.

Most of the analog monitors produced today are, to one extent or another, multisync. Because literally hundreds of manufacturers produce thousands of monitor models, it is impractical to discuss the technical aspects of each monitor model in detail. Suffice it to say that before investing in a monitor, you should check the technical specifications to make sure that the monitor meets your needs. If you are looking for a place to start, check out *PC Magazine*, which periodically features reviews of monitors. If you can't wait for a *PC Magazine* review, investigate monitors made by any of the following vendors:

- IBM
- Mitsubishi
- NEC
- Sony

Each of these manufacturers creates monitors that set the standards by which other monitors can be judged. Although you typically pay a bit more for these manufacturers' monitors, you never will be disappointed with their quality or with the service that you receive from them.

Many inexpensive monitors are curved because it's easier to send an electron beam across them. Flat-screen monitors, which are a bit more expensive, look better to most people. As a general rule, the less curvature a monitor has, the less glare it will reflect.

Consider the size of your desk before you think about a monitor 16 inches or larger. A 16-inch monitor typically is at least a foot and a half deep, and a 20-inch monitor takes up 2 square feet. (Typical 14-inch monitors are 16 to 18 inches deep.)

You also should check the dot pitch of the monitor. Smaller pitch values indicate sharper images. The original IBM PC color monitor had a dot pitch of 0.43mm, which is considered to be poor by almost any standard. The state-of-the-art displays marketed today have a dot pitch of 0.28mm or less. You can save money by picking a smaller monitor or one with a higher dot pitch. The tradeoff, of course, is clarity. Don't be too discerning; choosing a monitor with a 0.31mm dot pitch over one with a 0.28mm dot pitch may save you a good deal of money.

What resolution do you want for your display? Generally, the higher the resolution, the larger the display you will want. If you are operating at 640-by-480 resolution, for example, you should find a 14-inch monitor to be comfortable. At 1,024-by-768, you probably will find that the display of a 14-inch monitor is too small and therefore will prefer to use a larger one (such as a 17-inch monitor).

Get a monitor with positioning and image controls that are easy to reach. Look for more than just basic contrast and brightness controls; some monitors also enable you to adjust the width and height of your screen images. A tilt-swivel stand should be included with your monitor, enabling you to move the monitor to the best angle for your use.

A monitor is such an important part of your computer that it's not enough just to know its technical specifications. Knowing a monitor has a 0.28mm dot pitch doesn't necessarily tell you that it is ideal for you. It's best to "kick the tires" of your new monitor at a showroom or (with a liberal return policy) in the privacy of your office. To test your monitor:

- *Draw a circle with a graphics program.* If the result is an oval, not a circle, this monitor won't serve you well with graphics or design software.

- *Type some words in 8- or 10-point type* (1 point = 1/72 inch). If the words are fuzzy, or if the black characters are fringed with color, select another monitor.

- *Turn the brightness up and down* while examining the corner of the screen's image. If the image blooms or swells, it's likely to lose focus at high brightness levels.

- *Load Microsoft Windows to check for uniform focus.* Are the corner icons as sharp as the rest of the screen? Are the lines in the title bar curved or wavy? Monitors

III

Input/Output Hardware

usually are sharply focused at the center, but seriously blurred corners indicate a poor design. Bowed lines may be the result of a poor graphics card, so don't dismiss a monitor that shows those lines without using another card to double-check the effect. A good monitor will be calibrated so that rays of red, green, and blue light hit their targets (individual phosphor dots) precisely. If they don't, you have bad *convergence*. This is apparent when edges of lines appear to illuminate with a specific color. If you have good *convergence* then the colors will be crisp, clear, and true, provided there is not a predominant tint in the phosphor.

Video Cards

A video card provides signals that operate your monitor. With the PS/2 systems introduced in 1987, IBM developed new video standards that have overtaken the older display standards in popularity and support.

Most video cards follow one of several industry standards:

- MDA (Monochrome Display Adapter)
- CGA (Color Graphics Adapter)
- EGA (Enhanced Graphics Adapter)
- VGA (Video Graphics Adapter)
- SVGA (Super-VGA)
- XGA (eXtended Graphics Array)

These adapters and video standards are supported by virtually every program that runs on IBM or compatible equipment. Other systems are developing into de facto standards as well. For example, super-VGA (SVGA) offers different resolutions from different vendors, but 1,024-by-768 resolution is becoming a standard resolution for doing detailed work.

Most microcomputer monitors support at least one video standard, enabling you to operate them with video cards and software that are compatible with that standard. For example, a monitor that supports VGA may operate with VGA video cards and VGA software.

Although many types of display systems are considered to be standards, not all systems are considered to be viable standards for today's hardware and software. For example, the CGA standard works but is unacceptable for running the graphics-intensive programs on which many users rely. In fact, Microsoft Windows 3.1 does not work with any PC that has less-than-EGA resolution. The next several sections discuss the display adapters that are viewed as being obsolete in today's market.

Monochrome Display Adapter (MDA) and Display. The simplest (and first available) display type is the IBM Monochrome Display Adapter (MDA). (Actually, the MDA card doubles as a video and printer card.) The MDA video card can display text only at a resolution of 720 horizontal by 350 vertical pixels (720 by 350).

A character-only system, the display has no inherent graphics capabilities. The display originally was a top-selling option because it is fairly cost-effective. As a bonus, the MDA provides a printer interface, conserving an expansion slot.

The display is known for clarity and high resolution, making it ideal for business use—especially for businesses that use DOS-based word processing or spreadsheet programs.

Figure 10.1 shows the Monochrome Display Adapter pinouts.

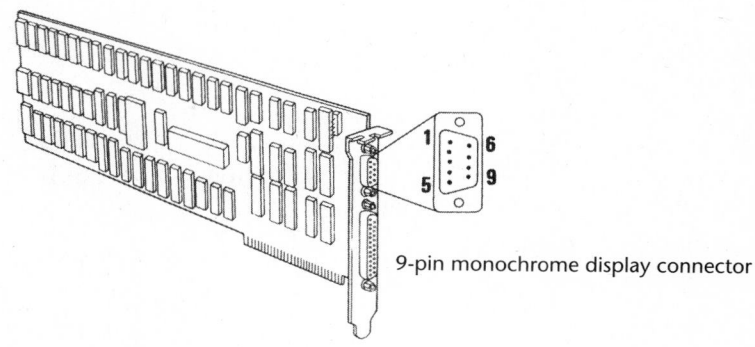

9-pin monochrome display connector

At Standard TTL Levels

IBM Monochrome Display			IBM Monochrome Display and Printer Adapter
	Ground	1	
	Ground	2	
	Not Used	3	
	Not Used	4	
	Not Used	5	
	+ Intensity	6	
	+ Video	7	
	+ Horizontal	8	
	− Vertical	9	

Fig. 10.1
Monochrome Display Adapter pinouts.

Because the monochrome display is a character-only display, you cannot use it with software that requires graphics. Originally, that drawback only kept the user from playing games on a monochrome display, but today, even the most serious business software uses graphics and color to great advantage. With the 9-by-14 dot character box (*matrix*), the IBM monochrome monitor displays attractive characters.

Table 10.1 summarizes the features of the MDA's single mode of operation.

Later, a company named Hercules released a video card called the Hercules Graphics Card (HGC). This card displays sharper text and can handle graphics, such as bar charts.

III

Input/Output Hardware

Table 10.1	IBM Monochrome Display Adapter (MDA) Specifications				
Video Standard	**Resolution**	**Number of Colors**	**Mode Type**	**BIOS Modes**	**Character Format**
MDA					
(08/12/81)	720 × 350	4	Text	07h	80 × 25

Colors refer to different display attributes such as regular, highlight, reverse video, and underlined.

Color Graphics Adapter (CGA) and Display. For many years, the Color Graphics Adapter (CGA) was the most common display adapter, although its capabilities now leave much to be desired. This adapter has two basic modes of operation: alphanumeric (A/N) or all points addressable (APA). In A/N mode, the card operates in 40-column by 25-line mode or 80-column by 25-line mode with 16 colors. In APA and A/N modes, the character set is formed with a resolution of 8-by-8 pixels. In APA mode, two resolutions are available: medium-resolution color mode (320 by 200), with four colors available from a palette of 16; and two-color high-resolution mode (640 by 200).

Figures 10.2 and 10.3 show the pinouts for the Color Graphics Adapter.

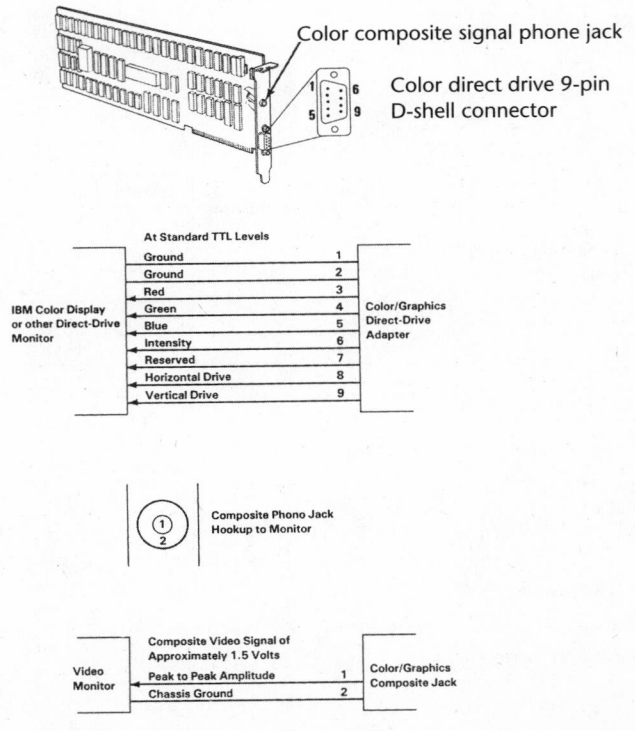

Fig. 10.2
CGA display connector specifications.

Character Box	Scan Frequency Vertical (Hz)	Horizontal (kHz)	Scan Mode
9 × 14	50	18.432	Std

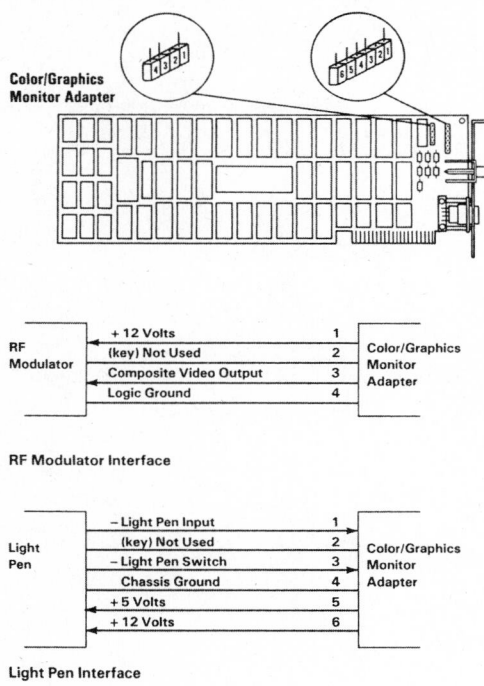

Fig. 10.3

CGA RF modulator and light-pen connector specifications.

Most of the monitors sold for the CGA are RGBs, not composite monitors. The color signal of a composite monitor contains a mixture of colors that must be decoded or separated. RGB monitors receive red, green, and blue separately, and combine the colors in different proportions to generate other colors. RGB monitors offer better resolution than composite monitors, and they do a much better job of displaying 80-column text.

One drawback of a CGA video card is that it produces flicker and snow. *Flicker* is the annoying tendency of the text to flash as you move the image up or down. *Snow* is the flurry of bright dots that can appear anywhere on the screen.

Most companies that sold CGA-type adapters have long since discontinued those products. When many VGA cards cost less than $100, recommending a CGA makes little sense.

Table 10.2 lists the specifications for all CGA modes of operation.

Table 10.2	IBM Color Graphics Adapter (CGA) Specifications				
Video Standard	**Resolution**	**Number of Colors**	**Mode Type**	**BIOS Modes**	**Character Format**
CGA					
(08/12/81)	320 × 200	16	Text	00/01h	40 × 25
	640 × 200	16	Text	02/03h	80 × 25
	160 × 200	16	APA	—	—
	320 × 200	4	APA	04/05h	40 × 25
	640 × 200	2	APA	06h	80 × 25

APA = All points addressable (graphics)
— = Not supported

Enhanced Graphics Adapter (EGA) and Display. The IBM Enhanced Graphics Adapter, discontinued when the PS/2 systems were introduced, consists of a graphics board, a graphics memory-expansion board, a graphics memory-module kit, and a high-resolution color monitor. The whole package originally cost about $1,800. The aftermarket gave IBM a great deal of competition in this area; you could put together a similar system from non-IBM vendors for much less money. One advantage of EGA, however, is that you can build your system in modular steps. Because the card works with any of the monitors IBM produced at the time, you can use it with the IBM Monochrome Display, the earlier IBM Color Display, or the IBM Enhanced Color Display.

With the EGA card, the IBM color monitor displays 16 colors in 320-by-200 or 640-by-200 mode and the IBM monochrome monitor shows a resolution of 640 by 350 with a 9-by-14 character box (text mode).

Figures 10.4 and 10.5 show the pinouts and P-2 connector of the Enhanced Graphics Display Adapter.

With the EGA card, the IBM Enhanced Color Display is capable of displaying 640-by-350 pixels in 16 colors from a palette of 64. The character box for text is 8 by 14, compared with 8 by 8 for the earlier CGA board and monitor. The 8-by-8 character box can be used, however, to display 43 lines of text. Through software, the character box can be manipulated up to the size of 8 by 32.

You can enlarge a RAM-resident, 256-member character set to 512 characters by using the IBM memory expansion card. A 1,024-character set is added with the IBM graphics memory-module kit. These character sets are loaded from programs.

All this memory fits in the unused space between the end of RAM user memory and the current display-adapter memory. The EGA has a maximum 128K of memory that maps into the RAM space just above the 640K boundary. If you install more than 640K, you probably will lose the extra memory after installing the EGA. The graphics memory-expansion card adds 64K to the standard 64K, for a total 128K. The IBM

Character Box	Scan Frequency Vertical (Hz)	Horizontal (kHz)	Scan Mode
8 × 8	60	15.75	Std
8 × 8	60	15.75	Std
—	60	15.75	Std
8 × 8	60	15.75	Std
8 × 8	60	15.75	Std

graphics memory-module kit adds another 128K, for a total 256K. This second 128K of memory is only on the card and does not consume any of the PC's memory space. (Because almost every aftermarket EGA card comes configured with the full 256K of memory, expansion options are not necessary.)

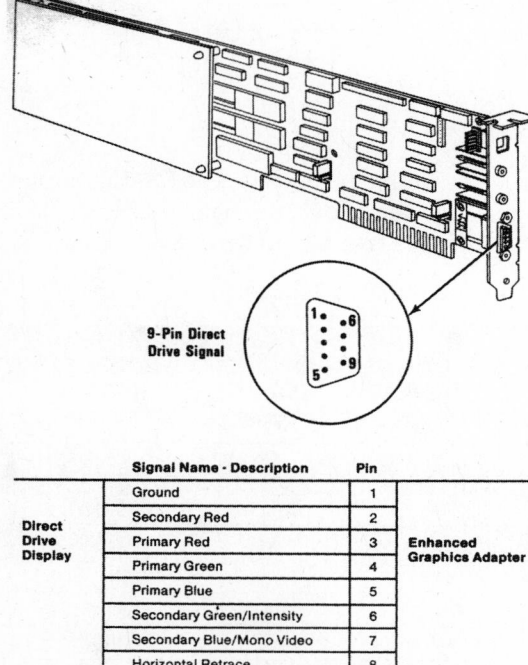

9-Pin Direct Drive Signal

	Signal Name - Description	Pin	
	Ground	1	
	Secondary Red	2	
Direct Drive Display	Primary Red	3	Enhanced Graphics Adapter
	Primary Green	4	
	Primary Blue	5	
	Secondary Green/Intensity	6	
	Secondary Blue/Mono Video	7	
	Horizontal Retrace	8	
	Vertical Retrace	9	

Fig. 10.4
EGA display connector specifications.

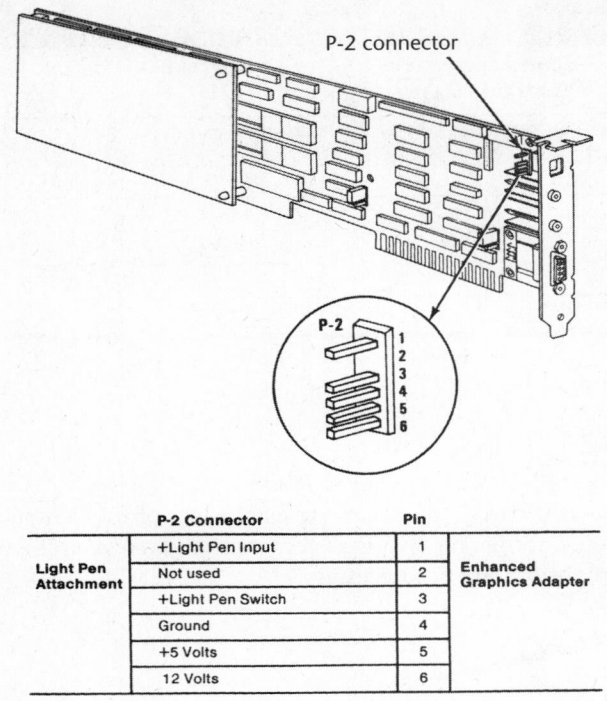

P-2 Connector		Pin	
	+Light Pen Input	1	
Light Pen Attachment	Not used	2	Enhanced Graphics Adapter
	+Light Pen Switch	3	
	Ground	4	
	+5 Volts	5	
	12 Volts	6	

Fig. 10.5
EGA light-pen connector specifications.

The VGA system supersedes the EGA in many respects. The EGA has problems emulating the earlier CGA or MDA adapters, and some software that works with the earlier cards will not run on the EGA until the programs are modified.

Table 10.3 shows the modes supported by the EGA adapter.

Table 10.3 IBM Enhanced Graphics Adapter (EGA) Specifications					
Video Standard	**Resolution**	**Number of Colors**	**Mode Type**	**BIOS Modes**	**Character Format**
EGA					
(09/10/84)	320 × 350	16	Text	00/01h	40 × 25
	640 × 350	16	Text	02/03h	80 × 25
	720 × 350	4	Text	07h	80 × 25
	320 × 200	16	APA	0Dh	40 × 25
	640 × 200	16	APA	0Eh	80 × 25
	640 × 350	4	APA	0Fh	80 × 25
	640 × 350	16	APA	10h	80 × 25

APA = All points addressable (graphics)

Professional Color Display and Adapter. The Professional Graphics Display System is a video display product that IBM introduced in 1984. At $4,290, the system was too expensive to become a mainstream product.

The system consists of a Professional Graphics Monitor and a Professional Graphics Card Set. When fully expanded, this card set uses three slots in an XT or AT system—which is a high price to pay, but the features are impressive. The Professional Graphics Adapter (PGA) offers three-dimensional rotation and clipping as a built-in hardware function. The adapter can run 60 frames of animation per second because the PGA uses a built-in dedicated microcomputer.

The Professional Graphics card and monitor targeted engineering and scientific applications rather than financial or business applications. This system, which was discontinued when the PS/2 was introduced, has been replaced by the VGA and other higher resolution graphics standards for these newer systems.

Table 10.4 lists all supported PGA modes.

VGA Adapters and Displays

When IBM introduced the PS/2 systems on April 2, 1987, it also introduced the Video Graphics Array display. On that day, in fact, IBM also introduced the lower-resolution MultiColor Graphics Array (MCGA) and higher-resolution 8514 adapters. The MCGA and 8514 adapters did not become standards like the VGA, and both were discontinued.

Digital versus Analog Signals. Unlike earlier video standards, which are digital, the VGA is an analog system. Why are displays going from digital to analog when most other electronic systems are going digital? Compact disc players (digital) have replaced most turntables (analog), and newer VCRs and camcorders have digital picture storage for smooth slow-motion and freeze-frame capability. With a digital television set, you can watch several channels on a single screen by splitting the screen or placing a picture within another picture.

Character Box	Scan Frequency Vertical (Hz)	Horizontal (kHz)	Scan Mode
8 × 14	60	21.8	Std
8 × 14	60	21.8	Std
9 × 14	50	18.432	Std
8 × 8	60	15.75	Std
8 × 8	60	15.75	Std
8 × 14	50	18.432	Std
8 × 14	60	21.85	Std

Table 10.4   IBM Professional Graphics Adapter (PGA) Specifications

Video Standard	Resolution	Number of Colors	Mode Type	BIOS Modes	Character Format
PGA					
(09/10/84)	320 × 200	16	Text	00/01	40 × 25
	640 × 200	16	Text	02/03	80 × 25
	320 × 200	4	APA	04/05	40 × 25
	640 × 200	2	APA	06	80 × 25
	640 × 480	256	APA	—	—

APA = All points addressable (graphics)
— = Not supported

Why, then, did IBM decide to change the video to analog? The answer is color.

Most personal-computer displays introduced before the PS/2 are digital. This type of display generates different colors by firing the red, green, and blue (RGB) electron beams in on-or-off mode. You can display up to eight colors (2 to the third power). In the IBM displays and adapters, another signal intensity doubles the number of color combinations from 8 to 16 by displaying each color at one of two intensity levels. This digital display is easy to manufacture and offers simplicity with consistent color combinations from system to system. The real drawback of the digital display system is the limited number of possible colors.

In the PS/2 systems, IBM went to an analog display circuit. Analog displays work like the digital displays that use RGB electron beams to construct various colors, but each color in the analog display system can be displayed at varying levels of intensity—64 levels, in the case of the VGA. This versatility provides 262,144 possible colors (64^3). For realistic computer graphics, color often is more important than high resolution, because the human eye perceives a picture that has more colors as being more realistic. IBM moved graphics into analog form to enhance the color capabilities.

MultiColor Graphics Array (MCGA). The MultiColor Graphics Array (MCGA) is a graphics adapter that is integrated into the motherboard of the PS/2 Models 25 and 30. The MCGA supports all CGA modes when an IBM analog display is attached, but any previous IBM display is not compatible. In addition to providing existing CGA mode support, the MCGA includes four additional modes.

Character Box	Scan Frequency Vertical (Hz)	Horizontal (kHz)	Scan Mode
8 × 8	60	15.75	Std
8 × 8	60	15.75	Std
8 × 8	60	15.75	Std
8 × 8	60	15.75	Std
—	60	30.48	Std

The MCGA uses as many as 64 shades of gray in converting color modes for display on monochrome displays, so that users who prefer a monochrome display still can execute color-based applications.

Video Graphics Array (VGA). PS/2 systems contain the primary display adapter circuits on the motherboard. The circuits, called the Video Graphics Array, are implemented by a single custom VLSI chip designed and manufactured by IBM. To adapt this new graphics standard to the earlier systems, IBM introduced the PS/2 Display Adapter. Also called a VGA card, this adapter contains the complete VGA circuit on a full-length adapter board with an 8-bit interface. IBM has since discontinued its VGA card, but many third-party units are available.

The VGA BIOS (basic input/output system) is the control software residing in the system ROM for controlling VGA circuits. With the BIOS, software can initiate commands and functions without having to manipulate the VGA directly. Programs become somewhat hardware-independent and can call a consistent set of commands and functions built into the system's ROM-control software.

Future implementations of the VGA will be different in hardware but will respond to the same BIOS calls and functions. New features will be added as a superset of the existing functions. The VGA, therefore, will be compatible with the earlier graphics and text BIOS functions that were built into the PC systems from the beginning. The VGA can run almost any software that originally was written for the MDA, CGA, or EGA.

In a perfect world, software programmers would write to the BIOS interface rather than directly to the hardware and would promote software interchanges between different types of hardware. More frequently, however, programmers want the software to perform better, so they write the programs to control the hardware directly. As a result, these programmers achieve higher-performance applications that are dependent on the hardware for which they first were written.

III

Input/Output Hardware

Table 10.5 lists the MCGA display modes.

Table 10.5	IBM MultiColor Graphics Array (MCGA) Specifications				
Video Standard	Resolution	Number of Colors	Mode Type	BIOS Modes	Character Format
MCGA					
(04/02/87)	320 × 400	16	Text	00/01h	40 × 25
	640 × 400	16	Text	02/03h	80 × 25
	320 × 200	4	APA	04/05h	40 × 25
	640 × 200	2	APA	06h	80 × 25
	640 × 480	2	APA	11h	80 × 30
	320 × 200	256	APA	13h	40 × 25

APA = All points addressable (graphics)
DBL = Double scan

When bypassing the BIOS, a programmer must ensure that the hardware is 100-percent compatible with the standard so that software written to a standard piece of hardware runs on the system. Note that just because a manufacturer claims this register level of compatibility does not mean that the product is 100-percent compatible or that all software runs as it would on a true IBM VGA. Most manufacturers have "cloned" the VGA system at the register level, which means that even applications that write directly to the video registers will function correctly. Also, the VGA circuits themselves emulate the older adapters even to the register level and have an amazing level of compatibility with these earlier standards. This compatibility makes the VGA a truly universal standard.

Table 10.6 lists the VGA display modes.

Table 10.6	IBM Video Graphics Array (VGA) Specifications				
Video Standard	Resolution	Number of Colors	Mode Type	BIOS Modes	Character Format
VGA					
(04/02/87)	360 × 400	16	Text	00/01h	40 × 25
	720 × 400	16	Text	02/03h	80 × 25
	320 × 200	4	APA	04/05h	40 × 25
	640 × 200	2	APA	06h	80 × 25
	720 × 400	16	Text	07h	80 × 25
	320 × 200	16	APA	0Dh	40 × 25
	640 × 200	16	APA	0Eh	80 × 25

Character Box	Scan Frequency Vertical (Hz)	Horizontal (kHz)	Scan Mode
8 × 16	70	31.5	Std
8 × 16	70	31.5	Std
8 × 8	70	31.5	Dbl
8 × 8	70	31.5	Dbl
8 × 16	60	31.5	Std
8 × 8	70	31.5	Dbl

The VGA displays up to 256 colors on-screen, from a palette of 262,144 (256K) colors. Because the VGA outputs an analog signal, you must have a monitor that accepts an analog input.

VGA displays come not only in color but also in monochrome VGA models, using color summing. With color summing, 64 gray shades are displayed in lieu of colors; the translation is performed in the ROM BIOS. The summing routine is initiated if the BIOS detects the monochrome display when the system is booted. This routine uses a formula that takes the desired color and rewrites the formula to involve all three color guns, producing varying intensities of gray. The color that would be displayed, for example, is converted to 30-percent red plus 59-percent green plus 11-percent blue to achieve the desired gray. Users who prefer a monochrome display, therefore, can execute color-based applications.

Character Box	Scan Frequency Vertical (Hz)	Horizontal (kHz)	Scan Mode
9 × 16	70	31.5	Std
9 × 16	70	31.5	Std
8 × 8	70	31.5	Dbl
8 × 8	70	31.5	Dbl
9 × 16	70	31.5	Std
8 × 8	70	31.5	Dbl
8 × 8	70	31.5	Dbl

(continues)

III

Input/Output Hardware

Video Standard	Resolution	Number of Colors	Mode Type	BIOS Modes	Character Format
Table 10.6 Continued					
VGA					
	640 × 350	4	APA	0Fh	80 × 25
	640 × 350	16	APA	10h	80 × 25
	640 × 480	2	APA	11h	80 × 30
	640 × 480	16	APA	12h	80 × 30
	320 × 200	256	APA	13h	40 × 25

APA = All points addressable (graphics)
Dbl = Double scan

8514 Display Adapter. The PS/2 Display Adapter 8514/A offers higher resolution and more colors than the standard VGA. This adapter, designed to use the PS/2 Color Display 8514, plugs into a Micro Channel slot in any PS/2 model so equipped.

All operation modes of the built-in VGA continue to be available. An IBM Personal System/2 8514 memory-expansion kit is available for the IBM Display Adapter 8514/A. This kit provides increased color and grayscale support.

The IBM Display Adapter 8514/A has these advantages:

■ Hardware assistance for advanced text, image, and graphics functions

■ New high-content display modes

■ Increased color and monochrome capability

■ Support for the new family of IBM displays

■ MDA, CGA, EGA, and VGA modes available

■ 256/256K colors and 64/64 grayscales with memory-expansion kit

Video Standard	Resolution	Number of Colors	Mode Type	BIOS Modes	Character Format
Table 10.7 IBM 8514 Specifications					
8514					
(04/02/87)	1024 × 768	256	APA	H-0h	85 × 38
	640 × 480	256	APA	H-1h	80 × 34
	1024 × 768	256	APA	H-3h	146 × 51

APA = All points addressable (graphics)
IL = Interlaced

Character Box	Scan Frequency Vertical (Hz)	Horizontal (kHz)	Scan Mode
8 × 14	70	31.5	Std
8 × 14	70	31.5	Std
8 × 16	60	31.5	Std
8 × 16	60	31.5	Std
8 × 8	70	31.5	Dbl

To take full advantage of this adapter, you should use the 8514 display, because it is matched to the capabilities of the adapter. Notice that IBM has discontinued the 8514/A adapter and specifies the XGA in its place. The 8514 display continues to be sold because it works well with the newer XGA.

Table 10.7 shows all 8514 modes.

Super-VGA (SVGA)

When IBM's XGA and 8514/A video cards were introduced, competing manufacturers chose not to clone these incremental improvements on VGA; instead, they began producing lower-cost adapters that offered even higher resolutions. These video cards fall into a category loosely known as *super-VGA* (SVGA).

SVGA provides capabilities that surpass those offered by the VGA adapter. Unlike display adapters discussed so far, super-VGA does not refer to a card that meets a particular specification but to a group of cards that have different capabilities.

For example, one card may offer two resolutions (800 by 600 and 1,024 by 768) that are greater than those achieved with a regular VGA, whereas another card may offer the same resolutions but also provide more color choices at each resolution. These cards have different capabilities; nonetheless, both of them are classified as super-VGA.

Character Box	Scan Frequency Vertical (Hz)	Horizontal (kHz)	Scan Mode
12 × 20	43.48	35.52	IL
8 × 14	60	31.5	Std
7 × 15	43.48	35.52	IL

Unlike the modes offered by IBM's CGA, EGA, and VGA standards, the new graphics modes are more or less proprietary. Because super-VGA cards are a category rather than a specification, the market at this level has been fractured. To take advantage of the enhanced capabilities of each card, you need special video-card drivers. To use an Orchid card with Microsoft Windows, for example, you need Orchid drivers. You cannot use an Orchid driver with a different SVGA card; you can use it only with Orchid models. This means that unlike VGA cards—which can have a single driver that works with all VGA cards, regardless of the vendor—each SVGA card must have a corresponding driver for each application you intend to use with it.

The SVGA cards look much like their VGA counterparts. They have the same connectors, including the feature adapter shown in figure 10.6.

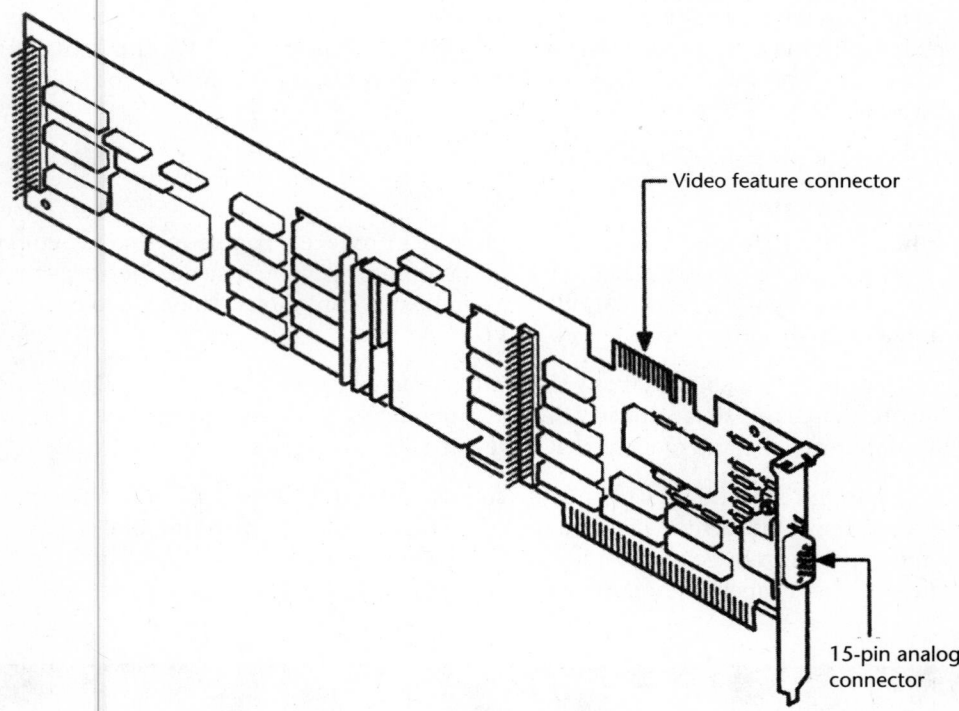

Fig. 10.6
The IBM PS/2 Display Adapter (VGA card).

Because the technical specifications from different SVGA vendors vary tremendously, it is impossible to provide a definitive technical overview in this book.

VESA SVGA Standards

In October 1989, the Video Electronics Standards Association (VESA), recognizing that programming for the many SVGA cards on the market is virtually impossible, proposed a standard for a uniform programmer's interface for SVGA cards. This association includes ATI Technologies, Genoa Systems, Orchid Technology, Renaissance GRX, STB Systems, Techmar, Headland Technology (formerly Video Seven), Western Digital Imaging/ Paradise Systems, and NEC.

The SVGA standard is called the VESA BIOS Extension. If a video card incorporates this standard, a program easily can determine the capabilities of the card and then access those capabilities. The benefit of the VESA BIOS Extension is that a programmer needs to worry about only one routine or driver to support SVGA. Different cards from different manufacturers are accessible through the common VESA interface.

This concept, when first proposed, met with limited acceptance. Several major SVGA manufacturers started supplying the VESA BIOS Extension as a separate memory-resident program that you could load when you booted your computer. Over the years, however, other vendors started supplying the VESA BIOS Extension as an integral part of their SVGA BIOS. Obviously, from a user's perspective, support for VESA in BIOS is a better solution. You don't need to worry about loading a driver or other memory-resident program whenever you want to use a program that expects the VESA extensions to be present.

Today, most SVGA cards support the VESA BIOS Extensions in one way or another. When you shop for an SVGA card, make sure that it supports the extensions in BIOS. Also, if you are interested in finding out more about programming for the VESA BIOS Extensions, check out the IBMPRO forum on CompuServe, or contact the Video Electronics Standards Association at (408)435-0333 for a copy of the VESA Programmer's Toolkit.

The current VESA super-VGA standard covers just about every video resolution and color-depth combination currently available, up to 1,280 by 1,024 with 16,777,216 (24-bit) colors. Even if a SVGA video adapter claims to be VESA-compatible, however, it still may not work with a particular driver, such as the 800-by-600, 256-color, super-VGA driver that comes with Microsoft Windows. In practice, however, manufacturers continue to provide their own driver software.

XGA and XGA-2

IBM announced the PS/2 XGA Display Adapter/A on October 30, 1990, and the XGA-2 in September 1992. Both adapters are high-performance, 32-bit bus-master adapters for Micro Channel-based systems. These video subsystems, evolved from the VGA, provide greater resolution, more colors, and much better performance.

III

Input/Output Hardware

Combine fast VGA, more colors, higher resolution, a graphics coprocessor, and bus mastering, and you have XGA. Being a bus-master adapter means that the XGA can take control of the system as though it were the motherboard. In essence, a bus master is an adapter with its own processor that can execute operations independent of the motherboard.

The XGA was introduced as the default graphics-display platform with the Model 90 XP 486 and the Model 95 XP 486. In the desktop Model 90, the XGA is on the motherboard; in the Model 95 (a tower unit), it is located on a separate add-in board. This board—the XGA Display Adapter/A—also is available for other 386- and 486-based Micro Channel systems. The XGA adapter can be installed in any MCA systems that have 80386, 80386SX, 80386SLC, 486SLC2, 486SLC3, or 80486 processors, including PS/2 Models 53, 55, 57, 65, 70, and 80.

The XGA comes standard with 512K of graphics memory, which can be upgraded to 1M with an optional video-memory expansion.

Following are some of the XGA adapter's features:

■ 1,024 by 768 with 256 colors (16 colors with standard memory)

■ 640 by 480 with 256 colors

■ DOS XGA adapter interface provides 8514/A compatibility

■ Integrates a 16-bit compatible VGA

■ Optimized for windowing operating systems

■ Includes device drivers for DOS, OS/2, and Windows

In addition to all VGA modes, the XGA adapter offers several new modes of operation, which are listed in table 10.8.

Table 10.8	XGA Unique Modes of Operation	
Maximum Resolution	**Maximum Colors**	**Required VRAM**
1,024 × 768	256 colors	1M
1,024 × 768	16 colors	512K
640 × 480	65,536 colors	1M
1,024 × 768	64 gray shades	1M
1,024 × 768	16 gray shades	512K
640 × 480	64 gray shades	512K

The 65,536-color mode provides almost photographic output. The 16-bit pixel is laid out as 5 bits of red, 6 bits of green, and 5 bits of blue (5-6-5)—in other words, 32 shades of blue, 64 shades of green, and 32 shades of blue. (The eye notices more variations in green than in red or blue.) One major drawback of the current XGA implementation is the interlacing that occurs in the higher-resolution modes. With interlacing, you can use a less expensive monitor, but the display updates more slowly, resulting in a slight flicker.

The XGA-2 improves on the performance of the XGA in several ways. To begin with, the XGA-2 increases the number of colors supported at 1,024-by-768 resolution to 64K. In addition, because of the circuitry of the XGA-2, it can process data at twice the speed of the XGA. The XGA-2 also works in noninterlaced mode, so it produces less flicker than the XGA does.

Both the XGA and XGA-2 support all existing VGA and 8514/A video modes. A large number of popular applications have been developed to support the 8514/A high-resolution 1,024-by-768 mode. These applications are written to the 8514/A Adapter interface, which is a software interface between the application and the 8514/A hardware. The XGA's extended graphics function maintains compatibility at the same level. Because of the power of the XGA and XGA-2, current VGA or 8514/A applications run much faster.

Much of the speed of the XGA and XGA-2 also can be attributed to its video RAM (VRAM), a type of dual-ported RAM designed for graphics-display systems. This memory can be accessed by both the processor on the graphics adapter and the system CPU simultaneously, providing almost instant data transfer. The XGA VRAM is mapped into the system's address space. The VRAM normally is located in the top addresses of the 386's 4G address space. Because no other cards normally use this area, conflicts should be rare. The adapters also have an 8K ROM BIOS extension that must be mapped somewhere in segments C000 or D000. (The motherboard implementation of the XGA does not require its own ROM, because the motherboard BIOS contains all the necessary code.)

Table 10.9 summarizes the XGA modes.

Table 10.9 IBM Extended Graphics Array (XGA) Specifications					
Video Standard	**Number Resolution**	**Mode of Colors**	**BIOS Type**	**Character Modes**	**Character Format**
XGA					
(10/30/90)	360 x 400	16	Text	00/01h	40 x 25
	720 × 400	16	Text	02/03h	80 × 25
	320 × 200	4	APA	04/05h	40 × 25
	640 × 200	2	APA	06h	80 × 25
	720 × 400	16	Text	07h	80 × 25
	320 × 200	16	APA	0Dh	40 × 25
	640× 200	16	APA	0Eh	80 × 25
	640 × 350	4	APA	0Fh	80 × 25
	640 × 350	16	APA	10h	80 × 25
	640 × 480	2	APA	11h	80 × 30
	640 × 480	16	APA	12h	80 × 30
	320 × 200	256	APA	13h	40 × 25
	1,056 × 400	16	Text	14h	132 × 25
	1,056 × 400	16	Text	14h	132 × 43
	1,056 × 400	16	Text	14h	132 × 56
	1,056 × 400	16	Text	14h	132 × 60
	1,024 × 768	256	APA	H-0h	85 × 38
	640 × 480	65,536	APA	H-1h	80 × 34
	1,024 × 768	256	APA	H-2h	128 × 54
	1,024 × 768	256	APA	H-3h	146 × 51

APA = All points addressable (graphics)
Dbl = Double scan
Il = Interlaced

Video Memory

A video card relies on memory in drawing your screen. Often, you can select how much memory you want on your video card—for example, 256K, 512K, 1M, or 2M. Finding 256K on a VGA card is rare, however; most cards come with at least 512K, if not 1M. The 512K and 1M of memory does not speed your video card; rather, it enables your monitor to display more colors and/or higher resolutions. For 256 colors drawn from a palette of 256,000, you need at least 512K of video memory. At 1,024 by 768 pixels, you need at least 1M.

A 24-bit (or true-color) video card can display photographic images by using 16.7 million colors. If you spend a lot of time working with graphics, you may want to invest in a

Scan Frequency Vertical Box	Horizontal (Hz)	Scan (kHz)	Mode
9 × 16	70	31.5	Std
9 × 16	70	31.5	Std
8 × 8	70	31.5	Dbl
8 × 8	70	31.5	Dbl
9 × 1	70	31.5	Std
8 × 8	70	31.5	Dbl
8 × 8	70	31.5	Dbl
8 × 14	70	31.5	Std
8 × 14	70	31.5	Std
8 × 16	60	31.5	Std
8 × 16	60	31.5	Std
8 × 8	70	31.5	Dbl
8 × 16	70	31.5	Std
8 × 9	70	31.5	Std
8 × 8	70	31.5	Std
8 × 6	70	31.5	Std
12 × 20	43.48	35.52	II
8 × 14	60	31.5	Std
8 × 14	43.48	35.52	II
7 × 15	43.48	35.52	II

24-bit video card. In 1992, true-color cards cost as much as a decent PC. Today, you can buy one for well under $1,000.

Improving Video Speed

Many efforts have been made recently to improve the speed of video adapters, due to the complexity and sheer data of the high-resolution displays used by today's software. The improvements in video speed are occurring along three fronts:

- Processor
- RAM
- Bus

The combination of these three is reducing the video bottleneck caused by the demands of graphical user interface software, such as Microsoft Windows.

III

Input/Output Hardware

The Video Processor. Three types of processors, or chipsets, can be used in creating a video card. The chipset used is, for the most part, independent of which video specification (VGA, SVGA, or XGA) the adapter follows.

The oldest technology used in creating a video adapter is known as *frame-buffer technology*. In this scheme, the video card is responsible for displaying individual frames of an image. Each frame is maintained by the video card, but the computing necessary to create the frame comes from the CPU of your computer. This arrangement places a heavy burden on the CPU, which could be busy doing other program-related computing.

At the other end of the spectrum is a chip technology known as *coprocessing*. In this scheme, the video card includes its own processor, which performs all video-related computations. This arrangement frees the main CPU to perform other tasks. Short of integrating video functions directly into the CPU, this chipset provides the fastest overall system throughput.

Between these two arrangements is a middle ground: a fixed-function accelerator chip. In this scheme, used in many of the graphics accelerator boards on the market today, the circuitry on the video card does many of the more time-consuming video tasks (such as drawing lines, circles, and other objects), but the main CPU still directs the card by passing graphics-primitive commands from applications, such as an instruction to draw a rectangle of a given size and color.

The Video RAM. Historically, most video adapters have used regular dynamic RAM (DRAM) to store video images. This type of RAM, although inexpensive, is rather slow. The slowness can be attributed to the need to constantly refresh the information contained within the RAM, as well as to the fact that DRAM cannot be read at the same time it is being written.

Newer video cards, however, use specialized video RAM (VRAM). This type of memory is optimized for video use, achieving faster throughput because it can be read from and written to at the same time. Such an arrangement can lead to impressive speed improvements, but it also costs more than DRAM.

The Bus. Earlier in this chapter, you learned that certain video cards are designed for certain buses. For example, the VGA was designed to be used with an MCA bus, and the XGA and XGA-2 still are intended for use with the MCA. The bus system that you are using in your computer (ISA, EISA, or MCA) affects the speed at which your system processes video information. The ISA offers a 16-bit data path at speeds of 8.33 MHz. The EISA or MCA buses can process 32 bits of data at a time, but they also run at speeds up to 10 MHz. (Don't confuse the bus speed with the CPU speed. Even though the CPU currently runs at speeds up to 100 MHz, the bus still can handle only a limited degree of speed.)

One improvement on this frontier is the VESA local bus (VL-Bus) standard. The VL-Bus standard typically is an addition to an existing bus technology. For example, you may have an ISA system that also contains a VL-Bus slot. Even if it is used in an ISA system, the VL-Bus processes 32 bits of data at a time and does so at the full-rated speed of the CPU: up to 40 MHz. Thus, you can achieve blinding speed by using a well-implemented VL-Bus in your system.

In July 1992, Intel Corporation introduced Peripheral Component Interconnect (PCI) as a blueprint for directly connecting microprocessors and support circuitry; it then extended the design to a full expansion bus with Release 2 in 1993. Popularly termed a mezzanine bus, PCI 2 combines the speed of a local bus with microprocessor independence. PCI video cards, like VL-Bus video cards, can increase video performance dramatically. PCI video cards, by their design, are meant to be *plug-and-play*, meaning that they require little configuration.

VL-Bus and PCI have some important differences, as table 10.10 shows.

Table 10.10   Local Bus Specifications

Feature	VL-Bus	PCI
Theoretical maximum throughput	132Mps	132Mps
Actual throughput in burst mode (on a 33 MHz 486)	107Mps	76Mps
Slots	3 (typical)	3 (typical)
Plug-and-play support	No	Yes
Cost	Inexpensive	Moderate, trailing off over time
Ideal use	Desktop 486s	High-end desktops and servers

The Fastest Speed Possible. Fortunately, you can choose the best of each area—chipset, RAM, and bus—to achieve the fastest speed possible. The faster you want your card to perform, the more money you will need to spend; it is not unusual to find high-performance video cards that cost close to $1,000. This price does not include the cost of a new motherboard, if you want to implement VL-Bus.

The trick to choosing a video subsystem is making an early decision. As you research specifications for your entire system, you should pay attention to the video and make sure that it performs the way you want it to. The best speeds can be achieved by a VL-Bus card that uses a coprocessor and VRAM, running in a system at higher CPU speeds (40 MHz or greater). At this writing, you can get the best performance from a card that uses the Weitek Power9000 chipset (make sure that you get an implementation that uses the VL-Bus or PCI bus with VRAM).

Video Card Buying Criteria

One trend is to display higher-resolution images on larger and larger monitors. The growth of multimedia also has encouraged users to invest in 24-bit video cards for photographic-quality images. Both of these trends mean that you may want your video card to produce its 17 million hues at high resolution—at least 1,024-by-768 pixels.

III

Input/Output Hardware

Better cards can produce high color (or 65,000 hues) at even finer resolutions of 1,280 by 1,024 and 256 colors at very high resolutions of 1,600 by 1,280. To avoid bothersome flickering images, make sure that your card supports at least 72 Hz vertical refresh rates at all resolutions (76 Hz is even better). To accomplish such tasks, you'll require at least 2M of video RAM (VRAM), although 4M is preferable.

True-color cards now appear in both VL-Bus and PCI versions. If you have an older system, plenty of ISA and MCA 24-bit cards still are available.

Whichever card you buy, make sure that it also has on-board VGA support so that you don't need an extra VGA card. Drivers for your particular operating system should be included, as should a utility for switching resolutions. Look for extras that better cards now include: auto-installation and mode-switching utilities. A Microsoft Windows utility should be provided to ease switching resolutions and colors.

If you are shopping for a video card to provide super-VGA resolutions, you need special software drivers for each of your software programs to take advantage of this resolution; otherwise, your video card will act as a typical VGA card. For example, if you use the desktop publishing program Ventura Publisher Gold (GEM version), you need a software driver for your SVGA video card to display more of the page on-screen.

When you shop for a higher-resolution video card, ensure that it has drivers that support the software packages you own; otherwise, your software will operate in the typical VGA mode. Don't expect many drivers to be available. Drivers usually are provided for only a few of the following programs: AutoCAD, Autoshade, CADKEY, Framework, GEM Desktop, Lotus 1-2-3, Microsoft Windows, Microsoft Word, P-CAD, Symphony, Ventura Publisher, VersaCAD, WordPerfect, WordStar, OS/2 Presentation Manager, and Quattro Pro.

Video Cards for Multimedia

Multimedia is the result of several different media working together. Video is just one, albeit important, element to be considered. Topics we have not yet discussed include animation, full-motion video (playback and capture), still-images, and graphics processing. Still images and video provide dazzling slides, while animation and full-motion video breathe life into any presentation.

A computer can mathematically animate sequences between *keyframes*. A *keyframe* identifies specific points. A bouncing ball, for example, can have three *keyframes*: up; down; up. Using these frames as a reference point, the computer will create all the images in-between. This creates a smooth bouncing ball.

More people are realizing the benefits of 3D animation. Prices are dropping and technology, once available only to high-end workstations, is now available on PCs. One example is the 64-bit graphics accelerator offered by Matrox Graphics. What makes this graphics accelerator card unique is the on-board 3D rendering engine. This allows smooth, photo realistic 3D images to be performed on a PC level at speeds exceeding low-end workstations.

Video Output Devices. When video technology was first introduced it was based upon television. There is a difference between the signals a television uses versus the signals used by a computer. In the U.S., color TV standards were established in 1953 by the *National Television System Committee (NTSC)*. Some countries, like Japan, followed this standard; other countries in Europe developed more sophisticated standards (Phase Alternate Line, PAL; SEquential Couleur Avec Memoire, SECAM). Table 10.11 shows the differences between these TV standards.

Table 10.11 Television versus Computer Monitors				
Standard	**Yr. Est.**	**Country**	**Lines**	**Rate**
Television				
NTSC	1953 (color) 1941 (b&w)	U.S., Japan	525	60 Hz
PAL	1941	Europe*	625	50 Hz
SECAM	1962	France	625	25 Hz
Computer				
VGA			640 × 480**	72 Hz

* *England, Holland, West Germany*
** *VGA is based upon more lines and uses pixels (480) versus lines; "gen-locking" is used to lock pixels into lines and synchronize computers with TV standards.*

A video-output (or VGA-to-NTSC) adapter lets you show computer screens on a TV set or record them onto videotape for easy distribution. These products fall into two categories: those with genlocking (which lets the board synchronize signals from multiple video sources or video with PC graphics) and those without. Genlocking provides the signal stability needed to obtain adequate results when recording to tape, but is not necessary for simply using a video display.

VGA-to-NTSC converters come as both internal boards—such as Magni Systems' VGA Producer Pro—or external boxes that you can port along with your laptop-based presentation—such as VideoLogic's Mediator LC. These latter devices do not replace your VGA adapter, but instead connect to your video adapter via an external cable that works with any type of VGA card. In addition to VGA input and output ports, a video-output board has a video output interface for S-Video and composite video.

VGA-to-TV converters support the standard NTSC television format and may also support the European PAL format. The resolution shown on a TV set or recorded on videotape is often limited to straight VGA at 640-by-480 pixels. Such boards may contain an "anti-flicker" circuit to help stabilize the picture, which often suffers from a case of the jitters in VGA-to-TV products.

III

Input/Output Hardware

Still-Image Video Capture Cards. Like a Polaroid camera, you can capture individual screen images for later editing and playback. One device, the Presenter Video Capture unit, plugs into a PC's parallel port. The unit captures still images from NTSC video sources like camcorders or VCRs. Although image quality is limited by the input signal, the results are still good enough for presentations and desktop publishing applications.

The Presenter Video Capture works with 8-, 16-, and 24-bit VGA cards, and accepts video input from VHS, Super VHS, and Hi-8 devices. The test unit performed well with a variety of cards, VCRs, and cameras. As you might expect, though, Super VHS and Hi-8 video sources give better results, as do Super VGA modes with more than 256 colors.

The Presenter Video Capture is easy to set up—one cable connects it to your PC and another to your video source. No memory-resident drivers are necessary, but you'll need to run a bundled Windows utility to capture and store images. The software displays incoming video at about one frame per second; when you see an image that you like, clicking the Capture button freezes it on the screen for saving as a BMP or DIB file. You have a choice of 16.7 million colors, 256 colors, or 256 gray levels.

You may want to invest in image-processing applications that offer features like image editing, file conversion, screen capture, and graphics file management.

Desktop Video (DTV) Boards. You can also capture NTSC (TV) signals to your computer system for display or editing. When capturing video, think in terms of digital versus analog. The biggest convenience of analog TV signals is efficiency; it's a compact way to transmit video information through a low-bandwidth pipeline. The disadvantage is that while you can control how the video is displayed, you can't edit it.

Actually capturing and recording video from external sources and saving the files onto your PC requires special technology. What is needed is a video capture board, which is also referred to as a video digitizer, or video grabber.

One of the most common uses for analog video is with interactive CBT programs in which your application sends start, stop, and search commands to a laserdisk player that plays disks you've mastered. The software controls the player via an interface that also converts the laserdisk's NTSC signal into a VGA-compatible signal for display on your computer's monitor. These types of applications require NTSC-to-VGA conversion hardware that ranges from adapters such as the VideoBlaster, ProMovie Spectrum, and VideoSpigot for Windows to Super VideoWindows, DVA-4000, or Matrox's Illuminator family.

While a computer can display up to 16 million colors, the NTSC standard only allows for approximately 32,000 colors. Affordable video is the Achilles' heel of multimedia. The images are often jerky or less than full-screen. Why? Full-motion video, such as you see on TV requires 30 images or frames per second (fps).

The typical computer screen was designed to display mainly static images. The storing and retrieving of these images requires managing huge files. Consider this: a single, full-screen color image requires almost 2M of disk space; a one-second video would require 45M. Also, any video transmission you may want to capture for use on your PC must be converted from an analog NTSC signal to a digital signal your computer can use. On top of that, the video signal must be moved inside your computer at 10 times the speed of the conventional ISA bus structure. You not only need a superior video card and monitor, but also an excellent expansion bus, such as VL-Bus or PCI.

Considering the fact that full-motion video can consume massive quantities of disk space (0.5 seconds = 15Meg), it becomes apparent that compression is needed. Compression and decompression (codec) applies to both video and audio. Not only does a compressed file take up less space, it also performs better; there is simply less data to process. When you're ready to replay the video/audio, you simply decompress the file during playback.

There are two types of codecs: 1) hardware dependent codecs; and, 2) software (hardware independent) codecs. Hardware codecs are typically better, however they do require additional hardware. Software codes don't require hardware for compression or playback, but they typically don't deliver the same quality or compression ratio. Two of the major codec algorithms are:

- *JPEG (Joint Photographic Experts Group).* Originally developed for still images, it was discovered that JPEG could be compressed and decompressed at rates acceptable for nearly full-motion video (30 fps). JPEG still uses a series of still-images, which is easier for editing. Typically *lossy* (but can be *lossless*), JPEG eliminates redundant data for each individual image (*intraframe*). Compression efficiency is approximately 30:1 (20:1–40:1).

- *MPEG (Motion Pictures Expert Group).* Since MPEG can compress up to 200:1 at high-quality levels it results in better, faster videos that require less space. MPEG is an interframe compressor. Since MPEG stores only incremental changes it is not used during editing phases.

If you will be capturing, compressing, and playing video then you will need Microsoft Video for Windows (VFW). Codecs are provided along with VFW:

- *Cinepak (also referred to Compact Video Coded (CVC)).* Although Cinepak can take longer to compress it can produce better quality and higher compression than Indeo.

- *Indeo.* Can outperform Cinepak and is capable of real-time compression (Intel Smart Video board required for real-time compression).

- *Microsoft Video 1.* Developed by MediaVision (MotiVE). Renamed to MS Video 1. A DCT based post-processor; file is compressed after capture.

To play or record video on your multimedia PC (MPC), you'll need some extra hardware and software:

- Video system software, such as Apple's QuickTime for Windows or Microsoft's Video for Windows.

III

Input/Output Hardware

■ A compression/digitization video card that allows you to digitize and play large video files.

■ An NTSC-to-VGA adapter that combines TV signals with computer video signals for output to a VCR. Video can come from a variety of sources: TV; VCR; video camera; or, a laser disc player. When an animation file is recorded it can be saved in a variety of different formats:

   • AVI: Audio Video Interleave

   • FLI: 320-by-200 pixel animation file

   • FLC: an animation file of any size

These files can then be incorporated into a multimedia presentation using authoring software like Icon Author from AIMTECH, or you can include the animated files as OLE! objects to be used with MS-Word, Excel, Access, or other OLE! compliant applications.

When you're connecting video devices it is recommended you use the S-Video (S-VHS) connector whenever available. This cable provides the best signal since separate signals are used for color (chroma) and brightness (luma). Otherwise, you will have to use *composite video* which mixes *luma* and *chroma*. This results in a lower quality signal. The better your signal the better your video quality will be.

You can get devices that just display NTSC signals on your computer. Soon, you won't know if you are using a computer screen or a television. Digital video, in screen-filling, full-motion color, has arrived on desktop platforms with titles, playback boards and encoding equipment. Sigma Designs' $449 ReelMagic is a MPEG playback controller. It is a complete motion-video decoder board for PCs that can display 32,000 colors and achieves a resolution of 1,024 by 768. ReelMagic can play (but not record) MPEG video and VideoCD ("White Book") movies, with CD-quality audio. Using OLE, Windows applications can call MPEG movies from within documents and business presentations. Soon, MPEG movie clip libraries will be the next form of clip art on CD-ROM.

Adapter and Display Troubleshooting

Solving most graphics adapter and monitor problems is fairly simple, although costly, because replacing the adapter or display is the usual procedure. A defective or dysfunctional adapter or display usually is replaced as a single unit, rather than repaired. Most of today's cards cost more to service than to replace, and the documentation required to service the adapters or displays properly is not always available. You cannot get schematic diagrams, parts lists, wiring diagrams, and so on for most of the adapters or monitors. Many adapters now are constructed with surface-mount technology that requires a substantial investment in a rework station before you can remove and replace these components by hand. You cannot use a $25 pencil-type soldering iron on these boards!

Servicing monitors is slightly different. Although a display often is replaced as a whole unit, many displays are too expensive to simply replace. Your best bet is to contact the company from which you purchased the display. If, for example, your NEC Multisync display goes out, a swap with another monitor can confirm that the display is the problem. After you narrow the problem to the display, call NEC for the location of the nearest factory repair depot. Third-party service companies can repair most displays; their prices often are much lower than "factory" service.

You usually cannot repair a display yourself. First, opening the case of a color display exposes you to as much as 35,000 volts of electricity, and if you don't follow recommended safety precautions, you easily can electrocute yourself. Second, the required documentation is not always available. Without schematic diagrams, board layouts, parts lists, or other documentation, even an experienced service technician may not be able to properly diagnose and repair the display.

> **Caution**
>
> You should not attempt to repair a display yourself. Touching the wrong item can be fatal. The display circuits sometimes hold extremely high voltages for hours, days, or even weeks after the power is shut off. A qualified service person should discharge the tube and power capacitors before proceeding.

For most displays, you are limited to making simple adjustments. For color displays, the adjustments can be quite formidable if you lack experience. Even factory service technicians often lack proper documentation and service information for newer models; they usually exchange your unit for another and repair the defective one later. Never buy a display for which no local factory repair depot is available.

If you have a problem with a display or adapter, it pays to call the manufacturer; the manufacturer may know about the problem and make repairs available, as occurred with the IBM 8513 display. Large numbers of the IBM 8513 color displays were manufactured with components whose values change over time and may exhibit text or graphics out of focus. This problem haunted the author's IBM 8513. Opening the monitor and adjusting the focus helped for a while, but the display became fuzzy again. The author discovered that IBM replaces these displays at no cost when focusing is a problem. If you have a fuzzy 8513 display, you should contact IBM to see whether your display qualifies for a free replacement.

You can call IBM at (800) IBM-SERV or contact an IBM-authorized dealer for assistance. This particular problem is covered under Engineering Change Announcement (ECA) 017.

Summary

This chapter discussed and examined the video portion of the original PC and its descendants. Monitor technologies and buying criteria were discussed. Video cards and standards were discussed, including techniques used to provide more graphics speed. Lastly, multimedia-related video cards were discussed, including NTSC-to-VGA, still-image capture, and video-in-window adapters and techniques.

III

Input/Output Hardware

Chapter 11

Communications and Networking

Most computer-to-computer connections occur through a serial port, a parallel port, or a network adapter. In this chapter, you explore ways to connect your PC to other computers. Such connections enable you to transfer and share files, send electronic mail, access software on other computers, and generally make two or more computers behave as a team.

Using Communications Ports and Devices

The basic communications ports in any PC system are the serial and parallel ports. The serial ports are used primarily for devices that must communicate bidirectionally with the system; such devices include modems, mice, scanners, digitizers, or any other device that "talks to" and receives information from the PC.

Parallel ports are used primarily for printers and operate normally as one-way ports, although sometimes they can be used bidirectionally. Several companies also manufacture communications programs that perform high-speed transfers between PC systems using serial or parallel ports. Several products currently on the market make untraditional use of the parallel port. You can purchase network adapters, floppy disk drives, or tape backup units that use the parallel port, for example.

Serial Ports

The asynchronous serial interface is the primary system-to-system communications device. *Asynchronous* means that no synchronization or clocking signal is present, so characters may be sent with any arbitrary time spacing, as when a typist is providing the data.

Each character is framed by a standard start and stop signal. A single 0 bit, called the *start bit*, precedes each character to tell the receiving system that the next eight bits constitute a byte of data. One or two stop bits follow the character to signal that the character has been sent. At the receiving end of the communication, characters are recognized by the start and stop signals instead of being recognized by the timing of their arrival. The asynchronous interface is character-oriented and has about 20 percent overhead for the extra information needed to identify each character.

Serial refers to data sent over one wire, with each bit lining up in a series as the bits are sent. This type of communication is used over the phone system, because this system provides one wire for data in each direction. Add-on serial ports for the PC are available from many manufacturers. You usually can find these ports on one of the available multifunction boards or on a board with at least a parallel port. Figure 11.1 shows the standard 9-pin AT-style serial port, and figure 11.2 shows the more conventional 25-pin version.

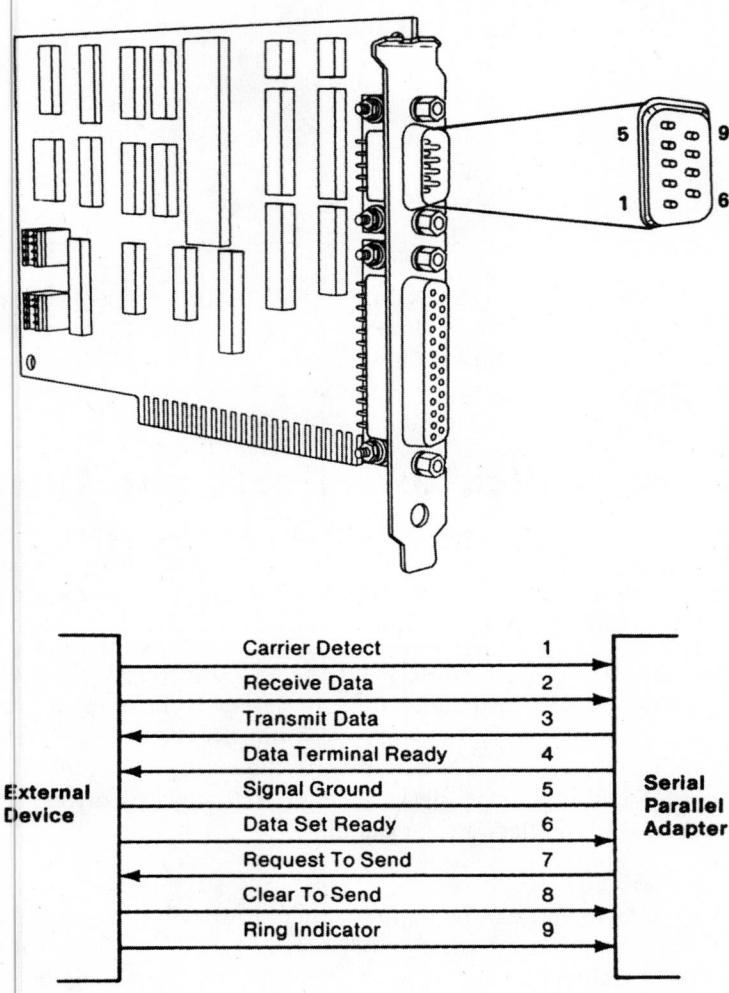

	Carrier Detect	1	
	Receive Data	2	
	Transmit Data	3	
	Data Terminal Ready	4	
External Device	Signal Ground	5	Serial Parallel Adapter
	Data Set Ready	6	
	Request To Send	7	
	Clear To Send	8	
	Ring Indicator	9	

Fig. 11.1
AT-style 9-pin serial-port connector specifications.

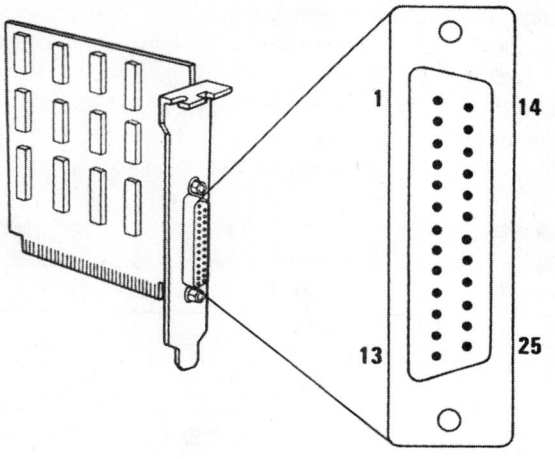

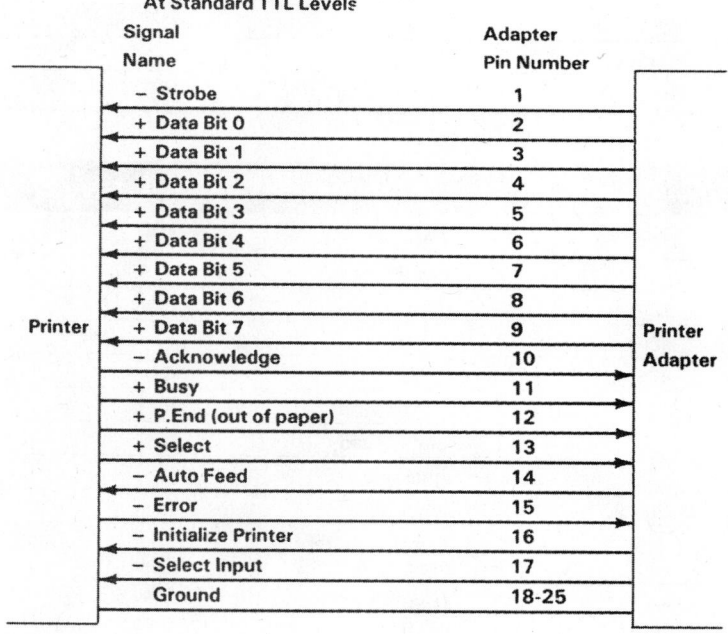

At Standard TTL Levels

	Signal Name	Adapter Pin Number	
	− Strobe	1	
	+ Data Bit 0	2	
	+ Data Bit 1	3	
	+ Data Bit 2	4	
	+ Data Bit 3	5	
	+ Data Bit 4	6	
	+ Data Bit 5	7	
	+ Data Bit 6	8	
Printer	+ Data Bit 7	9	Printer
	− Acknowledge	10	Adapter
	+ Busy	11	
	+ P.End (out of paper)	12	
	+ Select	13	
	− Auto Feed	14	
	− Error	15	
	− Initialize Printer	16	
	− Select Input	17	
	Ground	18-25	

Fig. 11.2
Standard 25-pin serial-port connector specifications.

Serial ports may connect to a variety of devices such as modems, plotters, printers, other computers, bar code readers, scales, and device control circuits. Basically, anything that needs a two-way connection to the PC uses the industry-standard Reference Standard number 232 revision c (RS-232c) serial port. This device enables data transfer between otherwise incompatible devices. Tables 11.1, 11.2, and 11.3 show the pinouts of the 9-pin (AT-style), 25-pin, and 9-pin-to-25-pin serial connectors.

Table 11.1   9-Pin (AT) Serial Port Connector

Pin	Signal	Description	I/O
1	CD	Carrier detect	In
2	RD	Receive data	In
3	TD	Transmit data	Out
4	DTR	Data terminal ready	Out
5	SG	Signal ground	—
6	DSR	Data set ready	In
7	RTS	Request to send	Out
8	CTS	Clear to send	In
9	RI	Ring indicator	In

Table 11.2   25-Pin (PC, XT, and PS/2) Serial Port Connector

Pin	Signal	Description	I/O
1	—	Chassis ground	—
2	TD	Transmit data	Out
3	RD	Receive data	In
4	RTS	Request to send	Out
5	CTS	Clear to send	In
6	DSR	Data set ready	In
7	SG	Signal ground	—
8	CD	Carrier detect	In
9	—	+Transmit current loop return	Out
11	—	−Transmit current loop data	Out
18	—	+Receive current loop data	In
20	DTR	Data terminal ready	Out
22	RI	Ring indicator	In
25	—	−Receive current loop return	In

Pins 9, 11, 18, and 25 are used for a Current Loop interface only. Current Loop is not supported on the AT Serial/Parallel Adapter or PS/2 systems.

Table 11.3	9-Pin to 25-Pin Serial Cable Adapter Connections		
9-Pin	**25-Pin**	**Signal**	**Description**
1	8	CD	Carrier detect
2	3	RD	Receive data
3	2	TD	Transmit data
4	20	DTR	Data terminal ready
5	7	SG	Signal ground
6	6	DSR	Data set ready
7	4	RTS	Request to send
8	5	CTS	Clear to send
9	22	RI	Ring indicator

UART Chips. The heart of any serial port is the Universal Asynchronous Receiver/Transmitter (UART) chip. This chip competely controls breaking the native parallel data within the PC into serial format, and later converting serial data back into the parallel format.

There are several types of UART chips on the market. The original PC and XT used the 8250 UART, which still is used in many low-price serial cards on the market. In the PC/AT (or other systems based on at least an 80286), the 16450 UART is used. The only difference between these chips is their suitability for high-speed communications. The 16450 is better suited for high-speed communications than the 8250; otherwise, both chips appear identical to most software.

The 16550 UART was the first serial chip used in the PS/2 line. This chip could function as the earlier 16450 and 8250 chips, but it also included a 16-byte buffer that aided in faster communications. Unfortunately, the 16550 also had a few bugs, particularly in the buffer area. These bugs were corrected with the release of the 16550A UART, which is used in all high-performance serial ports.

Because the 16550A is a faster, more reliable chip than its predecessors, it is best to look for serial ports that use it. If you are in doubt about which chip you have in your system, you can use the Microsoft MSD program (provided with Windows or DOS 6) to determine the type of UART you have.

Most UART chips used by IBM are made by National Semiconductor. You also can identify the chips by looking for the largest chip on the serial port card and reading the numbers on that chip. Usually the chips are socketed, and replacing only the chip may be possible. Table 11.4 provides a complete list of UART chips that may be in your system.

III

Input/Output Hardware

Note

The interrupt bug referred to in table 11.4 is a spurious interrupt generated by the 8250 at the end of an access. The ROM BIOS code in the PC and XT has been written to work around this bug. If a chip without the bug is installed, random lockups may occur. The 16450 or 16550(A) chips do not have the interrupt bug, and the AT ROM BIOS was written without any of the bug workarounds in PC or XT systems.

Table 11.4   UART Chips in PC or AT Systems

Chip	Description
8250	IBM used this original chip in the PC serial port card. The chip has several bugs, none of which is serious. The PC and XT ROM BIOS are written to anticipate at least one of the bugs. This chip was replaced by the 8250B.
8250A	Do not use the second version of the 8250 in any system. This upgraded chip fixes several bugs in the 8250, including one in the interrupt enable register, but because the PC and XT ROM BIOS expect the bug, this chip does not work properly with those systems. The 8250A should work in an AT system that does not expect the bug, but does not work adequately at 9600 bps.
8250B	The last version of the 8250 fixes bugs from the previous two versions. The interrupt enable bug in the original 8250, expected by the PC and XT ROM BIOS software, has been put back into this chip, making the 8250B the most desirable chip for any non-AT serial port application. The 8250B chip may work in an AT under DOS, but does not run properly at 9600 bps.
16450	IBM selected the higher-speed version of the 8250 for the AT. Because this chip has fixed the interrupt enable bug mentioned earlier, the 16450 does not operate properly in many PC or XT systems because they expect this bug to be present. OS/2 requires this chip as a minimum, or the serial ports do not function properly. It also adds a scratch-pad register as the highest register. The 16450 is used primarily in AT systems because of its increase in throughput over the 8250B.
16550	This newer UART improves on the 16450. This chip cannot be used in a FIFO (first in, first out) buffering mode because of problems with the design, but it does enable a programmer to use multiple DMA channels and thus increase throughput on an AT or higher class computer system. I highly recommend replacing the 16550 UART with the 16550A.
16550A	This chip is a faster 16450 with a built-in 16-character Transmit and Receive FIFO (first in, first out) buffer that works. It also allows multiple DMA channel access. You should install this chip in your AT system serial port cards if you do any serious communications at 9600 bps or higher. If your communications program makes use of the FIFO, which most do today, it can greatly increase communications speed and eliminate lost characters and data at the higher speeds.

Various manufacturers make versions of the 16550A; National Semiconductor was the first. Its full part number for the 40-pin DIP is NS16550AN or NS16550AFN. Make sure that the part you get is the 16550A, and not the older 16550. You can contact Fry's Electronics or Jameco Electronics to obtain the NS16550AN, for example.

Serial-Port Configuration

Each time a character is received by a serial port, it has to get the attention of the computer by raising an Interrupt Request Line (IRQ). Eight-bit ISA bus systems have eight of these lines, and systems with a 16-bit ISA bus have 16 lines. The 8259 interrupt controller chip usually handles these requests for attention. In a standard configuration, COM1 uses IRQ4, and COM2 uses IRQ3.

When a serial port is installed in a system, it must be configured to use specific I/O addresses (called ports), and interrupts (called IRQs for Interrupt ReQuest). The best plan is to follow the existing standards for how these devices should be set up. For configuring serial ports, you should use the addresses and interrupts indicated in table 11.5.

Table 11.5   Standard Serial I/O Port Addresses and Interrupts

System	COMx	Port	IRQ
All	COM1	3F8h	IRQ4
All	COM2	2F8h	IRQ3
ISA bus	COM3	3E8h	IRQ4
ISA bus	COM4	2E8h	IRQ3
ISA bus	COM3	3E0h	IRQ4
ISA bus	COM4	2E0h	IRQ3
ISA bus	COM3	338h	IRQ4
ISA bus	COM4	238h	IRQ3
MCA bus	COM3	3220h	IRQ3
MCA bus	COM4	3228h	IRQ3
MCA bus	COM5	4220h	IRQ3
MCA bus	COM6	4228h	IRQ3
MCA bus	COM7	5220h	IRQ3
MCA bus	COM8	5228h	IRQ3

A problem can occur when the ROM BIOS logs in these ports. If the Power-On Self-Test (POST) does not find a 3F8 serial port but does find a 2F8, then the 2F8 serial port is mistakenly assigned to COM1. The reserved IRQ line for COM1 is IRQ4, but this serial port of 2F8 is using COM2's address, which means that it should be using IRQ3 instead of IRQ4. If you are trying to use BASIC or DOS for COM1 operations, therefore, the serial port or modem cannot work.

Another problem is that IBM never built BIOS support in its original ISA bus systems for COM3 and COM4. Therefore, the DOS MODE command cannot work with serial ports above COM2 because DOS gets its I/O information from the BIOS, which finds out what is installed and where in your system during the POST. The POST in these older systems checks only for the first two installed ports. PS/2 systems have an improved BIOS that checks for as many as eight serial ports, although DOS is limited to handling only four of them.

To get around this problem, most communications software and some serial peripherals (such as mice) support higher COM ports by addressing them directly, rather than making DOS function calls. The communications program PROCOMM, for example, supports the additional ports even if your BIOS or DOS does not. Of course, if your system or software does not support these extra ports or you need to redirect data using the MODE command, trouble arises.

A couple of utilities enable you to append your COM port information to the BIOS, making the ports DOS-accessible. A program called Port Finder is one of the best, and is available in the "general hardware" data library of the IBMHW forum on CompuServe.

Port Finder activates the extra ports by giving the BIOS the addresses and providing utilities for swapping the addresses among the different ports. Address-swapping enables programs that don't support COM3 and COM4 to access them. Software that already directly addresses these additional ports usually is unaffected.

Extra ports, however, must use separate interrupts. If you are going to use two COM ports at one time, they should be on opposite interrupts. Using the standard port and interrupt configurations, the possibilities for simultaneous operation follow:

> COM1 (IRQ4) and COM2 (IRQ3)
>
> COM1 (IRQ4) and COM4 (IRQ3)
>
> COM2 (IRQ3) and COM3 (IRQ4)
>
> COM3 (IRQ4) and COM4 (IRQ3)

Divide your COM port inputs into these groups of two, pairing serial devices that will not be used simultaneously on the same interrupt, and devices that will be used at the same time on different interrupts. Note again that PS/2 Micro Channel Architecture systems are entirely exempt from these types of problems because they have a BIOS that looks for the additional ports, and because the MCA bus can share interrupts without conflicts.

To configure serial boards in ISA bus systems, you probably will have to set jumpers and switches. Because each board on the market is different, you always should consult the OEM manual for that particular card if you need to know how the card should or can be configured. IBM includes this information with each card's documentation. IBM also offers technical-reference options and adapters manuals as well as hardware-maintenance and service manuals, which also cover in detail all the jumper and switch settings for IBM adapter cards. Other manufacturers simply include with the card a manual that describes the card and includes the configuration information. The PS/2 MCA bus systems have an automatic or software-driven configuration that eliminates these configuration hassles.

Modem Standards

Bell Labs and the CCITT have set standards for modem protocols. Although the CCITT is actually a French term, it translates into English as the Consultative Committee on International Telephone and Telegraph. A *protocol* is a method by which two different entities agree to communicate. Bell Labs no longer sets new standards for modems, although several of its older standards still are used. Most modems built in the last few years conform to the CCITT standards. The CCITT is an international body of technical experts responsible for developing data communications standards for the world. The group falls under the organizational umbrella of the United Nations, and its members include representatives from major modem manufacturers, common carriers (such as AT&T), and governmental bodies.

The CCITT establishes communications standards and protocols in many areas, so one modem often adheres to several CCITT standards, depending on its various features and capabilities. Modem standards can be grouped into the following three areas:

- Modulation standards

    Bell 103
    Bell 212A
    CCITT V.21
    CCITT V.22bis
    CCITT V.29
    CCITT V.32
    CCITT V.32bis

- Error-correction standards

    CCITT V.42

- Data-compression standards

    V.42bis

Other standards have been developed by different companies, and not Bell Labs or the CCITT. These are sometimes called *proprietary standards*, even though most of these companies publish full specifications on their protocols so that other manufacturers can develop modems to work with them. The following list shows some of the proprietary standards that have become fairly popular:

- Modulation

    HST
    PEP
    DIS

- Error correction

    MNP 1-4
    Hayes V-series

- Data compression

    MNP 5
    CSP

III

Input/Output Hardware

Almost all modems today claim to be *Hayes compatible*, which does not refer to any communication protocol, but instead to the commands required to operate the modem. Because almost every modem uses the Hayes command set, this compatibility is a given and should not really affect your decisions about modems. Table 11.6 lists the command sets for the U.S. Robotics and Hayes brands of modems.

Table 11.6 U.S. Robotics and Hayes Modem Commands and Supported Features					
Command	**Modem Functions and Options**	**USR Dual**	**2400**	**Hayes 2400**	**1200**
&	See Extended Command Set	×			
%	See Extended Command Set	×			
A	Force Answer mode when modem has not received an incoming call	×	×	×	×
A/	Re-execute last command once	×	×	×	×
A>	Repeat last command continuously	×			
Any key	Terminate current connection attempt; exit Repeat mode	×	×		
AT	Attention: must precede all other commands except A/, A>, and +++	×	×	×	×
BN	Handshake options	×		×	
	BO CCITT answer sequence	×		×	
	B1 Bell answer tone	×		×	
Cn	Transmitter On/Off	×	×	×	×
	C0 Transmitter Off	×	×	×	×
	C1 Transmitter On-Default	×	×	×	×
Dn	Dial number n and go into originate mode. Use any of these options:	×	×	×	×
	P Pulse dial-Default	×	×	×	×
	T Touch-Tone dial	×	×	×	×
	, (Comma) Pause for 2 seconds	×	×	×	×
	; Return to command state after dialing	×	×	×	×
	"... Dial the letters that follow	×	×		
	! Flash switch-hook to transfer call	×	×	×	
	W Wait for 2nd dial tone (if X3 or higher is set)	×	×	×	
	@ Wait for an answer (if X3 or higher is set)	×	×	×	
	R Reverse frequencies	×	×	×	×
	S Dial stored number			×	
DL	Dial the last-dialed number	×			

Command	Modem Functions and Options		USR Dual	2400	Hayes 2400	1200
DSn	Dial number stored in NVRAM at position n		×			
En	Command mode local echo; not applicable after a connection has been made		×	×	×	×
	E0	Echo Off	×	×	×	×
	E1	Echo On	×	×	×	×
Fn	Local echo On/Off when a connection has been made		×	×	×	×
	F0	Echo On (Half duplex)	×	×	×	×
	F1	Echo Off (Full duplex)-Default	×	×	×	×
Hn	On/Off hook control		×	×	×	×
	H0	Hang up (go on hook)-Default	×	×	×	×
	H1	Go off hook	×	×	×	×
In	Inquiry		×	×	×	×
	I0	Return product code	×	×	×	×
	I1	Return memory (ROM) checksum	×	×	×	×
	I2	Run memory (RAM) test	×	×	×	
	I3	Return call duration/real time	×	×		
	I4	Return current modem settings	×	×		
	I5	Return NVRAM settings	×			
	I6	Return link diagnostics	×			
	I7	Return product configuration	×			
Kn	Modem clock operation		×			
	K0	ATI3 displays call duration-Default	×			
	K1	ATI3 displays real time; set with ATI3=HH:MM:SSK1	×			
Ln	Loudness of speaker volume;				×	
	L0	Low			×	
	L1	Low			×	
	L2	Medium			×	
	L3	High			×	
Mn	Monitor (speaker) control		×	×	×	×
	M0	Speaker always Off	×	×	×	×
	M1	Speaker On until carrier is established-Default	×	×	×	×
	M2	Speaker always On	×	×	×	×
	M3	Speaker On after last digit dialed, Off at carrier detect	×	×	×	×
O	Return on-line after command execution		×	×	×	×
	O0	Return on-line, normal	×	×	×	×
	O1	Return on-line, retrain	×	×	×	×

(continues)

Table 11.6   Continued

Command	Modem Functions and Options	USR Dual	2400	Hayes 2400	1200
P	Pulse dial	×	×	×	×
Qn	Result codes display	×	×	×	×
	Q0 Result codes displayed	×	×	×	×
	Q1 Result codes suppressed (quiet mode)	×	×	×	×
	Q2 Quiet in answer mode only	×			
Sr=n	Set register commands: r is any S-register; n must be a decimal number between 0 and 255.	×	×	×	×
Sr.b=n	Set bit .b of register r to n (0/Off or 1/On)	×			
Sr?	Query register r	×	×	×	×
T	Tone dial	×	×	×	×
Vn	Verbal/Numeric result codes	×	×	×	×
	V0 Numeric mode	×	×	×	×
	V1 Verbal mode	×	×	×	×
Xn	Result code options	×	×	×	×
Yn	Long space disconnect			×	
	Y0 Numeric mode			×	
	Y1 Enabled; disconnects after 1.5-second break			×	
Z	Software reset	×	×	×	×
+++	Escape code sequence, preceded and followed by at least one second of no data transmission	×	×		
/(Slash)	Pause for 125 msec	×			
>	Repeat command continuously or up to 10 dial attempts; cancel by pressing any key	×	×		
$	Online Help - Basic command summary	×	×		
&$	Online Help - Ampersand command summary	×			
%$	Online Help - Percent command summary	×			
D$	Online Help - Dial command summary	×	×		
S$	Online Help - S-register summary	×	×		
<Ctrl>-S	Stop/restart display of HELP screens			×	
<Ctrl>-C	Cancel display HELP screens			×	
<Ctrl>-K	Cancel display HELP screens			×	
Extended Command Set					
&An	ARQ result codes 14-17, 19	×			
	&A0 Supppress ARQ result codes	×			
	&A1 Display ARQ result codes-Default	×			
	&A2 Display HST and V.32 result codes	×			
	&A3 Display protocol result codes	×			

Command	Modem Functions and Options	USR Dual	2400	Hayes 2400	1200
Extended Command Set					
&Bn	Data Rate, terminal-to-modem (DTE/DCE)	×			
	&B0 DTE rate follows connection rate-Default	×			
	&B1 Fixed DTE rate	×			
	&B2 Fixed DTE rate in ARQ mode; variable DTE rate in non-ARQ mode	×			
&Cn	Carrier Detect (CD) operations	×		×	
	&C0 CD override	×		×	
	&C1 Normal CD operations	×		×	
&Dn	Data Terminal Ready (DTR) operations	×		×	
	&D0 DTR override	×		×	
	&D1 DTR Off; goes to command state			×	
	&D2 DTR Off; goes to command state and on hook	×		×	
	&D3 DTR Off; resets modem			×	
&F	Load factory settings into RAM	×		×	
&Gn	Guard tone	×		×	
	&G0 No guard tone; U.S., Canada-Default	×		×	
	&G1 Guard tone; some European countries	×		×	
	&G2 Guard tone; U.K., requires B0	×		×	
&Hn	Transmit Data flow control	×			
	&H0 Flow control disabled-Default	×			
	&H1 Hardware (CTS) flow control	×			
	&H2 Software (XON/XOFF) flow control	×			
	&H3 Hardware and software control	×			
&In	Received Data software flow control	×			
	&I0 Flow control disabled-Default	×			
	&I1 XON/XOFF to local modem and remote computer	×			
	&I2 XON/XOFF to local modem only	×			
	&I3 Host mode, Hewlett-Packard protocol	×			
	&I4 Terminal mode, Hewlett-Packard protocol	×			
	&I5 ARQ mode-same as &I2; non-ARQ mode; look for incoming XON/XOFF	×			
&Jn	Telephone Jack selection			×	
	&J0 RJ-11/RJ-41S/RJ-45S			×	
	&J1 RJ-12/RJ-13			×	

(continues)

III

Input/Output Hardware

Table 11.6   Continued

Command	Modem Functions and Options	USR Dual	2400	Hayes 2400	1200
Extended Command Set					
&Kn	Data compression	×			
	&K0 Disabled	×			
	&K1 Auto enable/disable-Default	×			
	&K2 Enabled	×			
	&K3 V.42bis only	×			
&Ln	Normal/Leased line operation	×		×	
	&L0 Normal phone line-Default	×		×	
	&L1 Leased line	×		×	
&Mn	Error Control/Synchronous Options	×		×	
	&M0 Normal mode, no error control	×		×	
	&M1 Synch mode	×		×	
	&M2 Synch mode 2 - stored number dialing			×	
	&M3 Synch mode 3 - manual dialing	×			
	&M4 Normal/ARQ mode-Normal if ARQ connection cannot be made-Default	×			
	&M5 ARQ mode-hang up if ARQ connection cannot be made	×			
&Nn	Data Rate, data link (DCE/DCE)	×			
	&N0 Normal link operations-Default	×			
	&N1 300 bps	×			
	&N2 1200 bps	×			
	&N3 2400 bps	×			
	&N4 4800 bps	×			
	&N5 7200 bps	×			
	&N6 9600 bps	×			
	&N7 12K bps	×			
	&N8 14.4K bps	×			
&Pn	Pulse dial make/break ratio	×		×	
	&P0 North America-Default	×		×	
	&P1 British Commonwealth	×		×	
&Rn	Received Data hardware (RTS) flow control	×		×	
	&R0 CTS tracks RTS	×		×	
	&R1 Ignore RTS-Default	×		×	
	&R2 Pass received data on RTS high; used Pass received data on RTS high; used	×			

Command	Modem Functions and Options	USR Dual 2400	Hayes 2400 1200
Extended Command Set			
&Sn	Data Set Ready (DSR) override	×	×
	&S0 DSR override (always On-Default)	×	×
	&S1 Modem controls DSR	×	×
	&S2 Pulsed DSR; CTS follows CD	×	
	&S3 Pulsed DSR	×	
&Tn	Modem Testing	×	×
	&T0 End testing	×	×
	&T1 Analog loopback	×	×
	&T2 Reserved	×	
	&T3 Digital loopback	×	×
	&T4 Grant remote digital loopback	×	×
	&T5 Deny remote digital loopback	×	×
	&T6 Initiate remote digital loopback	×	×
	&T7 Remote digital loopback with self test	×	×
	&T8 Analog loopback with self test	×	×
&W	Write current settings to NVRAM	×	×
&×n	Synchronous timing source	×	×
	&X0 Modem's transmit clock-Default	×	×
	&X1 Terminal equipment	×	×
	&X2 Modem's receiver clock	×	×
&Yn	Break handling. Destructive breaks clear the buffer; expedited breaks are sent immediately to remote system.	×	
	&Y0 Destructive, but don't send break	×	
	&Y1 Destructive, expedited-Default	×	
	&Y2 Nondestructive, expedited	×	
	&Y3 Nondestructive, unexpedited	×	
&Zn=L	Store last-dialed phone number in NVRAM at position n	×	
&Zn=s	Write phone number(s) to NVRAM at position n (0-3); 36 characters maximum	×	
&Zn?	Display phone number in NVRAM at position n (n=0-3)	×	×
%Rn	Remote access to Rack Controller Unit (RCU)	×	
	%R0 Disabled	×	
	%R1 Enabled	×	
%T	Enable Touch-Tone recognition	×	

(continues)

III

Input/Output Hardware

Command	Modem Functions and Options	USR Dual	2400	Hayes 2400	1200
Table 11.6 Continued					
Modem S-Register Functions and Defaults					
SO	Number of rings before automatic answering when DIP switch 5 is UP. Default = 1. SO = 0 disables Auto Answer, equivalent to DIP switch 5 Down	SW5	SW5	0	SW5
S1	Counts and stores number of rings from incoming call	0	0	0	0
S2	Define escape code character. Default = +.	43	43	43	43
S3	Define ASCII carriage return	13	13	13	13
S4	Define ASCII line feed	10	10	10	10
S5	Define ASCII Backspace	8	8	8	8
S6	Number of seconds modem waits before dialing	2	2	2	2
S7	Number of seconds modem waits for a carrier	60	30	30	30
S8	Duration (sec) for pause (,) option in Dial command and pause between command reexecutions for Repeat (>) command	2	2	2	2
S9	Duration (.1 sec units) of remote carrier signal before recognition	6	6	6	6
S10	Duration (.1 sec units) modem waits after loss of carrier before hanging up	7	7	7	7
S11	Duration and spacing (ms) of dialed Touch-Tones	70	70	70	70
S12	Guard time (in .02 sec units) for escape code sequence	50	50	50	50
S13	Bit-mapped register:	0			
	1 Reset when DTR drops				
	2 Auto answer in originate mode				
	4 Disable result code pause				
	8 DS0 on DTR low-to-high				
	16 DS0 on power up, ATZ				
	32 Disable HST modulation				
	64 Disable MNP Level 3				
	128 Watchdog hardware reset				
S15	Bit-mapped register:	0			
	1 Disable high-frequency equalization				
	2 Disable on-line fallback				
	4 Force 300-bps back channel				
	8 Set non-ARQ transmit buffer to 128 bytes				

Command	Modem Functions and Options	USR Dual	2400	Hayes 2400	1200
Modem S-Register Functions and Defaults					
	16 Disable MNP Level 4				
	32 Set Del as Backspace key				
	64 Unusual MNP incompatibilty				
	128 Custom applications only				
S16	Bit-mapped register:	0	0	0	
	1 Analog loopback				
	2 Dial test				
	4 Test pattern				
	8 Initiate remote digital loopback				
	16 Reserved				
	32 Reserved				
	64 Reserved				
	128 Reserved				
S18	&Tn Test timer, disabled when set to 0	0		0	
S19	Set inactivity timer in minutes	0			
S21	Length of Break, DCE to DTE, in 10ms units	10		0	
S22	Define ASCII XON	17		17	
S23	Define ASCII XOFF	19		19	
S24	Duration (20ms units) of pulsed DSR when modem is set to &S2 or &S3	150			
S25	Delay to DTR	5			
S26	Duration (10ms units) of delay between RTS and CTS, synchronous mode	1		1	
S27	Bit-mapped register:	0			
	1 Enable V.21 modulation, 300 bps				
	2 Enable unencoded V.32 modulation				
	4 Disable V.32 modulation				
	8 Disable 2100 Hz answer tone				
	16 Disable MNP handshake				
	32 Disable V.42 Detect phase				
	64 Reserved				
	128 Unusual software incompatibility				
S28	Duration (.1 sec units) of V.21/V.23 handshake delay	8			

(continues)

III

Input/Output Hardware

		USR		Hayes	
Command	**Modem Functions and Options**	**Dual**	**2400**	**2400**	**1200**
Modem S-Register Functions and Defaults					
S32	Voice/Data switch options:	1			
	0 Disabled				
	1 Go off hook in originate mode				
	2 Go off hook in answer mode				
	3 Redial last-dialed number				
	4 Dial number stored at position 0				
	5 Auto answer toggle On/Off				
	6 Reset modem				
	7 Initiate remote digital loopback				
S34	Bit-mapped register:	0			
	1 Disable V.32bis				
	2 Disable enhanced V.32 mode				
	4 Disable quick V.32 retrain				
	8 Enable V.23 modulation				
	16 Change MR LED to DSR				
	32 Enable MI/MIC				
	64 Reserved				
	128 Reserved				
S38	Duration (sec) before disconnect when DTR drops during an ARQ call	0			

ARQ = Automatic repeat request
ASCII = American Standard Code for Information Interchange
BPS = Bits per second
CCITT = Consultative Committee for International Telephone and Telegraph
CD = Carrier detect
CRC = Cyclic redundancy check
DCE = Data communications equipment
DTE = Data terminal equipment
EIA = Electronic Industries Association
HDLC = High-level data link control
HST = High-speed technology
Hz = Hertz
LAPM = Link access procedure for modems
MI/MIC = Mode indicate/Mode indicate common
MNP = Microcom networking protocol
NVRAM = Non-volatile memory
RAM = Random-access memory
ROM = Read-only memory
SDLC = Synchronous Data Link Control
MR = Modem ready
LED = Light-emitting diode
DTR = Data terminal ready
CTS = Clear to send
RTS = Ready to send
DSR = Data Set Ready

Modulation Standards. Modems start with *modulation*, which is the electronic signaling method used by the modem (from modulator to demodulator). Modems must use the same modulation method to understand each other. Each data rate uses a different modulation method, and sometimes more than one method exists for a particular rate.

The three most popular modulation methods are frequency-shift keying (FSK), phase-shift keying (PSK), and quadrature-amplitude modulation (QAM). FSK is a form of frequency modulation, otherwise known as FM. By causing and monitoring frequency changes in a signal sent over the phone line, two modems can send information. PSK is a form of phase modulation, in which the timing of the carrier signal wave is altered and the frequency stays the same. QAM is a modulation technique that combines phase changes with signal-amplitude variations, resulting in a signal that can carry more information than the other methods.

Baud versus Bits Per Second (bps). Baud rate and the bit rate often are confused in discussions about modems. *Baud rate* is the rate at which a signal between two devices changes in one second. If a signal between two modems can change frequency or phase at a rate of 300 times per second, for example, that device is said to communicate at 300 baud. Sometimes a single modulation change is used to carry a single bit. In that case, 300 baud also equals 300 bits per second (bps). If the modem could signal two bit values for each signal change, the bit-per-second rate would be twice the baud rate, or 600 bps at 300 baud. Most modems transmit several bits per baud, so that the actual baud rate is much slower than the bit-per-second rate. In fact, people usually use the term *baud* incorrectly. We normally are not interested in the raw baud rate, but in the bit-per-second rate, which is the true gauge of communications speed.

Bell 103. Bell 103 is a U.S. and Canadian 300-bps modulation standard. It uses frequency-shift-keying (FSK) modulation at 300 baud to transmit one bit per baud. Most higher-speed modems will communicate using this protocol, even though it is largely obsolete.

Bell 212A. Bell 212A is the U.S. and Canadian 1200-bps modulation standard. It uses differential phase-shift keying (DPSK) at 600 baud to transmit two bits per baud.

V.21. V.21 is an international data-transmission standard for 300-bps communications similar to Bell 103. Because of some differences in the frequencies used, Bell 103 modems are not compatible with V.21 modems. This standard is used primarily outside the United States.

V.22. V.22 is an international 1200-bps data-transmission standard. This standard is similar to the Bell 212A standard, but is incompatible in some areas, especially in answering a call. This standard was used primarily outside the United States.

V.22bis. V.22bis is a data-transmission standard for 2400-bps communications. *Bis* is Latin for *second*, indicating that this data transmission is an improvement to or follows V.22. This data transmission is an international standard for 2400 bps and is used inside and outside the United States. V.22bis uses quadrature-amplitude modulation (QAM) at 600 baud and transmits four bits per baud to achieve 2400 bps.

III

Input/Output Hardware

V.23. V.23 is a split data-transmission standard, operating at 1200 bps in one direction and 75 bps in the reverse direction. Therefore, the modem is only *pseudo-full-duplex*, meaning that it can transmit data in both directions simultaneously, but not at the maximum data rate. This standard was developed to lower the cost of 1200-bps modem technology, which was expensive in the early 1980s. This standard was used primarily in Europe.

V.29. V.29 is a data-transmission standard at 9600 bps, which defines a half duplex (one-way) modulation technique. This standard generally is used in Group III facsimile (fax) transmissions, and only rarely in modems. Because V.29 is a half-duplex method, it is substantially easier to implement this high-speed standard than to implement a high-speed full-duplex standard. As a modem standard, V.29 has not been fully defined, so V.29 modems of different brands seldom can communicate with each other. This does not affect fax machines, which have a fully defined standard.

V.32. V.32 is a full-duplex (two-way) data transmission standard at 9600 bps. It is a full modem standard, and also includes forward error-correcting and negotiation standards. V.32 uses TCQAM (trellis coded quadrature amplitude modulation) at 2400 baud to transmit 4 bits per baud, resulting in the 9600-bps transmission speed. The trellis coding is a special forward error-correction technique that creates an additional bit for each packet of 4. This extra check bit is used to enable on-the-fly error correction to take place at the other end. It also greatly increases the resistance of V.32 to noise on the line. In the past, V.32 has been expensive to implement because the technology it requires is complex. Because a one-way, 9600-bps stream uses almost the entire bandwidth of the phone line, V.32 modems implement *echo cancellation*, meaning that they cancel out the overlapping signal that their own modems transmit and just listen to the other modem's signal. This procedure is complicated and costly. Recent advances in lower-cost chipsets make these modems inexpensive, so they are becoming the *de facto* 9600-bps standard.

V.32bis. V.32bis is a relatively new 14,400-bps extension to V.32. This protocol uses TCQAM modulation at 2400 baud to transmit 6 bits per baud, for an effective rate of 14,400 bits per second. The trellis coding makes the connection more reliable. This protocol is also a full-duplex modulation protocol, with fallback to V.32 if the phone line is impaired. Although this high-speed standard is newly developed, it is rapidly becoming the communications standard for dial-up lines because of its excellent performance and resistance to noise. I recommend the V.32bis-type modem.

V.32fast. V.32fast is a new standard being proposed to the CCITT. V.32fast will be an extension to V.32 and V.32bis, but will offer a transmission speed of 28,800 bits per second. This standard, when approved, probably will be as advanced as modem communications ever gets. Looming on the horizon is that the phone system eventually will be digital. All further development on analog transmission schemes will end, and new digital modems will be developed. V.32fast will be the best and last of the analog protocols when it debuts.

Error-Correction Protocols. *Error correction* refers to a capability that some modems have to identify errors during a transmission, and to automatically resend data that appears to have been damaged in transit. For error correction to work, both modems must adhere to the same correction standard. Fortunately, most modem manufacturers follow the same error-correction standards.

V.42. V.42 is an error-correction protocol, with fallback to MNP 4. MNP stands for Microcom Networking Protocol (covered later in this section), and Version 4 is an error-correction protocol as well. Because the V.42 standard includes MNP compatibility through Class 4, all MNP 4 compatible modems can establish error-controlled connections with V.42 modems. This standard uses a protocol called LAPM (Link Access Procedure for Modems). LAPM, like MNP, copes with phone-line impairments by automatically retransmitting data corrupted during transmission, assuring that only error-free data passes through the modems. V.42 is considered to be better than MNP 4 because it offers about a 20 percent higher transfer rate due to more intelligent algorithms.

Data-Compression Standards. Data compression refers to a built-in capability in some modems to compress the data they're sending, thus saving time and money for long-distance modem users. Depending on the type of files that are sent, data can be compressed to 50 percent of its original size, effectively doubling the speed of the modem.

V.42bis. V.42bis is a CCITT data-compression standard similar to MNP Class 5, but providing about 35 percent better compression. V.42bis is not actually compatible with MNP Class 5, but nearly all V.42bis modems include the MNP 5 data-compression capability as well.

This protocol can sometimes quadruple throughput, depending on the compression technique used. This fact has led to some mildly false advertising: for example, a 2400-bps V.42bis modem might advertise "9600 bps throughput" by including V.42bis as well, but this would be possible in only extremely optimistic cases, such as in sending text files that are very loosely packed. In the same manner, many 9600-bps V.42bis makers now advertise "up to 38.4K bps throughput" by virtue of the compression. Just make sure that you see the truth behind such claims.

V.42bis is superior to MNP 5 because it analyzes the data first, and then determines whether compression would be useful. V.42bis only compresses data that needs compression. Files found on bulletin board systems often are compressed already (using ARC, PKZIP, and similar programs). Further attempts at compressing already compressed data can increase the size of the data and slow things down. MNP 5 always attempts to compress the data, which slows down throughput on previously compressed files. V.42bis, however, compresses only what benefits from the compression.

To negotiate a standard connection using V.42bis, V.42 also must be present. Therefore, a modem with V.42bis data compression is assumed to include V.42 error correction. These two protocols combined result in an error-free connection that has the maximum data compression possible.

Proprietary Standards. In addition to the industry-standard protocols for modulation, error correction, and data compression that generally are set forth or approved by the CCITT, several protocols in these areas were invented by various companies and included in their products without any official endorsement by the CCITT. Some of these protocols are quite popular and have become pseudo-standards of their own.

The most successful proprietary protocols are the MNP (Microcom Networking Protocols) that were developed by Microcom. These error-correction and data-compression protocols are supported widely by other modem manufacturers as well. Another company successful in establishing proprietary protocols as limited standards is U.S. Robotics, with its HST (high speed technology) modulation protocols. Because of an aggressive marketing campaign with bulletin board system operators, it captured a large portion of the market with its products.

This section examines these and other proprietary modem protocols.

HST. The HST is a 14400-bps and 9600-bps modified half-duplex proprietary modulation protocol used by U.S. Robotics. Although common in bulletin board systems, the HST probably is destined for extinction within the next few years as V.32 modems become more competitive in price. HST modems run at 9600 bps or 14400 bps in one direction, and 300 or 450 bps in the other direction. This is an ideal protocol for interactive sessions. Because echo-cancellation circuitry is not required, costs are lower.

U.S. Robotics also makes modems that use standard protocols as well as *dual standards*— modems that incorporate both V.32bis and HST protocols. This gives you the best of the standard and proprietary worlds and enables you to connect to virtually any other system at that system's maximum communications rate. I use and recommend the dual-standard modems.

DIS. The DIS is a 9600-bps proprietary modulation protocol by CompuCom, which uses dynamic impedance stabilization (DIS), with claimed superiority in noise rejection over V.32. Implementation appears to be very inexpensive, but like HST, only one company makes modems with the DIS standard. Because of the lower costs of V.32 and V.32bis, this proprietary standard will likely disappear.

MNP. MNP (Microcom Networking Protocol) offers end-to-end error correction, meaning that the modems are capable of detecting transmission errors and requesting retransmission of corrupted data. Some levels of MNP also provide data compression.

As MNP evolved, different classes of the standard were defined, describing the extent to which a given MNP implementation supports the protocol. Most current implementations support Classes 1 through 5. Higher classes usually are unique to modems manufactured by Microcom, Inc. because they are proprietary.

MNP generally is used for its error-correction capabilities, but MNP Classes 4 and 5 also provide performance increases, with Class 5 offering real-time data compression. The lower classes of MNP usually are not important to you as a modem user, but they are included for completeness in the following list:

- MNP Class 1 (block mode) uses asynchronous, byte-oriented, half-duplex (one-way) transmission. This method provides about 70 percent efficiency and error correction only, so it's rarely used today.

- MNP Class 2 (stream mode) uses asynchronous, byte-oriented, full-duplex (two-way) transmission. This class also provides error correction only. Because of *protocol overhead* (the time it takes to establish the protocol and operate it), throughput at Class 2 is only about 84 percent of that for a connection without MNP, delivering about 202 cps (characters per second) at 2400 bps (240 cps is the theoretical maximum). Class 2 is used rarely today.

■ MNP Class 3 incorporates Class 2 and is more efficient. It uses a synchronous, bit-oriented, full-duplex method. The improved procedure yields throughput about 108 percent of that of a modem without MNP, delivering about 254 cps at 2400 bps.

■ MNP Class 4 is a performance-enhancement class that uses Adaptive Packet Assembly and Optimized Data Phase techniques. Class 4 improves throughput and performance by about 5 percent, although actual increases depend on the type of call and connection, and can be as high as 25 percent to 50 percent.

■ MNP Class 5 is a data-compression protocol that uses a real-time adaptive algorithm. It can increase throughput up to 50 percent, but the actual performance of Class 5 depends on the type of data being sent. Raw text files allow the highest increase, although program files cannot be compressed as much and the increase is smaller. On precompressed data (files already compressed with ARC, PKZIP, and so on), MNP 5 *decreases* performance, and therefore is often disabled on BBS systems.

V-Series. The Hayes V-series is a proprietary error-correction protocol by Hayes that was used in some of its modems. Since the advent of lower cost V.32 and V.32bis modems (even from Hayes), the V-series has all but become extinct. These modems used a modified V.29 protocol, which is sometimes called a *ping-pong protocol* because it has one high-speed channel and one low-speed channel that alternate back and forth.

CSP. The CSP (CompuCom Speed Protocol) is an error-correction and data-compression protocol available on CompuCom DIS modems.

FAXModem Standards. Facsimile technology is a science unto itself, although it has many similarities to data communications. These similarities have led to the combination of data and faxes into the same modem. You now can purchase a single board that will send and receive both data and faxes; all the major modem manufacturers have models that support this capability.

Over the years, the CCITT has set international standards for fax transmission. This has led to the grouping of faxes into one of four groups. Each group (I through IV) uses different technology and standards for transmitting and receiving faxes. Groups I and II are relatively slow and provide results that are unacceptable by today's standards. Group III is the standard in use today by virtually all fax machines, including those combined with modems. Whereas Groups I through III are analog in nature (similar to modems), Group IV is digital and designed for use with ISDN or other digital networks. Because the telephone system has not converted to a digital system yet, there are very few Group IV fax systems available.

If you are interested in detailed information on the technical fax specifications, you can contact Telecommunications Industry Association or Global Engineering Documents.

III

Input/Output Hardware

Group III Fax. There are two general subdivisions within the Group III fax standard—Class 1 and Class 2. Many times you will hear about a FAXModem supporting Group III, Class 1 fax communications. This simply indicates the protocols that the board is able to send and receive. If your FAXModem does this, it can communicate with most of the other fax machines in the world. In FAXModems, the Class 1 specification is implemented by an additional group of modem commands that the modem translates and acts upon.

Earlier you learned about the V.29 modulation standard. As stated in that section, this standard is used for Group III fax transmissions.

Modem Recommendations. Today the cost of 9600-bps modems has dropped to just over $100 for one of these modems. You can even find 14400-bps modems for under $200.

Today, most modems come with multiple forms of error correction or data compression. Based on the discussions earlier in this chapter, you should search for the modem that offers the best combination of speed, error correction, and data compression. Probably the most universal modem is the U.S. Robotics Courier HST Dual Standard—a high-speed modem that uses both the industry standard ultra-high speed V.32bis protocol and U.S. Robotics' own transmission standard as well. This modem also includes V.42bis, which enables throughput to hit 38.4K bps with the right data. The multiple protocols and standards in this modem make possible connections to almost any other modem at its full capability. You are limited only by the speed and protocols of the modem you are calling. This device's only drawback is its price (which has been coming down lately), but its flexibility makes it cost effective.

Secrets of Modem Negotiation. If you are curious about the complex negotiations that occur when two modems connect, two detailed descriptions of *modem handshaking* follow. The two examples of connections use V.22bis and V.32. These sequences may differ slightly depending on your modem, and can get more complicated when you combine different modem types into one box. Making a V.22bis connection between two modems involves the following sequence of events:

1. The answering modem detects a ring, goes off-hook, and waits for at least two seconds of *billing delay* (required by phone company rules so that no data passes before the network recognizes that the call has been connected).

2. The answering modem transmits an *answer tone* (described in CCITT Recommendation V.25, occurs at 2100 Hz, and lasts 3.3 ± 0.7 seconds). The answer tone tells manual-dial originators that they have reached a modem and can put their calling modem in data mode, and informs the network that data is going to be transferred so that echo suppressors in the network can be disabled. If the echo suppressors remain enabled, you cannot transmit in both directions at the same time. (The originating modem remains silent throughout this period.)

3. The answering modem goes silent for 75 ± 20 milliseconds (ms) to separate the answer tone from the signals that follow.

4. The answering modem transmits unscrambled binary 1s at 1200 bits per second (USB1), which cause the static, or harsh sound, you hear after the answer tone.

This sound is slightly higher in pitch than the answer tone because the signal's major components are at 2250 Hz and 2550 Hz.

5. The originating modem detects the USB1 signal in 155 ± 10 ms, and remains silent for 456 ± 10 ms.

6. The originating modem transmits unscrambled double-digit 00s and 11s at 1200 bits (S1) for 100 ± 3 ms. A Bell 212 or V.22 modem does not transmit this S1 signal, and it is by the presence or absence of this single 100-ms signal that V.22bis knows whether to fall back to 1200-bps operation.

7. When the answering modem (which is still transmitting the USB1 signal) detects the S1 signal from the originator, it also sends 100 ms of S1 so that the originating modem knows that the answerer is capable of 2400-bps operation.

8. The originating modem then switches to sending scrambled binary 1s at 1200 bits (SB1). *Scrambling* has nothing to do with encryption or security, but is simply a method by which the signal is *whitened*, or randomized, to even out the power across the entire bandwidth. *White noise* is a term given by engineers to totally random noise patterns.

9. The answering modem switches to sending SB1 for 500 ms.

10. The answering modem switches to sending scrambled 1s at 2400 bps for 200 ms. After that, it is ready to pass data.

11. 600 ms after the originating modem hears SB1 from the answerer, it switches to sending scrambled 1s at 2400 bps. It does this for 200 ms, and then is ready to pass data.

The signals involved in a V.32 connection are more complicated than V.22bis because of the need to measure the total round-trip delay in the circuit so that the echo cancellers work. Making a V.32 connection involves the following sequence of events:

1. The answering modem detects a ring, goes off-hook, and waits two seconds (the billing delay).

2. The answering modem transmits a V.25 answer tone, but it is different from the preceding example. The phase of signal is reversed every 450 ms, which sounds like little clicks in the signal. These phase reversals inform the network that the modems themselves are going to do echo cancellation, and that any echo cancellers in the network should be disabled so as not to interfere with the modems.

3. The originating V.32 modem does not wait for the end of the answer tone. After one second, it responds with an 1800-Hz tone, which in V.32 is known as signal AA. Sending this signal before the end of the answer tone enables the answering modem to know, very early, that it is talking to another V.32 modem.

4. After the answer tone ends (3.3 ± 0.7 seconds), if the answering modem heard signal AA, it proceeds to try to connect as V.32 immediately. If it did not hear AA, it first tries, for three seconds, to connect as a V.22bis modem (sends signal USB1 and

III

Input/Output Hardware

waits for a response). If it does not get a response to USB1, it goes back to trying to connect as a V.32 modem because of the possibility that the calling V.32 modem didn't hear the answer tone, was manually dialed and switched to data mode late, or is an older V.32 model that does not respond to the answer tone.

5. To connect in V.32, the answering modem sends signal AC, which is 600 Hz and 3000 Hz sent together, for at least 64 *symbol intervals* (1/2400 of a second). It then reverses the phase of the signal, making it into signal CA.

6. When the originating modem detects this phase reversal, in 64 ± 2 symbol intervals, it reverses the phase of its own signal, making AA into CC.

7. When the answer modem detects this phase reversal (in 64 ± 2 symbol intervals), it again reverses the phase of its signal, making CA back into AC. This exchange of phase reversals enables the modems to accurately time the total propagation (round trip) delay of the circuit so that the echo cancellers can be set to properly cancel signal echoes.

8. The modems go into a half-duplex exchange of training signals to train the adaptive equalizers, test the quality of the phone line, and agree on the data rate to be used. The answering modem transmits first, from 650 ms to 3525 ms, and then goes silent.

9. The originating modem responds with a similar signal, but then leaves its signal on, while the answering modem responds one more time, establishing the final agreed-on data rate.

10. Both modems then switch to sending scrambled binary 1 (marks) for at least 128 symbol intervals, and then are ready to pass data.

As you can see, these procedures are quite complicated. Although you do not need to understand these communications protocols to use a modem, you can get an idea of what you're hearing when the connection is being established.

Parallel Ports

A parallel port has eight lines for sending all the bits for one byte of data, simultaneously, across eight wires. This interface is fast and usually is reserved for printers rather than computer-to-computer communications. The only problem with parallel ports is that cables cannot be extended for any great length without amplifying the signal, or errors occur in the data. Table 11.7 shows the pinout for a standard PC parallel port.

Table 11.7 25-Pin PC-Compatible Parallel Port Connector

Pin	Description	I/O
1	−Strobe	Out
2	+Data Bit 0	Out
3	+Data Bit 1	Out
4	+Data Bit 2	Out

Pin	Description	I/O
5	+Data Bit 3	Out
6	+Data Bit 4	Out
7	+Data Bit 5	Out
8	+Data Bit 6	Out
9	+Data Bit 7	Out
10	–Acknowledge	In
11	+Busy	In
12	+Paper End	In
13	+Select	In
14	–Auto Feed	Out
15	–Error	In
16	–Initialize Printer	Out
17	–Select Input	Out
18	–Data Bit 0 Return (GND)	In
19	–Data Bit 1 Return (GND)	In
20	–Data Bit 2 Return (GND)	In
21	–Data Bit 3 Return (GND)	In
22	–Data Bit 4 Return (GND)	In
23	–Data Bit 5 Return (GND)	In
24	–Data Bit 6 Return (GND)	In
25	–Data Bit 7 Return (GND)	In

Over the years, four types of parallel ports have evolved: Original, Type 1, Type 3, and Enhanced Parallel Port. The following sections discuss each of these types.

Original Unidirectional. The original IBM PC did not have different types of parallel ports available. The only port available was the parallel port used to send information from the computer to a device, such as a printer. This is not to say that bidirectional parallel ports were not available; indeed, they were common in other computers on the market and with hobbyist computers at the time.

The unidirectional nature of the original PC parallel port is consistent with its primary use—that is, sending data to a printer. There were times, however, when it was desirable to have a bidirectional port—for example, when you need feedback from a printer, which is common with PostScript printers. This could not be done with the original unidirectional ports.

Type 1 Bidirectional. With the introduction of the PS/2 in 1987, IBM introduced a bidirectional parallel port. This opened the way for true communications between the computer and the peripheral across the parallel port. This was done by defining a few of the previously unused pins in the parallel connector, and defining a status bit to indicate in which direction information was traveling across the channel.

III

Input/Output Hardware

In IBM documentation, this original PS/2 port became known as a Type 1 parallel port. Other vendors also introduced third-party ports that were compatible with the Type 1 port; they were based on chips from Chips & Technologies, Inc. Unless you specifically configure the port for bidirectional use, however, the PS/2 Type 1 port functions the same as the original unidirectional port in the PC. This configuration is done with the configuration disk that accompanies the PS/2.

Type 3 DMA. With the introduction of the PS/2 Models 57, 90, and 95, IBM introduced the Type 3 parallel port. This port featured greater throughput by use of direct memory access (DMA) techniques. You may be wondering why IBM skipped from Type 1 to Type 3. In reality, they did not. There is a Type 2 parallel port, and it served as a predecessor to the Type 3. It is only slightly less capable, but was never used widely in any IBM systems.

The types of parallel ports described earlier all use the CPU to control operations. In these ports, the CPU sends one byte to the I/O addresses used by the port, tests to see whether it was sent, and then sends the next. This process continues until all the information to be sent has been processed. The Type 3 port, however, enables you to define a block of memory that you want transmitted (perhaps a file stored in memory), and then enables the port controller to pace the sending of the information. This frees the CPU to perform other tasks, thereby increasing throughput.

Enhanced Parallel Port (EPP) Specification. This is a newer specification from Intel, sometimes referred to as the *Fast Mode parallel port*. While the IBM Type 3 port is designed to enable you to move large amounts of data without tying up the CPU, the Fast Mode port is aimed at quick bidirectional communication with intelligent peripherals. To do this, a Fast Mode port, when operating in that mode, redefines the parallel pins so they actually become bus control lines to augment communication and control between your system and the external device.

Parallel Port Configuration

Parallel-port configuration is not as complicated as it is for serial ports. Even the original IBM PC has BIOS support for three LPT ports, and DOS has always had this support as well. Table 11.8 shows the standard I/O address and interrupt settings for parallel port use.

Table 11.8 Parallel Interface I/O Port Addresses and Interrupts				
	LPTx		**I/O**	
System	**Std.**	**Alt.**	**Port**	**IRQ**
8-bit ISA		LPT1	3BCh	IRQ7
8-bit ISA	LPT1	LPT2	378h	None
8-bit ISA	LPT2	LPT3	278h	None
16-bit ISA		LPT1	3BCh	IRQ7
16-bit ISA	LPT1	LPT2	378h	IRQ5
16-bit ISA	LPT2	LPT3	278h	None

System	LPTx Std.	Alt.	I/O Port	IRQ
All MCA	LPT1		3BCh	IRQ7
All MCA	LPT2		378h	IRQ7
All MCA	LPT3		278h	IRQ7

Because the BIOS and DOS always have provided three definitions for parallel ports, problems with older systems are infrequent. Problems can arise, however, from the lack of available interrupt-driven ports for the ISA bus systems. Normally, an interrupt-driven port is not absolutely required for printing operations; in fact, many programs do not use the interrupt-driven capability. Many programs do use the interrupt, however, such as network print programs and other types of background or spooler-type printer programs. Also, any high-speed, laser-printer utility programs often would use the interrupt capabilities to allow for printing. If you use these types of applications on a port that is not interrupt driven, you see the printing slow to a crawl, if it works at all. The only solution is to use an interrupt-driven port. Note that because MCA bus PS/2 systems can share interrupts, they are completely exempt from this type of problem, and all parallel ports in these systems are interrupt driven on IRQ7.

To configure parallel ports in ISA bus systems, you probably will have to set jumpers and switches. Because each board on the market is different, you always should consult the OEM manual for that particular card if you need to know how the card should or can be configured. IBM includes this information with each card's documentation. IBM also offers technical-reference options and adapters manuals as well as hardware-maintenance and service manuals, which also cover in detail all the jumper and switch settings for IBM adapter cards. Other manufacturers simply include with the card a manual that describes the card and includes the configuration information. The PS/2 MCA bus systems have an automatic or software-driven configuration that eliminates these configuration hassles.

Parallel Port Devices. As already mentioned, the original IBM PC envisioned that the parallel port would be used only for communicating with a printer. Over the years, the number of devices that can be used with a parallel port has increased tremendously. You now can find everything from tape backup units to LAN adapters to CD-ROMs that connect through your parallel port.

Perhaps one of the most common uses for bidirectional parallel ports is to transfer data between your system and another, such as a laptop computer. If both systems utilize a Type 3 port, you can actually communicate at rates of up to 2M per second, which rivals the speed of some hard disk drives. This capability has led to an increase in software to serve this niche of the market. If you are interested in such software (and the parallel ports necessary to facilitate the software), you should refer to the reviews that periodically appear in sources such as *PC Magazine*.

Detecting Serial and Parallel Ports with DEBUG
If you cannot tell which ports (parallel and serial) the computer is using, check for the I/O ports by using DEBUG.

III

Input/Output Hardware

To use DEBUG, follow these steps:

1. Run DEBUG.

2. At the DEBUG prompt, type **D 40:0** and press Enter. This step displays the hexadecimal values of the active I/O port addresses—first serial and then parallel. Figure 11.3 shows a sample address.

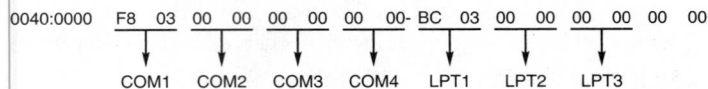

Fig. 11.3
DEBUG used to display installed serial and parallel port I/0 port addresses.

The address for each port is shown in the corresponding position. Because addresses are stored as words, the byte values are swapped and should be read backward. This example indicates one serial port installed at 03F8 and one parallel port installed at 03BC.

3. To exit DEBUG, press Q and press Enter.

Testing Serial Ports

You can perform several tests on serial and parallel ports. The two most common types of tests involve software only, or both hardware and software. The software-only tests are done with diagnostic programs such as Microsoft's MSD, while the hardware and software tests involve using a wrap plug to perform loopback testing.

Microsoft Diagnostics (MSD). MSD is a diagnostic program supplied with MS-DOS 6 or Microsoft Windows. Early versions of the program also were shipped with some Microsoft applications such as Microsoft Word for DOS.

To use MSD, switch to the directory in which it is located. This is not necessary, of course, if the directory containing the program is in your search path—which is often the case with the DOS 6- or Windows-provided versions of MSD. Then simply type **MSD** at the DOS prompt and press Enter. Soon you see the MSD screen.

Choose the Serial Ports option by pressing S. Notice that you are provided information about what type of serial chip you have in your system, as well as information about what ports are available. If any of the ports are in use (for example, a mouse), that information is provided as well.

MSD is helpful in at least determining whether your serial ports are responding. If MSD cannot determine the existence of a port, it does not provide the report indicating that the port exists. This sort of "look and see" test is the first action I usually take to determine why a port is not responding.

Advanced Diagnostics Using Loopback Testing. One of the most useful tests is the *loopback* test, which can be used to ensure the correct function of the serial port, as well as any attached cables. Loopback tests basically are internal (digital), or external (analog). Internal tests can be run simply by unplugging any cables from the port and executing the test via a diagnostics program.

The external loopback test is more effective. This test requires that a special loopback connector or wrap plug be attached to the port in question. When the test is run, the port is used to send data out to the loopback plug, which simply routes the data back into the port's receive pins so that the port is transmitting and receiving at the same time. A loopback or wrap plug is nothing more than a cable doubled back on itself. Most diagnostics programs that run this type of test include the loopback plug, and if not, these types of plugs can be purchased easily or even built. See Appendix A, "PC Technical Reference Section," for the necessary diagrams to construct your own wrap plugs.

If you want to purchase a wrap plug, I recommend the IBM tri-connector wrap plug. IBM sells this triple plug, as well as individual wrap plugs, under the following part numbers:

Description	IBM Part Number
Parallel-port wrap plug, 25-pin	8529280
Serial-port wrap plug, 9-pin (AT)	8286126
Tri-connector wrap plug	72X8546

As for the diagnostics software, IBM's own Advanced Diagnostics can be used to test serial ports. If you have a PS/2 system with Micro Channel Architecture, IBM already has given you the Advanced Diagnostics on the Reference Disk that came with the system. To activate this normally hidden Advanced Diagnostics, press Ctrl-A at the Reference Disk's main menu. For IBM systems that are not MCA, the Advanced Diagnostics must be purchased.

For any system, you can use the serial port tests in the comprehensive diagnostics packages sold by several companies as a replacement for the IBM- (or other manufacturer) supplied Advanced Diagnostics. Programs such as Micro-Scope from Micro 2000, Service Diagnostics from Landmark, or QA-Plus FE from Diagsoft all have this type of test as part of their package. All include the necessary three-wrap plugs as well. See Appendix B, "Vendor List," or Chapter 13, "Floppy Disk Drives and Controllers," for more information on these programs.

For testing serial ports, as well as any modems that are attached, I highly recommend an inexpensive ($19.95) program called the Modem Doctor. This comprehensive serial port and modem test program enables you to go beyond the simple loopback tests and test the complete communications system, including the cable and modem. The program is

III

Input/Output Hardware

especially useful with the U.S. Robotics modems or any other modem with a Hayes-compatible command structure. The program takes command of the modem and runs a variety of tests to determine whether it is functioning correctly.

Testing Parallel Ports

Testing parallel ports is, in most cases, simpler than testing serial ports. The procedures you use are effectively the same as those used for serial ports, except that when you use the diagnostics software, you choose the obvious choices for parallel ports rather than serial ports.

Not only are the software tests similar, but the hardware tests require the proper plugs for the loopback tests on the parallel port. You can use the tri-connector wrap plug recommended earlier, or you can purchase an individual parallel port wrap plug. If you want the individual plug, ask for IBM part number 8529228.

Diagnosing Problems with Serial and Parallel Ports

To diagnose problems with serial and parallel ports, you need diagnostics software and a wrap plug for each type of port. The diagnostics software works with the wrap plugs to send signals through the port. The plug wraps around the port so that the same port receives the information it sent. This information is verified to ensure that the port works properly. For further information, see Chapter 14, "Hard Disk Drives and Controllers."

You next turn your attention to local area network components and concepts.

Understanding the Components of a LAN

A local area network (LAN) enables you to share files, share applications, use multiuser software products, share printers, use electronic mail, share disk space, share modems, and otherwise make a collection of computers work as a team.

A LAN is a combination of computers, LAN cables, network adapter cards, network operating system software, and LAN application software. (You sometimes see *network operating system* abbreviated as *NOS*.) On a LAN, each personal computer is called a *workstation*, except for one or more computers designated as *file servers*. Each workstation and file server contains a network adapter card. LAN cables connect all the workstations and file servers. In addition to its local operating system (usually DOS), each workstation runs network software that enables the workstation to communicate with the file servers. In turn, the file servers run network software that communicates with the workstations and serves up files to those workstations. LAN-aware application software runs at each workstation, communicating with the file server when it needs to read and write files. Figure 11.4 illustrates the components that make up a LAN.

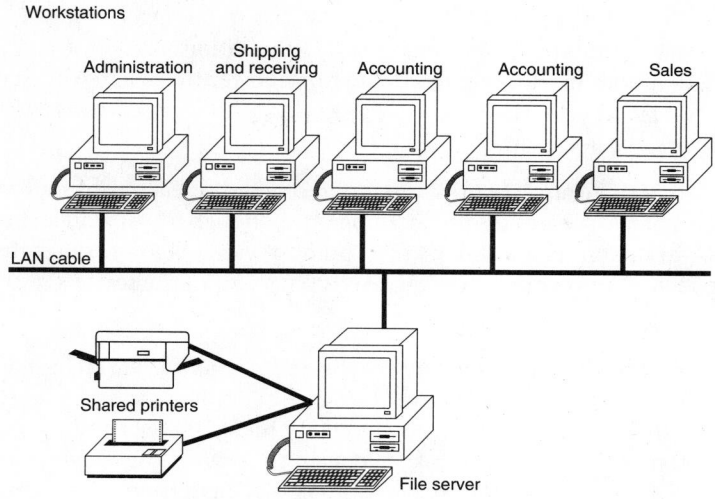

Workstations

Administration
Shipping and receiving
Accounting
Accounting
Sales

LAN cable

Shared printers

File server

Fig. 11.4
The components of a LAN.

Workstations

A LAN is made up of computers. You will find two kinds of computers on a LAN: the workstations, usually manned by people; and the file servers, usually located in a separate room or closet. The workstation works only for the person sitting in front of it, whereas a file server enables many people to share its resources. Workstations usually are intermediate-speed AT-class machines with an 80286 or better CPU, and they may have 1M to 4M of RAM. Workstations often have good-quality color or gray-scale VGA monitors, as well as high-quality keyboards, but these are characteristics that make them easy to use and are not required to make the LAN work. A workstation also usually has an inexpensive, slow, small hard disk.

Some workstations, called *diskless workstations*, do not have a disk drive of their own. Such workstations rely completely on the LAN for their file access.

File Servers

In contrast to the workstations, a *file server* is a computer that serves all the workstations—primarily storing and retrieving data from files shared on its disks. File servers usually are fast 386-, 486-, or Pentium-based computers, running at 25 MHz or faster and with 8M or more of RAM. File servers usually have only monochrome monitors and inexpensive keyboards, because people do not interactively use file servers. The file server normally operates unattended. A file server almost always has one or more fast, expensive, large hard disks, however.

Servers must be high-quality, heavy-duty machines because, in serving the whole network, they do many times the work of an ordinary workstation computer. In particular, the file server's hard disk(s) need to be durable and reliable.

III

Input/Output Hardware

You most often will see a computer dedicated to the task of being a file server. Sometimes, on smaller LANs, the file server doubles as a workstation. Serving an entire network is a big job that does not leave much spare horsepower to handle workstation duties, however, and if an end user locks up the workstation that serves as the file server, your network also locks up.

Under a heavy load, if there are 20 workstations and one server, each workstation can use only one-twentieth of the server's resources. In practice, though, most workstations are idle most of the time—at least from a disk-file-access point of view. As long as no other workstation is using the server, your workstation can use 100 percent of the server's resources.

LAN Cables

LAN cable comes in different varieties. You may use thin coaxial wire (referred to as *Thinnet* or *CheaperNet*) or thick coaxial wire (*ThickNet*). You may use shielded twisted pair (*STP*), which looks like the wire that carries electricity inside the walls of your house, or unshielded twisted pair (*UTP*), which looks like telephone wire. You may even use fiber optic cable. Fiber optic cable works more over longer distances than other types of cable, at faster speeds. Fiber optic cable installation and fiber-optic-based network adapters can be expensive, however. The kind of wire you use depends mostly on the kind of network adapter cards you choose. The next section discusses network adapter cards.

Each workstation is connected with cable to the other workstations and to the file server. Sometimes a single piece of cable wends from station to station, visiting all the servers and workstations along the way. This cabling arrangement is called a *bus* or *daisy-chain topology*, as shown in figure 11.5. (A *topology* is simply a description of the way the workstations and servers are physically connected.)

Sometimes separate cables run from a central place, such as a file server, to each workstation. Figure 11.6 shows this arrangement, called a *star*. Sometimes the cables branch out repeatedly from a root location, forming the *star-wired tree* shown in figure 11.7. Daisy-chained cabling schemes use the least cable but are the hardest to diagnose or bypass when problems occur.

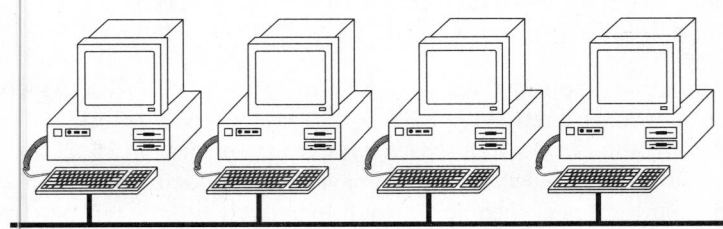

Fig. 11.5
The linear bus topology, attaching all network devices to a common cable.

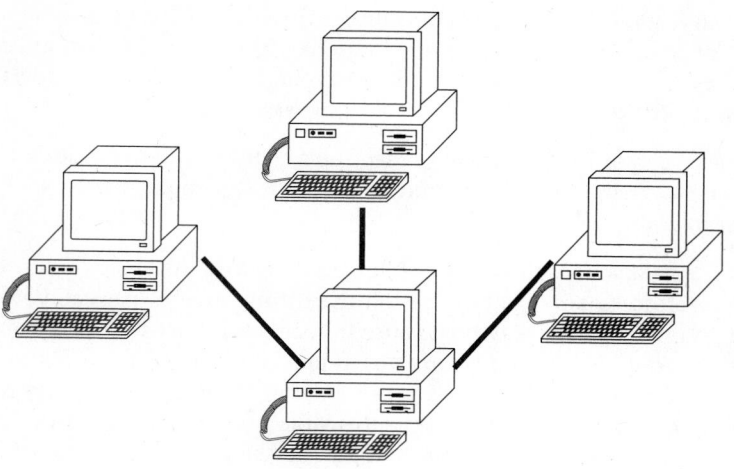

Fig. 11.6

The star topology, connecting the LAN's computers and devices with cables that radiate outward, usually from a file server.

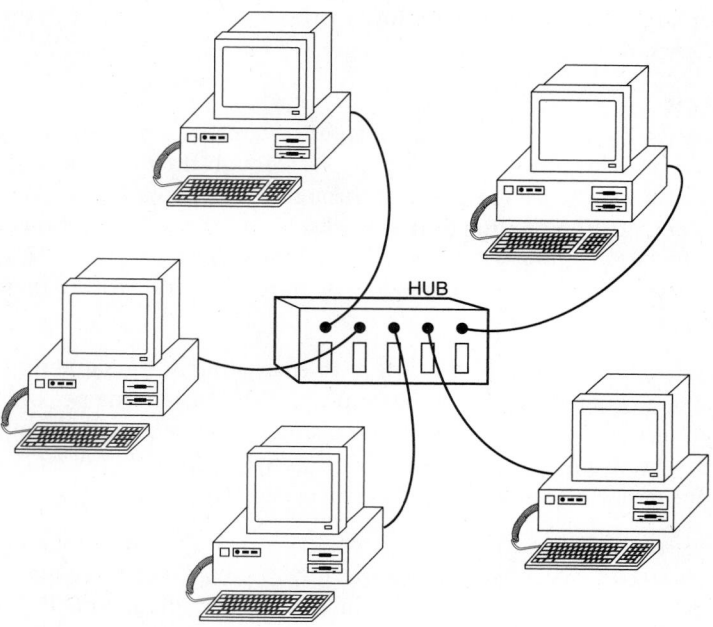

Fig. 11.7

The star-wired tree topology, linking the LAN's computers and devices to one or more central hubs, or access units.

If you have to run cables through walls or ceilings, installing the cable can be the most expensive part of setting up a LAN. At every branching point, special fittings connect the intersecting wires. Sometimes you also need various black boxes such as hubs, repeaters, or access units.

A few companies, such as Motorola, are pioneering a type of LAN that does not require cables at all. Such a *wireless LAN* uses infrared or radio waves to carry network signals from computer to computer.

Planning the cabling layout, cutting the cable, and installing the cables and fittings are jobs usually best left to experienced workers. If the fittings are not perfect, you may get electronic echoes on the network, which cause transmission errors. Coaxial cable costs about 15 cents per foot, whereas shielded twisted pair probably costs more than $1 per foot. This sounds like a big expense for a large LAN, but the cost of installing cable, at about $45 per hour, overshadows the cost of the cable itself. The only time you might consider installing LAN cable yourself is when you have a group of computers located on adjacent desks and you do not have to enter the walls or ceiling with the cable.

Building codes almost always require you to use fire-proof *plenum* cables. Chapter 5, "Bus Slots and Specifications," explains LAN cables in detail. For now, you should know that plenum cables are more fire-resistant than some other cables. You would be very upset if you installed ordinary cable and were later told by the building inspector to rip out the cable and start over with the proper kind.

Network Adapters

A network adapter card, like a video display adapter card, fits in a slot in each workstation and file server. Your workstation sends requests through the network adapter to the file server. The workstation receives responses through the network adapter when the file server delivers all or a portion of a file to that workstation. The sending of these requests and responses is the LAN's equivalent of reading and writing files on your PC's local hard disk. If you're like most people, you probably think of reading and writing files in terms of loading or saving your work.

Only two network adapters can communicate with each other at the same time on a LAN. This means that other workstations have to wait their turn if one person's workstation currently is accessing the file server (processing the requests and responses that deliver a file to the workstation). Fortunately, such delays are usually not noticeable. The LAN gives the appearance of many workstations accessing the file server simultaneously.

LANtastic adapters have two connectors on the back to attach the incoming and outgoing cables. Ethernet connectors have a single T connector, a D-shaped 15-pin connector, a connector that looks like a telephone jack, or sometimes a combination of all three. Token Ring adapters have a 9-pin connector and sometimes a telephone jack outlet. Figure 11.8 shows a high-performance Token Ring adapter with both kinds of connectors.

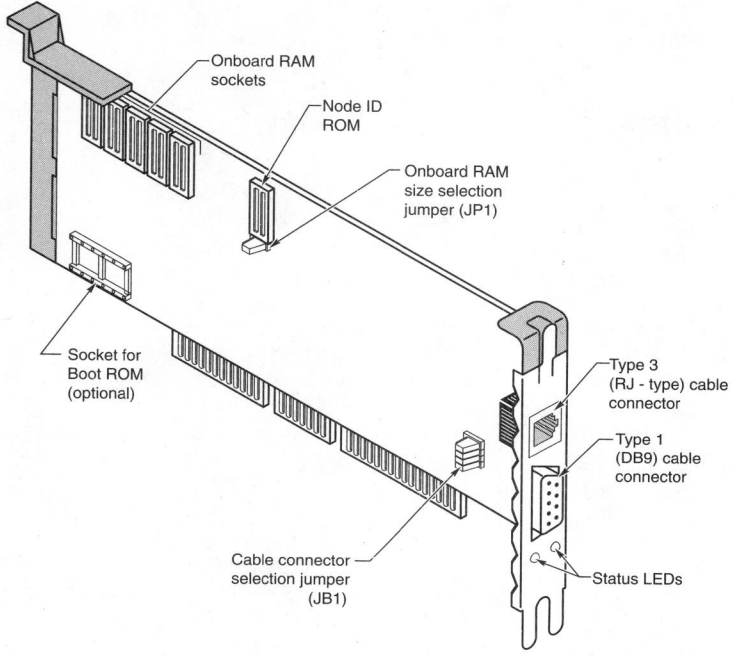

Onboard RAM
sockets

Node ID
ROM

Onboard RAM
size selection
jumper (JP1)

Socket for
Boot ROM
(optional)

Type 3
(RJ - type) cable
connector

Type 1
(DB9) cable
connector

Cable connector
selection jumper
(JB1)

Status LEDs

Fig. 11.8
The Thomas-Conrad 16/4 Token Ring adapter (with a 9-pin connector and a telephone wire connector).

Cards with two or more connectors enable you to choose from a wider variety of LAN cables. A Token Ring card with two connectors, for example, enables you to use shielded twisted pair (STP) or unshielded twisted pair (UTP, or telephone wire) cable.

The LAN adapter card listens to all the traffic going by on the cable, and filters out just the messages destined for your workstation. The adapter hands these messages over to your workstation when the workstation is ready to attend to the messages. When the workstation wants to send a request to a server, the adapter card waits for a break in the cable traffic and inserts your message into the stream. The workstation also verifies that the message arrived intact, and resends the message if it arrived garbled.

Adapters range in price from less than $100 to much more than $1,000. What do you get for your money? Primarily, speed. The faster adapters can push data faster onto the cable, which means that the file server gets a request more quickly and sends back a response more quickly.

III

Input/Output Hardware

Data-Transfer Speeds on a LAN

Electrical engineers and technical people measure the speed of a network in *megabits per second*. Because a byte of information consists of 8 bits, you can divide the megabits per second rating by 8 to find out how many millions of characters (bytes) per second the network can handle theoretically. Suppose that you want to transfer an entire 3 1/2-inch 720K floppy disk's worth of information across a LAN. The rated speed of the LAN is 4 megabits per second. Dividing 4 mbps by 8 tells you that the LAN theoretically can transmit 500 kilobytes (500K) of data per second. This is equivalent to an average hard disk's transfer rate. The data from the 720K floppy disk takes at least a few seconds to transfer, as you can see from these rough calculations.

In practice, a LAN is slower than its rated speed. In fact, a LAN is no faster than its slowest component. If you were to transfer 720K of data from one workstation's hard disk to the file server, the elapsed time would include not only the transmission time but also the workstation hard disk retrieval time, the workstation processing time, and the file server's hard disk and server CPU processing times. The transfer rate of your hard disk, which in this case is probably the slowest component involved in the copying of the data to the server, governs the rate at which data flows to the file server. Other people's requests interleave with your requests on the LAN, and the total transfer time may be longer because the other people are using the LAN at the same time you are.

If you transfer the data from a 720K floppy disk to the file server, you see that it takes even longer. Floppy disk drives, as you know, are slower than hard disks. Your workstation uses the network in small bursts as it reads the data from the floppy disk. The workstation cannot send data across the LAN, in this case, any faster than it can read the data from the disk.

LANtastic Adapters. Artisoft makes both Ethernet and its own proprietary network adapter cards. Artisoft's proprietary model is called a LANtastic adapter, which is a little confusing because Artisoft also makes a network operating system called LANtastic. The LANtastic adapter operates at a rate of 2 mbps, and it uses four-conductor cable strung out in a snaking path that connects to all the workstations. Installation is easy if you do not have to put the cable inside walls or the ceiling.

Ethernet and Token Ring are industry standards, while the LANtastic adapter has a proprietary design. Most people choose Ethernet or Token Ring network adapters when building a new LAN.

ARCnet Adapters. ARCnet is one of the oldest types of LAN hardware. It was originally a proprietary scheme of the Datapoint Corporation, but today many companies make ARCnet-compatible cards. ARCnet is a little slow, but it is forgiving of minor errors in installation. It is known for solid reliability, and ARCnet cable/adapter problems are easy to diagnose. ARCnet costs less than Ethernet. ARCnet operates something like Token Ring, but at the slower rate of 2.5 mbps. The section "Token Ring Adapters," later in this chapter, explains the basic principles on which ARCnet and Token Ring work.

Ethernet Adapters. Ethernet-based LANs enable you to interconnect a wide variety of equipment, including UNIX computers, Apple computers, IBM PCs, and IBM clones. You can buy Ethernet cards from dozens of competing manufacturers. Ethernet comes in three varieties (ThinNet, UTP, and ThickNet), depending on the thickness of the cabling you use. ThickNet cables can span a greater distance, but they are much more expensive. Ethernet operates at a rate of 10 mbps.

Between *data transfers* (requests and responses to and from the file server), Ethernet LANs remain quiet. After a workstation sends a request across the LAN cable, the cable falls silent again. What happens when two or more workstations (and/or file servers) attempt to use the LAN at the same time?

Suppose that one of the workstations wants to request something from the file server, just as the file server is sending a response to another workstation. A collision happens. (Remember that only two computers can communicate through the cable at a given moment.) Both computers—the file server and the workstation—back off and try again. Ethernet network adapters use something called *Carrier Sense, Multiple Access/Collision Detection* (CSMA/CD) to detect the collision, and they each back off a random amount of time. This method effectively enables one computer to go first. With higher amounts of traffic, the frequency of collisions rises higher and higher, and response times become worse and worse. An Ethernet network actually can spend more time recovering from collisions than sending data. IBM and Texas Instruments, recognizing Ethernet's traffic limitations, designed Token Ring to solve the problem.

Token Ring Adapters. Except for fiber optic cables/adapters, Token Ring is the most expensive type of LAN. Token Ring uses shielded or unshielded twisted pair cable. Token Ring's cost is justified when you have a great deal of traffic from many workstations. You find Token Ring in large corporations with large LANs, especially if the LANs are attached to mainframe computers. Token Ring operates at a rate of 4 mbps or 16 mbps.

Workstations on a Token Ring LAN continuously pass an electronic token among themselves. The *token* is just a short message indicating that the network is idle. If a workstation has nothing to send, as soon as it receives the token, it passes the token on to the next downstream workstation. Only when a workstation receives the token can it send a message on the LAN. If the LAN is busy, and you want your workstation to send a message to another workstation or server, you must wait patiently for the token to come around. Only then can your workstation send its message. The message circulates through the workstations and file servers on the LAN, all the way back to you, the sender. The sender then sends a token to indicate that the network is idle again. During the circulation of the message, one of the workstations or file servers recognizes that the message is addressed to it and begins processing that message.

Token Ring is not as wasteful of LAN resources as this description makes it sound. The token takes almost no time at all to circulate through a LAN, even with 100 or 200 workstations. It is possible to assign priorities to certain workstations and file servers so that they get more frequent access to the LAN. And, of course, the token-passing scheme is much more tolerant of high traffic levels on the LAN than the collision-sensing Ethernet.

ARCnet and Token Ring are not compatible with one another, but ARCnet uses a similar token-passing scheme to control workstation and server access to the LAN.

Sometimes a station fumbles and "drops" the token. LAN stations watch each other and use a complex procedure to regenerate a lost token. Token Ring is quite a bit more complicated than Ethernet, and the LAN adapter cards are correspondingly more expensive.

Evaluating File Server Hardware

A typical file server consists of a personal computer that you dedicate to the task of sharing disk space, files, and a printer. On a larger network, you may instead use a personal computer especially built for file server work (a superserver), a minicomputer, or even a mainframe. No matter what sort of computer you choose to use as a server, the server and the workstations communicate with each other through network adapter cards and LAN cables.

A file server does many times the work of an ordinary workstation. You may type on the server's keyboard only a couple of times a day, and you may glance at the server's monitor only a few times. The server CPU and hard disk, however, take the brunt of responding to the file-service requests of all the workstations on the LAN.

If you consider your LAN an important investment in your office (it is hard to imagine otherwise), you will want to get the highest quality computer you can afford for the file server. The CPU should be an 80486 or Pentium chip and should be one of the faster models. The hard disk should be large and fast. But the most important consideration is that the CPU, the motherboard on which the CPU is mounted, and the hard disk should be rugged and reliable. Do not skimp on these components. *Downtime* (when the network is not operating) can be expensive because people cannot access their shared files to get their work done. Higher quality components will keep the LAN running without failure for longer periods of time.

In the same vein, you will want to set up a regular maintenance schedule for your file server. Over a few weeks, the fan at the back of the computer can move great volumes of air through the machine to keep it cool. The air may contain dust and dirt, which accumulates inside the computer. You should clean out the "dust bunnies" in the server every month or two. You do not replace components in the server as part of your regular preventive maintenance, but you will want to know whether a part is beginning to fail. You may want to acquire diagnostic software or hardware to periodically check the health of your file server. (Chapter 19, "Maintaining Your System: Preventive Maintenance, Backups, and Warranties," discusses the tools you can use to keep your file server fit and trim.)

The electricity the file server gets from the wall outlet may, from time to time, vary considerably in voltage (resulting in *sags* and *spikes*). To make your file server as reliable as possible, you should install an uninterruptible power supply between the electric company and your server. The UPS not only provides electricity in case of a power failure, but also conditions the line to protect the server from sags and spikes.

In general, you want to do whatever you can to make your network reliable, including placing the server away from public access areas.

Evaluating the File Server Hard Disk

The hard disk is the most important component of a file server. The hard disk stores the files of the people who use the LAN. To a large extent, the reliability, access speed, and capacity of a server's hard disk determine whether people will be happy with the LAN and will use the LAN productively. The most common bottleneck in the average LAN is disk I/O time at the file server. And the most common complaint voiced by people on the average LAN is that the file server has run out of free disk space. Make sure that your file server's disk drives and hard disk controller are high-performance components, and that you have plenty of free disk space on your server's drives.

Evaluating the File Server CPU

The file server CPU tells the hard disk what to store and retrieve. The CPU is the next most important file server component after the hard disk. Unless your LAN will have only a few users and will never grow, a file server with a fast 80486 or Pentium CPU and plenty of RAM is a wise investment. The next section discusses server RAM.

The CPU chip in a computer executes the instructions given to it by the software you run. If you run an application, that application runs more quickly if the CPU is fast. Likewise, if you run a network operating system, that NOS runs more quickly if the CPU is fast.

Some network operating systems absolutely require certain types of CPU chips. NetWare Version 2, for example, requires at least an 80286 CPU. NetWare Versions 3 and 4 require at least an 80386. IBM LAN Server Version 2 and Microsoft LAN Manager Version 2 require that OS/2 1.3 be running on the server computer; OS/2 1.3 requires an 80286 or later CPU. LAN Server 3.0 requires that the file server use OS/2 2.x, which runs only on 80386 or later CPUs.

Evaluating Server RAM

The network operating system loads into the computer's RAM, just as any other application does. You need to have enough RAM in the computer for the NOS to load and run. On a peer LAN, a few megabytes of RAM might be enough, whereas on a server-based LAN, you might install 32M, 64M, or more in your file server.

You can realize significant performance gains with a faster CPU and extra RAM because of something called *caching*. If the file server has sufficient memory installed, it can "remember" those portions of the hard disk that it accessed previously. When the next user asks for the same file represented by those portions of the hard disk, the server can hand these to the next user without having to actually access the hard disk. Because the file server is able to avoid waiting for the hard disk to rotate into position, the server can do its job more quickly. The network operating system merely needs to look in the computer's RAM for the file data that a workstation has requested. Note that the network operating system's caching of file data is distinct from (and in addition to) any caching that might occur due to the hard disk or hard disk controller card having on-board memory.

Evaluating the Network Adapter Card

The server's network adapter card is the server's link to all the workstations on the LAN. All the requests for files enter the server through the network adapter, and all the response messages containing the requested files leave the server through the network adapter. Figure 11.9 shows a network adapter you might install in a file server. As you can imagine, a network adapter in a server is a busy component.

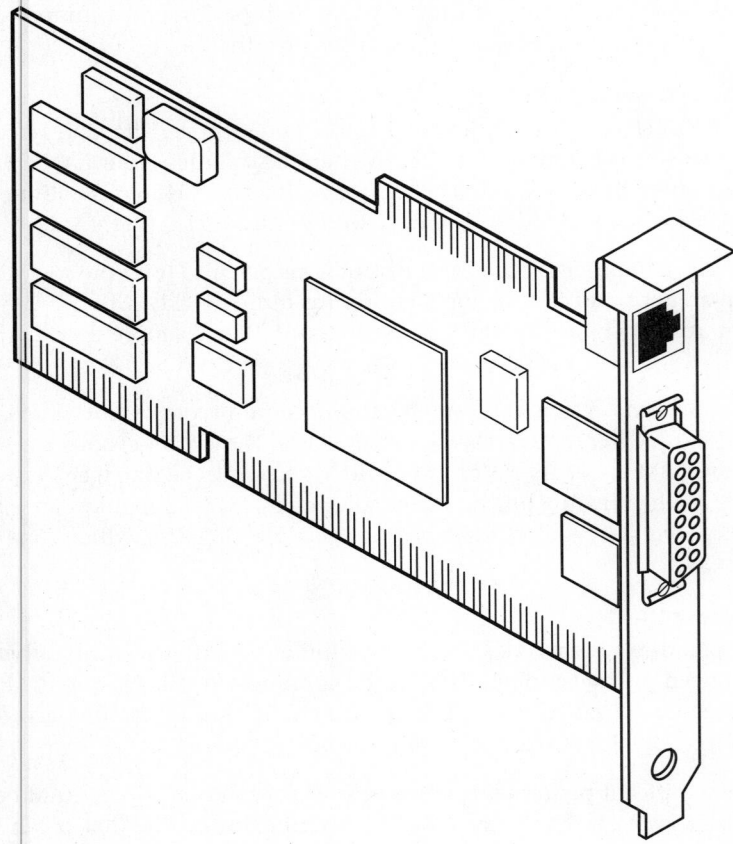

Fig. 11.9
The file server's network adapter sends and receives messages to and from all the workstations on the LAN.

All the network adapters on the LAN use Ethernet, Token Ring, ARCnet, or some other protocol. Within one of these protocols, however, you can find network adapters that perform better than others. A network adapter may be faster at processing messages because it has a large amount of on-board memory (RAM), because it contains its own microprocessor, or perhaps because the adapter uses one of the larger (longer) computer slots and thus can transfer more data between itself and the CPU at one time. A faster, more capable network adapter is an ideal candidate for installation in the file server.

Evaluating the Server's Power Supply

In a file server, the power supply is an important but often overlooked item. Power supply failures and malfunctions cause problems elsewhere in the computer and are difficult to diagnose. Your file server may display a message indicating that a RAM chip has failed, and then stop; the cause of the problem may indeed be a failed RAM chip, or the problem may be in the power supply.

The fan(s) in the power supply sometimes stop working or become obstructed with dust and dirt. The computer overheats and fails completely or acts strangely. Cleaning the fan(s)—after unplugging the computer from the wall outlet, of course—should be a part of the regular maintenance of your file server.

Power supplies vary considerably in quality. Some of the best power supplies are manufactured by the following company:

> PC Power and Cooling
> 31510 Mountain Way
> Bonsall, CA 92003
> (800) 722-6555

Evaluating the Keyboard, Monitor, and Mouse

The keyboard, monitor, and mouse (if any) are not significant components on a file server computer. Often you can use lower quality, less expensive components for these parts. A typical file server runs unattended and may go for hours or days without interaction from you. You can power off the monitor for these long periods.

Note one caution about the keyboard: you should tuck the keyboard away so that falling objects (pencils or coffee mugs, for example) do not harm your network's file server.

Examining Protocols, Frames, and Communications

The network adapter sends and receives messages among the LAN computers, and the cable carries the messages. The layer of protocols in each computer, however, turns the computers into a local area network.

At the lowest level, networked PCs communicate with one another and with the file server by using message packets, often called *frames*. These frames are the foundation on which all LAN activity is based. The network adapter, along with its support software, sends and receives these frames. Each computer has a unique address on the LAN to which frames can be sent.

You can send frames for various purposes, including the following:

- Opening a communications session with another adapter

- Sending data (perhaps a record from a file) to a PC

III

Input/Output Hardware

- Acknowledging the receipt of a data frame
- Broadcasting a message to all other adapters
- Closing a communications session

Figure 11.10 shows what a typical frame looks like. Different network implementations define frames in different ways, but the following data items are common to all implementations:

- The sender's unique network address
- The destination's unique network address
- An identification of the contents of the frame
- A data record or message
- A checksum or CRC for error-detection purposes

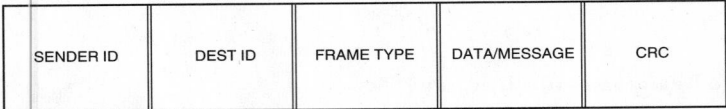

| SENDER ID | DEST ID | FRAME TYPE | DATA/MESSAGE | CRC |

Fig. 11.10
The basic layout of a frame.

Using Frames That Contain Other Frames

The layering of protocols is a powerful concept. The lowest layer knows how to tell the network adapter to send a message, but that layer is ignorant of file servers and file redirection. The highest layer understands file servers and redirection but knows nothing about Ethernet or Token Ring. Together, though, the layers give you a local area network. Frames always are layered (see fig. 11.11).

When the higher level file redirection protocol gives a message to a midlevel protocol (such as NetBIOS, for example) and asks that the message be sent to another PC on the network (probably a file server), the midlevel protocol puts an *envelope* around the message packet and hands it to the lowest level protocol, implemented as the network support software and network adapter card. This lowest layer, in turn, wraps the NetBIOS envelope in an envelope of its own and sends it out across the network. In figure 5.11, you see each envelope labeled *header* and *trailer*. On receipt, the network support software on the receiving computer removes the outer envelope and hands the result upward to the next higher level protocol. The midlevel protocol running on the receiver's computer removes its envelope and gives the message—now an exact copy of the sender's message—to the receiving computer's highest-level protocol.

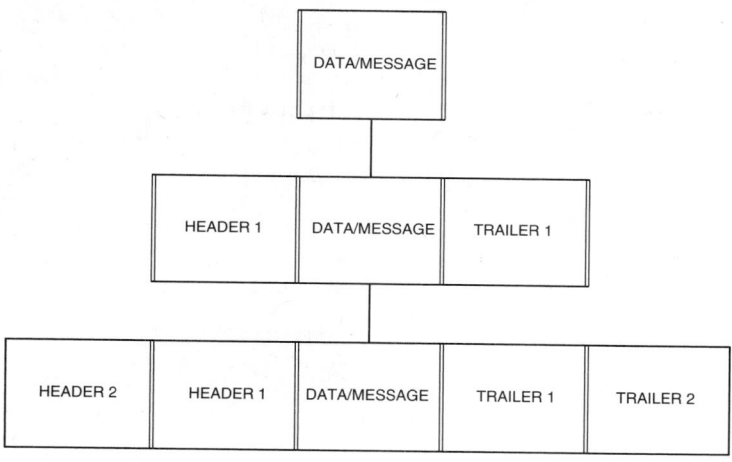

Fig. 11.11
Frame layers.

Different vendors split the LAN communications functions in different ways, but they all compare themselves to the OSI model.

Using the OSI Model

ISO, the International Standards Organization, has published a standard called the Open System Interconnection (OSI) model. Most vendors of LAN products endorse the OSI standard but have not yet implemented OSI fully. The OSI model divides LAN communications into seven layers. Most network operating system vendors use three or four layers of protocols.

The OSI model describes how communications between two computers should occur. Sometime in this decade, this theoretical standard will become a practical one as more and more vendors switch to OSI. The OSI model declares seven layers and specifies that each layer be insulated from the others by a well-defined interface. Figure 11.12 shows the seven layers.

Descriptions of the seven layers follow:

- *Physical.* This part of the OSI model specifies the physical and electrical characteristics of the connections that make up the network (twisted pair cables, fiber optic cables, coaxial cables, connectors, repeaters, and so on). You can think of this layer as the hardware layer. Although the rest of the layers may be implemented as chip-level functions rather than as actual software, the other layers are software in relation to this first layer.

- *Data Link.* At this stage of processing, the electrical impulses enter or leave the network cable. The network's electrical representation of your data (bit patterns, encoding methods, and tokens) is known to this layer, and only to this layer. It is at this point that errors are detected and corrected (by requesting retransmissions of corrupted packets). Because of its complexity, the Data Link layer often is subdivided into a Media Access Control (MAC) layer and a Logical Link Control (LLC) layer. The MAC layer deals with network access (token-passing or collision-sensing) and network control. The LLC layer, operating at a higher level than the MAC layer, is concerned with sending and receiving the user data messages.

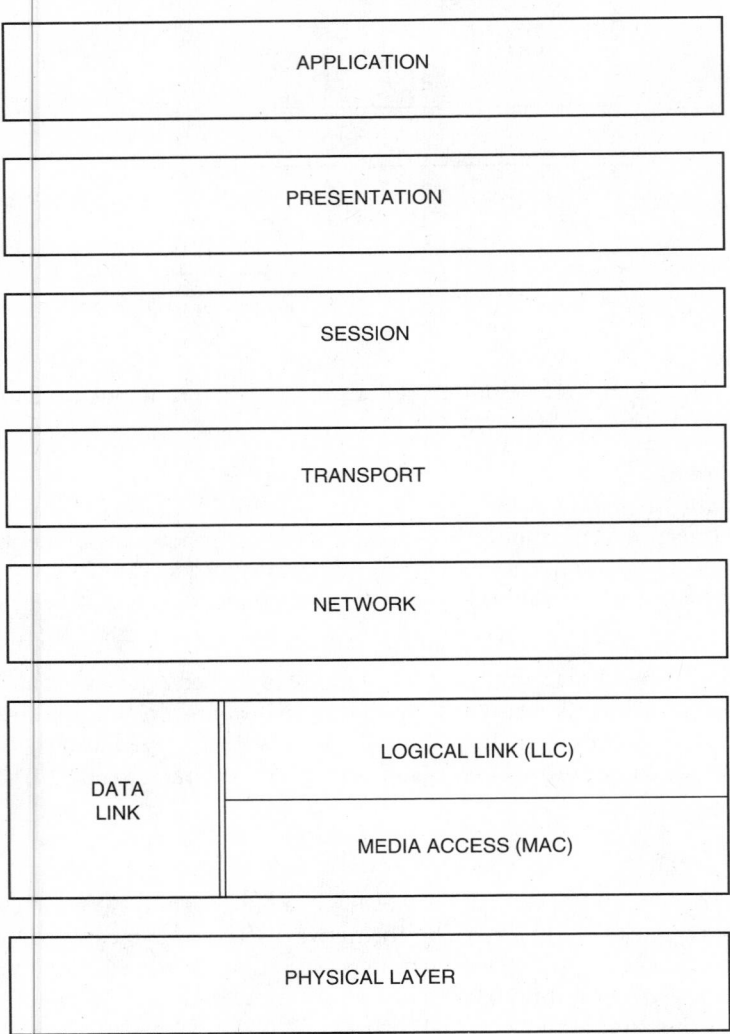

Fig. 11.12
The OSI model.

■ *Network*. This layer switches and routes the packets as necessary to get them to their destinations. This layer is responsible for addressing and delivering message packets.

■ *Transport*. When more than one packet is in process at any time, the Transport layer controls the sequencing of the message components and regulates inbound traffic flow. If a duplicate packet arrives, this layer recognizes it as a duplicate and discards it.

■ *Session*. The functions in this layer enable applications running at two workstations to coordinate their communications into a single session (which you can think of in terms of a highly structured dialog). The Session layer supports the creation of the session, the management of the packets sent back and forth during the session, and the termination of the session.

■ *Presentation*. When IBM, Apple, DEC, NeXT, and Burroughs computers want to talk to one another, obviously a certain amount of translation and byte reordering needs to be done. The Presentation layer converts data into (or from) a machine's native internal numeric format.

■ *Application*. This is the layer of the OSI model seen by an application program. A message to be sent across the network enters the OSI model at this point, travels downward toward layer 1 (the Physical layer), zips across to the other workstation, and then travels back up the layers until the message reaches the application on the other computer through its own Application layer.

One of the factors that makes the network operating system of each vendor proprietary (as opposed to having an *open architecture*) is the vendor's noncompliance with the OSI model.

Using Low-Level Protocols

Local area networks work in one of two basic ways: collision-sensing or token-passing. Ethernet is an example of a collision-sensing network; Token Ring is an example of a token-passing network.

The Institute of Electrical and Electronic Engineers (IEEE) has defined and documented a set of standards for the physical characteristics of both collision-sensing and token-passing networks. These standards are known as IEEE 802.3 (Ethernet) and IEEE 802.5 (Token Ring). Be aware, though, that there are minor differences between the frame definitions for true Ethernet and for true IEEE 802.3. In terms of the standards, IBM's 16-mbps Token Ring adapter card is an 802.5 Token Ring extension. You learn the definitions and layout of Ethernet and Token Ring frames in the sections "Using Ethernet" and "Using Token Ring," later in this chapter.

Some LANs don't conform to IEEE 802.3 or IEEE 802.5, of course. The most popular of these is ARCnet, available from such vendors as Datapoint Corporation, Standard Microsystems, and Thomas-Conrad. Other types of LANs include StarLan (from AT&T), VistaLan (from Allen-Bradley), LANtastic (from Artisoft), Omninet (from Corvus), PC Net (from IBM), and ProNet (from Proteon).

III

Input/Output Hardware

Fiber Distributed Data Interface (FDDI) is a new physical-layer LAN standard. FDDI uses fiber optic cable and a token-passing scheme similar to IEEE 802.5 to transmit data frames at a snappy 100 mbps.

Using Ethernet

In the collision-sensing environment, often referred to by the abbreviation CSMA/CD (carrier sense, multiple access, with collision detection), the network adapter card listens to the network when it has a frame to send. If the adapter hears that another card is sending a frame at that moment, the card waits a moment and tries again. Even with this approach, collisions (two workstations attempting to transmit at exactly the same moment) can and do occur. It is the nature of CSMA/CD networks to expect collisions and to handle them by retransmitting frames as necessary. These retransmissions are handled by the adapter card and are not seen or managed by you or your applications. Collisions generally happen and are handled in less than a microsecond.

> **Caution**
>
> Although many people blame poor CSMA/CD (Ethernet) network performance on the number of users currently on the network who are sending and receiving message traffic, the truth is that more than 90 percent of transmission problems on an Ethernet network are the result of faulty cables or malfunctioning adapter cards.

On an Ethernet network, data is broadcast throughout the network in all directions at the rate of 10 mbps. All machines receive every frame, but only those meant to receive a frame (by virtue of the frame's destination network address) respond with an acknowledgment. Figure 11.13 illustrates an Ethernet network.

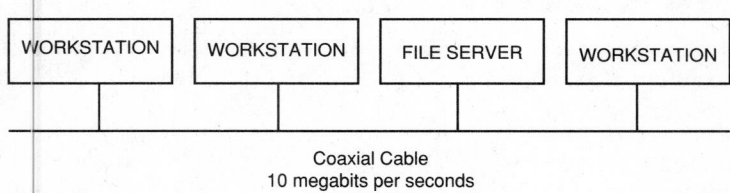

Coaxial Cable
10 megabits per seconds

Fig. 11.13
An Ethernet network.

Ethernet is a LAN standard that is based on the Experimental Ethernet network designed and built in 1975 by Xerox at the Palo Alto Research Center (PARC). Ethernet operates at 10 mbps over 50-ohm coaxial cable; the current version is 2.0, established in November, 1982.

IEEE 802.3 is a LAN standard similar to Ethernet. The first edition of IEEE 802.3 was published in 1985. The differences between the two Ethernet standards are in the areas of network architecture and frame formats.

In terms of network architecture, IEEE 802.3 distinguishes between MAC and LLC layers; true Ethernet lumps these layers together into a single Data Link layer. Ethernet also defines an Ethernet Configuration Test Protocol (ECTP) that is absent from the IEEE 802.3 standard. Note, however, that the important differences between the two are in the types and lengths of the fields that make up a frame. These differences can cause the two protocols to be incompatible. The Ethernet and IEEE 802.3 frames are discussed in the following sections.

Using Ethernet Frames. Figure 11.14 shows the layout and data field definitions for a true Ethernet frame (the original, non-IEEE Ethernet).

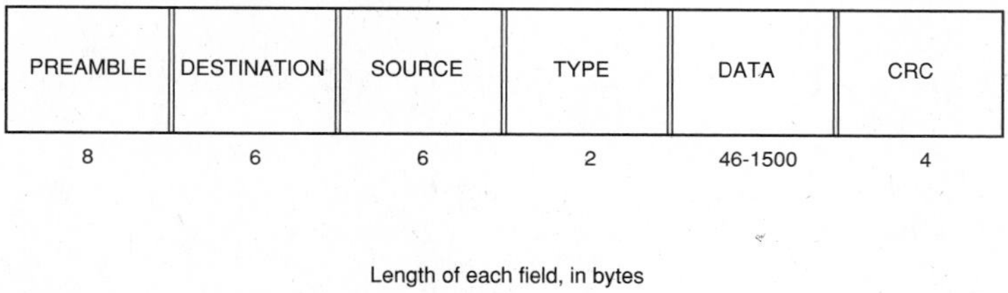

PREAMBLE	DESTINATION	SOURCE	TYPE	DATA	CRC
8	6	6	2	46-1500	4

Length of each field, in bytes

Fig. 11.14
An Ethernet frame.

Descriptions of the original Ethernet frame follow:

- *Preamble.* This field, used for synchronization and framing, is 8 bytes long (the standard refers to a byte as an *octet*, or *8 bits*; you can call them *bytes*). The Preamble always contains the bit pattern 10101010 in the first 7 bytes, with 10101011 in the last (8th) byte.

- *Destination Address.* This field is 6 bytes in size and contains the address of the workstation that will receive this frame. The first (leftmost) bit of the first byte has a special meaning. If the leftmost bit is a 0, the destination address is a physical address that is unique throughout the Ethernet universe. As a result of a naming scheme administered by Xerox Corporation, the first three bytes are a group address assigned by Xerox, and the last three are assigned locally. If the leftmost bit is a 1, it represents a broadcast frame. In this case, the rest of the destination address can refer to a group of logically related workstations or to all workstations on the network (all 1s).

- *Source Address.* This address field is also 6 bytes, and it identifies the workstation sending the frame. The leftmost bit of the first byte always is 0.

- *Type.* This field contains 2 bytes of information that identify the type of the higher-level protocol that issued (or wants to receive) this frame. The Type field is assigned by Xerox and is not interpreted by Ethernet. It enables multiple high-level protocols (referred to as *Client layers*) to share the network without running into one another's messages.

■ *Data Portion*. This portion of the frame can contain 46 to 1,500 bytes. It is the data message that the frame is intended to carry to the destination.

■ *CRC*. Finally, the frame contains 4 bytes of cyclic redundancy checksum remainder, calculated via a CRC-32 polynomial. The workstation that receives this frame performs its own CRC-32 calculation on the frame and compares the calculated value to the CRC field in the frame to find out whether the frame arrived intact or was damaged in transit.

Disregarding the preamble for a moment, you can see that an entire Ethernet frame is between 64 and 1,518 bytes in size. You can see also that the minimum size of a data message is 46 bytes.

Using IEEE 802.3 Frames. Figure 11.15 shows an IEEE 802.3 frame, which contains the following fields:

■ *Preamble*. This field contains 7 bytes of synchronization data. Each byte is the same bit pattern: 10101010.

■ *Start Frame Delimiter (SFD)*. The SFD consists of a single byte that has the bit pattern 10101011. (The Preamble and SFD IEEE 802.3 fields match the single Ethernet Preamble field.)

■ *Destination Address*. This field can contain 2 or 6 bytes, depending on which type of IEEE 802.3 network you install, and indicates the workstation for which the frame is intended. Note that all addresses on a particular network must be 2- or 6-byte addresses. The most popular type of IEEE 802.3, called 10BASE5, specifies 6-byte addresses. The first bit of the destination address is the individual/group bit. The I/G bit has a value of 0 if the address refers to a single workstation, or a 1 if it represents a group of workstations (a broadcast message). If the destination address is a 2-byte field, the rest of the bits form a 15-bit workstation address. If the destination address is a 6-byte field, however, the bit following the I/G bit is a universally/locally administered bit (the U/L bit). The U/L bit is a 0 for universally administered (global) addresses and is a 1 for locally administered addresses. The rest of the 6-byte field is a 46-bit workstation address.

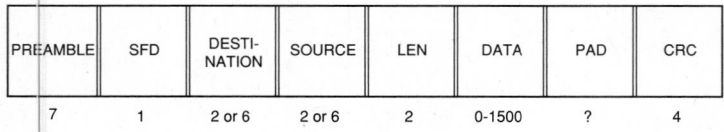

PREAMBLE	SFD	DESTI-NATION	SOURCE	LEN	DATA	PAD	CRC
7	1	2 or 6	2 or 6	2	0-1500	?	4

Length of each field, in bytes

Fig. 11.15
An IEEE 802.3 frame.

- *Source Address*. This is the 2- or 6-byte address of the sending workstation. The I/G (first) bit is always 0.

- *Length*. These two bytes express the length of the data portion of the frame.

- *Data Portion*. This field ranges from 0 to 1,500 bytes of data. If this field is less than 46 bytes, the next field (PAD) is used to fatten the frame to an acceptable (minimum) size.

- *Pad*. The Pad field contains enough bytes of filler to ensure that the frame has at least a certain overall size. If the data portion is large enough, the Pad field does not appear in the frame (Pad has zero length).

- *CRC*. The cyclic redundancy checksum remainder has 4 bytes of remainder from the CRC-32 algorithm—the same as for Ethernet.

The size of a frame under both true Ethernet and IEEE 802.3 Ethernet (assuming Type 10BASE5), excluding the Preamble and SFD, is the same: from 64 to 1,518 bytes. Under IEEE 802.3, however, it is permissible for the application (or an upper layer protocol) to send a data area that is less than 46 bytes, because the frame is padded automatically by the MAC layer. Under true Ethernet, data frames that are too small are considered to be error situations.

Using Token Ring

You can think of a token-passing network as a ring. Even though the network may be wired electrically as a star, data frames move around the network from workstation to workstation in ring fashion, as shown in figure 11.16. A workstation sends a frame to the MSAU (multistation access unit), which routes the frame to the next workstation.

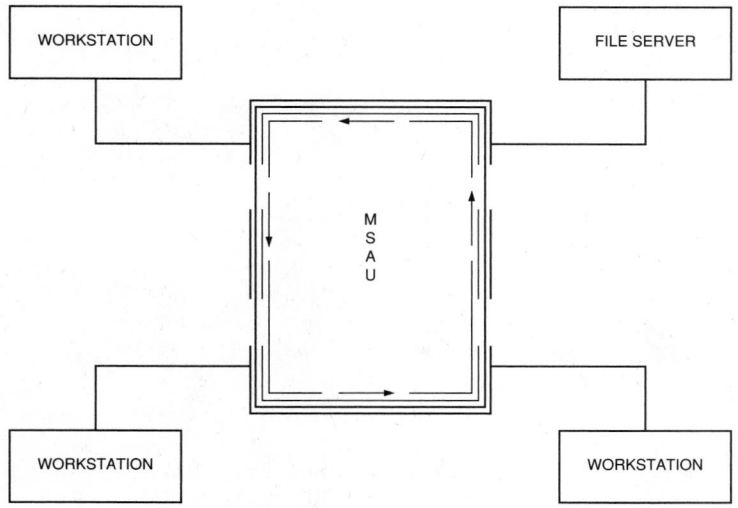

Fig. 11.16
A token ring network.

Each network adapter card receives a frame from its upstream neighbor, regenerates the electrical signals making up the frame, and passes the result along to the next (downstream) workstation. The frame may consist of some data that one computer is sending to another, or the frame may be a token. A *token* is a 3-byte message, indicating that the LAN is idle.

When a workstation wants to send a frame, the network adapter waits for the token. The adapter then turns the token into a data frame containing a protocol-layered message.

The frame travels along from adapter to adapter until it reaches its destination, which acknowledges reception of the frame by setting certain bits in the frame. The data frame continues its journey around the ring. When the sending station receives its own frame back, and if the frame was properly received, the sender relinquishes use of the LAN by putting a new token into circulation. A token-passing network is designed so that collisions never occur.

Early Token Release

Early Token Release (ETR) easily is misunderstood; Token Ring itself is a fairly complex subject. On a momentarily idle Token Ring LAN, workstations circulate a token. The LAN becomes busy (carries information) when a workstation receives a token and turns it into a data frame targeted at the file server (or targeted back at a file-needy workstation if originated by a server that is answering a file I/O request). After receipt by its target node, the data frame continues circulating around the LAN until it reaches its source node. The source node turns the data frame back into a token that circulates until a downstream node needs it. So far, so good—these are just standard Token Ring concepts.

A workstation needs to send only a few bytes to tell the file server that it needs some part of a file. If the signal must go into and out of many workstations to circulate the ring, and if the data frame is small, latency occurs. *Latency* is the unproductive delay that occurs while the source node waits for its upstream neighbor to return its data frame.

The source node appends idle characters onto the LAN following the data frame until the data frame circulates the entire LAN and arrives back at the source node. The typical latency of a 4-mbps ring is about 50 to 100 idle characters. On a 16-mbps ring, latency may reach 400 or more bytes' worth of LAN time.

With Early Token Release, available only on 16-mbps networks, the originating workstation transmits a new token immediately after sending its data frame. Downstream nodes pass along the data frame and then receive an opportunity to transmit data themselves—the new token. If you had a Token Ring microscope, you would see tokens and other data frames (instead of a long trail of idle characters) chasing the data frame. You would also know that your 16-mbps Token Ring LAN is using ETR to keep itself busy.

Using Token Ring Frames. In 1985, Texas Instruments and IBM jointly developed the TMS380 chipset (although IBM doesn't use the chipset; it builds its own proprietary chipset, which is mostly compatible with the TI/IBM set). The TMS380 chipset implements the IEEE 802.5 standards for the Physical and Data Link layers of the OSI model. The functions of both the MAC sublayer and the LLC sublayer of the Data Link layer are supported. Originally released as a set of five chips, the TI product now can be produced as a single chip.

Here are the TMS380 functions:

- *TMS38051 and 38052 chips*. These chips handle the lowest level: the ring interface itself. They perform the actual transmission/reception of data (frames), monitor cable integrity, and provide clocking functions.

- *TMS38020 chip*. This chip is the protocol handler. It controls and manages the 802.5 protocol functions.

- *ROM chip*. This chip has program code burned into it. The permanently stored software performs diagnostic and management functions.

- *TMS38010 chip*. This chip is a 16-bit dedicated microprocessor for handling communications; it executes the code in the ROM chip and has a 2.75K RAM buffer for temporary storage of transmitted and received data.

Although most people think of a Token Ring as a single piece of cable that all the workstations tap into, a Token Ring actually consists of individual point-to-point linkages. Joe's workstation sends the token (or a data frame) to your workstation, your workstation sends the token or frame downstream to the next workstation, and so on. Only the fact that one of your downstream neighbors also happens to be Joe's upstream neighbor makes it a ring. From a communications standpoint, the messages go directly from one PC to another.

Not all workstations on the ring are peers, although the differences are invisible to the outside world. One of the workstations is designated as the *active monitor*, which means that it assumes additional responsibilities for controlling the ring. The active monitor maintains timing control over the ring, issues new tokens (if necessary) to keep things going, and generates diagnostic frames under certain circumstances. The active monitor is chosen at the time the ring is initialized and can be any one of the workstations on the network. If the active monitor fails for some reason, there is a mechanism by which the other workstations (*standby monitors*) can decide which one becomes the new active monitor.

Three formats are defined for IEEE 802.5 Token Ring message packets: tokens, frames, and abort sequences. These formats are discussed in the following sections.

Using the Token. Figure 11.17 shows the first format of the IEEE 802.5 message packet: the token. In principle, the token is not a frame but simply a means by which each workstation can recognize when its turn to transmit has arrived.

III

Input/Output Hardware

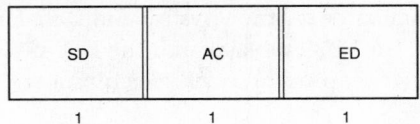

Length of each field, in bytes

Fig. 11.17
A token.

A token is 3 bytes long (24 bits) and contains the following three fields:

- Start Delimiter

- Access Control

- End Delimiter

The Start Delimiter (SD) field appears at the beginning of the token (as well as at the beginning of every message or frame that is sent across the network). The SD field consists not of just 0s and 1s, but of a unique series of electrical impulses that cannot be mistaken for anything other than a Start Delimiter field. Because the SD field contains four nondata symbols (each 1 bit long) and four (normal) 0 bits in the field, the field totals 1 byte in size.

Next, comes the Access Control (AC) field. This field is divided into four subfields:

P P P T M R R R

P P P are the priority bits, T is the token bit, M is the monitor bit, and R R R are the reservation bits.

A network adapter can prioritize a token or frame by setting the priority bits to a value ranging from 0 to 7 (with 7 being the highest priority). A workstation can use the network (that is, change a token into a frame) only if it receives a token with a priority less than or equal to the workstation's own priority. The workstation's network adapter sets the priority bits to indicate the priority of the current frame or token. Refer to the description of the reservation bits for more on how this works.

The token bit has a value of 1 for a token and has a value of 0 for a frame.

The monitor bit is set to 1 by the active monitor and set to 0 by any workstation transmitting a token or frame. If the active monitor sees a token or frame that contains a monitor bit of 1, it knows that this token or frame has been once around the ring without being processed by a workstation. Because a sending workstation is responsible for removing its own transmitted frames (by recirculating a new token), and because high-priority workstations are responsible for grabbing a token that they claimed previously, the active monitor detects that something is wrong if a frame or a prioritized token has circulated the ring without having been processed. The active monitor cancels the transmission and circulates a new token.

The reservation bits work hand in hand with the priority bits. A workstation can place its priority in the reservation bits (if its priority is higher than the current value of the reservation bits). The workstation then has reserved the next use of the network. When a workstation transmits a new token, the workstation sets the priority bits to the value that it found in the RRR field of the frame it just received. Unless preempted by an even higher priority workstation, the workstation that originally set the reservation bits will be the next station to turn the token into a frame.

The final field of the token is the End Delimiter (ED) field. As with the Start Delimiter field, this field contains a unique combination of 1s and special nondata symbols that cannot be mistaken for anything else. The ED field appears at the end of each token. Besides marking the end of the token, the ED field contains two subfields: the Intermediate Frame bit and the Error-Detected bit. These fields are discussed in the next section; they pertain more to frames than to tokens.

Using the Data Frame. Figure 11.18 shows the second format of the IEEE 802.5 message packet: the true data frame. Data frames can, of course, contain messages that a network operating system or an application sends to another computer on the ring. Data frames also sometimes contain internal messages used privately among the Token Ring network adapter cards for ring-management purposes.

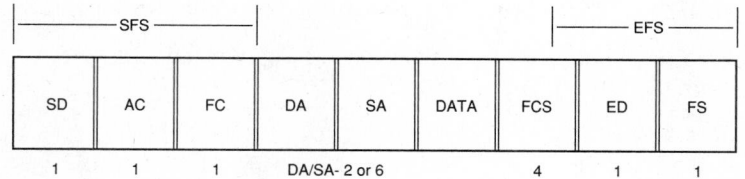

Length of each field, in bytes

Fig. 11.18
A token ring data frame.

A frame consists of several groups of fields: the Start Frame Sequence (SFS), the Destination Address (DA), the Source Address (SA), the data itself (DATA), the Frame Check Sequence (FCS), and the End Frame Sequence (EFS). Together, these fields form a message record (envelope) that is used to carry ring-management information (MAC data) or user data (LLC data). You already know about LLC data; these are the frames that contain application-oriented data, such as PC-to-PC messages or a portion of a disk file (from a file server) that is being shared through the network operating system. The network adapters use MAC frames internally, though, to control and manage the ring. The IEEE 802.5 standard defines six MAC control frames. The Frame Control field indicates the type of the frame (MAC or LLC); if it is a MAC frame, this field also indicates which of the six frames is represented by this particular frame.

The six MAC frames follow:

■ *Duplicate Address Test*. Sent by a workstation when it joins the ring to ensure that its address is unique.

■ *Active Monitor Present*. Circulated every so often by the active monitor to let other workstations know that it is still alive.

■ *Standby Monitor Present*. Sent by a monitor other than the active monitor.

■ *Claim Token*. If a standby monitor thinks that the active monitor may have died, it starts sending Claim Token frames. The standby monitors then go through a process of negotiation with one another to determine which one becomes the new active monitor.

■ *Beacon*. Sent in the event of a major network problem, such as a broken cable or a workstation that is transmitting without waiting for the token. By detecting which station is sending the Beacon frame, diagnostic software can localize the problem.

■ *Purge*. Sent after ring initialization and after a new active monitor establishes itself.

Each frame (MAC or LLC) begins with a start frame sequence, which contains three fields:

■ *Start Delimiter (SD)*. The definition of SD is the same for frames as for tokens.

■ *Access Control (AC)*. The definition is the same for frames as for tokens.

■ *Frame Control (FC)*. This is a 1-byte field containing two subfields—Frame Type and MAC Control ID:

        F F C C C C C C

The two frame type bits (FF) have a value of 00 for MAC frames and 01 for LLC frames (11 and 10 are reserved).

The MAC control ID bits identify the type of ring-management frame:

CCCCCC	MAC Frame
000011	Claim Token
000000	Duplicate Address Test
000101	Active Monitor Present
000110	Standby Monitor Present
000010	Beacon
000100	Purge

The Destination Address (DA) follows the Start Frame Sequence fields. The DA field can be 2 or 6 bytes. With 2-byte addresses, the first bit indicates whether the address is a group address or an individual address (just as in the collision-sensing IEEE 802.3 protocol). With 6-byte addresses, the first bit also is an I/G bit, and the second bit tells whether the address is assigned locally or globally (the U/L bit, which again is the same as in the IEEE 802.3 protocol). The rest of the bits form the address of the workstation to which the frame is addressed.

The Source Address (SA) field is the same size and format as the Destination Address field.

The data portion of the frame (DATA) can contain a user data message record intended for (or received from) a midlevel protocol such as IPX, TCP/IP, or NetBIOS. Or the Data field can contain one of the MAC frames just discussed. The Data field has no specified maximum length, although there are practical limits on its size based on how long a single workstation may have control of the ring.

The Frame Check Sequence (FCS) field is 4 bytes of remainder from the CRC-32 cyclic redundancy checksum algorithm. It is used for error detection.

The End Frame Sequence (EFS) is composed of two fields: the End Delimiter and the Frame Status. Descriptions of these fields follow:

- *End Delimiter (ED)*. You read about this field in relation to tokens; in a frame, however, this field takes on additional meaning. Besides consisting of a unique pattern of electrical impulses, it contains two subfields—each 1 bit in size. The intermediate frame bit is set to 1 if this frame is part of a multiple-frame transmission, and the bit is set to 0 if the frame is the last (or only) frame. The error-detected bit starts as a 0 when a frame is sent originally. Each workstation's network adapter, as it passes the frame along, checks for errors (verifying that the CRC in the Frame Check Sequence field still corresponds to the contents of the frame, for example). An adapter sets the error-detected bit to 1 if the adapter finds something wrong. The intervening network adapters that see an already set error-detected bit pass the frame along. The originating adapter notices that a problem occurred and tries again by retransmitting the frame.

- *Frame Status (FS)*. This 1-byte field contains four reserved bits (R) and two subfields—the address-recognized bit (A) and the frame-copied bit (C):

      A C R R A C R R

Because the calculated CRC does not encompass the Frame Status field, each of the 1-bit subfields is duplicated within frame status to ensure data integrity. A transmitting workstation sets the address-recognized bit to 0 when it originates a frame; the receiving workstation sets this bit to 1 to signal that it has recognized its destination address. The frame-copied bit also starts out as 0 but is set to 1 by the receiving (destination) workstation when it copies the contents of the frame into its own memory (when it actually receives the data). The data is copied (and the bit set) only if the frame is received without error. If the originating (source) workstation gets its frame back with both of these bits set, it knows that a successful reception occurred.

If, however, the address-recognized bit is not set by the time the frame gets back to the originating workstation, the destination workstation is no longer on the network; the other workstation must have crashed or powered off suddenly.

Another situation occurs when the destination address is recognized but the frame-copied bit is not set. This setting tells the originating workstation that the frame got damaged in transit (the error-detected bit in the end delimiter also will be set).

If the address-recognized bit and the frame-copied bit are both set, but the error-detected bit also is set, the originating workstation knows that the error occurred after the frame was received correctly.

Using the Abort Sequence. Figure 11.19 shows the third format of the IEEE 802.5 message packet: the abort sequence. An abort sequence can occur anywhere in the bit stream and is used to interrupt or terminate the current transmission.

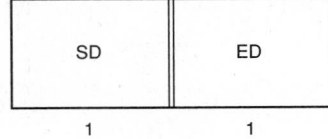

Length of each field, in bytes

Fig. 11.19
An abort sequence.

An abort sequence consists of a Start Delimiter followed by an End Delimiter. An abort sequence signals cancellation of the current frame or token transmission.

Using the Fiber Distributed Data Interface (FDDI)

The Fiber Distributed Data Interface (FDDI) is a much newer protocol than Ethernet or Token Ring. Designed by the X3T9.5 Task Group of ANSI (the American National Standards Institute), FDDI passes tokens and data frames around a ring of optical fiber at a rate of 100 mbps. FDDI was designed to be as much like the IEEE 802.5 Token Ring standard as possible. Differences occur only where necessary to support the faster speeds and longer transmission distances of FDDI.

If FDDI were to use the same bit-encoding scheme used by Token Ring, every bit would require two optical signals: a pulse of light and then a pause of darkness. This means that FDDI would need to send 200 million signals per second to have a 100-mbps transmission rate. Instead, the scheme used by FDDI—called 4B/5B—encodes 4 bits of data into 5 bits for transmission so that fewer signals are needed to send a byte of information. The 5-bit codes (symbols) were chosen carefully to ensure that network timing requirements are met. The 4B/5B scheme, at a 100-mbps transmission rate, actually causes 125 million signals per second to occur (this is 125 megabaud). Also, because each carefully selected light pattern symbol represents 4 bits (a half byte, or *nibble*), FDDI hardware can operate at the nibble and byte level rather than at the bit level, making it easier to achieve the high data rate.

Two major differences in the way the token is managed by FDDI and IEEE 802.5 Token Ring exist. In Token Ring, a new token is circulated only after a sending workstation gets back the frame that it sent. In FDDI, a new token is circulated immediately by the sending workstation after it finishes transmitting a frame. FDDI doesn't use the Priority and Reservation subfields that Token Ring uses to allocate system resources. Instead, FDDI classifies attached workstations as *asynchronous* (workstations that are not rigid about the time periods that occur between network accesses) and *synchronous* (workstations having very stringent requirements regarding the timing between transmissions). FDDI uses a complex algorithm to allocate network access to the two classes of devices.

Figure 11.20 shows an FDDI token. The token consists of Preamble, Start Delimiter, Frame Control, End Delimiter, and Frame Status fields. These fields have the same definition for tokens as for frames.

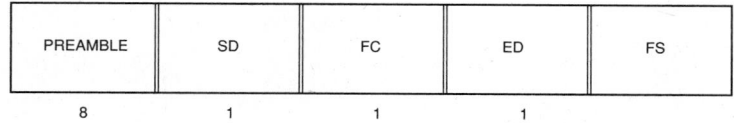

Length of each field, in bytes

Fig. 11.20
An FDDI token.

Figure 11.21 shows the layout of an FDDI frame. Notice the similarity to the IEEE 802.5 Token Ring frames just discussed. An FDDI frame, like its slower cousin, carries MAC control data or user data.

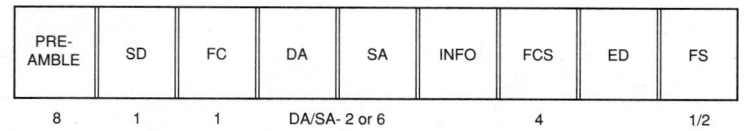

Length of each field, in bytes

Fig. 11.21
An FDDI frame.

The fields in an FDDI frame follow:

■ *Preamble.* This field is used for synchronization purposes. Although this field is initially 64 bits (16 symbol-encoded nibbles) in size, subsequent workstations can modify the Preamble's length dynamically according to their own clocking and synchronization requirements.

- *Start Delimiter (SD)*. A unique two-symbol (1-byte) field; its pattern identifies the start of the frame.

- *Frame Control (FC)*. A two-symbol (1-byte) field made up of the following subfields:

  C | L FF T T T T

  The C subfield designates the frame class, which tells whether the frame is being used for synchronous or asynchronous service. The L bit is the frame address length and indicates whether 16- or 48-bit addresses are being used (unlike with Ethernet and Token Ring, both kinds of addresses are possible on the same FDDI network). The FF bits are the Frame Format subfield, and express whether the frame is a MAC frame carrying ring-management information or an LLC frame carrying user data. If it is a MAC frame, the T T T T bits specify the type of the MAC control frame contained in the Info field.

- *Destination Address (DA)*. This field can be 16 bits or 48 bits and identifies the workstation to which this frame is being sent.

- *Source Address (SA)*. This field, which can be 16 or 48 bits, identifies the sending workstation.

- *Information (INFO)*. This field is the data portion of the frame. It contains a MAC control record or user data. This field can vary in length, but it cannot cause the overall length of the frame to exceed 4,500 bytes.

- *Frame Check Sequence (FCS)*. This field contains 4 bytes (8 symbols) of CRC data used for error-checking.

- *End Delimiter (ED)*. In a frame, this field is 1 nibble (1 symbol) long. In a token, it is 1 byte (2 symbols) long. This field uniquely identifies the end of the frame or token.

- *Frame Status (FS)*. This field is of arbitrary length, and contains the error-detected bit, the address-recognized bit, and the frame-copied bit. These subfields do the same job on an FDDI network as on a Token Ring network.

Using LAN Cables

Cabling systems for LANs vary widely in their appearance, characteristics, intended purpose, and cost. This chapter discusses the three most popular ways to tie computers together on a LAN: the IBM cabling system, the AT&T premises distribution system, and the Digital Equipment Corporation cabling concept called DECconnect.

Generally speaking, the cabling systems described in the next few sections use one of three distinct cable types. These are twisted pair (shielded and unshielded) cable, coaxial cable (thin and thick), and fiber optic cable.

Using Twisted Pair Cable

Twisted pair cable is just what its name implies: insulated wires with a minimum number of twists per foot. Twisting the wires reduces electrical interference (*attenuation*). *Shielded twisted pair* refers to the amount of insulation around the wire and therefore, its noise immunity. You are familiar with unshielded twisted pair; it is often used by the telephone company. Shielded twisted pair, however, is entirely different in appearance. Shielded twisted pair looks somewhat like the wire used to carry house current (110 volts) throughout your home or apartment. Appearances are deceiving, because shielded twisted pair actually carries a relatively low voltage signal. The heavy insulation is for noise reduction, not safety.

Figure 11.22 shows unshielded twisted pair cable; figure 11.23 illustrates shielded twisted pair cable.

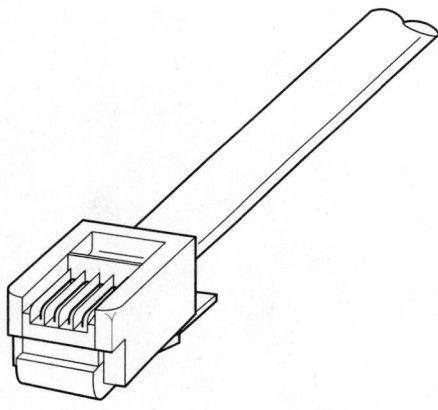

Unshielded twisted pair

Fig. 11.22
An unshielded twisted pair cable.

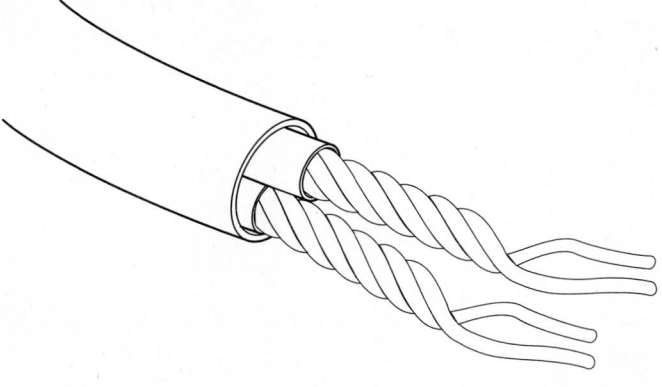

Fig. 11.23
A shielded twisted pair cable.

Using Coaxial Cable

Coaxial cable is fairly prevalent in your everyday life; you often find it connected to the backs of television sets and audio equipment. *Thin* and *thick*, of course, refer to the diameter of the coaxial cable. Standard Ethernet cable (thick Ethernet) is as thick as your thumb. The newer ThinNet (sometimes called CheaperNet) cable is about the size of your little finger. The thick cable has a greater degree of noise immunity, is more difficult to damage, and requires a *vampire tap* (a piercing connector) and a drop cable to connect to a LAN. Although thin cable carries the signal over shorter distances than the thick cable, ThinNet uses a simple BNC connector (a bayonet-locking connector for thin coaxial cables), is lower in cost, and has become a standard in office coaxial cable.

Figure 11.24 shows an Ethernet BNC coaxial connector, and figure 11.25 illustrates the design of coaxial cable.

Fig. 11.24
An Ethernet coaxial cable connector.

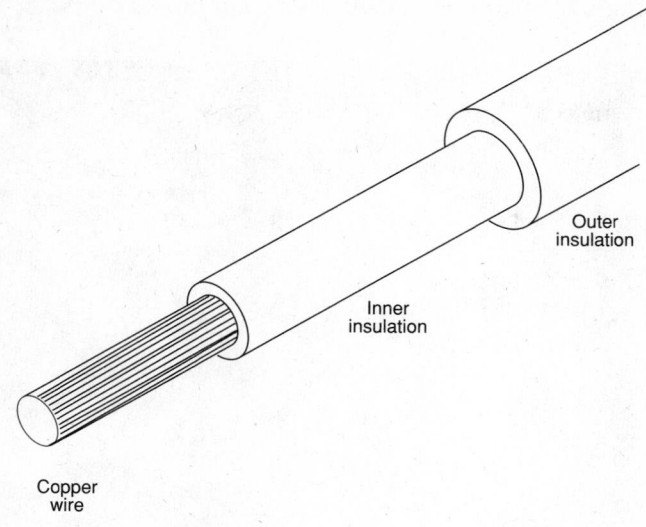

Outer
insulation

Inner
insulation

Copper
wire

Fig. 11.25
Coaxial cable.

Using Fiber Optic Cable

Fiber optic cable, as its name suggests, uses light rather than electricity to carry information. Fiber can send data over huge distances at high speeds, but it is expensive and difficult to work with. Splicing the cable, installing connectors, and using the few available diagnostic tools for finding cable faults are skills that very few people have.

Fiber optic cable is simply designed, but unforgiving of bad connections. Fiber cable usually consists of a core of glass thread, with a diameter measured in microns, surrounded by a solid glass cladding. This, in turn, is covered by a protective sheath. The first fiber optic cables were made of glass, but plastic fibers also have been developed. The light source for fiber optic cable is a light-emitting diode (LED); information usually is encoded by varying the intensity of the light. A detector at the other end of the cable converts the received signal back into electrical impulses. Two types of fiber cable exist: single mode and multimode. Single mode has a smaller diameter, is more expensive, and can carry signals for a greater distance.

III

Input/Output Hardware

Figure 11.26 illustrates fiber optic cables and their connectors.

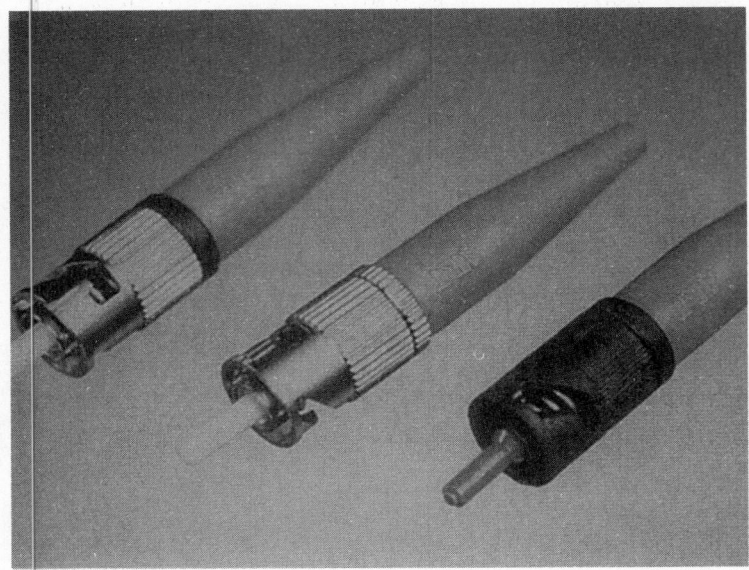

Fig. 11.26
Fiber optic cables use light to carry LAN messages. The ST connector is commonly used with fiber optic cables.

Using the IBM Cabling System

The IBM cabling system, ironically, is not manufactured or sold by IBM. This cabling system consists of a published IBM standard for wiring systems in office buildings that defines cabling system components and different cable types. When it was introduced in 1984, IBM described the IBM cabling system as the intended backbone of its Token Ring network. The first such cables to be manufactured by third-party companies were tested by IBM, verified to IBM specifications, and actually given IBM part numbers. At present, however, cable manufacturers have to rely on the ETL or UL independent testing laboratories or on industry-standard manufacturers (such as AMP) to verify compliance with the specifications published by IBM.

The IBM specification defines workstation faceplates, adapters/connectors, access units, and wiring-closet termination methods. The standard also defines the following cable types:

- *Type 1 data cable.* Copper-based, for data connections only. Available in nonplenum, plenum, and outdoor varieties. It consists of two twisted pairs of 22-gauge solid conductors, shielded with both foil and braid, and covered with a polyvinyl-chloride (PVC) sheath. Type 1 data cable is used for connecting terminal devices located in work areas to distribution panels located in wiring closets and for connecting between wiring closets. The plenum cable is installed in plenums, ducts, and spaces used for environmental air; in case of fire, it gives off less toxic fumes than nonplenum cable. The outdoor cable is protected in a corrugated metallic shield with a polyethylene sheath, and the core is filled with a jellylike compound to prevent moisture from entering.

■ *Type 2 data and telephone cable.* For both data and voice (telephone) applications. This cable is similar to Type 1 but has four additional twisted pairs (22-gauge). Type 2 cable comes in plenum and nonplenum varieties.

■ *Type 3 telephone twisted pair cable.* Consists of four-pair, 24-gauge wire in polyvinyl-chloride plastic. This cable is equivalent to the IBM Rolm specification and is available in plenum. This cable is unshielded and not as immune to noise as Type 1 cable when used for data.

■ *Type 5 fiber optic cable.* Contains two 100/140-micron multimode optical fibers (100-micron core surrounded by 140-micron cladding layer). This cable is not defined by IBM.

■ *Type 6 patch panel cable.* For connecting a workstation to a wall faceplate or making connections within a wiring closet. This cable is more flexible than Type 1 cable (hence, its use as patch cable). This cable consists of two twisted pairs of 26-gauge stranded conductors.

■ *Type 8 undercarpet cable.* An undercarpet cable useful for open office or workstation areas where there are no permanent walls. Type 8 cable consists of two pairs of 26-gauge solid conductors in a flat sheath.

■ *Type 9 low-cost plenum cable.* An economy version of Type 1 plenum cable, with a maximum transmission distance about two-thirds that of Type 1 cable. Type 9 cable consists of two twisted pairs of 26-gauge stranded conductors. This cable is not defined by IBM.

Connecting the Cables

In a token-passing network, the cables from the workstations (or from the wall faceplates) connect centrally to a multistation access unit (abbreviated MSAU, or sometimes just MAU). The MSAU keeps track of which workstations on the LAN are neighbors and which neighbor is upstream or downstream. It is an easy job; the MSAU usually does not even need to be plugged into a electrical power outlet. The exceptions to this need for external power are MSAUs that support longer cable distances, or the use of unshielded twisted pair (Type 3) cable in high-speed LANs. The externally powered MSAU helps the signal along by regenerating it.

An IBM MSAU has eight ports for connecting one to eight Token Ring devices. Each connection is made with a genderless data connector (as specified in the IBM cabling system). The MSAU has two additional ports, labeled RI (Ring-In) and RO (Ring-Out), that daisy-chain several MSAUs together when you have more than eight workstations on the LAN.

It takes several seconds to open the adapter connection on a Token Ring LAN (something you may have noticed). During this time, the MSAU and your Token Ring adapter card perform a small diagnostic check, after which the MSAU establishes you as a new neighbor on the ring. After being established as an active workstation, your computer is linked on both sides to your upstream and downstream neighbors (as defined by your position on the MSAU). In its turn, your Token Ring adapter card accepts the token or frame, regenerates its electrical signals, and gives the token or frame a swift kick to send it through the MSAU in the direction of your downstream neighbor.

In an Ethernet network, the number of connections (taps) and their intervening distances are limiting factors. Repeaters regenerate the signal every 500 meters or so. If repeaters were not used, *standing waves* (additive signal reflections) would distort the signal and cause errors. Because collision detection depends partly on timing, only five 500-meter segments and four repeaters can be placed in series before the propagation delay becomes longer than the maximum allowed period for the detection of a collision. Otherwise, the workstations farthest from the sender would be unable to determine whether a collision had occurred.

The people who design computer systems love to find ways to circumvent limitations. Manufacturers of Ethernet products have made it possible to create Ethernet networks in star, branch, and tree designs that overcome the basic limitations mentioned. You can have thousands of workstations on a complex Ethernet network.

Local area networks are local because the network adapters and other hardware components cannot send LAN messages more than about a few hundred feet. Table 11.9 reveals the distance limitations of different kinds of LAN cable. In addition to the limitations shown in the table, keep in mind that you cannot connect more than 30 computers on a ThinNet Ethernet segment, more than 100 computers on a ThickNet Ethernet segment, more than 72 computers on unshielded twisted pair Token Ring cable, or more than 260 computers on shielded twisted pair Token Ring cable.

Table 11.9   Network Distance Limitations

Network Adapter	Cable Type	Maximum	Minimum
Ethernet	Thin	607 ft.	20 in.
	Thick (drop cable)	164 ft.	8 ft.
	Thick (backbone)	1,640 ft.	8 ft.
	UTP	328 ft.	8 ft.
Token Ring	STP	328 ft.	8 ft.
	UTP	148 ft.	8 ft.
ARCnet (passive hub)		393 ft.	Depends on cable
ARCnet (active hub)		1,988 ft.	Depends on cable

Evaluating Fast Network Adapters

As mentioned earlier in this chapter, network adapters generally are collision-sensing or token-passing. A network adapter's design ties it to one of the low-level protocols—Ethernet, Token Ring, FDDI, ARCnet, or some other protocol.

If you have fast workstations and a fast file server, you want a fast network. Even 16 mbps may be too slow if your applications are data-intensive. TCNS, from Thomas-Conrad, operates at 100 mbps and doesn't cost much more than Token Ring. TCNS gives you all the advantages of FDDI without FDDI's high price tag. NetWare, LAN Manager, POWERLan, LANtastic, and other ARCnet-compatible network operating systems work well with TCNS. The only catch is that you have to use fast computers to realize performance gains with TCNS.

You can use the same shielded twisted pair (IBM Type 1) or coaxial (RG62A/U) cabling already in place for Token Ring or ARCnet, or you can install 62.5-micron fiber optic cable. You can mix and match cable types by using a TCNS Smart Hub with different connectors. You wire a TCNS network in a distributed star fashion, just as you would with ARCnet or Token Ring. TCNS adapters and hubs use ST connectors for fiber optic cable, BNC connectors for coaxial, and DB-9 connectors for STP.

A TCNS network adapter is register-compatible with an ARCnet adapter, which enables TCNSs to use industry-standard ARCnet software drivers. Thomas-Conrad also supplies "Accelerated Drivers" for an even greater performance boost. TCNS consists of network adapters with STP, coaxial, or fiber optic connectors; one or more Thomas-Conrad Smart Hubs; and software drivers. The adapters come in 16- and 32-bit, and ISA- and EISA-bus varieties. You can put up to 255 TCNS workstations on a single LAN segment, and you can span significant distances: 2,950 feet (hub to workstation) with fiber optic cable, 492 feet with shielded twisted pair cable, and 338 feet with RG62A/U coaxial cable.

Collision-sensing and token-passing adapters contain sufficient on-board logic to know when it is permissible to send a frame and to recognize frames intended for the adapters. With the adapter support software, both types of cards perform seven major steps during the process of sending or receiving a frame. Outbound, when data is being sent, the steps are performed in the order presented in the following list. Inbound, as data is received, however, the steps are reversed. Here are the steps:

1. *Data transfer*. Data is transferred from PC memory (RAM) to the adapter card or from the adapter card to PC memory via DMA, shared memory, or programmed I/O.

2. *Buffering*. While being processed by the network adapter card, data is held in a buffer. The buffer gives the card access to an entire frame at once, and the buffer enables the card to manage the difference between the data rate of the network and the rate at which the PC can process data.

III

Input/Output Hardware

3. *Frame formation.* The network adapter has to break up the data into manageable chunks (or, on reception, reassemble it). On an Ethernet network, these chunks are about 1,500 bytes. Token Ring networks generally use a frame size of about 4K. The adapter prefixes the data packet with a frame header and appends a frame trailer to it. The header and trailer are the Physical layer's envelope, which you learned about earlier in this chapter. At this point, a complete, ready-for-transmission frame exists. (Inbound, on reception, the adapter removes the header and trailer at this stage.)

4. *Cable access.* In a CSMA/CD network such as Ethernet, the network adapter ensures that the line is quiet before sending its data (or retransmits its data if a collision occurs). In a token-passing network, the adapter waits until it gets a token it can claim. (These steps are not significant to receiving a message, of course.)

5. *Parallel/serial conversion.* The bytes of data in the buffer are sent or received through the cables in serial fashion, with one bit following the next. The adapter card does this conversion in the split second before transmission (or after reception).

6. *Encoding/decoding.* The electrical signals that represent the data being sent or received are formed. Most network adapters use *Manchester encoding*. This technique has the advantage of incorporating timing information into the data through the use of *bit periods*. Instead of representing a 0 as the absence of electricity and a 1 as its presence, the 0s and 1s are represented by changes in polarity as they occur in relation to very small time periods.

7. *Sending/receiving impulses.* The electrically encoded impulses making up the data (frame) are amplified and sent through the wire. (On reception, the impulses are handed up to the decoding step.)

Of course, the execution of all of these steps takes only a fraction of a second. While you were reading about these steps, thousands of frames could have been sent across the LAN.

Network Adapter cards and the support software recognize and handle errors, which occur when electrical interference, collisions (in CSMA/CD networks), or malfunctioning equipment cause some portion of a frame to be corrupted. Errors generally are detected through the use of a cyclic redundancy checksum (CRC) data item in the frame. The CRC is checked by the receiver; if its own calculated CRC doesn't match the value of the CRC in the frame, the receiver tells the sender about the error and requests retransmission of the frame in error. Several products exist that perform network diagnostic and analysis functions on the different types of LANs, should you find yourself in need of such troubleshooting.

The different types of network adapters vary not only in access method and protocol, but also in the following elements:

- Transmission speed
- Amount of on-board memory for buffering frames and data

- Bus design (8-bit, 16-bit, or MicroChannel)
- Bus speed (some fail when run at high speeds)
- Compatibility with various CPU chipsets
- DMA usage
- IRQ and I/O port addressing
- Intelligence (some use an on-board CPU, such as the 80186)
- Connector design

Summary

This chapter gave you an understanding of serial, parallel, and network connectivity methods. You learned about the different types of UART chips, explored ways to diagnose serial and parallel ports, and considered local area network adapters, cables, and protocols.

In the next chapter, you turn your attention to sound cards as you discover how PCs can produce music and even speak words and phrases.

III

Input/Output Hardware

Chapter 12

Audio Hardware

For many years, the PC lacked a voice. While the Apple Macintosh and Commodore Amiga have long had standardized, high-quality sound, the typical PC features an impish two-inch speaker stuffed inside the computer's case.

Then the sound revolution came. PC owners can now buy sound cards, which give their software the capability to speak and sing. By buying the Sound Blaster Pro, Pro AudioStudio 16, Microsoft Sound System, or any of several other sound card models and makes, you can give your PC a voice.

At first, sound cards were used only for games. The first sound cards for the PC were the AdLib Music Synthesizer Card ($195) and the Roland MT-32 Sound Module ($500). In 1989, Creative Labs developed the Game Blaster, which was distributed by Brown-Wagh Publishing. The Game Blaster provided stereo sound to a handful of computer games. The question for many buyers was, "Why spend $100 for a card that adds sound to a $50 game?" More importantly, because no sound standards existed at the time, a sound card might be useless with other games.

A few months after releasing the Game Blaster, Creative Labs announced the Sound Blaster sound card, which originally sold for $239.95. The Sound Blaster was compatible with the AdLib sound card and Creative Labs' own Game Blaster card. It included a built-in microphone jack and a MIDI (Musicial Instrument Digital Interface) interface for connecting the PC to a musical synthesizer. Finally, the sound card had uses besides games.

Sound Card Applications

Unfortunately, sound cards have no standards. As in other aspects of the computer industry, the standard is developed by the market leader. For example, Hayes-compatible modems use the escape codes used by Hayes Microcomputer Products Inc. to connect two computers. (Hayes now collects royalties from many modem manufacturers who use their codes.)

Over the last few years, sound card manufacturers have fought for dominance. Today a sound card may be touted as AdLib-compatible or Sound Blaster-compatible. (The de facto standard is Sound Blaster.) Until the anemic speaker built into the PC is replaced by a standard sound chip, however, adding a Sound Blaster sound card hardly constitutes a standard.

Despite the lack of standards, a sound card has many uses, including the following:

- Adding stereo sound to entertainment (game) software
- Forming the backbone for multimedia
- Adding sound effects to business presentations and training software
- Creating music, using MIDI hardware and software
- Making screen savers talk
- Adding voice notes to Windows files
- Adding sound effects to Windows
- Giving a PC voice commands
- Turning a PC into a proofreader
- Playing audio CDs from DOS and from within Windows

Games

The sound card originally was designed to play games. In fact, many sound cards include *joystick ports*—connectors for adding a game joystick. Typically, you tell your game software that you have a sound card and to avoid using the PC's speaker (see fig. 12.1).

```
        Night Hawk F-117A Stealth Fighter 2.0 - Version 473.02

    Program & Audio-visual Copyright (C) 1991 by MicroProse Software,Inc.,
                          All Rights Reserved.




                          Select Sound Driver:

                          1) IBM Sound
                          2) Ad Lib Sound Board
                          3) Roland Sound Board
                          4) No Sound
```

Fig. 12.1
In many games, such as F-117A Stealth Fighter from MicroProse, you select the sound card you have.

The result is that the games take on human qualities. For example, the CD-ROM game *Sherlock Holmes, the Consulting Detective*, from Icom Simulations, uses recorded human voices and film clips. In this game you navigate through London, attempting to solve three different mysteries. Each new location brings up a 30- to 90-second film clip of actors portraying characters, including Holmes and Dr. Watson. The dialogue comes from the digitized voices of real actors.

Similarly, games such as *Monkey Island*, from LucasFilm Games, have beautiful musical scores. In Monkey Island, you become the character Guybrush Threepwood, roaming the Caribbean to become a pirate. To fit the tropical scenes, Monkey Island's musical score includes reggae music.

Multimedia

A sound card is a prerequisite if you want to turn your PC into a *multimedia* PC (MPC). What is multimedia? The term embraces a gamut of PC technologies. Basically, multimedia means the ability to merge voice, images, data, and video on a computer. Multimedia applications range from talking encyclopedias to databases of stored video clips.

An organization called the Multimedia PC (MPC) Marketing Council was formed to generate "standards" for multimedia. This group of hardware and software manufacturers already includes Tandy, Philips Electronics, NEC, and other big names. The group defines a multimedia PC as a computer having at least the following elements:

- 25-MHz 80486SX processor
- Double-speed CD-ROM drive that is CD-ROM XA ready
- 16-bit audio card
- 640 × 480 VGA card displaying 65,536 colors
- 4M RAM
- 160M hard disk
- A pair of speakers
- 1.44M (high-density) 3 1/2-inch disk drive
- MIDI interface
- Microsoft Windows 3.1

(This list is based on the second version of the MPC specifications, which are also called MPC-2 or MPC Level 2 specifications.)

The MPC-2 specifications are the *bare minimums*. In fact, the MPC Marketing Council sometimes raises these standards a notch or two.

A sound card is the backbone of an MPC. (In fact, many sound cards include a built-in connection for the CD-ROM drive.) What can you do with an MPC? Most multimedia software packages are designed for education, entertainment, or reference. With a CD-ROM disc's capability to hold so much information (up to 660M), you can provide the equivalent of volumes of static historical information on one disc. For example, one CD-ROM can hold the equivalent of an encyclopedia boot set.

III

Input/Output Hardware

One of the more impressive CD-ROM discs is Microsoft's *Multimedia Beethoven: The Ninth Symphony*. Professor Robert Winter, an authority on Beethoven, guides the user into appreciating Beethoven and his Ninth Symphony. Six sections focus on different aspects of the man and his work. The Art of Listening section, for example, teaches you how to appreciate music and applies those same principles to this particular symphony. You can select and listen to certain passages while the actual notes are displayed on the screen.

MIDI

If you're musically inclined, you'll enjoy MIDI (Musicial Instrument Digital Interface). Developed in the early 1980s, MIDI essentially is a powerful programming language that lets your computer store and edit or play back music in tandem with a MIDI-compatible electronic musical instrument, typically a keyboard synthesizer.

The MPC specs mentioned earlier call for MIDI support. With a MIDI interface, you can compose and edit music for presentations, learn about music theory, or turn your PC into a one-stop music mixing studio.

MIDI makes a musical note sound as though it comes from any of a wide array of instruments. The MPC specifications require a sound card to contain an FM MIDI synthesizer chip and be able to play at least six notes simultaneously.

To connect a MIDI device to a PC, you need a sound card that has two round serial ports in back—a MIDI input port and a MIDI output port. In addition to a keyboard, you'll need sequencing software to modify the tempo, sound, and volume of your recordings, or to cut and paste together various prerecorded music sequences.

Unlike other sound files, MIDI messages require little disk space. An hour of stereo music stored in MIDI requires less than 500K. (To contrast, a Microsoft Windows digital sound (WAV) file, consumes over 1,000 times that.)

Presentations

Businesses are discovering that combining graphics, animation, and sound is more impressive, and often less expensive, than a slide show. A sound card adds pizzazz to any presentation or classroom.

A variety of business-presentation software and high-end training and authoring packages already exist. And you don't have to be a programmer to get your own show on the road. Among the packages you can use to incorporate multimedia elements into your show are Asymetrix Corporation's Make Your Point and Macromedia's Action. Even such popular software packages as CorelDRAW! and PowerPoint now include rudimentary sound and animation features for their presentation files.

Some presentation software packages support MIDI. With these products you can synchronize sounds with objects. When a picture of a new product is displayed, for example, you can play a roaring round of applause. You can even pull in audio from a CD in your CD-ROM drive. Such presentation software programs include clip-media libraries.

A sound card can make tasks (such as learning how to use software) easier. PC software manufacturers have taken an early lead in this area. Microsoft and Lotus, for example, are already shipping special CD-ROM versions of some of their products. These versions include animated on-line help, replete with music.

You can even take your show on the road. Some special external sound cards attach to a laptop computer's parallel port to provide audio on the go. And some laptops include built-in audio. For example, Texas Instruments' line of 4000M laptops include multimedia capabilities.

Screen Savers

A *screen saver* is a software program that either blanks the screen or replaces it with moving images after a preset period of time. Why? If you leave your current work, such as a document, displayed on the screen, the monitor's electron beams may permanently etch the static image into the screen's phosphor surface. Screen savers often include passwords to protect your work from by prying eyes. Microsoft Windows 3.1, for example, has a built-in screen saver with password protection.

Your Microsoft Windows screen saver may blank the screen but not your ears. Some screen savers, such as After Dark for Windows and Intermission, now include sounds. In After Dark the nocturnal module howls and chirps, the aquatic scene bubbles, and the space toasters flap their wings. In Intermission you'll find a dancing pig and an ant farm.

Recording

Virtually all sound cards have an audio input jack. With a microphone, you can record your voice. Using the Microsoft Windows 3.1 Sound Recorder, you can play, edit, or record a sound file. These files are saved as WAV files, a type of file format. In the Windows Control Panel, you can assign certain Windows events a specific WAV file (see fig. 12.2). You might use a loud "Ta-da" to announce the starting of Windows, for example.

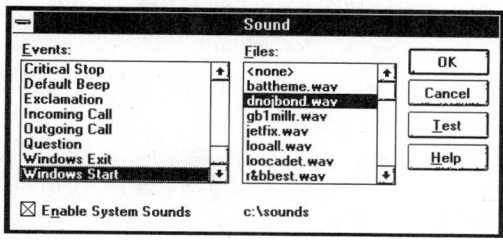

Fig. 12.2
The Sound section of the Windows Control Panel adds sound to different Windows events.

By recording your own sounds, you can create your own WAV files. Then you can use them for certain events. These are the standard events:

- Windows Start
- Windows Exit
- Default beep
- Asterisk
- Critical Stop
- Question
- Exclamation

Through the same audio input jack, you can attach your stereo system and record a song to a WAV file. You can also purchase prepackaged WAV files. Prerecorded WAV files can also be found on your local electronic bulletin board or on-line services such as CompuServe and America Online.

Voice Annotation

Using WAV files, you can record messages into your Windows documents and spreadsheets. For example, a business executive could pick up a microphone and, by embedding a message in a contract, give his or her secretary explicit instructions. This message is called a *voice annotation* (but think of it as a verbal Post-It note).

With voice annotation you can embed voice messages, suggestions, or questions in a document and send them to a colleague. To leave such messages, your Windows application must support Windows' Object Linking and Embedding (OLE) feature.

Imagine that you're editing a worksheet in Excel and want to insert a voice note next to a total that looks questionable. Place the cursor in the cell next to the total, then select **E**dit, **I**nsert, **O**bject, **S**ound to call up Windows' Sound Recorder. Click on the Record button and begin speaking.

Voice Recognition

Imagine giving your PC spoken commands from within Microsoft Windows. Some sound cards are capable of voice recognition. For example, the Pro AudioStudio 16, from Media Vision, includes voice-recognition software. You can also get voice recognition for your current sound card. IBM and Dragon Systems are marketing the Dragon Talk-To Plus software package ($149) for simple voice-command control of Windows applications. Voice-recognition technology is not perfect and you need a speedy computer, such as a 486DX4 or Pentium, for quick response times.

Proofreading

Sound cards can be used also as inexpensive proofreaders. Text-to-speech utilities can read back to you a list of numbers or text.

Monologue, a text-to-speech utility ($149) from First Byte Inc., is included with the Pro AudioStudio 16 sound card. You can have this text-to-speech utility loaded in the background while you are using your spreadsheet or word processor. Say, for example, that you are entering columns of numbers in Lotus 1-2-3. When you want to check your work, just highlight the numbers and press a hot key. Monologue begins to read back the highlighted numbers. Monologue can also read back an entire file.

You can change the speed and volume of Monologue's voice and change the pitch to resemble a male or female voice. You can even add words to a dictionary of exceptions in which you teach Monologue how to speak "correct" English. Windows versions of text-to-speech utilities also are available. Monologue for Windows ($149) reads back text you copy into the Windows Clipboard.

What are the practical uses for a text-to-speech utility? Forgotten words or awkward phrases may be easier to spot when you hear a letter read. Accountants can double-check spreadsheet numbers, and busy executives can listen to their E-mail while they are doing paperwork.

Audio CDs

Microsoft Windows can also play audio CDs while you are working on something else. The music can be piped not only through a pair of speakers but also through a headphone set plugged into the front of your CD-ROM drive.

Some sound cards include a DOS-based CD-player utility, although free versions are available on online services such as CompuServe. For example, the Sound Blaster Pro includes CD Player. With the DOS-based utility, however, you cannot use another program while the CD utility is in use (as you can with its Windows counterpart). However, you can exit the DOS CD utility, letting the audio CD play uncontrolled.

Sound Card Concepts and Terms

To understand sound cards, you need to understand various concepts and terms. Words like *16-bit*, *CD-quality*, and *MIDI port* are just a few. Concepts such as *sampling* and *digital-to-audio conversion (DAC)* are often sprinkled throughout stories about new sound products. The following sections describe some common sound card terms and concepts.

The Nature of Sound

To understand a sound card, you need to understand sound itself. Every sound is produced by vibrations that compress air or other substances. These sound waves travel in all directions, expanding in balloon-like fashion from the source of the sound. When these waves reach your ear, they cause vibrations that you perceive as sound.

III

Input/Output Hardware

The two basic properties of any sound are its *pitch* and its *intensity*.

Pitch is simply the rate at which vibrations are produced. It is measured in the number of hertz (Hz), or cycles per second. One cycle is a complete vibration back and forth. The number of Hz is the frequency of the tone; the higher the frequency, the higher the pitch.

You cannot hear all possible frequencies. Very few people can hear fewer than 16 Hz or more than about 20 kHz (*kilohertz;* 1 kHz equals 1,000 Hz). In fact, the lowest note on a piano has a frequency of 27 Hz, the highest note, a little more than 4 kHz. And frequency-modulation (FM) radio stations broadcast notes up to 15 kHz.

The intensity of a sound is called its *amplitude*. This intensity depends upon the strength of the vibrations producing the sound. A piano string, for example, vibrates gently when the key is struck softly. The string swings back and forth in a narrow arc and the tone it sends out is soft. If the key is struck forcefully, however, the string swings back and forth in a wider arc. The loudness of sounds is measured in *decibels* (db). The rustle of leaves is rated at 20db, average street noise at 70, and nearby thunder at 120.

Game Standards

Most sound cards support both of the current entertainment audio standards: *AdLib* and *Sound Blaster.* The Sound Blaster Pro is a sound card sold by Creative Labs; Ad Lib sells the Ad Lib Gold. To play most games, you must tell your game which of these sound card standards your sound card supports. (Some games support only one or the other.) Some sound devices support neither of these game sound standards. The Logitech AudioMan, for example, was meant for business, not fun.

Frequency Response

The quality of a sound card is often measured by two criteria: *frequency response* (or *range*) and *total harmonic distortion.*

The frequency response of a sound card is the range in which an audio system can record and/or play at a constant and audible amplitude level. Many cards support 30 Hz to 20 kHz. The wider the spread, the better the sound card.

The total harmonic distortion measures a sound card's linearity, the straightness of a frequency response curve. In laymen's terms, the harmonic distortion is a measure of accurate sound reproduction. Any nonlinear elements cause distortion in the form of harmonics. The smaller the percentage of distortion, the better.

Sampling

With a sound card, a PC can make noise in three ways. *Waveform audio* (also known as *sampled* or *digitized sound*) uses the PC as a tape recorder. Small computer chips built into a sound card, called *analog-to-digital converters* (ADCs), convert analog sound waves into digital bits the computer can understand. Likewise, *digital-to-analog converters* (DACs) convert the recorded sounds to something audible.

Sampling is the process of turning the original analog sound waves (see fig. 12.3) into digital (on/off) signals that can be saved and later replayed. Snapshots of the analog sounds are taken and saved. For example, at time X the sound may be measured with an amplitude of Y. The higher (or more frequent) the *sample rate*, the more accurate the digital sound is to its real-life source.

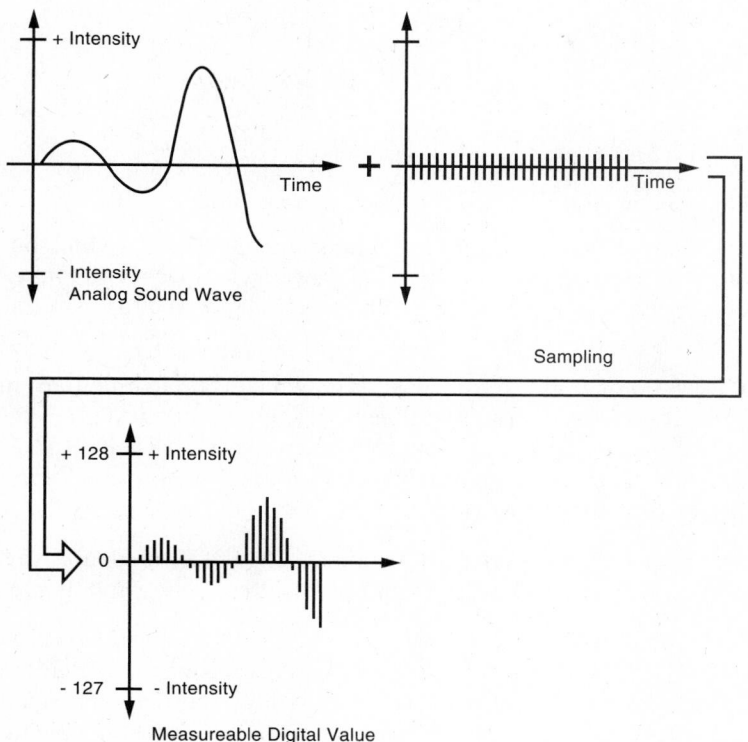

Fig. 12.3
Sampling turns a changing sound wave into measuerable digital values.

8-Bit versus 16-Bit
The original Multimedia PC (MPC) specifications required 8-bit sound. This doesn't mean the sound card must fit into an 8-bit instead of a 16-bit expansion slot. Rather, *8-bit audio* means that the sound card uses eight bits to digitize each sound sample. This translates into 256 possible digital values to which the sample can be pegged (less quality than the 65,536 values possible with a 16-bit sound card). Generally, 8-bit audio is adequate for recorded speech whereas 16-bit sound is best for the demands of music (see fig. 12.4).

III

Input/Output Hardware

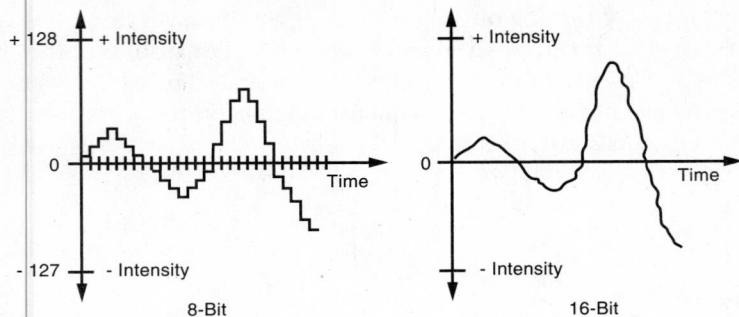

Fig. 12.4
16-bit resolution means more accurate sound reproduction than 8-bit resolution.

The Logitech AudioMan was designed as an 8-bit sound device with which business users could add voice notes to their Windows work. Likewise, Compaq Computer Corp.'s original Business Audio was 8-bit quality. (It has since been replaced by 16-bit Enhanced Business Audio.)

Whether you use 8-bit or 16-bit sound depends on which is more important to you: sound quality or disk space. The sampling frequency determines how often the sound card measures the level of the sound being recorded or played back. Basically, you have to sample at about two times the highest frequency you want to produce, plus an extra 10 percent to keep out unwanted signals.

Humans can hear up to 20,000 cycles per second, or 20 kHz. If you double this number and add 10 percent, you get a 44.1 kHz sampling rate, the same sampling rate used by high-fidelity audio CDs.

Sound recorded at 11 kHz (capturing 11,000 samples per second) is fuzzier than audio sampled at 22 kHz. A sound sampled in 16-bit stereo at 44 kHz (CD-audio quality) requires as much as *10.5M per minute* of disk space! The same sound sample in 8-bit mono at 11 kHz takes 1/16th the space. If you were to add a one-minute hi-fi voice annotation to your Excel spreadsheet, you'd find, when you finished recording, a spreadsheet whose size had at least quadrupled!

The CD-ROM Connection
Besides a sound card, the other foundation of multimedia is a CD-ROM (compact disc read-only memory) drive.

CD-ROM drives provide access to a wealth of text, graphics, sound, video, and animation. A single 4 3/4-inch compact disc can hold 660M of information. For example, a single CD-ROM can hold the equivalent information, along with pictures and sounds, of an encyclopedia set. Popping a CD-ROM into the drive is like piling 300,000 pages of information onto your bookshelves.

Many sound cards double as a CD-ROM controller, or interface card. Some sound cards, however, use a proprietary connection that accommodates only certain CD-ROM drives. For a wider selection of drives, consider a sound card that includes a SCSI (Small Computer Systems Interface) connector. By owning a SCSI sound card you can save both a slot in your PC and some money on a drive.

All CD-ROM players read all standard CD-ROM discs, just as the CD player in your stereo plays any CD you find in a record store. There's only one caveat: if you eventually want to play CD-ROMs recorded in the extended architecture (XA) format, you may need to upgrade your interface card.

If you want to use multimedia, your CD-ROM drive must also have an extra audio connection to send sound in analog form from the drive to the sound card.

Like a hard drive, a CD-ROM drive is measured by two criteria: *average access speed* and *data transfer rate*. The average access speed is the length of time the CD-ROM drive takes to find the information you request. This speed is measured in milliseconds (ms), or thousandths of a second. The data transfer rate indicates how fast the found information can be sent to your PC. This rate is measured in kilobytes transferred per second (KBps).

Make sure that the CD-ROM drive you buy meets the MPC (Multimedia PC) specifications for performance. The MPC recipe has changed since its debut: a drive must be double-speed (capable of a sustained 300KBps data transfer rate), with an access time of 400ms or less. The CD-ROM drive must use no more than 60 percent of the CPU's resources during a 300KBps read, and no more than 40 percent at 150KBps throughput. A 64K onboard memory buffer and read-ahead buffering are recommended but not mandated.

Triple- and quadruple-speed (abbreviated 3X and 4X, respectively) CD-ROM drives are also available. Triple-speed drives provide a minimum data transfer rate of 450Kbps. At the time of this writing, the triple-speed drives provide the best balance of performance versus price. However, some manufacturers such as Panasonic, Philips, Pioneer, and Sony are developing quad- but not triple-speed units. When buying a drive, you may be able to trade buffer size for access time or vice versa. If you know you will be mostly using reference materials, such as a magazine text-based database on CD-ROM, then you would prefer a faster access time (under 200–300 ms) and triple or quadruple speed. If you will be accessing large sound files, you would instead prefer a larger buffer of 256K. If primarily accessing graphics, such as stock photos on CD, insist on both a large 256K buffer and triple or quadruple speed.

Sound File Formats
There are several file formats for storing and editing digitized sound. The most notable is the WAV format supported by Windows 3.1. (WAV is short for waveform audio.) One audio minute saved to a WAV file requires 2.5M of disk space.

There are two other types of PC audio: synthesized sound and MIDI music. Synthesized sounds, like synthetic foods, are artificially created. Sound cards typically use one or two FM (frequency modulation) chips, such as those provided by Yamaha, to generate mono or stereo sounds without consuming as much disk space as WAV sound files.

The serious musician may prefer a high-end sound card, such as MultiSound from Turtle Beach. The MultiSound uses digitized sounds of actual instruments. These sounds are preserved in special ROM (read-only memory) chips. Using this *wave-table synthesis* technique, the Multisound plays genuine strings and trumpets instead of synthesized music that imitates sounds like strings and trumpets.

MIDI is a step above synthesized sound. MIDI, the acronym for Musical Instrument Digital Interface, allows your computer to store, edit, and play back music through a MIDI instrument such as a keyboard synthesizer. MIDI is more like a networking programming language, allowing you to add more instruments, including drum machines and special sound effects generators.

The MPC specs insist on MIDI support, although not all of us are musicians. Budget-priced sound cards such as the Microsoft Sound System do not provide a MIDI interface.

Compression/Decompression

Since one minute of stereo audio can consume up to 11M of disc space, several sound card makers use Adaptive Differential Pulse Code Modulation (ADPCM) compression to reduce file size by over 50 percent. However, a simple fact of audio life is that when you use such compression, you lose sound quality.

Because the sound quality can be degraded, there is no ADPCM standard. Creative Labs uses a proprietary hardware approach, while Microsoft is pushing the Business Audio ADPCM design developed with Compaq.

One emerging compression standard is the Motion Pictures Experts Group (MPEG) standard, which works with both audio and video compression and is gaining support in the non-PC world from products like the Philips CD-I player. With a potential compression ratio of 12:1 and full-motion-video MPEG CD-ROM titles expected soon, this standard may catch on.

Sound Card Characteristics

What are some key features to consider in a sound card? Although some aspects are subjective, the following sections describe some key buying points.

Compatibility

Although there are no official sound card standards, the popular Sound Blaster card has become a de facto standard. The Sound Blaster—the first widely distributed sound card—is supported by the greatest number of software programs. A sound card advertised as Sound Blaster-compatible should run virtually any application that supports sound.

Many sound cards also support the Multimedia PC (MPC) Level 2 specifications, allowing you to play sound files in Windows and more. Some sound cards, by excluding a MIDI interface, barely fall short of the MPC specs. Other compatibility standards to look for are Ad Lib and Pro AudioSpectrum.

Sampling

The most important sound card quality is its sampling capability. The rate at which the card samples (measured in kilohertz, or kHz) and the size of its sample (expressed in bits) determine the quality of the sound. The standard sampling rates for sound cards are 11.025 kHz, 22.050 kHz, and 44.1 kHz; sample sizes are 8, 12, and 16 bits.

Inexpensive monophonic cards generally sample at 8 bits up to speeds of 22.050 kHz, which is fine for recording voice messages. Some stereo-capable cards sample at 8 bits and run at speeds of 22.050 kHz in stereo and up to 44.1 kHz in mono. Other cards can sample 8 bits at 44.1 kHz speeds in both stereo and mono. The latest generation of cards do it all; they can record CD-quality audio of 16 bits at 44. 1kHz.

Don't expect a higher-sampling sound card to provide better sound. Very few software programs currently support 16-bit sound. Most computer games, for example, use 8-bit samples. Even the best-selling Sound Blaster Pro supports recording at 8 bits only. If price is your primary concern, a basic 8-bit card may meet your needs although it won't meet the MPC Level 2 specifications.

If you do buy a card that supports 16-bit sampling, make sure you have plenty of hard disk space. The higher the resolution of sampling, the more hard disk space needed to store the file. The sampling rate also affects file size; sampling at the next higher rate doubles the file size.

Stereo versus Mono

You'll also have to consider buying a monophonic or stereophonic sound card. Inexpensive sound cards are monophonic, producing sound from a single source. Still, monophonic cards produce better sound than your PC's speaker.

Stereophonic cards produce many voices, or sounds, concurrently and from two different sources. The more voices a card has, the higher the sound fidelity. Each stereo chip in a sound card is capable of 11 or more voices. To get 20 or more voices, manufacturers had to resort to two FM synthesizer chips. Today, a single chip produces 20 voices, providing truer stereo sound.

The number of voices a stereo card has is especially important for music files because the voices correspond to the individual instruments the card can play.

Most sound cards use FM synthesis to imitate the musical instruments played. Most use synthesizer chips developed by Yamaha. The least expensive sound cards use the monophonic 11-voice YM3812 or OPL3 chip. Better sound cards use the stereophonic 20-voice YMF262 or OPL3 chip.

III

Input/Output Hardware

Imitated musical instruments are not as impressive as the real thing. High-end sound cards use digital recordings of real instruments and sound effects. Often, several megabytes of these sound clips are embedded in ROM chips on the card. For example, some sound cards use the Ensoniq chipset (a type of circuit design) that does wave-table synthesis of musical instruments. Instead of pretending to play a trombone D flat, the Ensoniq chipset has a little digitized recording of an actual instrument playing that note.

If your primary interest in a sound card is for entertainment or use in educational or business settings, FM synthesis quality may be good enough.

Stereo sound cards vary in sampling rates and sizes. Some stereo cards do not work in mono mode. Also, moving from mono to stereo sound means an increase in the size of the sound files. As with 16-bit resolution, stereo sound is not supported by most software applications. However, a stereo card playing mono software does generate better sound than a mono card.

Another boon to buying the more expensive stereo cards is that they generally come with additional interfaces, such as connections to a SCSI device (such as a CD-ROM drive) or a MIDI device (such as a keyboard).

CD-ROM Connector

Most stereo sound cards not only provide great sound but also can operate your CD-ROM drive. Although many cards come with a SCSI port for any SCSI device, such as a CD-ROM drive, others support only a proprietary CD-ROM interface, such as just Mitsumi or Sony CD-ROM interfaces. If you own a CD-ROM drive, make sure it's compatible with the sound card you plan to buy. If you plan to add a CD-ROM drive or if you expect to upgrade your drive, keep in mind that a proprietary interface will limit your choices, perhaps to a single CD-ROM brand.

If you're seeking to add both a sound card and a CD-ROM drive, consider *multimedia upgrade kits*. These kits bundle a sound card, CD-ROM drive, CD-ROM titles, software, and cables in an attractively priced package. By buying a multimedia upgrade kit rather than disparate components, you may save some money. And you'll know that the components will work together, especially if the kit includes proper documentation.

Data Compression

The more-expensive cards produce CD-quality audio, which is sampled at 44.1 kHz. At this rate, recorded files (even of your own voice) can consume as many as 11M for every minute of recording. To counter this demand for disk space, many sound cards include a data-compression capability. For example, the Sound Blaster ASP 16 includes on-the-fly compression of sound in ratios of 2:1, 3:1, or 4:1.

MIDI Interface

The Musical Instrument Digital Interface (MIDI) is a standard for connecting musical instruments to PCs. Many stereo cards come with a MIDI interface, MIDI synthesizer, and sequencing software for composing music. Some cards include only a MIDI interface; you have to purchase the hardware separately to hook up other MIDI devices. Other sound cards may exclude the MIDI interface.

Bundled Software

Sound cards usually include several sound utilities so that you can begin using your sound card right away. Most of this software is DOS-based, but Windows-based versions are available with some cards. The possibilities include:

- Text-to-speech conversion programs
- Programs for playing, editing, and recording audio files
- Sequencer software, which helps you compose music (generally included with cards with MIDI interfaces)
- Various sound clips

Multi-Purpose Digital Signal Processors

One recent addition to many sound boards is the digital signal processor (DSP). DSPs add intelligence to your sound card, freeing your computer from work-intensive tasks, such as filtering noise from recordings or compressing audio on the fly.

About half of most general-purpose sound cards use DSPs. The Cardinal Technologies Sound Pro 16 and Sound Pro 16 Plus, for example, use the Analog Devices ADSP2115 digital signal processor. The Sound Blaster AWE32's programmable DSP features compression algorithms for processing text-to-speech data and enables the card's QSound surround-sound 3-D audio, along with reverb and chorus effects. DSPs allow a sound card to be a multi-purpose device. IBM uses its DSP to add a 14.4-kilobit-per-second modem, 9.6KBps fax, and a digital answering machine to its WindSurfer Communications Adapter.

Are DSPs worth the extra price? On low-powered PCs (those less powerful than a 486SX/25) or in true multitasking environments like Windows 3.1 or Windows NT, a DSP can make real-time compression possible—a valuable feature for voice annotation.

Sound Drivers

Most sound cards include universal drivers for DOS and Windows applications. Find out which drivers are included with your card. Windows 3.1 already includes drivers for the most popular sound cards, such as Sound Blaster. Other drivers are available on a separate driver disk available from Microsoft or from Microsoft's Product Support download service.

III

Input/Output Hardware

Connectors

Most sound cards have the same connectors. These 1/8-inch minijack connectors provide ways to pass sound from the sound card to speakers, headphones, and stereo systems; and to receive sound from a microphone, CD player, tape player, or stereo. The four types of connectors your sound card typically could or should have are shown in figure 12.5.

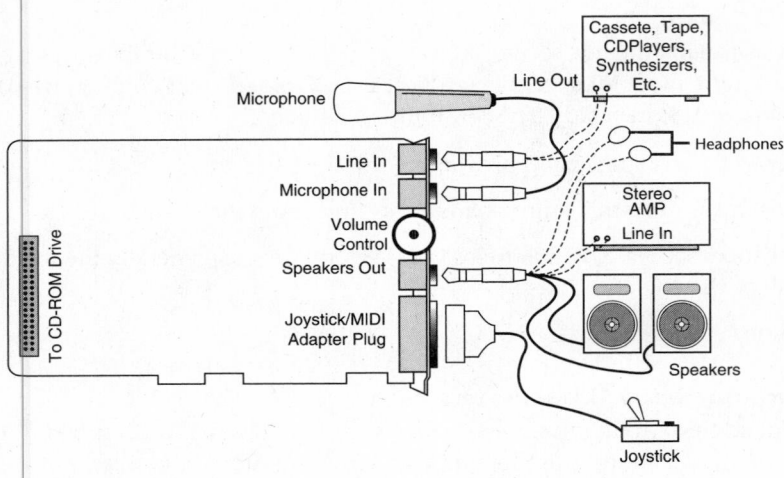

Fig. 12.5
The basic features most sound cards have in common.

- *Stereo line, or audio, out connector.* The line out is used to send sound signals from the sound card to a device outside the computer. The cables from the line out connector can be hooked up to stereo speakers, a headphone set, or your stereo system. If you hook up your stereo system, you can have amplified sound. Some sound cards, such as the Microsoft Windows Sound System, provide two jacks for line out. One is for the left channel of the stereo signal; the other is for the right channel.

- *Stereo line, or audio, in connector.* The line in connector is used to record, or mix, sound signals to the computer's hard disk.

- *Speaker/headphone connector.* The speaker/headphone connector is not always provided on a sound card. Instead, the line out (described earlier) doubles as a way to send stereo signals from the sound card to your stereo system or speakers. When both speaker/headphone and line out connectors are provided, the speaker/headphone connector provides an amplified signal that can power your headphones or small bookshelf speakers. Most sound cards can provide up to 4 watts of power to drive your speakers. Conversely, signals sent through the line out connector are not amplified. Using the line-out connector provides the best sound reproduction since the stereo system or amplified speakers will amplify the sounds.

■ *Microphone, or mono, in connector.* You connect a microphone to this 1/8-inch minijack to record your voice or other sounds to disk. This microphone jack records in mono, not in stereo. Many sound cards use Automatic Gain Control (AGC) to improve recordings. This feature adjusts the recording levels on the fly. A 600 to 10K ohm dynamic or condenser microphone works best with this jack. Some inexpensive sound cards use the line in connector instead of a separate microphone jack.

■ *Joystick/MIDI connector.* The joystick connector is a 15-pin, D-shaped connector. Two of the pins are used to control a MIDI device, such as a keyboard. Many sound card makers offer an optional MIDI connector.

Sometimes the joystick port can accommodate two joysticks if you order the optional Y-adapter. To use this connector as a MIDI interface, you'll need to buy the optional MIDI cable. Some sound cards do not provide a MIDI interface. If you're not interested in making music (and spending a few hundred dollars more for the MIDI keyboard), you may want to consider these models. And don't worry about the lack of a joystick port. Most PCs include one as part of the input/output (I/O) card; otherwise, you can buy a separate game card, such as the GameCard III Automatic from CH Products.

Volume Control

A thumbwheel control is provided on some sound cards, although sophisticated sound cards have no room for such a control. Instead, a combination of keys can be used to adjust the sound. Media Vision's Pro AudioStudio 16, for example, uses Ctrl-Alt-U to increase the volume and Ctrl-Alt-D to decrease it. By pressing these key combinations you adjust the volume from within a game, Windows program, or any other application.

Sound Card Options

You'll seldom buy just a sound card. You'll need—or want—other accessories that raise the cost of your PC sound system. At the very least, you'll have to invest in a set of speakers or headphones. At most, you may want to purchase a MIDI synthesizer keyboard.

Speakers

Successful business presentations, multimedia applications, and MIDI work demand external high-fidelity stereo speakers. Although you can use standard stereo speakers, they are too big to fit on or near your desk. Smaller bookshelf speakers are better.

Sound cards offer little or no power to drive external speakers. Although some sound cards have small 4-watt amplifiers, they are not powerful enough to drive quality speakers. Also, conventional speakers sitting near your display may create magnetic interference, which can distort colors and objects on-screen or jumble the data recorded on your nearby floppy disks.

III

Input/Output Hardware

To solve these problems, computer speakers need to be small, efficient, and self-powered. Also, you need to provide magnetic shielding, either in the form of added layers of insulation in the speaker cabinet or by electronically canceling out the magnetic distortion.

> **Note**
>
> Although most computer speakers are magnetically shielded, do not leave recorded tapes, watches, personal credit cards, or floppy disks in front of the speakers for long periods of time.

Quality sound depends on quality speakers. A 16-bit sound card may provide better sound to computer speakers, but even an 8-bit sound card sounds good from a good speaker. Conversely, an inexpensive speaker makes both 8-bit and 16-bit sound cards sound tinny.

The dozens of models on the market range from less expensive minispeakers from Sony and Koss to larger self-powered models from companies such as Bose. To evaluate speakers, you need to know the lingo. Speakers are measured by three criteria:

- *Frequency response.* A measurement of the range of high and low sounds a speaker can reproduce. The ideal range is from 20 Hz to 20 kHz, the range of human hearing. No speaker system reproduces this range perfectly. In fact, few people hear sounds above 18 kHz. An exceptional speaker may cover a range of 30 Hz to 23,000 kHz. Lesser models may cover only 100 Hz to 20,000 Hz. Frequency response is the most deceptive specification, because identically rated speakers can sound completely different.

- *Total Harmonic Distortion (THD).* THD, or just *distortion*, is an expression of the amount of distortion or noise created by amplifying the signal. Simply put, distortion is the difference between the sound sent to the speaker and the sound we hear. The amount of distortion is measured in percentages. An acceptable level of distortion is that below .1 percent (one-tenth of one percent). For some CD-quality recording equipment, a common standard is .05 percent. Some speakers have a distortion of 10 percent or more. Headphones often have a distortion of about 2 percent or less.

- *Watts.* Usually stated as *watts per channel*, this is the amount of amplification available to drive the speakers. Check that the company means "per channel" (or RMS) and not total power. Many sound cards have built-in amplifiers, providing up to 8 watts per channel. (Most provide 4 watts.) The wattage is not enough to provide rich sound, however, which is why many speakers have built-in amplifiers. With the flick of a switch or the press of a button, such speakers amplify the signals they receive from the sound card. If you do not want to amplify the sound, you typically leave the speaker switch set to "direct." In most cases, you'll want to amplify the signal.

Two or four C batteries are often used to power computer speakers. Because these speakers require so much power, you may want to invest in an AC adapter, although more expensive speakers include one. With an AC adapter, you won't have to buy new batteries every few weeks. If your speakers didn't come with an AC adapter, you can pick one up from your local Radio Shack or hardware store.

You can control your speakers in various ways, depending on their complexity and cost. Typically, each speaker has a volume knob, although some share one volume control. If one speaker is farther away than the other, you may want to adjust the volume accordingly. Many computer speakers include a dynamic bass boost (DBB) switch. This button provides a more powerful bass and clearer treble, regardless of the volume setting. Other speakers have separate bass and treble boost switches or a three-band equalizer to control low, middle, and high frequencies. When you rely on your sound card's power rather than your speaker's built-in amplifier, the volume and dynamic bass boost controls have no effect. Your speakers are at the mercy of the sound card's power.

A 1/8-inch stereo minijack connects from the sound card output jack to one of the speakers. The signal is then split and fed through a separate cable from the first speaker to the second one.

Before purchasing a set of speakers, check that the cables between the speakers are long enough for your computer setup. For example, a tower case sitting alongside one's desk may require longer speaker wires than a desktop computer.

Beware of speakers that have a tardy built-in "sleep" feature. Such speakers, which save electricity by turning themselves off when they are not in use, may have the annoying habit of clipping the first part of a sound after a period of inactivity.

Headphones are an option when you can't afford a premium set of speakers. Headphones provide privacy and allow you to play your sound card as loud as you like.

Microphone

Most sound cards do not include a microphone. You'll need one to record your voice to a WAV file. Selecting a microphone is quite simple. You need one that has a 1/8-inch minijack to plug into your sound card's microphone, or audio in, jack. Most have an on/off switch.

Like speakers, microphones are measured by their frequency range. This is not an important buying factor, however, since the human voice has a limited range. If you are recording only voices, consider an inexpensive microphone that covers a limited range of frequencies. An expensive microphone's recording capabilities extend to frequencies outside the voice's range. Why pay for something you won't be needing?

If you are recording music, invest in an expensive microphone, although an 8-bit sound card can record music just as well with an inexpensive microphone as an expensive one.

III

Input/Output Hardware

Your biggest decision is to select a microphone that suits your recording style. If you work in a noisy office, you may want a unidirectional microphone that will prevent extraneous noises from being recorded. An omnidirectional mike is best for recording a group conversation. If you want to leave your hands free, you may want to shun the traditional hand-held microphone for a lapel model.

Some sound cards include a microphone. For example, the Media Vision Pro AudioStudio 16 includes a small lapel microphone and a holster in which to place it. The Sound Blaster 16 ASP includes a hand-held microphone.

Joysticks

Many sound cards include a joystick, or game, port. (This joystick port often doubles as a connection to a MIDI device.) A joystick is ideally meant for game playing, such as simulating flying a Cessna aircraft. Joysticks, like speakers, are best chosen through hands-on experience.

A joystick has a fire button on top of a center wand you move in any of eight directions, with a second button or pair of buttons located on the base.

Good joysticks have resistance that increases the further you move the center wand from dead center. Some joysticks include suction cups that mount the unit on your desk. If you're short on desk space, you may prefer a smaller joystick that fits in your hand. If you are left-handed, look for an ambidextrous joystick, not one that is contoured for right-handers.

Some joysticks are meant especially for flight-simulation games. The ThrustMaster, from ThrustMaster Inc., provides additional buttons for firing and selecting missiles, turning radar on or off, and looking in different directions.

MIDI Connector

If you are interested in MIDI to create synthesized music, you'll need to connect your musical keyboard or other MIDI device to your sound card. The joystick port on sound cards has unused pins that can be used to send and receive MIDI data. By connecting a MIDI interface cable to the joystick port, you can connect your PC to a MIDI device. The cable has three connectors: a joystick connector, and MIDI In and Out connectors.

Media Vision sells an adapter box called MIDI Mate ($69.95) for adding Musical Instrument Digital Interface input, output, and throughput connectors to its boards. The Pro AudioSpectrum boards use a SCSI interface.

Creative Labs furnishes its MIDI Kit for its Sound Blaster family of sound cards. This kit includes a Voyetra Technologies sequencer program to record, edit, and play back your MIDI files, as well as an interface cable to attach your sound card to the keyboard.

Synthesizer

If you are considering MIDI, you will also have to get a MIDI keyboard synthesizer. To make MIDI scores, you need sequencer software to record, edit, and play back MIDI files. (Some sound cards include sequencing software.) You also need a sound synthesizer, which is included in the sound card. A MIDI keyboard simplifies the creation of musical scores. A MIDI file contains up to 16 channels of music data, so you can record many different instruments and play them back. Using the keyboard, you can enter the notes for various instruments.

To enhance MIDI sounds for the Sound Blaster 16 ASP sound card, consider the $249.95 Wave Blaster from Creative Labs. The Wave Blaster attaches to the Sound Blaster ASP 16. When MIDI music is played, it looks to the Wave Blaster for any of 213 CD-quality digitally recorded musical instrument sounds. Without the Wave Blaster, the Sound Blaster 16 ASP would imitate these sounds through FM synthesis. With the Wave Blaster, music sounds as though it's being played by real instruments—because it is.

Several MIDI keyboards are available, such as the Roland A-30 or PC-200 MK2. These keyboards range in price from $395 to more than $7,000.

Sound Card Installation

Installing a sound card is no more intimidating than installing an internal modem or a VGA card.

Typically, you follow these steps to install a sound card:

1. Open your computer.

2. Configure your sound card.

3. Install the sound card and attach the CD-ROM drive, if present.

4. Close your computer.

5. Install the sound card software.

6. Attach your speakers and other sound accessories.

III

Note

Some manufacturers use a different installation order than this. Microsoft Corporation's Windows Sound System has you install the software first to determine how it can best work in your PC.

Input/Output Hardware

Once your computer is open, you can install the sound card. Your sound card may be either an 8-bit or 16-bit expansion card. Select a slot that matches the type of card you have. You don't want to put a 16-bit card (one with dual edge connectors) into an 8-bit slot (one with a single edge connector). An 8-bit card, however, can fit in either an 8-bit or 16-bit slot.

If you have several empty slots from which to choose, you may want to place the new card in one as far away as possible from the others. This reduces any possible electromagnetic interference; that is, it reduces stray radio signals from one card that might affect the sound card.

Next, you must remove the screw that holds the metal cover over the empty expansion slot you've chosen. Remove your sound card from its protective packaging. When you open this bag, carefully grab the card by its metal bracket and edges. *Do not touch any of the components on the card.* Any static electricity you may transmit can damage the card. And do not touch the gold edge connectors. You may want to invest in a grounding wrist strap, which continually drains you of static build-up as you work on your computer.

You may have to set jumpers or DIP switches to configure your sound card to work best with your computer. For example, you may want to turn off your sound card's joystick port because your joystick is already connected elsewhere to your PC. See the instructions that came with your sound card.

If an internal CD-ROM drive is to be connected to the sound card, attach its cables. Attach your CD-ROM's striped ribbon cable to your sound card, placing the red edge of the CD-ROM cable on the side of the connector on which "0" or "1" printed. The cable must be placed this way for the CD-ROM drive to work.

The CD-ROM drive may also have an audio cable. Connect this cable to the audio connector on the sound card. This connector is keyed so that you can't insert it improperly.

Next, insert the card in the edge connector. First touch a metal object, such as the inside of the computer's cover, to drain yourself of static electricity. Then, holding the card by its metal bracket and edges, place it in the expansion slot. Attach the screw to hold the expansion card and then reassemble your computer.

You can connect small speakers to the speaker jack. Typically, sound cards provide four watts of power per channel to drive bookshelf speakers. If you are using speakers rated for less than four watts, do not turn up the volume on your sound card to the maximum; your speakers may burn out from the overload. You'll get better results if you plug your sound card into powered speakers, that is, speakers with built-in amplifiers.

Another alternative is to patch your sound card into your stereo system for greatly amplified sound. Check the plugs and jacks at both ends of the connection. Most stereos use pin plugs—also called RCA or phono plugs—for input. Although pin plugs are standard on some sound cards, most use miniature 1/8-inch phono plugs, which require an adapter when connecting to your stereo system. From Radio Shack, for example, you can purchase an audio cable that provides a stereo 1/8-inch miniplug on one end and a phono plug on the other (Cat. No. 42-2481A).

Make sure that you get stereo, not mono, plugs, unless your sound card supports mono only. To ensure that you have enough cable to reach from the back of your PC to your stereo system, get a six-foot long cable.

Hooking up your stereo to a sound card is simply a matter of sliding the plugs into jacks. If your sound card gives you a choice of outputs—speaker/headphone and stereo line out—choose the stereo line out jack for the connection. Choosing it will give you the best sound quality because the signals from the stereo line out jack are not amplified. The amplification is best left to your stereo system.

Connect this output to the auxiliary input of your stereo receiver, preamp, or integrated amplifier. If your stereo doesn't have an auxiliary input, other input options include—in order of preference—tuner, CD, or Tape 2. (Do not use phono inputs, however, because the level of the signals will be uneven.) You can connect the cable's single stereo miniplug to the sound card's Stereo Line Out jack, for example, and then connect the two RCA phono plugs to the stereo's Tape/VCR 2 Playback jacks.

The first time you use your sound card with a stereo system, turn down the volume on your receiver to prevent blown speakers. Barely turn up the volume control and then select the proper input (such as Tape/VCR 2) on your stereo receiver. Finally, start your PC. Never increase the volume to more than three-fourths of the way up. Any higher and the sound may become distorted.

Troubleshooting Sound Card Problems

To install a sound card, you need to select IRQ numbers, a base I/O address, or DMA channels that don't conflict with other devices. Most cards come already configured to use an otherwise idle set of ports, but problems occasionally arise. Troubleshooting may mean that you have to change board jumpers or switches, or even reconfigure your other cards. No one said life was fair.

Hardware Conflicts

The most common problem for sound cards is that they fight with other devices installed in your PC. You may notice that your sound card simply doesn't work, repeats the same sounds over and over, or causes your PC to freeze in Windows or DOS. This situation is called a *device*, or *hardware, conflict*. What are they fighting over? The same signal lines or channels used for talking to your PC. The sources of conflict are threefold:

■ *Interrupt requests (IRQs).* IRQs are used to "interrupt" your PC and get its attention.

■ *Direct memory access (DMA) channels.* DMA channels are the way to move information directly to your PC's memory, bypassing your PC's central brain. DMA channels allow sound to play while your PC is doing other work.

■ *Input/output (I/O) addresses.* An I/O address in your PC is used to channel information between your sound card and your PC. The address usually mentioned in a sound card manual is the starting address. Actually, your sound card may require several addresses, which together are called an *address segment*.

III

Input/Output Hardware

Your potential for problems is doubled or tripled because the Sound Blaster-compatible sound cards, and MIDI portions of many sound cards generally, also use an IRQ, DMA, and I/O address. For example, the Pro AudioStudio 16 by default uses DMA 5 and IRQ 7 for its "native" mode and DMA 1 and IRQ 5 for Sound Blaster compatibility. Also, you can have separate DMA and IRQ settings when your sound card is used with Windows.

Most sound cards include installation software that analyzes your PC and attempts to find settings that are not yet assigned to other devices. Although fairly reliable, this analysis is not complete because unless a device is operating during the analysis, detecting it is not always possible.

Resolving Interrupt Problems. Your sound card may support any of several interrupts, or IRQs (see table 12.1). Many of the 16 IRQs are reserved for parts of your PC, such as the keyboard (IRQ2). Some sound cards only work with certain IRQs. For example, the Windows Sound System supports IRQs 7, 9, 10, and 11 (the default), whereas the Logitech SoundMan 16 uses 2, 3, 5, 7, 10, 11, 12, or 15. The primary symptom of an interrupt conflict is that a sound skips, playing continuously.

Table 12.1   Interrupts and What They Control

Interrupt	Device	Comments
0	Timer	
1	Keyboard	
2	Unused	Used in AT-type computers as a gateway to IRQ 8/15 or for EGA/VGA video cards.
3	COM2 (second serial port)	Used for a modem or mouse.
4	COM1 (first serial port)	Used for a modem or mouse.
5	Hard disk	XT-type computers only; otherwise available for AT-type computers to use.
6	FDC (floppy disk drive controller)	
7	LPT1 (first parallel printer port)	
8	Clock	Interrupts 8 through 15 are available on AT-type computers only and often not to expansion cards.
9	PC network	
10–12	Unused	
13	Math coprocessor	Used for speeding mathematical calculations, such as those used in spreadsheet or computer-aided design (CAD) programs.
14	Hard disk	
15	Unused	

Correct DMA Channels. Your sound card also supports several DMA channels (see table 12.2). Many of the eight DMAs are reserved for parts of your PC, such as your floppy disk controller (DMA 2). DMA channels 5, 6, and 7 are used to provide the best performance under Windows. The primary symptom of a DMA conflict is that you hear no sound at all.

Table 12.2   DMA Channels and Their Purposes

DMA Channel	Purpose
0	Unused
1	Often reserved for Sound Blaster compatibility
2	Used by floppy disk controller
3	Unused
4	Refreshes computer's memory
5	Unused
6	Unused
7	Unused

Solving Hardware Conflicts. The best way to find a hardware conflict is to locate all of the documentation for your PC and its various devices, such as a tape backup interface card, CD-ROM drive, etc. Complete the list shown in table 12.3, adding the DMA, IRQ, and I/O address used by each device. By deduction and the following procedure, you can find which device is causing the problem.

Table 12.3   Hardware Conflict Worksheet

Device	DMA	IRQ	I/O Address
Timer	NA	0	
Keyboard	NA	1	
COM1	NA	4	
COM2	NA	3	
LPT1	NA	7	
Memory refresh	4	NA	
Floppy disk	2	6	
Hard disk	NA	14	
Math coprocessor	NA	13	
PC network	NA	9	
EGA/VGA card	NA	2	

Following are the most common causes of hardware conflicts:

- Network interface cards

- Tape drive interface cards

- Special printer controllers (such as a PostScript controllers)

- SCSI or other device controllers

- Modems and other serial devices

- Scanner interface cards

How do you find which device is conflicting with your sound card? Temporarily remove all of your expansion cards except the sound card and other essential cards (such as the video card). Then add each of the cards you removed, one at a time, until your sound card no longer works. The last card you added is the troublemaker.

Having found the card that's causing the conflict, you can either switch the settings for the device that is conflicting with your sound card or change the settings of the sound card. In either case, you will have to change the IRQ, DMA, or I/O address. To do this, you must set jumpers or DIP switches or use your sound card's setup software to change its settings.

Other Sound Card Problems

Sound card problems (like the common cold) have common symptoms. Use the following sections to diagnose your problem.

No Sound. If you don't hear anything from your sound card, consider these solutions:

- Are the speakers connected? Check that the speakers are plugged into the sound card's Stereo Line Out or Speaker jack.

- If you're using amplified speakers, are they powered on? Check the strength of the batteries or the adapter's connection to the electrical outlet.

  I once owned a pair of Sony amplified speakers. An avid computer game player, I needed a new set of batteries every week. The first time, I was surprised when I couldn't hear any sound. The batteries were so drained that they could not drive the speaker.

- Are the speakers stereo? Check that the plug inserted into the jack is a stereo plug, not mono.

- Are mixer settings high enough? Many sound cards include a mixer control for DOS and/or Microsoft Windows. The mixer controls the settings for various sound devices, such as a microphone or CD player. There may be controls for both recording and playback. Increase the master volume or speaker volume when you are in the play mode. In DOS, you can adjust the setting by either modifying your CONFIG.SYS file or pressing keys.

- Use your sound card's setup or diagnostic software to test and adjust the volume of the sound card. Such software usually includes sample sounds that play. For example, the Sound Blaster 16 ASP includes TESTSB16.

- Turn off your computer for one minute and then turn it back on. Such a hard reset (as opposed to pressing the reset button or pressing Ctrl-Alt-Del) may clear the problem.

- If your computer game lacks sound, check that it works with your sound card. For example, some games may require the exact settings of IRQ 7, DMA 1, and address 220 to be Sound Blaster compatible.

One-Sided Sound. If you hear sound coming from only one speaker, check out these possible causes:

- Are you using a mono plug in the stereo jack? A common mistake is to place a mono plug into the sound card's speaker or stereo out jacks. Seen from the side, a stereo connector has two darker stripes. A mono connector has only one stripe.

- Is the driver loaded? Some sound cards provide only left-channel sound if the driver is not loaded in the CONFIG.SYS file. Again, run your sound card's setup software.

Volume Is Low. If you can barely hear your sound card, try these solutions:

- Are the mixer settings too low? Again, adjust the volume level in your DOS or Windows mixer. If your sound card uses keystrokes to adjust the volume, use them.

- Is the initial volume too low? Some sound cards provide volume settings as part of the line in CONFIG.SYS that loads the sound card driver. The number for the volume may be set too low.

- Are the speakers too weak? Some speakers may need more power than your sound card can produce. Try other speakers or put a stereo amplifier between your sound card and speakers.

Scratchy Sound. If the sound is scratchy, consider the following possible problems:

- Is your sound card near other expansion cards? The sound card may be picking up electrical interference from other expansion cards inside the PC. Move the sound card to an expansion slot as far away as possible from other cards.

- Are your speakers too close to your monitor? The speakers may pick up electrical noise from your monitor. Move them farther away.

Your Computer Won't Start. If your computer won't start at all, you may not have inserted the sound card completely into its slot. Turn off the PC and then press firmly on the card until it is seated correctly.

III

Input/Output Hardware

Parity Error or Other Lockups. Your computer may display a memory parity error message or simply "crash." Several causes are possible:

■ Is there a DMA conflict? When your computer crashes, the crash is most likely caused by the sound card using the same DMA channel as another device, such as a disk, tape drive, or scanner. Use your sound card setup software to change the DMA channel.

■ Is there an I/O address conflict? Another card may be using some of the I/O addresses used by your sound card. Try to remove some of the other cards to see if that resolves the conflict. If so, change the address of either the offending card or your sound card.

■ Are you using certain DMA channels? Some sound cards work better with 16-bit DMA channels, such as 5, 6, or 7. Some computers, however, don't work well with these. Try using DMA 3, if available.

■ Are you using DMA 1 for Sound Blaster compatibility? Many games require Sound Blaster compatibility set to DMA 1. This may cause conflicts with other cards. Try to change the other boards, unless you can set the game to another DMA.

■ Should you try another Sound Blaster I/O port? You can change the I/O address required for Sound Blaster compatibility. The default setting is 220. But be sure to check that your game can accept a different value.

Joystick Won't Work. If your joystick won't work, consider the following list of cures:

■ Are you using two game ports? If you already have a game port installed in your PC, the joystick port provided on your sound card may conflict with it. To resolve this conflict, disable the joystick port on your sound card or the one already in your PC. On the Logitech SoundMan 16 and Pro AudioStudio 16 sound cards, the joystick can be turned on or off with a simple change to the device driver line in CONFIG.SYS. For example, this line is for the Pro AudioStudio 16:

```
DEVICE=C:\PASTUDIO\MVSOUND.SYS D:5 Q:7 S:1,220,1,5 M:1,330,2 J:0
```

The last switch (J:0) is used to turn the joystick on or off. On is J:1, off is J:0. If you have a separate game card or joystick port, change this setting to J:0.

■ Is your computer too fast? Some fast computers get confused by the inexpensive game ports. During the heat of battle, for example, you may find yourself flying upside down or spiraling out of control. This is one sign that your game port is inadequate. A dedicated game card, such as the CH Products GameCard III, can work with faster computers. Such game cards include software to calibrate your joystick and dual ports so that you can enjoy a game with a friend. Another solution is to run your computer at a slower speed, which is usually done by pressing some type of turbo button on your PC.

Unsolvable Problems. Unfortunately, some sound card problems cannot be solved. Your PC may be of a certain design that your sound card cannot support. For example, I initially could not get the Windows Sound System to work in my PC. It worked, but it either played the WAV files at "chipmunk" speed or with quality fit for the garbage disposal. A call to Microsoft's technical support staff helped to decipher the problem. The Windows Sound System was not tested with a PC that uses the Symphony chipset, a type of motherboard design. Apparently, this chipset handles the DMA channel differently than other motherboard designs. The solution was to wait for new software drivers and manually edit the SYSTEM.INI file.

Another solution to some sound card problems resides in the BIOS. In the AMI BIOS setup program the choice for the Timing Parameter Selection was set to 1, the best-case value. Somehow, this value affects the DMA timing. After the value is changed to 0, some sound cards work properly.

My main point here is that you shouldn't be frustrated if your sound card doesn't work. The PC "standard" is based loosely on the cooperation among a handful of companies. Something as simple as one vendor's BIOS or motherboard design can make the standard nonstandard.

Summary

This chapter introduced you to the uses of sound cards, including games, voice annotation, MIDI music-making, and voice recognition. The various facets of a sound card were discussed, such as the nature of sound, analog-to-digital (ADC) and digital-to-analog (DAC) conversion, and sampling. The chapter discussed the differences between 8- and 16-bit sound and how sound cards can double as CD-ROM interfaces. Sound standards such as Sound Blaster and AdLib were discussed as well as various sound file formats, such as WAV (waveform audio), FM and wave-table synthesis, and MIDI.

The chapter discussed the buying criteria for a sound card, such as bundled software, available driver, stereophonic versus monophonic cards, and connectors. Options were discussed, including speakers, MIDI keyboard synthesizers, joysticks and microphones. Finally, the chapter discussed installing a sound card and troubleshooting installation pitfalls. Most problems result from hardware conflicts involving DMA (direct memory access) channels, IRQs (interrupt request lines) and I/O addresses.

III

Input/Output Hardware

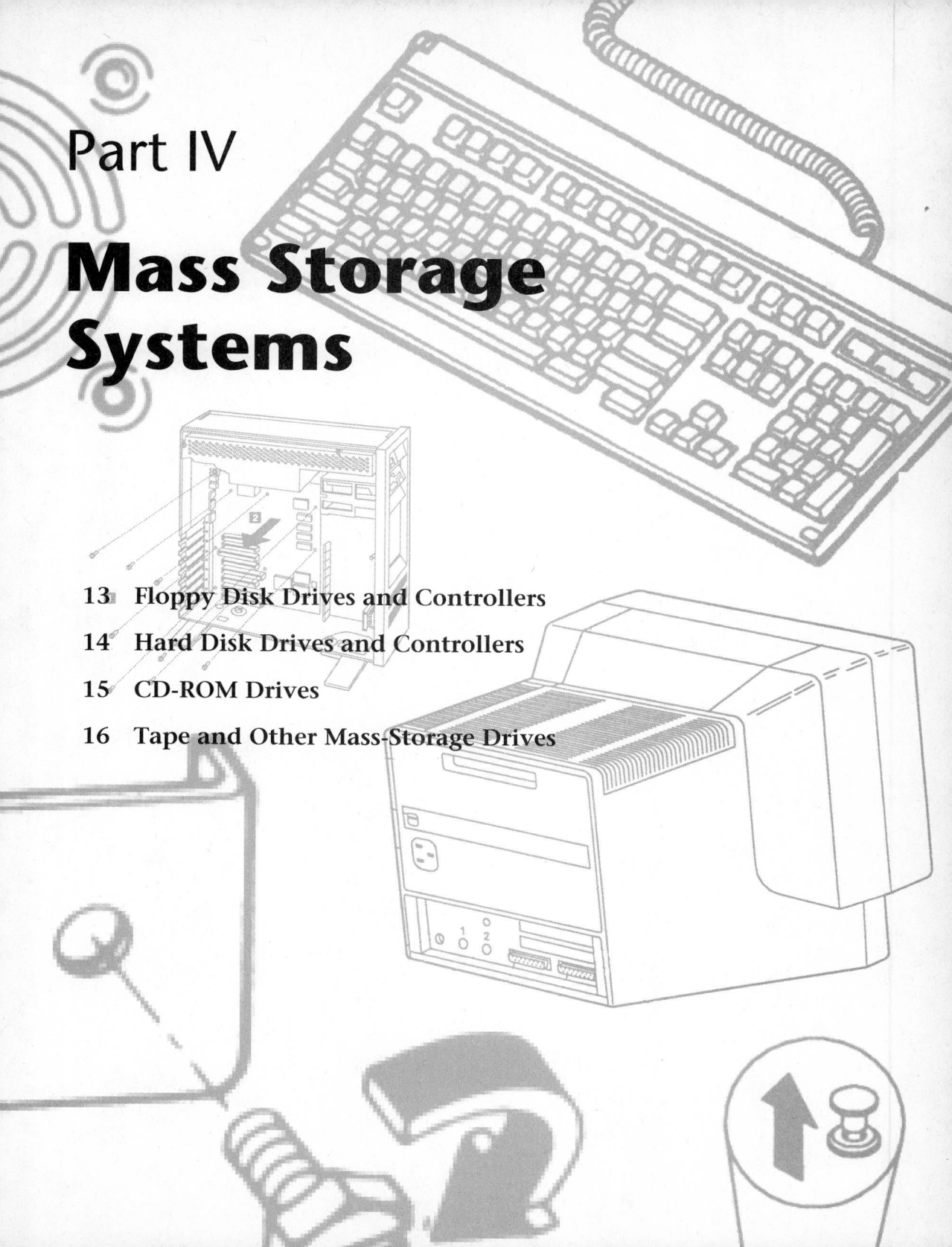

Part IV

Mass Storage Systems

13   Floppy Disk Drives and Controllers

14   Hard Disk Drives and Controllers

15   CD-ROM Drives

16   Tape and Other Mass-Storage Drives

Chapter 13

Floppy Disk Drives and Controllers

This chapter examines, in detail, floppy disk drives and disks. It explores how floppy disk drives and disks function, how DOS uses a disk, what types of disk drives and disks are available, and how to properly install and service drives and disks. You learn about all the types of drives available for today's personal computer systems; these drives include both the 5 1/4-inch and 3 1/2-inch drives in all different versions. The chapter discusses also the newer, extra-high density (ED) 3 1/2-inch disks. Also discussed are several upgrade options including the addition of the 3 1/2-inch drives to the early PC-family systems, which enables them to be compatible with many newer systems, as well as upgrading newer systems to support the ED drives and disks.

Development of the Floppy Disk Drive

Alan Shugart is generally credited with inventing the floppy drive while working for IBM in the late 60s. In 1967, he headed the disk drive development team at IBM's San Jose lab, where and when the floppy drive was created. One of Shugart's senior engineers, David Noble, actually proposed the flexible media (then 8 inches in diameter) and the protective jacket with the fabric lining. Shugart left IBM in 1969 and took more than 100 IBM engineers with him to Memorex. He was nicknamed "The Pied Piper" because of the loyalty exhibited by the many staff members who followed him. In 1973, he left Memorex, again taking with him a number of associates, and started Shugart Associates, to develop and manufacture floppy drives. The floppy interface developed by Shugart is still the basis of all PC floppy drives. IBM used this interface in the PC, enabling them to use off-the-shelf third-party drives instead of custom building their own solutions.

Shugart actually wanted to incorporate processors and floppy drives into complete microcomputer systems at that time, but the financial backers of the new Shugart Associates wanted him to concentrate on floppy drives only. He quit (or was forced to quit) Shugart Associates in 1974, right before they introduced the Mini-floppy (5.1/4-inch) diskette drive, which of course became the standard eventually used by personal computers, rapidly replacing the 8-inch drives. Shugart Associates also introduced the Shugart Associates System Interface (SASI), which was later renamed Small Computer Systems Interface (SCSI) when it was formally approved by the ANSI committee in 1986. After being forced to leave, Shugart attempted to legally force Shugart Associates to remove his name from the company, but failed. The remnants of Shugart Associates still operates today as Shugart Corporation.

For the next few years, Shugart took time off, ran a bar, and even dabbled in commercial fishing. In 1979, Finis Conner approached Shugart to create and market 5 1/4-inch hard disk drives. Together they founded Seagate Technology and by the end of 1979 had announced the ST-506 (6M unformatted, 5M formatted capacity) drive and interface. This drive is known as the father of all PC hard disk drives. Seagate then introduced the ST-412 (12M unformatted, 10M formatted capacity) drive, which was adopted by IBM for the original XT in 1983. IBM was Seagate's largest customer for many years. Today, Seagate Technology is the largest disk drive manufacturer in the world, second only to IBM.

When you stop to think about it, Alan Shugart has had a tremendous effect on the PC industry. He (or his companies) have created the floppy, hard disk, and SCSI drive and controller interfaces still used today. All PC floppy drives are still based on (and compatible with) the original Shugart designs. The ST-506/412 interface was the de facto hard disk interface standard for many years and served as the basis for the ESDI and IDE interfaces as well. Shugart also created the SCSI interface, used in both IBM and Apple systems today.

As a side note, in the late 80s Finis Conner left Seagate and founded Conner Peripherals, originally wholly owned and funded by Compaq. Conner became Compaq's exclusive drive supplier and gradually began selling drives to other system manufacturers as well. Compaq eventually cut Conner Peripherals free, selling off most (if not all) of their ownership of the company.

Drive Components

This section describes the components that make up a typical floppy drive and examines how these components operate together to read and write data—the physical operation of the drive. All floppy drives, regardless of type, consist of several basic common components. To properly install and service a disk drive, you must be able to identify these components and understand their function (see fig. 13.1).

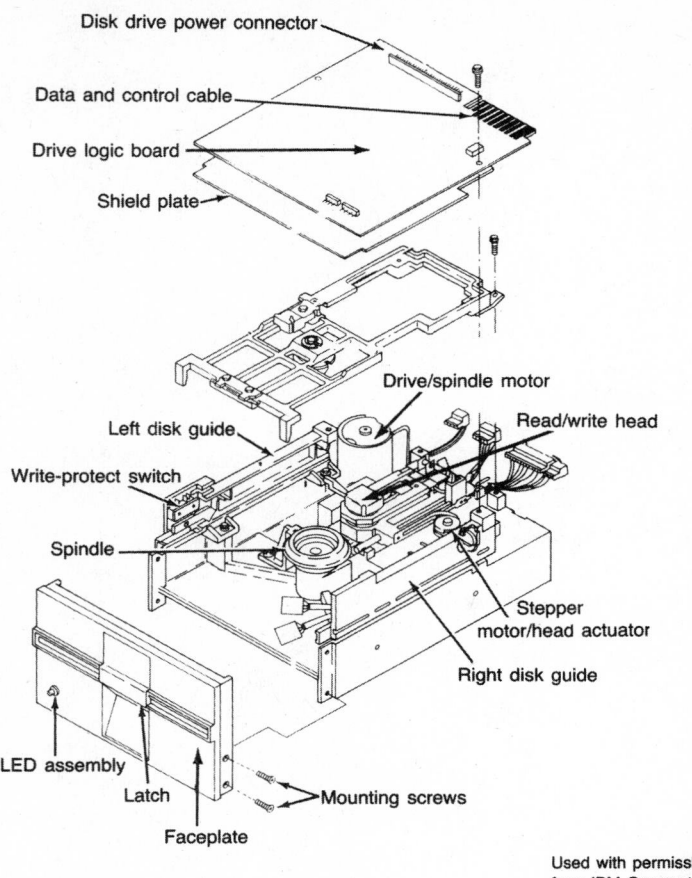

Disk drive power connector

Data and control cable

Drive logic board

Shield plate

Drive/spindle motor

Left disk guide

Read/write head

Write-protect switch

Spindle

Stepper motor/head actuator

Right disk guide

LED assembly

Latch

Mounting screws

Faceplate

Used with permission from IBM Corporation.

Fig. 13.1
A typical full-height disk drive.

Read/Write Heads

A floppy disk drive normally has two read/write heads, making the modern floppy disk drive a double-sided drive. A head exists for each side of the disk, and both heads are used for reading and writing on their respective disk sides. At one time, single-sided drives were available for PC systems (the original PC had such drives), but today single-sided drives are a fading memory (see fig. 13.2).

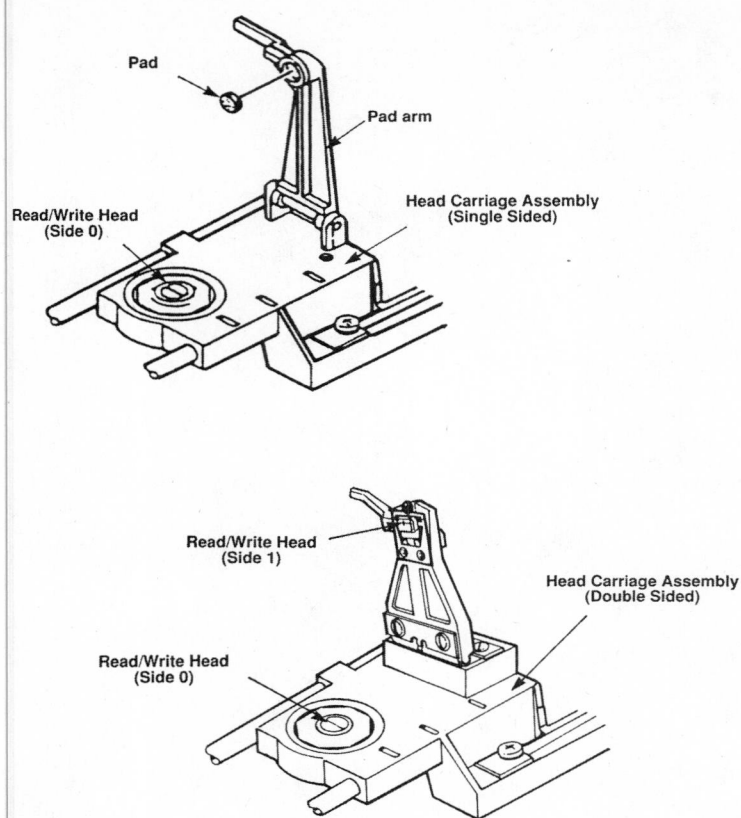

Fig. 13.2
Single- and double-sided drive head assemblies.

> **Note**
>
> Many people do not realize that the first head is the bottom one. Single-sided drives, in fact, use only the bottom head; the top head is replaced by a felt pressure pad (see fig 13.2). Another bit of disk trivia is that the top head (Head 1) is not directly over the bottom head—the top head is located either four or eight tracks inward from the bottom head, depending on the drive type. Therefore, what conventionally are called "cylinders" should more accurately be called "cones."

The head mechanism is moved by a motor called a *head actuator*. The heads can move in and out over the surface of the disk in a straight line to position themselves over various tracks. The heads move in and out tangentially to the tracks that they record on the disk. Because the top and bottom heads are mounted on the same rack, or mechanism, they move in unison and cannot move independently of each other. The heads are made of soft ferrous (iron) compounds with electromagnetic coils. Each head is a composite design, with a record head centered within two tunnel-erase heads in the same physical assembly (see fig. 13.3).

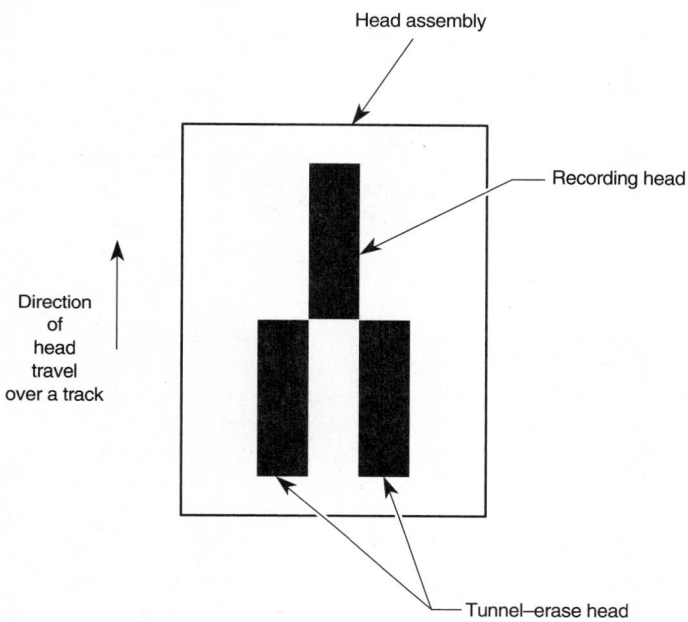

Fig. 13.3

Composite construction of a typical floppy drive head.

The recording method is called *tunnel erasure*; as the track is laid down, the trailing tunnel erase heads erase the outer bands of the track, trimming it cleanly on the disk. The heads force the data to be present only within a specified narrow "tunnel" on each track. This process prevents the signal from one track from being confused with the signals from adjacent tracks. If the signal were allowed to "taper off" to each side, problems would occur. The forcibly trimmed track prevents this problem.

Alignment is the placement of the heads with respect to the tracks they must read and write. Head alignment can be checked only against some sort of reference-standard disk recorded by a perfectly aligned machine. These types of disks are available, and you can use one to check your drive's alignment.

The two heads are spring-loaded and physically grip the disk with a small amount of pressure, which means that they are in direct contact with the disk surface while reading and writing to the disk. Because PC-compatible floppy disk drives spin at only 300 or 360 RPM, this pressure does not present an excessive friction problem. Some newer disks are specially coated with Teflon or other compounds to further reduce friction and enable the disk to slide more easily under the heads. Because of the contact between the heads and the disk, a buildup of the oxide material from the disk eventually forms on the heads. The buildup periodically can be cleaned off the heads as part of a preventive-maintenance or normal service program.

To read and write to the disk properly, the heads must be in direct contact with the media. Very small particles of loose oxide, dust, dirt, smoke, fingerprints, or hair can cause problems with reading and writing the disk. Disk and drive manufacturer's tests have found that a spacing as little as .000032 inches (32 millionths of an inch) between the heads and the media can cause read/write errors. You now can understand why it is important to handle diskettes carefully and avoid touching or contaminating the surface of the diskette media in any way. The rigid jacket and protective shutter for the head access aperture on the 3 1/2-inch disks is excellent for preventing problems with media contamination. 5 1/4-inch disks do not have the same protective elements, therefore more care must be exercised in their handling.

The Head Actuator

The *head actuator* is a mechanical motor device that causes the heads to move in and out over the surface of a disk. These mechanisms for floppy disk drives universally use a special kind of motor, a *stepper motor*, that moves in both directions an amount equal to or less than a single revolution. This type of motor does not spin around continuously; rather, the motor normally moves only a partial revolution in each direction. Stepper motors move in fixed increments, or *detents*, and must stop at a particular detent position. Stepper motors are not infinitely variable in their positioning. Each increment of motion, or a multiple thereof, defines each track on the disk. The motor can be commanded by the disk controller to position itself according to any relative increment within the range of its travel. To position the heads at track 25, for example, the motor is commanded to go to the 25th detent position.

The stepper motor usually is linked to the head rack by a coiled, split steel band. The band winds and unwinds around the spindle of the stepper motor, translating the rotary motion into linear motion. Some drives use a worm gear arrangement rather than a band. With this type, the head assembly rests on a worm gear driven directly off the stepper motor shaft. Because this arrangement is more compact, you normally find worm gear actuators on the smaller 3 1/2-inch drives.

Most stepper motors used in floppy drives can step in specific increments that relate to the track spacing on the disk. Most 48 Track Per Inch (TPI) drives have a motor that steps in increments of 3.6° (degrees). This means that each 3.6° of stepper motor rotation moves the heads from one track (or cylinder) to the next. Most 96 or 135 TPI drives have a stepper motor that moves in 1.8° increments, which is exactly half of what the 48 TPI drives use. Sometimes you see this information actually printed or stamped right on the stepper motor itself, which is useful if you are trying to figure out what type of drive you have. 5 1/4-inch 360K drives are the only 48 TPI drives available and use the 3.6°

increment stepper motor. All other drive types normally use the 1.8° stepper motor. On most drives, the stepper motor is a small cylindrical object near one corner of the drive.

A stepper motor usually has a full travel time of about 1/5 of a second—about 200 milliseconds. On average, a half-stroke is 100 milliseconds, and a one-third stroke is 66 milliseconds. The timing of a one-half or one-third stroke of the head-actuator mechanism often is used to determine the reported average-access time for a disk drive. *Average-access time* is the normal amount of time the heads spend moving at random from one track to another.

The Spindle Motor

The *spindle motor* spins the disk. The normal speed of rotation is either 300 or 360 RPM, depending on the type of drive. The 5 1/4-inch high-density (HD) drive is the only drive that spins at 360 RPM; all others, including the 5 1/4-inch double-density (DD), 3 1/2-inch DD, 3 1/2-inch HD, and 3 1/2-inch extra-high density (ED) drives, spin at 300 RPM. Most earlier drives used a mechanism on which the spindle motor physically turned the disk spindle with a belt, but all modern drives use a direct-drive system with no belts. The direct-drive systems are more reliable and less expensive to manufacture, as well as smaller in size. The earlier belt-driven systems did have more rotational torque available to turn a sticky disk because of the torque multiplication factor of the belt system. Most newer direct-drive systems use an automatic torque-compensation capability that automatically sets the disk-rotation speed to a fixed 300 or 360 RPM and compensates with additional torque for sticky disks or less torque for slippery ones. This type of drive eliminates the need to adjust the rotational speed of the drive.

Most newer direct-drive systems use this automatic-speed feature, but many earlier systems require that you periodically adjust the speed. Looking at the spindle provides you with one clue to the type of drive you have. If the spindle contains strobe marks for 50 Hz and 60 Hz strobe lights (fluorescent lights), the drive probably has an adjustment for speed somewhere on the drive. Drives without the strobe marks almost always include an automatic tachometer-control circuit that eliminates the need for adjustment. The technique for setting the speed involves operating the drive under fluorescent lighting and adjusting the rotational speed until the strobe marks appear motionless, much like the "wagon wheel effect" you see in old Western movies. The procedure is described later in this chapter, in the "Setting the Floppy Drive Speed Adjustment" section.

To locate the spindle-speed adjustment, you must consult the original equipment manufacturer's (OEM) manual for the drive. IBM provides the information for its drives in the *Technical Reference Options and Adapters* manual as well as in the hardware-maintenance reference manuals. Even if IBM had sold the drives, they most likely are manufactured by another company, such as Control Data Corporation (CDC), Tandon, YE-Data (C. Itoh), Alps Electric, or Mitsubishi. Contact these manufacturers for the original manuals for your drives.

Circuit Boards

A disk drive always incorporates one or more *logic* boards, circuit boards that contain the circuitry used to control the head actuator, read/write heads, spindle motor, disk sensors, and any other components on the drive. The logic board represents the drive's interface to the controller board in the system unit.

The standard interface used by all PC types of floppy disk drives is the Shugart Associates SA-400 interface. The interface, invented by Shugart in the 1970s, has been the basis of most floppy disk interfacing. The selection of this industry-standard interface is the reason that you can purchase "off-the-shelf" drives (raw, or bare, drives) that can plug directly into your controller. (Thanks, IBM, for sticking with industry-standard interfacing; it has been the foundation of the entire PC upgrade and repair industry!)

Some other computer companies making non-IBM-compatible systems (especially Apple, for example) have stayed away from industry standards in this and other areas, which can make tasks such as drive repair or upgrades a nightmare—unless, of course, you buy all your parts from them. For example, in both the Apple II series as well as the Mac, Apple used nonstandard proprietary interfaces for the floppy drives.

The Mac uses an interface based on a proprietary chip called either the IWM (Integrated Woz Machine) or the SWIM (Super Woz Integrated Machine) chip, depending on which Mac you have. These interfaces are incompatible with the industry standard SA-400 interface used in IBM-compatible systems, which is based on the non-proprietary NEC PD765 chip. In fact, the Apple drives use an encoding scheme called GCR (group-coded recording), which is very different from the standard MFM (modified frequency modulation) used in most other systems. The GCR encoding scheme, in fact, cannot be performed by the NEC-type controller chips, which is why it is impossible for IBM-compatible systems to read Mac floppy disks. To Apple's credit, the Mac systems with the SWIM chip include drives that can read and write both GCR and MFM schemes, enabling these systems to read and write IBM floppy disks.

Unfortunately, because the electrical interface to the drive is proprietary, you still cannot easily (or cheaply) purchase these drives as bare units from a variety of manufacturers, as you can for IBM-compatible systems. IBM uses true industry standards in these and other areas, which is why the PC, XT, AT, and PS/2 systems, as well as most IBM-compatible vendors' systems are so open to upgrade and repair.

Logic boards for a drive can fail and usually are difficult to obtain as a spare part. One board often costs more than replacing the entire drive. I recommend keeping failed or misaligned drives that might otherwise be discarded so that they can be used for their remaining good parts—such as logic boards. The parts can be used to restore a failing drive very cost-effectively.

The Faceplate

The *faceplate*, or bezel, is the plastic piece that comprises the front of the drive. These pieces, usually removable, come in different colors and configurations.

Most drives use a bezel slightly wider than the drive. These types of drives must be installed from the front of a system because the faceplate is slightly wider than the hole in the system-unit case. Other drive faceplates are the same width as the drive's chassis; these drives can be installed from the rear—an advantage in some cases. In the later-version XT systems, for example, IBM uses this design in its drives so that two half-height drives can be bolted together as a unit and then slid in from the rear, to clear the mounting-bracket and screw hardware. On occasion, I have filed the edges of a drive faceplate to install the drive from the rear of a system—which sometimes can make installation much easier.

Connectors

Nearly all disk drives have at least two connectors—one for power to run the drive and the other to carry the control and data signals to and from the drive. These connectors are fairly standardized in the computer industry; a four-pin in-line connector (called Mate-N-Lock, by AMP), in both a large and small style is used for power (see fig. 13.4); and a 34-pin connector in both edge and pin header designs are used for the data and control signals. 5 1/4-inch drives normally use the large style power connector and the 34-pin edge type connector, whereas most 3 1/2-inch drives use the smaller version of the power connector and the 34-pin header type logic connector. The drive controller and logic connectors and pinouts are detailed later in this chapter and in Appendix A.

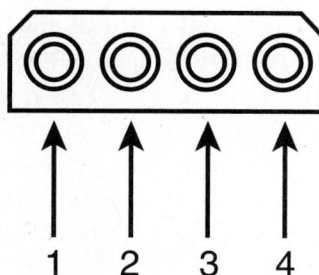

Fig. 13.4

A disk drive female power supply cable connector.

Both the large and small power connectors from the power supply are female plugs. They plug into the male portion, which is attached to the drive itself. One common problem with upgrading an older system with 3 1/2-inch drives is that your power supply only has the large style connectors, whereas the drive has the small style. An adapter cable is available from Radio Shack (Cat. No. 278-765) and other sources that converts the large style power connector to the proper small style used on most 3 1/2-inch drives.

The following chart shows the definition of the pins on the drive power-cable connectors.

Large Power Connector	Small Power Connector	Signal	Wire Color
Pin 1	Pin 4	+12 Vdc	Yellow
Pin 2	Pin 3	Ground	Black
Pin 3	Pin 2	Ground	Black
Pin 4	Pin 1	+5 Vdc	Red

Note that the pin designations are reversed between the large and small style power connectors. Also, it is important to know that not all manufacturers follow the wire color coding properly. I have seen instances in which all the wires are a single color (for example, black), or the wire colors are actually reversed from normal! For example, I once purchased the power connector adapter cables just mentioned that had all the wire colors backwards. This was not really a problem as the adapter cable was wired correctly from end to end, but it was disconcerting to see the red wire in the power supply connector attach to a yellow wire in the adapter (and vice versa)!

Not all drives use the standard separate power and signal connectors. IBM, for example, uses either a single 34-pin or single 40-pin header connector for both power and floppy controller connections in most of the PS/2 systems. In some older PS/2 systems, for example, IBM used a special version of a Mitsubishi 3 1/2-inch 1.44M drive called the MF-355W-99; which has a single 40-pin power/signal connector. Some newer PS/2 systems use a Mitsubishi 3 1/2-inch 2.88M drive called the MF356C-799MA, which uses a single 34-pin header connector for both power and signal connections.

Most standard IBM clone or compatible systems use 3 1/2-inch drives with a 34-pin signal connector and a separate small style power connector. For older PC- or AT-type systems, many drive manufacturers also sell 3 1/2-inch drives installed in a 5 1/4-inch frame assembly and have a special adapter built-in that allows the larger power connector and standard edge type signal connectors to be used. Mitsubishi, for example, sold 1.44M drives as the MF-355B-82 (black faceplate) or MF-355B-88 (beige faceplate). These drives included an adapter that enables the standard large style power connector and 34-pin edge type control and data connector to be used. Because no cable adapters are required and they install in a 5 1/4-inch half-height bay, these types of drives are ideal for upgrading earlier systems. Most 3 1/2-inch drive-upgrade kits sold today are similar and include the drive, appropriate adapters for the power and control and data cables, a 5 1/4-inch frame adapter and faceplate, and rails for AT installations. The frame adapter and faceplate enable the drive to be installed where a 5 1/4-inch half-height drive normally would go.

Drive-Configuration Devices

You must locate several items on a drive that you install in a system. These items control the configuration and operation of the drive and must be set correctly depending on which type of system the drive is installed in and exactly where in the system the drive is installed.

You must set or check the following items during installation:

- Drive select jumper

- Terminating resistor

- Diskette changeline jumper

- Media sensor jumper

You learn how to configure these items later in this chapter. In this section, you learn what function these devices perform.

Drive Select Jumper. Each drive in a controller and drive subsystem must have a unique drive number. The *drive select jumper* is set to indicate to the controller the logical number of a particular drive. The jumper indicates whether the specific drive should respond as drive 0 or 1 (A or B). Some idiosyncrasies can be found when you set this jumper in various systems because of strange cable configurations or other differences. Most drives allow four different settings, labeled DS1, DS2, DS3, and DS4. Some drives start with 0, and thus the four settings are labeled DS0, DS1, DS2, and DS3. On some drives, these jumpers are not labeled. If they are not labeled, you have several resources available for information about how to set the drive: the OEM manual, your experience with other similar drives, or simply an educated guess. First check the manual if it is available; if not, then perhaps you can rely on your past experiences and make an educated guess.

You might think that the first drive select position corresponds to A and that the second position corresponds to B, but in most cases you would be wrong. The configuration that seems correct is wrong because of some creative rewiring of the cable. IBM, for example, crosses the seven wires numbered 10 through 16 (the drive select, motor enable, and some ground lines) in the floppy interface cable between drives B: and A: to allow both drives to be jumpered the same way, as though they both were drive B:. This type of cable is shown later in this chapter.

When using a floppy cable with lines 10 through 16 twisted, you must set the DS jumper on both drives to the second (same) drive select position. This setup enabled dealers and installers to buy the drives pre-configured by IBM and install them with a minimum of hassle. Sometimes this setup confuses people who attempt to install drives properly without knowing about the twisted-cabling system. With this type of cable design, to swap drive A and B positions you can simply swap the cable connections between the drives with no jumper setting changes required. You still probably have to change the terminator resistor settings on the drives, however.

If the cable has a straight-through design, in which lines 10 through 16 are not twisted between the B and A connectors, you then need to jumper the drives as you might have thought originally—that is, drive A is set to the first drive select position, and drive B is set to the second drive select position.

If you install a drive and it either does not respond or responds in unison with the other drive in the system in calling for drive A, you probably have the drive select jumpers set incorrectly for your application. Check the DS jumpers on both drives as well as the cable for the proper setup.

Terminating Resistor. Any signal carrying electronic media or cable with multiple connections can be thought of as an electrical bus. In almost all cases, a bus must be terminated properly at each end with Terminating Resistors to allow signals to travel along the bus error free. Terminating resistors are designed to absorb any signals that reach the end of a cabling system or bus so that no reflection of the signal echoes, or bounces, back down the line in the opposite direction. Engineers sometimes call this effect *signal ringing*. Simply put, noise and distortion can disrupt the original signal and prevent proper communications between the drive and controller. Another function of proper termination is to place the proper resistive load on the output drivers in the controller and drive.

Most floppy disk cabling systems have the controller positioned at one end of the cable, and a terminating resistor network is built-in to the controller to properly terminate that end of the bus. IBM and IBM clone or compatible systems use a floppy controller design that normally allows up to two drives on a single cable. To terminate the other end of the bus properly, a terminating resistor must be set, or enabled, on the drive at the end of the cable farthest from the controller. In most systems, this drive also is the lowest-lettered drive (A) of the pair. The drive plugged into the connector in the center of the cable must have the terminating resistor (or terminator) removed or disabled for proper operation.

Because a terminating resistor is already installed in the controller to terminate the cable at that end, be concerned only with properly terminating the drive end. Sometimes a system operates even with incorrect terminator installation or configuration, but the system might experience sporadic disk errors. Additionally, with the wrong signal load on the controller and drives, you run the risk of damaging them by causing excessive power output because of an improper resistive load.

A terminating resistor usually looks like a memory chip—a 16-pin *dual in-line package* (DIP) device. The device is actually a group of eight resistors physically wired in parallel with each other to terminate separately each of the eight data lines in the interface subsystem. Normally, this "chip" is a different color from other black chips on the drive. Orange, blue, or white are common colors for a terminating resistor. Be aware that not all drives use the same type of terminating resistor, however, and it might be physically located in different places on different manufacturer's drive models. The OEM manual for the drive comes in handy in this situation because it shows the location, physical appearance, enabling and disabling instructions, and even the precise value required for the resistors. Do not lose the terminator if you remove it from a drive; you might need to reinstall it later if you relocate the drive to a different position in a system or even to a different system. Some drives use a resistor network in a *single in-line pin* (SIP) package, which looks like a slender device with eight or more pins in a line. Most terminating resistors have resistance values of 150 to 330 ohms.

Nearly all 5 1/4-inch floppy drives use a chip style terminator that must be physically installed or removed from the drive as required by the drive's position on the cable. Some 5 1/4-inch drives, especially those made by Toshiba, have a permanently installed terminating resistor enabled or disabled by a jumper labeled TR (Terminating Resistor). I prefer the jumper setup because you never have to actually remove (and possibly lose) the terminating resistor itself. Because some drives use different style and value resistors, if one is lost it can be a hassle to obtain a replacement of the correct type.

Most 3 1/2-inch drives have permanently installed, non-configurable terminating resistors. This setup is the best possible because you never have to remove or install them, and there are never any TR jumpers to set. Although some call this technique automatic termination, technically the 3 1/2-inch drives use a technique called *distributed termination*. With distributed termination, each 3 1/2-inch drive has a much higher value (1,000 to 1,500 ohm) terminating resistor permanently installed, and therefore carries a part of the termination load. These terminating resistors are fixed permanently to the drive and never have to be removed. This feature makes configuring these drives one step simpler. Because each drive is connected in parallel on the floppy cabling system, the total equivalent resistive load is calculated by the following formula:

$$1/R = 1/R1 + 1/R2 + 1/R3 + \text{etc.}$$

In a typical setup, a 330-ohm terminating resistor is permanently installed on the floppy controller, so the calculations for typical systems with one or two 3 1/2-inch drives (with built-in 1,500-ohm terminating resistors) is as follows:

$$1/R = 1/330 + 1/1,500 + 1/1,500 \text{ so } R = 229.17 \text{ ohms (two drives)}$$

$$1/R = 1/330 + 1/1,500 \text{ so } R = 270.5 \text{ ohms (one drive)}$$

Some confusion exists regarding the situation in which you have both 5 1/4-inch and 3 1/2-inch drives installed on a single cable. In this case, the 5 1/4-inch drive must have its terminating resistor configured as appropriate, which is to say either leave it installed or remove it depending on whether the drive is at the end of the cable. Nothing with regards to termination is done with the 3 1/2-inch drive because the terminating resistors are non-configurable. Although it sounds like mixing these might cause a problem with the termination, actually it works out quite well as the math shows. In this example, 33-ohm resistors are used both on the floppy controller and the 5 1/4-inch drive:

$1/R = 1/330 + 1/1,500$ so $R = 270.5$ ohms (3 1/2-inch drive at cable end)

$1/R = 1/330 + 1/330$ so $R = 165$ ohms (5 1/4-inch drive at cable end)

As long as a terminating resistor is at each end of the cable and the total equivalent resistance is between 100 to 300 ohms, the termination is normally considered correct. The drive in the center cable connector should not have a terminating resistor unless it employs distributed termination and has a resistor value of 1,000 ohms or higher. Note that in many cases even if the termination is improper a system seems to work fine, although the likelihood of read and write errors is greatly increased. In some cases, the drives do not work properly at all unless termination is properly configured. I have solved many intermittent floppy drive problems by correcting improper terminating resistor configurations, found even in brand new systems.

Diskette Changeline Jumper. In an XT-type system, pin 34 of the disk drive interface is not used, but in an AT system this pin is used to carry a signal called *Diskette Changeline*, or DC. Although the XT does not use pin 34, most drives that don't support the DC signal can optionally use the pin to carry a signal called *Ready* (usually labeled on the drive as RY, RDY, or SR). The Ready signal is actually never used in any IBM or IBM-compatible systems and should not be configured or in most cases the drive will not work properly.

The AT uses the Diskette Changeline signal to determine whether the disk has been changed, or more accurately, whether the same disk loaded during the previous disk access still is loaded in the floppy drive. *Disk Change* is a pulsed signal that changes a status register in the controller to let the system know that a disk has been either inserted or ejected. This register is set to indicate that a disk has been inserted or removed (changed) by default. The register is cleared when the controller sends a step pulse to the drive and the drive responds, acknowledging that the heads have moved. At this point, the system knows that a specific disk is in the drive. If the disk change signal is not received before the next access, the system can assume that the same disk is still in the drive. Any information read into memory during the previous access therefore can be reused without rereading the disk.

Because of this process, some systems can buffer or cache the contents of the file allocation table or directory structure of a disk in the system's memory. By eliminating unnecessary rereads of these areas of the disk, the apparent speed of the drive is increased. If you move the door lever or eject button on a drive that supports the disk change signal, the DC pulse is sent to the controller, thus resetting the register indicating that the disk has been changed. This procedure causes the system to purge buffered or cached data that had been read from the disk because the system then cannot be sure that the same disk is still in the drive.

AT class systems use the DC signal to increase significantly the speed of the floppy interface. Because the AT can detect whether you have changed the disk, the AT can keep a copy of the disk's directory and file allocation table information in RAM buffers. On every subsequent disk access, the operations are much faster because the information does not have to be reread from the disk in every individual access. If the DC signal has been reset (has a value of 1), the AT knows that the disk has been changed and appropriately rereads the information from the disk.

You can observe the effects of the DC signal by trying a simple experiment. Boot DOS on an AT-class system and place a formatted floppy disk with data on it in drive A. Drive A can be any type of drive except 5 1/4-inch double-density, although the disk you use can be anything the drive can read, including a double-density 360K disk, if you want. Then type the following command:

DIR A:

The disk drive lights up, and the directory is displayed. Note the amount of time spent reading the disk before the directory is displayed on-screen. Without touching the drive, enter the **DIR A:** command again, and watch the drive-access light and screen. Note again the amount of time that passes before the directory is displayed. The drive A directory should appear almost instantly the second time because virtually no time is spent actually reading the disk. The directory information was simply read back from RAM buffers or cache rather than read again from the disk. Now open and close the drive door and keep the same disk in the drive. Type the **DIR A:** command again. The disk again takes some time reading the directory before displaying anything because the AT "thinks" that you changed the disk.

The PC and XT controllers (and systems) are not affected by the status of the DC signal. These systems "don't care" about signals on pin 34. The PC and XT systems always operate under the assumption that the disk is changed before every access, and they reread the disk directory and file allocation table each time—one reason that these systems are slower in using the floppy disk drives.

A problem can occur when certain drives are installed in an AT system. As mentioned, some drives use pin 34 for a "Ready" signal. The RDY signal is sent when a disk is installed and rotating in the drive. If you install a drive that has pin 34 set to send RDY, the AT "thinks" that it is continuously receiving a disk change signal, which causes problems: usually the drive fails with a Drive not ready error and is inoperable.

A different but related problem occurs if the drive is not sending the DC signal on pin 34, and it should. If an AT class system is told (through CMOS setup) that the drive is any other type than a 360K (which cannot ever send the DC signal), then the system expects the drive to send DC whenever a disk has been ejected. If the drive is not configured properly to send the signal, then the system never recognizes that a disk has been changed. Therefore, even if you do change the disk, the AT still acts as though the first disk is in the drive and holds the first disk's directory and file allocation table information in RAM. This can be dangerous as the File Allocation Table (FAT) and directory information from the first disk can be partially written to any subsequent disks written to in the drive.

If you ever have seen an AT class system with a floppy drive that shows "phantom directories" of the previously installed disk, even after you have changed or removed it, you have experienced this problem firsthand. The negative side effect is that all disks after the first one you place in this system are in extreme danger. You likely will overwrite the directories and file allocation tables of many disks with information from the first disk. Data recovery from such a catastrophe can require quite a bit of work with utility programs such as the Norton Utilities. These problems with Disk Change most often are traced to an incorrectly configured drive. Another possibility is that the disk-eject sensor mechanism no longer operates correctly. A temporary solution to the problem is to press the Ctrl-Break or Ctrl-C key combination every time you change a floppy disk in the drive. These commands cause DOS to flush the RAM buffers manually and reread the directory and file allocation table during the next disk access.

All drives except 5 1/4-inch double-density (360K) drives support the Disk Change signal. Therefore, if your system thinks that one of these drives is installed, the drive is expected to provide the signal. If the system thinks that the installed drive is a 360K drive, no signal is expected on pin 34.

To summarize, PC and XT systems are not affected by pin 34, but on AT systems, non-360K drives must have pin 34 set to send Disk Change. If the drive is a 360K drive and you want to install it in an AT, pin 34 must be disabled (usually preconfigured as such, or set by removing a jumper). Never set a 360K drive (or any other drive for that matter) to send a signal called Ready (RDY) on pin 34 because IBM-compatible systems cannot use this signal. The only reason that the Ready signal exists on some drives is that it happens to be a part of the standard Shugart SA-400 disk interface that was not adopted by IBM.

Media Sensor Jumper. This configuration item exists only on the 3 1/2-inch 1.44M or 2.88M drives. The jumper selection, called the *media sensor (MS) jumper*, must be set to enable a special media sensor in the disk drive, which senses a media sensor hole found only in the 1.44M high-density and the 2.88M extra-high density floppy disks. The labeling of this jumper (or jumpers) varies greatly between different drives. In many drives, the jumpers are permanently set (enabled) and cannot be changed.

The three types of configurations with regards to media sensing are as follows:

- No media sense (sensor disabled or no sensor present)

- Passive media sense (sensor enabled)

- Active or intelligent media sense (sensor supported by Controller/BIOS)

Most systems use a *passive media sensor* arrangement. The passive media sensor setup enables the drive to determine the level of recording strength to use and is required for most installations of these drives because of a bug in the design of the Western Digital hard disk and floppy controllers used by IBM in the AT systems. This bug prevents the controller from properly instructing the drive to switch to double-density mode when you write or format double-density disks. With the media sensor enabled, the drive no longer depends on the controller for density mode switching and relies only on the drive's media sensor. Unless you are sure that your disk controller does not have this flaw, make sure that your HD drive includes a media sensor (some older or manufacturer-specific drives do not), and that it is properly enabled. The 2.88M drives universally rely on media sensors to determine the proper mode of operation. The 2.88M drives, in fact, have two separate media sensors because the ED disks include a media sensor hole in a different position than the HD disks.

With only a few exceptions, high-density 3 1/2-inch drives installed in most IBM-compatible systems do not operate properly in double-density mode unless the drive has control over the write current (recording level) via an installed and enabled media sensor. Exceptions are found primarily in systems with floppy controllers integrated on the motherboard, including most older IBM PS/2 and Compaq systems as well as most laptop or notebook systems from other manufacturers. These systems have floppy controllers without the bug referred to earlier, and can correctly switch the mode of the drive without the aid of the media sensor. In these systems, it technically does not matter whether you enable the media sensor. If the media sensor is enabled, the drive mode is controlled by the disk you insert, as is the case with most IBM-compatible systems. If the media sensor is not enabled, the drive mode is controlled by the floppy controller, which in turn is controlled by DOS.

If a disk is already formatted (correctly), DOS reads the volume boot sector to determine the current disk format, and the controller then switches the drive to the appropriate mode. If the disk has not been formatted yet, DOS has no idea what type of disk it is, and the drive remains in its native HD or ED mode.

When you format a disk in systems without an enabled media sensor (such as most PS/2s), the mode of the drive depends entirely on the FORMAT command issued by the user, regardless of the type of disk inserted. For example, if you insert a DD disk into an HD drive in an IBM PS/2 Model 70 and format the disk by entering FORMAT A:, the disk is formatted as though it is an HD disk because you did not issue the correct parameters to cause the FORMAT command to specify a DD format. On a system with the media sensor enabled, this type of incorrect format fails, and you see the Invalid media or Track 0 bad error message from FORMAT. In this case, the media sensor prevents an incorrect format from occurring on the disk, a safety feature most older IBM PS/2 systems lack.

Most of the newer PS/2 systems, including all those that come standard with the 2.88M drives, have what is called an active or intelligent media sensor setup. This means that the sensor not only detects what type of disk is in the drive and changes modes appropriately, but also the drive informs the controller (and the BIOS) about what type of disk is in the drive. Systems with an intelligent media sensor do not need to use the disk type parameters in the FORMAT command. In these systems, the FORMAT command automatically "knows" what type of disk is in the drive, and formats it properly. With an intelligent media sensor, you never have to know what the correct format parameters are for a particular type of disk, the system figures it out for you automatically. Many high-end systems such as the newer PS/2 systems as well as high-end Hewlett Packard PCs have this type of intelligent media sensor arrangement.

The Floppy Disk Controller

The floppy disk controller consists of the circuitry either on a separate adapter card or integrated on the motherboard, which acts as the interface between the floppy drives and the system. Most PC- and XT-class systems used a separate controller card that occupied a slot in the system. The AT systems normally had the floppy controller and hard disk controller built into the same adapter card and also plugged into a slot. In most of the more modern systems built since then, the controller is integrated on the motherboard. In any case, the electrical interface to the drives has remained largely static, with only a few exceptions.

The original IBM PC and XT system floppy controller was a 3/4-length card that could drive as many as four floppy disk drives. Two drives could be connected to a cable plugged into a 34-pin edge connector on the card, and two more drives could be plugged into a cable connected to the 37-pin connector on the bracket of this card. Figures 13.5 and 13.6 show these connectors and the pinouts for the controller.

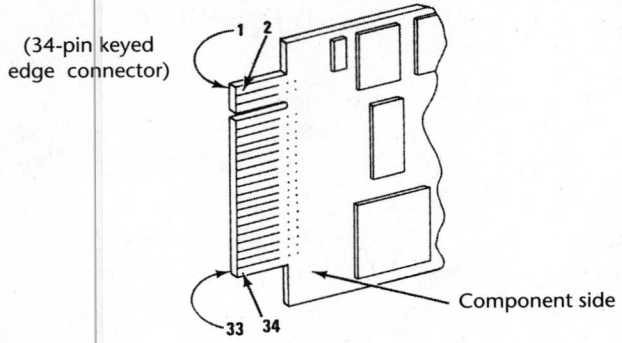

At Standard TTL Levels	Land Number	
Ground-Odd Numbers	1-33	
Unused	2,4,6	
Index	8	
Motor Enable A	10	
Drive Select B	12	
Drive Select A	14	
Motor Enable B	16	
Direction (Stepper Motor)	18	
Step Pulse	20	
Write Data	22	
Write Enable	24	
Track 0	26	
Write Protect	28	
Read Data	30	
Select Head 1	32	
Unused	34	

Diskette Drives / Drive Adapter

Fig. 13.5
A PC and XT floppy controller internal connector.

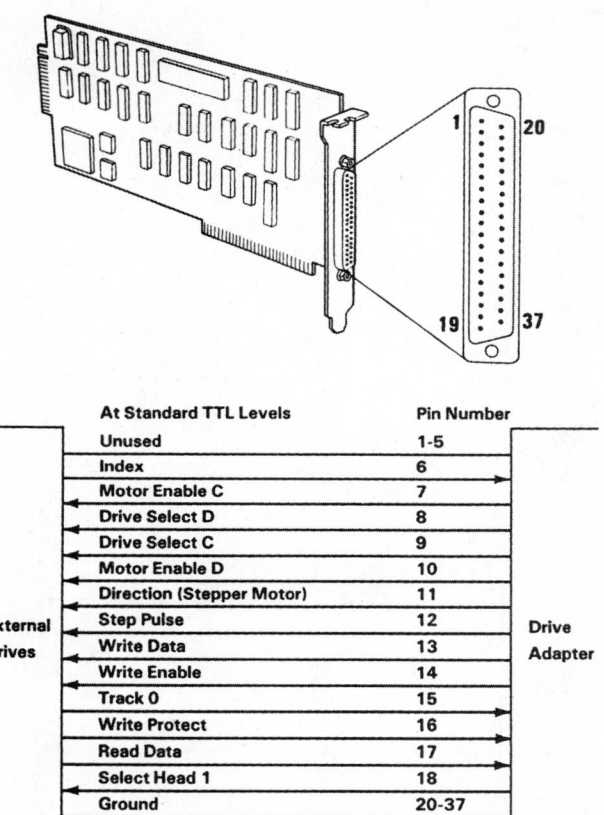

At Standard TTL Levels	Pin Number	
Unused	1-5	
Index	6	
Motor Enable C	7	
Drive Select D	8	
Drive Select C	9	
Motor Enable D	10	
Direction (Stepper Motor)	11	
Step Pulse	12	
Write Data	13	
Write Enable	14	
Track 0	15	
Write Protect	16	
Read Data	17	
Select Head 1	18	
Ground	20-37	

External Drives — Drive Adapter

Fig. 13.6
A PC and XT floppy controller external connector.

The AT used a board made by Western Digital, which included both the floppy and hard disk controllers in a single adapter. The connector location and pinout for the floppy controller portion of this card is shown in figure 13.7. IBM used two variations of this controller during the life of the AT system. The first one was a full 4.8 inches high, which used all the vertical height possible in the AT case. This board was a variation of the Western Digital WD1002-WA2 controller, sold through distributors and dealers. The second-generation card was only 4.2 inches high, which enabled it to fit into the shorter case of the XT-286 as well as the taller AT cases. This card was equivalent to the Western Digital WD1003-WA2, also sold on the open market.

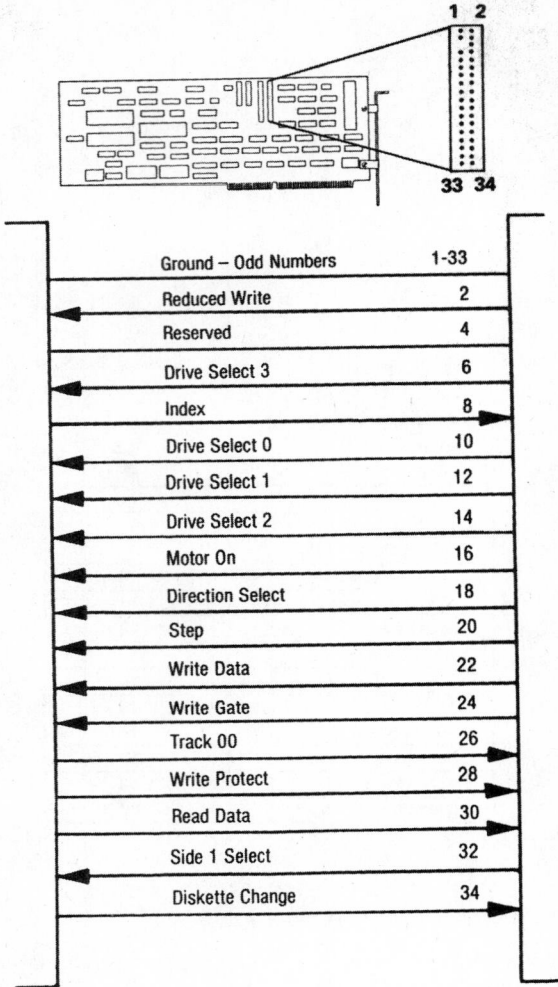

Fig. 13.7
An AT floppy controller connector.

Disk Physical Specifications and Operation

PC-compatible systems now use one of as many as five standard types of floppy drives. Also, five types of disks can be used in the drives. This section examines the physical specifications and operations of these drives and disks.

Drives and disks are divided into two classes: 5 1/4-inch and 3 1/2-inch. The physical dimensions and components of a typical 5 1/4-inch disk and a 3 1/2-inch disk are shown later in this chapter.

The physical operation of a disk drive is fairly simple to describe. The disk rotates in the drive at either 300 or 360 RPM. Most drives spin at 300 RPM, only the 5 1/4-inch 1.2M drives spin at 360 RPM (even when reading or writing 360K disks). With the disk spinning, the heads can move in and out approximately one inch and write either 40 or 80 tracks. The tracks are written on both sides of the disk and therefore sometimes are called *cylinders*. A single cylinder comprises the tracks on the top and bottom of the disk. The heads record by using a tunnel-erase procedure in which a track is written to a specified width and then the edges of the track are erased to prevent interference with any adjacent tracks.

The tracks are recorded at different widths for different drives. Table 13.1 shows the track widths in both millimeters and inches for the five types of floppy drives supported in PC systems.

Table 13.1 Floppy Drive Track-Width Specifications			
Drive Type	**No. of Tracks**	**Track Width**	
5 1/4-inch 360K	40 per side	0.300 mm	0.0118 in.
5 1/4-inch 1.2M	80 per side	0.155 mm	0.0061 in.
3 1/2-inch 720K	80 per side	0.115 mm	0.0045 in.
3 1/2-inch 1.44M	80 per side	0.115 mm	0.0045 in.
3 1/2-inch 2.88M	80 per side	0.115 mm	0.0045 in.

The differences in recorded track width can result in data-exchange problems between 5 1/4-inch drives. The 5 1/4-inch drives are affected because the double-density drives record a track width nearly twice that of the high-density drives. A problem occurs, therefore, if a high-density drive is used to update a double-density disk with previously recorded data on it.

Even in 360K mode, the high-density drive cannot completely overwrite the track left by an actual 360K drive. A problem occurs when the disk is returned to the person with the 360K drive: that drive reads the new data as embedded within the remains of the previously written track. Because the drive cannot distinguish either signal, an Abort, Retry, Ignore error message appears on-screen. The problem does not occur if a new disk (one that never has had data recorded on it) is first formatted in a 1.2M drive with the /4 option, which formats the disk as a 360K disk.

Note

You also can format a 360K disk in a 1.2M drive with the /N:9, /T:40, or /F:360 options, depending on the DOS version. The 1.2M drive then can be used to fill the brand-new and newly formatted 360K disk to its capacity, and every file will be readable on the 40-track, 360K drive.

I use this technique all the time to exchange data disks between AT systems that have only the 1.2M drive and XT or PC systems that have only the 360K drive. The key is to start with either a new disk or one wiped clean magnetically by a bulk eraser or degaussing tool. Just reformatting the disk does not work by itself because formatting does not actually erase a disk; instead it records data across the entire disk.

In addition to a track-width specification, specifications exist for the precise placement of tracks on a disk. A 5 1/4-inch DD disk has tracks placed precisely 1/48th of an inch apart. The outermost track on side 0 (the bottom of the disk) is the starting point for measurements, and this track (cylinder 0, head 0) has a radius of exactly 2.25 inches. Because Head 1 (the top of the disk) is offset by four tracks inward from Head 0, the radius of cylinder 0, Head 1 is 2.2500 inches – (1/48 * 4) = 2.1667 inches. Therefore, to calculate the exact track radius R in inches for any specified cylinder C and head position on a 360K disk, use these formulas:

For Head 0 (bottom): R = 2.2500 inches – C/48 inches

For Head 1 (top): R = 2.1667 inches – C/48 inches

That the tracks on top of the disk (Head 1) are offset toward the center of the disk from the tracks on the bottom of the disk (Head 0) might be surprising: in effect, the cylinders are cone shaped. Figure 13.8 shows the physical relationship between the top and bottom heads on a floppy drive. In this figure, both heads are positioned at the same cylinder. You can see that the top track of the cylinder is closer to the center of the disk than is the bottom track, resulting in cylinders shaped more like cones.

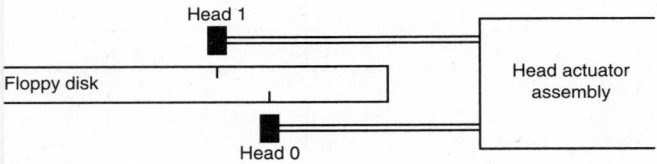

Fig. 13.8
Floppy disk drive head offset.

I first saw this track positioning in one of my data-recovery seminars. One of the experiments I perform in these courses is to stick a pin through a disk with data on it. The objective then is to recover as much data as possible from the disk. Normally, I can resolve the damage down to only a few unreadable sectors on either side of the disk and then easily recover all but these damaged sectors. As I was trying to determine the exact location of the hole by its cylinder, head, and sector coordinates, I noticed that I always had what seemed to be two groups of damaged sectors that were always located exactly four or eight (depending on the type of disk) cylinders apart. Because I had stuck the pin straight through the disk, I realized that any offset had to be in the tracks themselves. I then removed the disk from its jacket to look more closely at the holes.

When I want to "see" the tracks on a disk, I use a special type of solution called Magnetic Developer, a fine-powdered iron suspended in a trichloroethane solution. When this developer, which dries very quickly, is sprayed on the disk, the iron particles align themselves directly over magnetized areas of the disk and show very graphically the exact physical appearance and location of the tracks and sectors on the disk. You can see every individual track and sector on the disk "develop" right before your eyes! With a magnifier or low-powered microscope, I can locate the exact sectors and tracks damaged by the hole on either side of the disk. With this technique, it was easy to see that the tracks on top of the disk start and end farther toward the center of the disk. If you want to do similar experiments or simply "see" the magnetic image of your disks, you can obtain the Magnetic Developer solution from Sprague Magnetics (the address and phone number are in the "Vendor List" in Appendix B). By the way, after viewing this magnetic image, the disk "cookie" can be washed with distilled water or pure trichloroethane, placed back into a new jacket, and reused!

The high-density 5 1/4-inch disk track dimensions are similar to the double-density disk, except that the tracks are spaced precisely 1/96-inch apart, and the top head (Head 1) is offset eight tracks inward from the bottom head (Head 0). The physical head offset between Head 0 and Head 1 is the same as DD disks because twice as many tracks are in the same space as on a DD disk. The calculations for a given track radius R in inches for any cylinder C and head are as follows:

For Head 0 (bottom): $R = 2.2500$ inches $- C/96$ inches

For Head 1 (top): $R = 2.1667$ inches $- C/96$ inches

All the different 3 1/2-inch disks (DD, HD, ED) are dimensionally the same in track and cylinder spacing. The track and cylinder dimensions of these disks start with the radius of Cylinder 0, Head 0 (the bottom head outer track) defined as 39.5 millimeters. Tracks inward from this track are spaced precisely 0.1875 millimeters apart, and the top head (Head 1) is offset inward by eight tracks from Head 0. The radius, in millimeters, of the outer track on top of the disk (Cylinder 0, Head 1) therefore can be calculated as follows:

39.5 mm $- (0.1875 * 8) = 38.0$ mm

Now you can calculate the radius R in millimeters of any specified cylinder C and head using these formulas:

For Head 0 (bottom): $R = 39.5mm - (0.1875mm * C)$

For Head 1 (top): $R = 38.0mm - (0.1875mm * C)$

An interesting note about the dimensions of the 3 1/2-inch disks is that the dimensional standards all are based in the metric system, unlike the 5 1/4-inch disks. I could have converted these numbers to their English equivalents for comparison with the 5 1/4-inch disk figures, but rounding would have sacrificed some accuracy in the numeric conversion. For example, many texts often give the track spacing for 3 1/2-inch disks as 135 TPI (tracks per inch). This figure is an imprecise result of metric-to-English conversion and rounding. The true spacing of 0.1875 mm between tracks converts to a more precise figure of 135.4667 TPI. The figures presented here are the specifications as governed by the ANSI standards X3.125 and X3.126 for 360K and 1.2M disks, and by Sony, Toshiba, and Accurite, which all are involved in specifying 3 1/2-inch disk standards.

Disk Magnetic Properties

A subtle problem with the way a disk drive works magnetically is that the recording volume varies depending on the type of format you are trying to apply to a disk. The high-density formats use special disks that require a much higher volume level for the recording than do the double-density disks. My classes nearly always are either stumped or incorrect (unless they have read ahead in the book) when they answer this question: "Which type of disk is magnetically more sensitive: a 1.2M disk or a 360K disk?" If you answer that the 1.2M disk is more sensitive, you are wrong! The high-density disks are approximately half as sensitive magnetically as the double-density disks.

The high-density disks are called *high-coercivity disks* also because they require a magnetic field strength much higher than do the double-density disks. Magnetic field strength is measured in *oersteds*. The 360K floppy disks require only a 300-oersted field strength to record, and the high-density 1.2M disks require a 600-oersted field strength. Because the high-density disks need double the magnetic field strength for recording, you should not attempt to format a 1.2M high-density disk as though it were a 360K disk, or a 360K disk as though it were a 1.2M high-density disk.

The latter case in particular seems to appeal to people looking for an easy way to save money. They buy inexpensive 360K disks and format them in a 1.2M drive, to the full 1.2M capacity. Most of the time, this format seems to work, with perhaps a large amount of bad sectors; otherwise, most of the disk might seem usable. You should not store important data on this incorrectly formatted disk, however, because the data is recorded at twice the recommended strength and density. Eventually, the adjacent magnetic domains on the disk begin to affect each other and can cause each other to change polarity or weaken because of the proximity of these domains, and because the double-density disk is more sensitive to magnetic fields. This process is illustrated later in this chapter, in the "Media Coercivity and Thickness" section. Eventually, the disk begins to erase itself and deteriorates. The process might take weeks, months, or even longer, but the result is inevitable—a loss of the information stored on the disk.

Another problem results from this type of improper formatting: You can imprint the 360K disk magnetically with an image that is difficult to remove. The high-density format places on the disk a recording at twice the strength it should be. How do you remove this recording and correct the problem? If you attempt to reformat the disk in a 360K drive, the drive writes in a reduced write-current mode and in some cases cannot overwrite the higher-volume recorded image you mistakenly placed on the disk. If you attempt to reformat the disk in the high-density drive with the /4 (or equivalent) parameter, which indicates 360K mode, the high-density drive uses a reduced write-current setting and again cannot overwrite the recording.

You can correct the problem in several ways. You can throw away the disk and write it off as a learning experience, or you can use a bulk eraser or degaussing tool to demagnetize the disk. These devices can randomize all the magnetic domains on a disk and return it to an essentially factory-new condition. You can purchase a bulk-erasing device at electronic-supply stores for about $25.

The opposite problem with disk formatting is not as common, but some have tried it anyway: formatting a high-density disk with a double-density format. You should not (and normally cannot) format a 1.2M high-density disk to a 360K capacity. If you attempt to use one, the drive changes to reduced write-current mode and does not create a magnetic field strong enough to record on the "insensitive" 1.2M disk. The result in this case is normally an immediate error message from the FORMAT command: `Invalid media or Track 0 bad - disk unusable`. Fortunately, the system usually does not allow this particular mistake to be made.

The 3 1/2-inch drives don't have the same problems as the 5 1/4-inch drives—at least for data interchange. Because both the high-density and double-density drives write the same number of tracks and these tracks are always the same width, no problem occurs when one type of drive is used to overwrite data written by another type of drive. A system manufacturer therefore doesn't need to offer a double-density version of the 3 1/2-inch drive for systems equipped with the high-density or extra-high-density drive. The HD and ED drives can perfectly emulate the operations of the 720K DD drive, and the ED drive can perfectly emulate the 1.44M HD drive.

The HD and ED drives can be trouble, however, for inexperienced users who try to format disks to incorrect capacities. Although an ED drive can read, write, and format DD, HD, and ED disks, a disk should be formatted and written at only its specified capacity. An ED disk therefore should be formatted only to 2.88M, and never to 1.44M or 720K. *You must always use a disk at its designated format capacity.* You are asking for serious problems if you place a 720K disk in the A drive of a PS/2 Model 50, 60, 70, or 80 and enter FORMAT A:. This step causes a 1.44M format to be written on the 720K disk, which renders it unreliable at best and requires a bulk eraser to reformat it correctly. If you decide to use the resulting incorrectly formatted disk, you will eventually have massive data loss.

This particular problem could have been averted if IBM had used media sensor drives in all PS/2 systems. Drives that use the disk media-sensor hole to control the drive mode are prevented from incorrectly formatting a disk. The hardware causes the FORMAT command to fail with an appropriate error message if you attempt to format the disk to an incorrect capacity.

By knowing how a drive works physically, you can eliminate most of these user "pilot error" problems and distinguish this kind of easily solved problem from a more serious hardware problem. You will be a much better user as well as a troubleshooter of a system if you truly understand how a drive works.

Logical Operation

Each type of drive can create disks with different numbers of sectors and tracks. This section examines how DOS sees a drive. It gives definitions of the drives according to DOS and the definitions of cylinders and clusters.

How DOS Uses a Disk. A technical understanding of the way DOS maintains information on your disks is not necessary to use a PC, but you will be a more informed user if you understand the general principles.

To DOS, data on your PC disks is organized in tracks and sectors. Tracks are narrow, concentric circles on a disk. Sectors are pie-shaped slices of the disk. DOS versions 1.0 and 1.1 read and write 5 1/4-inch double-density disks with 40 tracks (numbered 0 through 39) per side and eight sectors (numbered 1 through 8) per track. DOS versions 2.0 and higher automatically increase the track density from eight to nine sectors, for greater capacity on the same disk. On an AT with a 1.2M disk drive, DOS 3.0 supports high-density 5 1/4-inch drives that format 15 sectors per track and 80 tracks per side; DOS 3.2 supports 3 1/2-inch drives that format 9 sectors per track and 80 tracks per side; DOS 3.3 supports 3 1/2-inch drives that format 18 sectors per track and 80 tracks per side. The distance between tracks and, therefore, the number of tracks on a disk is a built-in mechanical and electronic function of the drive. Tables 13.2 and 13.3 summarize the standard disk formats supported by DOS version 5.0 and higher.

Table 13.2   5 1/4-Inch Floppy Disk Drive Formats

	Double-Density 360K (DD)	High-Density 1.2M (HD)
Bytes per Sector	512	512
Sectors per Track	9	15
Tracks per Side	40	80
Sides	2	2
Capacity (KBytes)	360	1,200
Capacity (Megabytes)	0.352	1.172
Capacity (Million Bytes)	0.369	1.229

Table 13.3   3 1/2-Inch Floppy Disk Drive Formats

	Double-Density 720K (DD)	High-Density 1.44M (HD)	Extra-High Density 2.88M (ED)
Bytes per Sector	512	512	512
Sectors per Track	9	18	36
Tracks per Side	80	80	80
Sides	2	2	2
Capacity (KBytes)	720	1,440	2,880
Capacity (Megabytes)	0.703	1.406	2.813
Capacity (Million Bytes)	0.737	1.475	2.949

You can calculate the capacity differences between different formats by multiplying the sectors per track by the number of tracks per side together with the constants of two sides and 512 bytes per sector. Note that the disk capacity can actually be expressed in three different ways. The most common method is to refer to the capacity of a floppy by the number of KBytes (1,024 bytes equals 1K). This works fine for 360K and 720K disks, but is strange when applied to the 1.44M and 2.88M disks. As you can see, a 1.44M disk is really 1,440K, and not actually 1.44 megabytes. Because a megabyte is 1,024K, what we call a 1.44M disk is actually 1.406 megabytes in capacity. Another way of expressing disk capacity is in millions of bytes. In that case, the 1.44M disk has 1.475 million bytes of capacity. To add to the confusion over capacity expression, both megabyte and millions of bytes are abbreviated as MB or M. No universally accepted standard for the definition of M or MB exists, so throughout this book I will try to be explicit.

Like blank sheets of paper, new disks contain no information. Formatting a disk is similar to adding lines to the paper so that you can write straight across. Formatting places on the disk the information DOS needs to maintain a directory and file table of contents. Using the /S (system) option in the FORMAT command resembles making the paper a title page. FORMAT places on the disk the portions of DOS required to boot the system.

DOS reserves the track nearest to the outside edge of a disk (track 0) almost entirely for its purposes. Track 0, Sector 1 contains the DOS Boot Record (DBR) or Boot Sector, the system needs to begin operation. The next few sectors contain the File Allocation Tables (FATs), which act as the disk "room reservation clerk" that keeps records of which clusters or allocation units (rooms) on the disk have file information and which are empty. Finally, the next few sectors contain the root directory, in which DOS stores information about the names and starting locations of the files on the disk; you see most of this information when you use the DIR command.

In computer-industry jargon, this process is "transparent to the user," which means that you don't have to (and generally cannot) decide where information is stored on disks. That this process is "transparent," however, doesn't necessarily mean that you shouldn't be aware of the decisions DOS makes for you.

When DOS writes data, it always begins by attempting to use the earliest available data sectors on the disk. Because the file might be larger than the particular block of available sectors selected, DOS then writes the remainder of the file in the next available block of free sectors. In this manner, files can become fragmented as they are written to fill a hole on the disk created by the deletion of some smaller file. The larger file completely fills the hole; then DOS continues to look for more free space across the disk, from the outermost tracks to the innermost tracks. The rest of the file is deposited in the next available free space.

This procedure continues until eventually all the files on your disk are intertwined. This situation is not really a problem for DOS because it was designed to manage files in this way. The problem is a physical one: Retrieving a fragmented file that occupies 50 or 100 separate places across the disk takes much longer than if the file were in one piece. Also, if the files were in one piece, recovering data in the case of a disaster would be much easier. Consider unfragmenting a disk periodically simply because it can make recovery from a disk disaster much easier; many people, however, unfragment disks for the performance benefit in loading and saving files that are in one piece.

How do you unfragment a disk? DOS 6.0 and higher versions include a command called DEFRAG. This utility is actually a limited version of the Norton Utilities Speedisk program. It does not have some of the options of the more powerful Norton version and is not as fast, but it does work well in most cases. Earlier versions of DOS do not provide any easy method for unfragmenting a disk, although by backing up and restoring files, you can accomplish the goal. To unfragment a floppy disk for example, you can copy all the files one by one to an empty disk, delete the original files from the first disk, and then recopy the files. With a hard disk, you can back up all the files, reformat the disk, and restore the files. This procedure is time consuming, to say the least.

Because DOS versions earlier than 6.0 did not provide a good way to unfragment a disk, many software companies have produced utility programs that can easily unfragment disks in a clean and efficient manner. These programs can restore file contiguity without reformat and restore operations. My favorite for an extremely safe, easy, and *fast* unfragmenting program is the Vopt utility, by Golden Bow. In my opinion, no other unfragmenting utility even comes close to this amazing $50 package. Golden Bow's address and phone number are in Appendix B.

Caution

These unfragmenting programs, inherently dangerous by nature, do not eliminate the need for a good backup program. Before using an unfragmenting program, make sure that you have a good backup. What shape do you think your disk would be in if the power failed during an unfragmenting session? Also, some programs have bugs or are incompatible with new releases of DOS.

Cylinders. The term *cylinder* usually is used in place of *track*. A cylinder is all the tracks under read/write heads on a drive at one time. For floppy drives, because a disk cannot have more than two sides and the drive has two heads, normally there are two tracks per cylinder. Hard disks can have many disk platters, each with two (or more) heads, for many tracks per single cylinder.

Clusters or Allocation Units. A cluster also is called an *allocation unit* in DOS version 4.0 and higher. The term is appropriate because a single cluster is the smallest unit of the disk that DOS can allocate when it writes a file. A cluster or allocation unit consists of one or more sectors—usually two or more. Having more than one sector per cluster reduces the file-allocation table size and enables DOS to run faster because it has fewer individual allocation units of the disk with which to work. The tradeoff is in some wasted disk space. Because DOS can manage space only in the cluster size unit, every file consumes space on the disk in increments of one cluster. Table 13.4 lists the default cluster sizes used by DOS for different floppy disk formats. Chapter 14, "Hard Disk Drives and Controllers," discusses hard disk cluster or allocation unit sizes.

Table 13.4   DOS Default Cluster and Allocation Unit Sizes

Floppy Disk Capacity	Cluster/Allocation	Unit Size	FAT Type
5 1/4-inch, 360K	2 sectors	1,024 bytes	12-bit
5 1/4-inch, 1.2M	1 sector	512 bytes	12-bit
3 1/2-inch, 720K	2 sectors	1,024 bytes	12-bit
3 1/2-inch, 1.44M	1 sector	512 bytes	12-bit
3 1/2-inch, 2.88M	2 sectors	1,024 bytes	12-bit

K = 1,024 bytes
M = 1,048,576 bytes

The high-density disks normally have smaller cluster sizes, which seems strange because these disks have many more individual sectors than do double-density disks. The probable reason is that because these high-density disks are faster than their double-density counterparts, IBM and Microsoft thought that the decrease in wasted disk space cluster size and speed would be welcome. You learn later that the cluster size on hard disks can vary much more between different versions of DOS and different disk sizes. Table 13.5 shows the floppy disk logical parameters.

Types of Floppy Drives

Five types of standard floppy drives are available for an IBM-compatible system. The drives can be summarized most easily by their formatting specifications (refer to tables 13.2 and 13.3).

Most drive types can format multiple types of disks. For example, the 3 1/2-inch ED drive can format and write on any 3 1/2-inch disk. The 5 1/4-inch HD drive also can format and write on any 5 1/4-inch disk (although, as mentioned, sometimes track-width problems occur). This drive can even create some older obsolete formats, including single-sided disks and disks with eight sectors per track.

As you can see from table 13.5, the different disk capacities are determined by several parameters, some of which seem to remain constant on all drives, whereas others change from drive to drive. For example, all drives use 512-byte physical sectors, which remains true for hard disks as well. Note, however, that DOS treats the sector size as though it could be a changeable parameter, although the BIOS does not.

Note also that now all standard floppy drives are double-sided. IBM has not shipped PC systems with single-sided drives since 1982; these drives are definitely considered obsolete. Also, IBM never has utilized any form of single-sided 3 1/2-inch drives, although that type of drive appeared in the first Apple Macintosh systems in 1984. IBM officially began selling and supporting 3 1/2-inch drives in 1986 and has used only double-sided versions of these drives.

Table 13.5 Floppy Disk Logical DOS-Format Parameters

	Current Formats					Obsolete Formats		
Disk Size (in.)	3 1/2"	3 1/2"	3 1/2"	5 1/4"	5 1/4"	5 1/4"	5 1/4"	5 1/4"
Disk Capacity (K)	2,880	1,440	720	1,200	360	320	180	160
Media Descriptor Byte	F0h	F0h	F9h	F9h	FDh	FFh	FCh	FEh
Sides (Heads)	2	2	2	2	2	2	1	1
Tracks per Side	80	80	80	80	40	40	40	40

(continues)

Table 13.5   Continued

	Current Formats					Obsolete Formats		
Disk Size (in.)	3 1/2"	3 1/2"	3 1/2"	5 1/4"	5 1/4"	5 1/4"	5 1/4"	5 1/4"
Disk Capacity (K)	2,880	1,440	720	1,200	360	320	180	160
Sectors per Track	36	18	9	15	9	8	9	8
Bytes per Sector	512	512	512	512	512	512	512	512
Sectors per Cluster	2	1	2	1	2	2	1	1
FAT Length (Sectors)	9	9	3	7	2	1	2	1
Number of FATs	2	2	2	2	2	2	2	2
Root Dir. Length (Sectors)	15	14	7	14	7	7	4	4
Maximum Root Entries	240	224	112	224	112	112	64	64
Total Sectors per Disk	5,760	2,880	1,440	2,400	720	640	360	320
Total Available Sectors	5,726	2,847	1,426	2,371	708	630	351	313
Total Available Clusters	2,863	2,847	713	2,371	354	315	351	313

The 360K 5 1/4-Inch Drive

The 5 1/4-inch low-density drive is designed to create a standard-format disk with 360K capacity. Although I persistently call these low-density drives, the industry term is "double-density." I use "low-density" because I find the term "double-density" to be somewhat misleading, especially when I am trying to define these drives in juxtaposition to the high-density drives.

The term *double-density* arose from the use of the term *single-density* to indicate a type of drive that used frequency modulation (FM) encoding to store approximately 90 kilobytes on a disk. This type of obsolete drive never was used in any IBM-compatible systems, but was used in some older systems such as the original Osborne-1 portable computer. When drive manufacturers changed the drives to use Modified Frequency Modulation (MFM) encoding, they began using the term "double-density" to indicate it, as well as the (approximately doubled) increase in recording capacity realized from this encoding method. All modern floppy disk drives use MFM encoding, including all types listed in this section. Encoding methods such as FM, MFM, and RLL variants are discussed in Chapter 14, "Hard Disk Drives and Controllers."

The 360K 5 1/4-inch drive normally records 40 cylinders of two tracks each, with each cylinder numbered starting with 0 closest to the outside diameter of the floppy disk. Head position (or side) 0 is recorded on the underside of the floppy disk, and Head 1 records on the top of the disk surface. This drive normally divides each track into nine sectors, but it can optionally format only eight sectors per track to create a floppy disk compatible with DOS versions 1.1 or earlier. This type of format rarely (if ever) is used today.

The 360K 5 1/4-inch drives as supplied in the first IBM systems all were full-height units, which means that they were 3.25 inches tall. Full-height drives are obsolete now and have not been manufactured since 1986. Later units used by IBM and most compatible vendors have been the half-height units, which are only 1.6 inches tall. You can install two half-height drives in place of a single full-height unit. These drives, made by different manufacturers, are similar except for some cosmetic differences.

The 360K 5 1/4-inch drives spin at 300 RPM, which equals exactly five revolutions per second, or 200 milliseconds per revolution. All standard floppy controllers support a 1:1 interleave, in which each sector on a specific track is numbered (and read) consecutively. To read and write to a disk at full speed, a controller sends data at a rate of 250,000 bits per second. Because all low-density controllers can support this data rate, virtually any controller supports this type of drive, depending on ROM BIOS code that supports these drives.

All standard IBM-compatible systems include ROM BIOS support for these drives; therefore, you usually do not need special software or driver programs to use them. This statement might exclude some aftermarket (non-IBM) 360K drives for PS/2 systems that might require some type of driver in order to work. The IBM-offered units use the built-in ROM support to enable these drives to work. The only requirement usually is to run the Setup program for the machine to enable it to properly recognize these drives.

The 1.2M 5 1/4-Inch Drive

The 1.2M high-density floppy drive first appeared in the IBM AT system introduced in August 1984. The drive required the use of a new type of disk to achieve the 1.2M format capacity, but it still could read and write (although not always reliably) the lower-density 360K disks.

The 1.2M 5 1/4-inch drive normally recorded 80 cylinders of two tracks each, starting with cylinder 0, at the outside of the disk. This situation differs from the low-density 5 1/4-inch drive in its capability to record twice as many cylinders in approximately the same space on the disk. This capability alone suggests that the recording capacity for a disk would double, but that is not all. Each track normally is recorded with 15 sectors of 512 bytes each, increasing the storage capacity even more. In fact, these drives store nearly four times the data of the 360K disks. The density increase for each track required the use of special disks with a modified media designed to handle this type of recording. Because these disks initially were expensive and difficult to obtain, many users attempted incorrectly to use the low-density disks in the 1.2M 5 1/4-inch drives and format them to the higher 1.2M-density format, which results in data loss and unnecessary data-recovery operations.

A compatibility problem with the 360K drives stems from the 1.2M drive's capability to write twice as many cylinders in the same space as the 360K drives. The 1.2M drives position their heads over the same 40 cylinder positions used by the 360K drives through *double stepping*, a procedure in which the heads are moved every two cylinders to arrive at the correct positions for reading and writing the 40 cylinders on the 360K disks. The problem is that because the 1.2M drive normally has to write 80 cylinders in the same space in which the 360K drive writes 40, the heads of the 1.2M units had to be made dimensionally smaller. These narrow heads can have problems overwriting tracks produced by a 360K drive that has a wider head because the narrower heads on the 1.2M drive cannot "cover" the entire track area written by the 360K drive. This problem and possible solutions to it are discussed later in this chapter.

The 1.2M 5 1/4-inch drives spin at 360 RPM, or six revolutions per second, or 166.67 milliseconds per revolution. The drives spin at this rate no matter what type of disk is inserted—either low- or high-density. To send or receive 15 sectors (plus required over-head) six times per second, a controller must use a data-transmission rate of 500,000 bits per second (500 kilohertz, or kHz). All standard high- and low-density controllers support this data rate and, therefore, these drives. This support of course depends also on proper ROM BIOS support of the controller in this mode of operation. When a standard 360K disk is running in a high-density drive, it also is spinning at 360 RPM; a data rate of 300,000 bits per second (300 kHz) therefore is required in order to work properly. All standard AT-style low- and high-density controllers support the 250 kHz, 300 kHz, and 500 kHz data rates. The 300 kHz rate is used only for high-density 5 1/4-inch drives read-ing or writing to low-density 5 1/4-inch disks.

Virtually all standard AT-style systems have a ROM BIOS that supports the controller's operation of the 1.2M drive, including the 300 kHz data rate.

The 720K 3 1/2-Inch Drive

The 720K, 3 1/2-inch, double-density drives first appeared in an IBM system with the IBM Convertible laptop system introduced in 1986. In fact, all IBM systems introduced since that time have 3 1/2-inch drives as the standard supplied drives. This type of drive also is offered by IBM as an internal or external drive for the AT or XT systems. Note that outside the IBM-compatible world, other computer-system vendors (Apple, Hewlett Packard, and so on) offered 3 1/2-inch drives for their systems well before the IBM-compatible world "caught on."

The 720K, 3 1/2-inch, double-density drive normally records 80 cylinders of two tracks each, with nine sectors per track, resulting in the formatted capacity of 720 kilobytes. It is interesting to note that many disk manufacturers label these disks as 1-megabyte disks, which is true. The difference between the actual 1 megabyte of capacity and the usable 720K after formatting is that some space on each track is occupied by the header and trailer of each sector, the inter-sector gaps, and the index gap at the start of each track before the first sector. These spaces are not usable for data storage and account for the differences between the unformatted and formatted capacities. Most manufacturers re-port the unformatted capacities because they do not know on which type of system you will format the disk. Apple Macintosh systems, for example, can store 800K of data on the same disk because of a different formatting technique. Note also that the 720K of usable space does not account for the disk areas DOS reserves for managing the disk (boot sectors, FATs, directories, and so on) and that because of these areas, only 713K remains for file data storage.

IBM-compatible systems have used 720K, 3 1/2-inch, double-density drives primarily in XT-class systems because the drives operate from any low-density controller. The drives spin at 300 RPM, and therefore require only a 250 kHz data rate from the controller to operate properly. This data rate is the same as for the 360K disk drives, which means that any controller that supports a 360K drive also supports the 720K drives.

The only issue to consider in installing a 720K, 3 1/2-inch drive is whether the ROM BIOS offers the necessary support. An IBM system with a ROM BIOS date of 06/10/85 or later has built-in support for 720K drives and requires no driver in order to use them. If your system has an earlier ROM BIOS date, the DRIVER.SYS program from DOS 3.2 or higher—as well as the DRIVPARM config.sys command in some OEM DOS versions—is all you need to provide the necessary software support to operate these drives. Of course, a ROM BIOS upgrade to a later version negates the need for "funny" driver software and is usually the preferred option when you add one of these drives to an older system.

The 1.44M 3 1/2-Inch Drive

The 3 1/2-inch, 1.44M, high-density drives first appeared from IBM in the PS/2 product line introduced in 1987. Although IBM has not officially offered this type of drive for any of its older systems, most compatible vendors started offering the drives as options in systems immediately after IBM introduced the PS/2 system.

The drives record 80 cylinders consisting of two tracks each with 18 sectors per track, resulting in the formatted capacity of 1.44 megabytes. Most disk manufacturers label these disks as 2-megabyte disks, and the difference between this unformatted capacity and the formatted usable result is lost during the format. Note that the 1,440K of total formatted capacity does not account for the areas DOS reserves for file management, leaving only 1423.5K of actual file-storage area.

These drives spin at 300 RPM, and in fact must spin at that speed to operate properly with your existing high- and low-density controllers. To utilize the 500 kHz data rate, the maximum from most standard high- and low-density floppy controllers, these drives could spin at only 300 RPM. If the drives spun at the faster 360 RPM rate of the 5 1/4-inch drives, they would have to reduce the total number of sectors per track to 15 or else the controller could not keep up. In short, the 1.44M 3 1/2-inch drives store 1.2 times the data of the 5 1/4-inch 1.2M drives, and the 1.2M drives spin exactly 1.2 times faster than the 1.44M drives. The data rates used by both high-density drives are identical and compatible with the same controllers. In fact, because these 3 1/2-inch high-density drives can run at the 500 kHz data rate, a controller that can support a 1.2M 5 1/4-inch drive can support the 1.44M drives also. If you are using a low-density disk in the 3 1/2-inch high-density drive, the data rate is reduced to 250 kHz, and the disk capacity is 720K.

The primary issue in a particular system utilizing a 1.44M 3 1/2-inch drive is one of ROM BIOS support. An IBM system with a ROM BIOS date of 11/15/85 or later has built-in support for these drives and no external driver support program is needed. You might need a generic AT setup program because IBM's setup program doesn't offer the 1.44M drive as an option. Another problem relates to the controller and the way it signals the high-density drive to write to a low-density disk. The problem is discussed in detail in the following section.

The 2.88M 3 1/2-Inch Drive

The new 2.88M drive was developed by Toshiba Corporation in the 1980s, and officially announced in 1987. Toshiba began production manufacturing of the drives and disks in

1989, and then several vendors began selling the drives as upgrades for systems. IBM officially adopted these drives in the PS/2 systems in 1991, and virtually all PS/2s sold since then have these drives as standard equipment. Because a 2.88M drive can fully read and write 1.44M and 720K disks, the change was an easy one. DOS version 5.0 or higher is required to support the 2.88M drives.

To support the 2.88M drive, modifications to the disk controller circuitry were required because these drives spin at the same 300 RPM but have an astonishing 36 sectors per track. Because all floppy disks are formatted with consecutively numbered sectors (1:1 interleave), these 36 sectors have to be read and written in the same time it takes a 1.44M drive to read and write 18 sectors. This requires that the controller support a much higher data transmission rate of 1 MHz (1 million bits per second). Most of the older floppy controllers either found on an adapter card or built into the motherboard support only the maximum of 500 kHz data rate used by the 1.44M drives. To upgrade to 2.88M drives would require that the controller be changed to one that supports the higher 1 MHz data rate.

An additional support issue is the ROM BIOS. The BIOS must have support for the controller and the capability to specify and accept the 2.88M drive as a CMOS setting. Newer motherboard BIOS sets from companies like Phoenix, AMI, and Award have support for the new extra-high density controllers.

In addition to the newer IBM PS/2 systems, most newer IBM clone and compatible systems now have built-in floppy controllers and ROM BIOS software that fully supports the 2.88M drives. Adding or upgrading to a 2.88M drive in these systems is as easy as plugging in the drive and running the CMOS Setup program. For those systems who do not have this support built-in, this type of upgrade is much more difficult. Several companies offer new controllers and BIOS upgrades as well as the 2.88M drives specifically for upgrading older systems.

Although the 2.88M drives themselves are not much more expensive than the 1.44M drives they replace, the disk media is currently still very expensive. Although you can purchase 1.44M disks for around (or under) one dollar each, the 2.88M disks can cost more than $5 per disk! As the drives become more generally available, the disk media prices should fall. The 1.44M and even 1.2M disk media also was very expensive when first introduced.

Handling Recording Problems with 1.44M 3 1/2-Inch Drives

A serious problem awaits many users who use the 1.44M 3 1/2-inch drives: If the drive is installed improperly, any write or format operations performed incorrectly on 720K disks can end up trashing data on low-density disks. The problem is caused by the controller's incapability to signal the high-density drive that a low-density recording will take place.

High-density disks require a higher write-current or signal strength when they record than do the low-density disks. A low-density drive can record at only the lower write-current, which is correct for the low-density disks; the high-density drive, however, needs to record at both high and low write-currents depending on which type of disk is inserted in the drive. If a signal is not sent to the high-density drive telling it to lower or reduce the write-current level, the drive stays in its normal high write-current default mode, even when it records on a low-density disk. The signal normally should be sent to the drive by the controller, but many controllers do not provide this signal properly for the 1.44M drives.

The Western Digital controller used by IBM enables the reduced write-current (RWC) signal only if the controller also is sending data at the 300 kHz data rate, indicating the special case of a low-density disk in a high-density drive. The RWC signal is required to tell the high-density drive to lower the head-writing signal strength to be proper for the low-density disks. If the signal is not sent, the drive defaults to the higher write-current, which should be used for only high-density disks. If the controller is transmitting the 250 kHz data rate, the controller knows that the drive must be a low-density drive and therefore no RWC signal is necessary because the low-density drives can write only with reduced current.

This situation presented a serious problem for owners of 1.44M drives using 720K disks because the drives spin the disks at 300 RPM, and in writing to a low-density disk, use the 250 kHz data rate—not the 300 kHz rate. This setup "fools" the controller into "thinking" that it is sending data to a low-density drive, which causes the controller to fail to send the required RWC signal. Without the RWC signal, the drive then records improperly on the disk, possibly trashing any data being written or any data already present. Because virtually all compatibles use controllers based on the design of the IBM AT floppy disk controller, most share the same problem as the IBM AT.

Drive and disk manufacturers devised the perfect solution for this problem, short of using a redesigned controller. They built into the drives a *media sensor*, which, when it is enabled, can override the controller's RWC signal (or lack of it) and properly change the head-current levels within the drive. Essentially, the drive chooses the write-current level independently from the controller when the media sensor is operational.

The sensor is a small, physical or optical sensor designed to feel, or "see," the small hole on the high-density 3 1/2-inch disks located opposite the write-enable hole. The extra hole on these high-density or extra-high density disks is the media sensor's cue that the full write-current should be used in recording. If an ED disk is detected, the ED drive enables the vertical recording heads. Low-density disks do not have these extra holes; therefore, when the sensor cannot see a media-sensor hole, it causes the drive to record in the proper reduced write-current mode for a double-density disk.

Some people, of course, foolishly attempt to override the function of these sensors by needlessly punching an extra hole in a low-density disk, to fool the drive's sensor into acting as though an actual high-density disk has been inserted. Several "con artist" companies have made a fast buck by selling media sensor hole-punchers to unwary or misinformed people. These "shyster" disk-punch vendors try to mislead you into believing that no difference exists between the low- and high-density disks except for the hole, and that punching the extra hole makes the low-density disk a legitimate high-density disk. This, of course, is absolutely untrue: The high-density disks are very different from low-density disks. The differences between the disks are explained in more detail later in this chapter.

Another reason that this hole-punching is needless is that if you want to record a high-density format on a low-density disk, you only have to remove the jumper from the drive that enables the media sensor. Removing the media sensor jumper still allows the drive to work properly for high-density disks writing at the full write-current level, but unfortunately also allows the higher write-current to be used on low-density disks as well because then the drive has no way of knowing the difference. If you really want to risk your data to low-density disks formatted as high-density disks, you can save yourself the cost of the $40 hole-punchers. Note that even if you attempt to format or record properly on a 720K disk, you still will be working at the higher write-current and risk trashing the disk.

Many systems, including the IBM PS/2 series, Compaq, Toshiba laptops, and many others with floppy controllers built into the motherboard, do not need 1.44M drives with media sensors. Their controllers have been fixed to allow the RWC signal to be sent to the drive even when the controller is sending the 250 kHz data rate. This setup allows for proper operation no matter what type of disk or drive is used, as long as the user formats properly. Because these systems do not have a media sensor policing users, they easily can format low-density disks as high-density disks regardless of what holes are on the disk. This has caused problems for users of the older PS/2 systems who have accidentally formatted 720K disks as 1.44M disks. When passed to a system that has an enabled media sensor, the system refuses to read the disks at all because it is not correctly formatted. If you are having disk interchange problems, make sure that you are formatting your disks correctly.

The newer PS/2 and other high-end systems from other manufacturers (Hewlett Packard, for example) use an active media sensor setup in which the user no longer has to enter the correct FORMAT command parameters to format the disk. In these systems the media sensor information is passed through the controller to the BIOS, which properly informs the FORMAT command about which disk is in the drive. With these systems, it is impossible for a user to accidentally format a disk incorrectly, and it eliminates the user from having to know anything about the different disk media types.

Handling Recording Problems with 1.2M and 360K Drives

The 5 1/4-inch drives have their own special problems. One major problem resulting in needless data destruction is that the tracks sometimes are recorded at different widths for different drives. These differences in recorded track width can result in problems with data exchange between different 5 1/4-inch drives.

As shown in table 13.1, the recorded track-width difference affects only the 5 1/4-inch drives because the 5 1/4-inch low-density drives record a track width more than twice that of the 5 1/4-inch high-density drives. This difference presents a problem if a high-density drive is used to update a low-density disk with previously recorded data on it. The high-density drive, even in 360K mode, cannot completely overwrite the track left by the 40-track drive. The problem occurs when the disk is returned to the person with the 360K drive because that drive sees the new data as "embedded" within the remains of the previously written track. The 360K drive cannot distinguish either signal, and an Abort, Retry, Ignore error message results.

To avoid this problem, start with a brand-new disk that has never been formatted and format it in the 1.2M drive with the /4 (or equivalent) option. This procedure causes the 1.2M drive to place the proper 360K format on the disk. The 1.2M drive then can be used to fill the disk to its 360K capacity, and every file will be readable on the 40-track 360K drive because no previous wider data tracks exist to confuse the 360K drive. I use this trick all the time to exchange data disks between AT systems that have only a 1.2M drive and XT or PC systems that have only a 360K drive. The key is to start with a brand-new disk or a disk wiped clean magnetically by a bulk eraser. Simply reformatting the disk does not work because formatting actually writes data to the disk.

Note that because all the 3 1/2-inch drives write tracks of the same width, these drives have no disk-interchange problems related to track width.

Analyzing Floppy Disk Construction

The 5 1/4-inch and 3 1/2-inch disks each have unique construction and physical properties.

The flexible (or floppy) disk is contained within a plastic jacket. The 3 1/2-inch disks are covered by a more rigid jacket than are the 5 1/4-inch disks; the disks within the jackets, however, are virtually identical except, of course, for the size.

Differences and similarities exist between these two different-size disks. This section looks at the physical properties and construction of each disk type.

When you look at a typical 5 1/4-inch floppy disk, you see several things (see fig. 13.9). Most prominent is the large, round hole in the center. When you close the disk drive's "door," a cone-shaped clamp grabs and centers the disk through the center hole. Many disks come with *hub-ring reinforcements*—thin, plastic rings like those used to reinforce three-ring notebook paper—intended to help the disk withstand the mechanical forces of the clamping mechanism. The high-density disks usually lack these reinforcements because the difficulty in accurately placing them on the disk means that they will cause alignment problems.

On the right side, just below the center of the hub hole, is a smaller, round hole called the *index hole*. If you carefully turn the disk within its protective jacket, you see a small hole in the disk. The drive uses the index hole as the starting point for all the sectors on the disk—sort of the "prime meridian" for the disk sectors. A disk with a single index hole is a *soft-sectored* disk; the software (operating system) decides the actual number of sectors on the disk. Some older equipment, such as Wang word processors, use hard-sectored disks, which have an index hole to demarcate individual sectors. Do not use hard-sectored disks in a PC.

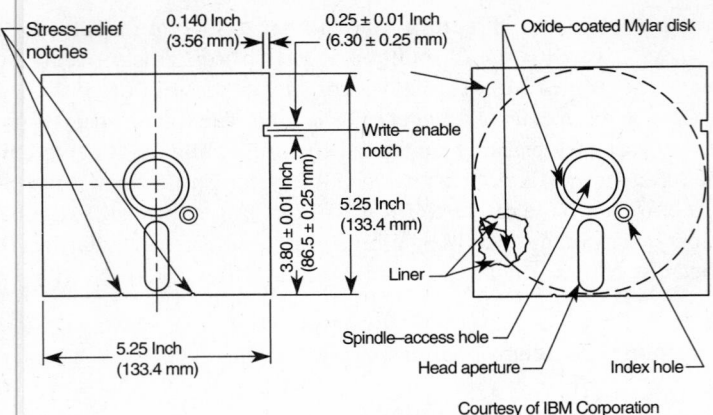

Fig. 13.9
Construction of a 5 1/4-inch floppy disk.

Below the hub hole is a slot shaped somewhat like a long racetrack through which you can see the disk surface. Through this *media-access hole*, the disk drive heads read and write information to the disk surface.

At the right side, about one inch from the top, is a rectangular punch from the side of the disk cover. If this *write-enable notch* is present, writing to the disk has been enabled. Disks without this notch (or with the notch taped over) are *write-protected* disks. The notch might not be on all disks, particularly those purchased with programs on them.

On the rear of the disk jacket, at the bottom, two very small, oval notches flank the head slot. The notches relieve stress on the disk and help prevent it from warping. The drive might use these notches also to assist in keeping the disk in the proper position in the drive.

Because the 3 1/2-inch disks use a much more rigid plastic case, which helps stabilize the disk, these disks can record at track and data densities greater than the 5 1/4-inch disks (see fig. 13.10). A metal shutter protects the media-access hole. The shutter is manipulated by the drive and remains closed whenever the disk is not in a drive. The media then is insulated from the environment and from your fingers. The shutter also obviates the need for a disk jacket.

Rather than an index hole in the disk, the 3 1/2-inch disks use a metal center hub with an alignment hole. The drive "grasps" the metal hub, and the hole in the hub enables the drive to position the disk properly.

On the lower-left part of the disk is a hole with a plastic slider—the write-protect/-enable hole (refer to fig. 13.9). When the slider is positioned so that the hole is visible, the disk is write-protected; the drive is prevented from recording on the disk. When the slider is positioned to cover the hole, writing is enabled, and you can record on the disk. For more permanent write-protection, some commercial software programs are supplied on disks with the slider removed so that you cannot easily enable recording on the disk.

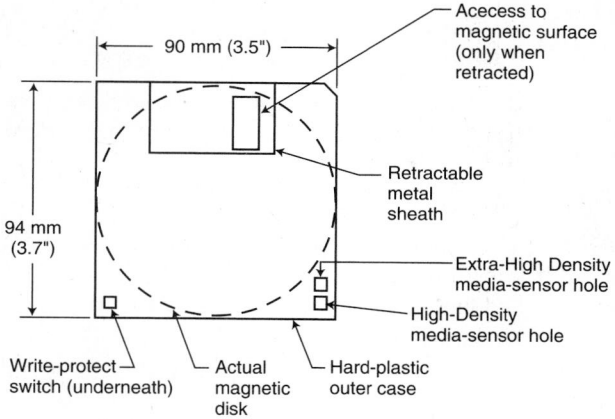

Fig. 13.10
Construction of a 3 1/2-inch floppy disk.

On the other (right) side of the disk from the write-protect hole, there might be in the disk jacket another hole called the *media-density-selector hole*. If this hole is present, the disk is constructed of a special media and is therefore a high-density or extra-high-density disk. If the media-sensor hole is exactly opposite the write-protect hole, it indicates a 1.44M HD disk. If the media-sensor hole is located more toward the top of the disk (the metal shutter is at the top of the disk), it indicates an ED disk. No hole on the right side means that the disk is a low-density disk. Most 3 1/2-inch drives have a media sensor that controls recording capability based on the existence or absence of these holes.

Both the 3 1/2-inch and 5 1/4-inch disks are constructed of the same basic materials. They use a plastic base (usually Mylar) coated with a magnetic compound. The compound is usually a ferric- (iron-) oxide-based compound for the standard density versions; a cobalt-ferric compound usually is used in the higher coercivity (higher density) disks. A newly announced disk type, called *extended density*, uses a barium-ferric compound. The rigid jacket material on the 3 1/2-inch disks often causes people to believe incorrectly that these disks are some sort of "hard disk" and not really a floppy disk. The disk "cookie" inside the 3 1/2-inch case is just as floppy as the 5 1/4-inch variety.

Floppy Disk Types and Specifications

This section examines all the types of disks you can purchase for your system. Especially interesting are the technical specifications that can separate one type of disk from another. This section defines all the specifications used to describe a typical disk.

Single- and Double-Sided Disks. Whether a disk is single- or double-sided is really an issue only for the lower-density disks. Because no single-sided high-density drives are manufactured, no need exists for disks to match the drives. The original IBM PC had single-sided drives, but they were discontinued in 1982.

A single-sided disk is constructed of the same material as a double-sided disk. The only difference seems to be that only the single-sided disks are "certified" (whatever that means) on only one side, and the double-sided disks are certified on both sides. Because the single-sided disks are cheaper than the double-sided versions, many PC users quickly determined that they could save some money if they used the single-sided disks even in double-sided drives.

This reasoning works because it is economically impractical for disk manufacturers to make some disks with recording surfaces on one side and other disks with recording surfaces on both sides. Today's single-sided disks look, and usually behave, exactly the same as double-sided disks. The result of this—depending on the brand of disks you buy—is that you can generally format and use "single-sided" disks successfully in double-sided drives, at a savings in disk costs. Unfortunately, the savings now are so small that this practice is obsolete, if not risky.

The danger in this practice is that some manufacturers do not burnish, or polish, the unused (top) side to the same level of smoothness as the used (bottom) side. This practice can cause accelerated wear on the top head. In single-sided drives, because the top head was replaced by a soft, felt pad, the rougher top side caused no problems. For the cost, it is not worth using with the wrong disks. I recommend the conservative route: Spend the small amount of extra money for double-sided disks of the correct density, and you will rarely have to recover damaged data.

Density. *Density*, in simplest terms, is a measure of the amount of information that can be packed reliably into a specific area of a recording surface. The keyword here is *reliably*.

Disks have two types of densities: longitudinal density and linear density. *Longitudinal density* is indicated by how many tracks can be recorded on the disk, often expressed as a number of tracks per inch (TPI). *Linear density* is the capability of an individual track to store data, often indicated as a number of bits per inch (BPI). Unfortunately, both types of densities often are interchanged incorrectly in discussing different disks and drives. Table 13.6 provides a rundown of each available type of disk.

Table 13.6   Floppy Disk Media Specifications

| Media Parameters | 5 1/4-Inch | | | 3 1/2-Inch | | |
	Double-Density (DD)	Quad-Density (QD)	High-Density (HD)	Double-Density (DD)	High-Density (HD)	Extra-High Density (ED)
Tracks Per Inch (TPI)	48	96	96	135	135	135
Bits Per Inch (BPI)	5,876	5,876	9,646	8,717	17,434	34,868
Media Formulation	Ferrite	Ferrite	Cobalt	Cobalt	Cobalt	Barium
Coercivity (Oersteds)	300	300	600	600	720	750
Thickness (Micro-In.)	100	100	50	70	40	100
Recording Polarity	Horiz.	Horiz.	Horiz.	Horiz.	Horiz.	Vert.

It is notable that IBM skipped the quad-density disk type—that is, no IBM system uses a quad-density drive or requires quad-density disks. Don't purchase a quad-density disk unless you just want a better-quality double-density disk.

Both the quad- and double-density disks store the same linear data on each track. They use the same formula for the magnetic coating on the disk, but the quad-density versions represent a more rigorously tested, higher-quality disk. The high-density disks are entirely different, however. To store the increased linear density, an entirely different magnetic coating was required. In both the 5 1/4-inch and 3 1/2-inch high-density disks, a high-coercivity coating is used to allow the tremendous bit density for each track. A high-density disk never can be substituted for a double- or quad-density disk because the write-current must be different for these very different media formulations and thicknesses.

The extra-high density 3 1/2-inch disk in the chart is newly available in some systems. This type of disk, invented by Toshiba, is available from several other vendors as well. The extra-high density disks use a barium-ferric compound to cover the disk with a thicker coating, which enables a vertical recording technique to be used. In vertical re-cording, the magnetic domains are recorded vertically rather than flat. The higher den-sity results from their capability to be stacked much more closely together. These types of drives can read and write the other 3 1/2-inch disks because of their similar track dimen-sions on all formats.

Media Coercivity and Thickness. The *coercivity specification* of a disk refers to the mag-netic-field strength required to make a proper recording on a disk. Coercivity, measured in oersteds, is a value indicating magnetic strength. A disk with a higher coercivity rating requires a stronger magnetic field to make a recording on that disk. With lower ratings, the disk can be recorded with a weaker magnetic field. In other words, *the lower the coer-civity rating, the more sensitive the disk.*

Another factor is the thickness of the disk. The thinner the disk, the less influence a region of the disk has on another adjacent region. The thinner disks therefore can accept many more bits per inch without eventually degrading the recording.

When I ask someone whether the high-density disks are more sensitive or less sensitive than the double-density disks, the answer is almost always "more sensitive." But you can see that this is not true. The high-density disks are in fact as much as half as sensitive as the double-density disks. A high-density drive can record with a much higher volume level at the heads than can the standard double-density drive. For these high-density drives to record properly on a double-density disk, the drive must be capable of using a reduced write-current mode and enable it whenever the lower-density disks are installed. A big problem with users and floppy disks then can occur.

Most users do not like paying more for the high-density disks their drives can use. These users, in an attempt to save money, are tempted to use the lower-density disks as a sub-stitute. Some users attempt to format the "regular" disk at the high-density capacity. This formatting is facilitated by DOS, which always attempts to format a disk to the maximum capacity of the drive's capabilities, unless specifically ordered otherwise through the use of proper parameters in the FORMAT command, or unless your system has an Active Media Sensor. If you use no parameters and simply enter FORMAT A:, however, the disk is formatted as though it were a high-density disk. Many users think that this procedure somehow is equivalent to using the single-sided disks in place of double-sided ones. I can assure you that this is not true—it is much worse. *Do not use double-density disks in place of high-density disks*, or you will experience severe problems and data loss from improper coercivity, media thickness, and write-current specifications.

The reasons for using the high-coercivity thin disks are simple. In designing the high-density drives, engineers found that the density of magnetic flux reversals caused adjacent flux reversals to begin to affect each other. The effect was that they started to cancel each other out, or cause shifts in the polarity of the domain. Data written at the high densities eventually began to erase itself. As an analogy, imagine a wooden track on which you place magnetic marbles, evenly spaced four inches apart in a specific pattern of magnetic polarity. At this distance, the magnetic forces from each marble are too weak to affect the adjacent marbles. Now imagine that the marbles must be placed only two inches apart. The magnetic attraction and repulsion forces now might start to work on the adjacent marbles so that they begin to rotate on their axis and thus change the direction of polarity and the data they represent.

You could eliminate the interaction of the magnetic domains by either spacing them farther apart or making the domains "weaker," therefore reducing their sphere of influence. If the marbles were made half as strong magnetically as they were before, you could get them twice as close together without any interaction between them. This is the principle behind the high-coercivity, thin media disks. Because they are weaker magnetically, they need a higher recording strength to store an image properly.

Try a simple experiment to verify this principle. Attempt to format a high-density disk in a low-density format. DOS responds with a Track 0 bad, Disk unusable message. The disk did not accept a recording in low-density mode because the low-density recording is also low volume. The disk cannot make a recording on the disk, and therefore the Track 0 bad message is displayed.

It is unfortunate for users that the opposite attempt appears to work: You can format a standard double-density disk as though it were a high-density disk, and the FORMAT command or DOS does not seem to be affected. You might notice a large number of "bad sectors," but DOS allows the format to be completed anyway.

This situation is unfortunate for two reasons. First, you are recording on the (low-density) disk with a density that requires weak magnetic domains to eliminate interaction between the adjacent domains. A low-density disk unfortunately stores magnetic domains twice as strong as they should be, and eventually they interact. You will experience mysterious data losses on this disk over the next few days, weeks, or months.

Second, you have just placed a recording on this disk at twice the signal strength it should be. This "industrial strength" recording might not be removable by a normal disk drive, and the disk might be magnetically saturated. You might not ever be able to reformat it correctly as a double-density disk because a double-density reformat uses reduced write-current. The reduced write-current might not be capable of overwriting the high write-current signal that had been recorded incorrectly. The best way to remove this "burned in" recording then is to use a bulk eraser to renew the disk by removing all magnetic information. In most cases, however, a fresh format can overcome the magnetic image of the previous one, even if the write-current had been incorrect.

Do not use the wrong media for the format you are attempting to perform. You must use the correct type of disk. Note that the 3 1/2-inch disks have a perfect mechanism—the media sensor for deterring users. If you are sure that all your high-density 3 1/2-inch drives contain this sensor, set to function (by way of a jumper or switch), you are saved from your own ignorance. A drive with a media sensor sets the write-current and operating mode by the actual disk inserted. You are prevented from taking a 720K disk and attempting to cram 1.44 megabytes on it. Remember that IBM did not make using this sensor a requirement because it fixed the controller problem that necessitated it; therefore, incorrectly formatting a disk is easy on the PS/2 system. Also, if you want to format a low-density 3 1/2-inch disk incorrectly with a high-density format using an IBM PS/2 system, you don't need one of the "disk converters" or hole punchers.

Soft and Hard Sectors. Floppy disks are either *soft sectored* or *hard sectored*. A soft-sectored disk has only one index hole on the disk surface. Once every revolution, the hole is visible through the hole in the protective jacket, and the drive, controller, and DOS use the hole to establish the location and timing of the first sector on a track. Individual sectors are defined by the controller and the software that runs the controller, hence the term soft sectored. Hard-sectored disks have an index hole as well as a separate hole for each sector on the disk marking the beginning of that sector. Hard-sectored disks are not used in IBM compatible PCs, but were used in some dedicated word processing systems and other proprietary computer systems. If you try to use a hard-sectored disk in a PC, the machine will get confused. Sometimes hard-sectored disks are not labeled specifically as hard-sectored, but rather specify "10 sectors" or "16 sectors." Because hard-sectored disks are not used in IBM-compatible systems, I have not seen these disks for sale in quite some time.

Formatting and Using High- and Low-Density Disks

This section describes how the different density capabilities of the high- and low-density drives sometimes can cause problems in formatting disks. You must always make sure that a disk initially is formatted to the density in which it was supposed to be run. In some cases, you should have a high-density drive format a low-density disk. You can perform this formatting with the correct format commands. The following section describes how to use DOS correctly so that your disks are formatted properly.

Reading and Writing 360K Disks in 1.2M Drives. Having 1.2M drives *read* or *write* to a 360K disk is a simple task. Just place a previously formatted 360K disk in the drive and use it normally. In other words, pretend that the drive is a 360K drive. Nothing special must be done. You can either read or write on the disk with absolutely no problems...yet.

You will have a problem if you decide to return the disk to a 360K drive and attempt to read it. Remember that the recorded track width of the 1.2M drive is half the track width of the 360K drive; therefore, if any tracks have been *previously recorded by an actual 360K drive*, the tracks are twice as wide as the tracks recorded by the 1.2M drive. If you write to the disk with the 1.2M drive, you cannot overwrite the entire track width—only the center portion of it. When you return this disk to a 360K drive, the wider head system in the 360K drive then sees two signals on any overwritten tracks, and the new data is nestled within the image of the old data that could not be completely covered by the 1.2M drive. An immediate Abort, Retry, Ignore error from DOS usually is displayed for any updated portions of the disk.

To solve this problem easily, if you want to record data in an AT 1.2M drive and later read it properly in a 360K drive, make sure that you use *brand-new* disks for recording in the 1.2M drive. Because a new disk has no magnetic information on it, the smaller recorded track width can be written on the 1.2M drive and read properly in the 360K drive: The more narrow track is written in "clean space." The 360K drive, therefore, no longer is confused by any "ghost images" of previously recorded wider tracks. Other than starting with a brand-new disk, your only other option is to use a disk erased by a bulk eraser. You cannot erase a disk by reformatting it if it has been in use. Formatting records actual data on the disk, and causes the track-width problem. The new or bulk-erased disk in fact must be formatted by the 1.2M drive for this procedure to work again. Remember the simple rule: Any track recorded by a 360K drive *cannot be overwritten* by a 1.2M drive, even in the 360K format.

How do you format a 360K disk in a 1.2M drive? If you just execute the FORMAT command without parameters, DOS attempts to format the disk to its maximum capacity. Because the 1.2M drive has no media-sensing capability, DOS assumes that the disk capability is equal to the maximum capability of the drive and attempts to create a 1.2M format on the disk. The write-current is increased also during a recording in this format, which is incompatible with the 360K media. To format the 360K disk correctly, therefore, look at the alternative command examples in table 13.7.

Table 13.7 Proper Formatting of 5 1/4-Inch 360K Disks in a 1.2M Drive							
Command	**DOS Version**						
	6.x	5.x	4.x	3.3	3.2	3.1	3.0
FORMAT d: /4	Yes	Yes	Yes	Yes	Yes	Yes	Yes
FORMAT d: /N:9 /T:40	Yes	Yes	Yes	Yes	Yes	No	No
FORMAT d: /F:360	Yes	Yes	Yes	No	No	No	No

d: = The drive to format
N = Number of sectors per track
T = Tracks per side
F = Format capacity

Note that DOS versions prior to 3.0 do not support 1.2M drives. Each example command accomplishes the same function, which is to place on a 360K disk a 40-track, 9-sector format using reduced write-current mode.

Reading and Writing 720K Disks in 1.44M and 2.88M Drives. The 3 1/2-inch drives do not have the same problems as the 5 1/4-inch disks—that is, at least not with data interchange. Because both the high- and low-density drives write the same number of tracks and are the same width, one type of drive can be used to overwrite data written by another type of drive. Because of this capability, IBM does not need to offer a low-density version of the 3 1/2-inch drives for the PS/2 systems. These systems (except Models 25 and 30) include only the HD or ED drives, which are capable of imitating perfectly the 720K drives in the Model 25 and Model 30. The high-density drives can be trouble, however, in the hands of an inexperienced (or cheapskate) user. You *must* make sure that you use only the 1.44M high-density disks in the 1.44M format, and only the 720K disks in the 720K format. You will encounter serious problems if you stick a 720K disk in a drive in a PS/2 without a media sensor drive and enter the command FORMAT A:. If you decide to use the formatted disk anyway, massive data loss eventually will occur.

Problems with incorrect formatting could have been averted if IBM had universally used disk drives that included the media sensor. This special switch senses the unique hole found only on the right side of high-density disks. Drives that use this hole to control the status of reduced write-current never can format a disk incorrectly. The hardware saves you by causing the FORMAT command to end in failure with an appropriate error message if you attempt to format the disk incorrectly. All the newer PS/2 systems from IBM include drives with an active media sensor that allows disks to be formatted correctly with no parameters on the FORMAT command. The information FORMAT needs about what type of disk is in the drive is supplied by the BIOS directly on these systems; no user supplied parameters are necessary.

The 1.44M drives and 720K drives do not have all the same problems as the 5 1/4-inch drives, primarily because all the 3 1/2-inch drives have the same recorded track width. The 1.44M or 2.88M drive has no problem recording 720K disks. For these reasons (and more), I applaud the industry move to the 3 1/2-inch drives. The sooner we stop using 5 1/4-inch disk drives, the better.

The only other problem with formatting, other than incorrectly selecting a drive without a media sensor or failing to enable it during the drive-installation procedure, is naive users attempting to format disks at a capacity for which they were not designed. *You must have a 720K (double-density) disk to write a 720K format; a 1.44M (high-density) disk to write a 1.44M format; and a 2.88M (extra-high density) disk to write an extra-high density format.* No ifs, ands, or buts. This chapter has explained already that this requirement stems from differences in the coercivity of the media and the levels of recording current used in writing the disks.

When you enter a standard FORMAT command with no parameters, DOS normally attempts to format the disk to the drive's maximum capacity as indicated by the BIOS. If you insert a 720K disk in a 1.44M drive, therefore, and enter the FORMAT command with no parameters, DOS attempts to create a 1.44M format on the disk. If the drive has a passive media sensor, the FORMAT command aborts with an error message. The media sensor does not communicate to DOS the correct information to format the disk—it just *prevents* incorrect formatting. You still must know the correct commands. If the system supports active media sensing, then no FORMAT command parameters are necessary as the BIOS will supply the correct parameters based on the type of disk in the drive. Table 13.8 shows the correct FORMAT command and parameters to use in formatting a 720K disk in a 1.44M drive.

Table 13.8   Proper Formatting of 3 1/2-Inch 720K Disks in a 1.44M or 2.88M Drive

| Command | DOS Version | | | |
	6.x	5.x	4.x	3.3
FORMAT d: /N:9 /T:80	Yes	Yes	Yes	Yes
FORMAT d: /F:720	Yes	Yes	Yes	No

d: = The drive to format
N = Number of sectors per track
T = Tracks per side
F = Format capacity

Note that DOS versions prior to 3.3 do not support 1.44M drives, and versions prior to 5.0 do not support 2.88M drives.

Reading and Writing 1.44M Disks in 2.88M Drives. The 2.88M extra-high density (ED) drive used in some newer systems, such as virtually the entire PS/2 line, is a welcome addition to any system. This drive offers a capacity twice as great as the standard 1.44M HD drive, and also offers full backward compatibility with the 1.44M HD drive and the 720K DD drive.

The 2.88M ED drive uses a technique called *vertical recording* to achieve its great linear density of 36 sectors per track. This technique increases density by magnetizing the domains perpendicular to the recording surface. By essentially placing the magnetic domains on their ends and stacking them side by side, density increases enormously.

The technology for producing heads that can perform a vertical or perpendicular recording has been around awhile. It is not the heads or even the drives that represent the major breakthrough in technology; rather, it is the media that is special. Standard disks have magnetic particles shaped like tiny needles that lie on the surface of the disk. Orienting these acicular particles in a perpendicular manner to enable vertical recording is very difficult. The particles on a barium-ferrite floppy disk are shaped like tiny, flat, hexagonal platelets that easily can be arranged to have their axis of magnetization perpendicular to the plane of recording. Although barium ferrite has been used as a material in the construction of permanent magnets, no one has been able to reduce the grain size of the platelets enough for high-density recordings.

Toshiba has perfected a glass-crystallization process for manufacturing the ultra fine platelets used in coating the barium-ferrite disks. This technology, patented by Toshiba, is being licensed to a number of disk manufacturers, all of whom are producing barium-ferrite disks using Toshiba's process. Toshiba also made certain modifications to the design of standard disk drive heads to enable them to read and write the new barium-ferrite disks as well as standard cobalt or ferrite disks. This technology is being used not only in floppy drives but also is appearing in a variety of tape drive formats.

The disks are called 4M disks in reference to their unformatted capacity. Actual formatted capacity is 2,880K, or 2.88M. Because of space lost in the formatting process, as well as space occupied by the volume boot sector, file-allocation tables, and root directory, the total usable storage space is 2,863K.

A number of manufacturers are making these drives, including Toshiba, Mitsubishi, Sony, and Panasonic. During the next few years, they should become more popular in higher-end systems. Table 13.9 shows the correct FORMAT command and parameters to use in formatting a 1.44M disk in a 2.88M drive, especially if your system does not support the active media sensor.

Table 13.9 Proper Formatting of 3 1/2-Inch 1.44M Disks in a 2.88M Drive		
Command	**DOS Version** 6.x	5.x
FORMAT d: /N:18 /T:80	Yes	Yes
FORMAT d: /F:1.44	Yes	Yes

d: = The drive to format
N = Number of sectors per track
T = Tracks per side
F = Format capacity

Note that DOS versions prior to 5.0 do not support the 2.88M drive. Also, most 2.88M installations have an active media sensor that automatically formats the disk correctly as determined by the media sensor. With active media sensing, the parameters indicating disk capacity are not necessary.

FORMAT Command Summary. This section is a short guide to the DOS FORMAT command. With newer DOS versions supporting more and different types of disk hardware, the once-simple FORMAT command has become more complex. Especially with the advent of DOS V5.0, the number of parameters and options available for the FORMAT command have increased dramatically. This section discusses the FORMAT command and these optional parameters. You see a simple guide to proper formatting of disks, as well as a thorough description of the FORMAT command parameters and options.

This chapter emphasized that a specific disk must always be formatted to its designated capacity. Formatting a disk to a capacity different from what it was designed for results only in an eventual loss of data from the disk. Because all the higher-density drives can format all the lower-density disks of the same form factor, knowing when a particular command option is required can be pretty complicated.

The basic rule is that a drive always formats in its native mode unless specifically instructed otherwise through the FORMAT command parameters. Therefore, if you insert a 1.44M HD disk in a 1.44M HD A drive, you then can format that disk by simply entering FORMAT A—no optional parameters are necessary in that case. If you insert any other type of disk (DD, for example), you absolutely *must* enter the appropriate parameters in the FORMAT command to change the format mode from the default 1.44M mode to the mode appropriate for the inserted disk. Even though the drive might have a media sensor that can detect which type of disk is inserted in the drive, in most cases the sensor does not communicate to the controller or DOS, which does not know which disk it is. An exception to this is the 2.88M drive installations that support active media sense. Most 2.88M drive installations support this advanced feature, which means that the media sensor will communicate the type of the inserted diskette to the controller and DOS. In this case no parameters are ever needed when formatting diskettes no matter what type is inserted. The FORMAT command will automatically default to the proper type as indicated by the active sensors on the 2.88M drive. I have even seen 1.44M drive installations with active media sensing (certain Hewlett Packard systems, for example), but this is rare.

In most cases of 1.44M drive installations, the media sensor in the drive is passive, and in effect all the sensor does is force the FORMAT command to fail if you do not enter the correct parameters for the inserted disk type.

Table 13.10 shows the proper format command for all possible variations in drive and disk types. It shows also which DOS versions support the various combinations of drives, disks, and FORMAT parameters.

To use this table, just look up the drive type and disk type you have. You then can see the proper FORMAT command parameters to use as well as the DOS versions that support the combination you want.

Table 13.10   Proper Disk Formatting

Drive Type	Disk Type	DOS Version	Proper FORMAT Command
5 1/4-inch 360K	DD 360K	DOS 2.0+	FORMAT d:
5 1/4-inch 1.2M	HD 1.2M	DOS 3.0+	FORMAT d:
5 1/4-inch 1.2M	DD 360K	DOS 3.0+	FORMAT d: /4
5 1/4-inch 1.2M	DD 360K	DOS 3.2+	FORMAT d: /N:9 /T:40
5 1/4-inch 1.2M	DD 360K	DOS 4.0+	FORMAT d: /F:360
3 1/2-inch 720K	DD 720K	DOS 3.2+	FORMAT d:
3 1/2-inch 1.44M	HD 1.44M	DOS 3.3+	FORMAT d:

Drive Type	Disk Type	DOS Version	Proper FORMAT Command
3 1/2-inch 1.44M	DD 720K	DOS 3.3+	FORMAT d: /N:9 /T:80
3 1/2-inch 1.44M	DD 720K	DOS 4.0+	FORMAT d: /F:720
3 1/2-inch 2.88M	ED 2.88M	DOS 5.0+	FORMAT d:
3 1/2-inch 2.88M	HD 1.44M	DOS 5.0+	FORMAT d: /F:1.44
3 1/2-inch 2.88M	DD 720K	DOS 5.0+	FORMAT d: /F:720

+ = Includes all higher versions
d: = Specifies drive to format
DD = double-density
HD = high-density
ED = extra-high density

Note

If the drive and installation you are using supports active (intelligent) media sense, no diskette type parameters are required. The drive will automatically communicate the type of the installed diskette to the FORMAT program. This is normal for most 2.88M drive installations.

With the advent of DOS 5.0, the FORMAT command has received a number of new functions and capabilities, all expressed through two new parameters: /Q (Quickformat) and /U (Unconditional). Precisely describing the effect of these parameters on the FORMAT command is difficult, especially considering that they have different effects on hard disks and floppy disks. Table 13.11 summarizes the functions of these new parameters and

relates the new functions to the older versions of DOS.

Table 13.11   DOS FORMAT Command Internal Operations

Hard Disk Format Operations:	DOS 2–4		DOS 5 and Higher			
FORMAT Command Parameters	Any	None	None	/Q	/U	/Q/U
Disk Previously Formatted?	–	Yes	No	Yes	Yes	Yes
Check Volume Boot Sector	No	Yes	Yes	Yes	No	Yes
Save UNFORMAT Information	No	Yes	No	Yes	No	No
Read Verify (Scan) Disk	Yes	Yes	Yes	No	Yes	No
Overwrite VBS, FATs & Root Dir.	Yes	Yes	Yes	Yes	Yes	Yes
Overwrite Data Area	No	No	No	No	No	No

(continues)

Table 13.11 Continued							
Floppy Disk Format Operations:		**DOS 2–4**	**DOS 5 and Higher**				
FORMAT Command Parameters		**Any**	**None**	**None**	**/Q**	**/U**	**/Q/U**
Disk Previously Formatted?		**–**	**Yes**	**No**	**Yes**	**Yes**	**Yes**
Check Volume Boot Sector	No	Yes	Yes	Yes	No	Yes	
Save UNFORMAT Information	No	Yes	No	Yes	No	No	
Read Verify (Scan) Disk	Yes	Yes	Yes	No	Yes	No	
Overwrite VBS, FATs & Root Dir.	Yes	Yes	Yes	Yes	Yes	Yes	
Overwrite Data Area	Yes	No	Yes	No	Yes	No	

/Q = Quick Format
/U = Unconditional Format
"–" = Does Not Matter
VBS = DOS Volume Boot Sector
FAT = File Allocation Table

From this table you should be able to discern the function of a specific FORMAT command relative to the use of the /Q and /U parameters. For example, suppose that you are using DOS V5.0 and you insert a brand-new 1.44M disk in a 1.44M drive A: on your system. If you enter the command FORMAT A: with no other parameters, what will happen? By looking at table 13.11, you can see that the default operation of the FORMAT command in this case would be as follows:

1. Check the DOS volume boot sector.

2. Perform a read verify (or scan) of the entire disk.

3. Overwrite the DVB, FATs, and the root directory.

4. Overwrite the entire data area of the disk.

These functions do not necessarily happen in this order; in fact, the last three items listed occur simultaneously as the format progresses. Now suppose that you write some files on this disk and reenter the same FORMAT A: command. As you can see from table 13.11, the functions of the FORMAT command are very different this time. The steps occur something like this:

1. Check the DOS volume boot sector.

2. Save UNFORMAT information.

3. Perform a read verify (or scan) of the entire disk.

4. Overwrite the DVB, FATs, and the root directory.

The default operation of FORMAT on a disk that is already formatted has changed dramatically with DOS V5.0. The biggest difference between this and older versions of DOS is that DOS V5.0 and higher versions (by default) save a backup copy of the disk's DOS volume boot sector, file-allocation tables, and root directory. This information, which is placed in a special format in sectors near the end of the disk, is designed to be utilized by the UNFORMAT command to restore these areas of the disk and therefore undo the work of the FORMAT command. In addition to saving this critical UNFORMAT information, the FORMAT command also defaults to *not* overwriting the data area of the disk; therefore, the UNFORMAT command can "restore" the disk data. The UNFORMAT does not actually restore the data—only the saved UNFORMAT information. The disk data is never lost. Older DOS versions do not check the disk to see whether it is formatted and always overwrite the entire floppy disk.

The /Q parameter stands for Quickformat. The basic function of /Q, to eliminate the (sometimes lengthy) read verify scan for disk defects that otherwise would occur, can be performed only on a disk that already is formatted. Any existing defect marks on the disk are preserved by using /Q. The net effect of /Q is to greatly speed up the formatting procedure for disks already formatted. It's a quick way to delete all the files from a disk quickly and efficiently.

The /U parameter stands for Unconditional. This parameter has two distinctly different effects depending on whether you are formatting a floppy disk or a hard disk. On a floppy disk, the /U parameter instructs the FORMAT command to overwrite the entire disk and skip saving UNFORMAT information because it would be useless anyway if the data were overwritten. On a hard disk, the purpose of /U is only to suppress saving UNFORMAT information. FORMAT on a hard disk *never* overwrites the data area of the disk, even with the /U parameter! If you have experience with the FORMAT command, you know that FORMAT never has overwritten data on a hard disk, no matter what version of IBM or MS-DOS you are using. (On some older OEM versions, such as Compaq and AT&T, DOS did overwrite the entire hard disk.)

When you combine the /Q and /U parameters, you get the fastest reformat possible. /Q prevents the scan for defects, which is the longest operation during formatting, and /U eliminates saving UNFORMAT information. The FORMAT command is restricted to simply erasing the DOS volume boot sector, FATs, and root directory, which it can do very quickly. In fact, a format using the /Q and /U parameters takes only a few seconds to complete no matter how large the disk.

For more information on the DOS FORMAT command, a master FORMAT command reference chart is in Appendix A. This explicit chart explains what all the FORMAT parameters do, and even describes some useful undocumented parameters I discovered.

Caring for and Handling Floppy Disks and Drives

Most computer users know the basics of disk care. Disks can be damaged or destroyed easily by the following:

- Touching the recording surface with your fingers or anything else
- Writing on a disk label with a ballpoint pen or pencil
- Bending the disk
- Spilling coffee or other substances on the disk

■ Overheating a disk (leaving it in the hot sun or near a radiator, for example)

■ Exposing a disk to stray magnetic fields

Despite all these cautions, disks are rather hardy storage devices; I can't say that I have ever destroyed one by just writing on it with a pen, because I do so all the time. I am careful, however, not to press too hard, which can put a crease in the disk. Also, simply touching a disk does not necessarily ruin it but rather gets the disk and your drive head dirty with oil and dust. The danger to your disks comes from magnetic fields that, because they are unseen, can sometimes be found in places you never dreamed of.

For example, all color monitors (and color TV sets) have, around the face of the tube, a degaussing coil used to demagnetize the shadow mask inside when the monitor is turned on. The coil is connected to the AC line and controlled by a thermistor that passes a gigantic surge of power to the coil when the tube is powered on, which then tapers off as the tube warms up. The degaussing coil is designed to remove any stray magnetism from the shadow mask at the front area of the tube. Residual magnetism in this mask can bend the electron beams so that the picture appears to have strange colors or be out of focus.

If you keep your disks anywhere near (within one foot) of the front of the color monitor, you expose them to a strong magnetic field every time you turn on the monitor. Keeping disks in this area is not a good idea because the field is designed to demagnetize objects, and indeed works well for demagnetizing disks. The effect is cumulative and irreversible.

Another major disk destructor is the telephone. The mechanical ringer in a typical telephone uses a powerful electromagnet to move the striker into the bell. The ringer circuit uses some 90 volts, and the electromagnetic fields have sufficient power to degauss a disk lying on the desk next to or partially underneath the phone. *Keep disks away from the telephone.* A telephone with an electronic ringer might not cause this type of damage to a disk, but be careful anyway.

Another source of powerful magnetic fields is an electric motor, found in vacuum cleaners, heaters or air conditioners, fans, electric pencil sharpeners, and so on. Do not place these devices near areas where you store disks.

Airport X-Ray Machines and Metal Detectors. People associate myths with things they cannot see, and we certainly cannot see data as it is stored on a disk, nor the magnetic fields that can alter the data.

One of my favorite myths to dispel is that the airport X-ray machine somehow damages disks. I have a great deal of experience in this area from having traveled around the country for the past ten years or so with disks and portable computers in hand. I fly about 150,000 miles per year, and my portable computer equipment and disks have been through X-ray machines more than 100 times each year.

Most people commit a fatal mistake when they approach the airport X-ray machines with disks or computers: they don't pass the stuff through! Seriously, X-rays are in essence just a form of light, and disks and computers are just not affected by X-rays at anywhere near the levels found in these machines. What can damage your magnetic media is the *metal detector*. Time and time again, someone with magnetic media or a portable computer approaches the security check. They freeze and say, "Oh no, I have disks and a computer—they have to be hand inspected." The person then refuses to place the disk and computer on the X-ray belt, and either walks through the metal detector with disks and computer in hand or passes the items over to the security guard, in very close proximity to the metal detector. Metal detectors work by monitoring disruptions in a weak magnetic field. A metal object inserted in the field area causes the field's shape to change, which the detector observes. This principle, which is the reason that the detectors are sensitive to metal objects, can be dangerous to your disks; the X-ray machine, however, is the safest area through which to pass either your disk or computer.

The X-ray machine is not dangerous to magnetic media because it merely exposes the media to electromagnetic radiation at a particular (very high) frequency. Blue light is an example of electromagnetic radiation of a different frequency. The only difference between X-rays and blue light is in the frequency, or wavelength, of the emission.

Electromagnetic radiation is technically a form of wave energy characterized by oscillating electric and magnetic fields perpendicular to one another. An electromagnetic wave is produced by an oscillating electric charge. This wave is not the same thing as a magnetic field. When matter intercepts electromagnetic energy, the energy is converted to thermal, electrical, mechanical, or chemical energy, but not to a magnetic field. Simply put, an electromagnetic wave generates either heat or an electrical alternating current in an object through which the wave passes.

I have been electrically shocked, for example, by touching metal objects in the vicinity of a high-powered amateur-radio transmitter. Your microwave oven induces thermal (kinetic) or even electrical energy in objects because of the same principle. Although a microwave oven is designed to induce kinetic energy in an irradiated substance's molecules, most of you know that when you place conductive (metal) objects in the microwave, an alternating electrical current also is generated, and you might even see sparks. This activity is a generation of electrical or mechanical energy, not of a magnetic field. Because a disk is not a good conductor, the only noticeable effect a high-powered electromagnetic field has on a floppy disk is the generation of kinetic (or thermal) energy. In other words, the only way that X-rays, visible light, or other radiation in these areas of the electromagnetic spectrum can damage a disk is by heating it.

Consider also that if electromagnetic radiation could truly magnetize a disk as a magnetic field can, all magnetic media (disks and tapes) in the world would be in danger. Much electromagnetic radiation is passing through you at this moment, and through all your disks and tapes as well. There is no danger of magnetic damage because the radiation's effect on an object is to impart electrical, thermal, mechanical, or chemical energy—*not to magnetize the object*. I am *not* saying that you cannot harm a disk with electromagnetic radiation, because you certainly can; the damage, however, is from the heating effects of the radiation.

You probably know what the sun's extremely powerful electromagnetic radiation can do to a disk. Just leave a disk lying in direct sunlight a while, and you can see the thermal effects of this radiation. A microwave oven would have basically the same cooking effect on a disk, only more intense! Seriously, at the levels of electromagnetic radiation to which we normally are exposed, or which are present in an airport X-ray machine, there is certainly no danger to your disks. The field strength is far too low to raise the temperature of the disk in any perceptible manner, and this radiation has no magnetic effect on a disk.

Some people worry about the effect of X-ray radiation on their system's EPROM (erasable programmable read-only memory) chips. This concern might actually be more valid than worrying about disk damage because EPROMs are erased by certain forms of electromagnetic radiation. In reality, however, you do not need to worry about this effect either. EPROMs are erased by direct exposure to very intense ultraviolet light. Specifically, to be erased, an EPROM must be exposed to a 12,000 uw/cm2 UV light source with a wavelength of 2,537 angstroms for 15 to 20 minutes, and at a distance of one inch. Increasing the power of the light source or decreasing the distance from the source can shorten the erasure time to a few minutes. The airport X-ray machine is different by a factor of 10,000 in wavelength, and the field strength, duration, and distance from the emitter source are nowhere near what is necessary for EPROM erasure. Be aware that many circuit-board manufacturers use X-ray inspection on circuit boards (with components including EPROMs installed) to test and check quality control during manufacture.

I have conducted my own tests: I passed one disk through different airport X-ray machines for two years, averaging two or three passes a week. The same disk still remains intact with all the original files and data, and never has been reformatted. I also have several portable computers with hard disks installed; one of them has been through the X-ray machines safely every week for more than four years. I prefer to pass computers and disks through the X-ray machine because it offers the best shielding from the magnetic fields produced by the metal detector standing next to it. Doing so also significantly lowers the "hassle factor" with the security guards because if I have it X-rayed, they usually do not require that I plug it in and turn it on.

Drive-Installation Procedures

The procedure for installing floppy drives is simple. You install the drive in two phases. The first phase is to configure the drive for the installation, and the second is to perform the physical installation. Of these two steps, the first one usually is the most difficult to perform, depending on your knowledge of disk interfacing and whether you have access to the correct OEM drive manuals.

Drive Configuration

Configuring a floppy drive consists of setting the jumpers and switches mounted on the drive to match the system in which the drive will be installed, as well as tailoring the function of the drive to the installer's requirements. Every drive has a stable of jumpers and switches, and many drives are different from each other. You will find no standards for what these jumpers and switches are called, where they should be located, or how they should be implemented. There are some general guidelines to follow, but to set up a specific drive correctly and know all the options available, you must have information from the drive's manufacturer, normally found in the original equipment manufacturer's (OEM) manual. The manual is a "must have" item when you purchase a disk drive.

Although additional options might be available, most drives have several configuration features that must be set properly for an installation. These standard options typically need attention during an installation procedure:

- Drive select jumper
- Terminating resistor
- Diskette changeline or ready jumper
- Media sensor jumper

Each configuration item was discussed in more detail earlier in this chapter. The following section describes how these items are to be set for various installations.

Floppy drives are connected by a cabling arrangement called a *daisy chain*. The name is descriptive because the cable is strung from controller to drive to drive in a single chain. All drives have a drive select (sometimes called DS) jumper that must be set to indicate a certain drive's physical drive number. The point at which the drive is connected on the cable does not matter; the DS jumper indicates how the drive should respond. Most drives allow four settings, but the controllers used in all PC systems support only two on a single daisy-chain cable. The PC and XT floppy controllers, for example, support four drives but only on two separate cables—each one a daisy chain with a maximum of two drives.

Every drive on a particular cable must be set to have unique drive select settings. In a normal configuration, the drive you want to respond as the first drive (A) is set to the first drive select position, and the drive you want to respond as the second drive (B) is set to the second drive-select position. On some drives, the DS jumper positions are labeled 0, 1, 2, and 3; other drives use the numbers 1, 2, 3, and 4 to indicate the same positions. For some drives then, a setting of DS0 is drive A. For others, however, DS1 indicates drive A. Likewise, some drives use a setting of DS1 for drive B, and others use a DS2 setting to indicate drive B. On some drives, the jumpers on the drive circuit board are unlabeled! In this case, consult the drive's manual to find out the descriptions of each jumper setting on the drive. A typical daisy-chain drive cable with this included "twist" is connected as shown in figure 13.11.

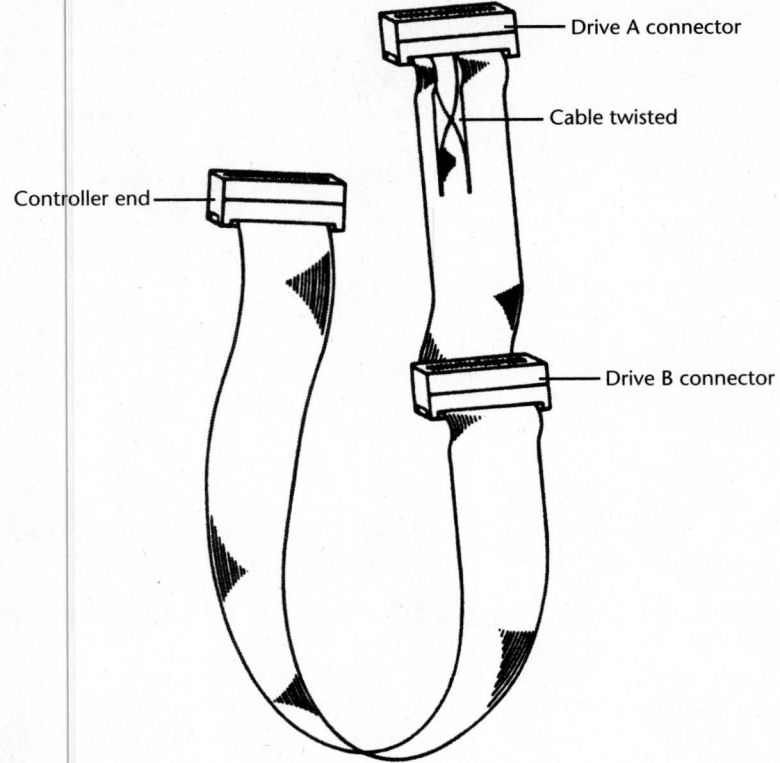

Drive A connector

Cable twisted

Controller end

Drive B connector

Fig. 13.11
A floppy controller cable showing the location of "the twist."

Make sure that the DS settings for every drive on a single daisy-chain cable are different, or both drives respond to the same signals. If you have incorrect DS settings, both drives respond simultaneously or neither drive responds at all.

The type of cable you use can confuse the drive select configuration. IBM puts in its cables a special twist that electrically changes the DS configuration of the drive plugged in after the twist. This twist causes a drive physically set to the first DS position (A) to appear to the controller to be set to the second DS position (B). If the first drive on the cable was before the twist in the cable and was set to the second DS position (B), the controller would see a conflict. To the controller, both drives would appear to be set to the second DS position (B), although physically they looked as though they were set differently. In essence, the system would think that two B drives were installed. The adjustment for this problem is simple: When this type of cable is used, both drives should be set to the second DS position. The drive plugged in to the connector farthest from the controller, which is after the twist in the cable, then would have the physical second-DS-position setting appear to be changed to a first-DS-position setting. Then the system would see this drive as A, and the drive plugged into the middle cable connector still would appear as B.

An IBM-style floppy cable is a 34-pin cable with lines 10 through 16 sliced out and cross-wired (twisted) between the drive connectors (refer to fig. 13.11). This twisting "cross-wires" the first and second drive-select and motor-enable signals, and therefore inverts the DS setting of the drive following the twist. All the drives in a system using this type of cable, therefore—whether you want them to be A or B, are physically jumpered the same way; installation and configuration are simplified because both floppies can be preset to the second DS position. Some drives used by IBM, in fact, have had the DS "jumper" setting permanently soldered into the drive logic board.

Most bare drives you purchase have the DS jumper already set to the second position, which is correct for the majority of systems that use a cable with the twisted lines. Although this setting is correct for the majority of systems, if you are using a cable with no twist, you will have to alter this setting on at least one of the two drives. Some systems come with only a single floppy drive and no provisions for adding a second one. These types of systems often use a floppy cable with only one drive connector attached. This type of cable does not have any twisted lines, so how do you set up a drive plugged into this cable? Because there is no twist, the DS setting you make on the drive is exactly what the controller sees. You can attach only one drive, and it should appear to the system as A—therefore, set the drive to the first DS position.

Most IBM-compatibles use a floppy cable with the twisted lines between the drive connectors. Drives plugged into this type of cable have their DS jumpers set to the second position. Drives on a single floppy cable or a cable with no twisted lines are set to the first DS position.

A terminating resistor should be placed (or enabled) in any drive plugged into the physical end of a cable. The function of this resistor is to prevent reflections or echoes of signals from reaching the end of the cable. All new drives have this resistor installed by default. The terminating resistor should be removed or disabled for drives that are not the farthest away from the controller. Most 3 1/2-inch floppy drives use the distributed-termination technique, in which the installed terminating resistors are permanently installed, and are non-removable and cannot be disabled. The resistor value in these drives is adjusted appropriately so that, in effect, the termination is distributed among both drives. When you mix 5 1/4-inch and 3 1/2-inch drives, you should enable or disable the terminators on the 5 1/4-inch drives appropriately, according to their position on the cable and ignore the non-changeable settings on the 3 1/2-inch drives.

In a typical cabling arrangement for two 5 1/4-inch floppies, for example, the terminating resistor is installed in drive A (at the end of the cable), and this resistor is removed from the other floppy drive on the same cable (B). The letter to which the drive responds is not important in relation to terminator settings; the important issue is that the drive at the end of the cable has the resistor installed and functioning and that other drives on the same cable have the resistor disabled or removed.

The terminating resistor usually looks like a memory chip; it might be white, blue, black, gray, or some other color, and memory chips usually are just black. IBM always labels the resistor with a T-RES sticker for easy identification. On some systems, the resistor is a built-in device enabled or disabled by a jumper or series of switches. If you have the removable type, make sure to store the resistor in a safe place because you might need it later. Figure 13.12 shows the location and appearance of the terminating resistor or switches on a typical floppy drive. Because most 3 1/2-inch drives have a form of automatic termination, there is no termination to configure; also, some 5 1/4-inch drives, such as Toshiba drives, have a permanently installed terminating resistor enabled or disabled by a jumper labeled TM.

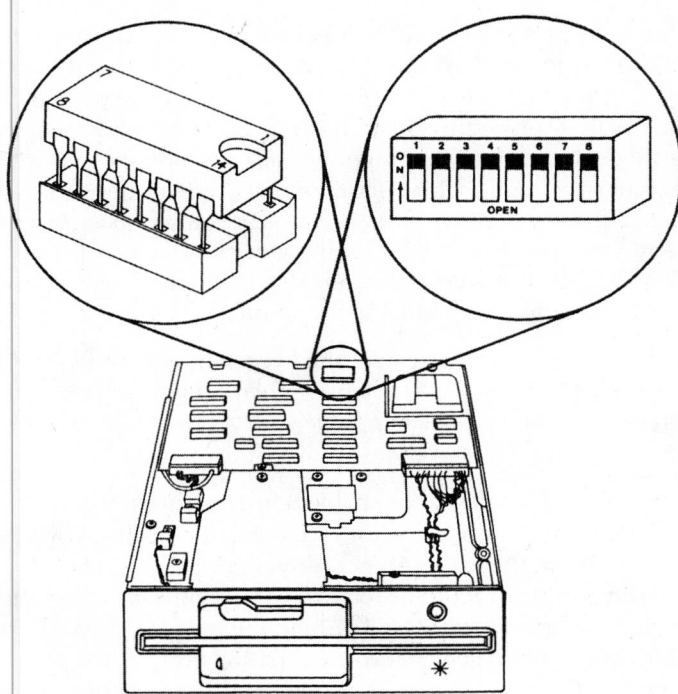

Fig. 13.12

A typical floppy drive terminating resistor, or termination switches.

Table 13.12 explains how a drive should be configured relative to the drive-select jumper and terminating resistor. You can use the table as a universal drive-select and terminating resistor configuration chart that applies to all types of drives, including floppy disk drives and hard disks.

Table 13.12   Configuring Drive-Select Jumpers and Terminating Resistors

Drive	Twisted Cable	Straight Cable
A: drive (end connector)	DS = second TR installed	DS = first TR installed
B: drive (center connector)	DS = second TR removed	DS = second TR removed

DS = Drive select position
TR = Terminating resistor

The assumption in table 13.12 is that you always plug drive B into the center connector on the cable and drive A into the end connector. This arrangement might seem strange at first, but it is virtually required if you ever assemble a single-drive system. The logical first (A) drive should be the end, or last, drive on the cable, and should be terminated. The twist in the cable is almost always between the two drive connectors on a cable and not between the controller and a drive.

Two other options might be available for you to set: the status of pin 34 on the drive's connector, and the function of a media-sensor feature. The guidelines for setting these options follow.

If the drive is a 5 1/4-inch 360K drive, set the status of pin 34 to Open (disconnected) regardless of the type of system in which you are installing the drive. The only other option normally found for pin 34 on 360K drives is Ready (RDY), which is incorrect. If you are using only a low-density controller, as in a PC or XT, pin 34 is ignored no matter what is sent on it. If the drive you are installing is a 5 1/4-inch 1.2M or 3 1/2-inch 720K, 1.44M, or 2.88M drive, be sure to set pin 34 to send the Disk Change (DC) signal. The basic rule is simple:

> For 360K drives only, pin 34 = Open (disconnected)
>
> For any other drive, pin 34 = Disk Change

The media-sensor setting is the easiest to describe. Only 1.44M and 2.88M drives have a media sensor. The best rule to follow is to set these drives so that the sensor is enabled; this step enables the sensor to control the drive's recording mode and, therefore, the drive's write-current level.

Physical Installation

When you physically install a drive, you plug in the drive. Here, your concerns are using the correct brackets and screws for the system and the correct drive you are installing.

IV

Mass Storage Systems

A special bracket usually is required whenever you install a half-height drive in place of an earlier full-height unit (see fig. 13.13). The brackets enable you to connect the two half-height drives together as a single full-height unit for installation. Remember also that nearly all floppy drives now use metric hardware; only the early, American-manufactured drives use the standard English threads.

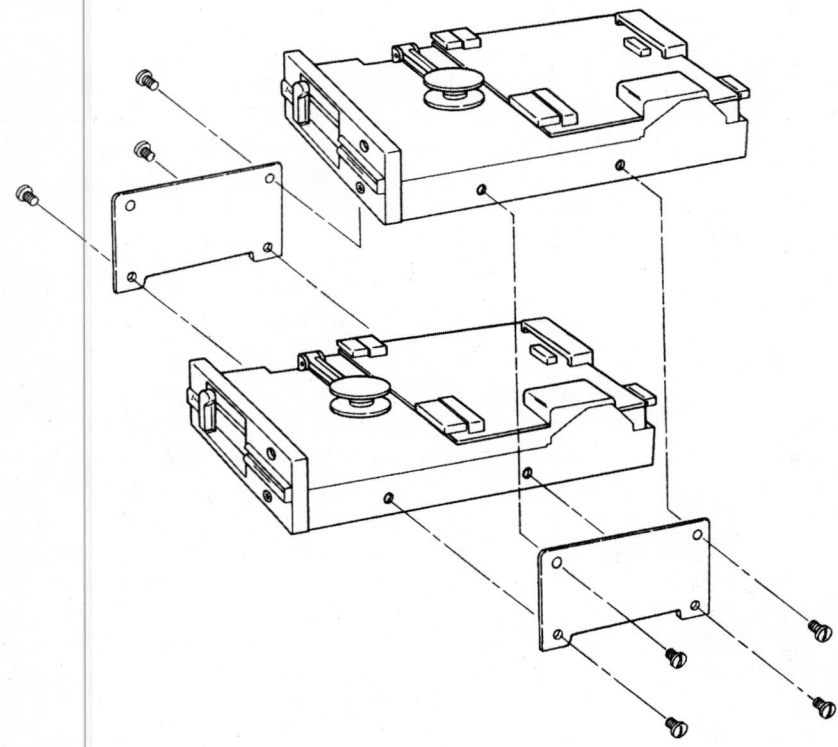

Fig. 13.13
Installing half-height drives in a full-height bay with adapter plates.

You can get these adapter plates from most vendors who sell drives, but sometimes they charge as much as $10 for basically a piece of sheet metal with four holes drilled in it! Several companies listed in Appendix B specialize in cables, brackets, screw hardware, and other items useful in assembling systems or installing drives. The template shown in figure 13.14 also will guide you if you want to make your own. I usually use a piece of galvanized sheet metal like that used in ventilation ductwork for the stock, which can be easily obtained at most hardware stores.

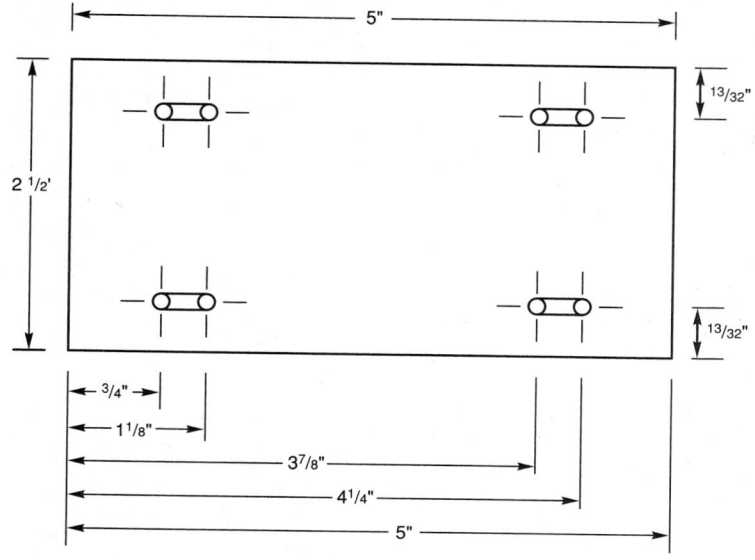

Fig. 13.14
The dimensions of a typical drive adapter plate.

Another piece of drive-installation paraphernalia you need is the rails used in installing disk drives in AT systems. Most IBM-compatible systems follow the IBM standard for rail design. Again, you can purchase these from some of the vendors listed in Appendix B. If you want to construct your own, figure 13.15 shows the construction of a typical IBM-style drive rail. These rails can be made from metal, but usually are made from plastic. They probably can even be made from wood. Drives installed in an AT are grounded to the system chassis through a separate ground wire and tab, which is why the rails do not need to be made from a conductive material. I find it more cost effective to purchase the rails rather than make them.

As you might expect, Compaq uses a slightly different rail construction. The vendors mentioned in Appendix B that sell cables, brackets, and other installation accessories also carry the Compaq-style rails.

When you connect a drive, make sure that the power cable is installed properly. The cable normally is keyed so that it cannot be plugged in backward. Also, install the data and control cable. If no key is in this cable, which allows only a correct orientation, use the colored wire in the cable as a guide to the position of pin 1. This cable is oriented correctly when you plug it in so that the colored wire is plugged into the disk drive connector toward the cut-out notch in the drive edge connector.

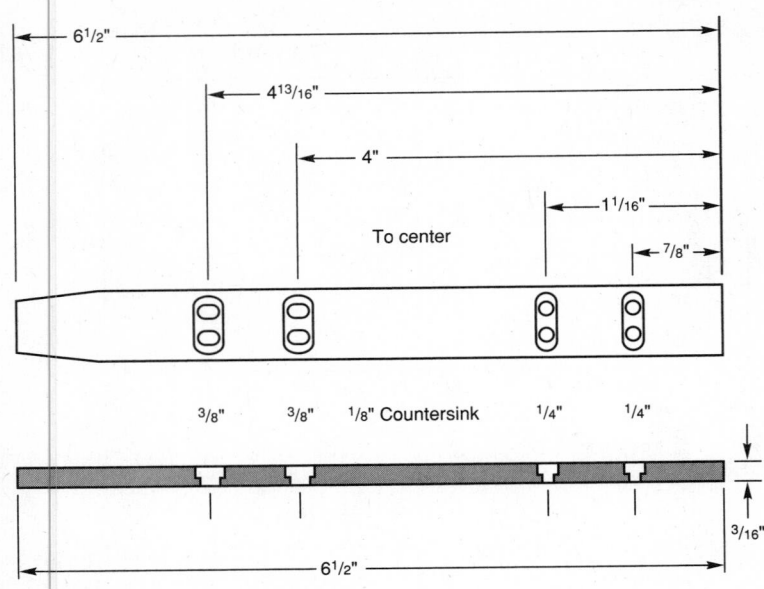

Fig. 13.15
A typical AT-drive mounting rail.

Floppy Drive Installation Summary

To install and set up a floppy drive properly, you must understand and set up primarily four different configuration items on the drive as follows:

- Drive select (DC) jumper setting

- Terminating resistor (TR) enabled or disabled

- Send disk change (DC) or no signal on pin 34

- Enable media sensor

This section explained the proper settings for these items in virtually any installation situation you might encounter.

For more information about configuring and installing a specific drive, you can use several resources. Obviously, this book contains much information about configuring and installing floppy disk drives—make sure that you have read it all! The best source of information about certain drives or controllers is the original equipment manufacturer's (OEM) documentation. These manuals tell you where all configuration items are located on the drive; what they look like; and how to set them. Unfortunately, most of the time you do not receive this detailed documentation when you purchase a drive or controller; instead, you must contact the OEM to obtain it.

Troubleshooting and Correcting Problems

The majority of floppy drive problems are caused primarily by improper drive configuration, installation, or operation. Unfortunately, floppy drive configuration and installation is much more complicated than the average technician seems to realize. Even if you had your drive "professionally" installed, it still might have been done incorrectly.

This section describes some of the most common problems that stem from improperly installing or configuring a drive. Also discussed are several problems that can occur from improperly using drives and disks. Solutions to these problems are presented also.

Handling the "Phantom Directory" (Disk Change)

One of the most common mistakes people make when installing a disk drive is incorrectly setting the signals sent by the drive on pin 34 of the cable to the controller. All drives *except* the 360K drive must be configured so that a Disk Change (DC) signal is sent along pin 34 to the controller.

If you do not enable the DC signal when the system expects you to, you might end up with trashed disks as a result. For example, a PC user with disk in hand might say to you, "Moments ago, this disk contained my document files, and now it seems as though my entire word processing program disk has mysteriously transferred to it. When I attempt to run the programs that now seem to be on this disk, they crash or lock up my system." Of course, in this case the disk has been damaged, and you will have to perform some data-recovery magic to recover the information for the user. My book, *Que's Guide to Data Recovery,* contains more information about data-recovery techniques. A good thing about this particular kind of problem is that recovering most—if not all—the information on the disk is entirely possible.

You also can observe this installation defect manifested in the "phantom directory" problem. For example, you place a disk with files on it in the A drive of your AT-compatible system and enter the **DIR A:** command. The drive starts spinning, the access light on the drive comes on, and after a few seconds of activity, the disk directory scrolls up the screen. Everything seems to be running well. Then you remove the disk and insert in drive A a different disk with different files on it and repeat the **DIR A:** command. This time, however, the drive barely (if at all) spins before the disk directory scrolls up the screen. When you look at the directory listing that has appeared, you discover in amazement that it is the same listing as on the first disk you removed from the drive.

Understand that the disk you have inserted in the drive is in danger. If you write on this disk in any way, you will cause the file-allocation tables and root-directory sectors from the first disk (which are stored in your system's memory) to be copied over to the second disk, thereby "blowing away" the information on the second disk. Most AT-compatible systems with high- or low-density controllers utilize a floppy disk caching system that buffers the FATs and directories from the floppy disk that was last read in system RAM. Because this data is kept in memory, these areas of the disk do not have to be reread as frequently. This system greatly speeds access to the disk.

Opening the door lever or pressing the eject button on a drive normally sends the Disk Change signal to the controller, which in turn causes DOS to flush out the floppy cache. This action causes the next read of the disk drive to reread the FAT and directory areas. If this signal is not sent, the cache is not flushed when you change a disk, and the system acts as though the first disk still is present in the drive. Writing to this newly inserted disk writes not only the new data but also either a full or partial copy of the first disk's FAT and directory areas. Also, the data is written to what was considered free space on the first disk, which might not be free on the subsequent disk and results in damaged files and data.

This problem has several simple solutions. One is temporary; the other is permanent. For a quick, temporary solution, press Ctrl-Break or Ctrl-C immediately after changing any disk, to force DOS to manually flush the floppy I/O buffers. This method is exactly how the old CP/M operating system used to work. After pressing Ctrl-Break or Ctrl-C, the next disk access rereads the FAT and directory areas of the disk and places fresh copies in memory. In other words, you must be sure that every time you change a disk, the buffer gets flushed. Because these commands work only from the DOS prompt, you must not change a disk while working in an application.

A more permanent and correct solution to the problem is simple—just correct the drive installation. In my experience, incorrect installation is the root cause of this problem nine out of ten times. Remember this simple rule: *If a jumper block is on the disk drive labeled DC, you should install a jumper there.* If you are absolutely certain that the installation was correct—for example, the drive has worked perfectly for some time, but then suddenly develops this problem—check the following list of items, all of which can prevent the Disk Change signal from being sent:

- Drive configuration/Setup. Make sure that the DC jumper is enabled; check CMOS Setup.

- Bad cable. Check for continuity on pin 34.

- Bad Disk Change sensor. Clean sensor or replace drive and retest.

- Bad drive logic board. Replace drive and retest.

- Bad controller. Replace controller and retest.

- Wrong DOS OEM version.

The last of these checklist items can stump you because the hardware seems to be functioning correctly. As a rule, you should use only the DOS supplied by the same OEM as the computer system on the system. For example, use IBM DOS on IBM systems, Compaq DOS on Compaq systems, Zenith DOS on Zenith systems, Toshiba DOS on Toshiba systems, Tandy DOS on Tandy systems, and so on. This problem is most noticeable with some laptop systems that apparently have a modified floppy controller design, such as some Toshiba laptops. On many of these systems, you *must* use the correct (Toshiba, for example) OEM version of DOS.

Handling Incorrect Media-Sensor Operation

Incorrect media-sensor operation occurs on only 1.44M or 2.88M, 3 1/2-inch, high-density drives—the only drives that have a media sensor. Again, this is largely a drive-configuration problem because the installer did not enable the sensor when it should have been enabled. You would think that the sensor would be set correctly when you purchase a drive, but that is not always the case. Never assume that a drive is preconfigured properly for your system. Remember that drive manufacturers sell drives for systems other than IBM-compatibles. Sometimes it is hard to remember that many other types of computers exist other than just IBMs or IBM clones.

If the media sensor is not operational, the controller likely will leave the drive in a state in which high write-current always is applied to the heads during write operations. This state is OK for high-density disks, but when low-density disks are used, random and sporadic read and write failures occur, usually ending with the DOS message `Abort, Retry, Ignore, Fail?`.

Another symptom of incorrect media-sensor operation is generating double-density disks that seem eventually to lose data—perhaps over a few weeks or months. This loss often can be traced back to an improperly configured media sensor on the drive. In some systems, the problem might be more obvious, such as not being capable of formatting or writing successfully on 720K disks. If your system can format a 720K disk to 1.44M without punching any extra holes in the disk, it is an immediate alert that the media sensor is not enabled.

Handling Problems Caused by Using Double-Density Disks at High Density

If you attempt to format a 5 1/4-inch, double-density disk at high-density format, you usually will hear several retries from the drive as DOS finds a large amount of bad sectors on the disk. When the format is completed, hundreds of kilobytes in bad sectors usually are reported. Most people would never use this disk. Because the 5 1/4-inch disks are so radically different from one another in terms of magnetic coercivity and media formulation, the double-density disks do not work well carrying a high-density format.

Problems are seen more often with the 3 1/2-inch disks because the double-density disks are not nearly as different from the high-density disks compared to the 5 1/4-inch versions, although they indeed are different. Because the 3 1/2-inch DD and HD disks differ less, however, a double-density, 3 1/2-inch disk usually accepts a high-density format with no bad sectors reported. This acceptance is unfortunate because it causes most users to feel that they are safe in using the disk for data storage.

A 3 1/2-inch, double-density disk with a 1.44M, high-density format initially seems to work with no problem. If you fill this type of double-density disk with 1.44M of data and store it on a shelf, you will notice that eventually the recording degrades, and the data becomes unreadable. Several months might pass before you can detect the degradation, but then it is too late. From talking to hundreds of my clients, I have found that the average "half life" of such a recording is approximately six months from the time the data is written to the time that one or more files suddenly have unreadable sectors. In six months to a year, much of the rest of the disk rapidly degrades until all the data and files have extensive damage. The recording simply destroys itself during this time. I have substantiated this situation with my own testing and my clients' experiences. If the data is reread and rewritten periodically before any degradation is noticeable, then the recording can be "maintained" for longer periods of time before data is lost.

The technical reasons for this degradation were explained earlier in this chapter. In a sense, the disk eventually performs a self-erasure operation. Again, the time frame for damage seems to be approximately six months to a year from the time the data is written. I certainly expect my disks to hold data for more than six months; in fact, data written properly to your disks should be readable many, many years from now.

If you have been using double-density, 3 1/2-inch disks with high-density formats, you are asking for problems. Using these types of disks for backup, for instance, is highly inappropriate! Many people use double-density disks as high-density disks to save money. You should realize that high-density disks are not very expensive anymore; *data-recovery services, however, are very expensive.*

If you have a disk that has been formatted improperly and is developing read problems, the first thing to do is DISKCOPY the disk immediately to another proper-density disk. Then you can survey the damage and make repairs to the new copy. For a more detailed investigation of the subject of data recovery, see *Que's Guide to Data Recovery.*

Handling Track-Width Problems from Writing on 360K Disks with a 1.2M Drive

As discussed earlier in this chapter, the 5 1/4-inch, high-density drives usually write a narrower track than the 5 1/4-inch, double-density drives. Therefore, when you use a high-density drive to update a double-density disk originally formatted or written in a double-density drive, the wider tracks written by the double-density drive are not completely overwritten by the high-density drive. Of course, if the double-density disk is newly formatted and subsequently written in only a high-density drive (although at the proper 360K format), there is no problem with overwrites—that is, until you update the disk with a double-density (wide-track) drive and then update it again with a high-density (narrow-track) drive. In that case, you again have a wider track with a narrow-track update embedded within—but not completely covering it.

You must remember *never* to use a high-density drive to write on a double-density disk previously written by a double-density drive. This procedure makes the disk unreadable by the double-density drive, but usually still readable by the high-density drive. In fact, the best way to recover information from a disk that has been incorrectly overwritten in this manner is to use a high-density disk drive to perform a DISKCOPY operation of the disk to a new, blank, never previously formatted, low-density disk.

Handling Off-Center Disk Clamping

Clamping the disk off-center in the drive has to be absolutely the most frequently encountered cause of problems with floppy drives. In my worldwide troubleshooting seminars, we run the PC systems with the lid off for most of the course. Whenever someone has a problem reading or booting from a floppy disk, I look down at the top of the exposed disk drive on the system while it is spinning to see whether the disk has been clamped by the drive hub in an off-center position. *More often than not, that is the problem.* I know that the disk is clamped off-center because the disk wobbles while it rotates. Ejecting and reinserting the disk so that it is clamped properly usually makes the disk reading or booting problem disappear immediately. This step might solve the problem in most cases, but it is not much help if you have formatted or written a disk in an off-center position. In that case, all you can do is try to DISKCOPY the improperly written disk to another disk and attempt various data-recovery operations on both disks.

I use a technique for inserting floppy disks that has eliminated this problem for me. After inserting a disk into a drive, I always take an extra half-second to wiggle the drive lever or door, first down, and then up, and then down again to clamp the disk rather than simply push the door or lever down once to clamp it. The reason is that the first partial closing of the lever serves to center the disk in its jacket so that the second motion allows the drive hub to clamp the disk properly in a centered position. If I were in charge of training for a large organization, I would make sure that all the basic PC starter classes taught proper disk handling, including insertion and on-center clamping in the drive.

Note that the 3 1/2-inch drives are virtually immune to this type of problem because of the different type of clamping and centering mechanisms they use. Some 5 1/4-inch drives have adopted a more reliable clamping mechanism similar to the 3 1/2-inch drives. Canon makes some of these new 5 1/4-inch drives, used by IBM and Compaq. The newest version used by IBM in some of its PS/2 systems is totally motorized. You merely slide the disk into the drive slot, and the drive grabs the disk and electrically pulls it in and centers it. These drives also include a motorized eject button.

Realigning Misaligned Drives

If your disk drives are misaligned, you will notice that other drives cannot read disks created in your drive, and you might not be able to read disks created in other drives. This situation can be dangerous if you allow it to progress unchecked. If the alignment is bad enough, you probably will notice it first in the incapability to read original application program disks, while still being able to read your own created disks. The Drive Probe program from Accurite for checking the alignment and operation of floppy drives is discussed later in this chapter.

To solve this problem, you can have the drive realigned. I don't always recommend realigning drives because of the low cost of simply replacing the drive compared to aligning one. Also, an unforeseen circumstance catches many people off guard: You might find that your newly aligned drive might not be able to read all your backup or data disks created while the drive was out of alignment. If you replace the misaligned drive with a new one and keep the misaligned drive, you can use it for DISKCOPY purposes to transfer the data to newly formatted disks in the new drive.

Repairing Floppy Drives

Attitudes about repairing floppy drives have changed over the years primarily because of the decreasing cost of drives. When drives were more expensive, people often considered repairing the drive rather than replacing it. With the cost of drives decreasing every year, however, certain labor or parts-intensive repair procedures have become almost as expensive as replacing the drive with a new one.

Because of cost considerations, repairing floppy drives usually is limited to cleaning the drive and heads and lubricating the mechanical mechanisms. On drives that have a speed adjustment, adjusting the speed to within the proper operating range also is common. Note that most newer half-height drives and virtually all 3 1/2-inch drives do not have an adjustment for speed. These drives use a circuit that automatically sets the speed at the required level and compensates for variations with a feedback loop. If such an auto-taching drive is off in speed, the reason usually is that the circuit failed. Replacement of the drive usually is necessary.

Cleaning Floppy Drives

Sometimes read and write problems are caused by dirty drive heads. Cleaning a drive is easy; you can proceed in two ways. In one method, you use one of the simple head-cleaning kits available from computer- or office-supply stores. These devices are easy to operate and don't require the system unit to be open for access to the drive. The other method is the manual method: You use a cleaning swab with a liquid such as pure alcohol, Freon, or trichloroethane. With this method, you must open the system unit to expose the drive and, in many cases (especially in earlier full-height drives), also remove and partially disassemble the drive. The manual method can result in a better overall job, but usually the work required is not worth the difference.

The cleaning kits come in two styles: The wet type uses a liquid squirted on a cleaning disk to wash off the heads; the dry kit relies on abrasive material on the cleaning disk to remove head deposits. I recommend that you never use the dry drive-cleaning kits. Always use a wet system in which a liquid solution is applied to the cleaning disk. The dry disks can prematurely wear the heads if used improperly or too often; wet systems are very safe to use.

The manual drive-cleaning method requires that you have physical access to the heads, in order to swab them manually with a lint-free foam swab soaked in a cleaning solution. This method requires some level of expertise: Simply jabbing at the heads incorrectly with a cleaning swab might knock the drive heads out of alignment. You must use a careful in-and-out motion, and lightly swab the heads. No side-to-side motion (relative to the way the heads travel) should be used; this motion can snag a head and knock it out of alignment. Because of the difficulty and danger of this manual cleaning, for most applications I recommend a simple wet-disk cleaning kit because it is the easiest and safest method.

One question that comes up repeatedly in my seminars is "How often should you clean a disk drive?" Only you can answer that question. What type of environment is the system in? Do you smoke cigarettes near the system? If so, cleaning would be required more often. Usually, a safe rule of thumb is to clean drives about once a year if the system is in a clean office environment in which no smoke or other particulate matter is in the air. In a heavy-smoking environment, you might have to clean every six months or perhaps even more often. In dirty industrial environments, you might have to clean every month or so. Your own experience is your guide in this matter. If DOS reports drive errors in the system by displaying the familiar DOS Abort, Retry, Ignore prompt, you should clean your drive to try to solve the problem. If cleaning does solve the problem, you probably should step up the interval between preventive-maintenance cleanings.

In some cases, you might want to place a (very small) amount of lubricant on the door mechanism or other mechanical contact points inside the drive. *Do not use oil;* use a pure silicone lubricant. Oil collects dust rapidly after you apply it and usually causes the oiled mechanism to gum up later. Silicone does not attract dust in the same manner and can be used safely. Use very small amounts of silicone; do not drip or spray silicone inside the drive. You must make sure that the lubricant is applied only to the part that needs it. If the lubricant gets all over the inside of the drive, it may cause unnecessary problems.

Setting the Floppy Drive Speed Adjustment

Most older 5 1/4-inch floppy disk drives, especially full-height drives, have a small variable resistor used to adjust the drive's rotational speed. In particular, the Tandon and CDC full-height drives used by IBM in the PC and XT systems have this adjustment. The location of this variable resistor is described in the hardware-maintenance reference manuals IBM sells for these systems.

If you have a Tandon drive, you make the adjustment through a small, brass screw on a variable resistor mounted on the motor control board, attached to the rear of the drive (see fig. 13.16). The resistor is usually blue, and the screw is brass. To gauge the speed, you can use a program such as Drive Probe, by Accurite; IBM's Advanced Diagnostics, supplied with the hardware-maintenance and service manual; or even a purely mechanical method that relies on a fluorescent light to act as a strobe.

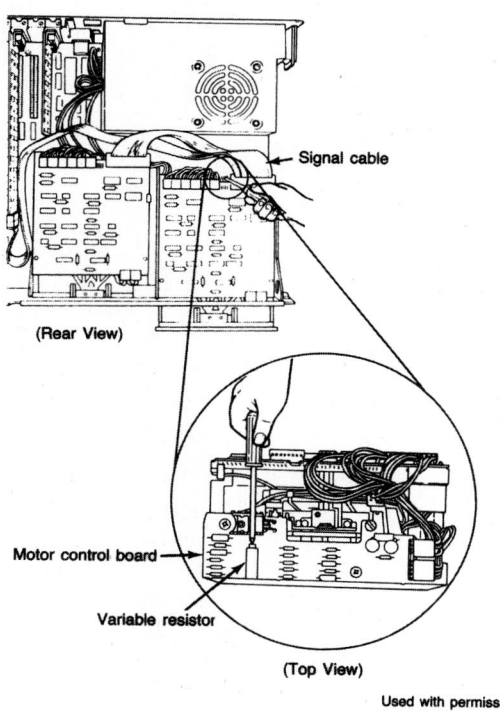

Signal cable

(Rear View)

Motor control board

Variable resistor

(Top View)

Used with permission
from IBM Corporation.

Fig. 13.16
The drive-speed adjustment for the Tandom TM-100 series drive.

The software methods use a disk to evaluate the running speed of the drive. Usually, you turn the screw until the speed reads correctly (300 RPM) according to the program you use. The mechanical method requires you to remove the drive from the system and place it upside down on a bench. Sometimes the drive is set sideways on the power supply so that the drive's case is grounded. Then the underside of the drive is illuminated by a standard fluorescent light. The light acts as a strobe that flashes 60 times per second because of the cycling speed of the AC line current. On the bottom of the drive spindle are strobe marks for 50 Hz and 60 Hz (see fig. 13.17). Because 60 Hz power is used in the United States, you should use the 60 Hz marks. The 50 Hz marks are used for (50 cycle) European power. While the drive is running, turn the small screw until the strobe marks appear to be stationary, much like the "wagon wheel effect" you see in old western movies. When the marks are completely stationary as viewed under the light, the drive's rotation speed is correct.

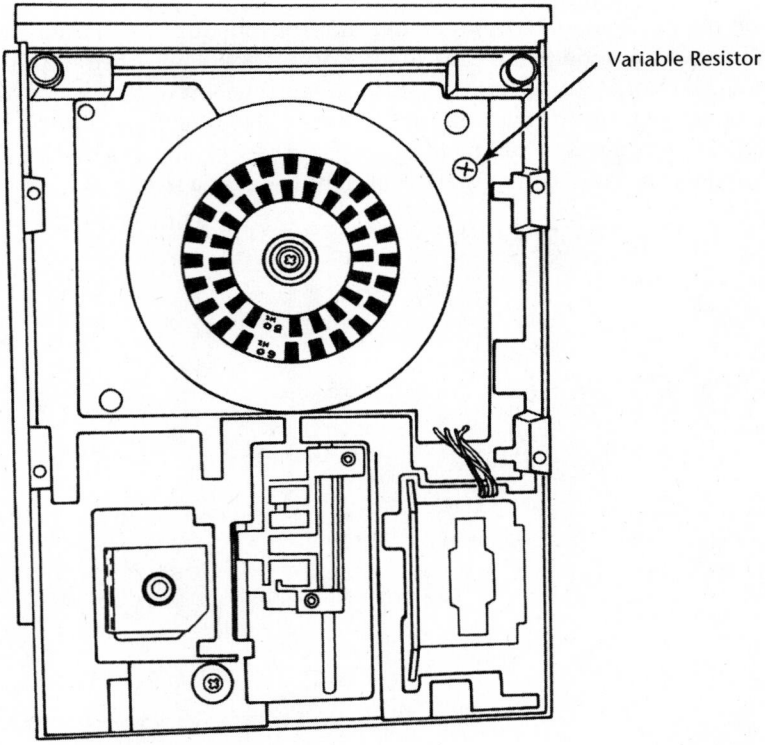

Variable Resistor

Fig. 13.17
Strobe marks and speed adjustment on a typical half-height drive.

With CDC drives, the adjustment resistor is mounted on the logic board, which is on top of the drive. The small, brass screw to the left of the board is the one you want. Other drives also might have an adjustment. The best way to tell whether a drive has a speed adjustment is to look for the telltale strobe marks on the spindle of the drive. If the marks are there, the drive probably has an adjustment; if the marks are not there, the drive probably has an automatic speed circuit and requires no adjustment. The OEM manual for the drive has information about all these adjustments (if any) and where you make them.

Aligning Floppy Disk Drives

Aligning disk drives is usually no longer done because of the high relative cost. To align a drive properly requires access to an oscilloscope (for about $500), a special analog-alignment disk ($75), and the OEM service manual for the drive; also, you must spend half an hour to an hour aligning the drive.

A new program, Drive Probe, by Accurite, uses special test disks called High-Resolution Diagnostic (HRD) disks. These disks are as accurate as the analog alignment disks (AAD) and eliminate the need for an oscilloscope to align a drive. You cannot use any program that relies on the older Digital Diagnostic Disk (DDD) or Spiral format test disks because they are not accurate enough to use to align a drive. The Drive Probe and HRD system can make an alignment more cost-effective than before, but it is still a labor-intensive operation. Figure 13.18 shows the main menu of the Accurite Drive Probe program, which offers various functions, including fully automatic or manual drive testing.

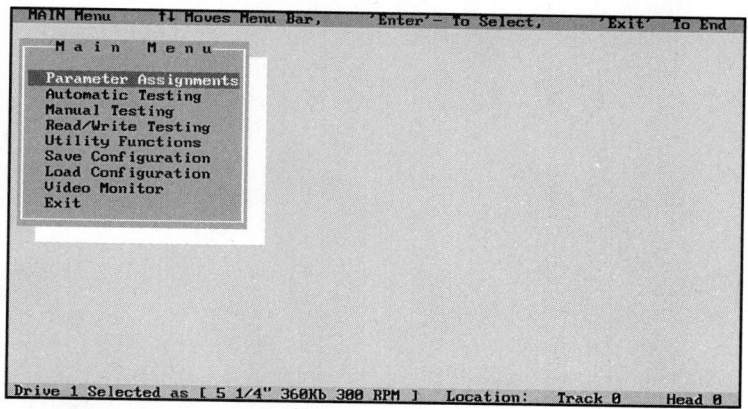

Fig. 13.18
The main menu screen from Accurite Drive Probe.

With the price of most types of floppy drives hovering at or below the $75 mark, aligning drives usually is not a cost-justified alternative to replacement. One exception exists. In a high-volume situation, drive alignment might pay off. Another alternative is to investigate local organizations that perform drive alignments, usually for $25 to $50. Weigh this cost against the replacement cost and age of the drive. I have purchased new 360K floppy drives for *as low as $30*. At these prices, alignment is no longer a viable option.

Summary

This chapter examined floppy drives and floppy media (disks) in great detail. One of the most important things to do when installing a drive in a system is to make sure that the drive is configured correctly. This chapter discussed drive configuration also. With this information, installing drives correctly should be an easy task.

This chapter also discussed many problems that confound floppy drive users, such as reading and writing double-density disks with high-density drives. It discussed thoroughly the differences between high- and double-density drives and disks, and mentioned the consequences of using the wrong type of disk in the wrong drive. Simple drive servicing, such as cleaning and speed adjustment, were explained so that these operations can be performed in-house. After reading this chapter, you should know much about floppy drives. Chapter 14 discusses hard disk drives and controllers.

Chapter 14

Hard Disk Drives and Controllers

To most users, the hard disk drive is the most important, yet most mysterious, part of a computer system. A *hard disk drive* is a sealed unit that holds the data in a system. When the hard disk fails, the consequences usually are very serious. To maintain, service, and expand a PC system properly, you must fully understand the hard disk unit.

Most computer users want to know how hard disk drives work and what to do when a problem occurs. Few books about hard disks, however, cover the details necessary for the PC technician or sophisticated user. This chapter corrects that situation.

This chapter thoroughly describes the hard disk, from the drives to the cables and controllers that run them. In particular, the chapter examines the construction and operation of a hard disk drive. You will learn about the various disk interfaces that you can select, and the shortcomings and strengths of each type, as well as the procedures for configuring, setting up, and installing various drives. The chapter introduces the basic procedures necessary to integrate a hard disk drive into a PC system.

Definition of a Hard Disk

A hard disk drive contains rigid, disc-shaped platters usually constructed of aluminum or glass. Unlike floppy disks, the platters cannot bend or flex—hence the term *hard disk*. In most hard disk drives, the platters cannot be removed; for that reason, IBM calls them *fixed disk drives*. Although removable-platter hard disk drives are available, their non-standard nature, higher cost, and reliability problems make them unpopular.

Hard disk drives often are called *Winchester drives*. This term dates back to the 1960s, when IBM developed a high-speed hard disk drive that had 30MB of fixed-platter storage and 30MB of removable-platter storage. The drive had platters that spun at high speeds and heads that floated over the platters while they spun in a sealed environment. That drive, the *30-30 drive*, soon received the nickname "Winchester," after the famous

Winchester 30-30 rifle. After that time, drives that used a high-speed spinning platter with a floating head also became known as Winchester drives. The term has no technical or scientific meaning; it is a slang term, synonymous with *hard disk*.

Hard Drive Advancements

In the 10 or more years that hard disks have commonly been used in PC systems, they have undergone tremendous changes. To give you an idea of how far hard drives have come in that time, the following are some of the most profound changes in PC hard disk storage:

- Maximum storage capacities have increased from the 10MB 5.25-inch full-height drives available in 1982 to 3GB or more for drives in that form factor and well over 2GB for small 3.5-inch half-height drives.

- Data transfer rates have increased from 102KB per second for the original IBM XT in 1983 to nearly 10MB per second for some of the fastest drives today.

- Average seek times have decreased from more than 85 ms for the 10MB XT hard disk in 1983 to fewer than 8 ms for some of the fastest drives today.

- In 1982, a 10MB drive cost more than $1,500 ($150 per megabyte). Today, the cost of hard drives has dropped to less than $1 per megabyte.

Areal Density

Areal density has been used as a primary technology-growth-rate indicator for the hard disk drive industry. *Areal density* is defined as the product of the linear bits per inch (BPI), measured along the length of the tracks around the disk, multiplied by the number of tracks per inch (TPI) measured radially on the disk. The results are expressed in units of Mb/sq-inch and are used as a measure of efficiency in drive recording technology. Current high-end drives record at areal densities of about 160 Megabits per square inch (Mb/sq-inch). Prototype models with densities as high as 1 Gb/sq-inch have been constructed, allowing for capacities of more than 1GB on a single 3.5-inch platter.

Areal density (and, therefore, drive capacity) has been doubling approximately every two to three years, and disk drives are likely to reach areal densities of 10 Gb/sq-inch before the year 2000. A drive built with this technology would be capable of storing 1GB of data on a single 1.3-inch platter, and the entire drive would be about the size of a large wristwatch. New media and head technologies, such as ceramic or glass platters and fluid suspension, are being developed to support these higher areal densities. Manufacturing drive heads and disks to operate at closer tolerances is the primary challenge in achieving higher densities.

It seems almost incredible that computer technology improves by doubling performance or capacity every two to three years. If only other industries could match that growth and improvement rate!

Hard Disk Drive Operation

The basic physical operation of a hard disk drive is similar to that of a floppy disk drive: a hard drive uses spinning disks with heads that move over the disks and store data in tracks and sectors. In many other ways, however, hard disk drives are different from floppy disk drives.

Hard disks usually have multiple platters, each with two sides on which data can be stored. Most drives have at least two or three platters, resulting in four or six sides, and some drives have up to 11 platters. The identically positioned tracks on each side of every platter together make up a *cylinder*. A hard disk drive has one head per platter side, and all the heads are mounted on a common carrier device, or *rack*. The heads move in and out across the disk in unison; they cannot move independently because they are mounted on the same rack.

Hard disks operate much faster than floppy drives. Most hard disks spin at 3,600 rpm—approximately 10 times faster than a floppy drive. Until recently, 3,600 rpm was pretty much a constant among hard drives. Now, however, quite a few hard drives spin even faster. One drive that I have, for example, spins at 4,318 rpm; others spin as fast as 5,600, 6,400, and even 7,200 rpm. High rotational speed combined with a fast head-positioning mechanism and more sectors per track make one hard disk faster than another, and all these features combine to make hard drives much faster than floppy drives in storing and retrieving data.

The heads in a hard disk do not (and should not!) touch the platters during normal operation. When the heads are powered off, however, they land on the platters as they stop spinning. While the drive is on, a cushion of air keeps each head suspended a short distance above or below the platter. If the cushion is disturbed by a particle of dust or a shock, the head may come into contact with the platter spinning at full speed. When contact with the spinning platters is forceful enough to do damage, the event is called a *head crash*. The result of a head crash may be anything from a few lost bytes of data to a totally trashed drive. Most drives have special lubricants on the platters and hardened surfaces that can withstand the daily "takeoffs and landings" as well as more severe abuse.

Because the platter assemblies are sealed and nonremovable, track densities can be very high. Many drives have 3,000 or more tracks per inch of media. Head Disk Assemblies (HDAs), which contain the platters, are assembled and sealed in clean rooms under absolutely sanitary conditions. Because few companies repair HDAs, repair or replacement of items inside a sealed HDA can be expensive. Every hard disk ever made will fail eventually. The only questions are when the hard disk will fail and whether your data is backed up.

Many PC users think that hard disks are fragile, and generally, they are one of the most fragile components in your PC. In my weekly PC Hardware and Troubleshooting or Data Recovery seminars, however, I have run various hard disks for days with the lids off, and have even removed and installed the covers while the drives were operating. Those drives continue to store data perfectly to this day with the lids either on or off.

Of course, I do not recommend that you try this test with your own drives; neither would I use it on my larger, more expensive drives.

The Ultimate Hard Disk Drive Analogy!

I'm sure that you have heard the traditional analogy that compares the interaction of the head and media in a typical hard disk as being similar in scale to a 747 flying a few feet off the ground at cruising speed (500-plus mph). I have heard this analogy used over and over again for years, and I've even used it in my seminars many times without checking to see whether the analogy is technically accurate with respect to modern hard drives.

One highly inaccurate aspect of the 747 analogy has always bothered me: the use of an airplane of any type to describe the head-and-platter interaction. This analogy implies that the heads fly very low over the surface of the disk—but technically, this is not true. The heads do not fly at all, in the traditional aerodynamic sense; instead, they float on a cushion of air that's being dragged around by the platters. A much better analogy would use a hovercraft instead of an airplane; the action of a hovercraft much more closely emulates the action of the heads in a hard disk drive. Like a hovercraft, the drive heads rely somewhat on the shape of the bottom of the head to capture and control the cushion of air that keeps them floating over the disk. By nature, the cushion of air on which the heads float forms only in very close proximity to the platter and is called an *air bearing* by the disk drive industry.

I thought it was time to come up with a new analogy that more correctly describes the dimensions and speeds at which a hard disk operates today. I looked up the specifications on a specific hard disk drive, and then equally magnified and rescaled all the dimensions involved to make the head floating height equal to 1 inch. For my example, I used a Seagate model ST-12550N Barracuda 2 drive, which is a 2GB (formatted capacity), 3.5-inch SCSI-2 drive. In fact, I intend to install this very drive in the P75 Portable on which I am writing this book, replacing the current 1.2GB drive. Table 14.1 shows the specifications of this drive, as listed in the technical documentation:

Table 14.1 Seagate ST-12550N Barracuda 2 2G, 3.5-Inch, SCSI-2 Drive Specifications		
Specification	**Value**	**Unit of Measure**
Linear density	52,187	Bits per inch (bpi)
Bit spacing	19.16	micro-inches (µ-in)
Track density	3,047	Tracks per inch (tpi)
Track spacing	328.19	micro-inches (µ-in)
Total tracks	2,707	tracks
Rotational speed	7,200	Revolutions per minute (rpm)
Average head linear speed	53.55	Miles per hour (mph)
Head slider length	0.08	inches
Head slider height	0.02	inches
Head floating height	5	micro-inches (µ-in)
Average seek time	8	milliseconds (ms)

By interpreting these specifications, you can see that in this drive. the heads are about 0.08 inch long and 0.02 inch high. The heads float on a cushion of air about 5 micro-inches (millionths of an inch) from the surface of the disk while traveling at an average speed of 53.55 mph (figuring an average track diameter of 2.5 inches). These heads read and write individual bits spaced only 19.16 micro-inches apart on tracks separated by only 328.19 micro-inches. The heads can move from one track to any other in only 8 ms during an average seek operation.

To create my new analogy, I simply magnified the scale to make the floating height equal to 1 inch. Because 1 inch is 200,000 times greater than 5 micro-inches, I scaled up everything else by the same amount.

Are you ready?

The heads of this "typical" hard disk, magnified to such a scale, would be more than 1,300 feet long and 300 feet high (about the size of the Sears Tower, lying sideways!), traveling at a speed of more than 10.7 million mph(178,500 miles per second!) only 1 inch above the ground, reading data bits spaced a mere 3.83 inches apart on tracks separated by only 5.47 feet. Additionally, each skyscraper-size head could move sideways to any track within a distance of 2.8 miles in an average 8 ms, resulting in an average sideways velocity of about 1,402 mph!

The speed of this imaginary head is difficult to comprehend, so I'll elaborate. The diameter of the Earth at the equator is 7,926 miles, which means a circumference of 24,900 miles. At 178,500 miles per second, this imaginary head would circle the Earth more than seven times per second!

This analogy should give you a new appreciation of the technological marvel that the modern hard disk drive actually represents. It makes the 747 analogy look rather pathetic (not to mention totally inaccurate), doesn't it?

Magnetic Data Storage

Learning how magnetic data storage works will help you develop a feel for the way that your disk drives operate and can improve the way that you work with disk drives and disks.

Nearly all disk drives in personal computer systems operate on magnetic principles. Purely optical disk drives often are used as a secondary form of storage, but the computer to which they are connected is likely to use a magnetic storage medium for primary disk storage. Due to the high performance and density capabilities of magnetic storage, optical disk drives and media probably never will totally replace magnetic storage in PC systems.

Magnetic drives, such as floppy disk drives and hard disk drives, operate by using *electromagnetism*. This basic principle of physics states that as an electric current flows through a conductor, a magnetic field is generated around the conductor. This magnetic field then can influence magnetic material in the field. When the direction of the flow of electric current is reversed, the magnetic field's polarity also is reversed. An electric motor uses electromagnetism to exert pushing and pulling forces on magnets attached to a rotating shaft.

Another effect of electromagnetism is that if a conductor is passed through a changing magnetic field, an electrical current is generated. As the polarity of the magnetic field changes, so does the direction of the electric current flow. For example, a type of electrical generator used in automobiles, called an *alternator*, operates by rotating electromagnets past coils of wire conductors in which large amounts of electrical current can be induced. The two-way operation of electromagnetism makes it possible to record data on a disk and read that data back later.

The read/write heads in your disk drives (both floppy and hard disks) are U-shaped pieces of conductive material. This U-shaped object is wrapped with coils of wire, through which an electric current can flow. When the disk drive logic passes a current through these coils, it generates a magnetic field in the drive head. When the polarity of the electric current is reversed, the polarity of the field that is generated also changes. In essence, the heads are electromagnets whose voltage can be switched in polarity very quickly.

When a magnetic field is generated in the head, the field jumps the gap at the end of the U-shaped head. Because a magnetic field passes through a conductor much more easily than through the air, the field bends outward through the medium and actually uses the disk media directly below it as the path of least resistance to the other side of the gap. As the field passes through the media directly under the gap, it polarizes the magnetic particles through which it passes so that they are aligned with the field. The field's polarity and, therefore, the polarity of the magnetic media are based on the direction of the flow of electric current through the coils.

The disk consists of some form of substrate material (such as Mylar for floppy disks or aluminum or glass for hard disks) on which a layer of magnetizable material has been deposited. This material usually is a form of iron oxide with various other elements added. The polarities of the magnetic fields of the individual magnetic particles on an erased disk normally are in a state of random disarray. Because the fields of the individual particles point in random directions, each tiny magnetic field is canceled by one that points in the opposite direction, for a total effect of no observable or cumulative field polarity.

Particles in the area below the head gap are aligned in the same direction as the field emanating from the gap. When the individual magnetic domains are in alignment, they no longer cancel one another, and an observable magnetic field exists in that region of the disk. This local field is generated by the many magnetic particles that now are operating as a team to produce a detectable cumulative field with a unified direction. The term *flux* describes a magnetic field that has a specific direction.

As the disk surface rotates below the drive head, the head can lay a magnetic flux over a region of the disk. When the electric-current flow through the coils in the head is reversed, so is the magnetic-field polarity in the head gap. This reversal also causes the polarity of the flux being placed on the disk to reverse. The *flux reversal* or *flux transition* is a change in polarity of the alignment of magnetic particles on the disk surface.

A drive head places flux reversals on a disk to record data. For each data bit (or bits) written, a pattern of flux reversals is placed on the disk in specific areas known as bit or transition cells. A *bit cell* or *transition cell* is a specific area of the disk controlled by the time and rotational speed in which flux reversals are placed by a drive head. The particular pattern of flux reversals within the transition cells used to store a given data bit or bits is called the *encoding method*. The drive logic or controller takes the data to be stored and encodes it as a series of flux reversals over a period of time, according to the encoding method used. Modified Frequency Modulation (MFM) and Run Length Limited (RLL) are popular encoding methods. All floppy disk drives use the MFM scheme. Hard disks use MFM or several variations of RLL encoding methods. These encoding methods are described in more detail later in this chapter.

During the write process, voltage is applied to the head, and as the polarity of this voltage changes, the polarity of the magnetic field being recorded also changes. The flux transitions are written precisely at the points where the recording polarity changes. Strange as it may seem, during the read process, a head does not output exactly the same signal that was written; instead, the head generates a voltage pulse or spike only when it crosses a flux transition. When the transition is from positive to negative, the pulse that the head would detect is negative voltage. When the transition changes from negative to positive, the pulse would be a positive voltage spike.

In essence, while reading the disk the head becomes a flux transition detector, emitting voltage pulses whenever it crosses a transition. Areas of no transition generate no pulse. Figure 14.1 shows the relationship between the read and write waveforms and the flux transitions recorded on a disk.

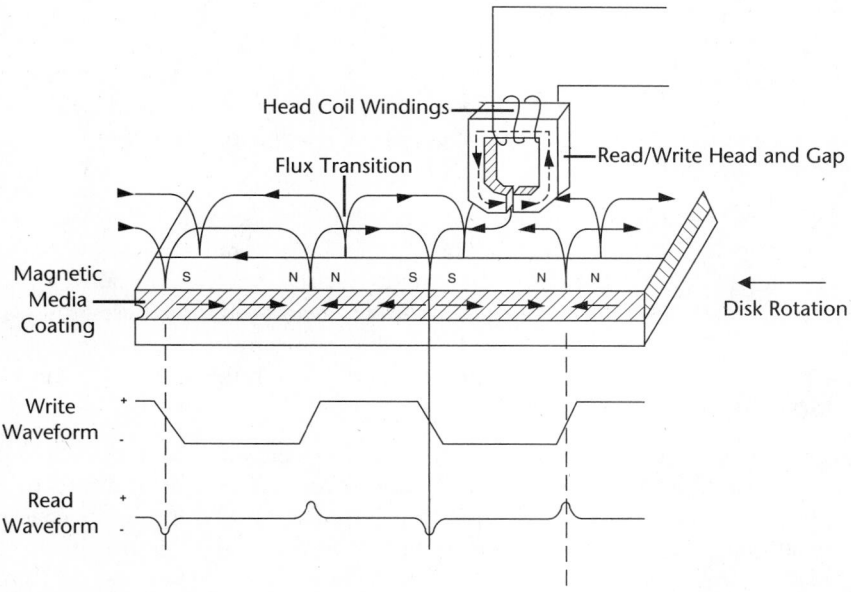

Fig. 14.1
Magnetic write and read processes.

You can think of the write pattern as being a square waveform that is at a positive or negative voltage level and that continuously polarizes the disk media in one direction or another. Where the waveform transitions go from positive to negative voltage, or vice versa, the magnetic flux on the disk also changes polarity. During a read, the head senses the flux transitions and outputs a pulsed waveform with a signal of zero volts unless a positive or negative transition is being detected. Pulses appear only when flux transitions occur on the disk media. By knowing the clock timing used, the drive or controller circuitry can determine whether a pulse (and therefore a flux transition) exists within a given transition cell.

The electrical pulse currents generated in the head while it is passing over a disk in read mode are very weak and can contain significant noise. Sensitive electronics in the drive and controller assembly then can amplify the signal above the noise level and decode the train of weak pulse currents back into data that is (theoretically) identical to the data originally recorded.

So as you now can see, disks are both recorded and read by means of basic electromagnetic principles. Data is recorded on a disk by passing electrical currents through an electromagnet (the drive head) that generates a magnetic field stored on the disk. Data on a disk is read by passing the head back over the surface of the disk; as the head encounters changes in the stored magnetic field, it generates a weak electrical current that indicates the presence or absence of flux transitions in the originally recorded signal.

Data Encoding Schemes

Magnetic media essentially is an analog storage medium. The data that we store on it, however, is digital information—that is, ones and zeros. When digital information is applied to a magnetic recording head, the head creates magnetic domains on the disk media with specific polarities. When a positive current is applied to the write head, the magnetic domains are polarized in one direction; when negative voltage is applied, the magnetic domains are polarized in the opposite direction. When the digital waveform that is recorded switches from a positive to a negative voltage, the polarity of the magnetic domains is reversed.

During a readback, the head actually generates no voltage signal when it encounters a group of magnetic domains with the same polarity, but it generates a voltage pulse every time it detects a switch in polarity. These magnetic-polarity switches are called *flux reversals*. Each flux reversal generates a voltage pulse in the read head; it is these pulses that the drive detects when reading data. A read head does not generate the same waveform that was written; instead, it generates a series of pulses, each pulse appearing where a magnetic flux transition has occurred.

To optimize the placement of pulses during magnetic storage, the raw digital input data is passed through a device called an *encoder/decoder (Endec),* which converts the raw binary information to a waveform that is more concerned with the optimum placement of the flux transitions (pulses). During a read operation, the Endec reverses the process and decodes the pulse train back into the original binary data. Over the years, several different schemes for encoding data in this manner have been developed; some are better or more efficient than others.

In any consideration of binary information, the use of timing is important. When interpreting a read or write waveform, the timing of each voltage transition event is critical. If the timing is off, a given voltage transition may be recognized at the wrong time, and bits may be missed, added, or simply misinterpreted. To ensure that the timing is precise, the transmitting and receiving devices must be in sync. This synchronization can be accomplished by adding a separate line for timing, called a *clock signal*, between the two devices. The clock and data signals also can be combined and then transmitted on a single line. This combination of clock and data is used in most magnetic data encoding schemes.

When the clock information is added in with the data, timing accuracy in interpreting the individual bit cells is ensured between any two devices. A *bit cell* is a window in time inside which a voltage transition will be placed to signify a bit. Clock timing is used to determine the start and end of each bit cell. Each bit cell is bounded by two clock cells where the clock transitions can be sent. First there is a clock transition cell, and then the data transition cell, and finally the clock transition cell for the data that follows. By sending clock information along with the data, the clocks will remain in sync, even if a long string of 0 bits are transmitted. Unfortunately, all the transition cells that are used solely for clocking take up space on the media that otherwise could be used for data.

Because the number of flux transitions that can be recorded on a particular medium is limited by the disk media and head technology, disk drive engineers have been trying various ways of encoding the data into a minimum number of flux reversals, taking into consideration the fact that some flux reversals, used solely for clocking, are required. This method permits maximum use of a given drive hardware technology.

Although various encoding schemes have been tried, only a few are popular today. Over the years, these three basic types have been the most popular:

■ Frequency Modulation (FM)

■ Modified Frequency Modulation (MFM)

■ Run Length Limited (RLL)

The following section examines these codes, discussing how they work, where they have been used, and any advantages or disadvantages that apply to them.

FM Encoding. One of the earliest techniques for encoding data for magnetic storage is called *Frequency Modulation* (FM) encoding. This encoding scheme, sometimes called *Single Density* encoding, was used in the earliest floppy disk drives that were installed in PC systems. The original Osborne portable computer, for example, used these Single Density floppy drives, which stored about 80K of data on a single disk. Although it was popular until the late 70s, FM encoding no longer is used today.

FM represents one of the simplest ways to encode zeros and ones on a magnetic surface. In each bit cell, a flux reversal is recorded to indicate a 1 bit, and no flux reversal is recorded to indicate a 0 bit. With no other modifications, problems would occur if you were recording a long series of zeros, in which case no flux transitions would be recorded. If no transitions occurred for a long period, the controller easily could get out of sync with the drive, resulting in a possible misinterpretation of the data. To keep the devices in sync, a clock signal is written onto the drive along with the data.

In FM encoding, each bit actually requires two transition cells. A 1 bit is recorded as a clock flux reversal followed by a data flux reversal, which the drive simply would see as two consecutive flux reversals. A 0 bit also is recorded in two transition cells. Only the clock cell, however, contains a flux reversal; the data cell is empty (no reversal). Whether you are recording a 1 or a 0, the initial flux reversal represents the clock signal, and the second transition cell would carry a reversal only if the data were a 1 bit.

Although this method is simple and inexpensive, it has one major disadvantage: each data bit requires two flux reversals, which reduces potential disk capacity by half. Table 14.2 shows how each bit cell is encoded.

Table 14.2   FM Data to Flux Transition Encoding

Data Bit Value	Flux Encoding
1	TT
0	TN

T = flux transition
N = no flux transition

MFM Encoding. *Modified Frequency Modulation* (MFM) encoding was devised to reduce the number of flux reversals used in the original FM encoding scheme and, therefore, to pack more data onto the disk. In MFM encoding, the use of the clock transition cells is minimized, leaving more room for the data. Clock transitions are recorded only if a stored 0 bit is preceded by another 0 bit; in all other cases, a clock transition is not required. Because the use of the clock transitions has been minimized, the actual clock frequency can be doubled from FM encoding, resulting in twice as many data bits being stored in the same number of flux transitions as in FM.

Because it is twice as efficient as FM encoding, MFM encoding also has been called *Double Density* recording. MFM is used in virtually all PC floppy drives today and was used in nearly all PC hard disks for a number of years. Today, most hard disks use RLL (Run Length Limited) encoding, which provides even greater efficiency than MFM.

Because MFM encoding places twice as many data bits in the same number of flux reversals as FM, the clock speed of the data is doubled, so that the drive actually sees the same number of total flux reversals as with FM. This doubling means that data is read and written at twice the speed in MFM encoding, even though the drive sees the flux reversals arriving at the same frequency as in FM. This method allows existing drive technology to store twice the data and deliver it twice as fast.

The only caveat is that MFM encoding requires improved disk controller and drive circuitry, because the timing of the flux reversals must be more precise than in FM. As it turned out, these improvements were not difficult to achieve, and MFM encoding became the most popular encoding scheme for a long period.

Table 14.3 shows the data bit to flux reversal translation in MFM encoding:

Table 14.3 MFM Data to Flux Transition Encoding	
Data Bit Value	**Flux Encoding**
1	NT
0 preceded by 0	TN
0 preceded by 1	NN

T = flux transition
N = no flux transition

RLL Encoding. Today's most popular encoding scheme, called *RLL (Run Length Limited)*, packs up to 50 percent more information on a given disk than even MFM does and three times as much information as FM. In RLL encoding, groups of bits are taken as a unit and combined to generate specific patterns of flux reversals. By combining the clock and data in these patterns, the clock rate can be further increased while maintaining the same basic distance between the flux transitions on the disk. By optimizing the code to limit the minimum and maximum distance between two flux transitions, the clock rate (and, therefore, storage density) can be increased—typically by three times over FM and one and a half times over MFM encoding.

IBM invented RLL encoding and first used the method in many of its mainframe disk drives. During the late 1980s, the PC hard disk industry began using RLL encoding schemes to increase the storage capabilities of PC hard disks. Today, virtually every drive on the market uses some form of RLL encoding.

Instead of encoding a single bit, RLL normally encodes a group of data bits at a time. The term *Run Length Limited* is derived from the two primary specifications of these codes, which is the minimum number (the run length) and maximum number (the run limit) of transition cells allowed between two actual flux transitions. Several schemes can be achieved by changing the length and limit parameters, but only two have achieved any real popularity: RLL 2,7 and RLL 1,7.

Even FM and MFM encoding can be expressed as a form of RLL. FM can be called RLL 0,1, because there can be as few as zero and as many as one transition cell separating two flux transitions. MFM can be called RLL 1,3, because as few as one and as many as three transition cells can separate two flux transitions. Although these codes can be expressed in RLL form, it is not common to do so.

RLL 2,7 initially was the most popular RLL variation because it offers a high density ratio (1.5 times that of MFM) with a transition detection window the same relative size as that in MFM. This method allows for high storage density with fairly good reliability. In very high-capacity drives, however, RLL 2,7 did not prove to be reliable enough. Most of today's highest-capacity drives use RLL 1,7 encoding, which offers a density ratio 1.27 times that of MFM and a larger transition detection window relative to MFM. Compared with RLL 2,7 the storage density is a little less, but the reliability is much higher. Because of the larger relative window size within which a transition can be detected, RLL 1,7 is a more forgiving and more reliable code, which is required when media and head technology are being pushed to their limits. With the greater need for reliability in high-capacity disk storage, it seems that RLL 1,7 soon will be the most popular code in use.

Another little-used RLL variation called *RLL 3,9*—sometimes called *ARLL (Advanced RLL)*—allowed an even higher density ration than RLL 2,7. Unfortunately, reliability suffered too greatly under the RLL 3,9 scheme; the method was used by only a few controller companies that have all but disappeared.

It is difficult to understand how RLL codes work without looking at an example. Because RLL 2,7 still is the most popular form of RLL encoding, I will use it as an example. Even within a given RLL variation such as RLL 2,7 or 1,7, many different tables can be constructed to show what groups of bits are encoded as what sets of flux transitions. For RLL 2,7 specifically, thousands of different translation tables could be constructed, but for my examples, I will use the encoder/decoder (Endec) table used by IBM because it is the most popular variation that you will find.

According to the IBM conversion tables, specific groups of data bits 2, 3, and 4 bits long are translated into strings of flux transitions 4, 6, and 8 transition cells long, respectively. The selected transitions coded for a particular bit sequence are designed to ensure that flux transitions do not occur too close together or too far apart.

It is necessary to limit how close two flux transitions can be because of the basically fixed resolution capabilities of the head and disk media. Limiting how far apart these transitions can be ensures that the clocks in the devices remain in sync.

Table 14.4 shows the IBM-developed encoding scheme for 2,7 RLL.

Table 14.4	RLL 2,7 (IBM Endec) Data to Flux Transition Encoding
Data Bit Values	**Flux Encoding**
10	NTNN
11	TNNN
000	NNNTNN
010	TNNTNN
011	NNTNNN
0010	NNTNNTNN
0011	NNNNTNNN

T = flux transition
N = no flux transition

In studying this table, you may think that encoding a byte such as 00000001b would be impossible because no combinations of data bit groups fit this byte. Encoding this type of byte is not a problem, however, because the controller does not transmit individual bytes; instead, the controller sends whole sectors, making it possible to encode such a byte simply by including some of the bits in the following byte. The only real problem occurs in the last byte of a sector if additional bits are needed to complete the final group sequence. In these cases, the encoder/decoder (Endec) in the controller simply adds excess bits to the end of the last byte. These excess bits are truncated during any reads so that the last byte always is correctly decoded.

Encoding Scheme Comparisons

Figure 14.2 shows an example of the waveform written to store an *X* ASCII character on a hard disk drive under three different encoding schemes.

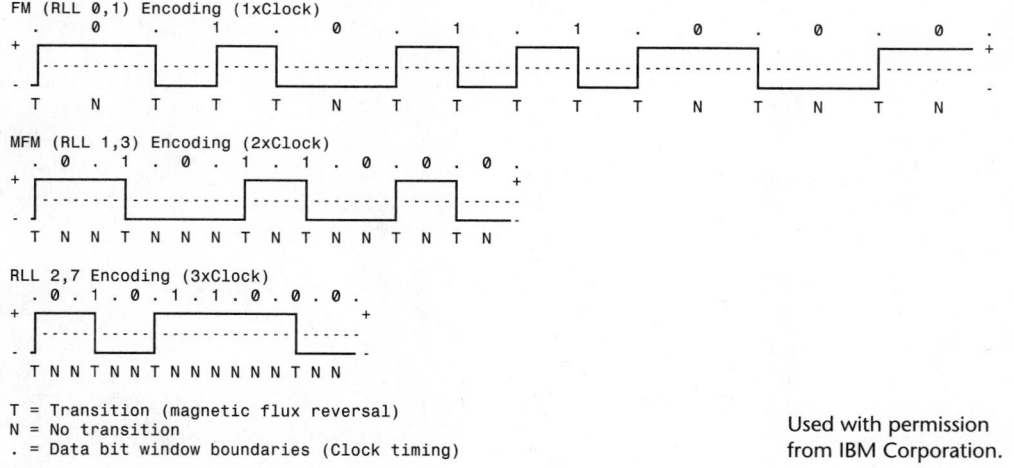

Fig. 14.2

ASCII *X* write waveforms using FM, MFM, and RLL 2,7 encoding.

In each of these encoding-scheme examples, the top line shows the individual data bits (01011000b) in their bit cells separated in time by the clock signal, which is shown as a period (.). Below that line is the actual write waveform, showing the positive and negative voltages as well as voltage transitions that result in the recording of flux transitions. The bottom line shows the transition cells, with T representing a transition cell that contains a flux transition and N representing a transition cell that is empty (no flux transition).

The FM encoding example is easy to explain. Each bit cell has two transition cells: one for the clock information and one for the data itself. All the clock transition cells contain flux transitions, and the data transition cells contain a flux transition only if the data is a 1 bit. No transition at all is used to represent a 0 bit. Starting from the left, the first data bit is 0, which decodes as a flux transition pattern of TN. The next bit is a 1, which decodes as TT. The next bit is 0, which decodes as TN, and so on. Using the FM encoding chart listed earlier, you easily can trace the FM encoding pattern to the end of the byte. Notice that in FM encoding, transitions can be written in adjacent transition cells, with no empty transition cells between them. This method is called a minimum run length of 0. Also, the maximum number of empty transition cells between any two flux transitions is 1, which is why FM encoding can be called RLL 0,1.

The MFM encoding scheme also has clock and data transition cells for each data bit to be recorded. As you can see, however, the clock transition cells carry a flux transition only when a 0 bit is stored after another 0 bit. Starting from the left, the first bit is a 0, and the preceding bit is unknown (assume 0), so the flux transition pattern is TN for that bit. The next bit is a 1, which always decodes to a transition-cell pattern of NT. The next bit is 0, which was preceded by 1, so the pattern stored is NN. Using the MFM encoding table listed earlier, you easily can trace the MFM encoding pattern to the end of the byte. You can see that the minimum and maximum number of transition cells between any two flux transitions is one and three, respectively; hence, MFM encoding also can be called RLL 1,3.

Notice that because half the total transitions used in FM are required, the clock rate can be doubled, so that the data takes up only half as much space. Also notice that even with the doubled clock rate, the minimum physical distance between any two flux transitions is exactly the same as with FM, meaning that the actual density of the write waveform is the same as with FM even though twice as much data is being encoded.

The RLL 2,7 pattern is more difficult to see because it relies on encoding groups of bits rather than each bit individually. Starting from the left, the first group that matches the groups listed in the encoder/decoder (Endec) table are the first three bits, 010. These bits are translated into a flux transition pattern of TNNTNN. The next two bits, 11, are translated as a group to TNNN; and the final group, 000 bits, is translated to NNNTNN to complete the byte. As you can see in this example, no additional bits were needed to finish the last group.

Notice that the minimum and maximum number of empty transition cells between any two flux transitions in this example are two and six, although a different example could show a maximum of seven empty transition cells. This is where the RLL 2,7 designation comes from. Because even fewer transitions are recorded than in MFM, the clock rate can be further increased to three times that of FM or one and a half times that of MFM, allowing more data to be stored in the same space on the disk. Notice, however, that the resulting write waveform itself looks exactly like a typical FM or MFM waveform in terms of the number and separation of the flux transitions for a given physical portion of the disk. In other words, the physical minimum and maximum distances between any two flux transitions remain the same in all three of these encoding-scheme examples.

Another new feature in high-end drives involves the disk read circuitry. Read channel circuits using Partial-Response, Maximum-Likelihood (PRML) technology allow disk drive manufacturers to increase the amount of data that can be stored on a disk platter by up to 40 percent. PRML replaces the standard "detect one peak at a time" approach of traditional analog peak-detect read/write channels with digital signal processing.

In digital signal processing, noise can be digitally filtered out, allowing flux change pulses to be placed closer together on the platter, achieving greater densities.

I hope that the examinations of these different encoding schemes and how they work have taken some of the mystery out of the way data is recorded on a drive. You can see that although schemes such as MFM and RLL can store more data on a drive, the actual density of the flux transitions remains the same as far as the drive is concerned.

Sectors

A disk track is too large to manage effectively as a single storage unit. Many disk tracks can store 50,000 or more bytes of data, which would be very inefficient for storing small files. For that reason, a disk track is divided into several numbered divisions known as *sectors*. These sectors represent slices of the track.

Different types of disk drives and disks split tracks into different numbers of sectors, depending on the density of the tracks. For example, floppy disk formats use 8 to 36 sectors per track, whereas hard disks usually store data at a higher density and can use 17 to 100 or more sectors per track. Sectors created by standard formatting procedures on PC systems have a capacity of 512 bytes, but this capacity may change in the future.

Sectors are numbered on a track starting with 1, unlike the heads or cylinders, which are numbered starting with 0. For example, a 1.44MB floppy disk contains 80 cylinders numbered from 0 to 79 and two heads numbered 0 and 1, and each track on each cylinder has 18 sectors numbered from 1 to 18.

When a disk is formatted, additional areas are created on the disk for the disk controller to use for sector numbering and identifying the start and end of each sector. These areas precede and follow each sector's data area, which accounts for the difference between a disk's unformatted and formatted capacities. For example, a 4MB floppy disk (3.5-inch) has a capacity of 2.88MB when it is formatted, and a 38MB hard disk has a capacity of only 32MB when it is formatted. All drives use some reserved space for managing the data that can be stored on the drive.

Although I have stated that each disk sector is 512 bytes in size, this statement technically is false. Each sector does allow for the storage of 512 bytes of data, but the data area is only a portion of the sector. Each sector on a disk typically occupies 571 bytes of the disk, of which only 512 bytes are usable for user data. The actual number of bytes required for the sector header and trailer can vary from drive to drive, but this figure is typical.

You may find it helpful to think of each sector as being a page in a book. In a book, each page contains text, but the entire page is not filled with text; rather, each page has top, bottom, left, and right margins. Information such as chapter titles (track and cylinder numbers) and page numbers (sector numbers) is placed in the margins. The "margin" areas of a sector are created and written to during the disk-formatting process. Formatting also fills the data area of each sector with dummy values. After the disk is formatted, the data area can be altered by normal writing to the disk. The sector header and trailer information cannot be altered during normal write operations unless you reformat the disk.

Each sector on a disk has a *prefix portion*, or header, that identifies the start of the sector and a sector number, as well as a *suffix portion*, or trailer, that contains a *checksum* (which helps ensure the integrity of the data contents). Each sector also contains 512 bytes of data. The data bytes normally are set to some specific value, such as F6h (hex), when the disk is physically (or low-level) formatted. (The following section explains low-level formatting.)

In many cases, a specific pattern of bytes that are considered to be difficult to write are written so as to flush out any marginal sectors. In addition to the gaps within the sectors, gaps exist between sectors on each track and also between tracks; none of these gaps contains usable data space. The prefix, suffix, and gaps account for the lost space between the unformatted capacity of a disk and the formatted capacity.

Table 14.5 shows the format for each track and sector on a typical hard disk with 17 sectors per track.

Table 14.5	Typical 17-Sector/17-Track Disk Sector Format	
Bytes	**Name**	**Description**
16	POST INDEX GAP	All 4Eh, at the track beginning after the Index mark
		Sector data; repeated 17 times for an MFM encoded track
13	ID VFO LOCK	All 00h; synchronizes the VFO for the sector ID
1	SYNC BYTE	A1h; notifies the controller that data follows
1	ADDRESS MARK	FEh; defines that ID field data follows
2	CYLINDER NUMBER	A value that defines the actuator position
1	HEAD NUMBER	A value that defines the head selected
1	SECTOR NUMBER	A value that defines the sector
2	CRC	Cyclic Redundancy Check to verify ID data
3	WRITE TURN-ON GAP	00h written by format to isolate the ID from DATA
13	DATA SYNC VFO LOCK	All 00h; synchronizes the VFO for the DATA
1	SYNC BYTE	A1h; notifies the controller that data follows
1	ADDRESS MARK	F8h; defines that user DATA field follows
512	DATA	The area for user DATA
2	CRC	Cyclic Redundancy Check to verify DATA
3	WRITE TURN-OFF GAP	00h; written by DATA update to isolate DATA
15	INTER-RECORD GAP	All 00h; a buffer for spindle speed variation
693	PRE-INDEX GAP	All 4Eh, at track end before Index mark

571   Total bytes per sector
512   Data bytes per sector
10,416 Total bytes per track
8,704   Data bytes per track

Table 14.5 refers to a hard disk track with 17 sectors. Although this capacity is typical, more advanced hard disks place as many as 100 or more sectors per track, and the specific formats of those sectors may vary slightly from the example.

As you can see, the usable space on each track is about 16 percent less than the unformatted capacity. This example is true for most disks, although some may vary slightly.

The Post Index Gap provides a head-switching recovery period so that when switching from one track to another, sequential sectors can be read without waiting for an additional revolution of the disk. In some drives running 1:1 interleave controllers, this time is not enough; additional time can be added by skewing the sectors so that the arrival of the first sector is delayed.

The Sector ID data consists of the Cylinder, Head, and Sector Number fields, as well as a CRC field to allow for verification of the ID data. Most controllers use bit 7 of the Head Number field to mark the sector as bad during a low-level format or surface analysis. This system is not absolute, however; some controllers use other methods to indicate a marked bad sector. Usually, though, the mark involves one of the ID fields.

Write Turn on Gap follows the ID field CRC bytes and provides a pad to ensure a proper recording of the following user data area as well as to allow full recovery of the ID CRC.

The user Data field consists of all 512 bytes of data stored in the sector. This field is followed by a CRC field to verify the data. Although many controllers use two bytes of CRC here, the controller may implement a longer Error Correction Code (ECC) that requires more than two CRC bytes to store. The ECC data stored here provides the possibility of Data-field read correction as well as read error detection. The correction/detection capabilities depend on the ECC code chosen and on the controller implementation. A write turn-off gap is a pad to allow the ECC (CRC) bytes to be fully recovered.

The Inter-Record Gap provides a means to accommodate variances in drive spindle speeds. A track may have been formatted while the disk was running slower than normal and then write updated while the disk was running faster than normal. In such cases, this gap prevents accidental overwriting of any information in the next sector. The actual size of this padding varies, depending on the speed of disk rotation when the track was formatted and each time the Data field is updated.

The Pre-Index Gap allows for speed tolerance over the entire track. This gap varies in size, depending on the variances in disk-rotation speed and write-frequency tolerance at the time of formatting.

This sector prefix information is extremely important, because it contains the numbering information that defines the cylinder, head, and sector. All this information except the Data field, Data CRC bytes, and Write Turn-Off Gap is written only during a low-level format. On a typical non-servo-guided (stepper-motor actuator) hard disk on which thermal gradients cause mistracking, the data updates that rewrite the 512-byte Data area and the CRC that follows may not be placed exactly in line with the sector header information. This situation eventually causes read or write failures of the Abort, Retry, Fail, Ignore variety. You can correct this problem by reformatting the disk; this process rewrites the header and data information together at the current track positions. Then, when you restore the data to the disk, the Data areas are written in alignment with the new sector headers.

Disk Formatting. You usually have two types of formats to consider:

■ Physical, or *low-level*

■ Logical, or *high-level*

When you format a floppy disk, the DOS FORMAT command performs both kinds of formats simultaneously. To format a hard disk, however, you must perform the operations separately. Moreover, a hard disk requires a third step, between the two formats, in which the partitioning information is written to the disk. *Partitioning* is required because a hard disk is designed to be used with more than one operating system. Separating the physical format in a way that is always the same, regardless of the operating system being used and regardless of the high-level format (which would be different for each operating system), makes possible the use of multiple operating systems on one hard drive. The partitioning step allows more than one type of operating system to use a single hard disk or a single DOS to use the disk as several volumes or logical drives. A volume or logical drive is anything to which DOS assigns a drive letter.

Consequently, formatting a hard disk involves three steps:

1. Low-level formatting (LLF)

2. Partitioning

3. High-level formatting (HLF)

During a low-level format, the disk's tracks are divided into a specific number of sectors. The sector header and trailer information is recorded, as are intersector and intertrack gaps. Each sector's data area is filled with a dummy byte value or test pattern of values. For floppy disks, the number of sectors recorded on each track depends on the type of disk and drive; for hard disks, the number of sectors per track depends on the drive and controller interface.

The original ST-506/412 MFM controllers always placed 17 sectors per track on a disk. ST-506/412 controllers with RLL encoding increase the number of sectors on a drive to 25 or 26 sectors per track. ESDI drives can have 32 or more sectors per track. IDE drives simply are drives with built-in controllers, and depending on exactly what type of controller design is built in, the number of sectors per track can range from 17 to 100 or more. SCSI drives essentially are IDE drives with an added SCSI Bus Adapter circuit, meaning that they also have some type of built-in controller; and like IDE drives, SCSI drives can have practically any number of sectors per track, depending on what controller design was used.

Most IDE and SCSI drives use a technique called *Zoned Recording,* which writes a variable number of sectors per track. The outermost tracks hold more sectors than the inner tracks do, because they are longer. Because of limitations in the PC BIOS, these drives still have to act as though they have a fixed number of sectors per track. This situation is handled by translation algorithms that are implemented in the controller.

Multiple Zone Recording. One way to increase the capacity of a hard drive is to format more sectors on the outer cylinders than on the inner ones. Because they have a larger circumference, the outer cylinders can hold more data. Drives without Zoned Recording store the same amount of data on every cylinder, even though the outer cylinders may be twice as long as the inner cylinders. The result is wasted storage capacity, because the disk media must be capable of storing data reliably at the same density as on the inner cylinders. With ST-506/412 and ESDI controllers, unfortunately, the number of sectors per track was fixed; drive capacity, therefore, was limited by the density capability of the innermost (shortest) track.

In a Zoned Recording, the cylinders are split into groups called *zones*, with each succes- sive zone having more and more sectors per track as you move out from the inner radius of the disk. All the cylinders in a particular zone have the same number of sectors per track. The number of zones varies with specific drives, but most drives have 10 or more zones.

Another effect of Zoned Recording is that transfer speeds will vary depending on what zone the heads are in. Since there are more sectors in the outer zones, but the rotational speed is always the same, the transfer rate will be highest.

Drives with separate controllers could not handle zoned recordings because there was no standard way to communicate information about the zones from the drive to the con- troller. With SCSI and IDE disks, it became possible to format individual tracks with different numbers of sectors, due to the fact that these drives have the disk controller built in. The built-in controllers on these drives can be made fully aware of the zoning that is used. These built-in controllers must then also translate the physical Cylinder, Head, and Sector numbers to logical Cylinder, Head, and Sector numbers so that the drive has the appearance of having the same number of sectors on each track. The PC BIOS was designed to only handle a single number of specific sectors per track through- out the entire drive, meaning that zoned drives always must run under a sector transla- tion scheme.

The use of Zoned Recording has allowed drive manufacturers to increase the capacity of their hard drives by between 20 percent and 50 percent compared with a fixed-sector- per-track arrangement. Nearly all IDE and SCSI drives today use Zoned Recording.

Partitioning. Partitioning segments the drive into areas, called *partitions*, that can hold a particular operating system's file system. Today, PC operating systems use three common file systems:

- *FAT (File Allocation Table).* This system is the standard file system used by DOS, OS/2, and Windows NT. FAT partitions support file names of 11 characters maxi- mum (eight plus a three-character extension), and a volume can be as large as 2GB.

- *HPFS (High Performance File System).* This UNIX-style file system is accessible only under OS/2 and Windows NT. DOS applications running under OS/2 or Windows NT can access files in HPFS partitions, but straight DOS cannot. File names can be 256 characters long, and volume size is limited to 8GB.

- *NTFS (Windows NT File System).* This UNIX-style file system currently is accessible only under Windows NT, but drivers should be available for OS/2 to access NTFS as well. DOS cannot access these partitions, but DOS applications running under Windows NT can. File names can be 256 characters long, and volume size is limited to 8GB.

Of these three file systems, the FAT file system still is by far the most popular (and recommended). The main problem with the FAT file system is that disk space is used in groups of sectors called *allocation units* or *clusters*. On large volumes, the larger cluster sizes required cause disk space to be used inefficiently. HPFS and NTFS always manage the disk space in sector increments, so there is no penalty of wasted disk space with large volumes.

The FAT file system is the most recommended for compatibility reasons. For example, few applications currently are compatible with the longer file names possible in the HPFS and NTFS file systems. All the operating systems can access FAT volumes, and the file structures and data-recovery procedures are well known. Data recovery can be difficult to impossible under the HPFS and NTFS systems; for those systems, good backups are imperative.

During partitioning, no matter what file system is specified, the partitioning software writes a special boot program and partition table to the first sector, called the Master Boot Sector (MBS). Because the term *record* sometimes is used to mean *sector*, this sector can also be called the Master Boot Record (MBR).

High-Level Format. During the high-level format, the operating system (such as DOS, OS/2, or Windows NT) writes the structures necessary for managing files and data. FAT partitions have a Volume Boot Sector (VBS), a file allocation table (FAT), and a root directory on each formatted logical drive. These data structures (discussed in detail in Chapter 15, "CD-ROM Drives") enable the operating system to manage the space on the disk, keep track of files, and even manage defective areas so that they do not cause problems.

High-level formatting is not really formatting, but creating a table of contents for the disk. In low-level formatting, which is the real formatting, tracks and sectors are written on the disk. As mentioned, the DOS FORMAT command can perform both low-level and high-level format operations on a floppy disk, but it performs only the high-level format for a hard disk. Hard disk low-level formats require a special utility, usually supplied by the disk-controller manufacturer.

Basic Hard Disk Drive Components

Many types of hard disks are on the market, but nearly all drives share the same basic physical components. Some differences may exist in the implementation of these components (and in the quality of materials used to make them), but the operational characteristics of most drives are similar. Following are the components of a typical hard disk drive (see fig. 14.3):

- Disk platters
- Read/write heads
- Head actuator mechanism
- Spindle motor
- Logic board
- Cables and connectors
- Configuration items (such as jumpers or switches)
- Bezel (optional)

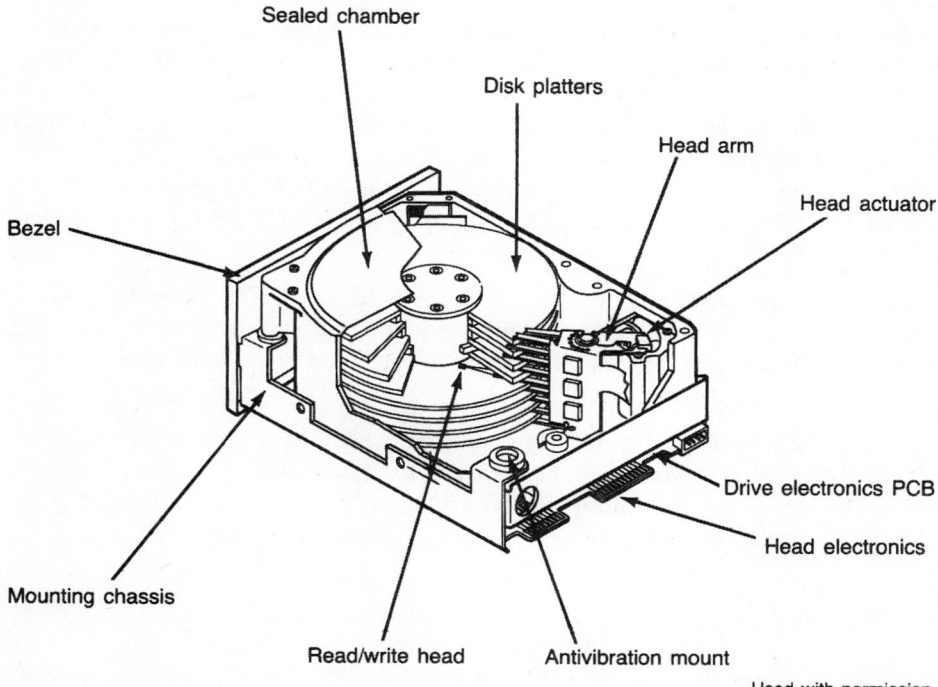

Used with permission from IBM Corporation.

Fig. 14.3

Hard disk drive components.

The platters, spindle motor, heads, and head actuator mechanisms usually are contained in a sealed chamber called the *Head Disk Assembly* (HDA). The HDA usually is treated as a single component; it rarely is opened. Other parts external to the drive's HDA—such as the logic boards, bezel, and other configuration or mounting hardware—can be disassembled from the drive.

Hard Disk Platters (Disks)

A typical hard disk has one or more platters, or *disks*. Hard disks for PC systems have been available in a number of form factors over the years. Normally, the physical size of a drive is expressed as the size of the platters. Following are the most common platter sizes used in PC hard disks today:

- 5.25-inch (actually, 130mm, or 5.12 inches)

- 3.5-inch (actually, 95mm, or 3.74 inches)

- 2.5-inch

- 1.8-inch

- 1.3-inch

Larger hard drives that have 8-inch, 14-inch, or even larger platters are available, but these drives typically have not been associated with PC systems. Currently, the 3.5-inch drives are the most popular for desktop and some portable systems, whereas the 2.5-inch and smaller drives are very popular in portable systems. The 1.3-inch drives entered the market most recently, and they truly are amazing. These drives, which are about the size of a large wristwatch, currently can store 40MB. Capacities of 100MB or more are not far away: the 1.3-inch drives are expected to reach 1GB capacity by the year 2000! Due to their small size, these drives are extremely rugged; they can withstand shocks of 100 g's *while operating* and double that when powered off.

I thought it was interesting to note that the 3.5-inch drives actually use platters that are 95mm or 3.74 inches in diameter, whereas the 5.25-inch drives' platters actually are 130mm or 5.12 inches in diameter. (This information could prove to be useful in your next Computer Trivia contest!)

Most hard drives have two or more platters, although some of the smaller drives have only one. The number of platters that a drive can have is limited by the drive's physical size vertically. So far, the maximum number of platters that I have seen in any 5.25-inch full-height drive is 11; some 3.5-inch drives have as many as 10 platters.

Platters traditionally have been made from an aluminum alloy, for strength and light weight. With manufacturers' desire for higher and higher densities and smaller drives, many drives now use platters made of glass (or, more technically, a glass-ceramic composite). One such material is called MemCor, which is produced by the Dow Corning glass company. MemCor is composed of glass with ceramic implants, which resists cracking better than pure glass.

Glass platters offer greater strength (rigidity) and therefore can be machined to one-half the thickness of conventional aluminum disks, or less. Glass platters also are much more thermally stable than aluminum platters, which means that they do not change dimensions (expand or contract) very much with any changes in temperature. Several hard disks made by companies such as Seagate, Toshiba, Areal Technology, Maxtor, and Hewlett Packard currently use glass or glass-ceramic platters. For most manufacturers, glass disks will replace the standard aluminum substrate over the next few years, especially in high-performance 2.5- and 3.5-inch drives.

Recording Media

No matter what substrate is used, the platters are covered with a thin layer of a magnetically retentive substance called *media* in which magnetic information is stored. Two popular types of media are used on hard disk platters:

- Oxide media
- Thin-film media

Oxide media is made of various compounds, containing iron oxide as the active ingredient. A magnetic layer is created by coating the aluminum platter with a syrup containing iron-oxide particles. This media is spread across the disk by spinning the platters at high speed; centrifugal force causes the material to flow from the center of the platter to the outside, creating an even coating of media material on the platter. The surface then is cured and polished. Finally, a layer of material that protects and lubricates the surface is added and burnished smooth. The oxide media coating normally is about 30 millionths of an inch thick. If you could peer into a drive with oxide-media-coated platters, you would see that the platters are brownish or amber.

As drive density increases, the media needs to be thinner and more perfectly formed. The capabilities of oxide coatings have been exceeded by most higher-capacity drives. Because oxide media is very soft, disks that use this type of media are subject to head-crash damage if the drive is jolted during operation. Most older drives, especially those sold as low-end models, have oxide media on the drive platters. Oxide media, which has been used since 1955, remained popular because of its relatively low cost and ease of application. Today, however, very few drives use oxide media.

Thin-film media is thinner, harder, and more perfectly formed than oxide media. Thin film was developed as a high-performance media that enabled a new generation of drives to have lower head floating heights, which in turn made possible increases in drive density. Originally, thin-film media was used only in higher-capacity or higher-quality drive systems, but today, virtually all drives have thin-film media.

Thin-film media is aptly named. The coating is much thinner than can be achieved by the oxide-coating method. Thin-film media also is known as *plated*, or *sputtered*, media because of the various processes used to place the thin film of media on the platters.

Thin-film plated media is manufactured by placing the media material on the disk with an electroplating mechanism, much the way chrome plating is placed on the bumper of a car. The aluminum platter then is immersed in a series of chemical baths that coat the platter with several layers of metallic film. The media layer is a cobalt alloy about 3 micro-inches (millionths of an inch) thick.

Thin-film sputtered media is created by first coating the aluminum platters with a layer of nickel phosphorus and then applying the cobalt-alloy magnetic material in a continuous vacuum-deposition process called *sputtering*. During this process, magnetic layers as thin as 1 or 2 micro-inches are deposited on the disk, in a fashion similar to the way that silicon wafers are coated with metallic films in the semiconductor industry. The sputtering technique then is used again to lay down an extremely hard, 1 micro-inch protective carbon coating. The need for a near-perfect vacuum makes sputtering the most expensive of the processes described here.

The surface of a sputtered platter contains magnetic layers as thin as 1 millionth of an inch. Because this surface also is very smooth, the head can float closer to the disk surface than was possible previously; floating heights as small as 3 micro-inches above the surface are possible. When the head is closer to the platter, the density of the magnetic flux transitions can be increased to provide greater storage capacity. Additionally, the increased intensity of the magnetic field during a closer-proximity read provides the higher signal amplitudes needed for good signal-to-noise performance.

Both the sputtering and plating processes result in a very thin, very hard film of media on the platters. Because the thin-film media is so hard, it has a better chance of surviving contact with the heads at high speed. In fact, modern thin-film media is virtually uncrashable. Oxide coatings can be scratched or damaged much more easily. If you could open a drive to peek at the platters, you would see that the thin-film media platters look like the silver surfaces of mirrors.

The sputtering process results in the most perfect, thinnest, and hardest disk surface that can be produced commercially. The sputtering process has largely replaced plating as the method of creating thin-film media. Having a thin-film media surface on a drive results increased storage capacity in a smaller area with fewer head crashes—and in a drive that will provide many years of trouble-free use.

Read/Write Heads

A hard disk drive usually has one read/write head for each platter side, and these heads are connected, or *ganged*, on a single movement mechanism. The heads, therefore, move across the platters in unison.

Mechanically, read/write heads are simple. Each head is on an actuator arm that is spring-loaded to force the head into a platter. Few people realize that each platter actually is "squeezed" by the heads above and below it. If you could open a drive safely and lift the top head with your finger, the head would snap back into the platter when you released it. If you could pull down on one of the heads below a platter, the spring tension would cause it to snap back up into the platter when you released it.

Figure 14.4 shows a typical hard disk head-actuator assembly from a voice coil drive.

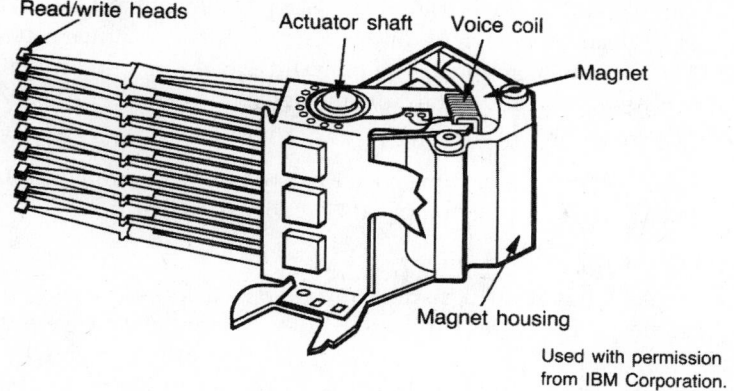

Used with permission
from IBM Corporation.

Fig. 14.4

Read/write heads and rotary voice coil actuator assembly.

When the drive is at rest, the heads are forced into direct contact with the platters by spring tension, but when the drive is spinning at full speed, air pressure develops below the heads and lifts them off the surface of the platter. On a drive spinning at full speed, the distance between the heads and the platter can be anywhere from 3 to 20 or more micro-inches (millionths of an inch).

In the early 1960s, hard disk drive recording heads operated at floating heights as large as 200 to 300 micro-inches; today's drive heads are designed to float as low as 3 to 5 micro-inches above the surface of the disk. To support higher densities in future drives, the physical separation between the head and disk is expected to be as little as 0.5 micro-inch by the end of the century.

Generally speaking, the older the drive and lower its capacity, the higher the heads float above the media. The small size of this gap is why the disk drive's Head Disk Assembly (HDA) should never be opened except in a clean-room environment: any particle of dust or dirt that gets into this mechanism could cause the heads to read improperly, or possibly even to strike the platters while the drive is running at full speed. The latter event could scratch the platter or the head.

To ensure the cleanliness of the interior of the drive, the HDA is assembled in a class-100 or better clean room. This specification is such that a cubic foot of air cannot contain more than 100 particles that measure up to 0.5 micron (19.7 micro-inch). A single person breathing while standing motionless spews out 500 such particles in a single minute! These rooms contain special air-filtration systems that continuously evacuate and refresh the air. A drive's HDA should not be opened unless it is inside such a room.

Although maintaining such an environment may seem to be expensive, many companies manufacture tabletop or bench-size clean rooms that sell for only a few thousand dollars. Some of these devices operate like a glove box; the operator first inserts the drive and any tools required, and then closes the box and turns on the filtration system. Inside the box, a clean-room environment is maintained, and a technician can use the built-in gloves to work on the drive.

In other clean-room variations, the operator stands at a bench where a forced-air curtain is used to maintain a clean environment on the bench top. The technician can walk in and out of the clean-room field simply by walking through the air curtain. This air curtain is much like the curtain of air used in some stores and warehouses to prevent heat from escaping in the winter while leaving a passage wide open.

Because the clean environment is very expensive to produce, few companies except those that manufacture the drives are prepared to service hard disk drives.

Read/Write Head Designs

As disk drive technology has evolved, so has the design of the Read/Write head. The earliest heads were simple iron cores with coil windings (essentially pure electromagnets). By today's standards the original head designs were enormous in physical size and operated at very low recording densities. Over the years many different head designs have evolved from the first simple Ferrite Core designs into several types and technologies available today. This section discusses the different types of heads found in PC type hard disk drives, including the applications and relative strengths and weaknesses of each.

Four types of heads have been used in hard disk drives over the years:

- Ferrite
- Metal-In-Gap (MIG)
- Thin Film (TF)
- Magneto-Resistive (MR)

Ferrite. *Ferrite heads*, the traditional type of magnetic-head design, evolved from the original IBM Winchester drive. These heads have an iron-oxide core wrapped with electromagnetic coils. A magnetic field is produced by energizing the coils; a field also can be induced by passing a magnetic field near the coils. This process gives the heads full read and write capability. Ferrite heads are larger and heavier than thin-film heads and therefore require a larger floating height to prevent contact with the disk.

Many refinements have been made in the original (monolithic) ferrite head design. A type of ferrite head called a *composite ferrite head* has a smaller ferrite core bonded with glass in a ceramic housing. This design permits a smaller head gap, which allows higher track densities. These heads are less susceptible to stray magnetic fields than are heads in the older monolithic design.

During the 1980s, composite ferrite heads were popular in many low-end drives, such as the popular Seagate ST-225. As density demands grew, the competing MIG and thin-film head designs were used in place of ferrite heads, which are virtually obsolete today. Ferrite heads cannot write to the higher coercivity media needed for high-density designs and have poor frequency response with higher noise levels. The main advantage of ferrite heads is that they are the cheapest type available.

Metal-In-Gap. *Metal-In-Gap* (MIG) heads basically are a specially enhanced version of the composite ferrite design. In MIG heads, a metal substance is sputtered into the recording gap on the trailing edge of the head. This material offers increased resistance to magnetic saturation, allowing higher-density recording. MIG heads also produce a sharper gradient in the magnetic field for a better-defined magnetic pulse. These heads permit the use of higher-coercivity thin-film disks and can operate at lower floating heights.

Two versions of MIG heads are available: single-sided and double-sided. Single-sided MIG heads are designed with a layer of magnetic alloy placed along the trailing edge of the gap. Double-sided MIG designs apply the layer to both sides of the gap. The metal alloy is applied through a vacuum-deposition process called sputtering. This alloy has twice the magnetization capability of raw ferrite and allows writing to the higher-coercivity thin-film media needed at the higher densities. Double-sided MIG heads offer even higher coercivity capability than the single-sided designs do.

Because of these increases in capabilities through improved designs, MIG heads for a time were the most popular head used in all but very high-capacity drives. Due to market pressures that have demanded higher and higher densities, however, MIG heads have been largely displaced in favor of Thin Film heads.

Thin Film. *Thin Film* (TF) heads are produced in the much the same manner as a semiconductor chip—that is, through a photolithographic process. In this manner, many thousands of heads can be created on a single circular wafer. This manufacturing process also results in a very small high-quality product.

TF heads offer an extremely narrow and controlled head gap created by sputtering a hard aluminum material. Because this material completely encloses the gap, this area is very well protected, minimizing the chance of damage from contact with the media. The core is a combination of iron and nickel alloy that is two to four times more powerful magnetically than a ferrite head core.

Thin film heads produce a sharply defined magnetic pulse that allows extremely high densities to be written. Because they do not have a conventional coil, TF heads are more immune to variations in coil impedance. The small, lightweight heads can float at a much lower height than the ferrite and MIG heads; floating height has been reduced to 2 micro-inches or less in some designs. Because the reduced height enables a much stronger signal to be picked up and transmitted between the head and platters, the signal-to-noise ratio increases, which improves accuracy. At the high track and linear densities of some drives, a standard ferrite head would not be able to pick out the data signal from the background noise. When Thin Film heads are used, their small size enables more platters to be stacked in a drive.

Until the past few years, TF heads were relatively expensive compared with older technologies, such as ferrite and MIG. Better manufacturing techniques and the need for higher densities, however, have driven the market to TF heads. The widespread use of these heads also has made them cost-competitive, if not cheaper than MIG heads.

Thin film heads currently are used in most high-capacity drives, especially in the smaller form factors. They have displaced MIG heads as the most popular head design being used in drives today. The industry is working on ways to improve TF head efficiency, so thin film heads are likely to remain popular for some time, especially in mainstream drives.

Magneto-Resistive. *Magneto-Resistive* (MR) heads are a relatively new technology. Invented and pioneered by IBM, magneto-resistive heads currently are the superior head design, offering the highest performance available. Most 3.5-inch drives with capacities in excess of 1G currently use MR heads. As areal densities continue to increase, the MR head eventually will become the head of choice for nearly all hard drives, displacing the popular MIG and TF head designs.

MR heads rely on the fact that the resistance of a conductor changes slightly when an external magnetic field is present. Rather than put out a voltage by passing through a magnetic-field flux reversal, as a normal head would, the MR head senses the flux reversal and changes resistance. A small current flows through the heads, and the change in resistance is measured by this sense current. This design enables the output to be three or more times more powerful than a thin film head during a read. In effect, MR heads are power-read heads, acting more like sensors than generators.

MR heads are more costly and complex to manufacture than other types of heads, because several special features or steps must be added. Among them:

- Additional wires must be run to and from the head to carry the sense current.

- Four to six more masking steps are required.

- Because MR heads are so sensitive, they are very susceptible to stray magnetic fields and must be shielded.

Because the MR principle can only read data and is not used for writing, MR heads really are two heads in one. A standard inductive thin film head is used for writing, and a magneto-resistive head is used for reading. Because two separate heads are built into one assembly, each head can be optimized for its task. Ferrite, MIG, and thin film heads are known as *single-gap heads* because the same gap is used for both reading and writing, whereas the MR head uses a separate gap for each operation.

The problem with single-gap heads is that the gap length always is a compromise between what is best for reading and what is best for writing. The read function needs a thin gap for higher resolution; the write function needs a thicker gap for deeper flux penetration to switch the media. In a dual-gap MR head, the read and write gaps can be optimized for both functions independently. The write (thin film) gap writes a wider track than the read (magneto-resistive) gap does. The read head then is less likely to pick up stray magnetic information from adjacent tracks.

Although MR heads have many good qualities, they do have some disadvantages. The primary disadvantage is cost. The cost actually is not too limiting, because these heads are primarily used in extremely high-capacity drives, for which cost is not as much of a concern. Another disadvantage is that MR heads are much more delicate than the other head designs. Handling MR heads during manufacturing requires more care due to their greater sensitivity to damage by ESD (Electro-Static Discharge). Finally, drives with MR heads require better shielding from stray magnetic fields, which can affect these heads more easily than they do the other head designs. All in all, however, the drawbacks are minor compared with the advantages that the MR heads offer.

Head Sliders

The term *slider* is used to describe the body of material that supports the actual drive head itself. The slider is what actually floats or slides over the surface of the disk, carrying the head at the correct distance from the media for reading and writing. Most sliders resemble a catamaran, with two outboard pods that float along the surface of the disk media and a central "rudder" portion that actually carries the head and read/write gap.

The trend toward smaller and smaller form factor drives has forced a requirement for smaller and smaller sliders as well. The typical mini-Winchester slider design is about .160 × .126 × .034 inch in size. Most head manufacturers now are shifting to 50 percent smaller nanosliders, which have dimensions of about .08 × .063 × .017 inch. The nanoslider is being used in both high-capacity and small-form-factor drives. Smaller sliders reduce the mass carried at the end of the head actuator arms, allowing for increased acceleration and deceleration, and leading to faster seek times. The smaller sliders also require less area for a landing zone, thus increasing the usable area of the disk platters. Further, the smaller slider contact area reduces the slight wear on the media surface that occurs during normal startup and spindown of the drive platters.

The newer nanoslider designs also have specially modified surface patterns that are designed to maintain the same floating height above the disk surface whether the slider is above the inner or outer cylinders. Conventional sliders increase or decrease their floating height considerably, according to the velocity of the disk surface traveling below them. Above the outer cylinders, the velocity and floating height are higher. This arrangement is undesirable in newer drives that use Zoned Recording, in which the same bit density is achieved on all the cylinders. Because the same bit density is maintained throughout the drive, the head floating height should be relatively constant as well for maximum performance. Special textured surface patterns and manufacturing techniques allow the nanosliders to float at a much more consistent height, making them ideal for Zoned Recording drives.

Head Actuator Mechanisms

Possibly more important than the heads themselves is the mechanical system that moves them: the *head actuator*. This mechanism moves the heads across the disk and positions them accurately above the desired cylinder. Many variations on head actuator mechanisms are in use, but all of them can be categorized as being one of two basic types:

- Stepper motor actuators
- Voice coil actuators

The use of one or the other type of positioner has profound effects on a drive's performance and reliability. The effect is not limited to speed; it also includes accuracy, sensitivity to temperature, position, vibration, and overall reliability. To put it bluntly, a drive equipped with a stepper motor actuator is much less reliable (by a large factor) than a drive equipped with a voice coil actuator.

The head actuator is the single most important specification in the drive. The type of head actuator mechanism in a drive tells you a great deal about the drive's performance and reliability characteristics. Table 14.6 shows the two types of hard disk drive head actuators and the affected performance parameters.

Table 14.6   Characteristics of Stepper Motor versus Voice Coil Drives

Characteristic	Stepper Motor	Voice Coil
Relative access speed	Slow	Fast
Temperature sensitive	Yes (very)	No
Positionally sensitive	Yes	No
Automatic head parking	Not usually	Yes
Preventive maintenance	Periodic format	None required
Relative reliability	Poor	Excellent

Generally, a stepper motor drive has a slow average access rating, is temperature-sensitive during read and write operations, is sensitive to physical orientation during read and write operations, does not automatically park its heads above a save zone during power-down, and usually requires annual or biannual reformats to realign the sector data with the sector header information due to mistracking. Overall, stepper motor drives are vastly inferior to drives that use voice coil actuators.

Some stepper motor drives feature automatic head parking at power-down. If you have a newer stepper motor drive, refer to the drive's technical reference manual to determine whether your drive has this feature. (Other than removing the lid and watching as you power-off—which is definitely *not* recommended—reading the documentation is the only reliable way to tell.) Sometimes, you hear a noise after power-down, but that can be deceptive; some drives use a solenoid-activated spindle break, which makes a noise as the drive is powered off and does not involve head parking.

Floppy disk drives position their heads by using a stepper motor actuator. The accuracy of the stepper mechanism is suited to a floppy drive, because the track densities usually are nowhere near those of a hard disk. Many of the less expensive, low-capacity hard disks also use a stepper motor system. Most hard disks with capacities of more than 40MB have voice coil actuators, as do all drives I have seen that have capacities of more than 100MB. In IBM's product line, a drive of 40MB or more always is a voice coil drive. On IBM systems with drives of less than 40MB (usually, 20MB or 30MB), both voice coil and stepper motor drives have been used.

This breakdown does not necessarily apply to other system manufacturers, but it is safe to say that hard disk drives with less than 80MB capacity may have either type of actuator and that virtually all drives with more than 80MB capacity have voice coil actuators. The cost difference between voice coil drives and stepper motor drives of equal capacity is marginal today, so there is little reason not to use a voice coil drive. Virtually no new stepper motor drives are being manufactured today.

Stepper Motor. A *stepper motor* is an electrical motor that can "step," or move from position to position, with mechanical detents or click stop positions. If you were to grip the spindle of one of these motors and spin it by hand, you would hear a clicking or buzzing sound as the motor passed each detent position with a soft click. The sensation is much like that of the volume control on some stereo systems which use a detented type control instead of something smooth and purely linear.

Stepper motors cannot position themselves between step positions; they can stop only at the predetermined detent positions. The motors are small (between 1 and 3 inches) and can be square, cylindrical, or flat. Stepper motors are outside the sealed HDA, although the spindle of the motor penetrates the HDA through a sealed hole. The stepper motor is located in one of the corners of the hard disk drive and usually is easy to see.

Mechanical Links. The stepper motor is mechanically linked to the head rack by a split-steel band coiled around the motor spindle or by a rack-and-pinion gear mechanism. As the motor steps, each detent, or click-stop position, represents the movement of one track through the mechanical linkage.

Some systems use several motor steps for each track. In positioning the heads, if the drive is told to move to track 100, the motor begins the stepping motion, proceeds to the 100th detent position, and stops, leaving the heads above the desired cylinder. The fatal flaw in this type of positioning system is that due to dimensional changes in the platter-to-head relationship over the life of a drive, the heads may not be precisely placed above the cylinder location. This type of positioning system is called a *blind system*, because the heads have no true way of determining the exact placement of a given cylinder.

The most widely used stepper motor actuator systems use a *split-metal-band mechanism* to transmit the rotary stepping motion to the in-and-out motion of the head rack. The band is made of special alloys to limit thermal expansion and contraction as well as stretching of the thin band. One end of the band is coiled around the spindle of the stepper motor; the other is connected directly to the head rack. The band is inside the sealed HDA and is not visible from outside the drive.

Some drives use a *rack-and-pinion gear mechanism* to link the stepper motor to the head rack. This procedure involves a small pinion gear on the spindle of the stepper motor that moves a rack gear in and out. The rack gear is connected to the head rack, causing it to move. The rack-and-pinion mechanism is more durable than the split-metal-band mechanism and provides slightly greater physical and thermal stability. One problem, however, is *backlash*: the amount of play in the gears. Backlash increases as the gears wear and eventually renders the mechanism useless.

Temperature Fluctuation Problems. Stepper motor mechanisms are affected by a variety of problems. The greatest problem is temperature. As the drive platters heat and cool, they expand and contract, respectively; the tracks then move in relation to a predetermined track position. The stepper mechanism does not allow the mechanism to move in increments of less than a single track to correct for these temperature-induced errors. The drive positions the heads to a particular cylinder according to a predetermined number of steps from the stepper motor, with no room for nuance.

The low-level formatting of the drive places the initial track and sector marks on the platters at the positions where the heads currently are located, as commanded by the stepper motor. If all subsequent reading and writing occur at the same temperature as during the initial format, the heads always record precisely within the track and sector boundaries.

At different temperatures, however, the head position does not match the track position. When the platters are cold, the heads miss the track location because the platters have shrunk and the tracks have moved toward the center of the disk. When the platters are warmer than the formatted temperature, the platters will have grown larger and the track positions are located outward. Gradually, as the drive is used, the data is written inside, on top of, and outside the track and sector marks. Eventually, the drive fails to read one of these locations, and a DOS Abort, Retry, Ignore error message usually appears.

The temperature sensitivity of stepper motor drives also may cause the "Monday morning blues." When the system is powered up cold (on Monday, for example), a 1701, 1790, or 10490 Power-On Self Test (POST) error occurs. If you leave the system on for about 15 minutes, the drive can come up to operating temperature, and the system then may boot normally. This problem sometimes occurs in reverse when the drive gets particularly warm, such as when a system is in direct sunlight or during the afternoon, when room temperature is highest. In that case, the symptom is a DOS error message with the familiar Abort, Retry, Ignore prompt.

Temperature-induced mistracking problems can be solved by reformatting the drive and restoring the data. Then the information is placed on the drive at the current head positions for each cylinder. Over time, the mistracking recurs, necessitating another reformat-and-restore operation, which is a form of periodic preventive maintenance for stepper motor drives. An acceptable interval for this maintenance is once a year (or perhaps twice a year, if the drive is extremely temperature-sensitive).

Reformatting a hard drive, because it requires a complete backup-and-restore operation, is inconvenient and time-consuming. To help with these periodic reformats, most low-level-format programs offer a special reformat option that copies the data for a specific track to a spare location, reformats the track, and then copies the data back to the original track. When this type of format operation is finished, you don't have to restore your data, because the program took care of that chore for you one track at a time.

> **Caution**
>
> *Never* use a so-called nondestructive format program without first making a complete backup. This type of program *does* wipe out the data as it operates. "Destructive-reconstructive" more accurately describes its operation. If a problem occurs with the power, the system, or the program (maybe a bug that stops the program from finishing), all the data will not be restored properly, and some tracks may be wiped clean. Although such programs save you from having to restore data manually when the format is complete, they do not remove your obligation to perform a backup first.

Beware of programs whose advertising is filled with marketing hype and miracle claims for making a hard disk "better than new." One company even boasted in its advertisements that by using its program, you will "never have any problems" with your hard disk—an outrageous claim indeed! What the ads don't say is that any real low-level format program performs these same feats of "magic" without the misleading or exaggerated claims and unnecessary hype. Many of these nondestructive formatters really cannot format a large number of drives that are available today. Also, you should note that annual or biannual formatting is not necessary with voice coil actuator drives, because they do not exhibit these types of mistracking errors.

Voice Coil. A *voice coil actuator* is found in all higher quality hard disk drives, including most drives with capacities greater than 40MB and virtually all drives with capacities exceeding 80MB. Unlike the blind stepper motor positioning system, a voice coil actuator uses a feedback signal from the drive to accurately determine the head positions and to adjust them, if necessary. This system allows for significantly greater performance, accuracy, and reliability than traditional stepper motor actuators offered.

A voice coil actuator works by pure electromagnetic force. The construction of this mechanism is similar to that of a typical audio speaker, from which the term *voice coil* is derived. An audio speaker uses a stationary magnet surrounded by a voice coil connected to the speaker's paper cone. Energizing the coil causes the coil to move relative to the stationary magnet, which produces sound from the speaker cone. In a typical hard disk voice coil system, the electromagnetic coil is attached to the end of the head rack and placed near a stationary magnet. No contact is made between the coil and the magnet; instead, the coil moves by pure magnetic force. As the electromagnetic coils are energized, they attract or repulse the stationary magnet and move the head rack. Such systems are extremely quick and efficient, and usually much quieter than systems driven by stepper motors.

Unlike a stepper motor, a voice coil actuator has no click-stops, or detent positions; rather, a special guidance system stops the head rack above a particular cylinder. Because it has no detents, the voice coil actuator can slide the heads in and out smoothly to any position desired, much like the slide of a trombone. Voice coil actuators use a guidance mechanism called a *servo* to tell the actuator where the heads are in relation to the cylinders and to place the heads accurately at the desired positions. This positioning system often is called a *closed loop, servo-controlled mechanism. Closed loop* indicates that the index (or servo) signal is sent to the positioning electronics in a closed-loop system. This loop sometimes is called a *feedback loop*, because the feedback from this information is used to position the heads accurately. *Servo-controlled* refers to this index or the servo information that is used to dictate or control head-positioning accuracy.

A voice coil actuator with servo control is not affected by temperature changes, as a stepper motor is. When the temperature is cold and the platters have shrunk (or when the temperature is hot and the platters have expanded), the voice coil system compensates because it never positions the heads in predetermined track positions. Rather, the voice coil system searches for the specific track, guided by the prewritten servo information, and can position the head rack precisely above the desired track at that track's current position, regardless of the temperature. Because of the continuous feedback of servo information, the heads adjust to the current position of the track at all times. For example, as a drive warms up and the platters expand, the servo information allows the heads to "follow" the track. As a result, a voice coil actuator often is called a *track following* system.

Two main types of voice-coil positioner mechanisms are available:

- Linear voice-coil actuators
- Rotary voice-coil actuators

The types differ only in the physical arrangement of the magnets and coils.

A *linear actuator* (see fig. 14.5) moves the heads in and out over the platters in a straight line, much like a tangential-tracking turntable. The coil moves in and out on a track surrounded by the stationary magnets. The primary advantage of the linear design is that it eliminates the head azimuth variations that occur with rotary positioning systems. (*Azimuth* refers to the angular measurement of the head position relative to the tangent of a given cylinder.) A linear actuator does not rotate the head as it moves from one cylinder to another, thus eliminating this problem.

Although the linear actuator seems to be a good design, it has one fatal flaw: the devices are much too heavy. As drive performance has increased, the desire for lightweight actuator mechanisms has become very important. The lighter the mechanism, the faster it can be accelerated and decelerated from one cylinder to another. Because they are much heavier than rotary actuators, linear actuators were popular only for a short time; they are virtually nonexistent in drives manufactured today.

Rotary actuators (see fig 14.4) also use stationary magnets and a movable coil, but the coil is attached to the end of an actuator arm, much like that of a turntable's tone arm. As the coil is forced to move relative to the stationary magnet, it swings the head arms in and out over the surface of the disk. The primary advantage of this mechanism is light weight, which means that the heads can be accelerated and decelerated very quickly, resulting in very fast average seek times. The disadvantage is that as the heads move from the outer to inner cylinders, they are rotated slightly with respect to the tangent of the cylinders. This rotation results in an azimuth error and is one reason why the area of the platter in which the cylinders are located is somewhat limited. By limiting the total motion of the actuator, the azimuth error can be contained to within reasonable specifications. Virtually all voice coil drives today use rotary actuator systems.

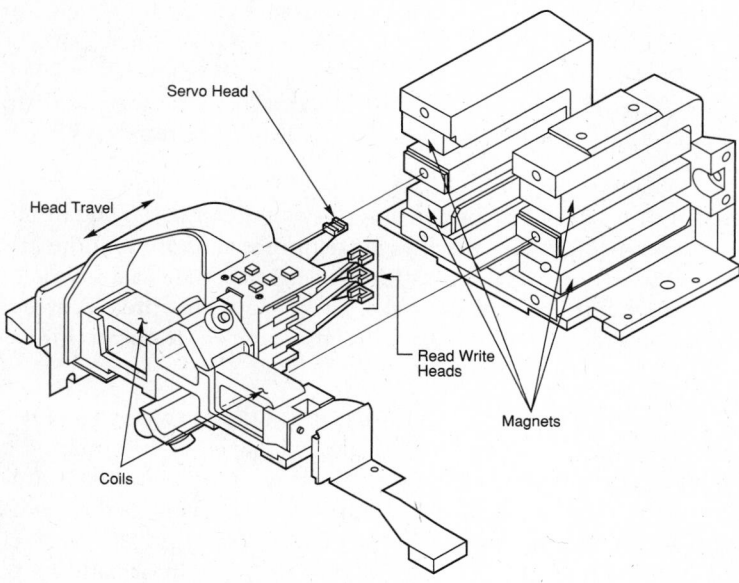

Fig. 14.5
A linear voice coil actuator.

Servo Control Mechanisms. Three servo mechanism designs have been used to control voice coil positioners over the years:

- Wedge servo
- Embedded servo
- Dedicated servo

These designs are slightly different, but they accomplish the same basic task: they enable the head positioner to adjust continuously so that it is precisely placed above a given cylinder in the drive. The main difference among these servo designs is where the gray code information is actually written on the drive.

All servo mechanisms rely on special information that is only written to the disk when the disk is manufactured. This information usually is in the form of a special code called a gray code. A *gray code* is a special binary notational system in which any two adjacent numbers are represented by a code that differs in only one bit place or column position. This system makes it easy for the head to read the information and quickly determine its precise position. This guidance code can be written only when the drive is manufactured; the code is used over the life of the drive for accurate positional information.

The servo gray code is written at the time of manufacture by a special machine called a *servowriter*: basically, a jig that mechanically moves the heads to a given reference position and then writes the servo information for that position. Many servowriters are themselves guided by a laser-beam reference that calculates its own position by calculating distances in wavelengths of light. Because the servowriter must be capable of moving the heads mechanically, this process is done with the lid of the drive off or through special access ports on the HDA. After the servowriting is complete, these ports usually are covered with sealing tape. You often see these tape-covered holes on the HDA, usually accompanied by warnings that you will void the warranty if you remove the tape. Because servowriting exposes the interior of the drive, it must be done in a clean-room environment.

A servowriter is an expensive piece of machinery, costing up to $50,000 or more, and often must be custom-made for a particular make or model of drive. Some drive-repair companies have servowriting capability, which means that they can rewrite the servo information on a drive if it becomes damaged. Lacking a servowriter, a drive with servo-code damage must be sent back to the drive manufacturer for the servo information to be rewritten.

Fortunately, it is impossible to damage the servo information through any normal reading and writing to a hard disk. Drives are designed so that servo information cannot be overwritten, even during low-level formatting of a drive. One myth that has been circulating (especially with respect to IDE drives) is that you can damage the servo information by improper low-level formatting. This is not true. An improper low-level format may compromise the performance of the drive, but the servo information is totally protected and cannot be overwritten.

The track-following capabilities of a servo-controlled voice coil actuator eliminates the positioning errors that occur over time with stepper motor drives. Voice coil drives simply are not affected by conditions such as thermal expansion and contraction of the platters. In fact, many voice coil drives today perform a special thermal-recalibration procedure at predetermined intervals while they run. This procedure usually involves seeking the heads from cylinder 0 to some other cylinder one time for every head on the drive. As this sequence occurs, the control circuitry in the drive monitors how much the track positions have moved since the last time the sequence was performed, and a thermal calibration adjustment is calculated and stored in the drive's memory. This information then is used every time the drive positions to ensure the most accurate positioning possible.

Most drives perform the thermal-recalibration sequence every five minutes for the first half-hour that the drive is powered on and then once every 25 minutes after that. With some drives (such as Quantum, for example), this thermal-calibration sequence is very noticeable; the drive essentially stops what it is doing, and you hear rapid ticking for a second or so. At this time, some people think that their drive is having a problem reading something and perhaps is conducting a read retry, but this is not true. Most of the newer intelligent drives (IDE and SCSI) employ this thermal-recalibration procedure for ultimate positioning accuracy.

While we are on the subject of automatic drive functions, most of the drives that perform thermal-recalibration sequences also automatically perform a function called a *disk sweep*. This procedure is an automatic head seek that occurs after the drive has been idle for a period of time (for example, nine minutes). The disk-sweep function moves the heads to a random cylinder in the outer portion of the platters, which is considered to be the high float-height area because the head-to-platter velocity is highest. Then, if the drive continues to remain idle for another period, the heads move to another cylinder in this area, and the process continues indefinitely as long as the drive is powered on.

The disk-sweep function is designed to prevent the head from remaining stationary above one cylinder in the drive, where friction between the head and platter eventually would dig a trench in the media. Although the heads are not in direct contact with the media, they are so close that the constant air pressure from the head floating above a single cylinder causes friction and excessive wear.

Wedge Servo. Some early servo-controlled drives used a technique called a *wedge servo*. In these drives, the gray-code guidance information is contained in a "wedge" slice of the drive in each cylinder immediately preceding the index mark. The index mark indicates the beginning of each track, so the wedge-servo information was written in the Pre-Index Gap, which is at the end of each track. This area is provided for speed tolerance and normally is not used by the controller. Figure 14.6 shows the wedge-servo information on a drive.

Some controllers, such as the Xebec 1210 that IBM used in the XT, had to be notified that the drive was using a wedge servo so that they could shorten the sector timing to allow for the wedge-servo area. If they were not correctly configured, these controllers would not work properly with such drives. Many people believed—erroneously—that the wedge-servo information could be overwritten in such cases by an improper low-level format. This is not the case, however; all drives using a wedge servo disable any write commands and take control of the head select lines whenever the heads are above the wedge area. This procedure protects the servo from any possibility of being overwritten, no matter how hard you try. If the controller tried to write over this area, the drive would prevent the write, and the controller would be unable to complete the format. Most controllers simply do not write to the Pre-Index Gap area and do not need to be configured specially for wedge-servo drives.

The only way that the servo information normally could be damaged is by a powerful external magnetic field (or perhaps by a head crash or some other catastrophe). In such a case, the drive would have to be sent in for repair.

One problem is that the servo information appears only one time every revolution, which means that the drive often needs several revolutions before it can accurately determine and adjust the head position. Because of these problems, the wedge servo never was a popular design; it no longer is used in drives.

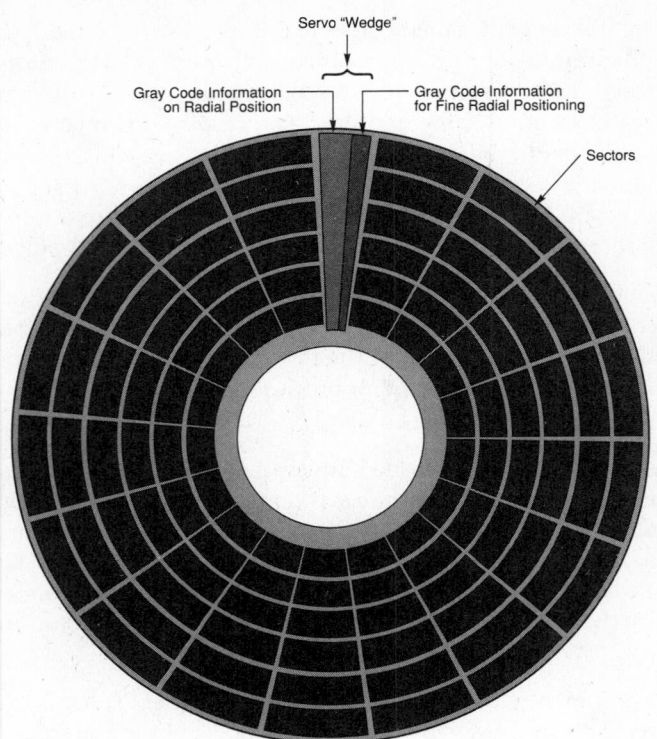

Fig. 14.6
A wedge servo.

Embedded Servo. An *embedded servo* (see fig. 14.7) is an enhancement of the wedge servo. Instead of placing the servo code before the beginning of each cylinder, an embedded servo design writes the servo information before the start of each sector. This arrangement enables the positioner circuits to receive feedback many times in a single revolution, making the head positioning much faster and more precise. Another advantage is that every track on the drive has this positioning information, so each head can quickly and efficiently adjust position to compensate for any changes in the platter or head dimensions, especially for changes due to thermal expansion or physical stress.

Most drives today use an embedded servo to control the positioning system. As in the wedge servo design, the embedded-servo information is protected by the drive circuits, and any write operations are blocked whenever the heads are above the servo information. Thus, it is impossible to overwrite the servo information with a low-level format, as many people incorrectly believed.

Although the embedded servo works much better than the wedge servo, because the feedback servo information is available several times in a single disk revolution, a system that offered continuous servo feedback information would be better.

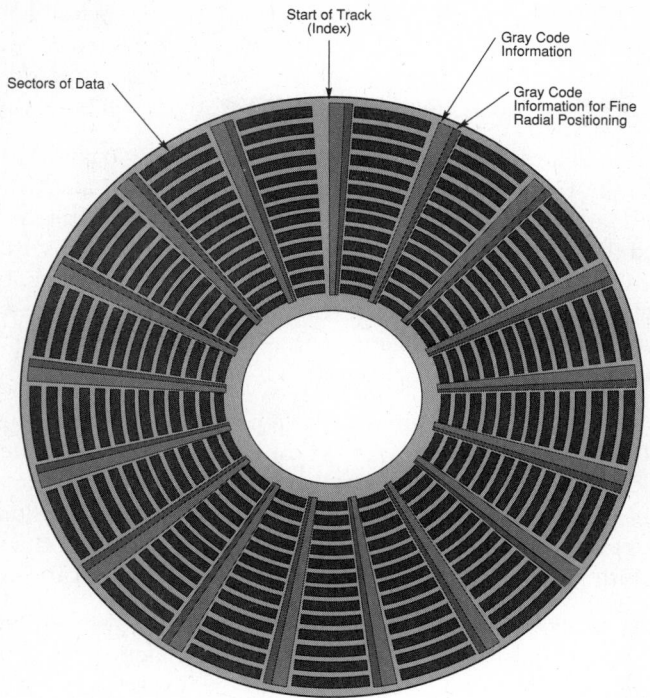

Fig. 14.7
An embedded servo.

Dedicated Servo. A *dedicated servo* is a design in which the servo information is written continuously throughout the entire track, rather than just one time per track or at the beginning of each sector. Unfortunately, if this procedure were performed on the entire drive, no room would be left for data. For this reason, a dedicated servo uses one side of one of the platters exclusively for the servo-positioning information. The term *dedicated* comes from the fact that this platter side is completely dedicated to the servo information and cannot contain any data. Although the dedicated-servo design may seem to be wasteful, none of the other platter sides carry any servo information, and you end up losing about the same amount of total disk real estate as with the embedded servo.

When a dedicated-servo drive is manufactured, one side of one platter is deducted from normal read/write usage; on this platter is recorded a special set of gray-code data that indicates proper track positions. Because the head that rests above this surface cannot be used for normal reading and writing, these marks can never be erased, and the servo information is protected, as in the other servo designs. No low-level format or other procedure can possibly overwrite the servo information.

When the drive is commanded to move the heads to a specific cylinder, the internal drive electronics use the signals received by the servo head to determine the position of the heads. As the heads are moved, the track counters are read from the dedicated servo surface. When the requested track is detected below the servo head, the actuator is stopped. The servo electronics then fine-tune the position so that before writing is allowed, the heads are positioned absolutely precisely above the desired cylinder. Although only one head is used for servo tracking, the other heads are attached to the same rigid rack, so if one head is above the desired cylinder, all the others will be as well.

One noticeable trait of dedicated servo drives is that they usually have an odd number of heads. For example, the Toshiba MK-538FB 1.2GB drive on which I am saving this chapter has eight platters but only 15 read/write heads; the drive uses a dedicated-servo positioning system, and the 16th head is the servo head. You will find that virtually all high-end drives use a dedicated servo because such a design offers servo information continuously, no matter where the heads are located. This system offers the greatest possible positioning accuracy. Some drives even combine a dedicated servo with an embedded servo, but this type of hybrid design is rare.

Automatic Head Parking. When a hard disk drive is powered off, the spring tension in each head arm pulls the heads into contact with the platters. The drive is designed to sustain thousands of takeoffs and landings, but it is wise to ensure that the landing occurs at a spot on the platter that contains no data. Some amount of abrasion occurs during the landing and takeoff process, removing just a "micro puff" from the media; but if the drive is jarred during the landing or takeoff process, real damage can occur.

One benefit of using a voice coil actuator is *automatic head parking*. In a drive that has a voice coil actuator, the heads are positioned and held by magnetic force. When power is removed from the drive, the magnetic field that holds the heads stationary over a particular cylinder dissipates, enabling the head rack to skitter across the drive surface and potentially cause damage. In the voice coil design, therefore, the head rack is attached to a weak spring at one end and a head stop at the other end. When the system is powered on, the spring normally is overcome by the magnetic force of the positioner. When the drive is powered off, however, the spring gently drags the head rack to a park-and-lock position before the drive slows down and the heads land. On many drives, you can actually hear the "ting...ting...ting...ting" sound as the heads literally bounce-park themselves, driven by this spring.

On a drive with a voice coil actuator, you can activate the parking mechanism simply by turning off the system; you do not need to run a program to park or retract the heads. In the event of a power outage, the heads park themselves automatically. (The drives unpark automatically when the system is powered on.)

Some stepper motor drives (such as the Seagate ST-251 series drives) park their heads, but this function is rare among stepper motor drives. The stepper motor drives that do park their heads usually use an ingenious system whereby the spindle motor actually is used as a generator after the power to the drive is turned off. The back EMF (Electro Motive Force), as it is called, is used to drive the stepper motor to park the heads.

Air Filters

Nearly all hard disk drives have two air filters. One filter is called the *recirculating filter*, and the other is called either a *barometric* or *breather filter*. These filters are permanently sealed inside the drive and are designed never to be changed for the life of the drive, unlike many older mainframe hard disks that had changeable filters. Many mainframe drives circulate air from outside the drive through a filter that must be changed periodically.

A hard disk on a PC system does not circulate air from inside to outside the HDA, or vice versa. The recirculating filter that is permanently installed inside the HDA is designed to filter only the small particles of media scraped off the platters during head takeoffs and landings (and possibly any other small particles dislodged inside the drive). Because PC hard disk drives are permanently sealed and do not circulate outside air, they can run in extremely dirty environments (see fig. 14.8).

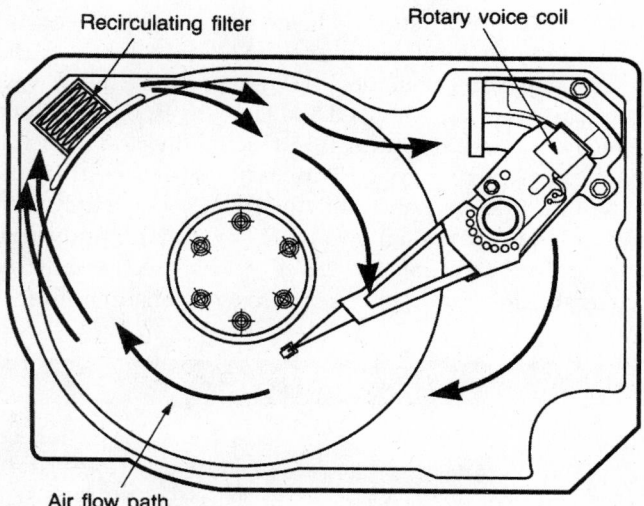

Recirculating filter

Rotary voice coil

Air flow path

Used with permission from IBM Corporation.

Fig. 14.8
Air circulation in a hard disk.

The HDA in a hard disk is sealed but not airtight. The HDA is vented through a barometric or breather filter element that allows for pressure equalization (breathing) between the inside and outside of the drive. For this reason, most hard drives are rated by the drive's manufacturer to run in a specific range of altitudes, usually from –1,000 to +10,000 feet above sea level. In fact, some hard drives are not rated to exceed 7,000 feet while operating, because the air pressure would be too low inside the drive to float the heads properly. As the environmental air pressure changes, air bleeds into or out of the drive so that internal and external pressures are identical. Although air does bleed through a vent, contamination usually is not a concern, because the barometric filter on this vent is designed to filter out all particles larger than 0.3 micron (about 12 micro-inches) to meet the specifications for cleanliness inside the drive. You can see the vent holes on most drives, which are covered internally by this breather filter. Some drives use even finer-grade filter elements to keep out even smaller particles.

I got a laugh when I read an article in one of the better known computer magazines, stating not only that hard drives are airtight, but also that the air is evacuated from the interior of the drive, and the heads and platters run in a vacuum! The person who wrote the article obviously does not understand even the most basic principles of hard disk operation. Air is required inside the HDA to float the heads, and this cushion of air (sometimes called an air bearing) is the primary principle in Winchester hard disk design.

I conducted a seminar in Hawaii several years ago, and several of the students were from the Mauna Kea astronomical observatory. They indicated that virtually all hard disks they had tried to use at the observatory site had failed very quickly, if they worked at all. This was no surprise, because the observatory is at the 13,800-foot peak of the mountain, and at that altitude, even people don't function very well! At the time, it was suggested that the students investigate solid-state (RAM) disks, tape drives, or even floppy drives as their primary storage medium. Since this time, IBM's Adstar division (which produces all IBM hard drives) introduced a line of rugged 3.5-inch drives that are in fact hermetically sealed (airtight), although they do have air inside the HDA. Because they carry their own internal air under pressure, these drives can operate at any altitude, and also can withstand extremes of shock and temperature. The drives are designed for military and industrial applications, such as aboard aircraft and in extremely harsh environments.

Caution

Airborne particulates such as cigarette smoke normally do not affect a PC hard disk drive, because any air that bleeds into the hard drive is filtered before entering the drive. However, many other components of the system (such as floppy drives, keyboards, connectors, and sockets) will sustain damage from contaminants such as cigarette smoke.

Hard Disk Temperature Acclimation

Although the HDA is sealed, it is not hermetically sealed, which means that it is not airtight and that there is air inside. To allow for pressure equalization, hard drives have a filtered port to bleed air into or out of the HDA as necessary.

This breathing also enables moisture to enter the drive, and after some period of time, it must be assumed that the humidity inside any hard disk is similar to that outside the drive. Humidity can become a serious problem if it is allowed to condense—and especially if the drive is powered up while this condensation is present. Most hard disk manufacturers have specified procedures for acclimating a hard drive to a new environment with different temperature and humidity ranges, especially for bringing a drive into a warmer environment in which condensation can form. This situation should be of special concern to users of laptop or portable systems with hard disks. If you leave a portable system in an automobile trunk during the winter, for example, it could be catastrophic to bring the machine inside and power it up without allowing it to acclimate to the temperature indoors.

The following text and Table 14.7 are taken from the factory packaging that Control Data Corporation (later Imprimis and eventually Seagate) used to ship its hard drives:

> If you have just received or removed this unit from a climate with temperatures at or below 50°F (10°C) do not open this container until the following conditions are met, otherwise condensation could occur and damage to the device and/or media may result. Place this package in the operating environment for the time duration according to the temperature chart.

Table 14.7   Hard Disk Drive Environmental Acclimation Table

Previous Climate Temp.	Acclimation Time
+40°F (+4°C)	13 hours
+30°F (–1°C)	15 hours
+20°F (–7°C)	16 hours
+10°F (–12°C)	17 hours
0°F (–18°C)	18 hours
–10°F (–23°C)	20 hours
–20°F (–29°C)	22 hours
–30°F (–34°C) or less	27 hours

As you can see from this chart, a hard disk that has been stored in a colder-than-normal environment must be placed in the normal operating environment for a specified amount of time to allow for acclimation before it is powered on.

Spindle Motors

The motor that spins the platters is called the *spindle motor* because it is connected to the spindle around which the platters revolve. Spindle motors in hard disks always are connected directly; no belts or gears are used. The motors must be free of noise and vibration; otherwise, they transmit to the platters a rumble that could disrupt reading and writing operations.

The motors also must be precisely controlled for speed. The platters on hard disks revolve at speeds ranging from 3,600 to 7,200 rpm or more, and the motor has a control circuit with a feedback loop to monitor and control this speed precisely. Because this speed control must be automatic, hard drives do not have a motor-speed adjustment. Some diagnostics programs claim to measure hard drive rotation speed, but all that these programs do is estimate the rotational speed by the timing at which sectors arrive.

There actually is no way for a program to measure hard disk rotational speed; this measurement can be made only with sophisticated test equipment. Don't be alarmed if some diagnostic program tells you that your drive is spinning at an incorrect speed; most likely the program is wrong, not the drive. Platter rotation and timing information is simply not provided through the hard disk controller interface. In the past, software could give approximate rotational speed estimates by performing multiple sector read requests and timing them, but this was valid only when all drives had the same number of sectors per track (17) and they all spun at 3,600 rpm. Zoned Recording combined with a variety of different rotational speeds found in modern drives, not to mention built-in buffers and caches means that these calculation estimates cannot be performed accurately.

On most drives, the spindle motor is on the bottom of the drive, just below the sealed HDA. Many drives today, however, have the spindle motor built directly into the platter hub inside the HDA. By using an internal hub spindle motor, the manufacturer can stack more platters in the drive, because the spindle motor takes up no vertical space. This method allows for more platters than would be possible if the motor were outside the HDA.

> **Note**
>
> Spindle motors, particularly on the larger form-factor drives, can consume a great deal of 12-volt power. Most drives require two to three times the normal operating power when the motor first spins the platters. This heavy draw lasts only a few seconds, or until the drive platters reach operating speed. If you have more than one drive, you should try to sequence the start of the spindle motors so that the power supply does not receive such a large load from all the drives at the same time. Most SCSI and IDE drives have a delayed spindle-motor start feature.

Spindle Ground Strap

Most drives have a special grounding strap attached to a ground on the drive and resting on the center spindle of the platter spindle motor. This device is the single most likely cause of excessive drive noise.

The *grounding strap* usually is made of copper and often has a carbon or graphite button that contacts the motor or platter spindle. The grounding strap dissipates static generated by the platters as they spin through the air inside the HDA. If the platters generate static due to friction with the air, and if no place exists for this electrical potential to bleed off, static may discharge through the heads or the internal bearings in the motor. When static discharges through the motor bearings, it can burn the lubricants inside the sealed bearings. If the static charge discharges through the read/write heads, the heads can be damaged or data can be corrupted. The grounding strap bleeds off this static buildup to prevent these problems.

Where the spindle of the motor contacts the carbon contact button (at the end of the ground strap) spinning at full speed, the button often wears, creating a flat spot. The flat spot causes the strap to vibrate and produce a high-pitched squeal or whine. The noise may come and go, depending on temperature and humidity. Sometimes, banging the side of the machine can jar the strap so that the noise changes or goes away, but this is not the way to fix the problem. *I am not suggesting that you bang on your system!* (Most people mistake this noise for something much more serious, such as a total drive-motor failure or bearing failure, which rarely occurs.)

If the spindle grounding strap vibrates and causes noise, you can remedy the situation in several ways:

- Dampen the vibration of the strap by attaching some foam tape or rubber to it.

- Lubricate the contact point.

- Tear off the strap (not recommended!).

On some drives, the spindle motor strap is easily accessible. On other drives, you have to partially disassemble the drive by removing the logic board or other external items to get to the strap.

Of these suggested solutions, the first one is the best. The best way to correct this problem is to glue (or otherwise affix) some rubber or foam to the strap. This procedure changes the harmonics of the strap and usually dampens vibrations. Most manufacturers now use this technique on newly manufactured drives. An easy way to do this is to place some foam tape on the back side of the ground strap.

You also can use a dab of silicone RTV (room-temperature vulcanizing) rubber or caulk on the back of the strap. If you try this method, be sure to use low-volatile (noncorrosive) silicone RTV sealer, which commonly is sold at auto-parts stores. The noncorrosive silicone will be listed on the label as being safe for automotive oxygen sensors. This low-volatile silicone also is free from corrosive acids that can damage the copper strap and is described as low-odor because it does not have the vinegar odor usually associated with silicone RTV. Dab a small amount on the back side of the copper strap (do not interfere with the contact location), and the problem should be solved permanently.

Lubricating the strap is an acceptable, but often temporary, solution. You will want to use some sort of conducting lube, such as a graphite-based compound (the kind used on frozen car locks). Any conductive lubricant (such as moly or lithium) will work as long as it is conductive, but do not use standard oil or grease. Simply dab a small amount of lubricant onto the end of a toothpick, and place a small drop directly on the point of contact.

The last solution is not acceptable. Tearing off the strap eliminates the noise, but it has several possible ramifications. Although the drive will work (silently) without the strap, an engineer placed it there for a reason. Imagine those ungrounded static charges leaving the platters through the heads, perhaps in the form of a spark—possibly even damaging the Thin Film heads. You should choose one of the other solutions.

I mention this last solution only because several people have told me that members of the tech-support staff of some of the hard drive vendors, and even of some manufacturers, told them to remove the strap, which—of course—I do not recommend.

Logic Boards

A disk drive, including a hard disk drive, has one or more logic boards mounted on it. The logic boards contain the electronics that control the drive's spindle and head actuator systems and that present data to the controller in some agreed-on form. In some drives, the controller is located on the drive, which can save on a system's total chip count.

Many disk drive failures occur in the logic board, not in the mechanical assembly. (This statement does not seem logical, but it is true.) Therefore, you can repair many failed drives by replacing the logic board, not the entire drive. Replacing the logic board, moreover, enables you to regain access to the data on the failed drive—something that replacing the entire drive precludes.

Logic boards can be removed or replaced because they simply plug into the drive. These boards usually are mounted with standard screw hardware. If a drive is failing and you have a spare, you may be able to verify a logic-board failure by taking the board off the known good drive and mounting it on the bad one. If your suspicions are confirmed, you can order a new logic board from the drive manufacturer. You also may be able to purchase a refurbished unit or even to trade in your old drive or logic board. The drive manufacturer will have details on what services it can offer.

To reduce costs further, many third-party vendors also can supply replacement logic-board assemblies. These companies often charge much less than the drive manufacturers for the same components. (See the "Vendor List" in Appendix B for vendors of drive components, including logic boards.)

Cables and Connectors

Most hard disk drives have several connectors for interfacing to the system, receiving power, and sometimes grounding to the system chassis. Most drives have at least these three types of connectors:

- Interface connector(s)
- Power connector
- Optional ground connector (tab)

Of these, the interface connectors are the most important, because they carry the data and command signals from the system to and from the drive. In many drive interfaces, the drive interface cables can be connected in a *daisy chain*, or bus-type configuration. Most interfaces support at least two drives, and SCSI (Small Computer System Interface) supports up to seven in the chain. Some interfaces, such as ST-506/412 or ESDI (Enhanced Small Device Interface), use a separate cable for data and control signals. These drives have two cables from the controller interface to the drive. SCSI and IDE (Integrated Drive Electronics) drives usually have a single data and control connector. With these interfaces, the disk controller is built into the drive (see fig. 14.9).

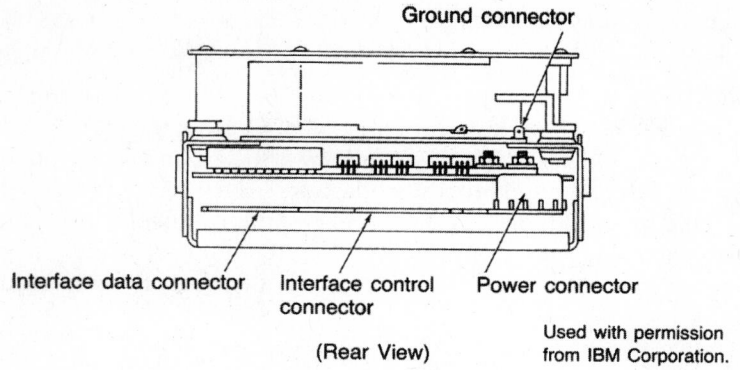

Ground connector

Interface data connector   Interface control
connector   Power connector

(Rear View)

Used with permission
from IBM Corporation.

IV

Mass Storage Systems

Fig. 14.9
Typical hard disk connections (ST-506/412 or ESDI shown).

The different interfaces and cable specifications are covered in the sections on drive interfaces later in this chapter. You also will find connector pinout specifications for virtually all drive interfaces and cable connections in this chapter.

The *power connector* usually is the same type that is used in floppy drives, and the same power-supply connector plugs into it. Most hard disk drives use both 5- and 12-volt power, although some of the smaller drives designed for portable applications use only 5-volt power. In most cases, the 12-volt power runs the spindle motor and head actuator, and the 5-volt power runs the circuitry. Make sure that your power supply can supply adequate power for the hard disk drives installed in your PC system; most hard drives draw quite a bit more power than a floppy drive.

The 12-volt-power consumption of a drive usually varies with the physical size of the unit. The larger the drive is and the more platters there are to spin, the more power is required. Also, the faster the drive spins, the more power will be required. For example, most of the 3.5-inch drives on the market today use roughly one-half to one-fourth the power (in watts) of the full-size 5.25-inch drives. Some of the very small (2.5-, 1.8-, or 1.3-inch) hard disks barely sip electrical power and actually use 1 watt or less!

Ensuring an adequate power supply is particularly important with some systems, such as the original IBM AT. These systems have a power supply with three disk drive power connectors, labeled P10, P11, and P12. The three power connectors may seem to be equal, but the technical-reference manual for these systems indicates that 2.8 amps of 12-volt current is available on P10 and P11 and that only 1 amp of 12-volt current is available on P12. Because most full-height hard drives draw much more power than 1 amp, especially at startup, the P12 connector can be used only by floppy drives or half-height hard drives. Some 5.25-inch drives draw as much as 4 amps of current during the first few seconds of startup. These drives also can draw as much as 2.5 amps during normal operation.

Sometimes, you can solve random boot-up failures simply by plugging the hard drive into a suitable power connector (P10 or P11 on the IBM AT). Most IBM-compatible PC systems have a power supply with four or more disk drive power connectors that provide equal power, but some use power supplies designed like those of the IBM AT.

A *grounding tab* provides a positive ground connection between the drive and the system's chassis. In a typical IBM PC or IBM XT system, because the hard disk drive is mounted directly to the chassis of the PC using screws, the ground wire is unnecessary. On AT-type systems from IBM and other manufacturers, the drives are installed on plastic or fiberglass rails, which do not provide proper grounding. These systems must provide a grounding wire, plugged into the drive at this grounding tab. Failure to ground the drive may result in improper operation, intermittent failure, or general read and write errors.

Configuration Items

To configure a hard disk drive for installation in a system, several jumpers (and, possibly, terminating resistors) usually must be set or configured properly. These items will vary from interface to interface and often from drive to drive as well. A complete discussion of the configuration settings for each interface appears in "Hard Disk Installation Procedures" later in this chapter.

The Faceplate or Bezel

Most hard disk drives offer as an option a front faceplate, or *bezel* (see fig. 14.10). A bezel usually is supplied as an option for the drive rather than as a standard item.

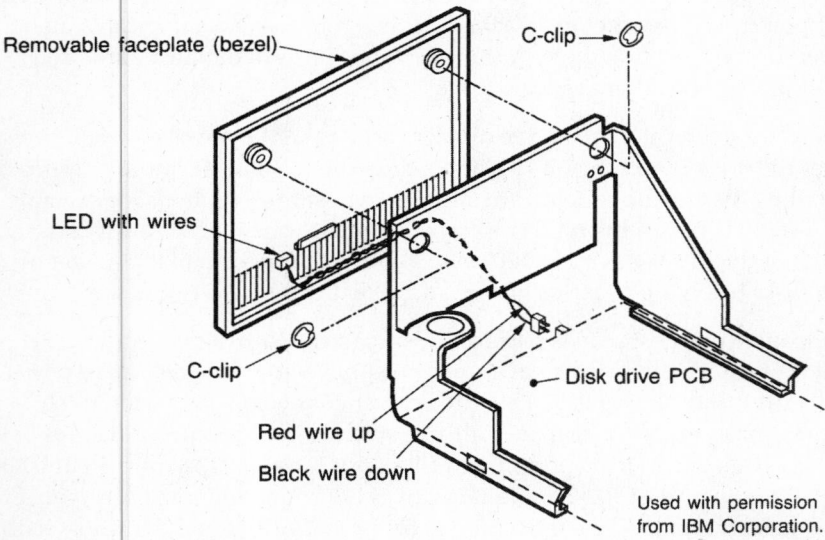

Removable faceplate (bezel)

C-clip

LED with wires

C-clip

Disk drive PCB

Red wire up

Black wire down

Used with permission from IBM Corporation.

Fig. 14.10

A typical hard drive faceplate (bezel).

Bezels often come in several sizes and colors to match various PC systems. For standard full-height, 5.25-inch, form-factor drives, you have only one choice of bezel. For half-height drives, bezels come in half-height and full-height forms. Using a full-height bezel on a half-height drive enables you to install a single drive in a full-height bay without leaving a hole in the front of the system. To add a second half-height drive, you may want to order the half-height bezels so that you can stack the old and new drives. Many faceplate configurations for 3.5-inch drives are available, including bezels that fit 3.5-inch drive bays as well as 5.25-inch drive bays. You even have a choice of colors (usually, black, cream, or white).

Some bezels feature a light-emitting diode (LED) that flickers when your hard disk is in use. The LED is mounted in the bezel; the wire hanging off the back of the LED plugs into the drive or perhaps the controller. In some drives, the LED is permanently mounted on the drive, and the bezel has a clear or colored window so that you can see the LED flicker while the drive is accessed.

One type of LED problem occurs with some AT-type-system hard disk installations: if the drive has an LED, the LED may remain on continuously, as though it were a "power-on" light rather than an access light. This problem happens because the controller in the AT has a direct connection for the LED, thus altering the drive LED function. Some controllers have a jumper that enables the controller to run the drive in what is called latched or unlatched mode. *Latched mode* means that the drive is selected continuously and that the drive LED remains lighted; in *unlatched mode* (to which we are more accustomed), the LED lights only when the drive is accessed. Check to see whether your controller has a jumper for changing this function; if so, you may be able to control the way that the LED operates.

In systems in which the hard disk is hidden by the unit's cover, a bezel is not needed. In fact, using a bezel may prevent the cover from resting on the chassis properly, in which case the bezel will have to be removed. If you are installing a drive that does not have a proper bezel, frame, or rails to attach to the system, check Appendix B of this book; several listed vendors offer these accessories for a variety of drives.

Hard Disk Features

To make the best decision in purchasing a hard disk for your system, or to understand what differentiates one brand of hard disk from another, you must consider many features. This section examines the issues that you should consider when you evaluate drives:

- Actuator mechanism
- Media
- Head parking
- Reliability
- Speed
- Shock mounting
- Cost

Actuator Mechanism

A drive with high performance and reliability has two basic physical properties:

- Voice coil actuator mechanism
- Thin-film media

Drives with stepper motor actuators should be used only when cost far outweighs other considerations. You should not use these drives in portable systems or in systems that must operate under extreme temperature, noise, or vibration conditions. Don't use these drives where preventive maintenance cannot be provided, because they require periodic reformats to maintain data integrity. Finally, you should not use these drives in demanding situations, such as in a network file server. Drives with stepper motor actuators perform adequately in low-volume-usage systems, as long as you provide preventive maintenance at least annually or semiannually and the environment can be controlled. Fortunately, stepper motor drives are virtually out of production today; nearly all new drives use voice coil actuators.

Voice coil actuator drives should be used wherever possible, especially if any real demands are placed on the drive. These drives are ideal for portable systems or for systems that suffer extreme temperatures, noise, or vibration. These drives are ideal when a fast drive is necessary. A voice coil drive requires little or no preventive maintenance, so the first low-level format usually is the only low-level format ever required. Less maintenance (no reformatting) enables this type of drive to be used for high-volume situations in which a single support person maintains many PC systems. Fortunately, virtually all drives manufactured today are voice coil drives, and they should be! Voice coil actuator technology is the only way to build a reliable, high-performance, low-maintenance drive.

Head Parking

Head parking is an often-misunderstood issue with hard disks. When a hard disk comes to a stop (actually, before it stops), the heads land on the media. This contact occurs as the drive slows, and in some drives, the distance that the heads skid before the platters stop may be many linear feet. The same skidding occurs when the drive is powered on and the platters begin to turn. In some drives, the heads land on whatever cylinder they were last positioned above—usually, an area of the disk that contains data.

Most drives today move the heads to a nondata area called the *landing zone* before the platters slow enough for the heads to come into contact with them. This procedure is called *automatic head parking*. Drives that do not park their heads automatically still can be parked, but it requires the manual execution of a program to move the heads before the system is powered down.

Drives with voice coil actuators offer automatic head parking. While the drive is running, an electric coil overcomes the spring tension and moves the head around the disk. When power is lost, the spring automatically pulls the head rack away from data areas of the disk to a special landing zone.

Most stepper motor drives do not have an automatic-parking function; instead they must be parked manually. To find out whether your drive autoparks, contact the drive manufacturer and ask for the technical or specification manual for the drive, which will contain the answer.

Some newer stepper drives do incorporate a parking mechanism. One example is the Seagate ST-251 series. This popular stepper drive autoparks the heads by using an ingenious system in which the drive spindle motor is used as a generator, powering the stepper motor to park the heads. When the drive is powered off, you hear the stepper motor drive the heads to the landing zone. Seagate seems to be using this type of mechanism in many of its newer stepper motor drives as well.

Software is available that enables you to park the heads of drives that lack the automatic-parking feature. The software is not quite as reliable as automatic parking, however, because it does not park the heads if the power goes off unexpectedly. If your system requires a head-parking program, the program usually comes on the configuration or setup utility disk that goes with the system. For example, IBM supplied a head-parking routine on the diagnostics disk supplied with its original XT and AT systems, as well as on the Advanced Diagnostics disk supplied with the hardware-maintenance service manual. Simply boot these disks and select the option Prepare System for Moving. This procedure invokes a program on the disk called SHIPDISK.COM. Different SHIPDISK.COM files exist for XT and AT systems. The heads of all attached disks are parked. Then you shut down the system.

As a note, several years ago IBM issued a warning to its dealers, recommending that they not run SHIPDISK.COM from the DOS prompt. IBM said that a slight chance exists that you can lose data, because the program can accidentally write random data on the drive. The memo indicated that SHIPDISK.COM should be run only from the menu. Apparently, the problem was that SHIPDISK.COM parks the disks and then executes a software interrupt to return to the diagnostics-disk menu, and unpredictable things can happen (including stray disk writes) if the program was not run from the diagnostics-disk menu.

For AT systems, IBM supplied a separate program, SHUTDOWN.EXE, that is designed to be run from the DOS prompt. This program is on the AT diagnostics and advanced-diagnostics disks. You can copy this program to the hard disk and enter the SHUTDOWN command at the DOS prompt. You see a graphic of a switch, which turns off as the heads are parked. The program then halts the system, requiring a complete power-down. This program works only on AT-type systems.

Note

It usually is not a good idea to run a hard disk parking program that is not designed for your system. Although no physical harm will occur, the heads may not be parked in the correct landing zone. (Many programs improperly position the heads above Cylinder 0—the last place where you want them!)

If your hard drive is a stepper motor actuator drive without automatic parking, it should come with a parking program. If you have an IBM system, this program comes on the diagnostics and setup disks that came with the system. If you have an IBM-compatible, you probably received such a program on your setup disk. Additionally, some public-domain programs park a stepper motor hard disk.

Should you park the heads every time you shut down the drive? Some people think so, but IBM says that you do not have to park the heads on a drive unless you are moving the drive. My experiences are in line with IBM's recommendations, although a more fail-safe approach is to park the heads at every shutdown. Remember that voice coil drives park their heads automatically every time and require no manual parking operations. I only park a stepper motor drive if I am moving the unit, but there is nothing wrong with parking the heads at every shutdown. The procedure is simple and cannot hurt.

Reliability

When you shop for a drive, you may notice a feature called the *mean time between failures* (MTBF) described in the brochures. MTBF figures usually range from 20,000 hours to 500,000 hours or more. I usually ignore these figures, because they usually are just theoretical—not actual—statistical values. Most drives that boast these figures have not even been manufactured for that length of time. One year of 5-day work weeks with 8-hour days equals 2,080 hours of operation. If you never turn off your system for 365 days and run the full 24 hours per day, you operate your system 8,760 hours each year; a drive with a 500,000-hour MTBF rating is supposed to last (on average) 57 years before failing! Obviously, that figure cannot be derived from actual statistics, because the particular drive probably has been on the market for less than a year.

Statistically, for the MTBF figures to have real weight, you must take a sample of drives, measure the failure rate for at least twice the rated figure, and measure how many drives fail in that time. To be really accurate, you would have to wait until all the drives fail and record the operating hours at each failure. Then you would average the running time for all the test samples to arrive at the average time before a drive failure. For a reported MTBF of 500,000 hours (common today), the test sample should be run for at least 1 million hours (114 years) to be truly accurate, yet the drive carries this specification on the day that it is introduced.

Manufacturers and vendors sometimes play with these numbers. For example, several years ago, CDC rated a Wren II half-height drive at 20,000 hours MTBF (this drive was one of the most reliable in the world at the time), but I saw a reseller rate the same unit at 50,000 hours. Some of the worst drives that I have used boasted high MTBF figures, and some of the best drives have lower ones. These figures do not necessarily translate to reliability in the field, and that is why I generally place no importance on them.

Performance

When you select a hard disk, an important feature to consider is the performance (speed) of the drive. Hard disks come in a wide range of performance capabilities. As is true of many things, one of the best indicators of a drive's relative performance is its price. An old saying from the automobile-racing industry is appropriate here: "Speed costs money. How fast do you want to go?"

You can measure the speed of a disk drive in two ways:

- Average seek time
- Transfer rate

Average seek time, normally measured in milliseconds, is the average amount of time it takes to move the heads from one cylinder to another cylinder a random distance away. One way to measure this specification is to run many random track-seek operations and then divide the timed results by the number of seeks performed. This method provides an average time for a single seek.

The standard way to measure average seek time used by many drive manufacturers involves measuring the time that it takes the heads to move across one-third of the total cylinders. Average seek time depends only on the drive; the type of interface or controller has little effect on this specification. (In some cases, the setup of the controller to the drive can affect seek times; this subject is discussed later in this chapter.) The rating is a gauge of the capabilities of the head actuator.

Be wary of benchmarks that claim to measure drive seek performance. Most IDE and SCSI drives use a scheme called sector translation, so any commands to the drive to move the heads to a specific cylinder do not actually cause the intended physical movement. This situation renders such benchmarks meaningless for those types of drives. SCSI drives also require an additional command, because the commands first must be sent to the drive over the SCSI bus. Even though these drives can have the fastest access times, because the command overhead is not factored in by most benchmarks, the benchmark programs produce poor performance figures for these drives.

I don't put too much faith in the benchmarks, and the drive manufacturers have been very honest in reporting their true performance figures over the years. The bottom line is that if you want to know the true seek performance of your drive, the most accurate way to find it is simply to look it up in the drive specification manual.

A slightly different measurement, called average access time, involves another element, called latency. *Latency* is the average time (in milliseconds) that it takes for a sector to be available after the heads have reached a track. On average, this figure is half the time that it takes for the disk to rotate one time, which is 8.33 ms at 3,600 rpm. A drive that spins twice as fast would have half the latency. A measurement of average access time is the sum of the average seek time and latency. This number provides the average amount of time required before a randomly requested sector can be accessed.

Latency is a factor in disk read and write performance. Decreasing the latency increases the speed of access to data or files, accomplished only by spinning the drive platters faster. I have a drive that spins at 4,318 rpm, for a latency of 6.95 ms. Some drives spin at 7,200 rpm or faster, resulting in an even shorter latency time of only 4.17 ms. In addition to increasing performance where real-world access to data is concerned, spinning the platters faster also increases the data-transfer rate after the heads arrive at the desired sectors.

The transfer rate probably is more important to overall system performance than any other specification. *Transfer rate* is the rate at which the drive and controller can send data to the system. The transfer rate depends primarily on the drive's HDA and secondarily on the controller. Transfer rate used to be more bound to the limits of the controller, meaning that drives that were connected to older controllers often outperformed those controllers. This situation is where the concept of interleaving sectors came from. *Interleaving* refers to the ordering of the sectors so that they are not sequential, enabling a slow controller to keep up without missing the next sector.

A following section discusses interleaving in more detail. For now, the point I am trying to make is that modern drives with integrated controllers are fully capable of keeping up with the raw drive transfer rate. In other words, they no longer have to interleave the sectors to slow the data for the controller.

Another performance issue is the raw interface performance, which, in IDE or SCSI drives, usually is far higher than any of the drives themselves are able to sustain. Be wary of quoted transfer specifications for the interface, because they may have little effect on what the drive can actually put out. The drive interface simply limits the maximum theoretical transfer rate; the actual drive and controller place the real limits on performance.

In older ST-506/412 interface drives, you sometimes can double or triple the transfer rate by changing the controller, because many of the older controllers could not support a 1:1 interleave. When you change the controller to one that does support this interleave, the transfer rate will be equal to the drive's true capability.

To calculate the true transfer rate of a drive, you need to know several important specifications. The two most important specifications are the true rotational speed of the drive (in RPM) and the average number of physical sectors on each track. I say "average" because most drives today use a Zoned Recording technique that places different numbers of sectors on the inner and outer cylinders. The transfer rate on Zoned Recording drives always is fastest in the outermost zone, where the sector per track count is highest. Also be aware that many drives (especially Zoned Recording drives) are configured with sector translation, so that the BIOS reported number of sectors per track has little to do with physical reality. You need to know the true physical parameters, rather than what the BIOS thinks.

When you know these figures, you can use the following formula to determine the maximum transfer rate in millions of bits per second (Mbps):

Maximum Data Transfer Rate (Mbps) = SPT × 512 bytes × RPM / 60 seconds / 1,000,000 bits

For example, the ST-12551N 2GB 3.5-inch drive spins at 7,200 RPM and has an average 81 sectors per track. The maximum transfer rate for this drive is figured as follows:

81 × 512 × 7,200 / 60 / 1,000,000 = 4.98Mbps

Using this formula, you can calculate the true maximum sustained transfer rate of any drive.

Cache Programs and Caching Controllers. At the software level, disk cache programs, such as SMARTDRV or PCKwik, can have a major effect on disk drive performance. These cache programs hook into the BIOS hard drive interrupt and then intercept the read and write calls to the disk BIOS from application programs and the device drivers of DOS.

When an application program wants to read data from a hard drive, the cache program intercepts the read request, passes the read request to the hard drive controller in the usual way, saves the data that was read in its cache buffer, and then passes the data back to the application program. Depending on the size of the cache buffer, numerous sectors are read into and saved in the buffer.

When the application wants to read more data, the cache program again intercepts the request and examines its buffers to see whether the data is still in the cache. If so, the data is passed back to the application immediately, without another hard drive operation. As you can imagine, this method speeds access tremendously and can greatly affect disk drive performance measurements.

Most controllers now have some form of built-in hardware buffer or cache that doesn't intercept or use any BIOS interrupts. Instead, the caching is performed at the hardware level and is invisible to normal performance-measurement software. Track read-ahead buffers originally were included in controllers to allow for 1:1 interleave performance. Some controllers have simply increased the sizes of these read-ahead buffers; others have added intelligence by making them a cache instead of a simple buffer.

Many IDE and SCSI drives have cache memory built directly into the drive. For example, the Toshiba MK-538FB 1.2GB drive on which I am saving this chapter has 512KB of built-in cache memory. Other drives have even more built-in caches, such as the Seagate Barracuda 2 2GB with 1MB of integral cache memory. I remember when 640KB was a lot of memory; now, tiny 3.5-inch hard disk drives have more than that built right in! These integral caches are part of the reason why most IDE and SCSI drives perform so well.

Although software and hardware caches can make a drive faster for routine transfer operations, a cache will not affect the true maximum transfer rate that the drive can sustain.

Interleave Selection. In a discussion of disk performance, the issue of interleave always comes up. Although traditionally, this was more a controller performance issue than a drive issue, most modern hard disks now have built-in controllers (IDE and SCSI) that are fully capable of taking the drive data as fast as the drive can send it. In other words, virtually all modern IDE and SCSI drives are formatted with no interleave (sometimes expressed as a 1:1 interleave ratio).

When a disk is low-level formatted, numbers are assigned to the sectors. These numbers are written in the Sector ID fields in the sector header and can be written or updated only by a low-level format. With older drive interfaces that used discrete controllers such as ST-506/412 or ESDI, you often had to calculate the best interleave value for the particular controller and system that you were using so you could low-level format the drive and number the sectors to offer optimum performance.

Notice that nearly all IDE and SCSI drives have their interleave ratios fixed at 1:1 and built-in controllers that can handle these ratios with no problem. In these drives, there no longer is a need to calculate or specify an interleave ratio, but knowing about interleaving can give you some further insight into the way that these drives function.

Many older ST-506/412 controllers could not handle the sectors as quickly as the drive could send them. Suppose that you have a standard ST-5096/412 drive with 17 sectors on each track and that you low-level formatted the drive, you specified a 1:1 interleave, which is to say that you numbered the sectors on each track consecutively.

Now suppose that you want to read some data from the drive. The controller commands the drive to position the heads at a specific track and to read all 17 sectors from that track. The heads move and arrive at the desired track. The time it takes for the heads to move is called the seek time. When the heads arrive at the desired track, you have to wait for an average half-revolution of the disk for the first sector to arrive. This wait is called latency. After an average latency of half of a disk revolution, the sector numbered 1 arrives below the heads. While the disk continues to spin at 3,600 rpm (60 revolutions per second), the data is read from sector 1, and as the data is being transferred from the controller to the system board, the disk continues to spin. Finally, the data is completely moved to the motherboard, and the controller is ready for sector 2. Figure 14.11 shows what is happening.

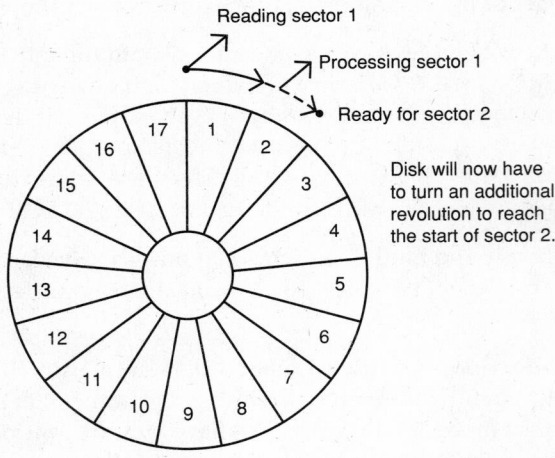

Fig. 14.11
A hard disk interleave ratio too low for the controller.

But wait—there's a problem here. Because the disk continues to spin at such a high rate of speed, the sector 2 passed below the head while the controller was working, and by the time that the controller is ready again, the heads will be coming to the start of sector 3. Because the controller needs to read sector 2 next, however, the controller must wait for the disk to spin a full revolution, or until the start of sector 2 comes below the heads. After this additional disk revolution, sector 2 arrives below the heads and is read. While the controller is transferring the data from sector 2 to the motherboard, sector 3 passes below the heads. When the controller finally is ready to read sector 3, the heads are coming to the start of sector 4, so another complete revolution is required, and the controller will have to get sector 3 on the next go-around. This scenario continues, with each new revolution allowing only one sector to be read and missing the next sector because that sector passes below the heads before the controller is ready.

As you can see, the timing of this procedure is not working out very well. At this pace, 17 full revolutions of the disk will be required to read all 17 sectors. Because each revolution takes 1/60 of 1 second, it will take 17/60 of 1 second to read this track, or almost one-third of a second—a very long time, by computer standards.

Can this performance be improved? You notice that after reading a specific sector from the disk, the controller takes some time to transfer the sector data to the motherboard. The next sector that the controller can catch in this example is the second sector away from the first one. In other words, the controller seems to be capable of catching every second sector.

I hope that you now can imagine the perfect solution to this problem: simply *number* the sectors out of order. The new numbering scheme takes into account how fast the controller works; the sectors are numbered so that each time the controller is ready for the next sector, the sector coming below the heads is numbered as the next sector that the controller will want to read. Figure 14.12 shows this new sector-numbering scheme.

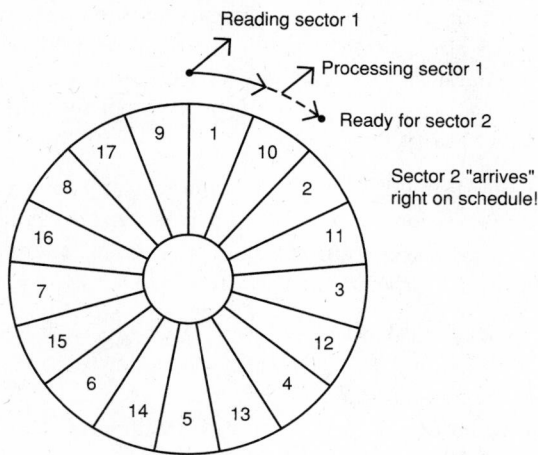

Fig. 14.12
A hard disk interleave ratio matching the controller's capabilities.

The new numbering system eliminates the extra disk revolution that previously was required to pick up each sector. Under the new scheme, the controller will read all 17 sectors on the disk in only two complete revolutions. Renumbering the sectors on the disk in this manner is called *interleaving*, which normally is expressed as a ratio. The interleave ratio in this example is 2 to 1 (also written as 2:1), which means that the next numbered sector is 2 sectors away from the preceding one; if the controller is capable of handling this, only two complete revolutions are needed to read an entire track. Thus, reading the track takes only 2/60 of one second at the 2:1 interleave, rather than the 17/60 of one second required to read the disk at the 1:1 interleave—an improvement of *800 percent* in the data transfer rate.

This example depicts a system in which the ideal interleave is 2:1. I used this example because most controllers that came in older AT systems worked in exactly this manner. If you set a controller for a 1:1 interleave, you likely would make the drive eight times slower than it should be. This situation, however, has changed with newer controller technology. Most disk controllers sold in the past couple of years support a 1:1 interleave on any AT-class system, even the slowest 6-MHz 286 versions. If you are purchasing or upgrading a system today, consider a disk subsystem with a 1:1 interleave controller to be a standard requirement. Fortunately, this is pretty much a non-issue; virtually all IDE or SCSI drives today have built-in controllers that easily handle a 1:1 interleave, and all these types of drives are preformatted at the factory in that manner. In many of these drives, it is not even possible to change the interleave to any value except 1:1.

The correct interleave for a system depends primarily on the controller and secondarily on the speed of the system into which the controller is plugged. A controller and system that can handle a *consecutive sector interleave* (a 1:1 interleave) must transfer data as fast as the disk drive can present it; this used to be quite a feat but now is commonplace.

Advances in controller technology have made a 1:1 interleave not only possible, but also affordable. Any 286 or faster system easily can handle the 1:1 interleave data transfer rate. The only types of systems that truly are too slow to handle a 1:1 interleave effectively are the original 4.77-MHz PC- and XT-type systems. Those systems have a maximum throughput to the slots of just under 400KB per second—not fast enough to support a 1:1 interleave controller.

Even with a 1:1 interleave, however, performance can vary significantly, and this is where the drive itself comes into play. A 1:1 interleave with a 17-sector disk is one thing, but with ESDI or SCSI drives spinning at 7,200 rpm and containing 81 or more sectors per track, the result is *nearly 5MB* of data transfer *each second.*

The interleave used in standard-issue IBM XT systems with hard drives was 6:1, whereas in IBM AT systems, it was 3:1. The best interleave for these systems actually is one lower than what was set up as standard in each case: In other words, the best interleave for the Xebec 1210 controller in a 4.77-MHz IBM PC or IBM XT is 5:1, and the best interleave for the Western Digital 1002 and 1003 controllers in a 6-MHz or 8-MHz IBM AT system is 2:1. If you redo the low-level format on these systems to the lower interleave number, you gain about 20 to 30 percent in data-transfer performance without changing any hardware and at no cost except some of your time.

Table 14.8 shows data transfer rates that were calculated for a variety of drives at a variety of different interleaves. The rows in this table represent a particular drive-and-controller combination with respect to the speed of revolution and the number of sectors per track. In all but the lowest-end setups, the interleave is 1:1, but I listed the other interleaves to show what the effect would be if they were used.

Table 14.8   Data-Transfer Rates (in K per Second) at Various Interleaves, Spindle Speeds, and Sector Densities

Speed (RPM)	Sectors /Track	1:1	2:1	Interleaves 3:1	4:1	5:1	6:1
3,600	17	510	255	170	128	102	85
3,600	25	750	375	250	188	150	125
3,600	26	780	390	260	195	156	130
3,600	27	810	405	270	203	162	135
3,600	32	960	480	320	240	192	160
3,600	33	990	495	330	248	198	165
3,600	34	1,020	510	340	255	204	170
3,600	35	1,050	525	350	263	210	175
3,600	36	1,080	540	360	270	216	180
3,600	37	1,110	555	370	278	222	185
3,600	38	1,140	570	380	285	228	190
3,600	39	1,170	585	390	293	234	195
4,500	50	1,875	938	625	469	375	313
3,600	81	2,430	1,215	810	608	486	405
4,500	70	2,625	1,313	875	656	525	438
5,400	70	3,150	1,575	1,050	788	630	525
6,300	90	4,725	2,363	1,575	1,181	945	788
7,200	81	4,860	2,430	1,620	1,215	972	810

Compare the 85KB-per-second transfer rate of the original IBM XT drive and controller (3,600 rpm, 17 sectors, and a 6:1 interleave standard) with the 4,860KB-per-second transfer rate of the Seagate Barracuda 2 drive (7,200 rpm, 81 sectors, and a 1:1 interleave). As you can see, we have come a long way in 10 years of disk and controller technology!

If you want to find out the current interleave setting of your drive, I usually recommend using Norton Utilities for performing hard disk drive interleave testing. The Calibrate program included with Norton Utilities can check, and possibly even change, the interleave on ST-506/412 interface drives through a nondestructive low-level format. Notice that in this case, nondestructive actually means that the format is performed one track at a time, with the data for that track being backed up and restored all the while. A full backup of the entire drive beforehand still is recommended, because if something goes wrong, one or more tracks can be wiped out.

Calibrate (and other utility programs like it) can change the interleave only on ST-506/412 and possibly some ESDI drives, and there can be problems even on drives that they can handle. If you really want to change the interleave of a drive through a new low-level format, I usually recommend whatever low-level format program the controller manufacturer specifies for the best possible job. In most modern drives (ESDI, IDE, or SCSI), it usually is not possible (or desirable) to change the interleave with a generic low-level format program such as Calibrate. With an ESDI-type drive, for example, you normally would need to use the controller's built-in (or supplied on disk) low-level format (LLF) program to re-set the interleave (most ESDI controllers support 1:1, so there should be little reason to change). IDE and SCSI drives have the disk controller built in, and most have the interleave permanently set (nonchangeable) to the best possible choice, eliminating any reason to change. Virtually all modern drive/controller combinations have a default 1:1 interleave anyway, so changing would not be beneficial.

Head and Cylinder Skewing. Most controllers today are capable of transferring data at a 1:1 sector interleave. This is especially true of controllers that are built in to IDE and SCSI drives. With a 1:1 interleave controller, the maximum data transfer rate can be maintained when reading and writing sectors to the disk. Although it would seem that there is no other way to further improve efficiency and the transfer rate, many people overlook two important factors that are similar to interleave: head and cylinder skewing.

When a drive is reading (or writing) data sequentially, first all of the sectors on a given track are read; then the drive must electronically switch to the next head in the cylinder to continue the operation. If the sectors are not skewed from head to head within the cylinder, no delay occurs after the last sector on one track and before the arrival of the first sector on the next track. Because all drives require some time (although a small amount) to switch from one head to another, and because the controller also adds some overhead to the operation, it is likely that by the time the drive is ready to read the sectors on the newly selected track, the first sector will already have passed by. By skewing the sectors from one head to another—that is, rotating their arrangement on the track so that the arrival of the first sector is delayed relative to the preceding track—you can ensure that no extra disk revolutions will be required when switching heads. This method provides the highest possible transfer rate when head switching is involved.

In a similar fashion, it takes considerable time for the heads to move from one cylinder to another. If the sectors on one cylinder were not skewed from those on the preceding adjacent cylinder, it is likely that by the time the heads arrive, the first sector will already have passed below them, requiring an additional revolution of the disk before reading of the new cylinder can begin. By skewing the sectors from one cylinder to the next, you can account for the cylinder-to-cylinder head-movement time and prevent any additional revolutions of the drive.

Head Skew. *Head skew* is the offset in logical sector numbering between the same physical sectors on two tracks below adjacent heads of the same cylinder. The number of sectors skewed when switching from head to head within a single cylinder is to compensate for head switching and controller overhead time. Think of it as the surface of each platter being rotated as you traverse from head to head. This method permits continuous read or write operation across head boundaries without missing any disk revolutions, thus maximizing system performance.

To understand head skew, you first need to know the order in which tracks and sectors are read from a disk. If you imagine a single-platter (two-head) drive with 10 cylinders and 17 sectors per track, the first sector that will be read on the entire drive is Cylinder 0,

Head 0, Sector 1. Following that, all the remaining sectors on that first track (Cylinder 0, Head 0) will be read until Sector 17 is reached. After that, two things could take place: one is that the heads could be moved so that the drive could continue reading the next track on the same side of the platter; or the second head could be selected, and therefore another entire track could be read with no head movement. Because head movement takes much longer than electronically selecting another head, all disk drives will select the subsequent heads on a cylinder before physically moving the heads to the next cylinder. Thus, the next sector to be read would be Cylinder 0, Head 1, Sector 1. Next, all the remaining sectors on that track are read (2 through 17), and then in our single platter example it is time to switch heads. This sequence continues until the last sector on the last track is read—in this example, Cylinder 9, Head 1, Sector 17.

If you could take the tracks off a cylinder in this example and lay them on top of one another, the tracks might look like this:

```
Cyl. 0, Head 0:    1- 2- 3- 4- 5- 6- 7- 8- 9-10-11-12-13-14-15-16-17
Cyl. 0, Head 1:    1- 2- 3- 4- 5- 6- 7- 8- 9-10-11-12-13-14-15-16-17
```

After reading all the sectors on head 0, the controller switches heads to head 1 and continues the read (looping around to the beginning of the track). In this example, the sectors were not skewed at all between the heads, which means that the sectors are directly above and below one another in a given cylinder.

Now the platters in this example are spinning at 3,600 rpm, so one sector is passing below a head once every 980 millionths of a second! This obviously is a very small timing window. It takes some time for the head switch to occur (usually, 15 millionths of a second), plus some overhead time for the controller to pass the head-switch command. By the time the head switch is complete and you are ready to read the new track, sector 1 has already gone by! This problem is similar to interleaving when the interleave is too low. The drive is forced to wait while the platter spins around another revolution so that it can begin to pick up the track, starting with Sector 1.

This problem is easy to solve: simply offset the sector numbering on subsequent tracks from those that precede them sufficiently to account for the head-switching and controller overhead time. That way, when Head 0, Sector 17 finishes and the head switches, Head 1, Sector 1 arrives right on time. The result looks something like this:

```
Cyl. 0, Head 0:    1- 2- 3- 4- 5- 6- 7- 8- 9-10-11-12-13-14-15-16-17
Cyl. 0, Head 1:   16-17- 1- 2- 3- 4- 5- 6- 7- 8- 9-10-11-12-13-14-15
```

Shifting the second track by two sectors provides time to allow for the head-switching overhead and is the equivalent to a head-skew factor of 2. In normal use, a drive switches heads much more often than it switches physical cylinders, which makes head skew more important than cylinder skew. Throughput can rise dramatically when a proper head skew is in place. Different head skews can account for different transfer rates among drives that have the same number of sectors per track and the same interleave.

A nonskewed MFM drive, for example, may have a transfer rate of 380KB per second, whereas the transfer rate of a drive with a head skew of 2 could rise to 425KB per second.

Notice that different controllers and drives have different amounts of overhead, so real-world results will be different in each case. In most cases, the head-switch time is very small compared with the controller overhead. As with interleaving, it is better to be on the conservative side to avoid additional disk revolutions.

Cylinder Skew. *Cylinder skew* is the offset in logical sector numbering between the same physical sectors on two adjacent tracks on two adjacent cylinders.

The number of sectors skewed when switching tracks from one cylinder to the next is to compensate for track-to-track seek time. In essence all of the sectors on adjacent tracks are rotated with respect to each other. This method permits continuous read or write operations across cylinder boundaries without missing any disk revolutions, thus maximizing system performance.

Cylinder skew is a larger numerical factor then head skew because more overhead exists. It takes much longer to move the heads from one cylinder to another than simply to switch heads. Also, the controller overhead in changing cylinders is higher as well.

The following is a depiction of our example drive with a head-skew factor of 2 but no cylinder skew.

```
Cyl. 0, Head 0:     1- 2- 3- 4- 5- 6- 7- 8- 9-10-11-12-13-14-15-16-17
Cyl. 0, Head 1:    16-17- 1- 2- 3- 4- 5- 6- 7- 8- 9-10-11-12-13-14-15
Cyl. 1, Head 0:     8- 9-10-11-12-13-14-15-16-17- 1- 2- 3- 4- 5- 6- 7
```

In this example, the cylinder-skew factor is 8. Shifting the sectors on the subsequent cylinder by eight sectors gives the drive and controller time to be ready for sector 1 on the next cylinder and eliminates an extra revolution of the disk.

Calculating Skew Factors. You can derive the correct head-skew factor from the following information and formula:

Head skew = (head-switch time/rotational period) × SPT + 2

In other words, the head-switching time of a drive is divided by the time required for a single rotation. The result is multiplied by the number of sectors per track, and 2 is added for controller overhead. The result should then be rounded up to the next whole integer (for example, 2.3 = 2, 2.5 = 3).

You can derive the correct cylinder-skew factor from the following information and formula:

Cylinder skew = (track-to-track seek time/rotational period) × SPT + 4

In other words, the track-to-track seek time of a drive is divided by the time required for a single rotation. The result is multiplied by the number of sectors per track, and 4 is added for controller overhead. Round the result up to a whole integer (for example, 2.3 = 2, 2.5 = 3).

The following example uses typical figures for an ESDI drive and controller. If the head-switching time is 15 μs (micro-seconds), the track-to-track seek is 3 ms, the rotational period is 16.67 ms (3,600 rpm), and the drive has 53 physical sectors per track:

Head skew = (0.015/16.67) × 53 +2 = 2 (rounded up)

Cylinder Skew = (3/16.67) × 53 + 4 = 14 (rounded up)

If you do not have the necessary information to make the calculations, contact the drive manufacturer for recommendations. Otherwise, you can make the calculations by using conservative figures for head-switch and track-to-track access times. If you are unsure, just as with interleaving, it is better to be on the conservative side, which minimizes the possibility of additional rotations when reading sequential information on the drive. In most cases, a default head skew of 2 and a cylinder skew of 16 work well.

Because factors such as controller overhead can vary from model to model, sometimes the only way to figure out the best value is to experiment. You can try different skew values and then run data-transfer rate tests to see which value results in the highest per-formance. Be careful with these tests, however; many disk benchmark programs will only read or write data from one track or one cylinder during testing, which totally eliminates the effect of skewing on the results. The best type of benchmark to use for this testing is one that reads and writes large files on the disk.

Most real (controller register level) low-level format programs are capable of setting skew factors. Those programs that are supplied by a particular controller or drive manufacturer usually already are optimized for their particular drives and controllers, and may not allow you to change the skew. One of the best general-purpose register-level formatters on the market that gives you this flexibility is the Disk Manager program by Ontrack. I highly recommend this program.

I normally do not recommend programs such as Norton Calibrate and Gibson Spinrite for re-interleaving drives, because these programs work only through the BIOS INT 13h functions rather than directly with the disk controller hardware. Thus, these programs cannot set skew factors properly, and using them actually may slow a drive that already has optimum interleave and skew factors.

Notice that most IDE and SCSI drives have their interleave and skew factors set to their optimum values by the manufacturer. In most cases, you cannot even change these val-ues; in the cases in which you can, the most likely result is a slower drive. For this rea-son, most IDE drive manufacturers recommend against low-level formatting their drives. With some IDE drives, unless you use the right software, you might alter the optimum skew settings and slow the drive. IDE drives that use Zoned Recording cannot ever have the interleave or skew factors changed, and as such, they are fully protected. No matter how you try to format these drives, the interleave and skew factors cannot be altered. The same can be said for SCSI drives.

Shock Mounting

Most hard disks manufactured today have a *shock-mounted* HDA, which means that a rubber cushion is placed between the disk drive body and the mounting chassis. Some drives use more rubber than others, but for the most part, a shock mount is a shock mount. Some drives do not have a shock-isolated HDA due to physical or cost con-straints. Be sure that the drive you are using has adequate shock-isolation mounts for the HDA, especially if you are using the drive in a portable PC system or in a system in which environmental conditions are less favorable than in a normal office. I usually never recommend a drive that lacks at least some form of shock mounting.

Cost

The cost of hard disk storage recently has fallen to the magic $1-per-megabyte barrier (or lower). You can purchase 2GB drives for $2,000, 1GB drives for $1,000, 500MB drives for $500, and so on. That places the value of the 10 MB drive that I bought in 1983 at about $10. (Too bad I paid $1,800 for it at the time!)

Of course, the cost of drives continues to fall, and eventually, even $1 per megabyte will seem expensive. Because of the low costs of disk storage today, not many drives that are less than 200MB are even being manufactured.

Capacity

Four figures commonly are used in advertising drive capacity:

- Unformatted capacity, in millions of bytes (MB)

- Formatted capacity, in millions of bytes (MB)

- Unformatted capacity, in megabytes (Meg or MB)

- Formatted capacity, in megabytes (Meg or MB)

Most manufacturers of IDE and SCSI drives now report only the formatted capacities, because these drives are delivered preformatted. Most of the time, advertisements refer to the unformatted or formatted capacity in millions of bytes (MB), because these figures are larger than the same capacity expressed in megabytes (Meg). This situation generates a great deal of confusion when the user runs FDISK (which reports total drive capacity in megabytes) and wonders where the missing space is. This question ranks as one of the most common questions that I hear during my seminars. Fortunately, the answer is easy; it only involves a little math to figure it out.

Perhaps the most common questions I get are concerning "missing" drive capacity. Consider the following example: "I just installed a new Western Digital AC2200 drive, billed as 212MB. When I entered the drive parameters (989 cylinders, 12 heads, 35 sectors per track), both the BIOS Setup routine and FDISK report the drive as only 203MB! What happened to the other 9MB?"

The answer is only a few calculations away. By multiplying the drive specification parameters, you get this result:

Cylinders:	989
Heads:	12
Sectors per track:	35
Bytes per sector:	512

Total bytes:	212.67MB
Total megabytes:	202.82Meg

The result figures to a capacity of 212.67MB (million bytes) or 202.82Meg. Drive manufacturers usually report drive capacity in millions of bytes, whereas your BIOS and FDISK usually report the capacity in megabytes. 1Meg equals 1,048,576 bytes (or 1,024KB, wherein each KB is 1,024 bytes). So the bottom line is that this 212.67MB drive also is a 202.82Meg drive! What is really confusing is that there is no industry wide accepted way of differentiating binary megabytes from decimal ones. Officially they are both abbreviated as "MB", so it is often hard to figure which one is being reported. Usually drive manufacturers will always report metric MBs, since they result in larger, more impressive sounding numbers! One additional item to note about this particular drive is that it is a Zoned Recording drive and that the actual physical parameters are different. Physically, this drive has 1,971 cylinders and 4 heads; however, the total number of sectors on the drive (and, therefore, the capacity) is the same no matter how you translate the parameters.

Although Western Digital does not report the unformatted capacity of this particular drive, unformatted capacity usually works out to be about 19 percent larger than a drive's formatted capacity. The Seagate ST-12550N drive, for example, is advertised as having the following capacities:

Unformatted capacity:	2,572.00MB
Unformatted capacity:	2,452.85Meg
Formatted capacity:	2,139.00MB
Formatted capacity:	2,039.91Meg

Each of these four figures is a correct answer to the question "What is the storage capacity of the drive?" As you can see, however, the numbers are very different. In fact, yet another number could be used. Divide the 2,039.91Meg by 1,024, and the drive's capacity is 1.99GB! So when you are comparing or discussing drive capacities, make sure that you are working with a consistent unit of measure, or your comparisons will be meaningless.

To eliminate confusion in capacity measurements. I have been using the abbreviation "Meg" in this section, which is not really industry standard. The true industry standard abbreviations for these figures are shown in table 14.9:

Table 14.9   Standard Abbreviations and Meanings

Abbreviation	Description	Decimal Meaning	Binary Meaning
Kb	Kilobit	1,000	1,024
KB	Kilobyte	1,000	1,024
Mb	Megabit	1,000,000	1,048,576
MB	Megabyte	1,000,000	1,048,576

(continues)

Table 14.9	Continued		
Abbreviation	**Description**	**Decimal Meaning**	**Binary Meaning**
Gb	Gigabit	1,000,000,000	1,073,741,824
GB	Gigabyte	1,000,000,000	1,073,741,824
Tb	Terabit	1,000,000,000,000	1,099,511,627,776
TB	Terabyte	1,000,000,000,000	1,099,511,627,776

Unfortunately there are no differences in the abbreviations when used to indicate metric verses binary values. In other words MB can be used to indicate both Millions of Bytes and Megabytes. In general, memory values are always computed using the binary derived meanings, while disk capacity goes either way. Unfortunately this often leads to confusion in reporting disk capacities. Note that bits and Bytes are distinguished by a lower- or uppercase "B" character. For example, Millions of bits are indicated by using a lowercase *b*, resulting in the abbreviation of Mbps for Million bits per second, while MBps indicates Million Bytes per second.

Specific Recommendations

If you are going to add a hard disk to a system today, I can give you a few recommendations. Starting with the actual, physical hard disk itself, you should demand the following features in a hard disk drive to ensure that you are getting a quality unit:

- Voice coil head actuator
- Thin-film media

For the drive interface, there really are only two types to consider today:

- IDE (Integrated Drive Electronics)
- SCSI (Small Computer System Interface)

Of these, I prefer SCSI because of its great expandability, cross-platform compatibility, high capacity, performance, and flexibility. IDE offers a very high-performance solution, but expansion, compatibility, capacity, and flexibility are severely limited compared with SCSI.

Hard Disk Interfaces

A variety of hard disk interfaces are available today. As time has passed, the number of choices has increased, and many of the older designs no longer are viable in newer systems. You need to know about all these interfaces, from the oldest to the newest designs, because you will encounter all of them whenever upgrading or repairing systems is necessary.

The interfaces have different cabling and configuration options, and the setup and format of drives will vary as well. Special problems may arise when you are trying to install more than one drive of a particular interface type or (especially) when you are mixing drives of different interface types in one system.

This section completely covers the different hard disk drive interfaces, giving you all the technical information you need to deal with them in any way: troubleshooting, servicing, upgrading, and even mixing the different types.

This section examines the standard controllers and describes how you can work with these controllers, as well as replace them with much faster units. Also discussed are the different types of drive interfaces: ST-506/412, ESDI, IDE, and SCSI. Choosing the proper interface is important, because your choice also affects your disk drive purchase and the ultimate speed of the disk subsystem.

The primary job of the hard disk controller or interface is to transmit and receive data to and from the drive. The different interface types limit how fast data can be moved from the drive to the system and offer different levels of performance. If you are putting together a system in which performance is a primary concern, you need to know how these different interfaces affect performance and what you can expect from them. Many of the statistics that appear in technical literature are not indicative of the real performance figures that you will see in practice. I will separate the myths presented by some of these overoptimistic figures from the reality of what you will actually see.

With regard to disk drives, and especially hard disk drives, the specification on which people seem to focus the most is the drive's reported average seek time: the (average) time it takes for the heads to be positioned from one track to another. Unfortunately, the importance of this specification often is overstated, especially in relation to other specifications, such as the data-transfer rate.

The transfer rate of data between the drive and the system is more important than access time, because most drives spend more time reading and writing information than they do simply moving the heads around. The speed at which a program or data file is loaded or read is affected most by the data-transfer rate. Specialized operations such as sorting large files, which involve a lot of random access to individual records of the file (and, therefore, many seek operations), are helped greatly by a faster-seeking disk drive, so seeking performance is important in these cases. Most normal file load and save operations, however, are affected most by the rate at which data can be read and written to and from the drive. The data-transfer rate depends on both the drive and the interface.

Several types of hard disk interfaces have been used in PC systems over the years:

- ST-506/412

- ESDI

- IDE

- SCSI

Of these interfaces, only ST-506/412 and ESDI are what you could call true disk-controller-to-drive interfaces. SCSI and IDE are system-level interfaces that usually incorporate a chipset-based variation of one of the other two types of disk controller interfaces internally. For example, most SCSI and IDE drives incorporate the same basic controller circuitry used in separate ESDI controllers. The SCSI interface adds another layer of interface that attaches the controller to the system bus, whereas IDE is a direct bus-attachment interface.

In data recovery, it helps to know the disk interface you are working with, because many data-recovery problems involve drive setup and installation problems. Each interface requires a slightly different method of installation and drive configuration. If the installation or configuration is incorrect or accidentally altered by the system user, it may prevent access to data on a drive. Accordingly, anyone who wants to become proficient in data recovery must be an expert on installing and configuring various types of hard disks and controllers.

IBM's reliance on industry-standard interfaces such as those listed here was a boon for everybody in the IBM-compatible industry. These standards allow a great deal of cross-system and cross-manufacturer compatibility. The use of these industry-standard interfaces allows us to pick up a mail-order catalog, purchase a hard disk for the lowest possible price, and be assured that it will work with our system. This *plug-and-play* capability results in affordable hard disk storage and a variety of options in capacities and speed.

The ST-506/412 Interface

The ST-506/412 interface was developed by Seagate Technologies around 1980. The interface originally appeared in the Seagate ST-506 drive, which was a 5MB formatted (or 6MB unformatted) drive in a full-height, 5.25-inch form factor. By today's standards, this interface is a tank! In 1981 Seagate introduced the ST-412 drive, which added a feature called *buffered seek* to the interface. This drive was a 10MB formatted (12MB unformatted) drive that also qualifies as a tank by today's standards. Besides the Seagate ST-412, IBM also used the Miniscribe 1012 as well the International Memories, Inc. (IMI) model 5012 drive in the XT. IMI and Miniscribe are long gone, but Seagate remains today as one of the largest drive manufacturers. Since the original XT, Seagate has supplied drives for numerous IBM systems, including the AT and many PS/2 models.

Most drive manufacturers that made hard disks for PC systems adopted the Seagate ST-506/412 standard, a situation that helped make this interface popular. One important feature is the interface's plug-and-play design. No custom cables or special modifications are needed for the drives, which means that virtually any ST-506/412 drive will work with any ST-506/412 controller. The only real compatibility issue with this interface is the level of BIOS support provided by the system.

When introduced to the PC industry by IBM in 1983, ROM BIOS support for this hard disk interface was provided by a BIOS chip on the controller. Contrary to what most believed, the PC and XT motherboard BIOS had no inherent hard disk support. When the AT system was introduced, IBM placed the ST-506/412 interface support in the motherboard BIOS and eliminated it from the controller. Since then, any system that is compatible with the IBM AT (which includes most systems on the market today) has an enhanced version of the same support in the motherboard BIOS as well. Because this support was somewhat limited, especially in the older BIOS versions, many disk controller manufacturers also placed additional BIOS support for their controllers directly on the controllers themselves. In some cases, you would use the controller BIOS and motherboard BIOS together; in other cases, you would disable the controller or motherboard BIOS and then use one or the other. These issues will be discussed more completely later in this chapter, in the section called System Configuration.

The ST-506/412 interface does not quite make the grade in today's high-performance PC systems. This interface was designed for a 5MB drive, and I have not seen any drives larger than 152MB (MFM encoding) or 233MB (RLL encoding) available for this type of interface. Because the capacity, performance, and expandability of ST-506/412 are so limited, this interface is obsolete and generally unavailable in new systems. However, many older systems still use drives that have this interface.

Encoding Schemes and Problems. As indicated earlier in this chapter in the section on Data Encoding Schemes, encoding schemes are used in communications for converting digital data bits to various tones for transmission over a telephone line. For disk drives, the digital bits are converted, or *encoded*, in a pattern of magnetic impulses, or *flux transitions* (also called flux reversals), which are written on the disk. These flux transitions are decoded later, when the data is read from the disk.

A device called an Endec (encoder/decoder) accomplishes the conversion to flux transitions for writing on the media and the subsequent reconversion back to digital data during read operations. The function of the Endec is very similar to that of a modem (modulator/demodulator) in that digital data is converted to an analog waveform, which then is converted back to digital data. Sometimes, the Endec is called a *data separator*, because it is designed to separate data and clocking information from the flux-transition pulse stream read from the disk.

One of the biggest problems with ST-506/412 was that this Endec resided on the disk controller (rather than the drive), which resulted in the possibility of corruption of the analog data signal before it reached the media. This problem became especially pronounced when the ST-506/412 controllers switched to using RLL Endecs to store 50 percent more data on the drive. With the RLL encoding scheme, the actual density of magnetic flux transitions on the disk media remains the same as with MFM encoding, but the timing between the transitions must be measured much more precisely.

The original ST-506/412 controllers used MFM encoding, for which the interface was designed. A few years after this interface had been out, several controller manufacturers started using RLL Endec circuits in their controllers. These newer controllers were fully compatible with the ST-506/412 interface drives, but they could put 50 percent more data on the drives, and transfer data to and from the drives 50 percent faster than the older MFM-variety controllers. Unfortunately, this situation caused many problems with the cheaper drives that were on the market at the time.

In RLL encoding, the intervals between flux changes are approximately the same as with MFM, but the actual timing between them is much more critical. As a result, the transition cells in which signals must be recognized are much smaller and more precisely placed than with MFM. RLL encoding places more stringent demands on the timing of the controller and drive electronics. With RLL encoding, accurately reading the timing of the flux changes is paramount. Additionally, because RLL encodes variable-length groups of bits rather than single bits, a single error in one flux transition can corrupt two to four bits of data. For these reasons, an RLL controller usually has a more sophisticated error-detection and error-correction routine than an MFM controller.

Most of the cheaper disk drives on the market did not have data-channel circuits that were designed to be precise enough to handle RLL encoding without problems. RLL encoding also is much more susceptible to noise in the read signal, and the conventional oxide media coatings did not have a sufficient signal-to-noise ratio for reliable RLL encoding. This problem often was compounded by the fact that many drives of the time used stepper motor head positioning systems, which are notoriously inaccurate, further amplifying the signal-to-noise ratio problem.

At this time, manufacturers starting RLL-certifying drives for use with RLL Endec controllers. This stamp of approval essentially meant that the drive had passed tests and was designed to handle the precise timing requirements that RLL encoding required. In some cases, the drive electronics were upgraded between a manufacturer's MFM and RLL drive versions, but the drives are essentially the same. In fact, if any improvements were made in the so-called RLL-certified drives, the same upgrades usually also were applied to the MFM version.

The bottom line is that other than improved precision, there is no real difference between an ST-506/412 drive that is sold as an MFM model and one that is sold as an RLL model. If you want to use a drive that originally was sold as an MFM model with an RLL controller, I suggest that you do so only if the drive uses a voice coil head actuator and thin-film media. Virtually any ST-506/412 drive with these qualities is more than good enough to handle RLL encoding with no problems.

Using MFM encoding, a standard ST-506/412 format specifies that the drive will contain 17 sectors per track, with each sector containing 512 bytes of data. A controller that uses an RLL Endec raises the number of sectors per track to 25 or 26.

The real solution to reliability problems with RLL encoding was to place the Endec directly on the drive rather than on the controller. This method reduces the susceptibility to noise and interference that can plague an ST-506/412 drive system running RLL encoding. ESDI, IDE, and SCSI drives all have the Endec (and, often, the entire controller) built into the drive by default. Because the Endec is attached to the drive without cables and with an extremely short electrical distance, the propensity for timing-and noise-induced errors is greatly reduced or eliminated. This situation is analogous to a local telephone call between the Endec and the disk platters. This local communication makes the ESDI, IDE, and SCSI interfaces much more reliable than the older ST-506/412 interface; they share none of the reliability problems that once were associated with RLL encoding over the ST-506/412 interface. Virtually all ESDI, IDE, and SCSI drives use RLL encoding today with tremendously increased reliability over even MFM ST-506/412 drives.

ST-506/412 Configuration and Installation. The ST-506/412 interface is characterized by a two- or three-cable arrangement, depending on whether one or two drives are connected. One 34-connector control cable is daisy-chained between up to two drives. The daisy-chain arrangement is much like that used for floppy drives. Each drive on the daisy chain is jumped to respond to a particular Drive Select (DS) line. In the controller implementation used in all PC systems, there are two available lines, called Drive Select 1 (DS1) and Drive Select 2 (DS2). Some drives support as many as four DS lines, but only the first two are usable. Although it may appear that you could string four drives on a single daisy-chain cable, the design of the PC system and controllers uses only the first two.

The control cable usually has lines 25 through 29 twisted between the drive D and C connectors. The first drive (drive C) normally is plugged into the last control cable connector at the end of the cable opposite the controller; an optional second drive (D) can be installed in the middle control-cable connector. The twist in the lines serves to reroute the Drive Select lines so that the drive plugged into the last cable position appears to the controller to be attached to Drive Select 1, even though the jumper on the drive is set for DS2. This arrangement is very similar to the one used for floppy drives; if the cable is twisted, both drives must be set to the DS2 jumper position. If the cable does not have the twisted lines, the drive at the end of the cable (C) must be set to DS1.

Another configuration item is the terminating resistor, which must be installed on the drive at the end of the cable (C) and must be removed from the optional second drive (D) attached to the middle control-cable connector. The controller has a permanently installed terminating resistor that never has to be adjusted. Although the control cable is similar in function and appearance to the 34-pin cable used for floppy drives, the cables generally are not interchangeable because different lines are twisted. Whereas pins 25 through 29 are inverted on the hard disk control cable, pins 10 through 16 are inverted on the floppy cable, rendering them incompatible.

The other two cables, called *data cables*, are 20-connector cables, each of which runs from the controller to a single drive, because this cable is not daisy-chained. A two-drive system therefore has one control cable from the controller to each of two drives in a daisy chain, plus two separate data cables—one for each drive. The controller has three connectors to support the two-drive maximum limit. As its name suggests, the data cable carries data to and from the drive.

If you are using a single drive, only the data cable connector closest to the control cable connector is used; the other is left unattached. Most ST-506/412 controllers also have an on-board floppy controller, which also will have a 34-pin connector for the floppy drives. Figures 14.13 and 14.14 show the control and data cable connectors on a typical combination ST-506/412 hard disk and floppy disk controller. Notice that some of these combination controllers allow the floppy controller portion to be disabled and others do not, which may cause a conflict if you have any other floppy controller in the system.

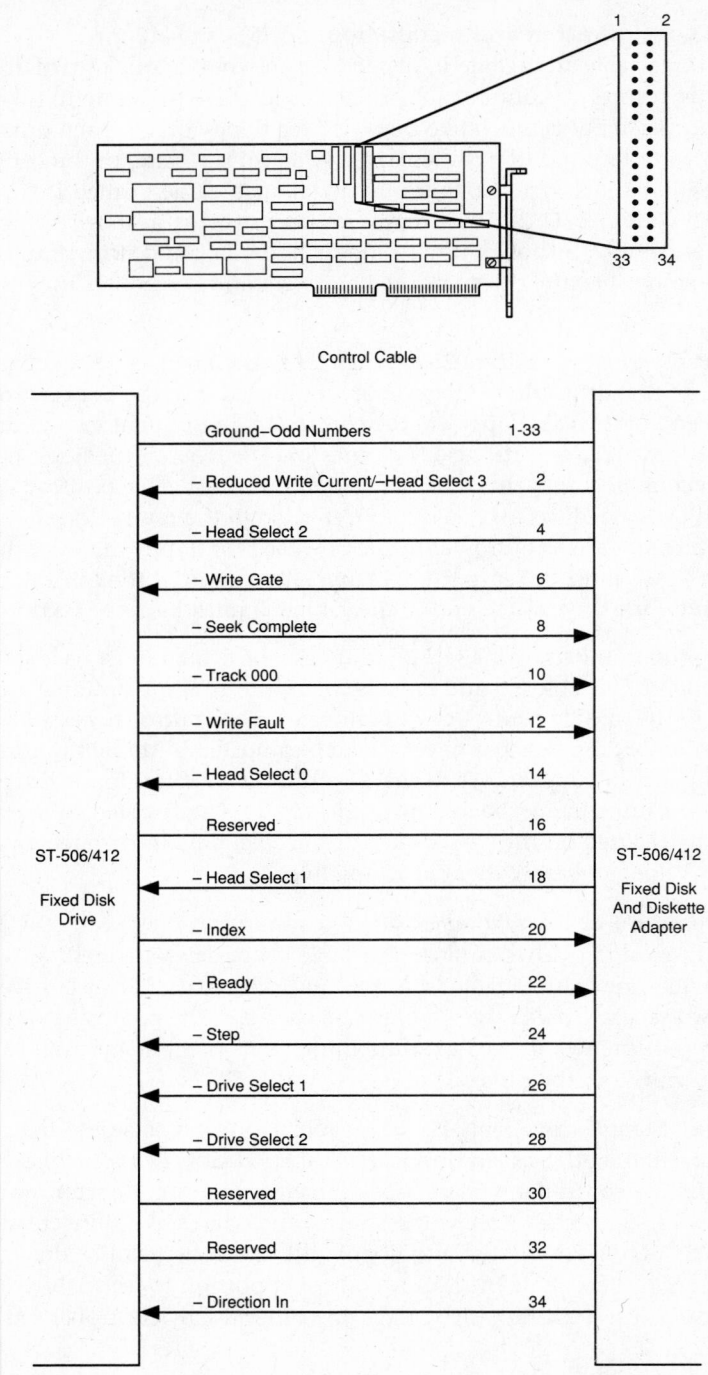

Fig. 14.13
ST-506/412 controller control cable connector.

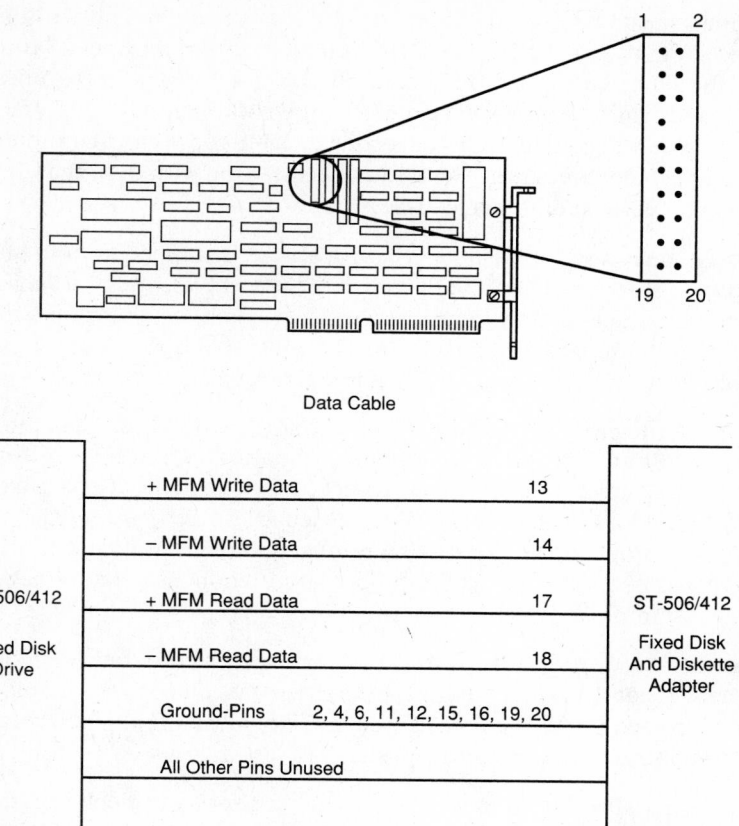

Data Cable

ST-506/412	+ MFM Write Data	13	ST-506/412
	− MFM Write Data	14	
Fixed Disk Drive	+ MFM Read Data	17	Fixed Disk And Diskette Adapter
	− MFM Read Data	18	
	Ground-Pins 2, 4, 6, 11, 12, 15, 16, 19, 20		
	All Other Pins Unused		

Fig. 14.14
ST-506/412 controller data cable connectors.

ST-506/412 Drive Configuration. With ST-506/412 and ESDI drives, you have to configure the following items on each drive:

■ Drive Select (DS) jumpers

■ Terminating resistor

These configuration items usually are located near the rear of the drive on the disk drive logic board.

Drive Select Jumpers. The *Drive Select jumper* selects the Drive Select (DS) signal to which the drive should respond. The drive controller sends control signals on two DS lines, one for each drive. Because each drive must be set to respond to a different DS signal, you can use only two drives per controller.

The DS jumpers must be set so that each drive responds to a different DS line from the controller (DS1 or DS2). If the 34-pin control cable has a twist in lines 25 through 29, both drives should be set to DS2. If the control cable is a straight-through design (no twist), the drive at the end of the cable opposite the controller (C) should be set to DS1, and a second drive attached to the middle control-cable connector (D) should be set to DS2. Notice that some drives label the DS jumpers starting with 0, so that DS1 would be labeled DS0 and DS2 would be labeled DS1.

Terminating Resistors. An ST-506/412 drive always is shipped from the factory with a terminating resistor installed. When you install these drives, you must ensure that the drive plugged into the end of the control-cable daisy chain has this terminator installed. Additionally, this terminator must be removed (or disabled with a jumper, in some cases) from the secondary drive installed in the center control-cable connector.

The functions of the terminating resistor are the same as those discussed for floppy drives. The idea is to provide electrical-signal termination so that the control signals to and from the drive and controller do not reflect back or echo along the cable. The terminating resistor provides the proper signal-to-noise ratio and the proper electrical load for the controller. Improper drive termination results in drives that do not function (or that do so only with excessive problems). Improper termination also may damage the controller because of improper electrical loads.

Control and Data Cables. The control cable connects to the controller and daisy chains to the secondary and primary drives, and separate data cables (20-pin) run from the controller to each drive. The data cable connector closest to the control-cable connector on the controller is used for the primary (C) drive.

When connecting cables, you should observe the proper pin-1 orientation from end to end. On ribbon cables, the pin-1 line usually is a different color from the other lines. (In most ribbon cables, for example, the pin-1 line is red or blue, and the rest of the cable is gray). You need to ensure that this pin-1 line is plugged into pin-1 of the controller and drive connectors. Both the controller and drive should have the pin-1 position on each connector marked. Sometimes the mark is the number 1; other times, it is a dot or some other symbol that is silkscreened on the circuit board. The cable connectors at the controller end may be keyed, in which case pin-15 will be missing from the control-cable connector on the controller connector, and the corresponding hole will be plugged in the control cable. The data cable connectors will be missing pin-8, and the corresponding hole also will be plugged in the data cables. The edge connectors used at the drive end normally are keyed to a notch in the drive connectors. The side of the connector with the notch cut out indicates the pin-1 orientation at the drive end.

Notice that the 34-pin control cable is very similar to the 34-pin control/data cable used for floppy drives; these cables, however, usually are not interchangeable. The ST-506/412 control cable has lines 25 through 29 twisted between the secondary and primary drive connectors, whereas the 34-pin floppy cable has lines 10 through 17 twisted. As a result, the cables are incompatible and therefore noninterchangeable.

ST-506/412 Interface Connectors. The ST-506/412 Interface uses two connections, a 34-pin Control connector and a 20-pin Data connector. Tables 14.10 and 14.11 show the pinouts for these connectors.

Table 14.10	ST-506/412 Hard Disk Interface 34-Pin Control Connector Pinout		
Signal Name	**Pin**	**Pin**	**Signal Name**
GROUND	1	2	-HD SLCT 3
GROUND	3	4	-HD SLCT 2
GROUND	5	6	-WRITE GATE
GROUND	7	8	-SEEK CMPLT
GROUND	9	10	-TRACK 0
GROUND	11	12	-WRITE FAULT
GROUND	13	14	-HD SLCT 0
KEY (no pin)	15	16	Not Connected
GROUND	17	18	-HD SLCT 1
GROUND	19	20	-INDEX
GROUND	21	22	-READY
GROUND	23	24	-STEP
GROUND	25	26	-DRV SLCT 0
GROUND	27	28	-DRV SLCT 1
GROUND	29	30	Not Connected
GROUND	31	32	Not Connected
GROUND	33	34	-DIRECTION IN

Table 14.11	ST-506/412 Hard Disk Interface 20-Pin Data Connector Pinout		
Signal Name	**Pin**	**Pin**	**Signal Name**
-DRV SLCTD	1	2	GROUND
Not Connected	3	4	GROUND
Not Connected	5	6	GROUND
Not Connected	7	8	KEY (no pin)
Not Connected	9	10	Not Connected
GROUND	11	12	GROUND
+MFM WRITE	13	14	-MFM WRITE
GROUND	15	16	GROUND
+MFM READ	17	18	-MFM READ
GROUND	19	20	GROUND

Power Cables. To complete the required cable connections to the hard drive, you need a spare power connector (table 14.12 shows the pinouts for the connector). Some older power supplies have only two-drive power connectors. Several companies sell a *power* *splitter cable,* or Y cable, that can adapt one cable from the power supply so that it powers two drives. If you add a power splitter to a system, make sure that the power supply can handle the load of the additional drive or drives.

Table 14.12	Disk Drive Power Connector Pinout	
Pin	**Wire Color**	**Signal**
1	Yellow	+12v
2	Black	Gnd
3	Black	Gnd
4	Red	+5v

If the original power supply is not adequate, purchase an aftermarket unit that can supply adequate power. Most better aftermarket supplies have four-drive power connectors, eliminating the need for the splitter cables. Power splitter cables are available from several of the cable and accessory vendors listed in Appendix B, as well as from electronic supply stores such as Radio Shack.

Historical Notes. The following sections list some information on the original ST-506/412 controllers used in the PC environment. These were the controllers that IBM supplied in the XT and AT systems. At the time of introduction, these controllers set standards that, especially in the case of the AT controller, we still live with today. In fact, the entire IDE interface standard is based on the controller that IBM designed and used in the AT. All the conventions and standards for the hard disk interfaces that we use today started with these controllers.

Original IBM 8-Bit Controllers. The first ST-506/412 controller standard sold for PC systems was the hard disk controller used in the original 10MB IBM XT. This controller actually was made for IBM by Xebec Corporation and also was sold under the Xebec name as the Xebec 1210 controller. The Xebec 1210 is an ST-506/412 controller that uses Modified Frequency Modulation (MFM) encoding to record data on a drive. This controller's ROM, produced by IBM, contains an 8KB hard disk BIOS with an internal table that had entries for four different drives. Each drive was selected by jumpers on the controller, which actually were soldered in the early IBM units. If you purchased the controller from Xebec, you got a slightly different but completely compatible ROM, and the jumpers were not soldered, so you easily could select one of the four BIOS table entries. Xebec also allowed system integrators to copy its ROM to modify the built-in drive tables for a specific drive.

Later IBM XT systems with a 20MB hard disk still used the Xebec 1210, but it had a new 4KB ROM that contained different drive tables, as well as jumpers like those found on the versions also sold separately by Xebec. Xebec never sold an autoconfigure version of this controller, which would have made integrating different drives easier.

The Xebec 1210 is one of the slowest ST-506/412 controllers ever made, supporting at best a 5:1 interleave on a stock IBM PC or IBM XT system. If you use the IBM Advanced

Diagnostics program for the IBM PC or IBM XT, the low-level formatter produces a standard 6:1 interleave, which results in a paltry 85KB-per-second data-transfer rate. By changing the interleave to 5:1, you can wring 102KB per second from this controller—still unbelievably slow by today's standards.

Xebec also made a Model 1220 that combined a hard disk and floppy disk controller, was hardware-compatible with the 1210, and works with the IBM or standard Xebec ROM. The separate floppy controller then could be removed from the system, and you could save a slot.

I recommend replacing this controller with an autoconfigure controller whenever you get the chance. Most other controllers also are significantly faster than the Xebec.

Original IBM 16-Bit Controllers. For the AT, IBM used two controllers made by Western Digital: the WD1002-WA2 and the WD1003A-WA2. The WD1003 is an upgraded WD1002 with a much lower chip count. The WD1003 also was shorter than the WD1002 to fit into the IBM XT 286.

The WD1002 is used in the IBM AT as a combination hard disk and floppy disk controller. The WD1002 and the WD1003 are standard ST-506/412 controllers that supply MFM encoding to the drive. Neither controller contains a ROM BIOS; instead, BIOS support is built into the motherboard ROM. Both controllers support a 2:1 interleave, even on a standard 6-MHz IBM AT system. The IBM Advanced Diagnostics low-level formatter can put down a 2:1 interleave, but the default is 3:1. Most users of these controllers can realize a performance gain if they simply reformat to the lower interleave.

The ESDI Interface

ESDI, or *Enhanced Small Device Interface*, is a specialized hard disk interface established as a standard in 1983, primarily by Maxtor Corporation. Maxtor led a consortium of drive manufacturers to adopt its proposed interface as a high-performance standard to succeed ST-506/412. ESDI later was adopted by the ANSI (American National Standards Institute) organization and published under the ANSI X3T9.2 Committee. The latest version of the ANSI ESDI document is known as X3.170a-1991. You can obtain this document, and other ANSI-standard documents, from ANSI itself or from Global Engineering Documents. These companies are listed in Appendix B.

Compared with ST-506/412, ESDI has provisions for increased reliability, such as building the Endec (encoder/decoder) into the drive. ESDI is a very-high-speed interface, capable of a maximum 24-megabits-per-second transfer rate. Most drives running ESDI, however, are limited to a maximum 10 or 15 megabits per second. Unfortunately, compatibility problems between different ESDI implementations, combined with pressure from low-cost, high-performance IDE interface drives have served to make the ESDI interface obsolete. Few, if any, new systems today include ESDI drives, although ESDI has become somewhat popular in high-end systems during the late '80s.

Enhanced commands enabled some ESDI controllers to read a drive's capacity parameters directly from the drive, as well as to control defect mapping, but several manufacturers had different methods for writing this information on the drive. When you install an ESDI drive, in some cases the controller automatically reads the parameter and defect information directly from the drive. In other cases, however, you still have to enter this information manually, as with ST-506/412.

The ESDI's enhanced defect-mapping commands provide a standard way for the PC system to read a defect map from a drive, which means that the manufacturer's defect list can be written to the drive as a file. The defect-list file then can be read by the controller and low-level format software, eliminating the need for the installer to type these entries from the keyboard and enabling the format program to update the defect list with new entries if it finds new defects during the low-level format or the surface analysis.

Most ESDI implementations have drives formatted to 32 sectors per track or more (80 or more sectors per track are possible)—many more sectors per track than the standard ST-506/412 implementation of 17 to 26 sectors per track. The greater density results in two or more times the data-transfer rate, with a 1:1 interleave. Almost without exception, ESDI controllers support a 1:1 interleave, which allows for a transfer rate of 1MB per second or greater.

Because ESDI is much like the ST-506/412 interface, it can replace that interface without affecting software in the system. Most ESDI controllers are register-compatible with the older ST-506/412 controllers, which enables OS/2 and other non-DOS operating systems to run with few or no problems. The ROM BIOS interface to ESDI is similar to the ST-506/412 standard, and many low-level disk utilities that run on one interface will run on the other. To take advantage of ESDI defect mapping and other special features, however, use a low-level format and surface-analysis utility designed for ESDI (such as the ones usually built into the controller ROM BIOS and called by DEBUG).

During the late '80s, most high-end systems from major manufacturers were equipped with ESDI controllers and drives. More recently, manufacturers have been equipping high end systems with SCSI. The SCSI interface allows for much greater expandability, supports more types of devices than ESDI does, and offers equal or greater performance. I no longer recommend installing ESDI drives unless you are upgrading a system that already has an ESDI controller.

ESDI Interface Connectors. ESDI (Enhanced Small Device Interface) uses two connections, a 34-pin Control connector and a 20-pin Data connector. Tables 14.13 and 14.14 show the pinouts for these connectors.

Table 14.13   ESDI (Enhanced Small Device Interface) 34-Pin Control Connector Pinout

Signal Name	Pin	Pin	Signal Name
GROUND	1	2	-HD SLCT 3
GROUND	3	4	-HD SLCT 2
GROUND	5	6	-WRITE GATE
GROUND	7	8	-CNFG/STATUS
GROUND	9	10	-XFER ACK

Signal Name	Pin	Pin	Signal Name
GROUND	11	12	-ATTENTION
GROUND	13	14	-HD SLCT 0
KEY (no pin)	15	16	-SECTOR
GROUND	17	18	-HD SLCT 1
GROUND	19	20	-INDEX
GROUND	21	22	-READY
GROUND	23	24	-XFER REQ
GROUND	25	26	-DRV SLCT 0
GROUND	27	28	-DRV SLCT 1
GROUND	29	30	Reserved
GROUND	31	32	-READ GATE
GROUND	33	34	-CMD DATA

Table 14.14   ESDI (Enhanced Small Device Interface) 20-Pin Data Connector Pinout

Signal Name	Pin	Pin	Signal Name
-DRV SLCTD	1	2	-SECTOR
-CMD COMPL	3	4	-ADDR MK EN
GROUND	5	6	GROUND
+WRITE CLK	7	8	-WRITE CLK
GROUND	9	10	+RD/REF CLK
-RD/REF CLK	11	12	GROUND
+NRZ WRITE	13	14	-NRZ WRITE
GROUND	15	16	GROUND
+NRZ READ	17	18	-NRZ READ
GROUND	19	20	-INDEX

ESDI Drive Configuration. The ESDI interface was modeled after the ST-506/412 interface and shares virtually all the same types of configuration items and procedures. The 34-pin control and 20-pin data cables are identical to those used in an ST-506/412 installation, and all the configuration procedures with regard to Drive Select jumpers, twisted cables, and terminating resistors are the same as with ST-506/412.

Follow the configuration procedures for ST-506/412 drives when configuring ESDI drives. Since ESDI was developed from the ST-506/412 interface it shares many characteristics including the type of cabling used as well as how it is configured.

The IDE Interface

Integrated Drive Electronics (IDE) is a generic term applied to any drive with an integrated (built-in) disk controller. The first drives with integrated controllers were Hardcards; today, a variety of drives with integrated controllers are available. In a drive with IDE, the disk controller is integrated into the drive, and this combination drive/controller assembly usually plugs into a bus connector on the motherboard or on a bus adapter card. Combining the drive and controller greatly simplifies installation, because there are no separate power or signal cables from the controller to the drive. Also, when the controller and the drive are assembled as a unit, the number of total components is reduced, signal paths are shorter, and the electrical connections are more noise-resistant, resulting in a more reliable design than is possible when a separate controller, connected to the drive by cables, is used.

Placing the controller (including Endec) on the drive gives IDE drives an inherent reliability advantage over interfaces with separate controllers. Reliability is increased because the data encoding, from digital to analog, is performed directly on the drive in a tight noise-free environment; the timing-sensitive analog information does not have to travel along crude ribbon cables that are likely to pick up noise and to insert propagation delays into the signals. The integrated configuration allows for increases in the clock rate of the encoder, as well as the storage density of the drive.

Integrating the controller and drive also frees the controller and drive engineers from having to adhere to the strict standards imposed by the earlier interface standards. Engineers can design what essentially are custom drive and controller implementations, because no other controller would ever have to be connected to the drive. The resulting drive and controller combinations can offer higher performance than earlier stand-alone controller and drive setups. IDE drives sometimes are called drives with *embedded controllers*.

The IDE connector on motherboards in many systems is nothing more than a stripped-down bus slot. In ATA IDE installations, these connectors contain a 40-pin subset of the 98 pins that would be available in a standard 16-bit ISA bus slot. The pins used are only the signal pins required by a standard-type XT or AT hard disk controller. For example, because an AT-style disk controller uses only interrupt line 14, the motherboard AT IDE connector supplies only that interrupt line; no other interrupt lines are needed. The XT IDE motherboard connector supplies interrupt line 5 because that is what an XT controller would use.

Many people who use systems with IDE connectors on the motherboard believe that a hard disk controller is built into their motherboard, but the controller really is in the drive. I do not know of any PC systems that have hard disk controllers built into the motherboard.

When IDE drives are discussed, the ATA IDE variety usually is the only kind mentioned, because it is so popular. But other forms of IDE drives exist, based on other buses. For example, several PS/2 systems came with Micro Channel (MCA) IDE drives, which plug directly into a Micro Channel Bus slot (through an angle adapter or Interposer card).

An 8-bit ISA form of IDE also exists but was never very popular. Most IBM-compatible systems with the ISA or EISA Bus use AT-Bus (16-bit) IDE drives. The ATA IDE interface is by far the most popular type of drive interface available.

The primary advantage of IDE drives is cost. Because the separate controller or host adapter is eliminated and the cable connections are simplified, IDE drives cost much less than a standard controller-and-drive combination. These drives also are more reliable, because the controller is built into the drive. Therefore, the Endec or *data separator* (the divisor between the digital and analog signals on the drive) stays close to the media. Because the drive has a short analog-signal path, it is less susceptible to external noise and interference.

Another advantage is performance. IDE drives are some of the highest-performance drives available—but they also are among the lowest-performance drives. This apparent contradiction is because all IDE drives are different. You cannot make a blanket statement about the performance of IDE drives, because each drive is unique. The high-end models, however, offer performance that is equal or superior to that of any other type of drive on the market for a single-user, single-tasking operating system.

The greatest drawbacks to the IDE interface are capacity and expandability. IDE drives are not suited for large, high-performance systems that require large-capacity, high-performance drives. Incompatibilities among different manufacturers' standards make it difficult to install more than one IDE drive on a system. Because the controller is mounted on the drive, to add a second drive you must disable its controller and have it use the controller on the first drive. This process can be difficult because of the many different kinds of controllers on the drives. In many cases, to add a second IDE drive, you must use one made by the same manufacturer as the first, for compatibility purposes.

An additional drawback to IDE drives is that they normally are locked into a specific type of bus. You cannot easily move IDE drives of one type to a system that does not have the corresponding type of bus. Also, IDE drives are specific to IBM-compatible systems and cannot be used in foreign environments, such as Apple Macintosh systems, UNIX systems, and other computing environments. Because of these drawbacks, I normally use SCSI drives myself, but in many situations, IDE is the logical choice for other people.

IDE Origins. Technically, the first IDE drives were Hardcards. Companies such as the Plus Development division of Quantum took small 3.5-inch drives (either ST-506/412 or ESDI) and attached them directly to a standard controller. The assembly then was plugged into a bus slot as though it were a normal disk controller. Unfortunately, the mounting of a heavy, vibrating hard disk in an expansion slot with nothing but a single screw to hold it in place left a lot to be desired—not to mention the possible interference with adjacent cards due to the fact that many of these units were much thicker than a controller card alone.

Several companies got the idea that you could redesign the controller to replace the logic-board assembly on a standard hard disk and then mount it in a standard drive bay just like any other drive. Because the built-in controller in these drives still needed to plug directly into the expansion bus just like any other controller, a cable was run between the drive and one of the slots.

These connection problems were solved in different ways. Compaq was the first to incorporate a special bus adapter in its system to adapt the 98-pin AT bus edge connector on the motherboard to a smaller 40-pin header style connector that the drive would plug into. The 40-pin connectors were all that were needed, because it was known that a disk controller never would need more than 40 of the bus lines.

In 1987, IBM developed its own MCA IDE drives and connected them to the bus through a bus adapter device called an interposer card. These bus adapters (sometimes called paddle boards) needed only a few buffer chips and did not require any real circuitry, because the drive-based controller was designed to plug directly into the bus. The paddle board nickname came from the fact that they resembled game paddle or joystick adapters, which do not have much circuitry on them. Another 8-bit variation of IDE appeared in 8-bit ISA systems such as the PS/2 Model 30. The XT IDE interface uses a 40-pin connector and cable that is similar to, but not compatible with, the 16-bit version.

IDE Bus Versions. Three main types of IDE interfaces are available, with the differences based on three different bus standards:

■ AT Attachment (ATA) IDE (16-bit ISA)

■ XT IDE (8-bit ISA)

■ MCA IDE (16-bit Micro Channel)

The XT and ATA versions have standardized on 40-pin connectors and cables, but the connectors have slightly different pinouts, rendering them incompatible with one another. MCA IDE uses a completely different 72-pin connector and is designed for MCA bus systems only.

In most cases, you must use the type of IDE drive that matches your system bus. This situation means that XT IDE drives work only in XT-class 8-bit ISA slot systems, AT IDE drives work only in AT-class 16-bit ISA or EISA slot systems, and MCA IDE drives work only in Micro Channel systems (such as the IBM PS/2 Model 50 or higher). A company called Silicon Valley offers adapter cards for XT systems that will run ATA IDE drives. Other companies, such as Arco Electronics and Sigma Data, have IDE adapters for Micro Channel systems that allow ATA IDE drives to be used on these systems. (You can find these vendors in Appendix B.) These adapters are very useful for XT or PS/2 systems, because there is a very limited selection of XT or MCA IDE drives, whereas the selection of ATA drives is virtually unlimited.

In most modern ISA and EISA systems, you will find an ATA connector on the motherboard. If your motherboard does not have one of these connectors and you want to attach an AT IDE drive to your system, you can purchase an adapter card that changes your 98-pin slot connector to the 40-pin IDE connector. These adapter cards are nothing more than buffered cables; they are not really controllers. The controller is built into the drive. Some of the cards offer additional features, such as an on-board ROM BIOS or cache memory.

ATA IDE. CDC, Western Digital, and Compaq actually created what could be called the first ATA type IDE interface drive and were the first to establish the 40-pin IDE connector pinout. The first ATA IDE drives were 5.25-inch half-height CDC 40M units (I believe that they had a green activity LED) with integrated WD controllers sold in the first Compaq 386 systems way back in '86. After that, Compaq helped found a company called Conner Peripherals to supply Compaq with IDE drives. Conner originally made drives only for Compaq but later, Compaq sold much of its ownership of Conner.

Eventually, the 40-pin IDE connector and drive interface method was placed before one of the ANSI standards committees, which, in conjunction with drive manufacturers, ironed out some deficiencies, tied up some loose ends, and published what is known as the CAM ATA (Common Access Method AT Attachment) interface. The CAM Committee was formed in October 1988, and the first working document of the AT Attachment interface was introduced in March 1989. Before the CAM ATA standard, many companies that followed CDC, such as Conner Peripherals, made proprietary changes to what had been done by CDC. As a result, many older ATA drives are very difficult to integrate into a dual-drive setup that has newer drives.

Some areas of the ATA standard have been left open for vendor-specific commands and functions. These vendor-specific commands and functions are the main reason why it is so difficult to low-level format IDE drives. To work properly, the formatter that you are using usually must know the specific vendor-unique commands for rewriting sector headers and remapping defects. Unfortunately, these and other specific drive commands differ from OEM to OEM, clouding the "standard" somewhat.

It is important to note that only the ATA IDE interface has been standardized by the industry. The XT IDE and MCA IDE never were adopted as industrywide standards and never became very popular. These interfaces no longer are in production, and no new systems of which I am aware come with these nonstandard IDE interfaces.

The CAM ATA Specification. The ATA specification was introduced in March 1989 by the ANSI CAM committee. You can obtain the current working-draft version of this standard, X3T9.2/791D Rev 4a or later, from Global Engineering Documents, which is listed in Appendix B. This standard has gone a long way toward eliminating incompatibilities and problems with interfacing IDE drives to ISA and EISA systems. The ATA specification defines the signals on the 40-pin connector, the functions and timings of these signals, cable specifications, and so on. The following section lists some of the elements and functions defined by the CAM ATA specification.

Dual-Drive Configurations. Dual-drive ATA installations can be problematic, because each drive has its own controller and both controllers must function while being connected to the same bus. There has to be a way to ensure that only one of the two controllers will respond to a command at a time.

The ATA standard provides the option of operating on the AT Bus with two drives in a daisy-chained configuration. The primary drive (drive 0) is called the *master*, and the secondary drive (drive 1) is the *slave*. You designate a drive as being master or slave by setting a jumper or switch on the drive or by using a special line in the interface called the Cable Select (CSEL) pin.

When only one drive is installed, the controller responds to all commands from the system. When two drives (and, therefore, two controllers) are installed, all commands from the system are received by both controllers. Each controller then must be set up to respond only to commands for itself. In this situation, one controller then must be designated as the master and the other as the slave. When the system sends a command for a specific drive, the controller on the other drive must remain silent while the selected controller and drive are functioning. You handle discrimination between the two controllers by setting a special bit (the DRV bit) in the Drive/Head Register of a command block.

ATA I/O Connector. The ATA interface connector is a 40-pin header-type connector that should be keyed to prevent the possibility of installing it upside down. A key is provided by the removal of pin 20, and the corresponding pin on the cable connector should be plugged to prevent a backward installation. The use of keyed connectors and cables is highly recommended, because plugging an IDE cable in backward can damage both the drive and the bus adapter circuits (although I have done it myself many times with no smoked parts yet!).

Table 14.15 shows the ATA-IDE interface connector pinout.

Table 14.15   ATA (AT Attachment) IDE (Integrated Drive Electronics) Connector Pinout

Signal Name	Pin	Pin	Signal Name
-RESET	1	2	GROUND
Data Bit 7	3	4	Data Bit 8
Data Bit 6	5	6	Data Bit 9
Data Bit 5	7	8	Data Bit 10
Data Bit 4	9	10	Data Bit 11
Data Bit 3	11	12	Data Bit 12
Data Bit 2	13	14	Data Bit 13
Data Bit 1	15	16	Data Bit 14
Data Bit 0	17	18	Data Bit 15
GROUND	19	20	KEY (pin missing)
DRQ 3	21	22	GROUND
-IOW	23	24	GROUND
-IOR	25	26	GROUND
I/O CH RDY	27	28	SPSYNC:CSEL
-DACK 3	29	30	GROUND
IRQ 14	31	32	-IOCS16
Address Bit 1	33	34	-PDIAG
Address Bit 0	35	36	Address Bit 2
-CS1FX	37	38	-CS3FX
-DA/SP	39	40	GROUND
+5 Vdc (Logic)	41	42	+5 Vdc (Motor)
GROUND	43	44	-TYPE (0=ATA)

ATA I/O Cable. A 40-conductor ribbon cable is specified to carry signals between the bus adapter circuits and the drive (controller). To maximize signal integrity and to eliminate potential timing and noise problems, the cable should not be longer than 0.46 meters (18 inches).

ATA Signals. The ATA interface signals and connector pinout are listed in Appendix A. This section describes some of the most important signals in more detail.

Pin 20 is used as a key pin for cable orientation and is not connected through the interface. This pin should be missing from any ATA connectors, and the cable should have the pin-20 hole in the connector plugged off to prevent the cable from being plugged in backward.

Pin 39 carries the Drive Active/Slave Present (DASP) signal, which is a dual-purpose, time-multiplexed signal. During power-on initialization, this signal indicates whether a slave drive is present on the interface. After that, each drive asserts the signal to indicate that it is active. Early drives could not multiplex these functions and required special jumper settings to work with other drives. Standardizing this function to allow for compatible dual-drive installations is one of the features of the ATA standard.

Pin 28 carries the Cable Select or Spindle Synchronization signal (CSEL or SPSYNC), which is a dual-purpose conductor; a given installation, however, may use only one of the two functions. The CSEL (Cable Select) function is the most widely used and is designed to control the designation of a drive as master (drive 0) or slave (drive 1) without requiring jumper settings on the drives. If a drive sees the CSEL as being grounded, the drive is a master; if CSEL is open, the drive is a slave.

You can install special cabling to ground CSEL selectively. This installation normally is accomplished through a Y-cable arrangement, with the IDE bus connector in the middle and each drive at opposite ends of the cable. One leg of the Y has the CSEL line connected through, indicating a master drive; the other leg has the CSEL line open (conductor interrupted or removed), making the drive at that end the slave.

ATA Commands. One of the best features of the ATA IDE interface is the enhanced command set. The ATA IDE interface was modeled after the WD1003 controller that IBM used in the original AT system. All ATA IDE drives must support the original WD command set (eight commands), with no exceptions, which is why IDE drives are so easy to install in systems today. All IBM-compatible systems have built-in ROM BIOS support for the WD1003, which means that essentially, they support ATA IDE as well.

In addition to supporting all the WD1003 commands, the ATA specification added numerous other commands to enhance performance and capabilities. These commands are an optional part of the ATA interface, but several of them are used in most drives available today and are very important to the performance and use of ATA drives in general.

Perhaps the most important is the *Identify Drive* command. This command causes the drive to transmit a 512-byte block of data that provides all details about the drive. Through this command, any program (including the system BIOS) can find out exactly what type of drive is connected, including the drive manufacturer, model number, operating parameters, and even the serial number of the drive. Many modern BIOSes use this information to automatically receive and enter the drive's parameters into CMOS memory, eliminating the need for the user to enter these parameters manually during system configuration. This arrangement helps prevent mistakes that later can lead to data loss when the user no longer remembers what parameters he or she used during setup.

The Identify Drive data can tell you many things about your drive, including the following:

- Number of cylinders in the recommended (default) translation mode
- Number of heads in the recommended (default) translation mode
- Number of sectors per track in the recommended (default) translation mode
- Number of cylinders in the current translation mode
- Number of heads in the current translation mode
- Number of sectors per track in the current translation mode
- Manufacturer and model number
- Firmware revision
- Serial number
- Buffer type, indicating sector buffering or caching capabilities

Several public-domain programs can execute this command to the drive and report the information on-screen. I use the IDEINFO program (which can be downloaded from the IBM Hardware Forum on CompuServe) or the IDEDIAG utility (which can be downloaded from the Western Digital BBS). Phone numbers for these information services appear in Appendix B. I find these programs especially useful when I am trying to install IDE drives and need to know the correct parameters for a user-definable BIOS type. These programs get the information directly from the drive itself.

Two other very important commands are the Read Multiple and Write Multiple commands. These commands permit multiple-sector data transfers and, when combined with block-mode Programmed I/O (PIO) capabilities in the system, can result in incredible data-transfer rates many times faster than single-sector PIO transfers.

> **Tip**
>
> If you want the ultimate in IDE performance and installation ease, make sure that your motherboard BIOS goes beyond supporting just the WD1003 command set and also supports block-mode Programmed I/O (PIO) and the Identify Drive commands. This support will allow your BIOS to execute data transfers to and from the IDE drive several times faster than normal, and also will make installation and configuration easier because the BIOS will be able to detect the drive-parameter information automatically. Block PIO and automatic detection of the drive type are included in the latest versions of most PC BIOSs.

There are many other enhanced commands, including room for a given drive manufacturer to implement what are called vendor-unique commands. These commands often
are used by a particular vendor for features unique to that vendor. Often, features such
as low-level formatting and defect management are controlled by vendor-unique
commands. This is why low-level format programs can be so specific to a particular
manufacturer's IDE drives and why many manufacturers make their own LLF programs
available.

ATA IDE Drive Categories. ATA-IDE drives can be divided into three main categories.
These categories separate the drives by function (such as translation capabilities) and
design (which can affect features such as low-level formatting). The three drive categories
are:

- Non-Intelligent ATA-IDE drives

- Intelligent ATA-IDE drives

- Intelligent Zoned Recording ATA-IDE drives

The following sections describe these categories.

Non-Intelligent IDE. As I stated earlier, the ATA standard requires that the built-in
controller respond exactly as though it were a Western Digital WD1003 controller. This
controller responds to a command set of eight commands. Early IDE drives supported
these commands and had few, if any, other options. These early drives actually were
more like regular ST-506/412 or ESDI controllers bolted directly to the drive than the
more intelligent drives that we consider today to be IDE.

These drives were not considered to be intelligent IDE drives; an intelligent drive is supposed to have several capabilities that these early IDE drives lacked. The drives could not
respond to any of the enhanced commands that were specified as (an optional) part of
the ATA IDE specification, including the Identify Drive command. These drives also did
not support sector translation, in which the physical parameters could be altered to appear as any set of logical cylinders, heads, and sectors. Enhanced commands and sector-
translation support are what make an IDE drive an intelligent IDE drive, and these features were not available in the early IDE drives.

These drives could be low-level formatted in the same manner as any normal ST-506/412
or ESDI drive. They were universally low-level formatted at the factory, with factory-
calculated optimum interleave (usually, 1:1) and head- and cylinder-skew factors. Also,
factory defects were recorded in a special area on the drive; they no longer were written
on a sticker pasted to the exterior. Unfortunately, this arrangement means that if you
low-level format these drives in the field, you most likely will alter these settings (especially the skew factors) from what the factory set as optimum, as well as wipe out the
factory-written defect table.

Some manufacturers released special low-level format routines that would reformat the
drives while preserving these settings, but others did not make such programs available.
Because they did not want you to overwrite the defect list or potentially slow the drive,
most manufacturers stated that you should never low-level format their IDE drives.

This statement started a myth that the drives could somehow be damaged or rendered inoperable by such a format, which truly is not the case. One rumor was that the servo information could be overwritten, which would mean that you would have to send the drive back to the manufacturer for re-servoing. This also is not true; the servo information is protected and cannot be overwritten. The only consequence of an improper low-level format of these drives is the possible alteration of the skew factors and the potential loss of the factory defect maps.

The Disk Manager program by Ontrack is the best special-purpose format utility to use on these drives for formatting, because it is aware of these types of drives and often can restore the skew factors and preserve the defect information. If you are working with a drive that already has had the defect map overwritten, Disk Manager can perform a very good surface analysis that will mark off any of these areas that it finds. Disk Manager allows you to specify the skew factors and to mark defects at the sector level so that they will not cause problems later. Other general-purpose diagnostics that work especially well with IDE drives such as this include the Microscope program by Micro 2000.

Intelligent IDE. Later IDE drives became known as intelligent IDE drives. These drives support enhanced ATA commands, such as the Identify Drive command, and sector-translation capabilities.

These drives can be configured in two ways: in raw physical mode or in translation mode. To configure the drive in raw physical mode, you simply enter the CMOS drive parameters during setup so that they match the true physical parameters of the drive. For example, if the drive physically has 800 cylinders, 6 heads, and 50 sectors per track, you enter these figures during setup. To configure the drive in translation mode, you simply enter any combination of cylinders, heads, and sectors that adds up to equal or less than the true number of sectors on the drive.

In the example that I just used, the drive has a total of 240,000 sectors ($800 \times 6 \times 50$). All I have to do is figure out another set of parameters that adds up to equal or less than 240,000 sectors. The simplest way to do this is to cut the number of cylinders in half and double the number of heads. Thus, the new drive parameters become 400 cylinders, 12 heads, and 50 sectors per track. This method adds up to 240,000 sectors and enables the drive to work in translation mode.

When these drives are in translation mode, a low-level format cannot alter the interleave and skew factors; neither can it overwrite the factory defect-mapping information. A low-level format program can, however, perform additional defect mapping or sector sparing while in this mode.

If the drive is in true physical mode, a low-level format will rewrite the sector headers and modify the head and cylinder skewing. If done incorrectly, the format can be repaired by a proper low-level format program that allows you to set the correct head and cylinder skew. This task can be accomplished automatically by the drive manufacturer's recommended low-level format program (if available) or by other programs, such as Disk Manager by Ontrack. When you use Disk Manager, you have to enter the skew values manually; otherwise, the program uses predetermined defaults. To get the correct skew values, it is best to contact the drive manufacturer's technical-support department. You can calculate the skew values if the manufacturer cannot provide them.

To protect the skew factors and defect information on intelligent IDE drives, all you have to do is run them in translation mode. In translation mode, this information cannot be overwritten.

Intelligent Zoned Recording IDE. The last and most sophisticated IDE drives combine intelligence with Zoned Recording. With Zoned Recording, the drive has a variable number sectors per track in several zones across the surface of the drive. Because the PC BIOS can handle only a fixed number of sectors on all tracks, these drives always must run in translation mode. Because these drives are always in translation mode, you cannot alter the factory-set interleave and skew factors or wipe out the factory defect information.

You still can low-level format these drives, however, and use such a format to map or spare additional defective sectors that crop up during the life of the drive. To low-level format intelligent Zoned Recording drives, you need either a specific utility from the drive manufacturer or an IDE-aware program, such as Disk Manager by Ontrack or Microscope by Micro 2000.

IDE Drive Configuration. IDE drives can be both simple and troublesome to configure. Single-drive installations usually are very simple, with few, if any, special jumper settings to worry about. Multiple-drive configurations, however, can be a problem. Jumpers have to be set on both drives; and the names, locations, and even functions of these jumpers can vary from drive to drive.

Because the CAM ATA (Common Access Method AT Attachment) IDE specification was ironed out only after many companies were already making and selling drives, many older IDE drives have problems in dual-drive installations, especially when the drives are from different manufacturers. In some cases, two particular drives may not function together at all. Fortunately, most of the newer drives follow the CAM ATA specification, which clears up this problem. Drives that follow the specification have no problems in dual-drive installations.

Cable Configuration. The cable connection to IDE drives usually is very simple. There is a single 40-pin cable that normally has three pin-header style connectors on it. One of the connectors plugs into the IDE interface connector; the other two plug into the primary and secondary drives. The cable normally runs from the IDE connector to both drives in a daisy-chain arrangement. On one end, this cable plugs into the IDE interface connector, which is located on the motherboard in many systems but also may be located on an IDE interface adapter card. The cable then connects to the secondary (D) and primary (C) drives in succession, with the primary drive usually (but not always) being at the end of the cable opposite the IDE interface connector.

There are no terminating resistors to set with IDE drives; instead a distributed termination circuit is built into all IDE drives. The last drive on the cable need not be the primary drive, so you actually may find the primary or secondary drive at either connector. Jumpers on the drives themselves normally control whether a drive responds as primary or secondary.

You may see a different arrangement of cable connections in some IDE installations. In some installations, the middle connector is plugged into the motherboard, and the primary and secondary drives are at opposite ends of the cable in a Y arrangement. If you see this arrangement, be careful; in some of these Y-cable installations, the cable, rather than jumpers on the drives, actually controls which drive is primary and which is secondary.

Controlling master/slave selection via the cable rather than jumpers on the drive is performed via a special signal on the IDE interface called *CSEL (Cable SELect)*, which is on pin 28 of the interface. If the CSEL line is connected through from the drive to the IDE interface connector, the drive automatically is designated as primary. If the CSEL line is open between a drive and the IDE interface connector, that drive automatically is designated as secondary.

In the Y-cable approach, the IDE interface connector is in the middle of the cable, and a separate length of cable goes to each drive. Study this type of cable closely. If one of the ends of the Y has line 28 open (usually, a hole in the cable through that wire), only the secondary drive can be plugged into that connector. HP Vectra PC systems use exactly this type of IDE cable arrangement. This type of setup eliminates the need to set jumpers on the IDE drives to configure them for primary or secondary operation, but the setup can be troublesome if you do not know about it.

IDE Drive Jumper Settings. Configuring IDE drives can be simple, as is the case with most single-drive installations, or troublesome, especially where it comes to mixing two drives from different manufacturers on a single cable.

Most IDE drives come in three configurations:

- Single-drive (master)
- Master (dual-drive)
- Slave (dual-drive)

Because each IDE drive has its own controller, you must specifically tell one drive to be the master and the other to be the slave. There's no functional difference between the two, except that the drive that's specified as the slave will assert the DASP signal after a system reset that informs the master that a slave drive is present in the system. The master drive then pays attention to the Drive Select line, which it otherwise ignores. Telling a drive that it's the slave also usually causes it to delay its spinup for several seconds, to allow the master to get going and thus to lessen the load on the system's power supply.

Until the ATA IDE specification, no common implementation for drive configuration was in use. Some drive companies even used different master/slave methods for different models of drives. Because of these incompatibilities, some drives work together only in a specific master/slave or slave/master order. This situation affects mostly older IDE drives that were introduced before the ATA specification.

Most drives that fully follow the ATA specification now need only one jumper (Master/ Slave) for configuration. A few also need a Slave Present jumper as well. Table 14.16 shows the jumper settings required by most ATA IDE drives.

Table 14.16 Jumper Settings for Most ATA IDE-Compatible Drives			
Jumper Name	Single-Drive	Dual-Drive Master	Dual-Drive Slave
Master (M/S)	On	On	Off
Slave Present (SP)	Off	On	Off

The Master jumper indicates that the drive is a master or a slave. Some drives also require a Slave Present jumper, which is used only in a dual-drive setup and then installed only on the master drive, which is somewhat confusing. This jumper tells the master that a slave drive is attached. With many ATA IDE drives, the Master jumper is optional and may be left off. Installing this jumper doesn't hurt in these cases and may eliminate confusion, so I recommend that you install the jumpers listed here.

Conner Peripherals Drives. Because they were introduced before the ATA IDE specification was formalized, Conner Peripherals drives often are different in configuration from many other-brand drives. When you mix and match IDE hard drives from different manufacturers, the drives are not always fully compatible. Table 14.17 shows the jumper settings that are correct for most Conner IDE drive installations.

Table 14.17 Jumper Settings for Conner Peripherals IDE Drives			
Jumper Name	Single Drive	Dual-Drive Master	Dual-Drive Slave
Master or Slave (C/D)	On	On	Off
Drive Slave Present (DSP)	Off	On	Off
Host Slave Present (HSP)	Off	Off	On
Drive Active (ACT)	On	On	Off

The C/D jumper is used to determine whether the drive is a master (drive C) or a slave (drive D). The drive is configured as master when this jumper is on. The DSP jumper indicates that a slave drive is present. The HSP jumper causes the drive to send the Slave Present signal to the master drive. The ACT jumper enables the master drive to signal when it is active.

Some Conner drives are not set up to support the industry-standard CAM ATA interface by default. The problems show up when you attempt to connect another manufacturer's drive to some Conner drives in either a master or slave role. Fortunately, you can correct many of these situations by changing the configuration of the drive.

You can make this change in two ways. One way is to use a special program to semipermanently change the mode of the drive. A special file available on the Conner BBS, called *FEATURE.COM*, contains a program that displays the current ISA/CAM setting and allows the setting to be changed. The change actually is stored in a feature byte in the firmware of the drive, and after this byte is changed, most other manufacturers' drives will work with the Conner drives. The program also can be used to reset the feature byte back to its original configuration, which is best when you are connecting to other Conner drives.

The second method for changing this configuration is available on some Conner drives. These drives also have a special jumper called ATA/ISA. This jumper almost always should be installed in the ATA position to provide compatibility with the ATA standard. If you are using only Conner drives, you can leave this jumper in ISA mode if you want. Some Conner drives have a separate jumper (E1) that can delay startup of the drive to minimize the load on the power supply. This jumper should be enabled on any drive that is configured as a slave. Most other drives automatically delay startup of the slave drive for a few seconds.

Most Conner drives also have a special 12-pin connector that is used to drive an optional LED (pin 1, LED +5v; and pin 2, ground), as well as to connect to special factory equipment for low-level formatting and configuration. A company called TCE (see Appendix B) sells a device called The Conner, which connects to this port and permits full factory-level initialization, formatting, and testing of Conner drives. I consider this piece of gear to be essential to anybody who services or supports a large number of Conner Peripherals drives. Notice that Compaq uses Conner drives in most of its systems.

For more information on any specific Conner drive, you can use the company's FaxBack system at (800) 4CONNER. Through this system, you can get drive information and jumper settings that are specific to Conner drives.

XT-Bus (8-Bit) IDE. Many systems with XT ISA bus architecture used XT IDE hard drives. The IDE interface in these systems usually is built into the motherboard. The IBM PS/2 Model 25, 25-286, 30, and 30-286 systems used an 8-bit XT IDE interface. These 8-bit XT IDE drives are difficult to find; few manufacturers other than IBM, Western Digital, and Seagate made them; and none of these drives were available in capacities beyond 40MB.

Since the ATA IDE interface is a 16-bit design, it could not be used in 8-bit (XT type) systems, so some of the drive manufacturers standardized on an XT-Bus (8-bit) IDE interface for XT class systems. These drives were never very popular, and were usually only available in capacities from 20MB to 40MB. Table 14.18 shows the industry standard 8-bit IDE connector pinout.

Table 14.18   XT-Bus IDE (Integrated Drive Electronics) Connector Pinout

Signal Name	Pin	Pin	Signal Name
-RESET	1	2	GROUND
Data Bit 7	3	4	GROUND
Data Bit 6	5	6	GROUND
Data Bit 5	7	8	GROUND
Data Bit 4	9	10	GROUND
Data Bit 3	11	12	GROUND
Data Bit 2	13	14	GROUND
Data Bit 1	15	16	GROUND
Data Bit 0	17	18	GROUND
GROUND	19	20	KEY (pin missing)
AEN	21	22	GROUND
-IOW	23	24	GROUND
-IOR	25	26	GROUND
-DACK 3	27	28	GROUND
DRQ 3	29	30	GROUND
IRQ 5	31	32	GROUND
Address Bit 1	33	34	GROUND
Address Bit 0	35	36	GROUND
-CS1FX	37	38	GROUND
-Drive Active	39	40	GROUND

Note that IBM used a custom version of the XT-Bus IDE interface in the PS/2 Model 25 and Model 30 systems. The pinout for the custom IBM XT-Bus IDE connector is shown in table 14.19.

Table 14.19   IBM Unique XT-Bus (PS/2 Model 25 and 30) IDE Connector Pinout

Signal Name	Pin	Pin	Signal Name
-RESET	1	2	-Disk Installed
Data Bit 0	3	4	GROUND
Data Bit 1	5	6	GROUND
Data Bit 2	7	8	GROUND
Data Bit 3	9	10	GROUND
Data Bit 4	11	12	GROUND
Data Bit 5	13	14	GROUND
Data Bit 6	15	16	GROUND
Data Bit 7	17	18	GROUND

(continues)

IV

Mass Storage Systems

Table 14.19   Continued

Signal Name	Pin	Pin	Signal Name
-IOR	19	20	GROUND
-IOW	21	22	GROUND
-CS1FX	23	24	GROUND
Address Bit 0	25	26	GROUND
Address Bit 1	27	28	GROUND
Address Bit 2	29	30	+5 Vdc
RESERVED	31	32	+5 Vdc
-DACK 3	33	34	GROUND
DRQ 3	35	36	GROUND
IRQ 5	37	38	GROUND
I/O CH RDY	39	40	+12 Vdc
Spare	41	42	+12 Vdc
Spare	39	44	+12 Vdc

The newer PS/1, PS/Valuepoint, and PS/2 systems with 16-bit ISA architecture use ATA IDE drives. Because nearly all hard disk manufacturers make a multitude of drives with the ATA IDE interface, these systems are easy to upgrade or repair. ATA IDE drives are available in capacities up to and beyond 1GB.

MCA IDE. The IBM PS/2 Models 50 and higher come with Micro Channel Architecture (MCA) bus slots. Although most of these systems now use SCSI drives, for some time IBM used a type of MCA IDE drive in these systems. MCA IDE is a form of IDE interface, but it is designed for the MCA bus and is not compatible with the more industry-standard ATA IDE interface. Few companies other than IBM and Western Digital make replacement MCA IDE drives for these systems. I recommend replacing these drives with ATA IDE drives, using adapters from Arco Electronics or Sigma Data, or switching to SCSI drives instead. The IBM MCA IDE drives are expensive for the limited capacity that they offer.

The pinout of the MCA IDE connector is shown in table 14.20.

Table 14.20   MCA (Micro Channel Architecture) IDE Connector Pinout

Signal Name	Pin	Pin	Signal Name
-CD SETUP	A1	B1	Address Bit 15
Address Bit 13	A2	B2	Address Bit 14
GROUND	A3	B3	GROUND
Address Bit 11	A4	B4	OSC (14.3 MHz)
Address Bit 10	A5	B5	GROUND
Address Bit 9	A6	B6	Address Bit 12
+5 Vdc	A7	B7	-CMD
Address Bit 8	A8	B8	-CD SFDBK

Signal Name	Pin	Pin	Signal Name
Address Bit 7	A9	B9	GROUND
Address Bit 6	A10	B10	Data Bit 1
+5 Vdc	A11	B11	Data Bit 3
Address Bit 5	A12	B12	Data Bit 4
Address Bit 4	A13	B13	GROUND
Address Bit 3	A14	B14	CHRESET
+5 Vdc	A15	B15	Data Bit 8
Address Bit 2	A16	B16	Data Bit 9
Address Bit 1	A17	B17	GROUND
Address Bit 0	A18	B18	Data Bit 12
+12 Vdc	A19	B19	Data Bit 14
-ADL	A20	B20	Data Bit 15
-PREEMPT	A21	B21	GROUND
-BURST	A22	B22	Data Bit 0
+5 Vdc	A23	B23	Data Bit 2
ARB 0	A24	B24	Data Bit 5
ARB 1	A25	B25	GROUND
ARB 2	A26	B26	Data Bit 6
+12 Vdc	A27	B27	Data Bit 7
ARB 3	A28	B28	Data Bit 10
+ARB/-GRANT	A29	B29	GROUND
-TC	A30	B30	Data Bit 11
+5 Vdc	A31	B31	Data Bit 13
-S0	A32	B32	-SBHE
-S1	A33	B33	GROUND
+M/-IO	A34	B34	-CD DS 16
GROUND	A35	B35	-IRQ 14
CD CHRDY	A36	B36	GROUND

Introduction to SCSI

SCSI (pronounced "scuzzy") stands for *Small Computer System Interface*. This interface has its roots in SASI, the *Shugart Associates System Interface*. SCSI is not a disk interface, but a systems-level interface. SCSI is not a type of controller, but a bus that supports as many as eight devices. One of these devices, the *host adapter*, functions as the gateway between the SCSI bus and the PC system bus. The SCSI bus itself does not talk directly with devices such as hard disks; instead, it talks to the controller that is built into the drive.

A single SCSI bus can support as many as eight *physical units*, usually called *SCSI IDs*. One of these units is the adapter card in your PC; the other seven can be other peripherals. You could have hard disks, tape drives, CD-ROM drives, a graphics scanner, or other devices (up to seven total) attached to a single SCSI host adapter. Most systems support up to four host adapters, each with seven devices, for a total 28 devices!

When you purchase a SCSI hard disk, you usually are purchasing the drive, controller, and SCSI adapter in one circuit. This type of drive usually is called an *embedded SCSI drive*; the SCSI interface is built into the drive. Most SCSI hard drives actually are IDE drives with SCSI bus adapter circuits added. You do not need to know what type of controller is inside the SCSI drive, because your system cannot talk directly to the controller as though it were plugged into the system bus, like a standard controller. Instead, communications go through the SCSI host adapter installed in the system bus. You can access the drive only with the SCSI protocols.

Apple originally rallied around SCSI as being an inexpensive way out of the bind in which it put itself with the Macintosh. When the engineers at Apple realized the problem in making the Macintosh a closed system (with no slots), they decided that the easiest way to gain expandability was to build a SCSI port into the system, which is how external peripherals can be added to the slotless Macs. Because PC systems always have been expandable, the push toward SCSI has not been as urgent. With eight bus slots supporting different devices and controllers in IBM and IBM-compatible systems, it seemed as though SCSI was not needed.

SCSI now is becoming popular in the IBM-based computer world because of the great expandability that it offers and the number of devices that are available with built-in SCSI. One thing that stalled acceptance of SCSI in the PC marketplace was the lack of a real standard; the SCSI standard was designed primarily by a committee. No single manufacturer has led the way, at least in the IBM arena; each company has its own interpretation of how SCSI should be implemented, particularly at the host-adapter level.

SCSI is a standard, in much the same way that RS-232 is a standard. The SCSI standard (like the RS-232 standard), however, defines only the hardware connections, not the driver specifications required to communicate with the devices. Software ties the SCSI subsystem into your PC, but unfortunately, most of the driver programs work only for a specific device and a specific host adapter. For example, a graphics scanner comes with its own SCSI host adapter to connect to the system; a CD-ROM drive comes with another (different) SCSI host adapter and driver software that works only with that SCSI adapter. On a system with those two SCSI adapters, you would need a third SCSI host adapter to run SCSI hard disk drives, because the host adapters supplied by the scanner and CD-ROM companies do not include a built-in, self-booting BIOS that supports hard disk drives.

SCSI has become something of a mess in the IBM world because of the lack of a host-adapter standard, a software interface standard, and standard ROM BIOS support for hard disk drives attached to the SCSI bus. Fortunately, some simple recommendations can keep you from living this compatibility nightmare!

The lack of capability to run hard disks off the SCSI bus, and to boot from these drives and use a variety of operating systems, is a problem that results from the lack of an interface standard. The standard IBM XT and AT ROM BIOS software was designed to talk to ST-506/412 hard disk controllers. The software easily was modified to work with ESDI because ESDI controllers are similar to ST-506/412 controllers at the register level.

(This similarity at the register level enabled manufacturers to easily design self-booting, ROM-BIOS-supported ESDI drives.). The same can be said of IDE, which completely emulates the WD1003 ST-506/412 controller interface and works perfectly with the existing BIOS as well. SCSI is so different from these other standard disk interfaces that a new set of ROM BIOS routines are necessary to support the system so that it can self-boot. The newer IBM PS/2 systems that come with SCSI drives have this support built into the motherboard BIOS or as an extension BIOS on the SCSI host adapter.

Companies such as Adaptec and Future Domain have produced SCSI cards with built-in ROM BIOS support for several years, but these BIOS routines were limited to running the drives only under DOS. The BIOS would not run in the AT-protected mode, and other operating systems included drivers for only the standard ST-506/412 and ESDI controllers. Thus, running SCSI was impossible under many non-DOS operating systems. This situation has changed significantly, however; IBM now supports many third-party SCSI host adapters in OS/2, especially those from Adaptec and Future Domain. For compatibility reasons, I usually recommend using SCSI adapters from these two companies, or any other adapters that are fully hardware-compatible with the Adapted and Future Domain adapters.

Because of the lead taken by Apple in developing systems software (operating systems and ROM) support for SCSI, peripherals connect to Apple systems in fairly standard ways. Until recently, this kind of standard-setting leadership was lacking for SCSI in the IBM world. This situation changed on March 20, 1990, when IBM introduced several "standard" SCSI adapters and peripherals for the IBM PS/2 systems, with complete ROM BIOS and full operating-system support.

IBM has standardized on SCSI for nearly all its high-end systems. In these systems, a SCSI host adapter card is in one of the slots, or the system has a SCSI host adapter built into the motherboard. This arrangement is similar in appearance to the IDE interface, because a single cable runs from the motherboard to the SCSI drive, but SCSI supports as many as seven devices (some of which may not be hard disks), whereas IDE supports only two devices, which must be either a hard disk or a tape drive. PS/2 systems with SCSI drives are easy to upgrade, because virtually any third-party SCSI drive will plug in and function.

The example set by IBM is causing other manufacturers to supply systems with either SCSI host adapters or SCSI interfaces integrated into the motherboards. As SCSI becomes more and more popular in the PC world, SCSI peripheral integration will be easier, due to better operating-system and device-driver support.

ANSI SCSI standards. The SCSI standard defines the physical and electrical parameters of a parallel I/O bus used to connect computers and peripheral devices in daisy-chain fashion. The standard supports devices such as disk drives, tape drives, and CD-ROM drives. The original SCSI standard (ANSI X3.131-1986) was approved in 1986; SCSI-2 was approved in January of 1994, and a new revision called SCSI-3, is being developed.

The SCSI interface is defined as a standard by ANSI (American National Standards Institute), an organization that approves and publishes standards. The X3 Task Group operates as an ASC (Accredited Standards Committee) under ANSI to develop Information Processing System standards. X3T9 is the I/O Interfaces group, and X3T9.2 specifically is in charge of low-level interfaces such as SCSI and ATA-IDE (among others). The original SCSI-1 standard was published by the X3T9 ANSI group in 1986 and is officially published by ANSI as X3.131-1986.

One problem with the original SCSI-1 document was that many of the commands and features were optional, and there was little or no guarantee that a particular peripheral would support the expected commands. This problem caused the industry as a whole to define a set of 18 basic SCSI commands called the Common Command Set (CCS), which would become the minimum set of commands supported by all peripherals. This Common Command Set became the basis for what is now the SCSI-2 specification.

In addition to formal support for the CCS, SCSI-2 provided additional definitions for commands to access CD-ROM drives (and their sound capabilities), tape drives, removable drives, optical drives, and several other peripherals. In addition, an optional higher speed called FAST SCSI-2 and a 16-bit version called WIDE SCSI-2 were defined. Another feature of SCSI-2 is command queuing, which enables a device to accept multiple commands and execute them in the order that the device deems to be most efficient. This feature is most beneficial when you are using a multitasking operating system that could be sending several requests on the SCSI bus at the same time.

The X3T9 group approved the SCSI-2 standard as X3.131-1990 in August 1990, but the document was recalled in December 1990 for changes before final ANSI publication. Final approval for the SCSI-2 document was finally made in January of 1994(!), although it has changed little from the original 1990 release. The SCSI-2 document is now called ANSI X3.131-1994. The official document is available from Global Engineering Documents or the ANSI committee, which are listed in Appendix B. You can also download working drafts of these documents from the NCR SCSI BBS, listed in the vendor list under NCR Microelectronics.

Most companies indicate that their host adapters follow both the ANSI X3.131-1986 (SCSI-1) as well as the x3.131-1994 (SCSI-2) standards. Note that since virtually all parts of SCSI-1 are supported in SCSI-2, virtually any SCSI-1 device is also considered SCSI-2 by default. Many manufacturers advertise that their devices are SCSI-2, but this does not mean that they support any of the additional *optional* features that were incorporated in the SCSI-2 revision.

For example, an optional part of the SCSI-2 specification includes a fast synchronous mode that doubles the standard synchronous transfer rate from 5MB per second to 10MB per second. This Fast SCSI transfer mode can be combined with 16-bit Wide or 32-bit Wide SCSI for transfer rates of up to 40MB per second. Currently, there are no 32-bit peripherals to speak of, and only a few 16-bit Wide SCSI devices and host adapters exist. Most SCSI implementations are 8-bit standard SCSI or Fast SCSI. Even devices which support none of the fast or wide modes can still be considered SCSI-2.

Table 14.21 shows the maximum transfer rates for the SCSI bus at various speeds and widths, as well as the cable type required for specific transfer widths.

IV

Table 14.21   SCSI Data-Transfer Rates

Bus Width	Std. SCSI	Fast SCSI	Cable Type
8-bit	5 MB/s	10 MB/s	A
16-bit	10 MB/s	20 MB/s	P
32-bit	20 MB/s	40 MB/s	P&Q

MB/s = Megabytes per second.

Note

The A cable is the standard 50-pin SCSI cable, whereas the P and Q cables are 68-pin cables designed for 16-bit and 32-bit Wide SCSI. For 32-bit SCSI, P and Q cables must be used together. Pinouts for these cable connections are listed in this chapter.

So-called SCSI-1 adapters have no problems with SCSI-2 peripherals. In fact, as was stated earlier, virtually any SCSI-1 device can also legitimately be called SCSI-2. You can't take advantage of Fast or Wide transfer capabilities, but the extra commands defined in SCSI-2 can be sent by means of a SCSI-1 controller. In other words, nothing is different between SCSI-1 and SCSI-2 compliant hardware. For example, I am running a Toshiba MK-538FB 1.2GB Fast SCSI-2 drive with my IBM SCSI host adapter, and it runs fine. Most adapters are similar, in that they actually are SCSI-2 compatible, even if they advertise only SCSI-1 support. Since the SCSI-2 standard was not actually approved before January 1994, any devices which claimed to be SCSI-2 before that time were not officially in compliance with the standard. This is really not a problem, however since the SCSI-2 document had not changed appreciably since it was nearly approved in 1990.

SCSI Hard Disk Evolution and Construction. SCSI is not a disk interface, but a bus that supports SCSI bus interface adapters connected to disk and other device controllers. The first SCSI drives for PCs simply were standard ST-506/412 or ESDI drives with a separate SCSI bus interface adapter (sometimes called a bridge controller) that converted the ST-506/412 or ESDI interfaces to SCSI. This interface originally was in the form of a secondary logic board, and the entire assembly often was mounted in an external case.

The next step was to build the SCSI bus interface "converter" board directly into the drive's own logic board. Today, we call these drives *embedded* SCSI drives, because the SCSI interface is built in.

At that point, there was no need to conform to the absolute specifications of ST-506/412 or ESDI on the internal disk interface, because the only other device that the interface ever would have to talk to was built in as well. Thus, the disk-interface and controller-chipset manufacturers began to develop more customized chipsets that were based on the ST-506/412 or ESDI chipsets already available but offered more features and higher performance. Today, if you look at a typical SCSI drive, you often can identify the chip or chipset that serves as the disk controller on the drive as being exactly the same kind that would be used on an ST-506/412 or ESDI controller or as being some evolutionary customized variation thereof.

Consider some examples. An ATA (AT Attachment interface) IDE drive must fully emulate the system-level disk-controller interface introduced with the Western Digital WD1003 controller series that IBM used in the AT. These drives must act as though they have a built-in ST-506/412 or ESDI controller; in fact, they actually do. Most of these built-in controllers have more capabilities than the original WD1003 series (usually in the form of additional commands), but they must at least respond to all the original commands that were used with the WD1003.

If you follow the hard drive market, you usually will see that drive manufacturers offer most of their newer drives in both ATA-IDE and SCSI versions. In other words, if a manufacturer makes a particular 500MB IDE drive, you invariably will see that the company also make a SCSI model with the same capacity and specifications, which uses the same HDA (Head Disk Assembly) and even looks the same as the IDE version. If you study these virtually identical drives, the only major difference you will find is the additional chip on the logic board of the SCSI version, called a SCSI Bus Adapter Chip (SBIC).

Figures 14.15 and 14.16 show the logic-block diagrams of the WD-AP4200 (a 200MB ATA-IDE drive) and the WD-SP4200 (a 200MB SCSI drive), respectively. These drives use the same HDA; they differ only in their logic boards, and even the logic boards are the same except for the addition of an SBIC (SCSI Bus Adapter Chip) on the SCSI drive's logic board.

Notice that even the circuit designs of these two drives are almost identical. Both drives use an LSI (Large Scale Integrated circuit) chip called the WD42C22 Disk Controller and Buffer manager chip. In the ATA drive, this chip is connected through a DMA control chip directly to the AT bus. In the SCSI version, a WD33C93 SCSI bus interface controller chip is added to interface the disk-controller logic to the SCSI bus. In fact, the logic diagrams of these two drives differ only in the fact that the SCSI version has a complete subset of the ATA drive, with the SCSI bus interface controller logic added. This essentially is a very condensed version of the separate drive and bridge controller setups that were used in the early days of PC SCSI!

To top off this example, study the following logic diagram for the WD 1006V-MM1, which is an ST-506/412 controller (see fig. 14.17).

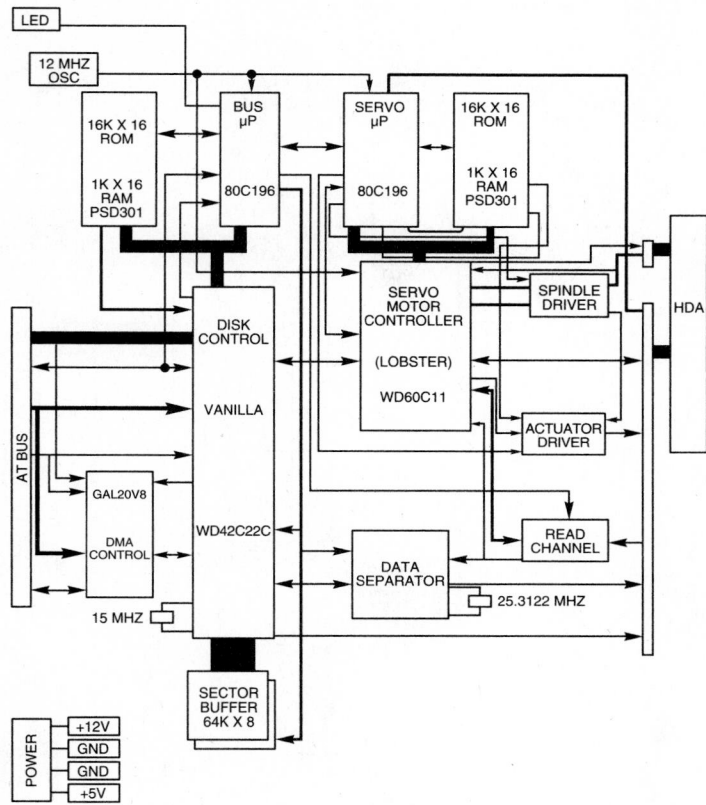

Fig. 14.15

Western Digital WD-AP4200 200MB ATA-IDE drive logic-board block diagram.

You can clearly see that the main LSI chip on board is the same WD42C22 disk controller chip used in the IDE and SCSI drives. Here is what the technical reference literature says about that chip:

> The WD42C22 integrates a high performance, low cost Winchester controller's architecture. The WD42C22 integrates the central elements of a Winchester controller subsystem such as the host interface, buffer manager, disk formatter/controller, encoder/decoder, CRC/ECC (Cyclic Redundancy Check/Error Correction Code) generator/checker, and drive interface into a single 84-pin PQFP (Plastic Quad Flat Pack) device.

The virtually identical design of ATA-IDE and SCSI drives is not unique to Western Digital. Most drive manufacturers design their ATA-IDE and SCSI drives the same way, often using these very same Western Digital chips as well as disk controller and SCSI bus interface chips from other manufacturers. You now should be able to understand that most SCSI drives simply are "regular" ATA-IDE drives with SCSI bus logic added. This fact will come up again later in this chapter, in the section called SCSI versus IDE that discusses performance and other issues differentiating these interfaces.

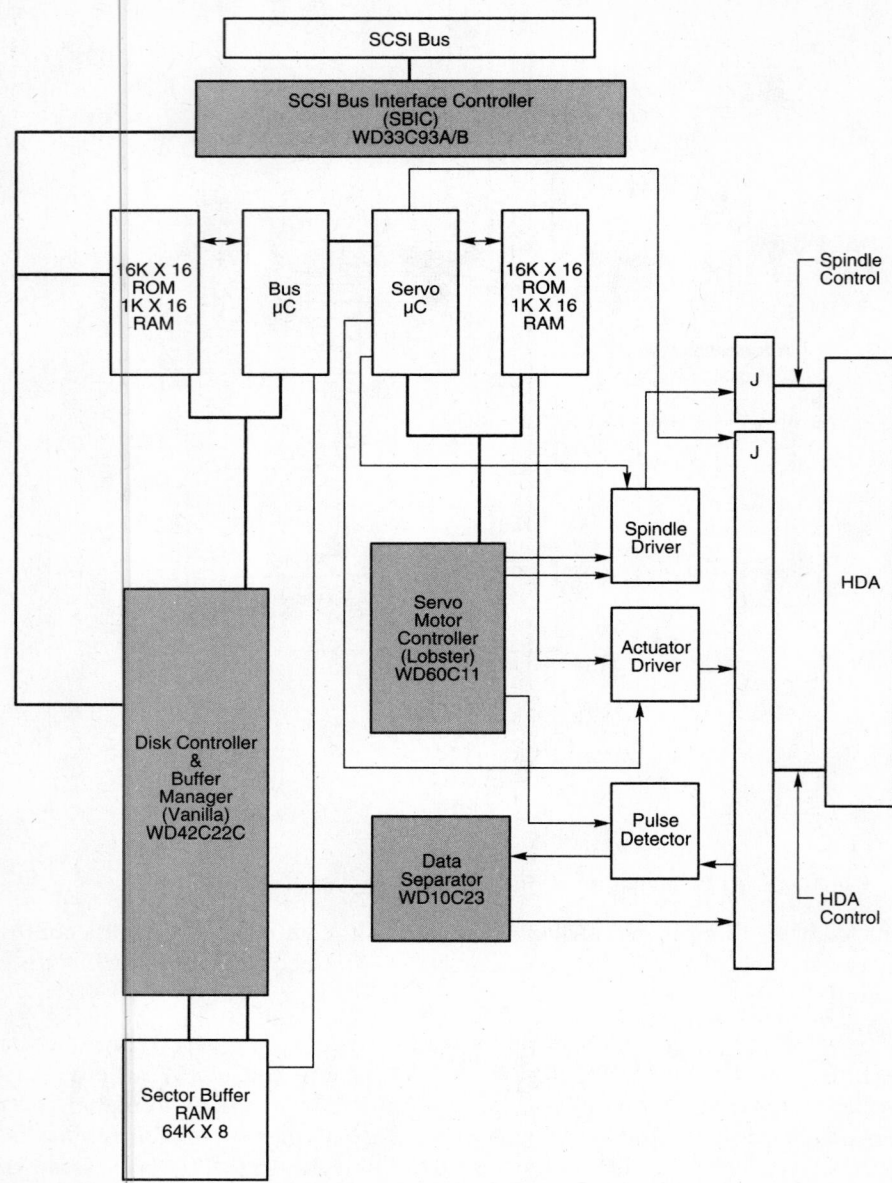

Fig. 14.16

Western Digital WD-SP4200 200MB SCSI drive logic-board block diagram.

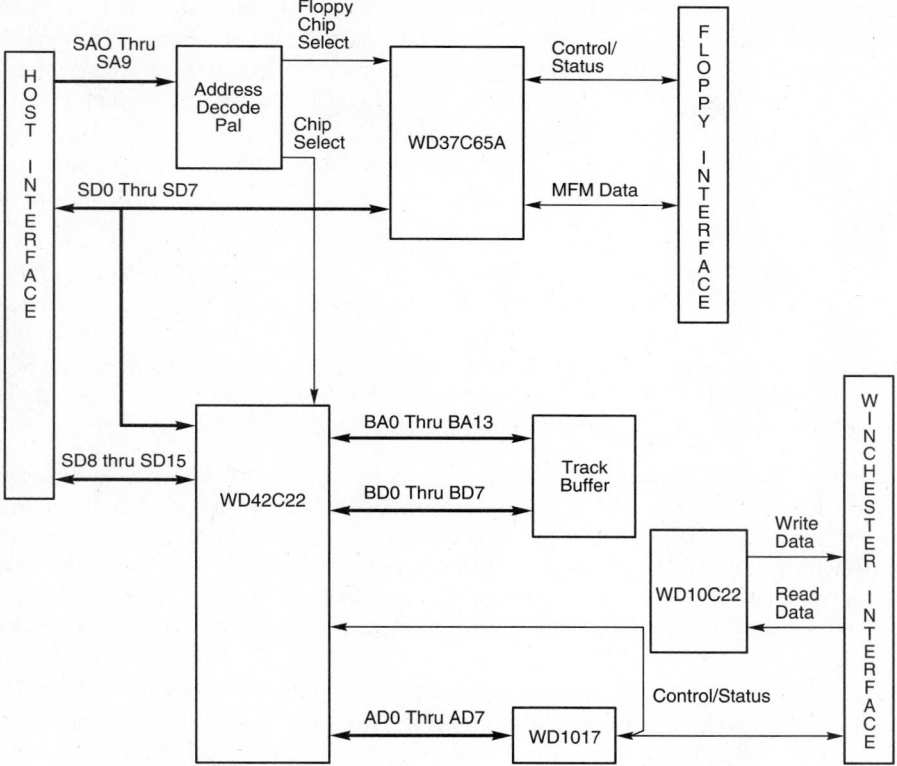

Fig. 14.17

Western Digital WD1006V-MM1 ST-506/412 Disk Controller block diagram.

For another example, I have several IBM 320MB and 400MB embedded SCSI-2 hard disks; each of these drives has on board a WD-10C00 Programmable Disk Controller in the form of a 68-pin PLCC (Plastic Leaded Chip Carrier) chip. The technical literature states, "This chip supports ST412, ESDI, SMD and Optical interfaces. It has 27-Mbit/sec maximum transfer rate and an internal, fully programmable 48- or 32-bit ECC, 16-bit CRC-CCITT or external user defined ECC polynomial, fully programmable sector sizes and 1.25 micron low power CMOS design."

In addition, these particular embedded SCSI drives include the 33C93 SCSI Bus Interface Controller chip, which also is used in the other SCSI drive that I mentioned. Again, there is a distinctly separate disk controller, and the SCSI interface is added on.

So again, most embedded SCSI drives have a built-in disk controller (usually based on previous ST-506/412 or ESDI designs) and additional logic to interface that controller to the SCSI bus (a built-in bridge controller, if you like). Now think about this from a performance standpoint. If virtually all SCSI drives really are ATA-IDE drives with a SCSI Bus Interface Controller chip added, what conclusions can you draw?

First, no drive can perform sustained data transfers faster than the data can actually be read from the disk platters. In other words, the HDA (Head Disk Assembly) limits performance to whatever it is capable of achieving. Drives can transmit data in short bursts at very high speeds, because they often have built-in cache or read-ahead buffers that store data. Many of the newer high-performance SCSI and ATA-IDE drives have 1MB or more of cache memory on board! No matter how big or intelligent the cache is, however, sustained data transfer still will be limited by the HDA.

Data from the HDA must pass through the disk controller circuits, which, as you have seen, are virtually identical between similar SCSI and ATA-IDE drives. In the ATA-IDE drive, this data then is presented directly to the system bus. In the SCSI drive, however, the data must pass through a SCSI Bus Interface adapter on the drive, travel through the SCSI bus itself, and then pass through another SCSI Bus Interface controller in the SCSI host adapter card in your system. The longer route that a SCSI transfer must take makes this type of transfer slower than the much more direct ATA-IDE transfer.

The conventional wisdom has been that SCSI always is much faster than IDE; unfortunately, this wisdom usually is wrong! This incorrect conclusion was derived by looking at the raw SCSI and ISA bus performance capabilities. An 8-bit Fast SCSI-2 bus can transfer data at 10MB (million bytes) per second, whereas the 16-bit ISA bus used directly by IDE drives can transfer data at rates ranging from 2MB to 8MB per second. Based on these raw transfer rates, SCSI seems to be faster, but the raw transfer rate of the bus is not the limiting factor. Instead, the actual HDA and disk-controller circuitry place the limits on performance. Another point to remember is that unless you are using a VL-Bus, EISA, or 32-bit MCA SCSI adapter, the SCSI data-transfer speeds will be limited by the host bus performance as well as by the drive performance.

Single-Ended or Differential SCSI. "Normal" SCSI also is called *single-ended* SCSI. For each signal that needs to be sent across the bus, a wire exists to carry it. With differential SCSI, for each signal that needs to be sent across the bus, a pair of wires exists to carry it. The first in this pair carries the same type of signal that the single-ended SCSI carries. The second in this pair, however, carries the logical inversion of the signal. The receiving device takes the difference of the pair (hence the name *differential*), which makes it less susceptible to noise and allows for greater cable length. Because of this, differential SCSI can be used with cable lengths up to 25 meters, whereas single-ended SCSI is good only for 6 meters with standard asynchronous or synchronous transfers or for only 3 meters for Fast SCSI.

You cannot mix single-ended and differential devices on a single SCSI bus; the result would be catastrophic. (That is to say that you probably will see smoke!) Notice that the cables and connectors are the same, so it's entirely possible to make this mistake. This usually is not a problem, however, because very few differential SCSI implementations exist. Especially with SCSI in the PC environment, single-ended is about all you will ever see. If, however, you come upon a peripheral that you believe might be differential, there are a few ways to tell. One way is to look for a special symbol on the unit; the industry has adopted different universal symbols for single-ended and differential SCSI. Figure 14.18 shows these symbols.

IV

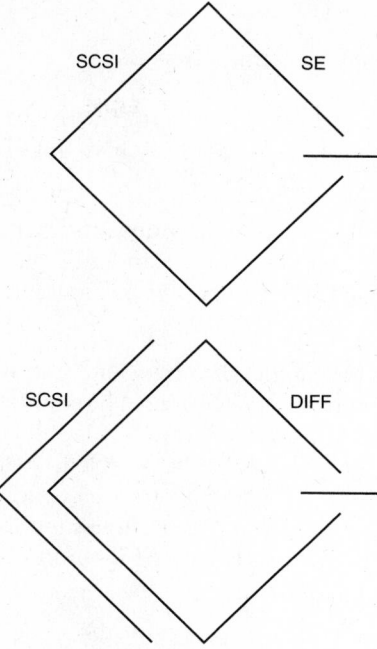

Fig. 14.18
Single-ended and differential SCSI universal symbols.

If you do not see such symbols, you can tell whether you have a differential device by using an ohm meter to check the resistance between pins 21 and 22 on the device connector. On a single-ended system, the pins should be tied together and also tied to Ground. On a differential device, the pins should be open or have significant resistance between them. Again, this generally should not be a problem, because virtually all devices used in the PC environment are single-ended.

SCSI-1 and SCSI-2. The SCSI-2 specification essentially is an improved version of SCSI-1 with some parts of the specification tightened and with several new features and options added. Normally, SCSI-1 and SCSI-2 devices are compatible, but SCSI-1 devices ignore the additional features in SCSI-2.

Some of the changes in SCSI-2 are very minor. For example, SCSI-1 allowed SCSI Bus parity to be optional, whereas parity must be implemented in SCSI-2. Another requirement is that initiator devices, such as host adapters, provide terminator power to the interface; most devices already did so.

SCSI-2 also has several optional features:

- Fast SCSI
- Wide SCSI
- Command queuing

■ High-density cable connectors

■ Improved Active (Alternative 2) termination

These features are not required; they are optional under the SCSI-2 specification. If you connect a standard SCSI host adapter to a Fast SCSI drive, for example, the interface will work, but only at standard SCSI speeds.

Fast SCSI. *Fast SCSI* refers to high-speed synchronous transfer capability. Fast SCSI achieves a 10MB per second transfer rate on the standard 8-bit SCSI cabling. When combined with a 16-bit or 32-bit Wide SCSI interface, this configuration results in data-transfer rates of 20 to 40MB per second.

Wide SCSI. Wide SCSI allows for parallel data transfer at bus widths of 16 and 32 bits. These wider connections require new cable designs. The standard 50-conductor 8-bit cable is called the A-cable. SCSI-2 originally defined a special 68-conductor B-cable that was supposed to be used in conjunction with the A cable for wide transfers, but the industry ignored this specification in favor of a newer 68-conductor P-cable that was introduced as part of the SCSI-3 specification. The P-cable superseded the A- and B-cable combination because the P-Cable can be used alone (without the A cable) for 16-bit Wide SCSI.

32-bit Wide SCSI has not found popularity and probably never will in the PC environment. Theoretically, 32-bit SCSI implementations require two cables: a 68-conductor P-cable and a 68-conductor Q-cable.

Termination. The single-ended SCSI bus depends on very tight termination tolerances to function reliably. Unfortunately, the original 132-ohm passive termination defined in the SCSI-1 document was not designed for use at the higher synchronous speeds now possible. These passive terminators can cause signal reflections to cause errors when transfer rates increase or when more devices are added to the bus. SCSI-2 defines an active (voltage-regulated) terminator that lowers termination impedance to 110 ohms and improves system integrity.

Command Queuing. In SCSI-1, an initiator device, such as a host adapter, was limited to sending one command per device. In SCSI-2, the host adapter can send as many as 256 commands to a single device, which will store and process those commands internally before responding on the SCSI bus. The target device even can resequence the commands to allow for the most efficient execution or performance possible. This feature is especially useful in multitasking environments, such as OS/2 and Windows NT, that can take advantage of this feature.

New Commands. SCSI-2 took the Common Command Set that was being used throughout the industry and made it an official part of the standard. The CCS was designed mainly for disk drives and did not include specific commands designed for other types of devices. In SCSI-2, many of the old commands are reworked and several new commands have been added. New command sets have been added for CD-ROMs, optical drives, scanners, communications devices, and media changers (jukeboxes).

SCSI-3. Even though the SCSI-2 specification has only recently been approved (although it has remained stable for some time), the SCSI-3 specification is already being developed. SCSI-3 will have everything that SCSI-2 has and definitely will add new commands, features, and implementations. For example, SCSI-3 will provide support for up to 32 devices on the bus instead of only 8.

One of the most exciting things about SCSI-3 is the proposed Serial SCSI, a scheme that may use only a six-conductor cable and that will be able to transfer data at up to 100MB per second! The switch to serial instead of parallel is designed to control the delay, noise, and termination problems that have plagued SCSI-2, as well as to simplify the cable connection. Serial SCSI will be capable of transferring more data over 6 wires than 32-bit Fast Wide SCSI-2 can over 128 wires! The intention is that Serial SCSI be implemented on the motherboard of future systems, giving them incredible expansion and performance capabilities.

Although Serial SCSI may not make the older host adapters and cables obsolete overnight, it does make future cabling possibilities even more of a puzzle. Serial SCSI offers the possibility of longer cable lengths; less electromagnetic interference; and easier connections on laptops, notebooks, and docking stations. Expect SCSI-3 to offer almost pain-free installations with automatic plug-and-play SCSI ID setup and termination schemes.

In any practical sense, SCSI-3 is still some ways away from being approved. Because the standard exists in draft documents before being officially approved, if the portions of the standard become stable, we may very well see products claiming SCSI-3 compatibility well before the standard truly exists. Since SCSI-3 actually incorporates all of what is in SCSI-2, technically anybody can call any SCSI-1 or SCSI-2 device a SCSI-3 device as well. Beware of product hype along these lines. Some of the new SCSI-3 features will likely be incompatible with previous SCSI implementations, and may take a while to appear on the market.

SCSI Cables and Connectors. The SCSI standards are very specific when it comes to cables and connectors. The most common connectors specified in this standard are the 50-position unshielded pin header connector for internal SCSI connections and the 50-position shielded Centronics latch-style connectors for external connections. The shielded Centronics style connector also is called Alternative 2 in the official specification. Passive or Active termination (Active is preferred) is specified for both single-ended and differential buses. The 50-conductor bus configuration is defined in the SCSI-2 standard as the A-cabled.

The SCSI-2 revision added a high-density, 50-position, D-shell connector option for the A-cable connectors. This connector now is called Alternative 1. The Alternative 2 Centronics latch-style connector remains unchanged from SCSI-1. A 68-conductor B-cable specification was added to the SCSI-2 standard to provide for 16- and 32-bit data transfers; the connector, however, had to be used in parallel with an A-cable. The industry did not widely accept the B-cable option, which has been dropped from the SCSI-3 standard.

To replace the ill-fated B-cable, a new 68-conductor P-cable was developed as part of the SCSI-3 specification. Shielded and unshielded high-density D-shell connectors are specified for both the A-cable and P-cable. The shielded high-density connectors use a squeeze-to-release latch rather than the wire latch used on the Centronics-style connectors. Active termination for single-ended buses is specified, providing a high level of signal integrity.

SCSI Cable and Connector Pinouts. The following section details the pinouts of the various SCSI cables and connectors. There are two electrically different version of SCSI, Single Ended and Differential. These two versions are electrically incompatible, and must not be interconnected or damage will result. Fortunately, there are very few Differential SCSI applications available in the PC industry, so you will rarely (if ever) encounter it. Within each electrical type (Single Ended or Differential), there are basically three SCSI cable types:

- A-Cable (Standard SCSI)
- P-Cable (16- and 32-bit Wide SCSI)
- Q-Cable (32-bit Wide SCSI)

The A-Cable is used in most SCSI-1 and SCSI-2 installations, and is the most common cable you will encounter. SCSI-2 Wide (16-bit) applications use a P-Cable instead, which completely replaces the A-Cable. You can intermix standard and wide SCSI devices on a single SCSI bus by interconnecting A- and P-Cables with special adapters. 32-bit wide SCSI-3 applications use both the P- and Q-Cables in parallel to each 32-bit device. Today there are virtually no PC applications for 32-bit Wide SCSI-3, and because of the two cable requirement, it is not likely to catch on.

The A-Cables can have Pin Header (Internal) type connectors or External Shielded connectors, each with a different pinout. The P- and Q-Cables feature the same connector pinout on either Internal or External cable connections.

The following tables show all of the possible interface, cable, and connector pinout specifications. A hyphen preceding a signal name indicates the signal is Active Low. The RESERVED lines have continuity from one end of the SCSI bus to the other. In an A-Cable bus, the RESERVED lines should be left open in SCSI devices (but may be connected to ground), and are connected to ground in the bus terminator assemblies. In the P- and Q-Cables, the RESERVED lines are left open in SCSI devices as well as in the bus terminator assemblies.

Single Ended SCSI Cables and Connectors. The single ended electrical interface is the most popular type for PC systems. The following tables show all of the possible single ended cable and connector pinouts. The A-Cable is available in both internal unshielded as well as external shielded configurations. Both are shown in tables 14.22 and 14.23.

IV

Mass Storage Systems

Table 14.22   A-Cable (Single Ended) Internal Unshielded Header Connector Pinout

Signal Name	Pin	Pin	Signal Name
GROUND	1	2	-DB(0)
GROUND	3	4	-DB(1)
GROUND	5	6	-DB(2)
GROUND	7	8	-DB(3)
GROUND	9	10	-DB(4)
GROUND	11	12	-DB(5)
GROUND	13	14	-DB(6)
GROUND	15	16	-DB(7)
GROUND	17	18	-DB(Parity)
GROUND	19	20	GROUND
GROUND	21	22	GROUND
RESERVED	23	24	RESERVED
Open	25	26	TERMPWR
RESERVED	27	28	RESERVED
GROUND	29	30	GROUND
GROUND	31	32	-ATN
GROUND	33	34	GROUND
GROUND	35	36	-BSY
GROUND	37	38	-ACK
GROUND	39	40	-RST
GROUND	41	42	-MSG
GROUND	43	44	-SEL
GROUND	45	46	-C/D
GROUND	47	48	-REQ
GROUND	49	50	-I/O

Table 14.23   A-Cable (Single Ended) External Shielded Connector Pinout

Signal Name	Pin	Pin	Signal Name
GROUND	1	26	-DB(0)
GROUND	2	27	-DB(1)
GROUND	3	28	-DB(2)
GROUND	4	29	-DB(3)
GROUND	5	30	-DB(4)
GROUND	6	31	-DB(5)
GROUND	7	32	-DB(6)
GROUND	8	33	-DB(7)

(continues)

Table 14.23   Continued

Signal Name	Pin	Pin	Signal Name
GROUND	9	34	-DB(Parity)
GROUND	10	35	GROUND
GROUND	11	36	GROUND
RESERVED	12	37	RESERVED
Open	13	38	TERMPWR
RESERVED	14	39	RESERVED
GROUND	15	40	GROUND
GROUND	16	41	-ATN
GROUND	17	42	GROUND
GROUND	18	43	-BSY
GROUND	19	44	-ACK
GROUND	20	45	-RST
GROUND	21	46	-MSG
GROUND	22	47	-SEL
GROUND	23	48	-C/D
GROUND	24	49	-REQ
GROUND	25	50	-I/O

IBM has standardized on the SCSI interface for virtually all PS/2 systems introduced since 1990. These systems use a Micro Channel SCSI adapter or have the SCSI Host Adapter built into the motherboard. In either case, IBM's SCSI interface uses a special 60-pin mini-Centronics type external shielded connector that is unique in the industry. A special IBM cable is required to adapt this connector to the standard 50-pin Centronics-style connector used on most external SCSI devices. The pinout of the IBM 60-pin mini-Centronics-style External Shielded connector is shown in table 14.24. In the following table, notice that although the pin arrangement is unique, the pin number to signal designations correspond with the standard unshielded internal pin header type of SCSI connector.

Table 14.24   IBM PS/2 SCSI External Shielded 60-Pin Connector Pinout

Signal Name	Pin	Pin	Signal Name
GROUND	1	60	Not Connected
-DB(0)	2	59	Not Connected
GROUND	3	58	Not Connected
-DB(1)	4	57	Not Connected
GROUND	5	56	Not Connected
-DB(2)	6	55	Not Connected
GROUND	7	54	Not Connected
-DB(3)	8	53	Not Connected

Signal Name	Pin	Pin	Signal Name
GROUND	9	52	Not Connected
-DB(4)	10	51	GROUND
GROUND	11	50	-I/O
-DB(5)	12	49	GROUND
GROUND	13	48	-REQ
-DB(6)	14	47	GROUND
GROUND	15	46	-C/D
-DB(7)	16	45	GROUND
GROUND	17	44	-SEL
-DB(Parity)	18	43	GROUND
GROUND	19	42	-MSG
GROUND	20	41	GROUND
GROUND	21	40	-RST
GROUND	22	39	GROUND
RESERVED	23	38	-ACK
RESERVED	24	37	GROUND
Open	25	36	-BSY
TERMPWR	26	35	GROUND
RESERVED	27	34	GROUND
RESERVED	28	33	GROUND
GROUND	29	32	-ATN
GROUND	30	31	GROUND

The P-Cable (Single-Ended) and connectors are used in 16-bit wide SCSI-2 applications (see table 14.25 for the pinout). This cable is used also in combination with the Q-cable for 32-bit SCSI applications.

Table 14.25   P-Cable (Single Ended) Internal or External Shielded Connector Pinout

Signal Name	Pin	Pin	Signal Name
GROUND	1	35	-DB(12)
GROUND	2	36	-DB(13)
GROUND	3	37	-DB(14)
GROUND	4	38	-DB(15)
GROUND	5	39	-DB(Parity 1)
GROUND	6	40	-DB(0)
GROUND	7	41	-DB(1)
GROUND	8	42	-DB(2)
GROUND	9	43	-DB(3)

(continues)

Table 14.25 Continued

Signal Name	Pin	Pin	Signal Name
GROUND	10	44	-DB(4)
GROUND	11	45	-DB(5)
GROUND	12	46	-DB(6)
GROUND	13	47	-DB(7)
GROUND	14	48	-DB(Parity 0)
GROUND	15	49	GROUND
GROUND	16	50	GROUND
TERMPWR	17	51	TERMPWR
TERMPWR	18	52	TERMPWR
RESERVED	19	53	RESERVED
GROUND	20	54	GROUND
GROUND	21	55	-ATN
GROUND	22	56	GROUND
GROUND	23	57	-BSY
GROUND	24	58	-ACK
GROUND	25	59	-RST
GROUND	26	60	-MSG
GROUND	27	61	-SEL
GROUND	28	62	-C/D
GROUND	29	63	-REQ
GROUND	30	64	-I/O
GROUND	31	65	-DB(8)
GROUND	32	66	-DB(9)
GROUND	33	67	-DB(10)
GROUND	34	68	-DB(11)

The Q-Cable (Single Ended) and connector is used only on 32-bit SCSI implementations, which also require a P-Cable as well (see table 14.26 for the pinout). 32-bit SCSI applications are rare to virtually nonexistant.

Table 14.26 Q-Cable (Single Ended) Internal or External Shielded Connector Pinout

Signal Name	Pin	Pin	Signal Name
GROUND	1	35	-DB(28)
GROUND	2	36	-DB(29)
GROUND	3	37	-DB(30)

Signal Name	Pin	Pin	Signal Name
GROUND	4	38	-DB(31)
GROUND	5	39	-DB(Parity 3)
GROUND	6	40	-DB(16)
GROUND	7	41	-DB(17)
GROUND	8	42	-DB(18)
GROUND	9	43	-DB(19)
GROUND	10	44	-DB(20)
GROUND	11	45	-DB(21)
GROUND	12	46	-DB(22)
GROUND	13	47	-DB(23)
GROUND	14	48	-DB(Parity 2)
GROUND	15	49	GROUND
GROUND	16	50	GROUND
TERMPWRQ	17	51	TERMPWRQ
TERMPWRQ	18	52	TERMPWRQ
RESERVED	19	53	RESERVED
GROUND	20	54	GROUND
GROUND	21	55	TERMINATED
GROUND	22	56	GROUND
GROUND	23	57	TERMINATED
GROUND	24	58	-ACKQ
GROUND	25	59	TERMINATED
GROUND	26	60	TERMINATED
GROUND	27	61	TERMINATED
GROUND	28	62	TERMINATED
GROUND	29	63	-REQQ
GROUND	30	64	TERMINATED
GROUND	31	65	-DB(24)
GROUND	32	66	-DB(25)
GROUND	33	67	-DB(26)
GROUND	34	68	-DB(27)

Differential SCSI Signals. Differential SCSI is not normally used in a PC environment, but is very popular with minicomputer installations due to the very long bus lengths that are allowed. Although not popular in PC systems, the interface connector specifications are shown here for reference.

The A-Cable (Differential) Connector is available in both an internal unshielded form as well as an external shielded form. Tables 14.27 and 14.28 show the pinouts for both.

Table 14.27   A-Cable (Differential) Internal Unshielded Header Connector Pinout

Signal Name	Pin	Pin	Signal Name
GROUND	1	2	GROUND
+DB(0)	3	4	-DB(0)
+DB(1)	5	6	-DB(1)
+DB(2)	7	8	-DB(2)
+DB(3)	9	10	-DB(3)
+DB(4)	11	12	-DB(4)
+DB(5)	13	14	-DB(5)
+DB(6)	15	16	-DB(6)
+DB(7)	17	18	-DB(7)
+DB(Parity)	19	20	-DP(Parity)
DIFFSENS	21	22	GROUND
RESERVED	23	24	RESERVED
TERMPWR	25	26	TERMPWR
RESERVED	27	28	RESERVED
+ATN	29	30	-ATN
GROUND	31	32	GROUND
+BSY	33	34	-BSY
+ACK	35	36	-ACK
+RST	37	38	-RST
+MSG	39	40	-MSG
+SEL	41	42	-SEL
+C/D	43	44	-C/D
+REQ	45	46	-REQ
+I/O	47	48	-I/O
GROUND	49	50	GROUND

Table 14.28   A-Cable (Differential) External Shielded Header Connector Pinout

Signal Name	Pin	Pin	Signal Name
GROUND	1	26	GROUND
+DB(0)	2	27	-DB(0)
+DB(1)	3	28	-DB(1)
+DB(2)	4	29	-DB(2)
+DB(3)	5	30	-DB(3)
+DB(4)	6	31	-DB(4)
+DB(5)	7	32	-DB(5)
+DB(6)	8	33	-DB(6)

Signal Name	Pin	Pin	Signal Name
+DB(7)	9	34	-DB(7)
+DB(Parity)	10	35	-DP(Parity)
DIFFSENS	11	36	GROUND
RESERVED	12	37	RESERVED
TERMPWR	13	38	TERMPWR
RESERVED	14	39	RESERVED
+ATN	15	40	-ATN
GROUND	16	41	GROUND
+BSY	17	42	-BSY
+ACK	18	43	-ACK
+RST	18	44	-RST
+MSG	20	45	-MSG
+SEL	21	46	-SEL
+C/D	22	47	-C/D
+REQ	23	48	-REQ
+I/O	24	49	-I/O
GROUND	25	50	GROUND

The P-Cable (Differential) and Connector is used for 16-bit and 32-bit wide SCSI connections. The pinout is shown in Table 14.29.

Table 14.29 P-Cable (Differential) Internal or External Shielded Connector Pinout

Signal Name	Pin	Pin	Signal Name
+DB(12)	1	35	-DB(12)
+DB(13)	2	36	-DB(13)
+DB(14)	3	37	-DB(14)
+DB(15)	4	38	-DB(15)
+DB(Parity 1)	5	39	-DB(Parity 1)
GROUND	6	40	GROUND
+DB(0)	7	41	-DB(0)
+DB(1)	8	42	-DB(1)
+DB(2)	9	43	-DB(2)
+DB(3)	10	44	-DP(3)
+DB(4)	11	45	-DB(4)
+DB(5)	12	46	-DB(5)
+DB(6)	13	47	-DB(6)
+DB(7)	14	48	-DB(7)
+DB(Parity 0)	15	49	-DB(Parity 0)

(continues)

Table 14.29 Continued

Signal Name	Pin	Pin	Signal Name
DIFFSENS	16	50	GROUND
TERMPWR	17	51	TERMPWR
TERMPWR	18	52	TERMPWR
RESERVED	19	53	RESERVED
+ATN	20	54	-ATN
GROUND	21	55	GROUND
+BSY	22	56	-BSY
+ACK	23	57	-ACK
+RST	24	58	-RST
+MSG	25	59	-MSG
+SEL	26	60	-SEL
+C/D	27	61	-C/D
+REQ	28	62	-REQ
+I/O	29	63	-I/O
GROUND	30	64	GROUND
+DB(8)	31	65	-DB(8)
+DB(9)	32	66	-DB(9)
+DB(10)	33	67	-DB(10)
+DB(11)	34	68	-DB(11)

The Q Cable (Differential) and connector is used only with 32-bit wide SCSI implementations, and in that case would also require a 16-bit wide P-cable. Table 14.30 shows the Q-Cable pinout.

Table 14.30 Q-Cable (Differential) Internal or External Shielded Connector Pinout

Signal Name	Pin	Pin	Signal Name
+DB(28)	1	35	-DB(28)
+DB(29)	2	36	-DB(29)
+DB(30)	3	37	-DB(30)
+DB(31)	4	38	-DB(31)
+DB(Parity 3)	5	39	-DB(Parity 3)
GROUND	6	40	GROUND
+DB(16)	7	41	-DB(16)
+DB(17)	8	42	-DB(17)
+DB(18)	9	43	-DB(18)
+DB(19)	10	44	-DP(19)
+DB(20)	11	45	-DB(20)

Signal Name	Pin	Pin	Signal Name
+DB(21)	12	46	-DB(21)
+DB(22)	13	47	-DB(22)
+DB(23)	14	48	-DB(23)
+DB(Parity 2)	15	49	-DB(Parity 2)
DIFFSENS	16	50	GROUND
TERMPWRQ	17	51	TERMPWRQ
TERMPWRQ	18	52	TERMPWRQ
RESERVED	19	53	RESERVED
TERMINATED	20	54	TERMINATED
GROUND	21	55	GROUND
TERMINATED	22	56	TERMINATED
+ACKQ	23	57	-ACKQ
TERMINATED	24	58	TERMINATED
TERMINATED	25	59	TERMINATED
TERMINATED	26	60	TERMINATED
TERMINATED	27	61	TERMINATED
+REQQ	28	62	-REQQ
TERMINATED	29	63	TERMINATED
GROUND	30	64	GROUND
+DB(24)	31	65	-DB(24)
+DB(25)	32	66	-DB(25)
+DB(26)	33	67	-DB(26)
+DB(27)	34	68	-DB(27)

Termination. All busses need to be electrically terminated at each end, and the SCSI bus is no exception. Improper termination still is one of the most common problems in SCSI installations. Three types of terminators typically are available for the SCSI bus:

- Passive

- Active (also called Alternative 2)

- Forced Perfect Termination (FPT)

Typical passive terminators (a network of resistors) allow signal fluctuations in relation to the terminator power signal on the bus. Usually, passive terminating resistors suffice over short distances, such as 2 or 3 feet, but for longer distances, active termination is a real advantage. Active termination is required with Fast SCSI.

An active terminator actually has one or more voltage regulators to produce the termination voltage, rather than resistor voltage dividers. This arrangement helps ensure that the SCSI signals always are terminated to the correct voltage level. The SCSI-2 specification recommends active termination on both ends of the bus and requires active termination whenever Fast or Wide SCSI devices are used.

A variation on active termination is available: Forced Perfect Termination. Forced Perfect Termination is an even better form of active termination, in which diode clamps are added to eliminate signal overshoot and undershoot. The trick is that instead of clamping to +5 and Ground, these terminators clamp to the output of two regulated voltages. This arrangement enables the clamping diodes to eliminate signal overshoot and undershoot, especially at higher signaling speeds and over longer distances.

Several companies make high-quality terminators for the SCSI bus, including Aeronics and the Data Mate division of Methode. Both of these companies make a variety of terminators, but Aeronics is well noted for some unique FPT versions that are especially suited to problem configurations that require longer cable runs or higher signal integrity. One of the best investments that you can make in any SCSI installation is in high-quality cables and terminators.

SCSI Drive Configuration. SCSI drives are not too difficult to configure, especially compared with IDE drives. The SCSI standard controls the way that the drives must be set up. You need to set two or three items when you configure a SCSI drive:

■ SCSI ID setting (0 through 7)

■ Terminating resistors

SCSI ID Setting. The SCSI ID setting is very simple. Up to eight SCSI devices can be used on a single SCSI bus, and each device must have a unique SCSI ID address. The host adapter takes one address, and up to seven SCSI peripherals take the others. Most SCSI host adapters are factory-set to ID 7, which is the highest-priority ID. All other devices must have unique IDs that do not conflict with one another. Some host adapters boot only from a hard disk set to a specific ID. In my system, for example, the IBM SCSI host adapter requires the boot drive to be set to ID 6. Newer IBM host adapters and systems enable you to boot from a hard disk at any SCSI ID. Older Adaptec host adapters required the boot hard disk to be ID 0; newer ones can boot from any ID.

Setting the ID usually involves changing jumpers on the drive itself. If the drive is installed in an external chassis, the chassis may have an ID selector switch that is accessible at the rear. This selector makes ID selection a simple matter of pressing a button or rotating a wheel until the desired ID number appears. If no external selector is present, you must open the external device chassis and set the ID via the jumpers on the drive.

Three jumpers are required to set the SCSI ID; the particular ID selected actually is derived from the binary representation of the jumpers themselves. For example, setting all three ID jumpers off results in a binary number of 000b, which translates to an ID of 0. A binary setting of 001b equals ID 1, 010b equals 2, 011b equals 3, and so on. Notice that as I list these values, I append a lowercase *b* to indicate binary numbers.

Unfortunately, the jumpers can appear either forward or backward on the drive, depending on how the manufacturer set them up. To keep things simple, I have recorded all the different ID jumper settings in Tables 14.31 and 14.32. One table is for drives that order the jumpers, with the Most Significant Bit (MSB) to the left; the other is for drives with the jumpers ordered so that the MSB is to the right.

IV

Table 14.31	SCSI ID Jumper Settings with the Most Significant Bit to the Left		
SCSI ID	**Jumper Settings**		
0	0	0	0
1	0	0	1
2	0	1	0
3	0	1	1
4	1	0	0
5	1	0	1
6	1	1	0
7	1	1	1

1 = Jumper On, 0 = Jumper Off

Table 14.32	SCSI ID Jumper Settings with the Most Significant Bit to the Right		
SCSI ID	**Jumper Settings**		
0	0	0	0
1	1	0	0
2	0	1	0
3	1	1	0
4	0	0	1
5	1	0	1
6	0	1	1
7	1	1	1

1 = Jumper On, 0 = Jumper Off

Termination. SCSI termination is very simple. Termination is required at both ends of the bus; there are no exceptions. If the host adapter is at one end of the bus, it must have termination enabled. If the host adapter is in the middle of the bus, and if both internal and external bus links are present, the host adapter must have its termination disabled, and the devices at each end of the bus must have terminators installed. Several types of terminators are available, differing both in quality and in appearance. Active terminators are the minimum recommended, and Forced Perfect Terminators (FPT) are considered the best available. For more information on the different types, see the previous section on Terminators in this chapter.

The rules are simple: use the best terminators possible, and make sure that only the ends of the SCSI bus are terminated. The majority of problems that I see with SCSI installations are the result of improper termination. Some devices have built-in termination resistors that are enabled or disabled through a jumper or by being physically removed. Other devices do not have built-in terminating resistors; these devices instead rely on external terminator modules for termination.

When installing an external SCSI device, you usually will find the device in a storage enclosure with both input and output SCSI connectors, so that you can use the device in a daisy chain. If the enclosure is at the end of the SCSI bus, an external terminator module most likely will have to be plugged into the second (outgoing) SCSI port to provide proper termination at that end of the bus (see fig. 14.19).

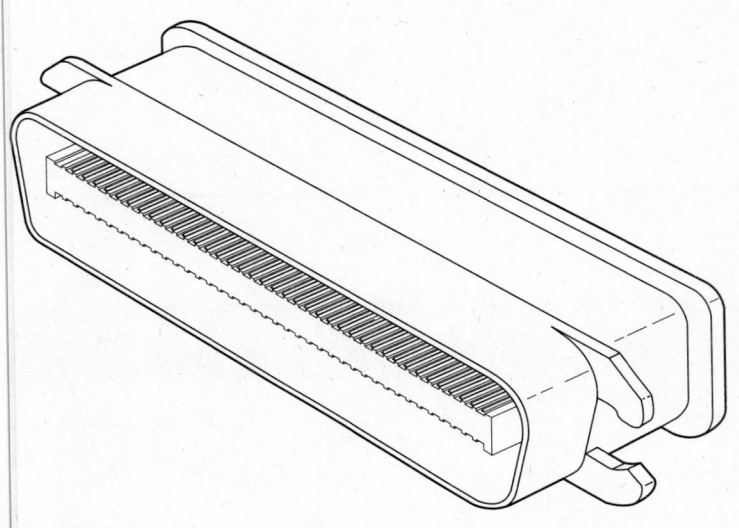

Fig. 14.19
External SCSI device terminator.

External terminator modules are available in a variety of connector configurations, including pass-through designs, which are needed if only one port is available. Pass-through terminators also are commonly used in internal installations in which the device does not have built-in terminating resistors. Many hard drives use pass-through terminators for internal installations to save space on the logic-board assembly (see fig. 14.20).

The pass-through models are required when a device is at the end of the bus and only one SCSI connector is available.

Remember to stick with high-quality active or Forced Perfect terminators at each end of the bus, and you will eliminate most common termination problems.

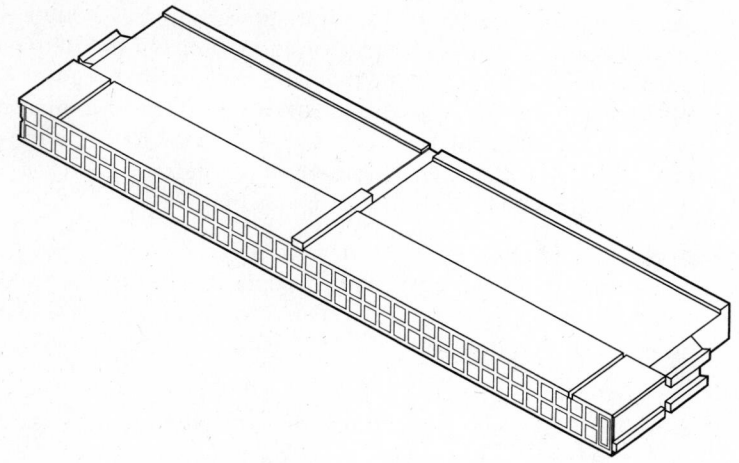

Fig. 14.20
Internal pin-header connector pass-through SCSI terminator.

Other Settings. Other configuration items on a SCSI drive can be set via jumpers. The following are several of the most common additional settings that you will find:

- Start on command (delayed start)
- SCSI parity
- Terminator power
- Synchronous negotiation

These configuration items are described in the following sections.

Start on Command (Delayed Start). If you have multiple drives installed in a system, it is wise to set them up so that all the drives do not start to spin immediately when the system is powered on. A hard disk drive can consume three or four times more power during the first few seconds after power-on then during normal operation. The motor requires this additional power to get the platters spinning quickly. If several drives are drawing all this power at the same time, the power supply may be overloaded, which can cause the system to hang or to have intermittent startup problems.

Nearly all SCSI drives provide a way to delay drive spinning so that this problem does not occur. When most SCSI host adapters initialize the SCSI bus, they send out a command called Start Unit to each of the ID addresses in succession. By setting a jumper on the hard disk, you can prevent the disk from spinning until it receives the Start Unit command from the host adapter. Because the host adapter sends this command to all the ID addresses in succession, from the highest-priority address (ID 7) to the lowest (ID 0), the higher-priority drives can be made to start first, with each lower-priority drive spinning up sequentially. Because some host adapters do not send the Start Unit command, some drives may simply delay spinup for a fixed number of seconds rather than wait for a command that never will arrive.

If drives are installed in external chassis with separate power supplies, you need not implement the delayed-start function. This function is best applied to internal drives that must be run from the same power supply that runs the system. For internal installations, I recommend setting Start on Command (delayed start) even if you have only one SCSI drive; this setting will ease the load on the power supply by spinning the drive up after the rest of the system has full power. This method is especially good for portable systems and other systems in which the power supply is limited.

SCSI Parity. SCSI parity is a limited form of error checking that helps ensure that all data transfers are reliable. Virtually all host adapters support SCSI parity checking, so this option should be enabled on every device. The only reason why it exists as an option is that some older host adapters do not work with SCSI parity, so the parity must be turned off.

Terminator Power. The terminators at each end of the SCSI bus require power from at least one device on the bus. In most cases, the host adapter supplies this terminator power; in some cases, however, it does not. For example, parallel port SCSI host adapters typically do not supply terminator power. It is not a problem if more than one device supplies terminator power, since each source is diode protected. For simplicity's sake, many will configure all devices to supply terminator power. If no device supplies terminator power, the bus will not be terminated correctly and will not function properly.

SCSI Synchronous Negotiation. The SCSI bus can run in two modes: asynchronous (the default) and synchronous. The bus actually switches modes during transfers through a protocol called *synchronous negotiation*. Before data is transferred across the SCSI bus, the sending device (called the *initiator*) and the receiving device (called the *target*) negotiate how the transfer will take place. If both devices support synchronous transfers, they will discover this fact through the negotiation, and the transfer will take place at the faster synchronous rate.

Unfortunately, some older devices do not respond to a request for synchronous transfer and actually can be disabled when such a request is made. For this reason, both host adapters and devices that support synchronous negotiation often have a jumper that can be used to disable this negotiation so that it can work with older devices. By default, all devices today should support synchronous negotiation, and this function should be enabled.

SCSI Drivers. Each SCSI peripheral that you add to your SCSI bus (other than hard disk drives) requires an external driver to make the device work. Hard disks are the exception; driver support for them normally is provided as part of the SCSI host adapter BIOS. These external drivers are specific not only to a particular device, but also to the host adapter.

Recently, two types of standard host adapter interface drivers have become popular, greatly reducing this problem. By having a standard host adapter driver to write to, peripheral makers can more quickly create new drivers that support their devices and then talk to the universal host adapter driver. This arrangement eliminates dependence on one particular type of host adapter. These primary or universal drivers link the host adapter and the operating system.

The Advanced SCSI Programming Interface (ASPI) currently is the most popular universal driver, with most peripheral makers writing their drivers to talk to ASPI. The *A* in ASPI used to stand for Adaptec, the company that introduced it, but other SCSI device vendors have licensed the right to use ASPI with their products. DOS does not support ASPI directly, but it does when the ASPI driver is loaded. OS/2 2.1 and later versions provide automatic ASPI support for several SCSI host adapters.

Future Domain and NCR have created another interface driver called the Common Access Method (CAM). CAM is an ANSI-approved protocol that enables a single driver to control several host adapters. In addition to ASPI, OS/2 2.1 and later versions currently offer support for CAM. Future Domain also provides a CAM-to-ASPI converter in the utilities that go with its host adapters.

SCSI Configuration Tips. When you are installing a chain of devices on a single SCSI bus, the installation can get complicated very quickly. Here are some tips for getting your setup to function quickly and efficiently.

- *Start by adding one device at a time.* Rather than plug numerous peripherals into a single SCSI card and then try to configure them at the same time, start by installing the host adapter and a single hard disk. Then you can continue installing devices one at a time, checking to make sure that everything works before moving on.

- *Keep good documentation.* When you add a SCSI peripheral, write down the SCSI ID address as well as any other switch and jumper settings, such as SCSI Parity, Terminator Power, and Remote Start. For the host adapter, record the BIOS addresses, Interrupt, DMA channel, and I/O Port addresses used by the adapter, as well as any other jumper or configuration settings (such as termination) that might be important to know later.

- *Use proper termination.* Each end of the bus must be terminated, preferably with active or Forced Perfect (FPT) terminators. If you are using any Fast SCSI-2 device, you must use active terminators rather than the cheaper passive types. Even with standard (slow) SCSI devices, active termination is highly recommended. If you have only internal or external devices on the bus, the host adapter and last device on the chain should be terminated. If you have external and internal devices on the chain, you generally will terminate the first and last of these devices but not the SCSI host adapter itself (which is in the middle of the bus).

- *Use high-quality shielded SCSI cables.* Make sure that your cable connectors match your devices. Use high-quality shielded cables, and observe the SCSI bus-length limitations. Use cables designed for SCSI use, and if possible, stick to the same brand of cable throughout a single SCSI bus. Different brands of cables have different impedance values; this situation sometimes causes problems, especially in long or high-speed SCSI implementations.

Following these simple tips will help minimize problems and leave you with a trouble-free SCSI installation.

IDE versus SCSI

When you compare the performance and capabilities of IDE (Integrated Drive Electronics) and SCSI (Small Computer System Interface) interfaced drives, you need to consider several factors. These two types of drives are the most popular drives used in PC systems today, and a single manufacturer may make identical drives in both interfaces. Deciding which drive type is best for your system is a difficult decision that depends on many factors.

In most cases, you will find that an IDE drive outperforms an equivalent SCSI drive at a given task or benchmark and that IDE drives usually cost less than SCSI drives, thus offering better value. In some cases, however, SCSI drives have significant performance and value advantages over IDE drives.

Performance. ATA (AT Attachment) IDE drives currently are used in most PC configurations on the market today, because the cost of an IDE-drive implementation is low and the performance capabilities are high. In comparing any given IDE and SCSI drive for performance, you have to look at the capabilities of the HDAs (Head Disk Assemblies) that are involved.

To minimize the variables in this type of comparison, it is easiest to compare IDE and SCSI drives from the same manufacturer that also use the identical HDA. You will find that in most cases, a drive manufacturer makes a given drive available in both IDE and SCSI forms. For example, Seagate makes the ST-3600A (ATA-IDE) and ST-3600N (Fast SCSI-2) drives, both of which use identical HDAs and which differ only in the logic board. The IDE version has a logic board with a built-in disk controller and a direct AT bus interface. The SCSI version has the same built-in disk controller and bus interface circuits, and also a SCSI Bus Interface Controller (SBIC) chip. The SBIC chip is a SCSI adapter that places the drive on the SCSI bus. What you will find, in essence, is that virtually all SCSI drives actually are IDE drives with the SBIC chip added.

The HDAs in these example drives are capable of transferring data at a sustained rate of 2.38MB to 4MB per second. Because the SCSI version always has the additional overhead of the SCSI bus to go through, in almost all cases the directly attached IDE version performs faster.

SCSI versus IDE: Advantages and Limitations. IDE drives have much less command overhead for a given sector transfer than SCSI drives do. In addition to the drive-to-controller command overhead that both IDE and SCSI must perform, a SCSI transfer involves negotiating for the SCSI bus; selecting the target drive; requesting data; terminating the transfer over the bus; and finally converting the logical data addresses to the required cylinder, head, and sector addresses.

This arrangement gives IDE an advantage in sequential transfers handled by a single-tasking operating system. In a multitasking system that can take advantage of the extra intelligence of the SCSI bus, SCSI can have the performance advantage.

SCSI drives offer significant architectural advantages over IDE and other drives. Because each SCSI drive has its own embedded disk controller that can function independently from the system CPU, the computer can issue simultaneous commands to every drive in the system. Each drive can store these commands in a queue and then perform the commands simultaneously with other drives in the system. The data could be fully buffered on the drive and transferred at high speed over the shared SCSI bus when a time slot was available.

Although IDE drives also have their own controllers, they do not operate simultaneously, and command queuing is not supported. In effect, the dual controllers in a dual-drive IDE installation work one at a time so as not to step on each other.

Although SCSI drives require an additional-cost host adapter card, more and more PCs require tape-backup, CD-ROM, or optical-drive support and thus must still be configured with a SCSI host bus adapter. This means that the incremental cost of supporting SCSI drives is virtually nil, because the SCSI host bus adapter is shared with other devices, such as tape and optical drives. In addition, all major operating systems today include software support for a wide range of SCSI devices.

What are the limitations of IDE?

- IDE does not support overlapped, multitasked I/O.
- IDE does not support command queuing.
- IDE does not support bus mastering.
- No more than two IDE drives can be supported without multiple IDE adapters.
- IDE drives normally are limited to 504MB per drive without an enhanced BIOS.
- IDE normally does not support other devices, such as tape or optical drives.

As you can see, SCSI has many advantages over IDE, especially where expansion is concerned, and also with regard to support for multitasking operating systems.

Recommended Aftermarket Controllers and Host Adapters

Many companies manufacture disk controllers for IBM and IBM-compatible systems. Many newer systems include IDE drives, which have built-in controllers and offer a high level of performance at a low cost. Other systems are using SCSI drives because of the inherent flexibility of the SCSI bus in supporting many drives and other peripherals.

I recommend IDE drives for most standard installations because the connections are simple and the drives are inexpensive for the power. For higher-end systems, or for systems in which upgradability and flexibility are most important, I recommend SCSI drives.

Silicon Valley makes a line of IDE adapters that are excellent for systems that do not have the special IDE connector on the motherboard. The company also makes a special adapter that enables you to put AT IDE drives in 8-bit XT systems, which few other cards do. Arco Electronics and Sigma Data make IDE adapters that enable you to install ATA IDE drives in PS/2 MCA bus systems. These companies even have unique versions for the Model 50z and 70 that replace the interposer card, therefore using no MCA slots in the system. All these companies are listed in Appendix B.

Recommended SCSI Host Adapters. For SCSI host adapters, I recommend IBM for MCA cards and Adaptec or Future Domain for ISA or EISA bus cards. All these adapters work well and come with the necessary formatting and operating software. OS/2 has built-in support for IBM and Adaptec SCSI adapters. This support is a consideration in many cases, because it frees you from having to deal with external drivers.

One example of a new breed of SCSI adapter is the Adaptec AHA-1540C and 1542C. The 1542 has a built-in floppy controller; the 1540 does not. These adapters are most notable for their ease of installation and use. Virtually all functions on the card can be configured and set through software. No more digging through manuals, looking for Interrupt, DMA, I/O Port, and other jumper settings—everything is controlled by software and saved in a flash memory module on the card. Following are some of the features of this card:

■ Complete configuration utility built into the adapter's ROM

■ Software-configurable IRQ, ROM Addresses, DMA, I/O Port Addresses SCSI Parity, SCSI ID, and other settings

■ Software-selectable termination (no resistors to pull out!)

■ Enhanced BIOS support for up to eight 7.88GB drives

■ No drivers required for more than two hard disks

■ Drive spinup on a per-drive basis available

■ Boots from any SCSI ID

The 1542C model includes an Intel 82077 floppy controller chip (which supports 2.88MB drives); 2.88MB BIOS support also must be provided by your motherboard BIOS. (see fig. 14.21)

All in all, this adapter is one of the easiest-to-install SCSI adapters that I have worked with. Most peripheral manufacturers write drivers for Adaptec's cards first, so you will not have many compatibility or driver-support problems with any Adaptec card.

If you are using the older AHA-1542B SCSI host adapter, the current ROM revision available is version 3.20, which adds Enhanced BIOS support for multiple drives up to 7.88GB with no drivers.

Future Domain also makes SCSI cards that are well supported throughout the industry. If compatibility is important, you can't go wrong with the Adaptec or Future Domain cards.

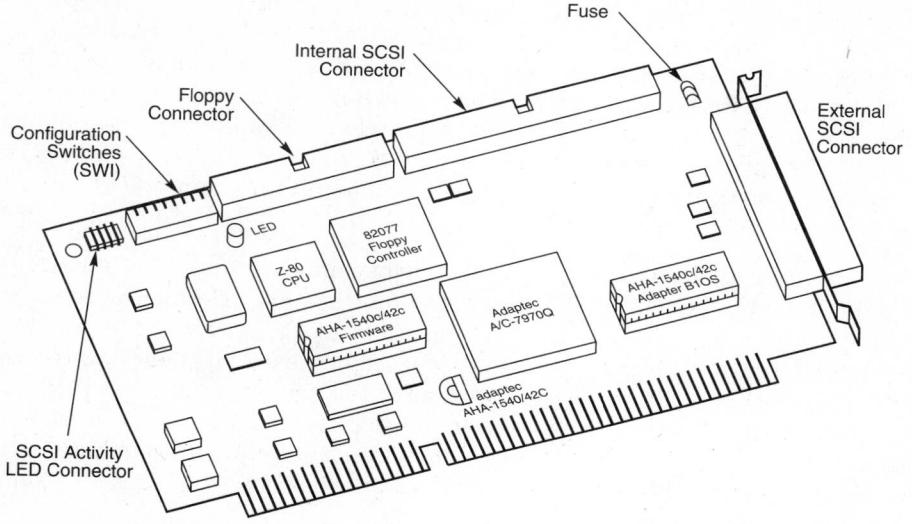

Fig. 14.21
An Adaptec AHA-1542C SCSI host adapter.

IBM SCSI Adapters. IBM has shipped several types of SCSI adapters since it introduced PC SCSI in 1990. Three basic types of adapters are available:

- 16-bit SCSI MCA adapter

- 32-bit SCSI MCA adapter with cache

- 16-bit Fast SCSI ISA adapter

The IBM host adapters (especially the MCA versions) are among the easiest to install and configure in the industry. Much of this ease comes from the Micro Channel architecture, which eliminates the need to worry about interrupts, DMA channels, I/O Port addresses, and even BIOS addresses. By virtue of MCA, these adapters are virtually self-configuring.

The only real problem is drivers. All these adapters have built-in support for hard disk drives, but no drivers are included for any other devices. This is important to know if you decide to attach external peripherals to these cards, because you will need drivers to make the peripherals work.

IBM makes DOS drivers available only for the peripherals that is sells. Amazingly, however, IBM OS/2 includes SCSI drivers not only for numerous IBM and non-IBM peripherals, but also for non-IBM SCSI host adapters. If you cannot use OS/2, one way around the driver-support problem is to use the same peripherals that IBM sells, in which case you can get the drivers from IBM. For example, IBM sells a CD-ROM drive that actually incorporates a Toshiba mechanism. If I purchase a Toshiba CD-ROM drive, I can make it work simply by using the drivers that IBM supplies with its (Toshiba) CD-ROM drive.

IBM makes its drivers available free for the downloading on the IBM NSC BBS (the phone number is in Appendix B). I am also using a Hewlett Packard DAT (digital audiotape) drive for backup, because that is the same mechanism that IBM sells in its own DAT drive. Again, I get the drivers from IBM. This system does not always work, however. For example, I want to attach a Hewlett Packard scanner to my IBM host adapter, but neither HP nor IBM (or anybody else so far) makes drivers to run the scanner with the IBM card. My only choice would be to use a different SCSI card to run the scanner—not a very good alternative, in my estimation.

The 16- and 32-bit MCA adapters have been available in two versions. The original version of the 16-bit (noncached) MCA adapter was known as FRU (Field Replacement Unit) # 15F6561 and was recalled for a defect. The replacement was labeled FRU # 85f0002. Some of the earlier cards were reworked and returned to the field without having the new FRU # applied over the old one. These repaired adapters can be identified by two yellow wires running from the upper to the lower side of the module (the module is labeled ZM10). If you have the original version of this card, getting the replacement is important (IBM should replace it free), because the original card could cause random lockups and data corruption.

The original 32-bit cached MCA adapter did not have a serious problem that required replacement, but it was updated over the years with improved functionality. The original SCSI adapter with cache does not support drive capacities greater than 1GB. If you install a drive larger than 1GB, the drive will work, but only the first 1GB will be recognized. A new version of this card has an improved BIOS that supports drives up to 8GB.

You can tell which SCSI adapter with cache you have by inspecting the adapter. The new adapter comes with an orange terminating resistor on the end of the card, similar to the noncached adapter. If you do not have both internal and external devices installed, this orange resistor should be located on the adapter. If you do have both internal and external devices, the resistor should be removed; there will be an empty socket on the adapter where the resistor originally was located. The new SCSI adapter with cache is sold under the part number 6451133 and known as FRU # 85F0063. If you have the original SCSI adapter with cache, you will not have either an orange resistor or an empty socket where the resistor is supposed to go. The original adapter does not implement termination on the card itself.

It is not widely known that you can upgrade the cache on the IBM SCSI adapter with cache from the standard 512KB to 2MB simply by replacing the 256KB (9-bit) SIMMs with 1MB SIMMs. The only caveat is that you must use the IBM-style 9-bit SIMMs, which have a slightly different pinout from so-called industry-standard 9-bit SIMMs. I have done this to my IBM SCSI card and have achieved perhaps a 10-percent improvement in throughput.

IBM also sells a new Fast/Wide MCA SCSI-2 adapter under part number G451280. IBM also has a Fast SCSI-2 adapter for ISA bus systems, which actually is made by Future Domain. This adapter is sold for use in ISA bus systems such as PS/1 and PS/Valuepoints. Because of Future Domain support, many more drivers are available for this adapter than for the MCA adapters, making it very easy to add a variety of peripherals under DOS as well as OS/2. This adapter also supports Fast SCSI transfers, whereas the original MCA IBM adapters do not.

Hard Disk Installation Procedures

This section describes the installation of a typical hard disk and its integration into a particular PC system. To install a hard drive in an IBM-compatible system, you must perform several procedures:

- Configure the drive

- Configure the controller or interface

- Physically install the drive

- Configure the system

- Low-level format the drive (not required with IDE and SCSI)

- Partition the drive

- High-level format the drive

Drive configuration was discussed earlier in this chapter, in the sections on interface types. For complete configuration information, consult the section that covers the type of drive that you are installing.

The following sections describe the other steps, which are simple to execute and, if done properly, result in the successful installation of a bootable hard disk. Special attention is given to issues of reliability and data integrity to ensure that the installation is long-lasting and trouble-free.

To begin the setup procedure, you need to know several details about the hard disk drive, controller or host adapter, and system ROM BIOS, as well as most of the other devices in the system. This information usually appears in the various OEM manuals that come with these devices. Make sure that when you purchase these items, the vendor includes these manuals. (Many vendors do not include the manuals unless you ask for them.) For most equipment sold today, you will get enough documentation from the vendor or reseller of the equipment to allow you to proceed.

If you are like me, however, and want all the technical documentation on the device, you will want to contact the original manufacturer of the device and order the technical specification manual. For example, if you purchase an IBM-compatible system that comes with a Western Digital IDE hard disk, the seller probably will give you some limited information on the drive, but not nearly the amount that the actual Western Digital technical specification manual provides. To get this documentation, you have to call Western Digital and order it. The same goes for any of the other components in most clones that are assembled rather than manufactured. I find the OEM technical manuals to be essential in providing the highest level of technical support possible.

Controller Configuration

Configuring a disk controller involves setting the different system resources that the controller requires. Some controllers have these resources fixed, which means that they cannot be altered. Other controllers provide jumpers, switches, or even software that enable you to reconfigure or change the resources used. Controllers with adjustable resource settings often can be used in conjunction with other controllers in a system, but controllers with fixed resources usually cannot coexist with others.

All hard disk controllers and SCSI host adapters require one or more of the following system resources:

- ROM addresses
- Interrupt Request Channel (IRQ)
- DMA channel (DRQ)
- I/O port addresses

Not all adapters use every one of these resources, but some will use them all. In most cases, these resources must be configured so that they are unique and cannot be shared among several adapters. For example, if a disk controller is using I/O port addresses from 1F0–1F7h, no other device in the system can use those addresses.

When a conflict in resource use occurs, not all of the adapters involved may function. In the case of disk controllers, the controller will not function, and disk access will be impossible or corrupted. You need to identify which boards in the system have overlapping resources and then change the configuration of one or more of those boards to eliminate the conflict. Before installing a board, you should know which resources the board will require, and you should make sure that these resources are not being used by other boards.

In most systems, this is a manual procedure that requires you to know exactly what every adapter in the system is using. In MCA and EISA systems, however, the procedure is under software control. MCA and EISA systems can automatically determine whether two adapters use the same resource and then change the configuration to eliminate the conflict. This method works on EISA systems only if you have all EISA 32-bit adapters. EISA systems also may have standard ISA adapters, which cannot be configured in this manner. MCA systems are universally self-configuring and are the easiest systems for the average user to configure.

For most systems, you need the documentation for every adapter in the system to ensure that no conflicts exist and to find out how to reconfigure a card to eliminate a conflict. Software such as Infospotter by Renasonce or MSD (Microsoft Diagnostics) can help when documentation is not available or is limited. Programs usually cannot identify direct conflicts, but if you install one board at a time, they can identify the addresses or resources that a given board is using. MSD comes free with Windows and MS-DOS 6.x; the excellent Infospotter program is available from Renasonce (listed in Appendix B).

Many system resources simply cannot be identified by software alone. A company called Allied Microcomputer manufactures a card called the Trapcard II that can be used to monitor interrupt and DMA channels. This board is very helpful in identifying which of these resources are used in your system. The company is listed in Appendix B.

ROM Addresses. Many disk controllers and SCSI host adapters require an on-board BIOS to function. An on-board BIOS can provide many functions, including the following:

- Low-level formatting
- Drive-type (parameter) control
- Adapter configuration
- Support for nonstandard I/O port addresses and interrupts

If the motherboard BIOS supports a hard disk controller, an on-board BIOS is not needed—and in fact is undesirable, because it uses memory in the Upper Memory Area (UMA). Fortunately, the on-board BIOS usually can be disabled if it is not required.

Only controllers that meet certain standards can run off the motherboard BIOS, including ST-506/412 controllers, ESDI controllers, and IDE bus adapters. These standards include the use of I/O port addresses 170–17Fh and interrupt 14. If you are installing a controller that uses other I/O port addresses or interrupt settings (such as when adding a second controller to a system), the motherboard BIOS will not be able to support it, and an on-board BIOS will be required. XT controllers universally need an on-board BIOS, because the motherboard BIOS has no hard disk support whatsoever.

SCSI adapters normally do not emulate the WD1003-type disk interface and almost always require an on-board BIOS to provide disk driver functions. This on-board BIOS supports any of the adapter's settings; and in most cases, multiple SCSI host adapters can use the BIOS of the first adapter, in which case the BIOSes on all but the first adapter can be disabled.

If an on-board BIOS is required and enabled, it will use specific memory address space in the UMA (Upper Memory Area). The UMA is the top 384KB in the first megabyte of system memory. The UMA is divided into three areas of two 64KB segments each, with the first and last areas being used by the video-adapter circuits and the motherboard BIOS, respectively. Segments C000h and D000h are reserved for use by adapter ROMs such as those found on disk controllers or SCSI host adapters.

You need to ensure that any adapters using space in these segments do not overlap with another adapter that uses this space. No two adapters can share this memory space. Most adapters have jumpers, switches, or even software that can adjust the configuration of the board and change the addresses that are used to prevent conflict.

Interrupt Request Channel (IRQ). All disk controllers and SCSI host adapters require an interrupt line to gain the system's attention. These devices invoke a hardware interrupt to gain timely access to the system for data transfers and control. The original 8-bit ISA systems have only 8 interrupt levels, with interrupts 2 through 7 available to any adapter. AT bus (16-bit ISA), EISA, and MCA systems have 16 interrupt levels, with interrupts 3 through 7, 9 through 12, and 14 through 15 available to any adapter cards. IRQs 10 through 12 and 14 through 15 are 16-bit interrupts available only to 16- or 32-bit adapters.

Tables 14.33 and 14.34 show the normally used and normally available interrupts in ISA, EISA, and MCA systems and in 8-bit ISA systems. The tables list the default use for each interrupt and indicate whether the interrupt is available in a bus slot.

Table 14.33   ISA, EISA, and MCA Default Interrupt Assignments

IRQ	Function	Bus Slot
0	System Timer	No
1	Keyboard Controller	No
2	Second IRQ Controller	No
8	Real-Time Clock	No
9	Available (Redirected IRQ 2)	Yes (8-bit)
10	Available	Yes (16-bit)
11	Available	Yes (16-bit)
12	Motherboard Mouse Port	Yes (16-bit)
13	Math Coprocessor	No
14	Hard Disk Controller	Yes (16-bit)
15	Available	Yes (16-bit)
3	Serial Port 2 (COM2:)	Yes (8-bit)
4	Serial Port 1 (COM1:)	Yes (8-bit)
5	Parallel Port 2 (LPT2:)	Yes (8-bit)
6	Floppy Disk Controller	Yes (8-bit)
7	Parallel Port 1 (LPT1:)	Yes (8-bit)

Table 14.34   XT-Bus (8-Bit ISA) Default Interrupt Assignments

IRQ	Function	Bus Slot
0	System Timer	No
1	Keyboard Controller	No
2	Available	Yes (8-bit)
3	Serial Port 2 (COM2:)	Yes (8-bit)
4	Serial Port 1 (COM1:)	Yes (8-bit)
5	Hard Disk Controller	Yes (8-bit)
6	Floppy Disk Controller	Yes (8-bit)
7	Parallel Port 1 (LPT1:)	Yes (8-bit)

Notice that some of the interrupts simply are not available in slots; they are reserved for use only by the indicated system function. Any interrupt that is listed as being in use by an item that is not installed in your system would be available. For example, if your system does not have a motherboard mouse port, IRQ 12 would be available; if your system does not have a second serial port, IRQ 3 would be available.

You must discover which interrupts currently are in use and which currently are available in a system, and then configure any new cards to use only the available interrupts. In a standard configuration, the hard disk controller uses interrupt (IRQ) 14. Any secondary controllers would have to use other interrupts. The suggested interrupt for a secondary controller is IRQ 15. Notice that any controllers that do not use IRQ 14 must have an on-board BIOS to function. The motherboard BIOS supports disk controllers only at IRQ 14.

Most adapters come preconfigured for IRQ 14, which is fine if the adapter is the only disk adapter in the system. Many SCSI host adapters, such as the Adaptec 1540/1542C, come configured to one of the other available 16-bit interrupts, because they never will be run off the motherboard BIOS. XT (8-bit) controllers normally use IRQ 5.

DMA Channel. Direct Memory Access (DMA) is a technique for transferring blocks of data directly into system memory without the complete attention of the main processor. The motherboard has DMA control circuits that orchestrate and govern DMA transfers. In the original 8-bit XT bus, DMA was the highest-performance transfer method, and XT hard disk controllers universally used DMA channel 3 for high-speed transfers.

In AT-bus (16-bit ISA) systems, most 16-bit disk controllers and SCSI host adapters do not use a DMA channel, partly because the performance of the AT bus DMA circuitry turned out to be very poor. Therefore, most adapters use a technique called Programmed I/O (PIO), which simply sends bytes of data through the I/O ports. PIO transfers are faster than DMA transfers in most cases, especially if the motherboard BIOS and device support block-mode PIO, such as with the new IDE drives. If an adapter does not use DMA, you can assume that PIO is used as the data-transfer method and that no DMA channel is required.

Some adapters have found a way around the poor performance of the ISA bus by becoming what is known as a bus master. A *bus master* actually takes control of the bus and can override the DMA controller circuitry of the motherboard to perform fast DMA transfers. These transfers can exceed the performance of a PIO transfer (even block-mode PIO), so you will find that many of the highest-performing controllers have bus-master capabilities.

You have to select a DMA channel for bus-master adapters to use. In an 8-bit ISA bus, normally only DMA channel 1 is available; in a 16-bit ISA bus, however, DMA channels 0 through 1, 3, and 5 through 7 are available. DMA channels 5 through 7 are 16-bit channels that most high-performance bus-master adapters would want to use. XT disk controllers always use DMA channel 3.

Tables 14.35 and 14.36 show the normally used and normally available DMA channels in ISA, EISA, and MCA systems and in 8-bit ISA systems. The tables list the default use for each DMA channel and indicate whether the DMA channel is available in a bus slot.

Table 14.35   ISA, EISA, and MCA Default DMA Channel Assignments

DMA	Function	Transfer	Bus Slot
0	Available	8-bit	Yes (16-bit)
1	Available	8-bit	Yes (8-bit)
2	Floppy Disk Controller	8-bit	Yes (8-bit)
3	Available	8-bit	Yes (8-bit)
4	First DMA Controller	N/A	No
5	Available	16-bit	Yes (16-bit)
6	Available	16-bit	Yes (16-bit)
7	Available	16-bit	Yes (16-bit)

Table 14.36   XT-Bus (8-Bit ISA) Default DMA Channel Assignments

DMA	Function	Transfer	Bus Slot
0	Dynamic RAM Refresh	N/A	No
1	Available	8-bit	Yes (8-bit)
2	Floppy Disk Controller	8-bit	Yes (8-bit)
3	Hard Disk Controller	8-bit	Yes (8-bit)

Notice that some of the DMA channels simply are not available in slots; they are reserved for use only by the indicated system function. Any DMA channel that is listed as being in use by an item that is not installed in your system would be available. For example, if your 8-bit ISA bus system does not have a hard disk controller, DMA channel 3 would be available.

MCA and EISA bus systems have additional DMA capabilities that support even faster transfers without the performance problems associated with non-bus-master cards. The MCA and EISA buses also provide even better support for bus-master devices that offer even higher performance.

To configure an adapter that requires a DMA channel, you first must find out which DMA channels currently are in use and which channels are available in your system. Unless you have a MCA or EISA system, software techniques for determining this are very limited. Most programs that claim to be capable of discovering which DMA channels are being used are only reporting what any standard configuration would be. In standard ISA systems, the only way to know for sure is to check the documentation for each adapter or to use a special hardware device that monitors DMA transfers. Allied

Electronics makes a card called the Trapcard II that monitors IRQ and DMA lines and can tell you for certain which are used and which are not. This inexpensive card plugs into a slot and monitors the bus, with LEDs indicating which resources are being used. Allied is listed in Appendix B.

After determining what DMA channels are free, you can set your adapter to any of those free channels. DMA conflicts usually result in improper operation or corrupted data transfers, so if you made a mistake, you usually will know quickly.

MCA and EISA systems automatically set up the boards so that no DMA conflicts exist. This method works fully only in EISA systems with all EISA 32-bit adapters installed.

I/O Port Addresses. I/O port addresses are like mailboxes through which data and commands are sent to and from an adapter. These addresses are different from memory addresses. I/O ports must be used exclusively and cannot be shared among different adapters. Each adapter usually uses a group of sequential port addresses for communication with the bus.

The standard I/O port addresses used by disk controllers are 1F0–1F7h. These are the only addresses that the motherboard BIOS supports, so if you have a disk controller at any other port address, it must have an on-board BIOS. Obviously, if you are adding a secondary controller to a system, that controller must use different I/O addresses and also must have an on-board BIOS. Most controllers use 170–177h as secondary I/O addresses, which would be used if another disk controller were in the system; however, you can use any I/O addresses that are free.

I/O port conflicts are rare unless you are installing multiple disk controllers in a system. In that case, each controller needs different I/O port address settings so as not to conflict with the others. To determine what I/O ports are currently in use, you normally have to refer to the documentation that comes with each device in your system. Software normally cannot identify all used I/O port addresses unless you have a Micro Channel or EISA system. When port conflicts exist, the devices in conflict do not function, or they function improperly.

Physical Installation

The procedure for physical installation of a hard disk is much the same as the procedure for installing a floppy drive. You must have the correct screws, brackets, and faceplates for the specific drive and system before you can install the drive.

IBM AT systems require plastic rails that are secured to the sides of the drives so that they can slide into the proper place in the system (see fig. 14.22). Compaq uses a different type of rail. When you purchase a drive, the vendor usually includes the IBM-type rails, so be sure to specify whether you need the special Compaq type. IBM PC-type and XT-type systems do not need rails, but they may need a bracket to enable double-stacking of half-height drives. Several companies listed in Appendix B specialize in drive-mounting brackets, cables, and other hardware accessories.

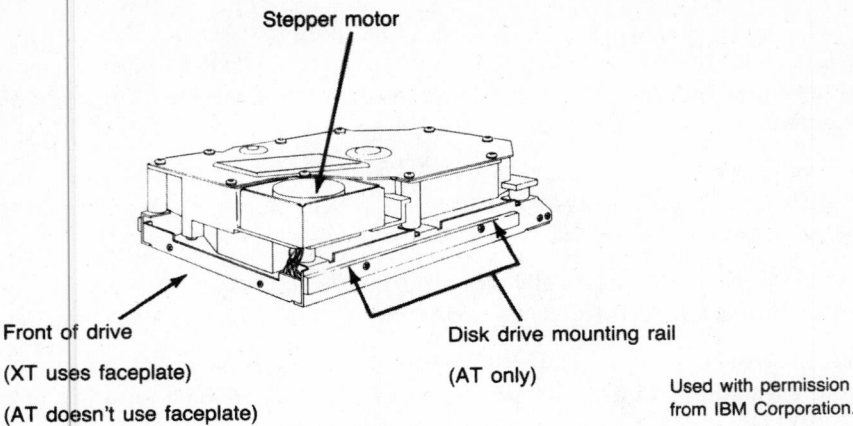

Stepper motor

Front of drive

(XT uses faceplate)

(AT doesn't use faceplate)

Disk drive mounting rail

(AT only)

Used with permission
from IBM Corporation.

Fig. 14.22
A full-height hard disk with AT mounting rails.

Different faceplate, or bezel, options are available; make sure that you have the correct bezel for your application. Some systems, for example, do not need a bezel; if a bezel is on the drive, it must be removed. If you are installing a half-height drive in a full-height bay, you may need a blank half-height bezel to fill the hole, or you may want to order a half-height drive with a full-height bezel so that no hole is created. Several vendors listed in Appendix B sell a variety of drive mounting kits, hardware, rails, adapters, and cables.

System Configuration

When the drive is physically installed, you can begin configuring the system to the drive. You have to tell the system about the drive so that the system can boot from it when it is powered on. How you set and store this information depends on the type of drive and system you have. Standard setup procedures are used for most hard disks except SCSI drives. SCSI drives normally follow a custom setup procedure that varies, depending on the host adapter that you are using. If you have SCSI drives, follow the instructions included with the host adapter to configure the drives.

AT-Class System Setup Program and Drive Types. If the system is an AT type and you are using the motherboard BIOS to support the hard disks, you need to know some information about the BIOS, such as what drives are supported in the hard drive table. Many BIOS versions now have user-definable drive types that enable you to enter any set of parameters required to match your drive. For IDE drives, many new BIOS versions have automatic typing, which interrogates the drive and automatically enters the parameter information returned by the drive. This procedure eliminates errors or confusion in parameter selection.

Normally, the information about the drive table appears in the technical manuals provided with the motherboard or the BIOS. Appendix A includes a list of drive types for many different BIOS versions. For systems that are not listed, you can find this information in the system's technical reference manual. Often, the BIOS setup program shows you all the available selections on-screen, enabling you to select the best choice interactively and eliminating the need to research this information.

After you collect the necessary information, the next step is to tell the system what kind of drive that is attached so that the system can boot from the drive (eventually). This chapter discusses the installation of an example drive in both an XT-type and an AT-type of system. The same drive is installed in both systems. With knowledge of drive interfacing, you can install just about any drive in any system.

The example drive is a Maxtor XT-1140, which is an ST-506/412 drive designed for MFM encoding. This drive is a full-height 5.25-inch platter drive that fits into any 5.25-inch full-height drive bay. The drive capacity is 140MB unformatted and 119.85MB formatted, with MFM encoding, or 183.31MB formatted, with RLL 2,7 encoding. You can use the drive in a system with an ST-506/412 interface controller. In its day, this drive was a fairly high-performance drive (as far as ST-506/412 drives go, anyway), with an advertised 27-ms seek time. This drive is a voice coil drive with thin-film media; it has 8 platters with 15 read/write heads and 1 dedicated servo head.

First, you need to read the drive manual and locate the required information. The manual for the example drive contains the following drive-parameter information:

- 918 cylinders

- 15 heads

- 17 or 26 sectors per track (MFM or RLL encoding)

- No write precompensation required

- 2 to 3,100μ head step pulse timing acceptable

- 2 to 13μ head step pulse timing optimum

- 7 defective tracks:

    Cyl 188, Head 7

    Cyl 217, Head 5

    Cyl 218, Head 5

    Cyl 219, Head 5

    Cyl 601, Head 13

    Cyl 798, Head 10

    Cyl 835, Head 5

To install this Maxtor XT-1140 in an IBM AT, I could simply use the original IBM AT controller (Western Digital WD1003A-WA2); however, I would have to live with the slow 2:1 interleave that this controller provides. A better choice is to upgrade the controller with a Data Technology Corporation DTC7287 controller. This controller not only supports a 1:1 interleave, but also has an RLL Endec, which will increase the storage capacity of the drive by 50 percent compared with the original MFM encoding controller. Because this drive is a high-quality voice coil actuated drive with thin-film media, it should work well with RLL encoding.

This controller also has an optional on-board ROM that can be used to set the drive type if the motherboard does not have a matching or user-definable type. The on-board ROM (if enabled) also has a low-level format program. For most systems, you set the drive type by looking up the drive information in the table of types located in the system ROM. You match the drive parameters to one of the table entries in the system ROM or set the parameters by using the user-definable drive type.

Following is the information required for installing the DTC7287 controller:

■ Interrupt Request Channel (IRQ) = 14

■ I/O ports = 1F0 to 1F7

■ Step pulse rate = 35µs (selected by BIOS)

■ Best interleave = 1:1

This controller uses Programmed I/O (PIO) transfers and does not require a DMA channel for the hard disk controller portion. Because this controller also contains a floppy controller, some additional information specific to the floppy controller portion of the card is required:

■ Interrupt Request Channel (IRQ) = 6

■ DMA channel (DRQ) = 2

■ I/O ports = 3F0 to 3F7

You need some of this information to ensure that the card is uniquely configured compared with other cards in the system. The system cannot have other cards using the same IRQ, DMA, ROM, or I/O ports as this card. Keep this information for future reference, and cross-check for conflicts when you add other cards to the system. The step pulse rates and interleave information are all that you need to complete the setup.

As mentioned earlier, the Maxtor XT-1140 manual states that the drive's seek performance degrades if step pulses are sent at intervals greater than 13µs. Unfortunately, the IBM AT ROM BIOS hard-codes this specification to 35µs, which slows the drive's performance. In my experience, the drive runs 25-ms seeks with the proper step pulse rate but an average 29-ms seeks with the slower step pulse rate selected in the IBM AT. If you want to bother with patching the AT ROM BIOS, you can change the controller's step pulse rate to 16µs; this change probably would make up a few milliseconds of average seek time. The instructions for making this patch appear in Chapter 17 "System Upgrades and Improvements," in the section "Upgrading the ROM BIOS." I made this modification to my own system to see whether it could be done, and I learned a lot in the process, but the results really are not worth the trouble.

After you find the information about the drive and controller, you need to match the drive's parameters to one of the drive-table entries in the motherboard ROM. ROM drive tables for IBM and many other compatible systems are listed in Appendix A, which also includes a detailed list of a large number of hard disk drives with parameter specifications. The information in Appendix A saved me several times when the original manuals were nowhere to be found.

With the drive tables and drive information in hand, try to find a table entry that matches on heads, cylinders, and write-precompensation starting cylinder. If you do not find an exact match for any of these values, use a type that has fewer cylinders and heads than your drive; you cannot use a type that has more. Remember that many compatible ROMs (such as those from Phoenix, Award, and AMI) have a user-definable drive type that enables you to support any drive parameters you want simply by typing them during setup.

Because the Maxtor XT-1140 drive has 918 cylinders and 15 heads, type 9, with 900 cylinders and 15 heads, is the best match in an IBM AT—if you are running an MFM controller, that is. Notice that all the types in an original AT BIOS have 17 sectors per track, whereas the drive actually has 26 sectors per track with RLL encoding. If the BIOS has a user-definable type entry (the original AT does not), you are home free; simply select the user-definable type and enter the exact parameters, including the correct number of sectors per track. If you select or define a type that indicates more cylinders, heads, or sectors than your drive has, you probably will see 1790 or 1791 Power-On Self Test (POST) error codes. These error codes indicate a fixed-disk 0 (or disk 1) read error, which most likely means that your selection is improper. If you are installing an intelligent IDE drive, it translates the parameters that you enter, which means that those parameters will work as long as they do not add up to more total sectors than the drive actually has.

The Maxtor XT-1140 drive requires no write precompensation. Type 9 in the original AT BIOS indicates a precompensation start cylinder of 65535—the largest number that can be stored with 16 bits. Essentially, this means that write precompensation never will be done, because you never will reach an actual cylinder number that high. For entries that have a value of 0 for the write-precompensation figure, write precompensation is performed on all cylinders, starting with 0.

The landing-cylinder designation is superfluous because this drive automatically parks and locks its heads at power-down, although it would be used if you ever ran a correctly written head-parking program.

Because there is no acceptable type in the original AT BIOS, and because there is no user-definable type either, this controller has an on-board BIOS that can override the motherboard BIOS and provide the drive-type information to the system. In this case, the motherboard BIOS is set to type 1, and the on-board controller BIOS takes over. To run the format program in the on-board BIOS, you use the DOS DEBUG program to point to the starting address of the BIOS format routine.

IBM AT Drive Type Tables. Rather than use a ROM on the controller card to support the card and drive tables, IBM incorporated the hard disk ROM BIOS into the main system ROM that resides on the motherboard. This ROM contains a hard disk table with at least 15 entries; later AT ROMs have tables with 23 entries. The XT 286 (really a late-model AT) has a table with 24 entries, and some PS/1 and PS/2 systems have as many as 44 entries. In each of these tables, entry 15 is reserved and not usable.

The tables are downward-compatible in the newer systems. For example, the PS/2 Model 80-111 has 32 table entries in its ROM, and the entries in the earlier systems match the specifications. Drive type 9, for example, is the same in all these systems, from the earliest AT to the newest PS/2 systems.

Notice that compatible systems are not consistent in regard to drive tables. Appendix A lists several hard disk drive tables for different compatible systems.

Table 14.37 lists the entries in the IBM motherboard ROM BIOS hard disk parameter table for AT or PS/2 systems using ST-506/412 (standard or IDE) controllers.

Table 14.37   IBM AT and PS/2 Hard Disk Drive Types

Type	Cyls	Heads	WPC	Ctrl	LZ	S/T	Meg	MB
1	306	4	128	00h	305	17	10.16	10.65
2	615	4	300	00h	615	17	20.42	21.41
3	615	6	300	00h	615	17	30.63	32.12
4	940	8	512	00h	940	17	62.42	65.45
5	940	6	512	00h	940	17	46.82	49.09
6	615	4	65,535	00h	615	17	20.42	21.41
7	462	8	256	00h	511	17	30.68	32.17
8	733	5	65,535	00h	733	17	30.42	31.90
9	900	15	65,535	08h	901	17	12.06	117.50
10	820	3	65,535	00h	820	17	20.42	21.41
11	855	5	65,535	00h	855	17	35.49	37.21
12	855	7	65,535	00h	855	17	49.68	52.09
13	306	8	128	00h	319	17	20.32	21.31
14	733	7	65,535	00h	733	17	42.59	44.66
15	0	0	0	00h	0	0	0	0
16	612	4	0	00h	663	17	20.32	21.31
17	977	5	300	00h	977	17	40.55	42.52
18	977	7	65,535	00h	977	17	56.77	59.53
19	1024	7	512	00h	1023	17	59.50	62.39
20	733	5	300	00h	732	17	30.42	31.90
21	733	7	300	00h	732	17	42.59	44.66
22	733	5	300	00h	733	17	30.42	31.90
23	306	4	0	00h	336	17	10.16	10.65
24	612	4	305	00h	663	17	20.32	21.31
25	306	4	65,535	00h	340	17	10.16	10.65
26	612	4	65,535	00h	670	17	20.32	21.31
27	698	7	300	20h	732	17	40.56	42.53

Type	Cyls	Heads	WPC	Ctrl	LZ	S/T	Meg	MB
28	976	5	488	20h	977	17	40.51	42.48
29	306	4	0	00h	340	17	10.16	10.65
30	611	4	306	20h	663	17	20.29	21.27
31	732	7	300	20h	732	17	42.53	44.60
32	1023	5	65,535	20h	1023	17	42.46	44.52
33	614	4	65,535	20h	663	25	29.98	31.44
34	775	2	65,535	20h	900	27	20.43	21.43
35	921	2	65,535	20h	1000	33	29.68	31.12
36	402	4	65,535	20h	460	26	20.41	21.41
37	580	6	65,535	20h	640	26	44.18	46.33
38	845	2	65,535	20h	1023	36	29.71	31.15
39	769	3	65,535	20h	1023	36	40.55	42.52
40	531	4	65,535	20h	532	39	40.45	42.41
41	577	2	65,535	20h	1023	36	20.29	21.27
42	654	2	65,535	20h	674	32	20.44	21.43
43	923	5	65,535	20h	1023	36	81.12	85.06
44	531	8	65,535	20h	532	39	80.89	84.82
45	0	0	0	00h	0	0	0.00	0.00
46	0	0	0	00h	0	0	0.00	0.00
47	0	0	0	00h	0	0	0.00	0.00

Type = drive type number
Cyls = total cylinders
Heads = total heads
WPC = write-precompensation starting cylinder
Ctrl = control byte; values as follows:
    Bit 0   01h, not used (XT = drive step rate)
    Bit 1   02h, not used (XT = drive step rate)
    Bit 2   04h, not used (XT = drive step rate)
    Bit 3   08h, more than 8 heads
    Bit 4   10h, not used (XT = embedded servo)
    Bit 5   20h, OEM defect map at (Cyls + 1)
    Bit 6   40h, disable disk retries
    Bit 7   80h, disable disk retries
LZ = landing-zone cylinder for head parking
S/T = number of sectors per track
Meg = drive capacity, in megabytes
MB = drive capacity, in millions of bytes

Table entry 15 is reserved as a CMOS pointer to indicate that the actual type is greater than 15.

IV

Mass Storage Systems

Type tables for compatible BIOS versions are listed in Appendix A. Notice that most IBM systems do not have every entry in this table. The maximum usable type number varies for each specific ROM version. The maximum usable type for each IBM ROM is indicated in table 14.38.

Table 14.38   Number of Drive Types in Various IBM BIOS Versions

System Description	ROM BIOS Date	ID Byte	Submodel Byte	Revision	No. of ST-506/ 412 Drive Types
PS/2 25	06/26/87	FA	01	00	26
PS/2 30	09/02/86	FA	00	00	26
PS/2 30	12/12/86	FA	00	01	26
PS/2 30	02/05/87	FA	00	02	26
PC-AT	01/10/84	FC	N/A	N/A	15
PC-AT	06/10/85	FC	00	01	23
PC-AT	11/15/85	FC	01	00	23
PC-XT 286	04/21/86	FC	02	00	24
PS/1	12/01/89	FC	0B	00	44
PS/2 25-286	06/28/89	FC	09	02	37
PS/2 30-286	08/25/88	FC	09	00	37
PS/2 30-286	06/28/89	FC	09	02	37
PS/2 35 SX	03/15/91	F8	19	05	37
PS/2 35 SX	04/04/91	F8	19	06	37
PS/2 40 SX	03/15/91	F8	19	05	37
PS/2 40 SX	04/04/91	F8	19	06	37
PS/2 L40 SX	02/27/91	F8	23	02	37
PS/2 50	02/13/87	FC	04	00	32
PS/2 50	05/09/87	FC	04	01	32
PS/2 50 Z	01/28/88	FC	04	02	33
PS/2 50 Z	04/18/88	FC	04	03	33
PS/2 55 SX	11/02/88	F8	0C	00	33
PS/2 60	02/13/87	FC	05	00	32
PS/2 65 SX	02/08/90	F8	1C	00	33
PS/2 70 386	01/29/88	F8	09	00	33
PS/2 70 386	04/11/88	F8	09	02	33
PS/2 70 386	12/15/89	F8	09	04	33
PS/2 70 386	01/29/88	F8	04	00	33
PS/2 70 386	04/11/88	F8	04	02	33
PS/2 70 386	12/15/89	F8	04	04	33
PS/2 70 386	06/08/88	F8	0D	00	33
PS/2 70 386	02/20/89	F8	0D	01	33

System Description	ROM BIOS Date	ID Byte	Submodel Byte	Revision	No. of ST-506/ 412 Drive Types
PS/2 P70 386	01/18/89	F8	0B	00	33
PS/2 80 386	03/30/87	F8	00	00	32
PS/2 80 386	10/07/87	F8	01	00	32

Numbers in the ID Byte, Submodel Byte, and Revision columns are in hexadecimal.

If you have an IBM-compatible, this table probably will be inaccurate for any of the entries past type 15. (Most compatibles follow the IBM table for at least the first 15 entries.) Several compatible-system drive tables appear in Appendix A of this book, including tables for compatible systems ranging from Compaq to Zenith.

Most IBM PS/2 systems' hard disk drives have the defect map written as data on the cylinder that is one cylinder beyond the highest reported cylinder. This special data is read by the IBM PS/2 Advanced Diagnostics low-level format program, which automates the entry of the defect list and eliminates the chance of human error (as long as you use only the IBM PS/2 Advanced Diagnostics program for hard disk low-level formatting).

This drive-table information does not apply to IBM ESDI or SCSI hard disk controllers, host adapters, and drives. Because ESDI and SCSI controllers and host adapters query the drive directly for the required parameters, no table-entry selection is necessary. The table for ST-506/412 drives, however, still appears in the ROM BIOS of most PS/2 systems, even if the model came standard with the ESDI or SCSI disk subsystem.

The manufacturers of most compatibles have enhanced the motherboard ROM BIOS tables in three ways:

- *Additional types.* The first thing that the manufacturers did was add more drive types to the table. Because the table had room for 47 or more entries, many compatible BIOS versions simply filled out all the entries with values that matched the most popular drives on the market, generally making drive installations easier. IBM tables often were short of the maximum number of possible entries.

- *User-definable drive types.* Most makers of compatibles then added a user-definable type, which used unused areas of the CMOS memory to store all the drive-parameter information. This was an excellent solution, because during setup, you can type a parameter that matches any drive on the market. The only drawback is that if the CMOS battery dies or the saved values are corrupted in some way, you would have to re-enter the information exactly as it was before to regain access to the drive. Many people did not write down the parameters that they used, or they used improper parameters that caused problems.

- *Automatic detection.* Most of the newer BIOS versions include a feature that is specific to IDE drives. Because most IDE drives are intelligent and will respond to a command called Identify Drive, the BIOS sends this command to the drive, which then responds with the correct parameters. This feature eliminates the need to type the parameters, because the BIOS will accept what the drive tells it.

Most of the newer compatible BIOS versions have both the user-definable type feature and automatic determination for IDE drives.

Drive-Table Alteration. Some drives do not match the table entries well. One way around the table-match problem is to purchase drives that match your tables. This solution can be limiting, however, especially if you have one of the earlier ROM-equipped systems. Most IBM-compatible systems have table entries all the way to type 47, but IBM AT systems stop much earlier than that.

ROM Patching. A second way around the drive-table limitation is to patch the correct entries for the desired drive and then reburn your own ROMs. This solution is illegal commercially and therefore is limited to "hacker" status, which means that you can do it to your own system but cannot legally sell patched IBM ROMs. For those who are so inclined, instructions for patching the BIOS are included in Chapter 17 "System Upgrades and Improvements."

ROM Replacement. A third way around the drive-table limits is to purchase and install a new ROM BIOS. A Phoenix ROM BIOS set, for example, costs about $50. These ROMs include a user-definable drive-type setting, which is the most elegant solution to this problem. A new set of ROMs probably will give you additional features, such as a built-in setup program, support for HD or ED 3.5-inch floppy drives, and Enhanced Keyboard support.

RLL/ESDI System Configuration. RLL and ESDI drives usually are not represented in the internal drive tables of older BIOS versions. Consequently, the controllers for these drives often have an on-board ROM BIOS that either contains an internal list of choices for the interface or enables you to dynamically configure (define) the controller to the specific geometry of the drive.

If you have a motherboard BIOS with a user-defined drive type (recommended), you can simply enter the correct parameters, and the drive will be supported. (Remember to write down the parameters that you use; if you lose them, you can lose access to the drive if you don't re-enter the parameters properly.) When using a user-definable type, you can disable the controller BIOS.

IDE System Configuration. Intelligent IDE drives can use the geometry that represents their true physical parameters, or they can translate to other drive geometries that have the same number of sectors or fewer. Simply select a type, or enter a user-definable type that is less than or equal to the total capacity of the drive.

SCSI System Configuration. Almost all SCSI drives use DRIVE TYPE 0 or NONE, because the host adapter BIOS and the drive communicate to establish the drive geometry. The low-level formatting routines usually are accessed on the host adapter through DEBUG or are on disk in the form of a configuration, setup, and format program. All SCSI drives are low-level formatted at the factory.

XT-Type System Drive Configuration. XT-type systems typically store the drive setup or type information in ROM. The IBM XT uses a controller with a ROM that contains the hard disk controller BIOS and a table of four drive types indicating the supported drives. You set jumpers or switches on that controller to indicate which of the four drives you are installing. XT systems lack the CMOS memory and setup methods used by AT-class systems.

Because the on-board BIOS in IBM's original XT controllers supported only four drives, most aftermarket controllers rapidly evolved into having an autoconfigure capability. This capability is essentially equivalent to the user-definable type in most later compatible AT BIOS versions, enabling you to dynamically configure the controller and drive by entering parameters through the controller BIOS configuration routine. These parameters often were stored in a hidden sector on the drive and were loaded each time the system was powered on. This technique was used because XT-class systems do not have CMOS memory in which to store information such as this.

XT-Class System Drive Selection. IBM XT hard disk controllers have used two different ROMs over the years, but each has only four entry tables, which means that a single ROM can support only four drives. Therefore, virtually every time you want to add a different type of hard disk to an IBM XT, you must reburn the ROM with the correct values for the new drive. You can try to anticipate future upgrades and burn in the values for those drives as well.

A new generation of controllers for the IBM PC and IBM XT alleviates the problem with the IBM XT disk controller. These new controllers request the type of drive being connected and store that information in a specially reserved track on the drive. Every time the system is booted, the information is read from that location, and the system has the correct drive type. Therefore, a drive table with an infinite number of entries is possible.

Regardless of the parameters of your drive, the system can support it because this "autoconfigure ROM" is built into the controller. No matter what type of disk drive you select, make sure that your controller is an *autoconfigure type;* it eliminates problems with table entries that do not match your drives.

Tables 14.39 and 14.40 list the ROM BIOS drive parameters in IBM XT (Xebec 1210) hard disk controllers.

Table 14.39 IBM 10MB Hard Disk Controller (Xebec 1210) Drive Parameter Tables									
Entry	**Type**	**Cyls**	**Heads**	**WPC**	**Ctrl**	**LZ**	**S/T**	**Meg**	**MB**
0	—	306	2	0	00h	00h	00h	5.08	5.33
1	—	375	8	0	05h	00h	00h	24.90	26.11
2	—	306	6	256	05h	00h	00h	15.24	15.98
3	—	306	4	0	05h	00h	00h	10.16	10.65

Table 14.40 IBM 20MB Hard Disk Controller (Xebec 1210) Drive Parameter Tables									
Entry	Type	Cyls	Heads	WPC	Ctrl	LZ	S/T	Meg	MB
0	1	306	4	0	05h	305	17	10.16	10.65
1	16	612	4	0	05h	663	17	20.32	21.31
2	2	615	4	300	05h	615	17	20.42	21.41
3	13	306	8	128	05h	319	17	20.32	21.31

Entry = controller table position
Type = drive-type number
Cyls = total cylinders
Heads = total heads
WPC = write-precompensation starting cylinder
Ctrl = control byte; values as follows:

    Bit 0   01h, drive step rate
    Bit 1   02h, drive step rate
    Bit 2   04h, drive step rate
    Bit 3   08h, more than eight heads
    Bit 4   10h, embedded servo drive
    Bit 5   20h, OEM defect map at (Cyls + 1)
    Bit 6   40h, disable ECC retries
    Bit 7   80h, disable disk access retries

Xebec 1210 Drive Step Rate Coding (control byte, bits 0–3)
    00h, 3-ms step rate
    04h, 200-microsecond buffered step
    05h, 70-microsecond buffered step
    06h, 30-microsecond buffered step
    07h, 15-microsecond buffered step
LZ = landing-zone cylinder for head parking
S/T = number of sectors per track
Meg = drive capacity, in megabytes
MB = drive capacity, in millions of bytes

The Landing Zone field and Sectors per Track fields are not used in the 10MB (original) controller and contain 00h values for each entry.

Note

MB and Meg sometimes are used interchangeably, but this is not exactly correct. MB is 1 million bytes, or 1,000,000 bytes. Meg (or M) is one megabyte, which is equal to 1,048,576 bytes. (1 megabyte = 1 kilobyte times 1 kilobyte, and 1 kilobyte = 1024 bytes. Thus, 1 megabyte = 1,024 × 1024 = 1,048,576.)

To select one of the drive-table entries in the IBM XT controllers (Xebec 1210), you would set the drive-table selection jumper (Jumper W5). Table 14.41 shows how these jumpers should be set to select a particular table entry. To select table entry 2 for drive 0 (C), for example, you would set the jumper off at position 1 and on at position 2.

Table 14.41 IBM XT Controller (Xebec 1210) Drive-Table Jumper (W5) Settings				
Drive 0 Table Entry	**1**	**2**	**3**	**4**
Jumper 1	On	On	Off	Off
Jumper 2	On	Off	On	Off
Drive 1 Table Entry	**1**	**2**	**3**	**4**
Jumper 3	On	On	Off	Off
Jumper 4	On	Off	On	Off

Autoconfigure Controllers. To install the example drive in an IBM XT, I could use the original IBM XT controller (Xebec 1210), but the built-in tables in that controller do not match my drive. I would have to download the ROM to disk and patch it to contain the correct drive-table values. If you can wield the DOS DEBUG program and have access to an EPROM burner, you can patch the correct table into one of the existing four table positions on the controller, and the controller will operate correctly with the drive. (I used this procedure on my vintage 1983 XT controller. The system works fine, but its best interleave is 5:1.)

Faster autoconfigure ROM controllers are available at such low prices that a better alternative is to purchase one. This example describes the installation of a Scientific Micro Systems Omti 5520A-10 controller, which has complete autoconfigure capability and supports a 2:1 interleave in the IBM PC and XT. Although this controller no longer is available, Data Technology Corporation (DTC) makes a DTC5150XL controller that offers even more features. The installation and configuration of all autoconfigure controllers are very similar.

DTC also makes a DTC5160XL controller that is an RLL version of the preceding controller. These controllers support co-residency, which means that they can be added to a system that already has an existing controller. These controllers can be installed with no hassle, run three times faster than the old Xebec controller, and cost less than $100. (Times have changed; an original Xebec 1210 cost me $795 in 1983.)

Following is the required information for the example installation:

- Interrupt Request Channel (IRQ) = 5
- DMA channel (DRQ) = 3

- ROM locations used = C8000 to C9FFF
- I/O ports = 320 to 32F
- Autoconfigure start location = C8006
- Step pulse rates = 10, 25, 50, 70, 200, and 3000µs
- Best interleave = 2:1 (4.77-MHz XT)

You need some of this information to ensure that the card is uniquely configured compared with other cards in the system. The system cannot have another card using the same IRQ, DMA, ROM, or I/O ports as this card. Keep this information for future reference, and cross-check for conflicts when you add other cards to the system. The autoconfigure start location, step pulse rates, and interleave information are necessary for completing the drive setup.

The next step is to activate the controller's built-in autoconfigure routine. When you do so, an autoconfigure controller prompts you for information about the drive (otherwise found in ROM tables) and then records the information directly on the drive in an area reserved by the controller on the first track. The advantage of the autoconfigure controller is that when you change drives, the controller can adapt. You never have to patch ROM-based tables with an EPROM burner, because this drive stores them on the drive dynamically. After the routine is completed, the controller reads this information every time the system is powered up and "knows" how to boot from the drive.

One potential problem with storing the parameters on the drive is that if they are accidentally overwritten, the drive is inaccessible. For this reason, you must be careful with any program that performs a low-level format on the drive. Most nondestructive formatters, such as the Norton Utilities Calibrate program, refuse to reformat the first track of any drive to avoid overwriting any of this special autoconfigure data.

To run the autoconfigure routine, follow these steps:

1. Boot DOS 3.3 or later.

2. Run the DOS DEBUG program.

3. At the DEBUG prompt, enter the information to tell DEBUG to move the system instruction pointer to the autoconfigure ROM start location. For this specific controller, you enter **G=C800:6**.

Because autoconfigure controllers from different manufacturers have different starting locations for the ROM BIOS format routine built into the controller, look in the manual to find the starting location for the specific controller that you are installing. Table 14.42 provides the controller BIOS low-level format addresses used with DEBUG for several popular controller brands.

Table 14.42   Controller BIOS Low-Level Format Addresses

Controller Manufacturer	Low-Level Format Address
Western Digital	g = XXXX:5
DTC	g = XXXX:5
Adaptec	g = XXXX:CCC
Seagate	g = XXXX:5
SMS-OMTI	g = XXXX:6

Replace the XXXX value with the starting segment address of the ROM as configured in the controller. Most controller ROMs can be configured for a variety of starting addresses in segments C000h and D000h. Most controllers have C800h or D800h as starting segment addresses, but you will have to consult the controller documentation and controller jumper settings to be sure. Note that when you enter this number, you do not type the "h", which is used here simply to indicate that these are hexadecimal numbers.

After you enter the last DEBUG instruction, the autoconfigure routine asks several questions about the drive and controller: how many heads and cylinders the drive has, what the starting write-precompensation cylinder is, and how quickly the step pulses should be sent. Use the information that you gathered about the drive and controller to answer these questions.

In the example, you would indicate that the controller should pulse the drive with step pulses spaced 10µs apart. To establish this figure, look at the range of spacing that the drive will accept, compare it with what the controller can send, and select the fastest rate that both can agree on. This procedure is similar to configuring a serial printer and serial port for 9600 bps transmission. Why not go as fast as the hardware will allow? The Maxtor XT-1140 manual states that seek performance on this particular drive degrades if step pulses are sent at intervals greater than 13µs. Setting this specification to a setting that is optimum for your drive can tweak a drive's seek performance.

The autoconfigure program also asks you to specify the desired interleave. An interleave of 2:1 is the best value for the example controller in a 4.77-MHz IBM PC or IBM XT system. This interleave value was determined by a simple trial-and-error testing session in which the disk was formatted at various interleaves, from 6:1 (the IBM XT default) down to 1:1. The transfer rate improved with each lower interleave until 1:1, at which point the transfer rate slowed by more than 800 percent. At 1:1, this controller cannot keep up with the rate at which the next sector passes below the heads; it requires 17 full revolutions of the disk to read a track, compared with 2 revolutions to read a track at a 2:1 interleave.

Finally, the autoconfigure program asks whether the drive has defects and gives you the opportunity to enter them. The example drive has seven defects (printed on a sticker on top of the drive, as well as included on a printed sheet). Entering this information causes the low-level format program to specially mark these tracks with invalid checksum figures, ensuring that these locations never are read or written to. Later, when DOS is used to high-level format the disk, the DOS format program will be unable to read these locations and will mark the file allocation table with information so that the locations never will be used. If you do not enter these locations properly, data or program files could use these defective tracks and become corrupted. Always mark these locations.

For the controller used in this example, the low-level format is part of the autoconfigure routine. After you answer the questions, the drive is low-level formatted, the defects are marked, and a scan is made for defects that were marked improperly or that became bad after the manufacturer's original tests. Finally, the autoconfigure information is written to a specially reserved track on the disk. When this process is complete, the drive is ready for DOS installation.

Formatting and Software Installation

Proper setup and formatting are critical to a drive's performance and reliability. This section describes the procedures used to format a hard disk drive correctly. Use these procedures when you install a new drive in a system or immediately after you recover data from a hard disk that has been exhibiting problems.

Three major steps complete the formatting process for a hard disk drive subsystem:

- Low-level formatting
- Partitioning
- High-level formatting

Considerations before Low-Level Formatting. In a low-level format (LLF), which is a "real" format, the tracks and sectors of the disk are outlined and written. During the LLF, data is written across the entire disk. An improper low-level format results in lost data and in many read and write failures. You need to consider several things before initiating a low-level format.

Data Backup. Low-level formatting is the primary standard repair procedure for hard disk drives that are having problems. Because data values are copied to the drive at every possible location during an LLF, necessary data-recovery operations must be performed *before* an LLF operation.

> **Caution**
>
> After an LLF has been performed, you cannot recover any information previously written to the drive.

Because an LLF overwrites all the data on a drive, it is a good way to erase an entire drive if you are trying to ensure that nobody will be able to get data from it. Government standards for this type of procedure actually require the data to be overwritten several times with different patterns, but for most intents and purposes, if the drive is overwritten one time, nobody will be able to read any data that was on it.

System Temperature. Sector header and trailer information is written or updated only during the LLF operation. During normal read and write activity, only the 512 bytes plus the CRC (Cyclic Redundancy Check) bytes in the trailer are written in a sector. Temperature-induced dimensional changes in the drive platters during read and write operations can become a problem.

When a 5.25-inch platter drive is low-level formatted five minutes after power-up at a relatively cold platter temperature of 70 degrees F, the sector headers and trailers and the 512-byte dummy data values are written to each track on each platter at specific locations.

Suppose that you save a file on a drive that has been running for several hours at a platter temperature of 140 degrees F. The data areas of only several sectors are updated. But with the drive platters as much as 70 degrees warmer than when the drive was formatted, each aluminum drive platter will have expanded in size by 2.5 thousandths of an inch (taking into account the coefficient of linear thermal expansion of aluminum). Each track, therefore, would have moved outward a distance of approximately 1.25 thousandths of an inch. Most 5.25-inch hard disks have track densities between 500 and 1,000 tracks per inch, with distances of only 1 to 2 thousandths of an inch between adjacent tracks. As a result, the thermal expansion of a typical 5.25-inch hard disk platter could cause the tracks to migrate from one-half to more than one full track of distance below the heads. If the drive head-movement mechanism does not compensate for these thermally induced dimensional changes in the platters, severe mistracking results.

When mistracking occurs, the data areas in each sector that have been updated at the higher temperature fail to line up with the sector header and trailer information. If the sector header and trailer information cannot be read properly, DOS usually issues an error message like this one:

```
Sector not found reading drive C
Abort, Retry, Ignore, Fail?
```

The data is misaligned with the sector boundaries on those tracks. This thermal effect also can work in reverse: if the drive is formatted and written to while it is extremely hot, it may not read properly while cold because of dimensional changes in the platters. This problem occurs with drives that have the "Monday-morning blues," in which they spin but cannot read data properly when they are first powered on, especially after being off for an extended period (over a weekend, for example). If you leave the power to the system on for some time so that the drive can warm up, the system then may boot and run normally.

If this happens, the next step is to back up the drive completely and initiate a new low-level format at the proper operating temperature (described next). This procedure enables the drive to work normally again until temperature-induced mistracking becomes great enough to cause the problem again.

Knowing that temperature fluctuations can cause mistracking, you should understand the reasons for the following basic rules of disk use:

- Leave the system's power on for at least 30 minutes before performing a low-level format on its hard disk. This step ensures that the platters are at a normal operating temperature and have stabilized dimensionally.

- If possible, allow a system some time to warm up after power-on before storing any data on the hard disk. This procedure is not required for voice coil drives.

If you have a cheap stepper motor drive that consistently exhibits temperature-related mistracking problems, you may want to consider running the drive constantly. Doing so would extend its trouble-free life span significantly, because the temperature and dimensions of the platters would stay relatively constant.

These kinds of temperature-fluctuation problems are more of a problem with drives that have open-loop stepper motor actuators (which offer no thermal compensation) than with the closed-loop voice coil actuators (which follow temperature-induced track migration and compensate completely, resulting in no tracking errors even with large changes in platter dimensions).

Modern voice coil actuator drives do not exhibit these dimensional instabilities due to thermal expansion and contraction of the platters, because they have a track-following servo mechanism. As the tracks move, the positioner automatically compensates. Many of these drives undergo a noticeable thermal compensation sequence every five minutes or so for the first 30 minutes after being powered on, and usually every 30 minutes after that. During these thermal-compensation routines, you hear the heads move back and forth as they measure and compensate for platter-dimension changes.

Drive Operating Position. Another consideration before formatting a drive is ensuring that the drive is formatted in the operating position it will have when it is installed in the system. Gravity can place on the head actuator different loads that can cause mistracking if the drive changes between a vertical and a horizontal position. This effect is minimized or even eliminated in most voice coil drives, but this procedure cannot hurt.

Additionally, drives that are not properly shock-mounted (such as the Seagate ST 2xx series) should be formatted only when they are installed in the system, because the installation screws exert twisting forces on the drive's Head Disk Assembly (HDA), which can cause mistracking. If you format the drive with the mounting screws installed tightly, it may not read with the screws out, and vice versa. Be careful not to overtighten the mounting screws, because doing so can stress the HDA. This usually is not a problem if the drive's HDA is isolated from the frame by rubber bushings.

In summary, for a proper low-level format, the drive should be

- At a normal operating temperature

- In a normal operating position

- Mounted in the host system (if the drive HDA is not shock-mounted or isolated from the drive frame by rubber bushings)

Because many different makes and models of controllers differ in the way that they write data to a drive, especially with respect to the encoding scheme, it is best to format the drive using the same make and model of controller as the controller that will be used in the host system. Some brands of controllers work exactly alike, however, so this is not an absolute requirement even if the interface is the same. This problem does not occur with IDE or SCSI drives, of course, because the controller is built into the drive. Usually, if the controller establishes the drive type by using its own on-board ROM rather than the system setup program, it will be incompatible with other controllers.

Low-Level Format. Of these procedures, the low-level format is most important to en-sure trouble-free operation of the drive. This format is the most critical of the operations and must be done correctly for the drive to work properly. The low-level format includes several subprocedures:

- Scanning for existing defect mapping
- Selecting the interleave
- Formatting and marking (or remarking) manufacturer defects
- Running a surface analysis

On some systems, such as the IBM PS/2, these subprocedures are performed automati-cally by the system's low-level format program and require no user intervention. On other systems, you must take the initiative.

To perform the drive defect mapping, to select an interleave, and to complete a surface analysis of the drive, you need information about the drive, the controller, and possibly the system. This information usually is provided in separate manuals or documents for each item; therefore, be sure that you get the complete documentation for your drive and controller products when you purchase them. The specific information required depends on the type of system, controller, and low-level format program that you are using.

Defect Mapping. Before formatting the disk, you need to know whether the drive has defects that have to be mapped out. Most drives come with a list of defects discovered by the manufacturer during the drive's final quality-control testing. These defects must be marked so that they are not used later to store programs or data.

Defect mapping is one of the most critical aspects of low-level formatting. To understand the defect-mapping procedures, you first must understand what happens when a defect is mapped on a drive.

The manufacturer's defect list usually indicates defects by cylinder and track. When this information is entered, the low-level format program marks these tracks with invalid checksum figures in the header of each of the sectors, ensuring that nothing can read or write to these locations. When DOS performs a high-level format of the disk, the DOS FORMAT program cannot read these locations, and it marks the involved clusters in the file allocation table (FAT) so that they never will be used.

The list of defects that the manufacturer gives you probably is more extensive than what a program could determine from your system, because the manufacturer's test equipment is far more sensitive than a regular disk controller. Do not expect a format program to find the defects automatically; you probably will have to enter them manually. An exception is the new IBM PS/2 systems, in which the defect list is encoded in a special area of the drive that normal software cannot access. The IBM PS/2 low-level format program (included on the Reference disk that comes with IBM PS/2 systems) reads this special map, thereby eliminating the need to enter these locations manually.

Most new drives are not low-level formatted by the manufacturer. Even if you bought a drive that had been low-level formatted, you would not know the temperature and the operating position of the drive when it was formatted. For best results, perform your own low-level format on a drive after you receive it. If you bought a system with a drive already installed by the manufacturer or dealer, a low-level format probably was done for you. To be safe, however, you might want to do a new low-level format in the system's new environment.

Although an *actual defect* is technically different from a *marked defect*, these defects should correspond to one another if the drive is formatted properly. For example, I can enter the location of a good track into the low-level format program as a defective track. The low-level format program then corrupts the checksum values for the sectors on that track, rendering them unreadable and unwriteable. When the DOS FORMAT program encounters that track, it finds the track unreadable and marks the clusters occupying that track as being bad. After that, as the drive is used, DOS ensures that no data ever is written to that track. The drive stays in that condition until you redo the low-level format of that track, indicate that the track is not to be marked defective, and redo the high-level format that no longer will find the track unreadable and therefore permit those clusters to be used. In general, unless an area is marked as defective in the low-level format, it will not be found as defective by the high-level format, and DOS will subsequently use it for data storage.

Defect mapping becomes a problem when someone formats a hard disk and fails to enter the manufacturer's defect list, which contains actual defect locations, so that the low-level format can establish these tracks or sectors as marked defects. Letting a defect go unmarked will cost you data when the area is used to store a file that you subsequently cannot retrieve. Unfortunately, the low-level format program does not automatically find and mark any areas on a disk that are defective. The manufacturer's defect list is produced by very sensitive test equipment that tests the drive at an analog level. Most manufacturers indicate areas as being defective even if they are just marginal. The problem is that a marginal area today may be totally unreadable in the future. You should avoid any area suspected as being defective by entering the location during the low-level format so that the area is marked; then DOS is forced to avoid the area.

Currently Marked Defects Scan. Most low-level format programs have the capability to perform a scan for previously marked defects on a drive. Some programs call this operation a defect scan; IBM calls it Read Verify in the IBM Advanced Diagnostics. This type of operation is nondestructive and reports by cylinder and head position all track locations marked bad. Do not mistake this for a true scan for defective tracks on a disk, which is a destructive operation normally called a surface analysis (discussed in "Surface Analysis" later in this chapter).

If a drive was low-level formatted previously, you should scan the disk for previously marked defects before running a fresh low-level format, for several reasons:

■ *To ensure that the previous low-level format correctly marked all manufacturer-listed defects.* Compare the report of the defect scan with the manufacturer's list, and note any discrepancies. Any defects on the manufacturer's list that were not found by the defect scan were not marked properly.

■ *To look for tracks that are marked as defective but are not on the manufacturer's list.* These tracks may have been added by a previously run surface-analysis program (in which case they should be retained), or they may result from the previous formatter's typographical errors in marking the manufacturer's defect. One of my drive manufacturer's lists showed Cylinder 514, Head 14 as defective. A defect scan, however, showed that track as good but Cylinder 814, Head 14 as bad. Because the latter location was not on the manufacturer's list, and because typing 5 instead of 8 would be an easy mistake to make, I concluded that a typographical error was the cause and then reformatted the drive, marking Cylinder 814, Head 14 as bad and enabling Cylinder 514, Head 14 to be formatted as a good track, thus "unmarking" it.

If you run a surface analysis and encounter defects in addition to those on the manufacturer's list, you can do one of two things. If the drive is under warranty, consider returning it. If the drive is out of warranty, grab a pen and write on the defect-list sticker, adding the bad tracks discovered by the surface-analysis program. (The IBM PS/2 low-level formatter built into the Reference disk automatically performs a surface analysis immediately after the low-level format; if it discovers additional defects, it automatically adds them to the defect list recorded on the drive.) Adding new defects to the sticker in this manner means that these areas are not forgotten when the drive is subsequently reformatted.

Manufacturer's Defect List. The manufacturer tests a new hard disk by using sophisticated analog test instruments that perform an extensive analysis of the surface of the platters. This kind of testing can indicate the functionality of an area of the disk with great accuracy, precisely measuring information such as the signal-to-noise ratio and recording accuracy.

Some manufacturers have more demanding standards than others about what they consider to be defects. Many people are bothered by the fact that when they purchase a new drive, it comes with a list of defective locations; some even demand that the seller install a defect-free drive. The seller can satisfy this request by substituting a drive made by a company with less-stringent quality control, but the drive will be of poorer quality. The manufacturer that produces drives with more listed defects usually has a higher quality product, because the number of listed defects depends on the level of quality control. What constitutes a defect depends on who is interpreting the test results.

To mark the manufacturer defects listed for the drive, consult the documentation for your low-level format program. For most drives, the manufacturer's defect list shows the defects by cylinder and head; other lists locate the defect down to the bit on the track that is bad, starting with the index location.

> **Caution**
>
> Make sure that all manufacturer's defects have been entered before proceeding with the low-level format.

Some systems automatically mark the manufacturer's defects, using a special defect file recorded on the drive by the manufacturer. For such a system, you need a special low-level format program that knows how to find and read this file. Automatic defect-map entry is standard for IBM PS/2 systems and for most ESDI and all SCSI systems. Consult the drive or controller vendor for the proper low-level format program and defect-handling procedures for your drive.

> **Note**
>
> Do not mark defective clusters on the disk with a data-recovery utility such as Norton, Mace, or PC Tools, because these utilities cannot mark the sectors or tracks at the low-level format level. The bad cluster marks that they make are stored only in the FAT and are erased during the next high-level format operation.

Surface Analysis. A *defect scan* is a scan for marked defects; a *surface analysis* is a scan for actual defects. A surface analysis ignores tracks already marked defective by a low-level format and tests the unmarked tracks. The surface-analysis program writes 512 bytes to each sector on the good tracks, reads the sectors back, and compares the data read to what was written. If the data does not verify, the program (like a low-level format) marks the track bad by corrupting the checksum values for each sector on that track. A proper surface analysis is like a low-level format program in that it should bypass the DOS and the BIOS so that it can turn off controller retry operations and also see when ECC (Error Correction Code) is invoked to correct soft errors.

Surface-analysis programs are destructive: they write over every sector except those that already are marked as bad. You should run a surface-analysis program immediately after running a low-level format, to determine whether defects have appeared in addition to the manufacturer's defects entered during the low-level format. A defect scan after the low-level format and the surface analysis shows the cumulative tracks that were marked bad by both programs.

If you have lost the manufacturer's defect list, you can use the surface-analysis program to indicate which tracks are bad, but this program never can duplicate the accuracy or sensitivity of the original manufacturer testing.

For example, if a spot in the sector were performing at 51 percent of capacity, it would be good enough to pass a PC surface analysis. The next day, due to variances in the drive and electronics, that same spot might perform at only 49 percent of capacity, failing a surface analysis. If you must use a surface analysis as your only source of defect information for a drive, be sure to use the option of increasing the number of times that each track will be tested, and run the program over an evening or weekend for a higher probability of catching an elusive or intermittent bad track.

Some low-level format and surface-analysis programs have hype-filled advertisements that make misleading and even false claims of performance and capability. Some programs even "unmark" defects that have been purposely marked by the initial, properly done low-level format according to the manufacturer's supplied list of defects, because the program determines that the area in question is not defective. (This is unbelievable!) If the drive is a good one, no surface-analysis program can possibly find all the defects on the manufacturer's list. Only factory testing at the analog level could indicate these defects, because most manufacturers include even slightly marginal areas on their list.

For example, I have a 40MB drive that has 27 manufacturer defects on the bad-track list; this drive probably is the highest quality 40MB sold. Most cheaper 40MB drives would have five or fewer defects on the bad-track list. I have run virtually every surface-analysis program on this drive, and none could find more than 5 of the 27 defects.

Although it is recommended if you have been experiencing any problems with a drive, on new drives I normally do not run a surface analysis after low-level formatting, for several reasons:

- Compared with formatting, surface analysis takes a long time. Most surface-analysis programs take two to five times longer than a low-level format. A low-level format of a 120MB drive takes about 15 minutes; a surface analysis of the same drive takes an hour or more. Moreover, if you increase the accuracy of the surface analysis by allowing multiple passes or multiple patterns, the surface analysis takes even longer.

- With high-quality drives, I never find defects beyond those that the manufacturer specified. In fact, the surface-analysis programs do not find all of the manufacturer's defects if I do not enter them manually. Because the high-quality (voice coil) drives that I use have been tested by the manufacturer to a greater degree than a program can perform on my system, I simply mark all the defects from the manufacturer's list in the low-level format. If I were using a low-quality (stepper motor) drive or installing a used and out-of-warranty drive, I would consider performing a surface analysis after the low-level format.

Defect-Free Drives. Although some manufacturers claim that the drives that they sell or install are defect-free, this really is not true. The defects are mapped out and replaced by spare sectors and tracks. This type of defect mapping, usually called *sector sparing*, insulates the operating system from having to handle the defects. IDE and SCSI drives universally use sector sparing to hide defects, so all these drives seem to be defect-free.

When you finish the low-level format and surface analysis of a hard disk in non-IDE or non-SCSI installations, several areas on the disk have been marked defective by corrupting the checksum values in the sector headers on the indicated tracks. When the high-level format scans the disk, it locates the defective sectors by failing to read them during the defect-scan portion of the high-level format operation. The clusters or allocation units that contain these unreadable sectors then are marked as bad in the FAT. When the CHKDSK command is executed, you get a report of how many of these bad clusters are on the disk. The CHKDSK report looks like this (although yours will have different numbers):

```
Volume DRIVE C   created 06-02-1990 9:14p
Volume Serial Number is 3311-1CD3

117116928 bytes total disk space
    73728 bytes in 3 hidden files
   593920 bytes in 268 directories
106430464 bytes in 4068 user files
   143360 bytes in bad sectors
  9875456 bytes available on disk

     2048 bytes in each allocation unit
    57186 total allocation units on disk
     4822 available allocation units on disk

   655360 total bytes memory
   561216 bytes free
```

The 143360 bytes in bad sectors really are only 70 clusters, or allocation units, because each allocation unit contains 2,048 bytes.

When I performed the low-level format of this disk, I entered 14 defects, which caused 14 tracks to be corrupted. This disk has 17 sectors per track; therefore, 238 total sectors (17 sectors times 14 tracks) have been corrupted by the low-level format program. Therefore, 121,856 total bytes have been marked bad (238 sectors times 512 bytes per sector).

This number does not agree with the total reported by CHKDSK, because DOS must mark entire allocation units, not individual sectors. Each allocation unit is made up of four sectors (2,048 bytes) on this disk. Therefore:

1 track = 17 sectors = 4 allocation units plus 1 extra sector

DOS must mark an entire allocation unit as being bad, even if only one sector in the unit is bad; therefore, DOS marks five allocation units for each marked track as being bad. In bytes, this becomes:

5 allocation units = 20 sectors = 10,240 bytes (20 sectors times 512 bytes)

Therefore, 10,240 bytes are marked as bad in the FAT for each track marked in the low-level format. And 10,240 bytes per track marked bad times 14 total marked tracks equals 143,360 total bytes marked bad.

From these calculations, you can see that all the correct defect mapping is in place. The bytes in bad sectors never will be used by files, so they won't bother you. This number should not change over the life of the drive unless new defects are entered during a subsequent low-level format or surface analysis.

The relationship between CHKDSK results and disk defects is not as clear with all drives and controllers. For example, I have an IBM PS/2 Model 70-121 that has a 120MB IBM drive and an MCA IDE drive with an embedded ESDI controller. (The controller is built into the drive.) I formatted this drive by using IBM Advanced Diagnostics for the IBM PS/2 (included free with the system). After finishing the high-level format, I ran CHKDSK, and it reported no bad sectors. Could this be true? Not really. In fact, this drive has more than 140 defects, and all have been correctly marked. How could that be? If the defects were marked, the high-level format should have been unable to read those locations, and CHKDSK would have reported the `xxxxxx bytes in bad sectors` message. The answer lies in how the drive and controller operate together.

IBM advertises this drive as having 32 sectors per track and 920 cylinders with 8 heads, but it actually has 33 sectors per track—or a spare sector on every track. When a defect location is given to the low-level format program, the program removes the defective sector from use by not numbering it as one of the 32 sectors on that track. Then the program gives the spare sector the number that the defective one would have been given; the defective sector becomes the spare. Through this technique, the disk can have up to one defect for every track on the drive (7,360 total) without losing capacity. Moreover, entire spare tracks are available on several spare cylinders past 920; if more than one sector on a track is defective, those extra tracks can be used. The disk has enough spare sectors and tracks to accommodate all possible defects.

Sector sparing is standard on all intelligent IDE and all SCSI drives; it also is an option on many ESDI controllers. This is why IDE and SCSI drives never seem to have any bytes in bad sectors. Of course they do, but they are replaced with good sectors from the spare-sector pool.

Why Low-Level Format? Even though it generally is not necessary (or even recommended) to low-level format IDE or SCSI drives, there are a few good reasons to consider a low-level format. One reason is that a low-level format will wipe out all the data on a drive, ensuring that other people will not be able to read or recover that data. This procedure is useful if you are selling a system and do not want your data to be readable by the purchaser. Another reason for wiping all the data from a drive is to remove corrupted or non-DOS operating-system partitions and even virus infections. The best reason is for defect management. As you may have noticed, most ATA-IDE drives appear to have no "bytes in bad sectors" under CHKDSK or any other software.

Any defects that were present on the drive after manufacturing were reallocated by the factory low-level format. Essentially, any known bad sectors are replaced by spare sectors stored in different parts of the drive. If any new defects occur, such as from a minor head/platter contact or drive mishandling, a proper IDE-aware low-level format program can map the new bad sectors to other spares, hiding them and restoring the drive to what appears to be defect-free status.

Because the IDE (ATA) specification is an extension of the IBM/WD ST-506/412 controller interface, the specification includes several new CCB commands that were not part of the original INT 13h/CCB support. Some of these new CCB commands are vendor-specific and are unique to each IDE drive manufacturer. Some manufacturers use these special CCB commands for tasks such as rewriting the sector headers to flag bad sectors, which in essence means LLF. When using these commands, the drive controller can rewrite the sector headers and data areas and then carefully step over any servo information (if the drive uses an embedded servo).

IDE drives *can* be low-level formatted, although some drives require special vendor-specific commands to activate certain low-level formatting features and defect-management options. Seagate, Western Digital, Maxtor, IBM, and others make specific low-level format and spare-sector defect-management software specific to their respective IDE drives. Conner drives are unique in that to actually low-level format them, you need a special hardware device that attaches to a diagnostic port connector on the Conner IDE drive. A company called TCE (800-383-8001 or 708-741-7200) sells such a device for $99. Coincidentally, this device is called The Conner. It includes software and the special adapter device that permits true low-level formatting (including rewriting all sectors and sector headers, as well as completely managing spare sector defects) at the factory level.

Other companies have developed low-level format software that recognizes the particular IDE drive and uses the correct vendor-specific commands for the low-level format and defect mapping. The best of these programs is Ontrack's Disk Manager. A general-purpose diagnostic program that also supports IDE-drive formatting is the MicroScope package by Micro 2000.

Intelligent IDE drives must be in nontranslating, or native, mode to low-level format them. Zoned Recording drives can perform only a partial low-level format, in which the defect map is updated and new defective sectors can be marked or spared, but the sector headers usually are rewritten only partially, and only for the purpose of defect mapping. In any case, you are writing to some of the sector headers in one form, and physical (sector-level) defect mapping and sector sparing can be performed. This procedure is, by any standard definition, an LLF.

On an embedded servo drive, all the servo data for a track is recorded at the same time by a specialized (usually, laser-guided) servowriter. This servo information is used to update the head position continuously during drive function, so that the drive automatically compensates for thermal effects. As a result, all the individual servo bursts are in line on the track. Because the servo controls head position, there is no appreciable head-to-sector drift, as there could be on a nonservo drive.

This is why even though it is possible to low-level format embedded servo drives, it rarely is necessary. The only purpose for performing an LLF on an embedded servo drive is to perform additional physical- (sector-) level defect mapping or sector sparing for the purpose of managing defects that occur after manufacture. Because no drift occurs, when a sector is found to contain a flaw, it should remain permanently marked bad, because a physical flaw cannot be repaired by reformatting.

Most IDE drives have three to four spare sectors for each physical cylinder of the drive. These hundreds of spare sectors are more than enough to accommodate the original defects and any subsequent defects. If more sectors are required, the drive likely has serious physical problems that cannot be fixed by software.

Software for Low-Level Formatting. You often can choose among several types of low-level format programs, but no single low-level format program works on all drives or all systems. Because low-level format programs must operate very closely with the controller, they often are specific to a controller or controller type. Therefore, ask the controller manufacturer for the formatting software that it recommends.

If the controller manufacturer supplies a low-level format program (usually in the controller's ROM), use that program, because it is the one most specifically designed for your system and controller. The manufacturer's program can take advantage of special defect-mapping features, for example. A different format program not only might fail to use a manufacturer-written defect map, but also might overwrite and destroy it.

IBM supplies a low-level format program for its PS/2 systems. For Models 50 and higher, the program is included in the Advanced Diagnostics portion of the Reference disk that comes with the system. For system models before 50, users can purchase the Advanced Diagnostics program separately.

For a general-purpose ST-506/412, ESDI, or IDE low-level format program, I recommend the Disk Manager program by Ontrack. For the ST-506/412 interface only, I recommend the IBM Advanced Diagnostics or the HDtest program by Jim Bracking, a user-supported product found on many electronic bulletin boards, including CompuServe. (These companies are listed in the vendor list at the back of this book.) For SCSI systems and systems on which the other recommended programs do not work, you normally use will the format program supplied with the SCSI host adapter.

Low-Level Format Software. There are several ways that a program can LLF (low-level format) a drive. The simplest way is to call the BIOS by using INT 13h functions such as the INT 13h, function 05h (Format Track) command. The BIOS then converts this command to what is called a CCB (Command Control Block) command: a block of bytes sent from the proper I/O ports directly to the disk controller. In this example, the BIOS would take INT 13h, 05h and convert it to a CCB 50h (Format Track) command, which would be sent through the Command Register Port (I/O address 1F7h for ST-506/412 or IDE). When the controller receives the CCB Format Track command, it may actually format the track or may simply fill the data areas of each sector on the track with a predetermined pattern.

The best way to LLF a drive is to bypass the ROM BIOS and send the CCB commands directly to the controller. Probably the greatest benefit in sending commands directly to the drive controller is being able to correctly flag defective sectors via the CCB Format Track command, including the capability to perform sector sparing. This is why IDE drives that are properly low-level formatted never show any bad sectors.

By using the CCB commands, you also gain the ability to read the Command Status and Error registers (which enable you to detect things such as ECC corrected data, which is masked by DOS INT 13h). You also can detect whether a sector was marked bad by the manufacturer or during a previous LLF and can maintain those marks in any subsequent Format Track commands, thereby preserving the defect list. I do not recommend unmarking a sector (returning it to "good" status), especially if the manufacturer previously marked it as bad.

When you use CCB commands, you can read and write sector(s) with automatic retries as well as ECC turned off. This capability is essential for any good surface analysis or LLF program, and this is why I recommend programs that use the CCB hardware interface rather than the DOS INT 13h interface.

Advanced Diagnostics Formatters. The standard low-level format program for IBM systems is the Advanced Diagnostics program. For IBM PS/2 Models 50 and higher, this formatting software is provided on the Reference disk included with the system. To get this software for other IBM PS/2 systems (lower than 50), you must purchase the hardware-maintenance service manuals, which cost several hundred dollars.

To access the Advanced Diagnostics portion of the Reference disk, press Ctrl-A (for Advanced) at the Reference disk main menu. The "secret" advanced diagnostics appear. IBM does not document this feature in the regular system documentation, because it does not want the average user wandering around in the software. The Ctrl-A procedure is documented in the service manuals.

The IBM PS/2 low-level format programs are excellent and are the only low-level format programs that you should use on these systems. Only the IBM-format tools know to find, use, and update the IBM-written defect map.

For standard IBM AT or IBM XT systems, the Advanced Diagnostics low-level format program is fine for formatting and testing hard disks; it has the standard features associated with this type of program. The AT version, however, does not allow an interleave setting of 1:1; this may not be a problem, but it renders the program useless if you upgrade to a controller that can handle a 1:1 interleave.

The IBM PC/XT version permits only a 6:1 interleave selection, which renders it useless on most IBM PC and IBM XT systems, because most controllers can handle between 2:1 and 5:1 interleaves. Using the IBM XT formatting program results in a very slow system. An additional problem with the IBM PC/XT version is that it does not permit the entry of the manufacturer's defect list—an unforgivable oversight that makes the IBM PC/XT low-level format program definitely *not* recommended. Fortunately, most PC- or XT-type system users use aftermarket autoconfigure-type controllers that come with a proper built-in ROM-based formatter.

IV

Ontrack Disk Manager. For AT-type systems and other systems with controllers that do not have an autoconfigure routine, the Disk Manager program from Ontrack is excellent. It probably is the most sophisticated hard disk format tool available and has many capabilities that make it a desirable addition to your toolbox.

Disk Manager is a true register-level format program that goes around the BIOS and manipulates the disk controller directly. This direct controller access gives it powerful capabilities that simply are not possible in programs that work through the BIOS.

Some of these advanced features include the capability to set head- and cylinder-skew factors. Disk Manager also can detect intermittent (soft) errors much better than most other programs can, because it can turn off the automatic retries that most controllers perform. The program also can tell when ECC (Error Correction Code) has been used to correct data, indicating that an error occurred, as well as directly manipulate the bytes that are used for ECC. Disk Manager has been written to handle most IDE drives and uses vendor-specific commands to unlock the capability to perform a true low-level format on IDE drives.

All these capabilities make Disk Manager one of the most powerful and capable LLF programs available. Ontrack also offers an excellent package of hard disk diagnostic and data-recovery utilities called DOS Utils. Anybody who has to support, maintain, troubleshoot, repair, or upgrade PCs needs a powerful disk formatter such as Disk Manager.

HDtest. HDtest is an excellent BIOS-level format program that will function on virtually any drive that has an INT 13h ROM BIOS interface, which includes most drives. HDtest does not have some of the capabilities of true register-level format programs, but it can be used when the additional capabilities of a register-level program are not required. For example, you can use this program to do a quick wipe of all the data on a drive, no matter what the interface or controller type is. HDtest also is good for BIOS-level read and write testing, and has proved to be especially useful in verifying the functions of disk interface BIOS code.

HDtest, by Jim Bracking, is a user-supported software program. This program is distributed through electronic bulletin boards and public-domain software libraries. You also can obtain the program from the Public Software Library, listed in Appendix B. It costs $35, but you can try it for free.

HDtest has an easy-to-use interface and pull-down menu system. The program offers all functions that normally are associated with a standard low-level format program, as well as some extras:

- Normal formatting
- Defect mapping
- Surface analysis
- Interleave test
- Nondestructive low-level reformat

■ Hard disk tests (duplicate of the IBM Advanced Diagnostics hard disk tests), including tests for drive seek, head selection, and error detection and correction, and well as a read/write/verify of the diagnostics cylinder. This program also can run low-level ROM BIOS commands to the controller.

HDtest includes most of what you would want in a generic low-level format program and hard disk diagnostics utility. Its real limitation is that it works only through the BIOS and cannot perform functions that a true register-level format program can. In some cases, the program cannot format a drive that a register-level program could format. Only register-level programs can perform defect mapping in most IDE and SCSI environments.

SCSI Low-Level Format Software. If you are using a SCSI drive, you must use the low-level format program provided by the manufacturer of the SCSI host adapter. The design of these devices varies enough that a register-level program can work only if it is tailored to the individual controller. Fortunately, all SCSI host adapters include such format software, either in the host adapter's BIOS or in a separate disk-based program.

The interface to the SCSI drive is through the host adapter. SCSI is a standard, but there are no true standards for what a host adapter is supposed to look like. This means that any formatting or configuration software will be specific to a particular host adapter. For example, IBM supplies formatting and defect-management software that works with the IBM PS/2 SCSI host adapters directly on the PS/2 Reference disk. That software performs everything that needs to be done to a SCSI hard disk connected to an IBM host adapter. IBM has defined a standard interface to its adapter through an INT 13h and INT 4Bh BIOS interface in a ROM installed on the card. The IBM adapters also include a special ABIOS (Advanced BIOS) interface that runs in the processor's protected mode of operation (for use under protected-mode operating systems such as OS/2).

Other SCSI host adapters often include the complete setup, configuration, and formatting software in the host adapter's on-board ROM BIOS. Most of these adapters also include an INT 13h interface in the BIOS. The best example is the Adaptec 1540/1542C adapters, which include software in ROM that completely configures the card and all attached SCSI devices.

Notice that SCSI format and configuration software is keyed to the host adapter and is not specific in any way to the particular SCSI hard disk drive that you are using.

IDE Low-Level Format Software. IDE drive manufacturers have defined extensions to the standard Western Digital 1002/1003 AT interface, which was further standardized for IDE drives as the CAM (Common Access Method) ATA (AT Adapter) interface. The CAM ATA specification provides for vendor-unique commands, which are manufacturer proprietary extensions to the standard. To prevent improper low-level formatting, many of these IDE drives have special codes that must be sent to the drive to unlock the format routines. These codes vary among manufacturers. If possible, you should obtain low-level format and defect-management software from the drive manufacturer; this software usually is specific to that manufacturer's products.

The custom nature of the ATA interface drives is the source of some myths about IDE. Many people say, for example, that you cannot perform a low-level format on an IDE drive, and that if you do, you will wreck the drive. This statement is untrue! What *can* happen is that in some drives, you may be able to set new head and sector skew factors that are not as optimal for the drive as the ones that the manufacturer set, and you also maybe able to overwrite the defect-map information. This situation is not good, but you still can use the drive with no problems, provided that you perform a proper surface analysis.

Most ATA IDE drives are protected from any alteration to the skew factors or defect map erasure because they are in a translated mode. Zoned Recording drives always are in translation mode and are fully protected. Most ATA drives have a custom command set that must be used in the format process; the standard format commands defined by the ATA specification usually do not work, especially with intelligent or Zoned Recording IDE drives. Without the proper manufacturer-specific format commands, you will not be able to perform the defect management by the manufacturer-specified method, in which bad sectors often can be spared.

Currently, the following manufacturers offer specific LLF and defect-management software for their own IDE drives:

- Seagate
- Western Digital
- Maxtor
- IBM

These utilities are available for downloading on the various BBSs run by these companies. The numbers appear in Appendix B.

Conner Peripherals drives are unique in that they cannot be low-level formatted through the standard interface; they must be formatted by a device that attaches to a special diagnostics and setup port on the drive. You see this device as a 12-pin connector on Conner drives. A company called TCE sells an inexpensive device that attaches your PC to this port through a serial port in your system, and includes special software that can perform sophisticated test, formatting, and surface-analysis operations. The product is called The Conner. (TCE is listed in Appendix B.)

For other drives, I recommend Disk Manager by Ontrack, as well as the MicroScope program by Micro 2000. These programs can format most IDE drives because they know the manufacturer-specific IDE format commands and routines. They also can perform defect-mapping and surface-analysis procedures.

Nondestructive Formatters. General-purpose, BIOS-level, nondestructive formatters such as Calibrate and SpinRite are not recommended in most situations for which a real low-level format (LLF) is required. These programs have several limitations and problems that limit their effectiveness; in some cases, they can even cause problems with the way defects are handled on a drive. These programs attempt to perform a track-by-track LLF by using BIOS functions, while backing up and restoring the track data as they go. These programs do not actually perform a complete LLF, because they do not even try to LLF the first track (Cylinder 0, Head 0) due to problems with some controller types that store hidden information on the first track.

These programs also do not perform defect mapping in the way that a standard LLF programs do, and they can even remove the carefully applied sector header defect marks applied during a proper LLF. This situation potentially allow data to be stored in sectors that originally were marked defective and may actually void the manufacturer's warranty on some drives. Another problem is that these programs work only on drives that are already formatted and can format only drives that are formattable through BIOS functions.

A true LLF program bypasses the system BIOS and send commands directly to the disk controller hardware. For this reason, many LLF programs are specific to the disk controller hardware for which they are designed. It is virtually impossible to have a single format program that will run on all different types of controllers. Many hard drives have been incorrectly diagnosed as being defective because the wrong format program was used and the program did not operate properly.

For example, I was helping somebody with an IBM PS/2 Model 30, which uses an 8-bit IDE interface 20MB drive. This drive was having serious problems reading and writing files. To start, CHKDSK showed about 40KB in bad sectors, and several programs would not load because they were corrupted. I could not copy files to the drive without getting Data error writing drive C: messages. Also, the system was having problems with booting; sometimes it would boot, and at other times it wouldn't, returning a Non-System disk or disk error message.

The owner first ran SpinRite II Version 2.0, using the deepest (level-4) pattern testing and formatting. This operation took an incredible 72 hours to complete, and it ended up marking more than 4MB of the drive as being bytes in bad sectors. SpinRite also indicated bad sectors in cylinders 00 and 01 in the FAT and root-directory areas. After SpinRite finished running, the drive owner tried running FDISK to repartition the drive from scratch, but FDISK crashed, displaying the error message No space to create a DOS partition. At this point, FDISK also had trashed the existing partition table. Fortunately, however, the owner was wise enough to have previously made a partition-table backup and stored it on a floppy disk with the MIRROR /PARTN command. The owner then recovered this partition table backup with the UNFORMAT /PARTN command, which reads the backup file from the floppy and uses it to restore the partition data.

At this point, even though SpinRite had marked out more than 4MB of the disk as being bad during a 72 hour test, the owner still could not load any additional software on the drive without getting write-error messages from DOS. At this point, many people would have considered the drive to be defective and replaced it with a new one. Fortunately, the owner did not do this; and called me instead!

I decided that we needed to low-level format the drive, and that this time, we would use a real LLF program that bypassed the BIOS routines and worked directly with the disk controller hardware registers.

IBM publishes a Hardware Maintenance Service package for the PS/2 Model 30 (about $60), which includes a troubleshooting pamphlet and a special Advanced Diagnostics disk. Notice that all Micro Channel-based PS/2 systems come with a free Advanced Diagnostics disk; for most of the ISA-bus systems, you have to purchase the disk separately. The IBM NSC BBS also makes many of these disks available free for the downloading (see Appendix B for the phone number), but the Model 30 disk was not available through the BBS.

Using the IBM Advanced Diagnostics, we ran an unconditional format and then a surface analysis; these operations together took less than an hour. During the surface analysis, only one sector was marked bad on the entire drive. After the format and surface analysis were complete, we ran FDISK (which worked perfectly this time) and, by accepting the defaults, partitioned the entire drive as a primary DOS partition and marked it as active. Then we formatted the drive with DOS 5, which picked up the sector flagged bad during the surface analysis and marked the cluster containing the flagged sector as bad in the FAT. When the DOS format was complete, we ran CHKDSK, and it showed only 2,048 bytes in bad sectors (equal to the single cluster marked bad in the FAT). The owner of the system then was able to reinstall all the software that had been on the drive with no problems or glitches, and the drive has been working flawlessly ever since!

The moral of this story (well, perhaps the most important part) is that you should not replace a hard disk unless you have tried to format it with a real register-level LLF program. I have little use for "partial" LLF programs and recommend that when a real format is needed, you use a program that works directly with the controller hardware registers. When in doubt, contact the manufacturer of the controller or drive; find out whether the manufacturer has something specific that you should use or can recommend something. If the manufacturer doesn't have its own special program, most controller and drive manufacturers recommend the Disk Manager program from Ontrack for real low-level formatting. I also highly recommend the Ontrack software (listed in Appendix B).

Drive Partitioning. *Partitioning* a hard disk is the act of defining areas of the disk for an operating system to use as a volume. To DOS, a volume is an area of a disk denoted as a drive letter; for example, drive C is volume C, drive D is volume D, and so on. Some people think that you have to partition a disk only if you are going to divide it into more than one volume. This is a misunderstanding; a disk must be partitioned even if it will be the single volume C.

When a disk is partitioned, a master partition boot sector is written at cylinder 0, head 0, sector 1—the first sector on the hard disk. This sector contains data that describes the partitions by their starting and ending cylinder, head, and sector locations. The partition table also indicates to the ROM BIOS which of the partitions is bootable and, therefore, where to look for an operating system to load. A single hard disk can have 1 to 24 partitions. This number includes all the hard drives installed in the system, which means that you can have as many as 24 separate hard disks with one partition each, a single hard disk with 24 partitions, or a combination of disks and partitions such that the total number of partitions is no more than 24. If you have more than 24 drives or partitions, DOS does not recognize them, although other operating systems may. What limits DOS is that a letter is used to name a volume, and the Roman alphabet ends with Z—the 24th volume, when you begin with C.

FDISK. The DOS FDISK program is the accepted standard for partitioning hard disks. Partitioning prepares the boot sector of the disk in such a way that the DOS FORMAT program can operate correctly; it also enables different operating systems to coexist on a single hard disk.

If a disk is set up with two or more partitions, FDISK shows only two total DOS partitions: the *primary partition* and the *extended partition*. The extended partition then is divided into *logical DOS volumes*, which are partitions themselves. FDISK gives a false impression of how the partitioning is done. FDISK reports that a disk divided as C, D, E, and F is set up as two partitions, with a primary partition having a volume designator of C and a single extended partition containing logical DOS volumes D, E, and F. But in the real structure of the disk, each logical DOS volume is a separate partition with an extended partition boot sector describing it. Each drive volume constitutes a separate partition on the disk, and the partitions point to one another in a daisy-chain arrangement.

Different versions of DOS have had different partitioning capabilities, as follows:

- DOS 1.x had no support whatsoever for hard disk drives.

- DOS 2.x was the first version to include hard disk support, including the capability to partition a drive as a single volume with a maximum partition size of 16MB. DOS versions 2.x support only 16MB-maximum partitions due to the limitations of the 12-bit FAT system. A 12-bit FAT can manage a maximum of only 4,096 total clusters on a disk.

  The limit of 16MB did not come from the FAT, but from the high-level DOS FORMAT command, which aborts with an `Invalid media` or `Track 0 bad - disk unusable` error message if the partition is larger than 16MB. On a disk that has no bad sectors beyond the first 16MB, you could ignore the error message and continue the setup of the disk with the SYS command. If the disk has defects beyond 16MB, those defects will not be properly marked in the FAT. Most vendors supplied modified high-level format programs that permitted partitions of up to 32MB to be formatted properly. Unfortunately, each cluster or minimum allocation unit on the disk then is 8,192 bytes (8KB) because of the 12-bit FAT.

- DOS 3.x increased the maximum partition and, therefore, volume size to 32MB but still could support only a single partition for DOS (assigned the C volume designator). The size limit is 32MB, due to the limit of 65,536 total sectors in a partition.

- DOS 3.3 introduced the concept of extended partitions, which enables DOS to see the drive as multiple volumes (drive letters). The extended partition's logical DOS volumes actually are partitions themselves. In the organization of the disk, the primary partition is assigned drive letter C, and the extended partitions are assigned letters sequentially from D through Z. Each drive letter (which is a volume or partition) can be assigned only as much as 32MB of disk space.

- DOS 4.x increased the size of a single DOS partition or volume to 2GB. FDISK was modified to allocate disk space in megabytes rather than in individual cylinders, as with previous versions of DOS. IBM DOS FDISK handled up to eight physical hard disk drives.

- DOS 5.x had no changes in partitioning capabilities, but MS-DOS now could universally handle up to eight physical hard drives. (IBM had this capability in IBM DOS 4.x.)

- DOS 6.x had no changes in partitioning capabilities, although both Microsoft and IBM added disk-compression software to DOS that created additional compressed volumes.

The minimum size for a partition in any version of DOS is one cylinder; however, FDISK in DOS 4 and later versions allocates partitions in megabytes, meaning that the minimum-size partition is 1MB. DOS 4.x and later versions permit individual partitions or volumes to be as large as 2GB, whereas versions of DOS earlier than 4.0 have a maximum partition size of 32MB.

The current DOS limits—8 physical hard disks with a maximum 24 total volumes between them, and up to 2GB per volume—do not seem to be too restrictive for most people

FDISK Undocumented Functions. FDISK is a very powerful program, and in DOS 5 and later versions, it gained some additional capabilities. Unfortunately, these capabilities were never documented in the DOS manual and remain undocumented even in DOS 6.x. The most important undocumented parameter in FDISK is the /MBR (Master Boot Record) parameter, which causes FDISK to rewrite the Master Boot Sector code area, leaving the partition tables intact. Beware: it will overwrite the partition tables if the two signature bytes at the end of the sector (55AAh) are damaged. This situation is highly unlikely, however. In fact, if these signature bytes were damaged, you would know; the system would not boot and would act as though there were no partitions at all.

The /MBR parameter seems to be tailor-made for eliminating boot-sector virus programs that infect the Master Partition Boot Sector (Cylinder 0, Head 0, Sector 1) of a hard disk. To use this feature, you simply enter

```
FDISK /MBR
```

FDISK then rewrites the boot sector code, leaving the partition tables intact. This should not cause any problems on a normally functioning system, but just in case, I recommend backing up the partition table information to floppy disk before trying it. You can do this with the following command:

```
MIRROR /PARTN
```

This procedure uses the MIRROR command to store partition-table information in a file called PARTNSAV.FIL, which should be stored on a floppy disk for safekeeping. To restore the complete partition-table information, including all the master and extended partition boot sectors, you would use the UNFORMAT command as follows:

```
UNFORMAT /PARTN
```

This procedure causes the UNFORMAT command to ask for the floppy disk containing the PARTNSAV.FIL file and then to restore that file to the hard disk.

FDISK also has three other undocumented parameters: /PRI:, /EXT:, and /LOG:. These parameters can be used to have FDISK create master and extended partitions, as well as logical DOS volumes in the extended partition, directly from the command line rather than through the FDISK menus. This feature was designed so that you can run FDISK in a batch file to partition drives automatically. Some system vendors probably use these parameters (if they know about them, that is!) when setting up systems on the production line. Other than that, these parameters have little use for a normal user, and in fact may be dangerous!

Other Partitioning Software. Since DOS 4 became available, there has been little need for aftermarket disk partitioning utilities, except in special cases. If a system is having problems that cause you to consider using a partitioning utility, I recommend that you upgrade to a newer version of DOS instead. Using nonstandard partitioning programs to partition your disk jeopardizes the data in the partitions and makes recovery of data lost in these partitions extremely difficult.

The reason why disk partitioning utilities other than FDISK even existed is that the maximum partition size in older DOS versions was restricted: 16MB for DOS 2.x and 32MB for DOS 3.x. These limits are bothersome for people whose hard disks are much larger than 32MB, because they must divide the hard disk into many partitions to use all the disk. Versions of DOS before 3.3 cannot even create more than a single DOS-accessible partition on a hard disk. If you have a 120MB hard disk and are using DOS 3.2 or an earlier version, you can access only 32MB of that disk as a C partition.

To overcome this limitation, several software companies created enhanced partitioning programs, which you can use rather than FDISK. These programs create multiple partitions and partitions larger than 32MB on a disk that DOS can recognize. These partitioning programs include a high-level format program, because the FORMAT program in DOS 3.3 and earlier versions can format partitions only up to 32MB.

Disk Manager by Ontrack, Speedstor by Storage Dimensions, and Vfeature Deluxe by Golden Bow are among the best-known of the partitioning utilities. These programs include low-level format capabilities, so you can use one of them as a single tool to set up a hard disk. The programs even include disk driver software that provides the capability to override the physical type selections in the system ROM BIOS, enabling a system to use all of a disk, even though the drive-type table in the system ROM BIOS does not have an entry that matches the hard disk.

Many drive vendors and integrators gave away these nonstandard partitioning and formatting programs, which makes some purchasers of such products feel that they must use those drivers to operate the drive. In most cases, however, better alternatives are available; nonstandard disk partitioning and formatting can cause more problems that it solves.

For example, Seagate shipped Ontrack Disk Manager with its drives larger than 32MB. One purpose of the program is to perform low-level formatting of the drive, which Disk Manager does well, and I recommend it highly for this function. If possible, however, you should avoid the partitioning and high-level formatting functions and stick with FDISK and FORMAT.

When you use a program other than standard FDISK and FORMAT to partition and high-level (DOS) format a drive, the drive is set up in a nonstandard way, different from pure DOS. This difference can cause trouble with utilities—including disk cache programs, disk test and interleave check programs, and data recovery or retrieval programs—written to function with a standard DOS disk structure. In many situations that a standard format would avoid, a nonstandard disk format can cause data loss and also can make data recovery impossible.

Caution

You should use only standard DOS FDISK and FORMAT to partition or high-level format your hard disks. If you use aftermarket partitioning software to create a nonstandard disk system, some programs that bypass DOS for disk access will not understand the disk properly and may write in the wrong place. Windows is an example of a program that bypasses DOS when you turn on the Use 32-bit Disk Access option in the Control Panel.

It is especially dangerous to use these partitioning programs to override your ROM BIOS disk-table settings. Consider the following disaster scenario.

Suppose that you have a Seagate ST-4096 hard disk, which has 1,024 cylinders and 9 heads, and requires that your controller never perform a data-write modification called *write precompensation* to cylinders of the disk. Some drives require this precompensation on the inner cylinders to compensate for the peak shifting that takes place because of the higher density of data on the (smaller) inner cylinders. The ST-4096 internally compensates for this effect and therefore needs no precompensation from the controller.

Now suppose that you install this drive in an IBM AT that does not have a ROM BIOS drive table that matches the drive. The best matching type you can select is type 18, which enables you to use only 977 cylinders and 7 heads—56.77MB of what should be a 76.5MB hard disk. If your IBM AT is one of the older ones with a ROM BIOS dated 01/10/84, the situation is worse, because its drive-table ends with type 14. In that case, you would have to select type 12 as the best match, giving you access to 855 cylinders and 7 heads, or only 49.68MB of a 76.5MB drive.

ROM BIOS drive tables are listed in Appendix A. Most IBM-compatibles have a more complete drive-type table and would have an exact table match for this drive, allowing you to use the full 76.5MB with no problems. In most compatibles with a Phoenix ROM BIOS, for example, you would select type 35, which would support the drive entirely.

Now suppose that you are not content with using only 50MB or 57MB of this 76.5MB drive. You invoke the SuperPartition aftermarket partitioning program that came with the drive and use it to low-level format the drive. Then you use the aftermarket program to override the type 18 or type 12 settings in the drive table. The program instructs you to set up a very small C partition (of only 1MB) and then partitions the remaining 75.5MB of the disk as D. This partitioning overrides the DOS 3.3 32MB partition limitation. (If you had an IBM-compatible system that did not require the drive-type override, you still would need to use the aftermarket partitioner to create partitions larger than the DOS 3.3 standard 32MB.) Following that, you use the partitioner to high-level format the C and D partitions, because the DOS high-level format in DOS 3.3 works only on volumes of 32MB or less.

Most aftermarket partitioners create a special driver file that they install in the CONFIG.SYS file through the DEVICE command. After the system boots from the C partition and loads the device driver, the 75.5MB D partition is completely accessible.

Along comes an innocent user of the system who always boots from her own DOS floppy disk. After booting from the floppy, she tries to log into the D partition. No matter what version of DOS this user boots from on the floppy disk, the D partition seems to have vanished. An attempt to log into that partition results in an Invalid drive specification error message. No standard version of DOS can recognize that specially created D partition if the device driver is not loaded.

An attempt by this user to recover data on this drive with a utility program such as Norton or PC Tools results in failure, because these programs interpret the drive as having 977 cylinders and 7 heads (type 18) or 855 cylinders and 7 heads (type 12). In fact, when these programs attempt to correct what seems to be partition-table damage, data will be corrupted in the vanished D partition.

Thinking that there may be a physical problem with the disk, the innocent user boots and runs the Advanced Diagnostics software to test the hard disk. Because Advanced Diagnostics incorporates its own special boot code and does not use standard DOS, it does not examine partitioning, but goes to the ROM BIOS drive-type table to determine the capacity of the hard disk. It sees the unit as having only 977 or 855 cylinders (indicated by the type 18 or 12 settings), as well as only 7 heads. The user then runs the Advanced Diagnostics hard disk tests, which use the last cylinder of the disk as a test cylinder for diagnostic read and write tests. This cylinder subsequently is overwritten by the diagnostics tests, which the drive passes because there is no physical problem with the drive.

This innocent user has just wiped out the D-drive data that happened to be on cylinder 976 in the type-18 setup or on cylinder 854 in the type-12 setup. Had the drive been partitioned by FDISK, the last cylinder indicated by the ROM BIOS drive table would have been left out of any partitions, being reserved so that diagnostics tests could be performed on the drive without damaging data.

Beyond the kind of disaster scenario just described, other potential problems can be caused by nonstandard disk partitioning and formatting, such as the following:

- Problems in using the 32-bit Disk Access feature provided by Windows, which bypasses the BIOS for faster disk access in 386 Enhanced Mode.

- Data loss by using OS/2, UNIX, XENIX, Novell Advanced NetWare, or other non-DOS operating systems that do not recognize the disk or the nonstandard partitions.

- Difficulty in upgrading a system from one DOS version to another.

- Difficulty in installing a different operating system, such as OS/2, on the hard disk.

- Data loss by using a low-level format utility to run an interleave test; the test area for the interleave test is the diagnostics cylinder, which contains data on disks formatted with Disk Manager.

- Data loss by accidentally deleting or overwriting the driver file and causing the D partition to disappear after the next boot.

- Data-recovery difficulty or failure because nonstandard partitions do not follow the rules and guidelines set by Microsoft and IBM, and no documentation on their structure exists. The sizes and locations of the FATs and root directory are not standard, and the detailed reference charts in this book (which are valid for an FDISK-created partition) are inaccurate for nonstandard partitions.

I could continue, but I think you get the idea. If these utility programs are used only for low-level formatting, they do not cause problems; it is the drive-type override, partitioning, and high-level format operations that cause difficulty. If you consider data integrity to be important, and you want to be able to perform data recovery, follow these disk support and partitioning rules:

- Every hard disk must be properly supported by system ROM BIOS, with no software overrides. If the system does not have a drive table that supports the full capacity of the drive, accept the table's limit, upgrade to a new ROM BIOS (preferably with a user-definable drive-type setting), or use a disk controller with an on-board ROM BIOS for drive support.

- Use only FDISK to partition a hard disk. If you want partitions larger than 32MB, use DOS 4 or a later version.

High-Level (Operating-System) Format. The final step in the software preparation of a hard disk is the DOS high-level format. The primary function of the high-level format is to create a FAT and a directory system on the disk so that DOS can manage files.

Usually, you perform the high-level format with the standard DOS FORMAT program, using the following syntax:

```
FORMAT C: /S /V
```

This step high-level formats drive C (or volume C, in a multivolume drive), places the hidden operating-system files in the first part of this partition, and prompts for the entry of a volume label to be stored on the disk at completion.

The high-level format program performs the following functions and procedures:

1. Scans the disk (read only) for tracks and sectors marked as bad during the low-level format, and notes these tracks as being unreadable.

2. Returns the drive heads to the first cylinder of the partition, and at that cylinder, head 1, sector 1, writes a DOS volume boot sector.

3. Writes a file allocation table (FAT) at head 1, sector 2. Immediately after this FAT, it writes a second copy of the FAT. These FATs essentially are blank except for bad-cluster marks noting areas of the disk that were found to be unreadable during the marked-defect scan.

4. Writes a blank root directory.

5. If the /S parameter is specified, copies the system files (IBMBIO.COM and IBMDOS.COM or IO.SYS and MSDOS.SYS, depending on which DOS you run) and COMMAND.COM files to the disk (in that order).

6. If the /V parameter is specified, prompts the user for a volume label, which is written as the fourth file entry in the root directory.

Now DOS can use the disk for storing and retrieving files, and the disk is a bootable disk.

During the first phase of the high-level format, a marked defect scan is performed. Defects marked by the low-level format operation show up during this scan as being unreadable tracks or sectors. When the high-level format encounters one of these areas, it automatically performs up to five retries to read these tracks or sectors. If the unreadable area was marked by the low-level format, the read fails on all attempts.

After five retries, the DOS FORMAT program gives up on this track or sector and moves to the next. Areas that remain unreadable after the initial read and the five retries are noted in the FAT as being bad clusters. DOS 3.3 and earlier versions can mark only entire tracks bad in the FAT, even if only one sector was marked in the low-level format. DOS 4 and later versions individually check each cluster on the track and recover clusters that do not involve the low-level format marked-bad sectors. Because most low-level format programs mark all the sectors on a track as bad, rather than the individual sector that contains the defect, the result of using DOS 3.3 or 4 is the same: all clusters involving sectors on that track are marked in the FAT as bad.

Note

Some low-level format programs mark only the individual sector that is bad on a track, rather than the entire track. This is true of the IBM PS/2 low-level formatters on the IBM PS/2 Advanced Diagnostics or Reference disk. In this case, high-level formatting with DOS 4 or later versions results in fewer lost bytes in bad sectors, because only the clusters that contain the marked bad sectors are marked bad in the FAT. DOS 4 and later versions display the `Attempting to recover allocation unit x` message (in which x is the number of the cluster) in an attempt to determine whether a single cluster or all the clusters on the track should be marked bad in the FAT.

If the controller and low-level format program together support sector and track sparing, the high-level format finds the entire disk defect-free, because all the defective sectors have been exchanged for spare good ones.

If a disk has been low-level formatted correctly, the number of bytes in bad sectors is the same before and after the high-level format. If the number does change after you repeat a high-level format (reporting fewer bytes or none), the low-level format was not done correctly. The manufacturer's defects were not marked correctly; or Norton, Mace, PC Tools, or a similar utility was used to mark defective clusters on the disk. The utilities cannot mark the sectors or tracks at the low-level format level; the bad-cluster marks that they make are stored only in the FAT and erased during the next high-level format operation. Defect marks made in the low-level format consistently show up as bad bytes in the high-level format, no matter how many times you run the format.

Only a low-level format or a surface-analysis tool can correctly mark defects on a disk; anything else makes only temporary bad-cluster marks in the FAT. This kind of marking may be acceptable temporarily, but when additional bad areas are found on a disk, you should run a new low-level format of the disk and either mark the area manually or run a surface analysis to place a more permanent mark on the disk.

Disk Hardware and Software Limitations

By studying the capabilities of the different disk interfaces as well as the ROM BIOS and operating systems, it is possible to determine the limits on disk storage. The following section details the limits under the different interfaces and operating systems.

Disk Interface Capacity Limitations

Different disk interfaces have different limitations on the theoretical maximum drive capacities that they may support. These limitations are due to variations in the way that each interface operates at the hardware level. It is important to note that even though a particular interface may permit access to a given amount of disk real estate, the BIOS and DOS usually are much more limiting and end up being the true limits for system disk capacity.

ST-506/412, ESDI, and IDE. To determine the capacity limits for the ST-506/412, ESDI, or IDE interface, you first need to determine the limits on the maximum number of cylinders, heads, and sectors per track. To do so, look at the size of the registers that hold this data in the controller. All these interfaces have the same controller register specifications, so the capacity limits calculated here apply to all of them. As you will see, the interface capacity limits are quite high. The drive parameter limits are as follows:

Cylinders (16 bits) = 65,536

Heads (4 bits) = 16

Sectors (8 bits) = 256

This calculates to a maximum theoretical drive size of:

65,536 Cyls × 16 Hds × 256 Secs × 512 Bytes = 137,438,953,472 Bytes (128GB)

Unfortunately, the maximum capacity—128GB—is limited by the BIOS. There are two different BIOS types with regards to disk size limitations. The standard BIOS built into most systems is limited to 1,024 cylinders, 16 heads, and 63 sectors per track. If the BIOS is an enhanced version, it will be limited to 1,024 cylinders, 256 heads, and 63 sectors per track. Combining the BIOS and interface limits results in the following maximum capacities (assuming 512-byte sectors):

Limit w/ Std. BIOS: 1,024 Cyls × 16 Hds × 63 Secs = 528,482,304 Bytes (504MB)

Limit w/ Enh. BIOS: 1,024 Cyls × 256 Hds × 63 Secs = 8,455,716,864 Bytes (7.88GB)

If you do not have enhanced BIOS support on your motherboard, then you could add an IDE bus adapter that has an on-board enhanced BIOS. To get around such BIOS problems, some IDE drive implementations over 528 million bytes split the drive to act as two physical units. In this case, the drive would appear on the IDE bus connector as being both master and slave, and could be used only as two 504MB-maximum-size drives.

SCSI. According to the SCSI specification, drives are not addressed by cylinders, heads, and sectors but instead by what is called a Logical Block Address (LBA). This is a sector number, in which all the sectors on the drive are numbered sequentially from start to finish. The LBA is specified by a 32-bit number an with 512-byte sectors, results in the following limitation:

4,294,967,296 LBAs (sectors) × 512 Bytes = 2,199,023,255,552 Bytes (2,048GB or 2 terabytes)

As you can see, SCSI drive capacity limits are extremely high. However, because the SCSI drive must appear to the BIOS as being a given number of cylinders, heads, and sectors per track, the BIOS limits SCSI capacity. Virtually all SCSI adapters have an enhanced BIOS that supports a maximum drive capacity as follows (assuming 512-byte sectors):

SCSI w/ Enh. BIOS: 1,024 Cyls × 256 Hds × 63 Secs = 8,455,716,864 Bytes (7.88GB)

If you do not have enhanced BIOS support in your SCSI adapter or motherboard, in some cases, you can load an external driver for your adapter to provide this support.

Most systems support up to 4 SCSI host adapters, each with up to 7 hard disk drives, for a total 28 physically installed drives.

ROM BIOS Capacity Limitations

In addition to the capacity limit of 504MB, the standard ROM BIOS is limited to supporting only two hard disk drives. The enhanced BIOS is limited to 128 drives maximum. Most SCSI and IDE adapters get around the two-drive standard BIOS limits by incorporating an enhanced BIOS on board that takes over the disk interface.

Operating-System Capacity Limitations

IBM and Microsoft officially say that DOS 5 and later versions will support up to eight physical hard disks. IBM says that OS/2 1.30.1 and later versions (including 2.x) support up to 24 physical hard disks, and because OS/2 includes DOS, that implies that DOS under OS/2 would support 24 physical drives as well. OS/2 HPFS (High Performance File System) also supports a maximum partition size of 8GB and a maximum single-file size of 2GB, whereas DOS and OS/2 FAT partitions have a maximum size of 2GB and a maximum single-file size of 2GB also. As you have seen, BIOS limitations currently limit the maximum physical hard disk size to about 7.88GB (or about 8.46 million bytes).

Doublespace Capacity Limitations. The current version of Microsoft's Doublespace disk-compression software limits the maximum size of a compressed volume to 512MB. Because a nearly 2:1 compression ratio is achieved, you should not use Doublespace to compress a drive larger than 256MB. The Doublespace compressed volume actually exists as a hidden file on your regular hard disk. Doublespace maintains its own FAT and directory structure within the hidden volume, making data recovery of any file inside one of these volumes difficult, if not impossible.

I do not use Doublespace myself and generally recommend against using most forms of data compression at the software level, with the possible exception of using the shareware PKZIP program to compress (zip) files that are not used often. In my opinion, the only reliable data compression is that which is built in to the hardware and is transparent. With hard disk real estate costing only $1 per megabyte, I find it much more cost-effective to purchase more disk real estate than to purchase and use clumsy, slow, and often dangerous software-compression schemes. About the only situation in which I would recommend using Doublespace (or anything like it) is for a laptop system for which larger hard disks might be unavailable. If you must use some form of compression, I recommend Stacker by Stac Electronics, which seems to be the most reliable and time-tested compression program on the market. The company also has an OS/2 version that Doublespace does not support.

Disk compression eventually will be built right into the hardware. Already, there are tape drives that offer built-in disk-compression hardware. When it is implemented in this fashion, the compression is totally transparent to any applications or operating software.

No funny drivers or special programs are required; the device simply stores more information transparently. Eventually, these compression chips will be implemented in hard disks. Until then, be careful when you use any of the software-compression schemes; they can be troublesome, and problems often result in lost data.

Hard Disk Drive Troubleshooting and Repair

If a hard disk drive has a problem inside its sealed HDA (Head Disk Assembly), repairing the drive usually is not feasible. If the failure is in the logic board, you can replace that assembly with a new or rebuilt assembly easily and at a much lower cost than replacing the entire drive.

Most hard disk problems really are not hardware problems; instead, they are *soft problems* that can be solved by a new low-level format and defect-mapping session. Soft problems are characterized by a drive that sounds normal but produces various read and write errors.

Hard problems are mechanical, such as when the drive sounds as though it contains loose marbles. Constant scraping and grinding noises from the drive, with no reading or writing capability, also qualify as hard errors. In these cases, it is unlikely that a low-level format will put the drive back into service. If a hardware problem is indicated, first replace the logic-board assembly. You can make this repair yourself, and if successful, you can recover the data from the drive.

If replacing the logic assembly does not solve the problem, contact the manufacturer or a specialized repair shop that has clean-room facilities for hard disk repair. (See Appendix B for drive manufacturers and companies that specialize in hard disk drive repair.)

The cost of HDA repair may be more than half the cost of a new drive, so you may want to consider replacing rather than repairing the drive. If the failed drive is an inexpensive 20MB or 30MB stepper motor drive, the better option is to purchase something better. If the drive is a larger, voice coil drive, however, it usually is more economical to repair the drive rather than replace it, because the replacement cost is much higher.

17xx, 104xx, and 210xxxx Hardware Error Codes

When a failure occurs in the hard disk subsystem at power-on, the Power-On Self Test (POST) finds the problem and reports it with an error message. The 17xx, 104xx, and 210xxxx errors during the POST or while running the Advanced Diagnostics indicate problems with hard disks, controllers, or cables. The 17xx codes apply to ST-506/412 interface drives and controllers; 104xx errors apply to ESDI drives and controllers; and 210xxxx errors apply to SCSI drives and host adapters.

Table 14.43 shows a breakdown of these error messages and their meanings.

Table 14.43   Hard Disk and Controller Diagnostic Error Codes

ST-506/412 Drive and Controller Error Codes

1701	Fixed disk general POST error
1702	Drive/controller time-out error
1703	Drive seek error
1704	Controller failed
1705	Drive sector not found error
1706	Write fault error
1707	Drive track 0 error
1708	Head select error
1709	Error Correction Code (ECC) error
1710	Sector buffer overrun
1711	Bad address mark
1712	Internal controller diagnostics failure
1713	Data compare error
1714	Drive not ready
1715	Track 0 indicator failure
1716	Diagnostics cylinder errors
1717	Surface read errors
1718	Hard drive type error
1720	Bad diagnostics cylinder
1726	Data compare error
1730	Controller error
1731	Controller error
1732	Controller error
1733	BIOS undefined error return
1735	Bad command error
1736	Data corrected error
1737	Bad track error
1738	Bad sector error
1739	Bad initialization error
1740	Bad sense error
1750	Drive verify failure
1751	Drive read failure
1752	Drive write failure
1753	Drive random read test failure
1754	Drive seek test failure
1755	Controller failure
1756	Controller Error Correction Code (ECC) test failure
1757	Controller head select failure

(continues)

Table 14.43   Continued

ST-506/412 Drive and Controller Error Codes

1780	Seek failure; drive 0
1781	Seek failure; drive 1
1782	Controller test failure
1790	Diagnostic cylinder read error; drive 0
1791	Diagnostic cylinder read error; drive 1

ESDI Drive and Controller Error Codes

10450	Read/write test failed
10451	Read verify test failed
10452	Seek test failed
10453	Wrong device type indicated
10454	Controller test failed sector buffer test
10455	Controller failure
10456	Controller diagnostic command failure
10461	Drive format error
10462	Controller head select error
10463	Drive read/write sector error
10464	Drive primary defect map unreadable
10465	Controller; Error Correction Code (ECC) 8-bit error
10466	Controller; Error Correction Code (ECC) 9-bit error
10467	Drive soft seek error
10468	Drive hard seek error
10469	Drive soft seek error count exceeded
10470	Controller attachment diagnostic error
10471	Controller wrap mode interface error
10472	Controller wrap mode drive select error
10473	Read verify test errors
10480	Seek failure; drive 0
10481	Seek failure; drive 1
10482	Controller transfer acknowledge error
10483	Controller reset failure
10484	Controller; head select 3 error
10485	Controller; head select 2 error
10486	Controller; head select 1 error
10487	Controller; head select 0 error
10488	Controller; read gate - command complete 2 error
10489	Controller; write gate - command complete 1 error
10490	Diagnostic area read error; drive 0
10491	Diagnostic area read error; drive 1
10499	Controller failure

SCSI Drive and Host Adapter Error Codes	
096xxxx	SCSI adapter with cache (32-bit) errors
112xxxx	SCSI adapter (16-bit without cache) errors
113xxxx	System board SCSI adapter (16-bit) errors
210xxxx	SCSI fixed disk errors

The first x in xxxx is the SCSI ID number.
The second x in xxxx is the logical unit number (usually, 0).
The third x in xxxx is the host adapter slot number.
The fourth x in xxxx is a letter code indicating drive capacity.
A list of all IBM SCSI error codes appears in Appendix A.

Most of the time, a seek failure indicates that the drive is not responding to the controller. This failure usually is caused by one of the following problems:

- Incorrect drive-select jumper setting
- Loose, damaged, or backward control cable
- Loose or bad power cable
- Stiction between drive heads and platters
- Bad power supply

If a diagnostics cylinder read error occurs, the most likely problems are these:

- Incorrect drive-type setting
- Loose, damaged, or backward data cable
- Temperature-induced mistracking

The methods for correcting most of these problems are obvious. If the drive-select jumper setting is incorrect, for example, correct it. If a cable is loose, tighten it. If the power supply is bad, replace it. You get the idea.

If the problem is temperature-related, the drive usually will read data acceptably at the same temperature at which it was written. Let the drive warm up for a while and then attempt to reboot it, or let the drive cool and reread the disk if the drive has overheated.

The stiction problem may not have an obvious solution; the next section addresses this problem.

Drive Spin Failure (Stiction)

Other than a faulty power-supply cable connection or a faulty power supply, stiction is the primary cause of a hard disk drive's failure to spin. *Stiction* (static friction) is a condition in which the drive heads are stuck to the platters in such a way that the platter motor cannot overcome the sticking force and spin the drive up for operation. This situation happens more frequently than you might imagine.

The heads stick to the platters in the same way that two very smooth pieces of glass might stick together. The problem is especially noticeable if the drive has been off for a week or more. It also seems to be more noticeable if the drive is operated under very hot conditions and then shut down. In the latter case, the excessive heat buildup in the drive softens the lubricant coating on the platter surface; after the drive is powered off, the platters cool rapidly and contract around the heads, which have settled in this lubricant coating. Drives that have more platters and heads are more susceptible to this problem than are drives that have fewer platters and heads.

To solve this problem, you must spin the platters with enough force to rip the heads loose from the platters. Usually, you accomplish this by twisting the drive violently in the same plane as the platters, using the platter's inertia to overcome the sticking force. The heavy platters tend to remain stationary while you twist the drive and essentially make the heads move around the platters.

Another technique is to spin the spindle motor manually, which rotates the platters inside the drive. To do this, you may have to remove the circuit board from the bottom of the drive to get to the spindle motor. In other cases, you can insert a thin wooden stick into the gap between the bottom of the drive and the circuit board, and push on the spindle motor drum with the stick. You probably will feel heavy resistance to rotation; then the platters will suddenly move free as the heads are unstuck.

Many drives today have spindle motors located inside the platter hub area, which is totally enclosed within the HDA. You will not be able to spin these platters by hand unless you open the HDA, which is recommended only in situations in which nothing else has worked. In most cases, simply twisting the entire drive in the same plane as the platters uses the inertia of the platters to jerk the heads free from their stuck position.

Another problem that can cause the appearance of stiction is a stuck spindle motor (platter) brake. Many drives use a solenoid actuated spindle motor brake to rapidly stop the platters when the drive is powered off (see fig. 14.23). This brake is designed to minimize the distance that the heads skid on the platter surface when the drive is powered down. When the brake solenoid fails, it does not release the spindle motor and can produce the same symptoms as stiction.

Because this device almost always is outside the HDA, you can easily remove if it fails, allowing the drive to spin freely. Because every drive is designed differently, consult the drive manual to see whether your drive has such a spindle braking system and where it is located. Of course, long-term reliability may be affected, because the heads will skid for a much longer distance every time the drive is powered off, accelerating wear of the heads and media.

After you free the platters, reapply the power; the drive should spin up normally. I have used these methods to solve stiction problems many times and have never lost data as long as I could get the drive to spin. If you cannot make the drive spin, you certainly will not be able to recover any data from it. Notice that most drive failures occur in the logic board, which also contains motor control circuits in most drives. This means that a no-spin situation can be caused by a defective logic board. Unless you have a spare drive with the same type of logic board to swap with, it is difficult to know whether the logic board is truly at fault.

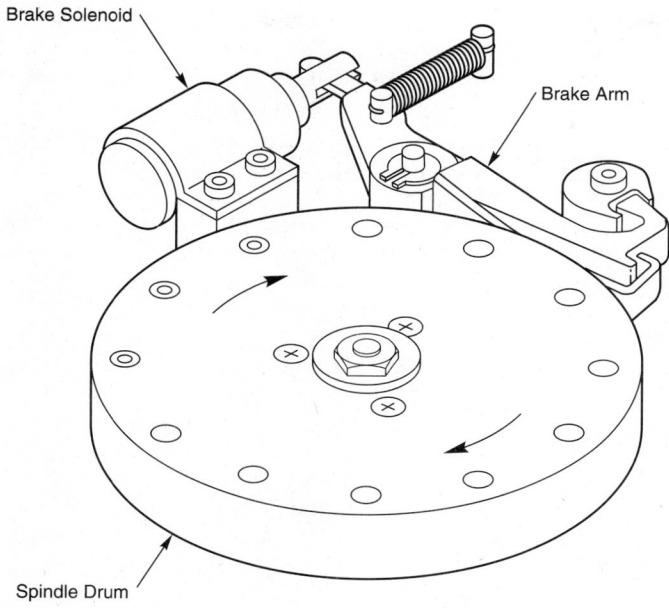

Fig. 14.23

A typical spindle motor solenoid and brake assembly.

Some drive manufacturers and repair depots sell logic boards individually, but I usually find it easier simply to purchase another (duplicate) entire drive. It is often cheaper to purchase a used drive exactly like the one that failed than to buy a single part, such as a logic board. You then can cannibalize the used drive for parts that can restore the failed drive to operation. This is not designed to be a cost-effective way to repair a drive, but it will allow you to possibly recover the data from the failed drive, which usually is worth much more than the drive itself. Most good data-recovery operations have a variety of functioning used drives available to be cannibalized for parts in recovering data from failed drives.

In some cases, I have had to open the HDA to forcibly spin the platters by hand so as to recover data. In many cases, this worked to free the platters and start the drive operation, after which I was able to close the HDA and back up all the data on the drive. If you are nervous about handling your drive in this manner, consult a professional drive repair facility.

I know that the impression that everybody normally has is that opening a drive will destroy or damage it in some way (head crash?), especially considering the extremely close proximity between the heads and the disk platters. I can say from experience, however, that most hard drives are much sturdier than people think. I have not only opened many functioning hard drives, but also operated them for extended periods while they were exposed in this manner, all the while reliably reading and writing data. In fact, I have several drives that I regularly use in my PC Hardware/Troubleshooting and Data Recovery seminars; I have been operating these drives with the lids off practically every week for several years now, with no lost data. Even more amazing is the fact that I often use the drives to perform torture demonstrations, in which I literally bend the HDA with my bare hands while the drive is reading files. This procedure instantly causes the file-read operation to fail (`Abort`, `Retry`, `Ignore`) due to the heads being forced away from their proper track positions. When I release the bending force, the heads return to normal track position, and the files can be read with no problem!

Although I use these seminar demonstrations to get people's attention, these lid-off techniques have helped me at times in extreme data-recovery situations. Of course, I am obligated to give you the standard "Don't try this at home" warning!

Logic Board Failures

A disk drive, including a hard disk drive, has one or more logic boards mounted on it. These boards contain the electronics that control the drive's spindle and head actuator systems and that present data to the controller. Some drives have built-in controllers.

Logic boards on hard disks fail more often than the mechanical components do. Most professional data-recovery companies stock a number of functional logic boards for popular drives. When a drive comes in for recovery, data-recovery professionals check the drive for problems such as installation or configuration errors, temperature mistracking, and stiction. If these situations are not the problem, the technicians replace the logic board on the drive with a known good unit. Often, the drive then works normally, and data can be read from it.

The logic boards on most hard disks can be removed and replaced easily; they simply plug into the drive and usually are mounted with standard screw hardware. If a drive is failing, and you have a spare of the same type, you may be able to verify a logic-board failure by removing the board from a known good drive and mounting it on the bad one. Then, if your suspicions are confirmed, in some cases you can order a new logic board from the drive's manufacturer. Be prepared for sticker shock; parts like this may cost more than replacing the entire drive with a new or refurbished unit.

A less-expensive option is buying a refurbished unit or trading in the old board (The drive manufacturer will have details on these options.) Purchasing a new logic board may not always be cost-effective, but borrowing one from a drive that works is one of the only ways to verify that the logic board has failed, and it may be the only way to recover all the data from the problem drive.

Summary

This chapter examined hard disks and controllers, and explored the physical and logical operations of the hard disk. You learned about configuring, installing, and troubleshooting hard disks and controllers. Now you can use this information to upgrade an existing system with a new hard disk or to troubleshoot and repair an existing configuration. A properly designed and installed hard disk system will give you fewer problems than a haphazardly installed system will. Most problems are related to software, installation, or formatting, so you can use the information in this chapter to restore many failing drives to normal operation.

The next chapter continues your tour through storage systems, focusing on CD-ROM drives.

Chapter 15

CD-ROM Drives

This chapter explains the technology behind CD-ROM drives and their storage technology, delineates the various recording formats used on PC CD-ROMs, and examines the performance characteristics of the typical CD-ROM drive. After showing you the process of selecting a good drive for a system upgrade, the chapter guides you through the installation of the CD-ROM interface card, the drive itself, and the software that must be added to your PC for the drive to communicate with the system.

What Is CD-ROM?

Within minutes of inserting a compact disc into your computer, you have access to information that might have taken you days, or even weeks, to find a few short years ago. Science, medicine, law, business profiles, and educational materials—every conceivable form of human endeavor or pursuit of knowledge—are making their way to aluminum-coated, five-inch plastic data discs called *CD-ROMs*, or *compact disc read-only memory*.

> **Note**
>
> The CD-ROM (compact disc read-only memory) is a read-only optical storage medium capable of holding 660 megabytes of data (approximately 500,000 pages of text), about 70 minutes of high-fidelity audio, or some combination of the two. The CD-ROM is very similar to the familiar audio compact disc, and can, in fact, play in a normal audio player. The result is noise unless audio accompanies the data on the CD-ROM. Accessing data from a CD-ROM is somewhat faster than from a floppy disk, but considerably slower than a modern hard drive. The term CD-ROM refers to both the discs themselves and the drive that reads them.

Although only dozens of CD-ROM discs, or titles, were published for personal computer users in all of 1988, the Software Publishers Association predicts that in 1994 publishers will offer over 4,800 individual titles, containing data and programs ranging from world-wide agricultural statistics to preschool learning games. Individual businesses, local and federal government offices, and small businesses also will publish thousands of their own limited-use titles.

CD-ROM, a Brief History

In 1978, the Philips and Sony Corporations joined forces to produce the current audio CD. Philips had already developed commercial laser-disc players, whereas Sony had a decade of digital recording research under its belt. The two companies were poised for a battle—the introduction of potentially incompatible audio laser disc formats—when they came to terms on a agreement to formulate a single audio technology.

Sony pushed for a 12-inch platter. Philips wanted to investigate smaller sizes, especially when it became clear that they could pack an astonishing 12 hours of music on the 12-inch discs.

By 1982, the companies announced the standard, which included the specifications for recording, sampling, and—above all—the five-inch format we live with today. To be specific, the discs are a full 12-centimeters in diameter. This size was chosen, legend has it, because it could contain Beethoven's Ninth Symphony.

With the continued cooperation of Sony and Philips through the 1980s, additional specifications were announced concerning the use of CD technology for computer data. These recommendations evolved into the computer CD-ROM drives in use today. Where once engineers struggled to find the perfect fit between disc form factor and the greatest symphony ever recorded, software developers and publishers are cramming these little discs with the world's information.

CD Technology

Although identical in appearance to audio CDs, computer CDs store data in addition to audio. The CD drives that read the data discs when attached to PCs also bear a strong resemblance to an audio CD player. How you must handle the CDs—insert them into the CD drive and eject them when finished—are all familiar to anyone who has used an audio CD. Both forms of CD operate on the same general mechanical principles.

The disc itself, nearly five inches in diameter, is made of a polycarbonate wafer. This wafer base is coated with a metallic film, usually an aluminum alloy. The aluminum film is the portion of the disc that the CD-ROM drive reads for information. The aluminum film or strata is then covered by plastic coating that protects the underlying data.

> **Note**
>
> CD-ROM media should be handled with the same care afforded a photographic negative. The CD-ROM is an optical device and degrades as its optical surface becomes dirty or scratched. If your drive uses a "caddy"—a container for the disc that does not require handling the disc itself—you should purchase a sufficient supply of these to reduce disc handling.

Mass-Producing CD-ROMs

Although a laser is used to etch data onto a master disc, this technique would be impractical for the reproduction of hundreds or thousands of copies. Each production of a master disc can take over one-half hour to encode. In addition, these master discs are made of materials that aren't durable enough for continued or prolonged use. In fact, unless you are using a CD-R (CD-Recordable) or CD-WO (CD-Write Once) for mastering discs or storing data, the material used for master CD discs is made of glass. Only the CD-R and CD-WO drives use metal-coated discs for making masters or writing data.

For limited run productions of CDs, an original master is coated with metal in a process similar to electroplating. After the metal is formed and separated from the master, the metal imprint of the original can be used to stamp copies, not unlike the reproduction of vinyl records. This process works effectively for small quantities—eventually the stamp wears out.

To produce a large volume of discs, the following three-step process is employed:

1. The master is, once again, plated and a stamp is produced.

2. This stamp is used to create a duplicate master, made of a more resilient metal.

3. The duplicate master can then be used to produce numerous stamps.

This technique allows a great many production stamps to be made from the duplicate master, preserving the original integrity of the first encoding. It also allows for the mass production to be made from inexpensive materials. The CDs you buy are coated with aluminum after they are stamped into polycarbonate, and then protected with a thin layer of plastic. The thin, aluminum layer coating the etched pits, as well as the smooth surfaces, enables the reading laser to determine the presence or absence of strongly reflected light, as described below.

This mass manufacturing process is identical for both data and audio CDs.

Reading the information back is a matter of reflecting a lower-powered laser off the aluminum strata. A receiver or light receptor notes where light is strongly reflected or where it is absent or diffused. Diffused or absent light is caused by the recorded pits in the CD. Strong reflection of the light indicates no pit—this is called a "land." The light receptors within the player collect the reflected and diffused light as it is refracted from the surface. As the light sources are collected from the refraction, they are passed along to microprocessors that translate the light patterns back into data or sound. The spiral of CD data is nearly three miles long.

When a CD—audio or data—seeks out a bit of data on the disc, it looks up the address of the data from a table of contents and positions itself near the beginning of this data across the spiral, waiting for the right string of bits to flow past the laser beam.

Inside Data CDs

The microprocessor that decodes the electrical impulses is the key difference between music and data compact players. Audio CDs can contain many differing degrees of light diffusion depending on how long a particular pit is stretched across the strata. These variations of diffusion carry important information for the reproduction of the original signal. Data encoding, however, based on the computer's native language of binary encoding, must be recorded strictly as the presence or absence of a signal.

CD-ROM drives operate in the following manner:

1. The laser diode emits a low-energy beam toward a reflecting mirror (see fig. 15.1).

2. The servo motor, on command from the microprocessor, positions the beam onto the correct track on the CD-ROM by moving the reflecting mirror.

3. When the beam hits the disc, its refracted light is gathered and focused through the first lens beneath the platter, bounced off the mirror, and sent toward the beam splitter.

4. The beam splitter directs the returning laser light toward another focusing lens.

5. The last lens directs the light beam to a photodetector that converts the light into electric impulses.

6. These incoming impulses are decoded by the microprocessor and sent along to the host computer as data.

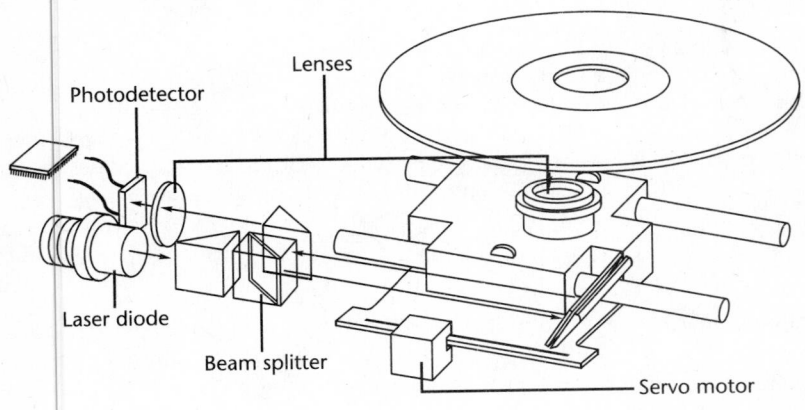

Fig. 15.1
Inside a CD-ROM drive.

Although the simplicity of data or binary language seems to imply that a data CD optical reader would need to be less sensitive to incoming signals, this is not the case. Because the encoding pits are uniform in size, the presence or absence of the pitting must be measured precisely, thereby signaling the 1 or 0 of binary code. Even one misreading of the space or pit would cause the entire data file to lose integrity, or become useless. Therefore, the tracking mechanisms—the motor that moves the laser beam across the surface and the receptors of the refracted light—must be more tightly integrated with each other and more accurate in reading the recording surface.

In the case of an audio CD, missing data can be *interpolated*—that is, the information follows a predictable pattern that allows the missing value to be guessed at. For example, if three values are stored on an audio disc, say 10, 13, and 20 appearing in a series, and the middle value is missing—due to damage or dirt on the CD's surface—you can interpolate a middle value of 15, which is midway between the 10 and 20 values. Although this is not exactly correct, in the case of audio recording it will not be noticeable to the listener. If those same three values appear on a CD-ROM in an executable program, there is no way to guess at the correct value for the middle sample. Interpolation cannot work on a CD-ROM because executable program data follows no natural law since the data is a series of values. To guess 15 in this situation is not just slightly off, it is completely wrong.

Because of the need for such precision, CD-ROM drives for use on PCs were later to market than their audio counterparts. When first introduced, CD-ROM drives were too expensive for widespread adoption. In addition, drive manufacturers were slow in adopting standards, causing a lag time for the production of CD-ROM titles. Without a wide base of software to drive the industry, acceptance was slow.

What Types of Drives Are Available?

When purchasing a CD-ROM drive for your PC, consider three distinct sets of attributes of CD-ROM drives, as follows:

- The drive's specifications.

- The interface it requires for connection to your PC.

- The format or formats it is capable of reading.

The variance in any of these categories is enormous; in fact, single vendors offer entire lines of drives that vary in performance specifications, format reading capability, and type of adapters that can interface with your PC. For these reasons, drive prices vary widely. First-generation CD-DA (Digital Audio) drives, for example, are available for as little as $190. You'll probably be disappointed in the drive's performance and capabilities, however, and would be better off looking elsewhere. So before you buy, know the drive's characteristics.

All three drive characteristics are discussed in this section, giving you a better understanding of what type of drive you need to buy.

CD-ROM Drive Specifications

Drive specifications tell you the drive's performance capabilities. If you're shopping for a sports car, for instance, and the dealer tells you the car can accelerate from a standing stop to 60 miles per hour in six seconds, you know you've got a hot car. The car's horsepower, displacement in liters, and number of cylinders and valves are also specifications you use to determine how fast it is.

CD-ROM drive specifications tell the shopper much the same thing. Typical performance figures published by manufacturers are the data transfer rate, access time, internal buffers (if any), and the interface used.

Data Transfer Rate. The data transfer rate tells you how much data the drive can read from a data CD and transfer to the host computer when reading one large, sequential chunk of data. The standard measurement in the industry is kilobytes per second, usually abbreviated as kb/s. If a manufacturer claims a drive can transfer data at 120 kb/s, it means that a drive reading a sequential stream of data from the CD will achieve 120 kilobytes a second after it has come up to speed. Note this is a sustained and sequential read, not access across the data disc from different portions of the platter. Obviously, the data transfer specification is meant to convey the drive's peak data reading capabilities. A higher rate of transfer might be better, but a number of other factors come into play.

First, a higher transfer rate might not be useful if the software accessing the data or the PC using the data do not need the information in such high volume. In addition, the drive's host adapter, which connects it to the PC, may not be capable of fast data transfers either.

Most 16-bit adapters and today's PCs are more than up to the task, however. If you expect to run a variety of CD-based software on your system, you need a drive with a high data transfer rate. Applications that employ full-motion video, animation, and sound require high transfer rates, and you'll be disappointed with the results of a slower drive. (Recommended transfer rate minimum: 150 kb/s.)

Access Time. A CD-ROM drive's access time is measured the same way as for PC hard drives. In other words, the access time is the delay between the drive receiving the command to read and its actual first reading of a bit of data. The time is recorded in milliseconds; a typical manufacturer's rating would be listed as 350 ms. This is an average access rate; the true access rate depends entirely on where the data is located on the disc. Positioning the read mechanism to a portion of the disc near the narrower center of the disc gives you a faster access rate than positioning it at the wider outer perimeter. Access rates quoted by many manufacturers are an average taken by calculating a series of random reads from a disc.

Obviously, a faster average access rate is desirable, especially when you are relying on the drive to locate and pull up data quickly. Access times for CD-ROM drives are steadily improving, and the advancements are discussed later in this chapter. Note that these average times are significantly slower than PC hard drives, ranging from 500 to 200 milliseconds when compared to 20 milliseconds found on your typical hard disk. Most of the speed difference lies in the construction of the drive itself; hard drives have multiple read heads and range over a smaller surface area of media. CD-ROM drives have only one laser read beam, and it must be positioned over the entire range of the disc. In addition, the data on a CD is organized in a long spiral from outer edge inward. When the drive positions its head to read a "track," it must estimate the distance into the disc and skip forward or backward to the appropriate point in the spiral. Reading off the outer edge requires a longer access time than the inner segments. (Recommended access time: 350 ms or better.)

Buffers. Some drives are shipped with internal buffers or caches of memory installed on-board. These buffers are actual memory chips installed on the drive's board, and they allow data to be staged or stored in larger segments before it is sent to the PC. A typical buffer for a CD-ROM drive is 64 kilobytes or KB. Having buffer memory on the CD-ROM drive offers a number of advantages. Buffers can ensure that the PC receives data at a constant rate; when an application requests data from the CD-ROM disc, the data is probably scattered across different segments of the disc. Because the drive has a relatively slow access time, the pauses between data reads can cause a drive to send data to the PC sporadically. You might not notice this in typical text applications, but a slower access rate drive coupled with no data buffering is very noticeable, even irritating, in the display of video or some audio segments. In addition, a drive's buffer, when under control of sophisticated software, can read and have ready the disc's table of contents, making the first request for data faster to find on the disc platter. (Recommended buffer: 64 KB or better.)

Interface

A CD-ROM's interface is the physical connection of the drive to the PC's expansion bus. The interface is the pipeline of data from the drive to the computer, and its importance shouldn't be minimized. Early 8-bit adapter interfaces compounded CD-ROM drive performance problems, making access to significant blocks of data, such as graphics, painfully slow. Most drives now come with or are compatible with popular 16-bit adapters. You should be aware of differences, however.

SCSI Standard Interfaces. SCSI (pronounced SKUH-zee), or the Small Computer System Interface, is a name given to a group of adapter cards that conform to a set of common commands. They also enable computer users to string a group of devices along a chain from the one adapter, avoiding the complication of inserting a new adapter card into the PC bus slots every time a new hardware device, such as a tape unit or additional CD-ROM drive, is added to the system. These traits make SCSI interfaces preferable for connecting peripherals such as your CD-ROM to your PC.

All SCSI adapters are not created equal, however. Although they may share a common command set, they can implement these commands differently, depending on how the adapter's manufacturer designed the hardware. Furthermore, although the adapter can use SCSI commands to operate the CD-ROM drive, it might not allow the chaining of devices, defeating one of the chief purposes of implementing a SCSI interface.

SCSI-2 and ASPI. SCSI-2 was implemented throughout the PC industry and intended to create a true standard; if an adapter card or peripheral conforms to the SCSI-2 standard, the commands and the capabilities will be uniform across adapter and peripheral manufacturer's products. Such SCSI-2 products are often referred to as ASPI-compatible, a term derived from the device driver used to communicate with the adapter card. ASPI stands for Advanced SCSI Programming Interface and was developed by Adaptec, Inc., a leader in the development of SCSI controller cards and adapters. The SCSI-2 specification also allows a broader array of commands to be used with the controller card and offers other performance enhancements.

Non-Standard SCSI. Some drive manufacturers ship their own controller cards with their drives. These controllers can be called SCSI, but may not be compatible with the ASPI and/or SCSI-2 specifications. When a manufacturer claims a drive has a SCSI interface, you might be getting far less than you might need. Make certain it is a standard SCSI interface, preferably ASPI compatible.

If you don't plan on installing multiple SCSI devices, however, a proprietary controller or adapter is acceptable. Just beware of the limitations on expansion and compatibility. (Recommended interface: SCSI-2, ASPI compatible.)

CD-ROM Disc and Drive Formats

Compact discs are pitted to encode the binary bits of 0 and 1. Without a logical organization to this disc full of digits, however, the CD-ROM drive and PC would be at a loss to find any discernible data amid all those numbers. To this end, the data is encoded to conform to particular standards. When a drive encounters particular patterns, it—and the PC—can "recognize" the organization of the disc and find its way around the platter. Without standard data formats, the CD-ROM industry would be dead in the water; vendors of particular discs and disc drives would be producing incompatible software discs and drives and thereby limiting the number of units that could be sold.

Formats are also needed to advance the technology. For instance, hard rubber wheels and no suspension were just fine for the first automobiles as they cruised along at the breakneck speed of thirty miles an hour. But hitting a pothole at sixty could cause serious damage to the vehicle—and the riders. Inflatable tires and shock absorbers became necessary components of the modern car.

Similarly, the standards for disc formats evolved as well. The first compact data discs stored only text information, which was relatively easy to encode onto a disc. Graphics produced a greater challenge, and the standards evolved to incorporate them. The use of animation with synchronized sound, and then live-motion video, called for other expansions to the standards in which CDs store data.

It is extremely important to note that advanced CD-ROM standards are in the process of evolution right now. Multiple vendors are deploying a number of different techniques for expanding the capabilities of CD-ROM technology. They may be incompatible with each other or are immature in their development, and acceptance of these newer standards by software vendors is essential to the widespread use of these newer standards. It is important that you are familiar with these issues before you purchase a drive; consider the formats it is capable of reading now—and in the future.

The majority of drives available today, however, do comply with earlier CD-ROM formats, ensuring that the vast library of CD-ROM applications available today can be used on these drives.

First Data Standard: ISO 9660. Manufacturers of the first CD-ROM data discs produced their discs for one particular drive. In other words, a data disc produced for company A's drive could not be read by anyone who had purchased company B's CD-ROM drive—the disc needed to be formatted for each manufacturer's drive. Obviously, this stalled the development of the industry. Philips and Sony—the original collaborators for the standards incorporated in audio CDs, developed the "Yellow Book" specifications for data CD-ROMs.

When Sony and Philips first published the audio CD specifications, the material was released in a red binder and became known as "Red Book." Subsequent CD-ROM specifications have been dubbed by color as well, such as "Orange Book" and "Green Book."

An extension of the way in which audio data was stored on disc, the Yellow Book specification details how data—rather than audio—can be organized on a disc for its later retrieval. The International Standards Organization refined this specification in such a way that every vendor's drive and disc would expect to find a table of contents for a data disc. This is known as a Volume Table of Contents (VTOC) and really is quite similar to a standard book's table of contents in theory. ISO 9660 did not completely solve compatibility problems, however. The incorporation of additional data to aid and refine the search for data on a disc and even how to format the data blocks were still left to each separate vendor's design.

High Sierra Format. It was in all manufacturers' interests to resolve this issue. In a meeting in 1985 at the High Sierra Hotel and Casino in Lake Tahoe, California, leading manufacturers of CD-ROM drives and CD-ROM discs came together to resolve the differences in their implementation of the ISO 9660 format. The agreement has become known as the High Sierra format and is now a part of the ISO 9660 specification document. This expansion enabled all drives to read all ISO 9660-compliant discs, opening the way for the mass production of CD-ROM software publishing. Adoption of this standard also enabled disc publishers to provide cross-platform support for their software, easily manufacturing discs for DOS, UNIX, and other operating system formats. Without this agreement, the maturation of the CD-ROM marketplace would have taken years longer and stifled the production of available CD ROM-based information.

The exact and entire specifications for how to format the CD media are complex, strewn with jargon you may never need, and superfluous to your understanding of drive capabilities. You should know the basics, however, because doing so gives you a glimpse of the inner workings of retrieving data so quickly from such an enormous well.

To put basic High Sierra format in perspective, the disc layout is roughly analogous to a floppy disk. A floppy has a system track that not only identifies itself as a floppy and its density and operating system, but also tells the computer how it's organized—into directories, and within the directories, files.

Basic CD-ROM formats are much the same. The initial track of a data CD identifies itself as a CD and begins synchronization between the drive and the disc. Beyond the synchronization lies a system level that details how the entire disc is structured; as a part of the system area, the disc identifies the location of the volume area—where the actual data is held. The system also contains the directories of this volume, with pointers or addresses to various named areas, as illustrated in figure 15.2. A significant difference between CD directory structures and that of DOS is that the system area also contains direct addresses of files within their subdirectories, allowing the CD to seek to a specific location on the spiral data track.

Because the CD data is all really on one long spiral track, when speaking of tracks in the context of a CD we're talking about sectors or segments of data along the spiral.

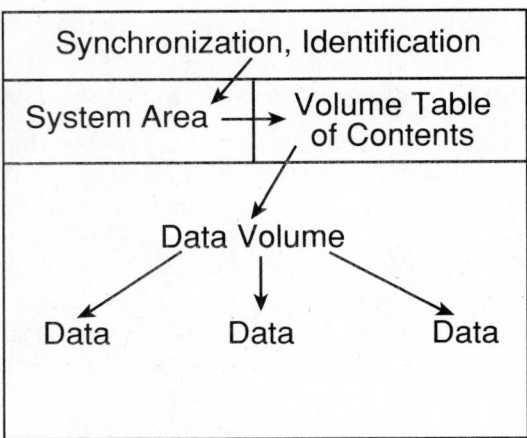

Fig. 15.2
CD-ROM basic organizational format.

CD-DA (Digital Audio). Data drives that can read data and audio are called CD-DA. Virtually any data drive now being sold reads both types of discs. When you insert a disc, the drive reads the first track of the disc to determine what type you loaded. Most drives ship with audio CD software, which enables you to play music CDs from your PC. You can use headphones, or with an installed sound card, connect speakers to the system. Some external drives ship with standard Left/Right audio plugs; just plug them into any external amplifier.

PhotoCD. First announced back in 1990, but not available until 1992, CD drives that display your own CD-ROM recorded photographs over your television are now being shipped in quantity by Kodak. You merely drop off a roll of film at a participating Kodak developer; later you take home a PhotoCD and drop it into your Kodak PhotoCD compatible disc player. But what's a PhotoCD compatible player?

The home unit is designed to play your PhotoCDs and your audio CDs as well. Because virtually all data-ready CD drives also can interpret audio, it's no mean feat for the Kodak CD players to play audio discs. The player merely reads off the first track and determines what type of disc you've fed it. The real breakthrough is in the drive's capability to determine whether one, two, or dozens of individual photo "sessions" are on the data disc.

CD Sessions. Remember from the High Sierra format discussion that each data disc holds a VTOC, or Volume Table of Contents, which tells the CD reader where—and how—the data is laid out on disc. CD data has, until this point, been single-session in its encoding. In other words, when a CD is mastered, all the data that will ever reside on the disc must be recorded in one session. The format, or the media, has no provision for returning later to append more information. The PhotoCD format—along with the XA and CD-I formats discussed later—not only allow for multiple sessions, but allow multiple sessions to be read back on a fully PhotoCD-capable CD-ROM drive. The drive must be capable of finding the multiple VTOCs associated with the appended sessions, however.

And this is where some confusion now reigns. When Kodak first released the PhotoCD, the company maintained that a drive must be CD-ROM XA-compliant to use PhotoCDs. An explanation of the XA spec follows. As of January 1992, however, Kodak has tested non-XA drives with new software drivers and approved them as single-session PhotoCD compatible. In other words, many of the drives shipping right now—in fact a majority— may be perfectly suited to reading PhotoCD discs that contain a single session of photos. The drive can recognize only the first session, and ignores any data or subsequent volume entries made after the initial session.

PC-based CD-ROM drives, if supplied with the proper device driver and Kodak-based software, can read single-session PhotoCD images. Kodak is licensing the "viewer" portion of its software so that it can be incorporated into existing software packages. Special filters—or decoders—will be added to desktop publishing, word processing, and PC paint software that allow them to import PhotoCD images into their documents.

Kodak has future plans to incorporate synchronized audio and text to the existing photo format. For these capabilities, the drive that reads these advanced discs must be XA-compatible. In addition, drives must be XA-compatible to read any disc that has multiple recordings.

PhotoCD Production

When you drop off your roll of film, the Kodak developers produce prints, just as they normally do. After prints are made, however, the process goes high-tech. Using high-speed UNIX operating system-based SUN SparcStations, the prints are scanned into the SparcStation at very high resolution using ultra-high resolution scanners. To give you an idea of the amount of information each scan carries, one color photograph can take 15–20 megabytes of storage. When the image is stored on disc, it is compressed using Kodak's own custom software. The compressed, stored images are then encoded onto special writable CD discs. The finished product is packaged in a familiar CD case and shipped back to your local developer for pickup.

Even though these scanned images occupy an enormous amount of media space, the capacity of CD technology can easily carry 100 photos, at the highest possible resolution. Because existing television, and even most home computers, cannot use these ultra-high resolutions, the typical home or PC-based PhotoCD can hold hundreds of images. See table 15.1 for more details. Because most of us rarely have that many photos developed at the same time, Kodak developed the system in conjunction with Philips so that multiple sessions can be recorded on one disc. You can have your Thanksgiving photos developed and recorded to disc in November, for example, and then bring the same disc back in late December to have your other holiday photos added to the remaining portion of the disc. Keep bringing the disc in until it fills up.

Table 15.1 PhotoCD Resolutions	
Resolution	**Description**
256 × 384 lines	Fine for most conventional TVs
512 × 768 lines	Good for S-VHS TVs and VGA PCs
1024 × 1536 lines	Beyond current TV technology, even Super VGA can't use all
2048 × 3072 lines	Beyond TV or current PC capacities

As of this writing, Kodak PhotoCD discs run fine in single session mode in many current CD-ROM drives—in Philips CD-I home entertainment systems as well as the Kodak systems.

For multisession capabilities and the capability to use audio and text on a PhotoCD for the PC, you must have an XA-compatible CD-ROM drive.

CD-ROM XA or Extended Architecture. CD-ROM XA, or Extended Architecture, is backwards compatible with the earlier High Sierra or ISO 9660 CD-ROMs. It adds another dimension to the world of CD-ROM technology.

Interleaving. CD-ROM XA drives employ a technique known as *interleaving*. The specification calls for the capability to encode on disc whether the data that is directly following an identification mark is graphics, sound, or text. Graphics can include standard graphics pictures, animation, or full-motion video. In addition, these blocks can be interleaved, or interspersed, with each other. For example, a frame of video may start a track followed by a segment of audio, which would accompany the video, followed by yet another frame of video. The drive picks up the audio and video sequentially, buffering the information in memory, and then sending it along to the PC for synchronization.

In short, the data is read off the disc in alternating pieces, and then synchronized at playback so that the result is a simultaneous presentation of the data.

Mode 1 and Mode 2, Form 1 and Form 2. To achieve this level of sophistication, the CD format is broken up so that the data types are layered. Mode 1 is CD data with error correction. Mode 2 is CD data without error correction. The Mode 2 track, however, allows what are called Form 1 and Form 2 tracks to exist one after the other on the Mode 2 track, thereby allowing the interleaving. These interleaved tracks may include their own error correction and can be any type of data. Figure 15.3 shows a visual representation of the breakdowns of Mode and Form structure.

For a drive to be truly XA-compatible, the Form 2 data encoded on the disc as audio must be ADPCM (Adaptive Differential Pulse Code Modulation) audio—specially compressed and encoded audio. This requires that the drive or the SCSI controller have a signal processor chip that can decompress the audio during the synchronization process.

What all this translates into is that drives currently available may be partially XA-compliant. They might be capable of the interleaving of data and reading of multisession discs, but may not have the ADPCM audio component on the disc or its controller.

Presently, the only drives with full XA compliance are produced by Sony and IBM. The Sony drive incorporates the ADPCM chip on its drive. The IBM XA drive is for IBM's proprietary micro channel bus and is designed for its high-end PS/2 Model computers.

Manufacturers may claim that their drives are "XA-ready," which means that they are capable of multiple sessions and Mode 1 and Mode 2, Form 1 and Form 2 reading, but they do not incorporate the ADPCM chip. Software developers, including Kodak, have yet to produce many XA software titles. IBM has a few under its Ultimedia program, but others have not yet hit the market.

If you get a drive that is fully mode and form compatible and is capable of reading multiple sessions, you may have the best available at this time. XA is a specification waiting for acceptance right now. Audio and video interleaving is possible without full XA compliance, as MPC applications under Microsoft Windows demonstrate.

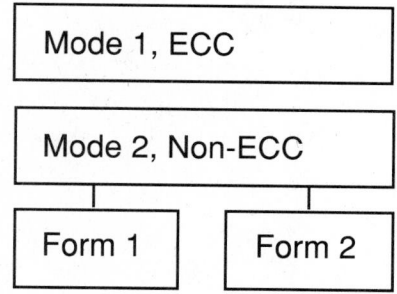

Fig. 15.3
Mode and Form format for CD-ROM XA.

CD-R. Sometimes known as CD-WORM and CD-WO, CD-R (CD-Recordable) enables you to write your own CDs.

As with mastering any CD, your data must be laid out or formatted before recording it to the CD-R unit. Often this layout is performed on a PC with large hard disks or other magnetic and removable media.

The CD-R is not quite the CD you might expect, however. Instead of the recording beam burning pits into a metallic or glass strata, the CD-R media is coated with a dye that has the same reflective properties as a "virgin" CD disc—in other words, a CD reader would see an unrecorded CD-R disc as one long land. When the recording laser begins to burn data into the CD-R media, it heats the gold layer and the dye layer beneath. The result of heating these areas causes the dye and gold areas to diffuse light in exactly the same way that a pit would on a glass master disc or a mass-produced CD. The reader is fooled into thinking a pit exists; there is no actual pit, however—just a spot of less-reflective disc caused by the chemical reaction of heating the dye and gold.

Many of the newer models support all the formats discussed—ISO 9660 all the way through CD-ROM XA. In addition, these drives read the formats as well, serving as a

ROM reader. Prices have fallen, but they're still around $5,000. A number of models may cost less than this by early 1995.

Multimedia CD-ROM

Multimedia is not a specific standard but a descriptive term. Any CD that incorporates text with graphics, sound, or video is by definition multimedia. Multimedia CDs exist for DOS, Macintosh System 7, AmigaDOS, Windows, OS/2, and UNIX operating systems and can be in many different formats.

MPC CD-ROMs. A consortium of hardware and software manufacturers led by Microsoft Corporation announced the formation of the Multimedia PC Marketing Council at Fall COMDEX in 1991. This council described the recommended platform for implementing multimedia on PC systems, and as more manufacturers joined the council, applications and hardware conformed to the prescribed specifications.

The MPC Council recommends minimum performance requirements for MPC-compatible CD-ROM drives, however. They are as follows:

- CD-DA drive with external audio output. (This can be as simple as a headphone jack. Most drives have headphone jacks and a 4-pin audio edge connector or standard RCS audio plugs.)

- 150 kb/s transfer rate, required for animation or video.

- 500ms access speed; this rate is unrealistically low, however. Most drives have much better access rates, and particularly with graphics and video, you'll want a drive with better performance than this.

Far from being an exact specification or format for data, MPC CD-ROM is a convention for storing audio, animation, video, and text for synchronization under the Microsoft Windows operating system from data received from an MPC-compliant CD-ROM. Microsoft has developed Windows Application Programmer's Interface software, which allows CD-ROM software manufacturers to organize the data on their CDs in such a way that information can be passed to Windows for processing.

Note that discs labeled as MPC only run under Microsoft Windows 3.0 or higher with the Microsoft Multimedia Extensions, or under OS/2 with MMPM. If a drive meets the minimum MPC Council recommendation for performance, it will run MPC CD-ROMs under Windows.

MultiSpin and High-Speed Drives. Audio drives deliver sound at a preset transfer rate to the amplifiers. MultiSpin drives, a term coined and patented by NEC, Inc., allow the drive to spin faster and deliver data at rates far higher than the audio equivalent. There is no reason why the computer must restrict itself to receiving data at this slower rate if the CPU, memory, and application software are capable of handling faster data rates.

NEC's line of high-speed drives was the first on the market in 1992 and delivers data to the PC at roughly twice the speed of previous CD-ROMs. Particular applications, such as live-motion video, especially benefit from this technology. Data is delivered in a constant stream, allowing the PC to process the video frames at a smoother rate. Some drives without high-speed technology, especially those that have no buffering capabilities, deliver video in a jerky and uneven manner.

A number of vendors are now supplying high-speed versions of their drives, including NEC, Texel, Toshiba, and Chinon.

The Pioneer mini-changer offers what the company calls QuadSpin—speeds up to four times the base delivery rate of data.

Other Drive Features

Although drive specifications are of the utmost importance, other factors and features should be taken into consideration as well. Besides quality of construction, the following criteria bear scrutiny when making a purchase decision:

- Drive sealing
- Caddy type
- Self-cleaning lenses
- Internal versus external drive

Drive Sealing. Dirt is your CD-ROM's biggest enemy. Dust or dirt, when it collects on the lens portion of the mechanism, can cause read errors or severe performance loss. Many manufacturers "seal" the lens and internal components in airtight enclosures from the drive bay. Other drives, although not sealed, have double dust doors—one external and one internal—to keep dust from the inside of the drive. All these features help prolong the life of your drive.

Caddy Type. Most CD-ROM drives require that you first insert the CD disc into a caddy, and then insert the caddy into the drive. Some drive manufacturers, however, have built-in caddies—drawers that slide out when the eject button is pushed. The disc is merely inserted into the drawer.

Both methods have pros and cons:

- *Caddiless.* Because these drive mechanisms don't require caddies, you spend much less time fumbling around with your CDs. There are two slight hitches here, though. First, you must make certain the CD drawer is kept very clean—the easiest way to foul the reading of a disc and potentially damage a drive is to introduce dirt into the mechanism. Second, if the drawer hinge fails, you must send the entire drive in for repair.

- *Caddy.* You need a phone number for a business in Los Angeles. You open the CD case for your American Business Phone Book CD. You eject the CD already in the drive, remove it, and replace it in its case. You take out the Phone Book CD and insert it into the caddy, and then...you get the picture. Using caddies is a time-consuming bother if you deal with a number of different CDs. This is the only drawback to using them, however. The individual caddies are easy to clean, and when they show signs of wear, throw them away. You can pick up caddies for around five or six dollars apiece, and it's worth the small investment to buy each of your most-used CDs its own caddy.

Self-Cleaning Lenses. If the laser lens gets dirty, so does your data. The drive will spend a great deal of time seeking and reseeking—or finally giving up. Lens cleaning discs are available, but built-in cleaning mechanisms are now included on some model drives. This may be a feature you'll want to consider, particularly if you work in a less than pristine work environment, or if you have trouble keeping your desk clean, let alone your CD-ROM drive lens.

Internal versus External Drives. When deciding whether you want an internal or external drive, think about where and how you're going to use your CD-ROM drive. What about the future expansion of your system? Both types of drives have pluses and minuses. The following lists some of the issues:

■ *External Enclosures.* These tend to be rugged, portable, and *large*—in comparison to their internal versions. Buy an external if you have the space and are considering or already own other external SCSI peripherals that you can chain to the same adapter. You might also consider an external if you want to move the drive from one PC to another easily. If each PC has its own SCSI adapter, all you need to do is unplug the drive from one adapter and plug it into the other.

■ *Internal Enclosures.* Internal drives will clear off a portion of your desk. Buy an internal if you already have internal SCSI devices you can chain to your adapter, have ample drive bay space, or plan on keeping the CD-ROM drive exclusively on one machine.

Installing Your Drive

You decided on the drive you want. You ordered it. Now it's arrived at your doorstep. What next?

Installation of a CD-ROM drive is as difficult—or easy—as you make it. If you know a little about SCSI interface devices, such as your CD drive, and plan ahead, the installation should go smoothly.

This section walks you through the installation of typical internal and external CD-ROM drives with tips that often aren't included in your manufacturer's installation manuals. Even after you install the hardware, it isn't enough to just turn on the drive and toss in a CD, though. Special software must be loaded onto your PC first.

Avoiding Conflict: Get Your Cards in Order

Regardless of your type of installation—internal or external drive—you need to check your CD-ROM drive's SCSI host adapter before installation.

Carefully remove the adapter card from its protective, antistatic bag.

IV

> **Note**
>
> Never handle the SCSI adapter card by its gold, edge connector contacts—a simple spark of static electricity sent to the card is enough to do potential damage.

Lay the card out on the antistatic bag with the IC chips, transistors, and processors face up and the external connector to your right. Virtually all documentation for adapter cards assumes that cards are oriented this way when you configure them.

The single most important step in installing any SCSI device, including this new CD-ROM drive, is the proper configuration, or settings, for the adapter card in front of you. If you pay special attention to this part of the installation, you avoid 90 percent of the problems with installing SCSI devices.

Check the adapter's documentation or pamphlet for the default settings for the card. These should be indicated by a list near the front, or by notation throughout the manual. DO NOT worry about pin settings, jumpers, or anything else other than copying the default settings to a piece of paper. Look for the following default settings:

- IRQ
- DMA channel
- I/O address or memory address
- Adapter SCSI ID

The following is a typical list of default settings for a SCSI adapter:

- IRQ   11
- DMA channel   5
- I/O address   330
- SCSI ID   7

Don't worry if your settings are different; each setting is discussed later in the chapter.

> **Note**
>
> Some proprietary SCSI host adapters may have some, all, or just a few of these settings available to you. In any case, jot down the defaults they list in the manual.

If you want to avoid hair-pulling, teeth-gnashing, and general frustration, check these default settings for your SCSI card for possible conflicts with other cards already installed in your PC. You CANNOT have two cards set for the same IRQ, DMA, or I/O address or the drive—and possibly your PC—will lock up or operate erratically.

The following are some typical cards you should check for IRQ, DMA, and I/O port address settings:

- Network interface cards (Ethernet, ARCNet, and so on)

- Sound cards

- Scanner interfaces

- Internal modems and fax-modems

- Other SCSI cards for hard drives, Bernoulli drives, or other added peripherals such as tape backup units

If you value your time and your sanity, it's a good idea to keep a record of these important settings for all your adapter cards handy. Write down the current settings on a piece of paper and tape it into your PC's owner manual, for example. Any time you add a new adapter card or must reconfigure one already installed, you'll have a reference. Otherwise, you might find yourself pulling out every peripheral adapter in your machine to check its settings. Obviously, any time you add a new card or change the settings of one installed, change your note card.

Make a note of any conflicts. It probably is easier to reset the defaults on your CD-ROM SCSI card—it's already out of the PC and sitting in front of you. Don't make changes yet. Just take notes.

The next step is to make sure that the defaults listed in the manual are, in fact, the defaults actually set on the board. Everyone makes mistakes, and your manufacturer is included. Although this is relatively uncommon, it's best to double-check things now, before you go too far into the installation.

Jumpers. Adapter card configurations are set with jumpers—tiny plastic-covered shunts that fit over pin-pairs on the adapter card (see fig. 15.4). These rows of jumper pins may run left to right or up and down across the card. Configuration is a matter of having the jumpers on or off a pair of pins.

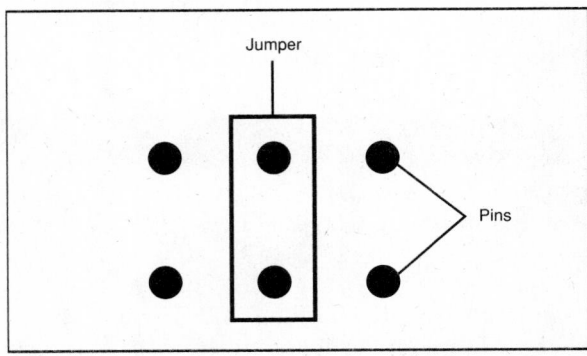

Fig. 15.4
A SCSI card with jumper banks.

These rows of jumper pins are labeled on the card as J5 or W1, for example. Your adapter card manual or pamphlet has a diagram of these jumper rows, or *blocks*, as they're called. Carefully check the pin settings against your manual. Make sure that pins are jumpered where they should be, and just as important, that no extra jumpers are on any of the pins.

> **Note**
>
> Some SCSI adapters, such as the Trantor 130, use rocker switches rather than jumpers to configure the cards.

If you believe you've found an error, double-check. You might have multiple jumper blocks on your card—make sure that you're checking the right ones.

After you make sure that you have the pins set to the correct defaults, you're ready to resolve any possible conflicts.

IRQ Conflicts. The most common cause of a system lock-up after an installation is an IRQ conflict. Avoid problems up front by making sure that you have no conflicts now. Table 15.2 lists common IRQ numbers and which ones are typically open. Remember, you may already have an installed card occupying one of the interrupt request lines.

Table 15.2 Common IRQ Assignments	
IRQ 0	**Use**
IRQ 0	Timer Interrupt
IRQ 1	Keyboard Interrupt
IRQ 2	Cascade to IRQ 9
IRQ 3	COM 2 and COM 4
IRQ 4	COM 1 and COM 3
IRQ 5	LPT 2 (parallel printer port)
IRQ 6	Floppy Disk
IRQ 7	LPT 1 (parallel printer port)
IRQ 8	Real Time Clock
IRQ 9	Cascade to IRQ 2
IRQ 10	Available to user
IRQ 11	Available to user
IRQ 12	Mouse Port on PS/2
IRQ 13	80X87 Math Coprocessor
IRQ 14	Hard Disk
IRQ 15	Available to user

If you find a conflict, consult your adapter card manual for selecting a different IRQ. At this point, remove or move a jumper from one pin pair to another. Although jumper blocks can be removed with your fingers, you risk handling chips that may be near the jumpers. It's better to use a pair of tweezers, especially those sold in a computer tool kit, to carefully remove the jumper. Reset the jumper blocks according to the manual's diagrams for the new IRQ.

DMA Conflicts. DMA, or Direct Memory Address, settings have less serious consequences when in conflict. A typical symptom of a DMA conflict is no response from one of the cards in conflict. For example, if you have a sound card and your CD-ROM SCSI card set for the same DMA channels, one—or both—of the cards might not function. Check DMA settings on the card, but be aware that the card may require that the DMA channel be set on a number of jumper blocks. The Adaptec 1540 SCSI card, for example, has a default DMA of 5, but jumpers pertaining to the DMA selection are on jumper block 5 as well as jumper block 9. For all DMA jumpers to be set, the Adaptec must have DMA Channel Select, DMA Request, DMA ACKnowledge, and DMA INTerrupt Request set on these two separate blocks.

> **Note**
>
> Direct Memory Access (DMA) is a technique that speeds up access to memory for expansion cards. Because it avoids the intervention of the CPU, this technique is "direct." Seven DMA channels are in an IBM-AT compatible machine.

Most SCSI cards come with a default of DMA channel 5 set. This should be fine for most PCs because few other adapter cards occupy these channels. Some of the newer, 16-bit sound cards have DMA channel 5 set as default, however, so they are likely culprits in any conflict.

Memory I/O Addresses. No two cards can live at the same memory address. More important, these I/O addresses are really base addresses—they describe the address start that the card occupies. The full range of the memory address must be taken into consideration when resolving conflict with other cards. For example, if a sound card occupies memory address 220, you might assume that the SCSI card could exist at 230. This is not necessarily so. If the sound card's memory range is 220–235, you've just introduced a conflict.

We've noticed some typical conflicts of late in the way types of adapter cards are shipped in their default state. Most SCSI cards ship with base memory I/O addresses of 300, 330, or 220. Many sound boards and internal fax modem cards may also occupy these addresses in their default configurations. Network interface cards are often set in the 300–360 range by default too. If you need to change your I/O address due to a conflict, make sure that you know the range of the possible conflict.

Typical symptoms of I/O conflict are similar to those with DMA—one or both of the cards in conflict will not respond. Another symptom of memory conflict is disconcerting, but harmless. Your machine may go through the boot process of checking memory, loading drivers, and so on, get to the end of the boot, and then reboot all over again. If this happens, you can be certain you have a memory conflict.

Selecting a Slot. After you configure your card correctly, resolve all potential conflicts, and are thoroughly tired of looking at the manual's hazy diagrams for jumper blocks, you're ready to insert the SCSI card into the PC.

Turn off the power. Unscrew the case cover and remove it. Look at the available or unoccupied slots in your PC bus. These card slots may come in 8-, 16-, or 32-bit lengths—with 8-bit being the shortest and the 32-bit slots the longest and usually the last slots in the case. If your CD SCSI adapter is an 8-bit adapter, it will have one set of gold edge connectors; the 16-bit cards have two sets—one short and one long. Make the most of the real estate inside your PC case. Don't put an 8-bit card in a 16-bit slot unless you have no other choice—you may want that 16-bit slot later on for a true 16-bit card. The main point is simple, though—you can put the SCSI card in any of the available slots in the case. Unscrew the slot cover for the bus slot you've selected from the back of the PC. Hang onto this screw.

Holding the card by its top edges, slide it firmly into the expansion bus, with the connector edge facing through the open slot in the back of the PC chassis. Press down firmly. You'll feel the card seat itself and pop into the connector. Be careful not to press down too hard—you might damage the motherboard below. Make sure that the card is evenly seated, front to back. Most SCSI cards have cable hooks on either side of the outside connector. These can get in the way when you put the card into the bus.

If one of these hooks gets caught between the chassis and the card, you'll have a difficult time seating the card properly (see fig. 15.5). Move the hooks straight up, parallel with the connector so that they'll slide easily through the slot in the back of the PC.

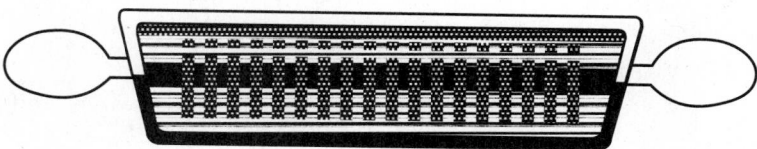

Fig. 15.5
A SCSI connector, showing hooks that can get in the way of installation.

Gently move the adapter flange with its slotted top away from the screw hole of the PC chassis. Put the screw from the slot plate into the hole and give it a few turns, enough to start it solidly. Slide the card flange under the screw head and secure it firmly. By starting the screw into the chassis first, and then sliding the card into place beneath it, you can avoid the problems of trying—often without luck—to align the adapter bracket flange and PC chassis hole with the screw. A common hassle here is dropping the screw into your PC case while attempting to secure the card. It's a good idea to have a flashlight around to peer between the cards to find dropped screws; those tweezers you used for changing jumpers might come in handy here to carefully remove the misplaced screws. If you've grounded yourself, you won't do any damage if you're careful in removing a dropped screw.

Never, under any circumstances, leave a loose or dropped screw in the case. It will inevitably short something out, doing severe damage to your main PC board and any cards in the expansion bus.

The worst part is over.

DO NOT replace the cover of the PC yet. If some lingering conflicts exist or the card is not fully seated in the slot, you might need to do more inside work. You can replace the PC case after you install the drive, reboot your system, install the driver software, and (whew!) test the drive—not before.

External CD-ROM Hook-Up

Unpack the CD-ROM carefully. With the purchase of an external drive, you should receive the following items:

- CD-ROM drive
- SCSI adapter cable
- SCSI adapter card

This is the bare minimum to get the drive up and running. You'll probably also find a CD caddy, a manual or pamphlet for the adapter card, and possibly a sampling of CDs to get you started.

Take a look at your work area and the SCSI cable that came with the drive. Where will the drive find a new home? You're limited by the length of the cable. Find a spot for the drive, and insert the power cable into the back of the unit; make sure that you have an outlet, or preferably, a free socket in a surge-suppressing power strip to plug in the new drive.

Plug one end of the supplied cable into the connector socket of the drive, and one into the SCSI connector on the adapter card. Most external drives have two connectors on the back—either connector can be hooked to the PC (see fig. 15.6). The following sections discuss the extra connector. Secure the cable with the guide hooks on both the drive and adapter connector, if provided. Some SCSI cables supplied with Future Domain 16-bit controllers have a micro-connector for the adapter end, and simply clip into place.

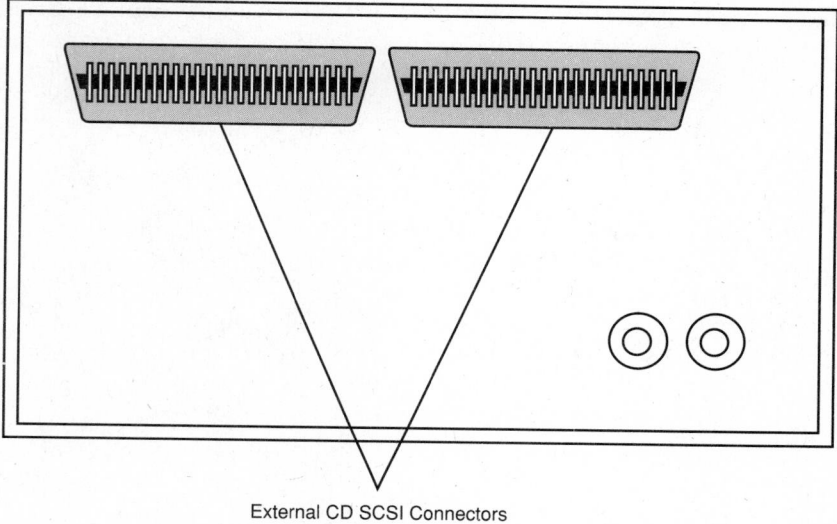

External CD SCSI Connectors

Fig. 15.6
External CD-ROM drive SCSI connectors.

Finally, your external CD-ROM drive should have a SCSI ID select switch on the back. This switch sets the identification number for the drive when hooked to a host adapter. The adapter, by most manufacturer's defaults, should be set for SCSI ID 7. Make sure that you set the SCSI ID for the CD-ROM drive to any other number—6, 5, or 4, for example. The only rule to follow is to make sure that you do not set the drive for an ID that is already occupied—by either the card or any other SCSI peripheral on the chain.

Internal Drive Installation

Unpack your internal drive kit. You should have the following pieces:

- The drive
- Power cord
- SCSI interface board
- Internal SCSI ribbon cable
- Floppy disks with device driver software and manual
- Drive rails and/or mounting screws

Your manufacturer also may have provided a power cable splitter—a bundle of wires with plastic connectors on each of three ends. A disc caddy and owner's manual may also be included.

Make sure that the PC is off and leave the cover off the PC for now. Before installing the card into the PC bus, however, connect the SCSI ribbon cable onto the adapter card (see fig. 15.7).

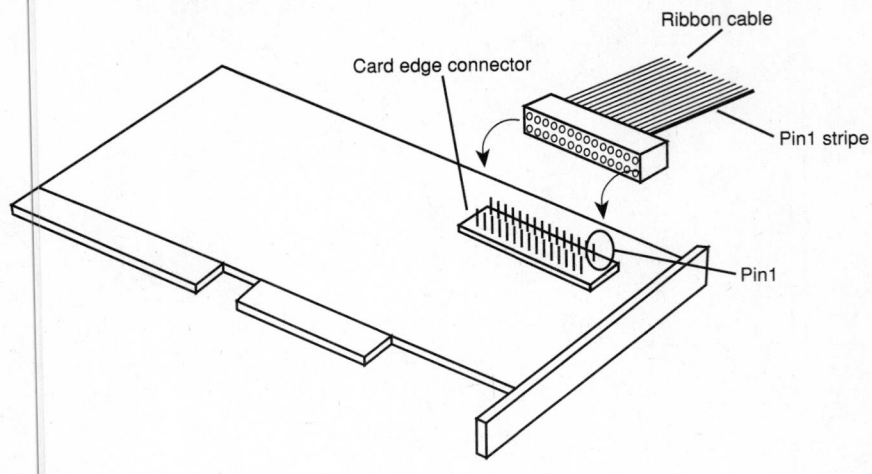

Ribbon cable

Card edge connector

Pin1 stripe

Pin1

Fig. 15.7
Ribbon cable connection to SCSI adapter.

Ribbon Cable and Card Edge Connector. The ribbon cable should be identical on both ends. You'll find a red stripe of dotted line down one side of the outermost edge of the cable. This stripe indicates a pin 1 designation, and ensures that the SCSI cable is connected properly into the card and into the drive. If you're lucky, the manufacturer supplied a cable with notches or keys along one edge of the connector. With such a key, you can insert the cable into the card and drive in only one way.

Unkeyed cable must be hooked up according to the pin 1 designation.

Along one edge of your SCSI adapter, you'll find a double row of fifty brass-colored pins. This is the card edge connector. In small print along the base of this row of pins you should find at least two numbers next to the pins—"1" and "50." Align the ribbon cable's marked edge over pin 1, and then carefully and evenly insert the ribbon cable connector.

Now insert the adapter card, leaving the drive end of the cable loose for the time being.

Choose a slot in the front bay for your internal drive. Make sure that it's easily accessible and not blocked by other items on your desk. You'll be inserting the CDs here, and you'll need the elbow room.

Remove the drive bay cover. Inside the drive bay you should find a metal enclosure with screw holes for mounting the drive. If the drive has mounting holes along its side and fits snugly into the enclosure, you won't need mounting rails. If it's a loose fit, however, mount the rails along the sides of the drive with the rail screws, and then slide the drive into the bay. Secure the drive into the bay with four screws—two on each side. If the rails or drive don't line up evenly with four mounting holes, make sure that you use at least two—one mounting screw on each side. Because you'll be inserting and ejecting many CDs over the years, mounting the drive securely is a must.

Once again, find the striped side of the ribbon cable and align it with pin 1 on the drive's edge connector. Either a diagram in your owner's manual or designation on the connector itself tells you which is pin 1.

The back of the CD drive has a power connector outlet. Inside the case of your PC, at the back of your floppy or hard disk, are power cords—bundled red and yellow wires with plastic connectors on them. You may already have a power connector lying open in the case. Take the open connector and plug it into the back of the power socket on the CD-ROM drive. These connectors only go in one way. If you do not have an open connector, use the splitter (see fig. 15.8). Disconnect a floppy drive power cord. Attach the splitter to the detached power cord. Plug one of the free ends into the floppy drive, the other into the CD-ROM drive.

> **Note**
>
> It's best to "borrow" juice from the floppy drive connector in this way. Your hard drive may require more power or be more sensitive to sharing this line than the floppy is. If you have no choice—the splitter and ribbon cable won't reach, for example—you can split off any power cord that hasn't already been split. Check the entire length of the power cord—power supply to drives—to ensure that you have a line not already overloaded with a split.

Again, DO NOT replace the PC cover yet—you need to make sure that everything is running perfectly before you seal the case. You're now ready to turn on the computer. For the drive to work, however, you need to install the software drivers.

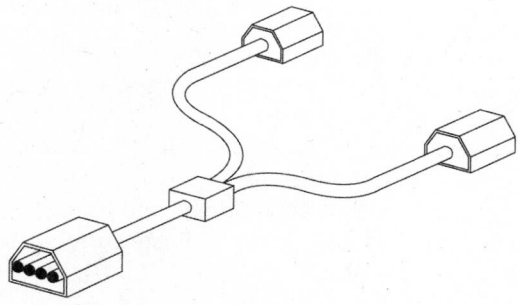

Fig. 15.8
Power cord splitter and connector.

SCSI Chains: Internal, External, a Little of Both

Remember, one of the primary reasons for using a SCSI controller for your CD-ROM drive is the capability to chain a string of peripherals from one adapter card—saving you card slots inside the PC, and limiting the nightmare of tracking IRQs, DMAs, and I/O memory addresses.

You can add scanners, tape backup units, and other SCSI peripherals to this chain (see fig. 15.9). You must keep a few things in mind; chief among them is SCSI termination.

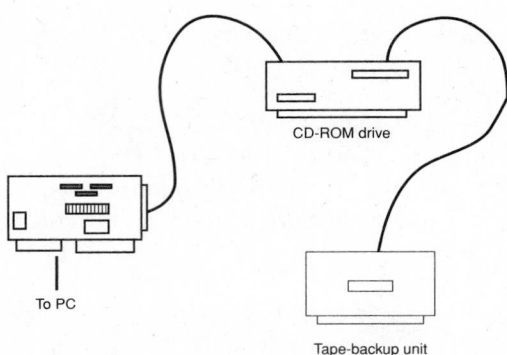

CD-ROM drive

To PC

Tape-backup unit

Fig. 15.9
A SCSI chain of devices on one adapter card.

Identify and Terminate with Care. The first rule of SCSI device chaining is simple: each end of the SCSI chain must be terminated. The first device must contain a termination resistor, and the last must also have a terminator attached. All devices between the first and last should be free of any terminator.

The second SCSI rule you must follow is that all SCSI devices must be set to a unique ID number. In the external drive installed earlier, the SCSI adapter is set for ID 7, and the CD-ROM drive is set for ID 6. Any additional SCSI devices added must then take IDs 1, 2, 3, 4, or 5. REMEMBER: the SCSI adapter takes an ID, and its default is usually ID 7.

Example One: All External SCSI Devices. Say that you installed your CD-ROM drive and added a tape device to the chain with the extra connector on the back of the CD-ROM drive. The first device in this SCSI chain is the adapter card itself. On all SCSI cards you find a series of long, reddish, ceramic-tipped components plugged into the board in a group of three. These are the terminating resistors for the card (see fig. 15.10). From the card, you ran an external cable to the CD-ROM drive, and from the CD-ROM drive, you added another cable to the back of the tape unit. The tape unit must then be terminated as well. Most external units are terminated with a SCSI cap—a small connector that plugs into the unused external SCSI connector. These external drive connectors come in two varieties: a SCSI cap and a pass-through terminator. The cap is just that; it plugs over the open connector and covers it. The pass-through terminator, however, plugs into the connector and has an open end that you can use to plug the SCSI cable into. This type of connector is essential if your external drive has only one SCSI connector; you can plug the drive in and make sure that it's terminated—all with one connector.

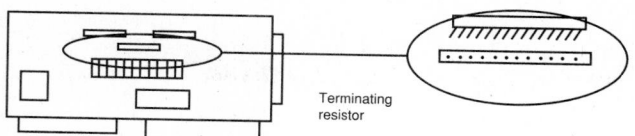

Terminating
resistor

Fig. 15.10
SCSI adapter card terminating resistors.

> **Note**
>
> Some external drives have internal termination. In other words, the manufacturer installed terminating resistors, much like the ones installed on the adapter card, onto the drive's IC board inside the drive case. If your drive has internal termination, you must not put a terminator cap on the external connector.

Example Two: Internal Chain and Termination. The same rules apply—all the internal devices must have unique SCSI ID numbers, and the first and last devices must be terminated. In the case of internal devices, however, you must check for termination. Internal devices have terminator packs or resistors similar to the ones installed on your adapter card. If you install a tape unit as the last device on the chain, it must have resistors on its circuit board. If you place your CD-ROM drive in the middle of this chain, its resistors must be removed. The adapter card, at the end of the chain, keeps its resistors intact.

> **Note**
>
> Most internal SCSI devices ship with terminating resistors on board. Check your user's manuals for their locations. Any given device may have one, two, or even three such resistors.

Example Three: Internal and External SCSI Devices. If you mix and match external as well as internal devices, follow the rules. The example shown in figure 15.11 has an internal CD-ROM drive, terminated and set for SCSI ID 6; the external tape unit also is terminated, and is assigned SCSI ID 5. The SCSI adapter itself is set for ID 7, and—most importantly—its terminating resistor packs have been removed.

> **Note**
>
> As with any adapter card, be careful when handling the card itself. Make sure that you ground yourself first. Chip pullers—specially made tweezers found in most computer tool kits—are especially useful in removing resistor packs from adapter cards and internal peripherals such as CD-ROM drives. The resistor packs have very thin teeth that are easily bent. Once bent, they're tough to straighten out and reinsert, so be careful when removing the packs.

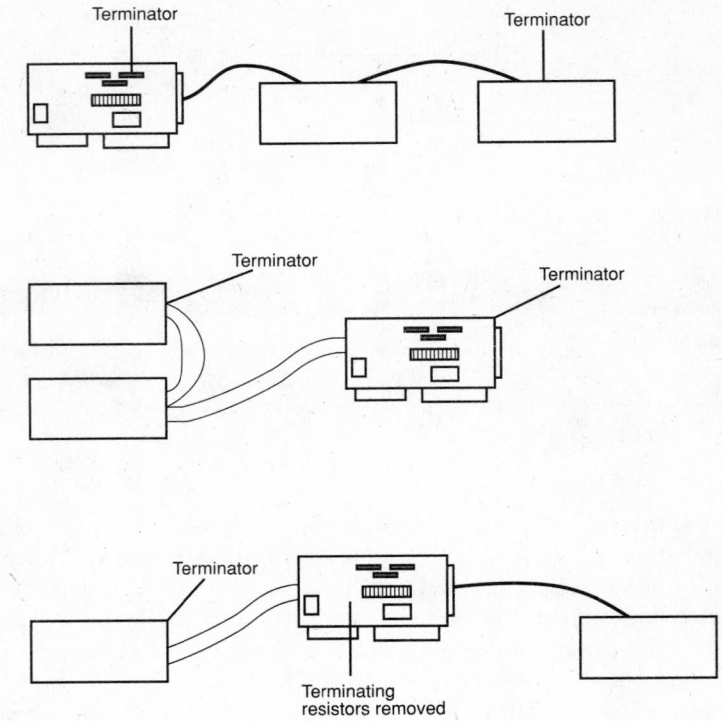

Fig. 15.11
Examples of SCSI termination.

CD-ROM Software on Your PC

After you configure the adapter card correctly, insert it into the PC, and make sure that the drives are connected and terminated properly, you're ready for the last step—installation of the CD-ROM software. The CD-ROM needs the following three software components for it to operate on a PC:

■ A SCSI adapter driver

■ A SCSI driver for the specific CD-ROM drive you've installed

■ MSCDEX—Microsoft CD Extensions for DOS

You can have the first two drivers—the SCSI adapter driver and CD-ROM driver—load into your system at startup by placing command lines in your CONFIG.SYS file. The MSCDEX, or DOS extension, is an executable file added into your system through your AUTOEXEC.BAT file.

SCSI Adapter Driver. Each SCSI adapter model has a specific driver that allows communications between the PC and the SCSI interface. This driver should have been provided with your SCSI drive and adapter kit. Documentation should also have been included that walks you through the installation of the software. You can manually add the SCSI device driver to your CONFIG.SYS file as follows:

At the front of the CONFIG.SYS file, add the name and path of the driver with the DEVICE= command:

```
DEVICE=C:\DRIVERS\MYSCSI.SYS
```

C:\DRIVERS is the subdirectory in which you copied the SCSI device driver. Some drivers have option switches or added commands that, for example, enable you to view the progress of the driver being loaded.

CD-ROM Device Driver. This driver, as well, should be a part of your basic installation kit. If not, contact the drive's manufacturer for the proper device driver for your SCSI card.

The device driver should come with an installation program that prompts you for the memory I/O address for the SCSI adapter on which you installed your CD-ROM drive. This device driver allows communication with the drive through the SCSI bus to your PC. Installation programs add a line similar to the following to your CONFIG.SYS file:

```
DEVICE=C:\DRIVERS\MYCDROM.SYS /D:mscd001
```

C:\DRIVERS is the subdirectory that contains the driver MYCDROM.SYS, the CD-ROM driver for your specific CD-ROM drive.

Note the /D:mscd001 option after the preceding statement. This designates this CD-ROM driver as controlling the first (001), and only, CD-ROM drive on the system. This portion of the device driver statement is for the Microsoft DOS Extension driver, which designates CD-ROM drives in this fashion.

MSCDEX: Adding CDs to DOS. The Microsoft CD Extensions for DOS allow the DOS operating system to identify and use data from CD-ROMs attached to the system. The original DOS operating system had no provisions for this technology, so "hooks" or handling of this unique media are not a part of the basic operating environment. Using these extensions is convenient for all involved, however. As CD-ROM technology changes, the MSCDEX can be changed, independent of the DOS system. For example, most PhotoCD, multiple session CD-ROM drives require MSCDEX.EXE version 2.21, which has been modified from earlier versions to accommodate the newer CD format.

MSCDEX.EXE should be in your software kit with your drive. If not, you can obtain the latest copy from Microsoft directly. The latest version of the DOS extension also is available on CompuServe in the Microsoft forum. If you are a registered user of the DOS operating system, the MSCDEX is free. Read the licensing agreement that appears on the disk or in your manual concerning the proper licensing of your MSCDEX files.

Your installation software should add a line similar to the following to your AUTOEXEC.BAT file:

```
C:\WINDOWS\MSCDEX.EXE /d:mscd001
```

C:\WINDOWS is the directory in which you copied the MSCDEX.EXE file. The /d:mscd001 portion of the command line tells the MSCDEX extension the DOS name of the device defined in the CD-ROM device driver of your CONFIG.SYS file.

> **Note**
>
> The MSCDEX and CD-ROM device driver names must match. The defaults that most installations provide are used in this example. As long as the two names are the same, the drivers can "find" one another.

Sounds complicated? Don't worry. As long as you have these three drivers—the SCSI adapter driver, the CD-ROM driver, and the DOS CD extensions—loaded properly in your system, the CD-ROM drive will operate as transparently as any other drive in your system.

MSCDEX.EXE has a variety of options or switches that you can add to its command line (see table 15.3).

Table 15.3 MSCDEX Command Line Options

Switch	Function
/V	Lists information about memory allocation, buffers, drive letter assignments, and device driver names on your screen at boot up when this option is added to the command line. This option is called Verbose.
/L: <letter>	Designates which DOS drive letter you will assign the drive. For instance, /L:G assigns the drive letter G: to your CD-ROM drive. Two conditions apply: first, you must not have another drive assigned to that letter; and second, your lastdrive= statement in your CONFIG.SYS file must be equal to or greater than the drive letter you're assigning. LASTDRIVE=G would be fine. LASTDRIVE=F would cause an error if you attempt to assign the CD-ROM drive to the G: drive through the /L: switch.
/M: <buffers>	Enables you to buffer the data from the CD-ROM drive. This is useful if you want faster initial access to the drive's directory. Buffers of 10 to 15 are more than enough for most uses. Any more is overkill. Each buffer, however, is equal to 2K of memory. So a /M:10 buffer argument, for instance, would take 20K of memory. Note that this does not significantly increase the overall performance of the drive, just DOS's initial access to the drive and the access of large data blocks when the drive is gulping down live-motion video, for example. You can't turn a 400 millisecond drive into a speed demon by adding a 200K buffer. With no /M: argument added, MSCDEX will add, as a default, 6 buffers anyway. That may be fine for most PCs and CD-ROM drives.
/E	Loads the aforementioned buffers into DOS high memory, freeing up space in the conventional 640K. Early versions of MSCDEX—anything below version 2.1—do not load into extended memory. You must have DOS 5.0 for this option to load.
/K	Kanji support.
/S	Enables you to share your CD-ROM drive on a peer-to-peer network, such as Windows for Workgroups.

Software Loaded, Ready to Run

As mentioned earlier, your drive should come with installation software that copies the device driver files to your hard drive and adds the necessary command lines to your CONFIG.SYS and AUTOEXEC.BAT files.

When this is accomplished, you can reboot your machine and look for signs that all went smoothly in the software installation.

Following is a series of sample portions of your boot up screens to give you an idea of what messages you'll receive when a given driver is properly loaded into the system.

When you're sure that the software is loaded correctly, try out the drive by inserting a CD into the disc caddy and loading it into the CD-ROM drive. Then get a directory of the disc from the DOS prompt by issuing the following command:

DIR/w G:

This command gives you a directory of the CD you've inserted, if your CD has been assigned the drive letter G (see fig. 15.12).

Fig. 15.12
The directory of a CD after installing the drive.

You can log in to the CD-ROM drive, just as you would any DOS drive. The only DOS commands not possible on a CD-ROM drive are those that write to the drive. CDs, remember, are media that cannot be overwritten, erased, or formatted.

If you logged in to the CD-ROM and received a directory of a sample CD, you're all set.

NOW you can power down the PC and replace the cover.

CD-ROM in Microsoft Windows. When your drive is added to your system, Windows already knows about it through DOS. Suddenly you'll find a few changes in your Windows environment. Open up your File Manager by double-clicking its file cabinet icon (see fig. 15.13). You see your CD-ROM drive among the old, familiar drive icons across the top. Notice that the CD-ROM drive icon is highlighted with a miniature CD disc, and the drive carries the title CD_ROM. Windows knows the media type your new drive is through the DOS extension discussed earlier.

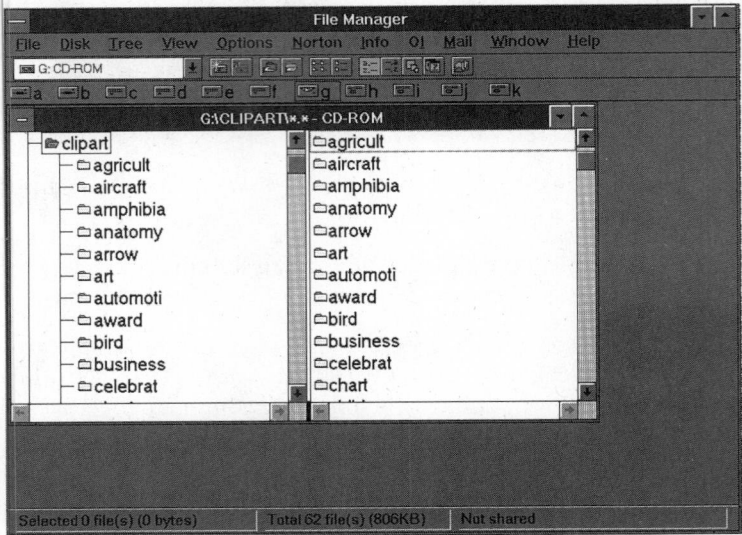

Fig. 15.13
The CD-ROM icon is automatically added to the Windows File Manager window.

Media Player

You can set your CD-ROM player to play audio CDs while you are working in Windows. You need to hook up your drive to a sound card and speakers or connect the CD's audio ports to a stereo first. Go to Window's Control Panel and select Drivers. If you do not see [MCI] CD Audio among the files in the driver's list, choose Add. Insert the Windows installation disk that contains the CDAUDIO driver. When the driver appears on the list, exit the Drivers and Control Panel windows.

Double-click on the Media Player icon. Under Devices, select CD. A listing of the track numbers on your audio CD appears along the bottom edge of the Media Player. The controls on Media Player are similar to those of an audio CD player, including track select, continuous play, and pause (see fig. 15.14).

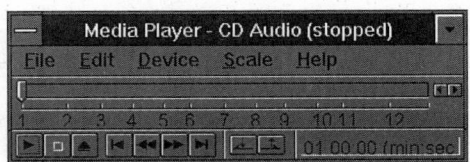

Fig. 15.14
The Media Player with an audio CD loaded.

Many drive manufacturers supply DOS-based CD audio players with their systems. Check your installation manual and software disks for these utilities.

Summary

This chapter should aid you in selecting, installing, and configuring a typical CD-ROM drive in a DOS- or Windows-based PC. When selecting a drive, remember to pay careful attention to drive specifications, drive quality, and other drive features such as self-cleaning lenses and tray versus caddy operations.

When installing your drive, make sure you follow the manufacturer's recommendations and instructions. What this chapter offers is a generic or basic guide for installation and tips on avoiding trouble spots and misconfiguration.

Finally, whenever possible update your SCSI, CD-ROM, and MSCDEX drivers to the latest revisions; these latest versions may increase performance and compatibility with other PC components and software.

Chapter 16

Tape and Other Mass-Storage Drives

The data backup needs on a personal computer can be overwhelming. People with large hard drives with numerous application programs installed, and those who generate a large amount of data, may find it necessary to back up their computers on a weekly or even a daily basis.

In addition, a critical need on today's PCs is data storage space. Sometimes it seems the storage requirements of a PC can never be satisfied. On nearly any PC used for business, study, or even for fun, the amount of software you need to install and the amount of data you need to store can overwhelm what just a short time before was considered a power user's jumbo hard drive.

This chapter focuses on tape backup drives and removable media disk drives, which increasingly are used to solve the problems of the growing need for data storage space and the need for a fast and efficient way to back up many megabytes of data.

Tape Backup Drives

Any computer book worth reading warns repeatedly that you should back up your system regularly. Backups are necessary because at any time a major problem, or even some minor ones, can corrupt the important information and the programs stored on your computer's hard drive, rendering this information useless. A wide range of problems can damage the data on your hard drive. Here is a list of some of these data-damaging problems:

1. Sudden fluctuations in the electricity that powers your computer (power spikes) resulting in data damage or corruption.

2. Overwriting a file by mistake.

3. Mistakenly formatting your hard disk when you meant to format a floppy.

4. Hard drive failure resulting in loss of data that has not been backed up. Not only do you have to install a new drive but, because you have no backup, you also must reinstall your software programs, disk by disk.

5. Catastrophic damage to your computer (storm, flood, lightning strike, fire, theft). A single lightning strike near your office or home can destroy the circuitry of your computer, including your hard drive. Theft of your computer, of course, is equally devastating. A recent, complete, backup greatly simplifies the process of setting up a replacement computer.

Backups are also the cure for such common headaches as a full hard drive and the need to transfer data between computers. By backing up data you rarely use, then deleting the original data from your hard drive, you free up the space once occupied by that data. If you later need a particular data file, you can retrieve that file from your backup. Sharing large amounts of data between computers—as when you send data from one city to another, for example—is more easily accomplished by backing up the data to a tape and sending the tape.

Regardless of how important regular backups are, many people avoid making them. A major reason for this lapse is that for many people, backing up their system is tedious work when they have to use their floppy disk drive. When you use your floppy drive, you may have to insert and remove as many as 150 high-density disks to back up 150M of programs and data, depending on whether your backup software includes *data compression*, the capability to specially encode backed up data in less space than it takes to store the same data on your hard drive.

Tape backup drives are the most simple and efficient device for backing up your system. With a tape backup drive installed in your system, you simply insert a tape into the drive, start your backup software, and select the drive and files you want to back up. The backup software copies your selected files onto the tape while you attend to other business. Later, when you need to retrieve some or all of the files on the backup tape, you insert the tape in the drive, start your backup program, and select the files you want to restore. The tape backup drive takes care of the rest of the job.

This section examines the various types of tape backup drives on the market, describing the capacities of different drives as well as the system requirements for installation and use of a tape drive. The following topics are covered in this section:

■ Common standards for tape backup drives, including QIC-40 and QIC-80 drives

■ Common backup tape capacities

■ Newer higher-capacity tape drives

■ Common tape drive interfaces

■ The QIC standards for tape backup drives

■ Portable tape drives

■ Tape backup software

The Origins of Tape Backup Standards

The evolution of tape backup standards is similar to that of standards for many computer components. Using tape to back up computer data became a common practice long before accepted tape backup standards existed. At first, reel-to-reel systems (somewhat similar to old reel-to-reel audio tape recorders) were used to store data. The most commonly used tape—quarter-inch—eventually developed into a de facto standard. But each tape system manufacturer used its own data-encoding specifications for backup tapes. Variations included not only the number of tracks and data density on the tape, but also the interface used to connect the drive to the computer.

In 1972, more than a decade before the introduction of the first IBM PC the 3M company introduced the first quarter-inch tape cartridge designed for data storage. The cartridge measured 6 by 4 by 5/8 inches. Inside this cartridge, the tape was threaded onto two reels. The tape was moved from one reel to another during the recording or read-back process by a drive belt. Because of the reliability of this tape cartridge, the demand for tape backup systems began to grow, despite the lack of established standards for storing data on these cartridges.

The result of this lack of standardization was that quarter-inch tapes written on one manufacturer's tape backup drive generally could not be read on another manufacturer's quarter-inch tape drive. One problem created by this situation was that the way particular manufacturers encoded data on a tape continued to change. If a particular model of tape drive became disabled and the manufacturer had discontinued that particular drive and no longer used its encoding format, the data stored on tapes written on the disabled drive could be unavailable until the drive had been sent for repairs. In the event the manufacturer could not repair the drive, the data was lost forever.

As with other computer components, such as hard drive interface cards, consumers were the force behind standardization. Consumers clamored for standardized tape drives that could read tapes created on different tape drives manufactured by different companies.

The QIC Standards

In response to this demand for standardization, the tape drive industry formed the Quarter-Inch Cartridge Drive Standards Inc., sometimes simply referred to as the Quarter-Inch Committee (QIC). In 1983–84, the first tape drive based on a QIC standard was shipped: the QIC-02, which stored 60M of data encoded in 9 data tracks on roughly 300 feet of tape.

As the technology improved, and because the 4-by-6-by-5/8-inch size of the first tape cartridges was difficult to adapt to the 5 1/2-inch drive bays in most IBM-compatible personal computers, QIC adopted a second standard for tape cartridges roughly the size of an audio cassette. These minicartridges measure roughly 3 1/4 by 2 1/2-by 3/5 inches.

These two cartridge sizes are currently used in various QIC-standard tape drives. A two-letter code at the end of the QIC standard number designates whether the tape standard is based on the full-sized cartridge or the minicartridge. These two-letter codes are shown in the following:

■ **DC** in a QIC standard number stands for data cartridge, the 4-by-6-by-5/8-inch cassette.

■ **MC** in a QIC standard number stands for minicartridge, the 3 1/4-by-2 1/2-by-3/5-inch cassette.

Table 16.1   Specifications of QIC-Standard Quarter-Inch Tape Cassettes and Minicartridges

QIC Minicartridge Tape Standards

DC-2000 QIC Tape Standards (Approximate Dimensions 3 1/4 by 2 1/2 by 3/5)

QIC Standard Number	Capacity (w/o Compression) (1)	Tracks	Data Transfer Rate (Approximate)
QIC-40	40M/60M	20	2M-to-8M/minute
QIC-80	80M/120M	28	3M-to-9M/minute
QIC-100 (obsolete)	20M/40M	12 or 24	—
QIC-128	86M/128M	32	—
QIC-3010	255M	40	9M/minute
QIC-3020	500M	40	9M/minute
QIC-3030	555M	40	—
QIC-3040	840M (3)	42 or 52	—
QIC-3050	750M	40	—
QIC-3060 (inactive)	875M	38	—
QIC-3070	4G	144	—
QIC-3080	1.6G	50	—
QIC-3110	2G	48	—
QIC-5010	13G	144	—

(1) Tape capacity may vary according to tape length.
(2) Tape lengths may vary by manufacturer.
(3) 1G with drives based on 0.315-inch tape cartridge
(4) SCSI: Small Computer Systems Interface

IV

The new QIC-5GB-DC, for example, is a 5G-capacity tape based on the QIC standard for the full-sized cartridge. The new QIC-5010-MC, which has 13G capacity, is based on the minicartridge standard.

Table 16.1 shows the common QIC-standard tape formats and their technical specifications.

Data Density	Tape Length (2)	Encoding Method	Interface Type
—	205 ft. or 307.5 ft.	MFM	Floppy or optional adapter card
—	205 ft. or 307.5 ft.	MFM	Floppy or optional adapter card
10,000bpi	—	MFM	SCSI (4) or QIC
16,000bpi	—	MFM	SCSI or QIC
22,000bpi	300 ft.	MFM	Floppy or IDE
42,000bpi	400 ft.	MFM	Floppy or IDE
51,000bpi	275 ft.	MFM	SCSI-2 or QIC
41,000bpi	400 ft.	RLL	SCSI-2 or QIC
—	295 ft.	RLL	SCSI-2 or QIC
—	295 ft.	RLL	—
68,000bpi	295 ft.	RLL	SCSI-2 or QIC
60,000bpi	—	RLL	SCSI-2 or QIC
—	—	RLL	SCSI-2 or QIC
—	—	RLL	SCSI-2 or QIC

(continues)

Table 16.1   Continued

QIC Full-Sized Data Cartridge Standards

DC-300a/DC-600/DC-6000 QIC Tape Standards (Approximate Dimensions 4 by 6 by 5/8

QIC Standard Number	Capacity (w/o Compression)	Tracks	Max. Data Transfer Rate (Approximate)
QIC-11 (DC-300)	45M	9	—
QIC-24	45M/60M	9	—
QIC-120	125M	15	—
QIC-150	150M/250M	18	—
QIC-525	320M/525M	26	12M/minute
QIC-1000	1G	30	18M/minute
QIC-1350	1.35G	30	18M/minute
QIC-2100	2.1G	30	18M/minute
QIC-2GB	2.0G	42	18M/minute
QIC-5GB	5G	44	18M/minute
QIC-5010	13G	144	18M/minute

(1) Tape capacity may vary according to tape length.
(2) Tape lengths may vary by manufacturer.

Unlike software whose version numbers (1.0, 1.1, 2.0, 2.1) tell you which version of the software is the most recent, the QIC number designation does not serve as an accurate guide to understanding which QIC-standard tape drives are the latest technology. The designations QIC-100 and QIC-128, for example, were used for tape drives marketed long before today's QIC-40 and QIC-80 drives. Furthermore, the QIC-standard version numbers frequently have no correlation with the capacity of the tape cassettes or minicartridges used with a drive bearing a QIC designation. For example, the QIC-40 tapes have a capacity of 60M; the QIC-80 tapes, a capacity of 120M.

QIC-standard backup tapes are magnetic media, primarily ferric oxide, and are recorded in a manner similar to the way data is encoded on your hard drive, using either modified frequency modulation (MFM) or run-length limited (RLL) technologies.

Common QIC Tape Backup Types

The most common QIC-standard drives, QIC-40 and QIC-80, are based on minicartridges. Millions of drives based on the QIC-40 and QIC-80 standards are currently installed in computer systems. There are several reasons for the success of QIC-40 and QIC-80, not the least of which is that these two standards resulted in the first generation of economically attractive tape drives which stored data in a manner compatible from one manufacturer to another. In other words, QIC-40 and QIC-80 tape drives and tapes are quite affordable and backups made on one QIC-40 or QIC-80 tape drive can be read in a tape drive built by another manufacturer.

Data Density	Tape Length (1)	Encoding Method	Interface Type
—	450 ft.	MFM	QIC-02
8,000	450 ft. or 600 ft.	MFM	SCSI or QIC-02
10,000	600 ft.	MFM	SCSI or QIC-02
10,000bpi	600 ft. or 1,000 ft.	MFM	SCSI or QIC-02
16,000bpi	1,000 ft.	MFM	SCSI or SCSI-2
36,000bpi	760 ft.	MFM	SCSI or SCSI-2
51,000bpi	760 ft.	RLL	SCSI-2
68,000bpi	875 ft.	RLL	SCSI-2
40,640bpi	900 ft.	MFM	SCSI-2
96,000bpi	1,200 ft.	RLL	SCSI-2
68,000bpi	—	RLL	SCSI-2

In addition, the compact size of the minicartridge used for QIC-40 and QIC-80 tapes has resulted in drives made by numerous manufacturers that fit easily into both 5 1/2-inch half-height drive bays and 3 1/2-by-1-inch drive bays. Portable tape drives that read and write QIC-40 and QIC-80 format tapes are quite common. Unlike a drive that is installed in a computer's drive bay, portable drives can be used to back up any number of computers.

Another reason for the success of QIC-40 and QIC-80 tape drives is that the cost of tapes themselves is considerably lower per megabyte than the cost of a stack of floppy disks that can store the same amount of backup data. For example, a name-brand QIC-80 tape that can hold 250M of data (with data compression) costs between $14 and $25. The street price of 13 boxes (of 10) name brand 1.44M 3 1/2-inch floppy disks, which hold roughly the same amount of compressed data, is about $90. The same number of generic, bulk floppy disks, which many people are hesitant to rely upon for backing up important data, costs nearly $50.

One major shortcoming of QIC-40 or QIC-80 tape drives is that the use of the floppy drive interface, especially on an 8-bit PC, makes the tape drive performance extremely slow. Data transfers occur at roughly the same slow rate as when data is written to a floppy disk. More recent drives, used on 386-, 486-, and Pentium-based systems using a 16-bit floppy drive interface and driven by backup software capable of using a Direct Memory Access channel (DMA), have improved this performance markedly.

In addition, drive manufacturers offer special interface cards that speed data transfer even more. It is not uncommon for a tape drive to achieve data transfer speeds of 2M to 4M per minute (with the floppy drive interface) or as high as 9M per minute (with a dedicated interface card).

Backup tapes, like floppy disks and hard drives, must be formatted before use. And one aspect of using a QIC-40 or QIC-80 tape drive—or any tape drive, for that matter—that has not improved is the time it takes to format a tape. Formatting a 60M-length QIC-40 tape can take quite a long time—90 minutes or more. Formatting a 125M length QIC-80 tape can take more than three hours. You can buy preformatted tapes but, as is true with many timesaving products, formatted tapes do cost slightly more than unformatted ones.

Data is stored on QIC-40 and QIC-80 tapes in Modified Frequency Modulation (MFM) format, the format used on floppy disks (and older hard drives). Another similarity in formatting a backup tape, floppy disks, or a hard drive is that the formatting process creates a record-keeping system. The record-keeping system used on QIC-40 and QIC-80 tapes is similar to that on a hard drive or floppy disk.

The QIC standard calls for a file allocation table (FAT) that keeps track of where data is stored on the tape and keeps bad sectors from being used for data storage. A QIC-40 tape is divided into 20 tracks, with each track divided into 68 segments of 29 sectors each. Each sector stores one kilobyte (1,024 bytes). This record-keeping system and the error-correcting system that ensures reliably stored backup data use a total of 30 percent or more of each QIC-40 tape.

Despite the slow backup speeds of tape backup drives on some computers and the time it takes to format tapes, the ease of using a backup tape drive makes it easy to understand the popularity of QIC-40 and QIC-80 tape drives. And that popularity has its benefits. Prices of QIC-80 tape drives—the smallest-capacity tape drives anyone should consider—have plunged in recent years. Name-brand QIC-80 tape backup drives often cost less than $150; sometimes you can buy them for as little as $100 by mail order, through a publication like *Computer Shopper* magazine.

QIC-40 Drives. The first tape backup drives to gain wide acceptance were based on the QIC-40 standard, adopted in 1986. Most early QIC-40 tape drives were built to fit a 5 1/2-inch drive bay, although models designed for 3 1/2-by-1-inch bays became available. The QIC-40-standard drives use an internal power connector and send and receive data through a cable linked to the floppy controller. The first QIC-40 tapes, which had a *native capacity* of 40M (they could hold 40M of data without data compression), were soon followed by QIC-40 tapes capable of holding 60M without data compression.

One disadvantage of the first QIC-40 tape drives was that, because a spare connector had to be used on the floppy drive cable, only one floppy drive could be used on a system in which a tape drive was installed. But with the use of a special cable, more recent QIC-40 drives are easily installed on systems with two floppy drives.

Although a major goal of the QIC organization was to achieve compatibility between tape backup systems, a tape created on one brand of tape drive could not necessarily be read in another brand. Manufacturers still clung to their individual arrangements for the physical placement of data on the tape. The goal of compatibility between tape backup systems became more of a reality with the introduction of QIC-80 drives.

QIC-80 Drives. The QIC-80 tape backup drive is the most popular tape backup drive on the market and the minimum any buyer should consider. QIC-80 tape drives generally are built to fit 3 1/2-by-1-inch bays, although they usually include a frame and faceplate that enable them to be used in a larger 5 1/2-inch bay. Like the QIC-40 drives, QIC-80 tape systems use an internal power connector. The data connection for a QIC-80 tape backup can be the same type of floppy disk controller connection used for QIC-40 drives, or a special high-speed interface installed in an available expansion slot on the mother-board. The use of a high-speed interface card can greatly increase the data transfer rate and decrease the amount of time needed for a backup.

Generally, a tape created on one brand of QIC-80 tape drive can be read and written to by another manufacturer's drive. This improved compatibility is due in large measure to the QIC-80 standard itself, which specifies not only the type of record-keeping system for each tape, but also the logical data structure of the tape. QIC-80-standard drives can read, but not write, QIC-40 tapes.

Portable Tape Drives. The portable tape drive is one of the most popular tape drive configurations because portables can be moved easily from system to system—desktops, laptops, a single system, or multisystem installations. Portable tape drives are particularly useful to people who use laptops (in which an internal tape backup drive will not fit) and those who want to back up a number of systems on a single tape backup drive. Portable tape drives are good also for people who want to use a tape backup drive for their desktop system but whose system has no available drive bay, as is often the case with small profile, or slimline, desktop systems.

Portable tape drives can meet so many needs because these drives are self-contained. The drive itself is contained in a rectangular box. The unit connects to the computer's parallel port and is powered by a transformer that plugs into a common AC socket.

To set up a portable tape drive, you simply plug the transformer cord into the system unit and an AC socket, connect the data cable to the computer's parallel port, and run the backup software. One limitation of portable units is availability of compatible backup software. Although portable tape drive manufacturers include software that operates the drive, some popular third-party backup software cannot be used with portable drives.

The most popular portable tape drives are available in QIC-40 and QIC-80 standards. The QIC-40 models ordinarily can achieve a data transfer rate of 1M to 3M per minute; the QIC-80 models, a rate of 3M to 6M per minute.

Newer High-Capacity QIC-Standard Drives
Using a QIC-40 or QIC-80 tape drive to back up a network server's 2G drive or other large hard drive packed with data can be as frustrating as swapping floppies during a backup

on a system with a more common 200M–500M drive. To back up a 2G network server hard drive with a QIC-40 tape drive without using data compression, for example, you need about 32 tapes. With data compression, the number of tapes drops to 16—but making the backup takes longer.

The solution to this tape-swapping problem is to use a larger-capacity tape drive system. QIC has established a number of standards for higher-capacity tape drive systems ranging from 86M to 13G. Generally, these larger-capacity systems pack data more densely on the tape, using as many as 144 tracks to pack 60,000 bits per inch (bpi) or more onto the tape (compared to the QIC-40's 20 tracks and 10,000 bpi). To achieve these higher capacities, QIC-standards call for tape media with a higher coercivity level of 1,300 oersted or more (compared to QIC-40 and QIC-80 tape media, which has a coercivity level of 550 oersted). High-capacity tapes are also longer. QIC-5010 tapes, for example, are 1,200 feet long (compared to QIC-40 and QIC-80 tapes, both of which are roughly 300 feet long).

> **Note**
>
> Just as the higher coercivity level of 1.44M floppy disks enables a high-density drive to use lower levels of power to write narrower tracks of data more closely together than is possible with 720K floppy disks, higher coercivity tape enables more precise tape drive head-positioning mechanisms to write narrower tracks of data to the tape.

Although tape systems based on the minicartridge dominate the market for lower capacity tape drives (the QIC-40 60M and QIC-80 120M systems), high-capacity tape backup systems are based on both minicartridge-sized tapes and full-sized data cartridge tapes. For example, the QIC-525 standard, which has a capacity of 525M (without data compression), is based on the full-sized (4-by-6-by-5/8) cartridge. The QIC-5010 standard is based on a minicartridge (3 1/4 by 2 1/2 by 3/5).

QIC-Tape Compatibility

Although QIC-standard drives are based on the standard minicartridge and the full-sized data cartridge, it would be a mistake to assume that tapes based on the same cartridge standard are always compatible. For example, QIC-5010-standard tapes are incompatible with QIC-40 and QIC-80 tape backup systems, although both standards are based on the minicartridge. Similarly, QIC-525-standard tapes are incompatible with earlier standards based on the full-sized data cartridge. The lack of compatibility between tapes based on the same sized cartridge is due to differences in tape drive mechanisms, as well as the coercivity differences between tape standards. Table 16.2 shows the compatibility of common QIC-standard backup tapes.

Table 16.2 QIC-Tape-Standard Compatibility

QIC Minicartridge Standard	Compatibility
QIC-40	—
QIC-80	QIC-40 (read-only)
QIC-100	—
QIC-128	QIC-100 (read-only)
QIC-3010	QIC-40 and QIC-80 (read only)
QIC-3030	QIC-3010 (read-only)
QIC-3070	QIC-3030 (read-only)

QIC Full-Sized Cartridge Standard	Compatibility
QIC-24	—
QIC-120	QIC-24 (read-only)
QIC-150	QIC-24 and QIC-120 (read-only)
QIC-525	QIC-24, QIC-120, and QIC-150 (read-only)
QIC-1000	QIC-120, QIC-150, and QIC-525 (read-only)
QIC-1350	QIC-525 and QIC-1000 (read-only)
QIC-2GB	QIC-120, QIC-150, QIC-525, and QIC-1000 (read-only)
QIC-2100	QIC-525 and QIC-1000 (read-only)
QIC-5GB	QIC-24, QIC-120, QIC-150, QIC-525, and QIC-1000 (read-only)
QIC-5010	QIC-150, QIC-525, and QIC-1000 (read-only)

Tape compatibility is an important issue to consider when you choose a tape backup system. For example, as you can see from table 16.2, the 4G QIC-3070-standard drive can read only its own tapes and those that conform to the QIC-3030 standard. If you have many QIC-80 tapes containing data you must be able to continue to access, a better choice might be a drive based on the 2G QIC-3010 standard. The QIC-3010 can read QIC-40 and QIC-80 tapes. This chapter's "Choosing a Tape Backup Drive" section covers similar issues to be considered when you purchase a new tape backup drive.

Other High-Capacity Tape Drive Standards

Although ferric oxide QIC-standard tapes continue to be popular, two other types of tape backup systems are becoming increasingly popular for backing up networks and other systems with large amounts of data: 4mm digital audio tape (DAT) and 8mm video tape.

Sony, which introduced both DAT tape and 8mm videotape, licenses DAT tape technologies to other manufacturers, in effect setting the standard for drives and tapes manufactured by those companies. Because the 8mm tape backup drive technologies have been developed by a variety of manufacturers, there is no recognized 8mm standard. For that reason, a QIC-standard or DAT tape drive might be a better choice for most potential buyers of backup tape systems. Table 16.3 shows the basic specifications of the DAT and 8mm technology tapes.

Table 16.3   DAT and 8mm Tape Specifications

Tape Standard	Capacity (w/o Compression)	Data Density	Tracks (Approximate)
DAT tape (4mm metal particle)	1.3G/2G/ square in.	114 megabits	1,869
8mm video tape (Sony-standard)	10G	NA	NA

(1) DDS: digital data storage

Helical scan recording is similar in many ways to the way video images are recorded to videotape. As with QIC-standard tape drives, DAT and 8mm tapes move past the recording heads, which are mounted on a drum. These read/write heads rotate at a slight angle to the tape, writing a section of a *helix*, or spiral. The tape drive mechanism wraps the tape about half way around the read/write heads, causing the heads to touch the tape at an angle. With helical scan technology, the entire surface of the tape is used to record data, unlike other technologies in which data tracks are separated by areas of unrecorded tape. This use of the entire tape surface enables helical scan backup drives to pack a much greater amount of data on a particular length of tape.

The DAT Tape Drive Standard. The technology behind the digital audio tape is similar in many ways to the techniques used to record music and encode it on musical compact discs (CDs). Data is not recorded on the tape in the MFM or RLL format used by QIC-standard drives; rather, bits of data received by the tape drive are assigned numerical values, or digits. Then these digits are translated into a stream of electronic pulses that are placed in the tape. Later, when information is being restored to a computer system from the tape, the DAT tape drive translates these digits back into binary bits that can be stored on the computer.

The most common capacity for DAT tapes is 1.3G, although increased tape length is making higher-capacity DAT backup drives and tapes more common. Two types of data formats—digital data storage (DDS) and DataDAT—are used for DAT tapes.

Thanks to the digital audio tape technology, the DAT tape backup drives are able to pack an incredible amount of information on the tiny cassettes (roughly 1/2 by 3 by 2 inches). DAT technology uses an extremely sensitive tape (1,450 oersted metal particle) that packs 114 megabits of data per square inch, the densest data storage of any backup tape technology.

The 8mm Tape Drive. A single manufacturer, Exabyte, offers tape backup drives that take advantage of 8mm videotape cartridges. These drives are offered in two capacities: 1.5G (3G, with hardware data compression), for the least expensive drives, and 5G (10G, with hardware compression) for the more expensive models. Although these drives use 8mm videotapes, video technology is not used in the process of recording computer data to these drives. Rather, Exabyte developed its own technology for encoding data on the tapes. The helical scan method is used to record data to the tape.

Tape Length	Recording Technology	Encoding Format	Interface
195 ft./300 ft.	Helical Scan DataDAT	DDS (1)	SCSI
2-hour video	Helical Scan/ proprietary	NTSC	Proprietary

The highest capacity 8mm tape backup drives are somewhat expensive. For example, one hardware vendor specializing in network hardware recently offered the 5G to 10G capacity Exabyte 8505i half-height internal drive for $2,265. That might seem expensive when the Exabyte drive is compared, gigabyte for gigabyte, with the 2G (4G, with software data compression) Colorado Memory Systems PowerDAT 6000 tape drive, offered by the same vendor for $1,295.

But the 30M per minute data throughput rate of the Exabyte 8mm tape backup drive, compared with the 10M per minute throughput of the DAT drive, makes the 8mm tape drive a more attractive choice. The extraordinary speed and huge capacity of these 8mm tape drives makes them extremely attractive for backing up network servers and for backing up workstations from the server. You can reach Colorado Memory Systems and Exabyte by writing or calling:

Colorado Memory Systems Inc.
800 S. Taft Avenue
Loveland, CO 80537
(800)845-7905
(800)451-4523

Exabyte Corporation
11100 West 82nd Street
Lexena, KS 66214
(913)492-6002
(800)825-4727

Choosing a Tape Backup Drive

Choosing a tape backup drive can be a simple job if you need to back up a single standalone system with a 500M (or smaller) hard drive. The decision becomes more complex if the system has a larger hard drive or if you must back up not only a desktop system, but also a laptop. Choosing a backup tape drive type can be an even more complex problem if you must back up a network server's 3G hard drive and perhaps even back up the workstations from the server. As you ponder which backup tape drive type you should choose, consider the following factors:

- The amount of data you must back up

- The data throughput you need

- The tape standard that is best for your needs
- The cost of the drive and tapes

By balancing the considerations of price, capacity, throughput, and tape standard, you can find a tape drive that best meets your needs.

> **Note**
>
> When purchasing a tape backup drive, take the time to look through a magazine like the *Computer Shopper*. Published monthly, the *Computer Shopper* is more a catalog than a magazine. It caters to people willing to spend money in the *direct channel* (often called *mail order*). Many of the vendors who advertise in direct channel magazines have cut their prices to the bone. By reading such publications, you can get an excellent idea of the drives available and the price you can expect to pay.

Capacity. The first rule for choosing a tape backup drive is to buy a drive whose capacity is large enough for your needs, now and for the forseeable future. The ideal is to buy a drive with enough capacity that you can start your backup software, insert a blank tape in the drive, walk away from the system (or go about other work), and find the backup completed when you return. You can safely store the tape and resume working.

Given that ideal, an internal QIC-80 drive might be just the ticket if you need to back up a single system with a hard drive of 250M or less. If you need to back up several systems, including laptops, with hard drives of 250M or less, a portable QIC-80 drive might be the solution.

But if you must back up a large network server hard drive, relying on a QIC-80 tape drive with its 125M capacity (250, with software data compression) is a bad idea. A better choice would be one of the larger-capacity tape backup drive systems detailed earlier in this chapter.

Tape Standards. The next most important consideration, after adequate capacity, is choosing a drive whose tapes meet a standard that is useful to you. For example, if you must be able to restore backup data using any of a number of different tape backup drives, you should ensure that all these drives can at least read the tapes. For this reason, if you have several systems to work with, you should choose a tape standard that will work in them all.

There is no quick, simple answer as to which standard is the best. Many people stick with QIC-standard drives because QIC created the first standards and continues to develop new standards for large-capacity tape backups. But if you need a large-capacity backup tape system, DAT or 8mm may be the correct choice.

If you need backward compatibility with tapes or tape drives you already have, you will need to buy drives that are the same standard or a higher compatible standard. For example, if you need a large-capacity tape drive that is backwardly compatible with your

QIC-80 tapes, you should consider the 2G-capacity QIC-3010, which reads QIC-40 and QIC-80 tapes. If, on the other hand, you don't have to worry about data already stored on old tapes, the important considerations may be capacity and performance. Therefore DAT or 8mm drives may be the best choice.

It is important that you make a choice you can live with. If you manage a large installation of computers, mixing QIC, DAT, and 8mm drives among systems is seldom a good idea.

Data Throughput. Without question, you should consider the 8mm drives if performance is more important to you than price or compatibility. These drives offer huge capacity and tremendous data throughput—as high as 30M per minute. Large-capacity drives based on newer QIC-standards are capable of 18M per minute throughput. DAT tape drives offer throughput of 10M per minute.

The low end of the tape backup drive performance spectrum is older QIC-80 standard drives. When linked to a floppy controller, these drives achieve 3M to 4M per minute throughput. Even with a dedicated interface card purchased at added cost, QIC-80 drives are lucky to achieve their advertised throughput of 9M per minute. Portable QIC-80 drives are advertised at 3M to 8M per minute, but 2M or 3M a minute is a more realistic figure.

The Cost of the Drive and Tapes. It pays to shop enthusiastically for price after you have settled on the type of drive you want to buy. The cost of tape drives and their tapes quite literally depends on where you buy. For example, the internal Colorado Memory Systems PowerDAT Series 6000 tape drive, purchased directly from Colorado, costs $1,695, a price close to that charged by many retail stores. The same DAT drive, advertised by several vendors in *Computer Shopper*, can be purchased for roughly $1,130, a savings of nearly $600. Regardless of where you buy the drive, the Colorado warranty remains in effect.

The cost of backup tapes also varies widely, depending on where you buy. The same name-brand DAT tape that costs as much as $14 from one vendor can cost $12 from another. The cost of a formatted name-brand QIC-80 (120M) tape can range from $15 to $26, depending on where you buy it. Because many computer retailers and direct channel vendors offer lower prices when you buy three or more tapes at a time, it pays to shop for price and buy the largest quantity of tapes you expect to need.

One point worth remembering when you evaluate whether to buy a tape drive is that the cost of the tapes and drive, taken as a whole, is nowhere near as high as the costs (in terms of frustration and lost productivity) of a single data-damaging hard drive problem. Considering that most people are more likely to back up their system if they have a tape drive installed than if they must use floppy disks for the backup, the cost of a drive and tapes is quite small, even on a stand-alone PC used mostly for fun.

Tape Drive Installation Issues

Each of the tape drive standards covered in this chapter provides a range of options for installation. These options include both internal and external installation. Whether to choose an internal or external drive, and which external drive to choose, if that appears to be the best choice for you, is not always a cut-and-dried issue. If you must back up a single computer with a relatively small hard drive (500M or less), an internal QIC-80 drive might be your best choice. If you have to back up several computers with 500M hard drives, or if you must be able to share data between several computers, you might be able to make do with a QIC-80 portable. If your backup needs are not that simple, however, here are some additional considerations:

- If your computer has a large hard drive and you back up often, or if you administer a large number of systems and want to minimize the amount of work you must do and the number of tapes you have to store for each computer, installing large-capacity QIC, DAT, or 8mm tape drives in each computer might be what you need to do.

- If your best choice is a large capacity QIC, DAT, or 8mm tape drive and almost all the computers you administer have an available drive bay, you might choose a portable DAT or 8mm tape system, which can be moved from system to system.

> **Caution**
>
> Steer away from nonstandard tape backup drives. For example, some drives may not conform to QIC, DAT, or Exabyte standards. Since Exabyte is the only manufacturer of 8mm tape backup drives, you can be confident that tapes made on this manufacturer's drives can be read on their drives. Also avoid drives based on VHS videotape. Many people consider these drives extremely unreliable.

Although some of the larger-capacity drives are available in external models, few models, except for QIC-80 portables like the Colorado Memory Systems Inc. Jumbo Trakker, can be considered truly portable. The reason is that most external tape drives require an interface card installed in a motherboard slot, whereas the QIC-40 and QIC-80 portables require only that the computer have a parallel port. The following sections cover some important installation issues for internally and externally mounted drives.

Internal Installation. Virtually all internal tape backup drives available today are designed to be installed in a half-height drive bay. Many are designed to be installed in either half-height drive bays or the smaller drive bays generally used for 3 1/2-inch floppy drives. Drives that can be installed in 3 1/2-inch floppy drive bays generally are shipped in a cage, or frame, that enables them to be installed in a 5 1/4-inch bay. To install the drive in a 3 1/2-inch bay, you remove the cage and the 5 1/4-inch bay faceplate. Most tape drives are between about 5 and 9 inches deep; they require approximately 5–9 inches of clearance inside the system case. To mount tape drives inside the system, use the same rails or cage apparatus used for floppy drives, hard drives, and devices such as CD-ROM drives.

> **Note**
>
> Half-height drive bays measure roughly 1.7 inches high by 5.9 inches wide. The smaller drive bays measure 1 by 4 inches.

Internal tape drives require a spare power connector, usually the larger connector used for hard drives, although some may require the smaller power connector common to 3 1/2-inch floppy drives. If a power connector is not available inside your system, you can buy a *power splitter* from a computer store or cable supply vendor. A power splitter looks like the letter Y and acts like an extension cord. You unplug the power connector from a device (such as a floppy drive) that's already installed. Then plug the bottom point of the Y into that power connector. The two arms of the Y then provide you with two power connectors.

Internal tape drives also require an interface to the system. QIC-40 and QIC-80 drives most often connect to the system through the floppy controller. On a system with only one floppy drive you connect the tape drive to an unused connector on the floppy disk data cable. On systems with two floppy disk drives you use a special cable linked to the floppy disk data cable which is in effect a splitter cable.

Internal drives other than QIC-40s and QIC-80s usually require a special adapter card, or they may link to a card already installed in your system. This card is usually one of the following: a QIC-standard adapter card, a Small Computer Systems Interface (SCSI) adapter, a SCSI-2 adapter card, or an Integrated Drive Electronics (IDE) card. When purchasing a drive, you must determine which interface you need; make sure that the drive kit includes the adapter card you need or that you purchase the correct card.

External Installation. If you want to move an external tape drive (except the portable QIC-40 and QIC-80 tape backup drives) from computer to computer, you must install an adapter card in each system on which you want to use the tape drive. Portable QIC-40 and QIC-80 tape backup drives like the Jumbo Trakker use the computer's parallel port connector. Adapter cards designed for use with external tape drives have a connector, somewhat similar to a parallel port connector, that is accessible from the back panel of the system unit. These cards generally are QIC-standard, SCSI, SCSI-2, or IDE.

When you buy an external tape backup drive that requires an adapter, you must ensure either that the drive includes the necessary adapter card or that you purchase the card at the same time you purchase the drive. In addition, if you plan to use the external tape drive to back up a number of systems, you must buy a card for each system on which you plan to use the drive.

Power is supplied to external units by a transformer that plugs into an ordinary 120v AC wall socket. Generally, the transformer connects to the external tape drive with a small connector. When you choose an external tape drive, be sure you have enough AC power sockets available for your computer, its peripherals, and the tape drive.

Tape Drive Backup Software

The most important decision you can make after you choose the tape standard and capacity of your backup tape drive is the backup software you will use with it. Most tape drives are shipped with backup software that generally is adequate for your basic backup needs.

Often, however, third-party software compatible with the drive you have chosen gives you greater flexibility and functionality. For example, some tape drives may be shipped with only DOS-based software. If you want to use one of these drives from within Windows, or on a system running OS/2 or UNIX, you may need to purchase third-party backup software. And if you will be backing up network workstations from a server, you must make sure that the drive is shipped with software capable of performing this function; otherwise, you will need to acquire third-party software.

One important issue with backup software is data compression. Most backup software offers data compression, special programming that stores data on the backup tape in less space than is needed on the original source disk. Some companies produce backup software that is well known for especially efficient data compression. In other words, backup software produced by these companies does a better job of compressing large data files into a small amount of space.

Note

Microsoft Backup (MSBACKUP.EXE) and Windows Backup (MWBACKUP.EXE), which are included with DOS 6.0 and later versions, do not work with tape drives. You must use either the software bundled with the drive or purchase third-party software. A similar problem is that some well-known third-party software does not work with the Colorado Jumbo Trakker portables. With these drives, you may need to use the excellent software for Windows and DOS provided by Colorado or purchase software that will work with remote tape drives.

You may want to take the time to read some articles on backup software in one of the many monthly computer magazines, such as *Byte* or *PCWorld*. These and other magazines frequently determine which backup software does the best job of compressing data; they also provide information on how quickly backup software programs perform a typical backup. The speed of the backup software and its data-compression capabilities are important considerations. Also of great importance is whether the software is easy to use. If your backup software makes backing up more difficult than it has to be, chances are you won't back up as often as you should.

Bundled Software. Before you buy a backup tape drive you should always check whether the drive includes software that will meet your needs. If it doesn't, be sure to buy third-party software that does the job. Generally, the software bundled with most tape backup drives will do the job for you—provided that you don't plan to place great demands on the tape drive.

The software included with a QIC-80 drive, for example, generally cannot be used to back up network workstations from the server. If you want to use a QIC-80 drive for this task, you may need to buy special software compatible with your network and the tape backup drive. If you use Windows, Windows NT, OS/2, or UNIX, your backup software must be compatible with your operating system as well as the drive, and you must determine whether the software shipped with the drive will do the job for you.

Third-Party Software. A large number of companies manufacture backup software designed for different types of tape drives and different uses. For example, many manufacturers design their backup software to be compatible with most networks. Others specialize in DOS and Windows backup software. Some specialize in OS/2 software. Others are well known among those whose computers run in UNIX. You may need to ask a trusted retailer or call the software company itself to determine whether a particular type of software is compatible not only with the tape drive you have chosen, but also with your network and operating environment.

Often, third-party software is easier to use than the software designed by a tape manufacturer. The tape manufacturer's software may have an unfamiliar interface or its commands may seem cryptic to you, even if you have used backup software for years. It is not uncommon for tape manufacturers to include inadequate or even incomplete documentation for the backup software included with the drive, although this generally is the case only with lower cost models. In such a case, you may be able to solve the problem by purchasing third-party software.

Third-party software often does a better job of data compression than the software designed by a tape manufacturer. In addition, third-party software often includes capabilities not included with the software bundled with many drives. Some of the capabilities you might want to look for include the following:

- *Unattended backup scheduling.* Enabling you to schedule a backup for a time when you won't need to use your computer

- *Macro capability.* For selecting options and the files to back up

- *A quick tape-erase capability.* For erasing the entire contents of a tape

- *Partial tape-erase capability.* For erasing only part of a tape

- *Tape unerase capability.* For recovering erased data

- *Password protect capability.* To protect backup data from access by unauthorized persons

The following is a short list of backup software manufacturers with a good reputation for programs that are easy to use, reliable, and do a good job with data compression.

Norton Backup
10201 Torre Avenue
Cupertino, CA 95014
(408)253-9600
(800)441-7234

Central Point Backup
15220 NW Greenbrier Parkway
Suite 150
Beaverton, OR 97006
(800)445-4208
(503)690-8088

FastBack Backup
Fifth Generation Systems
10049 N. Reiger Rd.
Baton Rouge, LA
(800)873-4384
(504)291-7221

You can find additional backup software manufacturers by reading some of the many monthly computer magazines, paying particular attention to their usability reviews. Generally, if a backup software product gets good reviews, works on a system configuration like yours, and has the features you need, it is worth the price you pay.

Removable Storage Drives

The reason for the shortage of storage space on today's PCs is easy enough to understand. Just take a look at the sheer number and size of the files stored in the two main directories used by Windows (usually C:\WINDOWS and C:\WINDOWS\SYSTEM). The amount of disk space used by the files in those two directories alone can quickly balloon to 40M or more after you also install a few Windows applications. The reason is simple: Nearly all Windows applications place files in one of the Windows directories that the application will use later. These files include those with extensions like DLL, 386, VBX, DRV, TTF, and many others. Similarly, Windows NT, OS/2, and UNIX, as well as the software applications that run in these operating systems, can require enormous amounts of storage space.

The remainder of this chapter focuses on some of the more advanced data storage options on the market: removable media large-capacity storage drives. Some removable media drives use media as small as a 1.44M floppy disk, others use media about the size of a 5 1/4-inch floppy.

These drives, whose capacities range from 35M to 270M, offer fairly speedy performance, the ability to store data or less frequently used programs on a removable disk, and the ability to easily transport huge data files—Computer Aided Drawing (CAD) files and graphics files, for example—from one computer to another. Or you can use a removable media disk to remove sensitive data from your office so that you can lock it safely away from prying eyes.

There are two commonly used types of removable media drives: magnetic media and optical media, also called *magneto-optical* media. Magnetic media drives use much the same technology used on a floppy disk or hard drive to encode data for storage. Magneto-optical media drives encode information on disk by using newer technology, a combination of traditional magnetic and laser technologies.

Magnetic media drives are considerably faster than magneto-optical drives and offer similar capacities. The SyQuest magnetic media drives, for example, offer 14ms average access times, compared to the 30ms (or slower) access times of magneto-optical drives. Magneto-optical drives can be more than twice as expensive as magnetic media drives. If you have a great deal of data to store, however, the comparative cost of using a magneto-optical drive drops because magneto-optical media cartridges are considerably less expensive than magnetic media. For example, when you buy 10, 270M SyQuest cartridges can cost roughly $80 each, and 150M Bernoulli cartridges can cost about $90 apiece. The 128M magneto-optical cartridges can cost as little as $25 apiece when you buy 10.

The following section provides information on magnetic media and magneto-optical drive types.

Magnetic Media Drives

A small group of companies dominate the market for magnetic removable media drives. One company, Iomega Bernoulli, always tops the list because it developed the first popular large-capacity removable magnetic media drives, and because its disk cartridges are known as the most rugged in the industry. Two other leading names in removable magnetic media drives are SyQuest and SyDOS (owned by SyQuest).

Both the Bernoulli and SyQuest designs are their own de facto standard. Other manufacturers market drives based on the Bernoulli and SyQuest designs (and some actually manufactured by Bernoulli or SyQuest). Generally these manufacturers' drives are somewhat less expensive than the Bernoulli and SyQuest models. If you are considering one of these compatible drives, however, make sure that the drive you are buying has the same performance characteristics (average access speed, and so on) as the original and that the drive manufacturer offers the same warranty as the original (Bernoulli, three years; SyQuest/SyDOS, two years).

Bernoulli Removable Media Drives. The disk used in the Bernoulli Drive is roughly the same size as a 5 1/4-inch floppy disk, although a large shutter, similar to the shutter on a 3 1/2-inch floppy disk, easily differentiates Bernoulli disks from floppy disks. Modern Bernoulli cartridges are available in 35M, 65M, 105M, and 150M capacities. The Iomega Bernoulli MultiDisk 150 drive, the company's newest model, reads and writes all of these drive capacities. In addition, the MultiDisk reads and writes to older Bernoulli 90M disks and reads older 40M disks. The MultiDisk is available in both internal and external models.

Bernoulli disks are widely known as the most durable of the removable media drive types. It is probably safer to mail a Bernoulli cartridge than another type of removable disk because the media is well protected inside the cartridge. Bernoulli encases a magnetic-media-covered flexible disk (in effect, a floppy disk) in a rigid cartridge in the same way the thin disk of a 1.44M floppy is encased in a rigid plastic shell.

When it rotates in the drive the disk floats on a cushion of air fractions of an inch from the read/write head. As the disk spins, the airflow generated by the disk movement encounters what is called a *Bernoulli plate,* a stationary plate designed to control the air flow so that the disk is pulled toward the read/write head but never touches the head itself. The disk itself spins at speeds approaching the 3,600 rpm of relatively slow hard drives. The drive has an average seek time of 18ms, not a great deal slower than today's medium-priced hard drives.

The Bernoulli MultiDisk 150 drive is available in an internal model, which requires a half-height drive bay, and an external model. The internal model connects to the IDE hard drive adapter already installed in your system. The external model requires a SCSI adapter card with an external connector. The external model is powered by a transformer that connects to a grounded AC wall plug.

SyQuest Removable Media Drives. SyQuest manufactures some drives that use 5 1/4-inch cartridges and others that use 3 1/2-inch cartridges. But the SyQuest disks, like the Bernoulli cartridges, are easily differentiated from floppy disks. The 5 1/4-inch 44M and 88M cartridges used in some SyDOS drives are encased in clear plastic, as are the SyDOS 3 1/2-inch 105M and SyQuest 270M cartridges. The disk spins inside the cartridge at several thousand rpm. SyQuest claims a 14ms average access time for the drives it manufactures.

The disks for the SyQuest and SyDOS drives are composed of a rigid platter inside a plastic cartridge but are not as well protected as the disk in a Bernoulli cartridge. Some people consider these disks fragile. If the SyQuest and SyDOS cartridges are not severely jostled or dropped, however, they can be transported safely. These cartridges must be carefully protected when they are mailed or shipped.

The SyQuest/SyDOS drives are available in internal and external models. The internal models require a connection to the existing IDE hard drive interface card. The external models require a SCSI interface card with an external connector and are powered by a transformer that connects to a grounded AC wall plug.

Floptical Drives

Floptical drives are another popular form of increased-capacity removable magnetic media drives. However, unlike Bernoulli and SyQuest drives, flopticals do not provide hard drive-sized storage capacities. Instead, flopticals pack 21M of data on the same sized disk as a 3 1/2-inch floppy. In addition, floptical drives can read and write 1.44M and 720K floppy disks (although they cannot handle 2.88M disks as of this writing). Because of their greatly increased storage capacity and ability to use common floppy disks, flopticals are considered by many to be the super floppy disk drive.

The name "floptical" might suggest the use of laser beams to burn or etch data onto the disk or to excite the media in preparation for magnetic recording—as is the case with the CD-ROM, Write-Once Read-Many (WORM), and magneto-optical disks discussed later in this chapter. But this suggestion is erroneous. The read/write heads of a floptical drive use magnetic recording technology, much like that of floppy drives. The floptical disk itself is composed of the same ferrite materials common to floppy and hard disks. Floptical drives are capable of such increased capacity because 755 tracks are packed on each disk, compared with the 80 tracks of a 1.44M floppy. Obviously, in order to fit so many tracks on the floptical disk, the tracks must be much more narrow than those on a floppy disk.

That's where optical technology comes into play. Flopticals use a special optical mechanism to properly position the drive read/write heads over the data tracks on the disk. The way this works, servo information, which specifically defines the location of each track, is embedded in the disk during the manufacturing process. Each track of servo information is actually etched or stamped on the disk and is never disturbed during the recording process. Each time the floptical drive writes to the disk, the recording mechanism (including the read/write heads) is guided by a laser beam precisely into place by this servo information. When the floptical drive reads the encoded data, this servo information again is used by the laser to guide the read/write heads precisely into place.

Each floptical disk track is formatted to 27 sectors of 512 bytes. The disks themselves revolve at 720 rpm. Flopticals are capable of nearly 10M-per-minute data throughput. These drives require a special interface. Most use an adaptation of the standard SCSI interface, although some brands require a proprietary interface. Many flopticals can be configured as drive A, so they can be used to boot your system. Each floptical drive comes with special software drivers and utilities that enable the drive to function properly on your system.

Magneto-Optical Drives

Magneto-optical drives, which are manufactured by a large number of companies, use an ingenious combination of magnetic and laser technology to pack data on 5 1/4-inch and 3 1/2-inch disks contained in cartridges. The media itself and the construction of the platter are similar in ways to the media of a CD-ROM disc. An aluminum base is covered with clear plastic, then a layer of magnetic, optically active media particles—an alloy of cobalt, iron, and terbium. A clear plastic coating seals the disk, rendering it nearly impervious to shock, contamination, and damage.

Although the magneto-optical disks are similar to CD-ROM discs, there is a world of difference in the way data is stored. When manufacturers write CD-ROM discs, the laser actually burns pits into the media to represent the data. These pits are read by the laser and translated into the form of computer data. In the case of magneto-optical disks, the magnetically/optically active media is not burned or pitted. Instead, during the writing process a magneto-optical drive focuses a laser beam onto a very tight track—a much thinner track than could be used to store data on a purely magnetic media platter. The laser beam heats the track and a weak magnetic signal is applied. The result is that only the thin track of heated media receives the magnetic signal and stores the data it contains.

Unlike a CD-ROM disc, a magneto-optical disk theoretically can be rewritten an infinite number of times because the media is never burned or pitted. When the time comes to erase data from or rewrite the disk, the disk is simply reheated with the laser and the old data removed magnetically so that new data can be recorded. When the magneto-optical drive reads the disk, the drive functions optically—that is, the laser reads the data from the disk (without heating the media).

Because of the thin tracks on which data is written to magneto-optical disks, the data is packed extremely densely: large amounts of data can be packed on a platter about the same size as common 3 1/2-inch and 5 1/4-inch floppy disks. The current maximum capacity of the 3 1/2-inch cartridges is 230M; the 5 1/2-inch cartridges can hold as much as a gigabyte of data. It is important to note, however, that capacity ratings of magneto-optical disks can be misleading. Magneto-optical disks are double sided, like floppy disks, but magneto-optical drives have only one read/write head. Therefore, to read or write to the second side you must manually flip over the cartridge. So only half the disk capacity is available at any one time.

For many applications, magneto-optical drives are tediously slow, although some drives—using refinements of the basic magneto-optical technology—offer data-access speeds that are inching more closely to those of removable magnetic media drives. One reason that magneto-optical drives are slow is that they typically spin the disk at roughly 2,000 rpm—much slower than the 3,600 rpm of a relatively slow hard drive. Another reason for the slow speeds is that the read/write head mechanism, although optically and magnetically advanced, is mechanically a kludge. The massive mechanism of a magneto-optical drive's read/write heads takes much longer to move and settle than the read/write heads of a hard drive or even a removable magnetic media drive.

Magneto-optical drives typically are rated with average access speeds of about 30ms. However, these average access speed figures do not tell the entire story. The process of rewriting a disk can take nearly twice the time it takes to read the disk. Because of the way magnetic-optical technology works, all the bias magnetic field of the area of the disk to be written must be oriented in a single direction during the write process. Because of this limitation, during the write process most magneto-optical drives must make a first pass over the disk to align the tracks of the disk that are to be rewritten. Then the drive makes a second pass over the disk to realign, or change the alignment of, the necessary areas. This alignment/realignment process is known as *two pass recording*.

New magneto-optical technologies are emerging which use single-pass recording of disks. If speed is an important factor in choosing a magneto-optical drive, you should be prepared to pay extra for a drive whose performance is not penalized by two-pass recording technology. In addition, several manufacturers are offering drives that spin the platter at speeds approaching the 3,600 rpm speeds of a hard drive. The performance boost offered by these drives is considerable, but this technology also boosts considerably the prices of these drives.

Most manufacturers adhere to the International Standards Organization specifications for magneto-optical disks and drives. The ISO standard calls for all drives to use a SCSI host adapter to interface with the computer. Under the ISO standard, 5 1/4-inch drives must be able to read two different disk formats: disks with 512-byte sectors and disks with 1,024-byte sectors. The disks with 512-byte sectors have a capacity of roughly

600M; those 1,024-byte sectors hold 650M of data. Under the ISO standard the 3 1/2-inch drives, which are quite popular among first-time purchasers, are required to read only the 128M disks. Some manufacturers, in addition to designing their drives to meet ISO standards, also design their drives to use a proprietary data format that can increase the capacity of 5 1/4-inch disks to about 1.3G. Both 5 1/4-inch and 3 1/2-inch drives are available as internal and external units.

Write-Once Read-Many (WORM) Drives

The removable media drive known as *write-once read-many* (WORM) is designed to serve as a nearly bulletproof data archival system. If you have extremely important data files that absolutely must remain in an unaltered state, perhaps accounting or database data, a WORM drive can provide the kind of security you are looking for. Data written to a WORM disk cannot be changed.

The WORM disk is encased in a high-impact cartridge with a sliding shutter similar to the shutter on a 3 1/2-inch floppy disk. The cartridge and the extremely durable nature of the disk inside make WORM disks worry free for data exchange. A WORM drive cartridge is very difficult to damage. The disk itself, with the media sandwiched in plastic, is not unlike a CD-ROM disc or a magneto-optical disk. The technology used to write a WORM disk, however, is more like the technology used for CD-ROM recording than that used for writing to magneto-optical disks. The WORM drive uses a laser to burn microscopic patches of darkness into the light-colored media.

A number of companies manufacture WORM drives but follow no single standard. Therefore, a WORM disk written on one manufacturer's drive is quite unlikely to be readable on another manufacturer's drive. Each manufacturer (sometimes small groups of manufacturers) uses its own proprietary data format and disk capacity and many use a cartridge size only their drives can handle. For example, most WORM drives are designed for 5 1/4-inch cartridges but some WORM drives handle only 12-inch disks. In addition, although most WORM drives interface the computer via a SCSI host adapter, others use different interfaces, some of them proprietary.

Certainly, at least in part because of these incompatibility problems, WORM drives are not big sellers. No more than several thousand are sold each year at prices soaring to the heights—some 5 1/4-inch drives cost several thousand dollars. The 5 1/4-inch-drive cartridges, which range in capacity from 650M to 1.3G, can cost more than $180.

The term *niche market* is used occasionally to describe a computer product or peripheral that lacks broad appeal or usefulness. Because of its cost and incompatibility problems, WORM drive technology is a niche market product. Unless you must be able to store massive amounts of data and ensure it can never be altered, you are better off buying a magneto-optical drive, or perhaps even a tape backup drive.

Summary

This chapter examined a wide range of data storage options, including backup tape drives and large-capacity removable media drives. The QIC standards for tape backup drives as well as DAT and 8mm tape drives also were covered. In addition, you were given some useful guidelines for choosing the tape backup drive that is right for your computer or the computer installation you administer.

In addition, this chapter covered magnetic media drives, such as those manufactured by Bernoulli and SyQuest, and discussed the similarities and the differences between these two de facto standards in large-capacity removable magnetic media drives. Floptical drives also were covered.

This chapter also discussed magneto-optical drives, detailing their strengths and weaknesses, explaining the technology of writing data to and reading it from magneto-optical disks, and offering some guidelines that may help you decide whether magneto-optical drive technology will meet your needs.

Finally, this chapter discussed WORM drives and their uses. It also discussed the incompatibilities between WORM drives, and different media, and explained why WORM drives are appropriate only for a small segment of computer users.

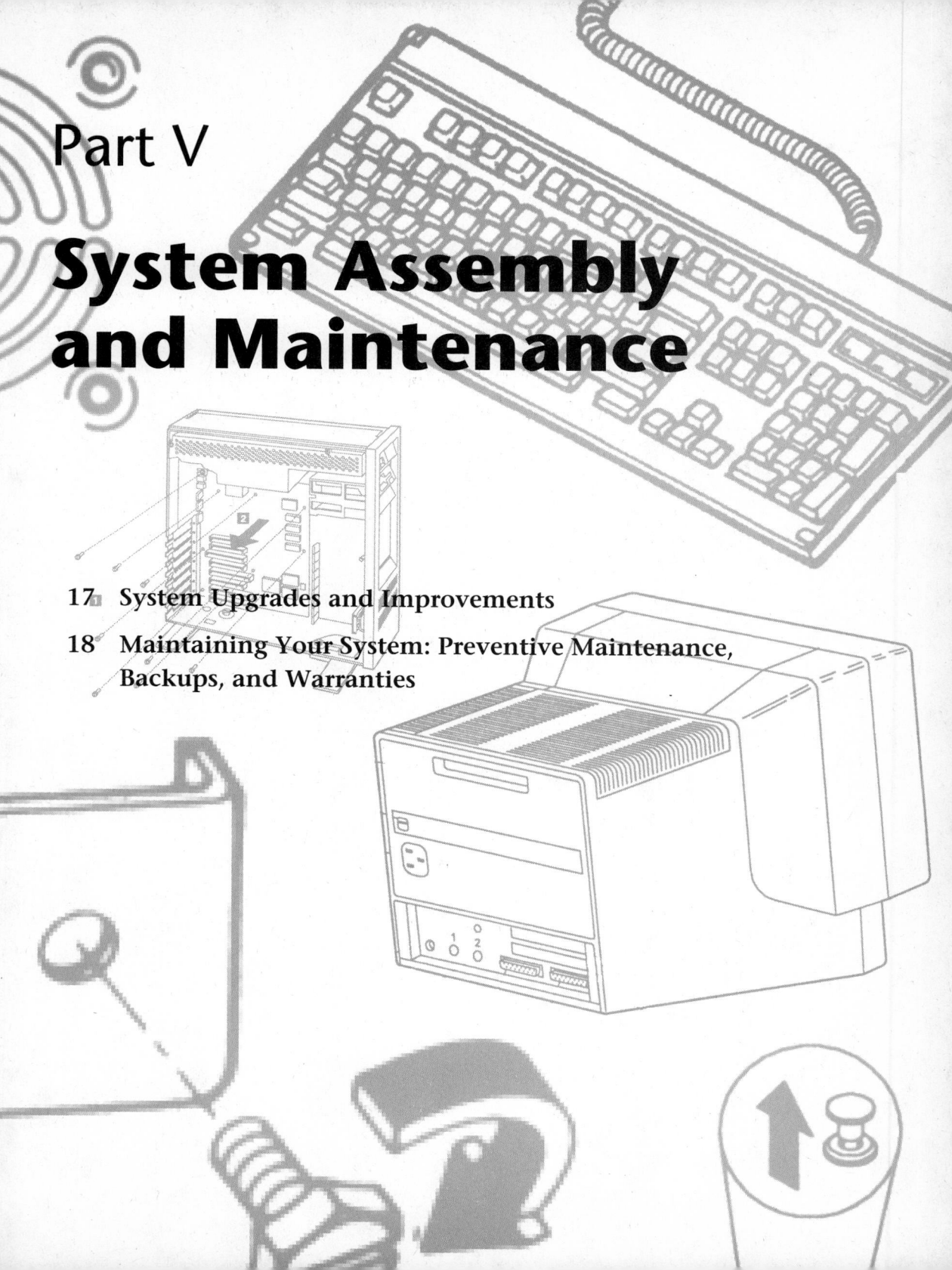

Part V

System Assembly and Maintenance

17 System Upgrades and Improvements

18 Maintaining Your System: Preventive Maintenance, Backups, and Warranties

Chapter 17

System Upgrades and Improvements

You want your PC to stay viable—even powerful—in a world of bigger, better, and faster machines. But how fast is fast?

- Do your software programs load quickly?

- Are you frustrated by waiting each time you save information to your hard disk?

- Does the cursor move when you want it to, where you want it to, as fast as you want it to?

- Do you find yourself watching the disk-drive lights as you wait?

Your computer's performance is measured by getting the most work done in as little time as possible. When your computer is slow, you have three options: stay with your current computer as is, upgrade it, or buy a new PC. Most often, upgrading is the preferred choice. Why? For several reasons:

- You can preserve your investment in a paid-for computer.

- You can expand your knowledge of computers by upgrading the PC yourself.

- You can save money by repairing and upgrading your computer until you can afford a new computer.

You can extend the life of older systems by adding functions and features that nearly match those of the newest systems on the market. You also can add new components to a modern system to squeeze cutting-edge performance out of what already is a premium system.

In this chapter, you learn about these types of system upgrades:

- Increasing system memory

- Upgrading a ROM BIOS

- Increasing disk storage

- Increasing system speed

- Improving a video subsystem

- Upgrading to a newer version of DOS

Caution

Avoid making radical upgrades. Sometimes, people throw far too much money and materials into an archaic system. You could upgrade a typical PC- or XT-class system to a 486 AT-class system, for example, but the result may be an expensive and lopsided system. The lightning speed of the processor would be slowed by the limping hard disk, and some expansion cards may not work with the new processor. You could spend hundreds of dollars to replace almost everything in an existing system, which may be more expensive than purchasing a new system. By making extensive changes in a system, you risk creating a Frankenstein system with strange quirks and eccentric—if not dangerous—operation. This type of system might be acceptable for personal use, but it is not recommended for use as a business system. In business, you have no time to coerce a reluctant "business partner."

Upgrading Goals

IBM and IBM-compatible systems are easy to upgrade and improve, not only because of support from IBM, but also because of the huge industry that has grown up around the IBM-compatible computer standard. For example, third-party manufacturers not only produce a wide range of complete IBM-compatible systems, but also make virtually every component for what are known as IBM *clones*. IBM uses many third-party components in its own systems as well. Because of the third-party support, a wide range of options is available for upgrading a system to achieve increased performance or expanded capabilities.

Although you can make many improvements to your PC, most of those improvements require you to open your computer. This situation is not unnatural; the first PC, unveiled in 1981, included five internal expansion slots for future enhancements. By buying various expansion cards for these slots, you can add more power and features to your PC. Also, you must open the system unit to add more memory, a new ROM BIOS chip, a new hard drive, and other items.

You should have a strategy for upgrading your PC. Upgrading isn't simply a matter of getting your PC to work faster and more reliably. When you travel, you can elect to take a bus, a car, a plane, or the subway; the decision depends on how far you have to go, how much money you want to spend, and how quickly you want to get there. The same is true of upgrading.

Consider what your PC keeps you from doing now. Is the screen too small to use for extended periods? Does the hard disk occasionally lose information? Is your machine not able to run the shareware programs that your brother-in-law passes on to you? Turn these weaknesses into goals that can be measured later with each improvement. If your goal can't be measured, you'll never know whether you achieved it.

Next, consider whether you can afford the upgrade today. If so, order right away. If not, you have the following choices:

- Wait to upgrade until you can afford it.

- Purchase another upgrade that is more in your financial ballpark. For example, you may forgo a new hard disk and instead get some extra memory, which costs less.

- Limit the features of your upgrade so that it is affordable. You can order a smaller hard disk, for example, and still benefit from its high speed.

Upgrading by Increasing System Memory

Adding memory to a system is one of the most useful upgrades that you can perform and also one of the least expensive, especially when you consider the increased capabilities of DOS, Microsoft Windows, and OS/2 when you give them access to more memory. In some cases, doubling the memory can virtually double the speed of a computer.

Memory chips come in different shapes and sizes, yet all memory chips in which you are interested are called *DRAM*, or dynamic random-access memory. DRAM chips are the most common type of memory. These chips are considered to be dynamic because they need to be energized hundreds of times per second to hold information. If you shut off the power, the information is lost.

You can add three primary types of memory to a system: conventional, extended, and expanded. (These types of memory are described in detail in Chapter 2, "Overview of System Features and Components," and Chapter 7, "Memory.")

This section discusses adding memory, including selecting memory chips, installing memory chips, and testing the installation.

Conventional Memory

Conventional memory is the memory within the first megabyte of a system's memory that can be used by DOS or application software. Conventional memory is accessible in the native mode of 8088 processors and in the real mode of operation of 80286 and higher processors. Today, virtually all systems are sold with the full 640K of usable conventional memory installed, if not more.

At this writing, 4M (4,096K) of memory is the bare minimum offered with most systems. If you have an older system and do not have the full complement of 640K conventional memory, you can add extended or expanded memory only after filling the 640K conventional-memory space.

Extended Memory

Extended memory is memory above 1M. This memory usually is not available to your computer directly, except through special software programs or drivers. This memory is available only in 80286 and higher computers.

PC and XT systems cannot use extended memory, because the 8088/8086 processors in PC and XT systems cannot run in protected mode. Expanded memory can enhance some of the capabilities—but generally not the speed—of these computer systems.

You can install both extended and expanded memory in AT-class systems. Extended memory is more useful than expanded memory. Windows and OS/2 can take full advantage of the 16M of available conventional- and extended-memory space. The need or desire for expanded memory in AT systems is virtually nonexistent because this expanded memory must be implemented in a slow and clumsy way. Fortunately, you easily can change almost any AT-type, 16-bit expanded memory board from expanded to extended memory by reconfiguring the adapter switches.

Expanded Memory

Expanded memory basically is converted extended memory. Introduced in 1985, expanded memory relies on a technical trick known as *paging* or *bank-switching*. Paging involves accessing large amounts of memory by swapping it, in 16K chunks, into and out of a 64K memory window. This window is placed in the unused memory space between 640K and 1M to access memory up to 32M.

Expanded memory is slow and clumsy for the system to use and generally is considered to be obsolete by today's standards. 80386 and higher systems can create expanded memory from extended memory, so normally, you only physically add extended memory to a system. Also, DOS, Windows, and OS/2 can use extended memory directly, but not expanded memory.

IBM and Microsoft have added limited expanded-memory support to DOS, starting with DOS 4.0. Expanded memory requires specialized hardware to implement the bank-switching techniques, so for PC and XT systems, you must purchase a special type of memory adapter that has built-in switching capability. If you decide to add one or more of these expanded-memory adapters to a PC- or XT-type system, be sure that the adapter meets Expanded Memory Specification 4.0 (EMS 4.0) or higher standards in the hardware and the software. Many older expanded-memory adapters meet only the inferior EMS 3.x standards in hardware, even though the software driver may comply with EMS 4.x. The major difference between the 3.x and 4.x EMS designs is that the newer 4.x versions provide a larger, variable-size paging area that can occupy a larger range of memory areas within the system memory map.

Because they use advanced AT chipsets, some 286 AT-class systems can use extended memory to emulate expanded memory. If your 286 system has this capability, check your system documentation for more information. An enhanced Setup program usually controls this capability.

Upgrade Strategies

Adding memory can be an inexpensive solution; at this writing, the cost of memory is about $45 per megabyte. A small dose can give your computer's performance a big boost.

How do you add memory to your PC? You have three options, listed in order of convenience and cost:

- Adding memory in vacant slots on your motherboard

- Replacing your current motherboard's memory with higher-capacity memory

- Purchasing a memory expansion card

Adding expanded memory to PC- or XT-type systems is not a good idea, mainly because an expanded memory board with a couple of megabytes of expanded memory installed can cost more than the entire system is worth. Also, this memory does not function for Windows, and a PC- or XT-class system cannot run OS/2. Instead, purchase a more powerful system—for example, an inexpensive 486SX—with greater expansion capabilities.

If you decide to upgrade to a more powerful computer system, you normally cannot salvage the memory from a PC or XT system. The 8-bit memory boards are useless in AT and Micro Channel systems, and the speed of the memory chips usually is inadequate for newer systems. Many new systems use high-speed SIMM modules rather than chips. A pile of 150-ns (nanoseconds), 64K or 256K chips is useless if your next system is a high-speed system that uses SIMMs or memory devices faster than 70 ns.

Be sure to weigh carefully your future needs for computing speed and for a multitasking operating system (OS/2, for example) with the amount of money that you spend to upgrade current equipment.

Adding Motherboard Memory

This section discusses *motherboard memory*—the memory actually installed on the motherboard—rather than the memory that resides on adapter boards. The first part of this section presents recommendations on selecting and installing chips. The last part of the section provides instructions for modifying an IBM XT Type 1 motherboard. This modification enables you to place a full 640K of memory on the motherboard, eliminating the need for memory-expansion boards. IBM's more recent XT Type 2 motherboards already include this modification.

Selecting and Installing Memory Chips or SIMMs

If you are upgrading a motherboard by adding memory, follow the manufacturer's guidelines on which memory chips or modules to purchase. As you learned in Chapter 7, "Memory," memory comes in various form factors, including individual chips known as DIP (dual in-line pin) memory chips, SIMMs (single in-line memory modules), and SIPPs (single in-line pin packages). Your computer may use one or possibly a mixture of these form factors.

The maker of your computer's motherboard determines what type of memory chips are used. The following list describes each chip or module type:

- *DIPs.* Early computers used DIP (dual in-line pin) memory chips. A DIP memory chip is a rectangular chip that has 16 metal legs, eight on each side. To install such a memory chip, you must plug it in place. DIP chips are installed in multiples of nine. For example, you must install 36 separate 256-kilobit chips to acquire 1M of memory. Sometimes, the DIPs are permanently soldered to your motherboard.

- *SIMMs.* Single in-line memory modules are like small circuit boards with chips soldered on them. Different numbers of chips can be mounted on the SIMM, and the chips can be mounted on one or both sides of the SIMM. A SIMM has a row of contacts on one edge of the board. The contacts can be tin- or gold-plated. SIMMs are retained in the system by special sockets with positive latching mechanisms that lock the SIMMs in place. SIMM connectors use a high-force wiping contact that is extremely resistant to corrosion.

  SIMMs are available in two types: 30-pin and 72-pin. The 30-pin modules come in 9-bit form with parity or 8-bit form for systems that lack parity checking. The 72-pin SIMMs are 36 bits wide with parity (32 data bits and 4 parity bits), or 32 bits wide without parity. Notice that the 9-bit and 36-bit SIMMs with parity always can be used in systems that lack parity checking and that the nonparity SIMMs cannot be used in normal systems that require parity bits. Systems that lack parity checking for memory are not recommended.

- *SIPPs.* Single in-line pin packages, sometimes called SIP, really are SIMMs with pins rather than contacts. The pins are designed to be installed in a long connector socket that is much cheaper than the standard SIMM socket. SIPPs are inferior to SIMMs because they lack the positive latching mechanism that retains the module, and the connector lacks the high-force wiping contacts that resist corrosion. SIPPs are rarely used today. For more information on the form factor of RAM chips, see Chapter 7, "Memory."

Whichever type of memory chips you have, the chips are installed in memory banks. A *memory bank* is a collection of memory chips that make up a block of memory. Each bank of memory is read by your processor in one pass. A memory bank does not work unless it is filled with memory chips.

Early 8088, 8086, and 80286 PCs have four memory banks that are nine chips wide. These memory banks may be labeled 0 through 3 or A through D. The first eight chips are for holding data. The ninth chip is a parity chip meant to ensure that the numbers of the other eight are correct. Each chip is measured in bits, and eight chips make up a byte. Imagine that you had the first two banks full of 256-kilobit chips. How much memory is that? Well, 18 chips (9 chips × 2 banks) of 256-kilobit memory equals 512K.

More modern 80286 computers usually can take four banks of 256-kilobit chips to make 1,024K (1M). Newer 80286 computers can handle up to 4M on the motherboard, using 1M chips. In 80386SX-based computers, four memory banks are used, requiring 18 chips, or sometimes two 9-bit SIMMs each. 80386DX, 80486SX, and 80486DX computers often have two memory banks, each using four 9-bit SIMMs or one 36-bit SIMM. Pentium computers usually have two memory banks using two 36-bit SIMMs.

Installing extra memory on your motherboard is the least expensive way to add memory to your computer. You may have a vacant memory bank in which you can install extra memory and use it to speed your computer.

RAM-Chip Type (Capacity). Individual RAM chips come in different capacities. The capacity determines the number of data bits that can be stored in a chip of a particular size. For example, RAM chips for the original IBM PC store 16 kilobits of data; these RAM chips are the smallest used in any IBM-compatible system. The RAM chips for the original version of the IBM XT store 64 kilobits of data. The standard chip for 386-based systems is the 1M chip (usually found in SIMMs). Today, 4- or 16-megabit chips (again, on SIMMs) are common in 486 and Pentium systems.

Before you add RAM to a system (or replace defective RAM chips), you must determine the memory chips required for your system. Your system documentation contains this information.

If you need to replace a defective RAM chip and do not have the system documentation, you can determine the correct chip for your system by inspecting the chips that are already installed. Each chip has markings that indicate the chip's capacity and speed. The following table lists the markings on individual 1M chips produced by various companies.

Markings	Manufacturer
TMS4C1024N/DJ	Texas Instruments
HM511000AP/AJP/AZP	Hitachi
MB81C1000P/PJ/PSZ	Fujitsu

If you do not have the documentation for your system and the manufacturer does not offer technical support, open your system case and carefully write down the markings that appear on your memory chips. Then contact a local computer store or mail-order chip vendor for help in determining the proper RAM chips for your system. Adding the wrong RAM chips to a system can make it as unreliable as leaving a defective chip on the motherboard and trying to use the system in that condition.

RAM-Chip Speed. RAM chips also come in various speeds. For example, 120-ns chips are used in older systems, and 60- or 70-ns chips are used in fast 486- and Pentium-based systems.

The motherboard manufacturer determines the correct speed of the memory chips installed in each system. IBM, for example, specifies different speed memory for different systems. Table 17.1 lists the required RAM-chip speeds and wait states for IBM motherboards.

Table 17.1 IBM Motherboard Memory Timing

System	CPU	Clock Speed (MHz)	Wait States	Memory-Access Time (ns)	Notes
PC	8088	4.77	1	200	
XT	8088	4.77	1	200	
AT	286	6	1	150	
AT	286	8	1	150	
XT-286	286	6	0	150	Zero wait
PS/1	286	10	1	120	
25	8086	8	0	150	Zero wait
30	8086	8	0	150	Zero wait
25-286	286	10	1	120	
30-286	286	10	1	120	
35 SX	386SX	20	0-2	85	Paged memory
40 SX	386SX	20	0-2	85	Paged memory
L40	386SX	20	0-2	80	Paged memory
50	286	10	1	150	
50Z	286	10	0	85	Zero wait
53 486SLC2	486SLC2	50	0-2	70	Interleaved memory, internal 16K cache
55 SX	386SX	16	0-2	100	Paged memory
56 486SLC3	486SLC3	75	0-2	70	Interleaved memory, internal 16K cache
57 SX	386SX	20	0-2	70	Paged memory
57 486SLC3	486SLC3	75	0-2	70	Interleaved memory, internal 16K cache
60	286	10	1	150	
65	386SX	16	0-2	100	Paged memory
70	386DX	16	0-2	85	Paged memory
70	386DX	20	0-2	85	Paged memory
70	386DX	25	0-5	80	External 64K cache
70	486DX	25	0-5	80	Internal 8K cache
P70	386DX	16	0-2	85	Paged memory
P70	386DX	20	0-2	85	Paged memory
P75	486DX	33	0-5	70	Internal 8K cache
76	486DX2	66	0-2	70	Interleaved memory, internal 8K cache
76	486SX	33	0-2	70	Interleaved memory, internal 8K cache

System	CPU	Clock Speed (MHz)	Wait States	Memory-Access Time (ns)	Notes
76	486DX4	100	0-2	70	Interleaved memory, internal 16K cache
77	486DX2	66	0-2	70	Interleaved memory, internal 8K cache
77	486SX	33	0-2	70	Interleaved memory, internal 8K cache
77	486DX4	100	0-2	70	Interleaved memory, internal 16K cache
80	386DX	16	0-2	80	Paged memory
80	386DX	20	0-2	80	Paged memory
80	386DX	25	0-5	80	External 64K cache
90	486SX	20	0-5	70	Interleaved memory, internal 8K cache
90	486SX	25	0-5	70	Interleaved memory, internal 8K cache
90	486DX	25	0-5	70	Interleaved memory, internal 8K cache, optional external 256K cache
90	486DX	33	0-5	70	Interleaved memory, internal 8K cache, optional external 256K cache
90	486DX	50	0-5	70	Interleaved memory, internal 8K cache, optional external 256K cache
95	486SX	20	0-5	70	Interleaved memory, internal 8K cache
95	486SX	25	0-5	70	Interleaved memory, internal 8K cache
95	486DX	25	0-5	70	Interleaved memory, internal 8K cache, optional external 256K cache
95	486DX	33	0-5	70	Interleaved memory, internal 8K cache, optional external 256K cache
95	486DX	50	0-5	70	Interleaved memory, internal 8K cache, optional external 256K cache

V

Assembly & Maintenance

It won't hurt to install chips that are faster than required for your motherboard or memory card; buying faster memory chips can be good if you intend to transplant them to a faster computer in the future. Unfortunately, the faster memory won't speed your computer; your computer's design anticipates working at a certain speed and no faster.

The speed of a memory chip is printed on the surface of the chip. On the memory chips—whether they are the DIP, SIPP, or SIMM type—you will find an identifying number. The last two digits after the dash (—) are especially important, because they indicate the speed of your memory.

In some cases, you can use slower-speed memory on an adapter than would normally be tolerated by the system motherboard. Many systems run the expansion slots at a fixed slower speed (8 MHz for most ISA bus systems) so that installed adapters function properly. The PS/2 system memory adapters may be capable of running more slowly than main memory because of the Micro Channel Architecture (MCA) interface's higher level of controls and capabilities. The MCA's asynchronous design enables adapters to remain independent of the processor's speed and to request additional wait states, as required, to accommodate the slower adapters. (A *wait state* is an idle cycle in which the processor and system essentially wait for a component, such as memory, to "catch up.")

All the memory adapters that IBM offers for the PS/2 50 and 60, for example, use 120-ns memory chips. These adapters also are specified for the Model 50Z, which normally runs with no wait states and requires 85-ns memory on the motherboard. If these slower 120-ns memory adapters are used in the Model 50Z, they cause the MCA in the 50Z to insert a wait state when the system accesses the adapter memory. Only the motherboard memory, therefore, runs with zero wait states. Several third-party board manufacturers offer special zero-wait-state boards for the 50Z, which requires memory faster than 120 ns.

In some systems, the motherboard memory speed can be controlled. Systems with adjustable wait-state settings enable you to choose optimal performance by purchasing the proper high-speed memory or to choose lower performance by purchasing cheaper memory. Many compatibles offer a wait-state jumper or configuration option, which controls whether the motherboard runs with wait states. Running with zero wait states may require faster-access-speed memory.

Other systems can configure themselves dynamically to the memory installed. The PS/2 Model 90 and 95 system boards check the speeds of the SIMMs installed on the system board and adjust the number of wait states accordingly. Most other PS/2 systems simply check the speed of SIMMs installed on the system board and flag an error condition if the minimum speed requirements are not met.

Systems that use 36-bit SIMMs can detect both the speed and capacity of the installed SIMMs through four special contacts called *presence detect pins*. The motherboard can use these pins to determine the installed SIMM's rated speed and capacity, in much the same way that many cameras can tell what speed film you have loaded by "reading" a series of contacts on the film canister. In the Model 90 and Model 95, if the SIMM is slower than 70 ns, the system adds wait states so that the rest of the memory can keep up. In other systems, such as the Model 70, if memory slower than the required 80 or 85 ns is installed, a 225 POST error message appears. If you look up this error code in the IBM error-code list in Appendix A, it says `Wrong-speed memory on system board`. This error message means that the installed memory is too slow for the system.

Systems with 16 MHz or faster clock speeds require extremely fast memory to keep up with the processor. In fact, the speeds that are required are so excessive that standard DRAM typically would be replaced by faster and more expensive static RAM (SRAM). One alternative—adding wait states to reduce the memory-speed requirements—greatly decreases performance, which is not what you want in a fast system.

RAM-Chip Architecture. Some special memory-architecture schemes have been devised to reduce the number of wait states required, boost overall system performance, and keep costs down. The following architecture schemes are most commonly used to increase memory performance:

- Paged memory
- Interleaved memory
- Memory caching

Paged memory is a simple scheme for improving memory performance that divides memory into pages ranging from 512 bytes to a few kilobytes long. The paging circuitry then enables memory locations within a page to be accessed with zero wait states. If the desired memory location is outside the current page, one or more wait states are added while the system selects the new page.

Paged memory has become common in higher-end 286 systems as well as in many 386 systems. For example, many PS/2 systems, such as the Model 70 and Model 80, use paged memory to increase performance so that slower 80- or 85-ns memory can be used.

Interleaved memory offers greater performance than paged memory. This higher-performance scheme combines two banks of memory into one, organized as even and odd bytes. With this combination, an access cycle can begin in the second bank while the first is already processing a previous access, and vice versa. By alternating access to even and odd banks, you can request data from one bank, and while the request is pending, the system can move to the next bank to process another request. The first request becomes available while the second request is still pending, and so on. By interleaving access to memory in this manner, a system can effectively double memory-access performance without using faster memory chips.

Many of the highest-performance systems use interleaved memory to achieve increased performance. Some systems that offer interleaved memory can use the interleaving function only if you install banks in matched-capacity pairs, which usually means adding two 36-bit SIMMs of equal capacity at a time. If you add only a single bank or add two banks of different capacity, the system still functions, but memory interleaving is disabled, and you pay a considerable performance penalty. Consult your system's technical-reference manual for more information.

Memory caching is the most popular and usually the most effective scheme for improving memory performance. This technique relies on a small amount (8K to 512K) of raw, high-speed memory fast enough to keep up with the processor with zero wait states. This small bank of cache memory often is rated at *15 ns or less* in access speed. Because this rate is faster than normal DRAM components can handle, a special type of memory is used. This memory is called *SRAM* (static RAM). SRAM devices do not need the constant refresh signals that DRAM devices require. This feature, combined with other design properties, results in extremely fast access times and very high costs.

Although SRAM chips are expensive, only a small number of SRAM chips are required in a caching scheme. SRAM is used by a special cache-controller circuit that stores frequently accessed RAM locations and also is preloaded with the RAM values that the cache controller expects to be accessed next. The cache acts as an intelligent buffer between the CPU and slower dynamic RAM.

A *cache hit* means that the particular data the CPU wanted was available in the cache RAM and that no additional wait states are available for retrieving this data. A *cache miss* means that the data the CPU wanted had not been loaded into the cache RAM and that wait states must be inserted while the data is retrieved. A good cache controller has a hit ratio of 95 percent or more (the system runs with zero wait states 95 percent of the time). The net effect is that the system acts as though nearly all the memory is 15 ns or less in speed, although most of the memory really is much slower (and, therefore, much less costly).

Systems based on the 486SX, SL, or DX processors include a cache controller and 8K of internal-cache RAM in the CPU that makes them much faster than earlier systems. The 486SLC CPU has a 1K internal cache, whereas the Pentium CPU includes two 8K internal caches: one for code and the other for data. 486DX4 processors have a 16K internal cache, while both the 486SLC2 and 486SLC3 processors have a 16K cache. Systems with 386SX or DX processors must use an external-cache controller with externally provided cache RAM; these systems have no internal cache. The 386SL provides a built-in cache controller, and the IBM-designed 386SLC incorporates virtually the same cache controller and 8K of built-in cache RAM as the 486 processors. IBM, therefore, can claim an 80 percent performance increase from the regular 386SX or DX chips for systems that use the 386SLC processor.

A CPU internal cache is called a primary or Level 1 (L1) cache, and an external cache is called a secondary or Level 2 (L2) cache. Typically, the larger the memory cache, the better the performance. A larger secondary processor cache, however, is no guarantee; you may find that the system with the least cache RAM can outperform a system with a greater amount of cache RAM. Actual performance depends on the efficiency of the cache controller and the system design; a cache integrated into a CPU, for example, can far outperform an external cache. For example, adding the 256K L2 cache RAM option to a PS/2 Model 90 or 95 with a 486DX processor offers only a small increase in performance relative to the 8K of L1 cache memory built into the 486 CPU chip, because the L1 cache integrated into the CPU can outperform an external (L2) cache. Also, adding cache RAM does not result in a proportional increase in performance. You often gain the best performance by using the middle amount of secondary cache that your computer can accept. A PC that can accommodate a 64K, 128K, or 256K secondary cache provides the most bang for the buck.

To get maximum system performance and reliability, the best recommendation for adding chips or SIMMs to a motherboard is to use memory rated at the speeds recommended by the manufacturer. Faster memory is likely to work in the system, but it creates no performance benefit and therefore is a waste of money.

The minimum access-time specification for motherboard memory in a specific system is listed in the system's technical-reference manual. If you have an IBM-compatible system that lacks proper documentation, you can refer to table 17.1 as a guide, because most compatibles follow IBM's requirements. Because of the variety of system designs on the market, however, you should try to acquire the proper documentation from the manufacturer.

Adding Adapter Boards

Memory expansion boards typically are a last-resort way to add memory. For many systems (such as older models from Compaq) with proprietary local bus memory-expansion connectors, you must purchase all memory-expansion boards from that company. Similarly, IBM used proprietary memory connectors in the PS/2 Model 80 systems. For other industry-standard systems that use nonproprietary memory expansion (such as the IBM PC, XT, and AT) and most IBM-compatible systems, as well as most PS/2 systems, you can purchase, from hundreds of vendors, memory-expansion boards that plug into the standard bus slots.

Unfortunately, any memory expansion that plugs into a standard bus slot runs at bus speed rather than at full system speed. For this reason, most systems today provide standard SIMM-connector sockets directly on the motherboard so that the memory can be plugged directly into the system's local bus. Using memory adapter cards in these systems only slows them. Other systems use proprietary local bus connectors for memory-expansion adapters, which can cause additional problems and expense when you have to add or service memory.

In some cases, an adapter board can use slower memory than would be required on the system motherboard. (Memory adapters for PS/2 Models 50 and 60, for example, use 120-ns memory chips.) Many systems run memory-expansion slots at a fixed slower speed—8 MHz for most ISA bus systems—so that installed adapters function properly. The PS/2 system memory adapters may be able to run more slowly than main memory because of the Micro Channel Architecture (MCA) interface's higher level of controls and capabilities. The MCA's asynchronous design enables adapters to remain independent of the processor's speed and to request additional wait states, as required, to accommodate the slower adapters.

Installing Memory

This section discusses installing memory chips—specifically, new RAM chips or memory modules. The section also covers the problems that you are most likely to encounter and how to avoid them; it also provides information on configuring your system to use new memory.

When you install or remove memory, you are most likely to encounter the following problems:

- Electrostatic discharge

- Broken or bent pins

- Incorrect switch and jumper settings

To prevent electrostatic discharge (ESD) when you install sensitive memory chips or boards, do not wear synthetic-fiber clothing or leather-soled shoes. Remove any static charge that you are carrying by touching the system chassis before you begin, or—better yet—wear a good commercial grounding strap on your wrist. You can order one from an electronics parts store or mail-order house. A grounding strap consists of a conductive wristband grounded at the other end by a wire clipped to the system chassis (usually with an alligator clip). Leave the system unit plugged in—but turned off—to keep it grounded.

Caution

Be sure to use a properly designed commercial grounding strap; *do not make one yourself*. Commercial units have a one-megohm resistor that serves as protection if you accidentally touch live power. The resistor ensures that you do not become the path of least resistance to the ground and therefore become electrocuted. An improperly designed strap can cause the power to conduct through you to the ground, possibly killing you.

Broken or bent leads are another potential problem associated with installing individual memory chips (DIPs) or SIPP modules. Sometimes, the pins on new chips are bent into a V, making them difficult to align with the socket holes. If you notice this problem on a DIP chip, place the chip on its side on a table, and press gently to bend the pins so that they are at a 90-degree angle to the chip. For a SIPP module, you may want to use needle-nose pliers to carefully straighten the pins so that they protrude directly down from the edge of the module, with equal amounts of space between pins; then you should install the chips in the sockets one at a time.

Caution

Straightening the pins on a DIP chip or SIPP module is not difficult work, but if you are not careful, you could easily break off one of the pins, rendering the chip or memory module useless. Use great care when you straighten the bent pins on any memory chip or module. You can use chip-insertion and pin-straightening devices to ensure that the pins are straight and aligned with the socket holes; these inexpensive tools can save you a great deal of time.

Each memory chip or module must be installed to point in a certain direction. Each chip has a polarity marking on one end. This marking may be a polarity notch, a circular indentation, or both. The chip socket may have a corresponding notch. Otherwise, the motherboard may have a printed legend that indicates the orientation of the chip. If the socket is not marked, you should use other chips as a guide. The orientation of the notch indicates the location of Pin 1 on the chip. Aligning this notch correctly with the others on the board ensures that you do not install the chip backward. Gently set each chip into a socket, ensuring that every pin is properly aligned with the connector into which it fits, and push the chip in firmly with both thumbs until the chip is fully seated.

SIMM memory is oriented by a notch on one side of the module that is not present on the other side. The socket has a protrusion that must fit into this notched area on one side of the SIMM. This protrusion makes it impossible to install a SIMM backward unless you break the connector. SIPP modules, however, do not plug into a keyed socket; you have to orient them properly. The system documentation can be helpful if the motherboard has no marks to guide you. You also can use existing SIPP modules as a guide.

Before installing memory, make sure that the system power is off. Then remove the PC cover and any installed cards. SIMMs snap easily into place, but chips can be more difficult to install. A chip-installation tool is not required, but it can make inserting the chips into sockets much easier. To remove chips, use a chip extractor or small screwdriver. Never try removing a RAM chip with your fingers because you can bend the chip's pins or poke a hole in your finger with one of the pins. You remove SIMMs by releasing the locking tabs and either pulling or rolling them out of their sockets.

After adding the memory chips and putting the system back together, you may have to alter motherboard switches or jumper settings. The original PC includes two switch blocks with eight switches per block. Switch positions 1 through 4 of a PC's second switch block must be set to reflect the total installed memory. The XT has only one switch block, which is set to reflect the number of memory banks installed on the system board but not the expansion-card memory. Appendix A, "PC Technical Reference Section," provides more detailed information about the PC and XT motherboard switch settings.

IBM AT and PS/2 systems have no switches or jumpers for memory. Rather, you must run a setup program to inform the system of the total amount of memory installed. IBM-compatible AT-type systems usually have a setup program built into the system ROM BIOS, and you must run this program after installing new memory to configure the system properly.

Most memory-expansion cards also have switches or jumpers that must be set. You often must make two settings when you configure a memory card. The first setting—a starting address for the memory on the card—usually enables the memory on the card to begin using system memory addresses higher than those used by any existing memory. The second setting is the total amount of memory installed on the card.

Because of the PS/2's influence in the market, many memory boards, as well as other types of adapter cards, are made without switches. Instead, these boards have a

V

Asssembly & Maintenance

configuration program that is used to set up the card. The configuration is stored in a special nonvolatile memory device contained on the card; after the settings are made, the card can remember the settings permanently. The Intel AboveBoard 286 and Plus versions, for example, have this switchless setup and configuration capability. Following a menu-driven configuration program is much easier than flipping tiny switches or setting jumpers located on a card. Another benefit of software configuration is that you don't even have to open the system to reconfigure a card.

After configuring your system to work properly with the additional memory, you should run a memory-diagnostics program to ensure the proper operation of the new memory. At least two and sometimes three memory-diagnostics programs are available for all systems. In order of accuracy, these programs are the following:

- POST (Power-On Self Test)
- User diagnostics disk
- Advanced diagnostics disk
- Aftermarket diagnostics software

The POST is used every time you power up the system; you can press Ctrl-A at the opening menu to access the advanced diagnostics on the reference disk.

PS/2 systems include the user diagnostics and advanced diagnostics programs on one reference disk. The disk ensures that PS/2 owners have all three memory-test programs.

Owners of standard IBM PC systems receive (in the guide-to-operations manual) a diagnostics disk that contains a good memory test. PC owners should purchase the advanced diagnostics disk as part of the hardware-maintenance service manual package. If you have purchased this package, you should use the advanced diagnostics program.

Many additional diagnostics programs are available from aftermarket utility software companies. Several companies listed in Appendix B have excellent diagnostics and test software for testing memory and other components of a system. These programs are especially useful when the manufacturer of the system does not provide its own diagnostics.

Installing 640K on an XT Motherboard

This section describes how to install 640K of RAM on the system board in an IBM XT and an IBM Portable. The upgrade essentially changes what IBM calls an XT Type 1 motherboard to a Type 2 motherboard.

The upgrade consists of installing two banks of 256K chips and two banks of 64K chips on the motherboard, and then enabling the memory chips by adding a multiplexer/decoder chip to an empty socket provided for it, as well as a jumper wire. The jumper wire enables an existing memory decoder chip (U44) to enable the additional memory. These modifications are relatively easy to perform and can be done with no soldering.

A memory-chip address is selected by two signals called *row-address select* (RAS) and *column-address select* (CAS). These signals determine where a value in a chip is located. You modify the signals by installing the jumper as indicated in this section so that the first two banks can be addressed four times deeper than they originally were, thus using the additional address locations in the 256K chips rather than in the original 64K chips.

To install 640K on an IBM XT motherboard, you must obtain the following parts from a chip vendor or electronics supply store (see Appendix B for sources):

- Eighteen 256K-by-1-bit, 200-ns (or faster) memory chips
- One 74LS158 (multiplexer/decoder) chip
- A small length of thin (30-gauge) jumper or wire-wrapping wire

After you have these parts, follow these steps:

1. Remove the motherboard (as explained in Chapter 4, "Motherboards").

2. Plug the 74LS158 chip into the socket labeled U84.

   All motherboard components are identified by an alphanumeric value. The letter usually indicates the type of component, and the number indicates a sequential component ID number for that type of component. The coding can differ among manufacturers, but most use this lettering scheme:

U	Integrated circuit
Q	Transistor
C	Capacitor
R	Resistor
T	Transformer
L	Coil
Y	Crystal
D	Diode

   Usually, component numbering follows a pattern in which the numbers increase as you move from left to right along the first row of components. Then the numbers begin again, at the left side and one row lower. You should be able to locate all the IC chips, starting with U1 in the upper-left corner of the board and ending with U90 in the lower-right corner.

3. Remove the IC installed in the socket labeled U44.

4. Install a jumper wire connecting Pin 1 to Pin 8 on the chip removed from position U44. To avoid making changes that you cannot undo later, it is easiest to wrap the ends of the jumper wire around the indicated IC pins. Be sure that the ends of the wire are wrapped securely around pins 1 and 8 and that the connection is good.

Route the wire on the underside of the IC so that the wire is held in place when you install the chip. Reinstall the chip with the jumper in place. The IC might sit slightly higher in the socket because of the wire underneath it, so make sure that it is seated as far as it goes.

> ### Caution
>
> Be careful with the U44: it is a unique IBM programmable array logic (PAL) chip that you cannot purchase separately. A PAL chip is burned with a circuit pattern, much as a ROM chip is burned with data values. The only way to obtain the chip is to purchase a new motherboard from IBM. Some chip houses, such as Microprocessors Unlimited (see Appendix B, the "Vendor List"), sell a copy of this PAL chip with the jumper wire modification burned in. Using one of these modified PAL chips is an alternative to adding the jumper wire manually, but be aware that most companies charge $20 for the chip. Adding the wire yourself is much cheaper.

Another alternative to adding the jumper wire to the chip in U44 is soldering two jumper pins into the plated holes numbered 1 and 2 in the jumper pad labeled E2. Using a standard plug-in jumper, you install a jumper across the two added pins. I normally do not recommend this method unless you are experienced with a soldering iron. All IBM XT Type 2 motherboards already have this modification built in.

5. Remove the 18 existing 64K-by-1-bit chips from banks 0 and 1. Reinstall the chips in banks 2 and 3 (if 64K chips are not already in these banks) or store them as spare chips.

6. Install the 18 new 256K-by-1-bit chips in banks 0 and 1.

7. Be sure that switches 3 and 4 of switch block SW1 are set to Off.

8. Replace the motherboard, and restore all other system components except memory cards.

   Remember that the motherboard now has 640K on it and that no other boards must address that space. If other memory cards were previously configured to supply memory in the first 640K area, you must reconfigure these cards or remove them from the system.

9. Power up the system, and test the installed memory for 640K without other memory-adapter cards.

If all operations are successful, you have performed an inexpensive memory upgrade that matches the capabilities of the Type 2 XT motherboard from IBM.

Upgrading the ROM BIOS

In this section, you learn that ROM BIOS upgrades can improve a system in many ways. You also learn that the upgrades can be difficult and may require much more than plugging in a generic set of ROM chips.

The *ROM BIOS*, or read-only memory basic input-output system, provides the crude brains that get your computer's components working together. A simple $30-to-$90 BIOS replacement can give your computer faster performance and more features.

The BIOS is the reason why DOS can operate on virtually any IBM-compatible system despite hardware differences. Because the BIOS communicates with the hardware, the BIOS must be specific to the hardware and match it completely. Instead of creating their own BIOSes, many computer makers buy a BIOS from specialists such as American Megatrends Inc. (AMI), Award Software, Microid Research, and Phoenix Technologies Ltd. A hardware manufacturer that wants to license a BIOS must undergo a lengthy process of working with the BIOS company to tailor the BIOS code to the hardware. This process is what makes upgrading a BIOS so difficult. The BIOS usually resides on ROM chips on the motherboard; some newer PS/2 systems from IBM, however, have a disk-loaded BIOS that is much easier to upgrade.

The BIOS is a collection of small computer programs embedded in an *EPROM* (erasable programmable read-only memory) chip or chips, depending on the design of your computer. That collection of programs is the first thing loaded when you start your computer, even before the operating system. Simply put, the BIOS has three main functions:

- Tests your computer's components when it is turned on. This test is called the Power-On Self-Test, or POST. The POST tests your computer's memory, motherboard, video adapter, disk controller, keyboard, and other crucial components.

- Finds the operating system and loads, or boots, it. This operation is called the bootstrap loader routine. If an operating system is found, it is loaded and given control of your computer.

- After an operating system is loaded, the BIOS works with your processor to give software programs easy access to your computer's specific features. For example, the BIOS tells your computer how to work with your video card and hard disk when a software program requires these devices.

In older systems, you often must upgrade the BIOS to take advantage of some other upgrade. To install some of the newer IDE (Integrated Drive Electronics) hard drives and 1.44M or 2.88M floppy drives in older machines, for example, you may need a BIOS upgrade. Machines still are being sold with older BIOSes that do not support the user-definable drive-type feature required for easy installation of an IDE drive or that may have timing problems associated with IDE drives.

V

Asssembly & Maintenance

The following list shows the primary functions of a ROM BIOS upgrade:

■ Adding 720K, 1.44M, or 2.88M 3 1/2-inch floppy drive support to a system

■ Eliminating controller- or device-driver-based hard disk parameter translation for MFM, RLL, IDE, or ESDI drives with 1,024 or fewer cylinders by using a user-definable hard drive type matched to the drive

■ Adding support for block-mode Programmed I/O (PIO) transfers for an ATA-IDE (AT Attachment-Integrated Drive Electronics) hard disk

■ Adding 101-key Enhanced Keyboard support

■ Adding compatibility for Novell networks

■ Adding compatibility for VGA displays

■ Adding support for additional serial (COM) ports and printer ports

■ Adding password protection

■ Adding virus protection

■ Adding support for additional floppy disk drives

■ Correcting known bugs or compatibility problems with certain hardware and software

Because of the variety of motherboard designs on the market, ordering a BIOS upgrade often is more difficult than it sounds initially. If you have a name-brand system with a well-known design, the process can be simple. For many lesser-known compatible systems, however, you must give the BIOS vendor information about the system, such as the type of manufacturer's chipset that the motherboard uses.

For most BIOS upgrades, you must obtain the following information:

■ The make and model of the system unit

■ The type of CPU (for example, 286, 386DX, 386SX, 486DX, 486SX, and so on)

■ The make and version of the existing BIOS

■ The part numbers of the existing ROM chips (you may have to peel back the labels to read this information)

■ The make, model, or part numbers of integrated motherboard chipsets, if used (for example, Chips & Technologies, SUNTAC, VLSI, OPTI, and others)

An *integrated chipset* is a group of chips on the original AT motherboard that can perform the functions of hundreds of discrete chips. Many chipsets offer customizable features that are available only if you have the correct BIOS. Most differences among systems today lie in the variety of integrated chipsets that are now used to manufacture PCs and in the special initialization required to operate these chips. Even IBM uses third-party integrated chipsets from VLSI in PS/2 ISA-bus systems such as Models 30-286, 35 SX, and 40 SX.

The BIOS also must support variations in keyboard-controller programming and in the way that nonstandard features such as speed switching are handled. A computer that uses the Chips & Technologies NEAT chipset, for example, must have a BIOS specifically made for it. The BIOS must initialize the NEAT chipset registers properly; otherwise, the machine does not even boot. The BIOS also must have support for this chipset's special features. Each of the 20 or more popular chipsets for 286, 386, 486, and 586 machines requires specific BIOS support for proper operation. A generic BIOS may boot some systems, but certain features, such as shifting to and from protected mode and speed switching, may not be possible without the correct BIOS.

Keyboard-Controller Chips

Besides the main system ROM, AT-class computers also have a keyboard controller or keyboard ROM, which is a keyboard-controller microprocessor with its own built-in ROM. The keyboard controller usually is an Intel 8042 microcontroller, which incorporates a microprocessor, RAM, ROM, and I/O ports. The keyboard controller usually is a 40-pin chip, often with a label that has a copyright notice identifying the BIOS code programmed into the chip.

The keyboard controller controls the reset and A20 lines and also deciphers the keyboard scan codes. The A20 line is used in extended memory and other protected-mode operations. In many systems, one of the unused ports is used to select the CPU clock speed. Because of the tie-in with the keyboard controller and protected-mode operation, many problems with keyboard controllers become evident when you use either Windows or OS/2. If you experience lockups or keyboard problems with either Windows or OS/2 software—or with any software that runs in protected mode, such as Lotus 1-2-3 Release 3.x—get a replacement from your BIOS vendor or system-board vendor.

IBM systems do not need a replacement of the keyboard controller for upgrade purposes. (Replacement is difficult because the chip normally is soldered in.) Most manufacturers of IBM-compatible systems install the keyboard-controller chip in a socket so that you can upgrade or replace it easily. If you upgrade the BIOS in your system, the BIOS vendor often includes a compatible keyboard controller as well. You usually do not have to buy the controller unless your old keyboard controller has a problem with the new BIOS.

BIOS Manufacturers and Vendors

Several BIOS manufacturers have developed ROM BIOS software for use in upgrading IBM or IBM-compatible systems. The following companies are the largest manufacturers of ROM BIOS software:

- Phoenix
- American Megatrends International (AMI)
- Microid Research (MR)
- Award

V

Asssembly & Maintenance

Phoenix pioneered the IBM-compatible BIOS and the legal means to develop a product that is fully compatible with IBM's BIOS without infringing on the corporation's copyright. Phoenix first introduced many new features, such as user-defined hard drive types and 1.44M drive support. The Phoenix BIOS has a very good Power-On Self Test; this thorough POST presents a complete set of failure codes for diagnosing problems, especially the ones that occur when a system seems to be dead. (Appendix A contains a complete list of Phoenix BIOS POST error codes.)

The Phoenix BIOS documentation, a complete three-volume reference package, is one of the product's most useful features. This documentation includes *System BIOS for IBM PC/ XT/AT Computers and Compatibles*, *CBIOS for IBM PS/2 Computers and Compatibles*, and *ABIOS for IBM PS/2 Computers and Compatibles*. I recommend these excellent reference works, published by Addison-Wesley, even if you do not have the Phoenix BIOS (although some of its specific information does not apply to other systems).

The BIOS produced by AMI is very popular and surpasses even Phoenix in new system installations. The AMI BIOS offers a less comprehensive Power-On Self Test than the Phoenix BIOS does, but it has an extensive diagnostics program in ROM. You even can purchase the program separately, as AMIDIAG. The in-ROM version, however, lacks the capability to test memory—a crucial capability if the failure is in the first bank. On the other hand, the BIOS is very compatible with the PC standard, available for several different chipsets and motherboards, and has been handled responsibly from the support level. When problems have occurred, AMI has fixed them, earning this program full compatibility with OS/2 and other difficult environments.

Because AMI manufactures its own motherboards, it has a distinct advantage over other BIOS companies. If the motherboard and BIOS are made by the same source, the single vendor probably can resolve any interaction problems between the BIOS and motherboard quickly, without shifting blame for the problem to another party. I recommend buying AMI's motherboards, because you generally don't have to worry about compatibility problems between the AMI BIOS and the AMI motherboard. Even if problems occur, AMI corrects them.

Microid Research is newer than some of the other BIOS manufacturers, but its BIOS has proved to be very compatible. The MR BIOS, as it is called, supports several CPU and motherboard chipset combinations. The MR BIOS offers one of the easiest and most informative setup programs available; this program does a good job of explaining the options. Some of you know that setting the advanced chipset functions is not always intuitive with the other BIOS vendors' products. In short, I recommend that you look at the MR BIOS if you are considering a BIOS upgrade or configuring a bare motherboard from scratch.

Award, the third-largest manufacturer of BIOS software, has made a name for itself with many system vendors, because it licenses the BIOS code to them for further modification. AST, for example, purchased the rights to the Award BIOS for its own systems and now can modify the BIOS internally, as though it created the BIOS from scratch. In a sense, AST could develop its own custom BIOS, using the Award code as a starting point.

Award also provides precustomized BIOS code for manufacturers. Although Award's BIOS is not yet as popular as the Phoenix and AMI BIOSes, it is very popular, and compatibility, even in tough environments such as OS/2, is ensured.

If you want to replace or upgrade your BIOS, you can obtain replacement chips directly from the BIOS manufacturer or from the following recommended distributors:

- *Micro Firmware Inc.* Micro Firmware offers an extensive line of Phoenix BIOS upgrades, with more than 50 common 8088, 286, 386, and 486 versions available. This company develops BIOS upgrades for specific hardware platforms, even when the original motherboard manufacturer is no longer in business. Many other BIOS vendors sell BIOSes developed by Micro Firmware for specific platforms.

- *Washburn & Company Distributors.* This licensed AMI distributor deals exclusively with AMI BIOS upgrades. Washburn has complete AMI motherboard and BIOS packages. A primary distributor for AMI, Washburn has great expertise in dealing with BIOS upgrade problems. The company also sells Second Nature, a disk drive support product that may eliminate the need for a BIOS if all you want is additional hard disk or floppy drive support.

- *Microid Research.* This company manufactures and sells its own MR BIOS direct, and offers technical support as well.

Alternatives to Upgrading the BIOS

Some companies, especially those that purchase only IBM systems, are timid about removing the BIOS and replacing it with a BIOS made by a company other than IBM. If you are leery of removing your system BIOS, another solution is available: you can purchase an accessory ROM to augment, rather than replace, your existing BIOS.

Second Nature is one of the best of these products. An accessory ROM for IBM and compatibles, Second Nature adds the following important features to a system:

- A greatly expanded BIOS hard disk parameter table

- Support for 720K and 1.44M drives

No software drivers or other memory-resident programs are used when Second Nature is installed. The hard disk parameters supplied by Second Nature overlay existing drive parameters in your system ROM BIOS. Second Nature is compatible with all popular operating systems (including DOS, Windows, and OS/2) and also has a built-in, low-level, format-and-verify utility.

Most AT-type computers have four 28-pin ROM sockets, two of which normally are occupied by the existing ROM BIOS chips. If no additional empty sockets are available (such as in the IBM XT-286 or some early IBM ATs), or if your computer cannot load accessory ROMs in the E000 memory segment (as in Sperry, Leading Edge, and some other AT clones), you can buy an optional card to install the Second Nature ROMs in any 8- or 16-bit slot. For more information about this product, contact Washburn & Company Distributors (see Appendix B).

Special ROM BIOS-Related Problems

Some known problems exist in certain ROM BIOS versions as well as in some systems sold during the past few years. Several of these problems have the potential to affect a large number of people, either because the problem is severe or many systems have the problem. This section describes some of the most important known BIOS- and system-interaction problems and also provides solutions for the problems.

Some systems with BIOSes even as recent as 1992 or 1993 may not start after you upgrade to DOS 6.x. Some of the older BIOSes came on line when DOS 3.3 or earlier was the current operating system. As a result, those older BIOSes often cannot take advantage of the advanced features of DOS 6.x.

If you use an AT&T 6300 system, you will want to use BIOS Version 1.43, which is the most recent one made for the system. This version solves many problems with older 6300 systems and also provides support for a 720K floppy disk drive. You can order BIOS Version 1.43 for about $35 from the AT&T National Parts Sales Center (see Appendix B) under part number 105203780.

Some systems with the AMI BIOS have had problems with IDE hard disk drives. IDE (Integrated Drive Electronics) drives have been touted as being fully port-compatible with existing ST-506/412 (MFM or RLL) and ESDI drives. Some IDE drives, however, take somewhat longer than they should after certain commands to present valid data at their ports. In late 1989, AMI received many reports of problems with IDE drives, especially Conner and Toshiba drives. Because of these timing problems, AMI BIOS versions dated earlier than April 9, 1990, are not recommended for use with IDE drives, and data loss can result if earlier versions are used. You may experience Drive C not ready errors with certain IDE drives, such as those from Conner Peripherals. If you have a computer with an IDE drive and an AMI BIOS dated earlier than 04/09/90, you should get a newer BIOS from the system vendor.

To make sure that you have the correct AMI BIOS version, look for this figure in the lower-left corner of the screen when you boot your computer:

```
xxxx-zzzz-040990-Kr
```

The 040990 indicates a BIOS date of April 9, 1990—the minimum version to use. Older versions are OK only if you are *not* using IDE drives. The xxxx-zzzz indicates the BIOS type code and an OEM (original equipment manufacturer) ID number. For AMI-manufactured motherboards, for example, the BIOS type code is DAMI-[model code]. The r indicates the keyboard-controller chip's revision level, which should be revision F or later to avert problems.

Changes to an Existing BIOS

If you have access to the correct tools and knowledge, you can perform some interesting modifications or upgrades to your system by altering your existing ROM BIOS. This section discusses several modifications that I have performed on my own systems. (These modifications have worked *for me*, and I am not necessarily recommending that anyone else perform them.) If nothing else, the research and development of these modifications taught me much about the way some things work in an IBM-compatible system, and I know that many of you are interested in some of this information.

Using EPROM Programming Equipment. You can accomplish some interesting modifications or upgrades and even repairs of a system by using an EPROM programmer (or *burner*, as it is sometimes called). *EPROM* stands for erasable programmable read-only memory—a type of chip that can have a program burned, or fused, into it by way of an EPROM programmer device. These devices cost anywhere from about $100 to several thousands of dollars, depending on the capabilities of the device.

Most cheaper EPROM programmers are more than adequate for burning PC ROMs. Both JDR Microdevices and Jameco Electronics sell EPROM programmers; I use and recommend one made by Andromeda Research (see Appendix B). These programmers either connect to a slot or use the standard serial or parallel ports for communications. The Andromeda Research EPROM burner connects to a system parallel port that gives it flexibility and performance that are not equaled in most other units. To erase an EPROM, you also need an EPROM eraser, an inexpensive device ($30 to $100) that exposes the EPROM chip to intense ultraviolet light for about three to five minutes. I recommend and use a simple unit made by DataRace (see Appendix B).

With an EPROM programmer, you can modify or customize your system ROM BIOS, as well as the ROM chips found on many expansion cards. You also can add hard drives to the drive table, change sign-on or error messages, and make specific changes to increase performance or otherwise customize your system. The ability to alter ROMs gives you an extra level of capability in upgrading and repairing systems.

Backing up Your BIOS. One often-overlooked benefit of an EPROM programmer is that you can use it to essentially back up your ROMs in case they are later damaged. Many hardware vendors, such as IBM, do not offer ROM upgrades for their systems, and the only way to repair a motherboard or card with a damaged ROM is to burn a new copy from a backup. The backup can be in the form of another EPROM chip with the original program burned in or even in the form of a disk file. I keep files containing images of the ROMs in each of my motherboards and expansion cards, in case I have to burn a new copy to repair one of my systems.

To create a disk-file copy of your motherboard ROM BIOS, you can place the ROM in an EPROM programmer and use the function provided by the device to read the EPROM into a disk file, or you can use the DOS DEBUG program to read your ROM BIOS from memory and transfer it to disk as a file. To use DEBUG in this manner, follow these instructions:

```
C:\>DEBUG                  ;Run DEBUG
-N SEG-F.ROM               ;Name the file
-R BX                      ;Change BX register (high-order file size)
BX 0000                    ;  from 0
:1                         ;   to 1 (indicates 64K file)
-M F000:0 FFFF CS:0        ;Move BIOS data to current code segment
-W 0                       ;Write file from offset 0 in code segment
Writing 10000 bytes        ;  10000h = 64K
-Q                         ;Quit DEBUG
```

These instructions save the entire 64K segment range from F000:0000 to 000:FFFF as a file by first setting up the name and size of the file to be saved and then moving (essentially, copying) the ROM BIOS code to the current code segment when DEBUG was loaded. The data then can be written to the disk. IBM AT systems and most compatibles have only 64K of BIOS, but IBM PS/2 systems normally have a full 128K of BIOS code that resides in both segment E000 and F000. For these systems, repeat the procedure, using E000:0 as the starting address in the Move command (rather than F000:0) and, of course, a different file name in the Name command. One important quirk of this procedure is that the commands should be entered in the order indicated here. In particular, the Name command must precede the Move command, or some of the data at the beginning of the current code-segment area will be trashed.

You also can use this routine to back up any adapter-board ROMs installed in your system. To back up the ROM on the IBM SCSI adapter with cache installed in my system, for example, a similar DEBUG session works. You must know the ROM's starting address and ending address or length to continue. My SCSI adapter ROM is located at D400:0 and is 16K, or 4,000H (hex) bytes long, which means that it ends at D400:3FFF. To save this ROM as a file, execute these instructions:

```
C:\>DEBUG                  ;Run DEBUG
-N SCSI.ROM                ;Name the file
-R CX                      ;Change CX register (low-order file size)
CX 0000                    ;   from 0
:4000                      ;   to 4000 (indicates 16K file)
-M D400:0 3FFF CS:0        ;Move BIOS data to current code segment
-W 0                       ;Write file from offset 0 in code segment
Writing 04000 bytes        ;  4000h = 16K
-Q                         ;Quit DEBUG
```

Most EPROM programmers are supplied with software that runs in your PC and enables you to control the unit. Available functions include the capability to read a ROM and save it as a disk file or write a ROM from a disk file, and the capability to copy or test ROMs. The software also should be capable of splitting a file into even and odd addresses for 16- or 32-bit systems, as well as combining two split files into one. Another requirement is the capability to calculate the proper checksum byte (usually, the last byte) in the ROM so that diagnostics passes it. All the programmers mentioned have these functions and more.

Removing the POST Speed Check. One problem in the IBM AT and XT-286 systems is that the clock speed is checked during the Power-On Self Test (POST). Checking the clock speed probably is a good idea, but it causes problems if you want to take advantage of the socketed clock crystal in these systems for a cheap and easy speedup. Most IBM compatibles do not have this speed check and can run at different clock rates, usually with no modifications of the BIOS required.

In IBM systems, the Verify Speed/Refresh Clock Rates test checks the system refresh rate (clock speed) to ensure that it is 6 or 8 MHz, depending on which IBM system you have. A marginally faster or slower rate causes the test to fail and results in a POST error of one long and one short beep, followed by a halt (HLT) instruction.

This test occurs at POST checkpoint 11h, which is sent to the manufacturer's test port 80h. A failure of this test, as indicated by one of the POST-card products that reads this port, can be identified by reading 11h as the last value sent to the manufacturer's test port. To eliminate the test and enable a faster-than-normal clock rate, you must patch the instruction at the proper location from a 73h (JAE—Jump if Above or Equal) to an EBh (JMP—Jump unconditionally); this patch causes the test for an abnormally high refresh rate (resulting in a low test value) to pass through the JAE instruction. When this instruction is changed to a JMP instruction, the test never passes through and falls into the error routine, no matter how fast the rate.

Notice that the test for a slow refresh rate still is intact and that it fails if the clock is below 6 or 8 MHz, depending on the system. The JAE instruction occurs at F000:05BC in IBM AT systems with the 06/10/85 or 11/15/85 ROM BIOS versions and at F000:05C0 in XT-286 systems. The original AT system with the 01/10/84 BIOS *does not have this test*. By creating a new set of chips with this value changed by an EPROM programmer, you can eliminate this speed check and enable faster clock rates.

Modifying ROM BIOS Hard Disk Drive Parameter Tables. Probably the most common change made to a BIOS is adding or changing drives in existing hard drive tables. For example, I have added two new drive types to one of my systems. Those types—25 and 26—have these parameters:

Type	Cylinders	Heads	WPC	Ctrl	LZ	S/T	Meg	MB
25	918	15	65535	08h	918	17	114.30	119.85
26	918	15	65535	08h	918	26	174.81	183.31

See Chapter 14, "Hard Disk Drives and Controllers," for more information about these parameters. In my old AT system, these table entries originally were unused (zeros), as are the remainder of types from 27 through 47. By burning a new set of ROMs with these two new completed entries, I can use my Maxtor XT-1140 drive to maximum capacity with an MFM controller (as type 25) or an RLL controller (as type 26). This setup precludes the need for a controller BIOS to override the motherboard table values and also saves me some memory in the C000 or D000 segments, where a hard disk controller ROM normally would reside. The procedure also makes my system more standard. If you are interested in performing this modification, get the *IBM AT Technical Reference Manual*, which documents the position and format of the drive tables in the BIOS.

Changing the Hard Disk Controller Head Step Rate. Another, more complicated modification that you can perform is to increase the stepping rate of the hard disk controller. The first edition of this book briefly mentioned this modification, and a reader wrote to me to express interest in it. This edition explains the precise nature of this modification and what is being changed, to give you greater insight into how the BIOS and disk controller work together. The performance gain, in fact, is relatively slight; I see making the change as being a learning experience more than anything else.

The Western Digital AT Controllers (1002/1003/1006) used by IBM in the original AT system, as well as in other compatible controllers (such as those from Data Technology Corporation and Adaptec), have a default head-stepping rate of 35μsec (microseconds). The fastest usable step rate is 16μsec—more than twice as fast. Most ST-506/412 hard disks have optimum stepping rates as low as 10μsec. By decreasing the rate to 16μsec, you can improve the seeking performance of the drive, resulting in an improvement of several milliseconds or more during an average seek. Because the standard rate is so slow compared with the optimum rate, many ST-506/412 drives—especially fast-seeking drives—do not perform to their manufacturer-rated seek performance unless the step rate from the controller is optimized in this manner.

You can decrease the step rate to 16μsec in two ways. The easiest and best way is to simply set a jumper on the controller card. Not all cards, however, support this option. In fact, only one of the many Western Digital ST-506/412 controllers—the WD1003-WAH (ST-506/412 MFM, no floppy support)—supports this option. None of the other WD cards for the AT permits you to change the step rate by way of a jumper. Adaptec, on the other hand, has a jumper for selecting the step rate on all its AT ST-506/412 controllers. Other than Adaptec's cards, most cards do not have a jumper and require other means of changing the step rate.

The second method of changing the step rate is universal and works with virtually all AT bus ST-506/412 controllers, regardless of whether they are MFM or RLL or whether they support floppy drives. You make the change by changing two bytes in the ROM BIOS hard disk support code, which alters the way that two specific commands are sent to the controller card.

First, consider a little background on the way that the BIOS and controller operate. When DOS reads or writes data to or from a hard disk, it accesses the disk through the ROM BIOS. Specifically, DOS uses the Int 13h (h = hexadecimal) functions provided in the BIOS. Int 13h functions are commands incorporated into the BIOS of an AT system that enable DOS (or any other software) to perform specific commands in relation to the drive. These Int 13h commands then are translated into direct controller-register-level commands by the BIOS. The direct controller commands are called *command control block* (CCB) commands, because each command must be presented to the controller in the form of a 7-byte command block with the command byte itself being the last (seventh) one. The other six bytes contain information such as the number of sectors on which to operate, as well as the cylinder and head positions where the command operates.

Sixteen Int 13h commands are available for hard disks in the IBM AT BIOS. Some of these commands, such as the Get Disk Type BIOS command, perform functions that do not involve accessing the controller or drive. Most other commands, however, are translated by the BIOS to the required code to send one of eight total CCB commands to the controller.

Table 17.2 shows the Int 13h BIOS commands and the specific CCB commands that the BIOS executes in the process.

Table 17.2   Int 13h AT Hard Disk BIOS and AT Controller CCB Commands

BIOS Command	Description	CCB Command	Description
00h	Reset Disk System	91h 10h	Set Parameters Recalibrate
01h	Get Status of Last Operation	—	—
02h	Read Sectors	20h	Read Sector
03h	Write Sectors	30h	Write Sector
04h	Verify Sectors	40h	Read Verify
05h	Format Track	50h	Format Track
08h	Read Drive Parameters	—	—
09h	Initialize Drive Characteristics	91h	Set Parameters
0Ah	Read Long	22h	Read Sector
0Bh	Write Long	32h	Write Sector
0Ch	Seek	70h	Seek
0Dh	Alternate Hard Disk Reset	10h	Recalibrate
10h	Test for Drive Ready	—	—
11h	Recalibrate Drive	10h	Recalibrate
14h	Controller Internal Diagnostic	80h	Diagnose
15h	Get Disk Type	—	—

Although only eight CCB commands are specific to the standard Western Digital (or compatible) AT hard disk controller, variations of some of the commands exist. Each CCB command consists of a single byte, with the most significant four bits (bits 4–7) of the byte indicating the actual command and the least significant four bits (bits 0–3) indicating various command options. For two of the CCB commands, the option bits indicate—and, in fact, set—the step rate for the controller. By changing these bits, you also change the default step rate.

Table 17.3 shows the eight standard CCB commands.

Table 17.3   WD1002/WD1003/WD1006 AT Hard Disk Controller CCB Commands

CCB Command	Description
10h-1Fh	Recalibrate
20h-23h	Read Sector
30h-33h	Write Sector
40h-41h	Read Verify
50h	Format Track
70h-7Fh	Seek
80h	Diagnose
91h	Set Parameters

In each of these commands, the CCB command byte is sent to the controller as the seventh byte of the total command block. The primary value is the first one listed in the chart. By setting the option bits, you can alter the command function. For example, the Read Sector command is 20h. By adding +1h to the command byte (making it 21h), you disable automatic retries in case of errors. This step prevents the controller from automatically rereading the sector as many as 19 additional times, in some cases; instead, the error is reported immediately. For error-correction code (ECC) errors, the controller simply attempts an immediate ECC correction, rather than rereading the sector as many as eight times in attempting to get a good read before making the ECC correction.

You can disable retries only for the Read Sector, Write Sector, and Read Verify commands. This capability is especially useful during low-level formatting, surface analyzing, or even just Read Verify testing of the drive, because any errors are reported more accurately without automatic retries taking place.

You can set another option for the Read Sector and Write Sector commands. This option involves the ECC bytes (an additional four bytes of data past the data area of the sector); it makes the sector read or write include a total 516 bytes instead of the normal 512. To set the "long" option, add +2h to the Read Sector or Write Sector CCB byte value. To change the standard Read Sector command (20h) to include the ECC bytes, for example, you add +2h, which results in a CCB command byte value of 22h. The option to include the ECC bytes during a read or write is especially useful in testing the ECC circuitry on the controller by specifically writing incorrect values and then reading them back to see the ECC in action.

For the Read Sector and Write Sector CCB commands, you can combine the disable-retries option with the long option by adding the two options (+1h and +2h = +3h), a procedure that results in a CCB command byte value of 23h (Read Sector) or 33h (Write Sector).

The last two commands—Recalibrate and Seek—have options that you can set through the option bits. For these two commands only, the option bits are used to set the stepping rate for subsequent seek commands to the drive. By adding a value from 1h through Fh to the CCB command byte for the Recalibrate or Seek commands, you can change the step rate from the default of 35μsec to something else.

The following table shows the different step rates that you can set by adding the step option to these commands.

Step Option	Step Rate (μsec)
0h	35
1h	500
2h	1,000
3h	1,500
4h	2,000
5h	2,500
6h	3,000
7h	3,500
8h	4,000
9h	4,500
Ah	5,000
Bh	5,500
Ch	6,000
Dh	6,500
Eh	3.2
Fh	16

In this case, you want to add Fh to change the step rate from the default 35μsec to 16μsec. Notice that the other possible values are much too slow (500 to 6,500μsec) and that the 3.2μsec rate is much too fast for most drives. To change the Recalibrate and Seek commands to use the 16μsec step rate, you must patch the BIOS, changing the 10h and 70h to 1Fh and 7Fh, respectively. You essentially are patching the code that is executed when an Int 13h, Function 11h (Recalibrate Drive), or Function 0Ch (Seek) BIOS command is executed. These BIOS routines contain the code that sends the 10h (Recalibrate) or 70h (Seek) CCB commands to the controllers. Because the other BIOS routines that also execute the CCB Recalibrate command do so by calling the same Int 13h Function 11h code, only one patch is required to change all occurrences of the CCB Recalibrate command.

Because these two commands can be in different positions in different BIOS, the following code shows you how to find them by using the DOS DEBUG command:

```
C:\>DEBUG                      ;Run DEBUG
-S F000:0 L 0 C6 46 FE 10      ;Search ROM for Recalibrate command
F000:30CF                      ; Found it!
```

```
-S F000:0 L 0 C6 46 FE 70      ;Search ROM for Seek command
F000:309A                      ; Found it!
-Q                             ;Quit
```

The first Search command locates the code sent to the controller for a CCB Recalibrate command, and the second Search locates the Seek command. The 10h (Recalibrate) command is at F000:30D2h in this example, because the address returned by the Search command points to the beginning of the search string, not to the end.

Remember to add 3 to each location returned for the actual location of the 10h or 70h command. The 70h byte, for example, is at F000:309Dh. These "found" locations vary from system to system; this example used an IBM AT Model 339 with an 11/15/85 BIOS. Therefore, you can change these bytes to 1Fh and 7Fh, respectively. You must have an EPROM programmer to record these changes in another set of chips.

This section examined some simple changes that you can make in a ROM BIOS with the help of an EPROM programmer. The steps involved in modifying or burning the ROMs were not described, because these instructions normally are included with the programmer device that you purchase.

Using a Flash BIOS. Flash ROM is a type of EEPROM chip that is included in several systems today. *EEPROM* (electrically erasable programmable read-only memory) is a type of ROM chip that you can erase and reprogram directly in the system without using ultraviolet light and an EPROM programmer device. Using Flash ROM enables a manufacturer to send out ROM upgrades on disk; you then can load the upgrade into the Flash ROM chip on the motherboard without removing and replacing the chip. This method saves time and money for both the system manufacturer and the end user.

Normally, the Flash ROM in a system is write-protected, and you must disable the protection before performing an update, usually by means of a jumper or switch that controls the lock on the ROM update. Without the lock, any program that knows the right instructions can rewrite the ROM in your system—not a comforting thought. Without the write protection, it is conceivable that virus programs could be written that copy themselves directly into the ROM BIOS code in your system! Fortunately, I have not seen an implementation of Flash that did not have write-protection capability.

Most manufacturers that use the Flash BIOS system notify their customers when they upgrade the BIOS for a particular system line. Usually, the cost of the upgrade is nominal; if your system is new enough, the upgrade may even be free.

Using IML System Partition BIOS. IBM uses a scheme similar to a Flash ROM called Initial Microcode Load (IML). IML is a technique in which the BIOS code is installed on the hard disk in a special hidden system partition and is loaded every time the system is powered up. Of course, the system still has a core BIOS on the motherboard, but all that BIOS does is locate and load updated BIOS code from the system partition. This technique enables IBM to distribute ROM updates on disk for installation in the system partition. The IML BIOS is loaded every time the system is reset or powered on.

Along with the system BIOS code, the system partition contains a complete copy of the Reference Diskette, which provides the option of running the setup and system-configuration software at any time during a reboot operation. This option eliminates the need to boot from the Reference Diskette to reconfigure the system and gives the impression that the entire Reference Diskette is contained in ROM.

One drawback to this technique is that the BIOS code is installed on the (SCSI) hard disk; the system cannot function properly without the properly set-up hard disk connected. You always can boot from the Reference Diskette floppy, should the hard disk fail or become disconnected, but you cannot boot from a standard floppy disk.

Upgrading Disk Drives

Interfacing a system with different types of floppy and hard disk drives sometimes is a problem because of the differences in controllers and support software. This section discusses adding floppy disk and hard disk drives to a system.

Upgrading a Floppy Disk Drive

To add floppy drives to an existing system, you must connect them to a controller board. Virtually every PC, XT, or AT comes with at least one floppy disk controller. The controllers and the system BIOS routines support different drives. Following are the floppy-drive types that are commonly installed on PCs:

- 5 1/4-inch double-density (DD) drive (360K)

- 5 1/4-inch high-density (HD) drive (1.2M)

- 3 1/2-inch double-density (DD) drive (720K)

- 3 1/2-inch high-density (HD) drive (1.44M)

- 3 1/2-inch extra-high-density (ED) drive (2.88M)

With 5 1/4-inch drives, you need to be concerned about the track-width differences. The 360K drives write wider tracks than 1.2M drives do. You must be careful when writing 360K disks in a 1.2M drive if those disks have been written on by a 360K drive because of these track-width differences. All 3 1/2-inch drives, however, write the same track width, so you need not be concerned about problems related to track width.

Because the ED or HD drives can read and write DD disks as well, a system with as few as two drives—one 5 1/4-inch HD drive and one 3 1/2-inch ED drive—can read and write any disk format. When you upgrade, therefore, you should add these higher-density drives whenever possible.

DOS versions 3.3 and later support both double-density and high-density drives. DOS versions 5.0 and later support the newer ED 3 1/2-inch drives. DOS versions earlier than 3.3 support fewer drives and probably should not be used anymore. Table 17.4 lists the floppy-disk support provided in each DOS version.

V

Asssembly & Maintenance

Chapter 17—System Upgrades and Improvements

Table 17.4 DOS Version Floppy-Disk-Format Support

Supported Disk Formats	DOS Version							
	1.0	1.1	2.0	3.0	3.2	3.3	5.0	6.x
5 1/4-inch DD (160K)	×	×	×	×	×	×	×	×
5 1/4-inch DD (180K)			×	×	×	×	×	×
5 1/4-inch DD (320K)		×	×	×	×	×	×	×
5 1/4-inch DD (360K)			×	×	×	×	×	×
5 1/4-inch HD (1.2M)				×	×	×	×	×
3 1/2-inch DD (720K)					×	×	×	×
3 1/2-inch HD (1.44M)						×	×	×
3 1/2-inch ED (2.88M)							×	×

Along with DOS support, the floppy drive controller is another issue of concern. Standard controllers in PC and XT systems support only double-density drives. To save money, consider adding only the double-density versions of the 5 1/4-inch and 3 1/2-inch drives to PC- or XT-type systems because they require no special controllers, cables, or software. DOS provides everything you need in the DRIVER.SYS driver file, which you can use to support the 3 1/2-inch 720K drive in systems that do not have built-in ROM support for that drive.

The HD drives use a higher data rate (500 kHz) than the DD drives (250 kHz) do. To use these higher-density drives, you must have a controller and software capable of supporting the higher data rate. Because the newer extra-high-density (ED) drives require a 1 MHz data rate—faster than most current controllers can support—you may need a controller upgrade to run those drives.

To use 1.2M or 1.44M drives in PC or XT systems, you must purchase a controller and software that can handle the high- or extra-high-density formats. Because the AT floppy controller already supports the 500 kHz data rate required by 1.2M or 1.44M high-capacity drives, no additional controller is necessary. To upgrade your system with a newer 2.88M drive, however, you must have a new controller that supports the 1 MHz data rate.

The final issue to consider when you upgrade a floppy disk drive is BIOS support. Many older systems do not have BIOS support for the newer floppy disk drives. Therefore, even if you have the correct drive, controller, and DOS version, you still cannot use the drive correctly unless your BIOS supports it.

Table 17.5 shows the IBM BIOS versions and the floppy disk drives that they support.

Table 17.5 IBM BIOS Floppy-Drive Support

System Description	ROM BIOS Date	ID Byte	Submodel Byte	Revision	5 1/4 DD	5 1/4 HD	3 1/2 DD	3 1/2 HD	3 1/2 ED
PC	04/24/81	FF	—	—	×				
PC	10/19/81	FF	—	—	×				
PC	10/27/82	FF	—	—	×				
PC-XT	11/08/82	FE	—	—	×				
PC-XT	01/10/86	FB	00	01	×		×		
PC-XT	05/09/86	FB	00	02	×		×		
PS/2 25	06/26/87	FA	01	00	×		×		
PS/2 30	09/02/86	FA	00	00	×		×		
PS/2 30	12/12/86	FA	00	01	×		×		
PS/2 30	02/05/87	FA	00	02	×		×		
PC-AT	01/10/84	FC	—	—	×		×		
PC-AT	06/10/85	FC	00	01	×	×	×		
PC-AT	11/15/85	FC	01	00	×	×	×	×	
PC-XT 286	04/21/86	FC	02	00	×	×	×	×	
PS/1	12/01/89	FC	0B	00	×	×	×	×	
PS/2 25-286	06/28/89	FC	09	02	×	×	×		
PS/2 30-286	08/25/88	FC	09	00	×	×	×	×	
PS/2 30-286	06/28/89	FC	09	02	×	×	×	×	
PS/2 35 SX	03/15/91	F8	19	05	×	×	×	×	×
PS/2 35 SX	04/04/91	F8	19	06	×	×	×	×	×
PS/2 40 SX	03/15/91	F8	19	05	×	×	×	×	×
PS/2 40 SX	04/04/91	F8	19	06	×	×	×	×	×
PS/2 L40 SX	02/27/91	F8	23	02	×	×	×	×	
PS/2 50	02/13/87	FC	04	00	×	×	×	×	
PS/2 50	05/09/87	FC	04	01	×	×	×	×	
PS/2 50Z	01/28/88	FC	04	02	×	×	×	×	
PS/2 50Z	04/18/88	FC	04	03	×	×	×	×	
PS/2 55 SX	11/02/88	F8	0C	00	×	×	×	×	
PS/2 57 SX	07/03/91	F8	26	02	×	×	×	×	×
PS/2 60	02/13/87	FC	05	00	×		×	×	
PS/2 65 SX	02/08/90	F8	1C	00	×		×	×	
PS/2 70 386	01/29/88	F8	09	00	×	×	×	×	
PS/2 70 386	04/11/88	F8	09	02	×	×	×	×	
PS/2 70 386	12/15/89	F8	09	04	×	×	×	×	
PS/2 70 386	01/29/88	F8	04	00	×	×	×	×	
PS/2 70 386	04/11/88	F8	04	02	×	×	×	×	

(continues)

V

Asssembly & Maintenance

Table 17.5	Continued				5 1/4		3 1/2		
System Description	ROM BIOS Date	ID Byte	Submodel Byte	Revision	DD	HD	DD	HD	ED
PS/2 70 386	12/15/89	F8	04	04	×	×	×	×	
PS/2 70 386	06/08/88	F8	0D	00	×	×	×	×	
PS/2 70 386	02/20/89	F8	0D	01	×	×	×	×	
PS/2 70 486	12/01/89	F8	0D	?	×	×	×	×	
PS/2 70 486	09/29/89	F8	1B	00	×	×	×	×	
PS/2 P70 386	?	F8	50	00	×	×	×	×	
PS/2 P70 386	01/18/89	F8	0B	00	×	×	×	×	
PS/2 P75 486	?	F8	52	00	×	×	×	×	×
PS/2 80 386	03/30/87	F8	00	00	×	×	×	×	
PS/2 80 386	10/07/87	F8	01	00	×	×	×	×	
PS/2 80 386	11/21/89	F8	80	01	×	×	×	×	
PS/2 90 XP 486	?	F8	2D	00	×	×	×	×	×
PS/2 90 XP 486	?	F8	2F	00	×	×			
PS/2 90 XP 486	?	F8	11	00	×	×			
PS/2 90 XP 486	?	F8	13	00	×	×			
PS/2 90 XP 486	?	F8	2B	00	×	×			
PS/2 95 XP 486	?	F8	2C	00	×	×	×		
PS/2 95 XP 486	?	F8	2E	00	×	×			
PS/2 95 XP 486	?	F8	14	00	×	×			
PS/2 95 XP 486	?	F8	16	00	×	×			
PS/2 95 XP 486	?	F8	2A	00	×	×			

? = Unavailable
The ID byte, submodel byte, and revision numbers are in hexadecimal form.

Table 17.5 shows that the original PC-AT (01/10/84) BIOS supports only the 5 1/4-inch drives and that the second revision (06/10/85) adds 720K drive support. The final AT BIOS (11/15/85) supports the 1.44M drive as well. Some of this information is undocumented by IBM; in fact, IBM states that the AT never supported the 1.44M drives. However, 1.44M drives have been installed on hundreds of AT systems with a BIOS date of 11/15/85.

If your BIOS does not support a 720K drive, DOS can add support for a 720K drive by adding a DRIVPARM command in CONFIG.SYS. You also can load DRIVER.SYS, by way of a command similar to DRIVPARM, for DOS versions that do not support the DRIVPARM command. To support a 3 1/2-inch floppy disk drive on an older system that does not have this support, you can use the following commands:

For a PC/XT-class system: DRIVPARM=/D:1 /F:2 /I

For an AT-class system: DRIVPARM=/D:1 /F:2 /I /C

The /D parameter indicates which physical drive unit is being specified; in this case, 1 equals B. The /F parameter indicates a 720K drive format. The /I parameter indicates that this drive is not supported in the BIOS. The /C parameter indicates that the drive has Disk Changeline support: the drive can alert the controller that the disk has been changed. Because the PC/XT controllers do not support a disk change, you cannot use /C with those systems.

As an alternative, especially if you are using versions of DOS 4.0 or earlier (which lack the DRIVPARM command), you can use DRIVER.SYS. The following example assumes that your DOS files are in C:\DOS.

> For a PC/XT-class system: DEVICE=C:\DOS\DRIVER.SYS /D:2 /F:2

> For an AT-class system: DEVICE=C:\DOS\DRIVER.SYS /D:2 /F:2 /C

Deciding whether to use DRIVPARM or DRIVER.SYS can be confusing for people who are new to personal computers. For example, the parameters for DRIVPARM and DRIVER.SYS are identical, and the commands have much the same effect. The primary difference between using DRIVPARM and using DRIVER.SYS occurs after you boot your machine.

When you use DRIVPARM, the B drive has the new, correct parameters and functions as a normal 720K drive, as though your BIOS fully supported the drive. If you place a disk in the new drive and enter **FORMAT B:**, the drive properly formats the disk as a 720K disk without additional parameters.

The procedure is not so simple if you use DRIVER.SYS. The new B drive acts as though it were a 360K drive—that is, if you execute a FORMAT B: command, DOS formats the 3 1/2-inch disk to 360K. This situation takes place because DRIVER.SYS creates a new drive letter to represent the 720K format of the new drive (one drive letter higher than your last hard disk partition letter) as a substitute for B. This new drive—which on a system with a C drive is D—operates properly as a 720K drive. When you execute the command FORMAT D:, the B drive operates in 720K mode.

To avoid this floppy-drive alphabet soup, use DRIVPARM if your DOS version supports it. The first IBM DOS version to support DRIVPARM is 5.0. MS-DOS versions (and original-equipment-manufacturer versions) as early as 3.2 support the command.

DRIVPARM and DRIVER.SYS work only for adding 720K support to a system that does not have that support for the BIOS. The DRIVPARM and DRIVER.SYS commands do not work for adding 1.44M or 2.88M support to a system that lacks that support in the BIOS, even though the DOS manual seems to indicate that they work. In these cases, you must purchase a third-party driver program or upgrade your BIOS to support the new drive. A BIOS upgrade is the recommended method of adding support for 1.44M or 2.88M drives.

PC and XT controllers can connect two floppy drives internally, through the supplied cable, and to two drives externally, through a cable that you can purchase. The AT controller supports two floppy drives and two hard disks. If you add large-capacity floppy drives to a PC or XT system, you must have a new controller card and driver programs that operate with the card to support high-density drives. Numerous vendors offer these special controllers and software drivers, as well as complete kits for installing 360K, 720K, 1.44M, and even 2.88M drives in any PC, XT, or AT system.

Adding a High-Density Floppy Drive to an XT System

Adding high-density floppy drives (1.2M or 1.44M) to an XT-class (8088) machine can be a problem. Some people incorrectly believe that a new motherboard BIOS is necessary. It's not, because the XT BIOS and system hardware does not support high-density floppy drive operation.

Special high-density floppy controllers for XTs are available. These controllers, however, include their own ROM BIOS extension that provides BIOS-level support tailored for their specific controller. The main BIOS normally has nothing to do with supporting a high-density drive on an XT.

The BIOS extension on an XT high-density controller may not work properly with some motherboard BIOS versions; ask the controller manufacturer for verification. You know that the controller BIOS is having problems when you see phantom-directory problems—that is, problems with the controller's recognizing the Disk Change signal. If you have this problem, contact the manufacturer of the controller. The manufacturer can recommend a solution, such as changing the BIOS on the controller card or installing a new motherboard BIOS. Of course, an incorrectly configured drive or bad cable also can cause these problems; be sure to check your installation thoroughly.

Adding a Hard Disk to a System

When you add hard disks to a system, purchase the entire package from one company unless you are familiar with disk drive interfaces. Because certain interfaces have emerged as industry standards, you can take the plug-and-play approach to selecting hard drives and interface cards. But for a novice to upgrading and repairing PCs, this process can be confusing. The key is that your hard drive and your disk controller or interface card must be matched perfectly so that they work together in your system.

For example, older ESDI drives and controllers often experience significant compatibility problems unless the drive and the controller card are matched. Nearly all SCSI hard drives work with any SCSI host adapter, but to get the maximum performance from the drive and adapter combination, you should ensure that they offer the same type of SCSI interface—for example, Standard SCSI, Fast SCSI, and Fast/Wide SCSI. The Fast and Fast/Wide versions sometimes are called SCSI-2, but not all drives or adapters advertised as SCSI-2 support Fast or Fast/Wide connections. Consult Chapter 14, "Hard Disk Drives and Controllers," for more information about the SCSI interface and hard disks.

An IDE drive is simple to install if it is the only drive in the system. Complications arise when you attempt to use two IDE drives on one cable or to install an IDE drive in a system that also uses some other type of drive. Because the IDE specification was relatively loose until 1990, many older IDE drives have problems sharing a cable with the newer, more standard drives.

If you are installing multiple IDE drives or installing IDE drives to coexist with other types of drives (ST-506/412, ESDI, or SCSI) in a single system, you may encounter some problems. You can solve some problems by using special IDE adapters that incorporate an on-board BIOS driver for support. Other problems, such as installing two different manufacturers' drives on a single cable, can require experimentation with master/slave jumpers and other jumper settings on the drive. In many cases, you have to contact the respective drive manufacturers, which can help you with the multiple-drive configuration.

Differences among SCSI, IDE, ESDI, and old-style ST-506/412 interfaces can complicate the process of upgrading your hard drive. To learn more about hard disk installations, be sure to familiarize yourself with the information in Chapter 14.

Speeding Up a System

This section examines ways to increase a system's speed. A common and easy way to increase a system's calculating performance is to add a math coprocessor. Products that are advertised as making your system run faster also are discussed in this section, along with indications of their relative performance gains.

Another type of performance improvement involves increasing the system clock rate, changing the processor for another type, or both. The idea of replacing the processor with a faster one can extend to replacing the entire motherboard. In this case, you do not really upgrade your system—you change it entirely. This extreme upgrade is not always recommended. This section also examines the cost benefit of these upgrades.

Math Coprocessors

The next-best thing to replacing the computer's brains is giving it a calculator. A math, or numeric, coprocessor will do just that. A *math coprocessor* is a computer chip that aids the CPU by relieving it of certain mathematical (also called *floating-point*) operations.

Not all math operations use the math coprocessor. Common operations such as addition, subtraction, multiplication, and division are performed by the processor. For sophisticated math operations—such as cosines, sines, tangents, and square roots—a math coprocessor can make the number-crunching up to 100 times faster, boosting overall performance by 200 to 1,000 percent.

Unfortunately, not all software programs can benefit from a math coprocessor; a program must be written to take advantage of this mathematical speed. Traditionally, spreadsheet, scientific, graphics, and computer-aided design (CAD) software receive a boost from a coprocessor. (For example, CAD software requires many calculations to track every dot on-screen.) Modeling and simulation software also require tremendous mathematical power. Usually, programs such as word processors do not need this power, although Microsoft Word for Windows supports a coprocessor.

About one in 10 software programs supports a math coprocessor. If your work involves software that accesses a math coprocessor, and if you do indeed use sophisticated mathematical functions, a math coprocessor can be a great addition (no pun intended). At a cost of less than $150, a math coprocessor becomes a very focused upgrade.

How do you add a math coprocessor to your computer? Most computers have a socket for a math coprocessor, usually located next to the main processor. Computers that have an 80486DX or Pentium processor do not require a math coprocessor; it's already built into the chip itself. Because of space limitations, some computers don't even have a coprocessor socket. The following table lists the coprocessors needed to assist your main processor.

Processor	Coprocessor
8086	8087
8088	8087
80286	80287
80386SX	80387SX
80386SL	80387SX
80386SLC	80387SX
80386DX	80387DX or Weitek 3167
80486SX	80487SX or Weitek 4167
80486DX	Built-in (no Intel coprocessor needed) or optional Weitek 4167
80486DX2	Built-in (no Intel coprocessor needed) or optional Weitek 4167
80486DX4	Built-in (no Intel coprocessor needed) or optional Weitek 4167
Pentium	Built-in (no Intel coprocessor needed) or optional Weitek 4167

As you can see, computers based on the 8088 and 8086 microprocessors require an 8087 coprocessor, systems based on the 80386DX require the 80387DX, and so on.

The type of coprocessor is not the only information you need to order one; you also need to know the speed needed by your computer's design. Like your processor, this speed is measured in megahertz (MHz). For example, the 8087 coprocessor originally came in three speeds: 5 MHz, 8 MHz, and 10 MHz. Each coprocessor speed is designed to match the speed of the computer. (You can now purchase an 8087XC that works at all three speeds. Be sure that the chip you purchase is designed to operate at the clock rate at which the system runs the math chip. Also, be careful about static discharges when you handle these chips; the chips are delicate and expensive. For detailed information about math coprocessors, refer to Chapter 6, "Microprocessor Types and Specifications."

As an upgrade, a math coprocessor is a very selective speed improvement. A math coprocessor works with software written specifically to recognize the coprocessor—and only in limited areas within a program. A spreadsheet program, for example, does not become faster in all mathematical operations.

There are four major manufacturers of math coprocessors. Intel Corporation, manufacturer of most microprocessors, is the leader in manufacturing math coprocessors. Other manufacturers of math coprocessors include Advanced Micro Devices (AMD), Cyrix, and Weitek Corporation.

After you choose a math coprocessor, installing it is easy. You simply buy the chip, plug it in, and flip a switch or run a setup program to recognize it.

To install a math coprocessor, follow these steps:

1. Turn off the system power.

2. Remove the system unit's cover assembly.

3. Touch the power supply to ensure that you have the same electrical potential as the system unit.

4. Remove as many plug-in adapter cards as necessary to access the coprocessor socket.

5. Locate the coprocessor socket on the motherboard. In almost all systems, the math-coprocessor socket is next to the main processor.

6. Remove the math coprocessor from its protective holder, place the coprocessor in the socket, and align Pin 1 of the processor with Pin 1 of the socket. To align the pins, look for a notch in the chip, and make sure that the notch faces in the same direction as the notches on other chips.

7. Carefully press the chip straight down, making sure that all the pins are seated in the socket. Be careful not to bend the pins.

8. If you are using a PC or XT, locate the DIP switch block of the PC on the system board, and flip switch position 2 to Off. On an AT or PS/2, run the Setup program so that the computer recognizes the addition of the coprocessor.

9. Reinstall all adapter boards that you removed.

10. Replace the system unit's cover.

11. Verify the operation of the math coprocessor by using the diagnostics or advanced diagnostics disk.

In the next few sections, we examine specific math coprocessors, from the original 8087 to the 487 chip. Each can perk up your computer's performance.

8087. The 8087 math coprocessor chip is designed for the 8088 (and 8086) CPU. Regardless of the clock speed of the 8088 chip in your system, the 8087 that you install must be rated to run at the same rate of speed as the main processor or faster; otherwise, the math coprocessor will fail. In 8088-based systems, the main CPU and the coprocessor run in synchronization, meaning that both must run at the same clock speed. In an IBM XT, for example, the 8088 runs at 4.77 MHz, and so does the 8087. Your system would work if you purchase an 8087 that is designed to run faster than 4.77 MHz, but not if you use one that is rated to run slower. To find the speed of the processor (and math coprocessor) for your system, consult your system documentation.

287. Unlike systems based on the 8088 processor chip, the 286 CPU chip and the 287 chip run asynchronously, which means that processor time is not wasted by linking the operation of the two chips for the sake of constant communication between them; instead, the two chips communicate at set time intervals. In addition, the 286 and 287 chips do not run at the same clock speed; the 80287 math chip runs at two-thirds the speed of the CPU. In a 6-MHz AT system, the math coprocessor runs at only 4 MHz.

Internally, the 287 chip is the same math chip as the 8087, meaning that the union of the 286/287 is not as effective a partnership as that of the 8088/8087. The 287 math chip, however, does effectively speed certain high-level math computations in software that is designed to take advantage of this chip. To determine the speed of the math chip supported by a particular 286-based system, consult the system documentation.

You have the additional option of adding an Intel 287XL or 287XLT math chip to these systems. The XL and XLT chips are offered in a single speed rating—12.5 MHz—but run at slower speeds on slower systems. The XL and XLT chips perform about 20 percent faster than an original 287, due to an improved die or mask design.

387. The 80387 math chip runs at the same clock speed as the main CPU, even though it runs asynchronously. The 80387 coprocessor is a high-performance math chip designed specifically to work with the 386 (unlike the 80287 coprocessor or an 8087 with different pins).

The 387 chip uses a low-power-consumption CMOS design and comes in two flavors: the 387DX, designed to work with the 386DX processor; and the 387SX, designed for the 386SX, SL, and SLC processors. Originally, Intel offered several speed versions of the 387DX coprocessor; the only version that Intel offers now is a 33-MHz version that can run at slower speeds on slower systems.

Notice that Intel improved the die design of the 33-MHz-rated 387 over all previous designs; this chip performs 10 to 20 percent faster than the slower-rated chips. This improvement was made mainly in response to competition; several other chip manufacturers began making clone 387 chips that originally outperformed Intel's. With the new mask, the Intel 387 has been brought back up to par with the clone chips, and performance differences among different manufacturers' versions of the 387 chip are minor.

487. As detailed in Chapter 6, "Microprocessor Types and Specifications," the 487SX chip is not a math coprocessor chip. Rather, the 487SX is a fully functional 486 chip, with the math coprocessor enabled, that is plugged into a vacant "overdrive" upgrade socket in what Intel calls 486SX systems. When you plug in a 487 chip, it disables the 486 chip and takes over all processing, including high-level math processing. In creating the 486SX, Intel disables the math coprocessor that is functional on a fully capable 486DX chip before releasing the chip to system manufacturers. Intel markets these chips more cheaply than it does 486DX chips, enabling system manufacturers to produce 486SX systems at roughly the same cost as 386 systems.

Main-CPU Upgrades or Replacements

You can use several methods to increase the calculating speed of a PC, including replacing the processor with a more efficient unit, replacing the processor with an In-Circuit Emulator, and replacing the entire motherboard. This section describes how to increase the calculating speed of a PC-type system, including systems based on the 8088, 286, 386, and 486 CPU chips. For detailed information on these processors, as well as on the Pentium, refer to Chapter 6.

8086 and 8088 System Processor. You have to replace your 8086 or 8088 CPU chip only if, by performing in-depth diagnostics on your system, you determine that the chip has gone bad. It is quite difficult to replace one clock speed of 8086 or 8088 CPU chip with another, along with the other components that are to be replaced, to gain what is a relatively small performance increase. This type of upgrade is not recommended.

Instead, if you use a system based on the 8086 or 8088 and want a performance increase, given the cost of new 386 and 486SX systems, you should think about buying a new system. If system replacement is not an option, the following sections describe some additional upgrade options.

NEC V20 and V30 Chip. A simple way to increase the performance of an 8088- or 8086-based system is to use the more efficient alternative processors produced by NEC: the NEC V20 and the NEC V30. These processors are plugged into the system as direct replacements for the original processors. The NEC unit that you should select varies, according to the original processor in the system. The processors are exchanged as follows:

Original Processor	Replacement Processor
Intel 8088	NEC V20
Intel 8086	NEC V30

These NEC chips were created several years ago, when Intel could not meet the demand for the production of 8086 and 8088 chips. Intel licensed other manufacturers to make these chips. NEC, which was one of the licensed manufacturers, was given the chip-mask specifications for the Intel chips and complete access to the Intel processors' source code. NEC then created a new processor that mimics the Intel units but that is more efficient in several instructions. Intel has attempted to restrain NEC from manufacturing and importing these devices, but they remain available.

One problem with the NEC processor upgrades is that they are not 100 percent compatible with Intel units. IBM PS/2 Models 25 and 30, for example, cannot use the NEC chips, and some of the special disk-duplicating programs that back up copy-protected disks do not work when the NEC chips are installed. In addition, the performance gain of upgrading to these chips is as little as 5 percent.

Because of the very small performance gain and the potential for both incompatibility and legal problems, business users probably should avoid purchasing NEC chips. You may want to consider this upgrade for a home or experimental system, however, because of its low cost. The following paragraphs provide information about the NEC processor upgrades for the 8088 chip.

The original processor in an IBM XT is a 4.77 MHz 8088. The replacement—the NEC V20—is rated to run at 8 MHz, but these chips operate properly on systems rated for the slower speed. The operating speed of the chip is controlled by the motherboard clock circuitry. The V30 chip works only in systems designed for the Intel 8086.

To install the NEC processor replacement, locate the 8088 or 8086 processor on the motherboard, remove the processor, and plug the NEC device into place. NEC chips are available for about $15 to $25, depending on the chip, the speed rating, and the retailer.

This processor upgrade is very inexpensive (about $15) and easy to install, but the speed increase is so small that it is difficult to detect. You should test-run applications and time different operations with a stopwatch to determine any time savings from using the new chip. The normal increase in performance is about 5 percent to 10 percent of the former speed. If an operation originally took 10 seconds to complete, the same operation would take 9 to 9 1/2 seconds with the new NEC chip. A 5 percent performance increase for only $15, however, is not bad.

Increasing the System Clock Rate. Another option for speeding your PC or XT system is increasing the processor's clock rate. This type of upgrade is difficult to implement for PC or XT systems, because the clock crystal cannot be easily altered or replaced. The crystal is soldered, not socketed, into place, and the crystal is multiplexed—that is, it is used for functions besides running the system clock.

The crystal in an IBM XT, for example, is a 14.31818-MHz unit whose frequency is divided by 3 by the timer circuits to generate the 4.77 MHz system clock. This 14.31818-MHz crystal frequency is on the system bus (slot) connectors at Pin B30. (This signal is one of the PC bus specifications.) Many cards, such as video boards, depend on this oscillator signal's presence for their operations. The oscillator signal is divided by 4 to obtain a 3.58-MHz signal used to drive circuits in the Color Graphics Adapter. An upgrade that attempts to increase the clock rate of the main processor, therefore, probably would interfere with the original crystal and its subset function of generating a 14.31818-MHz oscillator signal for the system bus.

Several years ago, some devices sold for PC and XT systems could increase the clock rate for the main processor without interfering with other circuits on the motherboard. These devices have been unavailable for some time. A much better alternative is installing an in-circuit emulator (ICE) board or a processor-enhancement card that has a 286 or 386 processor on board, or replacing the entire motherboard.

In-Circuit Emulator (ICE) Boards. You can upgrade your PC/XT system with an In-Circuit Emulator (ICE) board that serves as an entire replacement for the 8086 or 8088 CPU chip. An ICE board plugs into one of the system's expansion slots and has a cable that plugs into the microprocessor socket from which the CPU chip has been removed. The ICE board has a 286 or 386 processor running at a high clock rate, as well as high-speed 16- or 32-bit memory on board. The ICE board takes over the system as though it were a new processor.

These boards are a relatively economical system upgrade, given the fact that they provide a tremendous performance boost.

Another feature of some of the better ICE boards is that you can install your original 8086 or 8088 processor on the ICE board. For compatibility and reliability testing, you then can use the original processor to run the system.

To install an ICE board, follow these steps:

1. Remove the main processor from the motherboard. In some units, you install the processor on the speedup board. Other units require that you store the original processor for safekeeping.

2. Plug the speedup board into an open slot—preferably, next to the processor socket.

3. Run a cable from the board to the processor socket, and plug in the cable. The installation is complete.

These units have their own on-board memory, a full complement of 640K, or a small amount of cache memory. The high-speed memory is directly accessible by the 80286 or 80386 processor on the speedup board. Your system memory still is used in some of these units.

Most of these boards do not convert a PC or XT to an AT-type system with the capability to address 16M of memory and to run OS/2 or perform other AT functions, but they give a PC or XT system the speed of an AT system.

Replacing the PC/XT Motherboard. Another way to increase system speed is to replace the original PC/XT motherboard. Replacing the motherboard can convert a PC-type system to an AT design, but you must replace many other items to complete the procedure. By the time you pay for and complete this conversion, you probably could buy a complete AT-compatible system and leave your PC/XT alone. (You also could sell the PC or XT system and use the money for options on the new AT, or donate it to charity and take the tax break.)

Because of the cost, complexity, and numerous compatibility problems with other system components and accessories, you should consider replacing the motherboard in a PC- or XT-type system only in special cases—and then only if money is no object.

Complete motherboard replacements consist of placing a complete AT-type motherboard of 286-, 386-, or 486-based design in your original PC/XT case. The replacement motherboard usually has 16-bit ISA slots—or even 32-bit EISA slots.

The original AT motherboard was much larger than the PC or XT motherboards. Normally, you cannot find a full-size AT-style motherboard to fit a PC case, because the PC has openings for only five slots in the back of the case and the slot spacing is different from that of an XT or AT system. Replacement AT-type motherboards that fit an XT case usually are called "baby AT" designs.

Installing a replacement motherboard is relatively difficult, but only because you must disassemble the entire system to replace the motherboard and then reassemble the system. When you undertake this kind of task, it is important that you mark all data and control cables to remind yourself which cables work with which device. It also is a good idea to mark the power connectors, particularly those that plug into the motherboard itself (usually marked P8 and P9), to help you remember the orientation of these connectors. If you install the motherboard power connectors backward, you may ruin the new motherboard.

The idea of replacing the motherboard sounds attractive at first, especially when you see the low prices of some of the replacement motherboards. But problems occur when you reassemble the rest of your old system. For example, are you going to use that XT hard disk controller in what now is an AT system? If you do, you get XT hard drive performance on a fast AT system. Following are some additional issues and problems that you may encounter when you create a hybrid system that is part AT and part XT:

- You must tell the Setup program that no hard disks are installed so that your XT controller's built-in ROM BIOS can operate the card properly.

- The XT controller uses Interrupt 5, which conflicts with a second parallel port (LPT2) in the AT.

- Your XT floppy controller does not support the high-density drives required to boot and run OS/2 and other software.

- For proper AT and OS/2 operation, you must change all your serial ports to those that have a 16450 or 16550A UART chip.

- Any memory that you already have in the XT system—including both chips and complete memory cards—probably does not work properly in an AT.

Replacing the motherboard has other disadvantages over the ICE-board upgrade discussed in preceding sections. The biggest disadvantage is that you have many more items to replace or upgrade after you replace the motherboard. Many peripherals and components of XT systems that continue to work after you install an ICE board are not suitable for an AT-type system.

Another disadvantage is that you are losing your original system. If you encounter a compatibility problem that prompts you to switch back to your old system configuration, you have to remove the new motherboard and reinstall the old. No switch can enable you to use your old processor until you work out conflicts or other compatibility problems, as you can in some ICE-board designs.

286 Systems. Upgrading AT-class systems is much simpler than upgrading PC- or XT-type systems, because you have fewer alternatives to consider. Also, the motherboard-replacement upgrade in an AT system works well because you start and end with an AT-class system. You do not have to change other system components, such as disk controllers, drives, serial ports, memory, and keyboards.

AT-type systems have primarily three upgrade levels:

- Increase the clock rate of the CPU by replacing the crystal oscillator with a faster one.

- Replace the existing processor with an In-Circuit Emulator (ICE) board.

- Replace the motherboard with one that contains a more powerful processor.

These upgrades are described in the following sections.

Increasing an AT System's Clock Rate. IBM's decision to socket the clock crystal in the PC AT met with much interest and speculation when the machine first appeared. The ability to unplug and replace the crystal is the key factor in attempting to increase an AT's clock rate. Increasing the speed of the system beyond its original design can result in a somewhat unstable system; a lot depends on how far you want to push.

Increasing system speed from 6 MHz to 8 MHz, or from 8 MHz to 10 MHz, is relatively conservative and usually enables the system to operate without problems. Attempting to increase the speed beyond these levels, however, can result in erratic or flaky system operation. The type of upgrade described in this section is what I call a hacker upgrade— suitable for people who want to experiment with their systems, but probably unsuitable for people who use their systems in a business environment.

Because the crystal is not multiplexed, as it is in PC and XT systems (it does not perform functions other than regulating the system clock speed), replacing it does not disturb other areas of the system. The oscillator signal required for Pin B30 in the expansion-bus connectors is generated independently by a 14.31818-MHz crystal that is separate from the main clock crystal on the motherboard. To minimize radio interference, the bus oscillator crystal is under a large, square piece of metal shielding. Because the two oscillators are separate, you can replace the processor clock crystal with a faster one and not interfere with the rest of the system. Upgrading an AT system's clock crystal is inexpensive because you don't have to supply any additional clock circuitry.

The main system clock crystal is in a 1/2-inch-by-3/8-inch silver housing that plugs into the socket near the 80286 chip, behind the center opening for the hard disk. To remove the crystal, insert a small screwdriver between the crystal and the socket, push the crystal out of the socket, and lift the crystal up and out of the retaining clip. You can insert a faster crystal to increase the operating speed of the 80286 CPU chip driven at half the crystal's speed.

For a few dollars, you can buy a 16-MHz replacement crystal and plug it into the system in place of the original 12-MHz crystal used in the original AT Models 068 and 099. Remember that because the 80286 internally divides the system clock crystal frequency by 2, it runs at half the crystal speed. The system then runs at 8 MHz—a 30 percent improvement in processing speed. If the 16-MHz crystal works and your system runs well at 8 MHz, you can try different crystals of increasing speeds to see how far your system can go. Some systems can tolerate running at speeds as high as 10 MHz, depending on several factors. You know that you have exceeded your system's capabilities if it locks up or otherwise demonstrates erratic operation. If your system doesn't run at a certain speed, reinstall the last crystal that worked properly.

The type of crystal that IBM used in the AT has a large case and thick, gold-plated leads that may differ from what you find at your local electronic-parts store. The standard crystal that IBM used is a series-mode, AT-cut, fundamental crystal with an HC-25/U case and 0.01 percent frequency tolerance. (*AT-cut* refers to the angle at which the quartz inside the crystal is sliced and has nothing to do with AT-type computers.) Any good crystal vendor should be able to supply this type of crystal.

V

Asssembly & Maintenance

Installing Faster RAM in an AT. If you want to try for more speed than your system seems to allow, you can experiment further to increase the maximum running speed by replacing system memory with higher-speed RAM chips. The standard-speed chip in most AT systems is 150 ns. If you replace all the memory with 100- or 120-ns chips, you may be able to take the extra step to 10 MHz or more.

This upgrade, however, is ineffective and a waste of money. Replacing your system memory with faster RAM chips is likely to result in a faster system only if the system manufacturer installed slow RAM on a motherboard that is rated for fast RAM. For example, if a system rated for 80-ns RAM chips had 150-ns chips installed in the factory, you probably could get a significant performance boost by installing 80-ns chips. But remember that you have to replace all the RAM chips on the motherboard if you decide to try this upgrade.

Replacing an AT's CPU Chip. You can replace the processor on a slower AT with one that is rated to run at higher speeds. You can replace the 80286-6, for example, with an 80286-10 or 80286-12. This upgrade also requires the installation of a clock crystal of greater frequency than the one used by your 6-MHz 80286 chip. Don't forget that you also may have to replace the math coprocessor (if you have one) with a faster chip.

This simple crystal swap works only in the original AT models with ROM BIOS dated 01/01/84. You cannot change the crystal speed of systems with 06/10/85 or 11/15/85 ROM BIOS dates; the POST in these systems detects the crystal change and automatically fails the motherboard test. You hear the audio code for motherboard failure: one long and one short beep. Fortunately, this failure is only temporary; when you reinstall the original crystal, the system works. The failed POST results from intentional changes that IBM made in the POST routines in later ROM versions.

If you want to swap CPU chips and clock chips on systems with BIOSes dated later than 01/01/84, the simplest way around the POST speed check is replacing the IBM ROM BIOS with a BIOS from Phoenix, AMI, or Award. Alternatively, you can remove the test from the IBM BIOS by changing the ROM BIOS code and reprogramming a new chip, as described in "Removing the POST Speed Check" earlier in this chapter.

Several years ago, some companies developed variable-speed devices that throttled the system up and down when the user twisted a knob. These devices also could monitor the system-reset line to detect a reboot operation, and they automatically kicked the system into low gear until the POST was passed, thus working around the speed test. These devices, unfortunately, cost much more than a simple crystal change and have for the most part been discontinued.

386 and 486 Processor Upgrade Boards for AT Systems. Various manufacturers have produced modular-design AT-type computers that enable you to replace a small daughtercard that contains the processor. In this processor-complex design, the main processor and support chips reside on a replaceable card, with the majority of system circuits still residing on the motherboard. In effect, you have a modular motherboard design. You can replace this processor card (usually at considerable expense) with one that contains a more powerful processor. Some of these modular systems enable you to replace your 286 chip with a 386; others enable you to upgrade all the way to a 486, providing you a lengthy upgrade path.

If you have a processor-complex AT motherboard design, contact the manufacturer of the system to determine the cost of an upgrade.

In-Circuit Emulator (ICE) boards for ATs are not as diverse or complicated as the ICE boards for PC/XT type systems. AT upgrade boards normally serve as direct processor replacements: they plug into the processor socket and do not take up a slot, as ICE boards do. You install these processor upgrade boards by removing the 286 chip and installing an upgrade module in the 286 socket. Processor upgrade boards are available that use the 386SX, 386DX, 486SX, or 486DX chips running at various clock speeds. Some 386-based boards have sockets for math coprocessor chips.

Because some of these upgrade boards have had compatibility problems with the original IBM AT BIOS, most are supplied with a set of aftermarket BIOS chips as well. In many cases, these new BIOS chips also amount to an upgrade, because the new BIOS gives you the enhancements that were discussed in the previous section "Upgrading the ROM BIOS," including enhanced hard disk drive support and floppy drive support.

Several processor upgrade boards are on the market, including quality offerings from Intel, Kingston, and Sigma Data. The addresses and phone numbers of these companies appear in Appendix B.

These processor-upgrade modules are a relatively simple and effective way to double the performance of older AT computers.

Replacing the AT Motherboard. You can choose among many motherboard replacements for AT systems, most of which use 486 processors and some of which include Zero Insertion Force (ZIF) OverDrive sockets that will accept the Pentium OverDrive chip when it is released. Motherboard upgrades for an AT system do not present the same problems as upgrading an XT in this manner, because you do not have to worry about changing other system components to be compatible with the new motherboard. In general, because you are both starting and ending with an AT-class system, you do not have to worry about changing the existing disk controller, memory, serial ports, floppy controller, or floppy drives, because they already are AT devices.

Make sure that the board you purchase has the correct screw holes for mounting in the existing chassis. Most AT replacement motherboards include both AT and XT form-factor mounting holes, to enable the boards to be mounted in a variety of system chassis. Some higher-performance upgrade motherboards work only in an AT chassis, because they exploit the full AT motherboard form factor and are designed specifically for the larger AT case.

For a list of recommendations for what to look for in a motherboard, see Chapter 4 "Motherboards."

386 Systems. The modular-design AT-type computer became most popular when the 486 was introduced. Buyers of 386 machines often did not want to pay the high price of a 486 during its first months on the market, but they still wanted an upgrade path to the more powerful processor chip. As with 286-based modular systems, on a processor-complex 386 the CPU chip and some support circuitry are placed on a separate card that plugs into the motherboard.

Replacing the 386 CPU card with one equipped with a 486 chip can be quite expensive. Contact the manufacturer of the system to determine the cost of an upgrade.

Various manufacturers provide upgrades for 386-based systems. Among the most common are plug-in boards that contain a 486SX or 486DX chip. This plug-in card usually requires you to unplug the 386 from the motherboard and plug in a card that contains the new processor and support circuitry. Some upgrade cards also require you to plug an adapter board into one of your system slots with a cable running to the replacement CPU chip card. The cost of these upgrade cards varies, depending on the manufacturer.

You can, however, replace your processor with some special products. Cyrix Corporation's Cx486DRX2 is a 486 processor upgrade for 386-based machines that technically is not a 486 chip, but a clock-doubled chip with a 1K on-board cache. The upgrade kit includes a heat sink, chip-removal tool, and utility-software disk in addition to the processor itself. The documentation includes detailed diagrams showing you how to identify and replace the CPU.

Performance gains in an upgraded 33-MHz system are very impressive. The product brings 486-class performance to many 386 systems, and speed increases are noticeable in all but disk-intensive applications.

486 Systems. Upgrades for 486-based systems are so diverse that it almost takes a scorecard to keep up with them. Within the family of 486 chips, upgrades include a wide range of chips—a fact that, more than anything, reflects a desire on the part of computer buyers to remain on the cutting edge of technology in an age when the fastest computer chip changes every couple of years.

Upgrades for 486-based systems include these options:

- 486SX to 486DX (by way of the so-called 487 upgrade)

- 486SX to 486DX (through direct CPU-chip replacement)

- Slow-clock-speed 486 to faster 486 (for example, 25 MHz to 50 MHz)

- Normally clocked CPU chip to clock-doubled (DX2) chip

- Normally clocked CPU or clock-doubled CPU to clock-tripled CPU

- 486 to Pentium (by way of the Pentium OverDrive chip)

Sorting out all these chips and chip designation numbers is quite difficult for someone who has better things to do than read computer magazines all day. But the following sections provide some general guidelines on CPU upgrades for 486-based systems.

486SX to 486DX. Generally speaking, you can upgrade a system based on the 486SX chip in two ways. The most common way to upgrade a 486SX-based system is to fill the empty CPU socket known as the OverDrive socket with a 487 upgrade. As described in Chapter 7, "Memory," the 487 upgrade is a fully functional 486 chip (with math-coprocessor functions intact) that, when plugged into the OverDrive socket, disables the original SX chip.

The second route, supported on some 486SX-based systems but not all, involves removing the 486SX chip and replacing it with a 486DX chip. This option is available only if the motherboard was designed to accept not only the 486SX but also the 486DX. Upgrading these motherboards also may require you to replace the system clock chip.

For information on the compatibility of these two upgrade options with your system, contact the manufacturer.

Slow-Clock-Speed 486 to Faster 486. Some 486 motherboards enable you to replace a slower-clock-speed 486 CPU chip with a faster 486 chip. These motherboards can support an upgrade from, for example, a 25-MHz 486DX chip to a 50-MHz 486DX chip. Manufacturers often do not advertise the fact that their motherboards support this upgrade, but many computer makers use motherboards that accept various-speed 486 chips because it is less expensive to purchase a single motherboard design that supports all the chips the manufacturer plans to use than to purchase various CPU-speed-specific motherboard designs.

For information on whether your system supports a direct upgrade from a slower-clock-speed 486 CPU to a faster chip, consult your system documentation. If the motherboard manual discusses configuration for various-speed CPU chips, chances are that you can upgrade to the fastest CPU that the motherboard supports. (Remember, however, that this type of upgrade may require replacement of your system clock chip and ROM BIOS chip.)

If this kind of upgrade appeals to you, contact your motherboard manufacturer to find out what is involved in swapping CPU chips. When the time comes to purchase a new CPU chip, be sure to shop around. Mail-order chip vendors sell the same Intel CPU chips as system manufacturers, so shopping solely based on price is a good idea.

Normally Clocked CPU Chip to Clock-Doubled (DX2) Chip. The most common route to gaining greater speed and power in a 486-based system is upgrading from a normally clocked CPU chip—for example, upgrading a 33-MHz DX to a 66-MHz DX2. Intel designed the DX2 line of chips, which operate externally at the original 25-MHz or 33-MHz chip speed but that internally run at twice the speed, so that these chips would work in existing motherboard designs. The DX2 chip greatly speeds 486-based systems. The DX2 also comes in an SX model. The 486SX2 speeds up existing 486SX systems.

As mentioned in the preceding section, the motherboards of many computer systems accept various-speed 486 chips, so direct replacement of the CPU with its clock-doubled or clock-tripled version is possible. Upgrading a DX-based system to a DX2 chip, however, is not always a plug-and-play operation; replacing the existing CPU chip with its internally faster twin also can require you to replace the system clock chip and ROM BIOS chips. This replacement usually is not necessary, though, because externally, the

V

Assembly & Maintenance

CPU continues to communicate with system circuitry at the speed of the original CPU chip. You cannot perform this upgrade on some motherboards that do not support it.

Many manufacturers of systems that support upgrading from a normally clocked 486 chip to a fast 486DX2 include a special CPU chip socket on the motherboard. This socket, called a Zero Insertion Force (ZIF) socket, enables you to easily remove the old CPU chip and replace it with a faster one. Some manufacturers even allow you to trade in your old 486 CPU chip for the faster one.

486SX, DX, or DX/2 to DX4. The clock-tripled 486 CPU chip, or DX4, is another attempt to squeeze greater and greater speed out of existing motherboard designs. IBM currently is marketing a 99-MHz, clock-tripled 486 CPU chip called Blue Lightning. Like the Intel DX2 chips, Blue Lightning communicates externally with system peripherals at 33 MHz. Internally, however, Blue Lightning runs at 99 MHz. IBM is marketing the chip as being one-third faster for the same price as the DX2-66.

The company also is marketing a 25-MHz/75-MHz version of the chip. IBM's chip offers twice the internal cache of Intel's 486DX2, helping make this chip efficient at high speeds.

Some industry analysts expect Blue Lightning to compete with the Pentium for use in laptop systems. Blue Lightning uses only half the power and two-thirds the voltage of a DX2, making it ideal for laptop and notebook computers. Blue Lightning also conserves battery power through a sleep mode that enables the processor and other components to suspend active operation if the computer is idle for a certain time. The chip also is used in some non-IBM systems.

Intel released the 486DX4-75 and 486DX4-100—a clock-tripled chip based on the 25-MHz and 33-MHz DX 486, respectively. Although these clock-tripled CPU chips are most likely to be used in new midrange desktop systems and in high-end notebooks and laptops, they could be used as upgrades for systems based on normally clocked and clock-doubled CPU chips and for some 486SX systems, particularly those that have ZIF sockets. Some systems would require a new clock chip and ROM BIOS for the upgrade. Using this upgrade path may not be possible on some systems because of motherboard design limitations.

Upgrading to a clock-tripled chip should be attempted only by technically aware computer users. If you want to make this kind of upgrade, consult some of the more trustworthy computer magazines before purchasing the chip. Learning the pros and cons of this upgrade will be helpful.

486 to Pentium. For some time now, the hottest marketing tool for 486-system manufacturers has been the Pentium upgrade socket: a ZIF socket specifically designed to accept the Pentium OverDrive chip, which is expected to be released by the end of 1994.

Intel already is offering OverDrive chips that double the speed of its 486SX chips and is preparing to launch clock-tripling upgrades for 486DX units. The first 486DX2 system with a Pentium OverDrive socket shipped in 1992. Intel says that much of the two-year wait was due to overheating problems and to its desire to incorporate new technology from its 90-MHz and 100-MHz Pentiums into the chip.

Nearly every computer manufacturer is marketing systems with the promise that you can buy a 486 now and upgrade to a Pentium later. This upgrade is likely to be a simple plug-and-play operation in systems that are designed for it. You should be able to flip the lever on the ZIF socket, gently slide out the old CPU chip, orient and insert the new Pentium, and then enjoy the benefits of greatly enhanced system performance.

The compatibility problems involved in this upgrade, if any, are not known at this writing. Many system manufacturers, however, are relying heavily on the Pentium OverDrive's being easier to install than any previous CPU upgrade.

Adding High-Performance Video

Adding a high-resolution video adapter and monitor is a great way to breathe some life into a system. This type of upgrade, however, can be expensive. High-resolution, color-graphics monitors cost between $300 and several thousand dollars, depending primarily on the resolution and size of the monitor.

Video adapters usually cost less than monitors—anywhere from well under $150 to $300 or more—but some of today's cutting-edge video adapters are quite costly. For detailed information on video cards and monitors, refer to Chapter 10, "Video Display Hardware and Specifications."

At the core of your decision to upgrade your monitor and display adapter is how you plan to use your system. If you primarily use DOS-based text-mode applications, for example, you probably do not need one of today's large-screen edge-to-edge monitors or the high-end video adapters that drive them. If you use a graphical user interface such as Windows or OS/2, however, you will find that a large-screen monitor and a fast video card are near-necessities. Nothing in life seems to take as long as scrolling through a lengthy document in a Windows word processor that uses a common VGA adapter; the adapter card just cannot keep up with the incredible number of pixels that it takes to repaint a Windows screen. A problem with running Windows at normal VGA resolution (640 by 480 pixels) is that you constantly have to scroll from side to side in a document to read each line. In VGA resolution, word processors can display only about four-fifths the width of a page.

The hottest video adapters for Windows and other GUIs are VESA-Standard Local Bus (VLB) and Peripheral Component Interconnect (PCI) video cards. These cards plug into a special VESA or PCI slot, respectively, in motherboards that are designed for them, and they are capable of boosting video output to an incredible degree. The Diamond Viper (available in both PCI and VLB), for example, is one of the fastest of the Windows local bus video adapters; in real-world uses, it can paint as many as 43 million pixels per second on your screen. Other companies, such as ATI Technologies, also make extremely fast VLB and PCI video adapters.

If your system doesn't have a VLB slot, you can speed Windows and other GUIs by replacing your ISA-based video card with a graphics-accelerator video card. (These video cards also are called Windows accelerator cards.) If you have a graphics coprocessor on the video card, these accelerator cards free your PC's CPU to handle other work. The Diamond Speedstar 24X is one popular graphics-accelerator card. Numerous other companies market graphics-accelerator cards that are designed to speed your video in popular GUIs.

As mentioned earlier, running a GUI in 640 by 480 (VGA) resolution can be a problem that not only makes work harder, but also makes you less productive. Scrolling from side to side in a word processing program simply to read an entire line of a document, for example, is hardly a performance enhancement; in fact, it's the kind of thing that can make the workday seem as though it will never end.

Today's 17-inch high-resolution monitors enable you to run your system in Super VGA mode (typically, 800 by 600 resolution), which enables you to view an entire line of a document without scrolling back and forth, as well as to view more lines in the page.

Modern video adapters and high-resolution monitors not only make your work go faster, but also enable you to work with graphic images that contain millions of colors. Although not everyone needs the capability to view photographic images on his monitor, many computer users do make use of this capability.

Adding a Hardware Reset Switch

A switch that applies a full reset to your system keeps power moving to the system and rescues you from a system lockup. A reset switch saves you much time, as well as some of the wear and tear on your unit from using the power switch as a reset button. IBM and most vendors of compatibles have built reset circuitry into the motherboard and added reset switches to the front of the computer case. If your machine doesn't already have a reset switch, however, the following section teaches you how to add one. (The hardest part of adding a reset switch to your system is figuring out where to mount it.)

Adding a reset button is possible on any system, including all IBM systems, because it has a power supply that provides a Power Good signal. On most IBM-compatible computers, the Power Good signal is on the connector that plugs into the rearmost power-supply connectors. In PC and XT systems, this signal traces through the motherboard to the 8284a chip at Pin 11. When the line is shorted to ground and returned to normal, the 8284a (82284, in an AT) clock-timer chip generates a reset signal on Pin 10. The reset signal is sent to the 8088 at Pin 21, and the boot process begins. In other systems that have different processors and timer chips—for example, AT and PS/2 systems—the Power Good signal also initiates a reset if the signal is grounded and returned to normal, although the wiring details vary.

In all IBM-compatible systems, when the CPU is reset, it begins to execute code at memory location F000:FFF0, which is known as the power-up reset vector. An immediate jump instruction at this location sends the CPU's instruction pointer to the start location for the particular system ROM. The system then begins the POST. The processor and DMA chips are tested first, but before the system initiates the full POST memory test, it compares the memory location 0000:0472 with the value 1234h. If these values are equal, a *warm* start is indicated, and the POST memory tests are skipped. If any other value appears, a *cold* start occurs, forcing all memory to be tested.

This procedure is the basis of an effective reset switch. By setting the flag value at memory location 0000:0472, you can have the system perform either a cold or warm start when you press a reset button. The type of reset—a hardware reset—unfreezes a locked-up machine, unlike the Ctrl-Alt-Del software reset command.

To add a reset switch, you need these parts:

- Six inches of thin (about 20-gauge) insulated wire

- A single-pole, normally open, momentary-contact push-button switch

The idea behind installing a reset switch is to run a momentary-contact switch parallel with the Power Good line and ground. To do so, follow these steps:

1. Remove from the motherboard the power-supply connector that contains the Power Good signal.

> **Note**
>
> Check your technical-reference manual to make sure that you have the right connector and can identify the signal wire that contains the Power Good signal. Sometimes, this information also is on a sticker attached to the power supply.

2. Poke the stripped end of a wire into the hole in the power-supply connector in which the Power Good signal is carried.

3. Plug the connector, with the wire inserted, back into the motherboard.

4. Run the other end of the wire under one of the screws that secures the motherboard. The screw serves as a ground.

5. Cut the wire in the middle, bare the ends, and attach the stripped wire ends to the normally open, single-pole, momentary-contact push-button switch.

6. Run the wire and the switch outside the case.

You now should have a functioning reset button. You can mount the switch to an available place on the unit (such as an empty card bracket) in which you can drill a small hole to accept the switch.

A simple button and wire are sufficient for adding a reset switch, but as a safety precaution, you can place a 1/4-watt resistor with a value between 1K ohms and 2.7K ohms in-line with the wire from the Power Good line to the switch. The reason for adding the resistor is that the Power Good signal is provided by a PNP transistor inside the power supply, with its emitter connected to the +5 volt signal. Without the resistor, shorting the Power Good signal to ground for a long period can burn out the transistor.

When you press the switch, you initiate the boot sequence. The boot process that occurs (warm or cold) depends on the status of memory location 0000:0472. The value at this location is 0000h when you first power up the system and until you press Ctrl-Alt-Del for the first time. If the last boot operation was a cold boot (an initial power-on), every subsequent time that you press the reset button, a cold boot occurs. After you press Ctrl-Alt-Del once to initiate a manual warm-boot sequence, every subsequent time that you press the reset button, you initiate a warm boot that skips the memory tests.

To eliminate the need to press Ctrl-Alt-Del after you start the system every day to "set" the reset button for subsequent warm-boot operations, you can enter a program, using DEBUG, that produces a WARMSET.COM program to run in your AUTOEXEC.BAT file. This simple program quickly sets the memory flag to indicate that a warm boot should be initiated when the reset switch is pressed.

To create WARMSET.COM, make sure that you have the DEBUG program available in the path, and then enter these commands at the DOS prompt:

```
C:\>DEBUG
-N WARMSET.COM
-A 100
xxxx:0100 MOV AX,0040
xxxx:0103 MOV DS,AX
xxxx:0105 MOV WORD PTR [0072],1234
xxxx:010B INT 20
xxxx:010D
-R CX
CX 0000
:D
-W
Writing 0000D bytes
-Q
```

Unlike the Ctrl-Alt-Del combination, the hardware reset cannot be ignored by your system, no matter how locked up the system is.

The Phoenix BIOS sets the warm-boot flag during every boot sequence, regardless of whether the boot is warm or cold. Immediately after power-up, therefore, the flag is zero, which causes the standard POST test to run. Immediately after the POST, the Phoenix BIOS sets the flag for a warm boot, because many compatibles that use the Phoenix BIOS have a reset button integrated into the system. This reset button works the same way as the button that you can construct. Because of the warm-boot flag's automatic setting, a warm boot occurs every time you press the reset button, no matter what the last boot was. If you want a cold boot to occur (including POST), you can create a COLDSET.COM program, also using DEBUG.

To create COLDSET.COM, enter these commands:

```
C:\>DEBUG
-N COLDSET.COM
-A 100
xxxx:0100 MOV AX,0040
xxxx:0103 MOV DS,AX
```

```
xxxx:0105 MOV WORD PTR [0072],0000
xxxx:010B INT 20
xxxx:010D
-R CX
CX 0000
:D
-W
Writing 0000D bytes
-Q
```

This procedure causes a reset button to initiate a cold boot with POST tests, no matter which BIOS you have.

An interesting variation on these programs is to produce two additional companion programs called WARMBOOT.COM and COLDBOOT.COM. As their names indicate, these programs go one step further than the WARMSET.COM and COLDSET.COM programs: they not only set the flag, but also cause an immediate boot.

You may wonder why you would need that operation when you can just press Ctrl-Alt-Del, or turn the power off and on, to reboot the system. The answer is that with these programs, you can initiate the boot you want from a batch file, with no operator intervention.

I use the WARMBOOT.COM program in batch files that copy new CONFIG.SYS files to my root directory and then reboot the system automatically to initiate the new configuration. For example, one batch file copies a CONFIG.SYS file, which loads local-area network (LAN) drivers, as well as a new AUTOEXEC.BAT file, to the root directory of the C drive. The AUTOEXEC.BAT file has commands that automatically log on to the network. In seconds, my network is up and running, and I am automatically logged on, with only one command. You probably can come up with other uses for these programs.

Note

If you have DOS 6.x, you can create customized boot menus that replace this whole process. Both CONFIG.SYS and AUTOEXEC.BAT can have configuration blocks that allow you to pick one of several configurations.

To create WARMBOOT.COM, enter these commands:

```
C:\>DEBUG
-N WARMBOOT.COM
-A 100
xxxx:0100 MOV AX,0040
xxxx:0103 MOV DS,AX
xxxx:0105 MOV WORD PTR [0072],1234
xxxx:010B JMP FFFF:0
xxxx:0110
-R CX
CX 0000
:10
```

```
-W
Writing 00010 bytes
-Q
```

To create COLDBOOT.COM, enter these commands:

```
C:\>DEBUG
-N COLDBOOT.COM
-A 100
xxxx:0100 MOV AX,0040
xxxx:0103 MOV DS,AX
xxxx:0105 MOV WORD PTR [0072],0000
xxxx:010B JMP FFFF:0
xxxx:0110
-R CX
CX 0000
:10
-W
Writing 00010 bytes
-Q
```

Whether or not you have a reset button, the WARMBOOT.COM and COLDBOOT.COM programs can be useful.

Upgrading the DOS Version

An upgrade that many users overlook is an upgrade to a new version of an operating system. You can complicate a DOS upgrade by using different OEM versions of DOS, but normally, you should not have to reformat your hard disk when you upgrade from one version of DOS to another.

If you are using nonstandard drivers or other non-DOS support programs, you may have to format the disk, or use Norton Utilities or some other low-level utility to modify the disk's boot sector and root directory. This modification enables the SYS command in the new version to operate properly.

You can perform an operating-system upgrade in several ways. One way is to use the automatic installation and upgrade facility built into DOS. The automatic DOS upgrade and installation utility that comes with DOS 6.x, for example, works well. If you want to upgrade on your own, follow the simple instructions in the following section to complete the upgrade in a relatively short amount of time.

To repartition your hard disk at the same time that you upgrade to a new DOS version, you must back up your entire hard disk, repartition and reformat it, and then restore all your original files. Then you can install the new version of DOS over your original (restored) version. Depending on the type of backup hardware that you use, this procedure can be somewhat time-consuming.

Upgrading DOS the Easy Way

To perform a DOS-version upgrade the easy way, follow these steps:

1. Boot the new DOS version from drive A.

2. Transfer the system files to drive C, using this command:

   SYS C:

3. Locate the DOS disk with the REPLACE program, insert the disk into drive A, and execute this command:

   COPY REPLACE.* C:

4. Use the following command to replace all DOS transient files on drive C with new versions in all subdirectories and to enable read-only files to be overwritten:

   C:REPLACE A:*.* C: /S /R

> **Caution**
>
> This command replaces any file on the C drive with a file of the same name on the DOS disks, no matter where on the C drive the file is located. Any files on drive C that have the same name as any of the DOS files on drive A, therefore, are overwritten by this command.

5. Change the disk in drive A to the second DOS floppy disk, and repeat the preceding step until you have inserted all the DOS floppy disks.

6. Place the DOS boot disk back in drive A.

7. Use the following command to add any new DOS transient files to the C:\DOS directory (if you have a C:\DOS directory already in place on the hard disk):

   C:REPLACE A:*.* C:\DOS /A

8. Replace the boot disk with the second DOS floppy disk, and repeat the preceding step until you have inserted all the DOS floppy disks.

When you finish, the system is capable of booting the new DOS version from the hard disk. This method ensures that all previous DOS files are overwritten by new versions, no matter which subdirectories store those files.

> **Note**
>
> If you use a directory other than C:\DOS to store your DOS program files, replace C:\DOS in the preceding steps with that directory.

V

Asssembly & Maintenance

If you have problems with the SYS command, your original installation probably has a problem, which you must repair before you can proceed. Notice that the SYS commands in DOS 4.0 and later versions are more tolerant of different configurations on the destination drive. If you have problems, I recommend that you see *Que's Guide to Data Recovery* for additional information on this subject.

Upgrading DOS the Hard Way

To take advantage of the disk-formatting capabilities of newer DOS versions, you must use the more difficult method of upgrading the DOS version. A common use for this method is upgrading from DOS 3.3 to 6.x on a hard disk larger than 32M. Because DOS 3.3 could create disk partitions that were a maximum 32M, the disk must be currently partitioned into several volumes. Because DOS 6.x permits partitions as large as 2G (gigabytes), it's a good idea to use the upgrade as an opportunity to condense the multiple partitions into one partition that matches the total capacity of the drive.

This method requires that you first back up the data on all the partitions, because the existing partitions must be destroyed and re-created as a single partition.

To perform a DOS-version upgrade by using the full backup, format, and restore method, follow these steps:

1. Boot the system from the original (older) version of DOS.

2. Execute a complete backup of all partitions, using the backup method of your choice.

3. Boot the new version of DOS.

4. Use the new DOS FDISK command to remove the existing DOS partition or partitions.

5. Use the new DOS FDISK to create the new partition or partitions.

6. Perform a high-level format, and install the new DOS system files with this command:

   FORMAT C: /S

7. Restore the previous partition backups to the new partition, but do not restore the original system files (IBMBIO.COM and IBMDOS.COM). Your restore program should enable you to selectively ignore files such as these. BACKUP and RESTORE in DOS 3.3 and later always ignore the system files.

8. Locate the new DOS disk by using the REPLACE program, insert the disk into drive A, and execute this command:

   COPY REPLACE.EXE C:

9. Use the following command to replace all DOS transient files on drive C with new versions in all subdirectories and to enable read-only files to be overwritten:

   REPLACE A:*.* C: /S /R

> **Caution**
>
> This command replaces any file on the C drive with a file of the same name on the DOS disks, no matter where on C the file is located. Any files on drive C that have the same name as any of the DOS files on drive A, therefore, are overwritten by this command.

10. Place the second DOS floppy disk in drive A, and repeat the preceding step until you have inserted all DOS floppy disks.

11. Place the boot disk back in drive A.

12. Add new DOS transient files to the C:\DOS directory with this command:

    REPLACE A:*.* C:\DOS /A

13. Replace the boot disk with the second DOS floppy disk, and repeat the preceding step until you have inserted all DOS floppy disks.

When you finish, the system is capable of booting the new DOS version from the hard disk. (If you store program files in a directory other than C:\DOS, replace C:\DOS with that directory.) This method ensures that all previous DOS files are overwritten by new versions.

Backup procedures make this method very difficult unless you have a good backup system. You also must determine how to prevent your backup system from restoring the system files.

If you are using the DOS 3.3 or later BACKUP and RESTORE commands, preventing the system files from being overwritten is much simpler. Because RESTORE never can restore the files IBMBIO.COM, IBMDOS.COM, and COMMAND.COM, the chance of overwriting them is eliminated.

You must use the new DOS version's FDISK command to remove—and especially to create—the partitions to make the newer DOS version's partitioning capabilities available. One variation on this method is substituting a low-level format operation on the hard disk for step 4 of this procedure. One advantage of not repeating the low-level format is that any existing non-DOS partitions survive; in a low-level format, nothing is left on the disk. An advantage to the low-level format is that it rewrites the sectors and tracks, which might be a good idea for some older hard disks.

Summary

This chapter examined many types of system upgrades, including the upgrade of the system's most important chip: the central processing unit. The chapter also covered adding system memory, expanding hard drive storage, adding floppy drives, speeding a system, improving the video subsystem, adding a reset switch, and upgrading to a new version of DOS. You now should have some insight into ways to make your system faster and, therefore, more useful, as well as some useful recommendations on how to avoid upgrade pitfalls that other people have endured.

Upgrading a system can be a cost-effective way to keep up with the rest of the computing community and to extend the life of your system. By upgrading, however, you also can create a Frankenstein system that has compatibility problems before you realize how much money you have poured into the system. It is important to learn when to say no to more upgrades and to recognize when it's time to buy a new system. In some cases, the cost may be high; the cost is in installing new software and hardware and then getting it to work with the rest of your PC.

Chapter 18

Maintaining Your System: Preventive Maintenance, Backups, and Warranties

Preventive maintenance is the key to obtaining years of trouble-free service from your computer system. A properly administered preventive maintenance program pays for itself by reducing problem behavior, data loss, component failure, and by ensuring a long life for your system. In several cases, I have "repaired" an ailing system with nothing more than a preventive maintenance session. Preventive maintenance also increases your system's resale value because it will look and run better. This chapter describes preventive maintenance procedures and how often you should perform them.

You will also learn the importance of creating backup files of data and the various backup procedures available. A sad reality in the computer repair and servicing world is that hardware can always be repaired or replaced, but data cannot. Most hard disk troubleshooting and service procedures, for example, require that a low-level format be done. This low-level format overwrites any data on the disk.

Because data recovery depends a great deal on the type and severity of damage and the expertise of the recovery specialist, data-recovery services are very expensive. Most recovery services charge a premium and offer no guarantees that the data will be completely recovered. Backing up your system as discussed in this chapter is the only guarantee you have of seeing your data again.

Most of the discussion of backing up systems in this chapter is limited to professional solutions that require special hardware and software. Backup solutions that employ floppy disk drives, such as the DOS backup software, are insufficient and too costly in most cases for hard disk backups. It would take 1,456 1.44M floppy disks, for example, to backup the 2G hard disk in my portable system! That would cost more than $1,000 in disks, not to mention the time involved. A tape system can put 4G to 8G on a single $15 tape.

Finally, the last section in this chapter discusses the standard warranties and optional service contracts available for many systems. Although most of this book is written for people who want to perform their own maintenance and repair service, taking advantage of a good factory warranty that provides service for free definitely is prudent. Some larger computer companies, such as IBM, offer attractive service contracts that, in some cases, are cost-justified over self service. These types of options are examined in the final section.

Developing a Preventive Maintenance Program

Developing a preventive maintenance program is important to everyone who uses or manages personal computer systems. Two types of preventive maintenance procedures exist: active and passive.

Active preventive maintenance includes steps you apply to a system that promote a longer, trouble-free life. This type of preventive maintenance primarily involves periodic cleaning of the system and its components. This section describes several active preventive maintenance procedures, including cleaning and lubricating all major components, reseating chips and connectors, and reformatting hard disks.

Passive preventive maintenance includes steps you can take to protect a system from the environment, such as using power-protection devices; ensuring a clean, temperature-controlled environment; and preventing excessive vibration. In other words, passive preventive maintenance means treating your system well. This section also describes passive preventive maintenance procedures.

Active Preventive Maintenance Procedures

How often you should implement active preventive maintenance procedures depends on the system's environment and the quality of the system's components. If your system is in a dirty environment, such as a machine shop floor or a gas station service area, you might need to clean your system every three months or less. For normal office environments, cleaning a system every one to two years is usually fine. However, if you open your system after one year and find dust bunnies inside, you should shorten the cleaning interval.

Another active preventive maintenance technique discussed in this section is reformatting hard disks. Low-level reformatting restores the track and sector marks to their proper locations and forces you to back up and restore all data on the drive. Not all drives require this procedure, but if you are using drives with a stepper motor head actuator, periodic reformatting is highly recommended. Most drives with voice-coil head actuators run indefinitely without reformatting due to their track following servo mechanisms which prevent temperature induced mistracking.

Other hard disk preventive maintenance procedures include making periodic backups of critical areas such as Boot Sectors, File Allocation Tables, and Directory structures on the disk.

Cleaning a System. One of the most important operations in a good preventive maintenance program is regular and thorough cleaning of the system. Dust buildup on the internal components can lead to several problems. One is that dust acts as a thermal insulator which prevents proper system cooling. Excessive heat shortens the life of system components and adds to the thermal stress problem caused by wider than normal temperature changes between power-on and power-off states. Additionally, dust may contain conductive elements that can cause partial short circuits in a system. Other elements in dust and dirt can accelerate corrosion of electrical contacts and cause improper connections. In all, the removal of any layer of dust and debris from within a computer system benefits that system in the long run.

All IBM and IBM-compatible systems use a forced-air cooling system that allows for even cooling inside the system. A fan is mounted in, on, or near the power supply and pushes air outside. This setup depressurizes the interior of the system relative to the outside air. The lower pressure inside the system causes outside air to be drawn into openings in the system chassis and cover. This draw-through, or depressurization, is the most efficient cooling system that can be designed without an air filter. Air filters typically are not used with depressurization systems because there is no easy way to limit air intake to a single port that can be covered by a filter.

Some industrial computers from IBM and other companies use a forced-air system that uses the fan to pressurize, rather than to depressurize, the case. This system forces air to exhaust from any holes in the chassis and case or cover. The key to the pressurization system is that all air intake for the system is at a single location—the fan. The air flowing into the system therefore can be filtered by simply integrating a filter assembly into the fan housing. The filter must be cleaned or changed periodically. Because the interior of the case is pressurized relative to the outside air, airborne contaminants are not drawn into the system even though it may not be sealed. Any air entering the system must pass through the fan and filter housing, which removes the contaminants. Pressurization cooling systems are used primarily in industrial computer models designed for extremely harsh environments.

Most systems you have contact with are depressurization systems. Mounting any sort of air filter on these types of systems is impossible because air enters the system from too many sources. With any cooling system in which incoming air is not filtered, dust and other chemical matter in the environment is drawn in and builds up inside the computer. This buildup can cause severe problems if left unchecked.

One problem that can develop is overheating. The buildup of dust acts as a heat insulator, which prevents the system from cooling properly. Some of the components in a modern PC can generate an enormous amount of heat which must be dissipated for the component to function. The dust also might contain chemicals that conduct electricity. These chemicals can cause minor current shorts and create electrical signal paths where none should exist. The chemicals also cause rapid corrosion of cable connectors, socket-installed components, and areas where boards plug into slots. All can cause intermittent system problems and erratic operation.

> **Tip**
>
> Cigarette smoke contains chemicals that can conduct electricity and cause corrosion of computer parts. The smoke residue can infiltrate the entire system, causing corrosion and contamination of electrical contacts and sensitive components such as floppy drive read/write heads and optical drive lens assemblies. You should avoid smoking near computer equipment and encourage your company to develop and enforce a similar policy.

Floppy disk drives are particularly vulnerable to the effects of dirt and dust. Floppy drives are a large "hole" within the system through which air continuously flows. Therefore, they accumulate a large amount of dust and chemical buildup within a short time. Hard disk drives do not present quite the same problem. Because the head disk assembly (HDA) in a hard disk is a sealed unit with a single barometric vent, no dust or dirt can enter without passing through the barometric vent filter. This filter ensures that contaminating dust or particles cannot enter the interior of the HDA. Thus, cleaning a hard disk requires simply blowing the dust and dirt off from outside the drive. No internal cleaning is required.

Disassembly and Cleaning Tools. To properly clean the system and all the boards inside requires certain supplies and tools. In addition to the tools required to disassemble the unit (see Chapter 3, "System Teardown and Inspection"), you should have these items:

- Contact cleaning solution
- Canned air
- A small brush
- Lint-free foam cleaning swabs
- Antistatic wrist-grounding strap

You might also want to acquire these optional items:

- Foam tape
- Low-volatile room-temperature vulcanizing (RTV) sealer
- Silicone type lubricant
- Computer vacuum cleaner

These simple cleaning tools and chemical solutions will allow you to perform most common preventive maintenance tasks.

Chemicals. You can use several different types of cleaning solutions with computers and electronic assemblies. Most fall into the following categories:

■ Standard Cleaners

■ Contact Cleaner/Lubricants

■ Dusters

> **Tip**
>
> The makeup of many of the chemicals used for cleaning electronic components has been changing because many of the chemicals originally used are now considered environmentally unsafe. They have been attributed to damaging the Earth's ozone layer, a natural protective barrier in the strato-sphere which prevents harmful ultraviolet (UV-B) radiation from reaching Earth. Chlorine atoms from chlorofluorocarbons (CFCs) and chlorinated solvents attach themselves to ozone molecules and destroy them. Many of these chemicals are now strictly regulated by federal and international agencies in an effort to preserve the ozone layer. Most of the companies that produce chemicals used for system cleaning and maintenance have had to introduce environmentally safe replace-ments. The only drawback is that many of these safer chemicals cost more and usually do not work as well as those they replace.

Many specific chemicals are used in cleaning and dusting solutions, but five types are of particular interest. The EPA has classified ozone-damaging chemicals into two classes: Class I and Class II. Chemicals that fall into these two classes have their usage regulated. Other chemicals are nonregulated. Class I chemicals include:

■ Chlorofluorocarbons (CFCs)

■ Chlorinated solvents

Class I chemicals can only be sold for use in professional service and not to consumers. A new law that went into effect on May 15, 1993, requires that the containers for Class I chemicals be labeled with a warning that the product "Contains substances which harm public health and the environment by destroying ozone in the atmosphere." Addition-ally, electronics manufacturers and other industries must also apply a similar warning label to any products that use Class I chemicals in the production process. This means that any circuit board or computer that is manufactured with CFCs will have this label!

The most popular Class I chemicals are the various forms of Freon, which are CFCs. A very popular cleaning solution called 1,1,1 Trichloroethane is a chlorinated solvent and is also strictly regulated. Up until the last year or so, virtually all computer or electronic cleaning solutions contained one or both of these chemicals. While you can still pur-chase them, regulations and limited production have made them more expensive and more difficult to find.

Class II chemicals include hydrochlorofluorocarbons (HCFCs). These are not as strictly regulated as Class I chemicals because they have a lower ozone depletion potential. Many cleaning solutions have switched to HCFCs, because they do not require the restrictive labeling required by Class I chemicals and are not as harmful. Most HCFCs have only one tenth the ozone damaging potential of CFCs.

Other nonregulated chemicals include Volatile Organic Compounds (VOCs) and Hydrofluorocarbons (HFCs). These chemicals do not damage the ozone layer but actually contribute to ozone production, which, unfortunately, appears in the form of smog or ground level pollution. Pure isopropyl alcohol is an example of a VOC that is commonly used in electronic part and contact cleaning. HFCs are used as a replacement for CFCs because the HFCs do not damage the ozone layer.

The EPA has developed a method to measure the ozone damaging capability of a chemical. The Ozone Depletion Potential (ODP) of a chemical solution is the sum of the depletion potentials of each of the chemicals used in the solution by weight. The ODP of Freon R12 (Automotive Air Conditioning Freon), is 1.0 on this scale. Most modern CFC replacement chemicals have an ODP rating of 0.0 to 0.1, as opposed to those using CFCs and chlorinated solvents that usually have ODP ratings of 0.75 or higher.

Standard Cleaners. Standard cleaning solutions are available in a variety of types and configurations. You can use pure isopropyl alcohol, acetone, Freon, trichloroethane, or a variety of other chemicals. Most are now leaning to the alcohol, acetone, or others that do not cause ozone depletion and that comply with government regulations and environmental safety. You should be sure that your cleaning solution is designed to clean computers or electronic assemblies. In most cases this means that the solution should be chemically pure and free from contaminants or other unwanted substances. You should not, for example, use drugstore rubbing alcohol for cleaning electronic parts or contacts because it is not pure and could contain water or perfumes. The material must be moisture-free and residue-free. The solutions should be in liquid form, not a spray. Sprays can be wasteful and you almost never spray the solution directly on components. Instead, wet a foam or chamois swab used for wiping the component. These electronic-component cleaning solutions are available at any good electronics parts stores.

Contact Cleaner/Lubricants. These are very similar to the standard cleaners but include a lubricating component. The lubricant eases the force required when plugging and unplugging cables and connectors, which reduces strain on the devices. The lubricant coating also acts as a conductive protectant that insulates the contacts from corrosion. These chemicals can greatly prolong the life of a system by preventing intermittent contacts in the future.

Contact cleaner/lubricants are especially effective on I/O slot connectors, adapter card edge and pin connectors, disk drive connectors, power supply connectors, and virtually all connectors in the PC.

An excellent contact enhancer and lubricant is Stabilant 22. It is more effective than conventional contact cleaners or lubricants. This chemical is available in several forms. Stabilant 22 is the full strength concentrated version, while Stabilant 22a is a version diluted with isopropyl alcohol in a 4 to 1 ratio. An even more diluted 8 to 1 ratio version is sold in many high end stereo and audio shops under the name "Tweek." Just 15ml of Stabilant 22a sells for about $40, while a liter of the concentrate costs about $4,000. While Stabilant 22 is expensive, very little is required and an application can provide protection for a long time. Stabilant is manufactured by D. W. Electrochemicals, which is listed in Appendix B, the "Vendor List."

Dusters. Compressed gas often is used as an aid in system cleaning. The compressed gas is used as a blower to remove dust and debris from a system or component. Originally, these dusters used CFCs such as Freon, while modern dusters now use HFCs or carbon dioxide, neither of which is damaging to the ozone layer. Be careful when you use these devices because some of them can generate a static charge when the compressed gas leaves the nozzle of the can. Be sure that you are using the kind approved for cleaning or dusting off computer equipment, and consider wearing a static grounding strap as a precaution. The type of compressed-air cans used for cleaning camera equipment can sometimes differ from the type used for cleaning static-sensitive computer components.

Most older computer-grade canned gas dusters consisted of dichlorodifluoromethane (Freon R12), the same chemical used in many automotive air-conditioning systems built until 1995, when a ban of the manufacture and use of R12 takes place. In 1992 many automobile manufacturers began switching to an ozone safe chemical called R134a. Manufacturing of R12 will cease by 1995, and the regulations placed on its use have forced companies to use other products such as carbon dioxide for compressed gas dusters. In addition to the environmental concerns about depleting the ozone layer, Freon can be dangerous if exposed to an open flame.

> **Caution**
>
> If you use any chemical with the propellant Freon R12 (dichlorodifluoromethane), *do not expose the gas to an open flame or other heat source.* If you burn this substance, a highly toxic gas called *phosgene* is generated. Phosgene, used as a nerve gas in World War II, can be deadly.

Related to compressed-air products are chemical-freeze sprays. These sprays are used to quickly cool down a suspected failing component, which often temporarily restores it to operation. These substances are not used to repair a device, but to confirm that you have found a failed device. Often, a component's failure is heat-related and cooling it temporarily restores it to function. If the circuit begins operating normally, the device you are cooling is the suspect device.

Vacuum Cleaners. Some people prefer to use a vacuum cleaner instead of canned gas dusters for cleaning a system. Canned gas is usually better for cleaning in small areas. A vacuum cleaner is more useful when you are cleaning a system loaded with dust and dirt. You can use the vacuum cleaner to suck out dust and debris instead of blowing them on other components, which sometimes happens with canned air. For outbound servicing (when you are going to the location of the equipment instead of the equipment coming to you), canned air is easier to carry in a toolkit than a small vacuum cleaner.

V

Assembly & Maintenance

Brushes and Swabs. A small brush (makeup, photographic, or paint) can be used to carefully loosen accumulated dirt and dust before spraying with canned air or using the vacuum cleaner. Be careful about generating static electricity. In most cases the brushes should not be used directly on circuit boards but should be used instead on the case interior and other parts such as fan blades, air vents, and keyboards. Wear a grounded wrist strap if you are brushing on or near any circuit boards, and brush slowly and lightly to prevent static discharges from occurring.

Use cleaning swabs to wipe off electrical contacts and connectors, disk drive heads, and other sensitive areas. The swabs should be made of foam or synthetic chamois material that does not leave lint or dust residue. Unfortunately, proper foam or chamois cleaning swabs are more expensive than the typical cotton swabs. Do not use cotton swabs because they leave cotton fibers on everything they touch. Cotton fibers are conductive in some situations and can remain on drive heads, which can scratch disks. Foam or chamois swabs can be purchased at most electronics-supply stores.

One item to avoid is an eraser for cleaning contacts. Many people (including myself) have recommended using a soft pencil type eraser for cleaning circuit board contacts. Testing has proven this to be bad advice for several reasons. One is that any such abrasive wiping on electrical contacts generates friction and an electrostatic discharge (ESD). This ESD can be damaging to boards and components, especially with newer low voltage devices made using CMOS (Complimentary Metal Oxide Semiconductor) technology. These devices are especially static sensitive, and cleaning the contacts without a proper liquid solution is not recommended. Also the eraser will wear off the gold coating on many contacts, exposing the tin contact underneath, which will rapidly corrode when exposed to air. Some companies sell premoistened contact cleaning pads that are soaked in a proper contact cleaner and lubricant. These pads are safe to wipe on conductor and contacts with no likelihood of ESD damage or abrasion of the gold plating.

Foam Tape or RTV Sealer. Hard disks usually use a small copper strap to ground the spindle of the disk assembly to the logic board, thus bleeding off any static charge carried by the spinning disk platters. Unfortunately, this strap often can begin to harmonize, or vibrate, and result in an annoying squealing or whining noise. (Sometimes the noise is similar to fingernails dragged across a chalkboard.)

To eliminate the source of irritation, you can stop the strap from vibrating by weighting it. One method is to use a piece of foam tape cut to match the size of the strap and stuck to the strap's back side. Another way to dampen the vibration is to apply a low-volatile RTV sealer. You apply this silicone-type rubber to the back of the grounding strap. After it hardens to a rubber-like material, the sealer stops the vibrations that produce the annoying squeal. You can buy the RTV sealer from an automotive-supply house.

I prefer using the foam tape rather than the RTV because it is easier and neater to apply. If you use the RTV, be sure that it is the low-volatile type, which does not generate acid when it cures. This acid produces the vinegar smell common to the standard RTV sealer, and can be highly corrosive to the strap and anything else it contacts. The low-volatile RTV also eliminates the bad vinegar smell. You can purchase the foam tape at most electronics-supply houses, where it often is sold for attaching alarm switches to doors or windows. The low-volatile RTV is available from most auto-supply stores. To be sure that you buy low-volatile RTV, look for the packaging to state specifically that the product is either a low-volatile type or is compatible with automobile oxygen sensors.

Silicone Lubricants. Silicone lubricants are used to lubricate the door mechanisms on floppy disk drives and any other part of the system that may require clean, non-oily lubrication. Other items you can lubricate are the disk drive head slider rails or even printer-head slider rails, which allow for smooth operation.

Using silicone instead of conventional oils is important because silicone does not gum up and collect dust and other debris. Always use the silicone sparingly. Do not spray it anywhere near the equipment as it tends to migrate and will end up where it doesn't belong (such as on drive heads). Instead, apply a small amount to a toothpick or foam swab and dab the silicone on the components where needed. You can use a lint-free cleaning stick soaked in silicone lubricant to lubricate the metal print-head rails in a printer.

Remember that some of the cleaning operations described in this section might generate a static charge. You may want to use a static grounding strap in cases in which static levels are high to ensure that you do not damage any boards as you work with them.

Obtaining Required Tools and Accessories. Most cleaning chemicals and tools can be obtained from a number of electronics-supply houses, or even the local Radio Shack. A company called Chemtronics specializes in chemicals for the computer and electronics industry. These and other companies which supply tools, chemicals, and other computer and electronic cleaning supplies are listed in Appendix B, the "Vendor List." With all these items on hand, you should be equipped for most preventive maintenance operations.

Disassembling and Cleaning Procedures. To properly clean your system, it must at least be partially disassembled. Some people go as far as to remove the motherboard. Removing the motherboard results in the best possible access to other areas of the system but in the interest of saving time, you probably need to disassemble the system only to where the motherboard is completely visible.

All plug-in adapter cards must be removed, along with the disk drives. Although you can clean the heads of a floppy drive with a cleaning disk without opening the system unit's cover, you probably will want to do more thorough cleaning. In addition to the heads, you also should clean and lubricate the door mechanism and clean any logic boards and connectors on the drive. This procedure usually requires removing the drive.

Next, do the same procedure with a hard disk: clean the logic boards and connectors, as well as lubricate the grounding strap. To do so, you must remove the hard disk assembly. As a precaution, be sure it is backed up before removal.

Reseating Socketed Chips. A primary preventive maintenance function is to undo the effects of chip creep. As your system heats and cools, it expands and contracts, and the physical expansion and contraction causes components plugged into sockets to gradually work their way out of those sockets. This process is called *chip creep*. To correct its effects, you must find all socketed components in the system and make sure that they are properly reseated.

In most systems, all the memory chips are socketed or are installed in socketed SIMMs (Single Inline Memory Modules). SIMM devices are retained securely in their sockets by a positive latching mechanism and cannot creep out. Memory SIPP (Single Inline Pin Package) devices (SIMMs with pins rather than contacts) are not retained by a latching mechanism and therefore can creep out of their sockets. Standard socketed memory chips are prime candidates for chip creep. Most other logic components are soldered in. You can also expect to find the ROM chips, the main processor or CPU, and the math coprocessor in sockets. In most systems, these items are the only components that are socketed; all others are soldered in.

Exceptions, however, might exist. A socketed component in one system might not be socketed in another—even if both are from the same manufacturer. Sometimes this difference results from a parts-availability problem when the boards are manufactured. Rather than halt the assembly line when a part is not available, the manufacturer adds a socket instead of the component. When the component becomes available, it is plugged in and the board is finished. Many newer systems place the CPU in a Zero Insertion Force (ZIF) socket, which has a lever that can release the grip of the socket on the chip. In most cases there is very little creep with a ZIF socket.

To make sure that all components are fully seated in their sockets, place your hand on the underside of the board and then apply downward pressure with your thumb (from the top) on the chip to be seated. For larger chips, seat the chip carefully in two movements, and press separately on each end of the chip with your thumb to be sure that the chip is fully seated. (The processor and math coprocessor chips can usually be seated in this manner.) In most cases, you hear a crunching sound as the chip makes its way back into the socket. Because of the great force sometimes required to reseat the chips, this operation is difficult if you do not remove the board.

For motherboards, forcibly seating chips can be dangerous if you do not directly support the board from the underside with your hand. Too much pressure on the board can cause it to bow or bend in the chassis, and the pressure can crack it before seating takes place. The plastic standoffs that separate and hold the board up from the metal chassis are spaced too far apart to properly support the board under this kind of stress. Try this operation only if you can remove and support the board adequately from underneath.

You may be surprised to know that, even if you fully seat each chip, they might need reseating again within a year. The creep usually is noticeable within a year or less.

Cleaning Boards. After reseating any socketed devices that may have crept out of their sockets, the next step is to clean the boards and all connectors in the system. For this step, the cleaning solutions and the lint-free swabs described earlier are needed.

First, clean the dust and debris off the board and then clean any connectors on the board. To clean the boards, it is usually best to use a vacuum cleaner designed for electronic assemblies and circuit boards or a duster can of compressed gas. The dusters are especially effective at blasting any dust and dirt off the boards.

Also blow any dust out of the power supply, especially around the fan intake and exhaust areas. You do not need to disassemble the power supply to do this, just use a duster can and blast the compressed air into the supply through the fan exhaust port. This will blow the dust out of the supply and clean off the fan blades and grille which will help with system airflow.

> ### Caution
>
> Be careful with electrostatic discharge (ESD), which can damage components, when cleaning electronic components. Take extra precautions in the dead of winter in an extremely dry, high-static environment. You can apply antistatic sprays and treatments to the work area to reduce the likelihood of ESD damage.
>
> An antistatic wrist-grounding strap is recommended. This should be connected to a ground on the card or board you are wiping. This strap ensures that no electrical discharge occurs between you and the board. An alternative method is to keep a finger or thumb on the ground of the motherboard or card as you wipe it off. It is easier to ensure proper grounding while the motherboard is still installed in the chassis, so it is a good idea not to remove it.

Cleaning Connectors and Contacts. Cleaning the connectors and contacts in a system promotes reliable connections between devices. On a motherboard, you will want to clean the slot connectors, power-supply connectors, keyboard connector, and speaker connector. For most plug-in cards, you will want to clean the edge connectors that plug into slots on the motherboard as well as any other connectors, such as external ones mounted on the card bracket.

Submerge the lint-free swabs in the liquid cleaning solution. If you are using the spray, hold the swab away from the system and spray a small amount on the foam end until the solution starts to drip. Then, use the soaked foam swab to wipe the connectors on the boards. Pre-soaked wipes are the easiest to use. Simply wipe them along the contacts to remove any accumulated dirt and leave a protective coating behind.

On the motherboard, pay special attention to the slot connectors. Be liberal with the liquid; resoak the foam swab repeatedly, and vigorously clean the connectors. Don't worry if some of the liquid drips on the surface of the motherboard. These solutions are entirely safe for the whole board and will not damage the components.

Use the solution to wash the dirt off the gold contacts in the slot connectors, and then douse any other connectors on the board. Clean the keyboard connector, the grounding positions where screws ground the board to the system chassis, power-supply connectors, speaker connectors, battery connectors, and so on.

If you are cleaning a plug-in board, pay special attention to the edge connector that mates with the slot connector on the motherboard. When people handle plug-in cards, they often touch the gold contacts on these connectors. Touching the gold contacts coats them with oils and debris, which prevents proper contact with the slot connector when the board is installed. Make sure that these gold contacts are free of all finger oils and residue. It is a good idea to use one of the contact cleaners that has a conductive lubricant, which both allows connections to be made with less force, and also protects the contacts from corrosion.

> **Caution**
>
> Many people use a common pink eraser to rub the edge connectors clean. I do not recommend this procedure for two reasons. One, the eraser eventually removes some of the gold and leaves the tin solder or copper underneath exposed. Without the gold, the contact corrodes rapidly and requires frequent cleaning. The second reason to avoid cleaning with the eraser is that the rubbing action can generate a static charge. This charge can harm any component on the board. Rather than use an eraser, use the liquid solution and swab method described earlier.

You also will want to use the swab and solution to clean the ends of ribbon cables or other types of cables or connectors in a system. Clean the floppy drive cables and connectors, the hard disk cables and connectors, and any others you find. Don't forget to clean off the edge connectors that are on the disk drive logic boards as well as the power connectors to the drives.

Cleaning Floppy Drives. Because Chapter 13, "Floppy Disk Drives and Controllers," explains the procedure for cleaning floppy drives, the information is not repeated here. The basic idea is to use a canned gas duster to dust off the interior of the drive, use the silicone lubricant on whatever items need lubrication, and follow with a head cleaning, either manually with a foam swab or most likely with a chemical-soaked cleaning disk.

For hard disks, take this opportunity to dampen or lubricate the grounding strap if you have a noise problem as described earlier. Dampening is the recommended solution because if you lubricate this point, the lubricant eventually dries up and the squeal can come back. Because the dampening is usually a more permanent fix for this sort of problem, I recommend it whenever possible. Most newer hard disks have this dampening material applied at the factory and are not likely to generate noise like older drives.

Cleaning the Keyboard and Mouse. Keyboards and mice are notorious for picking up dirt and garbage. If you ever open an older keyboard, you often will be amazed at the junk you will find.

To prevent problems, it is a good idea to periodically clean out the keyboard with a vacuum cleaner. An alternative method is to turn the keyboard upside down and shoot it with a can of compressed gas. This will blow out the dirt and debris that has accumulated inside the keyboard and possibly prevent future problems with sticking keys or dirty keyswitches.

If a particular key is stuck or making intermittent contact, you can soak or spray that switch with contact cleaner. The best way to do this is to first remove the keycap and then spray the cleaner into the switch. This usually does not require complete disassembly of the keyboard. Periodic vacuuming or compressed gas cleaning will prevent more serious problems with sticking keys and keyswitches.

Most mice are easily cleaned. In most cases there is a twist off locking retainer that keeps the mouse ball retained in the body of the mouse. By removing the retainer, the ball will drop out. After removing the ball, you should clean it with one of the electronic cleaners. I would recommend a pure cleaner instead of a contact cleaner with lubricant because you do not want any lubricant on the mouse ball. Then you should clean off the rollers in the body of the mouse with the cleaner and some swabs.

Periodic cleaning of a mouse in this manner will eliminate or prevent skipping or erratic movement that can be frustrating. I also recommend a mouse pad for most ball type mice because the pad will prevent the mouse ball from picking up debris from your desk.

Mice often need frequent cleaning before they start sticking and jumping, which can be frustrating. If you never want to clean a mouse again, I suggest you look into the Honeywell mouse. These mice have a revolutionary new design that uses two external wheels rather than the conventional ball and roller system. The wheels work directly on the desk surface and are unaffected by dirt and dust. Because the body of the mouse is sealed, dirt and dust cannot enter it and gum up the positional sensors. I find this mouse excellent to use with my portable system because it works well on any surface. This mouse is virtually immune to the sticking and jumping that plague ball and roller designs and never needs to be cleaned, so it is less frustrating than conventional mice.

Hard Disk Maintenance

Certain preventive maintenance procedures protect your data and ensure that your hard disk works efficiently. Some of these procedures actually minimize wear and tear on your drive, which will prolong its life. Additionally, a high level of data protection can be implemented by performing some simple commands periodically. These commands provide methods for backing up (and possibly later restoring) critical areas of the hard disk that, if damaged, would disable access to all your files.

Defragmenting Files. Over time, as you delete and save files to a hard disk, the files become fragmented. This means that they are split into many noncontiguous areas on the disk. One of the best ways to protect both your hard disk and the data on it is to periodically defragment the files on the disk. This serves two purposes. One is that by ensuring that all of the files are stored in contiguous sectors on the disk, head movement and drive wear and tear will be minimized. This has the added benefit of improving the speed at which files will be retrieved from the drive by reducing the head thrashing that occurs every time a fragmented file is accessed.

The second major benefit, and in my estimation the more important of the two, is that in the case of a disaster where the File Allocation Tables (FATs) and Root Directory are severely damaged, the data on the drive can usually be recovered very easily if the files are contiguous. On the other hand, if the files are split up in many pieces across the drive, it is virtually impossible to figure out which pieces belong to which files without an intact File Allocation Table (FAT) and directory system. For the purposes of data integrity and protection, I recommend defragmenting your hard disk drives on a weekly basis, or immediately after you perform any major backup.

Three main functions are found in most defragmenting programs:

■ File Defragmentation

■ File Packing (Free Space Consolidation)

■ File Sorting

Defragmentation is the basic function but most other programs also add file packing. Packing the files is optional on some programs because it usually takes additional time to perform. This function packs the files at the beginning of the disk so that all free space is consolidated at the end of the disk. This feature minimizes future file fragmentation by eliminating any empty holes on the disk. Because all free space is consolidated into one large area, any new files written to the disk will be able to be written in a contiguous manner with no fragmentation necessary.

The last function, file sorting, is not usually necessary and is performed as an option by many defragmenting programs. This function adds a tremendous amount of time to the operation, and has little or no effect on the speed at which information is accessed. It can be somewhat beneficial for disaster recovery purposes because you will have an idea of which files came before or after other files if a disaster occurs. These benefits are minimal compared to having the files be contiguous no matter what their order. Not all defragmenting programs offer file sorting, and the extra time it takes is probably not worth any benefits you will receive. Other programs can sort the order that files are listed in directories, which is a quick and easy operation compared to sorting the file ordering the disk.

Several programs are available that can defragment the files on a hard disk but the one available to most people is the DEFRAG program built into DOS 6.x. This reduced function version of the SPEEDISK program is a part of the Symantec Norton Utilities. If you have the Norton Utilities, by all means use SPEEDISK instead of DEFRAG. The DOS DEFRAG program offers all three functions including defragmenting, packing, and sorting. The SPEEDISK program performs these operations faster and with more efficient use of memory. Many of these programs will have problems on very large disks, and SPEEDISK will work on drives as large as 2G (the maximum DOS volume size), while DEFRAG is limited to disks of about 512M or less due to memory constraints.

Several aftermarket defragmenting programs are more powerful or faster than the DOS DEFRAG program. They include:

■ SPEEDISK by Symantec (Norton Utilities)

■ Power Disk by PC-KWIK

■ Optune by Gazelle

■ VOPT by Golden Bow

All of these are highly recommended and usually perform much better than the DEFRAG program in DOS. The Power Disk, Optune, and VOPT programs are also much faster than

DEFRAG. The VOPT program is the simplest and quickest of these. It is a command line program not a menu driven program like the others and does not offer a sort capability while all the others do. What it does offer is the ultimate in speed and efficiency in defragmenting and packing files. Currently, most of these programs will work on drives up to 1G while some will handle drives of up to 2G. These programs are updated constantly; contact the manufacturer for more detailed specifications if you are interested. Each of these manufacturers is listed in Appendix B, the "Vendor List."

No matter which program you end up using, defragmenting and packing your disk helps to reduce drive wear and tear by minimizing the amount of work required to load files. It also greatly increases the chances for data recovery in the case of serious corruption in the File Allocation Tables (FATs) and directories on the disk.

Backing Up the FAT and Directory System. The operating system uses several areas on a formatted disk to manage the files stored on the disk. These areas are extremely critical. If they are damaged, all access to the drive volume may be compromised or completely disabled. In some cases, these critical areas can be rebuilt using known data recovery procedures and tools, but the easiest and best way to recover from damage to these areas is to simply have a backup of them to restore.

The critical areas of a hard disk file system are the following:

- Master (Partition) Boot Record (MBR)
- Extended (Partition) Boot Record (EBR)
- DOS Boot Record (DBR)
- File Allocation Tables (FATs)
- Root Directory

These areas are stored on the disk in the order listed, except that each volume starts with an MBR or EBR but not both. Unlike complete file backups of the entire hard disk, a backup of these system areas is relatively quick and easy. This is because these areas are very small in comparison to the remainder of the drive and normally occupy a fixed amount of space on the disk. For example, the MBR, EBRs and DBRs are only one sector long each, while the two FATs used on each volume cannot exceed 512 sectors (256K), and the Root Directory is limited to 32 sectors (15K). This means that even for the largest hard disk drive, these areas do not consume more than about 300K of space.

The boot record (sector) areas do not change during day to day usage of the disk. These areas will change only if you reformat, repartition, or change operating system versions. Because they are relatively constant, it makes good sense to back up these areas to a file on a floppy disk for later, to restore if necessary.

Each normal disk volume will have two File Allocation Tables and a single Root Directory. These areas change constantly as files are written and deleted from the disk. A backup of these areas is only good for temporary purposes and can be useful when trying to undelete files. Because of this, these backups are often written on the hard disk in a special hidden file near the end of the disk. Other recovery or restoration programs can then look for this special file and use the information within it to rebuild the FATs or directory system. Often this type of backup is very useful in a situation where files need to be undeleted.

DOS 5.0 provided the MIRROR command for backups of all of these areas. MIRROR has two functions: it can back up the boot sector areas on the hard disk to a file on a floppy disk as well as back up the FAT and directory areas to the end of the hard disk as a special hidden file that recovery programs can find. To use MIRROR to back up the boot sectors to a floppy disk, execute the command as follows:

MIRROR /PARTN

This will create a special file called PARTNSAV.FIL on a floppy disk you designate. This file contains an image of all of the boot sectors across all of the DOS accessible partitions on your hard disk. This information can later be restored by the UNFORMAT command as follows:

UNFORMAT /PARTN

The UNFORMAT program will ask for the disk containing the PARTNSAV.FIL file and restore the boot sector information to the hard disk.

MIRROR can also be used to backup the FATs and Directory structure to a special hidden file on the disk by simply executing the command with no parameters at all:

MIRROR

By executing the command in this manner, a special file called MIRROR.FIL, as well as a hidden file called MIRRORSAV.FIL, will be created in the root directory, and a copy of the FAT and Directory structures will be copied into some free space at the end of the drive. The actual FAT and Directory data is not stored in a normal file with a filename but is instead written to empty sectors at the end of the drive. These sectors will eventually be overwritten, which is why it is a good idea to run the MIRROR command frequently. The second time you run it, it will actually create a second backup and retain the first. Every subsequent run will retain the previous one as a secondary backup. It is a good idea to put the MIRROR command in your AUTOEXEC.BAT file so that these critical areas of the disk are backed up every time your system boots. Usually, MIRROR only takes a few seconds to perform its backup functions so there will be little delay in booting.

To restore the FAT and Directory area backups, you would use the UNFORMAT program, also with no parameters. This program will then search the disk for the MIRROR backups and prompt you for a possible restore. Be careful in restoring these areas as they may be out of sync somewhat with the actual files on your disk. You should always run MIRROR after defragmenting your drive because the defragmenting process moves many files on the disk, making the MIRROR backup obsolete.

There is one unfortunate problem with the MIRROR program; both Microsoft and IBM removed it from DOS 6. Fortunately, you can retain your copy of MIRROR from DOS 5, or you can download the DOS 6 supplemental disk from the MSDOS forum on CompuServe. This package will provide you with a number of utilities left out of DOS 6 but the MIRROR command is the most useful. You can also order this disk directly from Microsoft for $5 using an order form in the back of the DOS 6 manual from Microsoft.

Many other data recovery programs offer the ability to back up these areas on the disk. The Norton Utilities by Symantec is one of the best and most well known data recovery packages on the market. It offers this capability and does a much better job than DOS alone. Norton uses an IMAGE command instead of MIRROR, and also has a special program called RESCUE that creates a rescue disk with not only the boot sector areas on it, but copies of your AUTOEXEC.BAT and CONFIG.SYS files, the DOS system files, and the CMOS RAM data from your system. Also included on the rescue disk are copies of the appropriate Norton Utilities programs that can be used to restore these areas.

Checking for Virus Programs. Both Microsoft and IBM now provide standard anti-virus software in DOS 6.x. The Microsoft Anti-Virus program is actually a reduced function version of the Central Point Anti-Virus software. IBM has written a package called the IBM Anti-Virus program. Many aftermarket utility packages are available that will scan for and remove virus programs. One of the best known is the McAfee Associates SCANV program, which is also one of the easiest to run because it is a command line utility. The McAfee program is also distributed through BBS systems and is often site-licensed to large companies.

No matter which of these programs you use, it is a good idea to perform a scan for virus programs periodically, especially before making hard disk backups. This will help to ensure that you catch any potential virus problem before it spreads and becomes a major hassle.

Reformatting a Hard Disk. Periodically reformatting a hard disk is an operation often overlooked as part of a preventive maintenance plan. Reformatting serves two purposes. On non-servo controlled drives (stepper motor head actuators) the low level format re-writes the sector header information in alignment with current head positions, which can drift in stepper motor head actuator drives because of temperature- and stress-induced dimensional changes between the platters and heads. If these alignment variations continue unchecked, they eventually will cause read and write errors. Note that this reformatting operation applies to stepper motor head actuator drives only and not to voice-coil drives, which maintain their positional accuracy due to the closed loop servo control mechanism that guides the heads.

The second function of a Low Level Format is to locate and mark or spare out any new defective sectors. This can be accomplished during the Low Level Format and also by a subsequent surface analysis.

Reformatting a hard disk lays down new track and sector ID marks and boundaries, re-marks the manufacturer's defects, and performs a surface scan for new defects that might have developed since the last format. With Zone Recorded drives, only the defect mapping and surface analysis are performed. The sector headers are usually not completely rewritten. Temperature variations, case flexing, and physical positioning can add up to eventual read and write errors in a stepper motor head actuated hard disk. This type of failure sometimes appears as a gradually increasing number of disk retries and other read and write problems. You also might notice difficulties when you boot the disk for the first time each day or if the system has been turned off for some time. The cause of these problems is a mistracking between where the data has actually written on the drive and where the track and sector ID marks are located. If the drive is used in a variety of temperatures and environmental conditions, dimensional changes between the heads and platters can cause the data to be written at various improper offsets from the desired track locations.

The reformatting procedure for hard disks is the equivalent of aligning a floppy drive. For hard disks, however, the concern is not for the actual location of each track, but that the drive heads are positioned accurately to the same track location each time. Because of the inherent problems in tracking with stepper motor drives and the lack of a track-following system, mistracking errors accumulate and eventually cause a failure to read or write a particular location. To correct this problem, you must lay down a new set of track and sector ID marks that correspond as closely as possible to the position from which the heads actually read and write data. To do this (with stepper motor drives), you must perform a low-level format.

To make the new format effective, you must do it at the drive's full operating temperature and with the drive in its final mounted position. If the drive runs on its side when it is installed, the format must be done in that position.

For inexpensive drives that lack a proper shock-mounting system (such as the Seagate ST-225, -238, -251, or any ST-2XX drive), make sure that the drive is completely installed before beginning low-level formatting. When you attach the mounting screws to these drives, you are placing screws almost directly into the Head Disk Assembly (HDA), which can cause the HDA to bend or warp slightly depending on how much you tighten the screws. Turn the screws just until they are snug. Do not over tighten them, or your drive might fail if the screws ever loosen and the HDA stress is relaxed. Screws that are too tight can cause continuous read and write problems from stress in the HDA. Having this type of drive completely installed when you are formatting places the HDA under the same physical stress and distortion that it will be under when data is read and written, which makes the format much more accurate.

The frequency with which you should reformat a hard disk depends primarily on the types of drives you have. If the drives are inexpensive stepper motor types (the Seagate ST-2XX series, for example) you probably should reformat the drives once a year. People who must support large numbers of these cheaper drives become known as "hard disk reformatting specialists." A joke in the industry is that some of these drives require winter and summer formats because of temperature sensitivity. This joke, unfortunately, can be somewhat truthful in some cases.

High-quality voice-coil drives usually are formatted only once, either at the factory, as in the case of most IDE or SCSI drives, or by the installer, as is the case with most other types of hard disks. With these drives, a reformat is only performed when the drive begins to exhibit problems reading or writing any sectors on the disk. This might appear in the form of DOS "Abort, Retry, Fail, Ignore" error messages, or other read or write errors. Upon encountering difficulty with any sectors on the disk, it should be fully backed up and then a reformat should be performed. In this case, the reformat and subsequent surface analysis will locate and mark off or spare out the marginal sectors, thus restoring the drive to proper operation.

As mentioned earlier, voice-coil drives do not require reformatting the hard disk as do stepper motor drives. Voice-coil drives do not usually develop difficulties with *hysteresis,* a measurement of how accurately a drive can repeatedly locate to a specified position. Hysteresis is measured by commanding a drive to position itself at a particular cylinder and later (at a different temperature), commanding the drive to position itself at the same cylinder. The voice-coil drive always positions itself at the same position relative to the disk platter because of the track-following servo guide head. The stepper motor drive, however, is fooled by temperature and other environmental or physical stress changes because it is essentially a *blind* positioning system.

Refer to Chapter 14, "Hard Disk Drives and Controllers," which describes hard disk formatting procedures, for more information about the proper tools and procedures for reformatting the different types of hard disk drives.

Passive Preventive Maintenance Procedures

Passive preventive maintenance involves taking care of the system in an external manner: basically, providing the best possible environment—both physical as well as electrical—for the system to operate in. Physical concerns are conditions such as ambient temperature, thermal stress from power cycling, dust and smoke contamination, and disturbances such as shock and vibration. Electrical concerns are items such as electrostatic discharge (ESD), power line noise, and radio-frequency interference. Each of these environmental concerns is discussed in this section.

Examining the Operating Environment. Oddly enough, one of the most overlooked aspects of microcomputer preventive maintenance is protecting the hardware—and the sizable financial investment it represents—from environmental abuse. Computers are relatively forgiving, and they generally are safe in an environment that is comfortable for people. Computers, however, often are treated with no more respect than desktop calculators. The result of this type of abuse is a system failure.

Before you acquire a system, prepare a proper location for your new system, free of airborne contaminants such as smoke or other pollution. Do not place your system in front of a window: the system should not be exposed to direct sunlight or temperature variations. The environmental temperature should be as constant as possible. Power should be provided through properly grounded outlets, and should be stable and free from electrical noise and interference. Keep your system away from radio transmitters or other sources of radio frequency energy. This section examines these issues in more detail.

Heating and Cooling. Thermal expansion and contraction from temperature changes place stress on a computer system. Therefore, keeping the temperature in your office or room relatively constant is important to the successful operation of your computer system.

Temperature variations can lead to serious problems. You might encounter excessive chip creep, for example. If extreme variations occur over a short period, signal traces on circuit boards can crack and separate, solder joints can break, and contacts in the system can undergo accelerated corrosion. Solid-state components such as chips can be damaged also, and a host of other problems can develop.

Temperature variations can play havoc with hard disk drives also. Writing to a disk at different ambient temperatures can, on some drives, cause data to be written at different locations relative to the track centers. Read and write problems then might accelerate later.

To ensure that your system operates in the correct ambient temperature, you first must determine your system's specified functional range. Most manufacturers provide data about the correct operating temperature range for their systems. Two temperature specifications might be available, one indicating allowable temperatures during operation and another indicating allowable temperatures under non-operating conditions. IBM, for example, indicates the following temperature ranges as acceptable for most of its systems:

System on: 60 to 90 degrees Fahrenheit

System off: 50 to 110 degrees Fahrenheit

For the safety of the disk and the data it contains, avoid rapid changes in ambient temperatures. If rapid temperature changes occur—for example, when a new drive is shipped to a location during the winter and then brought indoors—let the drive acclimate to room temperature before turning it on. In extreme cases, condensation forms on the platters inside the drive head disk assembly—disastrous for the drive if you turn it on before the condensation can evaporate. Most drive manufacturers specify a timetable to use as a guide in acclimating a drive to room temperature before operating it. You usually must wait several hours to a day before a drive is ready to use after it has been shipped or stored in a cold environment.

Most office environments provide a stable temperature in which to operate a computer system, but some do not. Be sure to give some consideration to the placement of your equipment.

Power Cycling (On/Off). As you have just learned, the temperature variations a system encounters greatly stress the system's physical components. The largest temperature variations a system encounters, however, are those that occur during system warm-up when you initially turn it on. Turning on (also called powering on) a cold system subjects it to the greatest possible internal temperature variations. For these reasons, limiting the number of power-on cycles a system is exposed to greatly improves its life and reliability.

displays with low-persistence phosphors are the least susceptible. If you ever have seen a monochrome display with the image of some program permanently burned in—even with the display off—you know what I mean. Look at the monitors that display flight information at the airport—they usually show the effects of phosphor burn.

Screen savers or blankers will either blank the screen completely or display some sort of moving random image to prevent burn in. This can be accomplished by either a manual or automatic procedure as follows:

- *Manual.* Turn the brightness and contrast levels all the way down, or even power the display off completely. This technique is effective but it is a manual method; you must remember to do it.

- *Automatic.* Many types of programs can cause the screen to blank or display random images automatically at a predetermined interval. Screen savers are built into most Graphical User Interfaces (GUIs) such as Windows and OS/2. These can easily be enabled, and you can also specify the time delay before they activate. If you run under plain DOS, you can use a number of public domain as well as commercial screen saver programs. These programs usually run as terminate-and-stay-resident (TSR) programs. The program watches the clock as well as the keyboard and mouse ports. If several minutes pass with nothing typed at the keyboard or no mouse movement, the program activates and either shuts off all signals to the display or creates an image that moves around on the screen to prevent burn in.

Static Electricity. Static electricity can cause numerous problems within a system. The problems usually appear during the winter months when humidity is low or in extremely dry climates where the humidity is low year-round. In these cases, you might need to take special precautions to ensure that the system functions properly.

Static discharges outside a system-unit chassis are rarely a source of permanent problems within the system. The usual effect of a static discharge to the case, keyboard, or even in close proximity to a system, is a parity check (memory) error or a locked-up system. In some cases, I have been able to cause parity checks or system lockups by simply walking past a system. Most static-sensitivity problems such as this one are caused by improper grounding of the system power. Be sure that you always use a three-prong, grounded power cord plugged into a properly grounded outlet. If you are unsure about the outlet, you can buy an outlet tester at most electronics-supply or hardware stores for only a few dollars.

Whenever you open a system unit or handle circuits removed from the system, you must be much more careful with static. You can damage permanently a component with a static discharge if the charge is not routed to a ground. I usually recommend handling boards and adapters first by a grounding point such as the bracket to minimize the potential for static damage.

An easy way to prevent static problems is with good power-line grounding, which is extremely important for computer equipment. A poorly designed power-line grounding system is one of the primary causes of poor computer design. The best way to prevent static damage is to prevent the static charge from getting into the computer in the first place. The chassis ground in a properly designed system serves as a static guard for the computer, which redirects the static charge safely to ground. For this ground to be complete, therefore, the system must be plugged into a properly grounded three-wire outlet.

If the static problem is extreme, you can resort to other measures. One is to use a grounded static mat underneath the computer. Touch the mat first before you touch the computer, to ensure that any static charges are routed to ground and away from the system unit's internal parts. If problems still persist, you might want to check out the electrical building ground. I have seen installations in which three-wire outlets exist but are not grounded properly. You can use an outlet tester to be sure that the outlet is wired properly.

Power Line Noise. To run properly, a computer system requires a steady supply of clean, noise-free power. In some installations, however, the power line serving the computer serves heavy equipment also, and the voltage variations resulting from the on-off cycling of this equipment can cause problems for the computer. Certain types of equipment on the same power line also can cause voltage *spikes*—short transient signals of sometimes 1,000 volts or more—that can physically damage a computer. Although these spikes are rare, they can be crippling. Even a dedicated electrical circuit used only by a single computer can experience spikes and transients, depending on the quality of the power supplied to the building or circuit.

During the site-preparation phase of a system installation, you should be aware of these factors to ensure a steady supply of clean power:

- If possible, the computer system should be on its own circuit with its own circuit breaker. This setup does not guarantee freedom from interference but it helps.

- The circuit should be checked for a good, low-resistance ground, proper line voltage, freedom from interference, and freedom from brownouts (voltage dips).

- A three-wire circuit is a must but some people substitute grounding-plug adapters to adapt a grounded plug to a two-wire socket. This setup is not recommended; the ground is there for a reason.

- Power line noise problems increase with the resistance of the circuit, which is a function of wire size and length. To decrease resistance, therefore, avoid extension cords unless absolutely necessary, and then use only heavy-duty extension cords.

- Inevitably, you will want to plug in other equipment later. Plan ahead to avoid temptations to use too many items on a single outlet. If possible, provide a separate power circuit for noncomputer-related accessories.

Air conditioners, coffee makers, copy machines, laser printers, space heaters, vacuum cleaners, and power tools are some of the worst corrupters of a PC system's power. Any of these items can draw an excessive amount of current and play havoc with a PC system on the same electrical circuit. I've seen offices in which all the computers begin to crash at about 9:05 a.m. daily, which is when all the coffee makers are turned on!

Also, try to ensure that copy machines and laser printers do not share a circuit with other computer equipment. These devices draw a large amount of power.

Another major problem in some companies is partitioned offices. Many of these partitions are prewired with their own electrical outlets and are plugged into one another in a sort of power line daisy chain, similar to chaining power strips together. I pity the person in the cubicle at the end of the electrical daisy chain, who will have very flaky power!

As a real-world example of too many devices sharing a single circuit, I can describe several instances in which a personal computer had a repeating parity check problem. All efforts to repair the system had been unsuccessful. The reported error locations from the parity check message also were inconsistent, which normally indicates a problem with power. The problem could have been the power supply in the system unit or the external power supplied from the wall outlet. This problem was solved one day as I stood watching the system. The parity check message was displayed at the same instant someone two cubicles away turned on a copy machine. Placing the computers on a separate line solved the problem.

By following the guidelines in this section, you can create the proper power environment for your systems and help to ensure trouble-free operation.

Radio-Frequency Interference. Radio-frequency interference (RFI) is easily overlooked as a problem factor. The interference is caused by any source of radio transmissions near a computer system. Living next door to a 50,000-watt commercial radio station is one sure way to get RFI problems, but less powerful transmitters cause problems too. I know of many instances in which portable radio-telephones have caused sporadic random keystrokes to appear, as though an invisible entity were typing on the keyboard. I also have seen RFI cause a system to lock up. Solutions to RFI problems are more difficult to state because every case must be handled differently. Sometimes, reorienting a system unit eliminates the problem because radio signals can be directional in nature. At other times, you must invest in specially shielded cables for cables outside the system unit, such as the keyboard cable.

One type of solution to an RFI noise problem with cables is to pass the cable through a *toroidal iron core,* a doughnut-shaped piece of iron placed around a cable to suppress both the reception and transmission of electromagnetic interference (EMI). If you can isolate an RFI noise problem in a particular cable, you often can solve the problem by passing the cable through a toroidal core. Because the cable must pass through the center hole of the core, it often is difficult, if not impossible, to add a toroid to a cable that already has end connectors installed.

Radio Shack sells a special snap-together toroid designed specifically to be added to cables already in use. This toroid looks like a thick-walled tube that has been sliced in half. You just lay the cable in the center of one of the halves, and snap the other half over the first. This type of construction makes it easy to add the noise-suppression features of a toroid to virtually any existing cable.

IBM also makes a special 6-foot long PS/2 keyboard cable with a built-in toroid core (part number 27F4984) that can greatly reduce interference problems. This cable has the smaller 6-pin DIN (PS/2 style) connector at the system end and the standard SDL (Shielded Data Link) connector at the keyboard end; it costs about $40.

The best, if not the easiest, way to eliminate the problem probably is to correct it at the source. You likely won't convince the commercial radio station near your office to shut down but if you are dealing with a small radio transmitter that is generating RFI, sometimes you can add to the transmitter a filter that suppresses spurious emissions. Unfortunately, problems sometimes persist until the transmitter is either switched off or moved some distance away from the affected computer.

Note that your own computer systems can be a source of RFI. Computer equipment must meet one of these two classifications to be certified and salable, according to the FCC (Federal Communications Commission): Class A or Class B. The Class A specification applies to computing devices sold for use in commercial, business, and industrial environments. Class B indicates that the equipment has passed more stringent tests and can be used in residential environments, in addition to any environments allowed under Class A.

The FCC does not really police users or purchasers of computer equipment so much as it polices the equipment manufacturers or vendors. Therefore, if you are using a Class A-rated system in your home, you don't need to worry about radio police showing up at your door. You must obtain a Class B certification for systems that meet one of the following conditions:

- Marketed through retail or direct-mail outlets

- Sold to the general public rather than commercial users only

- Operates on battery or 120-volt AC electrical power

Notice that a system has to fit each of these three categories to be considered a personal computer and be subject to the stricter Class B rules. Notice also that the FCC considers all portable computer systems as meeting Class B standards because their portability makes them likely to be used in a residential setting.

The FCC standards for Class A and Class B certification govern two kinds of emissions: conductive emissions, radiated from the computer system into the power cord, and radio-frequency emissions, radiated from the computer system into space. Table 18.1 shows the conductive and radio-frequency emissions limitations to be eligible for both Class A and Class B ratings.

Table 18.1   FCC Class A and Class B Emission Limitations

Conductive Emissions: Maximum Signal Level (mv)

Frequency	Class A	Class B
0.45 to 1.705 MHz	1000	250
1.705 to 30.0 MHz	3000	250

Radiated Emissions: Maximum Field Strength (uv/M)

Frequency	Class A (10M)	Class B (3M0
30 to 88 MHz	90	100
88 to 216 MHz	150	150
217 to 960 MHz	210	200
960 MHz and up	300	500

MHz = Megahertz
10M = Measured at 10 meters
3M = Measured at 3 meters
mv = Millivolts
uv/M = Microvolts per meter

Notice that although some of the specific numbers listed for Class A seem lower than those required for Class B, you must consider that field strength measurements normally decline under the inverse square law: the strength of the signal decreases as the square of the distance from the source. A rating of 100 microvolts per meter at 3 meters, therefore, would be approximately equal to a rating of about 9 microvolts per meter at 10 meters. This calculation just means that the limits to pass Class B certification are much tougher than they look, and certainly are much tougher than Class A limits. Additionally, Class A certification is tested and verified entirely by the manufacturer; Class B certification requires a sample of the equipment to be sent to the FCC for testing.

IBM and most other responsible manufacturers ensure that all systems they sell meet the stricter Class B designations. One of the primary reasons for the Micro Channel Architecture design was to meet, and also greatly exceed these FCC classifications. IBM knew that as computing clock speeds go up, so do the radio emissions. As clock rates of 66, 75, and 100 MHz and higher become more common (and they will soon), IBM will have a distinct advantage over manufacturers still using the AT or EISA bus designs because vendors using ISA or EISA bus designs will have to invest in more expensive chassis and case shielding to combat the emission problem. IBM and other Micro Channel clones will gain a distinct manufacturing cost advantage.

Dust and Pollutants. Dirt, smoke, dust, and other pollutants are bad for your system. The power-supply fan carries airborne particles through your system, and they collect inside. If your system is used in an extremely harsh environment, you might want to investigate some of the industrial systems on the market designed for harsh conditions.

IBM used to sell industrial model XT and AT systems but discontinued them after introducing the PS/2. IBM has licensed several third-party companies to produce industrial versions of PS/2 systems.

Compatible vendors also have industrial systems; many companies make special *hardened* versions of their systems for harsh environments. Industrial systems usually use a different cooling system from the one used in a regular PC. A large cooling fan is used to pressurize the case rather than depressurize it, as most systems do. The air pumped into the case passes through a filter unit that must be cleaned and changed periodically. The system is pressurized so that no contaminated air can flow into it; air flows only outward. The only way air can enter is through the fan and filter system.

These systems also might have special keyboards impervious to liquids and dirt. Some flat-membrane keyboards are difficult to type on, but are extremely rugged; others resemble the standard types of keyboards, but have a thin, plastic membrane that covers all the keys. You can add this membrane to normal types of keyboards to seal them from the environment.

A new breed of humidifier can cause problems with computer equipment. This type of humidifier uses ultrasonics to generate a mist of water sprayed into the air. The extra humidity helps cure problems with static electricity resulting from a dry climate, but the airborne water contaminants can cause many problems. If you use one of these systems, you might notice a white ash-like deposit forming on components. The deposit is the result of abrasive and corrosive minerals suspended in the vaporized water. If these deposits collect on the disk drive heads, they will ruin the heads and scratch disks. The only safe way to run one of these ultrasonic humidifiers is with pure distilled water. If you use a humidifier, be sure it does not generate these deposits.

If you do your best to keep the environment for your computer equipment clean, your system will run better and last longer. Also, you will not have to open your unit as often for complete preventive maintenance cleaning.

Using Power-Protection Systems

Power-protection systems do just what the name implies: they protect your equipment from the effects of power surges and power failures. In particular, power surges and spikes can damage computer equipment, and a loss of power can result in lost data. In this section, you learn about the four primary types of power-protection devices available and under what circumstances you should use them.

Before considering any further levels of power protection, you should know that the power supply in your system (if your system is well-made) already affords you a substantial amount of protection. The power supplies in IBM equipment are designed to provide protection from higher-than-normal voltages and currents, and provide a limited amount of power line noise filtering. Some of the inexpensive aftermarket power supplies probably do not have this sort of protection; be careful if you have an inexpensive clone system. In those cases, further protecting your system might be wise.

IBM's PS/2 power supplies will stay within operating specifications and continue to run a system if any of these power line disturbances occur:

- Voltage drop to 80 volts for up to 2 seconds

- Voltage drop to 70 volts for up to .5 seconds

- Voltage surge of up to 143 volts for up to 1 second

IBM also states that neither their power supplies nor systems will be damaged by the following occurrences:

- Full power outage

- Any voltage drop (brownout)

- A spike of up to 2,500 volts

Because of the high quality power supply design that IBM uses, they state in their documentation that external surge suppressors are not needed for PS/2 systems. Most other high quality name brand manufacturers also use high quality power supply designs. Companies like Astec, PC Power and Cooling, and others make very high quality units.

To verify the levels of protection built into the existing power supply in a computer system, an independent laboratory subjected several unprotected PC systems to various spikes and surges up to *6,000 volts*—considered the maximum level of surge that can be transmitted to a system by an electrical outlet. Any higher voltage would cause the power to arc to ground within the outlet itself. Note that none of the systems sustained permanent damage in these tests; the worst thing that happened was that some of the systems rebooted or shut down if the surge was more than 2,000 volts. Each system restarted when the power switch was toggled after a shutdown.

I do not use any real form of power protection on my systems, and they have survived near-direct lightning strikes and powerful surges. The most recent incident, only 50 feet from my office, was a direct lightning strike to a brick chimney that *blew the top of the chimney apart*. None of my systems (which were running at the time) were damaged in any way from this incident; they just shut themselves down. I was able to restart each system by toggling the power switches. An alarm system located in the same office, however, was destroyed by this strike. I am not saying that lightning strikes or even much milder spikes and surges cannot damage computer systems—another nearby lightning strike did destroy a modem and serial adapter installed in one of my systems. I was just lucky that the destruction did not include the motherboard.

This discussion points out an important oversight in some power-protection strategies: you may elect to protect your systems from electrical power disturbances, but do not forget to provide similar protection also from spikes and surges on the phone line.

The automatic shutdown of a computer during power disturbances is a built-in function of most high-quality power supplies. You can reset the power supply by flipping the power switch from on to off and back on again. Some power supplies, such as those in most of the PS/2 systems, have an *auto-restart function.* This type of power supply acts the same as others in a massive surge or spike situation: it shuts down the system. The difference is that after normal power resumes, the power supply waits for a specified delay of three to six seconds and then resets itself and powers the system back up. Because no manual switch resetting is required, this feature is desirable in systems functioning as a network file server or in a system in a remote location.

The first time I witnessed a large surge cause an immediate shutdown of all my systems, I was extremely surprised. All the systems were silent, but the monitor and modem lights were still on. My first thought was that everything was blown, but a simple toggle of each system-unit power switch caused the power supplies to reset, and the units powered up with no problem. Since that first time, this type of shutdown has happened to me several times, always without further problems.

The following types of power-protection devices are explained in the sections that follow:

- Surge suppressors
- Line conditioners
- Standby power supplies (SPS)
- Uninterruptible power supplies (UPS)

Surge Suppressors (Protectors)

The simplest form of power protection is any of the commercially available surge protectors; that is, devices inserted between the system and the power line. These devices, which cost between $20 and $200, can absorb the high-voltage transients produced by nearby lightning strikes and power equipment. Some surge protectors can be effective for certain types of power problems, but they offer only very limited protection.

Surge protectors use several devices, usually metal-oxide varistors (MOVs), that can clamp and shunt away all voltages above a certain level. MOVs are designed to accept voltages as high as 6,000 volts and divert any power above 200 volts to ground. MOVs can handle normal surges, but powerful surges such as a direct lightning strike can blow right through them. MOVs are not designed to handle a very high level of power, and self-destruct while shunting a large surge. These devices, therefore, cease to function after a single large surge or a series of smaller ones. The real problem is that you cannot easily tell when they no longer are functional; the only way to test them is to subject the MOVs to a surge, which destroys them. Therefore, you never really know if your so-called surge protector is protecting your system.

Some surge protectors have status lights that let you know when a surge large enough to blow the MOVs has occurred. A surge suppressor without this status indicator light is useless because you never know when it has stopped protecting.

Underwriters Laboratories has produced an excellent standard that governs surge suppressors, called UL 1449. Any surge suppressor that meets this standard is a very good one, and definitely offers an additional line of protection beyond what the power supply in your PC already does. The only types of surge suppressors worth buying, therefore, should have two features: conformance to the UL 1449 standard and a status light indicating when the MOVs are blown. Units that meet the UL 1449 specification say so on the packaging or directly on the unit. If this standard is not mentioned, it does not conform, and you should avoid it.

Another good feature to have in a surge suppressor is a built-in circuit breaker that can be reset rather than a fuse. The breaker protects your system if the system or a peripheral develops a short. These better surge suppressors usually cost about $40.

Phone Line Surge Protectors

In addition to protecting the power lines, it is critical to provide protection to your systems from any phone lines that are connected. If you are using a modem or fax board which is plugged into the phone system, any surges or spikes that travel the phone line can potentially damage your system. In many areas, the phone lines are especially susceptible to lightning strikes, which is the largest cause of fried modems and computer equipment attached to them.

Several companies manufacture or sell simple surge protectors that plug between your modem and the phone line. These inexpensive devices can be purchased from most electronics supply houses. Most of the cable and communication product vendors listed in Appendix B sell these phone line surge protectors.

Line Conditioners

In addition to high-voltage and current conditions, other problems can occur with incoming power. The voltage might dip below the level needed to run the system and result in a brownout. Other forms of electrical noise other than simple voltage surges or spikes might be on the power line, such as radio-frequency interference or electrical noise caused by motors or other inductive loads.

Remember two things when you wire together digital devices (such as computers and their peripherals). A wire is an antenna and has a voltage induced in it by nearby electromagnetic fields, which can come from other wires, telephones, CRTs, motors, fluorescent fixtures, static discharge, and, of course, radio transmitters. Digital circuitry also responds with surprising efficiency to noise of even a volt or two, making those induced voltages particularly troublesome. The wiring in your building can act as an antenna and pick up all kinds of noise and disturbances. A line conditioner can handle many of these types of problems.

A line conditioner is designed to remedy a variety of problems. It filters the power, bridges brownouts, suppresses high-voltage and current conditions, and generally acts as a buffer between the power line and the system. A line conditioner does the job of a surge suppressor, and much more. It is more of an active device functioning continuously rather than a passive device that activates only when a surge is present. A line conditioner provides true power conditioning and can handle myriad problems. It contains transformers, capacitors, and other circuitry that temporarily can bridge a brownout or low-voltage situation. These units usually cost several hundreds of dollars, depending on the power-handling capacity of the unit.

Backup Power

The next level of power protection includes backup power-protection devices. These units can provide power in case of a complete blackout, which provides the time needed for an orderly system shutdown. Two types are available: the standby power supply (SPS) and the uninterruptible power supply (UPS). The UPS is a special device because it does much more than just provide backup power: it is also the best kind of line conditioner you can buy.

Standby Power Supplies (SPS). A standby power supply is known as an *off-line device*: it functions only when normal power is disrupted. An SPS system uses a special circuit that can sense the AC line current. If the sensor detects a loss of power on the line, the system quickly switches over to a standby battery and power inverter. The power inverter converts the battery power to 110-volt AC power, which then is supplied to the system.

SPS systems do work, but sometimes a problem occurs with the switch to battery power. If the switch is not fast enough, the computer system unit shuts down or reboots anyway, which defeats the purpose of having the backup power supply. A truly outstanding SPS adds to the circuit a *ferroresonant transformer,* a large transformer with the capability to store a small amount of power and deliver it during the switch time. Having this device is similar to having on the power line a buffer that you add to an SPS to give it almost truly uninterruptible capability.

SPS units also may or may not have internal line conditioning of their own; most cheaper units place your system directly on the regular power line under normal circumstances and offer no conditioning. The addition of a ferroresonant transformer to an SPS gives it additional regulation and protection capabilities due to the buffer effect of the transformer. SPS devices without the ferroresonant transformer still require the use of a line conditioner for full protection. SPS systems usually cost from $200 to several thousands of dollars, depending on the quality and power-output capacity.

Uninterruptible Power Supplies (UPS). Perhaps the best overall solution to any power problem is to provide a power source that is both conditioned and that also cannot be interrupted—which describes an uninterruptible power supply. UPSs are known as on-line systems because they continuously function and supply power to your computer systems. Because some companies advertise ferroresonant SPS devices as though they were UPS devices, many now use the term *true UPS* to describe a truly on-line system. A true UPS system is constructed much the same as an SPS system; however, because you always are operating from the battery, there is no switching circuit.

In a true UPS, your system always operates from the battery, with a voltage inverter to convert from 12 volts DC to 110 volts AC. You essentially have your own private power system that generates power independently of the AC line. A battery charger connected to the line or wall current keeps the battery charged at a rate equal to or greater than the rate at which power is consumed.

When power is disconnected, the true UPS continues functioning undisturbed because the battery-charging function is all that is lost. Because you already were running off the battery, no switch takes place and no power disruption is possible. The battery then begins discharging at a rate dictated by the amount of load your system places on the unit, which (based on the size of the battery) gives you plenty of time to execute an orderly system shutdown. Based on an appropriately scaled storage battery, the UPS functions continuously, generating power and preventing unpleasant surprises. When the line power returns, the battery charger begins recharging the battery, again with no interruption.

UPS cost is a direct function of both the length of time it can continue to provide power after a line current failure, and how much power it can provide; therefore, purchasing a UPS that gives you enough power to run your system and peripherals as well as enough time to close files and provide an orderly shutdown would be sufficient. In most PC applications, this solution is the most cost-effective because the batteries and charger portion of the system must be much larger than the SPS type of device, and will be more costly.

Many SPS systems are advertised as though they were true UPS systems. The giveaway is the unit's "switch time." If a specification for switch time exists, the unit cannot be a true UPS because UPS units never switch. Understand, however, that a good SPS with a ferroresonant transformer can virtually equal the performance of a true UPS at a lower cost.

Because of a UPS's almost total isolation from the line current, it is unmatched as a line conditioner and surge suppressor. The best UPS systems add a ferroresonant transformer for even greater power conditioning and protection capability. This type of UPS is the best form of power protection available. The price, however, can be very high. A true UPS costs from $1 to $2 per watt of power supplied. To find out just how much power your system requires, look at the UL sticker on the back of the unit. This sticker lists the maximum power draw in watts, or sometimes in just volts and amperes. If only voltage and amperage are listed, multiply the two figures to calculate a wattage figure.

As an example, the back of an IBM PC AT Model 339 indicates that the system can require as much as 110 volts at a maximum current draw of 5 amps. The maximum power this AT can draw is about 550 watts. This wattage is for a system with every slot full, two hard disks and one floppy—in other words, the maximum possible level of expansion. The system should never draw any more power than that; if it does, a 5-ampere fuse in the power supply blows. This type of system normally draws an average 300 watts; to be safe when you make calculations for UPS capacity, however, be conservative and use the 550-watt figure. Adding a monitor that draws 100 watts brings the total to 650 watts or more. To run two fully loaded AT systems, you need an 1,100-watt UPS. Don't forget two monitors, each drawing 100 watts; the total, therefore, is 1,300 watts. Using the $1 to $2 per watt figure, a UPS of at least that capacity or greater will cost from $1,300 to $2,600 dollars—expensive, but unfortunately what the best level of protection costs. Most companies can justify this type of expense for only a critical-use PC, such as a network file server.

In addition to the total available output power (wattage), several other factors can differentiate one UPS from another. The addition of a ferroresonant transformer improves a unit's power conditioning and buffering capabilities. Good units have also an inverter that produces a true sine wave output; the cheaper ones may generate a square wave. A square wave is an approximation of a sine wave with abrupt up-and-down voltage transitions. The abrupt transitions of a square wave signal are not compatible with some computer equipment power supplies. Be sure that the UPS you purchase produces a signal compatible with your computer equipment. Every unit has a specification for how long it can sustain output at the rated level. If your systems draw less than the rated level, you have some additional time. Be careful, though: most UPS systems are not designed for you to sit and compute for hours through an electrical blackout. They are designed to provide power to whatever is needed, to remain operating long enough to allow for an orderly shutdown. You pay a large amount for units that provide power for more than 15 minutes or so.

There are many sources of power protection equipment, but two of the best are Best Power and Tripp Lite. These companies sell a variety of UPS, SPS, line, and surge protectors. They are listed in Appendix B.

Using Data-Backup Systems

Making a backup of important data on a computer system is one thing that many users fail to do. A backup is similar to insurance: you need it only when you are in big trouble! Because of the cost in not only dollars, but also in time and effort, many users do not have adequate backup—which is not a problem until the day you have a catastrophe and suddenly find yourself without your important data or files. This section discusses several forms of backup hardware and software that can make the job both easier and faster, and—hopefully—cause more users to do it.

Backup is something a service technician should be aware of. After I repair a system that has suffered some kind of disk crash, I can guarantee that the disk subsystem will be completely functional. I cannot guarantee, however, that the original files are on the disks; in fact, the drive may have to be replaced. Without a backup, the system can be physically repaired, but the original data may be lost forever.

Nothing destroys someone's faith in computer technology faster than telling them that the last year or more of work (in the form of disk files) no longer exists. When I visit a customer site to do some troubleshooting or repair, I always tell my clients to back up the system before I arrive. They may be reluctant to do so at first, but it is better than paying a technician by the hour to do it. A backup must be done before I operate on a system, because I do not want to be liable if something goes wrong and data is damaged or lost. If the system is so dysfunctional that a backup cannot be performed, I make sure that the client knows that the service technician is not responsible for the data.

A good general rule is never to let a backup interval be longer than what you are willing to lose some day. You always can reload or even repurchase copies of software programs that might have been lost, but you cannot buy back your own data. Because of the extremely high value of data compared to the system itself, I have recommended for some time that service technicians become familiar with data-recovery principles and procedures. Being able to perform this valuable service gives you a fantastic edge over technicians who can only fix or replace the hardware.

Backup Policies

All users and managers of computer systems should develop a plan for regular disk backups. I recommend that one person in an office have the responsibility for performing these backups so that the job is not left undone.

A backup interval should be selected based on the amount of activity on the system. Some users find that daily backups are required, and others find that a weekly arrangement is more suitable. Backups rarely must be scheduled at more than weekly intervals. Some users settle on a mixed plan: perform weekly disk backups and daily backups of only the changed files.

The procedures for backing up and for dealing with copy protection are explained in the following sections.

Backup Procedures. You should back up to removable media such as cartridge or tape, which you remove from a system and store in a safe place. Backups performed on nonremovable media, such as another hard disk, are much more vulnerable to damage, theft, or fire; also, having multiple backups is much more expensive.

Because of the relatively low cost of hard disks, some users unfortunately install two hard disks and back up one to the other. Worse, some users split a single disk into two partitions and back up one partition to the other. These backups are false backups. If the system were subjected to a massive electrical surge or failure, the contents of both drives could be lost. If the system were stolen, again, both backups would be lost. Finally, if the system were physically damaged, such as in a fire or other mishap, both the data and the backup would be lost. These are good reasons that it is important to back up to removable media.

Perform your backups on a rotating schedule. I recommend using a tape-backup system with at least three tapes per drive, in which you back up data to the first tape the first week. The second week, you use a second tape. That way, if the second tape has been damaged, you can use the preceding week's backup tape to restore data. The third week, you should use still another, third, tape and place the first tape in a different physical location as protection against damage from fire, flood, theft, or another disaster.

The fourth week, you begin to rotate each tape so that the first (off-site) tape is used again for backup, and the second tape is moved off-site. This system always has two progressively older backups on-site, with the third backup off-site to provide for disaster insurance. Only removable media can provide this type of flexibility, and tape is one of the best forms of removable media for backup.

V

Assembly & Maintenance

Dealing with Copy Protection. One thing standing in the way of proper backups of some of your software is copy protection, a system in which the original disk the software is on is modified so that it cannot be copied exactly by your system. When the programs on the disk are run, they look for this unique feature to determine whether the original disk is in the system. Some software makers force you to use master copies of their programs by using this technique to require that the original disks be placed in the floppy drive for validation even though the system might have the software loaded on the hard disk.

Some forms of copy protection load the software on a hard disk only from an original disk, and modify the hard disk loaded version so that it runs only if it remains on the system in a specified set of sectors. If the program ever is moved on the disk, it fails to operate. Because these requirements make the software highly prone to failure, copy protection has no place on software used in a business environment.

My personal response to copy protection is to refuse to use, buy, or recommend any software from a company engaged in this practice. With rare exceptions, I simply do not buy copy-protected software. Unprotected alternatives always are available for whatever type of program you want. You might even discover that the unprotected alternative is a better program. If you don't make the software-purchasing decisions in your organization, however, you may have little choice in this matter.

Experienced computer users know that you never should use original disks when you install or configure software. After I purchase a new program, I first make a copy and store the original disks. In fact, I use the original disks solely for making additional backup copies. Following this procedure protects me if I make a mistake in installing or using the software. Because of the need for backup and the fact that copy protection essentially prevents proper backup, a solution has been devised.

When you must use a piece of protected software, you can purchase special programs that enable you to back up and even to remove the protection from most copy-protected programs on the market. Two such programs are CopyWrite, by Quaid Software Ltd., and Copy II PC, by Central Point Software. These programs cost about $50 and are absolutely necessary when you are forced to deal with copy-protected software.

Note that no matter what a software license agreement says, you have a legal right to back up your software; this right is guaranteed under US copyright law. Do not let a software license agreement bamboozle you into believing otherwise.

The best way to fight copy protection is with your wallet. Most companies respond to this economic pressure; many respond by removing the protection from their programs. Fortunately, because of this economic pressure by influential users, the scourge of copy protection has been almost eliminated from the business-software marketplace. Only a few remaining programs have this unfortunate defect; I hope that the protection will be eradicated from them as well.

Backup Software. In considering how to back up your system, you should be aware of both the hardware and software options available. This section first explores the software-only options; that is, using either what you get with DOS, or some more powerful aftermarket software to back up using a floppy drive. You will learn that the aftermarket software usually offers many features and capabilities that the standard DOS BACKUP program does not have. After discussing software alternatives, this section looks at complete, dedicated hardware and software backup systems. Using specialized hardware is the best way to have an easy, effective, and safe way of backing up your system.

The DOS BACKUP Command. The most basic backup software you can use are the DOS commands BACKUP and RESTORE. Since their introduction in Version 2.0 of DOS, and up to Version 3.3, these commands have frustrated users with their bugs and other problems. The versions supplied with DOS V4.0 and higher have been greatly improved, but they still do not offer what many aftermarket products offer. Because of the way BACKUP and RESTORE use the floppy drive as the hardware device, you can use this software only for backing up systems with low-capacity hard drives.

New Backup Software with DOS 6.x. Both Microsoft and IBM have included new backup software with their respective versions of DOS 6.x. These programs far outstrip the capabilities of the original BACKUP command and are much easier and safer to use.

In MS-DOS, Microsoft supplies a limited version of the Norton Backup software called MSBACKUP. This program is a full-featured menu-driven program that is designed to back up to floppy drives only. It is very easy to use, and represents a great leap from the older BACKUP and RESTORE commands. Because it is really a restricted version of the Norton Backup program by Symantec, you can easily upgrade to the more full-featured Norton Backup program and still retain compatibility with all of your existing backups.

IBM went a different route in PC DOS and supplies an only slightly limited version of the Central Point Backup program called CPBACKUP. This offers a great deal more functionality than the MSBACKUP program supplied by Microsoft. CPBACKUP can back up to a variety of different devices, including tape drives. It is also an easy to use menu-driven program, but can also be completely automated with an extensive number of command line options. Again, a more full-featured version can be obtained directly from Central Point which would be compatible with your existing backups.

Aftermarket Software for Floppy Backups. Most aftermarket software offers convenience and performance features not found in the DOS BACKUP and RESTORE commands. If you are relegated to using the floppy disk drive as your backup hardware, you should do yourself a favor and investigate some of the aftermarket software designed for backup. I recommend FASTBACK, by Fifth Generation Systems, as well as the Norton (Symantec) and Central Point backup programs. The latter two are included in utility packages from these companies, including Norton Desktop for Windows and PC Tools.

Even with these programs, however, backing up a hard disk larger than 20 to 40 megabytes is not recommended because it requires using a large number of floppy disks. To explain, consider the system I use. My main portable system has a 1-gigabyte disk drive, which requires *728* 1.44M floppy disks for backup. Some backup programs perform data compression that can reduce that number by a third to a half; optimistically, therefore, you still would need nearly 400 high-density disks. Because I always perform backups to a rotating set of media, with three backups in the rotation, I need somewhere from *1,200 to 2,184 HD disks for my backup.* That number handles only one of my systems; I have an aggregate of more than 1 gigabyte of disk space on several other systems as well. When you imagine trying to manage more than a thousand HD floppy disks, not to mention feeding 400 or more of them into a system for a day or so to perform each backup, you can see the problem associated with backing up large drives to floppy disks.

One solution is to back up the drive using either an 8mm videotape drive or a 4mm digital audio tape (DAT) drive. Either type of tape system easily backs up more than one gigabyte to a single tape and can perform a complete backup of a full drive in just over three hours. Partial backups take only seconds or minutes.

Another feature of a tape drive is that, because it is an external unit, I can carry it around and use it to back up all my systems. Also, the media costs for tape are much less than for floppy disks: the 4mm 1.3 gigabyte tapes cost only $20 or less. Therefore, I can have three backups that cost less than $60—using floppy media would cost from $1,000 to $2,000 or more. You may not have a gigabyte of on-line storage to back up, but any amount over 40 megabytes starts to become unwieldy when you are using a floppy drive.

For a total of about $1,500 for some of the less-expensive DAT or 8mm units, I have a reliable, complete, high-speed, and simple backup of every system I own. If you have more than 40M to back up—or more than one system—a tape-backup device is the best way. Various tape-backup products are discussed in the following section.

Dedicated Backup Hardware

As explained earlier, you can choose from software and hardware options when you consider backup equipment. In this section, you learn about dedicated backup hardware, usually a tape or cartridge device designed for high-speed, high-capacity backup purposes.

Backup Systems. A good, reliable backup is important when you're using a large hard disk. With a disk of 40M or more, you should consider some form of hardware backup device other than only the floppy drive. Tape backup is available in configurations easily supporting hundreds of megabytes and more. Tape backup is fast and accurate.

Because your data is probably worth much more to you than the physical hardware on which it is stored, it is important to develop a backup system you will use. A tape system makes the backup convenient and, therefore, helps to ensure that you will complete it. If backing up your system is a difficult, time-consuming operation, you or the person responsible for doing it probably will not do it regularly (if ever). Tape units also can be set to perform unattended automatic backups during times when you are not using your computer, such as during the middle of the night.

Basic parameters of different tape-backup devices include the following:

- Type of media used
- Hardware interface
- Backup software

These parameters are explained in the following sections.

QIC Standards. The Quarter-Inch Committee (QIC) issues standards for such things as tape-drive controller adapters, the tape cartridges, and commands that tape drives understand. You will find them listed in Appendix B, the "Vendor List."

The QIC organization was formed to develop standard formats for DC-600 and DC-2000 data cartridge tape drives. Because quarter-inch tapes typically have been the market leaders, even suppliers of other systems generally follow QIC standards, such as the SCSI command set in QIC-104, and QIC-122 or QIC-123, which define data-compression methods. Data compression allows you to store more data on a certain length of tape. Vendors can change their backup software so that the codes are inserted at the beginning of the tape. Then, if the tape is read back by other tape drives, the read back drive can determine the method used.

Tape Media. I like to use systems that employ industry-standard media. *Media* refers to the type of tape format used. The type of media you select dictates the capacity of the tape-unit storage. Many different types of systems use many different types of media, but I am concerned with only a handful of standard media types. Four primary standards are the 3M Data Cartridge 600 (or DC-600), the DC-2000, the 4mm digital audio tape (DAT), and the 8mm (video) cartridge media. I recommend any of these types, depending on your requirements for capacity and performance. This list shows the different media types:

■ *DC-600 cartridges.* Invented by 3M, the DC-600 cartridge is a relatively large tape, $4 \times 6 \times 0.665$ in L × W × D, and has a heavy metal base plate. This long-running standard was introduced in 1971. Many variations of the DC-600 tapes exist; longer lengths have capacities anywhere from 60M, at the low end, to 525M or more at the high end.

■ *DC-2000 cartridges.* Also invented by 3M, this cartridge is one of the most popular media for backup purposes. This tape is $2.415 \times 3.188 \times 0.570$ inches in L × W × D, with a heavy metal base plate. Although early versions held only 20M, the most common ones now hold 80M or more. A variety of capacities result from the different tape formats available.

■ *4mm DAT (digital audio tape) cartridges.* At first glance, this cartridge looks like a regular audiocassette but is slightly smaller. These cartridges come in several recording formats. The most widely used is digital data storage, or DDS for short. Another format, DataDAT, is also available. The recording technology is similar to digital audio tape decks and is done in a Helical-Scan format; it is licensed by Sony (the original DAT developer). DAT tapes can hold as much as 1.3 gigabytes (1 gigabyte = 1,024M).

■ *8mm cartridges.* These cartridges, which use the 8mm videotape developed by Sony for camcorders, comprise one of the highest-capacity backup systems available. Most units store 2.3G but larger-capacity units are available. The recording is done physically as a Helical-Scan, the same method used in a video recorder.

The DC-600 drives now store from 60M to 525M or more, depending on the format and quality of tape used. The DC-2000 media stores only 40M to 80M or more per tape and might be suitable for low-end (such as home) use. Because the larger-capacity 4mm and 8mm units store more than 1 or 2 gigabytes on a tape, they are ideal for network server applications. These large-capacity units can cost from $1,500 to $6,000 or more, depending on the features included and—of course—where you buy it.

Make sure that the system is capable of handling your largest drive either directly or through the use of multiple tapes. With this unit, you can change tapes in the middle of a backup session to accommodate greater capacities; because this method is inconvenient and requires an operator, however, you eliminate unattended, overnight backups. For network applications or large storage requirements, or anything else for which you need top performance and the most reliable backup, you should select DC-600 or the 4mm or 8mm rather than the DC-2000 media.

I recommend only tape systems that use these media because they offer the greatest value per dollar, are the most reliable, and hold a large amount of data. Stay away from devices that use the 3M DC-1000 tapes, Phillips audio tapes, or VHS VCR tape systems. These systems often are slow, error prone, and inconvenient to use; some do not handle larger capacities, and they are not standard.

Interfaces for Tape Backup Systems. Of the three primary hardware-interface standards, virtually all professional backup systems use the QIC-02 (for Quarter-Inch Committee 02) or SCSI (for *Small Computer Systems Interface*), and more recently, the parallel port interface. Some low-end systems use the Shugart Associates 400 (SA-400) interface, which is the standard floppy controller. The interface you select controls the backup speed, whether an adapter card and slot are required, and the reliability and capacity of the unit.

In the PC and XT systems with their 4-drive floppy controllers, you can use the extra connector on the back of the existing floppy controller for some tape-backup units. This connector saves the use of a slot in these systems. Unfortunately, the AT systems require some sort of multiplexer card to enable sharing one of the internal floppy ports or another complete floppy controller so that these systems can work.

I don't recommend these floppy interface systems in general because they are slow, and the floppy controller lacks any form of error-detection and correction capability, which can make the backups unreliable. A system using the SA-400 interface has a maximum data rate of 2M per minute, less than half the QIC-02 or SCSI interfaces. These floppy interface systems are suitable for home computer users on a tight budget but should not be used in business or professional environments. Another problem is that the interface limits the capacity to 40M, and you might have to format the tapes before using them.

The QIC-02 interface, designed specifically for tape-backup products, represents an industry standard. Many companies offer products that use this interface. The QIC-02 can back up at a rate of 5M per minute. The interface usually is a short adapter card that requires a free slot in the system. You can buy these adapters separately and enable many systems to use the same externally mounted drive. A free slot is required, however, and might not be available with a regular PC.

Perhaps the best hardware interface is the Small Computer Systems Interface (SCSI), which enables your PC to back up at high data rates. The data throughput of the SCSI interface is either 5MB or 10MB per minute for standard and fast 8-bit SCSI respectively. There are currently no tape drives or hard disks that can sustain this rate of transfer, so the performance is dictated by the drives rather than the SCSI interface. Because of the high speed of the SCSI interface relative to the tape and hard disk drives, when faster media and drives are available, SCSI can easily take advantage of the greater speed.

The SCSI interface is supplied as a SCSI host adapter card that plugs into the system unit and can connect to the tape drive. The SCSI host adapter requires an expansion slot, but it can connect to other devices such as hard disk drives or tape drives with embedded SCSI interfaces. The use of a single host adapter for as many as six hard disk drives and one tape unit is a strong case in favor of SCSI as a general disk and tape interface. The only real problem with SCSI is that you will need drivers which support both your particular tape drive as well as your particular host adapter. Most tape drivers support host adapters that have ASPI (Advanced SCSI Programming Interface) or CAM (Common Access Method) drivers. In other words, you will need the ASPI or CAM driver for your host adapter, and a tape driver that connects to ASPI or CAM for your tape drive. Although there can sometimes be problems getting the correct drivers for a particular system, SCSI is still the highest performance and most flexible interface for tape backup systems.

Another interface gaining wide acceptance is the parallel port. It is used for more than just printers, as several companies have introduced versions of their backup hardware and software systems that use the parallel port to connect to your system. The parallel port offers a high speed data transfer interface with easy configuration and cabling. Unlike serial ports, there is usually no confusion as to how the cables are wired for parallel port connections.

Several companies, like MicroSolutions and Colorado, offer complete external backup systems including all hardware, software, and cables needed to connect to the parallel port of any system. These types of backup systems offer independence from a particular type of system, which is especially useful in a mixed machine or mixed bus environment.

Other companies, like Trantor, offer parallel port SCSI adapters, to which you can connect any SCSI device including hard disk, CD-ROM, tape backup, scanners, and so on. If you are out of slots or desire to set up an external backup system that will attach to and back up several systems, I recommend using one of these parallel port SCSI adapters like the Trantor MiniSCSI Plus. Using a parallel port SCSI adapter and one of the higher performance DAT tape drives, you can set up a highly capable external backup system that can function on virtually any machine.

Tape Backup Drivers and Software. Now you need to consider the software that will run the tape system. Some manufacturers have written their own software, which is proprietary and used only by that manufacturer. In other words, even though you might be using a tape unit with the same media and interface, if the software is different you cannot interchange data between the units. One type of software does not recognize the data formats of another proprietary software system. Other tape software packages are designed to run on a variety of tape hardware rather than a single manufacturer's system. Several hardware independent backup software packages support a variety of tape drives such as SyTOS (Sytron Tape Operating System) by Sytron, Novaback by Novastor, and Central Point Backup by Central Point. All of these products work with a number of different tape drives. SyTOS is somewhat of an industry standard because it is endorsed (and sold) by IBM and many other vendors, as well as having versions that work on all major PC operating systems.

SyTOS has been selected by IBM as the standard software for its units. Because of market pressures to be compatible with IBM, Compaq and other system and tape-drive vendors are offering SyTOS with their tape systems. Because two systems that use the same media, interface, and software can read and write each other's tapes, you can have data interchangeability among different tape-unit manufacturers. You should consider using a system that runs SyTOS software for those reasons. Of course, the proprietary software is generally just as good, if not better. You can exchange data tapes only with other users of the same systems.

All software should be capable of certain basic operations. Make sure that your software does what you want, and consider buying only software that has these features:

- Can back up an entire DOS partition (full volume backup)
- Can back up any or all files individually (file-by-file backup)
- Allows a selective file-by-file restore from a volume backup as well as a file-by-file backup
- Can combine several backups on a single tape
- Can run the software as commands from DOS BATCH files
- Works under a network
- Can span a large drive on multiple tapes
- Can be completely verified

If the software you are considering does not have any of these essential features, look for another system.

Physical Location: Internal or External. Physical location of the tape-backup units is a simple factor often not considered in detail. I almost never recommend any tape-backup unit mounted internally in a system unit. I recommend that you buy a tape unit externally mounted in its own chassis and one that connects to the system unit through a cable and connectors.

Tape units are relatively expensive, and I never want to tie up a backup unit for only one system. The amount of time that just one system spends using the unit makes this proposition wasteful. With an external unit, many systems can share the backup unit. I just equip every system unit with the required interface, if they aren't already equipped. Extra QIC-02 cards are available for about $100 each, and SCSI host adapters are about $200. Note that many systems now include a SCSI host adapter as part of the mother-board, or as a card already installed. I already share my system among more than five computers and will continue adding systems to the backup pool. In some companies, the backup unit is mounted on a wheeled cart so that workers easily can move it from com-puter to computer.

If you have only one system or if all your data is stored in a single file-server system, you might have a legitimate argument for using an internal tape drive. You might wish that you had an external system, however, on the day a new system arrives, or when the server is down and you have to get a new one up and running.

Recommended Backup System

Although a variety of backup systems are available, I recommend units from any manu-facturer that meets these requirements:

> Type of media: DC-2000, DC-600, 4mm DAT, or 8mm

> Hardware interface: QIC-02, Parallel Port or SCSI

My preferences lean towards the 4mm DAT drives because of their high capacity (4G plus with built-in data compression) and relatively high performance. Also, the media cost is very low, around $15 per cartridge. DAT devices almost always use a SCSI interface, which means you would need a SCSI host adapter installed in the system. This could be either a standard type of SCSI host adapter in a slot (or integrated into the motherboard of some systems), or for a lower cost portable solution, you could run the SCSI DAT drive from a parallel port with one of the parallel to SCSI adapters like those from Trantor. The parallel port adapters make it easy to use a single external DAT drive to back up a variety of systems.

Purchasing Warranty and Service Contracts

Extended warranties are a recent trend in the computer industry. With the current fierce competition among hardware vendors, a good warranty is one way for a specific manu-facturer to stand out from the crowd. Although most companies offer a one year war-ranty on their systems, others offer longer warranty periods, such as two years or more.

In addition to extended-length warranties, some manufacturers offer free or nearly free on-site service during the warranty period. Many highly competitive mail-order outfits

V

Assembly & Maintenance

offer service such as this for little or no extra cost. Even IBM has succumbed to market pressure to lower service costs, and has an option for converting the standard one year warranty into a full-blown, on-site service contract for only $40. This same option can be extended to cover monitors and printers for only a small additional cost.

Tip

IBM and other companies are beginning to offer extended-length warranties and free or low-cost on-site service. IBM has a somewhat unknown option to upgrade the standard one year warranties on its PS/2 systems into a full-blown, on-site service contract. Under this option, you can upgrade the standard Customer Carry-in Repair warranty to an IBM On-site Repair warranty for only $40 for the first year.

If you have only the carry-in warranty, as its name implies you must carry in your computer to a depot for service; with the on-site warranty, the service technician comes to you. One car trip to a service center costs me more than $40 in wasted gasoline and time. I gladly pay the fee to have the service technician come to see me. Be sure to ask for this option when you buy your system. If your dealer is unfamiliar with it, ask that your order include IBM feature code #9805.

In most normal cases, service contracts are not worth the price. In the retail computer environment, a service contract is often a way for a dealer or vendor to add income to a sale. Most annual service contracts add 10 to 15 percent of the cost of the system. A service contract for a $5,000 system, for example, *costs $500 to $750 per year.* Salespeople in most organizations are trained to vigorously sell service contracts. Much like in the automobile sales business, these contracts are largely unnecessary except in special situations.

The high prices of service contracts also might affect the quality of service you receive. Technicians could try to make their work seem more complex than it actually is to make you believe that the contract's price is justified. For example, a service technician might replace your hard disk or entire motherboard with a spare when all you need is low-level formatting for the hard disk or a simple fix for the motherboard such as a single memory chip. A "defective" drive, for example, probably is just returned to the shop for low-level formatting. Eventually, it ends up in somebody else's system. Replacing a part is faster and leaves the impression that your expensive service contract is worth the price because you get a "new" part. You might be much less impressed with your expensive service contract if the service people visit, do a simple troubleshooting procedure, and then replace a single $2 memory chip or spend 15 minutes reformatting the hard disk.

With some basic troubleshooting skills, some simple tools, and a few spare parts, you can eliminate the need for most of these expensive service contracts. Unfortunately, some companies practice deceptive servicing procedures to justify the expensive service contracts they offer. Users are made to believe that these types of component failures are the norm, and they have a mistaken impression about the overall reliability of today's systems.

> **Tip**
>
> If you have many systems, you can justify carrying a spare-parts inventory, which can also eliminate the need for a service contract. For less than what a service contract costs for five to ten systems, you often can buy a complete spare system each year. Protecting yourself with extra equipment rather than service contracts is practical if you have more than ten computers of the same make or model. For extremely time-sensitive applications, you might be wise to buy a second system along with the primary unit—such as in a network file-server application. Only you can make the appropriate cost-justification analysis to decide whether you need a service contract or a spare system.

In some instances, buying a service contract can be justified and beneficial. If you have a system that must function at all times and is so expensive that you cannot buy a complete spare system, or for a system in a remote location far away from a centralized service operation, you might be wise to invest in a good service contract that provides timely repairs. Before contracting for service, you should consider your options carefully. These sources either supply or authorize service contracts:

■ Manufacturers

■ Dealers or vendors

■ Third parties

Although most users take the manufacturer or dealer service, sometimes a third-party tries harder to close the deal; for example, it sometimes includes all the equipment installed, even aftermarket items the dealers or manufacturers don't offer. In other cases, a manufacturer might not have its own service organization; instead, it makes a deal with a major third-party nationwide service company to provide authorized service.

After you select an organization, several levels of service often are available. Starting with the most expensive, these levels of service typically include:

■ Four-hour on-site response

■ Next-day on-site response

■ Courier service (a service company picks up and returns a unit)

■ Carry-in, or "depot," service

The actual menu varies from manufacturer to manufacturer. For example, IBM offers only a full 24-hours-a-day, 7-days-a-week, on-site service contract. IBM claims that a technician is dispatched usually within four hours of your call. For older systems, but not the PS/2, IBM also offers a courier or carry-in service contract. Warranty work, normally a customer carry-in depot arrangement, can be upgraded to a full on-site contract for only $40. After the first-year $40 contract upgrade expires, you can continue the full on-site service contract for standard rates. Table 18.2 lists the rates for IBM service contracts after the warranty has expired.

Table 18.2   PS/2 Service-Contract Fees after Warranty for Annual IBM On-Site Repair (IOR) Service

PS/2 Model	Contract	PS/2 Model	Contract
8525-x01/x02	$95	8570-0x1/1x1	$450
8525-x04/x05	$110	8570-Axx	595
8525-x06/x36	$210	8570-Bx1	645
8530-001	$190	8573-031/061	385
8530-002	$140	8573-121	385
8530-021	$190	8573-161	750
8530-E01/E21	$190	8573-401	850
8530-E31/E41	$190	8580-041	360
8535-all	$260	8580-071	425
8540-all	$400	8580-081	550
8543-044	$430	8580-111/121	500
8550-021	$220	8580-161	600
8550-031/061	$220	8580-311	575
8555-0x1	$260	8580-321	605
8555-LT0/LE0	$260	8580-A21	675
8557-045/049	$400	8580-A16/A31	785
8560-041	$310	8590-0G5/0G9	800
8560-071	$345	8590-0J5/0J9	850
8565-061	$425	8590-0KD	950
8565-121	$475	8595-0G9/0GF	1,400
8565-321	$550	8595-0Jx	1,450
8570-E61	$415	8595-0Kx	1,550

If you have bought a service contract in the past, these prices might surprise you. With the PS/2 systems, IBM has rewritten the rules for PC servicing. The same type of on-site annual contract for an earlier 20M AT system, for example, costs nearly $600 annually, compared with $220 for the PS/2 Model 50. Smaller third-party service companies are having difficulty competing with these newer prices. IBM claims that the PS/2 systems are five times more reliable than the earlier systems, and the service-contract pricing is about one-third what the earlier systems cost. If the claims of additional reliability are true, IBM is doing well even with lower pricing. If the claims are not true (which is unlikely), then IBM would be losing money on its service contracts.

> **Tip**
>
> In summary, for most standard systems, a service contract beyond what is included with the original warranty is probably a waste of money. For other systems that have not yet achieved commodity status, or for systems that must be up and running at all times, you might want to investigate a service-contract option, even though you might be fully qualified and capable of servicing the system.
>
> The PS/2 systems are a somewhat special case; they have low-priced, on-site warranty upgrades and fairly inexpensive service contracts compared to the costs of the systems. Remember, however, that you can buy most, if not all, parts for these systems from non-IBM sources; also, third-party companies that specialize in difficult items such as motherboards and power supplies can repair these items. Only after carefully weighing every option and cost involved can you decide how your systems should be serviced.

Summary

This chapter has presented the steps you can take to ensure proper operation of your system. It has examined active and passive preventive maintenance—the key to a system that gives many years of trouble-free service. You have learned about the procedures involved in preventive maintenance and the frequency with which these procedures should be performed.

Backup was discussed as a way to be prepared when things go wrong. The only guarantee for being able to retrieve data is to back it up. In this chapter, you also have learned about backup options.

Finally, you have learned about the commonly available warranty and service contracts provided by computer manufacturers. Sometimes the contracts can save you from worrying about tough-to-service systems or systems whose parts are largely unavailable on short notice.

V

Assembly & Maintenance

Part VI

Troubleshooting Hardware and Software Problems

19 Software and Hardware Diagnostic Tools

20 Operating Systems Software and Troubleshooting

Chapter 19

Software and Hardware Diagnostic Tools

Diagnostic software, the kind that comes with your computer as well as the types of available third-party software, is vitally important to you any time your computer malfunctions or you begin the process of upgrading a system component or adding a new device. Even when you attempt a simple procedure, such as adding a new adapter card, or begin the sometimes tedious process of troubleshooting a hardware problem that causes a system crash or lockup when you are working, you need to know more about your system than you can learn from the packing list sent with the system. Diagnostic software provides the portal through which you can examine your system hardware and the way your components are working.

This chapter describes three levels of diagnostic software (POST, system, and advanced) included with many computers, or available from your computer manufacturer. The chapter describes how you can get the most from this software. The chapter also details IBM's audio codes and error codes, which are similar to the error codes used by most computer manufacturers, and examines aftermarket diagnostics and public-domain diagnostic software.

Diagnostic Software

Several types of diagnostic software are available for IBM-compatible PCs, as well as the IBM PC, XT, AT, and PS/2. This software, some of which is included with the system when purchased, assists users in identifying many problems that can occur with a computer's components. In many cases, these programs can do most of the work in determining which PC component is defective. Three programs that can help you locate a problem are available; each program is more complex and powerful than the preceding one. The diagnostic programs include the following three items:

- *POST*. The Power-On Self Test operates whenever any PC is powered up (switched on).

- *General diagnostic software.* A suite of tests that thoroughly examines the system. IBM's general diagnostic software is on the diagnostics disk. Its accompanying problem-determination procedures are outlined in the guide-to-operations manual for each system. Many IBM-compatible systems come with their own manufacturer's version of this diagnostic software. Dell, for example, includes a diagnostics disk with each system.

- *Advanced diagnostic software.* This is included with IBM OS/2 systems in the hardware-maintenance service manual, but rarely included with other IBM systems or most IBM-compatible systems. However, the Advanced Diagnostics disk can be obtained from IBM for PC/XT and AT-type systems. To help IBM-compatible users fill this diagnostic software gap, this chapter covers software utilities such as Symantic's Norton Utilities 8, which provides detailed diagnostics of any IBM-compatible PC systems. The chapter also covers software from numerous other companies.

Many computer operators use the first and last of these software systems to test and troubleshoot most systems—the POST tests and either the IBM advanced diagnostic software or a third-party diagnostic package.

The IBM Advanced Diagnostics disk is included with the hardware-maintenance service manual. The manual and disk, along with the accompanying hardware-maintenance reference and assorted updates to both manuals, cost more than $400. Although this price might seem expensive, anyone supporting more than just a single IBM PC system quickly can recoup the expense in labor costs saved and avoid the trouble of carry-in service. Appendix A includes a catalog of these manuals.

Although the IBM service manuals are expensive, they are complete and represent the definitive work on the subject. Unlike many computer manufacturers, IBM provides truly in-depth system documentation. Indeed, this documentation is one of the primary reasons for the success of the IBM systems as the industry standard.

The Power-On Self Test (POST)

When IBM first began shipping the IBM PC in 1981, it included safety features that had never been seen in a personal computer. These features were the POST and parity-checked memory. The parity-checking feature is explained in Chapter 7, "Memory." The following sections provide much more detail on the POST, a series of program routines buried in the motherboard ROM-BIOS chip that tests all the main system components at power-on time. This program series causes the delay when you turn on an IBM-compatible system; the POST is executed before the computer loads the operating system.

What Is Tested?
Whenever you start up your computer, the computer automatically performs a series of tests that checks various components—the primary components—in your system.

Items such as the CPU, ROM, motherboard support circuitry, memory, and major peripherals (such as an expansion chassis) are tested. These tests are brief and not very thorough compared with available disk-based diagnostics. The POST process provides error or warning messages whenever a faulty component is encountered.

Although the diagnostics performed by the system POST are not always very thorough, they are the first line of defense, especially in handling severe motherboard problems. If the POST encounters a problem severe enough to keep the system from operating properly, it halts bootup of the system and produces an error message that often leads you directly to the cause of the problem. Such POST-detected problems are sometimes called *fatal errors*. The POST tests normally provide three types of output messages: audio codes, display-screen messages, and hexadecimal numeric codes to an I/O port address.

POST Audio Error Codes

POST audio error codes usually are audio codes consisting of a number of beeps that identifies the faulty component. If your computer is functioning normally, you hear one short beep when the system starts up. If a problem is detected, a different number of beeps sounds—sometimes in a combination of short and long beeps. These BIOS-dependent codes can vary among different BIOS manufacturers. Table 19.1 lists the beep codes for IBM systems and the problem indicated by each series of beeps.

Table 19.1	IBM POST Audio Error Codes and Indicated Problem	
Audio Code	**Sound**	**Problem (Fault domain)**
1 short beep	.	Normal POST-system OK
2 short beeps	..	POST error-error code
No beep		Power supply, system board
Continuous beep	——————	Power supply, system board
Repeating short beeps	......	Power supply, system board
One long, one short beep	-.	System board
One long, two short beeps	-..	Display adapter (MDA, CGA)
One long, three short beeps	-...	Enhanced Graphics Adapter (EGA)
Three long beeps	- - -	3270 keyboard card

. = short beep
- = long beep

Appendix A in this book lists the audio POST codes for the AMI BIOS and Phoenix BIOS, both of which have a much more detailed set of audio error codes than IBM's, which are much more helpful in diagnosing problems with a system motherboard. In particular, the Phoenix BIOS POST is so well done that many times I do not need to use any other diagnostics to isolate a problem—the BIOS does it for me. The sophisticated POST procedure is one of the reasons I like the Phoenix BIOS.

POST Visual Error Codes

On the XT, AT, PS/2, and most compatibles, the POST also displays on the system monitor the test of system memory. The last number displayed is the amount of memory that tested properly. For example, an XT might display the following:

```
640K OK
```

The number displayed by the memory test should agree with the total amount of memory installed on your system motherboard, including conventional and extended memory. On a system with 32M of memory, the POST displays 32768KB OK. The RAM on an expanded memory card is not tested by the POST and does not count in the numbers reported. However, if you are using an expanded memory driver such as EMM386.EXE or Quarterdeck's QEMM to configure extended memory installed on the motherboard as expanded, the POST executes before this driver is loaded so that all installed memory is counted. If the POST memory test stops short of the expected total, then the number displayed often indicates how far into system memory a memory error lies. This number alone is a valuable troubleshooting aid.

If an error is detected during the POST procedures, an error message is displayed on-screen. These messages usually are in the form of a numeric code several digits long; for example, 1790-Disk 0 Error. The information in the hardware-maintenance service manual identifies the malfunctioning component. I have researched all available IBM documentation and have included an abbreviated list of the on-screen error codes in this chapter, as well as a complete list in Appendix A. By looking in the error-code chart in Appendix A, you can see that a 1790 error code indicates a read error on the diagnostics cylinder for hard disk drive 0.

I/O Port POST Codes

A less-well-known feature of the POST is that at the beginning of each POST, the BIOS sends test codes to a special I/O port address. These POST codes can be read only by a special adapter card plugged into one of the system slots. These cards originally were designed to be used by the system manufacturers for burn-in testing of the motherboard during system manufacturing without the need for a video display adapter or display. Several companies now make these cards available to technicians. Micro 2000, Landmark, JDR Microdevices, Data Depot, Ultra-X, and MicroSystems Development (MSD) are just a few manufacturers of these POST cards.

When one of these adapter cards is plugged into a slot, during the POST you see two-digit hexadecimal numbers flash on a display on the card. If the system stops unexpectedly or hangs, you can just look at the two-digit display on the card for the code indicating the test in progress during the hang. This step usually identifies the failed part. A complete list of these POST codes is in Appendix A; the list covers several different manufacturers' BIOS, including IBM, AMI, Award, and Phoenix.

Most BIOS on the market that are in systems with an ISA or EISA bus output the POST codes to I/O port address 80h. Compaq is different; its systems send codes to port 84h. IBM PS/2 models with ISA bus slots, such as the Model 25 and 30, send codes to port 90h. Some EISA systems send codes to port 300h (most EISA systems also send the same codes to 80h). IBM MCA bus systems universally send codes to port 680h.

Several cards read only port address 80h. This port address is certainly the most commonly used and works in most situations, but the cards do not work in Compaq systems, some EISA systems, and IBM PS/2 systems. A POST card designed specifically for the PS/2 MCA bus needs to read only port address 680h because the card cannot be used in ISA or EISA bus systems anyway. With all these different addresses, make sure that the card you purchase reads the port addresses you need.

The two most common types of POST cards are those that plug into the 8-bit connector that is a part of the ISA or EISA bus, and those that plug into the MCA bus. Some companies offer both types of POST cards—one for MCA bus systems and one for ISA/EISA bus systems. Micro 2000 does not offer a separate card; rather, it includes with its POST Probe card a unique slot adapter that enables the card to work in MCA bus systems as well as in ISA and EISA systems. Most other companies offer only ISA/EISA POST cards and ignore the MCA bus.

To read a port address, a POST card needs to have only an 8-bit design; it does not have to be a 16-bit or 32-bit card. At least one manufacturer sells a separate EISA card that it claims is designed specifically for the EISA bus. However, because the EISA bus was designed to enable the use of 8-bit and 16-bit ISA adapter cards as well as 32-bit EISA cards, and only the 8-bit portion of the ISA bus is needed to read the required port addresses, it is unnecessary to have a separate card specific to EISA bus systems. As long as an ISA card is properly designed to latch the correct port addresses, there is no reason for it not to function perfectly in both ISA and EISA bus systems. There is absolutely no need for this separate (and expensive) EISA card.

POST-code cards are invaluable in diagnosing systems where the motherboard seems dead even though the power supply comes on (you can hear the fan). Just pop the card into a slot and observe the code on the card's display. Then look up the code in a list corresponding to the specific BIOS on the motherboard. These cards also can be very helpful with tough problems such as a memory-bit failure in Bank 0, which does not allow error codes to be displayed on a CRT in most EGA or VGA systems.

An important feature that separates the many POST cards on the market is that some provide extensive documentation of different BIOS, and others do not. Each computer manufacturer's BIOS runs different tests in a different sequence and even outputs different code numbers for the same tests. Therefore, without the proper documentation specific to the BIOS on the motherboard you are testing, the numbers shown on the POST card are meaningless.

The documentation supplied with the Micro 2000, Landmark, Data Depot, and Ultra-X cards offers excellent information covering a wide variety of different BIOS manufacturers' codes. One company, MicroSystems Development (MSD) supplies its POST Card documentation both in printed form and on a disk with a built-in POST code lookup program. This method is unique and desirable especially if you carry a laptop or portable system with you when you troubleshoot. The JDR Microdevices card offers less than most of the others in the way of documentation, but is also the least expensive card by a wide margin. Another thing that distinguishes the JDR card is that it is designed to be left in a system permanently. The two-digit display can be moved to the back bracket of the card so that it can be read outside the system. There is also a connector for an external two-digit display. The other cards have the display on the card only, which is impossible to read unless you open the system case.

Some cards have additional features worth mentioning. The Micro 2000 card (called the POST Probe) includes a built-in logic probe for testing signals on the major motherboard components. The POST Probe includes a series of separate LED readouts for several important bus signals as well as power-supply voltage levels. The separate LEDs enable these bus signals to be monitored simultaneously. Sometimes you can help to determine the cause of a failure by noting which bus LED is lit at a certain time. The power-supply LEDs verify the output of the +5, -5, +12, and -12 volt signals from the supply. Another feature is meter-probe attachment points on which you can easily connect a voltmeter to the card for more accurate measurements.

The Micro 2000 POST Probe is the only one that functions in every system on the market. The basic card functions in all ISA bus and EISA bus systems because of its capability to monitor all port addresses used for BIOS test codes. As mentioned, this card includes a unique adapter that enables it to function in MCA bus systems as well. The extensive documentation not only covers the expected POST codes for different BIOS versions, but also includes a detailed reference to the bus signals monitored by the card. A reference in the documentation enables even novices to use the included logic probe for some more-sophisticated motherboard tests. This card offers more features than others on the market.

The Data Depot Pocket POST is a unique card that includes an LED for monitoring bus signals. It can monitor a single signal at a time, which is selected by a jumper. The card includes LEDs for testing power-supply voltage levels and includes attachment points for a voltmeter as well. The Pocket POST is designed for ISA and EISA bus systems and can connect to any port addresses used in these systems for POST codes. As its name suggests, the card is small compared to most others, and therefore is easy to carry around. The entire package, including the comprehensive manual, fits in a standard (included) floppy disk case.

Ultra-X has two cards: the Quick-POST PC for ISA/EISA bus systems and the Quick-POST PS/2 for MCA bus systems. Because the Quick-POST cards monitor only one port address each—80h for the PC card and 680h for the PS/2 card—the ISA/EISA version is less flexible than some others. The included documentation is excellent and covers a variety of BIOS versions. Both cards also include LEDs used to monitor power-supply voltages.

As mentioned, the MicroSystems Development (MSD) card is unique because of its on-disk documentation. A printed manual is supplied also. This POST Code Master is capable of monitoring either port address 80h or 84h. It also includes voltage-test LEDS for checking the power supply.

A second type of diagnostics card goes beyond the function of a basic POST-code card. In addition to monitoring POST codes, these cards include an on-board ROM chip that contains a more sophisticated diagnostics program than the suite of tests in the motherboard ROM BIOS. Among the cards that offer this function are the Kickstart II card by Landmark and the RACER II card by Ultra-X. Both cards monitor POST codes as well as use their own on-board ROM-based diagnostics program. Because of the extra expense of having these programs and other options on-board, the cards are more expensive than the standard POST-code cards.

Although a higher-level diagnostics card can be handy, I normally do not recommend them because the standard POST-code cards provide 95 percent of the capabilities of these cards with no BIOS conflicts or other problems. In many cases, before you can use a higher-level diagnostics card, other adapters must be removed from the system to eliminate conflicts with ROMs on other cards. Although these cards are quite capable and function as a basic POST-code card if necessary, I find it more valuable to spend the extra money on a disk-based diagnostics program and stick to the basic POST-code cards. This way, I get the most functionality for my money.

IBM Diagnostics

IBM systems usually have two levels of diagnostics software. One is a general purpose diagnostics that is more user-oriented, and the second is a technician-level program that can be somewhat cryptic at times. In many cases, both of these programs are provided free with the system when it is purchased, and in some cases, the diagnostics and documentation have to be purchased separately. Since the troubleshooting procedures for most systems these days are fairly simple, most people have no problems running the diagnostics software without any official documentation. IBM runs a BBS system that has virtually all of its general and advanced diagnostics available free for downloading. You can find the number for this BBS in Appendix B. The following sections discuss the IBM diagnostics.

IBM System Diagnostics

Every IBM computer comes with a Guide To Operations (GTO) or Quick Reference manual. The GTO manual is in a reddish-purple binder; it includes a diagnostics disk to assist you in identifying problems. PS/2 computers are supplied with a much smaller quick-reference guide that includes a reference disk. The disk contains both the regular and advanced diagnostics, as well as the normal SETUP program.

The diagnostics disk and corresponding manual provide step-by-step instructions for testing various parts of the computer system, including the system unit and many installed options, such as the expansion unit, keyboard, display, and printer. Unfortunately, these diagnostics are a crippled version of the much more powerful advanced diagnostics IBM sells. Intended for use by customers who are not particularly technically oriented, the GTO diagnostics are lacking in many respects. For example, the tests cannot be run individually; whenever you start the tests you must always run all of them.

Many compatible-system vendors do not segregate the diagnostics software like IBM does; many include an advanced-type diagnostics disk free with the system. For example, AST includes its diagnostics program, called ASTute, free with every system. This program is similar to the IBM Advanced Diagnostics.

Before running the GTO tests, you must boot from the IBM diagnostics disk because a special version of DOS resides on the diagnostics disk. This DOS version suppresses memory parity checking during the boot process. Disabling parity checking might enable a defective system to limp through the diagnostics in a case where the system continually locks up with a parity-check error message. After the disk is loaded, the main diagnostics menu is displayed. The opening menu looks something like the following:

```
The IBM Personal Computer
DIAGNOSTICS
Version 2.06
Copyright IBM Corp. 1981,1986

SELECT AN OPTION
0 - SYSTEM CHECKOUT
1 - FORMAT DISKETTE
2 - COPY DISKETTE
3 - PREPARE SYSTEM FOR MOVING
4 - SETUP
9 - END DIAGNOSTICS
SELECT THE ACTION DESIRED
?
```

Options 0, 1, and 2 on the IBM diagnostics screen are part of the diagnostics procedures. These options, as well as options 3, 4, and 9, are detailed in the following paragraphs:

- *Option 0.* This option is used for general testing. When this option is selected, the diagnostics software loads from the disk various modules that perform a presence test to see whether the device to which the module corresponds is in the system. The option presents a list of installed devices, and you are asked whether the list is correct.

- *Option 1.* This option formats a disk with a special format to create a special scratch disk used by the diagnostics program when it is running tests on your system. The format is different from a normal DOS format and should not be used to format disks for normal use under DOS. Among other things, differences exist in the construction of the boot sector of the diagnostics scratch disk and a normal DOS disk.

- *Option 2.* Used to copy a disk, Option 2 creates a mirror-image copy of a disk using the same process as the DOS DISKCOPY command. This option is intended for copying the diagnostics disk that is used to boot your system before you run the GTO tests. (The diagnostics disk includes system files that enable the computer to boot without the presence of DOS.) The original diagnostics disk should not be used for testing. Instead, use a copy and place the original in a safe location.

The diagnostics disks can be copied by using DISKCOPY or a similar utility because these disks are not copy-protected, enabling you to make proper backups and keep the master disks safe.

- *Option 3.* This option is used to park, or secure, the heads on a hard disk so that the system unit can be moved safely without damaging the disk or its contents.

- *Option 4.* Present only on the AT version of the diagnostics, this option is used on the AT to identify installed options when you first set up your system.

- *Option 9.* This option is used to quit the diagnostics software and restart your system. You must remove the diagnostics disk from your floppy drive.

For several reasons, the list of installed devices does not always match the actual system configuration. The way the tests are designed, an installed device appears in the list only if a software module is included on the disk that can be used to test the device. For example, the IBM Token Ring network adapter does not appear in the list of installed devices even if you have this network card installed. This is because the diagnostics disk does not contain a module for testing an IBM Token Ring network adapter installed in your system. IBM provides a separate diagnostics program on a separate disk for this adapter.

Most standard devices should show up on the list, however, even if the particular device was not made by IBM. Your hard disk controller should show up, as should your video board, serial and parallel ports, conventional and extended memory, floppy drives, and motherboard. If you purchase a newer type of expansion item, such as a VGA graphics card, the diagnostics might instead identify this board as an EGA board, if the VGA testing module is not present on the disk. Because modules are not available for most expanded-memory boards, these boards almost never appear on the list, with the exception of IBM's XMA card. Nonstandard communications boards (boards containing other than normal serial or parallel ports) normally are not listed either.

If an installed device does not appear in the list and you know that the diagnostics software normally would find it, then it is safe to assume that the device is configured incorrectly or has a serious problem. In such a case, signify that the list is incorrect by answering No when you are asked whether the installed device list is correct. Then add the item to the list. If an item appears that is not installed, use the same procedure to remove the item from the list. This list represents all the tests that can be run; the only way you can test an item is to have it appear on this list.

After going through the installed-devices list, you see another menu, similar to this one:

```
0 - RUN TESTS ONE TIME
1 - RUN TESTS MULTIPLE TIMES
2 - LOG UTILITIES
3 - END SYSTEM CHECKOUT
```

Select Option 0 to test the devices installed in the system. Option 1 enables you to test these devices repetitively, as many times as you want, or forever. The forever option is handy because it enables you to run the diagnostics continuously overnight or over a weekend to find particularly troublesome problems. This method can be an easy way to identify the cause of an intermittent problem. To record errors that occur while you're not present, you first select Option 2, which can be used to set up an error log. The log records the date, time, and error message to a floppy disk or printer so that you can review them at a later time.

If an error occurs while these tests are running, a numerical error message appears along with the date and time. These numbers, listed in this chapter and in Appendix A, follow the same conventions as the numbers displayed by the POST, and are the same numbers in some cases. The diagnostic tests usually are much more powerful than the tests run in the POST.

Although the diagnostics do an excellent job of identifying specific problem areas or problem components, they provide limited assistance in telling you how to correct the cause of the errors. Little documentation is provided with these diagnostics; and, in fact, most often the advice provided on solving any problem is to have your system or the problem device serviced, which, if you want to service the system yourself, is akin to no advice at all. These diagnostics are a crippled version of the real diagnostics, which are part of the *Hardware Maintenance Service Manual*. If you plan to troubleshoot or upgrade your own system, or if you plan to administer a number of PCs, you should be using the advanced diagnostics; they are the diagnostics to which the remainder of this book refers.

IBM Advanced Diagnostics

For technician-level diagnostics, IBM sells hardware-maintenance and service manuals for each system, which include the Advanced Diagnostics disks for that system. These disks contain the real diagnostics programs and, combined with the hardware-maintenance service manuals, represent the de facto standard diagnostics information and software for IBM and compatible systems. For PS/2 machines, IBM includes the Advanced Diagnostics on the Reference Disk that comes with the system; however, the instructions for using the diagnostics are still found in the separately available service manuals.

If you need a copy of the Advanced Diagnostics for any IBM system, check the IBM National Support Center (NSC) Bulletin Board System (BBS). The IBM BBS has virtually all of the IBM Advanced Diagnostics and Reference Disks available for download at no charge! They are stored on the BBS in a compressed disk image format, and you will need one of two utilities to uncompress the file depending on how it was originally compressed. Follow the instructions presented on-line for more information on which uncompress program you need. The phone number for the IBM NSC BBS is listed in Appendix B under the IBM PC Company.

These programs produce error messages in the form of numbers you can use to identify the cause of a wide range of problems. The number codes used are the same as those used in the POST and general-diagnostics software. The meaning of the numbers is consistent across all IBM diagnostic programs. This section explores the Advanced Diagnostics and lists most of the known error-code meanings. IBM constantly adds to this error-code list as it introduces new equipment.

Using IBM Advanced Diagnostics. If you have a PS/2 system with the MCA (Micro Channel Architecture) bus slots (models produced later than the Models 25 to 40), you may already have IBM's Advanced Diagnostics, even if you don't know it. These diagnostics are usually hidden on the PS/2 Reference Disk. To access these diagnostics, boot the PS/2 Reference Disk. When the main menu is displayed, press Ctrl-A (for Advanced). The program changes to the Advanced Diagnostics menu. In some of the PS/2 systems, the Advanced Diagnostics were large enough to require a separate disk or disks. All of the PS/2 Reference and Diagnostics disks are available for downloading on the IBM NSC BBS (see Appendix B).

Hiding Advanced Diagnostics from average users is probably a good idea. For example, inexperienced users can easily wipe out all of their data by using this disk's option of low-level formatting the hard disk.

The PS/2 service manuals are fairly skimpy because the average PS/2 system doesn't have that many parts, and they are easy to repair. One drawback of the PS/2 service manuals is that they often end a troubleshooting session with this advice: Replace the system board. Although I recommend the hardware-maintenance and service manuals, if all you are looking for is the Advanced Diagnostics software (and you have a PS/2 system with the MCA bus), you already have it and do not need to purchase any additional items.

Non-MCA systems, such as the PS/2 25 to 40 systems, come with a Starter Disk, equivalent to the Setup and Diagnostics Disk that came with the original AT system. This Starter Disk includes the Setup program and limited diagnostics that lack many functions found in the Advanced Diagnostics. You get the Advanced Diagnostics for these systems included with the PS/2 *Hardware Maintenance and Service* (HMS) *Manual*, which includes the Advanced Diagnostics disks for Models 25, 30, and 30-286. If you want the diagnostics for later systems, such as Models 35 or 40, you must purchase the respective update package for the PS/2 HMS manual. These updates usually cost about $30. If all you need are the Advanced Diagnostics disks, they can be downloaded at no charge from the IBM NSC BBS (see the vendor list).

If you really want in-depth information about troubleshooting your system, you can purchase the IBM *Hardware Maintenance Service Manual*. This single book covers the earlier IBM systems, including the PC, XT, and AT. Updates cover the XT-286 and PS/2 Models 25 and 30. Later PS/2 systems have their own separate version of this book, called *PS/2 Hardware Maintenance and Service*. This book includes spare copies of the standard reference disks. The newer versions of the PS/2 book now cover also all PS/2 systems, those with ISA (Industry Standard Architecture) as well as MCA (Micro Channel Architecture) slots.

Although the guide-to-operations manual is good only for identifying a problem component, the HMS manual provides information for you to more accurately isolate and repair the failure of any field-replaceable unit (FRU).

The HMS manual includes an Advanced Diagnostics disk as well as provides maintenance-analysis procedures (MAPs), which are instructions to help you isolate and identify problem components. To run the advanced diagnostics tests, follow the procedures detailed in this section.

VI

Troubleshooting

After booting the Advanced Diagnostics disk for your particular system (PC or AT), a menu similar to this one appears:

```
The IBM Personal Computer
ADVANCED DIAGNOSTICS
Version 2.07
Copyright IBM Corp. 1981,1986

ROS P/N: 78X7462
ROS DATE: 04/21/86

SELECT AN OPTION

0 - SYSTEM CHECKOUT
1 - FORMAT DISKETTE
2 - COPY DISKETTE
3 - PREPARE SYSTEM FOR MOVING
4 - SETUP

9 - END DIAGNOSTICS

SELECT THE ACTION DESIRED

?
```

Note

If you are using the PC version, the fourth item is not displayed because PC systems do not have CMOS Setup memory.

The Advanced Diagnostics disks show the date of the ROM as well as the IBM part number for the particular chips in your system. The screen shows this information near the top as ROS (read-only software). The 04/21/86 date identifies the version of the ROM in this example. The date indicates an IBM XT Model 286. The part number, read directly from the ROM, is academic information because IBM does not sell the ROM chips separately—only with a complete motherboard swap.

After you select Option 0, which invokes the diagnostic routines, each module on the disk loads and executes a presence test to determine whether the applicable piece of hardware is truly in the system. In this example, the result looks like this:

```
THE INSTALLED DEVICES ARE

1 - SYSTEM BOARD
2 - 2688KB MEMORY
3 - KEYBOARD
6 - 2 DISKETTE DRIVE(S) AND ADAPTER
7 - MATH COPROCESSOR
9 - SERIAL/PARALLEL ADAPTER
9 - - PARALLEL PORT
11 - SERIAL/PARALLEL ADAPTER
11 - - SERIAL PORT
```

```
17 - 1 FIXED DISK DRIVE(S) AND ADAPTER
74 - PERSONAL SYSTEM/2 DISPLAY ADAPTER

IS THE LIST CORRECT (Y/N)

?
```

You then answer Yes or No depending on the accuracy of the list. Remember that not everything appears on this list. An IBM Token Ring network adapter never appears on this list because no software module designed for that option is present on the disk. The following list contains all items that could appear on the list as of version 2.07 of these diagnostics. This list is different for other versions.

```
 1  SYSTEM BOARD
 2  MEMORY
 3  KEYBOARD
 4  MONOCHROME & PRINTER ADAPTER
 5  COLOR/GRAPHICS MONITOR ADAPTER
 6  DISKETTE DRIVE(S)
 7  MATH COPROCESSOR
 9  SERIAL/PARALLEL ADAPTER - PARALLEL PORT
10  ALTERNATE SERIAL/PARALLEL ADAPTER - PARALLEL PORT
11  SERIAL/PARALLEL ADAPTER - SERIAL PORT
12  ALTERNATE SERIAL/PARALLEL ADAPTER - SERIAL PORT
13  GAME CONTROL ADAPTER
14  MATRIX PRINTER
15  SDLC COMMUNICATIONS ADAPTER
17  FIXED DISK DRIVE(S) AND ADAPTER
20  BSC COMMUNICATIONS ADAPTER
21  ALT BSC COMMUNICATIONS ADAPTER
22  CLUSTER ADAPTER(S)
24  ENHANCED GRAPHICS ADAPTER
29  COLOR PRINTER
30  PC NETWORK ADAPTER
31  ALT. PC NETWORK ADAPTER
36  GPIB ADAPTER(S)
38  DATA ACQUISITION ADAPTER(S)
39  PROFESSIONAL GRAPHICS CONTROLLER
71  VOICE COMMUNICATIONS ADAPTER
73  3.5" EXTERNAL DISKETTE DRIVE AND ADAPTER
74  PERSONAL SYSTEM/2 DISPLAY ADAPTER
85  EXPANDED MEMORY ADAPTER - 2 MB -
89  MUSIC FEATURE CARD(S)
```

After certifying that the list is correct, or adding or deleting items as necessary to make it correct, you can begin testing each item listed.

The tests performed by the Advanced Diagnostics disk are far more detailed and precise than the tests on the general diagnostics disk in the GTO. In addition to identifying the problem component, the Advanced Diagnostics further attempt to identify the specific malfunctioning part of the device.

After a problem is identified, the HMS manual provides detailed instructions for performing adjustments, preventive maintenance, and removal and replacement of the affected part. To help you, comprehensive hardware and design information is available, including parts lists that specify replacement-part numbers and internal design specifications.

VI

Troubleshooting

Examining Error Codes. Nearly all the personal computer error codes for the POST, general diagnostics, and advanced diagnostics are represented by the display of the device number followed by two digits other than 00. When the tests display the device number plus the number 00, it indicates a test was completed without an error being found.

The following list is a compilation from various sources including technical reference manuals, hardware-maintenance service manuals, and hardware-maintenance reference manuals. In each three-digit number, the first number indicates a device. The other two digits indicate the exact problem. For example, 7xx indicates the math coprocessor. A display of 700 means all is well. Any other number (701 to 799) indicates that the math coprocessor is bad or having problems. The last two digits (01 to 99) indicate what is wrong. Table 19.2 lists the basic error codes and their descriptions.

Table 19.2   Personal Computer Error Codes

Code	Description
1xx	System Board errors
2xx	Memory (RAM) errors
3xx	Keyboard errors
4xx	Monochrome Display Adapter (MDA) errors
4xx	PS/2 System Board Parallel Port errors
5xx	Color Graphics Adapter (CGA) errors
6xx	Floppy Drive/Controller errors
7xx	Math Coprocessor errors
9xx	Parallel Printer adapter errors
10xx	Alternate Parallel Printer Adapter errors
11xx	Primary Async Communications (serial port COM1) errors
12xx	Alternate Async Communications (serial COM2, COM3, and COM4) errors
13xx	Game Control Adapter errors
14xx	Matrix Printer errors
15xx	Synchronous Data Link Control (SDLC) Communications Adapter errors
16xx	Display Station Emulation Adapter (DSEA) errors (5520, 525x)
17xx	ST-506/412 Fixed Disk and Controller errors
18xx	I/O Expansion Unit errors
19xx	3270 PC Attachment Card errors
20xx	Binary Synchronous Communications (BSC) Adapter errors
21xx	Alternate Binary Synchronous Communications (BSC) Adapter errors
22xx	Cluster Adapter errors
23xx	Plasma Monitor Adapter errors
24xx	Enhanced Graphics Adapter (EGA) errors
24xx	PS/2 System Board Video Graphics Array (VGA) errors
25xx	Alternate Enhanced Graphics Adapter (EGA) errors

Code	Description
26xx	XT or AT/370 370-M (Memory) and 370-P (Processor) Adapter errors
27xx	XT or AT/370 3277-EM (Emulation) Adapter errors
28xx	3278/79 Emulation Adapter or 3270 Connection Adapter errors
29xx	Color/Graphics Printer errors
30xx	Primary PC Network Adapter errors
31xx	Secondary PC Network Adapter errors
32xx	3270 PC or AT Display and Programmed Symbols Adapter errors
33xx	Compact Printer errors
35xx	Enhanced Display Station Emulation Adapter (EDSEA) errors
36xx	General Purpose Interface Bus (GPIB) Adapter errors
38xx	Data Acquisition Adapter errors
39xx	Professional Graphics Adapter (PGA) errors
44xx	5278 Display Attachment Unit and 5279 Display errors
45xx	IEEE Interface Adapter (IEEE-488) errors
46xx	A Real-Time Interface Coprocessor (ARTIC) Multiport/2 Adapter errors
48xx	Internal Modem errors
49xx	Alternate Internal Modem errors
50xx	PC Convertible LCD errors
51xx	PC Convertible Portable Printer errors
56xx	Financial Communication System errors
70xx	Phoenix BIOS/Chip Set Unique Error Codes
71xx	Voice Communications Adapter (VCA) errors
73xx	3 1/2-inch External Diskette Drive errors
74xx	IBM PS/2 Display Adapter (VGA card) errors
74xx	8514/A Display Adapter errors
76xx	4216 PagePrinter Adapter errors
84xx	PS/2 Speech Adapter errors
85xx	2M XMA Memory Adapter or Expanded Memory Adapter/A errors
86xx	PS/2 Pointing Device (Mouse) errors
89xx	Musical Instrument Digital Interface (MIDI) Adapter errors
91xx	IBM 3363 Write-Once Read Multiple (WORM) Optical Drive/Adapter errors
096xxxx	SCSI Adapter with Cache (32-bit) errors
100xx	Multiprotocol Adapter/A errors
101xx	300/1200bps Internal Modem/A errors
104xx	ESDI Fixed Disk or Adapter errors
107xx	5 1/4-inch External Diskette Drive or Adapter errors
112xxxx	SCSI Adapter (16-bit w/o Cache) errors
113xxxx	System Board SCSI Adapter (16-bit) errors
129xx	Model 70 Processor Board errors; Type 3 (25 MHz) System Board

(continues)

VI

Troubleshooting

Table 19.2   Continued

Code	Description
149xx	P70/P75 Plasma Display and Adapter errors
165xx	6157 Streaming Tape Drive or Tape Attachment Adapter errors
166xx	Primary Token Ring Network Adapter errors
167xx	Alternate Token Ring Network Adapter errors
180xx	PS/2 Wizard Adapter errors
194xx	80286 Memory Expansion Option Memory Module errors
208xxxx	Unknown SCSI Device errors
209xxxx	SCSI Removable Disk errors
210xxxx	SCSI Fixed Disk errors
211xxxx	SCSI Tape Drive errors
212xxxx	SCSI Printer errors
213xxxx	SCSI Processor errors
214xxxx	SCSI Write-Once Read Multiple (WORM) Drive errors
215xxxx	SCSI CD-ROM Drive errors
216xxxx	SCSI Scanner errors
217xxxx	SCSI Optical Memory errors
218xxxx	SCSI Jukebox Changer errors
219xxxx	SCSI Communications errors

Appendix A in this book contains a detailed list of every IBM error code I have encountered. Also listed are charts I developed concerning SCSI errors. The SCSI interface has introduced a whole new set of error codes because of the large number and variety of devices that can be attached.

General Purpose Diagnostics Programs

One way to determine whether a system is fully IBM-compatible is to see whether it runs IBM's AT Advanced Diagnostics. IBM's diagnostics programs work just fine on fully compatible PCs produced by other manufacturers. Many system manufacturers offer their own diagnostics. Zenith, AT&T, and Tandy, for example, offer their own versions of service manuals and diagnostics programs for their systems. Many other system manufacturers include a version of a third-party diagnostic utilities package when you purchase their systems.

A large number of third-party diagnostics programs are available for IBM and compatible systems. Specific programs are available also to test memory, floppy drives, hard disks, video boards, and most other areas of the system. Although some of these utility packages should be considered essential in any tool kit, many fall short of the level needed by professional-level troubleshooters. Many products, geared more toward end users, lack the accuracy, features, and capabilities needed by technically proficient people who are serious about troubleshooting. In this section I present information about some of the diagnostics programs I recommend.

Most of the better diagnostics on the market offer several advantages over the IBM diagnostics. They usually are better at determining where a problem lies within a system, especially in IBM-compatible systems. Serial- and parallel-port loopback connectors, or *wrap plugs*, are often included in these packages, or are available for a separate charge. The plugs are required to properly diagnose and test serial and parallel ports. (IBM always charges extra for these plugs.)

Many of these programs can be run in a batch mode, which enables a series of tests to be run from the command line without operator intervention. You then can set up automated test suites, which can be especially useful in burning in a system or executing the same tests on many systems.

These programs test all types of memory including conventional (base) memory, extended memory, and expanded memory. Failures can usually be identified down to the individual chip or SIMM (bank and bit) level.

One question I commonly receive is about which diagnostic program I would recommend above all others. This is impossible to answer! There are so many programs available, and each seem to have strengths in some areas and weaknesses in others. I almost never rely on the "opinion" of one program, and usually try several to see if they corroborate the diagnosis. Having a second or third opinion in some cases is a good idea before replacing an expensive piece of equipment or getting involved in a lengthy repair procedure. Although many of these programs can be somewhat expensive for casual troubleshooters, if you work in a service or support role, then these professional-level programs can save you money in the long run with increased accuracy and capabilities in troubleshooting and servicing your systems.

The remainder of this section describes some of the different diagnostics programs I recommend.

AMIDiag

AMI (American Megatrends, Inc.) makes the most popular PC ROM BIOS software in use today. The AMI BIOS can be found on the majority of newer IBM-compatible systems that are currently being sold. If you have seen the AMI BIOS, then you know that most versions have a built-in diagnostics program. Few people know that AMI now markets an enhanced disk-based version of the same diagnostics that is built into the AMI ROM.

AMIDiag, as the program is called, has numerous features and enhancements not found in the simpler ROM version. AMIDiag is a comprehensive, general purpose diagnostics program that is designed for any IBM-compatible system, not just those with an AMI ROM BIOS.

Checkit Pro

Touchstone Software Corp.'s Checkit products offer an excellent suite of testing capabilities, including tests of the system CPU; conventional, extended and expanded memory;

hard and floppy drives; and video card and monitor (including VESA-standard cards and monitors, mouse, and keyboard). Several versions of the Checkit product are available—Checkit Pro Deluxe is the company's most complete hardware diagnostics program. Checkit Pro Analyst for Windows performs Windows-based diagnostics. Checkit Plus, which is included by some system manufacturers with their systems, is less complete.

Checkit Pro Deluxe provides limited benchmarking capabilities but gives detailed information about your system hardware such as the following: total installed memory, hard drive type and size, current memory allocation (including upper memory usage), IRQ availability and usage, modem/fax modem speed, and a variety of other tests important to someone troubleshooting a PC. Checkit Pro Deluxe includes a text-editing module that opens automatically to CONFIG.SYS and AUTOEXEC.BAT. If you use Windows, Checkit Pro's Windows option makes it easy to edit your Windows SYSTEM.INI and WIN.INI files.

Some of the testing performed by Checkit Pro is uncommon for diagnostic utility packages (for example, its capability to test modem/fax modem settings). Still, Checkit Pro lacks important features such as an easy-to-use listing of available DMA channels, which is crucial if you are trying to install a sound card and other hardware devices.

Micro-Scope

Micro-Scope by Micro 2000 is a full-featured general purpose diagnostics program for IBM-compatible systems. It has many features and capabilities that can be very helpful in troubleshooting or diagnosing hardware problems.

The Micro-Scope package is one of only a few diagnostics packages that are truly PS/2 aware. Micro-Scope not only helps you troubleshoot PS/2 systems, but also does some things that even IBM Advanced Diagnostics cannot do; for example, it can format industry-standard ESDI hard disk drives attached to the IBM PS/2 ESDI controller. When you attach an ESDI drive to the IBM ESDI controller, the BIOS on the controller queries the drive for its capacity and defect map information. IBM apparently chose a proprietary format for this information on its drives; if the controller cannot read the information, you cannot set up the drive or format it by using the PS/2 Reference Disk.

Although IBM used an ESDI controller in its PS/2 system, you could not get just any ESDI drive to work on that system. Some drive manufacturers produced special PS/2 versions of their drives that had this information on them. Another way around the problem was to use an aftermarket ESDI controller in place of the IBM controller so that you could use the IBM ESDI drive as well as any other industry-standard ESDI drive. With this method, however, you could not use the Reference Disk format program anymore because it works only with IBM's controller. Micro-Scope solves many of these problems because it can format an industry-standard ESDI drive attached to the IBM ESDI controller and save you from having to purchase an aftermarket controller or a special drive when you add drives to these systems.

Micro-Scope has also a hardware interrupt and I/O port address check feature that is more accurate than the same feature in most other software. It enables you to accurately identify the interrupt or I/O port address a certain adapter or hardware device in your system is using—a valuable capability in solving conflicts between adapters. Some user-level diagnostics programs have this feature, but the information they report can be grossly inaccurate, and they often miss items installed in the system. Micro-Scope goes around DOS and the BIOS; because the program has its own operating system and its tests bypass the ROM BIOS when necessary, it can eliminate the masking that occurs with these elements in the way. For this reason, the program also is useful for technicians who support PCs that run under non-DOS environments such as UNIX or on Novell file servers. For convenience, you can install Micro-Scope on a hard disk and run it under regular DOS.

Finally, Micro 2000 offers excellent telephone technical support. Its operators do much more than explain how to operate the software—they help you with real troubleshooting problems. This information is augmented by good documentation and on-line help built in to the software so that, in many cases, you don't have to refer to the manual.

Norton Diagnostics

When you consider that Norton Diagnostics (NDIAGS) comes with the Norton Utilities version 8.0, and that Norton Utilities is already an essential collection of system data safeguarding, troubleshooting, testing, and repairing utilities, NDIAGS probably is one of the best values in diagnostic programs.

If you already have a version of Norton Utilities earlier than 8.0, get the upgrade. If you don't already have Norton Utilities, you'll want to strongly consider this package, not only for NDIAGS, but also for enhancements to other utilities such as the Stacker 4.0-ready Speedisk, Disk Doctor, and Calibrate. These three hard drive utilities basically represent the state of the art in hard drive diagnostics and software-level repair. SYSINFO still handles benchmarking for the Norton Utilities, and it does as good a job as any other package on the market.

NDIAGS adds diagnostic capabilities that previously were not provided by the Norton Utilities, including comprehensive information about the overall hardware configuration of your system—the CPU, system BIOS, math coprocessor, video adapter, keyboard and mouse type, hard and floppy drive types, amount of installed memory (including extended and expanded), bus type (ISA, EISA, or MCA), and the number of serial and parallel ports. Unlike some other programs, loopback plugs do not come in the box for NDIAGS, but a coupon is included that enables you to get loopback plugs free. Note that this program uses wrap plugs that are wired slightly different than what has been commonly used by others. The different wiring allows you to run some additional tests. Fortunately, the documentation includes a diagram for these plugs, allowing you to make your own if you desire.

NDIAGS thoroughly tests the major system components and enables you to check minor details such as the NumLock, CapsLock, and ScrollLock LEDs on your keyboard. NDIAGS also provides an on-screen grid you can use to center the image on your monitor and test for various kinds of distortion that may indicate a faulty monitor. The Norton Utilities 8.0, as mentioned previously, is available for registered users of a previous version and can be purchased for $100 or less.

VI

Troubleshooting

PC Technician

PC Technician by Windsor Technologies is one of the longest running PC diagnostics products on the market. As such, it has been highly refined and continuously updated to reflect the changing PC market.

PC Technician is a full-featured, comprehensive hardware diagnostics and troubleshooting tool that tests all major areas of a system. Like several of the other high-end programs, PC Technician has its own operating system which isolates it from problems caused by software conflicts. The program is written in assembly language and has direct access to the hardware in the system for testing. This program also includes all of the wrap plugs needed for testing serial and parallel ports.

PC Technician has long been a favorite with field service companies, who equip their technicians with the product for troubleshooting. This program was designed for the professional service technician; however, it is easy to use for the amateur as well.

QAPlus/FE

QAPlus/FE by Diagsoft is one of the most advanced and comprehensive sets of diagnostics you can buy for 386, 486, or Pentium-based computers, including PS/2s. Its testing is extremely thorough, and its menu-based interface makes it downright easy to use, even for someone who is not particularly well-versed in diagnosing problems with personal computers. QAPlus/FE also includes some of the most accurate system benchmarks you can get, which can be used to find out if that new system you are thinking of buying is really all that much faster than the one you already have. More importantly, QAPlus/FE comes on bootable 3 1/2- and 5 1/4-inch disks that (regardless of whether your operating system is DOS, OS/2, or UNIX) can be used to start your system when problems are so severe that your system hardware cannot even find the hard drive. You also can install QAPlus/FE on your hard drive if you are using DOS 3.2 or later.

Many of you may already have a less comprehensive version of this program oriented towards end users called QAPlus. The basic QAPlus version is often included with systems sold by a number of different PC system vendors. Although the simple QAPlus program is OK, I much prefer the full-blown QAPlus/FE version for serious troubleshooting.

QAPlus/FE can be used to test your motherboard, system RAM (conventional, extended, and expanded), video adapter, hard drive, floppy drives, CD-ROM drive, mouse, keyboard, printer, and parallel and serial ports (the QAPlus/FE package includes loopback plugs for full testing of these ports). It also provides exhaustive information on your system configuration, including the hardware installed on your system, its CPU, and the total amount of RAM installed on your system. It provides full interrupt mapping—crucial when installing new adapter boards and other hardware devices—and gives you a full picture of the device drivers and memory resident programs loaded in CONFIG.SYS and AUTOEXEC.BAT, as well as other information about DOS and system memory use.

QAPlus/FE also includes various other utilities which are more likely to appeal to the serious PC troubleshooter than to the average PC user. These special capabilities include a CMOS editor that can be used to change system date and time, as well as the hard drive type; installed memory size and other CMOS information; a COM port debugger; a hard drive test and low-level formatting utility; a floppy drive test utility; and a configuration file editor that can be used to edit AUTOEXEC.BAT, CONFIG.SYS, a remote system communication host program that enables service people with the full remote package to operate your computer via modem, as well as other text files.

Unlike some diagnostics programs, QAPlus/FE has a system *burn-in* capability, meaning it can be used to run your system non-stop under a full load of computations and hardware activity for the purpose of determining whether any system component is likely to fail in real life use. Many people use a burn-in utility when they receive a new system, and then again just before the warranty runs out. A true system burn-in usually lasts 48 to 72 hours, or even longer. The amount of time QAPlus/FE can burn-in a system is user-configurable by setting the number of times the selected tests are to be run.

Service Diagnostics

The Service Diagnostics program by Landmark also has several features that distinguish it from other packages. This section describes these features.

The Service Diagnostics program is an excellent, all-around, comprehensive diagnostics package. The program has been around for awhile and has evolved to include nearly any test a troubleshooter could want. Service Diagnostics is known for its excellent memory tests, which are extremely thorough and accurate; it also gives you much control over the type of test to run. For example, you can optionally turn parity checking on or off during the tests, a feature not found in other programs. All memory errors are reported to the individual-bit level.

The Service Diagnostics program also has specific test routines for each different microprocessor that might be in a PC-compatible system. In other words, it detects the type of processor in your system and tests it by using specific routines designed for the processor. You can override the processor detection and specify the processor you have. The program can recognize and test specific Intel-based systems using 8088, 8086, 286, 386, 486, and Pentium CPUs. Also, Service Diagnostics specifically recognizes and tests Harris 80C88 and AMD 386 chips, as well as Intel, Cyrix, and IIT math coprocessors. The program also tests for several known bugs in 386 and 486 systems that have been known to cause problems in some systems.

Another Service Diagnostics feature is its floppy disk alignment diagnostics, which enable you to check the alignment of both 3 1/2- and 5 1/4-inch drives through the use of an included Digital Diagnostics Disk (DDD). These disks are accurate to a resolution of 500µ inches (micro-inches = millionths of an inch)—accurate enough for checking alignment, but not accurate enough for use in aligning a drive. For performing drive alignment, the program has a menu of analog alignment aids, designed to be used in conjunction with a more accurate Analog Alignment Disk (AAD) and an oscilloscope.

The Service Diagnostics program has an excellent hard disk, low-level format program for ST-506/412 drives. You can specify not only the interleave, but also the skew factor.

VI

Troubleshooting

Skew is the offset of sectors from one track to the next to allow for head-switching time. This process is possible because the low-level format routines in the Service Diagnostics work at the controller register level; the program bypasses DOS and the BIOS and interacts directly with the controller hardware. The program formats most ESDI drives, but cannot be used on SCSI or IDE drives.

A printer-test feature in the Service Diagnostics program enables test patterns to be sent to different printers. You can quickly verify the functionality of the port, cable, and printer in one simple operation.

I recommend diagnostics programs that accommodate the special features of IBM's PS/2 systems; Service Diagnostics meets this test. It has a separate stand-alone PS/2 version of the software designed specifically for PS/2 systems. This version recognizes PS/2 hardware differences and works correctly with the unique PS/2 CMOS RAM for adapter setup and configuration. The Service Diagnostics package includes excellent documentation that describes not only how to operate the software, but also how the software routines work. Landmark offers good technical support for its products.

Service Diagnostics packages also offer a special hardware-based diagnostics tool—diagnostics in ROM chips that can be plugged into the BIOS-chip sockets on a PC, XT, AT, or IBM-compatible motherboard. Such ROM-based diagnostics are useful in limited situations, particularly when you need to test a system that otherwise does not function. Note that these BIOS diagnostics do not function on all systems, but they can be useful on an IBM PC, XT, or AT, or a fully compatible system.

The Service Diagnostics program is available in three primary kits: the PC, XT, AT Kit with ROM POST modules, the PS/2 Complete Kit, and a Super Kit that includes everything. You also can buy special lower cost software-only modules for each specific type of system.

Disk Diagnostics

All of the general purpose diagnostics programs will test both floppy and hard disk drives. However, since these programs are general-purpose in nature, the drive tests are not always as complete as one would like. For this reason there are a number of specific programs designed expressly for performing diagnostics and servicing on disk drives. The following section discusses some of the best disk diagnostics and testing programs on the market and what they can do for you.

Drive Probe

Many programs on the market evaluate the condition of floppy disk drives by using a disk created or formatted on the same drive. A program that uses this technique cannot make a proper evaluation of a disk drive's alignment. A specially created disk produced by a tested and calibrated machine is required. This type of disk can be used as a reference standard by which to judge a drive. Accurite, the primary manufacturer of such reference standard floppy disks, helps specify floppy disk industry standards. Accurite produces the following three main types of reference standard disks used for testing drive function and alignment:

- Digital Diagnostic Diskette (DDD)
- High-Resolution Diagnostic Diskette (HRD)
- Analog Alignment Diskette (AAD)

The DDD disk, introduced in 1982, enables you to test drive alignment by using only software; no oscilloscope or special tools are needed. This disk is accurate to only 500μ-inches (millionths of an inch)—good enough for a rough *test* of drive alignment, but not nearly enough to use for *aligning* a drive.

The HRD disk, introduced in 1989, represents a breakthrough in floppy disk drive testing and alignment. The disk is accurate to within 50μ-inches (millionths of an inch)—accurate enough to use not only for precise testing of floppy drives, but also for aligning drives. With software that uses this HRD disk, you can align a floppy drive by using no special tools or oscilloscope. Other than the program and the HRD disk, you need only an IBM-compatible system to which to connect the drive. This product has lowered the cost of aligning a drive significantly and has eliminated much hassling with special test equipment.

The AAD disk has been the standard for drive alignment for many years. The disks, accurate to within 50μ inches (millionths of an inch), require that you use special test gear, such as an oscilloscope, to read the disk. These disks have no computer-readable data, only precisely placed analog tracks. Until HRD disks became available, using an AAD was the only way to align drives properly.

The Accurite program Drive Probe is designed to work with the HRD disks (also from Accurite). Drive Probe is *the* most accurate and capable floppy disk testing program on the market, thanks to the use of HRD disks. Until other programs utilize the HRD disks for testing, Drive Probe is my software of choice for floppy disk testing. Because the Drive Probe software also acts as a disk exerciser, for use with AAD disks and an oscilloscope, you can move the heads to specific tracks for controlled testing.

Disk Manager

Disk Manager by Ontrack stands today as the most comprehensive and capable hard disk test and format utility available. This program works with practically every hard disk and controller on the market, including the newer SCSI and IDE types.

The Disk Manager program allows testing of the controller as well as the drive. Read-only testing may be performed as well as read/write tests. One of the best features is the comprehensive low-level formatting capability, which allows a user to set not only interleave but skew factors as well. The low-level format portion is also capable of truly formatting most IDE drives, a feature that few other programs have.

If you do any testing and formatting of hard disks, this program should be in your utility library. I included more information about Disk Manager in Chapter 14, "Hard Disk Drives and Controllers."

VI

Troubleshooting

Data Recovery Utilities

There are several programs designed for data recovery rather than just hardware trouble-shooting and repair. These data recovery programs can troubleshoot and repair disk formatting structures (Boot Sectors, File Allocation Tables, and Directories) as well as files and file structures (database files, spreadsheet files, and so on).

Norton Utilities

The Norton Utilities by Symantec stands as perhaps the premier data recovery package on the market today. This package is very comprehensive and will automatically repair most types of disk problems.

What really makes this package stand out for me is the fantastic Disk Editor program. Currently there simply is no other program that is as comprehensive or as capable of editing disks at the sector level. For the professional PC troubleshooter or repair person, the Disk Editor included with the Norton Utilities can give you the ability to work directly with any sector on the disk. Unfortunately, this does require extensive knowledge of sector formats and disk structures. The documentation with the package is excellent and can be very helpful if you are learning data recovery on your own.

I find that data recovery is a lucrative service that the more advanced technician can provide. People are willing to pay much more to get their data back than to simply replace a hard drive. For more information on this subject, I have written a book called *Que's Guide to Data Recovery*, which is available from Que directly (see Appendix B).

For more automatic recovery that anybody can perform, Norton Utilities has several other useful modules. Disk Doctor and Calibrate are two of the modules included with the Norton Utilities version 8.0. Together, these two utilities provide exhaustive testing of the data structures and sectors of a hard drive. Disk Doctor works with both hard disks and floppies and tests the capability of the drive to work with the system in which it is installed, including the drive's boot sector, file allocation tables (FAT), file structure, and data areas. Calibrate, which is used for the most intensive testing of the data area of a drive, also tests the hard drive controller electronics.

Calibrate also can be used to perform deep-pattern testing of IDE, SCSI, and ST-506/412-interface drives—writing literally millions of bytes of data to every sector of the drive to see whether it can properly retain data, moving data if the sector where it is stored is flawed, and marking the sector as bad in the FAT.

Calibrate can perform a nondestructive low-level format of ST-506/412 drives, which means that the data stored on the drive is not destroyed as it is when you use the controller BIOS to perform a low-level format on these drives. Often, in performing deep-pattern testing and low-level formatting of ST-506/412 drives, Calibrate can refresh, or remagnetize, bad sectors and return them to service so that they can be safely used again for data storage. Calibrate also can be used to test for the optimal interleave on ST-506/412 drives and nondestructively change the format if system performance would benefit.

Due to the excellent Disk Editor, anybody serious about data recovery needs a copy of Norton Utilities. The many other modules that are included are excellent as well, and the latest versions now include NDIAGS, which is a comprehensive PC hardware diagnostic.

Others

Several other good data recovery packages are on the market. Some offer general purpose data recovery such as PC-Tools by Central Point Software. Others are designed to recover specific types of files, and due to their narrow focus, are much better than general purpose programs for this task. I highly recommend the dSALVAGE Professional by Comtech Publishing for recovering the database files used by most popular database programs.

Configuration Utilities

Many utilities that are on the market today specialize not only in hardware diagnostics, but also in hardware configuration. These programs are designed to tell you what type of hardware you have and how it is configured. I find this type of program to be one of the most useful, because most PC problems result from improper system configuration.

MSD (Microsoft Diagnostics)

Since the introduction of Windows 3.1 and now with DOS 6.0 and higher, Microsoft has included a little-known program called MSD (MicroSoft Diagnostics). MSD is not really a full-blown diagnostics program but is more of a system configuration utility. MSD provides quick answers to system configuration problems such as interrupt request line (IRQ) conflicts and memory address problems.

In addition, MSD provides basic information about the system it is running on, including the BIOS, processor type, video adapter, network (if any), the mouse, disk drives (including CD-ROM drives), parallel and serial ports, and the DOS version. Also provided is extensive information on any device drivers and memory resident programs loaded into memory. This information can be very useful in locating conflicts between two programs or especially when trying to fit different programs into different areas of memory. MSD can present in a visual manner the locations in memory each module occupies; this can be much more helpful than the text listings provided by the DOS MEM command.

MSD is provided free with Windows 3.1 and higher and with MS-DOS 6.0 and higher. This means that if you are not using Windows and are using other OEM versions of DOS such as IBM's PC-DOS, then you may not have MSD installed on your system. In that case, you can still get the program for free by downloading it from the Microsoft BBS (see Appendix B for the number). Microsoft has decided to treat MSD as a public domain program, and it can be downloaded for free by anyone with access to a modem. Although it may not be the greatest system configuration utility available, it certainly does a very good job, especially on memory, and the price is right!

InfoSpotter

One of my favorite configuration utilities is InfoSpotter by Renasonce. This program displays a great deal of information about a system, and is especially known for the intuitive way this information is formatted on-screen. I have used this program in my training seminars because the display makes the information easier to understand. In addition to configuration reports, InfoSpotter also includes some limited hardware diagnostics tests, which make it more useful than some of the others.

SysChk

SysChk by APS (Advanced Personal Systems) is also a favorite of mine. This program is distributed through the shareware concept, which makes it easy to try before you buy it. This program goes way beyond what simpler programs like MSD will do, and is much less expensive than some of the other commercial programs. You can get SysChk through CompuServe or virtually any other source of shareware software. SysChk also has a very intuitive user interface that displays the system configuration and hardware details in an easy to understand fashion.

Windows Diagnostic Software

With the startling success of Windows 3.0 and 3.1, software utility manufacturers have raced to fill what was perceived as a shortage of diagnostic programs that run under Windows. The results have been mixed. But some good utility packages have emerged.

For example, the Norton Desktop for Windows, which many users think of first as a replacement for Program Manager, includes SYSINFO, an excellent system hardware information program that offers details on your drives, available IRQs, memory, video adapter, printer, and other system information. SYSINFO also offers a benchmark that measures your CPU performance.

Another excellent Windows diagnostic program is WinSleuth, which benchmarks your system and performs extremely thorough testing of your system hardware. It also details your drives, memory, video adapter, printer, and other system components.

But a real treasure is WinSleuth's capability to tell you the IRQs available when Windows is running, and also the available direct memory access (DMA) channels. Although numerous DOS-based utility packages provide this information, few do so in Windows. And WinSleuth Gold can save you literally hours of scratching your head while trying to configure a sound board or other adapter to run in Windows.

Winprobe by Landmark is one of the most comprehensive of the Windows diagnostic utilities. Besides displaying system information and memory usage, Winprobe also helps you optimize your Windows configuration files (.INI files) and offers literally hundreds of tips for improving Windows performance. Winprobe can optimize Windows memory usage on the fly, which can be very helpful if you run many programs simultaneously.

Shareware and Public-Domain Diagnostics

Many excellent public-domain diagnostic programs are available, including programs for diagnosing problems with memory, hard disks, floppy disks, monitors and video adapters, as well as virtually any other part of the system. These programs can be excellent for users who do not perform frequent troubleshooting or who are on a budget.

Many programs assumed to be "public domain" are really not. These are often called shareware or user-distributed software. These programs are not free like true public domain programs, but are in fact commercial software that is merely distributed for free. In most cases you are allowed to try the program for a period of time before registering and paying for the software. Be sure to register; this will allow the author to stay in business, providing excellent software through the shareware concept, and you will then be notified of any updates or improvements. In some cases registration entitles you to the next version of the program for free, and may include other incentives such as an enhanced version of the program with additional features.

Shareware is a set of commercial-quality programs distributed under a *try now, pay later* concept. The authors of shareware programs depend on honest users to pay for the shareware they use (generally only a few dollars). *Public domain* software has been released by the author to be used by anyone without the payment of a fee of any kind to the author.

Most often, you obtain shareware programs by downloading them from a BBS by using a modem. However, some companies distribute shareware on disk. One of these companies stands out: the Public Software Library. This organization, which began as an outgrowth of a Houston computer users' group, has acquired the single best collection of public-domain and user-supported software. What makes this company extraordinary is that all the software is tested before entering the library, which eliminates virus or Trojan-horse programs that can damage a system. Buggy programs also usually don't make it into the Public Software Library. All the programs are the latest available versions, and earlier versions are purged from the library. Many other shareware disk distribution companies don't think twice about sending you a disk full of old programs.

The programs in this library are not sold but distributed. The authors are aware of how these programs are distributed, and no excessive fees are charged for the disk and copying services. This truly legitimate company has the program authors' approval to distribute software in this manner. All disks are guaranteed, unlike many comparable organizations that seem bent on making as much money as they can.

Besides the Public Software Library, you can find many shareware and public-domain programs on local Bulletin Board Systems (BBSs). If you have access to CompuServe, one of the best places to look for this type of software is in the IBMHW forum.

VI

Troubleshooting

Summary

This chapter examined the diagnostic hardware and software utilities you can use as a valuable aid in diagnosing and troubleshooting a system. First, the chapter described the three levels of diagnostic software (POST, system, and advanced) and explained how you can get the most from the POST each time your system boots. This chapter also included detailed information about IBM error codes and a reference chart showing the meanings of some of these codes.

In addition, this chapter covered diagnostic and benchmarking utility packages, such as IBM's system diagnostics and advanced diagnostics, as well as many other aftermarket general and special purpose diagnostics. Each of these packages, although taking different approaches to troubleshooting a PC, provides specialized diagnostics for particular areas of the system, such as system memory, hard drives, floppy drives, COM ports, parallel ports, video adapters, keyboards, the mouse, and other components.

Finally, this chapter included a discussion of diagnostic utilities distributed as shareware or released into the public domain. Shareware and public-domain software are a rich source of utilities that are relatively inexpensive, or free for the downloading.

Chapter 20

Operating Systems Software and Troubleshooting

This chapter focuses on the problems that occur in PC systems because of faulty or incompatible software. First, it describes the structure of DOS and how DOS works with hardware in a functioning system. Topics of particular interest are as follows:

- DOS file structure

- DOS disk organization

- DOS programs for data and disk recovery (their capabilities and dangers)

Additionally, the chapter examines two other important software-related issues: using memory-resident software (and dealing with the problems it can cause) and distinguishing a software problem from a hardware problem.

Disk Operating System (DOS)

Information about DOS may seem out of place in a book about hardware upgrade and repair, but if you ignore DOS and other software when you troubleshoot a system, you can miss a number of problems. The best system troubleshooters and diagnosticians know the entire system—hardware and software.

This book cannot discuss DOS in depth, but if you need to read more about it, Que Corporation publishes some good books on the subject (*Using MS-DOS 6.2*, Special Edition, for example).

This section describes the basics of DOS: where it fits into the PC system architecture, what its components are, and what happens when a system boots (starts up). Understanding the booting process can be helpful when diagnosing startup problems. This section also explains DOS configuration—an area in which many people experience problems—and the file formats DOS uses, as well as how DOS manages information on a disk.

Operating System Basics

DOS is just one component in the total system architecture. A PC system has a distinct hierarchy of software that controls the system at all times. Even when you are operating within an application program such as 1-2-3 or another high-level application software, several other layers of programs are always executing underneath. Usually the layers can be defined distinctly, but sometimes the boundaries are vague.

Communications generally occur only between adjoining layers in the architecture, but this rule is not absolute. Many programs ignore the services provided by the layer directly beneath them and eliminate the middleman by skipping one or more layers. An example is a program that ignores the DOS and ROM BIOS video routines and communicates directly with the hardware in the interest of the highest possible screen performance. Although the high-performance goal is admirable, many operating environments (such as OS/2 and Windows) no longer allow direct access to the hardware. Programs that do not play by the rules must be rewritten to run in these new environments.

The hardware is at the lowest level of the system hierarchy. By placing various bytes of information at certain ports or locations within a system's memory structure, you can control virtually anything connected to the CPU. Maintaining control at the hardware level is difficult; doing so requires a complete and accurate knowledge of the system architecture. The level of detail required in writing the software operating at this level is the most intense. Commands to the system at this level are in *machine language* (binary groups of information applied directly to the microprocessor). Machine language instructions are limited in their function: you must use many of them to perform even the smallest amount of useful work. The large number of instructions required is not really a problem because these instructions are executed extremely rapidly, wasting few system resources.

Programmers can write programs consisting of machine language instructions, but generally they use a tool—an *assembler*—to ease the process. They write programs using an *editor,* and then use the assembler to convert the editor's output to pure machine language. Assembler commands are still very low level, and using them effectively requires that programmers be extremely knowledgeable. No one (in his or her right mind) writes directly in machine code anymore; assembly language is the lowest level of programming environment typically used today. Even assembly language, however, is losing favor among programmers because of the amount of knowledge and work required to complete even simple tasks and because of its lack of portability between different kinds of systems.

When you start a PC system, a series of machine code programs, the ROM BIOS, assumes control. This set of programs, always present in a system, talks (in machine code) to the hardware. The BIOS accepts or interprets commands supplied by programs above it in the system hierarchy and translates them to machine code commands that then are passed on to the microprocessor. Commands at this level typically are called *interrupts* or *services.* A programmer generally can use nearly any language to supply these instructions to the BIOS. A complete list of these services is supplied in the IBM *BIOS Interface Technical Reference Manual.*

DOS itself is made up of several components. It attaches to the BIOS, and part of DOS actually becomes an extension of the BIOS, providing more interrupts and services for other programs to use. DOS provides for communication with the ROM BIOS in PCs and with higher-level software (such as applications). Because DOS gives the programmer interrupts and services to use in addition to those provided by the ROM BIOS, a lot of reinventing the wheel in programming routines is eliminated. For example, DOS provides an extremely rich set of functions that can open, close, find, delete, create, rename, and perform other file-handling tasks. When programmers want to include some of these functions in their programs, they can rely on DOS to do most of the work.

This standard set of functions that applications use to read from and write to disks makes data recovery operations possible. Imagine how tough writing programs and using computers would be if every application program had to implement its own custom disk interface, with a proprietary directory and file retrieval system. Every application would require its own special disks. Fortunately, DOS provides a standard set of documented file storage and retrieval provisions that all software can use; as a result, you can make some sense out of what you find on a typical disk.

Another primary function of DOS is to load and run other programs. As it performs that function, DOS is the *shell* within which another program can be executed. DOS provides the functions and environment required by other software—including operating environments such as GEM and Windows—to run on PC systems in a standard way.

The System ROM BIOS

Think of the system ROM BIOS as a form of compatibility glue that sits between the hardware and an operating system. Why is it that IBM can sell the same DOS to run on the original IBM PC *and* on the latest Pentium systems—two very different hardware platforms? If DOS were written to talk directly to the hardware on all systems, it would be a very hardware-specific program. Instead, IBM developed a set of standard services and functions each system should be capable of performing and coded them as programs in the ROM BIOS. Each system then gets a completely custom ROM BIOS that talks directly to the hardware in the system and knows exactly how to perform each specific function on that hardware only.

This convention enables operating systems to be written to what amounts to a standard interface that can be made available on many different types of hardware. Any applications written to the operating system standard interface can run on that system. Figure 20.1 shows that two very different hardware platforms can each have a custom ROM BIOS that talks directly to the hardware and still provides a standard interface to an operating system.

The two different hardware platforms described in figure 20.1 can run not only the exact same version of DOS, but also the same application programs because of the standard interfaces provided by the ROM BIOS and DOS. Keep in mind, however, that the actual ROM BIOS code differs among the specific machines and that it is not usually possible therefore to run a ROM BIOS designed for one system in a different system. ROM BIOS

VI

Troubleshooting

upgrades must come from a source that has an intimate understanding of the specific motherboard on which the chip will be placed because the ROM must be custom written for that particular hardware.

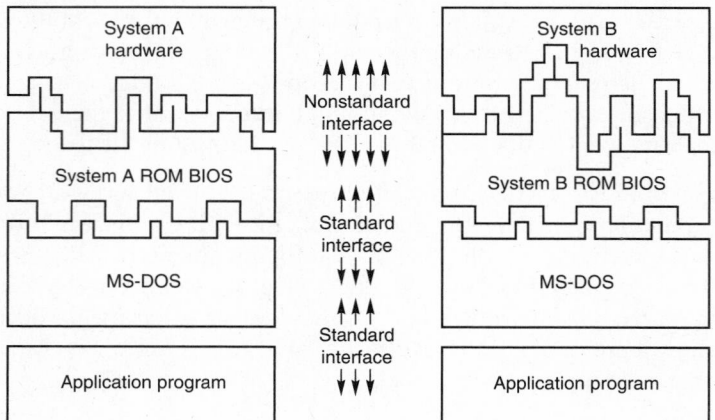

Fig. 20.1

A representation of the software layers in an IBM-compatible system.

The portion of DOS shown in figure 20.1 is the system portion, or core, of DOS. This core is found physically as the two system files on any bootable DOS disk. These hidden system files usually have one of two sets of names, IBMBIO.COM and IBMDOS.COM (used in IBM and Compaq DOS), or IO.SYS and MSDOS.SYS (used in MS-DOS and versions of DOS licensed from Microsoft by original equipment manufacturers [OEMs]). These files must be the first and second files listed in the directory on a bootable DOS disk.

Figure 20.1 represents a simplified view of the system; some subtle but important differences exist. Ideally, application programs are insulated from the hardware by the ROM BIOS and DOS, but in reality many programmers write portions of their programs to talk directly to the hardware, circumventing DOS and the ROM BIOS. A program therefore might work only on specific hardware, even if the proper DOS and ROM BIOS interfaces are present in other hardware.

Programs designed to go directly to the hardware are written that way mainly to increase performance. For example, many programs directly access the video hardware to improve screen update performance. These applications often have install programs that require you to specify exactly what hardware is present in your system so that the program can load the correct hardware-dependent routines into the application.

Additionally, some utility programs absolutely must talk directly to the hardware to perform their function. For example, a low-level format program must talk directly to the hard disk controller hardware to perform the low-level format of the disk. Such programs are very specific to a certain controller or controller type. Another type of system-specific utility, the driver programs, enables extended memory to function as expanded memory on an 80386-based system. These drivers work by accessing the 80386 directly and utilizing specific features of the chip.

Another way that reality might differ from the simple view is that DOS itself communicates directly with the hardware. In fact, much of the IBMBIO.COM file consists of low-level drivers designed to supplant and supersede ROM BIOS code in the system. People who own both IBM systems and compatibles might wonder why IBM never seems to have ROM BIOS upgrades to correct bugs and problems with its systems, although for vendors of most compatible systems, a ROM upgrade is at least a semiannual occurrence. The reason is simple: IBM distributes its ROM patches and upgrades in DOS. When IBM DOS loads, it determines the system type and ID information from the ROM and loads different routines depending on which version of ROM it finds. For example, at least four different hard disk code sections are in IBM DOS, but only one is loaded for a specific system.

I have taken a single DOS boot disk with only the system files (COMMAND.COM and CHKDSK.COM) on it, and booted the disk on both an XT and an AT system, each one with an identical 640K of memory. After loading DOS, CHKDSK reported different amounts of free memory, which showed that DOS had taken up different amounts of memory in the two systems. This is because of the different code routines loaded, based on the ROM ID information. In essence, DOS, the ROM BIOS, and the hardware are much more closely related than most people realize.

DOS Components

DOS consists of two primary components: the input/output (I/O) system and the shell. The I/O system consists of the underlying programs that reside in memory while the system is running; these programs are loaded first when DOS boots. The I/O system is stored in the form of two files hidden on a bootable DOS disk. The files are called IBMBIO.COM and IBMDOS.COM on an IBM DOS disk, but might go by other names for other manufacturers' versions of DOS. For example, IO.SYS and MSDOS.SYS are the MS-DOS file names. No matter what the exact names are, the function of these two files is basically the same for all versions of DOS. However, each individual system's ROM BIOS looks for the system files by name and often does not recognize them by another name. This is one reason that the OEM version of DOS you use must be the correct one for your system.

The user interface program, or shell, is stored in the COMMAND.COM file, which also is loaded during a normal DOS boot-up. The shell is the portion of DOS that provides the DOS prompt and that normally communicates with the user of the system.

The following sections examine the DOS I/O system and shell in more detail to help you properly identify and solve problems related to DOS rather than to hardware. Also included is a discussion on how DOS allocates disk file space.

The I/O System and System Files

This section briefly describes the two files that make up the I/O system: IBMBIO.COM and IBMDOS.COM.

VI

Troubleshooting

IBMBIO.COM (or IO.SYS). IBMBIO.COM is one of the hidden files that the CHKDSK command reports on any system (bootable) disk. This file contains the low-level programs that interact directly with devices on the system and the ROM BIOS. IBMBIO.COM usually is customized by the particular original equipment manufacturer (OEM) of the system to match perfectly with that OEM's ROM BIOS. The file contains low-level drivers loaded in accord with a particular ROM BIOS, based on the ROM ID information, as well as on a system initialization routine. During boot-up, the DOS volume boot sector loads the file into low memory and gives it control of the system (see the "DOS Volume Boot Sectors" section, later in this chapter). The entire file, except the system initializer portion, remains in memory during normal system operation.

The name used for the file that performs the functions just described varies among versions of DOS from different OEMs. Many versions of DOS, including Microsoft's MS-DOS, use IO.SYS as the name of this file. Some other manufacturers call the file MIO.SYS, and Toshiba calls it TBIOS.SYS. Using different names for this file is not normally a problem, until you try to upgrade from one OEM version of DOS to a different OEM version. If the different OEMs use different names for this file, the SYS command might fail with the error message `No room for system on destination`. Today, most OEMs use the standard IBMBIO.COM name for this file to eliminate problems in upgrading and otherwise remain standard.

For a disk to be bootable, IBMBIO.COM or its equivalent must be listed as the first file in the directory of the disk and must occupy at least the first cluster on the disk (cluster number 2). The remainder of the file might be placed in clusters anywhere across the rest of the disk (versions 3 and higher). The file normally is marked with hidden, system, and read-only attributes, and is placed on a disk by the FORMAT command or the SYS command.

IBMDOS.COM (or MSDOS.SYS). IBMDOS.COM, the core of DOS, contains the DOS disk handling programs. The routines present in this file make up the DOS disk and device handling programs. IBMDOS.COM is loaded into low memory at system boot-up by the DOS volume boot sector and remains resident in memory during normal system operation.

The IBMDOS.COM program collection is less likely to be customized by an OEM, but still might be present on a system by a name different from IBMDOS.COM. The most common alternative name, MSDOS.SYS, is used by Microsoft's MS-DOS and some OEM versions of DOS. Another name is TDOS.SYS (used by Toshiba). Most OEMs today stick to the IBM convention to eliminate problems in upgrading from one DOS version to another.

IBMDOS.COM or its equivalent must be listed as the second entry in the root directory of any bootable disk. This file usually is marked with hidden, system, and read-only attributes, and normally is placed on a disk by the FORMAT command or the SYS command. There are no special requirements for the physical positioning of this file on a disk.

The Shell or Command Processor (COMMAND.COM). The DOS command processor COMMAND.COM is the portion of DOS with which users normally interact. The commands can be categorized by function, but IBM DOS divides them into two types by how they are made available: *resident* or *transient*.

Resident commands are built into COMMAND.COM and are available whenever the DOS prompt is present. They are generally the simpler, frequently used commands such as CLS and DIR. Resident commands execute rapidly because the instructions for them are already loaded into memory. They are *memory-resident*.

When you look up the definition of a command in the DOS manual, you find an indication of whether the command is resident or transient. You then can determine what is required to execute that command. A simple rule is that, at a DOS prompt, all resident commands are instantly available for execution, with no loading of the program from disk required. Resident commands are also sometimes termed *internal*. Commands run from a program on disk are termed *external*, or *transient*, and also are often called *utilities*.

Transient commands are not resident in the computer's memory, and the instructions to execute the command must be located on a disk. Because the instructions are loaded into memory only for execution and then are overwritten in memory after they are used, they are called *transient commands*. Most DOS commands are transient; otherwise, the memory requirements for DOS would be astronomical. Transient commands are used less frequently than resident commands and take longer to execute because they must be found and loaded before they can be run.

Most executable files operate like transient DOS commands. The instructions to execute the command must be located on a disk. The instructions are loaded into memory only for execution and are overwritten in memory after the program is no longer being used.

DOS Commands. Tables 20.1 through 20.3 show all the resident, batch, and transient DOS commands and in which DOS version they are supported. If you are responsible for providing technical support, you should know what DOS commands are available to the users at the other end of the phone. These tables identify which commands are supported in any version of DOS released to date.

Table 20.1   Resident DOS Commands

Command Name	DOS Version Number										
	1.0	1.1	2.0	2.1	3.0	3.1	3.2	3.3	4.x	5.x	6.x
CD/CHDIR			×	×	×	×	×	×	×	×	×
CHCP									×	×	×
CLS			×	×	×	×	×	×	×	×	×
COPY	×	×	×	×	×	×	×	×	×	×	×
CTTY			×	×	×	×	×	×	×	×	×
DATE	×	×	×	×	×	×	×	×	×	×	×

(continues)

VI

Troubleshooting

Table 20.1   Continued

Command Name	DOS Version Number										
	1.0	1.1	2.0	2.1	3.0	3.1	3.2	3.3	4.x	5.x	6.x
DEL/ERASE	×	×	×	×	×	×	×	×	×	×	×
DIR	×	×	×	×	×	×	×	×	×	×	×
ExIT					×	×	×	×	×	×	×
ExPAND										×	×
LOADHI/LH										×	×
MD/MKDIR			×	×	×	×	×	×	×	×	×
PATH			×	×	×	×	×	×	×	×	×
PROMPT			×	×	×	×	×	×	×	×	×
RD/RMDIR			×	×	×	×	×	×	×	×	×
REN/RENAME	×	×	×	×	×	×	×	×	×	×	×
SET			×	×	×	×	×	×	×	×	×
TIME	×	×	×	×	×	×	×	×	×	×	×
TYPE	×	×	×	×	×	×	×	×	×	×	×
VER					×	×	×	×	×	×	×
VERIFY			×	×	×	×	×	×	×	×	×
VOL			×	×	×	×	×	×	×	×	×

Table 20.2   DOS Batch File Commands

Command Name	DOS Version Number										
	1.0	1.1	2.0	2.1	3.0	3.1	3.2	3.3	4.x	5.x	6.x
CALL								×	×	×	×
ECHO	×	×	×	×	×	×	×	×	×	×	×
FOR	×	×	×	×	×	×	×	×	×	×	×
GOTO	×	×	×	×	×	×	×	×	×	×	×
IF	×	×	×	×	×	×	×	×	×	×	×
PAUSE	×	×	×	×	×	×	×	×	×	×	×
REM	×	×	×	×	×	×	×	×	×	×	×
SHIFT	×	×	×	×	×	×	×	×	×	×	×

Table 20.3   Transient DOS Commands

Command Name	DOS Version Number										
	1.0	1.1	2.0	2.1	3.0	3.1	3.2	3.3	4.x	5.x	6.x
APPEND								×	×	×	×
ASSIGN			×	×	×	×	×	×	×	×	×
ATTRIB					×	×	×	×	×	×	×
BACKUP			×	×	×	×	×	×	×	×	×

Command Name	DOS Version Number										
	1.0	1.1	2.0	2.1	3.0	3.1	3.2	3.3	4.x	5.x	6.x
BASIC	×	×	×	×	×	×	×	×	×	×	×
BASICA	×	×	×	×	×	×	×	×	×	×	×
CHCP								×	×	×	×
CHKDSK	×	×	×	×	×	×	×	×	×	×	×
COMMAND			×	×	×	×	×	×	×	×	×
COMP	×	×	×	×	×	×	×	×	×	×	×
DEBUG	×	×	×	×	×	×	×	×	×	×	×
DISKCOMP	×	×	×	×	×	×	×	×	×	×	×
DISKCOPY	×	×	×	×	×	×	×	×	×	×	×
DOSKEY										×	×
DOSSHELL									×	×	×
EDIT										×	×
EDLIN	×	×	×	×	×	×	×	×	×	×	×
EMM386										×	×
EXE2BIN			×	×	×	×	×			×	×
FASTOPEN								×	×	×	×
FC										×	×
FDISK			×	×	×	×	×	×	×	×	×
FIND			×	×	×	×	×	×	×	×	×
FORMAT	×	×	×	×	×	×	×	×	×	×	×
GRAFTABL			×	×	×	×	×	×	×	×	×
GRAPHICS			×	×	×	×	×	×	×	×	×
HELP										×	
JOIN					×	×	×	×	×	×	×
KEYB								×	×	×	×
KEYBFR					×	×	×				
KEYBGR					×	×	×				
KEYBIT					×	×	×				
KEYBSP					×	×	×				
KEYBUK					×	×	×				
LABEL					×	×	×	×	×	×	×
LIB	×	×	×	×	×	×	×				
LINK	×	×	×	×	×	×	×				
MEM									×	×	×
MIRROR										×	×
MODE	×	×	×	×	×	×	×	×	×	×	×
MORE			×	×	×	×	×	×	×	×	×
NLSFUNC								×	×	×	×
PRINT			×	×	×	×	×	×	×	×	×

(continues)

Table 20.3 Continued

Command Name	DOS Version Number										
	1.0	1.1	2.0	2.1	3.0	3.1	3.2	3.3	4.x	5.x	6.x
QBASIC										×	
RECOVER			×	×	×	×	×	×	×	×	×
REPLACE					×	×	×	×	×	×	×
RESTORE			×	×	×	×	×	×	×	×	×
SETVER										×	×
SHARE						×	×	×	×	×	×
SORT			×	×	×	×	×	×	×	×	×
SUBST					×	×	×	×	×	×	×
SYS	×	×	×	×	×	×	×	×	×	×	×
TREE			×	×	×	×	×	×	×	×	×
UNDELETE										×	×
UNFORMAT										×	×
XCOPY								×	×	×	×

LIB, LINK, and EXE2BIN are included with the DOS technical-reference manual for DOS versions 3.3 and higher. EXE2BIN is included with DOS 5.0.

DOS Command File Search Procedure. DOS looks only in specific places for the instructions for a transient command, or a software application's executable file. The instructions that represent the command or program are in files on one or more disk drives. Files that contain execution instructions have one of three specific extensions to indicate to DOS that they are program files: .COM (command files), .EXE (executable files), or .BAT (batch files). .COM and .EXE files are machine code programs; .BAT files contain a series of commands and instructions using the DOS batch facilities. The places in which DOS looks for these files is controlled by the current directory and the PATH command.

In other words, if you type several characters, such as **WIN**, at the DOS prompt and press the Enter key, DOS attempts to find and run a program named WIN. DOS performs a two- or three-level search for program instructions (the file). The first step in looking for command instructions is to see whether the command is a resident one and, if so, run it from the program code already loaded. If the command is not resident, DOS looks in the current directory for .COM, .EXE, and .BAT files, in that order, and loads and executes the first file it finds with the specified name. If the command is not resident and not in the current directory, DOS looks in all the directories specified in the DOS PATH setting (which the user can control); DOS searches for the file within each directory in the extension order just indicated. Finally, if DOS fails to locate the required instructions, it displays the error message Bad command or filename. This error message might be misleading because the command instructions usually are missing from the search areas rather than actually being bad.

Suppose that, at the DOS prompt, I type the command **XYZ** and press Enter. This command sends DOS on a search for the XYZ program's instructions. If DOS is successful, the program starts running within seconds. If DOS cannot find the proper instructions, an error message is displayed. Here is what happens:

1. DOS checks internally to see whether it can find the XYZ command as one of the resident commands whose instructions are already loaded. It finds no XYZ command as resident.

2. DOS looks next in the current directory on the current drive for files named XYZ.COM, then for files named XYZ.EXE, and finally for files named XYZ.BAT. Suppose that I had logged in to drive C:, and the current directory is \ (the root directory); therefore, DOS did not find the files in the current directory.

3. DOS looks to see whether a PATH is specified. If not, the search ends here. In this scenario, I do have a PATH specified when my system was started, so DOS checks every directory listed in that PATH for the first file it can find named XYZ.COM, XYZ.EXE, or XYZ.BAT (in that order). My PATH lists several directories, but DOS does not find an appropriate file in any of them.

4. The search ends, and DOS gives me the message Bad command or filename.

For this search-and-load procedure to be successful, I must ensure that the desired program or command file exists in the current directory on the current drive, or I must set my DOS PATH to point to the drive and directory in which the program does exist. This is why the PATH is so powerful in DOS.

A common practice is to place all simple command files or utility programs in one directory and set the PATH to point to that directory. Then each of those programs (commands) is instantly available by simply typing its name, just as though it were resident.

This practice works well only for single-load programs such as commands and other utilities. Major applications software often consists of many individual files and might have problems if they are called up from a remote directory or drive using the DOS PATH. The reason is that when the application looks for its overlay and accessory files, the DOS PATH setting has no effect.

On a hard disk system, users typically install all transient commands and utilities in subdirectories and ensure that the PATH points to those directories. The path literally is a list of directories and subdirectories in the AUTOEXEC.BAT file that tells DOS where to search for files when these files are not in the same directory you are when you enter a command. The system then functions as though all the commands were resident because

DOS finds the necessary files without further thought or effort on the part of the user. A path on such a hard drive may look like this:

```
PATH=C:\DOS;C:\BAT;C:\UTILS;
```

It is important to know that when DOS loads each time you power up your system, it looks for two such text files. The first text file DOS looks for is CONFIG.SYS, which also can be edited by the system user. This file loads device drivers like ANSI.SYS. The following is an example of a common CONFIG.SYS file:

```
FILES=30
BUFFERS=17
SHELL=C:\DOS\COMMAND.COM C:\DOS /E:512 /P
LASTDRIVE=G
DEVICE=C:\DOS\ANSI.SYS
```

The second text file DOS looks for each time you power up your system is AUTOEXEC.BAT, which sets the PATH and loads memory-resident programs and performs other system configuration tasks like creating a C:\> prompt. A typical AUTOEXEC.BAT file might look like the following:

```
@ECHO OFF
PROMPT $P$G
PATH=C:\DOS;C:\BAT;C:\UTILS;
\DOS\MODE CON: RATE=32 DELAY=1
\DOS\DOSKEY
```

The PATH normally cannot exceed 128 characters in length (including colons, semi-colons, and backslashes). As a result of that limitation, you cannot have a PATH that contains all your directories if the directory names exceed 128 characters. For more information on the AUTOEXEC.BAT and CONFIG.SYS files, consult Que's *Using DOS 6.2, Special Edition*, or *Using IBM PC DOS 6.1*.

You can completely short-circuit the DOS command search procedure by simply entering at the command prompt the complete path to the file. For example, rather than include C:\DOS in the PATH and enter this command:

```
C:\>CHKDSK
```

You can enter the full name of the program:

```
C:\>C:\DOS\CHKDSK.COM
```

The latter command immediately locates and loads the CHKDSK program with no search through the current directory or PATH setting. This method of calling up a program speeds the location and execution of the program and works especially well to increase the speed of DOS batch file execution.

A few major software applications have problems if they are called up from a remote directory or drive using the DOS PATH. Such an application often is made up of many individual files, including overlay and accessory files. Problems can occur when an application expects you to run it from its own directory by making that directory current and then running the program's COM or EXE file. Such applications look for their own files in the current directory. If you did not change to the application's directory, because the program does not look for its files by checking the path, the program does not find its own files. The path entry in AUTOEXEC.BAT has no effect.

Such applications can be called up through batch files or aided by programs that "force-feed" a path-type setting to the programs; the software then works as though files are "here" even when they are in some other directory. The best utility for this purpose is the APPEND command in DOS 3.0 and later versions. For information on the use of the APPEND command see Que's *Using MS-DOS 6*.

DOS History

The following section details some of the differences between the DOS versions that have appeared over the years.

IBM and MS DOS 1.x to 3.x Versions. There have been many specific DOS versions in the 1.x to 3.x range from both IBM and Microsoft, as well as a few other OEMs. Table 20.4 lists the file dates and sizes for the major IBM and Microsoft DOS versions. You can see how DOS has grown over the years!

Table 20.4	System File Sizes			
DOS Version	File Dates	COMMAND.COM	IO.SYS IBMBIO.COM	MSDOS.SYS IBMDOS.COM
IBM PC 1.0	08-04-81	3,231	1,920	6,400
IBM PC 1.1	05-07-82	4,959	1,920	6,400
IBM PC 2.0	03-08-83	17,792	4,608	17,152
IBM PC 2.1	10-20-83	17,792	4,736	17,024
IBM PC 3.0	08-14-84	22,042	8,964	27,920
IBM PC 3.1	03-07-85	23,210	9,564	27,760
IBM PC 3.2	12-30-85	23,791	16,369	28,477
MS 3.2	07-07-86	23,612	16,138	28,480
IBM PC 3.3	03-17-87	25,307	22,100	30,159
MS 3.3	07-24-87	25,276	22,357	30,128

IBM DOS 4.xx Versions. DOS 4.xx has had many revisions since being introduced in mid-1988. Since the first release, IBM has released different Corrective Service Diskettes (CSDs), which fix a variety of problems with DOS 4. Each CSD is cumulative, which means that the later ones include all previous fixes. Note that these fixes are for IBM DOS and not for any other manufacturer's version.

Table 20.5 shows a summary of the different IBM DOS 4.xx releases and specific information about the system files and shell so that you can identify the release you are using. To obtain the latest Corrective Service Diskettes (CSDs) that update you to the latest release, contact your dealer—the fixes are free.

VI

Troubleshooting

Table 20.5   IBM DOS 4.xx Releases

File Name	Size	Date	Version	SYSLEVEL	Comments
IBMBIO.COM IBMDOS.COM COMMAND.COM	32810 35984 37637	06/17/88 06/17/88 06/17/88	4.00	—	Original release.
IBMBIO.COM IBMDOS.COM COMMAND.COM	32816 36000 37637	08/03/88 08/03/88 06/17/88	4.01	CSD UR22624	EMS fixes.
IBMBIO.COM IBMDOS.COM COMMAND.COM	32816 36000 37652	08/03/88 11/11/88 11/11/88	4.01	CSD UR24270	Date change fixed.
IBMBIO.COM IBMDOS.COM COMMAND.COM	33910 37136 37652	04/06/89 04/06/89 11/11/88	4.01	CSD UR25066	"Death disk" fixed.
IBMBIO.COM IBMDOS.COM COMMAND.COM	34660 37248 37765	03/20/90 02/20/90 03/20/90	4.01	CSD UR29015	SCSI support added.
IBMBIO.COM IBMDOS.COM COMMAND.COM	34660 37264 37765	04/27/90 05/21/90 06/29/90	4.01	CSD UR31300	HPFS compatibility.
IBMBIO.COM IBMDOS.COM COMMAND.COM	34692 37280 37762	04/08/91 11/30/90 09/27/91	4.01	CSD UR35280	HPFS and CHKDSK.

IBM DOS 5.xx Versions. DOS 5.xx has had several different revisions since being introduced in mid-1991. Since the first release, IBM has released various Corrective Service Diskettes (CSDs), which fix a variety of problems with DOS 5. Each CSD is cumulative, which means that the later ones include all previous fixes. Note that these fixes are for IBM DOS and not any other manufacturer's version. IBM typically provides more support in the way of fixes and updates than any other manufacturer. Note that IBM now supports the installation of IBM DOS on clone systems.

Table 20.6 shows a summary of the different IBM DOS 5.xx releases and specific information about the system files and shell so that you can identify the release you are using. To obtain the latest Corrective Service Diskettes (CSDs) that update you to the latest release, contact your dealer—the fixes are free.

Table 20.6   IBM DOS 5.xx Releases

File Name	Size	Date	Version	SYSLEVEL	Comments
IBMBIO.COM	33430	05/09/91	5.00	—	Original release.
IBMDOS.COM	37378	05/09/91			
COMMAND.COM	47987	05/09/91			
IBMBIO.COM	33430	05/09/91	5.00	CSD UR35423	XCOPY and
IBMDOS.COM	37378	05/09/91			QEDIT fixed.
COMMAND.COM	48005	08/16/91			
IBMBIO.COM	33430	05/09/91	5.00	CSD UR35748	SYS fixed.
IBMDOS.COM	37378	05/09/91			
COMMAND.COM	48006	10/25/91			
IBMBIO.COM	33446	11/29/91	5.00	CSD UR35834	EMM386, FORMAT,
IBMDOS.COM	37378	11/29/91			and BACKUP
COMMAND.COM	48006	11/29/91			fixed.
IBMBIO.COM	33446	02/28/92	5.00.1	CSD UR36603	Many fixes;
IBMDOS.COM	37378	11/29/91	Rev. A		clone support;
COMMAND.COM	48006	02/28/92			new retail version.
IBMBIO.COM	33446	05/29/92	5.00.1	CSD UR37387	RESTORE and
IBMDOS.COM	37362	05/29/92	Rev. 1		UNDELETE fixed;
COMMAND.COM	48042	09/11/92			>1GB HD fixed.
IBMBIO.COM	33718	09/01/92	5.02	—	New retail version;
IBMDOS.COM	37362	09/01/92	Rev. 0		several new
COMMAND.COM	47990	09/01/92			commands added.

IBM and MS DOS 6.xx Versions. There are several different versions of DOS 6.xx from both Microsoft and IBM. The original release of MS-DOS 6.0 came from Microsoft. One of the features included in 6.0 was the new DoubleSpace disk compression. Unfortunately, DoubleSpace had some problems with certain system configurations and hardware types. In the meantime, IBM took DOS 6.0 from Microsoft, updated it to fix several small problems, removed the disk compression, and sold it as IBM DOS 6.1. Microsoft had many problems with the DoubleSpace disk compression used in 6.0 and released 6.2 as a free bug fix upgrade. Microsoft then ran into legal problems in a lawsuit brought by Stacker Corporation. Microsoft was found to have infringed on the Stacker software and was forced to remove the DoubleSpace compression from DOS 6.2, which was released as 6.21. Microsoft then quickly developed a noninfringing disk compression utility called DriveSpace, which was released in 6.22, along with several minor bug fixes. IBM skipped over the 6.2 version number and released DOS 6.3 (now called PC DOS), which also included a different type of compression program than that used by Microsoft. By avoiding the DoubleSpace software, IBM also avoided the bugs and legal problems that Microsoft had encountered. Also included in the updated IBM releases are enhanced PCMCIA and power management commands.

VI

Troubleshooting

Table 20.7 shows a summary of the different IBM DOS 6.xx releases.

Table 20.7 IBM and Microsoft DOS 6.xx Releases

File Name	Size	Date	Version	SYSLEVEL	Comments
IO.SYS	40470	03/10/93	MS	—	Original Microsoft release.
MSDOS.SYS	38138	03/10/93	6.00		
COMMAND.COM	52925	03/10/93	Rev. A		
IBMBIO.COM	40694	06/29/93	IBM	—	Original IBM release. Has fixes over MS version.
IBMDOS.COM	38138	06/29/93	6.10		
COMMAND.COM	52589	06/29/93	Rev. 0		
IBMBIO.COM	40964	09/30/93	PC	—	SuperStor/DS compression; enhanced PCMCIA.
IBMDOS.COM	38138	09/30/93	6.10		
COMMAND.COM	52797	09/30/93	Rev. 0		
IO.SYS	40566	09/30/93	MS	—	DoubleSpace fixes. Enhanced cleanboot and data recovery.
MSDOS.SYS	38138	09/30/93	6.20		
COMMAND.COM	54619	09/30/93	Rev. A		
IO.SYS	40774	05/31/94	MS	—	New DriveSpace disk compression software and minor fixes.
MSDOS.SYS	38138	05/31/94	6.22		
COMMAND.COM	54645	05/31/94	Rev. A		
IBMBIO.COM	40758	12/31/93	IBM	—	Numerous bug fixes; new disk compression software.
IBMDOS.COM	38138	12/31/93	6.30		
COMMAND.COM	54804	08/12/94	Rev. 0		

The Boot Process

The term *boot* comes from the term *bootstrap* and describes the method by which the PC becomes operational. Just as you pull on a large boot by the small strap attached to the back, a PC can load a large operating system program by first loading a small program that then can pull in the operating system. A chain of events begins with the application of power and finally results in an operating computer system with software loaded and running. Each event is called by the event before it and initiates the event after it.

Tracing the system boot process might help you find the location of a problem if you examine the error messages the system displays when the problem occurs. If you can see an error message displayed only by a particular program, you can be sure that the program in question was at least loaded and partially running. Combine this information with the knowledge of the boot sequence, and you can at least tell how far along the system's startup procedure is. You usually want to look at whatever files or disk areas were being accessed during the failure in the boot process. Error messages displayed during the boot process as well as those displayed during normal system operation can be hard to decipher, but the first step in decoding an error message is to know where the message came from—what program actually sent or displayed the message. The following programs are capable of displaying error messages during the boot process:

- Motherboard ROM BIOS

- Adapter card ROM BIOS extensions

- Master partition boot sector

- DOS volume boot sector

- System files (IBMBIO.COM and IBMDOS.COM)
- Device drivers (loaded through CONFIG.SYS)
- Shell program (COMMAND.COM)
- Programs run by AUTOEXEC.BAT

This section examines the system startup sequence and provides a detailed account of many of the error messages that might occur during this process.

How DOS Loads and Starts

If you have a problem with your system during startup and you can determine where in this sequence of events your system has stalled, you know what events have occurred and you probably can eliminate each of them as a cause of the problem. The following steps occur in a typical system startup:

1. You switch on electrical power to the system.

2. The power supply performs a self-test. When all voltages and current levels are acceptable, the supply indicates that the power is stable and sends the Power Good signal to the motherboard. The time from switch-on to Power Good is normally between .1 and .5 seconds.

3. The microprocessor timer chip receives the Power Good signal, which causes it to stop generating a reset signal to the microprocessor.

4. The microprocessor begins executing the ROM BIOS code, starting at memory address FFFF:0000. Because this location is only 16 bytes from the very end of the available ROM space, it contains a JMP (jump) instruction to the actual ROM BIOS starting address.

5. The ROM BIOS performs a test of the central hardware to verify basic system functionality. Any errors that occur are indicated by audio codes because the video system has not yet been initialized.

6. The BIOS performs a video ROM scan of memory locations C000:0000 through C780:0000, looking for video adapter ROM BIOS programs contained on a video adapter card plugged into a slot. If a video ROM BIOS is found, it is tested by a checksum procedure. If it passes the checksum test, the ROM is executed; the video ROM code initializes the video adapter, and a cursor appears on-screen. If the checksum test fails, the following message appears:

   ```
   C000 ROM Error
   ```

7. If the BIOS finds no video adapter ROM, it uses the motherboard ROM video drivers to initialize the video display hardware, and a cursor appears on-screen.

8. The motherboard ROM BIOS scans memory locations C800:0000 through DF80:0000 in 2K increments for any other ROMs located on any other adapter cards. If any ROMs are found, they are checksum-tested and executed. These adapter ROMs can alter existing BIOS routines as well as establish new ones.

9. Failure of a checksum test for any of these ROM modules causes this message to appear:

    XXXX ROM Error

10. The address XXXX indicates the segment address of the failed ROM module.

11. The ROM BIOS checks the word value at memory location 0000:0472 to see whether this start is a cold start or a warm start. A word value of 1234h in this location is a flag that indicates a warm start, which causes the memory test portion of the POST (Power-On Self Test) to be skipped. Any other word value in this location indicates a cold start and full POST.

12. If this is a cold start, the POST executes. Any errors found during the POST are reported by a combination of audio and displayed error messages. Successful completion of the POST is indicated by a single beep.

13. The ROM BIOS searches for a DOS volume boot sector at cylinder 0, head 0, sector 1 (the very first sector) on the A drive. This sector is loaded into memory at 0000:7C00 and tested. If a disk is in the drive but the sector cannot be read, or if no disk is present, the BIOS continues with the next step.

14. If the first byte of the DOS volume boot sector loaded from the floppy disk in drive A is less than 06h, or if the first byte is greater than or equal to 06h, and the first nine words contain the same data pattern, this error message appears and the system stops:

    602-Diskette Boot Record Error

15. If the disk was prepared with FORMAT or SYS using DOS 3.3 or an earlier version and the specified system files are not the first two files in the directory, or if a problem was encountered loading them, the following message appears:

    Non-System disk or disk error
    Replace and strike any key when ready

16. If the disk was prepared with FORMAT or SYS using DOS 3.3 or an earlier version and the boot sector is corrupt, you might see this message:

    Disk Boot failure

17. If the disk was prepared with FORMAT or SYS using DOS 4.0 and later versions and the specified system files are not the first two files in the directory, or if a problem was encountered loading them, or the boot sector is corrupt, this message appears:

    Non-System disk or disk error
    Replace and press any key when ready

18. If no DOS volume boot sector can be read from drive A:, the BIOS looks for a master partition boot sector at cylinder 0, head 0, sector 1 (the very first sector) of the first fixed disk. If this sector is found, it is loaded into memory address 0000:7C00 and tested for a signature.

19. If the last two (signature) bytes of the master partition boot sector are not equal to 55AAh, software interrupt 18h (Int 18h) is invoked on most systems. On an IBM PS/2 system, a special character graphics message is displayed that depicts inserting a floppy disk in drive A: and pressing the F1 key. For non-PS/2 systems made by IBM, an Int 18h executes the ROM BIOS–based Cassette BASIC Interpreter. On any other IBM-compatible system, a message indicating some type of boot error is displayed. For example, systems with Phoenix AT ROM BIOS display this message:

```
No boot device available -
strike F1 to retry boot, F2 for setup utility
```

20. The master partition boot sector program searches its partition table for an entry with a system indicator byte indicating an extended partition. If the program finds such an entry, it loads the extended partition boot sector at the location indicated. The extended partition boot sector also has a table that is searched for another extended partition. If another extended partition entry is found, that extended partition boot sector is loaded from the location indicated, and the search continues until either no more extended partitions are indicated or the maximum number of 24 total partitions has been reached.

21. The master partition boot sector searches its partition table for a boot indicator byte marking an active partition.

22. On an IBM system, if none of the partitions is marked active (bootable), ROM BIOS–based Cassette BASIC is invoked. On most IBM-compatible systems, some type of disk error message is displayed.

23. If any boot indicator in the master partition boot record table is invalid, or if more than one indicates an active partition, the following message is displayed, and the system stops:

```
Invalid partition table
```

24. If an active partition is found in the master partition boot sector, the volume boot sector from the active partition is loaded and tested.

25. If the DOS volume boot sector cannot be read successfully from the active partition within five retries because of read errors, this message appears and the system stops:

```
Error loading operating system
```

26. The hard disk DOS volume boot sector is tested for a signature. If the DOS volume boot sector does not contain a valid signature of 55AAh as the last two bytes in the sector, this message appears and the system stops:

```
Missing operating system
```

27. The volume boot sector is executed as a program. This program checks the root directory to ensure that the first two files are IBMBIO.COM and IBMDOS.COM. If these files are present, they are loaded.

VI

Troubleshooting

28. If the disk was prepared with FORMAT or SYS using DOS 3.3 or an earlier version and the specified system files are not the first two files in the directory, or if a problem is encountered loading them, the following message appears:

```
Non-System disk or disk error
Replace and strike any key when ready
```

29. If the disk was prepared with FORMAT or SYS using DOS 3.3 or an earlier version and the boot sector is corrupt, you might see this message:

```
Disk Boot failure
```

30. If the disk was prepared with FORMAT or SYS using DOS 4.0 or a later version and the specified system files are not the first two files in the directory, or if a problem is encountered loading them, or the boot sector is corrupt, the following message appears:

```
Non-System disk or disk error
Replace and press any key when ready
```

31. If no problems occur, the DOS volume boot sector executes IBMBIO.COM.

32. The initialization code in IBMBIO.COM copies itself into the highest region of contiguous DOS memory and transfers control to the copy. The initialization code copy then relocates IBMDOS over the portion of IBMBIO in low memory that contains the initialization code, because the initialization code no longer needs to be in that location.

33. The initialization code executes IBMDOS, which initializes the base device drivers, determines equipment status, resets the disk system, resets and initializes attached devices, and sets the system default parameters.

34. The full DOS filing system is active, and the IBMBIO initialization code is given back control.

35. The IBMBIO initialization code reads CONFIG.SYS four times.

36. During the first read, all the statements except DEVICE, INSTALL, and SHELL are read and processed in a predetermined order. Thus, the order of appearance for statements other than DEVICE, INSTALL, and SHELL in CONFIG.SYS is of no significance.

37. During the second read, DEVICE statements are processed in the order in which they appear, and any device driver files named are loaded and executed.

38. During the third read, INSTALL statements are processed in the order in which they appear, and the programs named are loaded and executed.

39. During the fourth and final read, the SHELL statement is processed and loads the specified command processor with the specified parameters. If the CONFIG.SYS file contains no SHELL statement, the default \COMMAND.COM processor is loaded with default parameters. Loading the command processor overwrites the initialization code in memory (because the job of the initialization code is finished).

40. If AUTOEXEC.BAT is present, COMMAND.COM loads and runs AUTOEXEC.BAT. After the commands in AUTOEXEC.BAT have been executed, the DOS prompt appears (unless the AUTOEXEC.BAT calls an application program or shell of some kind, in which case the user might operate the system without ever seeing a DOS prompt).

41. If no AUTOEXEC.BAT is present, COMMAND.COM executes the internal DATE and TIME commands, displays a copyright message, and displays the DOS prompt.

These are the steps performed by IBM AT systems, and most IBM-compatible systems closely emulate them. Some minor variations from this scenario are possible, such as those introduced by other ROM programs in the various adapters that might be plugged into a slot. Also, depending on the exact ROM BIOS programs involved, some of the error messages and sequences might vary. Generally, however, a computer follows this chain of events in "coming to life."

You can modify the system startup procedures by altering the CONFIG.SYS and AUTOEXEC.BAT files. These files control the configuration of DOS and allow special startup programs to be executed every time the system starts. The *User's Guide and Reference* that comes with DOS 5 has an excellent section on DOS configuration.

File Management

DOS uses several elements and structures to store and retrieve information on a disk. These elements and structures enable DOS to communicate properly with the ROM BIOS as well as application programs to process file storage and retrieval requests. Understanding these structures and how they interact helps you to troubleshoot and even repair these structures.

DOS File Space Allocation

DOS allocates disk space for a file on demand (space is not preallocated). The space is allocated one *cluster* (or allocation unit) at a time. A cluster is always one or more sectors. (For more information about sectors, refer to Chapter 14, "Hard Disk Drives and Controllers.")

The clusters are arranged on a disk to minimize head movement for multisided media. DOS allocates all the space on a disk cylinder before moving to the next cylinder. It does this by using the sectors under the first head, and then all the sectors under the next head, and so on until all sectors of all heads of the cylinder are used. The next sector used is sector 1 of head 0 on the next cylinder. (You find more information on floppy disks and drives in Chapter 13, "Floppy Disk Drives and Controllers," and on hard disks in Chapter 14, "Hard Disk Drives and Controllers.")

DOS version 2.x uses a simple algorithm when it allocates file space on a disk. Every time a program requests disk space, DOS scans from the beginning of the FAT until it finds a free cluster in which to deposit a portion of the file; then the search continues for the next cluster of free space, until all the file is written. This algorithm, called the *First Available Cluster algorithm*, causes any erased file near the beginning of the disk to be overwritten during the next write operation because those clusters would be the first available to the next write operation. This system prevents recovery of that file and promotes file fragmentation because the first available cluster found is used regardless of whether the entire file can be written there. DOS simply continues searching for free clusters in which to deposit the remainder of the file.

The algorithm used for file allocation in DOS 3.0 and later versions is called the *Next Available Cluster algorithm*. In this algorithm, the search for available clusters in which to write a file starts not at the beginning of the disk, but rather from where the last write occurred. Therefore, the disk space freed by erasing a file is not necessarily reused immediately. Rather, DOS maintains a *Last Written Cluster pointer* indicating the last written cluster and begins its search from that point. This pointer is maintained in system RAM and is lost when the system is reset or rebooted, or when a disk is changed in a floppy drive.

In working with 360K drives, all versions of DOS always use the First Available Cluster algorithm because the Last Written Cluster pointer cannot be maintained for floppy disk drives that do not report a disk change (DC) signal to the controller, and because 360K drives do not supply the DC signal. With 360K floppy drives, therefore, DOS always assumes that the disk could have been changed, which flushes any buffers and resets the Last Written Cluster pointer.

The Next Available Cluster algorithm in DOS 3.0 and later versions is faster than the First Available Cluster algorithm and helps minimize fragmentation. Sometimes this type of algorithm is called *elevator seeking* because write operations occur at higher and higher clusters until the end of the disk area is reached. At that time, the pointer is reset, and writes work their way from the beginning of the disk again.

Files still end up becoming fragmented using the new algorithm, because the pointer is reset after a reboot, a disk change operation, or when the end of the disk is reached. Nevertheless, a great benefit of the newer method is that it makes unerasing files more likely to succeed even if the disk has been written to since the erasure, because the file just erased is not likely to be the target of the next write operation. In fact, it might be some time before the clusters occupied by the erased file are reused.

Even when a file is overwritten under DOS 3.0 and later versions, the clusters occupied by the file are not actually reused in the overwrite. For example, if you accidentally save on a disk a file using the same name as an important file that already exists, the existing file clusters are marked as available, and the new file (with the same name) is written to the disk in other clusters. It is possible, therefore, that the original copy of the file can still be retrieved. You can continue this procedure by saving another copy of the file with the same name, and each file copy is saved to higher numbered clusters, and each earlier version overwritten might still be recoverable on the disk. This process can continue until the system is rebooted or reset, or until the end of the available space is reached. Then the pointer is set to the first cluster, and previous file data is overwritten.

Because DOS always uses the first available directory entry when it saves or creates a file, the overwritten or deleted files whose data is still recoverable on the disk no longer appear in a directory listing. No commercial quick unerase or other unerase utilities therefore can find any record of the erased or overwritten file on the disk—true, of course, because these programs look only in the directory for a record of an erased file. Some newer undelete programs have a memory-resident delete tracking function that, in essence, maintains a separate directory listing from DOS. Unless an unerase program has a memory-resident delete tracking function, and that function has been activated before the deletion, no program can recall the files overwritten in the directory entry.

Because unerase programs do not look at the FAT, or at the data clusters themselves (unless they use delete tracking), they see no record of the files' existence. By scanning the free clusters on the disk one by one using a disk editor tool, you can locate the data from the overwritten or erased file and manually rebuild the FAT and directory entries. This procedure enables you to recover erased files even though files have been written to the disk since the erasure took place.

Interfacing to Disk Drives

DOS uses a combination of disk management components to make files accessible. These components differ slightly between floppies and hard disks and between disks of different sizes. They determine how a disk appears to DOS and to applications software. Each component used to describe the disk system fits as a layer into the complete system. Each layer communicates with the layer above and below it. When all the components work together, an application can access the disk to find and store data. Table 20.8 lists the DOS format specifications for floppy disks.

The four primary layers of interface between an application program running on a system and any disks attached to the system consist of software routines that can perform various functions, usually to communicate with the adjacent layers. These layers are shown in the following list:

- DOS Interrupt 21h (Int 21h) routines

- DOS Interrupt 25/26h (Int 25/26h) routines

- ROM BIOS disk Interrupt 13h (Int 13h) routines

- Disk controller I/O port commands

Each layer accepts various commands, performs different functions, and generates results. These interfaces are available for both floppy disk drives and hard disks, although the floppy disk and hard disk Int 13h routines differ widely. The floppy disk controllers and hard disk controllers are very different as well, but all the layers perform the same functions for both floppy disks and hard disks.

VI

Troubleshooting

Table 20.8   Floppy Disk Format Specifications

Disk Size (in.) Disk Capacity (KB)	Current Formats 3 1/2" 2,880	3 1/2" 1,440	3 1/2" 720
Media Descriptor Byte	F0h	F0h	F9h
Sides (Heads)	2	2	2
Tracks per Side	80	80	80
Sectors per Track	36	18	9
Bytes per Sector	512	512	512
Sectors per Cluster	2	1	2
FAT Length (Sectors)	9	9	3
Number of FATs	2	2	2
Root Dir. Length (Sectors)	15	14	7
Maximum Root Entries	240	224	112
Total Sectors per Disk	5,760	2,880	1,440
Total Available Sectors	5,726	2,847	1,426
Total Available Clusters	2,863	2,847	713

Interrupt 20h. The DOS Int 21h routines exist at the highest level and provide the most functionality with the least amount of work. For example, if an application program needs to create a subdirectory on a disk, it can call Int 21h, Function 39h. This function performs all operations necessary to create a subdirectory on the disk, including updating the appropriate directory and FAT sectors. The only information this function needs is the name of the subdirectory to create. DOS Int 21h would do much more work by using one of the lower-level access methods to create a subdirectory on the disk. Most applications programs you run access the disk through this level of interface.

Interrupt 25h and Int 26h. The DOS Int 25h and Int 26h routines provide much lower-level access to the disk than the Int 21h routines. Int 25h reads only specified sectors from a disk, and Int 26h only writes specified sectors to a disk. If you were to write a program that used these functions to create a subdirectory on a disk, the work required would be much greater than that required by the Int 21h method. For example, your program would have to perform all these tasks:

■ Calculate exactly which directory and FAT sectors need to be updated

■ Use Int 25h to read these sectors

■ Modify the sectors appropriately to contain the new subdirectory information

■ Use Int 26h to write the sectors back out

5 1/4" 1,200	5 1/4" 360	Obsolete Formats 5 1/4" 320	5 1/4" 180	5 1/4" 160
F9h	FDh	FFh	FCh	FEh
2	2	2	1	1
80	40	40	40	40
15	9	8	9	8
512	512	512	512	512
1	2	2	1	1
7	2	1	2	1
2	2	2	2	2
14	7	7	4	4
224	112	112	64	64
2,400	720	640	360	320
2,371	708	630	351	313
2,371	354	315	351	313

The number of steps would be even greater considering the difficulty in determining exactly what sectors have to be modified. According to Int 25/26h, the entire DOS-addressable area of the disk consists of sectors numbered sequentially from 0. A program designed to access the disk using Int 25h and Int 26h must know the location of everything by this sector number. A program designed this way might have to be modified to handle disks with different numbers of sectors or different directory and FAT sizes and locations. Because of all the overhead required to get the job done, most programmers would not choose to access the disk in this manner, and instead would use the higher-level Int 21h, which does all the work automatically.

Only disk- and sector-editing programs typically access a disk drive at the Int 25h and Int 26h level. Programs that work at this level of access can edit only areas of a disk that have been defined to DOS as a logical volume (drive letter). For example, DEBUG can read sectors from and write sectors to disks with this level of access.

Interrupt 13h. The next lower level of communications with drives, the ROM BIOS Int 13h routines, usually are found in ROM chips on the motherboard or on an adapter card in a slot; however, an Int 13h handler also can be implemented by using a device driver loaded at boot time. Because DOS requires Int 13h access to boot from a drive (and a device driver cannot be loaded until after boot-up), only drives with ROM BIOS–based Int 13h support can become bootable. Int 13h routines need to talk directly to the controller using the I/O ports on the controller. Therefore, the Int 13h code is very controller specific.

VI

Troubleshooting

Table 20.9 lists the different functions available at the Interrupt 13h BIOS interface. Some functions are available to floppy drives or hard drives only, whereas others are available to both types of drives.

Table 20.9 Int 13h BIOS Disk Functions

Function	Floppy Disk	Hard Disk	Description
00h	×	×	Reset disk system.
01h	×	×	Get status of last operation.
02h	×	×	Read sectors.
03h	×	×	Write sectors.
04h	×	×	Verify sectors.
05h	×	×	Format track.
06h		×	Format bad track.
07h		×	Format drive.
08h	×	×	Read drive parameters.
09h		×	Initialize drive characteristics.
0Ah		×	Read long.
0Bh		×	Write long.
0Ch		×	Seek.
0Dh		×	Alternate hard disk reset.
0Eh		×	Read sector buffer.
0Fh		×	Write sector buffer.
10h		×	Test for drive ready.
11h		×	Recalibrate drive.
12h		×	Controller RAM diagnostic.
13h		×	Controller drive diagnostic.
14h		×	Controller internal diagnostic.
15h	×	×	Get disk type.
16h	×		Get floppy disk change status.
17h	×		Set floppy disk type for format.
18h	×		Set media type for format.
19h		×	Park hard disk heads.
1Ah		×	ESDI—Low-level format.
1Bh		×	ESDI—Get manufacturing header.
1Ch		×	ESDI—Get configuration.

Table 20.10 shows the error codes that may be returned by the BIOS INT 13h routines. In some cases, you may see these codes be referred to when running a low-level format program, disk editor, or other program that can directly access a disk drive through the BIOS.

Table 20.10   INT 13h BIOS Error Codes

Code	Description
00h	No error.
01h	Bad command.
02h	Address mark not found.
03h	Write protect.
04h	Request sector not found.
05h	Reset failed.
06h	Media change error.
07h	Initialization failed.
09h	Cross 64K DMA boundary.
0Ah	Bad sector flag detected.
0Bh	Bad track flag detected.
10h	Bad ECC on disk read.
11h	ECC corrected data error.
20h	Controller has failed.
40h	Seek operation failed.
80h	Drive failed to respond.
AAh	Drive not ready.
BBh	Undefined error.
CCh	Write fault.
0Eh	Register error.
FFh	Sense operation failed.

If you design your own custom disk controller device, you need to write an IBM-compatible Int 13h handler package and install it on the card using a ROM BIOS that will be linked into the system at boot time. To use Int 13h routines, a program must use exact cylinder, head, and sector coordinates to specify sectors to read and write. Accordingly, any program designed to work at this level must be intimately familiar with the parameters of the specific disk on the system on which it is designed to run. Int 13h functions exist to read the disk parameters, format tracks, read and write sectors, park heads, and reset the drive.

A low-level format program for ST-506/412 drives needs to work with disks at the Int 13h level or lower. Most ST-506/412 controller format programs work with access at the Int 13h level because virtually any operation a format program needs is available through the Int 13h interface. This is not true, however, for other types of controllers (such as IDE, SCSI, or ESDI), for which defect mapping and other operations differ considerably from the ST-506/412 types. Controllers that must perform special operations during a low-level format, such as defining disk parameters to override the motherboard ROM BIOS drive tables, would not work with any formatter that used only the standard Int 13h interface. For these reasons, most controllers require a custom formatter designed to bypass the Int 13h interface. Most general purpose, low-level reformat programs that perform a nondestructive format (such as Norton Calibrate and SpinRite II) access the controller through the Int 13h interface (rather than going direct) and therefore cannot be used for an initial low-level format; the initial low-level format must be done by a controller-specific utility.

Few high-powered disk utility programs, other than some basic formatting software, can talk to the disk at the Int 13h level. The Kolod Research hTEST/hFORMAT utilities also can communicate at the Int 13h level, as can the DOS FDISK program. The Norton DISKEDIT and NU programs can communicate with a disk at the Int 13h level when these programs are in their absolute sector mode; they are two of the few utilities that can do so. These programs are important because they can be used for the worst data recovery situations, in which the partition tables have been corrupted. Because the partition tables as well as any non-DOS partitions exist outside the area of a disk that is defined by DOS, only programs that work at the Int 13h level can access them. Most utility programs for data recovery, such as the Mace Utilities MUSE program, work only at the DOS Int 25/26h level, which makes them useless for accessing areas of a disk outside of DOS domain.

Disk Controller I/O Port Commands. In the lowest level of interface, programs talk directly to the disk controller in the controller's own specific native language. To do this, a program must send controller commands through the I/O ports to which the controller responds. These commands are specific to the particular controller and sometimes differ even among controllers of the same type, such as different ESDI controllers. The ROM BIOS in the system must be designed specifically for the controller because the ROM BIOS talks to the controller at this I/O port level. Most manufacturer-type low-level format programs also need to talk to the controller directly because the higher-level Int 13h interface does not provide enough specific features for many of the custom ST-506/412 or ESDI and SCSI controllers on the market.

Figure 20.2 shows that most application programs work through the Int 21h interface, which passes commands to the ROM BIOS as Int 13h commands; these commands then are converted into direct controller commands by the ROM BIOS. The controller executes the commands and returns the results through the layers until the desired information reaches the application. This process enables applications to be written without worrying about such low-level system details, leaving such details up to DOS and the ROM BIOS. It also enables applications to run on widely different types of hardware, as long as the correct ROM BIOS and DOS support is in place.

Any software can bypass any level of interface and communicate with the level below it, but doing so requires much more work. The lowest level of interface available is direct communication with the controller using I/O port commands. As figure 20.2 shows, each different type of controller has different I/O port locations as well as differences among the commands presented at the various ports, and only the controller can talk directly to the disk drive.

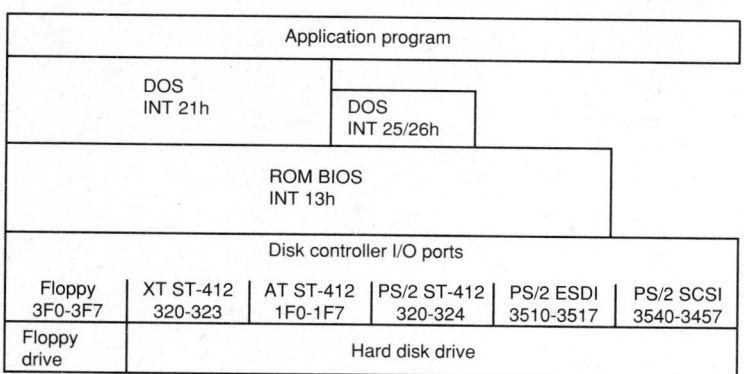

Fig. 20.2

Relationships between various interface levels.

If not for the ROM BIOS Int 13h interface, a unique DOS would have to be written for each available type of hard and floppy disk drive and disk. Instead, DOS communicates with the ROM BIOS using standard Int 13h function calls translated by the Int 13h interface into commands for the specific hardware. Because of the standard ROM BIOS interface, DOS can be written relatively independently of specific disk hardware and can support many different types of drives and controllers.

DOS Structures

To manage files on a disk and enable all application programs to see a consistent disk interface no matter what type of disk is used, DOS uses several structures. The following list shows all the structures and areas that DOS defines and uses to manage a disk, in roughly the order in which they are encountered on a disk:

- Master and extended partition boot sectors

- DOS volume boot sector

- Root directory

- File allocation tables (FAT)

- Clusters (allocation units)

- Data area

- Diagnostic read-and-write cylinder

A hard disk has all these DOS disk management structures allocated, and a floppy disk has all but the master and extended partition boot sectors and the diagnostic cylinder. These structures are created by the DOS FDISK program, which has no application on a floppy disk because floppy disks cannot be partitioned. Figure 20.3 is a simple diagram showing the relative locations of these DOS disk management structures on the 32M hard disk in an IBM AT Model 339.

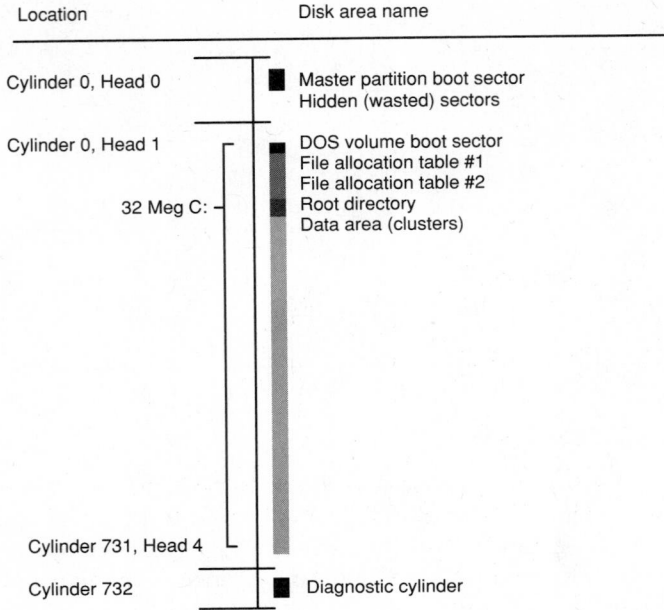

Location   Disk area name

Cylinder 0, Head 0   ■ Master partition boot sector
                              Hidden (wasted) sectors

Cylinder 0, Head 1   ■ DOS volume boot sector
                              File allocation table #1
                              File allocation table #2
        32 Meg C: ■ Root directory
                              Data area (clusters)

Cylinder 731, Head 4

Cylinder 732   ■ Diagnostic cylinder

Fig. 20.3
DOS disk management structures on an IBM AT Model 339 32M hard disk.

Each disk area has a purpose and function. If one of these special areas is damaged, serious consequences can result. Damage to one of these sensitive structures usually causes a domino effect and limits access to other areas of the disk or causes further problems in using the disk. For example, DOS cannot read and write files if the FAT is damaged or corrupted. You therefore should understand these data structures well enough to be able to repair them when necessary. Rebuilding these special tables and areas of the disk is essential to the art of data recovery.

Master Partition Boot Sectors. To share a hard disk among different operating systems, the disk might be logically divided into one to four master partitions. Each operating system, including DOS (through versions 3.2), might own only one partition. DOS 3.3 and later versions introduced the extended DOS partition, which allows multiple DOS partitions on the same hard disk. With the DOS FDISK program, you can select the size of each partition. The partition information is kept in several partition boot sectors on the disk, with the main table embedded in the master partition boot sector. The master partition boot sector is always located in the first sector of the entire disk (cylinder 0, head 0, sector 1). The extended partition boot sectors are located at the beginning of each extended partition volume.

Each DOS partition contains a DOS volume boot sector as its first sector. With the DOS FDISK utility, you might designate a single partition as active (or bootable). The master partition boot sector causes the active partition's volume boot sector to receive control when the system is started or reset. Additional master disk partitions can be set up for

Novell NetWare and for OS/2 HPFS, PCIX (UNIX), XENIX, CP/M-86, or other operating systems. None of these foreign operating system partitions can be accessible under DOS, nor can any DOS partitions normally be accessible under other operating systems. (OS/2 and DOS share FAT partitions, but high-performance file system [HPFS] partitions are exclusive to OS/2.)

A hard disk must be partitioned to be accessible by an operating system. You must partition a disk even if you want to create only a single partition. Table 20.11 shows the format of the Master Boot Record (MBR) with partition tables.

Table 20.11	Master Boot Record (Partition Table)	
Offset	**Length**	**Description**
Partition Table Entry #1		
1BEh 446	1 byte	Boot Indicator Byte (80h = Active, else 00h)
1BFh 447	1 byte	Starting Head (or Side) of Partition
1C0h 448	16 bits	Starting Cylinder (10 bits) and Sector (6 bits)
1C2h 450	1 byte	System Indicator Byte (see table 20.12)
1C3h 451	1 byte	Ending Head (or Side) of Partition
1C4h 452	16 bits	Ending Cylinder (10 bits) and Sector (6 bits)
1C6h 454	1 dword	Relative Sector Offset of Partition
1CAh 458	1 dword	Total Number of Sectors in Partition
Partition Table Entry #2		
1CEh 462	1 byte	Boot Indicator Byte (80h = Active, else 00h)
1CFh 463	1 byte	Starting Head (or Side) of Partition
1D0h 464	16 bits	Starting Cylinder (10 bits) and Sector (6 bits)
1D2h 466	1 byte	System Indicator Byte (see table 20.12)
1D3h 467	1 byte	Ending Head (or Side) of Partition
1D4h 468	16 bits	Ending Cylinder (10 bits) and Sector (6 bits)
1D6h 470	1 dword	Relative Sector Offset of Partition
1DAh 474	1 dword	Total Number of Sectors in Partition
Partition Table Entry #3		
1DEh 478	1 byte	Boot Indicator Byte (80h = Active, else 00h)
1DFh 479	1 byte	Starting Head (or Side) of Partition
1E0h 480	16 bits	Starting Cylinder (10 bits) and Sector (6 bits)
1E2h 482	1 byte	System Indicator Byte (see table 20.12)
1E3h 483	1 byte	Ending Head (or Side) of Partition
1E4h 484	16 bits	Ending Cylinder (10 bits) and Sector (6 bits)
1E6h 486	1 dword	Relative Sector Offset of Partition
1EAh 490	1 dword	Total Number of Sectors in Partition

VI

Troubleshooting

(continues)

Offset	Length	Description
Table 20.11 Continued		
Partition Table Entry #4		
1EEh 494	1 byte	Boot Indicator Byte (80h = Active, else 00h)
1EFh 495	1 byte	Starting Head (or Side) of Partition
1F0h 496	16 bits	Starting Cylinder (10 bits) and Sector (6 bits)
1F2h 498	1 byte	System Indicator Byte (see table 20.12)
1F3h 499	1 byte	Ending Head (or Side) of Partition
1F4h 500	16 bits	Ending Cylinder (10 bits) and Sector (6 bits)
1F6h 502	1 dword	Relative Sector Offset of Partition
1FAh 506	1 dword	Total Number of Sectors in Partition
Signature Bytes		
1FEh 510	2 bytes	Boot Sector Signature (55AAh)

A WORD equals two bytes read in reverse order, and a DWORD equals two WORDs read in reverse order.

Table 20.12 shows the standard values and meanings of the System Indicator Byte.

Value	Description
Table 20.12 Partition Table System Indicator Byte Values	
00h	No allocated partition in this entry
01h	Primary DOS, 12-bit FAT (Partition < 16M)
04h	Primary DOS, 16-bit FAT (16M <= Partition <= 32M)
05h	Extended DOS (Points to next Primary Partition)
06h	Primary DOS, 16-bit FAT (Partition > 32M)
07h	OS/2 HPFS Partition
02h	MS-XENIX Root Partition
03h	MS-XENIX usr Partition
08h	AIX File System Partition
09h	AIX Boot Partition
50h	Ontrack Disk Manager READ-ONLY Partition
51h	Ontrack Disk Manager READ/WRITE Partition
56h	Golden Bow Vfeature Partition
61h	Storage Dimensions Speedstor Partition
63h	IBM 386/ix or UNIX System V/386 Partition
64h	Novell NetWare Partition
75h	IBM PCIX Partition

Value	Description
DBh	Digital Research Concurrent DOS/CPM-86 Partition
F2h	Some OEM's DOS 3.2+ Second Partition
FFh	UNIX Bad Block Table Partition

DOS Volume Boot Sectors. The *volume boot sector* is the first sector on any area of a drive addressed as a volume (or logical DOS disk). On a floppy disk, for example, this sector is the first one on the floppy disk because DOS recognizes the floppy disk as a volume with no partitioning required. On a hard disk, the volume boot sector or sectors are located as the first sector within any disk area allocated as a nonextended partition, or any area recognizable as a DOS volume.

This special sector resembles the master partition boot sector in that it contains a program as well as some special data tables. The first volume boot sector on a disk is loaded by the system ROM BIOS for floppies or by the master partition boot sector on a hard disk. This program is given control; it performs some tests and then attempts to load the first DOS system file (IBMBIO.COM). The volume boot sector is transparent to a running DOS system; it is outside the data area of the disk on which files are stored.

You create a volume boot sector with the DOS FORMAT command (high-level format). Hard disks have a volume boot sector at the beginning of every DOS logical drive area allocated on the disk, in both the primary and extended partitions. Although all the logical drives contain the program area as well as a data table area, only the program code from the volume boot sector in the active partition on a hard disk is executed. The others are simply read by the DOS system files during boot-up to obtain their data table and determine the volume parameters.

The volume boot sector contains program code and data. The single data table in this sector is called the *media parameter block* or *disk parameter block*. DOS needs the information it contains to verify the capacity of a disk volume as well as the location of important features such as the FAT. The format of this data is very specific. Errors can cause problems with booting from a disk or with accessing a disk. Some non-IBM OEM versions of DOS have not adhered to the standards set by IBM for the format of this data, which can cause interchange problems with disks formatted by different versions of DOS. The later versions can be more particular, so if you suspect that boot sector differences are causing inability to access a disk, you can use a utility program such as DOS DEBUG or Norton Utilities to copy a boot sector from the newer version of DOS to a disk formatted by the older version. This step should enable the new version of DOS to read the older disk and should not interfere with the less particular older version. This has never been a problem in using different DOS versions from the same OEM, but might occur in mixing different OEM versions.

Table 20.13 shows the format and layout of the DOS Boot Record (DBR).

Table 20.13   DOS Boot Record (DBR) Format

Offset Hex	Dec	Field Length	Description
00h	0	3 bytes	Jump Instruction to Boot Program Code
03h	3	8 bytes	OEM Name and DOS Version ("IBM 5.0")
0Bh	11	1 word	Bytes / Sector (usually 512)
0Dh	13	1 byte	Sectors / Cluster (Must be a power of 2)
0Eh	14	1 word	Reserved Sectors (Boot Sectors, usually 1)
10h	16	1 byte	FAT Copies (usually 2)
11h	17	1 word	Maximum Root Directory Entries (usually 512)
13h	19	1 word	Total Sectors (If Partition <= 32M, else 0)
15h	21	1 byte	Media Descriptor Byte (F8h for Hard Disks)
16h	22	1 word	Sectors / FAT
18h	24	1 word	Sectors / Track
1Ah	26	1 word	Number of Heads
1Ch	28	1 dword	Hidden Sectors (If Partition <= 32M, 1 word only)
For DOS 4.0 or Higher Only, Else 00h			
20h	32	1 dword	Total Sectors (If Partition > 32M, else 0)
24h	36	1 byte	Physical Drive No. (00h=floppy, 80h=hard disk)
25h	37	1 byte	Reserved (00h)
26h	38	1 byte	Extended Boot Record Signature (29h)
27h	39	1 dword	Volume Serial Number (32-bit random number)
2Bh	43	11 bytes	Volume Label ("NO NAME" stored if no label)
36h	54	8 bytes	File System ID ("FAT12" or "FAT16")
For All Versions of DOS			
3Eh	62	450 bytes	Boot Program Code
1FEh	510	2 bytes	Signature Bytes (55AAh)

A WORD is two bytes read in reverse order, and a DWORD is two WORDs read in reverse order.

Root Directory. A *directory* is a simple database containing information about the files stored on a disk. Each record in this database is 32 bytes long, and no delimiters or separating characters are between the fields or records. A directory stores almost all the information that DOS knows about a file: name, attribute, time and date of creation, size, and where the beginning of the file is located on the disk. (The information a directory does *not* contain about a file is where the file continues on the disk and whether the file is contiguous or fragmented. The FAT contains that information.)

Two basic types of directories exist: the *root directory* and *subdirectories*. They differ primarily in how many there can be and in where they can be located. Any given volume can have only one root directory, and the root directory is always stored on a disk in a fixed location immediately following the two FAT copies. Root directories vary in size because of the varying types and capacities of disks, but the root directory of a given disk is fixed. After a root directory is created, it has a fixed length and cannot be extended to hold more entries. Normally, a hard disk volume has a root directory with room for 512 total entries. Subdirectories are stored as files in the data area of the disk and therefore have no fixed length limits.

Every directory, whether it is the root directory or a subdirectory, is organized in the same way. A directory is a small database with a fixed record length of 32 bytes. Entries in the database store important information about individual files and how files are named on a disk. The directory information is linked to the FAT by the starting cluster entry. In fact, if no file on a disk were longer than one single cluster, the FAT would be unnecessary. The directory stores all the information needed by DOS to manage the file, with the exception of all the clusters that the file occupies other than the first one. The FAT stores the remaining information about other clusters the file uses.

To trace a file on a disk, you start with the directory entry to get the information about the starting cluster of the file and its size. Then you go to the file allocation table. From there, you can follow the chain of clusters the file occupies until you reach the end of the file.

DOS Directory entries are 32 bytes long and are in the format shown in table 20.14.

Table 20.14   DOS Directory Format

Offset Hex	Dec	Field Length	Description
00h	0	8 bytes	File name
08h	8	3 bytes	File extension
0Bh	11	1 byte	File attributes
0Ch	12	10 bytes	Reserved (00h)
16h	22	1 word	Time of creation
18h	24	1 word	Date of creation
1Ah	26	1 word	Starting cluster
1Ch	28	1 dword	Size in bytes

VI

Troubleshooting

Table 20.15 describes the DOS Directory file attribute byte.

Table 20.15 DOS Directory File Attribute Byte		
Bit Positions Hex **7 6 5 4 3 2 1 0**	**Value**	**Description**
0 0 0 0 0 0 0 1	01h	Read-only file
0 0 0 0 0 0 1 0	02h	Hidden file
0 0 0 0 0 1 0 0	04h	System file
0 0 0 0 1 0 0 0	08h	Volume label
0 0 0 1 0 0 0 0	10h	Subdirectory
0 0 1 0 0 0 0 0	20h	Archive (updated since backup)
0 1 0 0 0 0 0 0	40h	Reserved
1 0 0 0 0 0 0 0	80h	Reserved
Examples		
0 0 1 0 0 0 0 1	21h	Read-only, archive
0 0 1 1 0 0 1 0	32h	Hidden, subdirectory, archive
0 0 1 0 0 1 1 1	27h	Read-only, hidden, system, archive

File Allocation Tables (FATs). The file allocation table (FAT) is a table of number entries describing how each cluster is allocated on the disk. The data area of the disk has a single entry for each cluster. Sectors in the nondata area on the disk are outside the range of the disk controlled by the FAT. The sectors involved in any of the boot sectors, file allocation table, and root directory are outside the range of sectors controlled by the FAT.

The FAT does not manage every data sector specifically, but rather allocates space in groups of sectors called *clusters* or *allocation units*. A cluster is one or more sectors designated by DOS as allocation units of storage. The smallest space a file can use on a disk is one cluster; all files use space on the disk in integer cluster units. If a file is one byte larger than one cluster, two clusters are used. DOS determines the size of a cluster when the disk is high-level formatted by the DOS FORMAT command.

You can think of the FAT as a sort of spreadsheet that controls the cluster use of the disk. Each cell in the spreadsheet corresponds to a single cluster on the disk; the number stored in that cell is a sort of code telling whether the cluster is used by a file and, if so, where the next cluster of the file is located.

The numbers stored in the FAT are hexadecimal numbers that are either 12 or 16 bits long. The 16-bit FAT numbers are easy to follow because they take an even two bytes of space and can be edited fairly easily. The 12-bit numbers are 1 1/2 bytes long, which presents a problem when most disk sector editors show data in byte units. To edit the FAT, you must do some hex/binary math to convert the displayed byte units to FAT numbers. Fortunately (unless you are using the DOS DEBUG program), most of the available tools and utility programs have a FAT editing mode that automatically converts the numbers for you. Most of them also show the FAT numbers in decimal form, which most people find easier to handle.

The DOS FDISK program determines whether a 12-bit or 16-bit FAT is placed on a disk, even though the FAT is written during the high-level format (FORMAT). All floppy disks use a 12-bit FAT, but hard disks can use either. On hard disk volumes with more than 16 megabytes (32,768 sectors), DOS creates a 16-bit FAT; otherwise, DOS creates a 12-bit FAT.

DOS keeps two copies of the FAT. Each one occupies contiguous sectors on the disk, and the second FAT copy immediately follows the first. Unfortunately, DOS uses the second FAT copy only if sectors in the first FAT copy become unreadable. If the first FAT copy is corrupted, which is a much more common problem, DOS does not use the second FAT copy. Even the DOS CHKDSK command does not check or verify the second FAT copy. Moreover, whenever DOS updates the first FAT, large portions of the first FAT automatically are copied to the second FAT. If, therefore, the first copy was corrupted and then subsequently updated by DOS, a large portion of the first FAT would be copied over the second FAT copy, damaging it in the process. After the update, the second copy is usually a mirror image of the first one, complete with any corruption. Two FATs rarely stay out of sync for very long. When they are out of sync and DOS writes to the disk and causes the first FAT to be updated, it also causes the second FAT to be overwritten by the first FAT. Because of all this, the usefulness of the second copy of the FAT is limited to manual repair operations, and even then it is useful only if the problem is caught immediately, before DOS has a chance to update the disk.

Clusters (Allocation Units). The term *cluster* was changed to *allocation unit* in DOS 4.0. The newer term is appropriate because a single cluster is the smallest unit of the disk that DOS can handle when it writes or reads a file. A cluster is equal to one or more sectors, and although a cluster can be a single sector, it is usually more than one. Having more than one sector per cluster reduces the size and processing overhead of the FAT and enables DOS to run faster because it has fewer individual units of the disk to manage. The trade-off is in wasted disk space. Because DOS can manage space only in full cluster units, every file consumes space on the disk in increments of one cluster.

Table 20.16 shows default cluster (or allocation unit) sizes used by DOS for the various floppy disk formats.

Table 20.16 Default Floppy Disk Cluster (Allocation Unit) Sizes

Drive Type	Cluster (Allocation Unit) Size
5 1/4-inch 360K	2 sectors (1,024 bytes)
5 1/4-inch 1.2M	1 sector (512 bytes)
3 1/4-inch 720K	2 sectors (1,024 bytes)
3 1/4-inch 1.44M	1 sector (512 bytes)
3 1/4-inch 2.88M	2 sectors (1,024 bytes)

It seems strange that the high-density disks, which have many more individual sectors than low-density disks, sometimes have smaller cluster sizes. The larger the FAT, the more entries DOS must manage, and the slower DOS seems to function. This sluggishness is due to the excessive overhead required to manage all the individual clusters; the more clusters to be managed, the slower things become. The trade-off is in the minimum cluster size.

Smaller clusters generate less *slack* (space wasted between the actual end of each file and the end of the cluster). With larger clusters, the wasted space grows larger. High-density floppy drives are faster than their low-density counterparts, so perhaps IBM and Microsoft determined that the decrease in cluster size balances the drive's faster operation and offsets the use of a larger FAT.

For hard disks, the cluster size can vary greatly among different versions of DOS and different disk sizes. Table 20.17 shows the cluster sizes IBM and most other OEM versions of DOS select for a particular volume size.

Table 20.17 Default Hard Disk Cluster (Allocation Unit) Sizes

Hard Disk Volume Size	Cluster (Allocation Unit) Size	FAT type
0M to less than 16M	8 sectors or 4,096 bytes	12-bit
16M through 128M	4 sectors or 2,048 bytes	16-bit
Over 128M through 256M	8 sectors or 4,096 bytes	16-bit
Over 256M through 512M	16 sectors or 8,192 bytes	16-bit
Over 512M through 1,024M	32 sectors or 16,384 bytes	16-bit
Over 1,024M through 2,048M	64 sectors or 32,768 bytes	16-bit

In most cases, these cluster sizes, selected by the DOS FORMAT command, are the minimum possible for a given partition size. Therefore, 8K clusters are the smallest possible for a partition size of greater than 256M. Although most non-IBM OEM versions of DOS work like the IBM version, some versions might use cluster sizes different from what this table indicates. For example, Compaq DOS 3.31 shifts to larger cluster sizes much earlier than IBM DOS does. Compaq DOS shifts to 4K clusters at 64M partitions, 8K clusters at 128M partitions, and 16K clusters at 256M partitions. A 305M partition that uses 8K clusters under IBM DOS has clusters of 16K under Compaq DOS 3.31.

The effect of these larger cluster sizes on disk use can be substantial. A drive containing about 5,000 files, with average slack of one-half of the last cluster used for each file, wastes about 20 megabytes [5000*(.5*8)K] of file space on a disk set up with IBM DOS or MS-DOS. Using Compaq DOS 3.31, this wasted space doubles to 40 megabytes for the same 5,000 files. Someone using a system with Compaq DOS 3.31 could back up, repartition, and reformat with IBM DOS, and after restoring all 5,000 files, gain 20 megabytes of free disk space.

Compaq DOS 3.31 does not use the most efficient (or smallest) cluster size possible for a given partition size because its makers were interested in improving the performance of the system at the expense of great amounts of disk space. Larger cluster sizes get you a smaller FAT, with fewer numbers to manage; DOS overhead is reduced when files are stored and retrieved, which makes the system seem faster. For example, the CHKDSK command runs much faster on a disk with a smaller FAT. Unfortunately, the trade-off for speed here is a tremendous loss of space on the disk. (Compaq DOS 4.0 and 5.0 use IBM DOS and MS-DOS conventions.)

The Data Area. The data area of a disk is the area that follows the boot sector, file allocation tables, and root directory on any volume. This area is managed by the FAT and the root directory. DOS divides it into allocation units sometimes called clusters. These clusters are where normal files are stored on a volume.

Diagnostic Read-and-Write Cylinder. The FDISK partitioning program always reserves the last cylinder of a hard disk for use as a special diagnostic read-and-write test cylinder. That this cylinder is reserved is one reason FDISK always reports fewer total cylinders than the drive manufacturer states are available. DOS (or any other operating system) does not use this cylinder for any normal purpose, because it lies outside the partitioned area of the disk.

On systems with IDE, SCSI, or ESDI disk interfaces, the drive and controller might allocate an additional area past the logical end of the drive for a bad-track table and spare sectors for replacing bad ones. This situation may account for additional discrepancies between FDISK and the drive manufacturer.

The diagnostics area enables diagnostics software such as the manufacturer-supplied Advanced Diagnostics disk to perform read-and-write tests on a hard disk without corrupting any user data. Low-level format programs for hard disks often use this cylinder as a scratch-pad area for running interleave tests or preserving data during nondestructive formats. This cylinder is also sometimes used as a head landing or parking cylinder on hard disks that do not have an automatic parking facility.

Potential DOS Upgrade Problems

You already know that the DOS system files have special placement requirements on a hard disk. Sometimes these special requirements cause problems when you are upgrading from one version of DOS to another.

If you have attempted to upgrade a PC system from one version of DOS to another, you know that you use the DOS SYS command to replace old system files with new ones. The SYS command copies the existing system files (stored on a bootable disk with hidden, system, and read-only attributes) to the disk in the correct position and with the correct names and attributes. The COPY command does not copy hidden or system files (nor would it place the system files in the required positions on the destination disk if their other attributes had been altered so that they could be copied using COPY).

In addition to transferring the two hidden system files from one disk to another, SYS also updates the DOS volume boot sector on the destination disk so that it is correct for the new version of DOS. Common usage of the SYS command is as follows:

    SYS C: (for drive C)

or

    SYS A: (to make a floppy in drive A bootable)

The syntax of the command is as follows:

    SYS[*d:*][*path*]***d:***

In this command line, *d:/path* specifies an optional source drive and path for the system files. If the source drive specification is omitted, the boot drive is used as the source drive. This parameter is supported in DOS 4.0 and later versions only. Versions of DOS older than 4.0 automatically look for system files on the default drive (not on the boot drive). The ***d:*** in the syntax specifies the drive to which you want to transfer the system files.

When the SYS command is executed, you usually are greeted by one of two messages:

    `System transferred`

or

    `No room for system on destination disk`

If a disk has data on it before you try to write the system files to it, the SYS command from DOS versions 3.3 and earlier probably will fail because these versions are not capable of moving other files out of the way. The SYS command in DOS 4.0 and higher versions rarely fails because these versions can and do move files out of the way.

Some users think that the cause of the `No room` message on a system that has an older version of DOS is that the system files in any newer version of DOS are always larger than the previous version, and that the new version files cannot fit into the space allocated for older versions. Such users believe that the command fails because this space cannot be provided at the beginning without moving other data away. This belief is wrong. The SYS command fails in these cases because you are trying to install a version of DOS that has file names different from the names already on the disk. There is no normal reason for the SYS command to fail when you update the system files on a disk that already has those files.

Although the belief that larger system files cannot replace smaller ones might be popular, it is wrong for DOS 3.0 and later versions. The system files can be placed virtually anywhere on the disk, except that the first clusters of the disk must contain the file IBMBIO.COM (or its equivalent). After that requirement is met, the IBMDOS.COM file might be fragmented and placed just about anywhere on the disk, and the SYS command implements it with no problems whatsoever. In version 3.3 or later, even the IBMBIO.COM file can be fragmented and spread all over the disk, as long as the first cluster of the file occupies the first cluster of the disk (cluster 2). The only other requirement is that the names IBMBIO.COM and IBMDOS.COM (or their equivalents) must use the first and second directory entries.

DOS 4.0 and Later Versions. Under DOS 4.0 and later versions, the SYS command is much more powerful than under previous versions. Because the system files must use the first two entries in the root directory of the disk as well as the first cluster (cluster 2) of the disk, the DOS 4.0 and later versions' SYS command moves any files that occupy the first two entries but that do not match the new system file names to other available entries in the root directory. The SYS command also moves the portion of any foreign file occupying the first cluster to other clusters on the disk. Whereas the SYS command in older versions of DOS would fail and require a user to make adjustments to the disk, the DOS 4.0 and later versions' SYS command automatically makes the required adjustments. For example, even if you are updating a Phoenix DOS 3.3 disk to IBM DOS 4.0, the IBM DOS SYS command relocates the Phoenix IO.SYS and MSDOS.SYS files so that the new IBMBIO.COM and IBMDOS.COM files can occupy the correct locations in the root directory as well as on the disk.

DOS 5.0 and 6.0. The SYS command in DOS versions 5.0 and 6.0 goes one step farther: it replaces old system files with the new ones. Even if the old system files had other names, DOS 5.0 and higher ensure that they are overwritten by the new system files. If you are updating a disk on which the old system file names match the new ones, the SYS command of any version of DOS overwrites the old system files with the new ones with no moving of files necessary. With the enhanced SYS command in DOS 4.0 and later versions, it is difficult to make a DOS upgrade fail.

DOS 3.3. The DOS 3.3 SYS command does not move other files out of the way (as SYS does in DOS 4.0 and later versions); therefore, you must ensure that the first two root directory entries are either free or contain names that match the new system file names. As in DOS 4.0 and later versions, the first cluster on the disk must contain the first portion of IBMBIO.COM; unlike DOS 4.0 and later versions, however, the SYS command under DOS 3.3 does not move any files for you. Necessary manual adjustments, such as clearing the first two directory entries or relocating a file that occupies the first cluster on the disk, must be done with whatever utility programs you have available. The DOS 3.3 system files can be fragmented and occupy various areas of the disk.

SYS under DOS 3.3 does not automatically handle updating from one version of DOS to a version that has different system file names. In that case, because the system file names are not the same, the new system files do not overwrite the old ones. If you are making this kind of system change, use a directory editing tool to change the names of the current system files to match the new names so that the system file overwrite can occur.

VI

Troubleshooting

DOS 3.2. DOS 3.2 or earlier requires that the entire IBMBIO.COM file be contiguous starting with cluster 2 (the first cluster) on the disk. The other system file (IBMDOS.COM) can be fragmented or placed anywhere on the disk; it does not have to follow the first system file physically on the disk.

DOS 2.x. DOS 2.x requires that both system files (IBMBIO.COM and IBMDOS.COM) occupy contiguous clusters on the disk starting with the first cluster (cluster 2). The DOS 2.1 system files are slightly larger than the DOS 2.0 files in actual bytes of size, but the size change is not enough to require additional clusters on the disk. A SYS change from DOS 2.0 to DOS 2.1, therefore, is successful in most cases.

Upgrading DOS from the Same OEM. Updating from one version of DOS to a later version from the same OEM by simply using the SYS command has never been a problem. I verified this with IBM DOS by installing IBM DOS 2.0 on a system with a hard disk through the normal FORMAT /S command. I copied all the subsequent DOS transient programs into a \DOS subdirectory on the disk and then updated the hard disk, in succession, to IBM DOS 2.1, 3.0, 3.1, 3.2, 3.3, 4.0, 5.0, and even 6.3 using nothing more than the SYS and COPY (or XCOPY or REPLACE) commands. Between each version change, I verified that the hard disk would boot the new version of DOS with no problems. Based on this experiment, I have concluded that you never have to use the FORMAT command to update one DOS version to a later version, as long as both versions are from the same OEM. I also verified the same operations on a floppy disk. Starting with a bootable floppy disk created by IBM DOS 2.0, I used SYS and COPY to update that disk to all subsequent versions of DOS through 6.3 without ever reformatting it. After each version change, the floppy disk was bootable with no problems.

You should be able to update a bootable hard disk or floppy disk easily from one DOS version to another without reformatting the disk. If you are having problems, you probably are attempting to upgrade to a version of DOS that uses names for the system files different from those used by the existing DOS, which means that you are moving from a DOS made by one OEM to a DOS made by a different company. If you are having trouble and this is not the case, carefully examine the list of requirements at the beginning of this section. Your problem must be that one of those requirements is not being met.

Downgrading DOS. One important and often overlooked function of the SYS command is its capability to update the DOS volume boot sector of a disk on which it is writing system files. Later versions of SYS are more complete than earlier versions in the way they perform this update; therefore, using SYS to go from a later version of DOS to an earlier version is sometimes difficult. For example, you cannot use SYS to install DOS 2.1 on a disk that currently boots DOS 3.0 and later versions. Changing from DOS 4.0 or higher versions back to DOS 3.3 usually works, if the partition is less than or equal to 32 megabytes in capacity. You probably will never see a problem with a later version of SYS updating a DOS volume boot sector created by an earlier version, but earlier versions might leave something out when they attempt to change back from a later version. Fortunately, few people ever attempt to install a lower version of DOS over a higher version.

Known Bugs in DOS

Few things are more frustrating than finding out that software you depend on every day has bugs. It's even worse when DOS does. Every version of DOS ever produced has had bugs, and users must learn to anticipate them. Some problems are never resolved; you must live with them.

Sometimes the problems are severe enough, however, that Microsoft, IBM, and other OEM distributors of DOS issue a patch disk that corrects the problems. If you use IBM DOS, you can get them from an IBM dealer or download them from the IBM National Support Center (NSC) BBS (the number is in Appendix B, the "Vendor List"). With MS-DOS, you can request a patch by calling the technical support number in the front of your DOS manual. Or, if you have a modem, you can download patches from the Microsoft Download Service BBS (see Appendix B).

If you have IBM PC DOS, check with your system vendor periodically to find out whether patches are available. You do not have to go to the dealer from which you purchased PC DOS; any dealer must provide the patches for free when you show you have a legal license for PC DOS. The proof-of-license page from the PC DOS 4.0 manual satisfies as a license check. If you ask a dealer who does not know about these patches, or who does not provide them for some reason, try another dealer. PC DOS is a warranted product, and the patches are part of the warranty service.

The following sections detail IBM patches for PC DOS 3.3, PC DOS 4.0, and IBM DOS 5.0. These versions have official IBM-produced patch disks available at no cost from your nearest IBM dealer, or available from the IBM BBS.

PC DOS 3.3 Bugs and Patches. The PC DOS 3.3 official patches and fixes from IBM originally were issued by IBM's National Support Center on September 9, 1987. A second update, issued October 24, 1987, superseded the first update. These disks fix the following two general problems with DOS 3.3:

- BACKUP did not work properly in backing up a large number of subdirectories in a given directory. A new version of BACKUP was created to resolve this problem.

- Systems that had slow serial printers with small input buffers sometimes displayed a false Out Of Paper error message when attempting to print. A new program, I17.COM, resolves this problem.

In addition to the two general problems resolved by this patch, IBM PS/2 systems had a particular problem between their ROM BIOS and DOS 3.3; a special DASDDRVR.SYS driver was provided on the patch disk to fix these BIOS problems. The versions of DASDDRVR.SYS supplied on the DOS 3.3 patch disks have been superseded by later versions supplied elsewhere; DASDDRVR.SYS was placed on the IBM PS/2 Reference disks for more widespread distribution, and you can obtain it directly from IBM on a special system update floppy disk. This driver and the problems it can correct are discussed later in this chapter, in the section "PS/2 BIOS Update."

PC DOS 4.0 and 4.01 Bugs and Patches. Six different versions of IBM DOS 4.0 have been issued, counting the first version and the five patch disks subsequently released. The disks are not called patch disks anymore; they are called *corrective service disks* (CSDs). Each level of CSD contains all the previous level CSDs. The first CSD issued for PC DOS 4.0 (UR22624) contained a series of problem fixes that later were incorporated into the standard release version of DOS 4.01. Several newer CSDs have been released since version 4.01 appeared. Unfortunately, these more recent updates were never integrated into the commercially packaged DOS. The only way to obtain these fixes is to obtain the CSDs from your dealer or from the IBM BBS.

The VER command in any level of IBM DOS 4.x always shows 4.00, which causes much confusion about which level of CSD fixes are installed on a specific system. To eliminate this confusion and allow for the correct identification of installed patches, the CSD UR29015 and later levels introduce to DOS 4.x a new command: SYSLEVEL. This command is resident in COMMAND.COM and is designed to identify conclusively to the user the level of corrections installed. On a system running PC DOS 4.x with CSD UR35284 installed, the SYSLEVEL command reports the following:

DOS Version: 4.00 U.S. Date: 06/17/88

CSD Version: UR35284 U.S. Date: 09/20/91

The following list notes each of the IBM DOS 4.0 Corrective Service Diskettes (CSDs) and when they first became available.

CSD	Date Available
UR22624	08/15/88 (this equals 4.01)
UR24270	03/27/89
UR25066	05/10/89
UR29015	03/20/90
UR31300	06/29/90
UR35284	09/20/91

These CSDs are valid only for the IBM version of DOS—PC DOS 4.0. Microsoft and OEM versions of DOS may not have corresponding patches. Some OEMs provide patches or corrections in different ways, and some may not even offer them. Because most OEMs released their versions of DOS after IBM, other manufacturers have had a chance to incorporate fixes in their standard version and may not need to provide patches. If you have a version of DOS by a manufacturer other than Microsoft or IBM, contact its source to find out which patch corrections have been applied to your version of DOS. With a system that can run standard MS-DOS, you can get patches from Microsoft. If you have an IBM, you must rely on a reputable dealer to get the latest version of DOS.

MS-DOS 4. Microsoft released its version of DOS 4 after IBM had fixed most of the bugs in PC DOS 4.0. Yet MS-DOS 4.01 introduced some bugs of its own. A patch for MS-DOS 4.x is available for download from the Microsoft Download Service or by calling

Microsoft technical service. The patch disk for MS-DOS 4.0x is available on the Microsoft Download service as PD0255.EXE.

IBM DOS 5.0 Bugs and Patches. With the release of its DOS version 5.0, IBM changed the product name from PC DOS to IBM DOS (version 6.0 of IBM's DOS has been changed back to PC DOS). IBM DOS version 5.0 has several CSDs that fix a couple of problems. The most significant is a defect in the XCOPY command that causes it to fail sometimes when it uses the /E or /S switches. The following list notes the IBM DOS 5.0 CSDs and indicates when they first became available:

CSD	Date available
UR35423	08/91
UR35748	10/91
UR35834	11/91
UR36603	02/92
UR37387	09/92

Table 20.18 lists the problems fixed by these patch disks.

Table 20.18   IBM DOS 5 Corrective Service Disks (CSDs)

CSD	Item	Problem
UR35423	XCOPY	Wrong output when using /E and /S switches.
UR35423	QBASIC	Enables QBASIC and QEDIT compatibility.
UR35748	SYS	Corrupted hard file after installing UR35423.
UR35834	DOSSHELL	DOSSHELL takes 27 seconds to load.
UR35834	MEUTOINI	4.0 .MEU to 5.0 .INI conversion incomplete.
UR35834	MEM	MEM switch hangs system with PC3270.
UR35834	IBMBIO	L40SX will not SUSPEND or RESUME.
UR35834	DOSSHELL	Can't edit dialog box if length is maximum.
UR35834	EMM386	Int 19H fails with EMM386 and DOS=HIGH.
UR35834	FORMAT	FORMAT on unpartitioned drive; rc = 0.
UR35834	REPLACE	REPLACE /A returns error.
UR35834	XCOPY	XCOPY /S incorrectly sets error level.
UR35834	GRAPHICS	PrtScr of graphics display produces garbage.
UR35834	DOSSHELL	DOSSHELL.INI corrupted from CTRL-ALT-DEL.
UR35834	BACKUP	BACKUP calls wrong FORMAT.COM from OS/2.
UR35834	MIRROR	MIRROR doesn't enable Interrupts correctly.
UR35834	BACKUP	BACKUP /A backs up too large a file.
UR36603	EDIT	Alt ### key combo doesn't work in EDIT.
UR36603	MIRROR	MIRROR fails with /T switch and DOS=UMB.
UR36603	IBMBIO	L40SX will not SUSPEND or RESUME if DOS=LOW.

(continues)

Table 20.18 Continued		
CSD	**Item**	**Problem**
UR36603	BACKUP	BACKUP fails to back up all files.
UR36603	QBASIC	QBASIC help msgs missing in nls versions.
UR36603	CHKDSK	CHKDSK data loss when sectors per FAT>256.
UR36603	EMM386	DMA transfer may not function on EISA systems.
UR36603	RECOVER	RECOVER can corrupt disks with 12-bit FAT.
UR36603	RECOVER	RECOVER may not adjust file size correctly.
UR36603	DOSSHELL	DOSSHELL incorrectly copies certain file sizes.
UR36603	DOSSWAP	Task Swapper destroys CX register.
UR36603	DOSSWAP	Task Swapper does not swap EMS memory.
UR36603	DOSSWAP	Task Swapper incorrectly swaps large XMS memory.
UR36603	DOSSWAP	DOSSHELL overwrites an interrupt vector.
UR36603	DOSSWAP	DOSSHELL random skip of swapping application memory.
UR36603	DOSSHELL	DOSSHELL uses environment var to set 2nd swap path.
UR37387	RESTORE	RESTORE fails to display backup files.
UR37387	IBMDOS	FASTOPEN causes bad FAT message.
UR37387	KEYB	Pause key doesn't work on PS/2 25 and 30.
UR37387	IBMDOS	Unmapped network drive returns error.
UR37387	MODE	MODE and off-line printer across net hangs.
UR37387	IBMDOS	RAMDRIVE errors with certain combinations.
UR37387	DOSSHELL	Unattended start mode—lose keyboard with DOSSHELL.
UR37387	COMMAND	Error with greater than 1G free space.
UR37387	IBMDOS	INT 27 returns no data after file create.
UR37387	IBMBIO	L40SX loses time during suspend.
UR37387	DOSSHELL	CTRL+ESC hangs when returning to DOSSHELL.
UR37387	IBMDOS	Extended File Open returns incorrect code.
UR37387	HIMEM	Device driver fails to load.
UR37387	HIMEM	HIMEM incorrectly identifies memory on EISA.
UR37387	UNDELETE	Doesn't work if partition is a multiple of 128M.
UR37387	UNDELETE	Doesn't handle foreign characters correctly.
UR37387	BACKUP	Restore does not ask for second diskette.
UR37387	KEYBOARD	Keyboard changes for Latin II countries.
UR37387	MEM	Finland MEM/C displays invalid characters.
UR37387	DOSSHELL	INT 33 DOSSHELL reentry problem with BASIC.
UR37387	MODE	MODE LPT1:, P reports Bad mode.
UR37387	BACKUP	Occasionally gets `Cannot Restore File` error.

MS-DOS 5.0 Bugs and Patches. As mentioned earlier, the Microsoft Download Service DOS files listing includes fixes for MS-DOS versions 4.0 and 5.0. When you call the Microsoft Download Service, you are asked to enter your name and city and to choose a password. Choose a password you will not forget because when you realize how simple it is to always have the most current bug fixes for MS-DOS, you will want to call back. After you enter your name and a password, the following screen appears:

```
*****************************************
****Microsoft Download Service****
****        Main Menu        ****
[I]nstructions on Using This Service
[D]ownload File
[F]ile Index

[W]indows 3.1 Driver Library Update
[N]ew Files & Complete File Listing

[M]icrosoft Information
[A]lter User Settings
[U]tilities - Comments
[L]ength of Call
[E]xit ... Logoff the System
[H]elp - System Instructions
Command:
```

At the command prompt choose **f** (for file) to display the following screen:

```
*****************************************
****  File Sections Available  ****
*****************************************
[1] Windows and MS-DOS
[2] Word, Excel and Multiplan
[3] PowerPoint, Publisher and Project
[4] LAN Manager and Microsoft Mail
[5] Languages and Windows SDK
[6] Works and Flight Simulator
[7] MS FOX, MS Access & MS Money
[8] MS Video for Windows

[F]ile Search

[-]Previous Menu
[M]ain Menu

[L]ength of Call
[E]xit ... Logoff the System

Command:
```

Choose **1** (for Windows and MS-DOS) to display the following screen:

```
Windows and MS-DOS Files
[1] Windows for Workgroups Appnotes
[2] Windows 3.1 Driver Library
[3] Windows 3.1 Application Notes
[4] Windows 3.1 Resource Kit
[5] Windows 3.0 Driver Library-SDL
[6] Windows 3.0 Application Notes
[7] Windows 3.0 Resource Kit
[8] MS DOS Files

[-]Previous Menu
[M]ain Menu

[L]ength of Call
[E]xit ... Logoff the System

Command:
```

Choose **8** (for MS-DOS files).

MS-DOS 5.0 fixes available on the Microsoft Download Service are as follows:

PD0445.EXE	Replacement DOSSWAP.EXE
PD0455.EXE	ADAPTEC.SYS Driver (for adaptec drives)
PD0488.EXE	8514.VID Video Driver for MS-DOS 5.0 Shell
PD0489.EXE	MS-DOS Messages Reference
PD0495.EXE	PRINTFIX.COM patch for PRINT problems
PD0646.EXE	Updated CHKDSK.EXE and UNDELETE.EXE
PD0315.EXE	BACKUP/RESTORE Supplemental Utilities

MS-DOS 6.0 and IBM PC DOS 6.1. As of this writing, there has been one bug fix for MS-DOS version 6.0—a new version of SmartDrive, which fixes a problem on some systems when SmartDrive is used at the same time as DoubleSpace. The fix can be used if you have experienced cross-linked files you think are related to upgrading to DOS 6.0. You can download the file, named PD0805.EXE, from the Microsoft Download Service. The Microsoft Download Service also enables you (free of charge) to download the MS-DOS 6.0 Supplemental Disk. This supplemental disk contains utilities helpful to the handicapped. The disk also contains new versions of various utilities that were part of DOS 5.0, but not included on the DOS 6.0 upgrade disks, including MIRROR, EDLIN, ASSIGN, JOIN, BACKUP (MSBACKUP is a new menu-based backup program included with DOS 6), COMP, PRINTER.SYS, and the DVORAK keyboard. Also available is a utility to fix a problem using the Shift key in Quick Basic 1.1, named PD0415.EXE.

In addition, numerous technical papers on setting up and running MS-DOS 6.0 are available on the download service. They are listed in table 20.19.

Table 20.19 MS-DOS Technical Papers

File Name	Subject
PD0456.TXT	Running MS-DOS in the High Memory Area
PD0457.TXT	HIMEM.SYS "ERROR: Unable to Control A20 Line"
PD0459.TXT	EMM386.EXE: No Expanded Memory Available
PD0460.TXT	Running Both Extended and Expanded Memory
PD0462.TXT	Mouse Doesn't Work with MS-DOS Shell
PD0463.TXT	Using the Setver Command
PD0465.TXT	Problems Formatting or Reading a Floppy Disk
PD0470.TXT	System Fails When You Are Using EMM.386
PD0471.TXT	Explanation of the WINA20.386 File
PD0473.TXT	Installing MS-DOS from Drive B
PD0474.TXT	Windows 3.0 Doesn't Run in 386 Enhanced Mode
PD0476.TXT	IBM PS/1 Fails After MS-DOS Is Installed
PD0477.TXT	Setup Stops Before Completing Upgrade to MS
PD0743.TXT	MS-DOS 6.0 Installation and Partition Q&A
PD0744.TXT	MS-DOS 6.0 General Installation Q&A
PD0745.TXT	DoubleSpace Questions and Answers
PD0746.TXT	MemMaker Questions and Answers
PD0747.TXT	MS-DOS 6.0 Configuration Q&A
PD0748.TXT	Backup and Miscellaneous Q&A
PD0771.TXT	Repartitioning Your Hard Disk To Upgrade to MS-DOS 6.0
PD0785.TXT	Upgrading DR DOS to MS-DOS 6

IBM has since released PC DOS 6.3, which has many fixes and updates. You can get a free upgrade from the IBM BBS if you have earlier versions of IBM DOS.

PS/2 BIOS Update (DASDDRVR.SYS)

The DASDDRVR.SYS (direct access storage device driver) file is a set of software patches that fixes various ROM BIOS bugs in several models of the IBM PS/2. DASDDRVR.SYS is required for specific PS/2 systems using IBM's PC DOS versions 3.30 or later, to correct several bugs in the IBM PS/2 ROM BIOS. Before IBM's PC DOS 4.00 was released, conflicting information indicated that PC DOS 4.00 would include the updates to correct the PS/2 ROM BIOS problems fixed by DASDDRVR.SYS under PC DOS 3.30. This information was not accurate, however. In fact, an IBM PS/2 system needs DASDDRVR.SYS with IBM DOS 5.00 (or any higher version of DOS) even with the most current corrective service disk (CSD) update.

The PS/2 needs the DASDDRVR.SYS fixes only in the DOS environment. Some users assume, therefore, that the PS/2 problems with DOS are DOS bugs; they are not. The DASDDRVR.SYS program is provided on the PS/2 Reference disk (included with every PS/2 system) and is available separately on a special PS/2 system update disk. The disks contain the device driver program (DASDDRVR.SYS) and an installation program.

The PS/2 ROM BIOS bugs in the following list are fixed by DASDDRVR.SYS (the problem numbers are shown in table 20.19, and more detailed information is provided later in this section):

1. Failures occur in reading some 720K program floppy disks (Models 8530, 8550, 8560, and 8580).

2. Intermittent Not ready or General failure error messages appear (Models 8550, 8560, and 8580).

3. 3 1/2-inch floppy disk format fails when user tries to format more than one floppy disk (Models 8550, 8560, 8570, and 8580).

4. Combined 301 and 8602 error messages appear at power-on or after power interruption (Models 8550 and 8560).

5. System clock loses time, or combined 162 and 163 errors appear during system initialization (Models 8550 and 8560).

6. User is unable to install Power-On Password program with DASDDRVR.SYS installed (Models 8550, 8560, and 8580).

7. Devices attached to COM2:, COM3:, or COM4: are not detected (Model 8530).

8. Devices that use Interrupt Request level 2 (IRQ2) fail (Model 8530).

9. System performance degradation occurs from processor intensive devices (Models 8550, 8555, and 8560).

10. Error occurs in a microcode routine that enhances long-term reliability of 60/120M disk drives (Models 8550, 8555, 8570, and 8573).

11. Time and date errors occur when user resets the time or date. Intermittent date changes occur when the system is restarted by pressing Ctrl-Alt-Del (Model 8530).

If you are an IBM PS/2-system user running PC DOS 3.3 or higher and experiencing any of these problems, load the DASDDRVR.SYS file. The problems are system specific, and DASDDRVR.SYS fixes the problems for only the systems listed. IBM requires its dealers to distribute the System Update disk containing DASDDRVR.SYS to anyone who requests it. Neither the dealer nor the customer pays a fee for the System Update disk. You also can obtain copies directly from IBM by calling (800) IBM-PCTB (800-426-7282) and ordering the PS/2 System Update disk.

Check table 20.20 for detailed descriptions of each of these problems and for the specific systems affected. Models not listed for a particular problem do not need DASDDRVR.SYS, and no benefit results from installing it.

Table 20.20   DASDDRVR.SYS Version Summary

Version	File Size	Problems Fixed	Source
1.10	648 bytes	1-3	DOS 3.3 Fix Disk (08/24/87)
1.20	698 bytes	1-5	Reference Disk, DOS 3.3 Fix Disk (09/09/87)
1.30	734 bytes	1-6	Reference Disk
1.56	1170 bytes	1-9	Reference Disk (03/90), System Update Disk 1.01 (part number 64F1500)
1.56	3068 bytes	1-11	Reference Disk (xx/xx), System Update Disk 1.02 (part number 04G3288)

The first three problem fixes originally were provided by the DASDDRVR.SYS version 1.10 file supplied on the first PC DOS 3.3 fix disk. Fixes for problems 4 and 5 were added in DASDDRVR.SYS version 1.20, included on all IBM PS/2 Reference disks (30-286, 50/60, and 70/80) version 1.02 or later, as well as on an updated version of the PC DOS 3.3 fix disk. The fix for problem 6 was added in DASDDRVR.SYS version 1.30, included on all 50/60 and 70/80 Reference disks version 1.03 or later. Fixes for problems 7 through 9 were added to DASDDRVR.SYS version 1.56, included on all IBM PS/2 Reference disks dated March 1990 or later. This version of DASDDRVR.SYS also was available separately, on the IBM PS/2 System Update disk version 1.01. The latest DASDDRVR.SYS (also called version 1.56, but dated January 1991) can be found on newer Reference disks or on the IBM PS/2 System Update disk version 1.02.

By using the DASDDRVR.SYS driver file, IBM can correct specific ROM BIOS problems and bugs without having to issue a new set of ROM chips for a specific system. Using this file eliminates service time or expense in fixing simple problems, but causes the inconvenience of having to load the driver. The driver does not consume memory, nor does it remain in memory (as does a typical driver or memory-resident program); it either performs functions on boot only and then terminates, or overlays existing code or tables in memory, thereby consuming no additional space. Because DASDDRVR.SYS checks the exact ROM BIOS by model, submodel, and revision, it performs functions only on those for which it is designed. If it detects a BIOS that does not need fixing, the program terminates without doing anything. You can load DASDDRVR.SYS on any system; it functions only on systems for which it is designed.

Because a system BIOS occasionally needs revising or updating, IBM used disk-based BIOS programs for most newer PS/2 systems. The Models 57, P75, 90, and 95, in fact, load the system BIOS from the hard disk every time the system is powered up, during a procedure called *initial microcode load* (IML). You can get a ROM upgrade for these systems by obtaining a new Reference disk and loading the new IML file on the hard disk. This system makes DASDDRVR.SYS or other such patches obsolete.

Installing DASDDRVR.SYS. To install DASDDRVR.SYS, you must update the CONFIG.SYS file with the following entry and restart the system:

DEVICE=[*d:\path*]DASDDRVR.SYS

The drive and path values must match the location and name of the DASDDRVR.SYS file on your system.

Detailed Problem Descriptions. This section gives a detailed description of the problems corrected by the most current release of DASDDRVR.SYS and indicates for which systems the corrections are necessary.

1. Failures occur in reading some 720K program disks.

   IBM PS/2 systems affected:

   Model 30 286 8530-E01, -E21

   Model 50 8550-021

   Model 60 8560-041, -071

   Model 80 8580-041, -071

   Intermittent read failures on some 720K original application software disks. Example: Not ready reading drive A: appears when a user attempts to install an application program. Attempting to perform DIR or COPY commands from the floppy disk also produces the error message.

2. Intermittent Not ready or General failure error messages are displayed.

   IBM PS/2 systems affected:

   Model 50 8550-021

   Model 60 8560-041, -071

   Model 80 8580-041, -071

   A very intermittent problem with a floppy disk drive Not ready or a fixed disk General failure message. This problem can be aggravated by certain programming practices that mask off (or disable) interrupts for long periods. The update ensures that interrupts are unmasked on each disk or floppy disk request.

3. A 3 1/2-inch floppy disk format fails when the user tries to format more than one disk.

   IBM PS/2 systems affected:

   Model 50 8550-021

   Model 60 8560-041, -071

   Model 70 8570-Axx (all)

   Model 80 8580-Axx (all)

The DOS FORMAT command fails when a user tries to format multiple 3 1/2-inch disks. The failure appears as an `Invalid media` or `Track 0 bad—disk unusable` message when the user replies **Y**es to the prompt `Format another (Y/N)?` after the format of the first disk is complete. The error message appears when the user tries to format the second disk. If a system is booted from a floppy disk, the problem does not occur. This problem occurs only with DOS 3.3, not with later versions.

4. Combined 301 and 8602 error messages at power-on or after power interruption.

   IBM PS/2 systems affected:

   > Model 50 8550-021

   > Model 60 8560-041, -071

   When power is interrupted momentarily or a system is otherwise switched on and off quickly, a 301 (keyboard) and 8602 (pointing device) error message may appear during the Power On Self Test (POST). This error occurs because the system powers on before the keyboard is ready. The problem is more likely to occur if the system was reset previously by pressing Ctrl-Alt-Del.

5. System clock loses time or combined 162 and 163 errors during system initialization.

   IBM PS/2 systems affected:

   > Model 50 8550-021

   > Model 60 8560-041, -071

   Intermittent 162 (CMOS checksum or configuration) and 163 (clock not updating) Power-On Self Test (POST) errors occur. Various time-of-day problems on specified IBM PS/2 Model 50 systems; for example, the user turns on the machine in the morning and finds the time set to the same time the machine was turned off the day before.

6. User is unable to install Power-On Password program with DASDDRVR.SYS installed.

   IBM PS/2 systems affected:

   > Model 50 8550-021

   > Model 60 8560-041, -071

   > Model 80 8580-041, -071

   When a user tries to install the Power-On Password feature with DASDDRVR.SYS version 1.3 or earlier installed, a message appears that states (incorrectly) that a password already exists. The user also may be prompted for a password (on warm boot), even though password security has not been implemented.

VI

Troubleshooting

7. Devices attached to COM2:, COM3:, or COM4: are not detected.

   IBM PS/2 systems affected:

   Model 30 286 8530-E01, -E21

8. Devices that use Interrupt Request level 2 (IRQ2) fail.

   IBM PS/2 systems affected:

   Model 30 286 8530-E01, -E21

9. System performance degradation occurs from processor intensive devices.

   IBM PS/2 systems affected:

   Model 50 8550-021, -031, -061

   Model 55 SX 8555-031, -061

   Model 60 8560-041, -071

10. Error occurs in a microcode routine that enhances long-term reliability of 60/120M disk drives.

    IBM PS/2 systems affected:

    Model 50 8550-061

    Model 55 SX 8555-061

    Model 70 8570-061, -121, -A61, -A21, -B61, -B21

    Model P70 8573-061, -121

11. Time and date errors occur when the user resets the time or date. Intermittent date changes occur when the system is restarted by pressing Ctrl-Alt-Del.

    IBM PS/2 systems affected:

    Model 30 8530 (all)

OS/2 versions 1.2 and earlier contained these BIOS fixes in the form of a .BIO file for each specific BIOS needing corrections. These files were automatically loaded by OS/2 at boot time, depending on the specific system on which it was being loaded.

OS/2 versions 1.3 and later contain the fixes directly in-line in the system files, not as separate files. When a system running one of these OS/2 versions is booted, OS/2 determines the model, submodel, and revision bytes for the particular BIOS under which it is running. Based on this information, OS/2 determines the correct .BIO file to load or the correct in-line code to run. For example, the IBM PS/2 55SX BIOS is Model F8, Submodel 0C, Revision 00, which causes IBM OS/2 version 1.2 to load the file F80C00.BIO automatically during boot-up. OS/2 versions 1.3 or later use this information to run the proper fix code contained in the system files. This procedure enables execution of only those BIOS fixes necessary for this particular system.

Any symptom described as being resolved by the DASDDRVR.SYS update may have other causes. If you install the DASDDRVR.SYS update and continue to have problems, consider the errors valid and follow normal troubleshooting procedures to find the causes.

DOS Disk and Data Recovery

The CHKDSK, RECOVER, and DEBUG commands are the DOS damaged disk recovery team. These commands are crude, and their actions sometimes are drastic, but at times they are all that is available or needed. RECOVER is best known for its function as a data recovery program, and CHKDSK usually is used for inspection of the file structure. Many users are unaware that CHKDSK can implement repairs to a damaged file structure. DEBUG, a crude, manually controlled program, can help in the case of a disk disaster, if you know exactly what you are doing.

The CHKDSK Command. The useful and powerful DOS CHKDSK command also is generally misunderstood. To casual users, the primary function of CHKDSK seems to be providing a disk space allocation report for a given volume and a memory allocation report. CHKDSK does those things, but its primary value is in discovering, defining, and repairing problems with the DOS directory and FAT system on a disk volume. In handling data recovery problems, CHKDSK is a valuable tool, although it is crude and simplistic compared to some of the after-market utilities that perform similar functions.

The output of the CHKDSK command which runs on a typical (well maybe not typical, but from my own) hard disk is as follows:

```
Volume 4GB_SCSI     created 08-31-1994 5:05p
Volume Serial Number is 1882-18CF

2,146,631,680 bytes total disk space
      163,840 bytes in 3 hidden files
   16,220,160 bytes in 495 directories
  861,634,560 bytes in 10,355 user files
1,268,613,120 bytes available on disk

       32,768 bytes in each allocation unit
       65,510 total allocation units on disk
       38,715 available allocation units on disk

      655,360 total bytes memory
      632,736 bytes free
```

A little known CHKDSK function is reporting a specified file's (or files') level of fragmentation. CHKDSK also can produce a list of all files (including hidden and system files) on a particular volume, similar to a super DIR command. By far, the most important CHKDSK capabilities are its detection and correction of problems with the DOS file management system.

The name of the CHKDSK program is misleading: it seems to be a contraction of CHECK DISK. The program does not actually check a disk, or even the files on a disk, for integrity. CHKDSK cannot even truly show how many bad sectors are on a disk, much less locate and mark them. The real function of CHKDSK is to inspect the directories and FATs to see whether they correspond with each other or contain discrepancies. CHKDSK does not detect (and does not report on) damage in a file; it checks only the FAT and directory areas (the table of contents) of a disk. Rather than CHKDSK, the command should have been called CKDIRFAT (for CHECK DIRECTORY FAT) because its most important job is to verify that the FATs and directories correspond with one another. The name of the program gives no indication of the program's capability to repair problems with the directory and FAT structures.

CHKDSK also can test files for contiguity. Files loaded into contiguous tracks and sectors of a disk or floppy disk naturally are more efficient. Files spread over wide areas of the disk make access operations take longer. DOS always knows the location of all of a file's fragments by using the pointer numbers in the file allocation table (FAT). These pointers are data that direct DOS to the next segment of the file. Sometimes, for various reasons, these pointers might be lost or corrupted and leave DOS incapable of locating some portion of a file. Using CHKDSK can alert you to this condition and even enable you to reclaim the unused file space for use by another file.

CHKDSK Command Syntax. The syntax of the CHKDSK command is as follows:

> **CHKDSK** [*d:\path*] [*filename*] [*/F*] [*/V*]

The *d:* specifies the disk volume to analyze. The *\path* and *filename* options specify files to check for fragmentation in addition to the volume analysis. Wild cards are allowed in the file-name specification, to include as many as all the files in a specified directory for fragmentation analysis. One flaw with the fragmentation analysis is that it does not check for fragmentation across directory boundaries, only within a specified directory.

The switch /F (Fix) enables CHKDSK to perform repairs if it finds problems with the directories and FATs. If /F is not specified, the program is prevented from writing to the disk, and all repairs were not really performed.

The switch /V (Verbose) causes the program to list all the entries in all the directories on a disk and give detailed information in some cases when errors are encountered.

The drive, path, and file specifiers are optional. If no parameters are given for the command, CHKDSK processes the default volume or drive and does not check files for contiguity. If you specify [*path*] and [*filename*] parameters, CHKDSK checks all specified files to see whether they are stored contiguously on the disk. One of two messages is displayed as a result:

```
All specified file(s) are contiguous
```

or

```
[filename] Contains xxx non-contiguous blocks
```

The second message is displayed for each file fragmented on the disk and displays the number of fragments the file is in. A *fragmented file* is one that is scattered around the disk in pieces rather than existing in one contiguous area of the disk. Fragmented files are slower to load than contiguous files, which reduces disk performance. Fragmented files are also much more difficult to recover if a problem with the FAT or directory on the disk occurs.

Utility programs that can defragment files are discussed in Chapter 19. But if you have only DOS, you have several possible ways to accomplish a full defragmentation. To defragment files on a floppy disk, you can format a new floppy disk and use COPY or XCOPY to copy all the files from the fragmented disk to the replacement. For a hard disk, you must completely back up, format, and then restore the disk. This procedure on a hard disk is time-consuming and dangerous, which is why so many defragmenting utilities have been developed.

CHKDSK Limitations. In several instances, CHKDSK operates only partially or not at all. CHKDSK does not process volumes or portions of volumes that have been created as follows:

- SUBST command volumes

- ASSIGN command volumes

- JOIN command subdirectories

- Network volumes

SUBST Problems. The SUBST command creates a virtual volume, which is actually an existing volume's subdirectory using another volume specifier (drive letter) as an alias. To analyze the files in a subdirectory created with SUBST, you must give the TRUENAME or actual path name to the files. TRUENAME is an undocumented command in DOS 4.0 and later versions that shows the actual path name for a volume that has been created by the SUBST command.

You also can use the SUBST command to find out the TRUENAME of a particular volume. Suppose that you use SUBST to create volume E: from the C:\AUTO\SPECS directory, as follows:

C:\>SUBST E: C:\AUTO\SPECS

After entering the following two commands to change to the E: volume and execute a CHKDSK of the volume and files there, you see the resulting error message:

C:\>E:

E:\>CHKDSK *.*

```
Cannot CHKDSK a SUBSTed or ASSIGNed drive
```

To run CHKDSK on the files on this virtual volume E:, you must find the actual path the volume represents. You can do so by entering the SUBST command (with no parameters):

E:\>SUBST

E: => C:\AUTO\SPECS

VI

Troubleshooting

You also can find the actual path with the undocumented TRUENAME command (in DOS 4.0 and later versions only), as follows:

    E:\>TRUENAME E:

    C:\AUTO\SPECS

After finding the path to the files, you can issue the appropriate CHKDSK command to check the volume and files:

    E:\>CHKDSK C:\AUTO\SPECS*.*

```
Volume 4GB_SCSI    created 08-31-1994 5:05p
Volume Serial Number is 1882-18CF

2,146,631,680 bytes total disk space
      163,840 bytes in 3 hidden files
   16,220,160 bytes in 495 directories
  861,634,560 bytes in 10,355 user files
1,268,613,120 bytes available on disk

       32,768 bytes in each allocation unit
       65,510 total allocation units on disk
       38,715 available allocation units on disk

      655,360 total bytes memory
      632,736 bytes free

All specified file(s) are contiguous
```

ASSIGN Problems. Similarly, CHKDSK does not process a disk drive that has been altered by the ASSIGN command. For example, if you have given the command ASSIGN A=B, you cannot analyze drive A: unless you first unassign the disk drive with the ASSIGN command, that is, ASSIGN A=A.

JOIN Problems. CHKDSK does not process a directory tree section created by the JOIN command (which joins a physical disk volume to another disk volume as a subdirectory), nor does it process the actual joined physical drive because such a drive is an invalid drive specification, according to DOS. On volumes on which you have used the JOIN command, CHKDSK processes the actual portion of the volume and then displays this warning error message:

```
Directory is joined
tree past this point not processed
```

This message indicates that the command cannot process the directory on which you have used JOIN. CHKDSK then continues processing the rest of the volume and outputs the requested volume information.

Network Problems. CHKDSK does not process a networked (shared) disk on either the server or workstation side. In other words, at the file server, you cannot use CHKDSK on any volume that has any portion of itself accessible to remote network stations. At any network station, you can run CHKDSK only on volumes physically attached to that specific station and not on any volume accessed through the network software. If you attempt to run CHKDSK from a server or a workstation on a volume shared on a network, you see this error message:

```
Cannot CHKDSK a network drive
```

If you want to run CHKDSK on the volume, you must go to the specific PC on which the volume physically exists and suspend or disable any sharing of the volume during the CHKDSK.

CHKDSK Command Output. CHKDSK normally displays the following information about a disk volume:

- Volume name and creation date

- Volume serial number

- Number of bytes in total disk space

- Number of files and bytes in hidden files

- Number of files and bytes in directories

- Number of files and bytes in user files

- Number of bytes in bad sectors (unallocated clusters)

- Number of bytes available on disk

- Number of bytes in total memory (RAM)

- Number of bytes in free memory

- Error messages if disk errors are encountered

By using optional parameters, CHKDSK also can show the following:

- Names and number of fragments in noncontiguous files

- Names of all directories and files on disk

If a volume name or volume serial number does not exist on a particular volume, that information is not displayed. If no clusters are marked as bad in the volume's FAT, CHKDSK returns no display of bytes in bad sectors.

For example, suppose that a disk was formatted under DOS 6.2 with the following command:

```
C:\>FORMAT A: /F:720 /U /S /V:floppy_disk
```

VI

Troubleshooting

The output of the FORMAT command looks like this:

```
Insert new diskette for drive A:
and press ENTER when ready...

Formatting 720K
Format complete.
System transferred


        730,112 bytes total disk space
        135,168 bytes used by system
        594,944 bytes available on disk

          1,024 bytes in each allocation unit.
            581 allocation units available on disk.

Volume Serial Number is 266D-1DDC

Format another (Y/N)?
```

The status report at the end of the FORMAT operation is similar to the output of the
CHKDSK command. The output of the CHKDSK command when run on this disk would
appear as follows:

```
C:\>CHKDSK A:

Volume FLOPPY_DISK created 01-16-1994 10:18p
Volume Serial Number is 266D-1DDC

        730,112 bytes total disk space
         79,872 bytes in 2 hidden files
         55,296 bytes in 1 user files
        594,944 bytes available on disk

          1,024 bytes in each allocation unit
            713 total allocation units on disk
            581 available allocation units on disk

        655,360 total bytes memory
        632,736 bytes free
```

In this case, CHKDSK shows the volume name and serial number information because
the FORMAT command placed a volume label on the disk with the /V parameter, and
FORMAT under DOS 4.0 and later versions automatically places the volume serial number on a disk. Note that three total files are on the disk, two of which have the HIDDEN
attribute. DOS versions earlier than 5.0 report the Volume Label "FLOPPY_DISK" as a
third hidden file. To see the names of the hidden files, you can execute the CHKDSK
command with the /V parameter, as follows:

```
C:\>CHKDSK A: /V

Volume FLOPPY_DISK created 01-16-1994 10:18p
Volume Serial Number is 266D-1DDC
Directory A:\
A:\IO.SYS
```

```
A:\MSDOS.SYS
A:\COMMAND.COM

      730,112 bytes total disk space
       79,872 bytes in 2 hidden files
       55,296 bytes in 1 user files
      594,944 bytes available on disk

        1,024 bytes in each allocation unit
          713 total allocation units on disk
          581 available allocation units on disk

      655,360 total bytes memory
      632,736 bytes free
```

With the /V parameter, CHKDSK lists the names of all directories and files across the entire disk, which in this example is only three total files. CHKDSK does not identify which of the files are hidden, it simply lists them all. Note that the DIR command in DOS versions 5.0 and higher can specifically show hidden files with the /AH parameter. The DOS system files are the first two files on a bootable disk and normally have HIDDEN, SYSTEM, and READ-ONLY attributes. After listing how many bytes are used by the hidden and normal files, CHKDSK lists how much total space is available on the disk.

If you are using DOS 4.0 or a later version, CHKDSK also tells you the size of each allocation unit (or cluster), the total number of allocation units present, and the number not currently being used.

Finally, CHKDSK counts the total amount of conventional memory or DOS-usable RAM (in this case, 640K or 655,360 bytes) and displays the number of bytes of memory currently unused or free. This information tells you the size of the largest executable program you can run.

CHKDSK under DOS versions 3.3 and earlier does not recognize the IBM PS/2 Extended BIOS Data Area (which uses the highest 1K of addresses in contiguous conventional memory) and therefore reports only 639K, or 654,336 bytes, of total memory. For most IBM PS/2 systems with 640K of contiguous memory addressed before the video wall, the Extended BIOS Data Area occupies the 640th K. DOS 4.0 and later versions provide the correct 640K report.

During the FORMAT of the disk in the example, the FORMAT program did not find any unreadable sectors. Therefore, no clusters were marked in the FAT as bad or unusable, and CHKDSK did not display the *xxxxxxxx* bytes in bad sectors message. Even if the disk had developed bad sectors since the FORMAT operation, CHKDSK still would not display any bytes in bad sectors because it does not test for and count bad sectors: CHKDSK reads the FAT and reports on whether the FAT says that there are any bad sectors. CHKDSK does not really count sectors; it counts clusters (allocation units) because that is how the FAT system operates.

Although bytes in bad sectors sounds like a problem or error message, it is not. The report is simply stating that a certain number of clusters are marked as bad in the FAT and that DOS therefore will never use those clusters. Because nearly all hard disks are

VI

Troubleshooting

manufactured and sold with defective areas, this message is not uncommon. In fact, the higher quality hard disks on the market tend to have more bad sectors than the lower quality drives, based on the manufacturer defect list shipped with the drive (indicating all the known defective spots). Many of the newest controllers allow for sector and track sparing, in which the defects are mapped out of the DOS readable area so that DOS never has to handle them. This procedure is almost standard in drives that have embedded controllers, such as IDE (Integrated Drive Electronics) or SCSI (Small Computer Systems Interface) drives.

Suppose that you use a utility program to mark two clusters (150 and 151, for example) as bad in the FAT of the 720K floppy disk formatted earlier. CHKDSK then reports this information:

```
Volume FLOPPY_DISK created 01-16-1994 10:18p
Volume Serial Number is 266D-1DDC

  730,112 bytes total disk space
   79,872 bytes in 2 hidden files
   55,296 bytes in 1 user files
    2,048 bytes in bad sectors
  592,896 bytes available on disk

    1,024 bytes in each allocation unit
      713 total allocation units on disk
      579 available allocation units on disk

  655,360 total bytes memory
  632,736 bytes free
```

CHKDSK reports 2,048 bytes in bad sectors, which corresponds exactly to the two clusters just marked as bad. These clusters, of course, are perfectly good—you simply marked them as bad in the FAT. Using disk editor utility programs such as those supplied with the Norton or Mace Utilities, you can alter the FAT in almost any way you want.

CHKDSK Operation. Although bytes in bad sectors do not constitute an error or problem, CHKDSK reports problems on a disk volume with a variety of error messages. When CHKDSK discovers an error in the FAT or directory system, it reports the error with one of several descriptive messages that vary to fit the specific error. Sometimes the messages are cryptic or misleading. CHKDSK does not specify how an error should be handled; it does not tell you whether CHKDSK can repair the problem or whether you must use some other utility, or what the consequences of the error and the repair will be. Neither does CHKDSK tell you what caused the problem or how to avoid repeating the problem.

The primary function of CHKDSK is to compare the directory and FAT to determine whether they agree with one another—whether all the data in the directory for files (such as the starting cluster and size information) corresponds to what is in the FAT (such as chains of clusters with end-of-chain indicators). CHKDSK also checks subdirectory file entries, as well as the special . and .. entries that tie the subdirectory system together.

The second function of CHKDSK is to implement repairs to the disk structure. CHKDSK patches the disk so that the directory and FAT are in alignment and agreement. From a repair standpoint, understanding CHKDSK is relatively easy. CHKDSK almost always modifies the directories on a disk to correspond to what is found in the FAT. In only a couple of special cases does CHKDSK modify the FAT; when it does, the FAT modifications are always the same type of simple change.

Think of CHKDSK's repair capability as a directory patcher. Because CHKDSK cannot repair most types of FAT damage effectively, it simply modifies the disk directories to match whatever problems are found in the FAT.

CHKDSK is not a very smart repair program and often can do more damage repairing the disk than if it had left the disk alone. In many cases, the information in the directories is correct and can be used (by some other utility) to help repair the FAT tables. If you have run CHKDSK with the /F parameter, however, the original directory information no longer exists, and a good FAT repair is impossible. You therefore should never run CHKDSK with the /F parameter without first running it in read-only mode (without the /F parameter) to determine whether and to what extent damage exists.

Only after carefully examining the disk damage and determining how CHKDSK would fix the problems do you run CHKDSK with the /F parameter. If you do not specify the /F parameter when you run CHKDSK, the program is prevented from making corrections to the disk. Rather, it performs repairs in a mock fashion. This limitation is a safety feature because you do not want CHKDSK to take action until you have examined the problem. After deciding whether CHKDSK will make the correct assumptions about the damage, you might want to run it with the /F parameter.

Sometimes people place a CHKDSK /F command in their AUTOEXEC.BAT file—*a very dangerous practice*. If a system's disk directories and FAT system become damaged, attempting to load a program whose directory and FAT entries are damaged might lock the system. If, after you reboot, CHKDSK is fixing the problem because it is in the AUTOEXEC.BAT, it can irreparably damage the file structure of the disk. In many cases, CHKDSK ends up causing more damage than originally existed, and no easy way exists to undo the CHKDSK repair. Because CHKDSK is a simple utility that makes often faulty assumptions in repairing a disk, you must run it with great care when you specify the /F parameter.

Problems reported by CHKDSK are usually problems with the software and not the hardware. You rarely see a case in which lost clusters, allocation errors, or cross-linked files reported by CHKDSK were caused directly by a hardware fault, although it is certainly possible. The cause is usually a defective program or a program that was stopped before it could close files or purge buffers. A hardware fault certainly can stop a program before it can close files, but many people think that these error messages signify fault with the disk hardware—almost never the case.

VI

Troubleshooting

I recommend running CHKDSK at least once a day on a hard disk system because it is important to find out about file structure errors as soon as possible. Accordingly, placing a CHKDSK command in your AUTOEXEC.BAT file is a good idea, but do not use the /F parameter. Also run CHKDSK whenever you suspect that directory or FAT damage could have occurred. For example, whenever a program terminates abnormally or a system crashes for some reason, run CHKDSK to see whether any file system damage has occurred.

Common Errors. All CHKDSK can do is compare the directory and FAT structures to see whether they support or comply with one another; as a result, CHKDSK can detect only certain kinds of problems. When CHKDSK discovers discrepancies between the directory and the FAT structures, they almost always fall into one of the following categories (these errors are the most common ones you will see with CHKDSK):

- Lost allocation units
- Allocation errors
- Cross-linked files
- Invalid allocation units

The RECOVER Command. The DOS RECOVER command is designed to mark clusters as bad in the FAT when the clusters cannot be read properly. When a file cannot be read because of a problem with a sector on the disk going bad, the RECOVER command can mark the FAT so that those clusters are not used by another file. Used improperly, this program is highly dangerous.

Many users think that RECOVER is used to recover a file or the data within the file in question. What really happens is that only the portion of the file before the defect is recovered and remains after the RECOVER command operates on it. RECOVER marks the defective portion as bad in the FAT and returns to available status all the data after the defect. Always make a copy of the file to be recovered before using RECOVER because the copy command can get all the information, including the portion of the file after the location of the defect.

Suppose that you are using a word processing program. You start the program and tell it to load a file called DOCUMENT.TXT. The hard disk has developed a defect in a sector used by this file, and in the middle of loading it, you see this message appear on-screen:

```
Sector not found error reading drive C
Abort, Retry, Ignore, Fail?
```

You might be able to read the file on a retry, so try several times. If you can load the file by retrying, save the loaded version as a file with a different name, to preserve the data in the file. You still have to repair the structure of the disk to prevent the space from being used again.

After ten retries or so, if you still cannot read the file, the data will be more difficult to recover. This operation has two phases, as follows:

- Preserve as much of the data in the file as possible.
- Mark the FAT so that the bad sectors or clusters of the disk are not used again.

Preserving Data. To recover the data from a file, use the DOS COPY command to make a copy of the file with a different name; for example, if the file you are recovering has the name DOCUMENT.TXT and you want the copy to be named DOCUMENT.NEW, enter the following at the DOS prompt:

    COPY document.txt document.new

In the middle of the copy, you see the Sector not found error message again. The key to this operation is to answer with the (I)gnore option. Then the bad sectors are ignored, and the copy operation can continue to the end of the file. This procedure produces a copy of the file with all the file intact, up to the error location and after the error location. The bad sectors appear as gibberish or garbage in the new copied file, but the entire copy is readable. Use your word processor to load the new copy and remove or retype the garbled sectors. If this file were a binary file (such as a part of a program), you probably would have to consider the whole thing a total loss because you generally do not have the option of retyping the bytes that make up a program file. Your only hope then is to replace the file from a backup. This step completes phase one, which recovers as much of the data as possible. Now you go to phase two, in which you mark the disk so that these areas will not be used again.

Marking Bad Sectors. You mark bad sectors on a disk by using the RECOVER command. After making the attempted recovery of the data, you can use the following RECOVER command at the DOS prompt to mark the sectors as bad in the FAT:

    RECOVER document.txt

In this case, the output of the RECOVER command looks like this:

    Press any key to begin recovery of the file(s) on drive C:
    XXXXX of YYYYY bytes recovered

The DOCUMENT.TXT file still is on the disk after this operation, but it has been truncated at the location of the error. Any sectors the RECOVER command cannot read are marked as bad sectors in the FAT and will show up the next time you run CHKDSK. You might want to run CHKDSK before and after running RECOVER, to see the effect of the additional bad sectors.

After using RECOVER, delete the DOCUMENT.TXT file because you have already created a copy of it that contains as much good data as possible.

This step completes phase two—and the entire operation. You now have a new file that contains as much of the original file as possible, and the disk FAT is marked so that the defective location will not be a bother.

VI

Troubleshooting

Caution

Be very careful when you use RECOVER. Used improperly, it can do much damage to your files and the FAT. If you enter the RECOVER command without a file name for it to work on, the program assumes that you want every file on the disk recovered, and operates on every file and subdirectory on the disk; it converts all subdirectories to files, places all file names in the root directory, and gives them new names (FILE0000.REC, FILE0001.REC, and so on). This process essentially wipes out the file system on the entire disk. *Do not use RECOVER without providing a file name for it to work on.* This program should be considered as dangerous as the FORMAT command.

When you get the `Sector not found error reading drive C:`, rather than using the DOS RECOVER command, use the Norton Disk Doctor, or a similar utility, to repair the problem. If the error is on a floppy disk, use Norton's DiskTool before you use Disk Doctor. DiskTool is designed to help you recover data from a defective floppy disk. Disk Doctor and DiskTool preserve as much of the data in the file as possible, and afterward mark the FAT so that the bad sectors or clusters of the disk are not used again. These Norton Utilities also save UNDO information, making it possible for you to reverse any data recovery operation.

The DEBUG Program

The DOS DEBUG program is a powerful debugging tool for programmers who develop programs in assembly language. The following list shows some of the things you can do with DEBUG:

- Display data from any memory location.
- Display or alter the contents of the CPU registers.
- Display the assembly source code of programs.
- Enter data directly into any memory location.
- Input from a port.
- Move blocks of data between memory locations.
- Output to a port.
- Perform hexadecimal addition and subtraction.
- Read disk sectors into memory.
- Trace the execution of a program.
- Write disk sectors from memory.
- Write short assembly language programs.

To use the DEBUG program, make sure that DEBUG.COM is in the current directory or in the current DOS PATH. The following is the DEBUG command syntax:

DEBUG [*d:*][*path*][*filename*][*arglist*]

Entering DEBUG alone at the DOS prompt launches DEBUG. The *d:* and *path* options represent the drive and directory where the file you want to debug is located. The *filename* entry represents the file you want to debug. When you want to use DEBUG to work on a file, the file name is mandatory. The *arglist* entry represents parameters and switches that are passed to a program being debugged and can be used only if the file name is present.

After DEBUG is executed, its prompt is displayed (the DEBUG prompt is a hyphen). At the DEBUG hyphen prompt, you can enter a DEBUG command.

Because more powerful programs are available for debugging and assembling code, the most common use for DEBUG is patching assembly language programs to correct problems, changing an existing program feature, or patching disk sectors.

DEBUG Commands and Parameters. The documentation for DEBUG no longer is provided in the standard DOS manual. If you are serious about using DEBUG, you should purchase the *DOS Technical Reference Manual*, which contains the information you need to use this program. Many third-party books also provide documentation of the DEBUG commands and parameters.

As a quick reference to the DEBUG program, the following is a brief description of each command:

A address assembles macro assembler statements directly into memory.

C range address compares the contents of two blocks of memory.

D address or *D range* displays the contents of a portion of memory.

E address displays bytes sequentially and enables them to be modified.

E address list replaces the contents of one or more bytes, starting at the specified address, with values contained in the list.

F range list fills the memory locations in the range with the values specified.

G processes the program you are debugging without breakpoints.

G =address processes instructions beginning at the address specified.

G =address address processes instructions beginning at the address specified. This command stops the processing of the program when the instruction at the specified address is reached (breakpoint), and displays the registers, flags, and the next instruction to be processed. As many as ten breakpoints can be listed.

H value value adds the two hexadecimal values and then subtracts the second from the first. It displays the sum and the difference on one line.

I portaddress inputs and displays (in hexadecimal) one byte from the specified port.

L address loads a file.

L address drive sector sector loads data from the disk specified by drive and places the data in memory beginning at the specified address.

M range address moves the contents of the memory locations specified by range to the locations beginning at the address specified.

N filename defines file specifications or other parameters required by the program being debugged.

O portaddress byte sends the byte to the specified output port.

P =address value causes the processing of a subroutine call, a loop instruction, an interrupt, or a repeat-string instruction to stop at the next instruction.

Q ends the DEBUG program.

R displays the contents of all registers and flags and the next instruction to be processed.

R F displays all flags.

R registername displays the contents of a register.

S range list searches the range for the characters in the list.

T =address value processes one or more instructions starting with the instructions at CS:IP, or at =address if it is specified. This command also displays the contents of all registers and flags after each instruction is processed.

U address unassembles instructions (translates the contents of memory into assembler-like statements) and displays their addresses and hexadecimal values, together with assembler-like statements.

W address enables you to use the WRITE command without specifying parameters or by specifying only the address parameter.

W address drive sector sector writes data to disk beginning at a specified address.

XA count allocates a specified number of expanded memory pages to a handle.

XD handle deallocates a handle.

XM lpage ppage handle maps an EMS logical page to an EMS physical page from an EMS handle.

XS displays the status of expanded memory.

Changing Disks and Files. DEBUG can be used to modify sectors on a disk. Suppose that you use the following DEBUG command:

    -L 100 1 0 1

This command loads into the current segment at an offset of 100h, sectors from drive B:\ (1), starting with sector 0 (the DOS volume boot sector), for a total of 1 or more sectors. You then could write this sector to a file on drive C:\ by using these commands:

```
-N C:\B-BOOT.SEC

-R CX

CX 0000

:200

-W

Writing 00200 bytes

-Q
```

The Name command sets up the name of the file to read or write.

The Register command enables you to inspect and change the contents of registers. The CX register contains the low-order bytes indicating the size of the file to load or save, and the BX register contains the high-order bytes. You would not need to set the BX register to anything but 0 unless the file was to be more than 65535 (64K) bytes in size. Setting the CX register to 200 indicates a file size of 200h, or 512 bytes.

The Write command saves 512 bytes of memory, starting at the default address of offset 100, to the file indicated in the Name command.

After quitting the program, your C:\ drive will have a file called B-BOOT.SEC that contains an image of the DOS volume boot sector on drive B:\.

Memory-Resident Software Conflicts

One area that gives many users trouble is a type of memory-resident software called Terminate and Stay Resident (TSR) or *pop-up utilities*. This software loads itself into memory and stays there, waiting for an activation key (usually a keystroke combination).

The problem with pop-up utilities is that they often conflict with each other, as well as with application programs and even DOS. Pop-up utilities can cause many types of problems. Sometimes the problems appear consistently, and at other times they are intermittent. Some computer users do not like to use pop-up utilities unless absolutely necessary because of their potential for problems.

Other memory-resident programs, such as MOUSE.COM, are usually loaded in AUTOEXEC.BAT. These memory-resident programs usually do not cause the kind of conflicts that pop-up utilities do, mainly because pop-up utilities are constantly monitoring the keyboard for the hotkey that activates them (and pop-up utilities are known to barge into memory addresses being used by other programs in order to monitor the keyboard, or to activate). Memory-resident programs like MOUSE.COM are merely installed in memory, do not poll the keyboard for a hotkey, and generally do not clash with the memory addresses used by other programs.

Device drivers loaded in CONFIG.SYS are another form of memory-resident software and can cause many problems.

If you are experiencing problems that you have traced to any of the three types of memory-resident programs, a common way to correct the problem is to eliminate the conflicting program. Another possibility is to change the order in which device drivers and memory-resident programs are loaded into system memory. Some programs must be loaded first, and others must be loaded last. Sometimes this order preference is indicated in the documentation for the programs, but often it is discovered through trial and error.

Unfortunately, conflicts between memory-resident programs are likely to be around as long as DOS is used. The light at the end of the tunnel is operating systems like Windows NT 3.1 and OS/2. The problem with DOS is that it establishes no real rules for how resident programs must interact with each other and the rest of the system. Windows NT and OS/2 are built on the concept of many programs being resident in memory at one time, and all multitasking. These operating systems should put an end to the problem of resident programs conflicting with each other.

Hardware Problems versus Software Problems

One of the most aggravating situations in computer repair is opening up a system and troubleshooting all the hardware just to find that the cause of the problem is a software program, not the hardware. Many people have spent large sums of money on replacement hardware such as motherboards, disk drives, adapter boards, cables, and so on, all on the premise that the hardware was causing problems, when software was actually the culprit. To eliminate these aggravating, sometimes embarrassing, and often expensive situations, you must be able to distinguish a hardware problem from a software problem.

Fortunately, making this distinction can be relatively simple. Software problems often are caused by device drivers and memory-resident programs loaded in CONFIG.SYS and AUTOEXEC.BAT on many systems. One of the first things to do when you begin having problems with your system is to boot the system from a DOS disk that has no CONFIG.SYS or AUTOEXEC.BAT configuration files on it. Then test for the problem. If it has disappeared, the cause was probably something in one or both of those files. To find the problem, begin restoring device drivers and memory-resident programs to CONFIG.SYS and AUTOEXEC.BAT one at a time (starting with CONFIG.SYS). For example, add one program back to CONFIG.SYS, reboot your system, and then determine if the problem has reappeared. When you discover the device driver or memory-resident program causing the problem, you might be able to solve the problem by editing CONFIG.SYS and AUTOEXEC.BAT to change the order in which device drivers and memory-resident programs are loaded, or you might have to eliminate the problem device driver or memory-resident program.

DOS can cause other problems, such as bugs or incompatibilities with certain hardware items. For example, DOS 3.2 does not support the 1.44M floppy drive format; therefore, using DOS 3.2 on a system equipped with a 1.44M floppy drive might lead you to believe (incorrectly) that the drive is bad. Make sure that you are using the correct version of DOS and that support is provided for your hardware. Find out whether your version of DOS has any official patches available; sometimes a problem you are experiencing might be one that many others have had, and IBM or Microsoft might have released a fix disk that takes care of the problem. For example, many PS/2 users have a floppy formatting problem under DOS 3.3. They get a `track 0 bad` message after answering Yes to the `Format another diskette` message. This problem is solved by a special driver file on the DOS 3.3 patch disk.

If you are having a problem related to a piece of application software, a word processor or spreadsheet, for example, contact the company that produces the software and explain the problem. If the software has a bug, the company might have a patched or fixed version available, or it might be able to help you operate the software in a different way to solve the problem.

Summary

This chapter examined the software side of your system. Often a system problem is in the software and is not hardware-related. The chapter also examined DOS and showed how DOS organizes information on a disk. You learned about the CHKDSK, RECOVER, and DEBUG commands to see how DOS can help you with data and disk recovery. Finally, the chapter described memory-resident software and some of the problems it can cause, and informed you how to distinguish a software problem from a hardware problem.

VI

Troubleshooting

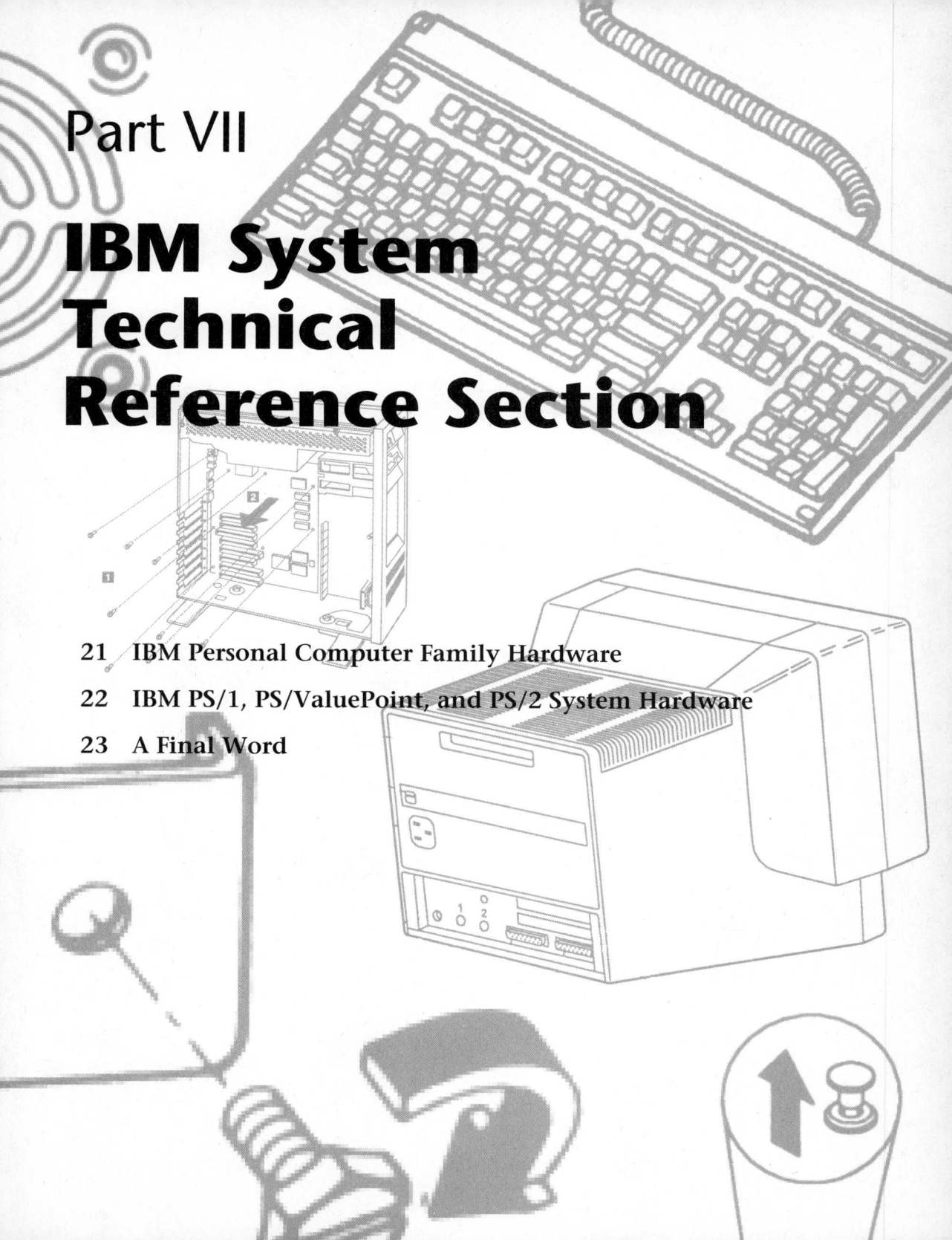

Part VII

IBM System Technical Reference Section

21   IBM Personal Computer Family Hardware

22   IBM PS/1, PS/ValuePoint, and PS/2 System Hardware

23   A Final Word

Chapter 21

IBM Personal Computer Family Hardware

This chapter serves as a technical reference to IBM's original family of personal computer system units and accessories. It separates and identifies each personal computer system originally offered by IBM, including the complete original line of PC systems that have been discontinued. Because the entire original line has been discontinued, much of this chapter can be considered a history lesson. The information still is valuable, however, because many people still own and manage these older systems, which are more likely to break down than newer ones. Also, nearly every IBM-compatible or clone system on the market today is based on one or more of these original IBM products. The original line of systems often are called Industry Standard Architecture (ISA) systems, or *Classic* PCs. IBM calls them *Family/1* systems. The PS/2 (or *Family/2*) systems are examined in the following chapter.

This chapter is a reference specific to the original line of true IBM PC, XT, and AT systems. For upgrade and repair purposes, most PC-compatible systems are treated in the same manner as IBM systems. Most compatible systems can exchange parts easily with IBM systems and vice versa. In fact, most of the parts that make up IBM systems are made by third-party companies, and you can purchase these same parts outside of IBM to save money.

In Chapter 2, "Overview of System Features and Components," you learned that all systems can be broken down into two basic types: PC/XT or AT. AT types of systems often are broken down into several subtypes. These subtypes can be classified as systems that use 286 or 386/486/Pentium processors and systems with Industry Standard Architecture (ISA), Extended Industry Standard Architecture (EISA), VL (Video Local) Bus, PCI (Peripheral Component Interconnect), or Micro Channel Architecture (MCA) slots. Use this chapter to compare a compatible system with a specific IBM system in a feature-by-feature comparison. This kind of comparison is often interesting because compatibles usually offer many more features and options at a lower price.

System-Unit Features by Model

In the following sections, you learn the makeup of all the various versions or models of the specific systems and also technical details and specifications of each system. Every system unit has a few standard parts. The primary component is the motherboard, which has the CPU (central processing unit, or microprocessor) and other primary computer circuitry. Each unit also includes a case with an internal power supply, a keyboard, certain standard adapters or plug-in cards, and usually some form of disk drive.

You receive an explanation of each system's various submodels and details about the differences between and features of each model. You learn about the changes from model to model and version to version of each system.

Included for your reference is part-number information for each system and option. This information is *for comparison and reference purposes only* because all these systems have been discontinued and generally are no longer available. IBM still stocks and sells component parts and assemblies, however, for even these discontinued units. You can (and usually should) replace failed components in these older systems with non-IBM replacement parts because you invariably can obtain upgraded or improved components compared to what IBM offers, and at a greatly reduced price.

An Introduction to the PC

IBM introduced the IBM Personal Computer on August 12, 1981, and officially withdrew the machine from marketing on April 2, 1987. During the nearly six-year life of the PC, IBM made only a few basic changes to the system. The basic motherboard circuit design was changed in April 1983 to accommodate 64K RAM chips. Three different ROM BIOS versions were used during the life of the system; most other specifications, however, remained unchanged. Because IBM no longer markets the PC system, and because of the PC's relatively limited expansion capability and power, the standard PC is obsolete by most standards.

The system unit supports only floppy disk drives unless the power supply is upgraded or an expansion chassis is used to house the hard disk externally. IBM never offered an internal hard disk for the PC but many third-party companies stepped in to fill this void with upgrades. The system unit included many configurations with single or dual floppy disk drives. Early on, one version even was available with no disk drives, and others used single-sided floppy drives. The PC motherboard was based on the 16-bit Intel 8088 microprocessor and included the Microsoft Cassette BASIC language built into ROM. For standard memory, the PC offered configurations with as little as 16K of RAM (when the system was first announced) and as much as 256K on the motherboard. Two motherboard designs were used. Systems sold before March 1983 had a motherboard that supported a maximum of only 64K of RAM, and later systems supported a maximum of 256K on the motherboard. In either case, you added more memory (as much as 640K) by installing memory cards in the expansion slots.

The first bank of memory chips in every PC is soldered to the motherboard. Soldered memory is reliable but not conducive to easy servicing because the solder prevents you from easily exchanging failing memory chips located in the first bank. The chips must be unsoldered and the defective chip replaced with a socket so that a replacement can be plugged in. When IBM services the defective memory, IBM advises you to exchange the entire motherboard. Considering today's value of these systems, replacing the motherboard with one of the many compatible motherboards on the market may be a better idea. Repairing the same defective memory chip in the XT system is much easier because all memory in an XT is socketed.

The only disk drive available from IBM for the PC is a double-sided (320 or 360K) floppy disk drive. You can install a maximum of two drives in the system unit by using IBM-supplied drives, or four using half-height third-party drives and mounting brackets.

The system unit has five slots that support expansion cards for additional devices, features, or memory. All these slots support full-length adapter cards. In most configurations, the PC included at least a floppy disk controller card. You need a second slot for a monitor adapter, which leaves three slots for adapter cards.

All models of the PC have a fan-cooled, 63.5-watt power supply. This low-output power supply doesn't support much in the way of system expansion, especially power-hungry items, such as hard disks. Usually, this low-output supply must be replaced by a higher-output unit, such as the one used in the XT. Figure 21.1 shows an interior view of a PC system unit.

An 83-key keyboard with an adjustable typing angle is standard equipment on the PC. The keyboard is attached to the rear of the system unit by a six-foot coiled cable. Figure 21.2 shows the back panel of the PC.

Most model configurations of the PC system unit included these major functional components:

- Intel 8088 microprocessor
- ROM-based diagnostics (POST)
- BASIC language interpreter in ROM
- 256 kilobytes of dynamic RAM
- Floppy disk controller
- One or two 360K floppy drives
- A 63.5-watt power supply
- Five I/O expansion slots
- Socket for the 8087 math coprocessor

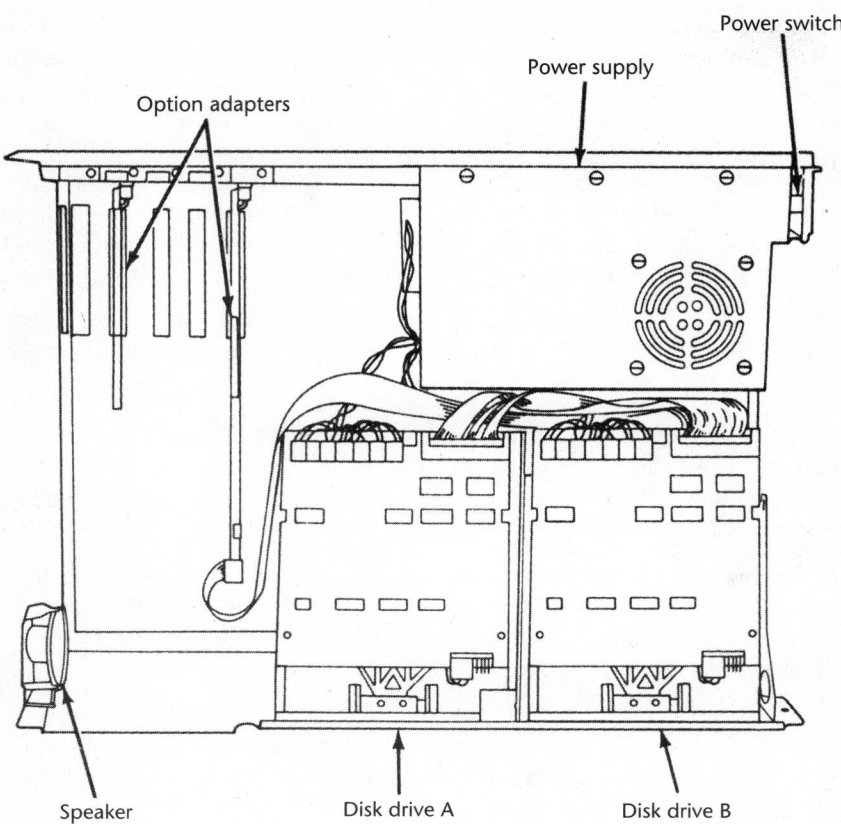

Fig. 21.1
The IBM PC interior view.

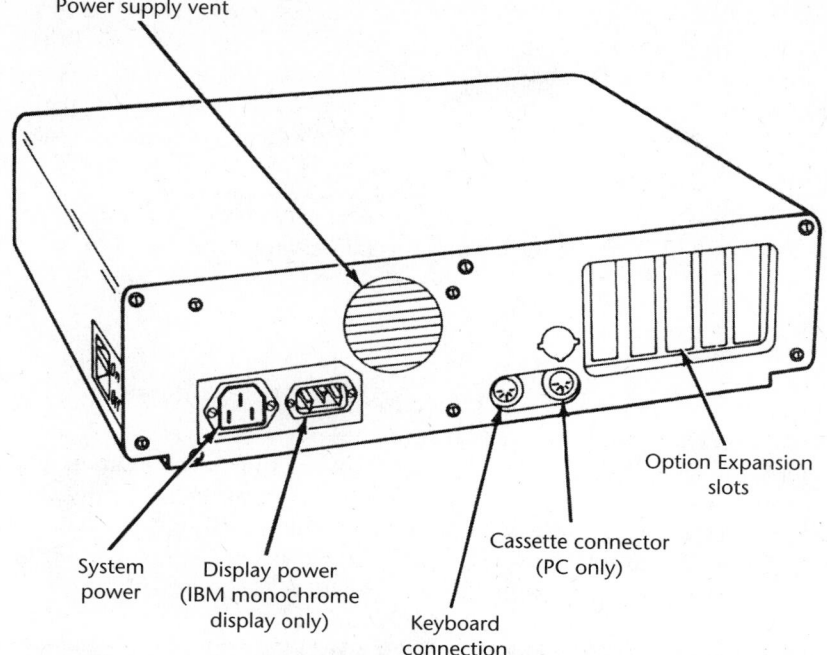

Power supply vent

Option Expansion
slots

Cassette connector
(PC only)

System
power

Display power
(IBM monochrome
display only)

Keyboard
connection

Fig. 21.2
The IBM PC rear view.

PC Models and Features

Although several early-model configurations of the IBM PC were available before March
1983, only two models were available after that time. The later models differ only in the
number of floppy drives: one or two. IBM designated these models as follows:

IBM PC 5150 Model 166: 256K RAM, one 360K drive

IBM PC 5150 Model 176: 256K RAM, two 360K drives

The PC never was available with a factory-installed hard disk, primarily because the system unit has a limited base for expansion and offered few resources with which to work.
After IBM started selling XTs with only floppy disk drives (on April 2, 1985), the PC became obsolete. The XT offered much more for virtually the same price. Investing in a PC
after the XT introduction was questionable.

IBM finally withdrew the PC from the market April 2, 1987. IBM's plans for the system
became obvious when the company didn't announce a new model with the Enhanced
Keyboard, as it did with other IBM systems.

With some creative purchasing, you can make a usable system of a base PC by adding the requisite components, such as a full 640K of memory and hard and floppy drives. You still may have a slot or two to spare. Unfortunately, expanding this system requires replacing many of the boards in the system unit with boards that combine the same functions in less space. Only you can decide when your money is better invested in a new system.

Before you can think of expanding a PC beyond even a simple configuration, and to allow for compatibility and reliability, you must address the following two major areas:

- ROM BIOS level (version)

- Power supply

In most cases, the power supply is the most critical issue because all PCs sold after March 1983 already have the latest ROM BIOS. If you have an earlier PC system, you also must upgrade the ROM because the early versions lack some required capabilities. Both problems, and also other expansion issues related to all systems in the PC family, are addressed in Chapter 4, "Motherboards," Chapter 8, "The Power Supply," Chapter 14, "Hard Disk Drives and Controllers," and Chapter 17, "System Upgrades and Improvements." Table 21.1 shows the part numbers for the IBM PC system unit.

Table 21.1 IBM PC Part Numbers	
Description	**Number**
PC system unit, 256K, one double-sided drive	5150166
PC system unit, 256K, two double-sided drives	5150176
Options	
PC expansion-unit Model 001 with 10M fixed disk	5161001
Double-sided disk drive	1503810
8087 math coprocessor option	1501002
BIOS update kit	1501005

PC Technical Specifications

Technical information for the Personal Computer system and keyboard is described in this section. Here, you find information about the system architecture, memory configurations and capacities, standard system features, disk storage, expansion slots, keyboard specifications, and physical and environmental specifications. This kind of information may be useful in determining what parts you need when you are upgrading or repairing these systems. Figure 21.3 shows the layout and components on the PC motherboard.

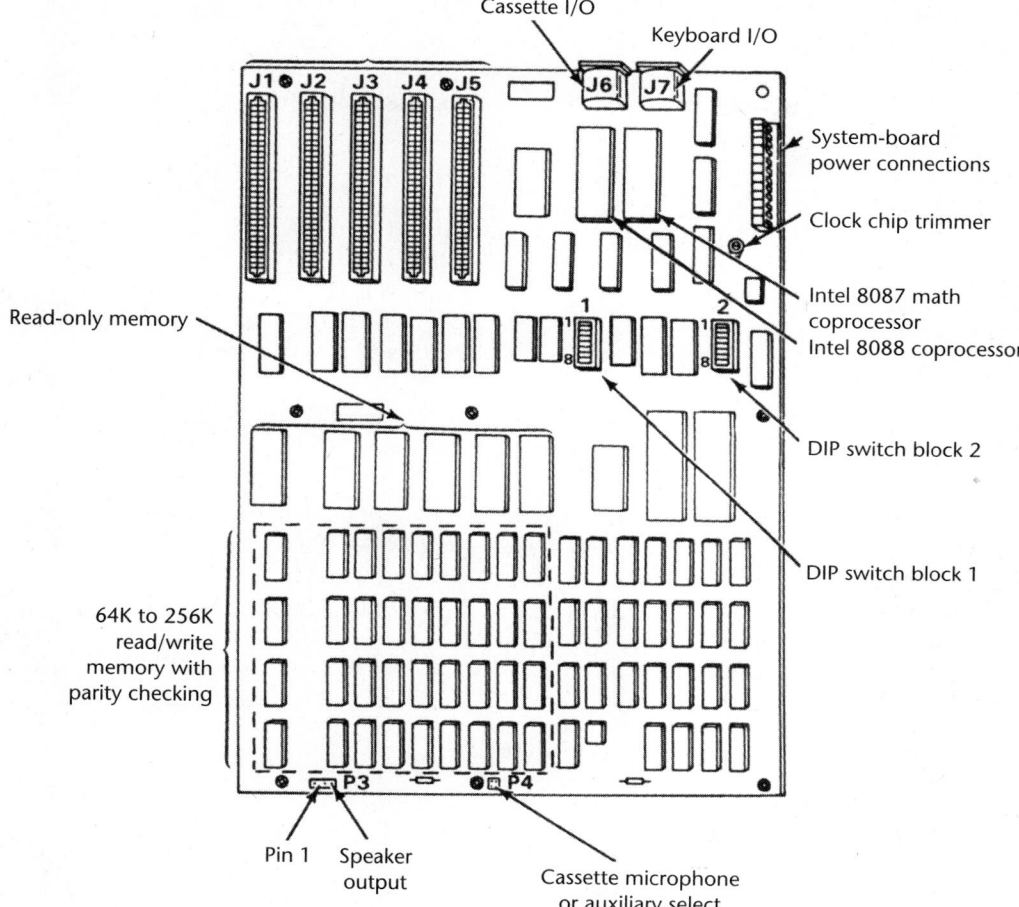

Fig. 21.3

The IBM PC motherboard.

System Architecture	
Microprocessor	8088
Clock speed	4.77 MHz
Bus type	ISA (Industry Standard Architecture)
Bus width	8-bit
Interrupt levels	8
Type	Edge-triggered
Shareable	No
DMA channels	3
DMA burst mode supported	No
Bus masters supported	No

(continues)

System Architecture

Upgradable processor complex	No

Memory

Standard on system board	16K, 64K, or 256K
Maximum on system board	256K
Maximum total memory	640K
Memory speed (ns) and type	200ns dynamic RAM
System board memory-socket type	16-pin DIP
Number of memory-module sockets	27 (3 banks of 9)
Memory used on system board	27 16K×1-bit or 64K×1-bit DRAM chips in 3 banks of 9, one soldered bank of 9 16K×1-bit or 64K×1-bit chips
Memory cache controller	No
Wait states: System board Adapter	 1 1

Standard Features

ROM size	40K
ROM shadowing	No
Optional math coprocessor Coprocessor speed	8087 4.77 MHz
Standard graphics	None standard
RS232C serial ports UART chip used Maximum speed (bits per second) Maximum number of ports supported	None standard NS8250B 9,600 bps 2
Pointing device (mouse) ports	None standard
Parallel printer ports Bi-directional Maximum number of ports supported	None standard No 3
CMOS real-time clock (RTC)	No
CMOS RAM	None

Disk Storage

Internal disk and tape drive bays Number of 3 1/2/5 1/4-inch bays	2 full-height 0/2
Standard floppy drives	1×360K

Disk Storage

Optional floppy drives:	
5 1/4-inch 360K	Optional
5 1/4-inch 1.2M	No
3 1/2-inch 720K	Optional
3 1/2-inch 1.44M	No
3 1/2-inch 2.88M	No
Hard disk controller included	None

Expansion Slots

Total adapter slots	5
Number of long and short slots	5/0
Number of 8-/16-/32-bit slots	5/0/0
Available slots (with video)	3

Keyboard Specifications

101-key Enhanced Keyboard	No, 83-key
Fast keyboard speed setting	No
Keyboard cable length	6 feet

Physical Specifications

Footprint type	Desktop
Dimensions:	
Height	5.5 inches
Width	19.5 inches
Depth	16.0 inches
Weight	25 pounds

Environmental Specifications

Power-supply output	63.5 watts
Worldwide (110/60, 220/50)	No
Auto-sensing/switching	No
Maximum current:	
104-127 VAC	2.5 amps
Operating range:	
Temperature	60–90 degrees F
Relative humidity	8–80 percent
Maximum operating altitude	7,000 feet
Heat (BTUs/hour)	505
Noise (Average dB, operating, 1m)	43
FCC classification	Class B

Tables 21.2 and 21.3 show the Switch Settings for the PC (and XT) motherboard. The PC has two eight-position switch blocks (Switch Block 1 and Switch Block 2), whereas the XT has only a single Switch Block 1. The PC uses the additional switch block to control the amount of memory the system would recognize, and the XT automatically counts up the memory amount.

Table 21.2   IBM PC/XT Motherboard Switch Settings

SWITCH BLOCK 1 (PC and XT)

	Switch 1	**IBM PC Function (PC Only):**
	Off	Boot From Floppy Drives
	On	Do Not Boot From Floppy Drives
	Switch 1	**IBM XT Function (XT Only):**
	Off	Normal POST (Power-On Self Test)
	On	Continuous Looping POST
	Switch 2	**Math Coprocessor (PC/XT):**
	Off	Installed
	On	Not Installed
Switch 3	**Switch 4**	**Installed Motherboard Memory (PC/XT):**
On	On	Bank 0 only
Off	On	Banks 0 and 1
On	Off	Banks 0, 1 and 2
Off	Off	All 4 Banks
Switch 5	**Switch 6**	**Video Adapter Type (PC/XT):**
Off	Off	Monochrome (MDA)
Off	On	Color (CGA) - 40x25 mode
On	Off	Color (CGA) - 80x25 mode
On	On	Any Video Card w/onboard BIOS (EGA/VGA)
Switch 7	**Switch 8**	**Number of Floppy Drives (PC/XT):**
On	On	1 floppy drive
Off	On	2 floppy drives
On	Off	3 floppy drives
Off	Off	4 floppy drives

Table 21.3   SWITCH BLOCK 2 (PC Only) Memory Settings

Memory	Switch Number (Switch Block 2, PC Only)							
	1	**2**	**3**	**4**	**5**	**6**	**7**	**8**
16K	On	On	On	On	On	Off	Off	Off
32K	On	On	On	On	On	Off	Off	Off
48K	On	On	On	On	On	Off	Off	Off
64K	On	On	On	On	On	Off	Off	Off

Memory	Switch Number (Switch Block 2, PC Only)							
	1	**2**	**3**	**4**	**5**	**6**	**7**	**8**
96K	Off	On	On	On	On	Off	Off	Off
128K	On	Off	On	On	On	Off	Off	Off
160K	Off	Off	On	On	On	Off	Off	Off
192K	On	On	Off	On	On	Off	Off	Off
224K	Off	On	Off	On	On	Off	Off	Off
256K	On	Off	Off	On	On	Off	Off	Off
288K	Off	Off	Off	On	On	Off	Off	Off
320K	On	On	On	Off	On	Off	Off	Off
352K	Off	On	On	Off	On	Off	Off	Off
384K	On	Off	On	Off	On	Off	Off	Off
416K	Off	Off	On	Off	On	Off	Off	Off
448K	On	On	Off	Off	On	Off	Off	Off
480K	Off	On	Off	Off	On	Off	Off	Off
512K	On	Off	Off	Off	On	Off	Off	Off
544K	Off	Off	Off	Off	On	Off	Off	Off
576K	On	On	On	On	Off	Off	Off	Off
608K	Off	On	On	On	Off	Off	Off	Off
640K	On	Off	On	On	Off	Off	Off	Off

An Introduction to the PC Convertible

IBM marked its entry into the laptop computer market on April 2, 1986, by introducing the IBM 5140 PC Convertible. The system superseded the 5155 Portable PC (IBM's transportable system), which no longer was available. The IBM 5140 system wasn't a very successful laptop system. Other laptops offered more disk storage, higher processor speeds, more readable screens, lower cost, and more compact cases, which pressured IBM to improve the Convertible. Because the improvements were limited to the display, however, this system never gained respect in the marketplace.

The PC Convertible was available in two models. The Model 2 had a CMOS 80C88 4.77 MHz microprocessor, 64 kilobytes of ROM, 256 kilobytes of Static RAM, an 80-column-by-25-line detachable liquid crystal display, two 3 1/2-inch floppy disk drives, a 78-key keyboard, an AC adapter, and a battery pack. Also included were software programs called Application Selector, SystemApps, Tools, Exploring the IBM PC Convertible, and Diagnostics. The Model 22 is the same basic computer as the Model 2 but with the diagnostic software only. You can expand either system to 512K of RAM by using 128K RAM memory-cards, and you can include an internal 1,200 bps modem in the system unit. With aftermarket memory expansion, the computers can reach 640K.

Although the unit was painfully slow at 4.77 MHz, one notable feature is the use of Static memory chips for the system's RAM. Static RAM does not require the refresh signal that normal Dynamic RAM requires, which would normally require about seven percent of the processor's time in a standard PC or XT system. This means that the Convertible is about seven percent faster than an IBM PC or XT even though they all operate at the same clock speed of 4.77 MHz. Because of the increased reliability of the Static RAM (compared to Dynamic RAM) used in the Convertible, as well as the desire to minimize power consumption, none of the RAM in the Convertible is parity checked.

At the back of each system unit is an extendable bus interface. This 72-pin connector enables you to attach the following options to the base unit: a printer, a serial or parallel adapter, and a CRT display adapter. Each feature is powered from the system unit. The CRT display adapter operates only when the system is powered from a standard AC adapter. A separate CRT display or a television set attached through the CRT display adapter requires a separate AC power source.

Each system unit includes a detachable liquid crystal display (LCD). When the computer is not mobile, the LCD screen can be replaced by an external monitor. When the LCD is latched in the closed position, it forms the cover for the keyboard and floppy disk drives. Because the LCD is attached with a quick-disconnect connector, you can remove it easily to place the 5140 system unit below an optional IBM 5144 PC Convertible monochrome or IBM 5145 PC Convertible color display. During the life of the Convertible, IBM offered three different LCD displays. The first display was a standard LCD, which suffered from problems with contrast and readability. Due to complaints, IBM then changed the LCD to a Super Twisted type LCD display, which had much greater contrast. Finally, in the third LCD they added a fluorescent backlight to the Super Twisted LCD display, which not only offered greater contrast, but made the unit usable in low light situations.

The PC Convertible system unit has these standard features:

- Complementary Metal-Oxide Semiconductor (CMOS) 80C88 4.77 MHz microprocessor

- Two 32K CMOS ROMs containing these items:

  POST (Power-On Self Test) of system components
  BIOS (basic input-output system) support
  BASIC language interpreter

- 256K CMOS static RAM (expandable to 512K)

- Two 3 1/2-inch 720K (formatted) floppy drives

- An 80-column-by-25-line detachable LCD panel (graphics modes: 640-by-200 resolution and 320-by-200 resolution)

- LCD controller

- 16K RAM display buffer

- 8K LCD font RAM
- Adapter for optional printer (#4010)
- Professional keyboard (78 keys)
- AC adapter
- Battery pack

The system-unit options for the 5140 are shown in this list:

- 128K Static RAM memory card (#4005)
- Printer (#4010)
- Serial/parallel adapter (#4015)
- CRT display adapter (#4020)
- Internal modem (#4025)
- Printer cable (#4055)
- Battery charger (#4060)
- Automobile power adapter (#4065)

The following two optional displays were available for the PC Convertible:

- IBM 5144 PC Convertible Monochrome Display Model 1
- IBM 5145 PC Convertible Color Display Model 1

PC Convertible Specifications and Highlights

This section lists some technical specifications for the IBM 5140 PC Convertible system. The weights of the unit and options are listed because weight is an important consideration when you carry a laptop system. Figure 21.4 shows the PC Convertible motherboard components and layout.

Dimensions	
Depth	360 mm (14.17 inches) 374 mm (14.72 inches) including handle
Width	309.6 mm (12.19 inches) 312 mm (12.28 inches) including handle
Height	67 mm (2.64 inches) 68 mm (2.68 inches) including footpads

(continues)

Weight	
Models 2 and 22 (including battery)	5.5 kg (12.17 pounds)
128K/256K memory card	40 g (1.41 ounces)
Printer	1.6 kg (3.50 pounds)
Serial/parallel adapter	470 g (1.04 pounds)
CRT display adapter	630 g (1.40 pounds)
Internal modem	170 g (6 ounces)
Printer cable	227 g (8 ounces)
Battery charger	340 g (12 ounces)
Automobile power adapter	113 g (4 ounces)
5144 PC Convertible monochrome display	7.3 kg (16 pounds)
5145 PC Convertible color display	16.9 kg (37.04 pounds)

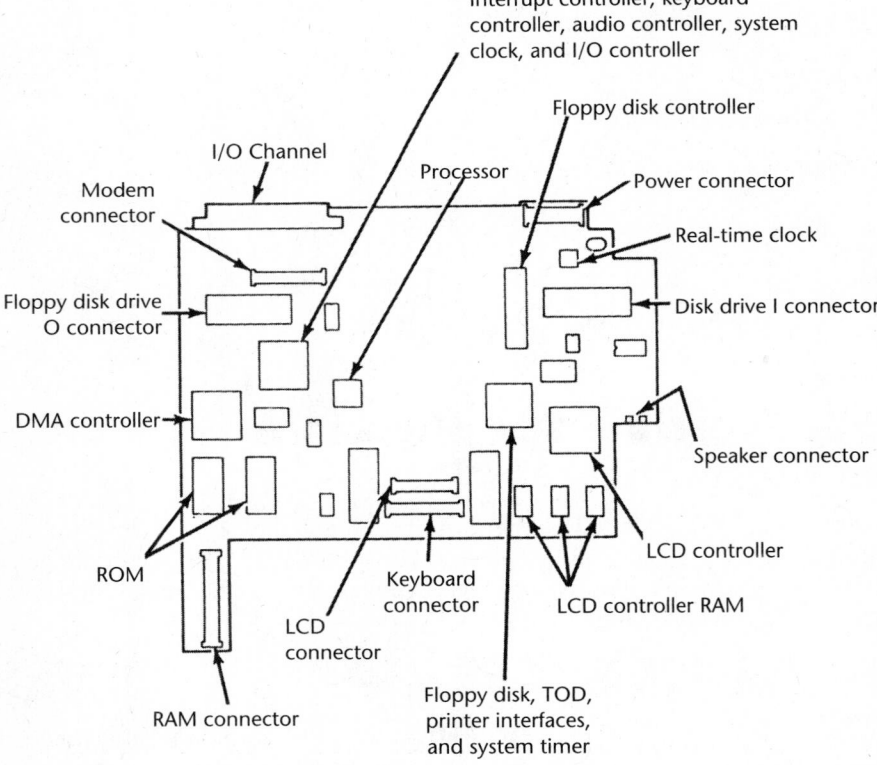

Fig. 21.4
The PC Convertible motherboard.

To operate the IBM 5140 PC Convertible properly, you must have PC DOS version 3.2 or later. Previous DOS versions aren't supported because they don't support the 720K floppy drive. Using the CRT display adapter and an external monitor requires that the system unit be operated by power from the AC adapter rather than from the battery.

PC Convertible Models and Features

This section covers the options and special features available for the PC Convertible. Several kinds of options were available, from additional memory to external display adapters, serial/parallel ports, modems, and even printers.

Memory Cards

A 128K or 256K memory card expands the base memory in the system unit. You can add two of these cards, for a system-unit total of 640K with one 256K card and one 128K card.

Optional Printers

An optional printer attaches to the back of the system unit or to an optional printer-attachment cable for adjacent printer operation. The printer's intelligent, microprocessor-based, 40 cps, non-impact dot-matrix design makes it capable of low-power operation. The optional printer draws power from and is controlled by the system unit. Standard ASCII 96-character, upper- and lowercase character sets are printed with a high-resolution, 24-element print head. A mode for graphics capability is provided also. You can achieve near-letter-quality printing by using either a thermal transfer ribbon on smooth paper or no ribbon on heat-sensitive thermal paper.

Serial/Parallel Adapters

A serial/parallel adapter attaches to the back of the system unit, a printer, or other feature module attached to the back of the system unit. The adapter provides an RS-232C asynchronous communications interface and a parallel printer interface, both compatible with the IBM personal computer asynchronous communications adapter and the IBM personal computer parallel printer adapter.

CRT Display Adapters

A CRT display adapter attaches to the back of the system unit, printer, or other feature module attached to the back of the system unit. This adapter enables you to connect a separate CRT display, such as the PC Convertible monochrome display or PC Convertible color display, to the system. By using optional connectors or cables, you can use the CRT display adapter also to attach a standard CGA monitor. Because composite video output is available, you also can use a standard television set.

Internal Modems

With an internal modem, you can communicate with compatible computers over telephone lines. It runs Bell 212A (1,200 bps) or Bell 103A (300 bps) protocols. The modem comes as a complete assembly, consisting of two cards connected by a cable. The entire assembly is installed inside the system unit. Over the life of the system, IBM made two different internal modems for the Convertible. The original modem was made for IBM by Novation, and did not follow the Hayes standard for commands and protocols. This rendered the modem largely incompatible with popular software designed to use the Hayes command set. Later, IBM changed the modem to one that was fully Hayes compatible, and this resolved the problems with software. IBM never introduced a modem faster than 1,200 bps for the Convertible. Fortunately, you still can operate a standard external modem through the serial port, although you lose the convenience of having it built in.

Printer Cables

The printer cable is 22 inches (0.6 meter) long with a custom 72-pin connector attached to each end. With this cable, you can operate the Convertible printer when it is detached from the system unit and place the unit for ease of use and visibility.

Battery Chargers

The battery charger is a 110-volt input device that charges the system's internal batteries. It does not provide sufficient power output for the system to operate while the batteries are being charged.

Automobile Power Adapters

An automobile power adapter plugs into the cigarette-lighter outlet in a vehicle with a 12-volt, negative-ground electrical system. You can use the unit while the adapter charges the Convertible's battery.

The IBM 5144 PC Convertible Monochrome Display

The 5144 PC Convertible monochrome display is a nine-inch (measured diagonally) composite video display attached to the system unit through the CRT display adapter. It comes with a display stand, an AC power cord, and a signal cable that connects the 5144 to the CRT display adapter. This display does not resemble—and is not compatible with—the IBM monochrome display for larger PC systems. The CRT adapter emits the same signal as the one supplied by the Color Graphics Adapter for a regular PC. This display is functionally equivalent to the display on the IBM Portable PC.

The IBM 5145 PC Convertible Color Display

The 5145 PC Convertible color display is a 13-inch color display attached to the system unit through the CRT display adapter. It comes with a display stand, an AC power cord, a signal cable that connects the 5145 to the CRT display adapter, and a speaker for external audio output. The monitor is a low-cost unit compatible with the standard IBM CGA display.

Special software available for the Convertible includes these programs:

- The *Application Selector* program, installed as an extension to DOS, provides a menu-driven interface to select and run applications software, the SystemApps, and Tools.

- The *SystemApps* program provides basic functions similar to many memory-resident programs on the market. This application, which includes Notewriter, Schedule, Phone List, and Calculator, is equivalent in function to the popular SideKick program.

- You can use the menu-driven *Tools* program as a front end for DOS to control and maintain the system (copying and erasing files, copying disks, and so on). With DOS, additional functions are available, including printing, formatting, and configuring the Application Selector function keys. This program presents many DOS functions in an easy-to-use menu format.

This additional software, except system diagnostics, is not included with the Model 22. Table 21.4 shows the part numbers of the IBM Convertible system units.

Table 21.4   IBM Convertible Part Numbers

5140 PC Convertible System Units	Number
Two drives, 256K with system applications	5140002
Two drives, 256K without system applications	5140022

An Introduction to the XT

Introduced March 8, 1983, the PC XT with a built-in 10M hard disk (originally standard, later optional) caused a revolution in personal computer configurations. At the time, having even a 10M hard disk was something very special. XT stands for eXTended. IBM chose this name because the IBM PC XT system includes many features not available in the standard PC. The XT has eight slots, allowing increased expansion capabilities; greater power-supply capacity; completely socketed memory; motherboards that support memory expansion to 640K without using an expansion slot; and optional hard disk drives. To obtain these advantages, the XT uses a different motherboard circuit design than the PC.

The system unit was available in several models, with a variety of disk drive configurations: one 360K floppy disk drive; two 360K floppy disk drives; one floppy disk and one hard disk drive; or two floppy disk drives and one hard disk drive. The floppy disk drives were full-height drives in the earlier models, and half-height drives in more recent models. With the four available drive bays, IBM had standard configurations with two floppy drives and a single hard disk, with room for a second hard disk provided all half-height units were used.

IBM offered 10M and 20M, full-height hard disks. In some cases they also installed half-height hard disks, but they were always installed in a bracket and cradle assembly that took up the equivalent space of a full-height drive. If you wanted half-height hard disks (to install two of them stacked, for example), then you had to use non-IBM supplied drives or modify the mounting of the IBM supplied half-height unit so that two could fit. Most aftermarket sources for hard disks had mounting kits that would work.

IBM also used double-sided (320/360K) floppy disk drives in full- or half-height configurations. A 3 1/2-inch 720K floppy disk drive was available in the more recent models. The 3 1/2-inch drives were available in a normal internal configuration or as an external device. You could install a maximum of two floppy disk drives and one hard disk drive in the system unit, using IBM-supplied drives. With half-height hard disks, you could install two hard drives in the system unit.

The XT is based on the same 8- and 16-bit Intel 8088 microprocessor (the CPU has 16-bit registers but only an 8-bit data bus) as the PC and runs at the same clock speed. Operationally, the XT systems are identical to the PC systems except for the hard disk. All models have at least one 360K floppy disk drive and a keyboard. For standard memory, the XT offers 256K or 640K on the main board. The hard disk models also include a serial adapter.

The system unit has eight slots that support cards for additional devices, features, or memory. Two of the slots support only short option cards because of physical interference from the disk drives. The XT has at least a disk drive adapter card in the floppy-disk-only models, and a hard disk controller card and serial adapter in the hard disk models. Either five or seven expansion slots (depending on the model) therefore are available. Figure 21.5 shows the interior of an XT.

All XT models include a heavy-duty, fan-cooled, 130-watt power supply to support the greater expansion capabilities and disk drive options. The power supply has more than double the capacity of the PC's supply, and can easily support hard disk drives as well as the full complement of expansion cards.

An 83-key keyboard was standard equipment with the early XT models, but was changed to an enhanced 101-key unit in the more recent models. The keyboard is attached to the system unit by a six-foot coiled cable.

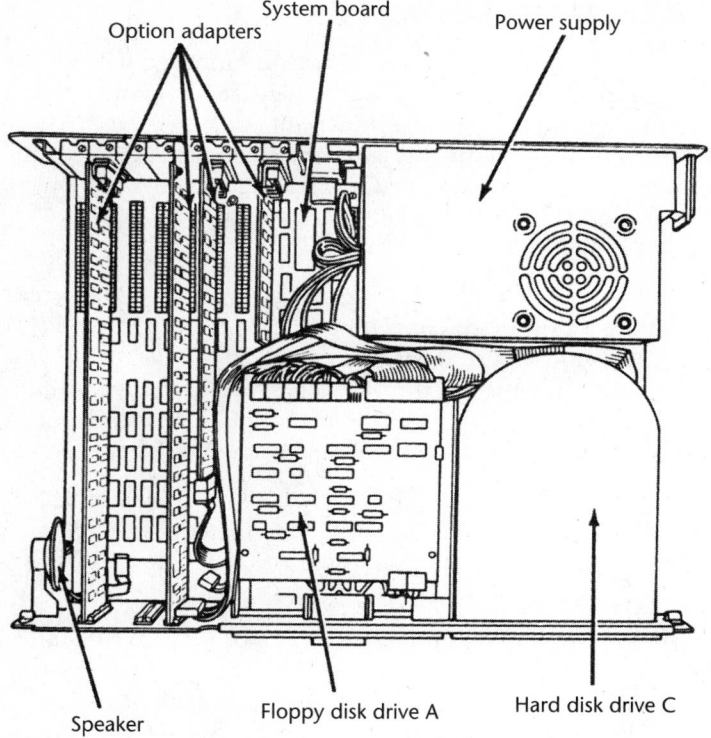

Option adapters System board Power supply

Speaker Floppy disk drive A Hard disk drive C

Fig. 21.5

The IBM PC XT interior.

All models of the PC XT system unit contain these major functional components:

- Intel 8088 microprocessor
- ROM-based diagnostics (POST)
- BASIC language interpreter in ROM
- 256K or 640K of dynamic RAM
- Floppy disk controller
- One 360K floppy drive (full- or half-height)
- 10M or 20M hard disk drive with interface (enhanced models)
- Serial interface (enhanced models)
- Heavy-duty, 135-watt power supply
- Eight I/O expansion slots
- Socket for 8087 math coprocessor

XT Models and Features

The XT was available in many different model configurations, but originally only one model was available. This model included a 10M hard disk, marking the first time that a hard disk was standard equipment in a personal computer and was properly supported by the operating system and peripherals. This computer helped change the industry standard for personal computers from normally having one or two floppy disk drives only to now including one or more hard disks.

Today, most people wouldn't consider a PC to be even remotely usable without a hard disk. The original XT was expensive, however, and buyers couldn't *unbundle*, or delete, the hard disk from the system at purchase time for credit and add it later. This fact distinguished the XT from the PC and misled many people to believe that the only difference between the two computers was the hard disk. People who recognized and wanted the greater capabilities of the XT without the standard IBM hard disk unfortunately had to wait for IBM to sell versions of the XT without the hard disk drive.

The original Model 087 of the XT included a 10M hard disk, 128K of RAM, and a standard serial interface. IBM later increased the standard memory in all PC systems to 256K. The XT reflected the change in Model 086, which was the same as the preceding 087 except for a standard 256K of RAM.

On April 2, 1985, IBM introduced new models of the XT without the standard hard disk. Designed for expansion and configuration flexibility, the new models enabled you to buy the system initially at a lower cost and add your own hard disk later. The XT therefore could be considered in configurations that previously only the original PC could fill. The primary difference between the PC and the XT is the XT's expansion capability, provided by the larger power supply, eight slots, and better memory layout. These models cost only $300 more than equivalent PCs, rendering the original PC no longer a viable option.

The extra expense of the XT was justified with the first power-supply replacement you made with an overworked PC. The IBM PC XT was available in two floppy disk models:

> 5160068 XT with one full-height 360K disk drive
>
> 5160078 XT with two full-height 360K disk drives

Both these models have 256K of memory and use the IBM PC XT motherboard, power supply, frame, and cover. The serial (asynchronous communications) adapter wasn't included as a standard feature with these models.

IBM introduced several more models of the PC XT on April 2, 1986. These models were significantly different from previous models. The most obvious difference, the Enhanced Keyboard, was standard with these newer computers. A 20M (rather than 10M) hard disk and high-quality, half-height floppy disk drives were included. The new half-height floppy disk drives allowed for two drives in the space that previously held only one floppy drive. With two drives, backing up floppy disks became easy. A new 3 1/2-inch floppy disk drive, storing 720K for compatibility with the PC Convertible laptop computer, was released also. These more recent XT system units were configured with a new memory layout allowing for 640K of RAM on the motherboard without an expansion slot. This feature conserved power, improves reliability, and lowered the cost of the system.

One 5 1/4-inch, half-height, 360K floppy disk drive and 256K of system-board memory were standard with the XT Models 267 and 268. Models 277 and 278 have a second 5 1/4-inch floppy disk drive. Models 088 and 089 are expanded PC XTs with all the standard features of the Models 267 and 268: a 20M hard disk, a 20M fixed disk drive adapter, a serial port adapter, and an additional 256K of system-board memory—a total of 512K.

The following list shows the highlights of these models:

- Enhanced Keyboard standard on Models 268, 278, and 089
- 101 keys

    Recappable

    Selectric typing section

    Dedicated numeric pad

    Dedicated cursor and screen controls

    Two additional function keys

    Nine-foot cable

- Standard PC XT keyboard on Models 267, 277, and 088
- More disk capacity (20M)
- Standard 5 1/4-inch, half-height, 360K floppy drive
- Available 3 1/2-inch, half-height, 720K floppy drive
- Capacity for four half-height storage devices within the system unit
- Capacity to expand to 640K bytes memory on system board without using expansion slots

These XT models have an extensively changed ROM BIOS. The BIOS is 64K and internally similar to the BIOS found in ATs. The ROM includes support for the keyboard and 3 1/2-inch floppy disk drives. The POST also was enhanced.

The new XTs were originally incompatible in some respects with some software programs. These problems centered on the new 101-key enhanced keyboard and the way the new ROM addressed the keys. These problems weren't major and were solved quickly by the software companies.

Seeing how much IBM changed the computer without changing the basic motherboard design is interesting. The ROM is different, and the board holds 640K of memory without a card in a slot. The memory trick is a simple one. IBM designed this feature into the board originally and chose to unleash it with these models of the XT.

During the past several years, I have modified many XTs to have 640K on the mother-board, using a simple technique designed into the system by IBM. A jumper and chip added to the motherboard can alter the memory addressing in the board to enable the system to recognize 640K. The new addressing is set up for 256K chips, installed in two of the four banks. The other two banks of memory contain 64K chips—a total of 640K. Chapter 17 has a set of detailed instructions for modifying an IBM XT in this way.

XT Technical Specifications

Technical information for the XT system, described in this section, provides information about the system architecture, memory configurations and capacities, standard system features, disk storage, expansion slots, keyboard specifications, and also physical and environmental specifications. This information can be useful in determining what parts you need when you are upgrading or repairing these systems. Figure 21.6 shows the layout and components on the XT motherboard.

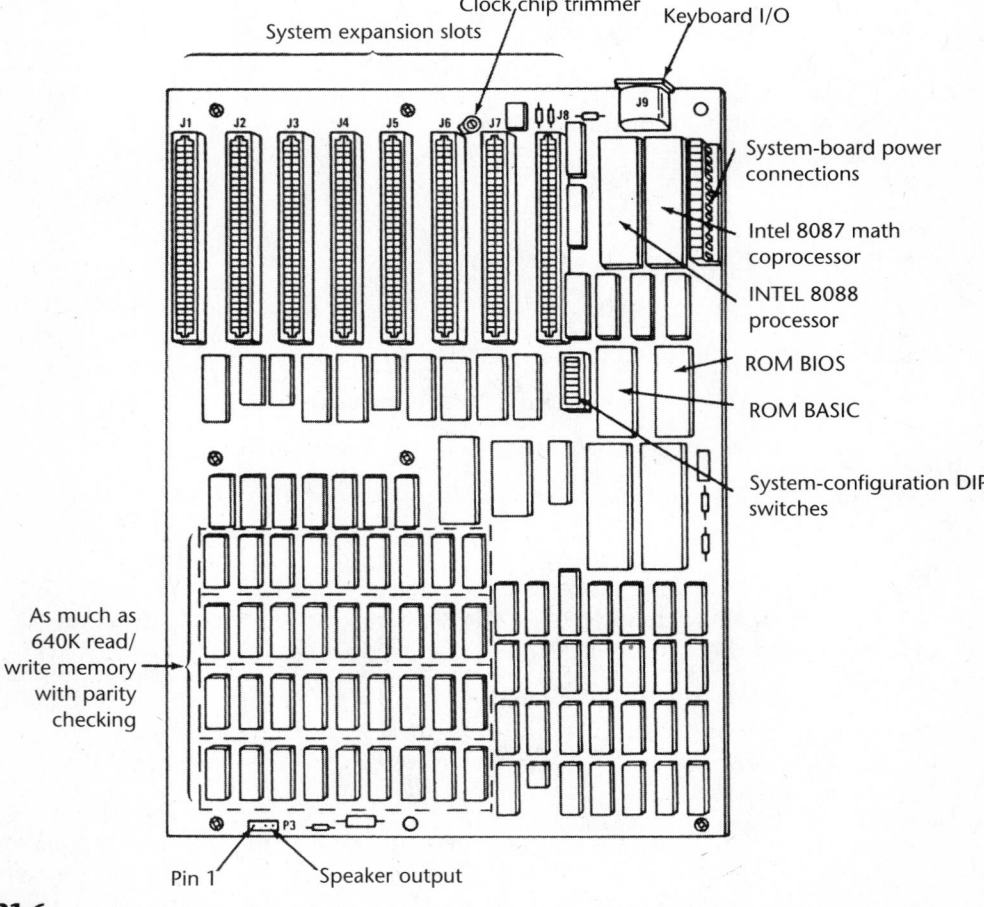

Fig. 21.6
The XT motherboard.

System Architecture

Microprocessor	8088
Clock speed	4.77 MHz
Bus type	ISA (Industry Standard Architecture)
Bus width	8-bit
Interrupt levels	8
Type	Edge-triggered
Shareable	No
DMA channels	3
DMA burst mode supported	No
Bus masters supported	No
Upgradable processor complex	No

Memory

Standard on system board	256K or 640K
Maximum on system board	256K or 640K
Maximum total memory	640K
Memory speed (ns) and type	200ns dynamic RAM
System board memory-socket type	16-pin DIP
Number of memory-module sockets	36 (4 banks of 9)
Memory used on system board	36 64K×1-bit DRAM chips in 4 banks of 9, or 2 banks of 9 256K×1-bit and 2 banks of 9 64K×1-bit chips
Memory cache controller	No
Wait states:	
System board	1
Adapter	1

Standard Features

ROM size	40K or 64K
ROM shadowing	No
Optional math coprocessor	8087
Coprocessor speed	4.77 MHz
Standard graphics	None standard
RS232C serial ports	1 (some models)
UART chip used	NS8250B
Maximum speed (bits per second)	9,600 bps
Maximum number of ports supported	2
Pointing device (mouse) ports	None standard
Parallel printer ports	1 (some models)
Bi-directional	No
Maximum number of ports supported	3
CMOS real-time clock (RTC)	No
CMOS RAM	None

(continues)

Disk Storage

Internal disk and tape drive bays	2 full-height or 4 half-height
Number of 3 1/2- or 5 1/4-inch bays	0/2 or 0/4
Standard floppy drives	1×360K
Optional floppy drives:	
5 1/4-inch 360K	Optional
5 1/4-inch 1.2M	No
3 1/2-inch 720K	Optional
3 1/2-inch 1.44M	No
3 1/2-inch 2.88M	No
Hard disk controller included	ST-506/412 (Xebec Model 1210)
ST-506/412 hard disks available	10/20M
Drive form factor	5 1/4-inch
Drive interface	ST-506/412

Drive capacity	10M	20M
Average access rate (ms)	85	65
Encoding scheme	MFM	MFM
BIOS drive type number	1	2
Cylinders	306	615
Heads	4	4
Sectors per track	17	17
Rotational speed (RPMs)	3600	3600
Interleave factor	6:1	6:1
Data transfer rate (kilobytes/second)	85	85
Automatic head parking	No	No

Expansion Slots

Total adapter slots	8
Number of long/short slots	6/2
Number of 8-/16-/32-bit slots	8/0/0
Available slots (with video)	4

Keyboard Specifications

101-key Enhanced Keyboard	Yes
Fast keyboard speed setting	No
Keyboard cable length	6 feet

Physical Specifications	
Footprint type	Desktop
Dimensions:	
Height	5.5 inches
Width	19.5 inches
Depth	16.0 inches
Weight	32 pounds

Environmental Specifications	
Power-supply output	130 watts
Worldwide (110/60, 220/50)	No
Auto-sensing/switching	No
Maximum current:	
90-137 VAC	4.2 amps
Operating range:	
Temperature	60–90 degrees F
Relative humidity	8–80 percent
Maximum operating altitude	7,000 feet
Heat (BTUs/hour)	717
Noise (Average dB, operating, 1m)	56
FCC classification	Class B

The following table shows the XT motherboard switch settings. The XT motherboard uses a single eight-position switch block to control various functions as detailed in table 21.5.

Table 21.5   IBM PC/XT Motherboard Switch Settings

SWITCH BLOCK 1 (PC and XT)

	Switch 1	IBM PC Function (PC Only):
	Off	Boot From Floppy Drives
	On	Do Not Boot From Floppy Drives
	Switch 1	**IBM XT Function (XT Only):**
	Off	Normal POST (Power-On Self Test)
	On	Continuous Looping POST
	Switch 2	**Math Coprocessor (PC/XT):**
	Off	Installed
	On	Not Installed
Switch 3	**Switch 4**	**Installed Motherboard Memory (PC/XT):**
On	On	Bank 0 only
Off	On	Banks 0 and 1

(continues)

Table 21.5   Continued

SWITCH BLOCK 1 (PC and XT)

On	Off	Banks 0, 1 and 2
Off	Off	All 4 Banks
Switch 5	**Switch 6**	**Video Adapter Type (PC/XT):**
Off	Off	Monochrome (MDA)
Off	On	Color (CGA) - 40x25 mode
On	Off	Color (CGA) - 80x25 mode
On	On	Any Video Card w/onboard BIOS (EGA/VGA)
Switch 7	**Switch 8**	**Number of Floppy Drives (PC/XT):**
On	On	1 floppy drive
Off	On	2 floppy drives
On	Off	3 floppy drives
Off	Off	4 floppy drives

Table 21.6 shows the part numbers of the XT system units.

Table 21.6   IBM XT Model Part Numbers

Description	Number
XT system unit/83-key keyboard, 256K:	
one full-height 360K drive	5160068
one half-height 360K drive	5160267
two full-height 360K drives	5160078
two half-height 360K drives	5160277
XT system unit/101-key keyboard, 256K:	
one half-height 360K drive	5160268
two half-height 360K drives	5160278
XT system unit/83-key keyboard, 256K, one serial, one full-height 360K drive, 10M hard disk	5160086
XT system unit/83-key keyboard, 640K, one serial, one half-height 360K drive, 20M fixed disk	5160088
XT system unit/101-key keyboard, 640K, one serial, one half-height 360K drive, 20M fixed disk	5160089
Option Numbers	
PC expansion-unit Model 002, 20M fixed disk	5161002
20M fixed disk drive	6450326
20M fixed disk adapter	6450327
10M fixed disk drive	1602500
10M fixed disk adapter	1602501
5 1/4-inch, half-height, 360K drive	6450325
5 1/4-inch, full-height, 360K drive	1503810
3 1/2-inch, half-height, 720K internal drive	6450258
3 1/2-inch, half-height, 720K external drive	2683190

Description	Number
Option Numbers	
8087 math coprocessor option	1501002
Asynchronous serial adapter	1502074
Enhanced Keyboard Accessories	
Clear keycaps (60) with paper inserts	6341707
Blank light keycaps	1351710
Blank dark keycaps	1351728
Paper inserts (300)	6341704
Keycap-removal tools (6)	1351717

An Introduction to the 3270 PC

On October 18, 1983, IBM announced a special version of the XT, the 3270 PC. The 3270 PC combines the functions of IBM's 3270 display system with those of the XT. This system was basically a standard XT system unit with three to six custom adapter cards added to the slots. The keyboard and display for this system also are special and attach to some of the special adapter cards. The 3270 PC Control Program runs all this hardware. This combination can support as many as seven concurrent activities: one local PC DOS session, four remote mainframe sessions, and two local electronic notepads. With the help of the 3270 PC Control Program, information can be copied between windows, but a PC DOS window cannot receive information.

The 3270 PC includes a new keyboard that addresses some complaints about the Personal Computer keyboard. The keyboard has more keys and an improved layout. The Enter and Shift keys are enlarged. The cursor keys are separate from the numeric keypad and form a small group between the main alphanumeric keys and the numeric keypad. At the top of the keyboard, 20 function keys are arranged in two rows of ten. To help clarify keystroke operations, the new keyboard is annotated. Blue legends designate PC-specific functions; black legends indicate 3270 functions. The keyboard is greatly improved, but most keys and features don't work in PC mode. Often, you must obtain special versions of programs or disregard most of the keys.

3270 PC Models and Features

The 3270 PC includes several specialized expansion boards that can be added to an XT. This section examines those expansion boards.

The 3270 System Adapter

The 3270 system adapter supports communication between the 3270 PC and the remote 3274 controller through a coaxial cable. One physical 3274 connection can support four logical connections.

The Display Adapter

A display adapter is used in place of the PC's monochrome or Color/Graphics Display Adapter and provides text-only displays in eight colors. The PC's extended-character graphics are available, but bit-mapped graphics capabilities are not supported unless you add the accessory extended graphics card.

The Extended Graphics Adapter

The Extended Graphics Adapter provides storage and controls necessary for displaying local graphics in high- or medium-resolution mode. High-resolution mode is available in two colors at 720-by-350 or 640-by-200 pixels. Note that this isn't the same as the newer XGA (eXtended Graphics Array), which is either available for, or included with, certain PS/2 systems.

Medium-resolution mode is available with a choice of two sets of four colors at 360-by-350 or 320-by-200 pixels. To run in medium-resolution mode, your system must have an available system-expansion slot adjacent to the display adapter card. If you install a Programmed Symbols feature (discussed in the following section) next to the display adapter, you must use the slot adjacent to the PS feature. Because the aspect ratio differs for each display monitor, applications programs must control the aspect ratio parameter; a circle on the 5150/5160 PC with the Color Graphics Adapter looks slightly elliptical on the 3270 PC with the XGA unless you change this parameter.

Programmed Symbols

The Programmed Symbols (PS) adapter provides graphics capabilities available on IBM 3278/3279 display stations. This card provides storage for as many as six 190-symbol sets whose shapes and codes are definable. Symbol sets are loaded (and accessed for display) under program control. To accept this board, your system must have an available system-expansion slot adjacent to the display adapter card. If an XGA feature is installed, you must use the slot adjacent to the XGA. The PS card is available in distributed-function terminal (DFT) mode only and can be used in only one of the four host sessions.

The Keyboard Adapter

You use the keyboard adapter to adapt the 3270-style keyboard to the system unit. The keyboard connects to this board rather than to the motherboard, as it does for the PC. The board is short and must be installed in the special eighth slot in the XT system unit.

The standard XT system unit provides eight expansion slots; at least five of the slots normally were filled upon delivery with the 3270 system adapter, the display adapter, the keyboard adapter, the disk drive adapter, and the hard disk controller. If you add options such as the graphics adapter and a memory multifunction card, you can see that even with the XT as a base, slots are at a premium in this system.

Software

The 3270 PC runs under control of the 3270 PC Control Program in conjunction with PC DOS and supports concurrent operation of as many as four remote-host interactive sessions, two local notepad sessions, and one PC DOS session. The Control Program enables users to associate sessions with display screen windows and to manage the windows by a set of functions that IBM named *advanced screen management*.

Windows

You can define windows that permit viewing of all (as many as 2,000 characters) or part of a presentation space. In IBM's vocabulary, a *presentation space* is a logical display area presented by a single host. PC DOS presentation spaces are 2,000 characters (25 lines by 80 characters); remote host spaces are as many as 3,440 characters; and notepad presentation spaces are 1,920 characters.

As many as seven windows can appear on-screen at one time. Every window is associated with a distinct presentation space. Windows can be as large as the screen or as small as one character and can be positioned at any point within their presentation space. A window 20 characters wide and four lines long, for example, shows the first 20 characters of the last four lines of a host session display. You can change window size and position in the presentation space at any time without affecting the content of the presentation space.

At any time, only one window on the 3270 PC screen can be the active window. When you enter information from the keyboard, the information is directed to the session associated with the active window. You can switch between active windows by using keystroke commands.

You can define the foreground and background colors of host session windows not using extended data-stream attributes. You can define the background color for the 5272 screen also (the color to be displayed in areas not occupied by windows).

Special Facilities

In addition to advanced screen-management functions, the Control Program offers a number of related special facilities that help you take further advantage of the 3270 environment.

Data can be copied within or between any presentation spaces except into the PC DOS screen. You copy by marking a block of data in one window and a destination in some other window, much the same as a block copy in a word processor.

Think of the notepads as local electronic scratch pads that you can use at your convenience. You can save and restore the contents of a notepad at any time by using PC DOS files as the storage medium.

You can define as many as ten screen configurations, each of which describes a set of windows configured in any way, and they can display on command any one configuration. Use PC DOS files to store the configuration information.

You can print a full copy of the display screen on a local printer. Similarly, you can print a full copy of a PC DOS presentation space on a local printer. You also can print a full copy of any host presentation space on a local printer, a 3274 attached printer, or a 43xx display/printer.

The Control Program maintains a status line at the bottom of the screen that displays current configuration information, including the name of the active window. The program includes a help function and displays active workstation functions and sessions and an on-line tutorial that explains and simulates system functions. The tutorial is a standard PC DOS program that can be run on any IBM PC.

The Control Program, assisted by a host-based IBM 3270 PC file-transfer program, can initiate transfers of ASCII, binary, and EBCDIC files to and from remote hosts.

A drawback to this software is that it is memory resident and consumes an enormous amount of space. The result is that in the PC DOS session, not many applications can run in the leftover workspace. Your only option—reboot the computer without loading the Control Program—is a clumsy and time-consuming procedure. Even with this tactic, the drastic differences in the display hardware and the keyboard still render this computer much less than "PC compatible." The AT version of this system offers a solution to the memory problem by enabling much of the Control Program to reside in the AT's extended memory, above the 1M memory limit of the PC and XT.

The Significance of the 3270

The 3270 PC is a great system to use if you are a corporate worker who deals every day with many information sources (most of which are available through an IBM mainframe SNA network). Corporate information managers greatly appreciate the concurrent access to several SNA-based databases. The 3270 PC provides essential tools for viewing, extracting, combining, and manipulating information: multiple concurrent-terminal sessions, cut-and-paste capability between sessions, PC productivity tools, and up- and downloading host files from PC DOS files.

For simple 3270 terminal-emulation capability, however, this system is more than you need. In addition, the display and keyboard make this system partially incompatible with the rest of the PC world. Many PC applications do not run properly on this system. If you depend more on PC DOS applications than on the mainframe, or if you consider the multiple mainframe sessions unimportant, using one of the simpler 3270 emulation adapters is more cost-effective.

An Introduction to the XT 370

On October 18, 1983, IBM introduced another special version of the XT, the XT 370, consisting of a standard PC XT chassis with three special cards added. These adapters are special S/370-emulation cards that enable the computer to execute the mainframe system 370 instruction set. The boards enable you to run VM/CMS and emulate 4M of virtual memory. You can download programs and compilers from the mainframe and execute them directly on the XT. You switch between 370 mode and the standard XT | by using a *hot key*, or special keystroke, sequence.

XT/370 Models and Features

The three cards that make up the XT 370—the PC 370-P card, the PC 370-M card, and the PC 3277-EM card—are examined in this section.

The P card implements an emulation of the 370 instruction set. The card has three microprocessors. One processor is a heavily modified Motorola 68000 produced under license to IBM. This chip implements the general-purpose registers, the PSW, instruction fetch and decode logic, and 72 commonly used S/370 instructions. Because Motorola manufactures the chip under license to IBM, the chip probably will not appear as a Motorola product.

A second processor is a slightly modified Motorola 68000, which is listed in Motorola's catalog. The chip emulates the remaining nonfloating-point instructions, manipulates the page table, handles exception conditions, and performs hardware housekeeping.

The third microprocessor, a modified Intel 8087 that executes S/370 floating-point instructions, is interfaced as a peripheral rather than the normal 8087 coprocessor linkage.

The M card has 512K of parity-checked RAM. You can access this memory from the P card or from the XT's native 8088 processor. Concurrent requests are arbitrated in favor of the 8088. The M card resides in an XT expansion slot but is connected to the P card by a special edge connector. Sixteen-bit-wide transfers between M card memory and the P card are carried out through this connector (normal XT memory transfers operate in 8-bit-wide chunks).

Operating in native PC mode, the M card's memory is addressed as contiguous memory beginning at the end of the 256K memory of the system's motherboard. In native PC mode, the XT 370 has 640K of usable RAM; some of the M card's memory is not used.

Operating in 370 mode, only the 512K RAM of the M card is usable. (The memory on the motherboard is not available.) The first 480K of this memory implements 480K of real S/370 space. The remaining 32K on the M card functions as a microcode control-storage area for the second P card microprocessor.

The first 64K (of 480K) of S/370 memory are consumed by VM/PC; 416K of real memory remains for user programs. User programs larger than 416K are handled through paging.

The PC 3277-EM card attaches the XT 370 to an S/370 mainframe by a local or remote 3274 control unit (connection through coaxial cable). When VM/PC is running, the EM card uses the IBM monochrome or color display. Under VM/PC, the EM card is used also to up- and download data between a host VM system and the XT 370.

The XT 370 can run in native PC XT mode or in S/370 mode under the VM/PC Control Program. Under VM/PC, the user can use a "hot key" to alternate between a local CMS session and a remote 3277 session (or, optionally, a 3101-emulation session). VM/PC does not offer a true VM-like environment. Rather, VM/PC provides an environment in which CMS applications can run. Non-CMS VM applications do not run on the XT 370.

The VM/PC system, which must be licensed, is provided on six floppy disks and includes the VM/PC Control Program, CMS, XEDIT, EXEC2, local and remote file-transfer utilities, and the 370 Processor Control package.

Estimations of the XT 370 CPU's performance indicate that it is about half of a 4331 when the XT 370 is running a commercial instruction mix. When the XT 370 is running scientific codes, you can expect twice the performance as from the 4331. The CPU generally is categorized as a 0.1 MIPS (million instructions per second) processor. This size does not sound impressive when you're used to multi-MIPS, single-chip microprocessors, but remember that 0.1-million S/370 instructions likely will produce substantially more computing than 0.1-million instructions of your standard microprocessor chip.

The XT 370 running in S/370 mode can access the 512K on the M card. Of this 512K, 32K is reserved for microcode control storage, and 65K is used by the VM/PC Control Program; 416K remains for user programs. If a user program requires more memory than 416K, VM/PC uses a paging area on the XT 370's hard disk and swaps pieces of the program in and out of memory according to use.

Swapping on the small 10M or 20M hard disks is considerably slower than on the large disks used with mainframes. Programs larger than 416K, therefore, probably will run very slowly. Field test users report long delays in loading large programs into memory, even when the programs are well under the maximum for nonpaging operation. Delays are due to the relatively slow operation of the XT 370 hard disks. Because of size and speed problems, many users of these systems should consider larger and faster hard disks.

An Introduction to the Portable PC

IBM introduced the Portable PC on February 16, 1984. The IBM Portable PC, a "transportable" personal computer, has a built-in, nine-inch, amber composite video monitor; one 5 1/4-inch, half-height floppy disk drive (with space for an optional second drive); an 83-key keyboard; two adapter cards; a floppy disk controller; and a Color Graphics Adapter (CGA). The unit also has a universal-voltage power supply capable of overseas operation on 220-volt power. Figure 21.7 shows the Portable PC exterior.

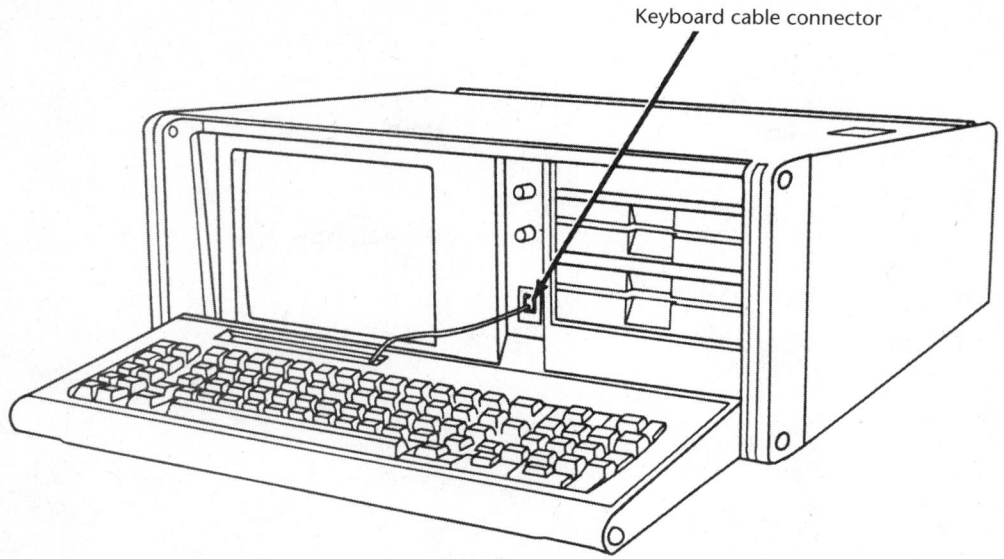

Keyboard cable connector

Fig. 21.7
The IBM Portable PC.

The system board used in the IBM Portable PC is the same board used in the original IBM XT, with 256K of memory. Because the XT motherboard is used, eight expansion slots are available for the connection of adapter boards, although only two slots can accept a full-length adapter card due to internal space restrictions. The power supply is basically the same as an XT's, with physical changes for portability and a small amount of power drawn to run the built-in monitor. In function and performance, the Portable PC system unit has identical characteristics to an equivalently configured IBM PC XT system unit. Figure 21.8 shows the Portable PC interior view.

IBM withdrew the Portable PC from the market on April 2, 1986, a date that coincides with the introduction of the IBM Convertible laptop PC. The Portable PC is rare because not many were sold. The system was largely misunderstood by the trade press and user community. Most did not understand that the system was really a portable XT and had more to offer than the standard IBM PC did. Maybe if IBM had called the system the Portable XT, it would have sold better.

The Portable PC system unit has these major functional components:

- Intel 8088 4.77 MHz microprocessor

- ROM-based diagnostics (POST)

- BASIC language interpreter in ROM

- 256K of dynamic RAM

- Eight expansion slots (two long slots, one 3/4-length slot, and five short slots)

- Socket for 8087 math coprocessor

- Color/Graphics Monitor Adapter

- 9-inch, amber, composite video monitor

- Floppy disk interface

- One or two half-height 360K floppy drives

- 114-watt universal power supply (115 V to 230 V, 50 Hz to 60 Hz)

- Lightweight 83-key keyboard

- Enclosure with carrying handle

- Carrying bag for the system unit

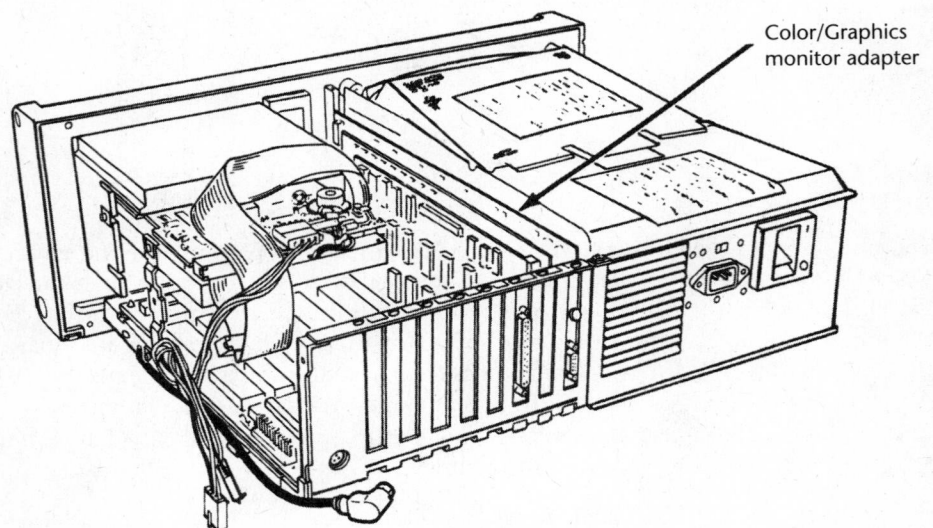

Color/Graphics
monitor adapter

Fig. 21.8
The IBM Portable PC interior.

Portable PC Technical Specifications

The technical data for the Portable PC system is described in this section, which includes information about the system architecture, memory configurations and capacities, standard system features, disk storage, expansion slots, keyboard specifications, and also physical and environmental specifications. This information can be useful in determining what kinds of parts you need when you are upgrading or repairing these systems. Figure 21.6 previously showed the XT motherboard, also used in the Portable PC.

System Architecture

Microprocessor	8088
Clock speed	4.77 MHz
Bus type	ISA (Industry Standard Architecture)
Bus width	8-bit
Interrupt levels	8
Type	Edge-triggered
Shareable	No
DMA channels	3
DMA burst mode supported	No
Bus masters supported	No
Upgradeable processor complex	No

Memory

Standard on system board	256K
Maximum on system board	256K
Maximum total memory	640K
Memory speed (ns) and type	200ns dynamic RAM
System board memory-socket type	16-pin DIP
Number of memory-module sockets	36 (4 banks of 9)
Memory used on system board	36 64K×1-bit DRAM chips in 4 banks of 9 chips
Memory cache controller	No
Wait states:	
System board	1
Adapter	1

Standard Features

ROM size	40K
ROM shadowing	No
Optional math coprocessor	8087
Coprocessor speed	4.77 MHz
Standard graphics	CGA adapter with built-in 9" amber CRT
RS232C serial ports	None standard
UART chip used	NS8250B
Maximum speed (bits per second)	9,600 bps
Maximum number of ports supported	2
Pointing device (mouse) ports	None standard
Parallel printer ports	None standard
Bi-directional	No
Maximum number of ports supported	3
CMOS real-time clock (RTC)	No
CMOS RAM	None

(continues)

Disk Storage

Internal disk and tape drive bays	2 half-height
Number of 3 1/2-/5 1/4-inch bays	0/2
Standard floppy drives	1 or 2×360K
Optional floppy drives:	
5 1/4-inch 360K	Optional
5 1/4-inch 1.2M	No
3 1/2-inch 720K	Optional
3 1/2-inch 1.44M	No
3 1/2-inch 2.88M	No
Hard disk controller included	None

Expansion Slots

Total adapter slots	8
Number of long/short slots	2/6
Number of 8-/16-/32-bit slots	8/0/0
Available slots (with video)	6

Keyboard Specifications

101-key Enhanced Keyboard	No
Fast keyboard speed setting	No
Keyboard cable length	6 feet

Physical Specifications

Footprint type	Desktop
Dimensions:	
Height	8.0 inches
Width	20.0 inches
Depth	17.0 inches
Weight	31 pounds

Environmental Specifications

Power-supply output	114 watts
Worldwide (110/60, 220/50)	Yes
Auto-sensing/switching	No
Maximum current:	
90-137 VAC	4.0 amps
Operating range:	
Temperature	60–90 degrees F
Relative humidity	8–80 percent
Maximum operating altitude	7,000 feet
Heat (BTUs/hour)	650
Noise (Average dB, operating, 1m)	42
FCC classification	Class B

Table 21.7 shows the part numbers for the Portable PC:

Table 21.7 IBM Portable PC Model Part Numbers	
Description	Number
256K, one 360K half-height drive	5155068
256K, two 360K half-height drives	5155076
Half-height 360K floppy disk drive	6450300

The disk drive used in the Portable PC was a half-height drive, the same unit specified for use in the PC*jr*. When the Portable PC was introduced, PC*jr* was the only one IBM sold with the half-height drive.

An Introduction to the AT

IBM introduced the Personal Computer AT (Advanced Technology) on August 14, 1984. The IBM AT system included many features previously unavailable in IBM's PC systems such as increased performance, an advanced 16-bit microprocessor, high-density floppy disk and hard disk drives, larger memory space, and an advanced coprocessor. Despite its new design, the IBM AT incredibly retained compatibility with most existing hardware and software products for the earlier systems.

In most cases, IBM AT system performance was from three to five times faster than the IBM XT for single applications running DOS on both computers. The performance increase was due to the combination of a reduced cycle count for most instructions by the 80286 processor, an increased system clock rate, 16-bit memory, and faster hard disk and controller.

The AT system unit has been available in several models: a floppy-disk-equipped base model (068) and several hard-disk-enhanced models. Based on a high-performance, 16-bit, Intel 80286 microprocessor, each computer includes Cassette BASIC language in ROM and a CMOS (Complementary Metal Oxide Semiconductor) clock and calendar with battery backup. All models are equipped with a high-density (1.2M) floppy disk drive, a keyboard, and a lock. For standard memory, the base model offers 256K, and the enhanced models offer 512K. In addition, the enhanced models have a 20M or a 30M hard disk drive and a serial/parallel adapter. Each system can be expanded through customer-installable options. You can add memory (to 512K) for the base model by adding chips to the system board. You can expand all models to 16M by installing memory cards.

Besides the standard drives included with the system, IBM only offered two different hard disks as upgrades for the AT: a 30M hard disk drive and a 20M hard disk drive. IBM also offered only three different types of floppy drives for the AT; a second, high-density (1.2M) floppy disk drive; a double-density (320/360K) floppy disk drive; and a new 3 1/2-inch 720K drive. The original 068 and 099 models of the AT did not support the 720K drive in the BIOS; you had to add a special driver (DRIVER.SYS—supplied with DOS) for the drive to work. The later model ATs also supported a 1.44M high-density 3 1/2-inch floppy drive, however IBM never sold or supported such a drive.

You can install as many as two floppy disk drives and one hard disk drive or one floppy disk drive and two hard disk drives in the system unit. To use the high-density 5 1/4-inch floppy disk drives properly, you must have special floppy disks—5 1/4-inch, high-coercivity, double-sided, soft-sectored disks. Due to track width problems between the high-density (1.2M) drives and the double-density (360K) drives, a double-density floppy disk drive (320/360K) was available for compatibility with the standard PC or XT systems. You can exchange disks reliably between the 1.2M and the standard 360K drives if you use the proper method and understand the recording process. For transferring data between a system with a 1.2M drive to a system with a 360K drive you must start with a blank, (never previously formatted), 360K disk, which must be formatted and written only by the 1.2M drive. There are no special precautions to transfer the data the other way. This information is covered in Chapter 13. For complete interchange reliability, however, IBM recommended you purchase the 360K drive.

The system unit has eight slots that support cards for additional devices, features, or memory. Six slots support the advanced 16-bit or 8-bit option cards. Two slots support only 8-bit option cards. All system-unit models, however, use one 16-bit slot for the fixed disk and floppy disk drive adapter. The enhanced models use an additional 8-bit slot for the serial/parallel adapter. The result is seven available expansion slots for the base model and six available expansion slots for enhanced models. Figure 21.9 shows the interior of an AT system unit.

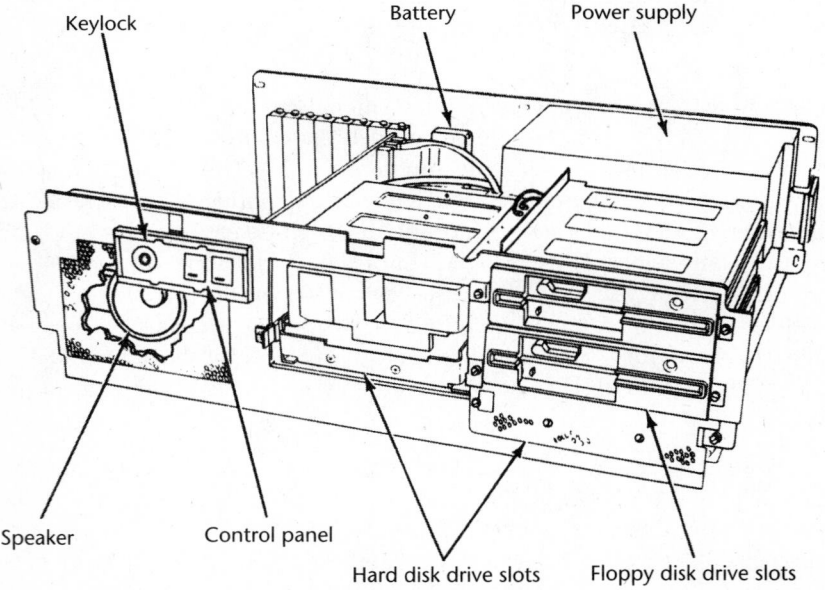

Fig. 21.9
The IBM AT unit interior.

All models include a universal power supply; a temperature-controlled, variable-speed cooling fan; and a security lock with key. The user selects the power supply for a country's voltage range. The cooling fan significantly reduces the noise in most environments; the fan runs slower when the system unit is cool and faster when the system unit is hot. When the system is locked, no one can remove the system-unit cover, boot the system, or enter commands or data from the keyboard, thereby enhancing the system's security.

The keyboard is attached to the system unit by a nine-foot, coiled cable that enables the AT to adapt to a variety of workspace configurations. The keyboard includes key-location enhancements and mode indicators for improved keyboard usability. Figure 21.10 shows the rear panel of an AT.

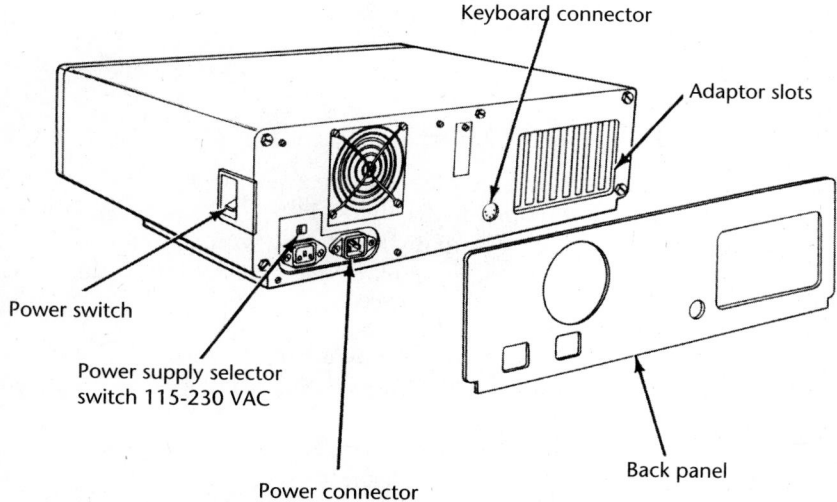

Fig. 21.10
The IBM AT rear panel.

Every system unit for the AT models has these major functional components:

- Intel 80286 (6 MHz or 8 MHz) microprocessor
- Socket for 80287 math coprocessor
- 8086-compatible real address mode
- Protected virtual address mode
- Eight I/O expansion slots (six 16-bit, two 8-bit)
- 256K of dynamic RAM (base model)
- 512K of dynamic RAM (enhanced models)
- ROM-based diagnostics (POST)

- BASIC language interpreter in ROM

- Hard/floppy disk controller

- 1.2M HD floppy drive

- 20M or 30M hard disk drive (enhanced models)

- Serial/parallel interface (enhanced models)

- CMOS clock-calendar and configuration with battery backup

- Keylock

- 84-key keyboard

- Enhanced, 101-key keyboard (standard on newer models)

- Switchable worldwide power supply

AT Models and Features

Since the introduction of the AT, several models became available. First, IBM announced two systems: a base model (068) and an enhanced model (099). The primary difference between the two systems is the standard hard disk that came with the enhanced model. IBM introduced two other AT systems since the first systems, each offering different features.

The first generation of AT systems have a 6 MHz system clock that dictates the processor cycle time. The *cycle time*, the system's smallest interval of time, represents the speed at which operations occur. Every operation in a computer takes at least one or (usually) several cycles to complete. Therefore, if two computers are the same in every way except for the clock speed, the system with the faster clock rate executes the same operations in a shorter time proportional to the difference in clock speed. Cycle time and clock speed are two different ways of describing the same thing. Discussions of clock speed are significant when you consider buying the AT because not all models have the same clock speed.

All models of the AT included a combination hard/floppy disk controller that was really two separate controllers on the same circuit board. The board was designed by IBM and Western Digital, and manufactured for IBM by Western Digital. This controller had no on-board ROM BIOS like the Xebec hard disk controller used in the XT. In the AT, IBM built full support for the hard disk controller directly into the motherboard ROM BIOS. To support different types of hard disks, IBM encoded a table into the motherboard ROM that listed the parameters of various drives that could be installed. In the first version of the AT, with a ROM BIOS dated 01/10/84, only the first 14 types in the table were filled in. Type 15 itself was reserved for internal reasons, and was not usable. Other table entries from 16 through 47 were left unused and were actually filled with zeros. Later versions of the AT added new drive types to the tables, starting from type 16 and up.

The first two AT models were the 068 (base) model, which had 256K on the motherboard and a single 1.2M floppy disk drive; and the model 099 (enhanced), which had a 20M hard disk drive, a serial/parallel adapter, and 512K on the motherboard. IBM designated the motherboard on these computers as Type 1, which is larger than the later Type 2 board and used an unusual memory layout. The memory is configured as four banks of 128K chips—a total of 512K on the board. This configuration sounds reasonable until you realize that a 128K chip does not really exist in the physical form factor that IBM used. IBM actually created this type of memory device by stacking a 64K chip on top of another one and soldering the two together. My guess is that IBM had many 64K chips to use, and the AT was available to take them.

On October 2, 1985, IBM announced a new model of the AT, the Personal Computer AT Model 239. The system has all the standard features of the AT Model 099, but also has a 30M hard disk rather than a 20M hard disk. A second, optional 30M hard disk drive expands the Model 239's hard disk storage to 60M. This unit's motherboard, a second-generation design IBM calls Type 2, is about 25 percent smaller than the Type 1 but uses the same mounting locations, for physical compatibility. All important items, such as the slots and connectors, remain in the same locations. Other major improvements in this board are in the memory. The 128K memory chips have been replaced by 256K devices. Now only two banks of chips were needed to get the same 512K on the board.

The AT Model 239 includes these items:

- 512K of RAM (standard)
- 6 MHz Type 2 motherboard with 256K memory chips
- Serial/parallel adapter (standard)
- 30M hard disk (standard)
- New ROM BIOS (dated 06/10/85)

> ROM supports 3 1/2-inch 720K floppy drives without using external driver programs
>
> ROM supports 22 hard disk types (up to type 23), including the supplied 30M disk
>
> POST fixes clock rate to 6 MHz

The Type 2 motherboard's design is much improved over Type 1's; the Type 2 motherboard improved internal-circuit timing and layout. Improvements in the motherboard indicated that the system would be pushed to higher speeds—exactly what happened with the next round of introductions.

In addition to obvious physical differences, the Model 239 includes significantly different ROM software from the previous models. The new ROM supports more types of hard and floppy disks, and its new POST prevents alteration of the clock rate from the standard 6 MHz models. Because support for the 30M hard disk is built into the new ROM, IBM sells also a 30M hard disk upgrade kit that includes the new ROM for the original AT systems. Unfortunately, this $1,795 kit represents the only legal way to obtain the newer ROM.

The 30M hard disk drive upgrade kit for the Personal Computer AT Models 068 and 099 includes all the features in the 30M hard disk drive announced for the AT Model 239. The upgrade kit also has a new basic input-output subsystem (BIOS), essential to AT operation. The new ROM BIOS supports 22 drive types (compared to the original 14 in earlier ATs), including the new 30M drive. To support the 30M hard disk drive, a new diagnostics floppy disk and an updated guide-to-operations manual were shipped with this kit.

The 30M update kit included these items:

- 30M hard disk drive
- Two new ROM BIOS modules
- Channel keeper bar (a bracket for the fixed disk)
- Data cable for the hard disk
- Diagnostics and Setup disk
- An insert to the AT guide-to-operations manual

Some people were upset initially that IBM had "fixed the microprocessor clock" to 6 MHz in the new model, thereby disallowing any possible "hot rod" modifications. Many people realized that the clock crystal on all the AT models was socketed so that the crystal could be replaced easily by a faster one. More important, because the AT circuit design is modular, changing the clock crystal does not have repercussions throughout the rest of the system, as is the case in the PC and PC XT. For the price of a new crystal (from $1 to $30) and the time needed to plug it in, someone easily could increase an AT's speed by 30 percent, and sometimes more. Because IBM now retrofits the ROM into earlier models or the 30M hard disk upgrade, you no longer can implement a simple speedup alteration without also changing the ROM BIOS as well.

Many people believed that this change was made to prevent the AT from being "too fast" and therefore competing with IBM's minicomputers. In reality, the earlier motherboard was run intentionally at 6 MHz because IBM did not believe that the ROM BIOS software and critical system timing was fully operational at a higher speed. Also, IBM used some components that were rated only for 6 MHz operation, starting of course with the CPU. Users who increased the speed of their early computers often received DOS error messages from timing problems, and in some cases, total system lockups due to components not functioning properly at the higher speeds. Many companies selling speedup kits sold software to help smooth over some of these problems, but IBM's official solution was to improve the ROM BIOS software and motherboard circuitry and to introduce a complete new system running at the faster speed. If you want increased speed no matter what model you have, several companies used to sell clock-crystal replacements that were frequency synthesizers rather than a fixed type of crystal. The units can wait until the POST is finished and change midstream to an increased operating speed. Unfortunately, I know of nobody still making or selling these upgrades. If you are really interested in speeding up your AT in this manner, Chapter 17, "System Upgrades and Improvements," discusses a technique for patching the existing ROM to ignore the speed test so that a faster crystal will still pass the POST procedure.

On April 2, 1986, IBM introduced the Personal Computer AT Models 319 and 339. These two similar systems were an enhancement of the earlier Model 239. The primary difference from the Model 239 is a faster clock crystal that provides 8 MHz operation. The Model 339 has a new keyboard, the Enhanced Keyboard, with 101 keys rather than the usual 84. Model 319 is the same as Model 339, but includes the original keyboard.

Highlights of the Models 319 and 339 are shown in this list:

- Faster processor speed (8 MHz)
- Type 2 motherboard, with 256K chips
- 512K of RAM (standard)
- Serial/parallel adapter (standard)
- 30M hard disk (standard)
- New ROM BIOS (dated 11/15/85)

    ROM support for 22 types (up to type 23) of hard disks

    ROM support for 3 1/2-inch drives, at both 720K and 1.44M capacities

    POST fixes clock rate to 8 MHz

- 101-key Enhanced Keyboard (standard on Model 339)

    Recappable keys

    Selectric typing section

    Dedicated numeric pad

    Dedicated cursor and screen controls

    12 function keys

    Indicator lights

    Nine-foot cable

The most significant physical difference in these new systems is the Enhanced Keyboard on the Model 339. The keyboard, similar to a 3270 keyboard, has 101 keys. It could be called the IBM "corporate" keyboard because it is standard on all new desktop systems. The 84-key PC keyboard still was available, with a new 8 MHz model, as the Model 319.

These new 8 MHz systems were available only in an enhanced configuration with a standard 30M hard drive. If you wanted a hard disk larger than IBM's 30M, you could either add a second drive or simply replace the 30M unit with something larger.

ROM support for 3 1/2-inch disk drives at both 720K and 1.44M exists only in Models 339 and 319. In particular the 1.44M drive, although definitely supported by the ROM

BIOS and controller, was not ever offered as an option by IBM. This means that the IBM Setup program found on the Diagnostics and Setup disk did not offer the 1.44M floppy drive as a choice when configuring the system! Anybody adding such a drive had to use one of the many Setup replacement programs available in the public domain, or "borrow" one from an IBM-compatible system that used a floppy disk-based setup program. Adding the 1.44M drive became one of the most popular upgrades for the AT systems because many newer systems came with that type of drive as standard equipment. Earlier AT systems still can use the 720K and 1.44M drives, but they need to either upgrade the ROM to support it (recommended) or possibly use software drivers to make them work.

AT Technical Specifications

Technical information for the AT system is described in this section. You will find information about the system architecture, memory configurations and capacities, standard system features, disk storage, expansion slots, keyboard specifications, as well as physical and environmental specifications. This type of information can be useful in determining what types of parts are needed when you are upgrading or repairing these systems. Figures 21.11 and 21.12 show the layout and components on the two different AT motherboards.

System Architecture	
Microprocessor	80286
Clock speed	6 or 8 MHz
Bus type	ISA (Industry Standard Architecture)
Bus width	16-bit
Interrupt levels	16
Type	Edge-triggered
Shareable	No
DMA channels	7
DMA burst mode supported	No
Bus masters supported	No
Upgradeable processor complex	No

Memory	
Standard on system board	512K
Maximum on system board	512K
Maximum total memory	16M
Memory speed (ns) and type	150ns dynamic RAM
System board memory-socket type	16-pin DIP
Number of memory-module sockets	18 or 36 (2 or 4 banks of 18)
Memory used on system board	36 128K×1-bit DRAM chips in 2 banks of 18, or 18 256K×1-bit chips in one bank
Memory cache controller	No
Wait states:	
System board	1
Adapter	1

Standard Features

ROM size	64K
ROM shadowing	No
Optional math coprocessor	80287
Coprocessor speed	4 or 5.33 MHz
Standard graphics	None standard
RS232C serial ports	1 (some models)
UART chip used	NS16450
Maximum speed (bits per second)	9,600 bps
Maximum number of ports supported	2
Pointing device (mouse) ports	None standard
Parallel printer ports	1 (some models)
Bi-directional	Yes
Maximum number of ports supported	3
CMOS real-time clock (RTC)	Yes
CMOS RAM	64 bytes
Battery life	5 years

Disk Storage

Internal disk and tape drive bays	1 full-height and 2 half-height	
Number of 3 1/2-/5 1/4-inch bays	0/3	
Standard floppy drives	1×1.2M	
Optional floppy drives:		
5 1/4-inch 360K	Optional	
5 1/4-inch 1.2M	Standard	
3 1/2-inch 720K	Optional	
3 1/2-inch 1.44M	Optional (8 MHz models)	
3 1/2-inch 2.88M	No	
Hard disk controller included:	ST-506/412 (Western Digital WD1002-WA2 or WD1003-WA2)	
ST-506/412 hard disks available	20/30M	
Drive form factor	5 1/4-inch	
Drive interface	ST-506/412	
Drive capacity	20M	30M
Average access rate (ms)	40	40
Encoding scheme	MFM	MFM
BIOS drive type number	2	20
Cylinders	615	733
Heads	4	5
Sectors per track	17	17
Rotational speed (RPMs)	3600	3600
Interleave factor	3:1	3:1
Data transfer rate (kilobytes/second)	170	170
Automatic head parking	Yes	Yes

(continues)

Expansion Slots

Total adapter slots	8
Number of long and short slots	8/0
Number of 8-/16-/32-bit slots	2/6/0
Available slots (with video)	5

Keyboard Specifications

101-key Enhanced Keyboard	Yes (8 MHz models)
Fast keyboard speed setting	Yes
Keyboard cable length	6 feet

Physical Specifications

Footprint type	Desktop
Dimensions:	
Height	6.4 inches
Width	21.3 inches
Depth	17.3 inches
Weight	43 pounds

Environmental Specifications

Power-supply output	192 watts
Worldwide (110/60, 220/50)	Yes
Auto-sensing/switching	No
Maximum current:	
90-137 VAC	5.0 amps
Operating range:	
Temperature	60–90 degrees F
Relative humidity	8–80 percent
Maximum operating altitude	7,000 feet
Heat (BTUs/hour)	1229
Noise (Average dB, operating, 1m)	42
FCC classification	Class B

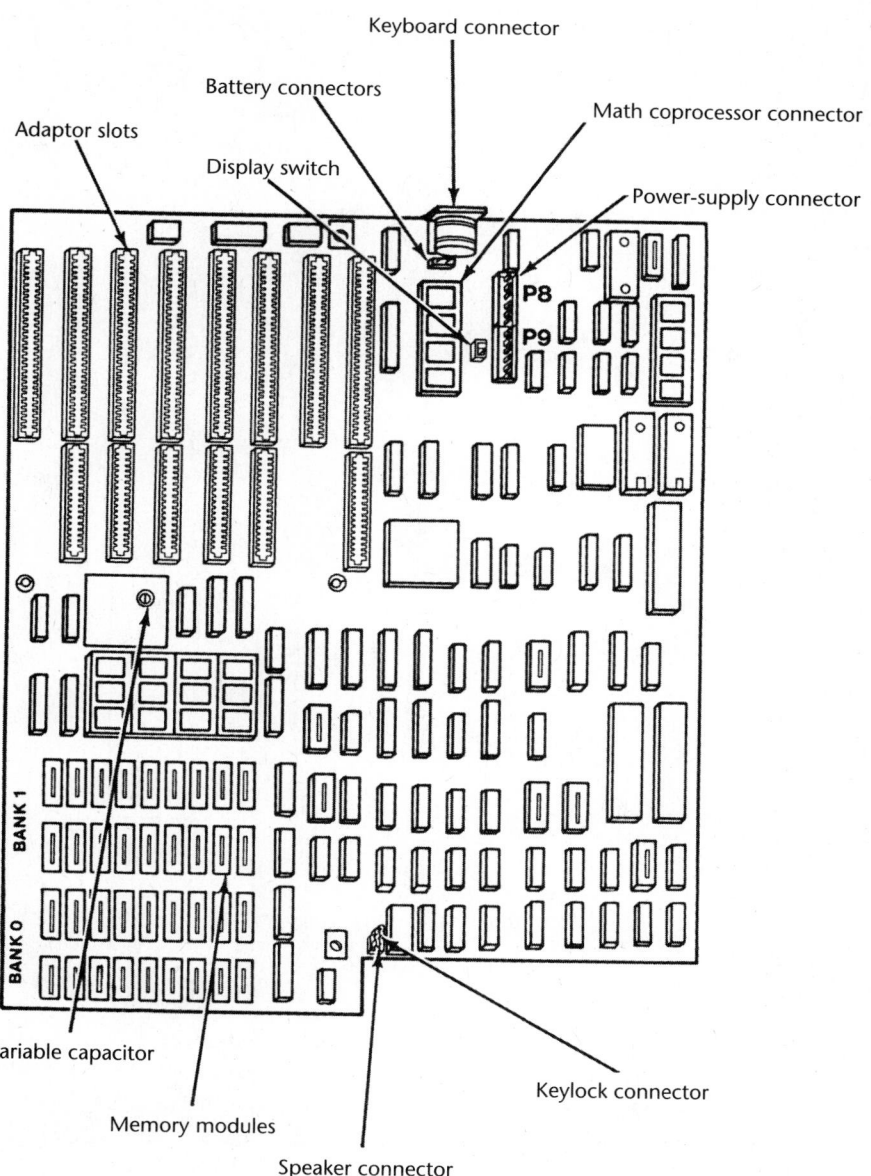

Keyboard connector

Battery connectors

Math coprocessor connector

Adaptor slots

Display switch

Power-supply connector

P8

P9

BANK 1

BANK 0

Variable capacitor

Memory modules

Speaker connector

Keylock connector

Fig. 21.11

The IBM AT Type 1 motherboard.

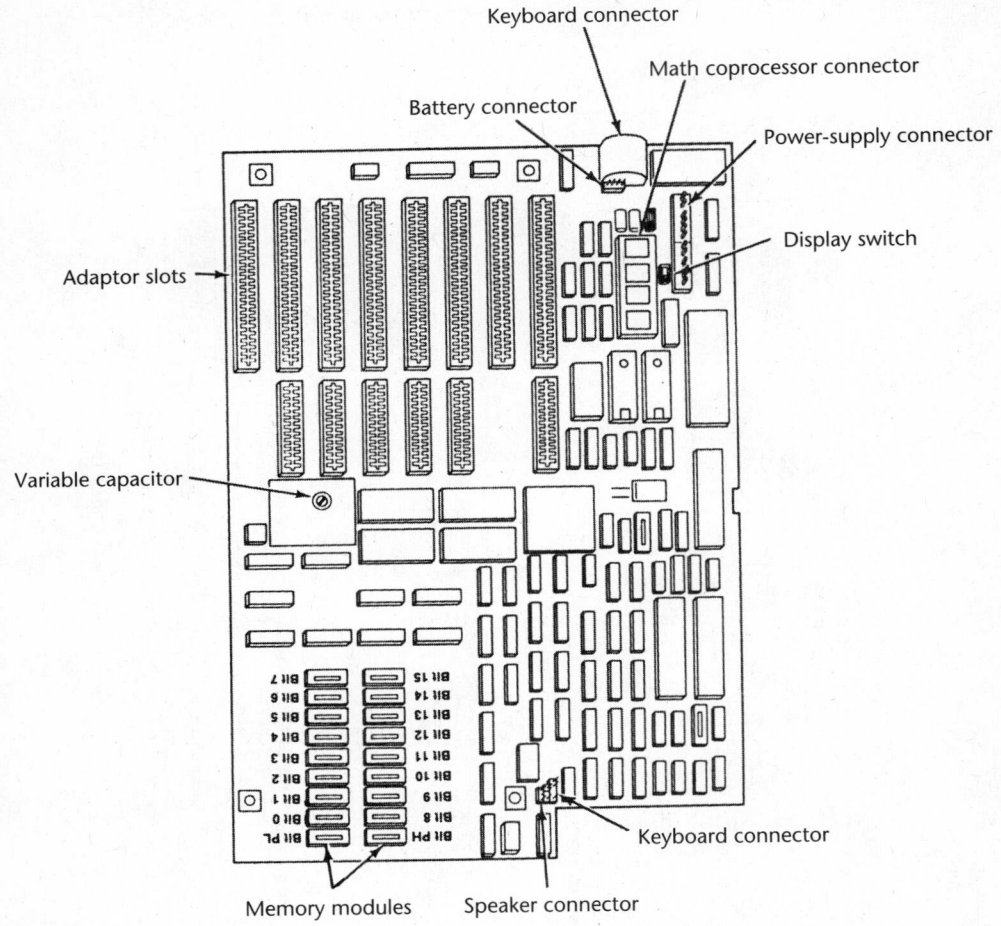

Fig. 21.12
The IBM AT Type 2 motherboard.

Table 21.8 shows the AT system-unit part-number information.

Table 21.8 IBM AT Model Part Numbers	
Description	**Number**
AT 6 MHz/84-key keyboard, 256K: one 1.2M floppy drive	5170068

AT 6 MHz/84-key keyboard, 512K, serial/parallel:
  one 1.2M floppy drive, 20M hard disk
  one 1.2M floppy drive, 30M hard disk
	5170099
	5170239

AT 8 MHz/84-key keyboard, 512K, serial/parallel: one 1.2M floppy drive, 30M hard disk	5170319
AT 8 MHz/101-key, 512K, serial/parallel: one 1.2M floppy drive, 30M hard disk	5170339

Description	Number
System Options	
20M fixed disk drive	6450205
30M fixed disk drive	6450210
30M fixed disk drive upgrade kit	6450468
360K half-height floppy disk drive (AT)	6450207
1.2M high-density drive	6450206
3 1/2-inch, half-height, 720K external drive (AT)	2683191
Serial/parallel adapter	6450215
80287 math coprocessor option	6450211
Floor-standing enclosure	6450218
Enhanced Keyboard Accessories	
Clear keycaps (60) with paper inserts	6341707
Blank light keycaps	1351710
Blank dark keycaps	1351728
Paper inserts (300)	6341704
Keycap-removal tools (6)	1351717

AT 3270

IBM announced the AT 3270 on June 18, 1985. This computer, basically the same as the original 3270 PC, is configured with an AT, rather than an XT, as the base. New software enhancements and adapter cards use the DOS memory space better than its predecessors and can place much of the Control Program in the extended-memory area, beyond the 1M boundary. Much of this capability comes from the *XMA card*, from IBM. Because much of the Control Program can reside in the area above 1M, DOS can find more room for applications software. Although this configuration doesn't eliminate the incompatibilities in the display hardware or keyboard, it at least makes available the memory needed to run an appli-cation.

The AT 3270 system has the same basic adapters as the standard 3270 PC. This system differs, however, in the capability of enabling the Control Program to reside in the memory space above 1M (*extended* memory), which doesn't exist on a standard PC or XT. IBM made several changes in the Control Program for this system and in special memory adapters, such as the XMA card. These changes enhanced the compatibility of the AT 3270 system over the original 3270 PC.

For more information about the AT 3270 system, refer to the section on the 3270 PC in this chapter.

The AT-370

The AT-370 is basically the same system as the XT-370 except for its use of an AT as the base unit. The same three custom processor boards that convert an XT into an XT-370 also plug into an AT. This system is at least two to three times faster than the XT version. The custom processor boards also were available as an upgrade for existing ATs. For a more complete description of this system, refer to the section "3270 PC Models and Features" earlier in this chapter.

An Introduction to the XT Model 286

On September 9, 1986, IBM introduced a new AT-type system disguised inside the chassis and case of an XT. This XT Model 286 system featured increased memory over its predecessors an Intel 80286 microprocessor, and as many as three internal drives standard. The computer combined an XT's cost-effectiveness, flexibility, and appearance with the high-speed, high-performance technology of the Intel 80286 microprocessor. This model looked like an XT, but underneath the cover, it was all AT.

The IBM XT Model 286 can operate as much as three times faster than earlier models of the XT in most applications. It has a standard 640K of memory. Various memory-expansion options enable users to increase its memory to 16M.

Standard features in this system include a half-height, 1.2M, 5 1/4-inch, high-density floppy disk drive; a 20M hard disk drive; a serial/parallel adapter card; and the IBM Enhanced Keyboard. You can select an optional, internal, second floppy disk drive from the following list:

- Half-height, 3 1/2-inch, 720K floppy drive
- Half-height, 3 1/2-inch, 1.44M floppy drive
- Half-height, 5 1/4-inch, 1.2M floppy drive
- Half-height, 5 1/4-inch, 360K floppy drive

The IBM XT Model 286's performance stems primarily from the AT motherboard design, with 16-bit I/O slots and an Intel 80286 processor running at 6 MHz. In addition to the type of processor used, clock speed and memory architecture are the primary factors in determining system performance. Depending on the model, the IBM AT's clock speed is 6 or 8 MHz, with one wait state; and the XT Model 286 processes data at 6 MHz, with zero wait states. The elimination of a wait state improves performance by increasing processing speed for system memory access. The zero-wait-state design makes the XT Model 286 definitely faster than the original AT models that ran at 6 MHz and about equal in speed to the 8 MHz AT systems. Based on tests, the XT Model 286 also is about three times faster than an actual XT.

Because the XT Model 286 is an AT-class system, the processor supports both real and protected modes. Operating in real address mode, the 80286 is 8088 compatible; therefore, you can use most software that runs on the standard PC systems. In real address mode, the system can address as much as 1M of RAM. Protected mode provides a number of advanced features to facilitate multitasking operations. Protected mode provides separation and protection of programs and data in multitasking environments. In protected mode, the 80286 can address as much as 16M of real memory and 1 gigabyte of virtual memory. In this mode, the XT Model 286 can run advanced operating systems such as OS/2 and UNIX. When the XT Model 286 was introduced, it was the least-expensive IBM system capable of running a true multitasking operating system.

The IBM XT Model 286 has a standard 640K of RAM. Memory options enable the system to grow to 15 1/2M, much higher than the 640K limit in other PC XTs. If you add an operating system such as OS/2 or Windows, you can take advantage of the larger memory capacities that the XT Model 286 provides.

A 20M hard disk drive is a standard feature in the XT Model 286, as is a 5 1/4-inch, 1.2M, high-density floppy disk drive. A similar floppy disk drive is standard on all models of the AT. Floppy disks formatted on a 1.2M floppy disk drive therefore can be read by an AT or an XT Model 286. The 1.2M floppy disk drive also can read floppy disks formatted with PC-family members that use a 360K floppy disk drive. Figure 21.13 shows the interior of an XT 286 system unit.

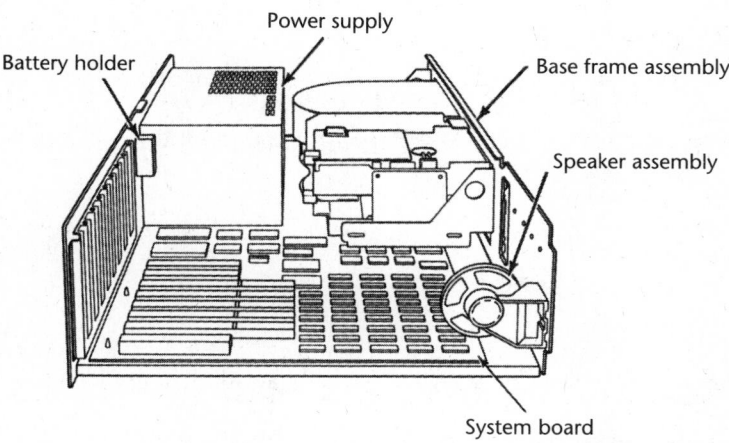

Fig. 21.13
The IBM XT Model 286 interior.

The XT Model 286 features the IBM Enhanced Keyboard with indicator lights. Many IBM personal computers use the Enhanced Keyboard, but the XT Model 286 was the first PC XT to feature keyboard indicator lights. The Caps Lock, Num Lock, and Scroll Lock lights remind users of keyboard status, which helps to prevent keyboard-entry errors.

The IBM XT Model 286 has eight I/O slots, to accommodate peripheral-device adapter cards and memory-expansion options. Five slots support the advanced 16-bit cards or 8-bit cards; three support only 8-bit cards. Two of the three 8-bit slots support only short cards.

A hard disk and floppy drive adapter card are standard features in the XT Model 286. This multifunction card takes only one 16-bit slot and supports as many as four disk drives (two floppy disk drives and two hard disk drives).

The serial/parallel adapter, another standard feature, is a combination card that requires only one slot (either type) and provides a serial and a parallel port. The parallel portion of the adapter has the capacity to attach devices, such as a parallel printer, that accept eight bits of parallel data. The fully programmable serial portion supports asynchronous communications from 50 bps to 9,600 bps, although even higher speeds are possible with the right software. The serial portion requires an optional serial-adapter cable or a serial-adapter connector. When one of these options is connected to the adapter, all the signals in a standard EIA RS-232C interface are available. You can use the serial port for interfacing a modem, a remote display terminal, a mouse, or other serial device. The XT Model 286 supports as many as two serial/parallel adapters.

A standard IBM XT Model 286 offers these features:

- 80286 processor at 6 MHz with 0 wait states
- 640K of motherboard memory
- 1.2M floppy drive
- 20M hard disk
- Five 16-bit and three 8-bit expansion slots
- Fixed disk/floppy disk drive adapter (occupies one 16-bit expansion slot)
- Serial/parallel adapter (occupies one 16-bit expansion slot)
- Enhanced Keyboard with indicator lights
- CMOS time-and-date clock with battery backup

XT Model 286 Models and Features

The XT Model 286 processor is as much as three times faster internally than the preceding XT family and as much as 25 percent faster than the AT Model 239, depending on specific applications. A 20M fixed disk and a 1.2M, 5 1/4-inch floppy disk drive were standard on the XT Model 286. One additional floppy disk drive can be installed internally as drive B. You can add as a second half-height floppy drive any type of floppy drive, including both the double and high-density versions of the 5 1/4- and 3 1/2-inch drives.

If you want to be able to read standard 5 1/4-inch data or program floppy disks created by the XT Model 286 on other PC systems, you might want to add a 5 1/4-inch 360K floppy disk drive, which provides full read/write compatibility with those systems. This is due to the fact that the 1.2M drives write a narrower track than the 360K drives, and are unable to properly overwrite a floppy disk first written on by a 360K drive. If full read/write compatibility with 360K drives is not important, you can add a second 1.2M high-density floppy disk drive.

You can add any 3 1/2-inch drive, including the 720K and 1.44M versions. Because the 1.44M does not have any read/write compatibility problems with the 720K drives, however, and the 1.44M drives always can operate in 720K mode, I suggest adding only the 1.44M 3 1/2-inch drives rather than the 720K versions. The higher-density drive is only a small extra expense compared to the double-density version. Most people do not know that full ROM BIOS support for these 1.44M drives is provided in the XT Model 286. Unfortunately, because IBM never offered the 1.44M drive as an option, the supplied Setup program does not offer the 1.44M drive as a choice in the Setup routine. Instead you have to use one of the many available public domain AT type setup programs, or "borrow" such a program from an AT-compatible system.

XT Model 286 Technical Specifications

The technical information for the XT 286 system described in this section covers the system architecture, memory configurations and capacities, standard system features, disk storage, expansion slots, keyboard specifications, and also physical and environmental specifications. You can use this information to determine the parts you need when you are upgrading or repairing these systems. Figure 21.14 shows the layout and components on the XT 286 motherboard.

System Architecture	
Microprocessor	80286
Clock speed	6 MHz
Bus type	ISA (Industry Standard Architecture)
Bus width	16-bit
Interrupt levels	16
Type	Edge-triggered
Shareable	No
DMA channels	7
DMA burst mode supported	No
Bus masters supported	No
Upgradeable processor complex	No
Memory	
Standard on system board	640K
Maximum on system board	640K
Maximum total memory	16M
Memory speed (ns) and type	150ns dynamic RAM
System board memory-socket type	9-bit SIMM
Number of memory-module sockets	2

(continues)

Memory

Memory used on system board	One bank of 4 64K×4-bit and 2 64K×1-bit DRAM parity chips, and one bank of 2 9-bit SIMMs
Memory cache controller	No
Wait states:	
System board	0
Adapter	1

Standard Features

ROM size	64K
ROM shadowing	No
Optional math coprocessor	80287
Coprocessor speed	4.77 MHz
Standard graphics	None standard
RS232C serial ports	1
UART chip used	NS16450
Maximum speed (bits per second)	9,600 bps
Maximum number of ports supported	2
Pointing device (mouse) ports	None standard
Parallel printer ports	1
Bi-directional	Yes
Maximum number of ports supported	3
CMOS real-time clock (RTC)	Yes
CMOS RAM	64 bytes
Battery life	5 years

Disk Storage

Internal disk and tape drive bays	1 full-height and 2 half-height
Number of 3 1/2-/5 1/4-inch bays	0/3
Standard floppy drives	1×1.2M
Optional floppy drives:	
5 1/4-inch 360K	Optional
5 1/4-inch 1.2M	Standard
3 1/2-inch 720K	Optional
3 1/2-inch 1.44M	Optional
3 1/2-inch 2.88M	No
Hard disk controller included:	ST-506/412 (Western Digital WD1003-WA2)
ST-506/412 hard disks available	20M
Drive form factor	5 1/4-inch
Drive interface	ST-506/412
Drive capacity	20M
Average access rate (ms)	65
Encoding scheme	MFM
BIOS drive type number	2
Cylinders	615

Disk Storage

Heads	4
Sectors per track	17
Rotational speed (RPMs)	3600
Interleave factor	3:1
Data transfer rate (kilobytes/second)	170
Automatic head parking	No

Expansion Slots

Total adapter slots	8
Number of long and short slots	6/2
Number of 8-/16-/32-bit slots	3/5/0
Available slots (with video)	5

Keyboard Specifications

101-key Enhanced Keyboard	Yes
Fast keyboard speed setting	Yes
Keyboard cable length	6 feet

Physical Specifications

Footprint type	Desktop
Dimensions:	
Height	5.5 inches
Width	19.5 inches
Depth	16.0 inches
Weight	28 pounds

Environmental Specifications

Power-supply output	157 watts
Worldwide (110v/60Hz,220v/50Hz)	Yes
Auto-sensing/switching	Yes
Maximum current:	
90-137 VAC	4.5 amps
Operating range:	
Temperature	60–90 degrees F
Relative humidity	8–80 percent
Maximum operating altitude	7,000 feet
Heat (BTUs/hour)	824
Noise (Average dB, operating, 1m)	42
FCC classification	Class B

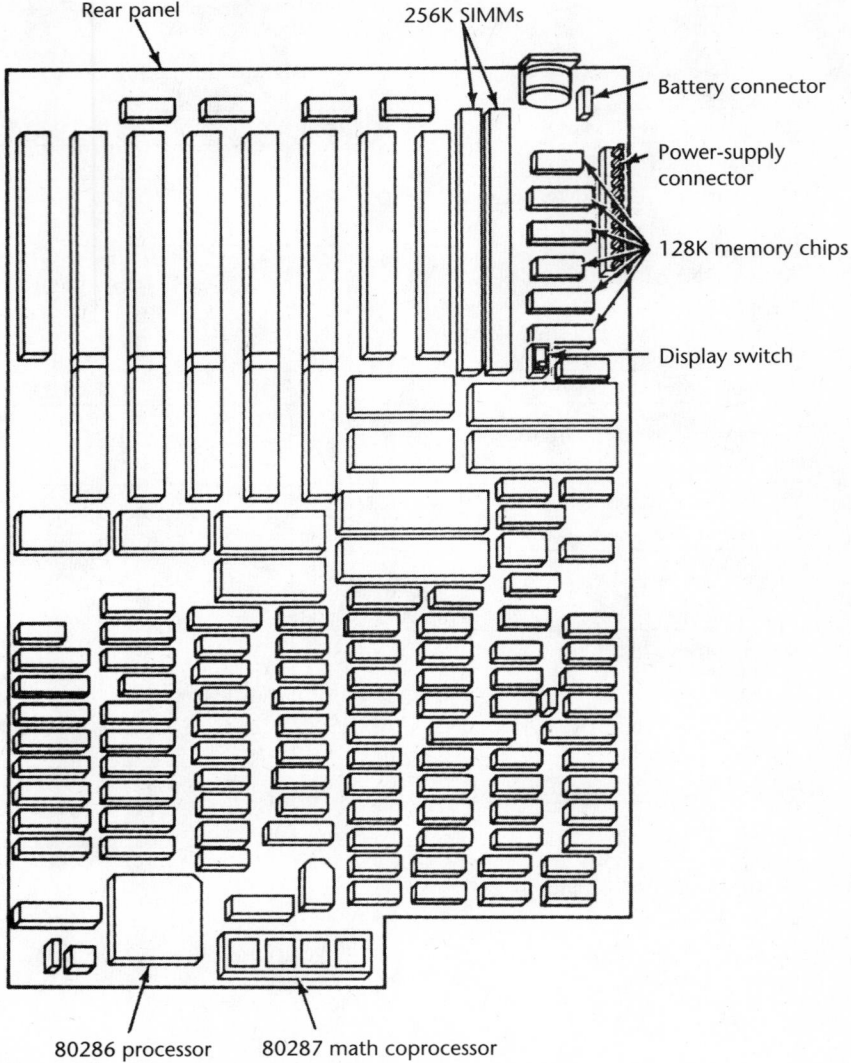

Fig. 21.14
The IBM XT 286 motherboard.

Table 21.9 lists the XT Model 286 system-unit part numbers.

Table 21.9 IBM XT-286 Model Part Numbers	
Description	**Number**
XT Model 286 system unit, 6 MHz 0 wait state, 640K, serial/parallel, 1.2M floppy drive, one 20M hard disk	5162286

Description	Number
Optional Accessories	
5 1/4-inch, half-height 360K drive	6450325
3 1/4-inch, half-height 720K internal drive	6450258
3 1/2-inch, half-height 720K external drive	2683190
80287 math coprocessor option	6450211
Enhanced Keyboard Accessories	
Clear keycaps (60) with paper inserts	6341707
Blank light keycaps	1351710
Blank dark keycaps	1351728
Paper inserts (300)	6341704
Keycap removal tools (6)	1351717

Summary

This chapter examined all the systems that make up the original line of IBM personal computers. Although these systems have long since been discontinued, I am amazed to find many of these systems still in everyday use. From individuals to large corporations to the United States government, I regularly encounter many of these old systems in my training and consulting practice. Because these systems still are used, and probably will be for years, the information in this chapter is useful as a reference tool. Much of this information also is a sort of history lesson; it is easy to see how far IBM-compatible computing has come when you look over the specifications of these older systems!

The chapter described the makeup of all the versions or models of each system, as well as their technical details and specifications. Each system unit's main components also were listed. Each system's submodels were discussed, which should help you better understand the differences among systems that might look the same on the outside but differ internally.

Chapter 22

IBM PS/1, PS/ValuePoint, and PS/2 System Hardware

This chapter identifies and describes each of the IBM Personal System/1 (PS/1), PS/ValuePoint, and Personal System/2 (PS/2) system units and standard features. (As a group, we'll call these the PS/x computers.) The chapter begins by explaining the major differences between the IBM PC and the PS/1, ValuePoint, and PS/2 systems and why each is so similar to, yet so different from, the classic PC line.

The chapter continues with a discussion of the primary PS/1, ValuePoint, and PS/2 models, which are based closely on the original PC line. These original systems sometimes are called Industry Standard Architecture (ISA) systems, and they include the standard ISA type of 8-bit and 16-bit I/O expansion slots. Others include more advanced EISA, PCI, and/or VESA Local Bus (VLB) buses. The chapter also examines the PS/x models and their respective submodels.

Differences between the PS/x Systems

The open architecture of IBM systems has allowed a variety of companies to introduce systems functionally identical to IBM's own. These compatible PCs strive to provide IBM PC performance for less-than-IBM prices. In fact, many exceed what IBM's own systems can do and offer higher performance, more features, or other benefits that the actual IBM systems lack. These non-IBM systems are usually called *IBM compatibles* or *IBM clones*. Because few systems actually duplicate IBM's own at the hardware level, the term *clone* is somewhat obsolete today. Most systems based on IBM designs are called *compatibles* because they are designed to work with the same basic software and peripheral components that IBM systems use.

IBM has done its best to keep the rest of the PC marketplace on its toes. IBM mounted an attack on several fronts, including introducing several lines of systems that cost much less than the premier PS/2 line. In September 1992, IBM formed the independent subsidiary, IBM Personal Computer Co., to develop and market various IBM personal computers. Another subsidiary, Ambra Computer Corp., was also formed to compete with low-end compatibles. IBM's lineup of PCs includes the following:

- PS/2

- PS/1

- PS/ValuePoint

- Ambra

Creating these brands is similar to the way General Motors sells Chevrolets and Buicks as well as Cadillacs. IBM's intent is to create products with performance and cost identities appropriate to different sorts of customers and distribution channels, as discussed in the following paragraphs.

PS/2

Introduced in April 1987, the PS/2 line targets large companies that expect to pay more for a premium product. The PS/2 line is generally more rugged than the PS/ValuePoint models and uses the less common but potent Micro Channel Architecture (MCA) bus (see table 22.4). PS/2s are positioned well as high-end desktops and servers. Also, service is better for the PS/2. Although the PS/ValuePoint line ships with 24-hour, seven-day-per-week, toll-free support via telephone and fax modem, the corporate-oriented PS/2 line includes all that plus on-site service that lasts for three years, under the latest warranty plan.

> **Note**
>
> We describe in detail the characteristics and strengths of the Micro Channel Architecture (MCA) bus in the PS/2 section found later in this chapter.

Some IBM PS/2s are sold under a variation called Ultimedia. The Ultimedia name is a multimedia version of the PS/2, although the name may apply to RISC and AS/400 computers. The first Ultimedia PS/2 was the M57 SLC, which is a special version of the PS/2 Model 57. The Ultimedia version included a built-in CD-ROM XA drive, an 80M hard drive, a 16-bit audio card, XGA video, and a "media control panel" on the front of the machine that includes a volume control and stereo output jacks.

PS/1

The PS/1 is IBM's low-cost line sold through retail outlets and superstores. The PS/1 was IBM's strategy to fight a two-front PC war. By introducing a more affordable PC, IBM was attempting to protect its premium line, the PS/2. There's little confusion between IBM's PS/2 and PS/1 lines because the former uses the Micro Channel, which is now clearly a proprietary architecture.

The focus of the PS/1—when first introduced, at least—was not all-out performance but ease of use for the first-time buyer. The PS/1s especially were designed for the new user who may even be intimidated by computer technology. IBM designed the PS/1 to be brought home as a learning tool or used in a small-business environment. Early models of the PS/1 included Windows and Microsoft Works preinstalled, including tutorials. Later, the PS/1 inherited Energy Star energy-saving compliance through a preinstalled Smart Energy System located on the motherboard. However, buyers noticed that value-line PCs such as the PS/1 didn't stack up as well against the compatibles. Often, the PS/1 had fewer slots and drive bays, proprietary video, and less CPU cache than found in other compatibles.

The PS/1 is targeted at definable customer sets. More than 40 remarketers are selling these new systems at over 3,000 outlets in the United States. The PS/1 Essential line, meant for small businesses, is sold through office warehouse stores such as Office Depot, Office Max, and Staples. The PS/1 Expert line, designed for advanced users, is sold through superstores such as Computer City, Elek-Tek, and BizMart. The PS/1 Consultant line, designed for home users, is sold through general merchandise and department stores such as Montgomery Ward, Sears, and Circuit City.

PS/ValuePoint

The PS/ValuePoint systems are virtually identical to the PS/1 systems, except that they offer greater expansion capabilities, higher performance versions, longer warranties, and are ordered, serviced, and supported directly through IBM. The PS/ValuePoint, or ValuePoint, line competes effectively with some clones, acting as a low-priced corporate desktop line. When first introduced in October 1992, they were called "clone-killers." (In fact, IBM's ValuePoint marketing literature talked about the "end of the Clone Age.") The ValuePoint line was designed as a line of budget business computers to be sold through IBM's new mail-order enterprise (IBM PC Direct) as well as through retailers and IBM-authorized dealers. It has helped IBM gain market share in areas in which it had not been successful. The ValuePoint line replaced the PS/1 Pro line of computers. In May 1994, the ValuePoint line was split into two lines: the more-powerful ValuePoint Performance Series and the mainstream ValuePoint Si Series.

Ambra

Ambra is a low-end PC line designed to be sold directly through mail order to compete with other high-end mail-order systems. The Ambra line was launched by Individual Computer Products International, a subsidiary started by IBM Europe. Ambra was then sold by Ambra Computer Corp. In the United States, Ambra is a line of mass market, low-end Asian desktop personal computers and notebooks. The subsidiary was kept virtually separate from its parent because IBM wanted to maintain its traditional image of being a supplier of high-quality corporate computers. Ambra machines are sold through retailers, dealers, and direct sales channels only. In the United States, the European division was closed down in spring of 1994.

> **Note**
>
> At the time of this writing, IBM decided to merge the marketing of the PS/2 and ValuePoint lines under a single name, tentatively called Commercial Desktop. The decision to market PS/2s and ValuePoint models under the same name is intended to sharpen marketing focus and eliminate unnecessary competition. Also, IBM announced in August 1994 that the Ambra line was being phased out.

The Major Differences

As you can see, each PS/x is aimed at a certain market, but the primary differences are fewer than you might think. The differences are categorized into the areas discussed in the following sections.

Construction. Few construction differences exist between the PS/2, PS/1, PS/ValuePoint, and Ambra lines. Overall, the PS/x line is the most sophisticated for design and construction. They were designed with automated assembly in mind. Because parts and components are modular, technicians and users can remove and reinstall most of them without using any tools.

The no-tool disassembly concept carries over to the floppy and hard disk drives. To remove the floppy disk drive, you hold the front of the drive while bending a plastic tab and pull the drive from the system unit. To replace the drive, slide the drive back into the case until it snaps into place. As a technician, you can amaze people unfamiliar with these systems when you open the system, remove a drive, replace it with a new unit, and close the system, all within 30 seconds. People who usually work on other types of systems, or who have never seen the inside of a PS/x system, are usually quite impressed.

A feature of the PS/2 and ValuePoint line is that several models contain no cables, which is amazing when you think of the earlier systems with their mazes of cables for carrying power and data. Eliminating cables makes components easier to install and also removes perhaps the largest single source of errors and problems. PS/2 systems are also much better shielded against stray signals because of their circuit and case design.

Parts and Availability. The small amount of labor required to service PS/x systems has changed the repair and service industry. The modular construction should make labor less expensive than parts on the repair bill. Parts pricing and availability are much more important when you service a PS/x.

The availability and price of parts, however, can be a problem. A PS/x system doesn't have many parts; the PS/x motherboard contains many components that other systems house on expansion adapter cards. For example, a PS/x integrates the mouse, serial, game, and parallel ports; video card; and floppy disk and hard disk controllers onto the motherboard. Occasionally, a certain bus video card, such as PCI, may be placed in an expansion slot. Having so much integration makes the PS/x computers much easier to repair, but may require replacing the motherboard more often than in earlier systems. Frequently, however, replacing an inexpensive adapter can solve a problem.

Because many of the custom chips used in the PS/x boards are unavailable separately, PS/x motherboards are very difficult to repair. Unlike motherboards in other systems, PS/x motherboards usually must be replaced (or exchanged) rather than repaired. Although very little motherboard repair occurs even with non-PS/2 systems because repairing a motherboard is usually more costly than replacing it, the repair or replacement issue is more important with the PS/xs because the PS/x motherboard contains so many more components (and therefore more potential places for things to go wrong) than other motherboards.

Design. The primary difference between the various PS/xs is the buses provided with each system. Typically, the PS/2 line offers only Micro Channel Architecture (MCA) buses. The PS/ValuePoint and Ambra lines offer a choice between PCI or VLB and a handful of ISA slots. PS/1 systems often offer all ISA slots with integrated local-bus video.

However, these bus distinctions are being blurred by IBM, precipitating the demise of some IBM subsidiaries. The ValuePoint Performance Series introduced in May 1994 incorporates IBM's SelectaBus feature. This technology allows ValuePoint customers to choose and upgrade the system's local bus to support either VESA or PCI, solving the PCI versus VLB dilemma. Although the motherboard is based on VESA's VLB, IBM figured out an intelligent way to support PCI as well, using a swappable backplane (called a riser) into which you plug add-in cards. The VL version of the swappable backplane adds one VL-Bus slot and four ISA slots. The PCI backplane has room for two PCI cards and two ISA cards. And, for maximum flexibility, you also can get a backplane that supports five ISA cards. Whereas the VLB version of the ValuePoint's backplane has room for only one VLB card, this is not a major snag because both video and hard disk controllers are already integrated onto the motherboard's VL-Bus.

Video. The three lines differ in video performance as well. The PS/2 video subsystem differs greatly from a PC subsystem. The original PC systems had a Monochrome Display Adapter (MDA), Color Graphics Adapter (CGA), or Enhanced Graphics Adapter (EGA) available as a plug-in board. The PS/2 Models 25 and 30 included a built-in video adapter on the motherboard called the MultiColor Graphics Array (MCGA). PS/2 Models 50 and up (as well as the 25-286 and 30-286) contain a built-in video subsystem: the Video Graphics Array (VGA), which is a higher-end system. The MCGA is a subset of the VGA and lacks color capability in the highest-resolution mode. Some newer systems, such as Models P75, 90, and 95, include eXtended Graphics Array (XGA) on either the motherboard or a card. The newer XGA standard is a super-VGA type of adapter that includes more resolution and colors than the standard VGA and retains backward compatibility.

The VGA and XGA support all video modes available in the earlier MDA, CGA, and EGA, as well as some newer VGA- and XGA-specific modes. Because this downward compatibility is almost 100 percent, few programs are unable to run on a VGA- or an XGA-equipped system, although programs not written specifically for VGA or XGA cannot take advantage of their extra resolution and color capability.

Because VGA and XGA supersede EGA and all other previous standards, IBM has stopped producing all other video adapters, including EGA. For a while, IBM sold a VGA card for upgrading PC systems to VGA; this 8-bit board, called the IBM PS/2 Display Adapter, plugged into any IBM PC or PC-compatible system. IBM discontinued the board, leaving only aftermarket boards available for upgrading older systems. Most video-card vendors have followed IBM's lead and have also discontinued EGA boards. These vendors have successfully cloned the VGA and XGA technology, providing many video-card choices for upgrading PC and PC-compatible systems.

In contrast to other graphics adapters, VGA and XGA have analog output and require displays that can accept this signal. Other graphics adapters use a digital signal and work with monitors designed to accept the signal. Therefore, if you are upgrading a system to VGA or XGA, you probably also need to add a new monitor to your shopping list. Some monitors, such as the NEC MultiSync and the Sony Multiscan, accept both digital and analog signals. These monitors offer a flexibility for working with older digital systems not found in IBM's monitors, but they can be more expensive. If you have such a monitor and are upgrading your system's video adapter to VGA or XGA, you do not need a new monitor.

The change to analog displays comes for two primary reasons: color and money. With an analog display, many colors become available without a big jump in cost. VGA is designed to display as many as 262,144 colors, which would require a digital interface design with at least 18 lines to transmit all this color information to the monitor. Using an interface with 18 digital driver circuits on the video card, running through a thick cable containing at least 18 shielded wires, to a monitor with 18 digital receiver circuits, would cost thousands of dollars. A much simpler and less costly approach is to convert the digital color information to analog information for transmission and use by the display. This approach reduces the amount of circuitry required and allows for a much smaller cable. Analog transmission can send the same color information through fewer wires and circuits.

With the recent iterations of the PS/2 Models 76 and 77, the XGA graphics chip was replaced by an S3-accelerated local-bus video chip. The new Models 76 and 77 include an S3 Inc. graphics chip in a local-bus design instead of the XGA standard of past PS/2 generations. IBM held onto XGA for several generations of PS/2 systems because many large customers developed applications that wrote directly to the XGA chip.

Repair and Support Policies. All PS/x lines include toll-free technical support, 24 hours a day, seven days a week. The differences between the lines are the length of warranty and availability of on-site service. The PS/2 line includes three years of on-site, same-day service, averaging a four-hour response time. The ValuePoint Performance series also includes three years of on-site service, but only for the next business day. The ValuePoint Si series includes a one-year warranty with next-day, on-site service. The IBM PS/1 comes with a one-year replacement policy via overnight shipping. The Ambra line includes a one-year, on-site warranty. However, there's a catch: Only the system unit is covered. A defective keyboard, mouse, or monitor must be shipped back for repair; Ambra promises a 48-hour turnaround.

Expandability. The more consumer-oriented the line, the less expandable it is. For example, the Ambra D4100I/VL, for example, offers no 32- or 8-bit slots. It includes five 16-bit slots and one VESA Local Bus (VLB) slot. Yet this is no hard and fast rule. The PS/2 Models 77i and 77s (a 66 MHz 486DX system) can hold a maximum of 64M of memory. The similarly configured ValuePoint Performance model can hold a maximum of 128M.

Energy Conservation. Most PS/x computers are Energy Star compliant, idling to less than 70 watts for both monitor and system unit. (Some PS/2 527M hard disk drive models do not meet compliance as well as faster ValuePoint Si Series models.) For the PS/1, for example, power management is controlled through a preinstalled Smart Energy System located on the motherboard. Energy Star compliance offers a deep-sleep standby mode and Rapid Resume, a feature that allows the last Window visible to return when the system quickly wakes up. In standby mode, power consumption in the PS/1's system unit drops from 38.0 watts to just 0.8; monitor power consumption, from 82.7 watts to 20.3. The Rapid Resume feature is possible only on the PS/1, however, because it is more than a simple software utility. It works hand-in-hand with IBM's own BIOS, dedicated circuitry on the motherboard, and a specialized power switch. The BIOS intercepts an off signal from the power switch, and, if applications or documents are open, writes the entire contents of the PC's memory to a file on the hard drive. When the PC reboots (regardless of when, even if you've unplugged or moved the machine), it swaps the contents of that file back into the system RAM. You're back in business without a perceptible delay.

Documentation. The Ambra line includes two well-organized, concise users' guides (beginner and advanced). The manuals include a table of contents but no index or glossary. The text is readable but not detailed. A basic troubleshooting section is included. The illustrations are useful, but few. An on-line help system is provided for the setup CMOS, but no on-line documentation is available. The ValuePoint's manuals demonstrate its corporate focus: Users get an "Intro to Computers" course, and administrators receive support information.

Micro Channel Architecture (MCA) Slots

As mentioned earlier, perhaps the most important difference between PS/2 systems and the other PS/x systems is the I/O adapter board interface bus, or slots. This difference is described in the following sections in more detail.

PS/2 Models 50 and higher incorporate a new bus interface called Micro Channel Architecture (MCA). MCA is a new slot design that is incompatible with the ISA slot system but offers improvements in many areas. The first consequence of this bus is that a design adapter that plugs into the ISA 8-bit or 8/16-bit slots cannot plug into MCA slots. MCA is both physically and electrically different from ISA.

MCA Advantages. MCA was designed to meet strict FCC regulations for Class B certification. These requirements are much more strict than for Class A, which covers allowable emissions in a location zoned as commercial or industrial. Class B requirements are for systems sold in residential environments and are designed to eliminate electrical interference with devices such as televisions and radios. Meeting Class B requirements should give these systems a distinct advantage as clock rates (speeds) go ever higher. People in the communications and radio industry know that as the frequency of an oscillator increases, so does the problem of noise emissions. MCA has many ground connections for shielding, including a ground pin no farther than one-tenth of an inch from any signal line in the slot. Appendix A includes a pinout diagram of ISA and MCA bus slots.

MCA is designed to eliminate the bane of adapter board installers: setting jumpers and switches to configure the adapters. In surveys, IBM found that as many as 60 percent of all technician service calls were "no problem" calls; they were switch- and jumper-setting sessions. No wonder switches and jumpers are a problem, considering the number of switches and jumpers on some memory and multifunction boards. Setting them correctly can be very difficult, and nearly impossible without the board's original manual because each manufacturer's board is different. If you buy new boards, you might save money if you buy whatever board is on sale; you probably will end up with many different adapter boards, however, most with hard-to-read manuals and a bunch of jumpers and switches to set.

IBM's answer to this problem is called Programmable Option Selection (POS), a built-in feature on all MCA-equipped systems. The POS uses a special file called an *Adapter Description File* (with the file extension ADF) that comes with each adapter. The ADF file contains all possible setting attributes for the board and is read in by the system start-up disk or reference disk. The reference disk contains a special configuration routine that reads all the files and decides on nonconflicting settings for each board. The operator might need to select particular settings when two boards conflict. When the settings are set, they are stored in CMOS (battery-saved memory) and are available every time the system is started. The settings can be stored on disk also for backup, in case of a battery failure, or to quickly restore a configuration to several systems. The POS feature saves much labor and time, and is affecting the upgrade and repair industry: Many manufacturers have established switchless setups for their adapters to make them more "PS/2-like."

This advantage of MCA might become a moot point, however. The Plug and Play (PnP) specification developed by Microsoft Corp. and Intel Corp. and to be supported by hundreds of vendors will allow sound and other expansion cards to be self-configuring. Just plug in the new card and available resources will be automatically detected, and the card will be configured with minimal work. However, your system BIOS, the add-in devices, and the operating system must all support PnP. PnP will become a popular feature supported by Microsoft Windows 4.0.

Finally, MCA-equipped systems are much more reliable than ISA-equipped systems for several reasons. The rest of this section discusses the reliability of the MCA system, particularly timing considerations.

MCA Reliability. One reason that MCA-equipped systems are more reliable than those with ISA bus interfaces is that the MCA is well-shielded. MCA-equipped systems therefore are more immune to noise from radio transmissions or any electrical noise.

This reason might be minor compared with the timing of the MCA bus. The MCA is asynchronous, which means that communication between adapters and the system board doesn't depend on timing. This feature solves a relatively common problem with bus systems. Have you ever had problems getting a system to work, only to find that moving a board to a different slot or switching two boards allows the system to operate normally? (By the way, I don't think that any IBM service manual officially suggests this solution.) The problem that moving or switching boards solves is one of timing. Each slot is supposed to carry the same signals as all the other slots, but that doesn't exactly happen. Effects on the bus, such as capacitance and signal propagation delays, can cause timing windows to "appear" differently in different slots, which can affect a board's functioning in that slot. MCA eliminates this type of problem; it is designed so that a board can tell it to "wait"—in effect, slowing the system by adding wait states until the board is ready.

Another timing-related problem is known to people who use some of the "turbo" IBM-compatible systems. In these "hypersystems," some boards cannot keep up with the system speed and do not work at all. On some systems, some of these boards can work if the system is slowed by adding wait states to operations or by reducing the speed of the system clock—but then the system doesn't really operate at its full performance capacity. Many communications, networking, and memory adapters can be speed-limiting in this way. With MCA, the bus cycles at a fixed, constant speed among all the systems, no matter what the microprocessor clock speed; the MCA always waits for a board, inserting wait states until the board is ready to proceed. Although this process might slow the system somewhat, the board and system work. Therefore, the same adapter functions in the 10 MHz Model 50 or the 50 MHz Model 90, regardless of their different clock speeds.

Other MCA design parameters for performance improvements exist, but they are more difficult to see. Most benchmarks have not proven any performance advantage in MCA systems over those with the standard ISA slots. IBM has demonstrated MCA coprocessing capabilities, however, which showed excellent performance. Taking full advantage of MCA's performance capabilities requires new bus master adapter designs. These new designs are adapters with processors that can function independently of the system or even take control of it. For now, MCA provides increased reliability and easy setup and use. The improvements incorporated into this bus make it the standard bus for the future; for now, however, many more systems in use still have the earlier ISA bus design (see table 22.3).

Fortunately, most troubleshooting techniques and methods apply equally to the MCA and the ISA bus systems. The MCA systems suffer fewer failures overall, and are much easier to set up and install. The real question is, how much are customers willing to pay for these features?

PS/2 System-Unit Features by Model

This section provides a reference to most PS/2 systems that IBM has produced. The standard parts included with each system unit include the items in this list:

■ Motherboard with the CPU (central processing unit, or microprocessor) and other primary computer circuitry

■ Case with internal power supply

■ Keyboard

■ Standard adapters or plug-in cards

■ Some form of disk drive (usually)

This section also includes the following various kinds of information about each system unit:

■ A listing of specific components

■ Technical data and specifications

■ An explanation of each submodel, with details about differences and features of each model, including changes from model to model and version to version

■ Price of each system and option

> **Note**
>
> Prices shown are the IBM list prices and usually do not reflect true purchase prices. Normally, a standard discount of 30 percent is subtracted from the retail price. On recent PS/x models, IBM has lowered margins to the point that they use a street price instead of a retail price. This means, in most cases, discounts are usually greater than 10 percent. Retail prices are provided for comparison and reference only. If a model has been discontinued, the price given represents the retail list price at the time the system was withdrawn.

Decoding PS/2 Model Numbers

With the large variety of PS/2 systems now available, you might have difficulty telling from the model number how one differs from another. IBM's model-designation scheme started out with some reasoning behind it; but the increasingly large number of models made the original scheme difficult to adhere to and resulted in many inconsistencies in model designations. To restore consistency and enable greater understanding of the product line, IBM recently created a new model-designation scheme. This section provides an explanation of the older, inconsistent scheme, as well as the new method.

The following list shows examples of the use of the old system:

Model	Meaning
Model 70-121	120M HD, one floppy disk drive
Model 30-E41	10 MHz 286, 45M HD, one floppy disk drive
Model 70-B61	25 MHz 486, 60M HD, one floppy disk drive

Table 22.1 describes the original PS/2 model designation meanings used by IBM for the PS/2 Models 25, 25-286, 30, 30-286, 50, 55, 60, 65, 70, P70, P75, and 80.

Table 22.1　PS/2 Model Designation Codes (for Original Models)

Model	Meaning
2	20M hard disk drive
3	30M hard disk drive (except A3*)
4	45M hard disk drive
6	60M hard disk drive
8	80M hard disk drive
**0	Medialess (no hard disk, no floppy disk drives)

(continues)

Table 22.1 Continued	
Model	**Meaning**
**1	1 floppy disk drive
**1	Monochrome display (25 only)
**2	2 floppy disk drives
**4	Color display (25, 25-286 only)
**6	10 MHz 286; 1 floppy disk (25-286 only)
0**	Space-saving keyboard (25-286 only)
12*	120M hard disk drive
A2*	25 MHz 386; 120M hard disk drive
B2*	25 MHz 486; 120M hard disk drive
16*	160M hard disk drive
A16	160M hard disk drive
32*	320M hard disk drive
40*	400M hard disk drive
A**	25 MHz 386 processor
A3*	25 MHz 386 processor; 320M hard disk drive
B**	25 MHz 486 processor
C**	Color display
E**	10 MHz 286 (30-286 only)
E6*	16 MHz 386; 60M hard disk drive (70 only)
G**	Enhanced keyboard
L0*	Token-Ring LAN adapter (25 only)
LE*	EtherNet LAN adapter (55 only)
LT*	16/4 Token-Ring LAN adapter (55 only)
M**	Monochrome display

Represents any number or letter

Table 22.2 describes the new model-designation meanings used by IBM for the PS/2 Models 35, 40, L40, 56, 56LS, 57, 76, 77, 90, and 95.

Table 22.2 PS/2 Model Designation Codes (for Models Introduced after 10/90)	
Model	**Meaning**
?**	Different hardware/software configurations
3	16 MHz 386SX
4	20 MHz 386SX
5	20 MHz 386SLC
6	25 MHz 386SLC
7	20 MHz 386SLC-LP
8	20 MHz 386DX

Model	Meaning
9	25 MHz 386SLC
B	50 MHz 486SLC2
D	33 MHz 486SLC
E	75 MHz 486SLC3
F	20 MHz 486DX
G	20 MHz 486SX
H	25 MHz 486SX
J	25 MHz 486DX
K	33 MHz 486DX
L	50 MHz 486DX2
M	50 MHz 486DX
N	66 MHz 486DX2
P	60 MHz Pentium
Q	66 MHz Pentium
T	100 MHz 486DX4
U	33 MHz 486SX
**0	No hard disk, one floppy disk drive
**2	20M hard disk drive
**3	40M hard disk drive
**4	60M hard disk drive
**5	80M hard disk drive
**6	100M or 104M hard disk drive
**7	120M hard disk drive
**9	160M or 170M hard disk drive
**A	200M, 208M, or 212M hard disk drive
**B	240M, 245M, or 250M hard disk drive
**C	270M hard disk drive
**D	320M, 340M, or 360M hard disk drive
**F	400M or 420M hard disk drive
**G	540M hard disk drive
**T	1G hard disk drive
**X	Medialess (no hard disk, no floppy disk drives)

The following list shows examples of the use of the new system:

Model	Meaning
Model 35-24X	Token ring, 20 MHz 386SX, no media
Model 40-040	20 MHz 386SX, 1 floppy disk drive, no hard disk
Model 9576-ATB	Model 76, 100 MHz DX4, 250M hard disk drive

Table 22.3 provides a reference list of all IBM PS/2 models that use the Industry Standard Architecture (ISA) bus and shows their standard.

Table 22.3   IBM PS/2 System Models with ISA Bus

| | | | PLANAR MEMORY | | STANDARD | |
Part Number	CPU	MHz	Std.	Max.	Floppy Drive	Hard Disk
25						
8525-001	8086	8	512K	640K	1×720K	—
8525-G01	8086	8	512K	640K	1×720K	—
8525-004	8086	8	512K	640K	1×720K	—
8525-G04	8086	8	512K	640K	1×720K	—
25 LS						
8525-L01	8086	8	640K	640K	1×720K	—
8525-L04	8086	8	640K	640K	1×720K	—
30						
8530-001	8086	8	640K	640K	1×720K	—
8530-002	8086	8	640K	640K	2×720K	—
8530-021	8086	8	640K	640K	1×720K	20M
PS/1 286						
2011-M01	286	10	512K	2.5M	1×1.44M	—
2011-C01	286	10	512K	2.5M	1×1.44M	—
2011-M34	286	10	1M	2.5M	1×1.44M	30M
2011-C34	286	10	1M	2.5M	1×1.44M	30M
PS/1 SX						
2121-C42	386SX	16	2M	6M	1×1.44M	40M
2121-B82	386SX	16	2M	6M	1×1.44M	80M
2121-C92	386SX	16	2M	6M	1×1.44M	129M
25 286						
8525-006	286	10	1M	4M	1×1.44M	—
8525-G06	286	10	1M	4M	1×1.44M	—
8525-036	286	10	1M	4M	1×1.44M	30M
8525-G36	286	10	1M	4M	1×1.44M	30M
25 SX						
8525-K00	386SX	16	1M	16M	1×1.44M	—
8525-K01	386SX	16	4M	16M	1×1.44M	—
8525-L01	386SX	16	4M	16M	1×1.44M	—

Bus Type	Total Available Slots	STANDARD		Date Introduced	Date Withdrawn
		Video	Keyboard		
ISA/8	2/2	MCGA	SS	08/04/87	—
ISA/8	2/2	MCGA	Enh	08/04/87	—
ISA/8	2/2	MCGA	SS	08/04/87	—
ISA/8	2/2	MCGA	Enh	08/04/87	—
ISA/8	2/1	MCGA	Enh	06/02/88	—
ISA/8	2/1	MCGA	Enh	06/02/88	—
ISA/8	3/3	MCGA	Enh	04/04/89	—
ISA/8	3/3	MCGA	Enh	04/02/87	—
ISA/8	3/3	MCGA	Enh	04/02/87	—
ISA/16	0	VGA	Enh	06/26/90	—
ISA/16	0	VGA	Enh	06/26/90	—
ISA/16	0	VGA	Enh	06/26/90	—
ISA/16	0	VGA	Enh	06/26/90	—
ISA/16	0	VGA	Enh	10/07/91	—
ISA/16	2/2	VGA	Enh	10/07/91	—
ISA/16	2/2	VGA	Enh	10/07/91	—
ISA/16	2/2	VGA	SS	05/10/90	—
ISA/16	2/2	VGA	Enh	05/10/90	—
ISA/16	2/2	VGA	SS	05/10/90	—
ISA/16	2/2	VGA	Enh	05/10/90	—
ISA/16	2/2	VGA	Enh	01/21/92	—
ISA/16	2/1	VGA	Enh	01/21/92	—
ISA/16	2/1	VGA	Enh	01/21/92	—

(continues)

Table 22.3   Continued

Part Number	CPU	MHz	PLANAR MEMORY Std.	Max.	STANDARD Floppy Drive	Hard Disk
30 286						
8530-E01	286	10	1M	4M	1×1.44M	—
8530-E21	286	10	1M	4M	1×1.44M	20M
8530-E31	286	10	1M	4M	1×1.44M	30M
8530-E41	286	10	1M	4M	1×1.44M	45M
35 SX						
8535-040	386SX	20	2M	16M	1×1.44M	—
8535-043	386SX	20	2M	16M	1×1.44M	40M
35 LS						
8535-14X	386SX	20	2M	16M	—	—
8535-24X	386SX	20	2M	16M	—	—
40 SX						
8540-040	386SX	20	2M	16M	1×1.44M	—
8540-043	386SX	20	2M	16M	1×1.44M	40M
8540-045	386SX	20	2M	16M	1×1.44M	80M
L40 SX						
8543-044	386SX	20	2M	18M	1×1.44M	60M
PS/2 Model E						
9533-DB7	486SLC2	50	4M	16M	1×1.44M	120M
9533-DBD	486SLC2	50	8M	16M	1×1.44M	120M
9533-DLA	486SLC2	50	8M	16M	1×2.88M	212M
9533-DLG	486SLC2	50	8M	16M	1×2.88M	540M
9533-GB7	486SLC2	50	8M	16M	1×1.44M	120M
9533-GBD	486SLC2	50	8M	16M	1×1.44M	340M
9533-GBX	486SLC2	50	4M	16M	1×1.44M	n/a
9533-2BX	486SLC2	50	4M	16M	n/a	n/a

* Sales of this system unit are limited to the educational market. Suggested pricing was not available before press time.

Bus Type	Total Available Slots	STANDARD		Date Introduced	Date Withdrawn
		Video	Keyboard		
ISA/16	3/3	VGA	Enh	09/13/87	05/04/92
ISA/16	3/3	VGA	Enh	09/13/88	09/11/91
ISA/16	3/3	VGA	Enh	09/26/89	01/17/92
ISA/16	3/3	VGA	Enh	04/23/91	05/04/92
ISA/16	3/3	VGA	Any	06/11/91	—
ISA/16	3/3	VGA	Any	06/11/91	—
ISA/16	3/2	VGA	Any	10/17/91	—
ISA/16	3/2	VGA	Any	06/11/91	—
ISA/16	5/5	VGA	Any	06/11/91	—
ISA/16	5/5	VGA	Any	06/11/91	—
ISA/16	5/5	VGA	Any	06/11/91	—
ISA/16	0	VGA	SS	03/26/91	07/21/92
ISA/16	2 PCMCIA	VGA	SS w/Trackpoint	06/14/93	—
ISA/16	2 PCMCIA	VGA	SS w/Trackpoint	06/14/93	—
ISA/16	2 PCMCIA	VGA	SS w/Trackpoint	06/14/93	—
ISA/16	2 PCMCIA	VGA	SS w/Trackpoint	06/14/93	—
ISA/16	2 PCMCIA	VGA	SS w/Trackpoint	06/14/93	—
ISA/16	2 PCMCIA	VGA	SS w/Trackpoint	06/14/93	—
ISA/16	2 PCMCIA	VGA	SS w/Trackpoint	06/14/93	—
ISA/16	2 PCMCIA	VGA	SS w/Trackpoint	06/14/93	—

Table 22.4   IBM PS/2 System Models with MCA Bus

Part Number	CPU	MHz	PLANAR MEMORY Std.	Max.	STANDARD Floppy Drive	Hard Disk
50						
8550-021	286	10	1M	1M	1×1.44M	20M
50Z						
8550-031	286	10	1M	2M	1×1.44M	30M
8550-061	286	10	1M	2M	1×1.44M	60M
53						
9553-0B7	486SLC2	50	4M	16M	1×1.44M	120M
9553-0BB	486SLC2	50	4M	16M	1×1.44M	250M
55 SX						
8555-031	386SX	16	2M	8M	1×1.44M	30M
8555-041	386SX	16	4M	8M	1×1.44M	40M
8555-061	386SX	16	2M	8M	1×1.44M	60M
8555-081	386SX	16	4M	8M	1×1.44M	80M
55 LS						
8555-LT0	386SX	16	4M	8M	—	—
8555-LE0	386SX	16	4M	8M	—	—
56 SX						
8556-043	386SX	20	4M	16M	1×2.88M	40M
8556-045	386SX	20	4M	16M	1×2.88M	80M
56 SLC						
8556-055	386SLC	20	4M	16M	1×2.88M	80M
8556-059	386SLC	20	4M	16M	1×2.88M	160M
56 LS						
8556-14x	386SX	20	4M	16M	—	—
8556-24x	386SX	20	4M	16M	—	—
56 SLC LS						
8556-15x	386SLC	20	4M	16M	—	—
8556-25x	386SLC	20	4M	16M	—	—
57 SX						
8557-045	386SX	20	4M	16M	1×2.88M	80M
8557-049	386SX	20	4M	16M	1×2.88M	160M

Bus Type	Total Available Slots	STANDARD		Date Introduced	Date Withdrawn
		Video	Keyboard		
MCA/16	4/3	VGA	Enh	04/02/87	05/03/89
MCA/16	4/3	VGA	Enh	06/07/88	07/23/91
MCA/16	4/3	VGA	Enh	06/07/88	07/23/91
MCA/16	3/3	XGA	Any	11/09/93	—
MCA/16	3/3	XGA	Any	11/09/93	—
MCA/16	3/3	VGA	Enh	05/09/89	09/11/91
MCA/16	3/3	VGA	Enh	06/11/91	05/25/92
MCA/16	3/3	VGA	Enh	05/09/89	09/11/91
MCA/16	3/3	VGA	Enh	06/11/91	05/25/92
MCA/16	3/2	VGA	Enh	10/09/90	05/25/92
MCA/16	3/2	VGA	Enh	10/09/90	05/25/92
MCA/16	3/3	VGA	Any	02/25/92	—
MCA/16	3/3	VGA	Any	02/25/92	—
MCA/16	3/3	VGA	Any	02/25/92	—
MCA/16	3/3	VGA	Any	02/25/92	—
MCA/16	3/2	VGA	Any	02/25/92	—
MCA/16	3/2	VGA	Any	02/25/92	—
MCA/16	3/2	VGA	Any	02/25/92	—
MCA/16	3/2	VGA	Any	02/25/92	—
MCA/16	5/5	VGA	Any	06/11/91	—
MCA/16	5/5	VGA	Any	06/11/91	—

(continues)

Table 22.4 Continued

Part Number	CPU	MHz	PLANAR MEMORY Std.	Max.	STANDARD Floppy Drive	Hard Disk
57 SLC						
8557-055	386SLC	20	4M	16M	1×2.88M	80M
8557-059	386SLC	20	4M	16M	1×2.88M	160M
M57 SLC						
8557-255	386SLC	20	4M	16M	1×2.88M	80M
8557-259	386SLC	20	4M	16M	1×2.88M	160M
60						
8560-041	286	10	1M	1M	1×1.44M	44M
8560-071	286	10	1M	1M	1×1.44M	70M
65 SX						
8565-061	386SX	16	2M	8M	1×1.44M	60M
8565-121	386SX	16	2M	8M	1×1.44M	120M
8565-321	386SX	16	2M	8M	1×1.44M	320M
70 386						
8570-E61	386DX	16	2M	6M	1×1.44M	60M
8570-061	386DX	20	2M	6M	1×1.44M	80M
8570-081	386DX	20	4M	6M	1×1.44M	80M
8570-121	386DX	20	2M	6M	1×1.44M	120M
8570-161	386DX	20	4M	6M	1×1.44M	160M
8570-A61	386DX	25	2M	8M	1×1.44M	60M
8570-A81	386DX	25	4M	8M	1×1.44M	80M
8570-A21	386DX	25	2M	8M	1×1.44M	120M
8570-A16	386DX	25	4M	8M	1×1.44M	160M
70 486						
8570-B61	486DX	25	2M	8M	1×1.44M	60M
8570-B21	486DX	25	2M	8M	1×1.44M	120M
P70 386						
8573-031	386DX	16	2M	8M	1×1.44M	30M
8573-061	386DX	20	4M	8M	1×1.44M	60M
8573-121	386DX	20	4M	8M	1×1.44M	120M
P75 486						
8573-161	486DX	33	8M	16M	1×1.44M	160M
8573-401	486DX	33	8M	16M	1×1.44M	400M

Bus Type	Total Available Slots	STANDARD		Date Introduced	Date Withdrawn
		Video	Keyboard		
MCA/16	5/5	VGA	Any	02/25/92	—
MCA/16	5/5	VGA	Any	02/25/92	—
MCA/16	5/3	XGA	Any	10/17/91	02/25/92
MCA/16	5/3	XGA	Any	02/25/92	—
MCA/16	8/7	VGA	Enh	04/02/87	10/31/90
MCA/16	8/7	VGA	Enh	04/02/87	10/31/90
MCA/16	8/7	VGA	Enh	03/20/90	07/23/91
MCA/16	8/7	VGA	Enh	03/20/90	07/23/91
MCA/16	8/7	VGA	Enh	10/30/90	07/23/91
MCA/32	3/3	VGA	Enh	06/07/88	07/23/91
MCA/32	3/3	VGA	Enh	09/26/89	09/11/91
MCA/32	3/3	VGA	Enh	06/11/91	—
MCA/32	3/3	VGA	Enh	09/26/89	09/11/91
MCA/32	3/3	VGA	Enh	06/11/91	—
MCA/32	3/3	VGA	Enh	09/26/89	09/11/91
MCA/32	3/3	VGA	Enh	06/11/91	01/17/92
MCA/32	3/3	VGA	Enh	09/26/89	09/11/91
MCA/32	3/3	VGA	Enh	06/11/91	—
MCA/32	3/3	VGA	Enh	09/26/89	09/11/91
MCA/32	3/3	VGA	Enh	06/20/89	09/11/91
MCA/32	2/2	VGA	Enh	03/20/90	07/23/91
MCA/32	2/2	VGA	Enh	05/09/89	07/23/91
MCA/32	2/2	VGA	Enh	05/09/89	—
MCA/32	4/4	XGA	Enh	11/12/90	—
MCA/32	4/4	XGA	Enh	11/12/90	—

(continues)

Table 22.4   Continued

Part Number	CPU	MHz	PLANAR MEMORY Std.	Max.	STANDARD Floppy Drive	Hard Disk
80 386						
8580-041	386DX	16	1M	4M	1×1.44M	44M
8580-071	386DX	16	2M	4M	1×1.44M	70M
8580-081	386DX	20	4M	4M	1×1.44M	80M
8580-111	386DX	20	2M	4M	1×1.44M	115M
8580-121	386DX	20	2M	4M	1×1.44M	120M
8580-161	386DX	20	4M	4M	1×1.44M	160M
8580-311	386DX	20	2M	4M	1×1.44M	314M
8580-321	386DX	20	4M	4M	1×1.44M	320M
8580-A21	386DX	25	4M	8M	1×1.44M	120M
8580-A16	386DX	25	4M	8M	1×1.44M	160M
8580-A31	386DX	25	4M	8M	1×1.44M	320M
90 XP 486						
8590-0G5	486SX	20	4M	64M	1×1.44M	80M
8590-0G9	486SX	20	4M	64M	1×1.44M	160M
8590-0H5	486SX	25	4M	64M	1×1.44M	80M
8590-0H9	486SX	25	4M	64M	1×1.44M	160M
8590-0J5	486DX	25	8M	64M	1×1.44M	80M
8590-0J9	486DX	25	8M	64M	1×1.44M	160M
8590-0K9	486DX	33	8M	64M	1×1.44M	320M
8590-0KD	486DX	33	8M	64M	1×1.44M	320M
8590-0KF	486DX	33	8M	64M	1×1.44M	400M
95 XP 486						
8595-0G9	486SX	20	4M	64M	1×1.44M	160M
8595-0GF	486SX	20	4M	64M	1×1.44M	400M
8595-0H9	486SX	25	8M	64M	1×1.44M	160M
8595-0HF	486SX	25	8M	64M	1×1.44M	400M
8595-0J9	486DX	25	8M	64M	1×1.44M	160M
8595-0JD	486DX	25	8M	64M	1×1.44M	320M
8595-0JF	486DX	25	8M	64M	1×1.44M	400M
8595-0KD	486DX	33	8M	64M	1×1.44M	320M
8595-0KF	486DX	33	8M	64M	1×1.44M	400M

Keyboards available include the Enhanced (101-key), Space-Saving (84-key), and Host-Connected (122-key). If "Any" is indicated, the purchaser can choose any of the three.

Bus Type	Total Available Slots	STANDARD		Date Introduced	Date Withdrawn
		Video	Keyboard		
MCA/32	8/7	VGA	Enh	04/02/87	10/31/90
MCA/32	8/7	VGA	Enh	04/02/87	10/31/90
MCA/32	8/7	VGA	Enh	10/30/90	—
MCA/32	8/7	VGA	Enh	04/02/87	12/27/90
MCA/32	8/7	VGA	Enh	03/20/90	01/29/91
MCA/32	8/7	VGA	Enh	10/30/90	—
MCA/32	8/7	VGA	Enh	08/04/87	12/27/90
MCA/32	8/7	VGA	Enh	03/20/90	—
MCA/32	8/7	VGA	Enh	03/20/90	01/29/91
MCA/32	8/7	VGA	Enh	10/30/90	—
MCA/32	8/7	VGA	Enh	03/20/90	—
MCA/32	4/3	XGA	Enh	04/23/91	01/17/92
MCA/32	4/3	XGA	Enh	04/23/91	01/17/92
MCA/32	4/3	XGA	Enh	10/17/91	—
MCA/32	4/3	XGA	Enh	10/17/91	—
MCA/32	4/3	XGA	Enh	10/30/90	01/17/92
MCA/32	4/3	XGA	Enh	10/30/90	01/17/92
MCA/32	4/3	XGA	Enh	10/17/91	—
MCA/32	4/3	XGA	Enh	10/30/90	—
MCA/32	4/3	XGA	Enh	10/17/91	—
MCA/32	8/6	XGA	Enh	04/23/91	01/17/92
MCA/32	8/6	XGA	Enh	04/23/91	01/17/92
MCA/32	8/6	XGA	Enh	10/17/91	—
MCA/32	8/6	XGA	Enh	10/17/91	—
MCA/32	8/6	XGA	Enh	10/30/90	01/17/92
MCA/32	8/6	XGA	Enh	10/30/90	01/17/92
MCA/32	8/6	XGA	Enh	04/23/91	01/17/92
MCA/32	8/6	XGA	Enh	10/30/90	—
MCA/32	8/6	XGA	Enh	04/23/91	—

Differences between PS/2 and PC Systems

Except for the obvious differences in appearance between PS/2 systems and the earlier "classic" (ISA) line of systems, they are quite similar. For troubleshooting and repair, you can consider the PS/2 systems as simply another type of PC-compatible system. All the troubleshooting techniques used on the other systems apply to the PS/2, although some repairs are conducted differently. For example, because each PS/2 motherboard includes a built-in floppy disk controller, if you determine that this controller is defective (using the same troubleshooting techniques as for the earlier systems), you must replace the entire motherboard. In contrast, on an IBM PC system with the same problem, you replace only the floppy controller card, a much less costly operation.

After working on a PS/2 system for some time, you will discover several positive features of these systems. The PS/2 is much more reliable than the earlier types of systems, for several reasons including the following:

- Robotic assembly of most of the system eliminates most human error during assembly.

- The presence of fewer cables than other systems—or no cables at all—eliminates one of the biggest problem areas for repairs.

- Better shielding than in other systems prevents reception and transmission of stray signals.

- The PS/2 systems have no switches or jumpers to set, a feature that eliminates many service calls due to operator installation or configuration errors.

- The systems can be taken apart and reassembled with no tools or only a few tools for special operations. Stripping down a PS/2 system to the motherboard usually takes less than one minute.

You will also discover several negative features as well:

- Because the motherboard includes so many features, it is likely to be replaced more often than in other systems.

- Parts are more expensive than for other systems, and items such as motherboards, power supplies, and floppy drives can be much more expensive. Because of greatly reduced frequency of repair and the decreased labor required for each repair, however, maintaining a PS/2 system costs about half as much as maintaining other systems.

The primary areas of difference between PS/2 and IBM PC systems are design and construction, video, and I/O adapter board slots.

PS/2 Model 25

The PS/2 Model 25, the lowest-priced PS/2 family member, was introduced August 11, 1987 (see fig. 22.1). The Model 25 (8525) is a general-purpose system that incorporates the PC-style 8-bit slot architecture, enabling this system to accept most current adapters.

The Model 25 uses the Intel 8086 processor and operates at 8 MHz with 0 wait states to read-only memory (ROM). This system is 40 percent smaller and more than twice as fast as the original IBM PC.

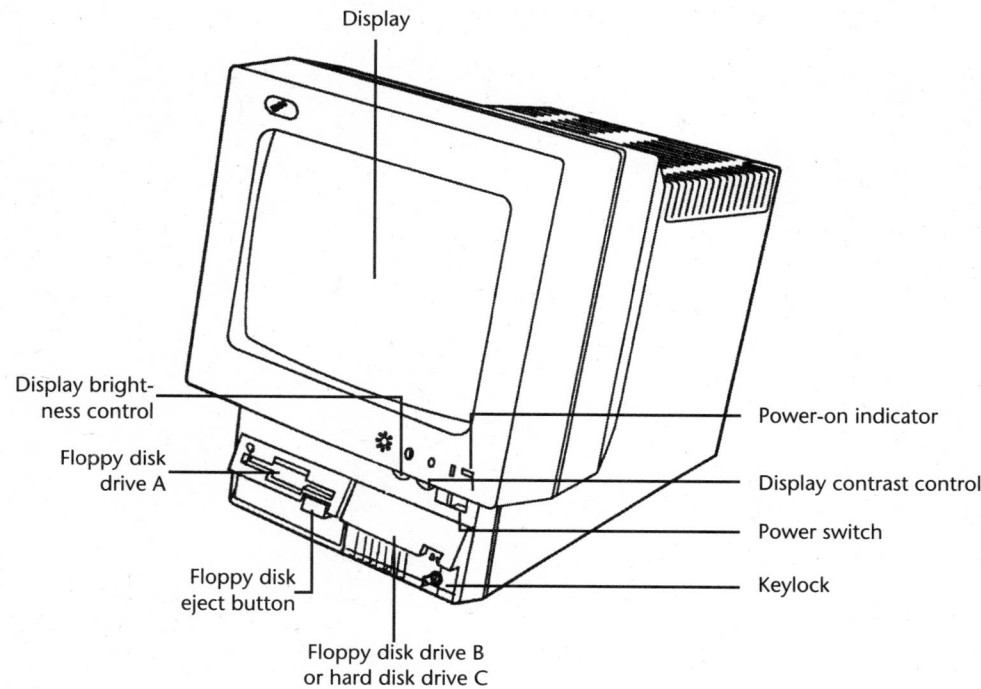

Fig. 22.1
PS/2 Model 25 (front view).

The Model 25's display is integrated into the system unit, which makes it look similar to the Apple Macintosh. With the Model 25, you can choose one of two keyboards: the IBM Space-Saving Keyboard or the IBM Enhanced Keyboard, which has a numeric keypad. You also can choose one of two displays: monochrome or color. A second 3 1/2-inch floppy disk drive, a 20M hard disk, and an additional 128K of RAM memory are available.

The Model 25 offers the same text and graphics capabilities as the IBM PS/2 Model 30. The built-in MultiColor Graphics Array (MCGA) can display as many as 256 colors on the system's color monitor (from a palette of more than 256,000 colors) or 64 shades of gray on the monochrome monitor.

Two 8-bit expansion slots enable you to attach many existing personal computer cards. A 12-inch analog display (color or monochrome), a display adapter, an RS-232C serial adapter, a parallel adapter, and a floppy disk drive adapter are standard, increasing the function of the standard unit. Figure 22.2 shows the rear panel of the Model 25.

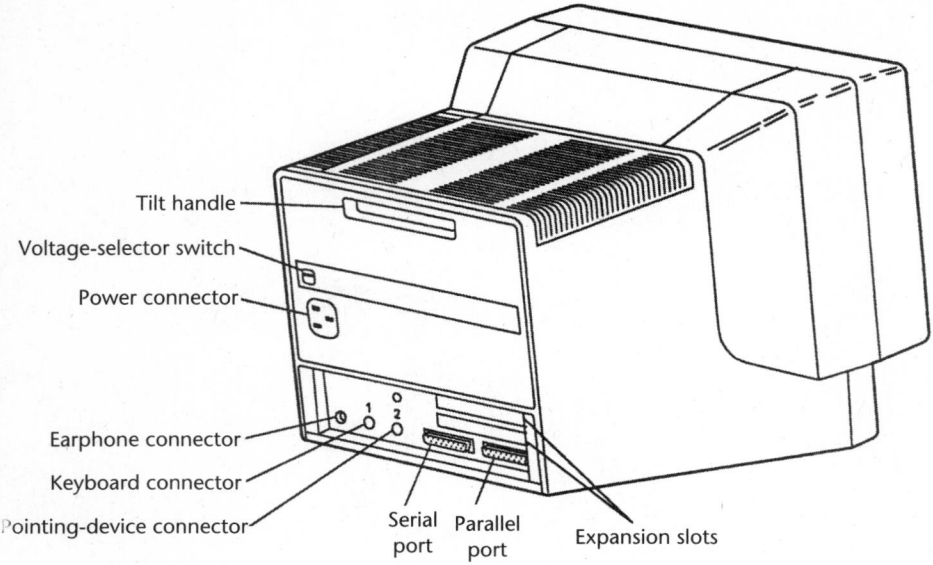

Tilt handle

Voltage-selector switch

Power connector

Earphone connector

Keyboard connector

Pointing-device connector

Serial port   Parallel port   Expansion slots

Fig. 22.2
PS/2 Model 25 (rear view).

Each model of the PS/2 Model 25 includes the following features:

- Approximately twice the speed of the IBM PC or IBM XT
- Two 8-bit expansion slots (one full-size and one 8-inch), which allow attachment of many existing PC cards
- Integrated MultiColor Graphics Array (MCGA) graphics

     Displays 256 colors from 262,144 possible colors

     Displays 64 shades of gray

- 512K of RAM standard, expandable to 640K on the motherboard
- Integrated floppy disk controller for as many as two 3 1/2-inch 720K drives
- One 3 1/2-inch (720K) floppy disk drive
- 12-inch analog display (color or monochrome)
- IBM Space-Saving Keyboard or Enhanced Keyboard
- Integrated serial port, parallel port, mouse port, and keyboard port

- Audio earphone connector
- Math coprocessor socket
- Advanced technology that eliminates jumpers and switches

Some PC adapters do not work in the Model 25 for various reasons. Because of the integrated functions on the Model 25 motherboard, certain options (such as PC types of memory upgrades, floppy controllers, and graphics adapters) might conflict with what is already present on the motherboard. Moreover, because of physical constraints, adapter cards thicker than 0.8 inch might not work, and one of the two slots is a half-length slot. The integrated MCGA does not support modes that support the 5151 Monochrome Display. The Model 25 has analog graphics output and does not support digital display devices. Figures 22.3 and 22.4 illustrate the locations of internal components of the PS/2 Model 25.

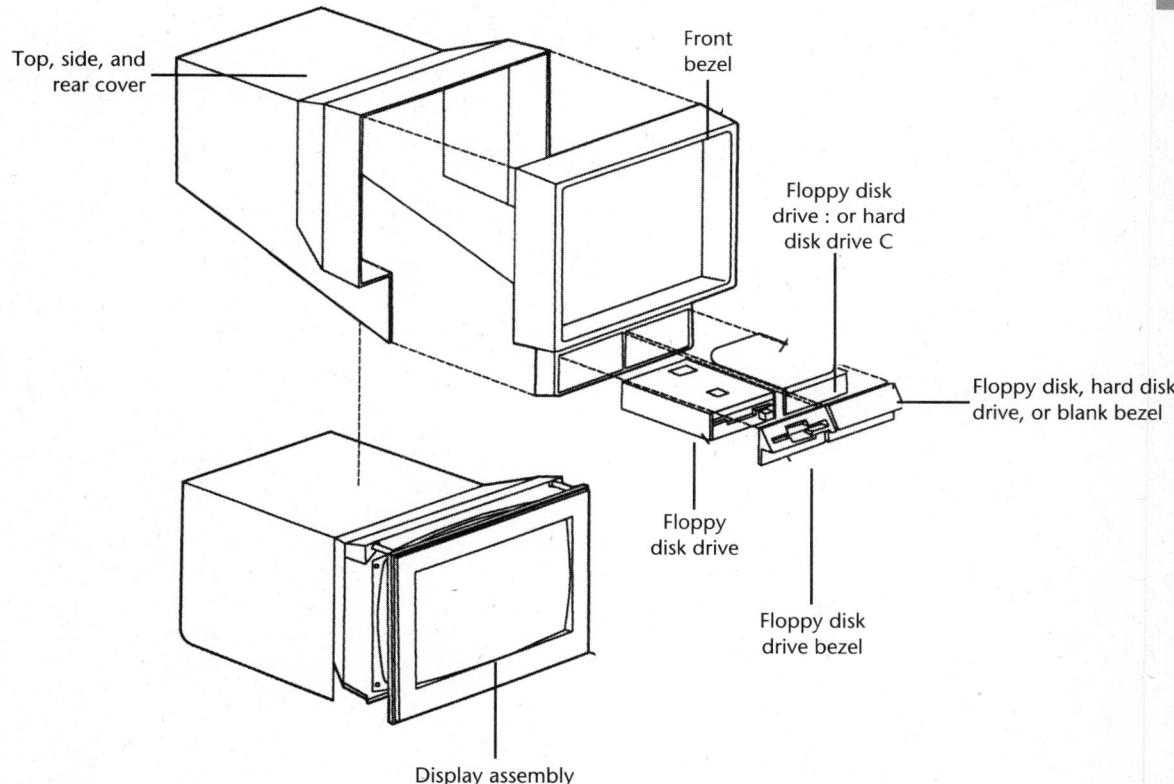

Fig. 22.3
PS/2 Model 25 interior (part 1).

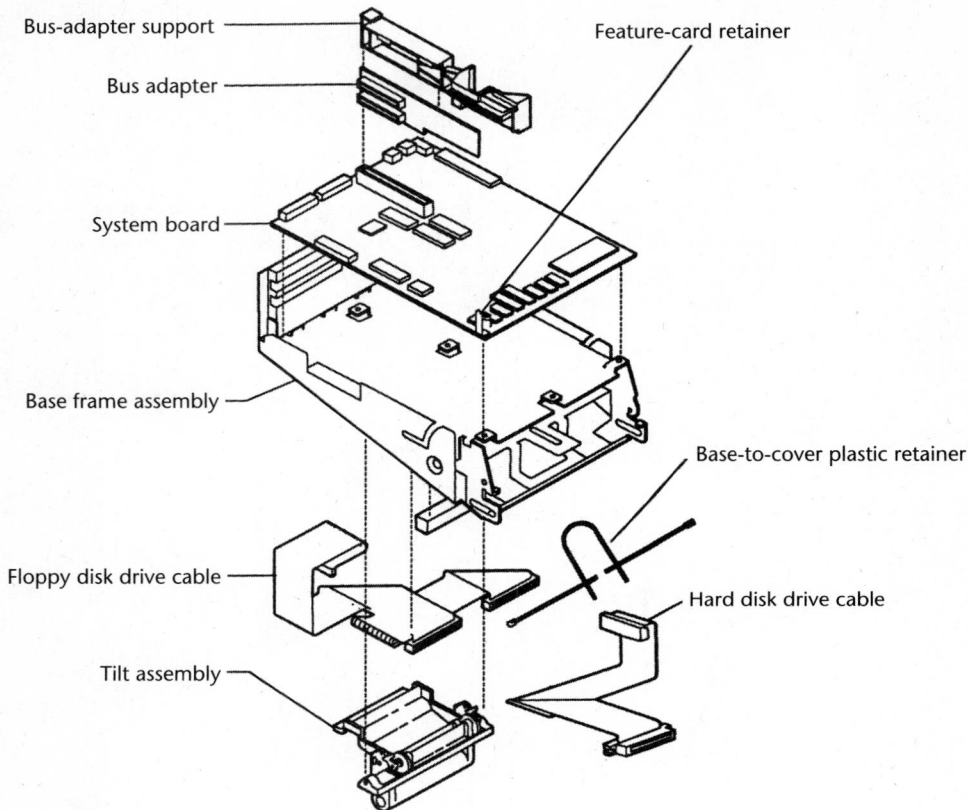

Fig. 22.4

PS/2 Model 25 interior (part 2).

IBM expanded the usefulness of the Model 25 in two main ways: by offering a version for use on a local area network (LAN) and by providing hard disks for data and program storage.

LAN Support. On June 2, 1988, IBM introduced a specially configured version of the Model 25, called the Model 25 LAN Station, or LS. This system is basically a standard Model 25 preconfigured with the IBM Token-Ring Network PC Adapter for use in a LAN. The Model 25 LS is available in both monochrome (8525-L01) and color (8525-L04) versions. The Models L01 and L04 include the Enhanced Keyboard and 640K of RAM. Because the Token-Ring Adapter II card uses the half-length expansion slot, the LS models have only a single full-length expansion slot remaining in the system unit for other adapter boards. Both models come with one 3 1/2-inch (720K) floppy disk drive. A second 720K floppy or a 20M hard drive is available.

LAN software for operating on a network is not supplied with this system and must be purchased separately. Because many people buy LAN software from a third party such as Novell, the fact that the software support is "unbundled" is beneficial. You then can choose which software to use.

Hard Disk Drives. For increased storage, IBM made a 20M hard disk drive for the Model 25. Each system has the capacity to use one hard disk drive. On models with two floppy disk drives, the 20M hard disk replaces the second floppy disk drive.

The IBM PS/2 Model 25 20M hard disk drive (78X8958) features 20M of storage, 3 1/2-inch hard disk technology, a stepper motor head-actuator mechanism, and a keylocked bezel, which disables the keyboard. It also has a built-in controller that plugs into a special port on the motherboard and does not occupy an expansion slot. (Because the controller is integrated on the drive, the term IDE—Integrated Drive Electronics— is used to describe this type of drive.) The hard disk drive is essentially the same one used in the Model 30. The built-in controller on this drive unit conserves a precious slot in the Model 25. Because the Model 25 has only two slots, conserving one of them is an important consideration.

IBM produced another hard disk for the Model 25—the 20M hard disk drive with adapter (27F4130). The controller uses RLL encoding and achieves higher data-transmission speeds than the built-in controller on the other hard drive. Like the currently available hard drive for the Model 25, the older drive uses 3 1/2-inch hard disk technology, a stepper motor head-actuator mechanism, and a keylocked bezel, which disables the keyboard. The older drive uses a higher-speed stepper motor and also has a special actuator that parks the heads automatically when the power is turned off. This drive, however, requires a separate controller, which occupies one of only two slots available in the Model 25; probably because of this limitation, IBM has discontinued production of this hard disk drive.

Table 22.5 lists the PS/2 Model 25 technical specifications; figure 22.5 shows the PS/2 Model 25 system board.

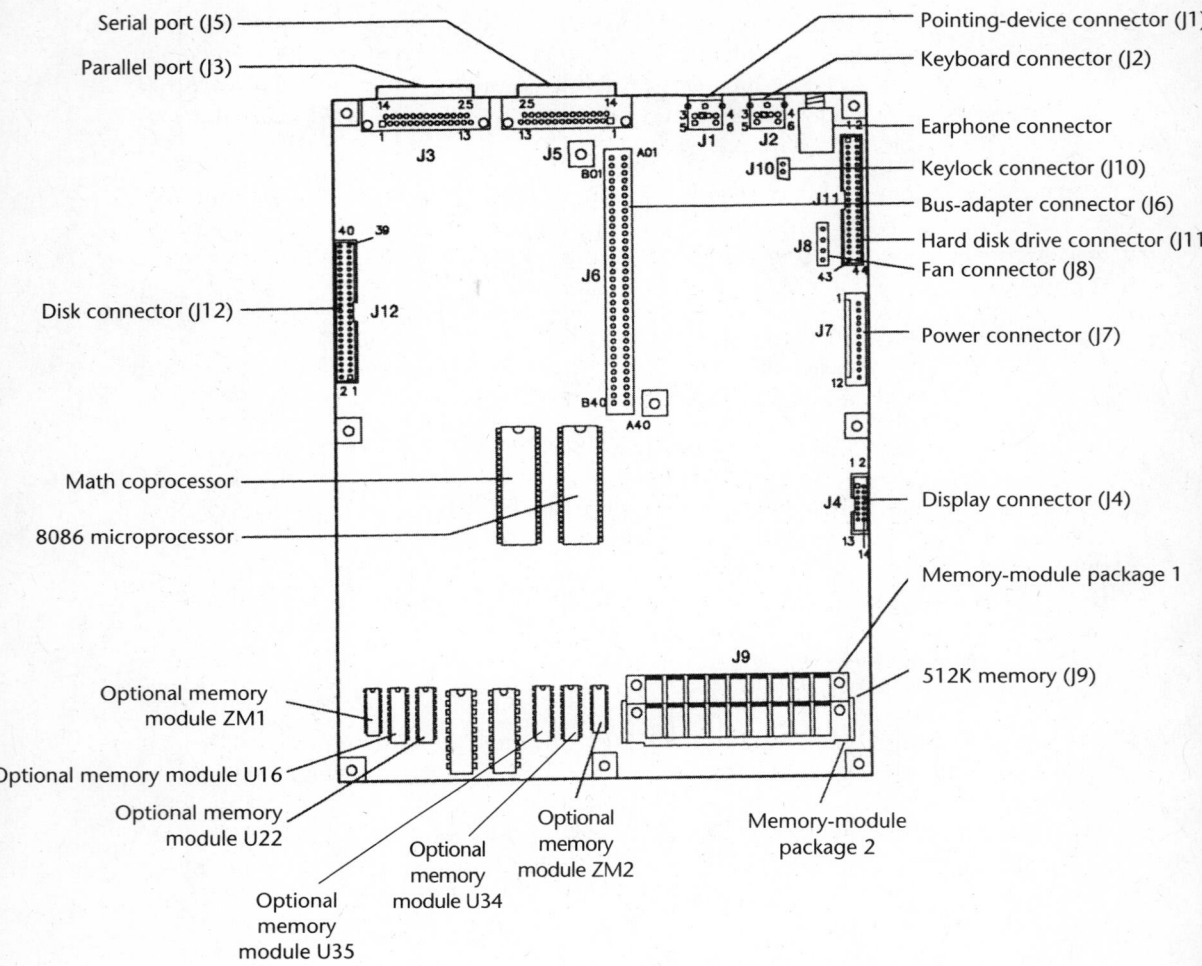

Fig. 22.5
The PS/2 Model 25 system board.

Table 22.5 PS/2 Model 25 Technical Specifications	
System Architecture	
Microprocessor	8086
Clock speed	8 MHz
Bus type	ISA (Industry Standard Architecture)
Bus width	8-bit
Interrupt levels	8
Type	Edge-triggered
Shareable	No
DMA channels	3
DMA burst mode supported	No

System Architecture

Bus masters supported	No
Upgradeable processor complex	No

Memory

Standard on system board	512K
Maximum on system board	640K
Maximum total memory	640K
Memory speed and type	150ns dynamic RAM
System board memory-socket type	9-bit SIMM (single in-line memory module)
Number of memory-module sockets	2
Number available in standard configuration	0
Memory used on system board	Two 256K 9-bit SIMMs, one socketed bank of four 64K×4-bit and two 64K×1-bit chips
Memory cache controller	No
Wait states:	
System board	0
Adapter	4

Standard Features

ROM size	64K
ROM shadowing	No
Optional math coprocessor	8087
Coprocessor speed	8 MHz
Standard graphics	MCGA (MultiColor Graphics Array)
Built-in display	Yes
Monochrome	Model 8525-xx1
Color	Model 82525-xx4
Dot pitch (mm)	0.38
Audio earphone jack	Yes
RS232C serial ports	1
UART chip used	NS8250B
Maximum speed	9,600 bps
Maximum number ports	2
Pointing device (mouse) ports	1
Parallel printer ports	1
Bidirectional	Yes
Maximum number ports	2
CMOS real-time clock (RTC)	No
CMOS RAM	None

Disk Storage

Internal disk and tape drive bays	2
Number of 3 1/2- and 5 1/4-inch bays	2/0
Standard floppy disk drives	15720K

(continues)

Table 22.5   Continued

Disk Storage

Optional floppy disk drives:	
5 1/4-inch 360K	Optional
5 1/4-inch 1.2M	No
3 1/2-inch 720K	Standard
3 1/2-inch 1.44M	No
3 1/2-inch 2.88M	No
Hard disk controller included	IDE connector on system board and/or an ST-506/412 RLL controller in the short slot
IDE/ST-506 hard disks available	20M
Drive form factor	3 1/2-inch

Drive interface	IDE	ST-506
Average access rate (ms)	80	3
Encoding scheme	MFM	RLL
BIOS drive type number	26	36
Cylinders	612	402
Heads	4	4
Sectors per track	17	26
Rotational speed (RPM)	3600	3600
Interleave factor	3:1	3:1
Data transfer rate (K/second)	170	260
Automatic head parking	No	Yes

Expansion Slots

Total adapter slots	2
Number of long and short slots	1/1
Number of 8-/16-/32-bit slots	2/0/0
Available slots	2

Keyboard Specifications

101-key Enhanced Keyboard	Yes (Gxx,Lxx)
84-key Space-Saving Keyboard	Yes (0xx)
Fast keyboard speed setting	No
Keyboard cable length:	
Space-Saving Keyboard	5 feet
Enhanced Keyboard	6 feet

Security Features

Keylock:	
Locks cover	Yes (with optional hard disk)
Locks keyboard	Yes
Keyboard password	No
Power-on password	No
Network server mode	No

Physical Specifications

Footprint type	Desktop
Dimensions:	
Height	15.0 inches
Width footprint	9.5 inches
Width display	12.6 inches
Depth	14.7 inches
Weight:	
001/G01	31.0 pounds
L01	32.0 pounds
004/G04	36.0 pounds
L04	37.0 pounds
Carrying case	Optional

Environmental Specifications

Power-supply output	90 watts (001/G01)
	115 watts (004/G04)
Worldwide (110/60,220/50)	Yes
Auto-sensing/switching	Manual switch
Maximum current:	
90-137 VAC	2.8 amps
80-259 VAC	1.7 amps
Operating range:	
Temperature	60-90 degrees F
Relative humidity	8-80 percent
Maximum operating altitude	7,000 feet
Heat (BTUs/hour)	683
Noise (Avg dB, operating, 1m)	44 dB
FCC classification	Class B

Table 22.6 shows the primary specifications of the different versions of PS/2 Model 25.

PS/2 Model 30

The IBM PS/2 Model 30 (IBM 8530), announced April 2, 1987, is a general-purpose system designed to offer more features and performance than the IBM PC and XT— especially in display graphics—and at a lower price. This system includes as standard many features built into the system board, including a graphics adapter, parallel port, serial port, clock calendar, 640K of RAM, and a mouse port. The Model 30 also uses many existing PC adapter cards for further expansion due to its ISA 8-bit slots. Figure 22.6 shows a front view, and figure 22.7 shows a rear-panel view of the Model 30. As of December 27, 1990, all versions of the PS/2 Model 30 have been discontinued and no longer are available.

Table 22.6   IBM PS/2 Model 25 Model Summary

Part Number	CPU	MHz	PLANAR MEMORY Std.	Max.	STANDARD Floppy Drive	Hard Disk
25						
8525-001	8086	8	512K	640K	1×720K	—
8525-G01	8086	8	512K	640K	1×720K	—
8525-004	8086	8	512K	640K	1×720K	—
8525-G04	8086	8	512K	640K	1×720K	—
25 LS						
8525-L01	8086	8	640K	640K	1×720K	—
8525-L04	8086	8	640K	640K	1×720K	—

Models that end in xx1 have the monochrome analog display as a built-in feature; models that end in xx4 have the color display. The 25LS models also include an IBM Token-Ring Adapter II card in the half-length slot.

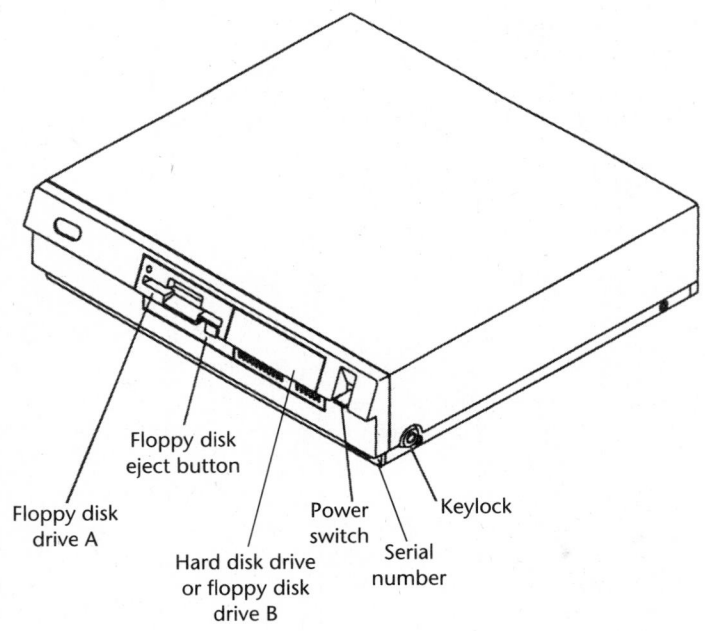

Fig. 22.6
PS/2 Model 30 (front view).

Bus Type	Total Available Slots	STANDARD		Date Introduced	Date Withdrawn
		Video	Keyboard		
ISA/8	2/2	MCGA	SS	08/04/87	—
ISA/8	2/2	MCGA	Enh	08/07/87	—
ISA/8	2/2	MCGA	SS	08/04/87	—
ISA/8	2/2	MCGA	Enh	08/04/87	—
ISA/8	2/1	MCGA	Enh	06/02/88	—
ISA/8	2/1	MCGA	Enh	06/02/88	—

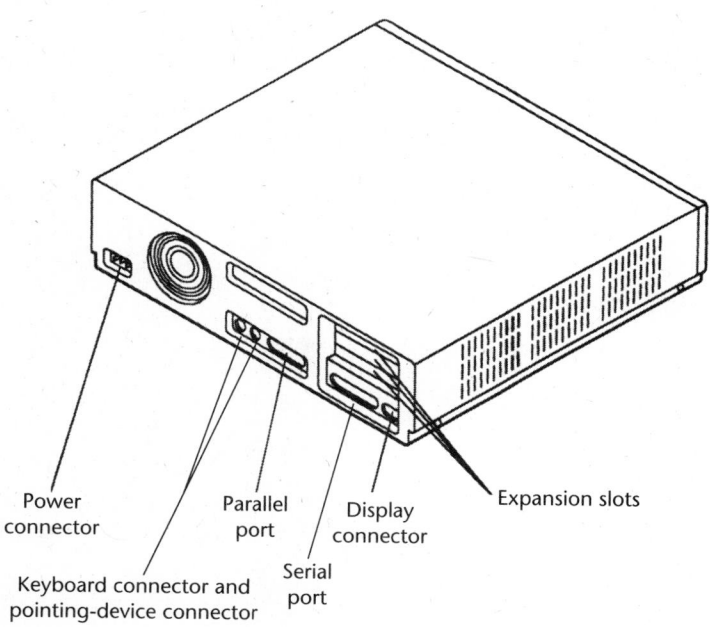

Power connector

Parallel port

Display connector

Expansion slots

Serial port

Keyboard connector and pointing-device connector

Fig. 22.7
PS/2 Model 30 (rear view).

The Model 30 is based on an 8086 microprocessor, running at 8 MHz with 0 wait states. Performance is enhanced by the use of a 16-bit-wide data path to the motherboard memory, which results in internal processing speed nearly comparable to a 6 MHz AT and more than twice as fast as the 8088-based PC or XT.

Major features of the Model 30 include the items in this list:

- Many functions integrated on the motherboard, including disk controllers, graphics, and ports

- Integrated MCGA graphics displays as many as 256 colors or 64 shades of gray

- Approximately twice the performance speed of 8088-based IBM PC and IBM XT systems

- Smaller design, with reduced power requirements

- Worldwide power supply

- Switchless installation and configuration

- 640K random-access memory (RAM)

- 16-bit access to motherboard memory

- Integrated floppy disk controller for two 720K drives

- Integrated serial port, parallel port, mouse port, and keyboard port

- IBM Enhanced Keyboard

- Time-of-day clock with extended-life battery

- Socket for a math coprocessor

- Three expansion slots to accommodate PC or XT 8-bit adapter cards

Figure 22.8 shows an interior view of the Model 30.

The Model 30 was available in three versions: the 30-001, with one 3 1/2-inch (720K) floppy drive; the 30-002, with two 3 1/2-inch (720K) floppy drives; and the 30-021, with a 20M hard disk drive and a single 3 1/2-inch (720K) floppy drive. All models included 640K RAM.

Graphics Adapter. MultiColor Graphics Array (MCGA), the graphics adapter function integrated into the Model 30 motherboard, supports all Color Graphics Adapter (CGA) modes when an analog PS/2 display is attached. Other digital displays are incompatible. In addition to providing existing CGA mode support, MCGA supports four expanded modes, a subset of the VGA processor on Models 50 and higher:

> 640×480 by 2 colors—all points addressable
>
> 320×200 by 256 colors—all points addressable

40×25 by 16 colors for text (8-by-16-character box)

80×25 by 16 colors for text (8-by-16-character box)

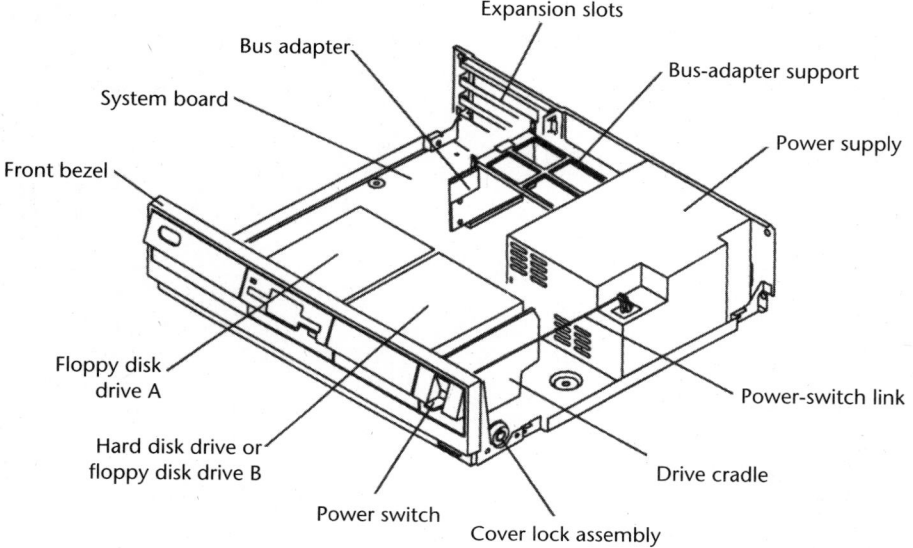

Fig. 22.8
PS/2 Model 30 interior.

The integrated graphics adapter automatically switches from color to 64 shades of gray when connected to a monochrome analog display. This feature enables users who prefer a monochrome display to execute color-based applications without compatibility problems or troublesome software reconfiguration.

Table 22.7 lists the PS/2 Model 30 technical specifications.

Table 22.7 PS/2 Model 30 Technical Specifications	
System Architecture	
Microprocessor	8086
Clock speed	8 MHz
Bus type	ISA (Industry Standard Architecture)
Bus width	8-bit
Interrupt levels	8
Type	Edge-triggered
Shareable	No
DMA channels	3
DMA burst mode supported	No
Bus masters supported	No
Upgradeable processor complex	No

(continues)

Table 22.7   Continued

Memory

Standard on system board	640K
Maximum on system board	640K
Maximum total memory	640K
Memory speed and type	150ns dynamic RAM
System board memory-socket type	9-bit SIMM (single in-line memory module)
Number of memory-module sockets	2
Number available in standard configuration	0
Memory used on system board	Two 256K 9-bit SIMMs, one soldered bank of four 64K×4-bit and two 64K×1-bit chips
Memory cache controller	No
Wait states:	
System board	0
Adapter	4

Standard Features

ROM size	64K
ROM shadowing	No
Optional math coprocessor	8087
Coprocessor speed	8 MHz

System Architecture

Standard graphics	MCGA (MultiColor Graphics Array)
RS232C serial ports	1
UART chip used	NS8250B
Maximum speed (bits per second)	9,600 bps
Maximum number of ports supported	2
Pointing device (mouse) ports	1
Parallel printer port	1
Bidirectional	Yes
Maximum number of ports supported	2
CMOS real-time clock (RTC)	Yes
CMOS RAM	None
Battery life	5 years
Replaceable	Yes (replace bus adapter)

Disk Storage

Internal disk and tape drive bays	2
Number of 3 1/2- and 5 1/4-inch bays	2/0
Standard floppy drives	15720K
	25720K (002)
Optional floppy drives:	
5 1/4-inch 360K	Optional
5 1/4-inch 1.2M	No
3 1/2-inch 720K	Standard
3 1/2-inch 1.44M	No
3 1/2-inch 2.88M	No
Hard disk controller included	IDE connector on system board
IDE hard disks available	20M
Drive form factor	3 1/2-inch
Controller type	IDE
Average access rate (ms)	80
Encoding scheme	MFM

Disk Storage	
BIOS drive type number	26
Cylinders	612
Heads	4
Sectors per track	17
Rotational speed (RPM)	3600
Interleave factor	3:1
Data transfer rate (K/second)	170
Automatic head parking	No

Expansion Slots	
Total adapter slots	3
Number of long and short slots	3/0
Number of 8-/16-/32-bit slots	3/0/0
Available slots	3

Keyboard Specifications	
101-key Enhanced Keyboard	Yes
Fast keyboard speed setting	No
Keyboard cable length	3 feet

Security Features	
Keylock:	
Locks cover	Yes
Locks keyboard	Yes
Keyboard password	No
Power-on password	No
Network server mode	No

Physical Specifications	
Footprint type	Desktop
Dimensions:	
Height	4.0 inches
Width	15.6 inches
Depth	16.0 inches
Weight:	
00x	17.5 pounds
021	21.0 pounds

Environmental Specifications	
Power-supply output	70 watts
Worldwide (110/60,220/50)	Yes
Auto-sensing/switching	Yes
Maximum current:	
90-137 VAC	1.5 amps
180-265 VAC	0.75 amps
Operating range:	
Temperature	60-90 degrees F
Relative humidity	8-80 percent
Maximum operating altitude	7,000 feet
Heat (BTUs/hour)	341
Noise (Average dB, operating, 1m)	37.5 dB
FCC classification	Class B

Table 22.8 shows the primary specifications of the different versions of PS/2 Model 30.

Table 22.8 IBM PS/2 Model 25 Model Summary						
			PLANAR MEMORY		**STANDARD** Floppy	Hard
Part Number	**CPU**	**MHz**	**Std.**	**Max.**	**Drive**	**Disk**
30						
8530-001	8086	8	640K	640K	1×720K	—
8530-002	8086	8	640K	640K	2×720K	—
8530-021	8086	8	640K	640K	1×720K	20M

All models of the 8530 have been discontinued and are no longer available from IBM.

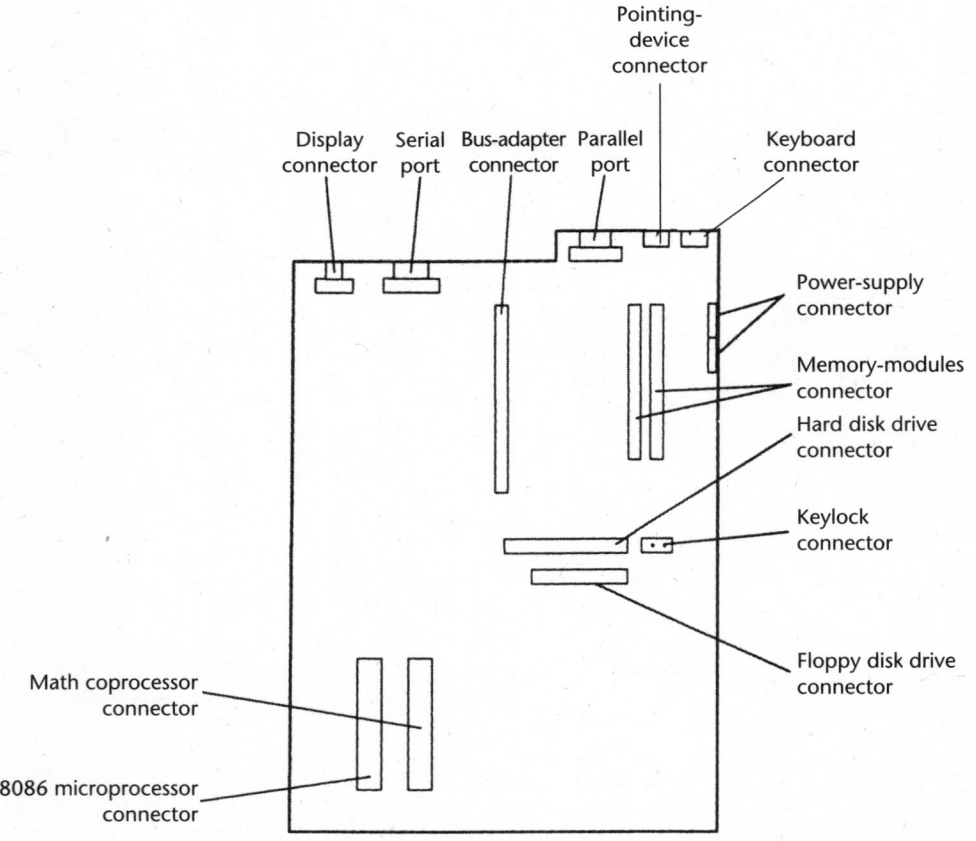

Fig. 22.9
PS/2 Model 30 (8530-001) system board.

Figures 22.9 and 22.10 show the system boards for the PS/2 Model 30 (8530-001) and the standard PS/2 Model 30.

Bus Type	Total Available Slots	STANDARD		Date Introduced	Date Withdrawn
		Video	Keyboard		
ISA/8	3/3	MCGA	Enh	04/04/89	12/27/90
ISA/8	3/3	MCGA	Enh	04/02/87	07/05/89
ISA/8	3/3	MCGA	Enh	04/02/87	12/27/90

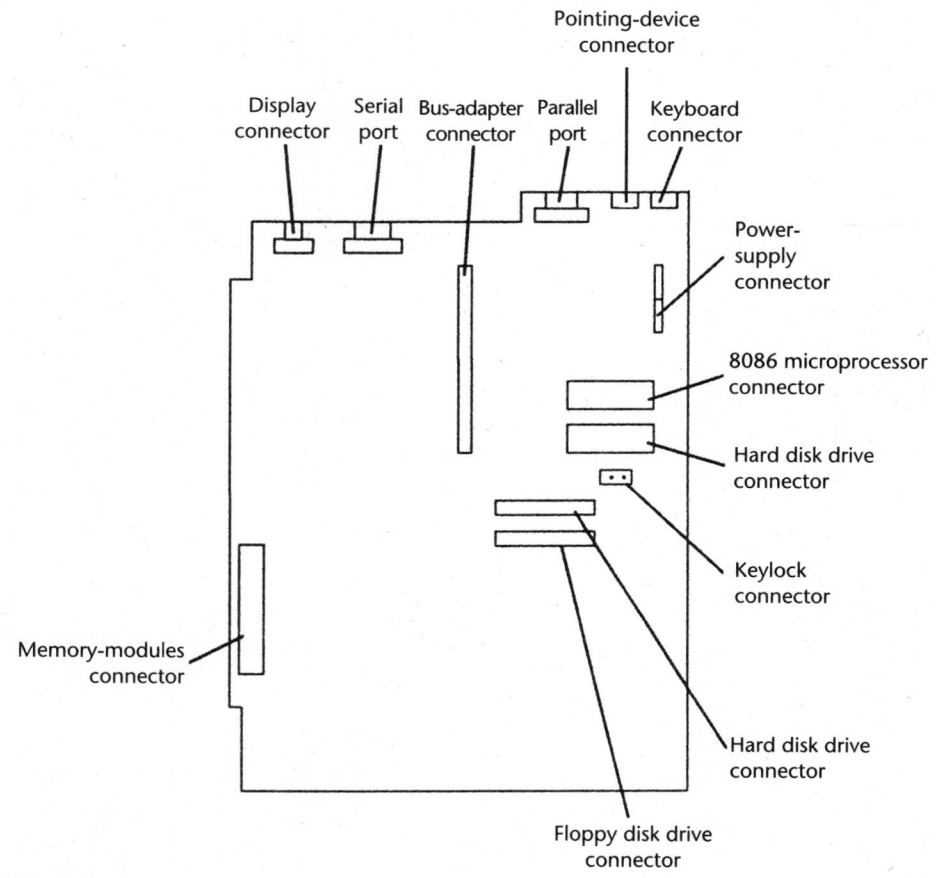

Fig. 22.10
Standard PS/2 Model 30 system board.

PS/2 Model 25 286

Introduced on May 10, 1990, the PS/2 Model 25 286 (8525) unit is an enhanced version of the PS/2 Model 25. It is a standard Model 25 with an upgraded motherboard that makes it an AT-type system. This system features an 80286 microprocessor, expanded system-board memory (1M to 4M), high-density 3 1/2-inch (1.44M) floppy disk drives, and an integrated 12-inch VGA color monitor. The Model 25 286 utilizes the 80286 processor operating at 10 MHz with 1 wait state to system memory and has the following integrated functions: parallel port, serial port, pointing device port, keyboard port, an audio earphone connector, 1.44M floppy disk drive support, and VGA graphics. The Model 25 286 is offered in floppy drive only and 30M hard disk models with the IBM Enhanced (101-key) or Space-Saving (84-key) Keyboard. It features 1M standard memory, with a maximum of 4M on the system board. The Model 25 286 is physically very similar to the Model 25 (see figures 22.1 through 22.4 earlier in this chapter, which show exterior and interior views of the Model 25).

The Model 25 286 differs significantly from the Model 25: It is a full AT-class system, and the original Model 25 is a PC-class system. They differ in virtually every way except appearance. (Refer to figures 22.1 through 22.4.) The Model 25 286 has a high-density floppy disk controller and a full VGA adapter integrated on the system board. An integrated color display is the only one offered. System memory can be increased to 4M on the system board and can address a maximum of 16M, providing functionality with DOS and Windows. As an AT-class system, the Model 25 286 is capable of running OS/2; the Model 25 is not. The Model 25 286 makes a perfect LAN workstation, although it is not sold preconfigured as one.

Like the Model 25, the Model 25 286 is compatible with the IBM AT at the BIOS interface level (although the BIOS is not identical) and at most hardware interfaces. Because many features are integrated on the motherboard in this system, many cards—graphics adapters, some disk controllers, and others—do not work with this system, and memory adapters that are not flexible in setting the starting memory address might not work either.

The motherboard in this system is identical to that of the Model 30 286. The BIOS is the same as the Model 30 286 as well, at least for the later versions.

The versions of this PS/2 model differ in type of keyboard (Enhanced or Space-Saving) and whether a 30M hard disk is included. Hard disks are available from IBM that will fit this system in sizes from 20M through 45M, but only the 30M is installed as standard. Hard disks are available from other manufacturers as well.

Figure 22.11 shows the Model 25 286 (and also 30 286) motherboard.

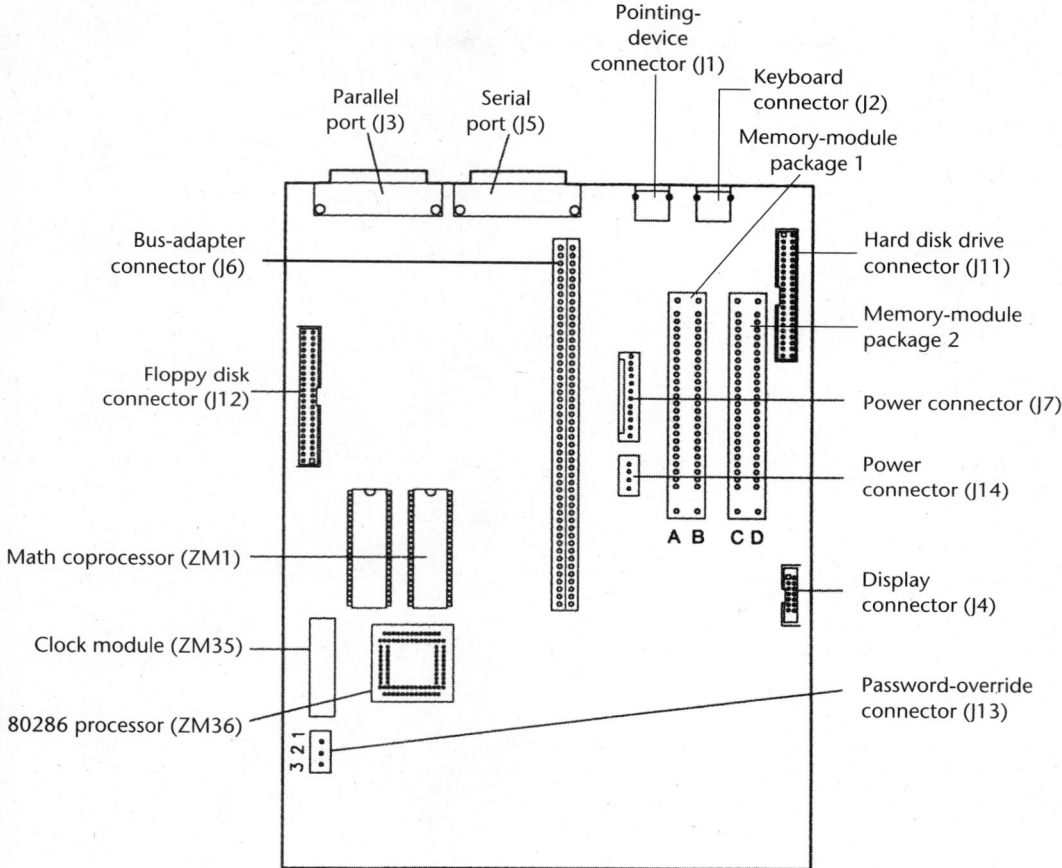

Fig. 22.11
PS/2 Model 25 286 (and 30 286) system board.

Table 22.9 lists the technical specifications for the PS/2 Model 25 286.

Table 22.9 PS/2 Model 25 286 Technical Specifications	
System Architecture	
Microprocessor	80286
Clock speed	10 MHz
Bus type	ISA (Industry Standard Architecture)
Bus width	16-bit
Interrupt levels	16
Type	Edge-triggered
Shareable	No
DMA channels	7
DMA burst mode supported	No
Bus masters supported	No
Upgradeable processor complex	No
Memory	
Standard on system board	1M
Maximum on system board	4M
Maximum total memory	16M
Memory speed and type	120ns dynamic RAM
System board memory-socket type	9-bit SIMM (single in-line memory module)
Number of memory-module sockets	4
Number available in standard configuration	2
Memory used on system board	256K/1M 9-bit SIMMs
Memory cache controller	No
Wait states:	
System board	1
Adapter	1
Standard Features	
ROM size	128K
ROM shadowing	No
Optional math coprocessor	80287
Coprocessor speed	6.67 MHz
Standard graphics	VGA (Video Graphics Array)
Built-in display	Yes
Monochrome	No
Color	(006,G06)
Dot pitch (mm)	.28
Audio earphone jack	Yes

Standard Features

RS232C serial ports	1
UART chip used	NS16450
Maximum speed	19,200 bps
Maximum number of ports supported	2
Pointing device (mouse) ports	1
Parallel printer ports	1
Bidirectional	Yes
Maximum number of ports supported	2
CMOS real-time clock (RTC)	Yes
CMOS RAM	64 bytes
Battery life	10 years
Replaceable	Yes (Dallas module)

Disk Storage

Internal disk and tape drive bays	2				
Number of 3 1/2- and 5 1/4-inch bays	2/0				
Standard floppy drives	1x1.44M				
Optional floppy drives:					
5 1/4-inch 360K	Optional				
5 1/4-inch 1.2M	No				
3 1/2-inch 720K	No				
3 1/2-inch 1.44M	Standard				
3 1/2-inch 2.88M	No				
Hard disk controller included	IDE connector on system board				
IDE hard disks available	20/30/45M				
Drive form factor	3 1/2-inch				
Drive interface	IDE				
Drive capacity	20M	20M	30M	30M	45M
Average access rate (ms)	80	27	27	19	32
Encoding scheme	MFM	RLL	RLL	RLL	RLL
BIOS drive type number	26	34	33	35	37
Cylinders	612	775	614	921	580
Heads	4	2	4	2	6
Sectors per track	17	27	25	33	26
Rotational speed (RPM)	3600	3600	3600	3600	3600
Interleave factor	2:1	3:1	3:1	4:1	3:1
Data transfer rate (K/second)	255	270	250	248	260
Automatic head parking	No	No	No	Yes	Yes

(continues)

Table 22.9 Continued

Expansion Slots

Total adapter slots	2
Number of long and short slots	1/1
Number of 8-/16-/32-bit slots	0/2/0
Available slots	2

Keyboard Specifications

101-key Enhanced Keyboard	Yes (Gxx)
84-key Space-Saving Keyboard	Yes (0xx)
Fast keyboard speed setting	Yes
Keyboard cable length:	
Space-Saving Keyboard	5 feet
Enhanced Keyboard	6 feet

Security Features

Keylock:	
Locks cover	Yes (x36)
Locks keyboard	No
Keyboard password	Yes
Power-on password	Yes
Network server mode	Yes

Physical Specifications

Footprint type	Desktop
Dimensions:	
Height	15.0 inches
Footprint width	9.5 inches
Display width	12.6 inches
Depth	14.7 inches
Weight:	
x06	35.3 lbs
x36	37.0 lbs
Carrying case	Optional

Environmental Specifications

Power-supply output	124.5 watts
Worldwide (110/60,220/50)	Yes
Auto-sensing/switching	Manual switch
Maximum current:	
90-137 VAC	3.0 amps
80-259 VAC	1.7 amps
Operating range:	
Temperature	60-90 degrees F
Relative humidity	8-80 percent
Maximum operating altitude	7,000 feet

Environmental Specifications	
Heat (BTUs/hour)	654
Noise (Average dB, operating, 1m)	51 dB
FCC classification	Class B

PS/2 Model 30 286

The IBM PS/2 Model 30 286 (8530), introduced September 13, 1988, was the first PS/2 system with the full 16-bit ISA slot design in the original IBM AT and IBM XT 286 systems. Some people considered the Model 30 286 a reintroduction of the IBM AT; in slot design, it was. IBM supports both original Industry Standard Architecture (ISA) and Micro Channel Architecture (MCA). MCA-equipped PS/2 systems, however, are still (and will be for some time) IBM's primary platform. Figure 22.12 shows a front view, and figure 22.13 shows a rear view of the Model 30 286.

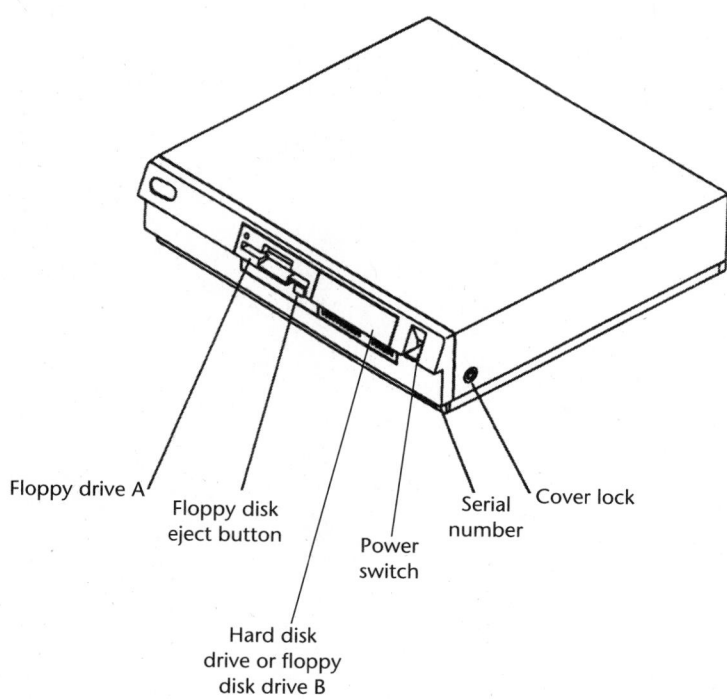

Floppy drive A

Floppy disk
eject button

Power
switch

Serial
number

Cover lock

Hard disk
drive or floppy
disk drive B

Fig. 22.12
PS/2 Model 30 286.

Table 22.10 shows the primary specifications of the different versions of PS/2 Model 25 286.

Table 22.10 IBM PS/2 Model 25 286 Model Summary						
Part Number	CPU	MHz	PLANAR MEMORY Std.	Max.	STANDARD Floppy Drive	Hard Disk
25 286						
8525-006	286	10	1M	4M	1×1.44M	—
8525-G06	286	10	1M	4M	2×1.44M	—
8525-036	286	10	1M	4M	2×1.44M	30M
8525-G36	286	10	1M	4M	2×1.44M	30M

Keyboards available include the Enhanced (101-key), Space-Saving (84-key), and Host-Connected (122-key). If "Any" is indicated, purchaser could choose any of the three.

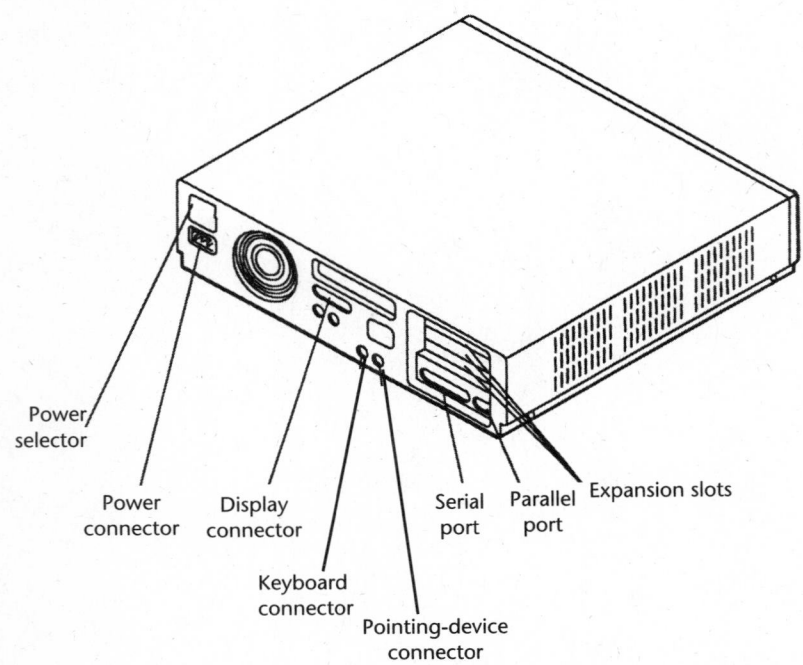

Fig. 22.13
PS/2 Model 30 286 (rear view).

Bus Type	Total Available Slots	STANDARD		Date Introduced	Date Withdrawn
		Video	Keyboard		
ISA/16	2/2	VGA	SS	05/10/90	—
ISA/16	2/2	VGA	Enh	05/10/90	—
ISA/16	2/2	VGA	SS	05/10/90	—
ISA/16	2/2	VGA	Enh	05/10/90	—

The PS/2 Model 30 286 is an 80286 version of the Model 30. Although it shares the shape and form of the Model 30, its motherboard and circuitry are very different. The Model 30 is a PC-type system, and the Model 30 286 is an AT-type system. The Model 30 286 has processor performance equal to the Model 50 and includes a 1.44M floppy disk drive and VGA graphics. The Model 30 286 uses the Intel 80286 processor and operates at 10 MHz with 1 wait state to ROM. In addition to accepting most IBM PC and XT adapter cards, the Model 30 286 accepts most AT adapter cards. Figure 22.14 shows an interior view of the Model 30 286.

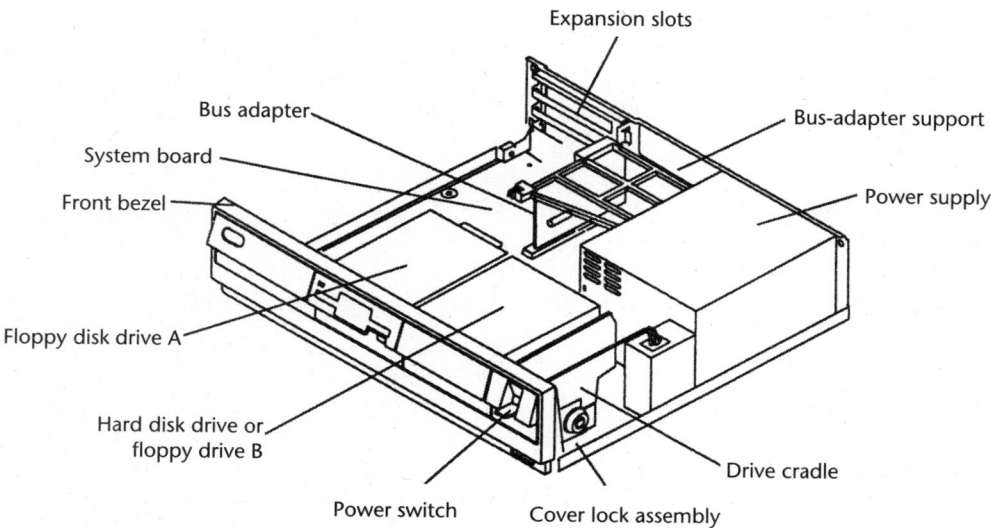

Fig. 22.14
PS/2 Model 30286 (interior view).

Think of the Model 30 286 as equal to the Model 50, except that it uses ISA slots rather than MCA slots. The Model 30 286 is very similar to the Model 25 286. In fact, the motherboards in the two systems are identical. The Models 25 286 and 30 286 can be considered identical systems in hardware and BIOS; they differ only in physical shape and form.

The PS/2 Model 30 286 includes these standard features:

- Greatly improved performance over the XT, the AT, and 8086-based versions of the Model 25 and Model 30

- 10 MHz 80286 16-bit microprocessor, 1 wait state

- Optional 80287 coprocessor

- 16-bit ISA bus for adapters

- Three full-sized slots

- 1M random-access memory (RAM) standard

- Memory expansion to 4M on the system board

- 1.44M, 3 1/2-inch floppy disk drive

- Universal, automatic voltage-sensing power supply

- Keyboard port, serial/asynchronous port, parallel port, mouse port, and Video Graphics Array (VGA) port

- IBM Enhanced Keyboard

- Switchless installation and configuration

Several versions of the Model 30 286 have been available. The Model E01 (8530-E01) was a single floppy disk drive version of the Model 30 286 (without a hard disk drive). An optional 3 1/2-inch 20M hard disk drive (27F4969) was available for this model. The second model (8530-E21) included the 20M drive as a standard feature. Otherwise, these models were identical. The 30 286 was then available with 30M and 45M IDE (Integrated Drive Electronics) hard disk drives that plug into a modified slot connector on the motherboard. As of May 4, 1992, even these newer models have been discontinued. Currently, all 8530 systems have been withdrawn from marketing by IBM.

The PS/2 Model 30 286 is compatible with the PC, XT, and AT at the BIOS level and at most hardware interfaces. Because many components are included on the motherboard, however, many boards that could be used in the standard PC, XT, or AT systems do not work in the Model 30 286, even though it has the ISA-style slots. Boards not likely to work include graphics adapters, some memory adapters (especially those not flexible in setting the starting memory address), and some other cards. Because of the built-in VGA, an analog display is required.

Available versions of this model differ only in the standard hard disk supplied with the unit. Available models offer no hard drive, a 30M hard drive, or a 45M hard drive. Hard disks for installation after you purchase the system are available from other manufacturers.

Table 22.11 lists the technical specifications for the PS/2 Model 30 286.

Table 22.11   PS/2 Model 30 286 Technical Specifications

System Architecture

Microprocessor	80286
Clock speed	10 MHz
Bus type	ISA (Industry Standard Architecture)
Bus width	16-bit
Interrupt levels	16
Type	Edge-triggered
Shareable	No
DMA channels	7
DMA burst mode supported	No
Bus masters supported	No
Upgradeable processor complex	No

Memory

Standard on system board	1M
Maximum on system board	4M
Maximum total memory	16M
Memory speed (ns) and type	120ns dynamic RAM
System board memory-socket type	9-bit SIMM (single in-line memory module)
Number of memory module sockets	4
Number available in standard configuration	2
Memory used on system board	256K/1M 9-bit SIMMs
Memory cache controller	No
Wait states:	
System board	1
Adapter	1

Standard Features

ROM size	128K
ROM shadowing	No
Optional math coprocessor	80287
Coprocessor speed	6.67 MHz
Standard graphics	VGA (Video Graphics Array)
RS232C serial ports	1
UART chip used	NS16450
Maximum speed (bits/second)	19,200 bps
Maximum number of ports	2

(continues)

Table 22.11   Continued

Standard Features

Pointing device (mouse) ports	1
Parallel printer ports	1
Bidirectional	Yes
Maximum number of ports	2
CMOS real-time clock (RTC)	Yes
CMOS RAM	64 bytes
Battery life	10 years
Replaceable	Yes (Dallas module)

Disk Storage

Internal disk and tape drive bays	2				
Number of 3 1/2- and 5 1/4-inch bays	2/0				
Standard floppy drives	1×1.44M				
Optional floppy drives:					
5 1/4-inch 360K	Optional				
5 1/4-inch 1.2M	No				
3 1/2-inch 720K	No				
3 1/2-inch 1.44M	Standard				
3 1/2-inch 2.88M	No				
Hard disk controller included	IDE connector on system board				
IDE hard disks available	20/30/45M				
Drive form factor	3 1/2-inch				
Drive interface	IDE				
Drive capacity	20M	20M	30M	30M	45M
Average access rate (ms)	80	27	27	19	32
Encoding scheme	MFM	RLL	RLL	RLL	RLL
BIOS drive type number	26	34	33	35	37
Cylinders	612	775	614	921	580
Heads	4	2	4	2	6
Sectors per track	17	27	25	33	26
Rotational speed (RPM)	3600	3600	3600	3600	3600
Interleave factor	2:1	3:1	3:1	4:1	3:1
Data transfer rate (K/second)	255	270	250	248	260
Automatic head parking	No	No	No	Yes	Yes

Expansion Slots

Total adapter slots	3
Number of long and short slots	3/0
Number of 8-/16-/32-bit slots	0/3/0
Available slots	3

Keyboard Specifications

101-key Enhanced Keyboard	Yes
Fast keyboard speed setting	Yes
Keyboard cable length	6 feet

Security Features

Keylock:	
Locks cover	Yes
Locks keyboard	No
Keyboard password	Yes
Power-on password	Yes
Network server mode	Yes

Physical Specifications

Footprint type	Desktop
Dimensions:	
Height	4.0 inches
Width	16.0 inches
Depth	15.6 inches
Weight	17.0 lbs (E01)
	19.0 lbs

Environmental Specifications

Power-supply output	90 watts
Worldwide (110/60, 220/50)	Yes
Auto-sensing/switching	Manual switch
Maximum current:	
90-137 VAC	2.5 amps
180-265 VAC	1.3 amps
Operating range:	
Temperature	60-90 degrees F
Relative humidity	8-80 percent
Maximum operating altitude	7,000 feet
Heat (BTUs/hour)	438
Noise (Average dB, operating, 1m)	46 dB
FCC classification	Class B

Table 22.12 shows the primary specifications of the various versions of PS/2 Model 30 286.

Table 22.12 IBM PS/2 Model 30 286 Model Summary						
			PLANAR MEMORY		**STANDARD**	
Part Number	**CPU**	**MHz**	**Std.**	**Max.**	**Floppy Drive**	**Hard Disk**
25 286						
8530-E01	286	10	1M	4M	1×1.44M	—
8530-E21	286	10	1M	4M	2×1.44M	20M
8530-E31	286	10	1M	4M	2×1.44M	30M
8530-E41	286	10	1M	4M	2×1.44M	40M

Note: *All the 30 286 models have been withdrawn and no longer are available from IBM.*

PS/2 Model 35 SX

The PS/2 Model 35 SX (8535), introduced June 11, 1991, uses the 80386SX microprocessor operating at 20 MHz with 0 to 2 wait states and has the following integrated functions: parallel port, serial port, pointing device port, video graphics array (VGA 16-bit) port, keyboard port, 1.44M (million bytes) floppy disk drive support, math coprocessor socket, and three single in-line memory module (SIMM) sockets (two available for memory expansion). The PS/2 Model 35 SX is a three-slot, two-bay system; it is offered in floppy disk drive only (040) and a 40M hard disk model (043). All models come with 2M memory (expandable to 16M) standard on the system board. This system uses the 16-bit ISA for expansion, and its slots are full length. IBM's first 386 system using the ISA bus shows that, although the company's emphasis is on the MCA bus, it continues to support and enhance its offerings in the ISA realm.

All versions of the PS/2 Model 35 are compatible with the IBM AT at the BIOS interface level (although the BIOS is not identical) and at most hardware interfaces. This system also uses the same motherboard as the PS/2 Model 40 SX. The only difference is that the bus adapter in the Model 40 supports five slots rather than three, as in the Model 35. Because many features are already integrated in these systems, many standard ISA adapters such as graphics, memory, disk controller, and other cards might not operate.

The PS/2 Floor Stand option is available if you want to install the system unit vertically.

LAN Version. A special version of the Model 35, the Model 35 LS, provides a local area network (LAN) workstation solution and is available with all the standard features of the Model 35 SX, with this exception: No disk devices of any kind are installed in this medialess system; rather, a 16/4 Token-Ring adapter or IBM EtherNet adapter with Remote Initial Program Load (RIPL) occupies one of the three adapter slots. The 35 LS-24X includes an IBM 16/4 Token-Ring adapter as a standard feature; the 35 LS-14X model includes an IBM EtherNet adapter as a standard feature.

Bus Type	Total Available Slots	STANDARD		Date Introduced	Date Withdrawn
		Video	Keyboard		
ISA/16	3/3	VGA	Enh	09/13/87	05/05/92
ISA/16	3/3	VGA	Enh	09/13/88	09/11/91
ISA/16	3/3	VGA	Enh	09/26/89	01/17/92
ISA/16	3/3	VGA	Enh	04/23/91	05/04/92

With the RIPL ROM, the system can "boot" DOS or OS/2 from the LAN server machine. The diskless Model 35 LS is fully upgradeable to the Model 35 SX configurations.

The Models 35 SX and LS both have a universal power supply with an autosense circuit. No manual switching is required. The Models 35 SX and LS, therefore, can easily be used worldwide.

Standard versions of Model 35 SX differ only in the choice of whether to have a hard disk; the LS version is completely diskless. In other respects, the models are similar.

Keyboard Options. Both the PS/2 Model 35 SX and 35 LS support the IBM Enhanced Keyboard (101/102 keys), Space-Saving Keyboard (84/85 keys), and the IBM Host-Connected Keyboard (122 keys). The Host-Connected Keyboard is similar to the 3270 keyboard offered with 3270 IBM PC and IBM AT systems. This keyboard is similar in design to that of a 3270 terminal keyboard and offers keys dedicated to 3270 functions. The Host-Connected Keyboard is supported by the BIOS in this system and cannot be retro-fitted to PS/2 systems that do not have the proper BIOS support. When you purchase a Model 35 SX or LS, you must choose any one of these three keyboards.

Floppy Drive Support. The Model 35 SX has BIOS support for the new 2.88M floppy drive. Although this drive does not come standard in this system, one is available from IBM. The Model 35 SX is one of the first systems to support this drive.

One very interesting feature of the Model 35 SX is its selectable-boot feature. As part of the system CMOS setup program, the user can specify which drive should be booted from and in which order the boot process should try each drive selected. The system supports an internally mounted 5 1/4-inch 1.2M drive in addition to the standard 3 1/2-inch 1.44M drive, and you can specify either drive as the primary boot device. You also can specify booting only from the hard disk, or even from a network file server (RIPL). This setup offers flexibility not found on many other systems.

The Model 35 SX system unit has two drive bays that can accommodate 5 1/4-inch or 3 1/2-inch devices, unlike many other PS/2 systems. Most older PS/2 systems cannot fit 5 1/4-inch devices internally.

Table 22.13 gives the specifications for the PS/2 model 35 SX.

Table 22.13   PS/2 Model 35 SX Technical Specifications

System Architecture

Microprocessor	80386SX
Clock speed	20 MHz
Bus type	ISA (Industry Standard Architecture)
Bus width	16-bit
Interrupt levels	16
Type	Edge-triggered
Shareable	No
DMA channels	7
DMA burst mode supported	No
Bus masters supported	No
Upgradeable processor complex	No

Memory

Standard on system board	2M
Maximum on system board	16M
Maximum total memory	16M
Memory speed and type	85ns dynamic RAM
System-board memory socket type	36-bit SIMM (single in-line memory module)
Number of memory-module sockets	3
Number available in standard configuration	2
Memory used on system board	1M/2M/4M/8M 36-bit SIMMs
Memory cache controller	No
Wait states:	
System board	0-2
Adapter	1

Standard Features

ROM size	128K
ROM shadowing	Yes
Optional math coprocessor	80387SX
Coprocessor speed	20 MHz
Standard graphics	VGA (Video Graphics Array)
8-/16-/32-bit controller	16-bit
Bus master	No
Video RAM (VRAM)	256K
RS232C serial ports	1
UART chip used	NS16450
Maximum speed (bits/second)	19,200 bps
Maximum number of ports	2

Standard Features

Pointing device (mouse) ports	1
Parallel printer ports	1
Bidirectional	Yes
Maximum number of ports	2
CMOS real-time clock (RTC)	Yes
CMOS RAM	64 bytes
CMOS battery life	10 years
Replaceable battery	Yes (Dallas module)

Disk Storage

Internal disk and tape drive bays	2	
Number of 3 1/2- and 5 1/4-inch bays	0/2	
Selectable boot drive	Yes	
Bootable drives	All physical drives	
Standard floppy drives	1×1.44M	
None (24X)		
Optional floppy drives:		
5 1/4-inch 360K	Optional	
5 1/4-inch 1.2M	Optional	
3 1/2-inch 720K	No	
3 1/2-inch 1.44M	Standard	
3 1/2-inch 2.88M	Optional	
Hard disk controller included	IDE connector on system board	
IDE hard drives available	40/80M	
Drive form factor	3 1/2-inch	
Drive interface	IDE	
Drive capacity	40M	80M
Average access rate (ms)	17	17
Read-ahead cache	32K	32K
Encoding scheme	RLL	RLL
Cylinders	1038	1021
Heads	2	4
Sectors per track	39	39
Rotational speed (RPM)	3600	3600
Interleave factor	1:1	1:1
Data transfer rate (K/second)	1170	1170
Automatic head parking	Yes	Yes

Expansion Slots

Total adapter slots	3
Number of long and short slots	3/0
Number of 8-/16-/32-bit slots	0/3/0
Available slots	3

(continues)

Table 22.13   Continued

Keyboard Specifications

Keyboard choices	122-key Host-Connected Keyboard 101-key Enhanced Keyboard 84-key Space-Saving Keyboard
Fast keyboard speed setting	Yes
Keyboard cable length	10 feet

Security Features

Keylock:	
Locks cover	Yes
Locks keyboard	No
Keyboard password	Yes
Power-on password	Yes
Network server mode	Yes

Physical Specifications

Footprint type	Desktop
Orientation	Horizontal (vertical with optional stand)
Dimensions:	
Height	4.5 inches
Width	14.2 inches
Depth	15.6 inches
Weight:	
24X	22.4 lbs
040	23.8 lbs
043	20.9 lbs

Environmental Specifications

Power-supply output	118 watts
Worldwide (110/60, 220/50)	Yes
Auto-sensing/switching	Yes
Maximum current:	
90-137 VAC	3.5 amps
180-265 VAC	1.75 amps
Operating range:	
Temperature	50-95 degrees F
Relative humidity	8-80 percent
Maximum operating altitude	7,000 feet
Heat (BTUs/hour):	
24X	123
040	130
043	144
FCC classification	Class B

PS/2 Model 40 SX

The PS/2 Model 40 SX (8540), introduced June 11, 1991, uses the 80386SX microprocessor operating at 20 MHz with 0 to 2 wait states to system memory. The Model 40 SX ships with 2M system board memory (expandable to 16M on planar), 3 1/2-inch drive options, and 16-bit VGA. The system also provides five full-size, customer-accessible, 8-/16-bit expansion card slots. The 80386SX microprocessor PS/2 Model 40 SX has the following integrated functions: parallel port, serial port, pointing device port, VGA port, keyboard port, 1.44M floppy disk drive support, math coprocessor socket, and three single in-line memory module (SIMM) sockets (two available for memory expansion).

The Model 40 SX has a universal power supply with an autosense circuit. No manual switching is required. Therefore, the Model 40 SX can easily be used worldwide.

The PS/2 Model 40 SX is compatible with the IBM AT at the BIOS interface level (although the BIOS is not identical) and at most hardware interfaces. This system also uses the same motherboard as the PS/2 Model 35 SX. The only difference is that the bus adapter in the Model 40 supports five slots rather than three, as in the Model 35. Because many features are already integrated in these systems, many standard ISA adapters such as graphics, memory, disk controller, and other cards might not operate.

The standard versions of the Model 40 SX differ only by whether and what kind of hard disk drive they provide: a floppy-drive-only model (8540-040), a 40M hard disk model (8540-043), or an 80M hard disk model (8540-045). In other respects the versions are similar.

The PS/2 Floor Stand option is available if you want to install the system unit vertically.

Keyboard Options. The PS/2 Model 40 SX supports the IBM Enhanced Keyboard (101/102 keys), Space-Saving Keyboard (84/85 keys), and the IBM Host-Connected Keyboard (122 keys). The Host-Connected Keyboard is similar to the 3270 keyboard offered with 3270 IBM PC and IBM AT systems. This keyboard is similar in design to a 3270 terminal keyboard and offers keys dedicated to 3270 functions. The Host-Connected Keyboard is supported by the BIOS in this system and cannot be retrofitted to PS/2 systems that do not have the proper BIOS support.

When you purchase a Model 40 SX, you can choose any of these three keyboards. The keyboard can be specified only in new equipment orders and cannot be ordered separately for on-order or installed equipment.

Floppy Drive Support. The Model 40 SX has BIOS support for the new 2.88M floppy drive. Although this drive does not come standard in this system, one is available from IBM. The Model 40 SX is one of the first systems to support this drive.

Table 22.14 shows the primary specifications of the various versions of PS2/ Model 35 SX and LS.

Table 22.14   IBM PS/2 Model 35 SX/LS Model Summary

Part Number	CPU	MHz	PLANAR MEMORY Std.	Max.	STANDARD Floppy Drive	Hard Disk
35 SX						
8535-040	386SX	20	2M	16M	1×1.44M	—
8535-043	386SX	20	2M	16M	2×1.44M	40M
35 LS						
8535-14X	386SX	20	2M	16M	—	—
8535-24X	386SX	20	2M	16M	—	—

Keyboards available include the Enhanced (101-key), Space-Saving (84-key), and Host-Connected (122-key). If "Any" is indicated, purchaser could choose any of the three.

One very interesting feature of the Model 40 SX is its selectable-boot feature. As part of the system CMOS setup program, you can specify from which drive it should be booted and in which order the boot process should try each drive selected. The system supports an internally mounted 5 1/4-inch 1.2M drive in addition to the standard 3 1/2-inch 1.44M drive; you can specify either drive as the primary boot device. You also can specify booting only from the hard disk, or even from a network file server (RIPL). This setup offers flexibility not found on many other systems.

The Model 40 SX has two or three available drive bays (depending on whether the model has a hard disk) and supports up to two hard disks and a variety of optional floppy disk devices, including a 5 1/4-inch internally mounted 1.2M floppy drive or a 2.88M 3 1/2-inch floppy drive. Because of a selectable boot feature, you can boot the system from any installed drive.

Table 22.15 lists the technical specifications for the PS/2 model 40 SX.

Table 22.15   PS/2 Model 40 SX Technical Specifications

System Architecture

Microprocessor	80386SX
Clock speed	20 MHz
Bus type	ISA (Industry Standard Architecture)
Bus width	16-bit
Interrupt levels	16
Type	Edge-triggered
Shareable	No
DMA channels	7
DMA burst mode supported	No
Bus masters supported	No
Upgradeable processor complex	No

Bus Type	Total Available Slots	STANDARD		Date Introduced	Date Withdrawn
		Video	Keyboard		
ISA/16	3/3	VGA	Any	06/11/91	—
ISA/16	3/3	VGA	Any	06/11/91	—
ISA/16	3/3	VGA	Any	10/17/91	—
ISA/16	3/3	VGA	Any	06/11/91	—

Memory

Standard on system board	2M
Maximum on system board	16M
Maximum total memory	16M
Memory speed and type	85ns dynamic RAM
System board memory-socket type	36-bit SIMM (single in-line memory module)
Number of memory-module sockets	3
Number available in standard configuration	2
Memory used on system board	1M/2M/4M/8M 36-bit SIMMs
Memory cache controller	No
Wait states:	
System board	0-2
Adapter	1

Standard Features

ROM size	128K
ROM shadowing	Yes
Optional math coprocessor	80387SX
Coprocessor speed	20 MHz
Standard graphics	VGA (Video Graphics Array)
8-/16-/32-bit controller	16-bit
Bus master	No
Video RAM (VRAM)	256K
RS232C serial ports	1
UART chip used	NS16450
Maximum speed (bits per second)	19,200 bps
Maximum number of ports	2

(continues)

Table 22.15   Continued

Standard Features

Pointing device (mouse) ports	1
Parallel printer ports	1
Bidirectional	Yes
Maximum number of ports	2
CMOS real-time clock (RTC)	Yes
CMOS RAM	64 bytes
CMOS battery life	10 years
Replaceable	Yes (Dallas module)

Disk Storage

Internal disk and tape drive bays	4	
Number of 3 1/2- and 5 1/4-inch bays	1/3	
Selectable boot drive	Yes	
Bootable drives	All physical drives	
Standard floppy drives	1×1.44M	
Optional floppy drives:		
5 1/4-inch 360K	Optional	
5 1/4-inch 1.2M	Optional	
3 1/2-inch 720K	No	
3 1/2-inch 1.44M	Standard	
3 1/2-inch 2.88M	Optional	
Hard disk controller included	IDE connector on system board	
IDE hard drives available	40/80M	
Drive form factor	3 1/2-inch	
Drive interface	IDE	
Drive capacity	40M	80M
Average access rate (ms)	17	17
Read-ahead cache	32K	32K
Encoding scheme	RLL	RLL
Cylinders	1038	1021
Heads	2	4
Sectors per track	39	39
Rotational speed (RPM)	3600	3600
Interleave factor	1:1	1:1
Data transfer rate (K/second)	1170	1170
Automatic head parking	Yes	Yes

Expansion Slots

Total adapter slots	5
Number of long and short slots	5/0
Number of 8-/16-/32-bit slots	0/5/0
Available slots	5

Keyboard Specifications

Keyboard choices	122-key Host-Connected Keyboard 101-key Enhanced Keyboard 84-key Space-Saving Keyboard
Fast keyboard speed setting	Yes
Keyboard cable length	10 feet

Security Features

Keylock:
    Locks cover
    Locks keyboard
	
	Yes
	No

Keyboard password	Yes
Power-on password Network server mode	Yes Yes

Physical Specifications

Footprint type	Desktop
Orientation	Horizontal/vertical (stand included)

Dimensions:
    Height
    Width
    Depth
	
	6.7 inches
	17.3 inches
	15.5 inches

Weight:	26.3 lbs (040) 27.8 lbs

Environmental Specifications

Power-supply output
    Worldwide (110/60, 220/50)
    Auto-sensing/switching
	197 watts
	Yes
	Manual switch

Maximum current:
    90-137 VAC
    180-265 VAC
	
	6.0 amps
	3.0 amps

Operating range:
    Temperature
    Relative humidity
    Maximum operating altitude
	
	50-95 degrees F
	8-80 percent
	7,000 feet

Heat (BTUs/hour)	190
FCC classification	Class B

Table 22.16 shows the primary specifications of the various versions of PS/2 Model 40 SX.

Table 22.16	IBM PS/2 Model 40 SX Model Summary					
			PLANAR MEMORY		**STANDARD**	
Part Number	**CPU**	**MHz**	**Std.**	**Max.**	**Floppy Drive**	**Hard Disk**
40 SX						
8540-040	386SX	20	2M	16M	1×1.44M	—
8540-043	386SX	20	2M	16M	1×1.44M	40M
8540-045	386SX	20	2M	16M	1×1.44M	80M

Keyboards available include the Enhanced (101-key), Space-Saving (84-key), and Host-Connected (122-key). If "Any" is indicated, the purchaser could choose any of the three.

PS/2 Model L40 SX

The PS/2 Model L40 SX, announced March 26, 1991, is a small, lightweight, battery-operated (AC/DC) portable laptop system. The PS/2 Model L40 SX is designed for people who want a high-function portable that is easy to carry and has the speed and capacity to support advanced applications. Standard features include a 20 MHz 80386SX processor; 2M of 80ns memory (expandable to 18M); 60M 2 1/2-inch hard disk; 3 1/2-inch 1.44M floppy disk drive; 10mm-thick, cold fluorescent, black-and-white LCD with VGA resolution; 84/85 key keyboard; and serial, parallel, keypad/mouse, VGA, and external expansion I/O ports for attaching external devices. In addition, each system includes an external 17-key numeric keypad, an AC adapter, a rechargeable battery pack, and a carrying case. Options for the PS/2 Model L40 SX include a one-slot expansion chassis, a data/fax modem (for the U.S. and Canada); a second serial adapter; a Trackpoint pointing device; 2M, 4M, or 8M memory upgrades; a quick charger; and a car-battery adapter.

The PS/2 Model L40 SX physical package is based on a clamshell design. It fits in most attaché cases and weighs 7.7 pounds, including the rechargeable battery pack. The PS/2 Model L40 SX features the familiar IBM keyboard size and layout; 80386SX architecture; large, easy-to-read display; high-capacity hard disk; and efficient battery-power management, while maintaining the light weight of a notebook portable. Compared to the IBM PS/2 Model P70, the PS/2 Model L40 SX adds battery operation, clamshell design, black-on-white LCD, and a smaller, lighter package.

System Expansion and Restrictions. The Model L40 SX is designed to be compatible with the IBM AT at the BIOS interface level and at most hardware interfaces, and the system is very expandable. Many I/O connections are provided as standard. An external numeric keypad, included with the unit, plugs into the standard mouse port. The numeric keypad has a mouse port to enable numeric keypad and mouse connections to operate concurrently. The L40 has a standard serial port, parallel port, VGA display port, and a special external expansion port reserved for an expansion chassis or base station called the Communications Cartridge I.

Bus Type	Total Available Slots	STANDARD		Date Introduced	Date Withdrawn
		Video	Keyboard		
ISA/16	5/5	VGA	Any	06/11/91	12/21/92
ISA/16	5/5	VGA	Any	06/11/91	12/21/92
ISA/16	5/5	VGA	Any	06/11/91	12/21/92

The PS/2 Communications Cartridge I is a one-slot expansion unit that you use with the Model L40 SX. The unit contains one half-size card slot especially designed to support Token-Ring, 3270, or 5250 communications adapter cards. Although the Communications Cartridge I was designed primarily for these communications adapters, other types of adapters should also work, but are technically not supported by IBM.

The expansion of the system has some limitations. Unless you purchase the Communications Cartridge I expansion chassis, for example, slots are available for attaching adapters and cards other than the specific IBM PS/2 Model L40 SX options. Also, when the VGA port is operational, the integrated LCD is not operational—a drawback when you use the system for presentations with a large-screen projector. Additionally, because the IBM PS/2 internal data/fax modem for Model L40 SX and the IBM PS/2 serial adapter for Model L40 SX use the same internal connector, only one of these options can be installed per system. Finally, external keyboards are not supported.

Power Management. The L40 boasts very efficient power management. A suspend-resume function is provided. You suspend an application by closing the clamshell and leaving the power switch on. When the clamshell is opened, the application resumes at the point at which it was suspended. During suspension, system components are automatically powered off, except for the real-time clock and application memory. The system can be set to resume at a specific time. An internal backup battery is provided to prevent disruption of the application or system when the rechargeable battery pack is being changed.

To reduce the frequency of recharging the batteries, trickle recharging occurs during AC operation. To conserve and prolong battery life between recharges, a switch is provided for user selection of system speed under manual or automatic control. In automatic mode, the hardware initiates low clock-speed operation during idle periods. In manual mode, the processor runs at the default clock speed set by the user when the system is configured. The clock-speed settings are 20 MHz, 10 MHz, and 5 MHz.

In an effort to conserve even more battery power, the hardware supports sleep mode. Sleep mode conserves battery power during idle times between clock cycles and keystrokes by putting system components in an idle state that results in low power usage. (Sleep mode is not operational when an external display is attached.) This function is exploited by DOS and OS/2. The L40 SX has an informative LCD display that uses international symbols that indicate operational and environmental status. These status indicators include: a battery gauge, humidity, temperature-limit indicator, modem carrier detect, Numeric Lock, Scroll Lock, speaker enabled, suspend mode, floppy disk drive in use, and hard drive in use indicators.

Environmental Protection. The system's temperature and humidity sensors do not allow the unit to operate under incorrect environmental conditions. This feature is essential considering that a laptop system may spend time in a parked car, garage, or some other environment unsuitable for computer use. Few other systems offer this kind of protection.

Imagine leaving your system in your car for a few hours in the winter. After bringing the system inside, condensation forms on the circuitry and even on the hard disk platters. If you power up the system, the circuits or the hard drive might be destroyed. The L40 intervenes and does not allow the system to operate until safe temperature and humidity exist in the system's environment.

Table 22.17 lists the technical specifications for the PS/2 model L40 SX.

Table 22.17 PS/2 Model L40 SX Technical Specifications

System Architecture	
Microprocessor	80386SX
Clock speed	20/10/5 MHz
Bus type	ISA (Industry Standard Architecture)
Bus width	16-bit
Interrupt levels	16
Type	Edge-triggered
Shareable	No
DMA channels	7
DMA burst mode supported	No
Bus masters supported	No
Upgradeable processor complex	No
Memory	
Standard on system board	2M
Maximum on system board	18M (16M + 2M EMS)
Maximum total memory	18M
Memory speed and type	80ns CMOS RAM

Memory

System board memory-socket type	36-bit CMOS SIMMs, specially keyed
Number system-board memory modules	2
Number available in standard configuration	2
Memory used on system board	2M soldered, and 2M/4M/8M 36-bit CMOS SIMMs
Memory cache controller	No
Wait states:	
System board	0-2

Standard Features

ROM size	128K
ROM shadowing	Yes
Optional math coprocessor	80387SX
Coprocessor speed	20 MHz
Standard graphics	VGA (Video Graphics Array)
8-/16-/32-bit controller	8-bit
Bus master	No
Video RAM (VRAM)	256K
Built-in display	Yes
Type	LCD
Dimensions (Diag/H×W)	10 inches/6 × 5 × 8 inches
Number of grayshades	32
Backlit/sidelit	Sidelit
Supertwisted	Yes
Contrast ratio	12:1
Detachable	No
External monitor port	Yes
External display disables LCD	Yes
LCD indicators	Yes
RS232C serial ports	1
UART chip used	NS16450
Maximum speed (bits/second)	19,200 bps
Maximum number of ports supported	2
Internal modem	Optional
Hayes-compatible	Yes
Asynchronous/synchronous	Yes/Yes
FAX capable	Yes
Group III compatible	Yes
FAX software included	Yes
Send/receive FAX	Yes/Yes
Maximum speed (bps):	
Data	2,400 bps
FAX	9,600 bps
Pointing device (mouse) ports	1

(continues)

Table 22.17   Continued

Standard Features

Parallel printer ports	1
Bidirectional	Yes
Maximum number of ports supported	1
CMOS real-time clock (RTC)	Yes
CMOS RAM	64 bytes
CMOS battery life	5 years
Replaceable	Yes

Disk Storage

Internal disk and tape drive bays	2
Number of 3 1/2- and 5 1/4-inch bays	1/0
Standard floppy drives	1×1.44M
Hard disk controller included	IDE connector on system board
IDE hard disks available	60M
Drive form factor	2 inches
Drive interface	IDE
Average access rate (ms)	19
Encoding scheme	RLL
Cylinders	822
Heads	4
Sectors per track	38
Rotational speed (RPM)	3600
Interleave factor	1:1
Data transfer rate (K/second)	1140
Automatic head parking	Yes

Expansion Slots

Total adapter slots	0
Available slots	0

Keyboard Specifications

101-key Enhanced Keyboard	Yes (with external keypad)
84-key keyboard	Yes
Fast keyboard speed setting	Yes
Keyboard detachable	No

Security Features

Keylock:	
Locks cover	No
Locks keyboard	No
Keyboard password	Yes
Power-on password	Yes
Network server mode	Yes

Physical Specifications

Footprint type	Laptop
Dimensions:	
Height	2.1 inches
Width	12.8 inches
Depth	10.7 inches
Weight: with battery	7.7 lbs
Carrying case	Leather, included

Environmental Specifications

Power supply:	
Worldwide (110/60, 220/50)	Yes
Auto-sensing/switching	Yes
Maximum current:	
90-265 VAC	2.7 amps
Operating range:	
Temperature	41-95 degrees F
Relative humidity	5-95 percent
Maximum operating altitude	8,000 feet
Heat (BTUs/hour)	136
Noise (Average dB, operating, 1m)	32 dB
FCC classification	Class B

Miscellaneous

A/C adapter included	Yes
Quick charger	Optional
Car cigarette lighter adapter	Optional
Battery pack included	Yes
Battery charge duration	3 hours
Setup and power-management software	Yes
Speed-setting switch and software	Yes

Table 22.18 shows the primary specifications of the PS/2 Model L40 SX.

Table 22.18   IBM PS/2 Model L40 SX Model Summary

| | | | PLANAR MEMORY | | STANDARD | |
Part Number	CPU	MHz	Std.	Max.	Floppy Drive	Hard Disk
L40 SX						
8543-044	386SX	20	2M	18M	1×1.44M	60M

Table 22.19 shows accessories available from IBM for the PS/2 Model L40 SX.

Table 22.19   IBM PS/2 Model L40 SX Special Accessories

Description	Part Number	Price	Notes
Communications Cartridge I	3541001	$595	One-slot expansion chassis
Rechargeable battery pack	79F0197	130	3 hours use/up to 500 charges
Quick charger	79F0192	132	Charges in 2 1/2 hours rather than 8 hours
Car battery adapter	79F1012	165	Lighter socket runs and recharges L40
Leather carrying case	79F3981	71	Included with L40SX, black leather
Deluxe carrying case	79F0981	115	Cloth case, pockets and compartments
Airline travel hard case	79F3844	247	Plastic, padded, wheels, storage
Serial adapter for L40 SX	79F0979	119	Second serial, N/A with internal FAX or modem

PS/2 Model 50

The IBM PS/2 Model 50, which uses MCA, was introduced April 2, 1987, as an entry-level desktop system in the PS/2 family. Figure 22.15 shows a front view of the Model 50. As of July 23, 1991, all models of the 50 and 50 Z were discontinued and no longer are available from IBM.

The Model 50 features a 10 MHz 286 processor running with 0 or 1 wait state, depending on the model version, and 1M of memory on the system board. System-board memory can be expanded to 2M on Model 50 Z systems, but is limited to 1M on the standard model (8550-021). As much as 16M of additional memory can be added with memory adapter cards. The IBM Model 50 comes standard with a 1.44M, 3 1/2-inch floppy disk drive; a 20M, 30M, or 60M hard disk drive (depending on the model); a serial port; a parallel port; a mouse port; and a Video Graphics Array (VGA) port. Figure 22.16 shows the rear panel of the Model 50.

Bus Type	Total Available Slots	STANDARD		Date Introduced	Date Withdrawn
		Video	Keyboard		
ISA/16	0	VGA	SS	03/26/91	07/21/92

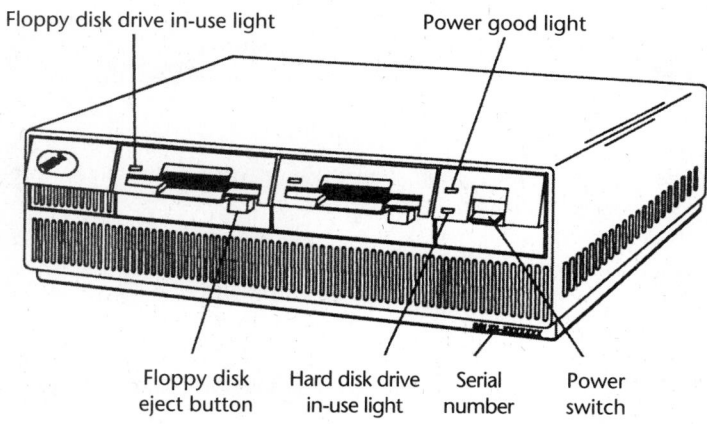

Fig. 22.15
PS/2 Model 50.

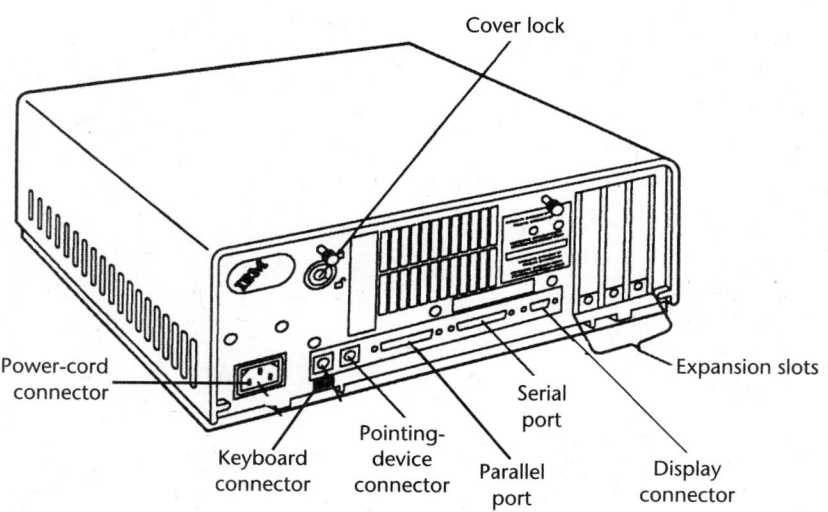

Fig. 22.16
PS/2 Model 50 rear panel view.

The 80286 10 MHz 16-bit microprocessor running with 1 wait state enables the 50-021 to perform approximately 20 percent faster than the IBM XT 286 or the IBM AT Model 339. The Model 50 Z systems (8550-031 and 8550-061) run with 0 wait states to motherboard memory access, which translates into an additional 20 percent performance increase for most computational tasks.

The Model 50 has two levels of BIOS, which total 128K: a Compatibility BIOS (CBIOS) with memory addressability of up to 1M provides support for real-mode-based application programs. An additional version of BIOS, Advanced BIOS (ABIOS), provides support for protected-mode-based multitasking operating systems and has extended memory addressability of up to 16M.

> **Note**
>
> Real mode is a mode in which the 80286 processor can emulate 8086 or 8088 processors for compatibility purposes. DOS runs under this mode. Protected mode, not found in the 8086 or 8088 processors, allows for specialized support of multitasking. Advanced multitasking operating systems such as OS/2 run under this mode.

Additional features of the system unit include four 16-bit I/O slots (with one slot occupied by the disk controller adapter); a 94-watt, automatic voltage-sensing, universal power supply; a time-and-date clock with battery backup; a socket for an 80287; an additional position for a second 3 1/2-inch floppy disk drive; and the IBM Enhanced Keyboard. Figure 22.17 shows an interior view of the Model 50.

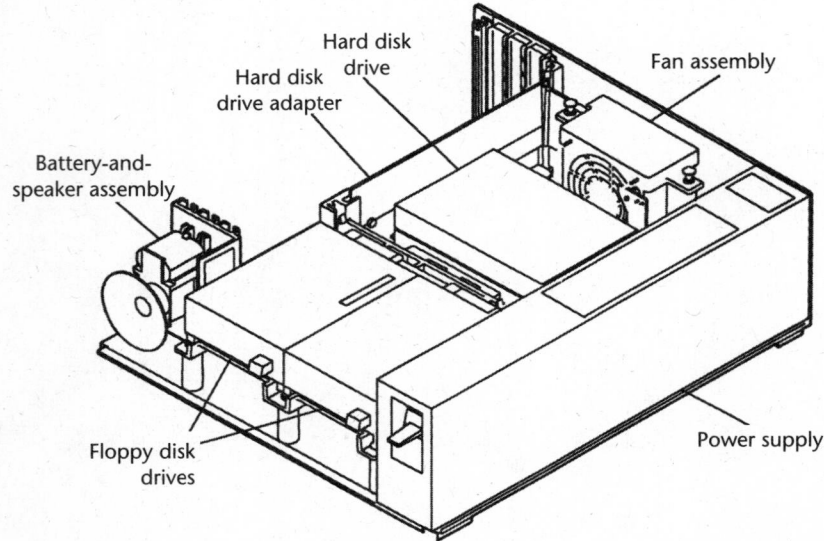

Fig. 22.17
PS/2 Model 50 interior view.

Model 50 Z. On June 2, 1988, IBM introduced the PS/2 Model 50 Z (actually the 8550-031 and the 8550-061). These models offer improved performance and greater hard disk capacity. Higher-speed (85ns) memory provides 0-wait-state processor performance and can be upgraded to 2M on the system board. The 50 Z comes with a 30M or 60M hard disk drive, which provides greater capacity and improved average access time over the standard 20M hard disk in Model 50-021.

Floppy Drive Support. The standard 1.44M drive in all the Model 50 systems can format, read, and write to either 720K (double density) or 1.44M (high density) floppy disks. In double-density mode, this drive is fully compatible with the 720K (3 1/2-inch) floppy disk drive. In high-density mode, the standard drive doubles the data capability to 1.44M and the data rate to 500K bits per second.

> **Note**
>
> Because of the capabilities and design of the disk media, you should not use the 1.44M drive to format a 720K (1M unformatted) disk as 1.44M, or to format a 1.44M (2M unformatted) disk as 720K.

A 5 1/4-inch external disk drive (360K) is available that enables you to convert or operate existing 5 1/4-inch applications. To operate, this drive requires the External Diskette Drive Adapter/A. The adapter card plugs into the connector for the 3 1/2-inch drive B. When the external drive is installed, it becomes drive B. Unfortunately, the external disk drive consumes one slot and the drive B position.

System Expansion. In response to user complaints about the storage capacity of the original 20M Model 50, IBM offers the PS/2 60M hard disk drive as an upgrade option. You can install this drive by replacing the existing 20M hard disk in the PS/2 Model 50 (8550-021) or 30M in the Model 50 Z (8550-031). No trade-in is available for the earlier drive. This drive provides 60M of storage and a faster access time of 27ms. The replacement adapter card required for the 50-021 is included.

For additional memory, IBM offers the PS/2 1-8M Memory Expansion Adapter/A and the PS/2 2-8M Memory Expansion Adapter/A—16-bit, full-length circuit cards. You can expand either card to a maximum of 8M by using optional memory kits. You can configure the adapter memory from 1M to 8M by using either the 0.5M memory module kit or the 2M memory module kit. These cards can be installed in any open expansion slot on the Model 50. The adapter is easy to set up because it contains no jumpers or hardware switches. An additional feature is an on-board ROM that contains a POST and microcode to initialize the card.

These memory cards also provide support for two different operating modes: expanded memory and extended memory. Used as expanded memory, the adapter card's memory is compatible with applications written to the LIM EMS V4.0 standard. In addition, you can use the adapter card's memory as extended memory for DOS or OS/2. By installing two adapters, each filled to 8M, a user can reach the system address limit of 16M for the Model 50.

Because of the 0 wait states on the 50 Z systems, IBM offers a special motherboard memory upgrade for only these systems. This upgrade consists of one 2M, 85ns memory kit, which you install on the system board of the 50-031 or 50-061, replacing the standard 1M of memory. This upgrade brings the system board to its maximum capacity of 2M for these models.

Table 22.20 lists the technical specifications for the PS/2 Model 50.

Table 22.20 PS/2 Model 50 Technical Specifications	
System Architecture	
Microprocessor	80286
Clock speed	10 MHz
Bus type	MCA (Micro Channel Architecture)
Bus width	16-bit
Interrupt levels	16
Type	Level-sensitive
Shareable	Yes
DMA channels	15
DMA burst mode supported	Yes
Bus masters supported	15
Upgradeable processor complex	No
Memory	
Standard on system board	1M
Maximum on system board	2M
	1M (021)
Maximum total memory	16M
Memory speed and type	85ns dynamic RAM
	150ns dynamic RAM (021)
System board memory-socket type	36-bit SIMM (single in-line memory module)
	9-bit SIMM (021)
Number of memory-module sockets	1
	2 (021)
Number available in standard configuration	0
Memory used on system board	1M/2M 36-bit SIMM
	512K 9-bit SIMMs (021)
Memory cache controller	No
Wait states:	
System board	0
	1 (021)
Adapter	0-1
Standard Features	
ROM size	128K
ROM shadowing	No
Optional math coprocessor	80287
Coprocessor speed	10 MHz

Standard Features

Standard graphics	VGA (Video Graphics Array)
8-/16-/32-bit controller	8-bit
Bus master	No
Video RAM (VRAM)	256K
RS232C serial ports	1
UART chip used	NS16550
Maximum speed (bits per second)	19,200 bps
FIFO mode enabled	No
Maximum number of ports	8
Pointing device (mouse) ports	1
Parallel printer ports	1
Bidirectional	Yes
Maximum number of ports	8
CMOS real-time clock (RTC)	Yes
CMOS RAM	64 bytes
Battery life	5 years
Replaceable	Yes

Disk Storage

Internal disk and tape drive bays	3		
Number of 3 1/2- and 5 1/4-inch bays	3/0		
Standard floppy drives	1×1.44M		
Optional floppy drives:			
5 1/4-inch 360K	Optional		
5 1/4-inch 1.2M	Optional		
3 1/2-inch 720K	No		
3 1/2-inch 1.44M	Standard		
3 1/2-inch 2.88M	No		
Hard disk controller included	IDE connector on Interposer Card ST-506 Controller (021)		
ST-506/IDE hard disks available	20/30/60M		
Drive form factor	3 1/2-inch		
Drive capacity	20M	30M	60M
Drive interface	ST-506	IDE	IDE
Average access rate (ms)	80	39	27
Encoding scheme	MFM	RLL	RLL
BIOS drive type number	30	33	None
Cylinders	611	614	762
Heads	4	4	6
Sectors per track	17	25	26
Rotational speed (RPM)	3600	3600	3600
Interleave factor	1:1	1:1	1:1
Data transfer rate (K/second)	510	750	780
Automatic head parking	No	No	Yes

(continues)

Table 22.20   Continued

Expansion Slots

Total adapter slots	3
Number of long and short slots	3/0
Number of 8-/16-/32-bit slots	0/3/0
Number of slots with video ext.	1
Available slots	3

Keyboard Specifications

101-key Enhanced Keyboard	Yes
Fast keyboard speed setting	Yes
Keyboard cable length	6 feet

Security Features

Keylock:	
Locks cover	Yes
Locks keyboard	No
Keyboard password	Yes
Power-on password	Yes
Network server mode	Yes

Physical Specifications

Footprint type	Desktop
Dimensions:	
Height	5.5 inches
Width	14.2 inches
Depth	16.5 inches
Weight	23.0 lbs
	21.0 lbs (021)

Environmental Specifications

Power-supply output	94 watts
Worldwide (110/60, 220/50)	Yes
Auto-sensing/switching	Yes
Maximum current:	
90-137 VAC	2.7 amps
180-265 VAC	1.4 amps
Operating range:	
Temperature	60-90 degrees F
Relative humidity	8-80 percent
Maximum operating altitude	7,000 feet
Heat (BTUs/hour)	494
Noise (Average dB, operating, 1m)	46 dB
FCC classification	Class B

Figures 22.18 and 22.19 show the layout and components on Model 50 and 50 Z motherboards, respectively.

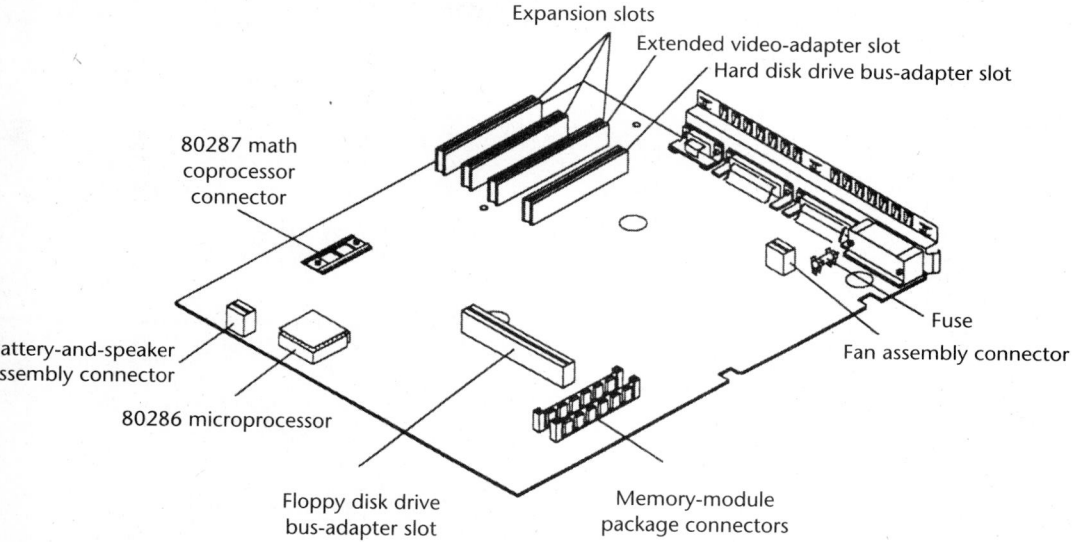

Fig. 22.18
PS/2 Model 50 system board.

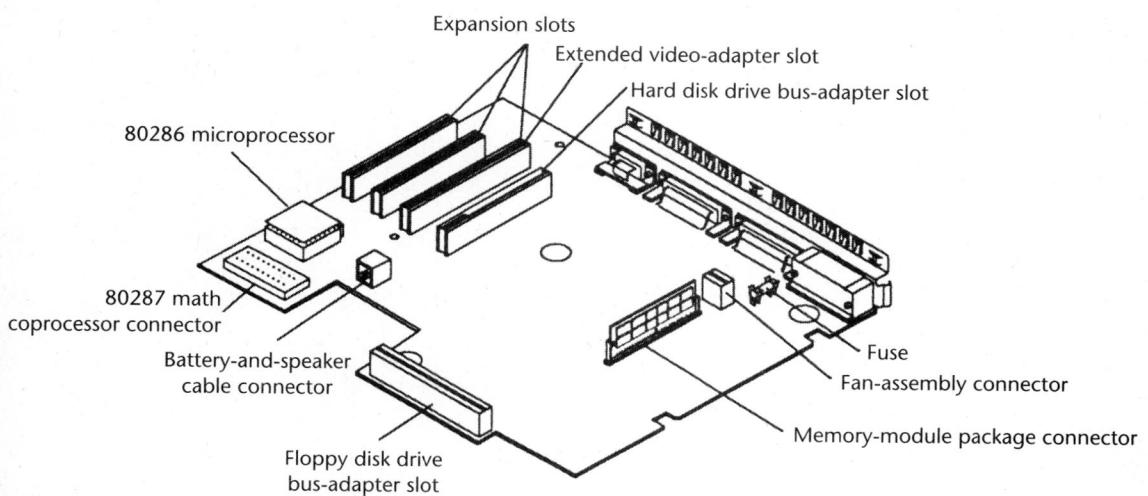

Fig. 22.19
PS/2 Model 50Z system board.

Table 22.21 shows the primary specifications of the different versions of PS/2 Model 50.

Table 22.21	**IBM PS/2 Model 50 Model Summary**						
				PLANAR MEMORY		**STANDARD**	
Part Number	**CPU**	**MHz**		**Std.**	**Max.**	**Floppy Drive**	**Hard Disk**
50							
8550-021	286	10		1M	1M	1×1.44M	20M
50 Z							
8550-031	286	10		1M	2M	1×1.44M	30M
8550-061	286	10		1M	2M	1×1.44M	60M

Note: *All 50 and 50 Z models have been withdrawn from marketing by IBM.*

PS/2 E

Introduced in the summer of 1993, the PS/2 E was designed to be a "green machine," running on only 24 watts (excluding monitor) and earning an EPA Energy Star rating. The system is designed to be used with a new 10.4-inch LCD thin-film transistor (TFT) monitor. One unique design feature of the PS/2 E is that all optional devices must be PCMCIA because no ISA slots are available. The PS/2 E is almost portfolio-size and light enough to carry under one arm. The PS/2 E uses 80486SLC2 processor running double-clocked at 50 MHz while communicating on the system bus at 25 MHz.

The PCMCIA bus accepts externally installed PCMCIA devices only. The PCMCIA slots can accommodate up to four Type I, up to four Type II, and up to two Type III devices. The exclusive use of PCMCIA adds to the compact design of the system and effectively eliminates any need to open it. The PS/2 E does not include a cooling fan.

The mouse is a built-in joystick-like stub positioned at the intersection of the G, H, and B keys on the keyboard. Although it sounds obtrusive, it isn't. It actually feels quite natural to use, partly because of the placement of the mouse buttons, which sit below the spacebar and are actuated without interfering with any of the keys. This is the same TrackPoint II mouse found on IBM laptops, although this one works more smoothly

Bus Type	Total Available Slots	STANDARD		Date Introduced	Date Withdrawn
		Video	Keyboard		
MCA/16	4/3	VGA	Enh	04/02/87	05/03/89
MCA/16	4/3	VGA	Enh	06/07/88	07/23/91
MCA/16	4/3	VGA	Enh	06/07/88	07/23/91

and precisely. The keyboard itself is small and very light. The keys are thinner than usual; travel is soft and quiet; and tactile feedback has been sacrificed. The arrangement of the keys is as close to normal as can be expected, although Delete, Home, and Insert will seem just slightly out of position. Spacing is good for its size and should pose no problem for anyone with normal-size hands.

The PS/2 E comes standard with 4M and is expandable to 16M. The on-board XGA-2 video controller is capable of 1,024 by 768 with 256 colors with its 1M of VRAM. The drives included on most variations of the PS/2 E include a 1.44M 3 1/2-inch disk drive and a 120M 2 1/2-inch form factor IDE hard drive with a 17-ms average seek time and built-in IDE controller.

The PS/2E is a suitable system for tight places with light Windows tasks. It is designed as a Windows computer, as evidenced by the built-in mouse, and performs well in this environment. It has the looks and credentials to fit into an educational situation, should IBM decide to market it as an educational tool, with its power management, silent operation, and compact size. This also makes it a good fit for hospital use and other institutions where power, noise, and space are concerns.

Table 22.22 lists the technical specifications for the PS/2 Model E.

Table 22.22 PS/2 Model E Technical Specifications	
System Architecture	
Microprocessor Clock speed	486SLC2 50 MHz
L1 Internal Memory Cache	16K
L2 External Memory	n/a
Math coprocessor	Optional
Bus type	MCA (Micro Channel Architecture)
Data path	16-bit
Upgradeable processor complex	No
Memory	
Standard on system board	4M
Maximum on system board	16M
Maximum total memory	16M
Memory speed and type	70ns dynamic RAM
System board memory-socket type	36-bit SIMM (single in-line memory module)
Standard Features	
Optional math coprocessor	80387SX

Standard graphics
    Video RAM (VRAM)
    Max. resolution
	Integrated XGA-2
	1M
	1280×1024

RS232C serial ports	1
Pointing device (mouse) ports	1
Parallel printer ports Bidirectional	1 Yes
Disk Storage	
Internal disk and tape drive bays Number of 3 1/2- and 5 1/4-inch bays	3 3/0
Standard floppy drives	1×1.44M

Disk Storage

Optional floppy drives:	
5 1/4-inch 360K	Optional
5 1/4-inch 1.2M	Optional
3 1/2-inch 720K	No
3 1/2-inch 1.44M	Standard
3 1/2-inch 2.88M	Yes

Hard disk controller included	IDE connector		
ST-506/IDE hard disks available	120M/212M/540M		
Drive form factor	3 1/2-inch		
Drive capacity	120M	212M	540M
Drive interface	IDE	IDE	IDE
Average access rate (ms)	17	17	17

Expansion Slots

Total adapter slots	4 PCMCIA Type I/II or 2 Type III
Number of long and short slots	n/a
Number of 8-/16-/32-bit slots	n/a
Available slots	4 PCMCIA Type I/II or 2 Type III

Keyboard Specifications

101-key Enhanced Keyboard	Yes
Fast keyboard speed setting	Yes
Keyboard cable length	6 feet

Security Features

Keylock:	
Locks cover	Yes
Locks keyboard	No
Keyboard password	Yes
Power-on password	Yes
Network server mode	Yes

Physical Specifications

Footprint type	Desktop
Dimensions:	
Height	2.5 inches
Width	12 inches
Depth	12 inches
Weight	10.0 lbs
FCC classification	Class B

Table 22.23 shows the primary specifications of the different versions of PS/2 Model E.

Table 22.23   IBM PS/2 Model E Model Summary

Part Number	CPU	MHz	PLANAR MEMORY Std.	Max.	STANDARD Floppy Drive	Hard Disk	Bus Type
E							
9533-DB7	486SLC2	50	4M	16M	1×1.44M	120M	ISA/16
9533-DBD	486SLC2	50	8M	16M	1×1.44M	120M	ISA/16
9533-DLA	486SLC2	50	8M	16M	1×2.88M	212M	ISA/16
9533-DLG	486SLC2	50	8M	16M	1×2.88M	540M	ISA/16
9533-GB7	486SLC2	50	8M	16M	1×44M	120M	ISA/16
9533-GBD	486SLC2	50	8M	16M	1×44M	340M	ISA/16
9533-GBX	486SLC2	50	4M	16M	1×44M	n/a	ISA/16
9533-2BX	486SLC2	50	4M	16M	n/a	n/a	ISA/16

PS/2 Model 53

The IBM PS/2 Model 53 broadened IBM's line of MCA desktop systems by offering this entry-level model on November 9, 1993. Besides the PS/2 E, the Model 53 was the first updating of the PS/2 line since September 1992. The system features the IBM 486SLC chip running at 50 MHz internally and 25 MHz externally. That processor, which has a 16K internal cache, is comparable to a 33-MHz 486SX chip. The PS/2 53 base models come standard with 4M of memory that can be upgraded to 16M on the system board. Hard disks range from 120M (9553-0B7) to 250M (9553-0BB).

Total Available Slots	STANDARD		Date Introduced	Date Withdrawn
	Video	Keyboard		
4 PCMCIA Type I/II or 2 Type III/4 PCMCIA Type I/II or 2 Type III	XGA-2	Any	07/94	—
4 PCMCIA Type I/II or 2 Type III/4 PCMCIA Type I/II or 2 Type III	XGA-2	Any	07/94	—
4 PCMCIA Type I/II or 2 Type III/4 PCMCIA Type I/II or 2 Type III	XGA-2	Any	07/94	—
4 PCMCIA Type I/II or 2 Type III/4 PCMCIA Type I/II or 2 Type III	XGA-2	Any	07/94	—
4 PCMCIA Type I/II or 2 Type III/4 PCMCIA Type I/II or 2 Type III	XGA-2	Any	07/94	—
4 PCMCIA Type I/II or Type III/4 PCMCIA Type I/II or 2 Type III	XGA-2	Any	07/94	—
4 PCMCIA Type I/II or 2 Type III/4 PCMCIA Type I/II or 2 Type III	XGA-2	Any	07/94	—
4 PCMCIA Type I/II or 2 Type III/4 PCMCIA Type I/II or 2 Type III	XGA-2	Any	07/94	—

With the video system's 1M of dynamic RAM, which is not upgradeable, users can get graphics resolutions as high as 1,024 by 768 with 256 colors. The PS/2 53 is available in four configurations.

The PS/2 Model 53LS is identical to the Model 53, but lacks internal drives. It was designed as a low-cost Token-Ring (9553-2BX) or 10Base-T EtherNet (9553-1BX) medialess model.

Table 22.24 lists the technical specifications for the PS/2 Model 53.

Table 22.24 PS/2 Model 53 Technical Specifications	
System Architecture	
Microprocessor	486SLC2
Clock speed	50 MHz
L1 Internal Memory Cache	16K
L2 External Memory	n/a
Math coprocessor	Optional
Bus type	MCA (Micro Channel Architecture)
Data path	16-bit
Upgradeable processor complex	No
Memory	
Standard on system board	4M
Maximum on system board	16M
Maximum total memory	16M
Memory speed and type	70ns dynamic RAM
System board memory-socket type	36-bit SIMM (single in-line memory module)
Number of memory-module sockets	3
Standard Features	
Optional math coprocessor	80387SX
Standard graphics	VESA SVGA (super-VGA)
8-/16-/32-bit controller	32-bit
Bus master	No
Video RAM (VRAM)	1M
Maximum resolution	1,024 × 768
RS232C serial ports	1
Pointing device (mouse) ports	1
Parallel printer ports	1
Bidirectional	Yes
Disk Storage	
Internal disk and tape drive bays	3
Number of 3 1/2- and 5 1/4-inch bays	3/0
Standard floppy drives	1×1.44M

Disk Storage

Optional floppy drives:	
5 1/4-inch 360K	Optional
5 1/4-inch 1.2M	Optional
3 1/2-inch 720K	No
3 1/2-inch 1.44M	Standard
3 1/2-inch 2.88M	Yes
Hard disk controller included	IDE connector
ST-506/IDE hard disks available	120M/250M
Drive form factor	3 1/2-inch
Drive capacity	120M 250M
Drive interface	IDE IDE
Average access rate (ms)	14 14

Expansion Slots

Total adapter slots	3
Number of long and short slots	3/0
Number of 8-/16-/32-bit slots	0/0/3
Available slots	3

Keyboard Specifications

101-key Enhanced Keyboard	Yes
Fast keyboard speed setting	Yes
Keyboard cable length	6 feet

Security Features

Keylock:	
Locks cover	Yes
Locks keyboard	No
Keyboard password	Yes
Power-on password	Yes
Network server mode	Yes

Physical Specifications

Footprint type	Desktop
Dimensions:	
Height	4.07 inches
Width	15.1 inches
Depth	16 inches
Weight	20.0 lbs
FCC classification	Class B

Table 22.25 shows the primary specifications of the different versions of PS/2 Model 53.

Table 22.25   IBM PS/2 Model 53 Model Summary

Part Number	CPU	MHz	PLANAR MEMORY Std.	Max.	STANDARD Floppy Drive	Hard Disk
53						
9553-0B7	486SLC2	50	4M	16M	1×1.44M	170M
9553-0BB	486SLC2	50	4M	16M	1×1.44M	250M
53LS						
9553LS-1BX	486SLC2	50	4M	16M	1×1.44M	n/a
9553LS-2BX	486SLC2	50	4M	16M	1×1.44M	n/a

PS/2 Model 55 SX

The PS/2 Model 55 SX, introduced May 9, 1989, has been one of IBM's top-selling systems because of the system's reasonable performance, modular construction, low price, and compact, efficient design. Model 55 SX systems use the 386 SX processor running at 16 MHz. They have 2M as standard memory in the 30M and 60M hard drive configurations, and 4M as standard memory in the 40M and 80M hard drive configurations. These Model 55 SX systems have the capability of supporting up to 16M of memory and have offered hard disks from 30M to 80M. Additional features include 1.44M, 3 1/2-inch floppy disk drive; ports (keyboard, pointing device, serial/asynchronous, parallel, VGA); three MCA I/O slots, and an Enhanced Keyboard. Figure 22.20 shows a front view, and figure 22.21 shows a rear panel view of a Model 55 SX.

Also available are special diskless versions of the Model 55 SX with preinstalled IBM Token-Ring or EtherNet Adapters. These "Lxx" versions are designed as LAN workstations and have the capability to boot directly from the LAN server system. The -LEx models include an IBM EtherNet Adapter, and the -LTx models include an IBM Token-Ring Network Adapter. Although these models come without any drives, they can be upgraded later with both floppy and hard disk drives.

The PS/2 Model 55 SX is designed to maintain compatibility with many software products currently operating under DOS and OS/2 on the IBM AT and the rest of the PS/2 family. These systems have full 80386 memory management capability, which means that they can operate in 32-bit software mode. Figure 22.22 shows an interior view of the Model 55 SX.

Bus Type	Total Available Slots	STANDARD		Date Introduced	Date Withdrawn
		Video	Keyboard		
MCA/16	3/3	VESA SVGA	Any	11/09/93	—
MCA/16	3/3	VESA SVGA	Any	11/09/93	—
MCA/16	3/3	VESA SVGA	Any	11/09/93	—
MCA/16	3/3	VESA SVGA	Any	11/09/93	—

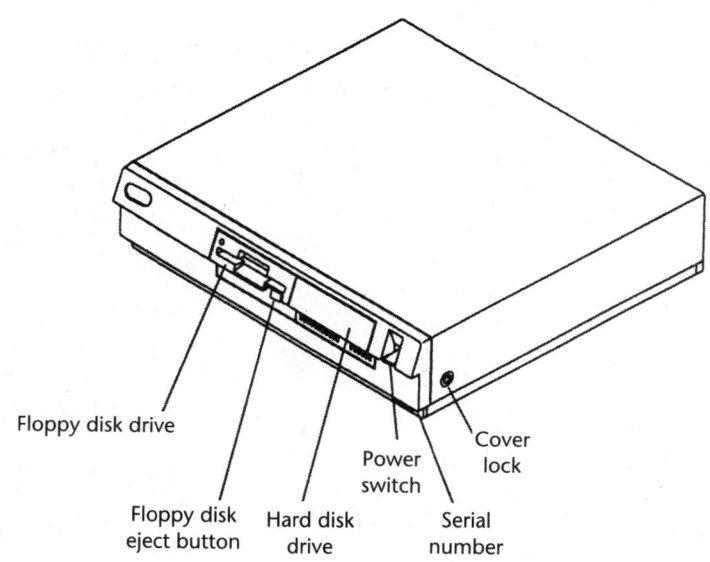

Floppy disk drive

Floppy disk eject button

Hard disk drive

Power switch

Serial number

Cover lock

Fig. 22.20
PS/2 Model 55 SX.

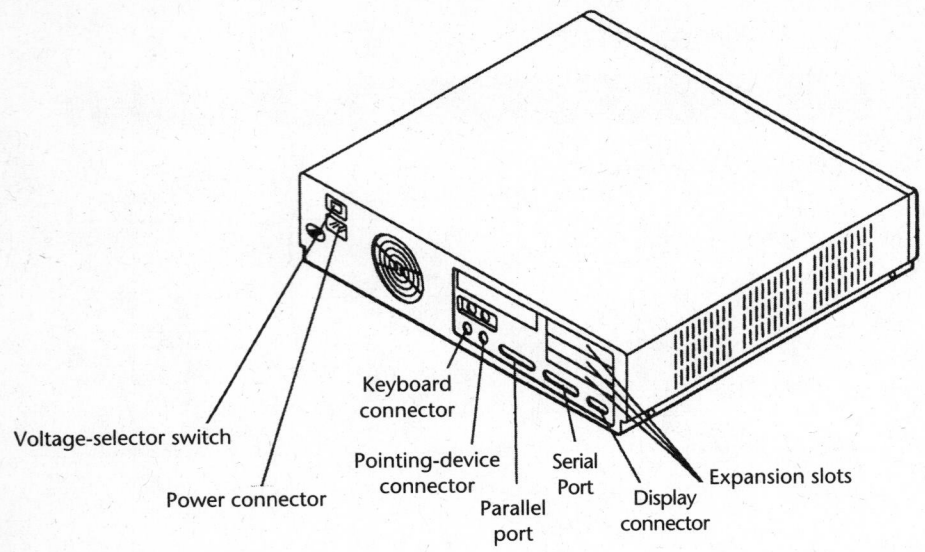

Fig. 22.21
PS/2 Model 55 SX rear panel view.

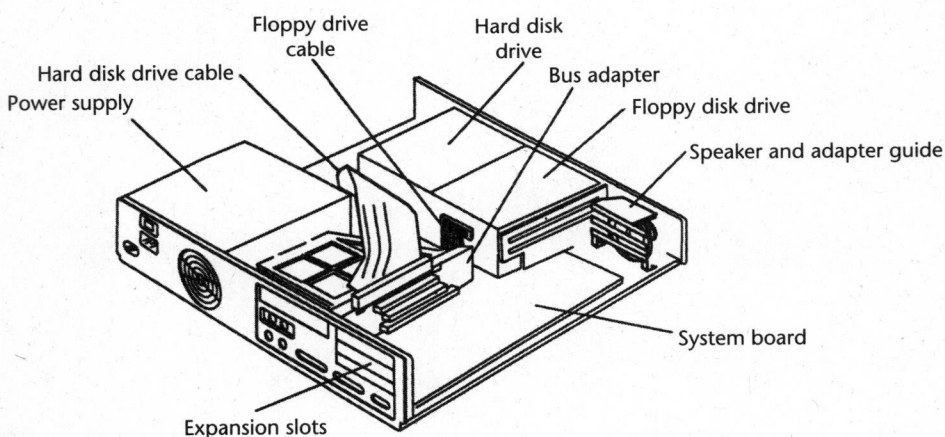

Fig. 22.22
PS/2 Model 55 SX interior view.

The various models of the 55 SX differ only in the size of the preinstalled hard disk. Models have been available with 30M, 40M, 60M, and 80M drives. The 30M and 60M drive models have been discontinued by IBM, and the 40M and 80M models have taken their place.

Table 22.26 lists the technical specifications for the PS/2 model 55SX.

Table 22.26 PS/2 Model 55 SX Technical Specifications

System Architecture

Microprocessor	80386SX
Clock speed	16 MHz
Bus type	MCA (Micro Channel Architecture)
Bus width	16-bit
Interrupt levels	16
Type	Level-sensitive
Shareable	Yes
DMA channels	15
DMA burst mode supported	Yes
Bus masters supported	15
Upgradeable processor complex	No

Memory

Standard on system board	4M
Maximum on system board	8M
Maximum total memory	16M
Memory speed and type	100ns dynamic RAM
System board memory socket type	36-bit SIMM (single in-line memory module)
Number of memory module sockets	2
Number available in standard configuration	1
Memory used on system board	1M/2M/4M 36-bit SIMMs
Memory cache controller	No
Wait states:	
System board	0-2
Adapter	0-4

Standard Features

ROM size	128K
ROM shadowing	Yes
Optional math coprocessor	80387SX
Coprocessor speed	16 MHz
Standard graphics	VGA (Video Graphics Array)
8-/16-/32-bit controller	8-bit
Bus master	No
Video RAM (VRAM)	256K
RS232C serial ports	1
UART chip used	NS16550A
Maximum speed (bits/second)	19,200 bps

(continues)

Table 22.26   Continued

Standard Features

FIFO mode enabled	Yes
Maximum number of ports	8
Pointing device (mouse) ports	1
Parallel printer ports	1
Bidirectional	Yes
Maximum number of ports supported	8
CMOS real-time clock (RTC)	Yes
CMOS RAM	64 bytes
Battery life	10 years
Replaceable	Yes (Dallas module)

Disk Storage

Internal disk and tape drive bays	2			
Number of 3 1/2- and 5 1/4-inch bays	2/0			
Standard floppy drives	1×1.44M			
None (LT0, LE0)				
Optional floppy drives:				
5 1/4-inch 360K	Optional			
5 1/4-inch 1.2M	Optional			
3 1/2-inch 720K	No			
3 1/2-inch 1.44M	Standard			
3 1/2-inch 2.88M	No			
Hard disk controller included	IDE connector on bus adapter			
IDE hard disks available	30M/40M/60M/80M			
Drive form factor	3 1/2-inch			
Drive interface	IDE			
Drive capacity	30M	40M	60M	80M
Average access rate (ms)	27	17	27	17
Read-ahead cache	No	32K	No	32K
Encoding scheme	RLL	RLL	RLL	RLL
BIOS drive type number	33	None	None	None
Cylinders	614	1038	762	1021
Heads	4	2	6	4
Sectors per track	25	39	26	39
Rotational speed (RPM)	3600	3600	3600	3600
Interleave factor	1:1	1:1	1:1	1:1
Actual transfer rate (K/second)	750	1170	780	1170
Automatic head parking	No	Yes	Yes	Yes

Expansion Slots

Total adapter slots	3
Number of long and short slots	3/0
Number of 8-/16-/32-bit slots	0/3/0
Number of slots with video ext.	1
Available slots	3
Keyboard specifications:	
101-key Enhanced Keyboard	Yes
Fast keyboard speed setting	Yes
Keyboard cable length	6 feet

Security Features

Keylock:	
Locks cover	Yes
Locks keyboard	No
Keyboard password	Yes
Power-on password	Yes
Network server mode	Yes

Physical Specifications

Footprint type	Desktop
Dimensions:	
Height	4.0 inches
Width	16.0 inches
Depth	15.6 inches
Weight	15.5 lbs (LT0, LE0)
	19.0 lbs

Environmental Specifications

Power-supply output	90 watts
Worldwide (110/60, 220/50)	Yes
Auto-sensing/switching	Manual switch
Maximum current:	
90-137 VAC	2.5 amps
180-265 VAC	1.3 amps
Operating range:	
Temperature	60-90 degrees F
Relative humidity	8-80 percent
Maximum operating altitude	7,000 feet
Heat (BTUs/hour)	438
Noise (Average dB, operating, 1m)	40 dB
FCC classification	Class B

Table 22.27 shows the primary specifications of the various versions of PS/2 Model 55 SX.

Table 22.27 IBM PS/2 Model 55 SX Model Summary						
Part Number	CPU	MHz	PLANAR MEMORY Std.	PLANAR MEMORY Max.	STANDARD Floppy Drive	Hard Disk
53						
8555-031	386SX	16	2M	8M	1×1.44M	30M
8555-041	386SX	16	4M	8M	1×1.44M	40M
8555-061	386SX	16	2M	8M	1×1.44M	60M
8555-081	386SX	16	4M	8M	1×1.44M	80M
55 LS						
8555-LT0	386SX	16	4M	8M	—	—
8555-LE0	386SX16	16	4M	8M	—	—

The LT0 model includes an IBM 16/4 Token-Ring Adapter, and the LE0 model includes an IBM EtherNet adapter. Both of these models are also diskless.

Figure 22.23 shows the Model 55 SX motherboard components and layout.

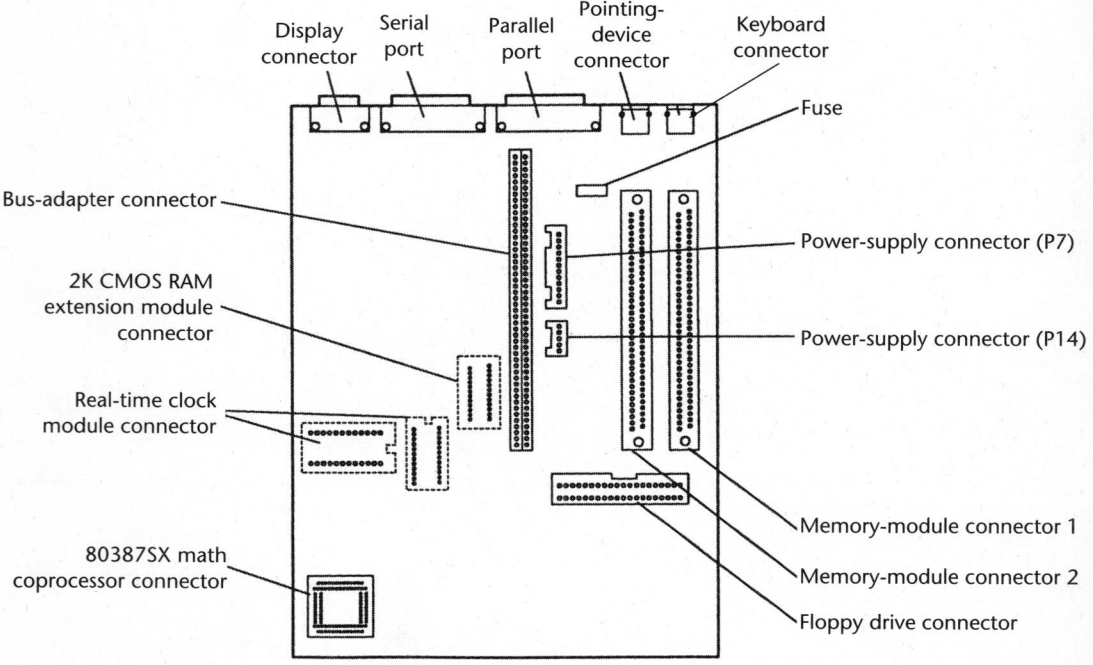

Fig. 22.23
PS/2 Model 55 SX system board.

Bus Type	Total Available Slots	STANDARD		Date Introduced	Date Withdrawn
		Video	Keyboard		
MCA/16	3/3	VGA	Enh	05/09/89	09/11/91
MCA/16	3/3	VGA	Enh	06/11/91	05/25/92
MCA/16	3/3	VGA	Enh	05/09/89	09/11/91
MCA/16	3/3	VGA	Enh	06/11/91	05/25/92
MCA/16	3/2	VGA	Enh	10/09/90	05/25/92
MCA/16	3/2	VGA	Enh	10/09/90	05/25/92

PS/2 Model 56 SX, SLC, LS, and LS SLC

The PS/2 Model 56, introduced February 25, 1992, is an MCA system designed to replace the PS/2 Model 55 SX. The system has a 386SX or 386SLC 20 MHz processor and offers improvements such as increased speed, configuration flexibility, and a Small Computer System Interface (SCSI) input/output interface. For improved graphics performance, video is provided through an enhanced 16-bit VGA controller integrated on the system board. Several models are offered including models with SCSI hard disk capacities of 80M and 160M, with or without the 386SLC processor option, and LAN versions with built-in Token-Ring or EtherNet adapters.

The SLC models use a new custom, high-speed processor. The new IBM 386SLC processor is designed and manufactured in IBM's Burlington, Vermont, semiconductor facility. The 386SLC chip powers the PS/2 cached processor option. This processor includes a built-in cache controller and 8K cache similar to 486 processors. The 386SLC is up to 88 percent faster than the standard 386SX processor. The standard Model 56 SX systems can be upgraded to the SLC processor by adding the PS/2 cached processor option.

The PS/2 Model 56 is designed for desktop operation but ships with a vertical stand, allowing the customer the flexibility of horizontal or vertical orientation. The mechanical package allows for expansion with three 16-bit slots for MCA adapters and two bays for I/O devices. One of the bays contains an extra-high-density 3 1/2-inch 2.88M (million bytes) media sense floppy disk drive. Another bay contains an SCSI hard disk.

SCSI Standard. The SCSI controller is integrated in the system board, so a slot is not required, and the controller can support up to seven SCSI devices (including the standard SCSI hard disk). Two of the additional SCSI devices can be attached internally and the remaining devices externally with the external SCSI connector.

System Memory. The system ships with one 4M single in-line memory module (SIMM) located in the first SIMM socket on the motherboard. The PS/2 Model 56 supports up to 16M of 70ns memory on the system board in three SIMM sockets, all of which are addressable by direct memory address (DMA). Because the system board supports the full 16M, memory should not be installed via adapter cards in the bus. The Model 56 supports 2M, 4M, and 8M memory SIMMs (70ns only). To take advantage of enhanced performance via interleaved memory, SIMMs should be installed using all 2M or all 4M SIMMs. One, two, or three 2M SIMMs provide memory interleaving. Two or three 4M SIMMs also provide memory interleaving. The 8M SIMMs do not provide interleaving, but do allow the maximum capacity of 16M to be reached.

Keyboard Options. The PS/2 Model 56 supports the IBM Enhanced Keyboard (101/102 keys), Space-Saving Keyboard (84/85 keys), and the IBM Host-Connected Keyboard (122 keys). The Host-Connected Keyboard is similar to the 3270 keyboard offered with 3270 IBM PC and IBM AT systems. This keyboard is similar in design to that of a 3270 terminal keyboard and offers keys dedicated to 3270 functions. The Host-Connected Keyboard is supported by the BIOS in this system and cannot be retrofitted to PS/2 systems that do not have the proper BIOS support.

When you purchase a Model 56, you can choose any of these three keyboards. The keyboard can be specified only in new equipment orders and cannot be ordered separately for on-order or installed equipment.

Floppy Drive Support. The Model 56 includes a standard 2.88M floppy disk drive. This drive is fully compatible with 1.44M and 720K floppy disk drives. The drive includes a media sensor that prevents accidentally formatting floppy disks to the wrong capacity (which can result in data loss).

DOS 5.0 is the minimum DOS version supported on this system. Because of the 2.88M floppy disk drive, versions of DOS prior to 5.0 (or other operating systems or applications) might not format floppy disk media correctly. Use of the proper level of operating system along with the new 2.88M floppy disk drive provides media sensing of 720K, 1.44M, and 2.88M floppy disks, giving greater ease in formatting, reading, and writing floppy disks.

Initial Microcode Load. One very special feature of the Model 56 is called Initial Microcode Load (IML). The ROM BIOS is stored on the hard disk in a protected 3M partition and loaded from the disk during a "pre-boot" process. The formatted capacity of the hard disk is reduced by 3M, and the total user-accessible capacity might vary slightly, based on operating environments. This partition is protected from normal access and does not appear to the system when it is running FDISK or FORMAT. In fact, the partition is so well protected that the system BIOS cannot even access this system partition with standard Int 13h commands. For all intents and purposes the hard disk is simply 3M smaller than it would normally be. The 3M system partition also contains a copy of the Reference disk, which means that the setup program is effectively in ROM as well! The setup program is accessed by pressing Ctrl-Alt-Ins when the cursor shifts to the right-hand portion of the screen during a boot operation.

Having a disk-based ROM offers an unprecedented level of control over the system compared to other models. For example, updating the ROM BIOS to a new version simply requires booting from a newer Reference disk and selecting the option that updates the system partition. This feature enables IBM to keep in step with ROM upgrades for new features and fix bugs in the BIOS without the expense and hassle of replacing ROM chips.

The optional 386SLC processor was designed, developed, and manufactured by IBM under a long-standing agreement with Intel. This chip has the same 32-bit internal, 16-bit external design as the Intel 386SX and is fully compatible with Intel 386 architecture. Intel participated in testing the 386SLC and determined the processor to be compatible with the Intel 386 architecture. IBM designed the 386SLC with 8K of internal cache and an internal cache controller, which improves performance by accessing data from high-speed cache memory rather than system memory, whenever possible. This is very similar to the 486 and is the primary reason for the increased performance. Performance has been further enhanced by optimizing commonly used instructions.

LS models are designed as LAN stations and include no disk drives. These diskless models are available in several versions, with or without the 386SLC processor. The -1xx models include an IBM EtherNet adapter in one of the three slots, and the -2xx models include an IBM Token-Ring network adapter in one of the three slots.

Table 22.28 lists the technical specifications for the PS/2 Model 56.

Table 22.28   PS/2 Model 56 Technical Specifications

System Architecture

Microprocessor	80386SX (04x)
	80386SLC (05x)
Optional microprocessor	80386SLC (04x)
Clock speed	20MHz
Bus type	MCA (Micro Channel Architecture)
Bus width	16-bit
Interrupt levels	16
Type	Level-sensitive
Shareable	Yes
DMA channels	15
DMA burst mode supported	Yes
Bus masters supported	15
Upgradeable processor complex	No

Memory

Standard on system board	4M
Maximum on system board	16M
Maximum total memory	16M

(continues)

Table 22.28   Continued

Memory

Memory speed and type	70ns dynamic RAM
System board memory socket type	36-bit SIMM (single in-line memory module)
Number of memory module sockets	3
Number available in standard configuration	2
Memory used on system board	2M/4M/8M 36-bit SIMMs
Memory interleaving	Yes (2M/4M SIMMs only)
Memory cache controller	No
Wait states:	
System board	0-2
Adapter	0-4

Standard Features

ROM size	128K
ROM shadowing	Yes
BIOS extensions stored on disk	Yes
Setup and Diagnostics stored on disk	Yes
Optional math coprocessor	80387SX
Coprocessor speed	20 MHz
Standard graphics	VGA
8-/16-/32-bit controller	16-bit
Bus master	No
Video RAM (VRAM)	256K
RS232C serial ports	1
UART chip used	Custom (compatible with NS16550A)
Maximum speed (bits/second)	345,600
FIFO mode enabled	Yes
Supports DMA data transfer	Yes
Maximum number of ports	8
Pointing device (mouse) ports	1
Parallel printer ports	1
Bidirectional	Yes
Supports DMA data transfer	Yes
Maximum number of ports	8
CMOS real-time clock (RTC)	Yes
CMOS RAM	64 bytes + 2K extension
Battery life	10 years
Replaceable	Yes (Dallas module)

Disk Storage

Internal disk and tape drive bays	4
Number of 3 1/2- and 5 1/4-inch bays	1/3

Disk Storage

Selectable boot drive	Yes					
Bootable drives	All physical drives					
Standard floppy drives	1×2.88M					
Optional floppy drives:						
5 1/4-inch 360K	Optional					
5 1/4-inch 1.2M	Optional					
3 1/2-inch 720K	No					
3 1/2-inch 1.44M	Optional					
3 1/2-inch 2.88M	Standard					
Hard disk controller included:	SCSI integrated on system board					
Bus master	Yes					
Devices supported per adapter	7					
Adapters supported per system	4					
SCSI hard disks available	60M/80M/120M/160M/320M/400M					
Drive form factor	3 1/2-inch					
Drive interface	SCSI					
Drive capacity	60M	80M	120M	160M	320M	400M
Average access rate (ms)	23	17	23	16	12.5	11.5
Read-ahead cache	32K	32K	32K	32K	64K	128K
SCSI transfer mode	Async	Async	Async	Async	Sync	Sync
Encoding scheme	RLL	RLL	RLL	RLL	RLL	RLL
Cylinders	920	1021	920	1021	949	1201
Heads	4	4	8	8	14	14
Sectors per track	32	39	32	39	48	48
Rotational speed (RPM)	3600	3600	3600	3600	4318	4318
Interleave factor	1:1	1:1	1:1	1:1	1:1	1:1
Data transfer rate (K/second)	960	1170	960	1170	1727	1727
Automatic head parking	Yes	Yes	Yes	Yes	Yes	Yes

Expansion Slots

Total adapter slots	3
Number of long and short slots	3/0
Number of 8-/16-/32-bit slots	0/3/0
Number of slots with video ext.	1
Available slots	3
	2 (1xx, 2xx)

Keyboard Specifications

Keyboard choices	122-key Host-Connected Keyboard
	101-key Enhanced Keyboard
	84-key Space-Saving Keyboard
Fast keyboard speed setting	Yes
Keyboard cable length	10 feet

(continues)

Table 22.28 Continued	
Security Features	
Keylock:	
Locks cover	Yes
Locks keyboard	No
Keyboard password	Yes
Power-on password	Yes
Network server mode	Yes
Physical Specifications	
Footprint type	Desktop
Orientation	Horizontal/vertical
Dimensions:	
Height	4.5 inches
Width	14.2 inches
Depth	15.6 inches
Weight	24 lbs
Environmental Specifications	
Power-supply output	118 watts
Worldwide (110/60, 220/50)	Yes
Auto-sensing/switching	Yes
Maximum current:	
90-137 VAC	3.5 amps
180-265 VAC	1.75 amps
Operating range:	
Temperature	50-95 degrees F
Relative humidity	8-80 percent
Maximum operating altitude	7,000 feet
Heat (BTUs/hour)	154
FCC classification	Class B

Table 22.30 shows the primary specifications of the different versions of PS/2 Model 56.

PS/2 Model 56 486SLC3, LS, and 57 486SLC3, M57 486SLC3 Ultimedia

The PS/2 Models 56 486SLC3 and 57 486SLC3 are revamped versions of the PS/2 Model 56 discussed earlier. The M57 486SLC3 Ultimedia is the multimedia version of the 57 486SLC3. Announced in October 1993, these models feature IBM's clock-tripled 75-MHz 486SLC processor and an MCA bus. Both models include XGA-2 local-bus graphics and "green," energy-saving capabilities. The 486SLC includes 16K cache, compared to the 8K found in Intel's 486SX and 486DX processors. The PS/2 Models 56 and 57 come standard with 8M RAM (4M for the LS variants) and are expandable to 16M on the system board. These systems are available in a variety of hard drive sizes, from 104M to 540M. Like the Model 56 SLC, the SCSI controller is integrated in the system board, and an external SCSI connector is available. These models come standard with one 2.88M floppy drive.

The M57 486SLC3 Ultimedia also includes IBM's Audiovation 16-bit sound card and a double-speed, multisession CD-ROM drive. This makes the M57 MPC Level 2 certified.

Table 22.29 lists the technical specifications for the PS/2 Model 56 486SLC3 and 57 486SLC3.

Table 22.29 PS/2 Model 56 486SLC3 and Model 57 486SLC3 Technical Specifications	
System Architecture	
Microprocessor	80486SLC3
Clock speed	75/25 MHz
L1/L2 cache	16K/n/a
Bus type	MCA (Micro Channel Architecture)
Bus width	16-bit
Upgradeable processor complex	No
Memory	
Standard on system board	8M (4M LS)
Maximum on system board	16M
Maximum total memory	16M
Memory speed and type	70ns dynamic RAM
System board memory socket type	36-bit SIMM (single in-line memory module)
Number of memory module sockets	3
Number available in standard configuration	3
Memory used on system board	2M/4M/8M 36-bit SIMMs
Memory interleaving	Yes (2M/4M SIMMs only)
Optional math coprocessor	80387SX
Standard graphics	XGA-2
Video RAM (VRAM)	1M
RS232C serial ports	1
UART chip used	Custom (compatible with NS16550A)
Pointing device (mouse) ports	1

(continues)

Table 22.29 Continued

Standard Features

Parallel printer ports	1
Bidirectional	Yes

Disk Storage

Internal disk and tape drive bays	3 (4 Model 57)
Number of 3 1/2- and 5 1/4-inch bays	1/3 (1/4 Model 57)
Standard floppy drives	1×2.88M
Optional floppy drives:	
5 1/4-inch 360K	Optional
5 1/4-inch 1.2M	Optional
3 1/2-inch 720K	No
3 1/2-inch 1.44M	Optional
3 1/2-inch 2.88M	Standard
Hard disk controller included	SCSI integrated on system board
Bus master	Yes
Devices supported per adapter	7
Adapters supported per system	4
SCSI hard disks available	170M/270M/340M/540M
Drive form factor	3 1/2-inch
Drive interface	SCSI

Drive capacity	170M	270M	340M	540M
Average access rate (ms)	13	12	13	8.5
Interleave factor	1:1	1:1	1:1	1:1
Automatic head parking	Yes	Yes	Yes	Yes

Expansion Slots

Total adapter slots	3
Number of long and short slots	3/0 (5/0 Model 57)
Number of 8-/16-/32-bit slots	0/3/0 (0/5/0 Model 57)
Available slots	3 (5 Model 57)

Keyboard Specifications

Keyboard choices	122-key Host-Connected Keyboard
	101-key Enhanced Keyboard
	84-key Space-Saving Keyboard
Fast keyboard speed setting	Yes

Keyboard Specifications

Keyboard cable length	10 feet

Security Features

Keylock:	
Locks cover	Yes
Locks keyboard	No
Keyboard password	Yes
Power-on password	Yes
Network server mode	Yes

Physical Specifications

Footprint type	Desktop
Orientation	Horizontal/vertical
Dimensions:	
Height	4.5 inches
Width	14.2 inches
Depth	15.6 inches
Weight	30 lbs
FCC classification	Class B

PS/2 Model 57 SX

The PS/2 Model 57 SX, introduced June 11, 1991, is an MCA system designed to complement and enhance the PS/2 Model 55 SX, the PS/2 Model 65 SX, and the low end of the PS/2 Model 70 386 family. The system has a 386SX 20 MHz processor and offers improvements such as increased speed, configuration flexibility, and a Small Computer System Interface (SCSI) input/output interface. For improved graphics performance, video is provided through an enhanced 16-bit VGA controller integrated on the system board. Several models are offered with SCSI hard disk capacities of 80M and 160M.

On October 17, 1991, IBM introduced a new custom, high-speed processor upgrade for the Model 57. The new upgrade option utilizes the powerful IBM 386SLC processor, designed and manufactured in IBM's Burlington, Vermont, semiconductor facility. The 386SLC chip powers the PS/2 cached processor option. This processor includes a built-in cache controller and 8K cache similar to 486 processors. The 386SLC is up to 88 percent faster than the standard 386SX processor.

Table 22.32 shows the primary specifications of the different versions of PS/2 Model 57 SX.

Table 22.30   IBM PS/2 Models 56 SX, 56 SLC, 56 LS, 56 SLC LS,

Part Number	CPU	MHz	PLANAR MEMORY Std.	Max.	STANDARD Floppy Drive	Hard Disk
56 SX						
8556-043	386SX	20	4M	16M	1×2.88M	40M
8556-045	386SX	20	4M	16M	1×2.88M	80M
56 SLC						
8556-055	386SLC	20	4M	16M	1×2.88M	80M
8556-059	386SLC	20	4M	16M	1×2.88M	160M
56 LS						
8556-14x	386SX	20	4M	16M	—	—
8556-24x	386SX	20	4M	16M	—	—
56 SLC LS						
8556-15x	386SLC	20	4M	16M	—	—
8556-25x	386SLC	20	4M	16M	—	—
56 486SLC3						
9556-DE9	486SLC3	75	8M	16M	1×2.88M	170M
9556-DEB	486SLC3	75	8M	16M	1×2.88M	270M
9556-DE9	486SLC3	75	8M	16M	1×2.88M	340M
56LS 486SLC						
9556LS-1EX	486SLC3	75	4M	16M	—	—
9556LS-2EX	486SLC3	75	4M	16M	—	—
57 486SLC3						
9557-DE9	486SLC3	75	8M	16M	1×2.88M	170M
9557-DEB	486SLC3	75	8M	16M	1×2.88M	270M
9557-DED	486SLC3	75	8M	16M	1×2.88M	340M
9557-DEG	486SLC3	75	8M	16M	1×2.88M	540M
M57 486SLC3 Ultimedia						
9557-6EB	486SLC3	75	8M	16M	1×2.88M	270M
9557-6EG	486SLC3	75	8M	16M	1×2.88M	540M
9557-7EB	486SLC3	75	8M	16M	1×2.88M	270M
9557-7EG	486SLC3	75	8M	16M	1×2.88M	540M

56 486SLC3, 56LS 486SLC, 57 486SLC3, and M57 486SLC3 Ultimedia Model Summary

Bus Type	Total Available Slots	STANDARD		Date Introduced	Date Withdrawn
		Video	Keyboard		
MCA/16	3/3	VGA	Any	02/25/92	—
MCA/16	3/3	VGA	Any	02/25/92	—
MCA/16	3/3	VGA	Any	02/25/92	—
MCA/16	3/3	VGA	Any	02/25/92	—
MCA/16	3/3	VGA	Any	02/25/92	—
MCA/16	3/3	VGA	Any	02/25/92	—
MCA/16	3/3	VGA	Any	02/25/92	—
MCA/16	3/3	VGA	Any	02/25/92	—
MCA/16	3/3	XGA-2	Any	02/01/94	—
MCA/16	3/3	XGA-2	Any	02/01/94	—
MCA/16	3/3	XGA-2	Any	02/01/94	—
MCA/16	3/3	XGA-2	Any	02/01/94	—
MCA/16	3/3	XGA-2	Any	02/01/94	—
MCA/16	5/5	XGA-2	Any	02/01/94	—
MCA/16	5/5	XGA-2	Any	02/01/94	—
MCA/16	5/5	XGA-2	Any	02/01/94	—
MCA/16	5/5	XGA-2	Any	02/01/94	—
MCA/16	5/3	XGA-2	Any	02/01/94	—
MCA/16	5/3	XGA-2	Any	02/01/94	—
MCA/16	5/3	XGA-2	Any	02/01/94	—
MCA/16	5/3	XGA-2	Any	02/01/94	—

The PS/2 Model 57 SX is designed for desktop operation but ships with a vertical stand, allowing the customer the flexibility of horizontal or vertical orientation. The mechanical package allows for expansion with five 16-bit slots for MCA adapters and four bays for I/O devices. One of the four bays contains an extra-high-density 3 1/2-inch 2.88M (million bytes) media sense floppy disk drive. Another bay contains a SCSI hard disk. Additional 5 1/4-inch and/or 3 1/2-inch devices, floppy disk drives, hard disks, tape and CD-ROM drives, and similar devices might be installed in the two remaining bays.

SCSI Standard. The SCSI controller is integrated in the system board, so a slot is not required, and the controller can support as many as seven SCSI devices (including the standard SCSI hard disk). Two of the additional SCSI devices can be attached internally and the remaining devices externally with the external SCSI connector.

System Memory. The system ships with one 4M single in-line memory module (SIMM) located in the first SIMM socket on the motherboard. The PS/2 Model 57 SX supports up to 16M of 70ns memory on the system board in three SIMM sockets, all of which are addressable by direct memory address (DMA). Because the system board supports the full 16M, memory should not be installed with adapter cards in the bus. The Model 57 SX supports 2M, 4M, and 8M memory SIMMs (70ns only). To take advantage of enhanced performance with interleaved memory, SIMMs should be installed using all 2M or all 4M SIMMs. One, two, or three 2M SIMMs provide memory interleaving. Two or three 4M SIMMs also provide memory interleaving. The 8M SIMMs do not provide interleaving, but do allow the maximum capacity of 16M to be reached.

Keyboard Options. The PS/2 Model 57 supports the IBM Enhanced Keyboard (101/102 keys), Space-Saving Keyboard (84/85 keys), and the IBM Host-Connected Keyboard (122 keys). The Host-Connected Keyboard is similar to the 3270 keyboard offered with 3270 IBM PC and IBM AT systems. This keyboard is similar in design to that of a 3270 terminal keyboard and offers keys dedicated to 3270 functions. The Host-Connected Keyboard is supported by the BIOS in this system and cannot be retrofitted to PS/2 systems that do not have the proper BIOS support.

When you purchase a Model 57, you can choose any of these three keyboards. The keyboard can be specified only in new equipment orders and cannot be ordered separately for on-order or installed equipment.

Floppy Drive Support. The Model 57 is the first system in the PC world to be shipped with a standard 2.88M floppy disk drive (although the drive is supported as an option in several other PS/2 systems). This drive is fully compatible with 1.44M and 720K floppy disk drives. The drive includes a media sensor that prevents accidentally formatting floppy disks to the wrong capacity (which can result in data loss).

DOS 5.0 is the minimum DOS version supported on this system. Because of the 2.88M floppy disk drive, versions of DOS prior to 5.0 (or other operating systems or applications) might not format floppy disk media correctly. Use of the proper level of operating system along with the new 2.88M floppy disk drive provides media sensing of 720K, 1.44M, and 2.88M floppy disks, making it easier to format, read, and write floppy disks.

Initial Microcode Load. One special feature of the Model 57 is called Initial Microcode Load (IML). The ROM BIOS is stored on the hard disk in a protected 3M partition and loaded from the disk during a "pre-boot" process. The formatted capacity of the hard disk is reduced by 3M, and the total user-accessible capacity might vary slightly, based on operating environments. This partition is protected from normal access and does not appear to the system when running FDISK or FORMAT. In fact, the partition is so well protected that the system BIOS cannot even access this system partition with standard Int 13h commands. For all intents and purposes the hard disk is 3M smaller than it would normally be. The 3M system partition also contains a copy of the Reference disk, which means that the setup program is effectively in ROM as well. The setup program is accessed by pressing Ctrl-Alt-Ins when the cursor shifts to the right-hand portion of the screen during a boot operation.

Having a disk-based ROM offers an unprecedented level of control over the system compared to other models. Updating the ROM BIOS to a new version, for example, simply requires booting from a newer Reference disk and selecting the option that updates the system partition. This feature enables IBM to keep in step with ROM upgrades for new features and fix bugs in the BIOS without the expense and hassle of replacing ROM chips.

The optional 386SLC processor was designed, developed, and manufactured by IBM under a long-standing agreement with Intel. This chip has the same 32-bit internal, 16-bit external design as the Intel 386SX and is fully compatible with Intel 386 architecture. Intel participated in testing the 386SLC and has determined the processor to be compatible with the Intel 386 architecture. IBM designed the 386SLC with 8K of internal cache and an internal cache controller that improves performance by accessing data from high-speed cache memory rather than system memory, whenever possible. This is very similar to the 486 and is the primary reason for the increased performance. Performance has been further enhanced by optimizing commonly used instructions.

Because of IBM's deal with Intel, you may see other compatible systems using the 386SLC processor. Until then, only IBM systems will contain the new chip. Because of the enhanced 486-like design, installation of this chip will allow the Model 57 to perform faster than nearly all 25 MHz 386DX-based systems from IBM and other manufacturers. The 386SLC processor option card installs easily in the math coprocessor socket on the Model 57 SX system board. A socket on the 386SLC module is available for installation of a math coprocessor if you want one, or if one has already been installed in the system.

On October 17, 1991, IBM pre-announced the PS/2 Ultimedia Model M57 SLC (8557-255). This enhanced version of the 57 includes the 386SLC processor module, for performance nearly double that of the standard Model 57. It also includes OS/2 2.0, whose availability coincides with the availability of this system in March 1992. This system also has complete multimedia capability. It adds the following standard product improvements to the model standard Model 57:

- Multimedia front panel with stereo headphone jack, mono microphone jack, volume control, and enhanced loudspeaker

- 16-bit eXtended Graphics Array (XGA) adapter card with 1M VRAM that supports 640×480 with 65,000 colors or 1024×768 with 256 colors

- 16-bit audio adapter card with I/O to the front panel that supports FM-quality stereo

- IBM PS/2 mouse

- 160M SCSI fixed disk

- A new CD-ROM/XA drive (PS/2 CD-ROM II) with connection to the multimedia front panel, supporting existing CD-ROM formats and enabled to support new CD-ROM/XA formats

- A CD containing three operating systems or environments, a variety of multimedia application samplers, and an "Introducing Ultimedia" demonstration

- Operating systems supplied on CD-ROM include IBM OS/2 Version 2.0, IBM DOS 5.0, and Microsoft Windows 3.0 with Microsoft Multimedia Windows Extensions 1.0.

The PS/2 Ultimedia Model M57 SLC (8557-255) includes the IBM 386 SLC microprocessor as a standard item. This system is designed for desktop and floor standing operation (a floor stand is included). The mechanical package has five Micro Channel slots and four bays for I/O devices. The Audio Capture and Playback Adapter and the XGA Adapter are installed in two of the slots, leaving three slots for future expansion. A 3 1/2-inch 2.88M media sense disk drive, an SCSI fixed disk, and a CD-ROM/XA drive are installed in three of the bays. An additional 5 1/4-inch or 3 1/2-inch device, optical disk drive, fixed disk drive, tape drive, CD-ROM drive, or a similar device can be installed in the one remaining bay.

The primary video in the Ultimedia is provided by the 16-bit IBM PS/2 XGA Display Adapter/A. Additionally, an enhanced VGA port is provided, for direct video display/ monitor connections or indirect connections via the video feature bus connections to Micro Channel slot #2.

With OS/2 Version 2.0 as a standard feature, users can run OS/2, DOS, and Windows applications. Multimedia applications supported in any of the operating systems can be used effectively by the PS/2 Ultimedia Model M57 SLC user. XGA graphics and CD-ROM/XA are leading-edge technologies. They offer capabilities yet to be exploited, making this one of the most advanced multimedia systems available. IBM introduced IBM multimedia extensions to OS/2 in 1992. These extensions exploit the CD-ROM Extended Architecture (CD-ROM/XA) capabilities for interleaved data and compressed audio enabled by the PS/2 CD-ROM II drive. IBM also has provided the new PS/2 CD-ROM II drive as an optional feature on all IBM SCSI-supported PS/2 systems in the future.

Table 22.31 lists the technical specifications for the PS/2 model 57 SX.

Table 22.31 PS/2 Model 57 SX Technical Specifications	
System Architecture	
Microprocessor	80386SX (04x)
	80386SLC (05x)
Optional microprocessor	80386SLC (04x)
Clock speed	20MHz
Bus type	MCA (Micro Channel Architecture)
Bus width	16-bit
Interrupt levels	16
Type	Level-sensitive
Shareable	Yes
DMA channels	15
DMA burst mode supported	Yes
Bus masters supported	15
Upgradeable processor complex	No
Memory	
Standard on system board	4M
Maximum on system board	16M
Maximum total memory	16M
Memory speed and type	70ns dynamic RAM
System board memory socket type	36-bit SIMM (single in-line memory module)
Number of memory module sockets	3
Number available in standard configuration	2
Memory used on system board	2M/4M/8M 36-bit SIMMs
Memory interleaving	Yes (2M/4M SIMMs only)
Memory cache controller	No
Wait states:	
System board	0-2
Adapter	0-4
Standard Features	
ROM size	128K
ROM shadowing	Yes
BIOS extensions stored on disk	Yes
Setup and Diagnostics stored on disk	Yes
Optional math coprocessor	80387SX
Coprocessor speed	20 MHz
Standard graphics	VGA
	XGA (255, 259)
8-/16-/32-bit controller	16-bit
Bus master	No
	Yes (XGA)
Video RAM (VRAM)	256K (1M on XGA)
RS232C serial ports	1

(continues)

Table 22.31   Continued

Standard Features

UART chip used	Custom (compatible with NS16550A)
Maximum speed (bits/second)	345,600
FIFO mode enabled	Yes
Supports DMA data transfer	Yes
Maximum number of ports	8
Pointing device (mouse) ports	1
Parallel printer ports	1
Bidirectional	Yes
Supports DMA data transfer	Yes
Maximum number of ports	8
CMOS real-time clock (RTC)	Yes
CMOS RAM	64 bytes + 2K extension
Battery life	5 years
Replaceable	Yes

Disk Storage

Internal disk and tape drive bays	4
Number of 3 1/2- and 5 1/4-inch bays	1/3
Selectable boot drive	Yes
Bootable drives	All physical drives
Standard floppy drives	1×2.88M
Optional floppy drives:	
5 1/4-inch 360K	Optional
5 1/4-inch 1.2M	Optional
3 1/2-inch 720K	No
3 1/2-inch 1.44M	Optional
3 1/2-inch 2.88M	Standard
Hard disk controller included	SCSI integrated on system board
Bus master	Yes
Devices supported per adapter	7
Adapters supported per system	4
SCSI hard disks available	60M/80M/120M/160M/320M/400M
Drive form factor	3 1/2-inch
Drive interface	SCSI

Drive capacity	60M	80M	120M	160M	320M	400M
Average access rate (ms)	23	17	23	16	12.5	11.5
Read-ahead cache	32K	32K	32K	32K	64K	128K
SCSI transfer mode	Async	Async	Async	Async	Sync	Sync
Encoding scheme	RLL	RLL	RLL	RLL	RLL	RLL
Cylinders	920	1021	920	1021	949	1201
Heads	4	4	8	8	14	14
Sectors per track	32	39	32	39	48	48
Rotational speed (RPM)	3600	3600	3600	3600	4318	4318
Interleave factor	1:1	1:1	1:1	1:1	1:1	1:1
Data transfer rate (K/second)	960	1170	960	1170	1727	1727
Automatic head parking	Yes	Yes	Yes	Yes	Yes	Yes

PS/2 Ultimedia Model M57 SLC (8557-255)

CD-ROM/XA drive characteristics:	
Formats	CD-DA, CD-ROM, CD-ROM/XA
Capacity	Typically 600M, media-dependent
Access time	380ms
Burst (64K) transfer rate	1.5M/sec
Sustained transfer rate	150K/second
Latency	56ms to 150ms

Expansion Slots

Total adapter slots	5
Number of long and short slots	5/0
Number of 8-/16-/32-bit slots	0/5/0
Number of slots with video ext.	1
Available slots	5

Keyboard Specifications

Keyboard choices	122-key Host-Connected Keyboard
	101-key Enhanced Keyboard
	84-key Space-Saving Keyboard
Fast keyboard speed setting	Yes
Keyboard cable length	10 feet

Security Features

Keylock:	
Locks cover	Yes
Locks keyboard	No
Keyboard password	Yes
Power-on password	Yes
Network server mode	Yes

Physical Specifications

Footprint type	Desktop
Orientation	Horizontal/vertical (stand included)
Dimensions:	
Height	6.7 inches
Width	17.3 inches
Depth	15.5 inches
Weight	32.0 lbs

Environmental Specifications

Power-supply output	197 watts
Worldwide (110/60, 220/50)	Yes
Auto-sensing/switching	Manual switch
Maximum current:	
90-137 VAC	6.0 amps
180-265 VAC	3.0 amps
Operating range:	
Temperature	50-95 degrees F
Relative humidity	8-80 percent
Maximum operating altitude	7,000 feet
Heat (BTUs/hour)	120
FCC classification	Class B

Table 22.32 shows the primary specifications of the various versions of PS/2 Model 57 SX.

Table 23.32 IBM PS/2 Model 57 SX Model Summary						
			PLANAR MEMORY		**STANDARD**	
					Floppy	**Hard**
Part Number	**CPU**	**MHz**	**Std.**	**Max.**	**Drive**	**Disk**
57 SX						
8557-045	386SX	20	4M	16M	1×2.88M	80M
8557-049	386SX	20	4M	16M	1×2.88M	160M
57 SLC						
8557-055	386SLC	20	4M	16M	1×2.88M	80M
8557-059	386SLC	20	4M	16M	1×2.88M	160M
M57 SLC						
8557-255	386SLC	20	4M	16M	1×2.88M	80M
8557-259	386SLC	20	4M	16M	1×2.88M	160M

*Keyboards available include the Enhanced (101-key), Space-Saving (84-key), and Host-Connected (122-key).
If "Any" is indicated, purchaser could choose any of the three.*

PS/2 Model 60

The IBM PS/2 Model 60, introduced April 2, 1987, is a mid-range, desk-side system in the PS/2 family using 16-bit MCA I/O slots. As of October 31, 1990, IBM has withdrawn all versions of the Model 60, and the system is no longer available. Figure 22.24 shows a front view of the Model 60.

The system unit features a 10 MHz microprocessor running with 1 wait state, enabling the Model 60 to perform approximately 20 percent faster than the IBM XT 286 or the IBM AT Model 339. The system-board limit of 1M memory is provided. The Model 60 comes standard with a 1.44M, 3 1/2-inch floppy disk drive; a 44M or a 70M hard disk drive; a disk controller; a serial port; a parallel port; a mouse port; a VGA port; and an 80287 coprocessor socket.

The system has two levels of BIOS, which total 128K: a Compatibility BIOS (CBIOS) with memory addressability of up to 1M provides support for real-mode-based application programs, and Advanced BIOS (ABIOS) provides support for protected-mode-based multitasking operating systems and has extended memory addressability up to 16M.

Additional features of the system unit include eight 16-bit MCA I/O slots (with one slot occupied by the disk controller adapter); an automatic voltage-sensing, universal power supply; a time-and-date clock with battery backup; an additional slot for a second 3 1/2-inch floppy disk drive; and the IBM Enhanced Keyboard. Figure 22.25 shows the rear panel, and figure 22.26 shows the interior view of a Model 60.

Bus Type	Total Available Slots	STANDARD		Date Introduced	Date Withdrawn
		Video	Keyboard		
MCA/16	5/5	VGA	Any	06/11/91	12/21/92
MCA/16	5/5	VGA	Any	06/11/91	12/21/92
MCA/16	5/5	VGA	Any	02/25/92	—
MCA/16	5/5	VGA	Any	02/25/92	—
MCA/16	5/3	XGA	Any	10/17/91	02/25/92
MCA/16	5/3	XGA	Any	02/25/92	—

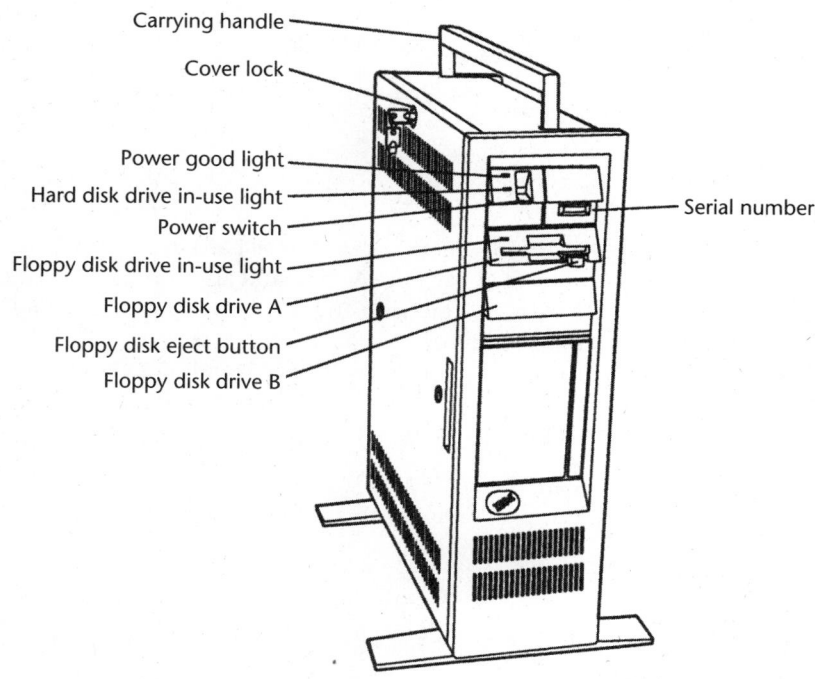

Carrying handle
Cover lock
Power good light
Hard disk drive in-use light
Power switch
Floppy disk drive in-use light
Floppy disk drive A
Floppy disk eject button
Floppy disk drive B
Serial number

Fig. 22.24
PS/2 Model 60.

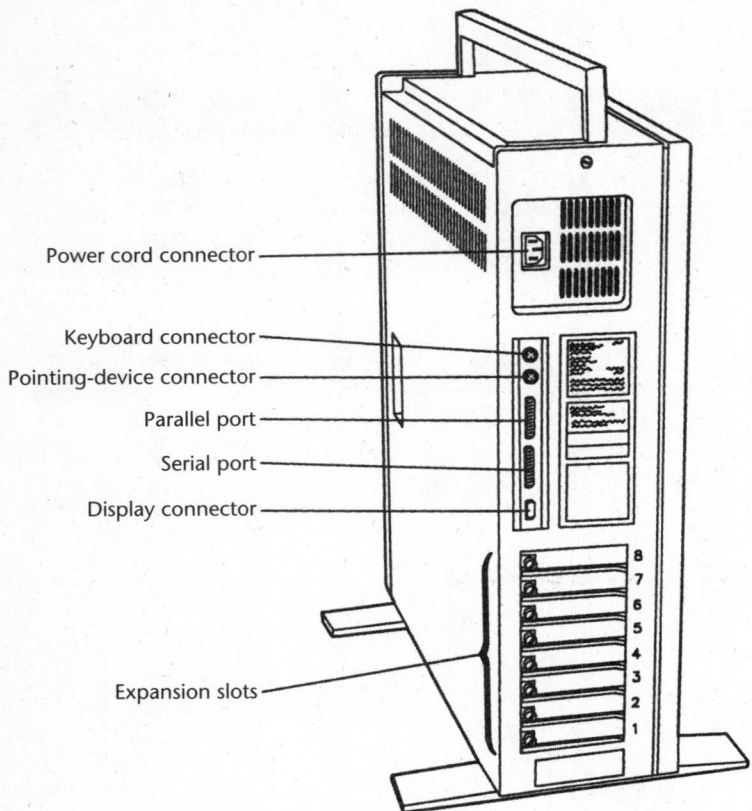

Power cord connector

Keyboard connector
Pointing-device connector
Parallel port
Serial port
Display connector

Expansion slots

Fig. 22.25
PS/2 Model 60 rear panel view.

IBM produced two versions of the Model 60, differing only in the hard disk and controller board supplied. The 70M drive is included with the 60-071 and also can be added as a second drive in that system. The 70M drive attaches using the high-performance Enhanced Small Device Interface (ESDI) disk adapter provided with the system unit and does not require an additional expansion slot. The ESDI adapter (standard in the 60-071) can connect up to two drives and allows for an extremely high data-transfer rate of 10 mbps (megabits per second) as well as increased reliability.

The standard Model 60-041 includes an ST-506/412 hard disk controller, which can connect up to two drives. The maximum transfer rate for this controller is 5 mbps (half that possible with the ESDI controller).

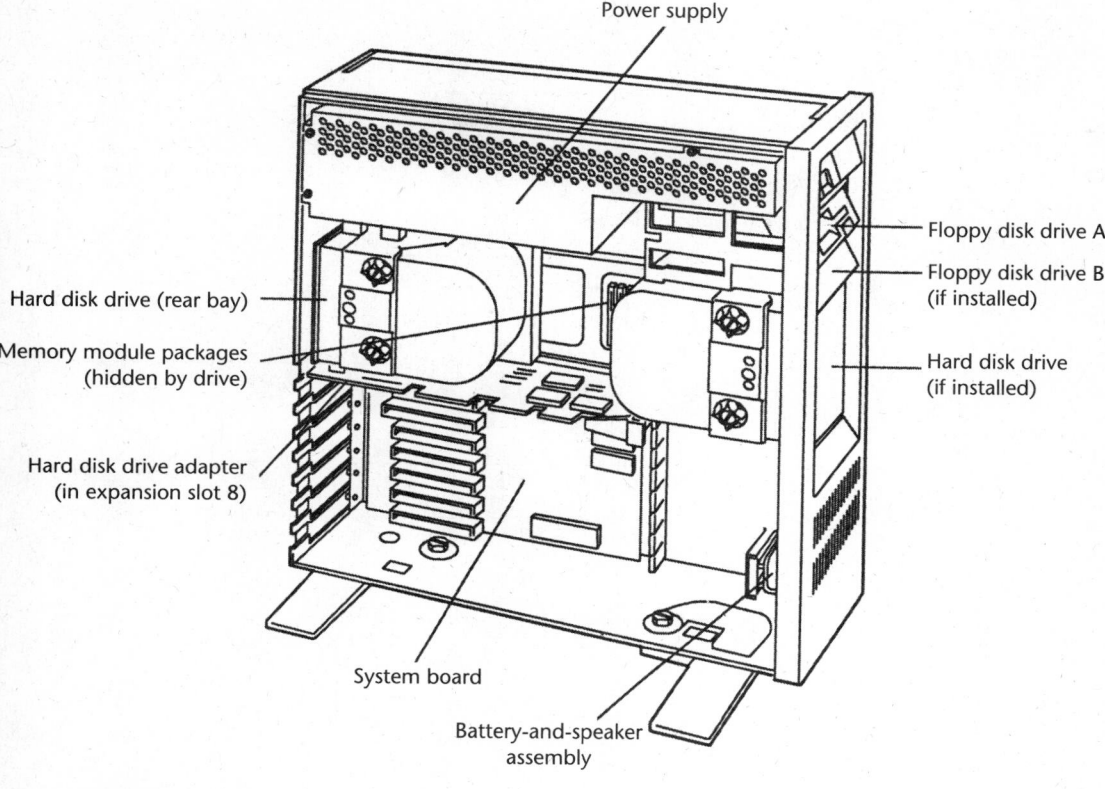

Power supply

Floppy disk drive A

Floppy disk drive B
(if installed)

Hard disk drive
(if installed)

Hard disk drive (rear bay)

Memory module packages
(hidden by drive)

Hard disk drive adapter
(in expansion slot 8)

System board

Battery-and-speaker
assembly

Fig. 22.26
PS/2 Model 60 (interior view).

Table 22.33 lists the technical specifications for the PS/2 Model 60.

Table 22.33 PS/2 Model 60 Technical Specifications	
System Architecture	
Microprocessor	80286
Clock speed	10 MHz
Bus type	MCA (Micro Channel Architecture)
Bus width	16-bit
Interrupt levels	16
Type	Level-sensitive
Shareable	Yes
DMA channels	15
DMA burst mode supported	Yes
Bus masters supported	15
Upgradeable processor complex	No
Memory	
Standard on system board	1M
Maximum on system board	1M

(continues)

Table 22.33   Continued

Memory

Maximum total memory	16M
Memory speed and type	150ns dynamic RAM
System board memory socket type	9-bit SIMM (single in-line memory module)
Number of memory module sockets	4
Number available in standard configuration	0
Memory used on system board	256K 9-bit SIMMs
Memory cache controller	No
Wait states:	
System board	1
Adapter	0-1

Standard Features

ROM size	128K
ROM shadowing	No
Optional math coprocessor	80287
Coprocessor speed	10 MHz
Standard graphics	VGA (Video Graphics Array)
8-/16-/32-bit controller	8-bit
Bus master	No
Video RAM (VRAM)	256K
RS232C serial ports	1
UART chip used	NS16550
Maximum speed (bits/second)	19,200 bps
FIFO mode enabled	No
Maximum number of ports	8
Pointing device (mouse) ports	1
Parallel printer ports	1
Bidirectional	Yes
Maximum number of ports	8
CMOS real-time clock (RTC)	Yes
CMOS RAM	64 bytes + 2K extension
Battery life	5 years
Replaceable	Yes

Disk Storage

Internal disk and tape drive bays	4				
Number of 3 1/2- and 5 1/4-inch bays	2/2				
Standard floppy drives	1×1.44M				
Optional floppy drives:					
5 1/4-inch 360K	Optional				
5 1/4-inch 1.2M	Optional				
3 1/2-inch 720K	No				
3 1/2-inch 1.44M	Standard				
3 1/2-inch 2.88M	No				
Hard disk controller included	ESDI controller ST-506 controller (041)				
ST-506/ESDI hard disks available	44M/70M/115M/314M				
Drive form factor	5 1/4-inch				
Drive capacity	44M	44M	70M	115M	314M
Drive interface	ST-506	ST-506	ESDI	ESDI	ESDI
Average access rate (ms)	40	40	30	28	23
Encoding scheme	MFM	MFM	RLL	RLL	RLL

Disk Storage

BIOS drive type	31	32	None	None	None
Cylinders	733	1024	583	915	1225
Heads	7	5	7	7	15
Sectors per track	17	17	36	36	34
Rotational speed (RPM)	3600	3600	3600	3600	3600
Interleave factor	1:1	1:1	1:1	1:1	1:1
Data transfer rate (K/second)	510	510	1080	1080	1020
Automatic head parking	Yes	Yes	Yes	Yes	Yes

Expansion Slots

Total adapter slots	8
Number of long and short slots	8/0
Number of 8-/16-/32-bit slots	0/8/0
Number of slots with video ext.	1
Available slots	7

Keyboard Specifications

101-key Enhanced Keyboard	Yes
Fast keyboard speed setting	Yes
Keyboard cable length	10 feet

Security Features

Keylock:	
Locks cover	Yes
Locks keyboard	No
Keyboard password	Yes
Power-on password	Yes
Network server mode	Yes

Physical Specifications

Footprint type	Floor-standing
Dimensions:	
Height	23.5 inches
Width	6.5 inches
Depth	19.0 inches
Weight	47.0 lbs

Environmental Specifications

Power-supply output	207 watts (041)
	225 watts (071)
Worldwide (110/60, 220/50)	Yes
Auto-sensing/switching	Yes
Maximum current:	
90-137 VAC	5.3 amps
180-265 VAC	2.7 amps
Operating range:	
Temperature	60-90 degrees F
Relative humidity	8-80 percent
Maximum operating altitude	7,000 feet
Heat (BTUs/hour)	1240
Noise (Average dB, operating, 1m)	46 dB
FCC classification	Class B

Table 22.34 shows the primary specifications of the various versions of PS/2 Model 60.

Table 22.34 IBM PS/2 Model 60 Model Summary

Part Number	CPU	MHz	PLANAR MEMORY Std.	Max.	STANDARD Floppy Drive	Hard Disk
60						
8560-041	286	10	1M	1M	1×1.44M	44M
8560-071	286	10	1M	1M	1×1.44M	70M

Figure 22.27 shows the motherboard components and layout of a Model 60.

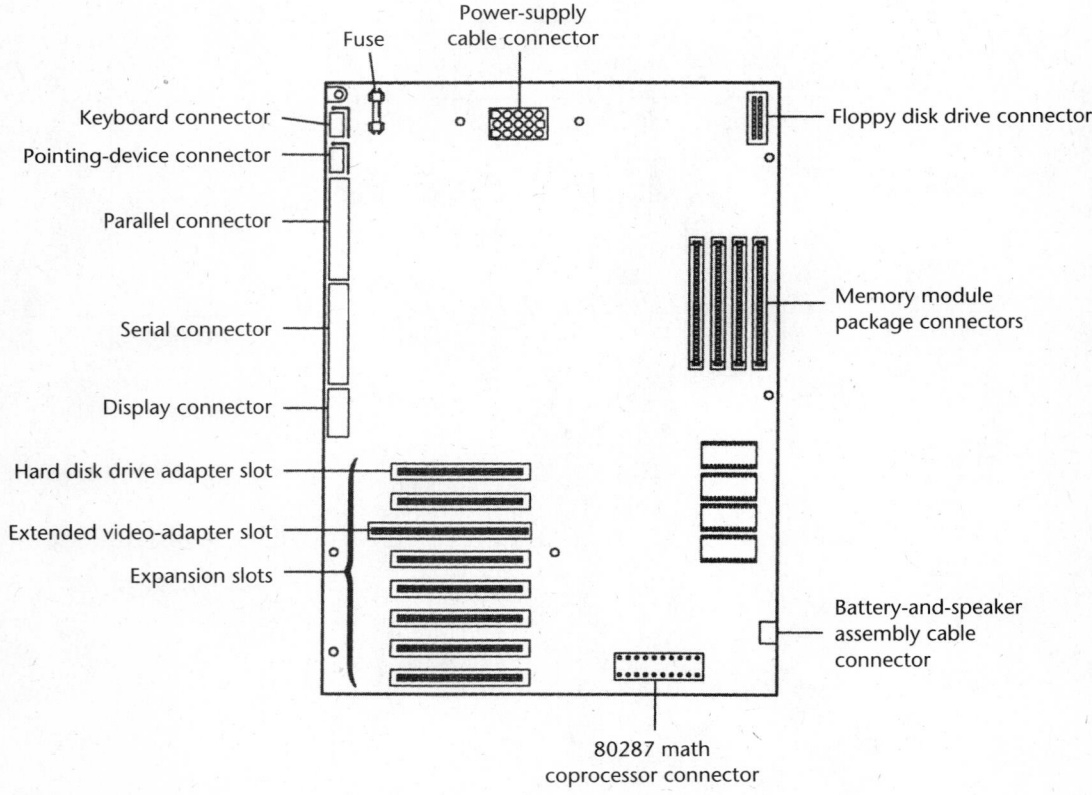

Fig. 22.27
PS/2 Model 60 system board.

Bus Type	Total Available Slots	STANDARD		Date Introduced	Date Withdrawn
		Video	Keyboard		
MCA/16	8/7	VGA	Enh	04/02/87	10/31/90
MCA/16	8/7	VGA	Enh	04/02/87	10/31/90

PS/2 Model 65 SX

The PS/2 Model 65 SX, introduced March 20, 1990, is based on the Intel 80386SX processor running at 16 MHz and uses 16-bit MCA I/O slots. All models of the Model 65 SX were discontinued on July 23, 1991, and are no longer available from IBM. Figure 22.28 and figure 22.29 show front and rear panel views of the Model 65, respectively.

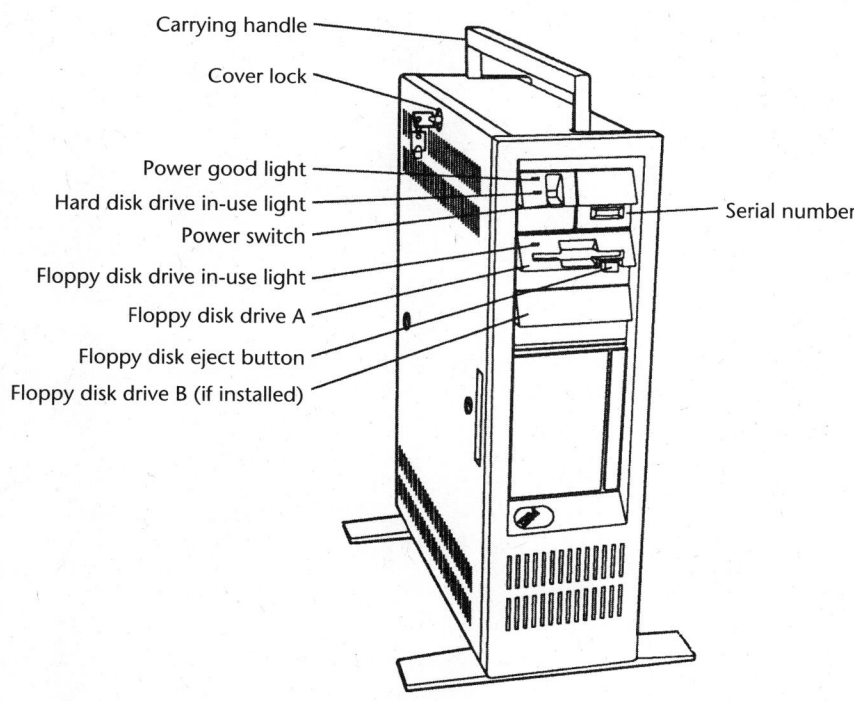

Fig. 22.28
PS/2 Model 65 SX.

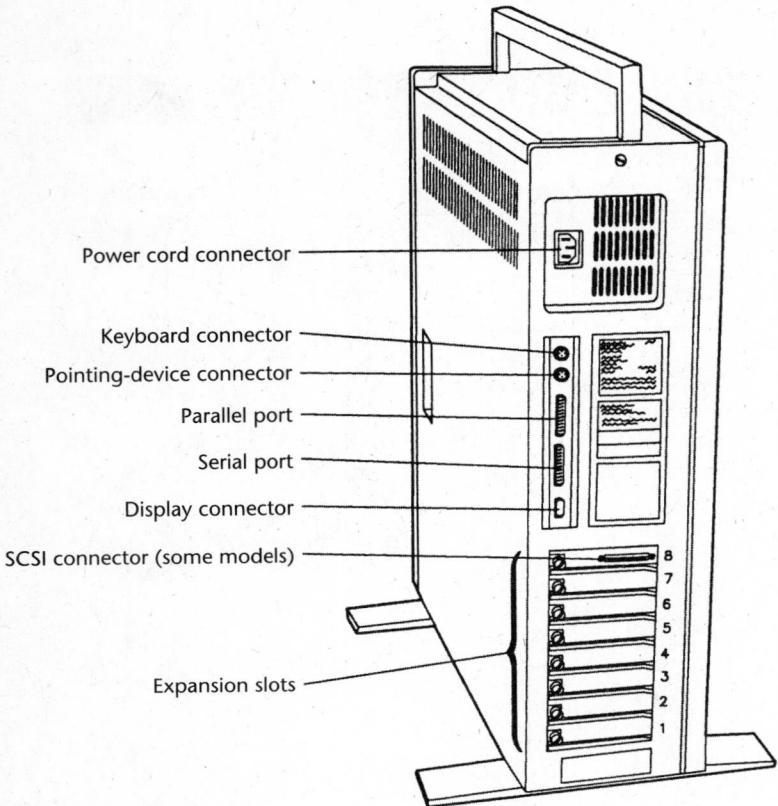

Power cord connector

Keyboard connector
Pointing-device connector
Parallel port
Serial port
Display connector
SCSI connector (some models)

Expansion slots

Fig. 22.29
PS/2 Model 65 SX rear panel view.

Standard features of the Model 65 SX include a 1.44M, 3 1/2-inch, half-height floppy disk drive; VGA graphics adapter; 2M of memory; a 250-watt power supply; a time-and-date clock with battery backup; and the IBM Enhanced PC Keyboard. Two memory SIMM sockets are provided on the system board; one contains 2M of 100ns memory. Both versions of the Model 65 SX can be expanded to 8M of memory on the system board and support up to 16M total system memory. This can be done by removing the standard 2M SIMM and using 4M SIMMs instead. Figure 22.30 shows an interior view of the Model 65.

The hard disk drive controller is the PS/2 Micro Channel SCSI (Small Computer System Interface) Adapter. This bus master adapter provides additional expansion capability and an interface for the 3 1/2-inch, half-height SCSI hard disk drives of either 60M (8565-061) or 120M (8565-121).

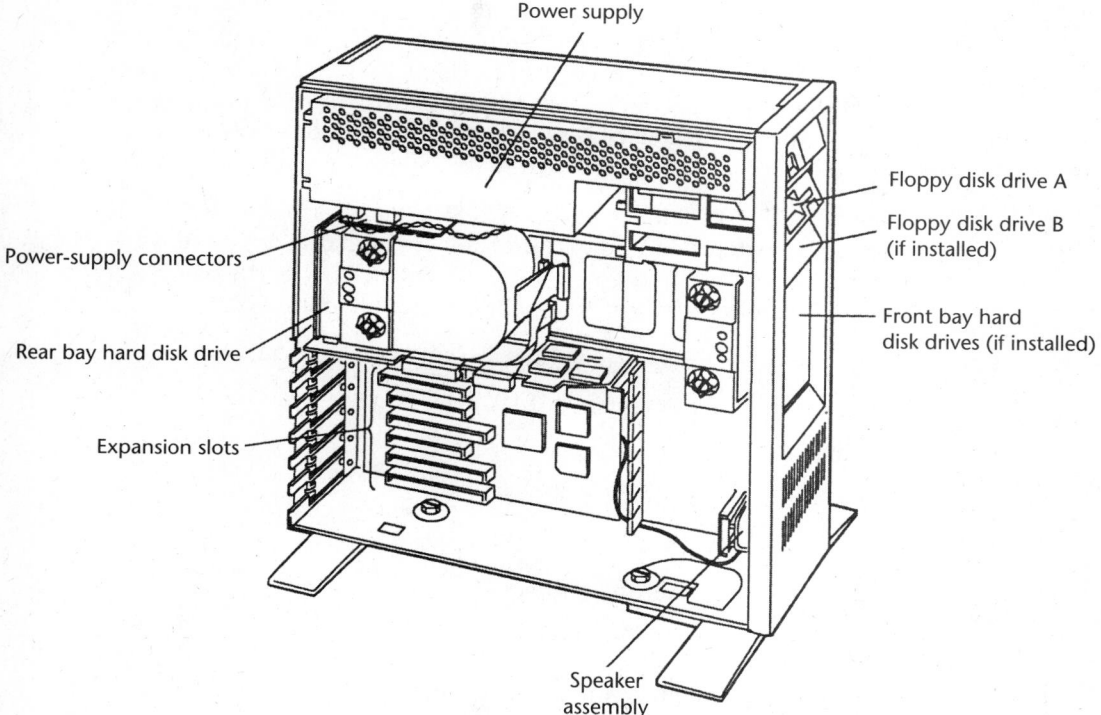

Fig. 22.30
PS/2 Model 65 SX (interior view).

The Model 65 SX has two levels of BIOS, which total 128K: a Compatibility BIOS (CBIOS) with memory addressability of up to 1M provides support for real-mode-based application programs, and Advanced BIOS (ABIOS) provides support for protected-mode-based multitasking operating systems and has extended memory addressability up to 16M.

Design enhancements to these systems offer significant advantages in configuration flexibility and expansion. In addition to providing seven available adapter slots, the standard configuration supports as many as five or six internal drives.

Drive Support. The PS/2 65 SX design provides five drive bays. The three bays in the front of the system are user-accessible; they can contain devices that require insertion and removal of media. The remaining two bays are designed for nonaccessible devices such as hard disks. The accessible bays consist of two 3 1/2-inch, half-height bays and one 5 1/4-inch, full-height bay. The top 3 1/2-inch, half-height bay contains a standard 1.44M floppy disk drive; the second 3 1/2-inch, half-height bay and the 5 1/4-inch, full-height bay are open for expansion purposes.

The standard hard disk drive configuration of the PS/2 Model 65 SX contains one SCSI hard disk drive located in one of the two nonaccessible bays. The other nonaccessible bay contains the necessary hardware to install a second IBM SCSI hard disk drive. The accessible 5 1/4-inch, full-height bay can be converted into two 3 1/2-inch, half-height bays through the use of the optional Fixed Disk Drive Kit A (1053) (6451053). This conversion allows the installation of third and fourth IBM SCSI hard disk drives.

The drive controller is the IBM PS/2 Micro Channel SCSI Adapter—a 16-bit MCA master adapter. Internal cabling is provided to support the standard hard disk drive and two additional internal SCSI devices. External SCSI devices attach directly to the IBM PS/2 Micro Channel SCSI Adapter external port, using the PS/2 card to option cable.

The specifications for the IBM PS/2 Micro Channel SCSI Adapter are as follows:

- Industry-standard interface (ANSI standard X3.131-1986)
- PS/2 16-bit intelligent bus master adapter
- Support for as many as seven physical SCSI devices
- Support for internal and external SCSI devices (single-ended)
- Micro Channel data transfer rate of up to 8.3M per second
- Support for asynchronous or synchronous SCSI devices

Table 22.35 lists the technical specifications for the PS/2 Model 65 SX.

Table 22.35 PS/2 Model 65 SX Technical Specifications	
System Architecture	
Microprocessor	80386SX
Clock speed	16 MHz
Bus type	MCA (Micro Channel Architecture)
Bus width	16-bit
Interrupt levels	16
Type	Level-sensitive
Shareable	Yes
DMA channels	15
DMA burst mode supported	Yes
Bus masters supported	15
Upgradeable processor complex	No
Memory	
Standard on system board	2M
Maximum on system board	8M
Maximum total memory	16M
Memory speed and type	100ns dynamic RAM

Memory

System board memory socket type	36-bit SIMM (single in-line memory module)
Number of memory module sockets	2
Number available in standard configuration	1
Memory used on system board	1M/2M/4M 36-bit SIMMs
Memory cache controller	No

Wait states:

System board	0-2
Adapters	0-4

Standard Features

ROM size	128K
ROM shadowing	Yes
Optional math coprocessor	80387SX
Coprocessor speed	16 MHz
Standard graphics	VGA
8-/16-/32-bit controller	8-bit
Bus master	No
Video RAM (VRAM)	256K
RS232C serial ports	1
UART chip used	NS16550A
Maximum speed (bits/second)	19,200 bps
FIFO mode enabled	Yes
Maximum number of ports	8
Pointing device (mouse) ports	1
Parallel printer ports	1
Bidirectional	Yes
Maximum number of ports	8
CMOS real-time clock (RTC)	Yes
CMOS RAM	64 bytes + 2K extension
Battery life	10 years
Replaceable	Yes (Dallas module)

Disk Storage

Internal disk and tape drive bays	5 or 6 (reconfigurable)
Number of 3 1/2- and 5 1/4-inch bays	4/1 or 6/0 (reconfigurable)
Standard floppy drives	1×1.44M

Optional floppy drives:

5 1/4-inch 360K	Optional
5 1/4-inch 1.2M	Optional
3 1/2-inch 720K	No
3 1/2-inch 1.44M	Standard
3 1/2-inch 2.88M	No
Hard disk controller included	16-bit SCSI adapter
Bus master	Yes
Devices supported per adapter	7
Adapters supported per system	4

(continues)

Table 22.35 Continued

Disk Storage

SCSI hard disks available	60M/80M/120M/160M/320M/400M					
Drive form factor	3 1/2-inch					
Drive interface	SCSI					
Drive capacity	60M	80M	120M	160M	320M	400M
Average access rate (ms)	23	17	23	16	12.5	11.5
Read-ahead cache	32K	32K	32K	32K	64K	128K
SCSI transfer mode	Async	Async	Async	Async	Sync	Sync
Encoding scheme	RLL	RLL	RLL	RLL	RLL	RLL
Cylinders	920	1021	920	1021	949	1201
Heads	4	4	8	8	14	14
Sectors per track	32	39	32	39	48	48
Rotational speed (RPM)	3600	3600	3600	3600	4318	4318
Interleave factor	1:1	1:1	1:1	1:1	1:1	1:1
Data transfer rate (K/sec)	960	1170	960	1170	1727	1727
Automatic head parking	Yes	Yes	Yes	Yes	Yes	Yes

Expansion Slots

Total adapter slots	8
Number of long and short slots	8/0
Number of 8-/16-/32-bit slots	0/8/0
Number of slots with video ext.	1
Available slots	7

Keyboard Specifications

101-key Enhanced Keyboard	Yes
Fast keyboard speed setting	Yes
Keyboard cable length	10 feet
Keylock:	
Locks cover	Yes
Locks keyboard	No
Keyboard password	Yes
Power-on password	Yes
Network server mode	Yes

Physical Specifications

Footprint type	Floor-standing
Dimensions:	
Height	23.5 inches
Width	6.5 inches
Depth	19.0 inches
Weight	52.0 lbs

Environmental Specifications

Power-supply output	250 watts
Worldwide (110/60, 220/50)	Yes
Auto-sensing/switching	Yes

Environmental Specifications	
Maximum current:	
90-137 VAC	5.3 amps
180-265 VAC	2.7 amps
Operating range:	
Temperature	60-90 degrees F
Relative humidity	8-80 percent
Maximum operating altitude	7,000 feet
Heat (BTUs/hour)	1218
Noise (Average dB, operating, 1m)	54 dB
FCC classification	Class B

Figure 22.31 shows the motherboard components and layout for the Model 65.

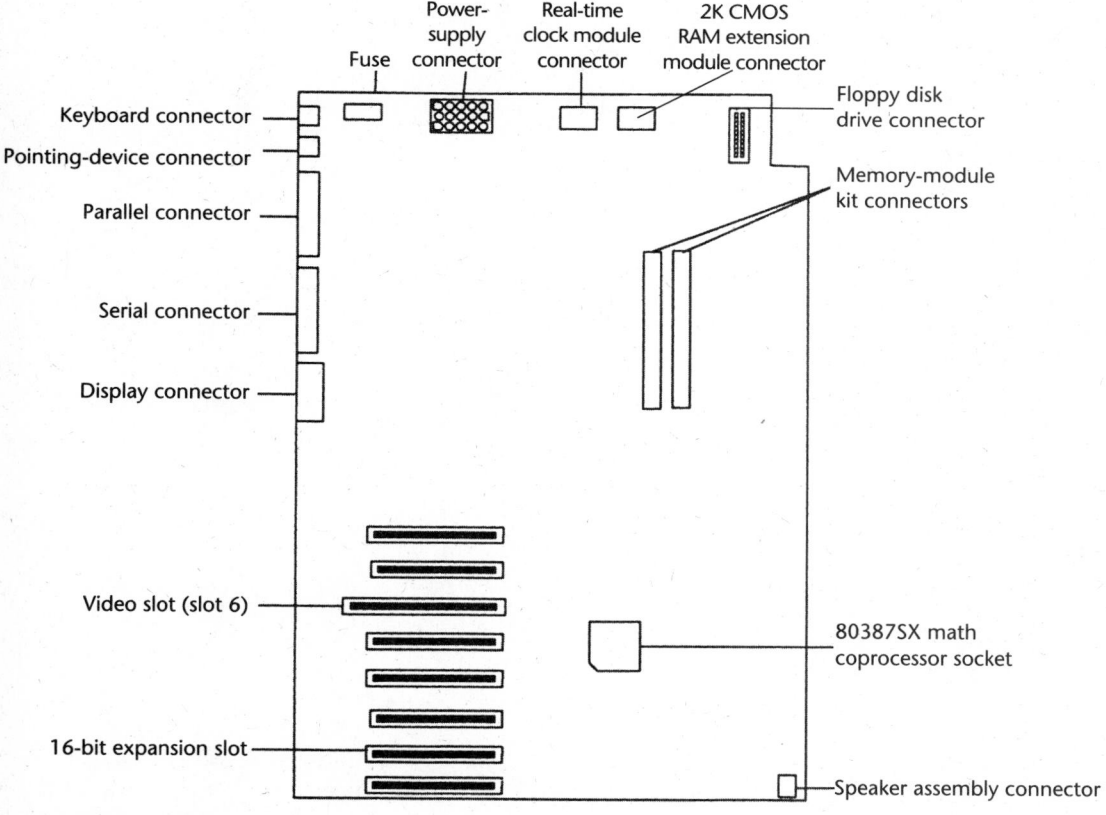

Fig. 22.31
PS/2 Model 65 SX system board.

Table 22.36 shows the primary specifications of the various versions of PS/2 Model 65 SX.

			PLANAR MEMORY		STANDARD	
Part Number	**CPU**	**MHz**	**Std.**	**Max.**	**Floppy Drive**	**Hard Disk**
65 SX						
8565-061	386SX	16	2M	8M	1×1.44M	60M
8565-121	386SX	16	2M	8M	1×1.44M	120M
8565-321	386SX	50	2M	8M	1×1.44M	320M

Table 22.36 IBM PS/2 Model 65 SX Model Summary

Note: *All Model 65 units are discontinued.*

PS/2 Model 70 386

The PS/2 Model 70 386, introduced June 2, 1988, is a desktop, high-end system in the PS/2 family. The Model 70 386 includes Micro Channel Architecture (MCA). Figure 22.32 shows a front view of the Model 70.

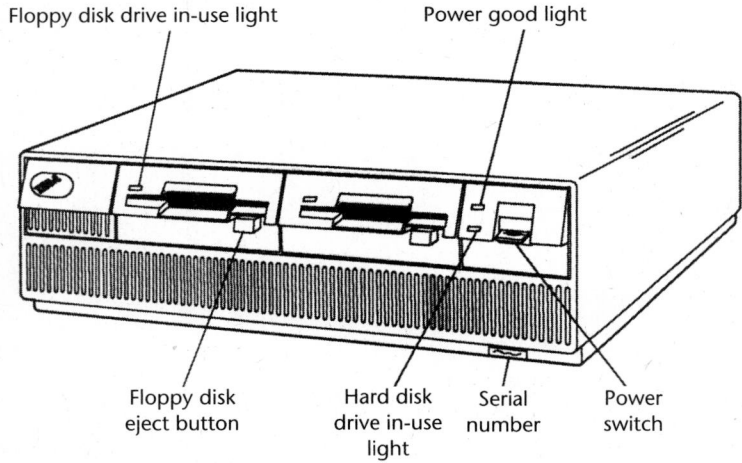

Fig. 22.32
PS/2 Model 70.

The basic system features a 16 MHz, 20 MHz, or 25 MHz 80386 microprocessor and 2M or 4M of high-speed memory on the motherboard. Motherboard memory is expandable to 6M or 8M depending on the model; you can expand total memory to 16M with memory adapters. The Model 70 386 comes with a 1.44M, 3 1/2-inch floppy disk drive and either a 60M or 120M hard disk drive with integrated controller (IDE) as standard. A serial port, parallel port, mouse port, and VGA port also are standard. Figure 22.33 shows a rear panel view of the Model 70.

Bus Type	Total Available Slots	STANDARD		Date Introduced	Date Withdrawn
		Video	Keyboard		
MCA/16	8/7	VGA	Enh	03/20/90	07/23/91
MCA/16	8/7	VGA	Enh	03/20/90	07/23/91
MCA/16	8/7	VGA	Enh	10/30/90	07/23/91

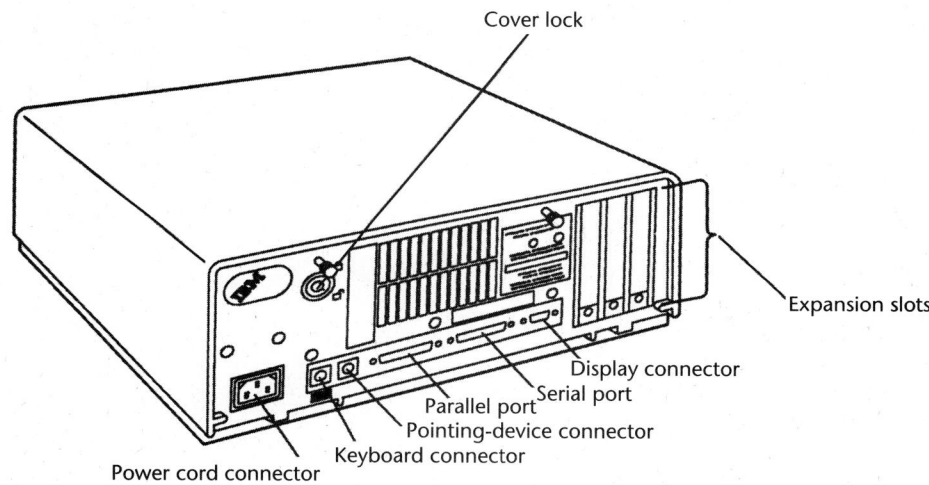

Cover lock

Expansion slots

Display connector

Serial port

Parallel port

Pointing-device connector

Keyboard connector

Power cord connector

Fig. 22.33
PS/2 Model 70 rear panel.

The top-of-the-line 70 386-Axx models feature a 25 MHz 80386 32-bit microprocessor and an Intel 82385 memory cache controller with a high-speed 64K static memory cache. This memory cache lets the Model 70 386 perform approximately 150 percent faster than the 20 MHz versions of the Model 80. The Model 70 386 is about 250 percent faster than the Model 50.

The Model 70 386 has two levels of BIOS, which total 128K: a Compatibility BIOS (CBIOS) with memory addressability of up to 1M provides support for real-mode-based application programs; and Advanced BIOS (ABIOS) provides support for protected-mode-based multitasking operating systems and has extended memory addressability up to 16M.

Additional features of the Model 70 386 include one 16-bit and two 32-bit I/O slots.

Because all the hard disks available with the Model 70 386 have integrated (embedded) controllers, no slot is lost to a disk controller card. The Model 70 386 also has a 132-watt, automatic voltage-sensing, universal power supply; a time-and-date clock with battery backup; an additional slot for a second 3 1/2-inch floppy disk drive; an optional 16 MHz, 20 MHz, or 25 MHz 80387 coprocessor; and the IBM Enhanced Keyboard. Figure 22.34 shows the interior view of the Model 70.

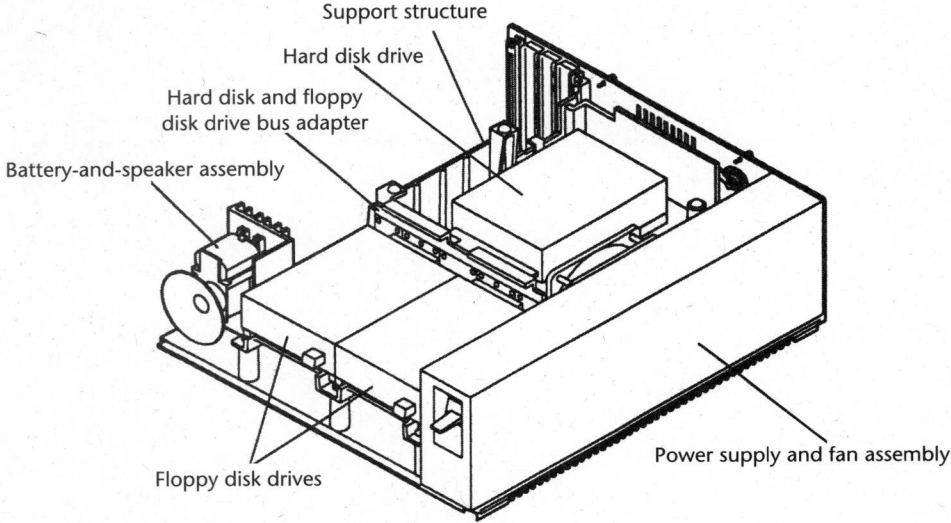

Fig. 22.34
PS/2 Model 70 interior view.

Several versions of the Model 70 386 are available. They differ mainly in clock speed, installed hard disk storage, and memory capabilities. Available system clock speeds are 16 MHz, 20 MHz, and 25 Mhz, and hard disks are available with 60M, 80M, 120M, and 160M of capacity. The 25 MHz models offer memory expansion to 8M on the system board and feature an upgradeable processor on a daughterboard (currently, only a single upgrade is available to a 25 MHz 80486DX processor).

The 25 MHz models have a few outstanding differences from the other models that give this system a higher-than-expected performance level. The 70 386-Axx models use an Intel 82385 cache controller chip, which manages 64K of extremely high-speed static memory. This memory is accessed at 0 wait states and uses a special algorithm to ensure an exceptionally high bit ratio for cache memory access. Because of this system's speed, this version of the Model 70 386 requires extremely fast (80ns) memory, which the other models do not need. Remember this requirement when you purchase additional memory for this system and when you make repairs.

The 80387 math coprocessor chip selected for each system unit must match the main processor in speed, and the 80387 chips (especially the 25 MHz chip) are expensive. These chips are no longer being sold by IBM and must be obtained from other sources.

Table 22.37 lists the technical specifications for the PS/2 Model 70 386.

Table 22.37   PS/2 Model 70 386 Technical Specifications

System Architecture

Microprocessor	80386DX
Clock speed	16 MHz (Exx)
	20 MHz (0xx,1xx)
	25 MHz (Axx)
Bus type	MCA (Micro Channel Architecture)
Bus width	32-bit
Interrupt levels	16
Type	Level-sensitive
Shareable	Yes
DMA channels	15
DMA burst mode supported	Yes
Bus masters supported	15
Upgradeable processor complex	No
	Yes (Axx)

Memory

Standard on system board	4M
Maximum on system board	6M
	8M (Axx)
Maximum total memory	16M
Memory speed and type	85ns dynamic RAM
	80ns dynamic RAM (Axx)
System board memory socket type	36-bit SIMM (single in-line memory module)
Number of memory module sockets	3
	4 (Axx)
Number available in standard configuration	1
	2 (Axx)
Memory used on system board	1M/2M 36-bit SIMMs
Paged memory logic	Yes
Memory cache controller	No
	Yes (Axx)
Internal/external cache	External
Standard memory cache size	64K
Cache memory speed and type	25ns static RAM
Wait states:	
System board	0-5 (Axx, 95 percent 0 wait states)
	0-2
Adapter	0-7 (Axx, 95 percent 0 wait states)
	0-4

(continues)

Table 22.37   Continued

Standard Features

ROM size	128K
ROM shadowing	Yes
Optional math coprocessor	80387DX
Coprocessor speed	16 MHz (Exx)
	20 MHz (0xx,1xx)
	25 MHz (Axx)
Standard graphics	VGA (Video Graphics Array)
8-/16-/32-bit controller	8-bit
Bus master	No
Video RAM (VRAM)	256K
RS232C serial ports	1
UART chip used	NS16550A
Maximum speed (bits/second)	19,200 bps
FIFO mode enabled	Yes
Maximum number of ports	8
Pointing device (mouse) ports	1
Parallel printer ports	1
Bidirectional	Yes
Maximum number of ports	8
CMOS real-time clock (RTC)	Yes
CMOS RAM	64 bytes + 2K extension
Battery life	5 years
Replaceable	Yes

Disk Storage

Internal disk and tape drive bays	3			
Number 3 1/2- and 5 1/4-inch bays	3/0			
Standard floppy drives	1×1.44M			
Optional floppy drives:				
5 1/4-inch 360K	Optional			
5 1/4-inch 1.2M	Optional			
3 1/2-inch 720K	No			
3 1/2-inch 1.44M	Standard			
3 1/2-inch 2.88M	No			
Hard disk controller included	IDE connector on Interposer Card			
IDE hard disks available	60M/80M/120M/160M			
Drive form factor	3 1/2-inch			
Drive interface	IDE			
Drive capacity	60M	80M	120M	160M
Average access rate (ms)	27	17	23	16
Read-ahead cache	No	32K	No	32K
Encoding scheme	RLL	RLL	RLL	RLL
Cylinders	762	1021	920	1021
Heads	6	4	8	8
Sectors per track	26	39	32	39
Rotational speed (RPM)	3600	3600	3600	3600

Disk Storage

Interleave factor	1:1	1:1	1:1	1:1
Data transfer rate (K/second)	780	1170	960	1170
Automatic head parking	Yes	Yes	Yes	Yes

Expansion Slots

Total adapter slots	3
Number of long and short slots	3/0
Number of 8-/16-/32-bit slots	0/1/2
Number of slots with video ext.	1
Available slots	3

Keyboard Specifications

101-key Enhanced Keyboard	Yes
Fast keyboard speed setting	Yes
Keyboard cable length	6 feet

Security Features

Keylock:	
Locks cover	Yes
Locks keyboard	No
Keyboard password	Yes
Power-on password	Yes
Network server mode	Yes

Physical Specifications

Footprint type	Desktop
Dimensions:	
Height	5.5 inches
Width	14.2 inches
Depth	16.5 inches
Weight	21.0 lbs

Environmental Specifications

Power-supply output	132 watts
Worldwide (110/60, 220/50)	Yes
Auto-sensing/switching	Yes
Maximum current:	
90-137 VAC	2.7 amps
180-265 VAC	1.4 amps
Operating range:	
Temperature	60-90 degrees F
Relative humidity	8-80 percent
Maximum operating altitude	7,000 feet
Heat (BTUs/hour)	751
Noise (average dB, operating, 1m)	40 dB
FCC classification	Class B

Figures 22.35, 22.36, and 22.37 show the components and layouts of the three different types of Model 70 motherboards.

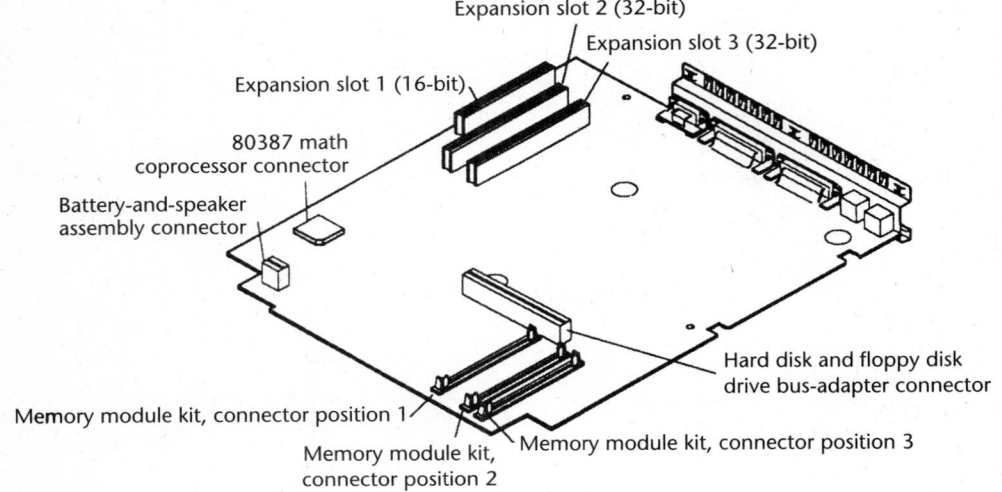

Fig. 22.35
PS/2 Model 70 386 system board (16 MHz and 20 MHz, type 1).

Table 22.38 shows the primary specifications of the various versions of PS/2 Model 70 386.

| Part Number | CPU | MHz | PLANAR MEMORY | | STANDARD | |
			Std.	Max.	Floppy Drive	Hard Disk
70 386						
8570-E61	386DX	16	2M	6M	1×1.44M	60M
8570-061	386DX	20	2M	6M	1×1.44M	60M
8570-081	386DX	20	4M	6M	1×1.44M	80M
8570-121	386DX	20	2M	6M	1×1.44M	120M
8570-161	386DX	20	4M	6M	1×1.44M	160M
8570-A61	386DX	25	2M	8M	1×1.44M	60M
8570-A81	386DX	25	4M	8M	1×1.44M	80M
8570-A21	386DX	25	2M	8M	1×1.44M	120M
8570-A16	386DX	25	4M	8M	1×1.44M	160M

Table 22.38   IBM PS/2 Model 70 386 Model Summary

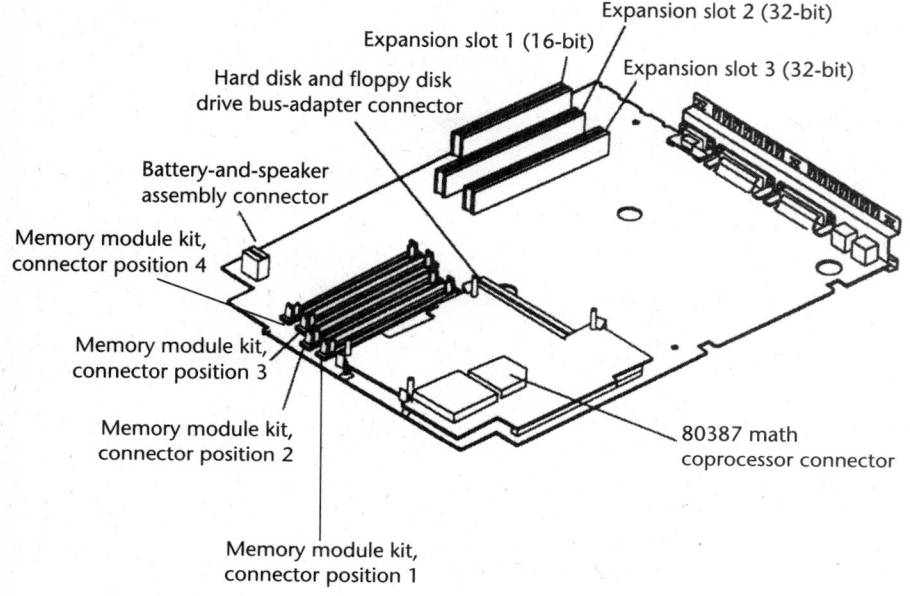

Expansion slot 2 (32-bit)

Expansion slot 1 (16-bit)

Hard disk and floppy disk
drive bus-adapter connector

Expansion slot 3 (32-bit)

Battery-and-speaker
assembly connector

Memory module kit,
connector position 4

Memory module kit,
connector position 3

Memory module kit,
connector position 2

80387 math
coprocessor connector

Memory module kit,
connector position 1

Fig. 22.36
PS/2 Model 70 386 system board (16 MHz and 20 MHz, type 2).

Bus Type	Total Available Slots	STANDARD		Date Introduced	Date Withdrawn
		Video	Keyboard		
MCA/32	3/3	VGA	Enh	06/07/88	07/23/91
MCA/32	3/3	VGA	Enh	09/26/89	09/11/91
MCA/32	3/3	VGA	Enh	06/11/91	—
MCA/32	3/3	VGA	Enh	09/26/89	09/11/91
MCA/32	3/3	VGA	Enh	06/11/91	—
MCA/32	3/3	VGA	Enh	09/26/89	09/11/91
MCA/32	3/3	VGA	Enh	06/11/91	01/17/92
MCA/32	3/3	VGA	Enh	09/26/89	09/11/91
MCA/32	3/3	VGA	Enh	06/11/91	—

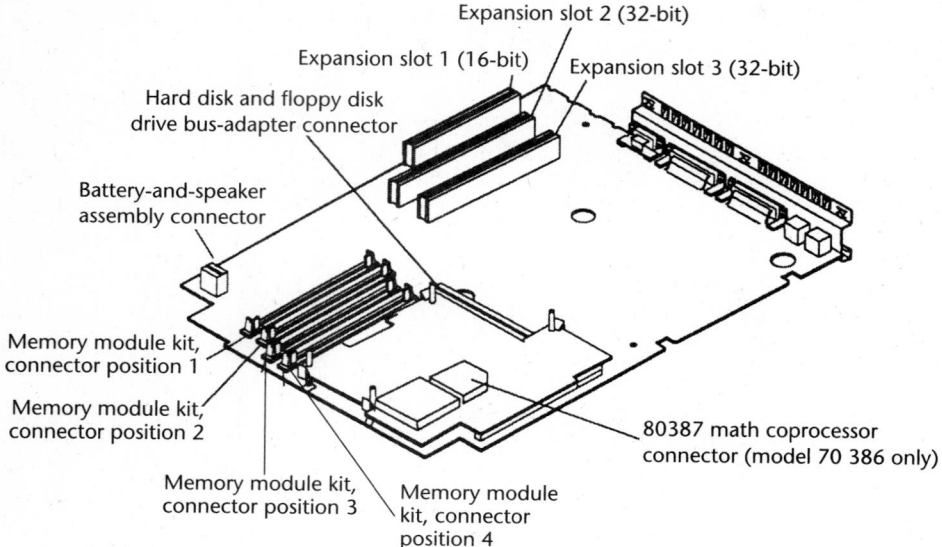

Fig. 22.37
PS/2 Model 70 386 system board (25 MHz, type 3).

PS/2 Model 70 486

The IBM PS/2 Model 70 486, introduced June 20, 1989, is essentially a Model 70 386-Axx with the 486 25 MHz Power Platform upgrade. The 25 MHz 80486 32-bit microprocessor replaces the 386 processor module standard in the Model 70 386. The Model 70 496 is no different from a Model 70 386 with the Power Platform added later.

The Model 70 486 has been discontinued by IBM as of 09/11/91 and is no longer available. The 486 Power Platform, however, is still available for upgrading existing 25 MHz Model 70 386 systems.

The basic system features a 25 MHz 80486 32-bit microprocessor with a built-in 8K memory cache. With this processor and memory cache, this unit can perform approximately 100 percent faster than the 386 version. Also included is 4M of high-speed memory on the motherboard, expandable to 8M, with total memory expandable to 16M (with memory adapters). This system comes with a 1.44M, 3 1/2-inch floppy disk drive and either a 60M or 120M hard disk drive with integrated controller (IDE) as standard. Also standard are a serial port, parallel port, mouse port, and VGA port.

The Model 70 486 has two levels of BIOS, which total 128K: A Compatibility BIOS (CBIOS) with memory addressability of up to 1M provides support for real-mode-based application programs; and an additional version of BIOS, Advanced BIOS (ABIOS), provides support for protected-mode-based multitasking operating systems and has extended memory addressability of up to 16M.

Additional features of the Model 70 486 include one 16-bit and two 32-bit I/O slots. Because all the hard disks available with the Model 70 have integrated (embedded) controllers, no slot is lost to a disk controller card. The Model 70 486 also has a 25 MHz 80387 math coprocessor; a 132-watt, automatic voltage-sensing, universal power supply; a time-and-date clock with battery backup; an additional slot for a second 3 1/2-inch floppy disk drive; and the IBM Enhanced Keyboard.

Table 22.39 lists the technical specifications for the PS/2 Model 70 486.

Table 22.39 PS/2 Model 70 486 Technical Specifications

System Architecture

Microprocessor	80486
Clock speed	25 MHz
Bus type	MCA (Micro Channel Architecture)
Bus width	32-bit
Interrupt levels	16
Type	Level-sensitive
Shareable	Yes
DMA channels	15
DMA burst mode supported	Yes
Bus masters supported	15
486 burst mode enabled	No
Upgradeable processor complex	Included

Memory

Standard on system board	2M
Maximum on system board	8M
Maximum total memory	16M
Memory speed and type	80ns dynamic RAM
System board memory socket type	36-bit SIMM (single in-line memory module)
Number of memory module sockets	4
Number available in standard configuration	3
Memory used on system board	2M 36-bit SIMMs
Paged memory logic	Yes
Memory cache controller	Yes
Internal/external cache	Internal
Standard memory cache size	8K
Optional external memory cache	No
Wait states:	
System board	0-5 (95 percent 0 wait states)
Adapter	0-7

Standard Features

ROM size	128K
ROM shadowing	Yes
Math coprocessor	Built-in
Coprocessor speed	25 MHz

(continues)

Table 22.39   Continued

Standard Features

Standard graphics	VGA
8-/16-/32-bit controller	8-bit
Bus master	No
Video RAM (VRAM)	256K
RS232C serial ports	1
UART chip used	NS16550A
Maximum speed (bits/second)	19,200 bps
FIFO mode enabled	Yes
Maximum number of ports	8
Pointing device (mouse) ports	1
Parallel printer ports	1
Bidirectional	Yes
Maximum number of ports	8
CMOS real-time clock (RTC)	Yes
CMOS RAM	64 bytes + 2K extension
Replaceable	Yes

Disk Storage

Internal disk and tape drive bays	3
Number of 3 1/2- and 5 1/4-inch bays	3/0
Standard floppy drives	1×1.44M
Optional floppy drives:	
5 1/4-inch 360K	Optional
5 1/4-inch 1.2M	Optional
3 1/2-inch 720K	No
3 1/2-inch 1.44M	Standard
3 1/2-inch 2.88M	No
Hard disk controller included	IDE connector on Interposer Card
IDE hard disks available	60M/80M/120M/160M
Drive form factor	3 1/2-inch
Drive interface	IDE

Drive capacity	60M	80M	120M	160M
Average access rate (ms)	27	17	23	16
Read-ahead cache	No	32K	No	32K
Encoding scheme	RLL	RLL	RLL	RLL
Cylinders	762	1021	920	1021
Heads	6	4	8	8
Sectors per track	26	39	32	39
Rotational speed (RPM)	3600	3600	3600	3600
Interleave factor	1:1	1:1	1:1	1:1
Data transfer rate (K/second)	780	1170	960	1170
Automatic head parking	Yes	Yes	Yes	Yes

Expansion Slots

Total adapter slots	3
Number of long and short slots	3/0
Number of 8-/16-/32-bit slots	0/1/2
Number of slots with video ext.	1
Available slots	3

Keyboard Specifications

101-key Enhanced Keyboard	Yes
Fast keyboard speed setting	Yes
Keyboard cable length	6 feet

Security Features

Keylock:	
Locks cover	Yes
Locks keyboard	No
Keyboard password	Yes
Power-on password	Yes
Network server mode	Yes

Physical Specifications

Footprint type	Desktop
Dimensions:	
Height	5.5 inches
Width	14.2 inches
Depth	16.5 inches
Weight	21.0 lbs

Environmental Specifications

Power-supply output	132 watts
Worldwide (110/60, 220/50)	Yes
Auto-sensing/switching	Yes
Maximum current:	
90-137 VAC	2.7 amps
180-265 VAC	1.4 amps
Operating range:	
Temperature	60-90 degrees F
Relative humidity	8-80 percent
Maximum operating altitude	7,000 feet
Heat (BTUs/hour)	751
Noise (Average dB, operating, 1m)	40 dB
FCC classification	Class B

Table 22.40 shows the primary specifications of the various versions of PS/2 Model 70 486.

Table 22.40 IBM PS/2 Model 70 486 Model Summary						
			PLANAR MEMORY		**STANDARD**	
Part Number	**CPU**	**MHz**	**Std.**	**Max.**	**Floppy Drive**	**Hard Disk**
70 486						
8570-B61	486DX	25	2M	8M	1×1.44M	60M
8570-B21	486DX	25	2M	8M	1×1.44M	120M

PS/2 Model P70 386

The PS/2 Model P70 386 (8573), introduced May 9, 1989, is a high-function, high-performance portable system designed to complement the PS/2 Model 70 386 desktop family of products. IBM has made the PS/2 Model P70 386 in 16 MHz and 20 MHz versions with 30M, 60M, and 120M hard disks. Effective July 23, 1991, IBM discontinued two versions of the Model P70 386: the 16 MHz model (031) and the 20 MHz, 60M disk model (061). The Model P70 386-121 (120M disk) continues to be sold. Figure 22.38 shows a front view of the Model P70.

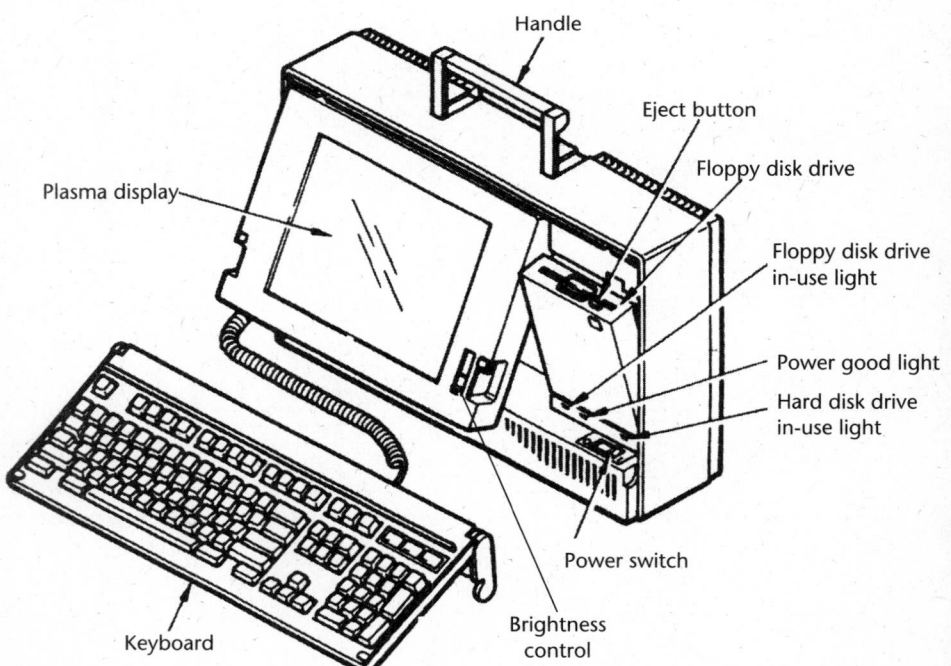

Fig. 22.38
PS/2 Model P70 386.

Bus Type	Total Available Slots	STANDARD		Date Introduced	Date Withdrawn
		Video	Keyboard		
MCA/32	3/3	VGA	Enh	09/26/89	09/11/91
MCA/32	3/3	VGA	Enh	06/20/89	09/11/91

The Model P70 386 includes MCA I/O slots, a VGA 16-grayscale plasma display, and a fully compatible PS/2 Enhanced Keyboard, all neatly integrated into a single package. It features an 80386DX processor, high-density memory technology, and a wide range of integrated features, supporting up to 16M of high-speed memory (4M standard, expandable up to 8M on system board), 120M or more disk storage, and an optional 80387 math coprocessor. Like most PS/2 systems, all models come standard with a 1.44M, 3 1/2-inch floppy disk drive, a pointing device port, a serial/asynchronous port, a parallel port, a VGA port, and an external storage device port. Figure 22.39 shows the rear panel view of the Model P70.

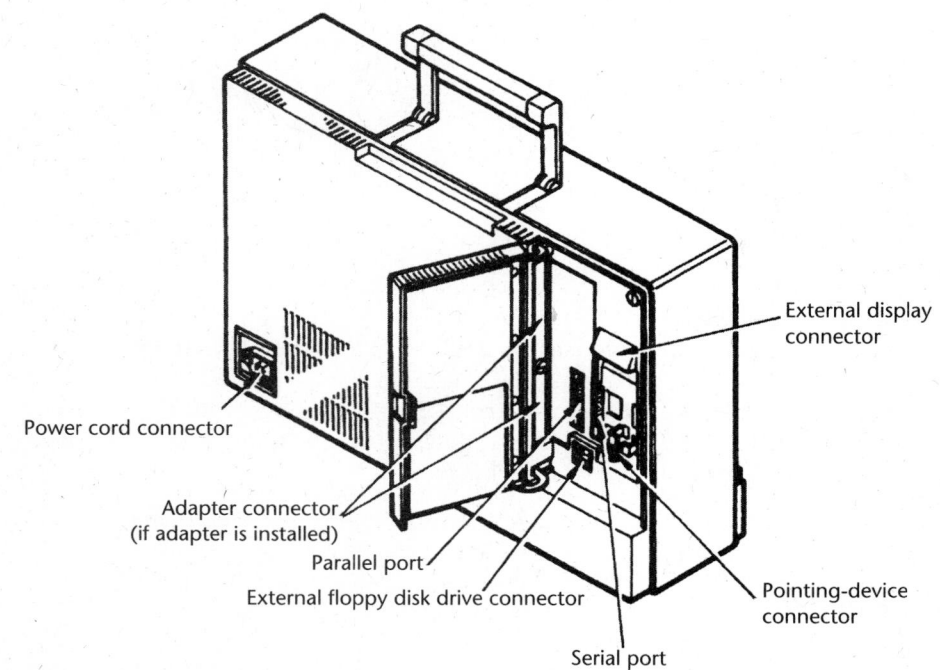

External display connector

Power cord connector

Adapter connector
(if adapter is installed)

Parallel port

External floppy disk drive connector

Serial port

Pointing-device connector

Fig. 22.39
PS/2 Model P70 386 rear panel view.

Exceptional features for a portable computer include the Model 70's two MCA expansion slots (one full and one half-length) and its ergonomic briefcase portable design. The expansion slots can be used for products such as the IBM PS/2 300/1200/2400 Internal Modem/A or P70 386 Token-Ring Adapter. Figure 22.40 shows the interior view of the P70.

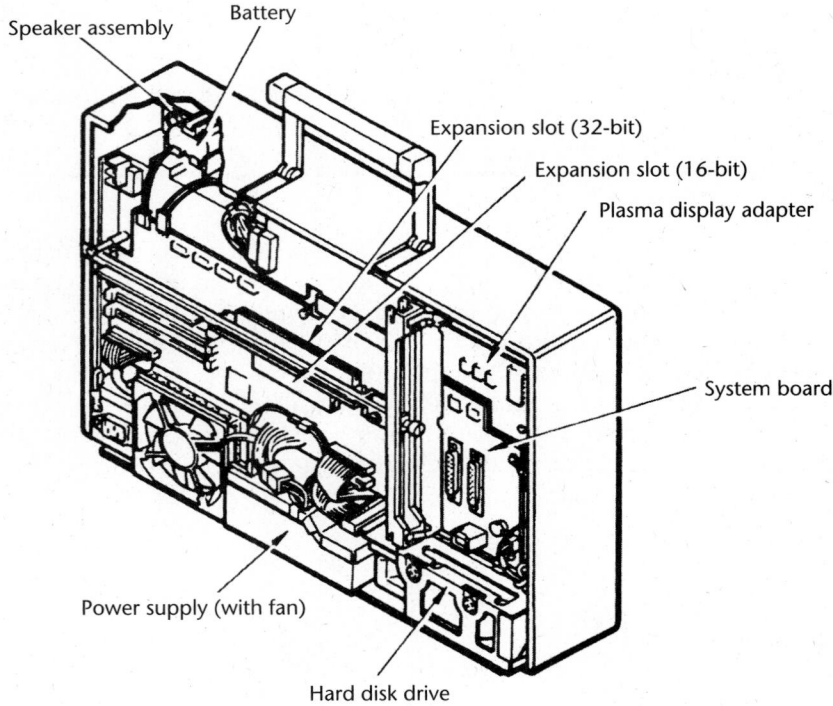

Fig. 22.40
PS/2 Model P70 386 interior view.

One exception to the norm is the external storage device port. The equivalent of the drive B internal floppy disk port, as found in the desktop Model 70, it permits attachment of externally powered devices, such as the IBM 360K external disk drive and some other manufacturers' backup devices. A cable (part number 23F2716) 35.5 centimeters or 14 inches long is available for attaching external drives. The cable features a Hoshiden Connector to attach to the P70 386 with an industry standard 37-pin D-shell connector that connects to the externally powered devices.

The VGA port supports all VGA graphics and text modes including 640 × 480 graphics, 320 × 200 graphics in 256 colors, and 720 × 400 text using any optional PS/2 VGA color display; and yet maintains compatibility with CGA and EGA modes. The gas plasma display normally shuts down when an external display is connected. You can override this feature and force both displays to operate simultaneously with the external display in monochrome mode, which is ideal for presentations using large-screen projection devices.

In addition, the system is designed for tool-free installation and includes security features in BIOS. The Model P70 386 has two levels of BIOS, which total 128K: A Compatibility BIOS (CBIOS) with memory addressability of up to 1M provides support for real-mode-based application programs; and an additional version of BIOS, Advanced BIOS (ABIOS), provides support for protected-mode-based multitasking operating systems and has extended memory addressability of up to 16M.

The P70 386 uses hard drives with integrated controllers (IDE). These drives plug directly into a special MCA IDE connector on the motherboard. All models use high-speed (85ns) memory and have memory paging and ROM shadowing to improve performance. Several accessories are available for the system, including three different carrying cases, the external storage device cable, and a keyboard extension cable.

Table 22.41 lists the technical specifications for the PS/2 Model P70 386.

Table 22.41   PS/2 Model P70 386 Technical Specifications

System Architecture	
Microprocessor	80386DX
Clock speed	20 MHz
	16 MHz (031)
Bus type	MCA (Micro Channel Architecture)
Bus width	32-bit
Interrupt levels	16
Type	Level-sensitive
Shareable	Yes
DMA channels	15
DMA burst mode supported	Yes
Bus masters supported	15
Upgradeable processor complex	No

Memory	
Standard on system board	4M
Maximum on system board	8M
Maximum total memory	16M
Memory speed and type	85ns dynamic RAM
System board memory socket type	36-bit SIMM (single in-line memory module)
Number of memory module sockets	4
Number available in standard configuration	2
Memory used on system board	1M/2M 36-bit SIMMs
Page memory logic	Yes
Memory cache controller	No
Wait states:	
System board	0-2
Adapter	0-4

Standard Features	
ROM size	128K
ROM shadowing	Yes

(continues)

Table 22.41 Continued

Standard Features

Optional math coprocessor	80387DX
Coprocessor speed	20 MHz
	16 MHz (031)
Standard graphics	VGA
8-/16-/32-bit controller	8-bit
Bus master	No
Video RAM (VRAM)	256K
Integrated display	Yes
Type	Gas plasma, orange
Size (diagonal measure)	10 inches
Grayshades	16
RS232C serial ports	1
UART chip used	NS16550A
Maximum speed (bits/second)	19,200 bps
FIFO mode enabled	Yes
Maximum number of ports	8
Pointing device (mouse) ports	1
Parallel printer ports	1
Bidirectional	Yes
Maximum number of ports	8
CMOS real-time clock (RTC)	Yes
CMOS RAM	64 bytes + 2K extension
Battery life	5 years
Replaceable	Yes

Disk Storage

Internal disk and tape drive bays	2		
Number of 3 1/2- and 5 1/4-inch bays	2/0		
Standard floppy drives	1×1.44M		
Optional floppy drives:			
5 1/4-inch 360K	Optional		
5 1/4-inch 1.2M	Optional		
3 1/2-inch 720K	No		
3 1/2-inch 1.44M	Standard		
3 1/2-inch 2.88M	No		
Auxiliary storage connector	Yes		
Drives supported	5 1/4-inch 360K		
Cable adapter	Optional		
Hard disk controller included	MCA IDE connector on system board		
IDE hard disks available	30M/60M/120M		
Drive form factor	3 1/2-inch		
Drive interface	MCA IDE		
Drive capacity	30M	60M	120M
Average access rate (ms)	19	27	23
Encoding scheme	RLL	RLL	RLL
Cylinders	920	762	920
Heads	2	6	8
Sectors per track	32	26	32
Rotational speed (RPM)	3600	3600	3600

Disk Storage

Interleave factor	1:1	1:1	1:1
Data transfer rate (K/second)	960	780	960
Automatic head parking	Yes	Yes	Yes

Expansion Slots

Total adapter slots	2
Number of long and short slots	1/1
Number of 8-/16-/32-bit slots	0/1/1
Number of slots with video ext.	0
Available slots	2

Keyboard Specifications

101-key Enhanced Keyboard	Yes
Fast keyboard speed setting	Yes
Keyboard cable length	1.2 feet (14 inches)
Keyboard extension cable	Optional, 6 feet

Security Features

Keylock:	
Locks cover	No
Locks keyboard	No
Keyboard password	Yes
Power-on password	Yes
Network server mode	Yes

Physical Specifications

Footprint type	Portable
Dimensions:	
Height	12.0 inches
Width	18.3 inches
Depth	16.5 inches
Weight	20.8 lbs
Carrying handle	Yes
Carrying case	Optional, three styles available

Environmental Specifications

Power-supply output	85 watts
Worldwide (110/60, 220/50)	Yes
Auto-sensing/switching	Yes
Maximum current:	
90-137 VAC	2.4 amps
180-264 VAC	1.2 amps
Operating range:	
Temperature	50-95 degrees F
Relative humidity	8-80 percent
Maximum operating altitude	7,000 feet
Heat (BTUs/hour)	480
Noise (Average dB, operating, 1m)	39 dB
FCC classification	Class B

Table 22.42 shows the primary specifications of the various versions of PS/2 Model P70 386.

Part Number	CPU	MHz	PLANAR MEMORY Std.	Max.	STANDARD Floppy Drive	Hard Disk
Table 22.42 IBM PS/2 Model P70 386 Model Summary						
70 386						
8573-031	386DX	16	2M	8M	1×1.44M	30M
8573-061	386DX	20	4M	8M	1×1.44M	60M
8573-121	386DX	20	4M	8M	1×1.44M	120M

Figure 22.41 shows the components and layout of the Model P70 motherboard.

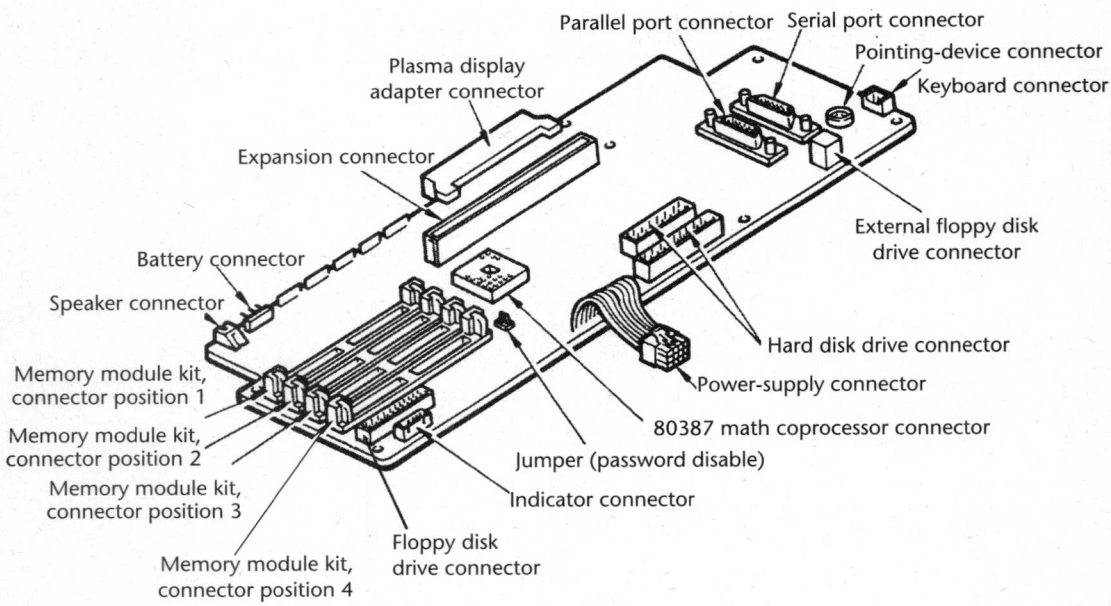

Fig. 22.41
PS/2 Model P70 386 system board.

Bus Type	Total Available Slots	STANDARD		Date Introduced	Date Withdrawn
		Video	Keyboard		
MCA/32	2/2	VGA	Enh	03/20/90	07/23/91
MCA/32	2/2	VGA	Enh	05/09/89	07/23/91
MCA/32	2/2	VGA	Enh	05/09/89	—

Table 22.43 shows accessories available from IBM for the PS/2 Model P70 386.

Table 22.43 IBM PS/2 Model P70 386 Special Accessories			
Description	**Part**	**Price**	**Notes**
Hartmann leather case	23F3192	$360	For P70 (not P75), pockets
Hartmann nylon case	23F3193	185	For P70 (not P75), pockets
Airline travel hard case	79F3205	299	Plastic, padded, wheels, storage
External storage device cable	23F2716	101	P70 360K, P75 360K/1.2M
Keyboard extension cable	79F3210	82	For P70/75, six-foot cable

PS/2 Model P75 486

The PS/2 Model P75 486, introduced November 12, 1990, is a high-end addition to IBM's portable computer family. The Model P75 486 features the powerful 486DX processor, operating at 33 MHz, and MCA slots. For several months after the introduction of this system, no other company had a portable as fast or as powerful. In fact, nearly every company that has tried to introduce a 33 MHz 486 portable has run into problems with the FCC in obtaining the proper Class B certification. This highlights one of the distinct advantages that IBM has with the Micro Channel Architecture: IBM can make systems faster and faster, while keeping them within noise-emission guidelines set by the FCC, because of the superior electrical characteristics of the MCA bus over the ISA or EISA bus.

The PS/2 Model P75 486 enables applications that require portability to run on a system that rivals many desktop or even floor-standing tower systems in capacity. This system allows a portable application to use the processing power of the 486DX processor operating at 33 MHz, up to 16M of main storage, hard disk capacity to 400M, an external SCSI port, and four MCA adapter slots. Because of the built-in SCSI interface, internal hard disk drives can be easily upgraded to well over 1 gigabyte in capacity. This system has one of the largest disk storage capabilities for a portable system.

The PS/2 Model P75 486 has the following features:

- 33 MHz 486DX processor on removable card

- 8M memory expandable to 16M

- Four slots (two full-length 32-bit, two half-length 16-bit)

- High-resolution eXtended Graphics Array (XGA) video port

- VGA 16-grayscale plasma display

- Choice of 160M or 400M disk drives

- Full-size PS/2 Enhanced Keyboard

- 3 1/2-inch 1.44M floppy disk drive

- External SCSI port

- AC operation (only)

- Maximum expansion

The PS/2 P75 486 offers power not previously available in a portable machine. It can be used as a network server or workstation for temporary offices at conventions, sporting events, and other temporary work locations. This system is ideal where a maximum system configuration must be carried along.

The PS/2 P75 486 does not run on batteries and has no "low-power" devices that would limit performance and expandability. Because of the extreme power and integration of this unit, it currently ranks as one of IBM's most expensive PCs.

In addition to the powerful processor, the PS/2 P75 486 features a SCSI hard disk drive up to 400M as standard. With 3 1/2-inch SCSI drives becoming available in the gigabyte-capacity range and higher, it will be easy to upgrade this system to even larger-capacity storage.

The XGA graphics adapter built-in on the unit offers graphics resolution of $1,024 \times 768$. Because this device also is configured as a bus master, the performance is far beyond a standard VGA, even at VGA resolution. A device driver package is included with drivers for many popular applications and environments, such as OS/2 and Windows.

Several accessories are available, including the IBM PS/2 travel case (part number 79F3205). This hard case is constructed of molded plastic with easy-rolling wheels and an integrated, telescopic handle for pulling. The interior is padded and provides space for the P75 (or P70 386), cables, and a mouse. The case is designed to provide an easy, safe way to transport the system. It conforms to FAA luggage regulations, so it can be carried on board an aircraft and stored under the seat.

Also available is a keyboard extension cable. The keyboard extension cable (part number 79F3210) gives users the flexibility of placing the keyboard and the system unit farther apart for more comfort and convenience.

Table 22.44 lists the technical specifications for the PS/2 Model P75 486.

Table 22.44 PS/2 Model P75 486 Technical Specifications

System Architecture

Microprocessor	80486DX
Clock speed	33 MHz
Bus type	MCA
Bus width	32-bit
Interrupt levels	16
Type	Level-sensitive
Shareable	Yes
DMA channels	15
DMA burst mode supported	Yes
Bus masters supported	15
486 burst mode enabled	No
Upgradeable processor complex	Yes

Memory

Standard on system board	8M
Maximum on system board	16M
Maximum total memory	16M
Memory speed and type	70ns dynamic RAM
System board memory socket type	36-bit SIMM (single in-line memory module)
Number of memory-module sockets	4
Number available in standard configuration	2
Memory used on system board	2M/4M 36-bit SIMMs
Paged memory logic	Yes
Memory cache controller	Yes
Internal/external cache	Internal
Standard memory cache size	8K
Optional external memory cache	No
Wait states:	
System board	0-5 (95 percent 0 wait states)
Adapter	0-7

Standard Features

ROM size	128K
ROM shadowing	Yes
Math coprocessor	Built-in to 486
Coprocessor speed	33 MHz
Standard graphics	XGA (eXtended Graphics Array)
8-/16-/32-bit controller	16/32-bit
Bus master	Yes
Video RAM (VRAM)	1M
Integrated display	Yes, VGA mode only
Type	Gas plasma, orange
Size (diagonal measure)	10 inches
Grayshades	16

(continues)

Table 22.44 Continued

Standard Features

RS232C serial ports	1
UART chip used	NS16550A
Maximum speed (bits/second)	19,200 bps
FIFO mode enabled	Yes
Maximum number of ports	8
Pointing device (mouse) ports	1
Parallel printer ports	1
Bidirectional	Yes
Maximum number of ports	8
CMOS real-time clock (RTC)	Yes
CMOS RAM	64 bytes + 2K extension
Battery life	5 years
Replaceable	Yes

Disk Storage

Internal disk and tape drive bays	2					
Number of 3 1/2- and 5 1/4-inch bays	2/0					
Standard floppy drives	1×1.44M					
Optional floppy drives:						
5 1/4-inch 360K	Optional					
5 1/4-inch 1.2M	Optional					
3 1/2-inch 720K	No					
3 1/2-inch 1.44M	Standard					
3 1/2-inch 2.88M	No					
Auxiliary storage connector	Yes					
Drives supported	5 1/4-inch 360K, 1.2M					
Cable adapter	Optional					
Hard disk controller included	SCSI integrated on system board					
Bus master	Yes					
Devices supported per adapter	7					
SCSI hard disks available	60M/80M/120M/160M/320M/400M					
Drive form factor	3 1/2-inch					
Drive interface	SCSI					
Drive capacity	60M	80M	120M	160M	320M	400M
Average access rate (ms)	23	17	23	16	12.5	11.5
Read-ahead cache	32K	32K	32K	32K	64K	128K
SCSI transfer mode	Async	Async	Async	Async	Sync	Sync
Encoding scheme	RLL	RLL	RLL	RLL	RLL	RLL
Cylinders	920	1021	920	1021	949	1201
Heads	4	4	8	8	14	14
Sectors per track	32	39	32	39	48	48
Rotational speed (RPM)	3600	3600	3600	3600	4318	4318
Interleave factor	1:1	1:1	1:1	1:1	1:1	1:1
Data transfer rate (K/second)	960	1170	960	1170	1727	1727
Automatic head parking	Yes	Yes	Yes	Yes	Yes	Yes

VII

Expansion Slots

Total adapter slots	4
Number of long and short slots	2/2
Number of 8-/16-/32-bit slots	0/2/2
Number of slots with video ext.	1
Available slots	4

Keyboard Specifications

101-key Enhanced Keyboard	Yes
Fast keyboard speed setting	Yes
Keyboard cable length	1.2 feet (14 inches)
Keyboard extension cable	Optional, 6 feet

Security Features

Keylock:	
Locks cover	No
Locks keyboard	No
Keyboard password	Yes
Power-on password	Yes
Network server mode	Yes

Physical Specifications

Footprint type	Portable
Dimensions:	
Height	12.0 inches
Width	18.3 inches
Depth	6.1 inches
Weight	22.1 lbs
Carrying handle	Yes
Carrying case	Optional hard-shell case

Environmental Specifications

Power-supply output	120 watts
Worldwide (110/60, 220/50)	Yes
Auto-sensing/switching	Yes
Maximum current:	
90-137 VAC	3.0 amps
180-264 VAC	1.5 amps
Operating range:	
Temperature	50-104 degrees F
Relative humidity	8-80 percent
Maximum operating altitude	7,000 feet
Heat (BTUs/hour)	751
Noise (average dB, operating, 1m)	39 dB
FCC classification	Class B

Table 22.45 shows the primary specifications of the various versions of PS/2 Model P75 486.

Table 22.45	IBM PS/2 Model P75 486 Model Summary						
				PLANAR MEMORY		**STANDARD**	
Part Number	**CPU**	**MHz**	**Std.**	**Max.**	**Floppy Drive**	**Hard Disk**
P75 486						
8573-161	486DX	33	8M	16M	1×1.44M	160M
8573-401	486DX	33	8M	16M	1×1.44M	400M

Table 22.46 shows accessories available from IBM for the PS/2 Model P75 486.

Table 22.46	IBM PS/2 Model P75 486 Special Accessories			
Description	**Part**	**Price**	**Notes**	
Airline-travel hard case	79F3205	$299	Plastic, padded, wheels, storage	
Keyboard extension cable	79F3210	82	For P70/75, 6-foot cable	
External storage device cable	23F2716	101	P70 360K, P75 360K/1.2M	

PS/2 Models 76, 77, and 77s Ultimedia

The PS/2 Models 76 and 77 use a series of processors: the Intel 33-MHz 486SX, the 66-MHz 486DX2, and the clock-tripled 100-MHz 486DX4. These systems were introduced June 13, 1994, after an aborted November 1993 ship date. The Models 76 and 77 were planned to use IBM's 33/99MHz "Blue Lightning" 486 CPU (a clock-tripled 486SLC3), but IBM felt customers were more comfortable with genuine Intel processors. The machines were first delayed by a shortage of Blue Lightning chips, and then later by a faulty controller IBM developed specifically for these models. Those models using DX4 chips can be upgraded to Intel Pentium P24T OverDrive processors, whereas the others accept 486 OverDrive and Pentium OverDrive upgrades.

These new systems are the first PS/2s that do not use IBM's internally developed XGA graphics chips. Instead, they come with S3-accelerated SVGA local-bus graphics and are capable of supporting resolutions as high as 1,280 by 1,024 with 256 colors. These new systems also use 32-bit Micro Channel Architecture slots, rather than the older 16-bit slots.

The 100-MHz 486DX4 models include a 16K L1 memory cache and a 256K L2 memory cache. The 486DX2-66 models include an 8K L1 cache and an external 128K cache. The 486SX versions have an 8K L1 cache and no L2 cache, which is optional. These systems come standard with 8M RAM and can accommodate up to 64M on the system board. The Models 76 and 77 come standard with 2.88M floppy disk drive. The hard disk drive may be either IDE or SCSI-2. Models with IDE are indicated by an "i" at the end of the model name, such as PS/2 Model 76i. SCSI models are indicated by an "s" ("PS/2 Model 76s"). Drive sizes range from 170M to 540M.

Bus Type	Total Available Slots	STANDARD		Date Introduced	Date Withdrawn
		Video	Keyboard		
MCA/32	4/4	XGA	Enh	11/12/90	—
MCA/32	4/4	XGA	Enh	11/12/90	—

The Model 77s is actually designed to be used as a server, and it will ship standard with ECC memory. Error-correcting code (ECC) memory detects and eliminates data errors without halting processing. Network managers consider ECC an extremely valuable component in any network server, although this feature is not cost-effective for systems based on low-power processors. For systems utilizing Intel's Pentium or DX4 chips, ECC is an excellent and inexpensive benefit. Unlike typical memory parity checking, which adds only one bit per byte, ECC generates multiple check bits to safeguard data against a variety of problems, including electrical noise, dynamic RAM (DRAM) errors, and rogue alpha particles.

The 77s Ultimedia is a multimedia version of the Model 77. The 77s Ultimedia includes a double-speed CD-ROM drive, an Audiovation sound card with IBM's programmable Mwave digital signal processor, and a MediaBurst movie card from VideoLogic Inc., in Cambridge, Mass.

Table 22.47 lists the technical specifications for the PS/2 Model 76 and 77.

Table 22.47 PS/2 Model 76 and 77 Technical Specifications	
System Architecture	
Microprocessor	80486SX (*U*)
	80486DX2 (*N*)
	80486DX4 (*T*)
Clock speed	33 MHz (*U*)
	66 MHz (*N*)
	100 MHz (*T*)
L1/L2 cache	8K/Optional (*U*)
	8K/128K (*N*)
	16K/256K (*T*)
Bus type	MCA
Bus width	32-bit
Upgradeable processor complex	No

(continues)

Table 22.47   Continued

Memory

Standard on system board	8M (16M on 9577-VTG)
Maximum on system board	64M
Maximum total memory	64M
Memory speed and type	70ns dynamic RAM

System board memory socket type
    Number of memory module sockets
    Number available in standard configuration
	36-bit SIMM (single in-line memory module)
	4
	4

Memory used on system board	2M/4M/8M/16M 36-bit SIMMs
Optional math coprocessor	80487SX (*U*) Standard (*N*) Standard (*T*)
Standard graphics Video RAM (VRAM)	S3-accelerated local-bus SVGA graphics 1M
RS232C serial ports	1
UART chip used	Custom (compatible with NS16550A)
Pointing device (mouse) ports	1

Standard Features

Parallel printer ports Bidirectional	1 Yes

Disk Storage

Internal disk and tape drive bays Number of 3 1/2- and 5 1/4-inch bays	3 (4 Model 77) 1/3 (1/4 Model 77)
Standard floppy drives	1×2.88M

Optional floppy drives:
    5 1/4-inch 360K
    5 1/4-inch 1.2M
    3 1/2-inch 720K
    3 1/2-inch 1.44M
    3 1/2-inch 2.88M
	
	Optional
	Optional
	No
	Optional
	Standard

Hard disk controller included:
    Bus master
    Devices supported per adapter
    Adapters supported per system
	SCSI or IDE integrated on system board
	Yes
	7
	4

SCSI hard disks available	170M/270M/540M
Drive form factor	3 1/2-inch

Disk Storage

Drive interface	IDE or SCSI		
Drive capacity	170M	270M	540M
Average access rate (ms)	12	12	8.5
Interleave factor	1:1	1:1	1:1
Automatic head parking	Yes	Yes	Yes

Expansion Slots

Total adapter slots	3 (5 Model 77)
Number of long and short slots	3/0 (5/0 Model 77)
Number of 8-/16-/32-bit slots	0/3/0 (0/5/0 Model 77)
Available slots	3 (5 Model 77)

Keyboard Specifications

Keyboard choices	122-key Host-Connected Keyboard 101-key Enhanced Keyboard 84-key Space-Saving Keyboard
Fast keyboard speed setting	Yes
Keyboard cable length	10 feet

Security Features

Keylock:	
Locks cover	Yes
Locks keyboard	No
Keyboard password	Yes
Power-on password	Yes
Network server mode	Yes

Physical Specifications

Footprint type	Desktop
Orientation	Horizontal/vertical
Dimensions:	
Height	4.5 inches (6.6 inches Model 77)
Width	14.2 inches (17.3 inches Model 77)
Depth	15.6 inches (15.5 inches Model 77)
Weight	30 lbs. (35 lbs. Model 77)
Power consumption	118 watts (195 watts Model 77)
FCC classification	Class B

Table 22.48 shows the primary specifications of the various versions of PS/2 Models 76 and 77.

Table 22.48   IBM PS/2 Model 76 and 77 Model Summary

| | | | PLANAR MEMORY | | STANDARD | | |
Part Number	CPU	MHz	Std.	Max.	Floppy Drive	Hard Disk	Bus Type
76i							
9576-AU9	486SX	33	8M	64M	1×2.88M	170M	MCA/32
9576-AUB	486SX	33	8M	64M	1×2.88M	270M	MCA/32
9576-ANB	486DX2	66	8M	64M	1×2.88M	270M	MCA/32
9576-ATB	486DX4	100	8M	64M	1×2.88M	270M	MCA/32
76s							
9576-BUB	486SX	33	8M	64M	1×2.88M	270M	MCA/32
9576-BNB	486DX2	66	8M	64M	1×2.88M	270M	MCA/32
9576-BTB	486DX4	100	8M	64M	1×2.88M	270M	MCA/32
77i							
9577-AUB	486SX	33	8M	64M	1×2.88M	270M	MCA/32
9577-ANB	486DX2	66	8M	64M	1×2.88M	270M	MCA/32
9577-ANG	486DX2	66	8M	64M	1×2.88M	527M	MCA/32
9577-ATB	486DX4	100	8M	64M	1×2.88M	270M	MCA/32
9577-ATG	486DX4	100	8M	64M	1×2.88M	527M	MCA/32
77s							
9577-BUB	486SX	33	8M	64M	1×2.88M	270M	MCA/32
9577-BNB	486DX2	66	8M	64M	1×2.88M	270M	MCA/32
9577-BNG	486DX2	66	8M	64M	1×2.88M	540M	MCA/32
9577-BTB	486DX4	100	8M	64M	1×2.88M	270M	MCA/32
9577-BTG	486DX4	100	8M	64M	1×2.88M	540M	MCA/32
9577-VTG	486DX4	100	16M	64M	1×2.88M	540M	MCA/32
77s Ultimedia							
9577s-6NB	486DX2	66	8M	64M	1×2.88M	270M	MCA/32
9577s-7NB	486DX2	66	8M	64M	1×2.88M	270M	MCA/32
9577s-6NG	486DX2	66	8M	64M	1×2.88M	540M	MCA/32
9577s-7NG	486DX2	66	8M	64M	1×2.88M	540M	MCA/32
9577s-6TG	486DX2	100	8M	64M	1×2.88M	540M	MCA/32
9577s-7TG	486DX2	100	8M	64M	1×2.88M	540M	MCA/32

Total Available Slots	STANDARD Video	Keyboard	Date Introduced	Date Withdrawn
3/3	S3-accelerated local-bus SVGA	Any	06/13/94	—
3/3	S3-accelerated local-bus SVGA	Any	06/13/94	—
3/3	S3-accelerated local-bus SVGA	Any	06/13/94	—
3/3	S3-accelerated local-bus SVGA	Any	06/13/94	—
3/3	S3-accelerated local-bus SVGA	Any	06/13/94	—
3/3	S3-accelerated local-bus SVGA	Any	06/13/94	—
3/3	S3-accelerated local-bus SVGA	Any	06/13/94	—
5/5	S3-accelerated local-bus SVGA	Any	06/13/94	—
5/5	S3-accelerated local-bus SVGA	Any	06/13/94	—
5/5	S3-accelerated local-bus SVGA	Any	06/13/94	—
5/5	S3-accelerated local-bus SVGA	Any	06/13/94	—
5/5	S3-accelerated local-bus SVGA	Any	06/13/94	—
5/5	S3-accelerated local-bus SVGA	Any	06/13/94	—
5/5	S3-accelerated local-bus SVGA	Any	06/13/94	—
5/5	S3-accelerated local-bus SVGA	Any	06/13/94	—
5/5	S3-accelerated local-bus SVGA	Any	06/13/94	—
5/5	S3-accelerated local-bus SVGA	Any	06/13/94	—
5/5	S3-accelerated local-bus SVGA	Any	06/13/94	—
5/3	S3-accelerated local-bus SVGA	Any	06/13/94	—
5/3	S3-accelerated local-bus SVGA	Any	06/13/94	—
5/3	S3-accelerated local-bus SVGA	Any	06/13/94	—
5/3	S3-accelerated local-bus SVGA	Any	06/13/94	—
5/3	S3-accelerated local-bus SVGA	Any	06/13/94	—
5/3	S3-accelerated local-bus SVGA	Any	06/13/94	—

PS/2 Model 80 386

IBM originally introduced the PS/2 Model 80 on April 2, 1987. Since then, many new models in the 80 family have been introduced and some have been discontinued. The Model 80 is a floor-standing, high-end system in the PS/2 family and includes MCA. Figure 22.42 shows a front view of the Model 80.

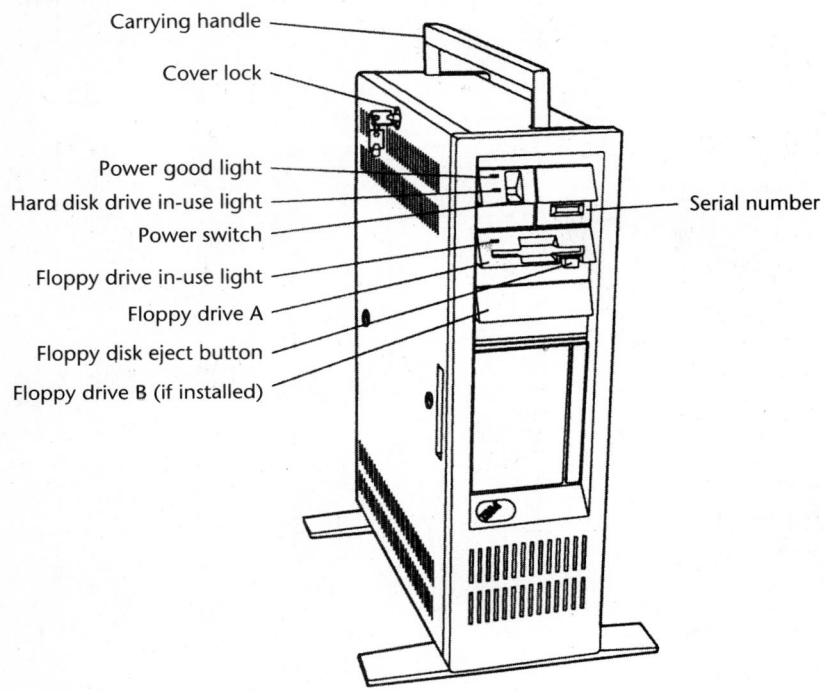

Carrying handle
Cover lock
Power good light
Hard disk drive in-use light
Power switch
Floppy drive in-use light
Floppy drive A
Floppy disk eject button
Floppy drive B (if installed)
Serial number

Fig. 22.42
PS/2 Model 80 386.

The basic Model 80 386 features a 16 MHz, 20 MHz, or 25 MHz 80386 microprocessor and 4M of high-speed (80ns) memory on the motherboard. Motherboard memory is expandable to 8M, depending on the model, and the total RAM can be expanded to 16M with memory adapters. This system comes standard with a 1.44M, 3 1/2-inch floppy disk drive and a wide variety of ST-506, ESDI, or SCSI hard disk drives ranging from 44M through 400M. Also standard are a serial port, parallel port, mouse port, and VGA port. Figure 22.43 shows the rear panel view of the Model 80.

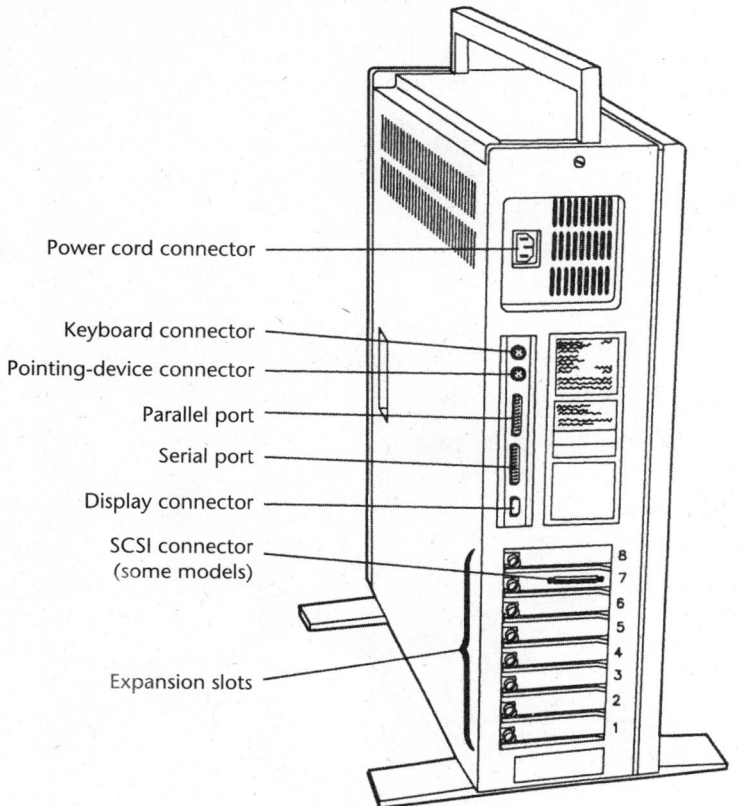

Power cord connector

Keyboard connector

Pointing-device connector

Parallel port

Serial port

Display connector

SCSI connector
(some models)

Expansion slots

Fig. 22.43
PS/2 Model 80 386 rear panel view.

The 80386 32-bit microprocessor running at 16 MHz, 20 MHz, or 25 MHz coupled with
the MCA and high-speed memory allows the Model 80 to perform three to four times
faster than the IBM AT Model 339. The 80387 math coprocessor running at the system
clock rate allows the Model 80 to perform math calculations four to five times faster than
an IBM AT Model 339 with an 80287 math coprocessor.

The Model 80 386 has two levels of BIOS, which total 128K: A Compatibility BIOS
(CBIOS) with memory addressability of up to 1M provides support for real-mode-based
application programs; and an additional version of BIOS, Advanced BIOS (ABIOS), provides support for protected-mode-based multitasking operating systems and has extended memory addressability of up to 16M.

Additional features of the system unit include eight I/O bus slots, of which five are 16-bit slots and three are 16/32-bit slots. Each system includes a hard disk controller that occupies one 16-bit slot. This controller is either an ST-506/412, ESDI, or SCSI controller. The Model 80 also has a 225-watt or 242-watt, automatic voltage-sensing, universal power supply with auto-restart; a time-and-date clock with battery backup; an additional position for a second 3 1/2-inch floppy disk drive; an additional position for a second full-height 5 1/4-inch hard disk; and the IBM Enhanced Keyboard. Figure 22.44 shows the interior view of the Model 80.

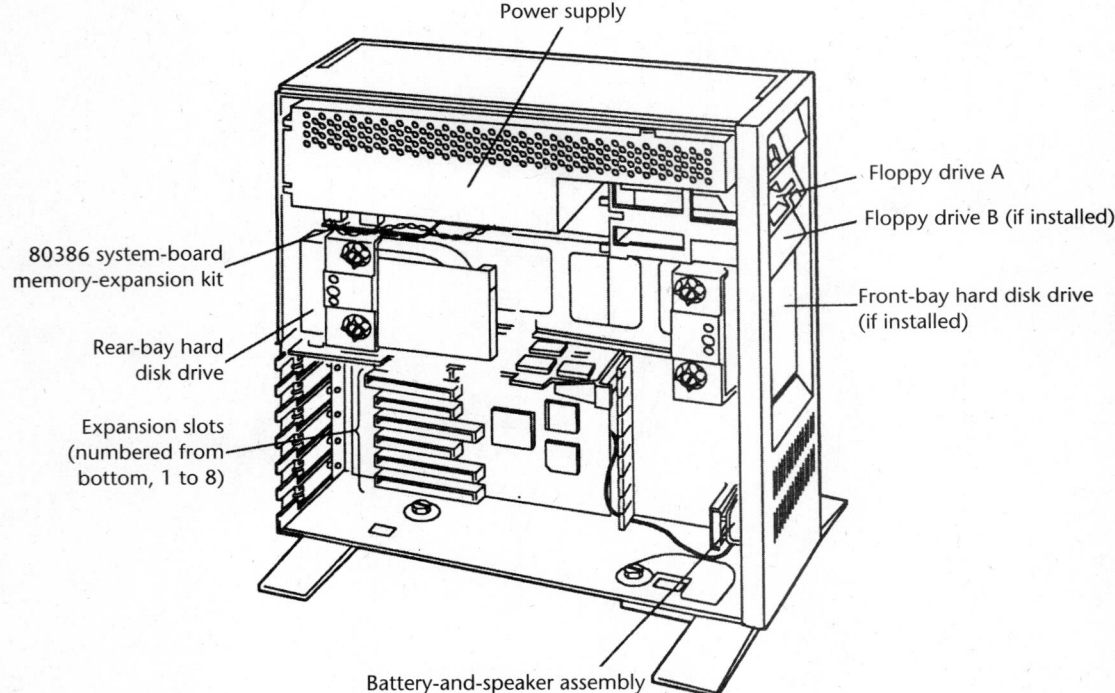

Fig. 22.44

PS/2 Model 80 386 interior view.

The auto-restart feature on the power supply enables the computer to restart automatically when AC power returns after a power decrease or outage. This feature enables the system to be programmed for unattended restart after power outages—a useful feature on a computer in a network file-server application.

Model 80 has a variety of configurations; three different Model 80 system boards are available. The motherboards differ primarily in the clock rate of the processor and the arrangement of the MCA slots. The 16 MHz and 20 MHz models have three 32-bit slots and five 16-bit MCA slots. One of the 16-bit slots includes a video extension connector. These motherboards also allow a maximum of 4M to be installed using two nonstandard memory connectors. None of the Model 80 systems used standard SIMM connectors; they use a custom-designed card, making the memory upgrades available only from IBM.

The 25 MHz model differs from the others in that it has four 32-bit slots and four 16-bit slots, with two of the 16-bit slots having the video extension connector. These systems also incorporate a 64K static RAM cache on the motherboard, which essentially makes these systems run at 0 wait states. These motherboards support a maximum of 8M using two custom 4M memory cards plugged directly into the motherboard. Any additional memory beyond these maximums must be installed using an adapter card.

The hard disk drive interfaces also differentiate the different models. Three different disk interfaces and drive types were supplied with the Model 80. The 041 model used an ST-506 type controller that handled up to two hard drives. The 071, 111, and 311 systems used an ESDI (Enhanced Small Device Interface) controller and drive. The ESDI controller supported up to two hard drives. The other (newer) models all include the IBM 16-bit MCA SCSI bus master adapter. This card provides an internal as well as external SCSI port for connecting devices. This card supports up to seven hard disks, and the system supports up to four of these cards. IBM has SCSI drives available from 60M through 400M to install in these systems. Also, because these drives are all in the 3 1/2-inch form factor (at least the ones from IBM), you can fit up to six of them inside the unit.

The 16 MHz systems also have a motherboard that always runs at 1 wait state, and does not offer ROM shadowing, in which the slower (150ns) ROM BIOS is copied into faster (80ns) motherboard memory chips. The ROM BIOS on this system board performs a ROM to RAM copy operation on startup that uses 128K of the total 16M of RAM. This copy then is used for all subsequent ROM operations, and because the ROM now effectively resides in 80ns RAM, access to these routines is improved significantly. The chips then are readdressed into the original BIOS locations and write protected. This means that you essentially have write-protected RAM acting as ROM, which can then run with fewer wait states. The 20 MHz systems incorporate a memory-paging scheme that reduces the number of wait states to 0 most of the time. All system board memory is accessed by a special paging scheme that allows for 0 wait state access to all 512 bytes within a single page. When access occurs outside the available page, you must perform a page swap requiring 2 wait states. Overall, this scheme allows for faster access to memory than a nonpaging, 1 wait state system. The 25 MHz systems incorporate a full-blown memory cache system that performs most operations in 25ns Static RAM. These systems are nearly always running at an apparent 0 wait states due to the efficiency of the cache.

Table 22.49 lists the technical specifications for the PS/2 Model 80 386.

Table 22.49 PS/2 Model 80 386 Technical Specifications

System Architecture

Microprocessor	80386DX
Clock speed	16 MHz (041, 071)
	20 MHz (081, 111, 121, 161, 311, 321)
	25 MHz (Axx)
Bus type	MCA (Micro Channel Architecture)
Bus width	32-bit
Interrupt levels	16
Type	Level-sensitive
Shareable	Yes
DMA channels	15
DMA burst mode supported	Yes
Bus masters supported	15
Upgradeable processor complex	No

Memory

Standard on system board	4M
Maximum on system board	4M
	8M (Axx)
Maximum total memory	16M
Memory speed and type	80ns dynamic RAM
System board memory socket type	Nonstandard memory card
Number of memory module sockets	2
Number available in standard configuration	1
Memory used on system board	1M/2M/4M card
Paged memory logic	Yes
	No (041,071)
Memory cache controller	No
	Yes (Axx)
Internal/external cache	External
Standard memory cache size	64K
Cache memory speed and type	25ns static RAM
Wait states:	
System board	0-5 (Axx, 95 percent 0 wait states)
	0-2 (081, 111, 121, 161, 311, 321)
	1 (041, 071)
Adapter	0-7 (Axx)
	0-4

Standard Features

ROM size	128K
ROM shadowing	Yes
	No (041, 071)
Optional math coprocessor	80387DX
	16 MHz (041, 071)
	20 MHz (081, 111, 121, 161, 311, 321)
	25 MHz (Axx)
Standard graphics	VGA (Video Graphics Array)
8-/16-/32-bit controller	8-bit
	No
Video RAM (VRAM)	256K
RS232C serial ports	1
UART chip used	NS16550A
	NS16550 (041, 071)
Maximum speed (bits/second)	19,200 bps
	Yes
	No (041, 071)
Maximum number of ports	8
Pointing device (mouse) ports	1
Parallel printer ports	1
Bidirectional	Yes
Maximum number of ports	8
CMOS real-time clock (RTC)	Yes
CMOS RAM	64 bytes + 2K extension
Battery life	5 years
Replaceable	Yes

Disk Storage

Internal disk and tape drive bays	5 or 6 (reconfigurable)
	4 (041, 071, 111, 311)
Number of 3 1/2- and 5 1/4-inch bays	4/1 or 6/0 (reconfigurable)
	2/2 (041, 071, 111, 311)
Floppy drives standard	1×1.44M
Optional floppy drives	
5 1/4-inch 360K	Optional
5 1/4-inch 1.2M	Optional
3 1/2-inch 720K	No
3 1/2-inch 1.44M	Standard
3 1/2-inch 2.88M	No
Hard disk controller included	SCSI adapter (081, 121, 161, 321, Axx)
	ESDI controller (071, 111, 311)
	ST-506 controller (041)
SCSI host adapter type	16-bit SCSI adapter
Bus master	Yes

(continues)

Table 22.49 Continued

Disk Storage

Devices supported per adapter	7				
Adapters supported per system	4				
ST-506/ESDI hard disks available	44M/70/115M/314M				
Drive form factor	5 1/4-inch				
Drive capacity	44M	44M	70M	115M	314M
Drive interface	ST-506	ST-506	ESDI	ESDI	ESDI
Average access rate (ms)	40	40	30	28	23
Encoding scheme	MFM	MFM	RLL	RLL	RLL
BIOS drive type	31	32	None	None	None
Cylinders	733	1023	583	915	1225
Heads	7	5	7	7	15
Sectors per track	17	17	36	36	34
Rotational speed (RPM)	3600	3600	3600	3600	3283
Interleave factor	1:1	1:1	1:1	1:1	1:1
Data transfer rate (K/second)	510	510	1080	1080	930
Automatic head parking	Yes	Yes	Yes	Yes	Yes

SCSI hard disks available	60M/80M/120M/160M/320M/400M					
Drive form factor	3 1/2-inch					
Drive interface	SCSI					
Drive capacity	60M	80M	120M	160M	320M	400M
Average access rate (ms)	23	17	23	16	12.5	11.5
Read-ahead cache	32K	32K	32K	32K	64K	128K
SCSI transfer mode	Async	Async	Async	Async	Sync	Sync
Encoding scheme	RLL	RLL	RLL	RLL	RLL	RLL
Cylinders	920	1021	920	1021	949	1201
Heads	4	4	8	8	14	14
Sectors per track	32	39	32	39	48	48
Rotational speed (RPM)	3600	3600	3600	3600	4318	4318
Interleave factor	1:1	1:1	1:1	1:1	1:1	1:1
Data transfer rate (K/sec.)	960	1170	960	1170	1727	1727
Automatic head parking	Yes	Yes	Yes	Yes	Yes	Yes

Expansion Slots

Total adapter slots	8
Number of long and short slots	8/0
Number of 8-/16-/32-bit slots	0/5/3
	0/4/4 (Axx)
Number of slots with video ext.	1
	2 (Axx)
Available slots	7

Keyboard Specifications

101-key Enhanced Keyboard	Yes
Fast keyboard speed setting	Yes
Keyboard cable length	10 feet

Security Features

Keylock:	
Locks cover	Yes
Locks keyboard	No
Keyboard password	Yes
Power-on password	Yes
Network server mode	Yes

Physical Specifications

Footprint type	Floor-standing
Dimensions:	
Height	23.5 inches
Width	6.5 inches
Depth	19.0 inches
Weight	45.3 lbs
	52.0 lbs (041, 071, 111, 311)

Environmental Specifications

Power-supply output	242 watts
	225 watts (041, 071, 111, 311)
Worldwide (110/60, 220/50)	Yes
Auto-sensing/switching	Yes
Maximum current:	
90-137 volts AC	5.3 amps
180-265 volts AC	2.7 amps
Operating range:	
Temperature	60-90 degrees F
Relative humidity	8-80 percent
Maximum operating altitude	7,000 feet
Heat (BTUs/hour)	1390
	1245 (041, 071, 111, 311)
Noise (average dB, operating, 1m)	40 dB
	46 dB (041, 071, 111, 311)
FCC classification	Class B

Figures 22.45 and 22.46 show the components and layout of the Model 80 type 1 and type 2 motherboards.

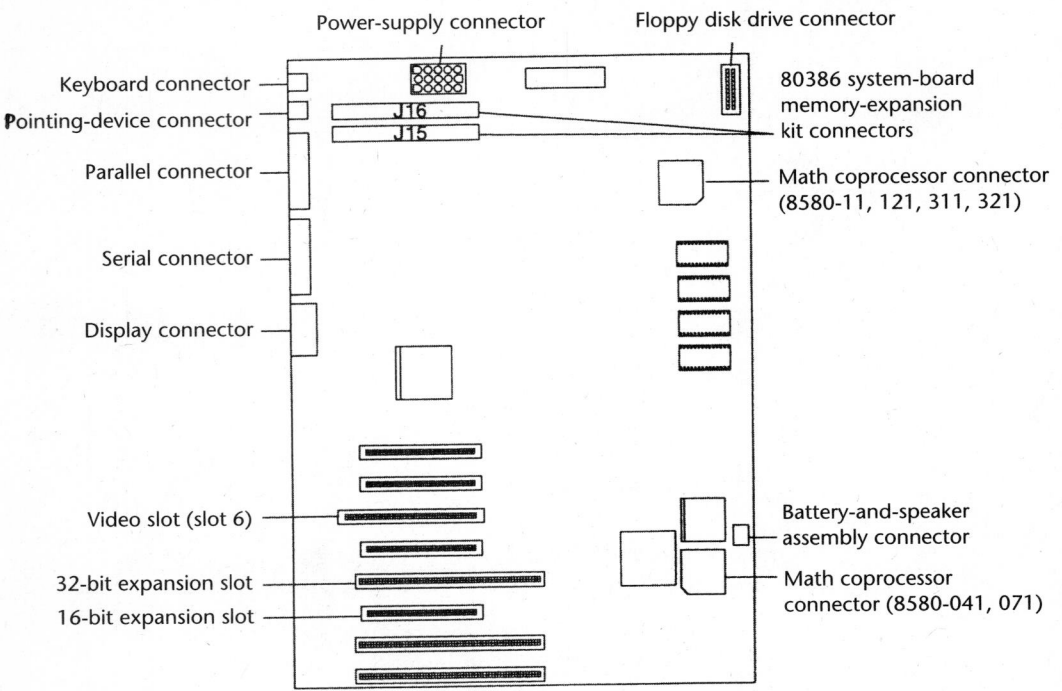

Fig. 22.45
PS/2 Model 80 386 system board (16 MHz and 20 MHz type 1).

Table 22.50	IBM PS/2 Model 80 386 Model Summary					
			PLANAR MEMORY **MEMORY**		**STANDARD**	
Part Number	**CPU**	**MHz**	**Std.**	**Max.**	**Floppy** **Drive**	**Hard** **Disk**
80 386						
8580-041	386DX	16	1M	4M	1×1.44M	44M
8580-071	386DX	16	2M	4M	1×1.44M	70M
8580-081	386DX	20	4M	4M	1×1.44M	80M
8580-111	386DX	20	2M	4M	1×1.44M	115M
8580-121	386DX	20	2M	4M	1×1.44M	120M
8580-161	386DX	20	4M	4M	1×1.44M	160M
8580-311	386DX	20	2M	4M	1×1.44M	314M
8580-321	386DX	20	4M	4M	1×1.44M	320M
8580-A21	386DX	25	4M	8M	1×1.44M	120M
8580-A16	386DX	25	4M	8M	1×1.44M	160M
8580-A31	386DX	25	4M	8M	1×1.44M	320M

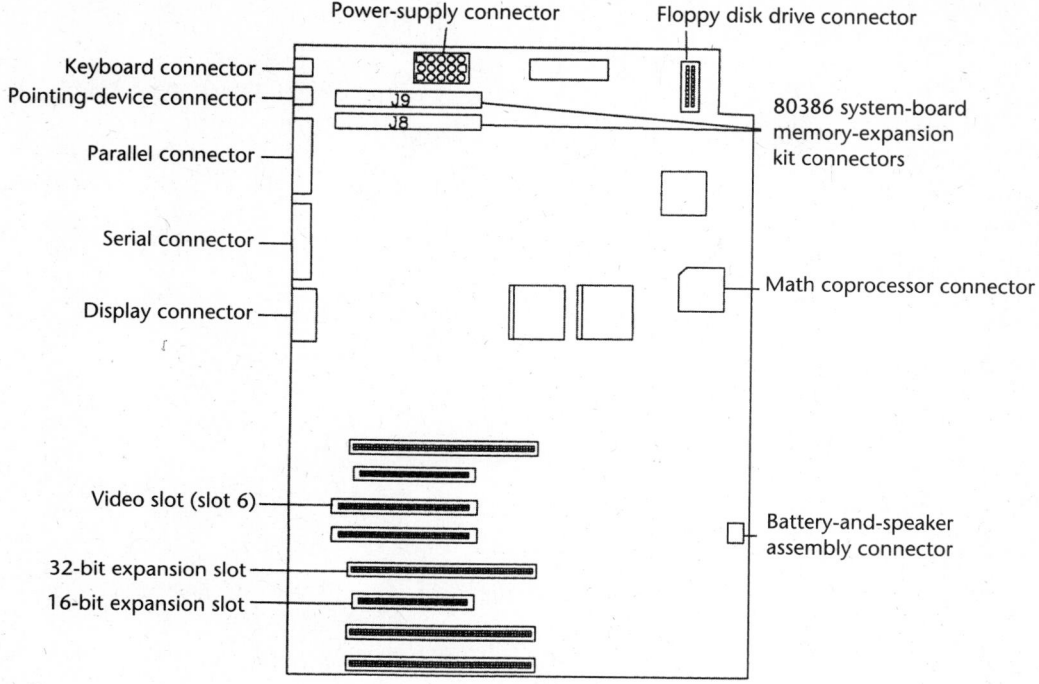

Fig. 22.46
PS/2 Model 80 386 system board (25 MHz type 2).

Table 22.50 shows the primary specifications of the various versions of PS/2 Model 80 386.

Bus Type	Total Available Slots	STANDARD Video	Keyboard	Date Introduced	Date Withdrawn
MCA/32	8/7	VGA	Enh	04/02/87	10/31/90
MCA/32	8/7	VGA	Enh	04/02/87	10/31/90
MCA/32	8/7	VGA	Enh	10/30/90	—
MCA/32	8/7	VGA	Enh	04/02/87	12/27/90
MCA/32	8/7	VGA	Enh	03/20/90	01/29/91
MCA/32	8/7	VGA	Enh	10/30/90	—
MCA/32	8/7	VGA	Enh	08/04/87	12/27/90
MCA/32	8/7	VGA	Enh	03/20/90	—
MCA/32	8/7	VGA	Enh	03/20/90	01/29/91
MCA/32	8/7	VGA	Enh	10/30/90	—
MCA/32	8/7	VGA	Enh	03/20/90	—

PS/2 Model 90 XP 486

The PS/2 Model 90 XP 486, introduced October 30, 1990, is a powerful and expandable MCA-based desktop system. Through an unusual design, the system's 32-bit 80486 processor is on a removable processor complex, allowing processor upgrade from the 25 MHz to the more powerful 33 MHz or 50 MHz system. This capability to upgrade can extend the life of the system as customer requirements for enhanced processor performance grow.

Highlights of the Model 90 include the following:

- Processor complex with 80486 20, 25, 33, or 50MHz processor

- 8M standard memory, expandable to 64M on the system board

- XGA graphics integrated on system board

- PS/2 SCSI 32-bit bus master adapter with cache

- Four internal storage device bays

- Four 32-bit Micro Channel expansion slots

- Two DMA serial ports and one DMA parallel port

- Selectable boot and disk loaded ROM BIOS

The PS/2 Model 90 XP 486 features the 20 MHz, 25 MHz, 33 MHz, or 50 MHz 80486 microprocessor. The processor includes an internal memory cache controller, an internal 8K memory cache, and an internal floating point processor unit. The PS/2 256K cache option provides additional memory cache capability beyond the 8K internal memory cache. The PS/2 256K cache option is supported on 486DX models of Model 90 and Model 95. This capability provides investment protection and flexibility for the user.

The Model 90 system provides four internal drive bays and four 32-bit MCA I/O slots (one slot is used for the IBM PS/2 Micro Channel SCSI Adapter with cache, leaving three available for expansion). The PS/2 Micro Channel SCSI adapter with cache allows up to seven SCSI devices to be attached to the Model 90. The Model 90 also supports an internal 5 1/4-inch floppy disk device. The 5 1/4-inch Slim High Disk Drive (part number 6451066) is an internal 5 1/4-inch, 1.2M floppy disk drive with electrical button eject. This drive does not require an attachment card or expansion slot for installation and is supported in Models 90 and 95.

The Model 90 memory subsystem has been designed for optimum performance with interleaved memory; it features parity memory checking for added reliability and data integrity. All system memory (up to 64M) is supported on the system board, eliminating the need for memory adapters in any of the expansion slots. Although the Model 90 supports a maximum of 64M of memory, only 16M of that is addressable by DMA. This effectively limits the use of memory past 16M to nonsystem operations such as caching, virtual memory, or other functions. The system board has a total of eight memory sockets, two of which are used by a pair of 2M SIMMs (single in-line memory modules) to provide the standard 4M of memory. Optional 2M, 4M, and 8M memory SIMMs (70ns, 80ns, and 85ns only) are supported in matched pairs to provide various memory configurations up to 64M. Although 80ns and 85ns memory SIMMs are supported, 70ns memory SIMMs provide optimum memory subsystem performance.

The eXtended Graphics Array (XGA), high-performance, 32-bit bus master video subsystem is a standard feature of the PS/2 Model 90 XP 486 system. The integrated XGA provides $1024 \times 768 \times 16$ colors or $640 \times 480 \times 256$ colors as standard and can be optionally expanded to $1024 \times 768 \times 256$ colors with the addition of one PS/2 video memory expansion option. XGA supports all VGA modes and is optimized for use with window managers and other graphical user interfaces, allowing for highly interactive pop-up icons and pull-down menus. XGA also provides hardware support for 132-character text mode (using 8515 or 8514 display) and 16-bit direct color mode (64K colors at 640×480 resolution). MCA slot 3 of the PS/2 Model 90 XP 486 system contains a video feature bus connector that can be used to install a video adapter.

Other features of the Model 90 include the dual direct memory address (DMA) serial ports and a DMA parallel port included as standard. One of the serial port connectors is standard 25-pin D-shell, and the other connector is 9-pin D-shell. The 9-pin D-shell connector requires an adapter for attaching devices with 25-pin D-shell connectors. The DMA serial port provides support for speeds from 300 bits per second to 345.6K bits per second. It reduces processor loading and overhead when used in high-speed communications and supports speeds up to 345.6K bits per second.

The Model 90 offers the selectable-boot feature. As part of the system CMOS setup program, the user can specify which drive should be booted from and in which order the boot process should try each drive (for example, boot first from drive A, and then drive C, and load BASIC). This step enables the user to boot or load a program from the optional 5 1/4-inch internal floppy disk drive as if it were drive A.

Initial Microcode Load. One special feature that the Model 90 has is called Initial Microcode Load (IML). The Model 90 stores the BIOS, configuration programs, and diagnostics on the hard disk in a protected 3M system partition and loaded from the disk during a "pre-boot" process. (The system programs also are provided on the PS/2 Model 90 XP 486 Reference Disk.) The formatted capacity of the hard disk is reduced by 3M, and the total user-accessible capacity might vary slightly, based on operating environments. This partition is not affected when the drive is formatted using the DOS or OS/2 FORMAT command.

The Initial Microcode Load (IML) loads the BIOS program from the hard disk drive into system memory. This process makes updating the BIOS an easy task when the time comes. Rather than pulling and replacing ROM chips on the motherboard, all you have to do is obtain a newer copy of the reference floppy disk and restore the system programs using that disk. Updates are available from your dealer or directly from IBM.

For example, a problem has been noted with Model 90 systems that have more than 8M of memory. To fix the problem, you need the Model 90 Reference Disk Version 1.02 or higher. To obtain the latest version, call 1-800-426-7282, weekdays between 8 a.m. and

8 p.m., Eastern Standard time. Specify the floppy disk for IBM PS/2 Model 90 XP 486. In Canada, call 1-800-465-1234 weekdays between 8 a.m. and 4:30 p.m. Eastern Standard time. In Alaska, call (414) 633-8108. The update will be sent to you and is installed in a menu-driven fashion. Because IBM sets the standards in this industry, you probably will see other compatible vendors adopting this disk-based BIOS approach as well. The flexibility and ease of upgrading are welcome.

On October 17, 1991, IBM enhanced the PS/2 Model 90 XP family with new Intel 486SX 25MHz (0Hx) models. The new systems come equipped with a new 486SX 25MHz processor complex, which provides improved performance over the previous 25MHz 486DX processor—and at a lower price. The new processor complex provides improved Micro Channel performance, better bus arbitration, and enhancements to the memory controller, making it ideal for multitasking or operating in heavily loaded networked environments. An improved physical design with fewer parts provides for greater reliability. The new processor complex also incorporates a conventional math coprocessor socket. Because of the improved price and performance of the new 25 MHz systems, earlier models using the 486SX 20MHz (0Gx) and 486 25MHz (0Jx) processor complex are being withdrawn. Because the 486SX lacks the integrated math coprocessor unit, a socket for the addition of the optional 487SX Math coprocessor is provided. In addition, these entry-level models can be upgraded to the more powerful 486/33MHz or the 486/50MHz processors with the IBM PS/2 486/33 and 486/50 processor upgrade options.

Table 22.51 lists the technical specifications for the PS/2 Model 90 XP 486.

Table 22.51 PS/2 Model 90 XP 486 Technical Specifications

System Architecture

Microprocessor and clock speed	80486SX 20 MHz (0Gx)
	80487SX 20 MHz
	80486SX 25 MHz (0Hx)
	80487SX 25 MHz
	80486DX 25 MHz (0Jx)
	80486DX 33 MHz (0Kx)
	80486DX 50 MHz
Bus type	MCA (Micro Channel Architecture)
Bus width	32-bit
Interrupt levels	16
Type	Level-sensitive
Shareable	Yes
DMA channels	15
DMA burst mode supported	Yes
Bus masters supported	15
486 burst mode enabled	Yes
Upgradeable processor complex	Yes
Processor upgrades available	20 MHz 487SX
	25 MHz 486SX
	25 MHz 486DX
	33 MHz 486DX
	50 MHz 486DX

Memory

Standard on system board	4M (0Gx) 8M (for all others)
Maximum on system board	64M
Maximum total memory	64M
Memory speed and type	70ns dynamic RAM
System board memory socket type 　Number of memory module sockets 　Number available in standard configuration 　Memory used on system board	36-bit SIMM (single in-line memory module) 8 6 (0Gx) 4 (for all others) 2M/4M/8M SIMMs
Memory interleaving	Yes
Paged memory logic	Yes
Memory cache controller 　Internal/external cache 　Standard memory cache size 　Optional external memory cache 　External cache size 　Cache memory speed and type	Yes Internal 8K No (0Gx, 0Hx) Yes 256K 17ns static RAM
Wait states: 　System board 　Adapter	 0-5 (95 percent 0 wait states) 0-7

System Features

ROM size 　ROM shadowing 　BIOS extensions stored on disk 　Setup and Diagnostics stored on disk	128K Yes Yes Yes
Optional math coprocessor	80487SX (0Gx) Built-in to 486DX
Coprocessor speed	20 MHz (0Gx) 25 MHz (0Jx) 33 MHz (0Kx) 50 MHz
Standard graphics 　8-/16-/32-bit controller 　Bus master 　Video RAM (VRAM)	XGA (eXtended Graphics Array) 32-bit Yes 512K
RS232C serial ports 　UART chip used 　Maximum speed (bits/second) 　FIFO mode enabled 　Supports DMA data transfer 　Maximum number of ports	2 Custom (compatible with NS16550A) 345,600 bps Yes Yes 8
Pointing device (mouse) ports	1
Parallel printer ports 　Bidirectional 　Supports DMA data transfer 　Maximum number of ports	1 Yes Yes 8

(continues)

Table 22.51 Continued

System Features

CMOS real-time clock (RTC)	Yes
CMOS RAM	64 bytes + 2K extension
Battery life	5 years
Replaceable	Yes

Disk Storage

Internal disk and tape drive bays	4					
Number of 3 1/2- and 5 1/4-inch bays	3/1					
Selectable boot drive	Yes					
Bootable drives	All physical drives					
Standard floppy drives	1×1.44M					
Optional floppy drives:						
5 1/4-inch 360K	Optional					
5 1/4-inch 1.2M	Optional					
3 1/2-inch 720K	No					
3 1/2-inch 1.44M	Standard					
3 1/2-inch 2.88M	No					
Hard disk controller included	32-bit SCSI adapter with 512K cache					
Bus master	Yes					
Devices supported per adapter	7					
Adapters supported per system	4					
SCSI hard disks available	60M/80M/120M/160M/320M/400M					
Drive form factor	3 1/2-inch					
Drive interface	SCSI					
Drive capacity	60M	80M	120M	160M	320M	400M
Average access rate (ms)	23	17	23	16	12.5	11.5
Read-ahead cache	32K	32K	32K	32K	64K	128K
SCSI transfer mode	Async	Async	Async	Async	Sync	Sync
Encoding scheme	RLL	RLL	RLL	RLL	RLL	RLL
Cylinders	920	1021	920	1021	949	1201
Heads	4	4	8	8	14	14
Sectors per track	32	39	32	39	48	48
Rotational speed (RPM)	3600	3600	3600	3600	4318	4318
Interleave factor	1:1	1:1	1:1	1:1	1:1	1:1
Data transfer rate (K/second)	960	1170	960	1170	1727	1727
Automatic head parking	Yes	Yes	Yes	Yes	Yes	Yes

Expansion Slots

Total adapter slots	4
Number of long and short slots	4/0
Number of 8-/16-/32-bit slots	0/0/4
Number of slots with video ext.	1
Available slots	3

Keyboard Specifications

101-key Enhanced Keyboard	Yes
Fast keyboard speed setting	Yes
Keyboard cable length	6 feet

Security Features

Keylock:	
Locks cover	Yes
Locks keyboard	No
Keyboard password	Yes
Power-on password	Yes
Network server mode	Yes

Physical Specifications

Footprint type	Desktop
Dimensions:	
Height	5.5 inches
Width	17.3 inches
Depth	16.9 inches
Weight	25.0 lbs

Environmental Specifications

Power-supply output	194 watts
Worldwide (110/60, 220/50)	Yes
Auto-sensing/switching	Yes
Maximum current:	
90-137 VAC	4.8 amps
180-264 VAC	2.4 amps
Operating range	
Temperature	50-95 degrees F
Relative humidity	8-80 percent
Maximum operating altitude	7,000 feet
Heat (BTUs/hour)	662
FCC classification	Class B

PS/2 Model 95 XP 486

The PS/2 Model 95 XP 486, introduced October 30, 1990, is a high-performance, highly expandable floor-standing system based on MCA. Like the Model 90, through an unusual design, this system's 32-bit 80486 processor is on a removable processor complex, allowing a processor upgrade from the 25 MHz to the more powerful 33 MHz or 50 MHz system. This capability to upgrade can extend the life of the system as customer requirements for enhanced processor performance grow.

Table 22.52 shows the primary specifications of the various versions of PS/2 Model 90 XP 486.

Table 22.52 IBM PS/2 Model 90 XP 486 Model Summary						
			PLANAR MEMORY		STANDARD	
Part Number	CPU	MHz	Std.	Max.	Floppy Drive	Hard Disk
90 XP 486						
8590-0G5	486SX	20	4M	64M	1×1.44M	80M
8590-0G9	486SX	20	4M	64M	1×1.44M	160M
8590-0H5	486SX	25	4M	64M	1×1.44M	80M
8590-0H9	486SX	25	4M	64M	1×1.44M	160M
8590-0J5	486SX	25	8M	64M	1×1.44M	80M
8590-0J9	486SX	25	8M	64M	1×1.44M	160M
8590-0K9	486SX	33	8M	64M	1×1.44M	320M
8590-0KD	486SX	33	8M	64M	1×1.44M	320M
8590-0KF	486SX	33	8M	64M	1×1.44M	400M

Highlights of the Model 95 include the following:

- Processor complex with 80486 20, 25, 33, or 50MHz processor
- 8M standard memory, expandable to 64M on the system board
- Enhanced Performance XGA Display Adapter/A standard
- PS/2 SCSI 32-bit bus master adapter with cache
- Seven internal storage device bays
- Eight 32-bit Micro Channel expansion slots
- One DMA serial port and one DMA parallel port
- Selectable boot and disk loaded ROM BIOS

The PS/2 Model 95 XP 486 features the 20, 25, 33, or 50 MHz 80486 microprocessor. The processor includes an internal memory cache controller, an internal 8K memory cache, and an internal floating point processor unit. The PS/2 256K cache option provides additional memory cache capability beyond the 8K internal memory cache. The PS/2 256K cache option is supported on 486DX models of Model 90 and Model 95. This capability provides investment protection and flexibility for the user.

The system provides a total of seven storage device bays: Two can accommodate 5 1/4-inch half-high drives and the other five support 3 1/2-inch devices. Up to five high-speed SCSI hard disk drives can be installed internally, and a variety of other storage devices can be installed, such as CD-ROM drives, 5 1/4-inch floppy disk drives, and tape backup devices. The PS/2 Micro Channel SCSI adapter with cache allows as many as seven SCSI devices to be attached to the PS/2 Model 95. The PS/2 Model 95 also supports

Bus Type	Total Available Slots	STANDARD Video	Keyboard	Date Introduced	Date Withdrawn
MCA/32	4/3	XGA	Enh	04/23/91	01/17/92
MCA/32	4/3	XGA	Enh	04/23/91	01/17/92
MCA/32	4/3	XGA	Enh	10/17/91	—
MCA/32	4/3	XGA	Enh	10/17/91	—
MCA/32	4/3	XGA	Enh	10/30/90	01/17/92
MCA/32	4/3	XGA	Enh	10/30/90	01/17/92
MCA/32	4/3	XGA	Enh	10/17/91	07/28/92
MCA/32	4/3	XGA	Enh	10/30/90	01/17/92
MCA/32	4/3	XGA	Enh	10/17/91	07/28/92

an internal 5 1/4-inch floppy disk device. The 5 1/4-inch Slim High Disk Drive (part number 6451066) is an internal 5 1/4-inch, 1.2M floppy disk drive with electrical button eject. This drive does not require an attachment card or expansion slot for installation and is supported in the Models 90 and 95.

The system provides eight 32-bit MCA slots: Two are used by the SCSI and XGA adapters, leaving six for other expansion adapters. A direct memory access (DMA) serial port and DMA parallel port are provided as standard. The Model 95 also features the capability of booting from any drive and an easy way to upgrade BIOS capability.

The Model 95 memory subsystem has been designed for optimum performance with interleaved memory; it features parity memory checking for added reliability and data integrity. All system memory (up to 64M) is supported on the system board, eliminating the need for memory adapters in any of the expansion slots. Although the Model 95 supports a maximum of 64M of memory, only 16M of that is addressable by DMA. This amount effectively limits the use of memory past 16M to nonsystem operations such as caching, virtual memory, or other functions. The system board has a total of eight memory sockets, two of which are used by a pair of 2M SIMMs (single in-line memory modules) to provide the basic standard 4M of memory. (Note that the amount of standard memory can vary according to the model from 4M to 8M.) Optional 2M, 4M, and 8M memory SIMMs (70ns, 80ns, and 85ns only) are supported in matched pairs to provide various memory configurations up to 64M. Although 80ns and 85ns memory SIMMs are supported, 70ns memory SIMMs provide optimum memory subsystem performance.

The Extended Graphics Array (XGA) Display Adapter/A with its high-performance 32-bit bus master video subsystem is a standard feature of the PS/2 Model 95 XP 486. The XGA adapter provides $1024 \times 768 \times 16$ colors or $640 \times 480 \times 256$ colors as standard and can be optionally expanded to $1024 \times 768 \times 256$ colors with the addition of one PS/2 video memory expansion option. XGA supports all VGA modes and is optimized for use with window managers and other graphical user interfaces, allowing for highly interactive pop-up icons and pull-down menus. XGA also provides hardware support for 132-character text mode (using 8515 or 8514 display) and 16-bit direct color mode (64K colors at 640×480 resolution).

Other specific features of the Model 95 include a direct memory address (DMA) serial port and a DMA parallel port as standard. The DMA serial port provides support for speeds from 300 bits per second to 345.6K bits per second, which reduces processor loading and overhead when used in high-speed communications.

The Model 95 offers the selectable-boot feature. As part of the system CMOS setup program, the user can specify which drive should be booted from and in which order the boot process should try each drive (for example, boot first from A drive, and then C drive, and load BASIC). This allows the user to boot or load a program from the optional 5 1/4-inch internal floppy disk drive as if it were drive A.

Initial Microcode Load. One special Model 95 feature is Initial Microcode Load (IML). The Model 95 stores the BIOS, configuration programs, and diagnostics on the hard disk in a protected 3M partition and loaded from the disk during a "pre-boot" process. (The system programs also are provided on the PS/2 Model 95 Reference Disk.) The formatted capacity of the hard disk is reduced by 3M, and the total user-accessible capacity might vary slightly, based on operating environments. This partition is not affected when the drive is formatted using the DOS or OS/2 FORMAT command.

The Initial Microcode Load (IML) loads the BIOS program from the hard disk drive into system memory. This step makes updating the BIOS an easy task when the time comes. Rather than pulling and replacing ROM chips on the motherboard, all you have to do is obtain a newer copy of the reference floppy disk and restore the system programs using that disk. Updates are available from your dealer or directly from IBM.

For example, a problem has been noted with Model 95 systems that have more than 8M of memory. To fix the problem, you need the Model 95 Reference Disk Version 1.02 or higher. To obtain the latest version, call 1-800-426-7282, weekdays between 8 a.m. and 8 p.m., Eastern Standard time. Specify the floppy disk for IBM PS/2 Model 90 XP 486. In Canada, call 1-800-465-1234 weekdays between 8 a.m. and 4:30 p.m. Eastern Standard time. In Alaska, call (414) 633-8108. The update will be sent to you and is installed in a menu-driven fashion. Because IBM sets the standards in the computer industry, other IBM-compatible vendors probably will adopt this disk-based BIOS approach. The flexibility and ease of upgrading are welcome.

On October 17, 1991, IBM enhanced the PS/2 Model 95 XP family with new Intel 486SX 25 MHz (0Hx) models. The new systems come equipped with a new 486SX 25 MHz processor complex, which provides improved performance over the previous 25 MHz 486DX processor at a lower price. The new processor complex provides improved Micro Channel performance, better bus arbitration, and enhancements to the memory controller, making it ideal for multitasking or operating in heavily loaded networked environments. An improved physical design with fewer parts provides greater reliability. The new processor complex also incorporates a conventional math coprocessor socket. Because of the improved price and performance of the new 25 MHz systems, earlier models using the 486SX 20MHz (0Gx) and 486 25 MHz (0Jx) processor complex are being withdrawn. Because the 486SX lacks the integrated math coprocessor unit, a socket for the addition of the optional 487SX math coprocessor is provided. In addition, these entry-level models may be upgraded to the more powerful 486/33MHz or the 486/50MHz processors with the IBM PS/2 486/33 and 486/50 processor-upgrade options.

Table 22.53 lists the technical specifications for the PS/2 model 95XP 486.

Table 22.53 PS/2 Model 95 XP 486 Technical Specifications	
System Architecture	
Microprocessor and clock speed	80486SX 20 MHz (0Gx)
	80487SX 20 MHz
	80486SX 25 MHz (0Hx)
	80487SX 25 MHz
	80486DX 25 MHz (0Jx)
	80486DX 33 MHz (0Kx)
	80486DX 50 MHz
Bus type	MCA (Micro Channel Architecture)
Bus width	32-bit
Interrupt levels	16
Type	Level-sensitive
Shareable	Yes
DMA channels	15
DMA burst mode supported	Yes
Bus masters supported	15
486 burst mode enabled	Yes
Upgradeable processor complex	Yes
Processor upgrades available	20 MHz 487SX
	25 MHz 486DX
	33 MHz 486DX
	50 MHz 486DX
Memory	
Standard on system board	4M (0Gx)
	8M (for all others)
Maximum on system board	64M
Maximum total memory	64M
Memory speed and type	70ns dynamic RAM
System-board memory socket type	36-bit SIMM (single in-line memory module)
Number of memory module sockets	8
Number available in standard configuration	6 (0Gx)
	4 (for all others)
Memory used on system board	2M/4M/8M SIMMs
Memory interleaving	Yes
Paged memory logic	Yes

(continues)

Table 22.53 Continued	
Memory	
Memory cache controller	Yes
Internal/external cache	Internal
Standard memory cache size	8K
Optional external memory cache	No (0Gx, 0Hx)
	Yes (for all others)
External cache size	256K
Cache memory speed and type	17ns static RAM
Wait states:	
System board	0-5 (95 percent 0 wait states)
Adapter	0-7
Standard Features	
ROM size	128K
ROM shadowing	Yes
BIOS extensions stored on disk	Yes
Setup and Diagnostics stored on disk	Yes
Optional math coprocessor	80487SX (0Gx)
	Built-in to 486DX
Coprocessor speed	20 MHz (0Gx)
	25 MHz (0Jx)
	33 MHz (0Kx)
	50 MHz
Standard graphics	XGA (eXtended Graphics Array)
8-/16-/32-bit controller	32-bit
Bus master	Yes
Video RAM (VRAM)	512K
RS232C serial ports	2
UART chip used	Custom (compatible with NS16550A)
Maximum speed (bits/second)	345,600 bps
FIFO mode enabled	Yes
Supports DMA data transfer	Yes
Maximum number of ports	8
Pointing device (mouse) ports	1
Parallel printer ports	1
Bidirectional	Yes
Supports DMA data transfer	Yes
Maximum number of ports	8
CMOS real-time clock (RTC)	Yes
CMOS RAM	64 bytes + 2K extension
Battery life	5 years
Replaceable	Yes
Disk Storage	
Internal disk and tape drive bays	7
Number of 3 1/2- and 5 1/4-inch bays	5/2
Selectable boot drive	Yes
Bootable drives	All physical drives
Standard floppy drives	1×1.44M

Disk Storage

Optional floppy drives:	
5 1/4-inch 360K	Optional
5 1/4-inch 1.2M	Optional
3 1/2-inch 720K	No
3 1/2-inch 1.44M	Standard
3 1/2-inch 2.88M	No
Hard disk controller included	32-bit SCSI adapter with 512K cache
Bus master	Yes
Devices supported per adapter	7
Adapters supported per system	4
SCSI hard disks available	60M/80M/120M/160M/320M/400M
Drive form factor	3 1/2-inch
Drive interface	SCSI

	60M	80M	120M	160M	320M	400M
Drive capacity	60M	80M	120M	160M	320M	400M
Average access rate (ms)	23	17	23	16	12.5	11.5
Read-ahead cache	32K	32K	32K	32K	64K	128K
SCSI transfer mode	Async	Async	Async	Async	Sync	Sync
Encoding scheme	RLL	RLL	RLL	RLL	RLL	RLL
Cylinders	920	1021	920	1021	949	1201
Heads	4	4	8	8	14	14
Sectors per track	32	39	32	39	48	48
Rotational speed (RPM)	3600	3600	3600	3600	4318	4318
Interleave factor	1:1	1:1	1:1	1:1	1:1	1:1
Data transfer rate (K/second)	960	1170	960	1170	1727	1727
Automatic head parking	Yes	Yes	Yes	Yes	Yes	Yes

Expansion Slots

Total adapter slots	8
Number of long and short slots	8/0
Number of 8-/16-/32-bit slots	0/0/8
Number of slots with video ext.	2
Adapter form factor	IBM RISC system/6000
Available slots	6

Keyboard Specifications

101-key Enhanced Keyboard	Yes
Fast keyboard speed setting	Yes
Keyboard cable length	6 feet
Keylock:	
Locks cover	Yes
Locks keyboard	No
Keyboard password	Yes
Power-on password	Yes
Network server mode	Yes

(continues)

Table 22.53 Continued	
Physical Specifications	
Footprint type	Floor-standing
Dimensions:	
Height	19.8 inches
Width	8.0 inches
Depth	20.0 inches
Weight	51.0 lbs
Environmental Specifications	
Power-supply output	329 watts
Worldwide (110/60, 220/50)	Yes
Auto-sensing/switching	Yes
Maximum current:	
90-137 VAC	8.3 amps
180-264 VAC	4.7 amps
Operating range:	
Temperature	50-95 degrees F
Relative humidity	8-80 percent
Maximum operating altitude	7,000 feet
Heat (BTUs/hour)	1123
FCC classification	Class B

Table 22.54 shows the primary specifications of the various versions of PS/2 Model 95 XP 486.

			PLANAR MEMORY		STANDARD	
Part Number	**CPU**	**MHz**	**Std.**	**Max.**	**Floppy Drive**	**Hard Disk**
95 XP 486						
8595-0G9	486SX	20	4M	64M	1×1.44M	160M
8595-0GF	486SX	20	4M	64M	1×1.44M	400M
8595-0H9	486SX	25	8M	64M	1×1.44M	160M
8595-0HF	486SX	25	8M	64M	1×1.44M	400M
8595-0J9	486SX	25	8M	64M	1×1.44M	160M
8595-0JD	486SX	25	8M	64M	1×1.44M	320M
8595-0JF	486SX	25	8M	64M	1×1.44M	400M
8595-0KD	486SX	33	8M	64M	1×1.44M	320M
8595-0KF	486SX	33	8M	64M	1×1.44M	400M

Table 22.54   IBM PS/2 Model 95 XP 486 Model Summary

PS/1 System-Unit Features by Model

Announced June 26, 1990, the IBM PS/1 Computer was designed for consumers who have little or no knowledge about computers and who intend to use their computers at home. The first PS/1 system was based on a 10 MHz 80286 processor with 512K or 1M of memory standard. The PS/1 was first made available in four basic models. The M01 was priced at $995 and included a monochrome VGA display and 512K of memory. The $1,499 M34 featured a 30M hard disk drive and 1M of standard RAM. These monochrome VGA configurations were available with color VGA monitors for $1,640 and $1,999, respectively.

On October 7, 1991, IBM expanded its PS/1 product line by introducing systems with 386SX processors. The $1,649 PS/1 SX C42 has a 16-MHz 386SX processor, 2M RAM (maximum of 6M), a 1.44M floppy disk drive, 12-inch VGA color monitor, and a 40M hard disk drive. The $2,199 PS/1 SX B82 model has all the features of the C42 but included an 80M hard disk drive. Both were 3 inches high, 11 inches wide, and 14 inches deep, weighing about nine pounds. A 2,400-bps modem was included along with Microsoft Works and Microsoft Windows 3.0. These newer models addressed a broader market, including small businesses and the advanced computing requirements of second-time buyers.

In September 1992, IBM introduced 21 new models of the PS/1, while segmenting the brand into three lines: PS/1 Essential models are for small businesses; the PS/1 Expert is for users who may already own microcomputers; and the PS/1 Consultant is targeted for students or those who take work home. Each line comprises a notebook model and six desktop machines.

Bus Type	Total Available Slots	STANDARD		Date Introduced	Date Withdrawn
		Video	Keyboard		
MCA/32	8/6	XGA	Enh	04/23/91	01/17/92
MCA/32	8/6	XGA	Enh	04/23/91	01/17/92
MCA/32	8/6	XGA	Enh	10/17/91	—
MCA/32	8/6	XGA	Enh	10/17/91	—
MCA/32	8/6	XGA	Enh	10/30/90	01/17/92
MCA/32	8/6	XGA	Enh	10/30/90	01/17/92
MCA/32	8/6	XGA	Enh	04/23/91	01/17/92
MCA/32	8/6	XGA	Enh	10/30/90	01/17/92
MCA/32	8/6	XGA	Enh	04/23/91	—

These 386SX and 486SX desktop models all came with DOS 5.0, Windows 3.1, Microsoft Works for Windows, and Prodigy preloaded. The 486DX models have OS/2 2.0 preloaded. Bundled with the PS/1 models are Microsoft's Works for Windows, Prodigy, and IBM-specific PS/2 Index, PS/1 Tutorial, and Promenade, a service for educating people on using their PS/1 computers. The PS/1 Essential line came bundled with Intuit's QuickBooks and Power Up's Express Publisher. The PS/1 Expert line included Power Up's Address Book Plus and Calendar Creator Plus. The PS/1 Consultant line comes with Intuit's Quicken for Windows' and Broderbund's The New Print Shop. The PS/note notebook, based on the IBM's SL processor, was also introduced, and included Prodigy, Promenade, and Delrina's WinFax Lite.

In October 1993, the PS/1 Consultant line was upgraded, adding multimedia and compliance with the EPA Energy Star conservation program. The special Rapid Resume utility is the most notable feature of the new systems. You can shut down your computer without having to save your documents or exit your applications. When the computer is re-started, everything loads just as you left it. The Rapid Resume feature is possible only on the PS/1, IBM contends, because it's more than a simple software utility. It works hand-in-hand with IBM's own BIOS, dedicated circuitry on the motherboard, and a specialized power switch. The BIOS intercepts an off signal from the power switch, and, if applications or documents are open, writes the entire contents of the PC's memory to a file on the hard drive. When the PC reboots (regardless of when, even if you've unplugged or moved the machine), it swaps the contents of that file back into the system RAM. You're back in business without a perceptible delay.

The multimedia features are also impressive, including a Sound Blaster 16 audio card and a front-loading double-speed CD-ROM drive. The PS/1 Multimedia Model comes with version 2.0 of Compton's Interactive Encyclopedia. Microsoft Windows and Works come preloaded on the hard drive, along with the software needed to log in to the America Online and Prodigy on-line services. The systems come with a unique one-year warranty: IBM will ship a new keyboard, monitor, or CPU via UPS within 24 hours of a mechanical mishap.

The PS/1 comes with three new software utilities: PS/1 Index, a concise tutorial that aids users with real-world applications; PS/1 Tutorial, which includes Windows Lessons and Software Descriptions; and PS/1 Fitness, which adds easy-to-understand dialog boxes to DOS utilities.

The $2,844 PS/1 Consultant 486DX2/66 uses a 66-MHz 80486DX microprocessor and comes in a minitower case with 8M of RAM, a 424M hard disk, and an internal fax mo-dem. The $2,144 PS/1 Consultant Multimedia desktop system uses a 25-MHz 80486SX processor and has 4M of RAM, a 256M hard disk, a double-speed CD-ROM drive, and a Sound Blaster 16 audio card.

Standby mode forces the system into a low-power state and blanks the screen after a user-defined period; Rapid Resume, which meets the Energy Star rating, turns the system off after a period of inactivity and restores it to its previous state when it is turned back on.

Recent iterations of the PS/1 include "beefier" processors, such as the 66-MHz 486DX2, 255M hard drive, and local-bus video. The PS/1 line is targeted to small- or home-business users. The systems are sold through different outlets, typically to nontechnical users. The focus is the mass retail channel (Staples, CompUSA), and systems come with exceptionally helpful and professional manuals and software. IBM plays a name game, with each PS/1 receiving a suffix indicating where it is available. Consultant LBL (general merchandisers), Expert (computer stores), and Essential (office superstores) are the current monikers, with new Advisor (mass merchandisers) and Investor (warehouse or membership clubs) lines in the works.

The original PS/1 system came with an IBM Enhanced Keyboard, VGA display, IBM mouse, 2,400 bps internal modem, IBM DOS, Microsoft Works, and tutorials that enable the purchaser to run a variety of applications immediately after setting up the system. Included with U.S. models is software to access the IBM PS/1 on-line Users' Club through the Prodigy on-line communications service. Several models are available so that you can select the type of display (monochrome or color) and the system-unit configuration (a single floppy drive with 512K of memory or a single floppy drive and 30M hard disk with 1M of memory). Highlights of the original PS/1 included these items:

- 10-MHz 80286 processor

- 12-inch Video Graphics Array (VGA) display (color or black-and-white)

- IBM mouse

- 101-key IBM keyboard

- Built-in 2,400 bits-per-second (bps) modem

- Free three-month subscription to Prodigy

- PS/1 Club, an on-line customer support service

- Microsoft Works integrated application software

- Ease of set-up and use

- Preloaded DOS 4.0 and menu interface (on hard disk models)

- Possibility of future expansion with PS/1 options

- Special IBM warranty

The 386SX models also offer the following additional features:

- 16-MHz 386SX processor

- 2M RAM, expandable to 6M on the system board

- 12-inch Color Video Graphics Array (VGA) display

Table 22.55 shows the primary specifications of the various versions of the PS/1.

Table 22.55   IBM PS/1 Model Summary

Part Number	CPU	MHz	PLANAR MEMORY Std.	Max.	STANDARD Floppy Drive	Hard Disk
PS/1 (June 1990)						
Model M01	286	10	512K	1M	1×1.44M	—
Model M34	286	10	1M	1M	1×1.44M	30M
PS/1 (October 1991)						
Model B82	386SX	16	2M	16M	1×1.44M	80M
Model C42	386SX	16	2M	16M	1×1.44M	40M
PS/1 Consultant						
2133-G11	386SX	25	2M	16M	1×1.44M	85M
2133-G13	386SX	25	2M	16M	1×1.44M, 1×1.2M	129M
2133-G14	386SX	25	2M	16M	1×1.44M, 1×1.2M	170M
2133-G43	486SX	20	4M	32M	1×1.44M	129M
2133-G44	486SX	20	4M	32M	1×1.44M, 1×1.2M	170M
2133-G76	486DX	33	8M	32M	1×1.44M, 1×1.2M	211M
PS/1 Essential						
2133-W11	386SX	25	2M	16M	1×1.44M	85M
2133-W13	386SX	25	2M	16M	1×1.44M, 1×1.2M	129M
2133-W14	386SX	25	2M	16M	1×1.44M, 1×1.2M	170M
2133-W43	486SX	20	4M	32M	1×1.44M	129M
2133-W44	486SX	20	4M	32M	1×1.44M, 1×1.2M	170M
2133-W76	486DX	33	8M	32M	1×1.44M, 1×1.2M	211M
PS/1 Expert						
2133-S11	386SX	25	2M	16M	1×1.44M	85M
2133-S13	386SX	25	2M	16M	1×1.44M, 1×1.2M	129M
2133-S14	386SX	25	2M	16M	1×1.44M, 1×1.2M	170M
2133-S43	486SX	20	4M	32M	1×1.44M	129M
2133-S44	486SX	20	4M	32M	1×1.44M, 1×1.2M	170M
2133-S76	486DX	33	8M	32M	1×1.44M, 1×1.2M	211M

Bus Type	Total Available Slots	STANDARD		Date Introduced	Date Withdrawn
		Video	Keyboard		
ISA/16	0	VGA	Enh	06/26/90	10/07/91
ISA/16	0	VGA	Enh	06/26/90	10/07/91
MCA/16	2/2	VGA	Enh	10/07/91	09/09/92
MCA/16	0	VGA	Enh	10/07/91	—
ISA/16	3/3	VGA	Enh	09/09/92	—
ISA/16	3/3	VGA	Enh	09/09/92	—
ISA/16	5/5	VGA	Enh	09/09/92	—
ISA/16	3/3	VGA	Enh	09/09/92	—
ISA/16	5/5	VGA	Enh	09/09/92	—
ISA/16	5/5	VGA	Enh	09/09/92	—
ISA/16	3/3	VGA	Enh	09/09/92	—
ISA/16	3/3	VGA	Enh	09/09/92	—
ISA/16	5/5	VGA	Enh	09/09/92	—
ISA/16	3/3	VGA	Enh	09/09/92	—
ISA/16	5/5	VGA	Enh	09/09/92	—
ISA/16	5/5	VGA	Enh	09/09/92	—
ISA/16	3/3	VGA	Enh	09/09/92	—
ISA/16	3/3	VGA	Enh	09/09/92	—
ISA/16	5/5	VGA	Enh	09/09/92	—
ISA/16	3/3	VGA	Enh	09/09/92	—
ISA/16	5/5	VGA	Enh	09/09/92	—
ISA/16	5/5	VGA	Enh	09/09/92	—

IBM introduced a special model (B84) of the PS/1 that is similar to the B82 but preloaded with OS/2 version 2.0. With OS/2 version 2.0, PS/1 users were able to run DOS, Windows, and OS/2 applications, exploiting virtually all software available, regardless of the environment for which the software was designed.

System Features. IBM designed the PS/1 to enable home consumers to buy everything in one convenient place. Most consumers can set up and use the PS/1 in 15 minutes. The setup is simple: Take the components out of the box, attach cables, plug in the system, and push one button. Because the user interface (in ROM) and DOS already are installed on the system, users select what they want to do from the first screen and (on the floppy-drive system) are prompted to insert the proper floppy disk or (on the hard-drive system) are presented with the program they select after the machine goes to the hard disk, on which all the software included with the PS/1 was preloaded.

One special feature of the PS/1 is its warranty. Although most repair service is available easily through IBM authorized dealers, you have also another option. IBM's Express Maintenance service provides parts directly to customers, normally within 48 hours. Because the PS/1 is a totally modular, snap-together unit, replacing any part of the system is a relatively easy task. You therefore have an alternate route for service if the dealer is too far away or does not have needed parts in stock.

With newer PS/1s, help is only a phone call away. All the systems come standard with IBM Online Housecall, a software program that enables an IBM technical support person to examine a user's system-control files and other files to fix software glitches and diagnose hardware failures over the telephone. A system can be viewed only with the user's permission because the user must start up the program before an IBM technician can access it.

All recent PS/1 models also include a 9,600/2,400 bps fax modem, PC-DOS 6.x, Microsoft Windows 3.x, Microsoft Works for Windows, the PS/1 Edition of American Online, Prodigy membership kit, a PS/1 Tutorial, PS/1 Index, PS/1 Fitness, and a choice of Quicken, Winfax Lite fax software, or The New Print Shop with America Online. All the software and DOS are preloaded, and everything is configured for an immediate start after you plug in the system.

The standard service and support provided with the PS/1 system is excellent. Although, if necessary, most repair service can be obtained easily through IBM authorized dealers, another route is available. IBM has a special toll-free service called Express Maintenance, which provides parts directly to the customer, normally within 48 hours. Support is available from the PS/1 Club, an on-line support service, exclusively available to PS/1 owners through Prodigy seven days a week, 365 days a year.

The PS/1 is compatible with the PS/2 Model 30-286 at the BIOS level (although the BIOS is not identical) and at most hardware interfaces. The PS/1 also is compatible with the original IBM AT system. The 286 PS/1 is about 50 percent faster than the IBM AT. All PS/1 systems incorporate many features that would have been extra-cost options on the original IBM AT system. Because the PS/1, like the PS/2, has many features integrated on its motherboard, many standard types of adapter cards—such as graphics adapters, some disk controllers, and many memory upgrades—do not work with it.

System Expansion and Restrictions. The PS/1 has some significant limitations and restrictions to expansion. The biggest limitation is that the system has no full-length expansion slots, although few expansion cards require the full 13-inch-long slot. Most PS/1 models include three 16-bit expansion slots and one local-bus expansion slot.

Early PS/1s had 512K or 2M of memory installed permanently on the motherboard, depending on the system. Current PS/1s accept up to either 32M or 64M of memory.

The limited number and kinds of possible expansion slots is a serious limitation, but less of a problem than it might seem at first, because of the special connectors the PS/1 provides for various options. The modem that comes with the system plugs into a special motherboard connector and does not require a slot.

On the PS/1, memory errors can go undetected more easily than in other IBM or IBM-compatible systems that do offer standard parity-checking. This statement might sound shocking and seem to reflect a seriously crippling feature of the system, but, in comparison, Apple Macintosh systems also do not have parity-checked memory as a standard feature. A computer does not require parity-checking to function, but the more "mission critical" that information accuracy is, the more parity-checking becomes an issue. The lack of parity-checking makes the PS/1 less suited for business applications use.

Table 22.56 describes the technical specifications for the 286 PS/1.

Table 22.56 PS/1 286 Technical Specifications	
System Architecture	
Microprocessor	80286
Clock speed	10 MHz
Bus type	ISA (Industry Standard Architecture)
Bus width	16-bit
Interrupt levels	16
Type	Edge-triggered
Shareable	No
DMA channels	7
DMA burst mode supported	No
Bus masters supported	No
Upgradeable processor complex	No

(continues)

Table 22.56   Continued

Memory

Standard on system board	512K (x01)
	1M (x34)
Maximum on system board	2.5M
Maximum total memory	8.5M
Memory speed and type	120ns dynamic RAM
System-board memory socket type	Proprietary card
Number of memory-module sockets	1
Number available in standard configurration	0 (x34)
	1 (x01)
Memory used on system board	Soldered 512K bank, 512K/2M cards
Parity-checked memory	No
Memory cache controller	No
Wait states:	
System board	1
Adapter	1

Standard Features

ROM size	256K
ROM shadowing	No
User interface menu in ROM	Yes
Optional math coprocessor	No
Standard graphics	VGA (Video Graphics Array)
Standard display	Included
Monochrome	(M01, M34)
Color	(C01, C34)
Audio earphone jack	Yes
2,400 bps modem	U.S./Canada only
Hayes-compatible	Yes
Phone cord and splitter included	Yes
RS232C serial ports	Optional (requires expansion chassis)
UART chip used	NS16450
Maximum speed (bits/second)	19,200 bps
DMA data transfer support	No
Maximum number of ports	1
Pointing device (mouse) ports	1
IBM mouse included	Yes
Parallel printer ports	1
Bidirectional	Yes
CMOS real-time clock (RTC)	Yes
CMOS RAM	64 bytes
Battery life	10 years
Replaceable	Yes (Dallas module)

Disk Storage

Internal disk and tape drive bays	2
Number of 3 1/2- and 5 1/4-inch bays	2/0
Standard floppy disk drives	1×1.44M

Disk Storage

Optional floppy disk drives:	
5 1/4-inch 360K	Optional
5 1/4-inch 1.2M	Optional
3 1/2-inch 720K	No
3 1/2-inch 1.44M	Standard
3 1/2-inch 2.88M	No
Hard disk controller included	IDE connector on system board
IDE hard disks available	30M
Drive form factor	3 1/2-inch
Drive interface	IDE
Average access rate (ms)	19
Encoding scheme	RLL
BIOS drive type number	35
Cylinders	921
Heads	2
Sectors per track	33
Rotational speed (RPM)	3600
Interleave factor	4:1
Data transfer rate (K/second)	248
Automatic head parking	Yes

Expansion Slots

Total adapter slots	0
Number of long and short slots	0/0
Number of 8-/16-/32-bit slots	0/0/0
Available slots	0
With optional expansion unit:	
Total adapter slots	3
Number of long and short slots	2/1
Number of 8-/16-/32-bit slots	0/3/0
Available slots	3

Keyboard Specifications

101-key Enhanced Keyboard	Yes
Fast keyboard speed setting	Yes
Keyboard cable length	6 feet

Security Features

Keylock:	
Locks cover	No
Locks keyboard	No
Keyboard password	No
Power-on password	No
Network server mode	No

(continues)

Table 22.56   Continued

Physical Specifications

Footprint type	Desktop
Dimensions:	
Height	14.25 inches
Width footprint	10.75 inches
Width display	12.0 inches
Depth	17.0 inches
Weight:	
Color display	38.0 pounds
Mono display	31.0 pounds

Environmental Specifications

Power supply:	
Worldwide (110/60, 220/50)	Yes
Auto-sensing and switching	Yes
Maximum current:	
90-137 VAC; color	2.5 amps
80-259 VAC; color	2.0 amps
90-137 VAC; mono	2.0 amps
80-259 VAC; mono	1.25 amps
Operating range:	
Temperature	50-95 degrees F
Relative humidity	8 to 80 percent
Heat (BTUs/hour)	358
FCC classification	Class B

Table 22.57 describes the technical specifications for the 386SX PS/1.

Table 22.57   PS/1 386SX Technical Specifications

System Architecture

Microprocessor	80386SX
Clock speed	16 MHz
Bus type	ISA (Industry Standard Architecture)
Bus width	16-bit
Interrupt levels	16
Type	Edge-triggered
Shareable	No
DMA channels	7
DMA burst mode supported	No
Bus masters supported	No
Upgradeable processor complex	No

Memory

Standard on system board	2M
Maximum on system board	6M
Maximum total memory	16M
Memory speed and type	100ns dynamic RAM
System-board memory socket type	Proprietary card
Number of memory-module sockets	1
Number available in standard configuration	1
Memory used on system board	Soldered 2M bank, 2M/4M cards
Parity-checked memory	No
Memory cache controller	No
Wait states:	
System board	0-2
Adapter	0-2

Standard Features

ROM size	256K
ROM shadowing	Yes
User interface menu in ROM	Yes
Optional math coprocessor	387SX
Coprocessor speed	16 MHz
Standard graphics	VGA (Video Graphics Array)
Standard display	Color, included
Audio earphone jack	Yes
2,400 bps modem	U.S./Canada only
Hayes-compatible	Yes
Phone cord and splitter included	Yes
RS232C serial ports	Optional
UART chip used	NS16450
Maximum speed (bits/second)	19,200 bps
DMA data transfer support	No
Maximum number of ports	1
Pointing device (mouse) ports	1
IBM mouse included	Yes
Parallel printer ports	1
Bidirectional	Yes
CMOS real-time clock (RTC)	Yes
CMOS RAM	64 bytes
Battery life	10 years
Replaceable	Yes (Dallas module)

(continues)

Table 22.57   Continued

Disk Storage

Internal disk and tape drive bays	2 (C42)
	3 (B82, C92)
Number of 3 1/2- and 5 1/4-inch bays	2/0 (C42)
	3/0 (B82, C92)
Standard floppy disk drives	1×1.44M
Optional floppy disk drives:	
5 1/4-inch 360K	Optional
5 1/4-inch 1.2M	Optional
3 1/2-inch 720K	No
3 1/2-inch 1.44M	Standard
3 1/2-inch 2.88M	No
Hard disk controller included	IDE connector on system board
IDE hard disks available	40M (C42)
	80M (B82)
	129M (C92)
Drive form factor	3 1/2-inch
Drive interface	IDE
Average access rate (ms)	21
Encoding scheme	RLL
Automatic head parking	Yes

Expansion Slots

Total adapter slots	0 (C42)
	2 (B82, C92)
Number of long and short slots	0/0 (C42)
	0/2 (B82, C92)
Number of 8-/16-/32-bit slots	0/0/0 (C42)
	0/2/0 (B82, C92)
Available slots	0 (C42)
	2 (B82, C92)
With optional expansion unit:	
Total adapter slots	3 (C42)
Number of long and short slots	2/1 (C42)
Number of 8-/16-/32-bit slots	0/3/0 (C42)
Available slots	3 (C42)

VII

Keyboard Specifications

101-key Enhanced Keyboard	Yes
Fast keyboard speed setting	Yes
Keyboard cable length	6 feet

Security Features

Keylock:	
Locks cover	No
Locks keyboard	No
Keyboard password	No
Power-on password	No
Network server mode	No

Physical Specifications

Footprint type	Desktop
Dimensions:	
Height	14.25 inches (C42)
	15.75 inches (B82, C92)
Width footprint	10.75 inches
Width display	12.0 inches
Depth	17.0 inches
Weight:	
Color display	39.0 pounds

Environmental Specifications

Power supply:	
Worldwide (110/60, 220/50)	Yes
Auto-sensing and switching	Yes
Maximum current:	
90-137 VAC; color	2.5 amps
80-259 VAC; color	2.0 amps
Operating range:	
Temperature	50-95 degrees F
Relative humidity	8 to 80 percent
Heat (BTUs/hour)	358
FCC classification	Class B

Table 22.58 shows the primary specifications and costs of the various PS/1 models, and table 22.59 shows the accessories available from IBM for the PS/1.

Table 22.58 PS/1 Model Summary						
			PLANAR MEMORY		STANDARD	
Part Number	CPU	MHz	Std.	Max.	Floppy Drive	Hard Disk
PS/1 286						
2011-M01	286	10	512K	2.5M	1×1.44M	—
2011-C01	286	10	512K	2.5M	1×1.44M	—
2011-M34	286	10	1M	2.5M	1×1.44M	30M
2011-C34	286	10	1M	2.5M	1×1.44M	30M
PS/1 SX						
2121-C42	386SX	16	2M	6M	1×1.44M	40M
2121-B82	386SX	16	2M	6M	1×1.44M	80M
2121-C92	386SX	16	2M	6M	1×1.44M	129M

Keyboards available include the Enhanced (101-key), Space-Saving (84-key), and Host-Connected (122-key). If "Any" is indicated, purchaser can choose any of the three.

Table 22.59 PS/1 Special Accessories		
Description	Part Number	Price
PS/1 286 to 386SX upgrade	93F2059	$1,045
PS/1 286 to 386SX upgrade	93F2059	845
PS/1 color display upgrade	1057108	699
PS/1 512K memory card	1057035	109
PS/12M memory card	1057660	279
PS/12M memory card	92F9935	279
PS/14M memory card	92F9694	549
5 1/4-inch 360K PS/1 286 drive	1057139	299
5 1/4-inch 360K PS/1 SX drive	92F9333	299
5 1/4-inch 1.2M PS/1 286 drive	1057191	299
5 1/4-inch 1.2M PS/1 SX drive	92F9334	299
3 1/2-inch 1.44M PS/1 drive	1057039	249
30M 3 1/2-inch IDE drive	1057036	599
80M 3 1/2-inch IDE drive	92F9937	1,060
129M 3 1/2-inch IDE drive	92F9938	1,500
PS/1 adapter expansion unit	1057028	169
AT serial/parallel adapter	6450215	161
Audio card/joystick connector	1057735	129
Audio card/joystick connector	92F9932	129
Audio card/joystick for 286	1057064	249
Second joystick	1057109	39
PS/1 two-piece dust cover set	95F1136	20

Bus Type	Total Available Slots	STANDARD		Date Introduced	Date Withdrawn
		Video	Keyboard		
ISA/16	0	VGA	Enh	06/26/90	—
ISA/16	0	VGA	Enh	06/26/90	—
ISA/16	0	VGA	Enh	06/26/90	—
ISA/16	0	VGA	Enh	06/26/90	—
ISA/16	0	VGA	Enh	10/07/91	—
ISA/16	2/2	VGA	Enh	10/07/91	—
ISA/16	2/2	VGA	Enh	10/07/91	—

PS/1 Models Mxx have a built-in monochrome analog display, and Models Cxx have the Color Analog Display.

Notes

Trade in x01 Model for B82 Model
Trade in x34 Model for B82 Model
Upgrade for mono systems
Upgrades to 1M on motherboard
Upgrades to 2.5M on motherboard
Upgrades to 4M on 386SX motherboard
Upgrades to 6M on 386SX motherboard
Attaches to PS/1
Attaches to PS/1
Attaches to PS/1
Attaches to PS/1
PS/1 internal drive
For PS/1-M01/C01
For PS/1 386SX
For PS/1 386SX
Three slots: two 11-inch, one 9.5-inch
Requires expansion unit
Attaches to 286 motherboard
Attaches to 386SX motherboard
Includes joystick, MIDI connector
Includes Y-cable for 1057064
Water-repellent, antistatic

PS/ValuePoint System-Unit Features by Model

IBM introduced its PS/ValuePoint line on October 20, 1992. At the time of the ValuePoint introduction, IBM's microcomputer market share had fallen from an estimated 30 percent in July 1991 to 18 percent in July 1992. The target of the ValuePoint line is corporate users desiring low-end microcomputers. The ValuePoint line was IBM's defense against Compaq Computer's affordable ProLinea line of computers, introduced in early 1992.

The new machines, which were first sold in Europe, are aimed at the middle ground between the entry-level PS/1 series and the increasingly upscale PS/2 machines. However, the prices of the ValuePoint line initially overlapped with those of PS/1 systems. Since 1992, the two have diverged to stake out their own niches. The ValuePoint PCs are available through IBM's sales force, resellers, and IBM PC Direct, the company's catalogue. They generally come with less software than the PS/1, but do have VESA local-bus graphics and 1M of video DRAM.

When first introduced, IBM unveiled four PS/ValuePoint machines. They start with the 325T, which contains an IBM 386SLC microprocessor running at 25 MHz and comes with 2M memory and a choice of 80M or 170M hard drive. The ValuePoint 425SX is equipped with an Intel 25-MHz 486SX, 8M RAM, and the same choice of drives as the 325T. The ValuePoint 433DX uses a 33-MHz 486DX chip, has 8M of memory, and a choice of either a 120M or 212M hard disk drive. The top of the line is the ValuePoint 466DX2, using Intel's clock-doubling 486DX2 66-MHz processor. This model comes with 8M of memory and a 212M hard disk drive. All ValuePoint machines come with five expansion slots and five bays for storage devices. Initially, they all used the ISA bus rather than the MCA bus found on PS/2 models. The PS/ValuePoint 325T came with DOS 5.0 preloaded, whereas the other models had IBM's OS/2 2.0.

Support

Initially, the ValuePoint systems did not come with the three-year warranty provided on some PS/2 models. Instead, they had a one-year warranty covering on-site service, with a promise of response within four hours. Since then, some high-end ValuePoint models now come with a three-year on-site warranty.

System Features

The IBM ValuePoint includes a ROM-based setup utility that provides menus and descriptions for various features. The cover's release latch located on the front of the system enables users to lift the cover on and off without any screws or tools. SIMMs install on the motherboard easily. The coprocessor socket resides on the motherboard, but you must remove the drive bracket assembly to access it.

In May 1994, the ValuePoint line was split into three lines: the ValuePoint P60/D (Pentium), the powerful ValuePoint Performance Series, and the mainstream ValuePoint Si Series. However, IBM intends to merge its PS/2 and ValuePoint lines into a unified solution for corporate customers. The resulting systems would move IBM toward industry-standard systems using the ISA and PCI buses with some of the PS/2's capabilities, such as IBM's plug and play features, data integrity, and built-in security. Table 22.61 shows the primary specifications of the early versions of the PS/ValuePoint.

Decoding ValuePoint Model Numbers

With the large variety of ValuePoint systems available, you might have difficulty telling from the model number how one differs from another.

Table 22.60 describes the model designation meanings used by IBM for its ValuePoint Performance Series, Si Series, and P60/D model.

Table 22.60 ValuePoint Model Designation Codes

Model	Meaning
6384-***	60-MHz Pentium series
64**-***	ValuePoint Performance Series
6381-***	ValuePoint Si Series
4-	PCI local-bus design
2-	ISA local-bus design
8*-*	Slimline (SpaceSaver) case (three slots, three bays)
8*-*	Desktop case (five slots, five bays)
9*-*	Mini-tower case (eight slots, six drive bays)
****-*0D	No hard drive
****-**F	Preinstalled IBM PC-DOS 6.3 and Windows 3.11
****-**G	Preinstalled OS/2 2.1
****-C**	33-MHz 486SX processor, Performance Series
****-H**	33-MHz 486DX processor, Performance Series
****-L**	66-MHz 486DX2 processor, Performance Series
****-X**	100-MHz 486DX4 processor, Performance Series
****-F**	25-MHz 486SX processor, Si Series
****-M**	33-MHz 486DX processor, Si Series
****-W**	66-MHz 486DX2 processor, Si Series

Table 22.61   First IBM PS/ValuePoints Model Summary

Part Number	CPU	MHz	PLANAR MEMORY Std.	Max.	STANDARD Floppy Drive	Hard Disk
PS/ValuePoint (October 1992)						
325T	386SLC	25	2M	8M	1×1.44M	80M
425SX	486SX	25	8M	16M	1×1.44M	80M
433DX	486DX	33	8M	16M	1×1.44M	120M
466DX2	486DX2	66	8M	16M	1×1.44M	120M

ValuePoint P60/D

The ValuePoint P60/D is IBM's foray into affordable Pentium-based PCs. The P60/D has a 60-MHz Pentium processor, which has a built-in 16K L1 cache. A 256K L2 cache comes standard, as well as 8M RAM (6384-193) or 16M RAM (6384-189, 6384-199). The P60/D uses 72-pin SIMM RAM for a maximum of 128M. Video graphics are provided through an onboard super-VGA PCI graphics chip. 1M video RAM comes standard, whereas an additional 2M is optional. A 1.44M disk drive comes standard, as well as either a 424M or 527M hard disk drive. A 1G hard disk is also available from IBM. The P60/D comes with various security features, including a key lock, power-on password, and administrator password.

The P60/D developed a reputation for an excellent keyboard, monitor, and mouse but not much else. (An optional keyboard with an integrated ThinkPoint II pointing device is available, similar to that found on IBM's popular ThinkPad line of notebooks.) Expandability is limited with the P60/D because of its small desktop case. No drive bays are free, and one of the ISA slots is difficult to access due to the tangle of cabling and proximity to the power supply. The machine comes with DOS 6.1 pre-installed. However, the P60/D does incorporate a unique riser-card design that allows additional expansion cards to be added. The riser card accommodates one half-size and one full-size ISA card and one full-size and one half-size 32-bit PCI card. The ValuePoint Performance Series takes this design one step farther by offering a choice of either VLB or PCI buses.

Table 22.62 lists the technical specifications for the ValuePoint P60/D.

Table 22.62   ValuePoint P60/D Technical Specifications

System Architecture	
Microprocessor 　Clock speed	Pentium 60 MHz
L1/L2 cache	16K/256K
Bus type 　Bus width	PCI 32-bit
Memory	
Standard on system board	16M (8M on 6384-193)
Maximum on system board	128M
Maximum total memory	128M

Bus Type	Total Available Slots	STANDARD		Date Introduced	Date Withdrawn
		Video	Keyboard		
ISA/16	5/5	ET4000 SVGA	Any	10/20/92	—
ISA/16	5/5	ET4000 SVGA	Any	10/20/92	—
ISA/16	5/5	ET4000 SVGA	Any	10/20/92	—
ISA/16	5/5	ET4000 SVGA	Any	10/20/92	—

Memory

Memory speed and type	70ns dynamic RAM
System board memory socket type	72-pin SIMM (single in-line memory module)
Number of memory module sockets	4
Number available in standard configuration	4
Memory used on system board	2M/4M/8M/16M 72-pin SIMMs
Optional math coprocessor	Standard
Standard graphics	Local-bus SVGA graphics
Video RAM (VRAM)	1M
RS232C serial ports	1
UART chip used	Custom (compatible with NS16550A)
Pointing device (mouse) ports	1

Standard Features

Parallel printer ports	1
Bidirectional	Yes

Disk Storage

internal disk and tape drive bays	5
Number of 3 1/2- and 5 1/4-inch bays	1/2
Standard floppy drives	1×1.44M
Optional floppy drives:	
5 1/4-inch 360K	Optional
5 1/4-inch 1.2M	Optional
3 1/2-inch 720K	No
3 1/2-inch 1.44M	Standard
3 1/2-inch 2.88M	Optional
Hard disk controller included	IDE integrated on system board
IDE hard disks available	424M/527M
Drive form factor	3 1/2-inch
Drive interface	IDE
Drive capacity	424M 527M
Average access rate (ms)	13 9
Interleave factor	1:1 1:1
Automatic head parking	Yes Yes

(continues)

Table 22.62   Continued

Expansion Slots

Total adapter slots	4
Number of long and short slots	4/0
Number of 8-/16-/32-bit slots	0/4/0
Available slots	4

Keyboard Specifications

Keyboard choices:	
122-key Host-Connected Keyboard	
101-key Enhanced Keyboard	
84-key Space-Saving Keyboard	
Fast keyboard speed setting	Yes
Keyboard cable length	10 feet

Security Features

Keylock:	
Locks cover	Yes
Locks keyboard	No
Keyboard password	Yes
Power-on password	Yes
Network server mode	Yes

Physical Specifications

Footprint type	Desktop
Orientation	Horizontal/vertical
Dimensions:	
Height	5.8 inches
Width	15.9 inches
Depth	16.5 inches
Weight	22 lbs.
Power consumption	200 watts
FCC classification	Class B

Table 22.63 shows the primary specifications of the ValuePoint P60/D models.

Table 22.63   IBM ValuePoint P60/D Model Summary

Part Number	CPU	MHz	PLANAR MEMORY Std.	Max.	STANDARD Floppy Drive	Hard Disk
ValuePoint P60/D						
6384-189	Pentium	60	16M	128M	1×1.44M	424M
6384-193	Pentium	60	8M	128M	1×1.44M	527M
6384-199	Pentium	60	16M	128M	1×1.44M	527M

ValuePoint Performance Series

The ValuePoint Performance Series is a revamped ValuePoint PC, offering flexibility to users. Instead of offering only PCI or VL-Bus models, the ValuePoint Performance Series, introduced in May 1994, offers the SelectaBus. This technology enables ValuePoint customers to choose and upgrade the system's local bus to support either VESA or PCI, solving the PCI versus VLB dilemma.

The Performance Series motherboard is based on VESA's VLB. However, a swappable backplane (called a riser) enables you to plug in expansion cards for one bus or the other. The VL version of the swappable backplane adds one VL-Bus slot and four ISA slots. The PCI backplane has room for two PCI cards and two ISA cards. And, for maximum flexibility, you also can get a backplane that supports five ISA cards. Whereas the VL-Bus version of the ValuePoint's backplane has room for only one VL-Bus card, this is not a major snag because both video and hard disk controllers are already integrated onto the motherboard's VL-Bus.

One promising aspect of the Performance Series is that 64-bit local-bus video is included directly on the motherboard. This video is upgradeable from 1M to 2M and supports resolutions up to 1280 × 1024. Unlike other desktop systems that have expandable video memory, the ValuePoint is one of the few with a motherboard that uses socketed DRAM (dynamic RAM) instead of a proprietary expansion board. The ValuePoint Performance Series is upgradeable with a Pentium OverDrive processor, and a ZIF socket enables you to upgrade straight to any 486DX2 OverDrive processor.

The Performance Series has good ergonomics, thanks to a Lexmark International Inc. keyboard, perhaps the best basic 101-key keyboard money can buy. Also, all models of the ValuePoint Performance Series meet the Energy Star energy-conservation specs, except those with 527M hard disk drives.

Like the PS/2, the ValuePoint Performance Series includes IBM's HelpWare, which includes a 30-day money-back guarantee, 24-hour-a-day HelpCenter technical support, as well as BBS and faxback services.

Bus Type	Total Available Slots	STANDARD		Date Introduced	Date Withdrawn
		Video	Keyboard		
PCI/32-bit, ISA/16	4/4	PCI SVGA	Any	10/18/93	—
PCI/32-bit, ISA/16	4/4	PCI SVGA	Any	10/18/93	—
PCI/32-bit, ISA/16	4/4	PCI SVGA	Any	10/18/93	—

Table 22.64 shows the primary specifications of the ValuePoint Performance Series models.

Part Number	CPU	MHz	PLANAR MEMORY Std.	Max.	STANDARD Floppy Drive	Hard Disk
ValuePoint Performance Series IntelDX4						
6482-X0D	486DX4	100	8M	128M	1×1.44M	—
6482-X4F	486DX4	100	8M	128M	1×1.44M	364M
6492-X0D	486DX4	100	8M	128M	1×1.44M	—
6492-X4F	486DX4	100	8M	128M	1×1.44M	364M
6484-X4G	486DX4	100	8M	128M	1×1.44M	364M
6484-X5F	486DX4	100	8M	128M	1×1.44M	527M
6484-X5G	486DX4	100	8M	128M	1×1.44M	527M
6494-X5F	486DX4	100	8M	128M	1×1.44M	527M
6494-X5G	486DX4	100	8M	128M	1×1.44M	527M
ValuePoint Performance Series IntelDX2 66						
6472-L0D	486DX2	66	8M	128M	1×1.44M	—
6472-L4F	486DX2	66	8M	128M	1×1.44M	364M
6472-L4G	486DX2	66	8M	128M	1×1.44M	364M
6482-L0D	486DX2	66	8M	128M	1×1.44M	—
6482-L4F	486DX2	66	8M	128M	1×1.44M	364M
6482-LPF	486DX2	66	8M	128M	1×1.44M	364M
6482-L5F	486DX2	66	8M	128M	1×1.44M	527M
6484-L4F	486DX2	66	8M	128M	1×1.44M	364M
6484-L5G	486DX2	66	8M	128M	1×1.44M	527M
6492-L0D	486DX2	66	8M	128M	1×1.44M	—
6492-L4F	486DX2	66	8M	128M	1×1.44M	364M
6492-L5F	486DX2	66	8M	128M	1×1.44M	527M
6494-L5F	486DX2	66	8M	128M	1×1.44M	527M
6494-L5G	486DX2	66	8M	128M	1×1.44M	527M
ValuePoint Performance Series IntelDX 33						
6472-H0D	486DX	33	8M	128M	1×1.44M	—
6472-H3B	486DX	33	8M	128M	1×1.44M	270M
6472-H4F	486DX	33	8M	128M	1×1.44M	364M
6482-H0D	486DX	33	8M	128M	1×1.44M	—
6482-H3B	486DX	33	8M	128M	1×1.44M	270M

Table 22.64   IBM ValuePoint Performance Series Model Summary

Bus Type	Total Available Slots	STANDARD Video	Keyboard	Date Introduced	Date Withdrawn
ISA/16-bit	5/5	VESA 64-bit SVGA	Any	05/23/94	—
ISA/16-bit	5/5	VESA 64-bit SVGA	Any	05/23/94	—
ISA/16-bit	8/8	VESA 64-bit SVGA	Any	05/23/94	—
ISA/16-bit	8/8	VESA 64-bit SVGA	Any	05/23/94	—
PCI/32-bit	5/5	VESA 64-bit SVGA	Any	05/23/94	—
PCI/32-bit	5/5	VESA 64-bit SVGA	Any	05/23/94	—
PCI/32-bit	5/5	VESA 64-bit SVGA	Any	05/23/94	—
PCI/32-bit	8/8	VESA 64-bit SVGA	Any	05/23/94	—
PCI/32-bit	8/8	VESA 64-bit SVGA	Any	05/23/94	—
ISA/16-bit	3/3	VESA 64-bit SVGA	Any	05/23/94	—
ISA/16-bit	3/3	VESA 64-bit SVGA	Any	05/23/94	—
PCI/32-bit	3/3	VESA 64-bit SVGA	Any	05/23/94	—
ISA/16-bit	5/5	VESA 64-bit SVGA	Any	05/23/94	—
ISA/16-bit	5/5	VESA 64-bit SVGA	Any	05/23/94	—
ISA/16-bit	5/5	VESA 64-bit SVGA	Any	05/23/94	—
PCI/32-bit	5/5	VESA 64-bit SVGA	Any	05/23/94	—
PCI/32-bit	5/5	VESA 64-bit SVGA	Any	05/23/94	—
PCI/32-bit	5/5	VESA 64-bit SVGA	Any	05/23/94	—
ISA/16-bit	8/8	VESA 64-bit SVGA	Any	05/23/94	—
ISA/16-bit	8/8	VESA 64-bit SVGA	Any	05/23/94	—
PCI/32-bit	8/8	VESA 64-bit SVGA	Any	05/23/94	—
PCI/32-bit	8/8	VESA 64-bit SVGA	Any	05/23/94	—
PCI/32-bit	8/8	VESA 64-bit SVGA	Any	05/23/94	—
ISA/16-bit	3/3	VESA 64-bit SVGA	Any	05/23/94	—
ISA/16-bit	3/3	VESA 64-bit SVGA	Any	05/23/94	—
ISA/16-bit	3/3	VESA 64-bit SVGA	Any	05/23/94	—
ISA/16-bit	5/5	VESA 64-bit SVGA	Any	05/23/94	—
ISA/16-bit	5/5	VESA 64-bit SVGA	Any	05/23/94	—

(continues)

Table 22.64 Continued

| Part Number | CPU | MHz | PLANAR MEMORY | | STANDARD | |
			Std.	Max.	Floppy Drive	Hard Disk
ValuePoint Performance Series IntelDX 33						
6482-H3G	486DX	33	8M	128M	1×1.44M	270M
6482-H4F	486DX	33	8M	128M	1×1.44M	364M
6484-H4B	486DX	33	8M	128M	1×1.44M	364M
6484-H4G	486DX	33	8M	128M	1×1.44M	364M
ValuePoint Performance Series IntelSX 33						
6472-C0D	486SX	33	8M	128M	1×1.44M	—
6472-C3B	486SX	33	8M	128M	1×1.44M	270M
6482-C0D	486SX	33	8M	128M	1×1.44M	—
6482-C3B	486SX	33	8M	128M	1×1.44M	270M
6482-CNB	486SX	33	8M	128M	1×1.44M	270M

ValuePoint Si Series

The ValuePoint Si Series became more affordable by reducing graphics power and upgradability. Although the ValuePoint Si systems feature VESA local bus on the motherboard, they don't include an available VL-bus slot. The Si's use inferior graphics accelerators and come with 512K DRAM, upgradeable to only 1M (rather than the 2M of earlier ValuePoints). The 1M limits you to a maximum of 256 colors at 1024×768 resolution. With 2M, you can view 65,536 colors.

Table 22.65 shows the primary specifications of the ValuePoint Si Series models.

Table 22.65 IBM ValuePoint Si Series Models

| Part Number | CPU | MHz | PLANAR MEMORY | | STANDARD | |
			Std.	Max.	Floppy Drive	Hard Disk
ValuePoint Si Series 466DX2/Si						
6381-W30	486DX2	66	4M	64M	1×1.44M	120M
6381-W50	486DX2	66	4M	64M	1×1.44M	212M
ValuePoint Si Series 433DX/Si						
6381-M30	486DX	33	4M	64M	1×1.44M	120M
6381-M50	486DX	33	4M	64M	1×1.44M	212M
ValuePoint Si Series 425SX/Si						
6381-F30	486SX	25	4M	64M	1×1.44M	120M
6381-F50	486SX	25	4M	64M	1×1.44M	212M

Bus Type	Total Available Slots	STANDARD Video	Keyboard	Date Introduced	Date Withdrawn
ISA/16-bit	5/5	VESA 64-bit SVGA	Any	05/23/94	—
ISA/16-bit	5/5	VESA 64-bit SVGA	Any	05/23/94	—
PCI/32-bit	5/5	VESA 64-bit SVGA	Any	05/23/94	—
PCI/32-bit	5/5	VESA 64-bit SVGA	Any	05/23/94	—
ISA/16-bit	3/3	VESA 64-bit SVGA	Any	05/23/94	—
ISA/16-bit	3/3	VESA 64-bit SVGA	Any	05/23/94	—
ISA/16-bit	5/5	VESA 64-bit SVGA	Any	05/23/94	—
ISA/16-bit	5/5	VESA 64-bit SVGA	Any	05/23/94	—
ISA/16-bit	5/5	VESA 64-bit SVGA	Any	05/23/94	—

There are other compromises in the Si series. The ValuePoint 425SX/Si does not offer an optional secondary cache or a Pentium OverDrive socket. The ValuePoint 433DX/Si does accept up to 256K of secondary cache and a Pentium OverDrive chip, but lacks a ZIF socket, making upgrading the CPU more difficult. All Si models accept up to 64M RAM, (using 16M SIMMs) and provide three open ISA slots and one open drive bay, as do small-footprint ValuePoints.

Bus Type	Total Available Slots	STANDARD Video	Keyboard	Date Introduced	Date Withdrawn
ISA/16-bit, VLB/32-bit	3/3	SVGA	Any	08/02/93	—
ISA/32-bit, VLB/32-bit	3/3	SVGA	Any	08/02/93	—
ISA/16-bit, VLB/32-bit	3/3	SVGA	Any	08/02/93	—
ISA/32-bit, VLB/32-bit	3/3	SVGA	Any	08/02/93	—
ISA/16-bit, VLB/32-bit	3/3	SVGA	Any	08/02/93	—
ISA/32-bit, VLB/32-bit	3/3	SVGA	Any	08/02/93	—

PS/2 BIOS Information

To uniquely identify each PS/2 system model through software, IBM encodes each system with a unique set of identifying information. By using this information and comparing it to a chart showing what versions have been available, you might be able to determine whether a system has an out-of-date ROM release that might be causing problems. A review of this information shows just how many different systems IBM has released.

To identify one system from another, one item that many technicians use is the ROM BIOS date of creation. The date is stored in the ROM at absolute address FFFF:5. To see this date, you can use the DOS DEBUG program as follows:

1. Run the DEBUG program by typing the DEBUG command at the C: prompt:

   ```
   C:\>DEBUG
   ```

2. When the debug prompt (-) appears, type the following command and press Enter:

   ```
   -D FFFF:5 L 8
   ```

   This command instructs debug to dump the memory in segment FFFF and offset 5, for a length of 8 bytes.

3. Read the screen display, which looks something like the following line, showing the BIOS date, unless the compatible BIOS is nonstandard and does not store the date there:

   ```
   FFFF:0000       30 31 2F-31 38 2F 38 39      01/18/89
   ```

4. To exit DEBUG, press Q.

The screen looks something like this when you are done:

```
C:\>DEBUG
-D FFFF:5 L 8
FFFF:0000       30 31 2F-31 38 2F 38 39   01/18/89
-Q
```

Although many people use the BIOS date of creation to identify a system, IBM uses other information in addition to the version of BIOS to uniquely identify the system. IBM has given each PS/2 system a model ID byte (or model byte), a submodel byte, and a revision byte. With these three pieces of information, you can clearly identify any PS/2 system by booting the Reference Disk and executing the "Display Revision Levels" option at the main menu. The display that results looks something like the following:

```
    Model Byte: F8
Sub-Model Byte: 0B
      Revision: 00
```

The values are in hexadecimal because they represent raw byte values. Many diagnostics programs can locate this information for a given system because a standard way to retrieve the information involves executing an Int 15h instruction with the AH register set to C0, which returns a pointer to the location of the desired information.

You also can find out this information by using DEBUG. The first step in the procedure involves (A)ssembling at memory offset 100h a short program that will (MOV)e the value C0 into the AH register. Then execute (Int)errupt 15h, and (Int)errupt 3h. The Int 15 function C0 causes the ES and BX registers to contain the address of the System Configuration Parameters table. This table is in memory and contains information about how the system is configured and the model ID information you are looking for. The Int 3 is a breakpoint instruction that causes the program to stop and display the register contents.

After the program is assembled in memory, the (G)o instruction tells DEBUG to run the program, which occurs until the Int 3 instruction is reached and causes the program to stop, gives DEBUG control of the system, and displays the current contents of the registers. The correct location of the System Configuration Table then is in the ES:BX registers. For my P70 system that would be E000:7CED, but the address varies for other systems. When you run these steps, make sure that you substitute whatever is reported on your system in the ES and BX registers for the address in the (D)ump command. The "L A" part of the (D)ump command says that the (L)ength of data to dump is Ah (10) bytes. This includes the first two bytes of the table, which is a word indicating the length of the remaining portion of the table. Normally this word has a value of 0008h, which means that the remainder of the table is 8 bytes long.

To find out the model byte, submodel byte, and revision number of your system, you can execute these steps using DOS DEBUG. Notice that the address given in the (D)ump instruction differs between systems. You must substitute whatever values are reported by the ES and BX registers:

```
C:\>DEBUG
-A 100
xxxx:0100 MOV AH,C0
xxxx:0102 INT 15
xxxx:0104 INT 3
xxxx:0105
-G

AX=00FF  BX=7CED  CX=0000  DX=0000  SP=FFEE  BP=0000  SI=0000  DI=0000
DS=269A  ES=E000  SS=269A  CS=269A  IP=0104    NV UP EI PL ZR NA PE NC
269A:0104 CC            INT    3
-D E000:7CED L A
E000:7CE0                                      08 00 F8              ...
E000:7CF0  0B 00 F6 40 00 00 00             ...@...
-Q
```

Starting with the address reported in the ES:BX registers, the third, fourth, and fifth bytes listed after the (D)ump command are the model byte, sub-model byte, and revision number, respectively. In this case they are F8, 0B, and 00.

Table 22.66 is a relatively complete compilation of IBM BIOS ID information. Some systems have had BIOS changes during their life span. One piece of information this table provides is the total number of ST-506 drive types each BIOS supports. These types often are used when installing ST-506 or IDE hard disk drives. If the BIOS of your system is included in table 22.66, you can look up the IBM BIOS Hard Drive Table in Appendix A and establish the exact drive types supported by your system.

Table 22.66   IBM ROM BIOS Model/Submodel/Revisions

System Drive Description	CPU	Clock Speed	Bus Type/ Width
PC	8088	4.77 MHz	ISA/8
PC	8088	4.77 MHz	ISA/8
PC	8088	4.77 MHz	ISA/8
PC-XT	8088	4.77 MHz	ISA/8
PC-XT	8088	4.77 MHz	ISA/8
PC-XT	8088	4.77 MHz	ISA/8
PCjr	8088	4.77 MHz	ISA/8
PC Convertible	80C8	4.77 MHz	ISA/8
PS/2 25	8086	8 MHz	ISA/8
PS/2 30	8086	8 MHz	ISA/8
PS/2 30	8086	8 MHz	ISA/8
PS/2 30	8086	8 MHz	ISA/8
PC-AT	286	6 MHz	ISA/16
PC-AT	286	6 MHz	ISA/16
PC-AT	286	8 MHz	ISA/16
PC-XT 286	286	6 MHz	ISA/16
PS/1	286	10 MHz	ISA/16
PS/2 25 286	286	10 MHz	ISA/16
PS/2 30 286	286	10 MHz	ISA/16
PS/2 30 286	286	10 MHz	ISA/16
PS/2 35 SX	386SX	20 MHz	ISA/16
PS/2 35 SX	386SX	20 MHz	ISA/16
PS/2 40 SX	386SX	20 MHz	ISA/16
PS/2 40 SX	386SX	20 MHz	ISA/16
PS/2 L40 SX	386SX	20 MHz	ISA/16
PS/2 50	286	10 MHz	MCA/16
PS/2 50	286	10 MHz	MCA/16
PS/2 50Z	286	10 MHz	MCA/16
PS/2 50Z	286	10 MHz	MCA/16
PS/2 55 SX	386SX	16 MHz	MCA/16
PS/2 57 SX	386SX	20 MHz	MCA/16
PS/2 60	286	10 MHz	MCA/16
PS/2 65 SX	386SX	16 MHz	MCA/16
PS/2 70 386	386DX	16 MHz	MCA/32
PS/2 70 386	386DX	16 MHz	MCA/32
PS/2 70 386	386DX	16 MHz	MCA/32
PS/2 70 386	386DX	20 MHz	MCA/32

ROM BIOS Date	ID Byte	Sub-Model Byte	Rev	ST506 Types
04/24/81	FF	—	—	—
10/19/81	FF	—	—	—
10/27/82	FF	—	—	—
11/08/82	FE	—	—	—
01/10/86	FB	00	01	—
05/09/86	FB	00	02	—
06/01/83	FD	—	—	—
09/13/85	F9	00	00	—
06/26/87	FA	01	00	26
09/02/86	FA	00	00	26
12/12/86	FA	00	01	26
02/05/87	FA	00	02	26
01/10/84	FC	—	—	15
06/10/85	FC	00	01	23
11/15/85	FC	01	00	23
04/21/86	FC	02	00	24
12/01/89	FC	0B	00	44
06/28/89	FC	09	02	37
08/25/88	FC	09	00	37
06/28/89	FC	09	02	37
03/15/91	F8	19	05	37
04/04/91	F8	19	06	37
03/15/91	F8	19	05	37
04/04/91	F8	19	06	37
02/27/91	F8	23	02	37
02/13/87	FC	04	00	32
05/09/87	FC	04	01	32
01/28/88	FC	04	02	33
04/18/88	FC	04	03	33
11/02/88	F8	0C	00	33
07/03/91	F8	26	02	None
02/13/87	FC	05	00	32
02/08/90	F8	1C	00	33
01/29/88	F8	09	00	33
04/11/88	F8	09	02	33
12/15/89	F8	09	04	33
01/29/88	F8	04	00	33

(continues)

Table 22.66   Continued

System Drive Description	CPU	Clock Speed	Bus Type/ Width
PS/2 70 386	386DX	20 MHz	MCA/32
PS/2 70 386	386DX	20 MHz	MCA/32
PS/2 70 386	386DX	25 MHz	MCA/32
PS/2 70 386	386DX	25 MHz	MCA/32
PS/2 70 486	486DX	25 MHz	MCA/32
PS/2 70 486	486DX	25 MHz	MCA/32
PS/2 P70 386	386DX	16 MHz	MCA/32
PS/2 P70 386	386DX	20 MHz	MCA/32
PS/2 P75 486	486DX	33 MHz	MCA/32
PS/2 80 386	386DX	16 MHz	MCA/32
PS/2 80 386	386DX	20 MHz	MCA/32
PS/2 80 386	386DX	25 MHz	MCA/32
PS/2 90 XP 486	486SX	20 MHz	MCA/32
PS/2 90 XP 486	487SX	20 MHz	MCA/32
PS/2 90 XP 486	486DX	25 MHz	MCA/32
PS/2 90 XP 486	486DX	33 MHz	MCA/32
PS/2 90 XP 486	486DX	50 MHz	MCA/32
PS/2 95 XP 486	486SX	20 MHz	MCA/32
PS/2 95 XP 486	487SX	20 MHz	MCA/32
PS/2 95 XP 486	486DX	25 MHz	MCA/32
PS/2 95 XP 486	486DX	33 MHz	MCA/32
PS/2 95 XP 486	486DX	50 MHz	MCA/32

The ID byte, submodel byte, and revision numbers are in hexadecimal.
None = Only SCSI drives are supported.

Summary of IBM Hard Disk Drives

The tables in this section are a complete reference to all the hard disk drives supplied by IBM in any XT, AT, or PS/2 system. This reference can be useful in determining which types of drives came with each system, and upgrades are possible.

You usually can easily install an upgraded drive of the same interface type in a given system. If I have a PS/2 Model 50Z that came with a 30M MCA IDE hard drive, for example, I easily can upgrade that system to any of the other MCA IDE drives that were available, such as the 120M or 160M units. Because the drives use the exact same interface, it would be a simple plug-in upgrade. Using this information, you can more easily "recycle" hard drives from systems that have since received upgrades.

ROM BIOS Date	ID Byte	Sub-Model Byte	Rev	ST506 Types
04/11/88	F8	04	02	33
12/15/89	F8	04	04	33
06/08/88	F8	0D	00	33
02/20/89	F8	0D	01	33
12/01/89	F8	0D	?	?
09/29/89	F8	1B	00	?
?	F8	50	00	?
01/18/89	F8	0B	00	33
10/05/90	F8	52	00	33
03/30/87	F8	00	00	32
10/07/87	F8	01	00	32
11/21/89	F8	80	01	?
?	F8	2D	00	?
?	F8	2F	00	?
?	F8	11	00	?
?	F8	13	00	?
?	F8	2B	00	?
?	F8	2C	00	?
?	F8	2E	00	?
?	F8	14	00	?
?	F8	16	00	?
?	F8	2A	00	?

— = This feature is not supported.
?=No information available.

Tables 22.67 through 22.80 list the standard and optional hard drives installed by IBM in its systems, grouped by interface.

Table 22.67 IBM-Installed ST-506/412 Hard Drives Used in the XT, AT, and PS/2 Model 25

Drive form factor	5 1/4	5 1/4	5 1/4	5 1/4	3 1/2
Capacity	10M	20M	20M	30M	20M
Physical/logical interface	ST506	ST506	ST506	ST506	ST506
Average access rate (ms)	85	65	40	40	38
Read-ahead cache (K)	—	—	—	—	—

(continues)

Table 22.67   Continued

Encoding scheme	MFM	MFM	MFM	MFM	RLL
BIOS drive type number	1	2	2	2	36
Cylinders	306	615	615	733	402
Heads	4	4	4	5	4
Sectors/track	17	17	17	17	26
Rotational speed (RPM)	3600	3600	3600	3600	3600
Standard interleave factor	6:1	3:1	3:1	3:1	3:1
Data transfer rate (K/second)	85	170	170	170	260
Automatic head parking	No	No	Yes	Yes	Yes

Table 22.68   IBM-Installed ST-506/412 Hard Drives Used in the XT, AT, and PS/2 Models 50, 60, and 80

Drive form factor	3 1/2	5 1/4	5 1/4
Capacity	20M	44M	44M
Physical/logical interface	ST506	ST506	ST506
Average access rate (ms)	80	40	40
Read-ahead cache (K)	—	—	—
Encoding scheme	MFM	MFM	MFM
BIOS drive type number	30	31	32
Cylinders	611	732	1023
Heads	4	7	5
Sectors/track	17	17	17
Rotational speed (RPM)	3600	3600	3600
Standard interleave factor	1:1	1:1	1:1
Data transfer rate (K/second)	510	510	510
Automatic head parking	No	Yes	Yes

Table 22.69   IBM-Installed XT IDE Drives Used in the PS/2 Models 25, 30, 25 286, and 30 286

Drive form factor	3 1/2	3 1/2	3 1/2	3 1/2	3 1/2
Capacity	20M	20M	30M	30M	45M
Physical interface	IDE	IDE	IDE	IDE	IDE
Logical interface	XT	XT	XT	XT	XT
Average access rate (ms)	80	27	27	19	32
Read-ahead cache (K)	—	—	—	—	—

Encoding scheme	MFM	RLL	RLL	RLL	RLL
BIOS drive type number	26	34	33	35	37
Cylinders	612	775	614	921	580
Heads	4	2	4	2	6
Sectors/track	17	27	25	33	26
Rotational speed (RPM)	3600	3600	3600	3600	3600
Standard interleave factor	2:1	3:1	3:1	4:1	3:1
Data transfer rate (K/second)	255	270	250	248	260
Automatic head parking	No	No	No	Yes	Yes

Table 22.70   IBM-Installed ATA IDE Drives Used in the PS/2 Models 35, 40, and L40

Drive form factor	2 1/2	3 1/2	3 1/2
Capacity	60M	40M	80M
Physical interface	IDE	IDE	IDE
Logical interface	ATA	ATA	ATA
Average access rate (ms)	19	17	17
Read-ahead cache (K)	—	32K	32K
Encoding scheme	RLL	RLL	RLL
BIOS drive type number		—	
Cylinders	822	1038	1021
Heads	4	2	4
Sectors/track	38	39	39
Rotational speed (RPM)	3600	3600	3600
Standard interleave factor	1:1	1:1	1:1
Data transfer rate (K/second)	1140	1170	1170
Automatic head parking	Yes	Yes	Yes

Table 22.71   IBM-Installed MCA IDE Drives Used in the PS/2 Models 50Z, 55, 70 386, and P70 386

Drive form factor	3 1/2	3 1/2	3 1/2	3 1/2	3 1/2	3 1/2	3 1/2	3 1/2
Capacity	30M	30M	30M	40M	60M	80M	120M	160M
Physical interface	IDE	IDE	IDE	IDE	IDE	IDE	IDE	IDE
Logical interface	ST506	ST506	ESDI	ESDI	ESDI	ESDI	ESDI	ESDI
Average access rate (ms)	39	27	19	17	27	17	23	16

(continues)

Table 22.71 Continued

Read-ahead cache (K)	—	—	—	32K	—	32K	—	32K
Encoding scheme	RLL	RLL	RLL	RLL	RLL	RLL	RLL	RLL
BIOS drive type number	33	33	—	—	—	—	—	—
Cylinders	614	614	920	1038	762	1021	920	1021
Heads	4	4	2	2	6	4	8	8
Sectors/track	25	25	32	39	26	39	32	39
Rotational speed (RPM)	3600	3600	3600	3600	3600	3600	3600	3600
Standard interleave factor	1:1	1:1	1:1	1:1	1:1	1:1	1:1	1:1
Data transfer rate (K/second)	750	750	960	1170	780	1170	960	1170
Automatic head parking	No	No	Yes	Yes	Yes	Yes	Yes	Yes

Table 22.72 IBM-Installed ESDI Drives Used in the PS/2 Models 60 and 80

Drive form factor	5 1/4	5 1/4	5 1/4
Capacity	70M	115M	314M
Physical/logical interface	ESDI	ESDI	ESDI
Average access rate (ms)	30	28	23
Read-ahead cache (K)	—	—	—
Encoding scheme	RLL	RLL	RLL
BIOS drive type number	—	—	—
Cylinders	583	915	1225
Heads	7	7	15
Sectors/track	36	36	34
Rotational speed (RPM)	3600	3600	3283
Standard interleave factor	1:1	1:1	1:1
Data transfer rate (K/second)	1080	1080	930
Automatic head parking	Yes	Yes	Yes

Table 22.75 PS/2 Processor/Coprocessor Upgrades

Description	Part Number	Price
16MHz 387SX Math Coprocessor	27F4676	$84
25MHz 486DX Power Platform	6450876	1,900
25MHz 487SX Chip Upgrade	6451243	840
25MHz 486SX Processor Complex	6450759	665
33MHz 486DX Processor Complex	6451094	985
33MHz 486DX Processor Complex	6451094	935
33MHz 486DX Processor Complex	6451094	935

Table 22.73   IBM-Installed SCSI Drives Used in the PS/2 Models 56, 57, 65, P75, 80, 90, and 95

Drive form factor	3 1/2	3 1/2	3 1/2	3 1/2	3 1/2	3 1/2
Capacity	60M	80M	120M	160M	320M	400M
Physical/logical interface	SCSI	SCSI	SCSI	SCSI	SCSI	SCSI
Average access rate (ms)	23	17	23	16	12.5	11.5
Read-ahead cache (K)	32K	32K	32K	32K	64K	128K
SCSI transfer mode	Async	Async	Async	Async	Sync	Sync
Encoding scheme	RLL	RLL	RLL	RLL	RLL	RLL
BIOS drive type number	—	—	—	—	—	—
Cylinders	920	1021	920	1021	949	1201
Heads	4	4	8	8	14	14
Sectors/track	32	39	32	39	48	48
Rotational speed (RPM)	3600	3600	3600	3600	4318	4318
Standard interleave factor	1:1	1:1	1:1	1:1	1:1	1:1
Data transfer rate (K/second)	960	1170	960	1170	1727	1727
Automatic head parking	Yes	Yes	Yes	Yes	Yes	Yes

Table 22.74   Standard PS/2 Accessories

Description	Part Number	Price	Notes
PS/2 mouse	6450350	$101	2-button mouse
Trackpoint	1397040	95	Mouse/trackball
Dual serial adapter/A	6451013	231	For 50-95, NS16550, 9-pin plug
Serial/parallel adapter	6450215	161	25-40 (not L40), NS16450, 9-pin
Floor stand	95F5606	45	Vertical mount for 35 LS/SX

Notes

For Model 55, 65
70-Axx, trade in 386DX-25
90/95, CPU only
90/95, trade in 486SX-20
90/95, trade in 486SX-20
90/95, trade in 486SX-25
90/95, trade in 486DX-25

(continues)

Table 22.75   Continued

Description	Part Number	Price
50MHz 486DX Processor Complex	6450757	$3,255
50MHz 486DX Processor Complex	6450757	3,200
50MHz 486DX Processor Complex	6450757	3,200
50MHz 486DX Processor Complex	6450757	2,800
50MHz 486DX2 CPU only	32G3374	665
50MHz 486DX2 Processor Complex	32G3491	1,335
50MHz 486DX2 Processor Complex	32G3491	935
50MHz 486DX Enhanced Complex	6451269	4,880
50MHz 486DX Enhanced Complex	6451269	4,825
50MHz 486DX Enhanced Complex	6451269	4,825
50MHz 486DX Enhanced Complex	6451269	4,425
50MHz 486DX Enhanced Complex	6451269	2,295
50MHz 486DX Enhanced Complex	6451269	3,825
50MHz 486DX Enhanced Complex	6451269	3,495
66MHz 486DX2 CPU only	32G3690	899
66MHz 486DX2 Processor Complex	32G3383	2,055
66MHz 486DX2 Processor Complex	32G3383	2,000
66MHz 486DX2 Processor Complex	32G3383	2,000
66MHz 486DX2 Processor Complex	32G3383	1,600
66MHz 486DX2 Processor Complex	32G3383	1,000
Processor Complex 256K Cache	6451095	1,595

Table 22.76   PS/2 Memory Modules and Adapters

Description	Part Number	Price	Notes
ISA 8-Bit Memory Adapters			
Expanded memory adapter (XMA)	2685193	$1,395	2M RAM, LPT port, XT/AT/30
ISA Bus 16-Bit Memory Adapters			
0-12M multifunction adapter	30F5364	495	COM/LPT port, 30 286
All ChargeCard	34F2863	495	Memory manager for 25/30 286
3M expanded memory adapter	34F2864	1,830	ChargeCard, 0-12M card, 3M RAM
4M expanded memory kit	34F2866	1,285	ChargeCard, 4M system-board RAM

Notes

90/95, trade in 486SX-20
90/95, trade in 486SX-25
90/95, trade in 486DX-25
90/95, trade in 486DX-33
90/95, CPU only
90/95, trade in 486SX-20
90/95, trade in 486DX-33
90/95, trade in 486SX-20
90/95, trade in 486SX-25
90/95, trade in 486DX-25
90/95, trade in 486DX-33
90/95, trade in 486DX-50
90/95, trade in 486DX2-50
90/95, trade in 486DX2-66
90/95, CPU only
90/95, trade in 486SX-20
90/95, trade in 486SX-25
90/95, trade in 486DX-25
90/95, trade in 486DX-33
90/95, trade in 486DX2-50
External Cache for 486DX

Description	Part Number	Price	Notes
MCA Bus 16-Bit Memory Adapters			
1-8M 80286 memory optional/85ns	6450685	$410	1M, EMS 4.0 for 50/55/60/65
2-8M 80286 memory optional/85ns	6450609	330	2M, EMS 4.0 for 50/55/60/65
MCA Bus 32-Bit Adapters			
2-14M enhanced adapter/85ns	87F9856	480	2M, for 70/P70/80
4-14M enhanced adapter/85ns	87F9860	600	4M, for 70/P70/80
Memory Module Kits (SIMMs)			
25 system board memory/120ns	78X8955	40	128K kit (6 chips) for 25

(continues)

Table 22.76   Continued

Description	Part Number	Price	Notes
512K memory module kit/120ns	30F5348	$140	2-256K SIMMs for 30F5364/1497259, 25/30 286 system board
2M memory module kit/120ns	30F5360	250	2-1M SIMMs for 30F5364/1497259, 34F2866 25/30 286 system board
1M memory module kit/85ns	6450603	80	1M SIMM for 6450605/6450609, 6450685/34F3077/34F3011, 50Z/55/65/70 386 (Not Axx/Bxx)/P70 386
2M memory module kit/85ns	6450604	150	2M SIMM for 6450605/6450609, 6450685/34F3077/34F3011, 50Z/55/65/ 70 (Not Axx/Bxx)/P70 386
4M memory module kit/85ns	87F9977	290	4M SIMM for 35/40/55/65 34F3011/34F3077
2M memory module kit/80ns	6450608	150	2M SIMM for 35/40/70 -Axx/Bxx
8M memory module kit/80ns	6450129	590	8M SIMM for 35/40
2M memory module kit/70ns	6450902	160	2M SIMM for 57/90/95
4M memory module kit/70ns	6450128	295	4M SIMM for 57/P75/90/95
8M memory module kit/70ns	6450130	695	8M SIMM for 35/40/57/P75/90/95
2M memory module kit/80ns	79F0999	215	2M CMOS SIMM for L40 (keyed)
4M memory module kit/80ns	79F1000	400	4M CMOS SIMM for L40 (keyed)
8M memory module kit/80ns	79F1001	785	8M CMOS SIMM for L40 (keyed)
1M system board kit/80ns	6450375	528	1M card for 80-041
2M system board kit/80ns	6450379	150	2M card for 80 (except Axx)
4M system board kit/80ns	6451060	280	4M card for 80-A21/A31

Table 22.77   PS/2 Floppy Drives, Adapters, and Cables

Description	Part Number	Price	Notes
5 1/4-Inch Floppy Drives			
5 1/4-inch external 360K drive	4869001	$489	For all PS/2s
5 1/4-inch external 1.2M drive	4869002	509	For 50-95, requires 6451007
5 1/4-inch internal 1.2M drive	6451006	365	For 60/65/80
5 1/4-inch internal 1.2M slim drive	6451066	310	For 35/40/57/90/95

Description	Part Number	Price	Notes
3 1/2-Inch Floppy Drives			
3 1/2-inch internal 720K drive	78X8956	$180	For 25 S/N < 100,000
3 1/2-inch internal 720K 1/3-height drive	6451056	159	For 25 S/N > 100,000
3 1/2-inch internal 720K 1/3-height drive	6451027	159	For 30-001
3 1/2-inch internal 1.44M 1/3-height drive	6451063	263	For 25-006/G06
3 1/2-inch internal 1.44M drive	6450353	263	For 30-E01/50-80, not 55/P70 386
3 1/2-inch internal 1.44M slim drive	6451130	263	35/40/57, not L40, media-sense
3 1/2-inch internal 1.44M 1/3-height drive	6451072	263	50-95, not 55/P70/30-E01
3 1/2-inch internal 2.88M slim drive	6451106	325	35/40/57, not L40, media-sense
Floppy Disk Drive Adapters			
5 1/4-inch external drive adapter	6450244	72	360K for 25-40, not L40
5 1/4-inch external drive adapter/A	6450245	72	360K for 50-80, not 55/P70 386
5 1/4-inch floppy disk drive adapter/A	6451007	216	For 1.2M/360K in 50-95
Cables and Miscellaneous			
5 1/4-inch external 360K cable	6451033	21	For 30-001/021 external drive
5 1/4-inch external 360K cable	27F4245	18	For 30-Exx external drive
5 1/4-inch external drive adapter cable	6451124	40	For 35/40 and 4869001
External storage device cable	23F2716	101	P70 360K, P75 360K/1.2M
3 1/2-inch internal drive kit	6451037	30	Cable/Bezel for 6451353
3 1/2-inch internal 1/3-height drive kit	6451034	25	Cable/Bezel for 6451072
3 1/2-inch internal 1/3-height drive kit B	6451035	30	For 6451026 in 55 LS
Drive upgrade kit for 35 LS	6451127	45	For 6451130/6451106/6451066
IBM Preformatted Floppy Disks			
5 1/4-inch 10 360K disks	6023450	44	Cardboard slipcase
5 1/4-inch 10 360K disks with case	6069769	45	Plastic library case/stand
5 1/4-inch 10 1.2M disks	6109660	54	Cardboard slipcase

(continues)

Table 22.77   Continued

Description	Part Number	Price	Notes
IBM Preformatted Floppy Disks			
5 1/4-inch 10 1.2M disks with case	6109661	$55	Plastic library case/stand
3 1/2-inch 10 720K disks with case	6404088	33	Plastic library case/stand
3 1/2-inch 10 1.44M disks with case	6404083	50	Plastic library case/stand
3 1/2-inch 10 2.88M disks with case	72X6111	99	Plastic library case/stand

Table 22.78   PS/2 Hard Disks, Adapters, and Cables

Description	Part Number	Price	Notes
IDE Hard Disk Drives			
20M 3 1/2-inch 80ms IDE drive	78X8958	$ 787	For 25
20M 3 1/2-inch 27ms IDE drive	6451075	787	For 25-xx6, Req 6451071
30M 3 1/2-inch 19ms IDE drive	6451076	695	For 25-xx6, Req 6451071
40M 3 1/2-inch 17ms IDE drive	6451047	290	For 55 LS
40M 3 1/2-inch 17ms IDE drive	6451073	290	For 35/40
80M 3 1/2-inch 17ms IDE drive	6451043	425	For 55 LS
80M 3 1/2-inch 17ms IDE drive	6451074	340	For 35/40
SCSI Hard Disk Drives			
60M 3 1/2-inch 23ms, 32K cache	6451049	1,000	Async, 1.25M/sec Xfer rate
80M 3 1/2-inch 17ms, 32K cache	6451045	340	Async, 1.25M/sec Xfer rate
120M 3 1/2-inch 23ms, 32K cache	6451050	1,670	Async, 1.5M/sec Xfer rate
160M 3 1/2-inch 16ms, 32K cache	6451046	580	Async, 1.5M/sec Xfer rate
320M 3 1/2-inch 12.5ms, 64K cache	6451234	1,625	Sync, 2.0M/sec Xfer rate
400M 3 1/2-inch 11.5ms, 128K cache	6451235	1,835	Sync, 2.0M/sec Xfer rate
IG 3 1/2-inch 11ms, 256K cache	0451052	5,000	Sync, 2.0M/sec Xfer rate

Description	Part Number	Price	Notes
SCSI Host Adapter			
SCSI adapter/A	6451109	$375	16-bit bus master
SCSI adapter/A with 512K cache	6451133	750	32/16-bit bus master
SCSI external terminator	6451039	110	For adapter with cache
Cables and Miscellaneous			
Fixed disk drive kit A	6451071	65	Installation kit for 25-xx6
Fixed disk upgrade kit/35	6451128	15	For 6451073/ 6451074 in 35 LS
SCSI installation kit A	6451053	90	For 3 1/2-inch drive in 60/65/80
Fixed disk drive kit D	6451120	20	For 60/120M drives in 90/95
SCSI card to option cable	6451139	220	Includes terminator, replaces 6451041
SCSI option to option cable	6451042	90	Connect external options
CD-ROM Drives			
Internal 600M CD-ROM drive	6451113	1,250	Requires SCSI adapter
External 600M CD-ROM drive	3510001	1,550	Requires SCSI adapter
CD-ROM installation kit/A	6450847	35	Install in 5 1/4-inch bay
3 1/2-inch 128M rewritable drive	6450162	1,795	Requires SCSI adapter
Optical drive kit A	6451126	29	For 6450162 in 60/ 80 (non-SCSI)
3 1/2-inch rewritable cartridge	38F8645	70	128M cartridge for 6450162
3 1/2-inch rewritable cartridge	38F8646	315	5-128M cartridges for 6450162
8mm Tape Backup Drives and Accessories			
2.3G internal SCSI drive	6451121	6,500	For 95/3511, requires SYTOS
2.3G external SCSI drive	6451121	6,915	Requires SCSI adapter and SYTOS
SCSI cable for external drive	31F4187	315	Connects tape drive to system

(continues)

Table 22.78   Continued

Description	Part Number	Price	Notes
8mm Tape Backup Drives and Accessories			
SCSI device-to-device cable	31F4186	$78	Chains tape to other devices
8mm data cartridge	21F8595	29	Stores 2.3 gigabytes
8mm cleaning cartridge	21F8593	40	For cleaning heads
SYTOS plus V1.3 for DOS	04G3375	150	Data compression
SYTOS plus V1.3 for OS/2 PM	04G3374	195	Data compression, FAT/HPFS
SCSI Expansion Units			
3510 external SCSI storage unit	35100V0	360	1 half-height, 3 1/2-inch, 5 1/4-inch bay
3511 external SCSI storage unit	3511003	3,845	7 bays, 3 1/2- and 5 1/4-inch, 320M drive

Table 22.79   PS/2 Video Displays and Adapters

Description	Part Number	Price	Notes
Analog Displays			
8504 12-inch VGA mono display	8504001	$245	640×480
8507 19-inch XGA mono display	8507001	600	1024×768
8604 16-inch XGA mono display	8604001	850	1024×768
PS/1 color display upgrade	1057108	699	Upgrade for mono systems
8512 14-inch color display	8512001	365	640×480, .41mm stripe
8513 12-inch VGA color display	8513001	665	640×480, .28mm dot, stand
8514 16-inch XGA color display	8514001	1,035	1024×768, .31mm dot, stand
8515 14-inch XGA color display	8515021	635	1024×768, .28mm dot, stand
8518 14-inch VGA color display	8518001	535	640×480, .28mm dot, stand
8516 14-inch XGA touch screen	8516001	1,200	1024×768, .28mm dot, stand
Analog Display Adapters			
XGA adapter/A	75X5887	210	1024×768, for 55-95 (not 60/P70)
Video memory expansion option	75X5889	60	512K Video RAM for XGA

Description	Part Number	Price	Notes
Analog Display Adapters			
8514/A display adapter	1887972	$980	1024×768×16, for 50-80 (not P70)
8514/A memory expansion kit	1887989	283	1024×768×256 colors
Miscellaneous Display Accessories			
Display Stand for 8512	1501215	36	Tilt-swivel stand
TouchSelect for 12-inch displays	91F7951	670	Adds Touch screen to 8513
Privacy filter for 8512	1053405	154	Prevents side view of display
Privacy filter for 8513	1053401	154	Prevents side view of display
Privacy filter for 8514	1053402	154	Prevents side view of display
Privacy filter for 8515	1053403	154	Prevents side view of display

Table 22.80	PS/2 Network Adapters and Accessories		
Description	**Part Number**	**Price**	**Notes**
ISA Bus Token-Ring Network (TRN) Adapters			
TRN Adapter II	25F9858	$395	4Mbps for 25-40 (not L40)
TRN 16/4 adapter	25F7367	895	16/4Mbps for 25-40 (not L40)
TRN 16/4 trace & performance	74F5121	1,220	16/4Mbps for 25-40 (not L40)
MCA Bus Token-Ring Network (TRN) Adapters			
TRN adapter/A (full-length)	69X8138	395	4Mbps, for 50-95
TRN adapter/A (half-length)	39F9598	448	4Mbps for P70/75 (and 50-95)
TRN 16/4 adapter/A	16F1133	895	16/4Mbps for 50-95
TRN 16/4 adapter/A (half)	74F9410	895	16/4Mbps, 50-95, 80 percent faster
TRN 16/4 trace & perf./A	74F5130	1,220	16/4Mbps for 50-95
TRN 16/4 busmaster server/A	74F4140	1,030	16/4Mbps for 50-95 servers only
MCA Bus EtherNet Network Adapters			
PS/2 EtherNet adapter/A	6451091	575	10Mbps for 50-95, including boot ROM

(continues)

Table 22.80   Continued

Description	Part Number	Price	Notes
Miscellaneous Network Adapter Accessories			
TRN adapter cable	6339098	$36	Connect card to LAN
TRN L-shaped connector cable	79F3229	50	For 74F9410 and P70/75
TRN 8230 4Mbps media filter	53F5551	55	For unshielded twisted pair
TRN adapter II boot ROM	83X7839	99	EPROM for 25F9858
TRN adapter/A boot ROM	83X8881	96	EPROM for 69X8138/ 39F9598
TRN 16/4 adapter/A boot ROM	25X8887	99	EPROM for 25F7367/ 16F1133

Summary

This chapter has presented information about the PS/2 line of systems from IBM, including information about all the various PS/2 models and submodels, from low-end to high-end systems. The low-end PS/2 systems—the PS/2 Models 25, 30, PS/1, 25 286, 30 286, 35 SX, 40 SX, and L40 SX—are based closely on the original PC line and include the standard ISA-type of expansion slots. The higher-end PS/2 Models 50, 50Z, 55 SX, 57 SX, 60, 65 SX, 70 386, P70 386, P75, 80, 90, 95, and their respective submodels use the newer MCA slot design, which is dramatically different from the original ISA bus. The newest Models 53, 56, 57, 76 and 77 indicate IBM's trend away from proprietary graphics chips and buses. The eventual merging of the ValuePoint line into the PS/2 line will provide customers with a choice of buses along with excellent performance and value.

Chapter 23

A Final Word

The contents of this book cover most of the components of an IBM-compatible personal computer system. In this book, you discover how all the components operate and interact and how these components should be set up and installed. You see the ways that components fail and learn the symptoms of these failures. You review the steps in diagnosing and troubleshooting the major components in a system so that you can locate and replace a failing component. You also learn about upgrades for components, including what upgrades are available, the benefits of an upgrade, and how to obtain and perform the actual upgrade. Because failing components so often are technically obsolete, it is often desirable to combine repair and upgrade procedures to replace a failing part with an upgraded or higher performance part.

The information I present in this book represents many years of practical experience with IBM and IBM-compatible systems. A great deal of research and investigation have gone into each section. This information has saved companies many thousands of dollars. By reading this book, you also take advantage of this wealth of information and may save you and your company time, energy, and, most importantly, money!

Bringing microcomputer service and support in-house is one of the best ways to save money. Eliminating service contracts for most systems and reducing down-time are just two of the benefits of applying the information presented in this book. As I indicate many times in this book, you can also save a lot of money on component purchases by eliminating the middleman and purchasing the components directly from distributors or manufacturers. The vendor list in Appendix B provides the best of these sources for you to contact. If you intend to build your own systems, the vendor list will be extremely useful as I list sources for all of the components needed to assemble a complete system from the screws and brackets all the way to the cases, power supplies and motherboards. I've found that this list is one of the most often used parts of the book. Many people have been unable to make direct purchases because doing so requires a new level of understanding of the components involved. Also, many of the vendors are unable to provide support for beginning users. I hope that this book gives you the deeper level of knowledge and understanding you need so that you can purchase the components you want directly from the vendors who manufacture and distribute them, saving a great deal of money in the long run.

I used many sources to gather the information in this book, starting with my own real world experiences. I also taught this information to thousands of people in seminars presented over the last 13 years by my company, Mueller Technical Research. During these seminars, I am often asked where more of this type of information can be obtained and whether I have any "secrets" for acquiring this knowledge. Well, I won't keep any secrets! I can freely share the following four key sources of information that can help you become a verifiable expert in PC upgrading and repairing:

- Manuals
- Machines
- Modems
- Magazines

Manuals

Manuals are the single most important source of computer information. Unfortunately, manuals also are one of the most frequently overlooked sources of information. Much of my knowledge has come from poring over technical-reference manuals and other original equipment manufacturer's (OEM) manuals. I would not even consider purchasing a system that does not have a detailed technical-reference manual available. This statement applies also to system components—whether it's a floppy drive, hard disk, power supply, motherboard, or memory card. I have to have a detailed reference manual to help me understand what future upgrades are possible and to provide valuable insight into the proper installation, use, and support of a product. Often times these manuals must be obtained from the OEM of the equipment you purchase, meaning the vendor or reseller will not supply them. Where possible, you should make an effort to discover who the real OEM of each component in your system is and try to obtain documentation from them on the product or component.

Large manufacturers such as IBM, Compaq, Hewlett Packard, and others both manufacture their own components as well as purchase components from other sources. Many of these manufacturers also make available complete libraries of technical documentation for their systems. I have included a list of IBM's technical documents in Appendix A, which are quite detailed, and unfortunately often fairly expensive. These are often excellent at detailing the operations of CPU, memory, bus, and other architectures in the system, and are even appropriate when discussing compatible systems because almost all systems must be compatible with IBM's in most elements. In other words, the IBM documentation would be interesting to those who do not even own a single piece of true IBM hardware. IBM also has extensive technical information available on-line in the form of a BBS, as well as a mainframe database and information retrieval system called IBMLINK. The number for the IBM National Support Center (NSC) BBS is listed in Appendix B. Contact your local IBM representative or dealer for information on how to get an account on IBMLINK.

Other companies, such as Compaq and HP, also have extensive documentation libraries. Compaq makes their complete technical library available in a CD-ROM version (called Quickfind), which is very convenient and easy to search. Quickfind contains detailed information about all of Compaq's models and is available from any Compaq dealer. Both Compaq and HP also have BBS services available for technical support, check the Vendor list for phone number information on these and other BBS systems.

A simple analogy explains the importance of manuals, as well as other issues concerning repair and maintenance of a system. Compare your business use of computers to a taxi-cab company. The company has to purchase automobiles to use as cabs. The owners purchase not one car but an entire fleet of cars. Do you think that they would purchase a fleet of automobiles based solely on reliability, performance, or even gas-mileage statistics? Would they neglect to consider on-going maintenance and service of these automobiles? Would they purchase a fleet of cars that could be serviced only by the original manufacturer and for which parts could not be obtained easily? Do you think that they would buy a car that did not have available a detailed service and repair manual? Would they buy an automobile for which parts were scarce and that was supported by a sparse dealer network with few service and parts outlets, making long waits for parts and service inevitable? The answer (of course) to all these questions is No, No, No!

You can see why most taxicab companies as well as police departments use "standard" automobiles such as the Chevrolet Caprice or Ford Crown Victoria. If ever there were "generic" cars, these models would qualify! Dealers, parts, and documentation for these particular models are everywhere, and they share parts with many other automobiles as well, making them easy to service and maintain.

Doesn't your business (especially if it is large) use what amounts to a "fleet" of computers? If so, why don't you think of this fleet as being similar to the cars of a cab company, which would go out of business quickly if these cars could not be kept running smoothly and inexpensively. Now you know why the Checker Marathon automobile used to be so popular with cab companies: its design barely changed from the time it was introduced in 1956 until it was discontinued in July 1982. (At last report, there were only eight still in service in New York City!) In many ways, the standard XT- and AT-compatible systems are like the venerable Checker Marathon. You can get technical information by the shelf-full for these systems. You can get parts and upgrade material from so many sources that anything you need is always immediately available and at a discounted price. I'm not saying that you should standardize on using older XT or AT systems, just that there are good reasons for standardizing on systems that follow the "generic" physical design of the XT or AT but use newer internal components. This results in systems that are completely modern in performance and capabilities and which are easily supported, repaired, and upgraded.

Even the PS/2 systems now are capable of being considered in this light because their installed base exceeds 14 million units. Many third parties now offer replacement and upgraded motherboards, power supplies, and disk drives for these systems. You can purchase everything from upgraded motherboards to disk drives, memory, video adapters, power supplies, and just about any other component in the system. Because PS/2 systems are easy to disassemble, the upgrade procedure also is usually very easy, even if you are replacing the motherboard.

It's amazing that people purchase computers that don't have technical documentation, use nonstandard form-factor components, or have parts available only through the dealers. The upgrade, repair, and maintenance of a company's computer systems always seem to take a back seat to performance and style.

In addition to the system OEM manuals, I like to collect documentation from the different Original Equipment Manufacturers that make the components used in various systems. For example, I recently worked with Gateway and Hewlett-Packard systems, both of which use Epson floppy drives. The OEM documentation for these systems did not include detailed information on the Epson floppy drives, so I called Epson and ordered the specification manual for these drives. I also ordered the specification manuals for several other drives used in these systems, including Western Digital and Quantum hard disks. I now have detailed information on these drives, which covers jumper settings, service and repair information, and other technical specifications not provided otherwise. I recommend that you inventory each major component of your system by manufacturer and model number. If you don't have the specification or technical reference manuals for these components, call the manufacturers (the vendor list in Appendix B will help) and ask for them. You'll be amazed at the wealth of information you can get.

If you're looking for more general purpose documentation, especially on operating systems or applications software, try Que Corporation, which specializes in this type of computer book. In particular, I recommend *Killer PC Utilities*, and *Que's Guide to Data Recovery*. These books combine basic hardware information with more extensive software and operating system coverage. Microsoft and IBM also publish books of interest to computer enthusiasts and technicians. For example, Microsoft sells the *DOS Resource Kit,* and IBM sells the *DOS Technical Reference Manual.* The Microsoft kit consists of a command reference book (Microsoft left the command reference out of the DOS 6 documentation), and a very useful disk of utilities that both Microsoft and IBM left out of DOS 6.22 and 6.3. Que also publishes the *IBM OS/2 Technical Reference* library (IBM calls them "Red Books" because the covers originally were red), which is recommended for anybody using OS/2. IBM has several other technical reference manuals for use with IBM Compatible systems. A detailed list of these manuals is included in Appendix A.

Machines

Machines refers to the systems themselves. Machines are one of my best sources of information. For example, suppose that I need to answer the question, "Will the XYZ SCSI host adapter work with the ABC tape drive?" The answer is as simple as plugging everything in and pressing the switch. (Simple to talk about, that is.) Seriously, experimenting with and observing running systems are some of the best learning tools at your disposal. I recommend that you try everything; rarely will anything you try harm the equipment. Harming valuable data is definitely possible, if not likely, however, so make regular backups as insurance. You should not use a system you depend on for day to day operations as an experimental system, if possible use a secondary machine. People sometimes are reluctant to experiment with systems that cost a lot of money, but much can be learned through direct tests and studies of the system. I often find that vendor claims about a product are somewhat misleading when I actually install it and run some tests. If you are unsure that something will really work, make sure that the company has a return policy that allows you to return the item for a refund should it not meet your expectations.

Support people in larger companies have access to quantities of hardware and software I can only dream about. Some larger companies have "toy stores," where they regularly purchase equipment solely for evaluation and testing. Dealers and manufacturers also have access to an enormous variety of equipment. If you are in this position, take advantage of this access to equipment, and learn from this resource. When new systems are purchased, take notes on their construction and components.

Every time I encounter a system I have not previously worked with, I immediately open it up and start taking notes. I want to know the make and model of all the internal components, such as disk drives, power supplies, and motherboards. As far as motherboards, I like to record the numbers of the primary IC chips on the board, such as the processor (of course), integrated chip sets, floppy controller chips, keyboard controller chips, video chipsets, and any other major chips on the board. By knowing which chip set your system uses, you can often infer other capabilities of the system, such as enhanced setup or configuration capabilities. I like to know which BIOS version is in the system, and I even make a copy of the BIOS on-disk for backup and further study purposes. I want to know the hard drive tables from the BIOS and any other particulars involved in setting up and installing a system. Write down the type of battery a system uses so that you can obtain spares. Note any unique brackets or construction techniques such as specialized hardware (Torx screws, for example) so that you can be prepared for servicing the system later. Some programs have been designed to help you maintain an inventory of systems and components, but I find that these fall far short of the detail I am talking about here.

This discussion brings up a pet peeve of mine. Nothing burns me up as much as reading a "review" of computer systems in a major magazine, in which reviewers test systems and produce benchmark and performance results for, let's say, the hard disks or video displays in a system. Then they do not just open up the machines and tell me (and the world) exactly which components the manufacturer of the system is using! I want to know *exactly* which disk controller, hard drive, BIOS, motherboard, video adapter, and so on are found in each system. Without this information, their review and benchmark tests are useless to me. Then they run a test of disk performance between two systems with the same disk controller and drives and say (with a straight face) that the one that came out a few milliseconds ahead of the other wins the test. With the statistical variation that normally occurs in any manufactured components, these results are meaningless. The point is perhaps to be very careful of what you trust in a normal magazine review. If it tells me exactly which components were tested, I can draw my own conclusions and even make comparisons to other systems not included in that review. The (now defunct) *PC Tech Journal* magazine always did *excellent* reviews and told readers what components were in the systems it tested. The review test data then was much more accurate and informative because it could be properly interpreted.

Modems

Modems refers to the use of public- and private-information utilities, which are a modem and a phone call away. With a modem, you can tie into everything from local electronic bulletin board systems (BBSs), vendor boards, and major information networks such as CompuServe. Many hardware and software companies offer technical support and even software upgrades over their own semi-public bulletin boards. The public-access information networks such as CompuServe and other BBS systems include computer enthusiasts and technical-support people from various organizations, as well as experts in virtually all areas of computer hardware and software. Bulletin boards are a great way to have questions answered and to collect useful utility and help programs that can make your job much easier. The world of public-domain and user-supported software awaits, as well as more technical information and related experiences than you can imagine.

Appendix B includes not only the name, address, and voice phone number for the company but also the BBS numbers where available. If you need more information on a vendor's products or need technical support, try using the vendor's BBS. Many companies run a BBS to provide updated software or driver files so that you can download them quickly and easily. One of the best examples of a BBS is the IBM National Support Center (NSC). This BBS not only provides information on all of IBM's products, but also serves as the source for Corrective Service disk patches to DOS, OS/2, and other IBM software. Also provided are fully downloadable copies of the reference and setup disks needed to configure IBM hardware. This BBS is the ideal way to get the latest versions of these disks directly from IBM at no charge. When a vendor provides a BBS service, I consider that service a major advantage in comparison to other vendors who do not provide such a service. Using vendor BBSs has saved me money and countless hours of time.

Many companies that provide a BBS do so through a public access utility, such as CompuServe, rather than running their own BBS. The CompuServe Information Service (CIS) is a public information access utility with an extensive network of dial-in nodes that allows you to log on to its cluster of mainframe systems (based in Ohio) from virtually anywhere in the world through a local telephone call. Among CompuServe's resources are the Forums sponsored or attended by most of the major software and hardware companies, as well as enthusiasts of all types. Some interesting discussions take place in the Forums. CompuServe, combined with a local electronic bulletin board or two, can greatly supplement the information you gather from other sources. In fact, CompuServe electronic mail is probably the most efficient method of reaching me. My CompuServe ID is 73145,1566, and if you have questions or just a comment or useful information you think I might be interested in, please send me a message. Because of the extra steps in processing, my standard mail can get backed up and it can take me awhile to answer a regular postal letter; electronic mail, however, involves fewer steps for me to send and always seems to have a higher priority. If you do send a regular letter, be sure to include a SASE (self-addressed stamped envelope) so that I will be able to reply.

Magazines

The last source of information, *magazines,* is one of the best sources of up-to-date reviews and technical data. Featured are "bug fixes," problem alerts, and general industry news. Keeping a printed book up-to-date with the latest events in the computer industry is extremely difficult or impossible. Things move so fast that the magazines themselves barely keep pace. I subscribe to most of the major computer magazines and am hard-pressed to pick one as the best. They all are important to me, and each one provides different information or the same information with a different angle or twist. Although the reviews usually leave me wanting, the magazines still are a valuable way to at least hear about products, most of which I never would have known about without the magazines' reports and advertisements. Most computer magazines are also available on CD-ROM, which can ease the frantic search for a specific piece of information you remember reading about. If CD-ROM versions are too much for your needs, be aware that you can access and search most major magazines on CompuServe. This capability is valuable when you want to research everything you can about a specific subject.

One of the best kept secrets in the computer industry is the excellent trade magazines that offer free subscriptions. Although many of these magazines are directed toward the wholesale or technical end of the industry, I like to subscribe to them. Some of my favorite magazines include the following:

- *The Processor*
- *Computer Hotline*
- *Computer Reseller News*
- *Electronic Buyer's News*
- *Electronic Engineering Times*
- *Computer Design*
- *Electronic Products*
- *Test and Measurement World*
- *Service News*

These magazines offer free subscriptions to anyone who qualifies. Aimed at people in the computer and electronics industries, these magazines offer a much greater depth and breadth of technical and industry information compared to the more "public" magazines that most people are familiar with. You'll find these and other recommended magazines in the "Vendor List" in Appendix B.

The Appendixes

Appendix A provides a collection of technical information, tables, charts, and lists especially useful to people in a computer support, troubleshooting, service, or upgrading role. Whether you're seeking the address and phone number of a company or vendor in the "Vendor List," or searching for something as technical as determining the pinout of the ISA bus connector, you'll most likely find the information in the appendixes.

The appendixes started out as a brief collection of essential information but has grown into a complete reference resource of its own. No other book currently on the market contains such a complete and informative technical reference, which is one reason why so many large companies and educational institutions have standardized on this book for their technicians and students. This book is currently being used as an official textbook for many corporate and college-level computer training courses, as well as my own PC training seminars, for which the book was originally designed.

I have recently released a new book which is actually an extension of the appendixes in this book. It is called *Upgrading and Repairing PCs, Quick Reference* and could be considered a sort of condensed version of this book. It contains all of the reference tables and charts found in the appendixes, as well as throughout the book, and even some new information. If you need a reference guide that is easier to carry, I highly recommend *Upgrading and Repairing PCs, Quick Reference.*

In Conclusion

I hope that *Upgrading and Repairing PCs*, 4th Edition, is beneficial to you, and I hope that you have enjoyed reading it as much as I have enjoyed writing it. If you have questions about this book, or if you have ideas for future versions, I can be reached at the following address:

> Scott Mueller
> Mueller Technical Research
> 21718 Mayfield Lane
> Barrington, IL 60010-9733
> (708)726-0709
> (708)726-0710 Fax
> 73145,1566 CompuServe ID

I am especially interested in any ideas you have for new topics and information to be included in future releases of this book. If you want a response through the mail, please include a self-addressed stamped envelope so that I can reply to you. If you are interested in one of our many intensive PC training seminars, just drop us a line.

Thank you again for reading this book, and a special thanks to those people who have been loyal readers since the first edition came out in January 1989.

Sincerely,

Scott Mueller

Appendixes

A PC Technical Reference Section

B Vendor List

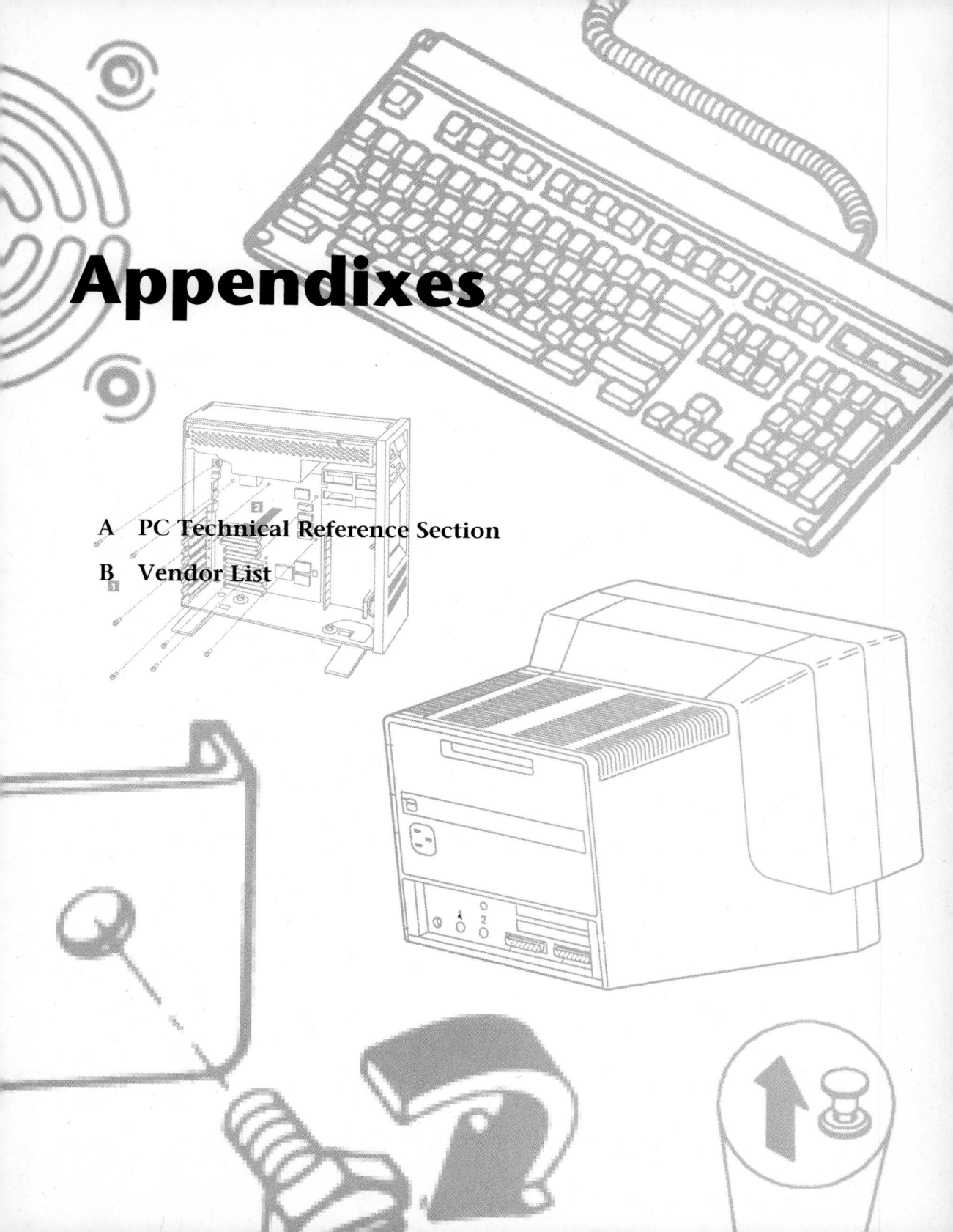

Appendix A

PC Technical Reference Section

This book has a great deal of useful information, primarily reference information, that is not designed to be read but to be looked up. Important technical information not provided in specific chapters is listed in this appendix. This type of information can be very useful in troubleshooting or upgrading sessions, but usually is spread out among many sources. In this edition of *Upgrading and Repairing PCs*, virtually all types of reference information you will need for troubleshooting and upgrading systems can be found quickly and easily.

This information is organized into charts and tables—in particular, information about the default interrupt, DMA channel, I/O port, and memory use of the primary system and most standard options. This information is invaluable if you install new boards or upgrade a system in any way, and can be important when you troubleshoot a conflict between two devices.

This book has information about various system connectors—from serial and parallel ports to power supply connections. Diagrams for making serial and parallel wrap (test) plugs are shown also.

Tables indicate the hard disk drive parameters found in XT, AT, PS/2, and other IBM-compatible systems. Many compatible BIOS drive tables are included. This information is often necessary when adding a hard disk to a system.

One of the most useful tables is a concise listing of the IBM diagnostic error codes. These codes can be generated by the POST and by the disk-based diagnostic programs. These error codes are not documented by IBM in tabular form; this compilation is the result of poring over hardware-maintenance service, technical-reference, and other manuals that IBM produces. Some of the codes come from reading the commented ROM listings in the technical-reference manuals. This information can be very useful in deciphering the codes quickly and efficiently, without having to look through a stack of books.

This book also has a listing of all the available IBM technical manuals and a description of all the documentation available. The included listing has part numbers and pricing information, as well as information useful in ordering this documentation.

Although all of this information comes from a wide range of sources, most of it comes from the technical-reference manuals and hardware-maintenance service manuals available for various systems from IBM and other manufacturers. These documents are invaluable if you want to pursue this topic more extensively.

General Information

ASCII Character Code Charts

Figure A.1 lists ASCII control character values. Figure A.2 shows the IBM extended ASCII line-drawing characters in an easy-to-use format. I frequently use these extended ASCII line-drawing characters for visual enhancement in documents I create.

DEC	HEX	CHAR	NAME	CONTROL CODE
0	00		Ctrl-@	NUL	Null
1	01	☺	Ctrl-A	SOH	Start of Heading
2	02	●	Ctrl-B	STX	Start of Text
3	03	♥	Ctrl-C	ETX	End of Text
4	04	♦	Ctrl-D	EOT	End of Transmit
5	05	♣	Ctrl-E	ENQ	Enquiry
6	06	♠	Ctrl-F	ACK	Acknowledge
7	07	●	Ctrl-G	BEL	Bell
8	08	◘	Ctrl-H	BS	Back Space
9	09	○	Ctrl-I	HT	Horizontal Tab
10	0A	■	Ctrl-J	LF	Line Feed
11	0B	♂	Ctrl-K	VT	Vertical Tab
12	0C	♀	Ctrl-L	FF	Form Feed
13	0D	♪	Ctrl-M	CR	Carriage Return
14	0E	♫	Ctrl-N	SO	Shift Out
15	0F	☼	Ctrl-O	SI	Shift In
16	10	►	Ctrl-P	DLE	Data Line Escape
17	11	◄	Ctrl-Q	DC1	Device Control 1
18	12	↕	Ctrl-R	DC2	Device Control 2
19	13	‼	Ctrl-S	DC3	Device Control 3
20	14	¶	Ctrl-T	DC4	Device Control 4
21	15	§	Ctrl-U	NAK	Negative Acknowledge
22	16	▬	Ctrl-V	SYN	Synchronous Idle
23	17	↨	Ctrl-W	ETB	End of Transmit Block
24	18	↑	Ctrl-X	CAN	Cancel
25	19	↓	Ctrl-Y	EM	End of Medium
26	1A	→	Ctrl-Z	SUB	Substitute
27	1B	←	Ctrl-[	ESC	Escape
28	1C	∟	Ctrl-\	FS	File Separator
29	1D	↔	Ctrl-]	GS	Group Separator
30	1E	▲	Ctrl-^	RS	Record Separator
31	1F	▼	Ctrl-_	US	Unit Separator

Fig. A.1
ASCII control codes.

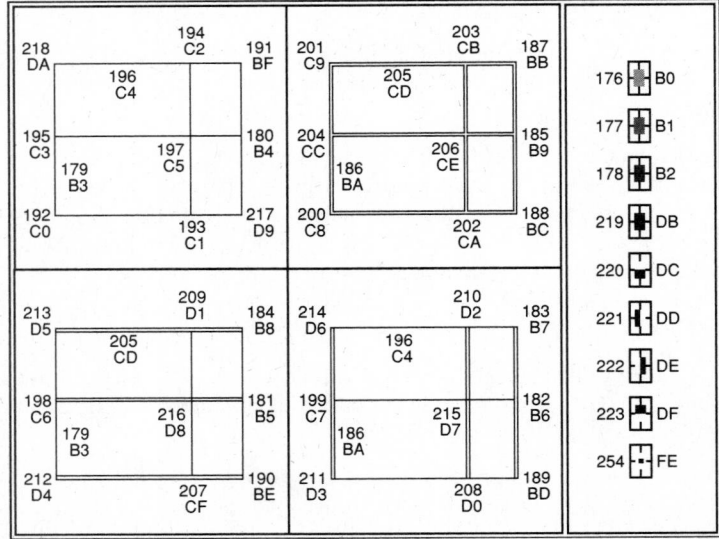

Fig. A.2
Extended ASCII line-drawing characters.

Hexadecimal/ASCII Conversions

Table A.1	**Hexadecimal/ASCII Conversions**				
Dec	**Hex**	**Octal**	**Binary**	**Name**	**Character**
0	00	000	0000 0000	blank	
1	01	001	0000 0001	happy face	☺
2	02	002	0000 0010	inverse happy face	●
3	03	003	0000 0011	heart	♥
4	04	004	0000 0100	diamond	♦
5	05	005	0000 0101	club	♣
6	06	006	0000 0110	spade	♠
7	07	007	0000 0111	bullet	•
8	08	010	0000 1000	inverse bullet	◘
9	09	011	0000 1001	circle	o
10	0A	012	0000 1010	inverse circle	◙
11	0B	013	0000 1011	male sign	♂
12	0C	014	0000 1100	female sign	♀
13	0D	015	0000 1101	single note	♪
14	0E	016	0000 1110	double note	♫
15	0F	017	0000 1111	sun	☼
16	10	020	0001 0000	right triangle	►
17	11	021	0001 0001	left triangle	◄
18	12	022	0001 0010	up/down arrow	↕
19	13	023	0001 0011	double exclamation	‼
20	14	024	0001 0100	paragraph sign	¶
21	15	025	0001 0101	section sign	§
22	16	026	0001 0110	rectangular bullet	■
23	17	027	0001 0111	up/down to line	↨
24	18	030	0001 1000	up arrow	↑
25	19	031	0001 1001	down arrow	↓
26	1A	032	0001 1010	right arrow	→
27	1B	033	0001 1011	left arrow	←
28	1C	034	0001 1100	lower left box	∟
29	1D	035	0001 1101	left/right arrow	↔
30	1E	036	0001 1110	up triangle	▲
31	1F	037	0001 1111	down triangle	▼
32	20	040	0010 0000	space	Space
33	21	041	0010 0001	exclamation point	!
34	22	042	0010 0010	quotation mark	"
35	23	043	0010 0011	number sign	#
36	24	044	0010 0100	dollar sign	$
37	25	045	0010 0101	percent sign	%
38	26	046	0010 0110	ampersand	&
39	27	047	0010 0111	apostrophe	'
40	28	050	0010 1000	opening parenthesis	(
41	29	051	0010 1001	closing parenthesis	)
42	2A	052	0010 1010	asterisk	*
43	2B	053	0010 1011	plus sign	+
44	2C	054	0010 1100	comma	,
45	2D	055	0010 1101	hyphen or minus sign	-
46	2E	056	0010 1110	period	.
47	2F	057	0010 1111	slash	/
48	30	060	0011 0000	zero	0
49	31	061	0011 0001	one	1
50	32	062	0011 0010	two	2
51	33	063	0011 0011	three	3
52	34	064	0011 0100	four	4
53	35	065	0011 0101	five	5
54	36	066	0011 0110	six	6
55	37	067	0011 0111	seven	7
56	38	070	0011 1000	eight	8
57	39	071	0011 1001	nine	9
58	3A	072	0011 1010	colon	:
59	3B	073	0011 1011	semicolon	;
60	3C	074	0011 1100	less-than sign	<

(continues)

Table A.1	**Continued**				
Dec	**Hex**	**Octal**	**Binary**	**Name**	**Character**
61	3D	075	0011 1101	equal sign	=
62	3E	076	0011 1110	greater-than sign	>
63	3F	077	0011 1111	question mark	?
64	40	100	0100 0000	at sign	@
65	41	101	0100 0001	capital A	A
66	42	102	0100 0010	capital B	B
67	43	103	0100 0011	capital C	C
68	44	104	0100 0100	capital D	D
69	45	105	0100 0101	capital E	E
70	46	106	0100 0110	capital F	F
71	47	107	0100 0111	capital G	G
72	48	110	0100 1000	capital H	H
73	49	111	0100 1001	capital I	I
74	4A	112	0100 1010	capital J	J
75	4B	113	0100 1011	capital K	K
76	4C	114	0100 1100	capital L	L
77	4D	115	0100 1101	capital M	M
78	4E	116	0100 1110	capital N	N
79	4F	117	0100 1111	capital O	O
80	50	120	0101 0000	capital P	P
81	51	121	0101 0001	capital Q	Q
82	52	122	0101 0010	capital R	R
83	53	123	0101 0011	capital S	S
84	54	124	0101 0100	capital T	T
85	55	125	0101 0101	capital U	U
86	56	126	0101 0110	capital V	V
87	57	127	0101 0111	capital W	W
88	58	130	0101 1000	capital X	X
89	59	131	0101 1001	capital Y	Y
90	5A	132	0101 1010	capital Z	Z
91	5B	133	0101 1011	opening bracket	[
92	5C	134	0101 1100	backward slash	\
93	5D	135	0101 1101	closing bracket	]
94	5E	136	0101 1110	caret	^
95	5F	137	0101 1111	underscore	_
96	60	140	0110 0000	grave	`
97	61	141	0110 0001	lowercase A	a
98	62	142	0110 0010	lowercase B	b
99	63	143	0110 0011	lowercase C	c
100	64	144	0110 0100	lowercase D	d
101	65	145	0110 0101	lowercase E	e
102	66	146	0110 0110	lowercase F	f
103	67	147	0110 0111	lowercase G	g
104	68	150	0110 1000	lowercase H	h
105	69	151	0110 1001	lowercase I	i
106	6A	152	0110 1010	lowercase J	j
107	6B	153	0110 1011	lowercase K	k
108	6C	154	0110 1100	lowercase L	l
109	6D	155	0110 1101	lowercase M	m
110	6E	156	0110 1110	lowercase N	n
111	6F	157	0110 1111	lowercase O	o
112	70	160	0111 0000	lowercase P	p
113	71	161	0111 0001	lowercase Q	q
114	72	162	0111 0010	lowercase R	r
115	73	163	0111 0011	lowercase S	s
116	74	164	0111 0100	lowercase T	t
117	75	165	0111 0101	lowercase U	u
118	76	166	0111 0110	lowercase V	v
119	77	167	0111 0111	lowercase W	w
120	78	170	0111 1000	lowercase X	x
121	79	171	0111 1001	lowercase Y	y
122	7A	172	0111 1010	lowercase Z	z
123	7B	173	0111 1011	opening brace	{
124	7C	174	0111 1100	vertical line		
125	7D	175	0111 1101	closing brace	}

Dec	Hex	Octal	Binary	Name	Character
126	7E	176	0111 1110	tilde	~
127	7F	177	0111 1111	small house	🏠
128	80	200	1000 0000	C cedilla	Ç
129	81	201	1000 0001	u umlaut	ü
130	82	202	1000 0010	e acute	é
131	83	203	1000 0011	a circumflex	â
132	84	204	1000 0100	a umlaut	ä
133	85	205	1000 0101	a grave	à
134	86	206	1000 0110	a ring	å
135	87	207	1000 0111	c cedilla	ç
136	88	210	1000 1000	e circumflex	ê
137	89	211	1000 1001	e umlaut	ë
138	8A	212	1000 1010	e grave	è
139	8B	213	1000 1011	I umlaut	ï
140	8C	214	1000 1100	I circumflex	î
141	8D	215	1000 1101	I grave	ì
142	8E	216	1000 1110	A umlaut	Ä
143	8F	217	1000 1111	A ring	Å
144	90	220	1001 0000	E acute	É
145	91	221	1001 0001	ae ligature	æ
146	92	222	1001 0010	AE ligature	Æ
147	93	223	1001 0011	o circumflex	ô
148	94	224	1001 0100	o umlaut	ö
149	95	225	1001 0101	o grave	ò
150	96	226	1001 0110	u circumflex	û
151	97	227	1001 0111	u grave	ù
152	98	230	1001 1000	y umlaut	ÿ
153	99	231	1001 1001	O umlaut	Ö
154	9A	232	1001 1010	U umlaut	Ü
155	9B	233	1001 1011	cent sign	¢
156	9C	234	1001 1100	pound sign	£
157	9D	235	1001 1101	yen sign	¥
158	9E	236	1001 1110	Pt	₧
159	9F	237	1001 1111	function	ƒ
160	A0	240	1010 0000	a acute	á
161	A1	241	1010 0001	I acute	í
162	A2	242	1010 0010	o acute	ó
163	A3	243	1010 0011	u acute	ú
164	A4	244	1010 0100	n tilde	ñ
165	A5	245	1010 0101	N tilde	Ñ
166	A6	246	1010 0110	a macron	ª
167	A7	247	1010 0111	o macron	º
168	A8	250	1010 1000	opening question mark	¿
169	A9	251	1010 1001	upper left box	⌐
170	AA	252	1010 1010	upper right box	¬
171	AB	253	1010 1011	1/2	½
172	AC	254	1010 1100	1/4	¼
173	AD	255	1010 1101	opening exclamation	¡
174	AE	256	1010 1110	opening guillemets	«
175	AF	257	1010 1111	closing guillemets	»
176	B0	260	1011 0000	light block	░
177	B1	261	1011 0001	medium block	▒
178	B2	262	1011 0010	dark block	▓
179	B3	263	1011 0011	single vertical	│
180	B4	264	1011 0100	single right junction	┤
181	B5	265	1011 0101	2 to 1 right junction	╡
182	B6	266	1011 0110	1 to 2 right junction	╢
183	B7	267	1011 0111	1 to 2 upper right	╖
184	B8	270	1011 1000	2 to 1 upper right	╕
185	B9	271	1011 1001	double right junction	╣
186	BA	272	1011 1010	double vertical	║
187	BB	273	1011 1011	double upper right	╗
188	BC	274	1011 1100	double lower right	╝
189	BD	275	1011 1101	1 to 2 lower right	╜
190	BE	276	1011 1110	2 to 1 lower right	╛
191	BF	277	1011 1111	single upper right	┐

Appendixes

(continues)

Table A.1   Continued

Dec	Hex	Octal	Binary	Name	Character
192	C0	300	1100 0000	single lower left	└
193	C1	301	1100 0001	single lower junction	┴
194	C2	302	1100 0010	single upper junction	┬
195	C3	303	1100 0011	single left junction	├
196	C4	304	1100 0100	single horizontal	─
197	C5	305	1100 0101	single intersection	┼
198	C6	306	1100 0110	2 to 1 left junction	╞
199	C7	307	1100 0111	1 to 2 left junction	╟
200	C8	310	1100 1000	double lower left	╚
201	C9	311	1100 1001	double upper left	╔
202	CA	312	1100 1010	double lower junction	╩
203	CB	313	1100 1011	double upper junction	╦
204	CC	314	1100 1100	double left junction	╠
205	CD	315	1100 1101	double horizontal	═
206	CE	316	1100 1110	double intersection	╬
207	CF	317	1100 1111	1 to 2 lower junction	╧
208	D0	320	1101 0000	2 to 1 lower junction	╨
209	D1	321	1101 0001	1 to 2 upper junction	╤
210	D2	322	1101 0010	2 to 1 upper junction	╥
211	D3	323	1101 0011	1 to 2 lower left	╙
212	D4	324	1101 0100	2 to 1 lower left	╘
213	D5	325	1101 0101	2 to 1 upper left	╒
214	D6	326	1101 0110	1 to 2 upper left	╓
215	D7	327	1101 0111	2 to 1 intersection	╫
216	D8	330	1101 1000	1 to 2 intersection	╪
217	D9	331	1101 1001	single lower right	┘
218	DA	332	1101 1010	single upper right	┌
219	DB	333	1101 1011	inverse space	█
220	DC	334	1101 1100	lower inverse	▄
221	DD	335	1101 1101	left inverse	▌
222	DE	336	1101 1110	right inverse	▐
223	DF	337	1101 1111	upper inverse	▀
224	E0	340	1110 0000	alpha	α
225	E1	341	1110 0001	beta	β
226	E2	342	1110 0010	Gamma	Γ
227	E3	343	1110 0011	pi	π
228	E4	344	1110 0100	Sigma	Σ
229	E5	345	1110 0101	sigma	σ
230	E6	346	1110 0110	mu	μ
231	E7	347	1110 0111	tau	τ
232	E8	350	1110 1000	Phi	Φ
233	E9	351	1110 1001	theta	θ
234	EA	352	1110 1010	Omega	Ω
235	EB	353	1110 1011	delta	δ
236	EC	354	1110 1100	infinity	∞
237	ED	355	1110 1101	phi	σ
238	EE	356	1110 1110	epsilon	ε
239	EF	357	1110 1111	intersection of sets	$\cap$
240	F0	360	1111 0000	is identical to	$\equiv$
241	F1	361	1111 0001	plus/minus sign	$\pm$
242	F2	362	1111 0010	greater/equal sign	$\geq$
243	F3	363	1111 0011	less/equal sign	$\leq$
244	F4	364	1111 0100	top half integral	$\lceil$
245	F5	365	1111 0101	lower half integral	$\rfloor$
246	F6	366	1111 0110	divide-by sign	$\div$
247	F7	367	1111 0111	approximately	$\approx$
248	F8	370	1111 1000	degree	$\circ$
249	F9	371	1111 1001	filled-in degree	$\bullet$
250	FA	372	1111 1010	small bullet	$\cdot$
251	FB	373	1111 1011	square root	$\sqrt{}$
252	FC	374	1111 1100	superscript n	^{n}
253	FD	375	1111 1101	superscript 2	^{2}
254	FE	376	1111 1110	box	■
255	FF	377	1111 1111	phantom space	

Extended ASCII Keycodes for ANSI.SYS

Table A.2   Extended ASCII Keycodes for ANSI.SYS

Code	Keystroke	Code	Keystroke	Code	Keystroke
0;1	\<Alt\> Esc	0;66	F8	0;116	\<Ctrl\> Right Arrow
0;3	Null Character	0;67	F9	0;117	\<Ctrl\> End
0;14	\<Alt\> Backspace	0;68	F10	0;118	\<Ctrl\> Page Down
0;15	\<Shift\> Tab	0;71	Home	0;119	\<Ctrl\> Home
0;16	\<Alt\> Q	0;72	Up Arrow	0;120	\<Alt\> 1
0;17	\<Alt\> W	0;73	Page Up	0;121	\<Alt\> 2
0;18	\<Alt\> E	0;74	\<Alt\> Keypad -	0;122	\<Alt\> 3
0;19	\<Alt\> R	0;75	Left Arrow	0;123	\<Alt\> 4
0;20	\<Alt\> T	0;76	Keypad 5	0;124	\<Alt\> 5
0;21	\<Alt\> Y	0;77	Right Arrow	0;125	\<Alt\> 6
0;22	\<Alt\> U	0;78	\<Alt\> Keypad +	0;126	\<Alt\> 7
0;23	\<Alt\> I	0;79	End	0;127	\<Alt\> 8
0;24	\<Alt\> O	0;80	Down Arrow	0;128	\<Alt\> 9
0;25	\<Alt\> P	0;81	Page Down	0;129	\<Alt\> 0
0;26	\<Alt\> [	0;82	Insert	0;130	\<Alt\> -
0;27	\<Alt\>]	0;83	Delete	0;131	\<Alt\> =
0;28	\<Alt\> Enter	0;84	\<Shift\> F1	0;132	\<Ctrl\> Page Up
0;30	\<Alt\> A	0;85	\<Shift\> F2	0;133	F11
0;31	\<Alt\> S	0;86	\<Shift\> F3	0;134	F12
0;32	\<Alt\> D	0;87	\<Shift\> F4	0;135	\<Shift\> F11
0;33	\<Alt\> F	0;88	\<Shift\> F5	0;136	\<Shift\> F12
0;34	\<Alt\> G	0;89	\<Shift\> F6	0;137	\<Ctrl\> F11
0;35	\<Alt\> H	0;90	\<Shift\> F7	0;138	\<Ctrl\> F12
0;36	\<Alt\> J	0;91	\<Shift\> F8	0;139	\<Alt\> F11
0;37	\<Alt\> K	0;92	\<Shift\> F9	0;140	\<Alt\> F12
0;38	\<Alt\> L	0;93	\<Shift\> F10	0;141	\<Ctrl\> Up Arrow
0;39	\<Alt\> ;	0;94	\<Ctrl\> F1	0;142	\<Ctrl\> Keypad -
0;40	\<Alt\> '	0;95	\<Ctrl\> F2	0;143	\<Ctrl\> Keypad 5
0;41	\<Alt\> '	0;96	\<Ctrl\> F3	0;144	\<Ctrl\> Keypad +
0;43	\<Alt\> \	0;97	\<Ctrl\> F4	0;145	\<Ctrl\> Down Arrow
0;44	\<Alt\> Z	0;98	\<Ctrl\> F5	0;146	\<Ctrl\> Insert
0;45	\<Alt\> X	0;99	\<Ctrl\> F6	0;147	\<Ctrl\> Delete
0;46	\<Alt\> C	0;100	\<Ctrl\> F7	0;148	\<Ctrl\> Tab
0;47	\<Alt\> V	0;101	\<Ctrl\> F8	0;149	\<Ctrl\> Keypad /
0;48	\<Alt\> B	0;102	\<Ctrl\> F9	0;150	\<Ctrl\> Keypad *
0;49	\<Alt\> N	0;103	\<Ctrl\> F10	0;151	\<Alt\> Home
0;50	\<Alt\> M`	0;104	\<Alt\> F1	0;152	\<Alt\> Up Arrow
0;51	\<Alt\> ,	0;105	\<Alt\> F2	0;153	\<Alt\> Page Up
0;52	\<Alt\> .	0;106	\<Alt\> F3	0;155	\<Alt\> Left Arrow
0;53	\<Alt\> /	0;107	\<Alt\> F4	0;157	\<Alt\> Right Arrow
0;55	\<Alt\> Keypad *	0;108	\<Alt\> F5	0;159	\<Alt\> End
0;59	F1	0;109	\<Alt\> F6	0;160	\<Alt\> Down Arrow
0;60	F2	0;110	\<Alt\> F7	0;161	\<Alt\> Page Down
0;61	F3	0;111	\<Alt\> F8	0;162	\<Alt\> Insert
0;62	F4	0;112	\<Alt\> F9	0;163	\<Alt\> Delete
0;63	F5	0;113	\<Alt\> F10	0;164	\<Alt\> Keypad /
0;64	F6	0;114	\<Ctrl\> Print Screen	0;165	\<Alt\> Tab
0;65	F7	0;115	\<Ctrl\> Left Arrow	0;166	\<Alt\> Keypad Enter

EBCDIC Character Codes

Table A.3   EBCDIC Character Codes

Dec	Hex	Octal	Binary	Name	Character
0	00	000	0000 0000	NUL	
1	01	001	0000 0001	SOH	
2	02	002	0000 0010	STX	
3	03	003	0000 0011	ETX	
4	04	004	0000 0100	SEL	

(continues)

Table A.3	Continued				
Dec	**Hex**	**Octal**	**Binary**	**Name**	**Character**
5	05	005	0000 0101	HT	
6	06	006	0000 0110	RNL	
7	07	007	0000 0111	DEL	
8	08	010	0000 1000	GE	
9	09	011	0000 1001	SPS	
10	0A	012	0000 1010	RPT	
11	0B	013	0000 1011	VT	
12	0C	014	0000 1100	FF	
13	0D	015	0000 1101	CR	
14	0E	016	0000 1110	SO	
15	0F	017	0000 1111	SI	
16	10	020	0001 0000	DLE	
17	11	021	0001 0001	DC1	
18	12	022	0001 0010	DC2	
19	13	023	0001 0011	DC3	
20	14	024	0001 0100	RES/ENP	
21	15	025	0001 0101	NL	
22	16	026	0001 0110	BS	
23	17	027	0001 0111	POC	
24	18	030	0001 1000	CAN	
25	19	031	0001 1001	EM	
26	1A	032	0001 1010	UBS	
27	1B	033	0001 1011	CU1	
28	1C	034	0001 1100	IFS	
29	1D	035	0001 1101	IGS	
30	1E	036	0001 1110	IRS	
31	1F	037	0001 1111	IUS/ITB	
32	20	040	0010 0000	DS	
33	21	041	0010 0001	SOS	
34	22	042	0010 0010	FS	
35	23	043	0010 0011	WUS	
36	24	044	0010 0100	BYP/INP	
37	25	045	0010 0101	LF	
38	26	046	0010 0110	ETB	
39	27	047	0010 0111	ESC	
40	28	050	0010 1000	SA	
41	29	051	0010 1001	SFE	
42	2A	052	0010 1010	SM/SW	
43	2B	053	0010 1011	CSP	
44	2C	054	0010 1100	MFA	
45	2D	055	0010 1101	ENQ	
46	2E	056	0010 1110	ACK	
47	2F	057	0010 1111	BEL	
48	30	060	0011 0000		
49	31	061	0011 0001		
50	32	062	0011 0010	SYN	
51	33	063	0011 0011	IR	
52	34	064	0011 0100	PP	
53	35	065	0011 0101	TRN	
54	36	066	0011 0110	NBS	
55	37	067	0011 0111	EOT	
56	38	070	0011 1000	SBS	
57	39	071	0011 1001	IT	
58	3A	072	0011 1010	RFF	
59	3B	073	0011 1011	CU3	
60	3C	074	0011 1100	DC4	
61	3D	075	0011 1101	NAK	
62	3E	076	0011 1110		
63	3F	077	0011 1111	SUB	
64	40	100	0100 0000	SP	
65	41	101	0100 0001	RSP	
66	42	102	0100 0010		
67	43	103	0100 0011		
68	44	104	0100 0100		

Dec	Hex	Octal	Binary	Name	Character
69	45	105	0100 0101		
70	46	106	0100 0110		
71	47	107	0100 0111		
72	48	110	0100 1000		
73	49	111	0100 1001		
74	4A	112	0100 1010		¢
75	4B	113	0100 1011		.
76	4C	114	0100 1100		<
77	4D	115	0100 1101		(
78	4E	116	0100 1110		+
79	4F	117	0100 1111		|
80	50	120	0101 0000		&
81	51	121	0101 0001		
82	52	122	0101 0010		
83	53	123	0101 0011		
84	54	124	0101 0100		
85	55	125	0101 0101		
86	56	126	0101 0110		
87	57	127	0101 0111		
88	58	130	0101 1000		
89	59	131	0101 1001		
90	5A	132	0101 1010		!
91	5B	133	0101 1011		$
92	5C	134	0101 1100		*
93	5D	135	0101 1101		)
94	5E	136	0101 1110		;
95	5F	137	0101 1111		¬
96	60	140	0110 0000		_
97	61	141	0110 0001		/
98	62	142	0110 0010		
99	63	143	0110 0011		
100	64	144	0110 0100		
101	65	145	0110 0101		
102	66	146	0110 0110		
103	67	147	0110 0111		
104	68	150	0110 1000		
105	69	151	0110 1001		
106	6A	152	0110 1010		|
107	6B	153	0110 1011		,
108	6C	154	0110 1100		%
109	6D	155	0110 1101		-
110	6E	156	0110 1110		>
111	6F	157	0110 1111		?
112	70	160	0111 0000		
113	71	161	0111 0001		
114	72	162	0111 0010		
115	73	163	0111 0011		
116	74	164	0111 0100		
117	75	165	0111 0101		
118	76	166	0111 0110		
119	77	167	0111 0111		
120	78	170	0111 1000		
121	79	171	0111 1001		`
122	7A	172	0111 1010		:
123	7B	173	0111 1011		#
124	7C	174	0111 1100		@
125	7D	175	0111 1101		'
126	7E	176	0111 1110		=
127	7F	177	0111 1111		"
128	80	200	1000 0000		
129	81	201	1000 0001		a
130	82	202	1000 0010		b
131	83	203	1000 0011		c
132	84	204	1000 0100		d

(continues)

Table A.3 Continued

Dec	Hex	Octal	Binary	Name	Character
133	85	205	1000 0101		e
134	86	206	1000 0110		f
135	87	207	1000 0111		g
136	88	210	1000 1000		h
137	89	211	1000 1001		i
138	8A	212	1000 1010		
139	8B	213	1000 1011		
140	8C	214	1000 1100		
141	8D	215	1000 1101		
142	8E	216	1000 1110		
143	8F	217	1000 1111		
144	90	220	1001 0000		
145	91	221	1001 0001		j
146	92	222	1001 0010		k
147	93	223	1001 0011		l
148	94	224	1001 0100		m
149	95	225	1001 0101		n
150	96	226	1001 0110		o
151	97	227	1001 0111		p
152	98	230	1001 1000		q
153	99	231	1001 1001		r
154	9A	232	1001 1010		
155	9B	233	1001 1011		
156	9C	234	1001 1100		
157	9D	235	1001 1101		
158	9E	236	1001 1110		
159	9F	237	1001 1111		
160	A0	240	1010 0000		
161	A1	241	1010 0001		~
162	A2	242	1010 0010		s
163	A3	243	1010 0011		t
164	A4	244	1010 0100		u
165	A5	245	1010 0101		v
166	A6	246	1010 0110		w
167	A7	247	1010 0111		x
168	A8	250	1010 1000		y
169	A9	251	1010 1001		z
170	AA	252	1010 1010		
171	AB	253	1010 1011		
172	AC	254	1010 1100		
173	AD	255	1010 1101		
174	AE	256	1010 1110		
175	AF	257	1010 1111		
176	B0	260	1011 0000		
177	B1	261	1011 0001		
178	B2	262	1011 0010		
179	B3	263	1011 0011		
180	B4	264	1011 0100		
181	B5	265	1011 0101		
182	B6	266	1011 0110		
183	B7	267	1011 0111		
184	B8	270	1011 1000		
185	B9	271	1011 1001		
186	BA	272	1011 1010		
187	BB	273	1011 1011		
188	BC	274	1011 1100		
189	BD	275	1011 1101		
190	BE	276	1011 1110		
191	BF	277	1011 1111		
192	C0	300	1100 0000		{
193	C1	301	1100 0001		A
194	C2	302	1100 0010		B

Dec	Hex	Octal	Binary	Name	Character
195	C3	303	1100 0011		C
196	C4	304	1100 0100		D
197	C5	305	1100 0101		E
198	C6	306	1100 0110		F
199	C7	307	1100 0111		G
200	C8	310	1100 1000		H
201	C9	311	1100 1001		I
202	CA	312	1100 1010	SHY	
203	CB	313	1100 1011		
204	CC	314	1100 1100		
205	CD	315	1100 1101		
206	CE	316	1100 1110		
207	CF	317	1100 1111		
208	D0	320	1101 0000		}
209	D1	321	1101 0001		J
210	D2	322	1101 0010		K
211	D3	323	1101 0011		L
212	D4	324	1101 0100		M
213	D5	325	1101 0101		N
214	D6	326	1101 0110		O
215	D7	327	1101 0111		P
216	D8	330	1101 1000		Q
217	D9	331	1101 1001		R
218	DA	332	1101 1010		
219	DB	333	1101 1011		
220	DC	334	1101 1100		
221	DD	335	1101 1101		
222	DE	336	1101 1110		
223	DF	337	1101 1111		
224	E0	340	1110 0000		\
225	E1	341	1110 0001	NSP	
226	E2	342	1110 0010		S
227	E3	343	1110 0011		T
228	E4	344	1110 0100		U
229	E5	345	1110 0101		V
230	E6	346	1110 0110		W
231	E7	347	1110 0111		X
232	E8	350	1110 1000		Y
233	E9	351	1110 1001		Z
234	EA	352	1110 1010		
235	EB	353	1110 1011		
236	EC	354	1110 1100		
237	ED	355	1110 1101		
238	EE	356	1110 1110		
239	EF	357	1110 1111		
240	F0	360	1111 0000		0
241	F1	361	1111 0001		1
242	F2	362	1111 0010		2
243	F3	363	1111 0011		3
244	F4	364	1111 0100		4
245	F5	365	1111 0101		5
246	F6	366	1111 0110		6
247	F7	367	1111 0111		7
248	F8	370	1111 1000		8
249	F9	371	1111 1001		9
250	FA	372	1111 1010		
251	FB	373	1111 1011		
252	FC	374	1111 1100		
253	FD	375	1111 1101		
254	FE	376	1111 1110		
255	FF	377	1111 1111	EO	

Appendixes

Metric System (SI) Prefixes

Table A.4 Metric System Prefixes			
Multiplier	**Exponent Form**	**Prefix**	**SI Symbol**
1 000 000 000 000 000 000	10^{18}	exa	E
1 000 000 000 000 000	10^{15}	peta	P
1 000 000 000 000	10^{12}	tera	T
1 000 000 000	10^{9}	giga	G
1 000 000	10^{6}	mega	M
1 000	10^{3}	kilo	K
100	10^{2}	hecto	h
10	10^{1}	deca	da
0.1	10^{-1}	deci	d
0.01	10^{-2}	centi	c
0.001	10^{-3}	milli	m
0.000 001	10^{-6}	micro	μ
0.000 000 001	10^{-9}	nano	n
0.000 000 000 001	10^{-12}	pico	p
0.000 000 000 000 001	10^{-15}	femto	f
0.000 000 000 000 000 001	10^{-18}	atto	a

Powers of 2

Table A.5 Powers of 2		
n	**2^n**	**Hexadecimal**
0	1	1
1	2	2
2	4	4
3	8	8
4	16	10
5	32	20
6	64	40
7	128	80
8	256	100
9	512	200
10	1,024	400
11	2,048	800
12	4,096	1000
13	8,192	2000
14	16,384	4000
15	32,768	8000
16	65,536	10000
17	131,072	20000
18	262,144	40000
19	524,288	80000
20	1,048,576	100000
21	2,097,152	200000
22	4,194,304	400000
23	8,388,608	800000
24	16,777,216	1000000
25	33,554,432	2000000
26	67,108,864	4000000

n	2^n	Hexadecimal
27	134,217,728	8000000
28	268,435,456	10000000
29	536,870,912	20000000
30	1,073,741,824	40000000
31	2,147,483,648	80000000
32	4,294,967,296	100000000
33	8,589,934,592	200000000
34	17,179,869,184	400000000
35	34,359,738,368	800000000
36	68,719,476,736	1000000000
37	137,438,953,472	2000000000
38	274,877,906,944	4000000000
39	549,755,813,888	8000000000
40	1,099,511,627,776	10000000000
41	2,199,023,255,552	20000000000
42	4,398,046,511,104	40000000000
43	8,796,093,022,208	80000000000
44	17,592,186,044,416	100000000000
45	35,184,372,088,832	200000000000
46	70,368,744,177,664	400000000000
47	140,737,488,355,328	800000000000
48	281,474,976,710,656	1000000000000
49	562,949,953,421,312	2000000000000
50	1,125,899,906,842,624	4000000000000
51	2,251,799,813,685,248	8000000000000
52	4,503,599,627,370,496	10000000000000
53	9,007,199,254,740,992	20000000000000
54	18,014,398,509,481,984	40000000000000
55	36,028,797,018,963,968	80000000000000
56	72,057,594,037,927,936	100000000000000
57	144,115,188,075,855,872	200000000000000
58	288,230,376,151,711,744	400000000000000
59	576,460,752,303,423,488	800000000000000
60	1,152,921,504,606,846,976	1000000000000000
61	2,305,843,009,213,693,952	2000000000000000
62	4,611,686,018,427,387,904	4000000000000000
63	9,223,372,036,854,775,808	8000000000000000
64	18,446,744,073,709,551,616	10000000000000000

Hardware and ROM BIOS Data

This section has an enormous amount of detailed reference information covering a variety of hardware and ROM BIOS topics. These figures and tables cover very useful information, such as IBM PC and XT motherboard switch settings (see fig. A.3), AT CMOS RAM addresses, and diagnostic status-byte information. This section also has a variety of other hardware information, such as BIOS version data, keyboard scan codes, and a great deal of information about the expansion buses— pinouts, resources such as interrupts, DMA channels, and I/O port addresses. Finally, this section has a number of connector pinouts for serial, parallel, keyboard, video, and other connectors.

Appendixes

IBM PC and XT Motherboard Switch Settings

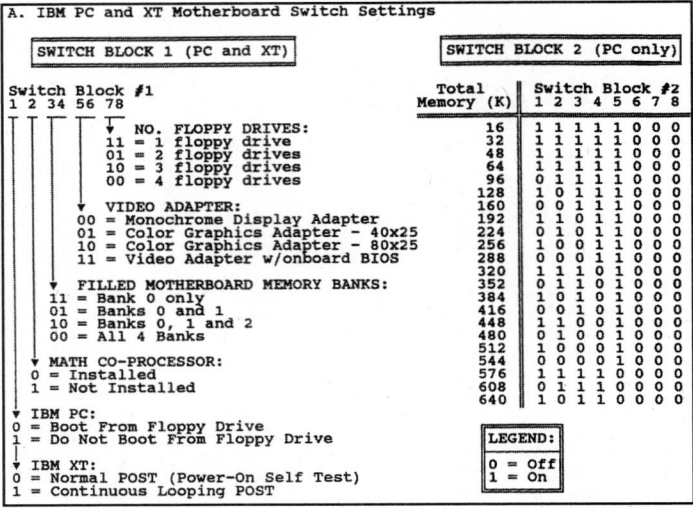

Fig. A.3

IBM PC and XT motherboard switch settings.

AT CMOS RAM Addresses

Table A.6 shows the information maintained in the 64-byte AT CMOS RAM module. This information controls the configuration of the system much like the switches control the PC and XT configurations. This memory is read and written by the system SETUP program.

Table A.6   AT CMOS RAM Addresses

Offset Hex	Offset Dec	Field Size	Function
00h	0	1 byte	Current second in binary coded decimal (BCD)
01h	1	1 byte	Alarm second in BCD
02h	2	1 byte	Current minute in BCD
03h	3	1 byte	Alarm minute in BCD
04h	4	1 byte	Current hour in BCD
05h	5	1 byte	Alarm hour in BCD
06h	6	1 byte	Current day of week in BCD
07h	7	1 byte	Current day in BCD
08h	8	1 byte	Current month in BCD
09h	9	1 byte	Current year in BCD

0Ah	10	1 byte	Status register A
			    Bit 7 = Update in progress
			        0 = Date and time can be read
			        1 = Time update in progress
			    Bits 6–4 = Time frequency divider
			        010 = 32.768 kHz
			    Bits 3–0 = Rate selection frequency
			        0110 = 1.024 kHz square wave frequency

Offset Hex	Offset Dec	Field Size	Function

0Bh	11	1 byte	Status register B
			Bit 7 = Clock update cycle
			    0 = Update normally
			    1 = Abort update in progress
			Bit 6 = Periodic interrupt
			    0 = Disable interrupt (default)
			    1 = Enable interrupt
			Bit 5 = Alarm interrupt
			    0 = Disable interrupt (default)
			    0 = Disable interrupt (default)
			    1 = Enable interrupt
			Bit 4 = Update-ended interrupt
			    0 = Disable interrupt (default)
			    1 = Enable interrupt
			Bit 3 = Status register A square wave frequency
			    0 = Disable square wave (default)
			    1 = Enable square wave
			Bit 2 = Date format
			    0 = Calendar in BCD format (default)
			    1 = Calendar in binary format
			Bit 1 = 24-hour clock
			    0 = 24-hour mode (default)
			    1 = 12-hour mode
			Bit 0 = Daylight Savings Time
			    0 = Disable Daylight Savings (default)
			    1 = Enable Daylight Savings

0Ch	12	1 byte	Status register C Bit 7 = IRQF flag Bit 6 = PF flag Bit 5 = AF flag Bit 4 = UF flag Bits 3–0 = Reserved

0Dh	13	1 byte	Status register D
			Bit 7 = Valid CMOS RAM bit
			    0 = CMOS battery dead
			    1 = CMOS battery power good
			Bits 6–0 = Reserved

0Eh	14	1 byte	Diagnostic status
			Bit 7 = Real-time clock power status
			    0 = CMOS *has not* lost power
			    1 = CMOS *has* lost power
			Bit 6 = CMOS checksum status
			    0 = Checksum is good
			    1 = Checksum is bad
			Bit 5 = POST configuration information status
			    0 = Configuration information is valid
			    1 = Configuration information is invalid
			Bit 4 = Memory size compare during POST
			    0 = POST memory equals configuration
			    1 = POST memory *not equal* to configuration
			Bit 3 = Fixed disk/adapter initialization
			    0 = Initialization good
			    1 = Initialization failed
			Bit 2 = CMOS time status indicator
			    0 = Time is valid
			    1 = Time is invalid
			Bits 1–0 = Reserved

(continues)

Table A.6 Continued			
Offset Hex	**Offset Dec**	**Field Size**	**Function**
0Fh	15	1 byte	Shutdown code 00h = Power on or soft reset 01h = Memory size pass 02h = Memory test pass 03h = Memory test fail 04h = POST end; boot system 05h = JMP double word pointer with EOI 06h = Protected mode tests pass 07h = Protected mode tests fail 08h = Memory size fail 09h = Int 15h block move 0Ah = JMP double word pointer without EOI 0Bh = used by 80386
10h	16	1 byte	Floppy disk drive types Bits 7–4 = Drive 0 type Bits 3–0 = Drive 1 type 0000 = None 0001 = 360K 0010 = 1.2M 0011 = 720K 0100 = 1.44M
11h	17	1 byte	Reserved
12h	18	1 byte	Hard disk types Bits 7–4 = Hard disk 0 type (0–15) Bits 3–0 = Hard disk 1 type (0–15)
13h	19	1 byte	Reserved
14h	20	1 byte	Installed equipment Bits 7–6 = Number of floppy disk drives 00 = 1 floppy disk drive 01 = 2 floppy disk drives Bits 5–4 = Primary display 00 = Use display adapter BIOS 01 = CGA 40-column 10 = CGA 80-column 11 = Monochrome Display Adapter Bits 3–2 = Reserved Bit 1 = Math coprocessor present Bit 0 = Floppy disk drive present
15h	21	1 byte	Base memory low-order byte
16h	22	1 byte	Base memory high-order byte
17h	23	1 byte	Extended memory low-order byte
18h	24	1 byte	Extended memory high-order byte
19h	25	1 byte	Hard Disk 0 Extended Type (0–255)
1Ah	26	1 byte	Hard Disk 1 Extended Type (0–255)
1Bh	27	9 bytes	Reserved

Offset Hex	Offset Dec	Field Size	Function
2Eh	46	1 byte	CMOS checksum high-order byte
2Fh	47	1 byte	CMOS checksum low-order byte
30h	48	1 byte	Actual extended memory low-order byte
31h	49	1 byte	Actual extended memory high-order byte
32h	50	1 byte	Date century in BCD

33h	51	1 byte	POST information flag
			Bit 7 = Top 128K base memory status
			  0 = Top 128K base memory not installed
			  1 = Top 128K base memory installed
			Bit 6 = Setup program flag
			  0 = Normal (default)
			  1 = Put out first user message
			Bits 5–0 = Reserved

34h	52	2 bytes	Reserved

Table A.7 shows the values that may be stored by your system BIOS in a special CMOS byte called the *diagnostics status byte*. By examining this location with a diagnostics program, you can determine whether your system has set "trouble codes," which indicates that a problem previously has occurred.

Table A.7   CMOS RAM (AT and PS/2) Diagnostic Status Byte Codes

Bit Number 7 6 5 4 3 2 1 0	Hex	Function
1	80	Real-time clock (RTC) chip lost power
. 1	40	CMOS RAM checksum is bad
. . 1	20	Invalid configuration information found at POST
. . . 1	10	Memory size compare error at POST
. . . . 1 . . .	08	Fixed disk or adapter failed initialization
. . . . . 1 . .	04	Real-time clock (RTC) time found invalid
. . . . . . 1 .	02	Adapters do not match configuration
. . . . 1	01	Time-out reading an adapter ID
. . . .	00	No errors found (Normal)

IBM BIOS Model, Submodel, and Revision Codes
Table A.8 shows information about the different ROM BIOS versions that have appeared in various IBM systems.

Table A.8 IBM BIOS Model, Submodel, and Revision Codes

System Description	CPU	Clock Speed	Bus Type /Width	ROM BIOS Date	ID Byte	Sub-model Byte	Rev.	ST506 Drive Types
PC	8088	4.77 MHz	ISA/8	04/24/81	FF	—	—	—
PC	8088	4.77 MHz	ISA/8	10/19/81	FF	—	—	—
PC	8088	4.77 MHz	ISA/8	10/27/82	FF	—	—	—
PC-XT	8088	4.77 MHz	ISA/8	11/08/82	FE	—	—	—
PC-XT	8088	4.77 MHz	ISA/8	01/10/86	FB	00	01	—
PC-XT	8088	4.77 MHz	ISA/8	05/09/86	FB	00	02	—
PCjr	8088	4.77 MHz	ISA/8	06/01/83	FD	—	—	—
PC Convertible	80C8	4.77 MHz	ISA/8	09/13/85	F9	00	00	—
PS/2 25	8086	8 MHz	ISA/8	06/26/87	FA	01	00	26
PS/2 30	8086	8 MHz	ISA/8	09/02/86	FA	00	00	26
PS/2 30	8086	8 MHz	ISA/8	12/12/86	FA	00	01	26
PS/2 30	8086	8 MHz	ISA/8	02/05/87	FA	00	02	26
PC-AT	286	6 MHz	ISA/16	01/10/84	FC	—	—	15
PC-AT	286	6 MHz	ISA/16	06/10/85	FC	00	01	23
PC-AT	286	8 MHz	ISA/16	11/15/85	FC	01	00	23
PC-XT 286	286	6 MHz	ISA/16	04/21/86	FC	02	00	24
PS/1	286	10 MHz	ISA/16	12/01/89	FC	0B	00	44
PS/2 25 286	286	10 MHz	ISA/16	06/28/89	FC	09	02	37
PS/2 30 286	286	10 MHz	ISA/16	08/25/88	FC	09	00	37
PS/2 30 286	286	10 MHz	ISA/16	06/28/89	FC	09	02	37
PS/2 35 SX	386SX	20 MHz	ISA/16	03/15/91	F8	19	05	37
PS/2 35 SX	386SX	20 MHz	ISA/16	04/04/91	F8	19	06	37
PS/2 40 SX	386SX	20 MHz	ISA/16	03/15/91	F8	19	05	37
PS/2 40 SX	386SX	20 MHz	ISA/16	04/04/91	F8	19	06	37
PS/2 L40 SX	386SX	20 MHz	ISA/16	02/27/91	F8	23	02	37
PS/2 50	286	10 MHz	MCA/16	02/13/87	FC	04	00	32
PS/2 50	286	10 MHz	MCA/16	05/09/87	FC	04	01	32
PS/2 50Z	286	10 MHz	MCA/16	01/28/88	FC	04	02	33
PS/2 50Z	286	10 MHz	MCA/16	04/18/88	FC	04	03	33
PS/2 55 SX	386SX	16 MHz	MCA/16	11/02/88	F8	0C	00	33
PS/2 55 LS	386SX	16 MHz	MCA/16	?	F8	1E	00	33
PS/2 57 SX	386SX	20 MHz	MCA/16	07/03/91	F8	26	02	None
PS/2 60	286	10 MHz	MCA/16	02/13/87	FC	05	00	32
PS/2 65 SX	386SX	16 MHz	MCA/16	02/08/90	F8	1C	00	33
PS/2 70 386	386DX	16 MHz	MCA/32	01/29/88	F8	09	00	33
PS/2 70 386	386DX	16 MHz	MCA/32	04/11/88	F8	09	02	33
PS/2 70 386	386DX	16 MHz	MCA/32	12/15/89	F8	09	04	33
PS/2 70 386	386DX	20 MHz	MCA/32	01/29/88	F8	04	00	33
PS/2 70 386	386DX	20 MHz	MCA/32	04/11/88	F8	04	02	33
PS/2 70 386	386DX	20 MHz	MCA/32	12/15/89	F8	04	04	33
PS/2 70 386	386DX	25 MHz	MCA/32	06/08/88	F8	0D	00	33
PS/2 70 386	386DX	25 MHz	MCA/32	02/20/89	F8	0D	01	33
PS/2 70 486	486DX	25 MHz	MCA/32	12/01/89	F8	0D	?	?

System Description	CPU	Clock Speed	Bus Type /Width	ROM BIOS Date	ID Byte	Sub-model Byte	Rev.	ST506 Drive Types
PS/2 70 486	486DX	25 MHz	MCA/32	09/29/89	F8	1B	00	?
PS/2 P70 386	386DX	16 MHz	MCA/32	?	F8	50	00	?
PS/2 P70 386	386DX	20 MHz	MCA/32	01/18/89	F8	0B	00	33
PS/2 P75 486	486DX	33 MHz	MCA/32	10/05/90	F8	52	00	33
PS/2 80 386	386DX	16 MHz	MCA/32	03/30/87	F8	00	00	32
PS/2 80 386	386DX	20 MHz	MCA/32	10/07/87	F8	01	00	32
PS/2 80 386	386DX	25 MHz	MCA/32	11/21/89	F8	80	01	?
PS/2 90 XP 486	486SX	20 MHz	MCA/32	?	F8	2D	00	?
PS/2 90 XP 486	487SX	20 MHz	MCA/32	?	F8	2F	00	?
PS/2 90 XP 486	486DX	25 MHz	MCA/32	?	F8	11	00	?
PS/2 90 XP 486	486DX	33 MHz	MCA/32	?	F8	13	00	?
PS/2 90 XP 486	486DX	50 MHz	MCA/32	?	F8	2B	00	?
PS/2 95 XP 486	486SX	20 MHz	MCA/32	?	F8	2C	00	?
PS/2 95 XP 486	487SX	20 MHz	MCA/32	?	F8	2E	00	?
PS/2 95 XP 486	486DX	25 MHz	MCA/32	?	F8	14	00	?
PS/2 95 XP 486	486DX	33 MHz	MCA/32	?	F8	16	00	?
PS/2 95 XP 486	486DX	50 MHz	MCA/32	?	F8	2A	00	?

The ID byte, Submodel byte, and Revision numbers are in hexadecimal.
— = This feature is not supported.
None = Only SCSI drives are supported.
? = Information unavailable.

Disk Software Interfaces

Figure A.4 shows a representation of the relationship between the different disk software interfaces at work in an IBM-compatible system. This figure shows the chain of command from the hardware, which is the drive controller, to the ROM BIOS, DOS, and, finally, an application program.

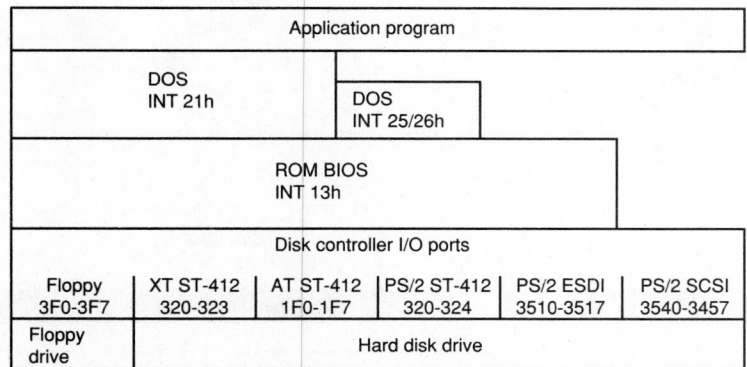

Fig. A.4
Disk software interface levels and relationships.

The following table shows the different functions available at the Interrupt 13h BIOS interface. Some functions are available to floppy drives or hard drives only, and others are available to both types of drives.

Table A.9 INT 13h BIOS Disk Functions

Function	Floppy Disk	Hard Disk	Description
00h	×	×	Reset disk system
01h	×	×	Get status of last operation
02h	×	×	Read sectors
03h	×	×	Write sectors
04h	×	×	Verify sectors
05h	×	×	Format track
06h		×	Format bad track
07h		×	Format drive
08h	×	×	Read drive parameters
09h		×	Initialize drive characteristics
0Ah		×	Read long
0Bh		×	Write long
0Ch		×	Seek
0Dh		×	Alternate hard disk reset
0Eh		×	Read sector buffer
0Fh		×	Write sector buffer
10h		×	Test for drive ready
11h		×	Recalibrate drive
12h		×	Controller RAM diagnostic
13h		×	Controller drive diagnostic
14h		×	Controller internal diagnostic
15h	×	×	Get disk type
16h	×		Get floppy disk change status
17h	×		Set floppy disk type for format
18h	×		Set media type for format
19h		×	Park hard disk heads
1Ah		×	ESDI—Low-level format
1Bh		×	ESDI—Get manufacturing header
1Ch		×	ESDI—Get configuration

The following table shows the error codes that may be returned by the BIOS INT 13h routines. In some cases you may see these codes referred to when running a low-level format program, disk editor, or other program that can directly access a disk drive through the BIOS.

Table A.10 INT 13h BIOS Error Codes

Code	Description
00h	No error
01h	Bad command
02h	Address mark not found
03h	Write protect

Code	Description
04h	Request sector not found
05h	Reset failed
06h	Media change error
07h	Initialization failed
09h	Cross 64K DMA boundary
0Ah	Bad sector flag detected
0Bh	Bad track flag detected
10h	Bad ECC on disk read
11h	ECC corrected data error
20h	Controller has failed
40h	Seek operation failed
80h	Drive failed to respond
AAh	Drive not ready
BBh	Undefined error
CCh	Write fault
0Eh	Register error
FFh	Sense operation failed

Motherboard Connectors

Table A.11 Battery Connector	
Pin	**Signal**
1	Gnd
2	Unused
3	KEY
4	+6v

Table A.12 LED and Keylock Connector	
Pin	**Signal**
1	LED Power (+5v)
2	KEY
3	Gnd
4	Keyboard Inhibit
5	Gnd

Table A.13 Speaker Connector	
Pin	**Signal**
1	Audio
2	KEY
3	Gnd
4	+5v

System Video Information

Table A.14 Video Adapter and Display Modes and Standards

Video Std.	Introduced	Resolution	No. of Colors	Scan Freq. Mode Type	BIOS Modes
MDA	08/12/81	720×350	4	Text	07h
CGA	08/12/81	320×200	16	Text	00/01h
		640×200	16	Text	02/03h
		160×200	16	APA	—
		320×200	4	APA	04/05h
		640×200	2	APA	06h
EGA	09/10/84	320×350	16	Text	00/01h
		640×350	16	Text	02/03h
		720×350	4	Text	07h
		320×200	16	APA	0Dh
		640×200	16	APA	0Eh
		640×350	4	APA	0Fh
		640×350	16	APA	10h
PGA	09/10/84	320×200	16	Text	00/01h
		640×200	16	Text	02/03h
		320×200	4	APA	04/05h
		640×200	2	APA	06h
		640×480	256	APA	—
MCGA	04/02/87	320×400	16	Text	00/01h
		640×400	16	Text	02/03h
		320×200	4	APA	04/05h
		640×200	2	APA	06h
		640×480	2	APA	11h
		320×200	256	APA	13h
VGA	04/02/87	360×400	16	Text	00/01h
		720×400	16	Text	02/03h
		320×200	4	APA	04/05h
		640×200	2	APA	06h
		720×400	16	Text	07h
		320×200	16	APA	0Dh
		640×200	16	APA	0Eh
		640×350	4	APA	0Fh
		640×350	16	APA	10h
		640×480	2	APA	11h
		640×480	16	APA	12h
		320×200	256	APA	13h
8514	04/02/87	1024×768	256	APA	H-0h
		640×480	256	APA	H-1h
		1024×768	256	APA	H-3h
XGA	10/30/90	360×400	16	Text	00/01h
		720×400	16	Text	02/03h
		320×200	4	APA	04/05h
		640×200	2	APA	06h
		720×400	16	Text	07h
		320×200	16	APA	0Dh
		640×200	16	APA	0Eh
		640×350	4	APA	0Fh

Char. Format	Char. Box	Vert. (Hz)	Horiz. (kHz)	Scan Mode
80×25	9×14	50	8.432	Std
40×25	8×8	60	15.75	Std
80×25	8×8	60	15.75	Std
—	—	60	15.75	Std
40×25	8×8	60	15.75	Std
80×25	8×8	60	15.75	Std
40×25	8×14	60	21.85	Std
80×25	8×14	60	21.85	Std
80×25	9×14	50	18.432	Std
40×25	8×8	60	15.75	Std
80×25	8×8	60	15.75	Std
80×25	8×14	50	18.432	Std
80×25	8×14	60	21.85	Std
40×25	8×8	60	15.75	Std
80×25	8×8	60	15.75	Std
40×25	8×8	60	15.75	Std
80×25	8×8	60	15.75	Std
—	—	60	30.48	Std
40×25	8×16	70	31.5	Std
80×25	8×16	70	31.5	Std
40×25	8×8	70	31.5	DBL
80×25	8×8	70	31.5	DBL
80×30	8×16	60	31.5	Std
40×25	8×8	70	31.5	DBL
40×25	9×16	70	31.5	Std
80×25	9×16	70	31.5	Std
40×25	8×8	70	31.5	DBL
80×25	8×8	70	31.5	DBL
80×25	9×16	70	31.5	Std
40×25	8×8	70	31.5	DBL
80×25	8×8	70	31.5	DBL
80×25	8×14	70	31.5	Std
80×25	8×14	70	31.5	Std
80×30	8×16	60	31.5	Std
80×30	8×16	60	31.5	Std
40×25	8×8	70	31.5	DBL
85×38	12×20	43.48	35.52	IL
80×34	8×14	60	31.5	Std
146×51	7×15	43.48	35.52	IL
40×25	9×16	70	31.5	Std
80×25	9×16	70	31.5	Std
40×25	8×8	70	31.5	DBL
80×25	8×8	70	31.5	DBL
80×25	9×16	70	31.5	Std
40×25	8×8	70	31.5	DBL
80×25	8×8	70	31.5	DBL
80×25	8×14	70	31.5	Std

Appendixes

(continues)

Table A.14   Continued

Video Std.	Introduced	Resolution	No. of Colors	Scan Freq. Mode Type	BIOS Modes
XGA	10/30/90	640×350	16	APA	10h
		640×480	2	APA	11h
		640×480	16	APA	12h
		320×200	256	APA	13h
		1056×400	16	Text	14h
		1056×400	16	Text	14h
		1056×400	16	Text	14h
		1056×400	16	Text	14h
		1024×768	256	APA	H-0h
		640×480	65536	APA	H-1h
		1024×768	256	APA	H-2h
		1024×768	256	APA	H-3h

MDA = Monochrome Display Adapter   EGA = Enhanced Graphics Adapter   MCGA = Multi-Color Graphics Arra
CGA = Color Graphics Adapter   PGA = Professional Graphics Adapter   VGA = Video Graphics Array

Note

The 8514/A adapter allows the System Board VGA signals to pass through via the Auxiliary Video Connector (slot); therefore, all VGA modes will function normally. The XGA Adapter shuts down the System Board VGA and contains a full 16-bit VGA adapter circuit onboard.

Monitor ID Pins

The following table shows the settings used for the Monitor ID bits for several different IBM displays. By sensing which of these four pins are grounded, the video adapter can determine what type of display is attached. This is especially used with regard to monochrome or color display detection. In this manner, the VGA or XGA circuitry can properly select the color mapping and image size to suit the display.

Table A.15   IBM Display Monitor ID Settings

Display	Size	Type	ID0	ID1	ID2	ID3
8503	12-inch	Mono	No Pin	Ground	No Pin	No Pin
8512	13-inch	Color	Ground	No Pin	No Pin	No Pin
8513	12-inch	Color	Ground	No Pin	No Pin	No Pin
8514	15-inch	Color	Ground	No Pin	Ground	No Pin
8515	14-inch	Color	No Pin	No Pin	Ground	No Pin
9515	14-inch	Color	No Pin	No Pin	Ground	No Pin
9517	17-inch	Color	Ground	No Pin	Ground	Ground
9518	14-inch	Color	Ground	No Pin	Ground	No Pin

Char. Format	Char. Box	Vert. (Hz)	Horiz. (kHz)	Scan Mode
80×25	8×14	70	31.5	Std
80×30	8×16	60	31.5	Std
80×30	8×16	60	31.5	Std
40×25	8×8	70	31.5	DBL
132×25	8×16	70	31.5	Std
132×43	8×9	70	31.5	Std
132×56	8×8	70	31.5	Std
132×60	8×6	70	31.5	Std
85×38	12×20	43.48	35.52	IL
80×34	8×14	60	31.5	Std
128×54	8×14	43.48	35.52	IL
146×51	7×15	43.48	35.52	IL

8514 = 8514/A Adapter *APA = All Points Addressable (Graphics)* *IL = Interlaced*
XGA = eXtended Graphics Array *DBL = Double Scan* *— = Not supported*

Modem Control Codes

This section lists the command and control codes for popular modems. If you have ever had to work with these devices without the original documentation, you will appreciate these tables. The following table shows the commands recognized by the popular Hayes and U.S. Robotics modems. These modems have a standard command set that can get quite complicated in the higher end models. This table comes in handy when you need to reconfigure a modem without the original manual. Even if your modem is not Hayes or U.S. Robotics, it probably follows most of these commands because this command set has become somewhat of a standard.

Table A.16 U.S. Robotics and Hayes Modem Commands and Supported Features

Command	Modem Functions and Options	USR Dual	2400	Hayes 2400	1200
&	See Extended Command Set	×			
%	See Extended Command Set	×			
A	Force Answer mode when modem has not received an incoming call	×	×	×	×
A/	Reexecute last command once	×	×	×	×
A>	Repeat last command continuously	×			
Any key	Terminate current connection attempt; exit Repeat mode	×	×		
AT	Attention: must precede all other commands, except A/, A>, and +++	×	×	×	×
Bn	Handshake options	×		×	
	B0 CCITT answer sequence	×		×	
	B1 Bell answer tone	×		×	
Cn	Transmitter On/Off	×	×	×	×
	C0 Transmitter Off	×	×	×	×
	C1 Transmitter On—Default	×	×	×	×

(continues)

Command	Modem Functions and Options	USR Dual	2400	Hayes 2400	1200
Dn	Dial number n and go into originate mode Use any of these options:	×	×	×	×
	P Pulse dial—Default	×	×	×	×
	T Touch-Tone dial	×	×	×	×
	' (Comma) Pause for 2 seconds	×	×	×	×
	; Return to command state after dialing	×	×	×	×
	"... Dial the letters that follow	×	×		
	! Flash switch-hook to transfer call	×	×	×	
	W Wait for 2nd dial tone (if X3 or higher is set)	×	×	×	
	@ Wait for an answer (if X3 or higher is set)	×	×	×	
	R Reverse frequencies	×	×	×	×
	S Dial stored number			×	
DL	Dial the last-dialed number	×			
DSn	Dial number stored in NVRAM at position n	×			
En	Command mode local echo; not applicable after a connection has been made	×	×	×	×
E0	Echo Off	×	×	×	×
E1	Echo On	×	×	×	×
Fn	Local echo On/Off when a connection has been made	×	×	×	×
F0	Echo On (Half duplex)	×	×	×	×
F1	Echo Off (Full duplex)—Default	×	×	×	×
Hn	On/Off hook control	×	×	×	×
H0	Hang up (go on hook)—Default	×	×	×	×
H1	Go off hook	×	×	×	×
In	Inquiry	×	×	×	×
I0	Return product code	×	×	×	×
I1	Return memory (ROM) checksum	×	×	×	×
I2	Run memory (RAM) test	×	×	×	
I3	Return call duration/real time	×	×		
I4	Return current modem settings	×	×		
I5	Return NVRAM settings	×			
I6	Return link diagnostics	×			
I7	Return product configuration	×			
Kn	Modem clock operation	×			
K0	ATI3 displays call duration—Default	×			
K1	ATI3 displays real time; set with ATI3=HH:MM:SSK1	×			
Ln	Loudness of speaker volume;			×	
L0	Low		×		
L1	Low		×		
L2	Medium			×	
L3	High		×		
Mn	Monitor (speaker) control	×	×	×	×
M0	Speaker always Off	×	×	×	×
M1	Speaker On until carrier is established—Default	×	×	×	×
M2	Speaker always On	×	×	×	×
M3	Speaker On after last digit dialed, Off at carrier detect	×	×	×	×
O	Return on-line after command execution	×	×	×	×
O0	Return on-line, normal	×	×	×	×
O1	Return on-line, retrain	×	×	×	×
P	Pulse dial	×	×	×	×

Command	Modem Functions and Options	USR Dual	2400	Hayes 2400	1200
Qn	Result codes display	×	×	×	×
	Q0 Result codes displayed	×	×	×	×
	Q1 Result codes suppressed (quiet mode)	×	×	×	×
	Q2 Quiet in answer mode only	×			
Sr=n	Set Register commands: r is any S-register; n must be a decimal number between 0 and 255.	×	×	×	×
Sr.b=n	Set bit .b of register r to n (0/Off or 1/On)	×			
Sr?	Query register r	×	×	×	×
T	Tone dial	×	×	×	×
Vn	Verbal/Numeric result codes	×	×	×	×
	V0 Numeric mode	×	×	×	×
	V1 Verbal mode	×	×	×	×
Xn	Result code options	×	×	×	×
	Long space disconnect			×	
	Y0 Disabled			×	
	Y1 Enabled; disconnects after 1.5-second break			×	
Z	Software reset	×	×	×	×
+++	Escape code sequence, preceded and followed by at least one second of no data transmission	×	×		
/(Slash)	Pause for 125 msec	×			
>	Repeat command continuously or up to 10 dial attempts. Cancel by pressing any key.	×	×		
$	Online Help—Basic command summary	×	×		
&$	Online Help—Ampersand command summary	×			
%$	Online Help—Percent command summary	×			
D$	Online Help—Dial command summary	×	×		
S$	Online Help—S-register summary	×	×		
<Ctrl>-S	Stop/restart display of HELP screens		×		
<Ctrl>-C	Cancel display HELP screens		×		
<Ctrl>-K	Cancel display HELP screens		×		
Extended Command Set					
&An	ARQ result codes 14–17, 19	×			
	&A0 Suppress ARQ result codes	×			
	&A1 Display ARQ result codes —Default	×			
	&A2 Display HST and V.32 result code	×			
	&A3 Display protocol result codes	×			
&Bn	Data Rate, terminal-to-modem (DTE/DCE)	×			
	&B0 DTE rate follows connection rate—Default	×			
	&B1 Fixed DTE rate	×			
	&B2 Fixed DTE rate in ARQ mode; variable DTE rate in non-ARQ mode	×			
&Cn	Carrier Detect (CD) operations	×		×	
	&C0 CD override	×		×	
	&C1 Normal CD operations	×		×	

(continues)

Command	Modem Functions and Options	USR Dual	2400	Hayes 2400	1200
Table A.16	**Continued**				
Extended Command Set					
&Dn	Data Terminal Ready (DTR) operations	×		×	
	&D0 DTR override	×		×	
	&D1 DTR Off; goes to command state			×	
	&D2 DTR Off; goes to command state and on hook	×		×	
	&D3 DTR Off; resets modem			×	
&F	Load factory settings into RAM	×		×	
&Gn	Guard tone	×		×	
	&G0 No guard tone; U.S., Canada—Default	×		×	
	&G1 Guard tone; some European countries	×		×	
	&G2 Guard tone; U.K., requires B0	×		×	
&Hn	Transmit Data flow control	×			
	&H0 Flow control disabled—Default	×			
	&H1 Hardware (CTS) flow control	×			
	&H2 Software (XON/XOFF) flow control	×			
	&H3 Hardware and software control	×			
&In	Received Data software flow control	×			
	&I0 Flow control disabled—Default	×			
	&I1 XON/XOFF to local modem and remote computer	×			
	&I2 XON/XOFF to local modem only	×			
	&I3 Host mode, Hewlett Packard protocol	×			
	&I4 Terminal mode, Hewlett Packard protocol	×			
	&I5 ARQ mode-same as &I2; non-ARQ mode; look for incoming XON/XOFF	×			
&Jn	Telephone jack selection			×	
	&J0 RJ-11/ RJ-41S/ RJ-45S			×	
	&J1 RJ-12/ RJ-13			×	
&Kn	Data compression	×			
	&K0 Disabled	×			
	&K1 Auto enable/disable—Default	×			
	&K2 Enabled	×			
	&K3 V.42bis only	×			
&Ln	Normal/Leased line operation	×		×	
	&L0 Normal phone line—Default	×		×	
	&L1 Leased line	×		×	
&Mn	Error Control/Synchronous Options	×		×	
	&M0 Normal mode, no error control	×		×	
	&M1 Synch mode	×		×	
	&M2 Synch mode 2—stored number dialing			×	
	&M3 Synch mode 3—manual dialing	×			
	&M4 Normal/ARQ mode-Normal if ARQ connection cannot be made Default	×			
	&M5 ARQ mode-hang up if ARQ connection cannot be made	×			
&Nn	Data Rate, data link (DCE/DCE)	×			
	&N0 Normal link operations—Default	×			
	&N1 300 bps	×			
	&N2 1200 bps	×			
	&N3 2400 bps	×			
	&N4 4800 bps	×			
	&N5 7200 bps	×			
	&N6 9600 bps	×			
	&N7 12K bps	×			
	&N8 14.4K bps	×			

Command	Modem Functions and Options	USR Dual	2400	Hayes 2400	1200
Extended Command Set					
&Pn	Pulse dial make/break ratio	×		×	
	&P1 British Commonwealth	×		×	
&Rn	Received Data hardware (RTS) flow control	×		×	
	&R0 CTS tracks RTS	×		×	
	&R1 Ignore RTS—Default	×		×	
	&R2 Pass received data on RTS high; used	×			
&Sn	Data Set Ready (DSR) override	×		×	
	&S0 DSR override (always On—Default)	×		×	
	&S1 Modem controls DSR	×		×	
	&S2 Pulsed DSR; CTS follows CD	×			
	&S3 Pulsed DSR	×			
&Tn	Modem Testing	×		×	
	&T0 End testing	×		×	
	&T1 Analog loopback	×		×	
	&T2 Reserved	×			
	&T3 Digital loopback	×		×	
	&T4 Grant remote digital loopback	×		×	
	&T5 Deny remote digital loopback	×		×	
	&T6 Initiate remote digital loopback	×		×	
	&T7 Remote digital loopback with self-test	×		×	
	&T8 Analog loopback with self-test	×		×	
&W	Write current settings to NVRAM	×		×	
&Xn	Synchronous timing source	×		×	
&X0	Modem's transmit clock—Default	×		×	
	&X1 Terminal equipment	×		×	
	&X2 Modem's receiver clock	×		×	
&Yn	Break handling. Destructive breaks clear the buffer; expedited breaks are sent immediately to remote system.	×			
&Y0	Destructive, but don't send break	×			
	&Y1 Destructive, expedited—Default	×			
	&Y2 Nondestructive, expedited	×			
	&Y3 Nondestructive, unexpedited	×			
&Zn=L	Store last-dialed phone number in NVRAM at position n	×			
&Zn=s	Write phone number(s) to NVRAM at position n (0–3); 36 characters maximum	×			
&Zn?	Display phone number in NVRAM at position n (n=0–3)	×		×	
%Rn	Remote access to Rack Controller Unit (RCU)	×			
	%R0 Disabled	×			
	%R1 Enabled	×			
%T	Enable Touch-Tone recognition	×			
Modem S-Register Functions and Defaults					
S0	Number of rings before automatic answering when DIP switch 5 is UP. Default = 1. S0 = 0 disables Auto Answer, equivalent to DIP switch 5 Down.	SW5	SW5	0	SW5
S1	Counts and stores number of rings from incoming call	0	0	0	0
S2	Define escape code character. Default = +	43	43	43	43

(continues)

Table A.16   Continued

Command	Modem Functions and Options	USR Dual	2400	Hayes 2400	1200
Modem S-Register Functions and Defaults					
S3	Define ASCII carriage return	13	13	13	13
S4	Define ASCII line feed	10	10	10	10
S5	Define ASCII Backspace	8	8	8	8
S6	Number of seconds modem waits before dialing	2	2	2	2
S7	Number of seconds modem waits for a carrier	60	30	30	30
S8	Duration (sec) for pause (,) option in Dial command and pause between command reexecutions for Repeat (>) command	2	2	2	2
S9	Duration (.1 sec units) of remote carrier signal before recognition	6	6	6	6
S10	Duration (.1 sec units) modem waits after loss of carrier before hanging up	7	7	7	7
S11	Duration and spacing (ms) of dialed Touch-Tones	70	70	70	70
S12	Guard time (in .02 sec units) for escape code sequence	50	50	50	50
S13	Bit-mapped register: 1 Reset when DTR drops 2 Auto answer in originate mode 4 Disable result code pause 8 DS0 on DTR low-to-high 16 DS0 on power up, ATZ 32 Disable HST modulation 64 Disable MNP Level 3 128 Watchdog hardware reset	0			
S15	Bit-mapped register: 1 Disable high-frequency equalization 2 Disable on-line fallback 4 Force 300-bps back channel 8 Set non-ARQ transmit buffer to 128 bytes 16 Disable MNP Level 4 32 Set Del as Backspace key 64 Unusual MNP incompatibility 128 Custom applications only	0			
S16	Bit-mapped register: 1 Analog loopback 2 Dial test 4 Test pattern 8 Initiate remote digital loopback 16 Reserved 32 Reserved 64 Reserved 128 Reserved	0		0	0
S18	&Tn Test timer, disabled when set to 0	0		0	
S19	Set inactivity timer in minutes	0			
S21	Length of Break, DCE to DTE, in 10ms units	10		0	
S22	Define ASCII XON	17		17	
S23	Define ASCII XOFF	19		19	

Command	Modem Functions and Options	USR Dual	2400	Hayes 2400	1200
Modem S-Register Functions and Defaults					
S24	Duration (20ms units) of pulsed DSR when modem is set to &S2 or &S3	150			
S25	Delay to DTR	5			
S26	Duration (10ms units) of delay between RTS and CTS, synchronous mode	1		1	
S27	Bit-mapped register:	0			
	1 Enable V.21 modulation, 300 bps				
	2 Enable unencoded V.32 modulation				
	4 Disable V.32 modulation				
	8 Disable 2100 Hz answer tone				
	16 Disable MNP handshake				
	32 Disable V.42 Detect phase				
	64 Reserved				
	128 Unusual software incompatibility				
S28	Duration (.1 sec units) of V.21/V.23 handshake delay	8			
S32	Voice/Data switch options:	1			
	0 Disabled				
	1 Go off hook in originate mode				
	2 Go off hook in answer mode				
	3 Redial last-dialed number				
	4 Dial number stored at position	0			
	5 Auto answer toggle On/Off				
	6 Reset modem				
	7 Initiate remote digital loopback				
S34	Bit-mapped register:	0			
	1 Disable V.32bis				
	2 Disable enhanced V.32 mode				
	4 Disable quick V.32 retrain				
	8 Enable V.23 modulation				
	16 Change MR LED to DSR				
	32 Enable MI/MIC				
	64 Reserved				
	128 Reserved				
S38	Duration (sec) before disconnect when DTR drops during an ARQ call	0			

ARQ = Automatic repeat request
ASCII = American Standard Code for Information Interchange
BPS = Bits per second
CCITT = Consultative Committee for International Telephone and Telegraph
CD = Carrier cetect
CRC = Cyclic redundancy check
DCE = Data communications equipment
DTE = Data terminal equipment
EIA = Electronic Industries Association
HDLC = High-level data link control
HST = High-speed technology
Hz = Hertz

LAPM = Link access procedure for modems
MI/MIC = Mode indicate/Mode indicate common
MNP = Microcom networking protocol
NVRAM = Non-volatile memory
RAM = Random-access memory
ROM = Read-only memory
SDLC = Synchronous Data Link Control
MR = Modem ready
LED = Light-emitting diode
DTR = Data terminal ready
CTS = Clear to send
RTS = Ready to send
DSR = Data set ready

Appendixes

Printer Control Codes

Table A.17 IBM Printer-Control Codes					
Function	Codes in ASCII	Codes In Hex	Pro-Printer	Graphics-Printer	Color-Printer
Job-Control Commands					
Escape (command start)	<ESC>	1B	×	×	×
Null (command end)	<NUL>	00	×	×	×
Ring bell	<BELL>	07	×	×	×
Cancel (clear printer buffer)	<CAN>	18	×	×	×
Select printer	<DC1>	11	×		×
Deselect printer *n*	<ESC>Q#	1B 51#	×		×
Deselect printer	<DC3>	13	×		×
Automatic ribbon band shift	<ESC>a	1B 61			×
Select ribbon band 1	<ESC>y	1B 79			×
Select ribbon band 2	<ESC>m	1B 6D			×
Select ribbon band 3	<ESC>c	1B 63			×
Select ribbon band 4 (black)	<ESC>b	1B 62			×
Home print head	<ESC><	1B 3C		×	
Form feed	<FF>	0C	×	×	×
Horizontal tab	<HT>	09	×	×	×
Backspace	<BS>	08	×		×
Initialize function On	<ESC>?<SOH>	1B 3F 01			×
Initialize function Off	<ESC>?<NUL>	1B 3F 00			×
Unidirectional printing On	<ESC>U<SOH>	1B 55 01	×	×	×
Unidirectional printing Off	<ESC>U<NUL>	1B 55 00	×	×	×
Space #/120 fwd to next character	<ESC>d#	1B 64 #			×
Space #/120 bwd to next character	<ESC>e#	1B 65 #			×
Set aspect ratio to 1:1	<ESC>n<SOH>	1B 6E 01			×
Set aspect ratio to 5:6	<ESC>n<NUL>	1B 6E 00			×
Select control values = binary	<ESC>@#<NUL>	1B 40 # 00			×
Select control values = ASCII	<ESC>@<SOH>	1B 40 01			×
Printer-Control Commands					
Ignore paper end On	<ESC>8	1B 38		×	
Ignore paper end Off	<ESC>9	1B 39		×	
Set length of page in lines (1–127)	<ESC>C#	1B 43 #	×	×	×
Set length of page in inches (1–22)	<ESC>C<SOH>#	1B 43 01 #	×	×	×
Automatic line justification On	<ESC>M<SOH>	1B 4D 01			×
Automatic line justification Off	<ESC>M<NUL>	1B 4D 00			×
Perforation skip On (1–127)	<ESC>N #	1B 4E #	×	×	×
Perforation skip Off	<ESC>O	1B 4F	×	×	×
Set top of page (form)	<ESC>4	1B 34	×		×
Set left and right margins	<ESC>X #	1B 58 #			×
Clear tabs (set to power-on defaults)	<ESC>R	1B 52	×		×
Set horizontal tab stops	<ESC>D # <NUL>	1B 44 # 00	×	×	×
Set vertical tab stops	<ESC>B # <NUL>	1B 42 # 00	×	×	×
Carriage return	<CR>	0D	×	×	×
Line feed	<LF>	0A		×	×

Function	Codes in ASCII	Codes In Hex	Pro-Printer	Graphics-Printer	Color-Printer
Printer-Control Commands					
Set n/72 lines per inch	<ESC>A #	1B 41 #	×	×	×
Set n/216 lines per inch	<ESC>3 #	1B 33 #	×	×	#/144"
Set 8 lines per inch	<ESC>0	1B 30	×	×	×
Set 7/72nd line per inch	<ESC>1	1B 31	×	×	6/72"
Start new line spacing	<ESC>2	1B 32	×	×	×
Vertical tab	<VT>	0B	×	×	×
Reverse line feed	<ESC>]	1B 5D			×
Automatic line feed On	<ESC>5<SOH>	1B 35 01	×		×
Automatic line feed Off	<ESC>5<NUL>	1B 35 00	×		×
Font Selection					
Select character set 1	<ESC>7	1B 37	×	×	×
Select character set 2	<ESC>6	1B 36	×	×	×
10 cpi (compressed Off)	<DC2>	12	×	×	×
17.1 cpi (compressed On)	<SI>	0F	×	×	×
Doublestrike On	<ESC>G	1B 47	×	×	×
Doublestrike Off	<ESC>H	1B 48	×	×	×
Doublewidth On (lines)	<ESC>W<SOH>	1B 57 01	×	×	×
Doublewidth Off (lines)	<ESC>W<NUL>	1B 57 00	×	×	×
Doublewidth by line On	<SO>	0E	×	×	×
Doublewidth by line Off	<DC4>	14	×	×	×
Emphasized printing On	<ESC>E	1B 45	×	×	×
Emphasized printing Off	<ESC>F	1B 46	×	×	×
Subscript On	<ESC>S<SOH>	1B 53 01	×	×	×
Superscript On	<ESC>S<NUL>	1B 53 00	×	×	×
Subscript/superscript Off	<ESC>T	1B 54	×	×	×
Set draft quality	<ESC>I<SOH>	1B 49 01			×
Set text quality (near-letter quality)	<ESC>I<STX>	1B 49 02	×		×
Set letter quality	<ESC>I<ETX>	1B 49 03			×
Proportional spacing On	<ESC>P<SOH>	1B 50 01			×
Proportional spacing Off	<ESC>P<NUL>	1B 50 00			×
12-characters-per-inch spacing	<ESC>:	1B 3A	×		×
Print all characters	<ESC>\ #	1B 5C #	×		×
Print next character	<ESC>^	1B 5E	×		×
Underline On	<ESC>-<SOH>	1B 2D 01	×	×	×
Underline Off	<ESC>-<NUL>	1B 2D 00	×	×	×
Graphics					
Graphics, 60 dots per inch (dpi)	<ESC>K #	1B 4B #	×	×	
Graphics, 70/84 dpi	<ESC>K #	1B 4B #			×
Graphics, 120 DPI half-speed	<ESC>L #	1B 4C #	×	×	
Graphics, 140/168 dpi half-speed	<ESC>L #	1B 4C #			×
Graphics, 120 dpi normal speed	<ESC>Y #	1B 59 #	×	×	
Graphics, 140/168 dpi normal speed	<ESC>Y #	1B 59 #			×
Graphics, 240 dpi half-speed	<ESC>Z #	1B 5A #	×	×	
Graphics, 280/336 dpi half-speed	<ESC>Z #	1B 5A #			×

 # indicates a variable number in the code.

Table A.18   Epson Printer-Control Codes

Function	Codes in ASCII	Codes in Hex
Job-Control Commands		
Ring bell	<BELL>	07
Clear line	<CAN>	18
Select printer	<DC1>	11
Deselect printer	<DC3>	13
Set justification	<ESC>a	1B 61
Cut sheet-feeder control	<ESC>	EM1B 19
Select character space	<ESC>	SP1B 20
Select mode combinations	<ESC>!	1B 21
Select active character set	<ESC>%	1B 25
Copies ROM to user RAM	<ESC>:	1B 3A
Defines user characters	<ESC>&	1B 26
Set MSB = 0	<ESC>>	1B 3E
Set MSB = 1	<ESC>=	1B 3D
Select international character set	<ESC>R#	1B 72#
Select 15 width	<ESC>g	1B 67
Select immediate print (typewriter mode)	<ESC>i	1B 69
Half-speed printing Off	<ESC>s<NUL>	1B 73 00
Half-speed printing On	<ESC>s<SOH>	1B 73 01
Set horizontal tab unit	<ESC>e<NUL>	1B 65 00
Set vertical tab unit	<ESC>e<SOH>	1B 6D 01
Special character-generator selection (control codes accepted)	<ESC>m<NUL>	1B 6D 00
Special character-generator selection (graphic characters accepted)	<ESC>m<SOH>	1B 6D 01
Unidirectional printing On	<ESC>U<SOH>	1B 55 01
Unidirectional printing Off	<ESC>U<NUL>	1B 55 00
Turn unidirectional (left to right) On	<ESC><	1B 3C
Form feed	<FF>	0C
Horizontal tab	<HT>	09
Initialize printer	<ESC>@	1B 40
Backspace	<BS>	08
Printer-Control Commands		
Ignore paper end On	<ESC>8	1B 38
Ignore paper end Off	<ESC>9	1B 39
Set length of page in lines (1–127)	<ESC>C#	1B 43#
Set length of page in inches (1–22)	<ESC>C<NUL>#	1B 43 00#
Set absolute tab	<ESC>$	1B 24
Set vertical tab	<ESC>/	1B 2F
Set vertical tab	<ESC>b	1B 62
Set horizontal tab unit	<ESC>e<NUL>	1B 65 00
Set vertical tab unit	<ESC>e<SOH>	1B 65 01
Set horizontal skip position	<ESC>f<NUL>	1B 66 00

Function	Codes in ASCII	Codes in Hex
Printer-Control Commands		
Set vertical skip position	<ESC>f<SOH>	1B 66 01
Perforation skip On (1–127)	<ESC>N#	1B 4E#
Perforation skip Off	<ESC>O	1B 4F
Set horizontal tab stop	<ESC>D	1B 44
Set vertical tab stop	<ESC>B	1B 42
Carriage return	<CR>	0D
Line feed	<LF>	0A
Set variable line feed to #/72 inch (1–85)	<ESC>A#	1B 41#
Set variable line feed to #/216 inch	<ESC>J#	1B 4A#
Set spacing at 1/8 inch	<ESC>0	1B 30
Set spacing at 7/72 inch	<ESC>1	1B 31
Set line spacing at 1/6 inch	<ESC>2	1B 32
Set #/216 inch line feed (0–225)	<ESC>3#	1B 33#
Vertical tab	<VT>	0B
Font Selection		
Deactivate high-order control codes	<ESC>6	1B 36
Turn alternate character (italics) On	<ESC>4	1B 34
10 CPI (compressed Off) spacing	<DC2>	12
17.1 CPI (compressed On) spacing	<SI>	0F
Doublestrike On	<ESC>G	1B 47
Doublestrike Off	<ESC>H	1B 48
Doublewidth On (lines)	<ESC>W<SOH>	1B 57 01
Doublewidth Off (lines)	<ESC>W<NUL>	1B 57 00
Enlarged print mode On	<SO>	0E
Enlarged print mode Off	<DC4>	14
Emphasized printing On	<ESC>E	1B 45
Emphasized printing Off	<ESC>F	1B 46
Turn alternate character (italics) On	<ESC>4	1B 34
Turn alternate character (italics) Off	<ESC>5	1B 35
Elite mode On (Pica mode off)	<ESC>M	1B 4D
Select family of type styles	<ESC>k	1B 6B
Proportional printing Off	<ESC>p<NUL>	1B 70 00
Proportional printing On	<ESC>p<SOH>	1B 70 01
Select letter- or draft-quality printing	<ESC>z	1B 7A
Subscript On	<ESC>S<SOH>	1B 53 01
Superscript On	<ESC>S<NUL>	1B 53 00
Subscript/superscript Off	<ESC>T	1B 54
Control code select	<ESC>I	1B 49
Elite mode Off (Pica mode On)	<ESC>P	1B 50
Nine-pin graphics mode	<ESC>^	1B 5E
Underline On	<ESC>-<SOH>	1B 2D 01
Underline Off	<ESC>-<NUL>	1B 2D 00

(continues)

Table A.18 Continued		
Function	**Codes in ASCII**	**Codes in Hex**
Graphics		
Normal-density bit image	<ESC>K	1B 4B##
Dual-density bit image	<ESC>L	1B 4C##
Double-speed, dual-density bit image	<ESC>Y	1B 59##
Quadruple-density bit image	<ESC>Z	1B 5A##

International character sets:

0 = U.S.	*6 = Italy*
1 = France	*7 = Spain*
2 = Germany	*8 = Japan*
3 = England	*9 = Norway*
4 = Denmark	*10 = Denmark II*
5 = Sweden	

Characters in brackets are ASCII code names.
 # indicates a variable numeric value.

Table A.19 HP LaserJet Printer-Control Codes			
Function type	**Function**	**Codes in ASCII**	**Codes in Hex**
Job-Control Commands			
Printer control	Reset printer	<ESC>E	1B 45
	Self-test mode	<ESC>z	1B 7A
	Number of copies	<ESC>&l#X	1B 26 6C # 58
	Long-edge (left) offset registration	<ESC>&l#U	1B 26 6C # 55
	Short-edge (top) offset registration	<ESC>&l#Z	1B 26 6C # 5A
Printer-Control Commands			
Paper source	Eject page	<ESC>&l0H	1B 26 6C 30 48
	Paper-tray auto feed	<ESC>&l1H	1B 26 6C 31 48
	Manual feed	<ESC>&l2H	1B 26 6C 32 48
	Manual envelope feed	<ESC>&l3H	1B 26 6C 33 48
	Feed from lower cassette	<ESC>&l4H	1B 26 6C 34 48
Page size	Executive	<ESC>&l1A	1B 26 6C 31 41
	Letter	<ESC>&l2A	1B 26 6C 32 41
	Legal	<ESC>&l3A	1B 26 6C 33 41
	A4	<ESC>&l26A	1B 26 6C 32 36 41
	Monarch (envelope)	<ESC>&l80A	1B 26 6C 38 30 41
	COM 10 (envelope)	<ESC>&l81A	1B 26 6C 38 31 41
	DL (envelope)	<ESC>&l90A	1B 26 6C 39 30 41
	C5 (envelope)	<ESC>&l91A	1B 26 6C 39 31 41
Orientation	Portrait mode	<ESC>&l0O	1B 26 6C 30 4F
	Landscape mode	<ESC>&l1O	1B 26 6C 31 4F
	Reverse portrait	<ESC>&l2O	1B 26 6C 32 4F
	Reverse landscape	<ESC>&l3O	1B 26 6C 33 4F
	Print direction	<ESC>&a#P	1B 26 61 # 50

Function type	Function	Codes in ASCII	Codes in Hex
Printer-Control Commands			
Page settings	Page length	\<ESC>&l#P	1B 26 6C # 50
	Top margin	\<ESC>&l#E	1B 26 6C # 45
	Text length	\<ESC>&l#F	1B 26 6C # 46
	Clear horizontal margins	\<ESC>9	1B 39
	Set left margin	\<ESC>&a#L	1B 26 61 # 4C
	Set right margin	\<ESC>&a#M	1B 26 61 # 4D
	Perforation skip enable	\<ESC>&l1L	1B 26 6C 31 4C
	Perforation skip disable	\<ESC>&l0L	1B 26 6C 30 4C
Line spacing	Vertical motion index	\<ESC>&l#C	1B 26 6C # 43
	Horizontal motion index	\<ESC>&k#H	1B 26 6B # 4B
	1 line/inch	\<ESC>&l1D	1B 26 6C 31 44
	2 lines/inch	\<ESC>&l2D	1B 26 6C 32 44
	3 lines/inch	\<ESC>&l3D	1B 26 6C 33 44
	4 lines/inch	\<ESC>&l4D	1B 26 6C 34 44
	6 lines/inch	\<ESC>&l6D	1B 26 6C 36 44
	8 lines/inch	\<ESC>&l8D	1B 26 6C 38 44
	12 lines/inch	\<ESC>&l12D	1B 26 6C 31 32 44
	16 lines/inch	\<ESC>&l16D	1B 26 6C 31 36 44
	24 lines/inch	\<ESC>&l24D	1B 26 6C 32 34 44
	48 lines/inch	\<ESC>&l48D	1B 26 6C 34 38 44
	Half line feed	\<ESC>=	1B 3D
Stacking position	Default	\<ESC>&l0T	1B 26 6C 30 54
	Toggle	\<ESC>&l1T	1B 26 6C 31 54
Cursor Positioning			
Vertical position	Number of rows	\<ESC>&a#R	1B 26 61 # 52
	Number of dots	\<ESC>*p#Y	1B 2A 70 # 59
	Number of decipoints	\<ESC>&a#V	1B 26 61 # 56
Horizontal position	Number of rows	\<ESC>&a#C	1B 26 61 # 43
	Number of dots	\<ESC>*p#X	1B 2A 70 # 58
	Number of decipoints	\<ESC>&a#H	1B 26 61 # 48
End-of-line	CR=CR; LF=LF; FF=FF	\<ESC>&k0G	1B 26 6B 30 47
	CR=CR+LF; LF=LF; FF=FF	\<ESC>&k1G	1B 26 6B 31 47
	CR=CR; LF=CR+LF; FF=CR+FF	\<ESC>&k2G	1B 26 6B 32 47
	CR=CR+LF; LF=CR+LF; FF=CR+FF	\<ESC>&k3G	1B 26 6B 33 47
Push/Pop position	Push position	\<ESC>&f0S	1B 26 66 30 53
	Pop position	\<ESC>&f1S	1B 26 66 31 53
Font Selection			
Font symbol set	Roman-8	\<ESC>(8U	1B 28 38 55
	USASCII	\<ESC>(0U	1B 28 30 55
	Danish/Norwegian	\<ESC>(0D	1B 28 30 44
	British (U.K.)	\<ESC>(1E	1B 28 31 45
	French	\<ESC>(1F	1B 28 31 46
	German	\<ESC>(1G	1B 28 31 47
	Italian	\<ESC>(0I	1B 28 30 49
	Swedish/Finnish	\<ESC>(0S	1B 28 30 53
	Spanish	\<ESC>(2S	1B 28 32 53
	Legal	\<ESC>(1U	1B 28 31 55
	Linedraw	\<ESC>(0B	1B 28 30 42
	Math8	\<ESC>(8M	1B 28 38 4D
	Math7	\<ESC>(0A	1B 28 30 41
	PiFont	\<ESC>(15U	1B 28 31 35 55
	ECMA-94 Latin	\<ESC>(0N	1B 28 30 4E
	PC-8	\<ESC>(10U	1B 28 31 30 55
	PC-8 D/N	\<ESC>(11U	1B 28 31 31 55
	PC 850	\<ESC>(12U	1B 28 31 32 55

Appendixes

(continues)

Table A.19 Continued

Function type	Function	Codes in ASCII	Codes in Hex
Primary spacing	Proportional	\<ESC\>(s1P	1B 28 73 31 50
	Fixed	\<ESC\>(s0P	1B 28 73 30 50
Character pitch	10 characters per inch	\<ESC\>(s10H	1B 28 73 31 30 48
	12 characters per inch	\<ESC\>(s12H	1B 28 73 31 32 48
	16.6 characters per inch	\<ESC\>(s16.6H	1B 28 73 31 36 2E 36 48
	Standard pitch (10 cpi)	\<ESC\>&k0S	1B 26 6B 30 53
	Compressed pitch (16.6 cpi)	\<ESC\>&k2S	1B 26 6B 32 53
	Elite (12.0)	\<ESC\>&k4s	1B 26 6B 34 53
Character point size	7 point	\<ESC\>(s7V	1B 28 73 37 56
	8 point	\<ESC\>(s8V	1B 28 73 38 56
	8.5 point	\<ESC\>(s8.5V	1B 28 73 38 2E 35 56
	10 point	\<ESC\>(s10V	1B 28 73 31 30 56
	12 point	\<ESC\>(s12V	1B 28 73 31 32 56
	14.4 point	\<ESC\>(s14.4V	1B 28 73 31 34 2E 34 56
Character style	Upright	\<ESC\>(s0S	1B 28 73 30 53
	Italic	\<ESC\>(s1S	1B 28 73 31 53
Character weight	Ultra thin	\<ESC\>(s-7B	1B 28 73 -37 42
	Extra thin	\<ESC\>(s-6B	1B 28 73 -36 42
	Thin	\<ESC\>(s-5B	1B 28 73 -35 42
	Extra light	\<ESC\>(s-4B	1B 28 73 -34 42
	Light	\<ESC\>(s-3B	1B 28 73 -33 42
	Demi light	\<ESC\>(s-2B	1B 28 73 -32 42
	Semi light	\<ESC\>(s-1B	1B 28 73 -31 42
	Medium (normal)	\<ESC\>(s0B	1B 28 73 30 42
	Semi bold	\<ESC\>(s1B	1B 28 73 31 42
	Demi bold	\<ESC\>(s2B	1B 28 73 32 42
	Bold	\<ESC\>(s3B	1B 28 73 33 42
	Extra bold	\<ESC\>(s4B	1B 28 73 34 42
	Black	\<ESC\>(s5B	1B 28 73 35 42
	Extra black	\<ESC\>(s6B	1B 28 73 36 42
	Ultra black	\<ESC\>(s7B	1B 28 73 37 42
Character typeface	Courier	\<ESC\>(s3T	1B 28 73 33 54
	Univers	\<ESC\>(s52T	1B 28 73 35 32 54
	Line printer	\<ESC\>(s0T	1B 28 73 30 54
	CG Times	\<ESC\>(s4101T	1B 28 73 34 31 30 31 54
	Helvetica	\<ESC\>(s4T	1B 28 73 34 54
	TMS RMN	\<ESC\>(s5T	1B 28 73 33 54
Font default	Primary font	\<ESC\>(3@	1B 28 33 40
	Secondary font	\<ESC\>)3@	1B 29 33 40
Underlining	Underline On	\<ESC\>&d#D	1B 26 64 30 44
	Underline floating	\<ESC\>&d3D	1B 26 64 33 44
	Underline Off	\<ESC\>&d@	1B 26 64 40
Transparent print	Number of bytes	\<ESC\>&p#X[Data]	1B 26 70 # 58

Font Management

Assign font ID	Font ID number	\<ESC\>*c#D	1B 2A 63 # 44
Font and character	Delete all fonts control	\<ESC\>*c0F	1B 2A 63 30 46
	Delete all temporary fonts	\<ESC\>*c1F	1B 2A 63 31 46
	Delete last font ID specified	\<ESC\>*c2F	1B 2A 63 32 46
	Delete last font ID and char code	\<ESC\>*c3F	1B 2A 63 33 46
	Make temporary font	\<ESC\>*c4F	1B 2A 63 34 46
	Make permanent font	\<ESC\>*c5F	1B 2A 63 35 46
	Copy/assign font	\<ESC\>*c6F	1B 2A 63 36 46
Select font (ID)	Primary font ID number	\<ESC\>(#X	1B 28 # 58
	Secondary font ID number	\<ESC\>)#X	1B 29 # 58

Soft Font Creation

Font descriptor	Create font	\<ESC\>)s#W[Data]	1B 29 73 # 57
	Download character	\<ESC\>(s#W[Data]	1B 28 73 # 57
	ASCII character code number	\<ESC\>*c#E	1B 2A 63 # 45

Function type	Function	Codes in ASCII	Codes in Hex
Graphics			
Vector graphics	Enter HP-GL/2 mode	<ESC>%0B	1B 25 30 42
	HP-GL/2 plot horizontal size	<ESC>%1B	1B 25 31 42
	HP-GL/2 plot vertical size	<ESC>*c#K	1B 2A 63 # 4B
	Set picture frame	<ESC>*0T	1B 2A 63 30 54
	Picture frame horizontal size	<ESC>*c#X	1B 2A 63 # 58
	Picture frame vertical size	<ESC>*c#Y	1B 2A 63 # 59
Raster resolution	75 dpi resolution	<ESC>*t75R	1B 2A 74 37 35 52
	100 dpi resolution	<ESC>*t100R	1B 2A 74 31 30 30 52
	150 dpi resolution	<ESC>*t150R	1B 2A 74 31 35 30 52
	300 dpi resolution	<ESC>*t300R	1B 2A 74 33 30 30 52
	Start at leftmost position	<ESC>*r0A	1B 2A 72 30 41
	Start at current cursor	<ESC>*r1A	1B 2A 72 31 41
Raster graphics	Rotate image presentation	<ESC>*r0F	1B 2A 72 30 46
	LaserJet landscape compatible	<ESC>*r3F	1B 2A 72 33 46
	Left raster graphics margin	<ESC>*r0A	1B 2A 72 30 41
	Current cursor	<ESC>*r1A	1B 2A 72 31 41
	Raster Y offset	<ESC>*b0M	1B 2A 62 # 59
Set raster	Uncoded compression	<ESC>*b0M	1B 2A 62 30 41
	Mode run-length encoded	<ESC>*b1M	1B 2A 62 31 41
	Tagged image file format	<ESC>*b2M	1B 2A 62 32 41
	Delta row	<ESC>*b3M	1B 2A 62 33 41
	Transfer graphic rows	<ESC>*b#W[Data]	1B 2A 62 # 57
	End graphics	<ESC>*rB	1B 2A 72 42
	Raster height	<ESC>*r#T	1B 2A 72 # 54
	Raster width	<ESC>*r#S	1B 2A 72 # 53
The Print Model			
Select pattern	Solid black (default)	<ESC>*v0T	1B 2A 76 30 54
	Solid white	<ESC>*v1T	1B 2A 76 31 54
	HP-defined shading pattern	<ESC>*v2T	1B 2A 76 32 54
	HP-defined cross-hatched pattern	<ESC>*v3T	1B 2A 76 33 54
Select source	Transparent	<ESC>*v0N	1B 2A 76 30 42
Transparency	Opaque	<ESC>*v1N	1B 2A 76 31 42
Select pattern	Transparent	<ESC>*v0O	1B 2A 76 30 43
Transparency	Opaque	<ESC>*v1O	1B 2A 76 31 43
Rectangle width	Horizontal # dots in pattern	<ESC>*c#A	1B 2A 63 # 41
	Horizontal # decipoints in pattern	<ESC>*c#H	1B 2A 63 # 48
Rectangle height	Vertical # dots in pattern	<ESC>*c#B	1B 2A 63 # 42
	Vertical # decipoints in pattern	<ESC>*c#V	1B 2A 63 # 56
Fill rectangular	Solid black	<ESC>*c0P	1B 2A 63 30 50
Area	Erase (solid white area fill)	<ESC>*c1P	1B 2A 63 31 50
	Shade fill	<ESC>*c2P	1B 2A 63 32 50
	Cross-hatched fill	<ESC>*c3P	1B 2A 63 33 50
	User defined	<ESC>*c4P	1B 2A 63 34 50
	Current pattern	<ESC>*c5P	1B 2A 63 35 50
Pattern ID	Percent of shading type of pattern	<ESC>*c#G	1B 2A 63 # 47
Shading	Print 2% grayscale	<ESC>*c2G	1B 2A 63 32 47
	Print 10% grayscale	<ESC>*c10G	1B 2A 63 31 30 47
	Print 15% grayscale	<ESC>*c15G	1B 2A 63 31 35 47
	Print 30% grayscale	<ESC>*c30G	1B 2A 63 33 30 47
	Print 45% grayscale	<ESC>*c45G	1B 2A 63 34 35 47
	Print 70% grayscale	<ESC>*c70G	1B 2A 63 37 30 47
	Print 90% grayscale	<ESC>*c90G	1B 2A 63 39 30 47
	Print 100% grayscale	<ESC>*c100G	1B 2A 63 31 30 30 47

Appendixes

(continues)

Table A.19 Continued

Function type	Function	Codes in ASCII	Codes in Hex
The Print Model			
Pattern	1 horizontal line	<ESC>*c1G	1B 2A 63 31 47
	2 vertical lines	<ESC>*c2G	1B 2A 63 32 47
	3 diagonal lines	<ESC>*c3G	1B 2A 63 33 47
	4 diagonal lines	<ESC>*c4G	1B 2A 63 34 47
	5 square grid	<ESC>*c5G	1B 2A 63 35 47
	6 diagonal grid	<ESC>*c6G	1B 2A 63 36 47
Macros			
Macro ID	Macro ID number	<ESC>&f#Y	1B 26 66 # 59
Macro control	Start macro	<ESC>&f0X	1B 26 66 30 58
	Stop macro definition	<ESC>&f1X	1B 26 66 31 58
	Execute macro	<ESC>&f2X	1B 26 66 32 58
	Call macro	<ESC>&f3X	1B 26 66 33 58
	Enable overlay	<ESC>&f4X	1B 26 66 34 58
	Disable overlay	<ESC>&f5X	1B 26 66 35 58
	Delete macros	<ESC>&f6X	1B 26 66 36 58
	Delete all temporary macros	<ESC>&f7X	1B 26 66 37 58
	Delete macro ID	<ESC>&f8X	1B 26 66 38 58
	Make temporary	<ESC>&f9X	1B 26 66 39 58
	Make permanent	<ESC>&f10X	1B 26 66 31 30 58
Programming Hints			
Display functions	Display functions On	<ESC>Y	1B 59
	Display functions Off	<ESC>Z	1B 5A
End-of-line wrap	Enable	<ESC>&s0C	1B 26 73 30 43
	Disable	<ESC>&s1C	1B 26 73 31 43

# indicates a variable numeric value.
[Data] indicates a bitstream of appropriate data.

DOS Disk Structures and Layout

Table A.20 Master Boot Record (Partition Table)

Offset	Length	Description
Partition Table Entry #1		
1BEh 446	1 byte	Boot Indicator Byte (80h = Active, else 00h)
1BFh 447	1 byte	Starting Head (or Side) of Partition
1C0h 448	16 bits	Starting Cylinder (10 bits) and Sector (6 bits)
1C2h 450	1 byte	System Indicator Byte (see table)
1C3h 451	1 byte	Ending Head (or Side) of Partition
1C4h 452	16 bits	Ending Cylinder (10 bits) and Sector (6 bits)
1C6h 454	1 dword	Relative Sector Offset of Partition
1CAh 458	1 dword	Total Number of Sectors in Partition

Offset	Length	Description
Partition Table Entry #2		
1CEh 462	1 byte	Boot Indicator Byte (80h = Active, else 00h)
1CFh 463	1 byte	Starting Head (or Side) of Partition
1D0h 464	16 bits	Starting Cylinder (10 bits) and Sector (6bits)
1D2h 466	1 byte	System Indicator Byte (see table)
1D3h 467	1 byte	Ending Head (or Side) of Partition
1D4h 468	16 bits	Ending Cylinder (10 bits) and Sector (6 bits)
1D6h 470	1 dword	Relative Sector Offset of Partition
1DAh 474	1 dword	Total Number of Sectors in Partition
Partition Table Entry #3		
1DEh 478	1 byte	Boot Indicator Byte (80h = Active, else 00h)
1DFh 479	1 byte	Starting Head (or Side) of Partition
1E0h 480	16 bits	Starting Cylinder (10 bits) and Sector (6 bits)
1E2h 482	1 byte	System Indicator Byte (see table)
1E3h 483	1 byte	Ending Head (or Side) of Partition
1E4h 484	16 bits	Ending Cylinder (10 bits) and Sector (6 bits)
1E6h 486	1 dword	Relative Sector Offset of Partition
1EAh 490	1 dword	Total Number of Sectors in Partition
Partition Table Entry #4		
1EEh 494	1 byte	Boot Indicator Byte (80h = Active, else 00h)
1EFh 495	1 byte	Starting Head (or Side) of Partition
1F0h 496	16 bits	Starting Cylinder (10 bits) and Sector (6 bits)
1F2h 498	1 byte	System Indicator Byte (see table)
1F3h 499	1 byte	Ending Head (or Side) of Partition
1F4h 500	16 bits	Ending Cylinder (10 bits) and Sector (6 bits)
1F6h 502	1 dword	Relative Sector Offset of Partition
1FAh 506	1 dword	Total Number of Sectors in Partition
Signature Bytes		
1FEh 510	2 bytes	Boot Sector Signature (55AAh)

A WORD equals two bytes which are read in reverse order, and a DWORD equals two WORDS which are read in reverse order.

Table A.21 Partition Table System Indicator Byte Values

Value	Description
00h	No Partition allocated in this entry
01h	Primary DOS, 12-bit FAT (Partition < 16M)
04h	Primary DOS, 16-bit FAT (16M <= Partition <= 32M)
05h	Extended DOS (Points to next Primary Partition)
06h	Primary DOS, 16-bit FAT (Partition > 32M)
07h	OS/2 HPFS Partition

(continues)

Value	Description
Table A.21	**Continued**
02h	MS-XENIX root Partition
03h	MS-XENIX usr Partition
08h	AIX File System Partition
09h	AIX Boot Partition
50h	Ontrack Disk Manager READ-ONLY Partition
51h	Ontrack Disk Manager READ/WRITE Partition
56h	Golden Bow Vfeature Partition
61h	Storage Dimensions Speedstor Partition
63h	IBM 386/ix or UNIX System V/386 Partition
64h	Novell Netware Partition
75h	IBM PCIX Partition
DBh	Digital Research Concurrent DOS/CPM-86 Partition
F2h	Some OEM's DOS 3.2+ second partition
FFh	UNIX Bad Block Table Partition

DOS Boot Record

Offset Hex	Offset Dec	Field Length	Description
Table A.22		**DOS Volume Boot Sector (DVB) Format**	
00h	0	3 bytes	Jump Instruction to Boot Program Code
03h	3	8 bytes	OEM Name and DOS Version ("IBM 5.0")
0Bh	11	1 word	Bytes/Sector (usually 512)
0Dh	13	1 byte	Sectors/Cluster (Must be a power of 2)
0Eh	14	1 word	Reserved Sectors (Boot Sectors, usually 1)
10h	16	1 byte	FAT Copies (usually 2)
11h	17	1 word	Maximum Root Directory Entries (usually 512)
13h	19	1 word	Total Sectors (If Partition <= 32M, else 0)
15h	21	1 byte	Media Descriptor Byte (F8h for hard disks)
16h	22	1 word	Sectors/FAT
18h	24	1 word	Sectors/Track
1Ah	26	1 word	Number of Heads
1Ch	28	1 dword	Hidden Sectors (If Partition <= 32M, 1 word only)
DOS 4.0 or Higher Only (Others 00h)			
20h	32	1 dword	Total Sectors (If Partition > 32M, else 0)
24h	36	1 byte	Physical Drive No. (00h=floppy, 80h=hard disk)
25h	37	1 byte	Reserved (00h)
26h	38	1 byte	Extended Boot Record Signature (29h)
27h	39	1 dword	Volume Serial Number (32-bit random number)
2Bh	43	11 bytes	Volume Label ("NO NAME" stored if no label)
36h	54	8 bytes	File System ID ("FAT12" or "FAT16")
All Versions of DOS			
3Eh	62	450 bytes	Boot Program Code
1FEh	510	2 bytes	Signature Bytes (55AAh)

A WORD is two bytes which are read in reverse order, and a DWORD is two WORDS which are read in reverse order.

Directory Structure

Table A.23   DOS Directory Entries

Offset Hex	Offset Dec	Field Length	Description
00h	0	8 bytes	Filename
08h	8	3 bytes	File Extension
0Bh	11	1 byte	File Attributes (see table)
0Ch	12	10 bytes	Reserved (00h)
16h	22	1 word	Time of Creation (see table)
18h	24	1 word	Date of Creation (see table)
1Ah	26	1 word	Starting Cluster
1Ch	28	1 dword	Size in Bytes

NOTE: File names and extensions are left-justified and padded with spaces (32h). The first byte of the filename indicates the file status as follows:

Hex	File Status
00h	Entry never used; entries past this point not searched.
05h	Indicates first character of file name is actually E5h.
E5h	"σ" (lowercase sigma) indicates file has been erased.
2Eh	"." (period) indicates this entry is a directory. If the second byte is also 2Eh, the cluster field contains the cluster number of parent directory (0000h if the parent is the Root).

DOS Directory File Attribute Byte

Bit Positions Hex 7 6 5 4 3 2 1 0	Value	Description
0 0 0 0 0 0 0 1	01h	Read Only file
0 0 0 0 0 0 1 0	02h	Hidden file
0 0 0 0 0 1 0 0	04h	System file
0 0 0 0 1 0 0 0	08h	Volume Label
0 0 0 1 0 0 0 0	10h	Subdirectory
0 0 1 0 0 0 0 0	20h	Archive (updated since backup)
0 1 0 0 0 0 0 0	40h	Reserved
1 0 0 0 0 0 0 0	80h	Reserved

Examples

	Value	Description
0 0 1 0 0 0 0 1	21h	Read Only, Archive
0 0 1 1 0 0 1 0	32h	Hidden, Subdirectory, Archive
0 0 1 0 0 1 1 1	27h	Read Only, Hidden, System, Archive

Hard Disk Drives

This section has a great deal of information concerning all aspects of hard disk drives, including a table that lists a large number of different drive parameters, organized by manufacturer. Because Seagate is the largest supplier of hard disks in the world, and its product line is so extensive, a separate table references Seagate's hard disk product line and shows the parameters of all of its drives. This section also shows BIOS hard drive parameter tables for a number of different ROM BIOS versions, including those from IBM, Compaq, AMI, Award, Phoenix, and Zenith. Finally, this section includes the pinouts of popular hard disk interfaces such as ST-506/412, ESDI, IDE, and SCSI.

The following table shows parameters and specifications for a large number of different hard disk drives. This table can be very helpful when you are trying to install one of these drives in a system with no documentation for the drive.

Table A.24 Hard Disk Drive Specifications

Make/Model	Capacity (MB)	Cyls	Hds	Sectors per Track	Write Precomp	Park Cyl
Atasi						
502	46.0	755	7	17	—	—
504	46.0	755	7	17	—	—
514	117.2	1,224	11	17	—	—
519MFM	159.8	1,224	15	17	—	—
519RLL	244.4	1,224	15	26	—	—
617	149.0	1,223	7	34	—	—
628	234.2	1,223	11	34	—	—
638	319.3	1,223	15	34	—	—
3046	39.3	645	7	17	323	644
3051	42.9	704	7	17	352	703
3051+	44.7	733	7	17	368	732
3085	71.3	1,024	8	17	0	—
V130	25.8	987	3	17	128	—
V150	43.0	987	5	17	128	—
V170	60.1	987	7	17	128	—
V185	71.0	1,166	7	17	128	—
Brand Technology						
BT8085	71.3	1,024	8	17	512	—
BT8128	109.1	1,024	8	26	—	—
BT8170E	142.5	1,023	8	34	—	—
Conner Peripherals						
CP-342	42.7	981	5	17	—	—
CP-344	42.9	805	4	26	—	—
CP-3024	21.4	634	2	33	—	—
CP-3044	43.1	526	4	40	—	—
CP-3102-A	104.9	776	8	33	—	—
CP-3102-B	104.3	772	8	33	—	—
CP-3104	104.9	776	8	33	—	—
CP-3184	84.3	832	6	33	—	—
CP-3204	209.8	1,348	8	38	—	—
CP-3204F	212.9	684	16	38	—	—
CP-30104	121.6	1,522	4	39	—	—
CMI						
CM-6626	22.3	640	4	17	256	615
CM-6640	33.4	640	6	17	256	615
Data-Tech Memories						
DTM-553	44.6	1,024	5	17	850	—
DTM-853	44.6	640	8	17	256	—
DTM-885	71.3	1,024	8	17	850	—

Make/Model	Capacity (MB)	Cyls	Hds	Sectors per Track	Write Precomp	Park Cyl
Fujitsu						
M2225D	21.4	615	4	17	—	615
M2227D	42.8	615	8	17	—	615
M2241AS	26.3	754	4	17	128	—
M2242AS	45.9	754	7	17	128	—
M2243AS	72.2	754	11	17	128	—
M2244E	71.5	822	5	34	—	—
M2245E	100.2	822	7	34	—	—
M2246E	143.1	822	10	34	—	—
M2247E	151.3	1,242	7	34	—	—
M2248E	237.8	1,242	11	34	—	—
M2249E	324.3	1,242	15	34	—	—
M2261E	359.7	1,657	8	53	—	—
M2263E	674.5	1,657	15	53	—	—
M2611T	45.1	1,334	2	33	—	—
M2612T	90.2	1,334	4	33	—	—
M2613T	135.2	1,334	6	33	—	—
M2614T	180.3	1,334	8	33	—	—
Hewlett Packard						
97544EF	339.9	1,456	8	57	128	—
97548EF	679.9	1,456	16	57	128	—
Hitachi						
DK511-3	30.4	699	5	17	300	699
DK511-5	42.6	699	7	17	300	699
DK511-8	71.6	823	10	17	256	—
DK512-8	71.5	822	5	34	—	—
DK512-10	85.9	822	6	34	—	—
DK512-12	100.2	822	7	34	—	—
DK512-17	143.1	822	10	34	—	—
DK514-38	329.7	902	14	51	—	—
DK522-10	85.9	822	6	34	—	—
Imprimis (CDC)						
9415-519	18.2	697	3	17	128	—
9415-536	30.3	697	5	17	128	—
9415-538	31.9	733	5	17	128	—
94155-48	40.3	925	5	17	128	—
94155-57	48.3	925	6	17	128	—
94155-67	56.4	925	7	17	128	—
94155-77	64.4	925	8	17	128	—
94155-85	71.3	1,024	8	17	—	—
94155-85P	71.3	1,024	8	17	128	—
94155-86	72.5	925	9	17	128	—
94155-96	80.2	1,024	9	17	—	—
94155-96P	80.2	1,024	9	17	128	—

(continues)

Table A.24 Continued

Make/Model	Capacity (MB)	Cyls	Hds	Sectors per Track	Write Precomp	Park Cyl
Imprimis (CDC)						
94155-120	102.2	960	8	26	—	—
94155-120P	102.2	960	8	26	128	—
94155-135	115.0	960	9	26	—	—
94155-135P	115.0	960	9	26	128	—
94156-48	40.3	925	5	17	128	—
94156-67	56.4	925	7	17	128	—
94156-86	72.5	925	9	17	128	—
94166-101	84.3	968	5	34	—	—
94166-141	118.0	968	7	34	—	—
94166-182	151.7	968	9	34	—	—
94186-383	319.3	1,411	13	34	—	—
94186-383H	319.3	1,223	15	34	—	—
94186-442H	368.4	1,411	15	34	—	—
94196-766	663.9	1,631	15	53	—	—
94204-65	65.5	941	8	17	128	—
94204-71	71.3	1,024	8	17	128	—
94205-51	43.0	989	5	17	128	—
94205-77	65.8	989	5	26	128	—
94211-106	89.0	1,023	5	34	—	—
94244-383	338.1	1,747	7	54	—	—
94246-383	331.7	1,746	7	53	—	—
94354-160	143.3	1,072	9	29	128	—
94354-200	177.8	1,072	9	36	—	—
94354-230	211.0	1,272	9	36	—	—
94355-100	84.0	1,072	9	17	128	—
94355-150	128.4	1,072	9	26	128	—
94356-111	93.2	1,071	5	34	—	—
94356-155	130.5	1,071	7	34	—	—
94356-200	167.8	1,071	9	34	—	—
Kalok						
KL320	21.4	615	4	17	—	660
KL330	32.7	615	4	26	—	660
KL343	42.5	670	4	31	—	669
Kyocera						
KC20A	21.4	616	4	17	0	—
KC20B	21.4	615	4	17	0	664
KC30A	32.8	616	4	26	0	—
KC30B	32.7	615	4	26	0	664
KC40GA	42.5	977	5	17	0	980
Lapine						
TITAN20	21.4	615	4	17	0	615

Make/Model	Capacity (MB)	Cyls	Hds	Sectors per Track	Write Precomp	Park Cyl
Maxtor						
LXT50S	48.0	733	4	32	—	—
LXT100S	96.1	733	8	32	—	—
LXT200A	200.5	816	15	32	—	—
LXT200S	212.9	1,320	7	45	—	—
LXT213A	212.6	683	16	38	—	—
LXT340S	352.2	1,560	7	63	—	—
LXT340AT	352.2	1,560	7	63	—	—
XT1050	39.3	902	5	17	—	—
XT1065	55.9	918	7	17	—	—
XT1085	71.3	1,024	8	17	—	—
XT1105	87.9	918	11	17	—	—
XT1120R	109.1	1,024	8	26	—	—
XT1140	119.9	918	15	17	—	—
XT1160	133.7	1,024	15	17	—	—
XT1240R	204.5	1,024	15	26	—	—
XT2085	74.6	1,224	7	17	—	—
XT2140	117.2	1,224	11	17	—	—
XT2190	159.8	1,224	15	17	—	—
XT4170E	149.2	1,224	7	34	—	—
XT4170S	149.2	1,224	7	34	—	—
XT4175	149.2	1,224	7	34	—	—
XT4230E	203.0	1,224	9	36	—	—
XT4280	234.4	1,224	11	34	—	—
XT4380E	338.4	1,224	15	36	—	—
XT4380S	338.4	1,224	15	36	—	—
XT8380E	361.0	1,632	8	54	—	—
XT8380S	361.0	1,632	8	54	—	—
XT8610E	541.5	1,632	12	54	—	—
XT8760E	676.8	1,632	15	54	—	—
XT8760S	676.8	1,632	15	54	—	—
XT8702S	617.9	1,490	15	54	—	—
XT8800E	694.7	1,274	15	71	—	—
Micropolis						
1323	35.7	1,024	4	17	—	—
1323A	44.6	1,024	5	17	—	—
1324	53.5	1,024	6	17	—	—
1324A	62.4	1,024	7	17	—	—
1325	71.3	1,024	8	17	—	—
1333	35.7	1,024	4	17	—	—
1333A	44.6	1,024	5	17	—	—
1334	53.5	1,024	6	17	—	—
1334A	62.4	1,024	7	17	—	—
1335	71.3	1,024	8	17	—	—
1353	71.2	1,023	4	34	—	—

(continues)

Appendixes

Table A.24   Continued

Make/Model	Capacity (MB)	Cyls	Hds	Sectors per Track	Write Precomp	Park Cyl
1353A	89.0	1,023	5	34	—	—
1354	106.9	1,023	6	34	—	—
1354A	124.7	1,023	7	34	—	—
1355	142.5	1,023	8	34	—	—
1551	149.0	1,223	7	34	—	—
1554	234.2	1,223	11	34	—	—
1555	255.5	1,223	12	34	—	—
1556	276.8	1,223	13	34	—	—
1557	298.1	1,223	14	34	—	—
1558	319.3	1,223	15	34	—	—
1568-15	663.9	1,631	15	53	—	—
1653-4	86.9	1,248	4	34	—	—
1653-5	108.6	1,248	5	34	—	—
1654-6	130.4	1,248	6	34	—	—
1654-7	152.1	1,248	7	34	—	—
1664-7	337.9	1,779	7	53	—	—
1743-5	110.9	1,140	5	38	—	—
Microscience						
HH-325	21.4	615	4	17	—	615
HH-725	21.4	615	4	17	—	615
HH-1050	44.6	1,024	5	17	—	—
HH-1060	68.2	1,024	5	26	—	—
HH-1075	62.4	1,024	7	17	—	—
HH-1090	80.1	1,314	7	17	—	—
HH-1095	95.4	1,024	7	26	—	—
HH-1120	122.4	1,314	7	26	—	—
HH-2120	124.7	1,023	7	34	—	—
HH-2160	155.4	1,275	7	34	—	—
4050	44.6	1,024	5	17	768	—
4060	68.2	1,024	5	26	768	—
4070	62.4	1,024	7	17	768	—
4090	95.4	1,024	7	26	768	—
5040-00	45.9	854	3	35	—	—
5070-00	76.5	854	5	35	—	—
5070-20	85.9	959	5	35	—	—
5100-00	107.1	854	7	35	—	—
5100-20	120.3	959	7	35	—	—
5160-00	159.3	1,270	7	35	—	—
7040-00	46.0	855	3	35	—	—
7070-00	76.6	855	5	35	—	—
7070-20	86.0	960	5	35	—	—
7100-00	107.3	855	7	35	—	—
7100-20	120.4	960	7	35	—	—

Make/Model	Capacity (MB)	Cyls	Hds	Sectors per Track	Write Precomp	Park Cyl
Miniscribe						
1006	5.3	306	2	17	128	336
1012	10.7	306	4	17	128	336
2006	5.3	306	2	17	128	336
2012	10.7	306	4	17	128	336
3012	10.7	612	2	17	128	656
3053	44.6	1,024	5	17	512	—
3085	71.3	1,170	7	17	512	—
3130E	112.0	1,250	5	35	—	—
3180E	156.8	1,250	7	35	—	—
3180S	161.9	1,255	7	36	—	—
3212	10.7	612	2	17	128	656
3412	10.7	306	4	17	128	336
3425	21.4	615	4	17	128	656
3425P	21.4	615	4	17	128	656
3438	32.7	615	4	26	128	656
3438P	32.7	615	4	26	128	656
3650	42.2	809	6	17	128	852
3650R	64.6	809	6	26	128	852
3675	64.6	809	6	26	128	852
4010	8.4	480	2	17	128	522
4020	16.7	480	4	17	128	522
6032	26.7	1,024	3	17	512	—
6053	44.6	1,024	5	17	512	—
6079	68.2	1,024	5	26	512	—
6085	71.3	1,024	8	17	512	—
6128	109.1	1,024	8	26	512	—
7040A	42.7	981	5	17	—	—
7080A	85.4	981	10	17	—	—
8051A	42.7	745	4	28	—	—
8051S	42.7	745	4	28	—	—
8212	10.7	615	2	17	128	656
8225	20.5	771	2	26	128	810
8225A	21.4	615	4	17	—	810
8225XT	21.4	805	2	26	—	820
8412	10.7	306	4	17	128	336
8425	21.4	615	4	17	128	664
8425F	21.4	615	4	17	128	664
8425S	21.4	615	4	17	—	664
8425XT	21.4	615	4	17	—	664
8438	32.7	615	4	26	128	664
8438F	32.7	615	4	26	128	664
8450	41.1	771	4	26	128	810
8450A	42.7	745	4	28	—	810

(continues)

Table A.24   Continued

Make/Model	Capacity (MB)	Cyls	Hds	Sectors per Track	Write Precomp	Park Cyl
Miniscribe						
8450XT	42.9	805	4	26	—	820
9380E	329.0	1,224	15	35	—	—
9380S	336.8	1,218	15	36	—	—
9780E	676.1	1,661	15	53	—	—
Mitsubishi						
MR522	21.3	612	4	17	300	612
MR535	42.5	977	5	17	0	—
MR535RLL	65.0	977	5	26	0	—
MR5310E	85.0	976	5	34	—	—
NEC						
D3126	21.4	615	4	17	256	664
D3142	44.7	642	8	17	128	664
D3146H	42.8	615	8	17	256	664
D3661	111.4	914	7	34	—	—
D3741	45.0	423	8	26	—	423
D5126	21.4	615	4	17	128	664
D5126H	21.4	615	4	17	128	664
D5127H	32.7	615	4	26	128	664
D5128	21.4	615	4	17	128	664
D5146H	42.8	615	8	17	128	664
D5147H	65.5	615	8	26	128	664
D5452	71.6	823	10	17	512	—
D5652	143.1	822	10	34	—	—
D5655	149.0	1,223	7	34	—	—
D5662	319.3	1,223	15	34	—	—
D5682	664.3	1,632	15	53	—	—
Newbury						
NDR320	21.4	615	4	17	—	615
NDR340	42.8	615	8	17	—	615
NDR360	65.5	615	8	26	—	615
NDR1065	55.9	918	7	17	—	—
NDR1085	71.3	1,024	8	17	—	—
NDR1105	87.9	918	11	17	—	—
NDR1140	119.9	918	15	17	—	—
NDR2190	159.8	1,224	15	17	—	—
NDR4170	149.0	1,223	7	34	—	—
NDR4380	319.3	1,223	15	34	—	—
Pacific Magtron						
4115E	114.6	1,599	4	35	—	—
4140E	143.3	1,599	5	35	—	—
4170E	171.9	1,599	6	35	—	—

Make/Model	Capacity (MB)	Cyls	Hds	Sectors per Track	Write Precomp	Park Cyl
Plus Development						
40AT	42.0	965	5	17	—	—
80AT	84.0	965	10	17	—	—
120AT	120.0	814	9	32	—	—
170AT	168.5	968	10	34	—	—
210AT	209.2	873	13	36	—	—
52AT/LP	52.3	751	8	17	—	—
80AT/LP	85.8	616	16	17	—	—
105AT/LP	105.1	755	16	17	—	—
Priam						
502	46.0	755	7	17	—	—
504	46.0	755	7	17	—	—
514	117.2	1,224	11	17	—	—
519	159.8	1,224	15	17	—	—
617	143.8	751	11	34	—	—
623	196.1	751	15	34	—	—
638	319.3	1,223	15	34	—	—
V130	25.8	987	3	17	128	—
V150	43.0	987	5	17	128	—
V170	60.1	987	7	17	128	—
V185	71.0	1,166	7	17	128	—
PTI						
PT225	21.4	615	4	17	410	—
PT234	28.5	820	4	17	547	—
PT338	32.1	615	6	17	410	—
PT351	42.8	820	6	17	547	—
PT238R	32.7	615	4	26	410	—
PT251R	43.7	820	4	26	547	—
PT357R	49.1	615	6	26	410	—
PT376R	65.5	820	6	26	547	—
Quantum						
40AT	42.0	965	5	17	—	—
80AT	84.0	965	10	17	—	—
120AT	120.0	814	9	32	—	—
170AT	168.5	968	10	34	—	—
210AT	209.2	873	13	36	—	—
LPS52	52.3	751	8	17	—	—
LPS80	85.8	616	16	17	—	—
LPS105	105.1	755	16	17	—	—
Q520	17.8	512	4	17	256	512
Q530	26.7	512	6	17	256	512
Q540	35.7	512	8	17	256	512

(continues)

Table A.24 Continued

Make/Model	Capacity (MB)	Cyls	Hds	Sectors per Track	Write Precomp	Park Cyl
Rodime						
203	16.8	321	6	17	132	321
204	22.4	321	8	17	132	321
202E	22.3	640	4	17	0	640
203E	33.4	640	6	17	0	640
204E	44.6	640	8	17	0	640
3099A	80.2	373	15	28	—	—
3139A	112.5	523	15	28	—	—
3259A	212.9	990	15	28	—	—
3000A-NAT	43.2	625	5	27	0	—
3000A-XLAT	43.2	992	5	17	0	—
3060R	49.9	750	5	26	0	—
3075R	59.9	750	6	26	0	—
3085R	69.9	750	7	26	0	—
5040	32.0	1,224	3	17	0	—
5065	53.3	1,224	5	17	0	—
5090	74.6	1,224	7	17	0	—
Samsung						
SHD2020	21.8	820	2	26	—	—
SHD2021	23.5	820	2	28	—	—
SHD2030	28.5	820	4	17	—	—
SHD2040	43.7	820	4	26	—	—
SHD2041	47.0	820	4	28	—	—
Siemens						
MF-1200	169.2	1,215	8	34	—	—
MF-1300	253.8	1,215	12	34	—	—
MF-4410	321.9	1,099	11	52	—	—
Syquest						
SQ312RD	10.7	612	2	17	0	615
SQ315F	21.3	612	4	17	0	615
SQ338F	32.0	612	6	17	0	615
Tandon						
TN262	21.4	615	4	17	0	615
TN362	21.4	615	4	17	0	615
TN703	25.2	578	5	17	0	615
TN703AT	31.9	733	5	17	0	733
TN705	41.9	962	5	17	0	962
TN755	42.7	981	5	17	128	981

Make/Model	Capacity (MB)	Cyls	Hds	Sectors per Track	Write Precomp	Park Cyl
Toshiba						
MK-53F	36.1	830	5	17	—	—
MK-53FRLL	55.2	830	5	26	—	—
MK-54F	50.6	830	7	17	—	—
MK-54FRLL	77.3	830	7	26	—	—
MK-56F	72.2	830	10	17	—	—
MK-56FRLL	110.5	830	10	26	—	—
MK-72PCMFM	72.2	830	10	17	—	—
MK-72PCRLL	110.5	830	10	26	512	—
MK-134FAMFM	44.7	733	7	17	—	—
MK-134FARLL	68.3	733	7	26	512	—
MK-153FA	72.2	829	5	34	—	—
MK-154FA	101.0	829	7	34	—	—
MK-156FA	144.3	829	10	34	—	—
MK-232FC	45.4	845	3	35	—	—
MK-234FC-I	106.0	845	7	35	—	—
MK-355FA	398.3	1,631	9	53	—	—
MK-358FA	663.9	1,631	15	53	—	—
MK-538FB	1229.0	1,980	15	80	—	—
Tulin						
TL226	22.3	640	4	17	—	640
TL240	33.4	640	6	17	—	640
Vertex						
V130	25.8	987	3	17	128	—
V150	43.0	987	5	17	128	—
V170	60.1	987	7	17	128	—
V185	71.0	1,166	7	17	128	—
Western Digital						
WD-93024A	21.6	782	2	27	—	—
WD-93028A	21.6	782	2	27	—	—
WD-93044A	43.2	782	4	27	—	—
WD-93048A	43.2	782	4	27	—	—
WD-95028A	21.6	782	2	27	—	—
WD-95044A	43.2	782	4	27	—	—
WD-95048A	43.2	782	4	27	—	—
WD-AC140	42.6	980	5	17	—	—
WD-AC280	85.3	980	10	17	—	—
WD-AP4200	212.2	987	12	35	—	—
WD-SP4200	209.7	1,280	8	40	—	—
WD-SC8320	326.5	949	14	48	—	—
WD-SC8400	413.2	1,201	14	48	—	—

— = *No write precompensation required, or no parking cylinder required (autopark)*

Appendixes

Table A.25 Seagate Hard Disk Drive Specifications

Seagate Model #	Imprimis Model #	Cyls	Hds	WPC	Park Cyl	Sectors/ Track	Capacity (MB)	Total Sectors
ST1057a		1024	6	-1	1024	17*	53.5	104448
ST1090a	94354-90	1072	5	-1	1072	29	79.6	155440
Opt. CMOS Values:		335	16	335	335	29	79.6	155440
ST1090n	94351-90	1068	5	-1	1068	29	79.3	154860
ST1096n		906	7	-1	906	26	84.4	164892
ST1100	94355-100	1072	9	-1	1072	17	84.0	164016
ST1102a		1024	10	-1	1024	17*	89.1	174080
ST1106r		977	7	-1	977	26	91.0	177814
ST1111a	94354-111	1072	5	-1	1072	36	98.8	192960
Opt. CMOS Values:		402	10	402	402	48	98.8	192960
ST1111e	94356-111	1072	5	-1	1072	36	98.8	192960
ST1111n	94351-111	1068	5	-1	1068	36	98.4	192240
ST11200n		1872	15	-1	1872	73*	1049.5	2049840
ST1126a	94354-126	1072	7	-1	1072	29	111.4	217616
Opt. CMOS Values:		469	16	469	469	29	111.4	217616
ST1126n	94351-125	1068	7	-1	1068	29	111.0	216804
ST1133a	94354-133	1272	5	-1	1272	36	117.2	228960
Opt. CMOS Values:		477	8	477	477	60	117.2	228960
ST1133n	94351-133s	1268	5	-1	1268	36	116.9	228240
ST1144a		1001	15	-1	1001	17*	130.7	255255
ST1150r	94355-150	1072	9	300	1072	26	128.4	250848
ST1156a	94354-156	1072	7	-1	1072	36	138.3	270144
Opt. CMOS Values:		536	9	536	536	56	138.3	270144
ST1156e	94356-156	1072	7	-1	1072	36	138.3	270144
ST1156n	94351-155	1068	7	-1	1068	36	137.8	269136
ST1156r	94355-156	1072	7	300	1072	36	138.3	270144
ST1162a	94354-162	1072	9	-1	1072	29	143.3	279792
Opt. CMOS Values:		603	16	603	603	29	143.3	279792
ST1162n	94351-160	1068	9	-1	1068	29	142.7	278748
ST1182e		972	9	-1	972	36	161.2	314928
ST1186a	94354-186	1272	7	-1	1272	36	164.1	320544
Opt. CMOS Values:		636	9	636	636	56	164.1	320544
ST1186n	94351-186	1268	7	-1	1268	36	163.6	319536
ST11950n		2706	15	-1	2706	99*	2057.4	4018410
ST1201a	94354-201	1072	9	-1	1072	36	177.8	347328
Opt. CMOS Values:		804	9	804	804	48	177.8	347328
ST1201e	94356-201	1072	9	-1	1072	36	177.8	347328
ST1201n	94351-200	1068	9	-1	1068	36	177.2	346032
ST1239a	94354-239	1272	9	-1	1272	36	211.0	412128
Opt. CMOS Values:		848	9	848	848	54	211.0	412128
ST1239n	94351-230	1268	9	-1	1268	36	210.3	410832
ST124		615	4	-1	670	17	21.4	41820
ST12400n		2626	19	-1	2626	82*	2094.7	4091308
ST125		615	4	-1	615	17	21.4	41820
ST125-1		615	4	-1	615	17	21.4	41820
ST12550N		2707	19	—	2707	81*	2133.0	4166073
ST12551N		2707	19	—	2707	81*	2133.0	4166073

Seagate Model #	Imprimis Model #	Cyls	Hds	WPC	Park Cyl	Sectors/ Track	Capacity (MB)	Total Sectors
ST12550ND		2707	19	—	2707	81*	2133.0	4166073
ST12551ND		2707	19	—	2707	81*	2133.0	4166073
ST125a Opt. CMOS Values:		404 615	4 4	-1 615	404 615	26 17	21.5 21.4	42016 41820
ST125n		407	4	-1	408	26	21.7	42328
ST137r		615	6	-1	670	26	49.1	95940
ST138		615	6	-1	615	17	32.1	62730
ST138a Opt. CMOS Values:		604 615	4 6	-1 615	604 615	26 17	32.2 32.1	62816 62730
ST138n		615	4	-1	615	26	32.7	63960
ST138r		615	4	-1	615	26	32.7	63960
ST1400a		1018	12	-1	1018	53*	331.5	647448
ST1400n		1476	7	-1	1476	62*	328.0	640584
ST1400ns		1476	7	-1	1476	62*	328.0	640584
ST1401a		726	15	-1	726	61*	340.1	664290
ST1401n		1100	9	-1	1100	66*	334.5	653400
ST1401ns		1100	9	-1	1100	66*	334.5	653400
ST1480a Opt. CMOS Values:		1474 1015	9 15	-1 1015	1474 1015	62* 54*	421.1 420.9	822492 822150
ST1480n		1476	9	-1	1476	62*	421.7	823608
ST1480ns		1476	9	-1	1476	62*	421.7	823608
ST1481n		1476	9	-1	1476	62*	421.7	823608
ST151		977	5	-1	977	17	42.5	83045
ST157a Opt. CMOS Values:		560 733	6 7	-1 733	560 733	26 17	44.7 44.7	87360 87227
ST157n		615	6	-1	615	26	49.1	95940
ST157r		615	6	-1	615	26	49.1	95940
ST1581n		1476	9	-1	1476	77*	523.7	1022868
ST177n		921	5	-1	921	26	61.3	119730
ST1980n		1730	13	-1	1730	74*	852.1	1664260
ST2106e	94216-106	1024	5	-1	1024	36	94.4	184320
ST2106n	94211-091	1024	5	-1	1024	36	94.4	184320
ST2106n	94211-106	1024	5	-1	1024	36	94.4	184320
ST2106nm	94211-106	1024	5	-1	1024	36	94.4	184320
ST212		306	4	128	319	17	10.7	20808
ST2125n	94221-125	1544	3	-1	1544	45*	106.7	208440
ST2125nm	94221-125	1544	3	-1	1544	45*	106.7	208440
ST2125nv	94221-125	1544	3	-1	1544	45*	106.7	208440
ST213		615	2	300	670	17	10.7	20910
ST2182e	94246-182	1453	4	-1	1453	54	160.7	313848
ST2209n	94221-209	1544	5	-1	1544	45*	177.9	347400
ST2209nm	94221-209m	1544	5	-1	1544	45*	177.9	347400
ST2209nv	94221-209	1544	5	-1	1544	45*	177.9	347400
ST224n		615	2	-1	615	17	10.7	20910
ST225		615	4	300	670	17	21.4	41820

(continues)

Table A.25   Continued

Seagate Model #	Imprimis Model #	Cyls	Hds	WPC	Park Cyl	Sectors/ Track	Capacity (MB)	Total Sectors
ST225n		615	4	-1	615	17	21.4	41820
ST225r		667	2	-1	670	31	21.2	41354
ST2274a	94244-274	1747	5	-1	1747	54	241.5	471690
Opt. CMOS Values:		536	16	536	536	55	241.5	471680
ST238		615	4	-1	670	26	32.7	63960
ST2383a	94244-383	1747	7	-1	1747	54	338.1	660366
Opt. CMOS Values:		737	16	737	737	56	338.1	660352
ST2383e	94246-383	1747	7	-1	1747	54	338.1	660366
ST2383n	94241-383	1260	7	-1	1260	74*	334.2	652680
ST2383nm	94241-383	1260	7	-1	1260	74*	334.2	652680
ST238r		615	4	-1	670	26	32.7	63960
ST2502n	94241-502	1756	7	-1	1755	69*	434.3	848148
ST2502nm	94241-502	1756	7	-1	1755	69*	434.3	848148
ST2502nv	94241-502	1756	7	-1	1755	69*	434.3	848148
ST250n		667	4	-1	670	31	42.3	82708
ST250r		667	4	-1	670	31	42.3	82708
ST251		820	6	-1	820	17	42.8	83640
ST251n-0		820	4	-1	820	26	43.7	85280
ST251n-1		630	4	-1	630	34	43.9	85680
ST252		820	6	-1	820	17	42.8	83640
ST253	94205-51	989	5	128	989	17	43.0	84065
ST274a	94204-74	948	5	-1	948	27	65.5	127980
ST277n-0		820	6	-1	820	26	65.5	127920
ST277n-1		628	6	-1	628	34	65.6	128112
ST277r		820	6	-1	820	26	65.5	127920
ST278r		820	6	-1	820	26	65.5	127920
ST279r	94205-77	989	5	-1	989	26	65.8	128570
ST280a	94204-71	1032	5	-1	1032	27	71.3	139320
Opt. CMOS Values:		1024	8	1024	1024	17	71.3	139264
ST280a	94204-81	1032	5	-1	1032	27	71.3	139320
Opt. CMOS Values:		1024	8	1024	1024	17	71.3	139264
ST296n		820	6	-1	820	34	85.6	167280
ST3051a		820	6	-1	820	17	42.8	83640
ST3096a		1024	10	-1	1024	17	89.1	174080
ST31200n		2626	9	-1	2626	79*	955.9	1867086
ST3120a		1024	12	-1	1024	17*	107.0	208896
ST3123a		1024	12	-1	1024	17*	107.0	208896
ST3144a		1001	15	-1	1001	17*	130.7	255255
ST3145a		1001	15	-1	1001	17*	130.7	255255
ST3195a		981	10	-1	981	34*	170.8	333540
ST3243a		1024	12	-1	1024	34*	213.9	417792
ST325a		615	4	-1	615	17	21.4	41820
ST325a/x		615	4	-1	615	17	21.4	41820
ST325n		654	2	-1	654	32	21.4	41856
ST325x		615	4	-1	615	17	21.4	41820
ST3283a		978	14	-1	978	35*	245.4	479220

Seagate Model #	Imprimis Model #	Cyls	Hds	WPC	Park Cyl	Sectors/ Track	Capacity (MB)	Total Sectors
ST3283n		1689	5	-1	1689	57*	246.5	481365
ST3290a		1001	15	-1	1001	34*	261.4	510510
ST3385a		767	14	-1	767	62*	340.9	665756
ST3390a		768	14	-1	768	62*	341.3	666624
ST3390n		2676	3	-1	2676	83*	341.2	666324
ST3500a		895	15	-1	895	62*	426.2	832350
ST351a		820	6	-1	820	17	42.8	83640
ST351a/x		820	6	-1	820	17	42.8	83640
ST351x		820	6	-1	820	17	42.8	83640
ST3550a		1018	14	-1	1018	62*	452.4	883624
ST3550n		2126	5	-1	2126	83*	451.7	882290
ST3600a Opt. CMOS Values:		1872 1024	7 16	-1 1024	1872 1024	79* 63*	530.0 528.5	1035216 1032192
ST3600n		1872	7	-1	1872	79*	530.0	1035216
ST3610n		1872	7	-1	1872	52*	348.9	681408
ST3655a		1024	16	-1	1024	63*	528.5	1032192
ST3655n		2676	5	-1	2676	79*	541.2	1057020
ST4026		615	4	-1	670	17	21.4	41820
ST4038		733	5	-1	733	17	31.9	62305
ST4038m		733	5	-1	733	17	31.9	62305
ST4051		977	5	-1	977	17	42.5	83045
ST4053		1024	5	-1	1024	17	44.6	87040
ST406		306	2	128	319	17	5.3	10404
ST4085		1024	8	-1	1024	17	71.3	39264
ST4086	94155-86	925	9	-1	925	17	72.5	141525
ST4086p	94155-86p	925	9	128	925	17	72.5	141525
ST4096		1024	9	-1	1024	17	80.2	156672
ST4097	94155-96	1024	9	-1	1024	17	80.2	156672
ST4097p	94155-96p	1024	9	128	1024	17	80.2	156672
ST412		306	4	128	319	17	10.7	20808
ST41200n	94601-12g	1931	15	-1	1931	71*	1052.9	2056515
ST41200nm	94601-12g	1931	15	-1	1931	71*	1052.9	2056515
ST41200nv	94601-12g	1931	15	-1	1931	71*	1052.9	2056515
ST4135r	94155-135	960	9	-1	960	26	115.0	224640
ST4144r		1024	9	-1	1024	26	122.7	239616
ST41520n		2101	17	-1	2101	77*	1408.1	2750209
ST41600n		2098	17	-1	2098	74*	1351.3	2639284
ST41650n		2110	15	-1	2110	88*	1426.0	2785200
ST41651n		2107	15	-1	2107	87*	1407.8	2749635
ST4182e	94166-155	969	9	-1	969	36	160.7	313956
ST4182e	94166-182	969	9	-1	969	36	160.7	313956
ST4182n	94161-182	967	9	-1	967	36	160.4	313308
ST4182nm	94161-182	967	9	-1	967	36	160.4	313308
ST419		306	6	128	319	17	16.0	31212

(continues)

Appendixes

Table A.25 Continued								
Seagate Model #	Imprimis Model #	Cyls	Hds	WPC	Park Cyl	Sectors/ Track	Capacity (MB)	Total Sectors
ST42000n		2624	16	-1	2624	83*	1784.2	3484672
ST42100n		2573	15	-1	2573	96*	1897.0	3705120
ST42400n		2624	19	-1	2624	83*	2118.7	4138048
ST425		306	8	128	319	17	21.3	41616
ST43400n		2735	21	-1	2735	99*	2911.3	5686065
ST4350n	94171-300	1412	9	-1	1412	46*	299.3	584568
ST4350n	94171-307	1412	9	-1	1412	46*	299.3	584568
ST4350n	94171-327	1412	9	-1	1412	46*	299.3	584568
ST4350n	94171-350	1412	9	-1	1412	46*	299.3	584568
ST4350nm	94171-327	1412	9	-1	1412	46*	299.3	584568
ST4376n	94171-344	1549	9	-1	1549	45*	321.2	627345
ST4376n	94171-376	1549	9	-1	1549	45*	321.2	627345
ST4376nm	94171-344	1549	9	-1	1549	45*	321.2	627345
ST4376nv	94171-344	1549	9	-1	1549	45*	321.2	627345
ST4383e	94186-383	1412	13	-1	1412	36	338.3	660816
ST4384e	94186-383h	1224	15	-1	1224	36	338.4	660960
ST4385n	94181-385h	791	15	-1	791	55*	334.1	652575
ST4385nm	94181-385h	791	15	-1	791	55*	334.1	652575
ST4385nv	94181-385h	791	15	-1	791	55*	334.1	652575
ST4442e	94186-442	1412	15	-1	1412	36	390.4	762480
ST4702n	94181-702	1546	15	-1	1546	50*	593.7	1159500
ST4702nm	94181-702	1546	15	-1	1546	50*	593.7	1159500
ST4766e	94196-766	1632	15	-1	1632	54	676.8	1321920
ST4766n	94191-766	1632	15	-1	1632	54	676.8	1321920
ST4766nm	94191-766	1632	15	-1	1632	54	676.8	1321920
ST4766nv	94191-766	1632	15	-1	1632	54	676.8	1321920
ST4767e		1399	15	-1	1399	63	676.9	1322055
ST4767n	94601-767h	1356	15	-1	1356	64*	666.5	1301760
ST4767nm	94601-767h	1356	15	-1	1356	64*	666.5	1301760
ST4767nv	94601-767h	1356	15	-1	1356	64*	666.5	1301760
ST4769e		1552	15	-1	1552	58	691.3	1350240
ST506		153	4	128	157	17	5.3	10404
ST9025a		1024	4	-1	1024	17	35.7	69632
ST9051a		1024	6	-1	1024	17	53.5	104448
ST9052a		980	5	-1	980	17*	42.6	83300
ST9077a		669	11	-1	669	17	64.1	125103
ST9080a		823	4	-1	823	38*	64.0	125096
ST9096a		980	10	-1	980	17*	85.3	166600
ST9100a		748	14	-1	748	16*	85.8	167552
ST9140a		980	15	-1	980	17*	127.9	249900
ST9144a		980	15	-1	980	17*	127.9	249900
ST9145a		980	15	-1	980	17*	127.9	249900

Seagate Model #	Imprimis Model #	Cyls	Hds	WPC	Park Cyl	Sectors/ Track	Capacity (MB)	Total Sectors
ST9190a		873	16	-1	873	24*	171.6	335232
ST9235a		985	13	-1	985	32*	209.8	409760
ST9235n		985	13	-1	985	32*	209.8	409760
ST——	9415-521	697	3	0	697	17	18.2	35547
ST——	9415-525	697	4	0	697	17	24.3	47396
ST——	9415-536	697	5	0	697	17	30.3	59245
ST——	9415-538	733	5	0	733	17	31.9	62305
ST——	94151-42	921	5	-1	921	17	40.1	78285
ST——	94151-62	921	7	-1	921	17	56.1	109599
ST——	94151-80	921	9	-1	921	17	72.1	140913
ST——	94155-48	925	5	-1	925	17	40.3	78625
ST——	94155-48p	925	5	128	925	17	40.3	78625
ST——	94155-57	925	6	-1	925	17	48.3	94350
ST——	94155-57p	925	6	128	925	17	48.3	94350
ST——	94155-67	925	7	-1	925	17	56.4	110075
ST——	94155-67p	925	7	128	925	17	56.4	110075
ST——	94155-92	989	9	-1	989	17	77.5	151317
ST——	94155-92p	989	9	128	989	17	77.5	151317
ST——	94155-130	024	9	128	1024	26	122.7	239616
ST——	94156-48	925	9	-1	925	17	72.5	141525
ST——	94156-67	925	7	-1	925	17	56.4	110075
ST——	94156-86	925	7	-1	925	17	56.4	110075
ST——	94161-86	969	5	-1	969	35	86.8	169575
ST——	94161-103	969	6	-1	969	35	104.2	203490
ST——	94161-121	969	7	-1	969	35	121.6	237405
ST——	94161-138	969	8	-1	969	35	138.9	271320
ST——	94166-86	969	5	-1	969	35	86.8	169575
ST——	94166-103	969	6	-1	969	35	104.2	203490
ST——	94166-121	969	7	-1	969	35	121.6	237405
ST——	94166-138	969	8	-1	969	35	138.9	271320
ST——	94244-219	1747	4	-1	1747	54	193.2	377352
Opt. CMOS Values:		536	16	536	536	44	193.2	377344

* Because these drives use zoned recording, the sectors-per-track value is an average, rounded down to the next-lower integer.
"Opt. CMOS Values" indicates optional translated values for the preceeding drive in the table which can be entered if the CMOS Setup program will not accept the actual values for the drive.

Seagate Model designations follow a specific format shown as follows:

ST-FXXXI PR-A

The various parts of each model number designation have meanings according to the following tables.

Table A.26 Hard Drive Model Number Code Legent

Code	Description
ST	Seagate Technologies
F	Form factor (see following table)
XXX	Unformatted capacity in MB
I	Interface type (see following table)
PR	Paired Solution (shipped with controller and installation software)
A	Access time; 0 = Standard, 1= Fast

Table A.27 F-Code Descriptions

F-Code	Description
1	3.5-inch, half-height (41mm)
2	5.25-inch, half-height (41mm)
3	3.5-inch, 1-inch high (25mm)
4	5.25-inch, full-height (82mm)
6	9-inch
8	8-inch
9	2.5-inch, .75-inch high (19mm)

Table A.28 I-Code Descriptions

I Code	Description
None	ST-412 MFM interface
R	ST-412 (RLL certified) interface
E	ESDI interface
A	ATA (AT Attachment) IDE interface
X	XT-Bus (8-bit) IDE interface
A/X	Switchable ATA IDE or XT-Bus interface
M or P	Modified Precompensation
N	SCSI Single Ended (SE) interface
NM	SCSI SE interface (Macintosh Plus)
NV	SCSI SE interface (Novell NetWare)
NS	SCSI SE interface (Synchronized Spindle)
ND	SCSI Differential interface

For example, the model designation ST112550N equates to a 3.5-inch half-height drive with an unformatted capacity of approximately 2550MB, and a SCSI Single Ended interface.

AT Motherboard BIOS Hard Drive Tables

This section consists of motherboard ROM BIOS hard disk parameters for AT systems. The following explains the column headings used in tables A.29–A.39:

Type = Drive type number

Cylinders = Total number of cylinders

Heads = Total number of heads

WPC = Write precompensation starting cylinder

65535 = No write precompensation

0 = Write precompensation on all cylinders

Ctrl = Control byte, with values according to the following table.

Bit Number	Hex	Meaning
Bit 0	01h	Not used (XT = drive step rate)
Bit 1	02h	Not used (XT = drive step rate)
Bit 2	04h	Not used (XT = drive step rate)
Bit 3	08h	More than eight heads
Bit 4	10h	Not used (XT = imbedded servo drive)
Bit 5	20h	OEM defect map at (cylinders + 1)
Bit 6	40h	Disable ECC retries
Bit 7	80h	Disable disk access retries

LZ = Landing-zone cylinder for head parking
S/T = Number of sectors per track
Meg = Drive capacity in megabytes
MB = Drive capacity in millions of bytes

Table A.29 shows the IBM motherboard ROM BIOS hard disk parameters for AT or PS/2 systems using ST-506/412 (standard or IDE) controllers.

Table A.29   IBM AT and PS/2 BIOS Hard Disk Table

Type	Cylinders	Heads	WPC	Ctrl	LZ	S/T	Meg	MB
1	306	4	128	00h	305	17	10.16	10.65
2	615	4	300	00h	615	17	20.42	21.41
3	615	6	300	00h	615	17	30.63	32.12
4	940	8	512	00h	940	17	62.42	65.45
5	940	6	512	00h	940	17	46.82	49.09
6	615	4	65535	00h	615	17	20.42	21.41
7	462	8	256	00h	511	17	30.68	32.17
8	733	5	65535	00h	733	17	30.42	31.90
9	900	15	65535	08h	901	17	112.06	117.50
10	820	3	65535	00h	820	17	20.42	21.41
11	855	5	65535	00h	855	17	35.49	37.21
12	855	7	65535	00h	855	17	49.68	52.09
13	306	8	128	00h	319	17	20.32	21.31
14	733	7	65535	00h	733	17	42.59	44.66
15	0	0	0	00h	0	0	0	0
16	612	4	0	00h	663	17	20.32	21.31
17	977	5	300	00h	977	17	40.55	42.52
18	977	7	65535	00h	977	17	56.77	59.53
19	1024	7	512	00h	1023	17	59.50	62.39
20	733	5	300	00h	732	17	30.42	31.90
21	733	7	300	00h	732	17	42.59	44.66
22	733	5	300	00h	733	17	30.42	31.90
23	306	4	0	00h	336	17	10.16	10.65
24	612	4	305	00h	663	17	20.32	21.31
25	306	4	65535	00h	340	17	10.16	10.65
26	612	4	65535	00h	670	17	20.32	21.31
27	698	7	300	20h	732	17	40.56	42.53

Appendixes

(continues)

Type	Cylinders	Heads	WPC	Ctrl	LZ	S/T	Meg	MB
Table A.29 Continued								
28	976	5	488	20h	977	17	40.51	42.48
29	306	4	0	00h	340	17	10.16	10.65
30	611	4	306	20h	663	17	20.29	21.27
31	732	7	300	20h	732	17	42.53	44.60
32	1023	5	65535	20h	1023	17	42.46	44.52
33	614	4	65535	20h	663	25	29.98	31.44
34	775	2	65535	20h	900	27	20.43	21.43
35	921	2	65535	20h	1000	33	29.68	31.12
36	402	4	65535	20h	460	26	20.41	21.41
37	580	6	65535	20h	640	26	44.18	46.33
38	845	2	65535	20h	1023	36	29.71	31.15
39	769	3	65535	20h	1023	36	40.55	42.52
40	531	4	65535	20h	532	39	40.45	42.41
41	577	2	65535	20h	1023	36	20.29	21.27
42	654	2	65535	20h	674	32	20.44	21.43
43	923	5	65535	20h	1023	36	81.12	85.06
44	531	8	65535	20h	532	39	80.89	84.82
45	0	0	0	00h	0	0	0.00	0.00
46	0	0	0	00h	0	0	0.00	0.00
47	0	0	0	00h	0	0	0.00	0.00

The landing zone and sectors per track fields are not used in the 10MB (original) controller and contain 00h values for each entry.

Table entry 15 is reserved to act as a pointer to indicate that the type is greater than 15. Most IBM systems do not have every entry in this table. The maximum usable type number varies for each particular ROM version. The maximum usable type for each IBM ROM is indicated in table A.8 on IBM ROM versions, earlier in this appendix. If you have a compatible, this table may be inaccurate for many of the entries past type 15. Instead, you should see whether one of the other tables listed here applies to your specific compatible ROM. Most compatibles follow the IBM table for at least the first 15 entries.

Most IBM PS/2 systems now are supplied with hard disk drives that have the defect map written as data on the cylinder one cylinder beyond the highest reported cylinder. This special data is read by the IBM PS/2 Advanced Diagnostics low-level format program. This process automates the entry of the defect list and eliminates the chance of human error, as long as you use only the IBM PS/2 Advanced Diagnostics for hard disk low-level formatting.

This type of table does not apply to IBM ESDI or SCSI hard disk controllers, host adapters, and drives. Because the ESDI and SCSI controllers or host adapters query the drive directly for the required parameters, no table-entry selection is necessary. Note, however, that the table for the ST-506/412 drives can still be found currently in the ROM BIOS of most of the PS/2 systems, even if the model came standard with an ESDI or SCSI disk subsystem.

Table A.30 shows the Compaq motherboard ROM BIOS hard disk parameters for the Compaq Deskpro 386.

Type	Cylinders	Heads	WPC	Ctrl	LZ	S/T	Meg	MB

Table A.30 Compaq Deskpro 386 Hard Disk Table

Type	Cylinders	Heads	WPC	Ctrl	LZ	S/T	Meg	MB
1	306	4	128	00h	305	17	10.16	10.65
2	615	4	128	00h	638	17	20.42	21.41
3	615	6	128	00h	615	17	30.63	32.12
4	1024	8	512	00h	1023	17	68.00	71.30
5	940	6	512	00h	939	17	46.82	49.09
6	697	5	128	00h	696	17	28.93	30.33
7	462	8	256	00h	511	17	30.68	32.17
8	925	5	128	00h	924	17	38.39	40.26
9	900	15	65535	08h	899	17	112.06	117.50
10	980	5	65535	00h	980	17	40.67	42.65
11	925	7	128	00h	924	17	53.75	56.36
12	925	9	128	08h	924	17	69.10	72.46
13	612	8	256	00h	611	17	40.64	42.61
14	980	4	128	00h	980	17	32.54	34.12
15	0	0	0	00h	0	0	0	0
16	612	4	0	00h	612	17	20.32	21.31
17	980	5	128	00h	980	17	40.67	42.65
18	966	6	128	00h	966	17	48.11	50.45
19	1023	8	65535	00h	1023	17	67.93	71.23
20	733	5	256	00h	732	17	30.42	31.90
21	733	7	256	00h	732	17	42.59	44.66
22	805	6	65535	00h	805	17	40.09	42.04
23	924	8	65535	00h	924	17	61.36	64.34
24	966	14	65535	08h	966	17	112.26	117.71
25	966	16	65535	08h	966	17	128.30	134.53
26	1023	14	65535	08h	1023	17	118.88	124.66
27	966	10	65535	08h	966	17	80.19	84.08
28	748	16	65535	08h	748	17	99.34	104.17
29	805	6	65535	00h	805	26	61.32	64.30
30	615	4	128	00h	615	25	30.03	31.49
31	615	8	128	00h	615	25	60.06	62.98
32	905	9	128	08h	905	25	99.43	104.26
33	748	8	65535	00h	748	34	99.34	104.17
34	966	7	65535	00h	966	34	112.26	117.71
35	966	8	65535	00h	966	34	128.30	134.53
36	966	9	65535	08h	966	34	144.33	151.35
37	966	5	65535	00h	966	34	80.19	84.08
38	611	16	65535	08h	611	63	300.73	315.33
39	1023	11	65535	08h	1023	33	181.32	190.13
40	1023	15	65535	08h	1023	34	254.75	267.13
41	1023	15	65535	08h	1023	33	247.26	259.27
42	1023	16	65535	08h	1023	63	503.51	527.97
43	805	4	65535	00h	805	26	40.88	42.86
44	805	2	65535	00h	805	26	20.44	21.43
45	748	8	65535	00h	748	33	96.42	101.11
46	748	6	65535	00h	748	33	72.32	75.83
47	966	5	128	00h	966	25	58.96	61.82

Table entry 15 is reserved to act as a pointer to indicate that the type is greater than 15.

Appendixes

Table A.31 shows the Compaq motherboard ROM BIOS hard disk parameters for the Compaq Deskpro 286 Revision F.

Table A.31	Compaq Deskpro 286 Revision F Hard Disk Table							
Type	**Cylinders**	**Heads**	**WPC**	**Ctrl**	**LZ**	**S/T**	**Meg**	**MB**
1	306	4	128	00h	305	17	10.16	10.65
2	615	4	128	00h	638	17	20.42	21.41
3	615	6	128	00h	615	17	30.63	32.12
4	1024	8	512	00h	1023	17	68.00	71.30
5	940	6	512	00h	939	17	46.82	49.09
6	697	5	128	00h	696	17	28.93	30.33
7	462	8	256	00h	511	17	30.68	32.17
8	925	5	128	00h	924	17	38.39	40.26
9	900	15	65535	08h	899	17	112.06	117.50
10	980	5	65535	00h	980	17	40.67	42.65
11	925	7	128	00h	924	17	53.75	56.36
12	925	9	128	08h	924	17	69.10	72.46
13	612	8	256	00h	611	17	40.64	42.61
14	980	4	128	00h	980	17	32.54	34.12
15	0	0	0	00h	0	0	0	0
16	612	4	0	00h	612	17	20.32	21.31
17	980	5	128	00h	980	17	40.67	42.65
18	966	6	128	00h	966	17	48.11	50.45
19	1023	8	65535	00h	1023	17	67.93	71.23
20	733	5	256	00h	732	17	30.42	31.90
21	733	7	256	00h	732	17	42.59	44.66
22	768	6	65535	00h	768	17	38.25	40.11
23	771	6	65535	00h	771	17	38.40	40.26
24	966	14	65535	08h	966	17	112.26	117.71
25	966	16	65535	08h	966	17	128.30	134.53
26	1023	14	65535	08h	1023	17	118.88	124.66
27	966	10	65535	08h	966	17	80.19	84.08
28	771	3	65535	00h	771	17	19.20	20.13
29	578	4	65535	00h	578	17	19.19	20.12
30	615	4	128	00h	615	25	30.03	31.49
31	615	8	128	00h	615	25	60.06	62.98
32	966	3	65535	00h	966	34	48.11	50.45
33	966	5	65535	00h	966	34	80.19	84.08
34	966	7	65535	00h	966	34	112.26	117.71
35	966	8	65535	00h	966	34	128.30	134.53
36	966	9	65535	08h	966	34	144.33	151.35
37	966	5	65535	00h	966	34	80.19	84.08
38	1023	9	65535	08h	1023	33	148.35	155.56
39	1023	11	65535	08h	1023	33	181.32	190.13
40	1023	13	65535	08h	1023	33	214.29	224.70
41	1023	15	65535	08h	1023	33	247.26	259.27
42	1023	16	65535	08h	1023	34	271.73	284.93

Type	Cylinders	Heads	WPC	Ctrl	LZ	S/T	Meg	MB
43	756	4	65535	00h	756	26	38.39	40.26
44	756	2	65535	00h	756	26	19.20	20.13
45	768	4	65535	00h	768	26	39.00	40.89
46	768	2	65535	00h	768	26	19.50	20.45
47	966	5	128	00h	966	25	58.96	61.82

Table entry 15 is reserved to act as a pointer to indicate that the type is greater than 15.

Table A.32 shows the Compaq motherboard ROM BIOS hard disk parameters for the Compaq Deskpro 286e Revision B (03/22/89).

Table A.32 Compaq Deskpro 286e Revision B Hard Disk Table								
Type	**Cylinders**	**Heads**	**WPC**	**Ctrl**	**LZ**	**S/T**	**Meg**	**MB**
1	306	4	128	00h	305	17	10.16	10.65
2	615	4	128	00h	638	17	20.42	21.41
3	615	6	128	00h	615	17	30.63	32.12
4	1024	8	512	00h	1023	17	68.00	71.30
5	805	6	65535	00h	805	17	40.09	42.04
6	697	5	128	00h	696	17	28.93	30.33
7	462	8	256	00h	511	17	30.68	32.17
8	925	5	128	00h	924	17	38.39	40.26
9	900	15	65535	08h	899	17	112.06	117.50
10	980	5	65535	00h	980	17	40.67	42.65
11	925	7	128	00h	924	17	53.75	56.36
12	925	9	128	08h	924	17	69.10	72.46
13	612	8	256	00h	611	17	40.64	42.61
14	980	4	128	00h	980	17	32.54	34.12
15	0	0	0	00h	0	0	0	0
16	612	4	0	00h	612	17	20.32	21.31
17	980	5	128	00h	980	17	40.67	42.65
18	966	5	128	00h	966	17	40.09	42.04
19	754	11	65535	08h	753	17	68.85	72.19
20	733	5	256	00h	732	17	30.42	31.90
21	733	7	256	00h	732	17	42.59	44.66
22	524	4	65535	00h	524	40	40.94	42.93
23	924	8	65535	00h	924	17	61.36	64.34
24	966	14	65535	08h	966	17	112.26	117.71
25	966	16	65535	08h	966	17	128.30	134.53
26	1023	14	65535	08h	1023	17	118.88	124.66
27	832	6	65535	00h	832	33	80.44	84.34
28	1222	15	65535	08h	1222	34	304.31	319.09
29	1240	7	65535	00h	1240	34	144.10	151.10
30	615	4	128	00h	615	25	30.03	31.49
31	615	8	128	00h	615	25	60.06	62.98
32	905	9	128	08h	905	25	99.43	104.26

(continues)

Appendixes

Table A.32 Continued								
Type	**Cylinders**	**Heads**	**WPC**	**Ctrl**	**LZ**	**S/T**	**Meg**	**MB**
33	832	8	65535	00h	832	33	107.25	112.46
34	966	7	65535	00h	966	34	112.26	117.71
35	966	8	65535	00h	966	34	128.30	134.53
36	966	9	65535	08h	966	34	144.33	151.35
37	966	5	65535	00h	966	34	80.19	84.08
38	611	16	65535	08h	611	63	300.73	315.33
39	1023	11	65535	08h	1023	33	181.32	190.13
40	1023	15	65535	08h	1023	34	254.75	267.13
41	1630	15	65535	08h	1630	52	620.80	650.96
42	1023	16	65535	08h	1023	63	503.51	527.97
43	805	4	65535	00h	805	26	40.88	42.86
44	805	2	65535	00h	805	26	20.44	21.43
45	748	8	65535	00h	748	33	96.42	101.11
46	748	6	65535	00h	748	33	72.32	75.83
47	966	5	128	00h	966	25	58.96	61.82

Table entry 15 is reserved to act as a pointer to indicate that the type is greater than 15.

Table A.33 shows the AMI ROM BIOS (286 BIOS version 04/30/89) hard disk parameters.

Table A.33 AMI ROM BIOS (286 BIOS Version 04/30/89) Hard Disk Table								
Type	**Cylinders**	**Heads**	**WPC**	**Ctrl**	**LZ**	**S/T**	**Meg**	**MB**
1	306	4	128	00h	305	17	10.16	10.65
2	615	4	300	00h	615	17	20.42	21.41
3	615	6	300	00h	615	17	30.63	32.12
4	940	8	512	00h	940	17	62.42	65.45
5	940	6	512	00h	940	17	46.82	49.09
6	615	4	65535	00h	615	17	20.42	21.41
7	462	8	256	00h	511	17	30.68	32.17
8	733	5	65535	00h	733	17	30.42	31.90
9	900	15	65535	08h	901	17	112.06	117.50
10	820	3	65535	00h	820	17	20.42	21.41
11	855	5	65535	00h	855	17	35.49	37.21
12	855	7	65535	00h	855	17	49.68	52.09
13	306	8	128	00h	319	17	20.32	21.31
14	733	7	65535	00h	733	17	42.59	44.66
15	0	0	0	00h	0	0	0	0
16	612	4	0	00h	663	17	20.32	21.31
17	977	5	300	00h	977	17	40.55	42.52
18	977	7	65535	00h	977	17	56.77	59.53
19	1024	7	512	00h	1023	17	59.50	62.39
20	733	5	300	00h	732	17	30.42	31.90
21	733	7	300	00h	732	17	42.59	44.66
22	733	5	300	00h	733	17	30.42	31.90
23	306	4	0	00h	336	17	10.16	10.65
24	925	7	0	00h	925	17	53.75	56.36

Type	Cylinders	Heads	WPC	Ctrl	LZ	S/T	Meg	MB
25	925	9	65535	08h	925	17	69.10	72.46
26	754	7	526	00h	754	17	43.81	45.94
27	754	11	65535	08h	754	17	68.85	72.19
28	699	7	256	00h	699	17	40.62	42.59
29	823	10	65535	08h	823	17	68.32	71.63
30	918	7	874	00h	918	17	53.34	55.93
31	1024	11	65535	08h	1024	17	93.50	98.04
32	1024	15	65535	08h	1024	17	127.50	133.69
33	1024	5	1024	00h	1024	17	42.50	44.56
34	612	2	128	00h	612	17	10.16	10.65
35	1024	9	65535	08h	1024	17	76.50	80.22
36	1024	8	512	00h	1024	17	68.00	71.30
37	615	8	128	00h	615	17	40.84	42.82
38	987	3	805	00h	987	17	24.58	25.77
39	987	7	805	00h	987	17	57.35	60.14
40	820	6	820	00h	820	17	40.84	42.82
41	977	5	815	00h	977	17	40.55	42.52
42	981	5	811	00h	981	17	40.72	42.69
43	830	7	512	00h	830	17	48.23	50.57
44	830	10	65535	08h	830	17	68.90	72.24
45	917	15	65535	08h	918	17	114.18	119.72
46	1224	15	65535	08h	1223	17	152.40	159.81
47	0	0	0	00h	0	0	0.00	0.00

Table entry 15 is reserved to act as a pointer to indicate that the type is greater than 15.
This BIOS uses type 47 as a user-definable entry.

Table A.34 shows the Award ROM BIOS (286 BIOS version 04/30/89) (Modular 286, 386SX, and 386 BIOS version 3.05) hard disk parameters.

Table A.34 Award ROM BIOS Version 3.05 Hard Disk Table								
Type	Cylinders	Heads	WPC	Ctrl	LZ	S/T	Meg	MB
1	306	4	128	00h	305	17	10.16	10.65
2	615	4	300	00h	615	17	20.42	21.41
3	615	6	300	00h	615	17	30.63	32.12
4	940	8	512	00h	940	17	62.42	65.45
5	940	6	512	00h	940	17	46.82	49.09
6	615	4	65535	00h	615	17	20.42	21.41
7	462	8	256	00h	511	17	30.68	32.17
8	733	5	65535	00h	733	17	30.42	31.90
9	900	15	65535	08h	901	17	112.06	117.50
10	820	3	65535	00h	820	17	20.42	21.41
11	855	5	65535	00h	855	17	35.49	37.21
12	855	7	65535	00h	855	17	49.68	52.09
13	306	8	128	00h	319	17	20.32	21.31
14	733	7	65535	00h	733	17	42.59	44.66

(continues)

Type	Cylinders	Heads	WPC	Ctrl	LZ	S/T	Meg	MB
Table A.34 Continued								
15	0	0	0	00h	0	0	0	0
16	612	4	0	00h	663	17	20.32	21.31
17	977	5	300	00h	977	17	40.55	42.52
18	977	7	65535	00h	977	17	56.77	59.53
19	1024	7	512	00h	1023	17	59.50	62.39
20	733	5	300	00h	732	17	30.42	31.90
21	733	7	300	00h	732	17	42.59	44.66
22	733	5	300	00h	733	17	30.42	31.90
23	306	4	0	00h	336	17	10.16	10.65
24	977	5	65535	00h	976	17	40.55	42.52
25	1024	9	65535	08h	1023	17	76.50	80.22
26	1224	7	65535	00h	1223	17	71.12	74.58
27	1224	11	65535	08h	1223	17	111.76	117.19
28	1224	15	65535	08h	1223	17	152.40	159.81
29	1024	8	65535	00h	1023	17	68.00	71.30
30	1024	11	65535	08h	1023	17	93.50	98.04
31	918	11	65535	08h	1023	17	83.82	87.89
32	925	9	65535	08h	926	17	69.10	72.46
33	1024	10	65535	08h	1023	17	85.00	89.13
34	1024	12	65535	08h	1023	17	102.00	106.95
35	1024	13	65535	08h	1023	17	110.50	115.87
36	1024	14	65535	08h	1023	17	119.00	124.78
37	1024	2	65535	00h	1023	17	17.00	17.83
38	1024	16	65535	08h	1023	17	136.00	142.61
39	918	15	65535	08h	1023	17	114.30	119.85
40	820	6	65535	00h	820	17	40.84	42.82
41	1024	5	65535	00h	1023	17	42.50	44.56
42	1024	5	65535	00h	1023	26	65.00	68.16
43	809	6	65535	00h	808	17	40.29	42.25
44	820	6	65535	00h	819	26	62.46	65.50
45	776	8	65535	00h	775	33	100.03	104.89
46	0	0	0	00h	0	0	0.00	0.00
47	0	0	0	00h	0	0	0.00	0.00

Table entry 15 is reserved to act as a pointer to indicate that the type is greater than 15.
This BIOS uses types 46 and 47 as user-definable entries.

Table A.35 shows the Award ROM BIOS hard disk parameters (modular 286, 386SX, and 386 BIOS version 3.1).

Type	Cylinders	Heads	WPC	Ctrl	LZ	S/T	Meg	MB
Table A.35 Award ROM BIOS Version 3.1 Hard Disk Table								
1	306	4	128	00h	305	17	10.16	10.65
2	615	4	300	00h	615	17	20.42	21.41
3	615	6	300	00h	615	17	30.63	32.12

Type	Cylinders	Heads	WPC	Ctrl	LZ	S/T	Meg	MB
4	940	8	512	00h	940	17	62.42	65.45
5	940	6	512	00h	940	17	46.82	49.09
6	615	4	65535	00h	615	17	20.42	21.41
7	462	8	256	00h	511	17	30.68	32.17
8	733	5	65535	00h	733	17	30.42	31.90
9	900	15	65535	08h	901	17	112.06	117.50
10	820	3	65535	00h	820	17	20.42	21.41
11	855	5	65535	00h	855	17	35.49	37.21
12	855	7	65535	00h	855	17	49.68	52.09
13	306	8	128	00h	319	17	20.32	21.31
14	733	7	65535	00h	733	17	42.59	44.66
15	0	0	0	00h	0	0	0	0
16	612	4	0	00h	663	17	20.32	21.31
17	977	5	300	00h	977	17	40.55	42.52
18	977	7	65535	00h	977	17	56.77	59.53
19	1024	7	512	00h	1023	17	59.50	62.39
20	733	5	300	00h	732	17	30.42	31.90
21	733	7	300	00h	732	17	42.59	44.66
22	733	5	300	00h	733	17	30.42	31.90
23	306	4	0	00h	336	17	10.16	10.65
24	977	5	65535	00h	976	17	40.55	42.52
25	1024	9	65535	08h	1023	17	76.50	80.22
26	1224	7	65535	00h	1223	17	71.12	74.58
27	1224	11	65535	08h	1223	17	111.76	117.19
28	1224	15	65535	08h	1223	17	152.40	159.81
29	1024	8	65535	00h	1023	17	68.00	71.30
30	1024	11	65535	08h	1023	17	93.50	98.04
31	918	11	65535	08h	1023	17	83.82	87.89
32	925	9	65535	08h	926	17	69.10	72.46
33	1024	10	65535	08h	1023	17	85.00	89.13
34	1024	12	65535	08h	1023	17	102.00	106.95
35	1024	13	65535	08h	1023	17	110.50	115.87
36	1024	14	65535	08h	1023	17	119.00	124.78
37	1024	2	65535	00h	1023	17	17.00	17.83
38	1024	16	65535	08h	1023	17	136.00	142.61
39	918	15	65535	08h	1023	17	114.30	119.85
40	820	6	65535	00h	820	17	40.84	42.82
41	1024	5	65535	00h	1023	17	42.50	44.56
42	1024	5	65535	00h	1023	26	65.00	68.16
43	809	6	65535	00h	852	17	40.29	42.25
44	809	6	65535	00h	852	26	61.62	64.62
45	776	8	65535	00h	775	33	100.03	104.89
46	684	16	65535	08h	685	38	203.06	212.93
47	615	6	65535	00h	615	17	30.63	32.12

Table entry 15 is reserved to act as a pointer to indicate that the type is greater than 15.
This BIOS uses types 48 and 49 as user-definable entries.

Table A.36 shows the Phoenix 286 ROM BIOS (80286 ROM BIOS version 3.01, dated 11/01/86) hard disk parameters.

Type	Cylinders	Heads	WPC	Ctrl	LZ	S/T	Meg	MB
Table A.36 Phoenix 286 (80286 ROM BIOS Version 3.01) Hard Disk Table								
1	306	4	128	00h	305	17	10.16	10.65
2	615	4	300	00h	638	17	20.42	21.41
3	615	6	300	00h	615	17	30.63	32.12
4	940	8	512	00h	940	17	62.42	65.45
5	940	6	512	00h	940	17	46.82	49.09
6	615	4	65535	00h	615	17	20.42	21.41
7	462	8	256	00h	511	17	30.68	32.17
8	733	5	65535	00h	733	17	30.42	31.90
9	900	15	65535	08h	901	17	112.06	117.50
10	820	3	65535	00h	820	17	20.42	21.41
11	855	5	65535	00h	855	17	35.49	37.21
12	855	7	65535	00h	855	17	49.68	52.09
13	306	8	128	00h	319	17	20.32	21.31
14	733	7	65535	00h	733	17	42.59	44.66
15	0	0	0	00h	0	0	0.00	0.00
16	612	4	0	00h	633	17	20.32	21.31
17	977	5	300	00h	977	17	40.55	42.52
18	977	7	65535	00h	977	17	56.77	59.53
19	1024	7	512	00h	1023	17	59.50	62.39
20	733	5	300	00h	732	17	30.42	31.90
21	733	7	300	00h	733	17	42.59	44.66
22	733	5	300	00h	733	17	30.42	31.90
23	0	0	0	00h	0	0	0.00	0.00
24	0	0	0	00h	0	0	0.00	0.00
25	0	0	0	00h	0	0	0.00	0.00
26	0	0	0	00h	0	0	0.00	0.00
27	0	0	0	00h	0	0	0.00	0.00
28	0	0	0	00h	0	0	0.00	0.00
29	0	0	0	00h	0	0	0.00	0.00
30	0	0	0	00h	0	0	0.00	0.00
31	0	0	0	00h	0	0	0.00	0.00
32	0	0	0	00h	0	0	0.00	0.00
33	0	0	0	00h	0	0	0.00	0.00
34	0	0	0	00h	0	0	0.00	0.00
35	0	0	0	00h	0	0	0.00	0.00
36	1024	5	512	00h	1024	17	42.50	44.56
37	830	10	65535	08h	830	17	68.90	72.24
38	823	10	256	08h	824	17	68.32	71.63
39	615	4	128	00h	664	17	20.42	21.41
40	615	8	128	00h	664	17	40.84	42.82
41	917	15	65535	08h	918	17	114.18	119.72
42	1023	15	65535	08h	1024	17	127.38	133.56
43	823	10	512	08h	823	17	68.32	71.63

Type	Cylinders	Heads	WPC	Ctrl	LZ	S/T	Meg	MB
44	820	6	65535	00h	820	17	40.84	42.82
45	1024	8	65535	00h	1024	17	68.00	71.30
46	925	9	65535	08h	925	17	69.10	72.46
47	1024	5	65535	00h	1024	17	42.50	44.56

Table entry 15 is reserved to act as a pointer to indicate that the type is greater than 15.

Table A.37 shows the Phoenix 286 ROM BIOS (286 BIOS Plus version 3.10) hard disk parameters.

Table A.37 Phoenix 286 ROM BIOS (286 BIOS Plus Version 3.10) Hard Disk Table

Type	Cylinders	Heads	WPC	Ctrl	LZ	S/T	Meg	MB
1	306	4	128	00h	305	17	10.16	10.65
2	615	4	300	00h	615	17	20.42	21.41
3	615	6	300	00h	615	17	30.63	32.12
4	940	8	512	00h	940	17	62.42	65.45
5	940	6	512	00h	940	17	46.82	49.09
6	615	4	65535	00h	615	17	20.42	21.41
7	462	8	256	00h	511	17	30.68	32.17
8	733	5	65535	00h	733	17	30.42	31.90
9	900	15	65535	08h	901	17	112.06	117.50
10	820	3	65535	00h	820	17	20.42	21.41
11	855	5	65535	00h	855	17	35.49	37.21
12	855	7	65535	00h	855	17	49.68	52.09
13	306	8	128	00h	319	17	20.32	21.31
14	733	7	65535	00h	733	17	42.59	44.66
15	0	0	0	00h	0	0	0	0
16	612	4	0	00h	663	17	20.32	21.31
17	977	5	300	00h	977	17	40.55	42.52
18	977	7	65535	00h	977	17	56.77	59.53
19	1024	7	512	00h	1023	17	59.50	62.39
20	733	5	300	00h	732	17	30.42	31.90
21	733	7	300	00h	732	17	42.59	44.66
22	733	5	300	00h	733	17	30.42	31.90
23	306	4	0	00h	336	17	10.16	10.65
24	0	0	0	00h	0	0	0.00	0.00
25	615	4	0	00h	615	17	20.42	21.41
26	1024	4	65535	00h	1023	17	34.00	35.65
27	1024	5	65535	00h	1023	17	42.50	44.56
28	1024	8	65535	00h	1023	17	68.00	71.30
29	512	8	256	00h	512	17	34.00	35.65
30	615	2	615	00h	615	17	10.21	10.71
31	989	5	0	00h	989	17	41.05	43.04
32	1020	15	65535	08h	1024	17	127.00	133.17
33	0	0	0	00h	0	0	0.00	0.00
34	0	0	0	00h	0	0	0.00	0.00
35	1024	9	1024	08h	1024	17	76.50	80.22

(continues)

Type	Cylinders	Heads	WPC	Ctrl	LZ	S/T	Meg	MB
Table A.37 Continued								
36	1024	5	512	00h	1024	17	42.50	44.56
37	830	10	65535	08h	830	17	68.90	72.24
38	823	10	256	08h	824	17	68.32	71.63
39	615	4	128	00h	664	17	20.42	21.41
40	615	8	128	00h	664	17	40.84	42.82
41	917	15	65535	08h	918	17	114.18	119.72
42	1023	15	65535	08h	1024	17	127.38	133.56
43	823	10	512	08h	823	17	68.32	71.63
44	820	6	65535	00h	820	17	40.84	42.82
45	1024	8	65535	00h	1024	17	68.00	71.30
46	925	9	65535	08h	925	17	69.10	72.46
47	699	7	256	00h	700	17	40.62	42.59

Table entry 15 is reserved to act as a pointer to indicate that the type is greater than 15. This BIOS uses types 48 and 49 as user-definable entries.

Table A.38 shows the Pheonix 386 ROM BIOS (A386 BIOS 1.01 Reference ID 08, dated 04/19/90) hard disk parameters.

Type	Cylinders	Heads	WPC	Ctrl	LZ	S/T	Meg	MB
Table A.38 Phoenix 386 ROM BIOS (A386 BIOS 1.01) Hard Disk Table								
1	306	4	128	00h	305	17	10.16	10.65
2	615	4	300	00h	615	17	20.42	21.41
3	615	6	300	00h	615	17	30.63	32.12
4	940	8	512	00h	940	17	62.42	65.45
5	940	6	512	00h	940	17	46.82	49.09
6	615	4	65535	00h	615	17	20.42	21.41
7	462	8	256	00h	511	17	30.68	32.17
8	733	5	65535	00h	733	17	30.42	31.90
9	900	15	65535	08h	901	17	112.06	117.50
10	820	3	65535	00h	820	17	20.42	21.41
11	855	5	65535	00h	855	17	35.49	37.21
12	855	7	65535	00h	855	17	49.68	52.09
13	306	8	128	00h	319	17	20.32	21.31
14	733	7	65535	00h	733	17	42.59	44.66
15	0	0	0	00h	0	0	0	0
16	987	12	65535	08h	988	35	202.41	212.24
17	977	5	300	00h	977	17	40.55	42.52
18	977	7	65535	00h	977	17	56.77	59.53
19	1024	7	512	00h	1023	17	59.50	62.39
20	733	5	300	00h	732	17	30.42	31.90
21	733	7	300	00h	732	17	42.59	44.66
22	1024	16	0	08h	0	17	136.00	142.61
23	914	14	0	08h	0	17	106.22	111.38
24	1001	15	0	08h	0	17	124.64	130.69

Type	Cylinders	Heads	WPC	Ctrl	LZ	S/T	Meg	MB
25	977	7	815	00h	977	26	86.82	91.04
26	1024	4	65535	00h	1023	17	34.00	35.65
27	1024	5	65535	00h	1023	17	42.50	44.56
28	1024	8	65535	00h	1023	17	68.00	71.30
29	980	10	812	08h	990	17	81.35	85.30
30	1024	10	0	08h	0	17	85.00	89.13
31	832	6	832	00h	832	33	80.44	84.34
32	1020	15	65535	08h	1024	17	127.00	133.17
33	776	8	0	00h	0	33	100.03	104.89
34	782	4	0	00h	862	27	41.24	43.24
35	1024	9	1024	08h	1024	17	76.50	80.22
36	1024	5	512	00h	1024	17	42.50	44.56
37	830	10	65535	08h	830	17	68.90	72.24
38	823	10	256	08h	824	17	68.32	71.63
39	980	14	65535	08h	990	30	200.98	210.74
40	615	8	128	00h	664	17	40.84	42.82
41	917	15	65535	08h	918	17	114.18	119.72
42	1023	15	65535	08h	1024	17	127.38	133.56
43	823	10	512	08h	823	17	68.32	71.63
44	820	6	65535	00h	820	17	40.84	42.82
45	1024	8	65535	00h	1024	17	68.00	71.30
46	0	0	0	00h	0	0	0.00	0.00
47	0	0	0	00h	0	0	0.00	0.00

Table entry 15 is reserved to act as a pointer to indicate that the type is greater than 15.
This BIOS uses types 46 and 47 as user-definable entries.

Table A.39 shows the Zenith motherboard BIOS (80286 Technical Reference 1988) hard disk parameters.

Table A.39	Zenith BIOS Hard Disk Table							
Type	Cylinders	Heads	WPC	Ctrl	LZ	S/T	Meg	MB
1	306	4	128	00h	305	17	10.16	10.65
2	615	4	300	00h	615	17	20.42	21.41
3	699	5	256	00h	710	17	29.01	30.42
4	940	8	512	00h	940	17	62.42	65.45
5	940	6	512	00h	940	17	46.82	49.09
6	615	4	65535	00h	615	17	20.42	21.41
7	699	7	256	00h	710	17	40.62	42.59
8	733	5	65535	00h	733	17	30.42	31.90
9	900	15	65535	08h	901	17	112.06	117.50
10	925	5	0	00h	926	17	38.39	40.26
11	855	5	65535	00h	855	17	35.49	37.21
12	855	7	65535	00h	855	17	49.68	52.09
13	306	8	128	00h	319	17	20.32	21.31

(continues)

Appendixes

Table A.39 Continued

Type	Cylinders	Heads	WPC	Ctrl	LZ	S/T	Meg	MB
14	733	7	65535	00h	733	17	42.59	44.66
15	0	0	0	00h	0	0	0	0
16	612	4	0	00h	663	17	20.32	21.31
17	977	5	300	00h	977	17	40.55	42.52
18	977	7	65535	00h	977	17	56.77	59.53
19	1024	7	512	00h	1023	17	59.50	62.39
20	733	5	300	00h	732	17	30.42	31.90
21	733	7	300	00h	732	17	42.59	44.66
22	733	5	300	00h	733	17	30.42	31.90
23	306	4	0	00h	336	17	10.16	10.65
24	612	2	65535	00h	611	17	10.16	10.65
25	615	6	300	00h	615	17	30.63	32.12
26	462	8	256	00h	511	17	30.68	32.17
27	820	3	65535	00h	820	17	20.42	21.41
28	981	7	65535	00h	986	17	57.00	59.77
29	754	11	65535	08h	754	17	68.85	72.19
30	918	15	65535	08h	918	17	114.30	119.85
31	987	5	65535	00h	987	17	40.96	42.95
32	830	6	400	00h	830	17	41.34	43.35
33	697	4	0	00h	696	17	23.14	24.27
34	615	4	65535	00h	615	17	20.42	21.41
35	615	4	128	00h	663	17	20.42	21.41
36	1024	9	65535	08h	1024	17	76.50	80.22
37	1024	5	512	00h	1024	17	42.50	44.56
38	820	6	65535	00h	910	17	40.84	42.82
39	615	4	306	00h	684	17	20.42	21.41
40	925	9	0	08h	924	17	69.10	72.46
41	1024	8	512	00h	1023	17	68.00	71.30
42	1024	5	1024	00h	1023	17	42.50	44.56
43	615	8	300	00h	615	17	40.84	42.82
44	989	5	0	00h	988	17	41.05	43.04
45	0	0	0	00h	0	0	0.00	0.00
46	0	0	0	00h	0	0	0.00	0.00
47	0	0	0	00h	0	0	0.00	0.00

Table entry 15 is reserved to act as a pointer to indicate that the type is greater than 15.

Troubleshooting Error Codes

The following sections list a variety of system error codes. Included are manufacturer test POST codes, display POST error codes, and advanced diagnostics error codes. This section includes also a detailed list of SCSI interface error codes, which can be very helpful in troubleshooting SCSI devices.

ROM BIOS Port 80h Power-On Self Test (POST) Codes

When the ROM BIOS is performing the Power-On Self Test, in most systems the results of these tests are sent to I/O Port 80h so they can be monitored by a special diagnostics card. These tests some-times are called *manufacturing tests* because they were designed into the system for testing systems on the assembly line without a video display attached. The POST-code cards have a two-digit hexadecimal display used to report the number of the currently executing test routine. Before executing each test, a hexadecimal numeric code is sent to the port, and then the test is run. If the test fails and locks up the machine, the hexadecimal code of the last test being executed remains on the card's display.

Many tests are executed in a system before the video display card is enabled, especially if the display is EGA or VGA. Therefore, many errors can occur that would lock up the system before the system could possibly display an error code through the video system. To most normal troubleshooting procedures, a system with this type of problem (such as a memory failure in Bank 0) would appear completely "dead." By using one of the commercially available POST-code cards, however, you can correctly diagnose the problem.

These codes are completely BIOS dependent because the card does nothing but display the codes sent to it. Some BIOSs have better Power-On Self Test procedures and therefore send more informative codes. Some BIOS versions also send audio codes that can be used to help diagnose such problems. The Phoenix BIOS, for example, sends the most informative set of audio codes, which eliminates the need for a Port 80h POST card. Tables A.46, A.47, and A.48 list the Port 80h codes and audio codes sent by a number of different BIOS manufacturers and versions.

AMI BIOS Audio and Port 80h Error Codes

Table A.40 AMI BIOS Audio POST Codes

Beep Code	Fatal Errors	Beep Code	Nonfatal Errors
1 short	DRAM refresh failure	1 long, 3 short	Conventional/extended memory failure
2 short	Parity circuit failure	1 long, 8 short	Display/retrace test failed
3 short	Base 64K RAM failure		
4 short	System timer failure		
5 short	Processor failure		
6 short	Keyboard controller Gate A20 error		
7 short	Virtual mode exception error		
8 short	Display memory Read/Write test failure		
9 short	ROM BIOS checksum failure		
10 short	CMOS Shutdown Read/Write error		
11 short	Cache Memory error		

Table A.41 AMI 286 BIOS Plus Port 80h POST Codes

Checkpoint	Meaning	Checkpoint	Meaning
01h	NMI disabled and 286 register test about to start	0Ch	Refresh and system timer OK
		0Dh	Refresh link toggling OK
02h	286 register test over	0Eh	Refresh period On/Off 50% OK
03h	ROM checksum OK	10h	Confirmed refresh On and about
04h	8259 initialization OK		to start 64K memory
05h	CMOS pending interrupt disabled	11h	Address line test OK
		12h	64K base memory test OK
06h	Video disabled and system timer counting OK	13h	Interrupt vectors initialized
		14h	8042 keyboard controller test OK
07h	CH-2 of 8253 test OK	15h	CMOS read/write test OK
08h	CH-2 of delta count test OK	16h	CMOS checksum/battery check
09h	CH-1 delta count test OK		OK
0Ah	CH-0 delta count test OK	17h	Monochrome mode set OK
0Bh	Parity status cleared	18h	Color mode set OK

(continues)

Table A.41   Continued

Checkpoint	Meaning	Checkpoint	Meaning
19h	About to look for optional video ROM	53h	DMA CH-2 base register test OK
		54h	About to test f/f latch for unit-1
1Ah	Optional video ROM control OK	55h	f/f latch test both unit OK
1Bh	Display memory R/W test OK	56h	DMA unit 1 and 2 programmed OK
1Ch	Display memory R/W test for alternate display OK	57h	8259 initialization over
1Dh	Video retrace check OK	58h	8259 mask register check OK
1Eh	Global equipment byte set for video OK	59h	Master 8259 mask register OK, about to start slave
1Fh	Mode set call for Mono/Color OK	5Ah	About to check timer and keyboard interrupt level
20h	Video test OK		
21h	Video display OK	5Bh	Timer interrupt OK
22h	Power-on message display OK	5Ch	About to test keyboard interrupt
30h	Virtual mode memory test about to begin	5Dh	ERROR! timer/keyboard interrupt not in proper level
31h	Virtual mode memory test started	5Eh	8259 interrupt controller error
32h	Processor in virtual mode	5Fh	8259 interrupt controller test OK
33h	Memory address line test in progress	70h	Start of keyboard test
		71h	Keyboard BAT test OK
34h	Memory address line test in progress	72h	Keyboard test OK
		73h	Keyboard global data initialization OK
35h	Memory below IMB calculated		
36h	Memory size computation OK	74h	Floppy setup about to start
37h	Memory test in progress	75h	Floppy setup OK
38h	Memory initialization over below IMB	76h	Hard disk setup about to start
		77h	Hard disk setup OK
39h	Memory initialization over above IMB	79h	About to initialize timer data area
		7Ah	Verify CMOS battery power
3Ah	Display memory size	7Bh	CMOS battery verification done
3Bh	About to start below 1M memory test	7Dh	About to analyze diagnostics test result for memory
3Ch	Memory test below 1M OK	7Eh	CMOS memory size update OK
3Dh	Memory test above 1M OK	7Fh	About to check optional ROM C000:0.
3Eh	About to go to real mode (shutdown)		
3Fh	Shutdown successful and entered in real mode	80h	Keyboard sensed to enable SETUP
		81h	Optional ROM control OK
40h	About to disable gate A-20 address line	82h	Printer global data initialization OK
41h	Gate A-20 line disabled successfully	83h	RS-232 global data initialization OK
42h	About to start DMA controller test	84h	80287 check/test OK
4Eh	Address line test OK	85h	About to display soft error message
4Fh	Processor in real mode after shutdown	86h	About to give control to system ROM E000.0
50h	DMA page register test OK	87h	System ROM E000.0 check over
51h	DMA unit-1 base register test about to start	00h	Control given to Int 19, boot loader
52h	DMA unit-1 channel OK, about to begin CH-2		

Table A.42   AMI Color BIOS Port 80h POST Codes

Port 80h Code	Test Description
01h	Processor register test about to start, and NMI to be disabled
02h	NMI is disabled; power-on delay starting
03h	Power-on delay complete; any initialization before keyboard BAT is in progress
04h	Any initialization before keyboard BAT is complete; reading keyboard SYS bit to check soft reset/power-on
05h	Soft reset/power-on determined; going to enable ROM (that is, disable shadow RAM/cache if any)

Port 80h Code	Test Description
06h	ROM enabled; calculating ROM BIOS checksum and waiting for KB controller input buffer to be free
07h	ROM BIOS checksum passed, KB controller I/B free; going to issue BAT command to keyboard controller
08h	BAT command to keyboard controller issued; going to verify BAT command
09h	Keyboard controller BAT result verified; keyboard command byte to be written next
0Ah	Keyboard-command byte code issued; going to write command byte data
0Bh	Keyboard controller command byte written; going to issue Pin-23,24 blocking/ unblocking command
0Ch	Pin-23,24 of keyboard controller blocked/unblocked; NOP command of keyboard controller to be issued next
0Dh	NOP command processing done; CMOS shutdown register test to be done next
0Eh	CMOS shutdown register R/W test passed; going to calculate CMOS checksum and update DIAG byte
0Fh	CMOS checksum calculation done and DIAG byte written; CMOS initialization to begin (If INIT CMOS IN EVERY BOOT is set.)
10h	CMOS initialization done (if any); CMOS status register about to initialize for date and time
11h	CMOS status register initialized; going to disable DMA and interrupt controllers
12h	DMA controller #1,#2, interrupt controller #1,#2 disabled; about to disable video display and init port-B
13h	Video display is disabled and port-B initialized; chipset init/auto memory detection to begin
14h	Chipset initialization/auto memory detection over; 8254 timer test about to start
15h	CH-2 timer test halfway; 8254 CH-2 timer test to be complete
16h	Ch-2 timer test over; 8254 CH-1 timer test to be complete
17h	CH-1 timer test over; 8254 CH-0 timer test to be complete
18h	CH-0 timer test over; about to start memory refresh
19h	Memory refresh started; memory refresh test to be done next
1Ah	Memory refresh line is toggling; going to check 15 micro-second On/Off time
1Bh	Memory refresh period 30 micro-second test complete; base 64K memory test about to start
20h	Base 64K memory test started; address line test to be done next
21h	Address line test passed; going to do toggle parity
22h	Toggle parity over; going for sequential data R/W test
23h	Base 64K sequential data R/W test passed; any setup before interrupt vector initialization about to start
24h	Setup required before vector initialization complete; interrupt vector initialization about to begin
25h	Interrupt vector initialization done; going to read I/O port of 8042 for turbo switch (if any)
26h	I/O port of 8042 is read; going to initialize global data for turbo switch
27h	Global data initialization is over; any initialization after interrupt vector to be done next
28h	Initialization after interrupt vector is complete; going for monochrome mode setting
29h	Monochrome mode setting is done; going for color mode setting
2Ah	Color mode setting is done; about to go for toggle parity before optional ROM test
2Bh	Toggle parity over; about to give control for any setup required before optional video ROM check

(continues)

Table A.42 Continued

Port 80h Code	Test Description
2Ch	Processing before video ROM control is done; about to look for optional video ROM and give control
2Dh	Optional video ROM control is done; about to give control to do any processing after video ROM returns control
2Eh	Return from processing after the video ROM control; if EGA/VGA not found, then do display memory R/W test
2Fh	EGA/VGA not found; display memory R/W test about to begin
30h	Display memory R/W test passed; about to look for the retrace checking
31h	Display memory R/W test or retrace checking failed; about to do alternate display memory R/W test
32h	Alternate display memory R/W test passed; about to look for the alternate display retrace checking
33h	Video display checking over; verification of display type with switch setting and actual card to begin
34h	Verification of display adapter done; display mode to be set next
35h	Display mode set complete; BIOS ROM data area about to be checked
36h	BIOS ROM data area check over; going to set cursor for power-on message
37h	Cursor setting for power-on message ID complete; going to display the power-on message
38h	Power-on message display complete; going to read new cursor position
39h	New cursor position read and saved; going to display the reference string
3Ah	Reference string display is over; going to display the Hit <Esc> message
3Bh	Hit <Esc> message displayed; virtual mode memory test about to start
40h	Preparation for virtual mode test started; going to verify from video memory
41h	Returned after verifying from display memory; going to prepare the descriptor tables
42h	Descriptor tables prepared; going to enter virtual mode for memory test
43h	Entered in virtual mode; going to enable interrupts for diagnostics mode
44h	Interrupts enabled (if diagnostics switch is on); going to initialize data to check memory wrap-around at 0:0
45h	Data initialized; going to check for memory wrap-around at 0:0 and find total system memory size
46h	Memory wrap-around test done; memory-size calculation over; about to go for writing patterns to test memory
47h	Pattern to be test-written in extended memory; going to write patterns in base 640K memory
48h	Patterns written in base memory; going to determine amount of memory below 1M memory
49h	Amount of memory below 1M found and verified; going to determine amount of memory above 1M memory
4Ah	Amount of memory above 1M found and verified; going for BIOS ROM data area check
4Bh	BIOS ROM data area check over; going to check <Esc> and clear memory below 1M for soft reset
4Ch	Memory below 1M cleared (Soft Reset); going to clear memory above 1M
4Dh	Memory above 1M cleared (Soft Reset); going to save the memory size
4Eh	Memory test started (No Soft Reset); about to display the first 64K memory test
4Fh	Memory size display started; will be updated during memory test; going for sequential and random memory test
50h	Memory test below 1M complete; going to adjust memory size for relocation and shadow
51h	Memory size adjusted due to relocation/shadow; memory test above 1M to follow

Port 80h Code	Test Description
52h	Memory test above 1M complete; going to prepare to go back to real mode
53h	CPU registers are saved including memory size; going to enter in real mode
54h	Shutdown successful, CPU in real mode; going to restore registers saved during preparation for shutdown
55h	Registers restored; going to disable Gate A20 address line
56h	A20 address line disable successful; BIOS ROM data area about to be checked
57h	BIOS ROM data area check halfway; BIOS ROM data area check to be complete
58h	BIOS ROM data area check over; going to clear Hit <ESC> message
59h	Hit <ESC> message cleared; <WAIT...> message displayed; about to start DMA and interrupt controller test
60h	DMA page-register test passed; about to verify from display memory
61h	Display memory verification over; about to go for DMA #1 base register test
62h	DMA #1 base register test passed; about to go for DMA #2 base register test
63h	DMA #2 base register test passed; about to go for BIOS ROM data area check
64h	BIOS ROM data area check halfway; BIOS ROM data area check to be complete
65h	BIOS ROM data area check over; about to program DMA unit 1 and 2
66h	DMA unit 1 and 2 programming over; about to initialize 8259 interrupt controller
67h	8259 initialization over; about to start keyboard test
80h	Keyboard test started, clearing output buffer, checking for stuck key; about to issue keyboard reset command
81h	Keyboard reset error/stuck key found; about to issue keyboard controller interface test command
82h	Keyboard controller interface test over; about to write command byte and initialize circular buffer
83h	Command byte written, global data initialization done; about to check for lock-key
84h	Lock-key checking over; about to check for memory-size mismatch with CMOS
85h	Memory size check done; about to display soft error and check for password or bypass setup
86h	Password checked; about to do programming before setup
87h	Programming before setup complete; going to CMOS setup program
88h	Returned from CMOS setup program and screen is cleared; about to do programming after setup
89h	Programming after setup complete; going to display power-on screen message
8Ah	First screen message displayed; about to display <WAIT...> message
8Bh	<WAIT...> message displayed; about to do main and video BIOS shadow
8Ch	Main and video BIOS shadow successful; Setup options programming after CMOS setup about to start
8Dh	Setup options are programmed, mouse check and initialization to be done next
8Eh	Mouse check and initialization complete; going for hard disk, floppy reset
8Fh	Floppy check returns that floppy is to be initialized; floppy setup to follow
90h	Floppy setup is over; test for hard disk presence to be done
91h	Hard disk presence test over; hard disk setup to follow
92h	Hard disk setup complete; about to go for BIOS ROM data area check
93h	BIOS ROM data area check halfway; BIOS ROM data area check to be complete
94h	BIOS ROM data area check over; going to set base and extended memory size
95h	Memory size adjusted due to mouse and hard disk type 47 support; going to verify display memory
96h	Returned after verifying display memory; going to do initialization before C800 optional ROM control

(continues)

Appendixes

Table A.42 Continued	
Port 80h Code	**Test Description**
97h	Any initialization before C800 optional ROM control is over; optional ROM check and control to be done next
98h	Optional ROM control is done; about to give control to do any required processing after optional ROM returns control
99h	Any initialization required after optional ROM test over; going to set up timer data area and printer base address
9Ah	Return after setting timer and printer base address; going to set the RS-232 base address
9Bh	Returned after RS-232 base address; going to do any initialization before coprocessor test
9Ch	Required initialization before coprocessor is over; going to initialize the coprocessor next
9Dh	Coprocessor initialized; going to do any initialization after coprocessor test
9Eh	Initialization after coprocessor test is complete; going to check extended keyboard, keyboard ID, and Num Lock
9Fh	Extended keyboard check is done, ID flag set, Num Lock on/off; keyboard ID command to be issued
A0h	Keyboard ID command issued; keyboard ID flag to be reset
A1h	Keyboard ID flag reset; cache memory test to follow
A2h	Cache memory test over; going to display any soft errors
A3h	Soft error display complete; going to set the keyboard typematic rate
A4h	Keyboard typematic rate set; going to program memory wait states
A5h	Memory wait states programming over; screen to be cleared next
A6h	Screen cleared; going to enable parity and NMI
A7h	NMI and parity enabled; going to do any initialization required before giving control to optional ROM at E000
A8h	Initialization before E000 ROM control over; E000 ROM to get control next
A9h	Returned from E000 ROM control; going to do any initialization required after E000 optional ROM control
AAh	Initialization after E000 optional ROM control is over; going to display the system configuration
00h	System configuration is displayed; going to give control to Int 19h boot loader

Award BIOS Port 80h POST Codes. Table A.43 provides information on the majority of Award POST codes displayed during the POST sequence. These POST codes are output to I/O port address 80h. Although this chart specifically lists all the POST codes output by the Award Modular BIOS, version 3.1, the codes are valid also for these Award Modular BIOS types:

> PC/XT Version 3.0 and greater

> AT Version 3.02 and greater

Not all these POST codes apply to all the BIOS types. Note that the POST tests do not necessarily execute in the numeric order shown. The POST sequence may vary depending on the BIOS.

Table A.43 Award BIOS Port 80h POST Codes	
Port 80h Code	**Code Meaning**
01h	Processor Test 1. Processor status verification. Tests the following processor-status flags; carry, zero, sign, and overflow. The BIOS sets each flag, verifies that they are set, and turns each flag off and verifies that it is off. Failure of a flag causes a fatal error.

Port 80h Code	Code Meaning
02h	Determine POST Type. This test determines whether the status of the system is manufacturing or normal. The status can be set by a physical jumper on some motherboards. If the status is normal, the POST continues through and, assuming no errors, boot is attempted. If manufacturing POST is installed, POST is run in continuous loop, and boot is not attempted.
03h	8042 Keyboard Controller. Tests controller by sending TEST_KBRD command (AAh) and verifying that controller reads command.
04h	8042 Keyboard Controller. Verifies that keyboard controller returned AAh, sent in test 3.
05h	Get Manufacturing Status. The last test in the manufacturing cycle. If test 2 found the status to be manufacturing, this POST triggers a reset and POSTs 1 through 5 are repeated continuously.
06h	Initialize Chips. POST 06h performs these functions: disables color and mono video, disables parity circuits, disables DMA (8237) chips, resets math co-processor, initializes timer 1 (8255), clears DMA chip, clears all page registers, and clears CMOS shutdown byte.
07h	Processor Test 2. Reads, writes, and verifies all CPU registers except SS, SP, and BP with data pattern FF and 00.
08h	Initialize CMOS Timer. Updates timer cycle normally.
09h	EPROM Checksum. Checksums EPROM; test failed if sum not equal to 0. Also checksums sign-on message.
0Ah	Initialize Video Interface. Initializes video controller register 6845 to the following: 80 characters per row 25 rows per screen 8/14 scan lines per row for mono/color First scan line of cursor 6/11 Last scan line of cursor 7/12 Reset display offset to 0
0Bh	Test Timer (8254) Channel 0. These three timer tests verify that the 8254 timer chip is functioning properly.
0Ch	Test Timer (8254) Channel 1.
0Dh	Test Timer (8254) Channel 2.
0Eh	Test CMOS Shutdown Byte. Uses a walking bit algorithm to check interface to CMOS circuit.
0Fh	Test Extended CMOS. On motherboards with chipsets that support extended CMOS configurations, such as Chips & Technologies, the BIOS tables of CMOS information are used to configure the chipset. These chipsets have an extended storage mechanism that enables the user to save a desired system configuration after the power is turned off. A checksum is used to verify the validity of the extended storage and, if valid, permit the information to be loaded into extended CMOS RAM.
10h	Test DMA Channel 0. These three functions initialize the DMA (direct memory access) chip and then test the chip using an AA, 55, FF, 00 pattern. Port addresses are used to check the address circuit to DMA page registers.
11h	DMA Channel 1.
12h	DMA Page Registers.
13h	Keyboard Controller. Tests keyboard controller interface.
14h	Test Memory Refresh. RAM must be refreshed periodically to keep the memory from decaying. This function ensures that the memory-refresh function is working properly.
15h	First 64K of System Memory. An extensive parity test is performed on the first 64K of system memory. This memory is used by the BIOS.
16h	Interrupt Vector Table. Sets up and loads interrupt vector tables in memory for use by the 8259 PIC chip.
17h	Video I/O Operations. This function initializes the video, either CGA, MDA, EGA, or VGA. If a CGA or MDA adapter is installed, the video is initialized by the system BIOS. If the system BIOS detects an EGA or VGA adapter, the option ROM BIOS installed on the video adapter is used to initialize and set up the video.

(continues)

Table A.43   Continued

Port 80h Code	Code Meaning
18h	Video Memory. Tests memory for CGA and MDA video boards. This test is not performed by the system BIOS on EGA or VGA video adapters—the board's own EGA or VGA BIOS ensures that it is functioning properly.
19h	Test 8259 Mask Bits—Channel 1. These two tests verify 8259 masked interrupts by alternately turning the interrupt lines off and on. Unsuccessful completion generates a fatal error.
1Ah	8259 Mask Bits—Channel 2.
1Bh	CMOS Battery Level. Verifies that the battery status bit is set to 1. A 0 value can indicate a bad battery or some other problem, such as bad CMOS.
1Ch	CMOS Checksum. This function tests the CMOS checksum data (located at 2Eh and 2Fh) and extended CMOS checksum, if present, to be sure that they are valid.
1Dh	Configuration from CMOS. If the CMOS checksum is good, the values are used to configure the system.
1Eh	System Memory. The system memory size is determined by writing to addresses from 0K to 640K, starting at 0 and continuing until an address does not respond. Memory size value then is compared to the CMOS value to ensure that they are the same. If they are different, a flag is set, and, at the end of POST an error message is displayed.
1Fh	Found System Memory. Tests memory from 64K to the top of the memory found by writing the pattern FFAA and 5500, and then reading the pattern back, byte by byte, and verifying that it is correct.
20h	Stuck 8259 Interrupt Bits. These three tests verify the functionality of the 8259 interrupt controller.
21h	Stuck NMI Bits (Parity or I/O Channel Check).
22h	8259 Function.
23h	Protected Mode. Verifies protected mode: 8086 virtual mode as well as 8086 page mode. Protected mode ensures that any data about to be written to extended memory (above 1M) is checked to ensure that it is suitable for storage there.
24h	Extended Memory. This function sizes memory above 1M by writing to addresses starting at 1M and continuing to 16M on 286 and 386SX systems, and to 64M on 386 systems until there is no response. This process determines the total extended memory, which is compared with CMOS to ensure that the values are the same. If the values are different, a flag is set and at the end of POST an error message is displayed.
25h	Found Extended Memory. This function tests extended memory using virtual 8086 paging mode and writing an FFFF, AA55, 0000 pattern.
26h	Protected Mode Exceptions. This function tests other aspects of protected mode operations.
27h	Cache Control or Shadow RAM. Tests for shadow RAM and cache controller (386 and 486 only) functionality. Systems with CGA and MDA adapters indicate that video shadow RAM is enabled, even though there is no BIOS ROM to shadow (this is normal).
28h	8242. Optional Intel 8242/8248 keyboard controller detection and support.
29h	Reserved.
2Ah	Initialize Keyboard. Initialize keyboard controller.
2Bh	Floppy Drive and Controller. Initializes floppy disk drive controller and any drives present.
2Ch	Detect and Initialize Serial Ports. Initializes any serial ports present.
2Dh	Detect and Initialize Parallel Ports. Initializes any parallel ports present.
2Eh	Initialize Hard Drive and Controller. Initializes hard drive controller and any drives present.
2Fh	Detect and Initialize Math Coprocessor. Initializes math coprocessor.
30h	Reserved.
31h	Detect and Initialize Option ROMs. Initializes any option ROMs present from C800h to EFFFh.
3Bh	Initialize Secondary Cache with OPTi chipset. Initializes secondary cache controller for systems based on the OPTi chipset (486 only).
CAh	Micronics Cache Initialization. Detects and initializes Micronics cache controller if present.

Port 80h Code	Code Meaning
CCh	NMI Handler Shutdown. Detects untrapped Non-Maskable Interrupts during boot.
EEh	Unexpected Processor Exception.
FFh	Boot Attempt. When the POST is complete, if all the system components and peripherals are initialized, and if no error flags were set (such as memory size error), then the system attempts to boot.

Phoenix BIOS Audio and Port 80h POST Codes. Table A.44 is a list of POST fatal errors that may be reported by the Phoenix BIOS. Table A.45 is a list of nonfatal errors. Fatal errors halt the system and prevent any further processing from occurring; nonfatal errors are less severe.

Table A.44 Phoenix BIOS Fatal System Board Errors

Beep Code	Code at Port 80h	Description
None	01h	CPU register test in progress
1-1-3	02h	CMOS write/read failure
1-1-4	03h	ROM BIOS checksum failure
1-2-1	04h	Programmable interval timer failure
1-2-2	05h	DMA initialization failure
1-2-3	06h	DMA page register write/read failure
1-3-1	08h	RAM refresh verification failure
None	09h	First 64K RAM test in progress
1-3-3	0Ah	First 64K RAM chip or data line failure, multibit
1-3-4	0Bh	First 64K RAM odd/even logic failure
1-4-1	0Ch	Address line failure first 64K RAM
1-4-2	0Dh	Parity failure first 64K RAM
2-1-1	10h	Bit 0 first 64K RAM failure
2-1-2	11h	Bit 1 first 64K RAM failure
2-1-3	12h	Bit 2 first 64K RAM failure
2-1-4	13h	Bit 3 first 64K RAM failure
2-2-1	14h	Bit 4 first 64K RAM failure
2-2-2	15h	Bit 5 first 64K RAM failure
2-2-3	16h	Bit 6 first 64K RAM failure
2-2-4	17h	Bit 7 first 64K RAM failure
2-3-1	18h	Bit 8 first 64K RAM failure
2-3-2	19h	Bit 9 first 64K RAM failure
2-3-3	1Ah	Bit 10 first 64K RAM failure
2-3-4	1Bh	Bit 11 first 64K RAM failure
2-4-1	1Ch	Bit 12 first 64K RAM failure
2-4-2	1Dh	Bit 13 first 64K RAM failure
2-4-3	1Eh	Bit 14 first 64K RAM failure
2-4-4	1Fh	Bit 15 first 64K RAM failure
3-1-1	20h	Slave DMA register failure
3-1-2	21h	Master DMA register failure
3-1-3	22h	Master interrupt mask register failure
3-1-4	23h	Slave interrupt mask register failure
None	25h	Interrupt vector loading in progress

(continues)

Table A.44 Continued		
Beep Code	**Code at Port 80h**	**Description**
3-2-4	27h	Keyboard controller test failure
None	28h	CMOS power failure/checksum calculation in progress
None	29h	Screen configuration validation in progress
3-3-4	2Bh	Screen initialization failure
3-4-1	2Ch	Screen retrace failure
3-4-2	2Dh	Search for video ROM in progress
None	2Eh	Screen running with video ROM
None	30h	Screen operable
None	31h	Monochrome monitor operable
None	32h	Color monitor (40 column) operable
None	33h	Color monitor (80 column) operable

Table A.45 Nonfatal System Board Errors		
Beep Code	**Code at Port 80h**	**Description**
4-2-1	34h	Timer tick interrupt test in progress or failure
4-2-2	35h	Shutdown test in progress or failure
4-2-3	36h	Gate A20 failure
4-2-4	37h	Unexpected interrupt in protected mode
4-3-1	38h	RAM test in progress or address failure > FFFFh
4-3-3	3Ah	Interval timer Channel 2 test or failure
4-3-4	3Bh	Time-of-day clock test or failure
4-4-1	3Ch	Serial port test or failure
4-4-2	3Dh	Parallel port test or failure
4-4-3	3Eh	Math coprocessor test or failure
Low 1-1-2	41h	System board select failure
Low 1-1-3	42h	Extended CMOS RAM failure

Low means that a lower pitched beep precedes the other tones.

Hewlett Packard POST and Diagnostics Error Codes

Table A.46 Hewlett Packard 386/N and 486/N POST Error Codes	
Code	**Description**
000F	Microprocessor test error. Check CPU and system board.
001x	ROM BIOS memory error. Check ROM BIOS and system board.
008x	Memory error in address range C000–C7FF. Check system board video ROM and/or video adapter.
009x, 00Ax, 00Bx	Memory error in address range C800–DFFF. Check adapter ROMs.
00C0	Memory error in address range E000–EFFF. Check adapters or system board LAN boot ROM.
011x	CMOS register test error; real-time clock (RTC) is not working correctly.
0120, 0130	CMOS real-time clock (RTC) failed or corrupted. Check battery.
0240	CMOS system configuration information corrupted by power failure. Check battery.
0250	CMOS system configuration information does not match system. Run Setup; check battery.

Code	Description
0241, 0280	CMOS power failure; check battery.
02C0, 02C1	EEPROM master configuration information corrupted or not set correctly. Check system board configuration switches. If the fifth switch (Clear EEPROM) is ON, set it to the OFF position, reset the system, and run Setup to reenter the system configuration.
030x, 0311, 0312, 03E0, 03E1, 03E2, 03E3, 03E4, 03EC	Keyboard/mouse controller failed to respond to a command. Check system board.
034x, 035x	Keyboard failed to respond during keyboard test. Check keyboard cable, keyboard, and system board.
03E5, 03E6, 03E7, 03E8, 03E9, 03EA, 03EB	Mouse test failure. Check mouse and cable.
0401	Protected mode switch failure. Check system board.
0503, 0505	Serial port failure or configuration error. Check setup and system board.
0543, 0545	Parallel port failure or configuration error. Check setup and system board.
0506, 0546	Serial or parallel port conflict. Check configuration.
06xx	Stuck key failure; *xx* = the scan code of the stuck key.
0800	System board LAN boot ROM conflict. Check memory address configurations.
0801	Cannot find LAN boot ROM declared in setup. Check configuration and boot ROM.
110x, 1200, 1201	System timer failure. Check the system board.
20xA	SIMM size mismatch; interleaved memory disabled. Check SIMM installation in the affected bank or banks as identified below: 201A = A 205A = A,C 209A = A,D 20DA = A,C,D 202A = B 206A = B,C 20AA = B,D 20EA = B,C,D 203A = A,B 207A = A,B,C 20BA = A,B,D 20FA = A,B,C,D 204A = C 208A = D 20CA = C,D
21xx, 22xx	DMA channel failure. Check system board.
4F01, 4F02, 4F03, 4F04, 4F05, 4F06, 4F07, 4F08	SIMM memory error. Check the defective SIMM as identified below: 4F01 = Bank A, slot 1 4F05 = Bank C, slot 1 4F02 = Bank A, slot 2 4F06 = Bank C, slot 2 4F03 = Bank B, slot 1 4F07 = Bank D, slot 1 4F04 = Bank B, slot 2 4F08 = Bank D, slot 2
61xx	Memory address line failure. Check SIMMs and system board.
63xx	Memory parity error. Check memory and system board.
6500	ROM BOS shadowing error. Check system memory and ROM BIOS
6510	Video ROM shadowing error. Check system memory and Video ROM BIOS.
6520	LAN option ROM shadowing error. Check system memory and LAN option ROM.
65A0, 65B0, 65C0, 65D0, 65E0, 65F0	ROM BIOS shadowing error; memory segment failure. Check system memory in the segment indicated by the third digit as identified below: A = A000, B = B000, C = C000, D = D000, E = E000, F = F000
66xx	ROM BIOS shadowing error. Check configuration or ROM checksum.
7xxx	Interrupt failure. Check system board.
8003, 8006	Hard drive configuration error; parameters do not match drive. Check configuration and cables.
8004, 8007	CMOS hard disk configuration error. Check drive and battery.
800D, 8010, 8012, 8020, 8021, 8038, 803C, 8040, 8045	Hard disk controller time-out (12 seconds without responding). Check drive and controller.

(continues)

Appendixes

Table A.46 Continued

Code	Description
800E	Hard disk boot failure. Check cables and disk drive failure.
800F	Hard disk CMOS configuration does not match drive.
8011, 8013, 8030, 8039, 803A, 803B, 8041, 8042, 8043, 8044, 8049, 804B, 8310, 8311, 8313	Hard drive does not respond to commands. Check drive, controller, and cables.
8048, 804A	System failed to identify installed hard disk drive. Check setup and cables.
8050	System failed to identify installed hard disk controller. Check configuration.
8400	Hard disk drive boot sector was corrupted or could not be loaded. Check drive partitions.
9x00, 9x01, 9x02, 9x03, 9x04, 9x05, 9x06, 9x07, 9x08, 9x09	Floppy drive error. Check drives and cables. Drive x not responding, where: $x = 1$ for drive 1 $x = 2$ for drive 2 $x = 3$ for drive 3 Check cables and drives.
9x10, 9x0A	CMOS floppy configuration error, where: $x = 0$ for drive 0 $x = 1$ for drive 1 $x = 2$ for drive 2 $x = 3$ for drive 3
A00x	Math coprocessor error. Check coprocessor and system board.
B300	Memory cache controller error.
Exxx	Memory adapter error. Check adapters or SIMMs.

Table A.47 Hewlett Packard 486/U POST Error Codes

Code	Description
00Ax, 00Bx, 00Cx, 00Dx	Adapter ROM (read-only memory) checksum error. Check configuration.
008x	Video ROM (read-only memory) checksum error. Check video ROM or adapter.
009x	Adapter ROM (read-only memory) checksum error in addresses between C8000h and CFFFFh. Check configuration and adapter.
0111x, 0120	CMOS real-time clock is not updating. Check battery and system board.
0130	CMOS real-time clock has invalid time and or date. Reset date and time.
0240, 0241	CMOS memory information is incorrect. Check the clear configuration switch on the system board; it should be OFF.
0250	CMOS configuration does not match installed devices.
0280, 0282	CMOS configuration information has been corrupted.
02C0	EEPROM memory has not been set or was corrupted.
0301, 0302, 0303, 0305, 0306, 0307, 0311, 0312, 03E0, 03E1, 03E2, 03E3, 03E4, 03E5, 03EE, 03EC	System board keyboard/mouse controller did not respond.
0342, 0343, 0344, 0345, 0346, 0350, 0351	System board keyboard/mouse controller self-test failure. Check keyboard controller.
0352, 0353	Keyboard not responding to POST tests. Check cable and keyboard controller.
0354	Keyboard self-test failure. Check keyboard.
03E6, 03E7, 03E8, 03E9	Mouse interface test failure. Check mouse, cable, or keyboard/mouse controller.
03EA, 03EB	Keyboard/mouse reset failure. Check mouse and cable.

Code	Description
0401	Gate A20 failure. Check keyboard/mouse controller (8042) on system board or the system board itself.
0503, 0505	Serial port error or conflict. Check system board or adapters.
0543, 0545	Parallel port or configuration failure. Check configuration, system board, or adapters.
06xx	Keyboard stuck key failure; xx = Scan code (hex) of the key.
1100, 1101	System timer failure. Check system board.
1300	Floppy controller conflict. Check configuration.
13x1	Adapter communications error; x = slot containing adapter (e.g. 1351 = slot 5).
13x2	CMOS indicates a slot is empty, but a board is installed; x = slot.
13x3	CMOS indicates a slot contains a board with no readable identification, but a board with a readable identification is present; x = slot.
13x4	CMOS configuration information does not match the board in slot x, where x = slot.
13x5	CMOS configuration information is incomplete.
2002	SIMM not detected. Check SIMMs and system board.
2003, 2005, 2007	Incorrect SIMM configuration; for example, when you have 2MB and 8MB memory modules installed at the same time, the 8MB modules must be in the first sockets.
21xx, 22xx	DMA (Direct Memory Access) controller is not functioning correctly. Check system board.
4F0x	SIMM error; x = SIMM socket (e.g. 4F02 = socket 2)
61xx	Memory addressing error. Check installed SIMMs.
62F0	Memory parity error. Check SIMMs or system board.
62F1	Memory controller error. Check system board.
6300	Adapter RAM error. Check installed adapters and memory.
6500	System board ROM BIOS shadowing error. Check system board and setup for conflicts.
6510	Video ROM shadowing error. Check system board or video adapter.
6520	Adapter ROM shadowing error. Check system board adapters and memory.
65C0, 65D0, 65E0	Reserved memory for shadowing failed tests. Segment indicated by third digit (e.g. 65D0 = segment D000h).
70xx, 71xx, 7400, 7500	Interrupt controller failure. Check system board and adapters.
8003, 8103	Hard disk configuration (number of sectors) is not correct.
8004, 8104	CMOS hard disk parameters are not correct, where 8004 = drive C, and 8104 = drive D.
8005, 8105	CMOS hard disk parameters not supported, where 8005 = drive C, and 8105 = drive D.
8x06	BIOS shadow RAM on your system board must be functioning if you have either a hard disk drive type 33 or type 34 installed.
8007, 8107	The number of hard disk drive cylinders specified for your type 33 or type 34 hard disk drive is not correct, where 8007 = drive C, and 8107 = drive D.
800D, 8010, 800E, 800F	Hard drive controller not responding. Check controller or cables.
8011	Hard disk test failure.
8012, 8013	Hard disk controller test failure.
8020, 8120	Hard drive not ready, where 8020 = drive C, and 8120 = drive D.
8021, 8121	Unable to communicate with hard disk controller, where 8021 = drive C, and 8121 = drive D is at fault.

(continues)

Code	Description
Table A.47 Continued	
Code	**Description**
8028	Hard disk controller is configured for drive splitting, but splitting is not supported or is not functioning. Check configuration.
8030, 8130	Identify drive failure, where 8030 = drive C, and 8130 = drive D is at fault. Check the EISA Configuration Manager Utility.
8038, 8138, 803A, 813A, 803B, 813B 803C, 813C	Hard disk (Recalibrate) error, where 8039, 803A, or 803C = hard disk or controller for drive C, and 8139, 8013A, or 813C = drive D or its controller is at fault.
8040, 8140, 8041, 8141, 8042, 8142, 8043, 8143, 8044, 8144, 8045, 8145	Hard disk (Read Verify) command failure, where $804x$ = hard disk drive or controller for C, and $814x$ = hard drive or controller for D.
8048, 8148, 804A, 814A	Hard disk (Drive Identify) command failure, where $804x$ = drive C, and $814x$ = drive D.
8049, 8149, 804B, 814B	Hard disk (Set Multiple Mode) command failure, where $804x$ = drive C, and $814x$ = drive D.
8400	No boot sector (or corrupted boot sector) on hard disk.
900A, 910A, 920A	CMOS floppy configuration does not match actual drives installed, where 900A = drive A, 910A = drive B, and 920A = a third floppy drive.
9000, 9100, 9200, 9001, 9101, 9201	Floppy controller communication error, where $90xx$ = drive A, $91xx$ = drive B, and $92xx$ = a third floppy drive.
9002, 9102, 9202	Floppy drive (Seek) error, where $90xx$ = drive A, $91xx$ = drive B, and 9202 = a third floppy drive.
9003, 9103, 9203	Floppy drive (Recalibrate) error, where $90xx$ = drive A, 9103 = drive B, and 9203 = a third floppy drive.
9005, 9105, 9205	Floppy drive (Reset) error, where 9005 = drive A, 9105 = drive as B, and 9205 = a third floppy drive.
9008, 9108, 9208	Floppy drive command error, where 9008 = drive A, 9108 = drive B, and 9208 = a third floppy drive.
9009, 9109, 9209	Floppy drive track zero error, where 9009 = drive A, 9109 = drive B, and 9209 = a third floppy drive.
A001, A002, A003, A004, A005, A006, A007, A008, A009, A00A, A00B, A00C, A00D, A00E	Math coprocessor failure.
B300	CPU Level 2 cache failure.
Exxx	Memory board failure (non-HP).

IBM POST and Diagnostics Display Error Codes

When an IBM or compatible system is first powered on, the system runs a Power-On Self Test (POST). If errors are encountered during the POST, they are displayed in the form of a code number and possibly some additional text. When you are running the IBM Advanced Diagnostics, which you can purchase from IBM or which is included on many of the PS/2 Reference Diskettes, similar codes are displayed if errors are encountered during the tests. IBM has developed a system in which the first part of the error code indicates the device the error involves, and the last part indicates the exact error meaning. One of the biggest problems with these error codes is that IBM does not publish a complete list of the errors in any single publication; instead, it details specific error codes in many different publications. I have researched these codes for many years; tables A.48 and A.49 represent all the codes I have found meanings for. These codes have been selected from a number of sources, including all of IBM's technical-reference and hardware-maintenance service manuals.

When diagnostics are run, any code ending in 00 indicates that the particular test has passed. For example, an error code of 1700 indicates that the hard disk diagnostic tests have passed.

After completing the Power-On Self Test (POST), an audio code indicates either a normal condition or that one of several errors has occurred. Table A.48 lists the audio codes for IBM systems, and table A.49 lists the IBM POST and diagnostics error codes.

Table A.48 IBM POST Audio Error Codes

Audio Code	Sound Graph	Fault Domain
1 short beep	o	Normal POST—system OK
2 short beeps	oo	POST error—error code on CRT
No beep		Power supply, system board
Continuous beep	————	Power supply, system board
Repeating short beeps	oooooo	Power supply, system board
1 long, 1 short beep	−o	System board
1 long, 2 short beeps	−oo	Display adapter (MDA, CGA)
1 long, 3 short beeps	−ooo	Enhanced Graphics Adapter (EGA)
3 long beeps	− − −	3270 keyboard card

Table A.49 IBM POST and Diagnostics Error-Code List

Code	Description
1xx	**System Board Errors**
101	System board interrupt failure (unexpected interrupt).
102	System board timer failure.
102	PS/2; real-time clock (RTC)/64 byte CMOS RAM test failure.
103	System board timer interrupt failure.
103	PS/2; 2KB CMOS RAM extension test failure.
104	System board protected mode failure.
105	System board 8042 keyboard controller command failure.
106	System board converting logic test failure.
107	System board Non-Maskable Interrupt (NMI) test failure; hot NMI.
108	System board timer bus test failure.
109	System board memory select error; low MB chip select test failed.
110	PS/2 system board parity check error (PARITY CHECK 1).
111	PS/2 I/O channel (bus) parity check error (PARITY CHECK 2).
112	PS/2 Micro Channel Arbitration error; watchdog time-out (NMI error).
113	PS/2 Micro Channel Arbitration error; DMA arbitration time-out (NMI error).
114	PS/2 external ROM checksum error.
115	Cache parity error, ROM checksum error or DMA error.
116	System board port read/write failure.
118	System board parity or L2-cache error during previous power-on.
119	"E" Step level 82077 (floppy controller) and 2.88MB drive installed (not supported).
120	Microprocessor self-test error.
121	256KB ROM checksum error (second 128KB bank).
121	Unexpected hardware interrupts occurred.
131	PC system board cassette port wrap test failure.
131	Direct memory access (DMA) compatibility registers error.
132	Direct memory access (DMA) extended registers error.

(continues)

Table A.49 Continued	
Code	**Description**
1xx System Board Errors	
133	Direct memory access (DMA) verify logic error.
134	Direct memory access (DMA) arbitration logic error.
151	Battery or CMOS RAM failure.
152	Real-time clock or CMOS RAM failure.
160	PS/2 system board ID not recognized.
161	CMOS configuration empty (dead battery).
162	CMOS checksum error or adapter ID mismatch.
163	CMOS error; date and time not set (clock not updating).
164	Memory size error; CMOS setting does not match memory.
165	PS/2 Micro Channel adapter ID and CMOS mismatch.
166	PS/2 Micro Channel adapter time-out error (card busy).
167	PS/2 CMOS clock not updating.
168	CMOS configuration error (math coprocessor).
169	System board and processor card configuration mismatch. Run Setup.
170	ASCII setup conflict error.
170	PC Convertible; LCD not in use when suspended.
171	Rolling-bit-test failure on CMOS shutdown address byte.
171	PC Convertible; base 128KB checksum failure.
172	Rolling-bit-test failure on NVRAM diagnostic byte.
172	PC Convertible; diskette active when suspended.
173	Bad CMOS/NVRAM checksum.
173	PC Convertible; real-time clock RAM verification error.
174	Bad configuration.
174	PC Convertible; LCD configuration changed.
175	Bad EEPROM CRC #1.
175	PC Convertible; LCD alternate mode failed.
176	Tamper evident.
177	Bad PAP (Privileged-Access Password) CRC.
177	Bad EEPROM.
178	Bad EEPROM.
179	NVRAM error log full.
180x	Sub Address data error, where x = the slot number that caused the error.
181	Unsupported configurations.
182	Privileged-access switch (JMP2) is not in the write-enable position.
183	PAP is needed to boot from the system programs.
183	Privileged-access password required.
184	Bad power-on password checksum—erase it.
184	Bad power-on password.
185	Bad startup sequence.
186	Password-protection hardware error.
187	Serial number error.
188	Bad EEPROM checksum CRC #2.
189	Excessive incorrect password attempts.
191	82385 cache controller test failure.
194	System board memory error.
199	User indicated INSTALLED DEVICES list is not correct.

Code	Description
2xx	**Memory (RAM) Errors**
20x	Memory error.
201	Memory test failure; error location may be displayed.
202	Memory address error; lines 00–15.
203	Memory address error; lines 16–23 (ISA) or 16–31 (MCA).
204	Memory remapped due to error (run diagnostics again).
205	Base 128KB memory error; memory remapped.
207	ROM failure.
210	System board memory parity error.
211	PS/2 memory; base 64KB on system board failed.
212	Watchdog time-out error (reported by NMI interrupt handler).
213	DMA bus arbitration time-out (reported by NMI interrupt handler).
215	PS/2 memory; base 64KB on daughter/SIP 2 failed.
216	PS/2 memory; base 64KB on daughter/SIP 1 failed.
221	PS/2 memory; ROM to RAM copy failed (ROM shadowing).
225	PS/2 memory; wrong-speed memory on system board, unsupported SIMM.
230	Overlapping adapter and planar memory (Family 1).
231	Non-contiguous adapter memory installed (Family 1).
231	2/4-16MB Enhanced 386 memory adapter; memory module 1 failed.
235	Stuck data line on memory module, microprocessor or system board.
241	2/4-16MB Enhanced 386 memory adapter; memory module 2 failed.
251	2/4-16MB Enhanced 386 memory adapter; memory module 3 failed.
3xx	**Keyboard Errors**
301	Keyboard reset or stuck key failure (SS 301, SS = scan code in hex).
302	System unit keylock is locked.
303	Keyboard-to-system board interface error; keyboard controller failure.
304	Keyboard or system board error; keyboard clock high.
305	Keyboard +5v dc error; PS/2 keyboard fuse (on system board) error.
306	Unsupported keyboard attached.
341	Keyboard error.
342	Keyboard cable error.
343	Keyboard LED card or cable failure.
365	Keyboard LED card or cable failure.
366	Keyboard interface cable failure.
367	Keyboard LED card or cable failure.
4xx	**Monochrome Display Adapter (MDA) Errors PS/2 System Board Parallel Port Errors**
401	Monochrome memory, horizontal sync frequency, or video test failure.
401	PS/2 system board parallel port failure.
408	User indicated display attributes failure.
416	User indicated character set failure.
424	User indicated 80525 mode failure.
432	Parallel port test failure; Monochrome Display Adapter.

(continues)

Table A.49 Continued

Code	Description
5xx	**Color Graphics Adapter (CGA) Errors**
*501	CRT error.
501	CGA memory, horizontal sync frequency, or video test failure.
503	CGA adapter controller failed.
508	User indicated display attribute failure.
516	User indicated character set failure.
524	User indicated 80×25 mode failure.
532	User indicated 40×25 mode failure.
540	User indicated 320×200 graphics mode failure.
548	User indicated 640×200 graphics mode failure.
556	User indicated light-pen test failed.
564	User indicated paging test failure.
6xx	**Floppy Drive/Controller Errors**
601	Floppy drive/controller Power-On Self Test failure; disk drive or controller error.
602	Diskette boot sector is not valid.
603	Diskette size error.
604	Non-media sense.
605	Diskette drive locked.
606	Diskette verify test failure.
607	Write protect error.
608	Drive command error.
610	Diskette initialization failure; track 0 bad.
611	Drive time-out error.
612	Controller chip (NEC) error.
613	Direct memory access (DMA) error.
614	Direct memory access (DMA) boundary overrun error.
615	Drive index timing error.
616	Drive speed error.
621	Drive seek error.
622	Drive cyclic redundancy check (CRC) error.
623	Sector not found error.
624	Address mark error.
625	Controller chip (NEC) seek error.
626	Diskette data compare error.
627	Diskette change error.
628	Diskette removed.
630	Index stuck high; drive A.
631	Index stuck low; drive A.
632	Track 0 stuck off; drive A.
633	Track 0 stuck on; drive A.
640	Index stuck high; drive B.
641	Index stuck low; drive B.
642	Track 0 stuck off; drive B.
643	Track 0 stuck on; drive B.
645	No index pulse.

Code	Description
6xx	**Floppy Drive/Controller Errors**
646	Drive track 0 detection failed.
647	No transitions on read data line.
648	Format test failed.
649	Incorrect media type in drive.
650	Drive speed error.
651	Format failure.
652	Verify failure.
653	Read failure.
654	Write failure.
655	Controller error.
656	Drive failure.
657	Write protect stuck protected.
658	Changeline stuck changed.
659	Write protect stuck unprotected.
660	Changeline stuck unchanged.
7xx	**Math Coprocessor Errors**
701	Math coprocessor presence/initialization error.
702	Exception errors test failure.
703	Rounding test failure.
704	Arithmetic test 1 failure.
705	Arithmetic test 2 failure.
706	Arithmetic test 3 (80387 only) failure.
707	Combination test failure.
708	Integer load/store test failure.
709	Equivalent expressions errors.
710	Exception (interrupt) errors.
711	Save state (FSAVE) errors.
712	Protected mode test failure.
713	Special test (voltage/temperature sensitivity) failure.
9xx	**Parallel Printer Adapter Errors**
901	Printer adapter data register latch error.
902	Printer adapter control register latch error.
903	Printer adapter register address decode error.
904	Printer adapter address decode error.
910	Status line(s) wrap connector error.
911	Status line bit 8 wrap error.
912	Status line bit 7 wrap error.
913	Status line bit 6 wrap error.
914	Status line bit 5 wrap error.
915	Status line bit 4 wrap error.
916	Printer adapter interrupt wrap error.
917	Unexpected printer adapter interrupt.
92x	Feature register error.

(continues)

Table A.49   Continued

Code	Description
10xx	**Alternate Parallel Printer Adapter Errors**
1001	Printer adapter data register latch error.
1002	Printer adapter control register latch error.
1003	Printer adapter register address decode error.
1004	Printer adapter address decode error.
1010	Status line(s) wrap connector error.
1011	Status line bit 8 wrap error.
1012	Status line bit 7 wrap error.
1013	Status line bit 6 wrap error.
1014	Status line bit 5 wrap error.
1015	Status line bit 4 wrap error.
1016	Printer adapter interrupt wrap error.
1017	Unexpected printer adapter interrupt.
102x	Feature register error.
11xx	**Primary Async Communications (Serial COM1:) Errors**
1101	16450/16550 chip error; serial port A error.
1102	Card selected feedback error.
1102	PC Convertible internal modem test failed.
1103	Port 102h register test failure.
1103	PC Convertible internal modem dial tone test 1 failed.
1104	PC Convertible internal modem dial tone test 2 failed.
1106	Serial option cannot be put to sleep.
1107	Cable error.
1108	Interrupt request (IRQ) 3 error.
1109	Interrupt request (IRQ) 4 error.
1110	16450/16550 chip register failure.
1111	Internal wrap test of 16450/16550 chip modem control line failure.
1112	External wrap test of 16450/16550 chip modem control line failure.
1113	16450/16550 chip transmit error.
1114	16450/16550 chip receive error.
1115	16450/16550 chip receive error; data not equal to transmit data.
1116	16450/16550 chip interrupt function error.
1117	16450/16550 chip baud rate test failure.
1118	16450/16550 chip receive external data wrap test failure.
1119	16550 chip first-in first-out (FIFO) buffer failure.
1120	Interrupt enable register error; all bits cannot be set.
1121	Interrupt enable register error; all bits cannot be reset.
1122	Interrupt pending; stuck on.
1123	Interrupt ID register; stuck on.
1124	Modem control register error; all bits cannot be set.
1125	Modem control register error; all bits cannot be reset.
1126	Modem status register error; all bits cannot be set.
1127	Modem status register error; all bits cannot be reset.
1128	Interrupt ID error.
1129	Cannot force overrun error.

Code	Description
11xx	**Primary Async Communications (Serial COM1:) Errors**
1130	No modem status interrupt.
1131	Invalid interrupt pending.
1132	No data ready.
1133	No data available interrupt.
1134	No transmit holding interrupt.
1135	No interrupts.
1136	No received sine status interrupt.
1137	No receive data available.
1138	Transmit holding register not empty.
1139	No modem status interrupt.
1140	Transmit holding register not empty.
1141	No interrupts.
1142	No interrupt 4.
1143	No interrupt 3.
1144	No data transferred.
1145	Maximum baud rate error.
1146	Minimum baud rate error.
1148	Time-out error.
1149	Invalid data returned.
1150	Modem status register error.
1151	No data set ready and delta data set ready.
1152	No data set ready.
1153	No delta data set ready.
1154	Modem status register not clear.
1155	No clear to send and delta clear to send.
1156	No clear to send.
1157	No delta clear to send.
12xx	**Alternate Async Communications (Serial COM2:, COM3:, and COM4:) Errors**
1201	16450/16550 chip error.
1202	Card selected feedback error.
1203	Port 102h register test failure.
1206	Serial option cannot be put to sleep.
1207	Cable error.
1208	Interrupt request (IRQ) 3 error.
1209	Interrupt request (IRQ) 4 error.
1210	16450/16550 chip register failure.
1211	Internal wrap test of 16450/16550 chip modem control line failure.
1212	External wrap test of 16450/16550 chip modem control line failure.
1213	16450/16550 chip transmit error.
1214	16450/16550 chip receive error.
1215	16450/16550 chip receive error; data not equal to transmit data.
1216	16450/16550 chip interrupt function error.
1217	16450/16550 chip baud rate test failure.
1218	16450/16550 chip receive external data wrap test failure.

(continues)

Appendixes

Table A.49 Continued	
Code	**Description**
12xx	**Alternate Async Communications (Serial COM2:, COM3:, and COM4:) Errors**
1219	16550 chip first-in first-out (FIFO) buffer failure.
1220	Interrupt enable register error; all bits cannot be set.
1221	Interrupt enable register error; all bits cannot be reset.
1222	Interrupt pending; stuck on.
1223	Interrupt ID register; stuck on.
1224	Modem control register error; all bits cannot be set.
1225	Modem control register error; all bits cannot be reset.
1226	Modem status register error; all bits cannot be set.
1227	Modem Status Register error; all bits cannot be reset.
1228	Interrupt ID error.
1229	Cannot force overrun error.
1230	No modem status interrupt.
1231	Invalid interrupt pending.
1232	No data ready.
1233	No data available interrupt.
1234	No transmit holding interrupt.
1235	No interrupts.
1236	No received sine status interrupt.
1237	No receive data available.
1238	Transmit holding register not empty.
1239	No modem status interrupt.
1240	Transmit holding register not empty.
1241	No interrupts.
1242	No interrupt 4.
1243	No interrupt 3.
1244	No data transferred.
1245	Maximum baud rate error.
1246	Minimum baud rate error.
1248	Time-out error.
1249	Invalid data returned.
1250	Modem status register error.
1251	No data set ready and delta data set ready.
1252	No data set ready.
1253	No delta data set ready.
1254	Modem status register not clear.
1255	No clear to send and delta clear to send.
1256	No clear to send.
1257	No delta clear to send.
13xx	**Game Control Adapter Errors**
1301	Game control adapter test failure.
1302	Joystick test failure.

Code	Description
14xx	**Matrix Printer Errors**
1401	Printer test failure.
1402	Printer not ready error.
1403	Printer no-paper error.
1404	System board time-out.
1405	Parallel adapter failure.
1406	Printer presence test failed.
15xx	**Synchronous Data Link Control (SDLC) Communications Adapter Errors**
1501	SDLC adapter test failure.
1510	8255 Port B failure.
1511	8255 Port A failure.
1512	8255 Port C failure.
1513	8253 Timer #1 did not reach terminal count.
1514	8253 Timer #1 stuck on.
1515	8253 Timer #0 did not reach terminal count.
1516	8253 Timer #0 stuck on.
1517	8253 Timer #2 did not reach terminal count.
1518	8253 Timer #2 stuck on.
1519	8273 Port B error.
1520	8273 Port A error.
1521	8273 command/read time-out.
1522	Interrupt Level 4 failure.
1523	Ring Indicate stuck on.
1524	Receive Clock stuck on.
1525	Transmit Clock stuck on.
1526	Test Indicate stuck on.
1527	Ring Indicate not on.
1528	Receive Clock not on.
1529	Transmit Clock not on.
1530	Test Indicate not on.
1531	Data Set Ready not on.
1532	Carrier Detect not on.
1533	Clear to Send not on.
1534	Data Set Ready stuck on.
1535	Carrier Detect stuck on.
1536	Clear to Send stuck on.
1537	Interrupt Level 3 failure.
1538	Receive interrupt results error.
1539	Wrap data compare error.
1540	Direct memory access Channel 1 error.
1541	Direct memory access Channel 1 error.
1542	8273 error-checking or status-reporting error.
1547	Stray interrupt Level 4.
1548	Stray interrupt Level 3.
1549	Interrupt presentation sequence time-out.

(continues)

Table A.49 Continued	
Code	**Description**
16xx	**Display Station Emulation Adapter (DSEA) Errors (5520, 525x)**
1604	DSEA or twinaxial network error.
1608	DSEA or twinaxial network error.
1624	DSEA error.
1634	DSEA error.
1644	DSEA error.
1652	DSEA error.
1654	DSEA error.
1658	DSEA error.
1662	DSEA interrupt level error.
1664	DSEA error.
1668	DSEA interrupt level error.
1669	DSEA diagnostics error; use 3.0 or higher.
1674	DSEA diagnostics error; use 3.0 or higher.
1674	DSEA station address error.
1684	DSEA device address error.
1688	DSEA device address error.
17xx	**ST-506/412 Fixed Disk and Controller Errors**
1701	Fixed disk general POST error.
1702	Drive/controller time-out error.
1703	Drive seek error.
1704	Controller failed.
1705	Drive sector not found error.
1706	Write fault error.
1707	Drive track 0 error.
1708	Head select error.
1709	Error-correction code (ECC) error.
1710	Sector buffer overrun.
1711	Bad address mark.
1712	Internal controller diagnostics failure.
1713	Data compare error.
1714	Drive not ready.
1715	Track 0 indicator failure.
1716	Diagnostics cylinder errors.
1717	Surface read errors.
1718	Hard drive type error.
1720	Bad diagnostics cylinder.
1726	Data compare error.
1730	Controller error.
1731	Controller error.
1732	Controller error.
1733	BIOS undefined error return.
1735	Bad command error.
1736	Data corrected error.
1737	Bad track error.
1738	Bad sector error.

Code	Description
17xx	**ST-506/412 Fixed Disk and Controller Errors**
1739	Bad initialization error.
1740	Bad sense error.
1750	Drive verify failure.
1751	Drive read failure.
1752	Drive write failure.
1753	Drive random read test failure.
1754	Drive seek test failure.
1755	Controller failure.
1756	Controller error-correction code (ECC) test failure.
1757	Controller head-select failure.
1780	Seek failure; drive 0.
1781	Seek failure; drive 1.
1782	Controller test failure.
1790	Diagnostic cylinder read error; drive 0.
1791	Diagnostic cylinder read error; drive 1.
18xxx	**I/O Expansion Unit Errors**
1801	I/O expansion unit POST failure.
1810	Enable/disable failure.
1811	Extender card wrap test failure; disabled.
1812	High-order address lines failure; disabled.
1813	Wait state failure; disabled.
1814	Enable/disable could not be set on.
1815	Wait state failure; disabled.
1816	Extender card wrap test failure; enabled.
1817	High-order address lines failure; enabled.
1818	Disable not functioning.
1819	Wait request switch not set correctly.
1820	Receiver card wrap test failure.
1821	Receiver high-order address lines failure.
19xx	**3270 PC Attachment Card Errors**
20xx	**Binary Synchronous Communications (BSC) Adapter Errors**
2001	BSC adapter test failure.
2010	8255 Port A failure.
2011	8255 Port B failure.
2012	8255 Port C failure.
2013	8253 Timer #1 did not reach terminal count.
2014	8253 Timer #1 stuck on.
2015	8253 Timer 2 did not reach terminal count.
2016	8253 Timer #2 output stuck on.
2017	8251 data set ready failed to come on.
2018	8251 clear to send not sensed.
2019	8251 data SET ready stuck on.
2020	8251 clear to send stuck on.
2021	8251 hardware reset failure.

Appendixes

(continues)

Table A.49	**Continued**
Code	**Description**
20xx	**Binary Synchronous Communications (BSC) Adapter Errors**
2022	8251 software reset failure.
2023	8251 software "error reset" failure.
2024	8251 transmit ready did not come on.
2025	8251 receive ready did not come on.
2026	8251 could not force "overrun" error status.
2027	Interrupt failure; no timer interrupt.
2028	Interrupt failure; transmit; replace card or planar.
2029	Interrupt failure; transmit; replace card.
2030	Interrupt failure; receive; replace card or planar.
2031	Interrupt failure; receive; replace card.
2033	Ring Indicate stuck on.
2034	Receive Clock stuck on.
2035	Transmit Clock stuck on.
2036	Test Indicate stuck on.
2037	Ring Indicate stuck on.
2038	Receive Clock not on.
2039	Transmit Clock not on.
2040	Test Indicate not on.
2041	Data Set Ready not on.
2042	Carrier Detect not on.
2043	Clear to Send not on.
2044	Data Set Ready stuck on.
2045	Carrier Detect stuck on.
2046	Clear to Send stuck on.
2047	Unexpected transmit interrupt.
2048	Unexpected receive interrupt.
2049	Transmit data did not equal receive data.
2050	8251 detected overrun error.
2051	Lost data set ready during data wrap.
2052	Receive time-out during data wrap.
21xx	**Alternate Binary Synchronous Communications (BSC) Adapter Errors**
2101	BSC adapter test failure.
2110	8255 Port A failure.
2111	8255 Port B failure.
2112	8255 Port C failure.
2113	8253 Timer #1 did not reach terminal count.
2114	8253 Timer #1 stuck on.
2115	8253 Timer 2 did not reach terminal count.
2116	8253 Timer #2 output stuck on.
2117	8251 Data Set Ready failed to come on.
2118	8251 Clear to Send not sensed.
2119	8251 Data Set Ready stuck on.
2120	8251 Clear to Send stuck on.
2121	8251 Hardware reset failure.
2122	8251 Software reset failure.

Code	Description
21xx	**Alternate Binary Synchronous Communications (BSC) Adapter Errors**
2123	8251 Software "error reset" failure.
2124	8251 Transmit Ready did not come on.
2125	8251 Receive Ready did not come on.
2126	8251 could not force "overrun" error status.
2127	Interrupt failure; no timer interrupt.
2128	Interrupt failure; transmit; replace card or planar.
2129	Interrupt failure; transmit; replace card.
2130	Interrupt failure; receive; replace card or planar.
2131	Interrupt failure; receive; replace card.
2133	Ring Indicate stuck on.
2134	Receive Clock stuck on.
2135	Transmit Clock stuck on.
2136	Test Indicate stuck on.
2137	Ring Indicate stuck on.
2138	Receive Clock not on.
2139	Transmit Clock not on.
2140	Test Indicate not on.
2141	Data Set Ready not on.
2142	Carrier Detect not on.
2143	Clear to Send not on.
2144	Data Set Ready stuck on.
2145	Carrier Detect stuck on.
2146	Clear to Send stuck on.
2147	Unexpected transmit interrupt.
2148	Unexpected receive interrupt.
2149	Transmit data did not equal receive data.
2150	8251 detected overrun error.
2151	Lost Data Set Ready during data wrap.
2152	Receive time-out during data wrap.
22xx	**Cluster Adapter Errors**
23xx	**Plasma Monitor Adapter Errors**
24xx	**Enhanced Graphics Adapter (EGA) or Video Graphics Array (VGA) Errors**
2401	Video adapter test failure.
2402	Video display error.
2408	User indicated display attribute test failed.
2409	Video display error.
2410	Video adapter error; video port error.
2416	User indicated character set test failed.
2424	User indicated 80×25 mode failure.
2432	User indicated 40×25 mode failure.
2440	User indicated 320×200 graphics mode failure.
2448	User indicated 640×200 graphics mode failure.
2456	User indicated light-pen test failure.
2464	User indicated paging test failure.

(continues)

Table A.49 Continued	
Code	Description
25xx	**Alternate Enhanced Graphics Adapter (EGA) Errors**
2501	Video adapter test failure.
2502	Video display error.
2508	User indicated display attribute test failed.
2509	Video display error.
2510	Video adapter error.
2516	User indicated character set test failed.
2524	User indicated 80×25 mode failure.
2532	User indicated 40×25 mode failure.
2540	User indicated 320×200 graphics mode failure.
2548	User indicated 640×200 graphics mode failure.
2556	User indicated light-pen test failure.
2564	User indicated paging test failure.
26xx	**XT or AT/370 370-M (Memory) and 370-P (Processor) Adapter Errors**
2601	370-M (memory) adapter error.
2655	370-M (memory) adapter error.
2657	370-M (memory) adapter error.
2668	370-M (memory) adapter error.
2672	370-M (memory) adapter error.
2673	370-P (processor) adapter error.
2674	370-P (processor) adapter error.
2677	370-P (processor) adapter error.
2680	370-P (processor) adapter error.
2681	370-M (memory) adapter error.
2682	370-P (processor) adapter error.
2694	370-P (processor) adapter error.
2697	370-P (processor) adapter error.
2698	XT or AT/370 diagnostic diskette error.
27xx	**XT or AT/370 3277-EM (Emulation) Adapter Errors**
2701	3277-EM adapter error.
2702	3277-EM adapter error.
2703	3277-EM adapter error.
28xx	**3278/79 Emulation Adapter or 3270 Connection Adapter Errors**
29xx	**Color/Graphics Printer Errors**
30xx	**Primary PC Network Adapter Errors**
3001	Processor test failure.
3002	ROM checksum test failure.
3003	Unit ID PROM test failure.
3004	RAM test failure.
3005	Host interface controller test failure.
3006	±12v test failure.
3007	Digital loopback test failure.

Code	Description
30xx	**Primary PC Network Adapter Errors**
3008	Host detected host interface controller failure.
3009	Sync failure and no Go bit.
3010	Host interface controller test OK and no Go bit.
3011	Go bit and no command 41.
3012	Card not present.
3013	Digital failure; fall through.
3015	Analog failure.
3041	Hot carrier; not this card.
3042	Hot carrier; this card!
31xx	**Secondary PC Network Adapter Errors**
3101	Processor test failure.
3102	ROM checksum test failure.
3103	Unit ID PROM test failure.
3104	RAM test failure.
3105	Host interface controller test failure.
3106	±12v test failure.
3107	Digital loopback test failure.
3108	Host detected host interface controller failure.
3109	Sync failure and no Go bit.
3110	Host interface controller test OK and no Go bit.
3111	Go bit and no command 41.
3112	Card not present.
3113	Digital failure; fall through.
3115	Analog failure.
3141	Hot carrier; not this card.
3142	Hot carrier; this card!
32xx	**3270 PC or AT Display and Programmed Symbols Adapter Errors**
33xx	**Compact Printer Errors**
35xx	**Enhanced Display Station Emulation Adapter (EDSEA) Errors**
3504	Adapter connected to Twinaxial cable during off-line test.
3508	Workstation address error.
3509	Diagnostic program failure.
3540	Workstation address invalid.
3588	Adapter address switch error.
3599	Diagnostic program failure.
36xx	**General-Purpose Interface Bus (GPIB) Adapter Errors**
3601	Adapter test failure.
3602	Serial poll mode register write error.
3603	Adapter address error.
3610	Adapter listen error.

(continues)

Table A.49	Continued
Code	**Description**
36xx	**General-Purpose Interface Bus (GPIB) Adapter Errors**
3611	Adapter talk error.
3612	Adapter control error.
3613	Adapter standby error.
3614	Adapter Asynchronous control error.
3615	Adapter Asynchronous control error.
3616	Adapter error; cannot pass control.
3617	Adapter error; cannot address to listen.
3618	Adapter error; cannot unaddress to listen.
3619	Adapter error; cannot address to talk.
3620	Adapter error; cannot unaddress to talk.
3621	Adapter error; cannot address to listen with extended addressing.
3622	Adapter error; cannot unaddress to listen with extended addressing.
3623	Adapter error; cannot address to talk with extended addressing.
3624	Adapter error; cannot unaddress to talk with extended addressing.
3625	Write to self error.
3626	Generate handshake error.
3627	Cannot detect "Device Clear" message error.
3628	Cannot detect "Selected Device Clear" message error.
3629	Cannot detect end with end of identify.
3630	Cannot detect end of transmission with end of identify.
3631	Cannot detect end with 0-bit end of string.
3632	Cannot detect end with 7-bit end of string.
3633	Cannot detect group execute trigger.
3634	Mode 3 addressing error.
3635	Cannot recognize undefined command.
3636	Cannot detect remote, remote changed, lockout, or lockout changed.
3637	Cannot clear remote or lockout.
3638	Cannot detect service request.
3639	Cannot conduct serial poll.
3640	Cannot conduct parallel poll.
3650	Adapter error; direct memory access (DMA) to 7210.
3651	Data error; error on direct memory access (DMA) to 7210.
3652	Adapter error; direct memory access (DMA) from 7210.
3653	Data error on direct memory access (DMA) from 7210.
3658	Uninvoked interrupt received.
3659	Cannot interrupt on address status changed.
3660	Cannot interrupt on address status changed.
3661	Cannot interrupt on command output.
3662	Cannot interrupt on data out.
3663	Cannot interrupt on data in.
3664	Cannot interrupt on error.
3665	Cannot interrupt on device clear.
3666	Cannot interrupt on end.
3667	Cannot interrupt on device execute trigger.

Code	Description
3668	Cannot interrupt on address pass through.
3669	Cannot interrupt on command pass through.
3670	Cannot interrupt on remote changed.
3671	Cannot interrupt on lockout changed.
3672	Cannot interrupt on service request In.
3673	Cannot interrupt on terminal count on direct memory access to 7210.
3674	Cannot interrupt on terminal count on direct memory access from 7210.
3675	Spurious direct memory access terminal-count interrupt.
3697	Illegal direct memory access configuration setting detected.
3698	Illegal interrupt level setting detected.

37xx System Board SCSI Controller Errors

38xx Data Acquisition Adapter Errors

Code	Description
3801	Adapter test failure.
3810	Timer read test failure.
3811	Timer interrupt test failure.
3812	Delay; binary input 13 test failure.
3813	Rate; binary input 13 test failure.
3814	Binary output 14; interrupt status—interrupt request test failure.
3815	Binary output 0; count-in test failure.
3816	Binary input strobe; count-out test failure.
3817	Binary output 0; binary output clear to send test failure.
3818	Binary output 1; binary input 0 test failure.
3819	Binary output 2; binary input 1 test failure.
3820	Binary output 3; binary input 2 test failure.
3821	Binary output 4; binary input 3 test failure.
3822	Binary output 5; binary input 4 test failure.
3823	Binary output 6; binary input 5 test failure.
3824	Binary output 7; binary input 6 test failure.
3825	Binary output 8; binary input 7 test failure.
3826	Binary output 9; binary input 8 test failure.
3827	Binary output 10; binary input 9 test failure.
3828	Binary output 11; binary input 10 test failure.
3829	Binary output 12; binary input 11 test failure.
3830	Binary output 13; binary input 12 test failure.
3831	Binary output 15; analog input CE test failure.
3832	Binary output strobe; binary output GATE test failure.
3833	Binary input clear to send; binary input HOLD test failure.
3834	Analog input command output; binary input 15 test failure.
3835	Counter interrupt test failure.
3836	Counter read test failure.
3837	Analog output 0 ranges test failure.
3838	Analog output 1 ranges test failure.
3839	Analog input 0 values test failure.
3840	Analog input 1 values test failure.

(continues)

Appendixes

Table A.49	Continued
Code	**Description**

38xx   Data Acquisition Adapter Errors

Code	Description
3841	Analog input 2 values test failure.
3842	Analog input 3 values test failure.
3843	Analog input interrupt test failure.
3844	Analog input 23 address or value test failure.

39xx   Professional Graphics Adapter (PGA) Errors

Code	Description
3901	PGA test failure.
3902	ROM1 self-test failure.
3903	ROM2 self-test failure.
3904	RAM self-test failure.
3905	Cold start cycle power error.
3906	Data error in communications RAM.
3907	Address error in communications RAM.
3908	Bad data reading/writing 6845-like register.
3909	Bad data in lower E0h bytes reading/writing 6845-like registers.
3910	Graphics controller display bank output latches error.
3911	Basic clock error.
3912	Command control error.
3913	Vertical sync scanner error.
3914	Horizontal sync scanner error.
3915	Intech error.
3916	Look-up table address error.
3917	Look-up table red RAM chip error.
3918	Look-up table green RAM chip error.
3919	Look-up table blue RAM chip error.
3920	Look-up table data latch error.
3921	Horizontal display error.
3922	Vertical display error.
3923	Light-pen error.
3924	Unexpected error.
3925	Emulator addressing error.
3926	Emulator data latch error.
3927	Base for error codes 3928–3930 (Emulator RAM).
3928	Emulator RAM error.
3929	Emulator RAM error.
3930	Emulator RAM error.
3931	Emulator horizontal/vertical display problem.
3932	Emulator cursor position error.
3933	Emulator attribute display problem.
3934	Emulator cursor display error.
3935	Fundamental emulation RAM problem.
3936	Emulation character set problem.
3937	Emulation graphics display error.
3938	Emulation character display problem.
3939	Emulation bank select error.
3940	Adapter RAM U2 error.

Code	Description
39xx	**Professional Graphics Adapter (PGA) Errors**
3941	Adapter RAM U4 error.
3942	Adapter RAM U6 error.
3943	Adapter RAM U8 error.
3944	Adapter RAM U10 error.
3945	Adapter RAM U1 error.
3946	Adapter RAM U3 error.
3947	Adapter RAM U5 error.
3948	Adapter RAM U7 error.
3949	Adapter RAM U9 error.
3950	Adapter RAM U12 error.
3951	Adapter RAM U14 error.
3952	Adapter RAM U16 error.
3953	Adapter RAM U18 error.
3954	Adapter RAM U20 error.
3955	Adapter RAM U11 error.
3956	Adapter RAM U13 error.
3957	Adapter RAM U15 error.
3958	Adapter RAM U17 error.
3959	Adapter RAM U19 error.
3960	Adapter RAM U22 error.
3961	Adapter RAM U24 error.
3962	Adapter RAM U26 error.
3963	Adapter RAM U28 error.
3964	Adapter RAM U30 error.
3965	Adapter RAM U21 error.
3966	Adapter RAM U23 error.
3967	Adapter RAM U25 error.
3968	Adapter RAM U27 error.
3969	Adapter RAM U29 error.
3970	Adapter RAM U32 error.
3971	Adapter RAM U34 error.
3972	Adapter RAM U36 error.
3973	Adapter RAM U38 error.
3974	Adapter RAM U40 error.
3975	Adapter RAM U31 error.
3976	Adapter RAM U33 error.
3977	Adapter RAM U35 error.
3978	Adapter RAM U37 error.
3979	Adapter RAM U39 error.
3980	Graphics controller RAM timing error.
3981	Graphics controller read/write latch error.
3982	Shift register bus output latches error.
3983	Addressing error (vertical column of memory; U2 at top).
3984	Addressing error (vertical column of memory; U4 at top).

(continues)

Appendixes

Table A.49 Continued

Code	Description
39xx	**Professional Graphics Adapter (PGA) Errors**
3985	Addressing error (vertical column of memory; U6 at top).
3986	Addressing error (vertical column of memory; U8 at top).
3987	Addressing error (vertical column of memory; U10 at top).
3988	Base for error codes 3989–3991 (horizontal bank latch errors).
3989	Horizontal bank latch errors.
3990	Horizontal bank latch errors.
3991	Horizontal bank latch errors.
3992	RAG/CAG graphics controller error.
3993	Multiple write modes, nibble mask errors.
3994	Row nibble (display RAM) error.
3995	Graphics controller addressing error.
44xx	**5278 Display Attachment Unit and 5279 Display Errors**
45xx	**IEEE Interface Adapter (IEEE-488) Errors**
46xx	**A Real-Time Interface Coprocessor (ARTIC) Multiport/2 Adapter Errors**
4611	ARTIC adapter error.
4612	Memory module error.
4613	Memory module error.
4630	ARTIC adapter error.
4640	Memory module error.
4641	Memory module error.
4650	ARTIC interface cable error.
48xx	**Internal Modem Errors**
49xx	**Alternate Internal Modem Errors**
50xx	**PC Convertible LCD Errors**
5001	LCD display buffer failure.
5002	LCD font buffer failure.
5003	LCD controller failure.
5004	User indicated PEL/drive test failed.
5008	User indicated display attribute test failed.
5016	User indicated character set test failed.
5020	User indicated alternate character set test failure.
5024	User indicated 80×25 mode test failure.
5032	User indicated 40×25 mode test failure.
5040	User indicated 320×200 graphics test failure.
5048	User indicated 640×200 graphics test failure.
5064	User indicated paging test failure.

Code	Description
51xx	**PC Convertible Portable Printer Errors**
5101	Portable printer interface failure.
5102	Portable printer busy error.
5103	Portable printer paper or ribbon error.
5104	Portable printer time-out.
5105	User indicated print-pattern test error.
56xx	**Financial Communication System Errors**
70xx	**Phoenix BIOS/Chipset-Unique Errors**
7000	Chipset CMOS failure.
7001	Chipset shadow RAM failure.
7002	Chipset CMOS configuration error.
71xx	**Voice Communications Adapter (VCA) Errors**
7101	Adapter test failure.
7102	Instruction or external data memory error.
7103	PC to VCA interrupt error.
7104	Internal data memory error.
7105	Direct memory access (DMA) error.
7106	Internal registers error.
7107	Interactive shared memory error.
7108	VCA to PC interrupt error.
7109	DC wrap error.
7111	External analog wrap and tone-output error.
7112	Microphone to speaker wrap error.
7114	Telephone attachment test failure.
73xx	**3 1/2-Inch External Diskette Drive Errors**
7301	Diskette drive/adapter test failure.
7306	Disk changeline failure.
7307	Diskette is write protected.
7308	Drive command error.
7310	Diskette initialization failure; track 0 bad.
7311	Drive time-out error.
7312	Controller chip (NEC) error.
7313	Direct memory access (DMA) error.
7314	Direct memory access (DMA) boundary overrun.
7315	Drive index timing error.
7316	Drive speed error.
7321	Drive seek error.
7322	Drive cyclic redundancy check (CRC) error.
7323	Sector not found error.
7324	Address mark error.
7325	Controller chip (NEC) seek error.

(continues)

Appendixes

Table A.49   Continued

Code	Description
74xx	**IBM PS/2 Display Adapter (VGA Card) Errors**
74xx	**8514/A Display Adapter Errors**
7426	8514 display error.
7440	8514/A memory module 31 error.
7441	8514/A memory module 30 error.
7442	8514/A memory module 29 error.
7443	8514/A memory module 28 error.
7444	8514/A memory module 22 error.
7445	8514/A memory module 21 error.
7446	8514/A memory module 18 error.
7447	8514/A memory module 17 error.
7448	8514/A memory module 32 error.
7449	8514/A memory module 14 error.
7450	8514/A memory module 13 error.
7451	8514/A memory module 12 error.
7452	8514/A memory module 06 error.
7453	8514/A memory module 05 error.
7454	8514/A memory module 02 error.
7455	8514/A memory module 01 error.
7460	8514/A memory module 16 error.
7461	8514/A memory module 27 error.
7462	8514/A memory module 26 error.
7463	8514/A memory module 25 error.
7464	8514/A memory module 24 error.
7465	8514/A memory module 23 error.
7466	8514/A memory module 20 error.
7467	8514/A memory module 19 error.
7468	8514/A memory module 15 error.
7469	8514/A memory module 11 error.
7470	8514/A memory module 10 error.
7471	8514/A memory module 09 error.
7472	8514/A memory module 08 error.
7473	8514/A memory module 07 error.
7474	8514/A memory module 04 error.
7475	8514/A memory module 03 error.
76xx	**4216 PagePrinter Adapter Errors**
7601	Adapter test failure.
7602	Adapter error.
7603	Printer error.
7604	Printer cable error.
84xx	**PS/2 Speech Adapter Errors**

Code	Description
85xx	**2MB XMA Memory Adapter or XMA Adapter/A Errors**
850x	Adapter error.
851x	Adapter error.
852x	Memory module error.
8599	Unusable memory segment found.
86xx	**PS/2 Pointing Device (Mouse) Errors**
8601	Pointing device error; mouse time-out.
8602	Pointing device error; mouse interface.
8603	Pointing device or system-bus failure; mouse interrupt.
8604	Pointing device or system board error.
8611	System bus error—I/F between 8042 and TrackPoint II.
8612	TrackPoint II error.
8613	System bus error or TrackPoint II error.
89xx	**Musical Instrument Digital Interface (MIDI) Adapter Errors**
91xx	**IBM 3363 Write-Once Read-Multiple (WORM) Optical Drive/Adapter Errors**
96xx	**SCSI Adapter with Cache (32-Bit) Errors**
100xx	**Multiprotocol Adapter/A Errors**
10001	Presence test failure.
10002	Card selected feedback error.
10003	Port 102h register rest failure.
10004	Port 103h register rest failure.
10006	Serial option cannot be put to sleep.
10007	Cable error.
10008	Interrupt request (IRQ) 3 error.
10009	Interrupt request (IRQ) 4 error.
10010	16550 chip register failure.
10011	Internal wrap test of 16550 chip modem control line failure.
10012	External wrap test of 16550 chip modem control line failure.
10013	16550 chip transmit error.
10014	16550 chip receive error.
10015	16550 chip receive error; data not equal to transmit data.
10016	16550 chip interrupt function error.
10017	16550 chip baud rate test failure.
10018	16550 chip receive external data wrap test failure.
10019	16550 chip first-in first-out (FIFO) buffer failure.
10026	8255 Port A error.
10027	8255 Port B error.
10028	8255 Port C error.
10029	8254 timer 0 error.
10030	8254 timer 1 error.

(continues)

Table A.49 Continued	
Code	**Description**
100xx	**Multiprotocol Adapter/A Errors**
10031	8254 timer 2 error.
10032	Binary sync data set ready response to data terminal ready error.
10033	Binary sync clear to send response to ready to send error.
10034	8251 hardware reset test failed.
10035	8251 function error.
10036	8251 status error.
10037	Binary sync timer interrupt error.
10038	Binary sync transmit interrupt error.
10039	Binary sync receive interrupt error.
10040	Stray interrupt request (IRQ) 3 error.
10041	Stray interrupt request (IRQ) 4 error.
10042	Binary sync external wrap error.
10044	Binary sync data wrap error.
10045	Binary sync line status/condition error.
10046	Binary sync time-out error during data wrap test.
10050	8273 command acceptance or results ready time-out error.
10051	8273 Port A error.
10052	8273 Port B error.
10053	SDLC modem status change logic error.
10054	SDLC timer interrupt request (IRQ) 4 error.
10055	SDLC modem status change interrupt request (IRQ) 4 error.
10056	SDLC external wrap error.
10057	SDLC interrupt results error.
10058	SDLC data wrap error.
10059	SDLC transmit interrupt error.
10060	SDLC receive interrupt error.
10061	Direct memory access (DMA) channel 1 transmit error.
10062	Direct memory access (DMA) channel 1 receive error.
10063	8273 status detect failure.
10064	8273 error detect failure.
101xx	**300/1200bps Internal Modem/A Errors**
10101	Presence test failure.
10102	Card selected feedback error.
10103	Port 102h register test failure.
10106	Serial option cannot be put to sleep.
10108	Interrupt request (IRQ) 3 error.
10109	Interrupt request (IRQ) 4 error.
10110	16450 chip register failure.
10111	Internal wrap test of 16450 modem control line failure.
10113	16450 transmit error.
10114	16450 receive error.
10115	16450 receive error data not equal transmit data.
10116	16450 interrupt function error.
10117	16450 baud rate test failure.

Code	Description
101xx	**300/1200bps Internal Modem/A Errors**
10118	16450 receive external data wrap test failure.
10125	Modem reset result code error.
10126	Modem general result code error.
10127	Modem S registers write/read error.
10128	Modem turn echo on/off error.
10129	Modem enable/disable result codes error.
10130	Modem enable number/word result codes error.
10133	Connect results for 300 baud not received.
10134	Connect results for 1200 baud not received.
10135	Modem fails local analog loopback test at 300 baud.
10136	Modem fails local analog loopback test at 1200 baud.
10137	Modem does not respond to escape/reset sequence.
10138	S-Register 13 does not show correct parity or number of data bits.
10139	S-Register 15 does not reflect correct bit rate.
104xx	**ESDI or MCA IDE Fixed Disk or Adapter Errors**
10450	Read/write test failed.
10451	Read verify test failed.
10452	Seek test failed.
10453	Wrong drive type indicated.
10454	Controller sector buffer test failure.
10455	Controller invalid failure.
10456	Controller diagnostic command failure.
10461	Drive format error.
10462	Controller head select error.
10463	Drive read/write sector error.
10464	Drive primary defect map unreadable.
10465	Controller; error-correction code (ECC) 8-bit error.
10466	Controller; error-correction code (ECC) 9-bit error.
10467	Drive soft seek error.
10468	Drive hard seek error.
10469	Drive soft error count exceeded.
10470	Controller attachment diagnostic error.
10471	Controller wrap mode interface error.
10472	Controller wrap mode drive select error.
10473	Read verify test errors.
10480	Seek failure; drive 0.
10481	Seek failure; drive 1.
10482	Controller transfer acknowledge error.
10483	Controller reset failure.
10484	Controller; head select 3 error.
10485	Controller; head select 2 error.
10486	Controller; head select 1 error.
10487	Controller; head select 0 error.
10488	Controller; read gate—command complete 2 error.
10489	Controller; write gate—command complete 1 error.

Appendixes

(continues)

Code	Description
Table A.49 Continued	
104xx	**ESDI or MCA IDE Fixed Disk or Adapter Errors**
10490	Diagnostic area read error; drive 0.
10491	Diagnostic area read error; drive 1.
10492	Controller error, drive 1.
10493	Reset error, drive 1.
10499	Controller failure.
107xx	**5 1/4-Inch External Diskette Drive or Adapter Errors**
112xx	**SCSI Adapter (16-Bit without Cache) Errors**
113xx	**System Board SCSI Adapter (16-Bit) Errors**
129xx	**Processor Complex (CPU Board) Errors**
129005	DMA error.
12901	Processor board; processor test failed.
12902	Processor board; cache test failed.
12904	Second level cache failure.
12905	Cache enable/disable errors.
12907	Cache fatal error.
12908	Cache POST program error.
12912x	Hardware failure.
12913x	Micro Channel bus time-out.
12914x	Software failure.
12915x	Processor complex error.
12916x	Processor complex error.
12917x	Processor complex error.
12918x	Processor complex error.
12919x	Processor complex error.
12940x	Processor complex failure.
12950x	Processor complex failure.
129900	Processor complex serial-number mismatch.
149xx	**P70/P75 Plasma Display and Adapter Errors**
14901	Plasma Display Adapter failure.
14902	Plasma Display Adapter failure.
14922	Plasma display failure.
14932	External display failure.
152xx	**XGA Display Adapter/A Errors**
164xx	**120MB Internal Tape Drive Errors**
165xx	**6157 Streaming Tape Drive or Tape Attachment Adapter Errors**
16520	Streaming tape drive failure.
16540	Tape attachment adapter failure.

Code	Description
166xx	**Primary Token Ring Network Adapter Errors**
167xx	**Alternate Token Ring Network Adapter Errors**
180xx	**PS/2 Wizard Adapter Errors**
18001	Interrupt controller failure.
18002	Incorrect timer count.
18003	Timer interrupt failure.
18004	Sync check interrupt failure.
18005	Parity check interrupt failure.
18006	Access error interrupt failure.
18012	Bad checksum error.
18013	Micro Channel interface error.
18021	Wizard memory compare or parity error.
18022	Wizard memory address line error.
18023	Dynamic RAM controller failure.
18029	Wizard memory byte enable error.
18031	Wizard memory-expansion module memory compare or parity error.
18032	Wizard memory-expansion module address line error.
18039	Wizard memory-expansion module byte enable error.
185xx	**DBCS Japanese Display Adapter/A Errors**
194xx	**80286 Memory-Expansion Option Memory-Module Errors**
200xx	**Image Adapter/A Errors**
208xx	**Unknown SCSI Device Errors**
209xx	**SCSI Removable Disk Errors**
210xx	**SCSI Fixed Disk Errors**

210PLSC	"PLSC" codes indicate errors
	P = SCSI ID number (Physical Unit Number or PUN)
	L = Logical unit number (LUN, usually 0)
	S = Host Adapter slot number
	C = SCSI Drive capacity:
	    A = 60MB
	    B = 80MB
	    C = 120MB
	    D = 160MB
	    E = 320MB
	    F = 400MB
	    H = 1,024MB (1GB)
	    I = 104MB
	    J = 212MB
	    U = Undetermined or non-IBM OEM Drive

(continues)

Appendixes

Table A.49 Continued	
Code	Description
211xx	SCSI Tape Drive Errors
212xx	SCSI Printer Errors
213xx	SCSI Processor Errors
214xx	SCSI Write-Once Read-Multiple (WORM) Drive Errors
215xx	SCSI CD-ROM Drive Errors
216xx	SCSI Scanner Errors
217xx	SCSI Magneto Optical Drive Errors
218xx	SCSI Jukebox Changer Errors
219xx	SCSI Communications Errors
243xxxx	XGA-2 Adapter/A Errors
I998xxxx	Dynamic Configuration Select (DCS) Information Codes
I998001x	Bad integrity of DCS master boot record.
I988002x	Read failure of DCS master boot record.
I988003x	DCS master boot record is not compatible with the planar ID.
I988004x	DCS master boot record is not compatible with the model/submodel byte.
I988005x	Bad integrity of CMOS/NVRAM (or internal process error).
I988006x	Read failure of header/mask/configuration record.
I988007x	Bad integrity of header/mask/configuration record.
I988008x	Hard disk does not support the command to set the maximum RBA.
I988009x	DCS master boot record is older than system ROM.
I9880402	Copyright notice in E000 segment does not match the one in DCS MBR.
I9880403	DCS MBR is not compatible with the system board ID or model/submodel byte.
I99900xx	Initial Microcode Load (IML) Errors
I999001x	Invalid disk IML record.
I999002x	Disk IML record load error.
I999003x	Disk IML record incompatible with system board.
I999004x	Disk IML record incompatible with processor/processor card.
I999005x	Disk IML not attempted.
I999006x	Disk stage II System Image load error.
I999007x	Disk stage II image checksum error.
I999008x	IML not supported on primary disk drive.
I999009x	Disk IML record is older than ROM.
I99900x1	Invalid diskette IML record.
I99900x2	Diskette IML record load error.
I99900x3	Diskette IML record incompatible with system board.

Code	Description
I99900xx	**Initial Microcode Load (IML) Errors**
I99900x4	Diskette IML record incompatible with processor card.
I99900x5	Diskette IML recovery prevented (valid password and CE override not set).
I99900x6	Diskette stage II image load error.
I99900x7	Diskette stage II image checksum error.
I99900x9	Diskette IML record older than ROM.
I99903xx	**No Bootable Device, Initial Program Load (IPL) Errors**
I9990302	Invalid disk boot record; unable to read IPL boot record from disk.
I9990303	IML System Partition boot failure.
I9990304	No bootable device with ASCII console.
I9990305	No bootable media found.
I9990306	Invalid SCSI Device boot record.
I99904xx	**IML-to-System Mismatch**
I9990401	Unauthorized access (manufacturing boot request with valid password).
I9990402	Missing ROM IBM Copyright notice.
I9990403	IML Boot Record incompatible with system board/processor card.
I99906xx	**IML Errors**

IBM SCSI Error Codes

With the new IBM SCSI adapter and SCSI devices comes a new set of error codes. This section contains tables describing all the known IBM SCSI Power-On Self Test (POST) and advanced diagnostics error codes. These codes can be used to determine the meaning of errors that occur on the IBM SCSI adapters and any attached SCSI devices. The error codes that occur during POST and diagnostic tests have the format shown in figure A.5.

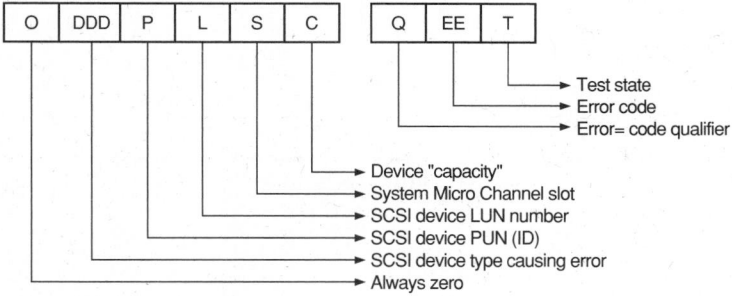

Fig. A.5

IBM SCSI POST and diagnostics error code format.

This section shows what each part of the error code indicates.

The DDD field in figure A.5 indicates the SCSI device causing the error. Table A.50 shows the device codes.

The P field indicates the SCSI device physical unit number (PUN) or SCSI ID. This value is between 0 and 7, with the host adapter normally set to 7 and the first (bootable) SCSI hard disk set to 6.

The L field indicates the SCSI device logical unit number (LUN). For most SCSI devices, it is 0 because normally there is only a single LUN per physical unit or SCSI ID.

The S field indicates the system Micro Channel Architecture (MCA) slot number containing the SCSI host adapter to which the device in error is connected. If S equals 0, the error is an adapter initialization error (there is no MCA slot 0). In this case, the DDD number is 096, 112, or 113, and you must use the following adapter initialization error chart to determine the error. The specific errors in this chart are indicated by the value in the L field, which immediately precedes the S field. In this case, the L does *not* represent the logical unit number (as it normally does), but instead shows a specific initialization error for the adapter. If S is not equal to 0, no error is on the adapter (or device attached to the adapter) in slot S. You can determine these standard errors by using the rest of the tables in this section.

Table A.50   SCSI Device Error Codes

DDDxxxx xxxx	Error
096xxxx xxxx	32-bit cached SCSI host adapter.
112xxxx xxxx	16-bit non-cached SCSI host adapter.
113xxxx xxxx	System board SCSI host adapter.
208xxxx xxxx	Unknown SCSI device type.
209xxxx xxxx	Direct access (disk) device with removable media and/or other than 512 byte blocks.
210xxxx xxxx	Direct access (disk) device with nonremovable media and 512 byte blocks (hard disk).
211xxxx xxxx	Sequential access device (magnetic tape).
212xxxx xxxx	Printer device.
213xxxx xxxx	Processor device (host to host).
214xxxx xxxx	Write-Once Read-Multiple device (optical WORM drive).
215xxxx xxxx	Read-only device (CD-ROM drive).
216xxxx xxxx	Scanner device.
217xxxx xxxx	Optical memory device (optical drive).
218xxxx xxxx	Media changer device (multiple tray CD-ROM or jukebox).
219xxxx xxxx	Communications device (LAN bridge).
DDD0LS0 0000	**SCSI Adapter Initialization Errors, Where S = 0**
DDD0100 0000	No extended CMOS setup data available. On systems with Non-Volatile RAM (NVRAM), this means that SCSI setup data was not located or the checksum did not verify. On systems without NVRAM (Model 50, for example), the setup data must be on the first non-SCSI fixed disk.
DDD0200 0000	No hard disk at PUN 6, LUN 0. (Also expect to see 161, 162, or 165 errors.)
DDD0300 0000	No space available in extended BIOS data area for SCSI data table.
DDD0400 0000	ROM modules not found on SCSI adapter.
DDD0500 0000	ROM checksum error in the second 16KB portion of 32KB SCSI adapter ROM space.

A value of x indicates any number or character.

The C field indicates the capacity of the device originating the error code. The capacity codes for each of the available IBM SCSI hard disk drives are listed in table A.51. In the case of error codes from a device with no capacity (such as a SCSI adapter or printer), this field is 0.

Table A.51 SCSI Device Capacity Codes	
DDDxxxC xxxx	**SCSI Device Capacity**
DDDxxx0 xxxx	Not a storage device
DDDxxxA xxxx	60MB
DDDxxxB xxxx	80MB
DDDxxxC xxxx	120MB
DDDxxxD xxxx	160MB
DDDxxxE xxxx	320MB
DDDxxxF xxxx	400MB
DDDxxxH xxxx	1,024MB (1GB)
DDDxxxI xxxx	104MB
DDDxxxJ xxxx	212MB
DDDxxxU xxxx	Undetermined device capacity, or non-IBM OEM drive

The Q field is the error code (EE field) qualifier. Q can have a value from 0 through 7. Depending on the value of Q, the error codes take on different meanings, because Q indicates what class of error occurred or what part of the SCSI system the error is coming from. To determine the error code meaning, use one of the following tables that correspond to the value of Q you have.

The Q value defines the origin of the EE code reported. Error codes with Q = 0 or 1 are generated by the SCSI host adapter, and all error codes with Q greater than 1 are developed using information returned by the adapter or a SCSI device. If Q = 2, the EE code indicates the value returned in the Command Error field (word 8, bits 15-8) of the SCSI Command Complete Status Block (CCSB) for values indicating hardware problems (codes of 20h or greater). If Q = 3, then EE also indicates the value returned in the Command Error field (word 8, bits 15-8) of the Command Complete Status Block (CCSB), but for values indicating software problems (codes less than 20h). If Q = 4, then EE indicates the value returned in the Sense Key field (byte 2, bits 3-0) of a Sense Data Block returned to the SCSI host adapter by a device following a SCSI Request Sense command. If Q = 5, then EE indicates the value returned in the Additional Sense Code field (byte 12) of a Sense Data Block returned by a Direct Access (Disk) device following a SCSI Request Sense command. If Q = 6, then EE indicates the value returned in the Device Error Code field (word 8, bits 7-0) of the Command Complete Status Block (CCSB). If Q = 7, a device error has occurred that normally would not be considered an error, but is now considered an error based on when the code was returned—for example, a Medium Corrupted error from a device with nonremovable media.

Although IBM has a unique format for displaying SCSI error codes, almost all except the adapter-specific errors are part of the SCSI specification. Because many of these codes come from the devices attached to the SCSI bus and not the host adapter, a new code not listed here possibly could appear because some errors can be dependent on the particular device, and some devices send manufacturer-specific errors. You then can look up the error code in the manufacturer's documentation for the device to determine the meaning. The tables in this section are standard as defined in the SCSI Common Command Set (CCS) of the ANSI SCSI-1 specification. Further information is in the IBM hardware-maintenance and service manual for the IBM SCSI adapter and the various SCSI devices.

Table A.52   SCSI Host Adapter Error Codes with Q = 0

DDDxxxx QEEx	Error Code
96xxxx 001x	80188 ROM test failure.
96xxxx 002x	Local RAM test failure.
96xxxx 003x	Power protection error (terminator or fuse).
96xxxx 004x	80188 internal peripheral test failure.
96xxxx 005x	Buffer control chip test failure.
96xxxx 006x	Buffer RAM test failure.
96xxxx 007x	System interface control chip test failure.
96xxxx 008x	SCSI interface test failure.
112xxxx 001x	8032 ROM test failure.
112xxxx 002x	Local RAM test failure.
112xxxx 003x	Power protection device error (terminator or fuse).
112xxxx 004x	8032 internal peripheral test failure.
112xxxx 005x	Buffer control chip test failure.
112xxxx 006x	Undefined error condition.
112xxxx 007x	System interface control chip test failure.
112xxxx 008x	SCSI interface test failure.
113xxxx 001x	Microprocessor ROM test failure.
113xxxx 002x	Local RAM test failure.
113xxxx 003x	Power protection device error (terminator or fuse).
113xxxx 004x	Microprocessor internal peripheral test failure.
113xxxx 005x	Buffer control chip test failure.
113xxxx 006x	Undefined error condition.
113xxxx 007x	System interface control chip test failure.
113xxxx 008x	SCSI interface test failure.

Table A.53   SCSI Adapter Error Codes with Q = 1

DDDxxxx QEEx	Error Code
DDDxxxx 107x	Adapter hardware failure.
DDDxxxx 10Cx	Command completed with failure.
DDDxxxx 10Ex	Command error (invalid command or parameter).
DDDxxxx 10Fx	Software sequencing error.
DDDxxxx 180x	Time-out.
DDDxxxx 181x	Adapter busy error.
DDDxxxx 182x	Unexpected interrupt presented by adapter.
DDDxxxx 183x	Adapter register test failure.
DDDxxxx 184x	Adapter reset (via basic control register) failure.
DDDxxxx 185x	Adapter buffer test failure (cached adapter only).
DDDxxxx 186x	Adapter reset count expired.
DDDxxxx 187x	Adapter registers not cleared on reset (power-on or channel reset).
DDDxxxx 188x	Card ID in adapter microcode did not match ID in POS registers.
DDDxxxx 190x	Expected device did not respond (target device not powered on).
DDDxxxx 190x	DMA arbitration level conflict (if device number is 096, 112, or 113).

Table A.54   SCSI Hardware Error Codes with Q = 2

DDDxxxx QEEx	Error Code
DDDxxxx 220x	Adapter hardware error.
DDDxxxx 221x	Global command time-out on adapter (device did not respond).
DDDxxxx 222x	Adapter DMA error.
DDDxxxx 223x	Adapter buffer defective.
DDDxxxx 224x	Command aborted by adapter.
DDDxxxx 280x	Adapter microprocessor detected error.

Table A.55   SCSI Software Error Codes with Q = 3

DDDxxxx QEEx	Error Code
DDDxxxx 301x	Invalid parameter in subsystem control block.
DDDxxxx 302x	Reserved.
DDDxxxx 303x	Command not supported.
DDDxxxx 304x	Command aborted by system.
DDDxxxx 305x	Command rejected (buffer not disabled).
DDDxxxx 306x	Command rejected (adapter diagnostic failure).
DDDxxxx 307x	Format rejected (sequence error).
DDDxxxx 308x	Assign rejected (command in progress on device).
DDDxxxx 309x	Assign rejected (device already assigned).
DDDxxxx 30Ax	Command rejected (device not assigned).
DDDxxxx 30Bx	Maximum logical block address exceeded.
DDDxxxx 30Cx	16-bit card slot address range exceeded.
DDDxxxx 313x	Invalid device for command.
DDDxxxx 3FFx	Status not returned by adapter.

Table A.56   SCSI Device Sense Key Error Codes with Q = 4

DDDxxxx QEEx	Error Code
DDDxxxx 401x	Recovered error (not considered an error condition).
DDDxxxx 402x	Device not ready.
DDDxxxx 403x	Device media error.
DDDxxxx 404x	Device hardware error.
DDDxxxx 405x	Illegal request for device.
DDDxxxx 406x	Device unit attention would not clear.
DDDxxxx 407x	Device data protect error.
DDDxxxx 408x	Device blank check error.
DDDxxxx 409x	Device vendor unique error.
DDDxxxx 40Ax	Device copy aborted.
DDDxxxx 40Bx	Command aborted by device.
DDDxxxx 40Cx	Device search data command satisfied.
DDDxxxx 40Dx	Device volume overflow (residual data still in buffer).
DDDxxxx 40Ex	Device miscompare (source and medium data don't match).
DDDxxxx 40Fx	Reserved.

Appendixes

Table A.57 SCSI Device Extended Sense Error Codes with Q = 5	
DDDxxxx QEEx	**Error Code**
DDDxxxx 501x	No index or sector signal.
DDDxxxx 502x	Seek incomplete.
DDDxxxx 503x	Write fault.
DDDxxxx 504x	Drive not ready.
DDDxxxx 505x	Drive not selected.
DDDxxxx 506x	No track 0 found.
DDDxxxx 507x	Multiple drives selected.
DDDxxxx 508x	Logical unit communication failure.
DDDxxxx 509x	Head positioning error (track following error).
DDDxxxx 50Ax	Error log overflow.
DDDxxxx 50Cx	Write error.
DDDxxxx 510x	CRC or ECC error on ID field.
DDDxxxx 511x	Unrecoverable read error.
DDDxxxx 512x	Address mark not found for ID field.
DDDxxxx 513x	Address mark not found for data field.
DDDxxxx 514x	Record not found.
DDDxxxx 515x	Seek error.
DDDxxxx 516x	Data synchronization mark error.
DDDxxxx 517x	Recovered read data with retries (without ECC).
DDDxxxx 518x	Recovered read data with ECC correction.
DDDxxxx 519x	Defect list error.
DDDxxxx 51Ax	Parameter list length overrun.
DDDxxxx 51Bx	Synchronous data transfer error.
DDDxxxx 51Cx	Primary defect list not found.
DDDxxxx 51Dx	Data miscompare during verify.
DDDxxxx 51Ex	Recovered ID read with ECC correction.
DDDxxxx 520x	Invalid command operation code.
DDDxxxx 521x	Illegal logical block address (out of range).
DDDxxxx 522x	Illegal function for device type.
DDDxxxx 524x	Invalid field in command descriptor block.
DDDxxxx 525x	Invalid logical unit number (LUN not supported).
DDDxxxx 526x	Invalid field in parameter list.
DDDxxxx 527x	Media write protected.
DDDxxxx 528x	Media changed error (ready went true).
DDDxxxx 529x	Power-on or bus device reset occurred (not an error).
DDDxxxx 52Ax	Mode select parameters changed (not an error).
DDDxxxx 52Bx	Copy command can't execute because host can't disconnect.
DDDxxxx 52Cx	Command sequence error.
DDDxxxx 52Fx	Tagged commands cleared by another initiator.
DDDxxxx 530x	Incompatible media (unknown or incompatible format).
DDDxxxx 531x	Medium format corrupted.
DDDxxxx 532x	Defect spare location unavailable.
DDDxxxx 537x	Rounded parameter error.
DDDxxxx 539x	Saving parameters not supported.
DDDxxxx 53Ax	Media not present.
DDDxxxx 53Cx	Link flag bit not supported.

DDDxxxx QEEx	Error Code
DDDxxxx 53Dx	Invalid bits in identify message.
DDDxxxx 53Ex	Logical unit has not self-configured.
DDDxxxx 53Fx	Target operating conditions have changed.
DDDxxxx 540x	Device RAM failure.
DDDxxxx 541x	Data path diagnostic failure.
DDDxxxx 542x	Device power-on diagnostic failure.
DDDxxxx 543x	Device message rejected.
DDDxxxx 544x	Target device internal controller error.
DDDxxxx 545x	Select/reselect failure (device unable to reconnect).
DDDxxxx 546x	Device soft reset unsuccessful.
DDDxxxx 547x	SCSI interface parity error.
DDDxxxx 548x	Initiator detected error.
DDDxxxx 549x	Illegal command or command out of sequence error.
DDDxxxx 54Ax	SCSI command phase error.
DDDxxxx 54Bx	SCSI data phase error.
DDDxxxx 54Cx	Logical unit failed self-configuration.
DDDxxxx 54Ex	Overlapped commands attempted.
DDDxxxx 560x	Status error from second-party copy command.
DDDxxxx 588x	Not digital audio track.
DDDxxxx 589x	Not CD-ROM data track.
DDDxxxx 58Ax	Drive not in play audio state.
DDDxxxx 5F0x	Format in progress (not an error).
DDDxxxx 5F1x	Spinup in progress.

Table A.58 SCSI Command Complete Status Block Errors with Q = 6

DDDxxxx QEEx	Error Code
DDDxxxx 601x	SCSI bus reset occurred.
DDDxxxx 602x	SCSI interface fault.
DDDxxxx 610x	SCSI selection time-out (device not available).
DDDxxxx 611x	Unexpected SCSI bus free.
DDDxxxx 612x	Mandatory SCSI message rejected.
DDDxxxx 613x	Invalid SCSI phase sequence.
DDDxxxx 620x	Short length record error.

Table A.59 SCSI Device Condition Error Codes with Q = 7

DDDxxxx QEEx	Error Code
DDDxxxx 702x	Device not ready (removable media devices).
DDDxxxx 704x	Device not ready (nonremovable media devices).
DDDxxxx 728x	Media changed error would not clear.
DDDxxxx 731x	Medium format corrupted (format unit interrupted—reissue format).
DDDxxxx 7F0x	Format in progress (prior format unit command being completed).
DDDxxxx 7F1x	Spinup in progress.

Appendixes

Table A.60 shows the diagnostic test state codes used when a failure occurs. Position *T* indicates the POST *or* diagnostic test state in which the failure occurred.

Table A.60 **SCSI Diagnostics Test State Codes**	
DDDxxxx xxxT	**Test State Code**
DDDxxxx xxx0	Not applicable for error code.
DDDxxxx xxxA	Adapter initialization.
DDDxxxx xxxB	Adapter reset.
DDDxxxx xxxC	Adapter register test.
DDDxxxx xxxD	Adapter buffer test Phase 1 (cached adapter only).
DDDxxxx xxxE	Adapter buffer test Phase 2 (cached adapter only).
DDDxxxx xxxF	Adapter buffer test Phase 3 (cached adapter only).
DDDxxxx xxxG	Adapter buffer test Phase 4 (cached adapter only).
DDDxxxx xxxH	Adapter information test state (buffer enable/size, retry enable, etc.).
DDDxxxx xxxI	Device assignment sequence.
DDDxxxx xxxJ	Device not ready (also initial unit attention clearing).
DDDxxxx xxxK	Device reset.
DDDxxxx xxxL	Device starting phase (appropriate devices only).
DDDxxxx xxxM	Device in process of starting (wait for device to become ready).
DDDxxxx xxxN	Device block size determination.
DDDxxxx xxxO	Device self-test.
DDDxxxx xxxP	Device single block (logical block address) read.
DDDxxxx xxxQ	Device double block (logical block address) read.
DDDxxxx xxxS	Error occurred after device testing had completed.

DOS Error Messages

Table A.61 **DOS Extended Error Codes**		
Hex Code	**Dec Code**	**Description**
01h	1	Invalid function number
02h	2	File not found
03h	3	Path not found
04h	4	Too many open files (no handles left)
05h	5	Access denied
06h	6	Invalid handle
07h	7	Memory control blocks destroyed
08h	8	Insufficient memory
09h	9	Invalid memory block address
0Ah	10	Invalid environment
0Bh	11	Invalid format
0Ch	12	Invalid access code
0Dh	13	Invalid data
0Eh	14	Reserved
0Fh	15	Invalid drive was specified
10h	16	Attempt to write on write-protected diskette
11h	17	Not same devise
12h	18	No more files

Hex Code	Dec Code	Description
13h	19	Attempt to write-protect diskette
14h	20	Unknown unit
15h	21	Drive not ready
16h	22	Unkown command
17h	23	Cyclic Redundancy Check (CRC) error
18h	24	Bad request structure length
19h	25	Seek error
1Ah	26	Unknown media type
1Bh	27	Sector not found
1Ch	28	Printer out of paper
1Dh	29	Write fault
1Eh	30	Read fault
1Fh	31	General failure
20h	32	Sharing violation
21h	33	Lock violation
22h	34	Invalid disk change
23h	35	FCB unavailable
24h	36	Sharing buffer overflow
25h	37	Reserved by DOS 5.0
26h	38	Unable to complete file operation
27h–31h	39–49	Reserved by DOS 5.0
32h	50	Network request not supported
33h	51	Remote computer not listening
34h	52	Duplicate name on network
35h	53	Network path not found
36h	54	Network busy
37h	55	Network device no longer exists
38h	56	NETBIOS command limit exceeded
39h	57	System error; NETBIOS error
3Ah	58	Incorrect response from network
3Bh	59	Unexpected network error
3Ch	60	Incompatible remote adapter
3Dh	61	Print queue full
3Eh	62	Note enough space for print file
3Fh	63	Print file was cancelled
40h	64	Network name was deleted
41h	65	Access denied
42h	66	Network device type incorrect
43h	67	Network name not found
44h	68	Network name limit exceeded
45h	69	NETBIOS session limit exceeded
46h	70	Sharing temporarily paused
47h	71	Network request not accepted
48h	72	Print or disk redirection is paused
49h–4Fh	73–79	Reserved

(continues)

Table A.61	Continued	
Hex Code	**Dec Code**	**Description**
50h	80	File exists
51h	81	Reserved
52h	82	Cannot make directory entry
53h	83	Fail on Interrupt 24
54h	84	Too many redirections
55h	85	Duplicate redirection
56h	86	Invalid password
57h	87	Invalid parameter
58h	88	Network data fault
59h	89	Function not supported by network
5Ah	90	Required system component not installed

Table A.62	DOS Parse Error Codes
Code	**Description**
1	Too many paramters
2	Required parameter missing
3	Invalid switch
4	Invalid keyword
6	Parameter value not in allowed range
7	Parameter value not allowed
8	Parameter value not allowed
9	Parameter format not correct
10	Invalid parameter
11	Invalid parameter combination

IBM Technical Manuals and Updates

IBM has an extensive array of documentation available to help a system troubleshooter responsible for upgrading and repairing any system. These manuals are primarily in three categories: Guide to Operations or Quick Reference Manuals, Hardware-Maintenance Manuals, and Technical-Reference Manuals. You purchase these manuals in basic form and then buy updates that reflect changes in newer systems as they are introduced. All the manuals together with the updates presents a bewildering—and expensive—array of documentation. If you are interested in obtaining any of this documentation, this section is very useful.

This section explains each manual type and gives information needed for ordering this documentation, and tables describe all the available manuals and updates, including part numbers and prices.

Guide to Operations and Quick-Reference Manuals

These publications contain instructions for system operation, testing, relocation, and option installation. A diagnostics floppy disk is included, which includes the Advanced Diagnostics for most PS/2 Model 50 and higher systems.

Table A.63 Guide to Operations and Quick Reference Manual Part Numbers and Prices

Description	Part Number	Price
Model 25	75X1051	$29.75
Model 25 286	15F2179	37.75
Model 30	68X2230	56.25
Model 30 286	15F2143	44.00
Model 35 SX	84F9844	35.75
Model 40 SX	84F7765	42.50
Model L40 SX	84F7577	81.50
Model 50	68X2321	56.25
Model N51 SX	04G5107	70.75
Model 55 SX	91F8575	49.50
Model 56 SX and 56 SLC	10G6001	66.25
Model 57 SX and 57 SLC	04G3382	64.75
Model 60	68X22I3	56.25
Model 65 SX	91F8622	28.75
Model 70	91F8577	50.50
Model 70 486	91F8619	57.75
Model P70 386	68X2380	17.00
Model P75 486	84F7590	39.25
Model 80	91F8580	50.50
Model 90 48	92F2685	90.25
Model 90 (Models 0H5 and 0H9 only)	41G8561	85.25
Model 90 (Models 0L9 and 0LF only)	41G8330	65.00
Model 95 486	92F2684	103.00
Model 95 (Models 0H9 and 0HF only)	41G8562	111.00
Models 95 (Model 0LF only)	41G8331	68.00
External Storage Enclosure for SCSI Devices	15F2159	15.25
FAX Concentrator Adapter/A	15F2260	31.50
Remote Program Load for Ethernet Networks	15F2292	29.00

PC Systems

Description	Part Number	Price
AT	6280066	$49.50
AT Model 339	6280102	80.00
PC	6322510	50.00
PC Convertible	6280629	71.50
PC*jr*	1502292	23.25
Portable PC	6936571	66.75
XT	6322511	50.00
XT Models 089 268 278	6280085	88.00
XT Model 286	6280147	65.00

Appendixes

Hardware-Maintenance Library

The Hardware-Maintenance Library consists of a two-part set of manuals, including a service manual, a reference manual, and supplements or updates.

The Hardware-Maintenance Service manuals contain all the information necessary to diagnose a failure. Maintenance-analysis procedures (MAPs), the parts catalog, and Reference Disks containing the advanced diagnostic tests are included with these manuals. The Hardware-Maintenance Reference contains product descriptions, field-replaceable unit (FRU) locations and removal procedures, and information about the diagnostic programs. To maintain an accurate library, you should add all available supplements.

Table A.64 PS/2 Hardware-Maintenance Service Manual Part Numbers and Prices		
Description	Part Number	Price
PS/2 Hardware-Maintenance Service Library (includes all of the following pamphlets):	SBOF-3988	N/A
General Information	15F2189	$3.70
Model 25/30	15F2191	3.70
Model 25 SX	10G6609	2.95
Model 25 286	15F2181	5.75
Model 30 286	91F9231	2.30
Model 35 SX	10G6621	2.05
Model 40 SX	84F7767	1.80
Model L40 SX	15F2266	1.65
Model 50	15F2193	1.60
Model N51 SX	04G5112	4.55
Model 55 SX	91F8637	2.40
Model 56 SX and 56 SLC	10G6003	3.40
Model 57 SX, 57 SLC, & M57 SLC	04G3383	2.70
Model 60	84F9825	3.55
Model 65 SX	84F8549	1.70
Model 70 (includes Model 70 486)	91F8635	2.40
Model P70 386	15F2198	1.60
Model P75 486	84F7593	5.55
Model 80	84F8547	1.70
Model 90 XP 486	04G3389	2.20
Model 95 XP 486	04G3394	2.20
Option Pamphlets		
Communications Cartridge (for L40 SX)	10G5993	$1.95
External Devices Parts Catalog	64F4022	3.55
External SCSI Devices	92F1656	4.65
300/1200/2400 Internal Modem/A	68X2384	10.75
Adapter/A for Ethernet Networks	84F9863	19.50
8504 Monochrome Display	15F2241	11.00
Host Connected Keyboard Errata Sheet	92F1682	6.55

Table A.65 PS/2 Hardware-Maintenance Reference Manual Part Numbers and Prices

Description	Part Number	Price
PS/2 Hardware-Maintenance Reference Library (includes all of the following manuals):	**SBOF-3989**	**N/A**
General Information Manual	64F3983	$5.95
Diagnostics for Micro Channel Systems	15F2245	6.00
Diagnostics for Non-Micro Channel Systems	64F3985	5.95
Model 25	64F3986	2.65
Model 25 SX	10G6610	2.80
Model 25 286	64F3811	2.65
Model 30	64F3987	2.65
Model 30 286	64F3988	2.65
Model 35 SX	10G6620	2.45
Model 40 SX	84F7768	5.10
Model L40 SX	15F2267	2.85
Model 50	64F3989	2.65
Model N51 SX	04G5111	5.25
Model 55 SX	15F2250	2.15
Model 56 SX	04G3295	3.55
Model 56 SX and 56 SLC	10G6002	3.55
Model 57 SX, 57 SLC, & M57 SLC	04G3384	2.95
Model 60	64F3991	2.65
Model 65 SX	64F3992	2.65
Model 70	64F3993	2.65
Model P70 386	64F3994	2.65
Model P75 486	84F8525	8.80
Model 80	84F8548	2.85
Model 90 XP 486	04G3388	2.50
Model 95 XP 486	04G3393	5.25
Options and Adapter Information	64F3996	2.65
Option Manuals		
Communications Cartridge (for L40 SX)	10G5992	$1.95
Adapter/A for Ethernet Networks	15F2290	2.20
5.25-Inch Slim High Diskette Drive	15F2274	1.55
1–8MB 286 Memory	85F1672	15.75
2.88MB Diskette Drive	85F1648	6.35
FAX Concentrator Adapter/A	15F2262	3.50
External Storage Enclosure for SCSI Devices	91F9233	2.20

Table A.66 PS/2 Hardware-Maintenance Library Update Part Numbers and Prices

Description	Part Number	Price
PS/2 Hardware-Maintenance Library Supplements (includes HMS and HMR update and diskette):		
Model 25 SX	10G6616	$36.00
Model 25 286	15F2180	17.00
Model 35 SX	92F2735	28.50
Model 40 SX	85F1645	13.75
Model L40 SX	15F2271	38.00
Model N51 SX and N51 SLC	04G5108	33.25
Model 56 SX and 56 SLC	10G6005	28.75
Model M57 SLC	10G3340	23.00
Model 57 SX and 57 SLC	04G3385	11.25
Model P70 386	15F2149	44.00
Model 90 486	04G3391	14.50
Model 95 486	04G3396	14.50
Communications Cartridge (for L40 SX)	10G5994	27.95
400MB Hard Disk Drive	15F2233	2.00
Image Adapter/A	15F2240	36.25
2.3GB Full Height SCSI Tape Drive	91F9250	20.00
Rewritable Optical Drive	91F9234	13.25
8517 Color Display	92F2676	11.75
8518 Color Display	85F1692	25.50
Cached Processor Option	04G5106	13.00
Manual Binders and Inserts		
Empty HMS (Service) Binder	85F8542	$41.00
HMS Vinyl Insert (pkg. of 6)	84F8543	11.75
Empty HMR (Reference) Binder	01F0200	17.00

Table A.67 PC Family Hardware-Maintenance Service Manual Part Numbers and Prices

Description	Part Number	Price
PC Hardware-Maintenance Service (PC,XT,AT,PPC)	6280087	$244.00
Supplements to 6280087		
AT Model 339	6280139	$12.00
XT Model 286	68X2211	12.00
XT Models 089, 268, 278	6280109	12.00
PS/2 Display Adapter (VGA Card)	68X2216	37.00
PC Music Feature	75X1049	52.00
2MB Expanded Memory Adapter	74X9923	67.25
3 1/2-Inch internal Floppy Disk Drive	6280159	7.05
3 1/2-Inch external Floppy Disk Drive	6280111	12.25
5 1/4-Inch external Floppy Disk Drive	68X2273	12.25
20MB Hard Disk Drive Model 25	01F0246	9.45
Empty supplement binder	1502561	9.45
Color Printer Model 5182	68X2237	$63.75

Description	Part Number	Price
Graphics and Compact Printer	6280079	43.00
PCjr	1502294	96.75
PC Convertible	6280641	101.00
Supplement to 6280641		
Speech Adapter	59X9964	$23.00

Table A.68   PC Family Hardware-Maintenance Reference Manual Part Numbers and Prices

Description	Part Number	Price
PC Hardware-Maintenance Reference (PC,XT,AT,PPC)	6280088	$187.00
Supplements to 6280088		
AT Model 339	6280138	$7.40
XT Model 286	68X2212	12.00
XT Models 089, 268, and 278	6280108	7.40
PS/2 Display Adapter (VGA Card)	68X2238	7.50
Color Display 8514	68X2218	7.50
3.5-Inch Internal Floppy Disk Drive	6280160	7.40
20MB Hard Disk Drive Model 25	01F0244	4.30
Empty supplement binder	01F0200	21.00

Technical-Reference Library

The publications listed in the following table provide system-specific hardware and software interface information for the IBM PC and PS/2 products. They are intended for developers who provide hardware and software products to operate with these systems. The library is divided into system, options and adapters, and BIOS interface publications.

Table A.69   PC and AT-Bus System Technical-Reference Manual Part Numbers and Prices

Description	Part Number	Price
Hardware Interface Technical-Reference AT-Bus Systems	85F1646	$63.00
Updates to 85F1646		
PS/2 Model 25 SX	10G6457	10.60
PS/2 Models 35 and 40	41G2950	10.60
Keyboard/Auxiliary Device and AT-Bus Architecture	41G5096	10.75
PS/2 Model L40 SX (Laptop)	15F2270	59.00
PS/2 Model 25	75X1055	35.75
Supplement to 75X1055		
20MB Hard Disk Drive	01F0245	4.20
PS/2 Model 30	68X2201	94.25
PS/2 Model 30 286	01F0237	30.25
Supplements to 01F0237		
PS/2 Model 25 286	15F2182	20.00
PC	6322507	37.50
PC AT	6280070	131.00

(continues)

Table A.69   Continued

Description	Part Number	Price
Supplements to 6280070		
PC AT Model 339	6280099	62.00
PC XT Model 286	68X2210	62.75
PC XT and Portable PC	6280089	62.00
PC Convertible	6280648	94.25
Supplements to 6280648		
Speech Adapter	59X9965	23.00
256KB Memory and Enhanced Modem	75X1035	5.20
PC*jr*	1502293	51.25

Hardware Interface Technical Reference. These publications provide interface and design information for the system units. Information is included for the system board, math coprocessor, power supply, video subsystem, keyboard, instruction sets, and other features of the system.

Table A.70   MCA-Bus Hardware Interface Technical-Reference Manual Part Numbers and Prices

Description	Part Number	Price
PS/2 Hardware Interface Technical-Reference Manuals		
System Specific Information Technical Reference	84F9807	$75.00
Updates to 84F9807		
Models 90, 95 and Model 57	04G3280	20.75
Models 56 SX and 56 SLC	41G2912	10.00
Supplements to 84F9807		
Model N51 SX	04G5120	16.75
Model P75 486	84F7592	35.50
Architectures Technical Reference	84F9808	55.00
Update to 84F9808		
Micro Channel Architecture and Setup.	04G3282	16.00
Supplements to 84F9808		
Subsystem Control Block Architecture	85F1678	15.00
Common Interfaces Technical Reference	84F9808	75.00
Update to 84F9809		
Floppy Controller, Keyboard, Keyboard/Auxiliary Device Controller, Serial Port Controller, Video Subsystem, and SCSI	04G3281	21.75
Supplement to 84F9809		
Model P70 386	68X2377	15.50

BIOS Interface Technical Reference. This publication provides basic input-output system (BIOS) interface information. It is intended for developers of hardware or software products that operate with the IBM PC and PS/2 products.

Table A.71 BIOS Interface Technical-Reference Manual Part Numbers and Prices		
Description	**Part Number**	**Price**
BIOS Interface Technical Reference (4th edition)	04G3283	$55.00

Options and Adapters Technical Reference. These publications provide interface and design information for the options and adapters available for various systems. This information includes a hardware description, programming considerations, interface specifications, and BIOS information (where applicable).

Table A.72 Options and Adapters Technical-Reference Manual Part Numbers and Prices		
Description	**Part Number**	**Price**

Options and Adapters Technical Reference, includes
    Asynchronous Communications Adapter
    Bisynchronous Communications Adapter
    Cluster Adapter
    Color Display
    Color/Graphics Monitor Adapter
    Color, Compact, and Graphics Printers
    Expansion Unit
    Hard Disk Drive Adapter
    Game Control Adapter
    Monochrome Display
    Monochrome/Printer Adapter
    Printer Adapter
    SDLC Adapter
    Slimline Floppy Disk Drive
    10MB Hard Disk Drive
    5.25-Inch Floppy Disk Drive and Adapter
    64/256KB Memory Option
	6322509	$156.00

Engineering/Scientific Adapters, includes
    Data Acquisition and Control Adapter (DAC)
    DAC Distribution Panel
    General Purpose Interface Bus Adapter
    Professional Graphics Controller
    Professional Graphics Display
	6280133	42.25

Personal Computer AT, includes
    Double-Sided Floppy Disk Drive
    Hard Disk and Floppy Disk Drive Adapter
    High-Capacity Floppy Disk Drive
    Serial/Parallel Adapter
    128KB Memory Expansion Option
    20MB Hard Disk Drive
    512KB Memory Expansion Option
	6280134	16.00

Communications		
Dual Async Adapter/A (Second Edition)	68X2315	$7.50
Multiprotocol Adapter/A (Second Edition)	68X2316	14.75
300/1200 Internal Modem/A	68X2275	7.50
300/1200/2400 Internal Modem/A	68X2378	6.40
Displays		
PS/2 Color Display 8514	68X2214	$7.50
PS/2 Display Adapter (VGA Card)	68X2251	12.25
PS/2 Display Adapter 8514/A	68X2248	12.25
PS/2 Displays 8503, 8512, and 8513	68X2206	7.50
EGA, EGA Display, and EGA Memory Expansion Card	6280131	12.00

(continues)

Appendixes

Table A.72   Continued

Description	Part Number	Price
Floppy Disk Drives and Adapters		
3.5-Inch External Drive	59X9945	$6.50
3.5-Inch External Drive Adapter	59X9946	6.50
3.5-Inch 720KB/1.44MB/2.88MB Drive	15F2258	11.50
5.25-Inch External Drive (360KB)	68X2272	12.25
5.25-Inch External Drive (1.2MB)	68X2348	11.75
5.25-Inch Internal Drive (1.2MB)	68X2350	11.75
5.25-Inch Drive Adapter (1.2MB)	68X2349	11.75
Floppy Disk Drive Half Height (XT, AT)	6280093	7.40
Hard Disk Drive and Adapters		
Hard Disk Drive Adapter/A	68X2226	$14.75
Hard Disk Drive Adapter/A, ESDI	68X2234	14.75
Hard Disk/Floppy Disk Adapter (for XT Model 286)	68X2215	7.50
20MB Drive (XT-089,-278,-286)	68X2208	8.75
20MB Adapter (XT-089,-268,-278)	6280092	7.40
20MB Drive and Adapter (Model 25)	01F0247	3.45
3.5-Inch 20MB Drive (Model 30)	68X2205	7.50
3.5-Inch 20MB Drive (Model 50)	68X2219	12.25
30MB Drive (AT)	68X2310	23.00
30MB Drive (Model 50-031)	68X2324	12.25
20/30/45MB Drive (Model 25 and 30)	92F1655	13.00
40MB/80MB Drive	91F9230	17.25
44MB Drive (Second Edition)	68X2317	7.50
60MB Adapter (50-021 and 50-031)	68X2343	4.95
60/120MB Drives (Models 50 and 70)	68X2314	11.00
70/115/314MB Drives	68X2236	7.50
Other Storage Devices and Adapters		
CD-ROM Drive	15F2134	$13.00
Rewritable Optical Drive	64F1513	17.50
2.3GB SCSI Tape Drive	84F9801	19.75
Micro Channel SCSI Adapter	68X2397	16.25
Micro Channel SCSI Adapter w/Cache	68X2365	17.25
FAX Concentrator Adapter/A Device Driver Reference	15F2263	18.00
FAX Concentrator Adapter/A Extended Device Driver Ref.	15F2276	30.00
Internal Data/FAX Modem for the L40 SX	15F2268	14.00
Memory		
128/640KB Memory Adapter	1502544	$7.40
256KB Memory Expansion	6280132	12.00
512KB/2MB Memory Adapter	6183075	7.40
2MB Expanded Memory Adapter	75X1086	10.75
Expanded Memory Adapter/A (0–8MB)	01F0228	7.80
80286 Memory Expansion Option	68X2227	7.50
80286 Memory Expansion Option 2–8MB	68X2356	7.60
80386 Memory Expansion Option 2–6MB	68X2257	12.25
80386 Memory Expansion Option 2–8MB	68X2339	14.75

Description	Part Number	Price
Other		
PS/2 Speech Adapter	68X2207	$15.75
Voice Communications Adapter	55X8864	7.40
PS/2 Mouse	68X2229	7.50
PC Music Feature	75X1048	21.75
Empty Options and Adapters Binder	6280115	9.30
Software Reference Manuals		
Basic Reference Version 3.30	6280189	$56.00
DOS Technical Reference Version 5.02	53G1686	85.00

Ordering Information

IBM technical and service publications can be ordered by calling toll-free, 1-800-IBM-PCTB (1-800-426-7282), Monday through Friday, 8 a.m. to 8 p.m. Eastern time. In Canada, call toll-free, 1-800-465-1234, Monday through Friday, from 8:30 a.m. to 4:30 p.m. Eastern time. In British Columbia, call toll-free, 112-800-465-1234. In Alaska, call 1-414-633-8108.

When you order by telephone, you can use a credit card. You also may call to request additional copies of the Technical Directory (catalog) or to inquire about the availability of technical information on newly announced products that may not be listed here.

Appendixes

Appendix B

Vendor List

One of the most frustrating things about supporting PCs is finding a specific adapter board, part, driver program, or whatever you need to make a system work. If you are supporting or installing products, you will often need access to technical support or documentation for products you may not have purchased yourself. Over the years I have compiled a list of companies whose products are popular or I have found to work exceptionally well. I use these contacts regularly to provide information and components to enable me to support PC systems effectively.

Many of these companies have been mentioned in this book, but others not specifically mentioned have been added here. These companies carry many computer products you often will have contact with, or I simply recommend. I have tried to list as many vendors as possible that are important in day-to-day work with PC systems. These vendors can supply documentation for components you have, provide parts and service, and be used as a source for new equipment and even software. This list is as up-to-date as possible, but companies move or go out of business all the time. If you find any information in this list that no longer is accurate, please call me or leave me a message on CompuServe. My address, phone number, and CIS ID are under the listing for Mueller Technical Research.

Many of the companies listed also provide support via electronic Bulletin Board Systems (BBSs). Ward Christensen (creator of the XModem protocol) and Randy Seuss created the first Computer-ized Bulletin Board System (CBBS) system that went on-line on February 16, 1978, and is still running today using the original software! You can call Ward and Randy's CBBS at (312)545-8086. Since that first BBS came on-line, BBS systems have proliferated throughout the world. While origi-nally exclusively the domain of computer enthusiasts, today many companies use BBS systems to provide a high level of technical support. Through a company-run BBS you often can receive de-tailed technical support on that company's products, as well as download product literature and reference materials. I usually find the level of support I can obtain through a BBS is superior to traditional phone support, especially since I don't have to wait on hold!

Many of these companies also provide on-line support and services through the CompuServe Infor-mation System (CIS). You will find many major hardware and software companies on CIS; however, most of these same companies also run standard BBS systems as well. Access to CIS is charged by the hour based on the connect speed (up to 9600 bps; 14,400 bps in some locations), but the phone call itself is usually a local one. If you want to access CIS, you can contact them via a voice line (see the vendor list) and request a startup kit.

With each company listing, I have included both standard phone numbers as well as 800 numbers where possible, so U.S. and international readers can easily contact these companies. Also included are fax and Bulletin Board System (BBS) numbers where available. I have not included any communications parameter settings, but virtually all BBS systems work with at least 2400 bps (V.22bis), 8 data bits, no parity, and 1 stop bit. Many of these systems also support faster communications rates up to 14,400 bps (V.32bis), or even 28,800 bps (V.34). Some companies run a FAXback system, an automated system through which you can request product and technical information to be sent directly to your own fax machine. FAXback systems are an excellent way to get immediate documentation or technical support to solve tough problems.

Finally, each listing also includes a short description of the products or services the company provides. I use this vendor list constantly myself; I hope you find this list as useful as I do!

3M Data Storage Products Division
3M Center Building
#223-5N-01
St. Paul, MN 55144
(612)736-1866

Manufactures magnetic disk and tape media. DC-600 and DC-2000 media are standards for tape backup data cartridges.

Accurite Technologies, Inc.
231 Charcot Ave.
San Jose, CA 95131
(408)433-1980

Manufactures Accurite Drive Probe floppy disk diagnostic program, as well as HRD, DDD, and ADD industry-standard test disks.

Acer America Corporation
2641 Orchard Parkway
San Jose, CA 95134
(408)432-6200
(800)733-2237
(800)637-7000 Technical Support
(408)922-2933 Fax
(800)239-2237 Sales

Manufactures PC-compatible systems, monitors, and printers.

Acme Electric/Safe Power
20 Water Street
Cuba, NY 14727
(716)968-2400
(800)325-5848

Manufactures uninterruptible power supplies (UPS) systems and power conditioners.

Adaptec
691 S. Milpitas Boulevard
Milpitas, CA 95035
(408)945-8600
(408)945-2550 Technical Support
(800)959-7274 Technical upport
(408)945-2766 Literature
(408)945-7727 BBS

Manufactures a variety of excellent hard disk controllers and SCSI host adapters. Its SCSI host adapters have become a de facto standard and have an enormous amount of third-party support.

Adaptive Technologies
127 N. Ventura Blvd.
Port Hueneme, CA 93041
(805)488-4890 Fax

Manufactures and sells the PROMPAQ automobile ECM chip selector. This device installs in General Motors automobiles and allows switching among as many as 4 EPROMS with different vehicle operating programs. The selected PROM is enabled as if it were plugged into the ECM. The switch can be changed even while the vehicle is running, instantly enabling the new PROM program! I used this device to install 4 custom EPROMS in one of my vehicles.

Addison-Wesley Publishing Co, Inc.
One Jacob Way
Reading, MA 01867
(617)944-3700

Publishes technical publications and books.

Adobe Systems, Inc.
1585 Charleston Road
Box 7900
Mountain View, CA 94039
(408)986-6500
(800)447-3577
(408)986-6560 Technical Support
(408)986-6587 Fax request
(800)83FONTS Sales

Manufactures (and created) the PostScript language and a variety of graphics software.

ADP Hollander Company
14800 28th Avenue N.
Suite 190
Plymouth, MN 55447
800-825-0644

Publishes automotive parts interchange manuals.

Advanced Digital Information Corporation
14737 NE 87th Street
Box 2996
Redmond, WA 98073-2966
(206)881-8004
(800)336-1233
(206)881-2296 Fax
(714)894-0893 BBS

Manufactures high-capacity tape-backup subsystems.

Advanced Logic Research (ALR)
9401 Jeronimo Street
Irvine, CA 92718
(714)581-6770
(800)444-4257
(714)581-9240 Fax
(714)458-1952 Technical Support
(714)458-6834 BBS

Manufactures PC compatibles featuring ISA, EISA, and MCA buses.

Advanced Micro Devices (AMD)
901 Thompson Place
Box 3453
Sunnyvale, CA 94088
(408)732-2400

Manufactures 386-compatible chips and math coprocessors.

Aeronics, Inc.
12741 Research Blvd.
Suite #500
Austin, TX 78759
(512)258-2303
(512)258-4392 Fax

Manufactures the highest quality active and forced perfect terminators for use in SCSI-bus systems. It is known for solving problems with longer distances or multiple-SCSI devices.

Aldus Corporation
411 1st Avenue South
Seattle, WA 98104
(206)622-5500
(800)333-2538

Manufactures PageMaker desktop publishing software and a variety of other graphical programs.

ALL Computers, Inc.
1220 Yonge Street
Second Floor
Toronto, ONT M4T1W1
CANADA
(416)960-0111
(416)960-0111 Technical Support
(416)960-5426 Fax
(416)960-8679 BBS

Manufactures the ALL Chargecard memory coprocessor.

Alliance Research
20120 Plummer Street
Chatsworth, CA 91311
(800)431-8124

Manufactures a complete line of switch boxes for parallel, serial, video, and many other connections.

Allied Computer Services, Inc.
3417 Center Point Road N.E.
Cedar Rapids, IA 52402
(319)378-1383
(319)378-1489 Fax

Manufactures and sells the Trapcard II IRQ and DMA diagnostic board.

AllMicro, Inc.
18220 US Highway 19 N
Suite 215
Clearwater, FL 34624
(813)539-7283

Manufacturer and distributor of the Rescue data recovery software and various other hardware and software diagnostic and troubleshooting tools.

Alloy Computer Products
25 Polter Rd.
Littleton, MA 01460
(508)486-0001
(508)486-3755 Fax
(508)486-4044 BBS

Manufactures tape-backup subsystems.

Alpha Research Corporation
8200 Mopac Expressway North
Park North Building, #120
Austin, TX 78759
(512)418-0220

Manufactures a complete line of caching and non-caching disk controllers, local bus motherboards, and video cards. Specializes in IDE and SCSI adapters that are fast and flexible.

ALPS America
3553 N. First Street
San Jose, CA 95134
(408)432-6000

Supplies 5 1/4-inch and
3 1/2-inch floppy drives to
IBM for use in the original XT,
AT, and now the PS/2 systems.
Also manufactures a line of
printers and scanners.

Altex Electronics, Inc.
300 Breesport
San Antonio, TX 78216
(800)531-5369

Supplies mail-order electronics
parts.

Ambra Computer Corporation
3200 Beechleaf Court
Suite 1000
Raleigh, NC 27604-1063
(919)713-1550
(800)25-AMBRA
(919)713-1599 Fax

An IBM company that manu-
factures and sells low-cost,
high-performance compatible
systems featuring Pentium and
IBM Blue Lightning processors
as well as other unique features.

Amdek Corporation
3471 N. First Street
San Jose, CA 95134
(408)473-1200
(800)722-6335
(408)435-2770 Technical
Support
(408)922-5729 Fax
(408)922-4400 BBS

Division of Wyse Technology
that manufactures monitors.

American Megatrends, Inc. (AMI)
6145-F Northbelt Parkway
Norcross, GA 30071
(404)263-8181
(800)828-9264
(404)246-8780 BBS

Manufactures IBM-compatible
BIOS, excellent ISA, EISA,
VL-Bus, and PCI local bus
motherboards, and diagnostic
software such as AMIDIAG,
SCSI DIAG, and Remote.

American National Standards Institute (ANSI)
11 West 42nd Street
13th Floor
New York, NY 10036
(212)642-4900

ANSI committees set stan-
dards throughout the com-
puter industry. Copies of any
ANSI-approved standard can
be ordered here.

AMP, Inc.
AMP Building
P.O. Box 3608
Harrisburg, PA 17105
(717)564-0100
(800)522-6752

Manufactures a variety of
computer connectors, sockets,
and cables used by many
OEMs, including IBM.

Andromeda Research
P.O. Box 222
Milford, OH 45150
(513)831-9708
(513)831-7562

Manufactures an excellent
EPROM programmer that runs
from a PC parallel port. The
device can program up to 4M
EPROMS and includes soft-
ware for menu driven operation on IBM-compatible systems.

Annabooks
11848 Bernardo Plaza Court
Suite 110
San Diego, CA 92128-2417

(619)673-0870
(800)462-1042
(619)673-1432 Fax

Publishes and sells an excellent
line of technical publications
and books especially for those
in PC hardware and software
design.

Anthem Technology Systems (ATS)
1160 Ridder Park Drive
San Jose, CA 95131
(408)441-7177
(800)359-3580
(800)359-9877 Fax

A large distributor of Hewlett
Packard DAT tape and hard
disk drives. It also distributes
other hard disk and storage
products.

Anvil Cases
15650 Salt Lake Avenue
Industry, CA 91745
(818)968-4100
(800)359-2684

Manufactures heavy-duty
equipment cases.

AOX, Inc.
486 Totten Pond Road
Waltham, MA 02154
(617)890-4402
(800)726-0269

Manufactures PS/2 MCA bus
master 386- and 486-processor
upgrade boards.

Apple Computer, Inc.
20525 Mariani Avenue
Cupertino, CA 95014
(408)996-1010
(800)538-9696

Manufactures a line of Apple-
compatible systems, peripherals, and software.

**Archive Technology/
Ardat, Inc.**
1650 Sunflower Avenue
Costa Mesa, CA 92626
(714)641-1230
(800)537-2724

Division of Conner Tape Products that manufactures high-capacity tape drives.

Arco Electronics, Inc.
2750 N. 29th Ave.
Suite 316
Hollywood, CA 33020
(305)925-2688
(305)925-2889 Fax
(305)925-2791 BBS

Manufactures a complete line of Micro Channel ATA IDE adapters used to upgrade IBM PS/2 systems.

Areal Technology, Inc.
2075 Zanker Road
San Jose, CA 95131
(408)436-6800

Manufactures high-capacity 3 1/2-inch hard disk drives.

Arrow Electronics, Inc.
25 Hub Drive
Melville, NY 11747
(516)391-1300
(800)447-5270

System and peripheral distributor.

Arrowfield International, Inc.
2822-C Walnut Ave.
Tustin, CA 92680
(714)669-0101
(714)669-0526 Fax

Manufactures an incredible array of disk drive brackets, rails, slides, cable adapters, bezels, cabinets, and complete drive upgrade and repair

assemblies for IBM, Compaq, and IBM-compatible systems.

AST Research, Inc.
16215 Alton Parkway
Irvine, CA 92713-9658
(714)727-4141
(800)876-4278
(714)727-4723 BBS

Manufactures an extensive line of adapter boards and peripherals for IBM and compatible computers, as well as a line of IBM-compatible systems.

Astec Standard Power
Division of Astec America, Inc.
401 Jones Road
Oceanside, CA 92054-1216
(619)757-1880
(619)439-4243 Fax

Manufactures high-end power supplies for PC systems as well as many other applications. Astec power supplies are used as OEM equipment in many of the top manufacturers' systems, including IBM and others.

AT&T
55 Corporate Drive
Bridgewater, NJ 08807
(404)446-4734
(800)247-1212
(201)769-6397 BBS

Manufactures a line of IBM-compatible computer systems.

AT&T National Parts Sales Center
2551 E. 40th Avenue
Denver, CO 80205
(800)222-7278

Supplies parts and components for AT&T computer systems. Call and ask for the free AT&T parts catalog.

ATI Technologies, Inc.
33 Commerce Valley Drive East
Thornhill, ONT L3T7N6
CANADA
(905)882-2600
(905)882-2626 Technical Support
(905)882-2620 Fax
(905)764-9404 BBS

Manufactures an excellent line of high-performance standard and local bus video cards and chipsets.

AutoDesk, Inc.
2320 Marinship Way
Sausalito, CA 94965
(415)332-2344
(800)445-5415

Manufactures AutoCAD software.

Award Software, Inc.
130 Knowles Drive
Los Gatos, CA 95030-1832
(415)968-4433
(408)370-3399 Fax
(408)370-3139 BBS

Manufactures a line of IBM-compatible ROM BIOS software.

Beckman Industrial
3883 Ruffin Road
San Diego, CA 92123
(619)495-3200
(800)854-2708

Division of Wave Tech that manufactures diagnostics and test equipment.

Belden Wire and Cable
P.O. Box 1980
Richmond, IN 47375
(317)983-5200
(800)235-3361

Manufactures cable and wire products.

Appendixes

Berkshire Products, Inc.
2180 Pleasant Hill Road
Suite A-5185
Duluth, GA 30136-4663
(404)271-0088
(404)932-0082 Fax

Manufactures a diagnostic monitoring product, called System Sentry, that continuously monitors power supply performance and system internal temperature as well as CMOS battery voltage, and BIOS POST codes. System Sentry is designed for diagnostic applications as well as for use in a file server application, where the internal serial port can transmit error information to another system via a modem. It also makes a high-speed buffered parallel port adapter.

Best Power Technology, Inc.
P.O. Box 280
Necedah, WI 54646
(608)565-7200
(800)356-5794
(608)565-2221 Fax

Manufactures an excellent line of computer power protection equipment from high-end Ferroresonent UPS systems to line conditioners and standby power protection systems.

Bitstream, Inc.
215 1st Street
Cambridge, MA 02142
(617)497-6222
(800)522-3668

Manufactures fonts and font software.

Black Box Corporation
P.O. Box 12800
Pittsburgh, PA 15241
(412)746-5530

Manufactures and distributes a variety of communications products, including network adapters, cables, and connectors for a variety of applications.

Boca Research, Inc.
6413 Congress Avenue
Boca Raton, FL 33487-2841
(407)997-6227
(407)241-8088 Technical Support
(407)997-0918 Fax
(407)241-1601 BBS

Manufactures a low-cost line of adapter card products for IBM compatibles.

Bondwell Industrial Company, Inc.
47485 Seabridge Drive
Fremont, CA 94538
(510)490-4300

Manufactures a line of laptop systems.

Borland International
100 Borland Way
Scotts Valley, CA 95066-3249
(800)331-0877
(408)431-1000 Technical Support
(408)822-4269 Technical Fax
(408)431-5096 BBS

Software manufacturer that features Turbo language products, Paradox, as well as dBASE IV, acquired from Ashton-Tate.

Boston Computer Exchange
55 Temple Place
Boston, MA 02111
(617)542-4414

A broker for used IBM and compatible computers.

Bracking, Jim
967 Pinewood Drive
San Jose, CA 95129
(408)725-0628

Manufactures the HDtest hard disk test and format program. This program, distributed as shareware, is excellent for testing and educational use.

Brightbill-Roberts
120 E. Washington Street
#421
Syracuse, NY 13202

Manufactures the ShowPartner FX presentation graphics program.

Buerg, Vernon D.
139 White Oak Circle
Petaluma, CA 94952
(707)778-1811
(707)778-8728 Fax
(707)778-8944 BBS

Manufactures an excellent line of utility programs, including the popular LIST program. Buerg Software is distributed through BBSs and CompuServe.

Bureau of Electronic Publishing
141 New Road
Parsippany, NJ 07054
(201)808-2700
(800)828-4766

Distributes and publishes software on CD-ROM disks.

Byte Information Exchange (BIX)
One Phoenix Mill Lane
Peterborough, NH 03458

An on-line computer information and messaging system.

Byte Magazine
One Phoenix Mill Lane
Peterborough, NH 03458
(603)924-9281
(617)861-9764 BBS

A monthly magazine covering
all lines of microcomputers.

C. Itoh Electronics, Inc.
19300 S. Hamilton Avenue
Box 9116
Torrance, CA 90508

Manufactures PC printers and
other peripherals.

Cable Connection
557 Salmar Avenue
Suite B
Campbell, CA 95008
(408)379-9224

Manufactures a variety of
cable, connector, and switch
products.

Cables To Go
1501 Webster Street
Dayton, OH 45404
(800)826-7904

Manufactures a variety of
cable, connector, and switch
products.

Cache Computers, Inc.
46600 Landing Parkway
Fremont, CA 94538

Manufactures a line of 386
and 486 motherboards.

Caig Laboratories
1175-0 Industrial Avenue
P.O. Box J
Escondido, CA 92025-0051

Manufactures and sells
Cramolin R-100L Red
liquid contact cleaner
and preservative.

Cal-Abco
6041 Variel Avenue
Woodland Hills, CA 91367
(800)669-2226
(818)704-7733 Fax

Distributes computer systems
and peripherals.

Canon USA, Inc.
One Canon Plaza
Lake Success, NY 11042
(516)488-6700
(800)221-3333
(516)354-5805 Fax
(516)488-6528 BBS

Manufactures a line of printer
and video equipment as well as
floppy drives. Supplies floppy
drives to Compaq and IBM.

Casio, Inc.
15 Gardner Road
Fairfield, NJ 07006

Manufactures personal data
systems and digital watches.

Central Point Software, Inc.
15220 NW Greenbrier Parkway
Beaverton, OR 97006-9937
(503)690-8088
(800)445-4208
(503)690-8083 Fax
(503)690-6650 BBS

Manufactures the PC Tools,
Copy II PC, and Central Point
Backup software. Central Point
supplies many of the utilities
found in IBM- and MS-DOS 5.0
and higher.

Chemtronics, Inc.
8125 Cobb Center Drive
Kennesaw, GA 30144
(404)424-4888
(404)424-4267 Fax

Manufactures and sells a complete line of computer and
electronic-grade chemicals,
materials, and supplies.

Cherry Electrical Products
3600 Sunset Avenue
Waukegan, IL 60087
(708)662-9200
(708)360-3566 Fax

Manufactures a line of
high-quality keyboards for
IBM-compatible systems.

Chicago Case Company
4446 S. Ashland Avenue
Chicago, IL 60609
(312)927-1600

Manufactures equipment-
shipping and travel cases.

Chilton Book Company
Chilton Way
Radnor, PA 19089-0230
(215)964-4000

Manufactures a number of
excellent automotive service
manuals and documentation.

Chinon America, Inc.
660 Maple Avenue
Torrance, CA 90503
(800)441-0222

Manufactures a line of floppy
disk and CD-ROM drives.

Chips & Technologies, Inc.
4950 Zanker Road
San Jose, CA 95134
(408)434-0600
(800)944-6284

Manufactures specialized
chipsets for compatible
motherboard manufacturers.

Chrysler Motors Service Publications
Service Publications
P.O. Box 360450
Strongsville, OH 44136
216-572-0725

Publishes Chrysler service manuals and documentation.

Ci Design Company
1711 Langley Avenue
Irvine, CA 92714
(714)556-0888

Manufactures custom-made 3 1/2-inch drive mounting kits used by Toshiba, Panasonic, and NEC for their drive products. Also makes drive faceplates, enclosures, and custom cable assemblies.

Cipher Data Products, Inc.
10101 Old Grove Road
San Diego, CA 92131
(714)641-1230
(800)424-7437

Division of Ioberlin Data that manufactures a line of tape-backup products. Also supplies tape-backup systems to IBM.

Ciprico, Inc.
2800 Campus Drive
Plymouth, MN 55441
(800)727-4669

Manufactures high-performance SCSI host adapters.

Citizen America Corporation
2450 Broadway
Suite 600
Santa Monica, CA 90404
(310)453-0614
(800)556-1234
(310)453-2814 Fax
(310)453-7564 BBS

Manufactures a line of printers and floppy disk drives.

CMD Technology, Inc.
1 Vanderbilt
Irvine, CA 92718
(714)454-0800
(800)426-3832
(714)455-1656 Fax

Manufactures EISA adapters, PCI and VL-Bus IDE, and SCSI disk adapters.

CMS Enhancements, Inc.
2722 Michelson Drive
Irvine, CA 92715
(714)222-6000

Division of Ameriquest that distributes a variety of system and peripheral products, and specializes in hard disk drives.

Colorado Memory Systems, Inc.
800 S. Taft Avenue
Loveland, CO 80537
(303)669-8000
(303)635-1500
(303)667-0997 Fax
(303)635-0650 BBS

Manufactures tape-backup subsystems specializing in QIC-80 and QIC-40 systems that attach through an interface card, floppy controller, or parallel port connection.

Columbia Data Products
1070B Rainer Drive
Altamonte Springs, FL 32714
(407)869-6700
(407)862-4725 Fax
(407)862-4724 BBS

Manufactures SCSI drivers for Western Digital FASST host adapters.

Comb
720 Anderson Avenue
Street Cloud, MN 56372
(612)612-535-4944
(800)328-0609

Liquidates and distributes a variety of discontinued products, including PC-compatible systems and peripherals.

Compaq Computer Corporation
20555 State Highway 249
Houston, TX 77070
(713)370-0670
(800)231-0900
(800)652-6672 Technical support
(713)378-1418 BBS

Manufactures high-end IBM-compatible computer systems.

CompUSA, Inc.
15151 Surveyor #A
Addison, TX 75244
(214)702-0055
(800)932-2667

Computer retail superstore and mail-order outlet.

CompuServe Information Service (CIS)
5000 Arlington Centre Boulevard
Columbus, OH 43220
(614)457-8600
(800)848-8990

Largest on-line information and messaging service; offers manufacturer- and vendor-sponsored forums for technical support.

Computer Component Source, Inc.
135 Eileen Way
Syosset, NY 11791-9022
(516)496-8727
(800)356-1227
(516)496-8984 Fax
(800)926-2062 Fax

Distributes a large number of computer components for repair. Specializes in display parts such as flyback transformers and other components.

Computer Design Magazine
PennWell Publishing Co.
Advanced Technology Group
119 Russell Street
P.O. Box 417
Littleton, MA 01460
(617)486-9501

An excellent industry magazine for electronic engineers and engineering managers, featuring articles on all types of computer components and hardware.

Computer Discount Warehouse
1020 E. Lake Cook Road
Buffalo Grove, IL 60089
(708)465-6000
(708)465-6800 Sales Fax
(708)465-6899 BBS

Computer retail superstore and mail order outlet offering a large selection of brand-name equipment at discount pricing.

Computer Graphics World Magazine
PennWell Publishing Co.
Advanced Technology Group
1714 Stockton Street
San Francisco, CA 94133

An industry magazine covering graphics hardware, software, and applications.

Computer Hotline Magazine
15400 Knoll Trail
#500
Dallas, TX 75248
(214)233-5131
(800)866-3241

A publication that features advertisers offering excellent sources of replacement and repair parts as well as new and used equipment at wholesale prices.

Computer Reseller News Magazine
CMP Publications, Inc.
600 Community Drive
Manhasset, NY 11030-3875
(516)562-5000
(516)562-5468

An excellent industry trade weekly news magazine featuring news for computer professionals involved in value-added reselling of computer equipment. Subscriptions are free to those who qualify.

Computer Retail Week Magazine
CMP Publications, Inc.
600 Community Drive
Manhasset, NY 11030-3875
(516)562-5000
(516)562-5468

An excellent industry trade weekly news magazine featuring news for computer superstores, mass merchants, and retailers. Subscriptions are free to those who qualify.

Computer Shopper Magazine
5211 S. Washington Avenue
Titusville, FL 32780
(305)269-3211

Monthly magazine for experimenters and bargain hunters; features a large number of advertisements.

Computer Technology Review Magazine
West World Productions, Inc.
924 Westwood Blvd.
Suite 650
Los Angeles, CA 90024-2910
(310)208-1335

An excellent monthly technical magazine for systems integrators, value-added resellers, and original equipment manufacturers. Subscriptions are free to those who qualify.

Comtech Publishing Ltd.
P.O. Box 12340
Reno, NV 89510
(702)825-9000
(800)456-7005
(702)825-1818 Fax

Manufactures dSalvage Professional, the best and most comprehensive xBASE data-recovery and file repair software available.

Connector Resources Unlimited (CRU)
1005 Ames Avenue
Milpitas, CA 95035
(408)957-5757

Manufactures a large variety of disk enclosures, mounting kits, cables, and connectors for IBM and Mac systems.

Appendixes

Conner Peripherals, Inc.
36 Skyline Dr.
Lake Mary, FL
(407)263-3500
(800)421-1879
(800)821-8782
(407)263-3502 BBS

Manufactures a line of tape-backup products from DC-2000 to DAT and 8mm units. Also supplies IBM with some tape-backup systems.

Core International, Inc.
7171 North Federal Hwy.
Boca Raton, FL 33487
(407)997-6055
(407)241-2929 BBS

Distributes a variety of different manufacturers' hard disk drives, including Seagate and Western Digital.

Corel Systems, Inc.
1600 Carling Avenue
Ottawa, ONT K1Z8R7
CANADA
(613)728-8200
(613)728-9790 Fax
(613)728-4752 BBS

Manufactures the CorelDRAW! graphics program as well as Corel SCSI, a SCSI driver kit featuring drivers for a variety of SCSI host adapters and devices.

Creative Labs, Inc.
2050 Duane Avenue
Santa Clara, CA 95054
(408)428-6600
(800)544-6146
(408)428-6622 Technical Support
(408)428-6011 Fax
(408)428-6660 BBS

Manufactures the Soundblaster series audio cards for multimedia and sound applications.

CS Electronics
1342 Bell Avenue
Tustin, CA 92680
(714)259-9100
(714)259-0911 Fax

Manufactures a very high-quality line of disk and tape drive cables, specializing in SCSI-1, SCSI-2, and SCSI-3 applications. It offers custom lengths, connectors, and impedances for a proper match with an existing installation, and uses the highest quality raw cable available.

Cumulus Corporation
23500 Mercantile Road
Cleveland, OH 44120
(216)464-3019 BBS

Manufactures processor-upgrade products and clone systems.

Curtis Manufacturing Co, Inc.
30 Fitzgerald Drive
Jaffrey, NH 03452
(603)532-4123
(800)955-5544

Manufactures a line of computer accessories, cables, and toolkits.

Cyrix Corporation
2703 N. Central Expressway
Richardson, TX 75080
(800)327-6284
(214)699-9857 Fax

Manufactures fast Intel-compatible processors and math coprocessors for 286-, 386SX-, and 386DX-based systems.

One product it makes is the 486DRx2, a clock-doubled 486 processor that is pin compatible with the Intel 386DX, and which can be used to upgrade existing 386DX systems.

D. W. Electrochemicals
9005 Leslie St.
Unit 106
Richmond Hill, ONT L4B1G7
Canada
(905)889-1522

Manufactures and sells Stabilant 22 contact enhancer and treatment. Stabilant 22 is the gel concentrate, and Stabilant 22a is a 4 to 1 isopropanol diluted form.

Dak Industries, Inc.
8200 Remmet Avenue
Canoga Park, CA 91304
(818)888-8220
(800)325-0800
(818)715-7153 BBS

Liquidates and distributes a variety of discontinued and/or unique products, including PC-compatible systems and peripherals.

Dallas Semiconductor
4401 S. Beltwood Parkway
Dallas, TX 75244
(214)450-0400

Manufactures real-time clock and nonvolatile RAM modules used by a number of OEMs, including IBM, Compaq, and others.

Damark International, Inc.
7101 Winnetka Avenue North
Minneapolis, MN 55429
(800)729-9000

Liquidates and distributes a variety of discontinued products, including PC-compatible systems and peripherals.

Data Based Advisor Magazine
Data Based Solutions
4010 Morena Blvd.
Suite 200
San Diego, CA 92117
(619)483-6400

An excellent magazine featuring articles on database applications software and programming routines.

Data Communications Magazine
McGraw-Hill Inc.
1221 Avenue of the Americas
New York, NY 10020
(212)512-2000

An excellent industry publication featuring articles on networking and communications.

Data Depot
1710 Drew Street
Clearwater, FL 34615-2151
(813)446-3402
(800)275-1913
(800)SOS-DIAGnostics
(767-3424)
(813)443-4377 Fax

Manufactures the PocketPOST diagnostic card for ISA and EISA systems, as well as several other excellent diagnostics hardware and software products.

Data Technology Corporation (DTC)
1515 Centre Pointe Drive
Milpitas, CA 95035-8010
(408)942-4000
(408)942-4027 Fax
(408)942-4197 BBS

Manufactures a complete line of hard disk controllers for ISA and EISA bus systems.

Datamation Magazine
Cahners Publishing Co.
44 Cook Street
Denver, CO 80206
(303)470-4000

An excellent industry publication, featuring articles on networking and communications.

Datastorm Technologies, Inc.
3212 Lemone Boulevard
Columbia, MO 65205
(314)443-3282
(314)875-0503 BBS

Manufactures ProCOMM and ProCOMM Plus communications software.

Dell Computer Corporation
9505 Arboretum Boulevard
Austin, TX 78759
(512)338-4400
(800)426-5150
(512)338-8528 BBS

Manufactures a line of low-cost, high-performance IBM-compatible computer systems.

DiagSoft, Inc.
5615 Scotts Valley Drive
Suite 140
Scotts Valley, CA 95066
(408)438-8247
(800)342-4763
(408)438-7113 Fax

Manufactures the QAPlus user-level PC diagnostic software, as well as the high-end QAPlus/FE (Field Engineer) software, which is an excellent program that includes complete high-resolution floppy drive testing and the Power Meter benchmarking utility.

Digi-Key Corporation
701 Brooks Ave. South
P.O. Box 677
Thief River Falls, MN
56701-0677
(800)344-4539
(218)681-3380 Fax

Sells an enormous variety of electronic and computer components, tools, and test equipment. Publishes a complete catalog listing all items.

Direct Drives
1107 Euclid Lane
Richton Park, IL 60471
(708)481-1111

Distributes an incredible selection of hard disk drives and controllers. Also publishes the *Hard Drive Buyer's Resource Guide*, the most comprehensive and accurate listing of drive and controller specifications available.

Distributed Processing Tech. (DPT)
140 Candace Drive
Maitland, FL 32751
(407)830-5522
(407)831-6432 BBS
(407)830-1070 BBS

Manufactures high-performance caching SCSI host adapters.

Diversified Technology
112 E. State Street
Ridgeland, MS 39158
(601)856-4121 Domestic
(201)891-8718 International
(800)443-2667

Manufactures industrial and rack-mount PC-compatible systems as well as a variety of backplane-design CPU boards and multifunction adapters.

Dr. Dobb's Journal of Software Tools
M&T Publishing
501 Galveston Drive
Redwood City, CA 94063

A long-running industry publication for programmers, featuring articles on various programming topics.

DTK Computer, Inc.
17700 Castleton Street
Industry, CA 91748
(818)810-8880
(818)333-6548 BBS

Manufactures PC-compatible systems and BIOS software.

Dukane Corporation
2900 Dukane Drive
St. Charles, IL 60174
(708)584-2300
(708)584-5156 Fax

Manufactures the best audio-visual overhead projectors on the market today. It specializes in portable high brightness units designed for LCD-panel projection applications.

D. W. Electrochemicals, Ltd.
97 Newkirk Road North
Unit 3
Richmond Hill, Ontario
L4C 3G4
(905)508-7500
(905)508-7502 Fax

Manufactures and sells Stabilant 22 contact enhancer and treatment. Stabilant 22 is the concentrate, and Stabilant 22a is a 4-to-1 isopropanol diluted form, which is recommended for most uses.

Dynatech Computer Power, Inc.
5800 Butler Lane
Scotts Valley, CA 95066
(800)638-9098

Manufactures a line of computer power-protection devices.

Edmund Scientific
101 E. Gloucester Pike
Barrington, NJ 08007
(609)573-6250

Supplies scientific supplies, including optical equipment and components, test equipment, and a variety of electronic components and gadgets. Its catalog is an experimenter's dream!

Electronic Buyers' News Magazine
CMP Publications, Inc.
600 Community Drive
Manhasset, NY 11030-3875
(516)562-5000
(516)562-5468

An excellent industry trade weekly magazine featuring news and information for those involved in electronics purchasing, materials, and management. Subscriptions are free to those who qualify.

Electronic Engineering Times Magazine
CMP Publications, Inc.
600 Community Drive
Manhasset, NY 11030-3875
(516)562-5000
(516)562-5468

An excellent industry trade weekly news magazine featuring news for engineers and technical management. Subscriptions are free to those who qualify.

Electronic Products Magazine
Hearst Business Communications, Inc.
645 Stewart Ave.
Garden City, NY 11530
(516)227-1300
(516)227-1444 Fax

An excellent industry trade magazine featuring engineering type information on electronic and computer components and in-depth technical articles. Subscriptions are free to those who qualify.

Elek-Tek, Inc.
7350 North Linder Avenue
Skokie, IL 60077
(708)677-7660
(800)395-1000

Computer retail superstore offering a large selection of brand-name equipment at discount pricing.

Emerson Computer Power
15041 Bake Parkway
#L
Irvine, CA 92718
(714)457-3600
(800)222-5877

Manufactures a line of computer power-protection devices.

Endl Publications
14426 Black Walnut Court
Saratoga, CA 95070
(408)867-6642
(408)867-2115

Publishes SCSI technical documentation such as *The SCSI Bench Reference* and *The SCSI Encyclopedia*.

Epson America, Inc. OEM Division
20770 Madrona Avenue
Torrance, CA 90509-2842
(213)782-5220 Fax
(800)922-8911 FAXback Information line
(408)782-4531 BBS

Manufactures printers, floppy disk drives, and complete PC-compatible systems.

Everex Systems, Inc.
5020 Brandin Ct.
Fremont, CA 94538
(510)498-1111
(800)821-0806 Sales
(510)498-4411 Technical Support
(510)226-9694 BBS

Manufactures PC-compatible systems and peripherals.

Exabyte Corporation
1685 38th Street
Boulder, CO 80301
(303)442-4333

Manufactures high-performance 8mm tape-backup systems.

Excel, Inc.
2200 Brighton-Henrietta Townline Road
Rochester, NY 14623

Distributes refurbished IBM PC, XT, AT, and PS/2 systems as well as printers, modems, displays, and so on.

Fedco Electronics, Inc.
184 W. 2nd Street
Fond du Lac, WI 54936
(414)922-6490
(800)542-9761

Manufactures and supplies a large variety of computer batteries.

Fessenden Technologies
116 N. 3rd Street
Ozark, MO 65721
(417)485-2501

Service company that offers hard disk drive and monitor repair and reconditioning. Also offers floppy disk and hard disk test equipment.

Fifth Generation Systems, Inc.
10049 N. Reiger Road
Baton Rouge, LA 70809
(504)291-7221
(800)873-4384
(504)295-3344 BBS

Manufactures a variety of software utility products, including FASTBACK, the Mace Utilities, and Brooklyn Bridge. Recently acquired by Symantec.

Fluke, John Manufacturing Company, Inc.
P.O. Box 9090
Everett, WA 98206-9090
(206)347-6100
(800)443-5853
(206)356-5116 Fax

Manufactures a line of high-end digital troubleshooting tools, including the 9000 series products designed to troubleshoot PC motherboards down to the component level. These systems are used by many motherboard manufacturers for design and manufacturing troubleshooting.

Forbin Project
P.O. Box 702
Cedar Falls, IA 50613

Manufactures the Qmodem communications software.

Fujitsu America, Inc.
3055 Orchard Drive
San Jose, CA 95134
(408)432-1300
(800)626-4686
(408)944-9899 BBS

Manufactures a line of high-capacity hard disk drives.

Future Domain Corporation
2801 McGaw Avenue
Irvine, CA 92714
(714)253-0400
(714)253-0913 Fax
(714)253-0432 BBS

Manufactures a line of high-performance SCSI host adapters and software.

Gateway 2000
P.O. Box 2000
610 Gateway Drive
North Sioux City, SD 57049
(605)232-2000
(800)523-2000
(605)232-2109 BBS

Manufactures a popular line of PC-compatible systems sold by mail order. Its systems use primarily Micronics Motherboards, Phoenix BIOS, and industry standard form factors.

Gazelle
305 North 500 West
Provo, Utah 84601
(801)377-1288
(800)RUN-FAST (786-3278)
(801)373-6933 Fax

Manufactures the Optune disk defragmenter and disk performance utility program.

GigaTrend, Inc.
2234 Rutherford Road
Carlsbad, CA 92008
(619)931-9122

Manufactures high-capacity tape drives.

Global Engineering Documents
15 Inverness Way East
Englewood, CO 80112-5704
(303)792-2181
(800)854-7179
(303)792-2192 Fax

A source for various ANSI and other industry standard documents, including SCSI-1, 2, and 3, ATA IDE, ESDI, and many others. Unlike ANSI, it sells draft documents of standards that are not yet fully ANSI approved.

Globe Manufacturing, Inc.
1159 Route 22
Mountainside, NJ 07092
(908)232-7301
(800)227-3258

Manufactures assorted PC adapter card brackets.

Golden Bow Systems
P.O. Box 3039
San Diego, CA 92163-1039
(619)298-9349
(800)284-3269

Manufactures VOPT, the best and fastest disk optimizer software available.

GoldStar Technology, Inc.
1000 Sylvan Ave.
Englewood Cliff, NJ 07632
(201)816-2000

Manufactures a line of color monitors.

GRACE Electronic Materials
77 Dragon Court
Woburn, MA 01888
(617)935-4850
(617)933-4318 Fax

Manufactures thermally conductive tapes and heat sinks.

Great Falls Computer Corp.
300 Brighton Dam Rd.
Brookville, MD
(301)774-0842
(301)774-3686 Fax

A service company specializing in computer repair and data recovery.

GSI (Great Software Ideas), Inc.
17951-H Skypark Circle
Irvine, CA 92714-6343
(714)261-7949
(800)486-7800
(714)757-1778 Fax

Manufactures an extremely flexible and powerful line of IDE adapters and floppy controllers, including units with security locks, and support for 2.88M drives. Also offers complete 2.88M drive upgrade kits. Its IDE controllers have a flexible on-board BIOS that allows them to coexist with other drive interfaces.

Harbor Electronics
650 Danbury Road
Ridgefield, CT 06877
(203)438-9625
(203)431-3001 Fax

Manufactures a line of high-quality SCSI-1, -2, and -3 interconnect cables.

Hauppauge Computer Works, Inc.
91 Cabot Court
Hauppauge, NY 11788
(516)434-1600
(800)443-6284

Manufactures upgrade motherboards for PC-compatible systems.

Hayes Microcomputer Products
P.O. Box 105203
Atlanta, GA 30348
(404)840-9200
(800)874-2937
(404)446-6336 BBS

Manufactures a complete line of modems.

Heathkit Education Systems
Heath Company
455 Riverview Dr.
Benton Harbor, MI 49023
(616)925-6000
(800)253-0570

Sells incredible kits for learning electronics and computer design.

Helm, Inc.
Publications Division
P.O. Box 07130
Detroit, MI 48207
313-865-5000

Publishes General Motors service manuals and documentation.

Hermann Marketing
1400 North Price Road
St. Louis, MO 63132-2308
(800)523-9009
(314)432-1818 Fax

Distributes a line of "Uniquely Intel" products and accessories. My favorites are the T-shirts, coffee cups, and especially the keychains containing actual Intel 386DX and 486DX processors encased in clear plastic.

Hewlett-Packard, San Diego Site
16399 W. Bernardo Drive
San Diego, CA 92127-1899
(619)592-4522
(800)333-1917 HP FIRST (Fax Information Retrieval System)
(208)344-4809 HP FIRST (Fax Information Retrieval System)

Manufactures an extensive line of excellent printers and PC-compatible systems.

Hewlett-Packard, Disk Memory Division
11413 Chinden Boulevard
Boise, ID 83714
(208)396-6000

Manufactures high-capacity 3 1/2-inch hard disk drives.

Hitatchi America, Ltd.
50 Prospect Avenue
Tarrytown, NY 10591
(914)332-5800

Manufactures computer peripherals, including hard disks and LCD devices.

Hypertech
1910 Thomas Road
Memphis, TN 38134
(901)382-8888

Manufactures and sells a wide variety of well-engineered, high-performance automotive computer EPROM replacements for many different types of vehicles.

Hyundai Electronics America
166 Baypointe Parkway
San Jose, CA 95134
(408)473-9200

Manufactures PC-compatible systems.

IBM Desktop Software
472 Wheelers Farm Road
Milford, CT 06460
(800)426-7699

Supports IBM PC applications software such as DisplayWrite and PC Storyboard.

IBM National Distribution Division (NDD)
101 Paragon Drive
Montvale, NJ 07645
(800)426-9397
(800)992-4777

Manufactures and supports IBM DOS and OS/2.

IBM OEM Division
1133 Westchester Avenue
White Plains, NY 10604
(914)288-3000

Manufactures and distributes IBM products such as high-capacity 3 1/2-inch hard disk drives, networking and chipset products.

IBM Parts Order Center
P.O. Box 9022
Boulder, CO 80301
(303)924-4100 Orders
(303)924-4015 Part Number ID and Lookup

IBM's nationwide service parts ordering center.

IBM PC Company
11400 Burnet Road
Austin, TX 78758
(512)823-2851
(800)IBM-3333
(800)426-7015 IBM PC Co. Factory Outlet (discontinued/used equipment)
(800)426-4329 IBM Fax Information Service (FAXback system)
(800)426-3395 IBM Tech

Support Fax Information (FAXback system)
(919)517-0001 IBM National Support Center BBS
(919)517-0095 IBM NSC BBS Status Line (voice)

Manufactures and supports IBM's PS/2, PS/Valuepoint, and PS/1 products.

IBM PC Direct
3039 Cornwallis Road
Building 203
Research Triangle Park, NC 27709-9766
(800)IBM-2YOU (426-2968)
(800)465-7999 Canada
(800)426-4182 Fax

IBM PC Company's direct mail-order catalog sales division. It sells IBM and approved third-party systems and peripherals at a discount from list price.

***IBM Personal Systems Technical Solutions* Magazine**
The TDA Group
P.O. Box 1360
Los Altos, CA 94023-1360
(800)551-2832
(415)948-4280 Fax

Publishes a bimonthly magazine on IBM Personal Computer systems and software.

IBM Technical Directory
P.O. Box 2009
Racine, WI 53404
(414)633-8108
(800)426-7282

The source for books, reference manuals, documentation, software toolkits, and language products for IBM systems.

Illinois Lock
301 West Hintz Road
Wheeling, IL 60090-5754
(708)537-1800
(708)537-1881 Fax

Manufactures keylocks in different IBM and IBM-compatible computer systems.

InfoChip Systems, Inc.
2840 San Tomas Expressway
Santa Clara, CA 95051
(408)727-0514
(408)727-2496 BBS

Manufactures the Expanz data-compression coprocessor products.

InfoWorld Magazine
375 Cochituate Road
Framingham, MA 01701
(508)879-0446 Fax

Publishes *InfoWorld* magazine, featuring excellent product reviews.

Inline, Inc.
1901 E. Lambert Rd.
Suite 110
La Habra, CA 90631
(310)690-6767
(800)882-7117

Manufactures a complete line of video-connection accessories, including distribution amplifiers, scan converters, line drivers, projector interfaces, and cables.

Inmac
2465 Augustine Rd.
Santa Clara, CA 95052
(408)727-1970

Distributes a large variety of computer supplies, floppy disks, cables, and so on.

Integrated Information Technology (IIT)
2445 Mission College Boulevard
Santa Clara, CA 95054
(408)727-1885

Manufactures fast, Intel-compatible math coprocessors for 286-, 386SX-, and 386DX-based systems.

Intel Corporation
3065 Bowers Avenue
Santa Clara, CA 95051
(408)765-8080
(800)548-4725

Manufactures microprocessors used in IBM and compatible systems. Also makes a line of memory and accelerator boards.

Intel PC Enhancement Operations
5200 NE Elam Young Parkway
Hillsboro, OR 97124
(503)629-7354
(503)696-8080
(800)538-3373
(503)645-6275 BBS

Manufactures a variety of PC upgrade products and expansion boards, including Overdrive CPU upgrades, AboveBoard memory adapters, SIMM memory modules, and modems.

Interface Group
300 First Avenue
Needham, MA 02194
(617)449-6600

Produces the annual COMDEX/Fall and COMDEX/Spring computer shows.

International Electronic Research Corp. (IERC)
135 W. Magnolia Boulevard
Burbank, CA 91502
(213)849-2481
(818)848-8872 Fax

Manufactures a line of excellent CPU heat sink products, including clip-on, low-profile models especially for 486 and Pentium processors that do not require a special socket.

Intex Solutions, Inc.
35 Highland Circle
Needham, MA 02194
(617)449-6222
(617)444-2318 Fax

Manufactures and distributes software, especially Lotus enhancement products such as the Rescue Plus Lotus spreadsheet Data Recovery program. Rescue is the most comprehensive and capable data recovery program for Lotus spreadsheet files.

Iomega Corporation
1821 West 4000 South
Roy, UT 84067
(801)778-1000
(800)777-6654 Sales
(801)392-9819 BBS

Manufactures the Bernoulli box removable-cartridge drive.

IQ Technologies, Inc.
13625 NE 126th Place
Kirkland, WA 98034
(206)823-2273
(800)277-2817

Manufactures PC interconnect cables and devices, including the SmartCable RS232 devices.

Jameco Computer Products
1355 Shoreway Road
Belmont, CA 94002
(415)592-8097

Supplies computer components, parts, and peripherals by mail order.

JDR Microdevices
2233 Branham Lane
San Jose, CA 95124
(408)494-1400
(800)538-5000
(408)559-0253 BBS

A vendor for chips, disk drives, and various computer and electronic parts and components.

Jensen Tools
7815 S. 46th Street
Phoenix, AZ 85044
(602)968-6231
(800)426-1194

Supplies and manufactures high-quality tools and test equipment.

Kalok Corporation
1289 Anvilwood Avenue
Sunnyvale, CA 94089
(408)747-1315

Division of JTS that manufactures a line of low-cost 3 1/2-inch hard disk drives.

Kenfil Distribution
16745 Saticoy Street
Van Nuys, CA 91406
(818)785-1181

Division of Ameriquest that is a major software distributor.

Kensington Microware, Ltd.
2855 Campus Drive
San Mateo, CA 94403
(415)572-2700

(415)572-9675 Fax
(800)535-4242

Manufactures and supplies computer accessories.

Key Power, Inc.
11853 East Telegraph Road
Santa Fe Springs, CA 90670
(310)948-2084
(310)942-0536 Fax

Manufacturers a line of power supplies, cases, installation kits, and other accessories used in building PC-compatible systems.

Key Tronic Corporation
North 4424 Sullivan Road
Spokane, WA 99216
(509)928-8000
(800)262-6006

Manufactures low-cost PC-compatible keyboards. It is known primarily as the manufacturer of Comaq's keyboards, but also supplies low-cost keyboards to a number of other compatible system manufacturers.

Kingston Technology Corporation
17600 Newhope Street
Fountain Valley, CA 92708
(714)435-2600
(800)835-6575
(714)435-2699 Fax

Manufactures an excellent line of direct processor upgrade modules for 286 and 386 IBM and Compaq systems, as well as the slot-based MCMaster bus master processor upgrade card for Micro Channel systems. It also sells numerous SIMM memory modules and disk upgrades for other systems.

Labconco Corporation
8811 Prospect
Kansas City, MO 64132
(816)333-8811
(800)821-5525
(816)363-0130 Fax

Manufactures a variety of clean room cabinets and clean benches for use in hard disk drive and other sensitive component repair.

***Lan* Magazine**
Telecon Library Inc.
12 W. 21st St.
New York, NY 10010
(212)691-8215
(800)677-3435

A publication featuring articles on various local area networking topics.

***LAN Times* Magazine**
Novell Inc.
122 E. 1700 S.
P.O. Box 5900
Provo, UT 84606
(801)379-5588
(800)526-7937

Publishes articles on various local area networking topics, centered around Novell software.

Landmark Research International
703 Grand Central Street
Clearwater, FL 34616
(813)443-1331
(800)683-6696

Manufactures the Service Diagnostics PC diagnostic program, as well as the Kickstart diagnostic adapter cards. Known also for the Landmark System Speed Test program.

Appendixes

Laser Magnetic Storage
4425 Arrowswest Drive
Colorado Springs, CO 80907
(719)593-7900
(800)777-5764

Division of DPMG that manufactures a variety of optical
disk products.

Lexmark
740 New Circle Road
Lexington, KY 40511-1876
(606)232-6814
(606)358-5835
(606)232-3000 Technical Support Hotline
(606)232-2380 FAXback Information
(606)232-5238 BBS

Manufactures IBM keyboards
and printers for retail distribution. Spun off from IBM in
1991, now sells to other OEMs
and distributors.

Lite-On, Inc.
720 S. HIllview Drive
Milpitas, CA 95035
(408)946-4873
(408)946-1751 Fax

Manufacturers a line of high-
quality keyboards with excellent tactile feedback, as well as
monitors and power supplies.

Liuski International, Inc.
10 Hub Drive
Melville, NY 11747
(516)454-8220

Hardware distributor that
carries a variety of peripherals
and systems.

Longshine Computer, Inc.
2013 N. Capitol Avenue
San Jose, CA 95132
(408)942-1746

Manufactures various PC
adapters, including floppy,
hard disk, SCSI, Token Ring,
Ethernet, and so on.

**Lotus Development
Corporation**
55 Cambridge Parkway
Cambridge, MA 02142
(617)577-8500
(800)343-5414

Manufactures Lotus 1-2-3,
Symphony, and Magellan
software.

LSI Logic, Inc.
1551 McCarthy Boulevard
Milpitas, CA 95035
(408)433-8000

Manufactures motherboard
logic and chipsets.

MacWEEK Magazine
Ziff Communications Co.
525 Brannon Street
San Francisco, CA 94107
415-882-7370

An excellent publication covering news in the Macintosh
universe.

Macworld Magazine
PC World Communications
Inc.
501 Second Street
Suite 600
San Francisco, CA 94107

An excellent publication covering news in the Macintosh
universe.

Manzana Microsystems, Inc.
P.O. Box 2117
Goleta, CA 93118

Manufactures floppy disk
upgrade subsystems and controllers.

Mastersoft, Inc.
6991 E. Camelback Road
Scottsdale, AZ 85251
(602)277-0900
(800)624-6107

Manufactures Word for Word,
a word processing file-conver-
sion program.

**Maxell Corporation of
America**
22-08 Route 208
Fair Lawn, NJ 07410
(800)533-2836

Manufactures magnetic media
products, including disks and
tape cartridges.

Maxi Switch, Inc.
2901 East Elvira Road
Tuscon, AZ 85706
(602)294-5450
(602)294-6890 Fax

Manufactures a line of high-
quality PC keyboards, including some designed for harsh or
industrial environments. Maxi
Switch keyboards are used by
many compatible system
manufacturers, including
Gateway 2000.

Maxoptix
2520 Junction Avenue
San Jose, CA 95134
(408)954-9700
(800)848-3092

Manufactures a line of optical
WORM and magneto-optical
drives. Joint venture with
Maxtor Corporation and
Kubota Corporation.

Maxtor Corporation
211 River Oaks Parkway
San Jose, CA 95134
(408)432-1700
(800)262-9867

(303)678-2222 BBS (2400bps)
(303)678-2020 BBS (9600+bps)

Manufactures a line of large-capacity, high-quality hard disk drives.

Maynard Electronics, Inc.
36 Skyline Drive
Lake Mary, FL 32746
(407)263-3500
(800)821-8782
(407)263-3502 BBS

Manufactures a line of tape-backup products.

McAfee Associates
4423 Cheeney Street
Santa Clara, CA 95054
(408)988-3832
(408)988-4044 BBS

Manufactures the SCAN virus-scanning software, which is nonresident and updated frequently to handle new viruses as they are discovered.

McGraw-Hill, Inc.
Princeton Road N-1
Highstown, NJ 08520
(800)822-8158

Publishes technical information and books.

McTronic Systems
7426 Cornwall Bridge Lane
Houston, TX 77041-1709
(713)462-7687

Manufactures the excellent Port Finder serial and parallel port diagnostic and utility program. This is a shareware utility available direct from them as well as through downloading from the IBMHW forum on CompuServe.

Megahertz Corporation
4505 S. Wasatch Boulevard
Salt Lake City, UT 84124
(801)320-7000
(800)527-8677

Makes laptop modems, external network adapters, and AT-speedup products.

Memorex Computer Supplies
1200 Memorex Drive
Santa Clara, CA 95050
(408)957-1000

Manufactures a line of computer disk media, tape cartridges, and other supplies.

Mentor Electronics, Inc.
7560 Tylor Boulevard
#E
Mentor, OH 44060
(216)951-1884

Supplies surplus IBM PC (10/27/82) ROM BIOS update chips.

Merisel
200 Continental Boulevard
El Segundo, CA 90245
(800)542-9955

A large distributor of PC hardware and software products from many manufacturers.

Meritec
1359 West Jackson Street
P.O. Box 8003
Painesville, OH 44077
(216)354-3148
(216)354-0509 Fax

Makes a line of SCSI 8-bit to 16-bit (Wide SCSI) adapters in a variety of configurations. These adapters allow Wide SCSI devices to be installed in a standard 8-bit SCSI bus and vice versa.

Merritt Computer Products, Inc.
5565 Red Bird Center Drive
#150
Dallas, TX 75237
(214)339-0753

Manufactures the SafeSkin keyboard protector.

Methode Electronics, Inc.
DataMate Division
7444 W. Wilson Ave.
Chicago, IL 60656
(708)867-9600
(708)867-3149 Fax

Manufactures and sells a complete line of SCSI terminators.

Micro 2000, Inc.
1100 E. Broadway
Third Floor
Glendale, CA 91205
(818)547-0125

Manufactures the MicroScope PC diagnostic program, as well as the POSTProbe ISA, EISA, and MCA POST diagnostics card. Is extending 25 percent discount to anyone who mentions this book when purchasing.

Micro Accessories, Inc.
2012 Hartog Drive
San Jose, CA 95131
(408)441-1242
(800)777-6687
(916)222-2528 Fax

Makes cables and disk drive mounting brackets and accessories, including PS/2 adapter kits.

Micro Channel Developers Association
2280 N. Bechelli Lane
Suite B
Redding, CA 96002
(916)222-2262
(800)GET-MCDA

An independent organization that facilitates the evolution of the Micro Channel Architecture as an industry-wide standard. Its primary focus is to assist developers in building compatible MCA products, and to explain to users the benefits of this architecture. It publishes the "International Catalog of Micro Channel Products and Services."

Micro Computer Cable Company, Inc.
12200 Delta Drive
Taylor, MI 48180
(313)946-9700
(313)946-9645 Fax

Manufactures and sells a complete line of computer cables, connectors, switchboxes, and cabling accessories.

Micro Design International
6985 University Boulevard
Winter Park, FL 32792
(407)677-8333
(800)228-0891

Manufactures the SCSI Express driver software for integration of SCSI peripherals in a variety of environments.

Micro House International
4900 Pearl East Circle
Suite 101
Boulder, CO 80301
(303)443-3389
(800)926-8299
(303)443-3323 Fax
(303)443-9957 BBS

Publishes the *Encyclopedia of Hard Disks*, an excellent reference book that shows hard disk drive and controller jumper settings.

Micro Solutions, Inc.
132 W. Lincoln Hwy.
DeKalb, IL 60115
(815)756-3411
(815)756-9100 BBS

Manufactures a complete line of floppy controllers and subsystems, including 2.88M versions. Also offers floppy drive and tape-backup systems that run from a standard parallel port, using no expansion slots.

Microcom, Inc.
500 River Ridge Drive
Norwood, MA 02062
(617)551-1000
(800)822-8224

Makes error-correcting modems, and develops the MNP communications protocols.

MicroComputer Accessories, Inc.
5405 Jandy Place
Los Angeles, CA 90066

Manufactures a variety of computer and office accessories.

Micrografx, Inc.
1303 E. Arapaho
Richardson, TX 75081
(800)733-3729

Manufactures the Micrografx Designer, Windows Draw, ABC Toolkit, Photomagic, and Charisma software. Specializes in Windows and OS/2 development.

Microid Research, Inc.
2336 Walsh Ave
Suite D
Santa Clara, CA 95051
(408)727-6991

Makes MR BIOS, one of the most flexible and configurable BIOS versions available. Versions are available for a variety of different chip sets and motherboards.

Microlink/Micro Firmware, Inc.
330 West Gray St.
Suite 170
Norman, OK 73069-7111
(800)767-5465
(405)321-3553 BBS

The largest distributor of Phoenix ROM BIOS upgrades. Develops custom versions for specific motherboards and supplies many other BIOS vendors with products.

Micron Technologies
2805 E. Columbia Road
Boise, ID 83706
(208)368-3900
(800)642-7661
(208)368-4530 BBS

Makes various memory chips, SIMMs, memory boards, and IBM-compatible systems.

Micronics Computers, Inc.
232 E. Warren Avenue
Fremont, CA 94539
(510)651-2300
(510)651-6837 BBS

Manufactures PC-compatible motherboards and complete laptop and portable systems. Micronics motherboards feature the Phoenix BIOS.

Micropolis Corporation
21211 Nordhoff Street
Chatsworth, CA 91311
(818)709-3300
(800)395-3000
(818)709-3310 BBS

Manufactures a line of high-capacity 5 1/4- and 3 1/2-inch hard disk drives.

Microprocessors Unlimited, Inc.
24000 S. Peoria Avenue
Beggs, OK 74421
(918)267-4961

Distributes memory chips, SIMMs, math coprocessors, UART chips, and other integrated circuits.

Microscience International Corporation
90 Headquarters Drive
San Jose, CA 95134
(800)334-3595

Manufactures hard disk drives.

Microsoft Corporation
One Microsoft Way
Redmond, WA 98052-6399
(206)882-8080
(800)426-9400
(206)936-6735 BBS

Manufactures MS-DOS, Windows, Windows NT, and a variety of applications software.

MicroSystems Development (MSD)
4100 Moorpark Avenue
Suite 104
San Jose, CA 95117
(408)269-4100
(408)296-5877 Fax
(408)296-4200 BBS

Manufactures the Port Test serial and parallel diagnostic test kit and the Post Code Master POST diagnostics card.

MicroWay, Inc.
Research Park
Box 79
Kingston, MA 02364
(508)746-7341

Manufactures a line of accelerator products for IBM and compatible systems. Also specializes in math coprocessor chips, math chip accelerators, and language products.

Mini Micro
2050 Corporate Ct.
San Jose, CA 95131
(408)456-9500
(800)275-4642
(408)434-9319 BBS

Makes 3 1/2-inch IDE and SCSI hard disk drives. Also, partly owned by Compaq, and supplies most of Compaq's hard drives. Wholesale distributor of Conner Peripherals, Inc.

Mitsubishi Electronics America, Inc.
991 Knox Street
Torrence, CA 90502
(310)217-5732
(800)843-2515

Manufactures monitors, printers, hard disks, and floppy disk storage products.

Motor Magazine
Hearst Corporation
645 Stewart Ave
Garden City, NY 11530
(516)227-1300
(800)AUTO-828
(516)227-1444 Fax

The essential trade magazine for the automotive technician, including troubleshooting tips and service product information. Subscriptions are free to those who qualify.

Motorola Inc.
6501 William Cannon Drive West
Austin, TX 78735
(512)891-2000

Manufactures microprocessors, memory components, real-time clocks, controller chips, and so on.

Mountain Network Solutions, Inc.
240 Hacienda Avenue
Campbell, CA 95008
(800)458-0300
(408)438-2665 BBS

Manufactures tape drives and backup subsystems, including hardware and software.

Mueller Technical Research
21718 Mayfield Lane
Barrington, IL 60010-9733
(708)726-0709
(708)726-0710 Fax

You found me! I run a service company that offers the best in PC hardware and software technical seminars and training, specializing in PC hardware and software troubleshooting and data recovery. My CompuServe ID is 73145,1566 (Scott Mueller).

Mustang Software
P.O. Box 2264
Bakersfield, CA 93303
(805)873-2500
(800)999-9619
(805)873-2400 BBS

Manufactures Wildcat! BBS software.

Appendixes

Mylex Corporation
34551 Ardenwood Boulevard
Fremont, CA 94555
(510)796-6100

Manufactures high-performance ISA and EISA motherboards and SCSI host adapters.

National Semiconductor Corporation
2900 Semiconductor Drive
Santa Clara, CA 95052
(408)721-5151 Fax
(408)245-0671 BBS

Manufactures chips for PC circuit applications. Known for its UART chips.

NCL America, Inc.
1221 Innsbruck Drive
Sunnyvale, CA 94086
(408)737-2496

Manufactures high-performance SCSI host adapters.

NCR Microelectronics
1635 Aeroplaza
Colorado Springs, CO 80916
(719)596-5795
(800)334-5454
(719)574-0424 BBS

Manufactures a variety of integrated circuits for PC systems, including SCSI protocol chips used by many OEMs. It also sponsors the SCSI BBS, an excellent source for standard documents covering SCSI, IDE, and other interfaces.

NEC Technologies, Inc.
1414 Massachusetts Avenue
Boxborough, MA 01719
(508)264-8000
(800)632-4636
(708)860-2602 BBS

Manufactures Multisync monitors, CD-ROM drives, video adapters, printers, and other peripherals as well as complete PC-compatible systems.

Newark Electronics
4801 N. Ravenswood Avenue
Chicago, IL 60640-4496
(312)784-5100
(312)907-5217 FAX
(800)298-3133 (Catalog requests)

A large distributor of electronic components, parts, assemblies, tools, and test equipment. It has an enormous catalog available on request.

Northgate Computer Systems, Inc.
7075 Flying Cloud Drive
Eden Prairie, MN 55344
(800)548-1993

Manufactures PC-compatible systems sold through mail order.

NovaStor Corporation
30961 Agoura Rd.
Suite 109
Westlake Village, CA 91361
(818)707-9900
(818)707-9902 Fax

Manufactures the Novaback tape backup software for SCSI tape drives. Supports 8mm, 4mm (DAT), 1/4-inch cartridge (QIC), IBM 3480 and 9-track tape drives.

Novell, Inc.
70 Garden Court
Monterey, CA 93940
(408)649-3896
(408)649-3443 BBS

Manufactures the Novell DOS operating system.

Novell, Inc.
122 E. 1700 South
Provo, UT 84601
(801)379-5588
(800)526-7937
(801)429-3030 BBS

Manufactures the NetWare LAN operating system.

Okidata
532 Fellowship Road
Mount Laurel, NJ 08054
(609)235-2600
(800)654-3282
(800)283-5474 BBS

Manufactures printers and modems.

Olivetti
765 US Hwy. 202
Somerville, NJ 08876
(908)526-8200

Manufactures Olivetti and many AT&T PC systems.

Ontrack Computer Systems, Inc.
6321 Bury Drive
Suites 15-19
Eden Prairie, MN 55346
(612)937-1107
(800)752-1333
(612)937-2121 Technical Support
(612)937-5161 Ontrack Data Recovery
(800)872-2599 Ontrack Data Recovery
(612)937-5750 Fax
(612)937-0860 BBS (2400bps)
(612)937-8567 BBS (9600+bps)

Manufactures the Disk Manager hard disk utilities for PC, PS/2, and Macintosh. Disk Manager is the most comprehensive and flexible low-level format program available, supporting even IDE drives.

Also provides extensive data recovery services.

Orchid Technology
45365 Northport Loop West
Fremont, CA 94538
(510)683-0300
(800)767-2443
(510)683-0329 BBS

Manufactures video and memory board products for IBM and compatible systems.

Osborne/McGraw Hill
2600 10th Street
Berkeley, CA 94710
(800)227-0900

Publishes computer books.

Pacific Data Products
9125 Rehco Road
San Diego, CA 92121
(619)552-0880
(619)452-6329 BBS

Manufactures the Pacific Page XL and PacificPage PE Postscript compatible enhancement products for HP LaserJet printers.

Pacific Magtron, Inc.
568-8 Weddell Drive
Sunnyvale, CA 94089
(408)774-1188

Manufactures hard disk drives.

Pacific Micro
201 Antonio Circle C250
Mountain View, CA 94040
(415)948-6200
(415)948-6296 FAX

Manufactures several software utility programs including Mac-In-DOS, a utility that allows bi-directional file transfer between the IBM and Mac environments.

Packard Bell
9425 Canoga Avenue
Chatsworth, CA 91311
(818)865-1555
(800)733-4411
(818)313-8601 BBS

Manufactures an excellent line of low-cost PC-compatible computer systems.

Panasonic Communications & Systems
2 Panasonic Way
Secaucus, NJ 07094
(201)348-7000
(800)233-8182
(201)863-7845 BBS

Manufactures monitors, optical drive products, floppy drives, printers, and PC-compatible laptop systems.

Parts Now, Inc.
810 Stewart Street
Madison, WI 53713
(608)276-8688

Sells a large variety of laser printer parts for HP, Canon, Apple, and other laser printers using Canon engines.

PC Connection
6 Mill Street
Marlow, NH 03456
(603)446-7721
(800)800-5555

Distributes many different hardware and software packages by way of mail order.

PC Magazine
One Park Avenue
New York, NY 10016
(212)503-5446

Magazine featuring product reviews and comparisons.

PC Power & Cooling, Inc.
5995 Avenida Encinas
Carlsbad, CA 92008
(619)931-5700
(800)722-6555
(619)931-6988 Fax

Manufactures a line of high-quality, high-output power supplies for IBM and compatible systems, including Compaq. Known for high-power output and quiet fan operation.

PC Repair Corporation
2010 State Street
Harrisburg, PA 17103
(717)232-7272

Service company and parts distributor that performs board repair of IBM PCs and PS/2s, printers, and typewriters as well as Compaq systems repair. Also offers an extensive parts line for these systems.

PC Week Magazine
10 Presidents Landing
Medford, MA 02155
(617)693-3753

Weekly magazine featuring industry news and information.

PC World Magazine
375 Chochituate Road
Framingham, MA 01701
(508)879-0700
(800)435-7766

A monthly magazine featuring product reviews and comparisons.

PC-Kwik Corporation
15100 S.W. Koll Parkway
Beaverton, OR 97006-6026
(503)644-5644
(800)759-5945
(503)646-8267 Fax

Appendixes

Formerly Multisoft, they manufacture the PC-Kwik Power Pak system performance utilities, Super PC-Kwik disk cache, and WinMaster Windows utility programs.

PC-SIG/Spectra Publishing
1030 E. Duane Avenue
#D
Sunnyvale, CA 94086
(408)730-9291
(800)245-6717

Publishes public-domain software and shareware available on CD-ROM.

PCI Special Interest Group
2111 NE 25th Ave.
Hillsboro, OR 97124
(503)696-6111
(800)433-5177
(503)234-6762 Fax

An independent group that owns and manages the PCI local bus architecture.

PCMCIA—Personal Computer Memory Card International Association
1030G East Duane Avenue,
Sunnyvale, CA 94086
(408)720-0107

An independent organization that maintains the PCMCIA bus standard for credit-card-sized expansion adapters.

Philips Consumer Electronics
One Philips Drive
Knoxville, TN 37914
(615)521-4366

Manufactures Magnavox PCs, monitors, and CD-ROM drives.

Phoenix Technologies, Ltd.
846 University Avenue
Norwood, MA 02062
(617)551-4000

Manufactures IBM-compatible BIOS software for ISA, EISA, and MCA systems.

Pivar Computing Services, Inc.
165 Arlington Heights Road
Buffalo Grove, IL 60089
(708)459-6010
(800)266-8378

Service company that specializes in data and media conversion.

PKWare, Inc.
9025 N. Deerwood Drive
Brown Deer, WI 53223
(414)354-8699
(414)354-8559 Fax
(414)354-8670 BBS

Manufactures the PKZIP, PKUNZIP, PKLite, and PKZMENU data compression software. Widely used on BBS systems and by manufacturers for software distribution.

Plus Development Corporation
1778 McCarthy Boulevard
Milpitas, CA 95035
(408)434-6900
(800)624-5545
(408)434-1664 BBS

Manufactures the Plus Hardcard product line. A division of Quantum Corporation.

Priam Systems Corporation
1140 Ringwood Court
San Jose, CA 95131
(408)441-4180

Division of AST Research that provides service and repair for Priam drives; original Priam has gone out of business.

***Processor* Magazine**
P.O. Box 85518
Lincoln, NE 68501
(800)247-4880

Publication that offers excellent sources of replacement and repair parts as well as new equipment at wholesale prices.

Procom Technology
2181 Dupont Drive
Irvine, CA 92715
(714)852-1000
(800)800-8600
(714) 261-8572 Fax
CompuServe: PCVEND

Manufactures a variety of products and kits, including SCSI adapters, PS/2 external floppy drives, and CD-ROM kits.

Programmer's Shop
90 Industrial Park Road
Hingham, MA 02043
(617)740-2510
(800)421-8006

Distributes programming tools and utility software.

PTI Industries
269 Mount Hermon Road
Scott Valley, CA 95066

Manufactures a line of computer power-protection devices.

Public Brand Software
P.O. Box 51315
Indianapolis, IN 46251
(317)856-7571
(800)426-3475

Publishes a public domain and shareware library.

Public Software Library
P.O. Box 35705-F
Houston, TX 77235
(713)524-6394
(800)242-4775

Top-notch distributor of high-
quality public domain and
shareware software. Its library
is the most well researched and
tested available. Also offers an
excellent newsletter that reviews the software.

Quadram
One Quad Way
Norcross, GA 30093
(404)923-6666
(404)564-5678 BBS

Manufactures a line of adapter
boards and upgrades for IBM
and compatible systems.

Quaid Software Limited
45 Charles Street East
Third Floor
Toronto, ON, M4Y1S2,
(519)942-0832

Manufactures the Quaid
Copywrite disk copy program
and other disk utilities.

Qualitas, Inc.
7101 Wisconsin Avenue
#1386
Bethesda, MD 20814
(301)907-6700
(301)907-8030 BBS

Manufactures the 386Max and
BlueMax memory-manager
utility programs.

Quantum Corporation
500 McCarthy Boulevard
Milpitas, CA 95035
(408)894-4000
(408)434-1664 BBS

Manufactures a line of 3 1/2-
inch hard disk drives. Supplies
drives to Apple Computer.

**Quarter-Inch Cartridge
Drive Standards, Inc. (QIC)**
311 East Carrillo Street
Santa Barbara, CA 93101
(805)963-3853
(805)962-1541 Fax

An independent industry
group that sets and maintains
Quarter Inch Cartridge (QIC)
tape drive standards for backup
and archiving purposes.

Quarterdeck Office Systems
150 Pico Boulevard
Santa Monica, CA 90405
(310)392-9851
(800)354-3260 Sales
(310) 314-3227 BBS

Manufactures the popular
DESQview, QEMM, and QRAM
memory-manager products.

Que Corporation
201 West 103rd Street
Indianapolis, IN 46290
(317)581-3500
(800)428-5331 Order Line
(800)448-3804 Sales Fax

Publishes the highest-quality
computer applications software and hardware books in
the industry, including this
one!

Qume Corporation
500 Yosemite Drive
Milpitas, CA 95035
(408)942-4000
(800)223-2479

Manufactures a variety of
peripherals, including displays,
printers, and printer supplies
such as toner cartridges. Qume
owns DTC, a disk controller
manufacturer.

Radio Shack
Division of Tandy Corporation
1800 One Tandy Center
Fort Worth, TX 76102
(817)390-3011
(817)390-2774 Fax

Manages the Radio Shack
electronics stores, which sell
numerous electronics devices,
parts, and supplies. Also manufactures a line of PC-compatible computers and computer
accessories and supplies.

Rancho Technology, Inc.
8632 Archibald Avenue
#109
Rancho Cucamonga, CA
91730

Manufactures an extensive
line of SCSI products, including host adapters for ISA,
EISA, and MCA bus systems,
SCSI extenders, and interface
software.

Renasonce Group, Inc.
5173 Waring Road
Suite 115
San Diego, CA 92120
(619)287-3348
(619)287-3554 Fax

Manufactures the excellent
InfoSpotter system inspection
and diagnostic program, as
well as RemoteRX and the
Skylight Windows trouble-
shooting program.

Reply Corporation
4435 Fortran Drive
San Jose, CA 95134
(408)942-4804
(800)955-5295
(408)942-4897 Fax

Designs and sells an exclusive
line of complete 386 and 486
motherboard upgrades for IBM

Appendixes

PS/2 systems, including the Model 30, 30-286, 50, 55, 60, 65, 70, and 80. These are new motherboards with integrated local bus SVGA adapters, Pentium Overdrive support, 2.88M floppy controller, Flash BIOS, built-in ATA IDE adapter, support for up to 32M of motherboard memory, and numerous other features. These upgrade boards are actually manufactured for Reply by IBM, and are fully IBM compatible.

Rinda Technologies Inc.
5112 N. Elston Ave.
Chicago, IL 60630
(312)736-6633

Manufactures the DIACOM General Motors and Chrysler automotive diagnostic and troubleshooting software. DIACOM includes a hardware adapter that connects your PC directly to the automobile diagnostic connector through a parallel port on your system, and essentially converts your PC into a professional SCAN tool. Vehicle data can then be observed live or stored for analysis and troubleshooting.

Robinson Nugent, Inc.
800 East 8th Street
New Albany, IN 47150
(812)945-0211
(812)945-0804 Fax

Manufactures a variety of computer connectors and sockets. It also manufactures the EPROM carriers used in GM Automotive applications from 1981–1993.

Roland Corporation U.S.
7200 Dominion Circle
Los Angeles, CA 90040-3696
(213)685-5141
(219)722-0911 Fax

Manufactures a variety of musical equipment and MIDI interfaces for computers.

Rotating Memory Repair, Inc.
23382-J Madero Road
Mission Viejo, CA 92691
(714)472-0159

Repair company that specializes in hard drive and floppy drive repair. Also repairs power supplies and displays.

Rotating Memory Services
4919 Windplay
El Dorado Hills, CA 95630

Repair company that specializes in hard disk drives.

Rupp Corporation
3228 East Indian School Road
Phoenix, AZ 85018
(602)224-9922
(800)852-7877
(602)224-0898 Fax

Developer of the DOS Interlink software used in MS- and PC DOS. Sells a commercial version called Fastlynx that offers many enhancements over Interlink. Also makes custom-length parallel transfer cables using a high-speed, 18-wire design.

Safeware Insurance Agency, Inc.
2929 N. High Street
Columbus, OH 43202
(614)262-0559
(800)848-3469

Insurance company that specializes in insurance for computer equipment.

SAMS
201 West 103rd Street
Indianapolis, IN 46290
(317)581-3500

Publishes technical books on computers and electronic equipment.

Seagate Technology
920 Disc Drive
Scotts Valley, CA 95066
(408)438-6550
(408)429-6356 Fax
(408)438-8111 Sales
(800)468-3472 Service
(408)438-2620 FAXback Information
(408)438-8771 BBS

The largest hard disk manufacturer in the world. Offers the most extensive product line of any disk manufacturer, ranging from low-cost units to the highest performance, capacity, and quality drives available.

***Service News* Magazine**
United Publications Inc.
38 Lafayette St.
P.O. Box 995
Yarmouth, ME 04096
(207)846-0600
(207)846-0657 Fax

Monthly newspaper for computer service and support people featuring articles covering PC service and repair products. Subscriptions are free to those who qualify.

SGS-Thomson Microelectronics/Inmos
1000 E. Bell Road
Phoenix, AZ 85022
(602)867-6100

Manufactures custom chipsets, and has been licensed by IBM to produce IBM-designed XGA chipsets for ISA, EISA, and MCA bus systems.

Sharp Electronics Corporation

Sharp Plaza
Mahwah, NJ 07430-2135
(201)529-8200
(201)529-8731 Sales Hotline
(201)529-9636 Fax

Manufactures a wide variety of electronic and computer equipment, including the best LCD monochrome and active matrix color displays and panels, as well as scanners, printers, and complete laptop and notebook systems.

Shugart Corporation

9292 Jeronimo Road
Irvine, CA 92714
(714)770-1100

Manufactures hard disk, floppy disk, and tape drives.

Sigma Data

Scytheville Row
P.O. Box 1790
New London, NH 03257
(603)526-6909
(800)446-4525
(603)526-6915 Fax

Distributes SIMM memory modules, hard drive, and processor upgrades. It is the sole distributor of a unique line of "Hyperace" direct processor upgrades for 286- and 386-based IBM PS/2 systems, including the Model 50, 60, 70, P70, and 80 systems. It also has a line of ATA IDE adapters and no-slot hard disk upgrades for IBM PS/2 systems.

Silicon Valley Computer

441 N. Whisman Road
Building 13
Mountain View, CA 94043
(415)967-1100
(415)967-0770 Fax
(415)967-8081 BBS

Manufactures a complete line of IDE interface adapters, including a unique model that supports 16-bit IDE (ATA) drives on PC and XT systems (8-bit ISA bus) and models, including floppy drive support as well as serial and parallel ports.

SMS Technology, Inc.

550 E. Brokaw Road
Box 49048
San Jose, CA 95161
(408)954-1633
(510)964-5700 BBS

Manufactures the OMTi disk controllers; formerly known as Scientific Micro Systems.

Softkey International, Inc.

201 Alameda del Prado
Novato, CA 94949
(617)494-1200
(800)227-5609

Manufactures the WordStar and WordStar 2000 programs.

SofTouch Systems, Inc.

1300 S. Meridian
Suite 600
Oklahoma City, OK 73108-1751
(405)947-8080
(405)632-6537 Fax

Manufactures the GammaTech Utilities for OS/2, which can undelete and recover files running under OS/2 even on an OS/2 HPFS partition.

Sola Electric

1717 Busse Road
Elk Grove, IL 60007
(708)439-2800
(800)289-7652

Manufactures a line of computer power-protection devices.

Solutronics Corp.

7255 Flying Cloud Drive
Eden Prairie, MN 55344
(612)943-1306
(800)875-2580
(612)943-1309 Fax

A depot repair company specializing in IBM, Compaq, and Apple motherboards; monitors; power supplies; keyboards; and disk drives. They offer 24-hour repair turn-around or advance exchange of most defective components. They also perform component level repair on other brand systems.

Sonera Technologies

P.O. Box 565
Rumson, NJ 07760
(908)747-5355
(800)932-6323
(908)747-4523 Fax

Manufactures the DisplayMate video display utility and diagnostic program. DisplayMate exercises, troubleshoots, and diagnoses video display adapter and monitor problems.

Sony Corporation of America

Sony Drive
Park Ridge, NJ 07656
(201)930-1000

Manufactures all types of high-quality electronic and computer equipment, including displays and magnetic- and optical-storage devices.

Specialized Products Company
3131 Premier Drive
Irving, TX 75063
(214)550-1923
(800)527-5018

Distributes a variety of tools and test equipment.

Sprague Magnetics, Inc.
15720 Stagg Street
Van Nuys, CA 91406
(818)994-6602
(800)553-8712

Manufactures a unique and interesting magnetic developer fluid that can be used to view sectors and tracks on a magnetic disk or tape. Also repairs tape drives.

Stac Electronics
5993 Avenida Encinas
Carlsbad, CA 92008
(619)431-7474
(800)522-7822
(800)225-1128
(619)431-0880 Fax
(619)431-5956 BBS

Makes the Stacker real-time data-compression adapter and software for OS/2 and DOS.

Standard Microsystems Corporation
35 Marcus Boulevard
Hauppauge, NY 11788
(516)273-3100
(800)992-4762

Manufactures ARCnet and EtherNet network adapters.

Star Micronics America, Inc.
200 Park Avenue
Pan Am Building
#3510
New York, NY 10166
(908)572-5550
(800)447-4700

Manufactures a line of low-cost printers.

STB Systems, Inc.
1651 N. Glenville
Richardson, TX 75085
(214)234-8750
(214)437-9615 BBS

Manufactures various adapter boards, and specializes in a line of high-resolution VGA video adapters.

Storage Dimensions, Inc.
2145 Hamilton Avenue
San Jose, CA 95125
(408)879-0300
(408)954-0710
(800)765-7895
(408)944-1220 BBS

Distributes Maxtor hard disk and optical drives as complete subsystems. Also manufactures the Speedstor hard disk utility software.

Symantec Corporation
10201 Torre Avenue
Cupertino, CA 95014
(408)253-9600
(800)441-7234
(408)973-9598 BBS

Manufactures a line of utility and applications software featuring the Norton Utilities for IBM and Apple systems.

SyQuest Technology
47071 Bayside Parkway
Fremont, CA 94538
(415)226-4000
(800)245-2278
(415)656-0470 BBS

Manufactures removable-cartridge hard disk drives.

Sysgen, Inc.
556 Gibraltar Drive
Milpitas, CA 95035
(800)821-2151
(408)946-5032 BBS

Manufactures a line of tape-backup storage devices.

Sytron
134 Flanders Road
P.O. Box 5025
Westboro, MA 01581-5025
(508)898-0100
(800)877-0016
(508)898-2677 Fax

Manufactures the SyTOS tape-backup software for DOS and OS/2, the most widely used tape software in the industry.

Tadiran
2975 Bowers Avenue
Santa Clara, CA 95051
(408)727-0300

Manufactures a variety of batteries for computer applications.

Tandon Corporation
405 Science Drive
Moorpark, CA 93021
(805)523-0340

Manufactures IBM-compatible computer systems and disk drives. Supplied to IBM most of the full-height floppy drives used in the original PC and XT systems.

Tandy Corporation/Radio Shack
1800 One Tandy Center
Fort Worth, TX 76102
(817)390-3700

Manufactures a line of IBM-compatible systems, peripherals, and accessories. Also distributes electronic parts and supplies.

Tatung Company of America, Inc.
2850 El Presidio Street
Long Beach, CA 90810
(213)979-7055
(800)827-2850

Manufactures monitors and complete compatible systems.

TCE Company
35 Fountain Square
5th Floor
Elgin, IL 60120
(708)741-7200
(800)383-8001
(708)741-1801 Fax

Manufactures an IDE drive formatter specifically for Conner Peripherals drives called "The Conner," consisting of a special hardware connector that plugs into the diagnostic port on Conner IDE drives, as well as special software to format the drive. It also specializes in power supply and power line monitoring and test equipment, and makes one of the best PC power supply test machines available.

TDK Electronics Corporation
12 Harbor Park Drive
Port Washington, NY 11050
(516)625-0100

Manufactures a line of magnetic and optical media, including disk and tape cartridges.

Teac America, Inc.
7733 Telegraph Road
Montebello, CA 90640
(213)726-0303

Manufactures a line of floppy and tape drives, including a unit that combines both 3 1/2-inch and 5 1/4-inch drives in one half-height package.

Tech Data Corporation
5350 Tech Data Drive
Clearwater, FL 34620
(813)539-7429
(800)237-8931

Distributes computer equipment and supplies.

Tech Spray Inc.
P.O. Box 949
Amarillo, TX 79105-0949
(806)372-8523

Manufactures computer and electronic cleaning chemicals and products.

Tecmar, Inc.
6225 Cochran Road
Solon, OH 44139
(216)349-0600
(800)344-4463
(216)349-0853 BBS

Manufactures a variety of adapter boards for IBM and compatible systems.

Test and Measurement World Magazine
275 Washington St.
Newton, MA 02158-1611
(617)558-4671

Thermalloy Inc.
2021 W. Valley View Lane
P.O. Box 810839
Dallas, TX 75381-0839
(214)243-4321
(214)241-4656 Fax

Manufactures a line of excellent CPU heat sink products, including versions with built-in fan modules.

Toshiba America, Inc.
9740 Irvine Boulevard
Irvine, CA 92718
(714)583-3000
(800)999-4823
(714)837-2116 BBS

Manufactures a complete line of 5 1/4- and 3 1/2-inch floppy and hard disk drives, CD-ROM drives, display products, printers, and a popular line of laptop and notebook IBM-compatible systems.

TouchStone Software Corporation
2130 Main Street
Suite 250
Huntington Beach, CA 92648
(714)969-7746
(800)531-0450
(714)960-1886 Fax

Manufactures the CheckIt user level and CheckIt Pro Deluxe high-end PC diagnostic and troubleshooting programs. CheckIt Pro Deluxe also includes their excellent CheckIt Sysinfo environmental diagnostic program.

Trantor Systems, Ltd.
5415 Randall Place
Fremont, CA 94538
(408)945-8600
(415)656-5159 BBS

Appendixes

Manufactures the MiniSCSI and MiniSCSI Plus Parallel Port SCSI adapters, including hard disk and CD-ROM drivers for a variety of devices.

Traveling Software, Inc.
18702 N. Creek Parkway
Bothell, WA 98011
(206)483-8088
(800)662-2652

Manufactures the LapLink file-transfer program for PC and Mac systems as well as several other utility programs.

Tripp Lite Manufacturing
500 N. Orleans
Chicago, IL 60610
(312)329-1777

Manufactures a complete line of computer power-protection devices.

Tseng Labs, Inc.
10 Pheasant Run
Newtown Commons
Newtown, PA 18940
(215)968-0502

Manufactures video controller chipsets, BIOS, and board design for OEMs.

Ultra-X, Inc.
P.O. Box 730010
San Jose, CA 95173-0010
(408)988-4721
(800)722-3789
(408)988-4849 Fax

Manufactures the excellent QuickPost PC, QuickPost PS/2, and Racer II diagnostic cards, as well as the Quicktech and Diagnostic Reference software packages. The Racer II is one of the most complete trouble-shooting hardware cards on the market today.

Ultrastor Corporation
15 Hammond Street
#310
Irvine, CA 92718
(714)453-8170

Manufactures a complete line of high-performance ESDI, SCSI, and IDE disk controllers for ISA and EISA bus systems.

UNISYS
Township Line and Union Meeting roads
Blue Bell, PA 19424
(800)448-1424

Manufactures PC-compatible systems that are part of the government Desktop IV contract.

Universal Memory Products
1378 Logan Avenue
#F
Costa Mesa, CA 92626

Distributes memory components, including chip and SIMM modules.

Upgrades Etc.
15251 NE 90th Street
Redmond, WA 98052
(714)640-5585
(800)541-1943

Distributes AMI, Award, and Phoenix BIOS upgrades.

U.S. Robotics, Inc.
8100 N. McCormick Boulevard
Skokie, IL 60076
(708)982-5010
(708)982-5151
(708)982-5092 BBS

Manufactures a complete line of modems and communications products. Its modems support more protocols than most others, including V.32bis, HST, and MNP protocols.

V Communications, Inc.
4320 Stevens Creek Boulevard
#275
San Jose, CA 95129
(408)296-4224

Manufactures the Sourcer disassembler and other programming tools.

Varta Batteries, Inc.
300 Executive Boulevard
Elmsford, NY 10523
(914)592-2500

Manufactures a complete line of computer batteries.

Verbatim Corporation
1200 WT Harris Boulevard
Charlotte, NC 28262
(704)547-6500

Manufactures a line of storage media, including optical and magnetic disks and tapes.

VESA—Video Electronic Standards Association
2150 North First St.
Suite 440
San Jose, CA 95131-2029
(408)435-0333
(408)435-8225 Fax

An organization of manufacturers dedicated to setting and maintaining video display, adapter, and bus standards. It has created the VESA video standards as well as the VESA Video Local Bus (VL-Bus) standard.

Visiflex Seels
16 E. Lafayette Street
Hackensack, NJ 07601
(201)487-8080

Manufactures form-fitting clear keyboard covers and other computer accessories.

VLSI Technology, Inc.
8375 S. River Parkway
Tempe, AZ 85284
(602)752-8574

Manufactures chipsets and circuits for PC-compatible motherboards and adapters. IBM uses these chipsets in some of the PS/2 system designs.

Volpe, Hank
P.O. Box 43214
Baltimore, MD 21236
(410)256-5767
(410)256-3631 BBS

Manufactures the Modem Doctor serial port and modem diagnostic program.

Walling Company
4401 S. Juniper
Tempe, AZ 85282
(602)838-1277

Manufactures the DataRase EPROM eraser, which can erase as many as four EPROM chips simultaneously using ultraviolet light.

Wang Laboratories, Inc.
One Industrial Avenue
Lowell, MA 01851
(508)656-1550
(800)225-0654

Manufactures a variety of PC-compatible systems, including some with MCA bus slots.

Wangtek, Inc.
41 Moreland Road
Simi Valley, CA 93065
(805)583-5525
(800)992-9916
(805)582-3620 BBS

Manufactures a complete line of tape-backup drives, including QIC, DAT, and 8mm drives for ISA, EISA, and MCA bus systems.

Warshawski/Whitney & Co.
1916 S. State Street
Chicago, IL 60680
(312)431-6100

Distributes an enormous collection of bargain-priced tools and equipment. Its products are primarily for automotive applications, but many of the tools have universal uses.

Washburn & Co.
3800 Monroe Avenue
Pittsford, NY 14534
(716)385-5200
(800)836-8026

The largest distributor of AMI BIOS and AMI motherboard products, known for providing very high-end technical information and support.

Watergate Software
2000 Powell Street
Suite 1200
Emeryville, CA 94608
(510)596-1770
(510)653-4784 Fax

Manufactures the excellent PC Doctor diagnostic program for PC troubleshooting and repair.

Wave Mate Inc.
2341 205th Street
#110
Torrance, CA 90501

Manufactures a line of high-speed replacement motherboards for IBM and compatible systems.

Weitek Corporation
1060 E. Arques
Sunnyvale, CA 94086
(408)738-8400

Manufactures high-performance math coprocessor chips.

Western Digital Corporation
8105 Irvine Center Drive
Irvine, CA 92718
(714)932-5000
(800)832-4778
(714)753-1234 BBS (2400bps)
(714)753-1068 BBS (9600+bps)

Manufactures many products, including IDE and SCSI hard drives; SCSI and ESDI adapters for ISA, EISA, and MCA bus systems; and EtherNet, Token Ring, and Paradise video adapters. Supplies IBM with IDE and SCSI drives for PS/2 systems.

Windsor Technologies, Inc.
130 Alto Street
San Rafael, CA 94901
(415)456-2200
(415)456-2244 Fax

Manufactures PC Technician, an excellent high-end technician level PC diagnostic and troubleshooting program.

WordPerfect Corporation
1555 N. Technology Way
Orem, UT 84057
(801)225-5000
(800)451-5151
(801)225-4414 BBS

Manufactures the popular WordPerfect word processing program.

Wyse Technology
3471 N. 1st Street
San Jose, CA 95134
(408)473-1200
(800)438-9973
(408)922-4400 BBS

Manufactures PC-compatible
systems and terminals.

Xebec
3579 Gordon
Carson City, NV 89701
(702)883-4000
(702)883-9264 BBS

Manufactures ISA disk controllers originally used by IBM in
the XT.

Xerox Corporation
Xerox Square
Rochester, NY 14644
(716)423-5078

Manufactures the Ventura
desktop publishing software, as
well as an extensive line of
computer equipment, copiers,
and printers.

Xidex Corporation
5100 Patrick Henry Drive
Santa Clara, CA 95050
(408)970-6574

Division of Hewlett Packard
that manufactures disk and
tape media.

Xircom
26025 Mureau Road
Calbasas, CA 91302
(800)874-7875
(818)878-7618 BBS

Manufactures external Token
Ring and EtherNet adapters
that attach to a parallel port.

Y-E Data America, Inc.
3030 Business Park Drive
#1
Norcross, GA 30071
(708)291-2340

Manufactures a line of floppy
disk drives, tape drives, and
printers. Supplied 5 1/4-inch
floppy drives to IBM for use in
XT, AT, and PS/2 systems.

Zenith Data Systems
2150 E. Lake Cook Road
Buffalo Grove, IL 60089
(800)553-0331

Manufactures a line of IBM-
compatible systems.

Zeos International, Ltd.
530 5th Avenue NW
St. Paul, MN 55112
(612)633-4591
(800)423-5891

Manufactures a line of good,
low-cost PC-compatible ISA
and EISA bus systems sold by
way of mail order.

Index

Symbols

1,1,1 trichloroethane, 32
1.2M 5 1/4-inch floppy
  disk drives, 545-546
  formatting 360K disks,
    558
  reading/writing 360K
    disks, 557-558, 580
  troubleshooting, 550-551
1.44M 3 1/2-inch floppy
  disk drives, 547
  formatting 720K floppy
    disks, 559-560
  reading/writing 720K
    floppy disks, 559
2.88M 3 1/2-inch floppy
  disk drives, 547-548
  formatting
    1.44M disks, 561
    720K floppy disks,
      559-560
  reading/writing
    1.44M disks, 560
    720K floppy disks, 559
3 1/2-inch floppy disk
  drives, 534
  1.44M 3 1/2-inch drives,
    547-550, 559-560
  2.88M 3 1/2-inch disk
    drives, 547-548,
    559-560
  720K 3 1/2-inch double-
    density drives, 546-547
3 1/2-inch floppy disks,
  551-552
  cylinder spacing, 537
  double-density, 554

extra-high density,
  554-555
high-density, 554
media-access hole, 552
media-sensor hole, 553
metal hub, 552
shutter, 552
tracks, 537
write-protect/-enable
  hole, 552
troubleshooting, 548-550
4-Way Set Associative
  Cache, 178
5 1/4-inch floppy disk
  drives, 534
  1.2M 5 1/4-inch floppy
    drives, 545-546
  360K 5 1/4-inch low-
    density drive, 544-545
  data-exchange, 535
  tracks, 537
  troubleshooting, 550-551
5 1/4-inch floppy disks,
  551
  double-density, 554
  high-density, 554
  hub hole, 551
  index hole, 551
  media-access hole, 552
  notches, 552
  quad-density, 554
8-bit sound cards, 491
8mm tape backup drives,
  817-819
9-Pin (AT) Serial Port
  Connector, 416
16-bit sound cards, 492

25-Pin (PC, XT, and PS/2)
  Serial Port Connector,
  416
25-Pin PC-Compatible
  Parallel Port Connector,
  438-439
32-bit internal registers,
  161
82-key PC and XT
  keyboards, 337
83-key keyboards
  AT, 337
  PC and XT , 327-328
    compatibility, 331
    key numbers, 340-342
    part numbers, 361
    scan codes, 340-342
84-key AT keyboards,
  327-329
  compatibility, 331
  key numbers, 343-345
  part numbers, 361
  scan codes, 343-345
101-key enhanced
  keyboards, 327, 329-330
  compatibility, 331-333
  cursor and screen
    controls, 331
  foreign language
    versions, 331
  function keys, 331
  key numbers, 346-354
  numeric keypad, 330
  part numbers, 361
  removeable keycaps, 331
  scan codes, 346-354
  typing area, 330

286 CPUs, 270
  upgrades, 880-883
287 math coprocessors, 875-876
360K 5 1/4-inch low-density drive, 544-545, 550-551
386DX CPUs, 173, 270
  upgrades, 883-884
386MAX memory manager, 269-270
386SL CPUs, 173-174, 270
387 math coprocessor chips, 876
486DX CPUs, 179-180, 270, 885-886
  upgrades, 884-887
487SX math coprocessor chip, 184-185, 876
720K 3 1/2-inch double-density drives, 546-547
8086 CPUs, 167-168, 270, 877
8087 math coprocessors, 214-216, 875
8088 CPUs, 167-168, 221-223, 270, 877
8250 UART chips, 417-418
8250A UART chips, 418
8250B UART chips, 418
8514/A Display Adapter cards, 396-397
16450 UART chips, 417-418
16550 UART chips, 417-418
16550A UART chips, 418
80186 CPUs, 168-169
80188 CPUs, 168-169
80286 CPUs, 169-171
80287 math coprocessors, 216-218
80386 CPUs, 171-173, 223-225
80387 math coprocessors, 218-219
80486 CPUs, 175-190
80487 math coprocessors, 220-221
82360SL CPUs, 174

A

AADs (analog alignment disks), 585
Abort, Retry, Ignore error message, 535
access keys (adapter cards), 103
access time
  CD-ROM drives, 778
  hard disk drives, 639
active preventive maintenance, 898-909
active-matrix LCD monitors, 377-378
actuators (hard disk drives), 615
  stepper motor, 615-626
  voice coil, 615-626, 636
Ad Lib Gold sound card, 490
Adaptec, 1474
adapter cards
  access keys, 103
  AT adapter cards, 105
  bus mouse, 366
  CD-ROM drives, 788-794
  EISA buses, 115
  hard disk drives, 711-715
  ISA buses, 102
  jumpers, 790
  MCA buses, 106
  memory
    BIOS memory areas, 150
    configuration, 150-151, 264
  memory-expansion adapter cards, 847
  NTSC-to-VGA adapter, 410
  plug-and-play, 155-156
  removing
    AT cases, 48
    PS/2 cases, 55, 62, 68
    Slimline cases, 40
    Tower cases, 48
    XT style cases, 40
  resource conflicts, 153-155, 265
  skirts, 105

VESA local buses, 125
VGA-to-NTSC adapters, 407-411
adapter plates (floppy disk drives), 574
adapter ROM, 230
ADCs (analog-to-digital converters) (sound cards), 490
address buses, 95, 98, 162-163
  SLC processors, 210
addresses (memory)
  linear addresses, 231
  segment addresses, 230
AdLib Music Synthesizer Card, 483
ADPCM (Adaptive Differential Pulse Code Modulation) (sound cards), 494
Advanced Diagnostics program, 583
advanced run length limited encoding, 598
air bearings (hard disk drive heads), 590-591
air filters (hard disk drives), 627-628, 899
alignment (floppy disk drives), 581, 585
allocation units (DOS)
  floppy disks, 542-543
  hard disks, 1011-1013
Altair, 10
Ambra, 1110
  see also IBM PS/x systems
AMD (Advanced Micro Devices), 212, 1475
American Megatrends, Inc. (AMI), 1476
  BIOS software, 86-89, 855-856
American National Standards Institute, see ANSI
AMI (American Megatrends, Inc.), 1476
  AMIDiag diagnostic software, 963

motherboards
BIOS error codes,
1411-1416
BIOS hard disk
parameters,
1402-1403
**AMIDiag diagnostic
software,** 963
amplitude (sound), 490
**analog alignment disks
(AAD),** 585
**analog-to-digital
converters (sound cards),**
490
Andromeda Research, 1476
EPROM programmers, 859
Annabooks, 1476
PC Keyboard Design, 362
**annotations (voice
annotations),** 488
**ANSI (American National
Standards Institute),**
683-684, 1476
**Anti-Virus program
(Microsoft),** 913
APPEND command, 982
Apple Computer, Inc., 11,
1476
architecture
I/O buses
EISA buses, 114-120
ISA buses, 100-105
local buses, 120-122
MCA buses, 106-114
VESA local buses,
122-127
memory chips, 845
interleaved memory,
845
memory caching,
846-847
paged memory, 845
motherboard memory,
270-271
operating systems,
976-977
ARCnet adapters, 450
**areal density (hard disk
drives),** 588

**ARLL (advanced run
length limited) encoding,**
598
ASCII characters
ANSI.SYS, 1343
EBCDIC characters,
1343-1347
hexadecimal to ASCII
conversions, 1339-1342
line-drawing characters,
1338
metric system prefixes,
1348
powers of 2, 1348-1349
**ASPI (Advances SCSI)
interface (CD-ROM
drives),** 779
ASSIGN command, 982
AT, see **IBM AT**
Atasi hard disk drives,
1380
ATTRIB command, 982
audio cards, see **sound
cards**
**audio CDs, playing on
CD-ROM drives,** 489
audio files, see **sound files**
audio systems
headphones, 501
microphones, 501-502
speakers, 499-501
MIDI (Musical
Instrument Digital
Interface), 502-503
sound cards, 483-499
**automobile power
adapters (IBM 5140 PC
Convertible),** 1064
**average access time (hard
disk drives),** 639
**average seek time (hard
disk drives),** 639
Award Software, Inc., 1477
BIOS software, 86-90,
855-856
motherboards
BIOS error codes,
1416-1419
BIOS hard disk
parameters,
1403-1405

B

Baby AT, 294
**back probing connectors
(power supply),** 314
backplane systems, 81-82
BACKUP command, 933,
982
backups, 807-808, 897,
930-931
backup software, 932-933
BIOS, 859-861
copy protection
(software), 932
floppy backups, 933-934
hard disk drives
EBR (Extended Boot
Record), 911
FATs (File Allocation
Tables), 911
MBR (Master Boot
Record), 911
root directory, 911
intervals, 931
power supply, 928-930
removable storage drives,
826
magnetic media
drives, 826-829
magneto-optical
drives, 826, 829-831
WORM (write-once
read-many) drives,
831
tape backup drives, 808,
934-939
8mm tape backup
drives, 817-819
buying, 819-821, 939
capacities, 815-816,
820
cassettes, 810-812
compatibility, 816-817
cost, 821
DAT (digital audio
tape) tape backup
drives, 817-818
data transfer rates,
814, 821
drivers, 937-938
external tape backup
drives, 938-939

formatting, 814
IBM PS/2, 1323
installation, 821-823
interfaces, 936-937
internal tape backup
  drives, 938-939
portables, 815
QIC-40 tape backup
  drives, 812-814
QIC-80 tape backup
  drives, 812-815
software, 824-826,
  937-938
standards, 809-812,
  817-820
bandwidths (processor
  buses), 96-97
bank-switching memory,
  838
barometric filters (hard
  disk drives), 627
BASIC command, 983
basic input-output system,
  see BIOS
BASICA command, 983
.BAT files, 984
battery chargers (IBM 5140
  PC Convertible), 1064
battery connectors
  (motherboards), 1357
battery-and-speaker
  assembly (IBM PS/2
  systems), 61, 69
baud rate (modems), 431
BBSes (bulletin board
  systems), 1332
  DOS patches, 1017
  IBM BBS, 956
  shareware, 973
Bell 103 modulation
  standard, 431
Bell 212A modulation
  standard, 431
Bell Labs modem
  standards, 420-438
benchmarks (hard disk
  drives), 639
Bernoulli removable media
  drives, 827-828
bezels
  floppy disk drives, 523
  hard disk drives, 634-635

LED (light-emitting
  diode), 635
IBM PS/2 systems,
  removing, 71
BiCMOS (Bipolar
Complementary Metal
Oxide Semiconductor)
Pentium processors, 206
BIOS (basic input-output
system)
  backups, 859-861
  BIOS Interface Technical-
    Reference manual, 22
  capacities, 763
  motherboards, 84
    AMI, 1402-1403
    Award, 1403-1405
    Compaq Deskpro 286
      Revision F,
      1400-1401
    Compaq Deskpro 286e
      Revision B,
      1401-1402
    Compaq Deskpro 386,
      1399
    error codes, 1411-1420
    IBM PS/2, 1308-1312,
      1397-1398
    memory requirements,
      230
    Phoenix 286,
      1406-1407
    Phoenix 386,
      1408-1409
    ROM compatibility,
      85-91
    Zenith, 1409-1410
  operating systems,
    977-979
  platforms, 977-979
  plug-and-play adapter
    cards, 156
  upgrades, 853-855, 858
    alternatives to an
      upgrade, 857
    EPROM programming,
      859-861
    Flash BIOS, 866
    IML system partition
      BIOS, 866-867
    keyboard-controller
      chips, 855

modifying hard disk
  controller head step
  rate, 862-866
modifying hard disk
  drive parameter
  tables, 861-862
software, 855-857
troubleshooting, 858
versions, 1353-1355
bit rate (modems), 431
bits, 9
blankers, *see* screen savers
Blue Lightning processors,
  210-211, 886
boards, *see* cards
booting, 890, 916-918
  cold boot, 889-892
  DOS (Disk Operating
    System), 990-991
  warm boot, 889-892
BPI (bits per inch) (floppy
  disks), 554
brackets (floppy disk
  drives), 574
Branch Target Buffer
  (BTB), 205
Brand Technology hard
  disk drives, 1380
brokers (Boston Computer
  Exchange), 1478
brushes (cleaning brushes),
  904
BTB (Branch Target
  Buffer), 205
buffers (CD-ROM drives),
  779
bugs (DOS), 1017-1023
burn-in (phosphor
  monitors), 918
bus adapter cards (IBM
  PS/2), 56
bus mastering
  EISA buses, 118
  MCA I/O buses, 106
bus mouse, 366-367
bus topology (networks),
  446
buses, 84, 95, 159-161
  address buses, 95, 98
  CACP (Central
    Arbitration Control
    Point), 106

I/O buses, 95-96
  EISA buses, 17, 114-120
  expansion slots, 98-99
  GUI (graphical user interfaces), 121
  ISA buses, 15, 100-105
  local buses, 120-122
  MCA buses, 16, 106-114, 291, 1114-1117
  PCI buses, 18, 127-138
  PCMCIA buses, 138-142
  VESA local buses, 122-127
  video cards, 404-411
IBM PS/x systems, 1111
local buses, 17
memory buses, 95, 97-98
  data widths, 98
power consumption, 307
processor buses, 95-96
  bandwidths, 96-97
buying
  CD-ROM drives, 777-788
  file servers, 452
  hard disk drives, 635-648
  modems, 436
  monitors, 382-384
  motherboards, 83-85
  sound cards, 494-499
  tape backup drives, 819-821, 939
  video cards, 405-406

C

C000 ROM Error error message, 991
cables
  disassembling, 39
  floppy disk drives
    data and control cables, 575
    power cables, 575
  IBM PS/2, 1321-1324
  keyboards, 354
    defective cables, 356

DIN (Deutsche Industrie Norm) connectors, 354-355
    part numbers, 361
    replacing, 359
    SDL (Shielded Data Link) connectors, 354-355
    testing, 356
  LANs, 446-448, 472
    coaxial cable, 474-475
    connecting, 477-478
    fiber optic cables, 475-476
    IBM Cabling System, 476-477
    installation, 448
    twisted pair cable, 472-473
  mouse, 363-364
    connectors, 356, 363
    mini-DIN connectors, 356
  printer cables (IBM 5140 PC Convertible), 1064
cache memory
  80486 CPUs, 178-179
  hard disk drives, 641
  motherboards, 83
caching controllers (hard disk drives), 641
CACP (Central Arbitration Control Point) (buses), 106
caddies (CD-ROM drives), 774, 787
calculating power consumption, 306-308
Calibrate program, 645
CALL command, 982
Cannot CHKDSK (network drive error message), 1033
cards
  bus mouse, 366
  cleaning, 906-907
  mothercards, 81
  riser cards, 99
  see also adapter cards; network adapter cards; sound cards; video cards

cassettes (tape backup drives), 810-812
CCITT (Consultative Committee on International Telephone and Telegraph) modem standards, 420-438
CD Extensions for DOS (Microsoft), 801-802
CD-DA (Digital Audio) drives, 777, 782
CD-R (CD-Recordable) drives, 775, 785-786
CD-ROM device drivers, 801
CD-ROM drives, 773, 775-777
  access time, 778
  audio CDs, playing, 489
  average access time, 493
  buffers, 779
  buying, 777-788
  caddies, 774, 787
  CD-DA (Digital Audio) drives, 777, 782
  CD-R (CD-Recordable) drives, 775, 785-786
  CD-ROM XA drives, 784-785
  data transfer rates, 493, 778
  drive sealing, 787
  external CD-ROM drives, 788
  IBM PS/2, 1323
  installation, 788
    adapter cards, 788-794
    external CD-ROM drives, 794-795
    internal CD-ROM drives, 795-797
    testing, 803-804
  interfaces, 779
    ASPI (Advances SCSI) interface, 779
    non-standard SCSI interfaces, 780
    SCSI interfaces, 779
    SCSI-2 interface, 779
  internal CD-ROM drives, 788
  Media Player, 804

MPCs (multimedia PCs), 493, 786-787
multimedia, 492-493
Multispin drives, 786
PhotoCD drives, 782-783
quadruple-speed CD-ROM drives, 493
self-cleaning lenses, 788
software
 CD Extensions for DOS (Microsoft), 801-802
 CD-ROM device drivers, 801
 SCSI adapter drivers, 801
sound cards, 492-493, 496
triple-speed CD-ROM drives, 493
CD-ROM XA drives, 784-785
CD-ROMs, 773-775
creating, 785-786
development, 774
interpolation, 776
PhotoCDs, 783-784
pits, 776
production, 775
standards, 780
 High Sierra format, 781
 ISO 9660 standard, 780-781
 Yellow Book standards, 781
VTOC (Volume Table of Contents), 781-782
CD-WO (CD-Write Once) drives, 775
CD/CHDIR command, 981
Central Arbitration Control Point (buses), 106
Central Point Backup software, 826
CGA (color graphics adapter) cards, 386-387
memory, 149
see also video cards
CGA (color graphics adapter) monitors, 386
see also monitors

CHCP command, 981-983
Checkit diagnostic software, 963-964
chemical-freeze sprays, 33, 903
chip creep, 283, 905
chips
memory chips, 271
 architectures, 845-847
 capacities, 841
 configuration, 849
 DIPs (Dual In-line Pin) chips, 271, 840
 installation, 847-849
 jumper settings, 849-850
 manufacturer's markings, 272, 841
 memory banks, 273-275
 parity checking, 275-279
 part numbers, 273
 removing, 849
 SIMMs (Single In-line Memory Modules), 279-287, 840, 844, 1319-1320
 SIPPs (Single In-line Pin Packages), 840
 speed, 287-288, 841-844
 switch settings, 849-850
seating, 906
TMS380 chips, 465
UART chips, 417-418
 16450, 417-418
 16550, 417-418
 16550A, 418
 8250, 417-418
 8250A, 418
 8250B, 418
 FIFO (first in, first out), 418
 identifying type, 417
see also CPUs; coprocessors
chipsets (motherboards), 85
CHKDSK command, 983, 1029-1038

cigarette smoke, 900
Cinepak, 409
circuit boards (floppy disk drives), 522
CISC (Complex Instruction Set Computer) chips, 204
classes (hardware)
comparing, 18
IBM AT, 16, 19-20
IBM PC/XT, 15, 19-20
keyboard interfaces, 19
cleaners, 901-902
contact cleaners, 902
dusters, 903
lubricants, 902, 905
Stabilant 22 contact cleaner/lubricant, 902
vendors, 905
cleaning, 32
brushes, 904
cards, 906-907
connectors, 906-908
contacts, 907-908
cooling systems, 899
dust, 899
erasers, 908
file servers, 452
floppy disk drives, 582-583, 908
foam tape, 904
hard disk drives, 908
keyboards, 359, 908
 dust, 359
 foam element key switches, 334
 liquid spills, 360
lubricants, 902, 905
mouse, 367, 909
RTV sealer, 904
swabs, 904
vaccuum cleaners, 903
clock speed, 163, 166
80486 processors, 177
increasing, 878, 881, 885
math coprocessors, 217
POST (Power-On Self Test), disabling, 861
CLS command, 981
clusters (DOS hard disks), 1011-1013

CMOS (Complementary Metal Oxide Semiconductor)
386DX processors, 173
486DX processors, 180
disassembling computers, 37
memory
IBM AT, 20, 1350-1353
Power_Good signal, 300
coaxial cables, 446, 474-475
codecs, 409
coercivity (floppy disks), 555
cold boot, 889-892
COLDSET.COM program, 890-892
color graphics adapter cards, *see* **CGA cards**
color graphics adapter monitors, *see* **CGA monitors**
color monitors, 378-379
Colorado Memory Systems, Inc., 819, 1480
COM files, 984
COM ports, *see* **serial ports**
COMMAND command, 983
command set (modems), 422-439
Hayes modems, 1361-1368
U.S. Robotics modems, 1361-1368
commands (DOS commands), 984-985
APPEND, 982
ASSIGN, 982
ATTRIB, 982
BACKUP, 982
BASIC, 983
BASICA, 983
CALL, 982
CD/CHDIR, 981
CHCP, 981, 983
CHKDSK, 983, 1029-1038
CLS, 981
COMMAND, 983
COMP, 983
COPY, 981

CTTY, 981
DATE, 981
DEBUG, 983, 1040-1043
DEL/ERASE, 982
DIR, 982
DISKCOMP, 983
DISKCOPY, 983
DOSBACKUP, 933
DOSKEY, 983
DOSSHELL, 983
ECHO, 982
EDIT, 983
EDLIN, 983
EMM386, 983
EXE2BIN, 983
EXIT, 982
EXPAND, 982
FASTOPEN, 983
FC, 983
FDISK, 983
FIND, 983
FOR, 982
FORMAT, 561-565, 983
GOTO, 982
GRAFTABL, 983
GRAPHICS, 983
HELP, 983
IF, 982
JOIN, 983
KEYB, 983
KEYBFR, 983
KEYBGR, 983
KEYBIT, 983
KEYBS, 983
KEYBUK, 983
LABEL, 983
LIB, 983
LINK, 983
LOADHI/LH, 982
MD/MKDIR, 982
MEM, 983
MIRROR, 912, 983
MODE, 983
MORE, 983
NLSFUNC, 983
PATH, 982
PAUSE, 982
PRINT, 983
PROMPT, 982
QBASIC, 984
RD/RMDIR, 982
RECOVER, 984, 1038-1039

REM, 982
REN/RENAME, 982
REPLACE, 984
resident commands, 981
RESTORE, 984
SET, 982
SETVER, 984
SHARE, 984
SHIFT, 982
SORT, 984
SUBST, 984
SYS, 984
TIME, 982
transient commands, 981
TREE, 984
TYPE, 982
UNDELETE, 984
UNFORMAT, 565-566, 984
VER, 982
VERIFY, 982
VOL, 982
XCOPY, 984
communications ports, 413
parallel ports, 413, 438-440
25-Pin PC-Compatible Parallel Port Connector, 438-439
configuration, 440-441
identifying, 441-442
original unidirectional parallel ports, 439
testing, 444
troubleshooting, 444
Type 1 Bidirectional parallel ports, 439
Type 3 DMA parallel ports, 440
serial ports, 413-418
9-Pin (AT) Serial Port Connector, 416
25-Pin (PC, XT, and PS/2) Serial Port Connector, 416
configuration, 419-420
identifying, 441-442
modems, 420-438
testing, 442-444
troubleshooting, 444
UART chips, 417-418

COMP command, 983
compact video coded, *see* CVC
Compaq Computer Corporation, 1480
  EISA (Extended Industry Standard Architecture) buses, 17
  motherboards, 1399-1402
  PC Power and Cooling, 324
Compaq Deskpro 286 Revision F motherboards, 1400-1401
Compaq Deskpro 286e Revision B motherboards, 1401-1402
Compaq Deskpro 386 motherboards, 1399
compatibility (sound cards), 494-495
Complex Instruction Set Computer chips, *see* CISC chips
compressed air, 33, 903
compression
  disks, 763-764
  full-motion video, 409
  sound cards, 496
    ADPCM (Adaptive Differential Pulse Code Modulation), 494
    MPEG (Motion Pictures Expert Group), 494
computers
  viewing computer screens on TV, 407-411
  see also PCs; computers by class, model
configuration, 38-39
  floppy disk drives, 568, 576
    daisy-chain configuration, 569
    disk change, 577-578
    drive select jumpers, 569-573
    media-sensor jumpers, 573, 579
    terminating resistors, 571-573

  troubleshooting, 577-581
hard disk drives, 715, 722-736
  controllers, 716-721
  ESDI interface, 665
  host adapters, 716-721
  IDE interface, 669-671, 675-681
  SCSI interface, 704-709
  ST-506/412 interface, 659-661
memory
  adapter cards, 150-151, 264
  EMM386.EXE program, 266
  HIMEM.SYS program, 266
  memory chips, 849
mouse, 370
parallel ports, 440-441
serial ports, 419
configuration utilities
  InfoSpotter, 972
  MSD (Microsoft Diagnostics), 971
  SysChk, 972
conflicts
  resources, 151-156
  adapter cards, 153-155, 265
  resolving, 152
  system-configuration template, 152-153
  software, 1043-1044
connecting
  cables for LANs, 477-478
  mouse
    I/O buses, 366-367
    motherboard mouse port, 365-366
    serial interface, 365-366
connectors
  cleaning, 906-908
  floppy disk drives
    drive controller connectors, 523-524
    logic connectors, 523-524

hard disk drives
  grounding tabs, 634
  interface connectors, 632
  power connectors, 633
motherboards
  battery connectors, 1357
  keylock connectors, 1357
  LED connectors, 1357
  speaker connectors, 1357
power supply, 295-299
  back probing, 314
  disk drives, 298
  physical connectors, 299
sound cards, 504-505
  CD-ROM connectors, 496
  joystick/MIDI connectors, 499
  microphone in connectors, 499
  MIDI connectors, 502
  speaker/headphone connector, 498
  stereo line in connectors, 498
  stereo line out connectors, 498
Conner Peripherals, Inc., 1482
  hard disk drives, 677-678, 1380-1381
Consultative Committee on International Telephone and Telegraph, *see* CCITT
contacts, cleaning, 907-908
control codes
  Epson printers, 1370-1372
  HP LaserJet printers, 1372-1376
  IBM printers, 1368-1370
control programs
  IBM 3270 PC, 1077-1078
  microprocessors, 10
controllers
  caching controllers
    hard disk drives, 641

hard disk drives, 711-715
  configuration, 716-721
  error codes, 764-767
  ESDI (enhanced small
    device interface),
    663-664
  IDE (Integrated Drive
    Electronics) interface,
    666
  ST-506/412 interface
    (hard disk drives),
    662-663
  motherboards, 98
controls (monitors), 383
**conventional (base)
  memory, 229, 837**
  conventional memory
    barrier, 227
  map, 228
cooling systems, 899
**coprocessors (math
  coprocessors)**
  287 math coprocessors,
    875-876
  387 math coprocessors,
    876
  487 math coprocessors,
    876
  8087 math coprocessors,
    875
  installation, 874-875
COPY command, 981
**copy protection (software),
  932**
**Corrective Service Disks
  (CSDs), 1019-1020**
corrosion, 899
covers
  IBM AT, 47
  IBM PS/2, 54, 60, 68
  IBM XT, 39-40
  Slimline cases, 39-40
  Tower cases, 47
**CP/M (Control Program
  for Microprocessors), 10**
CPBACKUP program, 933
**CPUs (central processing
  units), 270-271, 876**
  486 CPUs, 886
  486DX CPUs, 885
  8086 CPUs, 877
  8088 CPUs, 877

Blue Lightning chips, 886
chip creep, 906
DX2 CPUs, 885
file servers, 453
Intel chips, 167-209
NEC V20 CPUs, 877-878
NEC V30 CPUs, 877-878
Pentium chips, 886-887
power consumption, 307
seating, 906
upgrades, 882-883
see also processors
**CRT display adapters (IBM
5140 PC Convertible),
1063**
**CRTs (cathode ray tubes),
375**
**CSDs (Corrective Service
Disks), 1019-1020**
**CSMA/CD (carrier sense,
multiple access, with
collision detection),
460-463**
**CSP (CompuCom Speed
Protocol) standards, 435**
CTTY command, 981
**CVC (compact video
coded), 409**
cylinders, 542
  floppy disk drives, 535
  floppy disks, 539
    3 1/2-inch floppy
      disks, 537
    5 1/4 inch floppy
      disks, 537
  viewing, 536

D

**DACs (digital-to-analog
converters) (sound cards),
490**
daisy chains, 569
**DAT (digital audio tape)
tape backup drives,
817-818**
**data and control cables
(floppy disk drives), 575**
**data area (DOS hard disks),
1013**
**data buses (SLC
processors), 210**

Data Depot, 1483
  PC PowerCheck card,
    319-320
  POST cards, 952
data recovery
  DOS
    CHKDSK command,
      1029-1038
    DEBUG command,
      1040-1043
    RECOVER command,
      1038-1039
  utilities
    dSALVAGE, 971
    Norton Utilities,
      970-971
    PC-Tools, 971
**data widths (memory
buses), 98**
**data-compression
standards (modems), 421,
433**
**Data-Tech Memories hard
disk drives, 1381**
data-transfer rates
  CD-ROM drives, 778
  hard disk drives, 588
    cylinder skewing, 646,
      648
    head skewing, 646-648
    interleaving, 641-645
    SCSI interface, 685
  tape backup drives, 814,
    821
DATE command, 981
DBR (DOS Boot Record),
  see volume boot sectors
**DD (double-density)
floppy controllers, 19**
**DEBUG command,
441-442, 983, 1040-1043**
DEBUG utility, 222
**decompression (full-
motion video), 409**
**defect mapping (hard disk
drives), 739-740**
  defect scans, 740-741
  manufacturer's defect list,
    741-742
  sector sparing, 743-745
**defect scans (hard disk
drives), 740-741**

DEFRAG utility, 541, 910
defragmentation
   floppy disks, 541
   hard disk drives, 909-910
DEL/ERASE command, 982
density (floppy disks), 554
   double-density, 554
   extra-high density,
     554-555
   formatting, 579-580
   high-density, 554
   linear density, 554
   longitudinal density, 554
   quad-density, 554
depot repair (power
   supply), 321
desktop video cards, *see*
   DTV cards
diagnostic read-and-write
   cylinder (DOS hard
   disks), 1013
diagnostic utilities,
   947-948, 953, 962-963
   Advanced Diagnostics,
     583, 948, 956-962
     error codes, 960-962
   AMIDiag, 963
   Checkit, 963-964
   Disk Manager, 969
   Drive Probe, 583, 585,
     968-969
   IBM system diagnostics,
     953-956
   keyboards, 357
   memory, 289, 850
   Micro-Scope, 964-965
   Modem Doctor, 443
   MSD (Microsoft
     Diagnostics), 442
   Norton Desktop for
     Windows, 972
   Norton Diagnostics, 965
   PC Technician, 966
   POST (Power-On Self
     Test), 947-949
     audio error codes,
       949-950
     I/O port codes,
       950-953
     visual error codes, 950
   QAPlus/FE, 966-967

   Service Diagnostics,
     967-968
   Winprobe, 972
   WinSleuth, 972
Diamond Viper video card,
   887
Digital Multi-Meters, *see*
   DMMs
digital signal processors,
   see **DSPs**
Digital Volt-Ohm Meter
   (DVOMs), 313
digital-to-analog
   converters (sound cards),
   490
DIN (Deutsche Industrie
   Norm) connectors,
   354-355
DIPs (Dual In-line Pin)
   memory chips, 271, 840
   broken or bent pins, 848
   see also memory chips
DIR command, 982
Direct Drives, 1483
direct memory access
   channels, *see* **DMA**
   channels
directories, 985
   DOS, 1008-1010,
     1382-1390
   root directory backups,
     911
DIS (dynamic impedance
   stabilitzation), 434
disabling clock speed test
   (POST), 861
disassembling computers,
   35, 905
   cabling, 39
   ESD (Electro-Static
     Discharge), 36-37
   IBM AT cases
     adapter cards, 49
     covers, 47
     disk drives, 48-49
     motherboards, 52
     power supply, 49
   IBM PS/2 systems, 52-54
     adapter cards, 55, 62,
       68
     battery-and-speaker
       assembly, 61, 69

     bezels, 71
     bus adapter cards, 56
     covers, 54, 60, 68
     disk drives, 54-55, 64,
       71, 73-74
     fan assembly, 61
     motherboards, 60, 66,
       76
     power supply, 57, 65,
       71
     SIMMs, 59, 67-68
     support structures, 64
   IBM XT cases
     adapter boards, 40
     covers, 39-40
     disk drives, 41-42
     motherboards, 44-46
     power supply, 44
   keyboards, 358-359
   mouse, 367
   preparation, 35-39
   recording configuration,
     38-39
   setup programs, 37-38
   Slimline cases
     adapter boards, 40
     covers, 39-40
     disk drives, 41-42
     motherboards, 44-46
     power supply, 44
   Tower cases
     adapter boards, 48
     covers, 47
     disk drives, 48-49
     motherboards, 52
     power supply, 49
Disk Boot failure error
   message, 992, 994
disk change (floppy disk
   drive configuration),
   577-578
disk drives, *see* **drives**
Disk Manager diagnostic
   software, 649-674, 749,
   756, 969
Disk Operating System, *see*
   DOS
disk recovery (DOS)
   CHKDSK command,
     1029-1038
   DEBUG command,
     1040-1043

RECOVER command, 1038-1039
disk software interfaces, 1355-1357
DISKCOMP command, 983
DISKCOPY command, 983
diskette change line jumpers (floppy disk drives), 528-586
diskettes, *see* **disks**
disks
    compression, 763-764
        DOS, 1004-1013
display adapters (IBM 3270 PC), 1076
Display Power-Management Signaling (DPMS) spec, 380
DMA (Direct Memory Access) channels, 146-148
    IBM PCs, 11
    processors, 169
    see also resources
DMM (Digital Multi-Meters), 30, 313-316, 356
documentation, 20
    acquiring, 23-24
    hard disk drives, 715
    IBM, 1462
        GTO (Guide To Operations), 20-21, 953, 1462-1463
        Hardware-Maintenance Library, 22-23, 1463-1467
        ordering, 1471
        Quick-Reference Manuals, 1462-1463
        Technical-Reference Library, 21-22, 1467-1471
    IBM PS/x systems, 1114
    keyboards, 362
    magazines, 1333-1334
    manuals, 1328-1330
    motherboards, 84-85
    publishers
        Addison-Wesley Publishing Co., Inc., 1474
        ADP Hollander Company, 1475

Annabooks, 1476
Chilton Book Company, 1479
Chrysler Motors Service Publications, 1480
Direct Drives, 1483
Endl Publications, 1484
Global Engineering Documents, 1486
Heathkit Education Systems, 1486
Helm, Inc., 1486
IBM Technical Directory, 1487
McGraw-Hill, Inc., 1491
Micro House International, 1492
Osborne/McGraw Hill, 1495
Que Corporation, 1497
SAMS, 1498
DOS (Disk Operating System), 975-977
booting, 990-991
bugs, 1017-1023
commands, 981-987
    resident commands, 981
    transient commands, 981
CSDs (Corrective Service Diskettes), 987-988
DEBUG utility, 222
directories, 1382-1390
disk structures, 1377-1380
disk/data recovery
    CHKDSK command, 1029-1038
    DEBUG command, 1040-1043
    RECOVER command, 1038-1039
downgrades, 1016
DVB (DOS Volume Boot Sector), 1381-1390
error codes, 1460-1462

FATs (file allocation tables), 995-997
files, 995
    .BAT files, 984
    .COM files, 984
    directories, 985
    .EXE files, 984
floppy disks, 539-541
    allocation units, 542-543
    capacity, 540
    cylinders, 542
    DBR (DOS Boot Record), 541
    defragmentation, 541
    FATs (File Allocation Tables), 541
    formats, 539-540
    formatting, 541
    fragmentation, 541
hard disks
    allocation units, 1011-1013
    data area, 1013
    diagnostic read-and-write cylinder, 1013
    directories, 1008-1010
    FATs (File Allocation Tables), 1010-1011
    master partition boot sectors, 1004-1006
    volume boot sectors, 1007-1008
IBM PC DOS, 1017-1023
interfaces, 997-1003
I/O system, 979-987
MBR (master boot record), 1379-1380
Partition Table System Indicator Byte Values, 1380-1390
patches, 1017
shell, 979, 981-987
startup, 991-995
upgrades, 892-895, 1013-1016
versions, 987-990
DOS BACKUP command, 933
DOS Boot Record (DBR) (floppy disks), 541

DOSKEY command, 983
DOSSHELL command, 983
dot pitch (monitors), 380, 383
double-density encoding, *see* MFM encoding
double-density floppy controllers, 19
double-density floppy disks, 554
  formatting high-density format, 579-580
  magnetic sensitivity, 537
double-sided disks, 553-554
double-stacked expansion cards, 99
Doublespace disk compression software, 763-764
downgrading DOS, 1016
DPMS (Display Power-Management Signaling) spec, 380
DRAM (dynamic random-access memory), 837
Drive Probe diagnostic software, 583, 585, 968-969
drive sealing (CD-ROM drives), 787
drive select jumpers (floppy disk drives), 525-526, 569-573
drive spin failure (hard disk drives), 767-770
drivers
  CD-ROM drives
    CD-ROM device drivers, 801
    SCSI adapter drivers, 801
  hard disk drives, 708-709
  mouse, 364, 368
    installation, 369-370
    memory requirements, 369
  sound drivers (sound cards), 497
  tape backup drives, 937-938
  video cards, 398

XMS (extended memory specification) drivers, 258
drives
  floppy disk drives, 515
    3 1/2-inch drives, 534, 546-550
    5 1/4-inch drives, 534-535, 544-546, 550-551, 557-558
    aligning, 585
    circuit boards, 522
    cleaning, 582-583, 908
    configuration, 568-573, 576-581
    connectors, 523-524
    development, 515-516
    diagnostic software, 968-969
    disassembling, 905
    diskette change line jumpers, 528-529
    DOS interfaces, 998
    drive select jumper, 525-526
    realigning, 581
  removable storage drives, 826
    magnetic media drives, 826-829
    magneto-optical drives, 826, 829-831
    WORM (write-once read-many) drives, 831
  tape backup drives, 808, 934-939
    8mm tape backup drives, 817-819
    buying, 819-821, 939
    capacities, 815-816, 820
    cassettes, 810-812
    compatibility, 816-817
    cost, 821
    DAT (digital audio tape) tape backup drives, 817-818
    data transfer rates, 814, 821
    drivers, 937-938
    external tape backup drives, 938-939

    formatting, 814
    IBM PS/2, 1323
    installation, 821-823
    interfaces, 936-937
    internal tape backup drives, 938-939
    portables, 815
    QIC-40 tape backup drives, 812-814
    QIC-80 tape backup drives, 812-815
    software, 824-826, 937-938
    standards, 809-812, 817-820
dSALVAGE utility, 971
DSPs (digital signal processors) (sound cards), 497
DTV (desktop video) cards, 408
dust, 923-924
  chemical reactions, 899
  cleaning, 899
  floppy disk drives, 900
  hard disk drives, 900
  keyboards, 359, 924
  mouse, 367
  overheating, 899
dusters
  chemical-freeze sprays, 903
  compressed gas, 903
DVB (DOS Volume Boot Sector), 1381-1390
DVOMs (Digital Volt-Ohm Meters), 313
DX2 CPUs, 185-189, 885
DX4 CPUs, 198, 886

E

Early Token Release, *see* ETR
EBCDIC characters, 1343-1347
EBR (Extended Boot Record) backups, 911
ECHO command, 982
ED (extra-high density) floppy controllers, 19
EDIT command, 983

EDLIN command, 983
EEPROM chips (Flash BIOS), 866
EGA (enhanced graphics adapter) card, 388-411
    memory, 149
    see also video cards
EGA (enhanced graphics adapter) monitors, 388-411
    see also monitors
EISA (Extended Industry Standard Architecture) buses, 17, 114
    16-bit EISA buses, 145, 147-148
    32-bit EISA buses, 114-118
    automated setup, 118-120
    bus mastering, 118
    see also I/O buses
electricity
    ESD (electrostatic discharge), 848, 907
    grounding straps, 848
    static electricity, 919-920
    see also power supply
electro-static discharge, *see* ESD
electromagnetic fields (monitors)
    health concerns, 381
    standards
        MPR I, 381
        MPR II, 381
        SWEDAC, 381
        TCO, 381
electromagnetic radiation (floppy disks), 567-568
ELF (extremely low-frequency) elecromagnetic emissions (monitors), 381
EMM386 command, 983
EMM386.EXE program, 266
encoding (hard disk drives), 594-595, 655-656
    ESDI (enhanced small device interface), 663
    IDE (Integrated Drive Electronics) interface, 666

schemes
    ARLL (advanced run length limited) encoding, 598
    FM (frequency modulation) encoding, 595-596, 599
    MFM (modified frequency modulation) encoding, 596, 600
    RLL (run length limited) encoding, 597-598, 600-601
Endec (encoder/decoder)
    ESDI (enhanced small device interface), 663
    IDE (Integrated Drive Electronics) interface, 666
    ST-506/412 interface, 655
energy conservation (IBM PS/x systems), 1113
Energy Star requirements (monitors), 310, 323, 380-381
    IBM PS/x systems, 1113
English fasteners, 34-35
enhanced graphics adapter card, *see* EGA card
enhanced graphics adapter monitors, *see* EGA monitors
Enhanced Parallel Port (EPP) parallel ports, 440
enhanced small device interfaces, *see* ESDI
environmental considerations
    humidifiers, 924
    placement of systems, 915
    pollutants, 923-924
    RFI (radio frequency interference), 921-922
    static electricity, 919-920
    temperature, 916
Environmental Protection Agency (EPA) Energy Star program, 310, 323, 380-381
EPROM chips, 853
EPROM programmers, 859

BIOS backups, 859-861
Epson printers (control codes), 1370-1372
erasers (cleaning), 908
Errata 21 problem (80386 processors), 225
error codes, 960-962, 1410
    controllers, 764-767
    disk software interfaces, 1356-1357
    hard disk drives, 764-767
    POST (Power-On Self Test)
        AMI BIOS, 1411-1471
        Award BIOS, 1416-1419
        BIOS, 1410-1411
        DOS error codes, 1460-1462
        Hewlett Packard POST, 1420-1425
        IBM POST, 1424-1453
        IBM SCSI, 1453-1460
        keyboards, 357
        Phoenix BIOS, 1419-1420
Error loading operating system error message, 993
error messages
    Abort, Retry, Ignore, 535
    C000 ROM Error, 991
    Cannot CHKDSK a network drive, 1033
    Disk Boot failure, 992, 994
    Diskette Boot Record Error, 992
    Error loading operating system, 993
    Function not supported on this computer, 339
    I/O Card Parity Error at xxxxx, 278
    I/O card parity interrupt at xxxx:xxxx, 277
    Keyboard stuck key failure, 356
    Memory Parity Error at xxxxx, 278
    Memory parity interrupt at xxxx:xxxx, 277
    Missing operating system, 993

No boot device available—strike F1 to retry boot, F2 for setup utility, 993
No room for system on destination disk, 1014
Non-System disk or disk error, 992, 994
OFF BOARD PARITY ERROR ADDR (HEX) = (xxxxx), 278
ON BOARD PARITY ERROR ADDR (HEX) = (xxxxx), 278
Sector not found reading drive C, 737
XXXX ROM Error error message, 992
error-correction standards (modems), 421, 432
ESD (electro-static discharge) , 907
protection, 27, 36-37, 848
ESDI (enhanced small device interface) (hard disk drives), 663
configuration, 665
connectors
control connectors, 664-665
data connectors, 665
controllers, 663-664
encoding, 663
installation, 664-665
see also hard disk drives, interfaces
Ethernet
adapters, 450-451
frames, 461-462
LANs, 460-463
ETR (Early Token Release), 464
events (sound files), 488
Exabyte Corporation, 819, 1485
EXE files, 984
EXE2BIN command, 983
EXIT command, 982
EXPAND command, 982
expanded memory, 258-289

paging, 838
upgrades, 838-839
see also memory
expansion buses, *see* I/O **buses**
expansion slots (I/O buses), 98-99
8-bit ISA buses, 102
16-bit ISA buses, 103
double-stacked expansion cards, 99
EISA buses, 114
MCA buses, 107-114
VESA local buses, 124
Extended Boot Record (EBR), 911
extended graphics array card, *see* XGA card
extended graphics array monitors, *see* XGA **monitors**
extended graphics array-2 card, *see* XGA-2 card
Extended Industry Standard Architecture buses, *see* EISA buses
extended memory, 228, 255-289
high memory area (HMA), 257-258
map, 229
upgrades, 838
XMS (extended memory specification), 256-258
extended memory specification (XMS), 256-257
drivers, 258
map, 229
external (Level 2) secondary cache, 179
external CD-ROM drives, 788, 794-795
external tape backup drives, 938-939
extra-high density floppy controllers, 19
extra-high density floppy disks, 554-558
eye strain (monitors), 381

F

faceplates
floppy disk drives, 523
hard disk drives, 634-635
LED (light-emitting diode), 635
fans, 311-312
depressurized cooling systems, 899
IBM PS/2 systems, 61
pressurized cooling systems, 899
see also filters
Fast Mode parallel port, 440
FastBack Backup software, 826
FASTOPEN command, 983
FATs (File Allocation Tables)
backups, 911
DOS, 995-997
floppy disks, 541
hard disks, 1010-1011
hard disk partitioning, 605-606
FAXModem standards, 435-436
FC command, 983
FCC (Federal Communications Commission) RFI (radio frequency interference) certification, 922-923
FDDI (Fiber Distributed Data Interface), 460, 470-472
FDISK utility, 754-755, 983, 1013
ferrite heads (hard disk drives), 612
fiber optic cables, 446, 475-476
FIFO (first in, first out) (UART chips), 418
file allocation tables, *see* FATs
file servers
cleaning, 452
CPUs, 453

hard disk, 453
keyboards, 455
LANs, 444-446, 452
monitors, 455
mouse, 455
power supply, 452, 455
RAM, 453
files, 995
.BAT files, 984
.COM files, 984
.EXE files, 984
directories, 985
hard disk drives,
defragmenting, 909-910
IBMDOS.COM file, 980
filters (hard disk drives),
627-628, 899
see also fans
FIND command, 983
first-generation Pentium
processors, 207-208
fixed disk drives, 587
flicker (monitors), 376,
382, 387
floppy disk controller
(floppy disk drives),
532-534
floppy disk drives, 515
3 1/2-inch floppy disk
drives, 534
1.44 M 3 1/2-inch
drives, 547-550,
559-560
2.88M 3 1/2-inch
drives, 547-548,
559-561
720K 3 1/2-inch
drives, 546-547
5 1/4 inch floppy disk
drives, 534
1.2M 5 1/4-inch
drives, 544-546,
550-551, 557-558,
580
360K 5 1/4-inch low-
density drives,
550-551
aligning, 585
circuit boards, 522
cleaning, 582-583, 908
configuration, 568, 576
daisy-chain, 569

disk change, 577-578
drive select jumpers,
569-571, 573
media-sensor jumpers,
573, 579
terminating resistors,
571-573
troubleshooting,
577-581
connectors
drive controller
connectors, 523-524
logic connectors,
523-524
development, 515-516
diagnostic software,
968-969
disassembling, 905
diskette change line
jumpers, 528-529
DOS interfaces, 998
drive select jumper,
525-526
dust, 900
exchanging disks from
other drives, 535-536
faceplates, 523
floppy disk controller,
532-534
formatting disks,
537-539, 543-544
head actuator, 520-521
IBM PS/2, 1320-1322
installation, 573
adapter plates, 574
brackets, 574
cables, 575
rails, 575
troubleshooting,
577-581
media sensor jumpers,
530-531
off-center disk-clamping,
580-581
read/write heads, 517-520
repairing, 581-582
RPMs (rotations per
minute), 534
speed adjustments,
583-585
spindle motors, 521
stepper motors, 520-521

terminating resistors,
526-528
tracks, 535
tunnel erasure, 519
upgrades, 867-872
floppy disks, 515, 553
3 1/2-inch floppy disks,
551-552
cylinders, 537
media-access hole, 552
media-sensor hole, 553
metal hub, 552
shutter, 552
tracks, 537
write-protect/-enable
hole, 552
5 1/4-inch floppy disks,
551
cylinders, 537
hub hole, 551
index hole, 551
media-access hole, 552
notches, 552
allocation units, 542-543
backups, 933-934
capacity, calculating, 540
clusters, *see* allocation
units
coercivity, 555
cylinders, 542
defragmentation, 541
density, 19, 554
double-density, 537,
554
extra-high density,
554-555
high-density, 537, 554
linear density, 554
longitudinal density,
554
quad-density, 554
DOS, 539-541
allocation units,
542-543
capacity, 540
cylinders, 542
DBR (DOS Boot
Record), 541
defragmentation, 541
FATs (File Allocation
Tables), 541
formats, 539-540

formatting, 541
 fragmentation, 541
double-sided disks,
 553-554
electromagnetic
 radiation, 567-568
exchanging between
 drives, 535-536
formatting, 538-539,
 543-544, 555-557
 double-density disks at
  high-density,
  579-580
 troubleshooting, 151
fragmentation, 541
handling precautions,
 565-568
hard sectored, 557
magnetic fields, 537-539,
 566
metal detectors, 566
sectors, 536, 539
single-sided disks,
 553-554
soft sectored, 557
thickness, 555
tracks, 536, 539
X-ray machines, 566, 568
FM (frequency
 modulation) encoding,
 595-596, 599
foam tape, 904
FOR command, 982
foreign language
 keyboards, 331, 340
form factors
 motherboards, 84
  Baby-AT, 92
  full-size AT, 92
  LPX, 92-94
  Mini-LPX, 92-94
 power supply, 293-295,
  322
FORMAT command,
 561-565, 983
 /Q parameter
  (Quickformat), 563,
  565-566
 /U parameter
  (Unconditional), 563,
  565-566

formatting
 floppy disks, 538-539,
  543-544, 555-557
  1.44M floppy disks in
   2.88M drives, 561
  360K floppy disks in
   1.2M drives, 558
  720K floppy disks in
   1.44M drives,
   559-560
  720K floppy disks in
   2.88M drives,
   559-560
  DOS, 541
  double-density disks at
   high-density,
   579-580
  troubleshooting, 151
 hard disks, 604
  HLF (high-level
   formatting), 606,
   759-761
  LLF (low-level
   formatting), 604,
   736-753
 tape backup drives, 814
fragmentation (disks), 541
frames, 455-457
 Ethernet, 461-462
 Token Ring, 462-470
freon, 33
frequency modulation
 (FM) encoding, 595-596,
 599
frequency response (sound
 cards), 490
Fugitsu hard disk drives,
 1381
full-motion video, 408-410
 compression, 409
 decompression, 409
function, 1030
Function not supported on
 this computer error
 message, 339
functions, 1030
fuses, 321, 357
Future Pentium Overdrive
 Processors, 197

G

Game Blaster sound card,
 483
game control adapters,
 372-374
games
 joysticks, 502
 sound cards, 484-485,
  490
garbage (screen/printouts),
 troubleshooting, 151
gas-plasma monitors, 378
ghosts (monitors), 376
GOTO command, 982
GRAFTABL command, 983
graphical user interfaces,
 see GUIs
GRAPHICS command, 983
green PCs, 310, 323, 380
grounding straps, 630-632,
 848
grounding tabs (hard disk
 drives), 634
GTO (Guide To
 Operations) manuals,
 20-21, 953, 1462-1463
GUIs (graphical user
 interfaces)
 80486 processors, 175
 I/O buses, 121
 mouse, 363

H

hand tools, 25-28
handshaking modems,
 436-438
hard disk drives, 587, 1312
 air filters, 627-628
 areal density, 588
 Atasi drives, 1380
 average seek time, 639
 backups, 807-808
  removable storage
   drives, 826-831
  tape backup drives,
   808
 benchmarks, 639
 Brand Technology
  drives, 1380

buying, 635-648
cache programs, 641
capacities, 650-652
cleaning, 908
configuration, 715,
    722-736
connectors
    grounding tabs, 634
    interface connectors,
        632
    power connectors, 633
Conner Peripherals
    drives, 1380-1381
controllers, 711-715
    caching controllers,
        641
    configuration, 716-721
    error codes, 764-767
costs, 650
Data-Tech Memories
    drives, 1381
data-transfer rates, 588,
    640
    cylinder skewing,
        646-648
    head skewing, 646-648
    interleaving, 641-645
defect mapping, 743-745
defragmenting files,
    909-910
diagnostic software, 969
disassembling, 905
    IBM AT cases, 48-49
    IBM PS/2 systems,
        54-55, 61, 64, 71,
        73-74
    IBM XT style cases,
        41-42
    Slimline cases, 41-42
    Tower cases, 48-49
documentation, 715
drive spin failure,
    767-770
dust, 900
EBR (Extended Boot
    Record) backups, 911
error codes, 764-767
faceplates, 634-635
FATs (File Allocation
    Tables) backups, 911
file servers, 453
fixed disk drives, 587

formatting
    HLF (high-level
        formatting), 759-761
    LLF (low-level
        formatting), 736-753
Fugitsu drives, 1381
ground straps, 630-632
handling precautions,
    589-590
HDAs (head disk
    assemblies), 589, 608
head actuators, 615
    stepper motor,
        615-626
    voice coil, 615-626,
        636
head crashes, 589
head parking, 636-638
head sliders, 615
heads, 589
    air bearings, 590-591
    read/write heads,
        610-612
Hewlett Packard drives,
    1381
Hitachi drives, 1381-1382
host adapters, 711-721
IBM AT, 1313-1314
IBM PS/2, 1313-1324
IBM XT, 1313-1314
Imprimis (CDC) drives,
    1382-1383
installation, 721-722
interfaces, 652-654
    capacities, 761-763
    ESDI (enhanced small
        device interface),
        663-665
    IDE (Integrated Drive
        Electronics) interface,
        652, 666-681
    IDE vs. SCSI, 731-736
    SCSI (small computer
        system interface),
        652, 681-709
    ST-506/412 interface,
        654-663
Kalok drives, 1383
Kyocera drives, 1383
Lapine drives, 1383
latency, 639
LED (light-emitting
    diode), 635

logic boards, 632
    failures, 770
    replacement parts, 632
magnetic data storage,
    591-594
    capacities, 588
    encoding, 594-599
    PRML (Partial-
        Response, Maximum
        Likelihood), 600
Maxtor drives, 1383-1384
MBR (Master Boot
    Record) backups, 911
Micropolis drives, 1384
Microscience drives,
    1384-1385
Miniscribe drives,
    1385-1386
Mitsubishi drives, 1386
MTBF (mean time
    between failures), 638
NEC drives, 1386-1387
Newbury hard disk
    drives, 1387
Pacific Magtron drives,
    1387
partitioning, 753-759
platters, 587-589,
    608-609
    oxide media, 609
    thin-film media,
        609-610
Plus Development drives,
    1387
power consumption, 307
power supply connectors,
    298
Priam drives, 1387
PTI drives, 1387-1388
Quantum drives, 1388
read/write heads, 610-612
    ferrite, 612
    magneto-resistive
        (MR), 614-615
    metal-in-gap (MIG),
        613
    thin film (TF), 613-614
reformatting, 913-915
repairing, 764-770
Rodime drives, 1388
root directory backups,
    911

RPMs (rotations per minute), 589
Samsung drives, 1388-1389
scanning
   defect scans, 740-741
   surface analysis scans, 742-743
Seagate drives, 590, 1390-1396
sectors, 601-608
seek times, 588
shock mounting, 649-650
Siemens drives, 1389
spindle motors, 629-630
Syquest drives, 1389
Tandon drives, 1389
temperature sensitivity, 628-629
Toshiba drives, 1389
transfer rates, *see* data-transfer rates
troubleshooting, 764-770
Tulin drives, 1389
upgrades, 872-873
Vertex drives, 1389
Western Digital drives, 1390
whining noises, 631-632
zoned recording, 605
hard disks, 608-609
DOS
   clusters, 1011-1013
   data area, 1013
   diagnostic read-and-write cylinder, 1013
   directories, 1008-1010
   FATs (File Allocation Tables), 1010-1011
   master partition boot sectors, 1004-1006
   volume boot sectors, 1007-1008
formatting, 604
   HLF (high-level formatting), 606
   LLF (low-level formatting), 604
oxide media, 609
partitioning, 604-605
   FATs (File Allocation Tables), 605-606

HPFS (High Performance File System), 606
MBR (Master Boot Record), 606
NTFS (Windows NT File System), 606
sectors, 601-608
thin-film media, 609-610
hard sectored floppy disks, 557
hardware
classes
   comparing, 18
   IBM AT, 16
   IBM PC/XT, 15
fasteners, 34-35
keyboard interfaces, 19
types, 34
hardware interrupts, *see* IRQs
hardware reset switches, 888-892
booting, 890
   cold boot, 889-892
   warm boot, 889-892
installation, 889
Power Good signal, 888
Hardware-Maintenance (HM) manuals, 22-23, 1463-1467
Hayes modems, 422-430
command set, 1361-1368
see also modems
HD (high-density) floppy controllers, 19
HDAs (head disk assemblies), 589, 608
HDtest software, 749
head actuators
floppy disk drives, 520-521
hard disk drives, 615
   stepper motor, 615-626
   voice coil, 615-626, 636
headphones, 501
heads (hard disk drives), 589, 610-615
air bearings, 590-591

crashes, 589
head sliders, 615
parking, 636-638
health concerns (monitors)
electromagnetic emissions, 381
eye strain, 381
heat sinks, 28, 225
HELP command, 983
hertz (Hz), 163
Hewlett Packard
hard disk drives, 1381
HP LaserJet printers (control codes), 1372-1376
POST (Power-On Self Test), 1420-1425
high memory area, *see* HMA
High Sierra Format (CD-ROMs), 781
high-density floppy controllers, 19
high-density floppy disks, 537, 554
high-level formatting, *see* HLF
HIMEM.SYS program, 266
Hitatchi America, Ltd.,
hard disk drives, 1381-1382
HLF (high-level formatting) (hard disks), 606, 759-761
HMA (high memory area), 257-289
host adapters (hard disk drives), 711-721
HPFS (High Performance File System) (hard disks), 606
HR (Hardware-Maintenance) manuals, 22-23, 1463-1467
HST (high speed technology) standards, 434
humidifiers, 924
Hz (hertz), 163

I

I/O buses, 95-96
  DOS (Disk Operating
    System), 979-987
  EISA buses, 114
    16-bit EISA buses, 145,
      147
    32-bit EISA buses,
      114-118
    automated setup,
      118-120
    bus mastering, 118
    DMA channels,
      147-148
  expansion slots, 98-99
    double-stacked
      expansion cards, 99
  GUIs (graphical user
    interfaces), 121
  ISA buses, 100
    8-bit ISA buses,
      100-104, 144, 147
    16-bit ISA buses, 100,
      103-104, 145, 147
    32-bit ISA buses, 105
  local buses, 120-121
  MCA buses, 106
    16-bit MCA buses,
      107-109, 145, 147
    32-bit MCA buses,
      109-111
    adapter cards, 106
    bus mastering, 106
    DMA channels, 148
    memory-matched
      extensions, 112
    video extensions,
      112-114
  mouse, 366-367
  PCI buses, 127-138
  PCMCIA buses, 138-142
    pinouts, 140-141
    standards, 139
  VESA local buses,
    122-126
  video cards, 404-411
I/O Card Parity Error at
xxxxx error messages,
278

I/O card parity interrupt at
xxxx:xxxx error message,
277
I/O port addresses, 142-143
i486 local-bus I/O bus, 121
IBM, 11-12
  cables (keyboards), 361
  documentation, 1462
    GTO (Guide To
      Operations), 20-21,
      953, 1462-1463
    Hardware-
      Maintenance Library,
      22-23, 1463-1467
    ordering, 1471
    Quick-Reference
      Manuals, 1462-1463
    Technical-Reference
      Library, 21-22,
      1467-1471
  keyboards, 361
    IBM options keyboards
      part numbers, 361
    part numbers, 361
  NSC BBS (National
    Support Center Bulletin
    Board System), 202
  POST (Power-On Self
    Test)
    error codes, 1424-1453
    SCSI error codes,
      1453-1460
  processors, 209
    Blue Lightning,
      210-211
    SLC, 210
  technical support, 411
IBM 3270 PC, 1075, 1078
  Control Program,
    1077-1078
  keyboard adapters, 1076
  Programmed Symbols
    (PS) adapters, 1076
  software, 1077
  system adapters, 1075
  video cards, 1076
  windows, 1077
IBM 5140 PC Convertible,
1059-1061
  automobile power
    adapters, 1064
  battery chargers, 1064

  CRT display adapters,
    1063
  memory cards, 1063
  modems, 1064
  monitors, 1064-1065
  part numbers, 1065
  printer cables, 1064
  printers, 1063
  serial/parallel adapters,
    1063
  technical specifications,
    1061-1063
IBM 5155 Portable PC,
1059
IBM Advanced Diagnostics
software, 948, 956-962
IBM Ambra, 1110
  see also IBM PS/x systems
IBM AT, 16, 19, 1085-1088
  adapter cards, 48, 105
  Baby AT, 294
  CMOS RAM addresses,
    20, 1350-1353
  comparing to PC/XT
    class, 18
  covers, 47
  hard disk drives, 48-49,
    1313-1314
  models, 1089-1092
    AT 3270, 1097
    AT-270, 1098
    Model 068, 1088-1092
    Model 099, 1088-1092
    Model 239, 1089-1092
    Model 319, 1091-1092
    Model 339, 1091-1092
    upgrade kits, 1090
    XT Model 286,
      1098-1100
  motherboards
    removing, 52
    replacing, 883
  part numbers, 1096-1097
  power supply, 293-294
  ratings, 302
  technical specifications,
    1092-1097
IBM AT 3270, 1097
IBM AT-270, 1098
IBM BBS, 956
IBM Cabling System,
476-477

IBM Commercial Desktop, 1110

IBM PC 5150 Model 166, 1053-1054

IBM PC 5150 Model 176, 1053-1054

IBM PC DOS patches, 1017-1023

IBM PC XT, 15, 18-20, 1065-1067
  models, 1068
    3270 PC, 1075-1078
    Model 087, 1068
    Model 088, 1068-1070
    Model 089, 1068-1070
    Model 267, 1068-1070
    Model 268, 1068-1070
    Model 277, 1068-1070
    Model 278, 1068-1070
    Model 5160068, 1068
    Model 5160078, 1068
    XT 370, 1079-1080
    XT Model 286, 1098-1100
  part numbers, 1074-1075
  technical specifications, 1070-1075

IBM PC/2, 1130

IBM PCs, 1050-1053
  models
    IBM PC 5150 Model 166, 1053-1054
    IBM PC 5150 Model 176, 1053-1054
  part numbers, 1054
  technical specifications, 1054-1059

IBM Portable PC, 1080-1082
  part numbers, 1085
  technical specifications, 1082-1085

IBM printers (control codes), 1368-1370

IBM PS/1, 1107-1109, 1283-1296
  models
    Model 286, 1289-1292
    Model 386SX, 1292-1295
  PS/1 Consultant line, 1109

PS/1 Essential line, 1109
PS/1 Expert line, 1109
see also IBM PS/x systems

IBM PS/2, 1107-1108, 1116-1117
  accessories, 1317
  adapter cards, 55, 62, 68
  battery-and-speaker assembly, 61, 69
  bezels, 71
  BIOS, 1308-1312
  bus adapter cards, 56
  cables, 1321-1324
  CD-ROM drives, 1323
  covers, 54, 60, 68
  disassembling, 52-55, 61, 64, 71-74
  fan assembly, 61
  floppy disk drives, 1320-1322
  hard disk drives, 1313-1317, 1322-1324
  MCA (Micro Channel Architecture) buses, 1114-1117
  memory adapters, 1318-1320
  models, 1117-1128
    Model 25, 1130-1139, 1146, 1313-1315
    Model 25 286, 1148-1154, 1314-1315
    Model 30, 1139-1146, 1314-1315
    Model 30 286, 1153-1160, 1314-1315
    Model 35, 1315
    Model 35 LS, 1160, 1166
    Model 35 SX, 1160-1164, 1166
    Model 40, 1315
    Model 40 SX, 1165-1170
    Model 50, 1176-1184, 1314
    Model 50 Z, 1179, 1315-1316
    Model 53, 1188-1192

    Model 55, 1315-1316
    Model 55 SX, 1192-1204
    Model 56, 1201-1204, 1317
    Model 56 486SLC3, 1204-1208
    Model 56 LS, 1208
    Model 56 SLC, 1208
    Model 56 SLC LS, 1208
    Model 56 SX, 1208
    Model 56LS 486SLC, 1208
    Model 57, 1317
    Model 57 486SLC, 1208
    Model 57 486SLC3, 1204-1207
    Model 57 486SLC3 Ultimedia, 1204-1208
    Model 57 SX, 1207-1216
    Model 60, 1216-1222, 1314, 1316
    Model 65, 1317
    Model 65 SX, 1223-1230
    Model 70 386, 1230-1234, 1236, 1315-1316
    Model 70 486, 1238-1242
    Model 76, 1254-1258
    Model 77, 1254-1258
    Model 77s Ultimedia, 1254-1258
    Model 80, 1314, 1316-1317
    Model 80 386, 1260-1268
    Model 90, 1317
    Model 90 XP 486, 1270-1276
    Model 95, 1317
    Model 95 XP 486, 1275-1298
    Model E, 1184-1188
    Model L40, 1315
    Model L40 SX, 1170-1172, 1176

Model P70 386,
1245-1249,
1315-1316
Model P75, 1317
Model P75 486,
1249-1254
P70 386, 1242-1249
monitors, 1324-1325
motherboards, 60, 66, 76,
1397-1398
network adapters,
1325-1326
power supply
ratings, 303
removing, 57, 65, 71
specifications, 304-305
SIMMs, 59, 67-68,
1319-1320
support structures, 64
tape backup drives, 1323
Ultimedia PS/2, 1108
upgrades (processors/
coprocessors),
1316-1318
video cards, 149, 237,
1324-1325
see also IBM PS/x systems
IBM PS/ValuePoint, 1107,
1109, 1298
models, 1299-1300
Model P60/D,
1300-1302
ValuePoint
Performance Series,
1303-1306
ValuePoint Si Series,
1306-1307
warranties, 1298
see also IBM PS/x systems
IBM PS/x systems,
1107-1116
buses, 1111
construction, 1110
documentation, 1114
energy conservation,
1113
monitors, 1112-1113
repairs, 1113
replacement parts, 1111
technical support, 1113
upgrades, 1113
video cards, 1112-1113

IBM system diagnostics,
953-956
IBM XT
adapter boards, 40
covers, 39-40
disassembling, 41-42
hard disk drives,
1313-1314
motherboards, 44-46
memory upgrades,
850-852
switch settings, 1350
power supply, 293
disconnecting, 44
ratings, 302
upgrades, 872
IBM XT 286, 1098-1100
models, 1100-1101
part numbers, 1104-1105
technical specifications,
1101-1105
IBM XT 370, 1079-1080
IBMBIO.COM file, 980
IBMDOS.COM file, 980
IBM's Advanced
Diagnostics program, 583
IC (integrated circuit), 10
ICE (In-Circuit Emulator)
boards, 878-879, 883
iCOMP (Intel Comparative
Microprocessor
Performance) index, 165
ID settings, see
configuration
IDE (Integrated Drive
Electronics) interface
(hard disk drives), 652,
666
ATA version, 668-669
ATA I/O cable, 671
ATA I/O connector,
670
ATA signals, 671
CAM ATA
specifications, 669
command set, 671-673
dual-drive
configurations, 669
intelligent IDE drives,
674-675
intelligent zoned
recording IDE drives,
675

non-intelligent
ATA-IDE drives,
673-674
capacities, 667
compatibility, 667
configuration, 675-676
jumper settings,
676-678
controllers, 666
cost, 667
development, 667-668
encoding, 666
formatting, 750-751
MCA version, 668, 680
connectors, 680-681
performance, 667
v. SCSI, 750-761
XT version, 668-680
IDEDIAG utility, 672
IDEINFO program, 672
IEEE (Institute of Electrical
and Electronic
Engineers), 459
IEEE 802.3 standard,
459-460, 462-463
IEEE 802.5 standard, 459,
465-470
IF command, 982
IML system partition BIOS,
866-867
Imprimis (CDC) hard disk
drives, 1382-1383
In-Circuit Emulator
boards, see ICE boards
Industry Standard
Architecture buses, see
ISA buses
InfoSpotter utility, 972
inport mouse, 367
input devices, 327
joystick adapters, 372-374
keyboards, 327
82-key PC and XT
keyboards, 337
83-key AT keyboards,
337
83-key PC and XT
keyboards, 327-328,
331, 340-342
84-key AT keyboards,
327-329, 331,
343-345

101-key enhanced
keyboards, 327,
329-333, 346-354
cables, 354-356
documentation, 362
key matrix, 336
key numbers, 339-340
key switches, 333-335
LED indicators, 330
processors, 336
scan codes, 339-340
tactility, 333-336
troubleshooting,
356-362
typematic functions,
337-339
pointing devices
mouse, 363-367
Trackpoint II, 362,
370-372
installation
cables (LANs), 448
CD-ROM drives, 788
adapter cards, 788-794
external drives,
794-795
internal drives,
795-797
testing, 803-804
floppy disk drives, 573
adapter plates, 574
brackets, 574
cables, 575
rails, 575
troubleshooting,
577-581
hard disk drives, 721-722
ESDI (enhanced small
device interface),
664-665
IDE (Integrated Drive
Electronics) interface,
669-671
ST-506/412 interface
(hard disk drives),
657
hardware reset switches,
889
math coprocessors,
874-875
memory chips, 261-264,
847, 849

broken or bent pins,
848
ESD (electrostatic
discharge), 848
mouse drivers, 369-370
Overdrive processors,
199-200
sound cards, 503-505
tape backup drives,
821-823
**Institute of Electrical and
Electronic Engineers,** *see*
IEEE
integrated circuit (IC), 10
Intel Corporation, 10, 1488
iCOMP index, 165
processors, 167
386DX, 173
386SL, 174
386SX, 173-174
80186, 168-169
80188, 168-169
80286, 169-171
80386, 171-173
80486, 175-190
8086, 167-168
8088, 167-168
82360SL, 174
clones, 174-175
memory addressing,
163
Overdrive, 190-203
Pentium, 203-209
intensity (sound), 490
**interface connectors (hard
disk drives), 632**
interfaces
CD-ROM drives, 779
ASPI (Advances SCSI)
interface, 779
non-standard SCSI
interface, 780
SCSI interfaces, 779
SCSI-2 interface, 779
disk software interfaces,
1355-1357
hard disk drives, 652-654
capacities, 761-763
ESDI (enhanced small
device interface),
663-665

IDE (Integrated Drive
Electronics) interface,
652, 666-681
IDE vs. SCSI, 710
SCSI (small computer
system interface),
681-709
ST-506/412 interface,
654-663
motherboards, 84
operating systems (DOS),
997-1003
tape backup drives,
936-937
interlaced monitors, 380
interleaved memory, 845
interleaving
CD-ROM XA drives, 784
hard disk drives, 641-645
**internal (Level 1) cache
controllers, 178-179**
**internal CD-ROM drives,
788, 795-797**
internal registers, 161-162
**internal tape backup
drives, 938-939**
**interpolation (CD-ROMs),
776**
interrupt request channels,
see **IRQs**
**interrupts (mouse),
367-368**
**IRQs (interrupt request
channels), 143-146**
assignments, 791
conflicts, 146
parallel ports, 440-441
serial ports, 419-439
**ISA (Industry Standard
Architecture) buses, 15,
100**
8-bit ISA buses, 100-104
DMA channels, 147
IRQs, 144
pinouts, 101-102
16-bit ISA buses, 100, 103
DMA channels, 147
IRQs, 145
pinouts, 103-104
32-bit ISA buses, 105
power consumption, 307

ISO (International
Standards Organization)
  ISO 9660 standard
    (CD-ROMs), 780-781
  OSI (Open System
    Interconnection) model,
    457-459

J

Jameco Computer
Products, 1489
  EPROM programmers,
    859
JDR Microdevices, 1489
  EPROM programmers,
    859
JOIN command, 983
Joint Photographic Experts
Group codec, *see* JPEG
codec
joystick adapters, 372-374
joysticks, 502, 510
JPEG (Joint Photographic
Experts Group) codec,
409
jumpers
  adapter cards, 790
  see also configurations

K

Kalok Corporation, 1489
  hard disk drives, 1383
key matrix (keyboards),
336
key numbers (keyboards),
339-340
  83-key PC and XT
    keyboards, 340-342
  84-key AT keyboards,
    343-345
  101-key enhanced
    keyboards, 346-354
key switches (keyboards),
333
  capacitive key switches,
    335
  cleaning, 359
  foam element key
    switches, 333-334

cleaning, 334
  intermittent key
    strikes, 334
  tactility, 334
  membrane key switches,
    335
  pure mechanical key
    switches, 333
  rubber dome key
    switches, 333-335
  sticky keys, 340
KEYB command, 983
KEYBFR command, 983
KEYBGR command, 983
KEYBIT command, 983
keyboard adapters (IBM
3270 PC), 1076
keyboard interfaces, 19
Keyboard stuck key failure
error messages, 356
keyboard-controller chips,
855
keyboards, 327
  82-key PC and XT
    keyboards, 337
  83-key AT keyboards, 337
  83-key PC and XT
    keyboards, 327-328
    compatibility, 331
    key numbers, 340-342
    scan codes, 340-342
  84-key AT keyboards,
    327-329
    compatibility, 331
    key numbers, 343-345
    scan codes, 343-345
  101-key enhanced
    keyboards, 327, 329-330
    compatibility, 331-333
    cursor and screen
      controls, 331
    foreign language
      versions, 331
    function keys, 331
    key numbers, 346-354
    numeric keypad, 330
    removable keycaps,
      331
    scan codes, 346-354
    typing area, 330
  cables, 354
    defective cables, 356

DIN (Deutsche
  Industrie Norm)
  connectors, 354-355
  replacing, 359-361
  SDL (Shielded Data
    Link) connectors,
    354-355
  testing, 356
cleaning, 334, 359, 908
  dust, 359, 924
  liquid spills, 360
disassembling, 358-359
documentation, 362
failed keys, 354
file servers, 455
IBM/Lexmark keyboards,
  361
intermittent key strikes,
  334
key matrix, 336
key numbers, 339-340
key switches, 333
  capacitive key
    switches, 335
  foam element key
    switches, 333-334
  membrane key
    switches, 335
  pure mechanical key
    switches, 333
  rubber dome key
    switches, 333-335
  sticky keys, 340
LED indicators, 330
Lite-On keyboards, 362
Maxi-Switch, 362
part numbers, 361
POST (Power-On Self
  Test), 357
processors, 336
repairing, 359
replacement parts, 360
scan codes, 339-340
sticky keys, 354
tactility, 333-336
troubleshooting, 334
typematic functions, 337
  delay parameters, 339
  rate repeat parameters,
    338-339
  setting speed, 339

KEYBSP command, 983
KEYBUK command, 983
keycaps (removable keycaps), 331
keylock connectors (motherboards), 1357
Kodak PhotoCD, *see* **PhotoCD**
Kyocera hard disk drives, 1383

L

LABEL command, 983
LANs (local area networks), 444-445
  cables, 446-448, 472
    coaxial cable, 474-475
    connecting, 477-478
    fiber optic cables, 475-476
    IBM Cabling System, 476-477
    installation, 448
    twisted pair cable, 472-473
  data-transfer speeds, 450
  file servers, 444-446
    buying, 452
    cleaning, 452
    CPUs, 453
    hard disk, 453
    power supply, 452
    RAM, 453
  frames, 455-457
    Ethernet, 461-462
    FDDI, 471-472
    IEEE 802.3, 462-463
    Token Ring, 464-465
  network adapter cards, 448
    ARCnet adapters, 450
    Ethernet adapters, 450-451
    evaluating, 454, 479-481
    LANtastic adapters, 448, 450
    Token Ring adapters, 449, 451-452
  protocols, 456-457
  standards
    Ethernet, 460-463
    FDDI (Fiber Distributed Data Interface), 460, 470-472
    IEEE 802.3, 459-460
    IEEE 802.5, 459
    OSI (Open System Interconnection) model, 457-459
    Token Ring, 463-470
  topologies, 446
    bus topology, 446
    star topology, 447
    star-wired tree topology, 447
  wireless LANs, 448
  workstations, 444-445
LANtastic adapters, 448, 450
Lapine hard disk drives, 1383
laptops
  IBM 5140 PC Convertible, 1059-1061
    automobile power adapters, 1064
    battery chargers, 1064
    CRT display adapters, 1063
    memory cards, 1063
    modems, 1064
    monitors, 1064-1065
    part numbers, 1065
    printer cables, 1064
    printers, 1063
    serial/parallel adapters, 1063
    technical specifications, 1061-1063
  PCMCIA buses, 138-142
latency (hard disk drives), 639
LCD (liquid-crystal diode) monitors, 377
  active-matrix LCDs, 377-378
  color, 377-378
  monochrome, 377
  passive-matrix LCDs, 377
LED (light-emitting diode), 635
  connectors, 1357
  keyboards, 330
Lexmark, 1490
  keyboards, 360-361
LIB command, 983
LIF (low-insertion-force) sockets, 190
light-emitting diode, *see* **LED**
LIM (Lotus Intel Microsoft), 174
line conditioners, 927-928
linear addresses, 231-289
linear density (floppy disks), 554
LINK command, 983
Lite-On, Inc., 1490
  keyboards, 362
LLF (low-level formatting) (hard disks), 604, 736, 739, 745-747
  defect mapping, 739-742
  drive operating position, 738-739
  software, 747-753
  surface analysis scans, 742-743
  temperature sensitivity, 737-738
load resistors, 300-302, 316-318
LOADHI/LH command, 982
local area networks, *see* **LANs**
local buses, 17, 120-121
lock-ups, troubleshooting, 151
logic boards
  floppy disk drives, 522
  hard disk drives, 632
    failures, 770
    replacement parts, 632
logic probes, 31
Logitech
  AudioMan sound card, 490-492
  mouse, 363
longitudinal density (floppy disks), 554

loopback connectors, 30
loopback tests
    parallel ports, 444
    serial ports, 443
low-insertion-force (LIF)
    sockets, 190
low-level formatting, *see*
    LLF
lubricants, 902
    silicone lubricants, 905
    Stabilant 22 contact
        cleaner/lubricant, 902

M

magazines, 1333-1334
    Byte, 1479
    Computer Design, 1481
    Computer Graphics World,
        1481
    Computer Hotline, 1481
    Computer Reseller News,
        1481
    Computer Retail Week,
        1481
    Computer Shopper, 1481
    *Computer Technology
        Review*, 1481
    Data Based Advisor, 1483
    Data Communications,
        1483
    Datamation, 1483
    *Dr. Dobb's Journal of
        Software Tools*, 1484
    Electronic Buyers' News,
        1484
    Electronic Products, 1484
    *IBM Personal Systems
        Technical Solutions*, 1487
    InfoWorld, 1488
    Lan, 1489
    LAN Times, 1489
    MacWEEK, 1490
    Macworld, 1490
    Motor, 1493
    PC, 1495
    PC Week, 1495
    PC World, 1495
    Processor, 1496
    Service News, 1498
    *Test and Measurement
        World*, 1501

magnetic data storage
    (hard disk drives)
    capacities, 588
    encoding, 594-599
    PRML (Partial-Response,
        Maximum Likelihood),
        600
Magnetic Developer, 536
magnetic fields (floppy
    disks), 537-539, 566
magnetic media drives
    Bernoulli drives, 827-828
    floptical drives, 828-829
    SyDOS drives, 827-828
    SyQuest drives, 827-828
magneto-optical drives,
    826, 829-831
magneto-resistive (MR)
    heads (hard disk drives),
    614-615
Magni Systems (VGA
    Producer Pro), 407
main boards, *see*
    motherboards
maintenance, 897
    active preventive
        maintenance, 898-909
    passive preventive
        maintenance, 898,
        915-926
Maintenance-Analysis
    Procedures (MAPs), 22
manuals, 1328-1330
    see also documentation
maps (memory)
    Color Graphics Adapter
        (CGA), 234
    conventional (base)
        memory, 228
    Enhanced Graphics
        Adapter (EGA), 234
    extended memory, 229
    extended memory
        specification (XMS)
        memory, 229
    Monochrome Display
        Adapter (MDA), 233
    Super VGA (SVGA), 235
    upper memory area
        (UMA), 228-229
    Video Graphics Array
        (VGA), 235

MAPs (Maintenance-
    Analysis Procedures), 22
markings (memory chips),
    272, 841
maskable interrupts, 144
master boot record, *see*
    MBR
math coprocessors,
    212-214, 873-874
    287, 875-876
    387, 876
    486DX, 181
    487s, 876
    487SX, 184-185
    80287, 216-218
    80387, 218-219
    80486, 175
    80487, 220-221
    8087, 214-216, 875
    chip creep, 906
    clock speed, 217
    installation, 874-875
    Pentium processors, 207
    removing, 225
    seating, 906
    Weitek, 219-220
Maxi Switch, Inc., 1490
    keyboards, 362
Maxtor Corporation,
    1490-1491
    hard disk drives,
        1383-1384
MBR (Master Boot Record)
    backups, 911
    DOS, 1004-1006
    hard disk partitioning,
        606
MCA (Micro Channel
    Architecture) buses, 16,
    106
    16-bit MCA buses, 107
        DMA channels, 147
        IRQs, 145
        pinouts, 107-109
    32-bit MCA buses, 109
        pinouts, 109-111
    adapter cards, 106
    bus mastering, 106
    DMA channels, 148
    IBM PS/2, 62, 1114-1117
    power supply, 291

memory-matched extensions, 112
video extensions, 112-114
MCGA (multicolor graphics array) cards, 392-411
see also video cards
MCGA (multicolor graphics array) monitors, 391-397
see also monitors
MD/MKDIR command, 982
MDA (monochrome display adapter) cards, 384-411
memory, 149
see also video cards
MDA (monochrome display adapter) monitors, 384-411
see also monitors
mean time between failures, *see* **MTBF**
Media Player, 804
media sensor jumpers (floppy disk drive configuration), 530-531, 573, 579
Mediator LC (VideoLogic), 407
megahertz (MHz), 163
MEM command, 983
MEMMAKER utility, 266-268
memory, 227
adapter cards
configuration, 150-151, 264
BIOS memory areas, 150
addresses
linear addresses, 231-289
segment addresses, 230
buffers (CD-ROM drives), 779
configuration
EMM386.EXE program, 266

HIMEM.SYS program, 266
conventional (base) memory, 228-229
map, 228
upgrades, 837
conventional memory barrier, 227
CPUs, 270-271
expanded memory, 258-260
paging, 838
upgrades, 838-839
extended memory, 228, 255-257
high memory area (HMA), 257-258
map, 229
upgrades, 838
XMS (extended memory specification), 256-257
file servers, 453
installed memory v. usable memory, 261-264
motherboard architecture, 270-271
motherboards
cache memory, 83
SIMM memory, 84
ROM shadowing, 260-261
SRAM (static RAM), 845-846
testing, 288
diagnostic tests, 289
parity checking, 288
POST (Power-On Self Test), 288, 850
upgrades, 837-839
DRAM (dynamic random-access memory), 837
motherboard memory, 839-852
upper memory area (UMA), 230
adapter ROM, 230
free space, 230
map, 228-229

motherboard BIOS, 230
special purpose RAM, 230
video RAM, 230, 232-289
upper memory block (UMB)
mouse drivers, 369
video cards, 148, 402-403
video RAM, 404-411
memory adapters (IBM PS/2), 1318-1320
memory banks, 273-275, 840-841
memory buses, 95, 97-98
memory caching, 846-847
cache hit, 846
cache miss, 846
memory cards (IBM 5140 PC Convertible), 1063
memory chips, 271
architectures, 845
interleaved memory, 845
memory caching, 846-847
paged memory, 845
capacities, 841
chip creep, 283, 905
configuration, 849
DIPs (Dual In-line Pin) chips, 271, 840
installation, 847, 849
broken or bent pins, 848
ESD (electrostatic discharge), 848
jumper settings, 849-850
manufacturer's markings, 272, 841
memory banks, 273-275, 840-841
parity checking, 275-279
part numbers, 273
removing, 849
seating, 906
SIMMs (Single In-Line Memory Modules), 279-283, 840
IBM PS/2, 1319-1320
pinouts, 284-287

presence detect pins, 844
SIPPs (Single In-line Pin Packages), 840
speed, 287-288, 841-844
switch settings, 849-850
memory management units (MMUs), 171
memory managers
386MAX memory manager, 269-270
MEMMAKER, 266-268
QEMM, 266, 269
RAMBoost, 268
Memory Parity Error at xxxxx error message, 278
Memory parity interrupt at xxxx:xxxx error message, 277
memory-matched extensions (MCA buses), 112
messages, see error codes; error messages
metal detectors (floppy disks), 566
metal-in-gap (MIG) heads (hard disk drives), 613
meter (test equipment), 30-31
metric fasteners, 34-35
metric system prefixes, 1348
mezzanine buses, see PCI buses
MFM (modified frequency modulation) encoding, 596, 600
MHz (megahertz), 163
Micro 2000, Inc., 1491
POST cards, 952
Micro Channel Architecture buses, see MCA buses
Micro Firmware, Inc. BIOS chips, 857
Micro-Scope diagnostic software, 964-965
Microid Research, Inc., 1492
BIOS chips, 857
BIOS software, 855-856

microphones, 501-502
Micropolis Corporation, 1493
hard disk drives, 1384
microprocessors, see CPUs; processors
Microscience International Corporation, 1493
hard disk drives, 1384-1385
Microsoft Corporation, 1493
Anti-Virus program, 913
Backup software, 824
CD Extensions for DOS, 801-802
Microsoft Diagnostics (MSD), 368, 442, 971
Microsoft Video for Windows, 409
mouse, 363
MicroSystems Development (MSD), 1493
POST cards, 951-952
MIDI (Musical Instrument Digital Interface), 486
MPCs (multimedia PCs), 494
sound cards, 486, 494, 497
connectors, 502
synthesizers, 503
Wave Blaster, 503
MIG (metal-in-gap) heads (hard disk drives), 613
Mini Micro, 1493
mini-DIN connectors
mouse, 356
signals, 355
Miniscribe hard disk drives, 1385-1386
MIRROR command, 912, 983
Missing operating system error message, 993
MITS, 10
Mitsubishi Electronics America, Inc., 1493
hard disk drives, 1386
MMUs (Memory Management Units), 171

MNP (Microcom Networking Protocols), 434-435
MODE command, 983
Modem Doctor utility, 443
modems
baud rate, 431
bit rate, 431
buying, 436
command sets, 422-439
handshaking, 436-438
Hayes modem command set, 1361-1368
IBM 5140 PC Convertible, 1064
phone line surge suppressors, 927
standards, 420
data-compression standards, 421, 433
error-correction standards, 421, 432
modulation standards, 421, 431-432
proprietary standards, 433-436
U.S. Robotics modem command set, 1361-1368
modified frequency modulation (MFM) encoding, 596, 600
modulation standards (modems), 421, 431
Bell 103, 431
Bell 212A, 431
V.21, 431
V.22, 431
V.22bis, 431
V.23, 432
V.29, 432
V.32, 432
V.32bis, 432
V.32fast, 432
monitors, 375
backlighting, 378
buying, 382-384
CGA (color graphics adapter) monitors, 386
color monitors, 378-379
controls, 383

CRTs (cathode ray tubes), 375
curved monitors, 376
edgelighting, 378
EGA (enhanced graphics adapter) monitors, 388-411
electromagnetic emissions
  MPR I standard, 381
  MPR II standard, 381
  SWEDAC, 381
  TCO standard, 381
electromagnetic fields, 381
energy
  DPMS (Display Power-Management Signaling), 380
  Energy Star program, 380-381
file servers, 455
flat screens, 376
flicker, 376, 382, 387
gas-plasma screens, 378
ghosts, 376
health concerns, 381
IBM 5140 PC Convertible
  convertible color display, 1065
  convertible monochrome display, 1064
IBM PS/2, 1324-1325
IBM PS/x systems, 1112-1113
ID settings, 1360
landscape screens, 379
LCD (liquid-crystal diode) monitors, 377-378
MCGA (multicolor graphics array) monitors, 391-397
MDA (monochrome display adapter) monitors, 384-411
monochrome monitors, 378
multiple-frequency monitors, 376
phosphor burn-in, 918

portrait screens, 379
Professional Graphics monitors, 391
raster, 376
refresh rates, 376
repairing, 410-411
replacement parts, 410
resolution, 379-380, 383
  dot pitch, 380, 383
  interlaced mode, 380
  noninterlaced mode, 380
screen glare, 381
screen savers, 919
sizes, 379
snow, 387
SVGA (super-VGA) monitors, 397-398
upgrades, 887-888
VGA (video graphics array) monitors, 382, 391-397
video-output adapters, 407-411
WYSIWYG (what you see is what you get), 379
XGA (extended graphics array) monitors, 399-402
monochrome display adapter cards, *see* MDA cards
monochrome display adapter monitors, *see* MDA monitors
monochrome monitors, 378
monophonic sound cards, 495-496
MORE command, 983
motherboards
  advantages, 82
  architectures, 270-271
  BIOS (basic input/output system), 84
    error codes, 1411-1420
    memory requirements, 230
    ROM compatibility, 85-91
  bus type, 84

chipsets, 85
connectors
  battery connectors, 1357
  keylock connectors, 1357
  LED connectors, 1357
  speaker connectors, 1357
controllers, 98
disadvantages, 82
documentation, 84-85
form factors, 84
  Baby-AT, 92
  full-size AT, 92
  LPX, 92-94
  Mini-LPX, 92-94
fuses, 357
hard disk drive parameters
  AMI, 1402-1403
  Award, 1403-1425, 1404-1405
  Compaq Deskpro 286 Revision F, 1400-1401
  Compaq Deskpro 286e Revision B, 1401-1402
  Compaq Deskpro 386, 1399
  IBM PS/2, 1397-1398
  Phoenix 286, 1406-1425
  Phoenix 386, 1408-1409
IBM AT
  disassembling, 52
  replacing, 883
IBM PS/2, 60, 66, 76
IBM XT, 44-46
interfaces, 84
memory
  cache memory, 83
  SIMM memory, 84
ports, 98
  mouse port, 365-366
power consumption, 307
power management, 84
Power_Good signal, 292
processor sockets, 83

processors, 83, 91
repairs, 82
replacement parts, 82
riser-card slots, 99
Slimline cases, 44-46
speed, 83
switch settings, 1350
Tower cases, 52
upgrades, 82, 839
    adapter cards, 847
    IBM XT, 850-852
    memory chips,
        840-850
see also backplane
    systems
mothercards, 81
Motion Pictures Expert
    Group, *see* MPEG
mouse, 363, 365
    buttons, 363
    cables, 363-364
        connectors, 356, 363
        mini-DIN connectors,
            356
    cleaning, 367, 909
    connecting
        I/O buses, 366-367
        motherboard mouse
            ports, 365-366
        serial interfaces,
            365-366
    disassembling, 367
    drivers, 364, 368
        installation, 369-370
        memory requirements,
            369
    file servers, 455
    GUIs (graphical user
        interfaces), 363
    interrupt conflicts,
        367-368
    jerky mouse, 367
    Logitech mouse, 363
    Microsoft mouse, 363
    optical sensors, 364
    replacing, 368
    roller balls, 363
    rollers, 364
    rubber balls, 363
    software, 370

troubleshooting, 151
    unresponsive mouse, 368
MPCs (multimedia PCs)
    CD-ROM drives, 493,
        786-787
    MIDI, 494
    sound cards, 485-486
    video, 409-410
MPEG (Motion Pictures
    Expert Group)
    codecs, 409
    sound cards, 494
MPR I standard, 381
MPR II standard, 381
MR (magneto-resistive)
    heads (hard disk drives),
    614-615
MS Video 1, 409
MS-DOS
    bugs, 1021-1023
    patches, 1021-1023
MSBACKUP utility, 933
MSD (Microsoft
    Diagnostics) utility, 368,
    442, 971
MSD (MicroSystems
    Development), 1493
MTBF (mean time between
    failures) (hard disk
    drives), 638
multicolor graphics array
    card, *see* MCGA card
multicolor graphics array
    monitors, *see* MCGA
    monitors
multimedia
    CD-ROM drives, 492-493
    video cards, 406-411
multimedia PCs, *see* MPCs
multiple-frequency
    monitors, 376
MultiSound sound card,
    494
multispin CD-ROM drives,
    786
Musical Instrument Digital
    Interface, *see* MIDI

N

Nanao monitors, 381
National Support Center
    Bulletin Board System
    (NSC BBS), 202
National Television System
    Committee, *see* NTSC
NDIAGS utility, 289
NDP (numeric data
    processor), 214
NEC MultiSync 4FGe
    monitor, 376
NEC Technologies, Inc.,
    1494
    hard disk drives,
        1386-1387
    monitors, 376, 380
    Video Local Bus, 18
NEC V20 chips, 877-878
NEC V30 chips, 877-878
network adapter cards,
    448-452
    ARCnet adapters, 450
    Ethernet adapters,
        450-451
    evaluating, 454, 479-481
    IBM PS/2, 1325-1326
    LANtastic adapters, 448,
        450
    Token Ring adapters, 449,
        451-452
network operating system,
    see NOS
networks, *see* LANs (local
    area networks)
Newbury hard disk drives,
    1387
niche market products,
    831
NLSFUNC command, 983
NMIs (non-maskable
    interrupts), 277
No boot device available—
    strike F1 to retry boot, F2
    for setup utility error
    message, 993
No room for system on
    destination disk error
    message, 1014

non-maskable interrupts (NMI), 277
non-standard SCSI interfaces (CD-ROM drives), 780
Non-System disk or disk error error message, 992-994
noninterlaced monitors, 380
Norton Desktop for Windows, 972
Norton Utilities, 965, 970-971
   Backup, 825
   NDIAGS, 289
   Speedisk, 541
NOS (network operating system), 444
notebooks
   PCMCIA buses, 138-142
   see also laptops
NSC BBS (National Support Center Bulletin Board System), 202
NTFS (Windows NT File System) hard disk partitioning, 606
NTSC (National Television System Committee), 407
NTSC-to-VGA adapter, 410
numeric data processor (NDP), 214

O

OFF BOARD PARITY ERROR ADDR (HEX) = (xxxxx) error message, 278
off-center disk-clamping (floppy disk drives), 580-581
ON BOARD PARITY ERROR ADDR (HEX) = (xxxxx) error message, 278
Open System Interconnection model, *see* OSI model
operating systems
   architecture, 976-977

BIOS, 977-979
   capacities, 763-764
DOS (Disk Operating System), 975, 977
   booting, 990-991
   CSDs (Corrective Service Diskettes), 987-988
   directories, 1382-1390
   disk structures, 1377-1380
   DVB (DOS Volume Boot Sector), 1381-1390
   error codes, 1460-1462
   FATs (file allocation tables), 995-997
   files, 995
   hard disks, 1004-1013
   I/O system, 979-987
   interfaces, 997-1003
   MBR (master boot record), 1379-1380
   Partition Table System Indicator Byte Values, 1380-1390
   shell, 979, 981-987
   startup, 991-995
   upgrades, 892-895
   versions, 987-990
   plug-and-play features, 156
   upgrades, 892-895
optical media drives, *see* **magneto-optical drives**
optical sensors (mouse), 364
Options and Adapters Technical-Reference manual, 22
Optune program, 910
ordering IBM documentation, 1471
original unidirectional parallel ports, 439
OS/2, 170, 175
oscilloscopes, 585
OSI (Open System Interconnection) model, 457-459
   Application layer, 459
   Data Link layer, 457

Network layer, 459
   Physical layer, 457
   Presentation layer, 459
   Session layer, 459
   Transport layer, 459
outlet testers, 31-32
Overdrive processors, 185-189, 190-203
   compatibility, 201-202
   heat sinks, 226
   installing, 199-200
   Pentium, 203
overheating, 899
oxide media platters, 609

P

Pacific Magtron, Inc., 1495
   hard disk drives, 1387
paged memory, 838, 845
parallel ports, 413, 438-440
   25-Pin PC-Compatible Parallel Port Connector, 438-439
   configuration, 440-441
   Enhanced Parallel Port (EPP) parallel ports, 440
   I/O addresses, 143
   identifying, 441-442
   original unidirectional parallel ports, 439
   testing, 444
   troubleshooting, 444
   Type 1 Bidirectional parallel ports, 439
   Type 3 DMA parallel ports, 440
parity checking, 275-279, 288-289
part numbers
   Guide To Operations (GTO), 1463
   Hardware-Maintenance Library, 1463-1467
   IBM 5140 PC Convertible, 1065
   IBM AT, 1096-1097
   IBM keyboard cables, 361
   IBM keyboards, 361
   IBM PC XT, 1074-1075
   IBM Portable PC, 1085
   IBM PS/2, 1317

IBM XT Model 286,
1104-1105
memory chips, 273
Quick-Reference
Manuals, 1463
Technical-Reference
Library, 1467-1471
**partitioning (hard disks),
604-605, 753-759**
FATs (File Allocation
Tables), 605-606
HPFS (High Performance
File System), 606
MBR (Master Boot
Record), 606
NTFS (Windows NT File
System), 606
**passive preventive
maintenance, 898,
915-926**
**passive-matrix LCD
monitors, 377**
patches (DOS bugs), 1017
IBM PC DOS, 1017-1023
MS-DOS, 1021-1023
PATH command, 982
PAUSE command, 982
**PC Keyboard Design
(Annabooks), 362**
**PC Power & Cooling, Inc.,
324, 455, 1495**
**PC Power System Analyzer,
320-321**
**PC PowerCheck card,
319-320**
**PC Technician diagnostic
software, 966**
PC-Tools utility, 971
PC/XT, *see* IBM PC/XT
**PCI (Peripheral
Component
Interconnect) buses, 18,
127-138**
pinouts, 129-138
video cards, 405, 887
**PCMCIA (Personal
Computer Memory Card
International
Association) buses,
138-142**
pinouts, 140-141
standards, 139

PCs (personal computers)
developments, 12-13
disassembling, 35
cabling, 39
ESD (electro-static
discharge), 36-37
IBM AT, 46-52
IBM PS/2, 52-54
IBM XT, 39-46
preparation, 35-39
recording
configuration, 38-39
setup programs, 37-38
Slimline cases, 39-46
Tower cases, 46-52
history, 9-13
IBM, 11-12
see also computers; by
name, model
**Pentium processors,
203-209, 270-271,
886-887**
BiCMOS (Bipolar
Complementary Metal
Oxide Semiconductor),
206
BTB (Branch Target
Buffer), 205
caches, 206
compatibility, 203
first-generation design,
207-208
internal registers, 162
math coprocessors, 207
Overdrive processors,
192, 194, 197, 203
power consumption, 307
second-generation
design, 208-209
SIMMs, 206
**peripheral component
interconnect buses,** *see*
PCI buses
**Personal Computer
Memory Card
International Association
buses,** *see* **PCMCIA buses**
personal computers, *see*
**PCs; computers; by name,
model**
**PGA (professional graphics
adapter) card, 391**

**Philips Consumer
Electronics, 1496**
CD-ROMs, 774
**Phoenix Technologies,
Ltd., 1496**
BIOS software, 86, 90-91,
855-856
motherboards
286 motherboards,
1406-1425
386 motherboards,
1408-1409
BIOS error codes,
1419-1420
**phone line surge
suppressors, 927**
PhotoCD drives, 782
PhotoCDs, 783-784
sessions, 782-783
**physical connectors
(power supply), 299**
pitch (sound), 490
pits (CD-ROMs), 776
planars, *see* **motherboards**
platforms, *see* **operating
systems**
platters, 587-589, 608-609
formatting, 604
HLF (high-level
formatting), 606
LLF (low-level
formatting), 604
oxide media, 609
partitioning, 604-605
FATs (File Allocation
Tables), 605-606
HPFS (High
Performance File
System), 606
MBR (Master Boot
Record), 606
NTFS (Windows NT
File System), 606
sectors, 601-608
thin-film media, 609-610
**plug-and-play cards,
155-156**
**Plus Development
Corporation, 1496**
hard disk drives, 1387
pointing devices
mouse, 363-367

Trackpoint II, 362, 370-372
pollutants, 923-924
Port Finder, 420
Portable PC expansion slots (I/O buses), 102
portable tape backup drives, 815
ports
communications ports, 413
parallel ports, 143, 413, 438-442, 444
serial ports, 143, 146, 413-420, 441-444
motherboards, 98, 365-366
POST (Power-On Self Test), 288, 850, 947-949
AMI BIOS error codes, 1411-1471
audio error codes, 949-950
Award BIOS error codes, 1416-1419
BIOS error codes, 1410-1411
clock speed test, disabling, 861
DOS error codes, 1460-1462
Hewlett Packard POST error codes, 1420-1424
I/O port codes, 950-953
IBM POST error codes, 1424-1453
IBM SCSI error codes, 1453-1460
keyboard error codes, 357
Phoenix BIOS error codes, 1419-1420
visual error codes, 950
POST cards, 950-953
power cables (floppy disk drives), 575
power connectors (hard disk drives), 633
power cycling, 916-918
burn-in (phosphor picture tubes), 918
screen savers, 919
Power Disk program, 910

Power_Good signal, 888
power management (motherboards), 84
power supply, 291-292
connectors, 295-299
back probing, 314
disk drives, 298
physical connectors, 299
file servers, 452, 455
form factors, 293-295
fuses, 321
IBM 5140 PC Convertible automobile power adapters, 1064
battery chargers, 1064
IBM AT, 49
IBM PS/2, 57, 65, 71, 303
IBM XT, 44
load resistors, 300-302
outlet testers, 31-32
power consumption, calculating, 306-308
power line noise, 920-921
power-protection systems, 924-926
line conditioners, 927-928
phone line surge suppressors, 927
SPS (standby power supply), 928
surge suppressors, 926-927
UPS (uninterruptible power supply), 928-930
Power_Good signal, 292, 299-300
testing, 316
voltage, 298
ratings, 302-304
repairing, 321-322
replacing, 322-324
Slimline cases, 44, 294
specifications, 304-306
spikes, 920
test equipment
DMMs (Digital Multi-Meters), 313-316
load resistors, 316-318

PC Power System Analyzer, 320-321
PC PowerCheck card, 319-320
variable voltage transformers, 318-319
Tower cases, 49, 292-293
troubleshooting, 310-313
turning off, 309-310
vendors, 323-324
voltages, 298
see also electricity
Power-On Self Test, *see* **POST**
PPI (Programmable Peripheral Interface) chips, 19
presentations (sound cards), 486-487
Presenter Video Capture, 408
preventive maintenance, 897
active preventive maintenance, 898-909
passive preventive maintenance, 898, 915-926
Priam Systems Corporation, 1496
hard disk drives, 1387
PRINT command, 983
printer cables (IBM 5140 PC Convertible), 1064
printers
Epson printers control codes, 1370-1372
HP LaserJet printers control codes, 1372-1376
IBM 5140 PC Convertible, 1063
IBM printers control codes, 1368-1370
troubleshooting, 151
PRML (Partial-Response, Maximum Likelihood) hard disk drives, 600
processor buses, 95-97
processor sockets (motherboards), 83

processors
    386 clones, 174-175
    address buses, 162-163
    AMD, 212
    buses, 159-161
    Cyrix, 212
    heating/cooling, 225-226
    IBM, 209
        Blue Lightning,
            210-211
        SLC, 209-210
    identifying chips, 222
    Intel, 167
        386DX, 173
        386SL, 174
        386SX, 173-174
        80186, 168-169
        80188, 168-169
        80286, 169-171
        80386, 171-173
        80486, 175-190
        8086, 167-168
        8088, 167-168
        82360SL, 174
        Overdrive, 190-203
        Pentium, 203-209
    internal registers,
        161-162
    keyboards, 336
    math coprocessors,
        212-214
        80287, 216-218
        80387, 218-219
        80487, 220-221
        8087, 214-216
        clock speed, 217
        removing, 225
        Weitek, 219-220
    motherboards, 83, 91
    speed, 163-166
    testing, 221
        80386, 223-225
        8088, 221-223
    video cards, 404-411
    see also chips; CPUs
Professional Graphics
    Adapter card, see PGA
    card
Professional Graphics
    monitors, 391
Programmable Peripheral
    Interface chips (PPI), 19

Programmed Symbols (PS)
    adapters (IBM 3270 PC),
    1076
programs
    COLDSET.COM, 890-892
    CPBACKUP, 933
    DEFRAG, 910
    EMM386.EXE, 266
    FDISK, 1013
    HIMEM.SYS, 266
    Microsoft Anti-Virus, 913
    MSBACKUP, 933
    Optune, 910
    Power Disk, 910
    SCANV, 913
    SPEEDISK, 910
    TSR (terminate-and-stay
        resident) programs,
        1043-1044
    UNFORMAT, 912
    VOPT, 910-911
    WARMSET.COM,
        890-892
    see also utilities
PROMPT command, 982
proofreaders (sound cards),
    489
proprietary standards
    (modems), 421, 433-435
    CSP (CompuCom Speed
        Protocol) standards, 435
    DIS (dynamic impedance
        stabilization) standards,
        434
    FAXModem standards,
        435-436
    HST (high speed
        technology) standards,
        434
    MNP (Microcom
        Networking Protocol)
        standards, 434-435
    V-series standards, 435
protected mode
    80286 processors, 170
    80386 processors, 172
protocols, see standards
PS/1, see IBM PS/1
PS/2 Reference Diskette,
    202
PS/2, see IBM PS/2

PS/ValuePoint, see IBM PS/
    ValuePoint
PTI Industries, 1496
    hard disk drives,
        1387-1388
Public Software Library,
    973, 1497
publications
    magazines, 820,
        1333-1334
    manuals, 1328-1330
    see also documentation
pulsers, 31

Q

QAPlus/FE diagnostic
    software, 966-967
QBASIC command, 984
QEMM memory managers,
    266, 269
QIC (Quarter-Inch
    Cartridge Drive
    Standards, Inc.), 1497
    tape backup drives,
        809-812
QIC-40 tape backup drives,
    812-814
QIC-80 tape backup drives,
    812-815
quad-density floppy disks,
    554
Quadruple-speed CD-ROM
    drives, 493
Quantum Corporation,
    1497
    hard disk drives, 1388
Quarter-Inch Cartridge
    Drive Standards, Inc.,
    see QIC

R

radio-frequency
    interference (RFI),
    921-922
    Class A certification,
        922-923
    Class B certification,
        922-923

rails (floppy disk drives), 575

RAM, *see* conventional (base) memory

RAM chips, *see* memory chips

RAMBoost utility, 268

raster (monitors), 376

RD/RMDIR command, 982

Read Verify, *see* scanning

read/write heads
  floppy disk drives, 517-520
  hard disk drives, 610-612
    ferrite, 612
    magneto-resistive (MR), 614-615
    metal-in-gap (MIG), 613
    thin film (TF), 613-614

real mode
  80286 processors, 169
  80386 processors, 172

real-time clocks (IBM AT), 20

realigning floppy disk drives, 581

recirculating filters (hard disk drives), 627

recording sound files, 487-488

RECOVER command, 984, 1038-1039

ReelMagic (Sigma Designs), 410

reformatting hard disk drives, 913-915

refresh rates (monitors), 376

REM command, 982

removable keycaps, 331

removable storage drives, 826
  magnetic media drives, 826-827
    Bernoulli drives, 827-828
    floptical drives, 828-829
    SyDOS drives, 827-828
    SyQuest drives, 827-828

magneto-optical drives, 826, 829-831
  WORM (write-once read-many) drives, 831

removing memory chips, 849

removing, *see* disassembling computers

REN/RENAME command, 982

repairs
  floppy disk drives, 581-582
  hard disk drives, 589, 764-770
  IBM PS/x systems, 1113
  keyboards, 359
  monitors, 410-411
  motherboards, 82
  power supply, 321-322
  service contracts, 939-943
  warranties, 939-943

REPLACE command, 984

replacement parts
  HDAs (head disk assemblies), 589
  IBM PS/x systems, 1111
  keyboards, 358-361
  logic boards, 632
  monitors, 410
  motherboards, 82
  mouse, 368
  power supply, 322-324
  video cards, 410

reset switches, 888-892
  booting, 890
    cold boot, 889-892
    warm boot, 889-892
  installation, 889
  Power_Good signal, 888

resolution (monitors), 379-380, 383
  dot pitch, 380, 383
  interlaced mode, 380
  noninterlaced mode, 380

resources, 141-142
  conflicts, 151-156
    adapter cards, 153-155, 265
    resolving, 152
    system-configuration template, 152-153

DMA (direct memory access) channels, 146-148
  I/O port addresses, 142-143
  IRQs (interrupt request channels), 143-146
  memory, 148-151

RESTORE command, 984

RFI (radio-frequency interference), 921-922
  Class A certification, 922-923
  Class B certification, 922-923

riser cards, 99

RLL (run length limited) encoding, 597-601

Rodime hard disk drives, 1388

Roland MT-32 Sound Module card, 483

ROM (read-only memory)
  accessory ROMs, 857
  video adapters, 238
  see also BIOS

ROM shadowing, 260-261

root directory backups, 911

RPMs (rotations per minute)
  floppy disk drives, 534
  hard disk drives, 589

RTV sealer, 904

run length limited encoding, *see* RLL encoding

S

sampling (sound cards), 490-491, 495

Samsung hard disk drives, 1388-1389

scan codes (keyboards), 339-340
  83-key PC and XT keyboards, 340-342
  84-key AT keyboards, 343-345
  101-key enchanced keyboards, 346-354

scanning (hard disk drives)
defect scans, 740-741
surface analysis scans, 742-743
viruses, 913
SCANV program, 913
screen garbage, troubleshooting, 151
screen savers, 919
sound cards, 487
SCSI (Small Computer System Interface)
CD-ROM drives, 779, 801
chains, 798-800
hard disk drives, 652, 681-709
adapters, 685-695
cables, 693-703
capacities, 762-763
configuration, 704-709
connectors, 693-703
data-transfer rates, 685
differential SCSI, 690-691, 699-703
drivers, 708-709
formatting, 750
power consumption, 308
SCSI-1 specifications, 691-692
SCSI-2 specifications, 692
SCSI-3 specifications, 693
single-ended SCSI, 690-691, 694-699
standards, 683
termination, 703-706
v. IDE interface, 745-761
SDL (Shielded Data Link) connectors, 354-355
Seagate Technology, 1498
hard disk drives, 590, 1390-1396
seating chips, 906
Second Nature accessory ROM, 857
second-generation Pentium processors, 208-209

Sector not found reading drive C error message, 737
sector sparing (hard disk drives), 743-745
sectors
floppy disks, 536, 539
hard disks, 601-608
seek time (hard disk drives), 588, 639
segment addresses, 230
self-cleaning lenses (CD-ROM drives), 788
serial interface (mouse), connecting, 365-366
serial ports, 413-418
9-Pin (AT) Serial Port Connector, 416
25-Pin (PC, XT, and PS/2) Serial Port Connector, 416
configuration, 419-420
I/O addresses, 143
identifying, 441-442
IRQs, 146, 419-439
modems, 420-438
testing, 442-444
troubleshooting, 444
UART chips, 417-418
serial/parallel adapters (IBM 5140 PC Convertible), 1063
servers, *see* file servers
service contracts, 939-943
Service Diagnostics diagnostic software, 967-968
sessions (PhotoCD drives), 782-783
SET command, 982
SETUP programs, 37-38
math coprocessors, removing, 225
SETVER command, 984
shadowing ROMs, 260-261
SHARE command, 984
shareware, 973-974
shielded twisted pair cables, 446
SHIFT command, 982
SHIPDISK.COM program, 637

shock mounting (hard disk drives), 649-650
Shugart, Alan, 515-516
SHUTDOWN.EXE program, 637
Siemens hard disk drives, 1389
Sigma Designs ReelMagic, 410
signals (keyboard connectors), 355
silicone lubricants, 905
SIMMs (Single In-line Memory Modules), 279-283, 840
chip creep, 906
IBM PS/2, 1319-1320
removing, 59, 67-68
motherboards, 84
Pentium processors, 206
pinouts, 284-287
see also memory chips
single density encoding, *see* FM encoding
single-sided disks, 553-554
SIPPs (Single In-line Pin Packages), 840
broken or bent pins, 848
chip creep, 906
see also memory chips
skirts (adapter cards), 105
SL Enhanced chips, 181-183
SLC processors, 210
sliders (hard disk drives), 615
Slimline cases
adapter boards, 40
covers, 39-40
disk drives, 41-42
motherboards, 44-46
power supply, 294
disconnecting, 44
SMM (System Management Mode), 182
smoking, 900
SMS Technology, Inc., 1499
snow (monitors), 387
sockets (Intel processors), 190-203

soft sectored floppy disks, 557

software
backup software, 824-826, 932-933
Central Point Backup, 826
FastBack Backup, 826
Microsoft Backup, 824
Norton Backup, 825
third-party software, 824-826
Windows Backup, 824
BIOS, 86-91, 855-857
CD-ROM drives
CD Extensions for DOS (Microsoft), 801-802
CD-ROM device drivers, 801
SCSI adapter drivers, 800
conflicts, 1043-1044
copy protection, 932
diagnostic software, 947-948, 953, 962-963
AMIDiag, 963
Checkit Pro, 963-964
Disk Manager, 749, 969
Drive Probe, 968-969
HDtest, 749
IBM Advanced Diagnostics, 948, 956-962
IBM system diagnostics, 953-956
memory, 850
Micro-Scope, 964-965
Norton Desktop for Windows, 972
Norton Diagnostics, 965
PC Technician, 966
POST (Power-On Self Test), 947-953
QAPlus/FE, 966-967
Service Diagnostics, 967-968
Winprobe, 972
WinSleuth, 972
disk compression (Doublespace), 763-764

disk software interfaces, 1355-1357
head-parking software, 637-638
IBM 3270 PC, 1077
LLF (low-level formatting), 747-753
mouse configuration, 370
partitioning software
Disk Manager, 756
FDISK, 754-755
Speedstor, 756
Vfeature Deluxe, 756
shareware, 973-974
sound cards, 497
tape backup drives, 937-938
troubleshooting, 1044-1045
see also programs; utilities

soldering tools, 28-29

Sony Corporation of America, 1499-1500
CD-ROMs, 774

SORT command, 984

sound
intensity, 490
pitch, 490

Sound Blaster Pro sound card, 490

Sound Blaster sound card, 494

sound cards, 483-484
8-bit sound cards, 491
16-bit sound cards, 492
Ad Lib Gold sound card, 490
Ad Lib Music Synthesizer Card, 483
ADCs (analog-to-digital converters), 490
buying, 494-499
CD-ROM drives, 492-493
compatibility, 494-495
compression, 496
ADPCM (Adaptive Differential Pulse Code Modulation), 494
MPEG (Motion Pictures Expert Group), 494

connectors
CD-ROM connectors, 496
joystick/MIDI connectors, 499
microphone in connectors, 499
MIDI connectors, 502
speaker/headphone connector, 498
stereo line in connectors, 498
stereo line out connectors, 498
DACs (digital-to-analog converters), 490
DSPs (digital signal processors), 497
frequency response, 490
Game Blaster sound card, 483
games, 484-485, 490
installation, 503-505
Logitech AudioMan sound card, 490-492
MIDI, 486, 494, 497
monophonic, 495-496
MPCs (multimedia PCs), 485-486
MultiSound sound card, 494
presentations, 486-487
proofreaders, 489
recording sound files, 487-488
Roland MT-32 Sound Module card, 483
sampling, 490-491, 495
screen savers, 487
software, 497
Sound Blaster Pro sound card, 490
Sound Blaster sound card, 494
sound drivers, 497
sound quality, troubleshooting, 151
speakers, connecting, 504
stereophonic, 495-496
stereos, connecting, 505
synthesized sound, 494
total harmonic distortion, 490

troubleshooting, 511
  computer failure, 509
  hardware conflicts,
    505-508
  lockups, 510
  low volume, 509-511
  no sound, 508-509
  one-sided sound, 509
  scratchy sound, 509
  voice annotations, 488
  voice recognition, 488
  volume control, 499
**sound drivers (sound
  cards), 497**
sound files
  events, 488
  recording, 487-488
spare parts, *see*
  replacement parts
speakers, 499-501
  connecting, 504, 1357
special purpose RAM, 230
speed
  motherboards, 83, 91
  Overdrive processors, 199
  processors, 163-166
  upgrades
    286 systems, 880-883
    386 systems, 883-884
    486 systems, 884-887
    clock rate, 885
    CPU chips, 876-887
    ICE (In-Circuit
      Emulator) boards,
      878-879
    increasing clock rate,
      878
    math coprocessors,
      873-876
    motherboard
      replacements,
      879-880
    RAM, 882
SPEEDISK program, 910
Speedstor software, 756
spikes (power supply), 920
**spills on keyboards,
  cleaning, 360**
**spindle ground straps
  (hard disk drives),
  630-632**

spindle motors
  floppy disk drives, 521
  hard disk drives, 629-630
**SPS (standby power
  supply), 928**
**squealing (hard disk
  drives), 631-632**
**SRAM (static RAM),
  845-846**
**ST-506/412 interface (hard
  disk drives), 654-655**
  configuration, 657
    connectors, 661
    control cables, 660
    data cables, 660
    DS (drive select)
      jumpers, 659
    power cables, 661
    terminating resistors,
      660
  controllers, 662-663
  encoding, 655-656
  installation, 657
**Stabilant 22 contact
  cleaner/lubricant, 22,
  32-33, 902**
standards
  ANSI (American National
    Standards Institute),
    683-684, 1476
  CD-ROMs, 780-781
  LANs, 456-457
    Ethernet, 460-463
    FDDI (Fiber
      Distributed Data
      Interface), 460,
      470-472
    IEEE 802.3, 459-460
    IEEE 802.5, 459
    OSI (Open System
      Interconnection)
      model, 457-459
    Token Ring, 463-470
  modems, 420
    data-compression
      standards, 421, 433
    error-correction
      standards, 421, 432
    modulation standards,
      421, 431-432
    proprietary standards,
      433-436

  monitor-emissions
    MPR I, 381
    MPR II, 381
    SWEDAC, 381
    TCO, 381
  PCMCIA buses, 139
  SCSI (small computer
    system interface), 683
  tape backup drives, 809,
    820
    8mm tape backup
      drives, 817-819
    compatibility, 816-817
    DAT (digital audio
      tape), 817-818
    QIC (Quarter-Inch
      Committee)
      standard, 809-812
  TV (National Television
    System Committee),
    407
  video cards, 399,
    1358-1360
**standby power supply
  (SPS), 928**
**star topology (networks),
  447**
**star-wired tree topology
  (networks), 447**
start bits, 413
static electricity, 919-920
  ESD (electro-static
    discharge), 848, 907
  grounding straps, 848
static mats, 36
**static RAM (SRAM),
  845-846**
stepper motors
  floppy disk drives,
    520-521
  hard disk drives, 615-617
    automatic head
      parking, 626
    mechanical links, 617
    temperature
      sensitivity, 616-619
**stereophonic sound cards,
  495-496**
**stereos, connecting sound
  cards, 505**
**sticky keys (keyboards),
  340, 354**

stiction (hard disk drives), 767-770

stop bits, 413

storage (hard disk drives)
capacity, 588
magnetic data storage, 591-594

STP (shielded twisted pair) cables, 446, 473

SUBST command, 984

super-VGA cards, *see* SVGA cards

super-VGA monitors, *see* SVGA monitors

superscalar architecture, 204

support structures (IBM PS/2 systems), removing, 64

surface analysis scans (hard disk drives), 742-743

surge suppressors, 926-927

SVGA (super-VGA) cards, 397-398
drivers, 398
VESA standards, 399
see also video cards

SVGA (super-VGA) monitors, 397-398

swabs (cleaning swabs), 904

SWEDAC standards, 381

switch settings (motherboards), 1350

SyDOS removable media drives, 827-828

synthesized sound (sound cards), 494

synthesizers, 503

SyQuest Technology, 1500
hard disk drives, 1389
removable media drives, 827-828

SYS command, 984

SysChk utility, 972

Sysgen, Inc., 1500

system adapters (IBM 3270 PC), 1075

system boards, *see* motherboards

system failure (power supply), 312-313

System Management Mode (SMM), 182

system resources, *see* resources

system-configuration template (resource conflicts), 152-153

systems
disassembling, 905
testing, 1330-1331
see also computers; PCs; by name, model

T

tactility (keyboards)
capacitive key switches, 336
foam element key switches, 334
pure mechanical key switches, 333
rubber dome key switches, 335

Tandon Corporation, 1500
hard disk drives, 1389

tape backup drives, 808, 934-939
buying, 819-821, 939
capacities, 815-816, 820
cassettes, 810-812
cost, 821
data transfer rates, 814, 821
drivers, 937-938
external tape backup drives, 938-939
formatting, 814
IBM PS/2, 1323
installation, 821-823
interfaces, 936-937
internal tape backup drives, 938-939
portables, 815
QIC-40 tape backup drives, 812-814
QIC-80 tape backup drives, 812-815
software, 824-826, 937-938

standards, 809, 820
8mm tape backup drives, 817-819
compatibility, 816-817
DAT (digital audio tape), 817-818
QIC (Quarter-Inch Committee) standard, 809-812

TCE Company, 1501
PC Power System Analyzer, 320-321

TCO standard, 381

technical support
BBSes, 1332
IBM, 411, 1113

Technical-Reference (TR) manuals, 21-22, 1467-1471

temperature sensitivity (hard disk drives), 618-619, 628-629, 916

terminating resistors (floppy disk drives), 526-528, 571-573

test equipment, 29-30
chemicals, 32-33
DMMs (Digital Multi-Meters), 313-316
load resistors, 316-318
logic probes, 31
meters, 30-31
outlet testers, 31-32
PC Power System Analyzer, 320-321
PC PowerCheck card, 319-320
processors, 221
variable voltage transformers, 318-319
wrap plugs, 30
see also software

testing
CD-ROM drives, 803-804
keyboards, 356
memory, 288
diagnostic tests, 289
parity checking, 288
POST (Power-On Self Test), 288, 850
parallel ports, 444
serial ports, 442-444
systems, 1330-1331

Texas Instruments, 10
TF (thin film) heads (hard disk drives), 613-614
thermal expansion/ contraction, 309
thin-film media platters, 609-610
TIME command, 982
TMS380 chips, 465
Token Ring
  adapters, 449, 451-452
  frames, 464-465
  IEEE 802.5 standard, 463-470
tools
  ESD (Electro-Static Discharge) protection kits, 27
  hand tools, 25-28
  soldering tools, 28-29
topologies (LANs), 446
  bus topology, 446
  star topology, 447
  star-wired tree topology, 447
Torx screws, 34
Toshiba America, Inc., 1501
  hard disk drives, 1389
total harmonic distortion (sound cards), 490
Tower cases
  adapter boards, 48
  covers, 47
  disk drives, 48-49
  motherboards, 52
  power supply, 292-293
    disconnecting, 49
TPI (tracks per inch) (floppy disks), 554
TR (Technical-Reference) manuals, 21-22
Trackpoint II, 362, 370-372
tracks
  floppy disk drives, 535
  floppy disks, 539
    3 1/2-inch floppy disks, 537
    5 1/4 inch floppy disks, 537
    viewing, 536

transfer rates, *see* data transfer rates
TREE command, 984
Trinitron design (monitor screens), 376
Triple-speed CD-ROM drives, 493
troubleshooting
  DOS startup sequence, 991-995
  DOS upgrades, 1013-1016
  ESD (Electro-Static Discharge) protection kits, 27
  floppy disk drives, 151, 548-551
    configuration, 577-581
    installation, 577-581
  hard disk drives, 764-770
    whining noises, 631-632
  inaccurate data transfers, 151
  joysticks, 510
  keyboards
    defective cables, 356
    error codes, 357
    failed keys, 354
    intermittent key strikes, 334
    sticky keys, 340, 354
  lock-ups, 151
  motherboards, 357
  mouse, 151
    interrupt conflicts, 367-368
    jerky mouse, 367
    unresponsive mouse, 368
  parallel ports, 444
  power supply, 310-313
  printers, 151
    BIOS, 858
  screen garbage, 151
  serial ports, 444
  software, 1044-1045
  sound cards, 511
    computer failure, 509
    hardware conflicts, 505-508
    lockups, 510

    low volume, 509-511
    no sound, 508-509
    one-sided sound, 509
    scratchy sound, 509
    sound quality, 151
  test equipment, 29-30
    chemicals, 32-33
    logic probes, 31
    meters, 30-31
    outlet testers, 31-32
    wrap plugs, 30
  tools
    hand tools, 25-28
    soldering tools, 28-29
  see also error codes; error messages
TSR (terminate-and-stay resident) programs, 1043-1044
Tulin hard disk drives, 1389
tunnel erasure (floppy disk drives), 519
turning off power supply, 309-310
TV
  standards (National Television System Committee), 407
  viewing computer screens on TV, 407-411
twisted pair cables, 472-473
Type 1 Bidirectional parallel ports, 439
Type 3 DMA parallel ports, 440
TYPE command, 982
typematic functions (keyboards), 337
  delay parameters, 339
  rate repeat parameters, 338-339
  setting speed, 339

U

U.S. Robotics, Inc., 1502
  modems, 422-430, 1361-1368

UART (Universal Asynchronous Receiver/Transmitter) chips, 20, 417-418
   16450 UART chip, 417-418
   16550 UART chip, 417-418
   16550A UART chip, 418
   8250 UART chip, 417-418
   8250A UART chip, 418
   8250B UART chip, 418
   FIFO (first in, first out), 418
   identifying type, 417
Ultimedia PS/2, 1108
Ultra-X, Inc., 1502
   POST cards, 952
UMA, *see* upper memory area (UMA)
UMB, *see* upper memory blocks
UNDELETE command, 984
UNFORMAT command, 565, 912, 984
unfragmentation, *see* defragmentation
uninterruptible power supply, *see* UPS
Universal Asynchronous Receiver/Transmitter chips, *see* UART chips
UNIX processors, 170
unshielded twisted pair cables, 446
upgrades, 835-837
   BIOS, 853-855, 858
      alternatives to an upgrade, 857
      EPROM programming, 859-861
      Flash BIOS, 866
      IML system partition BIOS, 866-867
      keyboard-controller chips, 855
      modifying hard disk controller head step rate, 862-866
      modifying hard disk drive parameter tables, 861-862

software, 855-857
      troubleshooting, 858
   DOS, 892-895
      troubleshooting, 1013-1016
   drives
      floppy disk drives, 867-872
      hard disk drives, 872-873
   IBM AT, 883
   IBM PS/2, 1113
      processor/coprocessors, 1316-1318
   memory, 837, 839
      conventional memory, 837
      DRAM (dynamic random-access memory), 837
      expanded memory, 838
      extended memory, 838
      motherboard memory, 839-852
   monitors, 887-888
   motherboards, 82
   operating systems, 892-895
   speed
      286 systems, 880-883
      386 systems, 883-884
      486 systems, 884-887
      80486 processors, 189-190
      clock rate, 885
      CPUs, 876-887, 882-883
      ICE (In-Circuit Emulator) boards, 878-879
      increasing clock rate, 878
      math coprocessors, 873-876
      motherboard replacements, 879-880
      RAM, 882
   video cards, 887-888

upper memory area (UMA), 230
   adapter ROM, 230
   free space, 230
   map, 228-229
   motherboard BIOS, 230
   special purpose RAM, 230
   Video RAM, 230-232
upper memory block (UMB) (mouse drivers), 369
UPS (uninterruptible power supply), 452, 928-930
utilities
   Calibrate program, 645
   configuration utilities
      InfoSpotter, 972
      MSD (Microsoft Diagnostics), 971
      SysChk, 972
   data recovery utilities
      dSALVAGE, 971
      Norton Utilities, 289, 541, 970-971
      PC-Tools, 971
   Disk Manager utility, 649, 674
   IDEDIAG utility, 672
   IDEINFO utility, 672
   memory managers
      386MAX, 269-270
      MEMMAKER, 266-268
      QEMM, 266, 269
      RAMBoost, 268
   Vopt utility, 542
   see also programs; software
UTP (unshielded twisted pair) cables, 446, 473

V

V-series standards, 435
V.21 modulation standard, 411
V.22 modulation standard, 431
V.22bis modulation standard, 431

V.23 modulation standard, 432

V.29 modulation standard, 432

V.32 modulation standard, 432

V.32bis modulation standard, 432

V.32fast modulation standard, 432

V.42 error-correction standard (modems), 433

V.42bis data-compression standard, 433

vaccuum cleaners, 903

variable voltage transformers, 318-319

vendors, listing, 1473-1504

ventilation, 311-312

VER command, 982

VERIFY command, 982

Vertex hard disk drives, 1389

VESA (Video Electronics Standards Association), 18, 1502
  BIOS Extension, 399
  SBGA card standards, 399

VESA local buses, 122-124
  pinouts, 125-126

VESA-Standard Local Bus video cards, 887

Vfeature Deluxe software, 756

VFW (Video for Windows), 409

VGA (video graphics array) cards, 393-396
  memory, 149
  see also video cards

VGA (video graphics array) monitors, 382, 391-397
  see also monitors

VGA Producer Pro (Magni Systems), 407

VGA-to-NTSC adapters, 407-411

video
  full-motion video, 408-410

  compression, 409
  decompression, 409
  multimedia PCs, 409-410

video adapters, *see* video cards

video capture cards, 408-411

video cards, 384-391
  8514/A Display Adapter card, 396-397
  buying, 405-406
  CGA (color graphics adapter) card, 232, 386-387
  display modes, 1358-1360
  EGA (enhanced graphics adapter) card, 232, 388-411
  I/O buses, 404-411
  IBM 3270 PC, 1076
  IBM PS/2, 1324-1325
  IBM PS/x systems, 1112-1113
  MCGA (multicolor graphics array) card, 392-411
  MDA (monochrome display adapter) cards, 232, 384-411
  memory requirements, 148, 402-403
  multimedia, 406-411
  PCI (peripheral component interconnect) cards, 887
  PGA (professional graphics adapter) card, 391
  processors, 404-411
  replacing, 410
  ROM code, 238
  signals
    analog signals, 391-411
    digital signals, 391-411
  standards, 1358-1360
  SVGA (super-VGA) cards, 397-398
    drivers, 398

  VESA standards, 399
  memory requirements, 232
  upgrades, 887-888
  VESA-Standard Local Bus video cards, 404-411, 887
  VGA (video graphics array) card, 232, 393-396
  video RAM, 238, 404-411
  XGA (extended graphics array) card, 232, 399-402
  XGA-2 (extended graphics array) card, 399-402

Video Electronics Standards Association, *see* VESA

video extensions (MCA buses), 112-114

Video for Windows (Microsoft), 409

video graphics array cards, *see* VGA cards

video graphics array monitors, *see* VGA monitors

Video Local Bus, 18

video RAM, 230, 232
  video adapters, 238
  video cards, 404-411

VideoLogic Mediator LC, 407

ViewSonic monitors, 380

viruses, 151, 913

VL-Bus video cards, 404-411

VL-Buses, *see* VESA local buses

VLB (VESA-Standard Local Bus) video cards, 887

VLF (very-low-frequency) electromagnetic emissions (monitors), 381

voice annotations, 488

voice-coil actuators (hard disk drives), 615, 619-620, 636

automatic head parking, 626
linear voice-coil actuators, 620
rotary voice-coil actuators, 620
servo control mechanisms, 621-626
voice recognition, 488
VOL command, 982
volume boot sectors (DOS hard disks), 541, 1007-1008
volume control (sound cards), 499
Volume Table of Contents (VTOC) (CD-ROMs), 781-782
Vopt utility, 542, 910-911

W

warm boot, 889-890
WARMSET.COM program, 890-892
warranties, 898, 939-943
IBM PS/ValuePoint, 1298
Washburn & Co., 1503
BIOS chips, 857
WAV files, *see* sound files
Wave Blaster, 503
Weitek Corporation, 1503
math coprocessors, 219-220
Western Digital Corporation, 1503
hard disk drives, 1390
whining (hard disk drives), 631-632
Winchester drives, *see* hard disk drives
Windows
diagnostic software, 972
processors
80286, 171
80486, 175
windows (IBM 3270 PC), 1077
Windows Backup software, 824

Winprobe diagnostics software, 972
WinSleuth diagnostics software, 972
wireless networks, 448
workstations (LANs), 444-445
WORM (write-once read-many) drives, 831
wrap plugs, 30
parallel ports, 444
serial ports, 443
WYSIWYG (what you see is what you get), 379

X

X-ray machines (floppy disks), 566-568
XCOPY command, 984
XGA (extended graphics array) cards, 399-402
XGA (extended graphics array) monitors, 399-402
XGA-2 (extended graphics array) cards, 399-402
XMS (extended memory specification), 256-257
XT expansion slots (I/O buses), 102
XT, *see* IBM XT
XXXX ROM Error error message, 992

Y

Yellow Book standards (CD-ROMs), 781

Z

Zenith Data Systems, 1504
motherboards, 1409-1410
zero-insertion-force (ZIF) sockets, 29, 190
zoned recording (hard disk drives), 605